All-Time Rosters of Major League Baseball Clubs

All-Time Rosters of Major League Baseball Clubs

Revised Edition

By S. C. Thompson

Revisions by Pete Palmer

SOUTH BRUNSWICK
NEW YORK: A. S. BARNES and CO.
LONDON: THOMAS YOSELOFF LTD

Library of Congress Catalogue Card Number: 73-156

A. S. Barnes and Co., Inc.
Cranbury, New Jersey 08512

Thomas Yoseloff Ltd
108 New Bond Street
London W1Y OQX, England

ISBN 0-498-01380-4
Printed in the United States of America

Contents

Part 1, 1882–1964

Part 2, 1965–1972

All-Time Rosters of Major League Baseball Clubs

Key to Rosters

N-NATIONAL LEAGUE
A-AMERICAN LEAGUE
F-FEDERAL LEAGUE
AA-AMERICAN ASSOCIATION
P-PLAYER'S LEAGUE
U-UNION ASSOCIATION

The records of the National Association, the first major league in baseball, were destroyed in a fire and are therefore not available and are not included in the rosters in this volume.

THE "FROM" COLUMN:
- A-Indicates player's first appearance in Major Leagues.
- B-Indicates player played with same club in year immediately preceding.
- CLUB NAME, WITHOUT MARKING indicates player played with club so designated in year immediately preceding.
- CLUB NAME, PRECEDED BY "X" indicates player moved from club so designated in same year.
- CLUB NAME, WITH FIGURE indicates club and year of player's last previous appearance in Major Leagues.

THE "TO" COLUMN:
- C-Indicates player's last appearance in Major Leagues.
- CLUB NAME indicates player moved to club so designated in same year.

+Indicates separate Batting Average of player who was with another club in same league and in same year.

NOTE: WHILE IT WAS NOT CONSIDERED A MAJOR LEAGUE UNTIL 1901, THE AMERICAN LEAGUE ROSTERS FOR 1900 ARE INCLUDED TO BRIDGE THE GAP IN THE RECORDS OF CERTAIN WELL KNOWN PLAYERS WHO DESERTED THE NATIONAL LEAGUE FOR THE AMERICAN AND REMAINED THERE TO BECOME IMPORTANT FIGURES IN THE SUCCESS OF THE NEW MAJOR LEAGUE.

CLUB RECORD.

OTHER MAJOR LEAGUES

PHILADELPHIA

YEAR	TG	WON	LOST	PCT.	FINISHED	MANAGER
AMERICAN ASSOCIATION (ATHLETICS)						
1882	75	40	35	.533	3	Wm. J. Sharsig Chas. E. Mason
1883	98	66	32	.673	1	Alonzo P. Knight Chas. E. Mason Wm. J. Sharsig
1884	107	61	46	.570	7	Chas. E. Mason Wm. J. Sharsig
1885	112	55	57	.491	4	Alonzo Knight Chas. E. Mason Wm. J. Sharsig
1886	136	63	73	.467	6	Lewis Simmons Chas. E. Mason Wm. J. Sharsig
1887	133	64	69	.481	5	Frank Carter Bancroft Chas. E. Mason Wm. J. Sharsig
1888	133	81	52	.609	3	Wm. J. Sharsig
1889	133	75	58	.564	3	Wm. J. Sharsig
1890	132	54	78	.409	8	Wm. J. Sharsig
1891	139	73	66	.525	5	Wm. J. Sharsig George A. Wood Wm. S. Barnie
UNION ASSOCIATION						
1884	67	21	46	.313	DID NOT FINISH	Ferguson G. Malone Thomas J. Pratt
PLAYER'S LEAGUE						
1890	131	68	63	.519	5	Benjamin Franklin Hilt James G. Fogarty Chas. G. Buffington

American Association

WON 40 | LOST 35 | TG 75 — 1882. — FINISHED 3rd. PCT. .533

ATHLETICS

WM. J. SHARSIG — CHAS. E. MASON

WON	LOST	NAME	POS.	G.	BA	FROM	TO
		Arundel, John Thomas (OF1)	C1	1	.000	A	
		Birchall, A. Judson (2B1)	OF74	75	.263	A	
		Blakiston, Robert J. (2B1 OF34)	3B34	72	.242	A	
		Dorgan, Jeremiah F. (OF18)	C26	45	.287	WorN80	
		Greenwood, Wm. F. (2B1)	OF7	7	.290	A	
0	1	Holbrighter, Edward	P	1	.000	A	C
		Keinzil, Wm.	OF	9	.297	A	
1	1	Landis, Samuel H. (OF1)	P2	3	+.167	A	Balt
		Latham, George Warren (Juice)	1B72	75	.300	LvlleN77	
		Mann, Frederick I.	3B	29	.224	xWorN	
		Mansell, John	OF	32	.237	A	C
2	6	Mountain, Frank H. (OF1)	P8	9	.308	xWorN	WorN (return)
		O'Brien, John K. (1B1 OF20)	C41	62	.304	A	
1	1	Reynolds, Chas. E. (OF1)	P2	2	.125	A	C
		Richmond, John H.	OF	19	.173	xClevN	
		Say, James I.	SS	1	+.500	xLvlle	
		Say, Lewis I.	SS	71	.221	CinN80	
		Smith, Chas.Marvin (Pap) (2B3 SS4 OF4)	3B9	20	+.090	CinN80	Balt
1	0	Snyder, George T.	P	1	.333	A	C
		Straub, Joseph (OF1)	C7	8	.188	TroyN80	
1	0	Stricker, John A. (Cub) (P1 OF2)	2B73	74	.203	A	
8	11	Sweeney, Chas. J. (OF3)	P21	24	.175	A	
26	15	Weaver, Samuel H. (OF2)	P41	42	.240	MilN78	

WON 66 | LOST 32 | TG 98 — AMERICAN ASSOCIATION. 1883. — FINISHED 1st. PCT. .673

ATHLETICS

ALONZO P. KNIGHT — CHAS. E. MASON — WM. J. SHARSIG

WON	LOST	NAME	POS.	G.	BA	FROM	TO
5	4	Bakely, Edward (Enoch) (OF1)	P9	9	.139	A	
		Birchall, A. Judson	OF	95	.230	B	
		Blakiston, Robert J. (1B4 3B4)	OF40	40	.249	B	
17	7	Bradley, George Washington (P27 1B2 OF9)	3B44	77	.238	xClevN	
9	5	Corey, Frederick Harrison (P20 2B8 SS1 OF14)	3B31	71	.254	WorN	
		Crowley, Wm. Michael (1B1)	OF23	24	.265	BosN81	ClevN
5	2	Jones, Daniel Albion	P	7	.192	xDetN	C
		*Knight, Alonzo P. (Lon) MGR.	OF97	97	.237	DetN	
		Mason, Chas. E. MGR.	OF	1	.500	B	
30	14	Mathews, Robert T. (OF3)	P44	44	.173	BosN	
		Moynahan, Michael	SS	93	.283	DetN81	
		O'Brien, John K. (1B1 SS1 3B18 OF19)	C56	93	.281	B	
		#Rowan, W. Edward	C49	49	.227	BosN	
0	0	xStovey, Harry Duffield	1B	92	.318	WorN	
		Stricker, John A. (Cub) (C3 OF1)	2B89	89	.254	B	
		Hubbard, Allen (SS1)	C1	2	.286	A	C

*Knight also played 3 games at 2B and 3 games at 3B.
#Rowan also played 2 games at 2B, 1 game at 3B and 5 games in the OF.
xStovey also pitched 1 game, caught 1 game and played 2 games in the OF.

WON 61 | LOST 46 | TG 107 — AMERICAN ASSOCIATION 1884. — FINISHED 7th. PCT. .570

ATHLETICS

CHAS. E. MASON — WM. J. SHARSIG

WON	LOST	NAME	POS.	G.	BA	FROM	TO
11	11	Atkisson, Albert W.	P	22	.202	A	ChiUA
		Birchall, A Judson	OF	53	.262	B	C
		Blakiston, Robert J. (1B1 2B1 SS1 3B2)	CF28	33	+.266	B	Indpls
0	2	Coleman, John Francis (Jack) (P3)	OF26	30	.196	xPhilN	
		Corey, Frederick Harrison	3B	106	.273	B	
		Foster, Elmer E. (OF1)	C3	3	.167	A	PhilUA
2	1	Hilsey, Chas. (OF3)	P3	6	.261	PhilN	C
		Houck, Stephen Arnold Douglas (Sadie)	SS	110	.302	DetN	
0	1	Knight, Alonzo P. (Lon) (P1)	OF109	110	.275	B	
		Larkin, Henry E.	OF86	87	.296	A	
		Mansell, Michael R.	OF	20	+.194	xPitt	Rich
30	18	Mathews, Robert T.	P	49	.177	B	
		Milligan, John (Jack)	C65	66	.295	A	
		Moynahan, Michael	SS	1	.000	B	ClevN
		O'Brien, John K. (OF5)	C32	38	.300	B	
		Ringo, Frank C.	C	2	.000	xPhilN	
		Rowan, W. Edward	C	4	.400	B	C
		Siffel, Frank	C	7	.143	A	
0	1	Smith, John Francis	P	1	+.250	xBaltUA	Pitt
		Stovey, Harry Duffield	1B	106	.404	B	
		Stricker, John A. (Cub)	2B	109	.236	B	
18	12	Taylor, Wm. Henry	P	32	.271	xStLUA	

WON 55 | LOST 57 | TG 112 — AMERICAN ASSOCIATION. 1885. — FINISHED 4th. PCT. .491

ATHLETICS

ALONZO P. KNIGHT   CHAS. E. MASON   WM. J. SHARSIG

WON	LOST	NAME	POS.	G.	BA	FROM	TO
1	3	Coleman, John Francis (Jack) (P4)	OF93	97	.309	B	
1	1	Conway, James P. (OF1)	P2	2	.167	Bkn	
1	0	Corey, Frederick Harrison (P1)	3B95	95	.252	B	C
3	7	Cushman, Edgar Leander	P	10	+.194	MilUA	Met
0	3	Emslie, Robert Daniel (OF1)	P4	4	+.083	xBalt	C
		Fusselbach, Edward L.	C	5	.316	BaltUA	
		Houck, Stephen Arnold Douglas (Sadie)	SS	92	.259	B	
0	2	Hughes, Wm. W. (OF2)	P2	4	.188	WashUA	C
		Knight, Alonzo P. (Lon) MGR.	OF	28	.186	B	ProvN
7	6	Knouff, Edward (OF1)	P14	14	.204	A	
		Larkin, Henry E.	OF	108	.338	B	
7	8	Lovett, Thomas Joseph	P	16	.250	A	
30	17	Mathews, Robert T.	P	48	.162	B	
		Milligan, John (Jack)	C	7	.286	B	
		O'Brien, John K.	C41	61	.261	B	
		Powell, Martin J.	1B	18	.164	CinUA	C
0	1	Purcell, Wm. Aloysius (P1)	OF66	66	.298	PhilN	BosN
		Quinton, Marshall J.	C	7	.207	Rich	C
		Schaffer, George (Orator)	OF	2	.222	xStLN	
		Siffel, Frank (OF1)	C2	3	.100	B	C
0	1	Smith, John Francis	P	1	+.000	xBkn	
		Stovey, Harry Duffield (OF31)	1B81	112	.342	B	
		Stricker, John A. (Cub)	2B	106	.211	B	
		Strief, George Andrew (2B8 SS9)	3B14	44	.270	ClevN	C
1	5	Taylor, Wm. Henry	P	6	.182	B	
4	3	Vinton, Wm. M. (OF1)	P7	7	.192	xPhilN	C

WON 63   AMERICAN ASSOCIATION.   FINISHED 6th.
LOST 73
TG 136   1886.   PCT. .467

ATHLETICS

LEWIS SIMMONS   CHAS. E. MASON   WM. J. SHARSIG

WON	LOST	NAME	POS.	G.	BA	FROM	TO
25	17	Atkisson, Albert W.	P	43	.126	BaltUA84	
0	2	Aydelotte, Jacob S.	P	2	.000	IndpIsAA84	C
		Bierbauer, Louis W.	2B	137	.244	A	
		Bradley, George Washington	SS	13	.149	CinUA84	
0	1	Brown, James W. H.	P	1	.000	StPUA84	C
0	1	Clark, Edward C.	P	1	.000	A	
1	1	Coleman, John Francis (Jack) (P2)	OF120	122	+.252	B	Pitt
		Gleason, John Day	3B	76	.195	StLN	C
0	1	Gessner, Chas. J.	P	1	.250	A	C
		Greer, Edward C.	OF	72	+.197	xBalt	
9	13	Hart, Wm. Franklin	P	23	.145	A	
0	1	Hyndman, James Wm.	P	1	.000	A	C
		Irwin, John	SS	2	.333	BosUA84	
		Kelly, Chas. H.	SS	1	.000	PhilN83	C
5	15	Kennedy, Theodore A.	P	22	+.286	ChiN	Lvlle
		Larkin, Henry E.	OF	139	.327	B	
		Lyons, Dennis Patrick Aloysius	3B	32	.226	ProvN	
13	9	Mathews, Robert T.	P	23	.264	B	
10	9	Miller, Joseph H. (Cyclone)	P	21	.156	PhilN84	C
		Milligan, John (Jack) (1B29)	C41	76	.249	B	
		McGarr, James B. (Chippy)	SS	72	.271	ChiUA84	
		O'Brien, John K. (1B24 3B28)	C35	105	.257	B	
		Quest, Joseph L.	SS	41	.200	DetN	C
		Robinson, Wilbert (1B22)	C62	87	.205	A	
		Schaffer, George (Orator)	OF	21	.344	B	
0	1	Smith, Reginald	P	1	.000	A	C
		Stovey, Harry Duffield (OF46)	1B62	123	.317	B	
0	2	Weaver, Samuel H.	P	2	.143	PhilUA84	C

WON 64   AMERICAN ASSOCIATION.   FINISHED 5th.
LOST 69
TG 133   1887.   PCT. .481

ATHLETICS.

FRANK CARTER BANCROFT   CHAS. E. MASON   WM. J. SHARSIG

WON	LOST	NAME	POS.	G.	BA	FROM	TO
5	9	Atkisson, Albert W.	P	16	.281	B	C
		Bierbauer, Louis W.	2B	126	.302	B	
0	0	Casey, Wm. B.	P	1	.000	A	C
1	0	Chapman, Frederick James	P	1	.000	A	C
		Flanagan, Edward F.	1B	19	.277	A	
		Greer, Edward C.	OF	3	+.182	B	Bkn
1	2	Hart, Wm. Franklin	P	3	.077	B	
		Larkin Henry E. (1B20)	OF105	125	.374	B	
		Lyons, Dennis Patrick Aloysius	3B	137	.469	B	
		Mann, Frederick I.	OF	55	+.310	xClev	C
3	5	Mathews Robert T.	P	8	.276	B	C
		Milligan, John (Jack) (C47)	1B48	96	.344	B	
		McGarr, James. B. (Chippy)	SS	127	.331	B	
		Poorman, Thomas Iverson	OF	135	.316	BosN	
		Robinson, Wilbert	C	68	.286	B	
		Roseman, James J.	OF	21	+.325	Mets	Mets
		Roxburgh, James A.	C	2	.125	Balt84	C
25	24	Seward, Edward Wm.	P	75	.229	ProvN85	
		Stovey, Harry Duffield (1B46)	OF77	124	.402	B	
1	0	Taylor, Wm. Henry	P	1	.250	Balt	C
1	2	Titcomb, Ledell	P	3	.286	PhilN	NYN
		Townsend, George H.	C	34	.217	A	
27	27	Weyhing, August (Gus)	P	55	.229	A	

WON 81
LOST 52
TG 133

AMERICAN ASSOCIATION. 1888.

FINISHED 3rd. PCT. .609

ATHLETICS

WM. J. SHARSIG

WON	LOST	NAME	POS.	G.	BA	FROM	TO
		Bierbauer, Louis W.	2B122	134	.279	B	
1	4	Blair, Wm. Ellisworth	P	5	.308	A	C
		Farmer, Wm.	C	3	.167	xPittN	C
		Fennelly, Francis John	SS	15	+.239	xCin	
0	1	Gamble, Robert	P	1	.333	A	C
		Gibson, Leighton B.	C	1	.000	A	C
		Gleason, Wm. G.	SS121	123	.224	StL	
		Gunning, Thomas Francis	C	23	.217	PhilN	
		Larkin, Henry E.	1B121	135	.283	B	
		Lyons, Dennis Patrick Aloysius	3B	111	.325	B	
15	10	Mattimore, Michael J.	P26	41	.268	NYN	
		Poorman, Thomas Iverson	OF	85	.227	B	C
		Purcell, Wm. Aloysius (Blondy) (3B1)	OF17	18	+.167	xBalt	
		Robinson, Wilbert	C66	67	.268	B	
34	19	Seward, Edward Wm.	P57	64	.154	B	
2	0	Smith, John Francis	P	3	+.333	xBalt	
		Stovey, Harry Duffield	OF117	130	.318	B	
		Sullivan, Michael J. (Mike) (OF7)	3B21	28	.277	A	C
		Townsend, George H.	C	43	.150	B	
		Welch, Curtis Benton	OF135	136	.291	StL	
29	18	Weyhing, August	P48	49	.219	B	
		Zinn, Frank	C	2	.000	A	C

WON 75
LOST 58
TG 133

AMERICAN ASSOCIATION 1889.

FINISHED 3rd. PCT. .564

ATHLETICS

WM. J. SHARSIG

WON	LOST	NAME	POS.	G.	BA	FROM	TO
1	4	Bausewine, George	P	7	.045	A	C
		Bierbauer, Louis W.	2B	130	.313	B	
		Brennan, James A.	C	31	.214	K.C.	
3	2	Coleman, John Francis (Jack)	P	6	.048	PittN	
		Collins, Wm. J.	C	1	.200	Met87	
		Cross, LaFayette Napoleon (Lave)	C	55	.226	Lvlle	
		Fennelly, Francis John	SS	137	.259	B	
		Graham, Barney	3B	4	.167	A	C
		Gunning, Thomas Francis	C	5	.375	B	C
2	0	Knouff, Edward	P	3	.250	Clev	C
		Larkin, Henry E.	1B132	133	.324	B	
		Lyons, Dennis Patrick Aloysius	3B	131	.327	B	
2	2	Mattimore, Michael J. (P4)	OF19	23	+.257	B	K.C.
15	11	McMahon, John Joseph	P29	30	.143	A	
		Purcell, Wm. Aloysius (Blondy)	OF	130	.306	B	
		Robinson, Wilbert	C	69	.242	B	
21	16	Seward, Edward Wm.	P38	45	.219	B	
1	3	Smith, John Francis	P	4	.231	B	
		Stovey, Harry Duffield	OF	138	.330	B	
		Welch, Curtis Benton	OF	125	.273	B	
30	20	Weyhing, August (Gus)	P	53	.135	B	

WON 54
LOST 78
TG 132

AMERICAN ASSOCIATION 1890.

FINISHED 8th. PCT. .409

ATHLETICS

WM. J. SHARSIG

WON	LOST	NAME	POS.	G.	BA	FROM	TO
		Baldwin, Clarence Geoghan	C	24	.239	xCinN	C
		Campbell, Samuel	2B	2	.000	A	C
		Cantz, Bartholomew L.	C	5	.096	Balt	C
		Carmen, George W.	SS	25	.151	A	C
		Collins, Wm. J.	C	1	.000	B	
		Conroy, Benjamin Edward (2B16)	SS100	116	.175	A	C
		Crawford, George	OF	5	.111	A	C
0	1	Daly, Joseph John	P	20	.180	A	
7	8	Esper, Chas. H.	P	19	.285	A	PittN
		Esterday, Henry	SS	19	+.154	xCol	Lvlle
		Fitzgerald, Dennis S.	SS	2	.429	A	C
7	14	Green, Edward M.	P	39	.123	A	C
		Hasney, Peter James	OF	2	.125	A	C
1	0	Helmbold, Horace	P	1	.000	A	C
1	5	Hughes, Michael F.	P	6	.187	xBknN	C
		Kappel, Joseph	SS	57	.240	PhilN84	C
		Knox, Andrew Jackson	1B	21	.250	A	C
0	0	Luckey, Howard J.	P	1	.000	A	C
		Lyons, Dennis Patrick Aloysius	3B	88	.351	B	
		Macey,	C	1	.000	A	C
		Myers, Henry L. (3B2)	1B3	5	.167	A	C
		McBride, John F.	OF	1	.000	A	C
		McCaffrey, Chas. P.	C	1	.250	Col	C
29	17	McMahon, John Joseph	P	51	+.230	B	Balt
		O'Brien, John K.	1B	110	.270	Balt88	C
0	8	O'Neil, Edward J. (3B1 OF3)	P8	11	+.176	xTol	C
		Pabst, Edward D. A.	OF	8	+.345	A	StL
1	0	Price, Wm.	P	1	.333	A	C
		Purcell, Wm. Aloysius (Blondy)	OF	106	.287	B	C
		Riddle, John H. (OF1)	C	24	.115	WashN	C
		Robinson, Wilbert	C	83	+.236	B	Balt
		Sauters, Al	3B	14	.098	A	C
		Schaffer, George (Orator)	OF	106	.286	Ath86	C
		Schaffer, Taylor	2B	70	.178	A	C
6	13	Seward, Edward Wm.	P	27	.116	B	

WON	LOST	NAME	POS.	G.	BA	FROM	TO
		Snyder, Chas. (C4)	OF5	9	.419	A	C
		Stafford, Robert Lee	OF	1	.000	A	C
0	7	Stecher, Chas.	P	10	.233	A	C
0	1	Stine, Harry C.	P	1	.000	A	C
0	1	Sterling, John A.	P	1	.000	A	C
		Sweeney, Peter Jay	2B	14	+.157	xLvlle	C
		Sweigert,	OF	1	.000	A	C
		Welch, Curtis Benton	OF	106	+.283	B	Balt
2	3	Whitney, James E. (Grasshopper)	P	7	.318	IndplsN	C

WON 73
LOST 66
TG 139

AMERICAN ASSOCIATION. FINISHED 5th.

1891. PCT. .525

ATHLETICS

WM. J. SHARSIG GEORGE A. WOOD WM. S. BARNIE

WON	LOST	NAME	POS.	G.	BA	FROM	TO
		Beecher, Edward C.	OF	16	+.205	xWash	C
2	5	Bowman, Sumner Sallade (OF6)	P8	14	.215	PittN	C
5	7	Calihan, Wm. T.	P	16	.179	Roch	C
21	22	Chamberlain, Elton P.	P51	54	.195	Col	
		Clymer, Wm. Johnston	SS	3	.000	A	C
		Corcoran, Thomas W.	SS	132	.252	PittPL	
		Corkhill, John Stewart (Pop)	OF	83	.211	BknN	CinN
		Cross, LaFayette Napoleon (3B22 OF41) (Lave)	C44	109	.302	PhilPL	
		Friel, Patrick Henry	OF	2.	.286	Syr	C
		Hallman, Wm. White (Billy)	2B	140	.288	PhilPL	
		Larkin, Henry E. (OF20)	1B113	133	.277	ClevPL	
		Matthews, Robert	OF	1	.333	A	C
2	3	Meakim, George Clinton	P	6	.176	Lvlle	
		Milligan, John (Jack) (1B30)	C85	117	.300	PhilPL	
		Mulvey, Joseph H.	3B	112	.247	PhilPL	
		McGeachy, John Chas.	OF	46	+.217	BknPL	Bos
		McKeough, David J.	C	15	.278	Roch	C
		McTamany, James J.	OF	53	+.209	xCol	C
12	7	Sanders, Alexander Benjamin (OF20)	P21	41	.253	PhilPL	
0	2	Sullivan, Michael Joseph	P	2	+.000	ChiN	NYN
31	20	Weyhing, August (Gus)	P53	54	.117	BknPL	
		Wood, George A. MGR.	OF121	131	.302	PhilPL	

WON 19
LOST 54
TG 73

AMERICAN ASSOCIATION FINISHED 6th (LAST)

1882. PCT. .260

BALTIMORE.

HENRY C. MYERS

WON	LOST	NAME	POS.	G.	BA	FROM	TO
		Booth, Amos Smith	3B	1	+.000	CinN80	Lvlle
0	0	Brown, Thomas T. (P2)	OF46	46	.293	A	
		Burt, Frank J.	OF	10	.108	A	C
		Cline, John (2B1 SS7 3B1)	OF40	45	.222	A	
		East, Harry H.	3B	1	.000	A	C
		Evers, Thomas Francis	2B	1	.000	A	
4	9	Geiss, Emil M. (OF3)	P13	13	.159	A	
		Householder, Chas. W. (C2)	1B72	73	.244	A	
		Jacoby, Harry (OF9)	3B19	31	.213	A	
		Jones, (OF2)	C2	4	.067	A	
11	28	Landis, Samuel H. (OF15)	P43	51	+.160	xAth	C
2	1	Leary, John J. (OF1)	P3	4	+.167	xPitt	
0	2	Myers, Henry C. MGR. (P2)	SS67	69	.223	ProvN	
1	13	Nicholas, Frederick C. (Tricky) (OF13)	P14	27	.154	WorN80	C
		Pearce, Grayson S. (SS1 OF3)	2B39	42	+.210	xLvlle	
0	0	Rust, (OF1)	P1	1	.333	A	C
		Scharf, Edward T. (3B1)	OF9	10	.243	A	
		Shetzline, John Henry (2B20 SS1 OF1)	3B50	76	.226	A	C
		Smiley, Wm. B. (SS1)	2B16	16	+.113	xStL	C
		Smith, Chas. Marvin (Pap)	OF	1	+.000	xAth	Lvlle
		Waitt, Chas. C.	OF	72	.154	ChiN77	
		Whiting, Edward C. (1B3 OF2)	C72	73	.267	A	
1	1	Wise, Wm. E. (OF2)	P3	5	.150	A	

WON 28
LOST 68
TG 96

AMERICAN ASSOCIATION. FINISHED 8th (LAST)

1883. PCT. .292

BALTIMORE.

WM. S. BARNIE

WON	LOST	NAME	POS.	G.	BA	FROM	TO
		Allison, Douglass L. (Dona)	C	1	.500	ProvN79	C
		Baker, George F. (C2)	SS4	6	.227	A	
		Baker, Philip (SS1 OF11)	C19	27	.280	A	
		Barnie, Wm. S. MGR. (SS1 OF6)	C17	17	.200	A	
		Broughton, Cecil Calvert (OF1)	C8	9	.188	xClevN	
		Clinton, James L. (2B2)	OF94	94	.305	WorN	
1	1	Devine, Walter James (OF1)	P2	2	.222	A	
		Eggler, David Daniel	OF	53	.194	BuffN79	BuffN
9	16	Emslie, Robert Daniel (OF3)	P28	28	.153	A	
		Farrell, W.	SS	2	.000	A	C
6	14	Fox, John Joseph (1B1 OF4)	P23	23	.168	BosN81	

WON	LOST	NAME	POS.	G.	BA	FROM	TO
0	3	Gallagher, Wm. John (P6 SS4)	OF8	16	.159	A	PhilN
1	0	Gardner, Franklin W. (Gid) (P1 2B5 3B3)	OF35	42	.290	ClevN80	
10	30	Henderson, James Harding (SS1 3B1 OF9) (Hardie)	P45	50	.151	xPhilN	
		Ingraham, Chas.	C	1	.250	A	C
		Kelly, John Francis (OF13)	C36	46	.224	ClevN	PhilN
		Leary, John J.	2B	3	+.182	xLvlle	
		Loughlin, Wm. H.	OF	1	.400	A	C
		Manning, Timothy E.	2B	35	.233	ProvN	
		McCormick, John	3B	98	.261	A	
1	4	Neagle, John Henry (OF5)	P6	9	+.270	xPhilN	Pitt
		O'Brien, Thomas H. (OF1)	2B33	33	.294	WorN	
		Oldfield, David	C	1	.000	A	
		Reid, Wm. A. (SS1)	2B16	16	.285	A	
0	0	Rowe, David E. (P1 1B3 SS6)	OF54	59	.297	ClevN	
		Say, Lewis I.	SS	84	.260	Ath	
		Scharf, Edward T.	SS	3	.143	B	C
		Stearns, Daniel Eckford (OF1)	1B94	94	.248	Cin	
		Sweeney, John J. (C3 OF10)	2B12	25	.232	A	

WON 63
LOST 43
TG 106

AMERICAN ASSOCIATION — FINISHED 6th.

1884. — PCT. .594

BALTIMORE.

WM. S. BARNIE

WON	LOST	NAME	POS.	G.	BA	FROM	TO
		Ake, John Leckie (SS1 OF4)	3B9	13	.208	A	C
		Burns, Patrick	1B	6	.154	A	BalUA
0	0	Burns, Thomas P. (P2 2B10 3B2)	OF23	36	.304	xWilUA	
		Casey, Dennis Patrick	OF	38	.274	xWilUA	
		Clinton, James L.	OF104	105	.281	B	
		Dickerson, Lewis Pessano	OF	13	+.232	xStLUA	Lvlle
32	18	Emslie, Robert Daniel	P50	51	.199	B	
		Gardner, Franklin W. (Gid)	OF38	41	.203	B	ChiUA
3	1	Goldsmith, Frederick Ernest (1B1)	P4	4	.167	xChiN	C
27	22	Henderson, James Harding (Hardie)	P51	54	.222	B	
		Macullar, James F.	SS	108	.193	Cin	
		Manning, Timothy E.	2B	91	.207	B	
1	2	McLaughlin, James C. (OF3)	P3	5	.227	xKeyUA	C
		Pratt, Thomas J.	OF	1	.250	xWashUA	C
		Roxburgh, James A.	C	2	.333	A	
		Sommer, Joseph John (OF6)	3B98	107	.272	Cin	
		Stearns, Daniel Eckford	1B100	101	.241	B	
		Traffley, Wm. F. (OF6)	C47	54	.186	Cin	
		Trott, Samuel W.	C63	72	.254	DetN	
		York, Thomas J.	OF	84	.228	ClevN	

WON 41
LOST 68
TG 109

AMERICAN ASSOCIATION. — FINISHED 8th (LAST)

1885. — PCT. .376

BALTIMORE

WM. S. BARNIE

WON	LOST	NAME	POS.	G.	BA	FROM	TO
0	4	Brown, Joseph E.	P4	5	.158	ChiN	C
7	4	Burns, Thomas P. (P11 2B6 SS10)	OF43	76	.229	B	
		Casey, Dennis Patrick	OF	64	.282	B	
0	1	Derby, Eugene A. (P1 OF1)	C9	10	.129	A	C
2	10	Emslie, Robert Daniel	P	13	+.235	B	Ath
		Evans, Jacob	OF	20	.205	ClevN	C
		Field, James	1B	38	+.213	xPitt	
2	1	Foreman, Francis Isaiah (OF1)	P3	3	.286	KCUA	
0	1	Gardner, Franklin W. (Gid) (P1)	2B44	44	.219	BaltUA	
		Greer, Edward C. (C10)	OF45	55	.199	A	
26	35	Henderson, James Harding (Hardie)	P	61	.228	B	
2	6	Henry, John Michael (OF1)	P9	10	.273	ClevN	
		Jacoby, Harry	2B	11	.143	Balt82	C
		Levis, Chas. T.	1B	1	.333	Indpls	C
		Macullar, James F.	SS	100	.202	B	
		Manning, Timothy E.	2B	43	.201	B	ProvN
		Mappes, George Richard	2B	6	.211	A	
2	4	Mountjoy, Wm. R. (OF1)	P6	7	+.063	xCin	C
		Muldoon, Michael	3B	103	.250	ClevN	
		Nava, Vincent P.	C	8	.148	ProvN	
		O'Brien, Thomas H. (2B2)	1B6	8	.182	BosUA	
		Powers, Philip J. (OF1)	C8	9	+.121	xCin	C
		Sommer, Joseph John	OF	110	.250	B	
		Stearns, Daniel Eckford	1B	67	.186	B	BuffN
		Tener, John Kinley	OF	1	.000	A	
		Traffley, Wm. F.	C	70	.156	B	
		Trott, Samuel W.	C	20	.289	B	
		Visner, Joseph P.	OF	4	.214	A	
		Walker, Walter S.	OF	3	.000	DetN	C
0	2	Wetzel, George Wm.	P	2	.000	A	C
		York, Thomas J.	OF	22	.271	B	C

WON 48
LOST 83
TG 131

AMERICAN ASSOCIATION. — FINISHED 8th (LAST)

1886. — PCT. .366

BALTIMORE

WM. S. BARNIE

WON	LOST	NAME	POS.	G.	BA	FROM	TO
		Bligh, Edwin Forrest	C	3	.000	A	
		Clinton, James Lawrence	OF	23	.183	Cin	C

WON	LOST	NAME	POS.	G.	BA	FROM	TO
2	7	Conway, Richard Butler (Dick)	P	9	.206	A	
		Conway, Wm. F.	C	7	.142	PhilN84	C
		Davis, James J.	3B	59	.185	KCUA84	
		Dolan, Thomas J.	C	37	.153	xStLN	
		Farrell, Joseph F.	3B48	72	.212	DetN84	C
		Fulmer, Christopher	C	79	.251	WashUA84	
		Greer, Edward C.	OF8	10	+.139	B	Ath
		Hellman, Anthony J.	C	1	.000	A	C
3	16	Henderson, James Harding (Hardie)	P	19	+.250	B	Bkn
		Hoover, Wm. J. (Buster)	OF	40	.213	PhilN84	
		Houck, Stephen Arnold Douglas (Sadie)	SS	61	.203	Ath	WashN
0	1	Houseman, Frank	P	1	.250	A	C
29	34	Kilroy, Matthew Aloysius	P	69	.178	A	
0	1	Knouff, Edward	P	1	.000	Ath	
		Macullar, James F.	SS	76	.227	B	C
		Manning, John E.	OF	137	.227	PhilN	C
		Muldoon, Michael (3B43)	2B58	101	.205	B	C
11	12	McGinnis, George W.	P	26	+.186	xStL	
		Nava, Vincent P. (SS1)	C1	2	.200	B	C
		O'Connell, Patrick H.	OF	42	.186	A	
2	5	Powell, Chas. Abner (OF4)	P7	10	+.147	WashUA84	Cin
		Purcell, Wm. Aloysius (Blondy)	OF	27	.224	BosN	
		Scott, Milton Parker	1B	137	.192	Pitt	C
		Sommer, Joseph John (2B31)	OF94	139	.215	B	
		Sowders, Leonard	OF	23	.267	A	C
1	6	Taylor, Wm. Henry (OF1)	P7	10	.333	Ath	
		Traffley, Wm. F.	C	25	.224	B	C
0	1	Zay,	P	1	.000	A	C

WON 77
LOST 58
TG 135

AMERICAN ASSOCIATION. FINISHED 3rd.

1887. PCT. .570

BALTIMORE.

WM. S. BARNIE

WON	LOST	NAME	POS.	G.	BA	FROM	TO
		Burns, Thomas P. (3B42)	SS98	140	.401	Balt85	
		Daniels, Lawrence Long	C	47	.287	A	
		Davis, James J. (SS43)	3B87	130	.345	B	
		Fulmer, Christopher	C	56	.368	B	
0	1	Gardner, Frederick	P	4	.333	A	C
		Greenwood, Wm. F.	2B	119	.326	Bkn84	
		Griffin, Michael Joseph	OF	136	.368	A	
		Hayes, John J.	C	8	.143	WashN	
0	1	Keating, Edward	P	1	.250	A	C
46	20	Kilroy, Matthew Aloysius	P	73	.323	B	
0	6	Knouff, Edward	P	8	+.268	B	StL
		Purcell, Wm. Aloysius (Blondy)	OF	140	.305	B	
2	1	Shreve, Louis Leonard (Ledell)	P	6	.200	A	IndplsN
29	29	Smith, John Francis	P	62	.327	DetN	
		Sommer, Joseph John	OF	131	.355	B	
		Trott, Samuel W.	C	85	.302	Balt85	
		Tucker, Thomas Joseph	1B	136	.315	A	

WON 57
LOST 80
TG 137

AMERICAN ASSOCIATION. FINISHED 5th.

1888. PCT. .416

BALTIMORE.

WM. S. BARNIE

WON	LOST	NAME	POS.	G.	BA	FROM	TO
		Bradley, George Washington	SS	1	.000	Ath86	C
		Burns, Thomas P. (SS20)	OF57	77	+.308	B	Bkn
		Cantz, Bartholomew, L.	C33	37	.165	A	
22	29	Cunningham, Ellsworth Elmer	P	51	.188	Bkn	
		Farrell, John A. (2B47)	SS56	103	.197	WashN	
		Fulmer, Christopher	C46	51	.179	B	
		Goldsby, Walton Hugh	OF42	44	.227	WashN86	C
		Greenwood, Wm. F. (SS26)	2B87	113	.202	B	
		Griffin, Michael Joseph	OF	137	.261	B	
0	1	Harkins, John Joseph	P	1	.000	Bkn	C
16	21	Kilroy, Matthew Aloysius	P42	43	.166	B	
0	1	Kilroy, Michael Joseph	P	1	.000	A	
		O'Brien, John K.	C38	57	.224	Bkn	
		Peltz, John	OF	1	.250	Indpls84	
		Purcell, Wm. Aloysius (Blondy)	OF	101	+.233	B	Ath
2	4	Shaw, Samuel E.	P	6	.150	A	
		Shindle, Wm.	3B	135	.216	DetN	
15	20	Smith, John Francis	P	35	+.259	B	Ath
		Sommer, Joseph John (OF30)	SS34	79	.215	B	
		Trott, Samuel W.	C27	31	.275	B	
		Tucker, Thomas Joseph	1B129	136	.291	B	
1	3	Walker, George A.	P	4	.077	A	C
1	1	Whitaker, Wm. H.	P	2	.000	A	

WON 70
LOST 65
TG 135

AMERICAN ASSOCIATION FINISHED 5th.

1889. PCT. .519

BALTIMORE.

WM. S. BARNIE

WON	LOST	NAME	POS.	G.	BA	FROM	TO
		Cantz, Bartholomew L.	C19	21	.158	B	
15	19	Cunningham, Ellsworth Elmer	P37	40	.214	B	
		Dowie, Joseph E.	OF	20	.240	A	C
		Farrell, John A.	SS	42	.204	B	C
25	21	Foreman, Francis Isaiah	P51	54	.140	Balt85	
		Fulmer, Christopher	C	16	.278	B	C
1	0	Goetz, George Burt	P	1	.000	A	C
		Griffin, Michael Joseph (SS24)	OF109	137	.280	B	

WON	LOST	NAME	POS.	G.	BA	FROM	TO
		Holland, Willard A.	SS39	40	.182	A	C
		Hornung, Michael Joseph	OF134	135	.227	BosN	
		Kerins, John Nelson (C4 SS1 OF2)	1B9	16	+.283	xLvlle	
28	25	Kilroy, Matthew Aloysius	P59	65	.290	B	
		Mack, Joseph (Reddy)	2B135	136	.236	Lvlle	
		Miller, Chas. Bradley (Dusty)	OF	11	.125	A	
		McGarr, James B. (Chippy)	SS	3	+.143	xK.C.	
		Quinn, Thomas G.	C	54	.174	Pitt86	
		Ray, Irving Burton	SS21	27	.330	xBosN	
		Shindle, Wm.	3B	138	.315	B	
		Sommer, Joseph John	OF100	106	.224	B	
		Tate, Edward Christopher	C62	72	.178	BosN	
		Tucker, Thomas Joseph	1B123	134	.375	B	
1	0	Whitaker, Wm. H.	P	1	.250	B	C
		Wood, George A.	OF	3	.200	xPhilN	

WON 15
LOST 19
TG 34

AMERICAN ASSOCIATION — FINISHED 6th.

1890. — PCT. .441

BALTIMORE

WM. S. BARNIE

WON	LOST	NAME	POS.	G.	BA	FROM	TO
1	1	Baker, Norman Leslie	P	2	.000	Lvlle85	C
4	10	German, Lester S.	P	16	.113	A	
		Gilbert, Peter	3B	29	.262	A	
		Hill, Belden L.	3B	9	.133	A	C
		Johnson, Wm. T.	OF	24	.354	IndplsN87	
		Long, Daniel W.	OF	21	.177	Lvlle88	C
		Mack, Joseph (Reddy)	2B	26	.272	B	C
1	3	Morrison, Michael	P	4	+.111	xSyr	C
		McGuckin, Joseph W.	OF	10	.056	A	C
7	3	McMahon, John Joseph	P	12	+.132	xAth	
2	2	O'Rourke, Michael J.	P	9	.148	A	C
		Power, Thomas E.	1B	38	.211	A	C
		Ray, Irving Burton	SS	38	.347	B	
		Robinson, Wilbert (1B3)	C11	14	+.271	xAth	
		Sommer, Joseph John	OF	38	.239	xClevN	C
		Tate, Edward Christopher	C	20	.219	B	C
		Townsend, George H.	C	19	.214	Ath88	
		Welch, Curtis Benton (1B2)	OF17	19	+.122	xAth	

WON 71
LOST 64
TG 135

AMERICAN ASSOCIATION — FINISHED 4th.

1891. — PCT. .526

BALTIMORE.

WM. S. BARNIE — GEORGE E. VAN HALTREN

WON	LOST	NAME	POS.	G.	BA	FROM	TO
4	2	Bakely, Edward (Enoch)	P	13	+.211	xWash	C
11	14	Cunningham, Ellsworth Elmer	P	31	.149	BuffPL	
		Gilbert, Peter	3B	137	.229	B	
		Hardie, Lewis W.	OF	15	.232	BosN	C
8	12	Healy, John J. (Egyptian)	P	23	.141	Tol	
		Johnson, Wm. T.	OF	127	.269	B	
14	10	xMadden, Michael Joseph (Kid)	P31	36	+.257	xBos	C
		McGraw, John Joseph	SS21	31	.245	A	
34	25	McMahon, John Joseph	P	60	.201	B	
		O'Connell, John Joseph (2B2)	SS3	7	.172	A	
		Ray, Irving Burton (SS39)	OF64	103	.277	B	C
		Robinson, Wilbert	C92	93	.221	B	
		Townsend, George H.	C56	59	.178	B	C
0	1	Van Haltren, George E. (Pl SS58) MGR.	OF77	136	.316	BknPL	
		Walsh, Joseph A.	SS14	25	.189	A	C
		Welch, Curtis Benton	OF116	130	.278	B	
		Werden, Percival Wheritt (Perry)	1B	137	.292	Tol	
		Wise, Samuel Washington	2B	103	.250	BuffPL	

x - Madden also played 6 games in the outfield.

CLUB RECORD

OTHER MAJOR LEAGUES

BOSTON

YEAR	TG	WON	LOST	PCT.	FINISHED	MANAGER
UNION ASSOCIATION						
1884	109	58	51	.532	5	Timothy Hayes Murnane Thomas Furniss Jacob Chas. Morse
PLAYER'S LEAGUE						
1890	129	81	48	.628	1	Michael Joseph Kelly
AMERICAN ASSOCIATION						
1891	135	93	42	.689	1	Arthur Albert Irwin

WON 93
LOST 42
TG 135

AMERICAN ASSOCIATION

1891

FINISHED 1st.

PCT. .689

BOSTON

ARTHUR ALBERT IRWIN

WON	LOST	NAME	POS.	GA.	BA	FROM	TO
		Brouthers, Dennis (Dan)	1B	130	.352	BosPL	
		Brown, Thomas T.	OF	137	.323	BosPL	
27	9	Buffinton, Chas. G.	P46	56	.202	PhilPL	
		Cotter, Thomas B.	C	5	.273	A	C
9	5	Daley, Wm.	P19	20	.167	BosPL	C
		Donahue, Timothy Cornelius	C	3	.000	A	
		Dowd, Thomas Jefferson	OF	4	+.167	A	Wash
		Duffy, Hugh	OF124	127	.340	ChiPL	
		Farrell, Chas. A. (Duke) (C32 OF21)	3B65	122	.304	ChiPL	
2	1	Fitzgerald, John H.	P	6	.077	A	C
		Flynn, Michael E.	C	1	.000	A	C
3	1	Griffith, Clark Calvin	P	9	+.125	xStL	
33	11	Haddock, George Silas	P52	58	.238	BuffPL	
		Irwin, Arthur Albert MGR.	SS	5	.154	BosPL	
		Irwin, John (OF3)	3B17	20	+.192	BuffPL	Lvlle
		Joyce, Wm. Michael (Scrappy)	3B64	65	.317	BknPL	
		Kelly, Michael Joseph (King)	C	3	+.200	xCin	BosN
0	2	Madden, Michael Joseph (Kid)	P	4	+.500	BosPL	Balt
		McGeachy, John Chas.	OF	41	+.250	xAth	C
		Murphy, Morgan Edward	C105	107	.218	BosPL	
19	13	O'Brien, John F. (Darby)	P	41	.227	ClevPL	C
		Quinlan, Lawrence A.	C	2	.000	A	C
		Radford, Paul Revere	SS130	133	.257	ClevPL	
		Richardson, Arthur Harding	OF60	74	.264	BosPL	
		Stricker, John A. (Cub)	2B	139	.225	ClevPL	

CLUB RECORD

OTHER MAJOR LEAGUES

BROOKLYN

YEAR	TG	WON	LOST	PCT.	FINISHED	MANAGER
AMERICAN ASSOCIATION						
1884	104	40	64	.385	9	George J. Taylor
1885	112	53	59	.473	x 5(Lvlle)	Joseph J. Doyle Chas. M. Hackett Chas. H. Byrne
1886	137	76	61	.555	3	Chas. H. Byrne
1887	134	60	74	.448	6	Chas. H. Byrne
1888	140	88	52	.629	2	Wm. Henry McGunnigle
1889	137	93	44	.679	1	Wm. Henry McGunnigle
1890	99	26	73	.263	DID NOT FINISH	James C. Kennedy
PLAYER'S LEAGUE						
1890	132	76	56	.576	2	John Montgomery Ward
FEDERAL LEAGUE						
1914	154	77	77	.500	5	Wm. Joseph Bradley
1915	152	70	82	.461	7	Leo Christopher Magee John Henry Ganzel

WON 40
LOST 64
TG 104

AMERICAN ASSOCIATION

1884.

FINISHED 9th.

PCT. .385

BROOKLYN

GEORGE J. TAYLOR

WON	LOST	NAME	POS.	G.	BA	FROM	TO
		Benners, Isaac B.	OF	49	.209	A	WilUA
		Cassidy, John P.	OF101	106	.263	ProvN	
3	9	Conway, James P. (SS2 OF2)	P13	14	.133	A	
		Corcoran, John H.	C	52	.215	A	C
		Dorgan, Jeremiah F.	C	4	+.308	xIndpls	
		Farrow, John Jacob	C	16	.190	A	C
		Geer, Wm. Henry Harrison	SS106	107	.226	xKeyUA	
		Greenwood, Wm. F.	2B	92	.220	Ath82	
		Hayes, John J. (OF2)	C13	15	+.220	xPitt	
		Householder, Chas. W. (C30)	1B41	76	.242	Balt82	C
		Jones, Chas. F. (3B10)	2B13	24	.188	A	
18	20	Kimber, Samuel Jackson	P	41	.137	A	
		Knowles, James (3B11)	1B30	41	+.237	xPitt	
		Remsen, John Jay	OF	81	.238	xPhilN	C
19	35	Terry, Wm. J. (Adonis) (OF7)	P55	67	.235	A	
		Walker, Oscar (1B36)	OF59	95	.268	StL82	C
		Warner, Frederick John Rodney	3B	85	.212	PhilN	C
		Wilson, George Archibald W. (OF6)	C9	24	.214	A	C

WON 53
LOST 59
TG 112

AMERICAN ASSOCIATION.

1885.

FINISHED 5th.
(TIED WITH LVLLE)
PCT. .473

BROOKLYN

JOSEPH J. DOYLE CHAS. M. HACKETT CHAS. H. BYRNE

WON	LOST	NAME	POS.	G.	BA	FROM	TO
		Bell, Frank Gustav (3B2 OF4)	C5	10	.167	A	C
		Cassidy, John P.	OF	54	.211	B	C
14	21	Harkins, John Joseph	P	43	.256	ClevN	
		Hayes, John J.	P	42	.132	B	
		Hines, Michael C	OF	2	.167	xBosN	ProvN
		Hotaling, Peter James	OF	95	.277	ClevN	
		Krieg, Wm. Frederick	C	17	.150	xChiN	
		McClellan, Wm. Henry (2B56)	3B57	113	.251	PhilN	
		McTamany, James J.	OF	35	.238	A	
		McVey, George W. (1B3)	C3	6	.143	A	C
		Oldfield, David (OF2)	C9	10	.308	Balt83	
		Peoples, James E.	C	40	+.205	xCin	
		Phillips, Wm. B.	1B	100	.293	ClevN	
		Pinckney, George Burton (3B52)	2B57	111	.288	ClevN	
33	21	Porter, Henry	P	55	.200	MilUA	

WON	LOST	NAME	POS.	G.	BA	FROM	TO
		Robinson, Chas. Henry	C	12	.143	Indpls	C
		Schenck, Wm. G.	3B	1	.000	Rich	C
		Smith, George J. (Germany)	SS	109	.256	ClevN	
0	1	Smith, John Francis	P	1	+.333	Pitt	Ath
		Swartwood, Cyrus Edward	OF	100	.242	Pitt	
6	16	Terry, Wm. J. (Adonis) (P25)	OF45	70	.162	B	

WON 76
LOST 61
TG 137

AMERICAN ASSOCIATION.

FINISHED 3rd.

1886.

PCT. .555

BROOKLYN

CHAS. H. BYRNE

WON	LOST	NAME	POS.	G.	BA	FROM	TO
		Burch, Ernest W.	OF	114	.253	ClevN84	
		Clark, Robert H.	C	72	.228	A	
14	16	Harkins, John Joseph	P	41	.217	B	
10	4	Henderson, James Harding (Hardie)	P	14	+.180	xBalt	
		Kennedy, Edward	OF	6	.181	Mets	C
		McCauley, James A.	C	10	.233	ChiN	C
		McClellan, Wm. Henry	2B	142	.262	B	
		McTamany, James J.	OF	113	.248	B	
		Oldfield, David	C	14	.240	B	WashN
		Peoples, James E.	C	94	.221	B	
		Phillips, Wm. B.	1B	142	.281	B	
		Pinckney, George Burton	3B	142	.260	B	
28	20	Porter, Henry	P	48	.176	B	
		Schriver, Wm. F. (Pop)	C	9	.040	A	
		Smith, George J. (Germany)	SS	117	.249	B	
		Strauss, Joseph (C2)	OF7	9	+.235	xLvlle	C
		Swartwood, Cyrus Edward	OF	123	.262	B	
18	15	Terry, Wm. J. (Adonis) (P33)	OF42	75	.250	B	
6	6	Toole, Stephen J.	P	13	.392	A	
		Weaver, Wm. B.	C	1	.000	A	

WON 60
LOST 74
TG 134

AMERICAN ASSOCIATION.

FINISHED 6th.

1887.

PCT. .448

BROOKLYN

CHAS. H. BYRNE

WON	LOST	NAME	POS.	G.	BA	FROM	TO
		Burch, Ernest W.	OF	48	.400	B	C
		Clark, Robert H.	C	47	.289	B	
0	2	Cunningham, Ellsworth Elmer	P	3	.200	A	
		Greer, Edward C.	OF	88	+.302	xAth	C
10	14	Harkins, John Joseph	P	27	.298	B	
4	9	Henderson, James Harding (Hardie)	P	14	.224	B	
		McClellan, Wm. Henry	2B	136	.350	B	
		McTamany, James J.	OF	134	.354	B	
		O'Brien, John K.	C	30	.269	Ath	
		Otterson, Wm. John	SS	30	.269	A	C
		Peoples, James E.	C	73	.283	B	
		Phillips, Wm. B.	1B	132	.322	B	
		Pinckney, George Burton	3B	138	.326	B	
16	23	Porter, Henry	P	40	.250	B	
		Roseman, James J.	OF	1	+.250	xMets	
		Smith, George J. (Germany)	SS	104	.307	B	
		Swartwood, Cyrus Edward	OF	91	.344	B	
17	16	Terry, Wm. J. (Adonis) (OF30)	P40	86	.335	B	
13	10	Toole, Stephen J.	P	26	.257	B	

WON 88
LOST 52
TG 140

AMERICAN ASSOCIATION

FINISHED 2nd.

1888.

PCT. .629

BROOKLYN

WM. HENRY McGUNNIGLE

WON	LOST	NAME	POS.	G.	BA	FROM	TO
		Burdock, John Joseph	2B	69	.125	xBosN	
		Burns, Thomas P. (2B3 OF14)	SS35	52	+.286	xBalt	
		Bushong, Albert John	C68	69	.220	StL	
29	15	Caruthers, Robert Lee (OF31)	P45	94	.230	StL	
		Clark, Robert H.	C36	45	.245	B	
		Collins, Hubert B.	2B	12	+.295	xLvlle	
		Corkhill, John Stewart (Pop)	OF	19	+.386	xCin	
12	7	Foutz, David Luther (P19 1B42)	OF78	140	.283	StL	
		Holbert, Wm. H.	C	15	.115	Mets	C
25	13	Hughes, Michael F.	P	39	.150	A	
9	9	Mays, Albert C.	P	18	.095	Mets	
		McClellan, Wm. Henry (OF16)	2B59	75	+.214	B	Clev
		O'Brien, Wm. D. (Darby)	OF	136	.275	Mets	
		Orr, David L.	1B	95	.303	Mets	
		Peoples, James E.	C26	33	.198	B	
		Pinckney, George Burton	3B	143	.260	B	
		Radford, Paul Revere	OF84	91	.224	Mets	
		Silch, Edward	OF	13	.260	A	C
		Smith, George J. (Germany)	SS	103	.214	B	
13	8	Terry, Wm. J. (Adonis)	P24	30	.254	B	

WON 93
LOST 44
TG 137

AMERICAN ASSOCIATION

FINISHED 1st.

1889.

PCT. .679

BROOKLYN

WM. HENRY McGUNNIGLE

WON	LOST	NAME	POS.	G.	BA	FROM	TO
		Burns, Thomas P.	OF114	132	.316	B	
		Bushong, Albert John	C	25	.163	B	
40	12	Caruthers, Robert Lee	P55	57	.269	B	
		Clark, Robert H.	C	53	.265	B	
		Collins, Hubert B.	2B	138	.268	B	
		Corkhill, John Stewart (Pop)	OF	138	.258	B	
4	0	Foutz, David Luther (P4)	1B134	138	.286	B	
10	6	Hughes, Michael F.	P	19	.179	B	
18	10	Lovett, Thomas Joseph	P	30	.178	Ath85	
		O'Brien, Wm. D. (Darby)	OF	136	.312	B	
		Pinckney, George Burton	3B	138	.253	B	
		Reynolds, Chas. L.	C	11	+.222	xK. C.	
		Smith, George J. (Germany)	SS120	121	.233	B	
21	16	Terry, Wm. J. (Adonis)	P40	48	.293	B	
		Visner, Joseph P. (OF27)	C53	80	.249	Balt85	

WON 26 | LOST 73 | TG x99

AMERICAN ASSOCIATION 1890. FINISHED 9th (LAST) PCT. .263

BROOKLYN

JAMES C. KENNEDY

WON	LOST	NAME	POS.	G	BA	FROM	TO
		Bowes, Frank C.	C	62	.207	A	C
		Church, Hiram Lincoln	OF	3	.125	A	C
9	15	Daily, Edward M. (P30)	OF63	93	.250	Col	NYN
		Davis, James J.	3B	37	+.284	xStL	
		Fennelly, Francis John	SS	47	.251	Ath	C
0	6	Ford, Thomas W. (SS4)	P7	10	+.034	xCol	C
		Gerhardt, Joseph John	2B	97	+.211	Met87	StL
0	2	Lynch, John H.	P	2	.600	Met87	C
6	14	Mattimore, Michael J. (OF13)	P20	33	.126	K.C.	C
3	9	Murphy, Cornelius B. (Connie)	P	15	.166	xBknPL (return)	BknPL
4	20	McCullough, Chas.	P	22	+.184	A	Syr
		Nelson, Jackson W.	SS	60	.234	NYN87	C
		O'Brien, Wm. Smith	1B	95	.277	WashN	C
		O'Connell, Patrick H.	3B	11	.237	Balt86	C
		Peltz, John	OF	99	+.234	Balt88	Syr
		Pitz, Herman	C	61	+.129	A	Syr
1	2	Powers, James T.	P	4	.167	A	C
		Siefke, Frederick Edwin	3B	16	.137	A	C
		Simon, Henry J.	OF	90	+.247	Clev87	Syr
2	4	Toole, Stephen J.	P	6	.300	KC88	C
		Toy, James Madison	C	43	.172	Clev87	C
1	1	Williams, Augustine H.	P	2	.500	A	C

x - Club disbanded Aug. 25th. Succeeded by Baltimore Aug.27th.

CLUB RECORD

OTHER MAJOR LEAGUES

CINCINNATI

YEAR	TG	WON	LOST	PCT.	FINISHED	MANAGER
AMERICAN ASSOCIATION						
1882	80	54	26	.675	1	Chas. J. Fulmer
1883	98	62	36	.633	3	Chas. N. Snyder
1884	103	68	41	.624	5	Chas. N. Snyder / Wm. Henry White
1885	112	63	49	.563	2	Oliver Perry Caylor
1886	137	65	72	.471	5	Oliver Perry Caylor
1887	135	81	54	.600	2	Gustavus Heinrich Schmelz
1888	134	80	54	.597	4	Gustavus Heinrich Schmelz
1889	139	76	63	.547	4	Gustavus Heinrich Schmelz
1890	OUT OF LEAGUE					
1891	100	43	57	.430	DID NOT FINISH	Michael Joseph Kelly
UNION ASSOCIATION						
1884	103	68	35	.660	3	Daniel O'Leary / Samuel Newhall Crane

WON 54
LOST 26
TG 80

AMERICAN ASSOCIATION — FINISHED 1st.

1882. — PCT. .675

CINCINNATI

CHAS. J. FULMER

WON	LOST	NAME	POS.	G.	BA	FROM	TO
		Carpenter, Warren Wm. (Hick)	3B	80	.354	WorN	
		Fulmer, Chas. J. MGR.	SS	79	.277	BuffN80	
		Kemmler, Rudolph (OF1)	C3	3	+.091	ClevN	Pitt
		Luff, Henry T. (OF1)	1B27	28	.223	xDetN	
		Macullar, John F.	OF	79	.282	SyrN79	
13	12	McCormick, Patrick Henry (OF3)	P25	26	.126	WorN	
		McPhee, John Alexander (Bid)	2B	78	.218	A	
		Powers, Philip J. (1B5 OF1)	C8	15	.212	ClevN	
		Snyder, Chas. N. (1B2 OF1)	C70	72	.289	BosN	
		Sommer, Joseph John	OF	80	.280	CinN80	
		Stearns, Daniel Eckford (2B2 SS1 OF12)	1B34	49	.302	DetN80	
		Thompson, John P.F.	OF	1	.200	A	
1	2	Wheeler, Harry Eugene (P3 1B12)	OF62	75	.250	CinN80	
40	12	White, Wm. Henry (1B1 OF2)	P54	54	.264	DetN	
		Tiernay, Wm. J.	1B	1	.000	A	

WON 62
LOST 36
TG 98

AMERICAN ASSOCIATION — FINISHED 3rd.

1883. — PCT. .633

CINCINNATI

CHAS. N. SNYDER

WON	LOST	NAME	POS.	G.	BA	FROM	TO
		Carpenter, Warren Wm. (Hick)	3B	94	.308	B	
		*Corkhill, John Stewart (Pop)	OF86	86	.222	A	
10	8	#Deagle, Lorenzo Burrough (Ren)	P19	19	.130	A	
		Fulmer, Chas. J.	SS	82	.247	B	
		Jones, Chas. Wesley	OF	85	.285	BosN80	
		Macullar, John F. (SS1)	OF14	14	.151	B	
0	1	Mountjoy, Wm. R.	P	1	.000	A	
9	5	McCormick, Patrick Henry	P	14	.321	B	C
		%McPhee, John Alexander (Bid)	2B94	94	.235	B	
		Powers, Philip J. (OF13)	C16	29	.234	B	
		Reilly, John Good	1B	97	.289	CinN80	
		Snyder, Chas. N. MGR. (SS2)	C58	58	.245	B	
0	0	Sommer, Joseph John (P1 3B3)	OF94	97	.281	B	
		Traffley, Wm. F. (2B1 SS1)	C29	29	.200	ChiN78	
		Weihe, John Garibaldi (Podge)	OF	1	.250	A	
43	22	White, Wm. Henry	P	65	.222	B	

*Corkhill also played 2 games at 2B and 2 games at SS.
#Deagle also played 1 game at SS.
%McPhee also played 1 game as C.

WON 68
LOST 41
TG 109

AMERICAN ASSOCIATION — FINISHED 5th.

1884. — PCT. .624

CINCINNATI

CHAS. N. SNYDER — WM. HENRY WHITE

WON	LOST	NAME	POS.	G.	BA	FROM	TO
		Berkelbach, Frank P.	OF	6	.231	A	C
		#Carpenter, Warren Wm. (Hick)	3B	109	.265	B	
1	0	Corkhill, John Stewart (Pop) (P1 1B6 SS8 3B3)	OF94	111	.276	B	
2	1	Deagle, Lorenzo Burroughs (Ren)	P	3	+.000	B	Lvlle
		Fennelly, Francis John	SS	28	+.369	xWash	
		Fulmer, Chas. J. (3B1 OF2)	SS29	30	+.177	B	StL
		Jones, Chas. Wesley	OF	113	.322	B	
		Mansell, Thomas E.	OF	65	+.244	StL	Col
		Miller, George	C	6	.250	CinN77	C
20	12	Mountjoy, Wm. R. (OF2)	P32	34	.171	B	
		McPhee, John Alexander (Bid)	2B	113	.292	B	
		Peoples, James E. (C13 1B1 3B1 OF10)	SS48	70	.180	A	
		Powers, Philip J. (1B2 OF2)	C31	35	.158	B	
		Reilly, John Good (SS1 OF3)	1B103	106	.339	B	
11	10	Shallix, August	P	23	.049	A	
		*Snyder, Chas. N. MGR.	C66	68	.284	B	
		West, Milton Douglass	OF	33	.292	A	
34	18	White, Wm. Henry MGR.	P	54	.200	B	
		Woulffe, James Joseph (3B1)	OF7	8	+.118	A	Pitt
		Parsons, John S.	OF	1	.000	A	C
		Reeder, James Edward	OF	3	.143	A	Wash UA

*Snyder also played 2 games at 1B and 1 game in the OF.
#Carpenter also played 1 game in the OF.

WON 63
LOST 49
TG 112

AMERICAN ASSOCIATION — FINISHED 2nd.

1885. — PCT. .563

CINCINNATI

OLIVER PERRY CAYLOR

WON	LOST	NAME	POS.	G.	BA	FROM	TO
0	0	*Baldwin, Clarence Geoghan	C15	26	.147	KCUA	
		Carpenter, Warren Wm. (Hick)	3B	112	.291	B	
		Clinton, James Lawrence	OF	98	.239	Balt	
1	4	Corkhill, John Stewart (Pop) (P5 1B3)	OF107	112	.291	B	
		Fennelly, Francis John	SS	112	.259	B	

WON	LOST	NAME	POS.	G.	BA	FROM	TO
		Jones, Chas. Wesley	OF	112	.327	B	
0	0	Keenan, James W. (P1 1B3 OF1)	C27	32	.282	Indpls	
10	7	Mountjoy, Wm. R.	P	17	+.167	B	Balt
1	0	McCaffrey, Harry C.	P	1	.000	StL83	C
20	13	McKeon, Lawrence J. (OF1)	P33	33	.157	Indpls	
		McPhee, John Alexander (Bid)	2B	110	.275	B	
7	4	Pechiney, George Adolphe	P	11	.146	A	
0	2	Peoples, James E. (P2 OF1)	C4	7	+.136	B	Bkn
		Powers, Philip J.	C	15	+.267	B	Balt
		Reilly, John Good (OF7)	1B	106	.308	B	
7	4	Shallix, August (OF3)	P13	13	.128	B	C
		Snyder, Chas. N. (1B1)	C38	38	.250	B	
17	15	White, Wm. Henry	P	35	.177	B	

*Baldwin also pitched 2 games, played 2 games at 2B, 1 game at 3B and 6 games in the OF.

WON 65
LOST 72
TG 137

AMERICAN ASSOCIATION — FINISHED 5th.

1886. — PCT. .471

CINCINNATI

OLIVER PERRY CAYLOR

WON	LOST	NAME	POS.	G.	BA	FROM	TO
		Baldwin, Clarence Geoghan (OF6)	C80	86	.238	B	
1	0	Bickham, Daniel Denison	P	1	.250	A	C
		Boyle, John Anthony (Jack)	C	1	.250	A	
		Carpenter, Warren Wm.(Hick)	3B	111	.221	B	
0	0	#Corkhill, John Stewart (Pop)	OF	118	.283	B	
		Fennelly, Francis John	SS	132	.258	B	
0	2	Irwin, Wm. Franklin	P	2	.000	A	C
		Jones, Chas. Wesley	OF	127	.274	B	
0	0	Keenan, James W. (1B3 OF7)	C31	43	.278	B	
		Lewis, Frederick Miller	OF	67	.325	StLN	C
		Marr, Chas. W. (Lefty)	OF	7	.269	A	
		Maskrey, Samuel Leech	OF	27	+.204	xLvlle	C
31	27	Mullane, Anthony John (Tony) (1B4 2B1 SS1 OF23)	P71	103	.228	Tol84	
2	3	Murphy, Joseph Akin	P	5	.055	A	StLN
8	9	McKeon, Lawrence J. (1B3 2B1)	P17	18	.250	B	KCN
		McPhee, John Alexander (Bid)	2B	140	.272	B	
17	21	Pechiney, George Adolphe (OF5)	P38	43	.221	B	
0	1	Powell, Chas. Abner (P4 C1 SS6)	OF12	19	+.230	xBalt	C
0	1	Reardon, James Matthew (OF1)	P1	1	.000	xStLN	C
		Reilly, John Good (OF6)	1B109	115	.270	B	
0	1	Richmond, John Lee (P3)	OF7	8	.260	ProvN83	C
4	5	Smith, Elmer Ellsworth (OF1)	P9	9	.308	A	
		*Snyder, Chas. N.	C32	52	.195	B	
1	0	Stephens, Clarence Wright	P	1	.750	A	
		Sylvester, Louis J.	OF	14	+.156	xLvlle	
		Vaughn, Harry Francis	C	1	.000	A	
1	2	White, Wm. Henry	P	3	.100	B	C

*Snyder also played 19 games at 1B and 1 game in the OF.
#Corkhill also pitched in 1 game, played 1B in 7 games, and played 3 games at SS.

WON 81
LOST 54
TG 135

AMERICAN ASSOCIATION — FINISHED 2nd.

1887. — PCT. .600

CINCINNATI

GUSTAVUS HEINRICH SCHMELZ

WON	LOST	NAME	POS.	G.	BA	FROM	TO
		@Baldwin, Clarence Geoghan	C95	96	.262	B	
		Carpenter, Warren Wm. (Hick)	3B	127	.269	B	
0	0	*Corkhill, John Stewart (Pop)	OF122	127	.330	B	
		Fennelly, Francis John	SS	134	.368	B	
		Jones, Chas. Wesley	OF	41	+.374	B	Mets
		Kappel, Henry (SS2 3B10 OF6)	2B12	24	.294	A	
		Keenan, James W. (1B1)	C46	47	.297	B	
31	17	#Mullane, Anthony John (Tony)	P51	61	.284	B	
3	6	McGinnis, George W.	P	9	.219	Balt	C
		McPhee, John Alexander (Bid)	2B	129	.354	B	
		Nicol, Hugh N.	OF	126	.334	StL	
		O'Connor, John Joseph (OF7)	C5	12	.133	A	
		Reilly, John Good (OF9)	1B125	134	.334	B	
11	11	Serad, Wm. T. (OF1)	P22	22	.278	BuffN85	
1	1	Shea, Michael J.	P	2	.333	A	C
33	18	Smith, Elmer Ellsworth (OF1)	P51	52	.288	B	
0	0	Tebeau, George E. (P1)	OF87	88	.361	A	
1	1	Watson, Walter L. (OF1)	P2	2	.222	A	C
1	0	Widner, Wm. Waterfield	P	1	.250	A	

@Baldwin also played 1 game in the OF.
*Corkhill also pitched 5 games.
#Mullane also played 10 games in the OF.

WON 80
LOST 54
TG 134

AMERICAN ASSOCIATION — FINISHED 4th.

1888. — PCT. .597

CINCINNATI

GUSTAVUS HEINRICH SCHMELZ

WON	LOST	NAME	POS.	G.	BA	FROM	TO
		@Baldwin, Clarence Geoghan	C64	66	.220	B	
		Carpenter, Warren Wm. (Hick)	3B	135	.269	B	
0	0	*Corkhill, John Stewart (Pop)	OF115	118	+.271	B	Bkn
		%Fennelly, Francis John	SS104	112	+.191	B	Ath

WON	LOST	NAME	POS.	G.	BA	FROM	TO
		Kappel, Henry (2B10 3B1)	SS21	35	.254	B	
		Keenan, James W. (1B16)	C70	84	.229	B	
27	16	#Mullane, Anthony John (Tony)	P44	51	.251	B	
		McPhee, John Alexander (Bid)	2B	110	.230	B	
		Nicol, Hugh N. (2B12 SS1)	OF124	134	.236	B	
		O'Connor, John Joseph (C2)	OF34	36	.201	B	
		Reilly, John Good (OF10)	1B116	126	.324	B	
1	3	Serad, Wm. T.	P	6	.130	B	C
22	17	Smith, Elmer Ellsworth (OF1)	P39	40	.220	B	
		Tebeau, George E.	OF	121	.228	B	
27	14	Viau, Leon (OF1)	P41	41	.085	A	
3	4	Weyhing, John	P	8	.084	A	
		Bligh, Edwin Forrest (OF1)	C3	3	.000	Balt86	

@Baldwin also played 1 game at 1B and 2 games in the OF.
*Corkhill also pitched 1 game, played 1 game at 1B and 1 game at 2B.
%Fennelly also played 4 games at 2B and 4 games in the OF.
#Mullane also played 4 games at 1B, 2 games at 2B and 3 games in the OF.

WON 76 | AMERICAN ASSOCIATION | FINISHED 4th.
LOST 63
TG 139 | 1889. | PCT. .547

CINCINNATI

GUSTAVUS HEINRICH SCHMELZ

WON	LOST	NAME	POS.	G.	BA	FROM	TO
		@Baldwin, Clarence Geoghan	C55	60	.248	B	
		Beard, Oliver Perry	SS	141	.293	A	
		#Carpenter, Warren Wm. (Hick)	3B121	123	.257	B	
0	0	Conover, Theodore	P	1	.000	A	C
32	21	$Duryea, James Whitney (Jesse)	P54	55	.268	A	
		Earle, Wm. Moffat (1B5 OF22)	C24	53	.269	A	
		Holliday, James Wear (Bug)	OF	135	.343	A	
		Keenan, James W. (1B20 3B1)	C67	87	.287	B	
11	8	*Mullane, Anthony John (Tony)	P29	62	.307	B	
		%McPhee, John Alexander (Bid)	2B135	135	.269	B	
		Nicol, Hugh N. (2B6 3B3)	OF114	122	.246	B	
2	3	Petty, Chas. E.	P	5	.300	A	
		Reilly, John Good (OF2)	1B109	111	.261	B	
10	12	Smith, Elmer Ellsworth	P	29	.290	B	
		Tebeau, George E. (1B1)	OF134	135	.255	B	
21	19	Viau, Leon	P	47	.145	B	

@Baldwin also played 1 game at 1B, 1 game at 3B and 4 games in the OF.
#Carpenter also played 2 games at 1B.
$Duryea also played 3 games in the OF.
*Mullane also played 4 games at 1B, 18 games at 3B and 12 games in the OF.
%McPhee also played 1 game at 3B.

WON 43 | AMERICAN ASSOCIATION | FINISHED 7th.
LOST x 57
TG 100 | 1891. | PCT. .430

CINCINNATI

MICHAEL JOSEPH KELLY

WON	LOST	NAME	POS.	G.	BA	FROM	TO
		Andrews, George Edward	OF	83	.210	BknPL	C
		Bastian, Chas. J.	2B	1	.000	ChiPL	PhilN
1	0	Bell, Chas. C.	P	4	+.500	xLvlle	C
		Burke, Joseph M.	2B	1	.250	StL	C
		Canavan, James E.	SS	91	+.253	A	Mil
		Carney, John Joseph	1B	91	+.276	ClevPL	Mil
		Clingman, Wm. Frederick	2B	1	.200	CinN	
14	17	Crane, Edward Nicholas (OF3)	P32	34	.145	NYPL	CinN
13	18	#Dwyer, John Francis (Frank)	P29	34	+.250	ChiPL	Mil
		Hurley, Jeremiah F. (1B1 OF2)	C23	26	.220	PittPL	C
		Johnston, Richard Frederick	OF	99	.219	NYPL	C
0	1	Keenan, Harry Leon	P	1	.500	A	C
0	1	Kelly, Michael Joseph (King) (P3 1B5 2B6 SS1 3B7 OF7)	C46 MGR.	74	+.280	BosPL	Bos
1	4	Kilroy, Matthew Aloysius (OF1)	P7	8	.190	BosPL	
12	10	Mains, Willard Eben (OF1)	P26	27	+.280	ChiN88	Mil
		Marr, Chas. W. (Lefty)	OF	14	.204	xCinN	C
2	4	McGill, Wm. Vaness	P	16	+.050	ClevPL	StL
		Robinson, Wm. H. (Yank) (SS1)	2B96	97	.178	PittPL	
		Seery, John Emmett	OF	97	.282	BknPL	
0	0	Slagle, John A.	P	1	.000	A	C
0	0	*Vaughn, Harry Francis	C34	45	+.255	NYPL	Mil
		Whitney, Arthur Wilson	3B	86	+.200	NYPL	StL
0	1	Widner, Wm. Waterfield	P	1	.250	Col	C

#Dwyer also played 2 games at 2B and 3 games in the OF.
*Vaughn also pitched in 1 game, played 2 games at 1B, 2 games at 3B and 6 games in the OF.

xOne Game lost by forfeit.

CLUB RECORD

OTHER MAJOR LEAGUES

CLEVELAND

YEAR	TG	WON	LOST	PCT.	FINISHED	MANAGER
AMERICAN ASSOCIATION						
1887	131	39	92	.298	8 (Last)	James A. Williams
1888	132	50	82	.378	6	James A. Williams Thomas Joseph Leftus
PLAYER'S LEAGUE						
1890	130	55	75	.423	7	James S. Faatz Henry E. Larkin Oliver Wendell Tabeau
AMERICAN LEAGUE						
1900	136	63	73	.463	6	James Robert McAleer

WON 39
LOST 92
TG 131

AMERICAN ASSOCIATION 1887.

FINISHED 8th (LAST)
PCT. .298

CLEVELAND

JAMES A. WILLIAMS

WON	LOST	NAME	POS.	G.	BA	FROM	TO
		Allen, Myron S.	OF	117	.330	BosN	
		Carroll, John E.	OF	57	.252	BuffN85	
13	32	Crowell, Wm. Theodore	P	45	.195	A	
4	12	Daly, Hugh I. (One-Arm)	P	17	.123	WashN	C
		Flynn, Edward J.	3B	7	.215	A	C
6	5	Gilks, Robert James (P11)	OF16	22	.333	A	
		Herr, Edward Joseph	3B	11	.360	A	
		Hotaling, Peter James	OF	127	.367	Bkn85	
0	5	Kirby, John F.	P	5	.158	xIndplsN	
		Mann, Frederick I.	OF	64	+.375	Pitt	Ath
15	26	Morrison, Michael	P	41	.237	A	
		Munyan, John B.	OF	16	.276	A	
		McGlone, John T.	3B	21	.329	WashN	
		McKean, Edward John	SS	132	.364	A	
1	9	Pechiney, George Adolphe	P	10	.289	Cin	C
		Reccius, Philip	3B	62	+.295	xLvlle	
		Reipschlager, Christopher Frederick	C	63	.248	Mets	C
		Say, James I.	3B	15	.367	KCUA84	C
0	0	Sheibeck, Frank (P1)	3B2	3	.364	A	
		Simon, Henry J.	OF	3	.100	A	
		Snyder, Chas. N.	C	73	.276	Cin	
		Stricker, John A. (Cub)	2B	131	.333	Ath85	
0	3	Sweeney, Chas. J. (P3)	1B33	36	.329	StLN	C
		Toy, James Madison	1B	109	.239	A	
		Zimmer, Chas. Louis (Chief)	C	14	.321	Mets	

WON 50
LOST 82
TG 132

AMERICAN ASSOCIATION 1888.

FINISHED 6th.
PCT. .378

CLEVELAND

JAMES A. WILLIAMS THOMAS JOSEPH LOFTUS

WON	LOST	NAME	POS.	G.	BA	FROM	TO
		Alberts, August P. (3B48)	SS52	101	.192	WashUA84	
25	33	Bakely, Edward (Enoch)	P	60	.131	KCUA84	
0	12	Crowell, Wm. Theodore	P	18	+.085	B	Lvlle
		Faatz, Jay	1B	120	.264	Pitt84	
		Gilks, Robert James (3B26)	OF84	118	.232	B	
		Goodfellow, Michael J.	OF51	69	.250	StL	C
		Hogan, Robert Edward	OF	77	.236	Mets	C
		Hotaling, Peter James	OF	97	.250	B	C
3	3	Keas, Edward J.	P	6	.087	A	C
6	4	Knouff, Edward (2B1)	P10	10	+.143	xStL	

1	3	Morrison, Michael	P	4	.235	B	
		McClellan, Wm. Henry (2B5 SS1)	OF16	22	+.222	xBkn	C
		McGlone, John T.	3B48	55	.183	B	C
		McGuire, James Thomas	C16	25	.207	xDetN	
		McKean, Edward John (OF43)	SS75	130	.297	B	
1	2	Oberlander, Hartman Louis	P	3	.214	A	C
11	19	O'Brien, John F.	P30	31	.185	A	
3	4	Proeser, George	P	7	.304	A	
		Snyder, Chas. N.	C43	63	.216	B	
0	2	Stemmeyer, Wm.	P	3	.400	BosN	C
		Stricker, John A. (Cub)	2B122	126	.231	B	
		Van Zant, Richard	3B	10	.187	A	C
		Zimmer, Chas. Louis (Chief)	C56	63	.250	B	

CLUB RECORD

OTHER MAJOR LEAGUES

COLUMBUS

YEAR	TG	WON	LOST	PCT.	FINISHED	MANAGER
AMERICAN ASSOCIATION						
1883	97	32	65	.330	6	Horace B. Phillips
1884	108	69	39	.639	2	Gustavus Heinrich Schmelz
1885-1888		OUT OF LEAGUE				
1889	138	60	78	.435	6	Albert C. Buckenberger
1890	134	79	55	.590	2	Albert C. Buckenberger James P. Sullivan Gustavus Heinrich Schmelz
1891	137	61	76	.445	6	Gustavus Heinrich Schmelz

WON 32
LOST 65
TG 97

AMERICAN ASSOCIATION — 1883. — FINISHED 6th. — PCT. .330

COLUMBUS

HORACE B. PHILLIPS

WON	LOST	NAME	POS.	G.	BA	FROM	TO
0	2	Brown, Thomas T. (P2 SS1)	OF95	97	.276	Balt	
3	16	Dundon, Edward Joseph (2B1 OF7)	P19	25	.151	A	
		Field, James	1B	75	.239	A	
0	3	Fries, Peter J.	P	3	.273	A	
		Kemmler, Rudolph (OF1)	C85	85	.202	Pitt	
		Kuehne, Wm. J. (2B19 SS5 OF3)	3B68	96	.222	A	
		*Mann, Frederick I.	OF81	96	.230	Ath	
26	33	Mountain, Frank H. (OF12)	P60	71	.216	WorN	
1	1	McIntyre, Frank W.	P	2	.000	xDetN	C
		Pearce, Grayson S. (OF5)	2B6	11	.220	Balt	NYN
		Richmond, John H.	SS	91	.274	Ath	
		Schwartz, Wm. August (1B1)	C1	2	.250	A	
0	0	Smith, Chas. Marvin (Pap) (P2 3B24)	2B73	96	.258	Lvlle	
		Straub, Joseph (1B12 OF2)	C14	27	.135	Ath	C
2	9	Valentine, John G. (OF5)	P15	15	.294	A	C
0	1	Wheeler, Harry Eugene (P1)	OF83	83	.225	Cin	

*Mann also played 9 games at 1B, 1 game at SS, 5 games at 3B.

WON 69
LOST 39
TG 108

AMERICAN ASSOCIATION — 1884. — FINISHED 2nd. — PCT. .639

COLUMBUS

GUSTAVUS HEINRICH SCHMELZ

WON	LOST	NAME	POS.	G.	BA	FROM	TO
1	2	Bauers, Albert J.	P	3	.273	A	
1	1	Brown, Thomas T. (P2)	OF105	107	.275	B	
1	0	Cahill, John Francis (P1)	OF51	59	.210	A	
		Carroll, Frederick Herbert (OF12)	C54	69	.283	A	
5	4	Dundon, Edward Joseph (P10)	OF13	26	.139	B	C
		Field, James	1B	105	.229	B	
		Kemmler, Rudolph	C58	61	.202	B	
		Kuehne, Wm. J.	3B	110	.238	B	
		Mann, Frederick I.	OF97	99	.276	B	
		Mansell, Thomas E.	OF	23	+.211	xCin	C
35	13	Morris, Edward	P49	57	.181	A	
24	17	Mountain, Frank H. (OF8)	P43	58	.237	B	
		Richmond, John H.	SS	105	.237	B	
		Smith, Chas. Marvin (Pap)	2B	108	.240	B	
2	2	Sullivan, Thomas	P	4	.083	A	

WON 60
LOST 78
TG 138

AMERICAN ASSOCIATION — 1889. — FINISHED 6th. — PCT. .435

COLUMBUS

ALBERT C. BUCKENBERGER

WON	LOST	NAME	POS.	G.	BA	FROM	TO
26	34	Baldwin, Marcus, Elmore (Mark)	P63	64	.182	ChiN	
		Bligh, Edwin Forrest	C	27	.126	Cin	
		Crooks, John Chas. (Jack)	2B	12	.323	A	
		Daily, Edward M.	OF	137	.254	WashN	
		Doyle, John Joseph (Jack)	C	11	.355	A	
1	0	Easton, John E.	P	4	.000	A	
		Esterday, Henry	SS100	105	.175	K.C.	
11	13	Gastright, Henry Carl	P	31	.197	A	
0	0	George Wm. M. (OF3)	P3	5	.308	xNYN	C
		Greenwood, Wm. F.	2B	118	.219	Balt	
		Johnson, John Ralph (OF44)	3B71	117	.285	A	
		Kappel, Henry (3B23)	SS24	49	.269	Cin	C
		Kemmler, Rudolph	C	8	.134	StL86	C
		Marr, Chas. W. (Lefty) (SS27 OF45)	3B67	139	.303	Cin86	
9	9	Mays, Albert C.	P	22	.155	Bkn	
		McCaffrey, Chas. P.	C	2	.167	A	
		McTamany, James J.	OF	139	.279	K.C.	
		O'Connor, John Joseph	C84	107	.269	Cin	
		Orr, David L.	1B	134	.325	Bkn	
		Peoples, James E.	C21	28	.223	Bkn	C
		Reilly, Chas. Thomas	3B	6	.478	A	
0	0	Weyhing, John	P	1	.000	Cin	C
13	22	Widner, Wm. Waterfield	P39	40	.209	WashN	

WON 79
LOST 55
TG 134

AMERICAN ASSOCIATION — 1890. — FINISHED 2nd. — PCT. .590

COLUMBUS

ALBERT C. BUCKENBERGER   JAMES P. SULLIVAN
GUSTAVUS HEINRICH SCHMELZ

WON	LOST	NAME	POS.	G.	BA	FROM	TO
		Bligh, Edwin Forrest	C	8	+.214	B	Lvlle
13	7	Chamberlain, Elton P.	P	28	+.240	xStL	
		Crooks, John Chas. (Jack)	2B	135	.221	B	
1	0	Doyle, John Joseph (Jack) (P1)	C76	76	.272	B	
14	13	Easton, John E.	P	37	.217	B	
		Esterday, Henry	SS	52	+.145	B	Ath
0	1	Ford, Thomas W.	P	1	+.000	A	Bkn
26	14	Gastright, Henry Carl	P	50	.223	B	
		Johnson, John Ralph	OF	137	.354	B	
21	11	Knauss, Frank H.	P	33	.227	A	
		Lehane, Michael Patrick	1B	140	.185	WashUA84	
0	1	Mays, Albert C.	P	1	.000	B	C

WON	LOST	NAME	POS.	G.	BA	FROM	TO
		Munyan, John B.	OF	2	+.167	Clev87	StL
		McTamany, James J.	OF	125	.256	B	
		Nichol, Samuel Anderson	OF	14	.188	PittN88	C
		O'Connor, John Joseph (Jack)	C	118	.341	B	
		Reilly, Chas. Thomas	3B	137	.270	B	
		Sneed, John L.	OF	128	+.309	xTol	
		Wheelock, Warren H.	SS	59	.267	BosN87	
4	8	Widner, Wm. Waterfield	P	13	.205	B	

WON 61
LOST 76
TG 137

AMERICAN ASSOCIATION — FINISHED 6th.

1891. — PCT. .445

COLUMBUS

GUSTAVUS HEINRICH SCHMELZ

WON	LOST	NAME	POS.	G.	BA	FROM	TO
1	2	Clark, Edward C.	P	5	.091	Ath86	C
0	0	Clarke, Wm. H. (Dad)	P	5	.091	ChiN88	
		Cleveland, Elmer E.	3B	12	.142	PittN88	C
		Crooks, John Chas. (Jack)	2B	138	.240	B	
13	10	Dolan, John (Jack)	P27	28	.077	CinN	
		Donely, James B.	3B	17	.241	StL	
		Donahue, James Augustus	C75	77	.217	K.C.89	C
		Dowse, Thomas Jefferson	C51	55	.217	ClevN	
		Duffee, Chas. Edward	OF130	137	.302	StL	
5	13	Easton, John E. (P3)	P	15	+.204	B	StL
			P3 OF3	6	+.105	(& return)	
12	19	Gastright, Henry Carl	P	35	.197	B	
27	27	Knell, Philip H.	P58	66	.147	PhilPL	
		Kuehne, Wm. J.	3B	56	+.214	PittPL	Lvlle
		Lehane, Michael Patrick	1B	137	.217	B	C
2	3	Leiper, John Henry Thomas	P	6	.143	A	C
0	0	Lyston, Wm. Edward	P	1	.000	A	
		McTamany, James J.	OF	77	+.266	B	Ath
		O'Connor, John Joseph (Jack) (C20)	OF36	56	.260	B	
		O'Rourke, Timothy Patrick	3B	34	.261	Syr	
		Sneed, John L.	OF	99	.261	B	C
0	1	Sullivan, James E.	P	1	+.000	BosN	
1	1	Twitchell, Lawrence Grant (P2)	OF55	57	.275	BuffPL	
		Wheelock, Warren H.	SS	136	.230	B	C

WON 29
LOST 78
TG 107

AMERICAN ASSOCIATION — FINISHED 12th.

1884. — PCT. .271

INDIANAPOLIS

JAMES H. GIFFORD — WM. HENRY WATKINS

WON	LOST	NAME	POS.	G.	BA	FROM	TO
5	7	Aydelotte, Jacob S. (OF1)	P12	12	.114	A	
		Bahret, Frank J.	C4	5	.071	xBaltUA	C
3	11	Barr, Robert M. (OF2)	P16	18	+.188	xWash	
		Blakiston, Robert J. (OF1)	1B5	6	+.200	xAth	C
0	5	Bond, Thomas Henry (OF2)	P5	7	.136	xBosUA	C
		Butler, W. J.	OF	9	.206	A	C
		Callahan, Patrick J.	3B	61	.263	A	C
		Collins, Chas. (Chub)	2B	38	.229	xBuffN	
		Decker, Edward Harry	C	4	.286	StL82	KCUA
		Donely, James B. (SS8)	3B26	40	.249	xKCUA	
		Dorgan, Jeremiah F.	OF29	34	+.294	Ath82	Bkn
		Fries, Peter J.	OF	1	.250	Col	C
		Holdsworth, James	OF	5	.100	TroyN82	C
		Keenan, James W. (1B6)	C59	68	.305	Pitt82	
		Kerins, John Nelson	1B86	93	.210	A	
		Levis, Chas. T.	1B	3	.200	xWashUA	
		Locke, Marshall	OF	7	.241	A	C
		Merrill, Edward S.	2B	54	.183	WorN82	C
		Monroe, Frank	C	1	.000	A	C
0	2	Moriarity, Eugene John (P2 3B1)	OF7	10	.216	xBosN	
		Morrison, Jonathan W.	OF	43	.256	A	
		Mundinger, George	C	3	.200	A	C
1	5	McArthur, Malcolm	P	6	.091	A	C
2	7	McCauley, Allen B. (1B5)	P9	17	.189	A	
18	41	McKeon, Lawrence J. (1B5)	P61	70	.215	A	
		Peltz, John	OF	106	.213	A	
		Phillips, Marr B.	SS	97	.266	A	
		Reising, Chas.	OF	1	.000	A	C
		Robinson, Chas. Henry (SS2 OF1)	C17	19	.286	A	
		Sneed, John L.	OF	27	.105	A	
		Thompson, John P.F. (OF12)	C12	24	.204	Cin82	C
		Tray, James	C4	6	.261	A	C
		Watkins, Wm. Henry MGR. (2B11)	3B21	34	.211	A	
		Webber,	C	3	.000	A	C
		Weihe, John Garibaldi (Podge)	OF58	64	.261	Cin	C

WON 43
LOST 89
TG 132

AMERICAN ASSOCIATION 1888.

FINISHED 8th (LAST) PCT. .326

KANSAS CITY

DAVID E. ROWE SAMUEL WILSON BARKLEY WM. HENRY WATKINS

WON	LOST	NAME	POS.	G.	BA	FROM	TO
		Allen, Myron S.	OF33	37	.215	Clev	C
		Barkley, Samuel Wilson, MGR.	2B	116	.220	PittN	
		Brennan, James A.	C25	34	.174	StLN85	
		Briody, Chas. F.	C	13	.208	DetN	C
		Burns, James M.	OF	15	.273	A	
		Christman, H. B.	C	1	.250	A	C
		Cline, John	OF70	73	.243	Lvlle85	
		Daniels, Lawrence Long	C31	61	.205	Balt	C
		Davis, James J.	3B114	122	.266	Balt	
		Donahue, James Augustus	C66	87	.241	Mets	
4	3	Ehret, Philip Sydney (Red) (P7)	OF9	16	.186	A	
		Esterday, Henry	SS	114	.195	PhilUA84	
6	11	Fagan, Wm. A.	P17	18	.219	Mets	C
		Hamilton, Wm. Robert	OF29	35	.250	A	
		Hankinson, Frank Edward	2B	37	.175	Mets	C
3	9	Hoffman, Frank J.	P	12	.154	A	C
0	2	Hoffner, Wm.	P	2	.000	A	C
		Hoover, Chas.E.	C	3	.200	A	
		Jones, Chas. Wesley	OF	6	.250	Mets	C
1	5	Kirby, John F.	P	6	.071	Clev	C
		McTamany, James J.	OF	116	.251	Bkn	
		Phillips, Wm. B.	1B119	129	.235	Bkn	C
17	37	Porter, Henry	P	55	.137	Bkn	
		Rowe, David E. MGR.	OF	32	.195	KCN86	C
8	16	Sullivan, Thomas (OF16)	P24	28	.109	Lvlle86	
4	6	Toole, Stephen J.	P	13	.227	Bkn	
		Glenn, Edward C.	OF	3	.000	Pitt86	BosN

WON 55
LOST 82
TG 137

AMERICAN ASSOCIATION 1889.

FINISHED 7th. PCT. .401

KANSAS CITY

WM. HENRY WATKINS JAMES H. MANNING

WON	LOST	NAME	POS.	G.	BA	FROM	TO
		Alvord, Wm. C.	3B34	50	.221	StLN85	
		Barkley, Samuel Wilson	2B41	45	.277	B	C
0	1	Bates, Bush	P	1	.000	A	C
1	0	Bell, Chas. C.	P	1	.200	A	
		Bittman, Henry	2B	4	.286	A	C
		Burns, James M.	OF132	133	.303	B	
18	19	Conway, James P.	P	41	.208	Ath85	C
		Davis, James J.	3B	62	+.258	B	StL
		Donahue, James Augustus	C46	67	.238	B	
		Gunson, Joseph Brook	C32	34	.198	WashUA84	
		Hamilton, Wm. Robert	OF131	137	.301	B	
		Hoover, Chas. E.	C66	71	.247	B	C
0	0	LaDew, Stephen	P	2	.000	A	C
		Long, Herman C.	SS129	136	.280	A	
		Manning, James H. MGR. (2B63)	OF69	132	.204	DetN87	
1	1	Mattimore, Michael J. (P2)	OF19	19	+.147	xAth	
8	6	McCarty, John A.	P	20	.228	A	C
		McGarr, James B. (Chippy) (2B4 SS3 OF6)	3B12	25	+.287	StL	Balt
0	2	Pears, Frank T.	P	3	.100	A	
		Pickett, John Thomas	OF23	41	.223	A	
0	3	Porter, Henry	P	4	.111	B	C
		Reynolds, Chas. L.	C	1	+.250	A	Bkn
6	16	Sowders, John	P26	28	.230	IndplsN87	
		Stearns, Daniel Eckford	1B135	139	.288	BuffN85	C
2	8	Sullivan, Thomas	P	10	.151	B	C
19	26	Swartzel, Parke B.	P48	52	.151	A	C

WON 44
LOST 35
TG 79

AMERICAN ASSOCIATION — **FINISHED 2nd.**

1882. — **PCT. .557**

LOUISVILLE

JOHN F. DYLER — J. WM. RECCIUS — SAMUEL LEECH MASKREY

WON	LOST	NAME	POS.	G.	BA	FROM	TO
1	1	Bohn, Chas. (OF2)	P2	4	.154	A	C
		Booth, Amos Smith	2B	1	+.000	xBalt	C
		Browning, Louis Roger (Pete) (SS17 3B12)	2B40	69	.382	A	
		Crotty, Joseph	C	5	+.100	A	StL
		Dyler, John F. MGR.	OF	1	.000	A	C
7	5	Hecker, Guy Jackson (P12 (OF2)	1B65	78	.285	A	
		Mack, Dennis Joseph (2B22 OF5)	SS49	72	.193	BuffN80	
		Maskrey, Harry H.	OF	1	.000	A	C
		Maskrey, Samuel Leech MGR	OF76	76	.225	A	
31	23	Mullane, Anthony John (Tony) (1B12 2B2 OF8)	P55	77	.255	DetN	
		Pearce, Grayson S. (OF1)	2B9	9	+.294	LvlleN76	Balt
4	6	Reccius, John (P14)	OF64	73	.216	A	
		Reccius, Philip	OF	3	.091	A	
		Say, James I.	3B	1	+.500	A	Ath
1	0	Schenck, Wm. G. (P3 SS2 3B10 OF1)	3B56	59	.265	A	
		Smith, Chas. Marvin (Pap)	SS	3	+.182	xBalt	
		Strike, John (1B1 2B6 SS1 OF6)	C22	33	.142	A	
		Sullivan, Daniel C. (SS1 OF4)	C53	67	.284	A	
0	0	Wolf, Wm. V. (Chicken) (P1 1B1 SS7 3B1)	OF69	78	.294	A	

WON 52
LOST 45
TG 97

AMERICAN ASSOCIATION — **FINISHED 5th.**

1883. — **PCT. .536**

LOUISVILLE

J. WM. RECCIUS — SAMUEL LEECH MASKREY — JOSEPH JOHN GERHARDT

WON	LOST	NAME	POS.	G.	BA	FROM	TO
		Brown, Lewis J. (C1)	1B14	14	.197	xBosN	
		Browning, Louis Roger (Pete) (1B1 2B3 SS25 3B10)	OF58	83	.349	B	
		Gerhardt, Joseph John MGR.	2B	77	.270	DetN81	
		Gleason, John Day (SS1)	3B83	84	+.276	xStL	
28	25	Hecker, Guy Jackson (1B6 OF24)	P55	79	.264	B	
		Jones, Ryerson L. (SS1)	OF2	2	.000	A	
		Latham, George Warren (Juice) (2B13 SS9)	1B64	90	.248	Ath	
		Leary, John J.	SS	40	+.183	Balt	Balt
		Luff, Henry T. (OF2)	1B4	6	.174	Cin	
		Maskrey, Samuel Leech MGR.	OF96	96	.190	B	
		*McLaughlin, Thomas	SS18	42	.206	A	
		Prince, Walter F. (SS1 OF2)	1B2	4	.182	A	
0	0	Reccius, John (P1)	OF17	17	.154	B	C
		Reccius, Philip	OF	1	.333	B	
		#Sullivan, Daniel C.	C36	36	.225	B	
24	20	Weaver, Samuel H. (1B1 OF7)	P46	50	.195	Ath	
		@Whiting, Edward C.	C55	55	.295	Balt	
		Winkelman, George Edward	OF	4	.000	A	
		Wolf, Wm. V. (Chicken) (C18 2B1 SS5)	OF74	88	.250	B	

*McLaughlin also played 5 games at 1B, 2 games at 2B, 1 game at 3B and 17 games in the OF.
#Sullivan also played 1 game at SS, 2 games at 3B and 2 games in the OF.
@Whiting also played 1 game at 1B, 1 game at 3B and 4 games in the OF.

WON 68
LOST 40
TG 108

AMERICAN ASSOCIATION — **FINISHED 3rd.**

1884. — **PCT. .630**

LOUISVILLE

JOSEPH J. GERHARDT — MICHAEL F. WALSH

WON	LOST	NAME	POS.	G.	BA	FROM	TO
		Andrews, Wm. Walter	1B9	15	.185	A	
0	1	Browning, Louis Roger (Pete) (1B24 OF24)	3B52	105	.341	B	
		Cline, John (SS5)	OF86	94	.287	Balt82	
4	6	Deagle, Lorenzo Burroughs (Ren) (OF3)	P12	12	+.114	xCin	C
		Dickerson, Lewis Pessano	OF	8	+.138	xBalt	
7	6	Driscoll, John F. (OF1)	P13	13	.167	Pitt	
		Gerhardt, Joseph John MGR. (Moveup)	2B	108	.220	B	
52	20	Hecker, Guy Jackson	P76	79	.296	B	
		Hunter, Wm. Robert	C	2	.429	A	C
		Latham, George Warren (Juice)	1B	78	.161	B	C
		Maskrey, Samuel Leech	OF102	107	.247	B	
		McLaughlin, Thomas	SS96	100	.191	B	
5	7	Reccius, Philip (P13 SS9)	3B48	75	.249	B	
		Stockwell, Leonard C. (C1)	OF2	2	.111	ClevN79	
		Sullivan, Daniel C.	C63	64	.245	B	
		Whiting, Edward C.	C40	42	.220	B	
		Wolf, Wm. V. (Chicken) (C11)	OF98	112	.303	B	

WON 53 LOST 59 TG 112

AMERICAN ASSOCIATION 1885.

FINISHED 5th. (TIED WITH BKLYN) PCT. .473

LOUISVILLE

JAMES A. HART

WON	LOST	NAME	POS.	G.	BA	FROM	TO
13	12	Baker, Norman Leslie	P	25	.172	Pitt83	
		Browning, Louis Roger (Pete)	OF	113	.367	B	
		Cline, John (OF1)	3B1	2	.222	B	
1	3	Connor, John	P	4	.143	xBuffN	C
		Cross, Amos C.	C	35	.295	A	
		Crotty, Joseph	C	39	.172	CinUA	
		Geer, Wm. Henry Harrison	SS	14	.113	Bkn	C
30	24	Hecker, Guy Jackson (1B17)	P54	72	.274	B	
		Kerins, John Nelson (C15)	1B97	113	.243	Indpls	
		Krehmeyer, Chas. L. (1B1 OF2)	C4	7	.212	StL	StLN
		Mack, Joseph (Reddy)	2B	11	.244	A	
		Maskrey, Samuel Leech	OF	110	.230	B	
6	11	Mays, Albert C.	P	17	.216	A	
		Miller, Joseph A. (2B9 3B12)	SS76	97	.192	Tol	C
		Murray, Jeremiah J. (1B2)	C11	11	.162	ProvN	
		McLaughlin, Thomas	2B	113	.215	B	
3	4	Ramsey, Thomas A.	P	9	.129	A	
0	5	Reccius, Philip (P5)	3B100	105	.240	B	
		Strauss, Joseph (OF1)	C1	2	.167	KCUA	
		Sullivan, Daniel C.	C	13	+.156	B	StL
		Wolf, Wm. V. (Chicken)	OF	113	.288	B	

WON 66 LOST 70 TG 136

AMERICAN ASSOCIATION 1886.

FINISHED 4th. PCT. .485

LOUISVILLE

JAMES A. HART

WON	LOST	NAME	POS.	G.	BA	FROM	TO
		Browning, Louis Roger (Pete)	OF	112	.339	B	
0	3	Chamberlain, Elton P. (OF2)	P4	6	.150	A	
		Collins, Hubert B.	OF	27	.287	A	
		Cook, Paul (C19)	1B46	68	.205	PhilN84	
		Cross, Amos C. (1B22)	C52	74	.276	B	
0	4	Ely, Frederick Wm. (OF5)	P5	10	.147	BuffN84	
27	23	Hecker, Guy Jackson (1B21)	P50	84	.342	B	
		Heintzman, John P.	1B	1	.000	A	C
0	4	Kennedy, Theodore A.	P	4	+.077	xAth	C
		Kerins, John Nelson (1B50)	C62	119	.268	B	
		Mack, Joseph (Reddy)	2B	137	.244	B	
		Maskrey, Samuel Leech	OF	5	+.158	B	Cin
		Murphy, Clarence	OF	1	.000	A	C
0	1	Neal, Joseph H. (OF1)	P1	2	.000	A	
37	27	Ramsey, Thomas A.	P	66	.243	B	
0	1	Reccius, Philip (P1)	OF5	5	.267	B	
		Strauss, Joseph	OF	77	+.210	B	Bkn
2	7	Sullivan, Thomas	P	9	.083	Col84	
		Sylvester, Louis J.	OF	54	+.227	CinUA84	Cin
		Terrell, Thomas	C	1	.250	A	C
		Werrick, Joseph Abraham	3B	136	.250	StPUA84	
		White, Wm. Dighton	SS	135	.262	Pitt84	
		Wolf, Wm. V. (Chicken)	OF	129	.274	B	

WON 76 LOST 60 TG 136

AMERICAN ASSOCIATION 1887.

FINISHED 4th. PCT. .559

LOUISVILLE

JOHN O. KELLY

WON	LOST	NAME	POS.	G.	BA	FROM	TO
		Browning, Louis Roger (Pete)	OF	134	.471	B	
18	16	Chamberlain, Elton P.	P	37	.268	B	
		Collins, Hubert B.	OF	129	.349	B	
		Cook, Paul (1B20)	C43	63	.267	B	
		Cross, Amos C.	C	9	.257	B	C
		Cross, LaFayette Napoleon (Lave)	C	54	.327	A	
19	12	Hecker, Guy Jackson (P33)	1B42	91	.374	B	
		Hemp, Wm. H.	OF	1	.250	A	
		Kerins, John Nelson (C35)	1B74	112	.360	B	
		Mack, Joseph (Reddy)	2B	128	.410	B	
0	4	Neal, Joseph H.	P	5	.200	B	
39	27	Ramsey, Thomas A.	P	66	.240	B	
		Reccius, Philip (SS1)	OF10	11	+.341	B	Clev
0	1	Veach, Wm. Walter (Peek-a-boo)	P	1	.250	KCUA84	
		Werrick, Joseph Abraham	3B	136	.333	B	
		White, Wm. Dighton	SS	132	.311	B	
		Wolf, Wm. V. (Chicken)	OF	137	.324	B	

WON 48 LOST 87 TG 135

AMERICAN ASSOCIATION 1888.

FINISHED 7th. PCT. .360

LOUISVILLE

JOHN NELSON KERINS   MORDECAI H. DAVIDSON

WON	LOST	NAME	POS.	G.	BA	FROM	TO
		Andrews, Wm. Walter	1B	27	.202	ProvN85	C
		Browning, Louis Roger (Pete)	OF	99	.313	B	
		Burnett, Hercules H.	OF	1	.000	A	
9	8	Chamberlain, Elton P.	P	26	+.204	B	StL
		Collins, Hubert B. (2B30)	OF84	114	+.321	B	Bkn

WON	LOST	NAME	POS.	G.	BA	FROM	TO
		Cook, Paul	C50	53	.200	B	
		Cross, LaFayette Napoleon (Lave)	C38	47	.213	B	
5	2	Crowell, Wm. Theodore	P	7	+.000	xClev	C
		Esterbrook, Thomas Jefferson (Dude)	1B	23	.226	xIndplsN	
8	13	Ewing, John	P	21	.205	WashUA84	
		Fusselbach, Edward L.	OF	1	.250	Ath85	C
8	17	Hecker, Guy Jackson (1B27)	P28	55	.255	B	
		Kerins, John Nelson MGR. (C22)	OF35	81	.239	B	
		Long, Daniel W.	OF	1	.000	A	
		Mack, Joseph (Reddy)	2B	110	.228	B	
8	30	Ramsey, Thomas A.	P38	41	.123	B	
		Raymond, Harry H.	3B31	32	.208	A	
		Reccius, Philip	3B	2	.223	Clev	
		Smith, Samuel	1B	56	.246	A	C
10	17	Stratton, C. Scott (OF23)	P34	65	.266	A	
		Tomney, Philip H.	SS	34	.149	A	
		Vaughn, Harry Francis (OF20)	C25	49	.203	Cin86	
		Weaver, Wm. B.	OF	26	.274	Bkn86	
		Werrick, Joseph Abraham	3B89	109	.210	B	C
		White, Wm. Dighton (3B11)	SS38	49	+.283	B	StL
		Wolf, Wm. V. (Chicken) (SS38)	OF83	127	.298	B	

WON 27 | AMERICAN ASSOCIATION | FINISHED 8th (LAST)
LOST 111
TG 138 | 1889. | PCT. .195

LOUISVILLE

MORDECAI H. DAVIDSON ROBERT M. BROWN HENRY L. MEANS
BUCK McKINNEY DANIEL W. SHANNON JOHN CURTIS CHAPMAN
WM. V. WOLF

WON	LOST	NAME	POS.	G.	BA	FROM	TO
0	1	Anderson, Wm.	P	1	.333	A	C
		Browning, Louis Roger (Pete)	OF	83	.253	B	
		Carl, Frederick E. (OF7)	2B18	25	.202	A	C
		Cook, Paul	C73	81	.236	B	
9	29	Ehret, Philip Sydney (Red)	P47	66	.239	K.C.	
		Esterbrook, Thomas Jefferson (Dude)	1B	11	.309	B	
7	30	Ewing, John	P40	41	.179	B	
		Fisher, Harry C.	OF	1	.000	ClevN84	C
		Flanagan, Edward F.	1B	23	.247	Ath87	C
		Galligan, John T.	OF	31	.167	A	C
		Gaule, Michael John	OF	1	.000	A	C
		Gleason, Wm. G.	SS	15	.216	Ath	C
5	11	Hecker, Guy Jackson (P17)	1B66	82	.277	B	
		Kerins, John Nelson (C1)	OF2	2	+.333	B	Balt
1	7	McDermott, Michael Joseph	P	9	.172	A	
2	18	Ramsey, Thomas A.	P	20	+.259	B	StL
0	0	Raymond, Harry H. (P1)	3B129	130	.241	B	
		Ryan, John Bennett (Jack)	C	21	.163	A	
		Scherer, Harry	OF	1	.333	A	C
		Shannon, Daniel W. MGR.	2B	120	.262	A	
		Smith, Harry N.	C	1	1.000	A	C
0	1	Springer, Edward E.	P	1	.000	A	C
3	14	Stratton, C. Scott (P19)	OF43	62	.280	B	
		Tomney, Philip H.	SS	112	.215	B	
		Traffley, John	OF	1	.500	A	C
		Vaughn, Harry Francis	C57	90	.233	B	
		Weaver, Wm. B.	OF122	124	.290	B	
		Wolf, Wm. V. (Chicken) MGR.	OF85	130	.291	B	

WON 88 | AMERICAN ASSOCIATION | FINISHED 1st.
LOST 44
TG 132 | 1890 | PCT. .667

LOUISVILLE

JOHN CURTIS CHAPMAN

WON	LOST	NAME	POS.	G.	BA	FROM	TO
		Bligh, Edwin Forrest	C	24	+.154	xCol	C.
6	2	Daily, Edward M. (OF11)	P12	23	.244	xNYN	
24	13	Ehret, Philip Sydney (Red)	P	42	.190	B	
		Esterday, Henry	SS	7	+.087	xAth	C
10	6	Goodall, Herbert Frank	P	18	.422	A	C
		Hamburg, Chas. H.	OF	134	.265	A	C
4	0	Jones, Michael	P	4	.286	A	C
10	8	Meakim, George Clinton	P	30	.153	A	
		O'Connor, Daniel C.	1B	6	.480	A	C
		Phelan, Daniel B.	1B	8	.250	A	C
		Raymond, Harry H.	3B	122	.280	B	
		Roseman, James J.	OF	2	+.250	xStL	C
		Ryan, John Bennett	C	94	.219	B	
		Shinnick, Timothy James	2B	133	.267	A	
34	15	Stratton, C. Scott	P	54	.325	B	
		Sweeney, Peter Jay	2B	2	+.143	xStL	Ath
		Taylor, Harry Leonard	1B	134	.279	A	
		Tomney, Philip H.	SS	110	.264	B	C
		Weaver, Wm. B.	OF	130	.292	B	
		Weckbecker, Peter	C	30	.234	IndplsN	C
		Wolf, Wm. V. (Chicken)	OF	134	.366	B	

WON 55 | AMERICAN ASSOCIATION | FINISHED 8th.
LOST 84
TG 139 | 1891. | PCT. .396

LOUISVILLE

JOHN CURTIS CHAPMAN

WON	LOST	NAME	POS.	G.	BA	FROM	TO
		Beard, Oliver Perry	3B61	68	.247	CinN	C
3	8	Bell, Chas. C.	P	11	+.000	KC89	Cin
1	0	Boone, George M.	P	4	.250	A	C
		Briggs, Grant	C	1	.250	Syr	

0	1	Cahill, Thomas H. (P1 SS48)	C54	119	.263	A	C
		Cline, John	OF	19	.304	KC88	C
		Cook, Paul	C	39	+.232	BknPL	StL
4	8	Daily, Edward M. (OF7)	P15	22	+.277	B	Wash
1	0	Darragh, James S.	P	1	.500	A	C
		Donovan, Patrick Joseph	OF	98	+.319	BknN	Wash
5	9	Doran, John F.	P	17	.189	A	C
13	12	Ehret, Philip Sydney (Red)	P	26	.258	B	
12	17	Fitzgerald, John T.	P31	32	.192	Roch	
		Fox, George B.	3B	6	.105	A	C
		Gerhardt, Joseph John (Moveup)	2B	2	.000	StL	C
		Irwin, John	3B	14	+.038	xBos	
		Jennings, Hugh Ambrose (1B17)	SS68	87	.286	A	
		Kuehne, Wm. J.	3B	40	+.275	xCol	
		LaRoque, Samuel H. J.	2B	9	.333	xPittN	C
		Long, James M.	OF	6	.240	A	
10	17	Meekin, Jouett	P29	33	.221	A	
		Pettee, Patrick E.	2B	2	.167	A	C
		Raymond, Harry H.	SS	14	.207	B	
		Reeder, Nicholas	3B	1	.000	A	C
		Ryan, John Bennett (Jack)	C54	75	.212	B	
		Schellhasse, Albert Herman	C	6	.156	BosN	C
		Shinnick, Timothy James	2B118	135	.225	B	C
6	12	Stratton, C. Scott	P22	33	.239	xPittN	
		Taylor, Harry Leonard	1B	91	.289	B	
		Weaver, Wm. B.	OF131	133	.284	B	
		Wentz, John George	2B	1	.250	A	C
		Wolf, Wm. V. (Chicken)	OF130	136	.250	B	

CLUB RECORD

OTHER MAJOR LEAGUES

NEW YORK

YEAR	TG	WON	LOST	PCT.	FINISHED	MANAGER
AMERICAN ASSOCIATION (METROPOLITANS)						
1883	96	54	42	.563	4	James J. Mutrie
1884	107	75	32	.701	1	James J. Mutrie
1885	108	44	64	.407	7	James H. Gifford
1886	135	53	82	.393	7	James H. Gifford Robert V. Ferguson
1887	133	44	89	.331	7	Robert V. Ferguson Oliver Perry Caylor
PLAYER'S LEAGUE						
1890	131	74	57	.565	3	Wm. Ewing

WON 54
LOST 42
TG 96

AMERICAN ASSOCIATION 1883. FINISHED 4th. PCT. .563

METROPOLITANS

JAMES J. MUTRIE

WON	LOST	NAME	POS.	G.	BA	FROM	TO
		Brady, Stephen A. (OF17)	1B80	97	.280	A	
		Crane, Samuel Newhall (OF1)	2B97	97	.234	BuffN80	
		Esterbrook, Thomas Jefferson (Dude)	3B	41	.250	ClevN	
		Holbert, Wm. H. (2B1 OF4)	C67	71	.238	TroyN	
41	26	Keefe, Timothy J. (OF1)	P70	70	.220	TroyN	
		Kennedy, Edward	OF	97	.215	A	
13	16	Lynch, John H.	P	29	.155	BuffN81	
		Nelson, Jackson W.	SS	96	.291	WorN81	
		O'Rourke, John (1B1)	OF79	79	.256	BosN80	C
		Orr, David L.	1B	1	.250	A	NYN
		Orr, David L.	1B	12	.326	xNYN(returned)	
		Reipschlager, Christopher Frederick (OF7)	C29	35	.189	A	
		Roseman, James J. (1B2)	OF93	93	.260	TroyN	

WON 75
LOST 32
TG 107

AMERICAN ASSOCIATION 1884. FINISHED 1st. PCT. .701

METROPOLITANS

JAMES J. MUTRIE

WON	LOST	NAME	POS.	G.	BA	FROM	TO
1	0	Becannon, James Melville	P	1	.000	A	
		Brady, Stephen A.	OF109	112	.269	B	
		Esterbrook, Thomas Jefferson (Dude)	3B	112	.408	B	
		Holbert, Wm. H.	C59	65	.208	B	
35	18	Keefe, Timothy J.	P57	62	.252	B	
		Kennedy, Edward	OF	103	.184	B	
39	14	Lynch, John H.	P	54	.144	B	
		Murphy,	C	1	.333	A	C
		Nelson, Jackson W.	SS110	111	.259	B	
		Orr, David L.	1B	110	.352	B	
		Oxley, Henry Havelock	C	1	.000	xNYN	C
		Pearce, Grayson S. (OF3)	2B3	5	.250	NYN	C
		Reipschlager, Christopher Frederick	C52	59	.236	B	
		Roseman, James J.	OF105	107	.295	B	
		Troy, John Joseph (Dasher)	2B	107	.264	NYN	

WON 44
LOST 64
TG 108

AMERICAN ASSOCIATION 1885. FINISHED 7th. PCT. .407

METROPOLITANS

JAMES H. GIFFORD

WON	LOST	NAME	POS.	G.	BA	FROM	TO
2	8	Becannon, James Melville	P	10	.229	B	
4	9	Begley, Edward N. (OF4)	P15	15	.173	NYN	C
		Brady, Stephen A.	OF	108	.296	B	
		Broughton, Cecil Calvert	C	12	+.356	xStL	
7	11	Crothers, Douglas	P	18	.157	KCUA	C
8	14	Cushman, Edgar Leander	P	22	+.145	xAth	
		Forster, Thomas W.	2B	57	.220	Pitt	
		Hankinson, Frank Edward	3B	96	.241	NYN	
		Holbert, Wm. H.	C39	55	.190	B	
		Jones, Chas. F.	3B	1	.250	Bkn	C
		Kennedy, Edward	OF	96	.222	B	
23	21	Lynch, John H.	P	45	.196	B	
		Nelson, Jackson W.	SS	107	.251	B	
		Orr, David L.	1B	107	.366	B	
		Pierson, Edward David	2B	3	.091	A	C
		Reilly, Joseph J. (3B2)	2B8	10	.122	BosUA	C
		Reipschlager, Christopher Frederick	C	72	.234	B	
0	1	Roseman, James J. (P1)	OF101	101	.284	B	
		Troy, John Joseph (Dasher)	2B	46	.225	B	C

WON 53
LOST 82
TG 135

AMERICAN ASSOCIATION 1886. FINISHED 7th. PCT. .393

METROPOLITANS

JAMES H. GIFFORD — ROBERT V. FERGUSON

WON	LOST	NAME	POS.	G.	BA	FROM	TO
		Behel, Stephen Arnold Douglas	OF	59	.208	MilUA84	C
		Brady, Stephen A.	OF	123	.234	B	C
0	1	Brooks, F. Harry	P	1	.000	A	C
		Crotty, Joseph	C	12	.205	Lvlle	C
17	21	Cushman, Edgar Leander	P	38	.147	B	
		Donahue, James Augustus (C20)	OF21	50	.201	A	
		Forster, Thomas W.	2B	84	.205	B	C
		Foster, Elmer E.	OF	18	.206	PhilUA84	
		Hankinson, Frank Edward	3B	136	.240	B	
		Holbert, Wm. H.	C	48	.216	B	
20	30	Lynch, John H.	P	51	.162	B	
11	27	Mays, Albert C.	P	41	.113	Lvlle	
		Meister, John F.	2B	45	.240	Tol84	
		McLaughlin, Thomas	SS	74	.137	Lvlle	
		Nelson, Jackson W. (OF27)	SS73	109	.230	B	
		Orr, David L.	1B	136	.346	B	

WON	LOST	NAME	POS.	G.	BA	FROM	TO
		Reipschlager, Christopher Frederick	C	66	.221	B	
		Roseman, James J.	OF	134	.228	B	
5	3	Schafer, John W.	P	8	.200	A	
		Zimmer, Chas. Louis (Chief)	C	5	.187	DetN84	
		Connell, Peter J.	3B	1	.000	A	C

WON 44
LOST 89
TG 133

AMERICAN ASSOCIATION

1887.

FINISHED 7th.
PCT. .331

METROPOLITANS

ROBERT V. FERGUSON   OLIVER PERRY CAYLOR   DAVID L. ORR

WON	LOST	NAME	POS.	G.	BA	FROM	TO
		Collins, Wm. J.	C	1	.250	A	
		Cross, Clarence	SS	16	.245	KCUA84	C
11	14	Cushman, Edgar Leander	P	26	.311	B	
		Donahue, James Augustus	C	60	.345	B	
		Esterbrook, Thomas Jefferson (Dude)	SS	26	.224	NYN	
1	4	Fagan, Wm. A.	P	6	.143	A	
		Gerhardt, Joseph John (Moveup)	2B	85	.277	xNYN	
		Hall, Archibald W.	OF	3	.214	ClevN80	C
		Hankinson, Frank Edward	3B	127	.315	B	
		Hogan, Robert Edward	OF	32	.377	MilUA84	
		Holbert, Wm. H.	C	70	.252	B	
		Houck, Stephen Arnold Douglas (Sadie)	SS	10	.222	WashN	C
		Jones, Chas. Wesley	OF	63	+.302	xCin	
		Kinslow, Thomas F.	C	2	.000	WashN	
		Knowles, James	3B	16	.262	WashN	
7	15	Lynch, John H.	P	23	.239	B	
17	34	Mays, Albert C.	P	62	.240	B	
		Meister, John F.	OF	39	.282	B	C
		Morrison, Jonathan W.	OF	9	.231	Indpls84	C
1	2	McMullen, George	P	3	.167	A	C
		Nelson, Jackson W. (OF36)	SS59	68	.361	B	NYN
		O'Brien, Thomas H.	1B	29	.248	Balt85	
		O'Brien, Wm. D. (Darby)	OF	129	.353	A	
		O'Neill, Frederick J.	OF	5	.391	A	C
		Orr, David L. MGR.	1B	85	.403	B	
1	1	Parsons, Chas. J.	P	4	.188	BosN	
		Pike, Lipman E.	OF	1	.000	WorN81	C
		Radford, Paul Revere (OF32)	SS78	128	.404	KCN	
		Roseman, James J.	OF	59	+.281	xAth	Bkn
		Ryan, Daniel R.	1B	8	.285	A	
2	11	Schafer, John W.	P	13	.188	B	C
		Sommers, Joseph Andrew (Pete)	C	32	.219	A	
4	8	Weidman, George E. (OF3)	P	12	.229	xDetN	NYN

WON 21
LOST 15
TG 36

AMERICAN ASSOCIATION

1891.

FINISHED 3rd.
PCT. .583

MILWAUKEE

CHAS. H. CUSHMAN

WON	LOST	NAME	POS.	G.	BA	FROM	TO
		Alberts, August P.	3B	12	.100	Clev88	C
		Burke, Edward D.	OF	34	.224	PittN	
		Canavan, James E. (2B4)	SS30	34	+.268	xCin	
		Carney, John Joseph	1B	30	+.291	xCin	C
		Dalrymple, Abner Frank	OF	31	.315	PittN88	C
		Daly, James J.	OF	1	.000	A	
7	5	Davies, George Washington	P	12	.231	A	
5	4	Dwyer, John Francis (Frank)	P	10	+.278	xCin	
		Earl, Howard J.	OF25	30	.254	ChiN	C
		Grim, John Helm (Jack)	C16	28	.233	Roch	
1	1	Hughey, James Ulysses	P	2	.167	A	
8	3	Killen, Frank Bissell	P	11	.229	A	
		Letcher, Thomas F.	OF	6	.130	A	C
0	2	Mains, Willard Eben	P	2	+.600	xCin	
		Pettit, Robert Henry	3B	21	.174	ChiN88	C
		Shoch, George Quintus	2B32	34	.299	WashN89	
		Vaughn, Harry Francis (1B4)	C20	24	+.330	xCin	

CLUB RECORD

OTHER MAJOR LEAGUES

PITTSBURGH

YEAR	TG	WON	LOST	PCT.	FINISHED	MANAGER
AMERICAN ASSOCIATION (ALLEGHENY)						
1882	78	39	39	.500	4	Albert G. Pratt
1883	98	30	68	.306	7	Albert G. Pratt Ormond H. Butler
1884	108	30	78	.278	11	Joseph V. Battin George W. Creamer Robert V. Ferguson Henry Dennis McKnight Horace B. Phillips
1885	111	56	55	.505	3	Horace B. Phillips
1886	137	80	57	.584	2	Horace B. Phillips
PLAYER'S LEAGUE						
1890	128	60	68	.469	6	Edward Hugh Hanlon
FEDERAL LEAGUE						
1914	151	64	87	.424	7	Ennis Talmadge Oakes
1915	153	86	67	.562	3	Ennis Talmadge Oakes
UNION ASSOCIATION						
1884	11	6	5	.545	DID NOT FINISH	Joseph V. Battin Joseph J. Ellick

WON 39
LOST 39
TG 78

AMERICAN ASSOCIATION

1882.

FINISHED 4th.

PCT. .500

PITTSBURGH

ALBERT G. PRATT

WON	LOST	NAME	POS.	G.	BA	FROM	TO
4	10	Arundel, Harvey (SS1)	P14	14	.192	A	
		Battin, Joseph V.	3B	28	.207	StLN77	
1	0	Critchley, Morris A.	P	1	+.000	A	StL
13	9	Driscoll, John F.	P	22	.149	BuffN80	
		Goodman, Jacob	1B9	10	.316	MilN78	C
		Keenan, James W. (SS1 OF1)	C22	24	.206	BuffN80	
		Kemmler, Rudolph (OF1)	C24	25	+.218	xCin	
		Lane, George M. (C2 OF11)	1B40	54	.167	A	
1	0	Leary, John J. (P3 1B1 2B1 OF28)	3B33	61	+.293	DetN	Balt
		Mansell, Michael R.	OF	73	.283	CinN80	
		Morgan, Henry Wm. (C6)	OF10	16	.279	MilN78	
		Morton, Chas. Hazen (2B1 SS1 3B2)	OF23	23	+.278	A	StL
		McKelvy, Russell Errett	OF	1	.000	IndplsN78	C
		Peters, John Paul (2B1)	SS72	72	.278	BuffN	
20	19	Salisbury, Henry H. (OF1)	P39	39	.152	TroyN79	C
0	1	Seymour, Thomas	P	1	.000	A	C
		Strief, George Andrew (SS1)	2B73	73	.202	ClevN79	
		Swartwood, Cyrus Edward (1B4)	OF70	71	.319	BuffN	
0	0	Taylor, Wm. Henry (P1 1B23 3B12 OF8)	C26	65	.286	ClevN	
		Wylie,	OF	1	.000	A	C

WON 30
LOST 68
TG 98

AMERICAN ASSOCIATION

1883.

FINISHED 7th.

PCT. .306

PITTSBURGH

ALBERT G. PRATT ORMOND H. BUTLER JOSEPH V. BATTIN

WON	LOST	NAME	POS.	G.	BA	FROM	TO
0	2	Baker, Norman Leslie (OF2)	P3	4	.000	A	
6	18	Barr, Robert M. (1B3 OF10)	P24	28	.230	A	
0	0	Battin, Joseph V. (P1) MGR.	3B96	96	.202	B	
		Blogg, Wesley C. (1B1 OF3)	C6	9	.147	A	C
		Creamer, George W.	2B	89	.243	WorN	
		#Dickerson, Lewis Pessano	OF80	80	.283	WorN81	
18	21	Driscoll, John F. (C1 3B1 OF4)	P39	41	.185	B	
		Hayes, John J. (2B1 SS5 OF15)	C61	83	.263	WorN	
		Mack, Dennis Joseph (1B23)	SS36	60	.200	Lvlle	C
		Mansell, Michael R.	OF	90	.240	B	
		Morgan, Henry Wm. (C5 2B2 OF6)	SS30	30	.167	B	

WON	LOST	NAME	POS.	G.	BA	FROM	TO
0	0	*McLaughlin, Francis Edward	SS24	27	.200	A	
3	13	Neagle, John Henry (OF14)	P17	29	+.168	xBalt	
0	6	Nolan, Edward Sylvester (The Only) (OF1)	P7	7	.296	ClevN81	
		Overbeck, Henry A.	1B	2	+.222	A	StL
		Peters, John Paul	SS	8	.107	B	
		Swartwood, Cyrus Edward (C3 OF36)	1B57	95	.369	B	
3	8	Taylor, Wm. Henry (P11 C29 1B10)	OF33	83	.259	B	

#Dickerson also played 1 game at 2B and 7 games at SS.
*McLaughlin also played 2 games in OF, 2 at 2B and 1 as pitcher.

WON 30 — AMERICAN ASSOCIATION — FINISHED 11th.
LOST 78
TG 108 — 1884. — PCT. .278

PITTSBURGH

JOSEPH V. BATTIN GEORGE W. CREAMER ROBERT V. FERGUSON
HENRY DENNIS McKNIGHT HORACE B. PHILLIPS

WON	LOST	NAME	POS.	G.	BA	FROM	TO
		Alberts, August P	SS	2	.200	A	WashUA
		Battin, Joseph V. MGR.	3B	43	.178	B	PittUA
0	3	Beck, Frank J.	P	3	.364	A	BaltUA
		Colgan, Wm. H.	C44	48	.166	A	C
		Creamer, George W. MGR.	2B98	100	.185	B	C
		Dee, James D.	SS	13	.136	A	C
		Doyle, John A.	OF	23	.203	A	C
0	1	Eden, Chas. M. (P1)	OF31	32	.305	ClevN79	
		Faatz, Jay	1B	29	.230	A	
		Ferguson, Robert V. MGR. (1B3 3B1)	OF6	10	.154	PhilN	
		Forster, Thomas W. (3B5)	SS29	35	.212	DetN82	
1	6	Fox, John Joseph (SS1)	P7	8	.240	Balt	
1	2	Gorman, John F. (3B2 OF3)	P3	8	.133	xKCUA	C
		Gray, James W.	3B	1	1.000	A	C
		Hayes, John J. (1B5 2B1 OF3)	C25	34	+.220	B	Bkn
		Houtz, Chas. (OF2)	1B7	9	.226	A	C
		Knowles, James	1B	46	+.228	A	Bkn
0	2	Lauer, John Chas. (Chuck) (P3 1B1)	OF10	13	.109	A	
		Mansell, Michael R.	OF	27	+.131	B	Ath
		Miller, George Frederick (C36)	OF48	88	.222	A	
		McDonald, James A. (OF11)	3B22	38	.151	A	
11	26	Neagle, John Henry	P37	41	.148	B	C
1	2	Nelson, Wm. F.	P	3	.167	A	C
		Peters, John Paul	SS	1	.000	B	C
		Quest, Joseph L. (SS5)	2B7	12	+.209	xStL	
		Reid, Wm. A.	OF18	19	.246	Balt	C

WON	LOST	NAME	POS.	G.	BA	FROM	TO
		Smith, Frank L. (OF3)	C7	10	.263	A	C
0	1	Smith, John Francis	P	1	+.000	xAth	
16	35	Sullivan, Florence P.	P51	54	.151	A	C
		Swartwood, Cyrus Edward (1B22)	OF77	102	.330	B	
		Taylor, Edward S.	OF	41	.202	A	C
		White, Wm. Dighton (3B10)	SS61	74	.219	A	
		Whitney, Arthur Wilson	3B	22	.299	DetN82	
		Woulffe, James Joseph	OF	16	+.127	xCin	C

WON 56 — AMERICAN ASSOCIATION — FINISHED 3rd.
LOST 55
TG 111 — 1885. — PCT. .505

PITTSBURGH

HORACE B. PHILLIPS

WON	LOST	NAME	POS.	G.	BA	FROM	TO
		Brown, Thomas T.	OF	108	.304	Col	
		Carroll, Frederick Herbert	C	69	.263	Col	
1	2	Eden, Chas. M. (P3)	OF95	98	.264	B	C
		Field, James	1B	56	+.245	Col	Balt
3	8	Galvin, James F. (Jimmy) (OF1)	P11	11	.108	xBuffN	
0	2	Hofford, John Wm.	P	3	.123	A	
		Kemmler, Rudolph	C	18	.191	Col	
		Kuehne, Wm. J.	3B	105	.216	Col	
		Mann, Frederick I.	OF	100	.253	Col	
7	8	Meegan, Peter J.	P	19	.151	Rich	C
		Miller, George Frederick (Fog-Horn)	C	42	.161	B	
1	4	Mountain, Frank H.	P	5	.100	Col	
39	24	Morris, Edward	P	64	.102	Col	
5	7	O'Day, Henry F. (Hank)	P	14	.255	Tol	
		Phillips, Marr B.	SS	2	.375	xDetN	
		Richmond, John H.	SS	34	.206	Col	C
		Ringo, Frank C.	C	3	.182	xDetN	
		Scott, Milton Parker	1B	55	.241	xDetN	
		Smith, Chas. Marvin (Pap)	2B	106	.258	Col	
		Whitney, Arthur Wilson	SS	90	.227	B	

WON 80 — AMERICAN ASSOCIATION — FINISHED 2nd.
LOST 57
TG 137 — 1886. — PCT. .584

PITTSBURGH

HORACE B. PHILLIPS

WON	LOST	NAME	POS.	G.	BA	FROM	TO
		Barkley, Samuel Wilson	2B	122	.269	StL	
0	1	Bishop, Wm. R.	P	2	.143	A	
		Brown, Thomas T.	OF	114	.280	B	

		Carroll, Frederick Herbert (1B25)	C71	122	.292	B	
		Coleman, John Francis (Jack)	OF	10	+.333	xAth	
29	21	Galvin, James F. (Jimmie)	P	50	.251	B	
		Glenn, Edward C.	OF	71	.182	Rich84	
7	7	Handiboe, James Edward (OF2)	P14	14	.114	A	C
3	6	Hofford, John Wm.	P	9	.333	B	C
		Kuehne, Wm. J. (3B44)	OF73	117	.211	B	
		Mann, Frederick I.	OF	117	.259	B	
		Miller, George Frederick (Fog-Horn)	C	83	.258	B	
0	2	Mountain, Frank H. (P2)	1B16	18	.148	B	C
41	20	Morris, Edward	P	63	.174	B	
		Quinn, Thomas G.	C	3	.000	A	
		Ringo, Frank C.	C	16	.241	B	KCN
		Shomberg, Otto H.	1B	72	.295	A	
		Smith, Chas. Marvin (Pap) (2B28)	SS88	126	.223	B	
		Sullivan, Daniel C.	C	1	.000	StL	C
		Whitney, Arthur Wilson (SS42)	3B94	136	.225	B	

CLUB RECORD

OTHER MAJOR LEAGUES

RICHMOND

YEAR	TG	WON	LOST	PCT.	FINISHED	MANAGER
AMERICAN ASSOCIATION (VIRGINIA)						
1884	42	12	30	.286	10	Felix I. Moses

WON 12
LOST 30
TG 42

AMERICAN ASSOCIATION

1884.

FINISHED 10th.

PCT. .286

RICHMOND

FELIX I. MOSES

WON	LOST	NAME	POS.	G.	BA	FROM	TO
0	2	Curry, Wesley	P	2	.286	A	C
5	15	Dugan, Edward J. (2B2)	P20	21	.114	A	C
		Dugan, Wm. E.	C	8	.040	A	C
0	1	Firth, Theodore John	P	1	.333	A	C
		Ford, (SS1)	1B1	2	.000	A	C
		Glenn, Edward C.	OF	42	.250	A	
		Goldsby, Walton Hugh	OF	10	+.222	xWash	
		Hanna, John (SS1)	C21	22	+.206	xWash	C
		Johnston, Richard Frederick (SS2)	OF37	39	.286	A	
		Larkin, Frank	2B	39	.179	xWashUA	C
		Mansell, Michael R.	OF	29	+.301	xAth	C
7	12	Meegan, Peter J. (OF1)	P22	23	.156	A	
		Morgan, Henry Wm. (2B1 OF2)	C3	6	+.100	xWash	BaltUA
		Nash, Wm. Mitchell	3B	44	.188	A	
		Powell, James E.	1B	40	.243	A	C
		Quinton, Marshall J. (OF10)	C14	26	.231	A	
		Schenck, Wm. G. (2B2)	SS39	41	.218	Lvlle82	
		Swan, Albert D.	1B	3	+.500	xWash	C
		Williams, Washington J.	OF	2	.250	A	

CLUB RECORD

OTHER MAJOR LEAGUES

ROCHESTER

YEAR	TG	WON	LOST	PCT.	FINISHED	MANAGER
AMERICAN ASSOCIATION						
1890	126	63	63	.500	5	Patrick Thomas Powers

WON 63
LOST 63
TG 126

AMERICAN ASSOCIATION

1890.

FINISHED 5th.

PCT. .500

ROCHESTER

PATRICK THOMAS POWERS

WON	LOST	NAME	POS.	G.	BA	FROM	TO
28	25	Barr, Robert M.	P	57	.227	WashN86	
0	1	Blauvelt, Henry R.	P	2	.500	A	C
		Burke, Daniel F.	OF	30	+.286	A	Syr
18	13	Calihan, Wm. T.	P	48	.135	A	
		Field, James	1B	51	.190	Balt85	
3	8	Fitzgerald, John T.	P	12	.187	A	
		Greenwood, Wm. F.	2B	121	.226	Col	C
		Griffin, Tobias Chas. (Sandy)	OF	107	.305	NYN84	
2	0	Grim, John Helm (Jack) (P2 C17)	SS20	50	.254	PhiIN88	
		Knowles, James	3B	124	.281	Met87	
		Lyons, Harry P.	OF	132	.264	NYN	
3	8	Miller, Robert W.	P	13	.166	A	
		McGuire, James Thomas	C	87	.301	Clev88	
		McKeough, David J.	C	63	.218	A	
		O'Brien, Thomas H.	1B	73	.181	Met87	C
		Phillips, Marr B.	SS	65	.196	Pitt85	C
		Reccius, Philip	OF	1	.000	Lvlle88	C
		Scheffler, Theodore J.	OF	117	.239	DetN88	C
		Smith, Leo H.	SS	35	.190	A	C
9	8	Titcomb, Ledell	P	21	.106	NYN	C

CLUB RECORD

OTHER MAJOR LEAGUES

ST. LOUIS

YEAR	TG	WON	LOST	PCT.	FINISHED	MANAGER
AMERICAN ASSOCIATION						
1882	79	36	43	.456	5	Theodore Paul Sullivan
1883	98	65	33	.663	2	Theodore Paul Sullivan Chas. Albert Comiskey
1884	107	67	40	.626	4	James A. Williams Christopher Von der Ahe
1885	112	79	33	.705	1	Chas. Albert Comiskey
1886	139	93	46	.669	1	Chas. Albert Comiskey
1887	135	95	40	.704	1	Chas. Albert Comiskey
1888	135	92	43	.681	1	Chas. Albert Comiskey
1889	135	90	45	.667	2	Chas. Albert Comiskey
1890	136	78	58	.574	3	Thomas Francis M. McCarthy James J. Roseman Chas. C. Campau
1891	138	86	52	.623	2	Chas. Albert Comiskey
UNION ASSOCIATION						
1884	107	91	16	.850	1	Theodore Paul Sullivan Frederick C. Dunlap
FEDERAL LEAGUE						
1914	150	61	89	.407	8 (Last)	Mordecai Peter Centennial Brown Fielder Allison Jones
1915	154	87	67	.565	2	Fielder Allison Jones

WON 36 LOST 43 TG 79

AMERICAN ASSOCIATION 1882.

FINISHED 5th. PCT. .456

ST. LOUIS

EDGAR EDWARD CUTHBERT THEODORE PAUL SULLIVAN

WON	LOST	NAME	POS.	G.	BA	FROM	TO
0	0	Brown, Edward P. (P1 2B1)	OF16	17	.177	A	
0	1	Comiskey, Chas. Albert (P1)	1B77	78	.244	A	
0	3	Critchley, Morris A.	P	4	+.214	xPitt	C
		Crotty, Joseph (OF1)	C7	8	+.133	xLvlle	
		Cuthbert, Edgar Edward MGR.	OF	60	.219	CinN77	
		Decker, Edward Harry	2B	2	.250	SyrN79	
3	5	Dorr, Chas. Albert	P	8	.160	A	C
0	3	Doyle, Edward H.	P	3	.000	A	C
0	2	Fusselbach, Edward C. (P2 OF14)	C19	35	.219	A	
		Gleason, John Day (2B1 OF5)	3B73	78	.262	StLN77	
		Gleason, Wm. G.	SS	79	.286	A	
0	1	Hogan, Robert Edward	P	1	.333	A	
		Leonard, Andrew Jackson	OF	1	.250	CinN80	C
		Morton, Chas. Hazen (OF3)	2B7	9	+.059	xPitt	
		McCaffrey, Harry C. (1B1 2B9 3B6)	OF18	37	.268	A	
25	21	McGinnis, George W. (2B1 OF5)	P46	51	.227	A	
8	7	Schappert, John (OF1)	P15	15	.173	A	C
		Seward, George E. (C5)	OF6	38	.195	MutN76	C
		Shoup, John F.	2B	2	.000	TroyN79	
		Smiley, Wm. B. (SS1 OF1)	2B57	58	+.208	A	Balt
		Sullivan, Thomas Jefferson	C	51	.182	BosN	
		Walker, Oscar (1B1 2B1)	OF75	76	.233	BuffN80	
0	0	Mitchell, Robert McKasha (OF1)	P1	1	.000	ClevN79	C

WON 65 LOST 33 TG 98

AMERICAN ASSOCIATION 1883.

FINISHED 2nd. PCT. .663

ST. LOUIS

THEODORE PAUL SULLIVAN CHAS. ALBERT COMISKEY

WON	LOST	NAME	POS.	G.	BA	FROM	TO
		*Comiskey, Chas. Albert MGR.	1B95	95	.290	B	
		Cuthbert, Edgar Edward (1B1)	OF21	21	.158	B	
		Deasley, Thomas H. (Pat) (OF1)	C	53	.250	BosN	
0	0	Dolan, Thomas J. (P1 OF40)	C40	78	.222	BuffN	
		Ewing, John	OF	1	.000	A	
		Gleason, John Day (3B1)	OF9	9	+.205	B	Lvlle
		Gleason, Wm. G.	SS	95	.274	B	
		Gorman, John F. (OF1)	C1	1	.000	A	
1	1	Hodnet, Chas. (OF1)	P4	4	.154	A	
		Latham, Walter Arlington (Arlie)	3B	97	.228	BuffN80	
		Lewis, Frederick Miller	OF	50	.295	xPhilN	
		Loftus, Thomas Joseph	OF	6	.160	StLN77	
		Mansell, Thomas E.	OF	28	.370	xDetN	
35	17	Mullane, Anthony John (Tony) (1B2 2B3 OF27)	P52	77	.201	Lvlle	
		McCaffrey, Harry C.	OF	5	.053	B	
29	15	McGinnis, George W. (OF4)	P44	44	.211	B	
		Nicol, Hugh N. (2B9)	OF76	85	.263	ChiN	
		Overbeck, Henry A.	OF	4	+.000	xPitt	
		Quest, Joseph L.	2B	20	.253	xDetN	
		Strief, George Andrew (OF15)	2B66	78	.211	Pitt	
		Sullivan, Thomas Jefferson (OF1)	C7	8	.148	B	

*Comiskey also played 1 game in the OF.

WON 67 LOST 40 TG 107

AMERICAN ASSOCIATION 1884.

FINISHED 4th. PCT. 626

ST. LOUIS

JAMES A. WILLIAMS CHRISTIAN FREDERICK WILHELM VON DER AHE

WON	LOST	NAME	POS.	G.	BA	FROM	TO
		Alexander, Wm. Henry (OF1)	C1	1	.000	xKCUA	C
7	2	Caruthers, Robert Lee (OF16)	P13	23	.253	A	
		Comiskey, Chas. Albert	1B	108	.241	B	
11	12	Davis, John A.	P23	26	.168	A	BosN
		Deasley, Thomas H. (Pat)	C	73	.202	B	
		Dolan, Thomas J.	C33	35	.263	B	StLUA
15	6	Foutz, David Luther (OF7)	P23	32	.233	A	
		Fulmer, Chas J.	2B	1	+.000	xCin	C
		Gleason, Wm. G.	SS	110	.269	B	
		Goldsby, Walton Hugh	OF	5	+.211	A	Wash
		Kenzie, Walter H.	2B	2	.125	xChiN	C
		Krehmeyer, Chas. L. (C6)	OF8	20	.257	A	
		Latham, Walter Arlington (Arlie)	3B	110	.276	B	
		Lavin, John	OF15	16	.204	A	C
		Lewis, Frederick Miller	OF	72	.322	B	StLUA
		McCauley, James A.	C	1	.000	A	
24	16	McGinnis, George W.	P	40	.234	B	
		Nicol, Hugh N. (2B23)	OF87	110	.270	B	
10	4	O'Neill, James Edward (Tip) (P17)	OF58	77	.272	NYN	
		Quest, Joseph L.	2B	81	+.200	B	Pitt
		Strief, George Andrew	OF42	47	.193	B	KCUA
		Wheeler, Harry Eugene	OF	5	.200	Col	KCUA

WON 79
LOST 33
TG 112

AMERICAN ASSOCIATION 1885. FINISHED 1st. PCT. .705

ST. LOUIS

CHAS. ALBERT COMISKEY

WON	LOST	NAME	POS.	G.	BA	FROM	TO
		Barkley, Samuel Wilson (1B14)	2B82	96	.179	Tol	
		Broughton, Cecil Calvert	C	3	+.083	MilUA	Met
		Bushong, Albert John	C	85	.265	ClevN	
40	13	Caruthers, Robert Lee	P	60	.207	B	
		Comiskey, Chas. Albert MGR.	1B	83	.260	B	
		Drissel, Nicholas Michael	C	6	.056	A	C
33	14	Foutz, David Luther (1B15)	P47	65	.250	B	
		Gleason, Wm. G.	SS	112	.253	B	
		Latham, Walter Arlington (Arlie)	3B	110	.213	B	
6	6	McGinnis, George M.	P	13	.224	B	
		Nicol, Hugh N.	OF	112	.211	B	
		O'Neill, James Edward (Tip)	OF	51	.342	B	
		Robinson, Wm. H. (Yank) (C1 2B30)	OF47	78	.259	BaltUA	
		Sullivan, Daniel C.	C	17	+.138	xLvlle	
		Welch, Curtis Benton	OF	112	.266	Tol	

WON 93
LOST 46
TG 139

AMERICAN ASSOCIATION 1886. FINISHED 1st. PCT. .669

ST. LOUIS

CHAS. ALBERT COMISKEY

WON	LOST	NAME	POS.	G.	BA	FROM	TO
		Bushong, Albert John	C	107	.229	B	
30	14	Caruthers, Robert Lee (OF39)	P45	86	.342	B	
		Comiskey, Chas. Albert MGR.	1B	131	.260	B	
41	16	Foutz, David Luther (OF33)	P57	89	.282	B	
		Gleason, Wm. G.	SS	126	.267	B	
		Harding, Lewis Edward	C	1	.000	A	C
16	13	Hudson, Nathaniel P.	P	40	.223	A	
		Kemmler, Rudolph	C	35	.150	Pitt	
		Latham, Walter Arlington (Arlie)	3B	134	.303	B	
1	0	Murphy, Joseph Akin	P	1	.000	xStLN	
5	2	McGinnis, George W.	P	10	+.189	B	Balt
		McSorley, John Bernard	SS	5	.150	StLN	C
		Nicol, Hugh N.	OF	67	.204	B	
		O'Neill, James Edward (Tip)	OF	138	.329	B	
0	1	Robinson, Wm. H. (Yank) (Pl)	2B133	133	.279	B	
		Welch, Curtis Benton	OF	138	.285	B	

WON 95
LOST 40
TG 135

AMERICAN ASSOCIATION 1887. FINISHED 1st. PCT. .704

ST. LOUIS

CHAS. ALBERT COMISKEY

WON	LOST	NAME	POS.	G.	BA	FROM	TO
		Boyle, John Anthony (Jack)	C	88	.240	Cin	
		Bushong, Albert John	C	53	.295	B	
29	9	Caruthers, Robert Lee (P38)	OF44	98	.459	B	
		Comiskey, Chas. Albert MGR.	1B	125	.368	B	
24	12	Foutz, David Luther (P36)	OF51	103	.393	B	
		Gleason, Wm. G.	SS	135	.336	B	
		Goodfellow, Michael J.	C	1	.000	A	
3	5	Hudson, Nathaniel P.	P	13	.340	B	
34	11	King, Chas. Frederick	P	62	.280	KCN	
4	3	Knouff, Edward (P7)	OF10	16	+.190	xBalt	
		Latham, Walter Arlington (Arlie)	3B	136	.307	B	
		Lyons, Harry P.	2B	2	.125	xPhilN	
1	0	Murphy, Joseph Akin	P	1	.167	B	C
		O'Neill, James Edward (Tip)	OF	123	.495	B	
		Robinson, Wm. H. (Yank)	2B	124	.426	B	
		Sylvester, Louis J.	OF	28	.298	Cin	C
		Welch, Curtis Benton	OF	131	.307	B	

WON 92
LOST 43
TG 135

AMERICAN ASSOCIATION 1888. FINISHED 1st. PCT. .681

ST. LOUIS

CHAS. ALBERT COMISKEY

WON	LOST	NAME	POS.	G.	BA	FROM	TO
		Boyle, John Anthony (Jack)	C70	71	.245	B	
11	2	Chamberlain, Elton P. (OF1)	P20	20	+.080	xLvlle	
		Comiskey, Chas. Albert MGR.	1B133	137	.271	B	
6	5	Devlin, James H.	P	12	.306	PhilN	
		Dolan, Thomas J.	C	11	.194	Balt86	
0	1	Freeman, Julius B.	P	1	.333	A	C
		Herr, Edward Joseph	SS28	43	.266	Clev	
26	10	Hudson, Nathaniel P.	P37	55	.262	B	
44	21	King, Chas. Frederick	P	66	.212	B	
5	4	Knouff, Edward	P	9	+.097	B	Clev
		Latham, Walter Arlington (Arlie)	3B132	133	.264	B	
		Lyons, Harry P.	OF108	123	.190	B	
		Milligan, John (Jack)	C58	63	.252	Ath	
0	0	*McCarthy, Thomas Francis Michael (Pl)	OF118	131	.276	PhilN	
		McGarr, James B. (Chippy)	2B34	35	.187	Ath	
		O'Neill, James Edward (Tip)	OF	130	.332	B	
		Robinson, Wm. H. (Yank) (SS34)	2B100	134	.231	B	
		White, Wm Dighton	SS	69	+.176	xLvlle	C

WON 90
LOST 45
TG 135

AMERICAN ASSOCIATION — FINISHED 2nd.

1889. — PCT. .667

ST. LOUIS

CHAS. J. COMISKEY

WON	LOST	NAME	POS.	G.	BA	FROM	TO
		Bellman, John Chas.	C	1	.500	A	C
		Boyle, John Anthony (Jack)	C82	99	.250	B	
35	15	Chamberlain, Elton P.	P	53	.197	B	
		Comiskey, Chas. Albert MGR.	1B134	137	.288	B	
		Davis, James J. (OF1)	SS1	2	+.000	xK.C.	
4	2	Devlin, James H.	P	9	.178	B	C
		Duffee, Chas. Edward	OF132	137	.245	A	
		Fuller, Wm. Benjamin	SS	140	.228	WashN	
		Gettinger, Thomas L.	OF	3	.455	A	
		Gill, James C. (OF1)	2B1	2	.250	A	C
2	2	Hudson, Nathaniel P. (P4)	OF7	13	.245	B	C
33	17	King, Chas. Frederick	P	54	.225	B	
		Latham, Walter Arlington (Arlie)	3B116	118	.254	B	
		Meek, Frank J.	C	2	.500	A	
		Milligan, John (Jack)	C67	72	.370	B	
		McCarthy, Thomas Francis Michael	OF139	139	.297	B	
		O'Neill, James Edward (Tip)	OF	133	.337	B	
4	2	Ramsey, Thomas A.	P	6	+.313	xLvlle	
		Robinson, Wm. H. (Yank)	2B	132	.210	B	
12	7	Stivetts, John Elmer	P25	26	.228	A	
		Sweeney, Peter Jay	3B	9	.310	xWashN	

WON 78
LOST 58
TG 136

AMERICAN ASSOCIATION — FINISHED 3rd.

1890. — PCT. .574

ST. LOUIS

THOMAS FRANCIS MICHAEL McCARTHY — JAMES J. ROSEMAN
CHAS. C. CAMPAU

WON	LOST	NAME	POS.	G.	BA	FROM	TO
		Adams, James J.	C	1	.250	A	C
		Burke, Joseph M.	3B	2	.571	A	
		Campau, Chas. C. MGR.	OF	74	.274	DetN88	
		Cartwright, Edward H.	1B	75	.281	A	
2	3	Chamberlain, Elton P.	P	5	+.143	B	Col
		Creeley, August	SS	4	.000	A	C
		Davis, James J.	3B	21	+.250	B	Bkn
		Donely, James B.	3B	11	.344	WashN	
		Duffee, Chas. Edward	OF	98	.274	B	
		Earle, Wm. Moffat	C	23	.212	Cin	
		Fuller, Wm. Benjamin	SS	130	.271	B	
		Gerhardt, Joseph John (2B18) (Moveup)	3B19	37	+.260	xBkn	
		Gettinger, Thomas L.	OF	59	.260	B	
12	9	Hart, Joseph L.	P	28	.208	A	C
		Hartnett, Patrick J.	1B	13	.200	A	C
		Herr, Edward Joseph	2B	12	.233	StL88	C
		Higgins, Wm. H.	2B	64	+.251	BosN88	Syr
		Kane, Jeremiah	C	8	.160	A	C
		Kerins, John Nelson	C	19	.136	Balt	C
		Klussman, Wm. F.	1B	15	.275	BosN88	C
		Meek, Frank J.	C	4	.333	B	C
		Millard, Frank E.	2B	1	.000	A	C
		Miller, Chas. Brandley (Dusty)	OF	27	.203	Balt	
		Munyan, John B.	C	94	+.270	xCol	
		McCarthy, Thomas Francis Michael MGR.	OF	133	.332	B	
3	3	Neal, Joseph H.	P	10	.074	Lvlle87	
2	2	Nicol, George Edward	P	4	.286	A	
		Pabst, Edward D.A.	OF	4	+.143	xAth	C
22	14	Ramsey, Thomas A.	P	44	.211	B	C
		Roseman, James J. MGR.	OF	80	+.322	Bkn87	Lvlle
31	20	Stivetts, John Elmer	P	67	.277	B	
		Sweeney, Peter Jay	3B	49	+.162	B	Lvlle
		Trost, Michael J.	C	17	.250	A	
		Wells, Jacob	C	28	.238	DetN88	C
6	7	Whitrock, Wm. Franklin	P	13	.142	A	

WON x86
LOST 52
TG 138

AMERICAN ASSOCIATION — FINISHED 2nd.

1891. — PCT. 623

ST. LOUIS

CHAS. ALBERT COMISKEY

WON	LOST	NAME	POS.	G.	BA	FROM	TO
		Boyle, John Anthony (Jack)(SS25)	C91	120	.280	ChiPL	
0	1	Breitenstein, Theodore P.	P	5	.000	A	
3	2	Burrill, Harry J.	P	9	.227	A	C
		Comiskey, Chas. Albert MGR.	1B	139	.257	ChiPL	
		Cook, Paul	C	7	+.179	xLvlle	C
		Darling, Dell Conrad	C	17	.137	ChiPL	C
		Dolan, Thomas J.	C	1	.000	StL88	C
1	1	Duryea, James Whitney (Jesse)	P	4	.400	xCinN	
		Eagan, Wm. (Bad Bill)	2B	81	.222	A	
4	3	Easton, John E.	P	9	+.179	xCol	Col (return)
		Fuller, Henry W.	3B	1	.000	A	C
		Fuller, Wm. Benjamin (2B37)	SS98	135	.219	B	
		Geiss, Wm.	2B	76	.323	DetN84	C
11	8	Griffith, Clark Calvin	P	27	+.167	A	Bos
		Hoy, Wm. Ellsworth (Dummy)	OF	139	.288	BuffPL	
		Lyons, Dennis Patrick Aloysius	3B	120	.312	Ath	
		Munyan, John B.	C41	59	.234	B	C
		McCarthy, Thomas Francis Michael	OF107	135	.302	B	
19	9	McGill, Wm. Vaness (Billy)	P	28	+.176	xCin	

WON	LOST	NAME	POS.	G.	BA	FROM	TO
		McQuaid, James	2B	4	.333	A	
		McSweeney, Paul	2B	3	.250	A	C
6	4	Neal, Joseph H.	P	15	.122	B	C
		Newman, Chas. C.	C	1	.000	A	
		O'Neill, James Edward (Tip)	OF	127	.321	ChiPL	
10	3	Rettger, George Edward	P	15	.070	A	
		Ricks, John	3B	5	.158	A	
		Schultz,	C	1	.000	A	C
31	21	Stivetts, John Elmer (OF19)	P66	85	.305	B	
		Visner, Joseph P.	OF	5	+.136	xWash	C
		Whitney, Arthur Wilson	3B	2	+.000	xCin	C
		Zies, Wm.	C	1	.000	A	C

x-One game won by forfeit.

WON 55 AMERICAN ASSOCIATION FINISHED 7th.
LOST 72
TG 127 1890. PCT. .433

SYRACUSE

WALLACE CLIFTON FESSENDEN GEORGE KASSON FRAZER

WON	LOST	NAME	POS.	G.	BA	FROM	TO
		Battin, Joseph V.	3B	29	.194	BaltUA84	C
		Briggs, Grant	C	86	.179	A	
		Burke, Daniel F.	C	9	+.000	xRoch	
20	22	Casey, Daniel Maurice	P	48	.138	PhilN	C
		Childs, Clarence Algernon	2B	136	.344	PhilN88	
0	1	Dealey, Patrick E. (P1)	C17	18	.174	WashN87	C
		Dorgan, Michael Cornelius	OF	31	.219	NYN87	C
		Ely, Frederick Wm. (SS33)	OF65	118	.263	Lvlle86	
		Friel, Patrick Henry	OF	62	.238	A	
		Graff, Louis George	C	1	.400	A	C
		Hemp, Wm. H. (Ducky)	OF	9	.156	xPittN	C
		Higgins, Wm. H.	2B	1	+.250	xStL	C
14	23	Keefe, John T.	P	44	.195	A	C
0	1	Keffer, C. Frank	P	1	.250	A	C
		Leighton, John Atkinson	OF	7	.266	A	C
0	3	Lincoln, Ezra Perry	P	3	.000	xClevN	C
1	2	Lyons, Toby A.	P	3	.273	A	C
9	6	Mars, Edward	P	17	.252	A	C
7	8	Morrison, Michael (P15)	OF20	32	+.238	Clev88	Balt
2	2	McCullough, Chas.	P	5	+.100	xBkn	C
		McLaughlin, Bernard	SS	81	.260	PhilN87	C
		McQuery, Wm. Thomas	1B	120	.295	KCN86	
		O'Rourke, Thomas Joseph	C	43	.227	xNYN	C
		O'Rourke, Timothy Patrick	3B	82	.288	A	
		Peltz, John	OF	5	+.176	xBkn	Tol
		Pitz, Herman (SS1 OF1)	C27	29	+.216	xBkn	C
		Proeser, George	OF	13	.264	Clev88	C
		Simon, Henry J.	OF	37	+.294	xBkn	C
2	4	Sullivan, Wm. T.	P	6	.080	A	C
		Wright, Wm. S. (Rasty)	OF	89	.285	A	ClevN

CLUB RECORD

OTHER MAJOR LEAGUES

TOLEDO

YEAR	TG	WON	LOST	PCT.	FINISHED	MANAGER
AMERICAN ASSOCIATION						
1884	104	46	58	.442	8	Chas. H. Morton
1885-1889	OUT OF LEAGUE					
1890	132	68	64	.515	4	Chas. H. Morton

WON 46 LOST 58 TG 104 — AMERICAN ASSOCIATION 1884. — FINISHED 8th. PCT. .442

TOLEDO

CHAS. HAZEN MORTON

WON	LOST	NAME	POS.	G.	BA	FROM	TO
		Arundel, John Thomas (Tug)	C	14	.087	Ath82	
		Barkley, Samuel Wilson	2B102	104	.300	A	
		Brown, Edward P.	3B40	42	.174	StL82	C
		Ballas, Simon D. (OF1)	C12	13	.067	A	C
0	1	Kent, Edward C.	P	1	.000	A	C
		Lane, George M. (OF5)	1B44	56	.231	Pitt82	C
		Meister, John F.	3B	34	.199	A	
		Miller, Joseph A.	SS	105	.236	A	
		Miller, L. Edward	OF	8	.208	A	C
		Moffet, Joseph W. (3B11)	1B39	56	.207	A	C
0	1	Morton, Chas. H. (P1) MGR.	OF17	31	.188	StL82	
36	26	Mullane, Anthony John (Tony) (1B6 OF13)	P66	95	.276	StL	
		McGuire, James Thomas	C40	45	.184	A	
		McSorley, John Bernard	1B16	21	.249	A	
10	29	O'Day, Henry F. (Hank) (OF14)	P40	65	.209	A	
		Olin, Franklin Walter	OF	26	.271	xWashUA	
0	1	Poorman, Thomas Iverson (P1)	OF92	93	.224	ChiN80	
		Tilley, John C.	OF16	17	.182	ClevN82	StPUA
		Walker, Moses Fleetwood	C41	41	.251	A	C
		Welch, Curtis Benton	OF104	109	.224	A	
		Walker, Welday Wilberforce	OF	5	.222	A	C

WON 68 LOST 64 TG 132 — AMERICAN ASSOCIATION 1890. — FINISHED 4th. PCT. .515

TOLEDO

CHAS. HAZEN MORTON

WON	LOST	NAME	POS.	G.	BA	FROM	TO
1	2	Abbott, Leander Franklin	P	3	.143	A	C
		Alvord, Wm. C.	3B	120	.283	K.C.	
17	20	Cushman, Edgar Leander	P	39	.116	Met87	C
1	0	Doty, Elmer L.	P	1	.000	A	C
		Doyle, Cornelius J.	3B	1	.000	PhilN83	C
22	19	Healy, John J. (Egyptian)	P	47	.219	ChiN	
		Nicholson, Thomas C.	2B	133	.261	DetN88	
2	1	O'Neil, Edward J.	P	3	+.000	A	Ath
		Peltz, John	OF	18	+.227	xSyr	C
		Ritter,	C	1	.000	A	C
		Rogers, Emmett	C	35	.184	A	C
0	1	Sage, Henry (P1)	C57	58	.139	A	C

WON	LOST	NAME	POS.	G.	BA	FROM	TO
		Scheibeck, Frank S.	SS	134	.234	DetN88	
19	14	Smith, Frederick C.	P	37	.133	A	C
		Sneed, John L.	OF	9	+.167	Indpls84	Col
6	7	Sprague, Chas. Wellington (P14)	OF37	51	.245	ClevN	C
		Swartwood, Cyrus Edward	OF	126	.309	Bkn87	
		Tebeau, George E.	OF	96	.261	Cin	
		Van Dyke, Wm. Jennings	OF	128	.266	A	
		Welsh, James J. (Tub)	C	33	.263	A	
		Werden, Percival Wheritt (Perry)	1B	129	.283	WashN88	

WON 12 — AMERICAN ASSOCIATION — FINISHED 13th(LAST)
LOST 51 — (DID NOT FINISH)
TG 63 — 1884. — PCT. .190

WASHINGTON

JOHN SAMUEL HOLLINGSHEAD

WON	LOST	NAME	POS.	G.	BA	FROM	TO
9	24	Barr, Robert M. (1B2 OF5)	P33	39	+.152	Pitt	Indpls
		Beach, Jackson	OF	8	.094	A	C
		Dorgan,	OF	1	.000	A	C
		Drake,	OF	2	.286	A	C
		Farley, Thomas T.	OF	13	.213	A	C
		Fennelly, Francis John (2B3 OF1)	SS59	62	+.288	A	Cin
		Gardner, Alexander	C	1	.000	A	C
		Gladman, John H.	3B54	56	.158	PhilN83	
		Goldsby, Walton Hugh	OF	6	+.375	xStL	Rich
2	16	Hamill, John Alexander Chas.	P18	21	.101	A	C
		Hanna, John (OF6)	C19	24	+.113	A	Rich
		Hawkes, Thorndike Proctor	2B35	38	.256	TroyN79	C
		Humphries, John Henry (OF8)	C34	48	.178	NYN	NYN
		Kiley, John Frederick	OF	14	.203	A	
		King, Samuel Warren	1B	12	.174	PhilN	C
		Morgan, Henry Wm. (C12 2B2 SS2)	OF30	44	+.181	Pitt	Rich
		Mullin, Henry	OF32	34	.139	A	BosUA
		Murphy, Wm. N. (3B1)	OF4	5	.454	xClevN	BosUA
		Olin, Franklin Walter (OF11)	2B12	21	+.386	A	WashUA
		Prince, Walter F.	1B	43	.211	xDetN	WashUA
0	2	Smith, Edgar E. (P3)	OF12	14	.089	PhilN	
		Swan, Albert D. (3B2)	1B3	5	+.143	A	Rich
1	9	Trumbull, Edward J. (P10)	OF13	24	.109	A	C
		Wills,	OF	4	.133	A	KCUA
		Yewell, Edwin Leonard (3B6)	2B10	35	.258	A	WashUA

WON 44 — AMERICAN ASSOCIATION — FINISHED 9th (LAST)
LOST 91
TG 135 — 1891. — PCT. .326

WASHINGTON

SAMUEL W. TROTT CHAS. N. SNYDER DANIEL W. SHANNON
TOBIAS CHAS. GRIFFIN

WON	LOST	NAME	POS.	G.	BA	FROM	TO
		Alvord, Wm. C.	3B	81	.235	xClevN	
2	10	Bakely, Edward (Enoch)	P	12	+.194	ClevPL	Balt
		Beecher, Edward C.	OF	56	+.233	BuffPL	Ath
		Burns, James M.	OF	20	.313	KC89	C
14	33	Carsey, Wilfred (Kid)	P53	59	.158	A	
0	0	Cassian, Edwin	P	7	.307	xPhilN	C
		Curtiss, Irvine Duane	OF	29	.252	xCinN	C
0	0	Daily, Edward M. (P4)	OF13	17	+.206	xLvlle	C

		Davis, James J.	3B	18	.250	Bkn	C
		Donovan, Patrick Joseph	OF	17	+.200	xLvlle	
		Dowd, Thomas Jefferson	2B	105	+.252	xBos	
0	4	Duke, Martin F.	P	4	.100	A	C
		Dunlap, Frederick C.	2B	7	.200	NYPL	C
2	6	Eiteljorg, Edward Henry	P	8	.200	ChiN	C
22	22	Foreman, Francis Isaiah	P44	49	.217	xCinN	
0	0	Freeman, John F. (Buck)	P	6	.272	A	
		Griffin, Tobias Chas. (Sandy) MGR.	OF	19	.273	Roch	
		Hart, Thomas Henry (C4)	OF4	8	.130	A	C
0	2	Hatfield, Gilbert (P2 3B24)	SS106	132	.258	NYPL	
		Hines, Paul A.	OF48	54	.266	BosN	C
0	5	Keefe, George W.	P	5	.250	BuffPL	C
		Lohman, George F. (Pete)	C21	32	.200	A	C
0	4	Mace, Harry L.	P	5	.000	A	C
2	3	Miller, Robert W.	P	7	.111	Roch	C
		Murphy, Lawrence Patrick	OF	107	.255	A	C
		Murray, Jeremiah J.	C	2	.000	WashN88	C
		McCauley, Allen B.	1B	57	.283	PhilN	C
		McGuire, James Thomas	C93	111	.296	Roch	
		McLaughlin, Thomas	SS	14	.250	Met86	C
		McQuery, Wm. Thomas	1B	68	.256	Syr	C
2	2	Quarles, Wm. H.	P	4	.000	A	
		Shannon, Daniel W. MGR.	SS	19	.118	NYPL	
		Slattery, Michael J.	OF	15	.283	xCinN	C
		Smalley, Wm. D.	3B	9	.171	ClevN	C
		Smith, Chas. Marvin (Pap)	2B18	27	.161	BosN	C
		Sutcliffe, Edward Elmer (C20)	OF30	51	.365	ClevPL	
		Visner, Joseph P.	OF	13	+.229	PittPL	StL
		Snyder, Chas. N. MGR.	C	8	.179	ClevPL	C

CLUB RECORD

OTHER MAJOR LEAGUES

ALTOONA

YEAR	TG	WON	LOST	PCT.	FINISHED	MANAGER
UNION ASSOCIATION						
1884	25	6	19	.240	DID NOT FINISH	E. Curtis

WON 6
LOST 19
TG 25

Union Association

1884.

FINISHED 11th.
(DID NOT FINISH)
PCT. .240

ALTOONA

EDWIN R. CURTIS

WON	LOST	NAME	POS.	G.	BA	FROM	TO
		Berry, Chas. Joseph	2B	7	+.269	A	K.C.
2	9	Brown, James W. H. (P11)	OF14	21	+.239	A	NYN
		Carroll, Patrick (OF3)	C8	11	+.255	A	Phil
0	1	Connors, Joseph P. (3B1 OF1)	P1	3	+.100	A	K.C.
		Cross, Clarence	3B	2	+.572	A	Phi
		Daisey, George K.	OF	1	.000	A	C
		Dougherty, Chas. (SS1 3B1 OF7)	2B17	23	.259	A	C
		Grady, John J. (OF1)	1B8	9	.289	A	C
		Harris, Frank W. (OF7)	1B17	24	.242	A	C
		Koons, Harry M.	3B	20	.203	A	
0	3	Leary, John J. (P3 3B1)	OF7	8	+.088	BaltAA	Chi
		Manlove, Chas. Hale	C	1	.750	A	NYN
		Moore, Jeremiah S. (OF9)	C12	20	.298	A	ClevN
4	6	Murphy, Cornelius B. (Connie)	P	14	.153	A	PhilN
		Murphy, John H. (2B2)	OF11	13	+.158	A	Wil
		Noftsker, George W. (C3)	OF5	7	.042	A	C
		Shaffer, Frank (C2 3B1)	OF17	19	+.284	A	K.C.
0	0	Smith, George J. (Germany) (P1)	SS25	25	.307	A	ClevN

WON 56
LOST 48
TG 104

UNION ASSOCIATION

1884.

FINISHED 4th.

PCT. .538

BALTIMORE

CHAS. T. LEVIS — WM. C. HENDERSON

WON	LOST	NAME	POS.	G.	BA	FROM	TO
3	5	Atkisson, Albert W.	P	8	+.138	xPitt	
		Bahret, Frank J.	OF	1	.000	A	IndplsAA
		Battin, Joseph V. (2B1)	3B16	17	+.086	xPitt	
0	2	Beck, Frank J. (P2)	OF5	6	.208	xPittAA	C
		Burns, Patrick	1B	1	.500	xBalAA	C
		Cuff, John J.	C	3	.083	A	C
		Cuthbert, Edgar Edward (Ned)	OF	42	.193	StLAA	C
0	1	Dorsey, Jeremiah M. (P1)	OF2	2	.000	A	C
		Ellick, Joseph J. (OF1)	SS6	7	+.148	xK.C.	C
		Fusselbach, Edward L.	C	65	.286	StLAA82	
		Gardner, Franklin W.	SS	1	+.250	xPitt	
		Graham, Bernard (1B1)	OF41	42	+.271	xChi	C
5	8	Lee, Thomas F. (1B1 SS1 3B2 OF6)	P15	21	.300	xChiN	C
		Levis, Chas. T. (3B1) MGR.	1B87	88	+.228	A	Wash
		Meddlebrook,	OF	1	.667	A	C
		Morgan, Henry Wm. (2B1 OF1)	C1	2	.250	xRichAA	C
0	0	Morris, E. (OF1)	P1	1	.000	A	C
0	1	McFarland, Claude (P1)	OF3	3	.286	A	C
		O'Brien, John E.	OF	18	.256	A	C
0	0	Overbeck, Henry A. (P1 3B9)	OF27	33	+.159	StLAA	K.C.
		Phelan, James D.	2B	97	.254	A	
2	3	Robinson, Wm. H. (Yank) (P6 C10 SS14)	3B68	98	.269	DetN82	
3	2	Ryan, John A. (OF1)	P6	6	.095	A	C
		Say, Lewis I.	SS	79	+.236	BaltAA	K.C.
		Scott, (3B1)	OF13	13	.226	A	C
		Seery, John Emmett (C3 3B1)	OF105	107	+.309	A	K.C.
		Shaffer, Frank	OF	3	+.077	xK.C.	C
		Sheehan, Daniel	OF	1	.000	A	C
		Shoenick, Lewis N.	1B	16	+.283	xPitt	
		Skinner,	OF	1	+.333	A	Chi
3	5	Smith, John Francis (OF4)	P8	10	.158	A	AthAA
		Stanley, Joseph	OF	5	.217	A	C
		Suck, Anthony (Tony)	C	3	+.300	xPitt	C
		Sweeney, John J. (OF14)	C29	43	.239	BaltAA	
40	21	Sweeney, Wm. J.	P64	83	.220	A	C
		Tiernay, Wm. J.	OF	1	.333	CinA82	C
		Wheeler, Harry Eugene	OF	17	+.254	xPitt	C

WON 58
LOST 51
TG 109

UNION ASSOCIATION

1884.

FINISHED 5th.

PCT. .532

BOSTON

TIMOTHY HAYES MURNANE — THOMAS FURNISS — JACOB CHAS. MORSE

WON	LOST	NAME	POS.	G.	BA	FROM	TO
12	9	Bond, Thomas Henry	P23	36	.291	WorN82	IndplsAA
1	0	Brown, Lewis J. (P1 1B33 OF1)	C52	84	.236	LvlleAA	C
19	15	Burke, Walter R. (OF11)	P39	45	.212	BuffN	
		Butler, Frank E.	OF	70	.160	A	C
		Callahan, Edward J.	OF	4	+.357	xK.C.	C
0	2	Crane, Edward Nicholas (P2 C43) (Cannon-Ball)	OF60	99	.304	A	
0	2	Daniels, Chas. L. (OF1)	P2	3	.273	A	C
		Dow, Clarence G.	OF	1	.333	A	C
		Flynn, Joseph (1B1 OF4)	C6	9	+.233	xPhilUA	C
		Hackett, Walter Henry	SS	102	.248	A	
		Irwin, John	3B	104	.235	WorN82	
0	7	McCarthy, Thomas Francis Michael (P7)	OF47	53	.218	A	
		McKeever, James (OF4)	C12	16	.141	A	C
		Mullin, Henry	OF	2	.000	xWashAA	C
		Murnane, Timothy Hayes MGR. (OF14)	1B62	76	.235	ProvN78	C

WON	LOST	NAME	POS.	G.	BA	FROM	TO
		Murphy, Wm. N. (OF1)	C1	1	.000	xWashAA	C
		O'Brien, Thomas H.	2B	102	.265	BaltAA	
		Peak, Elias	OF	1	+.000	A	Phil
		Reilly, Joseph J. (3B1)	OF2	3	.000	A	
		Rudderham, John Edmund	OF	1	.250	A	C
		Scannell, John J.	OF	6	.304	A	C
22	15	Shaw, Frederick Lander (Dupee) (OF9)	P39	44	.235	xDetN	
		Sladen, Arthur	OF	2	.000	A	C
		Slattery, Michael J.	OF	105	.208	A	
4	1	Tenney, Frederick Clay	P	5	+.125	xWash	Wil

WON 33
LOST 35
TG 68

UNION ASSOCIATION

1884.

FINISHED 6th.
(DID NOT FINISH)
PCT. .459

CHICAGO

EDWARD S. HENGLE

WON	LOST	NAME	POS.	G.	BA	FROM	TO
5	7	Atkisson, Albert W. (OF2)	P12	12	+.278	xAthAA	Pitt
		Baker, Chas (2B1 SS2))	OF8	11	+.167	A	Pitts
		Baldwin, Charles Geoghan	C	1	+.000	xKC	KC
		Berry, Chas. Joseph	2B	5	+.118	xK.C.	Pitt
		Bishop, Frank (SS1)	3B3	4	.200	A	C
		Briggs, Chas. R. (2B12)	OF38	50	.171	A	C
2	0	Cady, Chas. B. (OF2)	P4	6	+.095	ClevN	KC
		Corrigan, (OF1)	2B1	2	.143	A	C
		Cronin, Daniel	2B	1	+.250	A	K.C.
22	25	Daly, Hugh I. (One-Arm) (2B2 SS1 OF1)	P47	47	+.235	ClevN	Pitt
		Ellick, Joseph J. (C1 2B4 SS15)	OF54	72	+.253	WorN80	Pitt
		Fisher, Harry C.	3B	1	+.667	xKC	ClevN
		Foley, Wm. B.	3B	18	.294	DetN81	C
1	0	Foreman, Francis Isaiah (OF1)	P3	3	+.091	A	K.C.
0	0	Gardner, Franklin W. (Gid) (P1 3B8)	OF12	20	+.173	BaltAA	Pitt
		Graham, Bernard	OF	2	+.500	A	Balt
		Gross, Emil M. (OF8)	C15	23	.326	PhilN	
		Hengle, Emory J.	2B	18	+.222	A	StPaul
3	3	Horan, John J. (OF9)	P11	20	.080	A	C
0	0	Householder, Chas. F. (P1 SS3 OF21)	3B40	64	+.232	A	Pitt
		Koons, Harry M.	3B	1	+.000	xAlt	C
		Krieg, Wm. Frederick (1B1 OF19)	C41	59	+.231	A	Pitt
0	0	Leary, John J. (P2 3B2 OF3)	2B4	10	+.184	xAlt	C
		Matthias, Stephen J.	SS	35	.274	A	C
0	0	Miller, Joseph H. (Cyclone)	P	1	.250	A	ProvN
		McGarr, James B. (Chippy)	2B	18	.160	A	
		McLaughlin, Francis Edward (SS1)	2B14	15	+.284	xCin	K.C.
		Richardson, Baker (2B1 SS2)	2B	1	.000	A	C
		Shoenick, Lewis N. (OF1)	1B70	70	+.315	A	Pitt
		Skinner,	OF	1	+.333	xBalt	C
		Suck, Anthony (Tony) (SS15 3B1 OF11)	C18	43	+.149	BuffN	Pitt
		Wheeler, Harry Eugene	OF	19	+.241	xK.C.	Pitt
		Wyman, Frank C.	1B	2	+.375	xK.C.	C

WON 68
LOST 35
TG 103

UNION ASSOCIATION

1884.

FINISHED 3rd.

PCT. .660

CINCINNATI

DANIEL O'LEARY SAMUEL NEWHALL CRANE

WON	LOST	NAME	POS.	G.	BA	FROM	TO
		Barber, Chas. D.	2B	48	.190	A	C
21	13	Bradley, George Washington (SS18)	P34	52	.202	AthAA	
		Briody, Chas. F.	C	23	.326	xClevN	
25	16	Burns, Richard Simon (OF27)	P41	68	.315	DetN	
		Cleveland, Elmer E.	2B	26	.281	A	
		Crane, Samuel Newhall MGR.	2B	68	.231	MetAA	
		Crotty, Joseph	C	20	.287	StLAA82	
		Ewing, John	OF	1	.000	StLAA	Was
		Glasscock, John Wesley (2B2)	SS37	39	.388	xClevN	
		Harbidge, Wm. Arthur	OF	65	.271	PhilN	C
		Hawes, Wm. Hildreth (1B19)	OF49	68	.260	BosN79	C
		Jones, Ryerson L.	SS	55	.265	LvlleAA	C
		Kelly, John Francis	C38	39	+.253	PhilN	Wash
		Kennedy, Chas. (SS4 OF1)	3B8	13	.213	A	C
		Meyers, Lewis Henry (OF1)	C1	1	.000	A	C
22	4	McCormick, James (OF3)	P26	28	.237	xClevN	
		McLaughlin, Francis Edward	SS	15	+.246	PittAA	Chi
		McQuery, Wm. Thomas	1B	32	.248	A	
		O'Leary, Daniel MGR.	OF	27	.252	WorN82	C
		Powell, Martin J.	1B	45	.314	DetN	
		Robinson, Frederic Henry	2B	3	.231	A	C
		Schwartz, Wm. August	C	24	.263	ColAA	C
0	2	Sylvester, Louis J. (P2)	OF70	70	.264	A	C

WON 14
LOST 63
TG 77

UNION ASSOCIATION

1884.

FINISHED 12th.

PCT. .182

KANSAS CITY

THEODORE PAUL SULLIVAN

WON	LOST	NAME	POS.	G.	BA	FROM	TO
		Alexander, William Henry (SS2 OF1)	C17	19	127	A	StLAA

WON	LOST	NAME	POS.	G.	BA	FROM	TO
2	2	Bakely, Edward (Enoch) (OF3)	P5	6	+.167	xWil	
		Baldwin, Clarence Geoghan (2B1 3B1 OF10)	C44	49	+.202	A	Chi & return
		Bastian, Chas. J.	2B	11	+.255	xWil	
		Berry, Chas. Joseph (3B1 OF9)	2B11	29	+.267	xAlt	Chi
3	9	Black, Robert Benjamin (P16 2B6 SS1)	OF19	38	.245	A	C
0	3	Blaisdell, Howard Carleton (Dick) (OF1)	P3	4	.295	A	C
		Cady, Charles B.	2B	1	.000	Chi	C
		Callahan, Edward J.	SS	1	+.250	xStL	Bos
0	1	Chatterton, James M. (P1 OF2)	1B2	4	.125	A	C
0	1	Connors, Joseph I. (OF2)	P2	3	+.091	xAlt	C
		Cross, Clarence	SS	25	+.212		xPhil
1	2	Crothers, Douglas (OF1)	P3	4	.200	A	
0	0	Cudworth, James Alaric (P1) (P1 OF12)	1B19	29	.134	A	C
		Davis, James J.	3B	7	.222	A	
		Deasley, James	SS	13	+.175	xWash	C
		Decker, Edward Harry (C11)	OF17	23	.136	xIndplsAA	
		Donely, James B. (C1)	3B5	6	.130	A	IndplsAA
		Dugan, E.	OF	3	.000	A	C
		Dwight, (OF2)	C11	12	.268	A	C
		Ellick, Joseph J. (OF1)	2B1	2	+.000	xPitt	Balt
		Fisher, Harry C. (SS2)	3B8	10	+.195	A	Chi
0	1	Foreman, Francis Isaiah	P	1	+.000	xChi	
		Gorman, John F. (3B4 OF5)	1B24	33	.275	StLAA	PittAA
3	13	Hickman, Ernest L.	P	18	.161	A	C
1	1	Hutchinson, James F.	P	2	.250	A	C
0	1	Kirby, John F. (OF1)	P2	2	.167	A	
0	1	Krieger,	P	1	.000	A	C
		Luff, Henry T. (3B4)	OF4	5	+.053	xPhil	C.
0	4	McLaughlin, Bernard (P6 2B12)	OF24	40	+.218	xWash	
1	1	McLaughlin, Francis Edward (P4 SS6 3B6 OF10)	2B10	33	+.219	xChi	C
		O'Brien, Wm. Smith (1B1)	3B3	4	+.235	xStP	
0	3	Overbeck, Henry A. (P4 1B2 OF6)	3B16	26	+.174	xBalt	C
		Porter, Henry	OF	3	+.083	A	Mil
		Say, James I.	3B	2	+.250	xWil	
		Say, Lewis I. (2B1)	SS16	17	+.217	xBalt	C
		Seery, John Emmett	OF	1	+.400	xBalt	
		Shaffer, Frank (C1 2B1 SS1 3B1)	OF40	43	+.172	xAlt	Balt
		Strauss, Joseph (C3 2B2 3B1)	OF9	15	.208	A	
		Strief, George Andrew	2B	14	+.094	xStLAA	Pitt
0	1	Sullivan, Patrick (P1 C1 OF9)	3B21	31	.193	A	C
		Sullivan, Theodore Paul MGR. (SS1)	OF2	3	+.333	xStL	
		Sweeney, Jeremiah H.	1B	30	.260	A	C
		Turbidy, Jeremiah	SS	12	.279	A	C
2	9	Veach, Wm. Walter (Peek-a-boo) (P14)	OF13	27	.127	A	
1	7	Voss, Alexander (OF8)	P8	14	+.089	xWash	C
0	1	Wheeler, Harry Eugene (P1)	OF13	14	+.246	StLAA	Chi
		Whitehead, Milton P. (SS2 3B1)	2B3	5	+.150	xStL	C
		Wills,	OF	5	.150	xWasAA	C
0	2	Wyman, Frank C. (P3 1B3 3B3)	OF25	30	+.203	A	Chi

WON 8
LOST 3
TG 11

UNION ASSOCIATION

1884.

FINISHED 2nd.
(DID NOT FINISH)
PCT. .727

MILWAUKEE

JANES F. McKEE

WON	LOST	NAME	POS.	G.	BA	FROM	TO
1	1	Baldwin, Chas. Busted (Lady) (P2)	OF5	7	.214	A	
		Behel, Stephen Arnold Douglas	OF	9	.222	A	
		Bignal, George Wm.	C	4	.222	A	C
		Broughton, Cecil Calvert (OF5)	C7	11	.308	BaltAA	
4	0	Cushman, Edgar Leander	P	4	.083	BuffN	
		Falch, Anton (C2)	OF3	5	.471	A	C
		Griffin, Thomas W.	1B	11	.295	A	C
		Hogan, Robert Edward	OF	11	.077	StLAA82	
		Morrissey, Thomas J.	3B	12	.174	A	C
		Myers, Albert	2B	12	.326	A	
3	2	Porter, Henry (1B1 OF3)	P6	10	+.278	xKC	
		Sexton, Thomas W.	SS	12	.229	A	C

WON 21
LOST 46
TG 67

UNION ASSOCIATION

1884.

FINISHED 9th.
(DID NOT FINISH)
PCT. .313

PHILADELPHIA

FERGUSON G. MALONE THOMAS J. PRATT

WON	LOST	NAME	POS.	G.	BA	FROM	TO
14	24	Bakely, Edward (Enoch) (1B3 OF2)	P39	43	+.134	AthAA	Wil
		Carroll, Patrick	C	5	+.158	xAlt	
		Clements, John T. (C20 SS1)	OF21	41	.289	A	PhilN
		Cross, Clarence	SS	2	+.143	xAlt	KC
		Dailey, Cornelius F. (Con)	C	2	.000	A	
0	0	Drew, David (P1)	2B2	2	+.444	A	Wash
		Esterday, Henry	SS	28	.250	A	
1	7	Fisher, (1B2)	P8	10	+.222	A	Wil
		Flynn, Joseph (C8 1B1 SS1)	OF42	50	+.244	A	Bos
		Foster, Elmer E.	C	1	.333	xAthAA	
1	2	Gallagher, Wm. John	P	3	.083	PhilN	C
		Johnson, Wm. T.	OF	1	.000	A	
		Jones, (OF1)	C4	4	.154	BalAA82	C

WON	LOST	NAME	POS.	G.	BA	FROM	TO
		Geer, Wm. Henry Harrison	SS	8	.226	WorN80	BknAA
		Gillen, Thomas J. (OF3)	C26	28	.149	A	PhilN
0	0	Hoover, Wm. J. (Buster) (Pl 1B4 2B5 SS15)	OF37	61	.355	A	PhilN
		Keinzil. Wm.	OF	61	.260	AthAA82	C
		Luff, Henry T. (OF11)	1B14	24	.266	LvlleAA	
		Malone, Ferguson G. MGR.	C	1	.250	AthN76	C
0	1	Maul, Albert Joseph	P	1	.000	A	
		Meyerle, Levi Samuel (OF1)	1B2	3	.091	CinN77	C
		McCormick, John (2B5 SS3 OF5)	3B53	66	+.296	BaltAA	Wash
		McGuinness, John J.	1B	52	.243	SyrN79	C
		O'Donnell,	C	1	.250	A	C
		Patterson, George	OF	2	.143	A	C
		Peak, Elias (SS2 OF5)	2B47	54	+.199	xBos	C
		Rickley, Christopher	SS	7	.207	A	C
		Siegel, John	3B	8	.226	A	C
5	12	Weaver, Samuel H.	P	20	.214	LvlleAA	

WON 7 — UNION ASSOCIATION — FINISHED 8th.
LOST 10 — (DID NOT FINISH)
TG 17 — 1884. — PCT. .412

PITTSBURGH

JOSEPH V. BATTIN — JOSEPH J. ELLICK

WON	LOST	NAME	POS.	G.	BA	FROM	TO
2	6	Atkisson, Albert W. (OF1)	P8	9	+.121	xChi	Balt
		x Baldwin, Clarence Geoghan	C	1	+1.000	xK.C.	K.C.
		Battin, Joseph V. MGR.	3B	18	+.197	xPittAA	Balt
		Berry, Chas. Joseph	2B	2	+.100	xChi	C
		Baker, Chas.	OF	3	+.083	xChi	C
5	4	Daly, Hugh I. (One-Arm)	P	10	+.111	xChi	Wash
		Ellick, Joseph J. MGR.	SS	18	+.167	xChi	K.C.
		Gardner, Franklin W. (Gid) (2B1)	OF15	16	+.254	xChi	Balt
		Householder, Chas. F.	OF	16	+.270	xChi	C
		Krieg, Wm. Frederick (OF1)	C9	10	+.350	xChi	
		Shoenick, Lewis N.	1B	18	+.276	xChi	Balt
		Strief, George Andrew	2B	15	+.182	xK.C.	ClevN
		Suck, Anthony (Tony)	C	10	+.182	xChi	Balt
		Wheeler, Harry Eugene	OF	17	+.236	xChi	Balt

x-Baldwin caught one game, filling in for Suck who was injured but never had a contract with Pittsburgh.

WON 91 — UNION ASSOCIATION — FINISHED 1st.
LOST 16
TG 107 — 1884. — PCT. .850

ST. LOUIS

THEODORE PAUL SULLIVAN — FREDERICK C. DUNLAP

WON	LOST	NAME	POS.	G.	BA	FROM	TO
		Baker, George F.	C	64	.471	BaltAA	
16	2	Boyle, Henry J. (P18)	OF36	49	.260	A	
		Brennan, James A. (OF15)	C30	45	.210	A	
		Callahan, Edward J.	OF	1	+.000	A	K.C.
1	1	Cattanach, John L.	P	2	.000	xProvN	C
		Cronin, Daniel	OF	1	+.000	xChi	C
		Dickerson, Lewis Pessano (3B5)	OF41	46	.357	PittAA	BaltAA
		Dolan, Thomas J. (3B3 OF2)	C15	20	.194	xStLAA	
0	0	Dunlap, Frederick C. MGR. (Pl OF1)	2B81	81	.420	ClevN	
		Gleason, John Day	3B	77	.312	LvlleAA	
12	1	Hodnet, Chas.	P	15	.113	StLAA	C
		Lewis, Frederick Miller	OF	8	.281	xStLAA	
1	0	Matterson, C. V. (OF1)	Pl	1	.000	A	C
		Quinn, Joseph J.	1B	82	.261	A	
1	0	Rowe, David E. (Pl SS15)	OF71	87	.292	BaltAA	
		Ryder, Thomas	OF	8	.214	A	C
		Schaffer, George (Orator)	OF	89	.354	BuffN	
1	0	Sullivan, Thomas Jefferson (C1)	Pl	2	.167	StLAA	C
24	8	Sweeney, Chas. J. (1B1 OF12)	P34	46	.307	xProvN	
24	2	Taylor, Wm. Henry (1B10 OF3)	P31	42	.371	PittAA	AthAA
11	1	Werden, Percival Wheritt (Perry) (OF7)	P15	18	.237	A	
0	1	Whitehead, Milton P. (Pl 2B1 3B1 OF1)	SS96	100	+.225	A	K.C.

WON 2 — UNION ASSOCIATION — FINISHED 10th.
LOST 6
TG 8 — 1884. — PCT. .250

ST. PAUL

A. M. THOMPSON

WON	LOST	NAME	POS.	G.	BA	FROM	TO
		Barnes, Wm. H.	OF	8	.161	A	C
1	3	Brown, James W. H. (1B1 OF1)	P6	6	+.313	xNYN	
		Carroll, John C. (3B4)	OF8	9	.083	A	
		Dealey, Patrick E. (OF1)	C4	5	.143	A	
		Dunn, Stephen (2B1)	1B9	9	.242	A	C
0	2	Galvin, Louis	P	3	.200	A	C
		Ganzel, Chas. Wm. (OF1)	C6	7	.208	A	
		Hengle, Emory J.	2B	9	+.132	xChi	
1	1	O'Brien, Wm. Smith (P3)	3B8	8	+.241	A	K.C.
		Tilley, John C.	OF	9	.148	xTolAA	C
		Werrick, Joseph Abraham	SS	9	.071	A	

WON 47 — UNION ASSOCIATION — FINISHED 7th.
LOST 66
TG 113 — 1884. — PCT. .416

WASHINGTON

MICHAEL B. SCANLON

WON	LOST	NAME	POS.	G.	BA	FROM	TO
		Alberts, August P.	SS	4	.250	xPittAA	
		Baker, Philip (C19)	1B37	83	.282	BaltAA	
		Bradley, J. Nicholas	OF	1	.000	A	C
		Carroll, E.	OF	4	.200	A	C
		Creegan, Martin	OF6	9	.152	A	C
		(C3 1B1 3B2)					
1	1	Daly, Hugh I. (One-Arm)	P	2	+.000	xPitt	
		Deasley, James	SS	31	+.216	A	K.C.
		Drew, David (1B5 OF1)	SS8	13	+.327	xPhil	C
		Evers, Thomas Francis	2B	106	.234	BaltAA82	C
		Ewing, John	OF	1	+.200	xCin	
		Franklin,	OF	1	.000	A	C
		Fulmer, Christopher	C32	47	.282	A	
		(1B5 OF16)					
11	9	Gagus, Chas. (SS3 OF21)	P21	42	.240	A	C
		Green, James R. (OF1)	3B9	10	.139	A	C
		Gunson Joseph Brook (OF11)	C33	44	.158	A	
		Halpin, James Nathaniel	SS	44	.182	WorN82	
		Hughes, Wm. W. (OF6)	1B9	14	.122	A	
		Joy, Aloysius C.	1B	35	.190	A	C
		Kalbfuss, Chas. Henry	OF	1	.200	A	C
		Kelly, John Francis (OF1)	C3	4	+.357	xCin	C
		Larkin, Frank	3B	17	.257	TroyN80	RichAA
		Lawlor, Michael H.	C	2	.000	TroyN80	C
		Lehane, Michael Patrick (3B1)	SS3	3	.333	A	
		Levis, Chas. T.	1B	1	+.000	xBalt	IndplsAA
1	9	Lockwood, Milo Hathaway	OF11	20	.209	A	C
		(P10 3B3)					
		Moore, Harry S.	OF	107	.337	A	C
		Morris, P.	SS	1	.000	A	C
		McCormick, John (SS4)	3B38	42	+.237	xPhil	C
		McDonald, (OF1)	C1	2	.167	A	C
		McGee, F. (C1 OF2)	3B2	4	.188	A	C
		McKee, (C1 3B2)	OF3	4	.188	A	C
		McKenna, Edward (OF10)	C22	32	.188	StLN77	C
		McLaughlin, Bernard	SS	10	+.189	WorN82	K.C.
		McLaughlin, James C.	SS9	10	.194	A	BaltAA
0	0	McRemer	P	1	.000	A	C
		Mulligan,	3B	1	.000	A	C
		Nusz,	OF	1	.000	A	C
		Olin, Franklin Walter	OF	1	.000	xWashAA	TolAA
		Pierce, Maurice	3B	2	.143	A	C
4	12	Powell, Chas. Abner (P19)	OF28	47	.270	A	
		Prince, Walter F.	1B	1	.250	xWashAA	C
		Reeder, James Edward	OF	3	.167	Cin.AA	C
		Rollinson,	C	1	.000	A	C
		Ryan, John M. (3B1)	OF7	743	+.143	A	Wil
		Shoup, John F.	OF	1	.750	StLAA82	C
		Tenney, Frederick Clay (1B4)	OF26	30	+.236	A	Bos
0	1	Thompson, Arthur J.	P	1	.000	A	C
7	14	Voss, Alexander	P26	63	+.190	A	K.C.
		(1B15 SS1 3B17 OF12)					
		Ward, E. John	OF	1	.250	A	
		White, Wm. Warren (3B1)	2B1	2	.000	A	C
		Wiley, (3B1)	OF1	1	.000	A	C
23	20	Wise, Wm. E. (OF34)	P44	78	.233	BaltAA82	
		Yewell, Edwin Leonard	3B	1	.000	xWashAA	C

WON 2
LOST 15
TG 17

UNION ASSOCIATION

1884.

FINISHED 13th (LAST)
(DID NOT FINISH)
PCT. .118

WILMINGTON

JOSEPH S. SIMMONS

WON	LOST	NAME	POS.	G.	BA	FROM	TO
0	2	Bakely, Edward (Enoch)	P	2	+.000	xPhil	K.C.
0	0	Bastian, Chas. J. (P1 SS1)	2B16	17	+.200	A	K.C.
		Benners, Isaac B.	OF	6	.045	xBknAA	C
		Burns, Thomas P.	SS	2	.143	A	BaltAA
1	1	Casey, Daniel Maurice	P	2	.250	A	
		Casey, Dennis Patrick	OF	2	.167	DetN82	BaltAA
		Cullen, John J. (SS3)	OF6	9	.194	A	C
		Cusick, Anthony Daniel	C6	11	.147	A	PhilN
		(2B1 SS3 3B1 OF3)					
		Fisher, (SS2)	OF6	+8	+.069	xPhil	
		Lynch, Thomas James	C8	16	.281	A	PhilN
		(1B1 OF8)					
		Munce, John	OF	7	.190	A	C
0	6	Murphy, John H.	P7	10	+.065	xAlt	C
		(2B1 SS2 3B1 OF2)					
		Myers, Henry C. (2B1)	SS5	6	.167	BaltAA82	C
		McCloskey, Wm. George (OF5)	C5	9	.133	A	C
0	1	McElroy, James D. (OF1)	P1	1	.000	xPhilN	C
1	4	Nolan, Edward Sylvester	P5	9	.242	PittAA	
		(The Only) (OF4)					
		Ryan, John M.	OF	2	.167	Wash	C
		Say, James I.	3B	16	+.220	AthAA82	K.C.
		Snyder, Emanuel Sebastian	1B16	17	.192	CinN76	C
		(OF1)					
0	1	Tenney, Frederick Clay	P	1	+.000	xBos	C

CLUB RECORD

OTHER MAJOR LEAGUES

ST. PAUL

YEAR	TG	WON	LOST	PCT.	FINISHED	MANAGER
1884	8	2	6	.250	DID NOT FINISH	Thompson

CLUB RECORD

OTHER MAJOR LEAGUES

WILMINGTON

YEAR	TG	WON	LOST	PCT.	FINISHED	MANAGER
UNION ASSOCIATION						
1884	17	2	15	.118	DID NOT FINISH	Joseph S. Simmons

Players League

1890.

WON 81
LOST 48
TG 129

FINISHED 1st.

PCT. .628

BOSTON

MICHAEL JOSEPH KELLY

WON	LOST	NAME	POS.	G.	BA	FROM	TO
		Brouthers, Dennis (Dan)	1B	123	.345	BosN	
		Brown, Thomas T.	OF	127	.277	BosN	
20	12	Daley, Wm.	P	47	.144	BosN	
22	9	Gumbert, Addison Courtney (Ad)	P	45	.253	ChiN	
		Hatfield, Gilbert	SS	3	+.143	xN.Y.	N.Y.
		Irwin, Arthur Albert	SS	96	.264	WashN	
		Johnston, Richard Frederick	OF	2	+.111	BosN	N.Y.
		Kelly, Michael Joseph (King) MGR. (SS27)	C54	90	.324	BosN	
10	13	Kilroy, Matthew Aloysius	P	31	.212	BaltAA	
3	2	Madden, Michael Joseph (Kid)	P	14	.166	BosN	
		Morrill, John Francis (SS1)	1B1	2	.143	WashN	C
		Murphy, Morgan Edward	C	60	.238	A	
		Nash, Wm. Mitchell	3B	129	.284	BosN	
		Quinn, Joseph J.	2B	129	.296	BosN	
26	12	Radbourn, Chas. (Hoss)	P	43	.243	BosN	
		Richardson, Arthur Harding	OF	130	.332	BosN	
		Stovey, Harry Duffield	OF	118	.308	AthAA	
		Swett, Chas. A.	C	37	.193	A	C

WON 76
LOST 56
TG 132

PLAYERS LEAGUE

1890.

FINISHED 2nd.

PCT. .576

BROOKLYN

JOHN MONTGOMERY WARD

WON	LOST	NAME	POS.	G.	BA	FROM	TO
		Andrews, George Edward	OF	95	.258	IndplsN	
		Bierbauer, Louis W.	2B	132	.319	AthAA	
		Cook, Paul (1B22)	C37	59	.242	LvlleAA	
		Dailey, Cornelius F. (Con) (1B6)	C40	46	.253	IndplsN	
		Hayes, John J.	C	12	.191	BaltAA87	C
7	5	Hemming, George Earl	P	16	+.200	xClev	
		Joyce, Wm. Michael (Scrappy)	3B	133	.269	A	
		Kinslow, Thomas F.	C	63	.277	MetAA87	
5	10	Murphy, Cornelius B. (Connie)	P	20	.242	PhilN84	BknAA
			P	2	.000	(& return)	C
		McGeachy, John Chas.	OF	104	.253	IndplsN	
		Orr, David L.	1B	107	.387	ColAA	C
		Seery, John Emmett	OF	104	.222	IndplsN	
18	16	Sowders, John	P	40	.190	KCAA	C
		Sunday, Arthur	OF	24	.292	A	C
15	10	Van Haltren, George E. (P26)	OF61	92	.346	ChiN	
		Ward, John Montgomery MGR.	SS	128	.371	NYN	
31	15	Weyhing, August	P	49	.184	AthAA	

WON 36
LOST 96
TG 132

PLAYERS LEAGUE

1890

FINISHED 8th (LAST)

PCT. .273

BUFFALO

JOHN CHAS. ROWE

WON	LOST	NAME	POS.	G.	BA	FROM	TO
2	5	Baldwin, Chas. Busted (Lady)	P	7	.286	xBknN	C
0	1	Beecher, Edward C. (P1)	OF	126	.357	WashN	
1	3	Buckley, John Edward	P	4	.067	A	C
		Carney, John Joseph	1B	28	+.262	WashN	Clev
		Clark, Owen F. (C15 2B22)	OF32	69	.268	WashN	C
0	1	Cotter, Daniel Joseph	P	1	.000	A	C
10	15	Cunningham, Ellsworth Elmer	P	29	+.255	xPhil	
0	1	Doe, Alfred George	P	1	+.000	A	Pitt
0	2	Duzen, William George	P	2	.250	A	C
		Faatz, Jay	1B	32	+.200	xClev	C
1	5	Ferson, Alexander	P	10	.212	WashN	
		Gillespie, James	OF	1	.000	A	C
9	26	Haddock, George Silas (OF7)	P35	42	.240	WashN	
		Halligan, Wm. E. (Jocko) (C18)	OF39	53	.268	A	
		Hoy, Wm. Ellsworth (Dummy)	OF	122	.299	WashN	
		Irwin, John (1B16)	3B61	77	.220	WashN	
5	17	Keefe, George W.	P	25	.205	WashN	
0	3	Krock, August H. (Gus)	P	4	.083	WashN	C
0	0	Lewis,	P	1	.200	A	C
		Mack, Connie	C	123	.268	WashN	
		Rainey, John Paul	OF35	42	.248	NYN87	C
		Rowe, John Chas. MGR.	SS	125	.250	PittN	C
		Smith, E. J.	(1B)	1	.000	A	C
3	9	Stafford, James Joseph	P	15	.184	A	
5	7	Twitchell, Lawrence Grant (P12)	OF37	44	+.216	xClev	
0	1	White, James Laurie (Deacon) (P1 1B58)	3B64	122	.264	PittN	C
		Wise, Samuel Washington	2B	119	.295	WashN	

WON 75
LOST 62
TG 137

PLAYERS LEAGUE

1890.

FINISHED 4th.

PCT. .547

CHICAGO

CHAS. ALBERT COMISKEY

WON	LOST	NAME	POS.	G.	BA	FROM	TO
32	21	Baldwin, Marcus Elmore (Mark)	P	58	.221	ColAA	
9	14	Bartson, Chas. Franklin	P	26	.164	A	C
		Bastian, Chas. J. (2B16)	SS64	80	.186	ChiN	

WON	LOST	NAME	POS.	G.	BA	FROM	TO
		Boyle, John Anthony (Jack) (SS15 3B31)	C47	100	.257	StLAA	
		Comiskey, Chas. Albert MGR.	1B	88	.248	StLAA	
		Darling, Dell Conrad (C5)	1B31	58	.259	ChiN	
		Duffy, Hugh	OF	137	.328	ChiN	
1	7	Dwyer, John Francis (Frank)	P	16	.250	ChiN	
		Farrell, Chas. A. (Duke) (1B22)	C88	117	.296	ChiN	
33	20	King, Chas. Frederick	P	57	.167	StLAA	
		Latham, Walter Arlington (Arlie)	3B	52	.241	StLAA	CinN
		O'Neill, James Edward (Tip)	OF	137	.302	StLAA	
		Pfeffer, Nathaniel Frederick	2B	123	.268	ChiN	
		Ryan, James E.	OF	118	.330	ChiN	
		Shugart, Wm. Frank	SS	29	.177	A	
		Williamson, Edward Nagle (SS21)	3B52	73	.204	ChiN	C

WON 55 — PLAYERS LEAGUE — FINISHED 7th.
LOST 75
TG 130 — 1890. — PCT. .423

CLEVELAND

JAY FAATZ — HENRY E. LARKIN — OLIVER WENDELL TEBEAU

WON	LOST	NAME	POS.	G.	BA	FROM	TO
13	26	Bakely, Edward (Enoch)	P	44	.206	ClevN	
		Brennan, James A. (3B15)	C44	59	.251	AthAA	C
		Browning, Louis Roger (Pete)	OF	118	.391	LvlleAA	
		Budd,	OF	1	.000	A	C
		Carney, John Joseph	OF	25	+.344	xBuff	
		Delahanty, Edward James (2B23 OF18)	SS74	115	.296	PhilN	
2	0	Dewald, Chas. H.	P	2	.375	A	C
		Faatz, Jay MGR.	(DID NOT PLAY)+			ClevN	Buff
0	1	Gleason, Wm.	P	1	.000	A	C
21	20	Gruber, Henry John	P	50	.217	ClevN	
0	3	Hemming, George Earl	P	3	+.182	A	Bkn
		Larkin, Henry E. MGR.	1B	125	.327	AthAA	
		McAleer, James Robert	OF	86	.272	ClevN	
11	9	McGill, Wm. Vaness (Billy)	P	24	.150	A	
8	16	O'Brien, John F.	P	26	.160	ClevN	
		Radford, Paul Revere (SS36)	OF43	122	.292	ClevN	
		Snyder, Chas. N.	C	12	.183	ClevN	
		Stricker, John A. (Cub)	2B	127	.248	ClevN	
		Stynes, Cornelius W.	C	2	.000	A	C
		Sutcliffe, Edward Elmer (OF17)	C82	99	.329	ClevN	
		Tebeau, Oliver Wendell (Pat) MGR.	3B	108	.292	ClevN	
0	0	Twitchell, Lawrence Grant (P3)	OF53	56	+.224	ClevN	Buff

WON 74 — PLAYERS LEAGUE — FINISHED 3rd.
LOST 57
TG 131 — 1890. — PCT. .565

NEW YORK

WM. EWING

WON	LOST	NAME	POS.	G.	BA	FROM	TO
		Brown, Willard (1B13)	C35	59	.274	NYN	
		Connor, Roger	1B	123	.372	NYN	
16	23	Crane, Edward Nicholas	P	44	.314	NYN	
		Dunlap, Frederick C.	2B·	1	.000	xPittN	
19	10	Ewing, John	P	35	.210	LvlleAA	
0	1	Ewing, Wm. MGR. (Buck) (P1)	C83	83	.349	NYN	
		Gore, George F.	OF	93	.335	NYN	
		Hatfield, Gilbert (SS10)	3B41	48	+.301	NYN	Bos
0	0	Hatfield, Gilbert (P2 3B4)	SS16	20	+.244	xBos (return)	
		Johnston, Richard Frederick	OF	75	+.257	xBos	
17	8	Keefe, Timothy J.	P	30	.205	NYN	
22	15	O'Day, Henry F. (Hank)	P	43	.235	NYN	
		O'Rourke, James Henry	OF	111	.366	NYN	
		Richardson, Daniel (Denny) (2B54)	SS69	123	.258	NYN	
		Shannon, Daniel W. (SS7 3B2)	2B74	83	+.238	xPhil	
		Slattery, Michael J.	OF	97	.290	NYN	
		Vaughn, Harry Francis	C	45	.248	LvlleAA	
		Whitney, Arthur Wilson (SS33)	3B86	119	.212	NYN	

WON 68 — PLAYERS LEAGUE — FINISHED 5th.
LOST 63
TG 131 — 1890. — PCT. .519

PHILADELPHIA

BENJAMIN FRANKLIN HILT — JAMES G. FOGARTY — CHAS. G. BUFFINTON

WON	LOST	NAME	POS.	G.	BA	FROM	TO
19	13	Buffinton, Chas. G. MGR.	P	41	.271	PhilN	
		Cross, LaFayette Napoleon (Lave)	C46	60	.299	AthAA	
3	10	Cunningham, Ellsworth Elmer	P	15	+.135	BaltAA	Buff
		Farrar, Sidney Douglas	1B	127	.251	PhilN	C
		Fogarty, James G. MGR.	OF	91	.251	PhilN	C
		Griffin, Michael Joseph	OF	115	.290	BaltAA	
		Hallman, Wm. White (Billy) (C27 2B14 3B10)	OF34	85	.278	PhilN	
5	10	Husted, Wm. J.	P	19	.109	A	C
20	11	Knell, Philip H.	P	35	.214	PittN88	
		Milligan, John (Jack)	C	62	.315	StLAA	
		Mulvey, Joseph H.	3B	120	.291	PhilN	
		Pickett, John Thomas	2B	100	.281	KCAA	
21	19	Sanders, Alexander Benjamin	P	44	.291	PhilN	

WON	LOST	NAME	POS.	G.	BA	FROM	TO
		Shanon, Daniel W.	2B	18	+.260	LvlleAA	N.Y.
		Shindle, Wm.	SS	132	.236	BaltAA	
		Wood, George A.	OF	132	.304	BaltAA	

WON 60
LOST 68
TG 128

PLAYERS LEAGUE

1890.

FINISHED 6th.

PCT. .469

PITTSBURGH

EDWARD HUGH HANLON

WON	LOST	NAME	POS.	G.	BA	FROM	TO
		Beckley, Jacob Peter (Jake)	1B	121	.325	PittN	
		Carroll, Frederick Herbert (OF48)	C56	111	.302	PittN	
		Corcoran, Thomas W.	SS	123	.219	A	
0	0	Doe, Alfred George	P	1	+.500	xBuff	C
		Fields, John James (C14 2B28)	OF81	127	.277	PittN	
11	12	Galvin, James F. (Jimmy)	P	26	.196	PittN	
		Gray, James D.	3B	2	.222	A	PittN
		Hanlon, Edward Hugh MGR.	OF	119	.284	PittN	
		Hurley, Jeremiah F.	C	8	.273	BosN	
		Kuehne, Wm. J.	3B	126	.243	PittN	
17	11	Maul, Albert Joseph (OF12)	P32	44	.265	PittN	
8	9	Morris, Edward	P	18	.146	PittN	C
		Quinn, Thomas G.	C	56	.207	BaltAA	C
		Robinson, Wm. H. (Yank)	2B	98	.239	StLAA	
21	23	Staley, Henry E.	P	47	.210	PittN	
3	13	Tener, John Kinley	P	19	.194	ChiN	C
		Visner, Joseph P.	OF	127	.265	BknAA	

WON 84
LOST 69
TG 153

Federal League

1914.

FINISHED 3rd.

PCT. .549

BALTIMORE

FRANZ OTTO KNABE

WON	LOST	NAME	POS.	G.	BA	FROM	TO
0	0	Allen, John Marshall	P	1	.500	A	C
7	9	Bailey, Wm. F.	P	19	.163	StLA12	
		Bates, John Wm.	OF	59	.307	xChiN	C
		Boucher, Medric T.	C	14	+.231	A	Pitt
		Chouinard, Felix George	OF	26	+.217	xBkn	
4	6	Conley, James Patrick (Snipe)	P	21	.118	A	
		Doolan, Michael Joseph	SS	144	.245	PhilN	
		Duncan, Vernon Van Duke	OF147	157	.287	PhilN	
0	0	Hughes, Vernon Alexander	P	3	.000	A	C
		Jacklitsch, Frederick Lawrence	C117	122	.275	PhilN10	
		Kerr, John Jonas	C	14	+.265	xPitt	
		Kirkpatrick, Enos Claire	3B36	55	.259	BknN	
		Knabe, Franz Otto MGR.	2B	146	.228	PhilN	
		Kommers, Frederick Raymond	OF	17	+.220	xStL	C
		Lobert, Frank John	3B6	10	.167	A	C
		Meyer, Benjamin (Benny)	OF131	141	.302	BknN	
		McCandless, John C.	OF7	11	.258	A	
26	14	Quinn, John Picus	P	48	.277	BosN	
0	0	Ridgeway, John A.	P	4	.000	A	C
		Russell, Harvey Holmes	C47	79	.247	A	
		Simmons, George Washington (2B25)	OF69	113	.269	NYA12	
10	8	Smith, Frank Elmer	P	33	.207	CinN12	
24	14	Suggs, George Franklin	P	43	.212	CinN	
		Swacina, Harry J.	1B	158	.276	PittN08	
		Walsh, Michael Timothy	3B	117	.310	PhilN	
12	17	Wilhelm, Irving Key (Kaiser)	P	42	.259	BknN10	
1	1	Yount, Herbert M.	P	14	.133	A	C
		Zinn, Guy	OF56	61	.277	BosN	

WON 47
LOST 107
TG 154

FEDERAL LEAGUE

1915.

FINISHED 8th (LAST)

PCT. .305

BALTIMORE

FRANZ OTTO KNABE

WON	LOST	NAME	POS.	G.	BA	FROM	TO
		Agler, Joseph Abram (2B3)	1B47	70	+.214	xBuffF	C
4	15	Bailey, Wm. F.	P	30	+.221	B	Chi
4	16	Bender, Chas. Albert (Chief)	P	23	.233	PhilA	
4	8	Black, David	P	12	+.200	xChiF	
1	4	Conley, James Patrick (Snipe)	P	20	.250	B	
		Crawford, Kenneth (OF1)	1B22	23	.244	A	C
		Doolan, Michael Joseph	SS	119	+.195	B	Chi

WON	LOST	NAME	POS.	G.	BA	FROM	TO
1	0	Douglas, Lawrence Howard	P	2	.000	A	C
		Duncan, Vernon Van Duke (3B19)	OF123	146	.269	B	C
		Eakle,	2B	2	.286	A	C
		Evans, Louis Richard	OF	87	+.319	xBknF	C
		Forsythe, Clarence	3B	1	.000	A	C
		Gallagher, John C.	2B	40	.200	A	C
		Hickman, David James	OF	20	.210	A	
		Jacklitsch, Frederick Lawrence	C	48	.237	B	
7	10	Johnson, Adam Rankin	P	20	+.163	xChiF	
		Kerr, John Jonas	C	3	.333	B	C
		Kirkpatrick, Enos Claire (2B19)	3B26	60	.241	B	C
		Knabe, Franz Otto MGR.	2B92	100	.251	B	
		Kolseth, Karl Dickey	1B	6	.217	A	C
0	6	Leclair, George L.	P	17	+.095	xBuffF	C
		Meisel,	C	1	.000	A	C
		Meyer, Benjamin (Benny)	OF	35	+.233	B	BuffF
		Miller, Chas. Hess		1	.000	A	C
		McCandless, John C.	OF105	116	.218	B	C
		Owens, Frank Walter	C	98	.245	BknF	C
9	22	Quinn, John Picus	P42	54	.263	B	
		Reinicker, Walter	3B	3	.125	A	C
		Russell, Harvey Holmes	C21	52	.243	B	C
		Simmons, George Washington	OF	39	.205	B	C
4	6	Smith, Frank Elmer	P	17	+.200	B	BknF
		Smith, James Lawrence	SS	33	+.191	xChiF	
11	17	Suggs, George Franklin	P	32	.221	B	C
		Swacina, Harry J.	1B78	85	.247	B	C
0	0	Vereker, Thomas	P	2	.000	A	C
		Walsh, Michael Timothy	3B	109	+.304	B	StL
0	0	Wilhelm, Irving Key (Kaiser)	P	1	.000	B	
2	3	Young Chas. V.	P	9	.222	A	C
		Zinn, Guy	OF84	100	.269	B	C

WON 77   FEDERAL LEAGUE   FINISHED 5th.
LOST 77
TG 154   1914.   PCT. .500

BROOKLYN

WM. JOSEPH BRADLEY

WON	LOST	NAME	POS.	G.	BA	FROM	TO
		Anderson, George Jendrus	OF91	97	.310	A	
4	4	Bluejacket, James	P	17	.130	A	
		Bradley, Wm. Joseph MGR.		7	.500	ClevA10	
3	6	Brown, Mordecai Peter Centennial	P	6	+.200	xStL	
0	0	Chaney, Esty Cleon	P	1	.000	BosA	C
4	2	Chappelle, Wm. Hogan	P	15	.000	CinN09	C
		Chouinard, Felix George	OF	15	+.366	xPitt	Balt
		Cooper, Claude Wm.	OF101	110	.239	NYN	
		Delahanty, James Christopher, Jr.	2B55	74	.284	DetA12	
		Evans, Louis Richard (1B27)	OF111	145	.355	StLN	
12	11	Finneran, Joseph Ignatius	P	23	.127	PhilN	
		Gagnier, Edward J.	SS89	94	.182	A	
		Griggs, Arthur J.	1B28	38	.282	ClevA12	
		Halt, Alva Wm.	SS70	80	.235	A	
		Hofman, Arthur Frederich (1B21 OF19)	2B106	147	.291	PittN	
2	6	Houck, Byron Simon	P	18	.233	xPhilA	
0	3	Juul, Earl Herbert	P	9	.222	A	C
18	15	LaFitte, Edward Francis	P	40	.252	DetA12	
		Land, Grover Cleveland	C98	103	.282	ClevA	
3	3	Marion, Donald G. M.	P	17	.222	A	
3	4	Maxwell, J. Albert	P	12	.091	NYN11	C
		Merson,		1	.000	A	C
		Myers, Ralph Edward	1B	89	.226	BosN	
		Murphy, Daniel Francis	OF43	50	.311	PhilA	
0	0	McGraw, James Leo	P	1	.000	A	C
		Owens, Frank Walter	C	55	.274	ChiA09	
1	1	Peters, Oscar C.	P	11	.091	ChiA12	C
25	14	Seaton, Thomas Gordon	P	44	.200	PhilN	
		Shaw, Albert Simpson	OF102	110	.321	StLN09	
2	7	Sommers, Rudolph	P	23	.250	ChiN12	
0	0	Vernon, Joseph Henry	P	1	.000	ChiN12	C
		Watson, Arthur	C	19	.289	A	
		Westerzil, George J.	3B	149	.253	A	
		Williams, Rinaldo Lewis	3B	4	.207	A	C
0	1	Wilson, Finis E.	P	2	.500	A	

WON 70   FEDERAL LEAGUE   FINISHED 7th.
LOST 82
TG 152   1915.   PCT. .461

BROOKLYN

LEO CHRISTOPHER MAGEE   JOHN HENRY GANZEL

WON	LOST	NAME	POS.	G.	BA	FROM	TO
		Anderson, George Jendrus	OF	134	.259	B	
10	11	Bluejacket, James	P	24	.136	B	
		Bradley, Hugh Frederick	1B22	37	+.246	xPittF	NwkF
		Chouinard, Felix George	OF	4	.500	BaltF	C
		Cooper, Claude Wm. (1B31)	OF121	152	.291	B	
		Delahanty, James Christopher Jr.	1B	16	.250	B	C
		Evans, Louis Richard	OF	63	+.289	B	Balt
7	8	Falkenberg, Frederick Peter (Cy)	P	16	+.077	xNwkF	
10	12	Finneran, Joseph Ignatius	P	34	.137	B	
		Gagnier, Edward J.	SS	19	+.260	B	Buff
		Griggs, Arthur J.	1B	27	.275	B	
		Halt, Alva Wm. (SS41)	3B110	151	.245	B	
		Helfrich, Emory Wilbur	2B34	40	.245	A	C
0	1	Herring, Wm. Francis	P	3	.000	A	C
		Howard, David Austin	2B	20	.222	WashA12	C
		Kane, Francis Thomas	OF	3	.200	A	
		Kauff, Benjamin Michael	OF	136	.344	Indpls	
7	9	LaFitte, Edward Francis	P	17	+.264	B	Buff
		Land, Grover Cleveland	C81	96	.261	B	C
		Magee, Leo Christopher (Lee) MGR.)	2B113	121	.330	StLN	
12	9	Marion, Donald G. M.	P	32	.171	B	C
		Myers, Ralph Edward	1B107	115	.282	B	C
		Murphy, Daniel Francis	OF	5	.166	B	C
		Pratt, Lester John	C	20	+.191	BosA	Nwk
		Reed, Milton D.	2B	10	.290	PhilN	C
7	7	Seaton, Thomas Gordon	P	26	+.242	B	Nwk
		Simon, Michael Edward (Mike)	C	47	.175	StLF	C
5	0	Smith, Frank Elmer	P	9	+.158	xBaltF	C
		Smith, Frederick Vincent	SS	109	+.245	xBuffF	
		Smith, James Harry	C19	25	.215	xNYN	
		Tesch, Albert John	2B3	7	.286	A	C
6	8	Upham, Wm. Lawrence	P	26	.108	A	
2	4	Walker, Frederick Mitchell	P	13	.222	PittF	C
		Watson, Arthur	C	8	+.294	B	Buff
		Westerzil, George J.	3B	36	+.311	B	ChiF
1	8	Wilson, Finis E.	P	18	.306	B	C
3	5	Wiltse, George LeRoy (Hooks)	P	19	.045	NYN	C
		Wright, Willard James (Dick)	C	4	.000	A	C

WON 80 LOST 71 TG 151

FEDERAL LEAGUE

1914.

FINISHED 4th. PCT. .530

BUFFALO

HARRY LAWRENCE SCHLAFLY

WON	LOST	NAME	POS.	G.	BA	FROM	TO
		Agler, Joseph Abram (OF53)	1B77	135	.272	WashA12	
		Allen, Artemus Ward (Nick)	C26	31	.235	A	
13	15	Anderson, John Frederick	P	36	.183	BosA	
		Blair, Walter Allan	C	127	.239	NYN11	
		Bonin, Ernest Luther	OF	21	.173	StLA	C
		Booe, Everett Little	OF	73	+.220	xIndpls	C
0	0	Brown, Robert M.	P	15	.222	A	C
		Chase, Harold Homer (Hal)	1B	75	.354	xChiA	
		Collins, Wm. Shirley	OF15	20	.146	BknN	C
		Delahanty, Frank George	OF	79	+.212	NYA08	Pitt
		Downey, Thomas Edward (SS16)	2B129	151	.223	ChiN12	
		Engle, Arthur Clyde	3B23	32	.259	xBosA	
21	6	Ford, Russell Wm.	P	30	.139	NYA	
		Hanford, Chas. Joseph	OF	156	.287	A	
0	1	Houser, Joseph	P	8	.286	A	C
16	14	Krapp, Eugene	P	37	.150	ClevA12	
		Lavigne, Arthur David	C33	45	.200	A	C
		Louden, Wm.	SS116	127	.313	DetA	
11	15	Moore, Earl Alonzo	P	33	.155	ChiN	C
10	7	Moran, Harry Edwin	P	30	.196	DetA12	
		McDonald, Chas. E.	OF	69	+.295	xPitt	
		Pettigrew, Jim Ned		2	.000	A	C
0	1	Porray, Edmund Joseph	P	3	.000	A	C
		Schlafly, Harry Lawrence MGR.	2B	52	.254	WashA07	
0	0	Schlitzer, Victor Joseph	P	3	1.000	BosA09	C
9	12	Schulz, Albert C.	P	24	.196	xNYA	
		Smith, Frederick Vincent (SS22)	3B124	146	.222	BosN	
		Snyder, John Wm.	C	1	.000	A	
		Wertz, Dwight Lewis (Del)	SS1	3	.000	A	C
0	0	Woodman, Daniel Courtney	P	13	.100	A	
		Young, Delmar John	OF37	79	.278	CinN09	

WON 74 LOST 78 TG 152

FEDERAL LEAGUE

1915.

FINISHED 6th. PCT. .487

BUFFALO

HARRY LAWRENCE SCHLAFLY WALTER ALLEN BLAIR HARRY DONALD LORD

WON	LOST	NAME	POS.	G.	BA	FROM	TO
		Agler, Joseph Abram	1B11	25	+.178	B	Balt
		Allen, Artemus Ward (Nick)	C	83	.205	B	

19	13	Anderson, John Frederick	P	33	.148	B	
16	18	Bedient, Hugh Carpenter	P	44	.107	BosA	C
		Blair, Walter Allan MGR.	C	98	.224	B	C
		Chase, Harold Homer (Hal)	1B	145	.284	B	
		Dalton, Talbot Percy	OF118	132	.294	BknN	
		Downey, Thomas Edward	2B49	90	.199	B	C
0	2	Ehmke, Howard John	P	16	.000	A	
		Engle, Arthur Clyde (2B21 3B16)	OF99	141	.263	B	
5	9	Ford, Russell Wm.	P	20	.286	B	C
		Gagnier, Edward J.	2B	2	+.000	xBknF	C
		Hofman, Arthur Frederich	OF81	108	.233	BknF	
9	19	Krapp, Eugene	P	34	.129	B	C
2	2	LaFitte, Edward Francis	P	14	+.118	xBknF	C
0	0	Leclair, George L.	P	1	+.000	xPittF	Balt
		Lord, Harry Donald MGR.	3B92	97	.273	ChiA	C
		Louden, Wm. (SS27 3B19)	2B86	137	.280	B	
2	1	Marshall, Roy DeVerne	P	21	.294	PhilN	C
		Meyer, Benjamin (Benny)	OF	93	+.237	xBaltF	
		McDonald, Chas. E.	OF65	87	.271	B	C
		Roach, Wilbur C.	SS	92	.270	WashA12	C
21	14	Schulz, Albert C.	P	42	.157	B	
		Smith, Frederick Vincent	SS	35	+.220	B	Bkn
0	0	Smith, Robert A.	P	1	.000	ChiA13	C
		Watson, Arthur	C	21	+.452	xBknF	C
0	0	Woodman, Daniel Courtney	P	6	.250	B	C
		Young, Delmar John	OF	12	.133	B	C

CLUB RECORD

OTHER MAJOR LEAGUES

CHICAGO

YEAR	TG	WON	LOST	PCT.	FINISHED	MANAGER
UNION ASSOCIATION						
1884	68	34	40	.459	DID NOT FINISH	Edward S. Hengle
PLAYER'S LEAGUE						
1890	137	75	62	.547	4	Chas. Albert Comiskey
FEDERAL LEAGUE						
1914	154	87	67	.565	2	Joseph Bert Tinker
1915	152	86	66	.566	1	Joseph Bert Tinker
AMERICAN LEAGUE						
1900	135	82	53	.608	1	Chas. Albert Comiskey

WON 87
LOST 67
TG 154

FEDERAL LEAGUE 1914.

FINISHED 2nd. PCT. .565

CHICAGO

JOSEPH BERT TINKER

WON	LOST	NAME	POS.	G.	BA	FROM	TO
		Beck, Frederick Thomas	1B	158	.279	PhilN11	
1	0	Black, David	P	9	.286	A	
		Block, James John	C33	45	.212	ChiA12	C
5	5	Brennan, Addison Foster (Ad)	P	15	.250	PhilN	
		Deniend,	C	1	.000	A	C
		Deniens, Clement Lambert	C	12	.154	A	
		Farrell, John J.	2B	157	.240	A	
12	12	Fisk, Maximilian Patrick	P	35	.232	A	C
		Flack, Max John	OF	135	.253	A	
		Fritz, Harry Koch	3B45	63	.229	PhilA	
29	10	Hendrix, Claude Raymond	P	48	.223	PittN	
		Jackson, Wm. Riley	1B	17	.040	A	
9	5	Johnson, Adam Rankin	P	17	.040	xBosA	
		Kading, John Fred		3	.000	PittN10	C
		Kavanagh, Leo Daniel	SS	5	.273	A	C
12	11	Lange, Irwin	P	31	.176	A	C
5	6	McGuire, Thomas Patrick	P20	37	.264	A	
5	9	Prendergast, Michael Thomas	P	23	.111	A	
		Roberts, Clarence Ashley	C	4	+.333	xPitt	Pitt
0	1	Sherman, Daniel	P	1	.000	A	C
		Smith, James Lawrence	SS	3	.500	A	
		Stanley, James F.	SS33	46	.206	A	C
		Tinker, Joseph Bert MGR.	SS	127	.259	CinN	
		Walsh, Austin	OF26	52	.235	A	C
9	8	Watson, Chas. J.	P	26	+.096	ChiN	StL
		Wickland, Albert	OF	158	.288	CinN	
		Wilson, Arthur Earl	C133	138	.287	NYN	
		Zeider, Rolla Hubert	3B	120	.263	NYA	
		Zwilling, Edward Harrison	OF	155	.308	ChiA10	

WON 86
LOST 66
TG 152

FEDERAL LEAGUE 1915.

FINISHED 1st. PCT. .566

CHICAGO

JOSEPH BERT TINKER

WON	LOST	NAME	POS.	G.	BA	FROM	TO
6	5	Bailey, Wm. F.	P	11	+.333	xBalt	
		Beck, Frederick Thomas	1B	121	.219	B	C
3	2	Black, David	P	21	+.154	B	Balt
3	9	Brennan, Addison Foster (Ad)	P	16	.185	B	
17	8	Brown, Mordecai Peter Centennial	P	35	.317	BknF	
		Clemens, Clement Lambert	C	11	.136	B	
		Doolan, Michael Joseph	SS	24	+.256	xBalt	
		Farrell, John J.	2B	69	.213	B	C
		Fischer, Wm. Chas.	C80	105	.326	BknN	
		Flack, Max John	OF	141	.315	B	
		Fritz, Harry Koch	3B66	72	.240	B	C
		Hanford, Chas. Joseph	OF43	74	.239	BuffF	C
		Hauser, Arnold J.	SS15	20	.222	StLN13	C
16	15	Hendrix, Claude Raymond	P37	46	.265	B	
		Jackson, Wm. Riley	1B36	48	.165	B	C
2	5	Johnson, Adam Rankin	P	11	+.043	B	Balt
		Mann, Leslie	OF130	135	.306	BosN	
25	10	McConnell, George Neely	P42	50	.248	ChiN	
		Pechous, Chas. Edward	3B	18	.220	A	
14	12	Prendergast, Michael Thomas	P	37	.075	B	
0	0	Rasmussen, Henry	P	2	.000	A	C
		Smith, James Lawrence	SS	94	+.217	B	Balt
		Strands, Lewis	2B	1	.000	A	C
		Tinker, Joseph Bert MGR.	SS15	30	.275	B	
		Weiss, Joseph Harold	1B	29	.239	A	C
		Westerzil, George J.	3B	7	+.250	xBkn & recall	StL C
		Wickland, Albert	OF	30	+.235	B	Pitt
		Wilson, Arthur Earl	C88	96	.309	B	
		Zeider, Rolla Hubert (SS17 3B30)	2B82	130	.233	B	
		Zwilling, Edward Harrison	OF	150	.291	B	

WON 88
LOST 65
TG 153

FEDERAL LEAGUE 1914.

FINISHED 1st. PCT. .575

INDIANAPOLIS

WM. CORCORAN PHILLIPS

WON	LOST	NAME	POS.	G.	BA	FROM	TO
8	7	Billiard, Harry P.	P	24	.179	NYA08	
		Booe, Everett Little	OF	19	+.233	PittN	Buff
		Campbell, Arthur Vincent	OF	133	.315	BosN12	
		Carr, Chas. Carbitt	1B	115	.292	CinN06	C
		Dolan, E. L.	1B	31	.223	A	C
		Esmond, James J.	SS	150	.295	CinN12	
25	16	Falkenberg, Frederick Peter(Cy)	P	46	.166	ClevA	
1	2	Harter, Frank Pierce	P	6	.000	CinN	C
1	0	Henderson, Edward J.	P	1	+.000	xPitt	C
		Kaiser, Albert Edward	OF50	59	.226	BosN12	C
17	10	Kaiserling, George	P	36	.112	A	
		Kauff, Benjamin Michael	OF	154	.366	NYA12	
1	0	Keifer, Sherman C.	P	1	.333	A	C
		LaPorte, Frank B.	2B	133	.311	WashA	
19	18	Moseley, Earl Victor	P	43	.099	BosA	
14	10	Mullin, George Joseph	P33	40	.295	WashA	
0	2	McConnaughey, Ralph J.	P	7	.125	A	C
		McKechnie, Wm. Boyd	3B	149	.305	NYA	
0	0	Ostendorf, Frederick K.	P	1	.000	A	C
		Rariden, Wm. Angel	C	132	.236	BosN	
		Rooney, Frank L.	1B	12	.212	A	C
		Roush, Edd J.	OF41	74	.333	ChiA	
		Scheer, Allen G.	OF101	117	.309	BknN	
		Textor, George B.	C	20	.179	A	
		Vandagrift, Carl Wm.	2B28	42	.246	A	C
		Warren, Wm. H.	C	23	.239	A	
2	0	Whitehouse, Chas. Evis	P	8	.000	A	
0	0	Wood,	P	2	.000	A	C

WON 69
LOST 84
TG 153

FEDERAL LEAGUE 1914.

FINISHED 6th. PCT. .451

KANSAS CITY

GEORGE THOMAS STOVALL

WON	LOST	NAME	POS.	G.	BA.	FROM	TO
4	9	Adams, Daniel Leslie	P	26	.152	A	
		Brown, Drummond N.	C23	30	.207	BosN	
		Chadbourne, Chester James	OF	147	.278	BosA07	
		Coles, Cadwallader R. (Cad)	OF38	77	.253	A	C
14	19	Cullop, Norman Andrew	P	41	.141	xClevA	
		Daringer, Clifford Clarence (3B18)	SS24	60	.247	A	C
		Easterly, Theodore Harrison (Ted)	C128	134	.331	ChiA	
		Enzenroth, Clarence Herman	C	24	.166	xStLA	
		Gilmore, Ernest Grover	OF132	138	.282	A	
		Goodwin, Claire Vernon (3B39)	SS65	111	.243	A	
7	7	Harris, Benjamin F.	P	27	.191	A	
5	9	Henning, Peter Herman	P	23	.159	A	
3	1	Hogan, George Emmet	P	4	.000	A	C
9	10	Johnson, George Murphy (Chief)	P	20	.122	xCinN	
		Kenworthy, Wm. Jennings	2B	146	.316	WashA12	
		Krueger, Arthur T.	OF	122	.250	ClevA10	
20	14	Packard, Eugene Milo	P	40	.246	CinN	
		Perring, George Wilson (1B38)	3B99	144	.282	ClevA10	
		Potts, John Frederick	OF30	40	.287	A	C
		Rawlings, John Wm.	SS	61	.209	xCinN	
7	14	Stone, Dwight Ely	P	34	.117	StLA	C
		Stovall, George Thomas MGR.	1B114	122	.270	StLA	
0	1	Swann, Henry	P	1	.000	A	C
		Van Tappen, W.	3B	18	.200	A	C

WON 81
LOST 72
TG 153

FEDERAL LEAGUE 1915.

FINISHED 4th. PCT. .533

KANSAS CITY

GEORGE THOMAS STOVALL

WON	LOST	NAME	POS.	G.	BA	FROM	TO
0	2	Adams, Daniel Leslie	P	11	.111	B	C
0	1	Blackburn, Foster Edwin	P	7	.000	A	
		Bradley, Wm. Joseph	3B60	66	.192	BknF	C
		Brown, Drummond N.	C65	77	.239	B	C
		Chadbourne, Chester James	OF	152	.224	B	
22	11	Cullop, Norman Andrew	P	40	.187	B	
		Easterly, Theodore Harrison (Ted)	C87	110	.267	B	C

		Enzenroth, Clarence Herman	C	14	.158	B	C
		Gilmore, Ernest Grover	OF	119	.282	B	C
0	0	Gingras, Joseph John E.	P	2	.000	A	C
		Goodwin, Claire Vernon (2B23)	SS40	81	.235	B	C
0	0	Harris, Benjamin F.	P	1	.000	B	C
9	15	Henning, Peter Herman	P	40	.203	B	C
17	17	Johnson, George Murphy (Chief)	P	39	.129	B	C
		Kenworthy, Wm. Jennings	2B106	121	.299	B	
		Krueger, Arthur T.	OF66	80	.234	B	C
13	14	Main, Miles Grant	P	32	.187	DetA	
20	12	Packard, Eugene Milo	P	39	.232	B	
		Perring, George Wilson (1B24 2B30)	3B99	153	.257	B	C
		Rawlings, John Wm.	SS	120	.213	B	
		Shaw, Albert Simpson	OF125	132	.279	BknF	C
		Stovall, George Thomas MGR.	1B	130	.233	B	C

CLUB RECORD

OTHER MAJOR LEAGUES

NEWARK

YEAR	TG	WON	LOST	PCT.	FINISHED	MANAGER
FEDERAL LEAGUE						
1915	152	80	72	.526	5	Wm. C. Phillips Wm. Boyd McKechnie

WON 80 LOST 72 TG 152 — FEDERAL LEAGUE 1915. — FINISHED 5th. PCT. .526

NEWARK

WM. CORCORAN PHILLIPS   WM. BOYD McKECHNIE

WON	LOST	NAME	POS.	G.	BA	FROM	TO
0	1	Billiard, Harry P.	P	14	.333	Indpls	
		Bradley, Hugh Frederick	1B	12	+.094	xBknF	C
1	1	Brandom, Chester Milton	P	16	.182	PittN09	C
		Campbell, Arthur Vincent	OF	127	.314	Indpls	
		Esmond, James J.	SS	155	.258	Indpls	C
4	6	Falkenberg, Frederick Peter (Cy)	P	16	+.053	Indpls	BknF
		Huhn, Emil Hugo (C16)	1B100	124	.227	A	
15	16	Kaiserling, Ge orge	P	38	.152	Indpls	C
		LaPorte, Frank B.	2B	148	.251	Indpls	C
		Mills, Rupert Frank	1B	41	.205	A	C
13	9	Moran, Harry Edwin	P	33	.175	BuffF	C
15	15	Moseley, Earl Victor	P	36	.148	Indpls	
2	2	Mullin, George Joseph	P	6	.100	Indpls	C
		McKechnie, Wm. Boyd MGR.	3B117	126	.257	Indpls	
		Pratt, Lester, John	C	5	+.500	xBknF	C
		Rariden, Wm. Angel	C	142	.278	Indpls	
		Reed, Ralph Edwin	3B	20	.247	A	C
21	10	Reulbach, Edward Marvin	P	33	.196	BknN	
		Roush, Edd J.	OF	145	.298	Indpls	
		Schaefer, Herman A. (Germany)	OF17	58	.214	WashA	
		Scheer, Allen G.	OF	155	.269	Indpls	C
7	10	Seaton, Thomas Gordon	P	18	+.174	xBknF	
		Strands, John Lawrence (2B6)	3B8	34	.187	A	C
		Textor, George B.	C	3	.333	Indpls	C
0	0	Trautman, Frederick Orlando	P	1	.000	A	C
		Warren, Wm. H.	C	5	.333	Indpls	C
2	2	Whitehouse, Chas. Evis	P	11	.000	Indpls	
		Whitehouse, Gilbert A.	OF28	35	.217	BosN12	C

WON 64 LOST 88 TG 152 — FEDERAL LEAGUE 1914. — FINISHED 7th. PCT. .421

PITTSBURGH

HARRY HOMER GESSLER   ENNIS TALMADGE OAKES

WON	LOST	NAME	POS.	G.	BA	FROM	TO
1	1	Adams, James Irwin	P	15	.067	StLA	
1	0	Allen, Frank Leon	P	1	.500	xBknN	
10	16	Barger, Eros Bollivar	P	33	.205	BknN12	
		Berry, Claude Elzy	C	124	.243	PhilA07	
		Boucher, Medric T.	C	1	+.000	xBalt	C
		Bradley, Hugh Frederick	1B	118	.302	BosA12	
14	19	Camnitz, Samuel Howard	P	36	.148	PhilN	
		Chouinard, Felix George	OF	5	+.440	ChiA11	Bkn
		Coulson, Robert Jackson	OF	18	.203	BknN11	C
		Delahanty, Frank George	OF	42	+.213	xBuff	
9	19	Dickson, Walter R.	P	37	.088	BosN	
0	3	Henderson, Edward J.	P	6	+.000	A	Indpls
		Holly, Edward Wm.	SS95	100	.246	StLN07	
		Jones, David Jefferson	OF	97	.272	ChiA	
		Kerr, John Jonas	C	41	+.254	A	Balt
20	12	Knetzer, Elmer Ellsworth	P	34	.099	BknN12	
5	2	Leclair, George L.	P	17	.148	A	
		Lennox, James Edgar	3B	124	.317	ChiN12	
		Lewis, John D.	2B	117	.234	BosA11	
		Madden,	C	2	.500	A	C
		Mattis, Ralph L.	OF24	35	.247	A	C
		Menoskey, Michael Wm.	OF38	60	.260	A	
		McDonald, Chas. E. (2B34)	3B37	67	+.318	BosN	Buff
		Oakes, Ennis Talmadge (Rebel) MGR.	OF	145	.311	StLN	
		Rheam, Kenneth Johnston (Cy)	1B43	72	.209	A	
		Roberts, Clarence Ashley	C20	32	+.226	StLN	Chi
				18	+.228		& return
		Savage, Harold James (3B1)	OF129	132	.285	PhilN12	
		Scott, James W.	SS	8	.250	A	C
4	16	Walker, Frederick Mitchell	P	31	.111	BknN	
		Yerkes, Stephen Douglas	SS	39	.333	xBosA	

WON 86 LOST 67 TG 153 — FEDERAL LEAGUE 1915. — FINISHED 3rd. PCT. .562

PITTSBURGH

ENNIS TALMADGE OAKES

WON	LOST	NAME	POS.	G.	BA	FROM	TO
23	13	Allen, Frank Leon	P	38	.079	B	
9	8	Barger, Eros Bollivar	P	28	.272	B	C
		Berghammer, Martin Andrew	SS	132	.238	CinN	C
		Berry, Claude Elzy	C	99	.192	B	C

WON	LOST	NAME	POS.	G.	BA	FROM	TO
		Bradley, Hugh Frederick	1B10	26	+.288	B	Bkn
0	0	Braithwood, Albert	P	1	.000	A	C
0	0	Burk, Charles Sanford	P	2	.167	StLN13	C
0	0	Camnitz, Samuel Howard	P	4	.143	B	C
3	3	Comstock, Ralph Remick	P	12	.000	xBosA	
		Delahanty, Frank George	OF	14	.238	B	C
7	5	Dickson, Walter R.	P	24	.133	B	C
6	11	Hearn, Bunn	P	26	.189	NYN13	
		Holly, Edward Wm.	SS	16	.262	B	C
		Jones, David Jefferson	OF	14	.327	B	
		Kelly, James Robert (Robert John Taggart)	OF	148	.290	PittN	
		Kerlin, Orie Milton	C	3	.000	A	C
18	14	Knetzer, Elmer Ellsworth	P	41	.130	B	
		Konetchy, Edward Joseph	1B	152	.310	PittN	
3	2	Leclair, George L.	P	14	+.154	B	Buff
		Lennox, James Edgar	3B	55	.321	B	C
		Lewis, John D.	2B43	77	.268	B	C
		Menosky, Michael Wm.	OF	16	100	B	
0	0	Miljus, John Kenneth	P	1	.000	A	
		Mowrey, Harry Harlan (Mike)	3B	151	.282	PittN	
		Oakes, Ennis Talmadge (Rebel) MGR.	OF	153	.281	B	C
		O'Connor, Patrick Francis	C	70	.224	StLN	
		Rheam, Kenneth Johnston (Cy)	OF20	27	.174	B	C
17	11	Rogge, F. Clinton	P	34	.175	A	
		Savage, Harold James	OF	14	.150	B	C
		Wickland, Albert	OF	110	+.303	xChi	
		Yerkes, Stephen Douglas	2B109	121	.286	B	

WON 61 LOST 89 TG 150

FEDERAL LEAGUE 1914.

FINISHED 8th (LAST) PCT. .407

ST. LOUIS

MORDECAI PETER CENTENNIAL BROWN FIELDER ALLISON JONES

WON	LOST	NAME	POS.	G.	BA	FROM	TO
		Boucher, Alexander Francis	3B	147	.232	A	C
		Bridwell, Albert Henry	SS105	117	.234	ChiN	
11	5	Brown, Mordecai Peter Centennial MGR.	P	26	+.233	CinN	Bkn
		Chapman, Harry E.	C50	59	.209	CinN	
12	9	Crandall, James Otis (Doc) (P26)	2B60	115	.312	NYN	
		Cueto, Manuel Melo (3B5)	SS6	15	.100	A	
10	15	Davenport, Arthur David	P	32	.088	xCinN	
		Drake, Delos Daniel (1B18)	OF116	138	.252	DetA11	
13	20	Groom, Robert	P	40	.126	WashA	
		Hartley, Grover Allen	C33	86	.286	NYN	
1	0	Herbert, Ernie Albert	P	25	.583	CinN	
		Jones, Fielder Allison MGR.		5	.333	ChiA08	
		Kirby, LaRue V.	OF	51	.253	NYN12	
		Kommers, Frederick Raymond	OF	75	+.308	PittN	Balt
7	20	Keupper, Henry	P	38	.253	A	C
		Marsans, Armando (SS2) (2B7)	OF	9	.350	xCinN	
		Mathes, Joseph John	2B	24	.298	PhilA12	
		Miller, Hugh Stanley	1B	132	.225	PhilN11	
		Miller, Ward Taylor	OF109	119	.295	ChiN	
		Misse, John B. (SS45)	2B51	97	.189	A	C
		Simon, Michael Edward (Mike)	C79	93	.219	PittN	
		Tobin, John Thomas	OF	135	.270	A	
3	4	Watson, Chas. J.	P	9	+.125	xChi	
0	0	Welch, Theodore	P	3	.000	A	C
4	16	Willett, Robert Edgar	P	27	.235	DetA	

WON 87 LOST 67 TG 154

FEDERAL LEAGUE 1915.

FINISHED 2nd. PCT. .565

ST. LOUIS

FIELDER ALLISON JONES

WON	LOST	NAME	POS.	G.	BA	FROM	TO
		Borton, Wm. Baker	1B	159	.289	NYA13	
		Bridwell, Albert Henry	2B39	63	.226	B	C
		Chapman, Harry E.	C53	62	.198	B	
		Compton, Albert Sebastian (Bash)	OF	2	.250	StLA13	BosN
21	15	Crandall, James Otis (Doc)	P48	81	.282	B	
22	18	Davenport, Arthur David	P	51	.092	B	
		Deal, Chas. Albert	3B	65	.314	BosN	
		Drake, Delos Daniel	OF94	99	.265	B	C

WON	LOST	NAME	POS.	G.	BA	FROM	TO
11	11	Groom, Robert	P	30	.149	B	
		Hartley, Grover Allen	C110	117	.271	B	
1	0	Herbert, Ernie Albert	P	12	.222	B	C
		Johnson, Ernest Rudolph	SS	152	.244	ChiA12	
		Jones, Fielder Allison MGR.	OF1	5	.000	B	
		Kirby, LaRue V.	OF52	59	.212	B	C
		Kores, Arthur Emil	3B	60	.229	A	C
		Marsans, Armando	OF	36	.177	B	
		Miller, Hugh Stanley	1B	6	.500	B	C
		Miller, Ward Taylor	OF	155	.307	B	
21	11	Plank, Edward Stewart	P	40	.259	PhilA	
		Tobin, John Thomas	OF	158	.299	B	
		Vaughn, Robert	2B126	144	.274	NYA09	C
		Walsh, Michael Timothy	3B	14	+.200	xBalt	C
9	9	Watson, Chas. J.	P	25	.122	B	C
		Westerzil, George J.	3B	50	+.240	xChi & return to Chi	
2	3	Willett, Robert Edgar	P	17	.118	B	C

National League

WON 14 LOST 45 TG 59

1876.

FINISHED 7th.

PCT. 237

ATHLETICS

ALFRED L. H. WRIGHT

WON	LOST	NAME	POS.	G.	BA	FROM	TO
		Berge, John Baptist	C	1	.000	A	
		Bushong, Albert John	C	5	.048	A	C
		Coons, Wilbur K. (C17)	OF29	54	.225	A	C
		Curren, Peter (OF1)	C2	3	.333	A	C
		Eggler, David Daniel	OF	39	.295	A	
		Fisler, Weston Dickson (1B13 2B21)	OF25	59	.286	A	C
		Force, David W.	SS59	60	.228	A	
		Fouser, Wm. C. (OF7)	2B14	21	.135	A	C
		Hall, George W.	OF	60	.355	A	
10	23	Knight, Alonzo P. (Lon) (1B10 OF9)	P33	55	.248	A	
0	1	Lafferty, Frank Bernard (Flip)	P	1	.000	A	
		Malone, Ferguson G.	C19	22	.229	A	
0	2	Meyerle, Levi Samuel (P2)	3B48	55	.336	A	
		Muller,	C	1	.000	A	C
		Paul,	C	3	.167	A	C
		Phelps, Cornelius Carman (Neal)	C	1	+.000	xMut	C
		Ritterson, E. W.	C12	15	.250	A	C
		Sutton, Ezra Ballou (2B15 3B7)	1B30	54	.293	A	
		Ward, James H.	C	1	.500	A	C
		Warner, Frederick John Rodney	OF	1	.000	A	
4	19	Zettlein, George (1B6)	P25	32	.211	A	C

CLUB RECORD

NATIONAL LEAGUE

BALTIMORE

YEAR	TG	WON	LOST	PCT.	FINISHED	MANAGER
1892	147	46	101	.313	12(Last)	George E. Van Haltren John J. Waltz Edward Hugh Hanlon
1893	130	60	70	.462	8	Edward Hugh Hanlon
1894	128	89	39	.695	1	Edward Hugh Hanlon
1895	129	86	43	.669	1	Edward Hugh Hanlon
1896	129	90	39	.698	1	Edward Hugh Hanlon
1897	130	90	40	.693	2	Edward Hugh Hanlon
1898	149	96	53	.644	2	Edward Hugh Hanlon
1899	142	84	58	.591	4	John Joseph McGraw

CLUB RECORD

OTHER MAJOR LEAGUES

BALTIMORE

YEAR	TG	WON	LOST	PCT.	FINISHED	MANAGER
AMERICAN ASSOCIATION						
1882	73	19	54	.260	6	Henry C. Myers
1883	96	28	68	.292	8(Last)	Wm. S. Barnie
1884	106	63	43	.594	6	Wm. S. Barnie
1885	109	41	68	.376	8(Last)	Wm. S. Barnie
1886	131	48	83	.366	8(Last)	Wm. S. Barnie
1887	135	77	58	.570	3	Wm. S. Barnie
1888	137	57	80	.416	5	Wm. S. Barnie
1889	135	70	65	.519	5	Wm. S. Barnie
1890	34	15	19	.441	6	Wm. S. Barnie
1891	136	71	64	.526	4	Wm. S. Barnie George E. Van Haltren
UNION ASSOCIATION						
1884	104	56	48	.538	4	Chas. T. Levis Wm. C. Henderson
FEDERAL LEAGUE						
1914	153	84	69	.549	3	Franz Otto Knabe
1915	154	47	107	.305	8(Last)	Franz Otto Knabe

WON 46
LOST 101
TG 147

NATIONAL LEAGUE — 1892. — FINISHED 12th (LAST) — PCT. .313

BALTIMORE

GEORGE E. VAN HALTREN EDWARD HUGH HANLON
JOHN J. WALTZ

WON	LOST	NAME	POS.	G.	BA	FROM	TO
5	8	Buffinton, Chas. G.	P	13	.349	BosAA	C
9	38	Cobb, George Washington	P47	49	.210	A	C
		Cross, Montford Montgomery (Monte)	SS	15	.160	A	
		Daly, James J.	OF	13	.229	MilAA	C
0	1	Ely, Frederick Wm.	P	1	.000	Bkn	
0	1	Ferson, Alexander	P	2	.000	BuffPL 90	C
0	2	Foreman, Francis Isaiah	P	5	+.167	xWash	
		Gilbert, Peter	3B	4	.200	BaltAA	
0	1	Gilbert, Wm.	P	2	.333	A	C
		Godar, John Michael	OF	5	.333	A	C
		Gunson, Joseph Brook (OF17)	C65	85	.223	KCAA89	
		Holligan, Wm. E. (Jocko)	OF	44	+.269	xCin	
		Hanlon, Edward Hugh MGR.	OF	8	.233	Pitt	
2	5	Healy, John J. (Egyptian)	P	9	+.115	BaltAA	Lvlle
		Hess, Thomas	C	1	.000	A	C
		Johnson, Wm. T.	OF	4	.133	BaltAA	C
		Kelley, Joseph James	OF	10	+.250	xPitt	
0	1	Kling, Wm.	P	2	.200	Phil	
		McGraw, John Joseph (OF31)	2B34	76	.267	BaltAA	
19	28	McMahon, John Joseph	P	47	.140	BaltAA	
		O'Rourke, Timothy Patrick	SS57	62	.317	ColAA	
		Pickett, John Thomas	2B	36	.208	PhilPL90	C
		Robinson, Wilbert	C	83	.270	BaltAA	
1	4	Schmidt, Frederick	P	7	.105	Pitt90	
		Shoch, George Quintus	SS56	75	.279	MilAA	
		Shindle, Wm.	3B134	143	.253	Phil	
1	0	Stephens, George Benjamin	P	5	.000	A	
		Stovey, Harry Duffield	OF	74	+.374	xBos	
		Stricker, John A. (Cub)	2B	72	+.275	xStL	
		Sutcliffe, Edward Elmer	1B	66	.275	WashAA	C
1	1	Terry, Wm. J. (Adonis)	P	6	+.000	Bkn	Pitt
		Van Haltren, George E. MGR.	OF	135	+.304	BaltAA	Pitt
8	11	Vickery, Thomas Gill	P	19	.246	Chi	
		Ward, Frank Gray (Piggy)	OF40	53	.282	Pitt	
		Welch, Curtis Benton	OF	63	+.233	BaltAA	Cin
		Whistler, Lewis	1B	52	+.227	N.Y.	Lvlle
		Wood, George A.	OF	20	+.183	AthAA	Cin

WON 60
LOST 70
TG 130

NATIONAL LEAGUE — 1893. — FINISHED 8th. — PCT. .462

BALTIMORE

EDWARD HUGH HANLON

WON	LOST	NAME	POS.	G.	BA	FROM	TO
3	10	Baker, Kirtly	P	19	.298	Pitt90	
		Brodie, Walter Scott	OF	25	+.372	xSt.L	
0	0	Brown, Richard P. (Stub)	P	11	.200	A	
		Brown, Willard	1B	7	+.129	Phil91	Lvlle
		Clarke, Wm. Jones	C36	47	.194	A	
		Gilks, Robert James	OF	15	.274	Clev90	C
11	17	Hawke, Wm. Victor	P	28	+.184	xStL	
		Jennings, Hugh Ambrose	SS	15	+.241	xLvlle	
		Kelley, Joseph James	OF	124	.312	B	
		Long, James M.	OF	55	.225	LvlleAA91	C
		Milligan, John (Jack) (Cl)	1B22	23	+.240	Wash	N.Y.
12	15	Mullane, Anthony John (Tony)	P	27	+.233	xCin	
		McGraw, John Joseph	SS117	127	.328	B	
23	16	McMahon, John Joseph	P	40	.262	B	
8	8	McNabb, Edgar J.	P	17	.209	A	C
		O'Rourke, Timothy Patrick	SS	31	+.379	B	Lvlle
		Reitz, Henry P.	2B	130	.297	A	
		Robinson, Wilbert	C	91	.338	B	
3	2	Schmidt, Frederick	P	9	+.288	B	N.Y.
		Shindle, Wm.	3B	125	.259	B	
		Stovey, Harry Duffield	OF7	8	+.167	B	Bkn
		Taylor, Harry Leonard	1B	88	.294	Lvlle	C
		Treadway, George B.	OF	114	.268	A	
0	2	Wadsworth, Wm. John	P	3	.600	Clev90	
		Ward, Frank Gray (Piggy)	OF	11	+.250	B	Cin
		Wright, Patrick W.	2B	1	.500	Chi90	C

WON 89 NATIONAL LEAGUE FINISHED 1st.
LOST 39
TG 128 1894. PCT. .695

BALTIMORE

EDWARD HUGH HANLON

WON	LOST	NAME	POS.	G.	BA	FROM	TO
0	0	Baker, Kirtly	P	2	.000	B	
		Bonner, Frank J.	2B24	27	.301	A	
		Brodie, Walter Scott	OF	129	.369	B	
		Brouthers, Dennis (Dan)	1B	123	.344	Bkn	
4	2	Brown, Richard P. (Stub)	P	9	.083	B	
		Clarke, Wm. Jones	C22	27	.270	B	
9	2	Esper, Chas. H.	P	16	+.217	xWash	
15	6	Gleason, Wm. J. (Kid)	P	23	+.384	xStL	
16	9	Hawke, Wm. Victor	P	25	.301	B	C
5	0	Hemming, George Earl	P	15	+.273	xLvlle	
0	1	Horner, Wm. Frank	P	2	.143	A	C
8	5	Inks, Albert Preston (Bert)	P	16	+.242	Wash92	Lvlle
		Jennings, Hugh Ambrose	SS	128	.332	B	
		Keeler, Wm. Henry	OF127	128	.367	Bkn	
		Kelley, Joseph James	OF	129	.391	B	
7	6	Mullane, Anthony John (Tony)	P	14	+.415	B	Clev
		McGraw, John Joseph	3B117	123	.340	B	
25	8	McMahon, John Joseph	P	34	.286	B	
		Reitz, Henry P.	2B100	109	.306	B	
		Robinson, Wilbert	C	106	.348	B	

WON 86 NATIONAL LEAGUE FINISHED 1st.
LOST 43
TG 129 1895. PCT. .669

BALTIMORE

EDWARD HUGH HANLON

WON	LOST	NAME	POS.	G.	BA	FROM	TO
		Bonner, Frank J.	3B	11	+.295	B	StL
		Bowerman, Frank Eugene	C	1	.000	A	
		Brodie, Walter Scott	OF	130	.365	B	
		Brouthers, Dennis (Dan)	1B	5	+.261	B	Lvlle
		Carey, George C.	1B121	123	.271	A	
		Clarke, Wm. Jones	C57	60	.297	B	
13	4	Clarkson, Arthur Hamilton	P	17	+.145	xStL	
12	12	Esper, Chas. H..	P24	27	.168	B	
3	1	Gleason, Wm. J. (Kid) (P4)	2B85	107	.323	B	
18	12	Hemming, George Earl	P	31	.290	B	
29	8	Hoffer, Wm. Leopold	P	38	.216	A	
		Jennings, Hugh Ambrose	SS	131	.386	B	
		Keeler, Wm. Henry	OF	131	.394	B	
		Kelley, Joseph James	OF	131	.370	B	
1	1	Kissinger, Wm. Francis	P	6	+.200	A	StL
		McGraw, John Joseph	3B	93	.374	B	
10	4	McMahon, John Joseph	P	15	.302	B	
0	1	Pond, Erasmus, Arlington	P	7	.333	A	
		Reitz, Henry P. (3B17)	2B46	63	.281	B	
		Robinson, Wilbert	C	74	.264	B	

WON 90 NATIONAL LEAGUE FINISHED 1st.
LOST 39
TG 129 1896 PCT. .698

BALTIMORE

EDWARD HUGH HANLON

WON	LOST	NAME	POS.	G.	BA	FROM	TO
		Bowerman, Frank Eugene	C	4	.125	B	
		Brodie, Walter Scott	OF	132	.294	B	
		Clarke, Wm. Jones	C64	77	.290	B	
3	2	Clarkson, Arthur Hamilton	P	7	.278	B	C
3	1	Corbett, Joseph	P	8	.200	Wash	
		Donely, James B.	3B	104	.330	ColAA91	
		Doyle, John Joseph (Jack)	1B	118	.345	N.Y.	
14	5	Esper, Chas. H.	P	19	.181	B	
15	7	Hemming, George Earl	P	25	.261	B	
26	7	Hoffer, Wm. Leopold	P	35	.301	B	
		Irwin, John	2B	1	.500	LvlleAA	C

WON	LOST	NAME	POS.	G.	BA	FROM	TO
		Jennings, Hugh Ambrose	SS	129	.397	B	
		Keeler, Wm. Henry	OF	127	.392	B	
		Keister, Wm. Hoffman	2B	13	.224	A	
		Kelley, Joseph James	OF	130	.370	B	
		McGraw, John Joseph	3B18	19	.356	B	
12	8	McMahon, John Joseph	P20	21	.126	B	
2	1	Nops, Jeremiah H.	P	3	+.111	xPhil	
15	8	Pond, Erasmus, Arlington	P	24	.243	B	
		Quinn, Joseph J.	2B	20	+.295	xStL	
		Reitz, Henry P.	2B116	119	.283	B	
		Robinson, Wilbert	C	66	.354	B	
0	0	Stocksdale, Otis H.	P	2	.333	Bos	C

WON 90 NATIONAL LEAGUE FINISHED 2nd.
LOST 40
TG 130 1897 PCT. .693

BALTIMORE

EDWARD HUGH HANLON

WON	LOST	NAME	POS.	G.	BA	FROM	TO
4	4	Amole, Morris George (Doc)	P	10	.120	A	
2	2	Blackburn, George W.	P	5	.167	A	C
		Bowerman, Frank Eugene	C	33	.323	B	
		Clarke, Wm. Jones	C59	63	.274	B	
0	0	Cogan, Richard Henry	P	1	.000	A	
24	8	Corbett, Joseph	P35	36	.257	B	
		Doyle, John Joseph (Jack)	1B	114	.356	B	
22	10	Hoffer, Wm. Leopold	P34	41	.238	B	
		Jennings, Hugh Ambrose	SS	115	.353	B	
		Keeler, Wm. Henry	OF	128	.432	B	
		Kelley, Joseph James	OF128	129	.389	B	
0	0	Maul, Albert Joseph	P	1	+.333	xWash	
		McGraw, John Joseph	3B	105	.326	B	
20	7	Nops, Jeremiah H.	P27	28	.217	B	
		O'Brien, Thomas F.	1B25	38	.268	A	
18	9	Pond, Erasmus, Arlington	P27	31	.244	B	
		Quinn, Joseph J. (SS21)	3B34	71	.264	B	
		Reitz, Henry P.	2B	127	.289	B	
		Robinson, Wilbert	C	47	.313	B	
		Stenzel, Jacob C. (Jake)	OF	131	.351	Pitt	

WON 96 NATIONAL LEAGUE FINISHED 2nd.
LOST 53
TG 149 1898. PCT. .644

BALTIMORE

EDWARD HUGH HANLON

WON	LOST	NAME	POS.	G.	BA	FROM	TO
		Ball, Arthur	3B	25	.175	StL94	C
		Bowerman, Frank Eugene	C4	5	+.438	B	Pitt
		Brodie, Walter Scott	OF	23	+.286	xPitt	
		Clarke, Wm. Jones	C68	77	.245	B	
		DeMontreville, Eugene Napoleon (SS28)	2B123	151	.325	Wash	
		Heydon, Michael Edward	C	3	.111	A	
0	5	Hoffer, Wm. Leopold (OF2)	P5	5	+.235	B	Pitt
		Holmes, Janes Wm. (Ducky)	OF	112	+.280	xStL	
21	11	Hughes, James Jay	P35	49	.236	A	
		Jennings, Hugh Ambrose (2B27)	SS114	143	.325	B	
		Keeler, Wm. Henry	OF	128	.379	B	
		Kelley, Joseph James	OF123	124	.328	B	
8	5	Kitson, Frank R.	P	23	.333	A	
20	7	Maul, Albert Joseph	P28	29	.202	B	
		McGann, Dennis L. (Dan)	1B	145	.298	Bos96	
		McGraw, John Joseph	3B137	141	.334	B	
27	14	McJames, James McCutchen	P	42	.172	Wash	
19	10	Nops, Jeremiah H.	P	29	.233	B	
		O'Brien, Thomas F.	OF16	19	+.217	B	Pitt
1	1	Pond, Erasmus, Arlington	P	2	.400	B	C
		Quinn, Joseph J. (2B1 OF1)	3B7	11	+.281	B	StL
		Robinson, Wilbert	C	77	.276	B	
		Stenzel, Jacob C. (Jake)	OF	35	+.254	B	StL
		Wilson, Henry C.	C	1	.000	A	C

WON x 84 NATIONAL LEAGUE FINISHED 4th.
LOST 58
TG 142 1899. PCT. .591

BALTIMORE

JOHN JOSEPH McGRAW

WON	LOST	NAME	POS.	G.	BA	FROM	TO
		Brodie, Walter Scott	OF	138	.309	B	
		Crisham, Patrick Lewis	1B25	44	.303	A	
		DeMontreville, Eugene Napoleon	2B	60	+.276	xChi	
		Fultz, David Lewis (3B21)	OF31	54	+.304	xPhil	
		Harris, Chas. Jenkins	3B	21	.283	A	C
3	4	Hill, Wm. C.	P	8	+.280	xClev	Bkn
		Holmes, James Wm. (Ducky)	OF	138	.315	B	
14	7	Howell, Harry	P25	28	.134	Bkn	
		Jennings, Hugh Ambrose	2B	2	+.375	xBkn	Bkn
		Keister, Wm. Hoffman (2B34)	SS90	134	.331	Bos	
20	16	Kitson, Frank R.	P38	40	.202	B	
		LaChance, George	1B	126	.307	Bkn	
		Magoon, George Henry	SS	61	+.252	Bkn	Chi
1	2	Miller, Ralph Darwin	P	6	.111	Bkn	C
27	13	McGinnity, Joseph Jerome	P43	47	.193	A	
		McGraw, John Joseph MGR.	3B	118	.390	B	
2	4	McKenna, James Wm.	P	9	.111	Bkn	
16	12	Nops, Jeremiah J.	P31	32	.269	B	
		O'Brien, John J.	2B	39	+.190	Wash97	Pitt

Robinson, Wilbert	C	105	.284	B	
Rothermel, Edward Hill	2B	10	.095	A	C
Ryan, John Bennett (Jack)	C	2	.500	Bkn	
Sheckard, Samuel James Tilden	OF	147	.298	Bkn	
Smith, Alexander Benjamin (Broadway) (1B1 OF2)	C36	41	+.383	xBkn	

x-One Game won by Forfeit.

CLUB RECORD

NATIONAL LEAGUE

BOSTON

YEAR	TG	WON	LOST	PCT.	FINISHED	MANAGER
1876	70	39	31	.557	4	Wm. Henry Wright
1877	60	42	18	.700	1	Wm. Henry Wright
1878	60	41	19	.683	1	Wm. Henry Wright
1879	78	49	29	.628	2	Wm. Henry Wright
1880	84	40	44	.476	6	Wm. Henry Wright
1881	83	38	45	.458	6	Wm. Henry Wright
1882	84	45	39	.536	x3(Buff)	John Francis Morrill
1883	98	63	35	.643	1	John Jay Burdock John Francis Morrill
1884	111	73	38	.658	2	John Francis Morrill
1885	112	46	66	.410	5	John Francis Morrill
1886	117	56	61	.478	5	John Francis Morrill
1887	121	61	60	.504	5	John Francis Morrill
1888	134	70	64	.522	4	John Francis Morrill
1889	128	83	45	.648	2	James A. Hart
1890	133	76	57	.571	5	Frank Gibson Selee
1891	138	87	51	.630	1	Frank Gibson Selee
1892	150	102	48	.680	1	Frank Gibson Selee
1893	130	86	44	.662	1	Frank Gibson Selee
1894	132	83	49	.629	3	Frank Gibson Selee
1895	131	71	60	.542	x5(Bkn)	Frank Gibson Selee
1896	131	74	57	.565	4	Frank Gibson Selee
1897	132	93	39	.705	1	Frank Gibson Selee
1898	149	102	47	.685	1	Frank Gibson Selee
1899	152	95	57	.625	2	Frank Gibson Selee
1900	138	66	72	.478	4	Frank Gibson Selee
1901	138	69	69	.500	5	Frank Gibson Selee
1902	137	73	64	.533	3	Albert C. Buckenberger
1903	138	58	80	.420	6	Albert C. Buckenberger
1904	153	55	98	.360	7	Albert C. Buckenberger
1905	154	51	103	.331	7	Frederick Tenney
1906	151	49	102	.324	8(Last)	Frederick Tenney
1907	148	58	90	.392	7	Frederick Tenney
1908	154	63	91	.409	6	Joseph James Kelley
1909	153	45	108	.294	8(Last)	Frank Eugene Bowerman Harry Thomas Smith
1910	153	53	100	.346	8(Last)	Frederick L. Lake
1911	151	44	107	.291	8(Last)	Frederick Tenney
1912	153	52	101	.340	8(Last)	John G. Kling
1913	151	69	82	.457	5	George Tweedy Stallings
1914	153	94	59	.614	1	George Tweedy Stallings
1915	152	83	69	.546	2	George Tweedy Stallings
1916	152	89	63	.586	3	George Tweedy Stallings
1917	153	72	81	.471	6	George Tweedy Stallings
1918	124	53	71	.427	7	George Tweedy Stallings
1919	139	57	82	.410	6	George Tweedy Stallings
1920	152	62	90	.408	7	George Tweedy Stallings
1921	153	79	74	.516	4	Frederick Francis Mitchell
1922	153	53	100	.346	8(Last)	Frederick Francis Mitchell
1923	154	54	100	.351	7	Frederick Francis Mitchell

1924	153	53	100	.346	8(Last)	David James Bancroft
1925	153	70	83	.458	5	David James Bancroft
1926	152	66	86	.434	7	David James Bancroft
1927	154	60	94	.390	7	David James Bancroft
1928	153	50	103	.327	7	John Thomas Slattery / Rogers Hornsby
1929	154	56	98	.364	8(Last)	Emil Edwin Fuchs / John Joseph Evers
1930	154	70	84	.455	6	Wm. Boyd McKechnie
1931	154	64	90	.416	7	Wm. Boyd McKechnie
1932	154	77	77	.500	5	Wm. Boyd McKechnie
1933	154	83	71	.539	4	Wm. Boyd McKechnie
1934	151	78	73	.517	4	Wm. Boyd McKechnie
1935	153	38	115	.248	8(Last)	Wm. Boyd McKechnie
1936	154	71	83	.461	6	Wm. Boyd McKechnie
1937	152	79	73	.520	5	Wm. Boyd McKechnie
1938	152	77	75	.507	5	Chas. Dillon Stengel
1939	151	63	88	.417	7	Chas. Dillon Stengel
1940	152	65	87	.428	7	Chas. Dillon Stengel
1941	154	62	92	.403	7	Chas. Dillon Stengel
1942	148	59	89	.399	7	Chas. Dillon Stengel
1943	153	68	85	.444	6	Chas. Dillon Stengel
1944	154	65	89	.422	6	Robert Hunter Coleman
1945	152	67	85	.441	6	Robert Hunter Coleman / Adelphia Louis Bissonette
1946	153	81	72	.529	4	Wm. Harrison Southworth
1947	154	86	68	.558	3	Wm. Harrison Southworth
1948	153	91	62	.595	1	Wm. Harrison Southworth
1949	154	75	79	.487	4	Wm. Harrison Southworth / John Walter Cooney
1950	154	83	71	.539	4	Wm. Harrison Southworth
1951	154	76	78	.494	4	Wm. Harrison Southworth / Thomas Francis Holmes
1952	153	64	89	.418	7	Thomas Francis Holmes / Chas. John Grimm

WON 39 / LOST 31 / TG 70

NATIONAL LEAGUE

FINISHED 4th.

1876.

PCT. .557

BOSTON

WM. HENRY WRIGHT

WON	LOST	NAME	POS.	G.	BA	FROM	TO
12	12	Borden, Joseph Emley	P24	32	.202	A	C
11	9	Bradley, George H.	P	22	.226	A	C
		Brown, Lewis J.	C44	45	.207	A	
		Leonard, Andrew Jackson (2B29)	OF35	64	.277	A	
15	6	Manning, John E. (P21)	OF47	70	.258	A	
		Morrill, John Francis (C23)	2B37	66	.260	A	
		Murnane, Timothy Hayes	1B65	69	.275	A	
0	4	McBride, James Dickson (Dick)	P	4	.188	A	C
		McGinley, Timothy S.	C	9	.150	A	C
1	0	Nicholas, Frederick C. (Tricky)	P	1	.000	A	
		O'Rourke, James Henry	OF68	70	.312	A	
		Parks, Wm. Robert		1	.000	A	C
		Schafer, Harry C.	3B	70	.248	A	
		Whitney, Frank Thomas	OF	34	.236	A	C
		Wright, George	SS68	70	.292	A	
		Wright, Samuel	SS	2	.125	A	
		Wright, Wm. Henry MGR.	OF	1	.000	A	

WON 42 / LOST 18 / TG 60

NATIONAL LEAGUE

FINISHED 1st.

1877.

PCT. .700

BOSTON

WM. HENRY WRIGHT

WON	LOST	NAME	POS.	G.	BA	FROM	TO
40	17	Bond, Thomas Henry (OF3)	P58	61	.228	Hart	
		Brown, Lewis J. (1B4)	C55	58	.253	B	
		Leonard, Andrew Jackson (SS21)	OF37	58	.286	B	
		Morrill, John Francis (1B18 2B3 OF11)	3B30	61	.302	B	
		Murnane, Timothy Hayes (1B5)	OF30	35	.279	B	
		O'Rourke, James Henry	OF60	61	.362	B	
		Schafer, Harry C. (SS1 3B9)	OF23	33	.277	B	
		Sutton, Ezra Ballou (3B22)	SS36	58	.292	Ath	
		White, James Laurie (Deacon) (C7 OF19)	1B35	59	.387	Chi	
2	1	White, Wm. Henry	P	3	.200	A	
		Wright, George (SS3)	2B58	61	.276	B	
		Wright, Wm. Henry MGR.	OF	1	.000	B	

WON 41
LOST 19
TG 60

NATIONAL LEAGUE

1878

FINISHED 1st.

PCT. .683

BOSTON

WM. HENRY WRIGHT

WON	LOST	NAME	POS.	G.	BA	FROM	TO
40	19	Bond, Thomas Henry	P	59	.211	B	
		Burdock, John Joseph	2B	60	.260	Hart	
		Leonard, Andrew Jackson	OF	60	.259	B	
1	0	Manning, John E. (P1)	OF59	60	.254	Cin	
		Morrill, John Francis	1B58	60	.240	B	
		O'Rourke, James Henry	OF56	60	.274	B	
		Schafer, Harry C.	OF	4	.235	B	
		Snyder, Chas. N.	C58	60	.212	Lvlle	
		Sutton, Ezra Ballou	3B59	60	.226	B	
		Wright, George	SS	59	.224	B	
		Wright, Wm. Henry MGR.	OF	1	.000	B	

WON 49
LOST 29
TG 78

NATIONAL LEAGUE

1879

FINISHED 2nd.

PCT. .628

BOSTON

WM. HENRY WRIGHT

WON	LOST	NAME	POS.	G.	BA	FROM	TO
42	19	Bond, Thomas Henry	P62	65	.238	B	
		Burdock, John Joseph	2B	84	.240	B	
		Cogswell, Edward	1B	49	.322	A	
5	8	Foley, Chas. Joseph (OF15)	P18	35	.313	A	
		Hawes, Wm. Hildreth	OF33	37	.200	A	
		Houck, Stephen Arnold Douglas (Sadie) (SS33)	OF47	80	.264	A	
		Jones, Chas. Wesley	OF	83	.315	Cin	
		Morrill, John Francis (1B33)	3B51	84	.281	B	
		O'Rourke, John	OF	70	.341	A	
1	0	Richmond, John Lee	P	1	.333	A	
		Snyder, Chas. N.	C80	81	.234	B	
		Sutton, Ezra Ballou (3B33)	SS51	84	.248	B	
1	2	Tyng, James Alexander	P	3	.357	A	

WON 40
LOST 44
TG 84

NATIONAL LEAGUE

1880

FINISHED 6th.

PCT. .476

BOSTON

WM. HENRY WRIGHT

WON	LOST	NAME	POS.	G.	BA	FROM	TO
		Bergh, John Babtist	C	11	.167	Ath76	C
26	29	Bond, Thomas Henry (1B1 OF18)	P56	74	.216	B	
		Burdock, John Joseph	2B	84	.256	B	
		Dignan, Stephen E.	OF	8	+.324	A	Wor
14	14	Foley, Chas. Joseph (P28 1B22)	OF30	78	.285	B	
		Houck, Stephen Arnold Douglas (Sadie)	OF	12	+.170	B	Prov
		Jones, Chas. Wesley	OF	64	.297	B	
0	1	Leary, John J. (OF1)	P1	1	.000	A	
0	0	Morrill, John Francis (P2 3B38)	1B45	84	.240	B	
		O'Leary, Daniel	OF	3	.250	Prov	
		O'Rourke, James Henry (C9 1B17 SS15 3B11)	OF34	84	.281	Prov	
		O'Rourke, John	OF	78	.282	B	
		Powers, Philip J. (OF2)	C34	35	.148	Chi78	
		Richmond, John H. (OF1)	SS30	31	.248	Syr	
		Sullivan, Dennis J.	C	1	.250	Prov	C
		Sutton, Ezra Ballou (3B36)	SS38	74	.250	B	
		Trott, Samuel W. (OF4)	C35	38	.197	A	
		Wright, George	SS	1	.250	Prov	

WON 38
LOST 45
TG 83

NATIONAL LEAGUE

1881.

FINISHED 6th.

PCT. .458

BOSTON

WM. HENRY WRIGHT

WON	LOST	NAME	POS.	G.	BA	FROM	TO
		*Barnes, Roscoe Conkling (Ross)	SS62	69	.271	Cin79	C
0	3	Bond, Thomas Henry	P	3	.200	B	
		Burkock, John Joseph (SS1)	2B72	73	.237	B	
		Crowley, Wm. Michael	OF	71	.254	Buff	
		Deasley, Thomas H. (1B2 SS7 OF7)	C28	43	.229	A	
6	8	Fox, John Joseph (1B6 OF12)	P17	30	.178	A	C
		Hornung, Michael Joseph	OF	83	.240	Buff	
		Lewis, Frederick Miller	OF	27	.195	A	
1	0	Mathews, Robert T. (P5)	OF18	19	+.169	xProv	
0	1	Morrill, John Francis (P1 2B5 3B2)	1B74	80	.289	B	
		Quinn, Joseph C.	1B	1	+.000	A	Wor
		Richmond, John H. (SS2)	OF24	26	.275	B	
		Snyder, Chas. N. (2B1 SS1 OF1)	C58	60	.228	Bos79	
		Sutton, Ezra Ballou (SS2)	3B78	83	.291	B	
31	33	#Whitney, James E. (Grasshopper)	P64	74	.255	A	
		Wright, Samuel	SS	1	.250	Cin	C
		Wright, George	SS	7	.179	B	

*Barnes also played 7 games at 2B.
#Whitney also played 2 games at 1B and 15 games in the OF.

WON 45 / LOST 39 / TG 84

NATIONAL LEAGUE 1882.

FINISHED 3rd. (TIED WITH BUFF) PCT. .536

BOSTON

JOHN FRANCIS MORRILL

WON	LOST	NAME	POS.	G.	BA	FROM	TO
2	3	Buffinton, Chas. G.	P15	15	.250	A	
		(1B5 OF7)					
		Burdock, John Joseph	2B	82	.239	B	
		Deasley, Thomas H.	C53	66	.267	B	
		(SS1 OF13)					
		Hornung, Michael Joseph	OF83	84	.301	B	
		(1B1)					
		Hotaling, Peter James	OF	83	.253	Wor	
19	14	Mathews, Robert T.	P34	45	.224	B	
		(SS1 OF11)					
0	0	Morrill, John Francis MGR.	1B75	82	.289	B	
		(P1 2B2 SS3 3B1 OF1)					
		McClure, Harold Murray	OF	2	.333	A	C
		Rowan, W. Edward	OF46	82	.245	A	
		(C31 SS6 3B1)					
		Sutton, Ezra Ballou (SS4)	3B76	80	.255	B	
24	22	Whitney, James E.(Grasshopper)	P46	60	.325	B	
		(1B5 OF14)					
		Wise, Samuel Washington	SS71	77	.225	Det	
		(3B6)					

WON 63 / LOST 35 / TG 98

NATIONAL LEAGUE 1883.

FINISHED 1st PCT. .643

BOSTON

JOHN JOSEPH BURKOCK JOHN FRANCIS MORRILL

WON	LOST	NAME	POS.	G.	BA	FROM	TO
		Brown, Lewis J.	1B	14	.236	Prov81	LvlleAA
24	13	Buffinton, Chas. G.	OF49	86	.237	B	
		(P37 1B2)					
		Burdock, John Joseph MGR.	2B	96	.330	B	
		Hackett, Mortimer Martin (OF3)	C42	46	.234	A	
		Hines, Michael P. (OF3)	C56	61	.228	A	
		Hornung, Michael Joseph	OF	98	.278	B	
1	0	Morrill, John Francis MGR.	1B80	97	.319	B	
		(P1 2B2 SS2 3B6 OF9)					
		Radford, Paul Revere	OF	71	.205	A	
		Smith, Albert Edgar	OF	29	.217	A	C
		*Sutton, Ezra Ballou	3B	94	.323	B	
38	22	Whitney, James E.(Grasshopper)	P62	96	.282	B	
		(1B2 OF32)					
		Wise, Samuel Washington	SS	95	.270	B	

*Sutton also played 1 game at SS and 1 game in the OF.

WON 73 / LOST 38 / TG 111

NATIONAL LEAGUE 1884.

FINISHED 2nd PCT. .658

BOSTON

JOHN FRANCIS MORRILL

WON	LOST	NAME	POS.	G.	BA	FROM	TO
		Annis, Wm. Perley	OF	26	.184	A	C
		Barrett, Martin	C	3	.000	A	C
40	14	Buffinton, Chas. G.	P65	84	.263	B	
		(1B6 OF19)					
		Burdock, John Joseph	2B	84	.267	B	
1	4	Connor, John	P	7	.080	A	
		Crowley, Wm. Michael	OF	103	.265	Clev	
1	3	Davis, John A. (OF1)	P5	5	.050	xStLAA	
		Gunning, Thomas Francis	C	12	.095	A	
		Hackett, Mortimer Martin	C67	68	.203	B	
		(3B1)					
		Hines, Michael P.	C	34	.181	B	
		Hornung, Michael Joseph	OF106	110	.266	B	
		(1B5)					
		*Manning, James H.	OF68	84	.241	A	
		Moriarity, Eugene John	OF	4	.063	A	IndplsAA
0	0	Morrill, John Francis MGR.	1B88	106	.265	B	
		(P1 2B15 3B2)					
		Sutton, Ezra Ballou	3B	106	.349q	B	
31	17	Whitney, James E.(Grasshopper)	P48	62	.260	B	
		(1B13 3B1 OF14)					
		Wise, Samuel Washington	SS103	109	.220	B	
		(2B6)					

*Manning also played 7 games at 2B, 8 games at SS and 1 game at 3B.

WON 46 / LOST 66 / TG 112

NATIONAL LEAGUE 1885.

FINISHED 5th. PCT. .410

BOSTON

JOHN FRANCIS MORRILL

WON	LOST	NAME	POS.	G.	BA	FROM	TO
23	27	Buffinton, Chas. G.	P50	82	.239	B	
		(1B15 OF16)					
		Burdock, John Joseph	2B	45	.142	B	
		Coliver, Wm. J.	OF	1	.000	A	C
5	6	Davis, John A.	P	11	.194	B	C
		*Dealey, Patrick E.	C27	34	.230	StPUA	
		Gunning, Thomas Francis	C	48	.184	B	
		Hackett, Mortimer Martin	C	33	.182	B	
		Hackett, Walter Henry	2B20	35	.184	BosUA	C
		(SS15)					
		Hines, Michael P.	OF	14	.250	B	BknAA

WON	LOST	NAME	POS.	G.	BA	FROM	TO
		Hornung, Michael Joseph	OF	25	.201	B	
		Johnston, Richard Frederick	OF	26	.238	RichAA	
		Manning, James H. (SS1)	OF84	84	+.206	B	Det
		Morrill, John Francis MGR. (2B17 3B2)	1B92	111	.225	B	
		McCarthy, Thomas Francis Michael	OF	40	.182	BosUA	
		Nash, Wm. Mitchell (2B8)	3B18	26	.255	RichAA	
		Poorman, Thomas Iverson	OF	55	.241	TolAA	
		Purcell, Wm. Aloysius (Blondy)	OF	21	.218	xAthAA	
1	1	Stemmeyer, Wm.	P	2	.500	A	
		Sutton, Ezra Ballou (1B1 SS15)	3B90	108	.312	B	
		Tate, Edward Christopher	C	4	.167	A	
		Whiteley, Gurdon (C1)	OF32	33	.185	Clev	C
17	32	Whitney, James E. (Grasshopper) (1B5 OF17)	P50	72	.234	B	
		Wise, Samuel Washington (2B22 OF5)	SS79	107	.283	B	

*Dealey also played 1 game at 1B, 2 games at SS and 3 games at 3B.

WON 56 NATIONAL LEAGUE FINISHED 5th.
LOST 61
TG 117 1886. PCT. .478

BOSTON

JOHN FRANCIS MORRILL

WON	LOST	NAME	POS.	G.	BA	FROM	TO
		Allen, Myron S.	2B	1	.000	NY83	
7	10	Buffinton, Chas. G. (P17)	1B19	44	.289	B	
		Burdock, John Joseph	2B	59	.217	B	
		Dailey, Cornelius F. (Con)	C49	50	.239	Prov	
		Dealey, Patrick E.	C	14	.333	B	
		Gunning, Thomas Francis	C	27	.224	B	
		Hornung, Michael Joseph	OF	94	.257	B	
		Johnston, Richard Frederick	OF	109	.239	B	
		Morrill, John Francis MGR. (1B41 2B20)	SS54	117	.246	B	
		Nash, Wm. Mitchell (SS17)	3B90	109	.280	B	
0	2	Parsons, Chas. J.	P	2	.375	A	
		Poorman, Thomas Iverson	OF	88	.261	B	
27	31	Radbourn, Chas. (Hoss)	P58	66	.237	Prov	
22	18	Stemmeyer, Wm.	P	41	.277	B	
		Sutton, Ezra Ballou (2B18 SS27 3B28)	OF43	116	.276	B	
		Tate, Edward Christopher	C	31	.226	B	
		Wise, Samuel Washington (2B20 SS18)	1B57	96	.289	B	

WON 61 NATIONAL LEAGUE FINISHED 5th.
LOST 60
TG 121 1887. PCT. .504

BOSTON

JOHN FRANCIS MORRILL

WON	LOST	NAME	POS.	G.	BA	FROM	TO
		Burdock, John Joseph	2B	64	.305	B	
9	15	Conway, Richard Butler (Dick)	P25	39	.320	BaltAA	
		Dailey, Cornelius F. (Con)	C	33	.217	B	
		Hornung, Michael Joseph	OF	97	.299	B	
		Johnston, Richard Frederick	OF	124	.283	B	
		Kelly, Michael Joseph (King) (C22 2B32)	OF55	114	.394	Chi	
22	14	Madden, Michael Joseph (Kid)	P	37	.305	A	
		Morrill, John Francis MGR.	1B	124	.331	B	
		Nash, Wm, Mitchell	3B114	118	.368	B	
		O'Rourke, Thomas Joseph	C19	21	.223	A	
24	23	Radbourn, Chas. (Hoss)	P	48	.297	B	
6	8	Stemmeyer, Wm.	P	14	.282	B	
		Sutton, Ezra Ballou (OF18)	SS34	74	.327	B	
		Tate, Edward Christopher	C50	55	.271	B	
		Wheelock, Warren H. (SS17)	OF23	44	.314	A	
		Wise, Samuel Washington (OF26)	SS70	110	.380	B	

WON 70 NATIONAL LEAGUE FINISHED 4th.
LOST 64
TG 134 1888. PCT. .522

BOSTON

JOHN FRANCIS MORRILL

WON	LOST	NAME	POS.	G.	BA	FROM	TO
		Brown, Thomas T.	OF	107	.247	Indpls	
		Burdock, John Joseph	2B	21	.202	B	BknAA
33	20	Clarkson, John Gibson	P	54	.195	Chi	
4	1	Conway, Richard Butler (Dick)	P	6	.167	B	C
		Glenn, Edward C.	OF	19	.154	xKCAA	C
		Higgins, Wm. H.	2B	14	.167	A	
		Hines, Michael P.	C	3	.167	Prov 85	C
		Hornung, Michael Joseph	OF	107	.239	B	
		Johnston, Richard Frederick	OF	135	.295	B	
		Kelly, Michael Joseph (King) (OF31)	C74	105	.318	B	
		Klussman, Wm. F.	2B	28	.168	A	
7	12	Madden, Michael Joseph (Kid)	P	19	.164	B	
		Morrill, John Francis MGR.	1B	134	.197	B	
		Nash, Wm. Mitchell (2B31)	3B104	135	.283	B	
		O'Rourke, Thomas Joseph	C	20	.175	B	
		Quinn, Joseph J.	2B	38	.301	StL83	
7	16	Radbourn, Chas. (Hoss)	P	24	.215	B	
		Ray, Irving Burton	SS47	50	.247	A	
		Sommers, Joseph Andrew (Pete)	C	4	.231	MetAA	
19	15	Sowders, Wm. Jefferson	P	35	.147	A	

WON	LOST	NAME	POS.	G.	BA	FROM	TO
		Sutton, Ezra Ballou	3B27	28	.218	B	C
		Tate, Edward Christopher	C	40	.229	B	
		Wise, Nicholas Joseph	C	1	.000	A	C
		Wise, Samuel Washington	SS89	104	.239	B	

WON 83 — LOST 45 — TG 128

NATIONAL LEAGUE 1889. FINISHED 2nd. PCT. .648

BOSTON

JAMES A. HART

WON	LOST	NAME	POS.	G.	BA	FROM	TO
		Bennett, Chas. Wesley	C	80	.230	Det	
		Brouthers, Dennis (Dan)	1B	126	.373	Det	
		Brown, Thomas T.	OF	88	.232	B	
48	19	Clarkson, John Gibson	P	72	.206	B	
3	3	Daley, Wm.	P	9	.158	A	
		Ganzel, Chas. Wm. (OF21)	C36	71	.265	Det	
		Hurley, Jeremiah F.	C	1	.000	A	
		Johnston, Richard Frederick	OF	131	.228	B	
		Kelly, Michael Joseph (King) (C16)	OF109	125	.293	B	
10	10	Madden, Michael Joseph (Kid)	P20	21	.290	B	
		Nash, Wm. Mitchell	3B	127	.274	B	
		Quinn, Joseph J. (2B47)	SS63	111	.261	B	
20	11	Radbourn, Chas. (Hoss)	P32	35	.188	B	
		Ray, Irving Burton	SS	9	.312	B	BaltAA
		Richardson, Arthur Harding (OF46)	2B86	132	.304	Det	
		Smith, Chas. Marvin (Pap)	SS	59	+.257	xPitt	
2	2	Sowders, Wm. Jefferson	P	4	+.000	B	Pitt

WON 76 — LOST 57 — TG 133

NATIONAL LEAGUE 1890. FINISHED 5th. PCT. .571

BOSTON

FRANK GIBSON SELEE

WON	LOST	NAME	POS.	G.	BA	FROM	TO
		Bennett, Chas. Wesley	C	85	.213	B	
		Brodie, Walter Scott	OF	132	.295	A	
26	18	Clarkson, John Gibson	P	44	.248	B	
		Donovan, Patrick Joseph	OF	32	+.245	A	Bkn
0	1	Fricken, Anthony	P	1	.000	A	C
		Ganzel, Chas. Wm.	C22	38	.269	B	
23	17	Getzein, Chas. H.	P	42	.231	Indpls	
		Hardie, Lewis W. (OF15)	C25	47	.227	Chi86	
		Hines, Paul A.	OF	69	+.266	xPitt	
0	1	Lawson, Albert W.	P	1	+.000	A	Pitt
		Long, Herman C.	SS	101	.250	KCAA	
		Lowe, Robert Lincoln (Link) (OF15)	SS24	52	.280	A	
		McGarr, James B. (Chippy)	3B115	121	.236	BaltAA	
27	19	Nichols, Chas. Augustus (Kid)	P	47	.247	A	
		Schellhasse, Albert Herman	C	9	.096	A	
		Smith, Chas. Marvin (Pap)	2B	134	.229	B	
		Sullivan, Martin J.	OF	121	.285	Indpls	
0	1	Taber, John Pardon	P	2	.000	A	C
		Tucker, Thomas Joseph	1B	132	.295	BaltAA	

WON 87 — LOST 51 — TG 138

NATIONAL LEAGUE 1891. FINISHED 1st. PCT. .630

BOSTON

FRANK GIBSON SELEE

WON	LOST	NAME	POS.	G.	BA	FROM	TO
		Bennett, Chas. Wesley	C	74	.215	B	
		Brodie, Walter Scott	OF	134	.266	B	
0	0	Brynan, Chas. R.	P	1	.000	Chi88	C
34	19	Clarkson, John Gibson	P	55	.223	B	
		Ganzel, Chas. Wm.	C59	68	.259	B	
4	6	Getzein, Chas. H. (OF2)	P11	13	+.189	B	Clev
		Kelley, Joseph James	OF	12	+.244	A	Pitt
		Kelly, Michael Joseph (King)	OF15	24	.239	xBosAA	
0	1	Kiley, John Frederick	P	1	.000	WashAA84	C
		Lake, Frederick Lovett	C	5	.142	A	
		Long, Herman C.	SS	139	.287	B	
		Lowe, Robert Lincoln (Link) (2B17)	OF105	124	.281	B	
		Nash, Wm. Mitchell	3B	139	.276	BosPL	
30	17	Nichols, Chas. Augustus (Kid)	P	50	.201	B	
		Quinn, Joseph J.	2B	123	.247	BosPL	
		Rooks, George Brinton McClellan	OF	5	.125	A	C
0	0	Ryan, Daniel R.	P	1	.000	MetAA87	C
19	8	Staley, Henry E.	P	27	+.168	xPitt	
		Stovey, Harry Duffield	OF	133	.279	BosPL	
0	0	Sullivan, James E.	P	1	.000	A	ColAA
		Sullivan, Martin J.	OF	17	+.224	B	Clev
		Tucker, Thomas Joseph	1B	140	.272	B	

WON 102 — LOST 48 — TG 150

NATIONAL LEAGUE 1892. FINISHED 1st. PCT. .680

BOSTON

FRANK GIBSON SELEE

WON	LOST	NAME	POS.	G.	BA	FROM	TO
		Bennett, Chas. Wesley	C	32	.201	B	

WON	LOST	NAME	POS.	G.	BA	FROM	TO
		Burke, Daniel F.	C	1	.000	SyrAA90	C
0	0	Clarkson, Arthur Hamilton	P	1	.000	N.Y.	
9	7	Clarkson, John Gibson	P	16	+.228	B	Clev
		Daly, Joseph John	C	1	.000	Clev	C
		Duffy, Hugh	OF	146	.302	BosAA	
		Ganzel, Chas. Wm.	C49	51	.270	B	
		Kelly, Michael Joseph (King)	C68	72	.201	B	
		Long, Herman C.	SS142	151	.286	B	
		Lowe, Robert Lincoln (Link)	OF89	124	.244	B	
		McCarthy, Thomas Francis Michael	OF	152	.244	StLAA	
		Nash, Wm. Mitchell	3B	135	.265	B	
35	16	Nichols, Chas. Augustus (Kid)	P53	54	.206	B	
		Quinn, Joseph J.	2B	142	.219	B	
24	11	Staley, Henry E.	P	35	.134	B	
33	14	Stivetts, John Elmer (OF17)	P47	64	.300	StLAA	
		Stovey, Harry Duffield	OF	38	+.171	B	Balt
		Tucker, Thomas Joseph	1B	148	.281	B	
1	0	Viau, Leon	P	2	+.000	xLvlle	C

WON 86 — NATIONAL LEAGUE — FINISHED 1st.
LOST 44
TG 130 — 1893. — PCT. .662

BOSTON

FRANK GIBSON SELEE

WON	LOST	NAME	POS.	G.	BA	FROM	TO
		Bennett, Chas. Wesley	C	58	.218	B	C
		Carroll, Samuel (Clifford)	OF	120	.234	StL	C
0	1	Coyle, Wm. Claude	P	1	.000	A	C
		Duffy, Hugh	OF	131	.378	B	
		Ganzel, Chas. Wm. (OF21)	C37	69	.282	B	
0	1	Garry, James Thomas	P	1	.000	A	
12	4	Gastright, Henry Carl	P	20	+.233	xPitt	
		Long, Herman C.	SS124	128	.294	B	
		Lowe, Robert Lincoln (Link)	2B116	120	.316	B	
		Merritt, Wm. Henry	C33	35	.363	Lvlle	
		McCarthy, Thomas Francis Michael	OF107	116	.360	B	
		Nash, Wm. Mitchell	3B	128	.304	B	
32	14	Nichols, Chas. Augustus (Kid)	P46	47	.239	B	
2	2	Quarles, Wm. H.	P	4	.400	WashAA91	C
19	10	Staley, Henry E.	P31	32	.280	B	
21	12	Stivetts, John Elmer	P33	41	.309	B	
		Tucker, Thomas Joseph	1B	121	.299	B	
		Van Dyke, Wm. Jennings	OF	3	.250	StL	C

WON 83 — NATIONAL LEAGUE — FINISHED 3rd.
LOST 49
TG 132 — 1894. — PCT. .629

BOSTON

FRANK GIBSON SELEE

WON	LOST	NAME	POS.	G.	BA	FROM	TO
		Bannon, James Henry	OF	127	.336	StL	
		Connaughton, Frank H.	SS32	38	.337	A	
		Duffy, Hugh	OF123	124	.438	B	
		Ganzel, Chas. Wm.	C55	65	.278	B	
0	0	Hawley, Scott	P	1	.000	A	C
4	3	Hodson, George S.	P	11	.103	A	
0	1	Lampe, Henry Joseph	P	2	.000	A	
		Long, Herman C.	SS99	103	.324	B	
7	4	Lovett, Thomas Joseph	P	15	.155	Bkn	C
		Lowe, Robert Lincoln (Link)	2B132	133	.341	B	
		Merritt, Wm. Henry (OF1)	C8	10	+.231	B	Pitt
		McCarthy, Thomas Francis Michael	OF124	126	.349	B	
		Nash, Wm. Mitchell	3B	132	.294	B	
33	13	Nichols, Chas. Augustus (Kid)	P	46	.282	B	
		Ryan, John Bennett (Jack)	C	49	.271	LvlleAA91	
0	0	Smith, Thomas E.	P	2	.000	A	
13	14	Staley, Henry E.	P	27	.238	B	
25	14	Stivetts, John Elmer	P41	57	.336	B	
1	0	Stultz, George Irvin	P	1	.333	A	C
		Tenney, Frederick	C18	24	.387	A	
		Tucker, Thomas Joseph	1B	122	.328	B	
0	0	West, Frank	P	1	.000	A	C

WON 71 — NATIONAL LEAGUE — FINISHED 5th. (TIED WITH BKLYN)
LOST 60
TG 131 — 1895. — PCT. .542

BOSTON

FRANK GIBSON SELEE

WON	LOST	NAME	POS.	G.	BA	FROM	TO
1	0	Banks, Wm. J. (Wm. Yerrick)	P	1	.000	A	
		Bannon, James Henry	OF	121	.339	B	
		Collins, James Joseph	3B	11	+.205	A	Lvlle
11	9	Dolan, Patrick Henry (Cozy)	P	23	.256	Wash92	
		Duffy, Hugh	OF	131	.352	B	
		Ganzel, Chas. Wm.	C71	74	.265	B	
		Harrington, Joseph C.	2B	18	.299	A	
		Long, Herman C.	SS	124	.319	B	
		Lowe, Robert Lincoln (Link)	2B	99	.301	B	
		McCarthy, Thomas Francis Michael	OF108	116	.291	B	
		Nash, Wm. Mitchell	3B	133	.296	B	
27	16	Nichols, Chas. Augustus (Kid)	P	43	.231	B	
		Nice, Chas. Reiff	SS	9	.229	A	C
		Ryan, John Bennett (Jack)	C43	49	.295	B	
1	4	Sexton, Frank Joseph	P	10	.269	A	C
16	16	Stivetts, John Elmer	P34	38	.211	B	
2	2	Stocksdale, Otis H. (1B1)	P7	8	+.308	xWash	
11	9	Sullivan, James E.	P25	26	.170	ColAA91	

WON	LOST	NAME	POS.	G.	BA	FROM	TO
		Tenney, Frederick (C18)	OF25	42	.276	B	
		Tucker, Thomas Joseph	1B	126	.254	B	
		Warner, John Joseph	C	3	+.143	A	Lvlle
2	4	Wilson, Frank Ealton (Zeke)	P	6	+.316	A	Clev

WON 74
LOST 57
TG 131

NATIONAL LEAGUE

1896.

FINISHED 4th.

PCT. .565

BOSTON

FRANK GIBSON SELEE

WON	LOST	NAME	POS.	G.	BA	FROM	TO
		Bannon, James Henry	OF74	87	.256	B	C
		Bergen, Martin	C	62	.267	A	
		Collins, James Joseph	3B78	83	.300	Lvlle	
1	4	Dolan, Patrick Henry (Cozy)	P	6	.144	B	
		Duffy, Hugh	OF120	131	.302	B	
		Ganzel, Chas. Wm.	C40	44	.262	B	
		Hamilton, Wm. Robert	OF	131	.363	Phil	
		Harrington, Joseph C.	3B48	53	.203	B	C
6	4	Klobedanz, Frederick Augustus	P	11	.317	A	
1	4	Lewis, Edward Morgan	P	6	.111	A	
		Long, Herman C.	SS	119	.334	B	
		Lowe, Robert Lincoln (Link)	2B	73	.320	B	
3	2	Mains, Willard Eben	P	10	.364	MilAA91	C
		McGann, Dennis L. (Dan)	2B	42	.315	Lvlle	
30	14	Nichols, Chas. Augustus (Kid)	P	45	.189	B	
		Ryan, John Bennett (Jack)	C	8	.094	B	
22	13	Stivetts, John Elmer	P39	59	.353	B	
11	13	Sullivan, James E.	P	24	.223	B	
		Tenney, Frederick (C26)	OF60	86	.342	B	
		Tucker, Thomas Joseph	1B	122	.304	B	
		Yeager, George E.	1B	2	.167	A	
0	3	Yerrick, Wm. J. (Banks, Wm. J.)	P	4	.272	B	C

WON 93
LOST 39
TG 132

NATIONAL LEAGUE

1897.

FINISHED 1st.

PCT. .705

BOSTON

FRANK GIBSON SELEE

WON	LOST	NAME	POS.	G.	BA	FROM	TO
		Allen, Robert Gilman	SS32	33	.309	Phi194	
		Bergen, Martin	C82	83	.247	B	
		Collins, James Joseph	3B	133	.346	B	
		Duffy, Hugh	OF127	134	.341	B	
		Ganzel, Chas. Wm.	C26	27	.274	B	C
		Hamilton, Wm. Robert	OF	125	.344	B	
0	0	Hickman, Chas. Taylor	P	2	.500	A	
25	8	Klobedanz, Frederick Augustus	P	38	.316	B	
		Lake, Frederick Lovett	C	17	.272	Lvlle94	
20	12	Lewis, Edward Morgan	P32	35	.254	B	
		Long, Herman C.	SS	106	.327	B	
		Lowe, Robert Lincoln (Link)	2B	121	.314	B	
		Mahoney, George W.	C1	2	.500	A	
32	11	Nichols, Chas. Augustus (Kid)	P	43	.264	B	
		Stahl, Chas. Sylvester (Chick)	OF	111	.359	A	
12	4	Stivetts, John Elmer (P16)	OF26	49	.388	B	
4	4	Sullivan, James E.	P	13	.167	B	C
		Tenney, Frederick	1B128	131	.325	B	
		Tucker, Thomas Joseph	1B	2	+.143	B	Wash
		Yeager, George E.	C	26	.239	B	

WON 102
LOST 47
TG 149

NATIONAL LEAGUE

1898.

FINISHED 1st.

PCT. .685

BOSTON

FRANK GIBSON SELEE

WON	LOST	NAME	POS.	G.	BA	FROM	TO
		Bergen, Martin	C119	120	.289	B	
		Bransfield, Wm. Edward (Kitty)	C	5	.222	A	
		Collins, James Joseph	3B	152	.337	B	
		Duffy, Hugh	OF	151	.319	B	
		Hamilton, Wm. Robert	OF	109	.367	B	
2	2	Hickman, Chas. Taylor	P	17	.259	B	
		Keister, Wm. Hoffman (SS4)	2B4	9	.200	Balt96	
19	10	Klobedanz, Frederick Augustus	P	32	.213	B	
		Ladd, Arthur Clifford Hiram	OF	1	+.000	xPitt	C
25	8	Lewis, Edward Morgan	P	34	.279	B	
		Long, Herman C.	SS	142	.275	B	
		Lowe, Robert Lincoln (Link)	2B	147	.272	B	
33	12	Nichols, Chas. Augustus (Kid)	P	45	.252	B	
		Pickett, David T.	OF	14	.272	A	C
		Smith, James A.	SS	3	.100	A	C
		Stafford, James Joseph (1B1)	OF35	37	+.270	xLvlle	
		Stahl, Chas. Sylvester (Chick)	OF	125	.311	B	
0	1	Stivetts, John Elmer (P1)	OF26	27	.252	B	
0	2	Sullivan, Michael Joseph (Mike)	P	3	.333	N.Y.	
		Tenney, Frederick	1B	117	.335	B	
23	12	Willis, Victor Gazaway	P	38	.147	A	
		Yeager, George E.	C36	57	.263	B	

WON 95
LOST 57
TG 152

NATIONAL LEAGUE

1899.

FINISHED 2nd.

PCT. .625

BOSTON

FRANK GIBSON SELEE

WON	LOST	NAME	POS.	G.	BA	FROM	TO

WON	LOST	NAME	POS.	G.	BA	FROM	TO
6	4	Bailey, Harvey Francis	P	12	.229	A	
		Bergen, Martin	C	71	.257	B	C
		Clarke, Wm. Jones	C	60	.229	Balt	
		Collins, James Joseph	3B	151	.275	B	
		Duffy, Hugh	OF	147	.279	B	
		Frisbee, Chas. Augustus	OF	39	.331	A	
1	0	Ging, Wm. Joseph	P	1	.000	A	C
		Hamilton, Wm. Robert	OF	81	.306	B	
		Hickey, Michael Edward	2B	1	.333	A	
7	0	Hickman, Chas. Taylor	P	18	.397	B	
7	5	Killen, Frank Bissell	P	12	+.171	xWash	
1	4	Klobedanz, Frederick Augustus	P	5	.182	B	
		Kuhns, Chas. B. (3B3)	SS4	6	.267	Pitt97	C
17	11	Lewis, Edward Morgan	P	28	.252	B	
		Long, Herman C.	SS142	145	.257	B	
		Lowe, Robert Lincoln (Link)	2B	152	.267	B	
7	6	Meekin, Jouett	P	17	+.167	xN.Y.	
		Merritt, Wm. Henry	C	1	.000	Pitt97	C
20	18	Nichols, Chas. Augustus (Kid)	P38	41	.181	B	
		Stafford, James Joseph	OF	50	+.313	B	Wash
		Stahl, Chas. Sylvester (Chick)	OF	148	.348	B	
1	0	Streit, Oscar W.	P	2	.000	A	
1	0	Sullivan, Michael Joseph (Mike)	P	1	.333	B	C
		Sulliven, Wm. Joseph (Billy)	C	22	.284	A	
		Tenney, Frederick	1B	150	.350	B	
27	9	Willis, Victor Gazaway	P38	40	.216	B	
		Yeager, George E.	C	2	.000	B	

WON 66 LOST 72 TG 138

NATIONAL LEAGUE 1900.

FINISHED 4th. PCT. .478

BOSTON

FRANK GIBSON SELEE

WON	LOST	NAME	POS.	G.	BA	FROM	TO
0	1	Bailey, Harvey Francis	P	4	.222	B	MinnA
		Barry, John C. (2B15 SS17)	OF23	66	.261	Wash	
0	0	Chambers, Rome J.	P	1	1.000	A	C
		Clarke, Wm. Jones	C66	71	.320	B	
		Clements, John T.	C	16	.307	Clev	C
		Collins, James Joseph	3B	142	.299	B	
		Connor, Joseph Francis	C	7	.200	A	
8	4	Cuppy, George Joseph (Nig)	P	17	.261	StL	
21	16	Dinneen, Wm. Henry	P	37	.287	Wash	
		Duffy, Hugh	OF49	50	.298	B	
		Freeman, John F. (Buck) (1B15)	OF94	109	.300	Wash	
		Hamilton, Wm. Robert	OF	135	.332	B	
13	12	Lewis, Edward Morgan	P	26	.125	B	
		Long, Herman C.	SS	124	.256	B	
		Lowe, Robert Lincoln (Link)	2B	127	.279	B	
13	14	Nichols, Chas. Augustus (Kid)	P	29	.207	B	
2	9	Pittinger, Chas. Reno	P	18	.152	A	
		Stahl, Chas. Sylvester (Chick)	OF	134	.293	B	
		Sullivan, Wm. Joseph (Billy)	C64	66	.267	B	
		Tenney, Frederick	1B108	111	.284	B	
9	16	Willis, Victor Gazaway	P	28	.136	B	

WON 69 LOST 69 TG 138

NATIONAL LEAGUE 1901.

FINISHED 5th. PCT. .500

BOSTON

FRANK GIBSON SELEE

WON	LOST	NAME	POS.	G.	BA	FROM	TO
		Barry, John C.	OF	11	+.179	B	Phil
		Brown, Frederick Herbert	OF	7	.125	A	
		Carney, Patrick Joseph	OF	13	.302	A	
		Cooley, Duff C. (Dick)	OF50	60	.270	Pitt	
		Crolius, Frederick Joseph	OF	50	.238	A	
		DeMontreville, Eugene Napoleon (3B20)	2B120	140	.305	Bkn	
16	19	Dinneen, Wm. Henry	P	40	.209	B	
		Gammons, John Ashley	OF	26	.211	A	C
		Grosart, George Albert	OF	7	.125	A	C
		Hamilton, Wm. Robert	OF	99	.292	B	C
		Hinton, John R	3B	4	.071	A	C
		Kittredge, Malachi Jedediah	C	113	.247	Wash99	
2	2	Lawson, Robert Baker	P	10	.142	A	
		Long, Herman C.	SS	138	.238	B	
		Lowe, Robert Lincoln (Link) (2B18)	3B111	129	.259	B	
		Lush, Wm. Lucas	OF	7	.185	Wash97	
		Moran, Patrick Joseph	C27	53	.216	A	
		Murphy, Frank Morton	OF	45	+.271	A	N.Y.
18	15	Nichols, Chas. Augustus (Kid)	P	46	.299	B	
15	16	Pittinger, Chas. Reno	P	32	.110	B	
		Rickert, Joseph Francis	OF	13	.175	Pitt98	C
		Slagle, James Franklin (Shorty)	OF	65	+.278	xPhil	
		Smith, Elmer Ellsworth	OF15	18	+.240	xPitt	C
		Tenney, Frederick	1B	113	.278	B	
18	17	Willis, Victor Gazaway	P	36	.192		B

WON 73 LOST 64 TG 137

NATIONAL LEAGUE 1902.

FINISHED 3rd. PCT. .533

BOSTON

ALBERT C. BUCKENBERGER

WON	LOST	NAME	POS.	G.	BA	FROM	TO
		Brown, Frederick Herbert	OF	1	.000	B	C
0	1	Carney, Patrick Joseph (P2)	OF137	137	.266	B	
		Cooley, Duff C. (Dick) (1B7)	OF127	134	.297	B	

WON	LOST	NAME	POS.	G.	BA	FROM	TO
		Courtney, Ernest E. (SS3)	OF37	40	.212	A	BaltA
0	0	Curran, Simon Francis	P	1	.000	A	C
		DeMontreville, Eugene Napoleon (SS10)	2B113	123	.269	B	
		Dexter, Chas. Dana (2B16 3B1 OF5)	SS18	49	+.257	xChi	
0	1	Dresser, Robert Nicholson	P	1	.250	A	C
9	14	Eason, Malcolm Wayne (Mal)	P	25	+.081	xChi	
		Gremminger, Lorenzo Edward	3B	140	.250	Clev95	
0	3	Hale, Roy L.	P	8	.000	A	BaltA
		Kittredge, Malachi Jedediah	C	72	.233	B	
1	0	Klobedanz, Frederick Augustus	P	1	.500	Bos99	C
		Long, Herman C. (2B13)	SS108	120	.227	B	
0	0	Long, Nelson	P	1	.000	A	C
		Lush, Wm. Lucas (3B1)	OF117	118	.231	B	
9	11	Malarkey, John S. (2B1)	P20	20	.210	Chi99	
		Moran, Patrick Joseph (1B3 OF1)	C70	72	.250	B	
27	15	Pittinger, Chas. Reno	P	44	.141	B	
		Tenney, Frederick	1B	134	.314	B	
27	19	Willis, Victor Gazaway	P	47	.154	B	

WON 58 LOST 80 TG 138

NATIONAL LEAGUE 1903. BOSTON

FINISHED 6th. PCT. .420

ALBERT C. BUCKENBERGER

WON	LOST	NAME	POS.	G.	BA	FROM	TO
		#Abbaticchio, Edward James	2B116	133	.227	MilA00	
		Aubrey, Harvey Herbert	SS	94	.212	A	C
		Bonner, Frank J. (SS22)	2B24	46	.220	PhilA	C
4	4	Carney, Patrick Joseph (P10)	OF92	102	.240	B	
		Cooley, Duff C. (Dick)	OF126	138	.289	B	
		Dexter, Chas. Dana	OF106	120	.223	Chi	C
		Gremminger, Lorenzo Edward	3B	140	.264	B	
		Kittredge, Malachi Jedediah	C	30	.212	B	WashA
11	15	Malarkey, John S.	P	32	.161	B	C
		Moran, Patrick Joseph	C107	108	.262	B	
		McCreery, Thomas Leavenworth	OF	23	+.217	xBkn	C
9	15	Piatt, Wiley Harlan	P	25	.225	ChiA	C
18	22	Pittinger, Chas. Reno	P	44	.109	B	
0	0	Stanley, Joseph Bernard (P1)	OF77	79	.250	WashA	
		Tenney, Frederick	1B	122	.313	B	
4	5	Williams, Walter Merrill	P	14	+.238	xPhil	C.
12	19	Willis, Victor Gazaway	P33	39	.188	B	

#Abbaticchio also played 17 games at SS.

WON 55 LOST 98 TG 153

NATIONAL LEAGUE 1904. BOSTON

FINISHED 7th. PCT. .360

ALBERT C. BUCKENBERGER

WON	LOST	NAME	POS.	G.	BA	FROM	TO
		Abbaticchio, Edward James	SS	154	.256	B	
		Barclay, George Oliver	OF	24	+.226	xStL	
		Cannell, Wirt Virgin	OF	93	.234	A	
0	2	Carney, Patrick Joseph (P5)	OF71	76	.204	B	C
		Cooley, Duff C. (Dick)	OF116	122	.272	B	
		Delahanty, James Christopher Jr. (2B18)	3B113	138	.285	NY02	
6	16	Fisher, Thomas Chalmers	P31	36	.212	DetA02	C
		Geier, Philip Louis	OF137	148	.243	MilA01	C
		Lauterborn, Wm. Bernard	2B	20	.275	A	
		Marshall, Wm. R. (Doc)	C	13	+.209	xN.Y. (returned)	N.Y.
		Moran, Patrick Joseph (3B39)	C72	111	.226	B	
		McAuliffe, Eugene Leo	C	1	.500	A	C
2	13	McNichol, Edward	P	17	.093	A	C
		Needham, Thomas J.	C77	78	.260	A	
		O'Hara, James Francis	OF	8	.207	A	C
14	21	Pittinger, Chas. Reno	P	38	.108	B	
		Raymer, Frederick Chas.	2B	114	.210	Chi01	
		Stanley, Joseph Bernard	OF	3	.000	B	
0	0	Stewart, Joseph Lawrence (Ace)	P	2	.200	A	C
		Sullivan, Andrew R.	SS	1	.000	A	C
		Tenney, Frederick	1B144	147	.270	B	
		White, John F.	OF	1	.000	ClevA00	C
15	21	Wilhelm, Irving Key (Kaiser)	P	39	.070	Pitt	
18	25	Willis, Victor Gazaway	P43	49	.182	B	

WON 51 LOST 103 TG 154

NATIONAL LEAGUE 1905. BOSTON

FINISHED 7th. PCT. .331

FREDERICK TENNEY

WON	LOST	NAME	POS.	G.	BA	FROM	TO
		Abbaticchio, Edward James	SS152	153	.279	B	
		Barclay, George Oliver	OF	28	.176	B	C
		Cannell, Wirt Virgin	OF	154	.247	B	C
		Delahanty, James Christopher Jr.	OF	124	.258	B	
		Dolan, Patrick Henry (Cozy)	OF	112	+.275	xCin	
15	21	Fraser, Chas. Carrolton (Chick)	P39	45	.224	Phil	
2	4	Harley, Henry Risk	P	7	.067	A	C
0	1	Hershey, Frank	P	2	.000	A	C

WON	LOST	NAME	POS.	G.	BA	FROM	TO
		Lauterborn, Wm. Bernard (2B23)	3B29	57	.185	B	C
		Moran, Patrick Joseph	C	78	.240	B	
		Murphy, David F. (3B1)	SS2	3	.167	A	C
		McCarthy, William John	C	1	.000	A	
		Needham, Thomas J.	C77	82	.218	B	
		Raymer, Frederick Chas.	2B134	136	.211	B	C
		Sharpe, Bayard Heston	OF42	45	.182	A	
		Street, Chas. Evard (Gabby)	C	3	+.167	xCin	Cin (return)
		Strobel, Albert Irving (OF1)	3B4	5	.105	A	
		Tenney, Frederick MGR.	1B	148	.288	B	
0	2	Volz, Jacob Phillip	P	3	.000	BosA01	
4	25	Wilhelm, Irving Key (Kaiser)	P34	38	.160	B	
10	29	Willis, Victor Gazaway	P	41	.153	B	
		Wolverton, Harry Sterling	3B	122	.225	Phil	
20	21	Young, Irving Melrose (Young Cy)	P	43	.103	A	

WON 49
LOST 102
TG 151

NATIONAL LEAGUE

1906.

FINISHED 8th (LAST)

PCT. .324

BOSTON

FREDERICK TENNEY

WON	LOST	NAME	POS.	G.	BA	FROM	TO
		Bates, John W.	OF	140	.252	A	
		Brain, David Leonard	3B	139	.250	Pitt	
		Bridwell, Albert Henry	SS119	120	.227	Cin	
		Brown, Samuel Wakefield	C35	65	.208	A	
0	0	Cameron, John Wm. (P2)	OF16	18	.180	A	C
		Connaughton, Frank H. (2B1)	SS11	12	.205	NY96	C
		Diehl, Ernest Guy	SS	3	.545	Pitt04	
		Dolan, Patrick Henry (Cozy)	OF144	152	.248	B	C
8	26	Dorner, Augustus	P	34	+.140	xCin	
		Good, Eugene J.	OF	34	.151	A	C
		Howard, George Elmer (2B45)	OF87	147	.261	Pitt	
12	23	Lindaman, Vivian Alexander	P	39	.132	A	
		Madden, Thomas J.	OF	4	.267	A	
0	3	Maroney, James Francis	P	3	.200	A	
0	0	McCarthy, Wm. Thomas	P	1	1.000	A	C
		Needham, Thomas J.	C76	81	.190	B	
		O'Neill, John Joseph (Jack)	C48	51	.180	Chi	C
13	22	Pfeffer, Francis Xavier	P35	50	.196	Chi	
		Schulte, David	SS	2	.000	A	C
		Spencer, Chester Arthur	OF	7	.148	A	C
		Strobel, Albert Irving	2B93	99	.202	B	C
		Tenney, Frederick MGR.	1B	143	.283	B	
0	3	Witherup, LeRoy Foster	P	8	.133	A	
16	25	Young, Irving Melrose (Young Cy)	P	43	.096	B	

WON 58
LOST 90
TG 148

NATIONAL LEAGUE

1907.

FINISHED 7th.

PCT. .392

BOSTON

FREDERICK TENNEY

WON	LOST	NAME	POS.	G.	BA	FROM	TO
		Asmussen, Thomas Wm. Sr.	C	2	.000	A	C
		Ball, James Chandler	C	11	.150	A	
1	0	Barberich, Frank	P	2	.000	A	
		Bates, John Wm	OF118	119	.260	B	
		Beaumont, Clarence Howeth	OF	149	.322	Pitt	
5	9	Boultes, Jake John	P24	29	.132	A	
		Brain, David Leonard	3B130	133	.279	B	
		Bridwell, Albert Henry	SS	140	.218	B	
		Brown, Samuel Wakefield	C63	65	.192	B	C
		Brush, Robert	1B	2	.000	A	C
		Burke, Frank Aloysius	OF32	36	.178	N.Y.	C
0	1	Dessau, Frank Rolland	P	2	.000	A	
12	16	Dorner, Augustus	P	36	.130	B	
12	15	Flaherty, Patrick Joseph	P27	35	.191	Pitt05	
1	3	Frock, Samuel W.	P	5	.000	A	
		Hoffman, Harry C.	OF15	19	.279	WashA04	C
		Howard, George Elmer	OF45	48	+.273	B	Chi
		Knotts, Joseph	C	3	.000	A	C
11	15	Lindaman, Vivian Alexander	P	34	.122	B	
0	0	Lindemann, Ernest	P	1	.500	A	C
		Needham, Thomas J.	C78	79	.196	B	
		Orndorf, Jesse Walwork Thayer	C	5	.100	A	C
6	8	Pfeffer, Francis Xavier	P	19	.250	B	
		Randall, Newton J.	OF59	73	+.213	xChi	C
		Ritchey, Claude Cassius	2B	144	.255	Pitt	
		Sweeney, Wm. John	3B23	57	+.262	xChi	
		Tenney, Frederick MGR.	1B	149	.273	B	
		Westerberg, Oscar	SS	3	.222	A	C
10	23	Young, Irving Melrose (Young Cy)	P	40	.163	B	

WON 63
LOST 91
TG 154

NATIONAL LEAGUE

1908.

FINISHED 6th.

PCT. .409

BOSTON

JOSEPH JAMES KELLEY

WON	LOST	NAME	POS.	G.	BA	FROM	TO
		Ball, James Chandler	C	6	.133	B	C
		Bates, John Wm.	OF101	117	.258	B	
		Beaumont, Clarence Howeth	OF	121	.267	B	
		Becker, Beals	OF	43	+.275	xPitt	
3	5	Boultes, Jake John	P	17	.143	B	
		Bowerman, Frank Eugene	C63	74	.228	N.Y.	
		Browne, George E.	OF126	138	.228	N.Y.	

WON	LOST	NAME	POS.	G.	BA	FROM	TO
2	4	Chappelle, Wm. Hogan	P	13	.048	A	
		Dahlen, Wm. Frederick (Bad Bill)	SS	144	.239	N.Y.	
8	19	Dorner, Augustus	P	38	.179	B	
11	11	Ferguson, George Cecil	P	37	.169	N.Y.	
12	18	Flaherty, Patrick Joseph	P	31	.140	B	
		Graham, George Frederick (Peaches)	C62	67	.274	Chi03	
		Hannifan, John Joseph	3B35	79	+.206	xN.Y.	C
		Kelley, Joseph James MGR.	OF38	62	.259	Cin06	C
12	16	Lindaman, Vivian Alexander	P	43	.176	B	
0	0	Maloney, Chas. Michael	P	1	.000	A	C
1	2	Mattern, Alonzo Albert	P	5	.125	A	
		Moran, Joseph Herbert	OF	8	.266	PhilA	
7	3	McCarthy, Thomas Patrick	P	14	+.171	xPitt	
		McGann, Dennis L. (Dan)	1B121	130	.240	N.Y.	C
0	0	Pfeffer, Francis Xavier	P	4	.000	B	
		Ritchey, Claude Cassius	2B	120	.273	B	
		Smith, Harry Thomas	C	38	.246	Pitt	
		Stem, Frederick B.	1B	19	.278	A	
		Sweeney, Wm. John	3B123	127	.244	B	
		Thomas, Walter W.	SS	5	.154	A	C
3	3	Tuckey, Thomas H.	P	8	.050	A	
0	1	Young, Harley E.	P	6	+.200	xPitt	C
4	9	Young, Irving Melrose (Young Cy)	P	16	+.156	B	Pitt

WON 45
LOST 108
TG 153

NATIONAL LEAGUE — 1909. — FINISHED 8th (LAST) — PCT. .294

BOSTON

FRANK EUGENE BOWERMAN HARRY THOMAS SMITH

WON	LOST	NAME	POS.	G.	BA	FROM	TO
		Autry, Wm. Askew (Chick)	1B	61	+.196	xCin	C
		Bates, John Wm.	OF	60	+.288	B	Phil
		Beaumont, Clarence Howeth	OF	111	.263	B	
		Beck, Frederick Thomas (1B33)	OF55	88	.198	A	
		Becker, Beals	OF	152	.245	B	
0	0	Boultes, Jake John	P	1	.500	B	C
		Bowerman, Frank Eugene MGR.	C	27	.212	B	C
4	8	Brown, Chas. Edward (Buster)	P	18	+.146	xPhil	
1	1	Chappelle, Wm. Hogan	P	5	+.364	B	Cin
		Coffey, John Francis	SS	73	.186	A	
0	0	Cooney, Wm. A.	P	5	.300	A	
4	5	Curtis, Clifton Garfield	P	10	.034	A	
		Dahlen, Wm. Frederick (Bad Bill)	SS49	57	.233	B	
		Dam, Elbridge Rust	OF	1	.500	A	C
		Diehl, Ernest Guy	OF	1	.500	Bos06	C
1	2	Dorner, Augustus	P	5	.167	B	C
0	3	Evans, Checkering F.	P	4	.000	A	

WON	LOST	NAME	POS.	G.	BA	FROM	TO
5	23	Ferguson, George Cecil	P	36	.204	B	
		Getz, Gustave	3B36	40	.223	A	
		Graham, George Frederick (Peaches)	C76	81	.239	B	
1	6	Lindaman, Vivian Alexander	P	15	.273	B	C
15	21	Mattern, Alonzo Albert	P	47	.168	B	
		Moran, Joseph Herbert	OF	8	.233	B	
1	5	More, Forest T.	P	10	+.067	xStL	C
0	5	McCarthy, Thomas Patrick	P	8	.125	B	C
		Rariden, Wm. Angel	C	13	.167	A	
7	7	Richie, Lewis A.	P	22	+.114	xPhil	
		Ritchey, Claude Cassius	2B	25	.172	B	C
		Shaw, Alfred L.	C	18	.100	ChiA	C
		Shean, David Wm.	2B	72	+.241	xPhil	
		Siner, Hosea John	3B	10	.130	A	C
		Smith, Harry Thomas MGR.	C	31	.168	B	
		Starr, Chas. Watkin	2B	61	+.222	Pitt	Phil
		Stem, Frederick B.	1B	68	.208	B	C
		Sweeney, Wm. John (SS26)	3B112	138	.243	B	
		Thomas, Roy Allen	OF	77	.263	Pitt	
0	9	Tuckey, Thomas H.	P	17	.138	B	C
6	13	White, Kirby	P	23	.160	A	

WON 53
LOST 100
TG 153

NATIONAL LEAGUE — 1910. — FINISHED 8th (LAST) — PCT. .346

BOSTON

FREDERICK LOVETT LAKE

WON	LOST	NAME	POS.	G.	BA	FROM	TO
		Abbaticchio, Edward James	SS	47	+.247	xPitt	C
		Beck, Frederick Thomas (1B19)	OF134	153	.275	B	
9	23	Brown, Chas. Edward (Buster)	P	46	.198	B	
		Burg, Joseph Peter (SS2)	3B11	13	.348	A	C
1	0	Burke, Wm. Ignatius	P19	20	.190	A	
		Collins, Wm. Shirley	OF	151	.241	A	
0	0	Cooney, Wm. A.	P	8	.250	B	C
6	24	Curtis, Clifton Garfield	P	43	.146	B	
		Elliott, Harold H.	C	1	.000	A	
1	1	Evans, Checkering F.	P	13	.100	B	C
7	7	Ferguson, George Cecil	P	26	.175	B	
12	19	Frock, Samuel W.	P	45	+.190	xPitt	
		Getz, Gustave	3B22	47	.194	B	
0	0	Good, Ralph Nelson	P	2	.000	A	C
		Good, Wilbur David	OF	23	.337	ClevA	
		Graham, George Frederick (Peaches)	C87	91	.282	B	
		Herzog, Chas. Lincoln (Buck)	3B	105	.250	N.Y.	
		Krueger, Arthur T.	OF	1	.000	xClevA	ClevA
		Lake, Frederick Lovett MGR.		3	.000	BosA	C
0	0	Liese, Frederick Richard	P	4	.000	A	C

WON	LOST	NAME	POS.	G.	BA	FROM	TO
		Martel, Leon Alphonse	1B	10	.000	Phil	C
16	19	Mattern, Alonzo Albert	P	51	.163	B	
		Miller, Roy Oscar (Doc)	OF	130	+.286	xChi	
		Moran, Joseph Herbert	OF	20	.119	B	
0	2	Parson, Wm. Edwin	P	10	.084	A	
		Rariden, Wm. Angel	C	49	.226	B	
0	3	Richie, Lewis A.	P	4	+.000	B	Chi
		Riley, James Joseph	OF	1	.000	A	C
		Sellers, Oliver	OF	12	.156	A	C
		Sharpe, Bayard Heston	1B	113	+.239	Bos05	Pitt
		Shean, David Wm.	2B	148	.239	B	
		Smith, Harry Thomas	C	38	.238	B	C
		Sweeney, Wm. John	SS110	147	.267	B	
		(1B17 3B21)					
0	0	Tyler, George Albert	P	4	.500	A	
1	2	White, Kirby	P	3	+.333	B	Pitt

WON 44
LOST 107
TG 151

NATIONAL LEAGUE — 1911. — FINISHED 8th (LAST) — PCT. .291

BOSTON

FREDERICK TENNEY

WON	LOST	NAME	POS.	G.	BA	FROM	TO
		Bridwell, Albert Henry	SS	51	+.291	xN.Y	
8	18	Brown, Chas. Edward (Buster)	P	42	.250	B	
0	1	Burke, Wm. Ignatius	P	2	1.000	B	C
		Butler, Arthur Edward	3B	19	.176	A	
		Clarke, Joshua Baldwin (Josh)	OF	30	.233	ClevA09	C
		Collins, Wm. Shirley	OF	17	+.149	B	Chi
1	8	Curtis, Clifton Garfield	P	12	+.250	B	Chi
		Donlin, Michael Joseph	OF	56	+.318	xN.Y.	
3	2	Donnelly, Edward	P	5	.071	A	
1	3	Ferguson, George Cecil	P	6	.250	B	C
0	2	Flaherty, Patrick Joseph	OF19	23	.287	Phil	C
		(P2)					
0	1	Frock, Samuel W.	P	4	.200	B	C
		Good, Wilbur David	OF	43	+.267	B	Chi
		Gowdy, Henry Morgan (Hank)	1B	29	+.289	xN.Y.	
		Graham, George Frederick	C	33	+.273	B	Chi
		(Peaches)					
0	6	Griffin, John Linton	P	15	+.233	xChi	
		Herzog, Chas. Lincoln (Buck)	3B	79	+.310	B	N.Y.
0	3	Hogg, Carter Bradley	P	8	.444	A	
		Houser, Benjamin Franklin	1B	20	.254	PhilA	
		Ingerton, Wm. John (OF43)	3B58	133	.250	A	C
		Jackson, George Christopher	OF	39	.347	A	
		Jones, Wm. Dennis	OF	18	.216	A	
		Kaiser, Albert Edward	OF	66	+.203	xChi	
		Kirke, Jay	OF	20	.360	DetA	
		Kling, John G.	C	75	+.224	xChi	
4	15	Mattern, Alonzo Albert	P	33	.175	B	
		Miller, Roy Oscar (Doc)	OF	146	.333	B	
		McDonald, Edward C.	3B53	54	.206	A	

WON	LOST	NAME	POS.	G.	BA	FROM	TO
0	5	McTigue, Wm. Percy	P	14	.100	A	
0	1	Parson, Wm. Edwin	P	7	.125	B	C
6	10	Perdue, Hubbard E. (Hub)	P	24	.208	A	
7	5	Pfeffer, Francis Xavier	P26	30	.196	Chi	C
		Rariden, Wm. Angel	C65	69	.228	B	
		Spratt, Henry Lee	SS26	41	.240	A	
		Steinfeldt, Harry M.	3B	19	.254	Chi	C
		Sweeney, Wm. John	2B	136	.314	B	
		Tenney, Frederick MGR.	1B96	98	.263	NY09	C
0	0	Thompson, Fuller Weidner	P	3	.000	A	C
7	10	Tyler, George Albert	P	28	.164	B	
3	12	Weaver, Orville F. (Orlie)	P	27	+.122	xChi	C
		Weeden, Chas. Albert		1	.000	A	C
4	5	Young, Denton True (Cy)	P10	11	.080	xClevA	C
		Young, Hermann John (SS3)	3B6	9	.230	A	C

WON 52
LOST 101
TG 153

NATIONAL LEAGUE — 1912. — FINISHED 8th (LAST) — PCT. .340

BOSTON

JOHN G. KLING

WON	LOST	NAME	POS.	G.	BA	FROM	TO
0	0	Brady, James Ward	P	2	.000	BosA08	C
0	0	Brady, Wm. A.	P	1	.000	A	C
		Bridwell, Albert Henry	SS	31	.236	B	
4	15	Brown, Chas. Edward (Buster)	P	31	.213	B	
		Campbell, Arthur Vincent	OF144	145	.296	Pitt	
		Devlin, Arthur McArthur	1B60	124	.289	N.Y.	
		(SS26 3B26)					
3	19	Dickson, Walter R.	P	36	.167	NY10	
5	10	Donnelly, Edward	P37	38	.275	B	C
		Gonzales, Miguel Angel Cordero	C	1	.000	A	
		Gowdy, Henry Morgan (Hank)	C22	44	.271	B	
0	0	Griffin, John Linton	P	3	.000	B	C
12	17	Hess, Otto C.	P	33	.245	ClevA08	
1	1	Hogg, Carter,Bradley	P	10	.091	B	
		Houser, Benjamin Franklin	1B83	108	.286	B	C
		Jackson, George Christopher	OF107	110	.262	B	
		Jones, Wm. Dennis	OF	2	.500	B	C
		Kaiser, Albert Edward	OF	4	.000	B	
		Kirke, Jay	OF71	103	.320	B	
		Kling, John G. MGR.	C74	81	.317	B	
0	0	Kroh, Floyd H.	P	3	.500	Chi10	C
		Maranville, Walter James	SS	26	.209	A	
		Vincent (Rabbitt)					
0	1	Mattern, Alonzo Albert	P	2	.000	B	C
		Miller, Roy Oscar (Doc)	OF	51	+.234	B	Phil
		McDonald, Edward C.	3B118	121	.259	B	
2	0	McTigue, Wm. Percy	P	10	.077	B	
		O'Rourke, Francis James	SS59	61	.122	A	
13	16	Perdue, Hubbard E. (Hub)	P	37	.138	B	
		Rariden, Wm. Angel	C73	79	.223	B	

WON	LOST	NAME	POS.	G.	BA	FROM	TO
		Schultz, Joseph Chas.	2B	4	.250	A	
		Schwind, Arthur E.	3B	1	.000	A	C
		Shean, David Wm.	SS	2	.400	Chi	
		Spratt, Henry Lee	SS23	27	.258	B	C
		Sweeney, Wm. John	2B	153	.344	B	
		Titus, John Franklin	OF	96	+.325	xPhil	
12	22	Tyler, George Albert	P	42	.198	B	
0	0	White, Stephen Vincent	P	3	.000	xWashA	C
		Whitehouse, Gilbert A.	C	1	.000	A	

WON 69
LOST 82
TG 151

NATIONAL LEAGUE

1913.

FINISHED 5th.

PCT. .457

BOSTON

GEORGE TWEEDY STALLINGS

WON	LOST	NAME	POS.	G.	BA	FROM	TO
0	0	Brown, Chas. Edward (Buster)	P	2	.000	B	C
		Brown, Drummond N.	C	15	.324	A	
		Bues, Arthur Frederick	3B	2	.000	A	
		Calhoun, Wm. Davitte (Red)	1B	6	.076	StL02	C
		Clymer, Otis Edgar	OF	14	+.324	xChi	C
0	1	Cochreham, Eugene	P	1	.000	A	
		Collins, Cyril Wilson	OF	16	.333	A	
		Connolly, Joseph Aloysius	OF124	126	.281	A	
0	0	Davis, George Allen Jr.	P	2	.000	NYA	
		Deal, Chas. Albert	3B	10	.309	xDetA	
		Devlin, Arthur McArthur	3B69	73	.229	B	C
		DeVogt, Rex Eugene	C	3	.000	A	C
6	7	Dickson, Walter R.	P	19	.178	B	
		Dugey, Oscar Joseph (SS1)	3B2	5	.250	A	
0	1	Gervais, Lucien Edward	P	6	.000	A	C
		Gowdy, Henry Morgan (Hank)	C	3	.600	B	
		Griffith, Thomas Herman	OF35	37	.252	A	
7	17	Hess, Otto C.	P29	35	.313	B	
		Jackson, George Christopher	OF	3	.300	B	C
6	10	James Wm. Lawrence	P	24	.255	A	
		Kirke, Jay	OF	18	.237	B	
		Lord, Bristol Robotham	OF62	73	.251	PhilA	C
		Mann, Leslie	OF	120	.253	A	
		Maranville, Walter James Vincent (Rabbitt)	SS	143	.247	B	
		Myers, Ralph Edward	1B135	140	.273	BosAll	
		Mitchell, Frederick Francis	C	4	.333	NYA10	
		McCleskey, Jefferson Lamar	3B	2	.000	A	C
		McDonald, Chas. E.	3B	62	+.353	xCin	
		McKechnie, Wm. Boyd	OF	1	.000	Pitt	NYA
0	0	McTigue, Wm. Percy	P	1	.000	B	
0	0	Noyes, Winfield Chas.	P	11	.250	A	
16	13	Perdue, Hubbard E. (Hub)	P	38	.104	B	
4	3	Quinn, John Picus	P	8	.191	NYA	
		Rariden, Wm. Angel	C87	95	.236	B	
14	13	Rudolph, Richard (Dick)	P33	35	.239	NY11	

WON	LOST	NAME	POS.	G.	BA	FROM	TO
		Schmidt, Chas. John	1B	22	.308	NYA09	
		Schultz, Joseph Chas.	OF	8	.222	B	
		Seymour, John Bentley (Cy)	OF18	39	.178	NY10	C
		Smith, Frederick Vincent	3B59	92	.228	A	
0	0	Strand, Paul Edward	P	7	.167	A	
		Sweeney, Wm. John	2B137	139	.257	B	
		Titus, John Franklin	OF75	87	.297	B	C
		Tragesser, Walter Joseph	C	1	.000	A	
16	17	Tyler, George Albert	P39	43	.206	B	
		Whaling, Albert (Bert)	C77	79	.242	A	
		Zinn, Guy	OF35	36	.297	NYA	

WON 94
LOST 59
TG 153

NATIONAL LEAGUE

1914.

FINISHED 1st.

PCT. .614

BOSTON

GEORGE TWEEDY STALLINGS

WON	LOST	NAME	POS.	G.	BA	FROM	TO
		Cather, Theodore P.	OF	50	+.296	xStL	
3	4	Cocreham, Eugene	P	15	.100	B	
		Collins, Cyril Wilson	OF19	27	.257	B	C
		Connolly, Joseph Aloysius	OF118	120	.306	B	
0	1	Cottrell, Ensign Stover	P	1	.000	PhilA	
5	6	Crutcher, Richard Louis	P	33	.148	A	
3	3	Davis, George Allen Jr.	P	9	.167	B	
		Deal, Chas. Albert	3B74	79	.210	B	
		Devore, Joshua (Josh)	OF	51	+.227	xPhil	C
		Dugey, Oscar Joseph (OF16)	2B16	58	.193	B	
		Evers, John Joseph	2B	139	.277	Chi	
		Gilbert, Lawrence Wm.	OF60	72	.268	A	
		Gowdy, Henry Morgan (Hank)	C115	128	.243	B	
		Griffith, Thomas Herman	OF	16	.104	B	
5	6	Hess, Otto C.	P	31	.234	B	
1	0	Hughes, Thomas L.	P	2	.000	NYA10	
26	7	James, Wm. Lawrence	P46	49	.256	B	
		Kraft, Clarence Otto	1B	3	.333	A	C
0	1	Luque, Adolfo	P	2	.000	A	
		Mann, Leslie	OF123	126	.247	B	
		Maranville, Walter James Vincent (Rabbitt)	SS	156	.246	B	
		Martin, John Christopher	3B26	33	+.212	NYA12	Phil
		Martin, Wm. Gloyd	SS	1	.000	A	C
		Moran, Joseph Herbert	OF	41	+.266	xCin	
		Murray, James O.	OF32	39	.232	StLA11	C
2	5	Perdue, Hubbard E. (Hub)	P	9	+.071	B	StL
27	10	Rudolph, Richard (Dick)	P42	43	.125	B	
		Schmidt, Chas. John	1B	147	.285	B	
		Smith, James Carlisle (Red)	3B	60	+.314	xBkn	
6	2	Strand, Paul Edward	P16	18	.333	B	
		Tyler, Frederick Franklin	C	6	.105	A	C
16	14	Tyler, George Albert	P	38	.202	B	
		Whaling, Albert (Bert)	C59	60	.209	B	
		Whitted, George Bostic	OF60	66	+.216	xStL	

WON 83
LOST 69
TG 152

NATIONAL LEAGUE

1915.

FINISHED 2nd.

PCT. .546

BOSTON

GEORGE TWEEDY STALLINGS

WON	LOST	NAME	POS.	G.	BA	FROM	TO
3	0	Barnes, Jesse Lawrence	P	9	.176	A	
		Blackburn, Earl Stuart	C	3	.167	Cin13	
		Cather, Theodore P.	OF32	40	.206	B	C
0	0	Cochreham, Eugene	P	1	.000	B	C
		Collins, John Edgar	OF	5	+.308	xPitt	
		Compton, Albert Sebastian (Bash)	OF31	35	.241	xStLF	
		Connolly, Joseph Aloysius	OF93	104	.298	B	
2	2	Crutcher, Richard Louis	P	14	.231	B	C
3	3	Davis, George Allen, Jr.	P	15	.261	B	C
		Egan, Richard Joseph (Dick) (2B22)	OF24	83	+.264	xBkn	
		Evers, John Joseph	2B82	83	.263	B	
		Fitzpatrick, Edward Henry (OF29)	2B71	105	.221	A	
		Gilbert, Lawrence Wm.	OF27	45	.151	B	C
		Gowdy, Henry Morgan (Hank)	C114	118	.247	B	
0	1	Hess, Otto C.	P	5	.400	B	C
16	14	Hughes, Thomas L.	P	50	.100	B	
5	4	James, Wm. Lawrence	P	14	.048	B	
		Low, Fletcher	3B	1	.250	A	C
0	0	Luque, Adolfo	P	2	.000	B	
		Magee, Sherwood Robert (Sherry) (1B21)	OF135	156	.280	Phil	
		Maranville, Walter James Vincent (Rabbitt)	SS	149	.244	B	
		Moran, Joseph Herbert	OF123	130	.200	B	C
5	4	Nehf, Arthur Neukom	P	12	.143	A	
16	12	Ragan, Don Carlos Patrick (Pat)	P	34	+.150	xBkn	
22	19	Rudolph, Richard (Dick)	P44	45	.198	B	
		Schmidt, Chas. John	1B	127	.251	B	C
		Shannon, Joseph Aloysius	OF	5	.200	A	C
		Shannon, Maurice Joseph	SS	1	.000	A	
		Smith, James Carlisle (Red)	3B	157	.264	B	
		Snodgrass, Fred Carlisle	OF	23	+.278	xN.Y.	
1	1	Strand, Paul Edward	P	24	.091	B	
		Tragesser, Walter Joseph	C	7	.000	Bos13	
10	9	Tyler, George Albert	P32	45	.261	B	
		Whaling, Albert (Bert)	C69	72	.221	B	C

WON 89
LOST 63
TG 152

NATIONAL LEAGUE

1916.

FINISHED 3rd.

PCT. .586

BOSTON

GEORGE TWEEDY STALLINGS

WON	LOST	NAME	POS.	G.	BA	FROM	TO
8	2	Allen, Frank Leon	P	19	.206	PittF	
		Bailey, Frederick Middleton	OF	6	.100	A	
6	14	Barnes, Jesse Lawrence	P	33	.188	B	
		Blackburn, Earl Stuart	C44	47	.273	B	
		Chappell, Lawrence A. (Larry)	OF	20	.226	xClevA	
		Collins, John Edgar	OF78	93	.209	B	
		Compton, Albert Sebastian (Bash)	OF	34	+.202	B	Pitt
		Connolly, Joseph Aloysius	OF31	62	.227	B	C
		Egan, Richard Joseph (Dick)	2B59	83	.223	B	C
		Evers, John Joseph	2B	71	.216	B	
		Fitzpatrick, Edward Henry (OF28)	2B46	83	.213	B	
		Gowdy, Henry Morgan (Hank)	C116	118	.252	B	
16	3	Hughes, Thomas L.	P	40	.192	B	
0	2	Knetzer, Elmer Ellsworth	P	2	+.000	PittF	Cin
		Konetchy, Edward Joseph	1B	158	.260	PittF	
		Magee, Sherwood Robert (Sherry)	OF120	122	.241	B	
		Maranville, Walter James Vincent (Rabbitt)	SS	155	.235	B	
		Mathes, Joseph John	2B	2	.000	PhilA12	C
7	5	Nehf, Arthur Neukom	P22	23	.125	B	
9	9	Ragan, Don Carlos Patrick (Pat)	P28	31	.217	B	
7	6	Reulbach, Edward Marvin	P	21	.091	NewF	
		Rico, Arthur Raymond	C	4	.000	A	
19	12	Rudolph, Richard (Dick)	P	41	.158	B	
		Smith, James Carlisle (Red)	3B	150	.259	B	
		Snodgrass, Fred Carlisle	OF110	112	.249	B	C
		Tragesser, Walter Joseph	C29	41	.204	B	
17	10	Tyler, George Albert	P34	39	.204	B	
		Wilhoit, Joseph Wm.	OF108	116	.230	A	

WON 72
LOST 81
TG 153

NATIONAL LEAGUE

1917.

FINISHED 6th.

PCT. .471

BOSTON

GEORGE TWEEDY STALLINGS

WON	LOST	NAME	POS.	G.	BA	FROM	TO
3	11	Allen, Frank Leon	P	29	.172	B	C
		Bailey, Frederick Middleton	OF27	50	.191	B	
13	21	Barnes, Jesse Lawrence	P50	53	.238	B	
		Chappell, Lawrence A. (Larry)	OF	3	.000	B	C
		Collins, John Edgar	OF	8	.148	B	
		Covington, Clarence Calvert	1B	17	.197	StLA13	
0	0	Crum, Calvin Carl	P	1	.000	A	
		Evers, John Joseph	2B	24	+.176	B	Phil
		Fitzpatrick, Edward Henry (3B15 OF19)	2B22	63	.253	B	C

WON	LOST	NAME	POS.	G.	BA	FROM	TO
		Gowdy, Henry Morgan (Hank)	C	49	.214	B	
5	3	Hughes, Thomas L.	P	13	.000	B	
		Jacklitsch, Frederick Lawrence	C	1	.000	BaltF15	C
		Kelly, Joseph Herbert	OF	116	.222	Chi	
		Konetchy, Edward Joseph	1B129	130	.272	B	
		Magee, Sherwood Robert	OF	72	+.255	B	Cin
		(Sherry)					
		Maranville, Walter James	SS	142	.260	B	
		Vincent (Rabbitt)					
		Massey, Wm. Herbert	2B25	31	.198	A	C
		Meyers, John Tortes (Chief)	C	25	+.246	xBkn	C
17	8	Nehf, Arthur Neukom	P	38	.171	B	
		Powell, Raymond Reath	OF	88	.272	DetA13	
6	9	Ragan, Don Carlos Patrick (Pat)	P	30	.125	B	
		Rawlings, John Wm. (SS17)	2B96	122	.256	KCF15	
		Rehg, Walter Phillip	OF86	87	.270	BosA15	
0	1	Reulbach, Edward Marvin	P	5	.000	B	C
		Rico, Arthur Raymond	C	13	.286	B	C
13	13	Rudolph, Richard (Dick)	P31	32	.230	B	
		Schreiber, Henry Ward (SS1)	3B1	2	.286	ChiA14	
1	2	Scott, John Wm. (Jack)	P	7	.125	Pitt	
		Smith, James Carlisle (Red)	3B	147	.295	B	
		Tragesser, Walter Joseph	C94	98	.222	B	
		Twombly, George Frederick	OF29	32	.186	Cin	
14	12	Tyler, George Albert	P32	61	.231	B	
0	1	Walsh, Edward Augustin	P	4	.250	ChiA	C
		Wilhoit, Joseph Wm.	OF	54	+.280	B	Pitt

WON 53
LOST 71
TG 124

NATIONAL LEAGUE — FINISHED 7th.

1918. — PCT. .427

BOSTON

GEORGE TWEEDY STALLINGS

WON	LOST	NAME	POS.	G.	BA	FROM	TO
		Bailey, Frederick Middleton	OF	9	.250	B	C
		Bass, Wm. O. (Doc)	OF	1	1.000	A	C
0	4	Canavan, Hugh Edward	P	16	.095	A	C
		Chadbourne, Chester James	OF	27	.260	KCF15	C
		Conway, Richard Daniel	2B	14	.167	A	C
		Covington, Clarence Calvert	OF	3	.333	B	C
1	2	Crandall, James Otis (Doc)	P	14	.285	StLA16	C
0	1	Crum, Calvin Carl	P	1	.000	B	C
7	6	Fillingim, Dana	P	14	.214	PhilA15	
1	5	George, Thomas Edward	P	10	.090	Cin15	C
5	6	Hearn, Bunn	P	17	.178	PittF15	
		Henry, John Park	C38	43	.206	WashA	C
		Herzog, Chas. Lincoln (Buck)	2B99	118	.228	N.Y.	
		(1B12 SS7)					
0	2	Hughes, Thomas L.	P	3	.333	B	C
		Johnson, Paul Oscar		1	.000	A	
		Kelly, Joseph Herbert	OF45	47	.232	B	
0	1	Konetchy, Edward Joseph	1B112	119	.236	B	
		(P1 OF6)					

WON	LOST	NAME	POS.	G.	BA	FROM	TO
		Maranville, Walter James	SS	11	.316	B	
		Vincent (Rabbitt)					
		Massey, Roy H.	OF49	66	.291	A	C
		(1B1 SS1 3B2)					
		Miller, Thomas Royall		2	.000	A	
		Murphy, Robert R.	OF	9	.375	A	
1	0	McQuillan, Hugh A.	P	1	.250	A	
15	15	Nehf, Arthur Neukom (OF2)	P32	35	.168	B	
5	1	Northrop, George Howard	P	7	.153	A	
		Powell, Raymond Reath	OF	53	.213	B	
8	17	Ragan, Don Carlos Patrick (Pat)	P	30	.183	B	
		Rawlings, John Wm.	SS71	111	.207	B	
		(2B20 OF18)					
		Rehg, Walter Phillip	OF38	40	.241	B	
9	10	Rudolph, Richard (Dick)	P	21	.185	B	
		Smith, James Carlisle (Red)	3B	119	.298	B	
		Smith, James Lawrence	2B10	34	.225	N.Y.	
		(SS9 3B5 OF6)					
		Taggart, Robert John	OF	35	.329	PittF15	C
		Terry, Zebulon Alexander (Zeb)	SS27	28	.305	ChiA	
		Tragesser, Walter Joseph	C	7	.000	B	
1	1	Upham, Wm. Lawrence	P	3	.222	BknF15	C
		Wagner, Wm. Joseph	C	13	.213	Pitt	C
		Wickland, Albert	OF	95	.262	PittF15	
		Wilson, Arthur Earl	C85	89	.211	Chi	

WON 57
LOST 82
TG 139

NATIONAL LEAGUE — FINISHED 6th.

1919. — PCT. .410

BOSTON

GEORGE TWEEDY STALLINGS

WON	LOST	NAME	POS.	G.	BA	FROM	TO
		Bailey, Arthur Eugene	OF	4	.333	PhilA17	
		Blackburne, Russell Aubrey	1B1	31	+.272	Cin	Phil
		(Lena) (2B1 SS1)					
		Boeckel, Norman D.	3B	95	+.249	xPitt	
		Carroll, Dorsey Lee	OF	15	.265	A	C
4	5	Causey, Cecil Algernon	P	10	+.095	xN.Y.	
0	2	Cheney, Lawrence Russell	P	8	+.200	xBkn	Phil
		Christenbury, Lloyd Reid	OF	7	.290	A	
		Cruise, Walton Edwin	OF	73	+.216	xStL	
6	6	Demaree, Albert Wentworth (Al)	P	25	.048	N.Y.	C
6	13	Fillingim, Dana	P	32	.246	B	
		Ford, Horace Hills	2B	10	.214	A	
		Gowdy, Henry Morgan (Hank)	C74	78	.279	Bos17	
		(1B1)					
		Herzog, Chas. Lincoln (Buck)	2B	73	+.276	B	Chi
		Holke, Walter Henry	1B136	137	.292	N.Y.	
0	0	James, Wm. Lawrence	P	1	.000	Bos15	C
7	11	Keating, Raymond Herbert	P22	24	.152	NYA	C
		Kelly, Joseph Herbert	OF16	18	.141	B	C
		King, Edward Lee	OF	2	.000	PhilA16	C

WON	LOST	NAME	POS.	G.	BA	FROM	TO
		Mann, Leslie	OF	40	+.285	xChi	
		Maranville, Walter James Vincent (Rabbitt)	SS	131	.267	B	
		Miller, Thomas Royall	OF	7	.333	B	C
2	3	McQuillan, Hugh A. (OF3)	P16	20	.222	B	
8	9	Nehf, Arthur Neukom (OF1)	P21	22	+.197	B	N.Y.
1	5	Northrop, George Howard	P	12	.364	B	C
		Nutter, Everett Clarence	OF	18	.212	A	C
4	2	Oeschger, Joseph Carl	P	7	+.087	xN.Y.	
		O'Neil, George Michael	C	11	.214	A	
		Pick, Chas. Thomas (1B2 OF3)	3B5	34	+.273	xChi	
		Powell, Raymond Reath	OF122	123	.236	B	
0	2	Ragan, Don Carlos Patrick (Pat)	P	4	+.250	B	N.Y.
		Rawlings, John Wm. (SS5 OF10)	2B58	77	.255	B	
		Riggert, Joseph Aloysius	OF61	63	.283	StL14	C
13	18	Rudolph, Richard (Dick)	P	37	.193	B	
6	6	Scott, John Wm. (Jack) (OF1)	P19	24	.175	Bos17	
		Smith, James Carlisle (Red) (3B23)	OF48	87	.245	B	C
		Thorpe, James Francis (1B2)	OF58	60	+.327	xN.Y.	C
		Tragesser, Walter Joseph	C	20	+.272	B	Phil
		White, Samuel	C	1	.000	A	C
		Wilson, Arthur Earl (1B1)	C64	71	.257	B	

WON 62
LOST 90
TG 152

NATIONAL LEAGUE — FINISHED 7th.

1920. — PCT. .408

BOSTON

GEORGE TWEEDY STALLINGS

WON	LOST	NAME	POS.	G.	BA	FROM	TO
		Bailey, Arthur Eugene	OF	13	.083	B	BosA
		Boeckel, Norman D.	3B149	153	.268	B	
		Christenbury, Lloyd Reid (2B2 OF6)	SS8	65	.208	B	
		Cruise, Walton Edwin	OF82	91	.278	B	
		Dugey, Oscar Joseph		5	.000	Phil17	C
1	2	Eayrs, Edwin (P7)	OF63	87	.328	Pitt13	
12	21	Fillingim, Dana	P37	38	.174	B	
		Ford, Horace Hills (SS18)	2B59	88	.241	B	
		Gowdy, Henry Morgan (Hank)	C74	80	.243	B	
0	3	Hearn, Bunn	P	11	.143	Bos18	C
		Holke, Walter Henry	1B143	144	.294	B	
1	0	Jones, John Paul	P	3	.250	N.Y.	C
		Mann, Leslie	OF110	115	.276	B	
		Maranville, Walter James Vincent (Rabbitt)	SS133	134	.266	B	
11	15	McQuillan, Hugh A.	P	38	.257	B	
15	13	Oeschger, Joseph Carl	P	38	.178	B	
		O'Neil, George Michael	C105	112	.283	B	
		Pick, Chas. Thomas	2B94	95	.274	B	C
1	1	Pierotti, Albert Felix	P	6	.250	A	
		Powell, Raymond Reath	OF	147	.225	B	
		Rawlings, John Wm.	2B	5	+.000	B	Phil
4	8	Rudolph, Richard (Dick)	P	18	.185	B	
10	21	Scott, John Wm. (Jack)	P	44	.212	B	
		Sullivan, John Lawrence	OF66	81	.296	A	
		Trophy, Walter Anthony	1B	3	.200	A	C
0	0	Townsend, Ira Dance	P	4	.000	A	
2	2	Townsend, Leo Alphonse	P	7	.167	A	
5	4	Watson, John Reeves	P	1	+.000	PhilA	Pitt
				12	+.130		(recall)
		Wilson, Arthur Earl	C	16	.053	B	
		Whelan, Thomas Joseph	1B	1	.000	A	C

WON 79
LOST 74
TG 153

NATIONAL LEAGUE — FINISHED 4th.

1921. — PCT. .516

BOSTON

FREDERICK FRANCIS MITCHELL

WON	LOST	NAME	POS.	G.	BA	FROM	TO
		Barbare, Walter Lawrence	SS121	134	.302	Pitt	
		Boeckel, Norman D.	3B	153	.313	B	
1	3	Braxton, Edgar Garland	P	17	.000	A	
		Christenbury, Lloyd Reid	2B32	62	.352	B	
0	1	Cooney, John Walter	P	8	.200	A	
		Cruise, Walton Edwin	OF102	108	.346	B	
0	0	Eayrs, Edwin	P2	15	+.067	B	Bkn
15	10	Fillingim, Dana	P44	45	.247	B	
		Ford, Horace Hills (SS33)	2B119	152	.279	B	
		Gibson, Frank Gilbert	C41	63	.264	DetA13	
		Gowdy, Henry Morgan (Hank)	C53	64	.299	B	
		Holke, Walter Henry	1B	150	.261	B	
1	1	Morgan, Cyril Arlon	P	17	.000	A	
13	17	McQuillan, Hugh A.	P	45	.205	B	
		Nicholson, Frederick	OF59	83	.327	Pitt	
		Nixon, Albert Richard	OF43	55	.239	Bkn18	
20	14	Oeschger, Joseph Carl	P	46	.255	B	
		O'Neil, George Michael	C95	98	.249	B	
0	1	Pierotti, Albert Felix	P	2	.000	B	C
		Powell, Raymond Reath	OF	149	.306	B	
15	13	Scott, John Wm. (Jack)	P47	51	.341	B	
		Southworth, Wm. Harrison	OF	141	.308	Pitt	
		Sullivan, John Lawrence	OF	5	+.000	B	Chi
0	0	Townsend, Ira Dance	P	4	.000	B	C
0	1	Townsend, Leo Alphonse	P	1	.000	B	C
14	13	Watson, John Reeves	P	44	.138	B	

WON 53
LOST 100
TG 153

NATIONAL LEAGUE — FINISHED 8th (LAST)

1922. — PCT. .346

BOSTON

FREDERICK FRANCIS MITCHELL

WON	LOST	NAME	POS.	G.	BA	FROM	TO
		Barbare, Walter Lawrence (1B14 3B33)	2B45	106	.231	B	C
		Boeckel, Norman D.	3B106	119	.289	B	
1	2	Braxton, Edgar Garland	P	25	.063	B	
		Christenbury, Lloyd Reid (2B5 3B2)	OF32	71	.250	B	C
1	2	Cooney, John Walter	P	4	.000	B	
		Cruise, Walton Edwin (1B2)	OF100	104	.278	B	
5	9	Fillingim, Dana	P	25	.158	B	
		Ford, Horace Hills (2B28)	SS115	143	.271	B	
		Gallagher, Lawrence Kirby	SS6	7	.045	A	C
0	2	Genewich, Joseph Edward	P	6	.167	A	
		Gibson, Frank Gilbert (1B20)	C29	66	.299	B	
		Gowdy, Henry Morgan (Hank) (1B1)	C72	92	.316	B	
		Henry, Frederick Marshall	1B	18	.197	A	
		Holke, Walter Henry	1B	105	.291	B	
2	3	Hulihan, Harry Joseph	P	7	.154	A	C
		Kopf, Wm. Lorenz (Larry) (SS33 3B13)	2B78	126	.266	Cin	
0	1	Lansing, Eugene Hewett	P	15	.000	A	C
11	15	Marquard, Richard Wm. (Rube)	P	39	.222	Cin	
0	1	Matthews, James Vincent	P	3	.000	A	C
11	13	Miller, Frank Lee	P	31	.118	Pitt19	
0	0	Morgan, Cyril Arlon	P	2	.000	B	C
3	4	McNamara, Timothy Aloysius	P	24	.118	A	
5	10	McQuillan, Hugh A.	P	28	+.167	B	N.Y.
		Nicholson, Frederick	OF63	78	.252	B	C
		Nixon, Albert Richard	OF79	86	.264	B	
6	21	Oeschger, Joseph Carl	P	46	.190	B	
		O'Neil, George Michael	C79	83	.223	B	
		Powell, Raymond Reath	OF136	142	.296	B	
		Roser, John Joseph	OF	32	.239	A	C
0	2	Rudolph, Richard (Dick)	P	3	.400	Bos20	
		Southworth, Wm. Harrison	OF41	43	.322	B	
8	14	Watson, John Reeves	P	41	.197	B	
0	1	Yeargin, James Almond	P	1	.000	A	

WON 54 NATIONAL LEAGUE FINISHED 7th.
LOST 100
TG 154 1923. PCT. .351

FREDERICK FRANCIS MITCHELL

WON	LOST	NAME	POS.	G.	BA	FROM	TO
		Bagwell, Wm. Mallory	OF22	56	.290	A	
10	14	Barnes, Jesse Lawrence	P	31	+.147	xN.Y.	
1	0	Batchelder, Joseph Edmund	P	4	.000	A	
5	9	Benton, Lawrence James (Larry)	P	35	.161	A	
		Boeckel, Norman D. (SS1)	3B147	148	.298	B	C
		Conlon, Arthur Joseph (Jocko) (SS6 3B4)	2B36	59	.218	A	C
3	5	Cooney, John Walter (1B1 OF11)	P23	42	.379	B	
		Cousineau, Edward Thomas	C	1	1.000	A	
		Cruise, Walton Edwin	OF9	21	.211	B	
		Emmerich, Robert G.	OF8	13	.083	A	C
		Felix, August Guenther (Gus) (2B5 3B4)	OF123	139	.273	A	
1	9	Fillingim, Dana	P35	36	.226	B	
		Ford, Horace Hills (SS19)	2B95	111	.271	B	
13	14	Genewich, Joseph Edward	P	43	.247	B	
		Gibson, Frank Gilbert	C20	41	.300	B	
		Gowdy, Henry Morgan (Hank)	C15	23	+.125	B	N.Y.
		Henry, Frederick Marshall	1B	11	.111	B	C
		Hermann, Albert Bartel (1B4 3B5)	2B15	31	.237	A	
		Kopf, Wm. Lorenz (Larry) (2B4)	SS37	39	.275	B	C
11	14	Marquard, Richard Wm. (Rube)	P	38	.140	B	
0	3	Miller, Frank Lee	P	8	.143	B	C
		McInnis, John Phaelen (Stuffy)	1B	154	.315	ClevA	
3	13	McNamara, Timothy Aloysius	P	32	.179	B	
		Nixon, Albert Richard	OF80	88	.274	B	
5	15	Oeschger, Joseph Carl	P	44	.231	B	
		O'Neil, George Michael	C95	96	.212	B	
		Padgett, Ernest Kitchen (2B1)	SS2	4	.182	A	
		Powell, Raymond Reath	OF84	97	.302	B	
1	2	Rudolph, Richard (Dick)	P	4	.000	B	
		Smith, Earl Sutton	C54	72	+.288	xN.Y.	
		Smith, Robert Eldridge (2B8)	SS101	115	.251	A	
		Southworth, Wm. Harrison (2B2)	OF151	153	.319	B	
1	2	Watson, John Reeves	P	11	+.250	B	N.Y.

WON 53 NATIONAL LEAGUE FINISHED 8th (LAST)
LOST 100
TG 153 1924. PCT. .346

BOSTON

DAVID JAMES BANCROFT

WON	LOST	NAME	POS.	G.	BA	FROM	TO
		Bancroft, David James MGR.	SS	79	.279	N.Y.	
15	20	Barnes, Jesse Lawrence	P	37	.222	B	
0	0	Batchelder, Joseph Edmund	P	3	.000	B	
5	7	Benton, Lawrence James (Larry)	P	30	.091	B	
8	9	Cooney, John Walter (1B1 OF16)	P34	55	.254	B	
		Cousineau, Edward Thomas	C	3	.000	B	
		Cruise, Walton Edwin	OF	9	.444	B	C
		Cunningham, Wm. Aloysius	OF109	114	.272	N.Y.	C
		Felix, August Guenther (Gus)	OF51	59	.211	B	
0	1	Gearin, Dennis John	P	1	+.000	xN.Y.	C

WON	LOST	NAME	POS.	G.	BA	FROM	TO
10	19	Genewich, Joseph Edward	P	34	.167	B	
		Gibson, Frank Gilbert (1B10 3B2)	C46	90	.310	B	
0	4	Graham, Kyle B.	P	5	.000	A	
		Hermann, Albert Bartel		1	.000	B	C
0	1	Kamp, Alphonse Francis (Ike)	P	1	.000	A	
		Kelleher, John Patrick	3B	1	.000	Chi	C
		Lane, James Hunter (2B1)	3B4	7	.067	A	C
		Lefler, Wade Hampton		1	.000	A	WashA
1	4	Lucas, Chas. Frederick (Red) (3B2)	P27	.33	.333	N.Y.	
		Mann, Leslie	OF28	32	.275	Cin	
1	2	Marquard, Richard Wm. (Rube)	P	6	.273	B	
0	0	Muich, Ignatius Andrew	P	3	.000	A	C
		McInnis, John Phaelen (Stuffy)	1B	146	.291	B	
8	12	McNamara, Timothy Aloysius	P	35	.140	B	
1	2	North, Louis Alexander	P	6	+.250	xStL	C
		O'Neil, George Michael	C	106	.246	B	
		Padgett, Ernest Kitchen (2B29)	3B113	138	.255	B	
		Phillips, Edward David	C1	3	.000	A	
		Powell, Raymond Reath	OF46	74	.261	B	C
		Shay, Arthur Joseph (SS1)	2B	19	.235	Chi16	C
		Smith, Earl Sutton	C13	33	+.271	B	Pitt
		Smith, Robert Eldridge (3B23)	SS80	106	.228	B	
		Sperber, Edwin George	OF17	24	.288	A	
		Stengel, Chas. Dillon (Casey)	OF126	131	.280	N.Y.	
3	8	Stryker, Sterling Albert	P	20	,217	A	
		Thomas, Herbert Mark	OF	32	.220	A	
		Tierney, James Arthur (3B22)	2B115	136	.259	Phil	
		Wilson, Francis Edward	OF55	61	.237	A	
1	11	Yeargin, James Almond	P	32	.143	Bos22	C

WON 70
LOST 83
TG 153

NATIONAL LEAGUE — FINISHED 5th.

1925. — PCT. .458

BOSTON

DAVID JAMES BANCROFT

WON	LOST	NAME	POS.	G.	BA	FROM	TO
0	0	Anderson, Wm. Edward	P	2	.000	A	C
		Bancroft, David James MGR.	SS125	128	.319	B	
11	16	Barnes, Jesse Lawrence	P	32	.198	B	
0	0	Batchelder, Joseph Edmund	P	4	.000	B	C
14	7	Benton, Lawrence James (Larry)	P31	32	.241	B	
		Burrus, Maurice Lennon	1B151	152	.340	PhilA20	
14	14	Cooney, John Walter (1B3 OF1)	P31	54	.320	B	
		Cousineau, Edward Thomas	C	1	.000	B	C

WON	LOST	NAME	POS.	G.	BA	FROM	TO
0	0	Edwards, Foster Hamilton	P	1	.000	A	
		Felix, August Guenther (Gus)	OF114	121	.307	B	
		Geautreau, Walter Paul	2B	68	.262	xPhilA	
12	10	Genewich, Joseph Edward	P	34	.273	B	
		Gibson, Frank Gilbert (1B2)	C86	104	.278	B	
7	12	Graham, Kyle B.	P	34	.136	B	
		Harris, David Stanley	OF90	92	.265	A	
		High, Andrew Aird (2B1)	3B60	60	+.288	xBkn	
		Hogan, James Francis (Shanty)	OF5	9	.286	A	
		Hood, Aubrey Lincoln	2B	5	.286	A	C
2	4	Kamp, Alphonse Francis (Ike)	P	24	.167	B	C
		Kibbie, Horace Kent (SS3)	2B8	11	.268	A	C
		Lucas, Chas. Frederick (Red)	2B	6	.150	B	
		Mann, Leslie	OF57	60	.342	B	
2	8	Marquard, Richard Wm. (Rube)	P	26	.136	B	C
		Marriott, Wm. Earl (OF1)	3B89	103	.268	Chi21	
0	0	McNamara, Timothy Aloysius	P	1	.000	B	
		Neis, Bernard Edmund	OF87	106	.285	Bkn	
0	0	Ogrodowski, Joseph Anthony	P	1	.000	A	C
		O'Neil, George Michael	C69	70	.258	B	
		Padgett, Ernest Kitchen (SS18 3B7)	2B47	86	.305	B	
2	8	Ryan, Wilfred Patrick Dolan (Rosy)	P37	38	.282	N.Y.	
		Siemer, Oscar Sylvester	C	16	.304	A	
5	3	Smith, Robert Eldridge (P13 2B15 OF1)	SS21	58	.282	B	
		Sperber, Edwin George	OF	2	.000	B	C
		Stengel, Chas. Dillon (Casey)	OF1	12	.077	B	
		Thomas, Herbert Mark	2B	5	.235	B	
1	1	Vargus, Wm. Fay	P	11	.250	A	
		Welsh, James D. (2B3)	OF116	122	.312	A	
		Wilson, Francis Edward	OF10	12	.419	B	C

WON 66
LOST 86
TG 152

NATIONAL LEAGUE — FINISHED 7th.

1926. — PCT. .434

BOSTON

DAVID JAMES BANCROFT

WON	LOST	NAME	POS.	G.	BA	FROM	TO
		Bancroft, David James MGR.	SS123	127	.311	B	
14	14	Benton, Lawrence James (Larry)	P43	45	.154	B	
		Brown, Edward Wm.	OF	153	.328	Bkn	
		Burrus, Maurice Lennon	1B128	131	.270	B	
3	3	Cooney, John Walter (P19)	1B31	64	.302	B	
2	0	Edwards, Foster Hamilton	P	3	.000	B	
		Geautreau, Walter Paul	2B74	79	.267	B	
8	16	Genewich, Joseph Edward	P	37	.164	B	
		Gibson, Frank Gilbert	C13	24	.340	B	
5	7	Goldsmith, Harold Eugene	P	19	.211	A	
3	3	Graham, Kyle B.	P	15	.167	B	

WON	LOST	NAME	POS.	G.	BA	FROM	TO
4	9	Hearn, Elmer LaFayette	P	34	.100	A	
		High, Andrew Aird (2B49)	3B81	130	.296	B	
		Hogan, James Francis (Shanty)	C	4	.286	B	
		Johnston, James Harle (Jimmy) (OF1)	3B14	23	+.246	Bkn	N.Y.
		Mann, Leslie	OF46	50	.302	B	
6	10	Mogridge, George Anthony	P39	40	.174	StLA	
		Moore, Graham Edward (SS14 3B1)	2B39	54	+.266	xPitt	
		Neis, Bernard Edmund	OF23	30	.215	B	
		Riconda, Harry Paul	3B	4	.167	PhilA24	
0	2	Ryan, Wilfred Patrick Dolan (Rosy)	P	7	.200	B	
		Siemer, Oscar Sylvester	C30	31	.205	B	C
		Smith, John W. (Jack)	OF83	96	+.311	xStL	
10	13	Smith, Robert Eldridge	P33	40	.298	B	
		Taylor, Edward James (SS33)	3B62	92	.268	A	C
		Taylor, James Wren (Zack)	C123	125	.255	Bkn	
0	0	Vargus, Wm. Fay	P	4	.000	B	C
		Welsh, James D.	OF129	134	.278	B	
11	9	Wertz, Henry Levi	P	32	.266	A	
		Wilson, Francis Edward	OF56	87	.237	B	
		Womack, Sidney Kirk	C	1	.000	A	C

WON 60 — NATIONAL LEAGUE — FINISHED 7th.
LOST 94
TG 154 — 1927. — PCT. .390

BOSTON

DAVID JAMES BANCROFT

WON	LOST	NAME	POS.	G.	BA	FROM	TO
		Bancroft, David James MGR.	SS104	111	.243	B	
4	2	Benton, Lawrence James (Larry)	P	11	+.222	B	N.Y.
		Brown, Edward Wm.	OF153	155	.306	B	
		Burrus, Maurice Lennon	1B61	72	.318	B	
		Clark, Bailey Earl Jr.	OF	13	.273	A	
0	0	Cooney, John Walter	P	10	.000	B	
2	8	Edwards, Foster Hamilton	P29	33	.045	B	
		Farrell, Edward Stephen (2B40 3B18)	SS57	110	+.292	xN.Y.	
		Fournier, Jacques Frank	1B102	122	.283	Bkn	C
		Geautreau, Walter Paul	2B57	87	.246	B	
11	8	Genewich, Joseph Edward	P	40	.193	B	
		Gibson, Frank Gilbert	C47	60	.222	B	C
1	3	Goldsmith, Harold Eugene	P	22	.238	B	
		Graves, Samuel Sidney	OF5	7	.250	A	C
11	14	Greenfield, Kent	P	27	+.172	xN.Y.	
0	2	Hearn, Elmer LaFayette	P	8	.400	B	
		High, Andrew Aird	3B89	113	.302	B	
		Hogan, James Francis (Shanty)	C61	71	.288	B	
0	0	Knight, Elma Russell (Jack)	P	3	.000	Phil	C
		Mann, Leslie	OF24	29	+.258	B	N.Y.
0	1	Mills, Arthur Grant	P	15	.000	A	
6	4	Mogridge, George Anthony	P	20	.200	B	C
		Moore, Graham Edward (2B39 OF16)	3B52	112	.302	B	
1	2	Morrison, Walter Guy	P	11	.125	A	
		McNamara, John Raymond	OF3	11	.000	A	
3	5	McQuillan, Hugh A.	P	13	+.227	xN.Y.	C
		Richbourg, Lancelot Clayton	OF110	115	.309	WashA24	
7	17	Robertson, Chas. Culbertson	P	28	.240	StLA	
0	0	Rudolph, Richard (Dick)	P	1	.000	Bos23	C
		Smith, John W. (Jack)	OF48	84	.317	B	
10	18	Smith, Robert Eldridge	P41	54	.248	B	
		Taylor, James Wren (Zack)	C27	30	+.240	B	N.Y.
		Thomas, Herbert Mark	2B17	24	+.230	Bos25	N.Y.
		Urban, Louis John (Luke)	C34	35	.288	A	
		Welsh, James D.	OF129	131	.288	B	
4	10	Wertz, Henry Levi	P	42	.163	B	

WON 50 — NATIONAL LEAGUE — FINISHED 7th.
LOST 103
TG 153 — 1928. — PCT. .327

BOSTON

JOHN THOMAS SLATTERY — ROGERS HORNSBY

WON	LOST	NAME	POS.	G.	BA	FROM	TO
2	7	Barnes, Virgil Jennings	P	16	+.059	xN.Y.	C
		Bell, Lester Rowland	3B	153	.277	StL	
0	0	Boggs, Raymond Joseph	P	4	.000	A	C
9	21	Brandt, Edward Arthur	P38	39	.243	A	
		Brown, Edward Wm.	OF129	142	.268	B	C
		Burrus, Maurice Lennon	1B32	64	.270	B	C
3	3	Cantwell, Benjamin Caldwell	P	22	+.172	xN.Y.	
		Clark, Bailey Earl Jr.	OF27	28	.304	B	
0	2	Clarkson, Wm. Henry	P	19	+.000	xN.Y.	
		Cooney, James Edward	SS11	18	.137	Phil	C
3	7	Cooney, John Walter	P24	33	.171	B	
		Cronin, Wm. Patrick	C1	3	.000	A	
9	17	Delaney, Arthur D.	P	39	.143	StL24	
2	1	Edwards, Foster Hamilton	P	21	.091	B	
		Fitzberger, Chas. Caspar		7	.286	A	C
		Farrell, Edward Stephen	SS132	134	.215	B	
		Freigau, Howard Earl (2B11)	SS14	52	+.257	xBkn	C
		Geautreau, Walter Paul	2B1	23	.278	B	C
3	7	Genewich, Joseph Edward	P	13	+.038	B	N.Y.
0	0	Goldsmith, Harold Eugene	P	4	.000	B	
3	11	Greenfield, Kent	P	32	.053	B	
		Harris, David Stanley	OF2	7	.118	Bos25	
1	0	Hearn, Elmer LaFayette	P	7	.000	B	
0	2	Hollingsworth, John Burnett	P	7	.167	Bkn24	C
		Hornsby, Rogers (Rajah) MGR.	2B	140	.387	N.Y.	
0	0	Mills, Arthur Grant	P	4	.000	B	C
		Moore, Graham Edward	OF54	68	.237	B	

WON	LOST	NAME	POS.	G.	BA	FROM	TO
0	0	Morrison, Walter Guy	P	1	.000	B	C
		Mueller, Clarence Franklin	OF41	42	.225	N.Y.	
		McNamara, John Raymond	OF2	9	.250	B	C
0	1	Palmero, Emilio A.	P	3	.000	WashA26	C
		Richbourg, Lancelot Clayton	OF	148	.337	B	
2	5	Robertson, Chas. Culbertson	P	13	.000	B	C
0	0	Sisler, George Harold (P1)	1B119	118	.340	xWashA	
		Smith, John W. (Jack)	OF65	96	.280	B	
13	17	Smith, Robert Eldridge	P38	39	.250	B	
		Spohrer, Alfred R.	C48	51	+.218	xN.Y.	
		Taylor, James Wren (Zack)	C124	125	.251	N.Y.	
0	0	Touchstone, Clayland Moffitt	P	5	.000	A	
		Urban, Louis John (Luke)	C10	15	.176	B	C
0	2	Wertz, Henry Levi	P	10	.333	B	
		Williams, Earl Baxter	C1	3	.000	A	C

WON 56 LOST 98 TG 154

NATIONAL LEAGUE 1929.

FINISHED 8th (LAST) PCT. .364

BOSTON

EMIL EDWARD FUCHS JOHN JOSEPH EVERS

WON	LOST	NAME	POS.	G.	BA	FROM	TO
		Barron, David Irenus	OF5	10	.190	A	
		Bell, Lester Rowland	3B127	139	.298	B	
		Boyle, Ralph Francis	OF	17	.263	A	
8	13	Brandt, Edward Arthur	P26	29	.234	B	
4	13	Cantwell, Benjamin Caldwell	P	27	.180	B	
		Clark, Bailey Earl Jr.	OF74	84	.315	B	
0	1	Clarkson, Wm. Henry	P	2	.500	B	C
		Collins, Tharon Patrick	C2	7	.000	NYA	C
2	3	Cooney, John Walter (P14)	OF16	41	.319	B	
		Cronin, Wm. Patrick	C2	6	.111	B	
		Cummings, John Wm.	C1	3	+.167	xN.Y.	C
4	6	Cunningham, Bruce Lee	P17	19	.148	A	
3	5	Delaney, Arthur D.	P	20	.143	B	C
		Dugan, Joseph Anthony (Jumping Joe)	3B24	60	.304	NYA	
		Dunlap, Wm. James	OF8	10	.414	A	
		Evers, John Joseph MGR.	2B	1	.000	ChiA24	C
		Farrell, Edward Stephen	2B	5	+.125	B	N.Y.
		Gowdy, Henry Morgan (Hank)	C	10	.438	NY25	
0	0	Greenfield, Kent	P	6	+.000	B	Bkn
		Harper, George Washington	OF130	136	.291	StL	C
2	0	Hearn, Elmer LaFayette	P	10	.000	B	C
		James, Robert Byrne	2B32	46	.307	A	
7	15	Jones, Percy Lee	P35	36	.148	Chi	
		Legett, Louis Alfred	C28	39	.160	A	
3	7	Leverett, Gorham Vance (Dixie)	P	24	.188	ChiA26	C
		Maguire, Frederick Edward	2B	138	.252	Chi	
		Maranville, Walter James Vincent (Rabbitt)	SS145	146	.284	StL	
		Mueller, Clarence Franklin	OF24	46	.204	B	
0	1	Peery, George A.	P	10	.214	Pitt27	C
		Peploski, Henry Stephen	3B1	6	.200	A	C
		Richbourg, Lancelot Clayton	OF134	139	.305	B	
		Robertson, Eugene Edward	3B6	8	.286	xNYA	
12	17	Seibold, Harry (Socks)	P	33	.286	PhilA19	
		Sisler, George Harold	1B	154	.326	B	
		Smith, John W. (Jack)	OF3	19	.250	B	C
11	17	Smith, Robert Eldridge	P34	39	.172	B	
		Spohrer, Alfred R.	C109	114	.272	B	
		Taylor, James Wren (Zack)	C31	34	+.248	B	Chi
0	0	Touchstone, Clayland Moffitt	P	1	1.000	B	
		Voyles, Philip Vance	OF	20	.235	A	C
		Welsh, James D.	OF51	53	+.290	xN.Y.	
0	0	Wertz, Henry Levi	P	4	1.000	B	C
		Weston, Alfred John		3	.000	A	C

WON 70 LOST 84 TG 154

NATIONAL LEAGUE 1930.

FINISHED 6th. PCT. .455

BOSTON

WM. BOYD McKECHNIE

WON	LOST	NAME	POS.	G.	BA	FROM	TO
		Berger, Walter Antone (Wally)	OF145	151	.310	A	
		Boyle, Ralph Francis	OF	1	.000	B	
4	11	Brandt, Edward Arthur	P	41	.240	B	
0	0	Brown, Robert Murray	P	3	.000	A	
9	15	Cantwell, Benjamin Caldwell	P31	34	.302	B	
		Chatham, Chas. L.	3B92	112	.267	A	
		Clark, Bailey Earl Jr.	OF63	82	.296	B	
0	0	Cooney, John Walter	P	4	.000	B	
		Cronin, Wm. Patrick	C64	66	.253	B	
5	6	Cunningham, Bruce Lee	P36	37	.194	B	
		Dunlap, Wm. James	OF5	16	.069	B	C
7	6	Frankhouse, Frederick Meloy	P	27	+.359	xStL	
		Gowdy, Henry Morgan (Hank)	C15	16	.200	B	
3	5	Grimes, Burleigh Arland	P	11	+.188	Pitt	StL
		James, Robert Byrne	2B2	8	.182	B	
0	1	Jones, Kenneth Frederick	P	8	.200	DetA24	C
		Kahn, Owen Earle		1	.000	A	C
		Maguire, Frederick Edward	2B	146	.267	B	
		Maranville, Walter Janes (Vincent (Rabbitt)	SS138	142	.281	B	
		Moore, Randolph Edward (Randy)	OF34	83	.288	ChiA28	
		Neun, John Henry	1B55	81	.325	DetA28	
		Rhiel, Wm. Joseph	3B13	20	.170	Bkn	
		Richbourg, Lancelot Clayton	OF128	130	.304	B	
		Robertson, Eugene Edward	3B17	21	.186	B	C
		Rollings, Wm. Russell (2B10)	3B28	52	.236	BosA28	C
15	16	Seibold, Harry (Socks)	P	36	.211	B	
6	5	Sherdel, Wm. Henry	P	21	+.095	xStL	
		Sisler, George Harold	1B107	116	.309	B	C
10	14	Smith, Robert Eldridge	P38	39	.235	B	

WON	LOST	NAME	POS.	G.	BA	FROM	TO
		Spohrer, Alfred R.	C108	112	.317	B	
		Welsh, James D.	OF110	113	.275	B	C
11	5	Zachary, Jonathan Thompson Walton (Tom)	P24	25	.241	xNYA	

WON 64
LOST 90
TG 154

NATIONAL LEAGUE

FINISHED 7th.

1931.

PCT. .416

BOSTON

WM. BOYD McKECHNIE

WON	LOST	NAME	POS.	G.	BA	FROM	TO
		Berger, Walter Antone (Wally)	OF	156	.323	B	
		Bool, Albert J.	C37	49	.188	Pitt	C
18	11	Brandt, Edward Arthur	P33	34	.256	B	
0	1	Brown, Robert Murray	P	3	.500	B	
7	9	Cantwell, Benjamin Caldwell	P33	40	.228	B	
		Chatham, Chas. L. (SS4)	3B4	17	.227	B	
		Clark, Bailey Earl Jr.	OF14	16	.220	B	
		Cronin, Wm. Patrick	C50	51	.206	B	C
3	12	Cunningham, Bruce Lee	P33	34	.071	B	
		Dreesen, Wm. R.	3B47	48	.222	A	C
8	8	Frankhouse, Frederick Meloy	P	26	.150	B	
0	2	Haid, Harold Augustine	P	27	.125	StL	
		Hunnefield, Wm. Fenton	2B4	11	+.286	xClevA	N.Y.
		Maguire, Frederick Edward	2B	148	.228	B	C
		Maranville, Walter James Vincent (Rabbitt) (2B11)	SS137	145	.260	B	
		Moore, Randolph Edward (Randy) (3B22)	OF29	83	.260	B	
0	1	McAfee, Wm. Fort Jr.	P	18	.000	Chi	
1	3	Moss, Raymond Earl	P	12	+.133	xBkn	C
		Neun, John Henry	1B36	79	.221	B	
		Richbourg, Lancelot Clayton	OF71	97	.287	B	
		Scalzi, F. John Anthony		2	.000	A	C
		Schulmerich, Edward Wesley	OF87	95	.309	A	
10	18	Seibold, Harry (Socks)	P	33	.129	B	
		Sheely, Earl Homer	1B143	147	.273	Pitt29	C
6	10	Sherdel, Wm. Henry	P	27	.304	B	
		Spohrer, Alfred R.	C111	114	.240	B	
		Urbanski, Wm. Michael (SS19)	3B68	82	.238	A	
		Veltman, Arthur Patrick (Pat)		1	.000	N.Y.29	
		Walters, Wm. Henry Jr. (Bucky) (2B2)	3B5	9	.211	A	
		Wilson, Chas. Woodrow	3B14	16	.190	A	
		Worthington, Robert Lee	OF124	128	.291	A	
11	15	Zachary, Jonathan Thompson Walton (Tom)	P	33	.167	B	

WON 77
LOST 77
TG 154

NATIONAL LEAGUE

FINISHED 5th.

1932.

PCT. .500

BOSTON

WM. BOYD McKECHNIE

WON	LOST	NAME	POS.	G.	BA	FROM	TO
		Akers, Wm.	3B20	36	.258	DetA	C
		Berger, Walter Antone (Wally) (1B11)	OF134	145	.307	B	
13	11	Betts Walter Martin (Huck)	P	31	.241	Phi125	
16	16	Brandt, Edward Arthur	P	35	.207	B	
14	7	Brown, Robert Murray	P	35	.194	B	
13	11	Cantwell, Benjamin Caldwell	P	37	.280	B	
		Clark, Bailey Earl Jr.	OF16	50	.250	B	
1	0	Cunningham, Bruce Lee	P	18	.222	B	C
		Eckhardt, Oscar George (Ox)		8	.250	A	
		Ford, Horace Hills (SS16)	2B20	40	+.274	xStL	
4	6	Frankhouse, Frederick Meloy	P37	40	.100	B	
		Hargrave, Wm. McKinley	C73	82	.263	WashA	
		Holland, Robert Clyde	OF	39	.295	A	
		Jordan, Baxter Byerly	1B	49	.321	WashA	
		Knothe, Wilfred Edgar	3B87	89	.238	A	
		Leach, Frederick M.	OF50	84	.247	N.Y.	C
0	0	Mangum, Leo Allen	P	7	.000	N.Y.28	
		Maranville, Walter James Vincent (Rabbitt)	2B	149	.235	B	
		Moore, Randolph Edward (Randy) (1B22 3B31)	OF41	107	.293	B	
1	5	Pruett, Hubert,Shelby (Hub)	P	18	.105	N.Y.30	C
		Schulmerich, Edward Wesley	OF101	119	.260	B	
		Schulte, John Clement	C	10	.222	xStLA	C
3	10	Seibold, Harry (Socks)	P	28	.152	B	
0	0	Sherdel, Wm. Henry	P	1	+.000	B	StL
		Shires, Arthur Lee (The Great)	1B80	82	.238	WashA30	C
		Spohrer, Alfred R.	C100	104	.269	B	
		Urbanski, Wm. Michael	SS	136	.272	B	
		Walters, Wm. Henry Jr. (Bucky)	3B	22	.187	B	
		Worthington, Robert Lee	OF104	105	.303	B	
12	11	Zachary, Jonathan Thompson Walton (Tom)	P32	33	.273	B	

WON 83
LOST 71
TG 154

NATIONAL LEAGUE

FINISHED 4th.

1933.

PCT. .539

BOSTON

WM. BOYD McKECHNIE

WON	LOST	NAME	POS.	G.	BA	FROM	TO
		Berger, Walter Antone (Wally)	OF136	137	.313	B	
11	11	Betts, Walter Martin (Huck)	P	35	.224	B	

WON	LOST	NAME	POS.	G.	BA	FROM	TO
18	14	Brandt, Edward Arthur	P41	47	.309	B	
0	0	Brown, Robert Murray	P	6	.000	B	
20	10	Cantwell, Benjamin Caldwell	P40	49	.141	B	
		Clark, Bailey Earl Jr.	OF	7	.348	B	
2	1	Fallenstein, Edward Joseph	P	11	.375	Phil31	C
		Ford, Horace Hills	SS	5	.067	B	C
16	15	Frankhouse, Frederick Meloy	P	43	.238	B	
		Gyselman, Richard Reynald (2B5 SS1)	3B42	58	.239	A	
		Hargrave, Wm. McKinley	C25	45	.178	B	C
		Hogan, J. Francis (Shanty)	C95	96	.253	N.Y.	
		Holland, Robert Clyde	OF	13	.258	B	
		Jordan, Baxter Byerly	1B150	152	.286	B	
		Knothe, Wilfred Edgar (SS9)	3B33	44	+.228	B	Phil
		Lee, Harold Burnham (Hal)	OF87	88	+.221	xPhil	
4	3	Mangum, Leo Allen	P	25	.091	B	
		Maranville, Walter James Vincent (Rabbitt)	2B142	143	.218	B	
		Moore, Randolph Edward (Randy) (1B10)	OF122	135	.302	B	
		Mowry, Joseph Aloysius	OF64	86	.221	A	
		Schulmerich, Edward Wesley	OF21	29	+.247	B	Phil
1	4	Seibold, Harry (Socks)	P	111	.000	B	C
4	3	Smith, Robert Eldridge	P	14	+.200	xCin	
		Spohrer, Alfred R.	C65	67	.250	B	
0	1	Starr, Raymond Francis	P	9	+.143	xN.Y.	
		Thompson, Rupert Luckhart	OF	24	.186	A	
		Urbanski, Wm. Michael	SS143	144	.251	B	
		Whitney, Arthur Carter (Pinkey) (2B18)	3B85	100	+.246	xPhil	
		Worthington, Robert Lee	OF10	17	.156	B	
		Wright, Albert E.	2B	4	1.000	A	C
7	9	Zachary, Jonathan Thompson Walton (Tom)	P26	27	.119	B	

WON 78 — NATIONAL LEAGUE — FINISHED 4th.
LOST 73
TG 151 — 1934. — PCT. .517

BOSTON

WM. BOYD McKECHNIE

WON	LOST	NAME	POS.	G.	BA	FROM	TO
		Berger, Walter Antone (Wally)	OF	150	.298	B	
17	10	Betts, Walter Martin (Huck)	P	40	.188	B	
16	14	Brandt, Edward Arthur	P40	48	.240	B	
1	3	Brown, Robert Murray	P	16	.238	B	
5	11	Cantwell, Benjamin Caldwell	P27	29	.279	B	
1	1	Elliott, James Thomas	P	7	+.250	xPhil	C
		Fletcher, Elburt Preston (Elbie)	1B	8	.500	A	
17	9	Frankhouse, Frederick Meloy	P	37	.200	B	
		Gyselman, Richard Reynald	3B15	24	.167	B	C
		Hogan, J. Francis (Shanty)	C90	92	.262	B	
		Jordan, Baxter Byerly	1B117	124	.311	B	
		Lee, Harold Burnham (Hal)	OF128	139	.292	B	
		Mallon, Leslie Clyde	2B	42	.295	Phil32	
5	3	Mangum, Leo Allen	P	29	.281	B	
		Moore, Randolph Edward (Randy) (1B37)	OF72	123	.284	B	
		Mowry, Joseph Aloysius	OF20	25	.215	B	
		McGee, Daniel Aloysius	SS	7	.136	A	C
		McManus, Martin Joseph (3B37)	2B73	119	.276	BosA	C
1	3	Oliver, Richard (Barrett)	P	15	.143	PhilA	
0	0	Pickrel, Clarence Douglas	P	10	.000	Phil	C
8	8	Rhem, Chas. Flint	P	25	+.058	xStL	
6	9	Smith, Robert Eldridge	P39	42	.250	B	
		Spohrer, Alfred R.	C98	100	.223	B	
		Thompson, Rupert Luckhart	OF82	105	.265	B	
		Tyler, John Anthony	OF1	3	.167	A	
		Urbanski, Wm. Michael	SS	146	.293	B	
		Whitney, Arthur Carter (Pinkey) (2B36)	3B111	146	.259	B	
		Worthington, Robert Lee	OF11	41	+.246	B	StL
1	2	Zachary, Jonathan Thompson Walton (Tom)	P	5	+.000	B	Bkn

WON 38 — NATIONAL LEAGUE — FINISHED 8th (LAST)
LOST 115
TG 153 — 1935. — PCT. .248

BOSTON

WM. BOYD McKECHNIE

WON	LOST	NAME	POS.	G.	BA	FROM	TO
2	3	Benton, Lawrence James (Larry)	P	29	.200	Cin	C
		Berger, Walter Antone (Wally)	OF149	150	.295	B	
2	9	Betts, Walter Martin (Huck)	P	44	.159	B	C
0	0	Blanche, Prosby Albert	P	6	.167	A	
5	19	Brandt, Edward Arthur	P29	31	.210	B	
1	8	Brown, Robert Murray	P15	16	.105	B	
4	25	Cantwell, Benjamin Caldwell	P39	41	.284	B	
		Coscarart, Joseph Marvin (2B15 SS27)	3B41	86	.236	A	
		Doll, Arthur James	C	3	.100	A	
		Fletcher, Elburt Preston (Elbie)	1B	39	.236	B	
11	15	Frankhouse, Frederick Meloy	P	40	.263	B	
		Hogan, J. Francis (Shanty)	C56	59	.301	B	
		Jordan, Baxter Byerly (3B8 OF2)	1B95	130	.279	B	
		Lee, Harold Burnham (Hal)	OF110	112	.303	B	
		Lewis, Wm. Henry	C1	6	.000	StL33	
5	13	MacFayden, Daniel Knowles (Danny)	P	28	+.157	xCin	
		Mallon, Leslie Clyde (3B36 OF1)	2B73	116	.274	B	C

WON	LOST	NAME	POS.	G.	BA	FROM	TO
0	0	Mangum, Leo Allen	P	3	.000	B	C
		Maranville, Walter James Vincent (Rabbitt)	2B20	23	.149	Bos33	C
		Moore, Randolph Edward (Randy) (1B21)	OF78	125	.275	B	
		Moriarity, Edward Jerome	2B	8	.324	A	
		Mowry, Joseph Aloysius	OF45	81	.265	B	C
		Mueller, Ray Coleman	C40	42	.227	A	
0	5	Rhem, Chas. Flint	P	10	.000	B	
		Ruth, George Herman (Babe)	OF26	28	.181	NYA	C
8	18	Smith, Robert Eldridge	P46	47	.270	B	
		Spohrer, Alfred R.	C90	92	.242	B	C
		Thompson, Rupert Luckhart	OF85	112	.273	B	
		Tyler, John Anthony	OF11	13	.340	B	C
		Urbanski, Wm. Michael	SS129	132	.229	B	
		Whitney, Arthur Carter (Pinkey) (2B49)	3B74	126	.273	B	

WON 71 NATIONAL LEAGUE FINISHED 6th.
LOST 83
TG 154 1936. PCT. .461

BOSTON

WM. BOYD McKECHNIE

WON	LOST	NAME	POS.	G.	BA	FROM	TO
0	0	Babich, John Chas.	P	3	.000	Bkn	
7	9	Benge, Raymond Adelphia	P	21	+.140	Bkn	Phil
		Berger, Walter Antone (Wally)	OF133	138	.288	B	
0	1	Blanche, Prosby Albert	P	11	.250	B	C
0	2	Brown, Robert Murray	P	2	.000	B	C
4	5	Bush, Guy Terrell	P	15	+.120	xPitt	
9	9	Cantwell, Benjamin Caldwell	P34	35	.195	B	
10	15	Chaplin, James Bailey	P	40	.202	NY31	C
		Coscarart, Joseph Marvin	3B97	104	.245	B	C
		Cuccinello, Anthony Francis (Tony)	2B	150	.308	Bkn	
0	1	Doll, Arthur James	P	1	.000	B	
0	0	Ford, Eugene Matthew	P	2	.000	A	
		Haslin, Michael Joseph (Mickey) (2B7)	3B17	36	+.279	xPhil	
		Jordan, Baxter Byerly	1B136	138	.323	B	
0	1	Kowalik, Fabian Lorenz	P1	2	+.400	xPhil	C
7	11	Lanning, John Young	P	28	.135	A	
		Larsen, Erling Arthur	2B2	3	.000	A	C
		Lee, Harold Burnham (Hal)	OF150	152	.253	B	C
		Lewis, Wm. Henry	C21	29	.306	B	C
		Lopez, Alfonso Ramon (Al)	C127	128	.242	Bkn	
17	13	MacFayden, Daniel Knowles (Danny)	P	37	.096	B	
		Moore, Eugene Jr. (Gene)	OF	151	.290	StL	
		Moriarity, Edward Jerome		6	.167	B	C
		Mueller, Ray Coleman	C23	24	.197	B	
0	0	Murray, Joseph Ambrose	P	4	.250	A	C

WON	LOST	NAME	POS.	G.	BA	FROM	TO
0	0	McCloskey, James Ellwood	P	4	.000	A	C
1	1	Osborne, Wayne Harold	P	5	.250	Pitt	C
		Pilney, Andrew James		3	.000	A	C
6	5	Reis, Robert Joseph Thomas	P35	37	.217	Bkn	
6	7	Smith, Robert Eldridge	P	35	.222	B	
		Thompson, Rupert Luckhart (1B25)	OF39	106	.286	B	
		Urbanski, Wm. Michael (3B38)	SS80	122	.261	B	
		Warstler, Harold Burton (Rabbitt)	SS	74	.211	xPhilA	
0	0	Weafer, Kenneth Albert	P	1	.000	A	C
4	3	Weir, Wm. Franklin	P12	13	.278	A	
		Whitney, Arthur Carter (Pinkey)	3B	10	+.175	B	Phil

WON 79 NATIONAL LEAGUE FINISHED 5th.
LOST 73
TG 152 1937. PCT. .520

BOSTON

WM. BOYD McKECHNIE

WON	LOST	NAME	POS.	G.	BA	FROM	TO
		Berger, Walter Antone (Wally)	OF28	30	+.274	B	N.Y.
8	15	Bush, Guy Terrell	P32	33	.111	B	
		Cuccinello, Anthony Francis (Tony)	2B151	152	.271	B	
		DiMaggio, Vincent Paul	OF130	132	.256	A	
		English, Gilbert Raymond	3B71	79	.290	xDetA	
20	10	Fette, Louis Henry Wm. (Lou)	P35	36	.239	A	
		Fletcher, Elburt Preston (Elbie)	1B	148	.247	Bos35	
0	0	Frasier, Victor Patrick	P	3	.000	DetA34	
4	7	Gabler, Frank Harold	P	19	+.182	xN.Y.	
		Garms, Debs C. (3B36)	OF81	125	.259	StLA35	
4	6	Hutchinson, Ira Kendall	P	31	.115	ChiA33	
		Johnson, Roy Cleveland	OF63	85	.277	xN.Y.A.	
		Jordan, Baxter Byerly	1B	8	+.250	B	Cin
5	7	Lanning, John Young	P	32	.121	B	
		Lopez, Alfonso Ramon (Al)	C102	105	.204	B	
14	14	MacFayden, Daniel Knowles (Danny)	P	32	.157	B	
		Mayo, Edward Joseph	3B50	65	.227	N.Y.	
		Moore, Eugene Jr. (Gene)	OF	148	.283	B	
		Mueller, Ray Coleman	C57	64	.251	B	
		McGowan, Frank Bernard	OF2	9	.083	StLA29	C
0	0	Reis, Robert Joseph Thomas (P4)	OF18	45	.244	B	
		Riddle, John Ludy	C	2	.000	xWashA	
3	1	Shoffner, Milburn James	P	6	.125	ClevA31	
0	1	Smith, Robert Eldridge	P18	19	.200	B	C
		Thevenow, Thomas Joseph Jr.	SS12	21	.118	Cin	
20	11	Turner, James Riley (Jim)	P33	39	.250	A	
		Urbanski, Wm. Michael		1	.000	B	C

WON	LOST	NAME	POS.	G.	BA	FROM	TO
		Warstler, Harold Burton (Rabbitt)	SS	149	.223	B	
		Wasem, Lincoln Wm.	C	2	.000	A	C
1	1	Weir, Wm. Franklin	P	10	.000	B	

WON 77
LOST 75
TG 152

NATIONAL LEAGUE 1938.

FINISHED 5th.
PCT. .507

BOSTON

CHAS. DILLON STENGEL

WON	LOST	NAME	POS.	G.	BA	FROM	TO
0	0	Balas, Mitchell Francis	P	1	.000	A	C
		Cooney, John Walter (1B13)	OF110	120	.271	Bkn	
		Cuccinello, Anthony Francis (Tony)	2B	147	.265	B	
		DiMaggio, Vincent Paul	OF149	150	.228	B	
0	0	Doll, Arthur James	P	3	1.000	Bos36	C
1	0	Earley, Thomas Francis Aloysius	P	2	.000	A	
		English, Gilbert Raymond	3B43	53	.248	B	
9	7	Errickson, Richard Merriwell (Leif)	P	34	.114	A	
11	13	Fette, Louis Henry Wm. (Lou)	P	33	.188	B	
		Fletcher, Elburt Preston (Elbie)	1B146	147	.272	B	
0	0	Gabler, Frank Harold	P	1	.000	B	ChiA
		Garms, Debs C. (3B54)	OF63	117	.315	B	
		Hitchcock, James Franklin	SS24	28	.171	A	C
9	8	Hutchinson, Ira Kendall	P	36	.173	B	
		Johnson, Roy Cleveland	OF	7	.172	B	C
		Kahle, Robert Wayne		8	.333	A	C
		Kane, Thomas Joseph	2B	2	.000	A	C
0	0	Kenney, Arthur Joseph	P	2	.000	A	C
8	7	Lanning, John Young	P	32	.188	B	
		Lopez, Alfonso Ramon (Al)	C	71	.267	B	
14	9	MacFayden, Daniel Knowles (Danny)	P	29	.117	B	
		Maggert, Harl Warren Jr.	OF10	66	.281	A	C
		Mayo, Edward Joseph (SS2)	3B6	8	.214	B	
		Moore, Eugene Jr. (Gene)	OF47	54	.272	B	
0	0	Moran, Albert Thomas	P	1	.000	A	
		Mueller, Ray Coleman	C75	83	.237	B	
		McLeod, Ralph Alton	OF1	6	.286	A	C
1	0	Niggeling, John Arnold	P	2	.000	A	
1	6	Reis, Robert Joseph Thomas (OF10)	P16	34	.184	B	C
0	0	Reis, Thomas Edward	P	4	+.000	xPhil	C
		Riddle, John Ludy	C	19	.281	B	
8	7	Shoffner, Milburn James	P26	27	.211	B	
		Stripp, Joseph Valentine	3B58	59	+.275	xStL	C
		Sutcliffe, Chas. Inigo	C	4	.250	A	C
14	18	Turner, James Riley (Jim)	P	35	.229	B	

WON	LOST	NAME	POS.	G.	BA	FROM	TO
		Walsh, Joseph Patrick	SS	4	.000	A	C
		Warstler, Harold Burton (Rabbitt)	SS135	142	.231	B	
1	0	Weir, Wm. Franklin	P	5	.333	B	
		West, Max Edward	OF109	123	.234	A	

WON 63
LOST 88
TG 151

NATIONAL LEAGUE 1939.

FINISHED 7th.
PCT. .417

BOSTON

CHAS. DILLON STENGEL

WON	LOST	NAME	POS.	G.	BA	FROM	TO
		Andrews, Stanley Joseph	C10	13	.231	A	
		Barkley, John Duncan (3B4)	SS7	12	.000	StLA37	
2	2	Barnicle, George Bernard	P	6	.000	A	
1	0	Callahan, Joseph Thomas	P	4	.000	A	
		Clemens, Chester Spurgeon	OF7	9	.217	A	
		Cooney, John Walter	OF116	118	.274	B	
		Cuccinello, Anthony Francis (Tony)	2B80	81	.306	B	
1	4	Earley, Thomas Francis Aloysius	P	14	.300	B	
6	9	Errickson, Richard Merriwell (Leif)	P	28	.227	B	
10	10	Fette, Louis Henry Wm. (Lou)	P	27	.061	B	
		Fletcher, Elburt Preston (Elbie)	1B31	35	+.245	B	Pitt
0	2	Frankhouse, Frederick Meloy	P	23	.000	Bkn	C
		Garms, Debs C. (3B37)	OF96	132	.298	B	
		Hassett, John Aloysius (Buddy) (OF23)	1B123	147	.309	Bkn	
		Hill, John Clinton		2	.500	A	C
		Hodgin, Elmer Ralph	OF9	32	.208	A	
		Huber, Otto (2B4)	3B4	11	.273	A	C
5	6	Lanning, John Young	P	37	.143	B	
		Lopez, Alfonso Ramon (Al)	C129	131	.252	B	
		Majeski, Henry	3B99	106	.272	A	
		Masi, Philip Samuel	C42	46	.254	A	
		Miller, Edward Robert	SS	77	.267	Cin37	
1	1	Moran, Albert Thomas	P	6	.200	B	C
8	14	MacFayden, Daniel Knowles (Danny)	P	33	.179	B	
		Outlaw, James Paulus	OF39	65	.263	Cin	
15	13	Posedel, Wm. John (Barnacle Bill)	P	33	.110	Bkn	
		Ross, Chester James	OF	11	.323	A	
		Rowell, Carvel Wm.	OF16	21	.186	A	
		Schuster, Wm. Chas. (SS1)	3B1	2	.000	Pitt37	
4	6	Shoffner, Milburn James	P	25	+.159	B	Cin
		Simmons, Aloysius Harry (Al)	OF82	93	+.282	WashA	Cin
		Sisti, Sebastian Daniel (Sibby) (SS10 3B17)	2B34	63	.226	A	

WON	LOST	NAME	POS.	G.	BA	FROM	TO
6	9	Sullivan, Joseph	P31	33	.300	DetA36	
4	11	Turner, James Riley (Jim)	P	25	.236	B	
0	1	Veigel, Allen Francis	P	2	.000	A	C
		Warstler, Harold Burton (Rabbitt) (2B43 3B21)	SS49	114	.243	B	
0	0	Weir, Wm. Franklin	P	2	.000	B	C
		West, Max Edward	OF124	130	.285	B	
		Wietelmann, Wm. Frederick	SS22	23	.203	A	

WON 65 LOST 87 TG 152

NATIONAL LEAGUE

1940.

FINISHED 7th.

PCT. .428

BOSTON

CHAS. DILLON STENGEL

WON	LOST	NAME	POS.	G.	BA	FROM	TO
		Andrews, Stanley Joseph	C14	19	.182	B	
1	0	Barnicle, George Bernard	P	13	.000	B	
		Berres, Raymond Frederick	C	85	+.192	xPitt	
		Broskie, Sigmund Theodore	C	11	.273	A	C
0	2	Callahan, Joseph Thomas	P	6	.000	B	C
1	5	Coffman, Samuel Richard (Dick)	P	31	.083	N.Y.	
		Cooney, John Walter (1B7)	OF99	108	.318	B	
		Cuccinello, Anthony Francis (Tony)	3B33	34	+.270	B	N.Y.
2	0	Earley, Thomas Francis Aloysius	P	4	.400	B	
12	13	Errickson, Richard Merriwell (Leif)	P	34	.157	B	
0	5	Fette, Louis Henry Wm. (Lou)	P	7	+.375	B	Bkn
		Glossop, Alban (SS1 3B18)	2B18	60	+.236	xN.Y.	
		Gremp, Lewis Edward	1B3	4	.222	A	
		Hassett, John Aloysius (Buddy) (OF13)	1B98	124	.234	B	
2	4	Javery, Alva Wm.	P	29	.087	A	
0	1	Johnson, Arthur Henry	P	2	.000	A	
1	0	LaManna, Frank	P	5	.200	A	
		Loane, Robert Kenneth	OF10	13	.227	WashA	C
		Lopez, Alfonso Ramon (Al)	C	36	+.294	B	Pitt
		Majeski, Henry		3	.000	B	
		Manno, Donald	OF2	3	.286	A	
		Masi, Philip Samuel	C52	63	.196	B	
		Miller, Edward Robert	SS	151	.276	B	
		Moore, Eugene Jr. (Gene)	OF94	103	+.292	xBkn	
2	5	Piechota, Aloysius Edward	P	21	.200	A	
12	17	Posedel, Wm. John (Barnacle Bill)	P	35	.171	B	
		Preibisch, Melvin Adolphus	OF	11	.225	A	
		Ross, Chester James	OF	149	.281	B	
		Rowell, Carvel Wm. (OF7)	2B115	130	.305	B	
10	9	Salvo, Manuel	P	21	.103	N.Y.	
		Scarsella, Leslie George (Les)	1B15	18	.300	Cin	C
		Sisti, Sebastian Daniel (Sibby) (2B16)	3B102	123	.251	B	
4	8	Strincevich, Nicholas Mihailovich	P32	33	.116	A	
10	14	Sullivan, Joseph	P	36	.197	B	
1	1	Swift, Wm. (Bill)	P	4	.000	Pitt	
7	3	Tobin, James Anthony	P15	20	.279	Pitt	
		Warstler, Harold Burton (Rabbitt)	2B24	33	+.211	B	Chi
		West, Max Edward (1B36)	OF102	139	.261	B	
		Wietelmann, Wm. Frederick (SS3 3B9)	2B15	35	.195	B	
		Wilborn, Claude Edward	OF3	5	.000	A	C
0	0	Williams, Robert Fulton	P	5	.000	A	

WON 62 LOST 92 TG 154

NATIONAL LEAGUE

1941.

FINISHED 7th.

PCT. .403

BOSTON

CHAS. DILLON STENGEL

WON	LOST	NAME	POS.	G.	BA	FROM	TO
		Averill, Howard Earl	OF4	8	.118	DetA	C
0	1	Barnicle, George Bernard	P	1	.000	B	C
		Berres, Raymond Frederick	C	120	.201	B	
		Bray, Clarence Wilbur	OF3	4	.091	A	C
0	0	Carnett, Edwin Elliott	P	2	.000	A	
		Cooney, John Walter (1B4)	OF111	123	.319	B	
		Dahlgren, Ellsworth Tenney (Babe) (3B5)	1B39	44	+.235	NYA	Chi
		Demaree, Joseph Franklin (Frank)	OF28	48	+.230	xN.Y.	
		Dudra, John Joseph (1B1 SS1 3B5)	2B5	14	.360	A	C
6	8	Earley, Thomas Francis Aloysius	P33	34	.234	B	
6	12	Errickson, Richard Merriwell (Leif)	P	38	.178	B	
2	1	Ferrell, Wesley Cheek (Wes)	P	4	.500	Bkn	C
		Gremp, Lewis Edward (C3 2B6)	1B21	37	.240	B	
		Hassett, John Aloysius (Buddy)	1B99	118	.296	B	
1	6	Hutchings, John Richard Joseph	P	36	+.148	xCin	
10	11	Javery, Alva Wm.	P	34	.103	B	
7	15	Johnson, Arthur Henry	P43	44	.145	B	
5	4	LaManna, Frank (OF4)	P35	47	.281	B	
		Majeski, Henry	3B11	19	.145	B	
		Manno, Donald (1B1 3B3)	OF5	22	.167	B	C
		Masi, Philip Samuel	C83	87	.222	B	
		Miller, Edward Robert	SS	154	.239	B	
		Montgomery, Alvin Atlas	C30	42	.192	A	C
		Moore, Eugene Jr. (Gene)	OF110	129	.272	B	
0	0	Piechota, Aloysius Edward	P	1	.000	B	C
4	4	Posedel, Wm. John (Barnacle Bill)	P	18	.320	B	

WON	LOST	NAME	POS.	G.	BA	FROM	TO
		Preibisch, Melvin Adolphus	OF2	5	.000	B	C
		Roberge, Joseph Albert Armand (SS2 3B5)	2B46	55	.216	A	
		Ross, Chester James	OF12	29	.120	B	
		Rowell, Carvel Wm. (3B2 OF14)	2B112	138	.267	B	
7	16	Salvo, Manuel	P	35	.113	B	
		Sisti, Sebastian Daniel (Sibby) (2B2 SS2)	3B137	140	.259	B	
0	0	Strincevich, Micholas Mihailovich	P	3	+.000	B	Pitt
2	2	Sullivan, Joseph	P	16	+.067	B	Pitt
12	12	Tobin, James Anthony	P33	43	.184	B	
		Waner, Lloyd James (Little Poison)	OF15	19	+.412	xPitt.	Cin
		Waner, Paul Glee (Bis Poison)	OF71	95	+.279	xBkn	
		West, Max Edward	OF132	138	.277	B	
		Wietelmann, Wm. Frederick (SS5 3B2)	2B10	16	.091	B	

WON x59
LOST 89
TG 148
xOne win by forfeit

NATIONAL LEAGUE 1942. FINISHED 7th. PCT. .399

BOSTON

CHAS. DILLON STENGEL

WON	LOST	NAME	POS.	G.	BA	FROM	TO
		Cooney, John Walter (1B23)	OF54	74	.207	B	
		Cuccinello, Anthony Francis (Tony) (2B14)	3B20	40	.202	NY40	
		Demaree, Joseph Franklin (Frank)	OF49	64	.225	B	
		Detweiler, Robert Sterling	3B	12	.318	A	
0	0	Diehl, George Krause	P	1	.000	A	
3	6	Donovan, Willard Earl	P	31	.240	A	
6	11	Earley, Thomas Francis Aloysius	P	27	.118	B	
2	5	Errickson, Richard Merriwell (Leif)	P	21	+.125	B	Chi
		Fernandez, Froilan (Nanny) (OF44)	3B98	145	.255	A	
		Gremp, Lewis Edward (3B1)	1B62	72	.217	B	C
0	1	Hickey, James Robert	P	1	.000	A	
		Holmes, Thomas Francis	OF140	141	.278	A	
1	0	Hutchings, John Richard Joseph	P	20	.050	B	
12	16	Javery, Alva Wm.	P	42	.105	B	
0	0	Johnson, Arthur Henry	P	4	.000	B	C
		Kluttz, Clyde Franklin	C57	72	.267	A	
0	1	LaManna, Frank	P5	10	.000	B	C
		Lombardi, Ernesto Natali (Schnozz)	C85	105	.330	Cin	

WON	LOST	NAME	POS.	G.	BA	FROM	TO
		Masi, Philip Samuel (OF4)	C39	57	.218	B	
		Miller, Edward Robert	SS	142	.244	B	
		McElyea, Frank	OF1	7	.000	A	C
		Roberge, Joseph Albert Armand (3B27)	2B29	74	.215	B	
		Ross, Chester James	OF57	76	.195	B	
4	7	Sain, John Franklin	P	40	.074	A	
7	8	Salvo, Manuel	P	25	.122	B	
		Sandlock, Michael Joseph	SS	2	1.000	A	
		Sisti, Sebastian Daniel (Sibby) (OF1)	2B124	129	.211	B	
0	0	Spahn, Warren Edward	P	4	.167	A	
12	21	Tobin, James Anthony	P37	47	.246	B	
10	10	Tost, Louis Eugene	P	35	.176	A	
1	3	Wallace, James Harold	P	19	.143	A	
		Waner, Paul Glee (Big Poison)	OF94	114	.258	B	
		West, Max Edward (OF50)	1B85	134	.255	B	
		Wietelmann, Wm. Frederick (2B1)	SS11	13	.206	B	

WON 68
LOST 85
TG 153

NATIONAL LEAGUE 1943. FINISHED 6th. PCT. .444

BOSTON

CHAS. DILLON STENGEL

WON	LOST	NAME	POS.	G.	BA	FROM	TO
14	20	Andrews, Nathan Hardy	P	36	.156	ClevA41	
12	18	Barrett, Chas. Henry (Red)	P	38	.136	Cin40	
		Brubaker, Wilbur Lee (Bill) (1B3)	3B5	13	.421	Pitt40	C
		Burns, Joseph James (OF4)	3B34	52	.208	A	
0	0	Cardoni, Armand Joseph	P	11	.000	A	
		Creedon, Cornelius Stephen		5	.250	A	C
		Cuccinello, Anthony Francis (Tony) (2B2 SS1)	3B4	13	.000	B	ChiA
1	0	Dagenhard, John Douglas	P	2	.000	A	C
0	0	Diehl, George Krause	P	1	.000	B	C
1	0	Donovan, Willard Earl	P	7	.333	B	C
		Etchison, Clarence Hampton	1B6	10	.316	A	
0	1	Farrell, Major Kirby (P5)	1B69	85	.268	A	
		Gentile, Samuel Christopher		8	.250	A	C
		Geraghty, Benjamin Raymond (SS1 3B1)	2B1	8	.000	Bkn36	
		Heltzel, Wm. Wade	3B	29	.151	A	
		Holmes, Thomas Francis	OF	152	.270	B	
17	16	Javery, Alva Wm.	P	41	.163	B	
1	2	Jeffcoat, George Edward	P	8	.500	Bkn39	C
		Joost, Edwin David (2B60 SS1)	3B67	124	.185	Cin	
		Kluttz, Clyde Franklin	C55	66	.246	B	
0	2	Lindquist, Carl Emil	P	2	.000	A	
2	1	MacFayden, Daniel Knowles (Danny)	P	10	.250	WashA41	C

WON	LOST	NAME	POS.	G.	BA	FROM	TO
0	0	Martin, Raymond Joseph	P	2	.000	A	
		Masi, Philip Samuel	C73	80	.273	B	
		McCarthy, John Joseph (Mac)	1B	78	.304	NY41	
		Nieman, Elmer LeRoy	OF93	101	.251	A	
0	3	Odom, David Everett	P	22	.000	A	C
		Poland, Hugh Reid	C38	44	+.191	xN.Y.	
		Ross, Chester James	OF73	94	.218	B	
		Ryan, Cornelius Joseph (3B30)	2B100	132	.212	N.Y.	
0	0	Salvo, Manuel	P	1	+1.000	B	Phil
5	7	Salvo, Manuel	P	20	.214	(& return)	C
1	0	Stout, Allyn McClelland	P	9	.000	NY35	C
0	0	Talcott, LeRoy Everett	P	1	.000	A	C
14	14	Tobin, James Anthony (1B1)	P33	46	.280	B	
0	1	Tost, Louis Eugene	P	3	.000	B	
		Wietelmann, Wm. Frederick	SS	153	.215	B	
		Workman, Chas. Thomas (1B3 3B1)	OF149	153	.249	ClevA41	

WON 65
LOST 89
TG 154

NATIONAL LEAGUE — 1944. — FINISHED 6th. — PCT. .422

BOSTON

ROBERT HUNTER COLEMAN

WON	LOST	NAME	POS.	G.	BA	FROM	TO
16	15	Andrews, Nathan Hardy	P	37	.114	B	
9	16	Barrett, Chas. Henry (Red)	P	42	.173	B	
		Capri, Patrick Nicholas	2B1	7	.000	A	C
0	6	Cardoni, Armand Joseph	P22	29	.235	B	
		Clemens, Chester Spurgeon	OF7	19	.176	Bos39	C
		Culler, Richard Broadus	SS	8	.071	ChiA	
		Drews, Frank John	2B	46	.206	A	
		Etchison, Clarence Hampton	1B85	109	.214	B	C
		Geraghty, Benjamin Raymond (3B3)	2B4	11	.250	B	C
		Gladu, Roland Edwin (OF3)	3B15	21	.242	A	C
0	0	Hickey, James Robert	P	8	.000	Bos42	C
		Hofferth, Stewart Edward	C47	66	.200	A	
		Holmes, Thomas Francis	OF	155	.309	B	
		Huston, Warren Llewellyn (2B5 SS4)	3B20	33	.200	PhilA37	C
1	4	Hutchings, John Richard Joseph	P	14	.067	Bos42	
9	7	Hutchinson, Ira Kendall	P	40	.138	StL41	
10	19	Javery, Alva Wm.	P	40	.152	B	
1	2	Klopp, Stanley Harold	P	24	.286	A	C
		Kluttz, Clyde Franklin	C58	81	.279	B	
0	0	Lindquist, Carl Emil	P	5	.000	B	C
0	0	Macon, Max Cullen (P1 OF22)	1B72	106	.273	Bkn	
0	0	MacPherson, Harry Wm.	P	1	.000	A	C
		Masi, Philip Samuel (1B12 3B2)	C63	89	.275	B	
		Nieman, Elmer LeRoy	OF126	134	.265	B	
		Patton, Eugene Tunney		1	.000	A	C
		Phillips, Damon Roswell (SS60)	3B90	140	.258	Cin42	
		Poland, Hugh Reid	C6	8	.130	B	
1	1	Rich, Woodrow Earl	P	7	.125	BosA41	C
		Ross, Chester James	OF38	54	.227	B	C
		Ryan, Cornelius Joseph (3B14)	2B80	88	.295	B	
		Sandlock, Michael Joseph (SS7)	3B22	30	.100	Bos42	
		Shemo, Stephen Stanley (3B2)	2B16	18	.290	A	
18	19	Tobin, James Anthony	P43	62	.190	B	
		Wietelmann, Wm. Frederick (2B23 3B1)	SS103	125	.240	B	
0	0	Woodend, George Anthony	P	3	.000	A	C
		Workman, Chas. Thomas (3B19)	OF103	140	.208	B	
		Wright, Albert Owen	OF47	71	.256	ClevA35	C

WON 67
LOST 85
TG 152

NATIONAL LEAGUE — 1945. — FINISHED 6th. — PCT. .441

BOSTON

ROBERT HUNTER COLEMAN ADELPHIA LOUIS BISSONETTE

WON	LOST	NAME	POS.	G.	BA	FROM	TO
		Aderholt, Morris Woodrow (2B1)	OF24	31	+.333	xBkn	C
7	12	Andrews, Nathan Hardy	P21	22	.209	B	
2	3	Barrett, Chas. Henry (Red)	P	9	+.222	B	StL
0	0	Cardoni, Armand Joseph	P	3	.000	B	C
7	4	Cooper, Morton Cecil	P	20	+.231	xStL	
1	0	Cozart, Chas. Rhubin	P	5	.000	A	C
		Culler, Richard Broadus (3B6)	SS126	136	.262	B	
		Drews, Frank John	2B48	49	.204	B	C
2	1	Earley, Thomas Francis Aloysius	P11	13	.214	Bos42	C
0	2	Fette, Louis Henry Wm. (Lou)	P	5	.000	Bkn40	C
		Gillenwater, Carden Edison	OF140	144	.288	Bkn43	
4	8	Hendrickson, Donald Williamson	P	37	.167	A	
1	0	Heving, Joseph Wm.	P	3	.000	ClevA	C
		Hofferth, Stewart Edward	C45	50	.235	B	
		Holmes, Thomas Francis	OF	154	.352	B	
7	6	Hutchings, John Richard Joseph	P	57	.241	B	
2	3	Hutchinson, Ira Kendall	P	11	.000	B	C
2	7	Javery, Alva Wm.	P.	17	.207	B	
		Joost, Edwin David (3B16)	2B19	35	.248	Bos43	
		Kluttz, Clyde Franklin	C19	25	+.296	B	N.Y.
6	3	Lee, Wm. Crutcher Jr. (Bill)	P	16	+.129	xPhil	

WON	LOST	NAME	POS.	G.	BA	FROM	TO
7	11	Logan, Robert Dean	P	34	.213	Cin41	C
		Mack, Joseph John	1B65	66	.231	A	C
		Masi, Philip Samuel (1B7)	C95	114	.272	B	
		Medwick, Joseph Michael (Ducky) (1B15)	OF38	66	+.284	xN.Y.	
		Nelson, Thomas Cousineau (2B12)	3B20	40	.165	A	C
		Nieman, Elmer LeRoy	OF57	97	.247	B	C
0	1	Pyle, Herbert Ewald	P	4	+.333	xN.Y.	C
		Ramsey, Wm. Thrace	OF43	78	.292	A	C
0	1	Schacker, Harold	P	6	.000	A	C
		Shemo, Stephen Stanley (SS1 3B3)	2B12	17	.239	B	C
		Shupe, Vincent Wm.	1B77	78	.269	A	C
1	4	Singelton, Bert Elmer	P	7	.000	A	
9	14	Tobin, James Anthony	P27	41	.143	B	DetA
		Ulisney, Michael Edward	C4	11	.389	A	C
		Wallen, Norman Edward	3B	4	.133	A	C
1	0	Wallace, James Harold	P5	6	.000	Bos42	
		Wentzel, Stanley Aaron	OF	4	.211	A	C
0	2	Whitcher, Robert Arthur	P6	9	.333	A	C
0	0	Wietelmann, Wm. Frederick (P1 SS39 3B2)	2B87	123	.271	B	
		Workman, Chas. Thomas (OF24)	3B107	139	.274	B	
8	3	Wright, Henderson Edward	P	15	.128	A	

WON 81 LOST 72 TG 153

NATIONAL LEAGUE 1946. FINISHED 4th. PCT. .529

BOSTON

WM. HARRISON SOUTHWORTH

WON	LOST	NAME	POS.	G.	BA	FROM	TO
2	4	Barrett, Francis Joseph	P	23	.000	BosA	
		Barrett, John Joseph	OF17	24	+.233	xPitt	C
		Brady, Robert Jay	C1	3	.200	A	
13	11	Cooper, Morton Cecil	P	28	.209	B	
		Culler, Richard Broadus	SS132	134	.255	B	
		Dark, Alvin Ralph (OF1)	SS12	15	.231	A	
		Detweiler, Robert Sterling (Ducky)		1	.000	Bos42	C
		Fernandez, Froilan (Nanny) (SS18 OF14)	3B81	115	.255	Bos42	
		Gillenwater, Carden Edison	OF78	99	.228	B	
0	1	Hendrickson, Donald Williamson	P	2	.000	B	C
		Herman, Wm. Jennings Bryan (Billy) (1B22 3B5)	2B44	75	+.306	xBkn	
		Hofferth, Stewart Edward	C15	20	.207	B	C
		Holmes, Thomas Francis	OF146	149	.310	B	
		Hopp, John Leonard (OF58)	1B68	129	.333	StL	
0	1	Hutchings, John Richard Joseph	P	1	.000	B	C
0	1	Javery, Alva Wm.	P	2	.000	B	C
6	5	Johnson, Silas Kenneth	P	28	+.135	xPhil	
0	1	Konstanty, Casimer James (Jim)	P	10	.000	Cin44	
10	9	Lee, Wm. Crutcher Jr. (Bill)	P	25	.170	B	
		Litwhiler, Daniel Webster (3B2)	OF65	79	+.292	xStL	
		Masi, Philip Samuel	C124	133	.267	B	
		McCarthy, John Joseph (Mac)	1B	2	.143	Bos43	
		McCormick, Myron Winthrop	OF48	59	+.262	xCin	
1	0	Mulligan, Richarc Chas.	P	4	+.000	xPhil	
		Neill, Thomas White	OF	13	.267	A	
2	5	Niggeling, John Arnold	P	8	.111	xWashA	C
		O'Dea, James Kenneth (Ken)	C	12	+.219	xStL	C
		Padgett, Donald Wilson (Don)	C26	44	+.255	xBkn	
		Phillips, Damon Roswell		2	.500	Bos44	C
		Poland, Hugh Reid	C2	4	.167	Bos44	
2	0	Posedel, Wm. John (Barnacle Bill)	P	19	.000	Bos41	C
1	0	Reid, Earl Percy	P	2	.000	A	C
		Roberge, Joseph Albert Armand	3B	48	.231	Bos42	C
1	1	Roser, Emerson Corey	P	14	.000	xN.Y.A	C
		Rowell, Carvel Wm.	OF85	95	.280	Bos41	
		Ryan, Cornelius Joseph (3B24)	2B120	143	.241	Bos44	
20	14	Sain, John Franklin	P37	40	.298	Bos42	
		Sanders, Raymond Floyd	1B77	80	.243	StL	
0	1	Singleton, Bert Elmer	P15	16	.000	B	
		Sisti, Sebastian Daniel (Sibby)	3B	1	.000	Bos42	
8	5	Spahn, Warren Edward	P	24	.163	Bos42	
3	3	Wallace, James Harold	P	27	.056	B	C
		West, Max Edward	1B	1	+.000	Bos42	Cin
0	1	White, Ernest Daniel	P12	14	.250	StL43	
0	0	Wietelmann, Wm. Frederick (P3 2B4 3B8)	SS16	44	.205	B	
0	0	Williams, Robert Fulton	P	1	.000	Bos40	C
		Workman, Chas. Thomas	OF12	25	+.167	B	Pitt
12	9	Wright, Henderson Edward	P	36	.305	B	

WON 86 LOST 68 TG 154

NATIONAL LEAGUE 1947. FINISHED 3rd. PCT. .558

BOSTON

WM. HARRISON SOUTHWORTH

WON	LOST	NAME	POS.	G.	BA	FROM	TO
11	12	Barrett, Chas. Henry (Red)	P	36	.111	StL.	
2	0	Beazley, John Andrew	P	9	.000	StL	
		Brady, Robert Jay		1	.000	B	C
		Camelli, Henry Richard	C51	52	.193	Pitt	C
2	5	Cooper, Morton Cecil	P	10	+.000	B	N.Y.
		Culler, Richard Broadus	SS	77	.248	B	
0	1	Elliott, Herbert Glenn	P	11	.500	A	

WON	LOST	NAME	POS.	G.	BA	FROM	TO
		Elliott, Robert Irving	3B148	150	.317	Pitt	
		Fernandez, Froilan (Nanny) (3B6 OF8)	SS62	83	.206	B	
		Holmes, Thomas Francis	OF147	150	.309	B	
		Hopp, John Leonard	OF125	134	.288	B	
6	8	Johnson, Silas Kenneth	P	36	.033	B	C
2	3	Karl, Anton Andrew	P	27	.167	Phil	C
4	4	LanFranconi, Walter Oswald	P36	37	.000	Chi41	C
0	0	Lanning, John Young	P	3	.000	Pitt	C
		Litwhiler, Daniel Webster	OF66	91	.261	B	
0	0	Macon, Max Cullen	P	1	.000	Bos44	C
1	0	Martin, Raymond Joseph	P	1	.000	Bos43	
		Masi, Philip Samuel	C123	126	.304	B	
0	0	Mulligan, Richard Chas.	P	1	.000	B	C
		Murtaugh, Daniel Edward (3B2)	2B2	3	.125	Phil	
		McCormick, Frank Andrew (Buck)	1B46	81	+.354	xPhil	
		McCormick, Myron Winthrop	OF79	92	.285	B	
		Neill, Thomas White	OF2	7	.200	B	C
		Rowell, Carvel Wm. (2B7 3B4)	OF100	113	.276	B	
		Ryan, Cornelius Joseph (SS1)	2B150	150	.265	B	
21	12	Sain, John Franklin	P38	40	.346	B	
5	3	Shoun, Clyde Mitchell	P	26	+.158	xCin	
		Sisti, Sebastian Daniel (Sibby) (2B1)	SS51	56	.281	B	
21	10	Spahn, Warren Edward	P40	41	.163	B	
		Torgeson, Clifford Earl	1B117	128	.281	A	
8	7	Voiselle, Wm. Symmes	P	22	+.170	xN.Y.	
0	0	White, Ernest Daniel	P	1	1.000	B	
3	3	Wright, Henderson Edward	P	23	.130	B	

WON 91 NATIONAL LEAGUE FINISHED 1st.
LOST 62
TG 153 1948 PCT. .595

BOSTON

WM. HARRISON SOUTHWORTH

WON	LOST	NAME	POS.	G.	BA	FROM	TO
0	0	Antonelli, John August	P	4	.000	A	
7	8	Barrett, Chas. Henry (Red)	P	34	.179	B	
0	1	Beazley, John Andrew	P	3	.000	B	
11	5	Bickford, Vernon Edgell	P	33	.204	A	
		Burris, Paul Robert	C	2	.500	A	
		Conatser, Clinton Astor	OF76	90	.277	A	
		Dark, Alvin Ralph	SS133	137	.322	Bos46	
1	0	Elliott, Herbert Glenn	P	1	.000	B	
		Elliott, Robert Irving	3B150	151	.283	B	
		Heath, John Geoffrey (Jeff)	OF106	115	.319	StLA	
8	2	Hogue, Robert Clinton	P	40	.095	A	
		Holmes, Thomas Francis	OF137	139	.325	B	
		Litwhiler, Daniel Webster	OF8	13	+.273	B	Cin

WON	LOST	NAME	POS.	G.	BA	FROM	TO
1	0	Lyons, Albert Harold (OF4)	P7	16	.167	Pitt	C
		McCormick, Frank Andrew (Buck)	1B50	75	.250	B	C
		McCormick, Myron Winthrop	OF100	115	.303	B	
0	0	Martin, Raymond Joseph	P	2	.000	B	C
		Masi, Philip Samuel	C109	113	.253	B	
5	2	Potter, Nelson Thomas	P	18	.379	xPhilA	
1	1	Prendergast, James Bartholomew	P	10	.000	A	C
		Rickert, Marvin August	OF	3	+.231	xCin	
		Russell, James Wm.	OF84	89	.264	Pitt	
		Ryan, Cornelius Joseph (3B4)	2B40	51	.213	B	
24	15	Sain, John Franklin	P42	43	.217	B	
		Salkeld, Wm. Franklin	C59	78	.242	Pitt	
		Sanders, Raymond Floyd		5	.250	Bos46	
5	1	Shoun, Clyde Mitchell	P	36	.190	B	
		Sisti, Sebastian Daniel (Sibby) (SS26)	2B44	83	.244	B	
15	12	Spahn, Warren Edward	P	36	.167	B	
		Stanky, Edward Raymond	2B66	67	.320	Bkn	
		Sturgeon, Robert Harwood (SS4 3B4)	2B18	34	.218	Chi	C
		Torgeson, Clifford Earl	1B129	134	.253	B	
13	13	Voiselle, Wm. Symmes	P	37	.097	B	
0	2	White, Ernest Daniel	P15	16	.000	B	C
0	0	Wright, Henderson Edward	P	3	.000	B	

WON 75 NATIONAL LEAGUE FINISHED 4th.
LOST 79
TG 154 1949. PCT. .487

BOSTON

WM. HARRISON SOUTHWORTH JOHN WALTER COONEY

WON	LOST	NAME	POS.	G.	BA	FROM	TO
3	7	Antonelli, John August	P	22	.120	B	
1	1	Barrett, Chas. Henry (Red)	P	23	.200	B	C
0	0	Beazley, John Andrew	P	1	.000	B	C
16	11	Bickford, Vernon Edgell	P	37	.185	B	
		Conatser, Clinton Astor	OF44	53	.263	B	C
		Crandall, Delmar Wesley	C63	67	.263	A	
		Dark, Alvin Ralph (3B4)	SS125	130	.276	B	
3	4	Elliott, Herbert Glenn	P	22	.059	B	C
		Elliott, Robert Irving	3B130	139	.280	B	
		Fletcher, Elburt Preston	1B121	122	.261	Pitt47	C
6	4	Hall, Robert Lewis (Elbie)	P	31	.364	A	
		Heath, John Geoffrey (Jeff)	OF31	36	.306	B	C
2	2	Hogue, Robert Clinton	P	33	.286	B	
		Holmes, Thomas Francis	OF103	117	.266	B	
		Kuczek, Stanislaw Leo		1	1.000	A	C
		Lakeman, Albert Wesley	1B2	3	.167	Phil	
		Livingston, Thompson Orville	C22	28	+.234	xN.Y.	
		Masi, Philip Samuel	C	37	+.210	B	Pitt
6	11	Potter, Nelson Thomas	P	41	.130	B	C

WON	LOST	NAME	POS.	G.	BA	FROM	TO
		Reiser, Harold Patrick (Pete) (3B4)	OF63	84	.272	Bkn	
		Rickert, Marvin August (1B12)	OF75	100	.292	B	
		Russell, James Wm.	OF120	130	.231	B	
		Ryan, Cornelius Joseph (1B3 2B16 SS18)	3B25	85	.250	B	
10	17	Sain, John Franklin	P37	39	.206	B	
		Salkeld, Wm. Franklin	C63	66	.255	B	
		Sanders, Raymond Floyd	1B7	9	.143	B	C
		Sauer, Edward	OF71	79	+.266	xStL	C
0	0	Shoun, Clyde Mitchell	P	1	.000	B	ChiA
		Sisti, Sebastian Daniel (Sibby) (2B21 SS18 3B1)	OF48	101	.257	B	
21	14	Spahn, Warren Edward	P38	40	.162	B	
		Stanky, Edward Raymond	2B135	138	.285	B	
		Thompson, Donald Newlin	OF2	7	.182	A	
		Torgeson, Clifford Earl	1B	25	.260	B	
7	8	Voiselle, Wm. Symmes	P	30	.115	B	

WON 83 NATIONAL LEAGUE FINISHED 4th.
LOST 71
TG 154 1950. PCT. .539

BOSTON

WM. HARRISON SOUTHWORTH

WON	LOST	NAME	POS.	G.	BA	FROM	TO
		Addis, Robert Gordon	OF7	16	.250	A	
2	3	Antonelli, John August	P	20	.125	B	
19	14	Bickford, Vernon Edgell	P	40	.138	B	
		Burris, Paul Robert	C8	10	.174	Bos48	
7	7	Chipman, Robert Howard	P	27	.154	Chi	
0	1	Cole, David Bruce	P	4	.000	A	
		Cooper, Wm. Walker	C88	102	+.329	xCin	
		Crandall, Delmar Wesley (1B1)	C75	79	.220	B	
0	2	Donovan, Richard Edward	P	10	.167	A	
		Elliott, Robert Irving	3B137	142	.305	B	
		Gordon, Sidney (3B10)	OF123	134	.304	N.Y.	
0	2	Haefner, Milton Arnold	P	8	.286	xChiA	C
0	2	Hall, Robert Lewis	P	21	.083	B	
		Hartsfield, Roy Thomas	2B96	107	.277	A	
3	5	Hogue, Robert Clinton	P	36	.231	B	
		Holmes, Thomas Francis	OF88	105	.298	B	
		Jethroe, Samuel	OF	141	.273	A	
2	0	Johnson, Ernest Thorwald	P	16	.500	A	
		Kerr, John Joseph	SS	155	.227	N.Y.	
		Linden, Walter Chas.	C	3	.400	A	C
0	0	Manville, Richard Wesley	P	1	.000	A	
		Marshall, Willard Warren	OF85	105	.235	N.Y.	
		Mauch, Eugene Wm. (SS5 3B7)	2B28	48	.231	Chi	
		Olmo, Luis Rodriguez (3B1)	OF55	69	.227	Bkn	
		Reiser, Harold Patrick (Pete) (3B1)	OF24	53	.205	B	
4	3	Roy, Norman Brooks	P	19	.167	A	C
		Ryan, Cornelius Joseph	2B	20	+.194	B	Cin
20	13	Sain, John Franklin	P	37	.206	B	
		Sisti, Sebastian Daniel (Sibby) (1B1 2B19 3B13 OF1)	SS23	69	.171	B	
21	17	Spahn, Warren Edward	P	41	.217	B	
5	2	Surkont, Maxim Constantine	P	9	.435	ChiA	
		Torgeson, Clifford Earl	1B	156	.290	B	
		Verban, Emil Matthew	2B2	4	+.000	xChi	C
0	0	Wall, Murray Wesley	P	1	.000	A	
0	0	Walters, Wm. Henry Jr. (Bucky)	P	1	.000	Cin	C

WON 76 NATIONAL LEAGUE FINISHED 4th.
LOST 78
TG 154 1951. PCT. .494

BOSTON

WM. HARRISON SOUTHWORTH THOMAS FRANCIS HOLMES

WON	LOST	NAME	POS.	G.	BA	FROM	TO
		Addis, Robert Gordon	OF46	85	.276	B	
11	9	Bickford, Vernon Edgell	P	25	.115	B	
0	0	Burdette, Selva Lewis	P	3	.000	NYA	
4	3	Chipman, Robert Howard	P	33	.100	B	
2	4	Cole, David Bruce	P	23	.353	B	
		Cooper, Wm. Walker	C90	109	.313	B	
0	1	Donnelly, Sylvester Urban (Blix)	P	6	.000	Phil	C
0	0	Donovan, Richard Edward	P	8	.333	B	
		Elliott, Robert Irving	3B127	136	.285	B	
0	1	Estock, George John	P	37	.286	A	C
		Gordon, Sidney (3B34)	OF122	150	.287	B	
		Hartsfield, Roy Thomas	2B114	120	.271	B	
0	0	Hogue, Robert Clinton	P	3	.500	B	StLA
		Holmes, Thomas Francis MGR.	OF3	27	.172	B	
		Jethroe, Samuel	OF140	148	.280	B	
		Kerr, John Joseph (2B5)	SS63	69	.186	B	C
		Logan, John	SS58	62	.219	A	
		Marquez, Luis Angel	OF43	68	.197	A	
		Marshall, Willard Warren	OF	136	.281	B	
		Mauch, Eugene Wm. (2B2 3B3)	SS10	19	.100	B	
		Mueller, Ray Coleman	C23	28	.157	Pitt	C
11	8	Nichols, Chester Raymond Jr.	P	33	.137	A	
		Olmo, Luis Rodriguez	OF16	21	.196	B	C
2	0	Paine, Phillips Steere	P	21	.000	A	
5	13	Sain, John Franklin	P	26	.212	B	NYA
0	2	Schacht, Sidney	P	5	.000	xStLA	C
		Sisti, Sebastian Daniel (1B1 2B52 3B6 OF1)	SS55	114	.279	B	
22	14	Spahn, Warren Edward	P39	42	.190	B	
		St.Claire, Edward Joseph	C62	72	.282	A	
12	16	Surkont, Maxim Constantine	P	37	.151	B	

WON	LOST	NAME	POS.	G.	BA	FROM	TO
		Thorpe, Benjamin Robert		2	.500	A	
		Torğeson, Clifford Earl	1B	155	.263	B	
7	7	Wilson, James Alger	P	20	.179	Phil A49	

WON 64 LOST 89 TG 153

NATIONAL LEAGUE

1952.

FINISHED 7th.

PCT. .418

BOSTON

THOMAS FRANCIS HOLMES CHAS. JOHN GRIMM

WON	LOST	NAME	POS.	G.	BA	FROM	TO
7	12	Bickford, Vernon Edgell	P	26	.176	B	
6	11	Burdette, Selva Lewis	P	45	.114	B	
		Burris, Paul Robert	C50	55	.220	Bos50	
1	1	Chipman, Robert Howard	P	29	.400	B	C
		Clarkson, James (3B2)	SS6	14	.200	A	C
1	1	Cole, David Bruce	P	22	.000	B	
0	3	Conley, Donald Eugene	P	4	.400	A	
		Cooper, Wm. Walker	C89	102	.235	B	
		Crowe, George Daniel	1B55	73	.258	A	
		Cusick, John Peter (3B3)	SS28	49	.167	Chi	C
		Daniels, Harold Jack	OF87	106	.187	A	C
		Dittmer, John Douglas	2B90	93	.193	A	
0	2	Donovan, Richard Edward	P	7	.000	B	
		Gordon, Sidney (3B2)	OF142	144	.289	B	
		Hartsfield, Roy Thomas	2B29	38	.262	B	C
0	0	Hoover, Richard Lloyd	P	2	.000	A	C
3	5	Jester, Virgil Milton	P	19	.211	A	
		Jethroe, Samuel	OF	151	.232	B	
6	3	Johnson, Ernest Thorwald	P	29	.091	Bos50	
1	4	Jones, Sheldon Leslie	P	39	.125	N.Y.	
		Klaus, Wm. Joseph	SS4	7	.000	A	
		Logan, John	SS	117	.283	B	
		Marshall, Willard Warren	OF16	21	+.227	B	Cin
		Mathews, Edwin Lee	3B142	145	.242	A	
		Reed, Wm. Joseph	2B14	15	.250	A	C
		Sisti, Sebastian Daniel (Sibby) (SS18 3B9 OF23)	2B33	90	.212	B	
14	19	Spahn, Warren Edward	P40	52	.161	B	
		St.Claire, Edward Joseph	C34	39	.213	B	
12	13	Surkont, Maxim Constantine	P	31	.111	B	
1	1	Thiel, Maynard Bert	P	4	.000	A	C
		Thorpe, Benjamin Robert	OF72	81	.260	B	
		Torgeson, Clifford Earl (OF5)	1B105	122	.230	B	
		Whisenant, Thomas Peter	OF14	24	.192	A	
12	14	Wilson, James Alger	P	33	.163	B	

CLUB RECORD

NATIONAL LEAGUE

BROOKLYN

YEAR	TG	WON	LOST	PCT.	FINISHED	MANAGER
1876	56	21	35	.375	6(MUTUALS)	G. Wm. H. Cammeyer
1877-1889		OUT OF LEAGUE				
1890	129	86	43	.667	1	Wm. Henry McGunnigle
1891	137	61	76	.445	6	John Montgomery Ward
1892	154	95	59	.617	3	John Montgomery Ward
1893	128	65	63	.508	x6(Cin)	David Luther Foutz
1894	131	70	61	.534	5	David Luther Foutz
1895	131	71	60	.542	x5(Bos)	David Luther Foutz
1896	131	58	73	.443	x9(Wash)	David Luther Foutz
1897	132	61	71	.462	x6(Wash)	Wm. S. Barnie
1898	145	54	91	.372	10	Wm. S. Barnie Michael Joseph Griffin Chas. Hercules Ebbets
1899	103	88	42	.667	1	Edward Hugh Hanlon
1900	136	82	54	.603	1	Edward Hugh Hanlon
1901	136	79	57	.581	3	Edward Hugh Hanlon
1902	138	75	63	.543	2	Edward Hugh Hanlon
1903	136	70	66	.515	5	Edward Hugh Hanlon
1904	153	56	97	.366	6	Edward Hugh Hanlon
1905	152	48	104	.316	8(Last)	Edward Hugh Hanlon
1906	152	66	86	.434	5	Patrick Joseph Donovan
1907	148	65	83	.439	5	Patrick Joseph Donovan
1908	154	53	101	.344	7	Patrick Joseph Donovan
1909	153	55	98	.359	6	Harry G. Lumley
1910	154	64	90	.416	6	Wm. Frederick Dahlen
1911	150	64	86	.427	7	Wm. Frederick Dahlen
1912	153	58	95	.379	7	Wm. Frederick Dahlen
1913	149	65	84	.436	6	Wm. Frederick Dahlen
1914	154	75	79	.487	5	Wilbert Robinson
1915	152	80	72	.527	3	Wilbert Robinson
1916	154	94	60	.610	1	Wilbert Robinson
1917	151	70	81	.464	7	Wilbert Robinson
1918	126	57	69	.452	5	Wilbert Robinson
1919	140	69	71	.493	5	Wilbert Robinson
1920	154	93	61	.604	1	Wilbert Robinson
1921	152	77	75	.507	5	Wilbert Robinson
1922	154	76	78	.494	6	Wilbert Robinson
1923	154	76	78	.494	6	Wilbert Robinson
1924	154	92	62	.597	2	Wilbert Robinson
1925	153	68	85	.444	x6(Phil)	Wilbert Robinson
1926	153	71	82	.464	6	Wilbert Robinson
1927	153	65	88	.425	6	Wilbert Robinson
1928	153	77	76	.503	6	Wilbert Robinson
1929	153	70	83	.458	6	Wilbert Robinson
1930	154	86	68	.558	4	Wilbert Robinson
1931	152	79	73	.520	4	Wilbert Robinson
1932	154	81	73	.526	3	Max George Carey
1933	153	65	88	.425	6	Max George Carey
1934	152	71	81	.467	6	Chas. Dillon Stengel
1935	153	70	83	.458	5	Chas. Dillon Stengel

1936	154	67	87	.435	7	Chas. Dillon Stengel
1937	153	62	91	.405	6	Burleigh Arland Grimes
1938	149	69	80	.463	7	Burleigh Arland Grimes
1939	153	84	69	.549	3	Leo Ernest Durocher
1940	153	88	65	.575	2	Leo Ernest Durocher
1941	154	100	54	.649	1	Leo Ernest Durocher
1942	154	104	50	.675	2	Leo Ernest Durocher
1943	153	81	72	.529	3	Leo Ernest Durocher
1944	154	63	91	.409	7	Leo Ernest Durocher
1945	154	87	67	.565	3	Leo Ernest Durocher
1946	156	96	60	.615	2	Leo Ernest Durocher
1947	154	94	60	.610	1	{Clyde LeRoy Sukeforth Burton Edwin Shotton
1948	154	84	70	.545	3	{Leo Ernest Durocher Burton Edwin Shotton
1949	154	97	57	.630	1	Burton Edwin Shotton
1950	154	89	65	.578	2	Burton Edwin Shotton
1951	157	97	60	.618	2	Chas. Walter Dressen
1952	153	96	57	.627	1	Chas. Walter Dressen
1953	154	105	49	.682	1	Chas. Walter Dressen
1954	154	92	62	.597	2	Walter Emmons Alston
1955	153	98	55	.641	1	Walter Emmons Alston
1956	154	93	61	.604	1	Walter Emmons Alston
1957	154	84	70	.545	3	Walter Emmons Alston

WON 86 NATIONAL LEAGUE FINISHED 1st.
LOST 43
TG 129 1890. PCT. .667

BROOKLYN

WM. HENRY McGUNNIGLE

WON	LOST	NAME	POS.	G.	BA	FROM	TO
1	0	Baldwin, Chas. Busted (Lady)	P	2	.000	Det88	BuffPL
		Burns, Thomas P.	OF116	119	.284	BknAA	
		Bushong, Albert John	C15	16	.234	BknAA	C
22	11	Caruthers, Robert Lee (P34)	OF39	71	.265	BknAA	
		Clark, Robert H.	C42	43	.218	BknAA	
		Collins, Hubert B.	2B	129	.278	BknAA	
		Corkhill, John Stewart (Pop)	OF48	51	.225	BknAA	
		Daly, Thomas Peter	C69	82	.243	Wash	
		Donovan, Patrick Joseph	OF	26	+.380	xBos	
3	1	Foutz, David Luther (P4)	1B113	129	.302	BknAA	
3	5	Hughes, Michael F.	P	8	.043	BknAA	AthAA
31	11	Lovett, Thomas Joseph	P43	44	.201	BknAA	
		O'Brien, Wm. D. (Darby)	OF	85	.314	BknAA	
		Pinckney, George Burton	3B	126	.309	BknAA	
		Reynolds, Chas. L.	(DID NOT PLAY)			BknAA	C
		Smith, George J. (Germany)	SS	129	.191	BknAA	
		Stallings, George Tweedy	C	4	.000	A	
26	15	Terry, Wm. J. (Adonis) (P44)	OF54	99	.278	BknAA	

WON 61 NATIONAL LEAGUE FINISHED 6th.
LOST 76
TG 137 1891. PCT. .445

BROOKLYN

JOHN MONTGOMERY WARD

WON	LOST	NAME	POS.	G.	BA	FROM	TO
		Burdock, John Joseph	2B	3	.083	BknAA88	C
		Burns, Thomas P.	OF113	122	.281	B	
17	17	Caruthers, Robert Lee	P34	47	.291	B	
		Collins, Hubert B. (OF35)	2B72	107	.284	B	
		Dailey, Cornelius F. (Con)	C49	53	.296	BknPL	
		Daly, Thomas Peter	C28	61	.293	B	
		Ely, Frederick Wm.	SS27	31	.171	SyrAA	
		Esterbrook, Thomas Jefferson (Dude)	2B	3	.375	N.Y.	C
3	3	Foutz, David Luther (P6)	1B123	130	.262	B	
		Griffin, Michael Joseph	OF	133	.272	PhilPL	
8	14	Hemming, George Earl	P	22	.169	BknPL	
3	9	Inks, Albert Preston (Bert)	P	13	.272	A	
		Kinslow, Thomas F.	C	59	.238	BknPL	
24	18	Lovett, Thomas Joseph	P	42	.184	B	
		O'Brien, John J.	2B	43	.251	A	
		O'Brien, Wm. D. (Darby)	OF	102	.260	B	
		Pinckney, George Burton	3B129	135	.278	B	

WON	LOST	NAME	POS.	G.	BA	FROM	TO
6	15	Terry, Wm. J. (Adonis)	P23	25	.202	B	
		Ward, John Montgomery MGR. (2B18)	SS86	104	.287	BknPL	

WON 95
LOST 59
TG 154

NATIONAL LEAGUE

1892.

FINISHED 3rd.

PCT. .617

BROOKLYN

JOHN MONTGOMERY WARD

WON	LOST	NAME	POS.	G.	BA	FROM	TO
		Brouthers, Dennis (Dan)	1B	152	.335	BosAA	
		Burns, Thomas P.	OF127	139	.310	B	
		Collins, Hubert B.	OF	20	.302	B	C
		Corcoran, Thomas W.	SS	151	.237	AthAA	
		Dailey, Cornelius F. (Con)	C70	78	.243	B	
		Daly, Thomas Peter (C23 OF30)	3B58	120	.255	B	
12	9	Foutz, David Luther (P22)	OF26	53	.199	B	
		Griffin, Michael Joseph	OF127	129	.276	B	
31	13	Haddock, George Silas	P	44	.173	BosAA	
7	10	Hart, Wm. Franklin	P25	29	.187	AthAA87	
5	1	Inks, Albert Preston (Bert)	P	9	+.375	B	Wash
		Joyce, Wm. Michael (Scrappy)	3B94	97	.249	BosAA	
13	8	Kennedy, Wm. V. (Brickyard)	P	22	.188	A	
		Kinslow, Thomas F.	C	63	.309	B	
		O'Brien, Wm. D. (Darby)	OF	121	.245	B	C
27	18	Stein, Edward F.	P	45	.218	Chi	
		Ward, John Montgomery MGR.	2B	148	.273	B	

WON 65
LOST 63
TG 128

NATIONAL LEAGUE

1893.

FINISHED 6th.
(TIED WITH CINCINNATI)
PCT. .508

BROOKLYN

DAVID LUTHER FOUTZ

WON	LOST	NAME	POS.	G.	BA	FROM	TO
		Brouthers, Dennis (Dan)	1B	75	.348	B	
		Burns, Thomas P.	OF	107	.279	B	
		Corcoran, Thomas W.	SS	115	.281	B	
0	2	Crane, Edward Nicholas	P	6	+.600	xN.Y.	C
		Dailey, Cornelius F. (Con)	C50	58	.286	B	
		Daly, Thomas Peter (3B44)	2B82	126	.306	B	
6	6	Daub, Daniel Wm.	P	12	.205	Cin	
		Foutz, David Luther MGR. (1B54)	OF76	130	.272	B	
		Griffin, Michael Joseph	OF	93	.304	B	
8	10	Haddock, George Silas	P18	26	.250	B	
		Hatfield, Gilbert	3B	33	.315	WashAA91	
		Keeler, Wm. Henry	3B	19	+.340	xN.Y.	
25	18	Kennedy, Wm. V. (Brickyard)	P	45	.275	B	
		Kinslow, Thomas F.	C75	77	.259	B	
		LaChance, George	C	11	.176	A	
3	6	Lovett, Thomas Joseph	P	18	.212	Bkn91	
		Richardson, Daniel (Denny)	2B44	51	.246	Wash	
		Shoch, George Quintus (3B36)	OF42	93	.276	Balt	
4	7	Sharrott, George Oscar	P	11	.207	A	
19	14	Stein, Edward F.	P	35	.243	B	
		Stovey, Harry Duffield	OF	45	+.266	xBalt	C

WON 70
LOST 61
TG 131

NATIONAL LEAGUE

1894.

FINISHED 5th.

PCT. .534

BROOKLYN

DAVID LUTHER FOUTZ

WON	LOST	NAME	POS.	G.	BA	FROM	TO
		Anderson, John Joseph	OF15	16	.301	A	
		Browning, Louis Roger (Pete)	OF	1	+1.000	xStL	C
		Burns, Thomas P.	OF	126	.358	B	
		Corcoran, Thomas W.	SS	129	.302	B	
		Dailey, Cornelius F. (Con)	C58	65	.269	B	
		Daly, Thomas Peter	2B	123	.338	B	
10	15	Daub, Daniel Wm.	P26	28	.226	B	
		Earle, Wm. Moffat (2B1)	C12	14	+.321	xLvlle	C
		Foutz, David Luther MGR.	1B	73	.310	B	
3	4	Gastright, Henry Carl	P	16	.184	Bos	
		Gilbert, Peter	3B	6	+.000	Balt92	Lvlle
		Griffin, Michael Joseph	OF	106	.365	B	
24	20	Kennedy, Wm. V. (Brickyard)	P	44	.300	B	
		Kinslow, Thomas F.	C	61	.298	B	
0	0	Korwan, James	P	1	.000	A	
		LaChance, George	1B56	65	.329	B	
4	3	Lucid, Cornelius Conrad (Con)	P	10	.212	Lvlle	
		Shoch, George Quintus	OF34	63	.320	B	
1	1	Sharrott, George Oscar	P	3	.570	B	C
		Shindle, Wm.	3B	117	.300	Balt	
0	1	Sommerville, Andrew	P	1	.000	A	C
26	14	Stein, Edward F.	P	41	.260	B	
		Treadway, George B.	OF	122	.336	Balt	
2	3	Underwood, Frederick G.	P	7	.389	A	C

WON 71*
LOST 60
TG 131

NATIONAL LEAGUE

1895.

FINISHED 5th.
(TIED WITH BOSTON)
PCT. .542

BROOKLYN

DAVID LUTHER FOUTZ

WON	LOST	NAME	POS.	G.	BA	FROM	TO

WON	LOST	NAME	POS.	G.	BA	FROM	TO
4	3	Abbey, Bert Wood	P	8	+.263	xChi	
		Anderson, John Joseph	OF	103	.296	B	
		Burns, Thomas P.	OF	17	+.192	B	N.Y.
		Burrell, Frank Andrew (Buster)	C	10	.160	NY91	
		Corcoran, Thomas W.	SS	128	.277	B	
0	0	Cronin, John J. (Jack)	P	2	.500	A	
		Dailey, Cornelius F. (Con)	C38	40	.233	B	
		Daly, Thomas Peter	2B	122	.289	B	
10	10	Daub, Daniel Wm.	P	20	.217	B	
		Foutz, David Luther MGR.	OF20	28	.304	B	
		Griffin, Michael Joseph	OF131	132	.335	B	
		Grim, John Helm (Jack)	C89	90	.288	Lvlle	
11	15	Gumbert, Addison Courtney (Ad)	P	26	.344	Pitt	
		Hines, Henry F.	OF	2	.250	A	C
19	13	Kennedy, Wm. V. (Brickyard)	P	36	.321	B	
		LaChance, George	1B125	128	.320	B	
11	6	Lucid, Cornelius Conrad (Con)	P18	21	+.283	B	Phil
		Mulvey, Joseph H.	3B	13	.327	Wash93	C
0	0	McDougal, John A.	P	5	.000	A	C
		Shoch, George Quintus	OF39	58	.263	B	
		Shindle, Wm.	3B	118	.278	B	
15	13	Stein, Edward F.	P	28	.283	B	
		Treadway, George B.	OF	85	.262	B	

*One game won by forfeit.

WON 58
LOST 73
TG 131

NATIONAL LEAGUE

1896.

FINISHED 9th.
(TIED WITH WASH)
PCT. .443

BROOKLYN

DAVID LUTHER FOUTZ

WON	LOST	NAME	POS.	G.	BA	FROM	TO
8	8	Abbey, Bert Wood	P	19	.174	B	C
		Anderson, John Joseph (1B38)	OF66	104	.314	B	
		Bonner, Frank J.	2B	7	.185	StL	
		Burrell, Frank Andrew (Buster)	C	58	.307	B	
		Corcoran, Thomas W.	SS	132	.299	B	
		Dailey, Cornelius F. (Con)	C	1	+.000	B	Chi
		Daly, Thomas Peter	2B	64	.280	B	
14	11	Daub, Daniel Wm.	P	27	.229	B	
		Foutz, David Luther MGR. (OF1)	1B1	2	.250	B	C
		Griffin, Michael Joseph	OF	122	.315	B	
		Grim, John Helm (Jack)	C76	80	.269	B	
0	4	Gumbert, Addison Courtney (Ad)	P	5	+.182	B	Phil
4	8	Harper, George B.	P	16	.176	Phil94	C
		Jones, Fielder Allison	OF	102	.353	A	
15	22	Kennedy, Wm. V. (Brickyard)	P	37	.197	B	
		LaChance, George	1B	89	.280	B	
		McCarthy, Thomas Francis Michael	OF	101	.253	Bos	C
14	13	Payne, Harley F.	P31	32	.218	A	
		Shoch, George Quintus	2B63	75	.278	B	
		Shindle, Wm.	3B	131	.281	B	
3	7	Stein, Edward F.	P	17	.250	B	

WON 61
LOST 71
TG 132

NATIONAL LEAGUE

1897.

FINISHED 6th.
(TIED WITH WASH)
PCT. .462

BROOKLYN

WM. S. BARNIE

WON	LOST	NAME	POS.	G.	BA	FROM	TO
		Anderson, John Joseph	OF114	116	.332	B	
0	2	Brown, John J. (Ad)	P	2	.500	A	C
		Burrell, Frank Andrew (Buster)	C27	31	.238	B	C
		Canavan, James E.	2B	63	.222	Cin94	C
5	11	Daub, Daniel Wm.	P17	18	.244	B	
16	9	Dunn, John Joseph (Jack)	P25	34	.228	A	
8	7	Fisher, Chauncey Burr	P15	18	.200	Cin	
		Griffin, Michael Joseph	OF	134	.320	B	
		Grim, John Helm (Jack)	C	76	.261	B	
		Hanifin, Patrick James	OF5	9	.200	A	C
		Jones, Fielder Allison	OF	135	.322	B	
19	21	Kennedy, Wm. V. (Brickyard)	P40	42	.269	B	
		LaChance, George	1B	125	.308	B	
0	0	McMahon, John Joseph	P	9	.167	Balt	C
13	21	Payne, Harley F.	P34	39	.232	B	
		Shoch, George Quintus	2B65	79	.290	B	C
		Sheckard, Samuel James Tilden (OF2)	SS11	13	.326	A	
		Shindle, Wm.	3B	134	.289	B	
		Smith, Alexander Benjamin (Broadway) (OF17)	C38	61	.309	A	
		Smith, George J. (Germany)	SS	113	.207	Cin	

WON 54
LOST 91
TG 145

NATIONAL LEAGUE

1898.

FINISHED 10th.

PCT. .372

BROOKLYN

WM. S. BARNIE MICHAEL J. GRIFFIN CHAS. H. EBBETS

WON	LOST	NAME	POS.	G.	BA	FROM	TO
		Anderson, John Joseph	OF	6	+.158	B	Wash
		(1B2)	OF17	19	+.275		(& return)
		Daly, Thomas Peter	2B	23	.329	Bkn96	
		Dresser, Edward	SS	1	.250	A	C
15	21	Dunn, John Joseph (Jack)	P37	45	.250	B	

WON	LOST	NAME	POS.	G.	BA	FROM	TO
1	1	Gaston, Welcome Thornburg	P	2	.125	A	
		Griffin, Michael Joseph MGR.	OF	134	.296	B	C
		Grim, John Helm (Jack)	C	50	.275	B	
		Hallman, Wm. White (Billy)	2B124	133	.245	StL	
0	1	Hansford, F. C.	P	1	.000	A	C
0	2	Hopper, C. F. (Lefty)	P	2	.000	A	C
0	1	Horton, Elmer E. (Herky-Jerky)	P	1	.250	Pitt96	C
2	0	Howell, Harry	P	2	.250	A	
		Jones, Fielder Allison	OF	147	.304	B	
16	22	Kennedy, Wm. V. (Brickyard)	P	38	.259	B	
		LaChance, George (SS48)	1B75	135	.243	B	
		Magoon, George Henry	SS	93	.227	A	
5	14	Miller, Ralph Darwin	P19	21	.197	A	
1	7	McKenna, James Wm.	P	14	.256	A	
1	0	Payne, Harley F.	P	1	.750	B	
		Ryan, John Bennett (Jack)	C79	82	.189	Bos96	
		Sheckard, Samuel James Tilden	OF	105	.290	B	
		Shindle, Wm.	3B	120	.228	B	C
		Smith, Alexander Benjamin (Broadway) (C20)	OF26	48	.260	B	
0	2	Stein, Edward F.	P	3	.400	Bkn96	C
		Tucker, Thomas Joseph	1B	73	+.278	Wash	StL
		Wagner, Albert Butts	3B	11	+.237	xWash	
13	20	Yeager, Joseph F.	P33	36	.178	A	

WON 88 NATIONAL LEAGUE FINISHED 1st.
LOST x42
TG 130 1899. PCT. .677

BROOKLYN

EDWARD HUGH HANLON

WON	LOST	NAME	POS.	G.	BA	FROM	TO
		Anderson, John Joseph	OF71	112	.274	Balt	
		Beck, Erwin Thomas	SS	7	.158	A	
		Casey, James Peter (Doc)	3B	136	+.267	xWash	
		Cassidy, Peter Francis	3B3	6	+.150	Lvlle96	Wash
		Dahlen, Wm. Frederick (Bad Bill)	SS	122	.276	Chi	
		Daly, Thomas Peter	2B	143	.312	B	
1	2	Donovan, Wm. Edward (Wild Bill)	P	4	.231	Wash	
21	12	Dunn, John Joseph (Jack)	P38	39	.244	B	
		Farrell, Chas. A. (Duke)	C	78	+.294	xWash	
0	1	Gaston, Welcome Thornburg	P	1	1.000	B	
		Grim, John Helm (Jack)	C	14	.271	B	
1	0	Hill, Wm. C.	P	1	+.500	xBalt	
25	5	Hughes, James Jay	P34	35	.261	Balt	
		Jennings, Hugh Ambrose	1B	10	+.200	Balt	Balt
		(SS1)	1B47	51	+.320		(& return)
		Jones, Fielder Allison	OF	95	.286	B	
		Keeler, Wm. Henry	OF	143	.376	Balt	
		Kelley, Joseph James	OF	144	.329	Balt	
18	8	Kennedy, Wm. V. (Brickyard)	P35	37	.241	B	
2	0	Maul, Albert Joseph	P	4	.273	Balt	
0	0	McFarlan, Anderson Daniel	P	1	+.000	Lvlle95	Wash
		McGann, Dennis L. (Dan)	1B	63	+.245	Balt	Wash
		McGuire, James Thomas	C	43	+.338	xWash	
17	11	McJames, James McCutchen	P	33	.162	Balt	
0	0	Reidy, Wm. Joseph	P	2	.000	NY96	
		Smith, Alexander Benjamin	C	16	+.164	B	Balt
		Wrigley, George Watson	SS	15	+.229	xN.Y.	C
3	2	Yeager, Joseph F.	P	15	.209	B	

x-One Game lost by Forfeit.

WON 82 NATIONAL LEAGUE FINISHED 1st.
LOST 54
TG 136 1900. PCT. .603

BROOKLYN

EDWARD HUGH HANLON

WON	LOST	NAME	POS.	G.	BA	FROM	TO
		Casey, James Peter (Doc)	3B	1	.333	B	DetA
		Cross, LaFayette Napoleon (Lave)	3B	117	+.292	xStL	
		Dahlen, Wm. Frederick (Bad Bill)	SS	134	.259	B	
		Daly, Thomas Peter	2B95	98	.313	B	
		DeMontreville, Eugene Napoleon	2B47	63	.250	Balt	
1	2	Donovan, Wm. Edward (Wild Bill)	P	5	.000	B	
3	5	Dunn, John Joseph (Jack)	P	8	+.273	B	Phil
		Farrell, Chas. A. (Duke)	C	73	.277	B	
6	3	Howell, Harry	P	21	.309	Balt	
		Jennings, Hugh Ambrose	1B110	112	.270	B	
		Jones, Fielder Allison	OF	136	.309	B	
		Keeler, Wm. Henry	OF	137	.366	B	
		Kelley, Joseph James (1B28)	OF78	118	.318	B	
22	15	Kennedy, Wm. V. (Brickyard)	P	37	.301	B	
14	13	Kitson, Frank R.	P30	33	.283	Balt	
29	9	McGinnity, Joseph Jerome	P	41	.185	Balt	
		McGuire, James Thomas	C	68	.280	B	
3	4	Nops, Jeremiah H.	P	9	.160	Balt	
		Sheckard, Samuel James Tilden	OF	75	.305	Balt	
		Smith, Alexander Benjamin (Broadway) (C1)	3B6	7	.240	Balt	
		Steelman, Morris James	C	1	.000	Lvlle	
3	2	Weyhing, August (Gus)	P	8	+.222	xStL	
1	1	Yeager, Joseph F. (3B1)	P2	3	.333	B	DetA & recalled

WON 79 NATIONAL LEAGUE FINISHED 3rd.
LOST 57
TG 136 1901. PCT. .581

BROOKLYN

EDWARD HUGH HANLON

WON	LOST	NAME	POS.	G.	BA	FROM	TO
1	0	Carsey, Wilfred (Kid)	P	2	.000	KCA	C
		Dahlen, Wm. Frederick	SS128	130	.261	B	
		(Bad Bill)					
		Daly, Thomas Peter	2B131	132	.310	B	
		Davis, Alfonzo DeFord (Lefty)	OF	25	+.209	MinnA	Pitt
		Dolan, Patrick Henry (Cozy)	OF	62	+.280	xChi	
25	15	Donovan, Wm. Edward	P	41	.200	B	
		(Wild Bill)					
		Farrell, Chas. A. (Duke)	C58	76	.293	B	
		(1B18)					
		Gatins, Frank Anthony	3B45	49	.229	Wash98	C
		Gochnaur, John Peter	SS	3	.363	A	
		Hearne, Hugh J.	C	2	.500	A	
17	12	Hughes, James Jay	P	30	.178	Bkn99	
		Irwin, Chas. E.	3B	64	+.223	xCin	
		Keeler, Wm. Henry	OF125	136	.355	B	
		Kelley, Joseph James	1B115	120	.309	B	
3	5	Kennedy, Wm. V. (Brickyard)	P	14	.167	B	
19	11	Kitson, Frank R.	P	32	.281	B	
2	3	McCann, Henry Eugene (Mike)	P	6	.000	MinnA	
		McCreery, Thomas Leavenworth	OF83	84	.302	Pitt	
		McGuire, James Thomas	C82	84	.293	B	
4	6	McJames, James McCutchen	P	13	.029	Bkn99	C
7	5	Newton, Eustace James (Doc)	P	13	+.220	xCin	
		Sheckard, Samuel James Tilden	OF120	133	.353	B	
		Steelman, Morris James	C	1	.333	B	PhilA
1	0	Wright, Clarence Eugene	P	1	.333	A	

WON 75 NATIONAL LEAGUE FINISHED 2nd.
LOST 63
TG 138 1902. PCT. .543

BROOKLYN

EDWARD HUGH HANLON

WON	LOST	NAME	POS.	G.	BA	FROM	TO
		Dahlen, Wm. Frederick (Bad Bill)	SS	136	.267	B	
		Deisel, Edward (Pat)	C	1	.667	A	
		Dolan, Patrick Henry (Cozy)	OF	140	.283	B	
17	15	Donovan, Wm. Edward	P32	46	.169	B	
		(Wild Bill) (1B8 2B1 OF4)					
5	6	Evans, LeRoy	P	13	+.265	xN.Y.	
		Farrell, Chas. A. (Duke)	C48	72	.237	B	
		(1B24)					
		Flood, Timothy A. (OF1)	2B131	131	.228	ClevA00	
		Fuller, Chas. F.	C	3	.000	A	C
1	1	Garvin, Virgil Lee	P	2	.142	xChiA	
		Hearne, Hugh J.	C	62	.281	B	
		Hildebrand, George Albert	OF	11	.227	A	C
15	11	Hughes, James Jay (OF1)	P29	29	.202	B	C
		Irwin, Chas. E. (SS1)	3B131	131	.273	B	C
		Keeler, Wm. Henry	OF	132	.342	B	
19	12	Kitson, Frank R.	P	31	.266	B	
		Latimer, Clifford Wesley	C	8	.041	BaltA	C
1	2	McCann, Henry Eugene (Mike)	P	3	.083	B	C
		McCreery, Thomas Leavenworth	1B107	111	.246	B	
		(OF4)					
2	2	McMackin, John Weaver	P	4	.153	A	C
15	14	Newton, Eustace James (Doc)	P30	32	.174	B	
		(1B2)					
		Ritter, Louis Elmer	C	16	.250	A	
		Sheckard, Samuel James Tilden	OF	122	.273	xBaltA	
		Wall, Joseph Francis	C	5	+.176	xN.Y.	C
		Ward, John A.	OF11	13	.290	A	C
		Wheeler, Edward W.	3B12	24	.128	DetA00	C
		(2B10 SS5)					
0	0	Winham, LaFayette Sylvester	P	1	.000	A	

WON 70 NATIONAL LEAGUE FINISHED 5th.
LOST 66
TG 136 1903. PCT. .515

BROOKLYN

EDWARD HUGH HANLON

WON	LOST	NAME	POS.	G.	BA	FROM	TO
		Broderick, Matthew L.	2B	2	.000	BuffA00	C
		Dahlen, Wm. Frederick	SS	138	.262	B	
		(Bad Bill)					
		Dobbs, John Gordon	OF	110	+.237	xChi	
0	0	Doscher, John Herman Jr.	P	3	+.000	xChi	
		Doyle, John Joseph (Jack)	1B	139	.313	WashA	
5	9	Evans, LeRoy	P	15	.172	B	StLA
		Flood, Timothy A.	2B84	87	.249	B	C
15	18	Garvin, Virgil Lee	P	38	.075	B	
		Gessler, Harry Homer	OF	43	.247	xDetA	
		Hearne, Hugh J.	C17	19	.281	B	C
		Householder, Edward H.	OF	12	.209	A	C
		Hug, Edward Ambrose	C	1	.000	A	C
		Jacklitsch, Frederick Lawrence	C53	55	.267	Phil	
		Jennings, Hugh Ambrose	OF	6	.235	Phil	
19	14	Jones, Oscar Winfield	P	38	.256	A	
		Jordan, Adolph Otto	2B54	77	.236	A	
		(3B18)					
		McCreedie, Walter Henry	OF	56	.324	A	C
		McCreery, Thomas Leavenworth	OF	38	+.262	B	Bos
		McManus, Francis E.	C	2	.000	KCA00	
0	0	Pounds, Wm. Chas.	P	1	.667	xClevA	C
6	7	Reidy, Wm. Joseph	P	15	.243	xStLA	
		Ritter, Louis Elmer	C74	75	.236	B	
22	13	Schmidt, Henry M.	P40	41	.196	A	C
		Sheckard, Samuel James Tilden	OF	139	.332	B	

WON	LOST	NAME	POS.	G.	BA	FROM	TO
		Strang, Samuel Nicklin	3B124	135	.272	Chi	
3	1	Thatcher, Ulysses Grant	P	4	.182	A	
0	3	Thielman, Henry Joseph	P	8	.217	Cin	C
0	1	Vickers, Harry Porter (Rube) (OF1)	P2	3	.000	Cin	

WON 56 — NATIONAL LEAGUE — FINISHED 6th.
LOST 97
TG 153 — 1904. — PXR. .366

BROOKLYN

EDWARD HUGH HANLON

WON	LOST	NAME	POS.	G.	BA	FROM	TO
		Babb, Chas. Amos	SS	151	.265	N.Y.	
		Batch, Emil Henry	3B	28	.255	A	
		Bergen, Wm. Aloysius	C93	94	.182	Cin	
11	22	Cronin, John J. (Jack)	P	40	.157	N.Y.	C
		Dillon, Frank Edward	1B	134	.258	BaltA02	C
		Dobbs, John Gordon	OF92	95	.248	B	
0	1	Doscher, John Herman Jr.	P	2	.333	B	
		Doyle, John Joseph (Jack)	1B	8	+.227	B	Phil
1	0	Durham, Louis G.	P	2	.250	A	
6	15	Garvin, Virgil Lee	P	23	.127	B	NYA
		Gessler, Harry Homer	OF88	89	.290	B	
		Jacklitsch, Frederick Lawrence	C	23	.234	B	
18	26	Jones, Oscar Winfield	P	46	.175	B	
		Jordon, Adolph Otto	2B70	85	.179	B	C
0	1	Koukalik, Joseph	P	1	.000	A	C
		Loudenschlager, Chas. E.	2B	1	.000	A	C
		Lumley, Harry G.	OF	150	.279	A	
2	4	Mitchell, Frederick Francis	P	8	+.292	xPhil	
		McCormick, Michael J.	3B104	105	.184	A	C
7	14	Poole, Edward I.	P	24	.129	Cin	C
0	4	Reidy, Wm. Joseph (2B5)	P6	11	.196	B	C
3	3	Reisling, Frank Carl	P	7	.000	A	
		Ritter, Louis Elmer	C57	63	.248	B	
7	7	Scanlan, Wm. Dennis (Doc)	P	14	+.143	xPitt	
		Sheckard, Samuel James Tilden	OF141	143	.239	B	
		Strang, Samuel Nicklin	2B63	76	.192	B	
1	0	Thatcher, Ulysses Grant	P	1	.250	B	C
		VanBuren, Edward Eugene	OF	1	+1.000	A	Phil

WON 48 — NATIONAL LEAGUE — FINISHED 8th (LAST)
LOST 104
TG 152 — 1905. — PCT. .316

BROOKLYN

EDWARD HUGH HANLON

WON	LOST	NAME	POS.	G.	BA	FROM	TO
		Babb, Chas. Amos (1B31)	SS36	74	.187	B	C
		Batch, Emil Henry	3B	145	.252	B	
		Bergen, Wm. Aloysius	C	76	.190	B	
		Dobbs, John Gordon	OF	123	.254	B	C
1	5	Doscher, John Herman Jr.	P	11	.095	B	
5	20	Eason, Malcolm Wayne (Mal)	P27	29	.173	DetA03	
		Gessler, Harry Homer	1B107	119	.290	B	
		Hall, Robert Prill	OF	52	+.236	xN.Y.	C
		Hummel, John Edwin	2B	30	.266	A	
7	14	Jones, Oscar Winfield	P29	30	.200	B	C
		Lewis, Philip	SS	118	.254	A	
		Lumley, Harry G.	OF	129	.293	B	
		Malay, Chas. Francis (OF25)	2B75	101	.252	A	C
3	7	Mitchell, Frederick Francis	P	25	.190	B	
		McGamwell, Edward M.	1B	4	.267	A	C
9	27	McIntire, Harry M.	P40	45	.246	A	
		Owens, Thomas Llewellyn	2B	43	.215	Phi199	C
0	0	Reisling, Frank Carl	P	2	.000	B	
		Ritter, Louis Elmer	C84	90	.219	B	
15	11	Scanlan, Wm. Dennis (Doc)	P	33	.167	B	
		Sheckard, Samuel James Tilden	OF	129	.292	B	
8	20	Stricklett, Elmer Griffin	P	33	.148	ChiA	
		Yale, Wm. M. (Ad)	1B	4	.076	A	C

WON 66 — NATIONAL LEAGUE — FINISHED 5th.
LOST 86
TG 152 — 1906. — PCT. .434

BROOKLYN

PATRICK JOSEPH DONOVAN

WON	LOST	NAME	POS.	G.	BA	FROM	TO
		Alperman, Chas. Augustus (SS24)	2B103	127	.252	A	
		Batch, Emil Henry	OF50	52	.256	B	
		Bergen, Wm. Aloysius	C	103	.161	B	
		Butler, John Albert	C	1	.000	StL04	
		Casey, James Peter (Doc)	3B	149	.233	Chi	
0	1	Doscher, John Herman Jr.	P	2	.000	B	
		Donovan, Patrick Joseph MGR.	OF	7	.238	WashA04	
10	17	Eason, Malcolm Wayne (Mal)	P34	36	.091	B	C
		Gessler, Harry Homer	1B	9	+.242	B	Chi
		Hummel, John Edwin (1B16 OF20)	2B50	86	.199	B	
		Jordan, Timothy Joseph	1B	126	.262	NYA03	
0	0	Knolls, Oscar Edward	P	2	.500	A	C
		Lewis, Philip	SS	135	.243	B	
		Lumley, Harry G.	OF	131	.324	B	
		Maloney, Wm. Alphonse	OF	151	.221	Chi	
		McCarthy, John A.	OF	86	.304	Chi	
0	1	McFarland, Chas. Edward (Chappie)	P	1	+.000	xPitt	C
13	21	McIntire, Harry M.	P39	42	.175	B	
10	14	Pastorius, James W.	P	29	.141	A	
		Reardon, Philip Michael	OF	5	.071	A	C

WON	LOST	NAME	POS.	G.	BA	FROM	TO
		Ritter, Louis Elmer	C53	67	.208	B	
18	13	Scanlan, Wm. Dennis (Doc)	P	38	.186	B	
14	18	Stricklett, Elmer Griffin	P	41	.206	B	
1	1	Whiting, Jesse W.	P	3	.300	Phi102	

WON 65 NATIONAL LEAGUE FINISHED 5th.
LOST 83
TG 148 1907. PCT. .439

BROOKLYN

PATRICK JOSEPH DONOVAN

WON	LOST	NAME	POS.	G.	BA	FROM	TO
		Alperman, Chas. Augustus	2B115	138	.233	B	
		Batch, Emil Henry	OF101	106	.247	B	C
8	16	Bell, George Glenn	P	35	.095	A	
		Bergen, Wm. Aloysius	C	51	.159	B	
		Burch, Albert Wm.	OF	36	+.292	xStL	
		Butler, John Albert	C28	29	.127	B	C
		Casey, James Peter (Doc)	3B	138	.231	B	C
		Donovan, Patrick Joseph MGR.	OF	1	.000	B	
1	5	Henley, Weldon	P	7	.222	PhilA05	C
		Hummel, John Edwin (OF21)	2B44	97	.234	B	
		Hurley, Patrick	C	1	.000	Cin01	C
		Jordan, Timothy Joseph	1B	143	.274	B	
		Lewis, Philip	SS	136	.248	B	
		Lumley, Harry G.	OF	118	.267	B	
		Maloney, Wm. Alphonse	OF	144	.229	B	
		McCarthy, John A.	OF	25	.220	B	C
7	15	McIntire, Harry M.	P	28	.217	B	
		McLane, Edward Cameron	OF	1	.000	A	C
16	12	Pastorius, James W.	P	28	.205	B	
		Ritter, Louis Elmer	C	89	.203	B	
15	13	Rucker, George Napoleon (Nap)	P	37	.155	A	
6	8	Scanlan, Wm. Dennis (Doc)	P	17	.265	B	
12	14	Stricklett, Elmer Griffin	P29	30	.148	B	C
0	0	Whiting, Jesse W.	P	2	.000	B	C

WON 53 NATIONAL LEAGUE FINISHED 7th.
LOST 101
TG 154 1908. PCT. .344

BROOKLYN

PATRICK JOSEPH DONOVAN

WON	LOST	NAME	POS.	G.	BA	FROM	TO
		Alperman, Chas. Augustus	2B42	57	.197	B	
4	15	Bell, George Glenn	P	29	.170	B	
		Bergen, Wm. Aloysius	C	99	.175	B	
		Burch, Albert Wm.	OF	116	.243	B	
		Catterson, Thomas Henry	OF	18	.191	A	
		Dunn, Joseph Edward	C	20	.172	A	
		Farmer, Alexander Johnson	C	12	.167	A	C
0	0	Finlayson, Pembroke	P	1	.000	A	
1	4	Holmes, James Scott	P	13	.077	PhilA06	C
		Hummell, John Edwin (2B43)	OF90	154	.241	B	
		Jordan, Timothy Joseph	1B	146	.247	B	
0	1	Kruger, Abraham (Abe)	P	1	.000	A	C
		Lewis, Philip	SS	116	.219	B	C
		Lumley, Harry G.	OF	116	.216	B	
		Maloney, Wm. Alphonse	OF95	107	.195	B	C
		Murch, Simeon T.	1B3	6	.181	StL05	C
11	20	McIntire, Harry M.	P	40	.200	B	
		McMillan, Thomas Law	SS29	43	.238	A	
4	20	Pastorius, James W.	P	28	.129	B	
		Pattee, Harry Ernest	2B	74	.216	A	C
		Ritter, Louis Elmer	C	37	.192	B	C
17	19	Rucker, George Napoleon (Nap)	P	42	.179	B	
		Sheehan, Thomas H.	3B	145	.214	Pitt	C
16	22	Wilhelm, Irving Key (Kaiser)	P	42	.108	Bos05	

WON 55 NATIONAL LEAGUE FINISHED 6th.
LOST 98
TG 153 1909. PCT. .359

BROOKLYN

HARRY G. LUMLEY

WON	LOST	NAME	POS.	G.	BA	FROM	TO
		Alperman, Chas. Augustus	2B	108	.248	B	C
16	15	Bell, George Glenn	P	33	.166	B	
		Bergen, Wm. Aloysius	C	112	.139	B	
		Burch, Albert Wm.	OF151	152	.271	B	
		Catterson, Thomas Henry	OF	9	.222	B	C
		Clement, Wallace Oakes	OF	88	+.256	xPhil	C
2	4	Dent, Elliott Estill	P	6	.067	A	
		Downey, Alexander Cummings	OF	19	.256	A	C
		Dunn, Joseph Edward	C5	7	.160	B	C
0	0	Finlayson, Pembroke	P	1	.000	B	C
0	1	Fletcher, Samuel S.	P	1	.000	A	
		Hummel, John Edwin (2B38 SS36 OF17)	1B54	145	.280	B	
4	10	Hunter, George Harrison (P16)	OF23	39	.228	A	
		Jordan, Timothy Joseph	1B	95	.273	B	
1	3	Knetzer, Elmer Ellsworth	P	5	.000	A	
		Kustus, Julius	OF	50	.145	A	C
		Lennox, James Edgar	3B	121	.262	PhilA06	
		Lumley, Harry G. MGR.	OF	52	.250	B	
		Marshall, Wm. R. (Doc)	C	47	.202	Chi	C
		Meyer, Lee	SS	7	.130	A	C
		McElveen, Pryor Mynatt	3B37	67	.198	A	
7	17	McIntire, Harry M.	P	32	.171	B	
		McMillan, Thomas Law	SS	108	.212	B	
		Myers, Henry Harrison (Hi)	OF	6	.227	A	

WON	LOST	NAME	POS.	G.	BA	FROM	TO
1	9	Pastorius, James W.	P	12	.080	B	C
		Redmond, Harry John	2B	6	.100	A	C
13	19	Rucker, George Napoleon (Nap)	P	38	.118	B	
8	7	Scanlan, Wm. Dennis (Doc)	P	19	.273	Bkn07	
		Sebring, James Dennison	OF	25	.099	Cin05	WashA
		Wheat, Zachary Davis (Zack)	OF	26	.304	A	
3	13	Wilhelm, Irving Key (Kaiser)	P	22	.228	B	

WON 64 — NATIONAL LEAGUE — FINISHED 6th.
LOST 90
TG 154 — 1910 — PCT. .416

BROOKLYN

WM. FREDERICK DAHLEN

WON	LOST	NAME	POS.	G.	BA	FROM	TO
15	15	Barger, Eros Bollivar	P	35	.231	NYA07	
10	27	Bell, George Glenn	P	44	.134	B	
		Bergen, Wm. Aloysius	C	89	.161	B	
		Burch, Albert Wm.	OF70	83	.236	B	
0	3	Burk, Charles Sanford	P3	4	.000	A	
		Coulson, Robert Jackson	OF	25	.247	Cin08	
0	0	Crable, George E.	P	2	.000	A	C
		Dahlen, Wm. Frederick MGR. (Bad Bill)		3	.000	Bos	
		Dalton, Talbot Percy	OF	72	.227	A	
		Daubert, Jacob Ellsworth (Jake)	1B	144	.264	A	
		Davidson, Wm. S.	OF	131	.238	Chi	
2	3	Dessau, Frank Rolland	P	19	.067	Bos07	C
		Erwin, Ross Emil	C	68	.188	DetA07	
		Hummel, John Edwin	2B	153	.244	B	
		Hunter, George Harrison	OF	1	.000	B	C
		Jordan, Timothy Joseph		5	.200	B	C
7	5	Knetzer, Elmer Ellsworth	P	20	.053	B	
		Lennox, James Edgar	3B	100	.259	B	
		Lumley, Harry G.	OF4	8	.100	B	C
1	1	Miller, Frederick Holman	P	3	.000	A	C
		Miller, Lowell Otto	C	28	.167	A	
		McElveen, Pryor Mynatt	3B54	64	.225	B	
		McMillan, Thomas Law	SS	23	+.176	B	Cin
17	18	Rucker, George Napoleon (Nap)	P	41	.209	B	
9	11	Scanlan, Wm. Dennis (Doc)	P	34	.203	B	
0	0	Schneiberg, Frank Frederick	P	1	.000	A	C
		Smith, Anthony (Tony)	SS100	106	.181	WashA07	
		Smith, Henry Joseph	OF	16	.237	A	C
		Stark, Monroe Randolph	SS	30	.165	ClevA	
		Wheat, Zachary Davis (Zack)	OF	156	.284	B	
3	7	Wilhelm, Irving Key (Kaiser)	P	15	.316	B	

WON 64 — NATIONAL LEAGUE — FINISHED 7th.
LOST 86
TG 150 — 1911. — PCT. .427

BROOKLYN

WM. FREDERICK DAHLEN

WON	LOST	NAME	POS.	G.	BA	FROM	TO
0	1	Aitchison, Raleigh Leonidas	P	1	.000	A	
11	15	Barger, Eros Bollivar	P30	42	.228	B	
5	6	Bell, George Glenn	P	19	.121	B	C
		Bergen, Wm. Aloysius	C	84	.132	B	C
		Browne, George E.	OF	7	.333	ChiA	
		Burch, Albert Wm.	OF43	46	.228	B	C
1	3	Burk, Charles Sanford	P	13	.095	B	
		Coulson, Robert Jackson	OF	145	.234	B	
		Dahlen, Wm. Frederick MGR. (Bad Bill)	SS	1	.000	B	
		Daley, Jud Lawrence	OF	16	.231	A	
		Daubert, Jacob Ellsworth (Jake)	1B	149	.307	B	
		Davidson, Wm. S.	OF	74	.233	B	C
2	1	Dent, Elliott Estill	P	5	.143	Bkn09	
		Erwin, Ross Emil	C	74	.271	B	
		Higgins, Robert Stone	C	4	.300	ClevA09	
		Hummel, John Edwin	2B127~	133	.270	B	
		Humphrey, Alfred W.	OF	8	.143	A	C
11	12	Knetzer, Elmer Ellsworth	P	35	.097	B	
		LeJeune, Sheldon Aldenbury	OF	6	.157	A	
		Miller, Lowell Otto	C	22	.210	B	
0	1	Miller, Walter W.	P	3	.000	A	C
		Myers, Henry Harrison (Hi)	OF	12	.179	Bkn09	
		McElveen, Pryor Mynett	2B	16	.193	B	C
		Northen, Hubbard Elwin	OF	19	+.316	xCin	
4	3	Ragan, Don Carlos Patrick (Pat)	P	22	.138	Chi09	
22	18	Rucker, George Napoleon (Nap)	P	48	.202	B	
0	1	Ryan, Jack	P	3	.000	BosA09	C
3	10	Scanlan, Wm. Dennis (Doc)	P	22	.121	B	C
5	15	Schardt, Wilburt	P	39	.169	A	
		Smith, Anthony (Tony)	SS	12	.138	B	C
		Smith, James Carlisle (Red)	3B	28	.261	A	
		Stark, Monroe Randolph (2B18)	SS34	55	.295	B	
0	0	Steele, Elmer Rae	P	5	+.000	xPitt	C
		Tooley, Albert R. (Bert)	SS	114	.206	A	
		Wheat, Zachary Davis (Zack)	OF	136	.287	B	
		Zimmerman, Edward Desmond	3B	122	.185	StL06	C

WON 58 — NATIONAL LEAGUE — FINISHED 7th.
LOST 95
TG 153 — 1912. — PCT. .379

BROOKLYN

WM. FREDERICK DAHLEN

WON	LOST	NAME	POS.	G.	BA	FROM	TO
3	9	Allen, Frank Leon	P	20	.167	A	
1	9	Barger, Eros Bollivar	P16	17	.189	B	

WON	LOST	NAME	POS	G.	BA	FROM	TO
0	0	Burk, Charles Sanford	P	2	+.250	B	StL
4	7	Curtis, Clifton Garfield	P	19	+.308	xPhil	
		Cutshaw, George Wm.	2B91	102	.280	A	
		Daley, Jud Lawrence	OF55	61	.256	B	C
		Daubert, Jacob Ellsworth (Jake)	1B143	145	.308	B	
0	0	Dent, Elliott Estill	P	1	.000	B	C
		Downs, Jerome Willis	2B	9	+.250	DetA08	Chi
		Erwin, Ross Emil	C41	59	.211	B	
		Fisher, Robert Tecumseh	SS74	82	.233	A	
		Higgins, Robert Stone	C	1	.000	B	C
		Hummel, John Edwin (OF43)	2B58	122	.282	B	
5	5	Kent, Maurice Allen	P	20	.229	A	
		Kirkpatrick, Enos Claire	3B29	32	.191	A	
7	9	Knetzer, Elmer Ellsworth	P	33	.135	B	
		Miller, Lowell Otto	C94	98	.278	B	
		Moran, Joseph Herbert	OF129	130	.276	Bos10	
		Northen, Hubbard Elwin	OF102	118	.282	B	C
		Phelps, Edward Joseph	C32	52	.288	StL10	
7	18	Ragan, Don Carlos Patrick (Pat)	P	36	.060	B	
18	21	Rucker, George Napoleon (Nap)	P	45	.245	B	
0	1	Schardt, Wilburt	P	7	.000	B	C
		Smith, James Carlisle (Red)	3B125	128	.286	B	
7	5	Stack, Wm. Edward	P	28	.135	Phil	
		Stark, Monroe Randolph	SS	8	.182	B	C
		Stengel, Chas. Dillon (Casey)	OF	17	.316	A	
		Tooley, Albert R. (Bert)	SS76	77	.234	B	C
		Wheat, Zachary Davis (Zack)	OF120	123	.305	B	
6	11	Yingling, Earl Hershey	P	25	.250	ClevA	

WON 65 NATIONAL LEAGUE FINISHED 6th.
LOST 84
TG 149 1913. PCT. .436

BROOKLYN

WM. FREDERICK DAHLEN

WON	LOST	NAME	POS.	G.	BA	FROM	TO
4	18	Allen, Frank Leon	P	34	.137	B	
0	0	Brown, Elmer Young	P	3	.000	StLA	
		Callahan, Leo David	OF	33	.171	A	
		Collins, Wm. Shirley	OF27	32	.189	Chill	
8	9	Curtis, Clifton Garfield	P	30	.122	B	C
		Cutshaw, George Wm.	2B	147	.267	B	
		Daubert, Jacob Ellsworth (Jake)	1B	139	.350	B	
		Erwin, Ross Emil	C	20	.258	B	
		Fischer, Wm. Chas.	C51	62	.267	A	
		Fisher, Robert Tecumseh	SS131	132	.262	B	
0	0	Hall, Wm. Bernard	P	3	.000	A	C
		Heckinger, Michael Vincent	C	9	+.222	xChi	C
		Hummel, John Edwin (SS16)	OF27	67	.242	B	
0	0	Kent, Maurice Allen	P	5	.000	B	C
		Kirkpatrick, Enos Claire	1B	48	.247	B	
		Meyer, Benjamin (Benny)	OF	38	.195	A	
		Miller, Lowell Otto	C	104	.272	B	
		Moran, Joseph Herbert	OF129	132	.266	B	
		Mowe, Raymond Benjamin	SS	5	.111	A	C
		McCarty, George Lewis	C	9	.192	A	
0	1	Pfeffer, Edward Joseph	P	5	.000	StLA11	
		Phelps, Edward Joseph	C	15	.222	B	C
15	18	Ragan, Don Carlos Patrick (Pat)	P	44	.165	B	
7	6	Reulbach, Edward Marvin	P	16	+.103	xChi	
14	15	Rucker, George Napoleon (Nap)	P	41	.241	B	
		Scheer, Allen G.	OF	6	.272	A	
		Smith, James Carlisle (Red)	3B	151	.296	B	
4	4	Stack, Wm. Edward	P	23	+.154	B	Chi
		Stengel, Chas. Dillon (Casey)	OF119	124	.272	B	
4	2	Wagner, Wm. George	P	18	.231	A	
1	3	Walker, Frederick Mitchell	P	10	.167	Cin10	
		Wheat, Zachary Davis (Zack)	OF135	138	.301	B	
8	8	Yingling, Earl Hershey	P26	40	.383	B	

WON 75 NATIONAL LEAGUE FINISHED 5th.
LOST 79
TG 154 1914. PCT. .487

BROOKLYN

WILBERT ROBINSON

WON	LOST	NAME	POS	G.	BA	FROM	TO
8	14	Allen, Frank Leon	P36	37	.128	B	PittF
12	7	Aitchison, Raleigh Leonidas	P	26	.196	Bkn11	
1	2	Brown, Elmer Young	P	11	.083	B	
		Cutshaw, George Wm.	2B	153	.257	Bkn10	
		Dalton, Talbot Percy	OF116	128	.319	B	
		Daubert, Jacob Ellsworth (Jake)	B	126	.329	B	
		Egan, Richard Joseph (Dick)	SS55	106	.226	Cin	
		Elberfeld, Norman Arthur (Kid)	SS18	30	.226	WashA11	C
1	0	Enzmann, John	P	7	.000	A	
		Erwin, Ross Emil	C	7	+.500	B	Cin
		Fischer, Wm. Chas.	C30	43	.257	B	
		Getz, Gustave	3B	55	.248	Bos10	
		Hummel, John Edwin (OF19)	1B36	73	.264	B	
		Miller, Lowell Otto	C50	54	.231	B	
		Myers, Henry Harrison (Hy)	OF60	70	.286	Bkn11	
		McCarty, George Lewis	C84	90	.254	B	
		O'Mara, Oliver Edward	SS63	67	.263	DetA12	
23	12	Pfeffer, Edward Joseph	P43	44	.198	B	
10	15	Ragan, Don Carlos Patrick (Pat)	P	38	.133	B	
11	18	Reulbach, Edward Marvin	P	44	.122	B	
		Riggert, Joseph Aloysius	OF	27	+.190	BosA11	StL
7	6	Rucker, George Napoleon (Nap)	P	16	.265	B	
1	3	Schmutz, Chas. Otto	P	18	.187	A	
		Smith, James Carlisle (Red)	3B	90	+.245	B	Bos
1	1	Steele, Wm. Mitchell	P	8	+.333	xStL	C
		Stengel, Chas. Dillon (Casey)	OF121	126	.316	B	
0	1	Wagner, Wm. George	P	6	.000	B	C
		Wheat, Zachary Davis (Zack)	OF144	145	.319	B	

WON 80 / LOST 72 / TG 152

NATIONAL LEAGUE 1915. BROOKLYN

FINISHED 3rd. PCT. .527

WILBERT ROBINSON

WON	LOST	NAME	POS.	G.	BA	FROM	TO
4	10	Appleton, Edward Sam	P	34	.159	A	
0	4	Aitchison, Raleigh Leonidas	P	7	.000	B	C
0	0	Brown, Elmer Young	P	1	.000	B	C
0	2	Cadore, Leon Joseph	P	7	.000	A	
0	2	Cheney, Lawrence Russell (Larry)	P	5	+.143	xChi	
15	10	Coombs, John Wesley (Jack)	P	29	.280	PhilA	
		Cutshaw, George Wm.	2B	154	.246	B	
		Daubert, Jacob Ellsworth (Jake)	1B	150	.301	B	
11	10	Dell, Wm. George	P	40	.152	StL12	
5	5	Douglas, Philip Brooks (Shufflin' Phil)	P	20	+.154	xCin	Chi
		Egan, Richard Joseph (Dick)	2B	3	+.000	B	Bos
		Getz, Gustave	3B128	130	.258	B	
		Hummel, John Edwin	OF21	53	.230	B	
		Karst, John Gottlieb	3B	1	.000	A	C
0	1	Mails, John Walter (Duster)	P	2	.000	A	
2	2	Marquard, Richard Wm. (Rube)	P	6	+.125	xN.Y.	
		Miller, Lowell Otto	C83	84	.224	B	
		Myers, Henry Harrison (Hy)	OF	153	.248	B	
		McCarty, George Lewis	C81	84	.239	B	
		Nixon, Albert Richard	OF	14	.231	A	
		Olson, Ivan Massie	3B8	18	+.077	xCin	
		O'Mara, Oliver Edward	SS	149	.244	B	
19	14	Pfeffer, Edward Joseph	P	40	.255	B	
1	0	Ragan, Don Carlos Patrick (Pat)	P	4	+.167	B	Bos
9	4	Rucker, George Napoleon (Nap)	P	19	.214	B	
0	0	Schmutz, Chas. Otto	P	1	.000	B	C
		Schultz, Joseph Chas.	3B	56	+.292	Bos13	Chi
14	8	Smith, Sherrod Malone (Sherry)	P	29	.246	Pitt12	
		Smyth, James Daniel	OF	19	.136	A	
		Stengel, Chas. Dillon (Casey)	OF129	132	.237	B	
		Wheat, McKinley Davis	C	8	.071	A	
		Wheat, Zachary Davis (Zack)	OF144	146	.258	B	
		Zimmerman, Wm. H.	OF18	22	.281	A	C

WON 94 / LOST 60 / TG 154

NATIONAL LEAGUE 1916. BROOKLYN

FINISHED 1st. PCT. .610

WILBERT ROBINSON

WON	LOST	NAME	POS.	G.	BA	FROM	TO
1	2	Appleton, Edward Sam	P	14	.167	B	C
0	0	Cadore, Leon Joseph	P	1	.000	B	
18	12	Cheney, Lawrence Russell (Larry)	P	41	.114	B	
13	8	Coombs, John Wesley (Jack)	P	27	.180	B	
		Cutshaw, George Wm.	2B	154	.260	B	
		Daubert, Jacob Ellsworth (Jake)	1B126	127	.316	B	
		Dede, Arthur Richard	C	1	.000	A	C
8	9	Dell, Wm. George	P	32	.091	B	
		Fabrique, Albert Lavern	SS	2	.000	A	
		Getz, Gustave	3B20	40	.219	B	
		Hickman, David James	OF	9	.200	BaltF	
		Johnston, James Harle (Jimmy)	OF106	118	.252	Chil4	
		Kelleher, John Patrick (SS1)	3B1	2	.000	StL12	
0	1	Mails, John Walter (Duster)	P	11	.250	B	
13	6	Marquard, Richard Wm. (Rube)	P	36	.143	B	
		Merkle, Frederick Chas.	1B	23	+.208	xN.Y.	
		Meyers, John Tortes (Chief)	C74	80	.247	N.Y.	
		Miller, Lawrence H. (Hack)	OF	3	.333	A	
		Miller, Lowell Otto	C69	73	.255	B	
		Mowrey, Harry Harlan (Mike)	3B	144	.244	PittF	
		Myers, Henry Harrison (Hy)	OF106	113	.262	B	
		McCarty, George Lewis (1B17)	C27	55	+.311	B	N.Y.
		Nixon, Albert Richard	OF	1	1.000	B	
		Olson, Ivan Massie	SS103	108	.254	B	
		O'Mara, Oliver Edward	SS51	72	.202	B	
25	11	Pfeffer, Edward Joseph	P41	43	.279	B	
2	1	Rucker, George Napoleon (Nap)	P	9	.091	B	C
14	10	Smith, Sherrod Malone (Sherry)	P36	38	.273	B	
		Smyth, James Daniel	OF	2	.000	B	
		Stengel, Chas. Dillon (Casey)	OF121	127	.279	B	
		Wheat, McKinley Davis	C	2	.000	B	
		Wheat, Zachary Davis (Zack)	OF	149	.312	B	

WON 70 / LOST 81 / TG 151

NATIONAL LEAGUE 1917. BROOKLYN

FINISHED 7th. PCT. .464

WILBERT ROBINSON

WON	LOST	NAME	POS.	G.	BA	FROM	TO
13	13	Cadore, Leon Joseph	P	37	.261	B	
8	12	Cheney, Lawrence Russell (Larry)	P	35	.206	B	
7	11	Coombs, John Wesley (Jack)	P31	32	.227	B	
		Cutshaw, George Wm.	2B134	135	.259	B	
		Daubert, Jacob Ellsworth (Jake)	1B	125	.261	B	
0	4	Dell, Wm. George	P	17	.063	B	C
0	0	Durning, Richard Knott	P	1	.000	A	
		Fabrique, Albert Lavern	SS21	25	.205	B	C
		Hickman, David James	OF101	114	.219	B	
		Johnston, James Harle (Jimmy)	OF92	103	.270	B	
		Krueger, Ernest George	C	31	+.272	x N.Y.	
		Leard, Wm. Wallace	2B1	3	.000	A	C
		Malone, Lewis Aloysius		1	.000	PhilA	

WON	LOST	NAME	POS.	G.	BA	FROM	TO
19	12	Marquard, Richard Wm. (Rube)	P	37	.200	B	
		Merkle, Frederick Chas.	1B	2	+.125	B	Chi
		Meyers, John Tortes (Chief)	C	47	+.214	B	Bos
0	1	Miljus, John Kenneth	P	4	.000	PittF15	
		Miller, Lowell Otto	C91	92	.230	B	
		Mowrey, Harry Harlan (Mike)	3B80	83	.214	B	C
		Myers, Henry Harrison (Hy) (1B22 2B19 3B15)	OF66	120	.268	B	
		Olson, Ivan Massie	SS133	139	.269	B	
		O'Rourke, Francis James	3B58	64	.237	Bos12	
11	15	Pfeffer, Edward Joseph	P30	31	.130	B	
0	1	Russell, John Albert (Jack)	P	5	.250	A	
12	12	Smith, Sherrod Malone (Sherry)	P38	43	.195	B	
		Smyth, James Daniel	OF	29	+.120	B	StL
		Snyder, John Wm.	C	7	.273	BuffF14	C
		Stengel, Chas. Dillon (Casey)	OF	150	.257	B	
0	0	Wachtel, Paul Horine	P	2	.333	A	C
		Wheat, McKinley Davis	C18	29	.133	B	
		Wheat, Zachary Davis (Zack)	OF98	109	.312	B	

WON 57
LOST 69
TG 126

NATIONAL LEAGUE — FINISHED 5th.

1918. — PCT. .452

BROOKLYN

WILBERT ROBINSON

WON	LOST	NAME	POS.	G.	BA	FROM	TO
		Archer, James Patrick	C	9	+.273	xPitt	Cin
		Bashang, Albert	OF	2	.200	DetA12	C
1	0	Cadore, Leon Joseph	P	2	.000	B	
11	13	Cheney, Lawrence Russell (Larry)	P	33	.242	B	
8	14	Coombs, John Wesley (Jack) (OF13)	P29	46	.168	B	
		Daubert, Jacob Ellsworth (Jake)	1B105	108	.308	B	
		Doolan, Michael Joseph	2B91	92	.179	NY16	C
0	0	Durning, Richard Knott	P	1	.000	B	C
19	9	Grimes, Burleigh Arland	P	41	.200	Pitt	
1	5	Griner, Daniel Dexter	P	12	.071	StL16	C
0	0	Hehl, Herman Jacob	P	1	.000	A	C
0	1	Heitman, Henry Anthony	P	1	.000	A	C
0	0	Hermann,	P	1	.000	A	C
		Hickman, David James	OF	53	.234	B	
		Johnston, James Harle (Jimmy) (1B21 2B1 3B4)	OF96	123	.281	B	
		Krueger, Ernest George	C23	30	.289	B	
0	1	Mamaux, Albert Leon	P	2	.000	Pitt	
9	18	Marquard, Richard Wm. (Rube)	P	34	.171	B	
		Miller, Lowell Otto (1B1)	C62	75	.193	B	
0	1	Mitchell, Clarence Elmer	P	10	.250	Cin	
		Myers, Henry Harrison (Hi)	OF	107	.256	B	
		Nixon, Albert Richard	OF	6	.454	Bkn16	
		Olson, Ivan Massie	SS	126	.239	B	
		O'Mara, Oliver Edward	3B	121	.213	Bkn16	
		O'Rourke, Francis James	2B	4	.167	B	
1	0	Pfeffer, Edward Joseph	P	1	.250	B	
0	0	Plitt, Norman Wm.	P	1	1 .000	A	
3	6	Robertson, Richard J.	P	14	.300	Cin13	
0	0	Russell, John Albert (Jack)	P	1	.000	B	
		Schmandt, Raymond Henry	2B	34	.307	StLA15	
		Sheridan, Eugene Anthony	2B	2	.250	A	
4	1	Smith, George Allen	P	8	+.067	xN.Y.	
		Ward, Chas. Wm.	SS	2	.333	Pitt	
		Wheat, McKinley Davis (OF7)	C38	57	.217	B	
		Wheat, Zachary Davis (Zack)	OF	105	.335	B	

WON 69
LOST 71
TG 140

NATIONAL LEAGUE — FINISHED 5th.

1919. — PCT. .493

BROOKLYN

WILBERT ROBINSON

WON	LOST	NAME	POS.	G.	BA	FROM	TO
		Allen, Horace Tanner	OF	4	.000	A	C
		Baird, Howard Douglas	3B	20	+.167	xStL	
14	12	Cadore, Leon Joseph	P35	37	.161	B	
1	3	Cheney, Lawrence Russell (Larry)	P	9	+.182	B	Bos
		Fitzsimmons, Thomas Wm.	3B	4	.000	A	C
		Griffith, Thomas Herman	OF	125	.281	Cin	
10	11	Grimes, Burleigh Arland	P25	26	.246	B	
0	0	Henion, LaFayette M.	P	1	.000	A	C
		Hickman, David James	OF29	57	.192	B	C
		Johnston, James Harle (1B2 SS1 OF14)	2B87	117	.281	B	
		Kilduff, Peter John (2B1)	3B31	32	+.301	xChi	
		Konetchy, Edward Joseph	1B	132	.298	Bos	
		Krueger, Ernest George	C66	80	.248	B	
		Magee, Leo Christopher (Lee)	2B	45	+.238	Cin	Chi
		Malone, Lewis Aloysius (2B2 SS2)	3B47	51	.204	Bkn17	C
10	12	Mamaux, Albert Leon	P	30	.175	B	
3	3	Marquard, Richard Wm. (Rube)	P	8	.261	B	
		Miller, Lowell Otto	C	51	.226	B	
7	5	Mitchell, Clarence Elmer	P23	34	.367	B	
		Myers, Henry Harrison (Hy)	OF131	133	.307	B	
		Olson, Ivan Massie	SS	140	.278	B	
		O'Mara, Oliver Edward	3B	2	.000	B	C
17	13	Pfeffer, Edward Joseph	P	30	.206	B	
		Schmandt, Raymond Henry (1B12 3B6)	2B18	47	.165	B	
7	12	Smith, Sherrod Malone (Sherry)	P	30	.148	Bkn17	
		Ward, Chas. Wm.	3B	45	.233	B	
		Wheat, McKinley Davis	C38	41	.205	B	
		Wheat, Zachary Davis (Zack)	OF	137	.297	B	

WON 93
LOST 61
TG 154

NATIONAL LEAGUE

1920.

FINISHED 1st.

PCT. .604

BROOKLYN

WILBERT ROBINSON

WON	LOST	NAME	POS.	G.	BA	FROM	TO
		Baird, Howard Douglas		6	+.333	B	N.Y.
15	14	Cadore, Leon Joseph	P	35	.220	B	
		Elliott, Harold H.	C39	41	.241	Chi18	C
		Griffith, Thomas Herman	OF92	93	.260	B	
23	11	Grimes, Burleigh Arland	P40	43	.306	B	
		Hood, Wallace James	OF	7	+.154	A	Pitt
		Johnston, James Harle (Jimmy)	3B146	155	.291	B	
		Kilduff, Peter John	2B134	141	.272	B	
		Konetchy, Edward Joseph	1B130	131	.308	B	
		Krueger, Ernest George	C46	52	.288	B	
		Lamar, Wm. Harmong	OF	24	.273	BosA	
12	8	Mamaux, Albert Leon	P	41	.167	B	
10	7	Marquard, Richard Wm. (Rube)	P	28	.169	B	
1	0	Miljus, John Kenneth	P	10	.333	Bkn17	
		Miller, Lowell Otto	C89	90	.289	B	
5	2	Mitchell, Clarence Elmer	P19	55	.234	B	
0	1	Mohart, George Benjamin	P	13	.125	A	
		Myers, Henry Harrison (Hi)	OF152	154	.304	B	
		McCabe, Wm. Francis	OF	41	+.147	xChi	C
		Neis, Bernard Edmund	OF83	95	.253	A	
		Olson, Ivan Massie (2B21)	SS125	143	.254	B	
16	9	Pfeffer, Edward Joseph	P	30	.243	B	
		Schmandt, Raymond Henry	1B20	28	.238	B	
		Sheehan, John Thomas	3B	4	.400	A	
		Sheridan, Eugene Anthony	SS	2	.000	Bkn18	C
11	9	Smith, Sherrod Malone (Sherry)	P	33	.233	B	
		Taylor, James Wren (Zack)	C	5	.167	A	
		Ward, Chas. Wm.	SS	19	.155	B	
		Wheat, Zachary Davis (Zack)	OF	148	.328	B	

WON 77
LOST 75
TG 152

NATIONAL LEAGUE

1921.

FINISHED 5th.

PCT. .507

BROOKLYN

WILBERT ROBINSON

WON	LOST	NAME	POS.	G.	BA	FROM	TO
0	0	Bailey, Abraham Lincoln	P	7	+.000	xChi	C
13	14	Cadore, Leon Joseph	P	35	.187	B	
0	0	Eayrs, Edwin	P	8	+.167	xBos	C
1	0	Gordonier, Raymond Chas.	P	3	.250	A	
		Griffith, Thomas Herman	OF124	129	.312	B	
22	13	Grimes, Burleigh Arland	P	37	.237	B	
		Hood, Wallace James	OF20	56	.262	Pitt	
		Janvrin, Harold Chandler (SS17)	1B17	44	+.196	xStL	
		Johnston, James Harle (Jimmy)	3B150	152	.325	B	
		Kilduff, Peter John	2B105	107	.288	B	C
		Konetchy, Edward Joseph	1B	55	+.269	B	Phil
		Krueger, Ernest George	C52	65	.264	B	
		Lamar, Wm. Harmong	OF	3	.333	B	
3	3	Mamaux, Albert Leon	P	12	.182	B	
6	3	Miljus, John Kenneth	P	28	.167	B	
		Miller, Lowell Otto	C	91	.234	B	
11	9	Mitchell, Clarence Elmer	P37	46	.264	B	
0	0	Mohart, George Benjamin	P	2	.500	B	C
		Myers, Henry Harrison (Hy) (2B21)	OF124	144	.288	B	
		Neis, Bernard Edmund	OF77	102	.257	B	
		Olson, Ivan Massie (2B20)	SS133	151	.267	B	
1	5	Pfeffer, Edward Joseph	P	6	+.000	B	StL
10	13	Ruether, Walter Henry (Dutch)	P36	49	.351	Cin	
		Schmandt, Raymond Henry	1B92	95	.306	B	
3	4	Schupp, Ferdinand Maurice	P	20	+.083	xStL	
		Sheehan, John Thomas	3B	5	.000	B	C
7	11	Smith, Sherrod Malone (Sherry)	P	35	.228	B	
		Taylor, James Wren (Zack)	C	30	.196	B	
		Ward, Chas. William	SS	12	.071	B	
		Wheat, Zachary Davis (Zack)	OF	148	.320	B	

WON 76
LOST 78
TG 154

NATIONAL LEAGUE

1922.

FINISHED 6th.

PCT. .494

BROOKLYN

WILBERT ROBINSON

WON	LOST	NAME	POS.	G.	BA	FROM	TO
8	15	Cadore, Leon Joseph	P	29	.267	B	
		Crane, Samuel Byren	SS	3	.250	Cin	C
		DeBerry, John Herman (Hank)	C81	85	.301	ClevA17	
3	4	Decatur, Arthur Rue	P	29	.080	A	
0	0	Gordonier, Raymond Chas.	P	5	.000	B	C
		Griffith, Bert Joseph (1B6)	OF77	106	.308	A	
		Griffith, Thomas Herman	OF82	99	.316	B	
17	14	Grimes, Burleigh Arland	P	36	.237	B	
		High, Andrew Aird (2B1 SS22)	3B130	153	.283	A	
		Hood, Wallace James	OF	2	.000	B	C
		Hungling, Bernard Herman	C36	39	.225	A	
		Janvrin, Harold Chandler (1B1 SS4 3B2 OF1)	2B15	30	.298	B	C
		Johnston, James Harle (Jimmy) (SS50 3B26)	2B62	138	.319	B	
1	4	Mamaux, Albert Leon	P	37	.235	B	
		Miller, Lowell Otto	C57	59	.261	B	C
0	3	Mitchell, Clarence Elmer (P5)	1B42	56	.290	B	
0	0	Murray, James Francis	P	4	.500	A	C
		Myers, Henry Harrison (Hy)	OF152	153	.317	B	

WON	LOST	NAME	POS.	G.	BA	FROM	TO
		(2B1)					
		Neis, Bernard Edmund	OF27	61	.229	B	
		Olson, Ivan Massie (SS51)	2B85	136	.272	B	
		Post, Samuel Gilbert	1B8	9	.280	A	C
21	12	Ruether, Walter Henry (Dutch)	P35	67	.208	B	
		Schmandt, Raymond Henry	1B	110	.267	B	C
0	0	Schreiber, Paul Frederick	P	1	.000	A	
4	6	Shriver, Harry Graydon	P	25	.037	A	
4	8	Smith, Sherrod Malone (Sherry)	P	28	.257	B	ClevA
		Taylor, James Wren (Zack)	C6	7	.214	B	
18	12	Vance, Clarence Arthur (Dazzy)	P	36	.224	NYA18	
		Ward, Chas. William	SS31	33	.274	B	C
		Wheat, Zachary Davis (Zack)	OF	152	.335	B	
		Whitted, George Bostic	OF	1	.000	Pitt	C

WON 76
LOST 78
TG 154

NATIONAL LEAGUE

1923.

FINISHED 6th.

PCT. .494

BROOKLYN

WILBERT ROBINSON

WON	LOST	NAME	POS.	G.	BA	FROM	TO
		Ainsmith, Edward Wilbur	C	2	+.200	xStL	
		Bailey, Arthur Eugene (1B5)	OF100	127	.265	BosA20	
		Barber, Samuel Turner	OF12	13	.217	Chi	C
		Berg, Morris (Moe) (2B1)	SS47	49	.186	A	
4	1	Cadore, Leon Joseph	P8	9	.077	B	ChiA
		DeBerry, John Herman (Hank)	C60	78	.285	B	
3	3	Decatur, Arthur Rue	P	36	.000	B	
8	12	Dickerman, Leo Louis	P	35	.250	A	
		Fournier, Jacques Frank	1B	133	.351	StL	
		French, Raymond Edward	SS30	43	.219	NYA20	
		Griffith, Bert Joseph	OF62	79	.294	B	
		Griffith, Thomas Herman	OF128	131	.293	B	
21	18	Grimes, Burleigh Arland	P39	40	.238	B	
		Hargreaves, Chas. Russell	C15	20	.281	A	
0	1	Harper, Harry Clayton	P	1	.000	NYA21	C
4	6	Henry, Frank John	P	17	.229	StLA	
		High, Andrew Aird (2B5 SS45)	3B80	123	.270	B	
		Hungling, Bernard Herman	C1	2	.000	B	
		Johnston, James Harle (Jimmy) (SS52 3B14)	2B84	151	.325	B	
0	2	Mamaux, Albert Leon	P	5	.500	B	
		Mullen, Wm. John	3B	4	.273	StLA21	
		McCarren, Wm. Joseph (OF1)	3B66	69	.245	A	C
		Neis, Bernard Edmund	OF111	126	.274	B	
		Olson, Ivan Massie (1B2 SS2 3B4)	2B72	82	.260	B	
15	14	Ruether, Walter Henry (Dutch) (1B1)	P34	49	.274	B	
		Schliebner, Frederick Paul	1B	19	.250	A	StLA
0	0	Schreiber, Paul Frederick	P	9	.000	B	
0	0	Shriver, Harry Graydon	P	1	.000	B	C
3	6	Smith, George Allen	P	25	.192	Phil	C
		Stewart, John Franklin (Stuffy)	2B3	4	.364	Pitt	
		Taylor, James Wren (Zack)	C84	96	.288	B	
18	15	Vance, Clarence Arthur (Dazzy)	P	37	.084	B	
		Wheat, Zachary Davis (Zack)	OF87	98	.375	B	

WON 92
LOST 62
TG 154

NATIONAL LEAGUE

1924.

FINISHED 2nd.

PCT. .597

BROOKLYN

WILBERT ROBINSON

WON	LOST	NAME	POS.	G.	BA	FROM	TO
		Bailey, Arthur Eugene	OF17	18	.239	B	C
		Brown, Edward Wm.	OF	114	.308	N.Y.21	
		DeBerry, John Herman(Hank)	C63	77	.243	B	
10	9	Decatur, Arthur Rue	P	31	.114	B	
0	0	Dickerman, Leo Louis	P	7	+.167	B	StL
11	5	Doak, Wm. Leopold	P	21	+.179	xStL	
5	3	Ehrhardt, Welton Claude (Rube)	P	15	.138	A	
		Fournier, Jacques Frank	1B153	154	.334	B	
0	1	Greene, Nelson George	P	4	.000	A	
		Griffith, Thomas Herman	OF139	140	.251	B	
22	13	Grimes, Burleigh Arland	P38	40	.298	B	
		Hargreaves, Chas. Russell	C9	15	.407	B	
1	2	Henry, Frank John	P	16	.250	B	
		High, Andrew Aird (SS17 3B1)	2B133	144	.328	B	
1	0	Hollingsworth, John Burnett	P	2	.000	WashA	
		*Johnston, James Harle (Jimmy)	SS63	86	.298	B	
		Johnston, Wilfred Ivy	2B	4	.250	A	C
		Jones, John Wm.	SS	10	.108	A	C
		Klugman, Joseph (SS1)	2B28	31	.165	Chi22	
		Loftus, Richard Joseph (1B1)	OF29	46	.272	A	
0	0	Long, Thomas Francis	P	1	.000	A	C
		Mitchell, John Franklin	SS	64	.263	BosA	
		Neis, Bernard Edmund	OF62	80	.303	B	
		Olson, Ivan Massie (2B2)	SS8	10	.222	B	C
6	5	Osborne, Ernest Preston	P	21	+.250	xChi	
0	3	Roberts, James Newsom Jr.	P	11	.143	A	
8	13	Ruether, Walter Henry (Dutch)	P29	33	.242	B	
		Stock, Milton Joseph	3B	142	.242	StL	
		Taylor, James Wren (Zack)	C93	99	.290	B	
28	6	Vance, Clarence Arthur (Dazzy)	P	35	.151	B	
		Wheat, Zachary Davis (Zack)	OF139	141	.375	B	
0	0	Wilson, Gomer Russell	P	2	.000	A	C
0	2	Yarrison, Byron Wordsworth	P	3	.000	PhilA22	C

*Johnston also played 4 games at 1B, 1 game at 2B, 1 game at 3B and 1 game in the OF.

WON 68 · LOST 85 · TG 153

NATIONAL LEAGUE 1925.

FINISHED 6th. (TIED WITH PHILA) PCT. .444

BROOKLYN

WILBERT ROBINSON

WON	LOST	NAME	POS.	G.	BA	FROM	TO
		Barrett, Robert Schley		1	+.000	xChi	
		Brown, Edward Wm.	OF	153	.306	B	
0	3	Brown, Lloyd Andrew	P	17	.087	A	
1	0	Cantrell, Guy Dewey	P	14	.000	A	C
		Corgan, Chas. Howard	SS	14	.170	A	
		Cox, Elmer Joseph	OF111	122	.329	A	
		DeBerry, John Herman (Hank)	C55	67	.259	B	
0	0	Decatur, Arthur Rue	P	1	+.000	B	Phil
10	14	Ehrhardt, Welton Claude (Rube)	P	36	.211	B	
0	2	Elliott, James Thomas	P	3	.000	StLA23	
		Ford, Horace Hills	SS	66	.273	Phil	
		Fournier, Jacques Frank	1B	145	.350	B	
2	0	Greene, Nelson George	P	11	.286	B	C
		Griffith, Thomas Herman	OF2	7	+.000	B	Chi
12	19	Grimes, Burleigh Arland	P33	34	.250	B	
		Hargreaves, Chas. Russell (1B2)	C18	45	.277	B	
		High, Andrew Aird (SS3 3B2)	2B11	44	+.200	B	Bos
3	6	Hubbell, Wilbert Wm.	P	33	+.150	xPhil	C
		Hutson, Roy Lee	OF4	7	.500	A	C
		Johnston, James Harle (Jimmy) (1B8 SS2 OF20)	3B81	123	.297	B	
		Loftus, Richard Joseph	OF38	51	.237	B	C
		Mitchell, John Franklin	SS90	97	.250	B	C
0	2	McGraw, Robert Emmett	P	2	.167	NYA20	
1	2	Oeschger, Joseph Carl	P	21	.125	Phil	C
8	15	Osborne, Ernest Preston	P	41	.246	B	C
9	9	Petty, Jesse Lee	P	28	.140	ClevA21	
0	0	Roberts, James Newsom Jr.	P	1	.000	B	C
0	1	Rush, Jesse Howard	P	4	.000	A	C
		Standaert, Jerome John		1	.000	A	
		Stock, Milton Joseph (3B5)	2B141	146	.328	B	
		Taylor, James Wren (Zack)	C96	109	.310	B	
0	3	Thormahlen, Herbert Ehler	P	5	.200	BosA21	C
		Tierney, James Arthur (1B1 2B1)	3B61	93	.257	Bos	C
22	9	Vance, Clarence Arthur (Dazzy)	P	31	.143	B	
		Wheat, Zachary Davis (Zack)	OF149	150	.359	B	

WON 71 · LOST 82 · TG 153

NATIONAL LEAGUE 1926.

FINISHED 6th. PCT. .464

BROOKLYN

WILBERT ROBINSON

WON	LOST	NAME	POS.	G.	BA	FROM	TO
10	11	Barnes, Jesse Lawrence	P	31	.237	Bos	
1	0	Boehler, George Henry	P10	11	.250	Pitt23	C
		Bohne, Samuel Arthur (3B15)	SS20	47	+.200	xCin	C
		Butler, John Stephen (3B42)	SS102	147	.269	A	
		Carey, Max George	OF	27	+.260	xPitt	
		Clabaugh, John Wm.	OF	11	.071	A	C
		Cox, Elmer Joseph	OF117	124	.296	B	C
		DeBerry, John Herman (Hank)	C37	48	.287	B	
		Dowd, Raymond Bernard	2B	2	.000	PhilA19	C
2	5	Ehrhardt, Welton Claude (Rube)	P	44	.250	B	
		Felix, August Guenther (Gus)	OF125	134	.280	Bos	
		Fewster, Wilson Lloyd	2B103	105	.243	ClevA	
		Fournier, Jacques Frank	1B64	87	.284	B	
12	13	Grimes, Burleigh Arland	P30	31	.222	B	
		Hargreaves, Chas. Russell	C70	85	.250	B	
		Herman, Floyd Caves (Babe) (OF36)	1B100	137	.319	A	
		Jacobson, Merwin John Wm.	OF86	110	.247	Chi16	
		Maranville, Walter James Vincent (Rabbitt) (2B18)	SS60	78	.235	Chi	
		Marriott, Wm. Earl	3B104	109	.267	Bos	
0	0	Moss, Raymond Earl	P	1	.000	A	
9	13	McGraw, Robert Emmett	P	33	.145	B	
11	13	McWeeney, Douglas Lawrence	P	42	.109	ChiA24	
		O'Neil, George Michael	C74	75	.209	Bos	
17	17	Petty, Jesse Lee	P	38	.175	B	
		Standaert, Jerome John (3B14)	2B21	66	.345	B	
		Stock, Milton Joseph	2B	3	.000	B	C
0	0	Stryker, Sterling Albert	P	2	.000	Bos24	C
9	10	Vance, Clarence Arthur (Dazzy)	P	22	.182	B	
		Wheat, Zachary Davis (Zack)	OF102	111	.290	B	
0	0	Williams, Leon Theo	P	12	.200	A	C
		Witt, Lawton Walter (Whitey)	OF23	63	.259	NYA	C

WON 65 · LOST 88 · TG 153

NATIONAL LEAGUE 1927.

FINISHED 6th. PCT. .425

BROOKLYN

WILBERT ROBINSON

WON	LOST	NAME	POS.	G.	BA	FROM	TO
2	10	Barnes, Jesse Lawrence	P	18	.217	B	C
		Barrett, Robert Schley	3B96	99	.259	Bkn25	
		Butler, John Stephen (3B60)	SS90	149	.238	B	
0	0	Cantrell, Guy Dewey	P	6	.333	Bkn25	PhilA
		Carey, Max George	OF141	144	.266	B	
7	2	Clark, Wm. Watson	P	27	.143	ClevA24	
		Corgan, Chas. Howard	2B13	19	.263	Bkn25	C

WON	LOST	NAME	POS.	G.	BA	FROM	TO
		DeBerry, John Herman (Hank)	C67	68	.234	B	
11	8	Doak, Wm. Leopold	P	27	.128	Bkn24	
3	7	Ehrhardt, Welton Claude (Rube)	P	46	.250	B	
6	13	Elliott, James Thomas	P	30	.141	Bkn25	
		Felix, August Guenther (Gus)	OF119	130	.265	B	C
		Fewster, Wilson Lloyd		4	.000	B	C
		Flowers, D'Arcy Raymond (Jake)	SS65	67	.234	StL	
		Hargreaves, Chas. Russell	C44	46	.286	B	
		Hendrick, Harvey (Gink) (1B53)	OF64	128	.310	ClevA25	
		Henline, Walter John (Butch)	C60	67	.266	Phil	
		Herman, Floyd Caves (Babe)	1B105	130	.272	B	
		Jacobson, Merwin John Wm.	OF1	11	.000	B	C
		Marriott, Wm. Earl	3B2	6	.111	B	C
		Meusel, Emil Frederick (Irish)	OF16	42	.243	N.Y.	C
1	0	Moss, Raymond Earl	P	1	.333	B	
0	1	McGraw, Robert Emmett	P	1	+.000	B	StL
4	8	McWeeney, Douglas Lawrence	P	34	.043	B	
		Partridge, James Bagg	2B140	146	.260	A	
13	18	Petty, Jesse Lee	P	42	.099	B	
2	6	Plitt, Norman Wm.	P	19	+.222	Bkn18	N.Y.
		Roettger, Oscar Frederick Louis	OF1	5	.000	NYA24	
		Statz, Arnold John (Jigger)	OF122	130	.274	Chi25	
		Tremper, Carlton Overton	OF18	26	.233	A	
16	15	Vance, Clarence Arthur (Dazzy)	P	34	.167	B	

WON 77
LOST 76
TG 153

NATIONAL LEAGUE — FINISHED 6th.

1928. — PCT. .503

BROOKLYN

WILBERT ROBINSON

WON	LOST	NAME	POS.	G.	BA	FROM	TO
		Bancroft, David James	SS	149	.247	Bos	
		Bissonette, Adelphia Louis (Del)	1B	155	.320	A	
		Bressler, Raymond Bloom (Rube)	OF137	145	.295	Cin	
		Carey, Max George	OF95	108	.247	B	
12	9	Clark, Wm. Watson	P	40	.152	B	
		DeBerry, John Herman (Hank)	C80	82	.252	B	
3	8	Doak, Wm. Leopold	P	28	.111	B	
1	3	Ehrhardt, Welton Claude (Rube)	P	28	.286	B	
9	14	Elliott, James Thomas	P	41	.176	B	
		Flowers, D'Arcy Raymond (Jake)	2B94	103	.274	B	
		Freigau, Howard Earl (SS1)	3B10	17	+.206	Chi	Bos
		Gilbert, Walter John	3B	39	.203	A	
		Gooch, John Beverly	C38	42	+.317	xPitt	
		Hargreaves, Chas. Russell	C	20	+.197	B	Pitt
		Harris, Joseph	OF16	55	+.236	xPitt	C
		Henline, Walter John (Butch)	C45	55	.212	B	
		Hendrick, Harvey (Gink) (OF17)	3B91	126	.318	B	
		Herman, Floyd Caves (Babe)	OF127	134	.340	B	
1	0	Koupal, Louis Laddie	P	17	.111	Pitt26	
		Lopez, Alfonso Ramon (Al)	C	3	.000	A	
0	3	Moss, Raymond Earl	P22	24	.320	B	
14	14	McWeeney, Douglas Lawrence	P	42	.173	B	
		Partridge, James Bagg	2B18	37	.247	B	C
15	15	Petty, Jesse Lee	P	40	.111	B	
		Riconda, Harry Paul (SS16 3B21)	2B53	92	.224	Bos26	
		Statz, Arnold John (Jigger)	OF52	77	.234	B	C
		Tremper, Carlton Overton	OF8	10	.194	B	C
		Tyson, Albert Thomas	OF55	59	.271	N.Y.	C
22	10	Vance, Clarence Arthur (Dazzy)	P	38	.177	B	
		West, Walter Maxwell	OF5	7	.286	A	

WON 70
LOST 83
TG 153

NATIONAL LEAGUE — FINISHED 6th.

1929. — PCT. .458

BROOKLYN

WILBERT ROBINSON

WON	LOST	NAME	POS.	G.	BA	FROM	TO
2	3	Ballou, Noble Winfred (Win)	P	25	.063	StLA27	C
		Bancroft, David James	SS102	104	.277	B	
		Bissonette, Adelphia Louis (Del)	1B113	116	.281	B	
0	0	Blethen, Clarence Waldo	P	2	.000	BosA23	C
0	0	Bradshaw, Joe Siah	P	2	.000	A	C
		Bressler, Raymond Bloom (Rube)	OF122	136	.318	B	
		Carey, Max George	OF2	19	.304	B	
16	19	Clark, Wm. Watson	P41	42	.165	B	
		Cullop, Henry Nicholas	OF11	13	.195	ClevA27	
		DeBerry, John Herman (Hank)	C	68	.262	A	
6	14	Dudley, Elzie Clise	P35	36	.098	B	
1	2	Elliott, James Thomas	P	6	.250	B	
0	1	Ferguson, James Alexander (Alex)	P	3	+1.000	xPhil	C
		Flowers, D'Arcy Raymond (Jake)	2B39	46	.200	B	
		Frederick, John Henry	OF143	148	.328	A	
		Gilbert, Walter John	3B142	143	.304	B	
		Gooch, John Beverly		1	+.000	B	Cin
0	0	Greenfield, Kent	P6	7	+.000	xBos	C
		Hendrick, Harvey (Gink) (1B39)	OF42	110	.354	B	
		Henline, Walter John (Butch)	C21	27	.242	B	
		Herman, Floyd Caves (Babe)	OF141	146	.381	B	
0	1	Koupal, Louis Laddie	P	18	+.071	Pitt26	Phil
		Moore, Graham Edward (SS36)	2B74	111	.296	Bos	
3	3	Moore, Wm. Austin	P	32	.188	A	
13	7	Morrison, John Dewey	P	39	.163	Pitt27	
11	6	Moss, Raymond Earl	P39	42	.076	B	
4	10	McWeeney, Douglas Lawrence	P	36	.104	B	

WON	LOST	NAME	POS.	G.	BA	FROM	TO
0	3	Newsom, Louis Norman (Buck)	P	3	.000	A	
0	1	Pattison, James Wells	P	6	.500	A	C
		Picinich, Valentine John (Val)	C85	93	.260	Cin	
		Rhiel, Wm. Joseph	2B47	76	.278	A	
0	0	Roy, Luther Franklin	P	2	+.000	xPhil	C
14	13	Vance, Clarence Arthur (Dazzy)	P	31	.135	B	
		Warner, John Ralph	SS	17	.274	DetA	
		West, Walter Maxwell	OF1	5	.250	B	C
		Wright, Forest Glenn	SS1	24	.200	Pitt	

WON 86 LOST 68 TG 154

NATIONAL LEAGUE 1930. FINISHED 4th. PCT. .558

BROOKLYN

WILBERT ROBINSON

WON	LOST	NAME	POS.	G.	BA	FROM	TO
		Bissonette, Adelphia Louis (Del)	1B	146	.336	B	
		Boone, Isaac Morgan	OF27	40	.297	ChiA27	
		Bressler, Raymond Bloom (Rube)	OF90	109	.299	B	
13	13	Clark, Wm. Watson	P	44	.206	B	
		DeBerry, John Herman (Hank)	C	35	.295	B	C
2	4	Dudley, Elzie Clise	P	21	.208	B	
10	7	Elliott, James Thomas	P	35	.147	B	
0	0	Faulkner, James LeRoy	P	2	.000	NY28	C
		Finn, Cornelius Francis (Mickey)	2B81	87	.278	A	
		Flowers, D'Arcy Raymond (Jake)	2B65	89	.320	B	
		Frederick, John Henry	OF	142	.334	B	
		Gilbert, Walter John	3B	150	.294	B	
0	2	Heimach, Fred Amos	P	13	.250	N.Y.A.	
		Hendrick, Harvey (Gink)	OF42	68	.257	B	
		Herman, Floyd Caves (Babe)	OF	153	.393	B	
		Lee, Harold Burnham (Hal)	OF12	22	.162	A	
		Lopez, Alfonso Ramon (Al)	C126	128	.309	Bkn28	
14	8	Luque, Adolfo	P	31	.240	Cin	
		Moore, Graham Edward (SS17 OF23)	2B23	76	.281	B	
0	0	Moore, Wm. Austin	P	1	.000	B	
1	2	Morrison, John Dewey	P	16	.000	B	C
9	6	Moss, Raymond Earl	P	36	.154	B	
0	0	Newsom, Louis Norman (Buck)	P	2	.000	B	
14	7	Phelps, Raymond Clifford	P	36	.147	A	
		Picinich, Valentine John (Val)	C22	23	.217	B	
		Slade, Gordon Leigh	SS21	25	.216	A	
6	4	Thurston, Hollis John (Sloppy)	P24	36	.200	WashA27	
17	15	Vance, Clarence Arthur (Dazzy)	P	35	.135	B	
		Warner, John Ralph	3B3	21	.320	B	
		Wright, Forest Glenn	SS134	135	.321	B	

WON 79 LOST 73 TG 152

NATIONAL LEAGUE 1931. FINISHED 4th. PCT. .520

BROOKLYN

WILBERT ROBINSON

WON	LOST	NAME	POS.	G.	BA	FROM	TO
		Bissonette, Adelphia Louis (Del)	1B	152	.290	B	
		Boone, Isaac Morgan		6	.200	B	
		Bressler, Raymond Bloom (Rube)	OF35	67	.281	B	
14	10	Clark, Wm. Watson	P	34	.250	B	
		Cohen, Alta Albert	OF	1	.667	A	
2	2	Day, Clyde Henry (Pea-Ridge)	P	22	.222	Cin26	C
		Finn, Cornelius Francis (Mickey)	2B112	118	.274	B	
		Flowers, D'Arcy Raymond (Jake) (SS1)	2B6	22	+.226	B	StL
		Frederick, John Henry	OF145	146	.270	B	
0	1	Gallivan, Philip Joseph	P	6	.000	A	
		Gilbert, Walter John	3B	145	.266	B	
9	7	Heimach, Fred Amos	P31	39	.197	B	
		Hendrick, Harvey (Gink)		1	+.000	B	Cin
		Herman, Floyd Caves (Babe)	OF150	151	.313	B	
		Lombardi, Ernesto Natali (Schnozz)	C50	73	.297	A	
		Lopez, Alfonso Ramon (Al)	C105	111	.269	B	
7	6	Luque, Adolfo	P	19	.133	B	
0	1	Mattingly, Lawrence Earl	P	8	.000	A	C
1	2	Moore, Wm. Austin	P	23	.154	B	
0	0	Moss, Raymond Earl	P	1	+.000	B	Bos
3	1	Mungo, Van Lingle	P	5	.250	A	
		O'Doul, Frank Joseph (Lefty)	OF132	134	.336	Phil	
7	9	Phelps, Raymond Clifford	P	28	.157	B	
		Picinich, Valentine John (Val)	C15	24	.267	B	
5	4	Quinn, John Picus	P	39	.200	PhilA	
		Reis, Robert Joseph Thomas (2B1)	3B4	6	.294	A	
		Rosenfeld, Max	OF	3	.222	A	
11	8	Shaute, Joseph Benjamin	P	25	.178	ClevA	
		Slade, Gordon Leigh	SS82	85	.239	B	
		Sothern, Dennis Elwood (Denny)	OF10	19	.161	Pitt	C
		Thompson, LaFayette Fresco Jr. (Chick) (SS10)	2B43	74	.265	Phil	
9	9	Thurston, Hollis John (Sloppy)	P	24	.217	B	
11	13	Vance, Clarence Arthur (Dazzy)	P	30	.134	B	
		Warner, John Ralph (SS1)	3B1	9	.500	B	
		Wright, Forest Glenn	SS75	77	.284	B	

WON 81 LOST 73 TG 154

NATIONAL LEAGUE 1932. FINISHED 3rd. PCT. .526

BROOKLYN

MAX GEORGE CAREY

WON	LOST	NAME	POS.	G.	BA	FROM	TO
		Boone, Isaac Morgan	OF3	13	.143	B	C
		Caldwell, Bruce	1B2	7	.091	ClevA28	C
		Clancy, John Wm.	1B	53	.306	ChiA30	
20	12	Clark, Wm. Watson	P	40	.216	B	
		Cohen, Alta Albert	OF7	9	.156	B	
		Cuccinello, Anthony Francis (Tony)	2B	154	.281	Cin	
		Finn, Cornelius Francis (Mickey)	3B50	65	.238	B	
		Frederick, John Henry	OF88	118	.299	B	
9	4	Heimach, Fred Amos	P36	37	.164	B	
1	3	Hoyt, Waite Chas.	P	8	+.000	PhilA	N.Y.
0	0	Jones, Arthur Lenox	P	1	.000	A	C
		Kelly, George Lange (Long George)	1B62	64	.243	Chi30	C
		Lopez, Alfonso Ramon (Al)	C125	126	.275	B	
0	3	Moore, Wm. Austin	P20	21	.214	B	
13	11	Mungo, Van Lingle	P	39	.203	B	
		O'Doul, Frank Joseph (Lefty)	OF	148	.368	B	
4	5	Phelps, Raymond Clifford	P	20	.087	B	
		Picinich, Valentine John (Val)	C24	41	.257	B	
0	1	Pipgras, Edward John	P	5	.000	A	C
3	7	Quinn, John Picus	P	42	.200	B	
		Reis, Robert Joseph Thomas	3B	1	.250	B	
		Richards, Paul Rapier	C	3	.000	A	
		Rosenfeld, Max	OF30	34	.359	B	
7	7	Shaute, Joseph Bemjamin	P34	35	.200	B	
		Seibert, Richard Walther (Dick)	1B	6	.286	A	
		Slade, Gordon Leigh (3B23)	SS55	79	.240	B	
		Stripp, Joseph Valentine (1B43)	3B93	138	.303	Cin	
		Sukeforth, Clyde LeRoy	C36	59	.234	Cin	
		Taylor, Daniel Turney	OF96	105	+.324	xChi	
0	1	Thomas, Fay Wesley	P	7	.000	ClevA	
		Thompson, LaFayette, Fresco Jr. (Chick)		3	.000	B	
12	8	Thurston, Hollis John (Sloppy)	P28	29	.304	B	
12	11	Vance, Clarence Arthur (Dazzy)	P	27	.089	B	
		Wilson, Lewis Robert (Hack)	OF125	135	.297	Chi	
		Wright, Forest Glenn	SS122	127	.274	B	

WON 65 NATIONAL LEAGUE FINISHED 6th.
LOST 88
TG 153 1933. PCT. .425

BROOKLYN

MAX GEORGE CAREY

WON	LOST	NAME	POS.	G.	BA	FROM	TO
12	20	Beck, Walter Wm. (Boom-Boom)	P	43	.189	StLA28	
10	17	Benge, Raymond Adelphia	P	37	.184	Phil	
		Bissonette, Adelphia Louis (Del)	1B32	35	.246	Bkn31	
		Blue, Luzerne Atwell (Lou)	1B	1	.000	ChiA	C
		Boyle, Ralph Francis	OF90	93	.299	Bos30	
13	15	Carroll, Owen Thomas	P33	34	.149	Cin	
2	4	Clark, Wm. Watson	P	11	+.154	B	N.Y.
		Cuccinello, Anthony Francis (Tony) (3B14)	2B120	134	.252	B	
		Delmas, Bert Chas.	2B10	12	.250	A	C
		Flowers, D'Arcy Raymond (Jake) (2B19 3B8 OF1)	SS36	78	.233	StL	
		Frederick, John Henry	OF138	147	.308	B	
		Frey, Linus Reinhard (Lonny)	SS	34	.319	A	
0	1	Heimach, Fred Amos	P	10	.200	B	C
		Hutcheson, Joseph Johnson	OF45	55	.234	A	C
		Jordan, James Wm. (2B11)	SS51	70	.256	A	
		Judge, Joseph Ignatius Jr.	1B28	42	.214	WashA	
2	3	Leonard, Emil John (Dutch)	P	10	.000	A	
		Leslie, Samuel Andrew	1B95	96	+.283	xN.Y.	
		Lopez, Alfonso Ramon (Al) (2B1)	C124	126	.301	B	
0	0	Lucas, Raymond Wesley	P	2	.000	N.Y.31	
16	15	Mungo, Van Lingle	P	41	.179	B	
		O'Doul, Frank Joseph (Lefty)	OF41	43	+.252	B	N.Y.
		Outen, Wm. Austin	C56	93	.248	A	C
		Picinich, Valentine John (Val)	C	6	+.167	B	Pitt
		Rosenfeld, Max Rosy	OF	5	.111	B	C
1	1	Ryan, Wilfred Patrick Dolan	P	30	.154	NYA28	C
3	4	Shaute, Joseph Benjamin	P	41	.222	B	
		Stripp, Joseph Valentine	3B140	141	.277	B	
		Sukeforth, Clyde LeRoy	C18	20	.056	B	
		Taylor, Daniel Turney	OF91	103	.285	B	
6	8	Thurston, Hollis John (Sloppy)	P	32	.159	B	C
		Wilson, Lewis Robert (Hack) (2B5)	OF90	117	.267	B	
		Wright, Forest Glenn (1B9 3B2)	SS51	71	.255	B	

WON 71 NATIONAL LEAGUE FINISHED 6th.
LOST 81
TG 152 1934. PCT. .467

BROOKLYN

CHAS. DILLON STENGEL

WON	LOST	NAME	POS.	G.	BA	FROM	TO
7	11	Babich, John Chas.	P	25	.140	A	
2	6	Beck, Walter Wm. (Boom-Boom)	P	22	.235	B	
14	12	Benge, Raymond Adelphia	P	36	.169	B	
		Berres, Raymond Frederick	C37	39	.215	A	
		Boyle, Ralph Francis	OF121	128	.305	B	
		Bucher, James Quinter	2B20	47	.226	A	
1	3	Carroll, Owen Thomas	P26	28	.240	B	C
		Chapman, Glenn Justice (2B14)	OF40	67	.280	A	C

WON	LOST	NAME	POS.	G.	BA	FROM	TO
2	0	Clark, Wm. Watson	P	17	+.125	xN.Y.	
		Cuccinello, Anthony Francis (Tony) (3B43)	2B101	140	.261	B	
		Frederick, John Henry	OF77	104	.296	B	C
		Frey, Linus Reinhard (Lonny) (3B13)	SS109	125	.284	B	
2	4	Herring, Arthur L.	P	14	.143	DetA	
		Hogg, Wilbert George	3B1	2	.000	A	C
		Jordan, James Wm. (2B41)	SS51	97	.266	B	
		Koenecke, Leonard George (Len)	OF121	123	.320	NY32	
14	11	Leonard, Emil John (Dutch)	P	44	.179	B	
		Leslie, Samuel Andrew	1B138	146	.332	B	
		Lopez, Alfonso Ramon (Al)	C137	140	.273	B	
1	1	Lucas, Raymond Wesley	P	10	.333	B	C
		Millies, Walter Louis	C	2	.000	A	
18	16	Mungo, Van Lingle	P45	46	.248	B	
3	7	Munns, Leslie Ernest	P33	34	.241	A	
		McCarthy, John Joseph (Mac)	1B13	17	.179	A	
1	0	Page, Philip Rausac Jr.	P	6	.000	DetA30	C
0	3	Perkins, Chas. Sullivan	P	11	.286	PhiIA30	C
1	1	Smythe, Wm. Harry	P	10	.333	xNYA	C
		Stripp, Joseph Valentine	3B96	104	.315	B	
		Sukeforth, Clyde LeRoy	C18	27	.163	B	
		Taylor, Daniel Turney	OF108	120	.299	B	
		Tremark, Nicholas Joseph	OF6	17	.250	A	
		Wilson, Lewis Robert (Hack)	OF43	67	+.262	B	Phil
5	6	Zachary, Jonathan Thompson Walton (Tom)	P22	24	+.184	xBos	

WON 70 — NATIONAL LEAGUE — FINISHED 5th.
LOST 83
TG 153 — 1935. — PCT. .458

BROOKLYN

CHAS. DILLON STENGEL

WON	LOST	NAME	POS.	G.	BA	FROM	TO
7	14	Babich, John Chas.	P	37	.184	B	
1	0	Baker, Thomas Calvin	P	11	.474	A	
0	0	Barr, Robert Alexander	P	2	.000	A	C
9	9	Benge, Raymond Adelphia	P	23	.191	B	
		Bordagaray, Stanley George	OF105	120	.282	ChiA	
		Boyle, Ralph Francis	OF124	127	.272	B	C
		Bucher, James Quinter (3B39 OF37)	2B41	123	.302	B	
13	8	Clark, Wm. Watson	P33	34	.177	B	B
		Cooney, John Walter	OF	10	.310	Bos30	
		Cuccinello, Anthony Francis (Tony) (3B36)	2B64	102	.292	B	
		Dedeaux, Raoul	SS	2	.250	A	C
3	12	Earnshaw, George Livingston (Moose)	P	25	.217	xChiA	
0	1	Eisenstat, Harry	P	2	.000	A	

WON	LOST	NAME	POS.	G.	BA	FROM	TO
		Frey, Linus Reinhard (Lonny) (2B4)	SS127	131	.262	B	
0	0	Green, Harvey G.	P	2	.000	A	C
		Jordan, James Wm. (SS28 3B5)	2B46	94	.278	B	
		Koenecke, Leonard George (Len)	OF91	100	.283	B	C
0	0	Lamanske, Frank James	P	2	.000	A	C
2	9	Leonard, Emil John (Dutch)	P	43	.025	B	
		Leslie, Samuel Andrew	1B138	142	.308	B	
0	1	Logan, Robert Dean	P	2	.000	A	
		Lopez, Alfonso Ramon (Al)	C126	128	.251	B	
		Mills, Colonel Buster	OF	17	.214	StL	
16	10	Mungo, Van Lingle	P37	44	.289	B	
1	3	Munns, Leslie Ernest	P21	22	.188	B	
		McCarthy, John Joseph (Mac)	1B19	22	.250	B	
		Ock, Harold David	C	1	.000	A	C
		Onis, Manuel Ralph	C	1	1.000	A	C
		Phelps, Ernest Goedon (Babe)	C34	47	.364	Chi	
3	2	Reis, Robert Joseph Thomas (P14 1B1 2B4 3B1)	OF21	52	.247	Bkn32	
		Sherlock, Vincent Thomas	2B	9	.462	A	C
		Skaff, Francis Michael	3B	6	.545	A	
		Stripp, Joseph Valentine (1B15 OF1)	3B88	109	.306	B	
		Taylor, Daniel Turney	OF99	112	.290	B	
		Taylor, James Wren (Zack)	C	26	.130	NYA	
		Tremark, Nicholas Joseph	OF4	10	.231	B	
3	2	Vance, Clarence Arthur (Dazzy)	P	20	.059	StL	C
7	12	Zachary, Jonathan Thompson Walton (Tom)	P	25	.135	B	

WON 67 — NATIONAL LEAGUE — FINISHED 7th.
LOST 87
TG 154 — 1936. — PCT. .435

BROOKLYN

CHAS. DILLON STENGEL

WON	LOST	NAME	POS.	G.	BA	FROM	TO
1	8	Baker, Thomas Calvin	P35	37	.233	B	
		Berres, Raymond Frederick	C	105	.240	Bkn34	
		Bordagaray, Stanley George (2B11)	OF92	125	.315	B	
11	13	Brandt, Edward Arthur	P38	43	.190	Bos	
		Bucher, James Quinter (2B32 OF30)	3B39	110	.251	B	
6	6	Butcher, Albert Maxwell (Max)	P38	42	.125	A	
7	11	Clark, Wm. Watson	P	33	.231	B	
		Cooney, John Walter	OF	130	.282	B	
4	9	Earnshaw, George Livingston (Moose)	P	19	+.242	B	StL
		Eckhardt, Oscar George (Ox)	OF10	16	.182	Bos32	C
1	2	Eisenstat, Harry	P	5	.333	B	

WON	LOST	NAME	POS.	G.	BA	FROM	TO
13	10	Frankhouse, Frederick Meloy	P41	42	.143	Bos	
		Frey, Linus Reinhard (Lonny) (2B30)	SS117	148	.279	B	
		Gautreaux, Sidney Allen	C15	75	.268	A	
		Geraghty, Benjamin Raymond	SS31	51	.194	A	
		Hassett, John Aloysius (Buddy)	1B	156	.310	A	
		Hudson, John Wilson	SS4	6	.167	A	
5	6	Jeffcoat, George Edward	P	40	.130	A	
		Jordan, James Wm.	2B98	115	.234	B	C
0	0	Leonard, Emil John (Dutch)	P	16	.400	B	
		Lindstrom, Frederick Chas.	OF	26	.264	Chi	C
		Moore, Randolph Edward (Randy)	OF21	42	.239	Bos	
18	19	Mungo, Van Lingle	P45	50	.179	B	
		Phelps, Ernest Gordon (Babe)	C98	115	.367	B	
		Radtke, Jack Wm.	2B14	33	.097	A	C
		Siebert, Richard Walther (Dick)	OF	2	.000	Bkn32	
		Stripp, Joseph Valentine	3B106	110	.317	B	
		Taylor, Daniel Turney	OF31	43	.293	B	C
		Tremark, Nicholas Joseph	OF	8	.250	B	C
		Watkins, George Archibald	OF98	105	+.256	xPhil	C
		Wilson, Edward Francis	OF47	52	.347	A	
		Winsett, John Thomas (Tom)	OF21	22	.235	StL	
1	3	Winston, Henry Randolph	P	14	.091	PhilA33	C
0	0	Zachary, Jonathan Thompson Walton (Tom)	P	1	+.000	B	Phil

WON 62   NATIONAL LEAGUE   FINISHED 6th.
LOST 91
TG 153   1937.   PCT. .405

BROOKLYN

BURLEIGH ARLAND GRIMES

WON	LOST	NAME	POS.	G.	BA	FROM	TO
0	1	Baker, Thomas Calvin	P	7	+.000	B	N.Y.
0	2	Birkofer, Ralph Joseph	P11	12	.273	Pitt	
		Brack, Gilbert Herman (Gib)	OF101	112	.274	A	
		Brown, John Lindsay	SS45	48	.270	A	C
		Bucher, James Quinter (3B43)	2B49	125	.253	B	
11	15	Butcher, Albert Maxwell (Max)	P39	40	.161	B	
0	0	Cantwell, Benjamin Caldwell	P	13	+.167	xN.Y.	
		Chervinko, Paul	C26	30	.146	A	
		Cisar, George	OF13	20	.207	A	C
0	0	Clark, Wm. Watson	P	2	.000	B	C
		Cooney, John Walter	OF111	120	.293	B	
		Daniel, Handley Jacob	1B7	12	.185	A	C
3	3	Eisenstat, Harry	P	13	.000	B	
		English, Elwood George (Woody) (2B11)	SS116	129	.238	Chi	
		Fallon, George Decatur	2B	4	.250	A	
4	8	Fitzsimmons, Frederick Landis	P	13	+.167	xN.Y.	
10	13	Frankhouse, Frederick Meloy	P33	39	.190	B	
		Gautreaux, Sidney Allen	C	11	.100	B	C
		Haas, Berthold John (Bert)	1B3	16	.400	A	
11	13	Hamlin, Luke Daniel (Hot Potato)	P39	41	.186	DetA34	
		Hassett, John Aloysius (Buddy)	1B131	137	.304	B	
5	12	Henshaw, Roy John	P42	43	.167	Chi	
7	7	Hoyt, Waite Chas.	P	27	+.083	xPitt	
		Hudson, John Wilson	SS11	13	.185	B	
1	3	Jeffcoat, George Edward	P	21	.000	B	
		Klumpp, Elmer Edward	C	5	.091	WashA34	C
		Lavagetto, Harry Arthur (Cookie) (3B45)	2B100	149	.282	Pitt	
0	1	Lindsey, James Kendrick	P	20	.167	StL34	C
		Malinosky, Anthony Francis (Tony) (SS11)	3B13	35	.228	A	C
		Manush, Henry Emmett (Heinie)	OF123	132	.333	BosA	
1	2	Marrow, Chas. Kennon	P	6	.000	DetA32	
		Moore, Randolph Edward (Randy)	C10	13	+.136	B	StL
		Morgan, Edwin Willis	OF7	31	.188	StL	C
9	11	Mungo, Van Lingle	P25	28	.250	B	
		Parks, Arthur Wm.	OF4	7	.313	A	
0	0	Peterson, James Niels	P	3	.000	PhilA33	C
		Phelps, Ernest Gordon (Babe)	C111	121	.313	B	
		Polly, Nicholas Joseph	3B7	10	.222	A	
		Rosen, Goodwin George (Goody)	OF21	22	.312	A	
		Spencer, Roy Hampton	C45	51	.205	N.Y.	
		Stripp, Joseph Valentine (1B14)	3B66	90	.243	B	
		Wilson, Edward Francis	OF21	36	.222	B	C
0	0	Winsett, John Thomas (Tom) (P1)	OF101	118	.237	B	

WON 69   NATIONAL LEAGUE   FINISHED 7th.
LOST 80
TG 149   1938.   PCT. .463

BROOKLYN

BURLEIGH ARLAND GRIMES

WON	LOST	NAME	POS.	G.	BA	FROM	TO
		Brack, Gilbert Herman (Gib)	OF13	40	+.214	B	Phil
5	4	Butcher, Albert Maxwell (Max)	P24	25	+.160	B	Phil
		Camilli, Adolph Louis	1B145	146	.251	Phil	
		Campbell, Wm. Gilthorpe (Gilly)	C44	54	.246	Cin	C
		Chervinko, Paul	C	12	.148	B	C
		Coscarart, Peter Joseph	2B27	32	.152	A	
		Cuyler, Hazen Shirley (Kiki)	OF68	82	.273	Cin	C
		Durocher, Leo Ernest	SS	141	.219	StL	
		English, Elwood George (Woody)	3B21	34	.250	B	C
11	8	Fitzsimmons, Frederick Landis	P	27	.171	B	

WON	LOST	NAME	POS.	G.	BA	FROM	TO
3	5	Frankhouse, Frederick Meloy	P30	31	.154	B	
2	0	Gaddy, John Wilson	P	2	.000	A	C
		George, Chas. Peter	C	7	.200	ClevA36	
		Haas, Berthold John (Bert)		1	.000	B	
12	15	Hamlin, Luke Daniel (Hot Potato)	P	44	.141	B	
		Hassett, John Aloysius (Buddy)	OF71	115	.293	B	
		Hayworth, Raymond Hall	C	5	.000	xDetA	
		Hockett, Oris Leon	OF17	21	.329	A	
0	3	Hoyt, Waite Chas.	P	6	.000	B	C
		Hudson, John Wilson	2B132	135	.261	B	
		Koy, Ernest Anyz (Chief)	OF135	142	.299	A	
0	1	LaMaster, Wayne Lee	P3	5	+.167	xPhil	C
		Lavagetto, Harry Arthur (Cookie)	3B132	137	.273	B	
		Manush, Henry Emmett (Heinie)	OF12	17	+.235	B	Pitt
0	1	Marrow, Chas. Kennon	P	15	.000	B	C
4	11	Mungo, Van Lingle	P24	32	.191	B	
1	0	Nahem, Samuel Ralph	P	1	.400	A	
		Phelps, Ernest Gordon (Babe)	C55	66	.308	B	
8	9	Posedel, Wm. John (Barnacle Bill)	P	33	.227	A	
0	0	Potter, Maryland Dykes	P	2	.000	A	C
11	14	Pressnell, Forest Chas. (Tot)	P	43	.143	A	
0	2	Rogers, Lee Otis	P12	14	.000	xBosA	C
		Rogers, Stanley Frank (2B3 SS7)	3B8	23	.189	A	C
		Rosen, Goodwin George (Goody)	OF113	138	.281	B	
		Shea, Mervyn David John	C47	48	.183	ChiA	
		Sington, Frederic Wm.	OF	17	.358	WashA	
		Spencer, Roy Hampton	C	16	.267	B	C
		Stainback, George Tucker (Tuck)	OF23	35	+.327	xPhil	
12	6	Tamulis, Vitautas Casimirus (Vito)	P38	39	.127	xStLA	
		Thomas, Raymond Joseph	C	1	.333	A	C
		Williams, Woodrow Wilson	SS18	20	.333	A	
0	1	Winford, James Harold	P	2	.000	StL	C
		Winsett, John Thomas (Tom)	OF	12	.300	B	C

WON 84
LOST 69
TG 153

NATIONAL LEAGUE — FINISHED 3rd.

1939. — PCT. .549

BROOKLYN

LEO ERNEST DUROCHER

WON	LOST	NAME	POS.	G.	BA	FROM	TO
		Almada, Melo Baldomero (Mel)	OF32	39	.214	xStLA	C
		Camilli, Adolph Louis	1B	157	.290	B	
15	10	Casey, Hugh Thomas	P	40	.203	Chi35	
		Coscarart, Peter Joseph	2B107	115	.277	B	
4	0	Crouch, Wm. Elmer	P	6	.133	A	
		Deal, Frederick Lindsay	OF	4	.000	A	C
1	2	Doyle, Wm. Carl	P	5	.167	PhilA36	
		Durocher, Leo Ernest MGR.	SS113	116	.277	B	
1	8	Evans, Russell Earl (Red)	P	24	.308	ChiA36	C
7	9	Fitzsimmons, Frederick Landis	P	27	.234	B	
20	13	Hamlin, Luke Daniel (Hot Potato)	P	40	.126	B	
		Hartje, Christian Henry	C	9	.313	A	C
		Hayworth, Raymond Hall	C18	21	+.154	B	N.Y.
		Hockett, Oris Leon	OF	9	.231	B	
1	2	Hollingsworth, Albert Wayne (Al)	P8	9	+.125	xPhil	
		Hudson, John Wilson (2B45)	SS50	109	.254	B	
5	2	Hutchinson, Ira Kendall	P	41	.037	Bos	
0	0	Jeffcoat, George Edward	P	1	.000	Bkn37	
		Koy, Ernest Anyz (Chief)	OF114	125	.278	B	
		Lary, Lynford Hobart (Lyn) (3B7)	SS12	29	+.161	xClevA	StL
		Lavagetto, Harry Arthur (Cookie)	3B149	153	.300	B	
		Lazzeri, Anthony Michael (Tony) (3B2)	2B11	14	+.282	Chi	N.Y.
		Moore, Eugene Jr. (Gene)	OF86	107	.225	Bos	
4	5	Mungo, Van Lingle	P14	29	.345	B	
		Parks, Arthur Wm.	OF65	71	.272	Bkn37	C
		Phelps, Ernest Gordon (Babe)	C92	98	.285	B	
0	0	Poffenberger, Cletus Elwood (Boots)	P	3	.000	DetA	C
9	7	Pressnell, Forest Chas. (Tot)	P	31	.196	B	
		Ripple, James Albert (Jimmy)	OF	28	+.330	xN.Y.	
		Rosen, Goodwin George (Goody)	OF47	54	.251	B	
0	0	Schott, Eugene Arthur	P	1	+.000	xPhil	C
		Sewell, James Luther (Luke)	(DID NOT PLAY)			ChiA	ClevA
		Sington, Frederic Wm.	OF22	32	.274	B	C
		Stainback, George Tucker (Tuck)	OF55	68	.269	B	
9	8	Tamulis, Vitautis Casimirus (Vito)	P	39	.182	B	
		Todd, Alfred Chester (Al)	C73	86	.277	Pitt	
		Walker, Fred (Dixie)	OF59	61	.280	xDetA	
8	3	Wyatt, John Whitlow (Whit)	P	16	.167	ClevA37	

WON 88
LOST 65
TG 153

NATIONAL LEAGUE — FINISHED 2nd.

1940. — PCT. .575

BROOKLYN

LEO ERNEST DUROCHER

WON	LOST	NAME	POS.	G.	BA	FROM	TO
		Camilli, Adolph Louis	1B140	142	.287	B	
6	6	Carleton, James Otto (Tex)	P	34	.186	Chi38	C
11	8	Casey, Hugh Thomas	P44	45	.250	B	
		Coscarart, Peter Joseph	2B140	143	.237	B	
		Cullenbine, Roy Joseph	OF19	22	.180	DetA	StLA

WON	LOST	NAME	POS.	G.	BA	FROM	TO
8	7	Davis, Curtis Benton (Curt)	P	22	+.128	xStL	
0	0	Doyle, Wm. Carl	P	3	+1 .000	B	StL
		Durocher, Leo Ernest MGR. (2B4)	SS53	62	.231	B	
0	0	Fette, Louis Henry Wm. (Lou)	P	2	+.000	xBos	
16	2	Fitzsimmons, Frederick Landis	P	20	.106	B	
0	0	Ferrell, Wesley Cheek (Wes)	P1	2	.000	NYA	
1	1	Flowers, Chas. Wesley	P	5	.200	A	
		Franks, Herman Louis	C43	65	.183	StL	
		Gallagher, Joseph Emmett	OF20	57	.264	xStLA	C
		Gilbert, Chas. Mader	OF43	57	.246	A	
		Giuliani, Angelo John (Tony)	C	1	.000	WashA	
2	5	Grissom, Leo Theo (Lee)	P	14	.217	xNYA	
9	8	Hamlin, Luke Daniel (Hot Potato)	P33	35	.086	B	
1	2	Head, Edward Marvin	P13	14	.182	A	
		Hudson, John Wilson (2B27 3B1)	SS38	85	.218	B	
3	1	Kimball, Newel W.	P	21	+.000	Chi38	StL
		Koy, Ernest Anyz (Chief)	OF19	24	+.229	B	StL
		Lavagetto, Harry Arthur (Cookie)	3B116	118	.257	B	
1	0	Macon, Max Cullen	P	21	.000	StL38	
		Mancuso, August Rodney (Gus)	C56	60	.229	Chi	
		Medwick, Joseph Michael (Ducky)	OF103	106	+.300	xStL	
		Moore, Eugene Jr. (Gene)	OF6	10	+.269	B	Bos
1	0	Mungo, Van Lingle	P7	8	.000	B	
		Phelps, Ernest Gordon (Babe) (1B1)	C99	118	.295	B	
6	5	Pressnell, Forest Chas. (Tot)	P	24	.000	B	
0	1	Rachunok, Stephen Stepanovich	P	2	.000	A	C
		Reese, Harold Henry (Pee-Wee)	SS83	84	.272	A	
		Reiser, Harold Patrick (Pete) (SS5 OF17)	3B30	58	.293	A	
		Ripple, James Albert (Jimmy)	OF3	7	+.231	B	Cin
		Ross, Donald Raymond	3B	10	.289	DetA38	
8	5	Tamulis, Vitautis Casimirus (Vito) (1B1)	P41	42	.130	B	
		Vosmik, Joseph Franklin	OF99	116	.282	BosA	
		Walker, Fred (Dixie)	OF136	143	.308	B	
		Wasdell, James Chas. (1B17)	OF42	77	.278	xWashA	
15	14	Wyatt, John Whitlow (Whit)	P	37	.175	B	

WON 100 NATIONAL LEAGUE FINISHED 1st.
LOST 54
TG 154 1941. PCT. .649

BROOKLYN

LEO ERNEST DUROCHER

WON	LOST	NAME	POS.	G.	BA	FROM	TO
0	2	Albosta, Edward John	P	2	.000	A	
3	0	Allen, John Thomas (Johnny)	P	11	.050	xStLA	
3	2	Brown, Mace Stanley	P	24	+.000	xPitt	
		Camilli, Adolph Louis	1B148	149	.285	B	
14	11	Casey, Hugh Thomas	P	45	.120	B	
1	0	Chipman, Robert Howard	P	1	.000	A	
		Coscarart, Peter Joseph (SS1)	2B19	43	.127	B	
13	7	Davis, Curtis Benton (Curt)	P28	31	.186	B	
1	1	Drake, Thomas Kendall (OF1)	P10	11	.400	ClevA39	
		Durocher, Leo Ernest MGR. (2B1)	SS12	18	.286	B	
6	1	Fitzsimmons, Frederick Landis	P	13	.143	B	
		Franks, Herman Louis (OF1)	C54	57	.201	B	
0	0	French, Lawrence Herbert (Larry)	P	6	+.250	xChi	
		Galan, August John (Augie)	OF6	17	+.259	xChi	
		Giuliani, Angelo John (Tony)	C	3	.000	B	
0	0	Grissom, Leo Theo (Lee)	P	4	+.500	B	Phil
8	8	Hamlin, Luke Daniel (Hot Potato)	P	30	.146	B	
		Herman, Wm. Jennings Bryan (Billy)	2B	133	+.291	xChi	
22	9	Higbe, Walter Kirby	P	48	.188	Phil	
		Kampouris, Alexis Wm.	2B15	16	.314	NY39	
3	1	Kimball, Newel W.	P	15	.214	StL	
		Lavagetto, Harry Arthur (Cookie)	3B120	132	.277	B	
		Medwick, Joseph Michael (Ducky)	OF131	133	.318	B	
0	0	Mungo, Van Lingle	P	2	.000	B	
		Owen, Arnold Malcolm (Mickey)	C	128	.231	StL	
		Pfister, George Edward	C	1	.000	A	C
		Phelps, ErnestGordon (Babe)	C11	16	.233	B	
		Reese, Harold Henry (Pee-Wee)	SS151	152	.228	B	
		Reiser, Harold Patrick (Pete)	OF133	137	.343	B	
		Riggs, Lewis Sidney (Lew)	3B43	77	.305	Cin	
3	0	Swift, Wm. (Bill)	P	9	.200	Bos	
0	0	Tamulis, Vitautis Casimirus (Vito)	P	12	+.000	xPhil	C
		Tatum, Thomas Vee Tee	OF4	8	.167	A	
		Vosmik, Joseph Franklin	OF18	25	.196	B	
		Walker, Fred (Dixie)	OF146	148	.311	B	
		Waner, Paul Glee (Big Poison)	OF9	11	+.171	Pitt	Bos
		Wasdell, James Chas.	OF54	94	.299	B	
1	2	Wicker, Kemp Caswell	P	16	.250	NYA38	C
22	10	Wyatt, John Whitlow (Whit)	P38	40	.239	B	

WON 104 NATIONAL LEAGUE FINISHED 2nd.
LOST 50
TG 154 1942. PCT. .675

BROOKLYN

LEO ERNEST DUROCHER

WON	LOST	NAME	POS.	G.	BA	FROM	TO
10	6	Allen, John Thomas (Johnny)	P	27	.179	B	

WON	LOST	NAME	POS.	G.	BA	FROM	TO
		Bordagaray, Stanley George	OF17	48	.241	NYA	
		Camilli, Adolph Louis	1B	150	.252	B	
6	3	Casey, Hugh Thomas	P	50	.148	B	
0	0	Chipman, Robert Howard	P	2	.000	B	
		Dahlgren, Ellsworth Tenney (Babe)	1B10	17	.173	xStLA	
		Dapper, Clifford Roland	C	8	.471	A	C
15	6	Davis, Curtis Benton (Curt)	P	32	.176	B	
0	0	Fitzsimmons, Frederick Landis	P	1	.500	B	
15	4	French, Lawrence Herbert (Larry)	P	38	.300	B	C
		Galan, August John (Augie) (1B4 2B3)	OF55	69	.263	B	
10	6	Head, Edward Marvin	P	36	.333	Bkn40	
		Herman, Wm. Jennings Bryan (Billy) (1B3)	2B153	155	.256	B	
16	11	Higbe, Walter Kirby	P	38	.104	B	
		Kampouris, Alexis Wm.	2B9	10	.238	B	
0	0	Kehn, Chester Lawrence	P	3	1.000	A	C
2	0	Kimball, Newel W.	P	14	.200	B	
5	3	Macon, Max Cullen	P14	26	.279	Bkn40	
		Medwick, Joseph Michael (Ducky)	OF140	142	.300	B	
2	2	Newsom, Louis Norman (Buck)	P	6	.000	xWashA	
		Owen, Arnold Malcolm (Mickey)	C	133	.259	B	
		Reese, Harold Henry (Pee-Wee)	SS	151	.255	B	
		Reiser, Harold Patrick (Pete)	OF	125	.310	B	
		Riggs, Lewis Sidney (Lew) (1B1)	3B46	70	.278	B	
		Rizzo, John Casta	OF70	78	.230	Phil	C
		Rojek, Stanley Andrew		1	.000	A	
1	0	Rowe, Lynwood Thomas (Schoolboy)	P9	14	.211	xDetA	
		Sullivan, Wm. Joseph Jr. (Billy)	C41	43	.267	DetA	
		Vaughan, Joseph Floyd (Arky) (2B1 SS5)	3B119	128	.277	Pitt	
		Walker, Fred (Dixie)	OF110	118	.290	B	
3	2	Webber, Lester Elmer	P	19	.071	A	
19	7	Wyatt, John Whitlow (Whit)	P	31	.182	B	

WON 81 | NATIONAL LEAGUE | FINISHED 3rd.
LOST 72
TG 153 | 1943. | PCT. .529

BROOKLYN

LEO ERNEST DUROCHER

WON	LOST	NAME	POS.	G.	BA	FROM	TO
5	1	Allen, John Thomas (Johnny)	P	17	+.429	B	N.Y.
		Ankenman, Frederick Norman Jr.	SS	1	.500	StL36	
		Barkley, John Duncan	SS18	20	.314	Bos39	C
2	2	Barney, Rex Edward	P	9	.056		
		Bartley, Boyd Owen	SS	9	.048	A	C
		Bordagaray, Stanley George (3B25)	OF53	89	.302	B	
		Bragan, Robert Randall (3B12)	C57	74	.264	Phil	
		Camilli, Adolph Louis	1B	95	.247	B	
		Campanis, Alexander Sebastian	2B	7	.100	A	C
0	0	Chipman, Robert Howard	P	1	.000	B	
		Cooney, John Walter	1B3	37	.206	Bos	
10	13	Davis, Curtis Benton (Curt)	P	31	.164	B	
		Durocher, Leo Ernest MGR.	SS	6	.222	B	
3	4	Fitzsimmons, Frederick Landis	P	9	+.071	B	Phil
		Galan, August John (Augie) (1B13)	OF124	139	.287	B	
		Gillenwater, Carden Edison	OF5	8	.176	StL40	
		Glossop, Alban (2B24 3B17)	SS33	87	.171	Phil	
0	3	Gregg, Harold Dana	P	5	.000	A	
		Hart, Wm. Woodrow	SS1	8	.158	A	
0	1	Haughey, Christopher Francis	P	1	.000	A	C
9	10	Head, Edward Marvin	P	47	.152	B	
		Herman, Wm. Jennings Bryan (Billy) (3B37)	2B117	153	.330	B	
		Hermanski, Eugene Victor	OF17	18	.300	A	
13	10	Higbe, Walter Kirby	P	35	.138	B	
		Hodges, Gilbert Raymond	SS	1	.000	A	
		Kampouris, Alexis Wm.	2B18	19	.227	B	WashA
1	1	Kimball, Newel W.	P	5	+.000	B	Phil
0	2	Lohrman, Wm. LeRoy (Bill)	P	6	+.143	xN.Y.	
7	5	Macon, Max Cullen (1B3)	P25	45	.164	B	
		Medwick, Joseph Michael (Ducky)	OF42	48	+.272	B	N.Y.
5	8	Melton, Reuben Franklin	P	30	.105	Phil	
		Moore, Dee Cee (3B9)	C15	37	+.253	Cin37	Phil
9	4	Newsom, Louis Norman (Buck)	P	22	.250	B	StLA
		Olmo, Luis Rodriguez	OF	57	.303	A	
		Orengo, Joseph Chas.	3B6	7	+.200	xN.Y.	
1	1	Ostermueller, Frederick Raymond (Fritz)	P7	8	.000	xStLA	
		Owen, Arnold Malcolm (Mickey) (SS1)	C100	106	.260	B	
		Peck, Harold Arthur		1	.000	A	
0	0	Sayles, Wm. Nisbeth	P	6	+.500	xN.Y.	C
		Schultz, Howard Henry	1B	45	.269	A	
		Vaughan, Joseph Floyd (Arky) (3B55)	SS99	149	.305	B	
		Walker, Fred (Dixie)	OF136	138	.302	B	
		Waner, Paul Glee (Big Poison)	OF57	82	.311	Bos	
2	2	Webber, Lester Elmer	P	54	.120	B	
14	5	Wyatt, John Whitlow (Whit)	P	27	.283	B	

WON 63 | NATIONAL LEAGUE | FINISHED 7th.
LOST 91
TG 154 | 1944. | PCT. .409

BROOKLYN

LEO ERNEST DUROCHER

WON	LOST	NAME	POS.	G.	BA	FROM	TO
		Aderholt, Morris Woodrow	OF13	17	.271	WashA41	
		Andrews, Stanley Joseph	C	4	.125	Bos40	
		Ankenman, Frederick Norman Jr. (SS2)	2B11	13	.250	B	C
		Basinski, Edwin Frank (SS3)	2B37	39	.257	A	
		Bolling, John Edward	1B27	56	.351	Phil39	C
		Bordagaray, Stanley George (OF25)	3B98	130	.281	B	
		Bragan, Robert Randall (C35 2B1)	SS51	94	.267	B	
0	2	Branca, Ralph Theodore Joseph	P	21	.000	A	
		Brown, Thomas Michael	SS	46	.164	A	
5	3	Chapman, Wm. Benjamin	P11	20	.368	ChiA41	
3	1	Chipman, Robert Howard	P	11	+.182	B	Chi
		Cooney, John Walter	OF2	7	.750	B	NYA
0	0	Crocker, Claude Arthur	P	2	1.000	A	
		Dantonio, John James	C	3	.143	A	
10	11	Davis, Curtis Benton (Curt)	P	31	.159	B	
		Durrett, Elmer Chas.	OF9	11	.156	A	
		English, Gilbert Raymond (2B2 3B11)	SS13	27	.152	Bos38	C
1	1	Flowers, Chas. Wesley	P	9	.600	Bkn40	C
0	0	Franklin, James Wilford (Jack)	P	1	.000	A	C
1	0	Fuchs, Chas. Thomas	P	8	.000	StLA	C
		Galan, August John (Augie) (2B2)	OF147	151	.318	B	
9	16	Gregg, Harold Dana	P39	42	.206	B	
		Hart, Wm. Woodrow (3B2)	SS25	29	.178	B	
		Hayworth, Raymond Hall	C6	7	.000	StLA42	
4	3	Head, Edward Marvin	P	9	.263	B	
3	4	Herring, Arthur L.	P	12	.200	ChiA39	
		Jarvis, LeRoy Gilbert	C	1	.000	A	
2	1	King, Clyde Edward	P	14	.200	A	
		Koch, Barney (SS1)	2B20	33	.219	A	C
0	0	Lohrman, Wm. LeRoy (Bill)	P	3	+.000	B	Cin
		Mauch, Eugene Wm.	SS	5	.133	A	
9	13	Melton, Reuben Franklin	P	37	.123	B	
		Miksis, Edward Thomas (SS10)	3B15	26	.220	A	
3	10	McLish, Calvin Coolidge	P23	31	.219	A	
		Olmo, Luis Rodriguez (2B42 3B31)	OF64	136	.258	B	
0	0	Osgood, Chas. Benjamin	P	1	.000	A	C
2	1	Ostermueller, Frederick Raymond (Fritz)	P10	11	+.154	B	Pitt
		Owen, Arnold Malcolm (Mickey) (2B1)	C125	130	.273	B	
		Rochelli, Louis Joseph	2B5	5	.176	A	C
		Rosen, Goodwin George (Goody)	OF65	89	.261	Bkn39	
		Schultz, Howard Henry	1B136	138	.255	B	
		Smyres, Clarence Melvin (Clancy)		5	.000	A	C
		Stanky, Edward Raymond (SS35 3B1)	2B58	89	+.276	xChi	
1	3	Sunkel, Thomas Jacob	P	12	.000	N.Y.	C
		Walker, Fred (Dixie)	OF140	147	.357	B	
		Waner, Lloyd James (Little Poison)	OF4	15	+.286	Phil42	Pitt
		Waner, Paul Glee (Big Poison)	OF32	83	.287	B	NYA
1	4	Warren, Thomas Gentry	P22	41	.256	A	C
7	8	Webber, Lester Elmer	P	48	.205	B	
0	2	Wells, John Frederick	P	4	.250	A	C
0	0	Wurm, Frank James	P	1	.000	A	C
2	6	Wyatt, John Whitlow (Whit)	P9	11	.154	B	
0	2	Zachary, Albert Myron	P	4	.000	A	C

WON 87 NATIONAL LEAGUE FINISHED 3rd.
LOST 67
TG 154 1945. PCT. .565

BROOKLYN

LEO ERNEST DUROCHER

WON	LOST	NAME	POS.	G.	BA	FROM	TO
		Aderholt, Morris Woodrow	OF8	39	+.217	B	Bos
		Andrews, Stanley Joseph	C	21	+.163	B	Phil
		Basinski, Edwin Frank (2B6)	SS101	108	.262	B	
		Bordagaray, Stanley George (OF22)	3B57	113	.256	B	C
5	6	Branca, Ralph Theodore Joseph	P	16	.100	B	
		Brown, Thomas Michael (OF1)	SS55	57	.245	B	
7	2	Buker, Cyril Owen	P	42	.188	A	C
3	3	Chapman, Wm. Benjamin	P10	13	+.136	B	Phil
		Corbitt, Claude Elliott	3B	2	.500	A	
0	0	Crocker, Claude Arthur	P	1	.000	B	C
		Dantonio, John James	C45	47	.250	B	C
10	10	Davis, Curtis Benton (Curt)	P	24	.137	B	
		Douglas, John Franklin	1B4	5	.000	A	C
		Durocher, Leo Ernest MGR.	2B	2	.200	B	
		Durrett, Elmer Chas.	OF4	8	.125	B	C
		Galan, August John (Augie) (3B40 OF49)	1B66	152	.307	B	
18	13	Gregg, Harold Dana	P	42	.220	B	
		Hart, Wm. Woodrow (SS8)	3B39	58	.230	B	C
0	1	Hathaway, Ray Wilson	P	4	.000	A	C
		Hayworth, Raymond Hall	C	2	.000	B	C
		Herman, Floyd Caves (Babe)	OF3	37	.265	DetA37	C
7	4	Herring, Arthur L.	P22	23	.095	B	
5	5	King, Clyde Edward	P42	43	.125	B	
10	11	Lombardi, Victor Alvin	P38	45	.183	A	
		Lund, Donald Andrew		4	.000	A	
1	0	Nitcholas, Otho James	P	7	.250	A	C
		Olmo, Luis Rodriguez (2B1 3B31)	OF106	141	.313	B	C
		Owen, Arnold Malcolm (Mickey)	C	24	.286	B	C
		Palica, Ervin Martin		2	.000	A	
		Peacock, John Gaston	C38	48	+.255	xPhil	C
3	2	Pfund, LeRoy Herbert	P	15	.182	A	C
		Rosen, Goodwin George (Goody)	OF141	145	.325	B	
1	0	Rudolph, Ernest Wm.	P	7	.000	A	C

WON	LOST	NAME	POS.	G.	BA	FROM	TO
		Sandlock, Michael Joseph (2B4 SS22 3B2)	C47	80	.282	Bos	
		Schultz, Howard Henry	1B38	39	.239	B	
10	7	Seats, Thomas Edward	P	31	.209	DetA40	C
		Stanky, Edward Raymond (SS1)	2B153	153	.258	B	
		Stevens, Edward Lee	1B	55	.274	A	
		Sukeforth, Clyde LeRoy	C13	18	.294	Bkn34	
		Walker, Fred (Dixie)	OF153	154	.300	B	
7	3	Webber, Lester Elmer	P	17	.091	B	
		White, Wm. Barney (3B1)	SS1	4	.000	A	C

WON 96 — NATIONAL LEAGUE — FINISHED 2nd.
LOST 60
TG 156 — 1946 — PCT. .615

BROOKLYN

LEO ERNEST DUROCHER

WON	LOST	NAME	POS.	G.	BA	FROM	TO
		Anderson, Ferrell Jack	C70	79	.256	A	
2	5	Barney, Rex Edward	P	16	.235	Bkn43	
11	5	Behrman, Henry Bernard	P	47	.095	A	
3	1	Branca, Ralph Theodore Joseph	P	24	.111	B	
11	5	Casey, Hugh Thomas	P	46	.136	Bkn42	
		Corriden, John Michael Jr.		1	.000	A	C
0	0	Davis, Curtis Benton (Curt)	P	1	.000	B	C
		Davis, Otis Allen		1	.000	A	C
		Edwards, Chas. Bruce	C91	92	.267	A	
		Furillo, Carl Anthony	OF112	117	.284	A	
		Galan, August John (Augie) (1B12 3B19)	OF60	99	.310	B	
		Graham, John Bernard	1B	2	+.200	A	N.Y.
6	4	Gregg, Harold Dana	P	26	.125	B	
14	11	Hatten, Joseph Hilarian	P	42	.076	A	
3	2	Head, Edward Marvin	P	13	.313	Bkn44	C
		Herman, Wm. Jennings Bryan (Billy) (2B16)	3B29	47	+.288	Bkn43	Bos
		Hermanski, Eugene Victor	OF34	64	.200	Bkn43	
7	2	Herring, Arthur L.	P	35	.182	B	
17	8	Higbe, Walter Kirby	P	42	.130	Bkn43	
		Lavagetto, Harry Arthur (Cookie)	3B67	88	.236	Bkn41	
13	10	Lombardi, Victor Alvin	P41	43	.230	B	
		Medwick, Joseph Michael (Ducky) (1B8)	OF18	41	.312	Bos	
6	3	Melton, Reuben Franklin	P	24	.107	Bkn44	
		Miksis, Edward Thomas (2B1)	3B13	23	.146	Bkn44	
0	1	Minner, Paul Edison	P	3	.000	A	
0	0	Moulder, Glen Herbert	P	1	.000	A	
0	0	McLish, Calvin Coolidge	P	1	.000	Bkn44	
		Naylor, Earl Eugene		3	.000	Phil43	C
		Padgett, Donald Wilson (Don)	C10	19	+.167	StL41	Bos

WON	LOST	NAME	POS.	G.	BA	FROM	TO
		Ramazotti, Robert Louis (2B16)	3B30	62	.208	A	
		Reese, Harold Henry (Pee-Wee)	SS	152	.284	Bkn42	
		Reiser, Harold Patrick (Pete) (3B15)	OF97	122	.277	Bkn42	
		Riggs, Lewis Sidney (Lew)	3B	1	.000	Bkn42	C
		Rojek, Stanley Andrew (2B6 3B4)	SS15	45	.277	Bkn42	
		Rosen, Goodwin George (Goody)	OF1	3	+.333	B	N.Y.
0	0	Roy, Jean Pierre	P	3	.000	A	C
		Sandlock, Michael Joseph (3B1)	C17	19	.147	B	
		Schultz, Howard Henry	1B87	90	.253	B	
		Stanky, Edward Raymond	2B141	144	.273	B	
		Stevens, Edward Lee	1B99	103	.242	B	
0	0	Taylor, James Harry	P	4	.000	A	
		Tepsic, Joseph John	OF	15	.000	A	C
		Walker, Fred (Dixie)	OF149	150	.319	B	
3	3	Webber, Lester Elmer	P	11	.100	B	ClevA
		Whitman, Dick Corwin	OF85	104	.260	A	

WON 94 — NATIONAL LEAGUE — FINISHED 1st.
LOST 60
TG 154 — 1947. — PCT. .610

BROOKLYN

CLYDE LEROY SUKEFORTH — BURTON EDWIN SHOTTON

WON	LOST	NAME	POS.	G.	BA	FROM	TO
0	0	Bankhead, Daniel Robert	P4	6	.250	A	
0	1	Banta, John Kay	P	3	.000	A	
5	2	Barney, Rex Edward	P	28	.111	B	
0	0	Behrman, Henry Bernard	P	2	+.000	B	Pitt
5	3			38	+.231	(& return)	
		Bragan, Robert Randall	C21	25	.194	Bkn44	
21	12	Branca, Ralph Theodore Joseph	P	43	.124	B	
		Brown, Thomas Michael (SS1 OF3)	3B6	15	.235	Bkn45	
10	4	Casey, Hugh Thomas	P	46	.056	B	
0	1	Chandler, Edward Oliver	P	15	.000	A	C
0	0	Dockins, George Woodrow	P	4	.000	StL45	C
		Edwards, Chas. Bruce	C128	130	.296	B	
		Furillo, Carl Anthony	OF121	124	.295	B	
		Gionfriddo, Albert Francis	OF17	37	+.177	xPitt	C
4	5	Gregg, Harold Dana	P	37	.265	B	
17	8	Hatten, Joseph Hilarian	P	42	.205	B	
1	0	Haugstad, Philip Donald	P	6	.000	A	
		Hermanski, Eugene Victor	OF66	79	.275	B	
2	0	Higbe, Walter Kirby	P	4	+.200	B	Pitt
		Hodges, Gilbert Raymond	C24	28	.156	Bkn43	
		Jorgensen, John Donald	3B128	129	.274	A	
6	5	King, Clyde Edward	P	29	.115	Bkn45	
		x Lavagetto, Harry Arthur (Cookie)	3B18	41	.261	B	C

WON	LOST	NAME	POS.	G.	BA	FROM	TO
12	11	Lombardi, Victor Alvin	P33	36	.242	B	
		Lund, Donald Andrew	OF5	11	.300	Bkn45	
0	1	Melton, Reuben Franklin	P	4	1.000	B	C
		Miksis, Edward Thomas (SS2 3B5 OF11)	2B13	45	.267	B	
0	1	Palica, Ervin Martin	P	3	.000	Bkn45	
		Rackley, Marvin Eugene	OF2	18	.222	A	
1	1	Ramsdell, James Willard	P	2	1.000	A	
		Reese, Harold Henry (Pee-Wee)	SS	142	.284	B	
		Reiser, Harold Patrick (Pete)	OF108	110	.309	B	
		Robinson, Jack Roosevelt	1B	151	.296	A	
		Rojek, Stanley Andrew (2B7 3B9)	SS17	32	.263	B	
		Schultz, Howard Henry	1B1	2	+.000	B	Phil
		Snider, Edwin Donald	OF25	40	.241	A	
		Stanky, Edward Raymond	2B	146	.252	B	
		Stevens, Edward Lee	1B4	5	.154	B	
		Tatum, Thomas Vee Tee	OF	4	+.000	Bkn41	Cin
10	5	Taylor, James Harry	P	33	.129	B	
0	0	Van Cuyk, John Henry	P	2	.000	A	
		Vaughan, Joseph Floyd (Arky) (3B10)	OF22	64	.325	Bkn43	
		Walker, Fred (Dixie)	OF147	148	.306	B	
		Whitman, Dick Corwin	OF3	4	.400	B	

x-Lavagetto also played 3 games at 1B.

WON 84 NATIONAL LEAGUE FINISHED 3rd.
LOST 70
TG 154 1948. PCT. .545

BROOKLYN

LEO ERNEST DUROCHER BURTON EDWIN SHOTTON

WON	LOST	NAME	POS.	G.	BA	FROM	TO
0	1	Banta, John Kay	P	2	.000	B	
15	13	Barney, Rex Edward	P	44	.167	B	
5	4	Behrman, Henry Bernard	P	34	.107	B	
		Bragan, Robert Randall	C5	9	.167	B	C
14	9	Branca, Ralph Theodore Joseph	P	36	.203	B	
		Brown, Thomas Michael (1B1)	3B43	54	.241	B	
		Campanella, Roy	C78	83	.258	A	
3	0	Casey, Hugh Thomas	P	22	.000	B	
		Cox, Wm. Richard (2B1 SS6)	3B70	88	.249	Pitt	
		Edwards, Chas. Bruce (1B1 3B14 OF21)	C48	96	.276	B	
6	3	Erskine, Carl Daniel	P	17	.095	A	
		Furillo, Carl Anthony	OF104	108	.297	B	
0	0	Hall, John Sylvester	P	3	.000	A	C
13	10	Hatten, Joseph Hilarian	P42	43	.206	B	
0	0	Haugstad, Philip Donald	P	1	.000	B	
		Hermanski, Eugene Victor	OF119	133	.290	B	
		Hodges, Gilbert Raymond (C38)	1B96	134	.249	B	
		Jorgensen, John Donald	3B24	31	.300	B	
0	1	King, Clyde Edward	P	9	.000	B	
		Lund, Donald Andrew	OF25	27	.188	B	StLA
		Mauch, Eugene Wm. (SS1)	2B7	12	+.154	Pitt	Chi
		Miksis, Edward Thomas (SS5 3B22)	2B54	86	.213	B	
4	3	Minner, Paul Edison	P28	31	.190	Bkn46	
6	6	Palica, Ervin Martin	P41	45	.128	B	
		Rackley, Marvin Eugene	OF74	88	.327	B	
		Ramazotti, Robert Louis	2B1	4	.000	Bkn46	
4	4	Ramsdell, James Willard	P	27	.091	B	
		Reese, Harold Henry(Pee-Wee)	SS149	151	.274	B	
		Reiser, Harold Patrick (Pete)	OF30	64	.236	B	
		Robinson, Jack Roosevelt (1B30)	2B116	147	.296	B	
12	8	Roe, Elwin Chas.	P	34	.098	Pitt	
0	0	Sexauer, Elmer George	P	2	.000	A	C
		Shuba, George Thomas	OF56	63	.267	A	
0	1	Sloat, Dwain Clifford	P	4	.000	A	
		Snider, Edwin Donald	OF47	53	.244	B	
2	7	Taylor, James Harry	P	17	.273	B	
0	0	Van Cuyk, John Henry	P	3	.000	B	
		Vaughan, Joseph Floyd (Arky) (3B8)	OF26	65	.244	B	C
		Ward, Preston Meyer	1B38	42	.260	A	
		Whitman, Dick Corwin	OF48	60	.291	B	

WON 97 NATIONAL LEAGUE FINISHED 1st.
LOST 57
TG 154 1949. PCT. .630

BROOKLYN

BURTON EDWIN SHOTTON

WON	LOST	NAME	POS.	G.	BA	FROM	TO
		Abrams, Calvin Ross	OF7	8	.083	A	
10	6	Banta, John Kay	P	48	.109	B	
9	8	Barney, Rex Edward	P	38	.213	B	
13	5	Branca, Ralph Theodore Joseph	P	34	.081	B	
		Brown, Thomas Michael	OF27	41	.303	B	
		Campanella, Roy	C127	130	.287	B	
		Connors, Kevin Joseph		1	.000	A	
		Cox, Wm. Richard	3B	100	.234	B	
		Edwards, Chas. Bruce (3B1 OF4)	C41	64	.209	B	
8	1	Erskine, Carl Daniel	P	22	.115	B	
		Furillo, Carl Anthony	OF	142	.324	B	
12	8	Hatten, Joseph Hilarian	P37	39	.179	B	
		Hermanski, Eugene Victor	OF77	87	.299	B	
		Hodges, Gilbert Raymond	1B	156	.285	B	

WON	LOST	NAME	POS.	G.	BA	FROM	TO
		Hopp, John Leonard (1B2)	OF4	8	+.000	xPitt	Pitt
		Jorgensen, John Donald	3B36	53	.269	B	
1	3	Martin, Morris Webster	P	10	.200	A	
		Miksis, Edward Thomas (1B1 2B3 SS4)	3B29	50	.221	B	
3	1	Minner, Paul Edison	P	27	.214	B	
		McCormick, Myron Winthrop	OF49	55	.209	Bos	
1	1	McGlothin, Ezra Mac	P	7	.000	A	
17	8	Newcombe, Donald	P38	39	.229	A	
		Olmo, Luis Rodriguez	OF34	38	.305	Bkn45	
8	9	Palica, Ervin Martin	P	49	.158	B	
0	1	Padbielan, Clarence Anthony	P	7	.000	A	
		Rackley, Marvin Eugene	OF9	9	.444	B	Pitt
			OF	54	+.291		& return
		Ramazzotti, Robert Louis	3B3	5	+.154	B	Chi
		Reese, Harold Henry (Pee-Wee)	SS	155	.279	B	
		Robinson, Jack Roosevelt	2B	156	.342	B	
15	6	Roe, Elwin Chas.	P	30	.114	B	
		Shuba, George Thomas		1	.000	B	
		Snider, Edwin Donald	OF145	146	.292	B	
0	0	Van Cuyk, John Henry	P	2	.000	B	C
		Whitman, Dick Corwin	OF11	23	.184	B	

WON 89
LOST 65
TG 154

NATIONAL LEAGUE — FINISHED 2nd.

1950. — PCT. .578

BROOKLYN

BURTON EDWIN SHOTTON

WON	LOST	NAME	POS.	G.	BA	FROM	TO
		Abrams, Calvin Ross	OF15	38	.205	B	
9	4	Bankhead, Daniel Robert	P	41	.231	Bkn47	
4	4	Banta, John Kay	P	16	.167	B	C
2	1	Barney, Rex Edward	P	20	.125	B	C
		Belardi, Carroll Wayne	1B1	10	.000	A	
7	9	Branca, Ralph Theodore Joseph	P	43	.118	B	
		Brown, Thomas Michael	OF16	48	.291	B	
		Campanella, Roy	C123	126	.281	B	
		Cox, Wm. Richard (2B13 SS9)	3B107	119	.257	B	
		Edwards, Chas. Bruce (1B2)	C38	50	.183	B	
0	0	Epperly, Albert Paul	P	5	.000	Chi38	C
7	6	Erskine, Carl Daniel	P	22	.243	B	
		Furillo, Carl Anthony	OF	153	.305	B	
2	2	Hatten, Joseph Hilarian	P23	27	.111	B	
		Hermanski, Eugene Victor	OF78	94	.298	B	
		Hodges, Gilbert Raymond	1B	153	.283	B	
		Jorgensen, John Donald	3B1	2	+.000	B	N.Y.
0	0	Labine, Clement Walter	P	1	.000	A	
0	0	Landrum, Joseph Butler	P	7	.000	A	
		Lembo, Stephen Neal	C	5	.167	A	
0	0	Loes, Wm.	P	10	.000	A	
0	0	Mallette, Malcolm Francis	P	2	.000	A	C
		Miksis, Edward Thomas (SS15 3B7)	2B15	51	.250	B	
		Morgan, Robert Morris (SS10)	3B52	67	.226	A	
0	0	McGlothin, Ezra Mac	P	1	.000	B	C
19	11	Newcombe, Donald	P	40	.247	B	
13	8	Palica, Ervin Martin	P43	48	.221	B	
5	4	Podbielan, Clarence Anthony	P	20	.107	B	
1	2	Ramsdell, James Willard	P	5	+.000	Bkn48	Cin
		Reese, Harold Henry(Pee-Wee) (3B7)	SS134	141	.260	B	
		Robinson, Jack Roosevelt	2B	144	.328	B	
19	11	Roe, Elwin Chas.	P	36	.154	B	
0	0	Romano, James King	P	3	.000	A	C
		Russell, James Wm.	OF55	77	.229	Bos	
		Shuba, George Thomas	OF27	34	.207	B	
		Snider, Edwin Donald	OF151	152	.321	B	
1	3	Van Cuyk, Christian Gerald	P	12	.100	A	

WON 97
LOST 60
TG 157

NATIONAL LEAGUE — FINISHED 2nd.

1951. — PCT. .618

BROOKLYN

CHAS. WALTER DRESSEN

WON	LOST	NAME	POS.	G.	BA	FROM	TO
		Abrams, Calvin Ross	OF34	67	.280	B	
0	1	Bankhead, Daniel Robert	P7	15	.000	B	C
		Belardi, Carroll Wayne		3	.333	B	
13	12	Branca, Ralph Theodore Joseph	P	42	.175	B	
		Bridges, Everett LaMar (2B10 SS9)	3B40	63	.254	A	
		Brown, Thomas Michael	OF5	11	+.160	B	Phila
		Campanella, Roy	C140	143	.325	B	
		Cox, Wm. Richard (SS1)	3B139	142	.279	B	
		Edwards, Chas. Bruce	C9	17	+.250	B	Chic.
		Edwards, Henry Albert		35	+.226	Chic.	Cin
16	12	Erskine, Carl Daniel	P	46	.131	B	
		Furillo, Carl Anthony	OF157	158	.295	B	
1	0	Hatten, Joseph Hilarian	P	11	+.135	B	Chic.
0	1	Haugstad, Philip Donald	P	21	.000	Bkn48	
		Hermanski, Eugene Victor	OF19	31	+.250	B	Chic.
		Hodges, Gilbert Raymond	1B	158	.268	B	
14	7	King, Clyde Edward	P	48	.138	Bkn48	
5	1	Labine, Clement Walter	P	14	.143	B	
		Livingston, Thompson Orville	C	2	.400	Bos49	C
		Miksis, Edward Thomas (2B1)	3B6	19	+.200	B	Chic.
0	0	Mossor, Earl Dalton	P	3	1.000	A	C
20	9	Newcombe, Donald	P	40	.223	B	
		Pafko, Andrew	OF76	84	+.249	xChic.	
2	6	Palica, Ervin Martin	P19	20	.154	B	
2	2	Podbielan, Clarence Anthony	P	27	.304	B	
		Reese, Harold Henry(Pee-Wee)	SS	154	.286	B	

WON	LOST	NAME	POS.	G.	BA	FROM	TO
		Robinson, Jack Roosevelt	2B150	153	.338	B	
22	3	Roe, Elwin Chas.	P	34	.112	B	
		Russell, James Wm.	OF4	16	.000	B	C
1	4	Schmitz, John Albert	P	16	+.222	xChic.	
		Snider, Edwin Donald	OF	150	.277	B	
		Terwilliger, Willard Wayne (3B1)	2B24	37	+.280	xChic.	
		Thompson, Donald Newlin	OF61	80	.229	Bos49	
1	2	Van Cuyk, Christian Gerald	P	9	.250	B	
		Walker, Albert Bluford	C22	36	+.243	xChic.	
		Williams, Richard Hirshfeld	OF15	23	.200	A	

WON 96 — NATIONAL LEAGUE — FINISHED 1st.
LOST 57
TG 153 — 1952. — PCT. .627

BROOKLYN

CHAS. WALTER DRESSEN

WON	LOST	NAME	POS.	G.	BA	FROM	TO
		Abrams, Calvin Ross	OF1	10	+.200	B	Cin
		Amoros, Edmunde Isasi	OF10	20	.250	A	
15	4	Black, Joseph	P56	57	.139	A	
4	2	Branca, Ralph Theodore Joseph	P	16	.158	B	
		Bridges, Everett LaMar (SS13 3B6)	2B24	51	.196	B	
		Campanella, Roy	C122	128	.269	B	
		Cox, Wm. Richard (2B9 SS10)	3B100	116	.259	B	
14	6	Erskine, Carl Daniel	P33	34	.152	B	
		Furillo, Carl Anthony	OF131	134	.247	B	
		Hodges, Gilbert Raymond	1B	153	.254	B	
		Holmes, Thomas Francis	OF6	31	+.111	xBos	C
2	1	Hughes, James Robert	P	6	.000	A	
2	0	King, Clyde Edward	P	23	.000	B	
8	4	Labine, Clement Walter	P25	26	.045	B	
1	3	Landrum, Joseph Butler	P	9	.125	Bkn50	C
1	2	Lehman, Kenneth Karl	P	4	.000	A	
		Lembo, Stephen Neal	C	2	.200	Bkn50	C
13	8	Loes, Wm.	P38	39	.092	Bkn50	
1	2	Moore, Raymond LeRoy	P	14	.000	A	
		Morgan, Robert Morris (2B5 SS4)	3B60	67	.236	Bkn50	
0	0	Negray, Ronald Alvin	P	4	.000	A	C
		Nelson, Glenn Richard	1B5	37	.256	ChiA	
		Pafko, Andrew (3B13)	OF139	150	.287	B	
0	0	Podbielan, Clarence Anthony	P3	4	+.000	B	Cin
		Reese, Harold Henry(Pee-Wee)	SS145	149	.272	B	
		Robinson, Jack Roosevelt	2B146	149	.308	B	
11	2	Roe, Elwin Chas.	P	27	.070	B	
7	7	Rutherford, John Wm.	P	22	.290	A	C
1	1	Schnitz, John Albert	P	10	.125	B	NYA

WON	LOST	NAME	POS.	G.	BA	FROM	TO
		Shuba, George Thomas	OF67	94	.305	Bkn50	
		Snider, Edwin Donald	OF141	144	.303	B	
5	6	Van Cuyk, Christian Gerald	P	23	.242	B	C
11	9	Wade, Benjamin Styron	P	37	.117	Chi48	
		Walker, Albert Bluford	C40	46	.259	B	
		Williams, Richard Hirshfeld (1B1 3B1)	OF25	36	.309	B	

WON 105 — NATIONAL LEAGUE — FINISHED 1st.
LOST 49
TG 154 — 1953. — PCT. .682

BROOKLYN

CHAS. WALTER DRESSEN

WON	LOST	NAME	POS.	G.	BA	FROM	TO
		Antonello, Wm. James	OF25	40	.163	A	C
		Belardi, Carroll Wayne	1B38	69	.239	Bkn51	
6	3	Black, Joseph	P	34	.235	B	
0	0	Branca, Ralph Theodore Joseph	P	7	.000	B	DetA
		Campanella, Roy	C140	144	.312	B	
		Cox, Wm. Richard (2B1 SS6)	3B89	100	.291	B	
20	6	Erskine, Carl Daniel	P39	43	.215	B	
		Furillo, Carl Anthony	OF131	132	.344	B	
		Gilliam, James Wm.	2B149	151	.278	A	
		Hodges, Gilbert Raymond (OF24)	1B127	141	.302	B	
		Howell, Homer Elliott		1	.000	Cin	
4	3	Hughes, James Robert	P	48	.286	B	
11	6	Labine, Clement Walter	P	37	.071	B	
14	8	Loes, Wm.	P	32	.125	B	
		Mauro, Carmen Louis	OF1	8	.000	Chi51	WashA
15	5	Meyer, Russell Chas.	P	34	.147	Phil	
0	1	Mickens, Glenn Roger	P	4	.000	A	C
8	4	Milliken, Robert Fogle	P	37	.118	A	
0	1	Moore, Raymond LeRoy	P	1	.000	B	
		Morgan, Robert Morris (SS21)	3B36	69	.260	B	
0	0	Palica, Ervin Martin	P	4	1.000	Bkn51	
9	4	Podres, John Joseph	P33	34	.306	A	
		Reese, Harold Henry (Pee-Wee)	SS135	140	.271	B	
		Robinson, Jack Roosevelt (1B6 2B9 SS1 3B44)	OF76	136	.329	B	
11	3	Roe, Elwin Chas.	P	25	.053	B	
		Shuba, George Thomas	OF44	74	.254	B	
		Snider, Edwin Donald	OF151	153	.336	B	
		Teed, Richard LeRoy		1	.000	A	C
		Thompson Donald Newlin	OF81	96	.242	Bkn51	
7	5	Wade, Benjamin Styron	P	32	.167	B	
		Walker, Albert Bluford	C28	43	.242	B	
		Williams, Richard Hirshfeld	OF24	30	.218	B	

WON 92 | NATIONAL LEAGUE | FINISHED 2nd.
LOST 62
TG 154 | 1954. | PCT. .597

BROOKLYN

WALTER EMMONS ALSTON

WON	LOST	NAME	POS.	G.	BA	FROM	TO
		Amoros, Edmundo Isasi	OF70	79	.274	Bkn52	
		Belardi, Carroll Wayne		11	.222	B	DetA
0	0	Black, Joseph	P	5	.000	B	
		Campanella, Roy	C	111	.207	B	
		Cox, Wm. Richard (2B11 SS8)	3B58	77	.235	B	
0	0	Darnell, Robert Jack	P	6	.000	A	
18	15	Erskine, Carl Daniel	P38	39	.159	B	
		Furillo, Carl Anthony	OF149	150	.294	B	
		Gilliam, James Wm. (OF4)	2B143	146	.282	B	
		Hoak, Donald Albert	3B75	88	.245	A	
		Hodges, Gilbert Raymond	1B	154	.304	B	
8	4	Hughes, James Robert	P	60	.188	B	
		Kress, Chas. Steven	1B1	13	.083	xDetA	C
7	6	Labine, Clement Walter	P	47	.033	B	
0	0	LaSorda, Thomas Chas.	P	4	.000	A	
13	5	Loes, Wm.	P	28	.118	B	
11	6	Meyer, Russell Chas.	P	36	.043	B	
5	2	Milliken, Robert Fogle	P	24	.176	B	C
		Moryn, Walter Joseph	OF20	48	.275	A	
9	8	Newcombe, Donald	P29	31	.319	Bkn51	
3	3	Palica, Ervin Martin	P25	28	.250	B	
11	7	Podres, John Joseph	P29	38	.283	B	
		Reese, Harold Henry (Pee-Wee)	SS140	141	.309	B	
		Robinson, Jack Roosevelt (2B4 3B50)	OF74	124	.311	B	
3	4	Roe, Elwin Chas.	P	15	.143	B	C
		Shuba, George Thomas	OF13	45	.154	B	
		Snider, Edwin Donald	OF148	149	.341	B	
2	0	Spooner, Karl Benjamin	P	2	.167	A	
		Thompson, Chas. Lemoine	C3	10	.154	A	
		Thomspon, Donald Newlin	OF29	34	.040	B	C
1	1	Wade, Benjamin Styron	P	23	+.000	B	StL
		Walker, Albert Bluford	C47	50	.181	B	
		Williams, Richard Hirshfeld	OF14	16	.147	B	
1	1	Wojey, Peter Paul	P	14	.000	A	
		Zimmer, Donald Wm.	SS13	24	.182	A	

WON 98 | NATIONAL LEAGUE | FINISHED 1st.
LOST 55
TG 153 | 1955 | PCT. .641

BROOKLYN

WALTER EMMONS ALSTON

WON	LOST	NAME	POS.	G.	BA	FROM	TO
		Amoros, Edmundo Isasi	OF109	119	.247	B	
8	1	Bessent, Fred Donald	P	24	.100	A	
1	0	Black, Joseph	P	6	+.333	B	Cin
		Borkowski, Robert Vilarian	OF	9	+.105	xCin	C
		Campanella, Roy	C121	123	.318	B	
5	3	Craig, Roger Lee	P	21	.077	A	
11	8	Erskine, Carl Daniel	P31	42	.203	B	
		Furillo, Carl Anthony	OF	140	.314	B	
		Gilliam, James Wm. (OF46)	2B99	147	.249	B	
		Hamric, Odbert Herman		2	.000	A	
		Hoak, Donald Albert	3B78	94	.240	B	
		Hodges, Gilbert Raymond (OF16)	1B139	150	.289	B	
		Howell, Homer Elliott	C13	16	.262	Bkn53	
0	2	Hughes, James Robert	P	24	.000	B	
		Kellert, Frank Wm.	1B22	39	.325	BaltA	
2	2	Koufax, Sanford	P	12	.000	A	
13	5	Labine, Clement Walter	P	60	.097	B	
0	0	LaSorda, Thomas Chas.	P	4	.000	B	
10	4	Loes, Wm.	P	22	.091	B	
6	2	Meyer, Russell Chas.	P	18	.037	B	
		Moryn, Walter Joseph	OF7	11	.263	B	
20	5	Newcombe, Donald	P34	57	.359	B	
9	10	Podres, John Joseph	P27	32	.183	B	
		Reese, Harold Henry (Pee-Wee)	SS142	145	.282	B	
		Robinson,Jack Roosevelt (1B1 2B1 OF10)	3B84	105	.256	B	
5	6	Roebuck, Edward Jack	P	47	.111	A	
		Shuba, George Thomas	OF9	44	.275	B	C
		Snider, Edwin Donald	OF146	148	.309	B	
8	6	Spooner, Karl Benjamin	P	29	.286	B	C
0	1	Templeton, Chas. Sherman	P	4	.000	A	
		Walker, Albert Bluford	C35	48	.252	B	
		Zimmer, Donald Wm. (SS21 3B8)	2B62	88	.239	B	

WON 93 | NATIONAL LEAGUE | FINISHED 1st.
LOST 61
TG 154 | 1956. | PCT. .604

BROOKLYN

WALTER EMMONS ALSTON

WON	LOST	NAME	POS.	G.	BA	FROM	TO
		Amoros, Edmundo Isasi	OF86	114	.260	B	
		Aspromonte, Robert Thomas		1	.000	A	
4	3	Bessent, Fred Donald	P	38	.111	B	
0	0	Branca, Ralph Theodore Joseph	P	1	.000	NYA54	C
		Campanella, Roy	C121	124	.219	B	
		Cimoli, Gino Nicholas	OF62	73	.111	A	
12	11	Craig, Roger Lee	P	35	.016	B	
0	0	Darnell, Robert Jack	P	1	.000	Bkn54	C
		Demeter, Donald Lee	OF1	3	.333	A	

WON	LOST	NAME	POS.	G.	BA	FROM	TO
5	5	Drysdale, Donald Scott	P25	26	.192	A	
13	11	Erskine, Carl Daniel	P31	32	.121	B	
		Fernandez, Humberto Perez	SS25	34	.227	A	
		Furillo, Carl Anthony	OF146	149	.289	B	
		Gilliam, James Wm. (OF56)	2B102	153	.300	B	
		Hodges, Gilbert Raymond (C1 OF30)	1B138	153	.265	B	
		Howell, Homer Elliott	C6	7	.231	B	C
0	0	Hughes, James Robert	P	5	+.000	B	Chi
		Jackson, Ransom Joseph	3B80	101	.274	Chi	
2	4	Koufax, Sanford	P	16	.118	B	
10	6	Labine, Clement Walter	P	62	.087	B	
2	3	Lehman, Kenneth Karl	P	25	.300	Bkn52	
0	1	Loes, Wm.	P	1	.000	B	BaltA
13	5	Maglie, Salvatore Anthony	P	28	.129	xClevA	
		Mitchell, Loren Dale	OF2	19	.292	xClevA	C
		Neal, Chas. Lenard (SS1)	2B51	62	.287	A	
		Nelson, Glenn Richard	1B25	31	+.208	ClevA54	StL
27	7	Newcombe, Donald	P38	52	.234	B	
		Reese, Harold Henry (Pee-Wee) (3B12)	SS136	147	.257	B	
		Robinson, Jack Roosevelt (1B9 2B22 OF2)	3B72	117	.275	B	C
5	4	Roebuck, Edward Jack	P	43	.333	B	
		Snider, Edwin Donald	OF150	151	.292	B	
0	1	Templeton, Chas. Sherman	P	6	.000	B	C
		Walker, Albert Bluford	C43	54	.212	B	
		Williams, Richard Hirshfeld		7	.286	Bkn54	BaltA
		Zimmer, Donald Wm. (2B1 3B3)	SS8	17	.300	B	

WON 84 NATIONAL LEAGUE FINISHED 3rd.
LOST 70
TG 154 1957. PCT. .545

BROOKLYN

WALTER EMMONS ALSTON

WON	LOST	NAME	POS.	G.	BA	FROM	TO
		Amoros, Edmundo Isasi	OF66	106	.277	B	
1	3	Bessent, Fred Donald	P	27	.250	B	
		Campanella, Roy	C100	103	.242	B	C
		Cimoli, Gino Nicholas	OF138	142	.293	B	
0	0	Collum, Jack Dean	P	3	+.000	xChi	
6	9	Craig, Roger Lee	P	32	.138	B	
17	9	Drysdale, Donald Scott	P34	37	.123	B	
0	0	Elston, Donald Ray	P	1	+.000	Chi53	Chi
5	3	Erskine, Carl Daniel	P15	21	.091	B	
		Furillo, Carl Anthony	OF107	119	.306	B	
		Gentile, James Edward	1B2	4	.167	A	
		Gilliam, James Wm. (OF2)	2B148	149	.250	B	
0	1	Harris, Wm. Thomas	P	1	.500	A	
		Hodges, Gilbert Raymond (2B1 3B2)	1B150	150	.299	B	
		Jackson, Ransom Joseph	3B34	48	.198	B	
		Kennedy, Robert Daniel (3B3)	OF9	19	.129	DetA	C
0	0	Kipp, Fred Leo	P	1	.000	A	
5	4	Koufax, Sanford	P	34	.000	B	
5	7	Labine, Clement Walter	P	58	.100	B	
0	0	Lehman, Kenneth Karl	P	3	.500	B	BaltA
6	6	Maglie, Salvatore Anthony	P	19	.034	B	NYA
7	4	McDevitt, Daniel Eugene	P	22	.154	A	
		Miller, Rodney Carter		1	.000	A	C
		Neal, Chas. Lenard (2B3 3B23)	SS100	128	.270	B	
11	12	Newcombe, Donald	P28	34	.230	B	
		Pignatano, Joseph Benjamin	C6	8	.214	A	
12	9	Podres, John Joseph	P31	35	.208	Bkn55	
		Reese, Harold Henry (Pee-Wee) (SS23)	3B75	103	.224	B	
8	2	Roebuck, Edward Jack	P	44	.238	B	
		Roseboro, John H. (1B5)	C19	35	.145	A	
		Snider, Edwin Donald	OF136	139	.274	B	
1	1	Valdes, Rene Gutierrez	P	5	.000	A	C
		Valo, Elmer Wm.	OF36	81	.273	Phil	
		Walker, Albert Bluford	C50	60	.181	B	
		Zimmer, Donald Wm. (2B5 SS37)	3B39	84	.219	B	

CLUB RECORD

NATIONAL LEAGUE

BUFFALO

YEAR	TG	WON	LOST	PCT.	FINISHED	MANAGER
1879	76	44	32	.579	x3(Chi)	Wm. Henry McGunnigle
1880	82	24	58	.293	7	Wm. Henry McGunnigle; Samuel Newhall Crane
1881	83	45	38	.542	3	James Henry O'Rourke
1882	84	45	39	.536	x3(Bos)	James Henry O'Rourke
1883	97	52	45	.536	5	James Henry O'Rourke
1884	111	64	47	.577	3	James Henry O'Rourke
1885	112	38	74	.339	7	John Curtis Chapman; George Hughson; James F. Galvin

CLUB RECORD

OTHER MAJOR LEAGUES

BUFFALO

YEAR	TG	WON	LOST	PCT.	FINISHED	MANAGER
PLAYER'S LEAGUE						
1890	132	36	96	.273	8(Last)	John Chas. Rowe
FEDERAL LEAGUE						
1914	151	80	71	.530	4	Harry Lawrence Schlafly
1915	152	74	78	.487	6	Harry Lawrence Schlafly; Walter Allan Blair; Harry Donald Lord
AMERICAN LEAGUE						
1900	139	61	78	.439	7	Daniel W. Shannon

WON 44
LOST 32
TG 76

NATIONAL LEAGUE
1879

FINISHED 3rd.
(TIED WITH CHIC.)
PCT. .579

BUFFALO

WM. HENRY McGUNNIGLE

WON	LOST	NAME	POS.	G.	BA	FROM	TO
		Clapp, John Edgar	C60	67	.265	Indpls	
		Crowley, Wm. Michael (C10)	OF39	59	.282	Lvlle77	
		Eggler, David Daniel	OF	77	.208	Chi77	
		Force, David W.	SS77	78	.209	StL77	
		Fulmer, Chas. J.	2B74	75	.266	Lvlle76	
37	27	Galvin, James F.	P65	66	.254	A	
		Hornung, Michael Joseph	OF77	78	.266	A	
7	5	McGunnigle, Wm. Henry MGR. (P13)	OF33	46	.180	A	
		Richardson, Arthur Harding	3B77	78	.278	A	
		Rowe, John Chas. (OF1)	C7	8	.382	A	
		Walker, Oscar	1B	70	.266	A	
		Libby, Stephen Augustus	1B	1	.000	A	C

WON 24
LOST 58
TG 82

NATIONAL LEAGUE
1880.

FINISHED 7th.
PCT. .293

BUFFALO

WM. HENRY McGUNNIGLE   SAMUEL NEWHALL CRANE

WON	LOST	NAME	POS.	G.	BA	FROM	TO
		Crane, Samuel Newhall MGR. (OF1)	2B10	10	.125	A	
		Crowley, Wm. Michael (C17)	OF69	82	.261	B	
1	3	Driscoll, John F. (P6)	OF14	18	.136	A	
		Esterbrook, Thomas Jefferson (Dude) (C1 2B6 SS1 OF14)	1B45	63	.241	A	
		Force, David W. (SS29)	2B49	78	.162	B	
		Fulmer, Chas. J.	2B	11	.152	B	
20	34	Galvin, James F. (OF16)	P55	64	.211	B	
0	0	*Hornung, Michael Joseph (P1)	OF64	82	.262	B	
		Latham, Walter Arlington (Arlie) (C1 OF10)	SS12	22	.125	A	
		Kearns, Thomas J. (OF1)	C9	9	.091	A	
		Keenan, James W.	C	2	.125	A	
		Mack, Dennis Joseph (2B1)	SS	17	.203	StL76	
		Moynahan, Michael	SS	27	.296	A	
2	3	McGunnigle, Wm. Henry MGR. (OF3)	P5	7	+.174	B	Wor
1	8	Poorman, Thomas Iverson (OF10)	P11	19	+.159	A	Chi
		Radbourn, Chas. (Hoss) (OF3)	2B3	6	.143	A	
		Richardson, Arthur Handing (C4)	3B78	80	.252	B	

WON	LOST	NAME	POS.	G.	BA	FROM	TO
		Rowe, John Chas. (3B3 OF21)	C54	77	.256	B	
		Stearns, Daniel Eckford (C9 2B1 SS1 3B5)	OF18	21	.232	A	
		Walker, Oscar	1B24	33	.230	B	
0	10	Weidman, George E. (OF12)	P17	23	.100	A	

*Hornung also played 12 games at 1B and 4 games at 2B.

WON 45 NATIONAL LEAGUE FINISHED 3rd.
LOST 38
TG 83 1881. PCT. .542

BUFFALO

JAMES HENRY O'ROURKE

WON	LOST	NAME	POS.	G.	BA	FROM	TO
		Brouthers, Dennis (Dan) (1B30)	OF35	65	.318	Troy	
2	4	Foley, Chas. Joseph (P6 1B28)	OF50	83	.256	Bos	
		Force, David W. (SS19 3B1 OF3)	2B53	75	.179	B	
29	24	Galvin, James F. (OF15)	P53	62	.211	B	
10	9	Lynch, John H. (OF6)	P19	23	.166	A	
		Manning, John E.	OF	1	.000	Cin	
		Morrissey, John H.	3B	12	.191	A	
		O'Rourke, James Henry MGR. (C8 1B1 SS 8 OF18)	3B56	83	.301	Bos	
		Peters, John Paul (OF1)	SS52	54	.214	Prov	
4	1	Purcell, Wm. Aloysius (Blondy) (P9)	OF25	30	+.267	xClev	
		*Richardson, Arthur Harding	OF78	83	.290	B	
		Rowe, John Chas. (SS7 3B8 OF3)	C43	61	.333	B	
		Smith, Chas. Marvin (Pap)	2B	3	+.000	xWor	
		Sullivan, Thomas Jefferson (OF4)	C29	31	.190	A	
		Swartwood, Cyrus Edward	OF	1	.250	A	
		White, James Laurie (Deacon) (C5 2B25 3B7 OF17)	1B25	78	.310	Cin	

*Richardson also played 5 games at 2B and 1 game at SS.

WON 45 NATIONAL LEAGUE FINISHED 3rd.
LOST 39 (TIED WITH BOSTON)
TG 84 1882. PCT. .536

BUFFALO

JAMES HENRY O'ROURKE

WON	LOST	NAME	POS.	G.	BA	FROM	TO
		Brouthers, Dennis (Dan)	1B	84	.367	B	
0	1	Burke, Walter R. (OF1)	P1	1	.000	A	
15	14	Daly, Hugh I. (One-Arm)	P	29	.163	A	
		Dolan, Thomas J. (3B2 OF3)	C17	22	.157	Chi79	
0	0	Foley, Chas. Joseph (P1)	OF84	84	.305	B	
		Force, David W. (2B1 3B10)	SS61	73	.241	B	
28	22	Galvin, James F. (OF6)	P50	54	.213	B	
		*O'Rourke, James Henry MGR.	OF79	84	.281	B	
2	2	Purcell, Wm. Aloysius (Blondy) (P4)	OF80	84	.276	B	
		Richardson, Arthur Harding	2B	83	.271	B	
		Rowe, John Chas. (SS22 3B7 OF2)	C44	75	.266	B	
		White, James Laurie (Deacon) (C20)	3B63	83	.281	B	

*O'Rourke also played 2 games as catcher, 2 games at SS and 2 games at 3B.

WON 52 NATIONAL LEAGUE FINISHED 5th.
LOST 45
TG 97 1883. PCT. .536

BUFFALO

JAMES HENRY O'ROURKE

WON	LOST	NAME	POS.	G.	BA	FROM	TO
0	0	Brouthers, Dennis (Dan) (P2 3B1)	1B96	97	.371	B	
0	0	Burke, Walter R. (OF1)	P1	1	.200	B	
4	3	Cushman, Edgar Leander (OF2)	P7	7	.200	A	
		Darling, Dell Conrad	C	5	.158	A	
3	11	Derby, George H. (OF3)	P15	15	.237	Det	C
		Eggler, David Daniel	OF	38	.245	xBaltAA	
1	0	Foley, Chas. Joseph (P1)	OF23	23	.270	B	
		Force, David W. (2B5 3B11)	SS77	95	.213	B	
44	29	Galvin, James F. (OF7)	P73	79	.220	B	
0	2	Hagan, Arthur F. (OF1)	P2	2	+.000	xPhil	
		Kennedy, Michael Joseph (Doc) (C2 1B1)	OF4	5	.286	Clev	C
0	0	Lillie, James J. (P1 2B1 3B1)	OF44	50	.231	A	
0	0	O'Rourke, James Henry MGR. (P1 C28 SS3 3B8)	OF56	93	.327	B	
		Richardson, Arthur Harding	2B	90	.310	B	
		Rowe, John Chas. (3B3) (SS17 3B3 OF22)	C45	86	.275	B	
		Schaffer, George (Orator)	OF	94	.292	Clev	
		Suck, Anthony (Tony) (OF1)	C1	2	.000	A	
		White, James Laurie (Deacon) (C18)	3B75	93	.289	B	

WON 64 — LOST 47 — TG 111

NATIONAL LEAGUE — 1884. — FINISHED 3rd. — PCT. .577

BUFFALO

JAMES HENRY O'ROURKE

WON	LOST	NAME	POS.	G.	BA	FROM	TO
		Brouthers, Dennis (Dan) (3B1)	1B89	90	.325	B	
		Collins, Chas. (Chub) (SS3)	2B42	45	.177	A	IndplsAA
0	0	Coughlan, Edward E. (OF1)	P2	2	.250	A	C
		Eggler, David Daniel	OF	58	.198	B	
0	1	Ely, Frederick Wm. (OF1)	P1	1	.000	A	
		Force, David W. (2B1)	SS101	102	.208	B	
46	21	Galvin, James F.	P	68	.182	B	
1	2	Hagan, Arthur F.	P	3	.500	B	C
0	1	Lillie, James J. (P1 C1)	OF109	110	.219	B	
		Myers, George D. (OF31)	C45	76	.186	A	
0	1	O'Rourke, James Henry MGR. (P4 C4 1B18 3B1)	OF81	104	.350	B	
		Richardson, Arthur Harding (1B3 3B5 OF24)	2B67	98	.301	B	
		Rowe, John Chas. (SS6 OF25)	C60	91	.310	B	
17	21	Serad, Wm. T. (OF2)	P38	38	.175	A	
		White, James Laurie (Deacon) (C3)	3B104	106	.325	B	

WON 38 — LOST 74 — TG 112

NATIONAL LEAGUE — 1885. — FINISHED 7th. — PCT. .339

BUFFALO

JOHN CURTIS CHAPMAN — GEORGE H. HUGHSON — JAMES F. GALVIN

WON	LOST	NAME	POS.	G.	BA	FROM	TO
		Brouthers, Dennis (Dan)	1B	98	.358	B	
		Carroll, John E. (2B1)	OF12	12	.056	StPUA	
0	1	Connor, John	P	1	.000	Bos	LvlleAA
10	17	Conway, Peter J. (1B1 SS1)	P27	29	.111	A	
		Crane, Edward Nicholas	OF	13	+.269	xProv	
		Crowley, Wm. Michael	OF	92	.241	Bos	C
		#Dickerson, Lewis Pessano	SS5	5	.048	LvlleAA	C
		Driscoll, John F.	2B	7	.158	LvlleAA	C
		Eggler, David Daniel	OF	6	.083	B	C
0	1	Fisher	P	1	.000	WilUA	C
		Force, David W. (3B6) (SS23 3B6)	2B42	71	.225	B	
12	19	Galvin, James F. MGR.	P	32	.188	B	PittAA
		Hatfield, Gilbert (2B3)	3B8	11	.125	A	
		Hengle, Emory J. (OF3)	2B5	7	.154	StPUA	C
		Lillie, James J. (1B1 SS2)	OF108	112	.248	B	
		Myers, George D. (OF20)	C69	89	.205	B	
		McCauley, James A. (OF3)	C24	24	+.205	St.LAA	Chi
		McDonald, James A. (OF1)	SS4	5	.000	PittAA	C
		Phelan, James D.	2B	4	+.133	BaltUA	StL
0	0	Richardson, Arthur Harding (P1 2B49 SS1)	OF48	96	.319	B	
		Ritter,	2B	2	.167	A	C
		Rowe, John Chas. (C22 OF12)	SS64	98	.289	B	
8	21	Serad, Wm. T.	P	29	.153	B	
		Staples, Joseph F. (2B1)	OF6	7	.045	A	C
		*Stearns, Daniel Eckford	SS18	30	.200	xBaltAA	
		White, James Laurie (Deacon)	3B	98	.292	B	
		Wood, Frederick S.	C	1	.250	Det	C
8	15	Wood, Peter Burke (1B2 OF5)	P23	28	.212	A	

*Stearns also played 2 games as catcher and 13 games at 1B.
#Dickerson also played 5 games in the OF.

CLUB RECORD

NATIONAL LEAGUE

CHICAGO

YEAR	TG	WON	LOST	PCT.	FINISHED	MANAGER
1876	66	52	14	.788	1	Albert Goodwill Spalding
1877	59	26	33	.441	5	Albert Goodwill Spalding
1878	60	30	30	.500	4	Robert V. Ferguson
1879	76	44	32	.579	x3(Buff)	Adrian Constantine Anson
1880	84	67	17	.798	1	Adrian Constantine Anson
1881	84	56	28	.667	1	Adrian Constantine Anson
1882	84	55	29	.655	1	Adrian Constantine Anson
1883	98	59	39	.602	2	Adrian Constantine Anson
1884	112	62	50	.554	x4(N.Y.)	Adrian Constantine Anson
1885	112	87	25	.776	1	Adrian Constantine Anson
1886	124	90	34	.725	1	Adrian Constantine Anson
1887	121	71	50	.587	3	Adrian Constantine Anson
1888	135	77	58	.578	2	Adrian Constantine Anson
1889	132	67	65	.508	3	Adrian Constantine Anson
1890	136	83	53	.610	2	Adrian Constantine Anson
1891	135	82	53	.607	2	Adrian Constantine Anson
1892	146	70	76	.479	7	Adrian Constantine Anson
1893	128	57	71	.445	9	Adrian Constantine Anson
1894	132	57	75	432	8	Adrian Constantine Anson
1895	130	72	58	.554	4	Adrian Constantine Anson
1896	128	71	57	.555	5	Adrian Constantine Anson
1897	132	59	73	.447	9	Adrian Constantine Anson
1898	150	85	65	.567	4	Thomas Everett Burns
1899	148	75	73	.507	8	Thomas Everett Burns
1900	140	65	75	.464	x5(StL)	Thomas Joseph Loftus
1901	139	53	86	.381	6	Thomas Joseph Loftus
1902	137	68	69	.496	5	Frank Gibson Selee
1903	138	82	56	.594	3	Frank Gibson Selee
1904	153	93	60	.608	2	Frank Gibson Selee
1905	153	92	61	.601	3	Frank Gibson Selee Frank LeRoy Chance
1906	152	116	36	.763	1	Frank LeRoy Chance
1907	152	107	45	.704	1	Frank LeRoy Chance
1908	154	99	55	.643	1	Frank LeRoy Chance
1909	153	104	49	.680	2	Frank LeRoy Chance
1910	154	104	50	.676	1	Frank LeRoy Chance
1911	154	92	62	.597	2	Frank LeRoy Chance
1912	150	91	59	.607	3	Frank LeRoy Chance
1913	153	88	65	.575	3	John Joseph Evers
1914	154	78	76	.506	4	Henry F. O'Day
1915	153	73	80	.477	4	Roger Patrick Bresnahan
1916	153	67	86	.438	5	Joseph Bert Tinker
1917	154	74	80	.481	5	Frederick Francis Mitchell
1918	129	84	45	.651	1	Frederick Francis Mitchell
1919	140	75	65	.536	3	Frederick Francis Mitchell
1920	154	75	79	.487	x5(StL)	Frederick Francis Mitchell
1921	153	64	89	.418	7	John Joseph Evers Wm. Lavier Killefer, Jr.
1922	154	80	74	.520	5	Wm. Lavier Killefer, Jr.
1923	154	83	71	.539	4	Wm. Lavier Killefer, Jr.
1924	153	81	72	.530	5	Wm. Lavier Killefer, Jr.
1925	154	68	86	.442	8(Last)	Wm. Lavier Killefer, Jr. Walter James Vincent Maranville George Gibson
1926	154	82	72	.532	4	Joseph Vincent McCarthy
1927	153	85	68	.556	4	Joseph Vincent McCarthy
1928	154	91	63	.591	3	Joseph Vincent McCarthy
1929	152	98	54	.645	1	Joseph Vincent McCarthy
1930	154	90	64	.584	2	Joseph Vincent McCarthy Rogers Hornsby
1931	154	84	70	.545	3	Rogers Hornsby
1932	154	90	64	.584	1	Rogers Hornsby Chas. John Grimm
1933	154	86	68	.558	3	Chas. John Grimm
1934	151	86	65	.570	3	Chas. John Grimm
1935	154	100	54	.649	1	Chas. John Grimm
1936	154	87	67	.565	x2(StL)	Chas. John Grimm
1937	154	93	61	.604	2	Chas. John Grimm
1938	152	89	63	.586	1	Chas. John Grimm Chas. Leo Hartnett
1939	154	84	70	.545	4	Chas. Leo Hartnett
1940	154	75	79	.487	5	Chas. Leo Hartnett
1941	154	70	84	.455	6	James Wilson
1942	154	68	86	.442	6	James Wilson
1943	153	74	79	.484	5	James Wilson
1944	154	75	79	.487	4	James Wilson Roy Cleveland Johnson Chas. John Grimm
1945	154	98	56	.636	1	Chas. John Grimm
1946	153	82	71	.536	3	Chas. John Grimm
1947	154	69	85	.448	6	Chas. John Grimm
1948	154	64	90	.416	8(Last)	Chas. John Grimm
1949	154	61	93	.396	8(Last)	Chas. John Grimm Frank Francis Frisch
1950	153	64	89	.418	7	Frank Francis Frisch
1951	154	62	92	.403	8(Last)	Frank Francis Frisch Philip Joseph Cavarretta
1952	154	77	77	.500	5	Philip Joseph Cavarretta
1953	154	65	89	.422	7	Philip Joseph Cavarretta
1954	154	64	90	.416	7	Stanley Camfield Hack
1955	153	72	81	.471	6	Stanley Camfield Hack
1956	154	60	94	.390	8(Last)	Stanley Camfield Hack
1957	154	62	92	.403	x7(Pitts)	Robert Boden Scheffing
1958	154	72	82	.468	x5(St.L)	Robert Boden Scheffing
1959	154	74	80	.481	x5(Cin)	Robert Boden Scheffing
1960	154	60	94	.390	7	Chas. John Grimm Louis Boudreau, Jr.
1961	154	64	90	.416	7	Avitus Bernard Himsl Harry Francis Craft Elvin Walter Tappe Louis Frank Klein
1962	162	59	103	.364	9	Elvin Walter Tappe Louis Frank Klein Charles Metro
1963	162	82	80	.506	7	Robert Daniel Kennedy
1964	162	76	86	.469	8	Robert Daniel Kennedy

YEAR	TG	WON	LOST	TIED	PCT.	FINISHED	MANAGER
1965	164	72	90	2	.444	8	ROBERT DANIEL KENNEDY
							LOUIS FRANK KLEIN
1966	162	59	103	0	.364	10 (LAST)	LEO ERNEST DUROCHER
1967	162	87	74	1	.540	3	LEO ERNEST DUROCHER
1968	163	84	78	1	.519	3	LEO ERNEST DUROCHER
1969	163	92	70	1	.568	2E	LEO ERNEST DUROCHER
1970	162	84	78	0	.519	2E	LEO ERNEST DUROCHER
1971	162	83	79	0	.512	X3E (NY)	LEO ERNEST DUROCHER
1972	156	85	70	1	.548	2E	LEO ERNEST DUROCHER
							CARROLL WALTER LOCKMAN

WON 52 — NATIONAL LEAGUE — FINISHED 1st.
LOST 14
TG 66 — 1876. — PCT. .788

CHICAGO

ALBERT GOODWILL SPALDING

WON	LOST	NAME	POS.	G.	BA	FROM	TO
		Addy, Robert Edward	OF	33	.272	A	
		Andrus, Frederick Hotham	OF	8	.306	A	
		Anson, Adrian Constantine (Pop)	3B	66	.343	A	
		Barnes, Roscoe Conkling (Ross)	2B	66	.404	A	
		Bielaski, Oscar	OF	31	.206	A	C
		Glenn, John W. (1B10)	OF56	66	.292	A	
		Hines, Paul A.	OF	64	.330	A	
6	0	McVey, Calvin Alexander (Cal) (P6)	1B55	63	.345	A	
		Peters, John Paul	SS	66	.348	A	
46	14	Spalding, Albert Goodwill MGR. (OF6)	P60	66	.306	A	
		White, James Laurie (Deacon)	C64	66	.335	A	

WON 26 — NATIONAL LEAGUE — FINISHED 5th.
LOST 33
TG 59 — 1877. — PCT. .441

CHICAGO

ALBERT GOODWILL SPALDING

WON	LOST	NAME	POS.	G.	BA	FROM	TO
		Anson, Adrian Constantine (C32) (Pop)	3B41	59	.337	B	
		Barnes, Roscoe Conkling (Ross)	2B	22	.272	B	
19	23	Bradley, George Washington (1B3 3B16 OF1)	P50	55	.243	StL	
		Eden, Chas. M.	OF	15	.218	A	
		Eggler, David Daniel	OF	33	.265	Ath	
		Fisher, Wm. Chas. (Cherokee)	3B	1	.000	Cin	
		Glenn, John W. (1B14)	OF36	50	.228	B	C
		Hallinan, James H.	OF	19	+.281	xCin	
		Hines, Paul A. (2B11)	OF49	60	.280	B	
		Jones, Chas. Wesley	OF	2	+.375	xCin	Cin
4	8	McVey, Calvin Alexander (Cal) (P17 1B1 2B1 3B17)	C41	60	.368	B	
		Quinn, Patrick	OF	4	.071	A	
		Peters, John Paul	SS	60	.317	B	
3	1	Reis, Lawrence P.	P	4	.125	A	
0	1	Rowe, David E. (P1)	OF2	2	.286	A	
		Smith, Chas. Henry (OF11)	2B13	24	+.202	A	Cin
0	0	Spalding, Albert Goodwill MGR. (P4 2B13 3B2)	1B45	60	.256	B	
		Waitt, Chas. C.	OF	10	.098	A	

WON 30
LOST 30
TG 60

NATIONAL LEAGUE

1878

FINISHED 4th.

PCT. .500

CHICAGO

ROBERT V. FERGUSON

WON	LOST	NAME	POS.	G.	BA	FROM	TO
		Anson, Adrian Constantine (Pop) (2B9)	OF44	59	.336	B	
		Cassidy, John P.	OF	60	.261	Hart	
		Ferguson, Robert V. MGR.	SS55	60	.334	Hart	
		Hallinan, James H. (2B4)	OF11	15	+.231	B	Indpls
0	1	Hankinson, Frank Edward (P1)	3B56	57	.268	A	
		Harbidge, Wm. Arthur (OF7)	C46	53	.298	Hart	
29	26	Larkin, Frank	P55	57	.289	Hart	
		McClellan, Wm. Henry	2B41	46	.221	A	
		Powers, Philip J. (OF1)	C8	9	.140	A	
1	3	Reis, Lawrence P. (OF1)	P4	5	.150	B	C
		Remsen, John Jay	OF	55	.233	StL	
		Spalding, Albert Goodwill	2B	1	.500	B	C
		Start, Joseph	1B	60	.345	Hart	
		Traffley, Wm. F.	C	2	.111	A	
		Sullivan, Wm.	OF	2	.000	A	C

WON 44
LOST 32
TG 76

NATIONAL LEAGUE

1879

FINISHED 3rd.
(TIED WITH BUFF)
PCT. .579

CHICAGO

ADRIAN CONSTANTINE ANSON

WON	LOST	NAME	POS.	G.	BA	FROM	TO
		Anson, Adrian Constantine (Pop) MGR.	1B	49	.407	B	
		Brown, Lewis J.	1B	6	+.273	xProv.	
		Dalrymple, Abner Frank	OF	67	.300	Mil.	
		Dolan, Thomas J.	C	1	.000	A	
		Flint, Frank Sylvester (Silver)	C74	75	.290	Indpls	
		Gore, George F.	OF52	60	.268	A	
14	9	Hankinson, Frank Edward (OF12)	P24	41	.183	B	
		Harbidge, Wm. Arthur	OF	1	.000	B	
30	23	Larkin, Frank	P55	58	.222	B	
		Peters, John Paul	SS	79	.254	Mil	
		Quest, Joseph L.	2B	79	.220	Indpls	
		Remsen, John Jay (1B10)	OF29	39	.248	B	
		Schaffer, George (Orator)	OF69	70	.319	Indpls	
		Stedrouske, (2B1)	3B3	4	.083	A	C
		Williamson, Edward Nagle	3B68	77	.299	Indpls	

WON 67
LOST 17
TG 84

NATIONAL LEAGUE

1880.

FINISHED 1st.

PCT. .798

CHICAGO

ADRIAN CONSTANTINE ANSON

WON	LOST	NAME	POS.	G.	BA	FROM	TO
		Anson, Adrian Constantine (Pop) MGR. (2B1 SS1 3B8)	1B77	84	.338	B	
		Beals, Thomas L. (2B3)	OF10	13	.149	A	C
0	0	*Burns, Thomas Everett (P1 C2)	SS73	82	.309	A	
43	14	Corcoran, Lawrence J. (Larry) (SS8 OF13)	P57	70	.221	A	
		Dalrymple, Abner Frank	OF	84	.332	B	
		%Flint, Frank Sylvester (Silver)	C62	71	.167	B	
22	3	Goldsmith, Frederick Ernest (1B4 OF10)	P25	35	.260	Troy	
		Gore, George F. (1B6)	OF71	75	.365	B	
1	0	Guth, Chas. J.	P	1	.200	A	C
0	0	Kelly, Michael Joseph (King) (P1 C13 SS1 3B7)	OF62	82	.292	Cin	
1	0	Poorman, Thomas Iverson (P2)	OF7	7	+.200	xBuff	
		Quest, Joseph L. (SS2)	2B78	80	.245	B	
		Williamson, Edward Nagle (C11 2B3)	3B61	74	.255	B	

*Burns also played 5 games at 3B.
%Flint also played 11 games in OF.

WON 56
LOST 28
TG 84

NATIONAL LEAGUE

1881.

FINISHED 1st.

PCT. .667

CHICAGO

ADRIAN CONSTANTINE ANSON

WON	LOST	NAME	POS.	G.	BA	FROM	TO
		Anson, Adrian Constantine (Pop) MGR. (C2 SS1)	1B83	84	.399	B	
		#Burns, Thomas Everett	SS79	84	.277	B	
31	14	%Corcoran, Lawrence J. (Larry)	P45	47	.222	B	
		Dalrymple, Abner Frank	OF	81	.323	B	
		*Flint, Frank Sylvester (Silver)	C77	80	.310	B	
25	13	Goldsmith, Frederick Ernest (OF3)	P38	40	.240	B	
		Gore, George F. (1B2 SS1)	OF71	73	.297	B	
		Kelly, Michael Joseph (King) (C7 3B7)	OF66	80	.323	B	
		Nicol, Hugh N. (SS1)	OF	26	.203	A	
		Piercy, Andrew J. (3B1)	2B1	2	.250	A	C

WON	LOST	NAME	POS.	G.	BA	FROM	TO
		Quest, Joseph L. (SS1)	2B76	77	.249	B	
0	1	Williamson, Edward Nagle	3B74	82	.268	B	
		(P1 2B4 SS2)					

#Burns also played 3 games at 2B and 4 games at 3B.
%Corcoran also played 2 games at SS and 3 games in the OF.
*Flint also played 1 game at 1B and 7 games in the OF.

WON 55 | LOST 29 | TG 84 — NATIONAL LEAGUE 1882. — FINISHED 1st. PCT. .655

CHICAGO

ADRIAN CONSTANTINE ANSON

WON	LOST	NAME	POS.	G.	BA	FROM	TO
		Anson, Adrian Constantine	1B82	82	.362	B	
		(Pop) MGR. (C1)					
		Burns, Thomas Everett (SS41)	2B43	84	.247	B	
27	13	*Corcoran, Lawrence J. (Larry)	P41	41	.207	B	
		Dalrymple, Abner Frank	OF	84	.294	B	
		#Flint, Frank Sylvester (Silver)	C79	81	.250	B	
28	16	Goldsmith, Frederick Ernest	P44	44	.229	B	
		(1B1)					
		Gore, George F.	OF	84	.318	B	
		Kelly, Michael Joseph (King)	SS41	84	.305	B	
		(C12 1B1 3B2 OF36)					
		Nicol, Hugh N. (SS8)	OF36	47	.198	B	
		Quest, Joseph L.	2B41	42	.201	B	
		Scott, Milton Parker	1B	1	.400	A	
0	0	Williamson, Edward Nagle	3B82	82	.281	B	
		(P1)					

*Corcoran also played 1 game at 3B.
#Flint also played 11 games in the OF.

WON 59 | LOST 39 | TG 98 — NATIONAL LEAGUE 1883. — FINISHED 2nd. PCT. .602

CHICAGO

ADRIAN CONSTANTINE ANSON

WON	LOST	NAME	POS.	G.	BA	FROM	TO
0	0	Anson, Adrian Constantine	1B98	98	.307	B	
		(Pop) MGR. (P2 C1)					
		Burns, Thomas Everett	SS79	97	.293	B	
		(2B17 OF1)					
31	21	#Corcoran, Lawrence J. (Larry)	P52	66	.207	B	
		Dalrymple, Abner Frank	OF	80	.297	B	
		%Flint, Frank Sylvester (Silver)	C77	84	.265	B	
28	18	*Goldsmith, Frederick Ernest	P46	60	.221	B	
		Gore, George F.	OF	91	.334	B	
0	0	Kelly, Michael Joseph (King)	OF74	98	.253	B	
		(P1 C20 2B1 3B1)					
		Pfeffer, Nathaniel Frederick	2B79	96	.234	Troy	
		(1B1 SS17 OF1)					
		Sunday, Wm. Ashley	OF	15	.259	A	
0	0	Williamson, Edward Nagle	3B97	98	.276	B	
		(P1 C1)					

#Corcoran also played 1 game at 2B, 2 games at SS and 13 games in the OF.
%Flint also played 21 games in the OF.
*Goldsmith also played 2 games at 1B and 17 games in the OF.

WON 62 | LOST 50 | TG 112 — NATIONAL LEAGUE 1884. — FINISHED 4th. (TIED WITH N.Y.) PCT. .554

CHICAGO

ADRIAN CONSTANTINE ANSON

WON	LOST	NAME	POS.	G.	BA	FROM	TO
0	0	Andrus, Frederick Hotham	P	1	.167	Chi76	C
0	0	Anson, Adrian Constantine	1B108	111	.337	B	
		(Pop) MGR. (P1 C2 SS1)					
3	2	Brown, Joseph E.	OF9	15	+.220	A	
		(P7 C1 1B1)					
		Burns, Thomas Everett (3B3)	SS79	82	.245	B	
10	3	%Clarkson, John Gibson	P20	20	.261	Wor82	
35	23	#Corcoran, Lawrence J. (Larry)	P59	63	.230	B	
0	1	Corcoran, M.	P	1	.000	A	C
1	2	Crosby, George W.	P	3	.308	A	C
		Dalrymple, Abner Frank	OF	110	.310	B	
		Flint, Frank Sylvester (Silver)	C	71	.207	B	
8	12	Goldsmith, Frederick Ernest	P21	22	.135	B	BaltAA
		(OF1)					
		Gore, George F.	OF	101	.316	B	
1	1	Hibbard, John Denison	P	2	.000	A	C
0	0	Kelly, Michael Joseph (King)	OF61	107	.341	B	
		(P2 C26 1B2 2B1 SS15 3B9)					
		Kenzie, Walter H. (3B2)	SS17	19	.158	Det82	StLAA
1	4	Lee, Thomas F. (SS1)	P5	6	.125	A	BaltUA
3	2	Lynch, Thomas S. (1B1)	P5	5	+.000	A	C
0	0	*Pfeffer, Nathaniel Frederick	2B111	111	.289	B	
		Sunday, Wm. Ashley	OF	43	.221	B	
		Sutcliffe, Edward Elmer	C	4	.200	A	
0	0	Williamson, Edward Nagle	3B98	106	.278	B	
		(P1 C10)					

%Clarkson also played 1 game at 1B, 3 games at 3B and 8 games in the OF.
#L.J.Corcoran also played 2 games at SS and 3 games in the OF.
*Pfeffer was in 1 game as P.

WON 87 | LOST 25 | TG 112 — NATIONAL LEAGUE 1885. — FINISHED 1st. PCT. .776

CHICAGO

ADRIAN CONSTANTINE ANSON

WON	LOST	NAME	POS.	G.	BA	FROM	TO
		Anson, Adrian Constantine (Pop) MGR. (C1)	1B	112	.310	B	
		Burns, Thomas Everett (2B1)	SS	111	.271	B	
52	16	Clarkson, John Gibson (3B1 OF1)	P70	72	.215	B	
5	2	Corcoran, Lawrence J. (Larry) (SS1)	P7	7	+.227	B	N.Y.
		Dalrymple, Abner Frank	OF	113	.274	B	
		*Flint, Frank Sylvester (Silver)	C67	67	.208	B	
		Gastfield, Edward	C	1	+.000	xDet	C
		Gore, George F.	OF	109	.312	B	
		Kelly, Michael Joseph (King) (C33 1B2 2B5 3B2)	OF67	107	.287	B	
7	2	Kennedy, Theodore A. (3B1)	P9	9	.065	A	
		Krieg, Wm. Frederick (OF1)	C1	1	.000	PittUA	BknAA
		McCauley, James A. (OF2)	C2	3	+.100	xBuff	
20	4	McCormick, James (OF1)	P25	25	+.231	xProv	
3	1	Pfeffer, Nathaniel Frederick (P4 OF1)	2B109	112	.240	B	
		Ryan, James E. (OF1)	SS2	3	.462	A	
		Sunday, Wm. Ashley	OF	42	.255	B	
		Sutcliffe, Edward Elmer (OF1)	C11	11	+.195	B	StL
0	0	Williams, Washington J. (OF1)	P1	1	.250	RichAA	C
0	0	Williamson, Edward Nagle (P2 C1)	3B111	112	.238	B	

*Flint also played 1 game in the OF.

WON 90 — NATIONAL LEAGUE — FINISHED 1st.
LOST 34
TG 124 — 1886. — PCT. .725

CHICAGO

ADRIAN CONSTANTINE ANSON

WON	LOST	NAME	POS.	G.	BA	FROM	TO
		Anson, Adrian Constantine (Pop) MGR.	1B121	125	.371	B	
		Burns, Thomas Everett	3B	111	.276	B	
35	17	Clarkson, John Gibson	P53	55	.233	B	
		Dalrymple, Abner Frank	OF	82	.232	B	
		Flint, Frank Sylvester (Silver)	C	49	.202	B	
24	6	Flynn, John A. (OF24)	P32	56	.200	A	
		Gore, George F.	OF	118	.304	B	
		Hardie, Lewis W.	C	16	.176	Phi184	
		Kelly, Michael Joseph (King) (C46)	OF54	118	.388	B	
		Moolic, George Henry	C	15	.145	A	C
31	11	McCormick, James	P	42	.235	B	
		Pfeffer, Nathaniel Frederick	2B	119	.263	B	
		Ryan, James E.	OF67	84	.306	B	
		Sunday, Wm. Ashley	OF	25	.242	B	
		Williamson, Edward Nagle	SS	121	.216	B	

WON 71 — NATIONAL LEAGUE — FINISHED 3rd.
LOST 50
TG 121 — 1887. — PCT. .587

CHICAGO

ADRIAN CONSTANTINE ANSON

WON	LOST	NAME	POS.	G.	BA	FROM	TO
		Anson, Adrian Constantine (Pop) MGR.	1B	122	.421	B	
19	17	Baldwin, Marcus Elmore (Mark)	P38	40	.241	A	
		Burns, Thomas Everett	3B107	115	.317	B	
38	21	Clarkson, John Gibson	P59	61	.279	B	
		Daly, Thomas Peter	C65	74	.269	A	
		Darling, Dell Conrad (C18)	OF20	38	.411	Buff83	
		Flint, Frank Sylvester (Silver)	C46	48	.282	B	
		Flynn, John A.	OF	1	.000	B	C
0	1	Geiss, Emil M.	P	3	.083	BaltAA82	C
		Pettit, Robert Henry	OF	32	.301	A	
		Pfeffer, Nathaniel Frederick	2B	123	.325	B	
1	3	Pyle, Harry Thomas	P	4	.188	Phil84	C
0	0	Ryan, James E. (P1)	OF120	126	.355	B	
1	1	Sprague, Chas. Wellington	P	3	.154	A	
		Sullivan, Martin J.	OF	115	.334	A	
		Sunday, Wm. Ashley	OF	48	.359	B	
		Tebeau, Oliver Wendell (Pat)	3B	20	.208	A	
12	7	Van Haltren, George E. (P19)	OF26	44	.278	A	
		Williamson, Edward Nagle	SS	127	.371	B	

WON 77 — NATIONAL LEAGUE — FINISHED 2nd.
LOST x 58
TG 135 — 1888. — PCT. .578

CHICAGO

ADRIAN CONSTANTINE ANSON

WON	LOST	NAME	POS.	G.	BA	FROM	TO
		Anson, Adrian Constantine (Pop) MGR.	1B	134	.343	B	
13	15	Baldwin, Marcus Elmore (Mark)	P28	30	.151	B	
4	5	Borchers, George B.	P	10	.059	A	
2	1	Brynan, Chas. R.	P	3	.091	A	
		Burns, Thomas Everett	3B	134	.238	B	
2	0	Clarke, Wm. H. (Dad)	P	3	.250	A	
		Daly, Thomas Peter	C62	65	.191	B	
		Darling, Dell Conrad	C	20	.213	B	
		Duffy, Hugh	OF67	71	.282	A	
4	1	Dwyer, John Francis (Frank)	P	5	.190	A	

WON	LOST	NAME	POS.	G.	BA	FROM	TO
		Farrell, Chas. A. (Duke) (OF31)	C31	63	.232	A	
		Flint, Frank Sylvester (Silver)	C	22	.181	B	
3	3	Gumbert, Addison Courtney (Ad)	P	7	.333	A	
25	14	Krock, August H.	P	39	.164	A	
1	1	Mains, Willard Eben	P	2	.125	A	
		Pettit, Robert Henry	OF	43	.254	B	
		Pfeffer, Nathaniel Frederick	2B	135	.249	B	
3	1	Ryan, James E. (P4)	OF125	130	.331	B	
		Sullivan, Martin J.	OF	75	.235	B	
7	5	Tener, John Kinley	P	14	.196	BaltAA85	
13	11	Van Haltren, George E. (P27)	OF54	81	.283	B	
		Williamson, Edward Nagle	SS	132	.250	B	

x-One game lost by forfeit.

WON 67   NATIONAL LEAGUE   FINISHED 3rd.
LOST 65
TG 132   1890.   PCT. 508

CHICAGO

ADRIAN CONSTANTINE ANSON

WON	LOST	NAME	POS.	G.	BA	FROM	TO
		Anson, Adrian Constantine (Pop) MGR.	1B	134	.341	B	
		Bastian, Chas. J.	SS45	46	.135	Phil	
0	0	Bishop, Wm. R.	P	2	.000	Pitt87	C
		Burns, Thomas Everett	3B	136	.257	B	
		Darling, Dell Conrad	C	35	.191	B	
		Duffy, Hugh	OF120	136	.311	B	
16	12	Dwyer, John Francis (Frank)	P29	33	.203	B	
		Farrell, Chas. A. (Duke) (OF25)	C75	100	.263	B	
		Flint, Frank Sylvester (Silver)	C	15	.232	B	C
14	13	Gumbert, Addison Courtney (Ad)	P29	49	.287	B	
3	4	Healy, John J. (Egyptian)	P	7	+.100	xWash	
16	17	Hutchinson, Wm. Forest	P	37	.158	A	
4	4	Krock, August H.	P	8	+.167	B	Indpls
		Pfeffer, Nathaniel Frederick	2B	134	.241	B	
		Ryan, James E. (SS29)	OF106	135	.324	B	
		Sommers, Joseph Andrew (Pete)	C	12	+.239	Bos	Indpls
14	15	Tener, John Kinley	P31	38	.273	B	
		Van Haltren, George E.	OF130	134	.322	B	
		Williamson, Edward Nagle	SS	47	.237	B	

WON 83   NATIONAL LEAGUE   FINISHED 2nd.
LOST 53
TG 136   1890.   PCT. .610

CHICAGO

ADRIAN CONSTANTINE ANSON

WON	LOST	NAME	POS.	G.	BA	FROM	TO
		Andrews, James F.	OF	53	.188	A	C
		Anson, Adrian Constantine (Pop) MGR.	1B135	139	.311	B	
		Burns, Thomas Everett	3B	139	.277	B	
		Carroll, Samuel (Clifford)	OF	136	.285	Pitt88	
		Cooney, James John	SS	135	.271	A	
4	7	Coughlin, Wm. E.	P	11	.243	A	
0	0	DeMarris, Frederick	P	1	.000	A	C
		Earl, Howard J. (2B36)	OF49	92	.247	A	
0	0	Eiteljorg, Edward Henry	P	1	.000	A	
		Foster, Elmer E.	OF	27	.247	N.Y.	
0	0	France, Osman B.	P	1	.000	A	C
1	0	Gibson, Chas. Robert	P	1	+.000	A	Pitt
		Glenalvin, Robert J.	2B	66	.268	A	
		Honan, Martin	C	1	.000	A	
		Hutchinson, Edward Forest	2B	7	.107	A	C
42	26	Hutchinson, Wm. F.	P	68	.203	B	
		Kittredge, Malachi Jedediah	C	96	.201	A	
		Lauer, John Chas. (Chuck)	C	2	.375	Pitt	C
20	8	Luby, John Perkins	P	30	.342	A	
		Lytle, Edward Benson (Dad)	OF	1	+.000	A	Pitt
		Nagle, Thomas G.	C33	38	.264	A	
		O'Brien, Peter F.	2B	27	.275	A	C
11	6	Stein, Edward F.	P	18	.152	A	
		Stenzel, Jacob C. (Jake) (OF5)	C6	11	.209	A	
5	6	Sullivan, Michael Joseph (Mike)	P	12	.153	Wash	
		Wilmot, Walter R.	OF	139	.278	Wash	
		Wright, Patrick W.	2B	1	.000	A	

WON 82   NATIONAL LEAGUE   FINISHED 2nd.
LOST 53
TG 135   1891.   PCT. .607

CHICAGO

ADRIAN CONSTANTINE ANSON

WON	LOST	NAME	POS.	G.	BA	FROM	TO
		Anson, Adrian Constantine (Pop) MGR.	1B	136	.294	B	
		Bowman, Wm. G.	C	15	.088	A	C
		Burns, Thomas Everett	3B52	57	.231	B	
		Carroll, Samuel (Clifford)	OF	130	.255	B	
		Cooney, James John	SS	118	.250	B	
		Dahlen, Wm. Frederick (Bad Bill) (SS15 OF36)	3B84	135	.263	A	
		Foster, Elmer E.	OF	4	.187	B	C
17	10	Gumbert, Addison Courtney (Ad)	P	29	.326	BosPL	
		Honan, Martin	C	5	.167	B	C
43	19	Hutchinson, Wm. Forest	P63	64	.179	B	
		Kittredge, Malachi Jedediah	C69	70	.202	B	
10	12	Luby, John Perkins	P22	24	.215	B	
		Merritt, Wm. Henry	C	11	.218	A	
		Nagle, Thomas G.	C	8	.120	B	C

WON	LOST	NAME	POS.	G.	BA	FROM	TO
0	1	Nicol, George Edward	P	3	.333	StLAA	
		Pfeffer, Nathaniel Frederick	2B	137	.246	ChiPL	
		Ryan, James E.	OF	118	.289	ChiPL	
		Schriver, Wm. F. (Pop)	C	25	.311	Phil	
6	6	Stein, Edward F.	P	13	.131	B	
6	5	Vickery, Thomas Gill	P	14	.154	Phil	
		Wilmot, Walter R.	OF	120	.285	B	

WON 70 NATIONAL LEAGUE FINISHED 7th.
LOST 76
TG 146 1892. PCT. .479

CHICAGO

ADRIAN CONSTANTINE ANSON

WON	LOST	NAME	POS.	G.	BA	FROM	TO
		Anson, Adrian Constantine	1B	147	.274	B	
		(Pop) MGR.					
		Canavan, James E.	2B114	118	.167	MilAA	
		Carroll, John E.	3B	1	.000	ClevAA87	C
		Connor, James Matthew	2B	10	.057	A	
		Cooney, James John	SS	84	+.171	B	Wash
		Dahlen, Wm. Frederick	SS74	143	.294	B	
		(Bad Bill) (3B68)					
		Decker, George A. (2B16)	OF63	79	.231	A	
		Dungan, Samuel Morrison	OF	113	.291	A	
0	0	Griffith, Edward	P	1	.000	A	C
23	18	**Gumbert, Addison** Courtney (Ad)	P44	48	.247	B	
0	1	Hollison, Henry John	P	1	.000	A	C
37	33	Hutchinson, Wm. Forest	P	71	.225	B	
		Kittredge, Malachi Jedediah	C	66	.187	B	
9	21	Luby, John Perkins	P30	40	.195	B	
0	1	Meakim, George Clinton	P	2	+.077	AthAA	Cin
1	2	Miller, Henry D.	P	4	.300	A	C
		Newman, Chas. C.	OF	14	+.148	xN.Y.	C
		Parrott, Walter E. (Jiggs)	3B	79	.215	A	
		Roat, Frederick	2B	8	.200	Pitt90	C
		Ryan, James E.	OF119	127	.289	B	
		Schriver, Wm. F. (Pop)	C80	89	.222	B	
		Wilmot, Walter R.	OF	92	.220	B	

WON 57 NATIONAL LEAGUE FINISHED 9th.
LOST 71
TG 128 1893. PCT. .445

CHICAGO

ADRIAN CONSTANTINE ANSON

WON	LOST	NAME	POS.	G.	BA	FROM	TO
3	5	Abbey, Bert Wood	P	8	.111	Wash	
		Anson, Adrian Constantine	1B100	101	.322	B	
		(Pop) MGR.					
		Camp, Llewellyn Robert	3B16	38	.268	StL	
0	0	Caruthers, Robert Lee	P	1	+.000	StL	Cin
5	3	Clausen, Frederick Wm.	P	10	+.094	xLvlle	
		Dahlen, Wm. Frederick	SS88	115	.311	B	
		(Bad Bill) (OF16)					
		Decker, George A.	OF34	81	.276	B	
		(1B27 2B20)					
3	1	Donnelly, Franklin Marion	P	6	.429	A	
		Dungan, Samuel Morrison	OF	107	.310	B	
		Eagan, Wm. (Bad Bill)	2B	6	.300	StLAA91	
		Glenalvin, Robert J.	2B	16	.400	Chi90	C
1	1	Griffith, Clark Calvin	P	3	.181	BosAA91	
0	1	Hughey, James Ulysses	P	1	.000	MilAA91	
16	24	Hutchinson, Wm. Forest	P40	41	.261	B	
		Irwin, Chas. E.	SS	21	.324	A	
0	0	Johnson, Abraham	P	1	.000	A	C
		Kitredge, Malachi Jedediah	C	67	.245	B	
		Lange, Wm. Alexander (OF39)	2B56	116	.288	A	
		Lynch, Henry W.	OF	4	.214	A	C
8	9	Mauck, Alfred Maris	P	18	.163	A	C
17	17	McGill, Wm. Vaness	P	35	.269	Cin	
2	6	McGinnis, August (Gus)	P	13	+.240	A	Phil
		O'Brien, John J.	2B	4	.416	Bkn91	
0	0	Parker, Harley Park (Dr)	P	1	.000	A	
0	4	Parrott, Thomas Wm.	P	12	+.357	A	Cin
		Parrott, Walter E. (Jiggs)	3B101	113	.252	B	
		Ryan, James E.	OF72	82	.304	B	
		Schriver, Wm. F. (Pop)	C56	59	.295	B	
1	0	Shaw, Samuel E.	P	2	.286	BaltAA88	C
		Wilmot, Walter R.	OF	93	.318	B	
1	0	Yost, Gus	P	1	.000	A	C

WON 57 NATIONAL LEAGUE FINISHED 8th.
LOST 75
TG 132 1894. PCT. .432

CHICAGO

ADRIAN CONSTANTINE ANSON

WON	LOST	NAME	POS.	G.	BA	FROM	TO
2	7	Abbey, Bert Wood	P	11	.132	B	
		Anson, Adrian Constantine	1B	83	.394	B	
		(Pop) MGR.					
		Camp, Llewellyn Robert	2B	8	.156	B	C
0	1	Camp, Winfield Scott	P	3	.000	Pitt92	C
0	1	Clausen, Frederick Wm.	P	2	.000	B	
		Dahlen, Wm. Frederick	SS66	121	.362	B	
		(Bad Bill) (3B55)					
		Decker, George A. (OF30)	1B48	89	.310	B	
0	0	Donnelly, Franklin Marion	P	1	.000	B	C
		Dungan, Samuel Morrison	OF	10	+.237	B	Lvlle
20	11	Griffith, Clark Calvin	P35	41	.244	B	
		Houseman, John Franklin	SS	4	.353	A	
16	18	Hutchinson, Wm. Forest	P	34	.323	B	

WON	LOST	NAME	POS.	G.	BA	FROM	TO
		Irwin, Chas. E. (SS62)	3B68	130	.302	B	
		Kittredge, Malachi Jedediah	C	50	.317	B	
		Lange, Wm. Alexander	OF110	112	.324	B	
6	19	McGill, Wm. Vaness	P	26	.229	B	
		Parrott, Walter E. (Jiggs)	2B125	126	.244	B	
		Ryan, James E.	OF	108	.359	B	
		Schriver, Wm. F. (Pop)	C86	94	.269	B	
9	6	Stratton, C. Scott	P	20	+.379	xLvlle	
4	12	Terry, Wm. J. (Adonis)	P	24	+.323	xPitt	
		Wilmot, Walter R.	OF	135	.331	B	

WON 72 — NATIONAL LEAGUE — FINISHED 4th.
LOST 58
TG 130 — 1895. — PCT. .554

CHICAGO

ADRIAN CONSTANTINE ANSON

WON	LOST	NAME	POS.	G.	BA	FROM	TO
0	1	Abbey, Bert Wood	P	2	+.250	B	Bkn
		Anson, Adrian Constantine (Pop) MGR.	1B	122	.338	B	
		Dahlen, Wm. Frederick (Bad Bill)	SS	131	.273	B	
		Decker, George A.	OF55	70	.291	B	
0	1	Dolan, John (Jack)	P	2	.000	StL93	C
		Donahue, Timothy Cornelius	C	62	.271	BosAA91	
		Everett, Wm. L.	3B130	133	.356	A	
2	2	Friend, Daniel Sebastian	P	5	.222	A	
25	14	Griffith, Clark Calvin	P	39	.319	B	
13	18	Hutchinson, Wm. Forest	P	34	.205	B	
		Irwin, Chas. E.	SS	3	.200	B	
		Kittredge, Malachi Jedediah	C	58	.244	B	
		Lange, Wm. Alexander	OF	122	.388	B	
		Moran, Wm. L.	C	15	.163	StL92	C
2	0	McFarland, LaMont A. (Monte)	P	2	.143	A	
4	3	Parker, Harley Park (Dr)	P	7	.318	Chi93	
		Parrott, Walter E. (Jiggs)	SS	3	.200	B	C
		Ryan, James E.	OF	108	.322	B	
		Stewart, Asa (Ace)	2B	97	.244	A	
2	3	Stratton, C. Scott	P	8	.222	B	C
21	14	Terry, Wm. J. (Adonis)	P37	39	.222	B	
3	2	Thornton, Walter Miller	P	9	.318	A	
		Truby, Harry Garvin	2B	33	.339	A	
		Wilmot, Walter R.	OF	108	.299	B	

WON 71 — NATIONAL LEAGUE — FINISHED 5th.
LOST 57
TG 128 — 1896. — PCT. .555

CHICAGO

ADRIAN CONSTANTINE ANSON

WON	LOST	NAME	POS.	G.	BA	FROM	TO
		Anson, Adrian Constantine (Pop) MGR.	1B96	106	.335	B	
12	8	Briggs, Herbert T.	P	22	.133	A	
		Dahlen, Wm. Frederick (Bad Bill)	SS	125	.361	B	
		Dailey, Cornelius F. (Con)	C	9	+.075	xBkn	C
		Decker, George A.	OF70	106	.281	B	
		Donahue, Timothy Cornelius	C	54	.226	B	
		Everett, Wm. L. (OF32)	3B99	131	.333	B	
		Flynn, George A.	OF	29	.267	A	
19	14	Friend, Daniel Sebastian	P	33	.240	B	
23	11	Griffith, Clark Calvin	P	36	.266	B	
		Kittredge, Malachi Jedediah	C	61	.223	B	
		Lange, Wm. Alexander	OF122	123	.333	B	
		McBride, Algernon Briggs (Algie)	OF	9	.233	A	
		McCormick, Wm. J. (Barry)	3B35	45	.219	Lvlle	
0	3	McFarland, Lamont A. (Monte)	P	3	.000	B	C
1	5	Parker, Harley Park (Dr)	P	10	.278	B	
		Pfeffer, Nathaniel Frederick	2B	95	+.244	xN.Y.	
		Reilly, Chas. (Josh)	2B	9	.205	A	C
		Ryan, James E.	OF	127	.312	B	
14	15	Terry, Wm. J. (Adonis)	P	29	.260	B	
2	1	Thornton, Walter Miller	P	9	.391	B	
		Truby, Harry Garvin	2B	27	+.266	B	Pitt

WON 59 — NATIONAL LEAGUE — FINISHED 9th.
LOST 73
TG 132 — 1897. — PCT. .447

CHICAGO

ADRIAN CONSTANTINE ANSON

WON	LOST	NAME	POS.	G.	BA	FROM	TO
		Anson, Adrian Constantine (Pop) MGR.	1B101	112	.302	B	C
5	17	Briggs, Herbert T.	P	22	.190	B	
13	10	Callahan, James Joseph (P23 SS16 OF20)	2B30	90	.308	Phi94	
		Connor, James Matthew	2B	77	.296	Chi92	
		Dahlen, Wm. Frederick (Bad Bill)	SS	75	.296	B	
		Decker, George A. (1B38)	OF72	109	.307	B	
3	6	Denzer, Roger	P	12	.154	A	
		Donahue, Timothy Cornelius	C	53	.234	B	
		Everett, Wm. L.	3B83	90	.314	B	
12	11	Friend, Daniel Sebastian	P23	24	.274	B	
18	18	Griffith, Clark Calvin	P40	46	.236	B	
		Hernon, Thomas H.	OF	4	.111	A	C
		Kittredge, Malachi Jedediah	C	77	.198	B	
1	2	Korwan, James	P	5	.000	Bkn94	C
		Lange, Wm. Alexander	OF	117	.352	B	
		McCormick, Wm. J. (Barry) (SS45)	3B53	100	.273	B	

WON	LOST	NAME	POS.	G.	BA	FROM	TO
		Pfeffer, Nathaniel Frederick	2B	32	.230	B	C
		Ryan, James E.	OF	135	.309	B	
0	0	Terry, Wm. J. (Adonis)	P	1	.000	B	C
6	9	Thornton, Walter Miller (P16)	OF58	71	.329	B	
1	0	Wright, David William	P	1	.333	Pitt95	C

WON 85 NATIONAL LEAGUE FINISHED 4th.
LOST 65
TG 150 1898. PCT. .567

CHICAGO

THOMAS EVERETT BURNS

WON	LOST	NAME	POS.	G.	BA	FROM	TO
1	4	Briggs, Herbert T.	P	5	.429	B	
20	11	Callahan, James Joseph	P31	42	.258	B	
		Chance, Frank LeRoy (Husk) (OF15)	C27	42	.288	A	
1	0	Clarke, Henry Tefft	P	2	.500	Cleve	C
		Connor, James Matthew	2B	136	.225	B	
		Dahlen, Wm. Frederick (Bad Bill)	SS	141	.290	B	
		Donahue, Timothy Cornelius	C	117	.236	B	
		Everett, Wm. L.	1B	149	.325	B	
0	2	Friend, Daniel Sebastian	P	2	.286	B	C
		Green, Edward (Danny)	OF	47	.328	A	
25	12	Griffith, Clark Calvin	P	37	.169	B	
4	6	Isbell, Wm. Frank (P10)	OF26	41	.235	A	
0	1	Katoll, John	P	2	.000	A	
6	6	Kilroy, Matthew Aloysius	P	25	.239	Lvlle94	C
		Lange, Wm. Alexander	OF109	111	.332	B	
		Martin, Frank	2B	1	.000	Lvlle	
		Mertes, Samuel Blair (Sandow)	OF58	70	.304	Phil96	
		McCormick, Wm. J. (Barry)	3B134	136	.248	B	
		Nichols, Arthur Francis	C	13	.264	A	
2	1	Phyle, Wm. Joseph	P	3	.111	A	
		Ryan, James E.	OF	143	.322	B	
5	0	Taylor, John W. (Jack)	P	5	.200	A	
12	9	Thornton, Walter Miller (P24)	OF34	56	.283	B	C
		Wolverton, Harry Sterling	3B	13	.327	A	
9	13	Woods, Walter Sydney	P22	41	.162	A	

WON 75 NATIONAL LEAGUE FINISHED 8th.
LOST 73
TG 148 1899. PCT. .507

CHICAGO

THOMAS EVERETT BURNS

WON	LOST	NAME	POS.	G.	BA	FROM	TO
		Bradley, Wm. Joseph	3B30	35	.307	A	
21	12	Callahan, James Joseph	P35	45	.255	B	
		Chance, Frank LeRoy (Husk)	C51	57	.289	B	
2	3	Cogan, Richard Henry	P	8	.200	Balt97	
		Connor, James Matthew (3B21)	2B45	66	.206	B	C
		Curley, Walter James	2B	10	.105	A	C
		DeMontreville, Eugene Napoleon	2B	83	+.286	Balt Balt	Balt
		Donahue, Timothy Cornelius	C	90	.250	B	
		Everett, Wm. L.	1B	136	.309	B	
9	13	Garvin, Virgil Lee	P	22	.147	Phil96	
		Green, Edward (Danny)	OF	114	.296	B	
21	13	Griffith, Clark Calvin	P36	39	.260	B	
1	1	Katoll, John	P	3	.000	B	
		Lange, Wm. Alexander	OF93	107	.324	B	C
		Magoon, George Henry	SS	59	+.235	xBalt	
0	1	Malarkey, John S.	P	1	.200	Wash96	
		Mertes, Samuel Blair (Sandow)	OF105	109	.305	B	
		McCormick, Wm. J. (Barry)	2B98	102	.234	B	
		Nichols, Arthur Francis	C	17	.277	B	
2	8	Phyle, Wm. T.	P	10	.171	B	
		Quinn, Frank J.	OF	12	.181	A	C
1	0	Roach, (Skel)	P	1	.000	A	C
		Ryan, James E.	OF	124	.301	B	
18	22	Taylor, John W. (Jack)	P41	42	.266	B	
		Wolverton, Harry Sterling	3B98	99	.295	B	

WON 65 NATIONAL LEAGUE FINISHED 5th.
LOST 75 (TIED WITH ST. LOUIS)
TG 140 1900. PCT. .464

CHICAGO

THOMAS JOSEPH LOFTUS

WON	LOST	NAME	POS.	G.	BA	FROM	TO
		Bradley, Wm. Joseph (1B15)	3B105	120	.288	B	
		Bresnahan, Roger Philip	C	1	.000	Wash97	
12	16	Callahan, James Joseph	P	33	.236	B	
		Chance, Frank LeRoy (Husk)	C	48	.304	B	
		Childs, Clarence Algernon	2B	138	.243	StL	
		Clingman, Wm. Frederick	SS	46	.201	Lvlle	KCA
5	3	Cunningham, Ellsworth Elmer	P	8	.192	Lvlle	
		Dexter, Chas. Dana	C20	35	.201	Lvlle	
		Dolan, Patrick Henry (Cozy)	OF	13	.205	Bos96	
		Donahue, Timothy Cornelius	C64	65	.239	B	
		Dungan, Samuel Morrison	OF	6	.266	Lvlle94	KCA
1	0	Eason, Malcolm Wayne (Mal)	P	1	.000	A	
		Everett, Wm. L.	1B	23	.236	B	
		Ganzel, John Henry	1B	78	.272	xKCA	
11	17	Garvin, Virgil Lee	P	28	.155	B	
		Green, Edward (Danny)	OF	100	.299	B	
14	13	Griffith, Clark Calvin	P	30	.250	B	
0	0	Harvey Erwin K.	P	2	.000	A	MinnA & return

WON	LOST	NAME	POS.	G.	BA	FROM	TO
1	1	Hughes, Thomas J.	P	3	.000	A	
3	3	Killen, Frank Bissell	P	6	.150	Bos	ChiA
		Kling, John G.	C	15	.294	A	
9	5	Menefee, John (Jock)	P	17	.102	NY98	
		Mertes, Samuel Blair (Sandow) (1B31)	OF86	125	.294	B	
		McCarthy, John A.	OF	123	.296	Pitt99	
		McCormick, Wm. J. (Barry) (3B21)	SS85	110	.215	B	
		Nichols, Arthur Francis	C	8	.208	B	MinnA & return
		Ryan, James E.	OF	106	.276	B	
		Strang, Samuel Nicklin	3B	25	.276	Lvlle96	
9	17	Taylor, John W. (Jack)	P	27	.225	B	
		Wolverton, Harry Sterling	3B	3	+.182	B	Phil

WON 53 LOST 86 TG 139

NATIONAL LEAGUE

1901.

FINISHED 6th. PCT. .381

CHICAGO

THOMAS JOSEPH LOFTUS

WON	LOST	NAME	POS.	G.	BA	FROM	TO
		Chance, Frank LeRoy (Husk)	OF48	63	.289	B	
		Childs, Clarence Algernon	2B	63	.257	B	C
		Childs, Peter Piene	2B	60	+.221	xStL	
		Croft, Henry T.	OF	3	.333	Phil99	C
0	1	Cunningham, Ellsworth Elmer	P	1	.000	B	C
		Delahanty, James Christopher Jr.	3B	16	.174	A	
		Dexter, Chas. Dana (3B28 OF19)	1B52	112	.278	B	
		Dolan, Patrick Henry (Cozy)	OF	43	+.262	B	Bkn
		Doyle, John Joseph (Jack)	1B	73	.241	N.Y.	
8	17	Eason, Malcolm Wayne (Mal)	P	25	.138	B	
0	0	Ferguson, Chas. Augustus	P	1	.000	A	C
		Gannon, Wm. G.	OF	15	.159	StL98	C
		Green, Edward (Danny)	OF	132	.317	B	
		Hartsel, Tullos Frederick (Topsy)	OF	140	.339	Cin	
		Hickey, Michael Edward	3B	10	.176	IndplsA	C
		Hoffman, Lawrence Chas.	3B	5	.315	A	C
10	23	Hughes, Thomas J.	P	33	.109	B	
		Kahoe, Michael Joseph	C	65	+.215	xCin	
		Kling, John G.	C69	70	.266	B	
8	12	Menefee, John (Jock) (P20)	OF22	46	.251	B	
		McCormick, Wm. J. (Barry)	SS112	115	.234	B	
		Raymer, Frederick Chas. (SS28)	3B82	118	.235	MilA	
		Schaefer, Herman A. (Germany)	2B	2	.375	KCA	
13	19	Taylor, John W. (Jack)	P	33	.217	B	
14	14	Waddell, George Edward (Rube)	P	31	+.263	xPitt	

WON 68 LOST 69 TG 137

NATIONAL LEAGUE

1902.

FINISHED 5th. PCT. .496

CHICAGO

FRANK GIBSON SELEE

WON	LOST	NAME	POS.	G.	BA	FROM	TO
		Chance, Frank LeRoy (Husk) (C29 OF4)	1B36	67	.284	B	
		Clark, Frederick R	1B	12	.186	A	C
		Congalton, Wm. Millar (Bunk)	OF	47	.245	A	
		Dexter, Chas. Dana (1B20 OF15)	3B35	70	+.227	B	Bos
		Dobbs, John Gordon	OF	59	+.310	xCin	
3	3	Eason, Malcolm Wayne (Mal)	P	6	+.200	B	Bos
		Evers, John Joseph (SS8)	2B18	25	.225	A	
1	2	Gardner, James Anderson	P	3	.200	IndplsA00	C
0	1	Glade, Frederick Monroe	P	1	.333	A	
		Glenn, Edward D.	SS	2	.000	NY98	C
2	2	Hardy, David Alexander (Alex)	P	4	.200	A	
		Hendricks, John Calhoun	OF	2	+.500	xN.Y.	
		Hildebrand, R. E.	OF	1	.000	A	C
		Hughes, Edward	OF	1	.000	A	C
		Jacobs, Morris Elmore	SS	5	.210	A	C
		Jones, David Jefferson	OF	63	.310	xStLA	
		Kahoe, Michael Joseph (SS1 3B2)	C4	7	.222	B	StLA
		Kennedy, Sherman Montgomery	OF	1	.000	A	C
		Kling, John G. (SS1)	C111	113	.286	B	
		Lamar, Pierre	C	2	.222	A	
		Lowe, Robert Lincoln (Link) (3B2)	2B119	121	.260	Bos	
9	9	Lundgren, Carl Leonard (SS2)	P18	19	.106	A	
		Lynch, Michael Joseph	OF	7	.166	A	C
12	10	Menefee, John (Jock) (1B19 2B1 3B2 OF20)	P22	64	.231	B	
		Miller, Dakin E.	OF	50	.225	A	C
0	3	Morrissey, Frank Frederick (3B2)	P5	7	.090	BosA	C
		Murray, James O.	OF	11	.166	A	
		O'Hagan, Harold P.	1B	33	+.188	WashN92	N.Y.
		Pedroes, Chas. P. (Chick)	OF1	2	.000	A	C
4	7	Rhoades, Robert Bruce	P	16	.222	A	
		Schaefer, Herman A. (Germany) (1B3 OF2)	3B74	80	.188	B	
		Schlafly, Harry Lawrence (2B4 SS1 3B2)	OF5	10	.333	A	
		Slagle, James Franklin (Shorty)	OF	114	.313	Bos	
		Strang, Samuel Nicklin (2B1)	3B2	3	.363	xChiA	
4	6	St. Vrain, James H.	P	12	.103	A	C
22	10	Taylor, John W. (Jack) (1B2 2B1 3B13 OF4)	P36	53	.239	B	
		Tinker, Joseph Bert (3B6)	SS127	133	.273	A	

WON	LOST	NAME	POS.	G.	BA	FROM	TO
		Williams, Arthur Frank (1B21)	OF28	49	.232	A	C
11	16	Williams, Walter Merrill (OF11)	P31	32	.194	Wash98	

WON 82 NATIONAL LEAGUE FINISHED 3rd.
LOST 56
TG 138 1903. PCT. .594

CHICAGO

FRANK GIBSON SELEE

WON	LOST	NAME	POS.	G.	BA	FROM	TO
		Casey, James Peter (Doc)	3B	112	.290	DetA	
		Chance, Frank LeRoy (Husk)	1B121	123	.327	B	
		Cook, James Fitchie	OF	8	.120	A	C
1	2	Currie, Clarence F.	P	6	+.417	xStL	C
		Dobbs, John Gordon	OF	16	+.230	B	Bkn
0	1	Doscher, John Herman Jr.	P	1	+.000	IndplsA00	Bkn
		Evers, John Joseph	2B110	123	.293	B	
0	1	Graham, George Frederick (Peaches)	P	1	.000	ClevA	
		Hanlon, Wm.	1B	8	.045	A	C
1	1	Hardy, David Alexander (Alex)	P	3	.143	B	C
		Harley, Richard Joseph	OF	103	.231	DetA	C
		Jones, David Jefferson	OF	130	.282	B	
		Kling, John G.	C	132	.297	B	
		Lowe, Robert Lincoln (Link)	2B22	28	.267	B	
11	9	Lundgren, Carl Leonard	P	27	.115	B	
8	10	Menefee, John (Jock)	P20	22	.203	B	C
		Moriarty, George Joseph	3B	1	.000	A	
		McCarthy, John A.	OF	24	.277	xClevA	
		McLean, John Bannerman(Larry)	C	1	.000	BosA01	
		Raub, Thomas Jefferson	C	27	.226	A	
		Slagle, James Franklin (Shorty)	OF	139	.298	B	
21	14	Taylor, John W. (Jack)	P37	39	.222	B	
		Tinker, Joseph Bert (3B19)	SS107	124	.241	B	
20	8	Weimer, John Wm.	P	35	.196	A	
20	9	Wicker, Robert Kitridge	P	32	+.245	xStL	
		Williams, Otto George	SS	37	+.223	xStL	
0	1	Williams, Walter Merrill	P	2	+.223	B	Phil

WON 93 NATIONAL LEAGUE FINISHED 2nd.
LOST 60
TG 153 1904. PCT. .608

CHICAGO

FRANK GIBSON SELEE

WON	LOST	NAME	POS.	G.	BA	FROM	TO
		Barry, John C. (1B18)	OF54	72	+.262	xPhil	
19	11	Briggs, Herbert T.	P	34	.170	Chi98	
15	9	Brown, Mordecai Peter Centennial	P26	27	.213	StL	
		Carney, Wm. J.	OF	2	.000	A	C
		Casey, James Peter (Doc)	3B134	136	.268	B	
		Chance, Frank LeRoy (Husk)	1B123	124	.310	B	
5	5	Corridon, Frank J.	P	19	+.224	A	Phil
		Evers, John Joseph	2B	152	.265	B	
0	2	Groth, Edward John	P	3	.000	A	C
		Hofman, Arthur Frederick	OF	7	.269	Pitt	
		Holmes, Frederick	C	1	.333	NYA	C
		Jones, David Jefferson	OF	97	.244	B	
		Kling, John G.	C104	120	.243	B	
17	10	Lundgren, Carl Leonard	P	31	.222	B	
		Moriarty, George Joseph (OF2)	3B3	5	.000	B	
		McCarthy, John A.	OF	115	.264	B	
		McChesney, Harry Vincent (Pud)	OF	22	.261	A	C
		O'Neill, John Joseph (Jack)	C	49	.214	StL	
		Rudolph, John Herman	OF	2	.250	Phil	C
		Schulte, Frank	OF	20	.286	A	
		Slagle, James Franklin (Shorty)	OF	120	.260	B	
		Smith, Alexander Benjamin (C1)	1B8	10	.173	BosA	
		Stanton, Harry Andrew	C	1	.000	StL00	C
		Tinker, Joseph Bert	SS140	141	.221	B	
		VanZandt, Chas. Isaac	OF	3	.000	NY01	
20	13	Weimer, John Wm.	P	37	.183	B	
17	10	Wicker, Robert Kitridge (OF20)	P30	50	.219	B	
		Williams, Otto George	OF21	54	.200	B	

WON 92 NATIONAL LEAGUE FINISHED 3rd.
LOST 61
TG 153 1905. PCT. .601

CHICAGO

FRANK GIBSON SELEE FRANK LEROY CHANCE

WON	LOST	NAME	POS.	G.	BA	FROM	TO
		Barry, John C.	1B	26	+.212	B	Cin
9	10	Briggs, Herbert T.	P	20	.053	B	C
17	9	Brown, Mordecai Peter Centennial	P	30	.140	B	
		Casey, James Peter (Doc)	3B	142	.232	B	
		Chance, Frank LeRoy (Husk) MGR.	1B	115	.316	B	
		Evers, John Joseph	2B	99	.276	B	
		Hofman, Arthur Frederich	2B59	83	.237	B	
		Kling, John G.	C106	110	.218	B	
		Lobert, John Bernard (Hans)	3B	14	.196	Pitt03	
13	4	Lundgren, Carl Leonard	P	23	.180	B	
		Maloney, Wm. Alphonse	OF	145	.260	Cin02	
		McCarthy, John A.	OF37	43	.276	B	

WON	LOST	NAME	POS.	G.	BA	FROM	TO
		O'Neill, John Joseph (Jack)	C	50	.198	B	
5	5	Pfeffer, Francis Xavier	P	15	.200	A	
17	13	Reulbach, Edward Marvin	P	34	.127	A	
		Schulte, Frank	OF	123	.274	B	
		Slagle, James Franklin (Shorty)	OF	155	.269	B	
		Tinker, Joseph Bert	SS	149	.247	B	
18	13	Weimer, John Wm.	P	33	.207	B	
13	7	Wicker, Robert Kitridge	P22	25	.139	B	

WON 116 — NATIONAL LEAGUE — FINISHED 1st.
LOST 36
TG 152 — 1906. — PCT. .763

CHICAGO

FRANK LEROY CHANCE

WON	LOST	NAME	POS.	G.	BA	FROM	TO
6	1	Beebe, Frederick Leonard	P	14	+.103	A	StL
26	6	Brown, Mordecai Peter Centennial	P	36	.204	B	
		Chance, Frank LeRoy (Husk)	1B	136	.319	B	
		Evers, John Joseph	2B152	154	.255	B	
		Gessler, Harry Homer	OF21	22	+.253	xBkn	
0	0	Harper, Chas. Wm. (Jack)	P	1	+.000	xCin	C
		Hofman, Arthur Frederich (1B20)	OF21	60	.256	B	
		Kling, John G.	C96	99	.312	B	
17	6	Lundgren, Carl Leonard	P27	28	.179	B	
		Moran, Patrick Joseph	C	61	.250	Bos	
		Noonan, Peter John	C	1	+.333	PhilA04	StL
12	3	Overall, Orval	P	18	+.170	xCin	
20	8	Pfiester, John Theodore Joseph (Jack)	P	31	.048	Pitt04	
19	4	Reulbach, Edward Marvin	P33	34	.157	B	
		Schulte, Frank	OF	146	.281	B	
		Sheckard, Samuel James Tilden	OF	149	.262	Bkn	
		Slagle, James Franklin (Shorty)	OF	127	.239	B	
		Smith, Louis O.		1	.000	Pitt04	
		Steinfeldt, Harry M.	3B150	151	.327	Cin	
12	3	Taylor, John W. (Jack)	P	17	+.208	xStL	
		Tinker, Joseph Bert	SS147	148	.233	B	
		Walsh, Thomas Joseph	C	2	.000	A	C
3	5	Wicker, Robert Kitridge	P	10	+.100	B	Cin

Won one game by forfeit vs. New York Aug. 7th.

WON 107 — NATIONAL LEAGUE — FINISHED 1st.
LOST 45
TG 152 — 1907. — PCT. .704

CHICAGO

FRANK LEROY CHANCE

WON	LOST	NAME	POS.	G.	BA	FROM	TO
20	6	Brown, Mordecai Peter Centennial	P34	35	.153	B	
		Chance, Frank LeRoy (Husk) MGR.	1B	109	.293	B	
0	1	Durbin, Blaine A.	P	10	.356	A	
		Evers, John Joseph	2B	151	.250	B	
8	5	Fraser, Chas. Carrolton (Chick)	P	22	.067	Cin	
		Hardy, John Doolittle	C	1	.250	ClevA03	
		Hofman, Arthur Frederich (1B18 SS42)	OF58	134	.268	B	
		Howard, George Elmer (OF8)	1B33	41	+.230	xBos	
		Kahoe, Michael Joseph	C	4	.286	Phil05	WashA
		Kling, John G.	C98	100	.284	B	
18	7	Lundgren, Carl Leonard	P	28	.106	B	
		Moran, Patrick Joseph	C	59	.227	B	
23	7	Overall, Orval	P	36	.213	B	
14	9	Pfiester, John Theodore Joseph (Jack)	P	30	.094	B	
		Randall, Newton J.	OF	21	+.205	A	Bos
17	4	Reulbach, Edward Marvin	P	27	.175	B	
		Schulte, Frank	OF91	92	.287	B	
		Sheckard, Samuel James Tilden	OF	142	.267	B	
		Slagle, James Franklin (Shorty)	OF132	136	.258	B	
		Steinfeldt, Harry M.	3B	151	.266	B	
		Sweeney, Wm. John	3B1	3	+.100	A	Bos
7	5	Taylor, John W. (Jack)	P	18	.191	B	C
		Tinker, Joseph Bert	SS	113	.221	B	
		Zimmerman, Henry (Heinie)	2B	3	.142	A	

WON 99 — NATIONAL LEAGUE — FINISHED 1st.
LOST 55
TG 154 — 1908. — PCT. .643

CHICAGO

FRANK LEROY CHANCE

WON	LOST	NAME	POS.	G.	BA	FROM	TO
29	9	Brown, Mordecai Peter Centennial	P	44	.207	B	
		Campbell, Arthur Vincent	OF	1	.000	A	
		Chance, Frank LeRoy (Husk) MGR.	1B	126	.272	B	
2	0	Coakley, Andrew James	P	4	+.000	xCin	
		Durbin, Blaine A.	OF6	14	.363	B	
		Evers, John Joseph	2B122	123	.300	B	
11	9	Fraser, Chas. Carrolton (Chick)	P	26	.120	B	
		Hayden, John Francis (Jack)	OF	11	.200	BosA06	C
		Hofman, Arthur Frederick (1B37 2B22)	OF50	116	.243	B	

WON	LOST	NAME	POS.	G.	BA	FROM	TO
		Howard, George Elmer (1B8)	OF81	89	.279	B	
		Kling, John G.	C117	125	.276	B	
0	0	Kroh, Floyd H.	P	2	.000	BosA	
6	9	Lundgren, Carl Leonard	P	23	.149	B	
0	0	Mack, Wm. Francis	P	2	.667	A	C
		Marshall, Wm. R. (Doc)	C	9	+.300	xStL	
		Moran, Patrick Joseph	C	45	.260	B	
15	11	Overall, Orval	P	37	.129	B	
12	10	Pfiester, John Theodore Joseph (Jack)	P	33	.101	B	
24	7	Reulbach, Edward Marvin	P	46	.232	B	
		Schulte, Frank	OF89	102	.236	B	
		Sheckard, Samuel James Tilden	OF	115	.231	B	
		Slagle, James Franklin (Shorty)	OF	101	.222	B	C
0	0	Sponsberg, Carl	P	1	.667	A	C
		Steinfeldt, Harry M.	3B	150	.241	B	
		Tinker, Joseph Bert	SS	157	.266	B	
		Zimmerman, Henry (Heinie)	2B20	30	.292	B	

WON 104 NATIONAL LEAGUE FINISHED 2nd.
LOST 49
TG 153 1909. PCT. .680

CHICAGO

FRANK LEROY CHANCE

WON	LOST	NAME	POS.	G.	BA	FROM	TO
		Archer, James Patrick	C	80	.230	DetA07	
27	9	Brown, Mordecai Peter Centennial	P	50	.176	B	
1	0	Brown, Paul Percival	P	1	.000	A	C
		Browne, George E.	OF	12	.200	Bos	WashA
		Chance, Frank LeRoy (Husk) MGR.	1B	92	.271	B	
0	1	Coakley, Andrew James	P	1	.000	B	
1	0	Cole, Leonard Leslie (King)	P	1	.750	A	
		Davidson, Wm. S.	OF	2	.142	A	
		Evers, John Joseph	2B	126	.263	B	
0	0	Fraser, Chas. Carrolton (Chick)	P	1	.000	B	C
4	4	Hagerman, Zeriah Zequiel (Rip)	P12	13	.130	A	
5	2	Higginbotham, Irving Clinton	P	19	+.231	xStL	C
		Hofman, Arthur Frederick	OF	153	.285	B	
		Howard, George Elmer	1B	57	.197	B	C
		Kane, John Francis	1B	15	.089	Cin	
9	4	Kroh, Floyd H.	P	17	.150	B	
		Luderus, Frederick Wm.	1B	11	.305	A	
0	1	Lundgren, Carl Leonard	P	2	.500	B	C
		Moran, Patrick Joseph	C	74	.219	B	
		Needham, Thomas J.	C	10	.200	N.Y.	
20	11	Overall, Orval	P	38	.229	B	
17	6	Pfiester, John Theodore Joseph (Jack)	P	29	.169	B	
0	0	Ragan, Don Carlos Patrick (Pat)	P	2	+.000	xCin	
19	10	Reulbach, Edward Marvin	P	35	.140	B	
		Schulte, Frank	OF	140	.264	B	
1	1	Schwenk, Rudolph C.	P	3	.250	A	C
		Sheckard, Samuel James Tilden	OF	148	.255	B	
		Stanley, Joseph Bernard	OF	16	.135	WashA06	C
		Steinfeldt, Harry M.	3B	151	.252	B	
		Tinker, Joseph Bert	SS	143	.256	B	
		Zimmerman, Henry (Heinie)	2B31	47	.273	B	

WON 104 NATIONAL LEAGUE FINISHED 1st.
LOST 50
TG 154 1910. PCT. .676

CHICAGO

FRANK LEROY CHANCE

WON	LOST	NAME	POS.	G.	BA	FROM	TO
		Archer, James Patrick (1B40)	C49	89	.259	B	
		Beaumont, Clarence Howeth	OF	56	.267	Bos	C
25	14	Brown, Mordecai Peter Centennial	P	46	.175	B	
0	0	Carson, Alexander James	P	2	.000	A	C
		Chance, Frank LeRoy (Husk) MGR.	1B	87	.298	B	
20	4	Cole, Leonard Leslie (King)	P	33	.231	B	
		Evers, John Joseph	2B	125	.263	B	
0	0	Foxen, Wm. A.	P	2	+.000	xPhil	
		Hofman, Arthur Frederick (1B24)	OF110	135	.325	B	
		Kane, John Francis	OF18	30	.242	B	C
		Kling, John G.	C	86	.269	Chi08	
3	1	Kroh, Floyd H.	P	6	.250	B	
		Luderus, Frederick Wm.	1B	17	+.204	B	Phil
		Miller, Roy Oscar (Doc)	OF	1	+.000	A	Bos
13	9	McIntire, Harry M.	P	28	.258	Bkn	
		Needham, Thomas J.	C27	28	.184	B	
12	6	Overall, Orval	P23	24	.122	B	
1	0	Pfeffer, Francis Xavier (OF1)	P13	14	.158	Bos08	
6	3	Pfiester, John Theodore Joseph (Jack)	P	14	.091	B	
12	8	Reulbach, Edward Marvin	P	24	.107	B	
11	4	Richie, Lewis A.	P	28	+.225	xBos	
		Schulte, Frank	OF	150	.301	B	
		Sheckard, Samuel James Tilden	OF	143	.256	B	
		Steinfeldt, Harry M.	3B	128	.252	B	
		Tinker, Joseph Bert	SS	132	.288	B	
1	1	Weaver, Orville F.	P	7	.154	A	
		Zimmerman, Henry (Heinie) (SS26 3B23)	2B32	86	.284	B	

WON 92 NATIONAL LEAGUE FINISHED 2nd.
LOST 62
TG 154 1911. PCT. .597

CHICAGO

FRANK LEROY CHANCE

WON	LOST	NAME	POS.	G.	BA	FROM	TO
		Archer, James Patrick	C102	112	.252	B	
		Bransfield, Wm. Edward (Kitty)	1B	3	+.400	xPhil	C
21	11	Brown, Mordecai Peter Centennial	P	53	.253	B	
		Chance, Frank LeRoy (Husk) MGR.	1B	29	.239	B	
1	0	Cheney, Lawrence Russell (Larry)	P	3	.250	A	
18	7	Cole, Leonard Leslie (King)	P	32	.152	B	
		Collins, Wm. Shirley	OF	7	+.333	xBos	
0	2	Curtis, Clifton Garfield	P	4	+.500	xBos	Phil
		Doyle, James Francis	3B	127	.282	Cin	C
		Evers, John Joseph	2B33	44	.226	B	
1	1	Foxen, Wm. A.	P	3	.250	B	C
		Good, Wilbur David	OF	58	+.269	xBos	
		Graham, George Frederick (Peaches)	C	36	+.239	xBos	
0	0	Griffin, John Linton	P	1	+.000	A	Bos
		Hofman, Arthur Frederick (1B36)	OF107	143	.252	B	
		Kaiser, Albert Edward	OF	26	+.250	A	Bos
		Kling, John G.	C	27	+.175	B	Bos
11	7	McIntire, Harry M.	P	25	.264	B	
		Needham, Thomas J.	C	23	.194	B	
0	0	Ovitz, Ernest Gayheart	P	1	.000	A	C
2	4	Pfiester, John Theodore Joseph (Jack)	P	6	.182	B	C
16	9	Reulbach, Edward Marvin	P	33	.090	B	
15	11	Richie, Lewis A.	P	36	.154	B	
1	3	Richter, Emil Henry	P	22	.100	A	C
0	0	Rowan, John Arthur	P	1	+.000	xPhil	
		Saier, Victor Sylvester	1B	73	.259	A	
		Schulte, Frank	OF	154	.300	B	
		Shean, David Wm. (SS19)	2B23	43	.193	Bos	
		Sheckard, Samuel James Tilden	OF	156	.276	B	
0	2	Slapnicka, Cyril Chas.	P	3	.222	A	
3	2	Smith, Chas. E.	P	7	.000	xBosA	
		Tinker, Joseph Bert	SS	143	.278	B	
1	1	Toney, Frederick Arthur	P	18	.111	A	
2	2	Weaver, Orville F. (Orlie)	P	6	+.059	B	Bos
		Zimmerman, Henry (Heinie) (3B20)	2B108	139	.307	B	

WON 91 NATIONAL LEAGUE FINISHED 3rd.
LOST 59
TG 150 1912. PCT. .607

CHICAGO

FRANK LEROY CHANCE

WON	LOST	NAME	POS.	G.	BA	FROM	TO
		Archer, James Patrick	C118	120	.283	B	
5	6	Brown, Mordecai Peter Centennial	P15	16	.290	B	
		Chance, Frank LeRoy (Husk) MGR.	1B	2	.200	B	
		Chapman, Harry E.	C	1	.250	A	
26	10	Cheney, Lawrence Russell (Larry)	P	42	.226	B	
1	2	Cole, Leonard Leslie (King)	P	8	+.400	B	Pitt
		Cotter, Richard Raphael	C24	26	.278	Phil	C
0	0	Cottrell, Ensign Stover	P	1	.000	Pitt	
		Downey, Thomas Edward	3B	13	+.182	xPhil	
		Downs, Jerome Willis	2B	43	+.263	xBkn	C
		Evers, John Joseph	2B	143	.341	B	
		Good, Wilbur David	OF	39	.143	B	
		Heckinger, Michael Vincent	C	2	.000	A	
		Hofman, Arthur Frederick	OF	36	+.272	B	Pitt
16	13	Lavender, James Sanford	P	42	.149	A	
		Leach, Thomas Wm.	OF	82	+.240	xPitt	
7	2	Leifield, Albert Peter (Lefty)	P	13	+.115	xPitt	
		Lennox, James Edgar	3B24	27	.235	Bkn10	
0	1	Lowdermilk, Grover Cleveland	P	2	.000	StL	
0	1	Madden, Leonard Joseph	P	6	.250	A	C
1	1	Maroney, James Francis	P	10	.500	Phil10	C
		Miller, Ward Taylor	OF64	86	.307	Cin10	
		Moore, Chas. Wesley (2B1)	3B1	5	.222	A	C
1	2	McIntire, Harry M.	P	7	.333	B	
		Needham, Thomas J.	C32	33	.178	B	
0	0	Pearce, George Thomas	P	3	.167	A	
0	0	Powell, Wm. Burruss	P	1	.000	Pitt10	
10	6	Reulbach, Edward Marvin	P	39	.109	B	
16	8	Richie, Lewis A.	P	39	.132	B	
		Saier, Victor Sylvester	1B120	122	.288	B	
		Schulte, Frank	OF	139	.264	B	
		Sheckard, Samuel James Tilden	OF	146	.245	B	
7	4	Smith, Chas. E.	P	21	.257	B	
0	1	Sommers, Rudolph	P	1	.000	A	
		Tinker, Joseph Bert	SS	142	.282	B	
1	2	Toney, Frederick Arthur	P	9	.000	B	
0	0	Vernon, Joseph Henry	P	1	.000	A	
		Williams, Frederick	OF22	28	.242	A	
		Yantz, George Webb	C	1	1.000	A	C
		Zimmerman, Henry (Heinie) (1B22)	3B121	145	.372	B	

WON 88 NATIONAL LEAGUE FINISHED 3rd.
LOST 65
TG 153 1913. PCT. .575

CHICAGO

JOHN JOSEPH EVERS

WON	LOST	NAME	POS.	G.	BA	FROM	TO
		Allison, Milo Henry	OF	2	.333	A	

WON	LOST	NAME	POS.	G.	BA	FROM	TO
		Archer, James Patrick	C103	111	.266	B	
		Bresnahan, Roger Philip	C58	69	.228	StL	
		Bridwell, Albert Henry	SS	136	.240	Bos	
21	14	Cheney, Lawrence Russell (Larry)	P54	56	.192	B	
		Clymer, Otis Edgar	OF	30	+.229	WashA09	Bos
		Corriden, John Michael (Red)	SS37	46	.175	DetA	
		Evers, John Joseph MGR.	2B	136	.285	B	
		Good, Wilbur David	OF26	49	.253	B	
		Hargrave, Eugene Franklin	C	3	.333	A	
		Heckinger, Michael Vincent	C	2	+.000	B	Bkn
16	4	Humpheries, Albert (Bert)	P	28	.194	Cin	
		Keating, Walter Francis	SS	2	.200	A	
		Knisely, Peter C.	OF	2	.000	Cin	
10	14	Lavender, James Sanford	P	40	.118	B	
		Leach, Thomas Wm.	OF129	131	.287	B	
0	1	Leifield, Albert Peter (Lefty)	P	6	.000	B	
		Miller, Ward Taylor	OF63	80	.236	B	
		Mitchell, Michael Francis (Mike)	OF	82	+.262	Cin	Pitt
		Mollwitz, Frederick August	1B	3	.428	A	
1	1	Moore, Earl Alonzo	P	7	+.125	xPhil	
		McDonald, Edward C.		1	.000	Box	C
		Needham, Thomas J.	C	20	.238	B	
4	5	Overall, Orval	P	10	.250	Chi10	C
		Phelan, Arthur Edward (3B38)	2B46	91	.249	Cin	
13	5	Pearce, George Thomas	P	25	.073	B	
1	3	Reulbach, Edward Marvin	P	9	+.250	B	Bkn
2	4	Richie, Lewis A.	P	16	.118	B	C
		Saier, Victor Sylvester	1B	149	.289	B	
		Schulte, Frank	OF130	132	.278	B	
7	9	Smith, Chas. E.	P	20	.089	B	
4	2	Stack, Wm. Edward	P	11	+.067	xBkn	
		Stewart, Chas. Eugene	OF	9	.125	A	
2	2	Toney, Frederick Arthur	P	7	.250	B	
5	1	Vaughn, James Leslie (Big Jim)	P	7	.190	WashA	
1	0	Watson, Chas. J.	P	1	.000	A	
		Williams, Frederick	OF44	49	.224	B	
1	0	Zabel, George Washington	P	1	.000	A	
		Zimmerman, Henry (Heinie)	3B	127	.313	B	

WON 78 NATIONAL LEAGUE FINISHED 4th.
LOST 76
TG 154 1914. PCT. .506

CHICAGO

HENRY F. O'DAY

WON	LOST	NAME	POS.	G.	BA	FROM	TO
		Allison, Milo Henry	OF	1	1.000	B	
		Archer, James Patrick	C76	79	.258	B	
		Bates, John Wm.	OF	9	+.125	xCin	BaltF
		Bresnahan, Roger Philip	C85	101	.278	B	
		Bronkie, Herman Chas.	3B	1	1.000	ClevA12	
		Bues, Arthur Frederick (2B1 3B12)	3B	14	.227	Bos	C
20	18	Cheney, Lawrence Russell (Larry)	P	50	.180	B	
		Corriden, John Michael (Red)	SS91	107	.230	B	
		Derrick, Claude Lester	SS	28	+.219	xCin	C
		Fisher, Robert Tecumseh	SS	15	.300	Bkn	
		Good, Wilbur David	OF	154	.272	B	
1	1	Hageman, Kurt R. Morris	P	16	+.353	xStL	C
		Hargrave, Eugene Franklin	C16	23	.222	B	
10	11	Humpheries, Albert (Bert)	P34	35	.236	B	
		Johnston, James Harle (Jimmy)	OF28	50	.228	ChiA11	
		Keating, Walter Francis	SS6	20	.100	B	
		Knisely, Peter C.	OF17	37	.130	B	
0	0	Koestner, Elmer Joseph	P	4	+.000	ClevA10	Cin
11	11	Lavender, James Sanford	P	37	.175	B	
		Leach, Thomas Wm. (3B16)	OF136	153	.263	B	
		Mollwitz, Frederick August	1B	12	+.143	B	Cin
0	1	McConnell, George Neely	P	1	.000	NYA	
		Needham, Thomas J.	C	9	.118	B	C
9	12	Pearce, George Thomas	P	30	.089	B	
		Phelan, Arthur Edward	SS	25	.283	B	
		Saier, Victor Sylvester	1B	153	.240	B	
		Schulte, Frank	OF134	137	.241	B	
2	4	Smith, Chas. E.	P	16	.091	B	C
0	1	Stack, Wm. Edward	P	6	.000	B	C
		Stewart, Chas. Eugene		1	.000	B	C
		Sweeney, Wm. John	2B	134	.218	Bos	C
		Tyree, Earl Carlton	C	1	.000	A	C
21	13	Vaughn, James Leslie (Big Jim)	P	42	.144	B	
		Williams, Frederick	OF27	55	.202	B	
4	4	Zabel, George Washington	P	29	.184	B	
		Zimmerman, Henry (Heinie) (SS15)	3B118	146	.296	B	

WON 73 NATIONAL LEAGUE FINISHED 4th.
LOST 80
TG 153 1915. PCT. .477

CHICAGO

ROGER PHILIP BRESNAHAN

WON	LOST	NAME	POS.	G.	BA	FROM	TO
1	9	Adams, Karl Tutweiler	P	26	.000	Cin	C
		Archer, James Patrick	C88	97	.243	B	
		Bresnahan, Roger Philip MGR.	C68	77	.204	B	C
8	9	Cheney, Lawrence Russell (Larry)	P	25	+.150	B	Bkn
		Corriden, John Michael (Red)	3B1	6	.000	B	
1	1	Douglas, Philip Brooks (Shufflin' Phil)	P	4	+.000	xBkn	
		Fisher, Robert Tecumseh	SS145	147	.287	B	

WON	LOST	NAME	POS.	G.	BA	FROM	TO
		Fluhrer, John L.	OF	7	.400	A	C
		Good, Wilbur David	OF125	128	.253	B	
		Hargrave, Eugene Franklin	C	15	.158	B	
1	0	Hogg, Carter Bradley	P	2	.000	Bos12	
8	13	Humpheries, Albert (Bert)	P	31	.174	B	C
		Keating, Walter Francis	SS	4	.000	B	
		Knisely, Peter C.	OF33	64	.246	B	C
10	16	Lavender, James Sanford	P	41	.134	B	
		Mulligan, Edward Joseph (SS9 3B1)	SS	11	.363	A	
		Murray, John Joseph (Red)	OF	51	+.299	xN.Y.	
		McCarthy, Alexander George	SS8	23	+.264	xPitt	
		McLarry, Paul Howard (Polly) (1B18)	2B21	68	.197	ChiA12	C
		O'Farrell, Robert Arthur	C	2	.667	A	
13	9	Pearce, George Thomas	P	36	.196	B	
		Phelan, Arthur Edward (2B24)	3B110	133	.219	B	C
		Saier, Victor Sylvester	1B139	144	.264	B	
0	0	Schorr, Edward Walter	P	2	.500	A	C
		Schulte, Frank	OF147	151	.249	B	
		Schultz, Joseph Chas.	3B	7	+.250	xBkn	
4	1	Standridge, Alfred Peter	P29	30	.225	StL11	C
20	12	Vaughn, James Leslie (Big Jim)	P41	43	.163	B	
		Wallace, C. E.	C	2	.285	A	C
		Williams, Frederick	OF149	151	.257	B	
0	0	Wright, Robert C.	P	2	.000	A	C
7	10	Zabel, George Washington	P36	37	.074	B	C
		Zimmerman, Henry (Heinie) (3B36)	2B100	139	.265	B	

WON 67 | NATIONAL LEAGUE | FINISHED 5th.
LOST 86
TG 153 | 1916. | PCT. .438

CHICAGO

JOSEPH BERT TINKER

WON	LOST	NAME	POS.	G.	BA	FROM	TO
		Allen, Artemus Ward (Nick)	C	5	.063	BuffF	
		Archer, James Patrick	C61	77	.220	B	
2	3	Brown, Mordecai Peter Centennial	P	12	.250	ChiF	
2	2	Carter, Paul Warren	P	8	.167	ClevA	
		Clemens, Clement Lambert	C	10	.000	ChiF	C
		Deal, Chas. Albert	3B	2	.250	xStLA	
		Doolan, Michael Joseph	SS	28	+.211	ChiF	N.Y.
		Doyle, Lawrence Joseph (Larry)	2B	9	+.436	xN.Y.	
		Elliott, Harold H.	C18	23	.255	Bos10	
		Fischer, Wm. Chas.	C	65	+.197	ChiF	Pitt
		Flack, Max John	OF136	141	.258	ChiF	
8	16	Hendrix, Claude Raymond	P36	45	.200	ChiF	
		Hofman, Arthur Frederick	OF	5	.313	xN.Y.A	C
		Hunter, Herbert Harrison		2	+.000	xN.Y.	
		Jacobson, Merwin John Wm.	OF	4	.231	N.Y.	
		Kelly, Joseph Herbert	OF46	54	.254	Pitt14	
		Knabe, Franz Otto	2B	51	+.274	xPitt	C
10	14	Lavender, James Sanford	P	36	.151	B	
		Mann, Leslie	OF115	127	.272	ChiF	
		Mollwitz, Frederick August	1B	33	+.268	xCin	
		Mulligan, Edward Joseph	SS	58	.153	B	
		McCarthy, Alexander George (SS3)	2B34	37	+.245	B	Pitt
4	12	McConnell, George Neely	P	28	.158	ChiF	C
		O'Connor, John J.	C	1	.000	A	C
		O'Farrell, Robert Arthur	C	1	.000	B	
10	6	Packard, Eugene Milo	P37	44	.130	K.C.F	
0	0	Pearce, George Thomas	P	4	.000	B	
		Pechous, Chas. Edward	3B	22	.145	ChiF	
2	1	Perry, Herbert Scott	P	4	.273	StLA	
6	11	Prendergast, Michael Thomas	P	35	.152	ChiF	
		Saier, Victor Sylvester	1B	147	.253	B	
		Schulte, Frank	OF	72	+.305	B	Pitt
6	6	Seaton, Thomas Gordon	P	31	.184	NewF	
		Shay, Arthur Joseph	2B	2	.286	A	
		Sicking, Edward Joseph	3B	1	.000	A	
		Smith, Earl Leonard	OF	14	.259	A	
		Tinker, Joseph Bert MGR.	2B2	7	.100	ChiF	C
17	15	Vaughn, James Leslie (Big Jim)	P	44	.135	B	
		Williams, Frederick	OF116	118	.279	B	
		Wilson, Arthur Earl	C	36	+.193	xPitt	
		Wortman, Wm. Lewis	SS	69	.201	A	
		Yerkes, Stephen Douglas	2B41	44	.263	PittF	C
		Zeider, Rollie Hubert (2B33)	3B55	98	.235	ChiF	
		Zimmerman, Henry (Heinie) (2B14)	3B85	107	+.294	B	N.Y.
		Zwilling, Edward Harrison	OF	35	.113	ChiF	C

WON 74 | NATIONAL LEAGUE | FINISHED 5th.
LOST 80
TG 154 | 1917. | PCT. .481

CHICAGO

FREDERICK FRANCIS MITCHELL

WON	LOST	NAME	POS.	G.	BA	FROM	TO
6	6	Aldridge, Victor Eddington	P	30	.138	A	
		Archer, James Patrick	C	2	.000	B	
		Barber, Samuel Turner	OF	7	.214	WashA	
		Blackburn, Earl Stuart	C	2	.000	Bos	C
5	8	Carter, Paul Warren	P	23	.171	B	
		Deal, Chas. Albert	3B130	135	.254	B	
5	9	Demaree, Albert Wentworth (Al)	P	24	+.122	Phil	N.Y.

WON	LOST	NAME	POS.	G.	BA	FROM	TO
		Dillhoefer, Wm. Martin (Pickles)	C37	42	.126	A	
14	20	Douglas, Philip Brooks (Shufflin' Phil)	P	51	.126	Chi15	
		Doyle, Lawrence Joseph (Larry)	2B128	135	.254	B	
		Driscoll, John Leo	2B5	13	.107	A	C
		Elliott, Harold H.	C73	85	.251	B	
		Flack, Max John	OF117	131	.248	B	
10	12	Hendrix, Claude Raymond	P40	48	.256	B	
		Hunter, Herbert Harrison (2B1)	3B1	3	.000	B	
		Kilduff, Peter John (2B5)	SS51	56	+.277	xN.Y.	
		Leslie, Roy Reid	1B	7	.211	A	
		Mann, Leslie	OF116	117	.273	B	
		Marriott, Wm. Earl		3	.000	A	
		Merkle, Frederick Chas.	1B	146	+.266	xBkn	
		O'Farrell, Robert Arthur	C	3	.375	B	
0	0	Packard, Eugene Milo	P	2	+.000	B	StL
		Pechous, Chas. Edward	SS	13	.244	B	C
3	6	Prendergast, Michael Thomas	P	35	.250	B	
2	0	Ruether, Walter Henry (Dutch)	P	31	+.286	A	Cin
		Saier, Victor Sylvester	1B	6	.238	B	
		Schick, Maurice Francis	OF	14	.147	A	C
5	4	Seaton, Thomas Gordon	P	16	.238	B	C
23	13	Vaughn, James Leslie (Big Jim)	P	41	.160	B	
0	1	Walker, James Roy	P	2	.000	ClevA15	
1	1	Weaver, Harry A.	P	4	.200	PhilA	
		Williams, Frederick	OF136	138	.241	B	
		Wilson, Arthur Earl	C75	81	.213	B	
		Wolfe, Harry	SS	5	+.333	A	Pitt
		Wolter, Harry Meigs	OF97	117	.249	NYA13	C
		Wortman, Wm. Lewis	SS65	75	.174	B	
		Zeider, Rollie Hubert (2B24 3B26)	SS48	108	.243	B	

WON 84 NATIONAL LEAGUE FINISHED 1st.
LOST 45
TG 129 1918. PCT. .651

CHICAGO

FREDERICK FRANCIS MITCHELL

WON	LOST	NAME	POS.	G.	BA	FROM	TO
0	1	Aldridge, Victor Eddington	P	3	.333	B	
2	1	Alexander, Grover Cleveland (Pete)	P	3	.100	Phil	
		Barber, Samuel Turner	OF41	55	.236	B	
3	2	Carter, Paul Warren	P	21	.240	B	
		Clarke, Thomas Aloysius	C	1	.000	Cin	C
		Daly, Thomas Daniel	C	1	.000	ClevA16	
		Deal, Chas. Albert	3B118	119	.239	B	
10	9	Douglas, Philip Brooks (Shufflin' Phil)	P	25	.255	B	
		Elliott, Harold H.	C	5	.000	B	
		Flack, Max John	OF121	123	.257	B	
20	7	Hendrix, Claude Raymond	P32	35	.264	B	
		Hollocher, Chas. Jacob	SS	131	.316	A	
		Kilduff, Peter John	2B	30	.204	B	
		Killefer, Wm. Lavier Jr.	C	104	.233	Phil	
		Lear, Frederick Francis	2B	2	.000	PhilA15	
		Mann, Leslie	OF	129	.288	B	
5	2	Martin, Elwood Goode	P	9	.187	StLA	
		Merkle, Frederick Chas.	1B	129	.297	B	
		McCabe, Wm. Francis (OF4)	2B13	29	.178	A	
0	0	Napier, Samuel LeRoy (Buddy)	P	1	.333	StLA12	
		O'Farrell, Robert Arthur	C45	52	.283	B	
		Paskert, George Henry (Dode) (3B6)	OF121	127	.286	Phil	
		Pick, Chas. Thomas (3B8)	2B20	29	.326	PhilA16	
19	8	Tyler, George Albert	P33	38	.210	Bos	
22	10	Vaughn, James Leslie (Big Jim)	P	35	.240	B	
1	3	Walker, James Roy	P	13	.000	B	
2	2	Weaver, Harry A.	P	8	.250	B	
		Wortman, Wm. Lewis (SS4)	2B8	17	.118	B	C
		Zeider, Rollie Hubert (1B1 3B1)	2B79	82	.223	B	C

WON 75 NATIONAL LEAGUE FINISHED 3rd.
LOST 65
TG 140 1919. PCT. .536

CHICAGO

FREDERICK FRANCIS MITCHELL

WON	LOST	NAME	POS.	G.	BA	FROM	TO
16	11	Alexander, Grover Cleveland (Pete)	P	30	.171	B	
3	5	Bailey, Abraham Lincoln	P	21	.389	A	
		Barber, Samuel Turner	OF68	76	.313	B	
5	4	Carter, Paul Warren	P28	29	.269	B	
		Daly, Thomas Daniel	C18	25	.220	B	
		Deal, Chas. Albert	3B	116	.289	B	
10	6	Douglas, Philip Brooks (Shufflin' Phil)	P	25	+.157	B	N.Y.
		Flack, Max John	OF	116	.294	B	
		Friberg, Bernard Albert	OF	8	.200	A	
10	14	Hendrix, Claude Raymond	P33	36	.192	B	
		Herzog, Chas. Lincoln (Buck)	2B	52	+.280	xBos	
		Hollocher, Chas. Jacob	SS	115	.270	B	
		Kilduff, Peter John (SS7)	2B8	31	+.273	B	Bkn
		Killefer, Wm. Lavier Jr.	C100	103	.286	B	
		Lear, Frederick Francis	2B	40	.224	B	
		Magee, Leo Christopher (Lee)	SS13	79	+.292	xBkn	C
		Mann, Leslie	OF	80	+.227	B	Bos
8	8	Martin, Elwood Goode	P	35	.182	B	
		Merkle, Frederick Chas. (2B1)	1B132	133	.267	B	

WON	LOST	NAME	POS.	G.	BA	FROM	TO
		McCabe, Wm. Francis (SS4 3B1)	OF20	33	.155	B	
0	0	Newkirk, Joel Ivan	P	1	.000	A	
		O'Farrell, Robert Arthur	C38	49	.216	B	
		Paskert, George Henry (Dode)	OF80	88	.196	B	
		Pick, Chas. Thomas	3B3	75	+.231	B	Bos
		Reilly, Harold J.	OF	1	.000	A	C
		Robertson, Davis Aydelotte	OF	27	+.208	xN.Y.	
2	2	Tyler, George Albert	P	6	.143	B	
21	14	Vaughn, James Leslie (Big Jim)	P	38	.173	B	
0	1	Weaver, Harry A.	P	2	.000	B	C

WON 75 — NATIONAL LEAGUE — FINISHED 5th. (TIED WITH ST. L.)
LOST 79
TG 154 — 1920. — PCT. .487

CHICAGO

FREDERICK FRANCIS MITCHELL

WON	LOST	NAME	POS.	G.	BA	FROM	TO
27	14	Alexander, Grover Cleveland (Pete)	P	46	.229	B	
1	2	Bailey, Abraham Lincoln	P	21	.143	B	
		Barber, Samuel Turner (OF17)	1B69	94	.265	B	
3	6	Carter, Paul Warren	P	31	.171	B	C
0	0	Cheeves, Virgil Earl	P	5	.000	A	
		Clarke, Sumpter Ellis	3B	1	.333	A	
		Daly, Thomas Daniel	C29	44	.311	B	
		Deal, Chas. Albert	3B128	129	.240	B	
		Flack, Max John	OF132	135	.302	B	
		Friberg, Bernard Albert (OF24)	2B24	50	.211	B	
1	1	Gaw, George Joseph (Chippy)	P	6	.250	A	C
9	12	Hendrix, Claude Raymond	P27	34	.181	B	C
		Herzog, Chas. Lincoln (Buck) (3B28)	2B59	91	.193	B	C
		Hollocher, Chas. Jacob	SS	80	.319	B	
0	0	Jaeger, Joseph P.	P	2	.000	A	C
0	0	Jones, Percy Lee	P	4	.000	A	
		Killefer, Wm. Lavier Jr.	C61	62	.220	B	
		Leathers, Harold Langford	SS	7	.319	A	C
		Marriott, Wm. Earl	2B	14	.279	Chi17	
4	15	Martin, Elwood Goode	P	35	.159	B	
		Merkle, Frederick Chas.	1B85	92	.285	B	
		McCabe, Wm. Francis	OF	3	+.500	B	Bkn
0	1	Newkirk, Joel Ivan	P	2	.000	B	C
		O'Farrell, Robert Arthur	C86	94	.248	B	
		Paskert, George Henry (Dode)	OF137	139	.279	B	
		Robertson, Davis Aydelotte	OF	134	.300	B	
		Terry, Zebulon Alexander (Zeb) (2B63)	SS70	133	.280	Pitt	
0	0	Turner, Theodore Holtop	P	1	.000	A	C
		Twombly, Clarence Edward	OF45	78	.235	A	
11	12	Tyler, George Albert	P27	29	.262	B	
19	16	Vaughn, James Leslie (Big Jim)	P	40	.216	B	

WON 64 — NATIONAL LEAGUE — FINISHED 7th.
LOST 89
TG 153 — 1921. — PCT. .418

CHICAGO

JOHN JOSEPH EVERS — WM. LAVIER KILLEFER JR.

WON	LOST	NAME	POS.	G.	BA	FROM	TO
15	13	Alexander, Grover Cleveland (Pete)	P	31	.305	B	
0	0	Bailey, Abraham Lincoln	P	3	+.000	B	Bkn
		Barber, Samuel Turner	OF123	127	.314	B	
11	12	Cheeves, Virgil Earl	P	37	.167	B	
		Daly, Thomas Daniel	C47	51	.238	B	C
		Deal, Chas. Albert	3B112	115	.289	B	C
		Elliott, Carter Ward	SS	12	.250	A	C
		Flack, Max John	OF130	133	.301	B	
9	10	Freeman, Alexander Vernon	P	38	.208	A	
0	0	Fuhr, Oscar Lawrence	P	1	.000	A	
		Grimes, Oscar Ray	1B	147	.321	BosA	
0	2	Hanson, Earl Sylvester	P	2	.000	A	C
		Hollocher, Chas. Jacob	SS137	140	.289	B	
3	5	Jones, Percy Lee	P	32	.222	B	
1	0	Kaufmann, Anthony Chas. (Tony)	P	2	.400	A	
0	3	Keen, Howard Victor	P	5	.000	PhilA18	
		Kelleher, John Patrick (2B27)	3B37	95	.309	Bkn16	
		Killefer, Wm. Lavier Jr. MGR.	C42	45	.323	B	
		Klugman, Joseph	2B	6	.286	A	
		Maisel, George John	OF108	111	.310	DetA16	
		Marriott, Wm. Earl	2B	30	.316	B	
11	15	Martin, Elwood Goode	P	37	.233	B	
		O'Farrell, Robert Arthur	C90	96	.250	B	
3	6	Ponder, Chas. Elmer	P	16	+.121	xPitt	C
		Robertson, Davis Aydelotte	OF	22	+.222	B	Pitt
0	1	Stueland, George Anton	P	2	.333	A	
		Sullivan, John Lawrence	OF	76	+.329	xBos	C
		Terry, Zebulon Alexander (Zeb)	2B122	123	.275	B	
		Thomas, Robert Wm.	OF	8	.267	A	C
		Twombly, Clarence Edward	OF45	87	.377	B	C
3	2	Tyler, George Albert	P	19	.231	B	C
3	11	Vaughn, James Leslie (Big Jim)	P	17	.244	B	C
		Warner, George Hoke	3B	14	.211	Pitt19	C
		Wirts, Elwood Vernon	C	7	.182	A	
5	9	York, James E.	P	40	.127	PhilA19	C

WON 80 — NATIONAL LEAGUE — FINISHED 5th.
LOST 74
TG 154 — 1922. — PCT. .520

CHICAGO

WM. LAVIER KILLEFER JR.

WON	LOST	NAME	POS.	G.	BA	FROM	TO
		Adams, Earl John (Sparky)	2B	11	.250	A	
16	15	Aldridge, Victor Eddington	P	36	.260	Chi18	
16	13	Alexander, Grover Cleveland (Pete)	P	33	.176	B	
		Barber, Samuel Turner	OF47	84	.309	B	
		Callaghan, Martin Francis	OF53	74	.257	A	
12	11	Cheeves, Virgil Earl	P	39	.210	B	
		Cotter, Harvey Louis	1B	1	1.000	A	
0	0	Eubanks, Uel Melvin	P	2	1.000	A	C
		Fitzgerald, Howard Chumney	OF6	10	.330	A	
		Flack, Max John	OF15	17	+.222	B	StL
0	1	Freeman, Alexander Vernon	P	11	.125	B	C
		Friberg, Bernard Albert (1B6 2B3 3B5)	OF74	97	.311	Chi20	
1	1	Fussell, Frederick Morris	P	3	.000	A	
		Golvin, Walter George	1B	2	.000	A	C
		Grantham, George Farley	3B5	7	.174	A	
		Grimes, Oscar Ray	1B	138	.354	B	
		Hartnett, Chas. Leo (Gabby)	C27	31	.194	A	
		Heathcote, Clifton Earl	OF60	76	+.276	xStL	
		Hollocher, Chas. Jacob	SS	152	.339	B	
8	9	Jones, Percy Lee	P	44	.085	B	
7	13	Kaufmann, Anthony Chas. (Tony)	P37	38	.200	B	
1	2	Keen, Howard Victor	P	7	.333	B	
		Kelleher, John Patrick (1B4 SS7)	3B46	63	.259	B	
		Klugman, Joseph	2B	2	.250	B	
		Krug, Martin John (2B23 SS1)	3B104	127	.275	BosA12	C
		Maisel, George John	OF26	38	.190	B	C
1	0	Martin, Elwood Goode	P	1	.000	B	C
		Miller, Lawrence H. (Hack)	OF116	122	.351	BosA18	
0	0	Morris, Edward	P	5	.250	A	
		O'Farrell, Robert Arthur	C125	128	.323	B	
9	5	Osborne, Ernest Preston	P	41	.134	A	
		Statz, Arnold John (Jigger)	OF	110	.297	BosA20	
9	4	Stueland, George Anton	P	35	.129	B	
		Terry, Zebulon Alexander (Zeb) (SS4 3B3)	2B125	131	.286	B	C
		Weis, Arthur John	OF	2	.500	A	
		Wirts, Elwood Vernon	C27	31	.172	B	

WON 83
LOST 71
TG 154

NATIONAL LEAGUE — FINISHED 4th.

1923. — PCT. .539

CHICAGO

WM. LAVIER KILLEFER JR.

WON	LOST	NAME	POS.	G.	BA	FROM	TO
		Adams, Earl John (Sparky) (OF1)	SS79	95	.289	B	
16	9	Aldridge, Victor Eddington	P	30	.268	B	
22	12	Alexander, Grover Cleveland (Pete)	P	39	.216	B	
		Barrett, Robert Schley		3	.333	A	
0	0	Bush, Guy Terrell	P	1	.000	A	
		Callaghan, Martin Francis	OF38	61	.225	B	
3	4	Cheeves, Virgil Earl	P	19	.174	B	
1	0	Collins, Philip Eugene	P	1	.000	A	
3	5	Dumovich, Nicholas (Nick)	P	28	.241	A	C
		Elliott, Allen Clifford	1B52	53	.250	A	
		Friberg, Bernard Albert	3B	146	.318	B	
3	5	Fussell, Frederick Morris	P	28	.200	B	
		Grantham, George Farley	2B150	152	.281	B	
		Grigsby, Denver Clarence	OF22	24	.292	A	
		Grimes, Oscar Ray	1B62	64	.329	B	
		Hartnett, Chas. Leo (Gabby) (1B31)	C39	85	.268	B	
		Heathcote, Clifton Earl	OF112	117	.249	B	
		Hollocher, Chas. Jacob	SS65	66	.342	B	
14	10	Kaufmann, Anthony Chas. (Tony)	P	33	.216	B	
12	8	Keen, Howard Victor	P	35	.151	B	
		Kelleher, John Patrick (2B6 SS14 3B11)	1B22	66	.306	B	
		Miller, Lawrence H. (Hack)	OF129	135	.301	B	
		Murray, Anthony Joseph	OF	2	.250	A	C
		O'Farrell, Robert Arthur	C124	131	.319	B	
8	15	Osborne, Ernest Preston	P	37	.200	B	
		Statz, Arnol John (Jigger)	OF	154	.319	B	
0	0	Stauffer, Chas. Edward	P	1	.000	A	
0	1	Stueland, George Anton	P	6	.000	B	
		Turgeon, Eugene Joseph	SS2	3	.167	A	C
		Vogel, Otto Henry (3B1)	OF24	41	.210	A	
		Weis, Arthur John	OF6	22	.231	B	
1	2	Wheeler, Floyd Clark	P	3	.111	Pitt	
		Wirts, Elwood Vernon	C3	5	.200	B	

WON 81
LOST 72
TG 153

NATIONAL LEAGUE — FINISHED 5th.

1924. — PCT. .530

CHICAGO

WM. LAVIER KILLEFER JR.

WON	LOST	NAME	POS.	G.	BA	FROM	TO
		Adams, Earl John (Sparky) (2B19)	SS89	117	.280	B	
15	12	Aldridge, Victor Eddington	P	32	.176	B	
12	5	Alexander, Grover Cleveland (Pete)	P	21	.231	B	
		Barrett, Robert Schley (1B10 3B8)	2B25	54	.241	B	

WON	LOST	NAME	POS.	G.	BA	FROM	TO
6	6	Blake, John Frederick (Sheriff)	P	29	.290	Pitt20	
0	0	Brett, Herbert James	P	1	.000	A	
2	5	Bush, Guy Terrell	P	16	.154	B	
		Churry, John	C3	6	.143	A	
		Cotter, Harvey Louis	1B90	98	.261	Chi22	C
		Elliott, Allen Clifford	1B	10	.143	B	C
		Fitzgerald, Howard Chumney	OF5	7	.158	Chi22	
		Friberg, Bernard Albert	3B	142	.279	B	
		Grantham, George Farley (3B6)	2B118	127	.316	B	
		Grigsby, Denver Clarence	OF121	124	.299	B	
		Grimes, Oscar Ray	1B50	51	.299	B	
		Hartnett, Chas. Leo (Gabby)	C105	111	.299	B	
		Heathcote, Clifton Earl	OF111	113	.309	B	
		Hollocher, Chas. Jacob	SS71	76	.245	B	C
11	12	Jacobs, Wm. Elmer	P	38	.111	StL20	
16	11	Kaufmann, Anthony Chas.(Tony)	P34	35	.316	B	
		Kearns, Edward Joseph	1B	4	.250	A	
15	14	Keen, Howard Victor	P	40	.156	B	
		Michaels, Ralph Joseph	SS4	8	.364	A	
		Miller, Lawrence H. (Hack)	OF30	53	.336	B	
1	1	Milstead, George Earl	P	13	.167	A	
		O'Farrell, Robert Arthur	C57	71	.241	B	
0	0	Osborne, Ernest Preston	P	2	+.000	B	Bkn
0	0	Pierce, Raymond Lester	P	6	.000	A	
		Statz, Arnold John (Jigger) (2B1)	OF131	135	.277	B	
		Vogel, Otto Henry (3B2)	OF53	70	.267	B	C
		Weis, Arthur John	OF36	37	.278	B	
3	6	Wheeler, Floyd Clark	P	29	.219	B	C

WON 68
LOST 86
TG 154

NATIONAL LEAGUE — 1925. — FINISHED 8th (LAST) — PCT. .442

CHICAGO

WM. LAVIER KILLEFER JR. — WALTER JAMES VINCENT MARANVILLE — GEORGE GIBSON

WON	LOST	NAME	POS.	G.	BA	FROM	TO
		Adams, Earl John (Sparky) (SS5)	2B144	149	.287	B	
15	11	Alexander, Grover Cleveland (Pete)	P	32	.241	B	
		Barrett, Robert Schley (2B4)	3B6	14	+.313	B	Bkn
10	18	Blake, John Frederick (Sheriff)	P	36	.152	B	
1	1	Brett, Herbert James	P	10	.000	B	C
		Brooks, Jonathan Joseph	OF89	90	.281	A	
0	0	Brown, Walter George (Jumbo)	P	2	.000	A	
6	13	Bush, Guy Terrell	P	42	.193	B	
		Churry, John	C	3	.500	B	
12	14	Cooper, Arley Wilbur	P	32	.207	Pitt	
		Freigau, Howard Earl (1B7 SS17)	3B96	117	+.307	xStL	
		Friberg, Bernard Albert (1B6)	3B26	44	+.257	B	Phil
		Gonzales, Miguel Angel Cordero	C50	70	+.264	xStL	
		Griffith, Thomas Herman	OF60	76	+.285	xBkn	C
		Grigsby, Denver Clarence	OF39	51	.255	B	C
		Grimm, Chas. John	1B139	141	.306	Pitt	
		Hartnett, Chas. Leo (Gabby)	C110	117	.289	B	
		Heathcote, Clifton Earl	OF99	109	.263	B	
2	3	Jacobs, Wm. Elmer	P	18	.231	B	
		Jahn, Arthur Chas.	OF	58	.301	A	
6	6	Jones, Percy Lee	P	28	.154	Chi22	
13	13	Kaufmann, Anthony Chas.(Tony)	P	31	.192	B	
		Kearns, Edward Joseph	1B	3	.500	B	C
2	6	Keen, Howard Victor	P	30	.240	B	
		Kerr, John Melville		1	.000	A	C
		Maranville, Walter James Vincent (Rabbitt) MGR. (2B1)	SS74	75	.233	Pitt	
		Metzler, Alexander	OF	9	.184	A	
		Michaels, Ralph Joseph (1B1 2B1 SS1)	3B15	22	.280	B	
		Miller, Lawrence H. (Hack)	OF21	24	.279	B	C
1	1	Milstead, George Earl	P	5	.000	B	
		Munson, Joseph Martin Napoleon	OF	9	.371	A	
		McAuley, James Earl	SS	37	.280	StL17	C
		O'Farrell, Robert Arthur	C3	17	+.182	B	StL
0	0	Osborn, Frank Robert	P	1	.000	A	
		Pittinger, Clark Alonzo (3B24)	SS24	59	.312	BosA23	
		Staley, Gale	2B	7	.423	A	C
		Statz, Arnold John (Jigger)	OF37	38	.257	B	
0	0	Stueland, George Anton	P	2	1.000	Chi23	C
		Taylor, C. L.	OF2	8	.000	A	C
		Weis, Arthur John	OF47	67	.267	B	C

WON 82
LOST 72
TG 154

NATIONAL LEAGUE — 1926. — FINISHED 4th. — PCT. .532

CHICAGO

JOSEPH VINCENT McCARTHY

WON	LOST	NAME	POS.	G.	BA	FROM	TO
		Adams, Earl John (Sparky) (3B19)	2B136	154	.309	B	
3	3	Alexander, Grover Cleveland (Pete)	P	7	+.467	B	StL
		Beck , Clyde Eugene	2B	30	.198	A	
11	12	Blake, John Frederick (Sheriff)	P	39	.215	B	
		Brooks, Jonathan Joseph	OF18	26	.188	B	C
13	9	Bush, Guy Terrell	P	35	.167	B	
		Churry, John	C	2	.000	B	
		Cooney, James Edward	SS	141	.251	StL	
2	1	Cooper, Arley Wilbur	P	8	.389	B	DetA
		Freigau, Howard Earl	3B135	140	.270	B	
		Gonzales, Miguel Angel Cordero	C78	80	.249	B	

WON	LOST	NAME	POS.	G.	BA	FROM	TO
		Graves, Joseph Ebenezer	3B	2	.000	A	C
		Grimm, Chas. John	1B	147	.277	B	
		Hartnett, Chas. Leo (Gabby)	C88	93	.275	B	
		Heathcote, Clifton Earl	OF133	139	.276	B	
1	1	Huntzinger, Walter Henry	P	11	+.143	xStL	C
12	7	Jones, Percy Lee	P	30	.260	B	
9	7	Kaufmann, Anthony Chas.(Tony)	P26	30	.250	B	
		Kelly, Joseph James	OF39	65	.335	A	
		Michaels, Ralph Joseph		2	.000	B	C
1	5	Milstead, George Earl	P	18	.053	B	C
		Munson, Joseph Martin Napoleon	OF28	33	.257	B	C
6	5	Osborn, Frank Robert	P	31	.146	B	
6	5	Piercy, Wm. Benton	P	19	.257	BosA24	C
18	17	Root, Chas. Henry	P	42	.143	StLA23	
		Schreiber, Henry Ward (2B1 SS1)	3B2	10	.056	N.Y.21	C
		Scott, Floyd John	OF60	77	.286	A	
		Shannon, Maurice Joseph	SS13	19	.333	PhilA21	C
		Stephenson, Jackson Riggs	OF74	82	.338	ClevA	
		Tolson, Chas. Julius	1B13	57	.313	ClevA	
0	0	Welch, John Vernon	P	3	1.000	A	
		Wilson, Lewis Robert (Hack)	OF140	142	.321	N.Y.	

WON 85 LOST 68 TG 153

NATIONAL LEAGUE 1927.

FINISHED 4th. PCT. .556

CHICAGO

JOSEPH VINCENT McCARTHY

WON	LOST	NAME	POS.	G.	BA	FROM	TO
		Adams, Earl John (Sparky) (SS40 3B53)	2B60	146	.292	B	
		Beck, Clyde Eugene (3B17)	2B99	117	.258	B	
13	14	Blake, John Frederick (Sheriff)	P	32	.193	B	
4	2	Brillheart, James Benson	P	32	.023	WashA23	
10	10	Bush, Guy Terrell	P	36	.123	B	
12	8	Carison, Harold Gust (Hal)	P	27	+.164	xPhil	
		Churry, John	C	1	1.000	B	C
		Cooney, James Edward	SS	33	+.242	B	Phil
0	0	Dean, Wayland Ogden	P	2	+.000	xPhil	C
		English, Elwood George (Woody)	SS84	87	.290	A	
		Freigau, Howard Earl	3B	30	.233	B	
		Gonzales, Miguel Angel Cordero	C35	39	.241	B	
0	0	Grampp, Henry Eckhardt	P	2	.000	A	
		Grimm, Chas. John	1B	147	.311	B	
		Haney, Fred Girard		4	.000	xBosA	
		Hartnett, Chas. Leo (Gabby)	C126	127	.294	B	
		Heathcote, Clifton Earl	OF57	83	.294	B	
7	8	Jones, Percy Lee	P	30	.350	B	
3	3	Kaufmann, Anthony Chas.(Tony)	P	9	+.313	B	Phil
1	1	Nehf, Arthur Neukom	P	8	+.429	xCin	
5	5	Osborn, Frank Robert	P	24	.205	B	
		Pick, Edgar Everett	3B49	54	.171	Cin24	C
26	15	Root, Chas. Henry	P	48	.221	B	
3	1	Roy, Luther Franklin	P	11	.333	ClevA25	
		Scott, Floyd John	OF36	71	.314	B	
		Sewell, Thomas Wesley		1	.000	A	C
		Stephenson, Jackson Riggs	OF146	152	.344	B	
		Tolson, Chas. Julius	1B7	39	.296	B	
		Webb, Earl Wm.	OF86	102	.301	NY25	
1	1	Weinert, Phillip Walter	P	5	.200	Phil24	
0	0	Welch, John Vernon	P	1	.000	B	
		Wilke, Harry Joseph	3B	3	.000	A	C
		Wilson, Lewis Robert (Hack)	OF	146	.318	B	
		Yoter, Elmer Ellsworth	3B11	13	.222	ClevA24	

WON 91 LOST 63 TG 154

NATIONAL LEAGUE 1928.

FINISHED 3rd. PCT. .591

CHICAGO

JOSEPH VINCENT McCARTHY

WON	LOST	NAME	POS.	G.	BA	FROM	TO
		Beck, Clyde Eugene (SS47)	3B87	131	.257	B	
17	11	Blake, John Frederick (Sheriff)	P34	35	.216	B	
15	6	Bush, Guy Terrell	P	42	.082	B	
		Butler, John Stephen	3B59	62	.270	Bkn	
3	2	Carlson, Harold Gust (Hal)	P	20	.263	B	
		Cuyler, Hazen Shirley (Kiki)	OF127	133	.285	Pitt	
		English, Elwood George (Woody)	SS114	116	.299	B	
		Gonzales, Miguel Angel Cordero	C45	49	.272	B	
		Grimm, Chas. John	1B	147	.294	B	
		Hartnett, Chas. Leo (Gabby)	C118	120	.302	B	
		Heathcote, Clifton Earl	OF39	67	.285	B	
0	0	Holley, Edward Edgar	P	13	.000	A	
		Jacobs, Raymond F.		2	.000	A	C
10	6	Jones, Percy Lee	P	39	.196	B	
		Kelly, Joseph James	1B10	32	.212	Chi26	C
		Maguire, Frederick Edward	2B138	140	.279	NY23	
18	13	Malone, Perce Leigh (Pat)	P	42	.189	A	
		Moore, John Francis		4	.000	A	
		McMillan, Norman Alexis (3B18)	2B19	49	.220	StLA24	
13	7	Nehf, Arthur Neukom	P	31	.190	B	
14	18	Root, Chas. Henry	P	40	.178	B	
		Stephenson, Jackson Riggs	OF135	137	.324	B	
0	0	Tincup, Austin Ben	P	2	.000	Phil18	C
		Webb, Earl Wm.	OF31	62	.250	B	
1	0	Weinert, Phillip Walter	P	10	.000	B	
0	0	Welch, John Vernon	P	3	.000	B	
		Wilson, Lewis Robert (Hack)	OF143	145	.313	B	
		Yoter, Elmer Ellsworth	3B	1	.000	B	C

WON 98
LOST 54
TG 152

NATIONAL LEAGUE — FINISHED 1st.

1929. — PCT. .645

CHICAGO

JOSEPH VINCENT McCARTHY

WON	LOST	NAME	POS.	G.	BA	FROM	TO
		Angley, Thomas Samuel	C	5	.250	A	C
		Beck, Clyde Eugene (SS14)	3B33	54	.211	B	
		Blair, Clarence Vick (1B6 2B2)	3B7	26	.319	A	
14	13	Blake, John Frederick (Sheriff)	P35	38	.173	B	
18	7	Bush, Guy Terrell	P	50	.165	B	
11	5	Carlson, Harold Gust (Hal)	P	31	.231	B	
		Cuyler, Hazen Shirley (Kiki)	OF129	139	.360	B	
5	4	Cvengros, Michael John	P32	33	.400	Pitt27	C
		English, Elwood George (Woody)	SS	144	.276	B	
		Gonzales, Miguel Angel Cordero	C	60	.240	B	
		Grace, Robert Earl	C	27	.250	A	
0	1	Grampp, Henry Eckhardt	P	1	.000	Chi27	C
		Grimm, Chas. John	1B	120	.298	B	
		Hartnett, Chas. Leo (Gabby)	C1	25	.273	B	
		Heathcote, Clifton Earl	OF52	82	.313	B	
1	1	Horne, Berlyn Dale	P	11	.400	A	C
		Hornsby, Rogers (Rajah)	2B	156	.380	Bos	
0	1	Jonnard, Claude Alfred	P	12	.200	StLA26	C
22	10	Malone, Perce Leigh (Pat)	P	40	.210	B	
		Moore, John Francis	OF15	37	.286	B	
		McMillan, Norman Alexis	3B120	124	.271	B	C
8	5	Nehf, Arthur Neukom	P	32	.289	B	C
0	0	Osborn, Frank Robert	P	3	.250	Chi27	
0	1	Penner, Wm. Kenneth	P	5	.250	ClevA16	C
19	6	Root, Chas. Henry	P	43	.156	B	
		Schulte, John Clement	C30	31	.261	Phil	
		Stephenson, Jackson Riggs	OF130	136	.362	B	
		Taylor, Daniel Turney	OF	2	.000	WashA26	
		Taylor, James Wren (Zack)	C	64	+.274	xBos	
		Tolson, Chas. Julius	1B31	32	.257	Chi27	
		Wilson, Lewis Robert (Hack)	OF	150	.345	B	

WON 90
LOST 64
TG 154

NATIONAL LEAGUE — FINISHED 2nd.

1930. — PCT. .584

CHICAGO

JOSEPH VINCENT McCARTHY — ROGERS HORNSBY

WON	LOST	NAME	POS.	G.	BA	FROM	TO
		Beck, Clyde Eugene (2B24)	SS57	83	.213	B	
		Bell, Lester Rowland	3B70	74	.278	Bos	
		Blair, Clarence Vick (3B13)	2B115	134	.273	B	
10	14	Blake, John Frederick (Sheriff)	P34	36	.227	B	
15	10	Bush, Guy Terrell	P	46	.282	B	
4	2	Carlson, Harold Gust (Hal)	P	8	.250	B	C
		Cuyler, Hazen Shirley (Kiki)	OF	156	.355	B	
		English, Elwood George (Woody) (SS78)	3B83	156	.335	B	
		Farrell, Edward Stephen	SS38	46	+.292	xStL	
		Grimm, Chas. John	1B113	114	.289	B	
		Hartnett, Chas. Leo (Gabby)	C136	141	.339	B	
		Heathcote, Clifton Earl	OF35	70	.260	B	
		Hornsby, Rogers (Rajah) MGR.	2B25	42	.308	B	
		Kelly, George Lange (Long George)	1B	39	+.331	xCin	
20	9	Malone, Perce Leigh (Pat)	P	45	.248	B	
0	0	Moss, Chas. Malcolm	P	12	.273	A	C
0	0	McAfee, Wm. Fort Jr.	P	2	.000	A	
3	2	Nelson, Lynn Bernard	P	37	.222	A	
10	6	Osborn Frank Robert	P	35	.095	B	
1	3	Petty, Jesse Lee	P	9	+.231	xPitt	C
16	14	Root, Chas. Henry	P	37	.263	B	
0	0	Shealy, Albert Berley	P	24	.600	NYA28	C
		Stephenson, Jackson Riggs	OF80	109	.367	B	
		Taylor, Daniel Turney	OF52	74	.283	B	
		Taylor, James Wren (Zack)	C28	32	.232	B	
11	4	Teachout, Arthur John	P40	42	.270	A	
		Tolson, Chas. Julius	1B4	13	.300	B	C
0	0	Warneke, Lonnie	P	1	.000	A	
		Wilson, Lewis Robert (Hack)	OF	155	.356	B	

WON 84
LOST 70
TG 154

NATIONAL LEAGUE — FINISHED 3rd.

1931. — PCT. .545

CHICAGO

ROBERS HORNSBY

WON	LOST	NAME	POS.	G.	BA	FROM	TO
		Adair, James Audrey	SS	18	.276	A	C
2	4	Baecht, Edward Joseph	P	22	.278	Phil28	
		Barton, Vincent David	OF61	66	.238	A	
		Bell, Lester Rowland	3B70	75	.282	B	C
		Blair, Clarence Vick (1B23)	2B44	86	.258	B	C
0	4	Blake, John Frederick (Sheriff)	P	16	+.500	B	Phil
16	8	Bush, Guy Terrell	P	39	.123	B	
		Cuyler, Hazen Shirley (Kiki)	OF153	154	.330	B	
		English, Elwood George (Woody) (3B18)	SS138	156	.319	B	
		Grace, Robert Earl	C2	7	+.111	Chi29	Pitt
		Grimm, Chas. John	1B144	146	.331	B	
		Hartnett, Chas. Leo (Gabby)	C105	116	.282	B	
		Hemsley, Ralston Burdett (Rollie)	C53	66	+.309	xPitt	
		Herman, Wm. Jennings Bryan (Billy)	2B	25	.327	A	

WON	LOST	NAME	POS.	G.	BA	FROM	TO
		Hornsby, Rogers (Rajah) MGR. (3B26)	2B69	100	.331	B	
		Jurges, Wm. Frederick (Bill) (2B33)	3B54	88	.201	A	
		Kreevich, Michael Andreas	OF	5	.167	A	
16	9	Malone, Perce Leigh (Pat)	P	36	.215	B	
5	5	May, Frank Spruell (Jake)	P	31	.227	Cin	
		Moore, John Francis	OF22	39	.240	Chi29	
17	14	Root, Chas. Henry	P	39	.222	B	
15	12	Smith, Robert Eldridge	P	36	.218	Bos	
		Stephenson, Jackson Riggs	OF66	80	.319	B	
8	7	Sweetland, Lester Leo	P26	29	.268	Phil	C
		Taylor, Daniel Turney	OF67	88	.300	B	
		Taylor, James Wren (Zack)	C1	8	.250	B	
1	2	Treachout, Arthur John	P27	37	.238	B	
2	4	Warneke, Lonnie	P	20	.263	B	
2	1	Welch, John Vernon	P	8	.417	Chi28	
		Wilson, Lewis Robert (Hack)	OF103	112	.261	B	

WON 90 NATIONAL LEAGUE FINISHED 1st.
LOST 64
TG 154 1932. PCT. .584

CHICAGO

ROGERS HORNSBY CHAS. JOHN GRIMM

WON	LOST	NAME	POS.	G.	BA	FROM	TO
0	0	Baecht, Edward Joseph	P	1	.000	B	
		Barton, Vincent David	OF34	36	.224	B	C
19	11	Bush, Guy Terrell	P	40	.179	B	
		Cuyler, Hazen Shirley (Kiki)	OF109	110	.291	B	
		Demaree, Joseph Franklin (Frank)	OF17	23	.250	A	
		English, Elwood George (Woody) (SS38)	3B93	127	.272	B	
6	11	Grimes, Burleigh Arland	P	30	.250	StL	
		Grimm, Chas. John MGR.	1B	149	.307	B	
0	0	Gudat, Marvin John (Pl)	OF14	60	.255	Cin29	C
		Hack, Stanley Camfield	3B51	72	.236	A	
		Hartnett, Chas. Leo (Gabby)	C117	121	.271	B	
		Hemsley, Ralston Burdett (Rollie)	C47	60	.238	B	
		Herman, Wm. Jennings Bryan (Billy)	2B	154	.314	B	
2	1	Herrmann, LeRoy George	P	7	.500	A	
		Hornsby, Rogers (Rajah) MGR.	OF10	19	.224	B	
		Jurges, Wm. Frederick (Bill)	SS108	115	.253	B	
		Koenig, Mark Anthony	SS31	33	.353	DetA	
15	17	Malone, Perce Leigh (Pat)	P	37	.179	B	
2	2	May, Frank Spruell (Jake)	P	35	.125	B	C
		Moore, John Francis	OF109	119	.305	B	
0	0	Newsom, Louis Norman (Buck)	P	1	.000	Bkn30	
		Richbourg, Lancelot Clayton	OF33	44	.257	Bos	C
15	10	Root, Chas. Henry	P	39	.171	B	
4	3	Smith, Robert Eldridge	P34	36	.238	B	
		Stephenson, Jackson Riggs	OF	147	.324	B	
		Taylor, Daniel Turney	OF	6	+.227	B	Bkn
		Taylor, Harry Warren	1B1	10	.125	A	C
		Taylor, James Wren (Zack)	C14	21	.200	B	
5	3	Tinning, Lyle Forrest	P	24	.087	A	
22	6	Warneke, Lonnie	P	35	.192	B	
0	0	Yerkes, Chas. Carroll	P	2	.333	PhilA29	

WON 86 NATIONAL LEAGUE FINISHED 3rd.
LOST 68
TG 154 1933. PCT. .558

CHICAGO

CHAS. JOHN GRIMM

WON	LOST	NAME	POS.	G.	BA	FROM	TO
20	12	Bush, Guy Terrell	P	41	.125	B	
		Camilli, Adolph Louis	1B	16	.224	A	
		Campbell, Wm. Gilthorpe (Gilly)	C20	46	.281	A	
		Cuyler, Hazen Shirley (Kiki)	OF69	70	.317	B	
		Demaree, Joseph Franklin (Frank)	OF133	134	.272	B	
		Douthit, Taylor Lee	OF18	27	+.225	xCin	C
		English, Elwood George (Woody) (SS1)	3B103	105	.261	B	
3	6	Grimes, Burleigh Arland	P	17	+.150	B	StL
		Grimm, Chas. John MGR.	1B104	107	.247	B	
		Hack, Stanley Camfield	3B17	20	.350	B	
		Hartnett, Chas. Leo (Gabby)	C	140	.276	B	
		Hendrick, Harvey (Gink) (3B1 OF8)	1B38	69	.291	Cin	
2	1	Henshaw, Roy John	P	21	.200	A	
		Herman, Floyd Caves (Babe)	OF131	137	.289	Cin	
		Hermann, Wm. Jennings Bryan (Billy)	2B	153	.279	B	
0	1	Herrmann, LeRoy George	P	9	.167	B	
		Jurges, Wm. Frederick (Bill)	SS	143	.269	B	
		Koenig, Mark Anthony (2B2 SS26)	3B37	80	.284	B	
10	14	Malone, Perce Leigh (Pat)	P	31	.159	B	
		Mosolf, James Frederick	OF22	31	.268	Pitt31	C
5	5	Nelson, Lynn Bernard	P24	29	.238	Chi30	
		Phelps, Ernest Gordon (Babe)	C	3	.286	WashA31	
0	0	Richmond, Berly Justice	P	5	.000	A	
15	10	Root, Chas. Henry	P	35	.094	B	
		Stephenson, Jackson Riggs	OF91	97	.329	B	
		Taylor, James Wren (Zack)	C12	16	.000	B	
13	6	Tinning, Lyle Forrest	P	32	.209	B	
18	13	Warneke, Lonnie	P36	39	.300	B	
0	0	Yerkes, Chas. Carroll	P	1	.000	B	C

WON 86 | NATIONAL LEAGUE | FINISHED 3rd.
LOST 65
TG 151 | 1934. | PCT. .570

CHICAGO

CHAS. JOHN GRIMM

WON	LOST	NAME	POS.	G.	BA	FROM	TO
18	10	Bush, Guy Terrell	P40	41	.229	B	
		Camilli, Adolph Louis	1B	32	+.275	B	Phil
		Cavarretta, Philip Joseph	1B	7	.381	A	
		Cuyler, Hazen Shirley (Kiki)	OF	142	.338	B	
		English, Elwood George (Woody) (3B46)	SS56	109	.278	B	
		Galan, August John (Augie)	2B43	66	.260	A	
		Grimm, Chas. John MGR.	1B74	75	.296	B	
		Hack, Stanley Camfield	3B109	111	.289	B	
		Hartnett, Chas. Leo (Gabby)	C129	130	.299	B	
		Herman, Floyd Caves (Babe)	OF113	125	.304	B	
		Herman, Wm. Jennings Bryan (Billy)	2B111	113	.303	B	
		Hurst, Frank O'Donnell (Don)	1B48	51	+.199	xPhil	C
0	1	Joiner, Roy Merrill	P	20	.200	A	
		Jurges, Wm. Frederick (Bill)	SS98	100	.246	B	
		Klein, Chas. Herbert (Chuck)	OF110	115	.301	Phil	
13	14	Lee, Wm. Crutcher Jr. (Bill)	P35	40	.132	A	
14	7	Malone, Perce Leigh (Pat)	P	34	.172	B	
0	1	Nelson, Lynn Bernard	P	2	.000	B	
		O'Farrell, Robert Arthur	C	22	+.224	xCin	
		Phelps, Ernest Gordon (Babe)	C18	44	.286	B	
4	7	Root, Chas. Henry	P	34	.175	B	
		Stainback, George Tucker (Tuck)	OF96	104	.306	A	
		Stephenson, Jackson Riggs	OF15	38	.216	B	C
		Tate, Henry Bennett	OF4	11	.125	BosA32	C
4	6	Tinning, Lyle Forrest	P	39	.179	B	
0	0	Ward, Richard O.	P	3	.000	A	
22	10	Warneke, Lonnie	P43	52	.195	B	
11	9	Weaver, James Dement	P	27	.058	xStLA	
0	0	Wiedemeyer, Chas. John	P	4	.000	A	C

WON 100 | NATIONAL LEAGUE | FINISHED 1st.
LOST 54
TG 154 | 1935. | PCT. .649

CHICAGO

CHAS. JOHN GRIMM

WON	LOST	NAME	POS.	G.	BA	FROM	TO
1	2	Bryant, Claiborne Henry (Clay)	P	12	.333	A	
11	8	Carleton, James Otto (Tex)	P	31	.129	StL	
0	0	Casey, Hugh Thomas	P	13	.167	A	
		Cavarretta, Philip Joseph	1B145	146	.275	B	
		Cuyler, Hazen Shirley (Kiki)	OF42	45	+.274	B	Cin
		Demaree, Joseph Franklin (Frank)	OF98	107	.325	Chi33	
		English, Elwood George (Woody) (SS12)	3B16	34	.202	B	
17	10	French, Lawrence Herbert (Larry)	P	42	.141	Pitt	
		Galan, August John (Augie)	OF	154	.314	B	
		Gill, John Wesley		3	.333	WashA	
		Grimm, Chas. John MGR.	1B	2	.000	B	
		Hack, Stanley Camfield (1B7)	3B111	124	.311	B	
		Hartnett, Chas. Leo (Gabby)	C110	116	.344	B	
13	5	Henshaw, Roy John	P	31	.255	Chi33	
		Herman, Wm. Jennings Bryan (Billy)	2B	154	.341	B	
0	0	Joiner, Roy Merrill	P	2	.000	B	
		Jurges, Wm. Frederick (Bill)	SS	146	.241	B	
		Klein, Chas. Herbert (Chuck)	OF111	119	.293	B	
2	2	Kowalik, Fabian Lorenz	P	20	.200	ChiA32	
20	6	Lee, Wm. Crutcher Jr. (Bill)	P	39	.235	B	
		Lindstrom, Frederick Chas. (3B33)	OF50	90	.275	Pitt	
		O'Dea, James Kenneth (Ken)	C63	76	.257	A	
15	8	Root, Chas. Henry	P	38	.203	B	
1	0	Shoun, Clyde Mitchell	P	5	.000	A	
		Stainback, George Tucker (Tuck)	OF28	47	.255	B	
		Stephenson, Walter McQueen	C	16	.385	A	
20	13	Warneke, Lonnie	P42	44	.220	B	

WON 87 | NATIONAL LEAGUE | FINISHED 2nd.
LOST 67 | | (TIED WITH ST. L.)
TG 154 | 1936. | PCT. .565

CHAS. JOHN GRIMM

WON	LOST	NAME	POS.	G.	BA	FROM	TO
		Allen, Ethan Nathan	OF89	91	+.295	xPhil	
1	2	Bryant, Claiborne Henry (Clay)	P26	32	.417	B	
14	10	Carleton, James Otto (Tex)	P	35	.233	B	
		Cavarretta, Philip Joseph	1B115	124	.273	B	
11	9	Davis, Curtis Benton (Curt)	P	24	+.151	xPhil	
		Demaree, Joseph Franklin (Frank)	OF	154	.350	B	
		English, Elwood George(Woody) (3B17)	SS42	64	.247	B	
18	9	French, Lawrence Herbert (Larry)	P	43	.212	B	
		Galan, August John (Augie)	OF	145	.264	B	
		Gill, John Wesley	OF41	71	.253	B	C
		Grimm, Chas. John MGR.	1B35	39	.250	B	
		Hack, Stanley Camfield (1B11)	3B140	149	.298	B	
		Hartnett, Chas. Leo (Gabby)	C114	121	.307	B	
6	5	Henshaw, Roy John	P	39	.136	B	
		Herman, Wm. Jennings Bryan (Billy)	2B	153	.334	B	

WON	LOST	NAME	POS.	G.	BA	FROM	TO
		Jurges, Wm. Frederick (Bill)	SS116	118	.280	B	
		Klein, Chas. Herbert (Chuck)	OF	29	+.294	B	Phil
0	2	Kowalik, Fabian Lorenz	P	6	+.000	B	Phil
18	11	Lee, Wm. Crutcher Jr. (Bill)	P	43	.138	B	
		Lillard, Robert Eugene (3B3)	SS4	19	.206	A	
		O'Dea, James Kenneth (Ken)	C55	80	.307	B	
3	6	Root, Chas. Henry	P	33	.333	B	
0	0	Shoun, Clyde Mitchell	P	4	.000	B	
		Stainback, George Tucker (Tuck)	OF26	44	.173	B	
		Stephenson, Walter McQueen	C4	6	.083	B	
16	13	Warneke, Lonnie	P	40	.202	B	

WON 93 NATIONAL LEAGUE FINISHED 2nd.
LOST 61
TG 154 1937. PCT. .604

CHICAGO

CHAS. JOHN GRIMM

WON	LOST	NAME	POS.	G.	BA	FROM	TO
		Bottarini, John Chas.	C18	26	.275	A	C
9	3	Bryant, Claiborne Henry (Clay)	P38	47	.311	B	
16	8	Carleton, James Otto (Tex)	P32	34	.169	B	
		Cavarretta, Philip Joseph (1B43)	OF55	106	.286	B	
		Collins, James Anthony (Rip)	1B111	115	.274	StL	
10	5	Davis, Curtis Benton (Curt)	P	28	.300	B	
		Demaree, Joseph Franklin (Frank)	OF	154	.324	B	
16	10	French, Lawrence Herbert (Larry)	P	42	.127	B	
		Frey, Linus Reinhard (Lonny) (2B13)	SS30	78	.278	Bkn	
		Galan, August John (Augie)	OF140	147	.252	B	
		Garbark, Robert Michael	C	1	.000	ClevA35	
		Hack, Stanley Camfield	3B150	154	.297	B	
		Hartnett, Chas. Leo (Gabby)	C103	110	.354	B	
		Herman, Wm. Jennings Bryan (Billy)	2B137	138	.335	B	
1	0	Higbe, Walter Kirby	P	1	.000	A	
		Jurges, Wm. Frederick (Bill)	SS128	129	.298	B	
0	0	Kimball, Newell W.	P	2	.000	A	
14	15	Lee, Wm. Crutcher Jr. (Bill)	P	42	.172	B	
0	0	Logan, Robert Dean	P	4	.000	xDetA	
		Marty, Joseph Anton	OF84	88	.290	A	
		Meyer, Lambert Dalton		1	.000	A	
		O'Dea, James Kenneth (Ken)	C64	83	.301	B	
7	8	Parmelee, LeRoy Earl	P33	37	.173	StL	
		Reynolds, Carl Nettles	OF2	7	.273	WashA	
13	5	Root, Chas. Henry	P	43	.179	B	
7	7	Shoun, Clyde Mitchell	P	37	.138	B	
		Stainback, George Tucker (Tuck)	OF49	72	.231	B	

WON 89 NATIONAL LEAGUE FINISHED 1st.
LOST 63
TG 152 1938. PCT. .586

CHICAGO

CHAS. JOHN GRIMM CHAS. LEO HARTNETT

WON	LOST	NAME	POS.	G.	BA	FROM	TO
		Asbell, James Marion	OF10	17	.182	A	C
19	11	Bryant, Claiborne Henry (Clay)	P44	50	.226	B	
10	9	Carleton, James Otto (Tex)	P	33	.231	B	
		Cavarretta, Philip Joseph (1B28)	OF52	92	.239	B	
		Collins, James Anthony (Rip)	1B135	143	.267	B	
7	1	Dean, Jay Hanna (Dizzy)	P	13	.192	StL	
		Demaree, Joseph Franklin (Frank)	OF125	129	.273	B	
2	0	Epperly, Albert Paul	P	9	.250	A	
10	19	French, Lawrence Herbert (Larry)	P	43	.210	B	
		Galan, August John (Augie)	OF103	110	.286	B	
		Garbark, Robert Michael	C20	23	.259	B	
		Hack, Stanley Camfield	3B	152	.320	B	
		Hartnett, Chas. Leo (Gabby) MGR.	C83	88	.274	B	
		Herman, Wm. Jennings Bryan (Billy)	2B151	152	.277	B	
0	0	Higbe, Walter Kirby	P	2	.000	B	
		Jurges, Wm. Frederick (Bill)	SS136	137	.245	B	
0	0	Kimball, Newell W.	P	1	.000	B	
		Lazzeri, Anthony Michael (Tony)	SS25	54	.267	NYA	
22	9	Lee, Wm. Crutcher Jr. (Bill)	P	44	.198	B	
0	2	Logan, Robert Dean	P	14	.000	B	
		Marty, Joseph Anton	OF68	76	.243	B	
		Mattick, Robert James	SS	1	1.000	A	
		Mesner, Stephan Mathias (Steve)	SS1	2	.250	A	
		O'Dea, James Kenneth (Ken)	C71	86	.263	B	
5	4	Page, Vance Linwood	P	13	.154	A	
		Reynolds, Carl Nettles	OF	125	.302	B	
8	7	Root, Chas. Henry	P	44	.167	B	
6	1	Russell, Jack Erwin	P	42	.219	DetA	
		Triplett, Herman Coaker	OF9	12	.250	A	

WON 84 NATIONAL LEAGUE FINISHED 4th.
LOST 70
TG 154 1939. PCT. .545

CHICAGO

CHAS. LEO HARTNETT

WON	LOST	NAME	POS.	G.	BA	FROM	TO

WON	LOST	NAME	POS.	G.	BA	FROM	TO
		Bartell, Richard Wm.	SS101	105	.238	N.Y.	
2	1	Bryant, Claiborne Henry (Clay)	P	28	.214	B	
		Cavarretta, Philip Joseph	1B13	22	.273	B	
6	4	Dean, Jay Hanna (Dizzy)	P	19	.147	B	
15	8	French, Lawrence Herbert (Larry)	P	36	.192	B	
		Galan, August John (Augie)	OF145	148	.304	B	
		Garbark, Robert Michael	C21	24	.143	B	
		Gleeson, James Joseph	OF91	111	.223	ClevA36	
		Hack, Stanley Camfield	3B	156	.298	B	
0	2	Harrell, Raymond James (Ray)	P	4	+.000	StL	Phil
		Hartnett, Chas. Leo (Gabby) MGR.	C86	97	.278	B	
		Herman, Wm. Jennings Bryan (Billy)	2B	156	.307	B	
2	1	Higbe, Walter Kirby	P	9	+.286	B	Phil
19	15	Lee, Wm. Crutcher Jr. (Bill)	P	37	.126	B	
		Leiber, Henry Edward (Hank)	OF98	112	.310	N.Y.	
3	5	Lillard, Robert Eugene	P20	23	.100	Chi36	
		Mancuso, August Rodney (Gus)	C76	80	.231	N.Y.	
		Marty, Joseph Anton	OF21	23	+.132	B	Phil
		Mattick, Robert James	SS48	51	.287	B	
		Mesner, Stephan Mathias (Steve)	SS12	17	.279	B	
		Nicholson, Wm. Beck	OF	58	.295	PhilA36	
1	0	Olsen, Vernon Jarl	P	4	.000	A	
7	7	Page, Vance Linwood	P	27	.255	B	
13	9	Passeau, Claude Wm.	P34	35	+.156	xPhil	
		Reynolds, Carl Nettles	OF72	88	.246	B	C
8	8	Root, Chas. Henry	P	35	.175	B	
		Russell, Glen David	1B	143	.273	A	
4	3	Russell, Jack Erwin	P39	43	.000	B	
4	7	Whitehill, Earl Oliver	P	24	.103	ClevA	C

WON 75   NATIONAL LEAGUE   FINISHED 5th.
LOST 79
TG 154   1940.   PCT. .487

CHICAGO

CHAS. LEO HARTNETT

WON	LOST	NAME	POS.	G.	BA	FROM	TO
0	0	Bonetti, Julio James Paul	P	1	.000	StLA38	C
		Bonura, Henry John (Zeke)	1B44	49	.264	xWashA	C
0	1	Bryant, Claiborne Henry (Clay)	P8	16	.333	B	C
		Cavarretta, Philip Joseph	1B52	65	.280	B	
		Collins, Robert Joseph	C42	47	.208	A	
3	3	Dean, Jay Hanna (Dizzy)	P	10	.222	B	
		Dallessandro, Nicholas Dominic	OF74	107	.268	BosA37	
14	14	French, Lawrence Herbert (Larry)	P	40	.165	B	
		Galan, August John (Augie) (2B2)	OF54	68	.230	B	
		Gleeson, James Joseph	OF123	129	.313	B	
		Hack, Stanley Camfield	3B148	149	.317	B	
		Hartnett, Chas. Leo (Gabby) MGR. (1B1)	C22	37	.266	B	
		Herman, Wm. Jennings Bryan (Billy)	2B	135	.292	B	
9	17	Lee, Wm. Crutcher Jr. (Bill)	P	37	.132	B	
		Leiber, Henry Edward (Hank) (1B12)	OF103	117	.302	B	
		Mattick, Robert James (3B1)	SS126	128	.218	B	
6	6	Mooty, Jacob T. (Jake)	P20	24	.263	Cin37	
		McCullough, Clyde Edward	C7	9	.154	A	
		Nicholson, Wm. Beck	OF123	135	.297	B	
13	9	Olsen, Vernon Jarl	P34	35	.263	B	
1	3	Page, Vance Linwood	P30	31	.308	B	
20	13	Passeau, Claude Wm.	P	46	.204	B	
7	9	Raffensberger, Kenneth David	P	43	.167	StL	
		Rogell, Wm. George (Billy) (2B3 3B9)	SS14	33	.136	DetA	C
2	4	Root, Chas. Henry	P	36	.129	B	
		Russell, Glen David (3B3)	1B51	68	.247	B	
		Sturgeon, Robert Harwood	SS	7	.190	A	
		Todd, Alfred Chester (Al)	C	104	.255	Bkn	
		Warstler, Harold Burton (Rabbitt) (2B17)	SS28	45	+.226	xBos	C

WON 70   NATIONAL LEAGUE   FINISHED 6th.
LOST 84
TG 154   1941.   PCT. .455

CHICAGO

JAMES WILSON

WON	LOST	NAME	POS.	G.	BA	FROM	TO
		Cavarretta, Philip Joseph (1B33)	OF66	107	.286	B	
		Dahlgren, Ellsworth Tenney (Babe)	1B98	99	+.281	xBos	
0	0	Dean, Jay Hanna (Dizzy)	P	1	.000	B	
		Dallessandro, Nicholas Dominic	OF131	140	.272	B	
3	3	Eaves, Vallie Ennis	P	12	.100	ChiA	
5	7	Erickson, Paul Wakefield	P	32	.152	A	
5	14	French, Lawrence Herbert (Larry)	P	26	+.191	B	Bkn
		Galan, August John (Augie)	OF31	65	+.208	B	Bkn
		George, Chas. Peter	C18	35	.156	Bkn38	
		Gilbert, Chas. Mader	OF22	39	.279	Bkn	
0	0	Gornicki, Henry Frank	P	1	+.000	xStL	
		Hack, Stanley Camfield (1B1)	3B150	151	.317	B	
		Herman, Wm. Jennings Bryan (Billy)	2B	11	+.194	B	Bkn
		Hudson, John Wilson (2B13 3B10)	SS17	50	.202	Bkn	
		Jelincich, Frank Anthony	OF2	4	.125	A	C
0	0	Kush, Emil Benedict	P	2	.000	A	

WON	LOST	NAME	POS.	G.	BA	FROM	TO
0	1	LanFranconi, Walter Oswald	P	2	.000	A	
8	14	Lee, Wm. Crutcher Jr. (Bill)	P	28	.186	B	
		Leiber, Henry Edward (Hank) (1B15)	OF29	53	.216	B	
0	1	Meers, Russell Harlan	P	1	.000	A	
		Merullo, Leonard Richard	SS	7	.353	A	
8	9	Mooty, Jacob T. (Jake)	P	33	.200	B	
		Myers, Wm. Harrison (Billy) (2B1)	SS19	24	.222	Cin	C
		McCullough, Clyde Edward	C119	125	.227	B	
		Nicholson, Wm. Beck	OF143	147	.254	B	
		Novikoff, Louis	OF54	62	.241	A	
		Olsen, Bernard Chas.	OF23	24	.288	A	C
10	8	Olsen, Vernon Jarl	P	37	.238	B	
2	2	Page, Vance Linwood	P	25	.286	B	C
14	14	Passeau, Claude Wm.	P	34	.221	B	
5	3	Pressnell, Forest Chas. (Tot)	P	29	.200	Bkn	
0	0	Quinn, Wellington Hunt	P	3	.500	A	C
0	1	Raffensberger, Kenneth David	P	10	.000	B	
8	7	Root, Chas. Henry	P	19	.152	B	C
		Russell, Glen David	1B5	6	.294	B	
		Scheffing, Robert Boden	C34	51	.242	A	
2	0	Schmitz, John Albert	P5	6	.571	A	
		Stringer, Louis Bernard	2B137	145	.246	A	
		Sturgeon, Robert Harwood (2B1 3B1)	SS126	129	.245	B	
		Todd, Alfred Chester (Al)		6	.167	B	
		Waitkus, Edward Stephen	1B9	12	.179	A	

WON 68
LOST 86
TG 154

NATIONAL LEAGUE

1942.

FINISHED 6th.

PCT. .442

CHICAGO

JAMES WILSON

WON	LOST	NAME	POS.	G.	BA	FROM	TO
0	0	Berry, Jonas Arthur	P	2	.000	A	
9	14	Bithorn, Hiram Gabriel	P	38	.123	A	
		Block, Seymour (Cy) (2B1)	3B8	9	.364	A	
0	0	Bowman, Robert James (Bob)	P	1	.000	N.Y.	C
		Cavarretta, Philip Joseph (1B61)	OF70	136	.270	B	
		Dahlgren, Ellsworth Tenney (Babe)	1B14	17	.214	B	StLA
		Dallessandro, Nicholas Dominic	OF66	96	.261	B	
0	0	Eaves, Vallie Ennis	P	2	.000	B	C
1	6	Erickson, Paul Wakefield	P	18	.143	B	
1	1	Errickson, Richard Merriwell (Leif)	P	13	+.000	xBos	C
		Felderman, Marvin Wilfred	C2	3	.167	A	C
5	6	Fleming, Leslie Fletcherd (Bill)	P	33	.051	BosA	
0	1	Flores, Jesse Sandoval	P	4	.000	A	

WON	LOST	NAME	POS.	G.	BA	FROM	TO
		Foxx, James Emory (Jimmie) (C1)	1B52	70	.205	xBosA	
		Gilbert, Chas. Mader	OF47	74	.184	B	
		Gillespie, Paul Allen	C4	5	.250	A	
		Hack, Stanley Camfield	3B139	140	.300	B	
1	1	Hanyzewski, Edward Michael	P	6	.200	A	
		Hernandez, Salvador Ramos	C43	47	.229	A	
0	0	Kush, Emil Benedict	P	1	.000	B	
13	13	Lee, Wm. Crutcher Jr. (Bill)	P	32	.159	B	
		Lowrey, Harry Lee	OF19	27	.190	A	
		Merullo, Leonard Richard	SS	143	.256	B	
2	5	Mooty, Jacob T. (Jake)	P	19	.214	B	
		McCullough, Clyde Edward	C97	109	.282	B	
		Nicholson, Wm. Beck	OF151	152	.294	B	
		Novikoff, Louis	OF120	128	.300	B	
6	9	Olsen, Vernon Jarl	P	32	.188	B	
19	14	Passeau, Claude Wm.	P	35	.181	B	
		Platt, Mizell George	OF	4	.063	A	
1	1	Pressnell, Forest Chas. (Tot)	P	27	.667	B	C
		Rickert, Marvin August	OF6	8	.269	A	
		Russell, Glen David (2B24 3B10 OF3)	1B35	102	.242	B	
		Scheffing, Robert Boden	C32	44	.196	B	
3	7	Schmitz, John Albert	P	23	.154	B	
		Stringer, Louis Bernard (3B1)	2B113	121	.236	B	
		Sturgeon, Robert Harwood (SS29 3B2)	2B32	63	.247	B	
5	7	Warneke, Lonnie	P	15	+.188	xStL	
2	1	Wyse, Henry Washington	P	4	.125	A	

WON 74
LOST 79
TG 153

NATIONAL LEAGUE

1943.

FINISHED 5th.

PCT. .484

CHICAGO

JAMES WILSON

WON	LOST	NAME	POS.	G.	BA	FROM	TO
0	1	Alderson, Dale Leonard	P	4	.000	A	
0	4	Barrett, Tracy Souter (Richard Oliver)	P	15	+.111	Bos34	Phil
		Becker, Heinz Reinhard	1B18	24	.145	A	
18	12	Bithorn, Hiram Gabriel	P	39	.174	B	
0	2	Burrows, John	P	23	.667	xPhilA	
		Cavarretta, Philip Joseph (OF7)	1B134	143	.291	B	
		Dallessandro, Nicholas Dominic	OF45	87	.222	B	
10	14	Derringer, Samuel Paul	P	32	.224	Cin	
		Elko, Peter	3B	9	.133	A	
1	3	Erickson, Paul Wakefield	P	15	.200	B	
0	1	Fleming, Leslie Fletcherd (Bill)	P	11	.000	B	
		Gilbert, Chas. Mader	OF6	8	.150	B	
		Goodman, Ival Richard	OF61	80	.320	Cin	

WON	LOST	NAME	POS.	G.	BA	FROM	TO
		Hack, Stanley Camfield	3B136	144	.289	B	
8	7	Hanyzewski, Edward Michael	P	33	.049	B	
		Hernandez, Salvador Ramos	C41	43	.270	B	C
		Holm, Wm. Frederick	C	7	.067	A	
		Johnson, Donald Spori	2B	10	.190	A	
		Kreitner, Albert Joseph	C	3	.375	A	
3	7	Lee, Wm. Crutcher Jr. (Bill)	P	13	+.269	B	Phil
		Livingston, Thompson Orville (1B4)	C31	36	+.261	xPhil	
		Lowrey, Harry Lee (2B3 SS16)	OF113	130	.292	B	
		Martin, Stuart McGuire (Stu) (1B2 3B8)	2B22	64	.220	Pitt	C
		Merullo, Leonard Richard	SS125	129	.254	B	
0	0	Mooty, Jacob T. (Jake)	P	2	.000	B	
		McCullough, Clyde Edward	C81	87	.237	B	
		Nicholson, Wm. Beck	OF	154	.309	B	
		Novikoff, Louis	OF61	78	.279	B	
		Ostrowski, John Theodore (3B4)	OF5	10	.207	A	
		Pafko, Andrew	OF	13	.379	A	
15	12	Passeau, Claude Wm.	P	35	.198	B	
		Platt, Mizell George	OF14	20	.171	B	
4	3	Prim, Raymond Lee	P	29	.167	Phi135	
		Sauer, Edward	OF13	14	.273	A	
		Schuster, Wm. Chas.	SS	13	.294	Bos39	
2	1	Signer, Walter Donald	P	4	.250	A	
		Stanky, Edward Raymond (SS12 3B2)	2B131	142	.245	A	
		Todd, Alfred Chester (Al)	C17	21	.133	Chi41	C
4	5	Warneke, Lonnie	P	21	.192	B	
9	7	Wyse, Henry Washington	P38	40	.080	B	

WON 75 NATIONAL LEAGUE FINISHED 4th.
LOST 79
TG 154 1944. PCT. .487

CHICAGO

JAMES WILSON ROY JOHNSON CHAS. JOHN GRIMM

WON	LOST	NAME	POS.	G.	BA	FROM	TO
0	0	Alderson, Dale Leonard	P	12	.000	B	C
		Brewster, Chas. Lawrence	SS	10	.250	Phil	
0	0	Burrows, John	P	3	.000	B	C
		Cavarretta, Philip Joseph (OF13)	1B139	152	.321	B	
9	9	Chipman, Robert Howard	P	26	+.104	xBkn	
		Dallessandro, Nicholas Dominic	OF106	117	.305	B	
7	13	Derringer, Samuel Paul	P	42	.158	B	
		Easterwood, Roy Chas.	C12	17	.212	A	C
		Elko, Peter	3B6	7	.227	B	C
5	9	Erickson, Paul Wakefield	P	33	.056	B	
9	10	Fleming, Leslie Fletcherd (Bill)	P39	40	.170	B	

WON	LOST	NAME	POS.	G.	BA	FROM	TO
		Foxx, James Emory (Jimmie) (C1)	3B2	15	.050	Chi42	
0	1	Gassaway, Chas. Cason	P	2	.250	A	
		Gillespie, Paul Allen	C7	9	.269	Chi42	
		Goodman, Ival Richard	OF35	62	.262	B	C
		Hack, Stanley Camfield (1B18)	3B75	98	.282	B	
2	5	Hanyzewski, Edward Michael	P	14	.059	B	
		Holm, Wm. Frederick	C50	54	.148	B	
		Hughes, Roy John (Jeep) (SS52)	3B66	126	.287	Phi140	
		Johnson, Donald Spori	2B	154	.278	B	
		Kreitner, Albert Joseph	C	39	.152	B	C
5	4	Lynn, Japhet Monroe	P	22	.207	NY40	C
		Mann, Ben Garth		1	.000	A	C
		Merullo, Leonard Richard (1B1)	SS56	66	.212	B	
0	0	Miklos, John Joseph	P	2	.000	A	C
		Nicholson, Wm. Beck	OF	156	.287	B	
		Novikoff, Louis	OF29	71	.281	B	
		Ostrowski, John Theodore	OF2	8	.154	B	
		Pafko, Andrew	OF123	128	.269	B	
15	9	Passeau, Claude Wm.	P	34	.163	B	
		Sauer, Edward	OF12	23	.220	B	
		Schuster, Wm. Chas. (2B6)	SS38	60	.221	B	
		Secory, Frank Edward	OF17	22	.321	Cin42	
		Stanky, Edward Raymond (SS3 3B3)	2B3	13	+.240	B	Bkn
		Stephenson, Joseph Chester	C3	4	.125	N.Y.	
0	0	Stewart, Wm. Macklin	P	8	.000	A	
7	4	Vandenberg, Harold Harris	P	35	.237	NY40	
		Williams, Dewey Edgar	C77	79	.240	A	
16	15	Wyse, Henry Washington	P	41	.178	B	
		York, Anthony B. (SS15)	3B12	28	.235	A	C

WON 98 NATIONAL LEAGUE FINISHED 1st.
LOST 56
TG 154 1945. PCT. .636

CHICAGO

CHAS. JOHN GRIMM

WON	LOST	NAME	POS.	G.	BA	FROM	TO
		Becker, Heinz Reinhard	1B28	67	.286	Chi43	
		Block, Seymour (Cy) (3B1)	2B1	2	.143	Chi42	
11	2	Borowy, Henry Ludwig	P	15	.171	xNYA	
		Cavarretta, Philip Joseph (OF11)	1B120	132	.355	B	
4	5	Chipman, Robert Howard	P	25	.176	B	
		Christopher, Loyd Eugene	OF	1	.000	xBosA	
0	2	Comellas, Jorge	P	7	.000	A	C
16	11	Derringer, Samuel Paul	P	35	.200	B	C
7	4	Erickson, Paul Wakefield	P	28	.156	B	
		Gillespie, Paul Allen (OF1)	C45	75	.288	B	C

WON	LOST	NAME	POS.	G.	BA	FROM	TO
		Hack, Stanley Camfield	3B146	150	.323	B	
		(1B5)					
0	0	Hanyzewski, Edward Michael	P	2	.000	B	
0	0	Hennessey, George	P	2	.000	Phil42	C
		Hughes, Roy John (Jeep)	SS36	69	.261	B	
		(1B2 2B21 3B9)					
		Johnson, Donald Spori	2B	138	.302	B	
		Livingston, Thompson Orville	C68	71	.254	Chi43	
		(1B1)					
		Lowrey, Harry Lee (SS2)	OF138	143	.283	Chi43	
		Merullo, Leonard Richard	SS118	126	.239	B	
		Moore, John Francis		7	.167	Phil37	C
		Nicholson, Wm. Beck	OF	151	.243	B	
		Ostrowski, John Theodore	3B4	7	.300	B	
		Otero, Regino Joseph	1B8	14	.391	A	C
		Pafko, Andrew	OF140	144	.298	B	
17	9	Passeau, Claude Wm.	P	34	.187	B	
13	8	Prim, Raymond Lee	P	34	.255	Chi43	
		Rice, Leonard Oliver	C29	32	.232	Cin	C
		Sauer, Edward	OF26	49	.258	B	C
		Schuster, Wm. Chas.	SS22	45	.191	B	C
		(2B3 3B1)					
		Secory, Frank Edward	OF12	35	.158	B	
0	0	Signer, Walter Donald	P	6	.000	Chi43	C
1	0	Starr, Raymond Francis	P	9	+.500	xPitt	C
0	1	Stewart, Wm. Macklin	P	16	.333	B	C
7	3	Vandenberg, Harold Harris	P	30	.125	B	C
0	1	Warneke, Lonnie	P	9	.000	Chi43	C
		Williams, Dewey Edgar	C54	59	.280	B	
22	10	Wyse, Henry Washington	P	38	.168	B	

WON 82 — NATIONAL LEAGUE — FINISHED 3rd.
LOST 71
TG 153 — 1946. — PCT. .536

CHICAGO

CHAS. JOHN GRIMM

WON	LOST	NAME	POS.	G.	BA	FROM	TO
0	1	Adams, Chas. Dwight	P	8	.000	A	C
2	1	Bauers, Russell Lee (Russ)	P	15	.300	Pitt41	
		Becker, Heinz Reinhard		9	.286	B	ClevA
6	5	Bithorn, Hiram Gabriel	P	26	.179	Chi43	
		Block, Seymour (Cy)	3B4	6	.231	B	C
12	10	Borowy, Henry Ludwig	P32	33	.181	B	
		Cavarretta, Philip Joseph	OF86	139	.294	B	
		(1B51)					
6	5	Chipman, Robert Howard	P	34	.061	B	
		Dallessandro, Nicholas Dominic	OF20	65	.225	Chi44	
9	7	Erickson, Paul Wakefield	P	32	.050	B	
0	1	Fleming, Leslie Fletcherd	P	14	.000	Chi44	C
		(Bill)					
		Garriott, Cecil Virgil		6	.000	A	C
		Gilbert, Chas. Mader	OF2	15	+.077	Chi43	Phil

WON	LOST	NAME	POS.	G.	BA	FROM	TO
		Glossop, Alban (SS2)	2B2	4	.000	Bkn43	C
		Hack, Stanley Camfield	3B90	92	.285	B	
1	0	Hanyzewski, Edward Michael	P	3	.000	B	C
		Johnson, Donald Spori	2B	83	.242	B	
		Jurges, Wm. Frederick	SS73	82	.222	N.Y.	
		(2B2 3B7)					
9	2	Kush, Emil Benedict	P	40	.211	Chi42	
0	2	Lade, Doyle Marion	P	3	.200	A	
		Livingston, Thompson Orville	C56	66	.256	B	
		Lowrey, Harry Lee (3B20)	OF126	144	.257	B	
		Maddern, James Clarence	OF2	3	.000	A	
0	1	Manders, Harold Carl	P	2	.000	xDetA	C
		McCullough, Clyde Edward	C89	95	.287	Chi43	
1	2	Meers, Russell Harlan	P	7	1.000	Chi41	
		Merullo, Leonard Richard	SS44	65	.151	B	
0	0	Meyer, Russell Chas.	P	4	.200	A	
		Nicholson, Wm. Beck	OF80	105	.220	B	
0	0	Olsen, Vernon Jarl	P	5	.000	Chi42	C
0	0	O'Neill, Robert Emmett	P	1	.000	BosA	ChiA
		Ostrowski, John Theodore	3B50	64	.213	B	
		(2B1)					
		Pafko, Andrew	OF64	65	.282	B	
9	8	Passeau, Claude Wm.	P	21	.204	B	
		Pawelek, Theodore John	C1	4	.250	A	C
2	3	Prim, Raymond Lee	P	14	.200	B	C
		Rickert, Marvin August	OF104	111	.263	Chi42	
		Scheffing, Robert Boden	C40	63	.278	Chi42	
		Schenz, Henry Leonard	3B5	6	.182	A	
11	11	Schmitz, John Albert	P41	42	.129	Chi42	
		Secory, Frank Edward	OF9	33	.233	B	C
		Stringer, Louis Bernard	2B62	80	.244	Chi42	
		(SS1 3B1)					
		Sturgeon, Robert Howard	SS72	100	.296	Chi42	
		(2B21)					
		Waitkus, Edward Stephen	1B106	113	.304	Chi41	
		Williams, Dewey Edgar	C2	4	.200	B	
14	12	Wyse, Henry Washington	P	40	.243	B	

WON 69 — NATIONAL LEAGUE — FINISHED 6th.
LOST 85
TG 154 — 1947. — PCT. .448

CHICAGO

CHAS. JOHN GRIMM

WON	LOST	NAME	POS.	G.	BA	FROM	TO
		Aberson, Clifford Alexander	OF40	47	.279	A	
8	12	Borowy, Henry Ludwig	P40	41	.125	B	
0	1	Carpenter, Robert Louis	P	4	+1.000	xN.Y.	C
		Cavarretta, Philip Joseph	OF100	127	.314	B	
		(1B24)					
7	6	Chipman, Robert Howard	P32	33	.091	B	
		Dallessandro, Nicholas Dominic	OF28	66	.287	B	C
7	12	Erickson, Paul Wakefield	P	40	.250	B	

WON	LOST	NAME	POS.	G.	BA	FROM	TO
		Frey, Linus Reinhard (Lonny)	2B9	24	.209	Cin	NYA
		Hack, Stanley Camfield	3B66	76	.271	B	
1	2	Hamner, Ralph Conant	P	3	.125	ChiA	
		Johnson, Donald Spori (3B6)	2B108	120	.259	B	
		Jurges, Wm. Frederick (Bill)	SS	14	.200	B	
8	3	Kush, Emil Benedict	P	47	.250	B	
11	10	Lade, Doyle Marion	P34	35	.217	B	
0	2	Lee, Wm. Crutcher Jr. (Bill)	P	14	.333	Bos	C
		Livingston Thompson Orville	C7	19	+.212	B	N.Y.
		Lowrey, Harry Lee	3B91	115	.281	B	
		(2B6 OF25					
		Mack, Raymond James	2B	21	.218	xNYA	C
		Madrid, Salvadore	SS	8	.125	A	C
2	0	Meers, Russell Harlan	P	35	.143	B	C
		Merullo, Leonard Richard	SS	108	.241	B	C
3	2	Meyer, Russell Chas.	P	23	.250	B	
1	2	Miller, John Anthony	P	4	.429	StLA	C
		McCullough, Clyde Edward	C64	86	.252	B	
		Nicholson, Wm. Beck	OF140	148	.244	B	
		Pafko, Andrew	OF127	129	.302	B	
2	6	Passeau, Claude Wm.	P	19	.000	B	C
		Rickert, Marvin August	OF30	71	.146	B	
		(1B7)					
		Scheffing, Robert Boden	C97	110	.264	B	
		Schenz, Henry Leonard	3B5	7	.071	B	
0	0	Schmidt, Frederick Albert	P	1	+.000	xPhil	C
13	18	Schmitz, John Albert	P	38	.132	B	
		Sturgeon, Robert Harwood	SS45	87	.254	B	
		(2B30 3B5)					
		Waitkus, Edward Stephen	1B126	130	.292	B	
		Williams, Dewey Edgar	C1	3	.000	B	
6	9	Wyse, Henry Washington	P	37	.111	B	

WON 64 NATIONAL LEAGUE FINISHED 8th (LAST)
LOST 90
TG 154 1948 PCT. .416

CHICAGO

CHAS. JOHN GRIMM

WON	LOST	NAME	POS.	G.	BA	FROM	TO
		Aberson, Clifford Alexander	OF8	12	.188	B	
5	10	Borowy, Henry Ludwig	P	39	.222	B	
0	0	Carlsen, Donald Herbert	P	1	.000	A	
		Cavarretta, Philip Joseph	1B41	111	.279	B	
		(OF40)					
2	9	Chambers, Clifford Day	P	29	.133	A	
2	1	Chipman, Robert Howard	P	34	.250	B	
		Cross, Joffre James (2B1)	SS9	16	+.100	xStL	C
		Culler, Richard Broadus (2B2)	SS43	48	.169	Bos	
7	2	Dobernic, Andrew Joseph	P	54	.200	ChiA39	
0	0	Erickson, Paul Wakefield	P	3	.000	B	Phil
0	1	Hacker, Warren Louis	P	3	.000	A	
5	9	Hamner, Ralph Conant	P	27	.182	B	

WON	LOST	NAME	POS.	G.	BA	FROM	TO
0	0	Jacobs, Anthony Robert	P	1	.000	A	
		Jeffcoat, Harold Bently	OF119	134	.279	A	
		Johnson, Donald Spori (3B2)	2B2	6	.250	B	C
1	4	Kush, Emil Benedict	P	34	.154	B	
5	6	Lade, Doyle Marion	P	19	.156	B	
		Lowrey, Harry Lee	OF103	129	.294	B	
		(2B2 SS1 3B9)					
		Lynch, Matthew Daniel Jr.	2B1	7	.286	A	C
		Maddern, James Clarence	OF55	80	.252	Chi46	
		Mauch, Eugene Wm. (SS19)	2B26	53	+.203	xBkn	
		Mauro, Carmen Louis	OF2	3	.200	A	
10	10	Meyer, Russell Chas.	P	29	.107	B	
4	13	McCall, Robert Leonard	P	30	.170	A	C
		McCullough, Clyde Edward	C51	69	.209	B	
		Nicholson, Wm. Beck	OF136	143	.261	B	
		Pafko, Andrew	3B139	142	.312	B	
5	11	Rush, Robert Ransom	P36	38	.128	A	
		Sawatski, Carl Ernest		2	.000	A	
		Scheffing, Robert Boden	C78	102	.300	B	
		Schenz, Henry Leonard (3B5)	2B78	96	.261	B	
18	13	Schmitz, John Albert	P	34	.131	B	
		Smalley, Roy Frederick	SS	124	.216	A	
		Verban, Emil Matthew	2B	56	+.295	xPhil	
0	1	Wade, Benjamin Styron	P	2	.000	A	
		Waitkus, Edward Stephen	1B116	139	.296	B	
		(OF20)					
		Walker, Albert Bluford	C44	79	.275	A	

WON 61 NATIONAL LEAGUE FINISHED 8th (LAST)
LOST 93
TG 154 1949. PCT. .396

CHICAGO

CHAS. JOHN GRIMM FRANK FRANCIS FRISCH

WON	LOST	NAME	POS.	G.	BA	FROM	TO
		Aberson, Clifford Alexander	OF1	4	.000	B	C
2	4	Adkins, John Dewey	P	30	.200	WashA43	C
		Baumholtz, Frank Conrad	OF43	58	+.226	xCin	
		Burgess, Forrest Harrill	C8	46	.268	A	
		Cavarretta, Philip Joseph	1B70	105	.294	B	
		(OF25)					
7	8	Chipman, Robert Howard	P	38	.125	B	
0	0	Cooper, Morton Cecil	P	1	.000	NY47	C
0	0	Dobernic, Andrew Joseph	P	4	+.000	B	Cin
6	9	Dubiel, Walter John	P32	33	.286	Phil	
		Edwards, Henry Albert	OF51	58	.290	xClevA	
		Gustine, Frank Wm. (2B16)	3B55	76	.226	Pitt	
5	8	Hacker, Warren Louis	P30	32	.184	B	
0	2	Hamner, Ralph Conant	P	6	.000	B	C
		Jeffcoat, Harold Bently	OF101	108	.245	B	
		Kirby, James Herschel		3	.500	A	C
3	3	Kush, Emil Benedict	P	26	.333	B	C
4	5	Lade, Doyle Marion	P	36	.219	B	

WON	LOST	NAME	POS.	G.	BA	FROM	TO
7	16	Leonard, Emil John (Dutch)	P	33	.203	Phil	
		Lowrey, Harry Lee (3B1)	OF31	38	+.270	B	Cin
		Maddern, James Clarence	1B1	10	.333	B	
		Mauch, Eugene Wm.	2B25	72	.247	B	
		(SS19 3B7)					
5	6	Muncrief, Robert Cleveland	P	34	+.286	xPitt	
1	1	McLish, Calvin Coolidge	P8	9	.333	Pitt	
		Novotney, Ralph Joseph	C20	22	.269	A	C
		Owen, Arnold Malcolm (Mickey)	C59	62	.273	Bkn45	
		Pafko, Andrew (3B49)	OF98	144	.281	B	
		Ramazzotti, Robert Louis	3B36	65	+.179	xBkn	
		(2B4 SS12)					
		Reich, Herman Chas. (OF16)	1B85	108	.280	xClevA	C
10	18	Rush, Robert Ransom	P	35	.032	B	
		Sauer, Henry John	OF	96	+.291	xCin	
		Scheffing, Robert Boden	C40	55	.268	B	
		Schenz, Henry Leonard	3B5	7	.429	B	
11	13	Schmitz, John Albert	P	36	.143	B	
		Serena, Wm. Robert	3B11	12	.216	A	
0	0	Sloat, Dwain Clifford	P	5	.000	Bkn	C
		Smalley, Roy Frederick	SS132	135	.245	B	
		Terwilliger, Willard Wayne	2B34	36	.223	A	
		Verban, Emil Matthew	2B88	98	.289	B	
		Walker, Albert Bluford	C43	56	.244	B	
		Walker, Harry Wm.	OF39	42	+.264	Phil	Cin

WON 64
LOST 89
TG 153

NATIONAL LEAGUE — FINISHED 7th.

1950. — PCT. .418

CHICAGO

FRANK FRANCIS FRISCH

WON	LOST	NAME	POS.	G.	BA	FROM	TO
		Borkowski, Robert Vilarian	OF65	85	.273	A	
		(1B1)					
		Cavarretta, Philip Joseph	1B67	82	.273	B	
		(OF3)					
		Chiti, Harry	C1	3	.333	A	
6	10	Dubiel, Walter John	P	39	.200	B	
		Edwards, Henry Albert	OF29	41	.364	B	
0	1	Hacker, Warren Louis	P	5	.000	B	
12	5	Hiller, Frank Walter	P	38	.114	NYA	
		Jackson, Ransom Joseph	3B27	34	.225	A	
		Jeffcoat, Harold Bently	OF53	66	.235	B	
2	9	Klippstein, John Calvin	P33	35	.333	A	
5	6	Lade, Doyle Marion	P	34	.286	B	C
5	1	Leonard, Emil John (Dutch)	P	35	.063	B	
		Mauro, Carmen Louis	OF49	62	.227	Chi48	
8	13	Minner, Paul Edison	P39	43	.215	Bkn	
		Northey, Ronald James	OF27	53	+.281	xCin	
		Owen, Arnold Malcolm (Mickey)	C	86	.243	B	
		Pafko, Andrew	OF144	146	.304	B	
		Ramazzotti, Robert Louis	2B31	61	.262	B	
		(SS3 3B10)					

WON	LOST	NAME	POS.	G.	BA	FROM	TO
13	20	Rush, Robert Ransom	P39	40	.167	B	
		Sauer, Henry John (1B18)	OF125	145	.274	B	
		Sawatski, Carl Ernest	C32	38	.175	Chi48	
		Scheffing, Robert Boden	C3	12	+.188	B	Cin
10	16	Schmitz, John Albert	P	39	.119	B	
		Serena, Wm. Robert	3B125	127	.239	B	
		Smalley, Roy Frederick	SS	154	.230	B	
		Terwilliger, Willard Wayne	2B126	133	.242	B	
		(1B1 3B1 OF1)					
3	4	Vander Meer, John Samuel	P32	35	.125	Cin	
0	0	Varga, Andrew Wm.	P	1	.000	A	
		Verban, Emil Matthew	2B8	45	+.108	B	Bos
		(SS3 3B1 OF1)					
0	4	Voiselle, Wm. Symmes	P	19	.077	Bos	C
		Walker, Albert Bluford	C62	74	.230	B	
		Ward, Preston Meyer	1B76	80	.253	Bkn48	

WON 62
LOST 92
TG 154

NATIONAL LEAGUE — FINISHED 8th (LAST)

1951. — PCT. .403

CHICAGO

FRANK FRANCIS FRISCH — PHILIP JOSEPH CAVARRETTA

WON	LOST	NAME	POS.	G.	BA	FROM	TO
		Baumholtz, Frank Conrad	OF140	146	.284	Chi49	
		Borkowski, Robert Vilarian	OF25	58	.157	B	
		Burgess, Forrest Harrill	C64	94	.251	Chi49	
		Cavarretta, Philip Joseph MGR.	1B53	89	.311	B	
		Chiti, Harry	C8	9	.355	B	
		Connors, Kevin Joseph	1B57	66	.239	Bkn49	C
		Cusick, John Peter	SS56	65	.177	A	
2	2	Dubiel, Walter John	P	22	.000	B	
		Edwards, Chas. Bruce (1B9)	C28	51	+.234	xBkn	
		Fondy, Dee Virgil	1B44	49	.271	A	
0	0	Hacker, Warren Louis	P	2	.000	B	
2	6	Hatten, Joseph Hilarian	P	23	+.235	xBkn	
		Hermanski, Eugene Victor	OF63	75	+.282	xBkn	
6	12	Hiller, Frank Walter	P	24	.125	B	
		Jackson, Ransom Joseph	3B143	145	.275	B	
		Jeffcoat, Harold Bently	OF87	113	.273	B	
7	4	Kelly, Robert Edward	P	35	.161	A	
6	6	Klippstein, John Calvin	P	35	.108	B	
10	6	Leonard, Emil John (Dutch)	P	41	.000	B	
4	9	Lown, Omar Joseph	P	31	.205	A	
		Mauro, Carmen Louis	OF6	13	.172	B	
		Miksis, Edward Thomas	2B	102	+.266	xBkn	
6	17	Minner, Paul Edison	P33	36	.254	B	
4	10	McLish, Calvin Coolidge	P30	31	.119	Chi49	
		Owen, Arnold Malcolm (Mickey)	C57	58	.184	B	
		Pafko, Andrew	OF48	49	+.264	B	Bkn
		Ramazzotti, Robert Louis	SS51	73	.247	B	
		(2B6 3B1)					

WON	LOST	NAME	POS.	G.	BA	FROM	TO
		Richards, Fred Chas.	1B9	10	.296	A	C
11	12	Rush, Robert Ransom	P	37	.191	B	
		Sauer, Henry John	OF132	141	.263	B	
1	2	Schmitz, John Albert	P	8	+.167	B	Bkn
3	6	Schultz, Robert Duffy	P	17	.138	A	
		Serena, Wm. Robert	3B12	13	.333	B	
		Smalley, Roy Frederick	SS74	79	.231	B	
		Terwilliger, Willard Wayne	2B49	50	+.214	B	Bkn
0	0	Varga, Andrew Wm.	P	2	.000	B	C
		Walker, Albert Bluford	C31	37	+.234	B	Bkn

WON 77 | NATIONAL LEAGUE | FINISHED 5th.
LOST 77
TG 154 | 1952. | PCT. .500

CHICAGO

PHILIP JOSEPH CAVARRETTA

WON	LOST	NAME	POS.	G.	BA	FROM	TO
		Addis, Robert Gordon	OF79	93	.295	Bos	
		Atwell, Maurice Dailey	C101	107	.290	A	
		Baumholtz, Frank Conrad	OF101	103	.325	B	
		Brinkopf, Leon Clarence	SS6	9	.182	A	C
		Brown, Thomas Michael (1B5 2B10)	SS39	61	+.320	xPhil	
		Cavarretta, Philip Joseph MGR.	1B13	41	.238	B	
		Chiti, Harry	C	32	.274	B	C
0	0	Dubiel, Walter John	P	1	.000	B	C
		Edwards, Chas. Bruce (2B1)	C22	50	.245	B	
0	0	Fear, Luvern Carl	P	4	.000	A	C
		Fondy, Dee Virgil	1B143	145	.300	B	
15	9	Hacker, Warren Louis	P33	34	.120	B	
		Hardin, Wm. Edgar (2B1)	SS2	3	.143	A	C
4	4	Hatten, Joseph Hilarian	P13	17	.067	B	C
		Hermanski, Eugene Victor	OF76	99	.255	B	
0	0	Howe, Calvin Earl	P	1	.000	A	C
		Jackson, Ransom Joseph (OF1)	3B104	116	.232	B	
		Jeffcoat, Harold Bently	OF95	102	.219	B	
4	9	Kelly, Robert Edward	P	31	.216	B	
9	14	Klippstein, John Calvin	P	41	.175	B	
2	2	Leonard, Emil John (Dutch)	P	45	.200	B	
4	11	Lown, Omar Joseph	P	33	.140	B	
0	0	Manville, Richard Wesley	P	11	.500	Bos50	C
		Midsis, Edward Thomas (SS40)	2B54	93	.232	B	
14	9	Minner, Paul Edison	P28	29	.234	B	
		Northey, Ronald James		1	.000	Chi50	C
		Pramesa, John Steven	C17	22	.283	Cin	C
		Ramazzotti, Robert Louis	2B	50	.284	B	
2	3	Ramsdell, James Willard	P	19	.056	Cin	C
17	13	Rush, Robert Ransom	P	34	.292	B	
		Sauer, Henry John	OF	151	.270	B	

WON	LOST	NAME	POS.	G.	BA	FROM	TO
6	3	Schultz, Robert Duffy	P	29	.222	B	
		Serena, Wm. Robert (2B49)	3B58	122	.274	B	
		Smalley, Roy Frederick	SS82	87	.222	B	
		Usher, Robert Royce		1	.000	Cin	

WON 65 | NATIONAL LEAGUE | FINISHED 7th.
LOST 89
TG 154 | 1953. | PCT. .422

CHICAGO

PHILIP JOSEPH CAVARRETTA

WON	LOST	NAME	POS.	G.	BA	FROM	TO
		Addis, Robert Gordon	OF3	10	+.167	B	Pitt
		Atwell, Maurice Dailey	C	24	+.230	B	Pitt
0	0	Baczewski, Frederick John	P	9	+.500	A	Cin
		Baker, Eugene Walter	2B6	7	.227	A	
		Banks, Ernest	SS	10	.314	A	
		Baumholtz, Frank Conrad	OF130	133	.306	B	
		Brown, Thomas Michael (OF6)	SS25	65	.196	B	C
		Cavarretta, Philip Joseph MGR.		27	.286	B	
4	5	Church, Emory Nicholas	P	27	+.212	xCin	
0	1	Elston, Donald Ray	P	2	.000	A	
		Fondy, Dee Virgil	1B149	150	.309	B	
		Garagiola, Joseph Henry	C68	74	+.272	xPitt	
12	19	Hacker, Warren Louis	P39	42	.218	B	
		Hermanski, Eugene Victor	OF13	18	+.150	B	Pitt
		Jackson, Ransom Joseph	3B133	139	.285	B	
		Jeffcoat, Harold Bently	OF100	106	.235	B	
0	2	Jones, Sheldon Leslie	P	22	.000	Bos	C
0	1	Kelly, Robert Edward	P	14	+.000	B	Cin
		Kiner, Ralph McPherran	OF116	117	+.283	xPitt	
10	11	Klippstein, John Calvin	P	48	.155	B	
2	3	Leonard, Emil John	P	45	.300	B	C
8	7	Lown, Omar Joseph	P	49	.125	B	
		Metkovich, George Michael (1B7)	OF38	61	+.234	xPitt	
		Miksis, Edward Thomas (SS53)	2B92	142	.251	B	
12	15	Minner, Paul Edison	P	31	.221	B	
0	0	Moisan, Wm. Joseph	P	3	.000	A	C
		McCullough, Clyde Edward	C73	77	.258	Pitt	
5	6	Pollet, Howard Joseph	P	25	+.129	xPitt	
		Ramazzotti, Robert Louis	2B18	26	.154	B	C
9	14	Rush, Robert Ransom	P	29	.111	B	
		Sauer, Henry John	OF105	108	.263	B	
		Sawatski, Carl Ernest	C15	43	.220	Chi50	
		Schramka, Paul Edward	OF1	2	.000	A	C
0	2	Schultz, Robert Duffy	P	7	+.000	B	Pitt
		Serena, Wm. Robert (3B28)	2B49	93	.251	B	
1	2	Simpson, Thomas Leo	P	30	.250	A	C
		Smalley, Roy Frederick	SS77	82	.249	B	
		Talbot, Robert Dale	OF7	8	.333	A	
		Ward, Preston Meyer (1B7)	OF27	33	+.230	Chi50	Pitt
2	1	Willis, James Gladden	P	13	.000	A	

WON 64 / LOST 90 / TG 154 — NATIONAL LEAGUE — FINISHED 7th.

1954. — PCT. .416

CHICAGO

STANLEY CAMFIELD HACK

WON	LOST	NAME	POS.	G.	BA	FROM	TO
		Baker, Eugene Walter	2B134	135	.275	B	
		Banks, Ernest	SS	154	.275	B	
		Baumholtz, Frank Conrad	OF71	90	.297	B	
		Bilko, Stephen Thomas	1B22	47	+.239	xStL	
1	0	Brosnan, James Patrick	P	18	.125	A	
1	3	Church, Emory Nicholas	P7	8	.000	B	
3	8	Cole, David Bruce	P18	19	.214	Milw.	
		Cooper, Wm. Walter	C48	57	+.310	xPitt	
11	7	Davis, James Bennett	P	46	.063	A	
		Edwards, Chas. Bruce		4	.000	Chi52	
		Fanning, Wm. James	C	11	.184	A	
		Fondy Dee Virgil	1B138	141	.285	B	
		Garagiola, Joseph Henry	C55	63	+.281	B	N.Y.
6	13	Hacker, Warren Louis	P39	43	.236	B	
		Jackson, Ransom Joseph	3B124	126	.273	B	
5	6	Jeffcoat, Harold Bently (OF3)	P43	56	.258	B	
		Kiner, Ralph McPherran	OF	147	.285	B	
		Kitsos, Christopher Anestos	SS	1	.000	A	C
4	11	Klippstein, John Calvin	P	36	.133	B	
0	0	Lary, Alfred Allen	P1	2	.500	A	
0	2	Lown, Omar Joseph	P15	16	.000	B	
		Marquez, Luis Angel	OF14	17	+.083	Bos51	Pitt
		Miksis, Edward Thomas (3B2 OF1)	2B21	38	.202	B	
11	11	Minner, Paul Edison	P32	33	.171	B	
		Morgan, Vernon Thomas	3B15	24	.234	A	
		McCullough, Clyde Edward (3B3)	C26	31	.259	B	
8	10	Pollet, Howard Joseph	P	20	.277	B	
0	1	Pyecha, John Nicholas	P	1	.000	A	C
		Rice, Harold Housten	OF24	51	+.153	xPitt	C
		Robertson, Donald Alexander	OF6	14	.000	A	C
13	15	Rush, Robert Ransom	P	33	.277	B	
		Sauer, Henry John	OF141	142	.288	B	
		Serena, Wm. Robert (2B2)	3B12	41	.159	B	C
		Talbot, Robert Dale	OF111	114	.241	B	C
		Tappe, Elvin Walter	C	46	.185	A	
1	2	Tremel, Wm. Leonard	P	33	.250	A	
0	1	Willis, James Gladden	P	14	.000	B	C
0	0	Zick, Robert George	P8	10	.250	A	C

WON 72 / LOST 81 / TG 153 — NATIONAL LEAGUE — FINISHED 6th.

1955. — PCT. .471

CHICAGO

STANLEY CAMFIELD HACK

WON	LOST	NAME	POS.	G.	BA	FROM	TO
0	1	Amor, Vicente Alvarez	P	4	.000	A	
0	1	Andre, John Edward	P	22	.111	A	C
		Baker, Eugene Walter	2B	154	.268	B	
		Banks, Ernest	SS	154	.295	B	
		Baumholtz, Frank Conrad	OF63	105	.289	B	
		Bolger, James Cyril	OF51	64	.206	Cin	
		Chiti, Harry	C	113	.231	Chi52	
0	0	Church, Emory Nicholas	P2	3	.000	B	C
0	0	Cohen, Hyman	P	7	.000	A	C
		Cooper, Wm. Walker	C31	54	.279	B	
7	11	Davis, James Bennett	P	42	.027	B	
		Fanning, Wm. James	C	5	.000	B	
		Fondy, Dee Virgil	1B147	150	.265	B	
		Friend, Owen Lacey (SS1)	3B2	6	.100	xBosA	
11	15	Hacker, Warren Louis	P	35	.250	B	
0	0	Hillman, Darius Dutton	P25	26	.100	A	
		Jackson, Ransom Joseph	3B134	138	.265	B	
8	6	Jeffcoat, Harold Bently	P50	52	.174	B	
14	20	Jones, Samuel	P	36	.182	ClevA52	
0	0	Kaiser, Clyde Donald	P	11	.000	A	
		King, James Hubert	OF93	113	.256	A	
		Lary, Alfred Allen		4	.000	B	
		Merriman, Lloyd Archer	OF47	72	.214	xChiA	C
		Miksis, Edward Thomas (3B18)	OF111	131	.235	B	
9	9	Minner, Paul Edison	P	22	.232	B	
		Morgan, Vernon Thomas	3B2	7	.143	B	C
		McCullough, Clyde Edward	C37	44	.198	B	
3	4	Perkowski, Harry Walter	P25	26	.154	Cin	C
4	3	Pollet, Howard Joseph	P	24	.400	B	
13	11	Rush, Robert Ransom	P	33	.110	B	
		Sauer, Henry John	OF68	79	.211	B	
		Speake, Robert Chas. (1B8)	OF55	95	.218	A	
		Tappe, Elvin Walter	C	2	.000	B	
		Tappe, Theodore Nash	OF15	23	.260	Cin51	C
0	0	Thorpe, Robert Joseph	P	2	.000	A	C
3	0	Tremel, Wm. Leonard	P	23	.286	B	
		Wade, Galeard Lee	OF	9	.182	A	

WON 60 / LOST 94 / TG 154 — NATIONAL LEAGUE — FINISHED 8th (LAST)

1956. — PCT. .390

CHICAGO

STANLEY CAMFIELD HACK

WON	LOST	NAME	POS.	G.	BA	FROM	TO
		Baker, Eugene Walter	2B	140	.258	B	
		Banks, Ernest	SS	139	.297	B	
0	0	Briggs, John Tift	P	3	.000	A	
5	9	Brosnan, James Patrick	P	30	.182	Chi54	

WON	LOST	NAME	POS.	G.	BA	FROM	TO
		Chiti, Harry	C67	72	.212	B	
5	7	Davis, James Bennett	P	46	.179	B	
2	4	Drabowsky, Myron Walter	P	9	.250	A	
		Drake, Solomon Louis	OF53	65	.256	A	
		Fanning, Wm. James	C	1	.250	B	
		Fondy, Dee Virgil	1B133	137	.269	B	
		Friend, Owen Lacey		2	.000	B	C
3	13	Hacker, Warren Louis	P	34	.148	B	
0	2	Hillman, Darius Dutton	P	2	.000	B	
		Hoak, Donald Albert	3B110	121	.215	Bkn	
1	3	Hughes, James Robert	P	25	+.286	xBkn	
		Irvin, Monford Merrill	OF96	111	.271	N.Y.	C
9	14	Jones, Samuel	P	33	.175	B	
4	9	Kaiser, Clyde Donald	P	27	.043	B	
		Kellert, Frank Wm.	1B27	71	.186	Bkn	C
		Kindall, Gerald Donald	SS18	32	.164	A	
		King, James Hubert	OF82	118	.249	B	
		Landrith, Hobert Neal	C99	111	.221	Cin	
9	8	Lown, Omar Joseph	P	61	.217	Chi54	
1	6	Meyer, Russell Chas.	P	20	+.083	Bkn	Cin
		Miksis, Edward Thomas (2B19 SS2 OF33)	3B48	114	.239	B	
2	5	Minner, Paul Edison	P	10	.250	B	C
		Moryn, Walter Joseph	OF141	147	.285	Bkn	
		Myers, Richard		4	.000	A	C
		McCullough, Clyde Edward	C7	14	.211	B	C
0	0	Piktuzis, George Richard	P	2	.000	A	C
13	10	Rush, Robert Ransom	P	32	.098	B	
		Tappe, Elvin Walter	C	3	.000	B	
0	0	Tremel, Wm. Leonard	P	1	.000	B	C
6	4	Valentinetti, Vito John	P	42	.100	ChiA54	
		Wade, Galeard Lee	OF3	10	.000	B	C
		Whisenant, Thomas Peter	OF93	103	.239	StL	
		Winceniak, Edward Joseph (2B1)	3B4	15	.118	A	

WON 62
LOST 92
TG 154

NATIONAL LEAGUE

1957.

FINISHED 7th.
(TIED WITH PITTSBURGH)
PCT. .403

CHICAGO

ROBERT BODEN SCHEFFING

WON	LOST	NAME	POS.	G.	BA	FROM	TO
		Adams, Robert Henry (2B1)	3B47	60	.251	BaltA	
0	1	Anderson, Robert Carl	P	8	.000	A	
		Baker, Eugene Walter	3B	12	+.250	B	Pitt
		Banks, Ernest (3B58)	SS100	156	.285	B	
		Bolger, James Cyril (3B3)	OF63	112	.275	Chi55	
0	1	Briggs, John Tift	P	3	.000	B	
5	5	Brosnan, James Patrick	P	41	.250	B	
1	1	Collum, Jack Dean	P	9	+.000	StL	Bkn
		Del Greco, Robert George	OF16	20	.200	StL	NYA
13	15	Drabowsky, Myron Walter	P	36	.183	B	
15	11	Drott, Richard Fred	P	38	.100	A	
6	7	Elston, Donald Ray	P	39	+.108	xBkn	
		Ernaga, Frank John	OF10	20	.314	A	
		Fanning, Wm. James	C35	47	.180	B	C
		Fondy, Dee Virgil	1B	11	+.314	B	Pitt
		Goryl, John Albert	3B	9	.211	A	
		Haas, George Edwin	OF4	14	.208	A	
6	11	Hillman, Darius Dutton	P32	36	.000	B	
0	0	Hobbie, Glen Frederick	P	2	.000	A	
2	6	Kaiser, Clyde Donald	P	20	.105	B	C
		Kindall, Gerald Donald (SS9 3B19)	2B28	72	.160	B	
		Lennon, Robert Albert	OF4	9	.143	N.Y.	
2	3	Littlefield, Richard Bernard	P	48	.182	N.Y.	
		Littrell, Jack Napier (2B6 3B5)	SS47	61	.190	KCA55	C
		Long, Richard Dale	1B104	123	+.305	xPitt	
5	7	Lown, Omar Joseph	P	67	.200	B	
		Massa, Gordon Richard	C	6	.467	A	
0	0	Mayer, Edwin David	P	3	.500	A	
		Mickelson, Edward Allen	1B2	6	.000	StLA53	C
		Morgan, Robert Morris (3B12)	2B116	125	+.207	xPhil	
		Moryn, Walter Joseph	OF147	149	.289	B	
		Neeman, Calvin Amandus	C118	122	.258	A	
1	7	Poholsky, Thomas George	P	28	.105	StL	C
6	16	Rush, Robert Ransom	P	31	.203	B	
		Silvera, Chas. Anthony Ryan	C	26	.208	NYA	C
0	1	Singleton, Bert Elmer	P5	6	.000	WashA50	
		Speake, Robert Chas. (1B39)	OF60	129	.232	Chi55	
		Tanner, Chas. Wm.	OF82	95	+.286	xMil	
0	0	Valentinetti, Vito John	P	9	.000	B	ClevA
		Walls, Ray Lee (3B1)	OF94	117	+.240	xPitt	
		Will, Robert Lee	OF30	70	.223	A	
		Winceniak, Edward Joseph (2B3 3B4)	SS5	17	.240	B	C
		Wise, Kendall Cole (SS5)	2B31	43	.179	A	
		Woods, James Jerome		2	.000	A	

WON 72
LOST 82
TG 154

NATIONAL LEAGUE

1958

FINISHED 5th.
(TIED WITH ST. LOUIS)
PCT. .468

CHICAGO

ROBERT BODEN SCHEFFING

WON	LOST	NAME	POS.	G.	BA	FROM	TO
		Adams, Robert Henry (2B7 3B9)	1B11	62	.281	B	
3	3	Anderson, Robert Carl	P	17	.118	B	
		Banks, Ernest	SS	154	.313	B	
		Bolger, James Cyril	OF37	84	.225	B	
5	5	Briggs, John Tift	P	20	.257	B	
3	4	Brosnan, James Patrick	P	8	+.105	B	StL

WON	LOST	NAME	POS.	G.	BA	FROM	TO
3	0	Buzhardt, John Wm.	P	6	.125	A	
		Dark, Alvin Ralph	3B111	114	+.295	xStL	
9	11	Drabowsky, Myron Walter	P	22	.156	B	
7	11	Drott, Richard Fred	P	39	.273	B	
0	1	Ellsworth, Richard Clark	P	1	.000	A	
9	8	Elston, Donald Ray	P	69	.357	B	
		Ernaga, Frank John		9	.125	B	C
1	1	Fodge, Eugene Arlen	P	16	.000	A	C
0	1	Freeman, Hershell Baskin	P	9	+.000	xCin	C
		Gabler, Wm. Louis		3	.000	A	C
		Goryl, John Albert (2B35)	3B44	83	.242	B	
5	4	Henry, Wm. Rodman	P	44	.235	BosA55	
4	8	Hillman, Darius Dutton	P31	32	.146	B	
10	6	Hobbie, Glen Frederick	P	55	.146	B	
		Jackson, Louis Clarence	OF12	24	.171	A	
		Johnson, Richard Allan		8	.000	A	C
		Kindall, Gerald Donald	2B	3	.167	B	
		King, Chas. Gilbert	OF7	8	.250	DetA56	
		Long, Richard Dale (C2)	1B137	142	.271	B	
0	0	Lown, Omar Joseph	P	4	+.000	B	Cin
		Marshall, Rufus James (OF11)	1B15	26	.272	xBaltA	
		Massa, Gordon Richard		2	.000	B	C
2	2	Mayer, Edwin David	P	19	.200	B	C
		Morgan, Robert Morris		1	.000	B	C
		Moryn, Walter Joseph	OF141	143	.264	B	
		Neeman, Calvin Amandus	C71	76	.259	B	
0	4	Nichols, Dolan Levon	P	24	.000	A	C
7	10	Phillips, Wm. Taylor	P	39	.056	Mil	
0	0	Rodriguez, Fernando Pedro	P	7	.000	A	
1	0	Singleton, Bert Elmer	P	2	.000	B	
		Smith, Paul Leslie	1B4	18	+.150	xPitt	C
3	3	Solis, Marcelino	P	15	.250	A	C
		Tanner, Chas. Wm.	OF15	73	.262	B	
		Tappe, Elvin Walter	C16	17	.214	Chi56	
		Taylor, Antonio Sanchez (3B1)	2B137	140	.235	A	
		Taylor, Samuel Douglas	C87	96	.259	A	
		Thacker, Morris Benton	C9	11	.250	A	
		Thomson, Robert Brown (3B4)	OF148	152	.283	N.Y.	
		Walls, Ray Lee	OF132	136	.304	B	
		Will, Robert Lee	OF1	6	.250	B	

WON 74 NATIONAL LEAGUE FINISHED 5th.
LOST 80 (TIED WITH CINCINNATI)
TG 154 1959. PCT. .481

CHICAGO

ROBERT BODEN SCHEFFING

WON	LOST	NAME	POS.	G.	BA	FROM	TO
		Adams, Robert Henry	1B1	3	.000	B	C
		Altman, George Lee	OF121	135	.245	A	
12	13	Anderson, Robert Carl	P	37	.075	B	
		Averill, Earl Douglas (2B2 3B13 OF5)	C32	74	.237	ClevA	

WON	LOST	NAME	POS.	G.	BA	FROM	TO
		Banks, Ernest	SS154	155	.304	B	
4	5	Buzhardt, John Wm.	P	31	.069	B	
5	5	Ceccarelli, Arthur Edward	P	18	.091	BaltA57	
		Dark, Alvin Ralph (1B4 SS1)	3B131	136	.264	B	
1	1	Donnelly, Edward Vincent	P	9	.000	A	C
5	10	Drabowsky, Myron Walter	P	31	.111	B	
1	2	Drott, Richard Fred	P	8	.125	B	
		Eaddy, Donald Johnson	3B1	15	.000	A	C
10	8	Elston, Donald Ray	P	65	.211	B	
		Goryl, John Albert (3B4)	2B11	25	.188	B	
9	8	Henry, Wm. Rodman	P	65	.194	B	
8	11	Hillman, Darius Dutton	P39	42	.150	B	
16	13	Hobbie, Glen Frederick	P	46	.114	B	
		Jackson, Louis Clarence		6	.250	B	C
		Jackson, Ransom Joseph (OF1)	3B22	41	.243	xClevA	C
0	0	Johnson, Benjamin Franklin	P	4	.000	A	
		King, Chas. Gilbert	OF1	7	+.000	B	StL
		Long, Richard Dale	1B85	110	.236	B	
		Marshall, Rufus James (OF8)	1B72	108	.252	B	
0	0	Martin, Morris Webster	P	3	.000	ClevA	C
0	1	Morehead, Seth Marvin	P	11	+.500	xPhil	
		Moryn, Walter Joseph	OF104	117	.234	B	
		Neeman, Calvin Amandus	C38	44	.162	B	
		Noren, Irving Arnold (1B1)	OF40	65	+.321	xStL	
0	2	Phillips, Wm. Taylor	P	7	+.000	B	Phil
0	0	Porterfield, Erwin Coolidge	P	4	+.091	xPitt	Pitt
1	0	Schaffernoth, Joseph Arthur	P	5	.000	A	
		Schult, Arthur Wm. (OF15)	1B23	42	.271	WashA57	
2	1	Singleton, Bert Elmer	P	21	.000	B	C
0	0	Smith, Robert Walkay	P	1	.000	BosA	ClevA
		Taylor, Antonio Sanchez (SS2)	2B149	150	.280	B	
		Taylor, Samuel Douglas	C109	110	.269	B	
		Thomson, Robert Brown	OF116	122	.259	B	
		Walls, Ray Lee	OF119	120	.257	B	
		Williams, Billy Lee	OF10	18	.152	A	

WON 60 NATIONAL LEAGUE FINISHED 7th.
LOST 94
TG 154 1960. PCT. .390

CHICAGO

CHAS. JOHN GRIMM LOUIS BOUDREAU

WON	LOST	NAME	POS.	G.	BA	FROM	TO
		Altman, George Lee (1B21)	OF79	119	.266	B	
9	11	Anderson, Robert Carl	P38	39	.169	B	
		Ashburn, Richie	OF146	151	.291	Phil	
		Averill, Earl Douglas (3B1 OF1)	C34	52	.235	B	ChiA
		Banks, Ernest	SS	156	.271	B	
		Bertell, Richard George	C	5	.133	A	
		Bouchee, Edward Francis	1B80	98	+.237	xPhil	

WON	LOST	NAME	POS.	G.	BA	FROM	TO
0	3	Brewer, James Thomas	P5	6	.167	A	
0	0	Burwell, Richard Matthew	P	3	.333	A	
8	14	Cardwell, Donald Eugene	P31	33	+.203	xPhil	
0	0	Ceccarelli, Arthur Edward	P	7	.000	B	C
3	1	Drabowsky, Myron Walter	P32	33	.000	B	
		Drake, Samuel Harrison (2B2)	3B6	15	.067	A	
0	6	Drott, Richard Fred	P	23	.100	B	
7	13	Ellsworth, Richard Clark	P	31	.042	Chi58	
8	9	Elston, Donald Ray	P	60	.125	B	
3	3	Freeman, Mark Price	P	30	.150	NYA	C
		Gernert, Richard Edward	1B18	52	.250	BosA	DetA
		(OF5)					
0	0	Goetz, John Hardy	P	4	.000	A	C
		Hatton, Grady Edgebert	2B8	28	.342	BaltA56	C
		Hegan, James Edward	C22	24	.209	S.F.	C
		Heist, Alfred Michael	OF33	41	.275	A	
16	20	Hobby, Glen Frederick	P	46	.151	B	
2	1	Johnson, Benjamin Franklin	P	17	.000	B	C
		Johnson, Louis Brown	OF25	34	.206	A	
		Kindall, Gerald Donald (SS2)	2B82	89	.240	Chi58	
		Mathews, Nelson Elmer	OF2	3	.250	A	
		McKnight, James Arthur (OF1)	2B1	3	.333	A	
2	9	Morehead, Seth Marvin	P	45	.138	B	
		Moryn, Walter Joseph	OF30	38	+.294	B	St.L.
		Murphy, Daniel Francis	OF21	31	.120	A	
		Neeman, Calvin Amandus	C	9	+.154	B	Phil
		Noren, Irving Arnold (OF1)	1B1	12	+.091	B	L.A.
		Rice, Delbert W.	C	18	+.231	Mil St.L.	
		Santo, Ronald Edward	3B94	95	.251	A	
2	3	Schaffernoth, Joseph Arthur	P	33	.286	B	
0	0	Schroll, Albert Bringhurst	P	2	1.000	BosA	
		Schult, Arthur Wm. (1B1)	OF4	12	.133	B	C
		Tappe, Elvin Walter	C49	51	.233	Chi58	
		Taylor, Antonio Sanchez	2B	19	+.263	B	Phil
		Taylor, Samuel Douglas	C43	74	.207	B	
		Thacker, Morris Benton	C50	54	.156	Chi58	
		Thomas, Frank Joseph	1B50	135	.238	Cin	
		(3B33 OF49)					
		Will, Robert Lee	OF121	.138	.255	Chi58	
		Williams, Billy Leo	OF	12	.277	B	
0	1	Wright, Melvin James	P	9	.000	StL55	
		Zimmer, Donald Wm.	2B75	132	.258	L.A.	
		(SS5 3B45 OF2)					

WON 64 NATIONAL LEAGUE FINISHED 7th.
LOST 90
TG 154 1961 PCT. .416

CHICAGO

AVITUS BERNARD HIMSL HARRY FRANCIS CRAFT
ELVIN WALTER TAPPE LOUIS FRANK KLEIN

WON	LOST	NAME	POS.	G.	BA	FROM	TO
		Altman, George Lee (1B3)	OF130	138	.303	B	
7	10	Anderson, Robert Carl	P	57	.143	B	
		Ashburn, Richie	OF76	109	.257	B	
		Banks, Ernest	SS104	138	.278	B	
		(1B7 OF23)					
		Barragan, Facundo Anthony	C	10	.214	A	
		Bertell, Richard George	C90	92	.273	B	
		Bouchee, Edward Francis	1B107	112	.248	B	
1	7	Brewer, James Thomas	P	36	.183	B	
		Brock, Louis Clark	OF3	4	.091	A	
0	0	Burwell, Richard Matthew	P	2	.000	B	C
15	14	Cardwell, Donald Eugene	P	40	.105	B	
10	13	Curtis, Jack Patrick	P	31	.167	A	
		Drake, Samuel Harrison	OF1	13	.000	B	
1	4	Drott, Richard Fred	P	35	.273	B	
10	11	Ellsworth, Richard Clark	P	37	.036	B	
6	7	Elston, Donald Ray	P	58	.182	B	
		Freese, George Walter		9	.286	Pitt55	C
		Heist, Alfred Michael	OF99	109	.255	B	
7	13	Hobbie, Glen Frederick	P	36	.167	B	
		Hubbs, Kenneth Douglass	2B8	10	.179	A	
		Kindall, Gerald Donald (SS47)	2B50	96	.242	B	
		Mathews, Nelson Elmer	OF2	3	.111	B	
		McAnany, James	OF1	11	.300	ChiA	
		Morhardt, Meredith Goodwin	1B	7	.278	A	
		Murphy, Daniel Francis	OF	4	.385	B	
		Roach, Melvin Earl (2B7)	1B7	23	+.128	xMilw	
		Rodgers, Kenneth Andre Ian	1B42	73	.266	S.F.	
		(2B1 SS24 OF2)					
		Santo, Ronald Edward	3B153	154	.284	B	
0	4	Schaffernoth, Joseph Arthur	P	21	.000	B	ClevA
7	6	Schultz, George Warren	P	41	.100	DetA59	
		Taylor, Samuel Douglas	C75	89	.238	B	
		Thacker, Morris Benton	C	25	.171	B	
		Thomas, Frank Joseph	OF10	15	+.260	B	Milw
		(1B6)					
		Will, Robert Lee (1B1)	OF30	86	.257	B	
		Williams, Billy Leo	OF135	146	.278	B	
0	1	Wright, Melvin James	P	11	.000	B	C
		Zimmer, Donald Wm.	2B116	128	.252	B	
		(3B5 OF1)					

WON 59 NATIONAL LEAGUE FINISHED 9th.
LOST 103
TG 162 1962. PCT. .364

CHICAGO

ELVIN WALTER TAPPE LOUIS FRANK KLEIN CHAS. METRO

WON	LOST	NAME	POS.	G.	BA	FROM	TO
		Altman, George Lee (1B16)	OF129	147	.318	B	
2	7	Anderson, Robert Carl	P	57	.130	B	
0	1	Balsamo, Anthony Fred	P	18	.200	A	C
		Banks, Ernest (3B3)	1B149	154	.269	B	
		Barragan, Facundo Anthony	C55	58	.201	B	

WON	LOST	NAME	POS.	G.	BA	FROM	TO
		Bertell, Richard George	C76	77	.302	B	
0	1	Brewer, James Thomas	P	6	.000	B	
		Brock, Louis Clark	OF106	123	.263	B	
12	13	Buhl, Robert Ray	P	34	+.000	xMil	
0	0	Burdette, Freddie Thomason	P	8	.000	A	
7	16	Cardwell, Donald Eugene	P	41	.148	B	
0	2	Curtis, Jack Patrick	P	4	+.250	B	Mil
9	20	Ellsworth, Richard Clark	P	37	.113	B	
4	8	Elston, Donald Ray	P	57	.000	B	
2	3	Gerard, David Frederick	P	39	.375	A	C
0	0	Gerberman, George Alois	P	1	.000	A	C
		Grammas, Alexander Peter (2B3)	SS13	23	+.233	xStL	
5	14	Hobbie, Glen Frederick	P	42	.122	B	
		Hubbs, Kenneth Douglass	2B159	160	.260	B	
10	10	Koonce, Calvin Lee	P	35	.094	A	
		Landrum, Donald Leroy	OF59	83	+.282	xStL	
0	1	Lary, Alfred Allen	P15	23	.167	Chi55	C
		Mathews, Nelson Elmer	OF14	15	.306	B	
		McAnany, James		7	.000	B	C
		McKnight, James Arthur (2B2)	OF5	60	.224	Chi60	C
		Morhardt, Meredith Goodwin		18	.125	B	C
		Murphy, Daniel Francis	OF5	14	.200	B	
		Ott, Wm. Joseph	OF7	12	.143	A	C
0	0	Prince, Donald Mark	P	1	.000	A	C
		Robertson, Daryl Berdene (3B1)	SS6	9	.105	A	C
		Rodgers, Kenneth Andre Ian (1B1)	SS133	138	.278	B	
		Santo, Ronald Edward (SS8)	3B157	162	.227	B	
5	5	Schultz, George Warren	P	51	.000	B	
		Smith, Bobby Gene	OF7	13	+.172	xN.Y.	StL
0	1	Steevens, Morris Dale	P	12	.000	A	
		Tappe, Elvin Walter (MGR)	C	26	.208	B	C
		Taylor, Samuel Douglas	C6	7	+.133	B	N.Y.
		Thacker, Morris Benton	C	65	.187	B	
3	1	Toth, Paul Louis	P	6	+.182	xStL	
0	0	Warner, Jack Dyer	P	7	.000	A	
		White, Elder Lafayette (3B1)	SS15	23	.151	A	C
		Will, Robert Lee	OF9	87	.239	B	
		Williams, Billy Leo	OF	159	.298	B	

WON 82 — NATIONAL LEAGUE — FINISHED 7th.
LOST 80
TG 162 — 1963. — PCT. .506

CHICAGO

ROBERT DANIEL KENNEDY

WON	LOST	NAME	POS.	G.	BA	FROM	TO
		Aspromonte, Kenneth Joseph (1B2)	2B7	20	.147	Mil	C
0	1	Baker, Thomas Henry	P	10	.000	A	C
		Banks, Ernest	1B125	130	.227	B	
		Barragan, Facundo Anthony	C	1	.000	B	C
		Bertell, Richard George	C99	100	.233	B	
		Boccabella, John Dominic	1B	24	.189	A	
		Boros, Steven A. (OF11)	1B14	41	.211	DetA	
		Brock, Louis Clark	OF140	148	.258	B	
3	2	Brewer, James Thomas	P	29	.000	B	
11	14	Buhl, Robert Ray	P	37	.108	B	
0	0	Burdette, Freddie Thomason	P	4	.000	B	
		Burke, Leo Patrick (1B4)	2B10	27	+.184	xStL	
		Burton, Ellis Narrington	OF90	93	.230	xClevA	
		Cowan, Billy Rolland	OF10	14	.250	A	
22	10	Ellsworth, Richard Clark	P	37	.096	B	
4	1	Elston, Donald Roy	P	51	.000	B	
		Grammas, Alexander Peter	SS13	16	.185	B	C
7	10	Hobbie, Glen Frederick	P	36	.080	B	
		Hubbs, Kenneth Douglass	2B152	154	.235	B	C
14	18	Jackson, Lawrence Curtis	P	37	.195	StL	
2	6	Koonce, Calvin Lee	P	21	.105	B	
		Landrum, Donald Leroy	OF57	84	.242	B	
0	1	LeMay, Richard Paul	P	9	.000	S.F.	C
		Mathews, Nelson Elmer	OF46	61	.157	B	
13	7	McDaniel, Lyndall Dale	P	57	.091	StL	
0	0	Mudrock, Philip Ray	P	1	.000	A	C
		Ranew, Merritt Thomas (1B9)	C37	78	.338	Hous	
		Rodgers, Kenneth Andre Ian	SS	150	.229	B	
		Santo, Ronald Edward	3B	162	.297	B	
		Schaffer, Jimmie Ronald	C54	57	.239	StL	
1	0	Schultz, George Warren	P	15	+.000	B	StL
		Stewart, James Franklin (2B1)	SS9	13	.297	A	
5	9	Toth, Paul Louis	P	27	.026	B	
0	1	Warner, Jack Dyer	P	8	.250	B	
		Will, Robert Lee	1B1	23	.174	B	C
		Williams, Billy Leo	OF160	161	.286	B	

WON 76 — NATIONAL LEAGUE — FINISHED 8th.
LOST 86
TG 162 — 1964. — PCT. .469

CHICAGO

ROBERT DANIEL KENNEDY

WON	LOST	NAME	POS.	G.	BA	FROM	TO
		Amalfitano, John Joseph (1B1 SS1)	2B86	100	.241	S.F.	
		Banks, Ernest	1B	157	.264	B	
		Bertell, Richard George	C110	112	.238	B	
		Boccabella, John Dominic (OF2)	1B5	9	.391	B	
		Brock, Louis Clark	OF	52	+.251	B	StL
4	7	Broglio, Ernest Gilbert	P	18	+.286	xStL	
15	14	Buhl, Robert Ray	P	36	.096	B	
1	0	Burdette, Freddie Thomason	P	18	1.000	B	C
9	9	Burdette, Selva Lewis	P	28	+.279	xStL	

		Burke, Leo Patrick (C1 1B2 2B5 3B4)	OF18	59	.262	B	
		Burton, Ellis Narrington	OF29	42	.190	B	
		Campbell, Ronald Thomas	2B	26	.272	A	
		Clemens, Douglas Horace	OF40	54	+.279	xStL	
		Cowan, Billy Rolland	OF134	139	.241	B	
14	18	Ellsworth, Richard Clark	P	37	.046	B	
2	5	Elston, Donald Ray	P	48	.167	B	C
0	1	Flavin, John Thomas	P	5	.000	A	C
		Gabrielson, Leonard Gary (1B8)	OF68	89	+.246	xMil	
0	0	Gregory, Grover Leroy	P11	19	.077	A	C
0	3	Hobbie, Glen Frederick	P	8	+.000	B	StL
24	11	Jackson, Lawrence Curtis	P	40	.175	B	
1	0	Jaeckel, Paul Henry	P	4	.000	A	C
		Kessinger, Donald Eulon	SS	4	.167	A	
3	0	Koonce, Calvin Lee	P	6	.000	B	
		Landrum, Donald Leroy	OF1	11	.000	B	
1	7	McDaniel, Lyndall Dale	P	63	.125	B	
0	4	Norman, Fred Hubert	P	8	.091	KCA	
		Ott, Wm. Joseph	OF10	20	.179	Chic62	C
		Popovich, Paul Edward		1	1.000	A	
		Ranew, Merritt Thomas	C9	16	+.091	B	Mil
		Rogers, Kenneth Andre Ian	SS126	129	.239	B	
		Roznovsky, Victor Joseph	C26	35	.197	A	
		Santo, Ronald Edward	3B	161	.313	B	
		Schaffer, Jimmie Ronald	C43	54	.205	B	
0	0	Schurr, Wayne Allen	P	26	.000	A	C
0	0	Scott, Richard Lewis	P	3	.000	L.A.	C
0	1	Shantz, Robert Clayton	P	20	+.000	xStL	Phil
2	4	Slaughter, Sterling E.	P	20	.083	A	C
0	0	Spring, Jack Russell	P	7	+.000	LAA	St.L
		Stewart, James Franklin (SS45 3B1 OF4)	2B61	132	.253	B	
0	2	Toth, Paul Louis	P	4	.333	B	C
0	0	Warner, Jack Dyer	P	7	.000	B	
		Williams, Billy Leo	OF	162	.312	B	

CLUB RECORD

NATIONAL LEAGUE

CINCINNATI

YEAR	TG	WON	LOST	PCT.	FINISHED	MANAGER
1876	65	9	56	.135	8(Last)	Chas. Harvey Gould
1877	57	15	42	.263	6(Last)	Lipman E. Pike Robert Addy
1878	60	37	23	.617	2	Calvin Alexander McVey
1879	74	38	36	.514	5	Jas. Laurie White Calvin Alexander McVey
1880	80	21	59	.263	8(Last)	John Edgar Clapp
1881-1889		OUT OF LEAGUE				
1890	133	78	55	.586	4	Thomas Joseph Loftus
1891	137	56	81	.409	7	Thomas Joseph Loftus
1892	150	82	68	.547	5	Chas. Albert Comiskey
1893	128	65	63	.508	x6(Bkn)	Chas. Albert Comiskey
1894	129	54	75	.419	10	Chas. Albert Comiskey
1895	130	66	64	.508	8	Wm. Ewing
1896	127	77	50	.606	3	Wm. Ewing
1897	132	76	56	.576	4	Wm. Ewing
1898	152	92	60	.605	3	Wm. Ewing
1899	150	83	67	.553	6	Wm. Ewing
1900	139	62	77	.446	7	Robert Gilman Allen
1901	139	52	87	.374	8(Last)	John Alexander McPhee
1902	140	70	70	.500	4	John Alexander McPhee Frank Carter Bancroft Joseph James Kelley
1903	139	74	65	.532	4	Joseph James Kelley
1904	153	88	65	.575	3	Joseph James Kelley
1905	153	79	74	.516	5	Joseph James Kelley
1906	151	64	87	.424	6	Edward Hugh Hanlon
1907	153	66	87	.431	6	Edward Hugh Hanlon
1908	154	73	81	.474	5	John Henry Ganzel
1909	153	77	76	.504	4	Clark Calvin Griffith
1910	154	75	79	.487	5	Clark Calvin Griffith
1911	153	70	83	.458	6	Clark Calvin Griffith
1912	153	75	78	.490	4	Henry F. O'Day
1913	153	64	89	.418	7	Joseph Bert Tinker
1914	154	60	94	.390	8(Last)	Chas. Lincoln Herzog
1915	154	71	83	.461	7	Chas. Lincoln Herzog
1916	153	60	93	.392	x7(StL)	Chas. Lincoln Herzog Ivy Brown Wingo Christopher Mathewson
1917	154	78	76	.506	4	Christopher Mathewson
1918	128	68	60	.531	3	Christopher Mathewson Henry Knight Groh
1919	140	96	44	.686	1	Patrick Joseph Moran
1920	153	82	71	.536	3	Patrick Joseph Moran
1921	153	70	83	.458	6	Patrick Joseph Moran
1922	154	86	68	.558	2	Patrick Joseph Moran
1923	154	91	63	.591	2	Patrick Joseph Moran
1924	153	83	70	.542	4	John Calhoun Hendricks
1925	153	80	73	.523	3	John Calhoun Hendricks
1926	154	87	67	.565	2	John Calhoun Hendricks

1927	153	75	78	.490	5	John Calhoun Hendricks
1928	152	78	74	.513	5	John Calhoun Hendricks
1929	154	66	88	.429	7	John Calhoun Hendricks
1930	154	59	95	.383	7	Daniel Philip Howley
1931	154	58	96	.377	8(Last)	Daniel Philip Howley
1932	154	60	94	.390	8(Last)	Daniel Philip Howley
1933	152	58	94	.382	8(Last)	Owen Joseph Bush
1934	151	52	99	.344	8(Last)	Robert Arthur O'Farrell
						Burton Edwin Shotton
						Chas. Walter Dressen
1935	153	68	85	.444	6	Chas. Walter Dressen
1936	154	74	80	.481	5	Chas. Walter Dressen
1937	154	56	98	.364	8(Last)	Chas. Walter Dressen
						Rhoderick John Wallace
1938	150	82	68	.547	4	Wm. Boyd McKechnie
1939	154	97	57	.630	1	Wm. Boyd McKechnie
1940	153	100	53	.654	1	Wm. Boyd McKechnie
1941	154	88	66	.571	3	Wm. Boyd McKechnie
1942	152	76	76	.500	4	Wm. Boyd MeKechnie
1943	154	87	67	.565	2	Wm. Boyd McKechnie
1944	154	89	65	.578	3	Wm. Boyd McKechnie
1945	154	61	93	.396	7	Wm. Boyd McKechnie
1946	154	67	87	.435	6	Wm. Boyd McKechnie
						Henry Morgan Gowdy
1947	154	73	81	.474	5	John Henry Neun
1948	153	64	89	.418	7	John Henry Neun
						Wm. Henry Walters
1949	154	62	92	.403	7	Wm. Henry Walters
						James Luther Sewell
1950	153	66	87	.431	6	James Luther Sewell
1951	154	68	86	.442	6	James Luther Sewell
1952	154	69	85	.448	6	James Luther Sewell
						Rogers Hornsby
1953	154	68	86	.442	6	Rogers Hornsby
						Colonel Buster Mills
1954	154	74	80	.481	5	George Robert Tebbetts
1955	154	75	79	.487	5	George Robert Tebbetts
1956	154	91	63	.591	3	George Robert Tebbetts
1957	154	80	74	.519	4	George Robert Tebbetts
1958	154	76	78	.494	4	George Robert Tebbetts
						James Joseph Dykes
1959	154	74	80	.481	x5(Chic)	Edward Mayo Smith
						Frederick Charles Hutchinson
1960	154	67	87	.435	6	Frederick Charles Hutchinson
1961	154	93	61	.604	1	Frederick Charles Hutchinson
1962	162	98	64	.605	3	Frederick Charles Hutchinson
1963	162	86	76	.531	5	Frederick Charles Hutchinson
1964	162	92	70	.568	x2(Phil)	Frederick Charles Hutchinson
						Richard Allan Sisler

YEAR	TG	WON	LOST	TIED	PCT.	FINISHED	MANAGER
1965	162	89	73	0	.549	4	RICHARD ALLAN SISLER
1966	160	76	84	0	.475	7	DONALD HENRY HEFFNER
							JAMES DAVID BRISTOL
1967	162	87	75	0	.537	4	JAMES DAVID BRISTOL
1968	163	83	79	1	.512	4	JAMES DAVID BRISTOL
1969	163	89	73	1	.549	3W	JAMES DAVID BRISTOL
1970	162	102	60	0	.630	1W (WP)	GEORGE LEE ANDERSON
1971	162	79	83	0	.488	X4W (HOU)	GEORGE LEE ANDERSON
1972	154	95	59	0	.617	1W (WP)	GEORGE LEE ANDERSON

WON 9
LOST 56
TG 65

NATIONAL LEAGUE

1876.

FINISHED 8th (LAST)

PCT. .135

CINCINNATI

CHAS. HARVEY GOULD

WON	LOST	NAME	POS.	G.	BA	FROM	TO
0	1	Booth, Amos Smith (P1 SS22 3B22)	C23	63	.253	A	
0	0	Clack, Robert S. (P1 1B4 2B8 3B2)	OF16	31	.154	A	C
4	26	Dean, Chas. Wilson (Dora) (SS1 OF4)	P30	34	.257	A	C
		Field, Samuel J. (2B2)	C2	4	.000	A	C
4	20	Fisher, Wm. Chas. (Cherokee) (1B1 SS1 OF10)	P25	35	.248	A	
		Foley, Wm. B. (C17)	3B43	58	.226	A	
0	0	Gould, Chas Harvey MGR. (P1)	1B61	61	.246	A	
		Jones, Chas. Wesley	OF	64	.279	A	
		Kessler, Henry (3B1 OF17)	SS44	59	.251	A	
0	1	Pearson, David P. (P1 C26)	OF31	56	.235	A	C
		Snyder, Emanuel Sebastian	OF	55	.150	A	
		Sweazy, Chas. James (OF1)	2B55	56	.203	A	
1	8	Williams, Elisha Alphonso (Dale)	P	9	.200	A	C

WON 15
LOST 42
TG 57

NATIONAL LEAGUE

1877.

FINISHED 6th. (LAST)

PCT. .263

CINCINNATI

LIPMAN E. PIKE ROBERT EDWARD ADDY

WON	LOST	NAME	POS.	G.	BA	FROM	TO
		Addy, Robert Edward MGR.	OF	57	.278	Chi	C
1	7	Booth, Amos Smith (C11 2B10 SS12 3B3 OF1)	P12	43	.170	B	
5	14	Cummings, Wm. Arthur (OF3)	P19	19	.200	Hart	C
		Cuthbert, Edgar Edward (Ned)	OF	12	.175	StL	
		Foley, Wm. B.	3B	56	.188	B	
		Gould, Chas. Harvey (OF1)	1B24	24	.275	B	C
		Hallinan, James H.	2B	16	+.370	Mut	Chi
		Hastings, Winfield Scott (OF1)	C20	20	.141	Lvlle	C
		Hicks, Nathaniel Woodhull (Nat)	C	8	.187	Mut	C
		Jones, Chas. Wesley (1B10)	OF10	20	+.329	B	Chi
			OF	35	.330	(& return)	
		Kessler, Henry (1B1)	C5	6	.100	B	C
0	4	Manning, John E. (P9 1B17 2B2 OF12)	SS27	58	.315	Bos	
3	12	Mathews, Robert T. (SS1 OF1)	P15	15	.169	Mut	
		Meyerle, Levi Samuel (2B12 OF1)	SS17	27	.327	Ath	
		Miller, George	C	11	.162	A	
6	5	Mitchell, Robert McKasha (OF2)	P12	13	.204	A	
		Pike, Lipman E. MGR. (2B22 SS2)	OF38	58	.297	StL	
		Redmond, Wm. T.	SS	3	.250	A	
		Ryan, John Joseph	OF	6	.154	Lvlle	C
		Smith, Chas. Henry (2B1 OF1)	C7	9	+.281	xChi	C
		Sullivan, John Frank (Chubb)	1B	8	.250	A	

WON 37
LOST 23
TG 60

NATIONAL LEAGUE

1878.

FINISHED 2nd.

PCT. .617

CINCINNATI

CALVIN ALEXANDER McVEY

WON	LOST	NAME	POS.	G.	BA	FROM	TO
		Dickerson, Lewis Pessano	OF	30	.309	A	
		Geer, Wm. Henry Harrison (2B2)	SS60	62	.215	A	
		Gerhardt, Joseph John	2B	61	.303	Lvlle	
		Jones, Chas. Wesley	OF	62	.297	B	
		Kelly, Michael Joseph (King) (C17 3B2)	OF46	61	.281	A	
7	2	Mitchell, Robert McKasha (SS2 OF2)	P9	14	.250	B	
1	0	#McVey, Calvin Alexander MGR.	3B61	62	.293	Chi	
		Pike, Lipman E.	OF	28	+.326	B	Prov
		Sullivan, John Frank (Chubb)	1B	62	.255	B	
		White, James Laurie (Deacon) (3B1 OF16)	C44	60	.313	Bos	
29	21	White, Wm. Henry (OF1)	P51	51	.132	Bos	

#McVey also pitched in 2 games and caught 3.

WON 38
LOST 36
TG 74

NATIONAL LEAGUE

1879.

FINISHED 5th.

PCT. .514

CINCINNATI

JAMES LAURIE WHITE CALVIN ALEXANDER McVEY

WON	LOST	NAME	POS.	G.	BA	FROM	TO
		Barnes, Roscoe Conkling (Ross) (2B15)	SS61	76	.256	Chi77	
		Burke, Michael E. (3B5 OF5)	SS19	29	.222	A	C

WON	LOST	NAME	POS.	G.	BA	FROM	TO
		Dickerson, Lewis Pessano	OF	80	.294	B	
		Foley, Wm. B. (2B4 OF25)	3B27	55	.213	Mil	
		Gerhardt, Joseph John (1B8 3B15)	2B56	78	.199	B	
		Hotaling, Peter James (C8 2B6 3B6)	OF65	80	.278	A	
		Kelly, Michael Joseph (King) (C21 OF31)	3B32	77	.348	B	
		Magner, Wm. John	OF	1	.000	A	C
0	2	McVey, Calvin Alexander MGR. (P3 C1 3B1 OF7)	1B71	80	.299	B	C
0	1	Neagle, John Henry (OF2)	P2	3	.167	A	
0	2	Purcell, Wm. Aloysius (Blondy) (P2)	OF10	12	+.231	xSyr.	
0	1	Wheeler, Harry Eugene (P1)	OF1	1	.000	Prov.	
		White, James Laurie (Deacon) MGR. (1B3 OF21)	C59	77	.330	B	
38	30	White, Wm. Henry	P	75	.137	B	
		Schafer, Harry C.	SS	1	.000	Bos	C

WON 21 — LOST 59 — TG 80

NATIONAL LEAGUE — 1880.

FINISHED 8th (LAST) — PCT. .263

CINCINNATI

JOHN EDGAR CLAPP

WON	LOST	NAME	POS.	G.	BA	FROM	TO
		Booth, Amos Smith	OF	1	.000	Cin77	
		Carpenter, Warren Wm. (Hick) (1B9)	3B67	76	.243	Syr	
		Clapp, John Edgar MGR. (OF8)	C74	79	.280	Buff	
		Leonard, Andrew Jackson (3B9 OF9)	SS24	33	.210	Bos78	
		Manning, John E. (1B1)	OF48	48	.216	Bos78	
		Mansell, Michael R.	OF	53	.192	Syr	
3	16	Purcell, Wm. Aloysius (Blondy) (P26 SS1)	OF54	76	.283	B	
		Reilly, John Good (OF3)	1B70	72	.195	A	
		Reilley, Chas. E. (C12 3B4)	OF16	29	.204	Troy	
		Say, Lewis I.	SS	47	.202	A	
		Smith, Chas. Marvin (Pap) (OF1)	2B82	82	.199	A	
		Sommer, Joseph John (SS1 3B1)	OF18	20	.182	A	
		Wheeler, Harry Eugene (3B1)	OF16	17	+.108	xClev	
		White, James Laurie (Deacon) (1B3 2B1)	OF33	34	.302	B	
18	43	White, Wm. Henry (OF3)	P61	61	.165	B	
		Wright, Samuel	SS	9	.058	Bos76	

WON 78 — LOST 55 — TG 133

NATIONAL LEAGUE — 1890.

FINISHED 4th. — PCT. .586

CINCINNATI

THOMAS JOSEPH LOFTUS

WON	LOST	NAME	POS.	G.	BA	FROM	TO
		Baldwin, Clarence Geoghan	C19	21	.153	CinAA	AthAA
		Beard, Oliver Perry	SS113	122	.268	CinAA	
		Clingman, Wm. Frederick	SS	7	.258	A	
1	1	Dolan, John (Jack)	P	2	.200	A	
17	13	Duryea, James Whitney (Jesse)	P31	32	.151	CinAA	
13	11	Foreman, Francis Isaiah	P	24	.133	BaltAA	
		Harrington, Jeremiah Peter	C	65	.246	A	
		Holliday, James Wear (Bug)	OF	131	.270	CinAA	
		Keenan, James W.	C50	54	.138	CinAA	
		Knight, Jonas Wm.	OF	127	.312	Phi84	C
		Latham, Walter Arlington (Arlie)	3B40	41	.250	xChiPL	
		Marr, Chas. W. (Lefty) (3B63)	OF64	130	.299	ColAA	
12	10	Mullane, Anthony John (Tony) (P22 3B21)	OF28	81	.276	CinAA	
		McPhee, John Alexander (Bid)	2B	132	.255	CinAA	
		Nicol, Hugh N.	OF46	50	.209	CinAA	
		Reilly, John Good	1B122	133	.300	CinAA	
28	17	Rhines, Wm. Pearl (Bunker)	P	45	.188	A	
7	3	Viau, Leon	P	12	+.135	CinAA	Clev

WON 56 — LOST 81 — TG 137

NATIONAL LEAGUE — 1891.

FINISHED 7th. — PCT. .409

CINCINNATI

THOMAS JOSEPH LOFTUS

WON	LOST	NAME	POS.	G.	BA	FROM	TO
		Browning, Louis Roger (Pete)	OF	51	+.362	xPitt	
		Clark, Robert H.	C	15	.132	Bkn	
		Corkhill, John Stewart (Pop)	OF	1	+.000	xAthAA	Pitt
2	10	Crane, Edward Nicholas	P	14	.071	xCinAA	
		Curtiss, Irvin Duane	OF	27	.266	A	WashAA
2	8	Duryea, James Whitney (Jesse)	P	11	.030	B	StLAA
0	0	Foreman, Francis Isaiah	P	1	.250	B	WashAA
		Halligan, Wm. E. (Jocko)	OF	61	.311	BuffPL	
		Harrington, Jeremiah Peter	C	90	.229	B	
		Holliday, James Wear (Bug)	OF	110	.318	B	
		Keenan, James W. (C33)	1B42	75	.203	B	C
		Latham, Walter Arlington (Arlie)	3B	135	.271	B	
		Marr, Chas. W. (Lefty)	OF71	72	.244	B	CinAA
24	23	Mullane, Anthony John (Tony)	P49	61	.150	B	

WON	LOST	NAME	POS.	G.	BA	FROM	TO
		McPhee, John Alexander (Bid)	2B	138	.257	B	
12	12	Radbourn, Chas. (Hoss)	P25	27	.179	BosPL	C
		Reilly, John Good (OF35)	1B98	133	.200	B	C
16	27	Rhines, Wm. Pearl (Bunker)	P	43	.124	B	
		Slattery, Michael J.	OF	41	.221	NYPL	WashAA
		Smith, George J. (Germany)	SS	138	.205	Bkn	
0	1	Stephens, Clarence Wright	P	1	.000	CinAA86	

WON 82 — LOST 68 — TG 150

NATIONAL LEAGUE

1892.

FINISHED 5th.

PCT. .547

CINCINNATI

CHAS. ALBERT COMISKEY

WON	LOST	NAME	POS.	G.	BA	FROM	TO
		Browning, Louis Roger (Pete)	OF	81	+.300	xLvlle	
		Burke, Edward D.	OF	14	+.139	MilAA	N.Y.
19	23	Chamberlain, Elton P.	P	44	.230	AthAA	
		Comiskey, Chas. Albert MGR.	1B	140	.223	StLAA	
1	1	Daub, Daniel Wm.	P	5	.000	A	
		Dowse, Thomas Jefferson	C	1	+.000	xLvlle	Phil
3	5	Duryea, James Whitney (Jesse) (OF1)	P9	11	+.111	B	Wash
20	10	Dwyer, John Francis (Frank)	P	46	+.156	xStL	
		Genins, C. Frank	SS	31	+.195	A	StL
		Halligan, Wm. E. (Jocko) (1B10)	OF16	26	+.287	B	Balt
		Harrington, Jeremiah Peter	C	18	.213	B	
0	0	Hemming, George Earl	P	1	+.333	Bkn	Lvlle
0	1	Holliday, James Wear (Bug) (P1)	OF148	149	.286	B	
		Hoover, Wm. J. (Buster)	OF	14	.176	BaltAA86	C
1	0	Jones, Chas. Leander (Bumpus)	P	1	.000	A	
0	1	Knauss, Frank H.	P	1	.333	Clev	
		Kuehne, Wm. J.	3B4	6	+.217	xStL (return)	StL
		Latham, Walter Arlington (Arlie)	3B142	150	.239	B	
		Mahaney, Daniel J.	C	5	.190	A	
1	1	Meakim, George Clinton	P	3	+.000	xChi	
20	14	Mullane, Anthony John (Tony)	P	34	.175	B	
		Murphy, Morgan Edward	C	69	.192	BosAA	
1	1	McGill, Wm. Vaness	P	3	.250	StLAA	
		McPhee, John Alexander (Bid)	2B	144	.294	B	
		O'Neill, James Edward (Tip)	OF	107	.250	StLAA	C
1	0	Rettger, George Edward (OF1)	P1	2	+.125	xClev	
3	4	Rhines, Wm. Pearl (Bunker)	P	12	.185	B	
		Smith, George J. (Germany)	SS	138	.248	B	
0	1	Stephens, Clarence Wright	P	2	+.000	B	C
12	6	Sullivan, Michael Joseph (Mike)	P	18	.175	N.Y.	
		Vaughn, Harry Francis	C69	85	.257	MilAA	
		Welch, Curtis Benton	OF	24	+.220	xBalt	
		Wood, George A.	OF	30	+.210	xBalt	C

WON 65 — LOST 63 — TG 128

NATIONAL LEAGUE

1893.

FINISHED 6th. (TIED WITH BKLYN)

PCT. .508

CINCINNATI

CHAS. ALBERT COMISKEY

WON	LOST	NAME	POS.	G.	BA	FROM	TO
		Canavan, James E.	OF114	118	.238	Chi	
		Caruthers, Robert Lee	OF	13	+.286	xChi	C
14	9	Chamberlain, Elton P.	P	27	.180	B	
		Comiskey, Chas. Albert MGR.	1B	62	.225	B	
0	2	Cross, George Lewis	P	2	.250	A	
2	1	Darby, George W.	P	4	+.273	A	Phil
		Duffee, Chas. Edward	OF	4	.200	Wash	C
18	14	Dwyer, John Francis (Frank)	P	32	.191	B	
		Henry, George Washington	OF	21	.273	A	C
		Holliday, James Wear (Bug)	OF121	122	.332	B	
1	3	Jones, Chas. Leander (Bumpus)	P	6	+.333	B	N.Y.
7	6	King, Chas. Frederick	P	13	+.222	xN.Y.	
		Latham, Walter Arlington (Arlie)	3B	125	.296	B	
		Motz, Frank H.	1B	42	.267	Phil90	
7	7	Mullane, Anthony John (Tony)	P	27	+.283	B	Balt
		Murphy, Cornelius David	C	3	.000	A	
		Murphy, Morgan Edward	C55	56	.234	B	
		McCarthy, John A.	OF46	48	.285	A	
		McPhee, John Alexander (Bid)	2B	127	.307	B	
9	8	Parrott, Thomas Wm.	P	17	+.163	xChi	
		Smith, George J. (Germany)	SS	130	.244	B	
		Smith, Judson Grant (Jud) (SS1 3B6)	OF9	16	+.233	A	StL
7	13	Sullivan, Michael Joseph (Mike)	P	22	.191	B	
		Ulrich, George F.	OF	1	.000	Wash	
		Vaughn, Harry Francis (1B21 OF23)	C75	119	.299	B	
		Ward, Frank Gray (Piggy)	OF	38	+.281	xBalt	

WON 54 — LOST 75 — TG 129

NATIONAL LEAGUE

1894.

FINISHED 10th.

PCT. .419

CINCINNATI

CHAS. ALBERT COMISKEY

WON	LOST	NAME	POS.	G.	BA	FROM	TO
0	1	Blank, Frederick August	P	1	.000	A	C
		Canavan, James E.	OF94	100	.293	B	
9	11	Chamberlain, Elton P.	P	20	.304	B	
		Comiskey, Chas. Albert MGR.	1B	59	.265	B	
2	4	Cross, George Lewis	P	9	.231	B	C
18	19	Dwyer, John Francis (Frank)	P39	49	.269	B	
2	10	Fisher, Chauncey Burr	P	12	+.209	xClev	

WON	LOST	NAME	POS.	G.	BA	FROM	TO
0	1	Flynn, Cornelius Francis Xavier	P	2	.000	A	
1	3	Fournier, F. Henry	P	6	.050	A	C
		Hogan, Martin T.	OF	6	+.174	A	StL
		Holliday, James Wear (Bug)	OF121	122	.383	B	
		Hoy, Wm. Ellsworth (Dummy)	OF	128	.312	Wash	
		Latham, Walter Arlington (Arlie)	3B129	130	.313	B	
		Massey, Wm. Harry	1B	13	.294	A	C
		Merritt, Wm. Henry (1B1 3B3 OF1)	C25	30	+.316	xPitt	
		Motz, Frank H.	1B	18	.204	B	C
		Murphy, Cornelius David	C	1	.000	B	C
		Murphy, Morgan Edward	C74	76	.268	B	
		McCarthy, John A. (1B15)	OF25	40	.267	B	
0	0	McGuire, Murray Mason	P	1	.250	A	C
		McPhee, John Alexander (Bid)	2B	128	.320	B	
19	19	Parrott, Thomas Wm.	P38	59	.329	B	
0	1	Pflann, Wm. F.	P	1	.000	A	C
		Smith, George J. (Germany)	SS	128	.266	B	
1	1	Tannehill, Jesse Niles	P	5	.000	A	
		Vaughn, Harry Francis (1B19)	C41	67	.309	B	
2	5	Whitrock, Wm. Franklin	P	17	+.242	xLvlle	

WON 66 — NATIONAL LEAGUE — FINISHED 8th.
LOST 64
TG 130 — 1895. — PCT. .508

CINCINNATI

WM. EWING

WON	LOST	NAME	POS.	G.	BA	FROM	TO
1	0	Bailey, Lemuel	P	1	.500	A	
		Burke, Edward D.	OF	56	+.279	xN.Y.	
18	13	Dwyer, John Francis (Frank)	P	34	.272	B	
		Ewing, Wm. (Buck) MGR.	1B	103	.316	Clev	
11	14	Foreman, Francis Isaiah	P	25	.312	NY93	
		Grey, Wm. Tobin	3B25	47	.301	Phil91	
		Hogriever, George C.	OF64	67	.278	A	
		Holliday, James Wear (Bug)	OF	31	.301	B	
		Hoy, Wm. Ellsworth (Dummy)	OF	107	.274	B	
		Kahoe, Michael Joseph	C	3	.000	A	
		Latham, Walter Arlington (Arlie)	3B107	110	.310	B	
		Merritt, Wm. Henry	C	21	+.213	B	Pitt
		Miller, Chas. Bradley (Dusty)	OF	132	.329	StLAA90	
		Murphy, Morgan Edward	C	22	.272	B	
		McPhee, John Alexander (Bid)	2B	114	.295	B	
11	20	Parrott, Thomas Wm.	P31	47	.340	B	
5	5	Phillips, Wm. Corcoran	P	17	.341	Pitt90	
20	12	Rhines, Wm. Pearl (Bunker)	P	32	.227	Lvlle93	
		Smith, George J. (Germany)	SS	127	.297	B	
		Spies, Henry	C	14	+.200	A	Lvlle
		Vaughn, Harry Francis	C75	88	.305	B	

WON 77 — NATIONAL LEAGUE — FINISHED 3rd.
LOST 50
TG 127 — 1896. — PCT. .606

CINCINNATI

WM. EWING

WON	LOST	NAME	POS.	G.	BA	FROM	TO
		Burke, Edward D.	OF	122	.342	B	
0	0	Davis, Wiley Anderson	P	2	.000	A	C
25	10	Dwyer, John Francis (Frank)	P	35	.254	B	
18	15	Ehret, Philip Sydney (Red)	P	33	.200	StL	
		Ewing, Wm. (Buck) MGR.	1B	67	.282	B	
9	7	Fisher, Chauncey Burr	P	20	.241	Cin94	
12	6	Foreman, Francis Isaiah	P	22	.261	B	
2	3	Foreman, John Davis (Brownie)	P	5	+.182	xPitt	C
0	1	Gastright, Henry Carl	P	2	.000	Bkn94	C
		Grey, Wm. Tobin	C	35	.216	B	
		Holliday, James Wear (Bug)	OF15	22	.346	B	
		Hoy, Wm. Ellsworth (Dummy)	OF	121	.296	B	
1	1	Inks, Albert Preston (Bert)	P	3	+.000	xPhil	C
		Irwin, Chas. E.	3B	127	.295	Chi	
		Miller, Chas. Bradley (Dusty)	OF	125	.318	B	
		McPhee, John Alexander (Bid)	2B	116	.299	B	
		Peitz, Henry Clement (Heinie)	C	67	.298	StL	
10	7	Rhines, Wm. Pearl (Bunker)	P	17	.196	B	
		Smith, George J. (Germany)	SS	119	.282	B	
		Vaughn, Harry Francis (1B56)	C57	113	.297	B	

WON 76 — NATIONAL LEAGUE — FINISHED 4th.
LOST 56
TG 132 — 1897. — PCT. .576

CINCINNATI

WM. EWING

WON	LOST	NAME	POS.	G.	BA	FROM	TO
		Beckley, Jacob Peter (Jake)	1B	96	+.336	xN.Y.	
23	12	Breitenstein, Theodore P.	P35	39	.270	StL	
0	2	Brown, Richard P. (Stub)	P	2	.000	Balt94	C
		Burke, Edward D.	OF	94	.269	B	
		Corcoran, Thomas W. (2B44)	SS64	108	.288	Bkn	
7	5	Damman, Wm. Henry A.	P	16	.167	A	
17	12	Dwyer, John Francis (Frank)	P33	35	.285	B	
10	10	Ehret, Philip Sydney (Red)	P22	27	.212	B	
		Ewing, Wm. (Buck) MGR.	1B	1	.000	B	
		Holliday, James Wear (Bug)	OF43	53	.328	B	
		Hoy, Wm. Ellsworth (Dummy)	OF	128	.290	B	
		Irwin, Chas. E.	3B	134	.293	B	
		Miller, Chas. Bradley (Dusty)	OF	119	.317	B	
		McPhee, John Alexander (Bid)	2B	80	.307	B	
		Peitz, Henry Clement (Heinie)	C72	73	.297	B	

WON	LOST	NAME	POS.	G.	BA	FROM	TO
19	15	Rhines, Wm. Pearl (Bunker)	P35	36	.168	B	
		Ritchey, Claude Cassius (OF20)	SS69	100	.288	A	
		Schriver, Wm. F. (Pop)	C	52	.310	NY95	
		Vaughn, Harry Francis	1B35	50	.305	B	

WON 92 — NATIONAL LEAGUE — FINISHED 3rd.
LOST 60
TG 152 — 1898. — PCT. .605

CINCINNATI

WM. EWING

WON	LOST	NAME	POS.	G.	BA	FROM	TO
		Beckley, Jacob Peter (Jake)	1B	116	.299	B	
21	14	Breitenstein, Theodore P.	P36	39	.219	B	
0	1	Coleman, Pierce D.	P	1	.000	StL	C
		Corcoran, Thomas W.	SS	153	.244	B	
16	8	Damman, Wm. Henry A.	P27	28	.218	B	
16	10	Dwyer, John Francis (Frank)	P27	29	.141	B	
0	0	Goar, Joshua Mercer (Jot)	P	1	.000	Pitt96	
26	12	Hawley, Emerson P. (Pink)	P40	42	.183	Pitt	
13	15	Hill, Wm. C.	P	28	.131	Lvlle	
		Holliday, James Wear (Bug)	OF	26	.240	B	C
		Irwin, Chas. E.	3B	135	.240	B	
		Miller, Chas. Bradley (Dusty)	OF	152	.299	B	
		McBride, Algernon Briggs (Algie)	OF	120	.300	Chi96	
		McFarland, Hermus W.	OF	15	.286	Lvlle96	
		McPhee, John Alexander (Bid)	2B128	131	.246	B	
		Peitz, Henry Clement (Heinie)	C	100	.281	B	
		Smith, Elmer Ellsworth	OF	122	.344	Pitt	
		Steinfeldt, Harry M. (OF28)	2B29	83	.289	A	
		Vaughn, Harry Francis (C33)	1B40	73	.303	B	
		Wood, Robert Lynn	C17	30	.280	A	

WON 83 — NATIONAL LEAGUE — FINISHED 6th.
LOST 67
TG 150 — 1899. — PCT. .553

CINCINNATI

WM. EWING

WON	LOST	NAME	POS.	G.	BA	FROM	TO
		Barrett, James Erigena	OF	26	.374	A	
		Beckley, Jacob Peter (Jake)	1B	135	.333	B	
14	10	Breitenstein, Theodore P.	P24	33	.339	B	
		Corcoran, Thomas W.	SS123	135	.279	B	
		Crawford, Samuel Earl	OF	31	.308	A	
2	2	Cronin, John J. (Jack)	P	5	.118	Pitt	
2	1	Damman, Wm. Henry A.	P	9	.105	B	
0	5	Dwyer, John Francis (Frank)	P	5	.273	B	
		Elberfeld, Norman Arthur (Kid)	SS23	41	.259	Phil	
3	6	Frisk, John Emil	P	9	.280	A	
23	8	Hahn, Frank George	P33	38	.147	A	
14	17	Hawley, Emerson P. (Pink)	P31	33	.222	B	
		Houtz, Fred Fritz (Lefty)	OF	5	.176	A	C
		Irwin, Chas. E.	3B78	87	.231	B	
		Kahoe, Michael Joseph	C	14	.167	Cin95	
		Miller, Chas. Bradley (Dusty)	OF	80	+.260	B	StL
		McBride, Algernon Briggs(Algie)	OF	62	.352	B	
		McPhee, John Alexander (Bid)	2B	106	.283	B	
		Peitz, Henry Clement (Heinie)	C	91	.271	B	
17	8	Phillips, Wm. Corcoran	P28	31	.135	Cin95	
		Selbach, Albert Carl (Kip)	OF	139	.302	Wash	
		Seybold, Ralph Orlando	OF	22	.221	A	
		Smith, Elmer Ellsworth	OF	87	.295	B	
		Steinfeldt, Harry M. (2B38)	3B61	107	.242	B	
		Stenzel, Jacob C. (Jake)	OF	9	+.321	xStL	C
8	10	Taylor, John Budd (Jack)	P21	24	.236	StL	C
		Vaughn, Harry Francis	1B21	28	.178	B	C
		Wood, Robert Lynn	C53	58	.317	B	

WON 62 — NATIONAL LEAGUE — FINISHED 7th.
LOST 77
TG 139 — 1900. — PCT. .446

CINCINNATI

ROBERT GILMAN ALLEN

WON	LOST	NAME	POS.	G.	BA	FROM	TO
		Allen, Robert Gilman MGR.	SS	5	.175	Bos97	C
		Barrett, James Erigena	OF	138	.316	B	
		Beckley, Jacob Peter (Jake)	1B	138	.343	B	
10	10	Breitenstein, Theodore P.	P22	33	.210	B	
		Corcoran, Thomas W.	SS125	128	.242	B	
		Crawford, Samuel Earl	OF	96	.270	B	
		Geier, Philip Louis	OF27	29	.273	Phil97	InplsA & return
16	21	Hahn, Frank George	P37	40	.205	B	
		Harley, Richard Joseph	OF	5	.450	xDetA	
		Hartsel, Tullos Frederick (Topsy)	OF	18	.328	xInplsA	
		Irwin, Chas. E. (SS16)	3B61	85	.271	B	
		Kahoe, Michael Joseph	C48	49	.186	B	
		McBride, Algernon Briggs (Algie)	OF	109	.277	B	
9	14	Newton, Eustace James (Doc)	P25	30	.198	A	
		Peitz, Henry Clement (Heinie)	C75	84	.251	B	
9	11	Phillips, Wm. Corcoran	P23	27	.167	B	
		Quinn, Joseph J.	2B	72	+.279	xStL	
17	20	Scott, Edward	P37	39	.154	A	
		Smith, Elmer Ellsworth	OF27	29	+.270	B	N.Y.
		Steinfeldt, Harry M. (2B66)	3B67	136	.247	B	

WON	LOST	NAME	POS.	G.	BA	FROM	TO
1	1	Stimmel, Archibald May	P	2	.200	A	InplsA
		Wood, Robert Lynn (3B15)	C19	34	.264	B	ChiA

WON 52 LOST 87 TG 139 — NATIONAL LEAGUE — FINISHED 8th (LAST)

1901. — PCT. .374

CINCINNATI

JOHN ALEXANDER McPHEE

WON	LOST	NAME	POS.	G.	BA	FROM	TO
		Bay, Harry Elbert	OF	34	.205	DetA	
		Beckley, Jacob Peter (Jake)	1B	140	.300	B	
		Bergen, Wm. Aloysius	C	82	.172	A	
1	2	Case, Chas. Emmett	P	3	.111	A	
		Corcoran, Thomas W.	SS	30	.184	B	
		Crawford, Samuel Earl	OF	124	.334	B	
		Dobbs, John Gordon	OF101	108	.276	A	
		Fox, Wm. H.	2B	44	.183	Wash97	C
1	4	Guese, Theodore	P	6	.188	IndpsA	C
		Haberer, Emil Karl	1B4	6	.167	A	
22	19	Hahn, Frank George	P	41	.173	B	
		Harley, Richard Joseph	OF	133	.268	B	
		Heileman, John George	3B	5	.133	A	C
0	1	Heismann, Christian Ernest	P	3	.500	A	
		Hurley, Patrick	C	7	.062	A	
		Irwin, Chas. E.	3B	67	+.226	B	Bkn
		Kahoe, Michael Joseph	C	4	+.267	B	Chi
		Krouse, Wm.	2B	1	.250	MinnA	C
		Magoon, George Henry	SS114	128	.251	InplsA	
		McBride, Algernon Briggs(Algie)	OF	30	+.254	B	N.Y.
3	4	McFadden, Bernard Joseph (Barney)	P	8	.190	A	
4	13	Newton, Eustace James (Doc)	P	20	+.130	B	Bkn
		O'Brien, Peter J.	2B	15	.208	A	
0	1	Parker, Harley Park (Dr)	P	1	.000	MinnA	C
		Peitz, Henry Clement (Heinie) (2B19)	C50	73	.311	B	
14	18	Phillips, Wm. Corcoran	P	33	.238	B	
0	1	Rusie, Amos Wilson	P	3	.125	NY98	C
0	2	Scott, Amos Richard	P	3	.000	A	C
		Steinfeldt, Harry M. (2B50)	3B55	105	.250	B	
4	14	Stimmel, Archibald May	P	20	.080	InplsA	
1	6	Sutthoff, John Gerhard (OF1)	P10	11	.121	StL99	
2	1	Swormstedt, Leonard Jordan	P	4	.000	A	
0	1	Weyhing, August (Gus)	P	1	.000	xClevA	C

WON 70 LOST 70 TG 140 — NATIONAL LEAGUE — FINISHED 4th.

1902. — PCT. .500

CINCINNATI

JOHN ALEXANDER McPHEE — FRANK CARTER BANCROFT

JOSEPH JAMES KELLEY

WON	LOST	NAME	POS.	G.	BA	FROM	TO
		Bay, Harry Elbert	OF3	6	.375	B	ClevA
		Beck, Erwin Thomas	2B31	43	.305	ClevA	DetA
0	1	Beckley, Jacob Peter (Jake) (P1)	1B129	129	.331	B	
		Bergen, Wm. Aloysius	C	89	.181	B	
		Corcoran, Thomas W. (2B1)	SS136	137	.251	B	
		Crawford, Samuel Earl	OF	140	.333	B	
3	4	Currie, Clarence F.	P	10	+.083	A	StL
		Dobbs, John Gordon	OF	63	+.287	B	Chi
0	0	Donlin, Michael Joseph (P1 SS1)	OF32	33	.294	BaltA	
5	6	Ewing, George Lemuel (Bob) (OF5)	P15	19	.171	A	
0	1	Glendon, Martin H.	P	1	.000	A	
23	12	Hahn, Frank George (1B1 OF1)	P36	37	.183	B	
2	1	Heismann, Christian Ernest	P	5	.214	B	BaltA
0	1	Hooker, Wm. E.	P	1	.000	BuffA00	
		Hoy, Wm. Ellsworth (Dummy)	OF	72	.294	ChiA	C
		Kelley, Joseph James MGR. (2B10 SS1 3B9)	OF19	37	.327	xBaltA	
		Magoon, George Henry (SS3)	2B41	44	.275	B	
		Maloney, Wm. Alphonse (C7)	OF18	24	.228	xStLA	
		Morrissey, John Albert (OF1)	2B11	12	.289	A	
		Peitz, Henry Clement (Heinie) (C46 1B6 3B6)	2B48	104	.313	B	
16	17	Phillips, Wm. Corcoran	P	33	.333	B	
12	4	Poole, Edward I.	P	16	+.117	xPitt	
0	0	Seymour, John Bentley (Cy) (P1 3B1)	OF59	60	.349	xBaltA	
		Steinfeldt, Harry M. (SS1 OF1)	3B128	128	.276	B	
0	4	Stimmel, Archibald May	P	4	.200	B	C
0	1	Swormstedt, Leonard Jordan	P	2	.166	B	
9	15	Thielman, Henry Joseph	P	29	+.116	xN.Y.	
0	3	Vickers, Harry Porter (Rube) (C1)	P3	4	.363	A	

WON 74 LOST 65 TG 139 — NATIONAL LEAGUE — FINISHED 4th.

1903. — PCT. .532

CINCINNATI

JOSEPH JAMES KELLEY

WON	LOST	NAME	POS.	G.	BA	FROM	TO
		Beckley, Jacob Peter (Jake)	1B	119	.327	B	
		Bergen, Wm. Aloysius	C	58	.227	B	
		Corcoran, Thomas W.	SS	115	.246	B	

WON	LOST	NAME	POS.	G.	BA	FROM	TO
		Cregan, Peter James	OF	6	.111	NY99	C
		Daly, Thomas Peter	2B	79	.293	xChiA	C
		DeArmond, Chas. Hommer	3B	11	.297	A	C
		Deisel, Edward (Pat)	C	2	.000	Bkn	C
		Dolan, Patrick Henry (Cozy)	OF	93	.288	xChiA	
		Donlin, Michael Joseph	OF118	124	.351	B	
14	13	Ewing, George Lumuel (Bob)	P29	31	.253	B	
		Fohl, Leo Alexander	C	4	.357	Pitt	
		Haberer, Emil Karl	C	5	.154	Cin01	
22	12	Hahn, Frank George	P	34	.161	B	
7	7	Harper, Chas. Wm. (Jack)	P	17	.250	StLA	
0	0	Hooker, Wm. E.	P	1	.000	B	C
		Kelley, Joseph James MGR.	OF67	104	.316	B	
		Kerwin, Daniel P.	OF	1	.750	A	C
		Magoon, George Henry	2B32	41	.216	B	ChiA
		Morrissey, John Albert (SS2)	2B17	27	.247	B	C
		Peitz, Henry Clement (Heinie)	C78	102	.260	B	
7	6	Phillips, Wm. Corcoran	P	16	.175	B	
8	13	Poole, Edward I.	P	25	.243	B	
0	2	Reagan, Arthur	P	3	.250	A	C
		Seymour, John Bentley (Cy)	OF	135	.342	B	
		Steinfeldt, Harry M.	3B104	118	.312	B	
16	11	Sutthoff, John Gerhard	P	30	.143	Cin01	
0	1	Wiggs, James Alvin	P	2	.000	A	
		Wood, Harry	OF	2	.000	A	C

WON 88 NATIONAL LEAGUE FINISHED 3rd.
LOST 65
TG 153 1904. PCT. .575

CINCINNATI

JOSEPH JAMES KELLEY

WON	LOST	NAME	POS.	G.	BA	FROM	TO
		Corcoran, Thomas W.	SS	150	.230	B	
		Dolan, Patrick Henry (Cozy) (1B24)	OF102	126	.284	B	
		Donlin, Michael Joseph	OF	59	+.356	B	N.Y.
4	6	Elliott, Claude J.	P	10	+.208	A	N.Y.
11	12	Ewing, George Lemuel (Bob)	P26	30	.258	B	
15	18	Hahn, Frank George	P	35	.172	B	
24	8	Harper, Chas. Wm. (Jack)	P	35	.159	B	
		Huggins, Miller James	2B	140	.263	A	
		Kelley, Joseph James MGR.	1B117	123	.281	B	
16	8	Kellum, Winford Ansley	P31	36	.159	BosA01	
		Odwell, Frederick Wm.	OF	126	.284	A	
		O'Neill, Philip Bernard	C	8	.267	A	C
		Peitz, Henry Clement (Heinie) (1B18)	C64	82	.243	B	
		Schlei, George Henry	C	88	.237	A	
		Sebring, James Dennison	OF	56	+.225	xPitt	
		Seymour, John Bentley (Cy)	OF	130	.312	B	
		Steinfeldt, Harry M.	3B	98	.244	B	
		Street, Chas. Evard (Gabby)	C	11	.121	A	
3	3	Sutthoff, John Gerhard	P	12	+.182	B	Phil
15	10	Walker, Thomas Wm.	P	25	.116	PhilA02	
		Woodruff, Orville Francis (2B17)	3B61	87	.190	ClevA01	

WON 79 NATIONAL LEAGUE FINISHED 5th.
LOST 74
TG 153 1905. PCT. .516

CINCINNATI

JOSEPH JAMES KELLEY

WON	LOST	NAME	POS.	G.	BA	FROM	TO
0	0	Baker, Ernest G.	P	1	.000	A	C
		Barry, John C.	1B	126	+.324	xChi	
		Blankenship, Clifford Douglas	1B	15	.196	A	
		Bridwell, Albert Henry (OF18)	3B43	74	.252	A	
13	13	Chech, Chas. Wm.	P	39	.191	ClevA00	
		Corcoran, Thomas W.	SS	151	.248	B	
		Dolan, Patrick Henry (Cozy)	1B	22	+.234	B	Bos
21	12	Ewing, George Lemuel (Bob)	P40	42	.262	B	
5	3	Hahn, Frank George	P	12	.190	B	
9	14	Harper, Chas. Wm. (Jack)	P	26	.167	B	
		Hinchman, Wm. White	OF	17	.255	A	
		Huggins, Miller James	2B	149	.273	B	
1	0	Johns, Oliver Tracy	P	4	.200	A	C
		Kelley, Joseph James MGR.	OF85	87	.277	B	
		Mowrey, Harry Harlan (Mike)	3B	7	.266	A	
		Odwell, Frederick Wm.	OF	126	.241	B	
17	23	Overall, Orval	P	42	.145	A	
		Phelps, Edward Joseph	C	44	.231	Pitt	
		Schlei, George Henry	C89	95	.226	B	
		Sebring, James Dennison	OF	56	.286	B	
		Seymour, John Bentley (Cy)	OF	149	.377	B	
		Siegle, John Herbert	OF	16	.304	A	
		Steinfeldt, Harry M.	3B103	106	.271	B	
		Street, Chas. Evard (Gabby)	C	2	+.000	B	Bos
				27	+.247		& return
3	3	Vowinkel, John Henry	P	6	.071	A	C
10	6	Walker, Thomas Wm.	P	23	.137	B	C

WON 64 NATIONAL LEAGUE FINISHED 6th.
LOST 87
TG 151 1906. PCT. .424

CINCINNATI

EDWARD HUGH HANLON

WON	LOST	NAME	POS.	G.	BA	FROM	TO
		Barrett, James Erigena	OF	5	.000	DetA	

WON	LOST	NAME	POS.	G.	BA	FROM	TO
		Barry, John C. (OF30)	1B43	73	+.287	B	StL
		Carr, Chas. Carbitt	1B	22	.191	ClevA	
1	4	Chech, Chas. Wm.	P	11	.208	B	
		Corcoran, Thomas W.	SS	117	.207	B	
		Deal, John Wesley	1B	65	.208	A	C
		Delahanty, James Christopher Jr.	3B105	112	.280	Bos	
0	0	Dorner, Augustus	P	2	+.000	ClevA03	Bos
6	8	Druhot, Carl A.	P	14	+.222	A	StL
1	1	Essick, Wm. Earl	P	6	.077	A	
13	14	Ewing, George Lemuel (Bob)	P	33	.139	B	
10	20	Fraser, Chas. Carrolton (Chick)	P	31	.171	Bos	
3	6	Hall, Chas. Louis (Sea-Lion)	P	16	.128	A	
0	3	Harper, Chas. Wm. (Jack)	P	5	+.273	B	Chi
		Hinchman, Wm. White	OF	16	.204	B	
0	0	Hafford, Leo Edgar	P	3	.222	A	C
		Huggins, Miller James	2B	146	.292	B	
		Jude, Frank	OF	80	.208	A	C
		Kelley, Joseph James	OF122	127	.228	B	
		Livingston, Patrick Joseph (Paddy)	C	47	.158	ClevA01	
		Lobert, John Bernard (Hans) (SS31)	3B35	76	.310	Chi	
0	1	Mason, Adelbert Wm. (Del)	P	2	.000	WashA04	
		Mowrey, Harry Harlan (Mike)	3B15	17	.321	B	
		McLean, John Bannerman (Larry)	C	12	.191	StL04	
		Odwell, Frederick Wm.	OF	57	.223	B	
4	5	Overall, Orval	P	13	+.194	B	Chi
		Phelps, Edward Joseph	C	12	+.275	B	Pitt
		Schlei, George Henry (1B21)	C91	112	.245	B	
		Seymour, John Bentley (Cy)	OF	79	+.257	B	N.Y.
		Siegle, John Herbert	OF	21	.118	B	C
		Smoot, Homer	OF	59	+.259	xStL	C
		Stanage, Oscar Harland	C	1	1.000	A	
0	0	Tiemeyer, Edward Carl	P	5	.181	A	
20	14	Weimer, John Wm.	P	41	.269	Chi	
6	11	Wicker, Robert Kitridge	P	20	+.180	xChi	C

WON 66 — NATIONAL LEAGUE — FINISHED 6th.
LOST 87
TG 153 — 1907. — PCT. .431

CINCINNATI

EDWARD HUGH HANLON

WON	LOST	NAME	POS.	G.	BA	FROM	TO
		Autry, Wm. Askew (Chick)	OF	7	.200	A	
2	0	Campbell, Wm. James (Billy)	P	3	.250	StL05	
17	16	Coakley, Andrew James	P	37	.071	PhilA	
		Davis, Alfonzo DeFord	OF69	70	.229	NYA03	C
0	2	Essick, Wm. Earl	P	3	.000	B	C
17	19	Ewing, George Lemuel (Bob)	P41	44	.154	B	
		Ganzel, John Henry	1B	143	.254	NYA04	
4	3	Hall, Chas. Louis (Sea-Lion)	P	12	.280	B	
6	10	Hitt, Roy Wesley	P	21	.179	A	C
		Huggins, Miller James	2B	156	.248	B	
		Kane, John Francis (3B25)	OF38	75	.248	A	
		Krueger, Arthur T.	OF	96	.233	A	
		Lamar, Pierre	C	1	.000	Chi02	C
1	1	Leary, Francis Patrick	P	2	.000	A	C
		Lobert, John Bernard (Hans)	SS142	147	.246	B	
5	12	Mason, Adelbert Wm. (Del)	P	25	.182	B	C
0	2	Minahan, Edmund Joseph	P	2	.000	A	C
		Mitchell, Michael Francis (Mike)	OF143	148	.292	A	
		Mowrey, Harry Harlan (Mike)	3B127	138	.252	B	
		McCarthy, William John	C	3	.125	Bos05	C
		McLean, John Bannerman (Larry)	C89	101	.289	B	
		Odwell, Frederick Wm.	OF76	84	.270	B	C
		O'Neill, Michael Joyce	OF	9	.069	StL04	C
		Paskert, George Henry (Dode)	OF	16	.280	A	
		Schlei, George Henry	C67	72	.272	B	
2	7	Smith, Frederick	P	18	.107	A	C
1	1	Spade, Robert	P	3	.286	A	
		Tiemeyer, Edward Carl		1	.000	B	
11	14	Weimer, John Wm.	P	29	.194	B	
		Wolter, Harry Meigs	OF	4	+.133	A	Pitt

WON 73 — NATIONAL LEAGUE — FINISHED 5th.
LOST 81
TG 154 — 1908. — PCT. .474

CINCINNATI

JOHN HENRY GANZEL

WON	LOST	NAME	POS.	G.	BA	FROM	TO
		Bayless, Harry Owen	OF17	19	.225	A	C
		Bescher, Robert Henry	OF	32	.272	A	
		Brain, David Leonard	OF	16	+.109	Bos	N.Y.
12	13	Campbell, Wm. James (Billy)	P	35	.083	B	
8	18	Coakley, Andrew James	P	32	+.092	B	Chi
		Coulson, Robert Jackson	OF	8	.333	A	
		Daley, Thomas Francis (Pete)	OF	13	.108	A	
1	3	Doscher, John Herman Jr.	P	6	.133	Bkn06	C
5	6	Dubuc, Jean Arthur	P	16	.138	A	
		Egan, Richard Joseph (Dick)	2B	18	.206	A	
17	15	Ewing, George Lemuel (Bob)	P	37	.149	B	
		Ganzel, John Henry MGR.	1B	108	.250	B	
		Hoblitzell, Richard Carleton	1B	32	.254	A	
		Huggins, Miller James	2B	135	.239	B	
		Hulswitt, Rudolph Edward	SS118	119	.228	Phil04	
		Kane, John Francis	OF120	127	.213	B	
		Lobert, John Bernard (Hans) (SS35 OF21)	3B99	155	.293	B	
		Mitchell, Michael Francis (Mike)	OF115	119	.222	B	

WON	LOST	NAME	POS.	G.	BA	FROM	TO
		Mowrey, Harry Harlan (Mike)	3B56	63	.220	B	
0	1	McCarthy, Thomas Patrick	P	1	+.000	A	Pitt
		McGilvray, Wm. Alexander		2	.000	A	C
		McLean, John Bannerman (Larry) (1B19)	C69	88	.217	B	
1	0	O'Toole, Martin James	P	3	.200	A	
		Paskert, George Henry (Dode)	OF101	116	.243	B	
		Pearce, Wm. C.	C	2	.000	A	
0	0	Rhodes, Chas. A.	P	1	+.000	StL06	StL
3	3	Rowan, John Arthur	P	8	.071	DetA06	
0	1	Savidge, Ralph Austin	P	4	.000	A	
		Schlei, George Henry	C	88	.220	B	
0	0	Sincock, Herbert Sylvester	P	1	.000	A	C
17	12	Spade, Robert	P	35	.195	B	
0	0	Tozier, Wm. Ralph	P	4	.000	A	C
1	2	Volz, Jacob Phillip	P	7	.250	Bos05	C
8	7	Weimer, John Wm.	P	15	.244	B	

WON 77   NATIONAL LEAGUE   FINISHED 4th.
LOST 76
TG 153   1909.   PCT. .504

CINCINNATI

CLARK CALVIN GRIFFITH

WON	LOST	NAME	POS.	G.	BA	FROM	TO
		Autry, Wm. Askew (Chick)	1B	9	+.182	Cin07	Bos
		Bescher, Robert Henry	OF	117	.240	B	
0	1	Bushelman, John Francis	P	1	.000	A	
7	11	Campbell, Wm. James (Billy)	P	30	.140	B	C
1	0	Cantwell, Thomas Aloysius	P	6	.428	A	
0	0	Carmichael, Chester Ralph	P	2	.000	A	C
1	1	Castleton, Roy J.C.	P	4	.667	NYA07	
0	0	Chappelle, Wm. Hogan	P	1	+.000	xBos	
		Charles, Raymond (2B6)	SS7	13	+.256	xStL	
		Clarke, Thomas Aloysius	C	17	.250	A	
		Dolan, Alvin James (Cozy)	3B	3	.167	A	
		Downey, Thomas Edward	SS	119	.231	A	
2	5	Dubuc, Jean Arthur	P	19	.167	B	
0	0	Durbin, Blaine A.	P	6	+.200	Chi	Pitt
		Egan, Richard Joseph (Dick)	2B116	126	.275	B	
		Ellam, Roy	SS	10	.190	A	
11	12	Ewing, George Lemuel (Bob)	P	31	.110	B	
19	13	Fromme, Arthur Henry	P	37	.191	StL	
19	11	Gaspar, Harry Lambert	P	44	.122	A	
0	1	Griffith, Clark Calvin MGR.	P	1	.000	NYA	
		Haberer, Emil Karl	C	5	.187	Cin03	C
		Hoblitzell, Richard Carleton	1B	142	.308	B	
		Huggins, Miller James (3B15)	2B31	46	.213	B	
		Johnston, Wheeler Rogers	1B	3	.000	A	
1	3	Karger, Edwin	P	9	.272	StL	BosA
		Konnick, Michael Aloysius	C	2	.400	A	
		Lobert, John Bernard (Hans)	3B	122	.212	B	

WON	LOST	NAME	POS.	G.	BA	FROM	TO
		Midkiff, Ezra Millington	3B	1	.000	A	
		Miller, Ward Taylor	OF	43	+.310	xPitt	
		Mitchell, Michael Francis (Mike)	OF	145	.310	B	
		Moriarty, Wm. Joseph	SS	6	.250	A	C
		Mowrey, Harry Harlan (Mike)	3B	35	+.191	B	StL
		McCabe, James Arthur	OF	4	.461	A	
		McLean, John Bannerman (Larry)	C	95	.256	B	
		Oakes, Ennis Talmadge (Rebel)	OF	113	.270	A	
		Paskert, George Henry (Dode)	OF82	88	.251	B	
		Patterson, Lorenzo Claire	OF	4	.125	A	C
		Pauxtis, Simon Francis	C	4	.125	A	C
		Pearce, Wm. C.	C	2	.000	B	C
0	1	Ragan, Don Carlos Patrick (Pat)	P	2	+.500	A	Chi
		Roth, Frank Charles	C	52	.238	ChiA06	
11	12	Rowan, John Arthur	P	38	.092	B	
0	0	Savidge, Ralph Austin	P	1	.000	B	C
5	5	Spade, Robert	P	14	.264	B	
		Young, Delmar John	OF	2	.286	A	

WON 75   NATIONAL LEAGUE   FINISHED 5th.
LOST 79
TG 154   1910.   PCT. .487

CINCINNATI

CLARK CALVIN GRIFFITH

WON	LOST	NAME	POS.	G.	BA	FROM	TO
		Altizer, David Tilden	SS	3	.600	ChiA	
0	0	Anderson, Wingo Charlie	P	7	.200	A	C
12	14	Beebe, Frederick Leonard	P	35	.164	StL	
0	1	Benton, John Cleveland (Rube)	P	12	.091	A	
		Bescher, Robert Henry	OF	150	.250	B	
		Burns, Joseph Francis		1	1.000	A	
8	13	Burns, Wm. Thomas	P	31	.262	xChiA	
0	0	Cantwell, Thomas Aloysius	P	2	.000	B	C
1	2	Castleton, Roy J. C.	P	4	.000	B	C
		Charles, Raymond	SS	4	.133	B	C
		Clarke, Thomas Aloysius	C	56	.278	B	
		Corcoran, Michael Joseph	3B	14	.217	A	C
1	1	Coveleskie, Harry Frank	P	7	.063	Phil	
		Crompton, Edward	OF	1	.000	StLA	C
		Downey, Thomas Edward (3B41)	SS68	109	.270	B	
		Doyle, James Francis	3B6	7	.191	A	
0	0	Doyle, Judd Bruce	P	5	.000	xNYA	C
		Egan, Richard Joseph (Dick)	2B131	134	.245	B	
3	4	Fromme, Arthur Henry	P	11	.133	B	
15	17	Gaspar, Harry Lambert	P	48	.115	B	
		Griffith, Clark Calvin MGR.		1	.000	B	
		Hoblitzell, Richard Carleton	1B148	155	.278	B	
		Konnick, Michael Aloysius	SS	1	.000	B	C
		Lobert, John Bernard (Hans)	3B	90	.309	B	

WON	LOST	NAME	POS.	G.	BA	FROM	TO
		Meinke, Robert Bernard	SS	2	.000	A	C
		Miller, Ward Taylor	OF	26	.238	B	
		Mitchell, Michael Francis (Mike)	OF149	156	.286	B	
		McCabe, James Arthur	OF9	13	.257	B	C
		McLean, John Bannerman (Larry)	C	119	.298	B	
		McMillan, Thomas Law	SS	82	+.185	xBkn	
		Paskert, George Henry (Dode)	OF139	141	.300	B	
		Phelan, Arthur Edward	3B	17	.214	A	
		Robinson, Clyde	3B	2	.000	DetA04	C
		Roth, Frank Charles	C5	27	.200	B	C
14	13	Rowan, John Arthur	P	42	.229	B	
0	0	Slagle, Walter John	P	1	.000	A	C
1	2	Spade, Robert	P	3	.000	B	StLA
20	12	Suggs, George Franklin	P	35	.165	DetA	
0	0	Walker, Frederick Mitchell	P	1	.000	A	
		Wheeler, George Harrison	OF	3	.000	A	C
		Woodruff, Orville Francis	3B17	21	.148	Cin06	C

WON 70 NATIONAL LEAGUE FINISHED 6th.
LOST 83
TG 153 1911. PCT. .458

CINCINNATI

CLARK CALVIN GRIFFITH

WON	LOST	NAME	POS.	G.	BA	FROM	TO
		Almeida, Rafael D.	3B28	29	.313	A	
		Altizer, David Tilden	SS23	26	.227	B	C
		Balenti, Michael Richard	SS	7	.250	A	
		Bates, John Wm.	OF	147	.292	Phil	
		Beck, Frederick Thomas	OF	41	+.184	Bos	Phil
3	3	Benton, John Cleveland (Rube)	P	6	.143	B	
		Bescher, Robert Henry	OF	153	.275	B	
3	3	Boyd, Raymond C.	P	7	.083	StLA	C
0	0	Burns, Wm. Thomas	P	6	+.429	B	Phil
		Clarke, Thomas Aloysius	C81	82	.241	B	
1	1	Compton, Harry LeRoy (Jack)	P	8	.500	A	C
		Downey, Thomas Edward	SS92	106	.261	B	
		Egan, Richard Joseph (Dick)	2B	152	.249	B	
		Esmond, James J.	SS43	59	.273	A	
10	11	Fromme, Arthur Henry	P	38	.189	B	
10	17	Gaspar, Harry Lambert	P	44	.153	B	
		Grant, Edward Leslie	3B122	133	.223	Phil	
		Hoblitzell, Richard Carleton	1B	158	.289	B	
4	1	Humpheries, Albert (Bert)	P	14	+.063	xPhil	
0	0	Juul, Herbert Victor	P	2	.000	A	C
12	13	Keefe, Robert Francis	P	39	.086	NYA07	
		Mahoney, Daniel Joseph		1	.000	A	C
		Marsans, Armando	OF34	36	.261	A	
		Mitchell, Michael Francis (Mike)	OF	140	.291	B	
		McLean, John Bannerman (Larry)	C	98	.287	B	
2	6	McQuillan, George Washington	P	19	.091	Phil	
		Northen, Hubbard Elwin	OF	1	+.000	StLA	Bkn
0	1	Schreiber, David (Barney)	P	3	.000	A	C
		Severeid, Henry Levai	C	22	.304	A	
10	14	Smith, Frank Elmer	P	34	.214	xBosA	
15	13	Suggs, George Franklin	P	36	.256	B	
0	0	Tannehill, Jesse Niles	P	1	.000	WashA09	C

WON 75 NATIONAL LEAGUE FINISHED 4th.
LOST 78
TG 153 1912. PCT. .490

CINCINNATI

HENRY F. O'DAY

WON	LOST	NAME	POS.	G.	BA	FROM	TO
		Almeida, Rafael D.	3B15	16	.220	B	
2	0	Bagby, James Chas. Jacob (Sarge)	P	5	.000	A	
		Bates, John Wm.	OF65	81	.289	B	
18	20	Benton, John Cleveland (Rube)	P	50	.135	B	
		Bescher, Robert Henry	OF143	145	.281	B	
		Blackburn, Earl Stuart	C	1	+.000	xPitt	
		Clarke, Thomas Aloysius	C63	72	.281	B	
0	0	Cramer, Wm. Wendell	P	1	.000	A	C
0	1	Davis, Frank Talmadge	P	7	.200	A	
0	0	Doak, Wm. Leopold	P	1	.000	A	
1	0	Donalds, Edward Alexander	P	1	.000	A	C
		Egan, Richard Joseph (Dick)	2B	149	.247	B	
		Esmond, James J.	SS74	82	.195	B	
0	0	Fletcher, Samuel S.	P	2	.500	Bkn09	C
1	0	Frill, John Edmond	P	3	.250	xStLA	C
16	19	Fromme, Arthur Henry	P	43	.087	B	
1	3	Gaspar, Harry Lambert	P	7	.250	B	C
		Grant, Edward Leslie (3B15)	SS56	96	.239	B	
2	0	Gregory, Frank E.	P	4	.200	A	C
1	2	Harter, Frank Pierce	P	6	.091	A	
		Hoblitzell, Richard Carleton	1B147	148	.294	B	
0	0	Horsey, Hanson	P	1	.000	A	C
9	11	Humpheries, Albert (Bert)	P	30	.137	B	
1	3	Keefe, Robert Francis	P	17	.167	B	C
		Knisely, Peter C.	OF	21	.328	A	
		Kyle, Andrew Ewing	OF	8	.350	A	C
		Marsans, Armando	OF98	110	.317	B	
		Mitchell, Michael Francis (Mike)	OF144	147	.283	B	
0	1	Moore, Eugene Sr.	P	5	.000	Pitt10	C
		McDonald, Chas. E.	SS42	61	.257	A	
1	0	McGraner, Howard	P	2	.250	A	C
		McLean, John Bannerman (Larry)	C98	102	.243	B	
1	0	Packard, Eugene Milo	P	1	.250	A	
		Phelan, Arthur Edward	3B127	130	.243	Cin10	

WON	LOST	NAME	POS.	G.	BA	FROM	TO
0	0	Prough, H. Clinton	P	1	.000	A	C
		Severeid, Henry Levai	C20	50	.237	B	
1	1	Smith, Frank Elmer	P	8	.000	B	
19	16	Suggs, George Franklin	P	42	.160	B	
0	0	Taylor, Benjamin	P	2	.000	A	C
0	0	Tompkins, Chas. Herbert	P	1	1.000	A	C
1	1	Works, Ralph Talmadge	P	3	.500	xDetA	

WON 64 NATIONAL LEAGUE FINISHED 7th.
LOST 89
TG 153 1913. PCT. .418

CINCINNATI

JOSEPH BERT TINKER

WON	LOST	NAME	POS.	G.	BA	FROM	TO
		Almeida, Rafael D.	3B37	50	.262	B	C
11	13	Ames, Leon Kessling	P	31	+.102	xN.Y.	
		Bates, John W.	OF111	131	.278	B	
		Becker, Beals	OF	30	+.296	N.Y.	Phil
11	7	Benton, John Cleveland (Rube)	P	23	.208	B	
		Berghammer, Martin Andrew	SS54	74	.218	ChiA11	
		Bescher, Robert Henry	OF138	141	.258	B	
0	0	Betts, Harold M.	P	1	.000	StL03	C
		Blackburn, Earl Stuart	C	17	.259	B	
11	12	Brown, Mordecai Peter Centennial	P	39	.204	Chi	
		Chapman, Harry E.	C	2	.500	Chi	
		Clarke, Thomas Aloysius	C100	114	.264	B	
		Devore, Joshua (Josh)	OF	66	+.267	xN.Y.	Phil
		Dodge, John Lewis	3B	94	+.243	xPhil	C
		Egan, Richard Joseph (Dick) (SS17)	2B37	60	.282	B	
1	4	Fromme, Arthur Henry	P	9	+.143	B	N.Y.
		Grant, Edward Leslie	3B	27	+.213	B	N.Y.
		Groh, Henry Knight (Heinie)	2B113	117	+.282	xN.Y.	
0	0	Harrington, Andrew Francis	P	1	.500	A	C
1	1	Harter, Frank Pierce	P	17	.143	B	
0	0	Herbert, Ernie Albert	P	6	.333	A	
		Hobbs, Wm. Lee	2B	2	.000	A	
		Hoblitzell, Richard Carleton	1B134	137	.285	B	
14	16	Johnson, George Murphy (Chief)	P	44	.114	A	
		Kling, John G.	C63	80	.273	Bos	C
		Marsans, Armando (1B22)	OF94	118	.297	B	
		Meister, Karl Daniel	OF	4	.285	A	C
0	1	Morgan, Harry Richard (Cy)	P	1	.000	PhilA	C
		McDonald, Chas. E.	SS	11	+.364	B	Bos
0	1	McIntire, Harry M.	P	1	.000	Chi	C
0	0	McManus, Joab Logan	P	1	.000	A	C
0	0	Nelson, Albert Francis	P	2	+.000	xPhil	C
		Niehoff, John Albert (Bert)	3B	2	.000	A	
7	11	Packard, Eugene Milo	P39	43	.180	B	
0	1	Powell, Wm. Burruss	P	1	.000	Chi	C
0	1	Robertson, Richard J.	P	2	.000	A	

WON	LOST	NAME	POS.	G.	BA	FROM	TO
0	4	Rowan, John Arthur	P	5	.182	Chi11	
		Severeid, Henry Levai	C7	8	.200	B	
		Sheckard, Samuel James Tilden	OF	47	+.190	xStL	C
0	1	Smith, John W.	P	5	.000	A	C
		Stewart, Mark	C	1	.000	A	C
8	15	Suggs, George Franklin	P	36	.254	B	
		Tinker, Joseph Bert MGR.	SS101	110	.317	Chi	
		Wickland, Albert	OF24	26	.215	A	
0	1	Works, Ralph Talmadge	P	4	.111	B	C

WON 60 NATIONAL LEAGUE FINISHED 8th (LAST)
LOST 94
TG 154 1914. PCT. .390

CINCINNATI

CHAS. LINCOLN HERZOG

WON	LOST	NAME	POS.	G.	BA	FROM	TO
0	0	Adams, Karl Tutweiler	P	4	.500	A	
15	23	Ames, Leon Kessling	P	47	.128	B	
		Bates, John Wm.	OF	58	+.252	B	Chi
16	18	Benton, John Cleveland (Rube)	P	41	.143	B	
		Berghammer, Martin Andrew	SS33	77	.223	B	
		Clarke, Thomas Aloysius	C106	113	.262	B	
		Daniels, Bertram Elmer	OF	71	.219	NYA	C
2	2	Davenport, Arthur David	P	10	.222	A	StLF
		Derrick, Claude Lester	SS	3	+.333	NYA	Chi
11	18	Douglas, Philip Brooks (Shufflin' Phil)	P	45	.137	ChiA12	
		Erwin, Ross Emil	C	14	+.306	xBkn	C
0	0	Fahrer, Clarence Willie (Pete)	P	5	.000	A	C
0	2	Fittery, Paul Clarence	P	11	.059	A	
		Glockson, Norman Stanley	C	7	.000	A	C
		Gonzales, Miguel Angel Cordero	C83	95	.233	Bos12	
		Graham, Dawson, Frank (Tiny)	1B	25	.230	A	C
0	0	Griffin, Patrick Richard	P	1	.000	A	C
		Groh, Henry Knight (Heinie)	2B134	139	.288	B	
		Herzog, Chas. Lincoln (Buck) MGR.	SS137	138	.281	N.Y.	
		Hoblitzell, Richard Carleton	1B75	78	.210	B	BosA
		Holden, Wm. Paul	OF	11	.214	xNYA	C
0	0	Ingersoll, Robert Randolph	P	4	1.000	A	C
0	0	Johnson, George Murphy (Chief)	P	1	.000	B	KCF
		Kellogg, Wm. Dearstyne	1B28	71	.175	A	C
		Killefer, Wade Hampton	OF37	42	.277	WashA10	
		Kippert, Edward A.	OF	2	.000	A	C
0	0	Koestner, Elmer Joseph	P	5	+.400	xChi	C
		LaRoss, Harry Raymond	OF20	22	.229	A	C
1	2	Lear, Chas. Bernard	P	17	.188	A	
		Lohr, Howard Sylvester	OF17	18	.213	A	
		Marsans, Armando	OF	36	.298	B	StLF
		Miller, Roy Oscar (Doc)	OF47	93	.255	Phil	C
		Mollwitz, Frederick August	1B	33	+.164	xChi	
		Moran, Joseph Herbert	OF	107	+.235	Bkn	Bos

WON	LOST	NAME	POS.	G.	BA	FROM	TO
		McLaughlin, James Anson (Kid)	OF1	3	.000	A	C
		Niehoff, John Albert (Bert)	3B134	142	.242	B	
		Rawlings, John Wm.	3B	33	.217	A	KCF
1	3	Rowan, John Arthur	P	12	.000	B	C
5	13	Schneider, Peter Joseph	P29	31	.178	A	
		Twombly, George Frederick	OF	68	.233	A	
		Uhler, Maurice W.	OF36	46	.214	A	C
		VonKolnitz, Alfred Holmes (Fritz)	3B20	41	.221	A	
9	13	Yingling, Earl Hershey	P34	61	.192	Bkn	

WON 71
LOST 83
TG 154

NATIONAL LEAGUE

1915.

FINISHED 7th.

PCT. .461

CINCINNATI

CHAS. LINCOLN HERZOG

WON	LOST	NAME	POS.	G.	BA	FROM	TO
2	4	Ames, Leon Kessling	P	17	+.050	B	StL
		Beall, John Woolf	OF	10	.232	ChiA13	
6	13	Benton, John Cleveland (Rube)	P	34	+.212	B	Pitt
0	2	Brown, Chas. Roy	P	9	.364	StLA13	C
0	0	Callahan, Ray James	P	3	.333	A	C
		Clarke, Thomas Aloysius	C72	96	.288	B	
0	0	Cochran, Alvin Jackson	P	1	.000	A	C
18	17	Dale, Emmett Eugene	P	49	.220	StL12	
		Dooin, Chas. Sebastian	C	10	+.323	Phil	N.Y.
1	5	Douglas, Philip Brooks (Shufflin' Phil)	P	8	+.118	B	Bkn
2	2	George, Thomas Edward	P	7	.363	ClevA12	
		Griffith, Thomas Herman	OF	160	.307	Bos	
		Groh, Henry Knight (Heinie) (2B29)	3B131	160	.290	B	
		#Herzog, Chas. Lincoln (Buck) MGR.	SS153	155	.264	B	
		Killefer, Wade Hampton (1B2)	OF150	155	.272	B	
		Leach, Thomas Wm.	OF96	107	.224	Chi	
6	10	Lear, Chas. Bernard	P	40	.170	B	C
		Mollwitz, Frederick August	1B	153	.259	B	
0	0	McCluskey, Harry Roberts	P	3	.000	A	C
5	5	McKenry, Frank Gordon	P	21	.152	A	
		Olson, Ivan Massie (1B9 3B15)	2B30	63	+.232	ClevA	Bkn
		%Rodgers, Wilbur Kincaid	2B56	72	.239	xBosA	
14	19	Schneider, Peter Joseph	P	48	.245	B	
17	6	Toney, Frederick Arthur	P	36	.095	Chi13	
		Twombly, George Frederick	OF24	46	.197	B	
		*VonKolnitz, Alfred Holmes (Fritz)	3B18	50	.192	B	
		@Wagner, Joseph Bernard	2B46	75	.178	A	C
		Williams, Kenneth Roy	OF62	71	.242	A	
		Wingo, Ivy Brown (OF2)	C98	119	.221	StL	

#Herzog also played 5 games at 1B.
%Rodgers also played 6 games at SS, 1 game at 3B and 1 game in the OF.
*VonKolnitz also played 2 games as C, 3 games at 1B, 6 games at SS and 1 game in the OF.
@Wagner also played 15 games at SS, 2 games at 3B and 2 games in the OF.

WON 60
LOST 93
TG 153

NATIONAL LEAGUE

1916.

FINISHED 7th.
(TIED WITH ST.LOUIS)
PCT. .392

CINCINNATI

CHAS. LINCOLN HERZOG CHRISTOPHER MATHEWSON
IVY BROWN WINGO

WON	LOST	NAME	POS.	G.	BA	FROM	TO
		Beall, John Woolf	OF	6	.333	B	
0	1	Bluejacket, James	P	3	.000	BknF	C
		Chase, Harold Homer (Hal) (2B16 OF25)	1B98	142	.339	BuffF	
		Clarke, Thomas Aloysius	C51	78	.237	B	
3	4	Dale, Emmett Eugene	P	17	.143	B	C
		Emmer, Frank Wm. (2B1 3B2 OF2)	SS29	42	.146	A	
		#Fisher, Robert Tecumseh	SS29	61	.272	Chi	
		Griffith, Thomas Herman	OF	155	.266	B	
		Groh, Henry Knight (Heinie) (2B33 SS5)	3B110	149	.269	B	
		xHerzog, Chas. Lincoln (Buck) MGR.	SS57	79	+.267	B	N.Y.
		Hobbs, Wm. Lee	SS	6	.182	Cin13	C
		Huhn, Emil Hugo (1B14 OF1)	C18	37	.255	NewF	
		Killefer, Wade Hampton	OF68	70	+.244	B	N.Y.
5	12	Knetzer, Elmer Ellsworth	P36	37	+.154	xBos	C
		Kopf, Wm. Lorenz (Larry)	SS	11	.275	PhilA	
		Louden, Wm. (SS23)	2B108	134	.219	BuffF	C
1	0	Mathewson, Christopher (Big Six) MGR.	P	1	+.600	xN.Y.	
11	10	*Mitchell, Clarence Elmer	P29	56	.239	DetA11	
		Mollwitz, Frederick August	1B	65	+.224	B	Chi
7	10	Moseley, Earl Victor	P	31	.087	NewF	C
1	1	McKenry, Frank Gordon	P	6	.400	B	C
		McKechnie, Wm. Boyd	3B	37	+.292	xN.Y.	
		Neale, Alfred Earle (Greasy)	OF133	138	.262	A	
		Rodgers, Wilbur Kincaid (SS1)	2B2	3	.000	B	C
		Roush, Edd J.	OF	69	+.287	xN.Y.	
10	19	Schneider, Peter Joseph	P44	49	.236	B	
8	19	Schulz, Albert C.	P	44	.125	BuffF	C
		Smith, Paul Stoner	OF	10	.227	A	C
14	17	Toney, Frederick Arthur	P	41	.121	B	
0	0	Twining, Howard Earle	P	1	.000	A	C
		Twombly, George Frederick	OF	3	.000	B	
		Williams, Kenneth Roy	OF	10	.111	B	
		Wingo, Ivy Brown MGR.	C107	119	.245	B	

#Fisher also played 7 games at 2B and 1 game in the OF.
xHerzog also played 22 games at 3B and 1 games in the OF.
*Mitchell also played 6 games at 1B and 5 games in the OF.

WON 78 — LOST 76 — TG 154

NATIONAL LEAGUE — 1917. — FINISHED 4th. — PCT. .506

CINCINNATI

CHRISTOPHER MATHEWSON

WON	LOST	NAME	POS.	G.	BA	FROM	TO
0	0	Bressler, Raymond Bloom (Rube)	P	3	.200	PhilA	
		Chase, Harold Homer (Hal)	1B151	152	.277	B	
		Clarke, Thomas Aloysius	C29	58	.291	B	
		Cueto, Manuel Melo (C5 2B6)	OF38	56	.200	StLF14	
10	5	Eller, Horace Owen (Hod)	P	37	.133	A	
0	1	Engel, Joseph Wm.	P	1	.000	WashA15	
		Getz, Gustave (2B3)	3B2	7	.286	Bkn	
		Griffith, Thomas Herman	OF100	115	.270	B	
		Groh, Henry Knight (Heinie) (2B2)	3B154	156	.304	B	
		Huhn, Emil Hugo (1B1)	C15	23	.196	B	C
0	0	Knetzer, Elmer Ellsworth	P	11	.000	B	C
		Kopf, Wm. Lorenz (Larry)	SS145	148	.255	B	
		*Magee, Sherwood Robert (Sherry)	OF45	45	+.324	xBos	
9	15	Mitchell, Clarence Elmer (1B6 OF6)	P32	47	.278	B	
		McKechnie, Wm. Boyd (SS13 3B4)	2B26	48	.254	B	
		Neale, Alfred Earle (Greasy)	OF119	121	.294	B	
0	0	Perry, Herbert Scott	P	4	.000	Chi	
0	0	Pillette, Herman Polycarp	P	1	.000	A	
11	10	Regan, Michael Joseph	P32	33	.200	A	
3	7	Ring, James Joseph	P	24	.077	A	
		Roush, Edd J.	OF134	136	.341	B	
1	2	Ruether, Walter Henry (Dutch)	P	19	+.192	xChi	
0	1	Sanders, Roy Garvin	P	3	.000	A	
20	19	Schneider, Peter Joseph	P46	49	.167	B	
		Shean, David Wm.	2B	131	.210	Bos12	
		Smith, James Harry	C	8	.118	BknF15	
		Thorpe, James Francis	OF	77	+.247	NY15	N.Y.
24	16	Toney, Frederick Arthur	P	43	.112	B	
		Wingo, Ivy Brown	C120	121	.266	B	

*Magee also played 2 games at 1B.

WON 68 — LOST 60 — TG 128

NATIONAL LEAGUE — 1918. — FINISHED 3rd. — PCT. .531

CINCINNATI

CHRISTOPHER MATHEWSON HENRY KNIGHT GROH

WON	LOST	NAME	POS.	G.	BA	FROM	TO
		Allen, Artemus Ward (Nick)	C31	37	.260	Chi16	
		Archer, James Patrick (1B1 OF1)	C8	9	+.219	xBkn	C
		Blackburne, Russell Aubrey (Lena)	SS	125	.228	ChiA15	
8	5	Bressler, Raymond Bloom (Rube) (OF3)	P17	23	.274	B	
		Chase, Harold Homer (Hal) (OF2)	1B67	74	.301	B	
2	0	Conley, James Patrick (Snipe)	P	5	.250	BaltF15	C
		Cueto, Manuel Melo (C6 2B10 SS9)	OF19	47	.296	B	
16	12	Eller, Horace Owen (Hod)	P	37	.157	B	
		Griffith, Thomas Herman	OF	118	.265	B	
		Groh, Henry Knight (Heinie) MGR.	3B	126	.320	B	
0	0	Haines, Jesse Joseph (Pop)	P	1	1.000	A	
0	1	Jacobus, Stuart Louis	P	5	.000	A	C
6	3	Luque, Adolfo	P13	13	.321	Bos15	
		Magee, Leo Christopher (Lee) (3B3)	2B114	119	.290	StLA	
		Magee, Sherwood Robert (Sherry) (2B6 OF38)	1B66	115	.297	B	
4	0	Mitchell, Albert Roy	P	5	.214	xChiA	
		Neale, Alfred Earle (Greasy)	OF102	107	.270	B	
9	5	Ring, James Joseph	P	21	.120	B	
5	5	Regan, Michael Joseph	P	23	.296	B	
		Roush, Edd J.	OF	113	.333	B	
0	1	Ruether, Walter Henry (Dutch)	P	2	.200	B	
10	15	Schneider, Peter Joseph	P34	36	.289	B	
2	3	Smith, George Allen	P	10	+.118	N.Y.	N.Y.
		Smith, James Harry	C	13	.185	B	C
6	10	Toney, Frederick Arthur	P	22	+.214	B	N.Y.
		Wingo, Ivy Brown (OF2)	C93	100	.254	B	

WON 96 — LOST 44 — TG 140

NATIONAL LEAGUE — 1919. — FINISHED 1st. — PCT. .686

CINCINNATI

PATRICK JOSEPH MORAN

WON	LOST	NAME	POS.	G.	BA	FROM	TO
		Allen, Artemus Ward (Nick)	C	15	.320	B	
2	4	Bressler, Raymond Bloom (Rube) (P13)	OF48	61	.206	B	
		Cueto, Manuel Melo (3B1)	OF25	29	.250	B	C
		Daubert, Jacob Ellsworth (Jake)	1B	140	.276	Bkn	
		Duncan, Louis Baird (Pat)	OF27	31	.244	Pitt15	
19	9	Eller, Horace Owen (Hod)	P	38	.280	B	

WON	LOST	NAME	POS.	G.	BA	FROM	TO
14	5	Fisher, Raymond Lyle	P	26	.271	NYA17	
1	0	Gerner, Edward Frederick	P	5	.167	A	C
		Groh, Henry Knight (Heinie)	3B121	122	.310	B	
		Kopf, Wm. Lorenz (Larry)	SS	135	.270	Cin17	
10	3	Luque, Adolfo (3B1)	P30	31	.125	B	
		Magee, Sherwood Robert (Sherry) (2B1 3B1)	OF47	56	.215	B	C
0	1	Mitchell, Albert Roy	P	7	.000	B	C
		Neale, Alfred Earle (Greasy)	OF138	139	.242	B	
		Rariden, Wm. Angel	C70	74	.216	N.Y.	
		Rath, Maurice Chas.	2B	138	.264	ChiA13	
0	0	Regan, Michael Joseph	P	1	.000	B	C
		Rehg, Walter Phillip	OF	5	.167	Bos	C
10	9	Ring, James Joseph	P	32	.097	B	
		Roush, Edd J.	OF	133	.321	B	
19	6	Ruether, Walter Henry (Dutch)	P33	42	.261	B	
21	7	Salle, Harry Franklin (Slim)	P	29	.189	N.Y.	
		Schreiber, Henry Ward (SS2)	3B17	19	.224	Bos17	
		See, Chas. Henry	OF	8	.286	A	
		*Smith, James Lawrence	SS5	28	.275	Bos	
		Wingo, Ivy Brown	C75	76	.273	B	
		Zitzmann, Wm. Arthur	OF	2	+.000	xPitt	

*Smith also played 1 game at 2B, 6 games at 3B and 4 games in the OF.

WON 82 — LOST 71 — TG 153

NATIONAL LEAGUE 1920. FINISHED 3rd. PCT. .536

CINCINNATI

PATRICK JOSEPH MORAN

WON	LOST	NAME	POS.	G.	BA	FROM	TO
		Allen, Artemus Ward (Nick)	C36	43	.271	B	C
2	1	Brenton, Lynn Davis	P	5	.250	ClevA15	
2	0	Bressler, Raymond Bloom (Rube) (1B2)	P21	21	.267	B	
0	1	@Coumbe, Frederick Nicholas	P5	5	.231	ClevA	
		*Crane, Samuel Byren	SS25	54	.215	WashA17	
		Daubert, Jacob Ellsworth (Jake)	1B140	142	.304	B	
		Duncan, Louis Baird (Pat)	OF	154	.295	B	
13	12	Eller, Horace Owen (Hod) (1B2 2B1)	P35	38	.253	B	
10	11	Fisher, Raymond Lyle	P	33	.243	B	C
		Groh, Henry Knight (Heinie)	3B144	145	.298	B	
		#Kopf, Wm. Lorenz (Larry)	SS123	126	.245	B	
0	0	Lowe, George Wesley	P	1	.000	A	C
13	9	Luque, Adolfo	P	37	.266	B	
4	2	Napier, Samuel LeRoy (Buddy)	P	9	.214	Chi18	
		Neale, Alfred Earle (Greasy)	OF	150	.255	B	
		Rariden, Wm. Angel	C37	39	.248	B	C
		Rath, Maurice Chas. (3B1 OF1)	2B126	129	.267	B	C
17	16	Ring, James Joseph	P	42	.198	B	
		Roush, Edd J. (1B11 2B1)	OF139	149	.339	B	
16	12	Ruether, Walter Henry (Dutch)	P37	45	.192	B	
5	6	Sallee, Harry Franklin (Slim)	P	21	+.171	B	N.Y.
0	0	See, Chas. Henry (P1)	OF17	47	.305	B	
		Sicking, Edward Joseph (SS10 3B6)	2B31	37	+.266	xN.Y.	C
0	1	Swartz, Monroe	P	1	.500	A	C
0	0	Theis, John Louis	P	1	.000	A	C
		Wingo, Ivy Brown (2B2)	C107	108	.264	B	

@Coumbe also played 2 games in the OF.
*Crane also played 4 games at 2B, 10 games at 3B and 3 games in the OF.
Kopf also played 2 games at 2B, 2 at 3B and 1 game in the OF.

WON 70 — LOST 83 — TG 153

NATIONAL LEAGUE 1921. FINISHED 6th. PCT. .458

CINCINNATI

PATRICK JOSEPH MORAN

WON	LOST	NAME	POS.	G.	BA	FROM	TO
		Bohne, Samuel Arthur (3B53)	2B102	153	.285	StL16	
1	8	Brenton, Lynn Davis	P	17	.133	B	C
		Bressler, Raymond Bloom (Rube)	OF85	109	.307	B	
0	1	Clarke, Alan Thomas	P	1	.000	A	C
3	4	Coumbe, Frederick Nicholas (Fritz)	P28	31	.320	B	C
		Crane, Samuel Byren	SS63	73	.233	B	
		Daubert, Jacob Ellsworth (Jake)	1B	136	.306	B	
7	6	Donohue, Peter Joseph	P	21	.211	A	
		Douglas, Astyanax Saunders	C	4	.143	A	
		Duncan, Louis Baird (Pat)	OF	145	.308	B	
2	2	Eller, Horace Owen (Hod)	P	13	.231	B	C
		Fonseca, Lewis Albert (1B16 OF16)	2B50	82	.276	A	
1	1	Geary, Robert Norton	P	10	.250	PhilA19	C
		Groh, Henry Knight (Heinie)	3B	97	.331	B	
		Hargrave, Eugene Franklin	C73	93	.289	Chi15	
		Hogan, Kenneth Timothy	OF	1	.000	A	
		Kimmick, Walter Lyons	3B	3	.167	StL19	
		Kopf, Wm. Lorenz (Larry)	SS93	107	.218	B	
17	19	Luque, Adolfo	P41	42	.270	B	
2	6	Markle, Clifford Monroe	P	10	.125	NYA16	
17	14	Marquard, Richard Wm. (Rube)	P	39	.200	Bkn	
0	2	Napier, Samuel LeRoy (Buddy)	P	22	.143	B	C
		Neale, Alfred Earle (Greasy)	OF	63	+.241	xPhil	
		Paskert, George Henry (Dode)	OF24	27	.174	Chi	C
19	18	Rixey, Eppa Jr.	P	40	.129	Phil	
1	2	Rogge, F. Clinton	P	6	.100	PittF15	C
		Roush, Edd J.	OF108	112	.352	B	
		See, Chas. Henry	OF30	37	.245	B	C

WON	LOST	NAME	POS.	G.	BA	FROM	TO
		Williams, Evon Daniel	OF	10	.000	A	
		Wingo, Ivy Brown	C92	97	.268	B	

WON 86 — NATIONAL LEAGUE — FINISHED 2nd.
LOST 68
TG 154 — 1922. — PCT. .558

CINCINNATI

PATRICK JOSEPH MORAN

WON	LOST	NAME	POS.	G.	BA	FROM	TO
		Bohne, Samuel Arthur (SS20)	2B85	112	.274	B	
		Bressler, Raymond Bloom (Rube) (OF2)	1B3	52	.264	B	
		Burns, George Joseph	OF	156	.285	N.Y.	
		Caveney, James Christopher	SS	118	.238	A	
16	9	Couch, John Daniel	P	43	.132	DetA17	
		Daubert, Jacob Ellsworth (Jake)	1B	156	.336	B	
18	9	Donohue, Peter Joseph	P	33	.181	B	
		Duncan, Louis Baird (Pat)	OF	151	.327	B	
		Fonseca, Lewis Albert	2B71	81	.361	B	
3	3	Gillespie, John Patrick	P	31	.133	A	C
		Hargrave, Eugene Franklin	C87	98	.315	B	
		Harper, George Washington	OF109	128	.339	DetA18	
7	6	Keck, Frank Joseph (Cactus)	P	27	.159	A	
		Kimmick, Walter Lyons (2B3 3B1)	SS30	39	.247	B	
13	23	Luque, Adolfo	P	39	.209	B	
		Lutz, Louis Wm. (Red)	C	1	1.000	A	C
4	5	Markle, Clifford Monroe	P	25	.150	B	
		Neale, Alfred Earle (Greasy)	OF16	25	.233	B	
		Pinelli, Ralph Arthur (Babe)	3B	156	.305	DetA20	
25	13	Rixey, Eppa Jr.	P	40	.192	B	
		Roush, Edd J.	OF43	49	.351	B	
0	0	Schnell, Karl Otto	P	10	.250	A	
0	0	Scott, John Wm. (Jack)	P	1	+.000	Bos	N.Y.
		Wingo, Ivy Brown	C78	80	.284	B	

WON 91 — NATIONAL LEAGUE — FINISHED 2nd.
LOST 63
TG 154 — 1923. — PCT. .591

CINCINNATI

PATRICK JOSEPH MORAN

WON	LOST	NAME	POS.	G.	BA	FROM	TO
0	0	Abrams, George Allen	P	3	1.000	A	C
14	10	Benton, John Cleveland (Rube)	P	33	.288	NY21	
		Bohne, Samuel Arthur (1B1 SS9 3B35)	2B96	139	.252	B	
		Bressler, Raymond Bloom (Rube) (OF6)	1B22	54	.277	B	
		Burns, George Joseph	OF	154	.274	B	
		Caveney, James Christopher	SS	138	.277	B	
2	7	Couch, John Daniel	P	19	+.174	B	Phil
		Daubert, Jacob Ellsworth (Jake)	1B121	125	.292	B	
21	15	Donohue, Peter Joseph	P	42	.250	B	
		Duncan, Louis Baird (Pat)	OF146	147	.327	B	
		Fonseca, Lewis Albert (1B14)	2B45	65	.278	B	
		Fowler, Joseph Chester	SS10	11	.333	A	
0	0	Gill, Harold Edmund	P	1	.000	A	C
		Hargrave, Eugene Franklin	C109	118	.333	B	
		Harper, George Washington	OF29	61	.256	B	
3	2	Harris, Wm. Milton	P	22	.353	A	
		Hock, Edward Francis	OF	2	.000	StL20	
3	6	Keck, Frank Joseph (Cactus)	P	35	.059	B	C
		Kimmick, Walter Lyons (SS1 3B4)	2B17	29	.225	B	
27	8	Luque, Adolfo	P41	43	.202	B	
		Mann, Leslie	OF	8	+.000	xStL	
1	0	McQuaid, Herbert George	P	12	.000	A	
		Pick, Edgar Everett	OF4	9	.375	A	
		Pinellie, Ralph Arthur (Babe)	3B114	117	.277	B	
20	15	Rixey, Eppa Jr.	P	42	.159	B	
		Roush, Edd J.	OF137	138	.351	B	
		Sanberg, Gustave E.	C5	7	.176	A	
0	0	Schnell, Karl Otto	P	1	.000	B	C
		Wingo, Ivy Brown	C57	61	.263	B	

WON 83 — NATIONAL LEAGUE — FINISHED 4th.
LOST 70
TG 153 — 1924. — PCT. .542

CINCINNATI

JOHN CALHOUN HENDRICKS

WON	LOST	NAME	POS.	G.	BA	FROM	TO
		Begley, James Lawrence	2B	2	.200	A	C
7	9	Benton, John Cleveland (Rube)	P	32	.261	B	
		Blott, John Leonard (Jack)	C1	2	.000	A	C
		Bohne, Samuel Arthur (SS40 3B12)	2B48	100	.255	B	
		Bressler, Raymond Bloom (Rube) (OF49)	1B50	115	.347	B	
		Burns, George Joseph	OF90	93	.256	B	
		Caveney, James Christopher (2B5)	SS90	95	.273	B	
		Critz, Hugh Melville (SS1)	2B96	102	.322	A	
		Daubert, Jacob Ellsworth (Jake)	1B	102	.281	B	C
3	0	Dibut, Pedro	P	7	.273	A	
16	9	Donohue, Peter Joseph	P35	36	.192	B	
		Duncan, Louis Baird (Pat)	OF83	96	.270	B	C
		Fonseca, Lewis Albert (1B6)	2B10	20	.228	B	
		Fowler, Joseph Chester (2B4 3B2)	SS32	59	.333	B	

WON	LOST	NAME	POS.	G.	BA	FROM	TO
		Hargrave, Eugene Franklin	C91	98	.301	B	
		Harper, George Washington	OF22	28	+.270	B	Phil
0	0	Harris, Wm. Milton	P	3	1.000	B	
		Hock, Edward Francis	OF2	16	.100	B	C
		Lee, Clifford Walker	OF1	6	+.333	xPhil	
10	15	Luque, Adolfo (OF1)	P31	33	.178	B	
3	3	May, Frank Spruell (Jake)	P	38	.111	StL21	
20	9	Mays, Carl Wm.	P37	38	.289	N.Y.A	
		Neale, Alfred Earle (Greasy)	OF2	3	.000	Cin22	C
		Pick, Edgar Everett	OF1	3	.000	B	
		Pinelli, Ralph Arthur (Babe)	3B143	144	.306	B	
15	14	Rixey, Eppa Jr.	P	35	.214	B	
		Roush, Edd J.	OF119	121	.348	B	
		Sanberg, Gustave E.	C	24	.173	B	C
9	11	Sheehan, Thomas Clancy	P39	41	.310	NYA21	
		Shorten, Chas. Henry	OF15	41	.275	StLA22	C
		Walker, Wm. Curtis	OF	109	+.300	xPhil	
		Wingo, Ivy Brown (1B1)	C65	66	.286	B	

WON 80 — NATIONAL LEAGUE — FINISHED 3rd.
LOST 73
TG 153 — 1925. — PCT. .523

CINCINNATI

JOHN CALHOUN HENDRICKS

WON	LOST	NAME	POS.	G.	BA	FROM	TO
9	10	Benton, John Cleveland (Rube)	P30	33	.200	B	C
0	1	Biemiller, Harry Lee	P	23	.000	WashA20	C
		Bohne, Samuel Arthur (1B2 2B10 3B2 OF4)	SS49	73	.257	B	
1	3	Brady, Cornelius Joseph (Neal)	P	20	.240	NYA17	C
		Bressler, Raymond Bloom (Rube) (OF38)	1B52	97	.348	B	
		Bruggy, Frank Leo	C	6	.214	PhilA	C
		Caveney, James Christopher	SS111	115	.249	B	C
		Critz, Hugh Melville	2B	144	.277	B	
0	0	Dibut, Pedro	P	1	.000	B	C
21	14	Donohue, Peter Joseph	P42	43	.294	B	
		Douglas, Astyanax Saunders	C	7	.176	Cin21	C
		Dressen, Chas. Walter (Chuck) (2B5 OF4)	3B47	76	.274	A	
		Fowler, Joseph Chester	SS	6	.400	B	
0	2	Goodwin, Marvin Mardo	P	4	.250	StL22	C
		Hargrave, Eugene Franklin	C84	87	.300	B	
		Holke, Walter Henry	1B	65	+.280	xPhil	C
		Hudgens, James Price	1B	3	.429	StL23	
		Klee, Ollie Chester	OF1	3	.000	A	C
		Krueger, Ernest George	C30	37	.307	Bkn21	C
16	18	Luque, Adolfo	P33	37	.255	B	
8	9	May, Frank Spruell (Jake)	P33	36	.186	B	
3	5	Mays, Carl Wm.	P	12	.250	B	
		Myers, Henry Harrison (Hy)	OF	3	+.167	xStL	StL
		Niehaus, Albert Bernard	1B45	51	+.299	xPitt	C
		Pinelli, Ralph Arthur (Babe) (SS17)	3B109	130	.283	B	
21	11	Rixey, Eppa Jr.	P36	39	.214	B	
		Roush, Edd J.	OF	134	.339	B	
		Schultz, Joseph Chas. (2B1)	OF15	33	+.323	xPhil	C
1	0	Sheehan, Thomas Clancy	P	10	+.200	B	Pitt
		Smith, Elmer John	OF80	96	.271	NYA23	C
		Sullivan, Thomas Brandon	C	1	.000	A	C
		Walker, Wm. Curtis	OF141	145	.318	B	
		Wingo, Ivy Brown	C	55	.205	B	
		Zitzmann, Wm. Arthur (SS1)	OF89	104	.252	Cin19	

WON 87 — NATIONAL LEAGUE — FINISHED 2nd.
LOST 67
TG 154 — 1926. — PCT. .565

CINCINNATI

JOHN CALHOUN HENDRICKS

WON	LOST	NAME	POS.	G.	BA	FROM	TO
		Allen, Ethan Nathan	OF9	18	.308	A	
		Bohne, Samuel Arthur	2B20	25	+.204	B	Bkn
		x Bressler, Raymond Bloom (Rube)	OF80	86	.357	B	
		Carter, John Howard (SS1)	2B3	5	.000	A	C
		Christenson, Walter Neils	OF93	114	.350	A	
		Critz, Hugh Melville	2B	155	.270	B	
0	0	Day, Clyde Henry (Pea Ridge)	P	4	.000	StL	
20	14	Donohue, Peter Joseph	P	47	.311	B	
		#Dressen, Chas. Walter (Chuck)	3B123	127	.266	B	
		Emmer, Frank Wm.	SS79	80	.196	Cin16	C
		Ford, Horace Hills	SS	57	.279	Bkn	
		Hargrave, Eugene Franklin	C93	105	.353	B	
0	0	Holland, Howard Arthur	P	3	.500	A	
		Hudgens, James Price	1B6	17	.250	B	C
8	5	Lucas, Chas. Frederick (Red) (2B1)	P39	66	.303	Bos	
13	16	Luque, Adolfo	P	34	.346	B	
13	9	May, Frank Spruell (Jake)	P	45	.146	B	
19	12	Mays, Carl Wm.	P	39	.224	B	
0	0	Meadows, Rufus Rivers	P	1	.000	A	C
0	2	Meeker, Chas. Roy	P	7	.000	PhilA24	C
0	1	Nehf, Arthur Neukom	P	7	+.200	xN.Y.	
		Picinich, Valentine John (Val)	C86	89	.263	BosA	
		Pinelli, Ralph Arthur (Babe) (2B3 SS27)	3B40	71	.222	B	
		Pipp, Walter Clement (Wally)	1B	155	.291	NYA	
		Prothro, James Thomson (Doc)	3B2	3	.200	BosA	
14	8	Rixey, Eppa Jr.	P	37	.226	B	
		Roush, Edd J. (1B1)	OF143	144	.323	B	
		Scott, Lewis Everett	SS	4	.667	xChiA	C
0	0	Springer, Bradford Louis	P	1	.000	StLA	C
		Sukeforth, Clyde LeRoy		1	.000	A	
		Walker, Wm. Curtis	OF152	155	.306	B	

WON	LOST	NAME	POS.	G.	BA	FROM	TO
		Wingo, Ivy Brown	C	7	.200	B	
		Zitzmann, Wm. Arthur	OF31	53	.245	B	

xBressler also played 4 games at 1B.
#Dressen also played 1 game at SS and 1 game in the OF.

WON 75 — NATIONAL LEAGUE — FINISHED 5th.
LOST 78
TG 153 — 1927. — PCT. .490

CINCINNATI

JOHN CALHOUN HENDRICKS

WON	LOST	NAME	POS.	G.	BA	FROM	TO
		Allen, Ethan Nathan	OF98	111	.295	B	
0	1	Beckman, James Joseph	P	4	.000	A	
		Bressler, Raymond Bloom(Rube)	OF120	124	.291	B	
		Christenson, Walter Neils	OF50	57	.254	B	C
		Critz, Hugh Melville	2B	113	.278	B	
6	16	Donohue, Peter Joseph	P	33	.250	B	
		Dressen, Chas. Walter (Chuck) (SS2)	3B142	144	.292	B	
		Ford, Horace Hills (2B12)	SS104	115	.274	B	
		Hargrave, Eugene Franklin	C92	102	.308	B	
2	1	Jablonowski, Peter Wm.	P	6	.545	A	
		Kelly, George Lange (Long George) (2B13 OF2)	1B49	61	.270	N.Y.	
3	3	Kolp, Raymond Carl	P	24	.200	StLA24	
18	11	#Lucas, Chas. Frederick (Red) (2B5)	P37	80	.313	B	
13	12	Luque, Adolfo	P	29	.217	B	
15	12	May, Frank Spruell (Jake)	P	44	.184	B	
3	7	Mays, Carl Wm.	P	14	.406	B	
3	5	Nehf, Arthur Neukom	P	21	+.077	B	Chi
		Picinich, Valentine John (Val)	C61	65	.254	B	
		Pinelli, Ralph Arthur (Babe) (2B5 SS9)	3B15	30	.197	B	C
		Pipp, Walter Clement (Wally)	1B114	122	.260	B	
		Pittinger, Clark Alonzo (SS9 3B2)	2B20	31	.274	Chi25	
		Purdy, Everett Virgil	OF16	18	.355	ChiA	
12	10	Rixey, Eppa Jr.	P	34	.247	B	
		Sukeforth, Clyde LeRoy	C24	38	.190	B	
		Walker, Wm. Curtis	OF141	146	.292	B	
		Wanninger, Paul Louis	SS	28	.247	xBosA	C
		White, John Peter (SS2)	2B3	5	.000	A	
		Wolf, Raymond Bernard	1B	1	.000	A	C
		Zitzmann, Wm. Arthur (SS8 3B3)	OF60	88	.284	B	

#Lucas also played 3 games at SS and 1 game in the OF.

WON 78 — NATIONAL LEAGUE — FINISHED 5th.
LOST 74
TG 152 — 1928. — PCT. .513

CINCINNATI

JOHN CALHOUN HENDRICKS

WON	LOST	NAME	POS.	G.	BA	FROM	TO
		Allen, Ethan Nathan	OF	129	.305	B	
3	3	Ash, Kenneth Lowther	P	9	.071	ChiA25	
0	1	Beckman, James Joseph	P	6	.000	B	C
		Callaghan, Martin Francis	OF69	81	.290	Chi23	
		Critz, Hugh Melville	2B	153	.296	B	
7	11	Donohue, Peter Joseph	P	23	.146	B	
		Dressen, Chas. Walter (Chuck)	3B	135	.291	B	
2	2	Edwards, James Corbette	P	18	.300	ChiA26	C
		Ford, Horace Hills	SS	149	.241	B	
		Hargrave, Eugene Franklin	C57	65	.295	B	
3	4	Jablonowski, Peter (OF1)	P31	32	.323	B	
0	0	Johnson, Silas Kenneth	P	3	.250	A	
		Kelly, George Lange (Long George) (OF13)	1B99	116	.296	B	
13	10	Kolp, Raymond Carl	P	44	.214	B	
13	9	Lucas, Chas. Frederick (Red)	P27	39	.315	B	
11	10	Luque, Adolfo	P	33	.119	B	
3	5	May, Frank Spruell (Jake)	P	21	.296	B	
4	1	Mays, Carl Wm.	P	14	.296	B	
		Picinich, Valentine John (Val)	C93	96	.302	B	
		Pipp, Walter Clement (Wally)	1B72	95	.283	B	C
		Pittinger, Clark Alonzo (2B4 3B4)	SS12	40	.237	B	
		Purdy, Everett Virgil	OF61	70	.309	B	
0	0	Pyle, Harlan Albert	P	2	.000	A	C
19	18	Rixey, Eppa Jr.	P	43	.173	B	
		Stripp, Joseph Valentine (SS1 3B17)	OF21	42	.288	A	
		Sukeforth, Clyde LeRoy	C26	33	.132	B	
		Walker, Wm. Curtis	OF122	123	.279	B	
		White, John Peter	2B	1	.000	B	C
		Zitzmann, Wm. Arthur (3B1)	OF78	101	.297	B	

WON 66 — NATIONAL LEAGUE — FINISHED 7th.
LOST 88
TG 154 — 1929. — PCT. .429

CINCINNATI

JOHN CALHOUN HENDRICKS

WON	LOST	NAME	POS.	G.	BA	FROM	TO
		Allen, Ethan Nathan	OF137	143	.292	B	
1	5	Ash, Kenneth Lowther (OF1)	P29	30	.143	B	
		Crabtree, Estel Crayton		1	.000	A	
		Critz, Hugh Melville (SS1)	2B106	107	.247	B	

WON	LOST	NAME	POS.	G.	BA	FROM	TO
		Dixon, Leo Michael	C	14	.167	StLA27	C
10	13	Donohue, Peter Joseph	P	32	.333	B	
		Dressen, Chas. Walter (Chuck) (2B8)	3B98	110	.244	B	
1	2	Ehrhardt, Welton Claude (Rube)	P	24	.182	Bkn	C
		Ford, Horace Hills (2B42)	SS108	148	.276	B	
1	2	Frey, Benjamin Rudolph	P	3	.375	A	
		Gooch, John Beverly	C86	92	+.300	xBkn	
1	1	Gudat, Marvin John	P	9	.200	A	
0	0	Johnson, Silas Kenneth	P	1	.000	B	
		Kelly, George Lange (Long George)	1B	147	.293	B	
0	0	Kemner, Herman John	P	9	.250	A	C
8	10	Kolp, Raymond Carl	P	30	.163	B	
19	12	Lucas, Chas. Frederick (Red)	P32	76	.293	B	
5	16	Luque, Adolfo	P	32	.278	B	
10	14	May, Frank Spruell (Jake)	P	41	.203	B	
		McMullen, Hugh Raphael	C	1	.000	WashA	C
		x Pittinger, Clark Alonzo (3B8)	SS50	77	.295	B	C
		Purdy, Everett Virgil	OF42	82	.271	B	C
10	13	Rixey, Eppa Jr.	P	35	.231	B	
		Shaner, Walter Dedaker (OF2)	1B7	13	.321	BosA27	C
		Stripp, Joseph Valentine (2B2)	3B55	64	.214	B	
		Sukeforth, Clyde LeRoy	C76	84	.354	B	
		Swanson, Ernest Evar	OF142	148	.300	A	
		Walker, Wm. Curtis	OF138	141	.313	B	
		Wingo, Ivy Brown	C	1	.000	Cin26	C
0	0	Zahniser, Paul Vernon	P	1	.000	BosA26	C
		Zitzmann, Wm. Arthur (1B5)	OF22	47	.226	B	C

xPittinger also played 4 games at 2B.

WON 59 NATIONAL LEAGUE FINISHED 7th.
LOST 95
TG 154 1930. PCT. .383

CINCINNATI

DANIEL PHILIP HOWLEY

WON	LOST	NAME	POS.	G.	BA	FROM	TO
		Allen, Ethan Nathan	OF15	21	+.271	B	N.Y.
2	0	Ash, Kenneth Lowther	P16	17	.182	B	C
7	12	Benton, Lawrence James (Larry)	P	35	+.177	xN.Y.	
		Callaghan, Martin Francis	OF54	79	.276	Cin28	C
2	4	Campbell, Archer Stewart (Archie)	P	23	.267	Wash	C
0	1	Carroll, Owen Thomas	P	3	.200	xN.Y.A.	
		Crawford, Clifford Rankin (1B13)	2B54	76	+.290	xN.Y.	
		Critz, Hugh Melville	2B	28	+.231	B	N.Y.
		Cuccinello, Anthony Francis (Tony) (2B15 SS4)	3B109	125	.312	A	
		Cullop, Henry Nicholas	OF5	7	.182	Bkn	
1	3	Donohue, Peter Joseph	P	8	+.100	B	N.Y.

WON	LOST	NAME	POS.	G.	BA	FROM	TO
		Dressen, Chas. Walter (Chuck) (2B3)	3B10	33	.211	B	
		Durocher, Leo Ernest (2B13)	SS103	119	.243	N.Y.A.	
0	1	Eckert, Albert George	P	2	.000	A	
		Ford, Horace Hills (2B66)	SS74	132	.231	B	
11	18	Frey, Benjamin Rudolph	P	44	.284	B	
		Gooch, John Beverly	C79	82	.243	B	
		Heilmann, Harry Edwin (1B19)	OF106	142	.333	DetA	
3	1	Johnson, Silas Kenneth	P	35	.235	B	
		Kelly, George Lange (Long George)	1B50	51	+.288	B	Chi
7	12	Kolp, Raymond Carl	P	37	.245	B	
14	16	Lucas, Chas. Frederick (Red)	P33	80	.336	B	
3	11	May, Frank Spruell (Jake)	P	26	.128	B	
		Meusel, Robert Wm.	OF112	113	.289	N.Y.A.	C
0	2	McWeeney, Douglas Lawrence	P	8	.143	Bkn	C
		Riconda, Harry Paul		1	.000	Pitt	C
9	13	Rixey, Eppa Jr.	P	32	.200	B	
		Stripp, Joseph Valentine (3B48)	1B75	130	.306	B	
		Styles, Wm. Graves (Lena) (1B1)	C5	7	.250	PhilA21	
		Sukeforth, Clyde LeRoy	C82	94	.284	B	
		Swanson, Ernest Evar	OF71	95	.309	B	
		Walker, Wm. Curtis	OF120	134	.307	B	C
0	1	Wysong, Harlan (Biff)	P	1	.000	A	

WON 58 NATIONAL LEAGUE FINISHED 8th (LAST)
LOST 96
TG 154 1931. PCT. .377

CINCINNATI

DANIEL PHILIP HOWLEY

WON	LOST	NAME	POS.	G.	BA	FROM	TO
		Asbjornson, Robert Anthony	C31	45	.305	BosA29	
		Beck, Clyde Eugene (SS6)	3B38	53	.154	Chi	C
10	15	Benton, Lawrence James (Larry)	P	38	.167	B	
3	9	Carroll, Owen Thomas	P29	30	.206	B	
		Crabtree, Estel Crayton (1B2 3B4)	OF101	117	.269	Cin29	
		Cuccinello, Anthony Francis (Tony)	2B	154	.315	B	
		Cullop, Henry Nicholas	OF83	104	.263	B	C
		Douthit, Taylor Lee	OF	95	+.262	xStL	
		Dressen, Chas. Walter (Chuck)	3B	5	.067	B	
		Durocher, Leo Ernest	SS120	121	.227	B	
0	1	Eckert, Albert George	P	14	.333	B	
		Fitzgerald, Raymond Francis		1	.000	A	C
		Ford, Horace Hills (2B3 3B1)	SS73	84	.229	B	

WON	LOST	NAME	POS.	G.	BA	FROM	TO
8	12	Frey, Benjamin Rudolph	P	34	.318	B	
		Heath, Minor Wilson (Mickey)	1B	7	.269	A	
		Heathcote, Clifton Earl	OF59	90	.258	Chi	
		Hendrick, Harvey (Gink)	1B	137	+.315	xBkn	
0	1	Hilcher, Walter Frank	P	2	.000	A	
11	19	Johnson, Silas Kenneth	P	42	.149	B	
4	9	Kolp, Raymond Carl	P	30	.125	B	
14	13	Lucas, Chas. Frederick (Red)	P29	97	.281	B	
		Moore, Eugene Jr. (Gene)	OF	4	.143	A	
4	8	Ogden, John Mahlon	P22	23	.148	StLA29	
4	7	Rixey, Eppa Jr.	P	22	.150	B	
		Roettger, Walter Henry	OF	44	+.351	N.Y.	StL
		Roush, Edd J.	OF88	101	.271	N.Y.29	C
		Sigafoos, Francis Leonard (SS2)	3B15	21	.169	ChiA29	C
0	0	Strelecki, Edward Harold	P	13	.200	StLA29	C
		Stripp, Joseph Valentine (1B9)	3B96	105	.324	B	
		Styles, Wm. Graves (Lena)	C31	34	.241	B	C
		Sukeforth, Clyde LeRoy	C106	112	.256	B	
0	2	Wysong, Harlan (Biff)	P	12	.250	B	

WON 60
LOST 94
TG 154

NATIONAL LEAGUE

1932.

FINISHED 8th (LAST)

PCT. .390

CINCINNATI

DANIEL PHILIP HOWLEY

WON	LOST	NAME	POS.	G.	BA	FROM	TO
		Asbjornson, Robert Anthony	C16	29	.172	B	C
6	13	Benton, Lawrence James (Larry)	P	35	.204	B	
		Bluege, Otto Adam		1	.000	A	
10	19	Carroll, Owen Thomas	P32	35	.208	B	
		Crabtree, Estel Crayton	OF95	108	.274	B	
		Douthit, Taylor Lee	OF88	96	.243	B	
		Durocher, Leo Ernest	SS142	143	.217	B	
4	10	Frey, Benjamin Rudolph	P	28	+.205	xStL	
		Gilbert Walter John	3B111	114	.214	Bkn	C
		Grantham, George Farley (1B10)	2B115	126	.292	Pitt	
		Hafey, Chas. James (Chick)	OF65	83	.344	StL	
		Heath, Minor Wilson (Mickey)	1B	39	.201	B	C
		Heathcote, Clifton Earl	OF	8	+.000	B	Phil
		Heilmann, Harry Edwin	1B6	15	.258	Cin30	C
		Hendrick, Harvey (Gink)	1B	94	+.327	xStL	
		Herman, Floyd Caves (Babe)	OF146	148	.326	Bkn	
		High, Andrew Aird (2B12)	3B46	84	.188	StL	
0	3	Hilcher, Walter Frank	P	11	.333	B	
13	15	Johnson, Silas Kenneth	P	42	.125	B	
6	10	Kolp, Raymond Carl	P	32	.184	B	
		Lombardi, Ernesto Natali (Schnozz)	C110	118	.303	Bkn	
13	17	Lucas, Chas. Frederick (Red)	P31	76	.287	B	
		Manion, Clyde Jennings	C47	49	.207	StLA30	

WON	LOST	NAME	POS.	G.	BA	FROM	TO
		Morrissey, Joseph Anselm (2B42 3B12)	SS45	89	.242	A	
2	2	Ogden, John Mahlon	P24	27	.167	B	C
5	5	Rixey, Eppa Jr.	P	25	.265	B	
		Roettger, Walter Henry	OF94	106	.277	StL	
		Shevlin, James Cornelius	1B	7	.208	DetA30	
1	0	Wysong, Harlan (Biff)	P	7	.000	B	C

WON 58
LOST 94
TG 152

NATIONAL LEAGUE

1933.

FINISHED 8th (LAST)

PCT. .382

CINCINNATI

OWEN JOSEPH BUSH

WON	LOST	NAME	POS.	G.	BA	FROM	TO
		Adams, Earl John (Sparky) (SS8)	3B132	137	+.262	xStL	
10	11	Benton, Lawrence James (Larry)	P	34	.170	B	
		Bluege, Otto Adam (2B10 3B1)	SS95	108	.213	B	C
		Bottomley, James LeRoy	1B	145	.250	StL	
		Crouch, Jack Albert	C	10	.125	xStLA	C
7	25	Derringer, Samuel Paul	P	33	+.184	xStL	
		Douthit, Taylor Lee	OF	1	+.000	B	Chi
		Durocher, Leo Ernest	SS	16	+.216	B	StL
6	4	Frey, Benjamin Rudolph	P37	38	.262	B	
		Grantham, George Farley (1B12)	2B72	87	.204	B	
		Hafey, Chas. James (Chick)	OF	144	.303	B	
		Hemsley, Ralston Burdett (Rollie)	C41	49	.190	Chi	StLA
		High, Andrew Aird (2B2)	3B11	24	.209	B	
		Hunter, Edward Franklin	3B	1	.000	A	C
7	18	Johnson, Silas Kenneth	P	34	.042	B	
6	9	Kolp, Raymond Carl	P	30	.156	B	
		Lombardi, Ernesto Natali (Schnozz)	C95	107	.283	B	
10	16	Lucas, Chas. Frederick (Red)	P29	75	.287	B	
		Manion, Clyde Jennings	C34	36	.167	B	
		Moore, John Francis	OF132	135	.263	Chi	
		Morrissey, Joseph Anselm (SS63 3B15)	2B88	148	.230	B	
0	1	Quinn, John Picus	P	14	.000	Bkn	C
		Rice, Harry Francis (3B1)	OF141	143	.261	WashA31	C
6	3	Rixey, Eppa Jr.	P	16	.257	B	C
		Robello, Thomas Vardasco (3B2)	2B11	14	.233	A	
		Roettger, Walter Henry	OF55	84	.239	B	
4	4	Smith, Robert Eldridge (SS1)	P16	23	+.200	Chi	Bos
2	3	Stout, Allyn McClelland	P	23	+.182	xStL	

WON 52 | LOST 99 | TG 151

NATIONAL LEAGUE

1934.

FINISHED 8th (LAST)

PCT. .344

CINCINNATI

ROBERT ARTHUR O'FARRELL   BURTON EDWIN SHOTTON
CHAS. WALTER DRESSEN

WON	LOST	NAME	POS.	G.	BA	FROM	TO
		Adams, Earl John (Sparky)	3B38	87	.252	B	C
0	0	Barnes, June Shoaf	P	2	.000	A	C
0	1	Benton, Lawrence James (Larry)	P	16	.286	B	
		Blakely, Lincoln Howard	OF28	34	.225	A	C
		Bottomley, James LeRoy	1B139	142	.284	B	
4	3	Brennan, James Donald (Don)	P	28	.227	NYA	
		Comorosky, Adam Anthony	OF122	127	.258	Pitt	
15	21	Derringer, Samuel Paul	P	47	.196	B	
0	0	Edwards, Sherman Stanley	P	1	.000	A	C
		Flowers, D'Arcy Raymond (Jake)		13	.333	Bkn	C
6	12	Freitas, Tony	P30	31	.191	PhilA	
11	16	Frey, Benjamin Rudolph	P39	41	.171	B	
0	1	Grissom, Leo Theo (Lee)	P	4	.000	A	
		Hafey, Chas. James (Chick)	OF	140	.293	B	
7	22	Johnson, Silas Kenneth	P	46	.139	B	
0	0	Johnson, Sylvester W.	P	2	+.500	StL	Phil
		Kampouris, Alexis Wm.	2B16	19	.197	A	
2	6	Kleinhans, Theodore Otto	P24	25	+.130	xPhil	
		Koenig, Mark Anthony (1B4 2B26 SS58)	3B64	151	.272	Chi	
0	2	Kolp, Raymond Carl	P	28	.083	B	C
0	0	Lindsey, James Kendrick	P	4	+.000	StL	StL
		Lombardi, Ernesto Natali (Schnozz)	C111	132	.305	B	
		Manion, Clyde Jennings	C24	25	.185	B	C
		Marshall, Wm. Henry	2B1	6	.125	BosA31	C
		Moore, John Francis	OF10	16	+.190	B	Phil
		McCormick, Frank Andrew (Buck)	1B	12	.313	A	
		McCurdy,*Harry Henry	1B1	3	.000	Phil	C
		O'Farrell, Robert Arthur MGR.	C42	44	+.244	StL	Chi
		Petoskey, Frederick Lee (Ted)	OF2	6	.000	A	
		Piet, Anthony Francis (Tony) (2B49)	3B51	106	.259	Pitt	
		Pool, Harlin Welty	OF94	99	.327	A	
1	2	Richmond, Beryl Justice	P	6	.000	Chi	C
		Robello, Thomas Vardasco		2	.000	B	C
		Schulmerich, Edward Wesley	OF56	74	+.263	xPhil	C
0	2	Shaute, Joseph Benjamin	P	8	.250	Bkn	C
		Shevlin, James Cornelius	1B10	18	.308	Cin32	C
		Shiver, Ivey Merwin	OF15	19	.203	DetA31	C
		Slade, Gordon Leigh (2B39)	SS97	138	.285	StL	
6	8	Stout, Allyn McClelland	P	41	.186	B	
0	2	Vance, Clarence Arthur (Dazzy)	P	6	+.250	StL	StL
0	1	Wistert, Francis Michael	P	3	.000	A	C

WON 68 | LOST 85 | TG 153

NATIONAL LEAGUE

1935.

FINISHED 6th.

PCT. .444

CINCINNATI

CHAS. WALTER DRESSEN

WON	LOST	NAME	POS.	G.	BA	FROM	TO
		Bottomley, James LeRoy	1B97	107	.258	B	
5	5	Brennan, James Donald (Don)	P	38	.100	B	
		Byrd, Samuel Dewey	OF115	121	.262	NYA	
		Campbell, Wm. Gilthorpe (Gilly) (1B5 OF1)	C66	88	.257	Chi33	
		Chapman, Calvin Louis (2B4)	SS12	15	.340	A	
		Comorosky, Adam Anthony	OF40	59	.248	B	C
		Cuyler, Hazen Shirley (Kiki)	OF57	62	+.251	xChi	
22	13	Derringer, Samuel Paul	P	45	.140	B	
		Erickson, Henry Nels	C25	37	.261	A	C
5	10	Freitas, Tony	P	31	.130	B	
6	10	Frey, Benjamin Rudolph	P	38	.344	B	
		Gamble, Lee Jesse	OF	2	.500	A	
		Goodman, Ival Richard	OF146	148	.269	A	
1	1	Grissom, Leo Theo (Lee)	P	3	.000	B	
		Hafey, Chas. James (Chick)	OF	15	.339	B	
		Herman, Floyd Caves (Babe) (1B14)	OF76	92	+.335	xPitt	
3	5	Herrmann, LeRoy George	P	29	.267	Chi33	C
2	0	Hilcher, Walter Frank	P	4	.167	Cin32	
6	13	Hollingsworth, Albert Wayne (Al)	P38	39	.148	A	
5	11	Johnson, Silas Kenneth	P	30	.024	B	
		Kampouris, Alexis Wm. (SS6)	2B141	148	.246	B	
		Lombardi, Ernesto Natali (Schnozz)	C82	120	.343	B	
1	2	MacFayden, Daniel Knowles	P	7	+.091	NYA	Bos
		Myers, Wm. Harrison (Billy)	SS112	117	.267	A	
4	4	Nelson, George Emmett (Ramrod)	P	19	.133	A	
		Petoskey, Frederick Lee (Ted)	OF	4	.400	B	C
		Piet, Anthony Francis (Tony)	OF1	6	.200	B	ChiA
		Pool, Harlin Welty	OF18	28	.176	B	C
		Riggs, Lewis Sidney (Lew)	3B135	142	.278	StL	
		Scarsella, Leslie George (Les)	1B2	6	.200	A	
8	11	Schott, Eugene Arthur	P33	36	.200	A	
		Slade, Gordon Leigh (2B19 3B7 OF8)	SS30	71	.281	B	C
		Sullivan, Wm. Joseph Jr. (Billy) (2B6 3B15)	1B40	85	.266	ChiA33	

WON 74 | LOST 80 | TG 154

NATIONAL LEAGUE

1936.

FINISHED 5th.

PCT. .481

CINCINNATI

CHAS. WALTER DRESSEN

WON	LOST	NAME	POS.	G.	BA	FROM	TO
5	2	Brennan, James Donald (Don)	P	41	.080	B	
		Byrd, Samuel Dewey	OF37	59	.248	B	C
		Campbell, Wm. Gilthorpe (Gilly) (1B1)	C71	89	.268	B	
		Chapman, Calvin Louis (2B23)	OF31	96	.247	B	C
		Cuyler, Hazen Shirley (Kiki)	OF140	144	.326	B	
8	8	Davis, Raymond Thomas (Peaches)	P	26	.163	A	
19	19	Derringer, Samuel Paul	P	51	.200	B	
0	2	Freitas, Tony	P	4	.000	B	C
10	8	Frey, Benjamin Rudolph	P31	32	.250	B	C
		Goodman, Ival Richard	OF120	136	.284	B	
1	1	Grissom, Leo Theo (Lee)	P	6	.000	B	
5	9	Hallahan, Wm. Anthony (Wild Bill)	P	23	+.191	xStL.	
		Handley, Lee Elmer (Jeep)	2B16	24	.308	A	
		Herman, Floyd Caves (Babe) (1B4)	OF92	119	.279	B	
1	2	Hilcher, Walter Frank	P	14	.000	B	C
9	10	Hollingsworth, Albert Wayne (Al)	P29	34	.315	B	
0	0	Johnson, Silas Kenneth	P	2	+.000	B	StL
		Joost, Edwin David (2B5)	SS7	13	.154	A	
		Kampouris, Alexis Wm.	2B119	122	.239	B	
		Lombardi, Ernesto Natali (Schnozz)	C105	121	.333	B	
		Miller, Edward Robert	SS4	5	.100	A	
0	0	Moore, Dee Cee (C1)	P	6	.400	A	
1	0	Moore, Lloyd Albert (Whitey)	P	1	.000	A	
0	0	Mooty, Jacob T. (Jake)	P	8	.000	A	
		Myers, Wm. Harrison (Billy)	SS	93	.269	B	
		McQuinn, George Hartley (Mac)	1B	38	.201	A	
1	0	Nelson, George Emmett (Ramrod)	P	6	.167	B	C
		Riggs, Lewis Sidney (Lew)	3B140	141	.257	B	
		Scarsella, Leslie George (Les)	1B	115	.313	B	
11	11	Schott, Eugene Arthur	P31	39	.300	B	
3	8	Stine, Lee Elbert	P	40	.296	ChiA	
		Thevenow, Thomas Joseph Jr. (2B33 3B12)	SS68	106	.234	Pitt	
		Walker, Harvey Willos (Hub) (C1 1B1)	OF73	92	.275	DetA	

WON 56 — NATIONAL LEAGUE — FINISHED 8th (LAST)

LOST 98

TG 154 — 1937. — PCT. .364

CINCINNATI

CHAS. WALTER DRESSEN   RHODERICK JOHN WALLACE

WON	LOST	NAME	POS.	G.	BA	FROM	TO
0	0	Barrett, Chas. Henry (Red)	P	1	.000	A	
1	1	Brennan, James Donald (Don)	P	10	+.000	B	N.Y.
		Brittain, August Schuster	C1	3	.167	A	C
1	0	Brown, Walter George (Jumbo)	P	4	+.000	NYA	N.Y.
		Campbell, Wm. Gilthorpe (Gilly)	C17	18	.275	B	
1	2	Cascarella, Joseph Thomas	P	11	.091	xWashA	
		Chozen, Harry Kenneth	C1	1	.250	A	C
		Craft, Harry Francis	OF	10	.310	A	
		Cuyler, Hazen Shirley (Kiki)	OF106	117	.271	B	
		Davis, George Willis (Kiddo)	OF35	40	+.257	xN.Y.	
11	13	Davis, Raymond Thomas (Peaches)	P	42	.128	B	
		Davis, Virgil Lawrence (Spud)	C59	76	.268	StL	
10	14	Derringer, Samuel Paul	P	43	.200	B	
		Dwyer, Joseph Michael		12	.273	A	C
		English, Chas. Dewie (2B2)	3B15	17	.238	N.Y.	C
0	1	Gehrman, Paul Arthur	P	2	.000	A	C
		Gelbert, Chas. Magnus (2B9 3B1)	SS37	43	.193	StL	DetA
		Goodman, Ival Richard	OF141	147	.273	B	
12	17	Grissom, Leo Theo (Lee)	P50	51	.109	B	
		Hafey, Chas. James (Chick)	OF64	89	.261	Cin35	C
3	9	Hallahan, Wm. Anthony (Wild Bill)	P	21	.095	B	
9	15	Hollingsworth, Albert Wayne (Al)	P43	46	.250	B	
		Joost, Edwin David	2B	6	.083	B	
		Jordan, Baxter Byerly	1B76	98	+.282	xBos	
		Jorgenson, Carl	OF4	6	.286	A	C
		Kampouris, Alexis Wm.	2B	146	.249	B	
1	2	Kleinhans, Theodore Otto	P	7	.250	N.Y.A.	
		Lombardi, Ernesto Natali (Schnozz)	C90	120	.334	B	
		Mele, Albert Ernest	OF5	6	.143	A	C
		Miller, Edward Robert (3B4)	SS30	36	.150	B	
		Moore, Dee Cee	C6	7	.077	B	
0	3	Moore, Lloyd Albert (Whitey)	P	13	.000	B	
0	3	Mooty, Jacob T. (Jake)	P14	15	.000	B	
		Moser, Arnold Robert		5	.000	A	C
		Myers, Wm. Harrison (Billy) (2B6)	SS121	124	.251	B	
		#McCormick, Frank Andrew (Buck)	1B20	24	.325	Cin34	
		Outlaw, James Paulus	3B41	49	.273	A	
		xRiggs, Lewis Sidney (Lew) (2B4)	3B100	122	.242	B	
		Scarsella, Leslie George (Les) (OF14)	1B65	110	.246	B	
4	13	Schott, Eugene Arthur	P37	50	.143	B	
3	5	Vander Meer, John Samuel	P19	21	.217	A	
		Walker, Harvey Willos (Hub) (2B3)	OF58	78	.249	B	
		Weintraub, Philip	OF47	49	+.271	N.Y.35	N.Y.

#McCormick also played 4 games at 2B and 1 game in the OF.

xRiggs also played one game at SS.

WON 82 LOST 68 TG 150 — NATIONAL LEAGUE 1938. — FINISHED 4th. PCT. .547

CINCINNATI

WM. BOYD McKECHNIE

WON	LOST	NAME	POS.	G.	BA	FROM	TO
2	0	Barrett, Chas. Henry (Red)	P	6	.143	B	
1	1	Benge, Raymond Adelphia	P	9	.333	Phil36	C
		Berger, Walter Antone (Wally)	OF98	99	+.307	xN.Y.	
		Bongiovanni, Anthony Thomas	OF	2	.286	A	
4	7	Cascarella, Joseph Thomas	P	33	.167	B	C
		Cooke, Allen Lindsey (Dusty)	OF51	82	.275	BosA36	
		Craft, Harry Francis	OF	151	.270	B	
		Davis, George Willis (Kiddo)	OF	5	.278	B	C
7	12	Davis, Raymond Thomas (Peaches)	P	29	.246	B	
		Davis, Virgil Lawrence (Spud)	C11	12	+.167	B	Phil
21	14	Derringer, Samuel Paul	P	41	.176	B	
		Frey, Linus Reinhard (Lonny) (SS3)	2B121	124	.265	Chi	
		Gamble, Lee Jesse	OF9	53	.320	Cin35	
		Goodman, Ival Richard	OF142	145	.292	B	
2	3	Grissom, Leo Theo (Lee)	P	14	.188	B	
		Hershberger, Willard McKee (2B1)	C39	49	.276	A	
2	2	Hollingsworth, Albert Wayne	P	9	+.250	B	Phil
		Jordan, Baxter Byerly		9	+.286	B	Phil
		Kampouris, Alexis Wm.	2B	21	+.257	B	N.Y.
0	0	Kleinhans, Theodore Otto	P	1	.000	B	C
		Lang, Donald Chas. (2B1)	3B15	21	.260	A	
		Lombardi, Ernesto Natali (Schnozz)	C123	129	.342	B	
6	4	Moore, Lloyd Albert (Whitey)	P	19	.077	B	
		Myers, Wm. Harrison (Billy) (2B11)	SS123	134	.253	B	
		McCormick, Frank Andrew (Buck)	1B	151	.326	B	
		Outlaw, James Paulus		4	.000	B	
		Richardson, Clifford Nolen	SS	35	.290	NYA35	
		Riggs, Lewis Sidney (Lew)	3B140	142	.252	B	
5	5	Schott, Eugene Arthur	P	31	.125	B	
		Stein, Justin Marion (2B2)	SS7	11	+.333	xPhil	C
15	10	Vander Meer, John Samuel	P32	33	.181	B	
11	6	Walters, Wm. Henry Jr. (Bucky)	P27	36	+.141	xPhil	
6	4	Weaver, James Dement	P	30	.205	xStLA	
		West, Richard Thomas		1	.000	A	

WON 97 LOST 57 TG 154 — NATIONAL LEAGUE 1939. — FINISHED 1st. PCT. .630

CINCINNATI

WM. BOYD McKECHNIE

WON	LOST	NAME	POS.	G.	BA	FROM	TO
0	0	Barrett, Chas. Henry (Red)	P	2	.000	B	
		Berger, Walter Antone (Wally)	OF95	97	.258	B	
		Bongiovanni, Anthony Thomas	OF39	66	.258	B	C
		Bordagaray, Stanley George (2B2)	OF43	63	.197	St.L.	
		Craft, Harry Francis	OF	134	.257	B	
1	0	Davis, Raymond Thomas (Peaches)	P	20	.333	B	C
25	7	Derringer, Samuel Paul	P	38	.209	B	
		DiMaggio, Vincent Paul	OF7	8	.071	Bos	
		Frey, Linus Reinhard (Lonny)	2B124	125	.291	B	
		Galatzer, Milton	1B2	3	.000	ClevA36	C
		Gamble, Lee Jesse	OF36	72	.267	B	
		Goodman, Ival Richard	OF123	124	.323	B	
9	7	Grissom, Leo Theo (Lee)	P	33	.085	B	
		Hafey, Daniel Albert	OF4	6	+.154	Pitt36	Phil
0	0	Jacobs, Arthur Evan	P	1	.000	A	C
0	3	Johnson, Henry Ward	P	20	.400	PhilA36	C
		Joost, Edwin David (SS6)	2B32	42	.252	Cin37	
		Hershberger, Willard McKee	C60	63	.345	B	
0	0	Livengood, Wesley Amos	P	5	.000	A	C
		Lombardi, Ernesto Natali (Schnozz)	C120	130	.287	B	
13	12	Moore, Lloyd Albert (Whitey)	P	42	.099	B	
		McCormick, Frank Andrew (Buck)	1B	156	.332	B	
		Myers, Wm. Harrison (Billy)	SS	151	.281	B	
0	0	Naktenis, Peter Ernest	P	3	.000	PhilA36	
2	1	Niggeling, John Arnold	P	10	.154	Bos	
		Richardson, Clifford Nolen	SS	1	.000	B	C
0	0	Riddle, Elmer Ray	P	1	.000	A	
		Riggs, Lewis Sidney (Lew)	3B11	22	.158	B	
		Scarsella, Leslie George (Les)		16	.143	Cin37	
2	2	Shoffner, Milburn James	P	10	+.091	xBos	
		Simmons, Aloysius Harry (Al)	OF4	9	+.143	xBos	
13	5	Thompson, Eugene Earl (Junior)	P	42	.229	A	
5	9	Vander Meer, John Samuel	P	30	.111	B	
27	11	Walters, Wm. Henry Jr.(Bucky)	P39	40	.325	B	
0	0	Weaver, James Dement	P	3	.000	B	C
		Werber, Wm. Murray (Bill)	3B	147	.289	PhilA	
		West, Richard Thomas (C1)	OF5	8	.211	B	
		Wilson, James	C1	4	.333	Phil	

WON 100 LOST 53 TG 153 — NATIONAL LEAGUE 1940. — FINISHED 1st. PCT. .654

CINCINNATI

WM. BOYD McKECHNIE

WON	LOST	NAME	POS.	G.	BA	FROM	TO
		Arnovich, Morris	OF60	62	+.284	xPhil	
		Baker, Wm. Presley	C24	27	.217	A	
1	0	Barrett, Chas. Henry (Red)	P	3	.000	B	
12	3	Beggs, Joseph Stanley	P	37	.190	NYA38	
		Berger, Walter Antone (Wally)		2	+.000	B	Phil
		Craft, Harry Francis (1B2)	OF109	115	.244	B	
		Dejan, Mike Dan	OF2	12	.188	A	C
20	12	Derringer, Samuel Paul	P	37	.167	B	
		DiMaggio, Vincent Paul	OF1	2	+.250	B	Pitt
		Frey, Linus Reinhard (Lonny)	2B	150	.266	B	
		Gamble, Lee Jesse	OF10	38	.143	B	C
		Goodman, Ival Richard	OF135	136	.258	B	
0	0	Guise, Witt Orison	P	2	.333	A	C
		Hershberger, Willard McKee	C37	48	.309	B	C
2	1	Hutchings, John Richard Joseph	P	19	.154	A	
		Joost, Edwin David (2B7 3B4)	SS78	88	.216	B	
		Lombardi, Ernesto Natali (Schnozz)	C101	109	.319	B	
8	8	Moore, Lloyd Albert (Whitey)	P	25	.128	B	
		Myers, Wm. Harrison (Billy)	SS88	90	.202	B	
		McCormick, Frank Andrew (Buck)	1B	155	.309	B	
		McCormick, Myron Winthrop (Mike)	OF107	110	.300	A	
1	2	Riddle, Elmer Ray	P	15	.143	B	
		Riggs, Lewis Sidney (Lew)	3B11	41	.292	B	
		Ripple, James Albert (Jimmy)	OF30	32	+.307	xBkn	
		Rizzo, John Costa	OF30	31	+.282	xPitt	Phil
1	0	Shoffner, Milburn James	P	20	.125	B	C
16	9	Thompson, Eugene Earl (Junior)	P	33	.228	B	
14	7	Turner, James Riley (Jim)	P24	25	.240	Bos	
3	1	Vander Meer, John Samuel	P10	12	.300	B	
22	10	Walters, Wm. Henry Jr. (Bucky)	P36	37	.205	B	
		Werber, Wm. Murray (Bill)	3B	143	.277	B	
		West, Richard Thomas	C	7	.393	B	
		Wilson, James	C	16	.243	B	

WON 88 — NATIONAL LEAGUE — FINISHED 3rd.
LOST 66
TG 154 — 1941. — PCT. .571

CINCINNATI

WM. BOYD McKECHNIE

WON	LOST	NAME	POS.	G.	BA	FROM	TO
		Aleno, Chas. (Chuck) (1B2)	3B40	54	.243	A	
		Baker, Wm. Presley	C1	2	+.000	B	Pitt
4	3	Beggs, Joseph Stanley	P	37	.300	B	
		Craft, Harry Francis	OF115	119	.249	B	
12	14	Derringer, Samuel Paul	P	29	.155	B	
		Frey, Linus Reinhard (Lonny)	2B145	146	.254	B	
		Gleeson, James Joseph	OF84	102	.233	Chi	
		Goodman, Ival Richard	OF40	42	.268	B	
0	0	Hutchings, John Richard Joseph	P	8	+.000	B	Bos
		Joost, Edwin David (1B2 2B4 3B1)	SS147	152	.253	B	
		Koy, Ernest Anyz (Chief)	OF49	67	+.250	xStL	
		Lamanno, Raymond Simon	C	1	.000	A	
0	1	Logan, Robert Dean	P	2	.000	Chi38	
		Lombardi, Ernesto Natali (Schnozz)	C116	117	.264	B	
		Lukon, Edward Paul	OF22	23	.267	A	
		Mattick, Robert James (2B1 3B5)	SS12	20	.183	Chi	
2	1	Moore, Lloyd Albert (Whitey)	P	23	.167	B	
		McCormick, Frank Andrew (Buck)	1B	154	.269	B	
		McCormick, Myron Winthrop (Mike)	OF101	110	.287	B	
1	3	Pearson, Marcellus Monte	P7	8	.000	NYA	C
19	4	Riddle, Elmer Ray	P	33	.225	B	
		Riddle, John Ludy	C	10	.300	Bos38	
		Ripple, James Albert (Jimmy)	OF25	38	.216	B	
		Sauer, Henry John	OF8	9	.303	A	
		Shokes, Edward Christopher		1	.000	A	
3	2	Starr, Raymond Francis	P	7	.182	Bos33	
6	6	Thompson, Eugene Earl (Junior)	P	27	.233	B	
6	4	Turner, James Riley (Jim)	P	23	.146	B	
16	13	Vander Meer, John Samuel	P33	35	.132	B	
19	15	Walters, Wm. Henry Jr. (Bucky)	P37	39	.189	B	
		Waner, Lloyd James (Little Poison)	OF44	55	+.256	xBos	
		Werber, Wm. Murray (Bill)	3B107	109	.239	B	
		West, Richard Thomas	C64	67	.215	B	
		Young, Lemuel Floyd (Pep)	3B3	4	+.167	Pitt	StL
		Zientara, Benedict Joseph	2B6	9	.286	A	

WON 76 — NATIONAL LEAGUE — FINISHED 4th.
LOST 76
TG 152 — 1942. — PCT. .500

CINCINNATI

WM. BOYD McKECHNIE

WON	LOST	NAME	POS.	G.	BA	FROM	TO
		Abreu, Joseph Lawrence (2B2)	3B6	9	.214	A	C
		Aleno, Chas. (Chuck) (2B1)	3B2	7	.143	B	

WON	LOST	NAME	POS.	G.	BA	FROM	TO
6	5	Beggs, Joseph Stanley	P	38	.000	B	
0	0	Blackwell, Ewell Jr.	P	2	.000	A	
		Craft, Harry Francis	OF33	37	.177	B	
10	11	Derringer, Samuel Paul	P	29	.132	B	
		Frey, Linus Reinhard (Lonny)	2B140	141	.266	B	
		Gleeson, James Joseph	OF5	9	.200	B	C
		Goodman, Ival Richard	OF57	87	.243	B	
		Haas, Berthold John (Bert) (1B6 OF2)	3B146	154	.239	Bkn38	
		Hemsley, Ralston Burdett (Rollie)	C34	36	.113	ClevA	NYA
		Joost, Edwin David (2B15)	SS130	142	.224	B	
		Kelleher, Francis Eugene	OF30	38	.182	A	
		Koy, Ernest Anyz (Chief)		3	.000	B	Phil
		Lakeman, Albert Wesley	C17	20	.158	A	
		Lamanno, Raymond Simon	C104	111	.264	B	
		Marshall, Milo Max	OF129	131	.255	A	
		Mattick, Robert James	SS3	6	.200	B	C
0	0	Moore, Lloyd Albert (Whitey)	P	1	+.000	B	StL
		McCormick, Frank Andrew (Buck)	1B144	145	.277	B	
		McCormick, Myron Winthrop	OF38	40	.237	B	
		Phillips, Damon Roswell	SS27	28	.202	A	
7	11	Riddle, Elmer Ray	P	29	.259	B	
		Sauer, Henry John	1B4	7	.250	B	
		Secory, Frank Edward	OF	2	.000	DetA40	
1	3	Shoun, Clyde Mitchell	P?	34	+.308	xStL	
15	13	Starr, Raymond Francis	P	37	.091	B	
4	7	Thompson, Eugene Earl (Junior)	P	29	.267	B	
		Tipton, Eric Gordon	OF58	63	.222	PhilA	
0	0	Turner, James Riley (Jim)	P	3	.000	B	NYA
18	12	Vander Meer, John Samuel	P33	37	.147	B	
		Vollmer, Clyde Frederick	OF11	12	.093	A	
		Walker, Gerald Holmes (Gee)	OF110	119	.230	ClevA	
15	14	Walters, Wm. Henry Jr. (Bucky) (OF1)	P34	40	.242	B	
		West, Richard Thomas (OF6)	C17	33	.177	B	

WON 87 NATIONAL LEAGUE FINISHED 2nd.
LOST 67
TG 154 1943. PCT. .565

CINCINNATI

WM. BOYD McKECHNIE

WON	LOST	NAME	POS.	G.	BA	FROM	TO
		Aleno, Chas. (Chuck)	OF2	7	.300	B	
7	6	Beggs, Joseph Stanley	P	39	.143	B	
		Brewster, Chas. Lawrence	2B2	7	+.125	A	Phil
		Clay, Dain Elmer	OF33	49	.269	A	
		Crabtree, Estel Crayton	OF65	95	.276	StL	
		DePhillips, Anthony Andrew	C	35	.100	A	C
		Frey, Linus Reinhard (Lonny)	2B	144	.263	B	
		Goldstein, Leslie Elmer	1B2	5	.200	A	
		Haas, Berthold John (Bert) (3B23 OF18)	1B44	101	.262	B	
4	3	Heusser, Edward Burlton	P	26	.185	PhilA40	
		Kelleher, Francis Eugene	OF1	9	.000	B	C
		Lakeman, Albert Wesley	C21	22	.255	B	
0	0	Malloy, Robert Paul	P	6	.667	A	
		Marshall, Milo Max	OF129	132	.236	B	
		Mesner, Stephan Mathias (Steve)	3B130	137	.272	StL41	
		Miller, Edward Robert	SS	154	.224	Bos	
		Mueller, Ray Coleman	C140	141	.260	Pitt40	
		McCormick, Frank Andrew (Buck)	1B120	126	.303	B	
		McCormick, Myron Winthrop	OF	4	.133	B	
0	0	Niemes, Jacob LeLand	P	3	.000	A	C
21	11	Riddle, Elmer Ray	P	36	.194	B	
14	5	Shoun, Clyde Mitchell	P	45	.310	B	
11	10	Starr, Raymond Francis	P	36	.122	B	
0	1	Stone, John Vernon	P	13	.250	A	C
		Tipton, Eric Gordon	OF139	140	.288	B	
15	16	Vander Meer, John Samuel	P36	40	.137	B	
		Walker, Gerald Holmes (Gee)	OF106	114	.245	B	
15	15	Walters, Wm. Henry Jr. (Bucky)	P34	37	.267	B	
		West, Richard Thomas		3	.000	B	C
		Williams, Woodrow Wilson (SS5 3B7)	2B12	30	.377	Bkn38	

WON 89 NATIONAL LEAGUE FINISHED 3rd.
LOST 65
TG 154 1944. PCT. .578

CINCINNATI

WM. BOYD McKECHNIE

WON	LOST	NAME	POS.	G.	BA	FROM	TO
		Aleno, Chas. (Chuck) (1B3 SS3)	3B42	50	.165	B	C
		Beeler, Joseph Sam (Jodie) (3B1)	2B1	3	.000	A	C
1	0	Beggs, Joseph Stanley	P	1	.000	B	
11	7	Carter, Arnold Lee	P33	37	.250	A	
		Clay, Dain Elmer	OF98	110	.250	B	
		Crabtree, Estel Crayton (1B2)	OF19	58	.286	B	C
		Criscola, Anthony Paul	OF35	64	.229	StLA	C
9	9	de la Cruz, Tomas	P34	36	.155	A	C
0	0	Eisenhardt, Jacob Henry	P	1	.000	A	C
0	0	Fausett, Robert Shaw (Buck) (P2)	3B6	13	.097	A	C
0	3	Ferguson, Robert Lester	P	9	.333	A	C
0	0	Fox, Howard Francis	P	2	.000	A	
10	8	Gumbert, Harry Edward	P	24	+.096	xStL	
13	11	Heusser, Edward Burlton	P	30	.217	B	

WON	LOST	NAME	POS.	G.	BA	FROM	TO
		Just, Joseph Erwin	C10	11	.182	A	
0	1	Katz, Robert Clyde	P	6	.000	A	C
6	4	Konstanty, Casimer James (Jim)	P	20	.294	A	
		Kosman, Michael Thomas		1	.000	A	C
		Lakeman, Albert Wesley		1	.000	B	
0	1	Lohrman, Wm. LeRoy	P	2	+.000	xBkn	C
1	1	Malloy, Robert Paul	P	9	.000	B	
		Marshall, Milo Max	OF59	66	.245	B	C
		Mesner, Stephan Mathias (Steve)	3B120	121	.242	B	
		Miller, Edward Robert	SS	155	.209	B	
		Mueller, Ray Coleman	C	155	.286	B	
		McCormick, Frank Andrew (Buck)	1B	153	.305	B	
0	0	Nuxhall, Joseph Henry Jr.	P	1	.000	A	
0	0	Peterson, Kent Franklin	P	1	.000	A	
		Ramos, Jesus Manuel Garcia	OF3	4	.500	A	C
		Rice, Leonard Oliver (ChuChu)	C5	10	.000	A	
2	2	Riddle, Elmer Ray	P	4	.125	B	
		Riddle, John Ludy	C	1	.000	Cin41	
13	10	Shoun, Clyde Mitchell	P	38	.224	B	
		Tipton, Eric Gordon	OF139	140	.301	B	
		Wahl, Kermit Emerson	3B1	4	.000	A	
		Walker, Gerald Holmes (Gee)	OF117	121	.278	B	
23	8	Walters, Wm. Henry Jr. (Bucky)	P34	37	.280	B	
		White, Joyner Clifford (Jo-Jo)	OF23	24	.235	xPhilA	
		Williams, Woodrow Wilson	2B	155	.240	B	

WON 61 — NATIONAL LEAGUE — FINISHED 7th.
LOST 93
TG 154 — 1945. — PCT. .396

CINCINNATI

WM. BOYD McKECHNIE

WON	LOST	NAME	POS.	G.	BA	FROM	TO
2	4	Beck, Walter Wm. (Boom-Boom)	P	11	+.214	DetA	Pitt
2	0	Bosser, Melvin Edward	P	7	.000	A	C
11	13	Bowman, Joseph Emil (Joe)	P25	29	.070	xBosA	C
0	0	Bush, Guy Terrell	P	4	.000	StL38	C
2	4	Carter, Arnold Lee	P13	19	.176	B	C
		Clay, Dain Elmer	OF152	153	.280	B	
4	5	Dasso, Francis Joseph Nicholas	P	16	.161	A	
		Flager, Walter Leonard	SS15	21	+.212	A	Phil
8	13	Fox, Howard Francis	P	45	.283	B	
2	4	Harrist, Earl	P	14	.000	A	
1	2	Hetki, John Edward	P	5	.091	A	
11	16	Heusser, Edward Burlton	P	31	.247	B	
		Just, Joseph Erwin	C	14	.147	B	C
5	12	Kennedy, Lloyd Vernon (Vern)	P	24	+.226	xPhil	C
		Lakeman, Albert Wesley	C74	76	.256	B	
0	0	Libke, Albert Walter (P4 1B2)	OF108	130	.283	A	

WON	LOST	NAME	POS.	G.	BA	FROM	TO
1	3	Lisenbee, Horace Milton	P	31	.000	PhilA36	C
		Lukon, Edward Paul	OF	2	.125	Cin41	
		McCormick, Frank Andrew (Buck)	1B151	152	.276	B	
		Medeiros, Ray Anton		1	.000	A	C
		Mesner, Stephan Mathias (Steve) (2B3)	3B148	150	.254	B	C
		Miller, Edward Robert	SS	115	.238	B	
1	2	Modak, Michael Joseph Aloysius	P	20	.100	A	C
1	4	Riddle, Elmer Ray	P	12	.273	B	
		Riddle, John Ludy	C	23	.178	B	
		Sauer, Henry John (1B3)	OF28	31	.293	Cin42	
		Sipek, Richard Francis	OF31	82	.244	A	C
		Tipton, Eric Gordon	OF83	108	.242	B	C
		Unser, Albert Bernard	C61	67	.265	DetA	C
		Wahl, Kermit Emerson (SS31 3B7)	2B32	71	.201	B	
		Walker, Gerald Holmes (Gee) (3B3)	OF67	106	.253	B	C
10	10	Walters, Wm. Henry Jr. (Bucky)	P22	24	.230	B	
0	1	Wehmeier, Herman Ralph	P2	3	.000	A	
		Williams, Woodrow Wilson	2B	133	.237	B	C

WON 67 — NATIONAL LEAGUE — FINISHED 6th.
LOST 87
TG 154 — 1946. — PCT. .435

CINCINNATI

WM. BOYD McKECHNIE HENRY MORGAN GOWDY

WON	LOST	NAME	POS.	G.	BA	FROM	TO
		Adams, Robert Henry (3B1 OF2)	2B74	94	.244	A	
2	4	Andrews, Nathan Hardy	P	7	+.071	Bos	N.Y.
12	10	Beggs, Joseph Stanley	P	28	.222	Cin44	
9	13	Blackwell, Ewell Jr.	P	33	.107	Cin42	
0	0	Burpo, George Harvie	P	2	.000	A	C
		Clay, Dain Elmer	OF120	121	.228	B	C
		Corbitt, Claude Elliott	SS77	82	.248	Bkn	
0	0	Dasso, Francis Joseph Nicholas	P	2	.000	B	C
0	0	Fox, Howard Francis	P	4	.000	B	
		Frey, Linus Reinhard (Lonny) (OF28)	2B65	111	.246	Cin43	
		Goldstein, Leslie Elmer		6	.000	Cin43	C
6	8	Gumbert, Harry Edward	P	36	.250	Cin44	
		Haas, Berthold John (Bert) (3B6)	1B140	140	.264	Cin43	
		Hatton, Grady Edgebert (OF2)	3B116	116	.271	A	
6	6	Hetki, John Edward	P	32	.333	B	
7	14	Heusser, Edward Burlton	P	29	.208	B	
		Lakeman, Albert Wesley	C6	23	.133	B	
		Lamanno, Raymond Simon	C61	85	.243	Cin42	
2	2	Lambert, Clayton Patrick	P	23	.154	A	

WON	LOST	NAME	POS.	G.	BA	FROM	TO
		Lawing, Garland Frederick	OF1	2	+.000	A	N.Y.
0	0	Libke, Albert Walter (P1)	OF115	124	.253	B	C
		Lukon, Edward Paul	OF83	102	.250	B	
2	5	Malloy, Robert Paul	P	27	.278	Cin44	
		McCormick, Myron Winthrop	OF21	23	+.216	Cin43	Bos
		Miller, Edward Robert	SS88	91	.194	B	
		Moss, Howard Glenn	OF6	7	.192	NY42	ClevA
		Mueller, Ray Coleman	C100	114	.254	Cin44	
		Shokes, Edward Christopher	1B29	31	.120	Cin41	C
1	6	Shoun, Clyde Mitchell	P	27	.095	Cin44	
		Usher, Robert Royce (3B1)	OF80	92	.204	A	
10	12	Vander Meer, John Samuel	P29	33	.247	Cin43	
		Vollmer, Clyde Frederick	OF7	9	.182	Cin42	
10	7	Walters, Wm. Henry Jr. (Bucky)	P22	24	.127	B	
		West, Max Edward	OF58	72	+.213	xBos	
		Zientara, Benedict Joseph (3B36)	2B39	78	.289	Cin41	

WON 73 NATIONAL LEAGUE FINISHED 5th.
LOST 81
TG 154 1947. PCT. .474

CINCINNATI

JOHN HENRY NEUN

WON	LOST	NAME	POS.	G.	BA	FROM	TO
		Adams, Robert Henry	2B69	81	.272	B	
		Baumholtz, Frank Conrad	OF150	151	.283	A	
0	3	Beggs, Joseph Stanley	P	11	+.091	B	N.Y.
22	8	Blackwell, Ewell Jr.	P	33	.123	B	
4	9	Erautt, Edward Lorenz Sebastian	P	36	.069	A	
		Galan, August John (Augie)	OF118	124	.314	Bkn	
10	10	Gumbert, Harry Edward	P	46	.273	B	
		Haas, Berthold John (Bert) (1B53)	OF69	135	.286	B	
		Hatton, Grady Edgebert	3B136	146	.281	B	
3	4	Hetki, John Edward	P	37	.222	B	
		Kluszewski, Theodore Bernard	1B2	9	.100	A	
		Kress, Chas. Steven	1B8	11	.148	A	
		Lakeman, Albert Wesley		2	+.000	B	Phil
		Lamanno, Raymond Simon	C109	118	.257	B	
0	0	Lambert, Clayton Patrick	P	3	.000	B	C
4	7	Lively, Everett Adrian	P	38	.188	A	
		Lukon, Edward Paul	OF55	86	.205	B	C
0	0	Malloy, Robert Paul	P	1	.000	B	
		Miller, Edward Robert	SS	151	.268	B	
		Mueller, Ray Coleman	C55	71	.250	B	
0	0	Perkowski, Harry Walter	P	3	.000	A	
6	13	Peterson, Kent Franklin	P	37	.068	Cin44	
		Poland, Hugh Reid	C3	16	+.333	xPhil	
0	0	Polivka, Kenneth Lyle	P	2	.000	A	C
6	5	Raffensberger, Kenneth David	P	19	+.162	xPhil	
1	0	Riddle, Elmer Ray	P	16	.000	Cin45	

WON	LOST	NAME	POS.	G.	BA	FROM	TO
0	0	Schultz, Wm. Michael	P	1	.000	A	C
0	0	Shoun, Clyde Mitchell	P	10	+.000	B	Bos
		Stallcup, Thomas Virgil	SS1	8	.000	A	
		Tatum, Thomas Vee Tee (2B1)	OF48	69	+.273	xBkn	C
		Usher, Robert Royce	OF8	9	.182	B	
9	14	Vander Meer, John Samuel	P30	31	.088	B	
		Vollmer, Clyde Frederick	OF66	78	.219	B	
		Wahl, Kermit Emerson (2B2 SS9)	3B20	39	.173	Cin45	
8	8	Walters, Wm. Henry Jr. (Bucky)	P	20	.267	B	
0	0	Wehmeier, Herman Ralph	P	1	.000	Cin45	
		Young, Norman Robert (Babe)	1B93	95	+.283	xN.Y.	
		Zientara, Benedict Joseph (3B13)	2B100	117	.258	B	

WON 64 NATIONAL LEAGUE FINISHED 7th.
LOST 89
TG 153 1948 PCT. .418

CINCINNATI

JOHN HENRY NEUN WM. HENRY WALTERS

WON	LOST	NAME	POS.	G.	BA	FROM	TO
		Adams, Robert Henry (3B7)	2B64	87	.298	B	
		Baumholtz, Frank Conrad	OF110	128	.296	B	
0	2	Blackburn, James Ray	P	16	.000	A	
7	9	Blackwell, Ewell Jr.	P	22	.229	B	
0	3	Burkhart, Wm. Kenneth	P	16	+.333	xStL	
		Corbitt, Claude Elliott (SS11 3B16)	2B52	87	.256	Cin46	
0	1	Cress, Walker James	P30	31	.500	A	
0	0	Erautt, Edward Lorenz Sebastian	P	2	.000	B	
		Filipowicz, Stephen Chas.	OF	7	.346	NY45	C
6	9	Fox, Howard Francis	P34	35	.200	Cin46	
		Galan, August John (Augie)	OF18	54	.286	B	
10	8	Gumbert, Harry Edward	P	61	.040	B	
		Hatton, Grady Edgebert (2B3 SS2 OF1)	3B123	133	.240	B	
0	1	Hetki, John Edward	P	3	.000	B	
0	0	Holcombe, Kenneth Edward	P	2	.000	NYA45	
0	4	Hughes, Thomas Owen	P	12	.143	Phil	C
		Kluszewski, Theodore Bernard	1B98	113	.275	B	
		Lamanno, Raymond Simon	C125	127	.242	B	C
		Litwhiler, Daniel Webster (3B15)	OF83	106	+.275	xBos	
0	0	Lively, Everett Adrian	P	10	.000	B	
		Mueller, Ray Coleman	C10	14	.206	B	
2	15	Peterson, Kent Franklin	P	43	.139	B	
		Poland, Hugh Reid		3	.333	B	C
11	12	Raffensberger, Kenneth David	P	40	.113	B	
		Rickert, Marvin August		8	+.167	Chi	Bos

WON	LOST	NAME	POS.	G.	BA	FROM	TO
		Sauer, Henry John (1B12)	OF132	145	.260	Cin45	
		Schultz, Howard Henry	1B26	36	+.167	xPhil	C
		Stallcup, Thomas Virgil	SS148	149	.228	B	
17	14	Vander Meer, John Samuel	P33	41	.141	B	
		Vollmer, Clyde Frederick	OF2	7	.111	B	WashA
0	3	Walters, Wm. Henry Jr. (Bucky) MGR.	P	7	.267	B	
11	3	Wehmeier, Herman Ralph	P33	36	.091	B	
		Williams, Dewey Edgar	C47	48	.168	Chi	C
		Wyrostek, John Barney	OF130	136	.273	Phil	
		*Young, Norman Robert (Babe)	1B31	49	+.231	B	StL
		Zientara, Benedict Joseph (SS2 3B3)	2B60	74	.187	B	C

*Young also played one game in the OF.

WON 62 NATIONAL LEAGUE FINISHED 7th.
LOST 92
TG 154 1949. PCT. .403

CINCINNATI

WM. HENRY WALTERS JAMES LUTHER SEWELL

WON	LOST	NAME	POS.	G.	BA	FROM	TO
		Adams, Robert Henry (3B14)	2B63	107	.253	B	
		Baumholtz, Frank Conrad	OF20	27	+.235	B	Chi
5	5	Blackwell, Ewell Jr.	P	30	.211	B	
		Bloodworth, James Henry (1B23 3B8)	2B92	134	.261	Pitt47	
0	0	Burkhart, Wm. Kenneth	P	11	.286	B	C
		Cooper, Wm. Walker	C77	82	+.280	xN.Y.	
		Corbitt, Claude Elliott (2B17 3B1)	SS18	44	.181	B	C
0	0	Cress, Walker James	P	3	.000	B	C
0	0	Dobernic, Andrew Joseph	P	14	+.000	xChi	C
4	11	Erautt, Edward Lorenz Sebastian	P	39	.174	B	
0	2	Fanovich, Frank Joseph	P	29	.000	A	
6	19	Fox, Howard Francis	P38	41	.236	B	
4	3	Gumbert, Harry Edward	P	29	+.000	B	Pitt
		Hatton, Grady Edgebert	3B136	137	.263	B	
		Howell, Homer Elliott	C56	64	.244	Pitt47	
0	1	Howell, Millard Fillmore	P5	9	.222	ClevA40	C
		Kluszewski, Theodore Bernard	1B134	136	.309	B	
		Kress, Chas. Steven	1B16	27	.207	Cin47	ChiA
		Litwhiler, Daniel Webster (3B3)	OF82	102	.291	B	
4	6	Lively, Everett Adrian	P	31	.154	B	C
		Lowrey, Harry Lee	OF78	89	+.224	xChi	
		Meeks, Samuel Mack (SS3)	2B8	16	.306	WashA	
		Merriman, Lloyd Archer	OF86	103	.230	A	
		Mueller, Ray Coleman	C31	32	+.274	B	N.Y.
1	1	Perkowski, Harry Walter	P	5	.333	Cin47	
4	5	Peterson, Kent Franklin	P	30	.056	B	

WON	LOST	NAME	POS.	G.	BA	FROM	TO
		Post, Walter Chas.	OF3	6	.250	A	
		Pramesa, John Steven	C13	17	.240	A	
18	17	Raffensberger, Kenneth David	P	41	.178	B	
		Sauer, Henry John (1B1)	OF39	42	+.237	B	Chi
		Stallcup, Thomas Virgil	SS	141	.254	B	
5	10	Vander Meer, John Samuel	P28	33	.077	B	
		Walker, Harry Wm. (1B1)	OF77	86	+.318	xChi	
11	12	Wehmeier, Herman Ralph	P33	36	.256	B	
		Wyrostek, John Barney	OF129	134	.249	B	

WON 66 NATIONAL LEAGUE FINISHED 6th.
LOST 87
TG 153 1950. PCT. .431

CINCINNATI

JAMES LUTHER SEWELL

WON	LOST	NAME	POS.	G.	BA	FROM	TO
		Adams, Robert Henry (3B42)	2B53	115	.282	B	
		Adcock, Joseph Wilbur (1B24)	OF75	102	.293	A	
0	0	Avrea, James Epherium	P	2	.000	A	C
17	15	Blackwell, Ewell Jr.	P	40	.146	B	
		Bloodworth, James Henry	2B	4	+.214	B	Phil
		Bolger, James Cyril	OF	2	.000	A	
0	1	Byerly, Eldred Wm.	P	4	.000	StL45	
		Cooper, Wm. Walker	C13	15	+.191	B	Bos
4	2	Erautt, Edward Lorenz Sebastian	P	33	.154	B	
11	8	Fox, Howard Francis	P34	35	.175	B	
		Hatton, Grady Edgebert (2B1 SS1)	3B126	130	.260	B	
1	2	Hetki, John Edward	P	22	.222	Cin48	
		Howell, Homer Elliott	C81	82	.223	B	
		Kluszewski, Theodore Bernard	1B131	134	.307	B	
		Landrith, Hobert Neal	C	4	.214	A	
		Litwhiler, Daniel Webster	OF29	54	.259	B	
		Lowrey, Harry Lee (2B1)	OF72	91	+.227	B	StL
		Meeks, Samuel Mack (3B2)	SS29	39	.284	B	
		Merriman, Lloyd Archer	OF84	92	.258	B	
		Northey, Ronald James	OF24	27	+.260	StL	Chi
0	0	Perkowski, Harry Walter	P22	32	.318	B	
0	3	Peterson, Kent Franklin	P	9	.333	B	
		Pramesa, John Steven	C73	74	.307	B	
		Rackley, Marvin Eugene		5	.500	Bkn	C
14	19	Raffensberger, Kenneth David	P	38	.134	B	
7	12	Ramsdell, James Willard	P	27	+.200	xBkn	
		Ryan, Cornelius Joseph	2B103	106	+.259	xBos	
		Scheffing, Robert Boden	C11	21	+.277	xChi	
2	7	Smith, Frank Thomas	P	38	.095	A	
		Stallcup, Thomas Virgil	SS	136	.251	B	
		Tappe, Theodore Nash		7	.200	A	
		Usher, Robert Royce	OF96	106	.259	Cin47	
10	18	Wehmeier, Herman Ralph	P41	54	.152	B	
		Wyrostek, John Barney (1B4)	OF129	131	.285	B	

WON 68 | LOST 86 | TG 154

NATIONAL LEAGUE 1951. FINISHED 6th. PCT. .442

CINCINNATI

JAMES LUTHER SEWELL

WON	LOST	NAME	POS.	G.	BA	FROM	TO
		Adams, Robert Henry (2B42 OF1)	3B60	125	.266	B	
		Adcock, Joseph Wilbur	OF107	113	.243	B	
0	0	Blackburn, James Ray	P	2	.000	Cin48	C
16	15	Blackwell, Ewell Jr.	P38	39	.293	B	
0	0	Blake, Edward James	P	3	.000	A	
		Bolger, James Cyril		2	.000	B	
2	1	Byerly, Eldred Wm.	P40	41	.000	B	
		Edwards, Henry Albert	OF34	41	+.315	xBkn	
0	0	Erautt, Edward Lorenz Sebastian	P	30	.000	B	
9	14	Fox, Howard Francis	P	40	.114	B	
		Hatton, Grady Edgebert (OF2)	3B87	96	.254	B	
		Howell, Homer Elliott	C73	77	.251	B	
		Kluszewski, Theodore Bernard	1B	154	.259	B	
		Landrith, Hobert Neal	C	4	.385	B	
		Litwhiler, Daniel Webster	OF7	12	.276	B	C
		Meeks, Samuel Mack (SS1)	3B4	23	.229	B	C
		Merriman, Lloyd Archer	OF102	114	.242	B	
		McCosky, Wm. Barney	OF11	25	.320	xPhilA	ClevA
		McMillan, Roy David (2B1 3B12)	SS54	85	.211	A	
3	6	Perkowski, Harry Walter	P35	37	.040	B	
1	1	Peterson, Kent Franklin	P	9	.000	B	
		Post, Walter Chas.	OF9	15	.220	Cin49	
		Pramesa, John Steven	C63	72	.229	B	
16	17	Raffensberger, Kenneth David	P	42	.122	B	
9	17	Ramsdell, James Willard	P	31	.155	B	
		Ryan, Cornelius Joseph (1B2 3B3 OF1)	2B121	136	.237	B	
		Scheffing, Robert Boden	C41	47	+.254	B	StL
5	5	Smith, Frank Thomas	P	50	.000	B	
		Stallcup, Thomas Virgil	SS117	121	.241	B	
		Tappe, Theodore Nash		4	.333	B	C
		Usher, Robert Royce	OF98	114	.208	B	
7	10	Wehmeier, Herman Ralph	P39	46	.288	B	
		Wyrostek, John Barney	OF139	142	.311	B	

WON 69 | LOST 85 | TG 154

NATIONAL LEAGUE 1952. FINISHED 6th. PCT. .448

CINCINNATI

JAMES LUTHER SEWELL ROGERS HORNSBY

WON	LOST	NAME	POS.	G.	BA	FROM	TO
		Abrams, Calvin Ross	OF46	71	+.278	xBkn	
		Adams, Robert Henry	3B	154	.283	B	
		Adcock, Joseph Wilbur (1B17)	OF85	117	.278	B	
3	12	Blackwell, Ewell Jr.	P	23	.156	B	NYA
0	0	Blake, Edward James	P	2	.000	B	
		Borkowski, Robert Vilarian (1B5)	OF103	126	.252	Chi	
0	1	Byerly, Eldred Wm.	P	12	.200	B	
5	9	Church, Emory Nicholas	P29	32	+.240	xPhil	
		Edwards, Henry Albert	OF51	74	.283	B	ChiA
		Greengrass, James Raymond	OF17	18	.309	A	
		Hatton, Grady Edgebert	2B120	128	.213	B	
0	0	Haugstad, Philip Donald	P	9	.000	Bkn	C
5	8	Hiller, Frank Walter	P28	29	.167	Chi	
		Howell, Homer Elliott	C16	17	.189	B	
0	1	Jordan, Niles Chapman	P	3	.000	Phil	C
		Kazak, Edward Terrance	1B1	13	+.067	xStL	C
		Kluszewski, Theodore Bernard	1B133	135	.320	B	
		Landrith, Hobert Neal	C14	15	.260	B	
		Marshall, Willard Warren	OF105	107	+.267	xBos	
		McMillan, Roy David	SS	154	.244	B	
1	4	Nuxhall, Joseph Henry	P	37	.087	Cin44	
		Pellagrini, Edward Chas. (1B8 SS1 3B1)	2B22	46	.170	Phil	
12	10	Perkowski, Harry Walter	P	33	.160	B	
4	5	Podbielan, Clarence Anthony	P	24	+.160	xBkn	
		Post, Walter Chas.	OF16	19	.155	B	
17	13	Raffensberger, Kenneth David	P	38	.107	B	
		Rossi, Joseph Anthony	C46	55	.221	A	C
1	0	Schmitz, John Albert	P	3	.000	xNYA	
		Seminick, Andrew Wasil	C99	108	.256	Phil	
		Sisler, Richard Allan	OF7	11	+.185	Phil	StL
12	11	Smith, Frank Thomas	P	53	.172	B	
		Stallcup, Thomas Virgil	SS1	2	+.000	B	StL
		Temple, John Ellis	2B22	30	.196	A	
9	11	Wehmeier, Herman Ralph	P33	41	.188	B	
		Westlake, Waldon Thomas	OF56	59	+.202	xStL	ClevA
		Wyrostek, John Barney (1B1)	OF29	30	+.236	B	Phil

WON 68 | LOST 86 | TG 154

NATIONAL LEAGUE 1953. FINISHED 6th. PCT. .442

CINCINNATI

ROGERS HORNSBY COLONEL BUSTER MILLS

WON	LOST	NAME	POS.	B.	BA	FROM	TO
		Adams, Robert Henry	3B	150	.275	B	
11	4	Baczewski, Frederick John	P	24	+.178	xChi	
		Bailey, Lonas Edgar	C	2	.375	A	
		Baldwin, Frank DeWitt	C6	16	.100	A	C
		Bell, David Russell	OF	151	.300	Pitt	
0	0	Blake, Edward James	P	1	.000	B	
		Borkowski, Robert Vilarian (1B2)	OF67	94	.269	B	

WON	LOST	NAME	POS.	G.	BA	FROM	TO
		Bridges, Everett LaMar (SS6 3B3)	2B115	122	.227	Bkn	
3	3	Church, Emory Nicholas	P11	12	+.267	B	Chi
7	11	Collum, Jack Dean	P	30	+.278	xStL	
0	0	Erautt, Edward Lorenz Sebastian	P	4	+.000	Cin51	StL
		Foiles, Henry Lee	C3	5	.154	A	ClevA
		Greengrass, James Raymond	OF153	154	.285	B	
		Hatton, Grady Edgebert (1B10 3B5)	2B35	83	.233	B	
0	1	Judson, Howard Kolls	P	10	.111	ChiA	
1	2	Kelly, Robert Edward	P	28	+.118	xChi	
3	6	King, Clyde Edward	P	35	.000	Bkn	C
		Kluszewski, Theodore Bernard	1B147	149	.316	B	
		Landrith, Hobert Neal	C47	52	.240	B	
		Lerchen, George Edward	OF1	22	.294	DetA	C
		Marquis, Robert Rudolph	OF10	40	.273	A	C
		Marshall, Willard Warren	OF95	122	.266	B	
0	0	Martin, Barney Robert	P	1	.000	A	C
		McMillan, Roy David	SS	155	.233	B	
0	0	Nevel, Ernie Wrye	P	10	.000	NYA51	C
9	11	Nuxhall, Joseph Henry	P	30	.327	B	
12	11	Perkowski, Harry Walter	P	33	.203	B	
6	16	Podbielan, Clarence Anthony	P	36	.125	B	
		Post, Walter Chas.	OF	11	.242	B	
7	14	Raffensberger, Kenneth David	P	26	.140	B	
		Seminick, Andrew Wasil	C112	119	.235	B	
8	1	Smith, Frank Thomas	P	50	.154	B	
		Szekely, Joseph	OF3	5	.077	A	C
		Temple, John Ellis	2B44	63	.264	B	
1	6	Wehmeier, Herman Ralph	P28	29	.200	B	

WON 74 NATIONAL LEAGUE FINISHED 5th.
LOST 80
TG 154 1954. PCT. .481

CINCINNATI

GEORGE ROBERT TEBBETTS

WON	LOST	NAME	POS.	G.	BA	FROM	TO
		Adams, Robert Henry (2B2)	3B93	110	.269	B	
6	6	Baczewski, Frederick John	P	29	.071	B	
		Bailey, Lonas Edgar	C61	73	.197	B	
		Bell, David Russell	OF	153	.299	B	
		Bolger, James Cyril	OF2	5	.333	Cin51	
		Borkowski, Robert Vilarian (1B3)	OF36	73	.265	B	
		Bridges, Everett LaMar (2B19 3B13)	SS20	53	.231	B	
7	3	Collum, Jack Dean	P	36	.231	B	
4	4	Drews, Karl August	P	22	+.167	xPhil	C
		Escalara, Saturnino Cuadrado (1B8 SS1)	OF14	73	.159	A	C
12	10	Fowler, John Arthur	P	40	.100	A	
		Greengrass, James Raymond	OF137	139	.280	B	
		Harmon, Chas. Byron (1B3)	3B67	94	.238	A	
		Hatton, Grady Edgebert		1	.000	B	ChiA
5	7	Judson, Howard Kolls	P	37	.083	B	C
		Kluszewski, Theodore Bernard	1B	149	.326	B	
		Landrith, Hobert Neal	C42	48	.198	B	
1	0	Lane, Jerald Hal	P	3	.000	WashA	
		Lipon, John Joseph		1	.000	StLA	C
		Merriman, Lloyd Archer	OF25	73	.268	Cin51	
		Murphy, Richard Lee		6	.000	A	C
		McMillan, Roy David	SS	154	.250	B	
12	5	Nuxhall, Joseph Henry	P35	36	.173	B	
1	0	Pearce, James Madison	P	2	.000	WashA	
2	8	Perkowski, Harry Walter	P	28	.160	B	
0	1	Picone, Mario Peter	P	4	+.000	xN.Y.	
7	10	Podbielan, Clarence Anthony	P	27	.143	B	C
		Post, Walter Chas.	OF116	130	.255	B	
0	2	Raffensberger, Kenneth David	P	6	.500	B	C
0	0	Ross, Clifford David	P	4	.000	A	C
		Ryan, Cornelius Joseph		1	.000	ChiA	C
0	2	Savransky, Morris	P	16	.500	A	C
		Seminick, Andrew Wasil	C82	86	.235	B	
5	8	Smith, Frank Thomas	P	50	.100	B	
		Temple, John Ellis	2B144	146	.307	B	
12	11	Valentine, Harold Lewis	P	36	.138	A	
0	3	Wehmeier, Herman Ralph	P12	13	+.000	B	Phil
0	0	Zuverink, George	P	2	.500	ClevA52	DetA

WON 75 NATIONAL LEAGUE FINISHED 5th.
LOST 79
TG 154 1955. PCT. .487

CINCINNATI

GEORGE ROBERT TEBBETTS

WON	LOST	NAME	POS.	G.	BA	FROM	TO
		Adams, Robert Henry (2B5)	3B42	64	.273	B	ChiA
0	0	Baczewski, Frederick John	P	1	.000	B	C
		Bailey, Lonas Edgar	C11	21	.205	B	
		Batts, Matthew Daniel	C21	26	.254	ChiA	
		Bell, David Russell	OF	154	.308	B	
5	2	Black, Joseph	P	32	+.100	xBkn	
		Borkowski, Robert Vilarian (1B1)	OF11	25	+.167	B	Bkn
		Bridges, Everett LaMar (2B9 SS26)	3B59	95	.286	B	
		Brovia, Joseph John		21	.111	A	C
		Burgess, Forrest Harrill	C107	116	+.306	xPhil	
9	8	Collum, Jack Dean	P	32	.250	B	
0	0	Fisher, Maurice Wayne	P	1	.000	A	C
11	10	Fowler, John Arthur	P	46	.200	B	
7	4	Freeman, Hershell Baskin (3B1)	P53	53	.167	xBosA	
		Gorbous, Glen Edward	OF5	8	+.333	A	Phil
		Greengrass, James Raymond	OF11	13	+.103	B	Phil

WON	LOST	NAME	POS.	G.	BA	FROM	TO
4	5	Gross, Donald John	P	17	.158	A	
		Harmon, Chas. Byron	3B39	96	.253	B	
		(1B4 OF32)					
		Hazle, Robert Sidney	OF3	6	.231	A	
0	2	Hooper, Robert Nelson	P	8	.000	ClevA	C
		Jablonski, Raymond Leo	3B28	74	.240	StL	
		(OF28)					
9	10	Klippstein, John Calvin	P	39	.065	Chi	
		Kluszewski, Theodore Bernard	1B	153	.314	B	
		Landrith, Hobert Neal	C27	43	.253	B	
0	2	Lane, Jerald Hal	P	8	.000	B	C
		Mele, Sabath Anthony (1B1)	OF13	35	.210	xBosA	
5	9	Minarcin, Rudy Anthony	P	41	.179	A	
		McMillan, Roy David	SS150	151	.268	B	
17	12	Nuxhall, Joseph Henry	P50	53	.198	B	
		Palys, Stanley Francis (1B1)	OF55	79	+.230	xPhil	
0	1	Pearce, James Madison	P	2	.000	B	C
1	2	Podbielan, Clarence Anthony	P	17	.400	B	
		Post, Walter Chas.	OF	154	.309	B	
0	3	Ridzik, Stephen George	P	13	+.167	xPhil	
		Seminick, Andrew Wasil	C5	6	+.133	B	Phil
		Silvera, Aaron Albert	OF1	13	.143	A	
		Smith, Milton (2B5)	3B28	36	.196	A	C
5	8	Staley, Gerald Lee	P	30	.056	StL	NYA
		Temple, John Ellis (SS1)	2B149	150	.281	B	
		Thurman, Robert Burns	OF36	82	.217	A	
2	1	Valentine, Harold Lewis	P	10	.000	B	C

WON 91 — NATIONAL LEAGUE — FINISHED 3rd.
LOST 63
TG 154 — 1956. — PCT. .591

CINCINNATI

GEORGE ROBERT TEBBETTS

WON	LOST	NAME	POS.	G.	BA	FROM	TO
4	3	Acker, Thomas James	P	29	.053	A	
		Bailey, Lonas Edgar	C106	118	.300	B	
		Balcena, Robert Rudolph	OF2	7	.000	A	C
		Batts, Matthew Daniel		3	.000	B	C
		Bell, David Russell	OF149	150	.292	B	
3	2	Black, Joseph	P32	34	.000	B	
		Bridges, Everett LaMar	3B51	71	.211	B	
		(2B8 SS7 OF1)					
		Burgess, Forrest Harrill	C55	90	.275	B	
		Crowe, George Daniel	1B32	77	.250	Milw	
		Dyck, James Robert (3B1)	1B1	18	.091	xBaltA	C
		Edwards, Chas. Bruce	C2	7	.200	WashA	C
		(2B1 3B1)					
		Flood, Curtis Chas.		5	.000	A	
11	11	Fowler, John Arthur	P	45	.146	B	
		Frazier, Joseph Filmore	OF4	10	+.235	xStL	BaltA
14	5	Freeman, Hershell Baskin	P	64	.056	B	
		Grammas, Alexander Peter	3B58	77	+.243	xStL	
		(2B5 SS12)					

WON	LOST	NAME	POS.	G.	BA	FROM	TO
3	0	Gross, Donald John	P	19	.105	B	
		Harmon, Chas. Byron (1B2)	OF6	13	+.000	B	StL
		Jablonski, Raymond Leo	3B127	130	.256	B	
		(2B1)					
2	3	Jansen, Lawrence Joseph	P	8	.000	NY54	C
8	2	Jeffcoat, Harold Bently	P38	49	.148	Chi	
0	0	Kennedy, Wm. Aulton	P	1	.000	BosA53	
12	11	Klippstein, John Calvin	P	37	.099	B	
		Kluszewski, Theodore Bernard	1B131	138	.302	B	
2	4	LaPalme, Paul Edmore	P	11	+.500	xStL	ChiA
19	10	Lawrence, Brooks Ulysses	P	49	.157	StL	
0	0	Meyer, Russell Chas.	P	1	+.000	xChi	
		McMillan, Roy David	SS	150	.263	B	
13	11	Nuxhall, Joseph Henry	P	44	.186	B	
		Oldham, John Hardin		1	.000	A	C
		Palys, Stanley Francis	OF10	40	.226	B	C
		Post, Walter Chas.	OF136	143	.249	B	
		Robinson, Frank	OF	152	.290	A	
0	1	Scantlebury, Patricio Athelstan	P6	8	.000	A	C
		Schult, Arthur Wm.	OF1	5	.429	NYA53	
		Silvera, Aaron Albert	OF	1	.000	B	C
0	0	Smith, Frank Thomas	P	2	.000	StL	C
		Temple, John Ellis (OF1)	2B154	154	.285	B	
		Thurman, Robert Burns	OF29	80	.295	B	

WON 80 — NATIONAL LEAGUE — FINISHED 4th.
LOST 74
TG 154 — 1957. — PCT. .519

CINCINNATI

GEORGE ROBERT TEBBETTS

WON	LOST	NAME	POS.	G.	BA	FROM	TO
10	5	Acker, Thomas James	P	49	.053	B	
1	2	Amor, Vecente Alvarez	P	9	.167	Chi55	C
		Bailey, Lonas Edgar	C115	122	.261	B	
		Bell, David Russell	OF	121	.292	B	
		Bridges, Everett LaMar	2B2	5	.000	B	WashA
		(SS1 3B1)					
		Burgess, Forrest Harrill	C45	90	.283	B	
		Crowe, George Daniel	1B120	133	.271	B	
		Dotterer, Henry John	C	4	.083	A	
		Durnbaugh, Robert Eugene	SS	2	.000	A	C
		Flood, Curtis Chas. (2B1)	3B2	3	.333	B	
3	0	Fowler, John Arthur	P	33	.176	B	
7	2	Freeman, Hershell Baskin	P	52	.200	B	
		Grammas, Alexander Peter	SS42	73	.303	B	
		(2B20 3B9)					
7	9	Gross, Donald John	P	43	.109	B	
3	2	Hacker, Warren Louis	P	15	+.125	Chi	Phil
		Henrich, Robert Edward	SS7	29	.200	A	
		(2B1 3B2 OF6)					
		Hoak, Donald Albert (2B1)	3B149	149	.293	Chi	
0	1	Hook, James Wesley	P	3	.000	A	
12	13	Jeffcoat, Harold Bently	P37	53	.203	B	

WON	LOST	NAME	POS.	G.	BA	FROM	TO
0	2	Kennedy, Wm. Aulton	P	8	.000	B	C
8	11	Klippstein, John Calvin	P	46	.073	B	
		Kluszewski, Theodore Bernard	1B23	69	.268	B	
16	13	Lawrence, Brooks Ulysses	P	49	.171	B	
		Lynch, Gerald Thomas (C2)	OF24	67	.258	Pitt	
		McMillan, Roy David	SS	151	.272	B	
10	10	Nuxhall, Joseph Henry	P39	42	.237	B	
0	0	Osteen, Claude Wilson	P	3	.000	A	
		Pavletich, Donald Stephen		1	.000	A	
0	1	Podbielan, Clarence Anthony	P	5	.000	Cin55	
		Post, Walter Chas.	OF124	134	.244	B	
0	1	Rabe, Chas. Henry	P	2	.000	A	
		Robinson, Frank (1B24)	OF136	150	.322	B	
3	2	Sanchez, Raul Guadalupe Rodriguez	P	38	.286	WashA52	
		Schult, Arthur Wm.	OF5	21	.265	B	WashA
0	0	Skaugstad, David Wendell	P	2	.000	A	C
		Taylor, Joe Cephus	OF27	33	.262	PhilA54	
		Temple, John Ellis	2B	145	.284	B	
		Thurman, Robert Burns	OF44	74	.247	B	
		Whisenant, Thomas Peter	OF43	67	.211	Chi	

WON 76
LOST 78
TG 154

NATIONAL LEAGUE

1958.

FINISHED 4th.

PCT. .494

CINCINNATI

GEORGE ROBERT TEBBETTS JAMES JOSEPH DYKES

WON	LOST	NAME	POS.	G.	BA	FROM	TO
4	3	Acker, Thomas James	P	38	.067	B	
		Bailey, Lonas Edgar	C99	112	.250	B	
		Bell, David Russell	OF107	112	.252	B	
		Bilko, Stephen Thomas	1B21	31	+.264	Chi54	LA
		Burgess, Forrest Harrill	C58	99	.283	B	
		Coles, Chas. Edward	OF4	5	.182	A	C
		Crowe, George Daniel (2B1)	1B93	111	.275	B	
		Dotterer, Henry John	C8	11	.250	B	
		Dropo, Walter	1B43	63	.290	xChiA	
		Fondy, Dee Virgil (OF22)	1B36	89	.218	Pitt	C
0	0	Freeman, Hershell Baskin	P	3	+.000	B	Chi
		Fridley, James Riley	OF2	5	.222	BaltA54	C
		Grammas, Alexander Peter (2B14 3B38)	SS61	105	.218	B	
8	7	Haddix, Harvey	P29	42	.180	Phil	
		Hatfield, Fred James (3B1)	2B1	3	.000	xClevA	C
0	0	Hayden, Eugene Franklin	P	3	.000	A	C
		Henrich, Robert Edward	SS2	5	.000	B	
		Hoak, Donald Albert (SS1)	3B112	114	.261	B	
0	1	Hook, James Wesley	P	1	.000	B	
6	8	Jeffcoat, Harold Bently (OF1)	P49	50	.556	B	
7	3	Kellner, Alexander Raymond	P	18	.357	xKCA	
0	0	Kelly, Robert Edward	P	2	.000	Cin53	ClevA
3	2	Klippstein, John Calvin	P	12	+.125	B	LA
8	13	Lawrence, Brooks Ulysses	P	46	.113	B	

WON	LOST	NAME	POS.	G.	BA	FROM	TO
0	2	Lown, Omar Joseph	P	11	+.000	xChi	ChiA
		Lynch, Gerald Thomas	OF101	122	.312	B	
		McMillan, Roy David	SS	145	.229	B	
		Miksis, Edward Thomas (1B1 2B7 SS5 3B14)	OF32	69	.140	xBaltA	C
		Morejon, Daniel Torres	OF11	12	.192	A	C
7	7	Newcombe, Donald	P20	39	+.350	xL.A.	
12	11	Nuxhall, Joseph Henry	P	36	.210	B	
0	1	O'Toole, James Jerome	P	1	.000	A	
1	0	Pena, Orlando Guevara	P	9	.000	A	
		Pinson, Vada Edward	OF	27	.271	A	
17	11	Purkey, Robert Thomas	P	37	.111	Pitt	
0	3	Rabe, Chas. Henry	P	9	.000	B	C
		Robinson, Frank (3B11)	OF138	148	.269	B	
3	5	Schmidt, Willard Raymond	P	41	.091	StL	
		Temple, John Ellis (1B1)	2B141	141	.306	B	
		Thurman, Robert Burns	OF41	94	.230	B	
		Whisenant, Thomas Peter (2B1)	OF66	85	.236	B	
0	0	Wieand, Franklin Delano Roosevelt	P	1	.000	A	
0	1	Wight, Wm. Robert	P	7	+.000	BaltA	StL

WON 74
LOST 80
TG 154

NATIONAL LEAGUE

1959.

FINISHED 5th.
(TIED WITH CHICAGO)
PCT. .481

CINCINNATI

EDWARD MAYO SMITH FREDERICK CHAS. HUTCHINSON

WON	LOST	NAME	POS.	G.	BA	FROM	TO
1	2	Acker, Thomas James	P	37	.111	B	C
1	0	Arroyo, Luis Enrique	P	10	.000	Pitt57	
0	1	Bailey, James Hopkins	P	3	.000	A	C
		Bailey, Lonas Edgar	C117	121	.264	B	
		Bell, David Russell	OF145	148	.293	B	
8	3	Brosnan, James Patrick	P	26	+.043	xStL	
		Cook, Raymond Clifford	3B	9	.381	A	
0	0	Cuellar, Miguel Santana	P	2	.000	A	C
		Dotterer, Henry John	C51	52	.267	B	
		Dropo, Walter	1B23	26	.103	B	BaltA
		Ennis, Delmer	OF3	5	.333	StL	ChiA
		Gilbert, Drew Edward	OF6	7	.150	A	C
		Henrich, Robert Edward (3B1)	SS5	14	.000	B	C
5	5	Hook, James Wesley	P17	19	.125	B	
0	1	Jeffcoat, Harold Bently	P	17	+1.000	B	St.L.
		Jones, Willie Edward	3B68	72	.249	xClevA	
		Kasko, Edward Michael (2B2 3B31)	SS84	118	.283	StL	
7	12	Lawrence, Brooks Ulysses	P	43	.150	B	
		Lockman, Carroll Walter (2B6 3B1 OF1)	1B20	52	.262	xBaltA	
		Lynch, Gerald Thomas	OF98	117	.269	B	
4	2	Mabe, Robert Lee	P	18	.000	StL	
		McMillan, Roy Da vid	SS73	79	.264	B	

WON	LOST	NAME	POS.	G.	BA	FROM	TO
13	8	Newcombe, Donald	P30	61	.305	B	
9	9	Nuxhall, Joseph Henry	P	28	.250	B	
0	0	Osteen, Claude Wilson	P	2	.000	Cin57	
5	8	O'Toole, James Jerome	P28	29	.135	B	
		Pavletich, Donald Stephen		1	.000	Cin57	
5	9	Pena, Orlando Guevara	P	46	.088	B	
		Pendleton, James Edward (SS3 3B16)	OF24	65	.257	Pitt	
		Pinson, Vada Edward	OF	154	.316	B	
		Powers, John Calvin	OF5	43	.256	Pitt	
13	18	Purkey, Robert Thomas	P	38	.167	B	
		Robinson, Frank (OF40)	1B125	146	.311	B	
0	0	Rudolph, Frederick Donald	P	5	.000	xChiA	
3	2	Schmidt, Willard Raymond	P	36	.083	B	C
		Temple, John Ellis	2B	149	.311	B	
		Thomas, Frank Joseph (1B14 OF33)	3B64	108	.225	Pitt	
		Thurman, Robert Burns		4	.250	B	C
		Whisenant, Thomas Peter	OF21	36	.239	B	

WON 67
LOST 87
TG 154

NATIONAL LEAGUE FINISHED 6th.

1960 PCT. .435

CINCINNATI

FREDERICK CHAS. HUTCHINSON

WON	LOST	NAME	POS.	G.	BA	FROM	TO
		Alvarez, Rogelio Hernandez	1B2	3	.111	A	
		Anderson, Harry Walter (OF4)	1B15	42	+.167	xPhil	
		Azcue, Jose Joaquin	C	14	.097	A	
		Bailey, Lonas Edgar	C129	133	.261	B	
		Bell, David Russell	OF131	143	.262	B	
4	0	Bridges, Marshall	P	14	+.250	xStL	
7	2	Brosnan, James Patrick	P	57	.200	B	
		Cardenas, Leonardo Alfonso Lazaro	SS47	48	.232	A	
		Chacon, Elio Rodriguez (OF2)	2B43	49	.181	A	
		Coleman, Gordon Calvin	1B	66	.271	ClevA	
		Cook, Raymond Clifford (OF4)	3B47	54	.208	B	
		Dotterer, Henry John	C31	33	.228	B	
		Gaines, Arnesta	OF3	11	.200	A	
		Gonzalez, Andres Antonio	OF31	39	+.212	A	Phil
2	2	Grim, Robert Anton	P	26	+.000	xClevA	St.L.
1	5	Henry, Wm. Rodman	P	51	.000	Chi	
11	18	Hook, James Wesley	P	36	.083	B	
		House, Henry Frank	C8	23	.179	KCA	
		Jones, Willie Edward (2B1)	3B46	79	.268	B	
		Kasko, Edward Michael (2B33 SS15)	3B86	126	.292	B	
1	0	Lawrence, Brooks Ulysses	P	7	.000	B	C
		Lockman, Carroll Walter	1B5	21	.200	B	C
		Lynch, Gerald Thomas	OF32	102	.289	B	
2	6	Maloney, James Wm.	P	11	.111	A	
		Martin, Alfred Manuel	2B97	103	.246	ClevA	
4	14	McLish, Calvin Coolidge	P	37	.049	ClevA	
		McMillan, Roy David (2B10)	SS116	124	.236	B	
4	6	Newcombe, Donald	P16	24	.139	B	ClevA
1	8	Nuxhall, Joseph Henry	P38	39	.077	B	
0	1	Osteen, Claude Wilson	P20	26	.083	B	
12	12	O'Toole, James Jerome	P	34	.106	B	
0	1	Pena, Orlando Guevara	P	4	.000	B	
		Pinson, Vada Edward	OF	154	.287	B	
		Post, Walter Chas.	OF67	77	+.281	xPhil	
17	11	Purkey, Robert Thomas	P	41	.133	B	
0	0	Richards, Duane Lee	P	2	.000	A	C
		Robinson, Frank (3B1 OF51)	1B78	139	.297	B	
1	0	Sanchez, Raul Guadalupe Rodriguez	P	8	.500	Cin57	C
		Walls, Ray Lee (1B2)	OF24	29	+.274	Chi	Phil
		Whisenant, Thomas Peter		1	.000	B	ClevA
0	1	Wieand, Franklin Delano Roosevelt	P	5	.000	Cin58	C

WON 93
LOST 61
TG 154

NATIONAL LEAGUE FINISHED 1st.

1961. PCT. .604

CINCINNATI

FREDERICK CHAS. HUTCHINSON

WON	LOST	NAME	POS.	G.	BA	FROM	TO
		Anderson, Harry Walter		4	.250	B	C
		Bailey, Lonas Edgar	C	12	+.302	B	S.F.
		Baumer, James Sloan	2B9	10	.125	ChiA49	C
		Bell, David Russell	OF75	103	.255	B	
		Bevan, Joseph Harold		3	.333	KCA55	C
		Blasingame, Donald Lee	2B116	123	+.222	xS.F.	
0	1	Bridges, Marshall	P	13	.000	B	
10	4	Brosnan, James Patrick	P	53	.154	B	
		Cardenas, Leonardo Alfonso Lazaro	SS63	74	.308	B	
		Chacon, Elio Rodriguez (OF7)	2B42	61	.265	B	
		Coleman, Gordon Calvin	1B	150	.287	B	
		Cook, Raymond Clifford	3B1	4	.000	B	
		Edwards, John Alban	C	52	.186	A	
		Freese, Eugene Lewis (2B1)	3B151	152	.277	ChiA	
		Gaines, Arnesta	OF3	5	.000	B	
		Gernert, Richard Edward	1B21	40	.302	xDetA	
2	1	Henry, Wm. Rodman	P47	48	.000	B	
1	3	Hook, James Wesley	P	22	.133	B	
9	10	Hunt, Kenneth Raymond	P	29	.179	A	C
21	10	Jay, Joseph Richard	P	34	.090	Milw	
		Johnson, Darrell Dean	C	20	+.315	xPhil	
6	2	Johnson, Kenneth Travis	P	15	.240	xKCA	

WON	LOST	NAME	POS.	G.	BA	FROM	TO
1	1	Jones, Sherman Jarvis	P	24	.182	S.F.	
		Jones, Willie Edward	3B1	9	.000	B	C
		Kasko, Edward Michael (2B6 3B12)	SS112	126	.271	B	
		Lynch, Gerald Thomas	OF44	96	.315	B	
6	7	Maloney, James Wm. (OF1)	P27	30	.379	B	
2	1	Nunn, Howard Ralph	P	24	.250	StL59	
0	0	Osteen, Claude Wilson (OF1)	P	1	.000	B	WashA
19	9	O'Toole, James Jerome	P	39	.172	B	
		Pinson, Vada Edward	OF153	154	.343	B	
		Post, Walter Chas.	OF81	99	.294	B	
16	12	Purkey, Robert Thomas	P	36	.100	B	
		Robinson, Frank (3B1)	OF150	153	.323	B	
		Schmidt, Robert Benjamin	C	27	+.129	xS.F.	
		Whisenant, Thomas Peter (C1 3B1)	OF12	26	.200	xMinnA	C
		Zimmerman, Gerald Robert	C	76	.206	A	

WON 98 — NATIONAL LEAGUE — FINISHED 3rd.
LOST 64
TG 162 — 1962. — PCT. .605

CINCINNATI

FREDERICK CHAS. HUTCHINSON

WON	LOST	NAME	POS.	G.	BA	FROM	TO
		Alvarez, Rogelio Hernandez	1B13	14	.214	Cin60	C
		Blasingame, Donald Lee	2B137	141	.281	B	
4	4	Brosnan, James Patrick	P	48	.000	B	
		Cardenas, Leonardo Alfonso Lazaro	SS149	153	.294	B	
		Coleman, Gordon Calvin	1B128	136	.277	B	
		Cook, Raymond Clifford	3B4	6	+.000	B	N.Y.
2	6	Drabowsky, Myron Walter	P	23	.000	Mil	K.C.A
		Edwards, John Alban	C130	133	.254	B	
2	2	Ellis, Samuel Joseph	P	8	.200	A	C
		Foiles, Henry Lee	C41	43	.275	BaltA	
		Freese, Eugene Lewis	3B10	18	.143	B	
		Gaines, Arnesta	OF13	64	.231	B	
		Gonder, Jesse Lemar		4	.000	N.Y.A	
		Harper, Thomas	3B	6	.174	A	
4	2	Henry, Wm. Rodman	P	40	.333	B	
0	0	Hillman, Darius Dutton	P	2	+.000	BosA	N.Y.
21	14	Jay, Joseph Richard	P	39	.167	B	
		Johnson, Darrell Dean	C	2	.000	B	BaltA
		Kasko, Edward Michael (SS21)	3B114	134	.278	B	
		Keough, Richard Martin (1B29)	OF71	111	.278	WashA	
7	6	Klippstein, John Calvin	P	40	.125	WashA	
		Lynch, Gerald Thomas	OF73	114	.281	B	
9	7	Maloney, James Wm.	P22	24	.186	B	
0	0	Miller, Robert Gerald	P	6	+.000	DetA56	N.Y.
0	0	Nunn, Howard Ralph	P	6	.000	B	C

WON	LOST	NAME	POS.	G.	BA	FROM	TO
5	0	Nuxhall, Joseph Henry	P	12	.269	xL.A.A	
16	13	O'Toole, James Jerome	P	36	.110	B	
		Pavletich, Donald Stephen (C2)	1B25	34	.222	Cin59	
		Pinson, Vada Edward	OF152	155	.292	B	
		Post, Walter Chas.	OF90	109	.263	B	
23	5	Purkey, Robert Thomas	P	37	.103	B	
		Robinson, Frank	OF161	162	.342	B	
		Rojas, Octavio Rivas (3B1)	2B30	39	.221	A	
4	3	Sisler, David Michael	P	35	.000	WashA	C
1	0	Tsitouris, John Philip	P	4	.000	KCA60	
0	2	Wills, Theodore Carl	P	26	.313	xBosA	
		Zimmer, Donald Wm. (SS1 2B17)	3B43	63	+.250	xN.Y.	

WON 86 — NATIONAL LEAGUE — FINISHED 5th.
LOST 76
TG 162 — 1963. — PCT. .531

CINCINNATI

FREDERICK CHAS. HUTCHINSON

WON	LOST	NAME	POS.	G.	BA	FROM	TO
		Blasingame, Donald Lee (3B2)	2B11	18	.161	B	WashA
		Bright, Harry James	1B	1	.000	WashA	NYA
0	1	Brosnan, James Patrick	P	6	.000	B	ChicA
		Cardenas, Leonardo Alfonso Lazaro	SS157	158	.235	B	
0	0	Coates, James Alton	P	9	.000	xWashA	
		Coleman, Gordon Calvin	1B107	123	.247	B	
		Edwards, John Alban	C	148	.259	B	
		Foiles, Henry Lee	C	1	.000	B	LAA
		Freese, Eugene Lewis (OF1)	3B62	66	.244	B	
		Gonder, Jesse Lemar	C7	31	+.313	B	N.Y.
		Green, Eugene Leroy	C8	15	.226	xCleveA	C
		Harper, Thomas (3B1)	OF118	129	.260	B	
1	3	Henry, Wm. Rodman	P	47	.167	B	
7	18	Jay, Joseph Richard	P	30	.160	B	
		Kasko, Edward Michael (2B1 SS15)	3B48	76	.241	B	
		Keough, Richard Martin (OF28)	1B46	95	.227	B	
		Lynch, Gerald Thomas	OF7	22	+.250	B	Pitt
23	7	Maloney, James Wm.	P33	34	.169	B	
		Neal, Chas. Lenard (2B1 SS1)	3B19	34	+.156	xN.Y.	C
15	8	Nuxhall, Joseph Henry	P	35	.158	B	
17	14	O'Toole, James Jerome	P	33	.149	B	
0	2	Owens, James Phillip	P	19	.125	Phil	
		Pavletich, Donald Stephen (C13)	1B57	71	.208	B	
		Pinson, Vada Edward	OF	162	.313	B	
		Post, Walter Chas.	OF1	5	.000	B	MinnA

WON	LOST	NAME	POS.	G.	BA	FROM	TO
6	10	Purkey, Robert Thomas	P	21	.098	B	
		Robinson, Frank (1B1)	OF139	140	.259	B	
		Rose, Peter Edward (OF1)	2B157	157	.273	A	
		Skinner, Robert Ralph	OF51	72	+.253	xPitt	
		Spencer, Daryl Dean	3B48	50	+.239	xL.A.	C
		Taylor, Samuel Douglas	C2	3	+.000	xN.Y.	C
12	8	Tsitouris, John Philip	P	30	.081	B	
		Walters, Kenneth Rogers (1B1)	OF21	49	.187	Phil61	C
4	4	Worthington, Allan Fulton	P	50	.083	ChicA60	
1	1	Zanni, Dominick Thomas	P	31	.333	xChicA	

WON 92 — NATIONAL LEAGUE — FINISHED 2nd.
LOST 70 — (TIED WITH PHILADELPHIA)
TG 162 — 1964. — PCT. .568

CINCINNATI

FREDERICK CHAS. HUTCHINSON — RICHARD ALLAN SISLER

WON	LOST	NAME	POS.	G.	BA	FROM	TO
		Boros, Steven A.	3B114	117	.257	Chic	
		Cardenas, Leonardo Alfonso Lazaro	SS	163	.251	B	
		Coker, Jimmie Goodwin	C	11	.313	S.F.	
		Coleman, Gordon Calvin	1B49	89	.242	B	
1	0	Dickson, James Edward	P	4	.000	Hous	
0	2	Duren, Rinold George	P	26	+.000	xPhila	
		Edwards, John Alban	C120	126	.281	B	
10	3	Ellis, Samuel Joseph	P	52	.083	Cin62	
		Harper, Thomas (3B2)	OF92	102	.243	B	
		Helms, Tommy Vann		2	.000	A	
2	2	Henry, Wm. Rodney	P37	38	.500	B	
11	11	Jay, Joseph Richard	P	34	.057	B	
		Johnson, Deron Roger (3B1 OF10)	1B131	140	.273	KCA62	
		Keough, Richard Martin (1B4)	OF81	109	.257	B	
		Klaus, Robert Francis (SS3 3B11)	2B18	40	.183	B	
15	10	Maloney, James Wm.	P	31	.151	B	
6	5	McCool, Wm. John	P	40	.000	A	
0	0	Nichols, Chester Raymond Jr.	P	3	.000	BosA	C
9	8	Nuxhall, Joseph Henry	P32	34	.130	B	
17	7	O'Toole, James Jerome	P	30	.100	B	
		Pavletich, Donald Stephen (1B1)	C27	34	.242	B	
		Perez, Atanasio Rigal	1B6	12	.080	A	
		Pinson, Vada Edward	OF	156	.266	B	
11	9	Purkey, Robert Thomas	P	34	.052	B	
		Queen, Melvin Douglas	OF20	48	.200	A	
		Robinson, Frank	OF	156	.306	B	
		Rose, Peter Edward	2B128	136	.269	B	
		Ruiz, Hiraldo Sablon (2B30)	3B49	77	.244	A	
		Skinner, Robert Ralph	OF12	25	+.220	B	StL
		Smith, Harold Wayne	C20	32	.121	Hous	C
		Temple, John Ellis		6	.000	Hous.	C
9	13	Tsitouris, John Philip	P	37	.190	B	
1	0	Worthington, Allan Fulton	P	6	.000	B	MinnA

CLUB RECORD

NATIONAL LEAGUE

CLEVELAND

YEAR	TG	WON	LOST	PCT.	FINISHED	MANAGER
1879	77	24	53	.312	7	James McCormick
1880	84	47	37	.559	3	James McCormick
1881	84	36	48	.429	7	James McCormick
1882	82	42	40	.512	5	J. Ford Evans
1883	97	55	42	.567	4	Frank Carter Bancroft
1884	112	35	77	.313	7	Chas. M. Hackett
1885-1888		OUT OF LEAGUE				
1889	133	61	72	.459	6	Thomas Joseph Loftus
1890	132	44	88	.333	7	Gustavus Heinrich Schmelz / Robert H. Leadley
1891	139	65	74	.468	5	Robert H. Leadley / Oliver Wendell Tebeau
1892	149	93	56	.624	2	Oliver Wendell Tebeau
1893	128	73	55	.570	3	Oliver Wendell Tebeau
1894	129	68	61	.527	6	Oliver Wendell Tebeau
1895	130	84	46	.646	2	Oliver Wendell Tebeau
1896	128	80	48	.625	2	Oliver Wendell Tebeau
1897	131	69	62	.527	5	Oliver Wendell Tebeau
1898	149	81	68	.544	5	Oliver Wendell Tebeau
1899	154	20	134	.129	12(Last)	LaFayette Napoleon Cross / Joseph J. Quinn

WON 24 LOST 53 TG 77

NATIONAL LEAGUE 1879. FINISHED 7th. PCT. .312

CLEVELAND

JAMES McCORMICK

WON	LOST	NAME	POS.	G.	BA	FROM	TO
		Allen, Cyrus Alban (Dick) (OF2)	3B14	16	+.117	xSyr.	C
		Carey, Thomas John	SS	80	.238	Prov	C
		Eden, Chas. M.	OF79	81	.272	Chi77	
		Gilligan, Andrew Bernard (Barney) (OF23)	C27	52	.170	A	
		Glasscock, John Wesley (3B15)	2B65	80	.209	A	
		Gunkle, Frederick W. (OF1)	C1	1	.000	A	C
		Hoffman, Chas.	C	1	.000	A	C
		Kennedy, Michael Joseph (Doc)	C44	47	.285	A	
4	13	Mitchell, Robert McKasha (OF8)	P22	30	.146	Cin	
20	40	McCormick, James MGR. (OF11)	P60	75	.219	Indpls	
		Phillips, Wm. B.	1B71	81	.271	A	
		Riley, Wm. J.	OF	43	.142	A	C
		Stockwell, Leonard C.	OF	2	.000	A	
		Strief, George Andrew (2B15)	OF56	71	.174	A	
		Warner, Frederick John Rodney (OF20)	3B54	76	.243	Indpls	

WON 47 LOST 37 TG 84

NATIONAL LEAGUE 1880. FINISHED 3rd. PCT. .559

CLEVELAND

JAMES McCORMICK

WON	LOST	NAME	POS.	G.	BA	FROM	TO
		Dunlap, Frederick C.	2B	84	.273	A	
2	7	Gardner, Franklin W. (OF1)	P9	10	.200	Troy	
		*Gilligan, Andrew Bernard (Barney)	C20	28	.179	B	
		Glasscock, John Wesley	SS	76	.247	B	
		Hall, Archibald W.	OF	2	.125	Troy	
1	1	Hankinson, Frank Edward (P2 OF14)	3B55	68	.209	Chi	
		Hanlon, Edward Hugh (SS4 3B1)	OF68	72	.247	A	
		Hotaling, Peter James	OF	77	.240	Cin	
		Kennedy, Michael Joseph (Doc)	C64	66	.200	B	
44	29	McCormick, James MGR. (OF9)	P73	77	.250	B	
		McGeary, Michael Henry (OF2)	3B29	31	+.233	xProv	
		Phillips, Wm. B.	1B	84	.255	B	
		Schaffer, George (Orator)	OF	82	.265	Chi	
		Wheeler, Harry Eugene	OF	1	+.250	Cin	Cin

*Gilligan also played 4 games at SS and 4 in OF.

WON 36 LOST 48 TG 84

NATIONAL LEAGUE 1881. FINISHED 7th. PCT. .429

CLEVELAND

JAMES McCORMICK

WON	LOST	NAME	POS.	G.	BA	FROM	TO
3	4	Bradley, George Washington (P7 SS6 OF1)	3B48	61	+.252	xDet	
		Clapp, John Edgar (OF20)	C45	65	.253	Cin	
		Doscher, John Herman Sr.	3B	5	.211	Troy79	
		Dunlap, Frederick C. (3B1)	2B78	78	.324	B	
		Glasscock, John Wesley (2B5)	SS79	84	.260	B	
		Kemmler, Rudolph	C	1	.000	Prov79	
		#Kennedy, Michael Joseph (Doc)	C34	38	.313	B	
		Moynahan, Michael (3B1)	OF32	33	+.255	Buff	Det
26	31	*McCormick, James MGR.	P57	69	.257	B	
		McGeary, Michael Henry	3B	10	.211	B	
7	13	Nolan, Edward Sylvester (The Only) (3B6 OF19)	P21	40	.251	Indpls78	
		Phillips, Wm. B.	1B	84	.270	B	
		Powers, Philip J. (3B1)	C5	6	.143	Bos	
		Purcell, Wm. Aloysius (Blondy)	OF	20	+.165	Cin	Buff
		Remsen, John Jay	OF	48	.174	Chi78	
		Schaffer, George (Orator)	OF	84	.257	B	
		Smith, Chas. Marvin (Pap)	3B	10	+.118	Cin	Wor
0	0	Taylor, Wm. Henry (P1 3B1)	OF24	25	+.222	xDet	

#Kennedy also played 1 game at 3B and 3 games in the OF.
*McCormick also played 2 games at 2B and 9 games in the OF.

WON 42 LOST 40 TG 82

NATIONAL LEAGUE 1882. FINISHED 5th. PCT. .512

CLEVELAND

J. FORD EVANS

WON	LOST	NAME	POS.	G.	BA	FROM	TO
7	10	Bradley, George Washington (1B6 3B12 OF8)	P17	29	.183	B	
		Briody, Chas. F.	C	52	.263	Troy80	
		*Doscher, John Herman Sr.	3B23	25	.240	B	C
		Dunlap, Frederick C.	2B	82	.278	B	
		Dwyer, John E. (OF1)	C1	1	.000	A	C
		Esterbrook, Thomas Jefferson (Dude) (1B2)	OF44	45	.246	Buff80	

WON	LOST	NAME	POS.	G.	BA	FROM	TO
		Glasscock, John Wesley	SS	82	.285	B	
		Kelly, John Francis	C	29	.134	Syr79	
		Kennedy, Michael Joseph (Doc)	C	1	.250	B	
		Muldoon, Michael (OF22)	3B60	82	.252	A	
35	29	McCormick, James (OF3)	P65	67	.216	B	
		McGunnigle, Wm. Henry	OF	1	.200	Wor80	
		Phillips, Wm. B. (C1)	1B75	76	.266	B	
		Richmond, John H.	OF	39	.154	Bos	AthAA
0	1	Rowe, David E. (P1)	OF22	23	.247	Chi77	
		Schaffer, George (Orator)	OF	82	.218	B	
		Tilley, John C.	OF	15	.089	A	
		Willigrod, Julius	OF	8	+.114	xDet	C

*Doscher also played 1 game in the OF.

WON 55 — NATIONAL LEAGUE — FINISHED 4th.
LOST 42
TG 97 — 1883. — PCT. .567

CLEVELAND

FRANK CARTER BANCROFT

WON	LOST	NAME	POS.	G.	BA	FROM	TO
		Bradley, George Washington	SS	4	.313	B	AthAA
		Briody, Chas. F.	C32	39	.232	B	
		(1B1 2B4 3B1)					
		Broughton, Cecil Calvert	C	4	.167	A	BaltAA
		Bushong, Albert John	C	61	.172	Wor	
0	1	Cady, Chas. B. (P1)	OF2	3	.000	A	
		Crowley, Wm. Michael	OF	11	.317	xAthAA	
24	18	Daly, Hugh I. (One-Arm) (OF1)	P42	42	.109	Buff	
		Dunlap, Frederick C.	2B	90	.328	B	
0	0	Evans, Jacob	OF84	89	.235	Wor	
		(P1 2B1 3B1)					
		Glasscock, John Wesley (2B3)	SS90	93	.290	B	
		Hotaling, Peter James	OF	97	.255	Bos	
0	0	Hunter, Robert Lemuel (OF1)	P1	1	.250	A	C
		Muldoon, Michael	3B	95	.224	B	
27	13	McCormick, James (1B1 OF1)	P40	41	.235	B	
		Phillips, Wm. B.	1B	94	.244	B	
4	10	Sawyer, Willard Newton	P	17	.019	A	C
		York, Thomas J.	OF	97	.255	Prov	

WON 35 — NATIONAL LEAGUE — FINISHED 7th.
LOST 77.
TG 112 — 1884. — PCT. .313

CLEVELAND

CHAS. M. HACKETT

WON	LOST	NAME	POS.	G.	BA	FROM	TO
		Ardner, Joseph A. (3B1)	2B25	26	.174	A	
		Briody, Chas. F. (OF1)	C43	43	.169	B	CinUA
		Burch, Ernest W.	OF	31	.201	A	
		Bushong, Albert John	C	60	.231	B	
		Evans, Jacob (2B3 SS2)	OF76	80	.258	B	
		Fisher, Harry C. (C1)	2B6	6	.130	xChiUA	
		Gilman, Pitkin Clark	OF	2	.100	A	
0	0	*Glasscock, John Wesley (P2)	SS68	72	.249	B	CinUA
12	32	Harkins, John Joseph	P45	60	.205	A	
		(SS1 3B1 OF15)					
1	4	Henry, John Michael (OF4)	P5	9	.154	A	
		Hotaling, Peter James (2B1)	OF101	101	.242	B	
3	19	Moffet, Samuel R.	OF40	66	.179	A	
		(P22 1B2 2B1 3B1)					
		Moore, Jeremiah S.	C	10	.235	xAltUA	
		Moynahan, Michael	2B6	12	.304	xAthAA	C
		(SS3 OF3)					
		Muldoon, Michael (2B1 OF1)	3B108	109	.239	B	
		Murphy, Wm. N. (SS1)	OF42	42	.226	A	WashAA
19	22	McCormick, James (OF8)	P41	48	.263	B	CinUA
		Phillips, Wm. B.	1B	110	.272	B	
		#Pinckney, George Burton	2B25	35	.309	A	
		Smith, George J. (Germany)	2B41	71	.258	xAltUA	
		(SS30)					
		Smith, Wm. E.	OF	1	.000	A	C
		Strief, George Andrew (3B2)	OF6	8	.241	xPittUA	
		Whiteley, Gurdon	OF	8	.147	A	

*Glasscock also played 3 games at 2B.
#Pinckney also played 10 games at SS.

WON 61 — NATIONAL LEAGUE — FINISHED 6th.
LOST 72
TG 133 — 1889. — PCT. .459

CLEVELAND

THOMAS JOSEPH LOFTUS

WON	LOST	NAME	POS.	G.	BA	FROM	TO
12	22	Bakely, Edward (Enoch)	P	34	.135	ClevAA	
20	14	Beatin, Ebenezer Ambrose	P	37	.115	Det	
		Faatz, Jay	1B	115	.230	ClevAA	
		Gilks, Robert James	OF29	52	.238	ClevAA	
7	16	Gruber, Henry John	P	23	.101	Det	
		McAleer, James Robert	OF	109	.235	A	
		McKean, Edward John	SS	123	.302	ClevAA	
22	17	O'Brien, John F. (Darby)	P	41	.250	ClevAA	
		Radford, Paul Revere	OF	136	.238	BknAA	
		Snyder, Chas. N.	C	21	.192	ClevAA	
		Sommers, Wm.	C	2	.000	A	
0	3	Sprague, Chas. Wellington	P	3	.143	Chi87	
		Stricker, John A. (Cub)	2B	136	.251	ClevAA	
		Sutcliffe, Edward Elmer	C50	65	.248	Det	
		Tebeau, Oliver Wendell (Pat)	3B	136	.282	Chi87	
		Twitchell, Lawrence Grant	OF	134	.275	Det	
		Zimmer, Chas. Louis (Chief)	C77	80	.258	ClevAA	

WON 44 / LOST 88 / TG 132

NATIONAL LEAGUE 1890. FINISHED 7th. PCT. .333

CLEVELAND

GUSTAVUS HEINRICH SCHMELZ — ROBERT H. LEADLEY

WON	LOST	NAME	POS.	G.	BA	FROM	TO
		Ardner, Joseph A.	2B	84	.223	Clev84	C
22	31	Beatin, Ebenezer Ambrose	P	53	.141	B	
		Daily, Vincent P.	OF	64	.288	A	C
		Davis, George Stacey	OF	134	.264	A	
		Davis, Thomas J.	OF	1	.000	A	C
		Delancy, Wm. L.	2B	36	.189	A	C
		Dowse, Thomas Jefferson	OF26	40	.207	A	
1	7	Garfield, Wm. Milton	P	8	.167	Pitt	C
2	2	Gilks, Robert James (P4)	OF123	130	.213	B	
3	10	Lincoln, Ezra Perry	P	15	.157	A	SyrAA
		Lyons, Patrick Jerry	2B	11	.052	A	C
		McKean, Edward John	SS134	136	.296	B	
0	1	Parsons, Chas. J.	P	2	.167	MetAA87	C
		Smalley, Wm. D.	3B	136	.213	A	
1	4	Smith, Edgar E.	P	7	.286	Prov85	C
0	1	Sommer, Joseph John (P1)	OF9	9	.294	BaltAA	BaltAA
		Stockwell, Leonard C.	C	2	.286	LvlleAA84	C
		Veach, Wm. Walter (Peek-a-boo)	1B	62	+.237	LvlleAA (87)	Pitt
4	10	Viau, Leon	P	14	+.140	xCin	
		Virtue, Jacob Kitchline	1B	62	.305	A	
2	15	Wadsworth, Wm. John	P	20	.178	A	
		West, Milton Douglass	OF	37	.245	CinAA84	C
		Wright, Wm. S. (Rasty)	OF	13	.106	xSyrAA	C
9	7	Young, Denton True (Cy)	P	17	.143	A	
		Zimmer, Chas. Louis (Chief)	C	125	.214	B	
		Sommers, Joseph Andrew (Pete) (OF1)	C7	8	+.192	xN.Y.	C

WON 65 / LOST 74 / TG 139

NATIONAL LEAGUE 1891. FINISHED 5th. PCT. .468

CLEVELAND

ROBERT H. LEADLEY — OLIVER WENDELL TEBEAU

WON	LOST	NAME	POS.	G.	BA	FROM	TO
		Alvord, Wm. C.	3B	13	.282	TolAA	WashAA
1	4	Beatin, Ebenezer Ambrose	P	5	.078	B	C
		Burkett, Jesse Cail	OF	40	.271	N.Y.	
		Childs, Clarence Algernon	2B	141	.295	SyrAA	
		Collins, Wm. J.	C	2	.000	AthAA	
		Daly, Joseph John	OF	1	.000	AthAA	
0	0	Davis, George Stacy (P1 3B21)	OF115	136	.292	B	
		Denny, Jeremiah D. (Jerry)	3B	36	+.229	xN.Y.	Phil
		Doyle, John Joseph (Jack) (3B18 OF21)	C25	64	.263	ColAA	
0	1	Getzein, Chas. H.	P	1	+.000	xBos	
16	21	Gruber, Henry John	P	38	.169	ClevPL	C
		Johnson, John Ralph	OF79	80	.263	ColAA	C
0	1	Killeen, Henry	P	1	.000	A	C
0	3	Knauss, Frank H.	P	3	.000	ColAA	
		McAleer, James Robert	OF	135	.246	ClevPL	
		McKean, Edward John	SS	141	.280	B	
1	0	Seward, Edward Wm.	P	7	.210	AthAA	C
1	4	Shearon, John M. (P6)	OF24	30	.234	A	
		Sullivan, Martin J.	OF	1	+.250	xBos	C
		Tebeau, Oliver Wendell MGR.	3B	61	.261	ClevPL	
18	20	Viau, Leon	P	39	.179	B	
		Virtue, Jacob Kitchline	1B	139	.262	B	
28	20	Young, Denton True (Cy)	P	50	.168	B	
		Zimmer, Chas. Louis (Chief)	C	116	.261	B	

WON 93 / LOST 56 / TG 149

NATIONAL LEAGUE 1892. FINISHED 2nd. PCT. .624

CLEVELAND

OLIVER WENDELL TEBEAU

WON	LOST	NAME	POS.	G.	BA	FROM	TO
		Burkett, Jesse Cail	OF	145	.277	B	
		Childs, Clarence Algernon	2B	144	.335	B	
17	10	Clarkson, John Gibson	P	27	+.140	xBos	
27	16	Cuppy, George Joseph (Nig)	P	43	.215	A	
10	15	Davies, George Washington	P	25	.130	MilAA	
		Davis, George Stacey (SS21 OF42)	3B78	143	.253	B	
		Doyle, John Joseph (Jack) (C8 1B1)	OF12	22	+.300	B	N.Y.
		McAleer, James Robert	OF	150	.241	B	
		McKean, Edward John	SS	128	.269	B	
		O'Connor, John Joseph (Jack) (C33)	OF106	139	.253	ColAA	
1	4	Rettger, George Edward	P	6	+.133	StLAA	Cin
		Tebeau, Oliver Wendell MGR.	3B75	84	.246	B	
1	0	Viau, Leon	P	1	+.000	B	Lvlle
		Virtue, Jacob Kitchline	1B	147	.282	B	
1	0	Williams, Thomas C.	P	3	.100	A	
36	11	Young, Denton True (Cy)	P	49	.163	B	
		Zimmer, Chas. Louis (Chief)	C	111	.268	B	

WON 73 / LOST 55 / TG 128

NATIONAL LEAGUE 1893. FINISHED 3rd. PCT. .570

CLEVELAND

OLIVER WENDELL TEBEAU

WON	LOST	NAME	POS.	G.	BA	FROM	TO
		Allen, Jesse Hall	C	1	.000	A	C
		Alvord, Wm. C.	3B	3	.250	WashAA91	C
		Boyd, Frank John	C	1	.200	A	C
		Burkett, Jesse Cail	OF	124	.372	B	
		Childs, Clarence Algernon	2B	122	.332	B	
16	16	Clarkson, John Gibson	P	34	.226	B	
17	11	Cuppy, George Joseph (Nig)	P	28	.257	B	
0	1	Davies, George Washington	P	3	+.333	B	N.Y.
		Ewing, Wm. (Buck)	OF110	114	.371	N.Y.	
0	2	Fisher, Chauncey Burr	P	3	.286	A	
		Gilman, Pitkin Clark	3B	2	.285	Clev84	C
		Gunson, Joseph Brook	C	21	+.296	xStL	C
4	6	Hastings, Chas. Morton	P	16	.179	A	
		McAleer, James Robert	OF	91	.253	B	
		McFarland, Edward Wm.	OF	9	.370	A	
		McGarr, James B. (Chippy)	3B	63	.309	Bos90	
		McKean, Edward John	SS	125	.325	B	
		O'Connor, John Joseph (OF41)	C52	93	.309	B	
1	1	Scheible, John G.	P	3	.142	A	
0	0	Stafford, John Henry	P	2	.000	A	C
		Tebeau, Oliver Wendell MGR. (3B56)	1B56	115	.359	B	
		Virtue, Jacob Kitchline	1B73	95	.287	B	
1	1	Williams, Thomas C.	P	8	.277	B	C
34	17	Young, Denton True (Cy)	P	51	.251	B	
		Zimmer, Chas. Louis (Chief)	C	55	.309	B	

WON 68
LOST 61
TG 129

NATIONAL LEAGUE — 1894. — FINISHED 6th. — PCT. .527

CLEVELAND

OLIVER WENDELL TEBEAU

WON	LOST	NAME	POS.	G.	BA	FROM	TO
		Blake, Henry C.	OF	73	.286	A	
		Burkett, Jesse Cail	OF	124	.357	B	
		Childs, Clarence Algernon	2B	117	.365	B	
8	8	Clarkson, John Gibson	P	16	.204	B	C
21	16	Cuppy, George Joseph (Nig)	P40	41	.253	B	
		Ewing, Wm. (Buck)	OF52	53	.255	B	
0	2	Fisher, Chauncey Burr	P	3	+.000	B	Cin
3	3	Griffith, Frank Wesley	P	7	.348	A	C
1	1	Knauss, Frank H.	P	2	.000	Cin92	
0	1	Lyston, Wm. Edward	P	1	.000	ColAA91	C
2	1	Mullane, Anthony John (Tony)	P	8	+.071	xBalt	C
		McAleer, James Robert	OF	64	.298	B	
		McGarr, James B. (Chippy)	3B	127	.272	B	
		McKean, Edward John	SS	130	.354	B	
		O'Connor, John Joseph (Jack) (OF31)	C42	80	.324	B	
0	2	Petty, Chas. E.	P	3	+.100	xWash	C
6	4	Sullivan, Michael Joseph (Mike)	P	12	+.295	xWash	
		Tebeau, George E.	OF	45	+.316	xWash	
		Tebeau, Oliver Wendell MGR.	1B107	110	.305	B	
		Virtue, Jacob Kitchline	OF20	23	.270	B	C
2	2	Wallace, Rhoderick John (Bobby)	P	4	.154	A	
25	21	Young, Denton True (Cy)	P47	48	.213	B	
		Zimmer, Chas. Louis (Chief)	C	88	.285	B	

WON 84
LOST 46
TG 130

NATIONAL LEAGUE — 1895. — FINISHED 2nd. — PCT. .646

CLEVELAND

OLIVER WENDELL TEBEAU

WON	LOST	NAME	POS.	G.	BA	FROM	TO
		Blake, Henry C.	OF	83	.280	B	
		Burkett, Jesse Cail	OF	132	.423	B	
		Childs, Clarence Algernon	2B	120	.312	B	
26	16	Cuppy, George Joseph (Nig)	P	40	.282	B	
		Donovan, Frederick M.	C	3	.083	A	C
		Gremminger, Lorenzo Edward	3B18	19	.275	A	
5	4	Knell, Philip H.	P	14	+.209	xLvlle	C
		McAleer, James Robert	OF	132	.291	B	
		McGarr, James B. (Chippy)	3B108	112	.270	B	
		McKean, Edward John	SS	132	.344	B	
		O'Connor, John Joseph (Jack) (1B41)	C47	88	.293	B	
		O'Meara, Thomas Edward	C	1	.000	A	
1	4	Sullivan, Michael Joseph (Mike)	P	5	.133	B	
		Tebeau, George E. (1B39)	OF47	87	.323	B	C
		Tebeau, Oliver Wendell MGR.	1B52	66	.329	B	
14	10	Wallace, Rhoderick John (Bobby)	P	27	.216	B	
5	2	Wilson, Frank Ealton (Zeke)	P	11	+.131	xBos	
33	10	Young, Denton True (Cy)	P45	46	.215	B	
		Zimmer, Chas. Louis (Chief)	C82	83	.336	B	

WON 80
LOST 48
TG 128

NATIONAL LEAGUE — 1896. — FINISHED 2nd. — PCT. .625

CLEVELAND

OLIVER WENDELL TEBEAU

WON	LOST	NAME	POS.	G.	BA	FROM	TO
		Blake, Henry C.	OF	102	.242	B	
		Burkett, Jesse Cail	OF	133	.410	B	
0	1	Chamberlain, Elton P.	P	2	.000	Cin94	C
		Childs, Clarence Algernon	2B	132	.348	B	
		Criger, Louis	C	2	.000	A	
25	15	Cuppy, George Joseph (Nig)	P40	41	.277	B	
		Delehanty, Thomas James	3B	15	+.216	Phil94	Pitt
0	2	Gear, Dale Dudley	P	2	.250	A	

WON	LOST	NAME	POS.	G.	BA	FROM	TO
		McAleer, James Robert	OF	116	.288	B	
0	0	McAllister, Lewis Wm. (C2 OF2)	P3	7	.185	A	
		McGarr, James B. (Chippy)	3B	111	.266	B	C
		McKean, Edward John	SS	133	.335	B	
		O'Connor, John Joseph	C37	60	.300	B	
		O'Meara, Thomas Edward	C	9	.148	B	C
		Shearon, John M.	OF	15	.174	Clev91	
		Tebeau, Oliver Wendell MGR.	1B122	132	.271	B	
9	6	Wallace, Rhoderick John	P15	33	.231	B	
17	10	Wilson, Frank Ealton (Zeke)	P	29	.262	B	
29	14	Young, Denton True (Cy)	P47	48	.304	B	
		Zimmer, Chas. Louis (Chief)	C	89	.273	B	

WON 69
LOST 62
TG 131

NATIONAL LEAGUE FINISHED 5th.

1897. PCT. .527

CLEVELAND

OLIVER WENDELL TEBEAU

WON	LOST	NAME	POS.	G.	BA	FROM	TO
		Belden, Ira A.	OF	8	.250	A	C
		Blake, Henry C.	OF	31	.256	B	
1	3	Brown, Chas. E.	P	4	.383	A	C
		Burkett, Jesse Cail	OF	128	1383	B	
		Childs, Clarence Algernon	2B	114	.336	B	
3	5	Clarke, Henry Tefft	P	8	.280	A	
		Cooke, Frederick B.	OF	5	.295	A	C
		Criger, Louis	C	38	.230	B	
10	6	Cuppy, George Joseph (Nig)	P	17	.148	B	
		Gear, Dale Dudley	OF	7	.167	B	
		McAleer, James Robert	OF	23	.224	B	
2	3	McAllister, Lewis Wm. (P7)	OF27	40	.211	B	
3	4	McDermott, Michael Joseph	P	9	+.320	Lvlle	StL
		McKean, Edward John	SS	127	.273	B	
		O'Connor, John Joseph (Jack) (1B33)	OF54	100	.290	B	
0	0	Pappalau, John Joseph	P	2	.200	A	C
		Pickering, Oliver Dan (2B1)	OF47	47	+.346	xLvlle	
15	9	Powell, John Joseph	P26	28	.202	A	
		Sockalexis, Louis Francis	OF	66	.331	A	
		Tebeau, Oliver Wendell MGR. (2B17)	1B91	111	.267	B	
		Wallace, Rhoderick John	3B130	131	.339	B	
14	14	Wilson, Frank Ealton (Zeke)	P29	35	.222	B	
21	18	Young, Denton True (Cy)	P40	45	.218	B	
		Zimmer, Chas. Louis (Chief)	C	81	.314	B	

WON 81
LOST 68
TG 149

NATIONAL LEAGUE FINISHED 5th.

1898. PCT. .544

CLEVELAND

OLIVER WENDELL TEBEAU

WON	LOST	NAME	POS.	G.	BA	FROM	TO
2	1	Bates, Frank Chas.	P	4	.111	A	
		Beecher, Edward	OF	8	.200	StL	C
		Blake, Henry C.	OF135	137	.245	B	
		Burke, James Timothy	3B	13	.111	A	
		Burkett, Jesse Cail	OF	148	.345	B	
		Childs, Clarence Algernon	2B	109	.289	B	
		Criger, Louis	C	81	.273	B	
9	7	Cuppy, George Joseph (Nig)	P	16	.130	B	
		Frank, Frederick	OF	17	.208	A	C
2	3	Fraser, Chas. Carrolton (Chick)	P	6	+.235	xLvlle	
		Heidrick, John Emmett	OF	19	.293	A	
4	4	Jones, Albert Edward	P	8	.080	A	
0	1	Kelb, George Francis	P	3	.167	A	C
		McAleer, James Robert	OF102	104	.235	B	
3	3	McAllister, Lewis Wm.	P	16	.255	B	
0	1	McBride, Peter Wm.	P	1	1.000	A	
		McKean, Edward John	SS	151	.285	B	
		O'Connor, John Joseph (Jack) (C47)	1B69	129	.262	B	
24	15	Powell, John Joseph	P	40	.131	B	
		Schreckengost, Ossee Freeman	C	5	.367	Lvlle	
		Sockalexis, Louis Francis	OF	20	.222	B	
		Tebeau, Oliver Wendell MGR. (2B34)	1B88	130	.254	B	
		Wallace, Rhoderick John	3B142	153	.269	B	
13	18	Wilson, Frank Ealton (Zeke)	P32	34	.161	B	
24	15	Young, Denton True (Cy)	P41	44	.253	B	
		Zimmer, Chas. Louis (Chief)	C	18	.250	B	

WON 20
LOST 134
TG 154

NATIONAL LEAGUE FINISHED 12th (LAST)

1899. PCT. .129

CLEVELAND

LAFAYETTE NAPOLEON CROSS JOSEPH J. QUINN

WON	LOST	NAME	POS.	G.	BA	FROM	TO
1	19	Bates, Frank Chas.	P	20	+.222	xStL	C
		Bristow, George	OF	3	.125	A	C
1	8	Carsey, Wilfred (Kid)	P	9	+.235	StL	Wash
		Clements, John T.	C	4	.167	StL	
1	11	Colliflower, James Harry	P	21	.311	A	C
		Cross, LaFayette Napoleon (Lave) MGR.	3B	38	+.263	StL	StL
		Dowd, Thomas Jefferson	OF	146	.275	StL	
		Duncan, James Wm.	C	30	+.231	xWash	C
		Harley, Richard Joseph	OF	145	.250	StL	
1	4	Harper, Chas. Wm. (Jack)	P	5	.182	A	
		Hemphill, Chas. Judson	OF	51	+.280	xStL	
3	6	Hill, Wm. C. (OF1)	P11	11	+.121	Cin	Balt

0	1	Kolb, Edward Wm.	P	1	.250	A	C
4	29	Hughey, James Ulysses	P33	35	.162	StL	
4	22	Knepper, Chas.	P26	27	.135	A	C
		Krueger, Oompaul Arthur	3B	13	.227	A	
		Lockhead, Harry P.	SS145	146	.223	A	
0	3	Maupin, Harry Carr	P	5	.000	StL	C
0	1	McAllister, Lewis Wm. (P1)	OF78	110	.238	B	
		Quinn, Joseph J. MGR.	2B	146	.292	StL	
2	17	Schmidt, Frederick	P19	21	.136	NY93	
		Schreckengost, Ossee Freeman (1B1 SS1 OF1) (Ossie)	C39	43	+.315	xStL	StL (return)
		Sockalexis, Louis Francis	OF	7	.252	B	C
0	4	Stivetts, John Elmer	P	18	.171	Bos	C
3	8	Sudhoff, John William	P	22	+.094	StL	StL
		Sugden, Joseph	C71	78	.281	StL	
		Sullivan, Suter G. (OF20)	3B100	126	.250	StL	
		Tucker, Thomas Joseph	1B	126	.237	StL	C
0	1	Wilson, Howard P.	P	1	.333	A	
		Ziegler, Chas. W. (2B1)	SS1	2	.250	A	
		Zimmer, Chas. Louis (Chief)	C	20	+.342	B	Lvlle

CLUB RECORD

NATIONAL LEAGUE

DETROIT

YEAR	TG	WON	LOST	PCT.	FINISHED	MANAGER
1881	84	41	43	.488	4	Frank Carter Bancroft
1882	83	42	41	.506	6	Frank Carter Bancroft
1883	98	40	58	.408	7	John Curtis Chapman
1884	112	28	84	.250	8(Last)	John Curtis Chapman
1885	108	41	67	.379	6	{Chas. H. Morton {Wm. Henry Watkins
1886	123	87	36	.707	2	Wm. Henry Watkins
1887	124	79	45	.637	1	Wm. Henry Watkins
1888	131	68	63	.519	5	{Wm. Henry Watkins {Robert H. Leadley

WON	41	NATIONAL LEAGUE	FINISHED 4th.
LOST	43		
TG	84	1881.	PCT. .488

DETROIT

FRANK CARTER BANCROFT

WON	LOST	NAME	POS.	G.	BA	FROM	TO
		Bennett, Chas. Wesley (OF6)	C67	76	.301	Wor	
		Bradley, George Washington	SS	1	+.000	Prov	Clev
		Brown, Lewis J.	1B	27	.243	Chi79	Prov
29	26	Derby, George H. (OF3)	P55	59	.186	A	
		Dorgan, Michael Cornelius (1B1 3B2)	OF5	8	+.229	xWor	
		Foley, Wm. B. (2B1)	3B4	5	.118	Cin79	
		Gerhardt, Joseph John (3B1)	2B80	80	.242	Cin79	
		Hanlon, Edward Hugh (3B2)	OF73	75	.278	Clev	
		Houck, Stephen Arnold Douglas (Sadie)	SS	75	.279	Prov	
		*Knight, Alonzo P. (Lon)	OF81	83	.270	Wor	
0	2	Leary, John J. (OF2)	P2	3	.273	Bos	
3	4	Mountain, Frank H.	P	7	.192	Troy	
1	4	Mullane, Anthony John (Tony)	P	5	.263	A	
		Moynahan, Michael	3B	2	+.333	xClev	
		O'Leary, Daniel	OF	2	.000	Bos	
		Powell, Martin J. (C1)	1B55	55	.310	A	
		Reilley, Chas. E. (1B1 SS3 3B2 OF4)	C10	18	+.179	Cin	Wor
		Stearns, Daniel Eckford	SS	3	.100	Buff	
		Taylor, Wm. Henry	3B	1	+.500	xWor	Clev
		Trott, Samuel W.	C	6	.192	Bos	
		Troy, John Joseph (Dasher) (2B4)	3B7	11	.304	A	
8	5	Weidman, George E.	P	13	.250	Buff	
0	2	White, Wm. Henry	P	2	.000	Cin	
		Whitney, Arthur Wilson	3B	58	.182	Wor	
		Wise, Samuel Washington	3B	1	.500	A	
		Wood, George A.	OF	80	.296	Wor	

*Knight also played 1 game at 1B and 1 game at 2B.

WON	42	NATIONAL LEAGUE	FINISHED 6th.
LOST	41		
TG	83	1882.	PCT. .506

DETROIT

FRANK CARTER BANCROFT

WON	LOST	NAME	POS.	G.	BA	FROM	TO
		*Bennett, Chas. Wesley	C62	80	.304	B	
		Casey, Dennis Patrick (2B1)	3B8	9	.231	A	
16	20	Derby, George H. (OF2)	P36	38	.202	B	
		Farrell, Joseph F. (2B17 SS9)	3B41	66	.246	A	
		Forster, Thomas W. (3B1)	2B20	20	.098	A	
		Hanlon, Edward Hugh (3B1)	OF	79	.236	B	
		Kearns, Thomas J.	2B	4	.308	Buff80	
		Kenzie, Walter H.	SS	13	.094	A	
		Knight, Alonzo P. (Lon) (1B2)	OF81	83	.204	B	
		Luff, Henry T. (OF1)	2B3	3	.273	A	CinAA
		Morrissey, John H.	3B	2	.286	Buff	C
		@McGeary, Michael Henry	SS32	33	.149	Clev	C
		Powell, Martin J.	1B	77	.247	B	
0	0	Robinson, Wm. H. (Yank) (P1 OF1)	SS11	11	.162	A	
		# Trott, Samuel W.	C21	30	.246	B	
		Troy, John Joseph (Dasher) (SS10)	2B31	39	+.232	B	Prov
26	20	Weidman, George E. (SS1 OF6)	P46	50	.217	B	
0	1	Whitney, Arthur Wilson (P3 SS8)	3B21	30	+.177	xProv	
		Willigrod, Julius (OF1)	SS1	2	+.286	A	Clev
		Wood, George A.	OF	81	.263	B	

*Bennett also played 1 game at 1B, 7 games at 2B and 10 games at 3B.
@McGeary also played 3 games at 2B.
#Trott also played 3 games at 1B, 2 games at 2B, 3 games at SS and 3 games in the OF.

WON	40	NATIONAL LEAGUE	FINISHED 7th.
LOST	58		
TG	98	1883.	PCT. .408

DETROIT

JOHN CURTIS CHAPMAN

WON	LOST	NAME	POS.	G.	BA	FROM	TO
		Bennett, Chas. Wesley (2B15 OF6)	C65	89	.301	B	
2	12	Burns, Richard Simon (P15)	OF21	36	.192	A	
		Farrell, Joseph F.	3B	98	.246	B	
		Guiney, Benjamin Franklin (OF1)	2B1	1	.200	A	
		Hanlon, Edward Hugh (2B9)	OF85	97	.245	B	
		Houck, Stephen Arnold Douglas (Sadie)	SS97	98	.251	Det81	
6	4	Jones, Daniel Albion (OF2)	P11	11	.243	A	AthAA
0	0	Mansell, Thomas E. (P1)	OF34	34	.213	Syr79	StLAA
1	0	McIntyre, Frank W.	P	1	.000	A	ColAA
		Powell, Martin J.	1B	97	.267	B	
		Quest, Joseph L.	2B	36	.204	Chi	StLAA
1	1	Radbourn, George B. (OF1)	P3	3	.154	A	C
11	18	Shaw, Frederick Lander (Dupee) (OF9)	P29	38	.189	A	
		Trott, Samuel W. (C32 1B1 OF4)	2B36	73	.233	B	

WON	LOST	NAME	POS.	G.	BA	FROM	TO
19	23	Weidman, George E. (2B4 OF26)	P45	76	.173	B	
0	0	Wood, George A. (P1)	OF95	96	.295	B	

WON 28 — NATIONAL LEAGUE — FINISHED 8th (LAST)
LOST 84
TG 112 — 1884. — PCT. .250

DETROIT

JOHN CURTIS CHAPMAN

WON	LOST	NAME	POS.	G.	BA	FROM	TO
		Beatle, David (OF1)	C1	1	.000	A	C
		*Bennett, Chas. Wesley	C77	88	.264	B	
2	10	Brill, John (OF1)	P12	13	.130	A	C
		Buker, Harry L. (OF11)	SS19	30	.136	A	C
		Cox, Frank Bernhardt	SS	27	.127	A	C
		Farrell, Joseph F.	3B	108	.225	B	
		Gastfield, Edward (1B2 OF2)	C18	22	.063	A	
0	0	Geiss, Wm. (P1 1B1 OF1)	2B72	75	.176	A	
5	12	Getzein, Chas. H.	P	17	.109	A	
		Guiney, Benjamin Franklin	C	2	.000	B	C
		Hanlon, Edward Hugh	OF	112	.268	B	
		Jones, Frank M. (2B16 SS8 OF12)	SS18	34	.209	A	C
		Kearns, Thomas J.	2B	18	.211	Det82	C
		Lowe,	C	1	.250	A	C
8	21	Meinke, Frank Louis (P33 2B3 3B2)	SS47	90	.167	A	
		Prince, Walter F.	OF	7	.130	LvlleAA	WashAA
		Santry, Edward (2B1)	SS5	6	.174	A	C
		Scott, Milton Parker	1B	108	.249	Chi82	
8	18	Shaw, Frederick Lander (Dupee) (OF12)	P26	36	.191	B	BosUA
		Walker, Walter S.	C	1	.250	A	
		Weber, Harry	OF	2	.000	A	C
5	22	Weidman, George E. (P27 2B1 SS2)	OF52	79	.162	B	
0	1	Wood, Frederick S. (P1 SS1 OF6)	C12	28	.221	A	
		Wood, George A. (3B2)	OF111	112	.251	B	
		Zimmer, Chas. Louis (Chief) (OF2)	C6	8	.071	A	

*Bennett also played 1 game at 1B, 1 game at 2B, 6 games at SS and 5 games in the OF.

WON 41 — NATIONAL LEAGUE — FINISHED 6th.
LOST 67
TG 108 — 1885. — PCT. .379

DETROIT

CHAS. HAZEN MORTON WM. HENRY WATKINS

WON	LOST	NAME	POS.	G.	BA	FROM	TO
11	9	#Baldwin, Chas. Busted (Lady)	P20	31	.241	MilUA	
		Bennett, Chas. Wesley (3B10 OF19)	C63	91	.269	B	
		Bryant,	2B	1	.000	A	C
4	8	Casey, Daniel Maurice	P	12	.103	WilUA	
		Collins, Chas. (Chub)	SS	14	.179	IndplsAA	C
		Crane, Samuel Newhall	2B	68	.191	CinUA	
		Donely, James B. (1B1)	3B	55	.232	IndplsAA	
		Dorgan, Jeremiah F.	OF	39	.285	BknAA	C
0	0	Gastfield, Edward	P	1	+.000	B	Chi
12	26	Getzein, Chas. H. (OF2)	P38	39	.211	B	
		Halpin, James Nathaniel	SS	15	.129	WashUA	C
		Hanlon, Edward Hugh (3B1)	OF105	106	.301	B	
		Kellogg, Nathaniel M.	SS	5	.118	A	C
		Manning, James H.	SS	20	+.269	xBos	
0	1	Meinke, Frank Louis (OF1)	P1	1	.000	B	C
		Moore, Jeremiah S.	C	5	.200	Clev	C
0	0	*Moriarity, Eugene John	OF5	11	.026	IndplsAA	
		Morton, Chas. Hazen MGR. (SS4)	3B18	22	.177	TolAA	
		McGuire, James Thomas (OF3)	C31	34	.190	TolAA	
		McQuery, Wm. Thomas	1B	70	.273	CinUA	
		Olin, Franklin Walter	3B	1	.500	TolAA	C
		Phillips, Marr B.	SS	33	.208	IndplsAA	PittAA
		Quest, Joseph L. (SS15)	2B39	55	.195	PittAA	
		Ringo, Frank C. (3B8 OF1)	C16	16	.246	AthAA	PittAA
		Scott, Milton Parker	1B	38	.263	B	PittAA
		Thompson, Samuel L.	OF	63	.303	A	
14	23	Weidman, George E. (OF8)	P38	43	.156	B	
0	0	Wood, George A. (P1 SS1 3B4)	OF71	82	.290	B	

#Baldwin also played 12 games in the OF.
*Moriarity also played 4 games at 3B, 1 game as Pitcher and 1 game at SS.

WON 87 — NATIONAL LEAGUE — FINISHED 2nd.
LOST 36
TG 123 — 1886. — PCT. .707

DETROIT

WM. HENRY WATKINS

WON	LOST	NAME	POS.	G.	BA	FROM	TO
42	13	Baldwin, Chas. Busted (Lady)	P56	57	.201	B	
		Bennett, Chas. Wesley	C67	69	.242	B	
		Brouthers, Dennis (Dan)	1B	121	.370	Buff	
6	5	Conway, Peter J.	P	11	+.237	xK.C.	
		Crane, Samuel Newhall	2B	49	+.139	B	StL
		Decker, Edward Harry (OF2)	C14	15	+.203	KCUA84	Wash
		Dunlap, Frederick C.	2B	49	+.284	xStL	
		Ganzel, Chas. Wm.	C42	53	+.276	xPhil	

WON	LOST	NAME	POS.	G.	BA	FROM	TO
31	11	Getzein, Chas. H.	P	43	.176	B	
		Gillen, Thomas J.	C	2	.400	Phil84	C
		Hanlon, Edward Hugh	OF125	126	.234	B	
		Manning, James H.	OF	26	.185	B	
		McGeachy, John Chas.	OF	7	+.333	A	StL
		Richardson, Arthur Harding (2B37)	OF81	125	.351	Buff	
		Rowe, John Chas.	SS109	111	.303	Buff	
		Shindle, Wm.	SS	5	.333	A	
1	1	Smith, John Francis	P	3	.111	AthAA	
5	4	Smith, Wm.	P	10	.184	A	C
		Thompson, Samuel L.	OF	122	.310	B	
2	2	Twitchell, Lawrence Grant	P	4	.000	A	
		White, James Laurie (Deacon)	3B	124	.289	Buff	

WON 79 NATIONAL LEAGUE FINISHED 1st.
LOST 45
TG 124 1887. PCT. .637

DETROIT

WM. HENRY WATKINS

WON	LOST	NAME	POS.	G.	BA	FROM	TO
13	10	Baldwin, Chas. Busted (Lady)	P	24	.347	B	
1	1	Beatin, Ebenezer Ambrose	P	2	.143	A	
		Bennett, Chas. Wesley	C	46	.363	B	
		Briody, Chas. F.	C	32	.277	K.C.	C
		Brouthers, Dennis (Dan)	1B	122	.419	B	
0	1	Burke, Walter R.	P	2	.250	BosUA84	C
8	10	Conway, Peter J.	P18	24	.247	B	
		Dunlap, Frederick C.	2B	64	.326	B	
		Ganzel, Chas. Wm.	C50	55	.285	B	
29	13	Getzein, Chas. H.	P	43	.240	B	
5	3	Gruber, Henry John	P	9	.308	A	
		Hanlon, Edward Hugh	OF	118	.316	B	
		Manning, James H.	OF	13	.250	B	
		Richardson, Arthur Harding (OF58)	2B62	120	.363	B	
		Rowe, John Chas.	SS	123	.363	B	
		Shindle, Wm.	3B19	20	.340	B	
		Thompson, Samuel L.	OF	127	.406	B	
10	1	Twitchell, Lawrence Grant (P11)	OF52	63	.352	B	
13	6	Weidman, George E.	P	21	.209	K.C.	MetAA
		White, James Laurie (Deacon)	3B106	111	.341	B	

WON 68 NATIONAL LEAGUE FINISHED 5th.
LOST 63
TG 131 1888. PCT. .519

DETROIT

WM. HENRY WATKINS ROBERT H. LEADLEY

WON	LOST	NAME	POS.	G.	BA	FROM	TO
3	3	Baldwin, Chas. Busted (Lady)	P	6	.261	B	
5	7	Beatin, Ebenezer Ambrose	P	16	.250	B	
		Bennett, Chas. Wesley	C	72	.263	B	
		Broughton, Cecil Calvert	C	1	.000	MetAA85	C
		Brouthers, Dennis (Dan)	1B	129	.306	B	
		Campau, Chas. C.	OF	70	.203	A	
31	14	Conway, Peter J.	P	45	.275	B	
		Ganzel, Chas. Wm. (C25)	2B51	93	.248	B	
18	26	Getzein, Chas. H.	P	45	.245	B	
		Gilligan, Andrew Bernard (Barney)	C	1	.200	Wash	C
11	13	Gruber, Henry John	P	27	.141	B	
		Hanlon, Edward Hugh	OF	108	.265	B	
		LaRoque, Samuel H. J.	2B	2	.444	A	
		McGuire, James Thomas	C	3	+.000	xPhil	ClevAA
		Nicholson, Thomas C.	2B	24	.259	A	
		Richardson, Arthur Harding	2B	57	.289	B	
		Rowe, John Chas.	SS	105	.277	B	
		Scheffler, Theodore J.	OF	27	.202	A	
		Scheibeck, Frank S.	SS	1	.000	ClevAA	
		Sutcliffe, Edward Elmer	SS24	49	.257	StL85	
		Thompson, Samuel L.	OF	55	.281	B	
		Twitchell, Lawrence Grant	OF129	130	.244	B	
		Wells, Jacob	C	16	.157	A	
		White, James Laurie (Deacon)	3B	125	.298	B	

CLUB RECORD

NATIONAL LEAGUE

HARTFORD

YEAR	TG	WON	LOST	PCT.	FINISHED	MANAGER
1876	68	47	21	.691	3	Robert V. Ferguson
1877	58	31	27	.534	3	Robert V. Ferguson

WON 47
LOST 21
TG 68

NATIONAL LEAGUE

1876.

FINISHED 3rd.

PCT. .691

HARTFORD

ROBERT V. FERGUSON

WON	LOST	NAME	POS.	G.	BA	FROM	TO
		Allison, Douglass L.	C38	43	.256	A	
32	13	Bond, Thomas Henry	P	45	.275	A	
		Burdock, John Joseph	2B	69	.248	A	
		Carey, Thomas John	SS	68	.301	A	
		Cassidy, John P.	OF8	12	.271	A	
15	8	Cummings, Wm. Arthur	P	24	.162	A	
		Ferguson, Robert V. MGR.	3B	69	.264	A	
		Harbidge, Wm. Arthur (OF6)	C20	30	.211	A	
		Higham, Richard (C11)	OF54	67	.325	A	
		Mills, Everett	1B	63	.259	A	C
		Remsen, John Jay	OF	69	.274	A	
		York, Thomas J.	OF	67	.249	A	

WON 31
LOST 27
TG 58

NATIONAL LEAGUE

1877.

FINISHED 3rd.

PCT. .534

HARTFORD

ROBERT V. FERGUSON

WON	LOST	NAME	POS.	G.	BA	FROM	TO
		Allison, Douglass L.	C	29	.148	B	
		Bass, John E.	OF	1	.250	A	C
		Bunce, Joshua	OF	1	.000	A	C
		Burdock, John Joseph (3B3)	2B55	58	.260	B	
		Carey, Thomas John	SS	60	.255	B	
1	1	Cassidy, John P. (P2)	OF58	60	.378	B	
1	1	Ferguson, Robert V. MGR. (P3)	3B56	58	.256	B	
		Harbidge, Wm. Arthur (2B4 OF5)	C32	41	.222	B	
		Holdsworth, James	OF	55	.254	Mut	
29	25	Larkin, Frank (2B1 3B2)	P56	58	.228	Mut	
		Maloney, John	OF	1	.250	Mut	
		Pike, J.	OF	1	.250	A	C
		Start, Joseph	1B	60	.332	Mut	
		Taylor, Wm. Henry	OF	2	.375	A	
		York, Thomas J.	OF	56	.283	B	

CLUB RECORD

NATIONAL LEAGUE

HOUSTON

YEAR	TG	WON	LOST	TIED	PCT.	FINISHED	MANAGER
1962	160	64	96		.400	8	Harry Francis Craft
1963	162	66	96		.407	9	Harry Francis Craft
1964	162	66	96		.407	9	Harry Francis Craft
							Chalmer Luman Harris
YEAR	TG	WON	LOST	TIED	PCT.	FINISHED	MANAGER
1965	162	65	97	0	.401	9	CHALMER LUMAN HARRIS
1966	163	72	90	1	.444	8	GRADY EDGEBERT HATTON
1967	162	69	93	0	.426	9	GRADY EDGEBERT HATTON
1968	162	72	90	0	.444	10 (LAST)	GRADY EDGEBERT HATTON
							HARRY WILLIAM WALKER
1969	162	81	81	0	.500	5W	HARRY WILLIAM WALKER
1970	162	79	83	0	.488	4W	HARRY WILLIAM WALKER
1971	162	79	83	0	.488	X4W (CIN)	HARRY WILLIAM WALKER
1972	153	84	69	0	.549	2W	HARRY WILLIAM WALKER
							FRANCIS JAMES PARKER *
							LEO ERNEST DUROCHER

WON 64
LOST 96
TG 160

NATIONAL LEAGUE — 1962. — FINISHED 8th. — PCT. .400

HOUSTON

HARRY FRANCIS CRAFT

WON	LOST	NAME	POS.	G.	BA	FROM	TO
		Amalfitano, John Joseph	2B110	117	.237	S.F.	
0	0	Anderson, John Chas.	P	10	+.000	xStL	C
		Aspromonte, Robert Thomas (2B1 SS11)	3B142	149	.266	L.A.	
		Browne, Prentice Almont	1B26	65	.210	A	C
10	9	Bruce, Robert James	P	32	.200	DetA	
2	4	Brunet, George Stuart	P	17	.059	Mil	
		Buddin, Donald Thomas	SS27	40	.163	BosA	DetA
		Busby, James Franklin (C1)	OF10	15	.182	BaltA	C
		Campbell, James Robert	C25	27	.221	A	
		Cerv, Robert Henry	OF6	19	.226	xNYA	C
0	0	Cicotte, Alva Warren	P	5	.000	StL	C
		Davis, Ronald Everette	OF5	6	.214	A	
1	0	Drott, Richard Fred	P	6	.000	Chi	
10	20	Farrell, Richard Joseph	P	43	.179	L.A.	
		Fazio, Ernest Joseph	SS10	12	.083	A	
		Gernert, Richard Edward	1B9	10	.208	Cin	C
2	3	Giusti, David John	P22	26	.292	A	C
7	11	Golden, James Edward	P37	43	.222	L.A.	
		Goodman, Wm. Dale (1B1 3B17)	2B31	82	.255	ChiA	C
		Hartman, Joe C.	SS48	51	.223	A	
		Heist, Alfred Michael	OF23	27	.222	Chi	C
7	16	Johnson, Kenneth Travis	P	33	.077	Cin	
5	3	Kemmerer, Russell Paul	P	36	.333	xChiA	
		Larker, Norman Howard (OF6)	1B135	147	.263	L.A.	
		Lillis, Robert Perry (2B33 3B9)	SS99	129	.249	StL	
5	5	MaMahon, Donald John	P	51	+.083	xMil	
		Mejias, Roman Gomez	OF142	146	.286	Pitt	
		Pendleton, James Edward (1B8 SS2 3B3)	OF90	117	.246	Cin59	C
		Ranew, Merritt Thomas	C58	71	.234	A	
		Roberts, David Leonard (1B6)	OF12	16	.245	A	C
1	1	Shantz, Robert Clayton	P3	7	+.000	Pitt	StL
		Smith, Harold Wayne (1B2)	C92	109	.235	Pitt	
		Spangler, Albert Donald	OF121	129	.285	Mil	
3	2	Stone, Darrah Dean	P	15	.250	StL59	ChiA
		Taussig, Donald Franklin	OF4	16	.200	StL	C
		Temple, John Ellis	2B26	31	.263	xBaltA	
2	4	Tiefenauer, Bobby Gene	P	43	.111	StL	
4	0	Umbricht, James	P	34	.111	Pitt	
		Warwick, Carl Wayne	OF128	130	+.260	xStL	
		Weekly, John	OF7	13	.192	A	
		Williams, George	2B3	5	.375	Phil	C

WON	LOST	NAME	POS.	G.	BA	FROM	TO
0	2	Witt, George Adrian	P	8	.250	xLAA	C
5	16	Woodeshick, Harold Joseph	P	31	.081	Det	

WON 66 LOST 96 TG 162 — NATIONAL LEAGUE — 1963. — FINISHED 9th. PCT. .407

HOUSTON

HARRY FRANCIS CRAFT

WON	LOST	NAME	POS.	G.	BA	FROM	TO
		Adlesh, David George	C	6	.000	A	
		Aspromonte, Robert Thomas (1B1)	3B131	136	.214	B	
		Bateman, John Alvin	C115	128	.210	A	
5	11	Brown, Hector Harold	P	26	.093	NYA	
5	9	Bruce, Robert James	P30	32	.127	B	
0	3	Brunet, George Stuart	P	5	.000	B	BaltA
		Campbell, James Robert	C42	55	.222	B	C
0	1	Cardinal, Conrad Seth	P	6	.000	A	C
0	0	Coombs, Daniel Bernard	P	1	.000	A	
0	1	Dahl, Jay Steven	P	1	.000	A	C
		Davis, Bryshear Barnett	OF14	34	.200	A	
0	1	Dickson, James Edward	P	13	.000	A	
2	12	Drott, Richard Fred	P	27	.130	B	C
14	13	Farrell, Richard Joseph	P	34	.143	B	
		Fazio, Ernest Joseph (SS1 3B1)	2B84	102	.184	B	
0	1	Golden, James Edward	P	3	.000	B	C
		Goss, Howard Wayne	OF123	133	.209	Pitt	C
		Grote, Gerald Wayne	C	3	.200	A	
		Hardy, Carroll Wm.	OF10	15	.227	BosA	
		Hartman, Joe C.	SS32	39	.122	B	C
0	0	Hoerner, Joseph Walter	P	1	.000	A	
		Jackson, Roland Thomas	SS	1	.000	A	
11	17	Johnson, Kenneth Travis	P37	38	.068	B	
0	0	Kemmerer, Russell Paul	P	17	.286	B	C
		Lillis, Robert Perry (2B19 3B6)	SS124	147	.198	B	
1	5	McMahon, Donald John	P	49	.083	B	
		Morgan, Joe Leonard	2B7	8	.240	A	
		Murrell, Ivan Augusto	OF	2	.200	A	
11	8	Nottebart, Donald Edward	P	31	.167	Mil	
		Paciorek, John Francis	OF	1	1.000	A	C
		Pointer, Aaron Elton	OF1	2	.200	A	
		Runnels, James Edward (2B36 3B3)	1B70	124	.253	BosA	
		Smith, Harold Wayne	C11	31	.241	B	
		Spangler, Albert Donald	OF113	120	.281	B	
		Staub, Daniel Joseph (OF49)	1B109	150	.224	A	
		Temple, John Ellis (3B29)	2B61	100	.264	B	
4	3	Umbricht, James	P	35	.111	B	C
		Vaughan, Glenn Edward	SS9	9	.167	A	C
		(3B1)					
		Warwick, Carl Wayne (1B2)	OF141	150	.254	B	
		Weekly, John	OF23	34	.225	B	
		White, Joyner Michael	2B2	3	.286	A	
11	9	Woodeshick, Harold James	P	55	.130	B	
		Wynn, James Sherman (SS21 3B2)	OF53	70	.244	A	
0	0	Yellen, Lawrence Alan	P	1	.000	A	
2	2	Zachary, Wm. Christopher	P	22	.000	A	

WON 66 LOST 96 TG 162 — NATIONAL LEAGUE — 1964. — FINISHED 9th. PCT. .407

HOUSTON

HARRY FRANCIS CRAFT CHALMER LUMAN HARRIS

WON	LOST	NAME	POS.	G.	BA	FROM	TO
		Adlesh, David George	C	3	.200	B	
		Aspromonte, Robert Thomas	3B155	157	.280	B	
		Bateman, John Alvin	C72	74	.190	B	
		Beauchamp, James Edward (1B2)	OF15	23	.164	StL	
		Bond, Walter Franklin (OF71)	1B76	148	.254	ClevA62	
0	2	Bradey, Donald Eugene	P	3	.000	A	C
3	15	Brown, Hector Harold	P	27	.128	B	C
15	9	Bruce, Robert James	P35	37	.190	B	
1	1	Coombs, Daniel Bernard	P	7	.000	B	
		Davis, Bryshear Barnett	OF	1	.000	B	
0	1	Dierker, Lawrence Edward	P	3	.000	A	
11	10	Farrell, Richard Joseph	P	32	.072	B	
		Fox, Jacob Nelson	2B115	133	.265	ChicA	
		Gaines, Arnesta	OF81	89	.254	xBaltA	
0	0	Giusti, David John	P	8	.286	Hous62	
		Grote, Gerald Wayne	C98	100	.181	B	
		Hardy, Carroll Wm.	OF41	46	.185	B	
		Hertz, Stephen Allan	3B2	5	.000	A	C
0	0	Hoerner, Joseph Walter	P	7	.000	B	
		Hoffman, John Edward	C5	6	.067	A	
		Jackson, Roland Thomas	SS7	9	.348	B	
11	16	Johnson, Kenneth Travis	P	35	.079	B	
0	1	Jones, Gordon Bassett	P	34	.250	KCA62	
		Kasko, Edward Michael (3B2)	SS128	133	.243	Cin	
4	8	Larsen, Donald James	P30	31	+.097	xS.F.	
		Lillis, Robert Perry (SS43 3B12)	2B52	109	.268	B	
		Morgan, Joe Leonard	2B	10	.189	B	
		Murrell, Ivan Augusto	OF5	10	.143	B	
6	11	Nottebart, Donald Edward	P	28	.064	B	
8	7	Owens, James Phillip	P	48	.103	Cin	
5	5	Raymond, Joseph Claude Marc	P38	41	.071	Mil	
		Roberts, David Leonard (OF4)	1B34	61	.184	Hous62	
		Runnels, James Edward	1B14	22	.196	B	C

		Spangler, Albert Donald	OF127	135	.245	B	
		Staub, Daniel Joseph (OF38)	1B49	89	.216	B	
		Weekly, John	OF5	6	.133	B	C
		White, Joyner Michael (2B10 3B3)	OF72	89	.271	B	
		Williams, Walter Allen	OF5	10	.000	A	
2	9	Woodeshick, Harold Joseph	P	61	.000	B	
		Wynn, James Sherman	OF64	67	.224	B	
0	0	Yellen, Lawrence Alan	P	13	.000	B	C
0	1	Zachary, Wm. Christopher	P	1	.000	B	

CLUB RECORD

NATIONAL LEAGUE

INDIANAPOLIS

YEAR	TG	WON	LOST	PCT.	FINISHED	MANAGER
1878	60	24	36	.400	5	John Edgar Clapp
1879-1887		OUT OF LEAGUE				
1887	126	37	89	.294	8(Last)	Horace S. Fogel George Walter Burnham Frederick L. Thomas
1888	135	50	85	.370	7	Harrison L. Spence
1889	134	59	75	.440	7	Frank Carter Bancroft John Wesley Glasscock

CLUB RECORD

OTHER MAJOR LEAGUES

INDIANAPOLIS

YEAR	TG	WON	LOST	PCT.	FINISHED	MANAGER
AMERICAN ASSOCIATION						
1884	107	29	78	.271	12(Last)	James H. Gifford Wm. Henry Watkins
FRDERAL LEAGUE						
1914	153	88	65	.575	1	Wm. C. Phillips
AMERICAN LEAGUE						
1900	135	71	64	.526	3	Wm. Henry Watkins

WON 24 | NATIONAL LEAGUE | FINISHED 5th.
LOST 36
TG 60 | 1878. | PCT. .400

INDIANAPOLIS

JOHN EDGAR CLAPP

WON	LOST	NAME	POS.	G.	BA	FROM	TO
		Clapp, John Edgar (1B12)	OF39	60	.296	StL	
		Croft, Arthur F. (OF9)	1B48	57	.162	StL	C
		Flint, Frank Sylvester (Silver)	C56	60	.228	A	
		Hallinan, James H.	OF	3	+.250	xChi	C
7	5	Healey, Thomas (OF3)	P12	13	+.204	xProv.	C
4	9	McCormick, James	P14	15	.143	A	
0	0	McKelvy, Russell Errett (P3)	OF57	60	.222	A	
		Nelson, Jackson W.	SS	18	.136	A	
13	22	Nolan, Edward Sylvester (The Only)	P	35	.259	A	
		Quest, Joseph L.	2B	59	.213	A	
		Schaffer, George (Orator)	OF	60	.344	Lvlle	
		Warner, Frederick John Rodney	SS39	41	.243	Ath76	
		Williamson, Edward Nagle	3B	60	.223	A	

WON 37 | NATIONAL LEAGUE | FINISHED 8th (LAST)
LOST 89
TG 126 | 1887. | PCT. .294

INDIANAPOLIS

HORACE S. FOGEL GEORGE WALTER BURNHAM FREDERICK L. THOMAS

WON	LOST	NAME	POS.	G.	BA	FROM	TO
		Arundel, John Thomas (Tug)	C42	43	.236	TolAA84	
		Bassett, Chas. Edwin	2B	119	.270	K.C.	
13	24	Boyle, Henry J.	P38	41	.240	StL	
		Brown, Thomas T.	OF	36	+.223	xPitt	
		Cahill, John Francis	OF52	68	.231	StL	C
0	2	Corcoran, Lawrence J. (Larry)	P	3	.250	Wash	C
		Denny, Jeremiah D. (Jerry)	3B116	122	.340	StL	
0	1	Fast,	P	4	.154	A	C
		Gardner, Franklin W. (Gid)	2B8	18	.306	BaltAA85	
		Glasscock, John Wesley	SS	121	.349	StL	
		Hackett, Mortimer Martin	C39	41	.272	K.C.	C
12	28	Healy, John J. (Egyptian)	P	40	.197	StL	
		Jackson, Henry Everett	1B	10	.263	A	C
		Johnson, Wm. T.	OF	11	.190	PhiUA84	
1	7	Kirby, John F.	P8	8	.138	StL	ClevAA
2	7	Leitner, George Aloysius	P	9	.143	A	C
1	5	Moffet, Samuel R.	P	11	.140	Clev84	
3	5	Morrison, Stephen Henry	P	8	.143	A	C
		Myers, George D.	C47	66	.284	StL	
		McGeachy, John Chas.	OF97	99	.278	StL	
		Polhemus, Mark S.	OF	19	.259	A	C
		Seery, John Emmett	OF	122	.326	StL	
		Shomberg, Otto H.	1B	112	.389	PittAA	
5	10	Shreve, Louis Leonard (Ledell)	P	15	.333	xBaltAA	
0	0	Sowders, John	P	1	.000	A	

WON 50 | NATIONAL LEAGUE | FINISHED 7th.
LOST 85
TG 135 | 1888. | PCT. .370

INDIANAPOLIS

HARRISON L. SPENCE

WON	LOST	NAME	POS.	G.	BA	FROM	TO
		Bassett, Chas. Edwin	2B	128	.241	B	
15	22	Boyle, Henry J.	P	37	.144	B	
		Buckley, Richard D. (Dick) (3B21)	C48	71	.273	A	
10	10	Burdick, Wm. B.	P	31	.147	A	
		Dailey, Cornelius F. (Con)	C42	57	.218	Bos	
		Denny, Jeremiah D. (Jerry) (SS23)	3B96	126	.261	B	
		Esterbrook, Thomas Jefferson (Dude)	1B61	64	.219	MetAA	LvlleAA
		Glasscock, John Wesley	SS109	112	.269	B	
12	24	Healy, John J. (Egyptian)	P	37	.229	B	
		Hines, Paul A.	OF124	132	.280	Wash	
2	5	Moffet, Samuel R. (OF3)	P7	10	.114	B	C
		Myers, George D.	C46	66	.238	B	
		McGeachy, John Chas.	OF117	118	.219	B	
		Seery, John Emmett	OF	133	.220	B	
		Shoenick, Lewis N.	1B	48	.237	BaltUA84	
		Shomberg, Otto H.	1B15	29	.214	B	C
11	24	Shreve, Louis Leonard (Ledell)	P35	36	.182	B	

WON 59 | NATIONAL LEAGUE | FINISHED 7th.
LOST 75
TG 134 | 1889. | PCT. .440

INDIANAPOLIS

FRANK CARTER BANCROFT JOHN WESLEY GLASSCOCK

WON	LOST	NAME	POS.	G.	BA	FROM	TO
0	1	Anderson, F. S.	P	1	.000	A	C
		Andrews, George Edward	OF	40	+.306	xPhil	
		Bassett, Chas. Edwin	2B	126	.253	B	
20	23	Boyle, Henry J.	P	44	.245	B	C
		Buckley, Richard D. (Dick)	C52	65	.258	B	
0	3	Burdick, Wm. B.	P	9	.176	B	C
		Dailey, Cornelius F. (Con)	C48	60	.251	B	
		Denny, Jeremiah D. (Jerry)	3B	133	.282	B	
0	1	Fanning, John Jacob	P	1	.000	A	
2	2	Fee, John	P	7	+.136	xPitt	C

19	22	Getzein, Chas. H.	P	41	.179	Det	
		Glasscock, John Wesley MGR.	SS131	134	.359	B	
		Hines, Paul A.	1B109	121	.304	B	
5	2	Krock, August H.	P	7	+.364	xChi	Wash
		Myers, George D. (C17)	OF22	39	.194	B	C
		McGeachy, John Chas.	OF	131	.267	B	
11	11	Rusie, Amos Wilson	P	26	.174	A	
		Seery, John Emmett	OF	127	.313	B	
		Shoenick, Lewis N.	1B	16	.242	B	C
0	3	Shreve, Louis Leonard (Ledell)	P	3	.000	B	C
		Sommers, Joseph Andrew (Pete)	C	19	+.241	xChi	
		Sullivan, Martin J.	OF64	69	.285	Chi	
		Weckbecker, Peter	C	1	.000	A	
2	7	Whitney, James E. (Grasshopper)	P	10	.400	Wash	

CLUB RECORD

NATIONAL LEAGUE

KANSAS CITY

YEAR	TG	WON	LOST	PCT.	FINISHED	MANAGER
1886	121	30	91	.247	7	David E. Rowe

CLUB RECORD

OTHER MAJOR LEAGUES

KANSAS CITY

YEAR	TG	WON	LOST	PCT.	FINISHED	MANAGER
UNION ASSOCIATION						
1884	77	14	63	.182	11	Theodore Paul Sullivan
AMERICAN ASSOCIATION						
1888	132	43	89	.326	8(Last)	David E. Rowe Samuel Wilson Barkley Wm. Henry Watkins
1889	137	55	82	.401	7	Wm. Henry Watkins James H. Manning
FEDERAL LEAGUE						
1914	152	69	84	.451	6	George Thomas Stovall
1915	153	81	72	.533	4	George Thomas Stovall
AMERICAN LEAGUE						
1900	139	69	70	.495	5	James H. Manning

WON 30 NATIONAL LEAGUE FINISHED 7th
LOST 91
TG 121 1886. PCT. .247

KANSAS CITY

DAVID E. ROWE

WON	LOST	NAME	POS.	G.	BA	FROM	TO
		Baker, George F.	C	1	.250	StL	C
		Bassett, Chas. Edwin	SS82	90	.260	Prov	
		Briody, Chas. F.	C53	55	.237	StL	
5	16	Conway, Peter J. (P21)	OF31	52	+.235	Buff	Det
0	1	Donely, James B. (P1)	3B	113	.201	Det	
		Dugdale, Daniel Edward	C6	12	.175	A	
		Hackett, Mortimer Martin	C50	62	.217	Bos	
1	3	King, Chas. Frederick	P	7	.045	A	
		Lillie, James J.	OF	114	.175	Buff	C
		Myers, Albert	2B	118	.276	Phil	
0	2	McKeon, Lawrence J.	P	2	.000	xCinAA	C
		McQuery, Wm. Thomas	1B	122	.247	Det	
		Radford, Paul Revere (SS30)	OF91	122	.229	Prov	
		Ringo, Frank C.	C	16	.232	PittAA	C
		Rowe, David E. MGR.	OF90	105	.240	StL	
12	37	Weidman, George E.	P49	51	.167	Det	
12	32	Whitney, James E. (Grasshopper) (OF20)	P46	67	.239	Bos	

CLUB RECORD

NATIONAL LEAGUE

LOS ANGELES

YEAR	TG	WON	LOST	PCT.	FINISHED	MANAGER
1958	154	71	83	.461	7	Walter Emmons Alston
1959	156	88	68	.564	1	Walter Emmons Alston
1960	154	82	72	.532	4	Walter Emmons Alston
1961	154	89	65	.578	2	Walter Emmons Alston
1962	165	102	63	.618	2	Walter Emmons Alston
1963	162	99	63	.611	1	Walter Emmons Alston
1964	162	80	82	.494	x6	Walter Emmons Alston

YEAR	TG	WON	LOST	TIED	PCT.	FINISHED	MANAGER
1965	162	97	65	0	.599	1	WALTER EMMONS ALSTON
1966	162	95	67	0	.586	1	WALTER EMMONS ALSTON
1967	162	73	89	0	.451	8	WALTER EMMONS ALSTON
1968	162	76	86	0	.469	X7 (PHI)	WALTER EMMONS ALSTON
1969	162	85	77	0	.525	4W	WALTER EMMONS ALSTON
1970	161	87	74	0	.540	2W	WALTER EMMONS ALSTON
1971	162	89	73	0	.549	2W	WALTER EMMONS ALSTON
1972	155	85	70	0	.548	3W	WALTER EMMONS ALSTON

WON 71 LOST 83 TG 154 — NATIONAL LEAGUE — 1958. — FINISHED 7th. — PCT. .461

LOS ANGELES

WALTER EMMONS ALSTON

WON	LOST	NAME	POS.	G.	BA	FROM	TO
1	0	Bessent, Fred Donald	P	19	.000	B	C
		Bilko, Stephen Thomas	1B25	47	+.208	xCin	
0	0	Birrer, Werner Joseph	P	16	.571	BaltA56	C
		Cimoli, Gino Nicholas	OF104	109	.246	B	
0	0	Collum, Jack Dean	P	2	.000	B	
2	1	Craig, Roger Lee	P	9	.000	B	
		Demeter, Donald Lee	OF39	43	.189	Bkn56	
12	13	Drysdale, Donald Scott	P44	47	.227	B	
4	4	Erskine, Carl Daniel	P31	32	.037	B	
		Fairly, Ronald Ray	OF	15	.283	A	
		Furillo, Carl Anthony	OF119	122	.290	B	
		Gentile, James Edward	1B8	12	.133	B	
1	1	Giallombardo, Robert Paul	P6	8	.167	A	C
		Gilliam, James Wm. (2B32 3B44)	OF75	147	.261	B	
		Gray, Richard Benjamin	3B55	58	.249	A	
		Hodges, Gilbert Raymond (C1 3B15 OF9)	1B122	141	.259	B	
		Howard, Frank Oliver	OF	8	.241	A	
		Jackson, Ransom Joseph	3B17	35	.185	B	ClevA
6	6	Kipp, Fred Leo	P40	42	.250	B	
3	5	Klippstein, John Calvin	P	45	+.050	xCin	
11	11	Koufax, Sanford	P	40	.122	B	
6	6	Labine, Clement Walter	P	52	.056	B	
		Larker, Norman Howard (1B25)	OF43	99	.277	A	
		Lillis, Robert Perry	SS19	20	.391	A	
1	1	Mauriello, Ralph	P	3	.000	A	C
2	6	McDevitt, Daniel Eugene	P	13	.133	B	
		Miles, Donald Ray	OF5	8	.182	A	C
		Neal, Chas. Lenard (SS9)	2B132	140	.254	B	
0	0	Negray, Ronald Alvin	P	4	.000	Phil56	C
0	6	Newcombe, Donald	P	11	+.417	B	Cin
		Pignatano, Joseph Benjamin	C57	63	.218	B	
13	15	Podres, John Joseph	P39	42	.127	B	
		Reese, Harold Henry (3B21)	SS22	59	.224	B	C
		Robinson, Earl John	3B6	8	.200	A	
0	1	Roebuck, Edward Jack	P	32	.500	B	
		Roseboro, John H. (OF5)	C104	114	.271	B	
0	0	Sherry, Lawrence	P	5	.000	A	
		Snider, Edwin Donald	OF92	106	.312	B	
		Valo, Elmer Wm.	OF26	65	.248	B	
		Walker, Albert Bluford	C20	25	.114	B	C
9	7	Williams, Stanley Wilson	P	27	.050	A	
		Zimmer, Donald Wm. (2B1 3B12 OF1)	SS114	127	.262	B	
		Wilson, Robert	OF1	3	.200	A	C

WON 88 LOST 68 TG 156 — NATIONAL LEAGUE — 1959. — FINISHED 1st. — PCT. .564

LOS ANGELES

WALTER EMMONS ALSTON

WON	LOST	NAME	POS.	G.	BA	FROM	TO
		Amoros, Edmundo Isasi		5	.200	Bkn57	
		Baxes, Dimitrios S.	3B10	11	.303	A	ClevA
3	2	Churn, Clarence Nottingham	P	14	.167	ClevA	C
11	5	Craig, Roger Lee	P	29	.058	B	
		Davis, Herman Thomas		1	.000	A	
		Demeter, Donald Lee	OF124	139	.256	B	
		Drake, Solomon Louis	OF4	9	+.250	Chi56	Phil
17	13	Drysdale, Donald Scott	P44	46	.165	B	
0	3	Erskine, Carl Daniel	P	10	.000	B	C
		Essegian, Chas. Abraham	OF10	24	+.304	xSt.L	
		Fairly, Ronald Ray	OF88	118	.238	B	
3	4	Fowler, John Arthur	P	36	.083	Cin57	
		Furillo, Carl Anthony	OF25	50	.290	B	
		Gilliam, James Wm. (2B8 OF3)	3B132	145	.282	B	
		Gray, Richard Benjamin	3B11	21	+.154	B	StL
0	0	Harris, Wm. Thomas	P	1	.000	Bkn57	C
		Hodges, Gilbert Raymond (3B4)	1B113	124	.276	B	
		Howard, Frank Oliver	OF6	9	.143	B	
0	0	Kipp, Fred Leo	P	2	.000	B	
4	0	Klippstein, John Calvin	P	28	.143	B	
8	6	Koufax, Sanford	P	35	.111	B	
5	10	Labine, Clement Walter	P	56	.000	B	
		Larker, Norman Howard (OF30)	1B55	108	.289	B	
		Lillis, Robert Perry	SS20	30	.229	B	
10	8	McDevitt, Daniel Eugene	P	39	.109	B	
		Moon, Wallace Wade (1B1)	OF143	145	.302	StL	
		Neal, Chas. Lenard (SS1)	2B151	151	.287	B	
		Pignatano, Joseph Benjamin	C49	52	.237	B	
14	9	Podres, John Joseph	P	34	.246	B	
		Repulski, Eldon John	OF31	53	.255	Phil	
		Roseboro, John H.	C117	118	.232	B	
7	2	Sherry, Lawrence	P	23	.219	B	
		Sherry, Norman Burt	C	2	.333	A	
		Snider, Edwin Donald	OF107	126	.308	B	
1	1	Snyder, Eugene Walter	P	11	.000	A	C
5	5	Williams, Stanley Wilson	P	35	.194	B	
		Wills, Maurice Morning	SS82	83	.260	A	
		Zimmer, Donald Wm. (2B1 3B5)	SS88	97	.165	B	

WON 82 LOST 72 TG 154 — NATIONAL LEAGUE — 1960. — FINISHED 4th. — PCT. .532

LOS ANGELES

WALTER EMMONS ALSTON

WON	LOST	NAME	POS.	G.	BA	FROM	TO
		Amoros, Edmundo Isasi	OF3	9	.143	B	DetA
		Aspromonte, Robert Thomas (3B4)	SS15	21	.182	Bkn56	
		Camilli, Douglas Joseph	C	6	.333	A	
8	3	Craig, Roger Lee	P	21	.056	B	
		Davis, Herman Thomas (3B5)	OF87	110	.276	B	
		Davis, Wm. Henry	OF	22	.318	A	
		Demeter, Donald Lee	OF62	64	.274	B	
15	14	Drysdale, Donald Scott	P	41	.157	B	
		Essegian, Chas. Abraham	OF18	52	.215	B	
		Fairly, Ronald Ray	OF13	14	.108	B	
		Furillo, Carl Anthony	OF2	8	.200	B	C
		Gilliam, James Wm. (2B30)	3B130	151	.248	B	
1	0	Golden, James Edward	P	1	.333	A	
		Hodges, Gilbert Raymond (3B10)	1B92	101	.198	B	
		Howard, Frank Oliver (1B4)	OF115	117	.268	B	
8	13	Koufax, Sanford	P	37	.123	B	
0	1	Labine, Clement Walter	P	13	.500	B	DetA
		Larker, Norman Howard (OF2)	1B119	133	.323	B	
		Lillis, Robert Perry (2B1 3B14)	SS23	48	.267	B	
0	4	McDevitt, Daniel Eugene	P	24	.200	B	
		Moon, Wallace Wade	OF127	138	.299	B	
		Neal, Chas. Lenard (SS3)	2B136	139	.256	B	
		Noren, Irving Arnold		26	+.200	xChi	C
0	0	Ortega, Filomeno Coronado	P	3	.000	A	
0	1	Palmquist, Edwin Lee	P	22	.000	A	
		Pignatano, Joseph Benjamin	C40	58	.233	B	
14	12	Podres, John Joseph	P	34	.136	B	
0	1	Rakow, Edward Chas.	P	9	.333	A	
		Repulski, Eldon John	OF2	4	.200	B	BosA
8	3	Roebuck, Edward Jack	P	58	.167	LA58	
		Roseboro, John H. (1B1 3B1)	C87	103	.213	B	
14	10	Sherry, Lawrence	P	57	.162	B	
		Sherry, Norman Burt	C44	47	.283	B	
		Smith, Chas. Wm.	3B	18	.167	A	
		Snider, Edwin Donald	OF75	101	.243	B	
14	10	Williams, Stanley Wilson	P	38	.141	B	
		Wills, Maurice Morning	SS145	148	.295	B	

WON 89 NATIONAL LEAGUE FINISHED 2nd.
LOST 65
TG 154 1961. PCT. .578

LOS ANGELES

WALTER EMMONS ALSTON

WON	LOST	NAME	POS.	G.	BA	FROM	TO
		Aspromonte, Robert Thomas (2B2 SS4)	3B9	47	.241	B	
		Camilli, Douglas Joseph	C12	13	.133	B	
5	6	Craig, Roger Lee	P	40	.148	B	
		Davis, Herman Thomas (3B59)	OF86	132	.278	B	
		Davis, Wm. Henry	OF114	128	.254	B	
		Demeter, Donald Lee	OF14	15	+.172	B	Phil
13	10	Drysdale, Donald Scott	P	40	.193	B	
		Fairly, Ronald Ray (1B23)	OF71	111	.322	B	
6	6	Farrell, Richard Joseph	P	50	+.000	xPhil	
		Gilliam, James Wm. (2B71 OF11)	3B74	144	.244	B	
1	1	Golden, James Edward	P	28	.000	B	
		Harkness, Thomas Wm.	1B2	5	.500	A	
		Hodges, Gilbert Raymond	1B100	109	.242	B	
		Howard, Frank Oliver (1B7)	OF65	92	.296	B	
18	13	Koufax, Sanford	P	42	.065	B	
		Larker, Norman Howard (OF1)	1B86	97	.270	B	
		Lillis, Robert Perry (2B1 SS1)	3B12	19	+.111	B	StL
		Moon, Wallace Wade	OF133	134	.328	B	
		Neal, Chas. Lenard	2B104	108	.235	B	
0	2	Ortega, Filomeno Coronado	P	4	.250	B	
0	1	Palmquist, Edwin Lee	P	5	.000	B	MinnA
7	5	Perranoski, Ronald Peter	P	53	.083	A	
18	5	Podres, John Joseph	P	32	.232	B	
2	0	Roebuck, Edward Jack	P	5	.000	B	
		Roseboro, John H.	C125	128	.251	B	
4	4	Sherry, Lawrence	P	53	.154	B	
		Sherry, Norman Burt	C45	47	.256	B	
		Smith, Chas. Wm. (SS3)	3B4	9	+.250	B	Phil
		Snider, Edwin Donald	OF66	85	.296	B	
		Spencer, Daryl Dean (SS3)	3B57	60	+.243	xStL	
		Warwick, Carl Wayne	OF12	19	+.091	A	StL
15	12	Williams, Stanley Wilson	P	41	.167	B	
		Wills, Maurice Morning	SS	148	.282	B	
		Windhorn, Gordon Ray	OF17	34	.242	NYA59	

WON 102 NATIONAL LEAGUE FINISHED 2nd.
LOST 63
TG 165 1962. PCT. .618

LOS ANGELES

WALTER EMMONS ALSTON

WON	LOST	NAME	POS.	G.	BA	FROM	TO
		Burright, Lawrence Allen (SS1)	2B109	115	.205	A	
		Camilli, Douglas Joseph	C39	45	.284	B	
		Carey, Andrew Arthur	3B42	53	.234	ChiA	C
		Davis, Herman Thomas (3B39)	OF146	163	.346	B	

WON	LOST	NAME	POS.	G.	BA	FROM	TO
		Davis, Wm. Henry	OF156	157	.285	B	
25	9	Drysdale, Donald Scott	P	43	.198	B	
		Fairly, Ronald Ray (OF48)	1B120	147	.278	B	
		Gilliam, James Wm.	2B113	160	.270	B	
		(3B90 OF1)					
		Harkness, Thomas Wm.	1B59	92	.258	B	
		Howard, Frank Oliver	OF131	141	.296	B	
0	0	Hunter, Willard Mitchell	P	1	+.000	A	N.Y.
14	7	Koufax, Sanford	P	28	.087	B	
		McMullen, Kenneth Lee	OF2	6	.273	A	
6	5	Moeller, Joseph Douglas	P	19	.212	A	
		Moon, Wallace Wade	OF36	95	.242	B	
		(1B32)					
0	2	Ortega, Filemeno Coronado	P	24	.000	B	
6	6	Perranoski, Ronald Peter	P	70	.071	B	
15	13	Podres, John Joseph	P	40	.159	B	
5	4	Richert, Peter Gerard	P	19	.080	A	
10	2	Roebuck, Edward Jack	P	64	.214	B	
		Roseboro, John H.	C	128	.249	B	
7	3	Sherry, Lawrence	P	58	.118	B	
		Sherry, Norman Burt	C34	35	.182	B	
0	0	Smith, Jack Hatfield	P	8	.000	A	
		Snider, Edwin Donald	OF39	80	.278	B	
		Spencer, Daryl Dean	3B57	77	.236	B	
		(SS10)					
		Tracewski, Richard Joseph	SS4	15	.000	A	
		Walls, Ray Lee	OF17	60	.266	Phil	
		(1B11 3B4)					
14	12	Williams, Stanley Wilson	P	40	.076	B	
		Wills, Maurice Morning	SS	165	.299	B	

WON 99 — NATIONAL LEAGUE — FINISHED 1st.
LOST 63
TG 162 — 1963. — PCT. .611

LOS ANGELES

WALTER EMMONS ALSTON

WON	LOST	NAME	POS.	G.	BA	FROM	TO
		Breeding, Marvin Eugene	2B17	20	.167	xWashA	C
		(SS1 3B1)					
3	1	Calmus, Richard Lee	P	21	.000	A	
		Camilli, Douglas Joseph	C47	49	.162	B	
		Davis, Herman Thomas	OF129	146	.326	B	
		(3B40)					
		Davis, Wm. Henry	OF153	156	.245	B	
19	17	Drysdale, Donald Scott	P	42	.167	B	
		Fairly, Ronald Ray (OF45)	1B110	152	.271	B	
		Ferrara, Alfred John	OF11	21	.159	A	
		Gilliam, James Wm.	2B119	148	.282	B	
		(3B55)					
		Gleason, Roy Wm.		8	1.000	A	C
		Griffith, Robert Derrell	2B	1	.000	A	
		Howard, Frank Oliver	OF111	123	.273	B	
25	5	Koufax, Sanford	P	40	.064	B	

WON	LOST	NAME	POS.	G.	BA	FROM	TO
		McMullen, Kenneth Lee	3B71	79	.236	B	
		(2B1 OF1)					
10	8	Miller, Robert Lane	P	42	.070	N.Y.	
		Moon, Wallace Wade	OF96	122	.262	B	
		Nen, Richard LeRoy	1B5	7	.125	A	
		Oliver, Nathaniel (SS2)	2B57	65	.239	A	
0	0	Ortega, Filomeno Coronado	P	1	.000	B	
16	3	Perranoski, Ronald Peter	P	69	.125	B	
14	12	Podres, John Joseph	P	37	.141	B	
5	3	Richert, Peter Gerard	P	20	.181	B	
2	4	Roebuck, Edward Jack	P	29	.250	B	WashA
		Roseboro, John H.	C134	135	.236	B	
1	1	Rowe, Kenneth Darrell	P	14	.000	A	
0	0	Scott, Richard Lewis	P	9	.000	A	
2	6	Sherry, Lawrence	P	36	.111	B	
		Skowron, Wm. Joseph	1B66	89	.203	NYA	
		(3B1)					
0	0	Smith, Jack Hatfield	P	4	.000	B	
		Spencer, Daryl Dean	3B3	7	+.111	B	Cin
		Tracewski, Richard Joseph	SS81	104	.226	B	
		(2B23)					
		Walls, Ray Lee	OF18	64	.233	B	
		(1B5 3B2)					
2	3	Willhite, Jon Nicholas	P	8	.300	A	
		Wills, Maurice Morning	SS109	134	.302	B	
		(3B33)					
		Zimmer, Donald Wm.	3B10	22	.217	Cin	WashA
		(2B1 SS1)					

WON 80 — NATIONAL LEAGUE — FINISHED 6th.
LOST 82 — (TIED WITH PITTSBURGH)
TG 162 — 1964. — PCT. .494

LOS ANGELES

WALTER EMMONS ALSTON

WON	LOST	NAME	POS.	G.	BA	FROM	TO
4	3	Brewer, James Thomas	P	34	.273	Chic	
		Camilli, Douglas Joseph	C46	50	.179	B	
		Crawford, Willie Murphy	OF4	10	.313	A	
		Davis, Herman Thomas	OF148	152	.275	B	
		Davis, Wm. Henry	OF155	157	.294	B	
18	16	Drysdale, Donald Scott	P	40	.173	B	
		Fairly, Ronald Ray	1B141	150	.256	B	
		Gilliam, James Wm.	3B86	116	.228	B	
		(2B25 OF2)					
		Griffith, Robert Derrell	3B35	78	.290	B	
		(OF29)					
		Howard, Frank Oliver	OF122	134	.226	B	
19	5	Koufax, Sanford	P	29	.095	B	
		McMullen, Kenneth Lee	1B13	24	.209	B	
		(3B4 OF3)					
4	8	Miller, Larry Don	P	16	.269	A	
7	7	Miller, Robert Lane	P	74	.158	B	

W	L	Name	Pos	G	Avg		
7	13	Moeller, Joseph Douglas	P	27	.067	LA62	
		Moon, Wallace Wade	OF23	68	.220	B	
		Oliver, Nathaniel (SS1)	2B98	99	.243	B	
7	9	Ortega, Filomeno Coronado	P34	35	.136	B	
		Parker, Maurice Wesley (1B31)	OF69	124	.257	A	
5	7	Perranoski, Ronald Peter	P	72	.105	B	
0	2	Podres, John Joseph	P	2	.000	B	
2	0	Purdin, John Nolan	P	3	.200	A	
3	4	Reed, Howard Dean	P	26	.100	A	
2	3	Richert, Peter Gerard	P	8	.091	B	
		Roseboro, John H.	C128	134	.287	B	
		Shirley, Barton Arvin (SS8)	3B10	18	.274	A	
0	1	Singer, Wm. Robert	P	2	.167	A	
		Torborg, Jeffrey Alan	C27	28	.233	A	
		Tracewski, Richard Joseph (SS19 3B30)	2B56	106	.247	B	
		Walls, Ray Lee (C1)	OF6	37	.179	B	C
		Werhas, John Chas.	3B28	29	.193	A	
2	4	Willhite, Jon Nicholas	P	10	.000	A	
		Wills, Maurice Morning (3B6)	SS149	158	.275	B	

CLUB RECORD

NATIONAL LEAGUE

LOUISVILLE

YEAR	TG	WON	LOST	PCT.	FINISHED	MANAGER
1876	66	30	36	.455	5	Chas. J. Fulmer
1877	60	35	25	.583	2	John Curtis Chapman
1878-1891		OUT OF LEAGUE				
1892	152	63	89	.414	9	Nathaniel Frederick Pfeffer John Curtis Chapman
1893	125	50	75	.400	11	Wm. S. Barnie
1894	130	36	94	.277	12(Last)	Wm. S. Barnie
1895	131	35	96	.267	12(Last)	John James McCloskey
1896	131	38	93	.290	12(Last)	John James McCloskey Wm. Henry McGunnigle
1897	130	52	78	.400	11	James P. Rogers Frederick Clifford Clarke
1898	151	70	81	.464	9	Frederick Clifford Clarke
1899	152	75	77	.493	9	Frederick Clifford Clarke

CLUB RECORD

OTHER MAJOR LEAGUES

LOUISVILLE

YEAR	TG	WON	LOST	PCT.	FINISHED	MANAGER
AMERICAN ASSOCIATION (ECLIPSE)						
1882	79	44	35	.557	2	John F. Dyler J. Wm. Reccius Samuel Leech Maskrey
1883	97	52	45	.536	5	J. Wm. Reccius Samuel Leech Maskrey Joseph John Gerhardt
1884	108	68	40	.630	3	Joseph John Gerhardt Michael F. Walsh
1885	112	53	59	.473	x5(Bkn)	James A. Hart
1886	136	66	70	.485	4	James A. Hart
1887	136	76	60	.559	4	John O. Kelly
1888	135	48	87	.360	7	John A. Kerins M. H. Davidson
1889	138	27	111	.195	8(Last)	M. H. Davidson Robert M. Brown Harry L. Means Buck McKinney Daniel W. Shannon Wm. V. Wolf John Curtis Chapman
1890	132	88	44	.667	1	John Curtis Chapman
1891	139	55	84	.396	7	John Curtis Chapman

WON 30
LOST 36
TG 66

NATIONAL LEAGUE — 1876. — FINISHED 5th. — PCT. .455

LOUISVILLE

CHAS. J. FULMER

WON	LOST	NAME	POS.	G.	BA	FROM	TO
		Allison, Arthur Algernon (1B8)	OF23	31	.205	A	C
		Bechtel, George A.	OF	14	+.182	A	Mut
		Carbine, John C.	1B	6	.150	A	C
		Chapman, John Curtis	OF	17	.235	A	
0	1	Clinton, James Lawrence (P2)	OF14	16	.338	A	
		Collins, Daniel Thomas	OF	7	.143	A	C
30	35	Devlin, James Alexander	P67	68	.312	A	
		Fulmer, Chas. J. MGR.	SS	66	.272	A	
		Gerhardt, Joseph John (Moveup) (2B6)	1B53	65	.258	A	
		Hague, Wm. L.	3B	67	.264	A	
		Hastings, Winfield Scott	OF63	67	.254	A	
		Holbert, Wm. H.	C	12	.256	A	
		McGuinness, John J.	2B	1	.000	A	
0	0	Pearce, Grayson S.	P	1	.000	A	
		Ryan, John Joseph	OF64	65	.247	A	
		Snyder, Chas. N.	C53	56	.195	A	
		Sommerville, Edward	2B63	64	.187	A	

WON 35
LOST 25
TG 60

NATIONAL LEAGUE — 1877. — FINISHED 2nd. — PCT. .583

LOUISVILLE

JOHN CURTIS CHAPMAN

WON	LOST	NAME	POS.	G.	BA	FROM	TO
		Craver, Wm. H.	SS	57	.263	Mut	C
		Crowley, Wm. Michael (C2 2B1 SS2 3B1)	OF58	61	.281	A	
35	25	Devlin, James Alexander	P	61	.269	B	C
		Gerhardt, Joseph John (1B1 SS1 OF1)	2B57	59	.304	B	
		Hague, Wm. L.	3B	59	.267	B	
		Hall, George W.	OF	61	.322	Ath	C
		Haldeman, John Avery	2B	1	.000	A	C
		Lafferty, Frank Bernard (Flip)	OF	4	.059	Ath	C
		Latham, George Warren (Juice)	1B	59	.290	A	
		Little, George Harry	2B	1	+.000	xStL	StL
		Nichols, Albert H. (1B1 SS1 3B1)	2B3	6	.211	Mut	C
		Schaffer, George (Orator) (1B1)	OF60	61	.285	A	
		Snyder, Chas. N. (SS1 OF1)	C61	61	.258	B	

WON 63
LOST 89
TG 152

NATIONAL LEAGUE — 1892. — FINISHED 9th. — PCT. .414

LOUISVILLE

NATHANIEL FREDERICK PFEFFER   JOHN CURTIS CHAPMAN

WON	LOST	NAME	POS.	G.	BA	FROM	TO
		Bassett, Chas. Edwin (2B2)	3B76	78	+.213	xN.Y.	C
		Brown, Thomas T.	OF	153	.232	BosAA	
		Browning, Louis Roger (Pete)	OF	21	+.260	Cin	Cin
9	13	Clausen, Frederick Wm.	P23	24	.180	A	
		Dooms, Harry E.	OF	1	.000	A	C
0	1	Dowse, Thomas Jefferson (P1)	C39	40	+.173	ColAA	Cin
1	3	Fitzgerald, John T.	P	4	.133	LvlleAA	C
		Grim, John Heim (Jack)	C69	95	.254	MilAA	
1	1	Healy, John J. (Egyptian)	P	8	+.286	xBalt	C
2	1	Hemming, George Earl	P	4	+.077	xCin	
		Jennings, Hugh Ambrose	SS145	152	.232	LvlleAA	
6	12	Jones, Alexander H.	P	18	+.145	Pitt89	Wash
		Kuehne, Wm. J.	3B	76	+.164	LvlleAA	StL
7	10	Meekin, Jouett	P	25	+.103	LvlleAA	Wash
		Merritt, Wm. Henry	C	45	.195	Chi91	
		McFarlan, Alexander Shepard	OF	14	.162	A	C
		Pfeffer, Nathaniel Frederick MGR.	2B115	124	.261	Chi	
12	17	Sanders, Alexander Benjamin (1B15)	P31	53	.267	AthAA	C
		Seery, John Emmett	OF	42	.194	CinAA	C
21	20	Stratton, C. Scott	P41	60	.275	LvlleAA	
		Taylor, Harry Leonard (1B34)	OF73	123	.274	LvlleAA	
4	11	Viau, Leon	P15	20	+.185	xClev	Bos
		Weaver, Wm. B.	OF122	136	.268	LvlleAA	
		Whistler, Lewis	1B	80	+.252	xBalt	

WON 50
LOST 75
TG 125

NATIONAL LEAGUE — 1893. — FINISHED 11th. — PCT. .400

LOUISVILLE

WM. S. BARNIE

WON	LOST	NAME	POS.	G.	BA	FROM	TO
		Brown, Thomas T.	OF	121	.253	B	
		Brown, Willard	1B	111	+.320	xBalt	
		Browning, Louis Roger (Pete)	OF	57	.371	Cin	

WON	LOST	NAME	POS.	G.	BA	FROM	TO
		Clark, Robert H.	C	11	.103	Cin91	C
1	3	Clausen, Frederick Wm.	P	9	+.231	B	Chi
		Denny, Jeremiah D. (Jerry)	SS41	44	.251	Phil91	
		Grim, John Helm (Jack)	C88	92	.287	B	
0	0	Gumbert, Wm. Skeen	P	1	1.000	Pitt	C
		Harrington, Jeremiah Peter	C	10	.121	Cin	C
18	18	Hemming, George Earl	P39	43	.234	B	
		Jennings, Hugh Ambrose	SS	23	+.148	B	Balt
3	2	Kilroy, Matthew Aloysius	P	5	.438	Wash	
0	1	Lucid, Cornelius Conrad (Con)	P	2	.250	A	
8	8	Menefee, John (Jock)	P17	21	.292	Pitt	
		O'Rourke, Timothy Patrick	SS	90	+.290	xBalt	
		Pfeffer, Nathaniel Frederick	2B	124	.269	B	
		Pinckney, George Burton	3B	118	.226	StL	C
1	3	Rhines, Wm. Pearl (Bunker)	P	5	.091	Cin	
5	12	Rhodes, Wm. Clarence	P	17	.149	A	C
12	24	Stratton, C. Scott (OF20)	P38	58	.252	B	
		Twitchell, Lawrence Grant	OF	45	.331	Wash	
		Weaver, Wm. B. (C21)	OF83	104	.309	B	
		Welch, Curtis Benton	OF	14	.181	Cin	C
		Whistler, Lewis	1B	13	+.222	B	StL
2	4	Whitrock, Wm. Franklin	P	8	.315	StLAA90	

WON 36
LOST 94
TG 130

NATIONAL LEAGUE — 1894.

FINISHED 12th (LAST) — PCT. .277

LOUISVILLE

WM. S. BARNIE

WON	LOST	NAME	POS.	G.	BA	FROM	TO
		Brown, Thomas T.	OF	130	.251	B	
		Brown, Willard	1B	13	+.192	B	StL
		Clarke, Frederick Clifford	OF	76	.275	A	
		Cote, Henry Joseph	C	10	.313	A	
		Denny, Jeremiah D. (Jerry)	3B	60	.274	B	C
		Dungan, Samuel Morrison	OF	8	+.333	xChi	
		Earle, Wm. Moffat	C	19	+.377	Pitt	Bkn
		Flaherty, Patrick Henry	3B	38	.295	A	C
		Gilbert, Peter	3B	28	+.287	xBkn	C
		Grim, John Helm (Jack) (2B24)	C75	107	.290	B	
11	20	Hemming, George Earl	P	32	+.254	B	Balt
2	6	Inks, Albert Preston (Bert)	P	11	+.444	xBalt	
0	6	Kilroy, Matthew Aloysius	P	6	.143	B	
7	22	Knell, Philip H.	P	30	+.293	xPitt	
		Lake, Frederick Lovett	C	16	.202	Bos91	
		Lutenberg, Chas. Wm.	1B68	70	.192	A	C
		Mares,	OF	1	.000	A	C
8	15	Menefee, John (Jock)	P	34	+.167	B	Pitt
3	3	Nicol, George Edward (P6)	OF22	28	+.345	xPitt	
		O'Rourke, Timothy Patrick	3B	55	+.284	B	StL
0	1	Pepper, Wm. Harrison	P	2	.000	A	C
		Pfeffer, Nathaniel Frederick (SS15)	2B89	104	.297	B	
		Richardson, Daniel (Denny)	SS107	116	.255	Bkn	C
		Smith, Oliver H.	OF	89	.288	A	C
1	3	Stratton, C. Scott (OF5)	P7	13	+.282	B	Chi
		Twitchell, Lawrence Grant	OF	51	.265	B	C
4	17	Wadsworth, Wm. John	P22	23	.243	Balt	
		Weaver, Wm. B.	C	60	+.206	B	Pitt
0	1	Whitrock, Wm. Franklin	P	2	+.000	B	Cin
		Zahner, Frederick Joseph	C	14	.204	A	

WON 35
LOST 96 *
TG 131

NATIONAL LEAGUE — 1895.

FINISHED 12th (LAST) — PCT. .267

LOUISVILLE

JOHN JAMES McCLOSKEY

WON	LOST	NAME	POS.	G.	BA	FROM	TO
0	1	Borchers, George B.	P	1	.000	Chi88	C
		Briggs, Grant	C	1	.000	StL92	C
		Brouthers, Dennis (Dan)	1B	24	+.296	xBalt	
		Burnett, Hercules H.	OF	5	.411	LvlleAA88	C
0	0	Childers,	P	1	.000	A	C
		Clarke, Frederick Clifford	OF	132	.354	B	
		Collins, James Joseph	3B	93	+.286	xBos	
		Cote, Henry Joseph	C	10	.265	B	C
11	16	Cunningham, Ellsworth Elmer	P28	31	.310	BaltAA91	
0	1	Gettinger, Thomas L. (P1)	OF60	60	.281	StLAA90	C
		Glasscock, John Wesley	SS	18	+.373	Pitt	Wash
		Hassamaer, Wm. Louis (OF8)	1B12	20	+.198	xWash	
		Hatfield, Gilbert	SS	5	.196	Bkn93	C
1	0	Holmes, James Wm. (Ducky) (P1)	OF28	39	.382	A	
7	19	Inks, Albert Preston (Bert)	P	27	.241	B	
		Kemmer, Wm. E.	3B	10	.139	A	C
0	0	Kling, Wm.	P	1	.000	Balt92	C
0	6	Knell, Philip H.	P	14	+.273	B	Clev
1	5	Luby, John Perkins	P	15	.272	Chi92	C
0	0	Meakim, George Clinton	P	1	.333	Cin92	C
		Minahan, Daniel Joseph	3B	8	.361	A	C
		Morrison, Thomas J. (SS3)	3B3	5	.272	A	
		McCormick, Wm. J. (Barry)	SS	3	.273	A	
3	2	x McCreery, Thomas Leavenworth	1B10	29	.336	A	
4	19	McDermott, Michael Joseph	P24	26	.155	LvlleAA89	
0	6	McFarlan, Anderson Daniel	P	7	.238	A	
		McGann, Dennis L. (Dan) (3B7)	SS10	17	.313	A	
		O'Brien, John J.	2B125	128	.262	Chi93	
		Pfeffer, Nathaniel Frederick (1B3 2B3)	SS5	11	.288	B	
		Preston, Walter B. (3B24)	OF25	49	.292	A	C
		Shugart, Wm. Frank (OF27)	SS85	112	.256	StL	
		Spies, Henry	C	69	+.268	xCin	
		Sweeney, Daniel J.	OF	21	.279	A	C

WON	LOST	NAME	POS.	G.	BA	FROM	TO
		Trost, Michael J.	1B	2	.111	StLAA90	C
0	1	Wadsworth, Wm. John	P	2	.200	B	C
		Warner, John Joseph	C	60	+.263	xBos	
		Welsh, James J. (Tub) (1B17)	C22	39	.224	TolAA90	C
8	19	Weyhing, August (Gus)	P	27	+.227	xPitt	
		Wright, Joseph	OF	59	.289	A	
		Zahner, Frederick Joseph	C	18	.234	B	C

xMcCreery also played 14 games in the OF and 5 as P.
*One game lost by forfeit.

WON 38 LOST 93 TG 131 — NATIONAL LEAGUE 1896. — FINISHED 12th (LAST) PCT. .290

LOUISVILLE

JOHN JAMES McCLOSKEY WM. HENRY McGUNNIGLE

WON	LOST	NAME	POS.	G.	BA	FROM	TO
		Boyle, Edward J.	C	3	+.111	A	Pitt
		Cassidy, Peter Francis	1B38	48	.221	A	
		Clarke, Frederick Clifford	OF	131	.327	B	
0	1	Clausen, Frederick Wm.	P	2	.000	Chi94	C
		Clingman, Wm. Frederick	3B	120	.230	Pitt	
		Crooks, John Chas. (Jack)	2B	37	+.232	xWash	
7	14	Cunningham, Ellsworth Elmer	P23	24	.267	B	
		Dexter, Chas. Dana (OF44)	C54	98	.284	A	
		Dolan, Joseph	SS	44	.219	A	
0	1	Emig, Chas. H.	P	1	.000	A	C
		Eustace, Frank John	SS22	25	.163	A	C
13	25	Fraser, Chas. Carrolton (Chick)	P41	43	.146	A	
		Friend, Frank B.	C	2	.200	A	C
		Hassamaer, Wm. Louis	1B	26	.248	B	C
3	5	Herman, Arthur	P	13	.118	A	
10	29	Hill, Wm. C.	P	39	.203	A	
0	2	Holmes, James Wm. (Ducky) (P4)	OF33	37	.276	B	
		Johnson, Albert J.	2B	24	.232	A	
		Kinslow, Thomas F.	C	8	.280	Pitt	
		Kostal, Joseph	C	2	.000	A	C
		Miller, George Frederick (Fog-Horn) (2B21)	C46	84	.273	StL	C
		Morrison, Thomas J.	3B	8	.107	B	C
0	1	McCreery, Thomas Leavenworth (P1)	OF110	110	.351	B	
2	7	McDermott, Michael Joseph	P	12	.307	B	
		McFarland, Hermus W.	OF24	25	.198	A	
		O'Brien, John J.	2B	49	+.333	B	Wash
		Pickering, Oliver Dan	OF	45	.303	A	
		Rogers, James F.	2B	74	+.256	xWash	
		Shannon, Frank E.	SS29	31	.161	Wash	C
1	5	Smith, Thomas E.	P	14	.200	Phil	
		Strang, Samuel Nicklin	SS	14	.222	A	

WON	LOST	NAME	POS.	G.	BA	FROM	TO
		Treadway, George B.	OF	2	.143	Bkn	C
		Warner, John Joseph (1B1)	C32	33	+.209	B	N.Y.
2	3	Weyhing, August (Gus)	P	6	.133	B	
		Wright, Joseph	OF	2	+.143	B	Pitt

WON 52 LOST 78 TG 130 — NATIONAL LEAGUE 1897. — FINISHED 11th. PCT. .400

LOUISVILLE

JAMES F. ROGERS FREDERICK CLIFFORD CLARKE

WON	LOST	NAME	POS.	G.	BA	FROM	TO
		Butler, Richard H.	C	10	.184	A	
3	3	Clark, Wm. H. (Dad)	P	7	+.217	xN.Y.	
		Clarke, Frederick Clifford MGR.	OF	129	.406	B	
		Clarke, Wm. Winfield	2B	4	.176	A	C
		Clingman, Wm. Frederick	3B	115	.232	B	
15	14	Cunningham, Ellsworth Elmer	P	30	.239	B	
		Delehanty, Thomas James	2B	1	.333	Pitt	
		Dexter, Chas. Dana (C24)	OF26	63	.292	B	
		Dolan, Joseph (SS18)	2B18	35	.210	B	
1	3	Dowling, Henry Peter	P	4	.200	A	
5	4	Evans, LeRoy	P	9	+.105	xStL	
15	17	Fraser, Chas. Carrolton (Chick)	P	36	.172	B	
		Hach, Irvin (Major) (3B3)	2B12	15	.163	A	C
3	5	Hemming, George Earl	P	8	.136	Balt	C
0	0	Herman, Arthur	P	3	.333	B	C
6	18	Hill, Wm. C.	P25	26	.095	B	
		Holmes, James Wm. (Ducky)	SS1	2	+.000	B	N.Y.
		Johnson, Albert J.	2B33	44	.251	B	C
0	0	Jones, James Tilford	P	2	.250	A	
4	13	Magee, Wm. M.	P17	20	.233	A	
		Martin, Frank	2B	2	.222	A	
0	0	Miller, Burt	P	4	.167	A	C
		McCreery, Thomas Leavenworth	OF	89	+.283	B	N.Y.
		Nance, Wm. G.	OF	34	.241	A	
		Pickering, Oliver Dan	OF	62	+.258	B	Clev
		Rogers, James F. MGR.	2B37	40	.148	B	C
		Schreckengost, Ossee Freeman	C	1	.000	A	
		Smith, George Henry	2B	21	.280	A	
		Stafford, James Joseph	SS	112	+.280	xN.Y.	
0	1	Waddell, George Edward (Rube)	P	2	.000	A	
		Wagner, John Peter (Hans)	OF52	61	.344	A	
		Werden, Percival Wheritt (Perry)	1B	134	.301	StL93	
		Wilson, Wm.	C105	106	.218	Pitt90	

WON 70 LOST 81 TG 151 — NATIONAL LEAGUE 1898. — FINISHED 9th. PCT. .464

LOUISVILLE

FREDERICK CLIFFORD CLARKE

WON	LOST	NAME	POS.	G.	BA	FROM	TO
3	4	Altrock, Nicholas	P	11	.280	A	
		Carey, George C.	1B	8	.187	Balt95	
0	1	Clark, Wm. H. (Dad)	P	1	.000	B	
		Clarke, Frederick Clifford MGR.	OF	147	.318	B	
		Clarke, Joshua Baldwin (Josh)	OF	6	.167	A	
		Clingman, Wm. Frederick (SS75)	3B79	154	.262	B	
28	15	Cunningham, Ellsworth Elmer	P	43	.229	B	
		Davis, Harry H. (2B1 OF1)	1B33	36	+.227	xPitt	Wash
		Decker, George A. (OF6)	1B32	42	+.315	xStL	
		Dexter, Chas. Dana	OF99	112	.311	B	
13	17	Dowling, Henry Peter	P	35	.202	B	
3	7	Ehret, Philip Sydney (Red)	P	12	.244	Cin	
7	19	Fraser, Chas. Carrolton (Chick)	P	26	+.173	B	Clev
		Hartsel, Tullos Frederick (Topsy)	OF	21	.319	A	
		Hoy, Wm. Ellsworth (Dummy)	OF	148	.318	Cin	
		Kittredge, Malachi Jedediah	C	88	.250	Chi	
		Leach, Thomas Wm.	3B	3	.300	A	
16	14	Magee, Wm. M.	P30	33	.144	B	
0	1	Mahaffy, Louis W.	P	2	.000	A	C
		Nance, Wm. G.	OF	22	.329	B	
		Powers, Michael Riley	C22	27	.298	A	
		Richter, John M.	3B	3	.154	A	
		Ritchey, Claude Cassius (2B73)	SS79	152	.259	Cin	
		Smith, George Henry	2B30	31	.207	B	
		Snyder, Frank C. (Cooney)	C	15	.169	A	C
		Stafford, James Joseph	OF	42	+.312	B	Bos
		Stouch, Thomas C.	2B	4	.377	A	C
		Taylor, Wallace Napoleon	3B	9	.200	A	C
0	3	Todd, Frank	P	3	.250	A	C
		Wagner, John Peter (Hans) (3B62)	1B76	148	.305	B	
		Wilson, Wm.	C29	30	.182	B	C

WON 75 NATIONAL LEAGUE FINISHED 9th.
LOST x77
TG 152 1899. PCT. .493

LOUISVILLE

FREDERICK CLIFFORD CLARKE

WON	LOST	NAME	POS.	G.	BA	FROM	TO
1	0	Brashear, Roy Parks	P	3	.333	A	
		Bayer, Christopher A.	SS	1	.000	A	C
		Clarke, Frederick Clifford MGR.	OF144	147	.348	B	
		Clingman, Wm. Frederick	SS	108	.267	B	
		Croft, Henry T.	OF	1	+.000	A	Phil
18	16	Cunningham, Ellsworth Elmer	P37	43	.258	B	
		Decker, George A.	1B	38	+.234	B	Wash
		Dexter, Chas. Dana	OF70	76	.262	B	
13	18	Dowling, Henry Peter	P34	35	.225	B	
1	0	Fauver, Clayton King	P	1	.000	A	
2	3	Flaherty, Patrick Joseph	P	7	.200	A	
		Hartsel, Tullos Frederick (Topsy)	OF	20	.261	B	
		Hoy, Wm. Ellsworth (Dummy)	OF	155	.306	B	
		Hulswitt, Rudolph Edward	SS	1	.000	A	
		Kelley, Michael Joseph	1B	76	.247	A	
		Ketcham, Frederick L.	OF	15	.311	A	
		Kittredge, Malachi Jedediah	C44	46	+.174	B	Wash
		Langsford, Robert Wm.	SS	1	.000	A	C
		Latimer, Clifford Wesley	C	8	.280	N.Y.	
		Leach, Thomas Wm. (SS25)	3B81	106	.289	B	
4	6	Magee, Wm. M.	P	11	+.111	B	Phil
		Messitt, Thomas John	C	2	.125	A	C
20	17	Phillippe, Chas. Louis (Deacon)	P39	42	.218	A	
		Powers, Michael Riley	C	41	+.211	B	Wash
		Ritchey, Claude Cassius	2B138	147	.309	B	
		Steelman, Morris James	C	5	.062	A	
7	2	Waddell, George Edward (Rube)	P	10	.235	Lvlle97	
		Wagner, John Peter (Hans) (OF58)	3B74	144	.359	B	
1	1	Wilhelm, Harry L.	P	4	.165	A	C
		Wills, Davis Bowles	1B	24	.255	A	C
8	13	Woods, Walter Sydney	P22	40	.174	Chi	
		Zimmer, Chas. Louis (Chief)	C	74	+.299	xClev	

x-One game lost by forfeit.

CLUB RECORD

AMERICAN LEAGUE

MILWAUKEE

YEAR	TG	WON	LOST	PCT.	FINISHED	MANAGER
1901	137	48	89	.350	8(Last)	Hugh Duffy

CLUB RECORD

OTHER MAJOR LEAGUES

MILWAUKEE

YEAR	TG	WON	LOST	PCT.	FINISHED	MANAGER
AMERICAN ASSOCIATION						
1891	36	21	15	.583	3	Chas. H. Cushman
UNION ASSOCIATION						
1884	11	8	3	.727	DID NOT FINISH	James F. McKee

MILWAUKEE

YEAR	TG	WON	LOST	PCT.	FINISHED	MANAGER
AMERICAN LEAGUE						
1900	137	79	58	.577	2	Connie Mack

CLUB RECORD

NATIONAL LEAGUE

MILWAUKEE

YEAR	TG	WON	LOST	PCT.	FINISHED	MANAGER
1878	60	15	45	.250	6(Last)	John Curtis Chapman
1953	154	92	62	.597	2	Chas. John Grimm
1954	154	89	65	.578	3	Chas. John Grimm
1955	154	85	69	.552	2	Chas. John Grimm
1956	154	92	62	.597	2	Chas. John Grimm Fred Girard Haney
1957	154	95	59	.617	1	Fred Girard Haney
1958	154	92	62	.597	1	Fred Girard Haney
1959	156	86	70	.551	2	Fred Girard Haney
1960	154	88	66	.571	2	Charles Walter Dressen
1961	154	83	71	.539	4	Chas. Walter Dressen George Robert Tebbetts
1962	162	86	76	.531	5	George Robert Tebbetts
1963	162	84	78	.519	6	Robert Randall Bragan
1964	162	88	74	.543	5	Robert Randall Bragan
1965	162	86	76	.531	5	Robert Randall Bragan

ATLANTA

CLUB TRANSFERRED FROM MILWAUKEE AFTER 1965 SEASON

YEAR	TG	WON	LOST	TIED	PCT.	FINISHED	MANAGER
1966	163	85	77	1	.525	5	ROBERT RANDALL BRAGAN WILLIAM CLYDE HITCHCOCK
1967	162	77	85	0	.475	7	WILLIAM CLYDE HITCHCOCK KENNETH JOSEPH SILVESTRI *
1968	163	81	81	1	.500	5	CHALMER LUMAN HARRIS
1969	162	93	69	0	.574	1W (LP)	CHALMER LUMAN HARRIS
1970	162	76	86	0	.469	5W	CHALMER LUMAN HARRIS
1971	162	82	80	0	.506	3W	CHALMER LUMAN HARRIS
1972	155	70	84	1	.455	4W	CHALMER LUMAN HARRIS EDWIN LEE MATHEWS

WON 15 | LOST 45 | TG 60

NATIONAL LEAGUE — 1878 — FINISHED 6th (LAST) — PCT. .250

MILWAUKEE

JOHN CURTIS CHAPMAN

WON	LOST	NAME	POS.	G.	BA	FROM	TO
		Bennett, Chas. Wesley	C30	48	.246	A	
		(OF18)					
		Bliss, F. E. (OF1)	3B1	2	.125	A	C
		Creamer, George W.	2B28	50	.212	A	
		(OF18)					
		Dalrymple, Abner Frank	OF	60	.356	A	
0	0	Ellick, Joseph J.	C2	3	.154	A	
		(P1 3B2)					
		Foley, Wm. B. (C7)	3B48	55	.271	Cin	
3	15	Golden, Michael Henry	OF35	54	.209	A	C
		(P18)					
		Goodman, Jacob	1B	59	.246	A	
		Holbert, Wm. H. (C18)	OF26	44	.184	Lvlle76	
		Jennings, Alfred	C	1	.000	A	C
		Knowdell, Jacob Augustus	C3	4	.000	A	C
		(OF1)					
		Morgan, Henry Wm.	OF11	14	.175	A	
		(2B1 3B4)					
		Peters, John Paul (SS22)	2B32	54	.311	Chi	
		Redmond, Wm. T. (OF6)	SS38	47	.229	Cin	C
12	30	Weaver, Samuel H.	P42	47	.205	A	

WON 92 | LOST 62 | TG 154

NATIONAL LEAGUE — 1953 — FINISHED 2nd. — PCT. .597

MILWAUKEE

CHAS. JOHN GRIMM

WON	LOST	NAME	POS.	G.	BA	FROM	TO
		Adcock, Joseph Wilbur	1B	157	.285	Cin	
12	12	Antonelli, John August	P	31	.177	Bos50	
2	5	Bickford, Vernon Edgell	P	20	.067	Bos	
		Bruton, Wm. Haron	OF150	151	.250	A	
13	8	Buhl, Robert Ray	P	30	.113	A	
15	5	Burdette, Selva Lewis	P	46	.170	Bos	
		Burris, Paul Robert	C	2	.000	Bos	
0	1	Cole, David Bruce	P	10	.500	Bos	
		Cooper, Wm. Walker	C35	53	.219	Bos	
		Crandall, Delmar Wesley	C108	116	.272	Bos50	
		Crowe, George Daniel	1B9	47	.286	Bos	
		Dittmer, John Douglas	2B	138	.266	Bos	
		Gordon, Sidney	OF137	140	.274	Bos	
		Hanebrink, Harry Aloysius	2B21	51	.238	A	
		(3B1)					
1	0	Jay, Joseph Richard	P	3	.000	A	
0	0	Jester, Virgil Milton	P	2	.000	Bos	
4	3	Johnson, Ernest Thorwald	P	36	.071	Bos	
0	1	Jolly, David	P	24	.500	A	
		Klaus, Wm. Joseph		2	.000	Bos	
7	6	Liddle, Donald Eugene	P	31	.088	A	
		Logan, John	SS	150	.273	Bos	
		Mathews, Edwin Lee	3B	157	.302	Bos	
		Pafko, Andrew	OF139	140	.297	Bkn	
		Pendleton, James Edward	OF105	120	.299	A	
		(SS7)					
		Roach, Melvin Earl	2B1	5	.000	A	
		Sisti, Sebastian Daniel	2B13	38	.217	Bos	
		(SS6 3B4)					
23	7	Spahn, Warren Edward	P35	38	.219	Bos	
		St.Claire, Edward Joseph	C27	33	.200	Bos	
11	5	Surkont, Maxim Constantine	P	28	.286	Bos	
		Thorpe, Benjamin Robert	OF18	27	.162	Bos	
4	9	Wilson, James Alger	P	20	.167	Bos	

WON 89 | LOST 65 | TG 154

NATIONAL LEAGUE — 1954. — FINISHED 3rd. — PCT. .578

MILWAUKEE

CHAS. JOHN GRIMM

WON	LOST	NAME	POS.	G.	BA	FROM	TO
		Aaron, Henry Louis	OF116	122	.280	A	
		Adcock, Joseph Wilbur	1B	133	.308	B	
		Bruton, Wm. Haron	OF141	142	.284	B	
2	7	Buhl, Robert Ray	P	31	.032	B	
15	14	Burdette, Selva Lewis	P38	39	.089	B	
		Calderone, Samuel Francis	C16	22	.379	N.Y.	
14	9	Conley, Donald Eugene	P	28	.156	Bos52	
		Crandall, Delmar Wesley	C136	138	.242	B	
1	0	Crone, Raymond Hayes	P	19	.200	A	
		Dittmer, John Douglas	2B55	66	.245	B	
0	1	Gorin, Chas. Perry	P	5	.000	A	
1	0	Jay, Joseph Richard	P	15	.000	B	
5	2	Johnson, Ernest Thorwald	P	40	.231	B	
11	6	Jolly, David	P47	48	.290	B	
1	1	Koslo, George Bernard	P	12	.000	xBaltA	
		Logan, John	SS	154	.275	B	
		Mathews, Edwin Lee	3B127	138	.290	B	
		(OF10)					
		Metkovich, George Michael	1B18	68	.276	Chi	
		(OF13)					
9	11	Nichols, Chester Raymond Jr.	P	35	.086	Bos51	
		O'Connell, Daniel Francis	2B103	146	.279	Pitt	
		(1B8 SS1 3B35)					
		Pafko, Andrew	OF	138	.286	B	
1	0	Paine, Phillips Steere	P	11	.000	Bos51	
		Pendleton, James Edward	OF50	71	.220	B	
		Queen, Wm. Eddleman	OF1	3	.000	A	
		Roach, Melvin Earl	1B1	3	.000	B	

		Sisti, Sebastian Daniel		9	.000	B	
		Smalley, Roy Frederick	SS9	25	.222	Chi	
		(1B2 2B7)					
21	12	Spahn, Warren Edward	P39	41	.208	B	
		Thomson, Robert Brown	OF26	43	.232	N.Y.	
		White, Chas.	C28	50	.237	A	
8	2	Wilson, James Alger	P	27	.159	B	

WON 85 | NATIONAL LEAGUE | FINISHED 2nd.
LOST 69
TG 154 | 1955. | PCT. .552

MILWAUKEE

CHAS. JOHN GRIMM

WON	LOST	NAME	POS.	G.	BA	FROM	TO
		Aaron, Henry Louis	OF126	153	.314	B	
		(2B27)					
		Adcock, Joseph Wilbur	1B78	84	.264	B	
		Bruton, Wm. Haron	OF	149	.275	B	
13	11	Buhl, Robert Ray	P	38	.105	B	
13	8	Burdette, Selva Lewis	P42	45	.233	B	
11	7	Conley, Donald Eugene	P	22	.204	B	
		Crandall, Delmar Wesley	C131	133	.236	B	
10	9	Crone, Raymond Hayes	P	33	.159	B	
		Crowe, George Daniel	1B79	104	.281	Mi153	
		Dittmer, John Douglas	2B28	38	.125	B	
0	0	Edelman, John Rogers	P	5	.000	A	
0	0	Gorin, Chas. Perry	P	2	.000	B	
0	0	Jay, Joseph Richard	P	12	.667	B	
5	7	Johnson, Ernest Thorwald	P	40	.100	B	
2	3	Jolly, David	P	36	.167	B	
0	1	Koslo, George Bernard	P	1	.000	B	
		Logan, John	SS	154	.297	B	
		Mathews, Edwin Lee	3B137	141	.289	B	
9	8	Nichols, Chester Raymond Jr.	P	34	.154	B	
		O'Connell, Daniel Francis	2B114	124	.225	B	
		(SS1 3B7)					
		Pafko, Andrew (3B12)	OF58	86	.266	B	
2	0	Paine, Phillips Steere	P	15	.333	B	
		Pendleton, James Edward	OF1	8	.000	B	
		(SS1 3B1)					
		Rice, Delbert W.	C22	27	+.197	xStL	
3	1	Robinson, Humberto Valentino	P	13	.077	A	
		Roselli, Robert Edward	C2	6	.222	A	
17	14	Spahn, Warren Edward	P39	40	.210	B	
		Tanner, Chas. Wm.	OF62	97	.247	A	
		Taylor, Eugene Benjamin	1B1	12	.100	DetA52	
		Thomson, Robert Brown	OF91	101	.257	B	
0	0	Vargas, Roberto Enrique	P	25	.500	A	
		White, Chas.	C10	12	.233	B	

WON 92 | NATIONAL LEAGUE | FINISHED 2nd.
LOST 62
TG 154 | 1956 | PCT. .597

MILWAUKEE

CHAS. JOHN GRIMM   FRED GIRARD HANEY

WON	LOST	NAME	POS.	G.	BA	FROM	TO
		Aaron, Henry Louis	OF152	152	.328	B	
		Adcock, Joseph Wilbur	1B129	137	.291	B	
		Atwell, Maurice Dailey	C10	15	+.167	xPitt	
		Bruton, Wm. Haron	OF145	147	.272	B	
18	8	Buhl, Robert Ray	P	38	.096	B	
19	10	Burdette, Selva Lewis	P39	45	.186	B	
8	9	Conley, Donald Eugene	P	31	.156	B	
		Covington, John Wesley	OF35	75	.283	A	
		Crandall, Delmar Wesley	C109	112	.238	B	
11	10	Crone, Raymond Hayes	P	35	.122	B	
		Dittmer, John Douglas	2B42	44	.245	B	
		Hersh, Earl Walter	OF2	7	.231	A	
4	3	Johnson, Ernest Thorwald	P	36	.250	B	
2	3	Jolly, David	P	29	.000	B	
		Logan, John	SS	148	.281	B	
		Mantilla, Felix LaMela	SS15	35	.283	A	
		(3B3)					
		Mathews, Edwin Lee	3B150	151	.272	B	
0	0	Murff, John Robert	P	14	.200	A	
0	1	Nichols, Chester Raymond Jr.	P	2	.000	B	
		O'Connell, Daniel Francis	2B138	139	.239	B	
		(SS1 3B4)					
		Pafko, Andrew	OF37	45	.258	B	
0	0	Paine, Phillips Steere	P	1	.000	B	
		Pendleton, James Edward	SS3	14	.000	B	
		(1B1 2B1 3B2)					
5	3	Phillips, Wm. Taylor	P	23	.000	A	
		Rice, Delbert W.	C65	71	.213	B	
0	0	Robinson, Humberto Valentino	P	1	.000	B	
		Roselli, Robert Edward	C3	4	.500	B	
2	2	Sleater, Louis Mortimer	P	25	.500	KCA	
20	11	Spahn, Warren Edward	P	39	.210	B	
		Tanner, Chas. Wm.	OF8	60	.238	B	
		Thomson, Robert Brown	OF136	142	.235	B	
		(3B3)					
		Torre, Frank Joseph	1B89	111	.258	A	
3	2	Trowbridge, Robert	P	19	.000	A	

WON 95 | NATIONAL LEAGUE | FINISHED 1st.
LOST 59
TG 154 | 1957. | PCT. .617

MILWAUKEE

FRED GIRARD HANEY

WON	LOST	NAME	POS.	G.	BA	FROM	TO

WON	LOST	NAME	POS.	G.	BA	FROM	TO
		Aaron, Henry Louis	OF150	151	.322	B	
		Adcock, Joseph Wilbur	1B56	65	.287	B	
		Bruton, Wm. Haron	OF	79	.278	B	
18	7	Buhl, Robert Ray	P	34	.082	B	
17	9	Burdette, Selva Lewis	P37	41	.148	B	
		Cole, Richard Roy (1B1 3B1)	2B10	15	.071	Pitt	
9	9	Conley, Donald Eugene	P	35	.196	B	
		Covington, John Wesley	OF89	96	.284	B	
		Crandall, Delmar Wesley (1B1 OF9)	C102	118	.253	B	
3	1	Crone, Raymond Hayes	P	11	+.182	B	N.Y.
		DeMerit, John Stephen	OF13	33	.147	A	
		Hanebrink, Harry Aloysius	3B2	6	.286	Mil53	
		Hazle, Robert Sidney	OF40	41	.403	Cin55	
0	0	Jay, Joseph Richard	P	1	.000	Mil55	
7	3	Johnson, Ernest Thorwald	P	30	.353	B	
1	1	Jolly, David	P	23	.600	B	
		Jones, Vernal LeRoy (OF1)	1B20	30	.266	Phil52	
		Logan, John	SS	129	.273	B	
		Malkmus, Robert Edward	2B7	13	.091	A	
		Mantilla, Felix LaMela (2B13 3B7 OF1)	SS35	71	.236	B	
		Mathews, Edwin Lee	3B147	148	.292	B	
2	3	McMahon, Donald John	P	32	.250	A	
2	2	Murff, John Robert	P	12	.000	B	
		O' Connell, Daniel Francis	2B	48	+.235	B	N.Y.
		Pafko, Andrew	OF69	83	.277	B	
0	0	Paine, Phillips Steere	P	1	.000	B	
3	2	Phillips, Wm. Taylor	P	27	.100	B	
5	6	Pizarro, Juan Cordova	P24	25	.250	A	
		Rice, Delbert W.	C48	54	.229	B	
		Roach, Melvin Earl	2B5	7	.167	Mil54	
		Sawatski, Carl Ernest	C28	58	.238	ChiA54	
		Schoendienst, Albert Fred (OF2)	2B92	93	+.310	xN.Y.	
		Shearer, Ray Solomon	OF1	2	.500	A	
21	11	Spahn, Warren Edward	P	39	.138	B	
		Tanner, Chas. Wm.	OF18	22	+.246	B	Chi
		Taylor, Robert Dale	C1	7	.000	A	
		Thomson, Robert Brown	OF38	41	+.236	B	N.Y.
		Torre, Frank Joseph	1B117	129	.272	B	
7	5	Trowbridge, Robert	P	32	.103	B	

WON 92 NATIONAL LEAGUE FINISHED 1st.
LOST 62
TG 154 1958. PCT. .597

MILWAUKEE

FRED GIRARD HANEY

WON	LOST	NAME	POS.	G.	BA	FROM	TO
		Aaron, Henry Louis	OF	153	.326	B	
		Adcock, Joseph Wilbur (OF22)	1B71	105	.275	B	
5	2	Buhl, Robert Ray	P	11	.200	B	
		Bruton, Wm. Haron	OF96	100	.280	B	
20	10	Burdette, Selva Lewis	P40	47	.242	B	
0	6	Conley, Donald Eugene	P	26	.188	B	
		Covington, John Wesley	OF82	90	.330	B	
		Crandall, Delmar Wesley	C124	131	.272	B	
		DeMerit, John Stephen	OF2	3	.667	B	
		Haas, George Edwin	OF3	9	.357	Chic	
		Hanebrink, Harry Aloysius (3B7)	OF33	63	.188	B	
		Hazle, Robert Sidney	OF	20	.179	B	DetA
7	5	Jay, Joseph Richard	P	18	.094	B	
3	1	Johnson, Ernest Thorwald	P	15	.000	B	
		Koppe, Joseph	SS3	16	.444	A	
0	1	Littlefield, Richard Bernard	P	4	.000	Chic	C
		Logan, John	SS144	145	.226	B	
		Mantilla, Felix Lamela (2B21 SS5 3B2)	OF43	85	.221	B	
		Mathews, Edwin Lee	3B	149	.251	B	
7	2	McMahon, Donald John	P	38	.111	B	
		Pafko, Andrew	OF93	95	.238	B	
6	4	Pizarro, Juan Cordova	P	16	.250	B	
		Rice, Robert W.	C38	43	.223	B	
		Roach, Melvin Earl (1B1 OF7)	2B27	44	.309	B	
2	4	Robinson, Humberto Valentino	P	19	.167	Mil56	
		Roselli, Robert Edward		1	.000	Mil56	
10	6	Rush, Robert Ransom	P	28	.200	Chic	
		Sawatski, Carl Ernest	C3	10	+.100	B	Phil
		Schoendienst, Albert Fred	2B105	106	.262	B	
22	11	Spahn, Warren Edward	P38	41	.333	B	
		Taylor, Robert Dale	OF	4	.125	B	
		Torre, Frank Joseph	1B122	138	.309	B	
1	3	Trowbridge, Robert	P	27	.111	B	
9	7	Willey, Carlton Francis	P	23	.104	A	
		Wise, Kendall Cole (SS7 3B1)	2B10	31	.197	Chic	

WON 86 NATIONAL LEAGUE FINISHED 2nd.
LOST 70
TG 156 1959. PCT. .551

MILWAUKEE

FRED GIRARD HANEY

WON	LOST	NAME	POS.	G.	BA	FROM	TO
		Aaron, Henry Louis (3B5)	OF152	154	.355	B	
		Adcock, Joseph Wilbur (OF21)	1B89	115	.292	B	
		Avila, Roberto Francisco Gonzalez	2B	51	.238	xBosA	C
		Boone, Raymond Otis	1B3	13	.200	xKCA	

WON	LOST	NAME	POS.	G.	BA	FROM	TO
		Bruton, Wm. Haron	OF	133	.289	B	
15	9	Buhl, Robert Ray	P	31	.057	B	
21	15	Burdette, Selva Lewis	P41	52	.202	B	
		Cottier, Chas. Keith	2B	10	.125	A	
		Covington, John Wesley	OF94	103	.279	B	
		Crandall, Delmar Wesley	C146	150	.257	B	
		DeMerit, John Stephen	OF4	11	.200	B	
1	0	Giggie, Robert Thomas	P	13	.000	A	
0	0	Hartman, Robert Louis	P	3	.000	A	
6	11	Jay, Joseph Richard	P	34	.086	B	
		Logan, John	SS	138	.291	B	
		Lopata, Stanley Edward (1B2)	C11	25	.104	Phil	
		Mantilla, Felix Lamela (SS23 3B9 OF7)	2B60	103	.215	B	
		Mathews, Edwin Lee	3B	148	.306	B	
		Maye, Arthur Lee	OF44	51	.300	A	
5	3	McMahon, Donald John	P	60	.222	B	
		Morgan, Joseph Michael	2B7	13	.217	A	K.C.A
		O'Brien, John Thomas	2B37	44	.198	StL	C
		Pafko, Andrew	OF64	71	.218	B	C
		Pisoni, James Pete	OF	9	.167	KCA57	NYA
6	2	Pizarro, Juan Cordova	P	29	.122	B	
		Rice, Delbert W.	C9	13	.207	B	
		Roach, Melvin Earl (3B1 OF4)	2B8	19	.097	B	
5	6	Rush, Robert Ransom	P	31	.188	B	
		Schoendienst, Albert Fred	2B4	5	.000	B	
		Slaughter, Enos Bradsher	OF5	11	.167	xNYA	C
21	15	Spahn, Warren Edward	P	40	.231	B	
		Spangler, Albert Donald	OF4	6	.417	A	
		Torre, Frank Joseph	1B87	115	.228	B	
1	0	Trowbridge, Robert	P	16	.000	B	
		Vernon, James Barton (OF4)	1B10	74	.220	ClevA	
5	9	Willey, Carlton Francis	P	26	.103	B	
		Wise, Kendall Cole (SS5)	2B20	22	.171	B	

WON 88
LOST 66
TG 154

NATIONAL LEAGUE — FINISHED 2nd.

1960. — PCT. .571

MILWAUKEE

CHAS. WALTER DRESSEN

WON	LOST	NAME	POS.	G.	BA	FROM	TO
		Aaron, Henry Louis (2B2)	OF153	153	.292	B	
		Adcock, Joseph Wilbur	1B136	138	.298	B	
		Boone, Raymond Otis	1B4	7	.250	B	BosA
2	0	Brunet, George Stuart	P	17	.091	xKCA	
		Bruton, Wm. Haron	OF149	151	.286	B	
16	9	Buhl, Robert Ray	P	36	.157	B	
19	13	Burdette, Selva Lewis	P45	46	.176	B	
		Cottier, Chas. Keith	2B92	95	.227	B	
		Covington, John Wesley	OF72	95	.249	B	

WON	LOST	NAME	POS.	G.	BA	FROM	TO
		Crandall, Delmar Wesley	C141	142	.294	B	
		Dark, Alvin Ralph (1B10 2B3 3B4)	OF25	50	+.298	xPhil	
0	0	Fox, Terrence Edward	P	5	.000	A	
		Gabrielson, Leonard Gary	OF1	4	.000	A	
0	0	Giggie, Robert Thomas	P	3	.000	B	K.C.A
		Haas, George Edwin	OF2	32	.219	Mil58	C
9	8	Jay, Joseph Richard	P	32	.156	B	
		Krsnich, Michael	OF3	4	.333	A	
		Lau, Chas. Richard	C16	21	.189	DetA	
		Logan, John	SS	136	.245	B	
		Lopata, Stanley Edward	C4	7	.125	B	C
0	1	MacKenzie, Kenneth Purvis	P	9	.000	A	
		Mantilla, Felix Lamela (SS25 OF8)	2B26	63	.257	B	
		Mathews, Edwin Lee	3B	153	.277	B	
		Maye, Arthur Lee	OF19	41	.301	B	
3	6	McMahon, Donald John	P	48	.000	B	
1	0	Nottebart, Donald Edward	P	5	.000	A	
3	5	Piche, Ronald Jacques	P	37	.000	A	
6	7	Pizarro, Juan Cordova	P21	23	.275	B	
		Roach, Melvin Earl (1B1 2B20 3B1)	OF21	48	.300	B	
2	0	Rush, Robert Ransom	P	10	.333	B	ChiA
		Schoendienst, Albert Fred	2B62	68	.257	B	
21	10	Spahn, Warren Edward	P	40	.147	B	
		Spangler, Albert Donald	OF92	101	.267	B	
		Torre, Frank Joseph	1B17	21	.205	B	
		Torre, Joseph Paul		2	.500	A	
6	7	Willey, Carlton Francis	P	28	.146	B	

WON 83
LOST 71
TG 154

NATIONAL LEAGUE — FINISHED 4th.

1961. — PCT. .539

MILWAUKEE

CHAS. WALTER DRESSEN GEORGE ROBERT TEBBETTS

WON	LOST	NAME	POS.	G.	BA	FROM	TO
		Aaron, Henry Louis (3B2)	OF154	155	.327	B	
		Adcock, Joseph Wilbur	1B148	152	.285	B	
1	0	Antonelli, John August	P	9	.000	xClevA	C
		Bolling, Frank Elmore	2B	148	.262	DetA	
		Boyd, Robert Richard	1B3	36	.244	xK.C.A	C
0	0	Brunet, George Stuart	P	5	.000	B	
9	10	Buhl, Robert Ray	P	32	.067	B	
18	11	Burdette, Selva Lewis	P40	42	.204	B	
		Chrisley, Barbra O'Neil		10	.222	DetA	C
		Cimoli, Gino Nicholas	OF31	37	+.197	xPitt	
7	2	Cloninger, Tony Lee	P	19	.167	A	
		Covington, John Wesley	OF5	9	.190	B	ChiA
		Crandall, Delmar Wesley	C5	15	.200	B	
		DeMerit, John Stephen	OF21	32	.162	Mil 59	
0	2	Drabowsky, Myron Walter	P	16	.250	Chi	
5	7	Hendley, Chas. Robert	P	19	.032	A	

WON	LOST	NAME	POS.	G.	BA	FROM	TO
		Jones, Mack	OF26	28	.231	A	
		Lau, Chas. Richard	C25	28	.207	B	BaltA
		Logan, John	SS2	18	+.105	B	Pitt
0	1	MacKenzie, Kenneth Purvis	P	5	.000	B	
		Mantilla, Felix Lamela (2B10 3B6 OF10)	SS19	45	.215	B	
		Martin, Alfred Manuel		6	.000	Cin	MinnA
		Mathews, Edwin Lee	3B151	152	.306	B	
		Maye, Arthur Lee	OF96	110	.271	B	
6	4	McMahon, Donald John	P	53	.188	B	
		McMillan, Roy David	SS	154	.220	Cin	
1	0	Morehead, Seth Marvin	P	12	.000	Chi	C
6	7	Nottebart, Donald Edward	P	38	.184	B	
0	0	Olivo, Frederico Emilio	P	3	.000	A	C
2	2	Piche, Ronald Jacques	P	12	.000	B	
1	0	Raymond, Joseph Claude Marc	P	13	.000	ChiA59	
		Roach, Melvin Earl (1B2)	OF9	13	+.167	B	Chi
		Roof, Phillip Anthony	C	1	.000	A	C
21	13	Spahn, Warren Edward	P38	39	.223	B	
		Spangler, Albert Donald	OF44	68	.268	B	
		Taylor, Robert Dale (C1)	OF5	20	.192	Mil 58	
		Thomas, Frank Joseph (1B11)	OF109	124	+.284	xChi	
		Torre, Joseph Paul	C112	113	.278	B	
		White, Samuel Chas.	C20	21	.222	BosA59	
6	12	Willey, Carlton Francis	P	35	.019	B	

WON 86 — NATIONAL LEAGUE — FINISHED 5th.
LOST 76
TG 162 — 1962. — PCT. .531

MILWAUKEE

GEORGE ROBERT TEBBETTS

WON	LOST	NAME	POS.	G.	BA	FROM	TO
		Aaron, Henry Louis (1B1)	OF153	156	.323	B	
		Aaron, Tommie Lee (2B1 3B1 OF42)	1B110	141	.231	A	
		Adcock, Joseph Wilbur	1B112	121	.248	B	
		Aspromonte, Kenneth Joseph	2B12	34	.291	xClevA	
		Bedell, Howard Wm.	OF45	58	.196	A	
		Bell, David Russell	OF58	79	+.285	xN.Y.	
		Blackaby, Ethan Allan	OF3	6	.154	A	C
		Bolling, Frank Elmore	2B119	122	.271	B	
0	1	Buhl, Robert Ray	P	1	+.000	B	Chi
10	9	Burdette, Selva Lewis	P37	39	.176	B	
2	0	Butler, Cecil Dean	P	9	.000	A	C
8	3	Cloninger, Tony Lee	P	24	.103	B	
1	1	Constable, James Lee	P	3	.000	WashA58	
		Crandall, Delmar Wesley (1B5)	C90	107	.297	B	
4	4	Curtis, Jack Patrick	P	30	+.222	xChi	
2	3	Fischer, Henry Wm.	P	29	.000	A	
11	13	Hendley, Chas. Robert	P35	36	.119	B	
		Johnson, Louis Brown	OF55	61	.282	LAA	
		Jones, Mack	OF	91	.255	B	
		Klimchock, Louis Stephen		8	.000	KCA	
		Krsnich, Michael (1B1 3B1)	OF3	11	.083	Mil60	C
3	4	Lemaster, Denver Clayton	P	17	.121	A	
		Mathews, Edwin Lee (1B7)	3B140	152	.265	B	
		Maye, Arthur Lee	OF94	99	.244	B	
0	1	McMahon, Donald John	P	2	+.000	B	Hous
		McMillan, Roy David	SS135	137	.246	B	
		Menke, Denis John (1B2 SS9 3B15 OF1)	2B20	50	.192	A	
2	2	Nottebart, Donald Edward	P	39	.333	B	
3	2	Piche, Ronald Jacques	P14	16	.056	B	
5	5	Raymond, Joseph Claude Marc	P	26	.000	B	
		Samuel, Amado Ruperto (2B28)	SS36	76	.206	A	
15	9	Shaw, Robert John	P	38	.137	KCA	
18	14	Spahn, Warren Edward	P34	36	.184	B	
		Taylor, Robert Dale	OF11	20	.255	B	
		Torre, Joseph Paul	C63	80	.282	B	
		Uecker, Robert George	C24	33	.250	A	
2	5	Willey, Carlton, Francis	P	30	.273	B	

WON 84 — NATIONAL LEAGUE — FINISHED 6th.
LOST 78
TG 162 — 1963. — PCT. .519

MILWAUKEE

ROBERT RANDALL BRAGAN

WON	LOST	NAME	POS.	G.	BA	FROM	TO
		Aaron, Henry Louis	OF	161	.319	B	
		Aaron, Tommie Lee (2B6 3B1 OF14)	1B45	72	.200	B	
		Bell, David Russell		3	.333	B	
0	0	Blasingame, Wade Allen	P	2	.000	A	
		Bolling, Frank Elmore	2B141	142	.244	B	
6	5	Burdette, Selva Lewis	P15	17	.038	B	
		Carty, Ricardo Adolfo, Jacobo		2	.000	A	
		Cline, Tyrone Alexander	OF62	72	.236	ClevA	
9	11	Cloninger, Tony Lee	P	41	.135	B	
		Crandall, Delmar Wesley (1B7)	C75	86	.201	B	
		Dillard, David Donald	OF30	67	.235	ClevA	
4	3	Fischer, Henry Wm.	P	31	.105	B	
3	3	Funk, Franklin Ray	P25	26	.000	ClevA	C
		Gabrielson, Leonard Gary (1B16 3B3)	OF22	46	.217	Milw60	
9	9	Hendley, Chas. Robert	P41	46	.106	B	
		Jones, Mack	OF80	93	.219	B	
		Klimchock, Louis Stephen	1B12	24	.196	xWashA	
		Larker, Norman Howard	1B42	64	+.177	Hous	S.F.
11	14	Lemaster, Denver Clayton	P	46	.189	B	

WON	LOST	NAME	POS.	G.	BA	FROM	TO
		Mathews, Edwin Lee (OF42)	3B121	158	.263	B	
		Maye, Arthur Lee	OF111	124	.271	B	
		McMillan, Roy David	SS94	100	.250	B	
		Menke, Denis John (1B1 2B22 3B51 OF1)	SS82	146	.234	B	
		Morton, Wycliffe Nathaniel	OF9	15	.179	xDetA	
		Oliver, Eugene George (C2 OF35)	1B55	95	+.250	xStL	
1	1	Piche, Ronald Jacques	P	37	.000	B	
4	6	Raymond, Joseph Claude Marc	P	45	.500	B	
5	7	Sadowski, Robert Francis	P	19	.057	A	
		Samuel, Amado Ruperto (2B4)	SS7	15	.176	B	
1	0	Schneider, Daniel Louis	P	30	.000	A	
7	11	Shaw, Robert John	P	48	.122	B	
23	7	Spahn, Warren Edward	P	33	.178	B	
		Taylor, Robert Dale	OF8	16	.069	B	
1	1	Tiefenauer, Bobby Gene	P	12	.000	Hous	
.		Torre, Joseph Paul (1B37 OF2)	C105	142	.293	B	
		Uecker, Robert George	C6	13	.250	B	
		Woodward, Wm. Frederick	SS5	10	.000	A	

WON 88 NATIONAL LEAGUE FINISHED 5th.
LOST 74
TG 162 1964. PCT. .543

MILWAUKEE

ROBERT RANDALL BRAGAN

WON	LOST	NAME	POS.	G.	BA	FROM	TO
		Aaron, Henry Louis (2B11)	OF139	145	.328	B	
		Alomar, Santos Conde	SS	19	.245	A	
		Alou, Felipe Rojas (1B18)	OF92	121	.245	S.F.	
		Bailey, Lonas Edgar	C80	95	.262	S.F.	
		Bell, David Russell		3	.000	B	C
		Blackaby, Ethan Allan	OF5	9	.083	Mil 62	C
9	5	Blasingame, Wade Allen	P28	29	.175	B	
		Bolling, Frank Elmore	2B117	120	.199	B	
0	0	Braun, John Paul	P	1	.000	A	C
0	0	Butler, Cecil Dean	P	2	.000	Mil62	C
2	0	Carroll, Clay Palmer	P	11	.000	A	
		Carty, Ricardo Adolfo Jacobo	OF121	133	.330	B	
19	14	Cloninger, Tony Lee	P	38	.241	B	
		Cline, Tyrone Alexander (1B6)	OF54	101	.302	B	
		de la Hoz, Miguel Angel (SS8 3B25)	2B25	78	.291	ClevA	
0	0	Eilers, David Louis	P	6	.000	A	
11	10	Fischer, Henry Wm.	P37	38	.154	B	
		Gabrielson, Leonard Gary (OF2)	1B12	24	.184	B	
4	0	Hoeft, Wm. Frederick	P	42	.222	S. F.	
0	0	Kelley, Richard Anthony	P	2	.000	A	
		Klimchock, Louis Stephen (2B2)	3B4	10	.333	B	
		Kolb, Gary Alan (C2 2B6 3B7)	OF14	36	.188	StL	
1	0	Lary, Frank Strong	P	5	+.000	xN.Y.	
17	11	Lemaster, Denver Clayton	P	39	.134	B	
		Mathews, Edwin Lee (1B7)	3B128	141	.233	B	
		Maye, Arthur Lee (3B5)	OF135	153	.304	B	
		McMillan, Roy David	SS	8	.308	B	
		Menke, Denis John (2B15 3B6)	SS141	151	.283	B	
0	0	Niekro, Philip Henry	P	10	.000	A	
		Oliver, Eugene George (C1)	1B76	93	.276	B	
2	1	Olivo, Frederico Emilio	P	38	.250	Mil 61	
		Ranew, Merritt Thomas	C3	9	+.118	xChic	
		Roof, Phillip Anthony	C	1	.000	Milw61	
9	10	Sadowski, Robert Francis	P	51	.154	B	
1	2	Schneider, Daniel Louis	P13	14	.000	B	
2	2	Smith, Jack Hatfield	P	22	.333	L.A.	C
		Southworth, Wm. Frederick	3B2	3	.286	A	C
6	13	Spahn, Warren Edward	P38	39	.186	B	
4	6	Tiefenauer, Bobby Gene	P	46	.000	B	
		Torre, Joseph Paul (1B70)	C96	154	.321	B	
1	0	Umbach, Arnold Wm.	P	1	.000	A	
		Woodward, Wm. Frederick (1B1 SS18 3B7)	2B40	77	.209	B	

CLUB RECORD

NATIONAL LEAGUE

NEW YORK

YEAR	TG	WON	LOST	PCT.	FINISHED	MANAGER
1883	96	46	50	.479	6	John Edgar Clapp
1884	112	62	50	.554	x4(Chi)	James L. Price
1885	112	85	27	.758	2	James J. Mutrie
1886	119	75	44	.630	3	James J. Mutrie
1887	123	68	55	.553	4	James J. Mutrie
1888	131	84	47	.641	1	James J. Mutrie
1889	126	83	43	.659	1	James J. Mutrie
1890	131	63	68	.481	6	James J. Mutrie
1891	132	71	61	.538	3	James J. Mutrie
1892	151	71	80	.470	8	Patrick Thomas Powers
1893	132	68	64	.515	5	John Montgomery Ward
1894	132	88	44	.667	2	John Montgomery Ward
1895	131	66	65	.504	9	George Stacey Davis John Joseph Doyle Harvey L. Watkins
1896	131	64	67	.489	7	Arthur Albert Irwin Wm. Michael Joyce
1897	131	83	48	.634	3	Wm. Michael Joyce
1898	150	77	73	.513	7	Wm. Michael Joyce Adrian Constantine Anson
1899	146	60	86	.411	10	John B. Day Frederick C. Hoey
1900	138	60	78	.435	8(Last)	Wm. Ewing George Stacey Davis
1901	137	52	85	.380	7	George Stacey Davis
1902	136	48	88	.353	8(Last)	Horace S. Fogel George Henry Smith John Joseph McGraw
1903	139	84	55	.604	2	John Joseph McGraw
1904	153	106	47	.693	1	John Joseph McGraw
1905	153	105	48	.686	1	John Joseph McGraw
1906	152	96	56	.632	2	John Joseph McGraw
1907	153	82	71	.536	4	John Joseph McGraw
1908	154	98	56	.636	x2(Pitt)	John Joseph McGraw
1909	153	92	61	.601	3	John Joseph McGraw
1910	154	91	63	.591	2	John Joseph McGraw
1911	153	99	54	.647	1	John Joseph McGraw
1912	151	103	48	.682	1	John Joseph McGraw
1913	152	101	51	.664	1	John Joseph McGraw
1914	154	84	70	.545	2	John Joseph McGraw
1915	152	69	83	.454	8(Last)	John Joseph McGraw
1916	152	86	66	.566	4	John Joseph McGraw
1917	154	98	56	.636	1	John Joseph McGraw
1918	124	71	53	.573	2	John Joseph McGraw
1919	140	87	53	.621	2	John Joseph McGraw
1920	154	86	68	.558	2	John Joseph McGraw
1921	153	94	59	.614	1	John Joseph McGraw
1922	154	93	61	.604	1	John Joseph McGraw
1923	153	95	58	.621	1	John Joseph McGraw
1924	153	93	60	.608	1	John Joseph McGraw
1925	152	86	66	.566	2	John Joseph McGraw
1926	151	74	77	.490	5	John Joseph McGraw
1927	154	92	62	.597	3	John Joseph McGraw
1928	154	93	61	.604	2	John Joseph McGraw
1929	151	84	67	.556	3	John Joseph McGraw
1930	154	87	67	.565	3	John Joseph McGraw
1931	152	87	65	.572	2	John Joseph McGraw
1932	154	72	82	.468	x6(StL)	John Joseph McGraw Wm. Harold Terry
1933	152	91	61	.599	1	Wm. Harold Terry
1934	153	93	60	.608	2	Wm. Harold Terry
1935	153	91	62	.595	3	Wm. Harold Terry
1936	154	92	62	.597	1	Wm. Harold Terry
1937	152	95	57	.625	1	Wm. Harold Terry
1938	150	83	67	.553	3	Wm. Harold Terry
1939	151	77	74	.510	5	Wm. Harold Terry
1940	152	72	80	.474	6	Wm. Harold Terry
1941	153	74	79	.484	5	Wm. Harold Terry
1942	152	85	67	.559	3	Melvin Thomas Ott
1943	153	55	98	.359	8(Last)	Melvin Thomas Ott
1944	154	67	87	.435	5	Melvin Thomas Ott
1945	152	78	74	.513	5	Melvin Thomas Ott
1946	154	61	93	.396	8(Last)	Melvin Thomas Ott
1947	154	81	73	.526	4	Melvin Thomas Ott
1948	154	78	76	.506	5	Melvin Thomas Ott Leo Ernest Durocher
1949	154	73	81	.474	5	Leo Ernest Durocher
1950	154	86	68	.558	3	Leo Ernest Durocher
1951	157	98	59	.624	1	Leo Ernest Durocher
1952	154	92	62	.597	2	Leo Ernest Durocher
1953	154	70	84	.455	5	Leo Ernest Durocher
1954	154	97	57	.630	1	Leo Ernest Durocher
1955	154	80	74	.519	3	Leo Ernest Durocher
1956	154	67	87	.435	6	Wm. Joseph Rigney
1957	154	69	85	.448	6	Wm. Joseph Rigney
1962	160	40	120	.250	10(Last)	Chas. Dillon Stengel
1963	162	51	111	.315	10(Last)	Chas. Dillon Stengel
1964	162	53	109	.327	10(Last)	Chas. Dillon Stengel

YEAR	TG	WON	LOST	TIED	PCT.	FINISHED	MANAGER
1965	164	50	112	2	.309	10 (LAST)	CHARLES DILLON STENGEL WESLEY NOREEN WESTRUM
1966	161	66	95	0	.410	9	WESLEY NOREEN WESTRUM
1967	162	61	101	0	.377	10 (LAST)	WESLEY NOREEN WESTRUM FRANCIS JAMES PARKER *
1968	163	73	89	1	.451	9	GILBERT RAYMOND HODGES
1969	162	100	62	0	.617	1E (WP)	GILBERT RAYMOND HODGES
1970	162	83	79	0	.512	3E	GILBERT RAYMOND HODGES
1971	162	83	79	0	.512	X3E (CHI)	GILBERT RAYMOND HODGES
1972	156	83	73	0	.532	3E	LAWRENCE PETER BERRA

WON 21 | LOST 35 | TG 56

NATIONAL LEAGUE

1876.

FINISHED 6th.

PCT. .375

MUTUALS

WM. HENRY CAMMEYER

WON	LOST	NAME	POS.	G.	BA	FROM	TO
		Bechtel, George A.	OF	2	+.273	xLvlle	C
		Booth, Edgar H.	OF53	57	.213	A	C
		Craver, Wm. H. (C11)	2B41	56	.222	A	
		Hallinan, James H.	SS50	54	.277	A	
		Hatfield, John Van Buren	2B	1	.250	A	C
		Hayes, Michael	OF	5	.182	A	C
		Heuble, George A.	1B	1	.000	A	C
		Hicks, Nathan Woodhull (Nat)	C	45	.230	A	
		Holdsworth, James	OF49	52	.264	A	
0	1	Larkin, Frank	P	1	.000	A	
		Maloney, John	OF	2	.286	A	
21	34	Mathews, Robert T.	P	56	.181	A	
		Nichols, Albert H.	3B	57	.177	A	
		Phelps, Cornelius Carman (Neal)	OF	1	+.000	A	Ath
		Seward, George E.	2B	1	.000	A	
		Shandley, James J.	OF	2	.125	A	C
		Start, Joseph	1B	56	.276	A	
		Thayer, Edward L.	2B	1	.000	A	C
		Treacey, Frederick	OF	57	.210	A	C
		Treacey, P.	SS	2	.167	A	C
		Valentine, Robert	C	1	.000	A	C
		West, Wm. Nelson	2B	1	.000	A	C

WON 46 | LOST 50 | TG 96

NATIONAL LEAGUE

1883.

FINISHED 6th.

PCT. .479

NEW YORK

JOHN EDGAR CLAPP

WON	LOST	NAME	POS.	G.	BA	FROM	TO
0	1	Allen, Myron S.	P	1	.250	A	
		Caskin, Edward James (2B13)	SS79	93	.238	Troy81	
		Clapp, John Edgar MGR. (OF4)	C15	19	.178	Clev81	C
		Connor, Roger	1B	96	.361	Troy	
		Cramer, Wm. B.	OF	2	.125	A	C
0	1	Dorgan, Michael Cornelius (P4 C1)	OF57	62	.235	Det81	
		*Ewing, Wm. (Buck) (2B12 SS3)	C60	85	.306	Troy	
		Gillespie, Patrick Peter	OF	95	.314	Troy	
		Hankinson, Frank Edward	3B90	91	.221	Troy81	
		Humphries, John Henry (OF10)	C16	26	.117	A	
7	13	O'Neill, James Edward (Tip) (OF3)	P20	23	.178	A	
		Orr, David L.	OF	1	.000	xMetAA	MetAA (return)
		Pearce, Grayson S. (2B1)	OF17	18	.095	xColAA	
		Troy, John Joseph (SS12)	2B70	82	.216	Prov	
12	14	Ward, John Montgomery (P33 2B1 SS2 3B5)	OF48	88	.258	Prov	
27	21	Welch, Michael F. (Mickey) (OF35)	P48	81	.239	Troy	

*Ewing also played 13 games in the OF.

WON 62 | LOST 50 | TG 112

NATIONAL LEAGUE

1884.

FINISHED 4th. (TIED WITH CHIC)

PCT. .554

NEW YORK

JAMES L. PRICE

WON	LOST	NAME	POS.	G.	BA	FROM	TO
12	18	Begley, Edward N. (OF3)	P31	32	.181	A	
0	1	Brown, James W. H.	P	1	+.000	xAltUA	StPUA
		Caskin, Edward James (C7)	SS92	97	.232	B	
		Connor, Roger (3B11 OF34)	2B67	112	.316	B	
8	6	Dorgan, Michael Cornelius (P14 C6 2B3)	OF59	79	.276	B	
0	1	Ewing, Wm. (Buck) (P1 SS3 OF12)	C74	88	.278	B	
		Gillespie, Patrick Peter	OF	97	.264	B	
		Griffin, Tobias Chas. (Sandy)	OF	15	.164	A	
		Hankinson, Frank Edward	3B	101	.235	B	
		Humphries, John Henry	C	19	.093	xWashAA	C
		Loughran, (OF1)	C8	8	.120	A	C
		Manlove, Chas. Hale	C	2	.000	AltUA	C
		McKinnon, Alexander J.	1B	112	.275	A	
		Oxley, Henry Havelock	C	2	.000	A	MetAA
		Richardson, Daniel (Denny) (SS17)	OF53	70	.259	A	
3	3	Ward, John Montgomery (P6 2B43)	OF59	109	.249	B	
39	21	Welch, Michael F. (Mickey) (OF9)	P60	67	.256	B	

WON 85 | LOST 27 | TG 112

NATIONAL LEAGUE

1885.

FINISHED 2nd.

PCT. .758

NEW YORK

JAMES J. MUTRIE

WON	LOST	NAME	POS.	G.	BA	FROM	TO
		Donnor, Roger	1B	110	.371	B	
1	1	*Corcoran, Lawrence J. (Larry)	P	2	+.375	xChi	
		Deasley, Thomas H. (Pat) (SS1)	C51	52	.256	StLAA	
		Dorgan, Michael Cornelius	OF87	88	.325	B	
		Esterbrook, Thomas Jefferson (Dude) (OF4)	3B84	88	.256	MetAA	
0	1	Ewing, Wm. (Buck) (P1 1B1 SS1 3B6 OF13)	C61	81	.304	B	
		Gerhardt, Joseph John (Moveup)	2B	112	.155	LvlleAA	
		Gillespie, Patrick Peter	OF	102	.292	B	
32	13	Keefe, Timothy J. (OF1)	P45	46	.162	MetAA	
		O'Rourke, James Henry (C7)	OF	112	.299	Buff	
5	1	Richardson, Daniel (Denny) (P9 OF18)	3B21	48	.262	B	
		Ward, John Montgomery	SS	111	.226	B	
47	11	Welch, Michael F. (Mickey) (OF1)	P58	58	.206	B	

*Corcoran also played 1 game in the OF.

WON 75
LOST 44
TG 119

NATIONAL LEAGUE

1886.

FINISHED 3rd.

PCT. .630

NEW YORK

JAMES J. MUTRIE

WON	LOST	NAME	POS.	G.	BA	FROM	TO
		Begley, Eugene I.	C	3	.111	A	C
		Caskin, Edward James	SS	1	.500	StL	C
		Connor, Roger	1B	118	.354	B	
		Corcoran, Lawrence J. (Larry)	OF	1	+.000	B	Wash
		Deasley, Thomas H. (Pat)	C26	38	.265	B	
		Devine, Walter James	OF	1	.000	BaltAA83	C
0	0	Devlin, James H.	P	1	.000	A	
		Dorgan, Michael Cornelius	OF116	118	.292	B	
		Esterbrook, Thomas Jefferson (Dude)	3B	123	.264	B	
		Ewing, Wm. (Buck) (OF20)	C48	70	.309	B	
		Finley, Wm. James (OF5)	C8	13	.188	A	C
		Gerhardt, Joseph John (Moveup)	2B	123	.190	B	
		Gillespie, Patrick Peter	OF	98	.272	B	
42	20	Keefe, Timothy J.	P63	64	.170	B	
		O'Rourke, James Henry (C44)	OF58	104	.309	B	
0	1	Richardson, Daniel (Denny) (P1)	OF58	64	.232	B	
		Ward, John Montgomery	SS	122	.273	B	
33	23	Welch, Michael F. (Mickey)	P58	59	.216	B	

WON 68
LOST 55
TG 123

NATIONAL LEAGUE

1887.

FINISHED 4th.

PCT. .553

NEW YORK

JAMES J. MUTRIE

WON	LOST	NAME	POS.	G.	BA	FROM	TO
		Becannon, James Melville	3B	1	.000	MetAA85	C
		Brown, Willard	C45	47	.261	A	
		Casey, Dennis Patrick	2B	1	.000	BaltAA85	C
		Connor, Roger	1B	127	.382	B	
		Deasley, Thomas H. (Pat)	C24	29	.362	B	
		Dorgan, Michael Cornelius	OF69	71	.295	B	
		Ewing, Wm. (Buck) (2B18)	3B51	76	.365	B	
3	9	George, Wm. M.	P	13	.176	A	
		Gerhardt, Joseph John (Moveup)	3B	1	.000	B	MetAA
		Gillespie, Patrick Peter	OF	74	.293	B	C
		Gore, George F.	OF	111	.348	Chi	
		Hatfield, Gilbert	3B	2	.429	Buff85	
35	20	Keefe, Timothy J.	P	56	.293	B	
3	4	Mattimore, Michael J.	P	8	.281	A	
		Murphy, Patrick J.	C	16	.245	A	
		Nelson, Jackson W.	3B	1	.000	xMetAA	
		O'Rourke, James Henry (3B36 OF29)	C37	103	.344	B	
		Rainey, John Paul	3B	17	.349	A	
		Richardson, Daniel (Denny)	2B108	122	.332	B	
0	1	Roach, John F.	P	1	.250	A	C
0	1	Swabach, Wm.	P	2	.000	A	C
		Tiernan, Michael Joseph	OF101	103	.340	A	
4	3	Titcomb, Ledell	P	9	.069	xAthAA	
		Ward, John Montgomery	SS	129	.371	B	
0	2	Weidman, George E.	P	2	.333	xMetAA	
23	15	Welch, Michael F. (Mickey)	P	40	.272	B	

WON x84
LOST 47
TG 131

NATIONAL LEAGUE

1888.

FINISHED 1st.

PCT. .641

NEW YORK

JAMES J. MUTRIE

WON	LOST	NAME	POS.	G.	BA	FROM	TO
		Brown, Willard	C	17	.271	B	
		Cleveland, Elmer E.	3B	10	+.270	CinUA84	Pitt
		Connor, Roger	1B133	134	.291	B	
5	6	Crane, Edward Nicholas	P	12	.181	Wash86	
		Ewing, Wm. (Buck) (3B21)	C78	103	.306	B	
		Foster, Elmer E.	OF	37	.147	MetAA86	
2	1	George, Wm. M. (P4)	OF5	9	.230	B	
		Gore, George F.	OF	64	.220	B	
		Hatfield, Gilbert	3B	27	.181	B	

WON	LOST	NAME	POS.	G.	BA	FROM	TO
35	12	Keefe, Timothy J.	P50	51	.127	B	
		Murphy, Patrick J.	C	28	.169	B	
		O'Rourke, James Henry	OF87	107	.273	B	
		Richardson, Daniel (Denny)	2B	135	.226	B	
		Slattery, Michael J.	OF	103	.245	BosUA84	
		Tiernan, Michael Joseph	OF	113	.293	B	
14	8	Titcomb, Ledell	P	23	.122	B	
		Ward, John Montgomery	SS	122	.251	B	
1	1	Weidman, George E.	P	2	.000	B	C
26	19	Welch, Michael F. (Mickey)	P	47	.189	B	
		Whitney, Arthur Wilson	3B	90	.219	Pitt	

x-One game won by forfeit.

WON 83 NATIONAL LEAGUE FINISHED 1st.
LOST 43
TG 126 1889. PCT. .659

NEW YORK

JAMES J. MUTRIE

WON	LOST	NAME	POS.	G.	BA	FROM	TO
		Brown, Willard	C30	33	.259	B	
		Connor, Roger	1B	131	.316	B	
14	10	Crane, Edward Nicholas	P	28	.204	B	
0	0	Ewing, Wm. (Buck) (P2)	C94	96	.326	B	
		Foster, Elmer E.	OF	2	.000	B	
		George, Wm. M.	OF	3	.267	B	ColAA
		Gore, George F.	OF	119	.305	B	
0	0	Hatfield, Gilbert (P6)	SS24	32	.184	B	
30	13	Keefe, Timothy J.	P	43	.154	B	
		Lyons, Harry P.	OF	5	.100	StLAA	
		Murphy, Patrick J.	C	8	.280	B	
9	6	O'Day, Henry F. (Hank)	P	15	+.107	xWash	
		O'Rourke, James Henry	OF	128	.320	B	
		Richardson, Daniel (Denny)	2B	124	.279	B	
		Slattery, Michael J.	OF	12	.286	B	
		Tiernan, Michael Joseph	OF	122	.334	B	
2	2	Titcomb, Ledell	P	4	.083	B	
		Ward, John Montgomery	SS107	114	.298	B	
28	12	Welch, Michael F. (Mickey)	P	41	.192	B	
		Whitney, Arthur Wilson	3B	129	.217	B	

WON 63 NATIONAL LEAGUE FINISHED 6th.
LOST 68
TG 131 1890. PCT. .481

NEW YORK

JAMES J. MUTRIE

WON	LOST	NAME	POS.	G.	BA	FROM	TO
		Bassett, Chas. Edwin	2B	100	.239	Indpls	
		Buckley, Richard D. (Dick)	C62	70	.255	Indpls	
3	11	Burkett, Jesse Cail (P14)	OF90	101	.309	A	
		Clark, Arthur Franklin (2B15 3B16 OF33)	C36	101	.225	A	
		Crane, Samuel Newhall (OF1)	1B1	2	+.000	Wash87	Pitt
			2B	2	+.000	(return)	C
2	1	Daily, Edward M.	P	4	.133	xBknAA	LvlleAA
		Denny, Jeremiah D. (Jerry)	3B106	114	.212	Indpls	
		Esterbrook, Thomas Jefferson (Dude)	1B	45	.289	LvlleAA	
		Glasscock, John Wesley	SS	124	.336	Indpls	
		Henry, John Michael	OF	37	.243	Wash86	C
		Hornung, Michael Joseph (OF77)	1B36	120	.238	BaltAA	C
		Howe, John (Shorty)	2B17	17	.172	A	
		Murphy, Patrick J.	C29	32	.235	B	C
1	1	Murphy, Robert J.	P	3	.167	A	C
		McMillan, George A. (Reddy)	OF	10	.138	A	C
		O'Rourke, Thomas Joseph	C	2	.000	Bos88	SyrAA
28	33	Rusie, Amos Wilson	P64	73	.278	Indpls	
		Scanlon M. J.	1B	3	.000	A	C
11	9	Sharrott, John Henry	P23	29	.201	A	
		Sommers, Joseph Andrew (Pete) (1B5 OF1)	C11	17	+.070	Indpls	Clev
		Tiernan, Michael Joseph	OF	133	.303	B	
18	13	Welch, Michael F. (Mickey)	P	35	.179	B	
		Whistler, Lewis	1B	45	.288	A	

WON 71 NATIONAL LEAGUE FINISHED 3rd.
LOST 61
TG 132 1891. PCT. .538

NEW YORK

JAMES J. MUTRIE

WON	LOST	NAME	POS.	G.	BA	FROM	TO
0	3	Barr, Robert M.	P	5	.125	RochAA	C
		Bassett, Chas. Edwin	3B122	130	.266	B	
		Buckley, Richard D. (Dick)	C66	67	.211	B	
		Burrell, Frank Andrew (Buster)	C	15	.075	A	
		Clark, Arthur Franklin	C40	46	.188	B	C
1	2	Clarkson, Arthur Hamilton	P	5	.307	A	
		Connor, Roger	1B	123	.293	NYPL	
3	4	Coughlin, Wm. E.	P	8	.130	Chi90	C
		Denny, Jeremiah D. (Jerry)	3B	4	+.250	B	Clev
0	0	Dunning, Andrew J.	P	1	.000	Pitt89	C
21	10	Ewing, John	P	31	.184	NYPL	C
		Ewing, Wm. (Buck) (C2)	2B8	14	.340	NYPL	
		Glasscock, John Wesley	SS	95	.243	B	
		Gore, George F.	OF	130	.285	NYPL	
2	5	Keefe, Timothy J.	P	8	+.095	NYPL	Phil
		O'Rourke, James Henry	OF123	136	.301	NYPL	
		Richardson, Daniel (Denny)	2B113	123	.262	NYPL	
34	20	Rusie, Amos Wilson	P	56	.247	B	

WON	LOST	NAME	POS.	G.	BA	FROM	TO
4	3	Sharrott, John Henry	P	10	.344	B	
1	2	Sullivan, Michael Joseph	P	3	.200	xAthAA	
0	1	Taylor, John Budd (Jack)	P	1	.000	A	
		Tiernan, Michael Joseph	OF	133	.303	B	
5	11	Welch, Michael F. (Mickey)	P18	19	.149	B	
		Whistler, Lewis (OF21)	SS32	71	.245	B	

WON 71 LOST 80 TG 151 — NATIONAL LEAGUE 1892. — FINISHED 8th. PCT. .470

NEW YORK

PATRICK THOMAS POWERS

WON	LOST	NAME	POS.	G.	BA	FROM	TO
		Bassett, Chas. Edwin (3B15)	2B19	34	+.185	B	Lvlle
		Boyle, John Anthony (Jack)	C77	116	.201	StLAA	
		Burke, Edward D. (OF25)	2B58	83	+.266	xCin	
14	26	Crane, Edward Nicholas	P	40	.242	Cin	
		Doyle, John Joseph (Jack) (2B34 OF3)	C49	86	+.295	xClev	
		Ewing, Wm. (Buck) (C29)	1B68	97	.319	B	
		Fields, John James	C	17	.268	Phil	C
		Fuller, Wm. Benjamin	SS	138	.236	StLAA	
		Gore, George F.	OF	53	+.254	B	StL
		Keeler, Wm. Henry	3B	13	.306	A	
24	24	King, Chas. Frederick	P	52	.214	Pitt	
		Knowles, James	3B	15	.169	RochAA90	C
		Lyons, Dennis Patrick Aloysius	3B	108	.260	StLAA	
		Lyons, Harry P.	OF	96	.245	RochAA90	
		Murphy, Daniel J.	C	8	.115	A	C
		McMahon, John Henry	1B	36	.239	A	
		Newman, Chas. C.	OF	2	+.375	StLAA	Chi
		O'Rourke, James Henry	OF109	112	.297	B	
		Richardson, Arthur Harding (OF21)	2B40	61	+.223	xWash	C
32	28	Rusie, Amos Wilson	P62	65	.214	B	
0	1	Sharrott, John Henry (P1)	OF4	5	.000	B	
		Tiernan, Michael Joseph	OF	114	.297	B	
1	1	Welch, Michael F. (Mickey)	P	2	.333	B	C

WON 68 LOST 64 TG 132 — NATIONAL LEAGUE 1893. — FINISHED 5th. PCT. .515

NEW YORK

JOHN MONTGOMERY WARD

WON	LOST	NAME	POS.	G.	BA	FROM	TO
12	19	Baldwin, Marcus Elmore (Mark)	P	35	+.146	xPitt	C
		Burke, Edward D.	OF	135	.289	B	
		Connor, Roger	1B	135	.322	Phil	
2	4	Crane, Edward Nicholas	P	10	+.500	B	Bkn
1	2	Davies, George Washington	P	4	+.400	xClev	C
		Davis, George Stacey	3B	133	.373	Clev	
0	1	Donahue, Francis Rostell (Red)	P	2	.000	A	
		Doyle, John Joseph (Jack) (OF28)	C46	80	.322	B	
0	1	Foreman, Francis Isaiah	P	2	.000	Balt	
		Fuller, Wm. Benjamin	SS	130	.247	B	
10	8	German, Lester S.	P18	20	.295	BaltAA90	
		Howe, John (Shorty)	3B	1	.500	NY90	C
0	1	Jones, Chas. Leander (Bumpus)	P	4	+.000	xCin	
		Keeler, Wm. Henry (2B2 SS2)	OF3	7	+.364	B	Bkn
		Kelly, Michael Joseph (King)	C	16	.314	Bos	C
5	3	King, Chas. Frederick	P	15	+.167	B	Cin
		Kinsler,	OF	1	.000	A	C
		Lyons, Harry P.	OF	46	.272	B	C
		Milligan, John (Jack)	C	40	+.243	xBalt	C
		McMahon, John Henry	C	11	.333	B	C
5	2	Petty, Chas. E.	P	9	.333	CinAA89	
33	21	Rusie, Amos Wilson	P54	55	.270	B	
0	2	Schmidt, Frederick	P	4	+.500	xBalt	
0	0	Sigsby, Seth DeWitt	P	1	.000	A	C
		Stafford, James Joseph	OF	67	.301	BuffPL90	
		Tiernan, Michael Joseph	OF	124	.327	B	
		Ward, John Montgomery MGR.	2B	134	.348	Bkn	
		Wilson, A. Parke	C	29	.280	A	

WON 88 LOST 44 TG 132 — NATIONAL LEAGUE 1894. — FINISHED 2nd. PCT. .667

NEW YORK

JOHN MONTGOMERY WARD

WON	LOST	NAME	POS.	G.	BA	FROM	TO
		Burke, Edward D.	OF	138	.299	B	
2	4	Clarke, Wm. H. (Dad)	P	16	.243	ColAA91	
		Connor, Roger (OF1)	1B21	22	+.293	B	StL
		Davis, George Stacey	3B	124	.345	B	
		Doyle, John Joseph (Jack)	1B99	105	.369	B	
		Farrell, Chas. A. (Duke)	C103	112	.282	Wash	
		Fuller, Wm. Benjamin	SS91	95	.282	B	
7	8	German, Lester S.	P17	19	.300	B	
36	10	Meekin, Jouett	P47	48	.281	Wash	
		Murphy, Wm. Henry (Yale) (OF20)	SS48	73	.271	A	
36	13	Rusie, Amos Wilson	P	50	.275	B	
		Stafford, James Joseph	3B	11	.229	B	
		Tiernan, Michael Joseph	OF	112	.282	B	
		VanHaltren, George E.	OF	139	.333	Pitt	
		Ward, John Montgomery MGR.	2B	136	.262	B	C
7	9	Westervelt, Huyler	P	18	.152	A	C

WON	LOST	NAME	POS.	G.	BA	FROM	TO
		Wilson, A. Parke	C32	45	.329	B	

WON 66 LOST 65 TG 131

NATIONAL LEAGUE 1895. FINISHED 9th. PCT. .504

NEW YORK

GEORGE STACEY DAVIS JOHN JOSEPH DOYLE
HARVEY L. WATKINS

WON	LOST	NAME	POS.	G.	BA	FROM	TO
		Bannon, Thomas Edward (1B16)	OF21	37	.266	A	
		Battam, Lawrence (Larry)	3B	2	.250	A	C
2	2	Boswell, Andrew Cottrell	P	5	+.187	A	Wash
		Burke, Edward D.	OF	39	+.256	B	Cin
		Burns, Thomas P.	OF	33	+.298	xBkn	C
		Butler, Frank Dean	OF	5	.272	A	C
18	14	Clark, Wm. H. (Dad)	P	32	.237	B	
		Clark, Wm. Otis	1B	22	.261	A	
		Davis, George Stacey MGR.	3B87	110	.330	B	
		Davis, Harry H.	1B	7	.333	A	
0	3	Doheny, Edward R.	P	3	.100	A	
		Doyle, John Joseph (Jack) MGR.	1B57	78	.316	B	
		Farrell, Chas. A. (Duke) (3B25)	C62	89	.283	B	
		Fuller, Wm. Benjamin	SS	126	.227	B	
7	13	German, Lester S.	P20	31	.245	B	
0	0	Knauss, Frank H.	P	1	.000	Clev	C
16	11	Meekin, Jouett	P	30	.290	B	
		Murphy, Wm. Henry (Vale)	OF32	47	.209	B	
23	22	Rusie, Amos Wilson	P	47	.254	B	
		Schriver, Wm. F. (Pop)	C18	24	.290	Chi	
		Stafford, James Joseph	2B109	123	.293	B	
		Tiernan, Michael Joseph	OF	119	.354	B	
		Van Haltren, George E.	OF	131	.338	B	
		Wilson, A. Parke	C51	62	.243	B	

WON 64 LOST 67 TG 131

NATIONAL LEAGUE 1896. FINISHED 7th. PCT. .489

NEW YORK

ARTHUR ALBERT IRWIN WM. MICHAEL JOYCE

WON	LOST	NAME	POS.	G.	BA	FROM	TO
		Bannon, Thomas Edward	OF	2	.143	B	C
		Beckley, Jacob Peter (Jake)	1B	45	+.297	xPitt	
0	1	Bowen, Sutherland McCoy	P	2	.333	A	C
0	1	Campfield, Wm. Holton	P	6	.167	A	C
16	27	Clark, Wm. H. (Dad)	P	43	.209	B	
		Clark, Wm. Otis	1B	65	.303	B	
		Connaughton, Frank H. (OF30)	SS53	83	.257	Bos94	
		Davis, George Stacey (SS45)	3B73	124	.315	B	
		Davis, Harry H.	1B	64	+.254	B	Pitt
7	7	Doheny, Edward R.	P	17	.150	B	
		Farrell, Chas. A. (Duke)	C	45	+.279	B	Wash
0	0	Flynn, Cornelius Francis Xavier	P	3	+.667	Cin94	Wash
		Foster, Oscar E.	OF	1	.000	A	C
		Fuller, Wm. Benjamin	SS	17	.180	B	C
1	1	German, Lester S.	P	3	+.000	B	Wash
1	0	Gettig, Chas. H.	P	6	.333	A	
		Gleason, Wm. J. (Kid)	2B130	133	.292	Balt	
		Joyce, Wm. Michael (Scrappy)	3B	49	+.350	xWash	
26	13	Meekin, Jouett	P	40	.293	B	
		Pfeffer, Nathaniel Frederick	2B	4	+.143	Lvlle	Chi
0	1	Reidy, Wm. Joseph	P	2	.000	A	
2	4	Seymour, John Bentley (Cy)	P	12	.258	A	
		Stafford, James Joseph	OF52	59	.282	B	
10	12	Sullivan, Michael Joseph	P	23	.216	Clev	
		Tiernan, Michael Joseph	OF	133	.361	B	
		Ulrich, George F.	OF	14	.178	Cin93	C
1	0	Van Haltren, George E. (P1)	OF132	133	.353	B	
		Warner, John Joseph	C	16	+.264	xLvlle	
		Wilson, A. Parke	C67	69	.230	B	
		Zearfoss, David William Tilden	C	16	.220	A	

WON 83 LOST 48 TG 131

NATIONAL LEAGUE 1897. FINISHED 3rd. PCT. .634

NEW YORK

WM. MICHAEL JOYCE

WON	LOST	NAME	POS.	G.	BA	FROM	TO
		Beckley, Jacob Peter (Jake)	1B	18	+.268	B	Cin
0	3	Clark, Wm. H. (Dad)	P	6	+.231	B	Lvlle
		Clark, Wm. Otis	1B110	118	.282	B	
		Davis, George Stacey	SS	131	.358	B	
6	4	Doheny, Edward R.	P	10	.200	B	
		Donely, James B.	3B	23	+.205	xPitt	
1	1	Gettig, Chas. H. (P2)	SS18	20	.203	B	
		Gleason, Wm. J. (Kid)	2B131	134	.311	B	
		Holmes, James Wm. (Ducky)	OF	78	+.288	xLvlle	
		Joyce, Wm. Michael (Scrappy) MGR.	3B108	110	.305	B	
20	11	Meekin, Jouett	P35	38	.280	B	
		Murphy, Wm. Henry (Yale)	SS	4	.000	NY95	C
		McCreery, Thomas Leavenworth (2B2)	OF47	49	+.290	xLvlle	
28	8	Rusie, Amos Wilson	P	37	.288	NY95	
20	14	Seymour, John Bentley (Cy)	P34	41	.248	B	
		Stafford, James Joseph (SS1)	OF6	7	+.091	B	Lvlle
8	7	Sullivan, Michael Joseph	P19	21	.277	B	
		Tiernan, Michael Joseph	OF	129	.331	B	

WON	LOST	NAME	POS.	G.	BA	FROM	TO
		VanHaltren, George E.	OF	131	.332	B	
		Warner, John Joseph	C	110	.274	B	
		Wilmot, Walter R.	OF	13	.242	Chi95	
		Wilson, A. Parke	C29	41	.310	B	
		Zearfoss, David William Tilden	C	5	.363	B	

WON 77 NATIONAL LEAGUE FINISHED 7th.
LOST 73
TG 150 1898. PCT. .513

NEW YORK

WM. MICHAEL JOYCE ADRIAN CONSTANTINE ANSON

WON	LOST	NAME	POS.	G.	BA	FROM	TO
3	1	Carrick, Wm. Martin	P	5	.167	A	
		Davis, George Stacey	SS	121	.306	B	
8	19	Doheny, Edward R.	P27	28	.167	B	
		Doyle, John Joseph (Jack)	1B	79	+.297	xWash	
		Foster, Clarence Francis (Pop)	OF20	31	.281	A	
5	4	Gettig, Chas. H. (OF18)	P37	55	.248	B	
		Gilbert, John Robert	OF	1	+.250	xWash	
		Gleason, Wm. J. (Kid)	2B143	149	.222	B	
		Glenn, Edward D.	SS	2	.167	A	
		Grady, Michael Wm. (OF27)	C47	83	.293	StL	
		Hartman, Frederick Orrin	3B	122	.267	StL	
		Joyce, Wm. Michael (Scrappy) MGR.	1B129	143	.253	B	C
		Latimer, Clifford Wesley	C	3	.400	A	
16	20	Meekin, Jouett	P	36	.218	B	
0	1	Menefee, John (Jock)	P	1	.000	Pitt95	
		McCreery, Thomas Leavenworth	OF	34	+.198	B	Pitt
		Puhl, John	3B	2	.250	A	
		Reagan, J.	OF	2	.200	A	C
20	11	Rusie, Amos Wilson	P35	36	.213	B	
25	17	Seymour, John Bentley (Cy) (OF34)	P44	78	.273	B	
		Tiernan, Michael Joseph	OF	103	.286	B	
		VanHaltren, George E.	OF	155	.315	B	
		Warner, John Joseph	C107	108	.259	B	
		Wilmot, Walter R.	OF	34	.246	B	
		Wilson, A. Parke	OF	1	.000	B	
		Zearfoss, David William Tilden	C	1	1.000	B	

WON x60 NATIONAL LEAGUE FINISHED 10th.
LOST x86
TG 146 1899. PCT. .411

NEW YORK

JOHN B. DAY FREDERICK C. HOEY

WON	LOST	NAME	POS.	G.	BA	FROM	TO
16	25	Carrick, Wm. Martin	P43	44	.139	B	
		Carsey, Wilfred (Kid) (SS2)	3B3	5	+.333	xWash	
4	5	Colcolough, Thomas Bernard (Thomas B. Coakley)	P	14	.256	Pitt95	
		Cregan, Peter James	OF	1	.000	A	
		Davis, George Stacey	SS	111	.348	B	
		Davis, J. Ira (1B2)	SS4	6	.250	A	C
14	16	Doheny, Edward R.	P34	35	.233	B	
		Doyle, John Joseph (Jack)	1B115	117	.308	B	
0	1	Fishel, Leo	P	1	.250	A	C
		Fleming, Thomas Vincent	OF	20	.257	A	
		Foster, Clarence Francis (Pop)	OF	88	.305	B	
0	1	Garoni, Wm.	P	3	.000	A	C
7	8	Gettig, Chas. H.	P15	31	.239	B	C
		Gleason, Wm. J. (Kid)	2B	148	.267	B	
		Grady, Michael Wm. (3B35)	C39	83	.336	B	
		Hardesty, Scott D.	SS	21	.228	A	C
		Hartman, Frederick Orrin	3B	52	.241	B	
0	0	Johnson, Thomas G.	P	1	.000	Phi197	C
		Martin, Frank	3B	17	.254	Chi	
5	11	Meekin, Jouett	P	16	+.224	B	Bos
0	0	McPartlin, Frank	P	1	.000	A	C
		O'Brien, Thomas F. (3B21)	OF131	152	.305	Pitt	
		O'Neill, John J.	C	2	.000	A	
		Puhl, John	3B	1	.000	B	C
0	0	Sechrist, Theodore O'Hara (Ted)	P	1	.000	A	C
13	18	Seymour, John Bentley (Cy)	P33	45	.337	B	
		Stuart, Wm. Alexander	2B	1	.000	Pitt95	C
		Tiernan, Michael Joseph	OF	36	.250	B	C
		VanHaltren, George E.	OF	153	.301	B	
		Warner, John Joseph	C82	83	.271	B	
		Wilson, A. Parke (1B22)	C29	93	.268	B	
		Woodruff, Orville Francis	OF	20	.246	A	
		Wrigley, George Watson	3B	4	+.133	Wash	Bkn

x-One game won by forfeit.
x-One game lost by forfeit.

WON 60 NATIONAL LEAGUE FINISHED 8th (LAST)
LOST 78
TG 138 1900. PCT. .435

NEW YORK

WM. EWING GEORGE STACEY DAVIS

WON	LOST	NAME	POS.	G.	BA	FROM	TO
		Bernard, Curtis Henry	OF18	19	.243	A	
		Bowerman, Frank Eugene	C	73	.256	Pitt	
19	21	Carrick, Wm. Martin	P	42	.167	B	
0	0	Cogan, Richard Henry	P	3	.125	Chi	C

WON	LOST	NAME	POS.	G.	BA	FROM	TO
		Davis, George Stacey MGR.	SS	113	.325	B	
4	14	Doheny, Edward R.	P	18	.236	B	ChiA & recall
		Doyle, John Joseph (Jack)	1B	130	.273	B	
		Foster, Clarence Francis (Pop)	OF	20	.286	B	
		Frisbee, Chas. Augustus	OF	4	.153	Bos	ClevA
		Gleason, Wm. J. (Kid)	2B	111	.257	B	
		Grady, Michael Wm.	C40	75	.222	B	
18	20	Hawley, Emerson P. (Pink)	P	39	.225	Cin	
		Hickman, Chas. Taylor	3B118	125	.313	Bos	
0	2	Mathewson, Christopher (Big Six)	P	6	.133	A	
13	16	Mercer, George Barclay (Winnie) (3B18)	P29	72	.308	Wash	
		Murphy, Daniel Francis	2B	21	.250	A	
		Selbach, Albert Carl (Kip)	OF	141	.345	Cin	
2	2	Seymour, John Bentley (Cy)	P	21	.263	B	ChiA & recall
		Sheehan, Daniel	SS	1	.000	xDetA	C
		Smith, Elmer Ellsworth	OF	87	+.274	xCin	
4	3	Taylor, Luther Haden	P	11	.142	A	
		VanHaltren, George E.	OF	141	.319	B	
		Warner, John Joseph	C30	31	.269	B	

WON 52 NATIONAL LEAGUE FINISHED 7th.
LOST 85
TG 137 1901. PCT. .380

NEW YORK

GEORGE STACEY DAVIS

WON	LOST	NAME	POS.	G.	BA	FROM	TO
		Bernard, Curtis Henry	OF	19	.192	B	C
		Bowerman, Frank Eugene	C43	52	.217	B	
		Buelow, Chas. John	3B17	19	.112	ClevA	C
		Davis, George Stacey MGR. (3B17)	SS113	130	.309	B	
0	2	Deegan, W. John	P	2	.000	A	C
2	5	Denzer, Roger	P	11	.091	ChiA	C
2	4	Doheny, Edward R.	P	9	+.462	B	Pitt
0	0	Felix, Harry	P	1	.000	A	
0	1	Fisher, Chauncey Burr	P	1	+.000	ChiA	StL
		Ganzel, John Henry	1B	139	.220	Chi	
0	1	Hesterfer, Lawrence	P	1	.000	A	C
3	5	Hickman, Chas. Taylor (P8 SS22 3B16)	OF48	101	.287	B	
0	1	Jones, James Tilford (P1)	OF20	21	.209	ClevA	
0	2	Leitner, George Michael	P	2	.143	PhilA	
0	2	Livingston, Albany	P	2	.167	A	C
0	3	Magee, Wm. M.	P	6	+.143	xStL	
20	16	Mathewson, Christopher (Big Six)	P	37	.211	B	
0	2	Maul, Albert Joseph	P	3	.375	Phil	C
		Miller, James (Rabbit)	2B	18	.136	A	C

WON	LOST	NAME	POS.	G.	BA	FROM	TO
0	2	Mills, Wm. Grant	P	2	.000	A	C
		Murphy, Daniel Francis	2B	5	.200	B	
		Murphy, Frank Morton	OF	34	+.143	xBos	C
		McBride, Algernon Briggs (Algie)	OF	62	+.277	xCin	C
		Nelson, Raymond N.	2B	36	.205	A	C
7	10	Phyle, Wm. Joseph	P	20	.178	Chi99	
		Selbach, Albert Carl (Kip)	OF	125	.292	B	
0	1	Smith, Alexander Benjamin (Broadway) (P1)	C25	29	.168	Bkn	
		Strang, Samuel Nicklin (2B37)	3B91	135	.291	Chi	
18	27	Taylor, Luther Haden	P	45	.125	B	
0	1	VanHaltren, George E. (P1)	OF	133	.342	B	
0	0	VanZandt, Chas. Isaac	P	3	.167	A	
		Wall, Joseph Francis	C	3	.286	A	
		Warner, John Joseph	C	77	.239	B	

WON 48 NATIONAL LEAGUE FINISHED 8th (LAST)
LOST 88
TG 136 1902. PCT. .353

NEW YORK

HORACE S. FOGEL GEORGE HENRY SMITH JOHN JOSEPH McGRAW

WON	LOST	NAME	POS.	G.	BA	FROM	TO
		Bean, Joseph Wm.	SS	50	.235	A	C
0	2	Blewett, Robert Lawrence	P	5	.000	A	C
		Bowerman, Frank Eugene (1B3)	C97	99	.253	B	
		Bresnahan, Roger Philip (C16 1B4 SS4 3B1)	OF27	50	.292	xBaltA	
		Brodie, Walter Scott	OF	109	.281	BaltA	C
		Browne, George E.	OF	55	+.348	xPhil	
0	1	Burke, John Patrick (OF2)	P2	4	.153	StL99	C
		Callahan, James J.	OF	1	.000	A	C
		Clark, Roy Elliott	OF	20	.139	A	C
5	6	Cronin, John J. (Jack) (OF7)	P13	19	.167	xBaltA	
		Delahanty, James Christopher Jr.	OF	7	.231	Chi	
		Doyle, John Joseph (Jack)	1B	50	.300	Chi	WashA
0	3	Dunn, John Joseph (Jack) (P3 SS36 2B2 3B18)	OF37	96	.211	BaltA	
8	11	Evans, LeRoy	P	19	+.143	WashN99	Bkn
		Hartley, Walter Scott	OF	1	.000	A	C
		Hendricks, John Calhoun	OF	7	+.240	A	Chi
		Jackson, James Benner	OF	35	.193	BaltA	
		Jones, James Tilford	OF	65	.236	B	C
1	4	Kennedy, Wm. V. (Brickyard)	P	6	.312	Bkn	
		Lauder, Wm. (OF5)	3B122	126	.239	PhilA	
0	0	Magee, Wm. M.	P	3	+.000	B	Phil
13	18	Mathewson, Christopher (Big Six) (1B3 OF4)	P34	41	.200	B	
1	8	Miller, Roscoe Clyde	P	10	.045	xDetA	

WON	LOST	NAME	POS.	G.	BA	FROM	TO
		McDonald, James	OF	2	.333	A	C
		McGann, Dennis L. (Dan)	1B	61	.301	xBaltA	
8	8	McGinnity, Joseph Jerome (2B1 OF4)	P16	19	.123	xBaltA	
		McGraw, John Joseph MGR.	SS	34	.226	xBaltA	
		O'Hagan, Harold P.	1B16	24	+.138	xChi (& return)	ClevA
		O'Neill, John J.	C	2	.000	NY99	C
		Robinson, John (Bridgeport)	C3	4	.000	A	C
		Smith, George Henry (Heinie) MGR.	2B	140	.248	Pitt99	
4	11	Sparks, Tully Frank	P	15	.154	MilA	BosA
8	15	Taylor, Luther Haden	P	23	.094	xClevA	
0	1	Thielman, Henry Joseph (OF2)	P5	6	+.111	A	Cin
		VanHaltren, George E.	OF	26	.250	B	
		Wagner, Chas. F.	SS	17	.214	A	
		Wall, Joseph Francis	OF	6	+.357	B	Bkn
		Washburn, Libe	OF3	6	.444	A	
		Yeager, George E. (1B3 OF1)	C26	29	.194	Pitt	BaltA

WON 84 — NATIONAL LEAGUE — FINISHED 2nd.
LOST 55
TG 139 — 1903. — PCT. .604

NEW YORK

JOHN JOSEPH McGRAW

WON	LOST	NAME	POS.	G.	BA	FROM	TO
2	0	Ames, Leon Kessling	P	2	.000	A	
		Babb, Chas. Amos	SS113	121	.248	A	
0	0	Bartley, Wm. Jackson	P	1	.000	A	
		Bowerman, Frank Eugene	C55	59	.276	B	
		Bresnahan, Roger Philip	OF84	111	.350	B	
		Browne, George E.	OF	141	.313	B	
6	4	Cronin, John J. (Jack)	P	20	.196	B	
		Davis, George Stacey	SS	4	.250	ChiA	
		Dunn, John Joseph (Jack) (2B19 3B25)	SS27	72	.241	B	
		Gilbert, Wm. Oliver	2B	128	.252	BaltA	
		Lauder, Wm.	3B	108	.281	B	C
30	13	Mathewson, Christopher (Big Six)	P	45	.226	B	
		Mertes, Samuel Blair (Sandow)	OF137	138	.280	ChiA	
2	5	Miller, Roscoe Clyde	P	15	.161	B	
		McGann, Dennis L. (Dan)	1B	129	.270	B	
31	20	McGinnity, Joseph Jerome	P	55	.206	B	
		McGraw, John Joseph MGR.	2B	12	.273	B	
13	13	Taylor, Luther Haden	P	33	.146	B	
		VanHaltren, George E.	OF	75	.257	B	C
		Warner, John Joseph	C	85	.284	BosA	

WON 106 — NATIONAL LEAGUE — FINISHED 1st.
LOST 47
TG 153 — 1904. — PCT. .693

NEW YORK

JOHN JOSEPH McGRAW

WON	LOST	NAME	POS.	G.	BA	FROM	TO
4	6	Ames, Leon Kessling	P	16	.125	B	
		Bowerman, Frank Eugene	C79	90	.232	B	
		Bresnahan, Roger Philip	OF93	107	.284	B	
		Brouthers, Dennis (Dan)	1B	2	.000	Phil96	C
		Browne, George E.	OF	149	.283	B	
		Dahlen, Wm. Frederick (Bad Bill)	SS	145	.268	Bkn	
		Devlin, Arthur McArthur	3B	130	.281	A	
		Donlin, Michael Joseph	OF	37	+.280	xCin	
0	0	Dunn, John Joseph (Jack) (P1)	3B28	55	.309	B	C
0	2	Elliott, Claude J.	P	3	+.200	xCin	
		Gilbert, Wm. Oliver	2B	146	.253	B	
		Marshall, Wm. R. (Doc)	C	1 10	+.000 +.353	xPhil (& return)	Bos
33	12	Mathewson, Christopher (Big Six)	P	48	.226	B	
		Mertes, Samuel Blair (Sandow)	OF147	148	.276	B	
0	1	Milligan, Wm. J.	P	5	.111	PhilA01	C
		McCormick, Harry Elwood (Moose)	OF	54	+.266	A	Pitt
		McGann, Dennis L. (Dan)	1B	141	.286	B	
35	8	McGinnity, Joseph Jerome	P	51	.176	B	
		McGraw, John Joseph MGR.	2B	3	.300	B	
		O'Rourke, James Henry	C	1	.250	Wash93	C
21	15	Taylor, Luther Haden	P	37	.157	B	
		Warner, John Joseph	C	86	.199	B	
13	3	Wiltse, George LeRoy (Hooks)	P	25	.224	A	

WON 105 — NATIONAL LEAGUE — FINISHED 1st.
LOST 48
TG 153 — 1905. — PCT. .686

NEW YORK

JOHN JOSEPH McGRAW

WON	LOST	NAME	POS.	G.	BA	FROM	TO
19	7	Ames, Leon Kessling	P	34	.144	B	
		Bowerman, Frank Eugene (1B17)	C72	90	.269	B	
		Bresnahan, Roger Philip	C87	95	.302	B	
		Browne, George E.	OF	127	.293	B	
		Clarke, Wm. Jones	1B15	27	.180	WashA	C
		Dahlen, Wm. Frederick (Bad Bill)	SS147	148	.242	B	

WON	LOST	NAME	POS.	G.	BA	FROM	TO
		Devlin, Arthur McArthur	3B	153	.246	B	
		Donlin, Michael Joseph	OF	150	.356	B	
2	1	Elliott, Claude J.	P	10	.133	B	C
		Gilbert, Wm. Oliver	2B	115	.247	B	
		Graham, Archibald Wright	OF	1	.000	A	C
		Hall, Robert Prill	OF	1	+.333	Phil	Bkn
32	8	Mathewson, Christopher (Big Six)	P	43	.236	B	
		Mertes, Samuel Blair (Sandow)	OF	150	.279	B	
		McGann, Dennis L. (Dan)	1B	136	.299	B	
22	16	McGinnity, Joseph Jerome	P	46	.233	B	
		McGraw, John Joseph MGR.	OF1	3	.000	B	
		Neal, Offa (2B1)	3B3	4	.077	A	C
		Strang, Samuel Nicklin (OF38)	2B47	96	.259	Bkn	
16	9	Taylor, Luther Haden	P	32	.130	B	
14	7	Wiltse, George LeRoy (Hooks)	P32	33	.278	B	

WON 96
LOST 56
TG 152

NATIONAL LEAGUE — FINISHED 2nd.

1906. — PCT. .632

NEW YORK

JOHN JOSEPH McGRAW

WON	LOST	NAME	POS.	G.	BA	FROM	TO
12	10	Ames, Leon Kessling	P	31	.066	B	
		Bowerman, Frank Eugene (1B20)	C67	87	.228	B	
		Bresnahan, Roger Philip (OF40)	C82	124	.281	B	
		Browne, George E.	OF	121	.264	B	
		Burke, Frank Aloysius	OF	8	.222	A	
		Dahlen, Wm. Frederick (Bad Bill)	SS	143	.240	B	
		Devlin, Arthur McArthur	3B	148	.299	B	
		Donlin, Michael Joseph	OF29	30	.314	B	
2	1	Ferguson, George Cecil	P	22	.333	A	
		Fitzgerald, Matthew Wm.	C	4	.500	A	
		Gilbert, Wm. Oliver	2B	98	.231	B	
		Hannifan, John Joseph (3B5)	SS5	10	.200	xPhilA	
		Marshall, Wm. R. (Doc)	OF16	29	+.167	NY04	StL
22	12	Mathewson, Christopher (Big Six)	P	38	.264	B	
0	1	Mathewson, Henry	P	2	.000	A	
		Mertes, Samuel Blair (Sandow)	OF	71	+.237	B	StL
		McGann, Dennis L. (Dan)	1B	133	.237	B	
27	12	McGinnity, Joseph Jerome	P	45	.130	B	
		McGraw, John Joseph MGR.	3B1	4	.000	B	
		Seymour, John Bentley (Cy)	OF	72	+.320	xCin	
		Shannon, Wm. Porter (Spike)	OF	76	+.254	xStL	
		Smith, Alexander Benjamin (1B1)	C9	14	.185	Chi04	C
		Strang, Samuel Nicklin (OF36)	2B59	104	.319	B	
17	9	Taylor, Luther Haden	P	31	.184	B	
16	11	Wiltse, George LeRoy (Hooks)	P38	40	.191	B	

WON 82
LOST 70
TG 152

NATIONAL LEAGUE — FINISHED 4th.

1907. — PCT. .536

NEW YORK

JOHN JOSEPH McGRAW

WON	LOST	NAME	POS.	G.	BA	FROM	TO
10	12	Ames, Leon Kessling	P	39	.174	B	
0	2	Beecher, LeRoy	P	2	.000	A	
		Bowerman, Frank Eugene (1B29)	C62	90	.260	B	
		Bresnahan, Roger Philip	C95	104	.253	B	
		Browne, George E.	OF	121	.260	B	
		Corcoran, Thomas W.	2B	62	.265	Cin	C
		Curtis, Harry Albert	C	6	.222	A	C
		Dahlen, Wm. Frederick (Bad Bill)	SS	143	.207	B	
		Devlin, Arthur McArthur	3B140	143	.277	B	
		Doyle, Lawrence Joseph (Larry)	2B	69	.260	A	
3	2	Ferguson, George Cecil	P	15	.055	B	
		Fitzgerald, Matthew Wm.	C	6	.133	B	C
		Hannifan, John Joseph	1B29	49	.228	B	
3	6	Lynch, Michael Joseph	P	12	+.296	xPitt	C
24	12	Mathewson, Christopher (Big Six)	P	41	.187	B	
0	0	Mathewson, Henry	P	1	.000	B	C
		Merkle, Frederick Chas.	1B	15	.255	A	
		McGann, Dennis L. (Dan)	1B	81	.298	B	
18	17	McGinnity, Joseph Jerome	P	47	.175	B	
		Pfyle, Meinhard Chas. (Monte)	1B	1	.000	A	C
		Seymour, John Bentley (Cy)	OF	126	.294	B	
		Shannon, Wm. Porter (Spike)	OF	155	.265	B	
		Shay, Daniel C.	SS15	24	.190	StL05	C
		Strang, Samuel Nicklin	OF69	95	.252	B	
11	7	Taylor, Luther Haden	P28	29	.125	B	
		Wade, Abraham Lincoln	OF	1	.000	A	C
13	12	Wiltse, George LeRoy (Hooks)	P33	34	.134	B	

WON 98
LOST 56
TG 154

NATIONAL LEAGUE — FINISHED 2nd. (TIED WITH PITTS)

1908. — PCT. .636

NEW YORK

JOHN JOSEPH McGRAW

WON	LOST	NAME	POS.	G.	BA	FROM	TO
7	4	Ames, Leon Kessling	P	18	.194	B	
		Barry, John C.	OF	31	+.149	xStL	C

WON	LOST	NAME	POS.	G.	BA	FROM	TO
0	0	Beecher, LeRoy	P	2	.323	B	C
		Brain, David Leonard	OF	9	+.076	xCin	C
		Bresnshan, Roger Philip	C	139	.283	B	
		Bridwell, Albert Henry	SS	147	.285	Bos	
12	12	Crandall, James Otis (Doc)	P	32	.222	A	
		Devlin, Arthur McArthur	3B	157	.253	B	
		Devore, Joshua (Josh)	OF	5	.167	A	
		Donlin, Michael Joseph	OF	155	.334	NY06	
		Doyle, Lawrence Joseph (Larry)	2B	102	.308	B	
0	0	Durham, Louis G.	P	1	.000	WashA	
		Evans, Louis Richard	OF	2	.333	A	
		Hannifan, John Joseph	2B	1	+.000	B	Bos
		Herzog, Chas. Lincoln (Buck)	2B42	59	.300	A	
0	2	Malarkey, Wm. John	P	15	.000	A	C
0	1	Marquard, Richard Wm. (Rube)	P	1	.000	A	
37	11	Mathewson, Christopher (Big Six)	P	56	.155	B	
		Merkle, Frederick Chas.	1B	18	.268	B	
		McCormick, Harry Elwood (Moose)	OF	65	+.302	xPhil	
11	7	McGinnity, Joseph Jerome	P	37	.180	B	C
		Needham, Thomas J.	C	47	.209	Bos	
		Seymour, John Bentley (Cy)	OF	155	.267	B	
		Shannon, Wm. Porter (Spike)	OF	74	+.224	B	Pitt
		Snodgrass, Frederick Carlisle	C	5	.250	A	
		Strang, Samuel Nicklin	3B	22	.094	B	C
8	5	Taylor, Luther Haden	P	27	.229	B	C
		Tenney, Frederick	1B	156	.256	Bos	
		Wilson, Arthur Earl	C	1	.000	A	
23	14	Wiltse, George LeRoy (Hooks)	P	44	.236	B	

WON 92 — NATIONAL LEAGUE — FINISHED 3rd.
LOST 61
TG 153 — 1909. — PCT. .601

NEW YORK

JOHN JOSEPH McGRAW

WON	LOST	NAME	POS.	G.	BA	FROM	TO
15	10	Ames, Leon Kessling	P	34	.074	B	
		Bridwell, Albert Henry	SS	145	.294	B	
6	4	Crandall, James Otis (Doc)	P	30	.244	B	
0	3	Daly, George Joseph	P	3	.111	A	C
		Devlin, Arthur McArthur	3B	143	.265	B	
		Devore, Joshua (Josh)	OF	23	.160	B	
		Doyle, Lawrence Joseph (Larry)	2B	144	.302	B	
2	1	Drucke, Louis Frank	P	3	.125	A	
0	0	Durham, Louis G.	P	4	.000	B	C
		Fletcher, Arthur	SS19	29	.214	A	
		Herzog, Chas. Lincoln (Buck)	OF30	38	.185	B	
1	1	Klawitter, Albert C.	P	6	.333	A	
		Latham, Walter Arlington (Arlie)	2B	4	.000	Wash99	C
5	13	Marquard, Richard Wm. (Rube)	P	29	.148	B	
25	6	Mathewson, Christopher (Big Six)	P	37	.263	B	
		Merkle, Frederick Chas.	1B70	71	.191	B	
		Meyers, John Tortes (Chief)	C	64	.277	A	
		Murray, John Joseph (Red)	OF	149	.263	StL	
		McCormick, Harry Elwood (Moose)	OF	110	.290	B	
		O'Hara, Wm. A.	OF	111	.236	A	
18	12	Raymond, Arthur Lawrence (Bugs)	P	39	.146	StL	
		Schlei, George Henry	C	89	.244	Cin	
		Seymour, John Bentley (Cy)	OF	73	.310	B	
		Shafer, Arthur Joseph	3B16	31	.179	A	
		Snodgrass, Frederick Carlisle	OF20	22	.300	B	
		Tenney, Frederick	1B	98	.235	B	
0	0	Waller, John Francis	P	1	.000	A	C
0	0	Weimer, John Wm.	P	1	.000	Cin	C
		Wilson, Arthur Earl	C	17	.238	B	
20	11	Wiltse, George LeRoy (Hooks)	P	37	.200	B	

WON 91 — NATIONAL LEAGUE — FINISHED 2nd.
LOST 63
TG 154 — 1910. — PCT. .591

NEW YORK

JOHN JOSEPH McGRAW

WON	LOST	NAME	POS.	G.	BA	FROM	TO
12	11	Ames, Leon Kessling	P	33	.177	B	
		Becker, Beals	OF45	46	.286	Bos	
		Bridwell, Albert Henry	SS	141	.276	B	
17	4	Crandall, James Otis (Doc)	P42	43	.342	B	
		Devlin, Arthur McArthur	3B	147	.260	B	
		Devore, Joshua (Josh)	OF	130	.304	B	
1	0	Dickson, Walter R.	P	12	.250	A	
		Doyle, Lawrence Joseph (Larry)	2B	151	.285	B	
12	10	Drucke, Louis Frank	P	34	.214	B	
		Fletcher, Arthur	SS22	44	.224	B	
		Gowdy, Henry Morgan (Hank)	1B	5	.214	A	
0	1	Hendricks, Edward	P	4	.000	A	C
		Keeler, Wm. Henry	OF2	17	.300	NYA	C
0	0	Klawitter, Albert C.	P	1	.000	B	
4	4	Marquard, Richard Wm. (Rube)	P	13	.115	B	
27	9	Mathewson, Christopher (Big Six)	P	38	.234	B	
		Merkle, Frederick Chas.	1B	144	.292	B	
		Meyers, John Tortes (Chief)	C	117	.285	B	
		Murray, John Joseph (Red)	OF	148	.277	B	
4	11	Raymond, Arthur Lawrence (Bigs)	P	19	.156	B	
0	1	Rudolph, Richard (Dick)	P	3	.250	A	
		Schlei, George Henry	C	49	.192	B	
		Seymour, John Bentley (Cy)	OF	76	.265	B	

WON	LOST	NAME	POS.	G.	BA	FROM	TO
		Shafer, Arthur Joseph	3B6	27	.182	B	
		Snodgrass, Frederick Carlisle	OF101	112	.321	B	
		Wilson, Arthur Earl	C	26	.269	B	
14	12	Wiltse, George LeRoy (Hooks)	P	36	.176	B	
		Zacher, Elmer Henry	OF	1	+.000	A	StL

WON 99 NATIONAL LEAGUE FINISHED 1st.
LOST 54
TG 153 1911. PCT. .647

NEW YORK

JOHN JOSEPH McGRAW

WON	LOST	NAME	POS.	G.	BA	FROM	TO
11	10	Ames, Leon Kessling	P	34	.094	B	
		Becker, Beals	OF	55	.262	B	
		Bridwell, Albert Henry	SS	76	+.270	B	Bos
		Burns, George Joseph	OF	6	.059	A	
15	5	Crandall, James Otis (Doc)	P41	50	.239	B	
		Devlin, Arthur McArthur	3B79	95	.278	B	
		Devore, Joshua (Josh)	OF	149	.280	B	
		Donlin, Michael Joseph	OF	12	+.333	NY08	Bos
		Doyle, Lawrence Joseph (Larry)	2B	141	.310	B	
4	4	Drucke, Louis Frank	P	15	.087	B	
0	0	Faust, Chas. Victor	P	2	.000	A	C
		Fletcher, Arthur (3B21)	SS74	108	.319	B	
		Gowdy, Henry Morgan (Hank)	1B	4	+.250	B	Bos
		Hartley, Grover Allen	C	10	.222	A	
		Herzog, Chas. Lincoln (Buck)	3B53	69	+.267	xBos	
24	7	Marquard, Richard Wm. (Rube)	P	45	.163	B	
26	13	Mathewson, Christopher (Big Six)	P	45	.196	B	
1	2	Maxwell, J. Albert	P	4	.111	PhilA08	
		Markle, Frederick Chas.	1B	148	.283	B	
		Meyers, John Tortes (Chief)	C	128	.332	B	
		Murray, John Joseph (Red)	OF	131	.291	B	
		Paulette, Eugene Edward	1B3	10	.167	A	
6	4	Raymond, Arthur Lawrence (Bugs)	P	17	.200	B	C
0	0	Rudolph, Richard (Dick)	P	1	1.000	B	
		Schlei, George Henry	C	1	.000	B	C
		Snodgrass, Frederick Carlisle	OF149	151	.294	B	
		Wilson, Arthur Earl	C	64	.302	B	
12	9	Wiltse, George LeRoy (Hooks)	P	30	.188	B	

WON 103 NATIONAL LEAGUE FINISHED 1st.
LOST 48
TG 151 1912. PCT. .682

NEW YORK

JOHN JOSEPH McGRAW

WON	LOST	NAME	POS.	G.	BA	FROM	TO
11	5	Ames, Leon Kessling	P	33	.224	B	
2	0	Bader, Loren Verne	P	2	.000	A	
		Becker, Beals	OF117	125	.264	B	
		Burns, George Joseph	OF23	29	.294	B	
13	7	Crandall, James Otis (Doc)	P37	50	.313	B	
1	0	Demaree, Albert Wentworth (Al)	P	2	.000	A	
		Devore, Joshua (Josh)	OF96	106	.275	B	
		Doyle, Lawrence Joseph (Larry)	2B	143	.330	B	
0	0	Drucke, Louis Frank	P	1	.000	B	C
		Fletcher, Arthur	SS126	129	.282	B	
0	0	Goulait, Theodore L.	P	1	.500	A	C
		Groh, Henry Knight (Heinie)	2B9	27	.271	A	
		Hartley, Grover Allen	C	25	.235	B	
		Herzog, Chas. Lincoln (Buck)	3B	140	.263	B	
1	0	Kirby, LaRue V.	P	3	.200	A	
26	11	Marquard, Richard Wm. (Rube)	P	43	.219	B	
23	12	Mathewson, Christopher (Big Six)	P	43	.264	B	
		Merkle, Frederick Chas.	1B	129	.309	B	
		Meyers, John Tortes (Chief)	C122	126	.358	B	
		Murray, John Joseph (Red)	OF	143	.277	B	
		McCormick, Harry Elwood (Moose)	OF	42	.333	NY09	
		Robertson, Davis Aydelotte (1B1)	OF1	3	.000	A	
		Shafer, Arthur Joseph	SS31	78	.288	NY10	
0	0	Shore, Ernest Grady	P	1	.000	A	
		Snodgrass, Frederick Carlisle (1B27)	OF116	146	.269	B	
17	7	Tesreau, Chas. Monroe (Jeff)	P	36	.146	A	
		Wilson, Arthur Earl	C61	65	.289	B	
9	6	Wiltse, George LeRoy (Hooke)	P	28	.326	B	

WON 101 NATIONAL LEAGUE FINISHED 1st.
LOST 51
TG 152 1913. PCT. .664

NEW YORK

JOHN JOSEPH McGRAW

WON	LOST	NAME	POS.	G.	BA	FROM	TO
2	1	Ames, Leon Kessling	P	8	+.250	B	Cin
		Burns, George Joseph	OF	150	.286	B	
		Cooper, Claude Wm.	OF15	27	.300	A	
4	4	Crandall, James Otis (Doc)	P	31	+.280	B	St.L.
				15	+.364	(and Recalled)	
13	4	Demaree, Albert Wentworth (Al)	P	31	.106	B	
		Devore, Joshua (Josh)	OF	16	+.190	B	Cin
		Doyle, Lawrence Joseph (Larry)	2B130	132	.280	B	
		Evers, Joseph Francis	3B	1	.000	A	C

WON	LOST	NAME	POS.	G.	BA	FROM	TO
		Fletcher, Arthur	SS	136	.297	B	
11	6	Fromme, Arthur Henry	P	26	+.171	xCin	
		Grant, Edward Leslie	3B	27	+.200	xCin	
		Groh, Henry Knight (Heinie)	2B	4	+.000	B	Cin
		Hartley, Grover Allen	C21	23	.316	B	
1	1	Hearn, Bunn	P	2	.400	StL11	
		Herzog, Chas. Lincoln (Buck)	3B84	96	.286	B	
23	10	Marquard, Richard Wm. (Rube)	P	42	.219	B	
25	11	Mathewson, Christopher (Big Six)	P	40	.184	B	
		Merkle, Frederick Chas.	1B	153	.261	B	
		Merritt, John Howard	OF	1	.000	A	C
		Meyers, John Tortes (Chief)	C116	120	.312	B	
		Murray, John Joseph (Red)	OF	147	.267	B	
		McCormick, Harry Elwood (Moose)	OF15	57	.275	B	C
		McLean, John Bannerman (Larry)	C	30	+.320	xStL	
0	1	Schauer, Alexander John (Rube)	P	3	.000	A	
0	0	Schupp, Ferdinand Maurice	P	5	.333	A	
		Shafer, Arthur Joseph (2B25 SS16 OF15)	3B81	138	.287	B	C
		Snodgrass, Frederick Carlisle	OF133	141	.291	B	
		Stock, Milton Joseph	SS	7	.176	A	
22	13	Tesreau, Chas. Monroe (Jeff)	P	41	.221	B	
		Thorpe, James Francis	OF9	19	.143	A	
		Wilson, Arthur Earl	C49	54	.190	B	
0	0	Wiltse, George LeRoy (Hooks)	P17	20	.208	B	

WON 84   NATIONAL LEAGUE   FINISHED 2nd.
LOST 70
TG 154   1914.   PCT. .545

NEW YORK

JOHN JOSEPH McGRAW

WON	LOST	NAME	POS.	G.	BA	FROM	TO
		Beatty, Desmond	3B	1	.000	A	C
		Bescher, Robert Henry	OF126	135	.270	Cin	
		Brainard, Frederick	2B	2	.510	A	
		Burns, George Joseph	OF	154	.303	B	
10	17	Demaree, Albert Wentworth (Al)	P	38	.132	B	
		Donlin, Michael Joseph	OF	35	.161	Pitt12	C
		Doyle, Lawrence Joseph (Larry)	2B	145	.260	B	
		Dyer, Benjamin Franklin (2B1)	SS6	7	.250	A	
0	1	Erickson, Eric George	P	1	.000	A	
		Fletcher, Arthur	SS	135	.286	B	
9	5	Fromme, Arthur Henry	P	38	.236	B	
		Grant, Edward Leslie (2B16 SS21)	3B52	88	.277	B	
		Holke, Walter Henry	1B	2	.333	A	
0	0	Huenke, Albert John	P	1	.000	A	C
		Johnson, Elmer Ellsworth	C	11	.166	A	C
12	22	Marquard, Richard Wm. (Rube)	P	39	.179	B	
24	13	Mathewson, Christopher (Big Six)	P	41	.219	B	
		Merkle, Frederick Chas.	1B	146	.258	B	
		Meyers, John Tortes (Chief)	C126	134	.286	B	
		Murray, John Joseph (Red)	OF49	86	.223	B	
		McLean, John Bannerman (Larry)	C74	79	.260	B	
1	1	O'Toole, Martin James	P	10	+.300	xPitt	C
		Piez, Chas. Wm. (Sandy)	OF	35	.375	A	C
1	0	Ritter, Wm. Herbert	P	1	.000	Phil12	
		Robertson, Davis Aydelotte	OF71	82	.266	NY12	
0	0	Schauer, Alexander John (Rube)	P	6	.143	B	
0	0	Schupp, Ferdinand Maurice	P	8	.000	B	
		Smith, James Harry	C	5	.428	A	
		Snodgrass, Frederick Carlisle	OF96	113	.263	B	
		Stock, Milton Joseph	3B113	115	.263	B	
26	10	Tesreau, Chas. Monroe (Jeff)	P	42	.239	B	
		Thorpe, James Francis	OF	30	.194	B	
1	1	Wiltse, George LeRoy (Hooks)	P20	21	.667	B	

WON 69   NATIONAL LEAGUE   FINISHED 8th (LAST)
LOST 83
TG 152   1915.   PCT. .454

NEW YORK

JOHN JOSEPH McGRAW

WON	LOST	NAME	POS.	G.	BA	FROM	YO
		Babington, Chas. Percy	OF	28	.242	A	C
		Baker, Howard Francis	3B	1	.000	xChiA	C
		Becker, Martin Henry	OF16	17	.250	A	C
3	5	Benton, John Cleveland (Rube)	P	10	+.190	xPitt	
		Brainard, Frederick (3B15)	1B43	91	.201	B	
		Burns, George Joseph	OF	155	.272	B	
		Dooin, Chas. Sebastian	C	46	+.218	xCin	
		Doyle, Lawrence Joseph (Larry)	2B147	150	.320	B	
		Dyer, Benjamin Franklin (SS1)	3B6	7	.211	B	
		Fletcher, Arthur	SS	149	.254	B	
0	1	Fromme, Arthur Henry	P	4	.333	B	C
		Grant, Edward Leslie	3B35	87	.208	B	C
1	1	Herbert, Frederick	P	2	.167	A	C
		Jacobson, Merwin John Wm.	OF	8	.083	A	
		Kelly, George Lange (Long George)	1B	17	.158	A	
		Kocher, Bradley Wilson	C	4	.455	DetA12	
		Lobert, John Bernard (Hans)	3B103	106	.251	Phil	
9	8	Marquard, Richard Wm. (Rube)	P	27	+.109	B	Bkn
8	14	Mathewson, Christopher (Big Six)	P	27	.157	B	
		Merkle, Frederick Chas. (OF30)	1B110	140	.299	B	
		Meyers, John Tortes (Chief)	C96	110	.232	B	
		Murray, John Joseph (Red)	OF	45	+.220	B	Chi

WON	LOST	NAME	POS.	G.	BA	FROM	TO
		McLean, John Bannerman (Larry)	C	13	.152	B	C
0	2	Palmero, Emilio A.	P	3	.250	A	
12	18	Perritt, Wm. Dayton (Pol)	P	35	.162	StL	
2	1	Ritter, Wm. Herbert	P	22	.125	B	
		Robertson, Davis Aydelotte	OF138	141	.294	B	
		Schang, Robert Martin	C	12	+.143	xPitt	
2	8	Schauer, Alexander John (Rube)	P	32	.077	B	
1	0	Schupp, Ferdinand Maurice	P	23	.200	B	
		Smith, James Harry	C18	21	.125	B	BknF
		Snodgrass, Frederick Carlisle	OF	80	+.151	B	Bos
12	9	Stroud, Ralph E.	P	32	.161	DetA10	
19	16	Tesreau, Chas. Monroe (Jeff)	P	43	.233	B	
		Thorpe, James Francis	OF15	17	.231	B	
		Wendell, Lewis Chas.	C18	20	.222	A	

WON 86 — NATIONAL LEAGUE — FINISHED 4th.
LOST 66
TG 152 — 1916. — PCT. .566

NEW YORK

JOHN JOSEPH McGRAW

WON	LOST	NAME	POS.	G.	BA	FROM	TO
9	13	Anderson, John Frederick	P	38	.138	BuffF	
16	8	Benton, John Cleveland (Rube)	P	38	.090	B	
		Brainard, Frederick	3B	2	.000	B	C
		Burns, George Joseph	OF	155	.279	B	
		Dooin, Chas. Sebastian	C	15	.118	B	C
		Doolan, Michael Joseph	SS	18	+.240	xChi	
		Doyle, Lawrence Joseph (Larry)	2B	113	+.264	B	Chi
		Fletcher, Arthur	SS	133	.286	B	
		Herzog, Chas. Lincoln (Buck) (SS9 3B27)	2B44	77	+.261	xCin	
		Holke, Walter Henry	1B	34	.351	NY14	
		Hunter, Herbert Harrison	3B 4	21	+.250	A	Chi
		Kauff, Benjamin Michael	OF	154	.264	BknF	
		Kelleher, Albert Aloysius	C	1	.000	A	C
		Kelly, George Lange (Long George)	1B9	49	.158	B	
		Killefer, Wade Hampton		2	+.500	xCin	C
		Kocher, Bradley Wilson	C30	34	.108	B	C
		Lobert, John Bernard (Hans)	3B20	48	.224	B	
3	4	Mathewson, Christopher (Big Six)	P	12	+.000	B	Cin
		Merkle, Frederick Chas.	1B	112	+.241	B	Bkn
		McCarty, George Lewis	C	25	+.400	xBkn	
		McKechnie, Wm. Boyd	3B	71	+.238	NewF	Cin
0	3	Palmero, Emilio A.	P	5	.000	B	
18	11	Perritt, Wm. Dayton (Pol)	P	40	.084	B	
		Rariden, Wm. Angel	C119	120	.222	NewF	
1	0	Ritter, Wm. Herbert	P	3	.000	B	C
		Robertson, Davis Aydelotte	OF144	150	.307	B	

WON	LOST	NAME	POS.	G.	BA	FROM	TO
		Rodriguez, Jose		1	.000	A	
		Roush, Edd J.	OF	39	+.188	NewF	Cin
9	4	Sallee, Harry Franklin (Slim)	P	15	+.257	xStL	
1	4	Schauer, Alexander John (Rube)	P	19	.222	B	
9	3	Schupp, Ferdinand Maurice	P	30	.098	B	
3	0	Smith, George Allen	P	9	.000	A	
		Stafford, Henry Alexander		1	.000	A	C
3	2	Stroud, Ralph E.	P	10	.071	B	C
14	14	Tesreau, Chas. Monroe (Jeff)	P40	41	.191	B	
		Wendell, Lewis Chas.	C	2	.000	B	
		Zimmerman, Henry (Heinie)	2B15	40	+.265	xChi	

WON 98 — NATIONAL LEAGUE — FINISHED 1st.
LOST 56
TG 154 — 1917. — PCT. .636

NEW YORK

JOHN JOSEPH McGRAW

WON	LOST	NAME	POS.	G.	BA	FROM	TO
8	8	Anderson, John Frederick	P	38	.071	B	
		Baird, Albert Wells	2B5	10	.292	A	
15	9	Benton, John Cleveland (Rube)	P	35	.167	B	
		Burns, George Joseph	OF	152	.302	B	
4	5	Demaree, Albert Wentworth (Al)	P	15	+.111	xChi	
		Fletcher, Arthur	SS	151	.260	B	
		Gibson, George	C	35	.171	Pitt	
		Hemingway, Edson M.	1B	7	.320	StLA14	
		Jerzog, Chas. Lincoln (Buck)	2B113	114	.235	B	
		Holke, Walter Henry	1B	153	.277	B	
		Kauff, Benjamin Michael	OF	153	.308	B	
1	0	Kelly, George Lange (Long George)	P1	11	+.000	B	Pitt
		Kilduff, Peter John (SS5)	2B21	31	+.205	A	Chi
		Krueger, Ernest George	C5	8	+.000	NYA15	Bkn
		Lobert, John Bernard (Hans)	3B21	50	.192	B	
1	1	Middleton, James Blaine	P	13	.000	A	
		Murray, John Joseph (Red)	OF	22	.045	Chi15	C
		McCarty, George Lewis	C54	56	.247	B	
		Onslow, John James	C	9	.250	DetA12	C
17	7	Perritt, Wm. Dayton (Pol)	P	35	.157	B	
		Rariden, Wm. Angel	C100	101	.271	B	
		Robertson, Davis Aydelotte	OF140	142	.259	B	
		Rodriguez, Jose	1B	7	.200	B	
18	7	Sallee, Harry Franklin (Slim)	P	34	.221	B	
21	7	Schupp, Ferdinand Maurice	P	36	.161	B	
0	3	Smith, George Allen	P	14	.000	B	
		Smith, James Lawrence	2B29	36	.229	Pitt	
0	1	Swigler, Adam Wm.	P	1	.000	A	C
13	8	Tresreau, Chas. Monroe (Jeff)	P	33	.230	B	
		Thorpe, James Francis	OF	26	+.200	xCin	
		Wilhoit, Joseph Wm.	OF	34	+.320	xPitt	
		Youngs, Ross Middlebrook (Pep)	OF	7	.346	A	
		Zimmerman, Henry (Heinie)	3B149	150	.297	B	

WON 71 | NATIONAL LEAGUE | FINISHED 2nd.
LOST 53
TG 124 | 1918. | PCT. .573

NEW YORK

JOHN JOSEPH McGRAW

WON	LOST	NAME	POS.	G.	BA	FROM	TO
4	2	Anderson, John Frederick	P	18	.000	B	C
6	1	Barnes, Jesse Lawrence	P	9	.222	Bos	
1	2	Benton, John Cleveland (Rube)	P	3	.142	B	
		Burns, George Joseph	OF	119	.290	B	
11	6	Causey, Cecil Algernon	P	29	.125	A	
		Compton, Albert Sebastian (Bash)	OF19	21	.217	Pitt16	C
8	6	Demaree, Albert Wentworth (Al)	P	26	.128	B	
		Doyle, Lawrence Joseph (Larry)	2B73	75	.261	Chi	
		Fletcher, Arthur	SS	124	.263	B	
		Gibson, George	C	4	.500	B	
		Holke, Walter Henry	1B	88	.252	B	
0	0	Hoyt, Waite Chas.	P	1	.000	A	
		Kauff, Benjamin Michael	OF	67	.315	B	
		Kirke, Jay	1B16	17	.250	ClevA15	C
		McCarty, George Lewis	C75	86	.269	B	
		Niehoff, John Albert (Bert)	2B	7	+.261	xStL	C
0	0	Ogden, John Mahlon	P	5	.000	A	
18	13	Perritt, Wm. Dayton (Pol)	P	36	.175	B	
		Rariden, Wm. Angel	C63	69	.224	B	
		Rodriguez, Jose (1B8 3B2)	2B40	50	.160	B	C
0	0	Ross, George Sidney	P	1	.000	A	C
8	8	Sallee, Harry Franklin (Slim)	P	18	.122	B	
0	1	Schupp, Ferdinand Maurice	P	10	.111	B	
		Sicking, Edward Joseph (2B18 SS3)	3B24	46	.250	Chi16	
2	3	Smith, George Allen	P	5	+.250	xCin	Bkn
3	5	Steele, Robert Wesley	P	12	+.286	xPitt	
4	4	Tesreau, Chas. Monroe (Jeff)	P	12	.312	B	C
		Thorpe, James Francis	OF44	58	.248	B	
6	2	Toney, Frederick Arthur	P	11	+.188	xCin	
		Wilhoit, Joseph Wm.	OF55	64	.274	B	
		Youngs, Ross Middlebrook (Pep) (2B1)	OF120	121	.302	B	
		Zimmerman, Henry (Heinie) (1B19)	3B100	121	.272	B	

WON 87 | NATIONAL LEAGUE | FINISHED 2nd.
LOST 53
TG 140 | 1919. | PCT. .621

NEW YORK

JOHN JOSEPH McGRAW

WON	LOST	NAME	POS.	G.	BA	FROM	TO
		Baird, Albert Wells (SS9 3B5)	2B24	38	.241	NY17	C
25	9	Barnes, Jesse Lawrence	P38	46	.267	B	
0	0	Barnes, Virgil Jennings	P	1	.000	A	
17	11	Benton, John Cleveland (Rube)	P	35	.194	B	
		Bowen, Emmons Joseph	OF	3	.201	A	C
		Burns, George Joseph	OF	139	.303	B	
9	3	Causey, Cecil Algernon	P	21	+.132	B	Bos
		Chase, Harold Homer (Hal)	1B107	110	.284	Cin	C
		Cooney, James Edward	SS	5	.214	BosA17	
2	4	Douglas, Philip Brooks (Shufflin' Phil)	P	8	+.000	xChi	
		Doyle, Lawrence Joseph (Larry)	2B100	113	.289	B	
6	4	Dubuc, Jean Arthur	P36	37	.143	BosA	C
		Fletcher, Arthur	SS	127	.277	B	
		Frisch, Frank Francis Jr. (SS1 3B20)	2B29	54	.226	A	
		Gonzales, Miguel Angel Cordero (1B4)	C52	58	.190	StL	
1	1	Hubbell, Wilbert Wm.	P	2	.125	A	
0	0	Jones, John Paul	P	2	.000	A	
		Kauff, Benjamin Michael	OF134	135	.277	B	
		Kelly, George Lange (Long George)	1B	32	.290	Pitt17	
		King, Lee	OF	21	.100	Pitt	
		Kinsella, Robert Francis	OF	3	.222	A	
		McCarty, George Lewis	C59	35	.281	B	
9	2	Nehf, Arthur Neukom	P	13	+.265	xBos	
0	1	Oeschger, Joseph Carl	P	5	+.000	xPhil	Bos
1	1	Perritt, Wm. Dayton (Pol)	P	11	.000	B	
1	0	Ragan, Don Carlos Patrick (Pat)	P	7	+.428	xBos	ChiA
		Robertson, Davis Aydelotte	OF	1	+.000	NY17	Chi
1	2	Ryan, Wilfred Patrick Dolan (Rosy)	P	4	.000	A	
1	3	Schupp, Ferdinand Maurice	P	9	+.333	B	StL
		Sicking, Edward Joseph (2B2)	SS2	6	+.333	B	Phil
		Smith, Earl Sutton	C	21	.250	A	
0	2	Smith, George Allen	P	3	+.000	Bkn	Phil
0	1	Snover, Colonel Lester	P	2	.000	A	C
		Snyder, Frank J. (Pancho)	C	32	+.228	xStL	
		Statz, Arnold John (Jigger) (2B1)	OF18	21	.300	A	
0	1	Steele, Robert Wesley	P	1	.000	B	C
		Thorpe, James Francis	OF	2	+.333	B	Bos
13	6	Toney, Frederick Arthur	P	24	.227	B	
1	2	Winters, Jesse Franklin	P	16	.000	A	
		Youngs, Ross Middlebrook (Pep)	OF	130	.311	B	
		Zimmerman, Henry (Heinie)	3B	123	.255	B	C

WON 86 | NATIONAL LEAGUE | FINISHED 2nd.
LOST 68
TG 154 | 1920. | PCT. .558

NEW YORK

JOHN JOSEPH McGRAW

WON	LOST	NAME	POS.	G.	BA	FROM	TO
		Baird, Howard Douglas	3B	7	+.125	xBkn	C
		Bancroft, David James	SS	108	+.308	xPhil	
20	15	Barnes, Jesse Lawrence	P43	45	.204	B	
0	1	Barnes, Virgil Jennings	P	1	.000	B	
9	16	Benton, John Cleveland (Rube)	P	33	.092	B	
		Brown, Edward Wm.	OF	3	.125	A	
		Burns, George Joseph	OF	154	.287	B	
0	0	Davenport, Claude Edwin	P	1	.000	A	C
14	10	Douglas, Philip Brooks (Shufflin' Phil)	P	46	.151	B	
		Doyle, Lawrence Joseph (Larry)	2B133	137	.285	B	C
		Fletcher, Arthur	SS	41	+.254	B	Phil
		Frisch, Frank Francis Jr.	3B109	110	.280	B	
		Gaston, Alexander Nathaniel	C	4	.100	A	
		Gonzales, Miguel Angel Cordero	C	11	.231	B	
		Griffin, Francis Arthur	OF	5	.250	PhilA17	C
0	1	Grubbs, Thomas Dillard	P	1	.000	A	C
		Grimes, Roy Austin	2B21	26	.158	A	C
0	1	Hubbell, Wilbert Wm.	P	14	+.200	B	Phil
		Kauff, Benjamin Michael	OF51	55	.274	B	C
		Kelly, George Lange (Long George)	1B	155	.266	B	
		King, Lee	OF84	93	.276	B	
		Kinsella, Robert Francis	OF	1	.333	B	C
		Lear, Frederick Francis	3B24	31	.253	Chi	C
		LeFevre, Alfred Modesto (2B2)	SS5	17	.148	A	C
		McCarty, George Lewis	C	36	+.132	B	StL
21	12	Nehf, Arthur Neukom	P	40	.268	B	
0	0	Perritt, Wm. Dayton (Pol)	P	8	.000	B	
0	1	Ryan, Wilfred Patrick Dolan (Rosy)	P	3	.000	B	
1	0	Sallee, Harry Franklin (Slim)	P	5	+.333	xCin	
		Sicking, Edward Joseph	3B14	46	+.172	Phil	Cin
		Smith, Earl Sutton	C82	91	.294	B	
		Snyder, Frank J. (Pancho)	C84	87	.250	B	
		Spencer, Vernon Murray	OF40	45	.200	A	C
		Statz, Arnold John (Jigger)	OF	16	.133	B	BosA
21	11	Toney, Frederick Arthur	P	42	.240	B	
		Walker, Wm. Curtis	OF	8	.000	NYA19	
0	0	Winters, Jesse Franklin	P	21	.000	B	
		Youngs, Ross Middlebrook (Pep)	OF	153	.351	B	

WON 94 NATIONAL LEAGUE FINISHED 1st.
LOST 59
TG 153 1921. PCT. .614

NEW YORK

JOHN JOSEPH McGRAW

WON	LOST	NAME	POS.	G.	BA	FROM	TO
		Bancroft, David James	SS	153	.319	B	
15	9	Barnes, Jesse Lawrence	P	42	.207	B	
5	2	Benton, John Cleveland (Rube)	P	18	.143	B	
		Berry, Joseph Howard Jr.	2B8	9	.333	A	
		Brown, Edward Wm.	OF30	70	.281	B	
		Burns, George Joseph	OF	149	.299	B	
1	1	Causey, Cecil Algernon	P	9	+.333	xPhil	
		Connolly, Joseph George	OF	2	.000	A	
		Cunningham, Wm. Aloysius	OF20	40	.276	A	
15	10	Douglas, Philip Brooks (Shufflin' Phil)	P	40	.198	B	
		Frisch, Frank Francis Jr. (2B61)	3B93	153	.341	B	
		Gaston, Alexander Nathaniel	C	20	.227	B	
		Gonzales, Miguel Angel Cordero (C1)	1B4	13	.375	B	
		Heinie, Wm. H.	2B	1	.000	A	C
		Henline, Walter John (Butch)	C	1	+.000	A	Phil
0	0	Jonnard, Claude Alfred	P	1	.000	A	
		Kelly, George Lange (Long George)	1B	149	.308	B	
		King, Lee	OF	39	+.223	B	Phil
		Kopf, Walter Henry	3B	2	.333	A	C
		Mahady, James B.	2B	1	.000	A	C
		Meusel, Emil Frederick (Irish)	OF	62	+.329	xPhil	
		Monroe, John Allen	2B	19	+.143	A	Phil
20	10	Nehf, Arthur Neukom	P41	42	.202	B	
		Patterson, Wm. Jennings Bryan	3B	23	.400	A	C
2	0	Perritt, Wm. Dayton (Pol)	P	5	.000	B	DetA
		Rapp, Joseph Aloysius (Goldie)	3B	58	+.215	A	Phil
		Rawlings, John Wm.	2B	86	+.267	xPhil	
7	10	Ryan, Wilfred Patrick Dolan (Rosy)	P	36	.200	B	
6	4	Sallee, Harry Franklin (Slim)	P	37	.364	B	C
		Schreiber, Henry Ward (SS2)	2B2	4	.167	Cin19	
5	2	Shea, Patrick Henry	P	9	.111	PhilA18	
		Smith, Earl Sutton	C78	89	.336	B	
		Snyder, Frank J. (Pancho)	C101	108	.320	B	
		Stengel, Chas. Dillon (Casey)	OF	18	+.227	xPhil	
18	11	Toney, Frederick Arthur	P	42	.209	B	
		Walker, Wm. Curtis	OF	64	+.286	B	Phil
		Youngs, Ross Middlebrook (Pep)	OF137	141	.327	B	
0	0	Zink, Walter Cyrus	P	2	.000	A	C

WON 93 NATIONAL LEAGUE FINISHED 1st.
LOST 61
TG 154 1922. PCT. .604

NEW YORK

JOHN JOSEPH McGRAW

WON	LOST	NAME	POS.	G.	BA	FROM	TO
		Bancroft, David James	SS	156	.321	B	
13	8	Barnes, Jesse Lawrence	P	37	.181	B	
1	0	Barnes, Virgil Jennings	P	22	.167	NY20	
		Berry, Joseph Howard Jr.		6	.000	B	C
1	0	Blume, Clinton Willis	P	1	1.000	A	
		Boone, Isaac Morgan	OF	2	.500	A	
4	3	Causey, Cecil Algernon	P24	25	.238	B	C
		Cunningham, Wm. Aloysius (3B1)	OF71	85	.327	B	
0	1	Cvengros, Michael John	P	1	.000	A	
		Dolan, Alvin James (Cozy)		1	.000	StL15	C
11	4	Douglas, Philip Brooks (Shufflin' Phil)	P	24	.206	B	C
		Frisch, Frank Francis Jr. (SS1 3B53)	2B85	132	.326	B	
		Gaston, Alexander Nathaniel	C13	16	.192	B	
		Groh, Henry Knight (Heinie)	3B110	115	.265	Cin	
		Higbee, Mahlon Jesse	OF	3	.400	A	C
2	1	Hill, Carmen Proctor	P	8	.182	Pitt19	
		Jackson, Travis Calvin	SS	3	.000	A	
0	2	Johnson, Frederick Edward	P	2	.000	A	
6	1	Jonnard, Claude Alfred	P	33	.042	B	
		Kelly, George Lange (Long George)	1B	151	.327	B	
		King, Lee (OF5)	1B5	20	+.176	xPhil	C
		MacPhee, Walter Scott	3B	2	.286	A	C
		Maguire, Frederick Edward	2B3	5	.333	A	
		Meusel, Emil Frederick (Irish)	OF	154	.330	B	
6	5	NcQuillan, Hugh A.	P	15	+.189	xBos	
19	13	Nehf, Arthur Neukom	P	37	.255	B	
		Rawlings, John Wm. (3B5)	2B77	88	.282	B	
		Robertson, Davis Aydelotte	OF8	42	.276	Pitt	C
17	12	Ryan, Wilfred Patrick Dolan (Rosy)	P	46	.193	B	
8	2	Scott, John Wm. (Jack)	P	17	+.267	xCin	
0	3	Shea, Patrick Henry	P	11	.000	B	C
		Shinners, Ralph Peter	OF37	56	.251	A	
		Smith, Earl Sutton	C75	90	.277	B	
		Snyder, Frank J. (Pancho)	C97	104	.343	B	
		Stengel, Chas. Dillon (Casey)	OF77	84	.368	B	
5	6	Toney, Frederick Arthur	P	13	.067	B	
		Youngs, Ross Middlebrook (Pep)	OF147	149	.330	B	

WON 95 NATIONAL LEAGUE FINISHED 1st.
LOST 58
TG 153 1923. PCT. .621

NEW YORK

JOHN JOSEPH McGRAW

WON	LOST	NAME	POS.	G.	BA	FROM	TO
		Bancroft, David James (2B11)	SS96	107	.304	B	
3	1	Barnes, Jesse Lawrence	P	12	+.273	B	Bos
2	3	Barnes, Virgil Jennings	P	22	.000	B	
13	8	Bentley, John Needles	P31	52	.427	WashA16	
2	0	Blume, Clinton Willis	P	12	.000	B	C
		Cunningham, Wm. Aloysius (2B4)	OF68	79	.271	B	
		Frisch, Frank Francis Jr. (3B17)	2B135	151	.348	B	
		Gaston, Alexander Nathaniel	C21	22	.205	B	
1	1	Gearin, Dennis John	P	6	.286	A	
		Gowdy, Henry Morgan (Hank)	C43	53	+.328	xBos	
		Groh, Henry Knight (Heinie)	3B118	123	.290	B	
0	1	Huntzinger, Walter Henry	P	2	.000	A	
		Jackson, Travis Calvin (2B1 3B31)	SS60	96	.275	B	
2	0	Johnson, Frederick Edward	P	3	.000	B	
4	3	Jonnard, Claude Alfred	P	45	.038	B	
		Kelly, George Lange (Long George)	1B	145	.307	B	
0	0	Lucas, Chas. Frederick (Red)	P	3	.000	A	
		Maguire, Frederick Edward (3B1)	2B16	41	.200	B	
		Meusel, Emil Frederich (Irish)	OF145	146	.297	B	
15	14	McQuillan, Hugh A.	P38	41	.171	B	
13	10	Nehf, Arthur Neukom	P	34	.190	B	
		O'Connell, James Joseph (1B8)	OF64	87	.250	A	
16	5	Ryan, Wilfred Patrick Dolan (Rosy)	P	45	.208	B	
16	7	Scott, John Wm. (Jack)	P	40	.316	B	
		Shinners, Ralph Peter	OF6	33	.154	B	
		Smith, Earl Sutton	C12	24	+.206	B	Bos
		Snyder, Frank J. (Pancho)	C112	120	.256	B	
		Solomon, Moses	OF	2	.375	A	C
		Stengel, Chas. Dillon (Casey)	OF57	75	.339	B	
		Terry, Wm. Harold	1B2	3	.143	A	
0	0	Walberg, George Elvin (Swede)	P	2	.000	A	PhilA
8	5	Watson, John Reeves	P	17	+.174	xBos	
		Wilson, Lewis Robert (Hack)	OF	3	.200	A	
		Youngs, Ross Middlebrook (Pep)	OF	152	.336	B	

WON 93 NATIONAL LEAGUE FINISHED 1st.
LOST 60
TG 153 1924. PCT. .608

NEW YORK

JOHN JOSEPH McGRAW

WON	LOST	NAME	POS.	G.	BA	FROM	TO
		Ainsmith, Edward Wilbur	C9	10	.600	Bkn	C
3	1	Baldwin, Howard Edward	P10	11	.364	A	
16	10	Barnes, Virgil Jennings	P	35	.182	B	

WON	LOST	NAME	POS.	G.	BA	FROM	TO
16	5	Bentley, John Needles	P28	46	.265	B	
0	0	Cadore, Leon Joseph	P	2	.000	ChiA	C
		Crump, Arthur Elliott	OF	1	.000	A	C
6	12	Dean, Wayland Ogden	P	26	.200	A	
		#Frisch, Frank Francis Jr.	2B143	145	.328	B	
1	2	Gearin, Dennis John	P6	10	+.333	B	Bos
		Gowdy, Henry Morgan (Hank)	C78	87	.325	B	
0	1	Greenfield, Kent	P	1	.000	A	
		Groh, Henry Knight (Heinie)	3B	145	.281	B	
		Hartley, Grover Allen	C3	4	.286	StLA17	
1	1	Huntzinger, Walter Henry	P	12	.500	B	
		Jackson, Travis Calvin	SS	151	.302	B	
4	5	Jonnard, Claude Alfred	P	34	.045	B	
		*Kelly, George Lange (Long George)	1B125	144	.324	B	
		Lindstrom, Frederick Chas. (3B11)	2B23	52	.253	A	
1	1	Maun, Ernest Gerald	P	22	.667	A	
		Meusel, Emil Frederick (Irish)	OF138	139	.310	B	
14	8	McQuillan, Hugh A.	P27	35	.209	B	
14	4	Nehf, Arthur Neukom (OF1)	P30	33	.228	B	
		O'Connell, James Joseph (2B1)	OF29	52	.317	B	C
2	0	Oeschger, Joseph Carl	P	10	+.429	Bos	Phil
8	6	Ryan, Wilfred Patrick Dolan (Rosy)	P	37	.139	B	
		Snyder, Frank J. (Pancho)	C110	118	.302	B	
		Southworth, Wm. Harrison	OF75	94	.256	Bos	
		Terry, Wm. Harold	1B35	77	.239	B	
7	4	Watson, John Reeves	P	22	.257	B	C
		Wilson, Lewis Robert (Hack)	OF103	107	.295	B	
		Youngs, Ross Middlebrook (Pep) (2B2)	OF	132	.355	B	

#Frisch also played 10 games at SS and 2 games at 3B.
*Kelly also played 5 games at 2B, 1 game at 3B and 14 games in the OF.

WON 86 — NATIONAL LEAGUE — FINISHED 2nd.
LOST 66
TG 152 — 1925. — PCT. .566

NEW YORK

JOHN JOSEPH McGRAW

WON	LOST	NAME	POS.	G.	BA	FROM	TO
0	0	Baldwin, Howard Edward	P	1	.000	B	C
15	11	Barnes, Virgil Jennings	P	32	.101	B	
11	9	Bentley, John Needles (1B1 OF3)	P29	64	.303	B	
		Carter, Otis Leonard	OF	1	.000	A	
0	0	Davies, Lloyd Garrison (OF1)	P2	4	.000	PhilA14	
10	7	Dean, Wayland Ogden	P	33	.235	B	
		Devine, Wm. Patrick (Mickey) (3B1)	C11	21	.273	BosA20	C
		Farrell, Edward Stephen (2B1 3B7)	SS13	27	.214	A	
6	3	Fitzsimmons, Frederick Landis	P	10	.310	A	
		Frisch, Frank Francis Jr. (2B42 SS39)	3B46	120	.331	B	
		Gowdy, Henry Morgan (Hank)	C41	47	.325	B	
12	8	Greenfield, Kent	P	29	.081	B	
		Groh, Henry Knight (Heinie) (2B2)	3B16	25	.231	B	
		Hartley, Grover Allen (1B8)	C37	46	.316	B	
5	1	Huntzinger, Walter Henry	P	26	.091	B	
		Jackson, Travis Calvin	SS110	112	.285	B	
		Kelly, George Lange (Long George) (1B25 OF17)	2B108	147	.309	B	
		Koehler, Horace Levering	OF3	12	.000	A	C
		Lindstrom, Frederick Chas. (2B1 SS1)	3B96	104	.287	B	
		Meusel, Emil Frederick (Irish)	OF126	135	.328	B	
		Moore, Albert James	OF	2	.125	A	
		McMullen, Hugh Raphael	C	5	.133	A	
2	3	McQuillan, Hugh A.	P14	16	.143	B	
11	9	Nehf, Arthur Neukom	P30	33	.216	B	
14	15	Scott, John Wm. (Jack)	P36	41	.241	NY23	
		Snyder, Frank J. (Pancho)	C96	107	.240	B	
		Southworth, Wm. Harrison	OF119	123	.292	B	
		Terry, Wm. Harold	1B126	133	.319	B	
		Walker, Chas. Franklin	OF21	39	.222	PhilA21	C
		Webb, Earl Wm.	OF	4	.000	A	
		Wilson, Lewis Robert (Hack)	OF50	62	.239	B	
0	0	Wisner, John Henry	P	24	.000	Pitt20	
		Youngs, Ross Middlebrook (Pep) (2B3)	OF127	130	.264	B	

WON 74 — NATIONAL LEAGUE — FINISHED 5th.
LOST 77
TG 151 — 1926. — PCT. .490

NEW YORK

JOHN JOSEPH McGRAW

WON	LOST	NAME	POS.	G.	BA	FROM	TO
8	13	Barnes, Virgil Jennings	P	31	.054	B	
0	0	Bentley, John Needles	P1	3	+.250	xPhil	
		Boyle, James John	C	1	.000	A	C
		Carter, Otis Leonard	OF	5	.235	B	C
		Cohen, Andrew Howard (Andy) (SS10)	2B10	32	.257	A	
		Connell, Joseph Bernard		2	.000	A	C
		Cote, Warren Peter		2	.000	A	C
		Cummings, John Wm.	C	7	.313	A	
2	4	Davies, Lloyd Garrison	P	38	.222	B	C
		Farrell, Edward Stephen	SS53	67	.287	B	

WON	LOST	NAME	POS.	G.	BA	FROM	TO
14	10	Fitzsimmons, Frederick Landis	P	37	.128	B	
		Florence, Paul Robert (Pep)	C	76	.229	A	C
		Frisch, Frank Francis Jr.	2B127	135	.314	B	
13	12	Greenfield, Kent	P	39	.092	B	
		Groh, Henry Knight (Heinie)	3B	12	.229	B	
		Hamby, James Sanford	C	1	.000	A	
		Hartley, Grover Allen	C	13	.048	B	
		Jackson, Travis Calvin	SS108	111	.327	B	
		Johnston, James Harle (Jimmy)	OF14	37	+.232	xBos	C
		Kelly, George Lange (Long George) (2B18)	1B114	136	.303	B	
		Lindstrom, Frederick Chas.	3B138	140	.302	B	
		Meusel, Emil Frederick (Irish)	OF112	129	.292	B	
		Moore, Albert James	OF20	28	.222	B	C
		Meuller, Clarence Franklin	OF82	85	+.249	xStL	
		McMullen, Hugh Raphael	C56	57	.187	B	
0	0	McNamara, Timothy Aloysius	P	6	.000	Bos	C
11	10	McQuillan, Hugh A.	P33	34	.132	B	
0	0	Nehf, Arthur Neukom	P	2	+.000	B	Cin
		Ott, Melvin Thomas (Mel)	OF10	35	.383	A	
0	1	Poetz, Joseph Frank	P	2	.000	A	C
0	0	Porter, Edward S. (Ned)	P	2	.000	A	
11	10	Ring, James Joseph	P	39	.143	Phil	
13	15	Scott, John Wm. (Jack)	P50	51	.337	B	
		Slayback, Elbert	2B	2	.000	A	C
0	0	Smith, Alfred Kendricks	P	1	.000	A	C
		Smith, Elwood Hope	OF	4	.143	A	C
		Snyder, Frank J. (Pancho)	C	55	.216	B	
		Southworth, Wm. Harrison	OF29	36	+.328	B	StL
		Terry, Wm. Harold (OF14)	1B38	98	.289	B	
		Thompson, LaFayette Fresco Jr. (Chick)	2B	2	.625	Pitt	
		Tyson, Albert Thomas	OF92	97	.293	A	
2	2	Wisner, John Henry	P	5	.200	B	C
		Youngs, Ross Middlebrook (Pep)	OF94	95	.306	B	C

WON 92 LOST 62 TG 154

NATIONAL LEAGUE 1927. FINISHED 3rd. PCT. .597

NEW YORK

JOHN JOSEPH McGRAW

WON	LOST	NAME	POS.	G.	BA	FROM	TO
14	11	Barnes, Virgil Jennings	P	35	.108	B	
0	0	Bentley, John Needles	P	8	.222	B	
13	5	Benton, Lawrence James (Larry)	P29	31	+.160	xBos	
0	0	Boney, Henry Tate	P	3	.000	A	C
1	1	Bush, Leslie Ambrose (Bullet Joe)	P	3	+.500	xPitt	
1	1	Cantwell, Benjamin Caldwell	P	5	.250	A	
0	0	Cheeves, Virgil Earl	P	3	.000	ClevA24	
3	9	Clarkson, Wm. Henry	P26	28	.050	A	
		Cummings, John Wm.	C34	43	.363	B	
		DeVormer, Albert E.	C54	68	.248	BosA23	C
		Farrell, Edward Stephen (3B2)	SS36	42	+.387	B	Bos
1	0	Faulkner, James LeRoy	P	3	.500	A	
17	10	Fitzsimmons, Frederick Landis	P	42	.207	B	
2	2	Greenfield, Kent	P	12	+.000	B	Bos
19	8	Grimes, Burleigh Arland	P	39	.188	Bkn	
		Hamby, James Sanford	C19	21	.192	B	C
		Harper, George Washington	OF142	145	.331	Phil	
11	6	Henry, Frank John	P	45	.236	Bkn24	
1	0	Holland, Howard Arthur	P	2	.000	Cin	
		Hornsby, Rogers (Rajah)	2B	155	.361	StL	
		Jackson, Travis Calvin	SS124	127	.318	B	
0	0	Jeanes, Ernest Lee	P	11	.300	WashA	C
0	0	Johnson, Arthur Gilbert	P	1	.000	A	C
		Jordan, Baxter Byerly		5	.200	A	
		Klinger, Joseph John	OF1	3	.400	A	
		Lindstrom, Frederick Chas. (OF51)	3B87	138	.306	B	
		Mann, Leslie	OF22	29	+.328	xBos	
		Meuller, Clarence Franklin	OF55	84	.289	B	
5	4	McQuillan, Hugh A.	P	11	+.211	B	Bos
		O'Neill, George Michael	C	16	.132	xWashA	C
		Ott, Melvin Thomas (Mel)	OF32	82	.282	B	
1	0	Plitt, Norman Wm.	P	3	+.000	xBkn	C
0	0	Porter, Edward S. (Ned)	P	1	.000	B	C
		Reese, Andrew Jackson (OF16)	3B64	97	.265	A	
		Roush, Edd J.	OF138	140	.304	Cin	
		Smith, Richard Paul	C	1	.000	A	C
3	5	Songer, Donald	P	22	+.300	xPitt	C
		Taylor, James Wren (Zack)	C81	83	+.233	xBos	
		Terry, Wm. Harold	1B	150	.326	B	
0	0	Thomas, Fay Wesley	P	9	.000	A	
		Thomas Herbert Mark	OF2	13	+.176	xBos	C
		Tyson, Albert Thomas	OF41	43	.264	B	
0	0	Walker, Wm. Henry	P	3	.000	A	

WON 93 LOST 61 TG 154

NATIONAL LEAGUE 1928. FINISHED 2nd. PCT. .604

NEW YORK

JOHN JOSEPH McGRAW

WON	LOST	NAME	POS.	G.	BA	FROM	TO
4	7	Aldridge, Victor Eddington	P	22	.275	Pitt	C
3	3	Barnes, Virgil Jennings	P	10	+.091	B	Bos
25	9	Benton, Lawrence James (Larry)	P	42	.143	B	
0	0	Buckeye, Garland Maiers	P	1	.500	xClevA	C
1	0	Cantwell, Benjamin Caldwell	P	7	+.500	B	Bos

WON	LOST	NAME	POS.	G.	BA	FROM	TO
0	2	Chaplin, James Bailey	P	12	.000	A	
0	0	Clarkson, Wm. Henry	P	4	+.000	B	Bos
		Cohen, Andrew Howard (Andy)	2B126	129	.274	NY26	
		Cummings, John Wm.	C1	33	.333	B	
9	8	Faulkner, James LeRoy	P	38	.231	B	
20	9	Fitzsimmons, Frederick Landis	P	40	.191	B	
		Foley, Raymond Kirwin		2	.000	A	C
		Fullis, Chas. Philip (Chick)	OF	11	.000	A	
11	4	Genewich, Joseph Edward	P	26	+.203	xBos	
		Haeffner, Wm. Bernard	C	2	.000	Pitt20	C
		Harper, George Washington	OF18	19	+.228	B	StL
3	6	Henry, Frank John	P	17	.158	B	
		Hogan, James Francis (Shanty)	C124	131	.333	Bos	
10	6	Hubbell, Carl Owen	P	20	.106	A	
		Jackson, Travis Calvin	SS149	150	.270	B	
		Jahn, Arthur Chas.	OF8	10	+.276	Chi25	Phil
		Lindstrom, Frederick Chas.	3B	153	.358	B	
0	0	Mangum, Leo Allen	P	1	1.000	ChiA25	
		Mann, Leslie	OF68	82	.264	B	C
0	0	Nichols Sr., Chester Raymond	P	3	.000	Pitt	
		O'Doul, Frank Joseph (Lefty)	OF94	114	.319	BosA23	
		O'Farrell, Robert Arthur	C63	75	+.195	xStL	
		Ott, Melvin Thomas (Mel)	OF115	124	.322	B	
		Price, Joseph Preston	OF	1	.000	A	C
		Reese, Andrew Jackson (2B26)	OF64	109	.308	B	
		Roush, Edd J.	OF39	46	.252	B	
4	1	Scott, John Wm. (Jack)	P	16	.267	Phil	
		Spohrer, Alfred R.	C	2	+.000	A	Bos
		Terry, Wm. Harold	1B	149	.326	B	
		Veltman, Arthur Patrick (Pat)	OF	1	.333	ChiA26	
3	6	Walker, Wm. Henry	P	22	.091	B	
		Welsh, James D.	OF117	124	.307	Bos	
		Wrightstone, Russell Guy		30	+.160	xPhil	C

WON 84
LOST 67
TG 151

NATIONAL LEAGUE

1929.

FINISHED 3rd.

PCT. .556

NEW YORK

JOHN JOSEPH McGRAW

WON	LOST	NAME	POS.	G.	BA	FROM	TO
11	17	Benton, Lawrence James (Larry)	P39	41	.105	B	
		Cohen, Andrew Howard (Andy)	2B94	101	.294	B	C
		Crawford, Clifford Rankin	1B4	65	.298	A	
		Cummings, John Wm.		3	+.333	B	Bos
		Farrell, Edward Stephen (2B25)	3B28	63	+.213	xBos	
15	11	Fitzsimmons, Frederick Landis	P	37	.183	B	
		Fullis, Chas. Philip (Chick)	OF78	86	.288	B	
3	7	Genewich, Joseph Edward	P21	25	.375	B	
5	6	Henry, Frank John	P	27	.250	B	
		Hogan, James Francis (Shanty)	C93	102	.300	B	
18	11	Hubbell, Carl Owen	P	39	.129	B	
		Jackson, Travis Calvin	SS	149	.294	B	
		Jordan, Baxter Byerly	1B1	2	.500	N.Y.27	
3	0	Judd, Ralph Wesley	P	18	.000	WashA27	
		Kaufmann, Anthony Chas. (Tony)	OF16	39	.031	StL	
		Leach, Frederick M.	OF95	113	.290	Phil	
		Leslie, Samuel Andrew	OF	1	.000	A	
		Lindstrom, Frederick Chas.	3B128	130	.319	B	
0	0	Lucas, Raymond Wesley	P	3	.500	A	
		Marshall, Edward Herbert	2B3	5	.400	A	
7	2	Mays, Carl Wm.	P	37	.353	Cin	C
		O'Farrell, Robert Arthur	C84	91	.306	B	
		Ott, Melvin Thomas (Mel)	OF149	150	.328	B	
1	0	Parmelee, LeRoy Earl	P	2	.500	A	
		Reese, Andrew Jackson	2B44	58	.263	B	
		Roush, Edd J.	OF107	115	.324	B	
		Schalk, Raymond Wm.	C1	5	.000	ChiA	C
7	6	Scott, John Wm. (Jack)	P	30	.308	B	C
0	0	Tennant, James McDonnell	P	1	.000	A	C
		Terry, Wm. Harold	1B149	150	.372	B	
		Veltman, Arthur Patrick (Pat)	C1	2	.000	B	
14	7	Walker, Wm. Henry	P	29	.115	B	
		Welsh, James D.	OF35	38	+.248	B	Bos

WON 87
LOST 67
TG 154

NATIONAL LEAGUE

1930.

FINISHED 3rd.

PCT. .565

NEW YORK

JOHN JOSEPH McGRAW

WON	LOST	NAME	POS.	G.	BA	FROM	TO
		Allen, Ethan Nathan	OF62	76	+.307	xCin	
		Bancroft, David James	SS4	10	.059	Bkn	C
1	3	Benton, Lawrence James (Larry)	P	8	+.300	B	Cin
2	6	Chaplin, James Bailey	P	19	.105	NY28	
		Crawford, Clifford Rankin (1B1)	2B18	25	+.276	B	Cin
		Critz, Hugh Melville	2B	124	+.265	xCin	
7	6	Donohue, Peter Joseph	P	18	+.273	xCin	
19	7	Fitzsimmons, Frederick Landis	P	41	.265	B	
		Fullis, Chas. Philip (Chick)	OF1	13	.000	B	
2	5	Genewich, Joseph Edward	P18	21	.150	B	C
		Healey, Francis Jeremiah	OF1	7	.000	A	
7	5	Heving, Joseph Wm.	P	41	.227	A	
		Hogan, James Francis (Shanty)	C96	122	.339	B	
17	12	Hubbell, Carl Owen	P	37	.151	B	
		Jackson, Travis Calvin	SS115	116	.339	B	
0	0	Judd, Ralph Wesley	P	2	.000	B	C

WON	LOST	NAME	POS.	G.	BA	FROM	TO
		Leach, Frederick M.	OF124	126	.327	B	
		Leslie, Samuel Andrew		2	.500	B	
		Lindstrom, Frederick Chas.	3B	148	.379	B	
0	0	Lucas, Raymond Wesley	P	6	.000	B	
		Marshall, Edward Herbert (2B17)	SS45	78	.309	B	
10	3	Mitchell, Clarence Elmer	P	24	+.255	xStL	
		More, Joseph Gregg (Jo-Jo)	OF	3	.200	A	
0	0	Morrell, Willard Blackmer	P	2	.000	WashA26	
		O'Farrell, Robert Arthur	C69	94	.301	B	
		Ott, Melvin Thomas (Mel)	OF146	148	.349	B	
0	1	Parmelee, LeRoy Earl	P	11	.250	B	
5	4	Pruett, Hubert Shelby (Hub)	P	45	.135	Phi128	
		Reese, Andrew Jackson (3B10)	OF32	67	.273	B	C
		Roettger, Walter Henry	OF114	121	.283	StL	
		Rosenberg, Harry	OF1	9	.000	A	C
		Terry, Wm. Harold	1B	154	.401	B	
17	15	Walker, Wm. Henry	P39	40	.186	B	

WON 87
LOST 65
TG 152

NATIONAL LEAGUE

1931.

FINISHED 2nd.

PCT. .572

NEW YORK

JOHN JOSEPH McGRAW

WON	LOST	NAME	POS.	G.	BA	FROM	TO
		Allen, Ethan Nathan	OF77	94	.329	B	
7	8	Berly, John Chambers	P	27	.171	StL24	
3	0	Chaplin, James Bailey	P	16	.182	B	
		Critz, Hugh Melville	2B54	66	.290	B	
0	1	Donohue, Peter Joseph	P	4	.000	B	ClevA
		English, Gilbert Raymond	3B2	3	.000	A	
18	11	Fitzsimmons, Frederick Landis	P	35	.228	B	
		Fullis, Chas. Philip (Chick)	OF68	89	.328	B	
		Healey, Francis Jeremiah	C1	6	.143	B	
1	6	Heving, Joseph Wm.	P	22	.125	B	
		Hogan, James Francis (Shanty)	C113	123	.301	B	
14	12	Hubbell, Carl Owen	P	36	.241	B	
		Hunnefield, Wm. Fenton	2B56	64	+.270	xBos	C
		Jackson, Travis Calvin	SS	145	.310	B	
		Leach, Frederick M.	OF125	129	.309	B	
		Leslie, Samuel Andrew	1B	53	.302	B	
		Lindstrom, Frederick Chas.	OF73	78	.300	B	
0	0	Lucas, Raymond Wesley	P	1	.000	B	
		Marshall, Edward Herbert (SS11)	2B47	68	.201	B	
13	11	Mitchell, Clarence Elmer	P	27	.219	B	
7	1	Mooney, Jim Irving	P	10	.160	A	
		Moore, Joseph Gregg (Jo-Jo)	OF	4	.250	B	
5	3	Morrell, Willard Blackmer	P	20	.111	B	C
		O'Farrell, Robert Arthur	C80	85	.224	B	
		Ott, Melvin Thomas (Mel)	OF131	138	.292	B	

WON	LOST	NAME	POS.	G.	BA	FROM	TO
2	2	Parmelee, LeRoy Earl	P	13	.200	B	
0	0	Planeta, Emil Joseph	P	2	.000	A	C
1	1	Schumacher, Harold Henry (Hal)	P	8	.143	A	
		Terry, Wm. Harold	1B	153	.349	B	
		Vergez, John Louis	3B	152	.278	A	
16	9	Walker, Wm. Henry	P	37	.065	B	

WON 72
LOST 82
TG 154

NATIONAL LEAGUE

1932.

FINISHED 6th.
(TIED WITH ST. L.)
PCT. .468

NEW YORK

JOHN JOSEPH McGRAW WM. HAROLD TERRY

WON	LOST	NAME	POS.	G.	BA	FROM	TO
		Allen, Ethan Nathan	OF24	54	.175	B	
8	4	Bell, Herman S.	P	35	.088	StL30	
		Critz, Hugh Melville	2B	151	.276	B	
		English, Gilbert Raymond (SS23)	3B39	59	.225	B	
11	11	Fitzsimmons, Frederick Landis	P	35	.221	B	
		Fullis, Chas. Philip (Chick)	OF55	96	.298	B	
4	8	Gibson, Samuel Braxton	P	41	.263	NYA30	C
		Healey, Francis Jeremiah	C11	14	.250	B	
		Hogan, James Francis (Shanty)	C136	140	.287	B	
5	7	Hoyt, Waite Chas.	P	18	+.097	xBkn	
18	11	Hubbell, Carl Owen	P	40	.241	B	
		Jackson, Travis Calvin	SS	52	.256	B	
		Koenecke, Leonard George	OF35	42	.255	A	
		Leslie, Samuel Andrew	1B	77	.293	B	
		Lindstrom, Frederick Chas.	OF128	144	.271	B	
6	7	Luque, Adolfo	P	38	.040	Bkn	
		Marshall, Edward Herbert	SS63	68	.248	B	C
1	3	Mitchell, Clarence Elmer	P	8	.200	B	C
6	10	Mooney, Jim Irving	P	29	.122	B	
		Moore, Graham Edward	SS21	37	.264	Bkn30	
		Moore, Joseph Gregg (Jo-Jo)	OF	86	.305	B	
		McLarney, Arthur James	SS6	9	.130	A	C
		O'Farrell, Robert Arthur	C41	50	.239	B	
		Ott, Melvin Thomas (Mel)	OF	154	.318	B	
0	3	Parmelee, LeRoy Earl	P	8	.400	B	
5	6	Schumacher, Harold Henry (Hal)	P27	30	.226	B	
		Terry, Wm. Harold MGR.	1B	154	.350	B	
		Tobin, John Martin		1	.000	A	C
		Veltman, Arthur Patrick (Pat)		2	.000	Bos	
		Vergez, John Louis	3B111	118	.261	B	
8	12	Walker, Wm. Henry	P	31	.135	B	

WON 91 | NATIONAL LEAGUE | FINISHED 1st.
LOST 61
TG 152 | 1933. | PCT. .599

NEW YORK

WM. HAROLD TERRY

WON	LOST	NAME	POS.	G.	BA	FROM	TO
6	5	Bell, Herman S.	P	38	.138	B	
3	4	Clark, Wm. Watson	P	16	+.273	xBkn	
		Critz, Hugh Melville	2B	133	.246	B	
		Danning, Harry (The Horse)	C	3	.000	A	
		Davis, George Willis (Kiddo)	OF120	126	.258	Phil	
		Dressen, Chas. Walter (Chuck)	3B	16	.222	Cin31	
16	11	Fitzsimmons, Frederick Landis	P	36	.200	B	
23	12	Hubbell, Carl Owen	P	45	.183	B	
		Jackson, Travis Calvin (3B21)	SS21	53	.246	B	
		James, Robert Byrne (SS6 3B5)	2B26	60	.224	Bos30	C
		Leiber, Henry Edward (Hank)	OF	6	.200	A	
		Leslie, Samuel Andrew	1B35	40	+.321	B	Bkn
8	2	Luque, Adolfo	P	35	.263	B	
		Malay, Joseph Chas.	1B	8	.125	A	
		Mancuso, August Rodney (Gus)	C142	144	.264	StL	
		Moore, Joseph Gregg (Jo-Jo)	OF	132	.292	B	
		O'Doul, Frank Joseph (Lefty)	OF63	78	+.306	xBkn	
		Ott, Melvin Thomas (Mel)	OF	152	.283	B	
13	8	Parmelee, LeRoy Earl	P32	33	.235	B	
		Peel, Homer Hefner	OF45	84	.257	StL30	
		Richards, Paul Rapier	C36	51	.195	Bkn	
		Ryan, John Collins (Blondy)	SS	146	.238	ChiA30	
0	2	Salveson, John Theodore	P	8	.111	A	
19	12	Schumacher, Harold Henry (Hal)	P35	39	.214	B	
2	1	Shores, Wm. David	P	8	.273	PhilA31	
0	2	Spencer, Glenn Edward	P	17	.167	Pitt	C
0	1	Starr, Raymond Francis	P	6	+.000	StL	Bos
		Terry, Wm. Harold MGR.	1B117	123	.322	B	
1	1	Uhle, George Ernest	P	8	.000	xDetA	NYA
		Vergez, John Louis	3B	123	.271	B	
		Weintraub, Philip	OF	8	.200	A	

WON 93 | NATIONAL LEAGUE | FINISHED 2nd.
LOST 60
TG 153 | 1934. | PCT. .608

NEW YORK

WM. HAROLD TERRY

WON	LOST	NAME	POS.	G.	BA	FROM	TO
4	3	Bell, Herman S.	P	22	.105	B	C
5	4	Bowman, Joseph Emil (Joe)	P30	31	.172	PhilA32	
1	0	Castleman, Clydell (Slick)	P	7	.250	A	
1	2	Clark, Wm. Watson	P	5	+.167	B	Bkn
		Critz, Hugh Melville	2B	137	.242	B	
		Danning, Harry (The Horse)	C37	53	.330	B	
18	14	Fitzsimmons, Frederick Landis	P	38	.232	B	
		Grantham, George Farley (3B1)	1B2	32	.241	Cin	C
21	12	Hubbell, Carl Owen	P	49	.197	B	
		Jackson, Travis Calvin	SS130	137	.268	B	
		Leiber, Henry Edward (Hank)	OF51	63	.241	B	
4	3	Luque, Adolfo	P	26	.286	B	
		Mancuso, August Rodney (Gus)	C	122	.245	B	
		Moore, Joseph Gregg (Jo-Jo)	OF131	139	.331	B	
		O'Doul, Frank Joseph (Lefty)	OF38	83	.316	B	C
		Ott, Melvin Thomas (Mel)	OF	153	.326	B	
10	6	Parmelee, LeRoy Earl	P	22	.200	B	
		Peel, Homer Hefner	OF10	21	.195	B	C
		Richards, Paul Rapier	C37	42	.160	B	
		Ryan, John Collins (Blondy) (2B25 SS30)	3B65	110	.242	B	
3	1	Salveson, John Theodore	P12	13	.300	B	
23	10	Schumacher, Harold Henry (Hal)	P41	44	.239	B	
3	5	Smith, Alfred John	P	30	.286	A	
		Terry, Wm. Harold MGR.	1B	153	.354	B	
		Thompson, LaFayette Fresco Jr. (Chick)		1	.000	Bkn32	C
		Vergez, John Louis	3B104	108	.200	B	
		Watkins, George Archibald	OF81	105	.247	StL	
		Weintraub, Philip	OF20	31	.351	B	

WON 91 | NATIONAL LEAGUE | FINISHED 3rd.
LOST 62
TG 153 | 1935. | PCT. .595

NEW YORK

WM. HAROLD TERRY

WON	LOST	NAME	POS.	G.	BA	FROM	TO
		Bartell, Richard Wm.	SS	137	.262	Phil	
15	6	Castleman, Clydell (Slick)	P	29	.179	B	
0	2	Chagnon, Leon Wilbur	P	14	.000	Pitt	C
		Critz, Hugh Melville	2B59	65	.187	B	C
		Cuccinello, Alfred Edward (3B2)	2B48	54	.248	A	C
		Danning, Harry (The Horse)	C44	65	.243	B	
		Davis, George Willis (Kiddo)	OF21	47	.264	Phil	
4	8	Fitzsimmons, Frederick Landis	P	18	.258	B	
2	1	Gabler, Frank Harold	P	26	.125	A	
1	2	Gumbert, Harry Edward	P	6	.000	A	
23	12	Hubbell, Carl Owen	P	42	.239	B	
		Jackson, Travis Calvin	3B	128	.301	B	
		Koenig, Mark Anthony (SS21 3B15)	2B64	107	.283	Cin	

WON	LOST	NAME	POS.	G.	BA	FROM	TO
		Leiber, Henry Edward (Hank)	OF	154	.331	B	
1	0	Luque, Adolfo	P	2	1.000	B	C
		Malay, Joseph Chas.		1	1.000	NY33	C
		Mancuso, August Rodney (Gus)	C126	128	.298	B	
		Moore, Joseph Gregg (Jo-Jo)	OF	155	.295	B	
1	0	Moore, Euel Walton	P	6	+.000	xPhil	
		Myatt, Glenn Calvin	C4	13	.222	xClevA	
		Ott, Melvin Thomas (Mel) (3B15)	OF137	152	.322	B	
14	10	Parmelee, LeRoy Earl	P	34	.209	B	
		Richards, Paul Rapier	C	7	.250	B	PhilA
19	9	Schumacher, Harold Henry (Hal)	P33	38	.196	B	
10	8	Smith, Alfred John	P	40	.118	B	
1	4	Stout, Allyn McClelland	P	40	.133	Cin	
		Terry, Wm. Harold MGR.	1B143	145	.341	B	
		Weintraub, Philip (OF7)	1B19	64	.241	B	

WON 92 — NATIONAL LEAGUE — FINISHED 1st.
LOST 62
TG 154 — 1936. — PCT. .597

NEW YORK

WM. HAROLD TERRY

WON	LOST	NAME	POS.	G.	BA	FROM	TO
		Bartell, Richard Wm.	SS144	145	.298	B	
4	7	Castleman, Clydell (Slick)	P29	30	.128	B	
7	5	Coffman, Samuel Richard (Dick)	P	42	.200	StLA	
		Danning, Harry (The Horse)	C24	32	.159	B	
		Davis, George Willis (Kiddo)	OF22	47	.239	B	
		English, Chas. Dewie	2B1	6	.000	ChiA33	
10	7	Fitzsimmons, Frederick Landis	P	28	.149	B	
9	8	Gabler, Frank Harold	P	43	.208	B	
11	3	Gumbert, Harry Edward	P	39	.250	B	
26	6	Hubbell, Carl Owen	P	42	.227	B	
		Jackson, Travis Calvin	3B116	126	.230	B	C
		Koenig, Mark Anthony	SS10	42	.276	B	C
		Leiber, Henry Edward (Hank)	OF86	101	.279	B	
		Leslie, Samuel Andrew	1B99	117	.295	Bkn	
		Mancuso, August Rodney (Gus)	C138	139	.301	B	
0	0	Marberry, Frederick (Firpo)	P	1	.000	DetA	WashA
		Martin, Wm. Joseph	3B	7	.267	A	
		Mayo, Edward Joseph	3B40	46	.199	A	
		Moore, Joseph Gregg (Jo-Jo)	OF149	152	.316	B	
		McCarthy, John Joseph (Mac)	1B	4	.438	Bkn	
		Ott, Melvin Thomas (Mel)	OF148	150	.328	B	
		Ripple, James Albert (Jimmy)	OF76	96	.305	A	
11	13	Schumacher, Harold Henry (Hal)	P35	46	.216	B	
		Sheehan, James Thomas	C	1	.000	A	C
14	13	Smith, Alfred John	P	43	.137	B	
		Spencer, Roy Hampton	C14	19	.278	ClevA34	
		Terry, Wm. Harold MGR.	1B56	79	.310	B	
		Whitehead, Burgess Urquhart (Whitey)	2B153	154	.278	StL	
		Young, Norman Robert (Babe)	1B	1	.000	A	

WON 95 — NATIONAL LEAGUE — FINISHED 1st.
LOST 57
TG 152 — 1937. — PCT. .625

NEW YORK

WM. HAROLD TERRY

WON	LOST	NAME	POS.	G.	BA	FROM	TO
1	0	Baker, Thomas Calvin	P	13	+.222	xBkn	
		Bartell, Richard Wm.	SS	128	.306	B	
		Berger, Walter Antone (Wally)	OF52	59	+.291	xBos	
1	0	Brennan, James Donald (Don)	P	6	+.000	xCin	C
1	0	Brown, Walter George (Jumbo)	P	4	+.000	xCin	
0	1	Cantwell, Benjamin Caldwell	P	1	+.000	Bos	Bkn
11	6	Castleman, Clydell (Slick)	P	23	.070	B	
		Chiozza, Louis Peo (OF12)	3B93	117	.232	Phil	
8	3	Coffman, Samuel Richard (Dick)	P	42	.368	B	
		Danning, Harry (The Horse)	C86	93	.288	B	
		Davis, George Willis (Kiddo)	OF37	56	+.263	B	Cin
2	2	Fitzsimmons, Frederick Landis	P	6	+.300	B	Bkn
0	0	Gabler, Frank Harold	P	6	+.000	B	Bos
10	11	Gumbert, Harry Edward	P	34	.181	B	
		x Haslin, Michael Joseph (Mickey)	SS9	27	.190	Bos	
22	8	Hubbell, Carl Owen	P	39	.216	B	
		Leiber, Henry Edward (Hank)	OF46	51	.293	B	
		Leslie, Samuel Andrew	1B44	72	.309	B	
1	0	Lohrman, Wm. LeRoy (Bill)	P	2	.000	Phil34	
		Madjeski, Edward Wm.	C	5	.200	ChiA34	C
		Mancuso, August Rodney (Gus)	C81	86	.279	B	
20	9	Melton, Clifford George (Cliff)	P	46	.122	A	
		Moore, Joseph Gregg (Jo-Jo)	OF140	142	.310	B	
		McCarthy, John Joseph (Mac)	1B110	114	.279	B	
		Ott, Melvin Thomas (Mel) (3B60)	OF91	151	.294	B	
		Ripple, James Albert (Jimmy)	OF111	121	.317	B	
		Ryan, John Collins (Blondy)	SS19	21	.240	NYA35	
13	12	Schumacher, Harold Henry (Hal)	P38	45	.222	B	
5	4	Smith, Alfred John	P	33	.120	B	
0	1	Vandenberg, Harold Harris	P	1	.000	BosA35	
		Weintraub, Philip	OF1	6	+.333	xCin	
		Whitehead, Burgess Urquhart (Whitey)	2B	152	.286	B	

xHaslin also played 4 games at 2B and 4 games at 3B.

WON 83 | LOST 67 | TG 150

NATIONAL LEAGUE 1938. NEW YORK

FINISHED 3rd. PCT. .553

WM. HAROLD TERRY

WON	LOST	NAME	POS.	G.	BA	FROM	TO
0	0	Baker, Thomas Calvin	P	2	.000	B	C
		Bartell, Richard Wm.	SS	127	.262	B	
		Berger, Walter Antone (Wally)	OF9	16	+.188	B	Cin
5	3	Brown, Walter George (Jumbo)	P	43	.186	B	
4	5	Castleman, Clydell (Slick)	P21	22	.097	B	
		Chiozza, Louis Peo (OF16)	2B34	57	.235	B	
		Cissell, Chalmer Wm.	2B33	38	.268	PhilA	C
8	4	Coffman, Samuel Richard (Dick)	P	51	.071	B	
		Danning, Harry (The Horse)	C114	120	.306	B	
0	0	Georgy, Oscar John	P	1	.000	A	C
15	13	Gumbert, Harry Edward	P38	40	.154	B	
		Haslin, Michael Joseph (Mickey) (2B13)	3B15	31	.324	B	C
13	10	Hubbell, Carl Owen	P	24	.155	B	
		Kampouris, Alexis Wm.	2B79	82	+.246	xCin	
		Leiber, Henry Edward (Hank)	OF89	98	.269	B	
		Leslie, Samuel Andrew	1B32	76	.253	B	C
9	6	Lohrman, Wm. LeRoy (Bill)	P	31	.082	B	
		Mancuso, August Rodney (Gus)	C44	52	.348	B	
14	14	Melton, Clifford George (Cliff)	P	36	.175	B	
		Moore, Joseph Gregg (Jo-Jo)	OF114	125	.302	B	
		Myatt, George Edward (3B19)	SS24	43	.306	A	
		McCarthy, John Joseph (Mac)	1B125	134	.272	B	
		Ott, Melvin Thomas (Mel) (OF37)	3B113	150	.311	B	
		Powers, Leslie Edwin		2	.000	A	
		Ripple, James Albert (Jimmy)	OF131	134	.261	B	
		Ryan, John Collins (Blondy) (SS2 3B3)	2B5	12	.208	B	C
13	8	Schumacher, Harold Henry (Hal)	P28	36	.239	B	
		Seeds, Robert Ira (Bob)	OF76	81	.291	NYA36	
0	1	Vandenberg, Harold Harris	P	6	.000	B	
2	3	Wittig, John Carl	P	13	.000	A	

WON 77 | LOST 74 | TG 151

NATIONAL LEAGUE 1939. NEW YORK

FINISHED 5th. PCT. .510

WM. HAROLD TERRY

WON	LOST	NAME	POS.	G.	BA	FROM	TO
		Bonura, Henry John (Zeke)	1B122	123	.321	WashA	
4	0	Brown, Walter George (Jumbo)	P	31	.364	B	
1	2	Castleman, Clydell (Slick)	P	12	.333	B	C
		Chiozza, Louis Peo	3B30	40	.268	B	C
1	2	Coffman, Samuel Richard (Dick)	P	28	.000	B	
		Danning, Harry (The Horse)	C132	135	.313	B	
		Demaree, Joseph Franklin (Frank)	OF	150	.304	Chi	
		Dickshot, John Oscar	OF	10	.235	Pitt	
		Glossop, Alban	2B	10	.188	A	
0	0	Gorman, Thomas David	P	4	.000	A	C
18	11	Gumbert, Harry Edward	P36	37	.200	B	
		Hafey, Thomas Francis	3B	70	.242	A	
		Hayworth, Raymond Hall	C	5	+.231	xBkn	
11	9	Hubbell, Carl Owen	P	29	.151	B	
		Jurges, Wm. Frederick (Bill)	SS137	138	.285	Chi	
		Kampouris, Alexis Wm. (3B11)	2B62	74	.249	B	
		Lazzeri, Anthony Michael (Tony)	3B	13	+.295	xBkn	C
12	13	Lohrman, Wm. LeRoy (Bill)	P	38	.233	B	
1	0	Lynn, Japhet Monroe	P	26	.000	xDetA	
12	15	Melton, Clifford George (Cliff)	P	41	.182	B	
		Moore, Joseph Gregg (Jo-Jo)	OF136	138	.269	B	
		Myatt, George Edward	3B14	22	.189	B	
		McCarthy, John Joseph (Mac)	1B12	50	.262	B	
		O'Dea, James Kenneth (Ken)	C30	52	.175	Chi	
		Ott, Melvin Thomas (Mel) (3B20)	OF96	125	.308	B	
		Ripple, James Albert (Jimmy)	OF23	66	+.228	B	Bkn
4	10	Salvo, Manuel	P	32	.098	A	
		Scalzi, Frank John (3B1)	SS5	11	.333	A	C
13	10	Schumacher, Harold Henry (Hal)	P29	30	.203	B	
		Seeds, Robert Ira (Bob)	OF50	63	.266	B	
0	0	Vandenberg, Harold Harris	P	2	.000	B	
		Whitehead, Burgess Urguhart (Whitey)	2B91	95	.239	N.Y.37	
0	2	Wittig, John Carl	P	5	.000	B	
		Young, Norman Robert (Babe)	1B	22	.307	N.Y.36	

WON 72 | LOST 80 | TG 152

NATIONAL LEAGUE 1940. NEW YORK

FINISHED 6th. PCT. .474

WM. HAROLD TERRY

WON	LOST	NAME	POS.	G.	BA	FROM	TO
2	4	Brown, Walter George (Jumbo)	P	41	.100	B	
2	0	Carpenter, Robert Louis	P	5	.100	A	
		Cuccinello, Anthony Francis (Tony) (3B37)	2B47	88	+.208	xBos	
		Danning, Harry (The Horse)	C131	140	.300	B	
4	4	Dean, Paul Dee (Daffy)	P	27	.115	St.L.	

WON	LOST	NAME	POS.	G.	BA	FROM	TO
		Demaree, Joseph Franklin (Frank)	OF119	121	.302	B	
		Glossop, Alban	2B24	27	+.209	B	Bos
12	14	Gumbert, Harry Edward	P	35	.195	B	
11	12	Hubbell, Carl Owen	P	31	.185	B	
0	1	Hudlin, George Willis	P	1	.000	xSt.L.A	
3	2	Joiner, Roy Merrill	P	30	.273	Chi35	C
		Jurges, Wm. Frederick (Bill)	SS	63	.252	B	
10	15	Lohrman, Wm. LeRoy (Bill)	P	31	.123	B	
4	3	Lynn, Japhet Monroe	P	33	.000	B	
		Maynard, James Walter	OF	7	.276	A	
10	11	Melton, Clifford George (Cliff)	P	37	.222	B	
		Moore, Joseph Gregg (Jo-Jo)	OF133	138	.276	B	
		McCarthy, John Joseph (Mac)	1B6	51	.239	B	
		O'Dea, James Kenneth (Ken)	C31	48	.240	B	
		Ott, Melvin Thomas (Mel) (3B42)	OF111	151	.289	B	
		Rucker, John Joel	OF57	86	.296	A	
13	13	Schumacher, Harold Henry (Hal)	P34	35	.192	B	
		Seeds, Robert Ira (Bob)	OF40	56	.290	B	C
		Stewart, Glen Weldon (SS5)	3B6	15	.138	A	
		Tramback, Stephen Joseph	OF1	2	.250	A	C
1	1	Vandenberg, Harold Harris	P	13	.125	B	
		Whitehead, Burgess Urquhart (Whitey) (2B57 SS4)	3B74	133	.282	B	
		Witek, Nicholas Joseph (Mickey) (2B32)	SS89	119	.256	A	
		Young, Norman Robert (Babe)	1B147	149	.286	B	

WON 74 — NATIONAL LEAGUE — FINISHED 5th.
LOST 79
TG 153 — 1941. — PCT. .484

NEW YORK

WM. HAROLD TERRY

WON	LOST	NAME	POS.	G.	BA	FROM	TO
4	1	Adams, Ace Townsend	P	38	.083	A	
		Aragon, Angel Valdes Jr. (Jack)		1	.000	A	C
		Arnovich, Morris	OF61	85	.280	Cin	
		Barna, Herbert Paul	OF	10	.214	PhilA38	
		Bartell, Richard Wm. (SS21)	3B84	104	.303	xDetA	
		Blaemire, Rae Bertram	C	2	.400	A	C
6	7	Bowman, Robert James (Bob)	P	29	.048	StL	
1	5	Brown, Walter George (Jumbo)	P	31	.111	B	C
11	6	Carpenter, Robert Louis	P	29	.156	B	
		Danning, Harry (The Horse) (1B1)	C116	130	.244	B	
		Davis, John Humphrey	3B	21	.214	A	C
0	0	Dean, Paul Dee (Daffy)	P	5	.000	B	
		Demaree, Joseph Franklin (Frank)	OF10	16	+.171	B	Bos
1	1	East, Gordon Hugh	P	2	.222	A	
1	1	Feldman, Harry	P	3	.167	A	
1	0	Fischer, Reuben Walter	P	2	.333	A	
		Gordon, Sidney	OF	9	.258	A	
1	1	Gumbert, Harry Edward	P	5	+.167	B	StL
1	0	Hadley, Irving Darius (Bump)	P	3	.000	NYA	PhilA
		Hale, Arvel Odell (Bad News)	2B29	41	.196	xBosA	C
		Hartnett, Chas. Leo (Gabby)	C34	64	.300	Chi	C
11	9	Hubbell, Carl Owen	P	26	.140	B	
		Jurges, Wm. Frederick (Bill)	SS	134	.293	B	
1	2	Koslo, George Bernard	P	4	.111	A	
9	10	Lohrman, Wm. LeRoy (Bill)	P	33	.229	B	
8	11	Melton, Clifford George (Cliff)	P	42	.115	B	
		Moore, Joseph Gregg (Jo-Jo)	OF116	121	.273	B	C
		McCarthy, John Joseph (Mac) (OF1)	1B8	14	.325	B	
2	9	McGee, Wm. Henry (Bill)	P	22	+.161	xStL	
		O'Dea, James Kenneth (Ken)	C14	59	.213	B	
		Orengo, Joseph Chas. (2B6 SS9)	3B59	77	.214	StL	
		Ott, Melvin Thomas (Mel)	OF145	148	.286	B	
		Rucker, John Joel	OF142	143	.288	B	
12	10	Schumacher, Harold Henry (Hal) (OF1)	P30	38	.152	B	
1	1	Sunkel, Thomas Jacob	P	2	.333	StL39	
		Whitehead, Burgess Urquhart (Whitey) (3B1)	2B104	116	.228	B	
		Witek, Nicholas Joseph (Mickey)	2B23	26	.362	B	
3	5	Wittig, John Carl	P	25	.200	NY39	
		Young, Norman Robert (Babe)	1B150	152	.265	B	

WON 85 — NATIONAL LEAGUE — FINISHED 3rd.
LOST x67
152 — 1942. — PCT. .559

NEW YORK

MELVIN THOMAS OTT

WON	LOST	NAME	POS.	G.	BA	FROM	TO
7	4	Adams, Ace Townsend	P	61	.100	B	
		Barna, Herbert Paul	OF89	104	.257	B	
		Bartell, Richard Wm. (SS31)	3B52	90	.244	B	
		Berres, Raymond Frederick	C	12	.188	Bos	
11	10	Carpenter, Robert Louis	P	28	.185	B	
		Danning, Harry (The Horse)	C116	119	.279	B	C
0	2	East, Gordon Hugh	P	4	.500	B	
7	1	Feldman, Harry	P	31	.282	B	
		Fox, Chas. Francis	C	3	.429	A	C
		Gordon, Sidney	3B	6	.316	B	
11	8	Hubbell, Carl Owen	P	24	.183	B	
		Jurges, Wm. Frederick (Bill)	SS124	127	.256	B	
3	6	Koslo, George Bernard	P	19	.120	B	
0	1	Leiber, Henry Edward (Hank) (P1)	OF41	58	.218	Chi	C
13	4	Lohrman, Wm. LeRoy (Bill)	P	26	+.120	xStL	

WON	LOST	NAME	POS.	G.	BA	FROM	TO
		Mancuso, August Rodney (Gus)	C38	39	+.193	xStL	
		Marshall, Willard Warren	OF107	116	.257	A	
		Maynard, James Walter (2B1 3B10)	OF58	89	.247	NY40	
11	5	Melton, Clifford George (Cliff)	P	23	.234	B	
		Mize, John Robert	1B138	142	.305	StL	
		Moss, Howard Glenn	OF3	7	.000	A	
1	2	Mungo, Van Lingle	P	9	.214	Bkn	
6	3	McGee, Wm. Henry (Bill)	P	31	.103	B	C
		Ott, Melvin Thomas (Mel) MGR.	OF	152	.295	B	
		Ryan, Cornelius Joseph	2B	11	.185	A	
12	13	Schumacher, Harold Henry (Hal)	P29	37	.173	B	
3	6	Sunkel, Thomas Jacob	P	19	.105	B	
0	1	Voiselle, Wm. Symmes	P	2	.000	A	
		Werber, Wm. Murray (Bill)	3B93	98	.205	Cin	C
		Witek, Nicholas Joseph (Mickey)	2B147	148	.260	B	
		Young, Norman Robert (Babe) (1B18)	OF54	101	.279	B	

x Lost one game forfeit.

WON 55 — NATIONAL LEAGUE — FINISHED 8th (LAST)
LOST 98
TG 153 — 1943. — PCT. .359

NEW YORK

MELVIN THOMAS OTT

WON	LOST	NAME	POS.	G.	BA	FROM	TO
11	7	Adams, Ace Townsend	P	70	.125	B	
1	3	Allen, John Thomas (Johnny)	P	15	+.000	xBkn	
		Barna, Herbert Paul	OF31	40	.204	B	BosA
		Bartell, Richard Wm. (SS33)	3B54	99	.270	B	
		Berres, Raymond Frederick	C17	20	.143	B	
		Bradford, Henry Victor	OF1	6	.200	A	C
4	12	Chase, Kendall Fay (Ken)	P21	23	.214	xBosA	C
0	1	Coombs, Raymond Frank	P	9	.000	PhilA33	C
1	3	East, Gordon Hugh	P13	17	.077	B	C
4	5	Feldman, Harry	P31	44	.133	B	
5	10	Fischer, Reuben Walter	P	22	.256	NY41	
		Gordon, Sidney (1B41 2B3 OF28)	3B53	131	.251	B	
4	4	Hubbell, Carl Owen	P	12	.200	B	C
		Jurges, Wm. Frederick (Bill) (3B28)	SS99	136	.229	B	
		Kerr, John Joseph	SS	27	.286	A	
5	6	Lohrman, Wm. LeRoy (Bill)	P17	21	+.037	B	Bkn
		Lombardi, Ernesto Natali (Schnozz)	C73	104	.305	Bos	
		Mancuso, August Rodney (Gus)	C77	94	.198	B	
		Maynard, James Walter (3B22)	OF74	121	.206	B	
		Mead, Chas. Richard	OF	37	.274	A	

WON	LOST	NAME	POS.	G.	BA	FROM	TO
		Medwick, Joseph Michael (Ducky) (1B3)	OF74	78	+.218	xBkn	
9	13	Melton, Clifford George (Cliff)	P	34	.148	B	
3	7	Mungo, Van Lingle	P45	49	.159	B	
		Orengo, Joseph Chas.	1B82	83	+.281	NY41	Bkn
		Ott, Melvin Thomas (Mel) MGR. (3B1)	OF111	125	.234	B	
		Poland, Hugh Reid	C	4	+.083	A	Bos
		Reyes, Napoleon Aguilera (3B1)	1B38	40	.256	A	
		Rucker, John Joel	OF117	132	.273	NY41	
1	3	Sayles, Wm. Nisbeth	P18	19	+.308	BosA39	Bkn
0	1	Seward, Frank Martin	P	1	.000	A	
		Stephenson, Joseph Chester	C6	9	.250	A	
0	1	Sunkel, Thomas Jacob	P	1	.000	B	
1	5	Trinkle, Kenneth Wayne	P	11	.250	A	
1	2	Voiselle, Wm. Symmes	P	4	.111	B	
		Witek, Nicholas Joseph	2B	153	.314	B	
5	15	Wittig, John Carl	P	40	.098	NY41	

WON 67 — NATIONAL LEAGUE — FINISHED 5th.
LOST 87
TG 154 — 1944. — PCT. .435

NEW YORK

MELVIN THOMAS OTT

WON	LOST	NAME	POS.	G.	BA	FROM	TO
8	11	Adams, Ace Townsend	P	65	.103	B	
4	7	Allen, John Thomas (Johnny)	P18	24	.083	B	C
1	1	Barthelson, Robert Edward	P	7	.000	A	C
		Berres, Raymond Frederick	C12	16	.471	B	
1	4	Brewer, John Herndon	P	14	.211	A	
0	1	Brondell, Kenneth LeRoy	P7	8	.000	A	C
11	13	Feldman, Harry	P40	54	.205	B	
		Filipowicz, Stephen Chas. (C1)	OF10	15	.195	A	
6	14	Fischer, Reuben Walter	P	38	.125	B	
		Gardella, Daniel Lewis	OF25	47	.250	A	
0	0	Gee, John Alexander Jr.	P	4	+.000	xPitt	
3	3	Hansen, Andrew Viggo Jr.	P23	24	.167	A	
		Housmann, George John	2B122	131	.268	A	
		Jurges, Wm. Frederick (2B1 SS10) (Bill)	3B61	85	.211	B	
		Kerr, John Joseph	SS149	150	.267	B	
		Lombardi, Ernesto Natali (Schnozz)	C100	117	.255	B	
		Luby, Hugh Max (1B1 2B45)	3B65	111	.254	PhilA36	C
		Mancuso, August Rodney (Gus)	C72	78	.251	B	
		Mead, Chas. Richard	OF23	39	.179	B	
		Medwick, Joseph Michael (Ducky)	OF122	128	.337	B	
2	2	Melton, Clifford George (Cliff)	P	13	.120	B	C
0	1	Miller, Kenneth Albert	P4	5	.000	A	C

WON	LOST	NAME	POS.	G.	BA	FROM	TO
		Nichols, Roy Jr. (3B1)	2B1	11	.222	A	C
0	0	Ockey, Walter Andrew	P	2	.000	A	C
		Ott, Melvin Thomas (Mel) MGR.	OF103	120	.288	B	
0	2	Polli, Louis Americo	P	19	.000	StLA32	C
7	10	Pyle, Herbert Ewald	P	31	.157	WashA	
		Reyes, Napoleon Aguilera (3B37 OF3)	1B63	116	.289	B	
0	0	Rosso, Francis James	P2	3	.000	A	C
		Rucker, John Joel	OF138	144	.244	B	
3	2	Seward, Frank Martin	P	25	.083	B	C
		Sloan, Bruce Adam	OF21	59	.269	A	C
		Treadway, Thadford Leon	OF38	50	.300	A	
21	16	Voiselle, Wm. Symmes	P43	44	.210	B	
		Weintraub, Philip	1B99	104	.316	Phil38	

WON 78 — LOST 74 — TG 152

NATIONAL LEAGUE — 1945. — FINISHED 5th. — PCT. .513

NEW YORK

MELVIN THOMAS OTT

WON	LOST	NAME	POS.	G.	BA	FROM	TO
11	9	Adams, Ace Townsend	P	65	.188	B	
0	0	Bain, Herbert Loren	P	3	.333	A	C
		Berres, Raymond Frederick	C	20	.167	B	C
8	6	Brewer, John Herndon	P	28	.179	B	
		Dekoning, Wm. Callahan	C2	3	.000	A	C
4	4	Emmerich, Wm. Peter	P	31	.120	A	
12	13	Feldman, Harry	P35	38	.097	B	
		Filipowicz, Stephen Chas.	OF31	35	.205	B	
3	8	Fischer, Reuben Walter	P	31	.211	B	
1	0	Fisher, Donald Raymond	P	2	.143	A	C
		Gardella, Alfred Steve (OF1)	1B8	17	.077	A	C
		Gardella, Daniel Lewis (1B15)	OF94	121	.272	B	
0	0	Gee, John Alexander Jr.	P	2	.000	B	
4	3	Hansen, Andrew Viggo	P	23	.000	B	
0	0	Harrell, Raymond James	P	12	.200	Pitt40	C
		Hausmann, George John	2B	154	.279	B	C
		Hudson, John Wilson (2B2)	3B5	28	.000	Chi41	C
		Jurges, Wm. Frederick (SS8) (Bill)	3B44	61	.324	B	
		Kerr, John Joseph	SS148	149	.249	B	
		Kluttz, Clyde Franklin	C57	73	+.279	xBos	
0	2	Lee, Roy Edwin	P	3	.000	A	C
		Lockman, Carroll Walter	OF	32	.341	A	
		Lombardi, Ernesto Natali (Schnozz)	C96	115	.307	B	
5	4	Maglie, Salvatore Anthony	P13	14	.167	A	
		Mallory, James Baugh III	OF21	37	+.298	xStL	C
		Mead, Chas. Richard	OF	11	.270	B	C
		Medwick, Joseph Michael (Ducky)	OF23	26	+.304	B	Bos
14	7	Mungo, Van Lingle	P26	28	.233	NY43	C

WON	LOST	NAME	POS.	G.	BA	FROM	TO
		Ott, Melvin Thomas MGR.	OF118	135	.308	B	
0	0	Phillips, John Stephen	P1	2	.500	A	C
0	0	Pyle, Herbert Ewald	P	6	+.000	B	Bos
		Reyes, Napoleon Aguilera (1B5)	3B115	122	.288	B	
		Rucker, John Joel	OF98	105	.273	B	
		Schemer, Michael	1B27	31	.333	A	
		Treadway, Thadford Leon	OF60	88	.241	B	C
14	14	Voiselle, Wm. Symmes	P	41	.127	B	
		Weintraub, Philip	1B77	82	.272	B	C
2	4	Zabala, Adrian	P	11	.231	A	
		Zimmerman, Roy Franklin (OF1)	1B25	27	.276	A	C

WON 61 — LOST 93 — TG 154

NATIONAL LEAGUE — 1946. — FINISHED 8th (LAST) — PCT. .396

NEW YORK

MELVIN THOMAS OTT

WON	LOST	NAME	POS.	G.	BA	FROM	TO
1	1	Abernathy, Virgil Woodrow	P	15	.000	A	
0	1	Adams, Ace Townsend	P	3	.000	B	C
1	0	Andrews, Nathan Hardy	P	3	+.500	xCin	C
		Arnovich, Morris	OF	1	.000	NY41	C
		Bartell, Richard Wm. (2B2)	3B4	5	.000	NY43	C
		Blattner, Robert Garnett (1B1)	2B114	126	.255	StL42	
0	0	Brewer, John Herndon	P	1	.000	B	C
2	3	Budnick, Michael Joe	P	35	.300	A	
0	0	Carden, John Bruton	P	1	.000	A	C
1	3	Carpenter, Robert Louis	P	12	.100	NY42	
		Cooper, Wm. Walker	C73	87	.268	StL	
		DiMaggio, Vincent Paul	OF13	15	+.000	xPhil	C
0	0	Emmerich, Wm. Peter	P	2	.000	B	C
0	2	Feldman, Harry	P	3	.000	B	C
1	2	Fischer, Reuben Walter	P	15	.111	B	C
2	4	Gee, John Alexander Jr.	P	13	.231	B	C
		Gladd, James Walter	C	4	.091	A	C
		Gordon, Sidney (3B30)	OF101	135	.293	NY43	
		Graham, John Bernard (1B7)	OF62	100	+.219	xBkn	
		Grasso, Newton Michael	C	7	.136	A	
0	2	Grissom, Marvin Edward	P	4	.200	A	C
1	2	Jones, Sheldon Leslie	P	6	.250	A	
3	4	Joyce, Robert Emmett	P	14	.158	PhilA39	C
9	10	Kennedy, Montia Calvin	P	38	.234	A	
		Kerr, John Joseph (3B18)	SS126	145	.250	B	
		Kluttz, Clyde Franklin	C2	5	+.375	B	StL
14	19	Koslo, George Bernard	P40	41	.125	NY42	
2	1	Kraus, John Wm.	P	17	.000	Phil	C
0	0	Kress, Ralph (Red)	P	1	.000	DetA40	C
		Lajeski, Richard Edward	2B4	6	.200	A	C
		Lawing, Garland Frederick	OF4	8	+.167	xCin	C

WON	LOST	NAME	POS.	G.	BA	FROM	TO
		Lombardi, Ernesto Natali (Schnozz)	C63	88	.290	B	
		Marshall, Willard Warren	OF125	131	.282	NY42	
		Maynard, James Walter	OF3	7	.000	NY43	C
		Mize, John Robert	1B	101	.337	NY42	
		Ott, Melvin Thomas (Mel) MGR.	OF16	31	.074	B	
		Pike, Jesse Willard	OF10	16	.171	A	C
		Rigney, Wm. Joseph (SS33)	3B73	110	.236	A	
		Rosen, Goodwin George (Goody)	OF84	100	+.281	xBkn	C
		Rucker, John Joel	OF54	95	.264	B	C
		Schemer, Michael		1	.000	B	C
4	4	Schumacher, Harold Henry (Hal)	P	24	.038	NY42	C
4	6	Thompson, Eugene Earl (Junior)	P	39	.143	Cin42	
		Thomson, Robert Brown	3B16	18	.315	A	
7	14	Trinkle, Kenneth Wayne	P	48	.079	NY43	
9	15	Voiselle, Wm. Symmes	P	36	.164	B	
		Warren, Benjamin Louis	C30	39	.159	Phil42	
		Witek, Nicholas Joseph (Mickey) (3B35)	2B42	82	.264	NY43	
		Young, Norman Robert (Babe) (OF24)	1B49	104	.278	NY42	

WON 81
LOST 73
TG 154

NATIONAL LEAGUE 1947. FINISHED 4th. PCT. .526

NEW YORK

MELVIN THOMAS OTT

WON	LOST	NAME	POS.	G.	BA	FROM	TO
0	0	Abernathy, Virgil Woodrow	P	1	.000	B	C
0	0	Andrews, Herbert Carl	P	7	.000	A	
0	3	Ayers, Wm. Oscar	P	13	.250	A	C
3	3	Beggs, Joseph Stanley	P	32	+.077	xCin	
		Blattner, Robert Garnett (3B11)	2B34	55	.261	B	
0	0	Budnick, Michael Joe	P	7	.250	B	C
0	0	Carpenter, Robert Louis	P	2	+.000	B	Chi
1	5	Cooper, Morton Cecil	P	8	+.429	xBos	
		Cooper, Wm. Walker	C132	140	.305	B	
		Gearhart, Lloyd Wm.	OF44	73	.246	A	C
		Gordon, Sidney	OF124	130	.273	B	
1	5	Hansen, Andrew Viggo Jr.	P	27	.190	NY45	
9	7	Hartung, Clinton Clarence (OF7)	P23	34	.309	A	
3	8	Iott, Clarence Eugene	P	20	.143	xStLA	C
21	5	Jansen, Lawrence Joseph	P	42	.186	A	
2	2	Jones, Sheldon Leslie	P	15	.125	B	
9	12	Kennedy, Montia Calvin	P	34	.167	B	
		Kerr, John Joseph	SS	138	.287	B	
15	10	Koslo, George Bernard	P	39	.128	B	
		Lafata, Joseph Joseph	OF19	62	.221	A	
		Livingston, Thompson Orville	C1	5	+.167	xChi	

WON	LOST	NAME	POS.	G.	BA	FROM	TO
		Lockman, Carroll Walter		2	.500	NY45	
		Lohrke, Jack Wayne	3B111	112	.240	A	
		Lombardi, Ernesto Natali (Schnozz)	C24	48	.282	B	C
		Marshall, Willard Warren	OF	155	.291	B	
		Mize, John Robert	1B	154	.302	B	
		Ott, Melvin Thomas MGR.		4	.000	B	
0	0	Picone, Mario Peter	P	2	.500	A	
4	3	Poat, Raymond Willis	P	7	.190	ClevA44	
		Rhawn, Robert John (3B5)	2B8	13	.311	A	
		Rigney, Wm. Joseph (SS24 3B41)	2B72	130	.267	B	
4	2	Thompson, Eugene Earl (Junior)	P	15	.000	B	C
		Thomson, Robert Brown (2B9)	OF127	138	.283	B	
8	4	Trinkle, Kenneth Wayne	P	62	.188	B	
1	4	Voiselle, Wm. Symmes	P	11	+.133	B	Bos
		Warren, Benjamin Louis	C	3	.200	B	C
		Westrum, Wesley Noreen	C2	6	.417	A	
		White, Albert Eugene		7	.231	StLA40	C
		Witek, Nicholas Joseph (Mickey)	2B40	51	.219	B	
		Young, Norman Robert (Babe)		14	+.071	B	Cin
		Yvars, Salvador Anthony	C	1	.200	A	

WON 78
LOST 76
TG 154

NATIONAL LEAGUE 1948. FINISHED 5th. PCT. .506

NEW YORK

MELVIN THOMAS OTT LEO ERNEST DUROCHER

WON	LOST	NAME	POS.	G.	BA	FROM	TO
0	0	Andrews, Herbert Carl	P	1	.000	B	C
		Bamberger, Harold Earl	OF3	7	.083	A	C
0	0	Beggs, Joseph Stanley	P	1	.000	B	C
		Blattner, Robert Garnett	2B7	8	.200	B	
		Conway, Jack Clements (SS6 3B3)	2B13	24	.245	ClevA	C
		Cooper, Wm. Walker	C79	91	.266	B	
0	0	Dreisewerd, Clement John	P	4	.250	xStLA	C
0	0	Erickson, Paul Wakefield	P	2	+.000	xPhil	C
		Frey, Linus Reinhard (Lonny)	2B13	29	.255	xNYA	C
		Gordon Sidney (OF23)	3B115	142	.299	B	
0	0	Hallett, Jack Price	P	2	.000	Pitt46	C
5	3	Hansen, Andrew Viggo Jr.	P	36	.050	B	
		Harshman, John Elvin	1B3	5	.250	A	
8	8	Hartung, Clinton Clarence	P36	43	.179	B	
18	12	Jansen, Lawrence Joseph	P	42	.137	B	
16	8	Jones, Sheldon Leslie	P	55	.203	B	
3	9	Kennedy, Montia Calvin	P25	26	.129	B	
		Kerr, John Joseph	SS143	144	.240	B	

WON	LOST	NAME	POS.	G.	BA	FROM	TO
2	3	Konikowski, Alexander James	P	22	.000	A	
8	10	Koslo, George Bernard	P	35	.114	B	
		Lafata, Joseph Joseph		1	.000	B	
		Layton, Lester Lee	OF20	63	.231	A	C
1	3	Lee, Thornton Starr (Lefty)	P	11	.091	ChiA	C
		Livingston, Thompson Orville	C42	45	.212	B	
		Lockman, Carroll Walter	OF144	146	.286	B	
		Lohrke, Jack Wayne (2B36)	3B50	97	.250	B	
0	0	Lombardo, Louis	P	2	.000	A	C
		Marshall, Willard Warren	OF142	143	.272	B	
		Milne, Wm. James (Pete)	OF9	12	.222	A	
		Mize, John Robert	1B	152	.289	B	
		Mueller, Donald Frederick	OF22	36	.358	A	
		McCarthy, John Joseph (Mac)	1B6	56	.263	Bos46	C
0	0	McGowan, Tullis Earl	P	3	.000	A	C
0	4	Newsom, Louis Norman (Buck)	P	11	.429	NYA	
11	10	Poat, Raymond Willis	P	39	.125	B	
		Rhawn, Robert John (3B7)	SS14	36	.273	B	
		Rigney, Wm. Joseph (SS7)	2B105	113	.264	B	
		Thomson, Robert Brown	OF125	138	.248	B	
4	5	Trinkle, Kenneth Wayne	P	53	.250	B	
2	1	Webb, Samuel Henry	P	5	.222	A	
		Westrum, Wesley Noreen	C63	66	.160	B	
		Yvars, Salvador Anthony	C	15	.211	B	

WON x73 | NATIONAL LEAGUE | FINISHED 5th.
LOST 81
TG 154 | 1949. | PCT. .474

NEW YORK

LEO ERNEST DUROCHER

WON	LOST	NAME	POS.	G.	BA	FROM	TO
3	3	Behrman, Henry Bernard	P	43	.077	Bkn	C
0	0	Bowman, Roger Clinton	P	2	.000	A	
		Cooper, Wm. Walker	C40	42	+.211	B	Cin
		Culler, Richard Broadus	SS	7	.000	Chi	C
		Franks, Herman Louis	C	1	.667	PhilA	C
		Galan, August John (Augie) (OF1)	1B3	22	.059	Cin	PhilA
		Gordon, Sidney (1B1 OF15)	3B123	141	.284	B	
		Haas, Berthold John (Bert) (3B11)	1B23	54	+.260	xPhil	
2	6	Hansen, Andrew Viggo Jr.	P	33	.000	B	
9	11	Hartung, Clinton Clarence	P33	38	.190	B	
2	0	Higbe, Walter Kirby	P	37	+.067	xPitt	
		Hofman, Robert George	2B16	19	.208	A	
		Hausmann, George John	2B13	16	.128	NY45	C
		Irvin, Monford Merrill (1B5 3B5)	OF10	36	.224	A	
15	16	Jansen, Lawrence Joseph	P	37	.165	B	
15	12	Jones, Sheldon Leslie	P	42	.121	B	
12	14	Kennedy, Montia Calvin	P38	39	.145	B	
		Kerr, John Joseph	SS89	90	.209	B	

WON	LOST	NAME	POS.	G.	BA	FROM	TO
11	14	Koslo, George Bernard	P38	39	.145	B	
		Lafata, Joseph Joseph	1B47	64	.236	B	C
		Livingston, Thompson Orville	C	19	+.298	B	Bos
		Lockman, Carroll Walter	OF	151	.301	B	
		Lohrko, Jack Wayne (SS15 3B19)	2B23	55	.267	B	
		Marshall, Willard Warren	OF138	141	.307	B	
		Milne, Wm. James	OF1	31	.241	B	
		Mize, John Robert	1B101	106	.263	B	N.Y.A
		Mueller, Donald Frederick	OF6	51	.232	B	
		Mueller, Ray Coleman	C	56	+.224	xCin	
0	0	Poat, Raymond Willis	P	2	+.000	B	Pitt
		Rhawn, Robert John	2B8	14	+.172	B	Pitt
		Rigney, Wm. Joseph (2B26 3B14)	SS81	122	.278	B	
		Rufer, Rudolph Joseph	SS	7	.067	A	
		Thompson, Henry Curtis (3B1)	2B69	75	.280	StLA47	
		Thomson, Robert Brown	OF	156	.309	B	
0	1	Tomasic, Andrew John	P	2	.000	A	C
1	1	Webb, Samuel Henry	P	20	.400	B	C
		Westrum, Wesley Noreen	C62	64	.243	B	
		Williams, David Carlous	2B	13	.240	A	
		Yvars, Salvador Anthony	C2	3	.000	B	
2	3	Zabala, Adrian	P	15	.077	NY45	C

x-One game won by forfeit.

WON 86 | NATIONAL LEAGUE | FINISHED 3rd.
LOST 68
TG 154 | 1950. | PCT. .558

NEW YORK

LEO ERNEST DUROCHER

WON	LOST	NAME	POS.	G.	BA	FROM	TO
		Blaylock, Marvin Edward		1	.000	A	C
		Calderone, Samuel Francis	C33	34	.299	A	
		Dark, Alvin Ralph	SS	154	.279	Bos	
		Gilbert, Harold Joseph	1B111	113	.220	A	
0	1	Hansen, Andrew Viggo Jr.	P	31	.000	B	
		Harshman, John Elvin	1B	9	.125	NY48	
3	3	Hartung, Clinton Clarence (1B1 OF2)	P20	32	.302	B	
11	3	Hearn, James Tolbert	P	16	+.136	xStL	
0	3	Higbe, Walter Kirby	P	18	.250	B	C
		Irvin, Monford Merrill (3B1 OF49)	1B59	110	.300	B	
19	13	Jansen, Lawrence Joseph	P	40	.167	B	
13	16	Jones, Sheldon Leslie	P	40	.105	B	
		Jorgensen, John Donald	3B5	24	+.135	xBkn	
5	4	Kennedy, Montia Calvin	P	36	.056	B	
13	15	Koslo, George Bernard	P	40	.123	B	
3	6	Kramer, John Henry	P	35	.100	BosA	
		Lockman, Carroll Walter	OF128	129	.295	B	
		Lohrke, Jack Wayne (2B1)	3B16	30	.186	B	
18	4	Maglie, Salvatore Anthony	P	47	.121	NY45	

WON	LOST	NAME	POS.	G.	BA	FROM	TO
		Maguire, Jack (1B2)	OF9	29	.175	A	
		Milne, Wm. James		4	.250	B	C
		Mueller, Donald Frederick	OF125	132	.291	B	
		Mueller, Ray Coleman	C	4	+.091	B	Pitt
		McCormick, Myron Winthrop		4	.000	Bkn	ChiA
		Reyes, Napoleon Aguilera	1B	1	.000	NY45	C
		Rigney, Wm. Joseph (3B11)	2B23	56	.181	B	
		Rufer, Rudolph Joseph	SS8	15	.091	B	C
1	0	Spencer, George Elwell	P	10	.000	A	
		Stanky, Edward Raymond	2B151	152	.300	Bos	
		Thompson, Henry Curtis	3B138	148	.289	B	
		(OF10)					
		Thomson, Robert Brown	OF	149	.252	B	
		Weatherly, Cyril Roy (Stormy)	OF15	52	.261	NYA46	C
		Westrum, Wesley Noreen	C139	140	.236	B	
		Yvars, Salvador Anthony	C	9	.143	B	

WON 98 NATIONAL LEAGUE FINISHED 1st.
LOST 59
TG 157 1951. PCT. .624

NEW YORK

LEO ERNEST DUROCHER

WON	LOST	NAME	POS.	G.	BA	FROM	TO
0	0	Bamberger, George Irvin	P	2	.000	A	
2	4	Bowman, Roger Clinton	P	9	.000	NY49	
5	1	Corwin, Elmer Nathan	P	15	.050	A	
		Dark, Alvin Ralph	SS	156	.303	B	
1	2	Gettel, Allen Jones	P	30	.083	WashA49	C
0	0	Hardy, Francis Joseph	P	2	.000	A	C
		Hartung, Clinton Clarence	OF12	21	.205	B	
17	9	Hearn, James Tolbert	P	34	.162	B	
		Irvin, Monford Merrill	OF112	151	.312	B	
		(1B39)					
23	11	Jansen, Lawrence Joseph	P	39	.094	B	
6	11	Jones, Sheldon Leslie	P	41	.097	B	
		Jorgensen, John Donald	OF11	28	.235	B	C
		(3B1)					
1	2	Kennedy, Montia Calvin	P	29	.200	B	
0	0	Konikowski, Alexander James	P	3	.000	NY48	
10	9	Koslo, George Bernard	P	39	.100	B	
0	0	Kramer, John Henry	P	4	.000	B	NYA
		Lockman, Carroll Walter	1B119	153	.282	B	
		(OF34)					
		Lohrke, Jack Wayne (SS1)	3B17	23	.200	B	
23	6	Maglie, Salvatore Anthony	P	42	.152	B	
		Maguire, Jack	OF8	16	+.400	B	Pitts
		Mays, Willie Howard	OF	121	.274	A	
		Mueller, Donald Frederick	OF115	122	.277	B	
		Noble, Rafael Miguel	C41	55	.234	A	
		Rapp, Earl Wellington		13	.091	ChiA49	StLA
		Rigney, Wm. Joseph (2B9)	3B12	44	.232	B	
		Schenz, Henry Leonard		8	+.000	xPitts	C
10	4	Spencer, George Elwell	P	57	.125	B	

WON	LOST	NAME	POS.	G.	BA	FROM	TO
		Stanky, Edward Raymond	2B140	145	.247	B	
		Thompson, Henry Curtis	3B71	87	.235	B	
		Thomson, Robert Brown	OF77	148	.294	B	
		(3B69)					
		Westrum, Wesley Noreen	C122	124	.219	B	
		Williams, David Carlous	2B22	30	.266	NY49	
		Wilson, Arthur Lee	2B3	19	.182	A	C
		(1B2 SS3)					
		Yvars, Salvador Anthony	C23	25	.317	B	

WON 92 NATIONAL LEAGUE FINISHED 2nd.
LOST 62
TG 154 1952. PCT. .597

NEW YORK

LEO ERNEST DUROCHER

WON	LOST	NAME	POS.	G.	BA	FROM	TO
0	0	Bamberger, George Irvin	P5	6	.000	B	
0	0	Bowman, Roger Clinton	P	2	.000	B	
5	0	Connelly, Wm. Wirt	P	11	.364	DetA50	
6	1	Corwin, Elmer Nathan	P21	23	.095	B	
		Dark, Alvin Ralph	SS150	151	.301	B	
		Diering, Chas. Edward Allen	OF36	41	.174	StL	
		Elliott, Robert Irving	OF65	98	.228	Bos	
		(3B13)					
0	1	Gregg, Harold Dana	P	16	.125	Pitt50	C
0	2	Harshman, John Elvin	P2	3	.000	NY50	
		Hartung, Clinton Clarence	OF24	28	.218	B	C
14	7	Hearn, James Tolbert	P	37	.182	B	
		Hofman, Robert George	2B21	32	.286	NY49	
		(1B1 3B2)					
		Howerton, Wm. Ray	OF8	11	+.067	xPitt	C
		Irvin, Monford Merrill	OF32	46	.310	B	
11	11	Jansen, Lawrence Joseph	P	34	.178	B	
		Katt, Raymond Frederick	C8	9	.222	A	
3	4	Kennedy, Montia Calvin	P31	34	.091	B	
10	7	Koslo, George Bernard	P	41	.037	B	
7	12	Lanier, Hubert Max	P37	38	.268	StL	
		Lockman, Carroll Walter	1B	154	.290	B	
18	8	Maglie, Salvatore Anthony	P	35	.072	B	
		Mays, Willie Howard	OF	34	.236	B	
		Mueller, Donald Frederick	OF120	126	.281	B	
		Noble, Rafael Miguel	C5	6	.000	B	
0	1	Picone, Mario Peter	P	2	.000	NY47	
		Rhodes, James Lamar	OF56	67	.250	A	
		Rigney, Wm. Joseph	3B10	60	.300	B	
		(1B1 2B9 SS4)					
		Spencer, Daryl Dean (3B3)	SS3	7	.294	A	
3	5	Spencer, George Elwell	P	35	.200	B	
		Thompson, Henry Curtis	OF72	128	.260	B	
		(2B4 3B46)					
		Thomson, Robert Brown	3B91	153	.270	B	
		(OF63)					
		Wakefield, Richard Cummings		3	.000	NYA50	C

WON	LOST	NAME	POS.	G.	BA	FROM	TO
		Westrum, Wesley Noreen	C112	114	.221	B	
15	3	Wilhelm, James Hoyt	P	71	.158	A	
		Williams, David Carlous	2B	138	.254	B	
		Wilson, George Washington (1B2)	OF21	62	.241	xChiA	
		Yvars, Salvador Anthony	C59	66	.245	B	

WON 70 LOST 84 TG 154 — NATIONAL LEAGUE 1953. — FINISHED 5th. PCT. .455

NEW YORK

LEO ERNEST DUROCHER

WON	LOST	NAME	POS.	G.	BA	FROM	TO
		Calderone, Samuel Francis	C31	35	.222	NY50	
0	1	Connelly, Wm. Wirt	P	8	.000	B	C
6	4	Corwin, Elmer Nathan	P48	54	.281	B	
0	0	Dark, Alvin Ralph (P1 2B26 3B8 OF17)	SS110	155	.300	B	
		Gilbert, Harold Joseph	1B44	70	.169	NY50	C
13	11	Gomez, Ruben Colon	P29	61	.208	A	
4	2	Grissom, Marvin Edward	P	21	.074	xBosA	
9	12	Hearn, James Tolbert	P36	37	.136	B	
2	1	Hiller, Frank Walter	P	19	.500	Cin	C
		Hofman, Robert George (2B17)	3B23	74	.266	B	
		Irvin, Monford Merrill	OF113	124	.329	B	
11	16	Jansen, Lawrence Joseph	P	36	.133	B	
		Katt, Raymond Frederick	C	8	.172	B	
0	0	Kennedy, Montia Ca lvin	P18	19	.000	B	C
6	12	Koslo, George Bernard	P	37	.033	B	
0	0	Lanier, Hubert Max	P	3	.000	B	StLA
		Lockman, Carroll Walter (OF30)	1B120	150	.295	B	
8	9	Maglie, Salvatore Anthony	P	27	.271	B	
		Mueller, Donald Frederick	OF122	131	.333	B	
		Noble, Rafael Miguel	C41	46	.206	B	C
		Rhodes, James Lamar	OF47	76	.233	B	
		Rigney, Wm. Joseph (2B1)	3B2	19	.250	B	
		Spencer, Daryl Dean (2B32 3B36)	SS53	118	.208	B	
0	0	Spencer, George Elwell	P	1	.000	B	
		Thompson, Henry Curtis (2B1 OF9)	3B101	114	.302	B	
		Thomson, Robert Brown	OF	154	.288	B	
		Westrum, Wesley Noreen (3B1)	C106	107	.224	B	
7	8	Wilhelm, James Hoyt	P	68	.152	B	
		Williams, David Carlous	2B95	112	.297	B	
		Wilson, George Washington		11	.125	B	
4	8	Worthington, Allan Fulton	P	20	.065	A	
		Yvars, Salvador Anthony	C20	23	+.277	B	StL

WON 97 LOST 57 TG 154 — NATIONAL LEAGUE 1954. — FINISHED 1st. PCT. .630

NEW YORK

LEO ERNEST DUROCHER

WON	LOST	NAME	POS.	G.	BA	FROM	TO
		Amalfitano, John Joseph (2B1)	3B4	9	.000	A	
21	7	Antonelli, John August	P	39	.163	Mil	
		Castleman, Foster Ephraim	3B2	13	.250	A	
1	3	Corwin, Elmer Nathan	P20	23	.000	B	
		Dark, Alvin Ralph	SS	154	.293	B	
		Evers, Walter Arthur	OF4	12	.091	xBosA	DetA
		Garagiola, Joseph Henry	C3	5	+.273	xChi	C
		Gardner, Wm. Frederick (2B13 SS5)	3B30	62	.213	A	
		Gentry, Harvey Wm.		5	.250	A	C
0	0	Giel, Pau; Robert	P	6	.000	A	
17	9	Gomez, Ruben Colon	P37	49	.173	B	
10	7	Grissom, Marvin Edward	P	56	.156	B	
8	8	Hearn, James Tolbert	P	29	.111	B	
		Hofman, Robert George (2B10 3B8)	1B21	71	.224	B	
		Irvin, Monford Merrill (1B1 3B1)	OF128	135	.262	B	
2	2	Jansen, Lawrence Joseph	P	13	.286	B	
		Katt, Raymond Frederick	C82	86	.255	B	
0	0	Konikowski, Alexander James	P	10	.000	NY51	C
		Lennon, Robert Albert		3	.000	A	
9	4	Liddle, Donald Eugene	P28	29	.189	Milw.	
		Lockman, Carroll Walter (OF2)	1B145	148	.251	B	
14	6	Maglie, Salvatore Anthony	P	34	.127	B	
		Mays, Willie Howard	OF	151	.345	NY52	
0	0	Monzant, Ramon Segundo	P	6	.000	A	
		Mueller, Donald Frederick	OF	153	.342	B	
2	5	McCall, John Wm.	P	33	.000	Pitt50	
0	0	Picone, Mario Peter	P	5	+.000	NY52	Cin
		Rhodes, James Lamar	OF37	82	.341	B	
		Rodin, Eric Chapman	OF3	5	.000	A	C
		Samford, Ronald Edward	2B3	12	.000	A	
1	0	Spencer, George Elwell	P	6	.000	B	
		St.Claire, Edward Joseph	C16	20	.262	Mil	C
		Taylor, Wm. Michael	OF9	55	.185	A	
		Thompson, Henry Curtis (2B2 OF1)	3B130	136	.263	B	
		Westrum, Wesley Noreen	C	98	.187	B	
12	4	Wilhelm, James Hoyt	P	57	.047	B	
		Williams, David Carlous	2B	142	.222	B	
0	2	Worthington, Allan Fulton	P	10	.000	B	

WON 80
LOST 74
TG 154

NATIONAL LEAGUE

1955.

NEW YORK

FINISHED 3rd.

PCT. .519

LEO ERNEST DUROCHER

WON	LOST	NAME	POS.	G.	BA.	FROM	TO
		Amalfitano, John Joseph (3B2)	SS5	36	.227	B	
14	16	Antonelli, John August	P	38	.207	B	
1	0	Burnside, Peter Willits	P	2	.200	A	
		Castleman, Foster Ephraim (3B1)	2B6	15	.214	B	
		Coan, Gilbert Fitzgerald	OF6	9	.154	xChiA	
0	1	Corwin, Elmer Nathan	P	13	.000	B	C
		Cark, Alvin Ralph	SS	115	.282	B	
		Gardner, Wm. Frederick (2B4 3B10)	SS38	59	.203	B	
4	4	Giel, Paul Robert	P	34	.053	B	
9	10	Gomez, Ruben Colon	P33	42	.300	B	
		Gordon, Sidney (OF17)	3B31	66	+.243	xPitts	C
		Grasso, Newton Michael	C	8	.000	ClevA	C
5	4	Grissom, Marvin Edward	P	55	.154	B	
		Harris, Boyd Gail	1B75	79	.232	A	
14	16	Hearn, James Tolbert	P39	41	.156	B	
		Hofman, Robert George (C19 2B19 3B5)	1B24	96	.266	B	
		Irvin, Monford Merrill	OF45	51	.253	B	
		Katt, Raymond Frederick	C122	124	.215	B	
10	4	Liddle, Donald Eugene	P	33	.185	B	
		Lockman, Carroll Walter (1B68)	OF81	147	.278	B	
9	5	Maglie, Salvatore Anthony	P	23	.125	B	ClevA
		Mays, Willie Howard	OF	152	.319	B	
4	8	Monzant, Ramon Segundo	P28	29	.125	B	
		Mueller, Donald Frederick	OF146	147	.306	B	
6	5	McCall, John Wm.	P	42	.118	B	
		Rhodes, James Lamar	OF45	94	.305	B	
0	0	Spencer, George Elwell	P	1	.000	B	
		Taylor, Wm. Michael	OF2	65	.266	B	
		Terwilliger, Willard Wayne (SS1 3B1)	2B78	80	.257	WashA	
		Thompson, Henry Curtis (2B7 SS1)	3B124	135	.245	B	
		Westrum, Wesley Noreen	C68	69	.212	B	
4	1	Wilhelm, James Hoyt	P	59	.158	B	
		Williams, David Carlous	2B71	82	.251	B	C

WON 67
LOST 87
TG 154

NATIONAL LEAGUE

1956.

NEW YORK

FINISHED 6th.

PCT. .435

WM. JOSEPH RIGNEY

WON	LOST	NAME	POS.	G.	BA	FROM	TO
20	13	Antonelli, John August	P41	49	.157	B	
		Brandt, John George	OF96	98	+.299	xStL	
		Bressoud, Edward Francis	SS48	49	.227	A	
		Castleman, Foster Ephraim (2B1 SS2)	3B107	124	.226	B	
		Coan, Gilbert Fitzgerald		4	.000	B	C
0	0	Constable, James Lee	P	3	.000	A	
		Dark, Alvin Ralph	SS	48	+.252	B	StL
7	17	Gomez, Ruben Colon (OF1)	P40	52	.183	B	
1	1	Grissom, Marvin Edward	P	43	.091	B	
		Harris, Boyd Gail	1B11	12	.132	B	
5	11	Hearn, James Tolbert	P30	32	.098	B	
		Hofman, Robert George (1B3 2B2 3B7)	C7	47	.179	B	
		Katt, Raymond Frederick	C	37	+.228	B	StL
		Lennon, Robert Albert	OF21	26	.182	NY54	
1	2	Liddle, Donald Eugene	P	11	+.167	B	StL
4	4	Littlefield, Richard Bernard	P	31	+.083	xStL	
		Lockman, Carroll Walter (1B7)	OF39	48	+.272	B	StL
		Mangan, James Daniel	C15	20	.100	Pitt54	C
6	6	Margoneri, Joseph Emanuel	P	23	.103	A	
		Mays, Willie Howard	OF	152	.296	B	
1	0	Monzant, Ramon Segundo	P4	6	.000	B	
		Mueller, Donald Frederick	OF117	138	.269	B	
3	4	McCall, John Wm.	P	46	.200	B	
0	1	McCormick, Michael Francis	P	3	.000	A	
		Rhodes, James Lamar	OF68	111	.217	B	
6	2	Ridzik, Stephen George	P41	44	.250	Cin	
		Sarni, Wm. F.	C	78	+.231	xStL	C
		Schoendienst, Albert Fred	2B85	92	+.296	xStL	
		Spencer, Daryl Dean (SS66 3B12)	2B70	146	.221	NY53	
2	2	Surkont, Maxim Constantine	P	8	+.111	xStL	
		Taylor, Wm. Michael	OF	1	.250	B	
		Terwilliger, Willard Wayne	2B6	14	.222	B	
		Thompson, Henry Curtis (SS1 OF10)	3B44	83	.235	B	C
		Virgil, Osvaldo Joseph	3B	3	.417	A	
		Westrum, Wesley Noreen	C67	68	.220	B	
		White, Wm. DeKova (OF2)	1B138	138	.256	A	
4	9	Wilhelm, James Hoyt	P	64	.222	B	
		Wilson, George Washington	OF8	53	.132	NY53	NYA
7	14	Worthington, Allan Fulton	P	28	.235	NY54	
0	1	Wright, Roy Earl	P	1	.000	A	C

WON 69
LOST 85
TG 154

NATIONAL LEAGUE

1957.

NEW YORK

FINISHED 6th.

PCT. .448

WM. JOSEPH RIGNEY

WON	LOST	NAME	POS.	G.	BA	FROM	TO
12	18	Antonelli, John August	P40	47	.153	B	
9	9	Barclay, Curtis Cordell	P	37	.190	A	
		Bressoud, Edward Francis (3B12)	SS33	49	.268	B	
1	4	Burnside, Peter Willits	P	10	.000	NY55	
		Castleman, Foster Ephraim (2B1 SS1)	3B7	18	.162	B	
1	1	Constable, James Lee	P	16	.000	B	
0	0	Consuegra, Sandalio Simeon Castellon	P	4	.000	xBaltA	C
4	8	Crone, Raymond Hayes	P	25	+.025	xMil	
1	0	Davis, James Bennett	P	10	+1.000	xStL	C
15	13	Gomez, Ruben Colon (OF1)	P38	54	.184	B	
4	4	Grissom, Marvin Edward	P	55	.167	B	
		Harris, Boyd Gail	1B61	90	.240	B	
		Hofman, Robert George		2	.000	B	C
		Jablonski, Raymond Leo (1B6 OF1)	3B70	107	.289	Cin	
0	1	Jones, Gordon Bassett	P	10	.500	StL	
		Katt, Raymond Frederick	C68	72	.230	B	
		Lockman, Carroll Walter (OF27)	1B102	133	.248	B	
1	1	Margoneri, Joseph Emanuel	P	13	.000	B	C
		Mays, Willie Howard	OF150	152	.333	B	
0	0	McCall, John Wm.	P	5	.000	B	C
3	1	McCormick, Michael Francis	P	24	.273	B	
7	9	Miller, Stuart Leonard	P	38	.057	Phil	
3	2	Monzant, Ramon Segundo	P	24	.300	B	
		Mueller, Donald Frederick	OF115	135	.258	B	
		O'Connell, Daniel Francis (3B30)	2B68	95	+.266	xMil	
		Rhodes, James Lamar	OF44	92	.205	B	
0	2	Ridzik, Stephen George	P15	16	.200	B	
		Rodgers, Kenneth Andre Ian (3B8)	SS20	32	.244	A	
		Sauer, Henry John	OF98	127	.259	StL	
		Schoendienst, Albert Fred	2B	57	+.307	B	Mil
		Spencer, Daryl Dean (2B36 3B6)	SS110	148	.249	B	
0	1	Surkont, Maxim Constantine	P	5	.000	B	C
		Taylor, Wm. Michael		11	.000	B	DetA
		Thomas, Valmy	C	88	.249	A	
		Thomson, Robert Brown (3B1)	OF71	81	+.242	xMil	
		Virgil, Osvaldo Joseph (SS1 OF24)	3B62	96	.235	B	
		Westrum, Wesley Noreen	C	63	.165	B	C
8	11	Worthington, Allan Fulton	P	55	.100	B	

WON 40
LOST 120
TG 160

NATIONAL LEAGUE — FINISHED 10th (LAST)

1962. — PCT. .250

NEW YORK

CHAS. DILLON STENGEL

WON	LOST	NAME	POS.	G.	BA	FROM	TO
3	17	Anderson, Norman Craig	P	50	.094	StL	
		Ashburn, Richie (2B2)	OF97	135	.306	Chi	C
		Bell, David Russell	OF26	30	+.149	Cin	Mil
		Bouchee, Edward Francis	1B19	50	.161	Chi	C
		Cannizzaro, Christopher John (OF1)	C56	59	.241	StL	
		Chacon, Elio Rodriquez (2B2)	SS110	118	.236	Cin	C
		Chiti, Harry	C14	15	.195	DetA	C
		Christopher, Joseph O'Neal	OF94	119	.244	Pitt	
1	1	Cisco, Galen Bernard	P	4	.000	xBosA	
		Coleman, Clarence	C44	55	.250	Phil	
		Cook, Raymond Clifford (OF10)	3B16	40	+.232	xCin	
10	24	Craig, Roger Lee	P	42	.053	L.A.	
1	5	Daviault, Raymond Joseph Robert	P	36	.067	A	C
		DeMerit, John Stephen	OF9	14	.188	Mil	C
		Drake, Samuel Harrison	2B10	25	.192	Chi	C
0	1	Foss, Larry Curtis	P	5	.000	Pitt	C
		Ginsberg, Myron Nathan	C	2	.000	BosA	C
		Herrscher, Richard Franklin (SS3 OF4)	1B10	35	.220	A	C
		Hickman, James Lucius	OF124	140	.245	A	
0	0	Hillman, Darius Dutton	P	13	+.000	xCin	C
		Hodges, Gilbert Raymond	1B47	54	.252	L.A.	
8	19	Hook, James Wesley	P37	41	.203	Cin	
1	6	Hunter, Willard Mitchell	P	27	+.231	xL.A.	
8	20	Jackson, Alvin Neil	P36	44	.068	Pitt	
0	4	Jones, Sherman Jarvis	P	8	.429	Cin	C
		Kanehl, Roderick Edwin (1B3 SS2 3B30 OF20)	2B62	133	.248	A	
		Kranepool, Edward Emil	1B	3	.167	A	
0	0	Labine, Clement Walter	P	3	.000	Pitt	C
		Landrith, Hobert Neal	C21	23	.289	S.F.	BaltA
5	4	MacKenzie, Kenneth Purvis	P	42	.083	Mil	
		Mantilla, Felix Lamela (2B14 SS25)	3B95	141	.275	Mil	
		Marshall, Rufus James (OF1)	1B5	17	+.344	S.F.	Pitt
2	2	Miller, Robert Gerald	P	17	+.000	xCin	C
1	12	Miller, Robert Lane	P33	40	.122	StL	
0	2	Mizell, Wilmer David	P	17	+.250	xPitt	C
0	1	Moford, Herbert	P	7	.250	BosA59	C
0	2	Moorhead, Chas. Robert	P	38	.045	A	
		Neal, Chas. Lenard (SS39 3B12)	2B85	136	.260	L. A.	
		Pignatano, Joseph Benjamin	C25	27	+.232	xS.F.	C
		Smith, Bobby Gene	OF6	8	+.136	Phil	Chi
		Taylor, Samuel Douglas	C50	68	+.222	xChi	
		Thomas, Frank Joseph (1B11 3B10)	OF126	156	.266	Mil	
		Throneberry, Marvin Eugene	1B97	116	.244	xBaltA	
		Woodling, Eugene Richard	OF48	81	.274	xWashA	C
		Zimmer, Donald Wm.	3B	14	+.077	Chi	Cin

WON 51 | LOST 111 | TG 162

NATIONAL LEAGUE 1963.

FINISHED 10th (LAST) PCT. .315

NEW YORK

CHAS. DILLON STENGEL

WON	LOST	NAME	POS.	G.	BA	FROM	TO
0	2	Anderson, Norman Craig	P	3	.333	B	
0	0	Bauta, Eduardo Galvez	P	9	+.000	xStL	
3	8	Bearnarth, Lawrence Donald	P	58	.200	A	
		Burright, Lawrence Allen (2B3 3B5)	SS19	41	.220	L.A.	
		Cannizzaro, Christopher John	C15	16	.242	B	
		Carmel, Leon James (1B18)	OF21	47	+.235	xStL	
		Christopher, Joseph O'Neal	OF45	64	.221	B	
7	15	Cisco, Galen Bernard	P	51	.132	B	
		Coleman, Clarence (OF1)	C91	106	.178	B	
		Cook, Raymond Clifford (1B5 3B9)	OF21	50	.142	B	C
5	22	Craig, Roger Lee	P	46	.087	B	
0	0	Dillon, Stephen Edward	P	1	.000	A	
		Fernandez, Humberto Perez (2B3 3B5)	SS45	58	.200	xDetA	C
		Gonder, Jesse Lemar	C31	42	+.302	xCin	
		Green, Elijah Jerry	3B16	17	.278	BosA	C
		Harkness, Thomas Wm.	1B106	123	.211	L.A.	
		Hickman, James Lucius (3B59)	OF82	146	.229	B	
		Hicks, Wm. Joseph	OF41	56	.226	WashA	C
		Hodges, Gilbert Raymond	1B10	11	.227	B	C
4	14	Hook, James Wesley	P	41	.237	B	
		Hunt, Ronald Kenneth (3B1)	2B142	143	.272	A	
13	17	Jackson, Alvin Neil	P37	49	.203	B	
		Jones, Cleon Joseph	OF5	6	.133	A	
		Kanehl, Roderick Edwin (1B3 2B12 3B13)	OF58	109	.241	B	
		Kranepool, Edward Emil (1B20)	OF55	86	.209	B	
3	1	MacKenzie, Kenneth Purvis	P	34	+.000	B	StL
		Moran, Richard Alan (3B1)	SS116	119	.193	A	
		Neal, Chas. Lenard (SS8)	3B66	72	+.225	B	Cin
		Piersall, James Anthony	OF38	40	.194	xWashA	LAA
1	1	Powell, Grover David	P	20	.200	A	C
0	0	Rowe, Donald Howard	P	26	.231	A	C
		Schreiber, Theodore Henry (2B3 SS9)	3B17	39	.160	A	C
		Sherry, Norman Burt	C61	63	.136	L.A.	C
		Smith, Richard Arthur (1B2)	OF10	20	.238	A	
		Snider, Edwin Donald	OF106	129	.243	L.A.	
6	17	Stallard, Evan Tracy	P	39	.063	BosA	
		Taylor, Samuel Douglas	C13	22	+.257	B	Cin
		Thomas, Frank Joseph (1B15 3B1)	OF96	126	.260	B	
		Thorneberry, Marvin Eugene	1B3	14	.143	B	C
9	14	Willey, Carlton Francis	P	30	.111	Mil	

WON 53 | LOST 109 | TG 162

NATIONAL LEAGUE 1964.

FINISHED 10th (LAST) PCT. .327

NEW YORK

CHAS. DILLON STENGEL

WON	LOST	NAME	POS.	G.	BA	FROM	TO
		Altman, George Lee	OF109	124	.230	StL	
0	1	Anderson, Norman Craig	P	4	.000	B	C
0	2	Bauta, Eduardo Galvez	P	8	.000	B	C
5	5	Bearnarth, Lawrence Donald	P	44	.143	B	
		Burright, Lawrence Allen	2B	3	.000	B	C
		Cannizzaro, Christopher John	C53	60	.311	B	
		Christopher, Joseph O'Neal	OF145	154	.300	B	
6	19	Cisco, Galen Bernard	P	36	.111	B	
0	0	Dillon, Stephen Edward	P	2	.000	B	C
		Elliott, Lawrence Lee	OF63	80	.228	Pitt	
10	17	Fisher, John Howard	P	40	.158	S.F.	
		Gonder, Jesse Lemar	C97	131	.270	B	
		Graham, Wayne Leon	3B11	20	.091	Phil	C
		Harkness, Thomas Wm.	1B32	39	.282	B	C
		Hickman, James Lucius (3B1)	OF113	139	.257	B	
0	2	Hinsley, Jerry Dean	P	9	.000	A	
0	1	Hook, James Wesley	P	3	.000	B	C
		Hunt, Ronald Kenneth (3B12)	2B109	127	.303	B	
3	3	Hunter, Willard Mitchell	P	41	1.000	NY62	C
11	16	Jackson, Alvin Neil	P40	50	.153	B	
		Kanehl, Roderick Edwin (1B2 3B19 OF25)	2B34	98	.232	B	C
		Klaus, Robert Francis (2B25 SS5)	3B28	56	+.244	xCin	
		Kranepool, Edward Emil (OF6)	1B104	119	.257	B	
0	1	Kroll, Gary Melvin	P	8	+.333	xPhila	
2	3	Lary, Frank Strong	P	13	+.118	DetA	Mil
1	2	Locke, Ronald Thomas	P	25	.000	A	C
		McMillan, Roy David	SS111	113	+.211	xMil	
		Moran, Richard Alan (3B1)	SS15	16	.227	B	C
1	2	Parsons, Thomas Anthony	P	4	.000	Pitt	
1	5	Ribant, Dennis Joseph	P14	17	.100	A	
		Samuel, Amado Ruperto *(2B3 3B17)	SS34	53	.232	Mil	C
		Smith, Chas. Wm. (SS36 OF13)	3B85	127	.239	xChicA	
		Smith, Richard Arthur (OF13)	1B18	46	.223	B	
10	20	Stallard, Evan Tracy	P	36	.190	B	
		Stephenson, John Herman (OF8)	3B14	37	.158	A	
0	0	Sturdivant, Thomas Virgil	P	16	.000	xKCA	C
0	3	Sutherland, Darrell Wayne	P	10	.200	A	
		Taylor, Robert Dale (OF16)	C45	92	.240	B	
		Thomas, Frank Joseph (1B19 3B2)	OF31	60	+.254	B	Phil
3	5	Wakefield, Wm. Sumner	P	62	.167	A	C
0	2	Willey, Carlton Francis	P	14	.000	B	

CLUB RECORD

NATIONAL LEAGUE

PHILADELPHIA

YEAR	TG	WON	LOST	PCT.	FINISHED	MANAGER
1876	59	14	45	.237	7 (ATHLETICS)	Alfred L. H. Wright
1877-1882		OUT OF LEAGUE				
1883	98	17	81	.173	8(Last)	Robert V. Ferguson
1884	112	39	73	.348	6	Wm. Henry Wright
1885	110	56	54	.509	3	Wm. Henry Wright
1886	114	71	43	.622	4	Wm. Henry Wright
1887	123	75	48	.610	2	Wm. Henry Wright
1888	130	69	61	.531	3	Wm. Henry Wright
1889	127	63	64	.496	4	Wm. Henry Wright
1890	131	78	53	.595	3	Wm. Henry Wright
1891	137	68	69	.496	4	Wm. Henry Wright
1892	153	87	66	.569	4	Wm. Henry Wright
1893	129	72	57	.558	4	Wm. Henry Wright
1894	127	71	56	.559	4	Arthur Albert Irwin
1895	131	78	53	.595	3	Arthur Albert Irwin
1896	130	62	68	.477	8	Wm. Mitchell Nash
1897	132	55	77	.417	10	George Tweedy Stallings
1898	149	78	71	.523	6	George Tweedy Stallings
						Wm. Joseph Shettsline
1899	152	94	58	.618	3	Wm. Joseph Shettsline
1900	138	75	63	.543	3	Wm. Joseph Shettsline
1901	140	83	57	.593	2	Wm. Joseph Shettsline
1902	137	56	81	.409	7	Wm. Joseph Shettsline
1903	135	49	86	.363	7	Chas. Louis Zimmer
1904	152	52	100	.342	8(Last)	Hugh Duffy
1905	152	83	69	.546	4	Hugh Duffy
1906	153	71	82	.464	4	Hugh Duffy
1907	147	83	64	.566	3	Wm. Jeremiah Murray
1908	154	83	71	.539	4	Wm. Jeremiah Murray
1909	153	74	79	.484	5	Wm. Jeremiah Murray
1910	153	78	75	.510	4	Chas. Sebastian Dooin
1911	152	79	73	.520	4	Chas. Sebastian Dooin
1912	152	73	79	.480	5	Chas. Sebastian Dooin
1913	151	88	63	.583	2	Chas. Sebastian Dooin
1914	154	74	80	.481	6	Chas. Sebastian Dooin
1915	152	90	62	.592	1	Patrick Joseph Moran
1916	153	91	62	.595	2	Patrick Joseph Moran
1917	152	87	65	.572	2	Patrick Joseph Moran
1918	123	55	68	.447	6	Patrick Joseph Moran
1919	137	47	90	.343	8(Last)	John Wesley Coombs
						Clifford Clarence Cravath
1920	153	62	91	.405	8(Last)	Clifford Clarence Cravath
1921	154	51	103	.331	8(Last)	Wm. Edward Donovan
						Irving Key Wilhelm
1922	153	57	96	.373	7	Irving Key Wilhelm
1923	154	50	104	.325	8(Last)	Arthur Fletcher
1924	151	55	96	.364	7	Arthur Fletcher
1925	153	68	85	.444	x6(Bkn)	Arthur Fletcher
1926	151	58	93	.384	8(Last)	Arthur Fletcher
1927	154	51	103	.331	8(Last)	John Phaelen McInnis
1928	152	43	109	.283	8(Last)	Burton Edwin Shotton
1929	153	71	82	.464	5	Burton Edwin Shotton
1930	154	52	102	.338	8(Last)	Burton Edwin Shotton
1931	154	66	88	.429	6	Burton Edwin Shotton
1932	154	78	76	.506	4	Burton Edwin Shotton
1933	152	60	92	.395	7	Burton Edwin Shotton
1934	149	56	93	.376	7	James Wilson
1935	153	64	89	.418	7	James Wilson
1936	154	54	100	.351	8(Last)	James Wilson
1937	153	61	92	.399	7	James Wilson
1938	150	45	105	.300	8(Last)	James Wilson
						John Bernard Lobert
1939	151	45	106	.298	8(Last)	James Thomson Prothro
1940	153	50	103	.327	8(Last)	James Thomson Prothro
1941	154	43	111	.279	8(Last)	James Thomson Prothro
1942	151	42	109	.278	8(Last)	John Bernard Lobert
1943	154	64	90	.416	7	Stanley Raymond Harris
						Frederick Landis Fitzsimmons
1944	153	61	92	.399	8(Last)	Frederick Landis Fitzsimmons
1945	154	46	108	.299	8(Last)	Frederick Landis Fitzsimmons
						Wm. Benjamin Chapman
1946	154	69	85	.448	5	Wm. Benjamin Chapman
1947	154	62	92	.403	x7(Pitt)	Wm. Benjamin Chapman
1948	154	66	88	.429	6	Wm. Benjamin Chapman
						Allen Lindsay Cooke
						Edwin Milby Sawyer
1949	154	81	73	.526	3	Edwin Milby Sawyer
1950	154	91	63	.591	1	Edwin Milby Sawyer
1951	154	73	81	.474	5	Edwin Milby Sawyer
1952	154	87	67	.565	4	Edwin Milby Sawyer
						Stephen Francis O'Neill
1953	154	83	71	.539	x3(StL)	Stephen Francis O'Neill
1954	154	75	79	.487	4	Stephen Francis O'Neill
						Terry Buford Moore
1955	154	77	77	.500	4	Edward Mayo Smith
1956	154	71	83	.461	5	Edward Mayo Smith
1957	154	77	77	.500	5	Edward Mayo Smith
1958	154	69	85	.448	8(Last)	Edward Mayo Smith
						Edwin Milby Sawyer
1959	154	64	90	.416	8(Last)	Edwin Milby Sawyer
1960	154	59	95	.383	8(Last)	Edwin Milby Sawyer
						Andrew Howard Cohen
						Eugene Wm. Mauch
1961	154	47	107	.305	8(Last)	Eugene Wm. Mauch
1962	161	81	80	.503	7	Eugene Wm. Mauch
1963	162	87	75	.537	4	Eugene Wm. Mauch
1964	162	92	70	.568	x2(Cin)	Eugene Wm. Mauch

YEAR	TG	WON	LOST	TIED	PCT.	FINISHED	MANAGER
1965	162	85	76	1	.528	6	EUGENE WILLIAM MAUCH
1966	162	87	75	0	.537	4	EUGENE WILLIAM MAUCH
1967	162	82	80	0	.506	5	EUGENE WILLIAM MAUCH
1968	162	76	86	0	.469	X7 (LA)	EUGENE WILLIAM MAUCH
							GEORGE EDWARD MYATT *
							ROBERT RALPH SKINNER
1969	162	63	99	0	.389	5E	ROBERT RALPH SKINNER
							GEORGE EDWARD MYATT *
1970	161	73	88	0	.453	5E	FRANK JOSEPH LUCCHESI
1971	162	67	95	0	.414	6E (LAST)	FRANK JOSEPH LUCCHESI
1972	156	59	97	0	.378	6E (LAST)	FRANK JOSEPH LUCCHESI
							PAUL FRANCIS OWENS

WON 17 | LOST 81 | TG 98

NATIONAL LEAGUE 1883. PHILADELPHIA

FINISHED 8th (LAST) PCT. .173

ROBERT V. FERGUSON

WON	LOST	NAME	POS.	G.	BA	FROM	TO
		Benedict, Arthur M.	2B	3	.267	A	C
0	1	Breitenstein, Alonzo	P	1	.000	A	C
13	48	Coleman, John Francis (Jack) (OF26)	P63	89	.232	A	
		Doyle, Cornelius J.	OF	16	.203	A	
		Farrar, Sidney Douglas	1B	98	.230	A	
0	0	Ferguson, Robert V. MGR. (P1)	2B	85	.256	Troy	C
		Gallagher, Wm. John	OF	2	.000	xBaltAA	
		Gladman, John H.	3B	1	.000	A	
		Gross, Emil M. (OF2)	C53	56	.312	Prov81	
1	16	Hagan, Arthur F.	P	17	+.085	A	Buff
		*Harbidge, Wm. Arthur	OF45	73	.221	Troy	
0	0	Henderson, James Harding (Hardie) (OF1)	P1	2	.250	A	BaltAA
0	3	Hilsey, Chas.	P	3	.200	A	
		Kelly, Chas. H.	3B	2	.143	A	
		Kelly, John Francis	OF	1	.000	xBaltAA	
		King, Samuel Warren	C	1	.000	A	
		Lewis, Frederick Miller	OF	38	.242	Bos81	StLAA
		Manning, John E.	OF	97	.265	Buff81	
		Mulvey, Joseph H.	3B	3	+.500	xProv	
		McClellan, Wm. Henry (OF2)	SS76	78	.230	Prov81	
1	4	Neagle, John Henry (P8)	OF12	18	.162	Cin79	BaltAA
		Pierre, Richard J.	SS	5	.158	A	C
2	8	Purcell, Wm. Aloysius (Blondy) (SS1 OF41)	3B47	96	.270	Buff	
		#Ringo, Frank C.	C38	57	.183	A	
0	1	Smith, Edgar E. (OF1)	P1	1	+.750	xProv	
		Waitt, Chas. C.	OF	1	.333	BaltAA	C
		Ward, Frank Gray (Piggy)	3B	1	.000	A	
		Warner, Frederick John Rodney	3B37	38	.233	Clev79	
		White, C. B.	3B	1	.000	A	C
		Wilsonholm, (OF1)	C2	3	.091	A	C

*Harbidge also played 6 games as C, 8 games at 2B, 12 games at SS and 5 games at 3B.

#Ringo also played 2 games at 2B, 7 games at SS, 4 games at 3B and 5 games in the OF.

WON 39 | LOST 73 | TG 112

NATIONAL LEAGUE 1884. PHILADELPHIA

FINISHED 6th. PCT. .348

WM. HENRY WRIGHT

WON	LOST	NAME	POS.	G.	BA	FROM	TO
		Allen, Hezekiah	C	1	.667	A	C
		Andrews, George Edward	2B	108	.221	A	
		Clements, John T.	C	8	.240	xPhilUA	
5	14	Coleman, John Francis (Jack) (P19 1B2)	OF22	43	.245	B	AthAA
		Conway, Wm. F.	C	1	.000	A	
		Cook, Paul	C	3	.083	A	
		Crawley, John A.	C	44	.244	A	C
		Cusick, Anthony Daniel	C	9	.143	xWilUA	
		DePaugher, Michael H.	C	2	.250	A	C
		Farrar, Sidney Douglas	1B	110	.246	B	
20	22	Ferguson, Chas. J. (OF7)	P46	51	.251	A	
0	0	*Fogarty, James G.	OF75	95	.211	A	
		Gillen, Thomas J.	C	1	.333	xPhilUA	
		Hardie, Lewis W.	C	2	.143	A	
		Hoover, Wm. J. (Buster)	OF	9	.211	xPhilUA	
		Kappel, Joseph	C	4	.067	A	
2	4	Knight, Jonas Wm.	P	6	.250	A	
0	1	Lynch, Thomas James (P1 C6)	OF7	12	+.318	xWilUA	
		Manning, John E.	OF	103	.272	B	
0	1	Miller, Joseph H. (Cyclone)	P	1	+.000	xProv	
0	2	Morton, Wm. H.	P	2	.375	A	C
		Mulvey, Joseph H.	3B	99	.229	B	
0	3	Murphy, Cornelius B. (Connie)	P	3	.000	xAltUA	
		McClellan, Wm. Henry	SS109	110	.256	B	
1	12	McElroy, James D. (OF1)	P13	13	.136	A	WilUA
2	5	Purcell, Wm. Aloysius (P7) (Blondy)	OF95	102	.244	B	
0	1	Pyle, Harry Thomas	P	1	.000	A	
		Remsen, John Jay	OF	10	.222	Clev81	BknAA
		Ringo, Frank C.	C	25	.132	B	AthAA
		Sixsmith, Edward	C	1	.000	A	C
		Vadeboncoeur, Eugene F.	C	4	.214	A	C
9	8	Vinton, Wm. M.	P	21	.115	A	

*Fogarty also played 1 game as P, 4 games at 2B, 3 games at SS and 13 games at 3B.

WON 56 | LOST 54 | TG 110

NATIONAL LEAGUE 1885. PHILADELPHIA

FINISHED 3rd. PCT. .509

WM. HENRY WRIGHT

WON	LOST	NAME	POS.	G.	BA	FROM	TO
		Andrews, George Edward (2B5)	OF98	103	.266	B	
		Bastian, Chas. J.	SS	104	.167	KCUA	
		Clements, John T. (OF11)	C41	52	.191	B	
		Cusick, Anthony Daniel (OF1)	C38	39	.177	B	

WON	LOST	NAME	POS.	G.	BA	FROM	TO
26	22	Daily, Edward M. (OF1)	P49	49	.206	A	
		Farrar, Sidney Douglas	1B	111	.245	B	
26	19	Ferguson, Chas. J. (OF13)	P46	59	.306	B	
		*Fogarty, James G.	OF89	111	.231	B	
		Ganzel, Chas. Wm. (OF1)	C32	33	.168	StPUA	
		Hiland, John W.	2B	3	.000	A	C
		Lynch, Thomas James (2B1)	OF13	13	.189	B	C
		Manning, John E.	OF	107	.256	B	
		Mulvey, Joseph H.	3B	106	.268	B	
		Myers, Albert	2B	93	.204	MilUA	
1	7	Nolan, Edward Sylvester (The Only) (OF1)	P8	8	.133	WilUA	C
3	6	Vinton, Wm. M.	P	9	.064	B	AthAA

*Fogarty also played 9 games at 2B, 7 games at SS and 5 games at 3B.

WON 71	NATIONAL LEAGUE	FINISHED 4th.
LOST 43		
TG 114	1886.	PCT. .622

PHILADELPHIA

WM. HENRY WRIGHT

WON	LOST	NAME	POS.	G.	BA	FROM	TO
		Andrews, George Edward	OF103	106	.249	B	
		Bastian, Chas. J.	2B86	104	.217	B	
25	19	Casey, Daniel Maurice	P	44	.152	Det	
		Clements, John T.	C48	54	.205	B	
		Cusick, Anthony Daniel	C22	27	.221	B	
13	9	Daily, Edward M. (P26)	OF52	78	.226	B	
		Farrar, Sidney Douglas	1B	118	.248	B	
		Farrell, John A.	2B	23	+.171	Prov	Wash
32	9	Ferguson, Chas. J. (OF29)	P43	71	.252	B	
		Fogarty, James G.	OF56	76	.292	B	
		Ganzel, Chas. Wm.	C	1	+.000	B	Det
		Irwin, Arthur Albert	SS	101	.233	Prov	
		Mulvey, Joseph H.	3B	105	.267	B	
		McCarthy, Thomas Francis Michael	OF	8	.185	Bos	
		McGuire, James Thomas	C47	48	.197	Det	
1	1	Strike, John	P	2	.000	LvlleAA82	C
0	5	Titcomb, Ledell	P	5	.100	A	
		Wood, George A.	OF96	106	.273	Det	

WON 75	NATIONAL LEAGUE	FINISHED 2nd.
LOST 48		
TG 123	1887.	PCT. .610

PHILADELPHIA

WM. HENRY WRIGHT

WON	LOST	NAME	POS.	G.	BA	FROM	TO
		Andrews, George Edward	OF99	103	.354	B	
		Bastian, Chas. J. (SS17)	2B39	60	.275	B	
21	17	Buffinton, Chas. G. (OF19)	P38	66	.296	Bos	
28	13	Casey, Daniel Maurice	P	44	.194	B	
		Clements, John T.	C58	63	.306	B	
		Cusick, Anthony Daniel	C	7	.358	B	C
0	4	Daily, Edward M. (P6)	OF21	25	+.306	B	Wash
0	2	Devlin, James H.	P	2	.375	N.Y.	
		Farrar, Sidney Douglas	1B	115	.344	B	
21	10	Ferguson, Chas. J. (2B25)	P33	69	.412	B	C
		Fogarty, James G.	OF120	126	.365	B	
		Gunning, Thomas Francis	C	27	.293	Bos	
		Irwin, Arthur Albert	SS	99	.339	B	
		Lyons, Harry P.	OF	1	.200	A	StLAA
5	2	Maul, Albert Joseph	P	16	.450	PhilUA84	
		Mulvey, Joseph H.	3B	109	.317	B	
		McCarthy, Thomas Francis Michael	OF	18	.208	B	
		McGuire, James Thomas	C	40	.354	B	
		McLaughlin, Bernard	2B	50	.259	KCUA84	
		Wood, George A.	OF105	113	.342	B	

WON 69	NATIONAL LEAGUE	FINISHED 3rd.
LOST 61		
TG 130	1888.	PCT. .531

PHILADELPHIA

WM. HENRY WRIGHT

WON	LOST	NAME	POS.	G.	BA	FROM	TO
		Andrews, George Edward	OF	123	.238	B	
		Bastian, Chas. J.	2B65	80	.192	B	
28	15	Buffinton, Chas. G.	P	44	.173	B	
14	19	Casey, Daniel Maurice	P	33	.152	B	
		Childs, Clarence Algernon	2B	2	.000	A	
		Clements, John T.	C84	85	.247	B	
		Delahanty, Edward James	2B56	74	.227	A	
		Farrar, Sidney Douglas	1B	130	.246	B	
		Fogarty, James G.	OF116	120	.235	B	
8	17	Gleason, Wm. J. (Kid)	P	24	.205	A	
		Grim, John Helm (Jack)	2B	2	.143	A	
		Hallman, Wm. White (Billy)	2B	16	.206	A	
		Irwin, Arthur Albert	SS121	124	.220	B	
		Mulvey, Joseph H.	3B	99	.215	B	
		McGuire, James Thomas	C	12	+.333	B	Det
19	10	Sanders, Alexander Benjamin (OF25)	P31	57	.245	A	
		Schriver, Wm. F. (Pop)	C27	39	.194	BknAA86	
0	0	Tyng, James Alexander	P	1	.000	Bos79	C
		Wagenhurst, Elwood Otto	3B	2	.125	A	C
		Wood, George A.	OF103	105	.230	B	

WON 63	NATIONAL LEAGUE	FINISHED 4th.
LOST 64		
TG 127	1889.	PCT. .496

PHILADELPHIA

WM. HENRY WRIGHT

WON	LOST	NAME	POS.	G.	BA	FROM	TO
0	2	Anderson, David S. (Varney)	P	3	.125	A	
		Andrews, George Edward (2B1)	OF9	10	+.282	B	Indpls
26	17	Buffinton, Chas. G.	P	43	.208	B	
8	10	Casey, Daniel Maurice	P	18	.234	B	
		Clements, John T.	C	78	.284	B	
0	3	Day, Wm.	P	3	.000	A	
		Decker, Edward Harry (C3)	2B7	11	.103	Wash86	
		Delahanty, Edward James (2B23)	OF29	54	.292	B	
		Farrar, Sidney Douglas	1B	130	.268	B	
		Fogarty, James G.	OF	128	.258	B	
9	14	Gleason, Wm. J. (Kid)	P25	28	.252	B	
		Hallman, Wm. White (Billy)	SS105	119	.253	B	
		Irwin, Arthur Albert	SS	18	+.219	B	Wash
		Mulvey, Joseph H.	3B	129	.288	B	
		Myers, Albert	2B	75	+.269	xWash	
19	17	Sanders, Alexander Benjamin	P40	41	.278	B	
		Schriver, Wm. F. (Pop)	C48	55	.265	B	
		Thompson, Samuel L.	OF	128	.296	Det	
		Ward, Frank Gray (Piggy)	2B	7	.160	Phil83	
		Wood, George A.	OF91	97	.251	B	BaltAA
1	1	Wood, Peter Burke	P	3	.000	Buff85	C

WON 78
LOST 53
TG 131

NATIONAL LEAGUE — FINISHED 3rd.

1890. — PCT. .595

PHILADELPHIA

WM. HENRY WRIGHT

WON	LOST	NAME	POS.	G.	BA	FROM	TO
		Allen, Robert Gilman	SS	133	.225	A	
1	2	Anderson, David S. (Varney)	P	6	+.000	B	Pitt
1	0	Bowman, Sumner Sallade	P	4	+.750	A	Pitt
		Burke, Edward D.	OF	100	+.280	A	Pitt
		Clements, John T.	C91	97	.315	B	
0	0	Coleman, John	P	1	.000	A	C
1	1	Day, Wm.	P	4	+.100	B	Pitt
		Decker, Edward Harry (C1 OF2)	1B2	5	+.368	B	Pitt
4	0	Esper, Chas. H.	P	6	+.157	xPitt	
39	17	Gleason, Wm. J. (Kid)	P56	58	.209	B	
		Grey, Wm. Tobin	C	32	.242	A	
		Hamilton, Wm. Robert	OF	123	.324	KCAA	
		Mayer, Edward H.	3B114	117	.241	A	
		Motz, Frank H.	1B	1	.000	A	
		Myers, Albert	2B	117	.277	B	
		McCauley, Allen B.	1B	112	.244	IndplsAA	
1	0	McFetridge, John R.	P	1	.750	A	
		Schriver, Wm. F. (Pop)	C34	57	.273	B	
7	15	Smith, John Francis	P	22	+.250	AthAA	Pitt
		Sunday, Wm. Ashley	OF	31	+.256	xPitt	C
		Thompson, Samuel L.	OF	132	.313	B	
24	18	Vickery, Thomas Gill	P	45	.207	A	

WON 68
LOST 69
TG 137

NATIONAL LEAGUE — FINISHED 4th.

1891. — PCT. .496

PHILADELPHIA

WM. HENRY WRIGHT

WON	LOST	NAME	POS.	G.	BA	FROM	TO
		Allen, Robert Gilman	SS	117	.227	B	
		Bastian, Chas. J.	SS	1	.000	xCinAA	C
		Brown, Willard	1B97	112	.242	NYPL	
1	3	Cassian, Edward	P	6	.118	A	WashAA
		Clements, John T.	C	105	.305	B	
		Delahanty, Edward James (1B28)	OF97	128	.249	ClevPL	
		Denny, Jeremiah D. (Jerry) (1B5)	3B14	19	+.301	xClev	
		Donohue, Joseph F.	OF	6	.317	A	C
20	13	Esper, Chas. H.	P	34	.232	B	
		Fields, John James	C	8	+.233	xPitt	
24	26	Gleason, Wm. J. (Kid)	P50	60	.244	B	
0	1	Gormley, Edward	p	1	.000	A	C
		Graulich, Lewis (1B3)	C4	7	.309	A	C
		Grey, Wm. Tobin	C	18	.264	B	
		Hamilton, Wm. Robert	OF	133	.338	B	
3	6	Keefe, Timothy J.	P	9	+.154	xN.Y.	
0	1	Kilroy, Michael Joseph	P	3	.400	BaltAA88	C
4	3	Kling, Wm.	P	13	.176	A	
		Mayer, Edward H. (OF26)	3B32	65	.201	B	C
		Morelock, A. Harry	3B	4	.071	A	
		Myers, Albert	2B	134	.238	B	C
		Plock, Walter S.	OF	2	.400	A	C
0	0	Saylor, Philip Andrew (Lefty)	P	1	.000	A	C
0	3	Schultze, John F.	P	6	.167	A	C
		Shindle, Wm.	3B101	103	.210	PhilPL	
1	2	Smith, John Francis	P	3	.375	Pitt	C
		Thompson, Samuel L.	OF	133	.295	B	
15	11	Thornton, John (Jack)	P	30	.145	Wash89	

WON 87
LOST 66
TG 153

NATIONAL LEAGUE — FINISHED 4th.

1892. — PCT. .569

PHILADELPHIA

WM. HENRY WRIGHT

WON	LOST	NAME	POS.	G.	BA	FROM	TO
		Allen, Robert Gilman	SS	148	.229	B	
19	16	Carsey, Wilfred (Kid)	P	35	.156	WashAA	
		Clements, John T.	C	102	.270	B	
		Connor, Roger	1B	153	.285	N.Y.	
		Connors, Jeremiah (Jerry)	OF	1	.000	A	C
		Cross, LaFayette Napoleon (Lave) (C34 OF23)	3B45	134	.262	AthAA	
		Delahanty, Edward James	OF118	120	.312	B	
		Dowse, Thomas Jefferson	C	16	+.170	xCin	Wash
13	6	Esper, Chas. H.	P	19	+.279	B	Pitt
		Hallman, Wm. White (Billy)	2B	136	.292	AthAA	
		Hamilton, Wm. Robert	OF	136	.330	B	
21	14	Keefe, Timothy J.	P	36	.105	B	
4	6	Knell, Philip H.	P	18	+.121	xWash	
		Morelock, A. Harry	3B	1	.000	B	C
		Mulvey, Joseph H.	3B	25	.142	AthAA	
		Reilly, Chas. Thomas	3B63	81	.201	Pitt	
		Stephenson, Reuben Crandol	OF	8	.277	A	C
2	0	Taylor, John Budd (Jack)	P	3	.167	N.Y.	
		Thompson, Samuel L.	OF	151	.303	B	
0	1	Thornton, John (Jack) (OF2)	P3	5	+.385	B	StL
28	23	Weyhing, August (Gus)	P53	54	.123	AthAA	

WON 72 — NATIONAL LEAGUE — FINISHED 4th.
LOST 57
TG 129 — 1893. — PCT, .558

PHILADELPHIA

WM. HENRY WRIGHT

WON	LOST	NAME	POS.	G.	BA	FROM	TO
		Allen, Robert Gilman	SS	123	.283	B	
		Boyle, John Anthony (Jack)	1B111	117	.305	N.Y.	
22	12	Carsey, Wilfred (Kid)	P35	36	.197	B	
		Clements, John T.	C	90	.290	B	
		Cross, LaFayette Napoleon (Lave) (3B29)	C40	94	.302	B	
0	0	Darby, George W.	P	4	+.000	xCin	C
		Delahanty, Edward James	OF114	132	.370	B	
		Hallman, Wm. White (Billy)	2B120	132	.328	B	
		Hamilton, Wm. Robert	OF	82	.395	B	
10	10	Keefe, Timothy J.	P	20	.237	B	C
1	3	McGinnis, August (Gus)	P	5	+.214	xChi	C
0	0	O'Connor, Frank Henry	P	3	1.000	A	C
		Reilly, Chas. Thomas	3B	104	.252	B	
2	3	Sharrott, John Henry (P8)	OF23	30	.254	N.Y.	C
8	8	Taylor, John Budd (Jack)	P17	19	.229	B	
		Thompson, Samuel L.	OF129	130	.377	B	
		Turner, George A. (Tuck)	OF	35	.324	A	
5	5	Vickery, Thomas Gill	P	14	.314	Balt	C
24	16	Weyhing, August (Gus)	P40	41	.158	B	

WON 71 — NATIONAL LEAGUE — FINISHED 4th.
LOST 56
TG 127 — 1894. — PCT. .559

PHILADELPHIA

ARTHUR ALBERT IRWIN

WON	LOST	NAME	POS.	G.	BA	FROM	TO
		Allen, Robert Gilman	SS	40	.253	B	
		Boyle, John Anthony (Jack)	1B	116	.291	B	
		Buckley, Richard D. (Dick)	C	39	+.302	xStL	
0	0	Burris, Alva Burton	P	1	.500	A	C
2	3	Callahan, James Joseph	P	9	.263	A	
16	14	Carsey, Wilfred (Kid)	P31	32	.277	B	
		Clements, John T.	C	47	.343	B	
		Cross, LaFayette Napoleon (Lave)	3B100	120	.388	B	
		Delahanty, Edward James	OF85	114	.400	B	
		Delehanty, Thomas James	2B	1	.250	A	
1	3	Fanning, John Jacob	P	6	.143	Indps89	C
0	1	Figgemeier, Frank Y.	P	1	.333	A	C
		Grady, Michael Wm.	C38	50	.363	A	
4	3	Haddock, George Silas	P	10	+.111	Bkn	Wash
		Hallman, Wm. White (Billy)	2B	119	.327	B	
		Hamilton, Wm. Robert	OF	131	.398	B	
5	3	Harper, George B.	P	12	.171	A	
		Irwin, Arthur Albert MGR.	SS	1	.000	Wash92	
1	3	Johnson, John Louis	P	4	.200	A	C
1	0	Jones, Alexander H.	P	1	.250	Wash92	
0	1	Lukens, Albert P.	P	3	.000	A	C
		Murray, Thomas	SS	1	.000	A	C
		Reilly, Chas. Thomas	3B27	36	.272	B	
0	1	Scheible, John G.	P	1	.000	Clev	C
		Sullivan, Joseph Daniel	SS	76	+.358	xWash	
24	10	Taylor, John Budd (Jack)	P33	34	.331	B	
		Thompson, Samuel L.	OF	102	.403	B	
		Turner, George (Tuck)	OF	77	.423	B	
17	14	Weyhing, August (Gus)	P	36	.168	B	
		Yingling, Joseph	SS	1	.333	Wash86	C

WON 78 — NATIONAL LEAGUE — FINISHED 3rd.
LOST 53
TG 131 — 1895. — PCT. .595

PHILADELPHIA

ARTHUR ALBERT IRWIN

WON	LOST	NAME	POS.	G.	BA	FROM	TO
0	2	Beam, Ernest	P	9	.182	A	C
		Boyle, John Anthony (Jack)	1B	133	.254	B	
		Buckley, Richard D. (Dick)	C	29	.255	B	
24	17	Carsey, Wilfred (Kid)	P	41	.281	B	
		Clements, John T.	C	84	.389	B	

WON	LOST	NAME	POS.	G.	BA	FROM	TO
		Cross, LaFayette Napoleon (Lave)	3B	124	.277	B	
		Delehanty, Edward James	OF100	116	.399	B	
		Grady, Michael Wm.	C32	33	.336	B	
		Hallman, Wm. White (Billy)	2B	124	.315	B	
		Hamilton, Wm. Robert	OF	121	.393	B	
0	2	Hodson, George S.	P	4	.000	Bos	C
0	2	Lampe, Henry Joseph	P	7	.125	Bos	C
6	3	Lucid, Cornelius Conrad (Con)	P	10	+.310	xBkn	
		Madison, Arthur M. (2B5)	SS6	10	.400	A	
10	8	McGill, Wm. Vaness	P	19	.250	Chi	
8	1	Orth, Albert Lewis	P	11	.364	A	
		Reilly, Chas. Thomas	SS31	44	.267	B	
3	3	Smith, Thomas E.	P	11	.273	Bos	
		Sullivan, Joseph Daniel	SS87	91	.340	B	
26	13	Taylor, John Budd (Jack)	P	40	.296	B	
		Thompson, Samuel L.	OF	118	.394	B	
		Turner, George A. (Tuck)	OF	48	.388	B	
0	2	Weyhing, August (Gus)	P	2	+.000	B	Pitt
1	0	White, George Frederick	P	3	.000	A	C

WON 62
LOST 68
TG 130

NATIONAL LEAGUE — FINISHED 8th.

1896. — PCT. .477

PHILADELPHIA

WM. MITCHELL NASH

WON	LOST	NAME	POS.	G.	BA	FROM	TO
		Boyle, John Anthony (Jack)	C28	39	.288	B	
		Brouthers, Dennis (Dan)	1B	57	.330	Lvlle	
11	13	Carsey, Wilfred (Kid)	P	24	.222	B	
		Clements, John T.	C	50	.362	B	
		Cooley, Duff C. (Dick)	OF	64	+.301	xStL	
		Cross, LaFayette Napoleon (Lave) (SS36)	3B63	106	.261	B	
		Delahanty, Edward James (1B21)	OF100	122	.394	B	
		Ellis, Benjamin F.	SS	4	.063	A	C
		Gallagher, Wm. H.	SS	14	.327	A	C
0	1	Garvin, Virgil Lee	P	2	.000	A	
		Geier, Philip Louis	OF	17	.232	A	
		Grady, Michael Wm.	C56	62	.333	B	
6	4	Gumbert, Addison Courtney	P	11	+.265	xBkn	C
		Hallman, Wm. White (Billy)	2B	120	.318	B	
		Hulen, Wm. Franklin	SS73	85	.268	A	
0	1	Inks, Albert Preston (Bert)	P	5	+.200	Lvlle	Cin
0	0	Jordan, Chas. T.	P	1	.500	A	C
2	10	Keener, Joshua Harry	P	15	.298	A	C
		Lajoie, Napoleon	1B	39	.328	A	
		Leahy, Daniel C.	SS	2	.333	A	C
1	4	Lucid, Cornelius Conrad (Con)	P	5	.118	B	
		Mertes, Samuel Blair (Sandow)	OF	35	.248	A	
4	4	McGill, Wm. Vaness	P	12	.233	B	
		Nash, Wm. Mitchell MGR.	3B	64	.242	Bos	
1	0	Nops, Jeremiah H.	P	1	+.000	A	Balt
15	9	Orth, Albert Lewis	P	24	.238	B	
		Sullivan, Joseph Daniel	OF37	38	+.269	B	StL
21	20	Taylor, John Budd (Jack)	P	44	.192	B	
		Thompson, Samuel L.	OF	119	.305	B	
		Turner, George A. (Tuck)	OF	11	+.231	B	StL
1	1	Wheeler, George L.	P	3	.111	A	
0	1	Whitrock, Wm. Franklin	P	2	.000	Cin94	C

WON 55
LOST 77
TG 132

NATIONAL LEAGUE — FINISHED 10th.

1897. — PCT. .417

PHILADELPHIA

GEORGE TWEEDY STALLINGS

WON	LOST	NAME	POS.	G.	BA	FROM	TO
		Abbaticchio, Edward James	2B	3	.300	A	
0	2	Becker, Robert Charles	P	5	.111	A	
		Boyle, John Anthony (Jack) (1B25)	C48	73	.259	B	
4	2	Carsey, Wilfred (Kid)	P	6	+.231	B	StL
		Clements, John T.	C48	49	.239	B	
		Cooley, Duff C. (Dick)	OF129	131	.327	B	
		Cross, LaFayette Napoleon (Lave) (2B41)	3B44	88	.261	B	
		Delahanty, Edward James	OF128	129	.377	B	
		Dowd, Thomas Jefferson	OF	90	+.290	xStL	
5	2	Dunkle, Edward Perks	P	7	.105	A	
4	20	Fifield, John Proctor (Jack)	P	24	.234	A	
		Geier, Philip Louis (2B37)	OF43	88	.285	B	
		Gillen, Samuel	SS69	74	.258	Pitt93	C
		Grady, Michael Wm.	1B	4	+.154	B	StL
		Hallman, Wm. White (Billy)	2B	31	+.248	B	StL
0	2	Johnson, Thomas G.	P	5	.077	A	
		Lajoie, Napoleon (OF18)	1B106	126	.363	B	
0	1	Lipp, Thomas C.	P	1	1.000	A	C
		Miller, Bert	2B	3	.200	A	C
		McFarland, EdwardWm.	C	36	+.221	xStL	
		Nash, Wm. Mitchell (SS19)	3B77	102	.258	B	
14	19	Orth, Albert Lewis	P33	42	.347	B	
		Shugart, Wm. Frank	SS	40	.251	Lvlle95	
0	1	Sparks, Tully Frank	P	1	.000	A	
		Stallings, George Tweedy MGR.	1B	1	.400	Bkn90	
18	18	Taylor, John Budd (Jack)	P36	37	.252	B	
		Thompson, Samuel L.	OF	3	.250	B	
10	10	Wheeler, George L.	P	25	.205	B	

WON 78
LOST 71
TG 149

NATIONAL LEAGUE — FINISHED 6th.

1898. — PCT. .523

PHILADELPHIA

WON	LOST	NAME	POS.	G.	BA	FROM	TO
		Abbaticchio, Edward James	3B17	20	.262	B	
0	0	Becker, Robert Charles	P	1	.000	B	C
		Boyle, John Anthony (Jack)	C	6	.091	B	C
0	0	Conn, Albert Thomas (Bert)	P	1	.333	A	
		Cooley, Duff C. (Dick)	OF	148	.317	B	
		Cross, Montford Montgomery (Monte)	SS	149	.259	StL	
		Delahanty, Edward James	OF	142	.334	B	
17	16	Donahue, Francis Rostell (Red)	P	34	.146	StL	
		Douglas, Wm. B.	1B	146	.266	StL	
3	3	Duggleby, Wm. James	P	9	.238	A	
1	5	Dunkle, Edward Perks	P	9	.217	B	
		Elberfeld, Norman Arthur (Kid)	3B	13	.228	A	
11	9	Fifield, John Proctor (Jack)	P	20	.125	B	
		Fisher, Newton	C	9	.154	A	
		Flick, Elmer Harrison	OF	133	.319	A	
		Fultz, David Lewis	OF	16	.196	A	
		Lajoie, Napoleon	2B146	147	.328	B	
		Lauder, Wm.	3B	97	.272	A	
1	3	Murphy, Edward J.	P	7	.357	A	
		Murphy, Morgan Edward	C	25	+.202	xPitt	
		McFarland, Edward Wm.	C	118	.274	B	
		Nash, Wm. Mitchell	3B	20	.232	B	C
15	12	Orth, Albert Lewis	P27	32	.279	B	
24	14	Piatt, Wiley Harlan	P	38	.269	A	
		Thompson, Samuel L.	OF	14	.365	B	
6	9	Wheeler, George L.	P	15	.228	B	

WON 94 NATIONAL LEAGUE FINISHED 3rd.
LOST 58
TG 152 1899. PCT. .618

PHILADELPHIA

WM. JOSEPH SHETTSLINE

WON	LOST	NAME	POS.	G.	BA	FROM	TO
6	5	Bernhard, Wm. Henry	P	17	.245	A	
		Chiles, Pearce Nuget (1B21)	OF42	81	.329	A	
		Cooley, Duff C. (Dick)	1B80	94	.280	B	
		Croft, Henry T.	2B	2	+.143	xLvlle	
		Cross, Montford Montgomery (Monte)	SS	153	.259	B	
		Delahanty, Edward James	OF	145	.408	B	
		Dolan, Joseph	2B	60	.256	Lvlle97	
22	7	Donahue, Francis Rostell (Red)	P32	34	.177	B	
		Douglas Wm. B.	C64	72	.264	B	
3	8	Fifield, John Proctor (Jack)	P	13	+.265	B	Wash
		Flick, Elmer Harrison	OF	125	.343	B	
21	13	Fraser, Chas. Carrolton (Chick)	P35	37	.176	Clev	
		Fultz, David Lewis (3B1)	SS1	2	+.400	B	Balt
		Goeckel, Wm. John	1B	35	.283	A	C
		Lajoie, Napoleon	2B67	72	.379	B	
		Lauder, Wm.	3B	149	.263	B	
3	5	Magee, Wm. M.	P	10	+.194	xLvlle	Wash
		McFarland, Edward Wm.	C	90	.333	B	
13	3	Orth, Albert Lewis	P	17	.245	B	
		Owens, Thomas Llewellyn	2B	8	.045	A	
23	15	Piatt, Wiley Harlan	P	39	.273	B	
		Thomas, Roy Allen	OF134	148	.324	A	
3	2	Wheeler, George L.	P	5	.267	B	

WON 75 NATIONAL LEAGUE FINISHED 3rd.
LOST 63
TG 138 1900. PCT. .543

PHILADELPHIA

WM. JOSEPH SHETTSLINE

WON	LOST	NAME	POS.	G.	BA	FROM	TO
14	11	Bernhard, Wm. Henry	P26	28	.158	B	
		Chiles, Pearce Nuget (OF8)	1B14	28	.220	B	C
0	1	Conn, Albert Thomas (Bert)	P	6	.333	Phil98	
		Cross, Montford Montgomery (Monte)	SS	130	.200	B	
		Delahanty, Edward James	1B	130	.319	B	
		Dolan, Joseph (2B29)	3B30	70	.194	B	
16	10	Donahue, Francis Rostell (Red)	P	26	.235	B	
		Douglas, Wm. B.	C	45	.306	B	
4	5	Dunn, John Joseph (Jack)	P	10	+.333	xBkn	
		Flick, Elmer Harrison	OF	138	.378	B	
16	10	Fraser, Chas. Carrolton (Chick)	P	26	.257	B	
		Jacklitsch, Frederick Lawrence	C	5	.181	A	MinnA & recall
		Lajoie, Napoleon	2B	102	.346	B	
2	3	Maul, Albert Joseph	P	5	.200	Bkn	
		Murphy, Morgan Edward	C	11	.277	Phil98	
		Meyers, J. Albert	3B	7	.185	Wash98	C
		McFarland, Edward Wm.	C	90	.307	B	
0	0	McLaughlin, Warren A.	P	1	.500	A	
14	14	Orth, Albert Lewis	P30	35	.307	B	
9	9	Piatt, Wiley Harlan	P	19	.265	B	
		Slagle, James Franklin (Shorty)	OF	141	.299	Wash	
0	0	Thomas, Roy Allen (P1)	OF139	139	.325	B	
		Wolverton, Harry Sterling	3B	98	+.280	xChi	
		Ziegler, Chas. W.	3B	3	.273	Clev	C

WON 83 NATIONAL LEAGUE FINISHED 2nd.
LOST 57
TG 140 1901. PCT. .593

PHILADELPHIA

WM. JOSEPH SHETTSLINE

WON	LOST	NAME	POS.	G.	BA	FROM	TO

WON	LOST	NAME	POS.	G.	BA	FROM	TO
		Barry, John C. (3B15)	OF30	63	+.245	xBos	
		Browne, George E.	OF	8	.192	A	
		Conn, Albert Thomas (Bert)	2B	5	.222	B	C
		Cross, Monford Montgomery (Monte)	SS	139	.197	B	
		Delahanty, Edward James (1B56)	OF82	138	.357	B	
		Dolan, Joseph	2B	5	.071	B	PhilA
20	13	Donahue, Francis Rostell (Red)	P	35	.097	B	
		Dougles, Wm. B.	C40	47	.333	B	
19	12	Duggleby, Wm. James	P	33	.166	Phil98	
0	1	Dunn, John Joseph (Jack)	P	2	1.000	B	BaltA
		Flick, Elmer Harrison	OF	138	.336	B	
		Hallman, Wm. White (Billy) (3B33)	2B89	122	.194	xClevA	
		Jacklitsch, Frederick Lawrence	C30	31	.252	B	
		Jennings, Hugh Ambrose	1B78	81	.274	Bkn	
		McFarland, Edward Wm.	C	72	.278	B	
21	12	Orth, Albert Lewis	P	35	.281	B	
		Slagle, James Franklin (Shorty)	OF	48	+.189	B	Bos
		Thomas, Roy Allen	OF	128	.305	B	
9	6	Townsend, John	P	18	.109	A	
14	13	White, Guy Harris (Doc)	P	28	.273	A	
		Wolverton, Harry Sterling	3B	92	.308	B	

WON 56 — NATIONAL LEAGUE — FINISHED 7th.
LOST 81
TG 137 — 1902. — PCT. .409

PHILADELPHIA

WM. JOSEPH SHETTSLINE

WON	LOST	NAME	POS.	G.	BA	FROM	TO
		Barry, John C. (1B1)	OF137	138	.302	B	
		Berry, Joseph Howard Sr.	C	1	.250	A	C
		Browne, George E.	OF	68	+.237	B	N.Y.
		Childs, Peter Piene	2B	120	.192	Chi	C
		Clay, Frederick C.	OF	3	.250	A	C
		Dooin, Chas. Sebastian (OF6)	C83	87	.228	A	
		Douglas, Wm. B. (C30 OF9)	1B69	107	.235	B	
11	17	Duggleby, Wm. James	P	31	.204	xPhilA	
1	3	Felix, Harry (3B7)	P9	16	.111	N.Y.	C
		Fleming, Thomas Vincent	OF	5	.375	NY99	
0	0	Fox, Henry H.	P	1	.000	A	C
12	13	Fraser, Chas. Carrolton (Chick)	P	27	.174	PhilA	
		Greene, Patrick Joseph	3B	19	.188	A	
		Hallman, Wm. White (Billy)	3B	73	.245	B	
		Hulswitt, Rudolph Edward	SS125	128	.272	Lvlle99	
11	19	Iburg, Herman Edward (Ham)	P	30	.140	A	C
		Jacklitsch, Frederick Lawrence (OF1)	C27	27	.200	B	
		Jennings, Hugh Ambrose (2B4 SS5)	1B69	78	.277	B	
		Krug, Henry C. (2B13 SS9 3B6)	OF28	53	.225	A	C
2	4	Magee, Wm. M.	P	8	+.250	xN.Y.	C
		Maher, F.	SS	2	.000	A	C
		Maher, Thomas	OF	1	.000	A	C
0	1	McFadden, Bernard Joseph (Barney)	P	1	.000	Cin	C
0	0	Salisbury, Wm. A.	P	2	.000	A	C
		Shea, John Edward	C	3	.111	A	C
		Thomas, Roy Allen	OF	138	.292	B	
		Thomas Wm. Miskey (1B1 2B1)	OF3	6	.176	A	C
3	2	Vorhees, Henry Bert (Cy)	P	10	.350	A	WashA
		Watkins, Edward	OF	1	.000	A	C
16	20	White, Guy Harris (Doc) (OF16)	P36	50	.274	B	
0	1	Whiting, Jesse W.	P	1	.333	A	
0	1	Wolfe, Wm.	P	1	.333	A	C
		Wolverton, Harry Sterling	3B	34	.284	xWashA	

WON 49 — NATIONAL LEAGUE — FINISHED 7th.
LOST 86
TG 135 — 1903. — PCT. .363

PHILADELPHIA

CHAS. LOUIS ZIMMER

WON	LOST	NAME	POS.	G.	BA	FROM	TO
		Barry, John C. (1B30)	OF107	138	.276	B	
		Brashear, Roy Parks	2B18	20	.227	Lvlle99	C
0	3	Burchell, Frederick Duff	P	6	.188	A	
		Dooin, Chas. Sebastian	C51	53	.218	B	
		Douglas, Wm. B.	1B	97	.255	B	
13	18	Duggleby, Wm. James	P	36	.231	B	
12	17	Fraser, Chas. Carrolton (Chick)	P31	32	.204	B	
		Gleason, Wm. J. (Kid)	2B102	106	.284	DetA	
		Hallman, Wm. White (Billy) (3B19)	2B22	57	.212	B	C
		Hulswitt, Rudolph Edward	SS	138	.247	B	
		Keister, Wm. Hoffman	OF	100	.320	WashA	C
11	14	Mitchell, Frederick Francis	P	28	.200	PhilA	
1	11	McFetridge, John R.	P	14	.176	Phil90	C
0	2	McLaughlin, Warren A.	P	3	.200	Pitt	C
		Roth, Frank Charles	C60	61	.273	A	
		Rudolph, John Herman		1	.000	A	
11	15	Sparks, Tully Frank	P	28	.109	BosA	
		Thomas, Roy Allen	OF	130	.327	B	
		Titus, John Franklin	OF	72	.286	A	
		Walsh, John	3B	1	.000	A	C
0	4	Washburn, Libe	P	8	.222	N.Y.	C
1	2	Williams, Walter Merrill	P	3	+.286	xChi	Bos
		Wolverton, Harry Sterling	3B	123	.308	B	

WON	LOST	NAME	POS.	G.	BA	FROM	TO
		Zimmer, Chas. Louis (Chief) MGR.	C	35	.220	Pitt	C

WON 52 LOST 100 TG 152

NATIONAL LEAGUE 1904. FINISHED 8th (LAST) PCT. .342

PHILADELPHIA

HUGH DUFFY

WON	LOST	NAME	POS.	G.	BA	FROM	TO
		Barry, John C.	OF30	33	+.205	B	Chi
0	1	Barry, Thomas Arthur	P	1	.000	A	C
0	2	Brackinridge, John Calhoun	P	7	.182	A	C
3	3	Caldwell, Ralph Grant	P	6	.444	A	
6	5	Corridon, Frank J.	P	12	+.171	xChi	
		Donahue, Chas. Michael (3B24)	SS32	56	+.215	xStL	C
		Dooin, Chas. Sebastian	C96	104	.242	B	
		Douglas, Wm. B.	1B	3	.333	B	C
		Doyle, John Joseph (Jack)	1B	64	+.220	xBkn	
		Duffy, Hugh MGR.	OF	16	.261	MilA01	
12	14	Duggleby, Wm. James	P	32	.170	B	
		Fleming, Thomas Vincent	OF	2	.000	Phi102	C
13	24	Fraser, Chas. Carrolton (Chick)	P42	44	.155	B	
		Gleason, Wm. J. (Kid)	2B152	153	.274	B	
		Hall, Robert Prill (SS15)	3B20	46	.160	A	
		Hulswitt, Rudolph Edward	SS	113	.244	B	
		Long, Herman C.	2B	1	.250	DetA	C
0	5	Lush, John Chas. (P7 OF33)	1B62	102	.276	A	
		Magee, Sherwood Robert (Sherry)	OF	95	.277	A	
		Marshall, Wm. R. (Doc)	C	8	+.100	A	N.Y.
4	8	Mitchell, Frederick Francis	P	25	+.207	B	Bkn
1	9	McPherson, John Jacob	P	15	.064	PhilA01	C
		Purnell, Jesse Rhoades	3B	7	.105	A	C
		Rementer, Willis J.	C	1	.000	A	C
		Roth, Frank Charles	C65	68	.258	B	
9	16	Sparks, Tully Frank	P	26	.105	B	
4	13	Sutthoff, John Gerhard	P	19	+.164	xCin	
		Thomas, Roy Allen	OF	139	.290	B	
		Titus, John Franklin	OF	140	.294	B	
		VanBuren, Edward Eugene	OF	12	+.233	xBkn	C
		Wolverton, Harry Sterling	3B	102	.266	B	

WON 83 LOST 69 TG 152

NATIONAL LEAGUE 1905. FINISHED 4th. PCT. .546

PHILADELPHIA

HUGH DUFFY

WON	LOST	NAME	POS.	G.	BA	FROM	TO
		Abbott, Frederick H.	C34	39	.195	ClevA	C
1	1	Brady, James Ward	P	2	.200	A	
		Bransfield, Wm. Edward (Kitty)	1B	151	.259	Pitt	
1	1	Caldwell, Ralph Grant	P	7	.000	B	C
11	13	Corridon, Frank J.	P	35	.208	B	
		Courtney, Ernest E.	3B	155	.275	DetA03	
		Dooin, Chas. Sebastian	C107	108	.250	B	
		Doolan, Michael Joseph	SS	135	.254	A	
		Duffy, Hugh MGR.	OF	15	.307	B	
18	16	Duggleby, Wm. James	P	38	.109	B	
		Gleason, Wm. J. (Kid)	2B	155	.247	B	
		Kahoe, Michael Joseph	C	15	.255	StLA	
1	1	Kane, Harry	P	2	.167	DetA03	
0	1	Krueger, Oompaul Arthur (Pl)	SS23	30	.184	Pitt	C
2	0	Lush, John Chas.	P	6	.267	B	
		Magee, Sherwood Robert (Sherry)	OF	155	.299	B	
		Munson, Clarence Hanford	C	9	.222	A	C
10	6	Nichols, Chas. Augustus	P	18	+.189	xStL	
23	16	Pittinger, Chas. Reno	P	46	.156	Bos	
13	11	Sparks, Tully Frank	P	34	.128	B	
3	3	Sutthoff, John Gerhard	P	13	.111	B	C
		Thomas, Roy Allen	OF	147	.317	B	
		Titus, John Franklin	OF	147	.308	B	
0	0	Washer, William	P	1	.000	A	C

WON 71 LOST 82 TG 153

NATIONAL LEAGUE 1906. FINISHED 4th. PCT. .464

PHILADELPHIA

HUGH DUFFY

WON	LOST	NAME	POS.	G.	BA	FROM	TO
		Bransfield, Wm. Edward (Kitty)	1B	139	.275	B	
		Courtney, Ernest E.	3B96	112	.236	B	
		Crist, Chester A.	C	5	.000	A	C
		Donovan, Jeremiah Francis	C	53	.199	A	C
		Dooin, Chas. Sebastian	C	107	.245	B	
		Doolan, Michael Joseph	SS	154	.230	B	
		Duffy, Hugh MGR.		1	.000	B	
13	19	Duggleby, Wm. James	P	42	.141	B	
		Gleason, Wm. J. (Kid)	2B	135	.227	B	
		Houston, Harry	C	2	.000	A	C
1	2	Kane, Harry	P	6	.000	B	C
18	15	Lush, John Chas. (OF22)	P37	61	.264	B	
		Magee, Sherwood Robert (Sherry)	OF	154	.282	B	
0	3	Moser, Walter F.	P	6	.000	A	
3	3	McCloskey, John J.	P	9	.176	A	
0	2	Nichols, Chas. Augustus	P	4	.000	B	C

WON	LOST	NAME	POS.	G.	BA	FROM	TO
8	10	Pittinger, Chas. Reno	P	20	.091	B	
9	11	Richie, Lewis A.	P	33	.050	A	
0	1	Roy, Chas. Robert	P	8	.000	A	C
		Sentelle, Leopold Theodore (2B19)	3B33	55	.229	A	
19	16	Sparks, Tully Frank	P	42	.154	B	
		Thomas, Roy Allen	OF	142	.254	B	
		Titus, John Franklin	OF	142	.267	B	
		Ward, Joseph A.	3B27	30	.295	A	

WON 82
LOST 64
TG 146

NATIONAL LEAGUE

1907.

FINISHED 3rd.

PCT. .566

PHILADELPHIA

WM. JEREMIAH MURRAY

WON	LOST	NAME	POS.	G.	BA	FROM	TO
		Bransfield, Wm. Edward (Kitty)	1B	92	.233	B	
8	5	Brown, Chas. Edward (Buster)	P	21	+.189	xStL	
17	14	Corridon, Frank J.	P37	38	.165	Phil05	
		Courtney, Ernest E. (1B48)	3B75	130	.243	B	
1	0	Coveleskie, Harry Frank	P	4	.000	A	
		Dooin, Chas. Sebastian	C94	96	.211	B	
		Doolan, Michael Joseph	SS	145	.204	B	
1	2	Duggleby, Wm. James	P	5	+.111	B	Pitt
		Gleason, Wm. J. (Kid)	2B26	35	.143	B	
		Grant, Edward Leslie	3B	74	.243	ClevA05	
		Jacklitsch, Frederick Lawrence	C58	65	.213	NYA05	
		Knabe, Franz Otto	2B121	126	.255	Pitt05	
5	6	Lush, John Chas.	P	12	+.200	B	StL
		Magee, Sherwood Robert (Sherry)	OF	139	.328	B	
11	18	Moren, Lewis Howard	P	37	.081	Pitt04	
0	0	McCloskey, John J.	P	2	.000	B	C
2	0	McQuillan, George Washington	P	6	.333	A	
		Osborn, Wilfred P.	OF26	37	.276	A	
9	5	Pittinger, Chas. Reno	P	16	.139	B	C
6	6	Richie, Lewis A.	P	25	.163	B	
		Sentelle, Leopold Theodore	SS1	3	.000	B	C
22	8	Sparks, Tully Frank	P	33	.034	B	
		Thomas, Roy Allen	OF	121	.243	B	
		Titus, John Franklin	OF	142	.275	B	

WON 83
LOST 71
TG 154

NATIONAL LEAGUE

1908.

FINISHED 4th.

PCT. .539

PHILADELPHIA

WM. JEREMIAH MURRAY

WON	LOST	NAME	POS.	G.	BA	FROM	TO
		Bransfield, Wm. Edward (Kitty)	1B	143	.304	B	
0	0	Brown, Chas. Edward (Buster)	P	4	.200	B	
		Clement, Wallace Oakes	OF	12	.242	A	
14	10	Corridon, Frank J.	P	27	.123	B	
		Courtney, Ernest E.	3B22	42	.181	B	C
4	1	Coveleskie, Harry Frank	P	6	.133	B	
		Deininger, Otto Chas.	OF	1	.000	BosA02	
		Dooin, Chas. Sebastian	C	132	.248	B	
		Doolan, Michael Joseph	SS	129	.234	B	
7	7	Foxen, Wm. A.	P	22	.094	A	
		Gleason, Wm. J. (Kid) (2B1)	OF1	2	.000	B	
		Grant, Edward Leslie	3B134	147	.244	B	
2	1	Hoch, Harry Keller	P	3	.200	A	
		Jacklitsch, Frederick Lawrence	C	30	.221	B	
		Johnson, Chas. Cleveland	OF	5	.214	A	C
		Knabe, Franz Otto	2B	151	.218	B	
		Magee, Sherwood Robert (Sherry)	OF	142	.283	B	
2	1	Moore, Earl Alonzo	P	3	.222	NYA	
8	9	Moren, Lewis Howard	P	28	.245	B	
		McCormick, Harry Elwood (Moose)	OF	5	+.091	Pitt04	N.Y.
23	17	McQuillan, George Washington	P	48	.151	B	
		Osborn, Wilfred P.	OF146	152	.267	B	
7	10	Richie, Lewis A.	P	25	.212	B	
		Shean, David Wm.	SS	14	.106	PhilA06	
16	15	Sparks, Tully Frank	P	33	.052	B	
		Thomas, Roy Allen	OF	6	+.167	B	Pitt
		Titus, John Franklin	OF	149	.286	B	

WON 74
LOST 79
TG 153

NATIONAL LEAGUE

1909.

FINISHED 5th.

PCT. .484

PHILADELPHIA

WM. JEREMIAH MURRAY

WON	LOST	NAME	POS.	G.	BA	FROM	TO
		Bates, John Wm.	OF	73	+.293	xBos	
		Bransfield, Wm. Edward (Kitty)	1B	138	.292	B	
0	0	Brown, Chas. Edward (Buster)	P	7	+.000	B	Bos
		Clement, Wallace Oakes	OF	3	+.000	B	Bkn
11	7	Corridon, Frank J.	P	27	.186	B	
6	10	Coveleskie, Harry Frank	P	24	.108	B	
		Deininger, Otto Chas.	OF45	46	.260	B	C
		Dooin, Chas. Sebastian	C	140	.224	B	
		Doolan, Michael Joseph	SS	147	.219	B	
3	7	Foxen, Wm. A.	P	18	.208	B	
		Froelich, Wm. Palmer	C	1	.000	A	C
		Grant, Edward Leslie	3B	154	.269	B	
		Jacklitsch, Frederick Lawrence	C	19	.310	B	

WON	LOST	NAME	POS.	G.	BA	FROM	TO
		Knabe, Franz Otto	2B110	111	.234	B	
		Magee, Sherwood Robert (Sherry)	OF	143	.270	B	
		Martel, Leon Alphonse	C	24	.268	A	
18	12	Moore, Earl Alonzo	P	38	.094	B	
16	15	Moren, Lewis Howard	P	40	.111	B	
		McDonough, Edward	C	1	.000	A	
13	16	McQuillan, George Washington	P	41	.118	B	
		Osborn, Wilfred P.	OF	54	.185	B	C
1	1	Richie, Lewis A.	P	11	+.250	B	Bos
0	0	Scanlan, Frank Aloysius	P	6	.000	A	C
		Shean, David Wm.	2B	29	+.232	B	Bos
6	11	Sparks, Tully Frank	P	24	.139	B	
		Starr, Chas. Watkin	2B	3	+.000	xBos	C
		Titus, John Franklin	OF	149	.270	B	
0	0	Van Dyke, Benjamin Harrison	P	2	.000	A	
		Ward, Joseph A.	2B48	63	.266	xNYA	

WON 78 — NATIONAL LEAGUE — FINISHED 4th.
LOST 75
TG 153 — 1910. — PCT. .510

PHILADELPHIA

CHAS. SEBASTIAN DOOIN

WON	LOST	NAME	POS.	G.	BA	FROM	TO
		Bates, John Wm.	OF	131	.305	B	
		Bransfield, Wm. Edward (Kitty)	1B	110	.239	B	
2	0	Brennan, Addison Foster (Ad)	P19	21	.280	A	
		Castle, John Francis	OF	2	.250	A	C
1	1	Chalmers, George W.	P3	4	.143	A	
		Cheek, Harry G.	C	2	.500	A	C
0	0	Culp, Wm. Edward	P	4	.000	A	C
		Dooin, Chas. Sebastian MGR.	C91	94	.242	B	
		Doolan, Michael Joseph	SS	148	.263	B	
16	14	Ewing, George Lemuel (Bob)	P	34	.222	Cin	
0	0	Flaherty, Patrick Joseph (OF1)	P1	2	.500	Bos08	
5	5	Foxen, Wm. A.	P	16	+.174	B	Chi
1	2	Girard, Chas. A.	P	7	.125	A	C
		Grant, Edward Leslie	3B	152	.268	B	
0	0	Humpheries, Albert (Bert)	P	5	.000	A	
		Jacklitsch, Frederick Lawrence	C	17	.196	B	
		Knabe, Franz Otto	2B	136	.261	B	
		Luderus, Frederick Wm.	1B	19	+.294	xChi	
		Magee, Sherwood Robert (Sherry)	OF	154	.331	B	
1	2	Maroney, James Francis	P	12	.000	Bos06	
22	15	Moore, Earl Alonzo	P	46	.230	B	
		Moran, Patrick Joseph	C	56	.236	Chi	
13	14	Moren, Lewis Howard	P	34	.149	B	C
		McDonough, Edward	C	4	.111	B	C
9	6	McQuillan, George Washington	P	24	.149	B	
2	6	Schettler, Louis Martin	P	27	.171	A	C
0	1	Slaughter, Byron Atkins	P	8	.200	A	C
0	2	Sparks, Tully Frank	P	3	.000	B	C
6	7	Stack, Wm. Edward	P	20	.083	A	
		Thomas, Roy Allen	OF	20	.183	Bos	
		Titus, John Franklin	OF	142	.241	B	
		Walsh, Michael Timothy (OF26)	2B26	67	.248	A	
		Ward, Joseph A.	1B32	33	.145	B	C

WON 79 — NATIONAL LEAGUE — FINISHED 4th.
LOST 73
TG 152 — 1911. — PCT. .520

PHILADELPHIA

CHAS. SEBASTIAN DOOIN

WON	LOST	NAME	POS.	G.	BA	FROM	TO
28	13	Alexander, Grover Cleveland (Pete)	P	48	.174	A	
		Beck, Frederick Thomas	OF	64	+.281	xCin	
3	3	Beebe, Frederick Leonard	P	9	.263	Cin	
		Bransfield, Wm. Edward (Kitty)	1B	23	+.256	B	Chi
3	1	Brennan, Addison Foster (Ad)	P	5	.222	B	
3	7	Burns, Wm. Thomas	P	21	+.150	xCin	
13	10	Chalmers, George W.	P	38	.178	B	
		Cotter, Richard Raphael	C	17	.283	A	
3	1	Curtis, Clifton Garfield	P	8	+.267	xChi	
		Dooin, Chas. Sebastian MGR.	C	74	.328	B	
		Doolan, Michael Joseph	SS	145	.238	B	
0	2	Ewing, George Lemuel (Bob)	P	4	.333	B	
0	1	Hall, Lewis C.	P	7	.333	A	C
3	3	Humpheries, Albert (Bert)	P	11	+.333	B	Cin
		Killefer, Wm. Lavier Jr.	C	6	.188	StLA	
		Kleinow, John Peter	C	4	.125	xBosA	C
		Knabe, Franz Otto	2B	142	.237	B	
		Lehr, Clarence Emanuel (2B4 OF1)	SS2	12	.148	A	C
		Lobert, John Bernard (Hans)	3B	147	.285	Cin	
		Luderus, Frederick Wm.	1B	146	.301	B	
		Madden, Thomas Francis	C	22	.276	xBosA	C
		Magee, Sherwood Robert (Sherry)	OF	120	.288	B	
		Mayes, Albert B.	OF	5	.000	A	C
		Miller, Hugh Stanley		1	.000	A	
15	19	Moore, Earl Alonzo	P	42	.109	B	
		Moran, Patrick Joseph	C	32	.184	B	
		Paskert, George Henry (Dode)	OF	153	.273	Cin	
0	0	Puckett, Troy Levi	P	1	.000	A	C
		Quinn, John Edward Pick	C	1	.000	A	C
3	4	Rowan, John Arthur	P	12	+.077	Cin	Chi
0	3	Shultz, Wallace Luther	P	5	.250	A	
0	0	Smith, Jacob G.	P	2	.000	A	C
		Spencer, Edward Russell	C	11	.156	BosA09	
5	5	Stack, Wm. Edward	P	12	.083	B	
0	1	Stanley, John Leonard	P	4	.250	A	C

WON	LOST	NAME	POS.	G.	BA	FROM	TO
		Thomas, Roy Allen	OF	21	.133	B	C
		Titus, John Franklin	OF	60	.284	B	
0	0	Walsh, Michael Timothy (Pl)	OF48	84	.270	B	
		Welchonce, Harry M.	OF	17	.212	A	C

WON 73
LOST 79
TG 152

NATIONAL LEAGUE FINISHED 5th.

1912. PCT. .480

PHILADELPHIA

CHAS. SEBASTIAN DOOIN

WON	LOST	NAME	POS.	G.	BA	FROM	TO
19	17	Alexander, Grover Cleveland	P	46	.186	B	
		(Pete)					
		Boyle, John Bellew (SS2)	3B13	15	.280	A	C
11	9	Brennan, Addison Foster (Ad)	P	27	.254	B	
		*Brinker, Wm. Hutchinson (Dode)	OF4	9	.222	A	C
		Browne, George E.		6	.200	Bkn	C
3	4	Chalmers, George W.	P	12	.188	B	
		Cravath, Clifford Carltone	OF113	130	.284	WashA09	
		(Cactus)					
2	5	Curtis, Clifton Garfield	P	10	+.000	B	Bkn
		Dodge, John Lewis	3B23	30	.120	A	
		(2B1 SS2)					
		Dolan, Alvin James (Cozy)	3B	11	.280	xNYA	
		Dooin, Chas. Sebastian MGR.	C58	69	.234	B	
		Doolan, Michael Joseph	SS	146	.258	B	
		Downey, Thomas Edward	3B	54	+.292	Cin	Chi
0	2	Finneran, Joseph Ignatius	P	14	.100	A	
		Graham, George Frederick	C19	24	.288	Chi	C
		(Peaches)					
		Killefer, Wm. Lavier Jr.	C	85	.224	B	
		Knabe, Franz Otto	2B123	126	.282	B	
		Loan, Wm. Joseph	C	1	.500	A	C
		Lobert, John Bernard (Hans)	3B64	65	.327	B	
		Luderus, Frederick Wm.	1B146	148	.257	B	
		Magee, Sherwood Robert	OF124	132	.306	B	
		(Sherry)					
		Mangus, George Graham	OF	10	.200	A	C
0	1	Marshall, Roy DeVerne	P	2	.000	A	
0	1	Mayer, James Erskine	P	7	.000	A	
		Miller, Roy Oscar (Doc)	OF	67	+.288	xBos	
9	14	Moore, Earl Alonzo	P	31	.107	B	
		Moran, Patrick Joseph	C	13	.115	B	
2	0	Nelson, Albert Francis	P	4	.100	xStLA	
0	0	Nicholson, Frank Collins	P	2	.000	A	C
		Paskert, George Henry (Dode)	OF141	145	.315	B	
0	0	Ritter, Wm. Herbert	P	3	.000	A	
10	10	Rixey, Eppa Jr.	P	23	.170	A	
		Savage, Harold James	2B	2	.000	A	
1	4	Shultz, Wallace Luther	P22	23	.238	B	C
16	12	Seaton, Thomas Gordon	P	44	.217	A	
		Steinbrenner, Eugene Gass	2B	3	.100	A	C
		Titus, John Franklin	OF	45	+.274	B	Bos

WON	LOST	NAME	POS.	G.	BA	FROM	TO
0	0	Wallace, Harry Clinton	P	4	.000	A	C
		Walsh, Michael Timothy	2B31	51	.267	B	

*Brinker also played 2 games at 3B.

WON 88
LOST 63
TG 151

NATIONAL LEAGUE FINISHED 2nd.

1913. PCT. .583

PHILADELPHIA

CHAS. SEBASTIAN DOOIN

WON	LOST	NAME	POS.	G.	BA	FROM	TO
22	8	Alexander, Grover Cleveland	P	47	.126	B	
		(Pete)					
		Becker, Beals	OF	88	+.324	xCin	
14	12	Brennan, Addison Foster (Ad)	P	40	.164	B	
		Burns, Edward James	C15	17	.200	StL	
		Byrne, Robert Mathew	3B	19	+.224	xPitt	
3	3	Camnitz, Samuel Howard	P	9	+.063	xPitt	
		Capron, Ralph E.	OF	5	.000	Pitt	C
3	10	Chalmers, George W.	P	26	.212	B	
		Cravath, Clifford Carlton	OF141	147	.341	B	
		(Cactus)					
		Devore, Joshua (Josh)	OF	23	+.282	xCin	
		Dodge, John Lewis	3B	3	+.333	B	Cin
		Dolan, Alvin James (Cozy)	3B	55	+.262	B	Pitt
		Dooin, Chas. Sebastian MGR.	C50	55	.256	B	
		Doolan, Michael Joseph	SS148	151	.218	B	
		Duncan, Vernon Van Duke	OF	8	.416	A	
0	0	Finneran, Joseph Ignatius	P	3	.667	B	
0	0	Haislip, James C.	P	1	.000	A	C
0	0	Hartranft, Raymond Chas.	P	1	.000	A	C
		Howley, Daniel Philip	C22	26	.125	A	
0	1	Imlay, Harry Miller	P	9	.000	A	C
		Killefer, Wm. Lavier Jr.	C	120	.244	B	
		Knabe, Franz Otto	2B	148	.263	B	
		Lobert, John Bernard (Hans)	3B145	150	.300	B	
		Luderus, Frederick Wm.	1B	155	.262	B	
		Magee, Sherwood Robert	OF123	138	.306	B	
		(Sherry)					
1	3	Marshall, Roy DeVerne	P	13	.111	B	
9	9	Mayer, James Erskine	P	39	.120	B	
		Miller, Roy Oscar (Doc)	OF6	69	.345	B	
0	0	Moore, Earl Alonzo	P	12	+.000	B	Chi
		Moran, Patrick Joseph	C	1	.000	B	
0	0	Nelson, Albert Francis	P	2	+.333	B	Cin
		Paskert, George Henry (Dode)	OF120	124	.262	B	
		Reed, Milton D. Jr. (2B3)	SS7	13	.240	StL11	
9	5	Rixey, Eppa Jr.	P	35	.191	B	
27	12	Seaton, Thomas Gordon	P	52	.109	B	
		Walsh, Michael Timothy	2B3	26	.333	B	

WON 74 LOST 80 TG 154

NATIONAL LEAGUE 1914. FINISHED 6th. PCT. .481

PHILADELPHIA

CHAS. SEBASTIAN DOOIN

WON	LOST	NAME	POS.	G.	BA	FROM	TO
27	15	Alexander, Grover Cleveland (Pete)	P46	48	.234	B	
2	2	Baumgartner, Stanwood Fulton	P	15	.053	A	
		Becker, Beals	OF126	138	.325	B	
		Burns, Edward James	C55	70	.259	B	
		Byrne, Robert Mathew (3B22)	2B101	126	.272	B	
0	3	Chalmers, George W.	P	3	.000	B	
		Cravath, Clifford Carlton (Cactus)	OF143	149	.298	B	
		Devore, Joshua (Josh)	OF	30	+.302	B	Bos
		Dooin, Chas. Sebastian MGR.	C40	53	.178	B	
		Fletcher, O. Frank		1	.000	A	C
		Hilly, Wm. Edward	OF	8	.300	A	C
		Irelan, Harold (Grump)	2B44	67	.236	A	C
1	3	Jacobs, Wm. Elmer	P	14	.000	A	
		Killefer, Wm. Lavier Jr.	C	98	.234	B	
		Lobert, John Bernard (Hans)	3B133	135	.275	B	
		Luderus, Frederick Wm.	1B	121	.248	B	
		Magee, Sherwood Robert (Sherry) (1B32 SS39)	OF67	146	.314	B	
6	7	Marshall, Roy DeVerne	P	27	.140	B	
		Martin, John Christopher	SS	83	+.253	xBos	C
3	2	Matteson, Henry Edson	P	15	.182	A	
21	19	Mayer, James Erskine	P	48	.194	B	
		Mollenkamp, Frederick Henry	1B	3	.125	A	C
		Moran, Patrick Joseph	C	1	.000	B	
		Murphy, Herbert C.	SS	9	.160	A	C
		McAvoy, George H.		1	.000	A	C
4	8	Oeschger, Joseph Carl	P	32	.075	A	
		Paskert, George Henry (Dode)	OF128	132	.264	B	
		Reed, Milton D. Jr.	SS22	44	.206	B	
2	11	Rixey, Eppa Jr.	P	24	.038	B	
8	10	Tincup, Austin Ben	P28	31	.170	A	

WON 90 LOST 62 TG 152

NATIONAL LEAGUE 1915. FINISHED 1st. PCT. .592

PHILADELPHIA

PATRICK JOSEPH MORAN

WON	LOST	NAME	POS.	G.	BA	FROM	TO
		Adams, John Bertram	C23	24	.111	ClevA12	
31	10	Alexander, Grover Cleveland (Pete)	P	49	.169	B	
		Bancroft, David James	SS	153	.254	A	
0	2	Baumgartner, Stanwood Fulton	P	16	.083	B	
		Becker, Beals	OF98	112	.246	B	C
		Burns, Edward James	C62	67	.241	B	
		Byrne, Robert Mathew	3B	105	.209	B	
8	9	Chalmers, George W.	P	26	.169	B	
		Cravath, Clifford Carlton (Cactus)	OF149	150	.285	B	
14	11	Demaree, Albert Wentworth (Al)	P	32	.176	N.Y.	
		Dugey, Oscar Joseph	2B5	42	.154	Bos	
		Killefer, Wm. Lavier Jr.	C104	105	.238	B	
		Luderus, Frederick Wm.	1B	141	.315	B	
21	15	Mayer, James Erskine	P	43	.239	B	
4	3	McQuillan, George Washington	P	9	+.043	xPitt	
		Niehoff, John Albert (Bert)	2B	148	.238	Cin	
1	0	Oeschger, Joseph Carl	P	6	.000	B	
		Paskert, George Henry (Dode)	OF92	109	.244	B	
11	12	Rixey, Eppa Jr.	P	29	.164	B	
		Stock, Milton Joseph	3B55	69	.260	N.Y.	
0	0	Tincup, Austin Ben	P	11	.000	B	
		Weiser, Harry Budson	OF20	37	.141	A	
		Whitted, George Bostic	OF119	128	.281	Bos	

WON 91 LOST 62 TG 153

NATIONAL LEAGUE 1916. FINISHED 2nd. PCT. .595

PHILADELPHIA

PATRICK JOSEPH MORAN

WON	LOST	NAME	POS.	G.	BA	FROM	TO
		Adams, John Bertram	C	11	.231	B	
33	12	Alexander, Grover Cleveland (Pete)	P48	49	.239	B	
		Bancroft, David James	SS	142	.212	B	
0	0	Baumgartner, Stanwood Fulton	P	1	.000	B	
7	7	Bender, Chas. Albert (Chief)	P27	28	.279	BaltF	
		Burns, Edward James	C75	78	.233	B	
		Byrne, Robert Mathew	3B40	48	.234	B	
1	4	Chalmers, George W.	P	12	.000	B	C
		Cooper, Claude Wm.	OF29	56	.192	BknF	
		Cravath, Clifford Carlton (Cactus)	OF130	137	.283	B	
19	14	Demaree, Albert Wentworth (Al)	P	39	.109	B	
		Dugey, Oscar Joseph	2B9	41	.220	B	
0	1	Fortune, Garrett Reese (Gary)	P	1	.000	A	
		Gandy, Robert Brinkley	OF	1	.000	A	C
		Good, Wilbur David	OF46	75	.250	Chi	
0	0	Kantlehner, Ervine Lester	P	3	+.000	xPitt	C
		Killefer, Wm. Lavier Jr.	C91	97	.217	B	
		Luderus, Frederick Wm.	1B	146	.281	B	
		Maharg, Wm.	OF	1	.000	DetA12	C
7	7	Mayer, James Erskine	P	28	.132	B	
1	7	McQuillan, George Washington	P	21	.091	B	

WON	LOST	NAME	POS.	G.	BA	FROM	TO
		Niehoff, John Albert (Bert)	2B144	146	.243	B	
1	0	Oeschger, Joseph Carl	P	14	.000	B	
		Paskert, George Henry (Dode)	OF146	149	.279	B	
22	10	Rixey, Eppa Jr.	P	38	.155	B	
		Stock, Milton Joseph (SS15)	3B117	132	.281	B	
0	0	Tincup, Austin Ben	P	1	.000	B	
		Weiser, Harry Budson	OF	4	.300	B	C
		Whitted, George Bostic (1B16)	OF136	147	.281	B	

WON 87
LOST 65
TG 152

NATIONAL LEAGUE — 1917. — FINISHED 2nd. — PCT. .572

PHILADELPHIA

PATRICK JOSEPH MORAN

WON	LOST	NAME	POS.	G.	BA	FROM	TO
		Adams, John Bertram	C38	43	.206	B	
30	13	Alexander, Grover Cleveland (Pete)	P45	47	.216	B	
		Bancroft, David James	SS120	127	.243	B	
8	2	Bender, Chas. Albert (Chief)	P	20	.205	B	
		Burns, Edward James	C15	20	.204	B	
		Byrne, Robert Mathew	3B1	13	.357	B	ChiA
		Cooper, Claude Wm.	OF	24	.103	B	C
		Cravath, Clifford Carltone (Cactus)	OF139	140	.280	B	
		Dugey, Oscar Joseph	2B15	44	.194	B	
		Evers, John Joseph	2B	56	+.231	xBos	
1	1	Fittery, Paul Clarence	P17	19	.091	Cin14	C
		Killefer, Wm. Lavier Jr.	C	125	.274	B	
6	8	Lavender, James Sanford	P	28	.139	Chi	C
		Luderus, Frederick Wm.	1B	154	.261	B	
11	6	Mayer, James Erskine	P	28	.196	B	
		McGaffigan, Martin A.	SS17	19	.167	A	
		Niehoff, John Albert (Bert)	2B96	114	.255	B	
15	14	Oeschger, Joseph Carl	P42	43	.114	B	
		Paskert, George Henry (Dode)	OF138	141	.251	B	
		Pearce, Harry James	SS	4	.250	A	
16	21	Rixey, Eppa Jr.	P	39	.191	B	
		Schulte, Frank	OF	64	+.213	xPitt	
		Stock, Milton Joseph (SS19)	3B133	150	.264	B	
		Whitted, George Bostic	OF141	149	.280	B	

WON 55
LOST 68
TG 123

NATIONAL LEAGUE — 1918. — FINISHED 6th. — PCT. .447

PHILADELPHIA

PATRICK JOSEPH MORAN

WON	LOST	NAME	POS.	G.	BA	FROM	TO
		Adams, John Bertram	C76	84	.176	B	
		Bancroft, David James	SS	125	.265	B	
		Burns, Edward James	C	68	.207	B	C
		Cravath, Clifford Carlton (Cactus)	OF118	121	.232	B	
0	2	Davis, Frank Talmadge	P17	18	.000	ChiA15	
		Devine, Wm. Patrick (Mickey)	C	4	.125	A	
		Dillhoefer, Wm. Martin (Pickles)	C	8	.090	Chi	
		Fitzgerald, Justin Howard	OF59	66	.293	NYA11	C
0	2	Fortune, Garrett Reese (Gary)	P	8	.200	Phi116	
		Hemingway, Edson M. (1B1 3B3)	2B25	33	.213	N.Y.	C
13	13	Hogg, Carter Bradley	P30	39	.228	Chi15	
9	5	Jacobs, Wm. Elmer	P	18	+.158	xPitt	
		Luderus, Frederick Wm.	1B	125	.288	B	
2	2	Main, Miles Grant	P	9	.090	KCF15	C
7	4	Mayer, James Erskine	P	13	+.216	B	Pitt
		Meusel, Emil Frederick (Irish) (2B4)	OF120	124	.279	WashA14	
		McGaffigan, Martin A. (SS1)	2B53	54	.203	B	C
6	18	Oeschger, Joseph Carl	P	30	.083	B	
		Pearce, Harry James (1B1 SS2)	2B55	60	.244	B	
		Pickup, Clarence Wm.	OF	1	1.000	A	C
13	14	Prendergast, Michael Thomas	P	33	.082	Chi	
		Stock, Milton Joseph	3B	123	.274	B	
0	1	Tincup, Austin Ben	P	11	.125	Phil16	
5	7	Watson, Milton W.	P	23	.075	StL	
		Whitted, George Bostic	OF22	24	.244	B	
		Williams, Frederick	OF91	94	.276	Chi	
0	0	Woodward, Frank Russell	P	2	.333	A	

WON 47
LOST 90
TG 137

NATIONAL LEAGUE — 1919. — FINISHED 8th (LAST) — PCT. .343

PHILADELPHIA

JOHN WESLEY COOMBS CLIFFORD CARLTON CRAVATH

WON	LOST	NAME	POS.	G.	BA	FROM	TO
		Adams, John Bertram (1B1)	C73	78	.233	B	C
0	2	Ames, Leon Kessling	P	3	+.400	xStL	C
		Baird, Howard Douglas	3B	66	+.260	StL	StL
		Bancroft, David James	SS88	92	.272	B	
		Blackburne, Russell Aubrey (Lena) (1B1)	3B71	72	+.197	xBos	
		Cady, Forrest LeRoy	C29	34	.214	BosA17	C
		Callahan, Leo David	OF58	81	.230	Bkn13	C
1	3	Cantwell, Michael Joseph	P	5	.222	NYA16	
		Cavanaugh, Patrick John	3B	1	.000	A	C
2	5	Cheney, Lawrence Russell (Larry)	P	9	+.095	xBos	C
		Clarke, Jay Justin (Nig)	C22	26	.242	StLA11	

WON	LOST	NAME	POS.	G.	BA	FROM	TO
		Cravath, Clifford Carlton (Cactus) MGR.	OF56	83	.341	B	
0	0	Faircloth, James Lamar	P	2	.000	A	C
5	12	Hogg, Carter Bradley	P22	25	.283	B	C
6	10	Jacobs, Wm. Elmer	P	17	+.178	B	StL
		LeBourveau, DeWitt Wiley (Bevo)	OF15	17	.270	A	
		Luderus, Frederick Wm.	1B	138	.293	B	
8	10	Meadows, Henry Lee	P	21	+.113	xStL	
		Meusel, Emil Frederick (Irish)	OF128	135	.305	B	
0	2	Murray, Patrick Joseph	P	8	.000	A	C
0	1	Oeschger, Joseph Carl	P	5	+.000	B	N.Y.
6	8	Packard, Eugene Milo	P21	27	.137	StL	C
		Pasquariello, Michael John	1B	1	+1.000	A	StL
		Paulette, Eugene Edward	OF10	67	+.259	xStL	
		Pearce, Harry James (SS23 3B2)	2B43	68	.180	B	C
0	1	Prendergast, Michael Thomas	P	5	.333	B	C
		Raymond, Louis Anthony	2B	1	.500	A	C
6	12	Rixey, Eppa Jr.	P	23	.149	Phil17	
		Sicking, Edward Joseph	3B1	61	+.216	xN.Y.	
5	11	Smith, George Allen	P	31	+.133	xN.Y.	
		Tragesser, Walter Joseph	C	35	+.164	xBos	
2	4	Watson, Milton W.	P	8	.063	B	C
0	0	Weinert, Phillip Walter	P	1	1.000	A	
		Whitted, George Bostic	2B	78	+.249	B	Pitt
		Williams, Frederick	OF108	109	.278	B	
6	9	Woodward, Frank Russell	P	17	+.200	B	StL
		Yeabsley, Robert Watson		2	.000	A	C
		Wallace, Frederick Renshaw	SS	2	.200	A	C

Stengel, Chas. Dillon (Casey) (suspended-did not play for Phila) xPitt

WON 62 LOST 91 TG 153

NATIONAL LEAGUE 1920. FINISHED 8th (LAST) PCT. .405

PHILADELPHIA

CLIFFORD CARLTON CRAVATH

WON	LOST	NAME	POS.	G.	BA	FROM	TO
		Bancroft, David James	SS	42	+.276	B	N.Y.
1	1	Betts, Walter Martin (Huck)	P	27	.080	A	
0	3	Cantwell, Michael Joseph	P	5	.143	B	C
7	14	Causey, Cecil Algernon	P34	44	.186	Bos	
		Cravath, Clifford Carlton (Cactus) MGR.	OF	46	.289	B	C
2	3	Enzmann, John	P16	17	.167	ClevA	C
		Fletcher, Arthur	SS	102	+.297	xN.Y.	
2	6	Gallia, Mervin Allys (Bert)	P18	19	.174	xStLA	C
9	9	Hubbell, Wilbert Wm.	P	24	+.132	xN.Y.	
0	0	Keenan, James Wm.	P	1	.000	A	
		LeBourveau, DeWitt Wiley (Bevo)	OF72	84	.257	B	
		Luderus, Frederick Wm.	1B	16	.156	B	C
16	14	Meadows, Henry Lee	P35	39	.171	B	
		Meusel, Emil Frederick (Irish)	OF129	138	.309	B	
		Miller, John Barney (3B17)	2B59	98	.254	StL	
		Miller, Ralph Joseph	3B91	97	.219	A	
		Paulette, Eugene Edward	1B139	143	.288	B	C
		Rawlings, John Wm.	2B	98	+.234	xBos	
11	22	Rixey, Eppa Jr.	P41	43	.248	B	
13	18	Smith, George Allen	P	43	.097	B	
		Stengel, Chas. Dillon (Casey)	OF118	129	.292	B	
		Tragesser, Walter Joseph	C52	62	.210	B	C
		Walsh, Walter Wm.		1	.000	A	C
1	1	Weinert, Phillip Walter	P	10	.000	B	
		Wheat, McKinley Davis	C74	78	.226	Bkn	
		Williams, Frederick	OF147	148	.325	B	
		Withrow, Frank Blaine	C48	48	.182	A	
		Wrightstone, Russell Guy	3B56	76	.262	A	

WON 51 LOST 103 TG 154

NATIONAL LEAGUE 1921. FINISHED 8th (LAST) PCT. .331

PHILADELPHIA

WM. EDWARD DONOVAN IRVING KEY WILHELM

WON	LOST	NAME	POS.	G.	BA	FROM	TO
3	6	Baumgartner, Stanwood Fulton	P22	31	.200	Phil16	
0	1	Behan, Chas. Frederick	P	2	.000	A	
3	7	Betts, Walter Martin (Huck)	P	32	.267	B	
		Bruggy, Frank Leo	C86	96	.310	A	
3	3	Causey, Cecil Algernon	P	8	+.150	B	N.Y.
		Henline, Walter John (Butch)	C32	33	+.306	xN.Y.	
9	16	Hubbell, Wilbert Wm.	P	36	.160	B	
1	2	Keenan, James Wm.	P	15	.000	B	C
		King, Lee	OF	64	+.269	xN.Y.	
		Konetchy, Edward Joseph	1B	72	+.321	xBkn	C
		LeBourveau, DeWitt Wiley (Bevo)	OF76	93	.295	B	
		Lee, Clifford Walker (OF27)	1B48	88	.308	Pitt	
11	16	Meadows, Henry Lee	P	28	.210	B	
		Meusel, Emil Frederick (Irish)	OF	84	+.353	B	N.Y.
		Miller, John Barney (1B38)	3B41	84	.297	B	C
		Miller, Ralph Joseph	SS46	57	.304	B	
		Monroe, John Allen	2B	41	+.286	xN.Y.	C
		Neale, Alfred Earle (Greasy)	OF	22	+.211	Cin	Cin
		Parkinson, Frank Joseph	SS105	108	.253	A	
		Peters, John Wm.	C44	55	.290	ClevA18	
		Rader, Donald Russell	SS	9	.281	ChiA13	C
		Rapp, Joseph Aloysius (Goldie)	3B	52	+.277	xN.Y.	
		Rawlings, John Wm.	2B	60	+.291	B	N.Y.
		Richbourg, Lancelot Clayton	2B1	10	.200	A	

WON	LOST	NAME	POS.	G.	BA	FROM	TO
10	19	Ring, James Joseph	P	34	.145	Cin	
1	3	Sedgwick, Henry Kenneth	P	16	.208	A	
4	20	Smith, George Allen	P	39	.056	B	
		Smith, James Lawrence	2B66	67	.231	Cin19	
		Stengel, Chas. Dillon (Casey)	OF	24	+.305	B	N.Y.
		Walker, Wm. Curtis	OF	21	+.338	xN.Y.	
1	0	Weinert, Phillip Walter	P	8	1.000	B	
		Wheat, McKinley Davis	C	10	.185	B	C
0	0	Wilhelm, Irving Key (Kaiser) MGR.	P	4	.000	BaltF15	
		Williams, Frederick	OF	146	.320	B	
5	10	Winters, Jesse Franklin	P	18	.128	N.Y.	
		Wrightstone, Russell Guy (OF37)	3B54	109	.296	B	

WON 57 NATIONAL LEAGUE FINISHED 7th.
LOST 96
TG 153 1922. PCT. .373

PHILADELPHIA

IRVING KEY WILHELM

WON	LOST	NAME	POS.	G.	BA	FROM	TO
1	1	Baumgartner, Stanwood Fulton	P	6	.333	B	
4	2	Behan, Chas. Frederick	P	7	.250	B	
		Benton. Stanley W.	2B5	6	.211	A	C
1	0	Betts, Walter Martin (Huck)	P	7	.000	B	
		Fletcher, Arthur	SS106	110	.280	Phil20	
		Henline, Walter John (Butch)	C119	125	.316	B	
7	15	Hubbell, Wilbert Wm.	P	35	.171	B	
		King, Lee	OF15	19	+.226	B	N.Y.
		LeBourveau, DeWitt Wiley (Bevo)	OF42	74	.269	B	
		Lee, Clifford Walker (1B18 3B1)	OF89	122	.322	B	
		Leslie, Roy Reid	1B139	141	.270	StL19	C
12	18	Meadows, Henry Lee	P	33	.313	B	
		Mokan, John Leo (3B2)	OF37	47	+.252	xPitt	
		Parkinson, Frank Joseph	2B139	141	.275	B	
		Peters, John Wm.	C39	55	.244	B	C
0	1	Pinto, Wm. Lerton	P	9	.111	A	
		Rapp, Joseph Aloysius (Goldie) (SS2)	3B117	119	.253	B	
12	18	Ring, James Joseph	P	40	.148	B	
1	10	Singleton, John Edward	P	22	.139	A	C
5	14	Smith, George Allen	P	42	.076	B	
		Smith, James Lawrence (2B13 3B1)	SS23	38	.219	B	C
0	0	Sullivan, Thomas A.	P	3	.250	A	C
		Walker, Wm. Curtis	OF147	148	.337	B	
8	11	Weinert, Phillip Walter	P	34	.241	B	
		Williams, Frederick	OF150	151	.308	B	
6	6	Winters, Jesse Franklin	P	34	.255	B	
		Withrow, Frank Blaine	C8	10	.333	Phil20	C
		Wrightstone, Russell Guy (1B2 SS35)	3B40	99	.305	B	

WON 50 NATIONAL LEAGUE FINISHED 8th (LAST)
LOST 104
TG 154 1923. PCT. .325

PHILADELPHIA

ARTHUR FLETCHER

WON	LOST	NAME	POS.	G.	BA	FROM	TO
3	12	Behan, Chas. Frederick	P30	34	.186	B	C
		Bennett, Joseph R.	3B	1	.000	A	C
2	4	Betts, Walter Martin (Huck)	P19	20	.097	B	
0	3	Bishop, James Morton	P	15	.000	A	
2	4	Couch, John Daniel	P11	12	+.250	xCin	
		Dennehy, Thomas Francis	OF	9	.250	A	C
0	0	Gardiner, Arthur Cecil	P	1	.000	A	C
7	14	Glazner, Chas. Franklin	P	28	+.170	xPitt	
0	0	Grant, James Ronald	P	2	.000	A	C
2	9	Head, Ralph	P	35	.071	A	C
		Henline, Walter John (Butch) (OF1)	C96	111	.324	B	
0	0	Holke, Walter Henry (P1)	1B146	147	.311	Bos	
1	6	Hubbell, Wilbert Wm.	P22	23	.235	B	
0	0	Jones, Jesse Frank	P	3	.500	A	C
		Leach, Frederick M.	OF26	52	.260	A	
		Lee, Clifford Walker (1B16)	OF83	107	.321	B	
		Lord, Carleton	3B14	17	.234	A	C
1	3	Meadows, Henry Lee	P	8	+.400	B	Pitt
		Metz, Leonard Raymond (SS6)	2B6	12	.216	A	
0	0	Miller, Leo Alphonso	P	1	.000	A	C
9	10	Mitchell, Clarence Elmer	P29	53	.269	Bkn	
		Mokan, John Leo (3B1)	OF105	113	.313	B	
		O'Brien, Frank Andrew	C9	15	.333	A	C
		Parker, Douglas Wooley (Dixie)	C2	4	.200	A	C
		Parkinson, Frank Joseph (SS15 3B11)	2B37	67	.242	B	
0	0	Ragan, Don Carlos Patrick (Pat)	P	1	.500	ChiA19	C
		Rapp, Joseph Aloysius (Goldie)	3B45	47	.263	B	C
18	16	Ring, James Joseph	P39	41	.106	B	
		Sand, John Henry (Heinie) (3B11)	SS120	132	.228	A	
		Tierney, James Arthur (3B2 OF7)	2B115	121	+.317	xPitt	
		Walker, Wm. Curtis (1B1)	OF137	140	.281	B	
4	17	Weinert, Phillip Walter	P38	39	.322	B	
		Williams, Frederick	OF135	136	.293	B	
		Wilson, James (OF2)	C69	85	.262	A	
1	6	Winters, Jesse Franklin	P	21	.160	B	C
		Woehr, Andrew Emil	3B	13	.341	A	
		Wrightstone, Russell Guy (2B9 SS21)	3B72	119	.273	B	

WON 55 | LOST 96 | TG 151

NATIONAL LEAGUE — 1924.

FINISHED 7th. PCT. .364

PHILADELPHIA

ARTHUR FLETCHER

WON	LOST	NAME	POS.	G.	BA	FROM	TO
7	10	Betts, Walter Martin (Huck)	P37	38	.156	B	
0	1	Bishop, James Morton	P	7	.200	B	C
8	17	Carlson, Harold Gust (Hal)	P38	39	.276	Pitt	
4	8	Couch, John Daniel	P	37	.204	B	
		Emery, Herrick Smith	OF1	5	.667	A	C
		Ford, Horace Hills	2B	145	.272	Bos	
7	16	Glazner, Chas. Franklin	P	35	.157	B	C
0	1	Hamilton, Earl A.	P	3	.000	Pitt	C
		Harper, George Washington	OF	109	+.295	xCin	
		Henline, Walter John (Butch) (OF2)	C83	115	.284	B	
		Henrich, Frank Wilde	OF32	36	.211	A	C
		Holke, Walter Henry	1B	148	.300	B	
10	9	Hubbell, Wilbert Wm.	P	36	.220	B	
		Leach, Frederick M.	OF7	8	.464	B	
		Lee, Clifford Walker (1B4 OF13)	OF	21	+.250	B	Cin
0	0	Lewis, Wm. Burton (Bert)	P	12	.000	A	C
		Metz, Leonard Raymond	SS6	7	.286	B	
6	13	Mitchell, Clarence Elmer	P29	69	.255	B	
		Mokan, John Leo	OF94	96	.260	B	
2	7	Oeschger, Joseph Carl	P	19	+.250	xN.Y.	
		Parkinson, Frank Joseph (2B10 SS21)	3B28	62	.212	B	C
0	0	Pinto, Wm. Lerton	P	3	.000	Phil22	C
10	12	Ring, James Joseph	P	32	.230	B	
		Sand, John Henry (Heinie)	SS	137	.245	B	
		Schultz, Joseph Chas.	OF76	88	+.285	xStL	
1	1	Steineder, Raymond J.	P	9	+.300	xPitt	C
		Walker, Wm. Curtis	OF20	24	+.291	B	Cin
0	1	Weinert, Phillip Walter	P	8	.000	B	
		Wendell, Lewis Chas.	C17	21	.250	N.Y.16	
		Williams, Frederick	OF145	148	.328	B	
		Wilson, James (1B2) (OF1)	C82	95	.279	B	
		Woehr, Andrew Emil (2B1)	3B44	50	.217	B	C
		*Wrightstone, Russell Guy	3B97	118	.307	B	

*Wrightstone also played 9 games at 2B, 5 games at SS and 1 game in the OF.

WON 68 | LOST 85 | TG 153

NATIONAL LEAGUE — 1925.

FINISHED 6th. (TIED WITH BKLYN) PCT. .444

PHILADELPHIA

ARTHUR FLETCHER

WON	LOST	NAME	POS.	G.	BA	FROM	TO
4	5	Betts, Walter Martin (Huck)	P35	37	.294	B	
		Burns, George Joseph	OF	88	.292	Cin	C
13	14	Carlson, Harold Gust (Hal)	P35	38	.183	B	
5	6	Couch, John Daniel	P	34	.161	B	C
0	0	Crumpler, Ray Maxton	P	3	.000	DetA20	C
4	13	Decatur, Arthur Rue	P	25	+.049	xBkn	
		Durning, George Warren	OF4	5	.357	A	C
1	0	Fillingim, Dana	P	5	.000	Bos23	C
		Fonseca, Lewis Albert (2B69)	1B55	126	.319	Cin	
0	0	Friberg, Bernard Albert (P1 SS2 3B14 OF12)	2B77	91	+.270	xChi	
		Harper, George Washington	OF126	132	.349	B	
		Hawks, Nelson Louis	1B90	105	.322	NYA21	C
		Henline, Walter John (Butch) (OF1)	C68	93	.304	B	
		Holke, Walter Henry	1B23	39	+.244	B	Cin
0	0	Hubbell, Wilbert Wm.	P	2	+.000	B	Bkn
		Huber, Clarence Bill	3B120	124	.284	DetA21	
		Kimmick, Walter Lyons (2B13 3B21)	SS28	70	.305	Cin23	
7	6	Knight, Elma Russell (Jack)	P33	40	.205	StL22	
		Leach, Frederick M.	OF	65	.312	B	
		Metz, Leonard Raymond (2B2)	SS9	11	.000	B	C
		Meyer, Benjamin (Benny)	2B	1	1.000	BuffF15	C
10	17	Mitchell, Clarence Elmer (1B2)	P32	52	.196	B	
		Mokan, John Leo	OF62	75	.330	B	
0	0	O'Neal, Oran Herbert	P	11	.167	A	
5	4	Pierce, Raymond Lester	P	23	.179	Chi	
14	16	Ring, James Joseph	P	38	.109	B	
		Sand, John Henry (Heinie)	SS143	148	.278	B	
		Schultz, Joseph Chas.	OF20	24	+.344	B	Cin
3	3	Ulrich, Frank W.	P	21	.125	A	
0	0	Vines, Robert Earl	P	3	.000	StL	C
		Wendell, Lewis Chas.	C9	18	.077	B	
		Williams, Frederick	OF96	107	.331	B	
2	1	Willoughby, Claude Wm.	P	3	.000	A	
		Wilson, James (OF1)	C89	108	.328	B	
		Wrightstone, Russell Guy (1B6 2B10 SS12 3B11)	OF45	92	.346	B	

WON 58 | LOST 93 | TG 151

NATIONAL LEAGUE — 1926.

FINISHED 8th (LAST) PCT. .384

PHILADELPHIA

ARTHUR FLETCHER

WON	LOST	NAME	POS.	G.	BA	FROM	TO
		Attreau, Richard Gilbert	1B	17	.230	A	
2	0	Baecht, Edward Joseph	P	28	.143	A	
0	2	Bentley, John Needles (P7)	1B56	75	+.258	N.Y.	N.Y.
		Buskey, Joseph Henry	SS	5	.000	A	C
17	12	Carlson, Harold Gust (Hal)	P35	38	.240	B	
		Cotter, Edward Christopher (3B8) (3B8)	SS9	17	.308	A	C

WON	LOST	NAME	POS.	G.	BA	FROM	TO
8	16	Dean, Wayland Ogden	P33	63	.265	N.Y.	
0	0	Decatur, Arthur Rue	P	2	.000	B	
		Dunham, Leland Huffield	1B	5	.250	A	C
		Friberg, Bernard Albert	2B	144	.268	B	
		Grimes, Oscar Ray	1B28	32	.297	Chi24	C
		Harper, George Washington	OF55	56	.314	B	
		Henline, Walter John (Butch)	C77	99	.283	B	
		Huber, Clarence Bill	3B115	118	.245	B	C
		Jonnard, Clarence James	C15	19	.118	Pitt22	
		Keating, Walter Francis	SS	4	.000	Chi15	C
0	0	Kelly, Michael J.	P	4	.000	A	C
		Kimmick, Walter Lyons (1B2 SS1)	3B3	20	.214	B	C
3	12	Knight, Elma Russell (Jack)	P35	40	.214	B	
		Leach, Frederick M.	OF123	129	.329	B	
1	4	Maun, Ernest Gerald	P	14	.250	NY24	C
9	14	Mitchell, Clarence Elmer	P28	39	.244	B	
		Mokan, John Leo	OF123	127	.303	B	
		Nixon, Albert Richard	OF88	93	.293	Bos23	
2	7	Pierce, Raymond Lester	P37	39	.125	B	C
0	0	Rambo, Warren Dawson	P	1	1.000	A	C
		Rice, Robert Turnbull	3B15	19	.148	A	C
		Sand, John Henry (Heinie)	SS	149	.272	B	
		Sothern, Dennis Elwood (Denny)	OF13	14	.245	A	
		Stutz, George	SS	6	.000	A	C
0	0	Taber, Edward Timothy	P	6	.000	A	
8	13	Ulrich, Frank W.	P	45	.245	B	
		Wendell, Lewis Chas.	C	1	.000	B	C
		Williams, Frederick	OF93	107	.345	B	
8	12	Willoughby, Claude Wm.	P	47	.212	B	
		Wilson, James	C79	90	.305	B	
		Wrightstone, Russell Guy (2B13 3B37)	1B53	112	.307	B	
0	1	Yarnell, Waldo Wm.	P	1	.000	A	C

WON 51
LOST 103
TG 154

NATIONAL LEAGUE — FINISHED 8th (LAST)

1927. — PCT. .331

PHILADELPHIA

JOHN PHAELEN McINNIS

WON	LOST	NAME	POS.	G.	BA	FROM	TO
		Attreau, Richard Gilbert	1B26	44	.205	B	C
0	1	Baecht, Edward Joseph	P	1	.000	B	
		Baldwin, Henry Clay (3B2)	SS3	6	.313	A	C
4	5	Carlson, Harold Gust (Hal)	P11	12	+.240	B	Chi
		Cooney, James Edward	SS74	76	+.270	xChi	
0	1	Dean, Wayland Ogden	P	3	+.667	B	Chi
3	5	Decatur, Arthur Rue	P	29	.222	B	C
		Dietrick, Wm. Alexander	SS1	5	.167	A	
8	16	Ferguson, James Alexander (Alex)	P	31	.100	WashA	
		Friberg, Bernard Albert	3B103	111	.233	B	
		Hohman, Wm. Henry	OF3	7	.278	A	C
		Jonnard, Clarence James	C41	53	.294	B	
0	3	Kaufmann, Anthony Chas. (Tony)	P5	8	+.143	xChi	StL
		Leach, Frederick M.	OF	140	.306	B	
1	1	Miller, Russell Lewis	P	2	.333	A	
6	3	Mitchell, Clarence Elmer	P13	18	.238	B	
		Mokan, John Leo	OF63	74	.286	B	C
		McInnis, John Phaelen MGR. (Stuffy)	1B	1	.000	Pitt	C
		Nixon, Albert Richard	OF44	54	.312	B	
		O'Donnell, Harry Herman	C12	16	.063	A	C
0	0	O'Neal, Oran Herbert	P	2	.000	Phil25	C
7	17	Pruett, Hubert Shelby (Hub)	P	31	.217	StLA24	
		Sand, John Henry (Heinie) (3B58)	SS86	141	.299	B	
9	21	Scott, John Wm. (Jack)	P48	83	.289	N.Y.	
		Spalding, Chas. Harry (Dick)	OF113	115	.296	A	
2	10	Sweetland, Lester Leo	P21	25	.316	A	
0	1	Taber, Edward Timothy	P	3	.000	B	C
		Thompson, LaFayette Fresco Jr. (Chick)	2B	153	.303	N.Y.	
8	11	Ulrich, Frank W.	P	32	.123	B	C
0	1	Walsh, August	P	1	.250	A	
		Williams, Frederick	OF130	131	.274	B	
3	7	Willoughby, Claude Wm.	P	35	.077	B	
		Wilson, James	C124	128	.275	B	
		Wrightstone, Russell Guy	1B136	141	.306	B	

WON 43
LOST 109
TG 152

NATIONAL LEAGUE — FINISHED 8th (LAST)

1928. — PCT. .283

PHILADELPHIA

BURTON EDWIN SHOTTON

WON	LOST	NAME	POS.	G.	BA	FROM	TO
1	1	Baecht, Edward Joseph	P	9	.143	B	
8	18	Benge, Raymond Adelphia	P40	42	.207	ClevA26	
1	4	Caldwell, Earle Welton	P	5	.111	A	
		Davis, Virgil Lawrence (Spud)	C49	67	+.282	xStL	
		Dietrick, Wm. Alexander	OF21	52	.200	B	C
5	10	Ferguson, James Alexander (Alex)	P	34	.026	B	
		Friberg, Bernard Albert	SS31	52	.202	B	
0	0	Green, June F.	P	11	.500	A	
		Hurst, Frank O'Donnell (Don)	1B104	107	.285	A	
		Jahn, Arthur Chas.	OF29	36	+.223	xN.Y.	C
		Kelly, Wm. Henry	1B	23	.169	PhilA20	C
		Klein, Chas. Herbert (Chuck)	OF63	64	.360	A	
		Leach, Frederick M. (1B25)	OF120	145	.304	B	
0	0	Lennon, Edward Francis	P	5	.000	A	C
		Lerian, Walter Irvin (Peck)	C74	96	.272	A	
0	12	Miller, Russell Lewis	P33	36	.148	B	C
2	5	Milligan, John Alexander	P	13	.050	A	
0	0	Mitchell, Clarence Elmer	P3	5	+.250	B	StL

WON	LOST	NAME	POS.	G.	BA	FROM	TO
		MacDonald, Harvey Forsyth	OF1	13	.250	A	C
7	8	McGraw, Robert Emmett	P	39	.111	StL	
		Nixon, Albert Richard	OF20	25	.234	B	C
2	4	Pruett, Hubert Shelby (Hub)	P	13	.208	B	
4	17	Ring, James Joseph	P	35	.183	StL	C
		Sand, John Henry (Heinie)	SS137	141	.211	B	C
		Schulte, John Clement	C34	65	.248	StL	
		Sothern, Dennis Elwood (Denny)	OF136	141	.285	Phi126	
3	15	Sweetland, Lester Leo	P37	41	.191	B	
		Thompson, LaFayette Fresco Jr. (Chick)	2B	152	.287	B	
0	1	Walker, Martin Van Buren	P	1	.000	A	C
4	9	Walsh, August S.	P38	39	.256	B	C
		Whitney, Arthur Carter (Pinkey)	3B149	151	.301	A	
		Williams, Frederick	OF69	99	.256	B	
6	5	Willoughby, Claude Wm.	P	35	.150	B	
		Wilson, James	C20	21	+.300	B	StL
		Wrightstone, Russell Guy	OF26	33	+.209	B	N.Y.

WON 71 — NATIONAL LEAGUE — FINISHED 5th.
LOST 82
TG 153 — 1929. — PCT. .464

PHILADELPHIA

BURTON EDWIN SHOTTON

WON	LOST	NAME	POS.	G.	BA	FROM	TO
11	15	Benge, Raymond Adelphia	P38	43	.203	B	
9	7	Collins, Philip Eugene	P43	59	.190	Chi23	
2	2	Dailey, Samuel L.	P	20	.059	A	C
		Davis, Virgil Lawrence (Spud)	C89	98	.342	B	
3	7	Elliott, Howard Wm.	P	40	.167	A	
1	2	Ferguson, James Alexander (Alex)	P	5	+.000	B	Bkn
		Friberg, Bernard Albert (OF40)	SS73	128	.301	B	
0	0	Green, June F.	P	21	.211	B	C
0	0	Holloway, James Madison	P	3	1.000	A	C
		Hurst, Frank O'Donnell (Don)	1B	154	.304	B	
		Klein, Chas. Herbert (Chuck)	OF	149	.356	B	
5	5	Koupal, Louis Laddie	P	15	+.125	xBkn	
		Lerian, Walter Irvin (Peck)	C103	105	.223	B	C
		Lyons, Terence Hilbert	1B	1	.000	A	C
0	1	Miller, Elmer LeRoy	P	31	.237	A	C
0	1	Milligan, John Alexander	P	8	.333	B	
5	5	McGraw, Robert Emmett	P	41	.200	B	C
		O'Doul, Frank Joseph (Lefty)	OF	154	.398	N.Y.	
		O'Rourke, Joseph Leo		3	.000	A	C
		Peel, Homer Hefner	OF39	53	.269	StL27	
3	6	Roy, Luther Franklin	P	21	+.281	Chi27	Bkn
		Sigman, Wesley Triplett	OF	10	.517	A	
4	6	Smythe, Wm. Harry	P19	20	.192	A	
		Sothern, Dennis Elwood (Denny)	OF71	76	.306	B	
		Susce, George Cyril Methodius	C11	17	.294	A	
		Thevenow, Thomas Joseph Jr.	SS	90	.227	StL	
		Thompson, LaFayette Fresco Jr. (Chick)	2B	148	.324	B	
		Whitney, Arthur Carter (Pinkey)	3B	154	.327	B	
		Williams, Frederick	OF11	66	.292	B	
15	14	Willoughby, Claude Wm.	P	49	.143	B	
13	11	Sweetland, Lester Leo	P43	53	.292	B	

WON 52 — NATIONAL LEAGUE — FINISHED 8th (LAST)
LOST 102
TG 154 — 1930. — PCT. .338

PHILADELPHIA

BURTON EDWIN SHOTTON

WON	LOST	NAME	POS.	G.	BA	FROM	TO
0	3	Alexander, Grover Cleveland (Pete)	P	9	.000	StL	C
11	15	Benge, Raymond Adelphia	P	38	.205	B	
		Brickell, George Frederick	OF	53	+.246	xPitt	
6	12	Collard, Earl Clinton	P30	31	.205	ClevA28	C
16	11	Collins, Philip Eugene	P47	55	.253	B	
		Davis, Virgil Lawrence (Spud)	C96	106	.313	B	
6	11	Elliott, Howard Wm.	P	48	.094	B	
		Friberg, Bernard Albert (SS12 OF35)	2B44	105	.341	B	
0	7	Hansen, Roy Emil	P	22	.111	A	
		Hurst, Frank O'Donnell (Don)	1B96	119	.327	B	
		Klein, Chas. Herbert (Chuck)	OF	156	.386	B	
0	4	Koupal, Louis Laddie	P	13	.083	B	
1	2	Milligan, John Alexander	P	9	.111	B	
		McCurdy, Harry Henry	C41	80	.331	ChiA28	
1	2	Nichols Sr., Chester Raymond	P16	26	.300	N.Y.28	
		O'Doul, Frank Joseph (Lefty)	OF131	140	.383	B	
0	0	Phillips, Albert Abernathy	P	14	.462	A	C
		Rensa, George Anthony	C49	54	.285	xDetA	
		Sherlock, John Clinton	1B70	92	.324	A	C
		Sigman, Wesley Triplett	OF19	52	.270	B	C
0	3	Smythe, Wm. Harry	P	25	.286	B	
		Sothern, Dennis Elwood (Denny)	OF84	90	+.280	B	Pitt
0	0	Speece, Byron Franklin	P	11	.333	ClevA26	C
		Spotts, James Russell	C1	3	.000	A	C
7	15	Sweetland, Lester Leo	P34	35	.281	B	
		Thevenow, Thomas Joseph Jr.	SS	156	.286	B	
		Thompson, LaFayette Fresco Jr. (Chick)	2B112	122	.282	B	
		Whitney, Arthur Carter (Pinkey)	3B148	149	.342	B	
		Williams, Frederick	OF1	21	.471	B	C
4	17	Willoughby, Claude Wm.	P	41	.104	B	

WON 66 — NATIONAL LEAGUE — FINISHED 6th.
LOST 88
TG 154 — 1931. — PCT. .429

PHILADELPHIA

BURTON EDWIN SHOTTON

WON	LOST	NAME	POS.	G.	BA	FROM	TO
0	1	Adams, Robert Andrew	P	1	.000	A	
		Arlett, Russell Louis (Buzz) (1B13)	OF94	121	.313	A	C
		Bartell, Richard Wm.	SS133	135	.289	Pitt	
14	18	Benge, Raymond Adelphia	P	38	.205	B	
4	5	Blake, John Frederick (Sheriff)	P	14	+.240	xChi	
3	12	Bolen, Stewart O'Neal	P	28	.156	StLA27	
		Brickell, George Frederick	OF122	130	.253	B	
12	16	Collins, Philip Eugene	P42	44	.168	B	
		Connell, Eugene Joseph	C3	6	.250	A	C
		Davis, Virgil Lawrence (Spud)	C114	120	.326	B	
8	14	Dudley, Elzie Clise	P30	44	.214	Bkn	
0	2	Elliott, Howard Wm.	P	16	.111	B	
19	14	Elliott, James Thomas	P	52	.122	Bkn	
0	0	Fallenstein, Edward Joseph	P	24	.200	A	
		Friberg, Bernard Albert (3B25)	2B64	103	.261	B	
		Hurst, Frank O'Donnell (Don)	1B135	137	.305	B	
		Klein, Chas. Herbert (Chuck)	OF	148	.337	B	
		Koster, Frederick Chas.	OF41	76	.225	A	C
		Lee, Harold Burnham (Hal)	OF38	44	.221	Bkn	
		Mallon, Leslie Clyde	2B97	122	.309	A	
0	0	Milligan, John Alexander	P	3	.000	B	
		McCurdy, Harry Henry	C45	66	.287	B	
0	1	Nichols Sr., Chester Raymond	P	3	.000	B	
		Rensa, George Anthony	C17	19	.103	B	
0	0	Schesler, Chas.	P	17	.111	A	C
1	0	Shields, Benjamin Cowan	P	4	.000	BosA	C
		Stevens, Robert Jordan	SS10	12	.343	A	C
0	0	Stoner, Ulysses Simpson Grant (Lil)	P	7	.000	Pitt	C
		Taitt, Douglas John	OF	38	.225	ChiA29	
5	5	Watt, Frank Marion	P	38	.205	A	C
		Whitney, Arthur Carter (Pinkey)	3B128	130	.287	B	
		Willingham, Thomas Hugh (1B1 3B1)	SS7	23	.257	ChiA	
0	0	Wiltse, Harold James	P	1	.000	StLA28	C

WON 78 — NATIONAL LEAGUE — FINISHED 4th.
LOST 76
TG 154 — 1932. — PCT. .506

PHILADELPHIA

BURTON EDWIN SHOTTON

WON	LOST	NAME	POS.	G.	BA	FROM	TO
0	0	Adams, Robert Andrew	P	4	.000	B	C
		Bartell, Richard Wm.	SS	154	.308	B	
13	12	Benge, Raymond Adelphia	P	41	.173	B	
1	2	Berly, John Chambers	P	21	.000	N.Y.	
0	0	Bolen, Stewart O'Neal	P	5	.143	B	C
		Bressler, Raymond Bloom (Rube)	OF18	27	+.229	Bkn	StL
		Brickell, George Frederick	OF12	45	.333	B	
14	12	Collins, Philip Eugene	P	43	.265	B	
		Davis, George Willis (Kiddo)	OF133	137	.309	NYA26	
		Davis, Virgil Lawrence (Spud)	C120	125	.336	B	
		Delker, Edward Albert	2B27	30	+.161	xStL	
1	1	Dudley, Elzie Clise	P13	23	.286	B	
2	4	Elliott, Howard Wm.	P	16	.167	B	C
11	10	Elliott, James Thomas	P	39	.197	B	
		Friberg, Bernard Albert	2B56	61	.240	B	
2	2	Grabowski, Reginald John	P	14	.000	A	
10	10	Hansen, Roy Emil	P	39	.127	Phi130	
		Heathcote, Clifton Earl	1B5	30	+.282	xCin	C
11	14	Holley, Edward Edgar	P	34	.132	Chi28	
		Hurst, Frank O'Donnell (Don)	1B	150	.339	B	
		Klein, Chas. Herbert (Chuck)	OF	154	.348	B	
		Knothe, George Bertram	2B2	6	.083	A	C
		Lee, Harold Burnham (Hal)	OF148	149	.303	B	
2	0	Liska, Adolph James (Ad)	P	8	.000	Wash	
		Mallon, Leslie Clyde	2B88	103	.259	B	
		McCurdy, Harry Henry	C42	62	.235	B	
0	2	Nichols Sr., Chester Raymond	P	11	.000	B	C
11	7	Rhem, Chas. Flint	P	26	+.113	xStL	
		Scarritt, Russell Mallory	OF1	11	.182	BosA	C
		Taitt, Douglas John		4	.000	B	C
		Todd, Alfred Chester (Al)	C25	33	.229	A	
		Whitney, Arthur Carter (Pinkey)	3B151	154	.298	B	
		Willingham, Thomas Hugh		4	.000	B	

WON 60 — NATIONAL LEAGUE — FINISHED 7th.
LOST 92
TG 152 — 1933. — PCT. .395

PHILADELPHIA

BURTON EDWIN SHOTTON

WON	LOST	NAME	POS.	G.	BA	FROM	TO
		Bartell, Richard Wm.	SS	152	.271	B	
2	3	Berly, John Chambers	P	13	.308	B	C
		Brickell, George Frederick	OF	8	.308	B	C
0	0	Butler, Chas. Thomas	P	1	.000	A	C
		Cohen, Alta Albert	OF4	19	.188	Bkn	C
8	13	Collins, Philip Eugene	P42	43	.132	B	
		Davis, Virgil Lawrence (Spud)	C132	141	.349	B	
		Delker, Edward Albert (3B4)	2B17	25	.171	B	C
		Dugas, Augustin Joseph (Gus) (OF1)	1B11	37	.169	Pitt	
6	10	Elliott, James Thomas	P35	36	.231	B	
		Finn, Cornelius Francis (Mickey)	2B	51	.237	Bkn	C
		Fullis, Chas. Philip (Chick) (3B1)	OF151	151	.309	N.Y.	

WON	LOST	NAME	POS.	G.	BA	FROM	TO
1	3	Grabowski, Reginald John	P	10	.125	B	
6	14	Hansen, Roy Emil	P32	33	.155	B	
		Haslin, Michael Joseph (Mickey)	2B	26	.236	A	
13	15	Holley, Edward Edgar	P	30	.162	B	
		Hurst, Frank O'Donnell (Don)	1B142	147	.267	B	
2	2	Jackson, John Lewis	P	10	.143	A	C
		Klein, Chas. Herbert (Chuck)	OF	152	.368	B	
		Knothe, Wilfred Edgar (2B4)	3B32	41	+.150	xBos	C
		Lee, Harold Burnham (Hal)	OF45	46	+.287	B	Bos
3	1	Liska, Adolph James (Ad) (OF1)	P45	47	.071	B	C
8	9	Moore, Wm. Austin	P	36	.063	Bkn	
		McCurdy, Harry Henry	C1	73	.278	B	
		McLeod, Soule James	3B67	67	.194	WashA	C
5	4	Pearce, Franklin Thomas	P	20	.192	A	
1	0	Pickrel, Clarence Douglas	P	9	.000	A	
0	4	Ragland, Frank Roland	P	11	.200	WashA	C
5	14	Rhem, Chas. Flint	P	28	.087	B	
		Schulmerich, Edward Wesley	OF	97	+.334	xBos	
		Todd, Alfred Chester (Al) (OF2)	C34	73	.206	B	
		Warner, John Ralph (SS1 3B30)	2B71	107	.224	Bkn31	C
		Whitney, Arthur Carter (Pinkey)	3B30	31	+.264	B	Bos
		Willingham, Thomas Hugh		1	.000	B	C

WON 56 NATIONAL LEAGUE FINISHED 7th.
LOST 93
TG 149 1934. PCT. .376

PHILADELPHIA

JAMES WILSON

WON	LOST	NAME	POS.	G.	BA	FROM	TO
		Allen, Ethan Nathan	OF	145	.330	StL	
		Bartell, Richard Wm.	SS	146	.310	B	
		Boland, Edward John	OF3	8	.300	A	
		Camilli, Adolph Louis	1B	102	+.212	xChi	
		Chiozza, Louis Peo (3B26 OF17)	2B85	134	.304	A	
		Clancy, John Wm.	1B10	20	.245	Bkn32	C
13	18	Collins, Philip Eugene	P45	48	.170	B	
2	6	Darrow, George F.	P	17	.133	A	C
19	17	Davis, Curtis Benton (Curt)	P	51	.211	A	
		Davis, George Willis (Kiddo)	OF	100	+.293	xStL	
0	1	Elliott, James Thomas	P	3	+.000	B	Bos
		Frink, Frederick Ferdinand	OF1	2	.000	A	C
		Fullis, Chas. Philip (Chick)	OF27	28	+.225	B	StL
1	3	Grabowski, Reginald John	P	27	.056	B	C
6	12	Hansen, Roy Emil	P	50	.233	B	
		Haslin, Michael Joseph (Mickey) (2B21)	3B26	72	.265	B	
		Hendrick, Harvey (Gink)	OF12	59	.293	Chi	C
		High, Andrew Aird	3B14	47	.206	Cin	C
		Holden, Joseph Francis	C2	10	.071	A	
1	8	Holley, Edward Edgar	P15	16	+.208	B	Pitt
		Hopkins, Meredith Hilliard	3B4	10	.120	A	ChiA
		Hurst, Frank O'Donnell (Don)	1B34	40	+.262	B	Chi
		Jeffries, Irvine Franklin	2B52	56	.246	ChiA31	C
5	9	Johnson, Sylvester W.	P	42	+.195	xCin	
0	0	Kleinhans, Theodore Otto	P	5	+.000	A	Cin
0	1	Lohrman, Wm. LeRoy (Bill)	P	4	.500	A	
0	0	Malis, Cyrus Sol	P	1	.000	A	C
		Moore, John Francis	OF115	116	+.365	xCin	
5	7	Moore, Euel Walton	P	35	.143	B	C
4	9	Moore, Wm. Austin	P	35	.143	B	
		Oana, Henry Kamehameha	OF	6	.238	A	
0	2	Pearce, Franklin Thomas	P	7	.667	B	
		Ruble, Wm. Arthur	OF14	19	.278	DetA27	C
		Schulmerich, Edward Wesley	OF13	15	+.250	B	Cin
		Todd, Alfred Chester (Al)	C82	91	.318	B	
0	0	Walters, Wm. Henry Jr. (Bucky) (P2)	3B80	83	.260	xBosA	
		Wilson, James MGR.	C77	91	.292	StL	
		Wilson, Lewis Robert (Hack)	OF6	7	+.100	xBkn	C

WON 64 NATIONAL LEAGUE FINISHED 7th.
LOST 89
TG 153 1935. PCT. .418

PHILADELPHIA

JAMES WILSON

WON	LOST	NAME	POS.	G.	BA	FROM	TO
		Allen, Ethan Nathan	OF	156	.307	B	
2	9	Bivin, James Nathaniel	P	47	.146	A	C
		Boland, Edward John	OF10	30	.213	B	
7	10	Bowman, Joseph Emil (Joe) (OF1)	P33	49	.194	N.Y.	
		Bramhall, Arthur Washington (3B1)	SS1	2	.000	A	C
		Camilli, Adolph Louis	1B	156	.261	B	
		Chiozza, Dino Joseph	SS	2	.000	A	C
		Chiozza, Louis Peo (3B2)	2B120	124	.284	B	
0	2	Collins, Philip Eugene	P	3	+.000	B	StL
16	14	Davis, Curtis Benton (Curt)	P44	46	.173	B	
		Gomez, Jose Luis Rodrigues (2B32)	SS36	67	.230	A	
0	1	Hansen, Roy Emil	P	2	.000	B	StLA
		Haslin, Michael Joseph (Mickey) (2B9 3B11)	SS87	110	.265	B	
		Holden, Joseph Francis	C	6	.111	B	
10	8	Johnson, Sylvester W.	P	37	.241	B	
		Jonnard, Clarence James	C	1	.000	StL29	C
10	15	Jorgens, Orville Edward	P	53	.097	A	
2	0	Kelleher, Harold Joseph	P	3	.375	A	
		Lucas, Frederick Warrington	OF10	20	.265	A	C
1	6	Moore, Euel Walton	P	15	+.400	B	N.Y.
		Moore, John Francis	OF150	153	.323	B	
1	5	Mulcahy, Hugh Noyes (OF1)	P18	19	.000	A	

WON	LOST	NAME	POS.	G.	BA	FROM	TO
0	0	Pearce, Franklin Thomas	P	5	.500	B	C
3	5	Pezzullo, John	P	41	.250	A	
3	4	Prim, Raymond Lee	P	29	.083	WashA	
		Ryan, John Collins (Blondy)	SS35	39	.264	N.Y.	NYA
0	1	Thomas, Alphonse Thomas Jr.	P	4	.000	xWashA	
		Todd, Alfred Chester (Al)	C87	107	.290	B	
		Vergez, John Louis (SS2)	3B148	148	.249	N.Y.	
9	9	Walters, Wm. Henry Jr.	P24	49	.250	B	
		(Bucky) (2B2 3B1 OF5)					
		Watkins, George Archibald	OF148	150	.270	N.Y.	
		Wilson, James MGR. (2B1)	C78	93	.279	B	

WON 54
LOST 100
TG 154

NATIONAL LEAGUE — 1936.

FINISHED 8th (LAST)
PCT. .351

PHILADELPHIA

JAMES WILSON

WON	LOST	NAME	POS.	G.	BA	FROM	TO
		Allen, Ethan Nathan	OF	30	+.296	B	Chi
		Arnovich, Morris	OF	13	.313	A	
		Atwood, Wm. Franklin	C53	71	.302	A	
		Bashore, Walter Franklin	OF6	10	.200	A	C
1	4	Benge, Raymond Adelphia	P	15	+.000	xBos	C
0	0	Bertrand, Roman Mathias	P	1	.000	A	C
9	20	Bowman, Joseph Emil (Joe)	P40	44	.195	B	
0	0	Burkart, Elmer Robert	P	2	.000	A	
		Camilli, Adolph Louis	1B150	151	.315	B	
		Chiozza, Louis Peo	OF90	144	.297	B	
		(2B33 3B26)					
		Corbett, Eugene Louis	1B	6	.143	A	
2	4	Davis, Curtis Benton (Curt)	P	11	+.154	B	Chi
		Gomez, Jose Luis Rodriguez	2B71	108	.232	B	
		(SS40)					
		Grace, Robert Earl	C65	86	.249	Pitt	
0	0	Harris, Herbert	P	4	.000	A	C
		Haslin, Michael Joseph	2B12	16	+.344	B	Bos
		(Mickey) (3B5)					
		Holden, Joseph Francis		1	.000	B	C
5	7	Johnson, Sylvester W.	P	39	.250	B	
8	8	Jorgens, Orville Edward	P	39	.200	B	
0	5	Kelleher, Harold Joseph	P	14	.167	B	
		Klein, Chas. Herbert (Chuck)	OF	117	+.309	xChi	
1	5	Kowalik, Fabian Lorenz	P23	42	+.228	xChi	Bos
2	3	Moore, Fuel Walton	P	20	.222	N.Y.	C
		Moore, John Francis	OF112	124	.328	B	
1	1	Mulcahy, Hugh Noyes	P	3	.250	B	
		Norris, Leo John (2B38)	SS121	154	.265	A	
11	15	Passeau, Claude Wm.	P49	50	.282	Pitt	
0	0	Pezzullo, John	P	1	.000	B	C
		Sheerin, Chas. Joseph	2B17	39	.264	A	C
3	4	Sivess, Peter	P	17	.120	A	
		Sperry, Stanley Kenneth	2B15	20	.135	A	
		Sulik, Ernest Richard	OF105	122	.287	A	C

WON	LOST	NAME	POS.	G.	BA	FROM	TO
		Vergez, John Louis	3B12	15	+.275	B	StL
11	21	Walters, Wm. Henry Jr. (Bucky)	P40	64	.240	B	
		Watkins, George Archibald	OF17	19	+.243	B	Bkn
		Whitney, Arthur Carter	3B111	114	+.294	xBos	
		(Pinkey)					
		Wilson, James MGR.	C63	85	.278	B	
0	3	Zachary, Jonathan Thompson	P	8	+.333	xBkn	C
		Walton (Tom)					

WON 61
LOST 92*
TG 153

NATIONAL LEAGUE — 1937.

FINISHED 7th.
PCT. .399

PHILADELPHIA

JAMES WILSON

WON	LOST	NAME	POS.	G.	BA	FROM	TO
0	1	Allen, Robert Earl	P	3	.333	A	C
		Andrus, Wm. Morgan	3B1	3	.000	WashA31	C
		Arnovich, Morris	OF107	117	.290	B	
		Atwood, Wm. Franklin	C80	87	.244	B	
		Browne, James Wm. Earle	OF54	105	.292	Pitt	
		(1B23)					
0	0	Burkart, Elmer Robert	P	7	.000	B	
0	0	Burke, Robert James	P	2	.000	WashA35	C
		Camilli, Adolph Louis	1B	131	.339	B	
		Corbett, Eugene Louis (2B1)	3B3	7	.333	B	
0	0	Crawford, Chas. Lowrie	P	6	.000	A	C
		Gorman, Howard Paul	OF7	13	.211	A	
		Grace, Robert Earl	C64	80	.211	B	C
4	10	Johnson, Sylvester W.	P	32	.146	B	
3	4	Jorgens, Orville Edward	P	52	.143	B	C
2	4	Kelleher, Harold Joseph	P27	30	.176	B	
		Klein, Chas. Herbert (Chuck)	OF103	115	.325	B	
15	19	LaMaster, Wayne Lee	P50	51	.190	A	
		Martin, Hershel Ray	OF139	141	.283	A	
0	0	Masters, Walter Thomas	P	1	.000	WashA31	
		Moore, John Francis	OF74	96	.319	B	
8	18	Mulcahy, Hugh Noyes	P	56	.151	B	
		Norris, Leo John	2B74	116	.257	B	C
		(SS20 3B24)					
14	18	Passeau, Claude Wm.	P	50	.196	B	
0	1	Pettit, Leon Arthur	P	3	.000	WashA35	C
		Scharein, George Albert (Tom)	SS	146	.241	A	
1	1	Sivess, Peter	P	6	.000	B	
		Stephenson, Walter McQueen	C	10	.261	Chi	C
		Tauby, Fred Joseph	OF10	11	.000	ChiA35	C
14	15	Walters, Wm. Henry Jr.	P37	56	.277	B	
		(Bucky)					
		Whitney, Arthur Carter	3B130	138	.341	B	
		(Pinkey)					
		Wilson, James MGR.	C22	39	.276	B	
		Young, Delmar Edward	2B108	109	.194	A	

*One game lost by Forfeit.

WON 45 LOST 105 TG 150 — NATIONAL LEAGUE 1938. — FINISHED 8th (LAST) PCT. .300

PHILADELPHIA

JAMES WILSON — JOHN BERNARD LOBERT

WON	LOST	NAME	POS.	G.	BA	FROM	TO
		Arnovich, Morris	OF133	139	.275	B	
		Atwood, Wm. Franklin	C94	102	.196	B	
		Brack, Gilbert Herman (Gib)	OF68	72	+.287	xBkn	
		Browne, James Wm. Earle	1B16	21	.257	B	C
0	1	Burkart, Elmer Robert	P	2	.000	B	
4	8	Butcher, Albert Maxwell (Max)	P	12	+.257	xBkn	
		Clark, John Carroll	C29	52	.257	A	C
		Corbett, Eugene Louis	1B22	24	.080	B	C
		Davis, Virgil Lawrence (Spud)	C63	70	+.247	xCin	
		Feinberg, Edward (OF2)	SS4	10	.150	A	
		Gorman, Howard Paul		1	.000	B	C
1	8	Hallahan, Wm. Anthony (Wild Bill)	P	21	.192	Cin	C
0	0	Heusser, Edward Burlton	P	1	.000	StL36	
5	16	Hollingsworth, Albert Wayne (Al)	P	24	+.224	xCin	
2	7	Johnson, Sylvester W.	P	22	.034	B	
		Jordan, Baxter Byerly (1B17)	3B58	87	+.300	xCin	C
0	0	Kelleher, Harold Joseph	P	6	.500	B	C
		Klein, Chas. Herbert (Chuck)	OF119	129	.247	B	
4	7	LaMaster, Wayne Lee	P	18	+.409	B	Bkn
0	1	Lanning, Thomas Newton	P	3	1.000	A	C
		Martin, Hershel Ray	OF116	120	.298	B	
		Mueller, Emmett Joseph (3B21)	2B111	136	.250	A	
10	20	Mulcahy, Hugh Noyes	P46	47	.170	B	
11	18	Passeau, Claude Wm.	P44	45	.163	B	
		Pitko, Alexander	OF	7	.316	A	
		Rebel, Arthur Anthony	OF3	7	.222	A	
0	1	Reis, Thomas Edward	P	4	+.000	A	Bos
		Scharein, George Albert (Tom) (2B39)	SS77	117	.238	B	
3	6	Sivess, Peter	P	39	.188	B	C
1	4	Smith, Alfred John	P	37	.000	N.Y.	
		Stainback, George Tucker (Tuck)	OF25	30	+.259	xStL.	Bkn
		Stein, Justin Marion (2B3)	3B7	11	+.256	A	Cin
		Stoviak, Raymond Thomas	OF4	10	.000	A	C
4	8	Walters, Jr. Wm. Henry (Bucky)	P12	15	+.286	B	Cin
		Weintraub, Philip	1B98	100	.311	N.Y.	
		Whitney, Arthur Carter (Pinkey)	3B75	102	.277	B	
		Wilson, James MGR.	C	3	.000	B	
		Young, Delmar Edward (2B17)	SS87	108	.229	B	

WON 45 LOST 106 TG 151 — NATIONAL LEAGUE 1939. — FINISHED 8th (LAST) PCT. .298

PHILADELPHIA

JAMES THOMSON PROTHRO

WON	LOST	NAME	POS.	G.	BA	FROM	TO
		Arnovich, Morris	OF132	134	.324	B	
		Atwood, Wm. Franklin	C	4	.000	B	
		Bates, Hubert Edgar	OF14	15	.259	A	C
7	14	Beck, Walter Wm. (Boom-Boom)	P	34	.132	Bkn34	
		Benjamin, Alfred Stanley (3B5)	OF8	12	.140	A	
		Bolling, John Edward	1B48	69	.289	A	
		Brack, Gilbert Herman (Gib) (1B19)	OF48	91	.289	B	C
0	4	Bruner, Walter Roy	P	4	.111	A	
1	0	Burkart, Elmer Robert	P	5	1.000	B	C
2	13	Butcher, Albert Maxwell (Max)	P	19	+.184	B	Pitt
		Coble, David LaMar	C13	15	.280	A	C
		Davis, Virgil Lawrence (Spud)	C85	87	.307	B	
		Feinberg, Edward (SS1)	2B4	6	.222	B	C
		Gabrielson, Leonard Hilbourne	1B	5	.222	A	C
0	0	Hafey, Daniel Albert (P2)	OF13	18	+.176	xCin	C
3	7	Harrell, Raymond James (Ray)	P	22	+.115	xChi	
0	1	Henry, James Francis	P	9	.000	BosA37	C
10	14	Higbe, Walter Kirby	P	34	+.167	xChi	
0	0	Hoffman, Wm. Joseph	P	3	.000	A	C
1	9	Hollingsworth, Albert Wayne (Al)	P	15	+.100	B	Bkn
		Hughes, Roy John (Jeep)	2B	65	.228	xStLA	
8	8	Johnson, Sylvester W.	P	22	.152	B	
0	2	Kerksieck, Wayman Wm.	P23	25	.082	A	C
		Klein, Chas. Herbert (Chuck)	OF11	25	+.191	B	Pitt
		Kracher, Joseph Peter	C2	5	.200	A	C
		Letchas, Charlie	2B	12	.227	A	
		Martin, Hershel Ray	OF95	111	.282	B	
0	0	Marty, Joseph Anton (P1)	OF79	91	+.254	xChi	
		May, Merrill Glend (Pinky)	3B132	135	.287	A	
		Millies, Walter Louis	C	84	.234	WashA37	
		Mueller, Emmett Joseph (3B17 OF17)	2B51	115	.279	B	
9	16	Mulcahy, Hugh Noyes	P	38	.158	B	
2	4	Passeau, Claude Wm.	P	8	+.200	B	Chi
2	13	Pearson, Isaac Overton	P26	27	.054	A	
0	0	Poindexter, Chester Jennings	P	11	.200	BosA36	C
		Powers, Leslie Edwin	1B13	19	.346	N.Y.	C
		Scharein, George Albert (Ton)	SS117	118	.238	B	
0	1	Schott, Eugene Arthur	P	8	+.333	Cin	Bkn
		Scott, Legrant, Edward	OF55	76	.280	A	C
		Shilling, James Robert (SS3 3B2)	2B5	11	.303	xClevA	C
0	0	Smith, Alfred John	P	5	.000	B	
		Suhr, August Richard (Gus)	1B	60	+.318	xPitt	
		Warren, Benjamin Louis	C17	18	.232	A	
		Watwood, John Clifford	1B	2	.167	BosA33	C

WON	LOST	NAME	POS.	G.	BA	FROM	TO
		Whitney, Arthur Carter (Pinkey)	1B12	34	.187	B	C
		Young, Delmar Edward (2B17)	SS55	77	.263	B	

WON 50
LOST 103
TG 153

NATIONAL LEAGUE — FINISHED 8th (LAST)

1940. — PCT. .327

PHILADELPHIA

JAMES THOMSON PROTHRO

WON	LOST	NAME	POS.	G.	BA	FROM	TO
		Arnovich, Morris	OF37	39	+.199	B	Cin
		Atwood, Wm. Franklin	C69	78	.192	B	C
4	9	Beck, Walter Wm. (Boom-Boom)	P	29	.056	B	
		Benjamin, Alfred Stanley	OF2	8	.222	B	
		Berger, Walter Antone (Wally)	OF11	20	+.317	xCin	C
4	3	Blanton, Darrell Elijah (Cy)	P	13	.083	Pitt	
		Bragan, Robert Randall (3B2)	SS132	132	.222	A	
1	3	Brown, Lloyd Andrew	P	18	.077	ClevA37	C
0	0	Bruner, Walter Roy	P	2	.500	B	
		File, Lawrence Samuel (3B1)	SS6	7	.077	A	C
0	6	Frye, Chas. Andrew	P15	18	.263	A	C
14	19	Higbe, Walter Kirby	P	41	.165	B	
1	0	Hoerst, Frank Joseph	P	6	.000	A	
		Hughes, Roy John (Jeep)	2B	1	.000	B	
5	14	Johnson, Silas Kenneth	P	37	.140	St.L38	
2	2	Johnson, Sylvester W.	P	17	.000	B	C
		Jumonville, George Benedict	SS10	11	.088	A	
		Klein, Chas. Herbert (Chuck)	OF96	116	.218	Pitt	
		Levy, Edward Clarence		1	.000	A	
		Litwhiler, Daniel Webster	OF34	36	.345	A	
0	0	Mahan, Arthur Leo (P1)	1B145	146	.244	A	C
		Marnie, Harry Sylvester	2B	11	.176	A	
		Martin, Hershel Ray	OF23	33	.253	B	
		Marty, Joseph Anton	OF118	123	.270	B	
0	0	Masterson, Paul Nickalis	P	2	.000	A	
		May, Merrill Glend (Pinky) (SS1)	3B135	136	.293	B	
		Mazzera, Melvin Leonard (Mike) (1B11)	OF42	69	.237	StLA	C
		Millies, Walter Louis	C24	26	.070	B	
		Monchak, Alex (2B1)	SS9	19	.143	A	C
		Mueller, Emmett Joseph (1B2 3B13 OF31)	2B34	97	.247	B	
13	22	Mulcahy, Hugh Noyes	P36	37	.202	B	
3	14	Pearson, Isaac Overton	P	29	.205	B	
1	3	Podgatny, John Sigmund	P	4	.167	A	
		Rizzo, John Costa	OF91	103	+.292	xCin	
		Scharein, George Albert (Tom)	SS	7	.294	B	C
		Schulte, Herman Joseph (SS1)	2B119	120	.236	A	C
2	8	Smoll, Clyde Hetrick	P	33	.161	A	C
		Stewart, Walter Nesbitt Jr.	OF9	10	.129	A	C
		Suhr, August Richard (Gus)	1B7	10	.160	B	C
		Warren, Benjamin Louis (1B1)	C97	106	.246	B	

WON	LOST	NAME	POS.	G.	BA	FROM	TO
0	0	Wilson, Chas. Max	P	3	.000	A	
		Young, Delmar Edward (2B5)	SS6	15	.242	B	C

WON 43
LOST 111
TG 154

NATIONAL LEAGUE — FINISHED 8th (LAST)

1941. — PCT. .279

PHILADELPHIA

JAMES THOMSON PROTHRO

WON	LOST	NAME	POS.	G.	BA	FROM	TO
1	9	Beck, Walter Wm. (Boom-Boom)	P	34	.120	B	
		Benjamin, Alfred Stanley (1B8 2B2 3B1)	OF110	129	.235	B	
6	13	Blanton, Darrell Elijah (Cy)	P	28	.118	B	
		Bragan, Robert Randall (2B2 3B1)	SS154	154	.251	B	
0	3	Bruner, Walter Roy	P	13	.000	B	C
		Busby, Paul Muller	OF3	10	.313	A	
		Carlin, James Arthur (3B2)	OF9	16	.143	A	C
2	3	Crouch, Wm. Elmer	P	20	+.091	Bkn39	StL
		Etten, Nicholas Raymond Thomas	1B150	151	.311	PhilA39	
2	13	Grissom, Leo Theo (Lee)	P	29	+.167	xBkn	C
0	0	Harman, Wm. Bell (C5)	P5	15	.071	A	C
3	10	Hoerst, Frank Joseph	P	37	.182	B	
9	14	Hughes, Thomas Owen	P34	37	.200	A	
5	12	Johnson, Silas Kenneth	P	39	.149	B	
0	1	Jones, Dale Eldon	P	2	.333	A	C
		Jumonville, George Benedict (SS1)	2B1	6	.429	B	C
		Klein, Chas. Herbert (Chuck)	OF14	50	.123	B	
0	1	Lambert, Eugene Marion	P	2	.000	A	
		Litwhiler, Daniel Webster	OF150	151	.305	B	
		Livingston, Thompson Orville (1B1)	C71	95	.203	WashA38	
		Marnie, Harry Sylvester (SS16 3B3)	2B39	61	.241	B	
		Marty, Joseph Anton	OF132	137	.268	B	C
1	0	Masterson, Paul Nickalis	P	2	.000	B	
		May, Merrill Glend (Pinky)	3B140	142	.267	B	
1	5	Melton, Reuben Franklin	P	25	.105	A	
		Millies, Walter Louis	C	1	.000	B	C
		Mueller, Emmett Joseph (3B19 OF21)	2B29	93	.227	B	C
		Murtaugh, Daniel Edward (SS1)	2B85	85	.219	A	
		Nagel, Wm. Taylor (3B1 OF2)	2B12	17	.143	PhilA39	
4	14	Pearson, Isaac Overton	P	46	.125	B	
9	12	Podgajny, John Sigmund	P34	35	.129	B	
		Rizzo, John Costa (3B2)	OF62	99	.217	B	
0	1	Tamulis, Vitautis Casimirus (Vito)	P	6	+.000	Bkn	Bkn
		Warren, Benjamin Louis	C110	1wl	.121	B	

WON 42 | LOST 109 | TG 151

NATIONAL LEAGUE 1942.

FINISHED 8th (LAST) PCT. .278

PHILADELPHIA

JOHN BERNARD LOBERT

WON	LOST	NAME	POS.	G.	BA	FROM	TO
0	1	Beck, Walter Wm. (Boom-Boom)	P26	27	.333	B	
		Benjamin, Alfred Stanley (1B15)	OF45	78	.224	B	
0	4	Blanton, Darrell Elijah (Cy)	P	6	.125	B	C
		Bragan, Robert Randall (C22 2B4 3B3)	SS78	109	.218	B	
		Burich, Wm. Max (3B3)	SS19	25	.288	A	
		Culp, Benjamin Baldy	C	1	.000	A	
		Etten, Nicholas Raymond Thomas	1B135	139	.264	B	
0	0	Flitcraft, Hildreth Milton	P	3	.000	A	C
		Freed, Edward Chas.	OF11	13	.303	A	C
		Glossop, Alban (3B1)	2B118	121	.225	Bos40	
1	1	Hennessey, George	P	5	.000	StLA37	
		Hodge, Edward Burton	3B2	8	.182	A	C
4	16	Hoerst, Frank Joseph	P	33	.152	B	
12	18	Hughes, Thomas Owen	P40	42	.100	B	
8	19	Johnson, Silas Kenneth	P	39	.103	B	
		Klein, Chas. Herbert (Chuck)		14	.071	B	
		Koy, Ernest Anyz (Chief)	OF78	91	+.244	xCin	C
0	0	Lambert, Eugene Marion	P	1	.000	B	C
0	2	Lapihuska, Andrew	P	3	.286	A	
		Litwhiler, Daniel Webster	OF	151	.271	B	
		Livingston, Thompson Orville (1B6)	C78	89	.205	B	
		Marnie, Harry Sylvester (SS7 3B1)	2B11	24	.167	B	C
0	0	Masterson, Paul Nickalis	P	4	.000	B	C
		May, Merrill Glend (Pinky)	3B107	115	.238	B	
9	20	Melton, Reuben Franklin	P	42	.123	B	
		Murphy, Edward Joseph	1B8	13	.250	A	C
		Murtaugh, Daniel Edward (2B32 3B53)	SS60	144	.241	B	
1	3	Nahem, Samuel Ralph	P	35	.100	StL	
0	5	Naylor, Earl Eugene (P20)	OF34	76	.196	A	
		Northey, Ronald James	OF109	127	.251	A	
1	6	Pearson, Isaac Overton	P	35	.043	B	
		Peterman, Wm. David	C	1	1.000	A	C
6	14	Podgajny, John Sigmund	P43	44	.183	B	
		Waner, Lloyd James (Little Poison)	OF75	101	.261	Cin	
		Warren, Benjamin Louis (1B1)	C78	90	.209	B	

WON 64 | LOST 90 | TG 154

NATIONAL LEAGUE 1943.

FINISHED 7th. PCT. .416

PHILADELPHIA

STANLEY RAYMOND HARRIS FREDERICK LANDIS FITZSIMMONS

WON	LOST	NAME	POS.	G.	BA	FROM	TO
		Adams, Elvin Clark	OF107	111	+.256	xStL	
10	9	Barrett, Tracy Souter (Richard Oliver)	P	23	+.143	xChi	
0	0	Beck, Walter Wm. (Boom-Boom)	P	4	.500	B	
		Brewster, Chas. Lawrence	SS46	49	+.220	xCin	
		Busby, Paul Miller	OF10	26	.250	Phil41	C
2	7	Conger, Richard	P	13	.063	Pitt	C
		Culp, Benjamin Baldy	C	10	.208	B	
		Dahlgren, Ellsworth Tenney (Babe) (C1 SS25 3B35)	1B73	136	.288	Bkn	
		DelSavio, Garton Orville	SS	4	.091	A	C
1	1	Dietz, Lloyd Arthur	P	21	+.167	xPitt	C
0	0	Donahue, John Stephen Michael	P	2	.000	A	
0	0	Eyrich, George Lincoln	P	9	.000	A	C
		Finley, Robert Edward	C24	28	.259	A	
2	7	Fuchs, Chas. Thomas	P	17	.091	DetA	StLA
10	19	Gerheauser, Albert	P	38	.113	A	
		Hamrick, Raymond Bernard (SS12)	2B31	44	.200	A	
8	3	Johnson, Silas Kenneth	P	21	.182	B	
1	2	Karl, Anton Andrew	P9	11	.250	xBosA	
1	6	Kimball, Newel W.	P	34	+.188	xBkn	C
		Klein, Chas. Herbert (Chuck)		12	.100	B	
9	15	Kraus, John Wm.	P34	35	.067	A	
0	0	Lapihuska, Andrew	P	1	.000	B	C
1	5	Lee, Wm. Crutcher Jr. (Bill)	P	13	+.059	xChi	
		Litwhiler, Daniel Webster	OF34	36	+.258	B	StL
		Livingston, Thompson Orville (1B2)	C84	84	+.249	B	Chi
1	0	McKee, Rogers Hornsby	P	4	.200	A	
0	3	Matthewson, Dale Wesley	P11	12	.000	A	
		May, Merrill Glend (Pinky)	3B132	137	.282	B	C
		Moore, Dee Cee (1B1 3B5)	C21	37	+.239	xBkn	
		Murtaugh, Daniel Edward	2B113	113	.273	B	
		Naylor, Earl Eugene	OF	33	.175	B	
		Northey, Ronald James	OF145	147	.278	B	
		Padden, Thomas Francis	C16	17	.293	Pitt37	WashA
4	4	Podgajny, John Sigmund	P	13	+.250	B	Pitt
0	1	Raffensberger, Kenneth David	P	1	.000	Chi41	
14	8	Rowe, Lynwood Thomas (Schoolboy)	P27	82	.300	Bkn	
0	0	Salvo, Manuel	P	1	+.000	xBos (returned)	Bos
		Seminick, Andrew Wasil	C	22	.181	A	
		Stewart, Glen Weldon (C1 1B8 2B18)	SS77	110	.211	NY40	
		Triplett, Herman Coaker	OF90	105	+.272	xStL	
		Wasdell, James Chas. (OF56)	1B82	141	+.261	xPitt	
0	0	Webb, Wm. Frederick	P	1	.000	A	C

WON 61 LOST 92 TG 153

NATIONAL LEAGUE 1944.

FINISHED 8th (LAST) PCT. .399

PHILADELPHIA

FREDERICK LANDIS FITZSIMMONS

WON	LOST	NAME	POS.	G.	BA	FROM	TO
		Adams, Elvin Clark	OF	151	.283	B	
		Antolik, Joseph	C3	4	.333	A	C
12	18	Barrett, Tracy Souter (Richard Oliver)	P	37	.216	B	
		Caballero, Ralph Joseph	2B2	4	.000	A	
		Cieslak, Thaddeus Walter (OF5)	3B48	85	.245	A	C
1	1	Covington Chester Roger	P	19	.000	A	C
		Culp, Benjamin Baldy	C1	4	.000	B	C
0	2	Donahue, John Stephen Michael	P	6	.000	B	C
0	0	Fick, John Ralph	P	4	.000	A	C
		Finley, Robert Edward	C74	94	.249	B	C
8	16	Gerheauser, Albert	P30	32	.231	B	
		Goulish, Nicholas Edward		1	.000	A	
		Hamner, Granville Wilbur	SS	21	.247	A	
		Hamrick, Raymond Bernard	SS	74	.205	B	C
		Heltzel, Wm. Wade	SS10	11	.182	Bos	C
3	2	Karl, Anton Andrew	P38	42	.200	B	
1	5	Kennedy, Lloyd Vernon (Vern)	P12	14	.286	xClevA	
		Klein, Chas. Herbert (Chuck)	OF1	4	.143	B	C
10	11	Lee, Wm. Crutcher Jr. (Bill)	P	31	.194	B	
		Letchas, Charlie (SS29 3B32)	2B47	116	.238	WashA41	
0	0	Lucier, Louis Joseph	P	1	.000	xBosA	
		Lupien, Ulysses John	1B151	153	.283	BosA	
0	0	Matthewson, Dale Wesley	P	17	.333	B	C
		Mullen, Ford Parker (3B1)	2B114	118	.267	A	C
0	1	Mussill, Bernard James	P	16	.000	A	C
0	0	McKee, Rogers Hornsby	P	1	.000	B	C
		Northey, Ronald James	OF151	152	.288	B	
		Peacock, John Gaston (2B1)	C73	83	.225	xBosA	
13	20	Raffensberger, Kenneth David	P37	38	.138	B	
		Riley, Leon Francis	OF3	4	.083	A	C
0	0	Ripple, Chas. Dawson	P	1	1.000	A	
13	16	Schanz, Charley Murrell	P	40	.148	A	
		Seminick, Andrew Wasil (OF7)	C11	22	.222	B	
		Shea, Mervyn David John	C6	7	.267	DetA39	C
0	0	Shuman, Harry	P	18	.000	Pitt	C
		Stewart, Glen Weldon (2B1 SS32)	3B83	118	.220	B	C
		Triplett, Herman Coaker	OF44	84	.234	B	
		Tyson, Cecil Washington		1	.000	A	C
0	0	Verdel, Alfred Albert	P	1	.000	A	C
		Wasdell, James Chas. (1B4)	OF121	133	.277	B	

WON 46 LOST 108 TG 154

NATIONAL LEAGUE 1945.

FINISHED 8th (LAST) PCT. .299

PHILADELPHIA

FREDERICK LANDIS FITZSIMMONS WM. BENJAMIN CHAPMAN

WON	LOST	NAME	POS.	G.	BA	FROM	TO
		Adams, Elvin Clark	OF	14	+.232	B	StL
		Andrews, Stanley Joseph	C12	13	+.333	xBkn	C
		Antonelli, John Lawrence (1B1 2B23 SS1)	3B108	125	+.256	xStL	C
8	20	Barrett, Tracy Souter (Richard Oliver)	P	36	.145	B	C
		Caballero, Ralph Joseph	3B5	9	.000	B	
0	0	Chapman, Wm. Benjamin MGR. (P3 3B4)	OF10	24	+.314	xBkn	
0	0	Chetkovich, Mitchell	P	4	.000	A	C
2	1	Coffman, Samuel Richard (Dick)	P	14	.250	Bos40	C
		Crawford, Glenn Martin (2B14 SS34)	OF33	82	+.295	xStL	
		Daniels, Frederick Clinton (3B1)	2B75	76	.200	A	C
		DiMaggio, Vincent Paul	OF121	127	.257	Pitt	
		Dinges, Vance George Jr. (1B42)	OF65	109	.287	A	
		Flager, Walter Leonard (2B1)	SS48	49	+.250	xCin	C
1	0	Foxx, James Emory (Jimmie) (P9 3B14)	1B40	89	.268	Chi	C
		Goulish, Nicholas Edward	OF2	13	.273	B	C
0	1	Grate, Donald	P4	5	.000	A	
		Hamner, Granville Wilbur	SS13	14	.171	B	
		Hamner, Wesley Garvin (SS9 3B1)	2B21	32	.198	A	C
		Hasenmayer, Donald Irvin (3B1)	2B4	5	.111	A	
5	4	Judd, Thomas Wm. Oscar	P23	27	.267	xBosA	
8	8	Karl, Antone Andrew	P	67	.143	B	
0	3	Kennedy, Lloyd Vernon (Vern)	P12	13	+.182	B	Cin
4	9	Kraus, John Wm.	P	19	.120	Phil43	
3	6	Lee, Wm. Crutcher Jr. (Bill)	P	13	+.167	B	Bos
0	4	Leon, Isidore Juan	P	14	.111	A	C
0	1	Lucier, Louis Joseph	P	13	.250	B	C
		Lupien, Ulysses John	1B	15	.315	B	
		Mancuso, August Rodney (Gus)	C	70	.199	N.Y.	C
6	10	Mauney, Richard	P20	22	.146	A	
0	0	Monteagudo, Rene Miranda (P14)	OF35	114	.301	WashA	C
		Mott, Elisha Matthew (2B27 3B7)	SS63	90	.222	A	C
1	3	Mulcahy, Hugh Noyes	P	5	.000	Phil40	
		Peacock, John Gaston	C23	33	+.203	B	Bkn
		Picciuto, Nicholas Thomas (2B4)	3B30	36	.135	A	C

WON	LOST	NAME	POS.	G.	BA	FROM	TO
		Powell, Alvin Jacob (Jake)	OF44	48	.231	xWashA	C
0	3	Raffensberger, Kenneth David	P	5	.000	B	
0	1	Ripple, Chas. Dawson	P	4	.000	B	
4	15	Schanz, Charley Murrell	P	35	.154	B	
0	2	Scott, Marshall	P	8	.000	A	C
		Seminick, Andrew Wasil (3B4 OF1)	C70	80	.239	B	
		Spindel, Harold Stewart	C31	36	.230	StLA39	
4	10	Sproull, Chas. Wm.	P	34	.143	A	C
		Triplett, Herman Coaker	OF92	120	.240	B	C
		Walczak, Edwin Joseph (SS2)	2B17	20	.211	A	C
		Wasdell, James Chas. (1B63)	OF65	134	.300	B	
0	7	Wyatt, John Whitlow (Whit)	P	10	.125	Bkn	C

WON 69 NATIONAL LEAGUE FINISHED 5th.
LOST 85
TG 154 1946. PCT. .448

PHILADELPHIA

WM. BENJAMIN CHAPMAN

WON	LOST	NAME	POS.	G.	BA	FROM	TO
		Burich, Wm. Max	3B1	2	.000	Phil42	C
0	0	Chapman, Wm. Benjamin MGR.	P	1	.000	B	
		Crawford, Glenn Martin		1	.000	B	C
		DiMaggio, Vincent Paul	OF	6	+.211	B	N.Y.
		Dinges, Vance George Jr. (OF1)	1B26	50	.308	B	C
3	4	Donnelly, Sylvester Urban (Blix)	P	12	+.280	xStL	
		Ennis, Delmer	OF138	141	.313	A	
		Gilbert, Chas. Mader	OF69	88	+.242	xChi	
1	0	Grate, Donald	P	3	.000	B	C
		Hamner, Granville Wilbur	SS	2	.143	B	
		Hasenmayer, Donald Irvin	3B3	6	.083	B	C
		Hemsley, Ralston Burdett (Rollie)	C45	49	.223	NYA44	
0	1	Hodkey, Aloysius Joseph	P	2	.000	A	C
1	6	Hoerst, Frank Joseph	P	18	.059	Phil42	
		Hughes, Roy John (Jeep) (1B1 2B7 3B31)	SS34	89	.236	Chi	C
6	9	Hughes, Thomas Owen	P	29	.097	Phil42	
0	0	Humphries, John Wm.	P	10	.250	ChiA	C
0	0	Johnson, Silas Kenneth	P	1	+1.000	Phil43	Bos
11	12	Judd, Thomas Wm. Oscar	P30	46	.316	B	
4	3	Jurisich, Alvin Joseph	P	13	.130	StL	
3	7	Karl, Anton Andrew	P	39	.100	B	
0	1	Koecher, Richard Finlay	P	1	.000	A	
		Letchas, Charlie	2B4	6	.231	Phil44	C
0	1	Lopatka, Arthur Joseph	P	4	.000	StL	C
6	4	Mauney, Richard	P24	25	.167	B	
		McCormick, Frank Andrew (Buck)	1B134	135	.284	Cin	
0	0	Milnar, Albert Joseph	P	1	.000	xStLA	C
		Moore, Dee Cee (1B2)	C6	11	.077	Phil43	C
2	4	Mulcahy, Hugh Noyes	P	16	.188	B	
2	2	Mulligan, Richard Chas.	P	19	+.000	WashA41	Bos
		Murtaugh, Daniel Edward	2B	6	.211	Phil43	
		Newsome, Ashby Lamar (2B3 3B2)	SS107	112	.232	BosA	
		Northey, Ronald James	OF111	128	.249	Phil44	
		Novikoff, Louis	OF3	17	.304	Chi44	C
		O'Neil, John Francis	SS32	46	.266	A	C
1	0	Pearson, Isaac Overton	P	5	.200	Phil42	
1	2	Possehl, Louis Thomas	P	4	.000	A	
8	15	Raffensberger, Kenneth David	P	39	.167	B	
		Richardson, Kenneth Franklin	2B	6	.150	PhilA42	C
1	0	Ripple, Chas. Dawson	P	6	.000	B	C
11	4	Rowe, Lynwood Thomas (Schoolboy)	P17	30	.180	Phil43	
6	6	Schanz, Charley Murrell	P	32	.083	B	
		Seminick, Andrew Wasil	C118	124	.264	B	
		Spindel, Harold Stewart	C	1	.333	B	C
2	4	Stanceu, Chas.	P	14	.000	xNYA	C
		Tabor, James Reubin	3B	124	.268	BosA44	
		Verban, Emil Matthew	2B	138	+.275	xStL	
		Wasdell, James Chas. (1B2)	OF11	26	.255	B	ClevA
		Wyrostek, John Barney	OF	145	.281	Pitt43	

WON 62 NATIONAL LEAGUE FINISHED 7th.
LOST 92 (TIED WITH PITTSBURGH)
TG 154 1947. PCT. .403

PHILADELPHIA

WM. BENJAMIN CHAPMAN

WON	LOST	NAME	POS.	G.	BA	FROM	TO
		Adams, Elvin Clark	OF51	69	.247	B	C
		Albright, John Harold	SS33	41	.232	A	C
		Caballero, Ralph Joseph (3B1)	2B2	2	.143	Phil45	
4	6	Donnelly, Sylvester Urban (Blix)	P	38	.063	B	
		Ennis, Delmer	OF135	139	.275	B	
		Etten, Nicholas Raymond Thomas	1B11	14	.244	NYA	C
		Finney, Louis Klopsche		4	.000	StLA	C
		Gilbert, Chas. Mader	OF37	83	.237	B	C
		Hamner, Granville Wilbur	SS	2	.286	B	
		Handley, Lee Elmer (Jeep) (2B3 SS1)	3B83	101	.253	Pitt	C
7	10	Heintzelman, Kenneth Alphonse	P	24	+.116	xPitt	
		Hemsley, Ralston Burdett (Rollie)	C	2	.333	B	C
1	1	Hoerst, Frank Joseph	P	4	.500	B	C
4	11	Hughes, Thomas Owen	P29	32	.050	B	
		Jones, Willie Edward	3B17	18	.226	A	

WON	LOST	NAME	POS.	G.	BA	FROM	TO
4	15	Judd, Thomas Wm. Oscar	P32	44	.188	B	
1	7	Jurisich, Alvin Joseph	P	34	.032	B	C
0	2	Koecher, Richard Finlay	P	3	.000	B	
		Lakeman, Albert Wesley (C23)	1B29	55	+.159	xCin	
		LaPointe, Ralph John	SS54	56	.308	A	
17	12	Leonard, Emil John (Dutch)	P	32	.175	WashA	
		Levan, Jesse Roy	OF	2	.444	A	
0	0	Mauney, Richard	P9	15	.000	B	C
		McCormick, Frank Andrew (Buck)	1B12	15	+.225	B	Bos
		Newsome, Ashby Lamar (2B6 3B3)	SS85	95	.229	B	C
		Northey, Ronald James	OF	13	+.255	B	StL
		Padgett, Donald Wilson (Don)	C39	75	.316	Bos	
		Poland, Hugh Reid	C2	4	+.000	Bos	Cin
0	0	Possehl, Louis Thomas	P	2	.000	B	
2	6	Raffensberger, Kenneth David	P	10	+.267	B	Cin
14	10	Rowe, Lynwood Thomas (Schoolboy)	P31	43	.278	B	
2	4	Schanz, Charley Murrell	P	34	.148	B	
5	8	Schmidt, Frederick Albert	P	29	+.050	xStL	Chi
		Schultz, Howard Henry	1B	114	+.223	xBkn	
		Seminick, Andrew Wasil	C107	111	.252	B	
1	0	Simmons, Curtis Thomas	P	1	.500	A	
0	0	Spragins, Homer Franklin	P	4	.000	A	C
		Tabor, James Reubin	3B67	75	.235	B	C
		Verban, Emil Matthew	2B	155	.285	B	
		Walker, Harry Wm. (1B4)	OF127	130	+.371	xStL	
		Wyrostek, John Barney	OF126	128	.273	B	

WON 66 NATIONAL LEAGUE FINISHED 6th.
LOST 88
TG 154 1948. PCT. .429

PHILADELPHIA

WM. BENJAMIN CHAPMAN ALLEN LINDSAY COOKE EDWIN MILBY SAWYER

WON	LOST	NAME	POS.	G.	BA	FROM	TO
		Ashburn, Richie	OF116	117	.333	A	
0	1	Bicknell, Chas. Stephen	P	17	.000	A	
		Blatnik, John Louis	OF105	121	.260	A	
		Caballero, Ralph Joseph (2B23)	3B79	113	.245	B	
5	7	Donnelly, Sylvester Urban (Blix)	P	26	.222	B	
8	10	Dubiel, Walter John	P37	38	.167	NYA45	
		Ennis, Delmer	OF151	152	.290	B	
2	0	Erickson, Paul Wakefield	P	4	+.143	xChi	N.Y.
0	0	Grasmick, Louis Junior	P	2	1.000	A	C
		Haas, Berthold John (Bert) (1B35)	3B54	95	.282	Cin	
		Hamner, Granville Wilbur (SS37 3B3)	2B87	129	.260	B	
6	11	Heintzelman, Kenneth Alphonse	P	27	.135	B	

WON	LOST	NAME	POS.	G.	BA	FROM	TO
3	2	Heusser, Edward Burlton	P	33	.158	Cin46	C
		Jones, Willie Edward	3B	17	.333	B	
0	2	Judd, Thomas Wm. Oscar	P	4	.167	B	C
0	1	Koecher, Richard Finlay	P	3	.000	B	C
1	0	Konstanty, Casimer James (Jim)	P	6	.000	Bos46	
0	0	Lakeman, Albert Wesley (P1)	C22	32	.162	B	
12	17	Leonard, Emil John (Dutch)	P	34	.145	B	
		Lopata, Stanley Edward	C4	6	.133	A	
		Mayo, John Lewis	OF11	12	.229	A	
		Miller, Edward Robert	SS122	130	.246	Cin	
3	3	Nahem, Samuel Ralph	P	28	.154	Phil42	C
		Padgett, Donald Wilson (Don)	C19	36	.230	B	C
1	1	Possehl, Louis Thomas	P3	4	.250	B	
0	0	Porto, Alfred	P	3	.000	A	C
7	9	Roberts, Robin Evan	P20	21	.250	A	
10	10	Rowe, Lynwood Thomas (Schoolboy)	P30	31	.192	B	
		Rowell, Carvel Wm. (2B12 OF17)	3B18	77	.240	Bos	C
		Schultz, Howard Henry	1B3	6	+.077	B	Cin
		Seminick, Andrew Wasil	C124	125	.225	B	
7	13	Simmons, Curtis Thomas	P	31	.137	B	
		Sisler, Richard Allan	1B120	121	.274	StL	
0	1	Strincevich, Nicholas Mihailovich	P	6	+.000	xPitt	C
1	0	Thompson, John Samuel	P	2	.000	A	
		Verban, Emil Matthew	2B54	55	+.231	B	Chi
		Wagner, Harold Edward	C1	3	.000	xDetA	
		Walker, Harry Wm. (1B4 3B1)	OF81	112	.292	B	

WON 81 NATIONAL LEAGUE FINISHED 3rd.
LOST x73
TG 154 1949. PCT. .526

PHILADELPHIA

EDWIN MILBY SAWYER

WON	LOST	NAME	POS.	G.	BA	FROM	TO
		Ashburn, Richie	OF	154	.284	B	
0	0	Bicknell, Chas. Stephen	P	13	.000	B	C
		Blatnik, John Louis	OF2	6	.125	B	
		Blattner, Robert Garnett (SS1 3B12)	2B15	64	.247	N.Y.	C
12	12	Borowy, Henry Ludwig	P	28	.213	Chi	
		Caballero, Ralph Joseph (SS1)	2B21	29	.279	B	
2	1	Donnelly, Sylvester Urban (Blix)	P	23	.174	B	
		Ennis, Delmer	OF	154	.302	B	
		Glynn, Wm. Vincent	1B1	8	.200	A	
		Goliat, Mike Mitchel (1B5)	2B50	55	.212	A	
		Haas, Berthold John (Bert)		2	+.000	B	N.Y.
		Hamner, Granville Wilbur	SS	154	.263	B	

WON	LOST	NAME	POS.	G.	BA	FROM	TO
17	10	Heintzelman, Kenneth Alphonse	P	33	.157	B	
		Hollmig, Stanley Ernest	OF66	81	.255	A	
		Jones, Willie Edward	3B145	149	.245	B	
9	5	Konstanty, Casimer James (Jim)	P	53	.176	B	
		Lopata, Stanley Edward	C58	83	.271	B	
		Mayo, John Lewis	OF25	45	.128	B	
17	8	Meyer, Russell Chas.	P	37	.143	Chi	
		Miller, Edward Robert (SS1)	2B82	85	.207	B	
0	0	Miller, Robert John	P	3	.000	A	
		Nicholson, Wm. Beck	OF91	98	.234	Chi	
15	15	Roberts, Robin Evan	P	43	.075	B	
3	7	Rowe, Lynwood Thomas (Schoolboy)	P	23	.235	B	C
		Sanicki, Edward Robert	OF6	7	.231	A	
		Seminick, Andrew Wasil	C98	109	.243	B	
		Silvestri, Kenneth Joseph (2B1 SS1)	C1	4	.000	NYA47	
4	10	Simmons, Curtis Thomas	P38	39	.171	B	
		Sisler, Richard Allan	1B96	121	.289	B	
1	3	Thompson, John Samuel	P8	9	.182	B	
1	1	Trinkle, Kenneth Wayne	P	42	.000	N.Y.	C
		Wagner, Harold Edward	C	1	.000	B	C
		Waitkus, Edward Stephen	1B	54	.306	Chi	

x-One game lost by forfeit.

WON 91 — NATIONAL LEAGUE — FINISHED 1st.
LOST 63
TG 154 — 1950. — PCT. .591

PHILADELPHIA

EDWIN MILBY SAWYER

WON	LOST	NAME	POS.	G.	BA	FROM	TO
		Ashburn, Richie	OF147	151	.303	B	
		Blatnik, John Louis	OF1	4	+.250	B	St.L.
		Bloodworth, James Henry (1B7 3B2)	2B27	54	+.229	xCin	
0	0	Borowy, Henry Ludwig	P	3	+.000	B	Pitt
0	0	Brittin, John Albert	P	3	.000	A	
		Caballero, Ralph Joseph (SS2 3B4)	2B5	46	.167	B	
1	0	Candini, Mario Cain	P	18	.167	WashA	
8	6	Church, Emory Nicholas	P31	39	.182	A	
2	4	Donnelly, Sylvester Urban (Blix)	P	14	.200	B	
		Ennis, Delmer	OF149	153	.311	B	
		Goliat, Mike Mitchel	2B	145	.234	B	
		Hamner, Granville Wilbur	SS	157	.270	B	
3	9	Heintzelman, Kenneth Alphonse	P	23	.053	B	
		Hollmig, Stanley Ernest	OF3	11	.250	B	
4	1	Johnson, Kenneth Carstensen	P14	21	+.158	xSt.L.	
		Jones, Willie Edward	3B	157	.267	B	
16	7	Konstanty, Casimer James (Jim)	P	74	.108	B	
		Lopata, Stanley Edward	C51	58	.209	B	
		Mayo, John Lewis	OF15	18	.222	B	
9	11	Meyer, Russell Chas.	P	32	.140	B	
11	6	Miller, Robert John	P	35	.180	B	
		Nicholson, Wm. Beck	OF15	41	.224	B	
0	0	Ridzik, Stephen George	P	1	.000	A	
20	11	Roberts, Robin Evan	P	40	.118	B	
		Seminick, Andrew Wasil	C124	130	.288	B	
		Silvestri, Kenneth Joseph	C9	11	.250	B	
17	8	Simmons, Curtis Thomas	P	34	.156	B	
		Sisler, Richard Allan	OF137	141	.296	B	
0	0	Stuffel, Paul Harrington	P	3	.000	A	
0	0	Thompson, John Samuel	P	2	.000	B	
		Waitkus, Edward Stephen	1B	154	.284	B	
		Whitman, Dick Corwin	OF32	75	.250	B	

WON 73 — NATIONAL LEAGUE — FINISHED 5th.
LOST 81
TG 154 — 1951. — PCT. .474

PHILADELPHIA

EDWIN MILBY SAWYER

WON	LOST	NAME	POS.	G.	BA	FROM	TO
		Ashburn, Richie	OF	154	.344	B	
		Bloodworth, James Henry (1B6)	2B8	21	.143	B	C
0	0	Brittin, John Albert	P	3	.000	B	C
		Brown, Thomas Michael (1B12 2B14 3B1)	OF32	78	+.219	xBkn	
		Caballero, Ralph Joseph (SS1 3B3)	2B54	84	.186	B	
1	0	Candini, Mario Cain	P	15	.333	B	C
15	11	Church, Emory Nicholas	P38	39	.256	B	
		Clark, Melvin Earl	OF7	10	.323	A	
1	1	Cristante, Leo Dante	P	10	.167	A	C
1	0	Drews, Karl August	P	5	.250	StLA49	
		Ennis, Delmer	OF135	144	.267	B	
		Goliat, Mike Mitchel (3B2)	2B37	41	.225	B	StLA
		Hamner, Granville Wilbur	SS	150	.255	B	
3	1	Hansen, Andrew Viggo Jr.	P	24	.333	N.Y.	
6	12	Heintzelman, Kenneth Alphonse	P	35	.107	B	
		Hollmig, Stanley Ernest		2	.000	B	C
5	8	Johnson, Kenneth Carstensen	P20	36	.143	B	
		Jones, Willie Edward	3B147	148	.285	B	
2	3	Jordan, Niles Chapman	P	5	.077	A	
4	11	Konstanty, Casimer James	P	58	.158	B	
		Lopata, Stanley Edward	C1	3	.000	B	
		Mayo, John Lewis	OF5	9	.143	B	
8	9	Meyer, Russell Chas.	P	28	.104	B	
2	1	Miller, Robert John	P	17	.429	B	
		Nicholson, Wm. Beck	OF41	85	.241	B	
		Pellagrini, Edward Chas. (SS8 3B6)	2B53	86	.234	StLA49	

WON	LOST	NAME	POS.	G.	BA	FROM	TO
0	1	Possehl, Louis Thomas	P	2	.000	Phi148	
21	15	Roberts, Robin Evan	P	44	.172	B	
		Sanicki, Edward Robert	OF10	13	.500	Phil49	C
		Seminick, Andrew Wasil	C91	101	.227	B	
		Silvestri, Kenneth Joseph (2B1)	C3	4	.222	B	C
		Sisler, Richard Allan	OF111	125	.287	B	
4	8	Thompson, John Samuel	P29	30	.103	B	C
		Waitkus, Edward Stephen	1B144	145	.257	B	
		Whitman, Dick Corwin	OF6	19	.118	B	C
		Wilber, Delbert Quentin	C73	84	.278	StL49	
		Young, Richard Ennis	2B	15	.235	A	

WON 87 — NATIONAL LEAGUE — FINISHED 4th.
LOST 67
TG 154 — 1952. — PCT. .565

PHILADELPHIA

EDWIN MILBY SAWYER — STEPHEN FRANCIS O'NEILL

WON	LOST	NAME	POS.	G.	BA	FROM	TO
		Ashburn, Richie	OF	154	.282	B	
		Brown, Thomas Michael (OF3)	1B3	18	+.160	B	Chi
		Burgess, Forrest Harrill	C104	110	.296	Chi	
		Caballero, Ralph Joseph (2B7 3B7)	SS8	35	.238	B	C
0	0	Church, Emory Nicholas	P	2	+.000	B	Cin
		Clark, Melvin Earl (3B1)	OF38	47	.335	B	
14	15	Drews, Karl August	P	33	.110	B	
		Ennis, Delmer	OF149	151	.289	B	
2	7	Fox, Howard Francis	P	13	.048	Cin	
		Hamner, Granville Wilbur	SS	151	.275	B	
5	6	Hansen, Andrew Viggo	P	43	.182	B	
1	3	Heintzelman, Kenneth Alphonse	P	23	.000	B	C
		Jones, Vernal LeRoy	1B	8	.167	StL	
		Jones, Willie Edward	3B	147	.250	B	
5	3	Konstanty, Casimer James	P	42	.071	B	
		Lohrke, Jack Wayne (2B1 3B3)	SS5	25	.207	N.Y.	
		Lopata, Stanley Edward	C55	57	.274	B	
		Mayo, John Lewis (1B6)	OF27	50	.244	B	
13	14	Meyer, Russell Chas.	P	37	.089	B	
0	1	Miller, Robert John	P	3	.000	B	
		Nicholson, Wm. Beck	OF19	55	.273	B	
0	0	Peterson, Kent Franklin	P	3	.000	Cin	
0	1	Possehl, Louis Thomas	P	4	.000	B	C
4	2	Ridzik, Stephen George	P	24	.136	Phil50	
28	7	Roberts, Robin Evan	P	39	.125	B	
		Ryan, Cornelius Joseph	2B	154	.241	Cin	
14	8	Simmons, Curtis Thomas	P	28	.164	Phil50	
1	0	Stuffel, Paul Harrington	P	2	.000	Phil50	
		Waitkus, Edward Stephen	1B	146	.289	B	
		Wilber, Delbert Quentin		2	.000	B	BosA
		Wyrostek, John Barney	OF88	98	+.274	xCin	
		Young, Richard Ennis	2B2	5	.222	B	C

WON 83 — NATIONAL LEAGUE — FINISHED 3rd.
LOST 71 — (TIED WITH ST. LOUIS)
TG 154 — 1953. — PCT. .539

PHILADELPHIA

STEPHEN FRANCIS O'NEILL

WON	LOST	NAME	POS.	G.	BA	FROM	TO
		Ashburn, Richie	OF	156	.330	B	
		Burgess, Forrest Harrill	C95	102	.292	B	
		Clark, Melvin Earl	OF51	60	.298	B	
9	10	Drews, Karl August	P	47	.119	B	
		Ennis, Delmer	OF150	152	.285	B	
		Glaviano, Thomas Giatano (2B12 SS1)	3B14	53	.203	StL q	C
		Hamner, Granville Wilbur (SS71)	2B93	154	.276	B	
0	2	Hansen, Andrew Viggo	P	30	.286	B	C
		Jones, Willie Edward	3B147	149	.225	B	
		Kazanski, Theodore Stanley	SS	95	.217	A	
3	3	Kipper, Thornton John	P	20	.091	A	
14	10	Konstanty, Casimer James	P	48	.220	B	
1	1	Lindell, John Harlan (OF2)	P5	11	+.389	xPitt	
		Lohrke, Jack Wayne (SS2 3B1)	2B2	12	.154	B	C
		Lopata, Stanley Edward	C80	81	.239	B	
		Mayo, John Lewis	OF1	5	.000	B	C
8	9	Miller, Robert John	P	35	.182	B	
		Nicholson, Wm. Beck	OF12	38	.210	B	C
		Palys, Stanley Francis	OF1	2	.000	A	
0	1	Peterson, Kent Franklin	P	15	.000	B	C
0	0	Qualters, Thomas Francis	P	1	.000	A	
9	6	Ridzik, Stephen George	P	42	.194	B	
23	16	Roberts, Robin Evan	P	44	.179	B	
		Ryan, Cornelius Joseph (1B2)	2B65	90	.296	B	ChiA
16	13	Simmons, Curtis Thomas	P	32	.140	B	
0	0	Stuffel, Paul Harrington	P	2	.000	B	C
		Torgeson, Clifford Earl	1B105	111	.274	Bos	
		Waitkus, Edward Stephen	1B59	81	.291	B	
		Wyrostek, John Barney	OF110	125	.271	B	

WON 75* — NATIONAL LEAGUE — FINISHED 4th.
LOST 79
TG 154 — 1954. — PCT. .487

PHILADELPHIA

STEPHEN FRANCIS O'NEILL — TERRY BUFORD MOORE

WON	LOST	NAME	POS.	G.	BA	FROM	TO
		Ashburn, Richie	OF	153	.313	B	
		Baker, Floyd Wilson (2B2)	3B7	23	.227	xBosA	
		Burgess, Forrest Harrill	C91	108	.368	B	
		Clark, Melvin Earl	OF63	83	.240	B	
		Command, James Dalton	3B6	9	.222	A	

WON	LOST	NAME	POS.	G.	BA	FROM	TO
10	20	Dickson, Murry Monroe	P	40	.190	Pitt	
1	0	Drews, Karl August	P	8	+.000	B	Cin
		Ennis, Delmer (1B1)	OF142	145	.261	B	
1	2	Greenwood, Robert Chandler	P11	12	.000	A	
		Hamner, Granville Wilbur (SS1)	2B152	152	.299	B	
		Jok, Stanley Edward		3	.000	A	ChiA
		Jones, Willie Edward	3B141	142	.271	B	
		Kazanski, Theodore Stanley	SS38	39	.135	B	
0	0	Kipper, Thornton John	P	11	.000	B	
2	3	Konstanty, Casimer James	P	33	.000	B	NYA
		Lindell, John Harlan		7	.200	B	C
		Lopata, Stanley Edward (1B1)	C75	86	.290	B	
		Micelotta, Robert Peter	SS1	13	.000	A	
7	9	Miller, Robert John	P	30	.160	B	
		Morgan, Robert Morris (2B5 3B8)	SS129	135	.262	Bkn	
1	1	Mrozinski, Ronald Frank	P	15	.083	A	
		Niarhos, Constantine Gregory	C	3	.200	BosA	
		Palys, Stanley Francis	OF1	2	.250	B	
1	1	Penson, Paul Eugene	P	5	.000	A	C
4	5	Ridzik, Stephen George	P	35	.227	B	
23	15	Roberts, Robin Evan	P	45	.123	B	
		Schell, Clyde Daniel	OF69	92	.283	A	
14	15	Simmons, Curtis Thomas	P34	38	.176	B	
		Torgeson, Clifford Earl	1B133	135	.271	B	
10	8	Wehmeier, Herman Ralph	P	25	+.120	xCin	
		Wyrostek, John Barney (1B22)	OF55	92	.239	B	C

*Won one game by forfeit vs. St. Louis July 18 (2nd game).

WON 77 — NATIONAL LEAGUE — FINISHED 4th.
LOST 77
TG 154 — 1955. — PCT. .500

PHILADELPHIA

EDWARD MAYO SMITH

WON	LOST	NAME	POS.	G.	BA	FROM	TO
		Ashburn, Richie	OF	140	.338	B	
		Baker, Floyd Wilson	3B1	5	.000	B	C
		Blaylock, Marvin Edward (OF6)	1B77	113	.208	NY50	
		Bowman, Robert LeRoy	OF2	3	.000	A	
		Burgess, Forrest Harrill	C6	7	+.190	B	Cin
		Clark, Melvin Earl	OF8	10	.156	B	
0	3	Cole, David Bruce	P	7	.200	Chi	C
		Command, James Dalton		5	.000	B	C
12	11	Dickson, Murry Monroe	P	36	.220	B	
		Easton, John David		1	.000	A	
		Ennis, Delmer	OF145	146	.296	B	
		Gorbous, Glen Edward	OF57	91	+.237	xCin	
		Greengrass, James Raymond (3B2)	OF83	94	+.272	xCin	

WON	LOST	NAME	POS.	G.	BA	FROM	TO
0	0	Greenwood, Robert Chaldler	P	1	.000	B	C
		Hamner, Granville Wilbur (SS32)	2B82	104	.257	B	
		Jones, Willie Edward	3B	146	.258	B	
		Kazanski, Theodore Stanley (3B4)	SS4	9	.083	B	
0	1	Kipper, Thornton John	P	24	.333	B	C
1	0	Kuzava, Robert LeRoy	P	17	.143	xBaltA	
		Lopata, Stanley Edward (1B24)	C66	99	.271	B	
0	1	Lovenguth, Lynn Richard	P	14	.000	A	
		Lowrey, Harry Lee (1B1 2B2)	OF28	54	.189	StL	C
6	11	Meyer, John Robert	P	50	.100	A	
		Micelotta, Robert Peter	SS2	4	.000	B	C
8	4	Miller, Robert John	P	40	.278	B	
		Morgan, Robert Morris (1B1 SS41 3B6)	2B88	136	.232	B	
0	2	Mrozinski, Ronald Frank	P	22	.000	B	C
4	3	Negray, Ronald Alvin	P	19	.000	Bkn52	
		Niarhos, Constantine Gregory	C	7	.111	B	C
0	2	Owens, James Philip	P	3	.000	A	
		Palys, Stanley Francis	OF	15	+.288	B	Cin
0	1	Ridzik, Stephen George	P	3	+.000	B	Cin
23	14	Roberts, Robin Evan	P41	51	.252	B	
5	3	Rogovin, Saul Walter	P12	13	.250	xBaltA	
		Schell, Clyde Daniel		2	.000	B	C
		Seminick, Andrew Wasil	C88	93	+.246	xCin	
8	8	Simmons, Curtis Thomas	P25	27	.174	B	
		Smalley, Roy Frederick (2B1 3B1)	SS87	92	.196	Mil	
0	1	Spring, Jack Russell	P	2	.000	A	
		Torgeson, Clifford Earl	1B43	47	.267	B	DetA
		Van Dusen, Frederick Wm.	–	1	.000	A	C
		Waitkus, Edward Stephen	1B31	33	.280	xBaltA	C
10	12	Wehmeier, Herman Ralph	P31	34	.278	B	
		Westlake, James Patrick		1	.000	A	C

WON 71 — NATIONAL LEAGUE — FINISHED 5th.
LOST 83
TG 154 — 1956. — PCT. .461

PHILADELPHIA

EDWARD MAYO SMITH

WON	LOST	NAME	POS.	G.	BA	FROM	TO
		Ashburn, Richie	OF	154	.303	B	
		Baumholtz, Frank Conrad	OF15	76	.270	Chi	
		Blaylock, Marvin Edward (OF1)	1B124	136	.254	B	
		Bouchee, Edward Francis	1B6	9	.273	A	
		Bowman, Robert LeRoy	OF5	6	.188	B	
		Burk, Mack Edwin	C1	15	1.000	A	
0	3	Dickson, Murry Monroe	P	3	+.333	B	StL
		Ennis, Delmer	OF	153	.260	B	

WON	LOST	NAME	POS.	G.	BA	FROM	TO
0	1	Farrell, Richard Joseph	P	1	.000	A	
0	2	Flowers, Bennett	P	32	+.000	xStL	C
		Gorbous, Glen Edward	OF8	15	.182	B	
		Greengrass, James Raymond	OF62	86	.205	B	C
12	8	Haddix, Harvey	P31	46	+.237	xStL	
0	1	Hamner, Granville Wilbur (P3 2B11)	SS110	122	.224	B	
		Hemus, Solomon Joseph (3B1)	2B49	78	+.289	xStL	
		Jones, Willie Edward	3B	149	.277	B	
		Kazanski, Theodore Stanley (SS1)	2B116	117	.211	B	
0	0	LiPetri, Michael Angelo	P	6	.000	A	
		Lonnett, Joseph Paul	C7	16	.182	A	
		Lopata, Stanley Edward (1B39)	C102	146	.267	B	
7	11	Meyer, John Robert	P	41	.200	B	
3	6	Miller, Robert John	P	49	.091	B	
5	8	Miller, Stuart Leonard	P24	29	+.160	xStL	
		Morgan, Robert Morris (2B3)	3B5	8	+.200	B	StL
2	3	Negray, Ronald Alvin	P	39	.429	B	
0	4	Owens, James Philip	P	10	.167	B	
0	0	Pillette, Duane Xavier	P	20	.000	BaltA	C
19	18	Roberts, Robin Evan	P	43	.200	B	
7	6	Rogovin, Saul Walter	P	22	.111	B	
0	0	Ross, Floyd Robert	P	3	.000	WashA51	C
1	0	Sanford, John Stanley	P	3	.333	A	
		Seminick, Andrew Wasil	C54	60	.199	B	
15	10	Simmons, Curtis Thomas	P33	39	.236	B	
		Smalley, Roy Frederick	SS60	65	.226	B	
		Valo, Elmer Wm.	OF87	98	.289	xKCA	
0	2	Wehmeier, Herman Ralph	P	3	+.000	B	StL
		Westlake, Waldon Thomas		5	.000	BaltA	C

WON 77 NATIONAL LEAGUE FINISHED 5th.
LOST 77
TG 154 1957. PCT. .500

PHILADELPHIA

EDWARD MAYO SMITH

WON	LOST	NAME	POS.	G.	BA	FROM	TO
		Anderson, Harry Walter	OF109	118	.268	A	
		Ashburn, Richie	OF	156	.297	B	
		Baumholtz, Frank Conrad		2	.000	B	C
		Blaylock, Marvin Edward (OF1)	1B12	37	.154	B	C
		Bouchee, Edward Francis	1B	154	.293	B	
		Bowman, Robert LeRoy	OF81	99	.266	B	
4	8	Cardwell, Donald Eugene	P	30	.200	A	
10	2	Farrell, Richard Joseph	P	52	.111	B	
		Fernandez, Humberto Perez	SS	149	.262	Bkn	
		Gorbous, Glen Edward		3	.500	B	C
4	4	Hacker, Warren Louis	P	20	+.261	xCin	
10	13	Haddix, Harvey	P27	41	.309	B	
0	0	Hamner, Granville Wilbur (P1 SS5)	2B125	133	.227	B	
		Harmon, Chas. Byron (1B2 3B5)	OF25	57	+.256	xStL	C
5	1	Hearn, James Tolbert	P	36	.000	N.Y.	
		Hemus, Solomon Joseph	2B24	70	.185	B	
		Jones, Willie Edward	3B126	133	.218	B	
		Kazanski, Theodore Stanley (2B22 SS3)	3B36	62	.265	B	
		Kennedy, John Irvin	3B2	5	.000	A	C
		Landrum, Donald Leroy	OF	2	.143	A	
		Lonnett, Joseph Paul	C65	67	.169	B	
		Lopata, Stanley Edward	C108	116	.237	B	
0	2	Meyer, John Robert	P	19	.167	B	
2	5	Miller, Robert John	P	32	.250	B	
1	1	Morehead, Seth Marvin	P	34	.000	A	
		Morgan, Robert Morris	2B1	2	+.000	B	Chi
		Northey, Ronald James		33	.269	xChiA	C
0	0	Qualters, Thomas Francis	P	6	.000	Phi153	
		Repulski, Eldon John	OF130	134	.260	StL	
10	22	Roberts, Robin Evan	P	39	.163	B	
0	0	Rogovin, Saul Walter	P	4	.000	B	C
19	8	Sanford, John Stanley	P	33	.169	B	
		Seminick, Andrew Wasil	C	8	.091	B	C
12	11	Simmons, Curtis Thomas	P32	38	.239	B	
		Smalley, Roy Frederick	SS20	28	.161	B	

WON 69 NATIONAL LEAGUE FINISHED 8th (LAST)
LOST 85
TG 154 1958. PCT. .448

PHILADELPHIA

EDWARD MAYO SMITH EDWIN MILBY SAWYER

WON	LOST	NAME	POS.	G.	BA	FROM	TO
		Anderson, Harry Walter (1B49)	OF87	140	.301	B	
0	0	Anderson, John Chas.	P	5	.000	A	
		Ashburn, Richie	OF	152	.350	B	
		Bouchee, Edward Francis	1B	89	.257	B	
		Bowman, Robert LeRoy	OF57	91	.288	B	
		Burk, Mack Edwin		1	.000	Phi156	C
3	6	Cardwell, Donald Eugene	P	16	.211	B	
		Coker, Jimmie Goodwin	C	2	.167	A	
0	0	Conley, Robert Burns	P	2	.000	A	
0	1	Erickson, Donald Lee	P	9	.000	A	C
		Essegian, Chas. Abraham	OF30	39	.246	A	
8	9	Farrell, Richard Joseph	P	54	.208	B	
		Fernandez, Humberto Perez	SS	148	.230	B	
0	0	Gray, John Leonard	P	15	.000	ClevA	C
0	1	Hacker, Warren Louis	P	9	.000	B	
		Hamner, Granville Wilbur (2B11 SS3)	3B22	35	.301	B	
5	3	Hearn, James Tolbert	P	39	.000	B	

WON	LOST	NAME	POS.	G.	BA	FROM	TO
		Hegan, James Edward	C	25	.220	xDetA	
		Hemus, Solomon Joseph (3B1)	2B84	105	.284	B	
		Herrera, Juan Francisco (1B11)	3B16	29	.270	A	
		Jones, Willie Edward (1B1)	3B110	118	.271	B	
		Kazanski, Theodore Stanley (SS22 3B16)	2B59	95	.228	B	C
0	0	LiPetri, Michael Angelo	P	4	.000	Phil56	C
		Lonnett, Joseph Paul	C15	17	.140	B	
		Lopata, Stanley Edward	C80	86	.248	B	
0	0	Mason, Henry	P	1	.000	A	
3	6	Meyer, John Robert	P	37	.278	B	
1	1	Miller, Robert John	P	27	.182	B	C
1	6	Morehead, Seth Marvin	P	27	.182	B	
1	0	Owens, James Philip	P	1	.000	Phil56	
		Philley, David Earl (1B18)	OF24	91	.309	DetA	
		Post, Walter Chas.	OF91	110	.282	Cin	
0	0	Qualters, Thomas Francis	P	1	.000	B	ChiA
		Repulski, Eldon John	OF56	85	.244	B	
17	14	Roberts, Robin Evan	P35	36	.202	B	
10	13	Sanford, John Stanley	P	38	.169	B	
		Sawatski, Carl Ernest	C53	60	+.230	xMil	
13	11	Semproch, Roman Anthony	P	36	.095	A	
7	14	Simmons, Curtis Thomas	P29	38	.203	B	
		Smalley, Roy Frederick	SS	1	.000	B	C
		Young, Robert George	2B21	32	.233	ClevA56	C

WON 64
LOST 90
TG 154

NATIONAL LEAGUE — 1959. — FINISHED 8th (LAST) — PCT. .416

PHILADELPHIA

EDWIN MILBY SAWYER

WON	LOST	NAME	POS.	G.	BA	FROM	TO
		Anderson, George Lee	2B	152	.218	A	C
		Anderson, Harry Walter	OF137	142	.240	B	
		Ashburn, Richie	OF149	153	.266	B	
		Bolger, James Cyril	OF9	35	.083	xClevA	C
		Bouchee, Edward Francis	1B134	136	.285	B	
0	1	Bowman, Robert LeRoy (P5)	OF20	57	.127	B	C
9	10	Cardwell, Donald Eugene	P25	26	.055	B	
12	7	Conley, Donald Eugene	P	25	.239	Mil	
		Drake, Solomon Louis	OF37	67	+.145	xL.A.	C
		Easton, John David		3	.000	Phil55	C
1	6	Farrell, Richard Joseph	P	38	.167	B	
		Fernandez, Humberto Perez (2B2)	SS40	45	.211	B	
		Freese, Eugene Lewis (2B6)	3B109	132	.268	StL	
3	8	Gomez, Ruben Colon	P20	24	.176	S.F.	
		Hamner, Granville Wilbur (3B1)	SS15	21	.297	B	ClevA
		Hanebrink, Harry Aloysius (3B9 OF1)	2B15	57	.258	Mil	C
0	2	Hearn, James Tolbert	P	6	.000	B	C
		Hegan, James Edward	C	25	+.196	B	S.F.
		Jones, Willie Edward	3B46	47	.269	B	ClevA
0	3	Keegan, Edward Chas.	P	3	.000	A	
		Koppe, Joseph (2B11)	SS113	126	.261	Mil	
		Lonnett, Joseph Paul	C	43	.172	B	C
5	3	Meyer, John Robert	P	47	.071	B	
0	2	Morehead, Seth Marvin	P	3	+.000	B	Chi
12	12	Owens, James Philip	P	31	.120	B	
		Philley, David Earl (1B24)	OF34	99	.291	B	
1	4	Phillips, Wm. Taylor	P	32	+.091	xChi	
		Post, Walter Chas.	OF120	132	.254	B	
15	17	Roberts, Robin Evan	P	35	.191	B	
2	4	Robinson, Humberto Valentino	P	31	.231	xClevA	
0	0	Rodriguez, Fernando Pedro	P	1	.000	Chi	C
		Sawatski, Carl Ernest	C69	74	.293	B	
1	1	Schroll, Albert Bringhurst	P	3	.250	BosA	BosA
3	10	Semproch, Roman Anthony	P	30	.176	B	
0	0	Short, Christopher Joseph	P	3	.000	A	
0	0	Simmons, Curtis Thomas	P7	8	.000	B	
		Thomas Valmy (3B1)	C65	66	.200	S.F.	

WON 59
LOST 95
TG 154

NATIONAL LEAGUE — 1960. — FINISHED 8th (LAST) — PCT. .383

PHILADELPHIA

EDWIN MILBY SAWYER — ANDREW HOWARD COHEN — EUGENE WM. MAUCH

WON	LOST	NAME	POS.	G.	BA	FROM	TO
		Amaro, Ruben Mora	SS	92	.231	StL58	
		Anderson, Harry Walter (1B12)	OF16	38	+.247	B	Cin
		Bouchee, Edward Francis	1B	22	+.262	B	Chi
5	16	Buzhardt, John Wm.	P30	32	.161	Chi	
		Callison, John Wesley	OF86	99	.260	Chi	
1	2	Cardwell, Donald Eugene	P	5	+.250	B	Chi
		Coker, Jimmie Goodwin	C76	81	.214	Phil58	
8	14	Conley, Donald Eugene	P	29	.127	B	
		Curry, George Anthony	OF64	95	.261	A	
		Dalrymple, Clayton Errol	C48	82	.272	A	
		Dark, Alvin Ralph (1B1)	3B53	55	+.242	Chi	Milw
		Del Greco, Robert George	OF89	100	.237	NYA58	
10	6	Farrell, Richard Joseph	P	59	.200	B	
0	3	Gomez, Ruben Colon	P	22	.083	B	
		Gonzalez, Andres Antonio	OF67	78	+.299	xCin	
3	6	Green, George Dallas	P23	24	.206	A	
		Herrera, Juan Francisco (2B17)	1B134	145	.281	Phil58	
		Koppe, Joseph (3B2)	SS55	58	.171	B	
		Lepcio, Thaddeus Stanley (2B5 SS14)	3B50	69	.227	DetA	

WON	LOST	NAME	POS.	G.	BA	FROM	TO
7	3	Mahaffey, Arthur	P	14	.100	A	
		Malkmus, Robert Edward (2B23 3B12)	SS29	79	.211	WashA	
0	0	Mason, Henry	P	3	.000	Phi158	C
3	1	Meyer, John Robert	P	7	.125	B	
		Morgan, Joseph Michael	3B24	26	.133	KCA	ClevA
		Neeman, Calvin Amandus	C52	59	+.181	xChi	
0	0	Neiger, Alvin Edward	P	6	.500	A	C
4	14	Owens, James Phillip	P	31	.068	B	
		Philley, David Earl (1B2)	OF3	14	+.333	B	S.F.
0	1	Phillips, Wm. Taylor	P	10	.000	B	
		Post, Walter Chas.	OF22	34	+.286	B	Cin
12	16	Roberts, Robin Evan	P	35	.152	B	
0	4	Robinson, Humberto Valentino	P	33	.167	B	C
6	9	Short, Christopher Joseph	P	42	.000	B	
0	0	Simmons, Curtis Thomas	P	4	+.000	B	St.L.
		Smith, Bobby Gene (3B1)	OF70	98	.286	StL	
		Taylor, Antonio Sanchez (3B4)	2B123	127	+.287	xChi	
		Walls, Ray Lee (1B7 OF13)	3B34	65	+.199	xCin	
		Walters, Kenneth Rogers	OF119	124	.239	A	
		Wine, Robert Paul	SS	4	.143	A	
		Woods, James Jerome	3B	11	.176	Chi57	

WON 47 — LOST 107 — TG 154

NATIONAL LEAGUE — FINISHED 8th (LAST)

1961. — PCT. .305

PHILADELPHIA

EUGENE WM. MAUCH

WON	LOST	NAME	POS.	G.	BA	FROM	TO
		Amaro, Ruben Mora (1B3 2B1)	SS132	135	.257	B	
5	3	Baldschun, Jack Edward	P	65	.000	A	
0	1	Brown, Paul Dwayne	P	5	.500	A	
6	18	Buzhardt, John Wm.	P	41	.105	B	
		Callison, John Wesley	OF124	138	.266	B	
		Coker, Jimmie Goodwin	C	11	.400	B	
		Coleman, Clarence	C14	34	.128	A	
		Covington, John Wesley	OF45	57	.303	xK.C. A	
		Curry, George Anthony	OF8	15	.194	B	
		Dalrymple, Clayton Errol	C122	129	.220	B	
		Del Greco, Robert George (2B1 3B1)	OF32	41	.259	B	K.C.A
		Demeter, Donald Lee (1B22)	OF79	106	+.257	xL.A.	
2	1	Farrell, Richard Joseph	P	5	+.500	B	L.A.
5	12	Ferrarese, Donald Hugh (OF1)	P42	43	.171	ChiA	
		Gonzalez, Andres Antonio	OF118	126	.277	B	
2	4	Green, George Dallas	P	42	.152	B	
		Herrera, Juan Francisco	1B115	126	.258	B	C
		Johnson, Darrell Dean	C	21	+.230	StL	Cin
		Kenders, Albert Daniel George	C	10	.174	A	C
		Koppe, Joseph	SS5	6	.000	B	L.A.A
1	1	Lehman, Kenneth Karl	P41	42	.000	BaltA58	C

WON	LOST	NAME	POS.	G.	BA	FROM	TO
11	19	Mahaffey, Arthur	P	36	.127	B	
		Malkmus, Robert Edward (SS34 3B25)	2B58	121	.231	B	
0	0	Meyer, John Robert	P	1	.000	B	C
		Neeman, Calvin Amandus	C	19	.226	B	
5	10	Owens, James Philip (OF1)	P20	21	.074	B	
1	10	Roberts, Robin Evan	P	26	.091	B	
		Sadowski, Robert Frank	3B14	16	.130	StL	
6	12	Short, Christopher Joseph (C1)	P39	40	.162	B	
		Smith, Bobby Gene	OF47	79	.253	B	
		Smith, Chas. Wm. (SS14)	3B94	112	+.248	xL.A.	
3	16	Sullivan, Franklin Leal	P	49	.152	BosA	
		Taylor, Antonio Sanchez (3B3)	2B91	106	.250	B	
		Valo, Elmer Wm.	OF1	50	.186	xMinnA	C
		Walls, Ray Lee (3B26 OF17)	1B28	91	.280	B	
		Walters, Kenneth Rogers (1B5 3B1)	OF56	86	.228	B	
		Williams, George	2B15	17	.250	A	
		Woods, James Jerome	3B15	23	.229	B	C

WON 81 — LOST 80 — TG 161

NATIONAL LEAGUE — FINISHED 7th.

1962. — PCT. .503

PHILADELPHIA

EUGENE WM. MAUCH

WON	LOST	NAME	POS.	G.	BA	FROM	TO
		Amaro, Ruben Mora (1B1)	SS78	79	.243	B	
12	7	Baldschun, Jack Edward	P	67	.063	B	
9	9	Bennett, Dennis John	P	31	.127	A	
0	0	Boozer, John Morgan	P	9	.000	A	
0	6	Brown, Paul Dwayne	P	23	.154	B	
		Callison, John Wesley	OF152	157	.300	B	
		Coker, Jimmie Goodwin		5	.000	B	
		Consolo, Wm. Angelo		13	.400	MinnA	LAA
		Covington, John Wesley	OF88	116	.283	B	
		Dalrymple, Clayton Errol	C119	123	.276	B	
		Davis, Jacke Sylvesta	OF26	48	.213	Aq	C
		Demeter, Donald Lee (1B1 OF63)	3B105	153	.307	B	
0	1	Ferrarese, Donald Hugh	P	5	+1.000	B	StL
		Gonzalez, Andres Antonio	OF114	118	.302	B	
6	6	Green, George Dallas	P37	47	.063	B	
9	12	Hamilton, Jack Edwin	P	41	.056	A	
		Herrnstein, John Ellett	OF1	6	.200	A	
0	0	Keegan, Edward Chas.	P4	5	.000	KCA	C
		Klaus, Wm. Joseph (2B11 SS30)	3B53	102	.206	WashA	
1	0	Locke, Lawrence Donald	P	5	+.286	xStL	
19	14	Mahaffey, Arthur	P41	42	.141	B	
		Malkmus, Robert Edward	SS1	8	.200	B	C

WON	LOST	NAME	POS.	G.	BA	FROM	TO
11	5	McLish, Calvin Coolidge	P	32	.08	ChiA	
		Oldis, Robert Carl	C30	38	.078	Pitt	
2	4	Owens, James Phillip	P	23	.143	B	
		Roach, Melvin Earl	3B26	65	.190	Chi	C
		(1B4 2B9 OF3)					
		Savage, Theodore E.	OF109	127	.266	A	
11	9	Short, Christopher Joseph	P47	48	.222	B	
		Sievers, Roy Edward (OF7)	1B130	144	.262	ChiA	
1	5	Smith, Wm. Garland	P	24	.182	StL59	C
0	2	Sullivan, Franklin Leal	P	19	.000	B	MinnA
		Taylor, Antonio Sanchez	2B150	152	.259	B	
		(SS2)					
		Torre, Frank Joseph	1B76	108	.310	Mil60	
		White, Samuel Chas.	C40	41	.216	Mil	C
		Wine, Robert Paul (3B20)	SS89	112	.244	Phil60	

WON 87
LOST 75
TG 162

NATIONAL LEAGUE

1963.

FINISHED 4th.

PCT. .537

PHILADELPHIA

EUGENE WM. MAUCH

WON	LOST	NAME	POS.	G.	BA	FROM	TO
		Allen, Richard Anthony	OF7	10	.292	A	
		(1B5 3B1)					
		Amaro, Ruben Mora	SS63	115	.217	B	
		(3B45)					
		Averill, Earl Douglas	C20	47	.268	LAA	C
		(1B1 3B1 OF8)					
11	7	Baldschun, Jack Edward	P	65	.000	B	
9	5	Bennett, Dennis John	P	23	.225	B	
3	4	Boozer, John Morgan	P	26	.143	B	
0	1	Brown, Paul Dwayne	P	6	.500	B	
		Callison, John Wesley	OF	157	.284	B	
		Covington, John Wesley	OF101	119	.303	B	
14	11	Culp, Raymond Leonard	P	34	.136	A	
		Dalrymple, Clayton Errol	C	142	.252	B	
		Demeter, Donald Lee	OF119	154	.258	B	
		(1B26 3B43)					
6	2	Duren, Rinold George	P33	34	.143	LAA	
		Emery, Calvin Wayne	1B2	16	.158	A	C
		Gonzalez, Andres Antonio	OF151	155	.306	B	
		Graham, Wayne Leon	OF6	10	.182	A	
7	5	Green, George Dallas	P40	42	.086	B	
2	1	Hamilton, Jack Edwin	P	19	.000	B	
		Harrington, Chas. Michael		1	.000	A	C
		Herrnstein, John Ellett	OF2	15	.167	B	
		(1B1)					
		Hoak, Donald Albert	3B106	115	.231	Pitt	
		Klaus, Wm. Joseph	SS5	11	.056	B	C
		(3B3)					
5	6	Klippstein, John Calvin	P	49	.038	Cin	
		Lemon, James Robert	OF18	31	.271	xMinnA	ChicA

WON	LOST	NAME	POS.	G.	BA	FROM	TO
0	0	Locke, Lawrence Donald	P	9	.000	B	
1	0	Lopez, Marcelino Pons	P4	5	.000	A	
7	10	Mahaffey, Arthur	P	26	.200	B	
13	11	McLish, Calvin Coolidge	P32	33	.203	B	
		Oldis, Robert Carl	C43	47	.224	B	C
		Rojas, Octavio Rivas	2B25	64	.221	Cin	
		(OF1)					
9	12	Short, Christopher Joseph	P	38	.106	B	
		Sievers, Roy Edward	1B126	138	.240	B	
		Taylor, Antonio Sanchez	2B149	157	.281	B	
		(3B13)					
		Torre, Frank Joseph	1B56	92	.250	B	C
		Wine, Robert Paul	SS132	142	.215	B	
		(3B8)					

WON 92
LOST 70
TG 162

NATIONAL LEAGUE

1964.

FINISHED 2nd.
(TIED WITH CINCINNATI)
PCT. .568

PHILADELPHIA

EUGENE WM. MAUCH

WON	LOST	NAME	POS.	G.	BA	FROM	TO
		Allen, Richard Anthony	3B	162	.318	B	
		Amaro, Ruben Mora	1B58	129	.264	B	
		(2B3 SS44 3B3 OF1)					
6	9	Baldschun, Jack Edward	P	71	.250	B	
0	0	Bennett, David Hans	P	1	.000	A	C
12	14	Bennett, Dennis John	P	41	.197	B	
3	4	Boozer, John Morgan	P22	23	.077	B	
		Briggs, John Edward	OF19	61	.258	A	
		(1B1)					
19	8	Bunning, James Paul David	P	41	.121	DetA	
		Callison, John Wesley	OF	162	,274	B	
		Cater, Daniel Anderson	OF39	60	.296	A	
		(1B7 3B1)					
		Corrales, Patrick		2	.000	A	
		Covington, John Wesley	OF108	129	.280	B	
8	7	Culp, Ray Leonard	P	30	.114	B	
		Dalrymple, Clayton Errol	C124	127	.238	B	
0	0	Duren, Rinold George	P	2	+.000	B	Cin
		Gonzalez, Andres Antonio	OF119	131	.278	B	
2	1	Green, George Dallas	P25	26	.000	B	
		Herrnstein, John Ellett	OF69	125	.234	B	
		(1B68)					
		Hoak, Donald Albert		6	.000	B	C
		Johnson, Alexander	OF35	43	.303	A	
2	1	Klippstein, John Calvin	P	11	.000	B	
0	0	Kroll, Gary Melvin	P	2	+.000	A	N.Y.
0	0	Locke, Lawrence Donald	P	8	.000	B	
12	9	Mahaffey, Arthur	P	34	.120	B	
0	1	McLish, Calvin Coolidge	P	2	.000	B	C
		Phillips, Adolfo Emilio	OF4	13	.231	A	
		Lopez					

		Power, Victor Pellot	1B17	18	.208	xLAA	
5	3	Roebuck, Edward Jack	P	60	.000	xWashA	
		Rojas, Octavio Rivas (C1 2B20 SS18 3B1)	OF70	109	.291	B	
1	1	Shantz, Robert Clayton	P	14	+.000	xChic	C
		Shockley, John Costen	1B9	11	.229	A	
17	9	Short, Christopher Joseph	P42	44	.108	B	
		Sievers, Roy Edward	1B33	49	.183	B	WashA
0	0	Steevens, Morris Dale	P	4	.000	Chic62	
		Taylor, Antonio Sanchez	2B150	154	.251	B	
		Thomas, Frank Joseph	1B36	39	+.294	xN.Y.	
		Triandos, Gus (1B1)	C64	73	.250	DetA	
		Wine, Robert Paul (3B16)	SS108	126	.212	B	
5	3	Wise, Richard Chas.	P	25	.294	A	

CLUB RECORD

NATIONAL LEAGUE

PITTSBURGH

YEAR	TG	WON	LOST	PCT.	FINISHED	MANAGER
1887	124	55	69	.444	6	Horace B. Phillips
1888	134	66	68	.493	6	Horace B. Phillips
1889	132	61	71	.462	5	Horace B. Phillips Frederick C. Dunlap Edward Hugh Hanlon
1890	137	23	114	.168	8(Last)	Guy Jackson Hecker
1891	135	55	80	.407	8(Last)	Edward Hugh Hanlon Wm. Henry McGunnigle
1892	153	80	73	.523	6	Thomas Everett Burns Albert C. Buckenberger
1893	129	81	48	.628	2	Albert C. Buckenberger
1894	130	65	65	.500	7	Albert C. Buckenberger Connie Mack
1895	132	71	61	.538	7	Connie Mack
1896	129	66	63	.512	6	Connie Mack
1897	131	60	71	.458	8	Patrick Joseph Donovan
1898	148	72	76	.486	8	Wm. Henry Watkins
1899	149	76	73	.510	7	Wm. Henry Watkins Patrick Joseph Donovan
1900	139	79	60	.568	2	Frederick Clifford Clarke
1901	139	90	49	.647	1	Frederick Clifford Clarke
1902	139	103	36	.741	1	Frederick Clifford Clarke
1903	140	91	49	.650	1	Frederick Clifford Clarke
1904	153	87	66	.569	4	Frederick Clifford Clarke
1905	153	96	57	.627	2	Frederick Clifford Clarke
1906	153	93	60	.608	3	Frederick Clifford Clarke
1907	154	91	63	.591	2	Frederick Clifford Clarke
1908	154	98	56	.636	x2(N.Y.)	Frederick Clifford Clarke
1909	152	110	42	.724	1	Frederick Clifford Clarke
1910	153	86	67	.562	3	Frederick Clifford Clarke
1911	154	85	69	.552	3	Frederick Clifford Clarke
1912	151	93	58	.616	2	Frederick Clifford Clarke
1913	149	78	71	.523	4	Frederick Clifford Clarke
1914	154	69	85	.448	7	Frederick Clifford Clarke
1915	154	73	81	.474	5	Frederick Clifford Clarke
1916	154	65	89	.422	6	James Joseph Callahan
1917	154	51	103	.331	8(Last)	James Joseph Callahan John Peter Wagner Hugo Frank Bezdek
1918	125	65	60	.520	4	Hugo Frank Bezdek
1919	139	71	68	.511	4	Hugo Frank Bezdek
1920	154	79	75	.513	4	George Gibson
1921	153	90	63	.588	2	George Gibson
1922	154	85	69	.552	x3(StL)	George Gibson Wm. Boyd McKechnie
1923	154	87	67	.565	3	Wm. Boyd McKechnie
1924	153	90	63	.588	3	Wm. Boyd McKechnie
1925	153	95	58	.621	1	Wm. Boyd McKechnie
1926	153	84	69	.549	3	Wm. Boyd McKechnie

1927	154	94	60	.610	1	Owen Joseph Bush
1928	152	85	67	.559	4	Owen Joseph Bush
1929	153	88	65	.575	2	{ Owen Joseph Bush
						{ Jewel Willoughby Ens
1930	154	80	74	.519	5	Jewel Willoughby Ens
1931	154	75	79	.487	5	Jewel Willoughby Ens
1932	154	86	68	.558	2	George Gibson
1933	154	87	67	.565	2	George Gibson
1934	150	74	76	.493	5	George Gibson
						Harold Joseph Traynor
1935	153	86	67	.562	4	Harold Joseph Traynor
1936	154	84	70	.545	4	Harold Joseph Traynor
1937	154	86	68	.558	3	Harold Joseph Traynor
1938	150	86	64	.573	2	Harold Joseph Traynor
1939	153	68	85	.444	6	Harold Joseph Traynor
1940	154	78	76	.506	4	Frank Francis Frisch
1941	154	81	73	.526	4	Frank Francis Frisch
1942	147	66	81	.449	5	Frank Francis Frisch
1943	154	80	74	.519	4	Frank Francis Frisch
1944	153	90	63	.588	2	Frank Francis Frisch
1945	154	82	72	.532	4	Frank Francis Frisch
1946	154	63	91	.409	7	Frank Francis Frisch
						Virgil Lawrence Davis
1947	154	62	92	.403	x7 (Phila)	Wm. Jennings Bryan Herman
						Wm. Edwin Burwell
1948	154	83	71	.539	4	Wm. Adam Meyer
1949	154	71	83	.461	6	Wm. Adam Meyer
1950	153	57	96	.373	8(Last)	Wm. Adam Meyer
1951	154	64	90	.416	7	Wm. Adam Meyer
1952	154	42	112	.273	8(Last)	Wm. Adam Meyer
1953	154	50	104	.325	8(Last)	Fred Girard Haney
1954	154	53	101	.344	8(Last)	Fred Girard Haney
1955	154	60	94	.390	8(Last)	Fred Girard Haney
1956	154	66	88	.429	7	Robert Randall Bragan
1957	154	62	92	.403	x7(Chic)	Robert Randall Bragan
						Daniel Edward Murtaugh
1958	154	84	70	.545	2	Daniel Edward Murtaugh
1959	154	78	76	.506	4	Daniel Edward Murtaugh
1960	154	95	59	.617	1	Daniel Edward Murtaugh
1961	154	75	79	.487	6	Daniel Edward Murtaugh
1962	161	93	68	.578	4	Daniel Edward Murtaugh
1963	162	74	88	.457	8	Daniel Edward Murtaugh
1964	162	80	82	.494	x6 (L.A.)	Daniel Edward Murtaugh

YEAR	TG	WON	LOST	TIED	PCT.	FINISHED	MANAGER
1965	163	90	72	1	.556	3	HARRY WILLIAM WALKER
1966	162	92	70	0	.568	3	HARRY WILLIAM WALKER
1967	163	81	81	1	.500	6	HARRY WILLIAM WALKER
							DANIEL EDWARD MURTAUGH
1968	163	80	82	1	.494	6	LAWRENCE WILLIAM SHEPARD
1969	162	88	74	0	.543	3E	LAWRENCE WILLIAM SHEPARD
							ALEXANDER PETER GRAMMAS *
1970	162	89	73	0	.549	1E (LP)	DANIEL EDWARD MURTAUGH
1971	162	97	65	0	.599	1E (WP)	DANIEL EDWARD MURTAUGH
1972	155	96	59	0	.619	1E (LP)	WILLIAM CHARLES VIRDON

WON 55 — NATIONAL LEAGUE — FINISHED 6th.
LOST 69
TG 124 — 1887. — PCT. .444

PITTSBURGH

HORACE B. PHILLIPS

WON	LOST	NAME	POS.	G.	BA	FROM	TO
		Barkley, Samuel Wilson (2B37)	1B53	90	.286	PittAA	
		Beecher, Edward C.	OF	40	.272	A	
0	4	Bishop, Wm. R.	P	4	.154	PittAA	
		Brown, Thomas T.	OF	46	+.284	PittAA	Indpls
		Carroll, Frederick Herbert (C39 1B17)	OF44	101	.380	PittAA	
		Coleman, John Francis (Jack)	OF114	115	.334	PittAA	
		Dalrymple, Abner Frank	OF	92	.300	Chi	
		Fields, John James	OF23	39	.298	A	
28	20	Galvin, James F. (Jimmy)	P	49	.220	PittAA	
		Kuehne, Wm. J.	SS91	101	.322	PittAA	
		Miller, George Frederick (Fog-Horn) (OF15)	C71	87	.313	PittAA	
14	22	Morris, Edward	P	37	.229	PittAA	
13	23	McCormick, James	P	36	.253	Chi	C
		McKinnon, Alexander J.	1B	48	.365	StL	C
		Smith, Chas. Marvin (Pap) (SS34)	2B88	122	.263	PittAA	
		Whitney, Arthur Wilson	3B	119	.343	PittAA	

WON 66 — NATIONAL LEAGUE — FINISHED 6th.
LOST x68
TG 134 — 1888. — PCT. .493

PITTSBURGH

HORACE B. PHILLIPS

WON	LOST	NAME	POS.	G.	BA	FROM	TO
		Beckley, Jacob Peter (Jake)	1B	71	.342	A	
		Carroll, Frederick Herbert (OF38)	C53	96	.243	B	
		Carroll, Samuel (Clifford)	OF	7	.107	Wash	
		Cleveland, Elmer E.	3B	30	+.204	xN.Y.	
		Coleman, John Francis (Jack) (1B25)	OF90	115	.230	B	
		Dalrymple, Abner Frank	OF	56	.224	B	
		Dunlap, Frederick C.	2B	81	.261	Det	
		Farmer, Wm.	C	2	.000	A	AthAA
		Fields, John James	OF29	44	.195	B	
23	25	Galvin, James F.	P	50	.143	B	
1	3	Henderson, James Harding (Hardie)	P	5	.282	BknAA	C
1	2	Knell, Philip H.	P	4	.091	A	
		Kuehne, Wm. J. (SS63)	3B74	137	.234	B	

WON	LOST	NAME	POS.	G.	BA	FROM	TO
0	1	Maul, Albert Joseph (P2 OF34)	1B37	73	.211	Phil	
		Miller, George Frederick (Fog-Horn) (OF32)	C68	103	.277	B	
29	24	Morris, Edward	P	54	.102	B	
		McShannick, Peter Robert	3B	26	.194	A	C
		Nichol, Samuel Anderson	OF	8	.045	A	
		Smith, Chas. Marvin (Pap) (2B56)	SS74	130	.207	B	
12	12	Staley, Henry E.	P	24	.129	A	
		Sunday, Wm. Ashley	OF	119	.233	Chi	
		Yaik, Henry	C	2	.333	A	C

x-One game lost by forfeit.

WON 61 | NATIONAL LEAGUE | FINISHED 5th.
LOST 71
TG 132 | 1889. | PCT. .462

PITTSBURGH

HORACE B. PHILLIPS FREDERICK C. DUNLAP EDWARD HUGH HANLON

WON	LOST	NAME	POS.	G.	BA	FROM	TO
1	1	Beam, Alexander Rodger	P	2	.250	A	C
		Beckley, Jacob Peter (Jake)	1B122	123	.300	B	
		Carroll, Frederick Herbert (OF39)	C43	90	.330	B	
2	1	Conway, Peter J.	P	3	.091	Det	C
		Dunlap, Frederick C. MGR.	2B	121	.235	B	
0	2	Dunning, Andrew J.	P	2	.000	A	
		Fee, John	(DID NOT PLAY)			A	Indpls
		Fields, John James (C16)	OF58	74	.311	B	
23	17	Galvin, James F.	P	40	.187	B	
0	2	Garfield, Wm. Milton	P	4	.000	A	
		Hanlon, Edward Hugh MGR.	OF	115	.238	Det	
1	0	Jones, Alexander H.	P	1	.250	A	
0	1	Krumm, Albert	P	1	.000	A	C
		Kuehne, Wm. J.	3B75	97	.246	B	
		Lauer, John Chas. (Chuck)	C	4	.231	PittAA84	
1	3	Maul, Albert Joseph (P6)	OF61	67	.276	B	
		Miller, George Frederick (Fog-Horn) (OF25)	C73	102	.267	B	
7	14	Morris, Edward	P	21	.097	B	
		Rowe, John Chas.	SS	74	.258	Det	
		Smith, Chas. Marvin (Pap)	SS	72	+.210	B	Bos
5	4	Sowders, Wm. Jefferson (OF2)	P12	14	+.256	xBos	
21	26	Staley, Henry E.	P48	49	.161	B	
		Sunday, Wm. Ashley	OF	80	.239	B	
		White, James Laurie (Deacon)	3B52	55	.253	Det	

WON 23 | NATIONAL LEAGUE | FINISHED 8th (LAST)
LOST 114
TG 137 | 1890. | PCT. .168

PITTSBURGH

GUY JACKSON HECKER

WON	LOST	NAME	POS.	G.	BA	FROM	TO
2	11	Anderson, David S. (Varney)	P	13	+.098	xPhil	
2	19	Baker, Kirtly	P	23	.147	A	
		Berger, John Henry (Tun) (C21 SS33)	OF41	104	.266	A	
2	7	Bowman, Sumner Sallade	P	10	+.263	xPhil	
		Burke, Edward D.	OF	32	+.225	xPhil	
		Clements, Edward	SS	1	.000	A	C
0	2	Coleman, John Francis (Jack)	P	3	.182	AthAA	C
		Crane, Samuel Newhall (SS7)	2B15	22	+.200	xN.Y.	N.Y.
2	2	Daniels, Peter J.	P	4	.250	A	
0	7	Day, Wm.	P	7	+.042	xPhil	C
		Decker, Edward Harry	C	90	+.273	xPhil	C
		Dunlap, Frederick C.	2B	17	.172	B	NYPL
0	2	Esper, Chas. H.	P	2	+.143	xAthAA	Phil
0	2	Gibson, Chas. Robert (OF2)	P3	3	+.231	xChi	C
		Gilbert, Harry	2B	2	.250	A	C
		Gilbert, John G.	SS	2	.000	A	C
0	3	Gray, Chas.	P	5	.267	A	C
		Gray, James D.	SS	1	.000	xPittPL	
4	4	Gumbert, Wm. Skeen	P	10	.243	A	
0	6	Heard, Chas. H.	P	12	.186	A	C
2	12	Hecker, Guy Jackson MGR. (P14)	1B66	86	.226	LvlleAA	C
		Hemp, Wm. H. (Ducky)	OF	21	.213	LvlleAA87	SyrAA
		Hines, Paul A. (OF15)	1B16	31	+.172	Indpls	Bos
0	0	Heyner, John	P	1	.000	A	C
2	2	Jones, Henry M.	P	4	.250	A	C
		Jordan, Michael J.	OF	37	.096	A	C
		Kelty, John E. Joseph	OF	59	.236	A	C
		LaRoque, Samuel H. J. (SS31)	2B76	111	.242	Det88	
0	1	Lawson, Albert W.	P	2	+.000	xBos	C
		Lytle, Edward Benson (Dad) (OF7)	2B8	15	+.123	xChi	C
		Miller, George Frederick (Fog-Horn) (OF25)	3B85	138	.273	B	
		McGinn, Frank J.	OF	1	.000	A	C
0	6	Osborne, Frederick W. (P6)	OF35	41	.238	A	C
1	9	Phillips, Wm. Corcoran	P	15	.234	A	
		Roat, Frederick	3B44	57	.223	A	
		Routcliffe, Philip J.	OF	1	.250	A	C
		Sales, Edward A.	SS	51	.228	A	C
1	9	Schmidt, Frederick	P	11	.086	A	
2	3	Smith, John Francis	P	5	+.412	xPhil	
3	7	Sowders, Wm. Jefferson	P	17	.196	B	C
		Sunday, Wm. Ashley	OF	85	+.268	B	Phil
		Traux, Frederick W.	OF	1	.333	A	C

WON	LOST	NAME	POS.	G.	BA	FROM	TO
		Veach, Wm. Walter (Peek-a-boo)	1B	8	+.300	xClev	C
		Wilson, Wm. (1B18 OF25)	C38	83	.213	A	
		Youngman, Henry	2B	13	.167	A	C
0	0	Ziegler, George J.	P	1	.000	A	C

x-One game lost by forfeit.

WON 55 NATIONAL LEAGUE FINISHED 8th (LAST)
LOST 80
TG 135 1891. PCT. .407

PITTSBURGH

EDWARD HUGH HANLON WM. HENRY McGUNNIGLE

WON	LOST	NAME	POS.	G.	BA	FROM	TO
20	28	Baldwin, Marcus Elmore (Mark)	P51	54	.147	ChiPL	
		Beckley, Jacob Peter (Jake)	1B	129	.291	PittPL	
		Berger, John Henry (Tun) (C15)	2B16	37	.240	B	
		Bierbauer, Louis W.	2B	117	.202	BknPL	
		Browning, Louis Roger (Pete)	OF	50	+.287	ClevPL	Cin
		Carroll, Frederick Herbert	OF	87	.228	PittPL	C
		Corkhill, John Stewart (Pop)	OF	41	+.231	xCin	
		Fields, John James	C	19	+.239	PittPL	Phil
15	13	Galvin, James F. (Jimmy)	P	28	.176	PittPL	
		Hanlon, Edward Hugh MGR.	OF	115	.274	PittPL	
		Kelley, Joseph James	OF	2	+.143	xBos	
17	31	King, Chas. Frederick	P	48	.171	ChiPL	
		Lally, Daniel J.	OF	41	.225	A	
		LaRoque, Samuel H. J.	2B	1	.000	B	LvlleAA
		Mack, Connie	C68	71	.210	BuffPL	
1	2	Maul, Albert Joseph (P6)	OF38	40	.194	PittPL	
		Miller, George Frederick (Fog-Horn) (SS33 3B32 OF22)	C42	131	.285	B	
		Newell, John A.	3B	5	.111	A	C
		Reilly, Chas. Thomas	3B97	110	.211	ColAA	
		Shugart, Wm. Frank	SS	75	.285	ChiPL	
		Spurney, Edward Frederick	SS	3	.285	A	C
2	4	Staley, Henry E.	P	9	+.233	PittPL	Bos
0	2	Stratton, C. Scott	P	3	.125	LvlleAA	LvlleA
		Ward, Frank Gray (Piggy)	OF	5	.333	Phil89	

WON 80 NATIONAL LEAGUE FINISHED 6th.
LOST 73
TG 153 1892. PCT. .523

PITTSBURGH

THOMAS EVERETT BURNS ALBERT C. BUCKENBERGER

WON	LOST	NAME	POS.	G.	BA	FROM	TO
25	27	Baldwin, Marcus Elmore (Mark)	P	57	.105	B	
		Beckley, Jacob Peter (Jake)	1B	152	.250	B	
		Bierbauer, Louis W.	2B	153	.240	B	
		Burns, Thomas Everett MGR. (OF5)	3B7	12	.210	Chi	
0	2	Camp. Winfield Scott	P	4	.091	A	
		Cargo, Robert J.	SS	2	.200	A	C
		Corkhill, John Stewart (Pop)	OF	67	.191	B	C
		Donovan, Patrick Joseph	OF	88	+.311	xWash	
		Earle, Wm. Moffat	C	5	.500	StLAA90	
18	19	Ehret, Philip Sydney (Red)	P	40	.273	LvlleAA	
1	0	Esper, Chas. H.	P	11	+.000	xPhil	
		Farrell, Chas. A. (Duke) (OF19)	3B133	152	.230	BosAA	
5	6	Galvin, James F.	P	11	+.136	B	StL
3	2	Gumbert, Wm. Skeen	P	7	.118	Pitt90	
		Kelley, Joseph James	OF	56	+.245	B	Balt
		Mack, Connie	C83	86	.257	B	
0	0	Menefee, John (Jock)	P	2	.000	A	
		Miller, George Frederick (Fog-Horn) (C60 SS17)	OF70	147	.268	B	
		Raymond, Harry H.	3B	11	+.083	LvlleAA	Wash
		Shugart, Wm. Frank	SS136	137	.276	B	
7	6	Smith, Elmer Ellsworth (P13)	OF123	136	.282	CinAA89	
		Stenzel, Jacob C. (Jake)	OF	2	.000	Chi90	
		Swartwood, Cyrus Edward	OF	12	.263	TolAA90	C
20	7	Terry, Wm. J. (Adonis)	P	27	+.198	xBalt	
0	1	Thompson, Will McLain	P	1	.000	A	C
		Van Haltren, George E.	OF	13	+.212	xBalt	
1	3	Woodcock, Frederick Wayland	P	7	.214	A	C

WON 81 NATIONAL LEAGUE FINISHED 2nd.
LOST 48
TG 129 1893. PCT. .628

PITTSBURGH

ALBERT C. BUCKENBERGER

WON	LOST	NAME	POS.	G.	BA	FROM	TO
1	1	Baldwin, Marcus Elmore (Mark)	P	5	+.000	B	N.Y.
		Beckley, Jacob Peter (Jake)	1B	128	.324	B	
		Bierbauer, Louis W.	2B	129	.298	B	
2	1	Colcolough, Thomas Bernard	P	8	.143	A	
		Donovan, Patrick Joseph	OF	110	.331	B	
		Earle, Wm. Moffat	C	26	.317	B	
17	17	Ehret, Philip Sydney (Red)	P	36	.193	B	
3	2	Gastright, Henry Carl	P	9	+.048	Wash	Bos
		Gillen, Samuel	SS	3	.000	A	
		Glasscock, John Wesley	SS	66	+.380	xStL	
		Gray, James D.	SS	2	.500	Pitt90	C
13	6	Gumbert, Addison Courtney (Ad)	P19	24	.250	Chi	
33	14	Killen, Frank Bissell	P	47	.291	Wash	
		Lyons, Dennis Patrick Aloysius	3B	131	.318	N.Y.	

WON	LOST	NAME	POS.	G.	BA	FROM	TO
		Mack, Connie	C	36	.325	B	
		Miller, George Frederick (Fog-Horn)	C	40	.194	B	
		Shugart, Wm. Frank (OF1)	SS51	52	+.274	B	StL
		Smith, Elmer Ellsworth	OF	128	.366	B	
		Stenzel, Jacob C. (Jake)	OF40	51	.409	B	
		Sugden, Joseph	C	25	.273	A	
12	7	Terry, Wm. J. (Adonis)	P	21	.283	B	
		Van Haltren, George E.	OF110	123	.350	B	

WON 65 — NATIONAL LEAGUE — FINISHED 7th.
LOST 65
TG 130 — 1894. — PCT. .500

PITTSBURGH

ALBERT C. BUCKENBERGER CONNIE MACK

WON	LOST	NAME	POS.	G.	BA	FROM	TO
		Beckley, Jacob Peter (Jake)	1B	132	.344	B	
		Bierbauer, Louis W.	2B	131	.301	B	
7	7	Colcolough, Thomas Bernard	P15	19	.214	B	
		Cross, Montford Montgomery (Monte)	SS	13	.404	Balt92	
		DeMontreville, Eugene Napoleon	SS	2	.250	A	
		Donovan, Patrick Joseph	OF	133	.306	B	
0	1	Easton, John E.	P	3	.000	StL92	C
18	22	Ehret, Philip Sydney (Red)	P	41	.172	B	
		Glasscock, John Wesley	SS	86	.282	B	
18	14	Gumbert, Addison Courtney (Ad)	P32	33	.303	B	
		Hartman, Frederick Orrin	3B	49	.311	A	
1	0	Jordan, Harry J.	P	1	.000	A	
14	10	Killen, Frank Bissell	P	24	.256	B	
0	0	Knell, Philip H.	P	4	+.000	Phil92	Lvlle
		Lyons, Dennis Patrick Aloysius	3B	72	.311	B	
		Mack, Connie MGR.	C	63	.257	B	
3	8	Menefee, John (Jock)	P	13	+.255	xLvlle	
		Merritt, Wm. Henry	C	26	+.300	xBos	Cin
4	2	Nicol, George Edward	P	9	+.391	Chi91	Lvlle
		Ritz, James L.	3B	1	.000	A	C
		Scheibeck, Frank (2B2 3B3 OF9)	SS11	26	+.347	TolAA90	Wash
		Smith, Elmer Ellsworth	OF	125	.352	B	
		Steere, Frederick Eugene	SS	10	.184	A	C
		Stenzel, Jacob C. (Jake)	OF	131	.351	B	
		Sugden, Joseph	C30	39	.333	B	
0	1	Terry, Wm. J. (Adonis)	P	6	+.000	B	Chi
		Weaver, Wm. B. (SS12 3B5 OF1)	C14	30	+.352	xLvlle	

WON 71 — NATIONAL LEAGUE — FINISHED 7th.
LOST 60
TG 131 — 1895. — PCT. .538

PITTSBURGH

CONNIE MACK

WON	LOST	NAME	POS.	G.	BA	FROM	TO
		Beckley, Jacob Peter (Jake)	1B	131	.324	B	
		Bierbauer, Louis W.	2B	119	.255	B	
		Clingman, Wm. Frederick	3B	108	.261	CinAA91	
1	1	Colcolough, Thomas Bernard	P	8	.278	B	
		Corcoran, John A. (3B2)	SS3	6	.150	A	C
		Cross, Montford Montgomery (Monte)	SS	108	.255	B	
		Donovan, Patrick Joseph	OF	126	.316	B	
8	7	Foreman, John Davis (Brownie)	P16	19	.143	A	
0	0	Gannon, James Edward	P	1	.000	A	C
8	2	Gardner, James Anderson	P	10	.242	A	
		Genins, C. Frank (3B15)	OF27	64	.253	StL92	
14	15	Hart, Wm. Franklin	P	31	.233	Bkn92	
29	21	Hawley, Emerson P. (Pink)	P	53	.324	StL	
1	0	Hewitt, Chas. Jacob	P	3	.500	A	C
0	2	Jordan, Harry J.	P	2	.167	B	C
7	6	Killen, Frank Bissell	P	14	.342	B	
		Kinslow, Thomas F.	C	17	.230	Bkn	
		Mack, Connie MGR.	C	14	.362	B	
0	1	Menefee, John (Jock)	P	2	.000	B	
		Merritt, Wm. Henry	C	66	+.273	xCin	
2	5	Moran, Samuel	P	10	.130	A	C
		Niles, Wm. A.	3B	11	.205	A	C
		Smith, Elmer Ellsworth	OF	124	.296	B	
		Stenzel, Jacob C.	OF	131	.384	B	
		Stuart, Wm. Alexander	SS17	19	.259	A	
		Sugden, Joseph	C	45	.310	B	
1	0	Weyhing, August (Gus)	P	3	+.250	xPhil	Lvlle
0	0	Wright, David Wm.	P	1	.000	A	

WON 66 — NATIONAL LEAGUE — FINISHED 6th.
LOST 63
TG 129 — 1896. — PCT. .512

PITTSBURGH

CONNIE MACK

WON	LOST	NAME	POS.	G.	BA	FROM	TO
		Beckley, Jacob Peter (Jake)	1B	54	+.244	B	N.Y.
		Bierbauer, Louis W.	2B	57	.277	B	
		Boyle, Edward J.	C	2	+.000	xLvlle	C
		Davis, Harry H. (OF10)	1B34	43	+.206	xN.Y.	
		Delehanty, Thomas James	SS	1	+.333	xClev	
		Donovan, Patrick Joseph	OF	129	.316	B	
		Ely, Frederick Wm.	SS	126	.287	StL	
3	4	Foreman, John Davis (Brownie)	P	9	+.150	B	Cin
0	0	Goar, Joshua Mercer (Jot)	P	3	.167	A	
5	9	Hastings, Chas. Morton	P	17	.211	Clev93	
21	21	Hawley, Emerson P. (Pink)	P	48	.234	B	

WON	LOST	NAME	POS.	G.	BA	FROM	TO
0	2	Horton, Elmer E. (Herky-Jerky)	P	3	.000	A	
6	8	Hughey, James Ulysses	P	21	.222	Chi93	
31	19	Killen, Frank Bissell	P	50	.235	B	
		Lezotte, Abel	1B	7	.104	A	C
		Lyons, Dennis Patrick Aloysius	3B	116	.306	StL	
		Mack, Connie MGR. (C5)	1B25	30	.207	B	
		Merritt, Wm. Henry	C60	70	.296	B	
		Padden, Richard J.	2B	60	.239	A	
		Smith, Elmer Ellsworth	OF	120	.358	B	
		Smith, Judson Grant (Jud)	3B	4	.333	StL93	
		Stenzel, Jacob C. (Jake)	OF	112	.366	B	
		Sugden, Joseph	C65	77	.298	B	
		Truby, Harry Garvin	2B	8	+.156	xChi	C
		Wright, Joseph	OF	15	+.308	xLvlle	C

WON 60 — NATIONAL LEAGUE — FINISHED 8th.
LOST 71
TG 131 — 1897. — PCT. .458

PITTSBURGH

PATRICK JOSEPH DONOVAN

WON	LOST	NAME	POS.	G.	BA	FROM	TO
		Brodie, Walter Scott	OF	100	.298	Balt	
		Davis, Harry H. (3B32)	1B62	107	.309	B	
		Donely, James B.	3B	43	+.177	Balt	N.Y.
		Donovan, Patrick Joseph MGR.	OF	120	.326	B	
		Ely, Frederick Wm.	SS	133	.282	B	
5	5	Gardner, James Anderson	P	28	.153	Pitt95	
7	3	Hastings, Chas. Morton	P	15	.216	B	
18	19	Hawley, Emerson P. (Pink)	P	37	.216	B	
		Hoffmeister, Jesse H.	3B	47	.312	A	C
6	13	Hughey, James Ulysses	P	20	.115	B	
16	23	Killen, Frank Bissell	P40	41	.257	B	
		Kuhns, Chas. B.	3B	2	.000	A	
		Leahy, Thomas Joseph	OF	23	+.242	A	Wash
		Lyons, Dennis Patrick Aloysius	1B34	36	.206	B	C
		Merritt, Wm. Henry	C53	56	.270	B	
		Padden, Richard J.	2B	135	.281	B	
		Rothfuss, John	1B30	31	.348	A	C
		Smith, Elmer Ellsworth	OF121	122	.311	B	
		Sugden, Joseph	C81	83	.219	B	
8	8	Tannehill, Jesse Niles (P17)	OF32	53	.266	Cin94	

WON 72 — NATIONAL LEAGUE — FINISHED 8th.
LOST 76
TG 148 — 1898. — PCT. .486

PITTSBURGH

WM. HENRY WATKINS

WON	LOST	NAME	POS.	G.	BA	FROM	TO
		Bowerman, Frank Eugene	C	62	+.278	xBalt	
		Brodie, Walter Scott	OF	42	+.274	B	Balt
		Clark, Wm. Otis	1B	57	.310	N.Y.	
2	2	Cronin, John J. (Jack)	P	4	.100	Bkn95	
		Davis, Harry H.	1B	58	+.290	B	Lvlle
		Donovan, Patrick Joseph	OF	147	.302	B	
		Eagan, Wm. (Bad Bill)	2B	16	.328	Chi93	C
		Ely, Frederick Wm.	SS	148	.210	B	
		Ganzel, John Henry	1B	14	.111	A	
10	13	Gardner, James Anderson	P23	32	.165	B	
		Grey, Wm. Tobin	3B	137	.232	Cin96	
6	9	Hart, Wm. Franklin	P	15	.225	StL	
4	9	Hastings, Chas. Morton	P15	18	.238	B	
3	0	Hoffer, Wm. Leopold	P	4	+.100	xBalt	
10	12	Killen, Frank Bissell	P	22	+.254	B	Wash
		Ladd, Arthur Clifford Hiram	OF	1	+.000	A	Bos
		Lake, Frederick Lovett	1B	5	.083	Bos	
1	0	Leever, Samuel W.	P	4	.250	A	
		Murphy, Morgan Edward	C	5	+.125	StL	Phil
		McCarthy, John A.	OF	137	.289	Cin94	
		McCreery, Thomas Leavenworth	OF	51	+.304	xN.Y.	
		O'Brien, Thomas F. (1B20)	OF85	104	+.259	xBalt	
		Padden, Richard J.	2B	128	.256	B	
12	15	Rhines, Wm. Pearl (Bunker)	P30	31	.151	Cin	
		Rickert, Joseph Francis	OF	2	.167	A	
0	2	Rosebrough, E. E.	P	4	.333	A	
		Schriver, Wm. F. (Pop)	C	93	.227	Cin	
24	14	Tannehill, Jesse Niles	P38	45	.294	B	

WON 76 — NATIONAL LEAGUE — FINISHED 7th.
LOST 73
TG 149 — 1899. — PCT. .510

PITTSBURGH

WM. HENRY WATKINS — PATRICK JOSEPH DONOVAN

WON	LOST	NAME	POS.	G.	BA	FROM	TO
		Beaumont, Clarence Howeth	OF100	104	.350	A	
		Bowerman, Frank Eugene (1B28)	C79	107	.269	B	
6	9	Chesbro, John Dwight (Jack)	P17	19	.140	A	
		Clark, Wm. Otis	1B	79	.282	B	C
		Dillon, Frank Edward	1B	30	.258	A	
		Donovan, Patrick Joseph MGR.	OF	123	.296	B	
		Ely, Frederick Wm.	SS132	138	.288	B	
		Fox, George (Paddy)	C	13	.243	A	C
4	3	Gray, George Edward (Chummy)	P	9	.125	A	
1	1	Gardner, James Anderson	P	7	.267	B	
8	9	Hoffer, Wm. Leopold	P19	30	.200	B	
20	23	Leever, Samuel W.	P48	50	.241	B	
		Madison, Arthur M. (2B16)	SS17	33	.269	Phil95	
		McCarthy, John A.	OF137	139	.307	B	

WON	LOST	NAME	POS.	G.	BA	FROM	TO
		McCreery, Thomas Leavenworth	OF98	113	.325	B	
		O'Brien, John J.	2B	76	+.223	xBalt	C
0	0	Parker, Jay	P	1	.000	A	C
1	3	Payne, Harley F.	P	4	.100	Bkn	C
		Reitz, Henry P.	2B	35	.263	Wash	
4	3	Rhines, Wm. Pearl (Bunker)	P	10	.417	B	C
0	1	Rosebrough, E. E.	P	2	.000	B	C
		Schriver, Wm. F. (Pop)	C75	84	.297	B	
		Smith, George Henry	2B	15	.264	Lvlle	
9	7	Sparks, Tully Frank	P17	25	.133	Phil97	
23	14	Tannehill, Jesse Niles	P38	40	.246	B	
		Williams, James Thomas Williams	3B151	153	.352	A	

WON 79 NATIONAL LEAGUE FINISHED 2nd.
LOST 60
TG 139 1900. PCT. .568

PITTSBURGH

FREDERICK CLIFFORD CLARKE

WON	LOST	NAME	POS.	G.	BA	FROM	TO
		Beaumont, Clarence Howeth	OF	138	.282	B	
15	13	Chesbro, John Dwight (Jack)	P	29	.165	B	
		Clarke, Frederick Clifford MGR.	OF	103	.281	Lvlle	
		Cooley, Duff C. (Dick)	1B	65	.200	Phil	
		Dillon, Frank Edward	1B	5	.111	B	DetA
		Donahue, John Augustus (Jiggs)	C	3	.200	A	
		Ely, Frederick Wm.	SS	130	.242	B	
0	1	Flaherty, Patrick Joseph	P	4	.000	Lvlle	
0	0	Husting, Berthold Juneau	P	2	.000	xMilA	
		Latimer, Clifford Wesley	C	4	.333	Lvlle	
		Leach, Thomas Wm.	3B31	45	.215	Lvlle	
15	13	Leever, Samuel W.	P	28	.207	B	
0	2	Meekin, Jouett	P	2	.000	Bos	C
		McCreery, Thomas Leavenworth	OF	33	.223	B	
		O'Brien, Thomas F. (OF24)	1B65	94	.294	N.Y.	C
		O'Connor, John Joseph (Jack)	C	38	+.242	xStL	
18	14	Phillippe, Chas. Louis (Deacon)	P	32	.181	Lvlle	
1	0	Poole, Edward I.	P	2	.500	A	
		Ritchey, Claude Cassius	2B	123	.295	Lvlle	
		Schriver, Wm. F. (Pop)	C	23	.317	B	
20	7	Tannehill, Jesse Niles	P28	32	.342	B	
10	10	Waddell, George Edward (Rube)	P	22	.160	Lvlle & return	MilA
		Wagner, John Peter (Hans)	OF117	134	.380	Lvlle	
		Williams, James Thomas Williams	3B104	106	.266	B	
0	0	Woods, Walter Sidney	P	1	.000	Lvlle	C
		Zimmer, Chas. Louis (Chief)	C78	80	.298	Lvlle	

WON 90 NATIONAL LEAGUE FINISHED 1st.
LOST 49
TG 139 1901. PCT. .647

PITTSBURGH

FREDERICK CLIFFORD CLARKE

WON	LOST	NAME	POS.	G.	BA	FROM	TO
		Beaumont, Clarence Howeth	OF	132	.328	B	
		Bransfield, Wm. Edward (Kitty)	1B	139	.274	Bos98	
		Burke, James Timothy	3B	34	.211	xChiA	
		Carr, Lewis Smith	SS	9	.233	A	C
21	9	Chesbro, John Dwight (Jack)	P	33	.210	B	
		Clarke, Frederick Clifford MGR.	OF127	128	.316	B	
		Davis, Alfonzo DeFord (Lefty)	OF	88	+.308	xBkn	
6	3	Doheny, Edward R.	P	11	+.097	xN.Y.	
		Donahue, John Augustus (Jiggs)	C	2	.000	B	MilA
		Eagan, Chas. Eugene (Truck)	SS	4	.083	A	ClevA
		Ely, Frederick Wm.	SS	62	.219	B	PhilA
		Leach, Thomas Wm.	3B90	93	.298	B	
14	5	Leever, Samuel W.	P	19	.169	B	
3	0	Merritt, George Washington	P	4	.272	A	
		O'Connor, John Joseph (Jack)	C	56	.200	B	
22	12	Phillippe, Chas. Louis (Deacon)	P	34	.211	B	
5	4	Poole, Edward I.	P	23	.237	B	
		Ritchey, Claude Cassius	2B	140	.298	B	
		Smith, Elmer Ellsworth	OF	4	+.000	N.Y.	Bos
		Smith, Judson Grant (Jud)	3B	6	.130	BuffA	C
18	10	Tennehill, Jesse Niles	P	40	.226	B	
		Turner, Terrence LaMont (Terry)	3B	2	.428	A	
0	2	Waddell, George Edward	P	2	+.000	B	Chi
		Wagner, John Peter (Hans) (3B26 OF54)	SS61	141	.352	B	
1	4	Wiltse, Lewis DeWitt	P	7	.158	A	PhilA
		Yeager, George E.	C19	24	.267	xClevA	
		Zimmer, Chas. Louis (Chief)	C	67	.222	B	

WON 103 NATIONAL LEAGUE FINISHED 1st.
LOST 36
TG 139 1902. PCT. .741

PITTSBURGH

FREDERICK CLIFFORD CLARKE

WON	LOST	NAME	POS.	G.	BA	FROM	TO
		Beaumont, Clarence Howeth	OF	131	.357	B	
		Bransfield, Wm. Edward (Kitty)	1B	100	.308	B	
		Burke, James Timothy (SS4 3B9 OF15)	2B23	55	.296	B	
27	6	Chesbro, John Dwight (Jack)	P	34	.179	B	
		Clarke, Frederick Clifford MGR.	OF	114	.321	B	

WON	LOST	NAME	POS.	G.	BA	FROM	TO
		Conroy, Wm. Edward (Wid) (OF2)	SS93	95	.241	MilA	
		Crolius, Frederick Joseph	OF	9	.263	Bos	C
0	4	Cushman, Harvey Barnes	P	4	.200	A	C
		Davis, Alfonzo DeFord (Lefty)	OF55	59	.291	B	
17	4	Doheny, Edward R.	P	21	.169	B	
		Fohl, Leo Alexander	C	1	.000	A	
		Hopkins, John Winton	C	1	1.000	A	
		Leach, Thomas Wm.	3B	135	.280	B	
16	7	Leever, Samuel W. (OF1)	P26	26	.178	B	
0	0	Merritt, George Washington (P1)	OF2	2	.333	B	
		Miller, Wm.	OF	1	.200	A	C
3	0	McLaughlin, Warren A.	P	3	.363	Phil00	
		O'Connor, John Joseph (Jack) (1B6)	C39	45	.292	B	
		Phelps, Edward Joseph (1B5)	C13	18	.197	A	
20	9	Phillippe, Chas. Louis (Deacon)	P	30	.221	B	
0	0	Poole, Edward I.	P	1	+.250	B	Cin
		Richey, Claude Cassius (OF1)	2B114	114	.275	B	
		Sebring, James Dennison	OF	19	.338	A	
		Smith, Harry Thomas	C	49	.187	PhilA	
20	6	Tannehill, Jesse Niles (OF16)	P27	41	.289	B	
0	0	Wagner, John Peter (Hans) (P1 1B31 2B1 SS45)	OF59	137	.329	B	
		Zimmer, Chas. Louis (Chief) (1B1)	C40	40	.268	B	

WON 91 — NATIONAL LEAGUE — FINISHED 1st.
LOST 49
TG 140 — 1903. — PCT. .650

PITTSBURGH

FREDERICK CLIFFORD CLARKE

WON	LOST	NAME	POS.	G.	BA	FROM	TO
		Beaumont, Clarence Howeth	OF	141	.341	B	
		Bransfield, Wm. Edward (Kitty)	1B	127	.265	B	
		Carisch, Frederick Behlmer	C	5	.352	A	
		Clarke, Frederick Clifford MGR.	OF101	102	.351	B	
		Curtis, Eugene	OF	5	.421	A	C
		Diehl, Ernest Guy	OF	1	.333	A	
16	8	Doheny, Edward R.	P	27	.209	B	C
1	5	Falkenberg, Frederick Peter (Cy)	P	10	.190	A	
		Gertenrich, Louis Wilhelm	OF	1	.000	MilA01	C
		Gray, Wm.	OF	2	.333	A	C
		Hofman, Arthur Frederich	OF1	3	.000	A	
9	6	Kennedy, Wm. V. (Brickyard)	P	18	.362	N.Y.	C
		Krueger, Oompaul Arthur (OF28)	SS29	71	.246	StL	
		Leach, Thomas Wm.	3B	127	.298	B	
25	7	Leever, Samuel W.	P	36	.165	B	
		Lobert, John Bernard (Hans)	3B	5	.077	A	
		Marshall, Joseph H. (2B1)	OF9	9	.261	A	
0	0	Merritt, George Washington	P	8	.148	B	C
0	1	Moren, Lewis Howard	P	1	.000	A	
0	3	Pfiester, John Theodore Joseph (Jack)	P	3	.000	A	
		Phelps, Edward Joseph	C76	79	.282	B	
25	9	Phillippe, Chas. Louis (Deacon)	P36	37	.210	B	
		Ritchey, Claude Cassius	2B	137	.287	B	
0	1	Scanlan, Wm. Dennis (Doc)	P	1	.000	A	
		Sebring, James Dennison	OF	124	.277	B	
		Smith, Harry Thomas	C60	61	.175	B	
2	2	Thompson, John (Gus)	P	5	.250	A	
5	3	Veil, Frederick Wm. (Bucky)	P	12	.207	A	
		Wagner, John Peter (Hans)	SS111	129	.355	B	
		Weaver, Arthur Coggshall	C	15	+.239	xStL	
5	3	Wilhelm, Irving Key (Kaiser)	P	13	.088	A	
3	1	Winham, LaFayette Sylvester	P	5	.071	Bkn	C

WON 87 — NATIONAL LEAGUE — FINISHED 4th.
LOST 66
TG 153 — 1904. — PCT. .569

PITTSBURGH

FREDERICK CLIFFORD CLARKE

WON	LOST	NAME	POS.	G.	BA	FROM	TO
		Archer, James Patrick	C	7	.157	A	
		Beaumont, Clarence Howeth	OF	153	.301	B	
		Bransfield, Wm.Edward (Kitty)	1B	139	.223	B	
1	2	Camnitz, Samuel Howard	P	10	.063	A	
		Carisch, Frederick Behlmer	C22	36	.248	B	
10	5	Case, Chas. Emmett	P	18	.170	Cin01	
		Cassady, Harry D.	OF	11	.214	A	
		Clarke, Frederick Clifford MGR.	OF	70	.306	B	
		Diehl, Ernest Guy (SS4)	OF8	12	.162	B	
19	9	Flaherty, Patrick Joseph	P29	31	.212	xChiA	
		Gilbert, John Robert	OF	25	.241	NY98	C
		Krueger, Oompaul Arthur (SS32)	OF33	75	.194	B	
		Leach, Thomas Wm.	3B	146	.257	B	
1	2	Lee, Wyatt Arnold	P	8	.333	WashA	C
18	12	Leever, Samuel W.	P	34	.263	B	
		Lowe, Robert Lincoln (Link)		1	.000	Chi	DetA
14	11	Lynch, Michael Joseph	P	27	.230	A	
7	9	Miller, Roscoe Clyde	P	19	.043	N.Y.	C
0	0	Moren, Lewis Howard	P	1	.000	B	
		McCormick, Harry Elwood (Moose)	OF	66	+.290	xN.Y.	
1	1	Pfiester, John Theodore Joseph (Jack)	P	3	.167	B	

WON	LOST	NAME	POS.	G.	BA	FROM	TO
		Phelps, Edward Joseph	C91	92	.242	B	
10	10	Phillippe, Chas. Louis (Deacon)	P	21	.123	B	
		Rafter, John Cornelius	C	1	.000	A	C
		Ritchey, Claude Cassius	2B	156	.263	B	
5	3	Robertaille, Anthony F. (Chick)	P	9	.083	A	
1	2	Scanlan, Wm. Dennis (Doc)	P	4	+.000	B	Bkn
		Sebring, James Dennison	OF	80	+.269	B	Cin
		Smith, Harry Thomas	C44	47	.248	B	
		Smith, Louis O.	OF	13	.142	A	
		Stankard, Thomas Francis	3B	2	.000	A	C
0	0	Veil, Frederick Wm. (Bucky)	P	1	1.000	B	C
		Wagner, John Peter (Hans)	SS121	132	.349	B	

WON 96 NATIONAL LEAGUE FINISHED 2nd.
LOST 57
TG 153 1905. PCT. .627

PITTSBURGH

FREDERICK CLIFFORD CLARKE

WON	LOST	NAME	POS.	G.	BA	FROM	TO
		Beaumont, Clarence Howeth	OF	97	.328	B	
		Brain, David Leonard (SS6)	3B76	82	+.257	xStL	
		Carisch, Frederick Behlmer	C	30	.206	B	
12	10	Case, Chas. Emmett	P	31	.103	B	
		Clancey, Wm. Edward	1B52	56	.229	A	C
		Clarke, Frederick Clifford MGR.	OF	137	.299	B	
		Clymer, Otis Edgar	OF89	90	.296	A	
10	10	Flaherty, Patrick Joseph	P27	29	.197	B	
		Flanagan, James Paul (Steamer)	OF	7	.280	A	C
		Ganley, Robert Stephen	OF	32	.315	A	
		Gibson, George	C	44	.178	A	
4	2	Hillebrand, Homer Hiller Henry (P10)	1B16	36	.236	A	
		Howard, George Elmer (OF28)	1B90	119	.292	A	
0	1	Kinsella, Edward Wm.	P	3	.000	A	
		Knabe, Franz Otto	3B	3	.300	A	
		Leach, Thomas Wm. (3B58)	OF71	131	.257	B	
19	6	Leever, Samuel W.	P	33	.102	B	
5	2	Leifield, Albert Peter (Lefty)	P	8	.450	A	
17	7	Lynch, Michael Joseph	P	33	.136	B	
0	0	Moore, George Raymond	P	1	.000	A	C
		McBride, George Florian	3B17	25	+.218	MilA01	StL
		Peitz, Henry Clement (Heinie)	C87	88	.223	Cin	
22	13	Phillippe, Chas. Louis (Deacon)	P	38	.093	B	
		Ritchey, Claude Cassius	2B	153	.255	B	
7	6	Robertaille, Anthony F. (Chick)	P	17	.133	B	C
		Smith, Harry Thomas	C	1	.000	B	
		Wagner, John Peter (Hans)	SS145	147	.363	B	
		Wallace, James L.	OF	7	.214	A	C

WON 93 NATIONAL LEAGUE FINISHED 3rd.
LOST 60
TG 153 1906. PCT. .608

PITTSBURGH

FREDERICK CLIFFORD CLARKE

WON	LOST	NAME	POS.	G.	BA	FROM	TO
		Abstein, Wm. Henry (Big Bill)	OF	8	.200	A	
		Beaumont, Clarence Howeth	OF	78	.265	B	
1	1	Brady, James Ward	P	3	.100	Phil	
1	0	Camnitz, Samuel Howard	P	2	.000	Pitt04	
		Carisch, Frederick Behlmer	C	4	.083	B	
1	1	Case, Chas. Emmott	P	2	.600	B	C
		Clarke, Frederick Clifford MGR.	OF	110	.309	B	
		Clymer, Otis Edgar	OF	11	.244	B	
		Ganley, Robert Stephen	OF	134	.268	B	
		Gibson, George	C	81	.258	B	
		Hallman, Wm. Harry	OF	23	.270	ChiA03	
3	2	Hillebrand, Homer Hiller Henry	P	7	.250	B	
2	3	Karger, Edwin	P	5	+.091	A	StL
		Leach, Thomas Wm. (OF60)	3B65	126	.286	B	
22	7	Leever, Samuel W.	P	36	.211	B	
18	13	Leifield, Albert Peter (Lefty)	P	37	.125	B	
6	5	Lynch, Michael Joseph	P	18	.205	B	
0	0	Manske, Louis	P	2	.000	A	C
0	1	Maxwell, J. Albert	P	1	.000	A	
		Meier, Arthur Ernst (SS17)	OF52	68	.256	A	C
1	3	McFarland, Chas. Edward (Chappie)	P	6	+.385	xStL	Bkn
0	1	McIlveen, Henry Cooke	P	5	.286	A	
		Nealon, James Joseph	1B	154	.255	A	
		Peitz, Henry Clement (Heinie)	C	38	.240	B	
		Phelps, Edward Joseph	C	40	+.237	xCin	
15	10	Phillippe, Chas. Louis (Deacon)	P	33	.244	B	
		Ritchey, Claude Cassius	2B	151	.269	B	
		Sheehan, Thomas H.	3B	90	.241	A	
		Smith, Harry Thomas	C	1	.000	B	
		Storke, Alan Marshall (SS1)	3B2	5	.250	A	
		Wagner, John Peter (Hans)	SS137	140	.339	B	
23	13	Willis, Victor Gazaway	P	41	.174	Bos	

WON 91 NATIONAL LEAGUE FINISHED 2nd.
LOST 63
TG 154 1907. PCT. .591

PITTSBURGH

FREDERICK CLIFFORD CLARKE

WON	LOST	NAME	POS.	G.	BA	FROM	TO
		Abbaticchio, Edward James	2B	147	.262	Bos05	

WON	LOST	NAME	POS.	G.	BA	FROM	TO
2	2	Adams, Chas. Benjamin (Babe)	P	4	.286	StL	
		Anderson, Edward John (Goat)	OF115	121	.206	A	C
0	0	Brady, James Ward	P	1	.000	B	
13	8	Camnitz, Samuel Howard	P	31	.050	B	
		Campbell, Marc Thaddeus	SS	2	.250	A	C
		Clarke, Frederick Clifford MGR.	OF	144	.289	B	
		Clymer, Otis Edgar	OF15	16	.227	B	WashA
0	2	Duggleby, Wm. James	P	9	+.154	xPhil	C
		Gibson, George	C	110	.220	B	
		Hallman, Wm. Harry	OF73	84	.222	B	C
		Kelsey, George W.	C	2	.400	A	C
		Leach, Thomas Wm. (3B33)	OF109	149	.303	B	
14	9	Leever, Samuel W.	P	31	.151	B	
20	16	Leifield, Albert Peter (Lefty)	P	40	.147	B	
2	2	Lynch, Michael Joseph	P	7	+.250	B	N.Y.
5	1	Maddox, Nicholas (Nick)	P	6	.308	A	
		Maggart, Harl Vess	OF	3	.000	A	
		Moeller, Daniel Edward	OF	11	.285	A	
		McKechnie, Wm. Boyd	2B	3	.125	A	
		Nealon, James Joseph	1B	104	.257	B	C
0	1	Otey, Wm. Tilford	P	3	.200	A	
		Philps, Edward Joseph	C35	36	.212	B	
14	11	Phillippe, Chas. Louis (Deacon)	P	35	.185	B	
		Sheehan, Thomas H.	3B57	67	.274	B	
		Smith, Harry Thomas	C	18	.263	B	
		Storke, Alan Marshall (1B23)	3B67	102	.258	B	
		Swacina, Harry J.	1B	26	.200	A	
		Wagner, John Peter (Hans)	SS138	142	.350	B	
0	0	Walsh, Cornelius	P	1	.000	A	C
21	11	Willis, Victor Gazaway	P	39	.136	B	
0	0	Wolter, Harry Meigs	P	1	+.000	xCin	StL

WON 98 — NATIONAL LEAGUE — FINISHED 2nd.
LOST 56 — (TIED WITH N.Y.)
TG 154 — 1908. — PCT. .636

PITTSBURGH

FREDERICK CLIFFORD CLARKE

WON	LOST	NAME	POS.	G.	BA	FROM	TO
		Abbaticchio, Edward James	2B	144	.250	B	
		Becker, Beals	OF	17	+.154	A	Bos
1	0	Brandom, Chester Milton	P	3	.143	A	
16	9	Camnitz, Samuel Howard	P	38	.083	B	
		Clarke, Frederick Clifford MGR.	OF150	151	.265	B	
		Gibson, George	C	140	.228	B	
		Gill, Warren Darst	1B	25	.224	A	C
0	0	Hillebrand, Homer Hiller Henry	P	1	.000	Pitt06	C
		Kane, James J.	1B	40	.241	A	C
		Leach, Thomas Wm.	3B150	152	.259	B	
15	7	Leever, Samuel W.	P	38	.148	B	
15	14	Leifield, Albert Peter (Lefty)	P	34	.227	B	
23	8	Maddox, Nicholas (Nick)	P	36	.266	B	
		Moeller, Daniel Edward	OF23	27	.193	B	
0	0	McCarthy, Thomas Patrick	P	2	+.000	xCin	Bos
		O'Connor, Patrick Francis	C	12	.187	A	
		Phelps, Edward Joseph	C	20	.234	B	
0	0	Phillippe, Chas. Louis (Deacon)	P	5	.250	B	
		Shannon, Wm. Porter (Spike)	OF	32	+.197	xN.Y.	C
		Shaw, Royal N.	OF	1	.000	A	
		Starr, Chas. Watkin	SS	19	.186	StLA05	
		Storke, Alan Marshall	1B49	56	.252	B	
		Sullivan, John Eugene	C	1	.000	DetA05	C
		Swacina, Harry J.	1B	50	.216	B	
		Thomas, Roy Allen	OF	101	+.256	xPhil	
1	2	Vail, Robert Garfield	P	4	.250	A	C
		Wagner, John Peter (Hans)	SS	151	.354	B	
23	11	Willis, Victor Gazaway	P	41	.165	B	
		Wilson, John Owen	OF143	144	.227	A	
0	2	Young, Harley E.	P	8	+.083	A	Bos
4	3	Young, Irving Melrose (Young Cy)	P	16	+.200	xBos	

WON 110 — NATIONAL LEAGUE — FINISHED 1st.
LOST 42
TG 152 — 1909. — PCT. .724

PITTSBURGH

FREDERICK CLIFFORD CLARKE

WON	LOST	NAME	POS.	G.	BA	FROM	TO
		Abbaticchio, Edward James	SS18	23	.230	B	
		Abstein, Wm. Henry (Big Bill)	1B	135	.260	Pitt06	
12	3	Adams, Chas. Benjamin (Babe)	P	25	.051	Pitt07	
		Barbeau, Wm. Joseph (Jap)	3B	85	+.220	ClevA06	StL
1	0	Brandom, Chester Milton	P	13	.100	B	
		Byrne, Robert Mathew	3B	46	+.256	xStL	
0	0	Camnitz, R. Harry	P	1	.000	A	
25	6	Camnitz, Samuel Howard	P	41	.138	B	
		Clarke, Frederick Clifford MGR.	OF	152	.287	B	
0	0	Durbin, Blaine A.	P	1	+.000	xCin	C
2	1	Frock, Samuel W.	P	8	.142	Bos07	
		Gibson, George	C	150	.265	B	
		Hyatt, Robert Hamilton (Ham)	OF	49	.299	A	
		Leach, Thomas Wm.	OF138	151	.261	B	
8	1	Leever, Samuel W.	P	19	.167	B	
19	8	Leifield, Albert Peter (Lefty)	P	32	.192	B	
13	8	Maddox, Nicholas (Nick)	P	31	.224	B	
		Miller, John Barney	2B	150	.279	A	
		Miller, Ward Taylor	OF	14	+.143	A	Cin
0	0	Moore, Eugene Sr.	P	1	.000	A	
		O'Connor, Patrick Francis	C	9	.312	B	
8	3	Phillippe, Chas. Louis (Deacon)	P	22	.071	B	
0	1	Powell, Wm. Burruss	P	3	.000	A	
		Shaw, Royal N.		1	.000	B	C
		Simon, Michael Edward	C	12	.167	A	

WON	LOST	NAME	POS.	G.	BA	FROM	TO
		Storke, Alan Marshall	1B	32	+.254	B	StL
0	0	Wacker, Chas.	P	1	.000	A	C
		Wagner, John Peter (Hans)	SS136	137	.339	B	
22	11	Willis, Victor Gazaway	P	39	.136	B	
		Wilson, John Owen	OF	154	.273	B	

WON 86 — NATIONAL LEAGUE — FINISHED 3rd.
LOST 67
TG 153 — 1910. — PCT. .562

PITTSBURGH

FREDERICK CLIFFORD CLARKE

WON	LOST	NAME	POS.	G.	BA	FROM	TO
		Abbaticchio, Edward James	SS	1	+.000	B	Bos
18	9	Adams, Chas. Benjamin (Babe)	P	34	.193	B	
		Byrne, Robert Mathew	3B	148	.296	B	
		Campbell, Arthur Vincent	OF	74	.326	Chi08	
12	13	Camnitz, Samuel Howard	P	38	.125	B	
		Carey, Max George	OF	2	.500	A	
		Clarke, Frederick Clifford MGR.	OF	118	.263	B	
0	0	Dowd, James Joseph	P	1	.000	A	C
1	2	Ferry, John Francis	P	6	.333	A	
		Flynn, John Anthony	1B	93	.274	A	
0	0	Frock, Samuel W.	P	1	+.000	B	Bos
		Gibson, George	C	143	.259	B	
		Hyatt, Robert Hamilton (Ham)	1B38	41	.263	B	
		Kading, John Fred	1B	8	.304	A	
		Leach, Thomas Wm.	OF131	133	.270	B	
6	5	Leever, Samuel W.	P25	26	.065	B	C
15	13	Leifield, Albert Peter (Lefty)	P	40	.183	B	
2	3	Maddox, Nicholas (Nick)	P	20	.214	B	C
0	0	Mercer, John Locke	P	1	.000	A	
		Miller, John Barney	2B	119	.227	B	
2	1	Moore, Eugene Sr.	P	4	.000	B	
		McCarthy, Alexander George	SS	3	.084	A	
		McKechnie, Wm. Boyd	2B36	60	.217	Pitt07	
		O'Connor, Patrick Francis	C	1	.250	B	
14	2	Phillippe, Chas. Louis (Deacon)	P	31	.220	B	
4	6	Powell, Wm. Burruss	P	12	.261	B	
		Sharpe, Bayard Heston	1B	4	+.188	xBos	C
		Simon, Michael Edward	C14	20	.213	B	
0	3	Steele, Elmer Rae	P	3	.000	BosA	
		Wagner, John Peter (Hans)	SS137	150	.320	B	
2	1	Webb, Cleon Earl	P	7	.200	A	C
10	9	White, Kirby	P	30	+.261	xBos	
		Wilson, John Owen	OF	146	.276	B	

WON 85 — NATIONAL LEAGUE — FINISHED 3rd.
LOST 69
TG 154 — 1911. — PCT. .552

PITTSBURGH

FREDERICK CLIFFORD CLARKE

WON	LOST	NAME	POS.	G.	BA	FROM	TO
22	12	Adams, Chas. Benjamin (Babe)	P	40	.252	B	
		Byrne, Robert Mathew	3B	152	.259	B	
20	15	Camnitz, Samuel Howard	P	40	.143	B	
		Campbell, Arthur Vincent	OF	21	.312	B	
		Carey, Max George	OF	122	.258	B	
		Clarke, Frederick Clifford MGR.	OF	101	.324	B	
0	0	Cottrell, Ensign Stover	P	1	.000	A	
		Dorsey, Jeremiah (Jerry)	OF	2	.000	A	C
6	4	Ferry, John Francis	P	26	.310	B	
		Flynn, John Anthony (3B12)	1B20	32	.214	B	
1	1	Gardner, Harry	P	13	.214	A	
		Gibson, George	C	98	.209	B	
4	6	Hendrix, Claude Raymond	P	22	.098	A	
		Hunter, Frederick Creighton	1B	61	.254	A	C
		Keene, Wm. Brown	1B	5	.000	A	C
		Keliher, Maurice Michael	1B	3	.000	A	
		Kelly, Wm. J.	C	6	.125	StL	
		Leach, Thomas Wm.	OF89	102	.238	B	
16	16	Leifield, Albert Peter (Lefty)	P42	43	.235	B	
		Miller, John Barney	2B	129	.268	B	
		McCarthy, Alexander George	SS33	46	.240	B	
		McKechnie, Wm. Boyd (2B17)	1B57	92	.227	B	
4	2	Nagle, Walter Harold	P	8	.143	A	BosA
3	2	O'Toole, Martin James	P	5	.357	Cin08	
0	0	Phillippe, Chas. Louis (Deacon)	P	3	1.000	B	C
0	1	Robinson, John Henry	P	5	.000	A	
		Shovelin, John Joseph		2	.000	A	
		Simon, Michael Edward	C	68	.228	B	
0	0	Smith, Sherrod Malone (Sherry)	P	1	.000	A	
9	9	Steele, Elmer Rae	P	31	+.180	B	Bkn
		Wagner, John Peter (Hans) (1B28)	SS101	130	.334	B	
0	1	White, Kirby	P	2	.000	B	C
		Wilson, John Owen	OF	146	.300	B	

WON 93 — NATIONAL LEAGUE — FINISHED 2nd.
LOST 58
TG 151 — 1912. — PCT. .616

PITTSBURGH

FREDERICK CLIFFORD CLARKE

WON	LOST	NAME	POS.	G.	BA	FROM	TO
11	8	Adams, Chas. Benjamin (Babe)	P	28	.226	B	
		Bisland, Rivington Martin		1	.000	A	
		Blackburn, Earl Stuart	C	1	+.000	A	Cin
		Butler, Arthur Edward	2B	43	.273	Bos	
		Byrne, Robert Mathew	3B	130	.288	B	
22	12	Camnitz, Samuel Howard	P	41	.235	B	

WON	LOST	NAME	POS.	G.	BA	FROM	TO
		Capron, Ralph E.	OF	1	.000	A	
		Carey, Max George	OF	150	.302	B	
		Clarke, Frederick Clifford MGR.	(DID NOT PLAY)			B	
2	2	Cole, Leonard Leslie (King)	P	12	+.133	xChi	
3	0	Cooper, Arley Wilbur	P	6	.154	A	
		Dodd, Ona Melvin	2B	5	.000	A	C
		Donlin, Michael Joseph	OF62	77	.316	Bos	
		Edington, Jacob Frank	OF	15	.302	A	C
2	0	Ferry, John Francis	P	11	.077	B	
0	0	Gardner, Harry	P	1	.000	B	C
		Gibson, George	C94	95	.240	B	
		Gray, Stanley	1B5	7	.250	A	C
24	9	Hendrix, Claude Raymond	P39	46	.322	B	
		Hofman, Arthur Frederich	OF	17	+.283	xChi	
		Hyatt, Robert Hamilton (Ham)	OF15	46	.289	Pitt10	
		Keliher, Maurice Michael		2	.000	B	C
		Kelly, Wm. J.	C39	48	.318	B	
		Leach, Thomas Wm.	OF	28	+.299	B	Chi
1	2	Leifield, Albert Peter (Lefty)	P	6	+.143	B	Chi
		Mensor, Edward E.	OF32	39	.263	A	
		Miller, John Barney	1B147	148	.275	B	
		McCarthy, Alexander George	2B105	111	.277	B	
		McKechnie, Wm. Boyd (2B4)	SS12	24	.247	B	
		Nicholson, Ovid	OF	6	.454	A	C
15	17	O'Toole, Martin James	P	37	.222	B	
		Rehg, Walter Phillip	OF	7	.000	A	
12	7	Robinson, John Henry	P	33	.254	B	
		Simon, Michael Edward	C40	42	.301	B	
0	0	Smith, Sherrod Malone (Sherry)	P	3	.000	B	
		Viox, James Harry	3B9	33	.186	A	
		Wagner, John Peter (Hans)	SS143	145	.324	B	
1	1	Warner, Edward Emory	P	11	.133	A	C
		Wilson, John Owen	OF	152	.300	B	

WON 78 NATIONAL LEAGUE FINISHED 4th.
LOST 71
TG 149 1913. PCT. .523

PITTSBURGH

FREDERICK CLIFFORD CLARKE

WON	LOST	NAME	POS.	G.	BA	FROM	TO
21	10	Adams, Chas. Benjamin (Babe)	P	43	.289	B	
		Booe, Everett Little	OF22	29	.200	A	
		Britton, Stephen Gilbert	SS	3	.000	A	C
		Butler, Arthur Edward (SS26)	2B28	82	.280	B	
		Byrne, Robert Mathew	3B	113	+.270	B	Phil
6	17	Camnitz, Samuel Howard	P	36	+.153	B	Phil
		Carey, Max George	OF	154	.277	B	
		Clarke, Frederick Clifford MGR.	OF8	9	.077	B	
		Coleman, Robert Hunter	C	24	.180	A	
0	1	Conzelman, Joseph Harrison	P	2	.000	A	

WON	LOST	NAME	POS.	G.	BA	FROM	TO
5	3	Cooper, Arley Wilbur	P	30	.077	B	
		Dolan, Alvin James (Cozy)	3B	35	+.203	xPhil	
0	0	Duffy, Barney A.	P	3	.250	A	C
0	0	Eayrs, Edwin	P	4	.167	A	
1	0	Ferry, John Francis	P	4	.000	B	C
		Gibson, George	C	48	.280	B	
14	15	Hendrix, Claude Raymond	P42	53	.273	B	
		Hofman, Arthur Frederich	OF24	28	.229	B	
		Hyatt, Robert Hamilton (Ham)	OF	63	.333	B	
		Kafora, Frank Jacob	C	1	.000	A	
		Kelly, Wm. J.	C40	48	.268	B	C
		Kommers, Frederick Raymond	OF	40	.232	A	
3	1	Luhrsen, Wm. Ferdinand	P	5	.000	A	C
0	0	Mamaux, Albert Leon	P	1	.000	A	
		Mensor, Edward E.	OF18	44	.179	B	
		Miller, John Barney	1B150	154	.272	B	
		Mitchell, Michael Francis	OF	54	+.271	xChi	
		McCarthy, Alexander George	SS	31	.203	B	
8	6	McQuillan, George Washington	P	25	.103	Cinll	
6	8	O'Toole, Martin James	P	26	.132	B	
14	9	Robinson, John Henry	P	43	.180	B	
0	1	Scheneberg, John B.	P	1	.500	A	
		Simon, Michael Edward	C	92	.247	B	
		Viox, James Harry	2B124	137	.317	B	
		Wagner, John Peter (Hans)	SS105	114	.300	B	
		Wilson, John Owen	OF	155	.266	B	
		Wood, Roy Winton	OF	14	.285	A	

WON 69 NATIONAL LEAGUE FINISHED 7th.
LOST 85
TG 154 1914. PCT. .448

PITTSBURGH

FREDERICK CLIFFORD CLARKE

WON	LOST	NAME	POS.	G.	BA	FROM	TO
13	16	Adams, Chas. Benjamin (Babe)	P	40	.165	B	
		Berger, Clarence	OF	5	.083	A	C
0	0	Bohen, Leo J. (Pat)	P	1	.000	PhilA	C
		Brenegan, Selmar G.	C	1	.000	A	C
		Carey, Max George	OF154	156	.243	B	
		Clarke, Frederick Clifford MGR.		2	.000	B	
		Coleman, Robert Hunter	C72	73	.266	B	
		Collins, John Edgar	OF	49	.242	A	
5	6	Conzelman, Joseph Harrison	P	33	.111	B	
16	15	Cooper, Arley Wilbur	P	40	.207	B	
		Costello, Daniel Francis	OF20	21	.297	NYA	
		Gerber, Walter	SS	17	.241	A	
		Gibson, George	C101	102	.285	B	
0	0	Falsey, Peter James	P	3	.000	A	C
13	17	Harmon, Robert Green	P37	44	.140	StL	
		Hyatt, Robert Hamilton (Ham)	OF	74	.215	B	
		Kafora, Frank Jacob	C17	21	.130	B	C
3	2	Kantlehner, Ervine Lester	P	21	.067	A	
0	2	Kelly, Herbert Barrett	P	5	.222	A	

WON	LOST	NAME	POS.	G.	BA	FROM	TO
		Kelly, James Robert	OF	32	.227	A	
		(Robert John Taggart)					
		Kelly, Joseph Herbert	OF139	141	.222	A	
		Kilhullen, Joseph Isadore	C	1	.000	A	C
		Konetchy, Edward Joseph	1B	154	.249	StL	
		Leonard, Joseph Howard	3B38	53	.198	A	
5	2	Mamaux, Albert Leon	P	13	.250	B	
		Mensor, Edward E.	OF25	44	.202	B	C
		Mitchell, Michael Francis	OF	76	.234	B	WashA
		Mowrey, Harry Harlan (Mike)	3B78	79	.254	StL	
0	0	McArthur, Oliver Alexander	P	1	.000	A	C
		McAuley, James Earl	SS12	15	.125	A	
		(2B1 3B2)					
		McCarthy, Alexander George	3B36	57	.150	B	
13	17	McQuillan, George Washington	P	45	.068	B	
1	8	O'Toole, Martin James	P	19	+.167	B	N.Y.
		Schang, Robert Martin	C	10	.250	A	
		Scheeren, Frederick (Fritz)	OF	11	.267	A	
		Shafer, Ralph Newton		1	.000	A	C
		Siglin, Wesley Peter	2B	14	.154	A	
		Smith, Sydney	C	4	.300	ClevAll	
		Viox, James Harry	2B138	143	.265	B	
		Wagner, John Peter (Hans)	SS132	150	.252	B	
		(3B17)					
		Wagner, Wm. Joseph	C	3	.000	A	

WON 73 — NATIONAL LEAGUE — FINISHED 5th.
LOST 81
TG 154 — 1915. — PCT. .474

PITTSBURGH

FREDERICK CLIFFORD CLARKE

WON	LOST	NAME	POS.	G.	BA	FROM	TO
14	14	Adams, Chas. Benjamin (Babe)	P	40	.141	B	
		Baird, Howard Douglas	3B120	145	.219	A	
		(OF20)					
		Barney, Edmund J.	OF26	32	.273	xN.Y.A	
0	0	Benton, John Cleveland (Rube)	P	1	+.333	xCin	N.Y.
		Carey, Max George	OF139	140	.254	B	
		Clarke, Frederick Clifford	OF	1	.500	B	C
		MGR.					
		Collins, John Edgar	OF	101	+.293	B	Bos
1	1	Conzelman, Joseph Harrison	P	18	.091	B	C
5	16	Cooper, Arley Wilbur	P	38	.117	B	
		Costello, Daniel Francis	OF22	71	.216	B	
		Daubert, Harry J.	SS	1	.000	A	C
		Duncan, Louis Baird (Pat)	OF	3	.200	A	
		Gerber, Walter (SS21)	3B23	56	.194	B	
		Gibson, George	C118	120	.251	B	
16	17	Harmon, Robert Green	P37	42	.147	B	
2	1	Hill, Carmen Proctor	P	8	.154	A	
		Hinchman, Wm. White	OF	156	.307	ClevA09	
		Johnston, Wheeler Rogers	1B	147	.265	ClevA	
5	12	Kantlehner, Ervine Lester	P	29	.288	B	

WON	LOST	NAME	POS.	G.	BA	FROM	TO
1	1	Kelly, Herbert Barrett	P	5	.500	B	C
		Lejeune, Sheldon Aldenbury	OF	18	.169	Bknll	C
21	8	Mamaux, Albert Leon	P	38	.163	B	
		Murphy, Leo Joseph	C20	31	.098	A	C
		McAuley, James Earl	SS	5	.133	B	
		McCarthy, Alexander George	2B	21	+.204	B	Chi
8	10	McQuillan, George Washington	P	31	+.091	B	Phil
		Schang, Robert Martin	C	56	+.184	B	N.Y.
		Scheeren, Frederick (Fritz)	OF	4	.000	B	C
		Siglin, Wesley Peter	2B	6	.285	B	
0	0	Slattery, Philip Richard	P	3	.000	A	C
		Smith, Sydney		1	.000	B	C
0	1	Vance, Clarence Arthur (Dazzy)	P	1	.000	A	NYA
		Viox, James Harry	2B134	150	.256	B	
		Wagner, John Peter (Hans)	SS131	156	.274	B	
		Wagner, Wm. Joseph	C	5	.000	B	

WON 65 — NATIONAL LEAGUE — FINISHED 6th.
LOST 89
TG 154 — 1916. — PCT. .422

PITTSBURGH

JAMES JOSEPH CALLAHAN

WON	LOST	NAME	POS.	G.	BA	FROM	TO
2	9	Adams, Chas. Benjamin (Babe)	P	16	.273	B	
		Altenburg, Jesse Howard	OF	8	.429	A	
		Baird, Howard Douglas	3B80	128	.216	B	
		(2B29 OF16)					
		Barney, Edmund J.	OF40	45	.197	B	C
		Batsch, Wm. McKinley		1	.000	A	C
		Bigbee, Carson Lee (OF19)	2B23	43	.250	A	
		Carey, Max George	OF	154	.264	B	
0	0	Carpenter, Paul Calvin	P	5	.000	A	C
		Compton, Albert Sebastian	OF	5	+.100	xBos	
		(Bash)					
12	11	Cooper, Arley Wilbur	P42	44	.215	B	
		Costello, Daniel Francis	OF41	60	.239	B	C
2	5	Evans, Wm. James	P	13	.150	A	
		Farmer, John Floyd (OF15)	2B31	55	.271	A	
		Fischer, Wm. Chas.	C	42	+.254	xChi	
		Fisher, Wilbur McCullough		1	.000	A	C
		Gibson, George	C29	33	.202	B	
		Gleason, Wm. Patrick	2B	1	.000	A	
2	3	Grimes, Burleigh Arland	P	6	.176	A	
		Halliday, Newton	1B	1	.000	A	C
8	11	Harmon, Robert Green	P31	35	.109	B	
0	0	Hill, Carmen Proctor	P	2	.000	B	
		Hinchman, Wm. White (1B31)	OF124	152	.315	B	
6	10	Jacobs, Wm. Elmer	P	34	.075	Phil14	
		Johnston, Wheeler Rogers	1B110	114	.213	B	
5	15	Kantlehner, Ervine Lester	P	34	+.174	B	Phil
		King, Lee	OF	8	.111	A	
		Knabe, Franz Otto	2B	28	+.193	BaltF	Chi
		Madden, Eugene	OF	1	.000	A	C

WON	LOST	NAME	POS.	G.	BA	FROM	TO
21	15	Mamaux, Albert Leon	P	45	.191	B	
7	10	Miller, Frank Lee	P	30	.137	ChiA13	
		McAuley, James Earl	SS	4	.250	B	
		McCarthy, Alexander George (2B7)	SS39	50	+.197	xChi	
		O'Brien, Raymond Joseph	OF	16	.211	A	C
		Schmidt, Walter Joseph	C57	64	.190	A	
		Schulte, Frank	OF	55	+.241	xChi	
		Schultz, Joseph Chas. (3B24)	2B24	77	.260	Chi	
0	0	Scott, John Wm. (Jack)	P	3	.000	A	
		Siglin, Wesley Peter	2B	3	.250	B	C
		Smith, James Lawrence	SS27	36	.188	BaltF	
		Smykal, Frank John	SS3	6	.300	A	C
		Viox, James Harry	2B25	43	.250	B	C
		Wagner, John Peter (Hans) (1B24)	SS92	123	.287	B	
		Wagner, Wm. Joseph	C15	19	.237	B	
		Warner, George Hoke	3B42	44	.238	A	
		Wilson, Arthur Earl	C	53	+.258	ChiF	Chi

WON 51 LOST 103 TG 154 — NATIONAL LEAGUE 1917. — FINISHED 8th (LAST) PCT. .331

PITTSBURGH

JAMES JOSEPH CALLAHAN JOHN PETER WAGNER HUGO FRANK BEZDEK

WON	LOST	NAME	POS.	G.	BA	FROM	TO
		Altenburg, Jesse Howard	OF2	11	.176	B	C
		Baird, Howard Douglas	3B	43	+.259	B	StL
		Bigbee, Carson Lee (2B16)	OF107	133	.239	B	
		Blackwell, Frederick Wm.	C	3	.200	A	
		Boeckel, Norman D.	3B62	64	.265	A	
		Brief, Anthony Vincent (Bunny)	1B34	36	.217	ChiA15	C
		Carey, Max George	OF153	155	.296	B	
7	11	Carlson, Harold Gust (Hal)	P	34	.122	A	
		Caton, James Howard	SS	14	.211	A	
17	11	Cooper, Arley Wilbur	P40	41	.204	B	
		Debus, Adam Joseph (3B18)	SS21	38	.229	A	C
0	4	Evans, Wm. James	P	8	.111	B	
		Fischer, Wm. Chas.	C69	95	.286	B	C
		Flinn, Don Raphiel	OF8	14	.298	A	C
		Gleason, Wm. Patrick	2B	14	.167	B	
3	16	Grimes, Burleigh Arland	P37	42	.232	B	
		Hinchman, Wm. White (1B20)	OF48	69	.189	B	
		Jackson, Chas. Herbert	OF36	41	.240	ChiA15	C
6	19	Jacobs, Wm. Elmer	P	38	.179	B	
		Kelly, George Lange (Long George)	1B	8	+.087	xN.Y.	
		King, Lee	OF102	111	.249	B	
2	11	Mamaux, Albert Leon	P	16	.226	B	
10	19	Miller, Frank Lee	P38	39	.118	B	
		Miller, Raymond P.	1B	6	.148	xCleveA	C
		Mollwitz, Frederick August	1B	36	.257	Chi	
		McCarthy, Alexander George	3B26	49	.219	B	C
		Pitler, Jacob Albert	2B106	109	.233	A	
1	1	Ponder, Chas. Elmer	P	3	.000	A	
		Reilly, Archer E.	3B	1	.000	A	C
		Schmidt, Walter Joseph	C61	72	.246	B	
		Schulte, Frank	OF	30	+.216	B	Phil
		Shaw, Benjamin Nathaniel	OF	2	.000	A	
		Smith, Willard Jehu	C4	11	.143	A	
5	11	Steele, Robert Wesley	P	33	+.224	xStL	
		Wagner, John Peter (Hans) MGR. (3B18)	1B47	74	.265	B	C
		Wagner, Wm. Joseph	C37	53	.205	B	
		Ward, Chas. Wm.	SS112	125	.236	A	
		Warner, George Hoke	3B	3	.200	B	
		Webb, Wm. Joseph (SS2)	2B3	5	.200	A	C
		Wilhoit, Joseph Wm.	OF	9	+.200	xBos	N.Y.
		Wolfe, Harry	2B	2	+.000	xChi	C

WON 65 LOST 60 TG 125 — NATIONAL LEAGUE 1918. — FINISHED 4th. PCT. .520

PITTSBURGH

HUGO FRANK BEZDEK

WON	LOST	NAME	POS.	G.	BA	FROM	TO
1	1	Adams, Chas. Benjamin (Babe)	P	3	.333	Pitt16	
		Archer, James Patrick (1B1)	C23	24	+.155	Chi	Bkn
		Bigbee, Carson Lee	OF	92	.255	B	
		Blackwell, Frederick Wm.	C	8	.153	B	
		Boone, Lute Joseph (2B1)	SS25	27	.198	NYA16	C
		Carey, Max George	OF	126	.274	B	
0	1	Carlson, Harold Gust (Hal)	P	3	.200	B	
		Caton, James Howard	SS79	80	.234	B	
5	6	Comstock, Ralph Remick	P	15	.192	PittF15	C
19	14	Cooper, Arley Wilbur	P	38	.242	B	
		Cutshaw, George Wm.	2B	126	.285	Bkn	
		Ellam, Roy	SS	26	.130	Cin09	C
		Getz, Gustave	3B	7	.200	xClevA	C
6	0	Hamilton, Earl A.	P	6	.285	StLA	
2	7	Harmon, Robert Green	P17	18	.148	Pitt16	C
2	3	Hill, Carmen Proctor	P	6	.166	Pitt16	
		Hinchman, Wm. White (1B3)	OF40	50	.234	B	
0	1	Jacobs, Wm. Elmer	P	8	+.286	B	Phil
		King, Lee	OF	36	.232	B	
		Leach, Thomas Wm. (SS3)	OF23	30	.194	Cin15	C
9	3	Mayer, James Erskine	P	15	+.167	xPhil	
11	8	Miller, Frank Lee	P	23	.105	B	
		Mollwitz, Frederick August	1B	119	.269	B	
		McKechnie, Wm. Boyd	3B	126	.255	Cin	
		Pitler, Jacob Albert	2B	3	.000	B	C

WON	LOST	NAME	POS.	G.	BA	FROM	TO
7	9	Sanders, Roy Garvin	P	28	.151	Cin	C
		Schmidt, Walter Joseph	C104	105	.238	B	
		Shaw, Benjamin Nathaniel	C	21	.194	B	C
1	4	Slapnicka, Cyril Chas.	P	7	.071	Chill	C
		Smith, Willard Jehu	C	15	.167	B	C
		Southworth, Wm. Harrison	OF	64	.341	ClevA15	
2	3	Steele, Robert Wesley	P	10	+.125	B	N.Y.
		Stengel, Chas. Dillon (Casey)	OF37	39	.246	Bkn	

WON 71 NATIONAL LEAGUE FINISHED 4th.
LOST 68
TG 139 1919. PCT. .511

PITTSBURGH

HUGO FRANK BEZDEK

WON	LOST	NAME	POS.	G.	BA	FROM	TO
17	10	Adams, Chas. Benjamin (Babe)	P	34	.185	B	
		Barbare, Walter Lawrence	3B80	85	.273	BosA	
		Bigbee, Carson Lee	OF124	125	.276	B	
		Blackwell, Frederick Wm.	C22	24	.215	B	C
		Boeckel, Norman D.	3B	45	+.250	Pitt17	Bos
		Carey, Max George	OF63	66	.307	B	
8	10	Carlson, Harold Gust (Hal)	P	22	.163	B	
		Caton, James Howard (OF2)	3B14	39	.176	B	
19	13	Cooper, Arley Wilbur	P35	36	.287	B	
		Cutshaw, George Wm.	2B	139	.242	B	
0	4	Evans, Wm. James	P	7	.000	Pitt17	C
		Grimm, Chas. John	1B	14	.318	StL	
8	11	Hamilton, Earl A.	P	28	.135	B	
0	0	Hill, Carmen Proctor	P	4	.000	B	
		Lee, Clifford Walker (OF6)	C28	42	.196	A	
5	3	Mayer, James Erskine	P	18	.207	B	ChiA
13	12	Miller, Frank Lee	P	32	.106	B	
		Mollwitz, Frederick August (OF1)	1B53	56	+.167	B	StL
		Nicholson, Frederick (1B1)	OF17	30	.273	DetA17	
0	5	Ponder, Chas. Elmer	P	9	.400	Pitt17	
		Saier, Victor Sylvester	1B51	58	.223	Chi17	C
		Schmidt, Walter Joseph	C	85	.251	B	
		Southworth, Wm. Harrison	OF	121	.280	B	
		Stengel, Chas. Dillon (suspended by Phila)	OF87	89	+.293	B	Phil
		Sweeney, Edward Francis	C15	17	.095	NYA15	C
		Terry, Zebulon Alexander (Zeb)	SS127	129	.227	Bos	
		Warner, George Hoke	3B	6	.125	Pitt17	
		Whitted, George Bostic (3B2)	OF25	35	+.398	xPhil	
1	0	Wisner, John Henry	P	4	.000	A	
		Zitzmann, Wm. Arthur	OF	11	+.192	A	Cin

WON 79 NATIONAL LEAGUE FINISHED 4th.
LOST 75
TG 154 1920. PCT. .513

PITTSBURGH

GEORGE GIBSON

WON	LOST	NAME	POS.	G.	BA	FROM	TO
17	13	Adams, Chas. Benjamin (Babe)	P	35	.146	B	
		Barbare, Walter Lawrence	SS34	57	.274	B	
		Barnhart, Clyde Lee	3B	12	.326	A	
		Bigbee, Carson Lee	OF133	137	.280	B	
0	0	Blake, John Frederick (Sheriff)	P	6	.250	A	
		Carey, Max George	OF129	130	.289	B	
14	13	Carlson, Harold Gust (Hal)	P	39	.271	B	
		Caton, James Howard	SS96	98	.236	B	C
		Clarke, Jay Justin (Nig)	C	3	.000	Phil	C
24	15	Cooper, Arley Wilbur	P	44	.221	B	
		Cutshaw, George Wm.	2B129	131	.252	B	
0	0	Glazner, Chas. Franklin	P	2	.000	A	
		Grimm, Chas. John	1B	148	.227	B	
		Haeffner, Wm. Bernard	C52	54	.194	PhilA15	
10	13	Hamilton, Earl A.	P	39	.149	B	
		Hinchman, Wm. White	OF	18	.188	Pitt18	C
		Hood, Wallace James	OF	2	+.000	xBkn	
		Lee, Clifford Walker	C19	37	.237	B	
0	2	Meador, John Davis	P	12	.167	A	C
1	0	Morrison, John Dewey	P	2	.000	A	
		McKechnie, Wm. Boyd	3B20	40	.218	Pitt18	
		Nicholson, Frederick	OF58	99	.360	B	
11	15	Ponder, Chas. Elmer	P	33	.119	B	
		Schmidt, Walter Joseph	C92	94	.277	B	
		Southworth, Wm. Harrison	OF142	146	.284	B	
		Summa, Homer Wayne	OF	10	.318	A	
		Tierney, James Arthur	2B	12	.260	A	
		Traynor, Harold Joseph (Pie)	SS	17	.212	A	
0	0	Watson, John Reeves	P	5	+.000	xBos & return	
		Whitted, George Bostic	3B125	134	.261	B	
1	3	Wisner, John Henry	P	17	.000	B	
1	1	Zinn, James Edward	P	8	.200	PhilA	

WON 90 NATIONAL LEAGUE FINISHED 2nd.
LOST 63
TG 153 1921. PCT. .588

PITTSBURGH

GEORGE GIBSON

WON	LOST	NAME	POS.	G.	BA	FROM	TO
14	5	Adams, Chas. Benjamin (Babe)	P	25	.254	B	
		Barnhart, Clyde Lee	3B118	124	.258	B	
		Bigbee, Carson Lee	OF146	147	.323	B	
0	0	Bigbee, Lyle Randolph	P	5	.000	PhilA	C
		Brottem, Anton Christian	C29	30	.242	xWashA	C
		Carey, Max George	OF139	140	.309	B	
4	8	Carlson, Harold Gust (Hal)	P	31	.294	B	
22	14	Cooper, Arley Wilbur	P	38	.254	B	

WON	LOST	NAME	POS.	G.	BA	FROM	TO
		Cutshaw, George Wm.	2B84	98	.340	B	
		Cuyler, Hazen Shirley (Kiki)	OF	1	.000	A	
14	5	Glazner, Chas. Franklin	P	36	.132	B	
		Gooch, John Beverly	C	13	.237	A	
		Grimm, Chas. John	1B150	151	.274	B	
13	15	Hamilton, Earl A.	P	35	.160	B	
0	0	Hughes, Wm. Nesbert	P	1	.000	A	C
		Maranville, Walter James Vincent (Rabbitt)	SS	153	.294	Bos	
		Mokan, John Leo	OF15	19	.269	A	
9	7	Morrison, John Dewey	P	21	.119	B	
0	0	Morrison, Philip Melvin	P	1	.000	A	C
2	0	Ponder, Chas. Elmer	P	8	+.000	B	Chi
0	0	Rader, Drew Leon	P	1	.000	A	C
		Robertson, Davis Aydelotte	OF	60	+.322	xChi	
		Rohwer, Ray	OF	30	.250	A	
		Schmidt, Walter Joseph	C111	114	.282	B	
		Skiff, Wm. Franklin	C	16	.289	A	
		Tierney, James Arthur (3B32)	2B72	117	.299	B	
		Traynor, Harold Joseph (Pie)	3B	7	.263	B	
		Warwick, Firmin Newton	C	1	.000	A	
0	0	Wheeler, Floyd Clark	P	1	.000	A	
		Whitted, George Bostic	OF102	108	.280	B	
		Wilson, Samuel Marshall	C	5	.000	A	C
5	3	Yellowhorse, Moses J.	P	10	.000	A	
7	6	Zinn, James Edward	P32	33	.224	B	

WON 85
LOST 69
TG 154

NATIONAL LEAGUE

1922.

FINISHED 3rd.
(TIED WITH ST. L.)
PCT. .552

PITTSBURGH

GEORGE GIBSON — WM. BOYD McKECHNIE

WON	LOST	NAME	POS.	G.	BA	FROM	TO
8	11	Adams, Chas. Benjamin (Babe)	P	27	.285	B	
		Barnhart, Clyde Lee (OF26)	3B30	75	.330	B	
		Bigbee, Carson Lee	OF	150	.350	B	
3	1	Brown, Myrl L.	P	7	.273	A	C
		Carey, Max George	OF	155	.329	B	
9	12	Carlson, Harold Gust (Hal)	P	39	.267	B	
23	14	Cooper, Arley Wilbur	P	41	.268	B	
		Cuyler, Hazen Shirley (Kiki)		1	.000	B	
		Ens, Jewel Willoughby (1B2 SS1 3B3)	2B29	47	.295	A	
11	12	Glazner, Chas. Franklin	P	33	.246	B	
		Gooch, John Beverly	C103	105	.328	B	
		Grimm, Chas. John	1B	154	.292	B	
11	7	Hamilton, Earl A.	P	33	.155	B	
		Hammond, Walter Chas.	2B4	9	.273	xClevA	C
0	0	Hollingsworth, John Burnett	P	9	.000	A	
		Jonnard, Clarence James	C	10	.238	ChiA20	
		Lovelace, Grover Thomas	OF	1	.000	A	C
		Maranville, Walter James Vincent (Rabbitt) (2B18)	SS138	155	.294	B	
		Mattox, James Powell	C21	29	.294	A	
		Merewether, Arthur Francis	2B	1	.000	A	C
		Miller, Jacob George	OF	3	.091	A	C
		Mokan, John Leo	OF23	31	+.258	B	Phil
17	11	Morrison, John Dewey	P	45	.198	B	
		Mueller, Walter John	OF31	32	.270	A	
		McNamara, Thomas Henry		1	.000	A	C
		Rohwer, Ray	OF30	53	.294	B	C
		Russell, Ewell Albert (Reb)	OF	60	.368	ChiA19	
		Schmidt, Walter Joseph	C	40	.328	B	
		Stewart, John Franklin (Stuffy)	2B	3	.154	StLA	
		Tierney, James Arthur (SS1 3B1 OF2)	2B105	122	.345	B	
		Traynor, Harold Joseph (Pie) (SS18)	3B124	142	.281	B	
0	0	Wheeler, Floyd Clark	P	1	.000	B	
3	1	Yellowhorse, Moses J.	P	28	.315	B	C
0	0	Zinn, James Edward	P	5	.000	B	

WON 87
LOST 67
TG 154

NATIONAL LEAGUE

1923.

FINISHED 3rd.
PCT. .565

PITTSBURGH

WM. BOYD McKECHNIE

WON	LOST	NAME	POS.	G.	BA	FROM	TO
13	7	Adams, Chas. Benjamin (Babe)	P	26	.273	B	
		Adams, Spencer Dewey (SS6)	2B11	25	.250	A	
3	2	Bagby, James Chas. Jacob (Sarge)	P	21	.050	ClevA	C
		Barnes, Everett Duane	1B1	2	.500	A	
		Barnhart, Clyde Lee	OF92	114	.324	B	
		Bigbee, Carson Lee	OF122	123	.299	B	
1	3	Boehler, George Henry	P	10	.300	StLA21	
		Carey, Max George	OF	153	.308	B	
0	0	Carlson, Harold Gust (Hal)	P	4	.000	B	
17	19	Cooper, Arley Wilbur	P	39	.262	B	
		Cuyler, Hazen Shirley (Kiki)	OF	11	.250	B	
		Ens, Jewel Willoughby (3B3)	1B4	12	.267	B	
2	1	Glazner, Chas. Franklin	P	7	+.333	B	Phil
		Gooch, John Beverly	C	66	.277	B	
		Grimm, Chas. John	1B	152	.345	B	
7	9	Hamilton, Earl A.	P	28	.173	B	
1	2	Kunz, Earl Dewey	P	21	.083	A	C
		Luce, Frank Edward	OF5	9	.500	A	C
		Maranville, Walter James Vincent (Rabbitt)	SS	141	.277	B	
		Mattox, James Powell	C8	22	.188	B	C
16	10	Meadows, Henry Lee	P	31	+.250	xPhil	
		Moore, Graham Edward	SS	6	.269	A	
25	13	Morrison, John Dewey	P	42	.183	B	

WON	LOST	NAME	POS.	G.	BA	FROM	TO
		Mueller, Walter John	OF26	40	.306	B	
		Rawlings, John Wm.	2B	119	.284	N.Y.	
		Russell, Ewell Albert (Reb)	OF76	94	.289	B	C
		Schmidt, Walter Joseph	C96	97	.248	B	
2	0	Steineder, Raymond J.	P	15	.467	A	
0	1	Stone, Edwin Arnold	P	9	.000	A	
		Tierney, James Arthur	2B	29	+.292	B	Phil
		Traynor, Harold Joseph (Pie)	3B	153	.338	B	

WON 90 LOST 63 TG 153

NATIONAL LEAGUE FINISHED 3rd.

1924. PCT. .588

PITTSBURGH

WM. BOYD McKECHNIE

WON	LOST	NAME	POS.	G.	BA	FROM	TO
3	1	Adams, Chas. Benjamin (Babe)	P	9	.182	B	
		Barnes, Everett Duane	1B1	2	.000	B	C
		Barnhart, Clyde Lee	OF88	102	.276	B	
		Bigbee, Carson Lee	OF75	89	.262	B	
		Carey, Max George	OF	149	.297	B	
20	14	Cooper, Arley Wilbur	P	38	.346	B	
		Cuyler, Hazen Shirley (Kiki)	OF114	117	.354	B	
		Ens, Jewel Willoughby	1B	5	.300	B	
		Gooch, John Beverly	C69	70	.290	B	
		Grimm, Chas. John	1B	151	.288	B	
		Knox, Clifford H.	C	6	.222	A	C
18	10	Kremer, Remy (Ray)	P41	42	.151	A	
0	1	Lundgren, Ebin Delmar	P	8	.000	A	
		Maranville, Walter James Vincent (Rabbitt)	2B	152	.266	B	
0	0	May, Wm. Herbert	P	1	.000	A	C
13	12	Meadows, Henry Lee	P	36	.195	B	
		Moore, Graham Edward (2B4 3B13)	OF35	72	.359	B	
11	16	Morrison, John Dewey	P	41	.169	B	
		Mueller, Walter John	OF15	30	.260	B	
5	3	Pfeffer, Edward Joseph	P	15	+.240	xStL	C
		Rawlings, John Wm.		3	.333	B	
0	0	Sale, Frederick Link	P	1	.000	A	C
		Schmidt, Walter Joseph	C57	58	.243	B	
		Smith, Earl Sutton	C35	39	+.369	xBos	
0	0	Songer, Donald	P	4	.000	A	
0	1	Steineder, Raymond J.	P	5	+.000	B	Phil
4	2	Stone, Edwin Arnold	P	26	.133	B	C
		Traynor, Harold Joseph (Pie)	3B141	142	.294	B	
		Wright, Forest Glenn	SS	153	.287	A	
16	3	Yde, Emil Ogden	P33	50	.239	A	

WON 95 LOST 58 TG 153

NATIONAL LEAGUE FINISHED 1st.

1925. PCT. .621

PITTSBURGH

WM. BOYD McKECHNIE

WON	LOST	NAME	POS.	G.	BA	FROM	TO
6	5	Adams, Chas. Benjamin (Babe)	P	33	.226	B	
15	7	Aldridge, Victor Eddington	P	30	.233	Chi	
		Barnhart, Clyde Lee	OF138	142	.325	B	
		Bigbee, Carson Lee	OF42	66	.238	B	
		Carey, Max George	OF130	133	.343	B	
0	1	Culloton, Bernard Aloysius	P	9	.000	A	
		Cuyler, Hazen Shirley (Kiki)	OF	153	.357	B	
		Ens, Jewel Willoughby	1B	3	.200	B	
		Gooch, John Beverly	C76	79	.298	B	
		Grantham, George Farley	1B102	114	.326	Chi	
		Haas, George Wm. (Mule)	OF2	4	.000	A	
0	0	Koupal, Louis Laddie	P6	7	.000	A	
17	8	Kremer, Remy (Ray)	P	40	.197	B	
19	10	Meadows, Henry Lee	P	35	.175	B	
		Moore, Graham Edward (3B3 OF15)	2B122	142	.298	B	
17	14	Morrison, John Dewey	P	44	.178	B	
		McInnis, John Phaelen (Stuffy)	1B46	59	.368	Bos	
		Niehaus, Albert Bernard	1B15	17	+.219	A	Cin
3	2	Oldham, John Cyrus	P	11	.333	DetA22	
		Rawlings, John Wm.	2B29	36	.282	B	
1	1	Sheehan, Thomas Clancy	P23	24	+.150	xCin	
		Smith, Earl Sutton	C96	109	.313	B	
0	1	Songer, Donald	P	8	.000	B	
		Spencer, Roy Hampton	C11	14	.214	A	
		Thompson, LaFayette Fresco Jr. (Chick)	2B12	14	.243	A	
		Traynor, Harold Joseph (Pie) (SS1)	3B150	150	.320	B	
		Wright, Forest Glenn (3B1)	SS153	153	.308	B	
17	9	Yde, Emil Ogden	P33	47	.191	B	

WON 84 LOST 69 TG 153

NATIONAL LEAGUE FINISHED 3rd.

1926. PCT. .549

PITTSBURGH

WM. BOYD McKECHNIE

WON	LOST	NAME	POS.	G.	BA	FROM	TO
2	3	Adams, Chas. Benjamin (Babe)	P	19	.222	B	C
10	13	Aldridge, Victor Eddington	P	30	.225	B	
		Barnhart, Clyde Lee	OF61	76	.192	B	
		Bigbee, Carson Lee	OF21	42	.221	B	C
		Brickell, George Frederick	OF14	24	.345	A	
6	6	Bush, Leslie Ambrose (Bullet Joe)	P19	28	.265	WashA	
		Carey, Max George	OF82	86	+.222	B	Bkn
		Comorosky, Adam Anthony	OF	8	.267	A	

WON	LOST	NAME	POS.	G.	BA	FROM	TO
		Cronin, Joseph Edward	2B27	38	.265	A	
0	0	Culloton, Bernard Aloysius	P	4	.000	B	C
		Cuyler, Hazen Shirley (Kiki)	OF	157	.321	B	
		Gooch, John Beverly	C80	86	.271	B	
		Grantham, George Farley	1B132	141	.319	B	
3	3	Hill, Carmen Proctor	P	6	.176	NY22	
0	2	Koupal, Louis Laddie	P	6	.250	B	
20	6	Kremer, Remy (Ray)	P	37	.253	B	
0	0	Mahaffey, Lee Roy	P	4	.000	A	
20	9	Meadows, Henry Lee	P	36	.227	B	
		Moore, Graham Edward (SS1 3B9)	2B24	43	+.227	B	Bos
6	8	Morrison, John Dewey	P	26	.077	B	
		Mueller, Walter John	OF15	19	.242	Pitt24	C
		Murphy, Joseph Edward	OF	16	.118	ChiA21	C
		McInnis, John Phaelen (Stuffy)	1B40	47	.299	B	
0	0	Nichols, Chester Raymond Sr.	P	3	.333	A	
2	2	Oldham, John Cyrus	P	17	.222	B	C
		Rawlings, John Wm.	2B59	61	.232	B	C
		Rhyne, Harold (Hal) (SS44)	2B66	109	.251	A	
0	2	Sheehan, Thomas Clancy	P	9	.111	B	C
		Smith, Earl Sutton	C98	105	.346	B	
7	8	Songer, Donald	P	35	.105	B	
		Spencer, Roy Hampton	C12	28	.395	B	
		Traynor, Harold Joseph (Pie)	3B148	152	.317	B	
		Waner, Paul Glee (Big Poison)	OF139	144	.336	A	
		Wright, Forest Glenn	SS116	119	.308	B	
8	7	Yde, Emil Ogden	P37	43	.230	B	

WON 94 — NATIONAL LEAGUE — FINISHED 1st.
LOST 60
TG 154 — 1927. — PCT. .610

PITTSBURGH

OWEN JOSEPH BUSH

WON	LOST	NAME	POS.	G.	BA	FROM	TO
15	10	Aldridge, Victor Eddington	P	35	.219	B	
		Barnhart, Clyde Lee	OF94	108	.319	B	
		Bartell, Richard Wm.	SS	1	.000	A	
		Brickell, George Frederick	OF2	32	.286	B	
1	2	Bush, Leslie Ambrose (Bullet Joe)	P	10	+.600	B	N.Y.
		Comorosky, Adam Anthony	OF16	18	.230	B	
		Cronin, Joseph Edward	SS	12	.227	B	
		Cuyler, Hazen Shirley (Kiki)	OF73	85	.309	B	
2	1	Cvengros, Michael John	P	23	.158	ChiA25	
3	7	Dawson, Ralph Fenton	P	20	.200	ClevA24	
		Gooch, John Beverly	C91	101	.258	B	
		Grantham, George Farley (1B29)	2B124	151	.305	B	
		Groh, Henry Knight (Heinie)	3B12	14	.286	N.Y.	C
		Harris, Joseph	1B116	129	.326	WashA	
22	11	Hill, Carmen Proctor	P43	44	.212	B	
19	8	Kremer, Remy (Ray)	P	35	.169	B	
		Layne, Herman	OF1	11	.000	A	C
1	0	Mahaffey, Lee Roy	P	2	.400	B	
19	10	Meadows, Henry Lee	P	40	.157	B	
8	3	Miljus, John Kenneth	P	19	.179	Bkn21	
3	2	Morrison, John Dewey	P	21	.154	B	
0	3	Nichols, Sr. Chester Raymond	P	8	.111	B	
0	0	Peery, George A.	P	1	.000	A	
		Rhyne, Harold (Hal) (3B10)	2B45	62	.274	B	
		Sicking, Edward Joseph	2B2	6	.143	Cin20	C
		Smith, Earl Sutton	C61	66	.270	B	
0	0	Songer, Donald	P	2	+.000	B	N.Y.
		Spencer, Roy Hampton	C34	38	.283	B	
		Traynor, Harold Joseph (Pie)	3B143	149	.342	B	
		Waner, Lloyd James (Little Poison)	OF	150	.355	A	
		Waner, Paul Glee (Big Poison) (1B14)	OF143	155	.380	B	
		Wright, Forest Glenn	SS	143	.281	B	
1	3	Yde, Emil Ogden	P	23	.167	B	

WON 85 — NATIONAL LEAGUE — FINISHED 4th.
LOST 67
TG 152 — 1928. — PCT. .559

PITTSBURGH

OWEN JOSEPH BUSH

WON	LOST	NAME	POS.	G.	BA	FROM	TO
		Adams, Earl John (Sparky) (SS27)	2B107	135	.276	Chi	
		Barnhart, Clyde Lee	OF48	61	.296	B	C
		Bartell, Richard Wm. (SS27)	2B39	72	.305	B	
0	0	Bartholomew, Lester Justin	P	6	.143	A	
0	2	Blankenship, Homer	P	5	.375	ChiA23	C
7	4	Brame, Ervin Beckham	P24	35	.265	A	
		Brickell, George Frederick	OF50	81	.322	B	
1	0	Burwell, Wm. Edwin	P	4	.222	StLA21	
		Comorosky, Adam Anthony	OF49	51	.295	B	
7	7	Dawson, Ralph Fenton	P	31	.279	B	
8	9	Fussell, Frederick Morris	P	28	.121	Chi23	
		Gooch, John Beverly	C	31	+.238	B	Bkn
		Grantham, George Farley	1B119	124	.323	B	
25	14	Grimes, Burleigh Arland	P	48	.321	N.Y.	
		Hargreaves, Chas. Russell	C77	79	+.285	xBkn	
		Harris, Joseph	1B4	16	+.391	B	Bkn
		Hemsley, Ralston Burdett (Rollie)	C49	50	.271	A	
16	10	Hill, Carmen Proctor	P	36	.233	B	
		Hillis, Malcolm David	2B	11	.250	NYA24	C
		Jones, Coburn D.	SS	1	.500	A	
15	13	Kremer, Remy (Ray)	P	34	.179	B	
1	1	Meadows, Henry Lee	P	4	.500	B	
5	7	Miljus, John Kenneth	P	21	.308	B	ClevA

WON	LOST	NAME	POS.	G.	BA	FROM	TO
		Mulligan, Edward Joseph (2B1)	3B8	27	.233	ChiA22	C
		O'Connell, John Chas.	C	1	.000	A	
		Scott, Floyd John	OF42	60	.311	Chi	C
		Smith, Earl Sutton	C28	32	+.247	B	StL
0	0	Spencer, Glenn Edward	P	4	.000	A	
0	0	Tauscher, Walter Edward	P	17	.167	A	
		Traynor, Harold Joseph (Pie)	3B	144	.337	B	
0	0	Tutweiler, Elmer S.	P	2	.000	A	C
		Waner, Lloyd James (Little Poison)	OF	152	.335	B	
		Waner, Paul Glee (Big Poison) (1B24)	OF131	152	.370	B	
		Windle, Willis Brewer	1B	1	1.000	A	
		Wright, Forest Glenn	SS101	108	.310	B	

WON 88
LOST 65
TG 153

NATIONAL LEAGUE

1929.

FINISHED 2nd.

PCT. .575

PITTSBURGH

OWEN JOSEPH BUSH JEWELL WILLOUGHBY ENS

WON	LOST	NAME	POS.	G.	BA	FROM	TO
		Adams, Earl John (Sparky) (2B20 3B15)	SS30	74	.260	B	
		Bartell, Richard Wm. (2B70)	SS97	143	.302	B	
16	11	Brame, Ervin Beckham	P37	59	.310	B	
		Brickell, George Frederick	OF27	60	.314	B	
0	0	Chagnon, Leon Wilbur	P	1	.000	A	
		Clarke, Wm. Stuart (3B15)	SS41	57	.264	A	
		Comorosky, Adam Anthony	OF121	127	.321	B	
0	1	Dawson, Ralph Fenton	P	4	.500	B	C
0	0	Erickson, Ralph Lief	P	1	.000	A	
		Flagstead, Ira	OF9	26	.280	xWashA	
7	5	French, Lawrence Herbert (Larry)	P	30	.190	A	
2	2	Fussell, Frederick Morris	P	21	.250	B	C
		Grantham, George Farley (1B12 OF19)	2B76	110	.307	B	
17	7	Grimes, Burleigh Arland	P	33	.286	B	
		Hargreaves, Chas. Russell	C101	102	.268	B	
		Hemsley, Ralston Burdett (Rollie)	C80	88	.289	B	
2	3	Hill, Carmen Proctor	P	27	+.036	B	StL
		Ingram, Melvin David		3	.000	A	C
		Jones, Coburn D.	SS15	25	.254	B	C
18	10	Kremer, Remy (Ray)	P	34	.128	B	
		Linton, Claude C.	C1	17	.111	A	C
0	0	Meadows, Henry Lee	P	1	.000	B	C
7	6	Meine, Henry Wm. (Heinie)	P	22	.103	StLA22	
		Mosolf, James Frederick	OF2	8	.462	A	
		O'Connell, John Chas.	C	2	.143	B	C
11	10	Petty, Jesse Lee	P	36	.104	Bkn	
		Riconda, Harry Paul	SS4	8	.467	Bkn	

WON	LOST	NAME	POS.	G.	BA	FROM	TO
		Sankey, Benjamin Turner	SS	2	.143	A	
		Sheely, Earl Homer	1B	139	.293	ChiA27	
		Stroner, James M.	3B2	6	.375	A	C
8	10	Swetonic, Stephen Albert (Steve)	P41	42	.271	A	
		Traynor, Harold Joseph (Pie)	3B	130	.356	B	
		Waner, Lloyd James (Little Poison)	OF	151	.353	B	
		Waner, Paul Glee (Big Poison)	OF143	151	.336	B	
		Windle, Willis Brewer	1B1	2	.000	B	C

WON 80
LOST 74
TG 154

NATIONAL LEAGUE

1930.

FINISHED 5th.

PCT. .519

PITTSBURGH

JEWEL WILLOUGHBY ENS

WON	LOST	NAME	POS.	G.	B A	FROM	TO
		Bartell, Richard Wm.	SS126	129	.320	B	
0	0	Bednar, Andrew F.	P	2	.000	A	
		Bool, Albert J.	C65	78	.259	WashA28	
17	8	Brame, Ervin Beckham	P32	50	.353	B	
		Brickell, George Frederick	OF61	68	+.297	B	Phil
0	3	Chagnon, Leon Wilbur	P	18	.200	B	
		Clarke, Wm. Stuart	2B2	4	.444	B	C
		Comorosky, Adam Anthony	OF	152	.313	B	
		Dugas, Augustin Joseph (Gus)	OF6	9	.290	A	
		Engle, Chas.	3B24	67	.264	PhilA26	C
1	0	Erickson, Ralph Lief	P	7	.250	B	C
		Flagstead, Ira	OF40	44	.250	B	C
17	18	French, Lawrence Herbert (Larry)	P	42	.242	B	
		Grantham, George Farley	2B141	146	.324	B	
		Grosskloss, Howard Hoffman	SS1	2	.333	A	
		Hargreaves, Chas. Russell	C	11	.226	B	C
		Hemsley, Ralston Burdett (Rollie)	C98	104	.253	B	
0	1	Jones, Percy Lee	P	9	.000	Bos	C
20	12	Kremer, Remy (Ray)	P	39	.157	B	
0	0	Lang, Martin John	P	2	.000	A	C
6	8	Meine, Henry Wm. (Heinie)	P	20	.122	B	
0	0	Mosolf, James Frederick (P1)	OF12	40	.333	B	
1	6	Petty, Jesse Lee	P	10	+.083	B	Chi
		Sankey, Benjamin Turner (2B2)	SS5	13	.167	B	
		Sothern, Dennis Elwood (Denny)	OF13	17	+.176	xPhil	
8	9	Spencer, Glenn Edward	P	41	.113	Pitt28	
0	0	Stoner, Ulysses Simpson Grant (Lil)	P	5	.000	DetA	
		Suhr, August Richard (Gus)	1B	151	.286	A	
6	6	Swetonic, Stephen Albert (Steve)	P	23	.111	B	
		Traynor, Harold Joseph (Pie)	3B	130	.366	B	
0	0	Walter, James Bernard	P	1	.000	A	C

WON	LOST	NAME	POS.	G.	BA	FROM	TO
		Waner, Lloyd James (Little Poison)	OF65	68	.362	B	
		Waner, Paul Glee (Big Poison)	OF143	145	.368	B	
4	3	Wood, Chas. Asher Jr.	P	9	.250	A	

WON 75 NATIONAL LEAGUE FINISHED 5th.
LOST 79
TG 154 1931. PCT. .487

PITTSBURGH

JEWEL WILLOUGHBY ENS

WON	LOST	NAME	POS.	G.	BA	FROM	TO
0	0	Bednar, Andrew F.	P	3	.000	B	C
		Bennett, James Fred	OF21	32	.281	StLA28	C
9	13	Brame, Ervin Beckham	P26	48	.274	B	
		Comorosky, Adam Anthony	OF90	99	.243	B	
		Finney, Harold Wilson	C6	10	.308	A	
15	13	French, Lawrence Herbert (Larry)	P	39	.179	B	
		Grace, Robert Earl	C45	47	+.280	xChi	
0	0	Grant, George Addison	P	11	.000	ClevA29	C
		Grantham, George Farley (2B51)	1B78	127	.305	B	
		Grosskloss, Howard Hoffman	2B39	53	.280	B	
2	2	Harris, Wm. Milton	P	4	.091	Cin24	
		Hemsley, Ralston Burdett (Rollie)	C9	10	+.171	B	Chi
		Jensen, Forrest Ducenus (Woody)	OF67	73	.243	A	
11	15	Kremer, Remy (Ray)	P	30	.227	B	
19	13	Meine, Henry Wm. (Heinie)	P	36	.146	B	
		Mosolf, James Frederick	OF1	39	.250	B	
		McClanahan, Peter		7	.500	A	C
6	1	Osborn, Frank Robert	P	27	.167	Chi	C
		Phillips, Edward David	C103	106	.232	DetA29	
		Piet, Anthony Francis (Tony)	2B	44	.299	A	
		Regan, Wm. Wright	2B	28	.202	BosA	C
		Sankey, Benjamin Turner	SS49	57	.227	B	C
11	12	Spencer, Glenn Edward	P	38	.096	B	
		Steinecke, Wm. Robert	C1	4	.000	A	C
		Suhr, August Richard (Gus)	1B76	87	.211	B	
0	2	Swetonic, Stephen Albert (Steve)	P	14	.143	B	
		Thevenow, Thomas Joseph Jr.	SS	120	.213	Phil	
		Traynor, Harold Joseph (Pie)	3B	155	.298	B	
		Waner, Lloyd James (Little Poison)	OF153	154	.314	B	
		Waner, Paul Glee (Big Poison) (1B10)	OF138	150	.322	B	
0	2	Willoughby, Claude Wm.	P	9	.286	Phil	C
2	6	Wood, Chas. Asher Jr.	P	15	.227	B	C

WON 86 NATIONAL LEAGUE FINISHED 2nd.
LOST 68
TG 154 1932. PCT. .558

PITTSBURGH

GEORGE GIBSON

WON	LOST	NAME	POS.	G.	BA	FROM	TO
		Barbee, David Monroe	OF78	97	.257	PhilA26	C
3	1	Brame, Ervin Beckham	P23	26	.250	B	C
		Brenzel, Wm. Richard	C7	9	.042	A	
		Brubaker, Wilbur Lee (Bill)	3B	7	.417	A	
9	6	Chagnon, Leon Wilbur	P	30	.225	Pitt30	
		Comorosky, Adam Anthony	OF92	108	.286	B	
		Dugas, Augustin Joseph (Gus)	OF20	55	.237	Pitt30	
		Finney, Harold Wilson	C11	31	.212	B	
18	16	French, Lawrence Herbert (Larry)	P	47	.207	B	
		Grace, Robert Earl	C114	115	.274	B	
		Grosskloss, Howard Hoffman	SS1	17	.100	B	C
10	9	Harris, Wm. Milton	P	37	.182	B	
		Jensen, Forrest Ducenus (Woody)	OF	7	.000	B	
4	3	Kremer, Remy (Ray)	P	11	.105	B	
12	9	Meine, Henry Wm. (Heinie)	P	28	.164	B	
		Padden, Thomas Francis	C43	47	.263	A	
		Piet, Anthony Francis (Tony)	2B	154	.282	B	
1	0	Smith, Harold Laverne	P	2	.000	A	
4	8	Spencer, Glenn Edward	P	39	.162	B	
		Suhr, August Richard (Gus)	1B	154	.263	B	
11	6	Swetonic, Stephen Albert (Steve)	P	24	.093	B	
14	10	Swift, Wm. (Bill)	P	39	.192	A	
		Thevenow, Thomas Joseph Jr. (3B22)	SS29	59	.237	B	
		Traynor, Harold Joseph (Pie)	3B127	135	.329	B	
		Vaughan, Joseph Floyd (Arky)	SS128	129	.318	A	
		Waner, Lloyd James (Little Poison)	OF131	134	.333	B	
		Waner, Paul Glee (Big Poison)	OF	154	.341	B	

WON 87 NATIONAL LEAGUE FINISHED 2nd.
LOST 67
TG 154 1933. PCT. .565

PITTSBURGH

GEORGE GIBSON

WON	LOST	NAME	POS.	G.	BA	FROM	TO
4	2	Birkofer, Ralph Joseph	P	9	.318	A	
		Brubaker, Wilbur Lee (Bill)	3B	2	.000	B	
6	4	Chagnon, Leon Wilbur	P	39	.048	B	
		Comorosky, Adam Anthony	OF30	64	.284	B	
0	0	Dudley, Elzie Clise	P	1	.000	Phil	C

WON	LOST	NAME	POS.	G.	BA	FROM	TO
		Finney, Harold Wilson	C47	56	.233	B	
18	13	French, Lawrence Herbert (Larry)	P	47	.149	B	
		Grace, Robert Earl	C88	93	.289	B	
4	4	Harris, Wm. Milton	P	31	.000	B	
5	7	Hoyt, Waite Chas.	P	36	.156	N.Y.	
		Jensen, Forrest Ducenus (Woody)	OF40	70	.296	B	
1	0	Kremer, Remy (Ray)	P	7	.000	B	C
		Lindstrom, Frederick Chas.	OF130	138	.310	N.Y.	
15	8	Meine, Henry Wm. (Heinie)	P	32	.173	B	
		Nonnenkamp, Leo Wm. (Red)		1	.000	A	
		Padden, Thomas Francis	C27	30	.211	B	
		Picinich, Valentine John (Val)	C	16	+.250	xBkn	C
		Piet, Anthony Francis (Tony)	2B97	107	.323	B	
8	7	Smith, Harold Laverne	P	28	.128	B	
		Suhr, August Richard (Gus)	1B	154	.267	B	
12	12	Swetonic, Stephen Albert (Steve)	P	31	.200	B	
14	10	Swift, Wm. (Bill)	P	37	.244	B	
		Thevenow, Thomas Joseph Jr. (SS3 3B1)	2B61	73	.312	B	
		Traynor, Harold Joseph (Pie)	3B	154	.304	B	
		Vaughan, Joseph Floyd (Arky)	SS	152	.314	B	
		Waner, Lloyd James (Little Poison)	OF114	121	.276	B	
		Waner, Paul Glee (Big Poison)	OF	154	.309	B	
		Young, Lemuel Floyd (Pep) (SS1)	2B1	25	.300	A	

WON 74 NATIONAL LEAGUE FINISHED 5th.
LOST 76
TG 150 1934. PCT. .493

PITTSBURGH

GEORGE GIBSON HAROLD JOSEPH TRAYNOR

WON	LOST	NAME	POS.	G.	BA	FROM	TO
11	12	Birkofer, Ralph Joseph	P	41	.227	B	
0	1	Blanton, Darrell Elijah (Cy)	P	1	.000	A	
		Brubaker, Wilbur Lee (Bill)	3B	3	.333	B	
4	1	Chagnon, Leon Wilbur	P	33	.231	B	
		Finney, Harold Wilson	C1	5	.000	B	
12	18	French, Lawrence Herbert (Larry)	P	49	.190	B	
		Grace, Robert Earl	C83	95	.270	B	
1	2	Grimes, Burleigh Arland	P	8	+.143	xStL	NYA
0	0	Harris, Wm. Milton	P	11	.500	B	
0	3	Holley, Edward Edgar	P	5	+1.000	xPhil	C
15	6	Hoyt, Waite Chas.	P	48	.179	B	
		Jensen, Forrest Ducenus (Woody)	OF66	88	.290	B	
0	0	Johnson, Lloyd Wm.	P	1	.000	A	C
		Lavagetto, Harry Arthur (Cookie)	2B83	87	.220	A	
		Lindstrom, Frederick Chas.	OF92	97	.290	B	
10	9	Lucas, Chas. Frederick (Red)	P29	68	.219	Cin	
7	6	Meine, Henry Wm. (Heinie)	P	26	.107	B	C
		Padden, Thomas Francis	C76	82	.321	B	
		Roettger, Walter Henry	OF23	47	.245	Cin	C
3	4	Smith, Harold Laverne	P	20	.059	B	
0	1	Struss, Clarence Herbert	P	1	.333	A	C
		Suhr, August Richard (Gus)	1B	151	.283	B	
11	13	Swift, Wm. (Bill)	P	37	.214	B	
		Thevenow, Thomas Joseph Jr. (3B44)	2B75	122	.271	B	
		Traynor, Harold Joseph (Pie) MGR.	3B110	119	.309	B	
		Vaughan, Joseph Floyd (Arky)	SS	149	.333	B	
		Veltman, Arthur Patrick (Pat)	C11	12	.107	NY32	C
		Waner, Lloyd James (Little Poison)	OF139	140	.283	B	
		Waner, Paul Glee (Big Poison)	OF145	146	.362	B	
		Young, Lemuel Floyd (Pep) (2B1)	SS1	19	.235	B	

WON 86 NATIONAL LEAGUE FINISHED 4th.
LOST 67
TG 153 1935. PCT. .562

PITTSBURGH

HAROLD JOSEPH TRAYNOR

WON	LOST	NAME	POS.	G.	BA	FROM	TO
9	7	Birkofer, Ralph Joseph	P37	38	.241	B	
18	13	Blanton, Darrell Elijah (Cy)	P	35	.134	B	
4	1	Brown, Mace Stanley	P	18	.167	A	
		Browne, James Wm. Earle	1B	9	.250	A	
		Brubaker, Wilbur Lee (Bill)	3B	6	.000	B	
11	11	Bush, Guy Terrell	P	41	.127	Chi	
		Epps, Aubrey Lee	C	1	.750	A	C
		Grace, Robert Earl	C69	77	.263	B	
		Hafey, Daniel Albert	OF47	58	.228	xChiA	
		Herman, Floyd Caves (Babe)	OF15	26	+.235	Chi	Cin
7	11	Hoyt, Waite Chas.	P	39	.259	B	
		Jensen, Forrest Ducenus(Woody)	OF140	143	.324	B	
		Lavagetto, Harry Arthur (Cookie) (3B15)	2B42	78	.290	B	
8	6	Lucas, Chas. Frederick (Red)	P20	47	.318	B	
0	0	Osborne, Wayne Harold	P	3	.000	A	
		Padden, Thomas Francis	C94	97	.272	B	
0	1	Passeau, Claude Wm.	P	1	.000	A	
0	1	Salveson, John Theodore	P	5	.000	N.Y.	ChiA
0	0	Smith, Harold Laverne	P	1	.000	B	C
		Suhr, August Richard (Gus) (OF2)	1B149	153	.272	B	
0	0	Swetonic, Stephen Albert (Steve)	P	1	.000	Pitt33	C
15	8	Swift, Wm. (Bill)	P	39	.244	B	

WON	LOST	NAME	POS.	G.	BA	FROM	TO
		Thevenow, Thomas Joseph Jr. (2B8 SS13)	3B82	110	.238	B	
		Traynor, Harold Joseph (Pie) MGR. (1B1)	3B49	57	.279	B	
		Vaughan, Joseph Floyd (Arky)	SS	137	.385	B	
		Waner, Lloyd James (Little Poison)	OF121	122	.309	B	
		Waner, Paul Glee (Big Poison)	OF136	139	.321	B	
14	8	Weaver, James Dement	P	33	.071	Chi	
		Young, Lemuel Floyd (Pep) (SS4 3B6 OF6)	2B107	128	.265	B	

WON 84 NATIONAL LEAGUE FINISHED 4th.
LOST 70
TG 154 1936. PCT. .545

PITTSBURGH

HAROLD JOSEPH TRAYNOR

WON	LOST	NAME	POS.	G.	BA	FROM	TO
0	0	Bauers, Russell Lee (Russ)	P	1	.000	A	
7	5	Birkofer, Ralph Joseph	P	34	.220	B	
13	15	Blanton, Darrell Elijah (Cy)	P	44	.155	B	
10	11	Brown, Mace Stanley	P	47	.167	B	
		Browne, James Wm. Earl (1B1)	OF4	8	.304	B	
		Brubaker, Wilbur Lee (Bill)	3B	145	.289	B	
1	3	Bush, Guy Terrell	P	16	+.333	B	Bos
		Dickshot, John Oscar	OF	9	.222	A	
		Finney, Harold Wilson	C14	21	.000	Pitt34	C
		Hafey, Daniel Albert	OF29	39	.212	B	
7	5	Hoyt, Waite Chas.	P	22	.154	B	
		Jensen, Forrest Ducenus (Woody)	OF	153	.283	B	
		Lavagetto, Harry Arthur (Cookie) (3B13)	2B37	60	.244	B	
15	4	Lucas, Chas. Frederick (Red)	P27	69	.241	B	
		Padden, Thomas Francis	C87	88	.249	B	
		Schulte, Fred Wm.	OF55	74	.261	WashA	
		Suhr, August Richard (Gus)	1B	156	.312	B	
16	16	Swift, Wm. (Bill)	P	45	.295	B	
1	3	Tising, John Joseph	P	10	.273	A	C
		Todd, Alfred Chester (Al)	C70	76	.273	Phil	
		Vaughan, Joseph Floyd (Arky)	SS	156	.335	B	
		Waner, Lloyd James (Little Poison)	OF92	106	.321	B	
		Waner, Paul Glee (Big Poison)	OF145	148	.373	B	
14	8	Weaver, James Dement	P	38	.101	B	
0	0	Welch, John Vernon	P	9	.286	xBosA	C
		Young, Lemuel Floyd (Pep)	2B123	125	.248	B	

WON 86 NATIONAL LEAGUE FINISHED 3rd.
LOST 68
TG 154 1937. PCT. .558

PITTSBURGH

HAROLD JOSEPH TRAYNOR

WON	LOST	NAME	POS.	G.	BA	FROM	TO
13	6	Bauers, Russell Lee (Russ)	P	34	.217	B	
		Berres, Raymond Frederick	C	2	.167	Bkn	
14	12	Blanton, Darrell Elijah (Cy)	P	36	.165	B	
8	8	Bowman, Joseph Emil (Joe)	P30	35	.213	Phil	
11	10	Brandt, Edward Arthur	P	33	.169	Bkn	
7	2	Brown, Mace Stanley	P	50	.300	B	
		Brubaker, Wilbur Lee (Bill)	3B115	120	.254	B	
		Dickshot, John Oscar	OF64	82	.254	B	
		Handley, Lee Elmer (Jeep)	2B126	127	.250	Cin	
1	0	Heintzelman, Kenneth Alphonse	P	1	.000	A	
1	2	Hoyt, Waite Chas.	P	11	+.083	B	Bkn
		Jensen, Forrest Ducenus (Woody)	OF120	124	.279	B	
8	10	Lucas, Chas. Frederick (Red)	P20	59	.268	B	
		Padden, Thomas Francis	C34	35	.286	B	
		Schulte, Fred Wm.	OF4	29	.100	B	C
		Schuster, Wm. Chas.	SS2	3	.500	A	
		Suhr, August Richard (Gus)	1B	151	.278	B	
9	10	Swift, Wm. (Bill)	P	36	.167	B	
6	3	Tobin, James Anthony	P20	21	.441	A	
		Todd, Alfred Chester (Al)	C128	133	.307	B	
		Traynor, Harold Joseph (Pie) MGR.	3B	5	.167	B	
		Vaughan, Joseph Floyd (Arky) (OF12)	SS108	126	.322	B	
		Waner, Lloyd James (Little Poison)	OF123	129	.330	B	
		Waner, Paul Glee (Big Poison)	OF150	154	.354	B	
8	5	Weaver, James Dement	P	32	.148	B	
		Young, Lemuel Floyd (Pep) (2B30 3B39)	SS45	113	.260	B	

WON 86 NATIONAL LEAGUE FINISHED 2nd.
LOST 64
TG 150 1938. PCT. .573

PITTSBURGH

HAROLD JOSEPH TRAYNOR

WON	LOST	NAME	POS.	G.	BA	FROM	TO
13	14	Bauers, Russell Lee (Russ)	P	40	.239	B	
		Berres, Raymond Frederick	C	40	.230	B	
11	7	Blanton, Darrell Elijah (Cy)	P	29	.203	B	
3	4	Bowman, Joseph Emil (Joe)	P17	18	.333	B	
5	4	Brandt, Edward Arthur	P	24	.297	B	C

WON	LOST	NAME	POS.	G.	BA	FROM	TO
15	9	Brown, Mace Stanley	P	51	.132	B	
		Brubaker, Wilbur Lee (Bill)	3B18	45	.295	B	
		Dickshot, John Oscar	OF10	29	.229	B	
		Handley, Lee Elmer (Jeep)	3B136	139	.268	B	
0	0	Heintzelman, Kenneth Alphonse	P	1	.000	B	
		Jensen, Forrest Ducenus (Woody)	OF38	68	.200	B	
12	5	Klinger, Robert Harold (Bob)	P	28	.167	A	
6	3	Lucas, Chas. Frederick (Red)	P13	33	.109	B	C
		Manush, Henry Emmett (Heinie)	OF	15	+.308	xBkn	
		Rizzo, John Costa	OF140	143	.301	A	
0	1	Sewell, Truett Banks (Rip)	P	17	.088	DetA32	
		Suhr, August Richard (Gus)	1B	145	.294	B	
7	5	Swift, Wm. (Bill)	P	36	.200	B	
		Thevenow, Thomas Joseph Jr. (SS4 3B1)	2B10	15	.200	Bos	C
14	12	Tobin, James Anthony	P40	56	.243	B	
		Todd, Alfred Chester (Al)	C132	133	.265	B	
		Vaughan, Joseph Floyd (Arky)	SS147	148	.322	B	
		Waner, Lloyd James (Little Poison)	OF144	147	.313	B	
		Waner, Paul Glee (Big Poison)	OF147	148	.280	B	
		Young, Lemuel Floyd (Pep)	2B	149	.278	B	

WON 68 NATIONAL LEAGUE FINISHED 6th.
LOST 85
TG 153 1939. PCT. .444

PITTSBURGH

HAROLD JOSEPH TRAYNOR

WON	LOST	NAME	POS.	G.	BA	FROM	TO
2	4	Bauers, Russell Lee (Russ)	P	15	.211	B	
		Bell, Fern Lee	OF67	83	.286	A	
		Berres, Raymond Frederick	C80	81	.229	B	
2	3	Blanton, Darrell Elijah (Cy)	P	10	.286	B	
10	14	Bowman, Joseph Emil (Joe)	P37	70	.344	B	
9	13	Brown, Mace Stanley	P	47	.109	B	
		Brubaker, Wilbur Lee (Bill) (3B32)	2B65	100	.232	B	
4	4	Butcher, Albert Maxwell (Max)	P	14	+.097	xPhil	
0	1	Clemensen, John Wm. Melville	P	12	.333	A	
		Elliott, Robert Irving	OF30	32	.333	A	
		Fletcher, Elburt Preston (Elbie)	1B101	102	+.303	xBos	
1	2	Gee, John Alexander Jr.	P	3	.000	A	
		Gustine, Frank Wm.	3B	22	.186	A	
		Handley, Lee Elmer (Jeep)	3B100	101	.285	B	
1	1	Heintzelman, Kenneth Alphonse	P	17	.222	B	
		Jensen, Forrest Ducenus (Woody)	OF	12	.167	B	C
		Juelich, John Walter (Jack)	2B10	17	.239	A	C
		Klein, Chas. Herbert (Chuck)	OF66	85	+.300	xPhil	
14	17	Klinger, Robert Harold (Bob)	P	37	.202	B	

WON	LOST	NAME	POS.	G.	BA	FROM	TO
		Manush, Henry Emmett (Heinie)	OF	10	.000	B	C
		Mueller, Ray Coleman	C81	86	.233	Bos	
0	0	Rambert, Elmer Donald	P	2	.000	A	
		Rizzo, John Costa	OF86	94	.261	B	
		Schultz, Joseph Chas. Jr.	C	4	.286	A	
10	9	Sewell, Truett Banks (Rip)	P	52	.200	B	
		Suhr, August Richard (Gus)	1B52	63	+.289	B	Phil
		Susce, George Cyril Methodius	C	31	.227	DetA32	
5	7	Swift, Wm. (Bill)	P	36	.238	B	
1	1	Swigart, Oadis Vaughn	P	3	.250	A	
9	9	Tobin, James Anthony	P25	43	.243	B	
		Van Robays, Maurice Rene	OF25	27	.314	A	
		Vaughan, Joseph Floyd (Arky)	SS	152	.306	B	
		Waner, Lloyd James (Little Poison)	OF92	112	.285	B	
		Waner, Paul Glee (Big Poison)	OF106	125	.328	B	
		Young, Lemuel Floyd (Pep)	2B	84	.276	B	
		Yount, Floyd Edwin	OF	2	.000	PhilA37	C

WON 78 NATIONAL LEAGUE FINISHED 4th.
LOST 76
TG 154 1940. PCT. .506

PITTSBURGH

FRANK FRANCIS FRISCH JR.

WON	LOST	NAME	POS.	G.	BA	FROM	TO
0	2	Bauers, Russell Lee (Russ)	P	15	.286	B	
		Bell, Fern Lee		6	.000	B	C
		Berres, Raymond Frederick	C	21	+.188	B	Bos
9	10	Bowman, Joseph Emil (Joe)	P32	57	.244	B	
10	9	Brown, Mace Stanley	P	48	.115	B	
		Brubaker, Wilbur Lee (Bill) (1B4 SS8)	3B19	38	.192	B	
8	9	Butcher, Albert Maxwell (Max)	P35	36	.300	B	
		Davis, Virgil Lawrence (Spud)	C	99	.326	Phil	
0	1	Dietz, Lloyd Arthur	P4	6	.143	A	
		DiMaggio, Vincent Paul	OF108	110	+.289	xCin	
		Elliott, Robert Irving	OF147	148	.292	B	
		Fernandes, Edward Paul	C	28	.121	A	
		Fletcher, Elburt Preston (Elbie)	1B	147	.273	B	
		Garms, Debs C. (OF19)	3B64	103	.355	Bos	
		Gustine, Frank Wm.	2B130	133	.281	B	
		Handley, Lee Elmer (Jeep) (2B2)	3B80	98	.281	B	
0	0	Harrell, Raymond James (Ray)	P	3	.000	Phil	
8	8•	Heintzelman, Kenneth Alphonse	P39	41	.167	B	
		Kalin, Frank Bruno	OF2	3	.000	A	
8	13	Klinger, Robert Harold (Bob)	P	39	.143	B	
6	8	Lanahan, Richard Anthony	P	40	.118	WashA37	
8	4	Lanning, John Young	P	38	.200	Bos	
		Leip, Edgar Ellsworth	2B2	3	.200	WashA	
		Lopez, Alfonso Ramon (Al)	C	59	+.259	xBos	

WON	LOST	NAME	POS.	G.	BA	FROM	TO
		Mueller, Ray Coleman	C	4	.333	B	
5	4	MacFayden, Daniel Knowles (Danny)	P	35	.179	Bos	
0	1	Rambert, Elmer Donald	P	3	.000	B	C
		Rizzo, John Costa	OF7	9	+.179	B	Cin
		Schultz, Joseph Chas. Jr.	C	16	.194	B	
16	5	Sewell, Truett Banks (Rip)	P33	47	.192	B	
0	2	Swigart, Oadis Vaughn	P	7	.200	B	C
		VanRobays, Maurice Rene (1B1)	OF143	145	.273	B	
		Vaughan, Joseph Floyd (Arky) (3B2)	SS155	156	.300	B	
		Waner, Lloyd James (Little Poison)	OF42	72	.259	B	
		Waner, Paul Glee (Big Poison) (1B8)	OF45	89	.290	B	
		Young, Lemuel Floyd (Pep) (SS7 3B5)	2B33	54	.250	B	

WON 81 LOST 73 TG 154

NATIONAL LEAGUE

1941.

FINISHED 4th.

PCT. .526

PITTSBURGH

FRANK FRANCIS FRISCH JR.

WON	LOST	NAME	POS.	G.	BA	FROM	TO
		Anderson, Alfred Walton	SS58	70	.215	A	
		Baker, Wm. Presley	C33	35	+.224	xCin	
1	3	Bauers, Russell Lee (Russ)	P	8	.357	B	
3	2	Bowman, Joseph Emil (Joe)	P18	22	.258	B	
0	1	Brandt, Wm. George	P	2	.000	A	
0	0	Brown, Mace Stanley	P	1	+.000	B	Bkn
17	12	Butcher, Albert Naxwell (Max)	P	33	.183	B	
1	0	Clemensen, John Wm. Melville	P	2	.000	Pitt39	
		Collins, James Anthony (Rip) (OF3)	1B11	49	.210	Chi38	C
0	0	Conger, Richard	P	2	.000	DetA	
		Cox, Wm. Richard	SS	10	.270	A	
		Davis, Virgil Lawrence (Spud)	C49	57	.252	B	
7	2	Dietz, Lloyd Arthur	P	33	.160	B	
		DiMaggio, Vincent Paul	OF	151	.267	B	
		Elliott, Robert Irving	OF139	141	.273	B	
		Fletcher, Elburt Preston (Elbie)	1B	151	.288	B	
		Garms, Debs C. (OF24)	3B29	83	.264	B	
0	2	Gee, John Alexander Jr.	P	3	.333	Pitt39	
		Gustine, Frank Wm. (3B15)	2B104	121	.270	B	
		Handley, Lee Elmer (Jeep)	3B114	124	.288	B	
11	11	Heintzelman, Kenneth Alphonse	P	35	.127	B	
9	4	Klinger, Robert Harold (Bob)	P	35	.250	B	
0	1	Lanahan, Richard Anthony	P	7	.000	B	C
11	11	Lanning, John Young	P	34	.107	B	
		Leip, Edgar Ellsworth (3B1)	2B7	15	.200	B	

WON	LOST	NAME	POS.	G.	BA	FROM	TO
		Lopez, Alfonso Ramon (Al)	C	114	.265	B	
		Martin, Stuart McGuire (Stu) (1B1 3B2)	2B53	88	.304	StL	
		Rikard, Culley	OF5	6	.200	A	
		Schultz, Joseph Chas. Jr.	C	2	.500	B	
14	17	Sewell, Truett Banks (Rip)	P39	42	.174	B	
		Smith, Vincent Ambrose	C	9	.303	A	
		Stewart, Edward Perry	OF41	73	.267	A	
1	2	Strincevich, Nicholas Mihailovich	P	12	+.429	xBos	
4	1	Sullivan, Joseph	P	16	+.364	xBos	C
		VanRobays, Maurice Rene	OF121	129	.282	B	
		Vaughan, Joseph Floyd (Arky) (3B3)	SS97	106	.316	B	
		Waner, Lloyd James (Little Poison)	OF1	3	+.250	B	Bos
2	4	Wilkie, Aldon Jay	P	26	.292	A	

WON 66 LOST 81 TG 147

NATIONAL LEAGUE

1942.

FINISHED 5th.

PCT. .449

PITTSBURGH

FRANK FRANCIS FRISCH JR.

WON	LOST	NAME	POS.	G.	BA	FROM	TO
		Anderson, Alfred Walton	SS48	54	.271	B	
		Baker, Wm. Presley	C11	18	.118	B	
		Barrett, John Joseph	OF94	111	.247	A	
1	1	Brandt, Wm. George	P	3	.143	B	
5	8	Butcher, Albert Maxwell (Max)	P	24	.143	B	
		Colman, Frank Loyd	OF8	10	.135	A	
0	0	Conger, Richard	P2	3	.000	B	
		Coscarart, Peter Joseph (2B25)	SS108	133	.228	Bkn	
6	9	Dietz, Lloyd Arthur	P	40	.200	B	
		DiMaggio, Vincent Paul	OF138	143	.238	B	
		Elliott, Robert Irving (OF1)	3B142	143	.297	B	
		Fletcher, Elburt Preston (Elbie)	1B144	145	.289	B	
		Geary, Eugene Francis Joseph	SS8	9	.227	A	
5	6	Gornicki, Henry Frank	P	25	.114	Chi	
		Gustine, Frank Wm. (C1 SS2 3B2)	2B108	115	.229	B	
0	1	Hallett, Jack Price	P	3	.375	ChiA	
4	4	Hamlin, Luke Daniel (Hot Potato)	P	23	.243	Bkn	
8	11	Heintzelman, Kenneth Alphonse	P	27	.086	B	
0	0	Jungels, Kenneth Peter	P6	9	.500	ClevA	C
8	11	Klinger, Robert Harold (Bob)	P	37	.200	B	
6	8	Lanning, John Young	P	34	.138	B	
		Leip, Edgar Ellsworth		3	.000	B	C
		Lopez, Alfonso Ramon (Al)	C99	103	.256	B	

WON	LOST	NAME	POS.	G.	BA	FROM	TO
		Martin, Stuart McGuire (Stu) (1B1 SS1)	2B30	42	.225	B	
		Phelps, Ernest Gordon (Babe)	C72	95	.284	Bkn	C
		Rikard, Cully	OF16	38	.192	B	
		Russell, James Wm.	OF3	5	.071	A	
17	15	Sewell, Truett Banks (Rip)	P40	41	.149	B	
0	0	Shuman, Harry	P	1	.000	A	
		Stewart, Edward Perry (2B6 3B10)	OF34	82	.219	B	
0	0	Strincevich, Nicholas Mihailovich	P	7	.000	B	
		VanRobays, Maurice Rene	OF84	100	.232	B	
		Wasdell, James Chas. (1B7)	OF97	122	.259	Bkn	
6	7	Wilkie, Aldon Jay	P35	36	.263	B	
		Wyrostek, John Barney	OF8	9	.114	A	

WON 80 NATIONAL LEAGUE FINISHED 4th.
LOST 74
TG 154 1943. PCT. .519

PITTSBURGH

FRANK FRANCIS FRISCH JR.

WON	LOST	NAME	POS.	G.	BA	FROM	TO
		Baker, Wm. Presley	C56	63	.273	B	
		Barrett, John Joseph	OF99	130	.231	B	
4	1	Brandt, Wm. George	P	29	.143	B	C
10	8	Butcher, Albert Maxwell (Max)	P	33	.164	B	
		Camelli, Henry Richard	C	1	.000	A	
		Colman, Frank Loyd	OF11	32	.271	B	
		Coscarart, Peter Joseph (SS47 3B1)	2B85	133	.242	B	
0	1	Cuccurullo, Arthur Joseph	P	1	.000	A	
0	3	Dietz, Lloyd Arthur	P8	10	+.000	B	Phil
		DiMaggio, Vincent Paul (SS1)	OF156	157	.248	B	
		Elliott, Robert Irving (2B2 SS1)	3B151	156	.315	B	
		Fletcher, Elburt Preston (Elbie)	1B	154	.283	B	
		Geary, Eugene Francis Joseph	SS	46	.151	B	C
4	4	Gee, John Alexander Jr.	P	15	.115	Pitt41	
9	13	Gornicki, Henry Frank	P	42	.175	B	
		Gustine, Frank Wm. (1B1 2B40)	SS68	112	.290	B	
1	2	Hallett, Jack Price	P	9	.286	B	
10	11	Hebert, Wallace Andrew	P34	35	.220	StLA33	C
11	8	Klinger, Robert Harold (Bob)	P	33	.246	B	
4	1	Lanning, John Young	P	12	.167	B	
		Lopez, Alfonso Ramon (Al) (3B1)	C116	118	.263	B	
		O'Brien, Thomas Edward (3B9)	OF48	89	.310	A	
		Ordenana, Antonio Rodriquez	SS	1	.500	A	C
0	4	Podgajny, John Sigmund	P15	21	+.143	xPhil	

WON	LOST	NAME	POS.	G.	BA	FROM	TO
6	9	Rescigno, Xavier Frederick	P	37	.143	A	
		Rubeling, Albert Wm. (3B1)	2B44	47	.262	PhilA41	
		Russell, James Wm. (1B6)	OF134	146	.259	B	
21	9	Sewell, Truett Banks (Rip)	P35	41	.286	B	
0	0	Shuman, Harry	P	11	.000	B	
		VanRobays, Maurice Rene	OF60	69	.288	B	
		Wasdell, James Chas.		4	+.500	B	Phil
		Wyrostek, John Barney (1B1 2B1 3B2)	OF20	51	.152	B	

WON 90 NATIONAL LEAGUE FINISHED 2nd.
LOST 63
TG 153 1944. PCT. .588

PITTSBURGH

FRANK FRANCIS FRISCH JR.

WON	LOST	NAME	POS.	G.	BA	FROM	TO
		Barnhart, Victor Dee	SS	1	.500	A	
		Barrett, John Joseph	OF147	149	.269	B	
13	11	Butcher, Albert Maxwell (Max)	P35	36	.190	B	
		Camelli, Henry Richard	C61	63	.296	B	
		Colman, Frank Loyd (1B6)	OF53	99	.270	B	
		Coscarart, Peter Joseph (SS4 OF1)	2B136	139	.264	B	
2	1	Cuccurullo, Arthur Joseph	P32	36	.368	B	
		Dahlgren, Ellsworth Tenney (Babe)	1B	158	.289	Phil	
		Davis, Virgil Lawrence (Spud)	C35	54	.301	Pitt41	
		DiMaggio, Vincent Paul (3B1)	OF101	109	.240	B	
		Elliott, Robert Irving (SS1)	3B140	143	.298	B	
0	0	Gee, John Alexander Jr.	P	4	+.500	B	N.Y.
0	1	Gilmore, Leonard Preston	P	1	.000	A	C
		Gionfriddo, Albert Francis	OF1	4	.167	A	
		Gustine, Frank Wm. (2B11 3B1)	SS116	127	.230	B	
		Handley, Lee Elmer (Jeep) (SS3 3B11)	2B19	40	.221	Pitt41	
		Lopez, Alfonso Ramon (Al)	C	115	.230	B	
		O'Brien, Thomas Edward (3B1)	OF48	85	.250	B	
11	7	Ostermueller, Frederick Raymond (Fritz)	P28	29	+.250	xBkn	
10	8	Rescigno, Xavier Frederick	P	48	.091	B	
		Rodgers, Wm. Sherman	OF1	2	.250	A	
13	11	Roe, Elwin Chas.	P	39	.132	StL38	
		Rubeling, Albert Wm. (2B17 3B16)	OF18	92	.245	B	C
		Russell, James Wm.	OF149	152	.312	B	
21	12	Sewell, Truett Banks (Rip)	P38	44	.223	B	
6	5	Starr, Raymond Francis	P	27	.136	Cin	
14	7	Strincevich, Nicholas Mihailovich	P	40	.158	Pitt42	

WON	LOST	NAME	POS.	G.	BA	FROM	TO
		Sweeney, Henry Leon	1B	1	.000	A	C
0	0	Vitelli, Joseph Anthony	P	4	.000	A	
		Waner, Lloyd James (Little Poison)	OF7	19	+.357	xBkn	
0	0	Wise, Roy Ogden	P	2	.000	A	C
		Zak, Frank Tom	SS67	87	.300	A	

WON 82 LOST 72 TG 154 — NATIONAL LEAGUE — FINISHED 4th.

1945. — PCT. .532

PITTSBURGH

FRANK FRANCIS FRISCH JR.

WON	LOST	NAME	POS.	G.	BA	FROM	TO
		Barnhart, Victor Dee (3B4)	SS60	71	.269	B	
		Barrett, John Joseph	OF132	142	.256	B	
6	1	Beck, Walter Wm. (Boom-Boom)	P	14	+.125	xCin	C
10	8	Butcher, Albert Maxwell (Max)	P	28	.222	B	C
		Camelli, Henry Richard	C	1	.000	B	
		Colman, Frank Loyd (OF12)	1B22	77	.209	B	
		Coscarart, Peter Joseph (SS1)	2B122	123	.242	B	
1	3	Cuccurullo, Arthur Joseph	P	29	.214	B	C
		Dahlgren, Ellsworth Tenney (Babe)	1B	144	.250	B	
		Davis, Virgil Lawrence (Spud)	C13	23	.242	B	
		Elliott, Robert Irving (OF61)	3B81	144	.290	B	
11	7	Gables, Kenneth Harlin	P	29	.103	A	
5	10	Gerheauser, Albert	P	32	.250	Phil	
		Gionfriddo, Albert Francis	OF106	122	.284	B	
		Gustine, Frank Wm. (C1 2B29)	SS104	128	.280	B	
		Handley, Lee Elmer (Jeep)	3B79	98	.298	B	
0	0	Lanning, John Young	P	1	.000	Pitt43	
		Lopez, Alfonso Ramon (Al)	C	91	.218	B	
		O'Brien, Thomas Edward	OF45	58	.335	B	
5	4	Ostermueller, Frederick Raymond (Fritz)	P	14	.321	B	
3	5	Rescigno, Xavier Frederick	P	44	.133	B	C
		Rodgers, Wm. Sherman		1	1.000	B	C
14	13	Roe, Elwin Chas.	P	33	.107	B	
		Russell, James Wm.	OF140	146	.284	B	
		Salkeld, Wm. Franklin	C86	95	.311	A	
		Saltzgaver, Otto Hamlin (Jack) (3B1)	2B31	52	.325	NYA37	C
11	9	Sewell, Truett Banks (Rip)	P33	35	.313	B	
0	2	Starr, Raymond Francis	P	4	+1.000	B	Chi
16	10	Strincevich, Nicholas Mihailovich	P	36	.202	B	
		Vitelli, Joseph Anthony		1	.000	B	C
		Waner, Lloyd James (Little Poison)	OF3	23	.263	B	C
		Zak, Frank Tom (2B1)	SS10	15	.143	B	

WON 63 LOST 91 TG 154 — NATIONAL LEAGUE — FINISHED 7th.

1946. — PCT. .409

PITTSBURGH

FRANK FRANCIS FRISCH JR. VIRGIL LAWRENCE DAVIS

WON	LOST	NAME	POS.	G.	BA	FROM	TO
0	6	Albosta, Edward John	P	17	.125	Bkn41	C
		Anderson, Alfred Walton		2	.000	Pitt42	C
8	6	Bahr, Edson Garfield	P27	29	.178	A	
		Baker, Wm. Presley (1B1)	C41	53	.239	Pitt43	
		Barnhart, Victor Dee		2	.000	B	C
		Barrett, John Joseph	OF21	32	+.169	B	Bos
		Brown, James Roberson (2B21 3B9)	SS30	79	.241	StL43	C
		Camelli, Henry Richard	C39	42	.208	B	
0	0	Clemensen, John Wm. Melville	P	1	.000	Pitt41	C
		Colman, Frank Loyd (1B2)	OF8	26	.170	B	NYA
		Coscarart, Peter Joseph	SS1	3	.500	B	C
		Cox, Wm. Richard	SS114	121	.290	Pitt41	
		Elliott, Robert Irving (3B43)	OF92	140	.263	B	
		Fletcher, Elburt Preston (Elbie)	1B147	148	.256	Pitt43	
2	4	Gables, Kenneth Harlin	P	32	.250	B	
2	2	Gerheauser, Albert (OF1)	P35	36	.333	B	
		Gionfriddo, Albert Francis	OF33	64	.255	B	
0	0	Gornicki, Henry Frank	P	7	.000	Pitt43	C
		Guintini, Benjamin John	OF1	2	.000	A	
		Gustine, Frank Wm. (SS13 3B7)	2B113	131	.259	B	
5	7	Hallett, Jack Price	P	35	.231	Pitt43	
		Handley, Lee Elmer (Jeep) (2B3)	3B102	116	.238	B	
8	12	Heintzelman, Kenneth Alphonse	P	32	.136	Pitt42	
0	1	Hopper, James McDaniel	P	2	.000	A	C
0	1	Howard, Lee Vincent	P	3	.000	A	
		Jarvis, LeRoy Gilbert	C1	2	.250	Bkn44	
		Kiner, Ralph McPherran	OF140	144	.247	A	
4	5	Lanning, John Young	P	27	.143	B	
		Lopez, Alfonso Ramon (Al)	C	56	.307	B	
13	10	Ostermueller, Frederick Raymond (Fritz)	P27	28	.328	B	
3	8	Roe, Elwin Chas.	P	21	.067	B	
		Russell, James Wm. (1B5)	OF134	146	.277	B	
		Salkeld, Wm. Franklin	C51	69	.294	B	
8	12	Sewell, Truett Banks (Rip)	P25	26	.180	B	
		Smith, Vincent Ambrose	C	7	.190	Pitt41	C
10	15	Strincevich, Nicholas Mihailovich	P	32	.154	B	
0	1	Tate, Alvin Walter	P	2	.333	A	C
		Van Robays, Maurice Rene (1B2)	OF37	59	.212	Pitt43	C
0	1	Walsh, James Gerald	P	4	.000	A	
		Whitehead, Burgess Urquhart (SS1 3B4)	2B30	55	.220	NY41	C

WON	LOST	NAME	POS.	G.	BA	FROM	TO
0	0	Wilkie, Aldon Jay	P	7	.000	Pitt42	C
		Workman, Chas. Thomas (3B1)	OF40	58	+.221	xBos	C
		Zak, Frank Tom	SS10	21	.200	B	C

WON 62
LOST 92
TG 154

NATIONAL LEAGUE

1947.

FINISHED 7th.
(TIED WITH PHILADELPHIA)
PCT. .403

PITTSBURGH

WM. JENNINGS BRYAN HERMAN WM. EDWIN BURWELL

WON	LOST	NAME	POS.	G.	BA	FROM	TO
5	4	Bagby, James Chas. Jr.	P	37	.219	BosA	C
3	5	Bahr, Edson Garfield	P19	21	.087	B	C
		Basinski, Edwin Frank	2B	56	.199	Bkn45	C
0	2	Behrman, Henry Bernard	P	10	+.000	xBkn	Bkn
		Bloodworth, James Henry	2B87	88	.250	DetA	
11	8	Bonham, Ernest Edward	P	33	.156	NYA	
		Castiglione, Peter Paul	SS129	13	.280	A	
		Cox, Wm. Richard	SS120	132	.274	B	
		Fletcher, Elburt Preston (Elbie)	1B50	69	.242	B	
0	0	Gables, Kenneth Harlin	P	1	.000	B	C
		Gionfriddo, Albert Francis		1	+.000	B	Bkn
		Greenberg, Henry Benjamin (Hank)	1B119	125	.249	DetA	C
		Gustine, Frank Wm.	3B	156	.297	B	
0	0	Heintzelman, Kenneth Alphonse	P	2	+.000	B	Phil
		Herman, Wm. Jennings Bryan (Billy) MGR. (1B2)	2B10	15	.213	Bos	C
1	3	Herring, Arthur L.	P	11	.000	Bkn	C
11	17	Higbe, Walter Kirby	P	46	+.139	xBkn	
0	0	Howard, Lee Vincent	P	2	.000	B	C
		Howell, Homer Elliott	C74	76	.276	A	
		Jarvis, LeRoy Gilbert	C15	18	.156	B	C
		Kiner, Ralph McPherran	OF	152	.313	B	
		Kluttz, Clyde Franklin	C69	73	.302	StL	
1	2	Lyons, Albert Harold	P13	15	.200	xNYA	
		Mauch, Eugene Wm. (SS4)	2B6	16	.300	Bkn44	
0	0	Mulcahy, Hugh Noyes	P	2	.333	Phil	C
0	0	McLish, Calvin Coolidge	P	1	.000	Bkn	
1	3	Nagy, Stephen	P	6	.250	A	
12	10	Ostermueller, Frederick Raymond (Fritz)	P	26	.188	B	
3	7	Queen, Melvin Joseph	P	14	.077	xNYA	
		Rikard, Culley	OF79	109	.287	Pitt42	C
4	15	Roe, Elwin Chas.	P	38	.125	B	
		Russell, James Wm.	OF119	128	.253	B	
		Salkeld, Wm. Franklin	C15	47	.213	B	
6	4	Sewell, Truett Banks (Rip)	P	24	.125	B	
2	2	Singleton, Bert Elmer	P36	41	.308	Bos	
1	6	Strincevich, Nicholas Mihailovich	P	32	.048	B	

WON	LOST	NAME	POS.	G.	BA	FROM	TO
		Sullivan, Wm. Joseph Jr. (Billy)	C12	38	.255	Bkn42	C
0	0	Tost, Louis Eugene	P	1	.000	Bos43	C
		Westlake, Waldon Thomas	OF109	112	.273	A	
		Wietelmann, Wm. Frederick (1B1 2B14 3B6)	SS22	48	.234	Bos	C
1	4	Wolff, Roger Francis	P	13	.000	xClevA	C
		Woodling, Eugene Richard	OF21	22	.266	ClevA	

WON 83
LOST 71
TG 154

NATIONAL LEAGUE

1948.

FINISHED 4th.

PCT. .539

PITTSBURGH

WM. ADAM MEYER

WON	LOST	NAME	POS.	G.	BA	FROM	TO
		Basgall, Romanus	2B22	38	.216	A	
		Beard, Cramer Theodore	OF22	25	.198	A	
		Bockman, Joseph Edward (2B1)	3B51	70	.239	ClevA	
6	10	Bonham, Ernest Edward	P	22	.163	B	
		Castiglione, Peter Paul	SS1	4	.000	B	
14	6	Chesnes, Robert Vincent	P25	39	.275	A	
		FitzGerald, Edward Raymond	C96	102	.267	A	
2	4	Gregg, Harold Dana	P	22	.273	Bkn	
		Gustine, Frank Wm.	3B118	131	.267	B	
		Gutteridge, Donald Joseph		4	.000	BosA	C
8	7	Higbe, Walter Kirby	P	56	.208	B	
		Hopp, John Leonard (1B25)	OF80	120	.278	Bos	
		Kiner, Ralph McPherran	OF154	156	.265	B	
		Kluttz, Clyde Franklin	C91	94	.221	B	
10	9	Lombardi, Victor Alvin	P38	39	.208	Bkn	
1	1	Main, Forrest Harry	P	17	.000	A	
		Murtaugh, Daniel Edward	2B	146	.290	Bos	
0	0	McLish, Calvin Coolidge	P2	3	.000	B	
8	11	Ostermueller, Frederick Raymond (Fritz)	P	23	.182	B	C
4	4	Queen, Melvin Joseph	P	25	.059	B	
12	10	Riddle, Elmer Ray	P28	29	.188	Cin	
		Riddle, John Ludy	C	10	.200	Cin45	C
		Rojek, Stanley Andrew	SS	156	.290	Bkn	
13	3	Sewell, Truett Banks (Rip)	P	21	.143	B	
4	6	Singleton, Bert Elmer	P	38	.087	B	
		Stevens, Edward Lee	1B117	128	.254	Bkn	
0	0	Strincevich, Nicholas Mihailovich	P	3	+.000	B	Phil
		Turner, Earl Edwin	C1	2	.000	A	
		Walker, Fred (Dixie)	OF112	129	.316	Bkn	
1	0	Walsh, James Gerald	P	2	.000	Pitt46	
		West, Max Edward (OF16)	1B32	87	.178	Cin46	C
		Westlake, Waldon Thomas	OF125	132	.285	B	
		Wilson, Grady Herbert	SS7	12	.100	A	C

WON 71
LOST 83
TG 154

NATIONAL LEAGUE — 1949. — FINISHED 6th. — PCT. .461

PITTSBURGH

WM. ADAM MEYER

WON	LOST	NAME	POS.	G.	BA	FROM	TO
		Basgall, Romanus (3B3)	2B98	107	.218	B	
		Beard, Cramer Theodore	OF10	14	.083	B	
		Bockman, Joseph Edward	3B68	79	.223	B	C
		(2B5)					
7	4	Bonham, Ernest Edward	P	18	.045	B	C
4	1	Casey, Hugh Thomas	P	33	.333	Bkn	NYA
		Cassini, Jack Dempsey		8	.000	A	C
		Castiglione, Peter Paul	3B98	118	.268	B	
		(SS17 OF2)					
13	7	Chambers, Clifford Day	P	34	.236	Chi	
7	13	Chesnes, Robert Vincent	P27	42	.250	B	
12	14	Dickson, Murry Monroe	P	44	.202	StL	
		FitzGerald, Edward Raymond	C56	75	.263	B	
		Fleming, Leslie Harvey	1B5	24	.258	ClevA47	C
1	1	Gregg, Harold Dana	P	8	.000	B	
1	4	Gumbert, Harry Edward	P	16	+.250	xCin	
0	2	Higbe, Walter Kirby	P	7	+.000	B	N.Y.
		Hopp, John Leonard (OF16)	1B77	20	+.218	B	Bkn
				85	.335	& return	
		Judnich, Walter Franklin	OF8	10	.229	ClevA	C
		Kiner, Ralph McPherran	OF	152	.310	B	
5	5	Lombardi, Victor Alvin	P34	43	.347	B	
		Masi, Philip Samuel (1B2)	C44	48	+.274	xBos	
1	5	Muncrief, Robert Cleveland	P	13	+.143	ClevA	Chi
		Murtaugh, Daniel Edward	2B74	75	.203	B	
		McCullough, Clyde Edward	C90	91	.237	Chi	
		Phillips, Jack Dorn (3B1)	1B16	18	.232	xN.Y.A	
0	1	Poat, Raymond Willis	P	11	+.100	xN.Y.	C
		Rackley, Marvin Eugene	OF8	11	+.314	xBkn	Bkn
		Restelli, Dino Paul (1B1)	OF61	72	.250	A	
		Rhawn, Robert John	3B2	3	+.143	xN.Y.	ChiA
1	8	Riddle, Elmer Ray	P	16	.136	B	C
		Rojek, Stanley Andrew	SS	144	.244	B	
		Saffell, Thomas Judson	OF53	73	.322	A	
6	1	Sewell, Truett Banks (Rip)	P	28	.063	B	C
		Stevens, Edward Lee	1B58	67	.262	B	
		Walker, Fred (Dixie) (1B3)	OF39	88	.282	B	C
1	4	Walsh, James Gerald	P	9	.000	B	
12	13	Werle, Wm. George	P	35	.117	A	
		Westlake, Waldon Thomas	OF143	147	.282	B	

WON 57
LOST 96
TG 153

NATIONAL LEAGUE — 1950. — FINISHED 8th (LAST) — PCT. .373

PITTSBURGH

WM. ADAM MEYER

WON	LOST	NAME	POS.	G.	BA	FROM	TO
1	2	Barrett, Francis Joseph	P	5	.000	Bos46	C
		Beard, Cramer Theodore	OF49	61	.232	B	
		Bell, David Russell	OF104	111	.282	A	
		Berardino, John (3B3)	2B36	40	.206	xClevA	
1	3	Borowy, Henry Ludwig	P	11	+.167	xPhil	
		Castiglione, Peter Paul	3B35	94	.255	B	
		(1B3 2B9 SS29)					
12	15	Chambers, Clifford Day	P	37	.289	B	
3	3	Chesnes, Robert Vincent	P	9	.154	B	C
		Coogan, Dale Roger	1B32	53	.240	A	C
10	15	Dickson, Murry Monroe	P51	52	.256	B	
		Dillinger, Robert Bernard	3B51	58	.288	xPhilA	
		Fernandez, Froilan	3B52	65	.258	Bos47	C
		FitzGerald, Edward Raymond	C5	6	.067	B	
0	1	Gregg, Harold Dana	P	5	.000	B	
0	0	Gumbert, Harry Edward	P	1	1.000	B	C
		Hopp, John Leonard (OF7)	1B70	106	.340	B	NYA
		Kiner, Ralph McPherran	OF	150	.272	B	
7	9	Law, Vernon Sanders	P	27	.073	A	
0	5	Lombardi, Victor Alvin	P39	42	.250	B	C
8	10	MacDonald, Wm. Paul	P	32	.122	A	
1	0	Main, Forrest Harry	P	12	.400	Pitt48	
		Mueller, Ray Coleman	C63	67	+.269	xN.Y.	
		Murtaugh, Daniel Edward	2B108	118	.294	B	
0	0	McCall, John Wm.	P	2	.000	BosA	
		McCullough, Clyde Edward	C100	103	.254	B	
		O'Connell, Daniel Francis	SS65	79	.292	A	
		(3B12)					
0	0	Papish, Frank Richard	P	4	.000	ClevA	C
0	0	Phillips, Jack Dorn	1B54	69	.293	B	
		(P1 3B3)					
0	2	Pierro, Wm. Leonard	P12	13	.222	A	C
5	14	Queen, Melvin Joseph	P	33	.057	Pitt48	
		Rickert, Marvin August	OF3	17	.150	Bos	ChiA
		Rojek, Stanley Andrew (2B3)	SS68	76	.257	B	
		Saffell, Thomas Judson	OF43	67	.203	B	
		Schenz, Henry Leonard	2B21	58	.228	Chi	
		(SS4 3B12)					
		Stevens, Edward Lee	1B12	17	.196	B	C
		Strickland, George Bevan	SS19	23	.111	A	
		(3B1)					
		Turner, Earl Edwin	C34	40	.243	Pitt48	C
1	1	Walsh, James Gerald	P	38	.167	B	
8	16	Werle, Wm. George	P	48	.194	B	
		Westlake, Waldon Thomas	OF123	139	.285	B	

WON 64
LOST 90
TG 154

NATIONAL LEAGUE — 1951. — FINISHED 7th. — PCT. .416

PITTSBURGH

WM. ADAM MEYER

WON	LOST	NAME	POS.	G.	BA	FROM	TO
		Basgall, Romanus	2B	55	.209	Pitt49	C
		Beard, Cramer Theodore	OF15	22	.188	B	
		Bell, David Russell	OF145	149	.278	B	
2	3	Carlsen, Donald Herbert	P	7	.250	Chi48	
		Castiglione, Peter Paul (SS28)	3B99	132	.261	B	
3	6	Chambers, Clifford Day	P	10	+.333	B	StL
		Cole, Richard Roy (SS8)	2B34	42	+.236	xStL	
0	2	Dempsey, Cornelius Francis	P	3	.000	A	C
20	16	Dickson, Murry Monroe	P45	46	.273	B	
		Dillinger, Robert Bernard	3B10	12	.233	B	ChiA
0	1	Dusak, Ervin Frank (P3 2B2 3B2)	OF12	21	+.308	xStL	
		Fisher, Harry Devereux		3	.000	A	
		Fitz Gerald, Edward Raymond	C38	55	.227	B	
6	10	Friend, Robert Bartmess	P	34	.091	A	
		Garagiola, Joseph Henry	C61	72	+.255	xStL	
		Howerton, Wm. Ray (3B4)	OF53	80	+.274	xStL	
		Kiner, Ralph McPherran (1B58)	OF94	151	.309	B	
0	1	Koski, Wm. John	P	13	.000	A	C
1	5	LaPalme, Paul Edmore	P	22	.100	A	
6	9	Law, Vernon Sanders	P	28	.344	B	
		Long, Richard Dale	1B1	10	.167	A	StLA
		Maguire, Jack (3B1)	2B1	8	+.000	xN.Y.	StLA
		Merson, John Warren	2B	13	.360	A	
		Metkovich, George Michael (1B37)	OF69	120	.293	ChiA49	
0	2	Muir, Joseph Allen	P	9	.000	A	
		Murtaugh, Daniel Edward (3B3)	2B65	77	.199	B	C
		McCullough, Clyde Edward	C87	92	.297	B	
		Nelson, Glenn Richard (OF12)	1B32	71	+.267	xStL	ChiA
0	0	Pettit, George Wm. Paul	P	2	.000	A	
		Phillips, Jack Dorn (3B4)	1B53	70	.237	B	
6	10	Pollet, Howard Joseph	P	21	+.139	xStL	
7	9	Queen, Melvin Joseph	P	39	.106	B	
		Reiser, Harold Patrick (Pete) (3B5)	OF27	74	.271	Bos	
		Restelli, Dino Paul	OF11	21	.184	Pitt49	C
		Rojek, Stanley Andrew	SS	8	+.188	B	StL
		Saffell, Thomas Judson	OF17	49	.200	B	C
		Schenz, Henry Leonard (3B2)	2B19	25	+.213	B	N.Y.
		Smith, Richard Harrison	3B	12	.174	A	
		Strickland, George Bevan (2B13)	SS125	138	.216	B	
		Tnomas, Frank Joseph	OF37	39	.264	A	
1	4	Walsh, James Gerald	P	36	.143	B	C
8	6	Werle, Wm. George	P	59	.300	B	
		Westlake, Waldon Thomas (OF11)	3B34	50	+.282	B	StL
3	5	Wilks, Theodore	P	48	+.083	xStL	
1	1	Yochim, Leonard Joseph	P	2	.000	A	

WON 42
LOST 112
TG 154

NATIONAL LEAGUE

FINISHED 8th (LAST)

1952.

PCT. .273

PITTSBURGH

WM. ADAM MEYER

WON	LOST	NAME	POS.	G.	BA	FROM	TO
		Bartirome, Anthony Joseph	1B118	124	.220	A	C
		Beard, Cramer Theodore	OF13	15	.182	B	
		Bell, David Russell	OF123	131	.250	B	
0	1	Bell, Wm. Samuel	P	4	.000	A	C
		Berardino, John	2B18	19	.143	xClevA	C
0	1	Carlsen, Donald Herbert	P	5	.333	B	C
		Castiglione, Peter Paul (1B1 OF1)	3B57	67	.266	B	
		Davis, Robert Brandon	OF29	55	.179	A	
		Del Greco, Robert George	OF93	99	.217	A	
14	21	Dickson, Murry Monroe	P43	47	.224	B	
0	0	Dunn, James Wm.	P	3	.000	A	C
		Dusak, Ervin Frank	OF11	20	.222	B	C
1	2	Fisher, Harry Devereux	P8	15	.333	B	C
		Fitz Gerald, Edward Raymond (3B2)	C18	51	.233	B	
7	17	Friend, Robert Bartmess	P	35	.058	B	
		Garagiola, Joseph Henry	C105	118	.273	B	
		Groat, Richard Morrow	SS94	95	.284	A	C
		Hall, Richard Wallace (3B5)	OF14	26	.138	A	
1	8	Hogue, Calvin Grey	P	19	.250	A	
		Howerton, Wm. Ray	3B1	13	+.320	B	N.Y.
		Kiner, Ralph McPherran	OF	149	.244	B	
0	7	Kline, Ronald Lee	BS	27	.000	A	C
		Koshorek, Clement John (2B27 3B26)	SS33	98	.261	A	
1	2	LaPalme, Paul Edmore	P	31	.100	B	
2	12	Main, Forrest Harry	P	48	.054	Pitt50	
		Mangan, James Daniel	C4	11	.154	A	
		Merson, John Warren (3B27)	2B81	111	.246	B	
		Metkovich, George Michael (OF33)	1B72	125	.271	B	
2	3	Muir, Joseph Allen	P	12	.111	B	C
0	3	Munger, George David	P	5	+.100	xStL	
		McCullough, Clyde Edward (1B1)	C61	66	.233	B	
1	6	Necciai, Ronald Andrew	P	12	.059	A	C
		Phillips, Jack Dorn	1B	1	.000	B	
7	16	Pollet, Howard Joseph	P	31	.191	B	
0	2	Queen, Melvin Joseph	P	2	.000	B	C
		Senerchia, Emanuel Robert	3B28	29	.220	A	C
		Smith, Richard Harrison (2B4 SS4)	3B16	29	.106	B	
		Strickland, George Bevan (1B1 SS28 3B1)	2B45	76	.177	B	ClevA
0	0	Suchecki, James Joseph	P	5	.000	StLA	C
		Tnomas Frank Joseph	OF5	6	.095	B	
		Walls, Ray Lee	OF19	32	.188	A	

WON	LOST	NAME	POS.	G.	BA	FROM	TO
1	6	Waugh, James Elden	P	17	.100	A	
0	0	Werle, Wm. George	P	5	+.000	B	StL
5	5	Wilks, Theodore	P	44	.125	B	ClevA
0	0	Wolfe, Edward Anthony	P	3	.000	A	C

WON 50
LOST 104
TG 154

NATIONAL LEAGUE

1953.

FINISHED 8th (LAST)

PCT. .325

PITTSBURGH

FRED GIRARD HANEY

WON	LOST	NAME	POS.	G.	BA	FROM	TO
		Abrams, Calvin Ross	OF112	119	.286	Cin	
		Addis, Robert Gordon		4	+.000	xChi	C
		Atwell, Maurice Dailey	C45	53	+.245	xChi	
		Bernier, Carlos Rodriquez	OF86	105	.213	A	C
0	4	Bowman, Roger Clinton	P	30	.286	N.Y.	
		Castiglione, Peter Paul	3B43	45	+.208	B	StL
		Cole, Richard Roy	SS77	97	.272	Pitt51	
		(1B1 2B7)					
		Davis, Robert Brandon	OF9	12	.205	B	C
10	19	Dickson, Murry Monroe	P	45	.115	B	
6	8	Face, Elroy Leon	P41	43	.133	A	
		Fitz Gerald, Edward Raymond	C5	6	.118	B	WashA
8	11	Friend, Robert Bartmess	P	32	.135	B	
		Garagiola, Joseph Henry	C22	27	+.233	B	Chi
		Hall, Richard Wallace	2B	7	.167	B	
3	12	Hall, Robert Louis	P	37	.158	Bos50	C
		Hermanski, Eugene Victor	OF13	41	+.177	xChi	C
3	6	Hetki, John Edward	P	54	.208	StLA	
1	1	Hogue, Calvin Grey	P	3	.000	B	
		Janowicz, Victor Felix	C35	42	.252	A	
		Kiner, Ralph McPherran	OF	41	+.270	B	Chi
		Koback, Nicholas Nicholia	C6	7	.125	A	
		Koshorek, Clement John		1	.000	B	C
8	16	LaPalme, Paul Edmore	P	35	.085	B	
5	16	Lindell, John Harlan (1B2)	P27	58	+.286	StL50	Phil
0	1	MacDonald, Wm. Paul	P	4	.000	Pitt50	C
0	0	Main, Forrest Harry	P	2	.000	B	C
		Metkovich, George Michael	1B5	26	+.146	B	Chi
		(OF4)					
		Montemayor, Felipe Angel	OF12	28	.109	A	
		Naton, Peter Alphonsus	C4	6	.167	A	C
		O'Brien, Edward Joseph	SS81	89	.238	A	
		O'Brien, John Thomas (SS1)	2B77	89	.247	A	
		O'Connell, Daniel Francis	3B104	149	.294	Pitt50	
		(2B47)					
		Pellagrini, Edward Chas.	2B31	78	.253	Cin	
		(SS3 3B12)					
1	2	Pettit, George Wm. Paul	P10	11	.250	Pitt51	C
1	1	Pollet, Howard Joseph	P	5	+.333	B	Chi
		Rice, Harold Housten	OF70	78	+.311	xStL	
		Sandlock, Michael Joseph	C	64	.231	Bkn46	C
0	2	Schultz, Robert Duffy	P	11	+.000	xChi	

WON	LOST	NAME	POS.	G.	BA	FROM	TO
		Shepard, Jack Leroy	C	2	.250	A	
		Smith, Paul Leslie (OF19)	1B74	118	.283	A	
		Smith, Richard Harrison	SS	13	.163	B	
		Thomas, Frank Joseph	OF118	128	.255	B	
		Ward, Preston Meyer	1B78	88	+.210	xChi	
4	5	Waugh, James Eldon	P	29	.227	B	C

WON 53
LOST 101
TG 154

NATIONAL LEAGUE

1954.

FINISHED 8th (LAST)

PCT. .344

PITTSBURGH

FRED GIRARD HANEY

WON	LOST	NAME	POS.	G.	BA	FROM	TO
		Abrams, Calvin Ross	OF13	17	.143	B	BaltA
		Allie, Gair Roosevelt (3B19)	SS95	121	.199	A	C
		Atwell, Maurice Dailey	C88	96	.289	B	
		Cole, Richard Roy	SS66	138	.270	B	
		(2B17 3B55)					
		Cooper, Wm. Walker	C2	14	+.200	Mil	Chi
7	12	Friend, Robert Bartmess	P	35	.275	B	
		Gordon, Sidney (3B40)	OF73	131	.306	Mil	
		Hall, Richard Wallace	OF102	112	.239	B	
		Hall, Wm. Lemuel	C1	5	.000	A	
		Henley, Gail Curtice	OF9	14	.300	A	C
4	4	Hetki, John Edward	P	58	.222	B	C
0	1	Hogue, Calvin Grey	P	3	.000	B	C
		Janowicz, Victor Felix	3B18	41	.151	B	C
		(OF1)					
		Jethroe, Samuel	OF1	2	.000	Bos	C
0	0	King, Nelson Joseph	P	4	.000	A	
		Koback, Nicholas Nicholia	C	4	.000	B	
4	10	LaPalme, Paul Edmore	P	33	.143	B	
9	13	Law, Vernon Sanders (OF1)	P39	50	.231	Pitt51	
10	11	Littlefield, Richard Bernard	P	23	.163	xBaltA	
		Lynch, Gerald Thomas	OF83	98	.239	A	
		Mangan, James Daniel	C7	14	.192	Pitt52	
		Marquez, Luis Angel	OF4	14	+.111	xChi	C
3	9	O'Donnell, George Dana	P	21	.087	A	C
0	0	Page, Joseph Francis	P	7	.000	NYA50	C
		Pellagrini, Edward Chas.	3B31	73	.216	B	C
		(2B7 SS1)					
1	5	Pepper, Hugh McLaurin	P	14	.235	A	
3	8	Purkey, Robert Thomas	P	36	.077	A	
		Rice, Harold Housten	OF24	28	+.173	B	Chi
		Roberts, Curtis Benjamin	2B131	134	.232	A	
		Shepard, Jack Leroy	C67	82	.304	B	
		Skinner, Robert Ralph (OF2)	1B118	132	.249	A	
		Smith, Richard Harrison	3B9	12	.097	B	
9	18	Surkont, Maxim Constantine	P	33	.167	Mil	
3	9	Thies, Vernon Arthur	P	33	.030	A	
		Thomas, Frank Joseph	OF	153	.298	B	
		Ward, Preston Meyer	1B48	117	.269	B	
		(3B11 OF42)					

0	1	Yochim, Leonard Joseph	P	10	.500	Pitt51	C

WON 60
LOST 94
TG 154

NATIONAL LEAGUE 1955. FINISHED 8th (LAST) PCT. .390

PITTSBURGH

FRED GIRARD HANEY

WON	LOST	NAME	POS.	G.	BA	FROM	TO
		Atwell, Maurice Dailey	C67	71	.213	B	
0	0	Bell, Wm. Samuel	P	1	.000	Pitt52	C
0	3	Bowman, Roger Clinton	P	7	.500	Pitt53	C
		Clemente, Roberto Walker	OF118	124	.255	A	
		Cole, Richard Roy	3B33	77	.226	B	
		(2B24 SS12)					
4	6	Donoso, Lino Galata	P	25	.185	A	
5	7	Face, Elroy Leon	P42	43	.115	Pitt53	
		Freese, Eugene Lewis	3B65	134	.253	A	
		(2B57)					
		Freese, George Walter	3B50	51	.257	DetA53	
14	9	Friend, Robert Bartmess	P	44	.164	B	
		Gordon, Sidney (OF4)	3B8	16	+.170	B	N.Y.
		Groat, Richard Morrow	SS149	151	.267	Pitt52	
0	0	Grunwald, Alfred Henry	P	3	.500	A	
6	6	Hall, Richard Wallace	P15	21	.175	B	
		(OF3)					
1	3	King, Nelson Joseph	P	17	.000	B	
6	13	Kline, Ronald Lee (3B1)	P36	37	.132	Pitt52	
		Koback, Nicholas Nicholia	C2	5	.286	B	C
10	10	Law, Vernon Sanders	P43	44	.254	B	
5	12	Littlefield, Richard Bernard	P	35	.176	B	
		Long, Richard Dale	1B119	131	.291	StLA51	
		Lynch, Gerald Thomas (C2)	OF71	88	.284	B	
0	1	Martin, Paul Chas.	P	7	.000	A	C
		Mejias, Roman Gomez	OF44	71	.216	A	
		Montemayor, Felipe Angel	OF28	36	.211	Pitt53	C
		O'Brien, Edward Joseph	OF56	75	.233	Pitt53	
		(SS4 3B7)					
		O'Brien, John Thomas	2B78	84	.299	Pitt53	
0	1	Pepper, Hugh McLaurin	P	14	.000	B	
		Peterson, Harding Wm.	C31	32	.247	A	
		Powers, John Calvin	OF	2	.250	A	
2	7	Purkey, Robert Thomas	P	14	.316	B	
		Roberts, Curtis Benjamin	2B	6	.118	B	
		Saffell, Thomas Judson	OF47	73	.168	Pitt51	KCA
		Shepard, Jack Leroy	C77	94	.239	B	
		Smith, Earl Calvin	OF	5	.063	A	C
		Smith, Richard Harrison	SS1	4	.000	B	C
7	14	Surkont, Maxim Constantine	P	35	.140	B	
0	0	Swanson, Arthur Leonard	P	1	.000	A	
0	1	Thies, Vernon Arthur	P	1	.000	B	C
		Thomas, Frank Joseph	OF139	142	.245	B	
0	1	Wade, Benjamin Styron	P	11	.000	StL	C
		Wade, Preston Meyer (OF1)	1B48	84	.212	B	

0	0	Waters, Fred Warren	P	2	.000	A	

WON 66
LOST 88
TG 154

NATIONAL LEAGUE 1956. FINISHED 7th. PCT. .429

PITTSBURGH

ROBERT RANDALL BRAGAN

WON	LOST	NAME	POS.	G.	BA	FROM	TO
3	3	Arroyo, Luis Enrique	P	18	.500	StL	
		Atwell, Maurice Dailey	C9	12	+.111	B	Mil
		Clemente, Roberto Walker	OF139	147	.311	B	
		(2B2 3B1)					
		Cole, Richard Roy	3B18	72	.212	B	
		(2B12 SS6)					
		Del Greco, Robert George	OF7	14	+.200	Pitt52	StL
		(3B3)					
0	0	Donoso, Lino Galata	P	3	.000	B	C
12	13	Face, Elroy Leon	P68	69	.192	B	
		Foiles, Henry Lee	C73	79	.212	xClevA	
		Freese, Eugene Lewis	3B47	65	.208	B	
		(2B26)					
17	17	Friend, Robert Bartmess	P	49	.165	B	
0	0	Garber, Robert Mitchell	P	2	.000	A	C
		Groat, Richard Morrow (3B2)	SS141	142	.273	B	
0	7	Hall, Richard Wallace (1B1)	P19	33	.345	B	
		Hall, Wm. Lemuel	C	1	.000	Pitt54	
		Jacobs, Forrest Vandergrift	2B	11	.162	xKCA	C
4	1	King, Nelson Joseph	P	38	.000	B	
14	18	Kline, Ronald Lee	P	44	.127	B	
		Kravitz, Daniel (3B2)	C26	32	.265	A	
8	16	Law, Vernon Sanders	P	39	.175	B	
0	0	Littlefield, Richard Bernard	P	6	+.000	B	StL
		Long, Richard Dale	1B138	148	.263	B	
		Lynch, Gerald Thomas	OF1	19	.158	B	
		Mazeroski, Wm. Stanley	2B	81	.243	A	
3	4	Munger, George David	P	35	.107	Pitt52	C
0	0	McMahan, Jack Wally	P	11	.000	A	KCA
1	2	Naranjo, Lazaro Ramon	P	17	.143	A	C
		Gonzalo Naranjo Couto					
0	0	O'Brien, Edward Joseph	SS23	63	.264	B	
		(P1 2B2 3B4 OF6)					
1	0	O'Brien, John Thomas	2B53	73	.173	B	
		(P8 SS1)					
1	1	Pepper, Hugh McLaurin	P	11	.000	B	
0	4	Pollet, Howard Joseph	P	19	.000	xChiA	C
		Powers, John Calvin	OF5	11	.048	B	
0	0	Purkey, Robert Thomas	P	2	.000	B	
		Roberts, Curtis Benjamin	2B27	31	.177	B	C
		Shepard, Jack Leroy (1B2)	C86	100	.242	B	C
		Skinner, Robert Ralph	OF36	113	.202	Pitt54	
		(1B23 3B1)					
0	0	Surkont, Maxim Constantine	P	1	+.000	B	StL
0	0	Swanson, Arthur Leonard	P9	10	.000	B	

WON	LOST	NAME	POS.	G.	BA	FROM	TO
		Thomas, Frank Joseph (2B4 OF56)	3B111	157	.282	B	
		Virdon, Wm. Chas.	OF130	133	+.334	xStL	
		Walls, Ray Lee (3B1)	OF133	143	.274	Pitt52	
		Ward, Preston Meyer (OF5)	3B5	16	.333	B	ClevA
2	2	Waters, Fred Warren	P	23	.050	B	C

WON 62 NATIONAL LEAGUE FINISHED 7th.
LOST 92 (TIED WITH CHICAGO)
TG 154 1957. PCT. .403

PITTSBURGH

ROBERT RANDALL BRAGAN DANIEL EDWARD MURTAUGH

WON	LOST	NAME	POS.	G.	BA	FROM	TO
3	11	Arroyo, Luis Enrique	P54	56	.156	B	
		Baker, Eugene Walter (2B13 SS28)	3B60	111	+.266	xChi	
0	0	Churn, Clarence Nottingham	P	5	.000	A	
		Clemente, Roberto Walker	OF109	111	.253	B	
0	1	Daniels, Bennie	P	1	.000	A	
3	3	Douglas, Chas. Wm.	P	11	.063	A	C
4	6	Face, Elroy Leon	P	59	.125	B	
		Foiles, Henry Lee	C	109	.270	B	
		Fondy, Dee Virgil	1B73	95	+.313	xChi	
		Freese, Eugene Lewis (2B10 OF10)	3B74	114	.283	B	
14	18	Friend, Robert Bartmess	P	40	.184	B	
		Groat, Richard Morrow (3B2)	SS123	125	.315	B	
0	0	Hall, Richard Wallace	P8	10	.000	B	
		Hamlin, Kenneth Lee	SS1	2	.000	A	
2	1	King, Nelson Joseph	P	36	.000	B	C
9	16	Kline, Ronald Lee	P	40	.061	B	
		Kravitz, Daniel	C15	19	.146	B	
0	0	Kuzava, Robert LeRoy	P	4	+.000	Phil55	StL
10	8	Law, Vernon Sanders	P31	34	.190	B	
		Long, Richard Dale	1B	7	+.182	B	Chi
		Mazeroski, Wm. Stanley	2B144	148	.283	B	
		Mejias, Roman Gomez	OF42	58	.275	Pitt55	
1	0	O'Brien, Edward Joseph	P	3	.000	B	
0	3	O'Brien, John Thomas (2B2 SS8)	P16	34	.314	B	
0	1	Pepper, Hugh McLaurin	P5	7	.000	B	C
		Pendleton, James Edward (SS1 3B2)	OF9	46	.305	Mil	
		Peterson, Harding Wm.	C	30	.301	Pitt55	
		Powers, John Calvin	OF9	20	.286	B	
		Pritchard, Harold Wm. (OF3)	SS10	23	.091	A	C
11	14	Purkey, Robert Thomas	P	48	.111	B	
		Rand, Richard Hilton	C57	60	.219	StL55	C
		Skinner, Robert Ralph (1B9 3B1)	OF93	126	.305	B	
		Smith, Paul Leslie (1B1)	OF33	81	.253	Pitt53	
2	4	Smith, Robert Gilchrist	P	20	+.077	xStL	
3	3	Swanson, Arthur Leonard	P	32	.000	B	C
		Thomas, Frank Joseph (3B31 OF59)	1B71	151	.290	B	
0	2	Trimble, Joseph Gerard	P	5	.143	BosA55	C
		Virdon, Wm. Chas.	OF141	144	.251	B	
		Walls, Ray Lee	OF7	8	+.182	B	Chi
0	1	Witt, George Adrian	P	1	.000	A	

WON 84 NATIONAL LEAGUE FINISHED 2nd.
LOST 70
TG 154 1958. PCT. .545

PITTSBURGH

DANIEL EDWARD MURTAUGH

WON	LOST	NAME	POS.	G.	BA	FROM	TO
		Baker, Eugene Walter (2B3)	3B11	29	.250	B	
2	1	Blackburn, Ronald Hamilton	P	38	.286	A	
		Bright, Harry James	3B7	15	.250	A	
		Clemente, Roberto Walker	OF135	140	.289	B	
0	3	Daniels, Bennie	P	8	.125	B	
5	2	Face, Elroy Leon	P	57	.000	B	
		Foiles, Henry Lee	C103	104	.205	B	
		Freese, Eugene Lewis	3B1	17	+.167	B	StL.
22	14	Friend, Robert Bartmess	P	38	.106	B	
		Groat, Richard Morrow	SS149	151	.300	B	
5	7	Gross, Donald John	P	40	.056	Cin	
		Hall, Wm. Lemuel	C	51	.284	Pitt56	C
13	16	Kline, Ronald Lee	P32	33	.027	B	
		Kluszewski, Theodore Bernard	1B72	100	.292	Cin	
		Kravitz, Daniel	C37	45	.240	B	
14	12	Law, Vernon Sanders	P35	36	.194	B	
		Mazeroski, Wm. Stanley	2B	152	.275	B	
		Mejias, Roman Gomez	OF57	76	.268	B	
0	0	O'Brien, Edward Joseph	P	1	.000	B	C
		O'Brien, John Thomas		3	+.000	B	StL.
		Pendleton, James Edward		3	.333	B	
0	1	Perez, George Thomas	P	4	.000	A	C
		Peterson, Harding Wm.	C	2	.333	B	
4	6	Porterfield, Erwin Coolidge	P	37	.050	xBosA	
		Powers, John Calvin	OF14	57	.183	B	
8	4	Raydon, Curtis Lowell	P	31	.026	A	C
		Schofield, John Richard (3B2)	SS5	26	+.148	xStL	
		Skinner, Robert Ralph	OF141	144	.321	B	
		Smith, Paul Leslie		6	+.333	B	Chi
2	2	Smith, Robert Gilchrist	P	35	.091	B	
		Stevens, R. C.	1B52	59	.267	A	
		Stuart, Richard Lee	1B64	67	.268	A	
		Thomas, Frank Joseph (1B2 OF8)	3B139	149	.281	B	
		Virdon, Wm. Chas.	OF143	144	.267	B	
0	0	Williams, Donald Fred	P	2	.000	A	
9	2	Witt, George Adrian	P	18	.154	B	

WON 78 LOST 76 TG 154

NATIONAL LEAGUE 1959. FINISHED 4th. PCT. .506

PITTSBURGH

DANIEL EDWARD MURTAUGH

WON	LOST	NAME	POS.	G.	BA	FROM	TO
1	1	Blackburn, Ronald Hamilton	P	26	.200	B	C
		Bright, Harry James (2B1 3B3)	OF4	40	.250	B	
		Burgess, Forrest Harrill	C101	114	.297	Cin	
		Christopher, Joseph O'Neal	OF9	15	.000	A	
		Clemente, Roberto Walker	OF104	105	.296	B	
7	9	Daniels, Bennie	P34	36	.310	B	
18	1	Face, Elroy Leon	P57	58	.231	B	
		Foiles, Henry Lee	C51	53	.225	B	
8	19	Friend, Robert Bartmess	P	35	.164	B	
0	0	Giel, Paul Robert	P	4	.000	S.F.	
1	2	Green, Fred Allan	P	17	.000	A	
		Groat, Richard Morrow	SS145	147	.275	B	
1	1	Gross, Donald John	P	21	.000	B	
12	12	Haddix, Harvey	P	31	.145	Cin	
0	0	Hall, Richard Wallace	P	2	.000	Pitt57	
		Hamlin, Kenneth Lee	SS	3	.125	Pitt57	
		Hoak, Donald Albert	3B	155	.294	Cin	
0	0	Jackson, Alvin Neil	P	8	.200	A	
11	13	Kline, Ronald Lee	P33	38	.136	B	
		Kluszewski, Theodore Bernard	1B20	60	.262	B	ChiA
		Kravitz, Daniel	C45	52	.253	B	
18	9	Law, Vernon Sanders	P34	38	.167	B	
		Mazeroski, Wm. Stanley	2B133	135	.241	B	
		Mejias, Roman Gomez	OF85	96	.236	B	
		Nelson, Glenn Richard (OF2)	1B56	98	.291	StL56	
		Peterson, Harding Wm.	C	2	.000	B	C
1	2	Porterfield, Erwin Coolidge	P	36	+.000	B	Chi
						(& return)	C
		Schofield, John Richard (SS8 OF3)	2B28	81	.234	B	
		Simpson, Harry Leon	OF3	9	.267	xChiA	
		Skinner, Robert Ralph (1B1)	OF142	143	.280	B	
0	0	Smith, Robert Gilchrist	P	20	.000	B	DetA
		Stevens, R. C.	1B1	3	.286	B	
		Stuart, Richard Lee (OF1)	1B105	118	.297	B	
0	0	Umbricht, James	P	1	.000	A	
		Virdon, Wm. Chas.	OF	144	.254	B	
0	0	Williams, Donald Fred	P	6	.333	B	
0	7	Witt, George Adrian	P	15	.000	B	

WON 95 LOST 59 TG 154

NATIONAL LEAGUE 1960. FINISHED 1st. PCT. .617

PITTSBURGH

DANIEL EDWARD MURTAUGH

WON	LOST	NAME	POS.	G.	BA	FROM	TO
		Baker, Eugene Walter (2B1)	3B7	33	.243	Pitt58	
		Barone, Richard Anthony	SS2	3	.000	A	C
		Bright, Harry James		4	.000	B	
		Burgess, Forrest Harrill	C89	110	.294	B	
2	2	Cheney, Thomas Edgar	P	11	.176	StL	
		Christopher, Joseph O'Neal	OF17	50	.232	B	
		Cimoli, Gino Nicholas	OF91	101	.267	StL	
		Clemente, Roberto Walker	OF142	144	.314	B	
1	3	Daniels, Bennie	P	10	.188	B	
10	8	Face, Elroy Leon	P	68	.412	B	
1	0	Francis, Earl Coleman	P	7	.000	A	
18	12	Friend, Robert Bartmess	P	38	.068	B	
4	2	Gibbon, Joseph Chas.	P	27	.211	A	
2	0	Giel, Paul Robert	P	16	.000	B	
8	4	Green, Fred Allan	P	45	.375	B	
		Groat, Richard Morrow	SS136	138	.325	B	
0	0	Gross, Donald John	P	5	.000	B	C
11	10	Haddix, Harvey	P	29	.254	B	
		Hoak, Donald Albert	3B	155	.282	B	
		Kravitz, Daniel	C1	8	.000	B	K.C.A
3	0	Labine, Clement Walter	P	15	.000	xDetA	
20	9	Law, Vernon Sanders	P	35	.181	B	
		Mazeroski, Wm. Stanley	2B	151	.273	B	
		Mejias, Roman Gomez		3	.000	B	
13	5	Mizell, Wilmer David	P	23	+.137	xStL	
		Nelson, Glenn Richard	1B73	93	.300	B	
		Oldis, Robert Carl	C	22	.200	WashA55	
0	0	Olivo, Diomedes Antonio	P	4	.000	A	
		Schofield, John Richard (2B10 3B1)	SS23	65	.333	B	
		Skinner, Robert Ralph	OF141	145	.273	B	
		Smith, Harold Wayne	C71	77	.295	KCA	
		Stevens, R. C.	1B7	9	.000	B	
		Stuart, Richard Lee	1B108	122	.260	B	
1	2	Umbricht, James	P	17	.333	B	
		Vernon, James Barton		9	.125	Mil	C
		Virdon, Wm. Chas.	OF109	120	.264	B	
1	2	Witt, George Adrian	P	10	.000	B	

WON 75 LOST 79 TG 154

NATIONAL LEAGUE 1961. FINISHED 6th. PCT. .487

PITTSBURGH

DANIEL EDWARD MURTAUGH

WON	LOST	NAME	POS.	G.	BA	FROM	TO
		Baker, Eugene Walter	3B3	9	.100	B	C
		Burgess, Forrest Harrill	C92	100	.303	B	
0	0	Cheney, Thomas Edgar	P	1	.000	B	WashA
		Christopher, Joseph O'Neal	OF55	76	.263	B	
		Cimoli, Gino Nicholas	OF19	21	+.299	B	Mil

WON	LOST	NAME	POS.	G.	BA	FROM	TO
		Clemente, Roberto Walker	OF144	146	.351	B	
		Clendenon, Donn Alvin	OF8	9	.314	A	
6	12	Face, Elroy Leon	P	62	.273	B	
1	1	Foss, Lawrence Curtis	P	3	.167	A	
2	8	Francis, Earl Coleman	P	23	.107	B	
14	19	Friend, Robert Bartmess	P	41	.139	B	
13	10	Gibbon, Joseph Chas.	P30	31	.136	B	
0	0	Green, Fred Allen	P	13	.000	B	
		Groat, Richard Morrow (3B1)	SS144	148	.275	B	
10	6	Haddix, Harvey	P29	31	.143	B	
		Hoak, Donald Albert	3B143	145	.298	B	
1	0	Jackson, Alvin Neil	P3	5	.000	Pitt59	
4	1	Labine, Clement Walter	P	56	.100	B	
3	4	Law, Vernon Sanders	P	11	.263	B	
		Leppert, Donald George	C21	22	.267	A	
		Logan, John (SS6)	3B7	27	+.231	xMil	
		Mazeroski, Wm. Stanley	2B	152	.265	B	
3	2	McBean, Alvin Neil	P27	28	.267	A	
		Mejias, Roman Gomez	OF2	4	.000	B	
7	10	Mizell, Wilmer David	P	25	.130	B	
		Moryn, Walter Joseph	OF11	40	+.200	xStL	C
		Nelson, Glenn Richard	1B35	75	.197	B	C
		Oldis, Robert Carl	C	4	.000	B	
		Schofield, John Richard (2B5 SS9 OF3)	3B11	60	.192	B	
6	3	Shantz, Robert Clayton	P43	44	.438	NYA	
		Skinner, Robert Ralph	OF97	119	.268	B	
		Smith, Harold Wayne	C65	67	.223	B	
		Stuart, Richard Lee (OF1)	1B132	138	.301	B	
5	2	Sturdivant, Thomas Virgil	P	13	.250	xWashA	
0	0	Umbricht, James	P	1	1.000	B	
		Virdon, Wm. Chas.	OF145	146	.260	B	
0	1	Witt, George Adrian	P	9	.500	B	

WON 93 NATIONAL LEAGUE FINISHED 4th.
LOST 68
TG 161 1962. PCT. .578

PITTSBURGH

DANIEL EDWARD MURTAUGH

WON	LOST	NAME	POS.	G.	BA	FROM	TO
		Bailey, Robert Sherwood	3B12	14	.167	A	
		Burgess, Forrest Harrill	C101	103	.328	B	
0	0	Butters, Thomas Arden	P	4	.000	A	
		Clemente, Roberto Walker	OF142	144	.312	B	
		Clendenon, Donn Alvin (OF19)	1B52	80	.302	B	
		Elliot, Lawrence Lee	OF3	8	.300	A	
8	7	Face, Elroy Leon	P	63	.083	B	
9	8	Francis, Earl Coleman	P	36	.164	B	
18	14	Friend, Robert Bartmess	P	39	.121	B	
3	4	Gibbon, Joseph Chas.	P	19	.176	B	
		Goss, Howard Wayne	OF66	89	.243	A	
		Groat, Richard Morrow	SS	161	.294	B	
9	6	Haddix, Harvey	P	28	.250	B	
		Hoak, Donald Albert	3B116	121	.241	B	
3	1	Lamabe, John Alexander	P	46	.000	A	
10	7	Law, Vernon Sanders	P	23	.311	B	
		Leppert, Donald George	C44	45	.266	B	
		Logan, John	3B19	44	.300	B	
		Marshall, Rufus James	1B26	55	+.220	xN.Y.	C
		Mazeroski, Wm. Stanley	2B	159	.271	B	
15	10	McBean, Alvin O'Neal	P33	34	.209	B	
		McFarlane, Orlando Jesus	C	8	.087	A	C
1	1	Mizell, Wilmer David	P	4	+.000	B	N.Y.
		Neeman, Calvin Amandus	C	24	.180	Phil	
5	1	Olivo, Diomedes Antonio	P	62	.188	Pitt60	
		Plaskett, Elmo Alexander	C4	7	.286	A	
1	0	Priddy, Robert Simpson	P	2	.000	A	C
		Schofield, John Richard (2B2 SS1)	3B20	54	.288	B	
0	2	Sisk, Thomas Wayne	P	5	.200	A	
		Skinner, Robert Ralph	OF139	144	.302	B	
		Stargell, Wilver Dornel	OF9	10	.290	A	
		Stuart, Richard Lee	1B101	114	.228	B	
9	5	Sturdivant, Thomas Virgil	P	49	.182	B	
		Veal, Orville Inman		1	.000	WashA	
2	2	Veale, Robert Andrew	P	11	.250	A	
		Virdon, Wm. Chas.	OF	156	.247	B	

WON 74 NATIONAL LEAGUE FINISHED 8th.
LOST 88
TG 162 1963. PCT. .457

PITTSBURGH

DANIEL EDWARD MURTAUGH

WON	LOST	NAME	POS.	G.	BA	FROM	TO
		Alley, Leonard Eugene (2B4 SS4)	3B7	17	.216	A	
		Bailey, Robert Sherwood (SS3)	3B153	154	.228	B	
		Brand, Ronald George (2B2 3B2)	C33	46	.288	A	
		Burgess, Forrest Harrill	C72	91	.280	B	
0	0	Butters, Thomas Arden	P	6	.333	B	
13	15	Cardwell, Donald Eugene	P	33	.085	Chic	
		Clemente, Roberto Walker	OF151	152	.320	B	
		Clendenon, Donn Alvin	1B151	154	.275	B	
		Elliot, Lawrence Lee		4	.000	B	
3	9	Face, Elroy Leon	P	56	.250	B	
4	6	Francis, Earl Coleman	P33	34	.308	B	
17	16	Friend, Robert Bartmess	P	39	.105	B	
5	12	Gibbon, Joseph Chas.	P37	40	.093	B	
		Gotay, Julio Enrique	2B1	4	.500	StL	
3	4	Haddix, Harvey	P49	50	.182	B	
4	5	Law, Vernon Sanders	P18	21	.217	B	
		Logan, John (3B4)	SS44	81	.232	B	C
		Lynch, Gerald Thomas	OF64	88	+.266	xCin	
		Mazeroski, Wm. Stanley	2B138	142	.245	B	

WON	LOST	NAME	POS.	G.	BA	FROM	TO
13	3	McBean, Alvin O'Neal	P55	59	.194	B	
		Mota, Manuel Rafael (2B1)	OF37	59	.270	S.F.	
		Pagliarone, James Vincent	C85	92	.230	BosA	
0	1	Parsons, Thomas Anthony	P	1	.000	A	
		Plaskett, Elmo Alexander (3B1)	C5	10	.143	B	C
		Savage, Theodore E.	OF47	85	.195	Phil	
		Schofield, John Richard (2B20 3B1)	SS117	138	.246	B	
6	12	Schwall, Donald Bernard	P	33	.160	BosA	
1	3	Sisk, Thomas Wayne	P	57	.063	B	
		Skinner, Robert Ralph	OF32	34	+.270	B	Cin
		Stargell, Wilver Dornel (1B16)	OF65	108	.243	B	
0	0	Sturdivant, Thomas Virgil	P	3	.000	B	DetA
5	2	Veale, Robert Andrew	P34	35	.087	B	
		Virdon, Wm. Chas.	OF	142	.269	B	

WON 80 — NATIONAL LEAGUE — FINISHED 6th.
LOST 82 — (TIED WITH LOS ANGELES)
TG 162 — 1964. — PCT. .494

PITTSBURGH

DANIEL EDWARD MURTAUGH

WON	LOST	NAME	POS.	G.	BA	FROM	TO
		Alley, Leonard Eugene (2B1 3B31)	SS61	81	.211	B	
		Bailey, Robert Sherwood (SS2 OF35)	3B105	143	.281	B	
5	8	Blass, Stephen Robert	P	24	.067	A	
2	2	Bork, Frank Bernard	P	33	.200	A	C
		Burgess, Forrest Harrill	C44	68	.246	B	ChicA
2	2	Butters, Thomas Arden	P	28	.182	B	
1	2	Cardwell, Donald Eugene	P	4	.143	B	
		Clemente, Roberto Walker	OF154	155	.339	B	
		Clendenon, Donn Alvin	1B119	133	.282	B	
3	3	Face, Elroy Leon	P	55	.000	B	
0	1	Francis, Earl Coleman	P	2	.000	B	
		Freese, Eugene Lewis	3B72	99	.225	Cin	
13	18	Friend, Robert Bartmess	P	35	.070	B	
0	0	Gelnar, John Richard	P	7	.000	A	
10	7	Gibbon, Joseph Chas.	P28	29	.255	B	
		Gotay, Julio Snachez		3	.500	B	
0	0	Green, Fred Allan	P	8	.000	WashA62	C
		Johnston, Rex David	OF8	14	.000	A	C
12	13	Law, Vernon Sanders	P35	36	.311	B	
		Lynch, Gerald Thomas	OF78	114	.273	B	
		May, Jerry Lee	C	11	.258	A	
		Mazeroski, Wm. Stanley	2B	162	.268	B	
8	3	McBean, Alvin O'Neal	P	58	.083	B	
		McFarlane, Orlando Jesus (OF1)	C35	37	.244	Pitt62	
		Mota, Manuel Rafael (C1 2B1)	OF93	115	.277	B	
		Pagliaroni, James Vincent	C96	97	.295	B	
1	2	Priddy, Robert Simpson	P	19	.000	Pitt62	
		Schofield, John Richard	SS111	121	.246	B	
4	3	Schwall, Donald Bernard	P15	16	.263	B	
1	4	Sisk, Thomas Wayne	P	42	.000	B	
		Stargell, Wilver Dornel (1B50)	OF59	117	.273	B	
18	12	Veale, Robert Andrew	P40	41	.156	B	
		Virdon, Wm. Chas.	OF134	145	.243	B	
		Wissman, David Alvin	OF10	16	.148	A	C
0	2	Wood, Wilbur Forrester	P	3	.000	xBosA	

CLUB RECORD

NATIONAL LEAGUE

PROVIDENCE

YEAR	TG	WON	LOST	PCT.	FINISHED	MANAGER
1878	60	33	27	.550	3	George Ware
1879	78	55	23	.705	1	George Wright
1880	84	52	32	.619	2	James Leonard Bullock
1881	84	47	37	.559	2	James Leonard Bullock Robert Morrow
1882	84	52	32	.619	2	Wm. Henry Wright
1883	98	58	40	.592	3	Wm. Henry Wright
1884	112	84	28	.750	1	Frank Carter Bancroft
1885	110	53	57	.481	4	Frank Carter Bancroft

WON 33   NATIONAL LEAGUE   FINISHED 3rd.
LOST 27
TG 60   1878.   PCT. .550

PROVIDENCE

GEORGE WARE

WON	LOST	NAME	POS.	G.	BA	FROM	TO
		Allison, Douglass L. (Dona)	C17	18	.267	Hart	
0	0	Brown, Lewis J. (P1 1B15 OF1)	C44	57	.315	Bos	
		Carey, Thomas John	SS	59	.251	Hart	
1	3	Corey, Frederick Harrison (1B1 2B2)	P4	6	.125	A	
0	1	Fisher, Wm. Chas. (Cherokee)	P	1	.000	Chi	C
		Hague, Wm. L.	3B	60	.207	Lvlle	
		Higham, Richard	OF	60	.315	Hart76	
		Hines, Paul A.	OF59	60	.351	Chi	
0	2	Healey, Thomas	P	2	+.000	A	Indpls
		Murnane, Timothy Hayes (OF1)	1B47	48	.245	Bos	
4	7	Nichols, Frederick C. (Tricky)	P	11	.183	StL	
		Pike, Lipman E.	2B	5	+.227	xCin	
		Sweazy, Chas. James	2B	54	.178	Cin76	C
22	13	Ward, John Montgomery	P	35	.203	A	
6	1	Wheeler, Harry Eugene	P	7	.148	A	
		York, Thomas J.	OF	60	.302	Hart	

WON 55   NATIONAL LEAGUE   FINISHED 1st.
LOST 23
TG 78   1879.   PCT. .705

PROVIDENCE

GEORGE WRIGHT

WON	LOST	NAME	POS.	G.	BA	FROM	TO
		Allison, Douglass L.(Dona)	C	1	.000	B	
		Brown, Lewis J. (OF6)	C46	51	+.262	B	Chi
		Farrell, John A.	2B	12	+.260	xSyr.	
		Gross, Emil M.	C	30	.379	A	
		Hague, Wm. L.	3B	50	.227	B	C
		Hines, Paul A.	OF	84	.357	B	
		Kemmler, Rudolph	C	2	.143	A	
11	5	Mathews, Robert T. (OF19)	P19	42	.200	Cin77	
		McGeary, Michael Henry (3B12)	2B72	84	.276	StL77	
		O'Leary, Daniel	OF	2	.429	A	
		O'Rourke, James Henry (1B19)	OF54	80	.351	Bos	
		Start, Joseph	1B64	65	.318	Chi	
		Sullivan, Dennis J.	3	5	.250	A	
44	18	Ward, John Montgomery (3B10)	P65	82	.287	B	
		White, Wm. Edward	1B	1	.250	A	C

WON	LOST	NAME	POS.	G.	BA	FROM	TO
		Wright, George MGR.	SS	84	.281	Bos	
		York, Thomas J.	OF	80	.307	B	

WON 52 — NATIONAL LEAGUE — FINISHED 2nd.
LOST 32
TG 84 — 1880. — PCT. .619

PROVIDENCE

JAMES LEONARD BULLOCK

WON	LOST	NAME	POS.	G.	BA	FROM	TO
12	9	Bradley, George Washington (P22 1B2 OF5)	3B47	78	.226	Troy	
0	0	*Dorgan, Michael Cornelius (P1)	OF74	76	.246	Syr	
		Farrell, John A.	2B	77	.270	B	
		Gross, Emil M.	C	84	.255	B	
		Hines, Paul A. (1B3 2B6)	OF73	82	.306	B	
		Houck, Stephen Arnold Douglas (Sadie)	OF	48	+.197	xBos	
		McGeary, Michael Henry (2B2 SS1)	3B15	17	+.129	B	Clev
		Peters, John Paul	SS	83	.230	Chi	
		Start, Joseph	1B	79	.280	B	
40	23	Ward, John Montgomery (3B2 OF1)	P63	82	.226	B	
		York, Thomas J.	OF	50	.211	B	

*Dorgan also played 2 games at 3B.

WON 47 — NATIONAL LEAGUE — FINISHED 2nd.
LOST 37
TG 84 — 1881. — PCT. .559

PROVIDENCE

JAMES LEONARD BULLOCK ROBERT MORROW

WON	LOST	NAME	POS.	G.	BA	FROM	TO
		Brown, Lewis J. (1B5)	OF13	18	.228	Det	
		Denny, Jeremiah D. (Jerry)	3B	84	.240	A	
		Farrell, John A. (OF2)	2B81	83	.237	B	
		*Gilligan, Andrew Bernard (Barney)	C34	45	.218	Clev	
		Gross, Emil M.	C50	51	.274	B	
		Hines, Paul A. (2B3)	OF76	79	.283	B	
4	7	Mathews, Robert T. (OF4)	P13	15	+.155	Prov79	Bos
		Myers, Henry C.	SS	1	.000	A	
		McClellan, Wm. Henry (2B1 OF14)	SS50	65	.164	Chi78	
25	12	Radbourn, Chas. (Hoss) (2B1 SS14 OF21)	P37	70	.221	Buff	
		Start, Joseph	1B	79	.327	B	

WON	LOST	NAME	POS.	G.	BA	FROM	TO
18	18	Ward, John Montgomery (SS13 OF35)	P36	83	.241	B	
		York, Thomas J.	OF	84	.304	B	

*Gilligan also played 1 game at 2B, 7 games at SS and 2 games in the OF.

WON 52 — NATIONAL LEAGUE — FINISHED 2nd.
LOST 32
TG 84 — 1882. — PCT. .619

PROVIDENCE

WM. HENRY WRIGHT

WON	LOST	NAME	POS.	G.	BA	FROM	TO
		Carroll, Samuel (Clifford)	OF	10	.121	A	
		Denny, Jeremiah D. (Jerry)	3B	84	.246	B	
		Farrell, John A.	2B	84	.254	B	
		*Gilligan, Andrew Bernard (Barney)	C53	55	.223	B	
		Hines, Paul A. (1B2)	OF82	84	.308	B	
		Manning, Timothy E. (C3)	SS17	19	.105	A	
		Nava, Vincent P. (OF1) (Irwin Sandy)	C26	27	.206	A	
33	19	Radbourn, Chas. (Hoss) (SS1 OF29)	P54	83	.239	B	
		Reilley, Chas. E.	C	3	.182	Wor	C
		Start, Joseph	1B	82	.328	B	
		Sweeney, Chas. J.	OF	1	.000	xAthAA	
		Troy, John Joseph (Dasher)	SS	4	+.235	xDet	
19	13	Ward, John Montgomery (P32 SS5)	OF49	83	.245	B	
		Whitney, Arthur Wilson	SS	11	+.071	Det	Det
		Wright, George	SS	45	.162	Bos	C
		York, Thomas J.	OF	81	.267	B	

*Gilligan also played 2 games at SS.

WON 58 — NATIONAL LEAGUE — FINISHED 3rd.
LOST 40
TG 98 — 1883. — PCT. .592

PROVIDENCE

WM. HENRY WRIGHT

WON	LOST	NAME	POS.	G.	BA	FROM	TO
		Carroll, Samuel (Clifford)	OF	58	.264	B	
		Cassidy, John P. (1B1 2B1)	OF89	89	.237	Troy	
		Denny, Jeremiah D. (Jerry)	3B	98	.274	B	
		Farrell, John A.	2B	93	.304	B	
		Gilligan, Andrew Bernard (Barney)	C	72	.198	B	
		Hines, Paul A. (1B8)	OF97	97	.298	B	

WON	LOST	NAME	POS.	G.	BA	FROM	TO
		Irwin, Arthur Albert (2B4)	SS94	98	.285	Wor	
		Mulvey, Joseph H. (2B1)	SS3	4	+.053	A	Phil
		Nava, Vincent P. (OF1) (Irwin Sandy)	C26	27	.240	B	
44	23	Radbourn, Chas. (Hoss) (1B2 OF15)	P72	89	.283	B	
3	8	Richmond, John Lee (P11)	OF37	48	.283	Wor	
		Smith, Edgar E. (OF2)	1B2	2	+.222	WashAA	Phil
		Start, Joseph	1B	87	.283	B	
11	9	Sweeney, Chas. J. (OF7)	P21	21	.218	B	

WON 84 NATIONAL LEAGUE FINISHED 1st.
LOST 28
TG 112 1884. PCT. .750

PROVIDENCE

FRANK CARTER BANCROFT

WON	LOST	NAME	POS.	G.	BA	FROM	TO
1	0	Arundel, Harvey	P	1	.333	PittAA82	C
		$Bassett, Chas. Edwin	3B13	21	.144	A	
		Carroll, Samuel (Clifford)	OF	112	.261	B	
0	1	Cattanach, John L. (OF1)	P1	1	.000	A	StLUA
4	4	Conley, Edward J.	P	8	.107	A	C
		*Denny, Jeremiah D. (Jerry)	3B96	118	.251	B	
		Farrell, John A. (3B3)	2B106	109	.220	B	
		%Gilligan, Andrew Bernard (Barney)	C79	80	.244	B	
0	0	Hines, Paul A. (P1 1B6)	OF108	112	.304	B	
0	0	Irwin, Arthur Albert (P1)	SS99	99	.245	B	
2	4	&Miller, Joseph H. (Cyclone)	P6	6	+.045	xChiUA	Phil
		Murray, Jeremiah J. (1B1 OF1)	C7	8	.185	A	
		@Nava, Vincent P. (Irwin Sandy)	C26	32	.089	B	
60	12	#Radbourn, Chas. (Hoss)	P72	85	.233	B	
0	0	Radford, Paul Revere (P2 1B1 SS1)	OF94	96	.202	Bos	
		Start, Joseph	1B	90	.273	B	
17	7	Sweeney, Chas. J. (1B1 OF15)	P25	40	.302	B	StLUA

$Bassett also played 1 game at 2B, 7 games at SS, and 2 games in the OF.
*Denny also played 1 game as C, 10 games at 1B and 3 games at 2B.
%Gilligan also played 1 game at 1B and 1 game at 3B.
&Miller also played 3 games in the OF.
@Nava also played 1 game at 2B, 2 games at SS and 1 game in the OF.
#Radbourn also played 5 games at 1B, 1 game at 2B, 2 games at SS, 3 games at 3B and 4 games in the OF.

WON 53 NATIONAL LEAGUE FINISHED 4th.
LOST 57
TG 110 1885. PCT. .481

PROVIDENCE

FRANK CARTER BANCROFT

WON	LOST	NAME	POS.	G.	BA	FROM	TO
		Andrews, Wm. Walter	3B	1	.000	LvlleAA	
		Bassett, Chas. Edwin (SS21 3B21)	2B39	81	.143	B	
		Carroll, Samuel (Clifford)	OF	104	.232	B	
0	0	Crane, Edward Nicholas (OF1)	P1	1	+.000	BosUA	Buff
		*Dailey, Cornelius F. (Don)	C47	59	.260	PhilUA	
		Denny, Jeremiah D. (Jerry)	3B	83	.223	B	
		Farrell, John A.	2B	67	.206	B	
0	1	Foley, Chas. Joseph	P	1	.000	Buff83	C
		#Gilligan, Andrew Bernard (Barney)	C62	69	.214	B	
0	1	Hallstrom, Chas. E.	P	1	.000	A	C
		Hines, Michael P.	C	1	.000	xBknAA	
		%Hines, Paul A.	OF92	98	.270	B	
		Irwin, Arthur Albert (2B1)	SS58	59	.179	B	
0	1	Kimber, Samuel Jackson	P	1	.000	BknAA	C
0	0	Knight, Alonzo P. (Lon) (P1)	OF24	25	.160	xAthAA	C
		Lyons, Dennis Patrick Aloysius	3B	4	.125	A	
		Manning, Timothy E.	SS	10	.086	xBaltAA	C
1	3	McCormick, James	P	4	+.200	CinUA	Chi
28	21	Radbourn, Chas. (Hoss) (2B2 OF16)	P49	65	.232	B	
0	1	Radford, Paul Revere (P2 SS16)	OF87	105	.242	B	
0	1	Seward, Edward Wm.	P	1	.000	A	
23	26	@Shaw, Frederick Lander (Dupee)	P	49	.133	BosUA	
1	0	Smith, Wm. Edgar	P	1	.000	Clev	
0	1	Stalberger, Wm.	P	1	.000	A	C
		Start, Joseph	1B	99	.275	B	
0	1	Ward, E. John	P	1	.000	WashUA	C

*Dailey also played 8 games at 1B and 5 games in the OF.
#Gilligan also played 2 games at SS and 1 game in the OF.
%Hines also played 3 games at 1B, 1 game at 2B, 1 game at SS and 1 game at 3B.
@Shaw also played 3 games in the OF.

CLUB RECORD
NATIONAL LEAGUE
ST. LOUIS

YEAR	TG	WON	LOST	PCT.	FINISHED	MANAGER
1876	64	45	19	.703	2	S. Mason Graffen
1877	60	28	32	.467	4	J. R. C. Lucas
						George McManus
1878-1884	OUT OF LEAGUE					
1885	108	36	72	.333	8(Last)	Frederick C. Dunlap
						Benjamin J. Fine
						Henry V. Lucas
1886	122	43	79	.352	6	Gustavus Heinrich Schmelz
1887-1891	OUT OF LEAGUE					
1892	150	56	94	.373	11	Christopher Von der Ahe
1893	132	57	75	.432	10	Wm. Henry Watkins
1894	132	56	76	.424	9	George Frederick Miller
1895	131	39	92	.298	11	Albert C. Buckenberger
						Joseph J. Quinn
						Lewis G. Phelan
						Christopher Von der Ahe
1896	130	40	90	.308	11	Henry H. Diddlebock
						Walter Arlington Latham
						Roger Connor
						Thomas Jefferson Dowd
1897	131	29	102	.221	12(Last)	Thomas Jefferson Dowd
						Hugh N. Nicol
						Wm. White Hallman
						Christopher Von der Ahe
1898	150	39	111	.260	12(Last)	Timothy Carroll Hurst
1899	149	83	66	.557	5	Oliver Patrick Tebeau
1900	140	65	75	.464	x5(Chi)	Oliver Patrick Tebeau
						Louis Wilbur Heilbroner
1901	140	76	64	.543	4	Patrick Joseph Donovan
1902	134	56	78	.418	6	Patrick Joseph Donovan
1903	137	43	94	.314	8(Last)	Patrick Joseph Donovan
1904	154	75	79	.422	5	Chas. Arthur Nichols
1905	154	58	96	.377	6	Chas. Arthur Nichols
						James Timothy Burke
						Matthew Stanley Robison
1906	150	52	98	.347	7	John James McCloskey
1907	153	52	101	.340	8(Last)	John James McCloskey
1908	154	49	105	.318	8(Last)	John James McCloskey
1909	152	54	98	.355	7	Roger Patrick Bresnahan
1910	153	63	90	.412	7	Roger Patrick Bresnahan
1911	149	75	74	.503	5	Roger Patrick Bresnahan
1912	153	63	90	.412	6	Roger Patrick Bresnahan
1913	150	51	99	.340	8(Last)	Miller James Huggins
1914	153	81	72	.529	3	Miller James Huggins
1915	153	72	81	.471	6	Miller James Huggins
1916	153	60	93	.392	x7(Cin)	Miller James Huggins
1917	152	82	70	.539	3	Miller James Huggins
1918	129	51	78	.395	8(Last)	John Calhoun Hendricks
1919	137	54	83	.394	7	Wesley Branch Rickey
1920	154	75	79	.487	x5(Chi)	Wesley Branch Rickey
1921	153	87	66	.569	3	Wesley Branch Rickey
1922	154	85	69	.552	x3(Pitt)	Wesley Branch Rickey
1923	153	79	74	.516	5	Wesley Branch Rickey
1924	154	65	89	.422	6	Wesley Branch Rickey
1925	153	77	76	.503	4	Wesley Branch Rickey
						Rogers Hornsby
1926	154	89	65	.578	1	Rogers Hornsby
1927	153	92	61	.601	2	Robert Arthur O'Farrell
1928	154	95	59	.617	1	Wm. Boyd McKechnie
1929	152	78	74	.513	4	Wm. Boyd McKechnie
						Wm. Harrison Southworth
1930	154	92	62	.597	1	Chas. Evard Street
1931	154	101	53	.656	1	Char. Evard Street
1932	154	72	82	.468	x6(N.Y.)	Chas. Evard Street
1933	153	82	71	.536	5	Chas. Evard Street
						Frank Francis Frisch
1934	153	95	58	.621	1	Frank Francis Frisch
1935	154	96	58	.623	2	Frank Francis Frisch
1936	154	87	67	.565	x2(Chi)	Frank Francis Frisch
1937	154	81	73	.526	4	Frank Francis Frisch
1938	151	71	80	.470	6	Frank Francis Frisch
						Miguel Angel Gonzales
1939	153	92	61	.601	2	Francis Raymond Blades
1940	153	84	69	.549	3	Francis Raymond Blades
						Miguel Angel Gonzales
						Wm. Harrison Southworth
1941	153	97	56	.634	2	Wm. Harrison Southworth
1942	154	106	48	.688	1	Wm. Harrison Southworth
1943	154	105	49	.682	1	Wm. Harrison Southworth
1944	154	105	49	.682	1	Wm. Harrison Southworth
1945	154	95	59	.617	2	Wm. Harrison Southworth
1946	156	98	58	.628	1	Edwin Hawley Dyer
1947	154	89	65	.578	2	Edwin Hawley Dyer
1948	154	85	69	.552	2	Edwin Hawley Dyer
1949	154	96	58	.623	2	Edwin Hawley Dyer
1950	153	78	75	.510	5	Edwin Hawley Dyer
1951	154	81	73	.526	3	Martin Whitford Marion
1952	154	88	66	.571	3	Edward Raymond Stanky
1953	154	83	71	.539	x3(Phil)	Edward Raymond Stanky
1954	154	72	82	.468	6	Edward Raymond Stanky
1955	154	68	86	.442	7	Edward Raymond Stanky
						Harry Wm. Walker
1956	154	76	78	.494	4	Frederick Chas. Hutchinson
1957	154	87	67	.565	2	Frederick Chas. Hutchinson
1958	154	72	82	.468	x5(Chic)	Frederick Chas. Hutchinson
						Stanley Camfield Hack
1959	154	71	83	.461	7	Solomon Joseph Hemus
1960	154	86	68	.558	3	Solomon Joseph Hemus
1961	154	80	74	.519	5	Solomon Joseph Hemus
						John Joseph Keane
1962	162	84	78	.519	6	John Joseph Keane
1963	162	93	69	.574	2	John Joseph Keane
1964	162	93	69	.574	1	John Joseph Keane

YEAR	TG	WON	LOST	TIED	PCT.	FINISHED	MANAGER
1965	162	80	81	1	.497	7	ALBERT FRED SCHEONDIENST
1966	162	83	79	0	.512	6	ALBERT FRED SCHEONDIENST
1967	161	101	60	0	.627	1	ALBERT FRED SCHEONDIENST
1968	162	97	65	0	.599	1	ALBERT FRED SCHEONDIENST
1969	162	87	75	0	.537	4E	ALBERT FRED SCHEONDIENST
1970	162	76	86	0	.469	4E	ALBERT FRED SCHEONDIENST
1971	163	90	72	1	.556	2E	ALBERT FRED SCHEONDIENST
1972	156	75	81	0	.481	4E	ALBERT FRED SCHEONDIENST

WON 45 / LOST 19 / TG 64 — NATIONAL LEAGUE — 1876. — FINISHED 2nd. — PCT. .703

ST. LOUIS

S. MASON GRAFFEN

WON	LOST	NAME	POS.	G.	BA	FROM	TO
		Battin, Joseph V.	3B63	64	.294	A	
		Blong, Joseph Myles	OF	62	.233	A	
45	19	Bradley, George Washington	P	64	.246	A	
		Clapp, John Edgar	C61	64	.298	A	
		Cuthbert, Edgar Edward (Ned)	OF	62	.242	A	
		Dehlman, Harmon J.	1B	64	.178	A	
		Mack, Dennis Joseph	SS41	48	.204	A	
		Miller, Thomas P.	C (DID NOT PLAY)			A	C
		McGeary, Michael Henry	2B55	60	.259	A	
		Pearce, Richard J. (Dickey)	SS23	25	.200	A	
		Pike, Lipman E.	OF61	63	.314	A	

WON 28 / LOST 32 / TG 60 — NATIONAL LEAGUE — 1877. — FINISHED 4th. — PCT. .467

ST. LOUIS

JOHN R. C. LUCAS — GEORGE McMANUS

WON	LOST	NAME	POS.	G.	BA	FROM	TO
0	0	Battin, Joseph V. (P1 2B21 OF5)	3B32	57	.199	B	
10	9	Blong, Joseph Myles (P25 2B1)	OF40	58	.216	B	C
		Clapp, John Edgar (1B1 OF10)	C53	60	.316	B	
		Croft, Arthur F. (2B1 OF26)	1B28	54	.233	A	
		Dehlman, Harmon J. (OF1)	1B31	32	.185	B	C
		Dorgan, Michael Cornelius (C12 SS1 3B2)	OF59	60	.308	A	
		Force, David W. (3B8)	SS50	58	.258	Ath	
		Gleason, John Day	OF	1	.250	A	
		Lee, Leonidas P. (SS1)	OF4	4	.278	A	C
		Little, George Harry	OF	1	+.200	A	Lvlle
			OF	2	+.364	(& return)	
		Loftus, Thomas Joseph	OF	3	.182	A	
		McGeary, Michael Henry (3B19)	2B39	57	.253	B	
		McKenna, Edward	OF	1	.200	A	
		Newell, T. E.	SS	1	.000	A	C
18	23	Nichols, Frederick C. (Tricky) (OF16)	P42	51	.168	Bos	
		Pearce, Richard J. (Dickey)	SS	8	.172	B	C
		Remsen, John Jay	OF	33	.260	Hart	

WON 36 / LOST 72 / TG 108 — NATIONAL LEAGUE — 1885. — FINISHED 8th (LAST) — PCT. .333

ST. LOUIS

FREDERICK C. DUNLAP — BENJAMIN J. FINE — HENRY V. LUCAS

WON	LOST	NAME	POS.	G.	BA	FROM	TO
		Alvord, Wm. C.	3B	2	.000	A	
		*Baker, George F.	C34	39	.122	StLUA	
15	25	Boyle, Henry J. (2B1 OF28)	P42	72	.201	StLUA	
		Brennan, James A. (3B1)	OF2	3	.100	StLUA	
		Briody, Chas. F. (2B1 3B1)	C59	61	.195	CinUA	
0	0	Burns, Richard Simon (P1)	OF14	14	.218	CinUA	C
		#Caskin, Edward James	3B67	70	.179	N.Y.	
3	8	Daly, Hugh I. (One-Arm)	P	11	.088	WashUA	
		Dolan, Thomas J.	C	3	.222	StLUA	
		Dunlap, Frederick C. MGR.	2B	106	.269	StLUA	
		Fogarty, Joseph J.	OF	2	.125	A	C
		Glasscock, John Wesley (2B2)	SS109	111	.280	CinUA	
		Gleason, John Day	3B	2	.143	StLUA	
1	7	Healy, John J. (Egyptian)	P	8	.042	A	
5	8	Kirby, John F.	P	14	.061	KCUA	
		Krehmeyer, Chas. L. (C1)	OF1	1	.000	xLvlleAA	C
		Lewis, Frederick Miller	OF	45	.292	StLUA	
		McKinnon, Alexander J.	1B	100	.270	N.Y.	
		McSorley, John Bernard	3B	2	.500	TolAA	
0	4	Palmer,	P	4	.091	A	C
		Phelan, James D.	3B	2	+.250	xBuff	C
		Quinn, Joseph J. (1B11 3B31)	OF55	97	.212	StLUA	
		Rowe, David E.	OF	16	.161	StLUA	
		Schaffer, George (Orator)	OF	69	.194	StLUA	AthAA
		Seery, John Emmett (3B1)	OF58	58	.162	KCUA	
		Sutcliffe, Edward Elmer (OF2)	C15	15	+.140	xChi	
12	20	Sweeney, Chas. J. (P33)	OF38	73	.207	StLUA	
		Sweeney, John J. (Rooney) (C1)	OF2	3	.091	BaltUA	C

*Baker also played 1 game at 2B, 4 games at 3B and 1 game in the OF.
#Caskin also played 2 games as C and 2 games at SS.

WON 43 / LOST 79 / TG 122 — NATIONAL LEAGUE — 1886. — FINISHED 6th. — PCT. .352

ST. LOUIS

GUSTAVUS HEINRICH SCHMELZ

WON	LOST	NAME	POS.	G.	BA	FROM	TO
0	4	Bauers, Albert J.	P	4	.143	ColAA84	C

WON	LOST	NAME	POS.	G.	BA	FROM	TO
9	15	Boyle, Henry J.	P24	30	.250	B	
		Cahill, John Francis	OF122	125	.198	ColAA84	
		Connelly, John M.	OF	2	.000	A	C
		Crane, Samuel Newhall	2B	37	+.175	xDet	
		Denny, Jeremiah D. (Jerry)	3B117	119	.257	Prov	
		Dolan, Thomas J.	C	15	.250	B	BaltAA
		Dunlap, Frederick C.	2B	73	+.281	B	Det
		Glasscock, John Wesley	SS120	121	.325	B	
		Graves, Frank M.	C39	41	.152	A	C
		Gross, Emil M.	C	1	.000	ChiUA84	C
17	24	Healy, John J. (Egyptian)	P41	42	.096	B	
12	25	Kirby, John F.	P38	41	.110	B	
		Mappes, George Richard	C	6	.143	BaltAA	C
0	4	Murphy, Joseph Alin	P	4	.214	xCinAA	StLAA
		Myers, George D.	C71	78	.189	Buff	
		McGeachy, John Chas.	OF	58	+.216	xDet	
		McKinnon, Alexander J.	1B119	122	.301	B	
		Pelouze,	OF	1	.000	A	C
		Quinn, Joseph J. (2B15)	OF48	75	.232	B	
0	1	Reardon, James Matthew	P	1	.250	A	CinAA
		Seery, John Emmett	OF	126	.238	B	
5	6	Sweeney, Chas. J.	P	17	.250	B	

WON 56 — NATIONAL LEAGUE — FINISHED 11th.
LOST 94
TG 150 — 1892. — PCT. .373

CHRISTIAN FREDERICK WILHELM VON DER AHE JR.

WON	LOST	NAME	POS.	G.	BA	FROM	TO
		Bird, Frank Zepherin	C	17	.196	A	C
14	20	Breitenstein, Theodore P.	P34	38	.124	StLAA	
		Briggs, Grant	C	23	.070	LvlleAA	
		Brodie, Walter Scott (2B16)	OF136	154	.256	Bos	
		Buckley, Richard D. (Dick)	C104	106	.220	N.Y.	
		Camp, Llewellyn Robert	3B40	43	.204	A	
		Carpenter, Warren Wm. (Hick)	3B	1	.333	CinAA89	C
		Carroll, Samuel (Clifford)	OF	100	.273	Chi	
2	8	Caruthers, Robert Lee (P10)	OF121	142	.277	Bkn	
		Collins, Wm. J.	OF	1	.000	Clev	C
		Crooks, John Chas. (Jack) (3B25)	2B102	127	.213	ColAA	
		DeMiller, Henry	SS	1	.000	A	C
2	6	Dwyer, John Francis (Frank)	P	14	+.136	MilAA	Cin
2	3	Easton, John E.	P	5	.188	ColAA	
5	6	Galvin, James F.	P	15	+.028	xPitt	C
		Genins, C. Frank	SS	14	+.167	xCin	
5	9	Getzein, Chas. H.	P	14	.222	Clev	C
		Glasscock, John Wesley	SS	139	.273	N.Y.	
16	24	Gleason, Wm. J. (Kid)	P44	63	.215	Phil	
		Gore, George F.	OF	20	+.200	xN.Y.	C
		Haigh, Edward E.	OF	1	.250	A	C
4	5	Hawke, Wm. Victor	P	15	.089	A	
6	13	Hawley, Emerson P. (Pink)	P	19	.200	A	
		Kuehne, Wm. J. (SS1)	3B5	6	+.167	xLvlle	Cin
			3B	1	+.000	(& return)	C

WON	LOST	NAME	POS.	G.	BA	FROM	TO
		Leonard,	OF	1	.000	A	C
		Moran, Wm. L.	C20	22	.153	A	
		Moriarity, Eugene John	OF	46	.175	Det85	C
		McCormick, James Ambrose	2B	2	.000	A	C
		McCrellis, Mark	3B	1	.000	A	C
		Peitz, Joseph	OF	1	.000	A	
		Pinckney, George Burton	3B77	78	.172	Bkn	
		Stricker, John A. (Cub) (SS1)	2B27	28	+.206	BosAA	Balt
		Thornton, John (Jack)	OF	1	+.000	xPhil	C
		Van Dyke, Wm. Jennings	OF	3	.000	TolAA90	
		Werden, Percival Wheritt (Perry)	1B	148	.255	BaltAA	
		Wolf, Wm. V. (Chicken)	OF	4	.220	LvlleAA	C
0	0	Young, J. D.	P	1	.000	A	C

WON 57 — NATIONAL LEAGUE — FINISHED 10th.
LOST 75
TG 132 — 1893. — PCT. .432

ST. LOUIS

WM. HENRY WATKINS

WON	LOST	NAME	POS.	G.	BA	FROM	TO
0	1	Bannon, James Henry (P2)	OF21	23	.363	A	
19	20	Breitenstein, Theodore P.	P	41	.177	B	
		Brodie, Walter Scott	OF	107	+.336	B	Balt
		Buckley, Richard D. (Dick)	C	7	.057	B	
12	9	Clarkson, Arthur Hamilton	P	21	.139	Bos	
		Cooley, Duff C. (Dick)	OF	26	.359	A	
		Crooks, John Chas. (Jack)	3B123	128	.251	B	
0	2	Dolan, John (Jack)	P	3	.143	ColAA91	
		Dowd, Thomas Jefferson	OF	131	.294	Wash	
		Ely, Frederick Wm.	SS	44	.263	Balt	
		Frank, Chas.	OF	40	.331	A	
		Glasscock, John Wesley	SS	48	+.301	B	Pitt
21	25	Gleason, Wm. J. (Kid)	P46	55	.266	B	
		Goodenough, Wm. B.	OF	10	.178	A	C
		Griffin, Tobias Chas. (Sandy)	OF	23	.204	WashAA91	C
		Gunson, Joseph Brook	C	37	+.280	Balt	Clev
0	1	Hawke, Wm. Victor	P	3	+.333	B	Balt
5	17	Hawley, Emerson P. (Pink)	P	33	.295	B	
		McCauley, Patrick M.	C	5	.067	A	
		O'Neill, Dennis	1B	7	.120	A	C
0	0	Pears, Frank T.	P	1	.000	KCAA89	C
		Peitz, Henry Clement (Heinie)	C72	94	.266	A	
		Quinn, Joseph J.	2B	135	.241	Bos	
		Shugart, Wm. Frank (OF25)	SS32	57	+.297	xPitt	
		Smith, Judson Grant (Jud)	3B	4	+.067	xCin	
		Sommers, Wm.	C	2	.000	Clev89	C
		Twineham, Arthur W.	C	14	.325	A	
		Werden, Percival Wheritt (Perry)	1B	124	.284	B	
		Whistler, Lewis	1B	10	+.243	xLvlle	C

WON 56 | NATIONAL LEAGUE | FINISHED 9th.
LOST 76
TG 132 | 1894. | PCT. .424

ST. LOUIS

GEORGE FREDERICK MILLER

WON	LOST	NAME	POS.	G.	BA	FROM	TO
		Ball, Arthur	2B	1	.333	A	
27	25	Breitenstein, Theodore P.	P	53	.229	B	
		Brown, Willard	1B	117	+.257	xLvlle	C
		Browning, Louis Roger (Pete)	OF	2	+.143	Lvlle	Bkn
		Buckley, Richard D. (Dick)	C	28	+.169	B	Phil
9	18	Clarkson, Arthur Hamilton	P	27	.118	B	
		Connor, Roger	1B	99	+.318	xN.Y.	
		Cooley, Duff C. (Dick)	OF38	52	.299	B	
		Dowd, Thomas Jefferson	OF115	123	.267	B	
		Ely, Frederick Wm.	SS	127	.305	B	
		Frank, Chas.	OF77	80	.246	B	C
2	6	Gleason, Wm. J. (Kid)	P	10	+.200	B	Balt
18	25	Hawley, Emerson P. (Pink)	P47	48	.273	B	
		Hogan, Martin T.	OF	23	+.288	xCin	
0	2	Mason, Ernest	P	4	.250	A	C
		Miller, George Frederick (Fog-Horn) (C39 2B18) MGR.	3B52	125	.341	Pitt	
		O'Rourke, Timothy Patrick	OF	18	+.274	xLvlle	Wash
		Paynter, George Washington	OF	1	.000	A	C
		Peitz, Henry Clement (Heinie) (C38 1B18)	3B43	100	.274	B	
		Peitz, Joseph	OF	5	.421	StL92	C
		Quinn, Joseph J.	2B	106	.274	B	
		Ricks, John	3B	1	.000	StLAA91	C
		Russell, Benjamin Paul	OF	3	.100	A	C
		Shugart, Wm. Frank	OF119	133	.285	B	
		Twineham, Arthur W.	C	31	.314	B	C

WON 39 | NATIONAL LEAGUE | FINISHED 11th.
LOST 92
TG 131 | 1895. | PCT. .298

ST. LOUIS

ALBERT C. BUCKENBERGER JOSEPH J. QUINN
LEWIS G. PHELAN CHRISTIAN FREDERICK WILHELM VON DER AHE JR.

WON	LOST	NAME	POS.	G.	BA	FROM	TO
		Adkinson, Henry Magee	OF	1	.400	A	C
		Bonner, Frank J.	SS	14	+.132	xBalt	
18	30	Breitenstein, Theodore P.	P51	66	.190	B	
		Brown, Thomas T.	OF	87	+.226	Lvlle	Wash
1	6	Clarkson, Arthur Hamilton	P	11	+.050	B	Balt
0	1	Coleman, John	P	2	.200	A	C
		Connor, Roger	1B	104	.326	B	
		Connor, Joseph	3B	2	.000	A	C
		Cooley, Duff C. (Dick)	OF125	132	.340	B	
0	1	Donahue, Francis Rostell (Red)	P	1	.000	NY93	
		Dowd, Thomas Jefferson	OF113	127	.325	B	
6	20	Ehret, Philip Sydney (Red)	P30	31	.208	Pitt	
		Ely, Frederick Wm.	SS	118	.260	B	
		Fagin, Frederick H.	C	1	.333	A	C
		Hogan, Martin T.	OF	5	.150	B	C
		Kinlock, Walter	3B	1	.333	A	C
5	10	Kissinger, Wm. Francis	P	23	+.258	xBalt	
		Lyons, Dennis Patrick Aloysius	3B	33	.290	Pitt	
		Miller, George Frederick (Fog-Horn) (3B42 OF21)	C44	123	.290	B	
4	11	McDougal, John H.	P	15	.154	A	
		McFadden, Guy	1B	4	.200	A	C
		Otten, Joseph G.	C22	24	.233	A	C
		Peitz, Henry Clement (Heinie)	C70	90	.288	B	
		Quinn, Joseph J. MGR.	2B	134	.309	B	
		Ryan, J.	3B	2	.000	A	C
		Samuels, Samuel Earl	3B19	22	.186	A	C
		Sheehan, Timothy James	OF38	49	.324	A	
5	13	Staley, Henry E.	P	18	.164	Bos	C
		Young, David	3B	1	.400	A	C

WON 40 | NATIONAL LEAGUE | FINISHED 11th.
LOST 90
TG 130 | 1896. | PCT. .308

ST. LOUIS

HENRY H. DIDDLEBOCK WALTER ARLINGTON LATHAM
ROGER CONNOR THOMAS JEFFERSON DOWD

WON	LOST	NAME	POS.	G.	BA	FROM	TO
17	26	Breitenstein, Theodore P.	P43	48	.268	B	
		Connor, Roger MGR.	1B	126	.282	B	
		Cooley, Duff C. (Dick)	OF	40	+.302	B	Phil
		Cross, Montford Montgomery (Monte)	SS	124	.264	Pitt	
7	23	Donahue, Francis Rostell (Red)	P	33	.157	B	
		Douglas, Wm. B.	OF74	79	.268	A	
		Dowd, Thomas Jefferson MGR. (OF48)	2B77	125	.266	B	
13	26	Hart, Wm. Franklin	P40	46	.196	Pitt	
2	13	Kissinger, Wm. Francis	P19	22	.315	B	
		Latham, Walter Arlington (Arlie) MGR.	3B	8	.229	Cin	
		Murphy, Morgan Edward	C	48	.251	Cin	
		Meyers, J. Albert	3B	122	.258	A	
0	1	McDougal, John H.	P	3	.000	B	C
		McFarland, Edward Wm.	C	80	.239	Clev93	
		Niland, Thomas James (SS4)	OF14	18	.162	A	C
1	1	Parrott, Thomas Wm. (P6)	OF112	118	.288	Cin	C
		Quinn, Joseph J.	2B	48	+.231	B	Balt
		Sheehan, Timothy James	OF	5	.133	B	C
		Sullivan, Joseph Daniel	OF	60	+.287	xPhil	C
		Turner, George A. (Tuck)	OF	48	+.255	xPhil	
0	0	Wood, John B.	P	1	.000	A	C

WON 29 / LOST 102 / TG 131

NATIONAL LEAGUE — FINISHED 12th (LAST)

1897. — PCT. .221

ST. LOUIS

THOMAS JEFFERSON DOWD HUGH N. NICOL WM. WHITE HALLMAN
CHRISTIAN FREDERICK WILHELM VON DER AHE, JR.

WON	LOST	NAME	POS.	G.	BA	FROM	TO
		Beecher, Edward	OF	3	.333	A	
		Bierbauer, Louis W.	2B	12	.217	Pitt	
1	7	Carsey, Wilfred (Kid)	P12	13	+.302	xPhil	
1	5	Coleman, Pierce D.	P	12	.222	A	
		Connor, Roger	1B	22	.229	B	C
		Cross, Montford Montgomery (Monte)	SS	130	.288	B	
11	33	Donahue, Francis Rostell (Red)	P	44	.216	B	
		Douglas, Wm. B. (1B17 OF43)	C61	127	.327	B	
		Dowd, Thomas Jefferson MGR. (2B5)	OF30	35	+.267	B	Phil
1	6	Esper, Chas. H.	P	8	.320	Balt	
0	1	Evans, Le Roy	P	2	+.000	A	Lvlle
		Grady, Michael Wm.	1B	83	+.281	xPhil	
0	2	Grimes, John C.	P	3	.286	A	C
		Hallman, Wm. White (Billy) MGR.	2B	81	+.252	xPhil	
		Harley, Richard Joseph	OF	89	.288	A	
9	23	Hart, Wm. Franklin	P37	43	.245	B	
		Hartman, Frederick Orrin	3B	126	.301	Pitt94	
		Houseman, John Franklin (OF33)	2B36	76	.232	Chi94	C
		Huelsman, Frank Elmer	SS	2	.286	A	
1	4	Hutchinson, Wm. Forest	P	6	.278	Chi95	C
0	4	Kissinger, Wm. Francis	P	11	.345	B	C
		Lally, Daniel J.	OF85	87	.278	Pitt91	
1	5	Lucid, Cornelius Conrad (Con)	P	6	.158	Phil	C
		Murphy, Morgan Edward	C51	55	.177	B	
3	4	McDermott, Michael Joseph	P	7	+.222	xClev	C
		McFarland, Edward Wm. (1B2 2B1 OF3)	C24	31	+.324	B	Phil
1	8	Sudhoff, John William	P	11	.238	A	
		Turner, George A. (Tuck)	OF	102	.289	B	

WON 39 / LOST 111 / TG 150

NATIONAL LEAGUE — FINISHED 12th (LAST)

1898. — PCT. .260

ST. LOUIS

TIMOTHY CARROLL HURST

WON	LOST	NAME	POS.	G.	BA	FROM	TO
		Bierbauer, Louis W.	2B	4	.000	B	
0	2	Callahan, James W.	P	2	.000	A	C
1	12	Carsey, Wilfred (Kid)	P	33	.200	B	
		Clements, John T.	C	85	+.268	xPhil	
		Crooks, John Chas. (Jack)	2B65	71	.238	Lvlle96	
		Cross, LaFayette Napoleon (Lave)	3B149	151	.314	Phil	
1	6	Daniels, Peter J.	P	10	.167	Pitt90	C
		Decker, George A.	1B	64	+.263	Chi	Lvlle
		Donely, James B.	3B	1	1.000	N.Y.	C
		Dowd, Thomas Jefferson	OF132	139	.243	Phil	
3	5	Esper, Chas. H.	P	10	.400	B	C
0	1	Gannon, Wm. G.	P	1	.333	A	
0	1	Gilpatrick, George F.	P	7	.125	A	C
		Hall, Russell P.	SS35	39	.252	A	
		Harley, Richard Joseph	OF141	142	.248	B	
		Holmes, James Wm. (Ducky)	OF	23	+.276	N.Y.	Balt
7	24	Hughey, James Ulysses	P33	34	.111	Pitt	
		Kinslow, Thomas F.	C	14	+.278	xWash	C
		Mahoney, George W.	1B	2	.000	Bos	C
0	2	Maupin, Harry Carr	P	2	.429	A	
		Quinn, Joseph J.	2B	99	+.250	xBalt	
		Smith, George J. (Germany)	SS	51	.156	Bkn	
0	1	Smith, Thomas E. (Pl)	OF50	51	.156	Lvlle96	C
		Stenzel, Jacob C. (Jake)	~OF	105	+.287	xBalt	
11	26	Sudhoff, John William	P	38	.161	B	
		Sugden, Joseph	C59	80	.259	Pitt	
		Sullivan, Suter G.	SS25	40	.225	A	
16	31	Taylor, John Budd (Jack)	P47	49	.242	Phil	
		Tucker, Thomas Joseph	1B	72	+.238	xBkn	
		Turner, George A. (Tuck)	OF	34	.210	B	C

WON x83 / LOST 66 / TG 149

NATIONAL LEAGUE — FINISHED 5th.

1899. — PCT. .557

ST. LOUIS

OLIVER WENDELL TEBEAU

WON	LOST	NAME	POS.	G.	BA	FROM	TO
0	0	Bates, Frank Chas.	P	4	+.333	Clev	Clev
		Blake, Henry C.	OF86	94	.238	Clev	C
		Buelow, Frederick Wm.	C	7	.285	A	
		Burke, John Patrick	2B	2	.333	A	
		Burkett, Jesse Cail	OF	138	.402	Clev	
		Childs, Clarence Algernon	2B	125	.266	Clev	
		Criger, Louis	C	75	.256	Clev	
		Cross, LaFayette Napoleon (Lave)	3B	103	+.304	xClev	
10	8	Cuppy, George Joseph (Nig)	P	21	.174	Clev	
0	0	Donlin, Michael Joseph (Pl)	OF50	67	.329	A	
		Flood, Timothy A.	2B	9	.333	A	
		Heidrick, John Emmett	OF	147	.329	Clev	
		Hemphill, Chas. Judson	OF	11	+.243	A	Clev
6	5	Jones, Albert Edward	P	14	.172	Clev	
		Miller, Chas. Bradley (Dusty)	OF	10	+.231	xCin	C
2	5	McBride, Peter Wm.	P	11	.174	Clev	C

WON	LOST	NAME	POS.	G.	BA	FROM	TO
		McKean, Edward John	SS42	67	.281	Clev	C
		O'Connor, John Joseph (Jack) (1B24)	C55	79	.261	Clev	
		Parent, Frederick Alfred	2B	2	.125	A	
23	21	Powell, John Joseph	P44	46	.198	Clev	
		Schreckengost, Ossee Freeman (Ossie) (OF1)	1B1 C	6 60	+.000 +.306	Clev & return	Clev
		Stenzel, Jacob C. (Jake)	OF	32	+.270	B	Cin
12	10	Sudhoff, John William	P	22	+.228	xClev	
1	1	Sutthoff, John Gerhard	P	2	.167	Wash	
		Tebeau, Oliver Wendell MGR.	1B67	76	.253	Clev	
1	1	Thomas, Thomas W.	P	4	.250	A	
		Wallace, Rhoderick John (Boddy) (3B53)	SS98	151	.302	Clev	
1	1	Wilson, Frank Ealton (Zeke)	P	5	.000	Clev	
26	14	Young, Denton True (Cy)	P42	43	.216	Clev	

x-One game won by forfeit.

WON 65 NATIONAL LEAGUE FINISHED 5th.
LOST 75 (TIED WITH CHICAGO)
TG 140 1900. PCT. .464

ST. LOUIS

OLIVER WENDELL TEBEAU LOUIS WILBER HEILBRONER

WON	LOST	NAME	POS.	G.	BA	FROM	TO
		Buelow, Frederick Wm.	C	7	.235	B	
		Burkett, Jesse Cail	OF	142	.360	B	
		Criger, Louis	C75	76	.266	B	
		Cross, LaFayette Napoleon (Lave)	3B	16	+.300	B	Bkn
		Dillard, Robert Lee (3B20)	OF22	44	.237	A	ChiA
		Donlin, Michael Joseph	1B21	77	.327	B	
		Donovan, Patrick Joseph	OF	127	.324	Pitt	
0	1	Harper, Chas. Wm. (Jack)	P	1	.000	Clev	
		Heidrick, John Emmett	OF	83	.301	B	
5	8	Hughey, James Ulysses	P	20	.209	Clev	C
13	20	Jones, Albert Edward	P34	38	.178	B	
		Keister, Wm. Hoffman	2B119	128	.298	Balt	
		Krueger, Oompaul Arthur	2B	12	.400	Clev	
		McGann, Dennis L. (Dan)	1B	124	.301	Wash	
		McGraw, John Joseph	3B	98	.337	Balt	
		O'Connor, John Joseph (Jack)	C	10	+.219	B	Pitt
		Quinn, Joseph J. (SS6 3B1)	2B14	22	+.259	Clev	Cin
17	18	Powell, John Joseph	P35	37	.275	B	
		Robinson, Wilbert	C	56	.255	Balt	
		Stanton, Harry Andrew	C	1	.000	A	
6	8	Sudhoff, John William	P	32	.190	B	
		Tebeau, Oliver Wendell (Pat) MGR.	1B	1	.000	B	C
1	0	Thomas, Thomas W.	P	5	.100	B	KCA
		Wallace, Rhoderick John	SS127	129	.272	B	

WON	LOST	NAME	POS.	G.	BA	FROM	TO
3	4	Weyhing, August (Gus)	P	7	+.143	Wash	Bkn
20	16	Young, Denton True (Cy)	P	39	.185	B	

WON 76 NATIONAL LEAGUE FINISHED 4th.
LOST 64
TG 140 1901. PCT. .543

ST. LOUIS

PATRICK JOSEPH DONOVAN

WON	LOST	NAME	POS.	G.	BA	FROM	TO
0	3	Breitenstein, Theodore P.	P	3	.250	Cin	C
		Burkett, Jesse Cail	OF	142	.382	B	
0	0	Burns, James	P	1	.000	A	C
		Childs, Peter Piene	2B	8	+.609	A	Chi
		Donovan, Patrick Joseph MGR.	OF	129	.294	B	
0	0	Fisher, Chauncey Burr	P	1	+.000	xN.Y.	C
23	13	Harper, Chas. Wm. (Jack)	P	36	.172	B	
		Hazleton, Willard Carpenter	1B	7	.125	A	
		Heidrick, John Emmett	OF	115	.339	B	
		Heydon, Michael Edward	C	14	.244	InplsA	
2	6	Jones, Albert Edward	P	10	.148	B	C
		Krueger, Oompaul Arthur	3B	142	.274	B	
0	1	Magee, Wm. M.	P	1	+.667	Wash99	N.Y.
10	9	Murphy, Edward J.	P	20	.250	Phil98	
		McGann, Dennis L. (Dan)	1B	113	.288	B	
		Nichols, Arthur Francis (OF36)	C46	82	.247	Chi	
2	2	O'Neill, Michael Joyce	P	6	.429	A	
		Padden, Richard J.	2B115	123	.253	ChiA	
19	18	Powell, John Joseph	P	37	.161	B	
		Richardson, Wm. H.	1B	15	.211	A	C
		Ryan, John Bennett (Jack)	C62	80	.196	DetA	
		Schriver, Wm. F. (Pop) (1B19)	C25	44	.286	Pitt	C
17	11	Sudhoff, John William	P	33	.171	B	
		Wallace, Rhoderick John (Bobby)	SS	135	.322	B	
0	0	Wicker, Robert Kitridge	P	3	.200	A	
3	1	Yerkes, Stanley	P	4	.091	xBaltA	

WON 56 NATIONAL LEAGUE FINISHED 6th.
LOST 78
TG 134 1902. PCT. .418

ST. LOUIS

PATRICK JOSEPH DONOVAN

WON	LOST	NAME	POS.	G.	BA	FROM	TO
0	0	Adams, Joseph Edward	P	1	.000	A	C
		Barclay, George Oliver	OF	137	.301	A	
		Brashear, Robert Norman (2B21 SS3 OF15)	1B67	106	.284	A	C

WON	LOST	NAME	POS.	G.	BA	FROM	TO
		Calhoun, John Chas. (1B5 OF1)	3B12	17	.156	A	C
7	5	Currie, Clarence F.	P	13	+.196	xCin	
		Donovan, Patrick Joseph MGR.	OF	126	.309	B	
2	3	Dunham, Wiley H.	P	7	.083	A	C
		Farrell, John Stephen (SS20)	2B119	139	.255	WashA	
0	4	Hackett, James Joseph (OF2)	P4	6	.285	A	
		Hartman, Frederick Orrin (1B3 SS4)	3B105	112	.221	ChiA	C
		Hazelton, Willard Carpenter	1B	7	.130	B	C
		Kling, Rudolph A.	SS	4	.200	A	C
		Krueger, Oompaul Arthur (3B18)	SS107	125	.264	B	
10	6	Murphy, Edward J.	P18	19	.277	B	
		Murphy, John P.	3B	1	.600	A	
0	1	McFarland, Chas. Edward (Chappie)	P	2	.000	A	
		Nichols, Arthur Francis (C11 OF4)	1B57	69	.272	B	
		O'Neill, John Joseph (Jack)	C	56	.154	A	
16	15	O'Neill, Michael Joyce (OF3)	P33	36	.318	B	
2	6	Pearson, Alexander Franklin	P	11	.264	A	
2	6	Popp, Wm. Peter	P	9	.047	A	C
		Ryan, John Bennett (Jack) (1B4 2B2 SS1 3B4)	C64	74	.177	B	
		Smoot, Homer	OF	129	.313	A	
		Weaver, Arthur Coggshall	C	11	.171	A	
5	11	Wicker, Robert Kitridge (OF3)	P19	22	.234	B	
		Williams, Otto George	SS	2	.400	A	
12	21	Yerkes, Stanley	P	36	.130	B	

WON 43
LOST 94
TG 137

NATIONAL LEAGUE — FINISHED 8th (LAST)

1903. — PCT. .314

ST. LOUIS

PATRICK JOSEPH DONOVAN

WON	LOST	NAME	POS.	G.	BA	FROM	TO
		Barclay, George Oliver	OF	107	.248	B	
		Berte, Harry (SS1)	2B3	4	.357	A	C
0	1	Betts, Harold M.	P	1	.000	A	
		Brain, David Leonard (3B46)	SS72	118	.231	ChiA01	
9	13	Brown, Mordecai Peter Centennial	P	26	.195	A	
		Burke, James Timothy (2B15)	3B93	113	.285	Pitt	
		Coveney, John Patrick	C	3	.200	A	C
4	12	Currie, Clarence F.	P	22	+.085	B	Chi
		DeMontreville, Leon (Lee)	SS15	20	.243	A	C
		Donovan, Patrick Joseph MGR.	OF	105	.327	B	
6	8	Dunleavy, John Francis (P14)	OF38	52	.249	A	

WON	LOST	NAME	POS.	G.	BA	FROM	TO
		Farrell, John Stephen	2B118	130	.272	B	
1	3	Hackett, James Joseph (P5)	1B89	96	.228	B	C
0	1	Hynes, Patrick J.	P	1	.000	A	
0	0	Lovett, John	P	3	.333	A	C
0	0	Milton S. Lawrence	P	1	.500	A	C
0	1	Moran, Chas. Barthel (SS1)	P3	4	.429	A	
4	8	Murphy, Edward J.	P16	24	.203	B	C
9	19	McFarland, Chas. Edward (Chappie)	P	28	.108	B	
		Nichols, Arthur Francis	1B25	33	.192	B	C
		O'Neill, John Joseph (Jack)	C	74	.236	B	
4	13	O'Neill, Michael Joyce	P19	32	.227	B	
5	8	Rhoades, Robert Bruce	P17	18	.140	Chi	ClevA
		Ryan, John Bennett (Jack) (1B18)	C47	66	.238	B	
1	6	Sanders, Warren W. (War)	P	8	.067	IndplsA00	
		Smoot, Homer	OF	129	.296	B	
0	0	Taylor, Edward	P	1	.000	A	C
		Ury, Louis	1B	2	.142	A	C
		Weaver, Arthur Coggshall	C	16	+.245	B	Pitt
0	0	Wicker, Robert Kitridge	P	1	+.000	B	Chi
		Williams, Otto George	SS	53	+.203	B	Chi
0	1	Yerkes, Stanley	P	1	.000	B	C

WON 75
LOST 79
TG 154

NATIONAL LEAGUE — FINISHED 5th.

1904. — PCT. .422

ST. LOUIS

CHAS. AUGUSTUS NICHOLS

WON	LOST	NAME	POS.	G.	BA	FROM	TO
		Barclay, George Oliver	OF	103	+.200	B	Bos
		Beckley, Jacob Peter (Jake)	1B	142	.325	Cin	
		Brain, David Leonard (3B30 OF19)	SS59	125	.266	B	
		Burke, James Timothy	3B	118	.227	B	
		Butler, John Albert	C	12	.167	A	
		Byers, John Wm.	C16	17	.217	A	C
5	9	Corbett, Joseph	P	14	.209	MinnA00	C
		Donahue, Chas. Michael	SS	4	+.213	A	Phil
1	4	Dunleavy, John Francis (P7)	OF44	51	.236	B	
		Farrell, John Stephen	2B	130	.255	B	
		Grady, Michael Wm.	C77	92	.313	WashA01	
		Hill, Hugh Ellis	OF	23	.226	ClevA	C
		Murch, Simeon T. (2B4)	3B8	13	.137	A	
13	18	McFarland, Chas. Edward (Chappie)	P	32	.131	B	
2	1	McGinley, James Wm.	P	3	.091	A	
		McLean, John Bannerman (Larry)	C	24	.167	Chi	
20	12	Nichols, Chas. Augustus (Kid) MGR.	P	36	.156	Bos01	
10	14	O'Neill, Michael Joyce	P25	28	.231	B	
1	2	Sanders, Warren W. (War)	P	4	.000	B	C

WON	LOST	NAME	POS.	G.	BA	FROM	TO
		Shannon, Wm. Porter (Spike)	OF	133	.280	A	
		Shay, Daniel C.	SS97	98	.256	ClevA01	
		Smoot, Homer	OF	137	.281	B	
		Swindell, Chas. Jay	C	3	.125	A	C
22	19	Taylor, John W. (Jack)	P	41	.211	Chi	
		Zearfoss, David William Tilden	C	25	.213	NY98	

WON 58 NATIONAL LEAGUE FINISHED 6th.
LOST 96
TG 154 1905. PCT. .377

ST. LOUIS

CHAS. AUGUSTUS NICHOLS JAMES TIMOTHY BURKE
MATTHEW STANLEY ROBISON

WON	LOST	NAME	POS.	G.	BA	FROM	TO
		Arndt, Harry A.	2B90	111	.243	BaltA02	
		Beckley, Jacob Peter (Jake)	1B	134	.286	B	
		Brain, David Leonard (3B7)	SS34	41	+.228	B	Pitt
8	11	Brown, Chas. Edward (Buster)	P	23	.092	A	
		Burke, James Timothy MGR.	3B	122	.225	B	
1	1	Campbell, Wm. James (Billy)	P	2	.143	A	
		Clarke, Joshua Baldwin (Josh) (2B16)	OF26	46	.257	Lvlle98	
		DeGroff, Edward Arthur	OF	15	.250	A	
		Dunleavy, John Francis	OF118	119	.241	B	C
5	16	Egan, Aloysius Jerome	P	23	.102	DetA02	
		Farrell, John Stephen	2B	6	.182	B	C
		Grady, Michael Wm. (1B20)	C71	91	.286	B	
		Himes, John H.	OF	12	.156	A	
0	1	Hoelskoetter, Arthur H. (P1)	3B20	24	.241	A	
3	3	Kellum, Winford Ansley	P	11	.200	Cin	C
		Leahy, Thomas Joseph	C	29	.227	MilA01	C
		Murch, Simeon T. (SS1)	2B2	4	.111	B	
		McBride, George Florian	SS	81	+.253	xPitt	
1	4	McDougall, James A.	P	5	.077	A	C
9	18	McFarland, Chas. Edward (Chappie)	P	31	.165	B	
0	1	McGinley, James Wm.	P	1	1.000	B	C
1	5	Nichols, Chas. Augustus (Kid) MGR.	P	8	+.227	B	Phil
		Shannon, Wm. Porter (Spike)	OF	140	.268	B	
		Shay, Daniel C. (SS39)	2B39	78	.238	B	
		Shea, Gerald J.	C	2	.333	A	C
		Smoot, Homer	OF	138	.311	B	
15	20	Taylor, John W. (Jack)	P37	39	.190	B	
15	16	Thielman, John Peter (Jake)	P32	33	.231	A	
		Warner, John Joseph	C	41	.255	N.Y.	DetA
		Zearfoss, David William Tilden	C	19	.157	B	C

WON 52 NATIONAL LEAGUE FINISHED 7th.
LOST 98
TG 150 1906. PCT. .347

ST. LOUIS

JOHN JAMES McCLOSKEY

WON	LOST	NAME	POS.	G.	BA	FROM	TO
0	1	Adams, Chas. Benjamin (Babe)	P	1	.000	A	
		Arndt, Harry A.	3B65	67	.270	B	
		Barry, John C. (1B20)	OF42	62	+.249	xCin	
		Beckley, Jacob Peter (Jake)	1B	85	.247	B	
9	9	Beebe, Frederick Leonard	P	20	+.172	xChi	
		Bennett, Justin Titus	2B	153	.262	A	
8	16	Brown, Chas. Edward (Buster)	P	32	.165	B	
		Burch, Albert Wm.	OF	91	.266	A	
		Crawford, Forrest A.	SS39	45	.207	A	
		DeGroff, Edward Arthur	OF	1	.000	B	C
2	1	Druhot, Carl A.	P	5	+.232	xCin	
2	9	Egan, Aloysius Jerome	P	16	.069	B	C
1	4	Fromme, Arthur Henry	P	5	.222	A	
		Grady, Michael Wm. (1B35)	C57	92	.250	B	C
1	6	Higginbotham, Irving Clinton	P	7	.222	A	
		Himes, John H.	OF	40	.271	B	C
1	0	Hoelskoetter, Arthur H. (P1 SS16)	3B53	94	.224	B	
		Holly, Edward Wm.	SS	9	.067	A	
		Holmes, Howard Elbert	C	9	.185	A	C
5	16	Karger, Edwin	P	25	+.233	xPitt	
		Marshall, Joseph H.	OF23	27	.158	Pitt03	C
		Marshall, Wm. R. (Doc)	C	38	+.276	xN.Y.	
		Mertes, Samuel Blair (Sandow)	OF	53	+.246	xN.Y.	C
		Murray, John Joseph (Red)	OF34	41	.257	A	
		McBride, George Florian	SS	90	.169	B	
		McCarthy, Joseph N.	C	14	.237	NYA	C
3	4	McFarland, Chas. Edward (Chappie)	P	7	+.133	B	Pitt
4	2	McGlynn, Ulysses Simpson Grant (Stoney)	P	6	.063	A	
		Noonan, Peter John (1B16)	C23	39	+.168	xChi	
		O'Hara, Thomas F.	OF	14	.321	A	
		Phyle, Wm. Joseph	3B	21	.178	NY01	C
2	2	Puttman, Ambrose Nicholas	P	4	.333	NYA	C
		Raub, Thomas Jefferson	C	22	.282	Chi03	C
4	5	Rhodes, Chas. A.	P	9	.176	A	
		Shannon, Wm. Porter (Spike)	OF	80	+.258	B	N.Y.
		Slattery, John Thomas	C	2	.000	ChiA03	
		Smoot, Homer	OF	86	+.248	B	Cin
8	9	Taylor, John W. (Jack)	P	19	+.208	B	Chi
0	3	Thielman, John Peter (Jake)	P	3	.500	B	
2	11	Thompson, John Gus	P	17	.176	Pitt03	C
		Zimmerman, Edward Desmond	3B	5	.213	A	

WON 52 NATIONAL LEAGUE FINISHED 8th (LAST)
LOST 101
TG 153 1907. PCT. .340

ST. LOUIS

JOHN JAMES McCLOSKEY

WON	LOST	NAME	POS.	G.	BA	FROM	TO
		Arndt, Harry A.	1B	9	.130	B	C
		Barry, John C.	OF	81	.248	B	
		Baxter, John	1B	6	.190	A	C
		Beckley, Jacob Peter (Jake)	1B	32	.209	B	C
7	19	Beebe, Frederick Leonard	P	31	.128	B	
		Bennett, Justin Titus	2B83	86	.222	B	C
2	7	Brown, Chas. Edward (Buster)	P	9	+.269	B	Phil
		Burch, Albert Wm.	OF	48	+.227	B	Bkn
		Burnett, John P.	OF	59	.238	A	C
		Byrne, Robert Mathew	3B148	149	.256	A	
		Crawford, Forrest A.	SS	7	.227	B	C
		Delahanty, Joseph Nicholas	OF	6	.303	A	
0	2	Druhot, Carl A.	P	2	.000	B	C
5	13	Fromme, Arthur Henry	P	23	.182	B	
		Hoelskoetter, Arthur H. (1B27)	2B73	118	.247	B	
		Holly, Edward Wm.	SS147	150	.229	B	
		Hopkins, John Winton	OF	15	.136	Pitt02	C
15	19	Karger, Edwin	P	39	.179	B	
		Kelly, John B.	OF	52	.188	A	C
		Konetchy, Edward Joseph	1B	91	.251	A	
5	9	Lush, John Chas.	P	16	+.271	xPhil	
		Marshall, Wm. R. (Doc)	C	83	.202	B	
		Murray, John Joseph (Red)	OF124	131	.262	B	
14	25	McGlynn, Ulysses Simpson Grant (Stoney)	P	45	.200	B	
		Noonan, Peter John	C	70	.224	B	C
		O'Hara, Thomas F.	OF	47	.237	B	C
3	4	Raymond, Arthur Lawrence	P	10	.090	DetA04	
		Shaw, Albert Simpson	OF	8	.303	A	
0	3	Shields, Chas. Jessamine	P	3	.000	StLA02	C
0	0	Wolter, Harry Meigs	P	12	+.340	xPitt	

WON 49 — NATIONAL LEAGUE — FINISHED 8th (LAST)
LOST 105
TG 154 — 1908. — PCT. .318

ST. LOUIS

JOHN JAMES McCLOSKEY

WON	LOST	NAME	POS.	G.	BA	FROM	TO
1	3	Baldwin, O. F.	P	4	.000	A	C
		Barry, John C.	OF	71	+.228	B	N.Y.
5	13	Beebe, Frederick Leonard	P	29	.125	B	
		Bliss, John Joseph Alfred	C	43	.213	A	
		Byrne, Robert Mathew	3B122	126	.191	B	
		Charles, Raymond (SS31 3B23)	2B65	119	.205	A	
		Delahanty, Joseph Nicholas	OF	138	.255	B	
5	13	Fromme, Arthur Henry	P	20	.139	B	
0	0	Gaiser, Frederick Jacob	P	1	.000	A	C
		Gilbert, Wm. Oliver	2B	89	.214	NY06	
3	8	Higginbotham, Irving Clinton	P	19	.132	StL06	
		Hoelskoetter, Arthur H.	C41	45	.232	B	C
4	9	Karger, Edwin	P	22	.241	B	
		Konetchy, Edward Joseph	1B	154	.248	B	
		Ludwig, Wm. Lawrence	C	62	.182	A	C
11	18	Lush, John Chas.	P	38	.169	B	
		Marshall, Wm. Riddle (Doc)	C	6	+.071	B	Chi
		Moran, Chas. Barthel	C	16	.175	StL03	C
		Morris, John Walter	SS	23	.178	A	C
		Murdock, Wilbur E.	OF	16	.258	A	C
		Murray, John Joseph (Red)	OF	154	.282	B	
1	6	McGlynn, Ulysses Simpson Grant (Stoney)	P	16	.077	B	C
		McLaurin, Ralph Edgar	OF	8	.227	A	C
		O'Rourke, Joseph Patrick	SS	53	.195	A	C
		O'Steen, James Champ	SS17	29	.196	NYA04	
15	25	Raymond, Arthur Lawrence (Bugs)	P	48	.189	B	
		Reilly, Thomas H.	SS	29	.173	A	
1	2	Rhodes, Chas. A.	P	4	+.250	xCin	
3	8	Sallee, Harry Franklin (Slim)	P	25	.049	A	
		Shaw, Albert Simpson	OF89	96	.264	B	

WON 54 — NATIONAL LEAGUE — FINISHED 7th.
LOST 98
TG 152 — 1909. — PCT. .355

ST. LOUIS

ROGER PHILIP BRESNAHAN

WON	LOST	NAME	POS.	G.	BA	FROM	TO
3	11	Backman, Lester John	P	21	.102	A	
		Barbeau, Wm. Joseph (Jap)	3B	44	+.251	xPitt	
15	21	Beebe, Frederick Leonard	P	44	.167	B	
0	0	Bernard, Joseph	P	1	.000	A	C
		Blank,	C	1	.000	A	C
		Bliss, John Joseph Alfred	C	32	.221	B	
		Bresnahan, Roger Philip MGR.	C59	69	.244	N.Y.	
		Byrne, Robert Mathew	3B	105	+.214	B	Pitt
		Charles, Raymond (SS16)	2B83	99	+.236	B	Cin
		Delahanty, Joseph Nicholas (2B48)	OF63	111	.214	B	C
		Ellis, George Wm.	OF	145	.268	A	
		Enwright, Chas. Michael	SS	3	.142	A	C
		Evans, Louis Richard	OF141	143	.259	N.Y.	
		Gilbert, Wm. Oliver	2B	12	.172	B	C
6	11	Harmon, Robert Green	P	21	.255	A	
1	0	Higginbotham, Irving Clinton	P	3	+.000	B	Chi
3	3	Higgins, Festus Edward	P	16	.190	A	
		Hulswitt, Rudolph Edward	SS65	77	.280	Cin	
		James, Berton Hulon	OF	6	.285	A	C
		Konetchy, Edward Joseph	1B	152	.286	B	
0	2	Lowdermilk, Grover Cleveland	P	7	.111	A	
11	18	Lush, John Chas.	P34	45	.239	B	
0	1	Melter, Stephen B.	P	23	.133	A	C

WON	LOST	NAME	POS.	G.	BA	FROM	TO
1	5	More, Forest T.	P	15	+.154	A	Bos
		Mowrey, Harry Harlan (Mike)	3B	8	+.241	xCin	
		Murphy, Howard	OF	19	.200	A	C
		O'Steen, James Champ	SS	16	.199	B	C
		Phelps, Edward Joseph	C	83	.248	Pitt	
1	10	Raleigh, John Austin	P	15	.087	A	
		Reilly, Thomas H.	SS	4	.167	B	
3	5	Rhodes, Chas. A.	P	12	.211	B	C
10	11	Sallee, Harry Franklin (Slim)	P	32	.113	B	
		Shaw, Albert Simpson	OF	92	.248	B	
		Storke, Alan Marshall	SS	48	+.282	xPitt	C
0	0	Sullivan, Harry Andrew	P	2	.000	A	C

WON 63 LOST 90 TG 153

NATIONAL LEAGUE 1910.

FINISHED 7th. PCT. .412

ST. LOUIS

ROGER PHILIP BRESNAHAN

WON	LOST	NAME	POS.	G.	BA	FROM	TO
		Abbott, Ody Cleon	OF	21	.186	A	C
1	2	Alberts, Frederick Joseph	P	4	.000	A	C
6	7	Backman, Lester John	P	26	.114	B	C
		Barbeau, Wm. Joseph (Jap) (2B1 OF1)	3B6	7	.227	B	C
		Betcher, Franklin Lyle	SS	27	.202	A	C
		Bliss, John Joseph Alfred	C13	16	.063	B	
		Bresnahan, Roger Philip MGR.	C77	78	.278	B	
0	0	Chambers, Wm. Christopher	P	1	.000	A	C
6	14	Corridon, Frank J.	P	30	.196	Phil	C
		Ellis, George Wm.	OF	141	.258	B	
		Evans, Louis Richard	OF141	151	.241	B	
0	1	Geyer, Jacob Bowman	P	4	.000	A	
2	3	Golden, Roy K.	P	7	.267	A	
13	15	Harmon, Robert Green	P	43	.184	B	
		Hauser, Arnold J.	SS117	118	.205	A	
1	3	Hearn, Bunn	P	5	.133	A	
0	1	Higgins, Festus Edward (OF1)	P	2	.400	B	C
		Huggins, Miller James	2B	151	.265	Cin	
		Hulswitt, Rudolph Edward	SS30	32	.248	B	C
		Kelly, Wm. J.	C	2	.000	A	
0	0	Konetchy, Edward Joseph (P1)	1B	144	.302	B	
		Lush, Ernest Benjamin	OF	1	.000	A	C
14	13	Lush, John Chas.	P	36	.226	B	C
		Mowrey, Harry Harlan (Mike)	3B	141	.282	B	
		Oakes, Ennis Talmadge (Rebel)	OF	127	.252	Cin	
0	0	O'Hara, Wm. A. (P1 1B1)	OF5	9	.150	N.Y.	C
0	0	Patton, Harry C.	P	1	.000	A	C
		Phelps, Edward Joseph	C	80	.263	B	
0	0	Pickett, Chas. A.	P	2	.000	A	C
0	0	Raleigh, John Austin	P	3	.000	B	C
0	2	Reiger, Elmer Jay	P	13	.000	A	C
7	8	Sallee, Harry Franklin (Slim)	P	18	.108	B	
4	4	Steele, Wm. Mitchell	P	9	.267	A	

WON	LOST	NAME	POS.	G.	BA	FROM	TO
9	12	Willis, Victor Gazaway	P	33	.167	Pitt	C
		Zacher, Elmer Henry	OF	38	+.212	xN.Y.	C
0	5	Zmich, Edward A.	P	9	.077	A	

WON 75 LOST 74 TG 149

NATIONAL LEAGUE 1911.

FINISHED 5th. PCT. .503

ST. LOUIS

ROGER PHILIP BRESNAHAN

WON	LOST	NAME	POS.	G.	BA	FROM	TO
		Bliss, John Joseph Alfred	C84	85	.229	B	
		Bresnahan, Roger Philip MGR.	C77	78	.278	B	
1	0	Camnitz, R. Harry	P	2	.000	Pitt09	C
		Clark, James F.	OF	14	.176	A	
		Conwell, Edward James	3B	1	.000	A	C
0	2	Dale, Emmett Eugene	P	5	.400	A	
		Ellis, George Wm.	OF	148	.250	B	
		Evans, Louis Richard	OF	150	.294	B	
9	6	Geyer, Jacob Bowman	P	29	.228	B	
		Gilhooley, Frank Patrick	OF	1	.000	A	
4	9	Golden, Roy K.	P	30	.114	B	C
23	16	Harmon, Robert Green	P	51	.153	B	
		Hauser, Arnold J.	SS134	136	.241	B	
0	0	Hearn, Bunn	P	2	.000	B	
		Huggins, Miller James	2B	136	.261	B	
		Konetchy, Edward Joseph	1B	158	.289	B	
0	1	Lowdermilk, Grover Cleveland	P	11	.111	StL09	
3	4	Lowdermilk, Louis Bailey	P	16	.111	A	
		Magee, Leo Christopher (Lee)	2B18	21	.261	A	
		Morse, Peter R. (OF1)	SS2	4	.000	A	C
		Mowrey, Harry Harlan (Mike)	3B134	135	.267	B	
0	0	McAdams, George D. John (Jack)	P	6	.000	A	C
		McGeehan, Daniel DeSales	2B	3	.222	A	C
		McIvor, E. Otto	OF	17	.226	A	C
		Oakes, Ennis Talmadge (Rebel)	OF	151	.263	B	
0	0	Radabaugh, Roy	P	2	.000	A	C
		Reed, Milton D. Jr.		1	.000	A	
0	0	Reis, Harrie Crane	P	3	.000	A	C
15	9	Sallee, Harry Franklin (Slim)	P	36	.169	B	
		Smith, Wallace H. (SS25)	3B26	60	.216	A	
0	0	Standridge, Alfred Peter	P	2	.000	A	
18	19	Steele, Wm. Mitchell	P	43	.208	B	
		Wilie, Dennis Ernest	OF	15	.235	A	
0	1	Willis, Joseph	P	2	.000	xStLA	
		Wingo, Ivy Brown	C	18	.211	A	
1	5	Woodburn, Eugene Stewart	P	11	.166	A	
0	2	Zackert, George	P	4	.000	A	
1	0	Zmich, Edward A.	P	4	.250	B	C

WON 63 | LOST 90 | TG 153

NATIONAL LEAGUE 1912. FINISHED 6th. PCT. .412

ST. LOUIS

ROGER PHILIP BRESNAHAN

WON	LOST	NAME	POS.	G.	BA	FROM	TO
		Bliss, John Joseph Alfred	C41	49	.246	B	C
		Bresnahan, Roger Philip MGR.	C28	48	.333	B	
1	3	Burk, Charles Sanford	P	12	+.000	xBkn	
		Burns, Edward James	C	1	.000	A	
		Cather, Theodore P.	OF	5	.421	A	
		Clark, James F.	OF	2	.000	B	C
0	5	Dale, Emmett Eugene	P19	20	.273	B	
0	0	Dell, Wm. George	P	3	.000	A	
		Ellis, George Wm.	OF76	109	.269	B	C
		Evans, Louis Richard	OF134	135	.283	B	
0	0	Ewing, George Lemuel (Bob)	P	1	.000	Phil	C
		Galloway, James Cato	2B16	21	.185	A	C
7	14	Geyer, Jacob Bowman	P	41	.208	B	
		Gilhooley, Frank Patrick	OF	13	.224	B	
3	4	Griner, Daniel Dexter	P	12	.077	A	
18	18	Harmon, Robert Green	P43	46	.232	B	
		Hauser, Arnold J.	SS132	133	.259	B	
0	0	Howell, Roland Boatner	P	3	.000	A	C
		Huggins, Miller James	2B114	120	.304	B	
		Kelleher, John Patrick	3B	6	.363	A	
		Konetchy, Edward Joseph	1B142	143	.314	B	
1	1	Lowdermilk, Louis Bailey	P	4	+.250	B	C
		Magee, Leo Christopher (Lee) (2B23)	OF85	128	.290	B	
		Mercer, John Locke	1B	1	.000	Pitt10	C
		Miller, Elmer	OF	12	.189	A	
		Mowrey, Harry Harlan (Mike)	3B108	114	.255	B	
		Murphy, Michael Jerome	C	1	.000	A	
		Oakes, Ennis Talmadge (Rebel)	OF	136	.281	B	
1	1	Perritt, Wm. Dayton (Pol)	P	6	.222	A	
2	1	Redding, Philip Hayden	P	3	.000	A	
		Rolling, Raymond Copeland	2B	5	.200	A	C
16	17	Sallee, Harry Franklin (Slim)	P	48	.136	B	
		Smith, Wallace H. (SS22)	3B32	75	.256	B	
		Snyder, Frank J. (Pancho)	C	11	.111	A	
9	13	Steele, Wm. Mitchell	P	41	.180	B	
		Whitted, George Bostic	3B	12	.282	A	
		Wilie, Dennis Ernest	OF16	30	.229	B	
4	9	Willis, Joseph	P	31	.158	B	
		Wingo, Ivy Brown	C92	100	.265	B	
1	4	Woodburn, Eugene Stewart	P	20	.000	B	C
0	0	Zackert, George	P	1	.000	B	C

WON 51 | LOST 99 | TG 150

NATIONAL LEAGUE 1913. FINISHED 8th (LAST) PCT. .340

ST. LOUIS

MILLER JAMES HUGGINS

WON	LOST	NAME	POS.	G.	BA	FROM	TO
		Beck, Zinn Bertram	3B	10	.218	A	
0	2	Burk, Charles Sanford	P	19	.091	B	
		Cabrera, Alfredo A.	SS	1	.000	A	C
		Callahan, Wesley LeRoy	SS	7	.285	A	C
0	0	Cather, Theodore P. (P1 1B1)	OF57	67	.213	B	
0	0	Crandall, James Otis (Doc)	P	2	+.000	xN.Y.	N.Y. (Recall)
2	8	Doak, Wm. Leopold	P	15	.032	Cin	
		Evans, Louis Richard	OF74	97	.249	B	
1	5	Geyer, Jacob Bowman	P	30	.091	B	C
10	22	Griner, Daniel Dexter	P	34	.259	B	
8	21	Harmon, Robert Green	P42	46	.261	B	
		Hauser, Arnold J.	SS	22	.289	B	
		Hildebrand, Palmer Marion	C	26	.164	A	C
0	3	Hopper, Wm. Booth	P	3	.375	A	
		Huggins, Miller James MGR.	2B113	121	.285	B	
0	1	Hunt, Benjamin Franklin	P	2	.000	BosA10	C
1	0	Konetchy, Edward Joseph (P1)	1B140	140	.276	B	
		Magee, Leo Christopher (Lee) (2B22)	OF108	137	.267	B	
0	1	Marbet, Walter	P	3	.000	A	C
		Miller, Chas. M.	OF	4	.091	A	
		Mowrey, Harry Harlan (Mike) (Larry)	3B131	132	.260	B	
		McLean, John Bannerman	C	48	+.270	Cin	N.Y.
0	2	Niehaus, Richard J.	P	3	.286	A	
		Oakes, Ennis Talmadge (Rebel)	OF145	147	.293	B	
		O'Leary, Chas. Timothy (2B15)	SS103	121	.217	DetA	
		Peitz, Henry Clement (Heinie) (OF1)	C2	3	.333	Pitt06	C
6	14	Perritt, Wm. Dayton (Pol)	P	36	.203	B	
		Quinlan, Thomas Finners	OF	13	.160	A	
0	0	Redding, Philip Hayden	P	1	.000	B	C
		Roberts, Chester A.	C16	26	.146	A	
19	15	Sallee, Harry Franklin (Slim)	P	50	.211	B	
		Sheckard, Samuel James Tilden	OF	52	+.199	Chi	Cin
		Snyder, Frank J. (Pancho)	C	7	.190	B	
4	4	Steele, Wm. Mitchell	P	12	.056	B	
0	1	Trekell, Harry R.	P	7	.111	A	C
		Vann, John Silas		1	.000	A	C
		Whelan, James Frank	OF	1	.000	A	C
		Whitted, George Bostic (SS38 3B22)	OF41	123	.220	B	
0	0	Willis, Joseph	P	2	.000	B	C
		Wingo, Ivy Brown	C98	112	.254	B	

WON 81 | LOST 72 | TG 153

NATIONAL LEAGUE 1914.

FINISHED 3rd. PCT. .529

ST. LOUIS

MILLER JAMES HUGGINS

WON	LOST	NAME	POS.	G.	BA	FROM	TO
		Beck, Zinn Bertram (SS16)	3B122	137	.232	B	
		Betzel, Albert John Henry (3B1)	2B5	7	.000	A	
		Butler, Arthur Edward	SS83	86	.201	Pitt	
		Cather, Theodore P.	OF	39	+.273	B	Bos
		Cruise, Walton Edwin	OF81	95	.227	A	
		Daringer, Rolla Harrison	SS	2	.500	A	
19	6	Doak, Wm. Leopold	P	36	.118	B	
		Dolan, Alvin James (Cozy) (3B27)	OF96	126	.240	Pitt	
		Dressen, Lee August	1B38	46	.233	A	
9	13	Griner, Daniel Dexter	P	37	.255	B	
2	4	Hageman, Kurt R. Morris	P	12	+.214	BosA12	Chi
0	0	Hopper, Wm. Booth	P	3	.000	B	
		Huggins, Miller James MGR.	2B147	148	.263	B	
		Magee, Leo Christopher (Lee) (1B39)	OF102	142	.284	B	
		Miller, Chas. M.	OF	36	.194	B	C
		Miller, John Barney (SS60)	1B91	155	.290	Pitt	
		Nash, Kenneth Leland (1B1 2B3 3B6)	SS11	24	.275	ClevA12	C
1	0	Niehaus, Richard J.	P	8	.500	B	
		O'Connor, Patrick Francis	C	10	.000	Pitt10	
8	8	Perdue, Hubbard E. (Hub)	P	22	+.167	xBos	
16	13	Perritt, Wm. Dayton (Pol)	P	41	.141	B	
		Riggert, Joseph Aloysius	OF	34	+.216	xBkn	
7	8	Robinson, John Henry	P	26	.171	Pitt	
		Roche, John Joseph (Jack)	C	12	.667	A	
18	17	Sallee, Harry Franklin (Slim)	P	46	.231	B	
		Snyder, Frank J. (Pancho)	C98	100	.230	B	
1	2	Steele, Wm. Mitchell	P	17	+.294	B	Bkn
		Whitted, George Bostic	OF3	20	+.129	B	Bos
0	1	Williams, Rees Geppert	P	6	.000	A	
		Wilson, John Owen	OF	154	.259	Pitt	
		Wingo, Ivy Brown	C70	80	.300	B	

WON 72 | LOST 81 | TG 153

NATIONAL LEAGUE 1915.

FINISHED 6th. PCT. .471

ST. LOUIS

MILLER JAMES HUGGINS

WON	LOST	NAME	POS.	G.	BA	FROM	TO
9	3	Ames, Leon Kessling	P	15	+.114	xCin	
		Beck, Zinn Bertram	3B62	70	.233	B	
		Bescher, Robert Henry	OF129	130	.263	N.Y.	
		Betzel, Albert John Henry	3B105	117	.251	B	
1	0	Boardman, Chas. Louis	P	3	.286	PhilA	C
		Brown, James Donaldson (Moose)	OF	1	.500	A	
		Butler, Arthur Edward	SS125	130	.254	B	
		Daringer, Rolla Harrison	SS	10	.087	B	C
16	18	Doak, Wm. Leopold	P	38	.174	B	
		Dolan, Alvin James (Cozy)	OF98	111	.280	B	
		Glenn, Harry M.	C	6	.312	A	C
		Gonzales, Miguel Angel Cordero	C32	51	.227	Cin	
5	11	Griner, Daniel Dexter	P37	39	.269	B	
		Hornsby, Rogers (Rajah)	SS	18	.246	A	
		Huggins, Miller James MGR.	2B105	107	.241	B	
		Hyatt, R. Hamilton (Ham) (OF25)	1B64	106	.268	Pitt	
0	0	Lamline, Frederick Arthur	P	4	.125	ChiA12	C
		Long, Thomas Augustus	OF136	140	.294	WashA12	
13	11	Meadows, Henry Lee	P	39	.096	A	
		Miller, John Barney (2B55)	1B94	150	.264	B	
2	1	Niehaus, Richard J.	P	15	.071	B	
6	12	Perdue, Hubbard E. (Hub)	P	31	.111	B	C
7	8	Robinson, John Henry	P	32	.106	B	
		Roche, John Joseph (Jack)	C	46	.205	B	
13	17	Sallee, Harry Franklin (Slim)	P	46	.120	B	
		Smith, John W.(Jack)	OF	4	.187	A	
		Snyder, Frank J. (Pancho)	C142	144	.298	B	
		Wilson, John Owen	OF105	107	.276	B	

WON 60 | LOST 93 | TG 153

NATIONAL LEAGUE 1916.

FINISHED 7th (TIED WITH CINCINNATI) PCT. .392

ST. LOUIS

MILLER JAMES HUGGINS

WON	LOST	NAME	POS.	G.	BA	FROM	TO
11	16	Ames, Leon Kessling	P	45	.176	B	
		Beck, Zinn Bertram	3B52	62	.223	B	
		Bescher, Robert Henry	OF	151	.235	B	
		Betzel, Albert John Henry (3B33)	2B118	142	.233	B	
		Bohne, Samuel Arthur	SS	14	.237	A	
		Brottem, Anton Christian (OF2)	C15	26	.182	A	
		Butler, Arthur Edward	OF15	86	.209	B	C
		Corhan, Roy	SS84	92	.210	ChiA11	C
		Cruise, Walton Edwin	OF	3	.667	StLI4	
0	0	Currie, Murphy	P	6	.000	A	C
12	8	Doak, Wm. Leopold	P	29	.129	B	
		Gonzales, Miguel Angel Cordero	C93	118	.239	B	
0	0	Griner, Daniel Dexter	P	4	.250	B	
0	4	Hall, Chas. Louis (Sea-Lion)	P	10	.143	BosA13	

WON	LOST	NAME	POS.	G.	BA	FROM	TO
		Hornsby, Rogers (Rajah) (1B15 SS46)	3B83	139	.313	B	
		Huggins, Miller James MGR.	2B2	18	.333	B	
5	6	Jasper, Harry W. (Hi)	P	21	.212	ChiA	
		Long, Thomas Augustus	OF106	119	.293	B	
0	3	Lotz, Joseph Peter	P	12	.333	A	C
12	23	Meadows, Henry Lee	P	51	.158	B	
		Miller, John Barney (2B38 SS21)	1B93	143	.238	B	
5	5	Sallee, Harry Franklin (Slim)	P	16	+.167	B	N.Y.
		Smith, John W. (Jack)	OF120	130	.244	B	
		Snyder, Frank J. (Pancho) (1B46)	C72	132	.259	B	
5	15	Steele, Robert Wesley	P	29	.196	A	
		Stewart, John Franklin (Stuffy)	2B4	9	.176	A	
0	0	Warmoth, Wallace Walter (Cy)	P	3	.000	A	
4	6	Watson, Milton W.	P	18	.219	A	
6	7	Williams, Rees Geppert	P	36	.208	B	C
		Wilson, John Owen	OF113	120	.239	B	C

WON 82 — NATIONAL LEAGUE — FINISHED 3rd.
LOST 70
TG 152 — 1917. — PCT. .539

ST. LOUIS

MILLER JAMES HUGGINS

WON	LOST	NAME	POS.	G.	BA	FROM	TO
15	10	Ames, Leon Kessling	P	43	.188	B	
		Baird, Howard Douglas	3B	104	+.253	xPitt	
		Bescher, Robert Henry	OF32	42	.155	B	
		Betzel, Albert John Henry (OF23)	2B75	106	.217	B	
		Brock, John Roy	C	7	.400	A	
		Cruise, Walton Edwin	OF152	153	.295	B	
		DeFate, Clyde	SS	14	.143	A	DetA
16	20	Doak, Wm. Leopold	P	44	.126	B	
		Gonzales, Miguel Angel Cordero (1B18)	C68	106	.262	B	
6	4	Goodwin, Marvin Mardo	P	14	.174	WashA	
0	0	Hitt, Bruce O.	P	2	.000	A	C
		Hornsby, Rogers (Rajah)	SS144	145	.327	B	
9	4	Horstman, Oscar Theodore	P	35	.196	A	
		Livingston, Patrick Joseph (Paddy)	C	7	.200	ClevA12	C
		Long, Thomas Augustus	OF137	144	.232	B	C
0	0	May, Frank Spruell (Jake)	P	15	.000	A	
15	9	Meadows, Henry Lee	P	43	.101	B	
		Miller, John Barney (1B46)	2B92	148	.248	B	
0	0	Murchison, Thomas Malcolm	P	1	.000	A	
		McAuley, James Earl	SS	3	.286	Pitt	
0	0	North, Louis Alexander	P	5	.000	DetA13	
9	6	Packard, Eugene Milo	P	36	+.288	xChi	
		Paulette, Eugene Edward	1B93	95	.265	xStLA	

WON	LOST	NAME	POS.	G.	BA	FROM	TO
1	1	Pearce, George Thomas	P	5	.000	Chi	C
		Roche, John Joseph (Jack)	C	1	.000	StL15	C
		Smith, Frederick Vincent	3B51	56	.182	BknF15	C
		Smith, John W. (Jack)	OF128	137	.297	B	
		Smyth, James Daniel	OF	38	+.211	xBkn	
		Snyder, Frank J. (Pancho)	C94	115	.237	B	
1	3	Steele, Robert Wesley	P	12	+.385	B	Pitt
		Stewart, John Franklin (Stuffy)	2B1	13	.000	B	
		xWallace, Rhoderick John (Bobby)	SS2	8	.100	StLA	
10	13	Watson, Milton W.	P	41	.098	B	

xWallace also played 1 game at 3B.

WON 51 — NATIONAL LEAGUE — FINISHED 8th (LAST)
LOST 78
TG 129 — 1918. — PCT. .395

ST. LOUIS

JOHN CALHOUN HENDRICKS

WON	LOST	NAME	POS.	G.	BA	FROM	TO
9	14	Ames, Leon Kessling	P	27	.156	B	
		Anderson, George Jendrus	OF	35	.295	BknF15	C
		Baird, Howard Douglas (OF1)	3B81	82	.247	B	
		Beall, John Woolf	OF18	19	.224	Cin16	C
		Betzel, Albert John Henry	3B34	76	.222	B	C
		Brock, John Roy (OF1)	C18	27	.212	B	C
		Bronkie, Herman Chas.	3B	18	.221	Chi14	
		Brottem, Anton Christian	1B	2	.000	StL16	
		Cruise, Walton Edwin	OF65	70	.271	B	
		Distel, George Adam (SS1)	2B3	8	.176	A	C
9	15	Doak, Wm. Leopold	P	31	.182	B	
		Fisher, Robert Tecumseh	2B	63	.317	Cin16	
		Gonzales, Miguel Angel Cordero (1B2 OF5)	C100	117	.252	B	
		Grimm, Chas. John (3B1 OF2)	1B42	50	.220	PhilA16	
		Heathcote, Clifton Earl (1B1)	OF87	88	.259	A	
		Hornsby, Rogers (Rajah) (OF3)	SS109	115	.281	B	
0	2	Horstman, Oscar Theodore	P	9	.000	B	
0	0	Howard, Earl N.	P	1	.000	A	C
1	1	Johnson, Adam Rankin	P	6	.200	BaltF15	C
		Kavanagh, Martin Joseph	2B9	12	.181	xClevA	DetA
		Larmore, Robert McKahan	SS2	4	.285	A	C
		Mattick, Walter Joseph	OF	8	.142	ChiA13	C
5	6	May, Frank Spruell (Jake)	P	29	.067	B	
		Maynard, Richard Wheeler	OF	5	.000	A	C
8	14	Meadows, Henry Lee	P30	31	.127	B	
		Menze, Theodore Chas.	OF	2	.000	A	C
		McHenry, Austin Bush	OF	80	.261	A	
		Niehoff, John Albert (Bert)	2B	22	+.176	Phil	N.Y.
12	12	Packard, Eugene Milo	P30	36	.174	B	

WON	LOST	NAME	POS.	G.	BA	FROM	TO
0	0	Paulette, Eugene Edward (P1 2B7 SS12 3B2 OF5)	1B97	125	.273	B	
6	12	Sherdel, Wm. Henry	P	35	.242	A	
		Smyth, James Daniel (2B11)	OF25	40	.212	B	C
		Smith, John W. (Jack)	OF	42	.211	B	
		Snyder, Frank J. (Poncho) (1B3)	C27	39	.250	B	
1	2	Tuero, Oscar Monzon	P	12	.250	A	
		Wallace, Rhoderick John (Bobby) (SS12 3B1)	2B17	32	.153	B	

WON 54
LOST 83
TG 137

NATIONAL LEAGUE

1919.

FINISHED 7th.
PCT. .394

ST. LOUIS

WESLEY BRANCH RICKEY

WON	LOST	NAME	POS.	G.	BA	FROM	TO
3	5	Ames, Leon Kessling	P	23	+.222	B	Phil
		Baird, Howard Douglas (2B1 OF1)	3B14	16	+.260	xPhil	Bkn
0	1	Bolden, Wm. Horace	P	3	.323	A	C
		Clemons, Vernon James	C75	88	.264	StLA16	
		Cruise, Walton Edwin (1B2)	OF7	9	+.095	B	Bos
		Dillhoefer, Wm. Martin (Pickles)	C39	45	.213	Phil	
13	14	Doak, Wm. Leopold	P	31	.109	B	
		Fishburne, Samuel (1B1)	2B1	9	.333	A	C
		Fisher, Robert Tecumseh	2B	3	.273	B	C
11	9	Goodwin, Marvin Mardo	P33	34	.200	StL17	
		Heathcote, Clifton Earl (1B2)	OF101	114	.279	B	
		Hornsby, Rogers (Rajah) (1B5 2B25 SS37)	3B72	138	.318	B	
0	1	Horstman, Oscar Theodore	P	6	.500	B	C
3	6	Jacobs, Wm. Elmer	P	17	+.348	xPhil	
		Janvrin, Harold Chandler	2B	7	.214	xWashA	
		Kimmick, Walter Lyons	SS	2	.000	A	
0	0	Koenigsmark, Willis T.	P	1	.000	A	C
		Lavan, John Leonard	SS99	100	.242	WashA	
		Leslie, Roy Reid	1B	12	.208	Chi17	
3	12	May, Frank Spruell (Jake)	P	28	.162	B	
4	10	Meadows, Henry Lee	P	22	+.111	B	Phil
		Miller, John Barney (2B28)	1B68	101	.231	StL17	
		Mollwitz, Frederick August	1B	25	+.241	xPitt	C
		McHenry, Austin Bush (2B6 3B1)	OF103	110	.286	B	
0	0	Parker, Roy W.	P	2	.000	A	C
		Pasquariello, Michael John		1	+.000	xPhil	C
		Paulette, Eugene Edward	SS8	43	+.215	B	Phil
0	0	Reinhart, Arthur Conrad	P	1	.000	A	
		Schultz, Joseph Chas.	OF49	88	.253	Pitt16	
4	4	Schupp, Ferdinand Maurice	P	10	+.050	xN.Y.	
5	9	Sherdel, Wm. Henry	P36	40	.271	B	

WON	LOST	NAME	POS.	G.	BA	FROM	TO
		Shotton, Burton Edwin	OF67	85	.285	WashA	
		Smith, John W. (Jack)	OF111	119	.223	B	
		Snyder, Frank J. (Pancho) (1B1)	C49	50	+.182	B	N.Y.
		Stock, Milton Joseph (3B58)	2B77	135	.307	Phil	
5	7	Tuero, Oscar Monzon	P	45	.205	B	
3	5	Woodward, Frank Russell	P	17	+.048	xPhil	

WON 75
LOST 79
TG 154

NATIONAL LEAGUE

1920.

FINISHED 5th.
(TIED WITH CHICAGO)
PCT. .487

ST. LOUIS

WESLEY BRANCH RICKEY

WON	LOST	NAME	POS.	G.	BA	FROM	TO
		Clemons, Vernon James	C103	112	.281	B	
		Dillhoefer, Wm. Martin (Pickles)	C74	76	.263	B	
20	12	Doak, Wm. Leopold	P	39	.114	B	
		Fournier, Jacques Frank	1B138	141	.306	NYA18	
		Gilham, George Lewis	C	1	.000	A	
0	0	Glenn, Burdette (Bob)	P	2	.000	A	C
3	8	Goodwin, Marvin Mardo	P	32	.200	B	
		Greisenbeck, Carlos Timothy	C	5	.331	A	C
13	20	Haines, Jesse Joseph (Pop)	P47	48	.176	Cin18	
		Heathcote, Clifton Earl	OF129	133	.284	B	
		Hock, Edward Francis	OF	1	.000	A	
		Hornsby, Rogers (Rajah)	2B	149	.370	B	
4	8	Jacobs, Wm. Elmer	P	23	.192	B	
		Janvrin, Harold Chandler (1B25 OF20)	SS27	87	.274	B	
0	0	Kime, Harold Lee	P	4	.000	A	C
2	1	Kircher, Michael Andrew	P	9	.273	PhilA	
		Knode, Kenneth Thomson	OF	42	.231	A	C
		Lavan, John Leonard	SS138	142	.289	B	
2	1	Lyons, George Tony	P	7	.143	A	
1	4	May, Frank Spruell (Jake)	P	16	.227	B	
		Mueller, Clarence Franklin	OF	4	.318	A	
		McCarty, George Lewis	C	5	+.286	xN.Y.	
		McHenry, Austin Bush	OF133	137	.282	B	
3	2	North, Louis Alexander	P24	26	.226	StL17	
		Schindler, Wm. Gibbons	C	1	.000	A	C
		Schultz, Joseph Chas.	OF80	99	.263	B	
0	0	Schulz, Walter Frederick	P	2	.000	A	C
16	13	Schupp, Ferdinand Maurice	P38	39	.256	B	
0	0	Scott, George Wm.	P	2	.000	A	C
11	10	Sherdel, Wm. Henry	P43	49	.222	B	
		Shotton, Burton Edwin	OF51	62	.228	B	
		Smith, John W. (Jack)	OF83	91	.332	B	
		Stock, Milton Joseph	3B	155	.319	B	
0	0	Tuero, Oscar Monzon	P	2	.000	B	C

WON 87
LOST 66
TG 153

NATIONAL LEAGUE — 1921. — FINISHED 3rd. — PCT. .569

ST. LOUIS

WESLEY BRANCH RICKEY

WON	LOST	NAME	POS.	G.	BA	FROM	TO
		Ainsmith, Edward Wilbur	C23	27	.290	xDetA	
2	5	Bailey, Wm. F.	P	19	.091	DetA18	
		Clemons, Vernon James	C107	117	.320	B	
		Dillhoefer, Wm. Martin (Pickles)	C	76	.241	B	C
15	6	Doak, Wm. Leopold	P	32	.143	B	
		Ewing, Reuben	OF	3	.000	A	C
		Fournier, Jacques Frank	1B	149	.343	B	
		Gilham, George Lewis	C	1	.000	B	C
1	2	Goodwin, Marvin Mardo	P	14	.000	B	
18	12	Haines, Jesse Joseph (Pop)	P37	39	.181	B	
		Heathcote, Clifton Earl	OF51	62	.244	B	
		Hornsby, Rogers (Rajah)	2B142	154	.397	B	
		Hunter, Herbert Harrison	1B1	9	.000	BosA	C
		Irwin, Walter Kingsley		4	.000	A	C
		Janvrin, Harold Chandler	1B	18	+.281	B	Bkn
		Jones, Howard	OF	3	.000	B	C
0	1	Kircher, Michael Andrew	P	3	.000	B	C
		Lavan, John Leonard	SS	150	.259	B	
		Mann, Leslie	OF97	7	.328	Bos	
1	3	May, Frank Spruell (Jake)	P	5	.333	B	
		Mueller, Clarence Franklin	OF54	55	.352	B	
		McCarty, George Lewis	C	1	.000	B	C
		McHenry, Austin Bush	OF	152	.350	B	
		Niebergall, Chas. Arthur	C	5	.167	A	
4	4	North, Louis Alexander	P	40	.158	B	
14	10	Pertica, Wm. Andrew	P	38	.143	BosA18	
9	3	Pfeffer, Edward Joseph	P	18	+.138	xBkn	
1	0	Riviere, Arthur Bernard (Tink)	P	18	.375	A	
		Schultz, Joseph Chas.	OF67	92	.309	B	
2	0	Schupp, Ferdinand Maurice	P	9	+.214	B	Bkn
9	8	Sherdel, Wm. Henry	P33	39	.114	B	
		Shotton, Burton Edwin	OF	38	.250	B	
		Smith, John W. (Jack)	OF103	116	.328	B	
		Stock, Milton Joseph	3B	149	.307	B	
		Toporcer, George (Specs)	2B	22	.264	A	
11	12	Walker, James Roy	P	38	.204	Chi18	

WON 85
LOST 69
TG 154

NATIONAL LEAGUE — 1922. — FINISHED 3rd. (TIED WITH PITTS) — PCT. .552

ST. LOUIS

WESLEY BRANCH RICKEY

WON	LOST	NAME	POS.	G.	BA	FROM	TO
		Ainsmith, Edward Wilbur	C116	119	.293	B	
0	2	Bailey, Wm. F.	P	12	.286	B	C
4	5	Barfoot, Clyde Raymond	P	42	.353	A	
0	0	Benton, Sidney Wright	P	1	.000	A	C
		Blades, Francis Raymond (SS4 3B1)	OF29	37	.300	A	
		Bottomley, James LeRoy	1B34	37	.325	A	
		Clemons, Vernon James	C63	71	.256	B	
11	13	Doak, Wm. Leopold	P	37	.130	B	
0	0	Dyer, Edwin Hawley	P2	6	.333	A	
		Flack, Max John	OF	66	+.292	xChi	
0	0	Fournier, Jacques Frank (P1)	1B109	128	.294	B	
		Freigau, Howard Earl (3B1)	SS2	3	.000	A	
		Gainor, Delos Chas. (OF10)	1B26	43	.268	BosA19	C
0	0	Goodwin, Marvin Mardo	P	2	.000	B	
11	9	Haines, Jesse Joseph (Pop) (1B1)	P29	30	.167	B	
		Heathcote, Clifton Earl	OF32	34	+.245	B	Chi
		Hornsby, Rogers (Rajah)	2B	154	.401	B	
0	0	Knight, Elma Russell (Jack)	P	1	.500	A	
		Lavan, John Leonard (3B5)	SS82	89	.227	B	
		Mann, Leslie	OF57	84	.347	B	
		Moore, Guy W.	OF	1	.000	A	C
		Mueller, Clarence Franklin	OF44	61	.270	B	
		McCurdy, Harry Henry (1B2)	C9	13	.296	A	
		McHenry, Austin Bush	OF61	64	.303	B	C
10	3	North, Louis Alexander	P	53	.234	B	
8	8	Pertica, Wm. Andrew (SS1)	P34	35	.181	B	
19	12	Pfeffer, Edward Joseph	P44	45	.244	B	
		Schultz, Joseph Chas.	OF89	112	.313	B	
4	2	Sell, Lester Elwood	P	7	.333	A	
17	13	Sherdel, Wm. Henry	P47	48	.193	B	
		Shotton, Burton Edwin	OF3	34	.200	B	
		Smith, John W. (Jack)	OF136	143	.309	B	
		Stock, Milton Joseph (SS1)	3B149	151	.304	B	
0	0	Stuart, John Davis	P	2	.000	A	
		Toporcer, George (Specs) (2B1 3B6 OF1)	SS91	116	.323	B	
		Vick, Henry Arthur	C	3	.333	A	
1	2	Walker, James Roy	P	12	.143	B	C

WON 79
LOST 74
TG 153

NATIONAL LEAGUE — 1923. — FINISHED 5th. — PCT. .516

ST. LOUIS

WESLEY BRANCH RICKEY

WON	LOST	NAME	POS.	G.	BA	FROM	TO
		Ainsmith, Edward Wilbur	C80	82	+.213	B	Bkn
3	3	Barfoot, Clyde Raymond	P33	37	.189	B	
		Bell, Lester Rowland	SS	15	.373	A	
		Blades, Francis Raymond (3B4)	OF83	98	.246	B	

WON	LOST	NAME	POS.	G.	BA	FROM	TO
		Bottomley, James LeRoy	1B130	134	.371	B	
		Clemons, Vernon James	C41	57	.285	B	
8	13	Doak, Wm. Leopold	P	30	.045	B	
		Douthit, Taylor Lee	OF7	9	.185	A	
2	1	Dyer, Edwin Hawley (P4)	OF8	35	.267	B	
		Flack, Max John	OF121	128	.291	B	
		Flowers, D'Arcy Raymond (Jake) (2B2 3B2)	SS7	13	.094	A	
		Freigau, Howard Earl (1B9 2B16 3B1 OF1)	SS87	113	.263	B	
20	13	Haines, Jesse Joseph (Pop)	P	37	.202	B	
		Hornsby, Rogers (Rajah) (1B10)	2B96	107	.384	B	
		Hudgens, James Price (2B1)	1B3	6	.250	A	
		Kopshaw, George Chas.	C1	2	.200	A	C
		Lavan, John Leonard (1B3 2B1 3B4)	SS40	50	.198	B	
		Mann, Leslie	OF26	38	+.371	B	Cin
		Mueller, Clarence Franklin	OF74	78	.343	B	
		Myers, Henry Harrison (Hy)	OF87	96	.300	Bkn	
		McCurdy, Harry Henry	C58	67	.265	B	
		Niebergall, Chas. Arthur	C7	9	.107	StL21	
3	4	North, Louis Alexander	P	34	.182	B	
0	0	Pertica, Wm. Andrew	P	1	.000	B	C
8	9	Pfeffer, Edward Joseph	P	26	.127	B	
		Schultz, Joseph Chas.	OF	2	.286	B	
0	1	Sell, Lester Elwood	P	5	.000	B	C
15	13	Sherdel, Wm. Henry	P39	45	.337	B	
		Shotton, Burton Edwin	OF	1	.000	B	
		Smith, John W. (Jack)	OF109	124	.310	B	
		Stock, Milton Joseph (2B1)	3B150	151	.289	B	
0	0	Stone, Wm. Arthur (P1)	OF4	5	1.000	A	C
9	5	Stuart, John Davis	P	37	.246	B	
11	12	Toney, Frederick Arthur	P	29	.116	N.Y.	C
		Toporcer, George (Specs) (1B1 SS33 3B1)	2B52	97	.254	B	
		Walker, Joseph Richard	1B	2	.286	A	C
0	0	Wiginton, Frederick Thomas	P	4	.000	A	C

WON 65 | NATIONAL LEAGUE | FINISHED 6th.
LOST 89
TG 154 | 1924. | PCT. .422

ST. LOUIS

WESLEY BRANCH RICKEY

WON	LOST	NAME	POS.	G.	BA	FROM	TO
3	8	Bell, Herman S.	P	28	.065	A	
		Bell, Lester Rowland	SS	17	.246	B	
0	0	Berly, John Chambers	P	4	.000	A	
		*Blades, Francis Raymond	OF109	131	.311	B	
		#Bottomley, James LeRoy	1B133	137	.316	B	
		Bratcher, Joseph Warlick	OF1	4	.000	A	C
		Clemons, Vernon James	C17	25	.321	B	C
		Clough, Edgar George	OF6	7	.071	A	
		Cooney, James Edward (3B7)	SS99	110	.295	N.Y.19	
1	1	Day, Clyde Henry (Pea Ridge)	P	3	.125	A	
1	0	Delaney, Arthur D.	P	8	.286	A	
7	4	Dickerman, Leo Louis	P	18	+.231	xBkn	
2	1	Doak, Wm. Leopold	P	11	+.200	B	Bkn
		Douthit, Taylor Lee	OF50	53	.277	B	
8	11	Dyer, Edwin Hawley (OF1)	P31	50	.237	B	
		Flack, Max John	OF52	67	.263	B	
1	1	Fowler, Jesse Peter	P	13	.222	A	C
		Freigau, Howard Earl (SS2)	3B98	98	.269	B	
		Gonzales, Miguel Angel Cordero	C119	120	.296	N.Y.21	
		Hafey, Chas. James (Chick)	OF	24	.253	A	
8	19	Haines, Jesse Joseph (Pop)	P	35	.189	B	
		%Holm, Roscoe Albert(Wattie)	OF64	81	.294	A	
		Hornsby, Rogers (Rajah)	2B	143	.424	B	
		@Lavan, John Leonard	SS	4	.000	B	C
		Mueller, Clarence Franklin (1B27)	OF53	92	.264	B	
		¢Myers, Henry Harrison (Hy)	OF22	43	.210	B	
		Niebergall, Chas. Arthur	C34	40	.293	B	C
0	0	North, Louis Alexander	P	9	+.111	B	Bos
4	5	Pfeffer, Edward Joseph	P	16	+.115	B	Pitt
2	2	Rhem, Chas. Flint	P	6	.167	A	
		Schultz, Joseph Chas.	OF2	12	+.167	B	Phil
		Shepherdson, Raymond Francis	C	3	.000	A	C
8	9	&Sherdel, Wm. Henry	P38	49	.200	B	
1	1	Shields, Vincent Wm.	P2	3	.400	A	C
		Smith, John W. (Jack)	OF114	124	.283	B	
10	16	Sothoron, Allen Sutton	P	29	.194	ClevA22	
9	11	Stuart, John Davis (3B1)	P28	30	.204	B	
		Thevenow, Thomas Joseph Jr.	SS	23	.202	A	
		Toporcer, George (Specs) (2B3 SS25)	3B33	70	.313	B	
		Vick, Henry Arthur	C	16	.348	StL22	
0	0	Vines, Robert Earl	P	2	.000	A	

*Blades also played 7 games at 2B and 7 games at 3B.
#Bottomley also played 1 game at 2B.
%Holm also caught 9 games and played 4 games at 3B.
@Lavan also played 2 games at 2B and 2 games at SS.
¢Myers also played 3 games at 2B and 12 games at 3B.
&Sherdel also played 2 games in the OF.

WON 77 | NATIONAL LEAGUE | FINISHED 4th.
LOST 76
TG 153 | 1925. | PCT. .503

ST. LOUIS

WESLEY BRANCH RICKEY ROGERS HORNSBY

WON	LOST	NAME	POS.	G.	BA	FROM	TO
		Bell, Lester Rowland (SS1)	3B153	153	.285	B	
		Blades, Francis Raymond (3B1)	OF114	122	.342	B	

WON	LOST	NAME	POS.	G.	BA	FROM	TO
		Bottomley, James LeRoy	1B	153	.367	B	
0	1	Clough, Edgar George	P	3	.250	B	
		Cooney, James Edward (2B15 OF1)	SS37	54	.273	B	
2	4	Day, Clyde Henry (Pea Ridge)	P	17	.154	B	
4	11	Dickerman, Leo Louis	P	29	.114	B	C
		Douthit, Taylor Lee	OF21	30	.274	B	
4	3	Dyer, Edwin Hawley	P27	31	.097	B	
		Flack, Max John	OF59	79	.249	B	C
		Freigau, Howard Earl	SS7	9	+.154	B	Chi
		Gonzales, Miguel Angel Cordero	C5	22	+.310	B	Chi
		Hafey, Chas. James (Chick)	OF88	93	.302	B	
13	14	Haines, Jesse Joseph (Pop)	P	29	.176	B	
1	0	Hallahan, Wm. Anthony (Wild Bill)	P	6	.333	A	
		Holm, Roscoe Albert (Wattie)	OF	13	.207	B	
		Hornsby, Rogers (Rajah) MGR.	2B136	138	.403	B	
7	7	Mails, John Walter (Duster)	P	21	.133	ClevA22	
		Mueller, Clarence Franklin	OF72	78	.313	B	
		Myers, Henry Harrison (Hy)	OF	1	+.000	B	Cin
				1	+1.000	recalled	C
		O'Farrell, Robert Arthur	C92	94	+.278	xChi	
0	0	Paulson, Paul Guilford	P	1	.000	A	C
11	5	Reinhart, Arthur Conrad	P20	28	.328	StL19	
8	13	Rhem, Chas. Flint	P	30	.237	B	
		Schmidt, Walter Joseph	C31	37	.253	Pitt	C
15	6	Sherdel, Wm. Henry	P32	33	.205	B	
		Shinners, Ralph Peter	OF66	74	.295	NY23	C
		Smith, John W. (Jack)	OF64	80	.251	B	
10	10	Sothoron, Allen Sutton	P	28	.196	B	
2	2	Stuart, John Davis	P	15	.250	B	C
		Thevenow, Thomas Joseph Jr.	SS	50	.269	B	
		Toporcer, George (Specs) (2B7)	SS66	83	.284	B	
		Vick, Henry Arthur	C9	14	.188	B	
		Warwick, Firmin Newton	C	13	.293	Pitt21	

WON 89 NATIONAL LEAGUE FINISHED 1st.
LOST 65
TG 154 1926. PCT. .578

ST. LOUIS

ROGERS HORNSBY

WON	LOST	NAME	POS.	G.	BA	FROM	TO
9	7	Alexander, Grover Cleveland (Pete)	P	23	+.120	xChi	
6	6	Bell, Herman S.	P	27	.120	StL24	
		Bell, Lester Rowland	3B	155	.325	B	
		Blades, Francis Raymond	OF105	107	.305	B	
		Bottomley, James LeRoy	1B	154	.299	B	
0	0	Clough, Edgar George	P	1	.000	B	C
		Douthit, Taylor Lee	OF138	139	.308	B	
1	0	Dyer, Edwin Hawley	P	6	.500	B	
		Flowers, D'Arcy Raymond (Jake)	2B11	40	.270	StL23	
		Hafey, Chas. James (Chick)	OF64	78	.271	B	
13	4	Haines, Jesse Joseph (Pop)	P	33	.213	B	
1	4	Hallahan, Wm. Anthony (Wild Bill)	P	19	.250	B	
		Holm, Roscoe Albert (Wattie)	OF39	55	.285	B	
		Hornsby, Rogers (Rajah) MGR.	2B	134	.317	B	
0	4	Huntzinger, Walter Henry	P	9	+.000	N.Y.	Chi
0	3	Johnson, Sylvester W.	P	19	.000	DetA	
10	9	Keen, Howard Victor	P	26	.057	Chi	
0	1	Mails, John Walter (Duster)	P	1	.000	B	C
		Mueller, Clarence Franklin	OF51	52	+.267	B	N.Y.
		O'Farrell, Robert Arthur	C146	147	.293	B	
10	5	Reinhart, Arthur Conrad	P27	40	.317	B	
20	7	Rhem, Chas. Flint	P	34	.188	B	
16	12	Sherdel, Wm. Henry	P34	36	.244	B	
		Smith, John W. (Jack)	OF	1	+.000	B	Bos
3	3	Sothoron, Allen Sutton	P	15	.231	B	
		Southworth, Wm. Harrison	OF	99	+.317	xN.Y.	
		Thevenow, Thomas Joseph Jr.	SS	156	.256	B	
		Toporcer, George (Specs)	2B27	64	.250	B	
		Vick, Henry Arthur	C23	24	.196	B	C
		Warwick, Firmin Newton	C	9	.357	B	C

WON 92 NATIONAL LEAGUE FINISHED 2nd.
LOST 61
TG 153 1927. PCT. .601

ST. LOUIS

ROBERT ARTHUR O'FARRELL

WON	LOST	NAME	POS.	G.	BA	FROM	TO
21	10	Alexander, Grover Cleveland (Pete)	P	37	.245	B	
1	3	Bell, Herman S.	P	25	.091	B	
		Bell, Lester Rowland (SS10)	3B100	115	.259	B	
		Blades, Francis Raymond	OF50	61	.317	B	
		Bottomley, James LeRoy	1B	152	.303	B	
		Clark, Daniel Curran	OF8	58	.236	BosA24	C
		Douthit, Taylor Lee	OF125	130	.262	B	
0	0	Dyer, Edwin Hawley	P	1	.000	B	C
5	1	Frankhouse, Frederick Meloy	P	8	.250	A	
		Frisch, Frank Francis Jr.	2B	153	.337	N.Y.	
		Hafey, Chas. James (Chick)	OF94	103	.330	B	
24	10	Haines, Jesse Joseph (Pop)	P	38	.202	B	
		Holm, Roscoe Albert (Wattie)	OF97	110	.286	B	
0	0	Johnson, Sylvester W.	P	2	.000	B	
0	0	Kaufmann, Anthony Chas. (Tony)	P	1	+.000	xPhil	
2	1	Keen, Howard Victor	P	21	.250	B	C
3	1	Littlejohn, Chas. Carlisle	P14	15	.417	A	
		Maranville, Walter James Vincent (Rabbitt)	SS	9	.241	Bkn	
4	5	McGraw, Robert Emmett	P	18	+.182	xBkn	

WON	LOST	NAME	POS.	G.	BA	FROM	TO
		O'Farrell, Robert Arthur MGR.	C53	61	.264	B	
		Orsatti, Ernest Ralph	OF26	27	.315	A	
		Peel, Homer Hefner	OF1	2	.000	A	
5	2	Reinhart, Arthur Conrad	P21	27	.313	B	
10	12	Rhem, Chas. Flint	P	27	.068	B	
0	4	Ring, James Joseph	P	13	.375	N.Y.	
		Roettger, Walter Henry	OF1	5	.000	A	
		Schang, Robert Martin	C1	3	.200	NY15	C
		Schuble, Henry George (Heinie)	SS	65	.257	A	
		Schulte, John Clement	C59	64	.288	StLA23	
17	12	Sherdel, Wm. Henry	P	39	.194	B	
		Snyder, Frank J. (Pancho)	C62	63	.258	N.Y.	C
		Southworth, Wm. Harrison	OF83	92	.301	B	
		Thevenow, Thomas Joseph Jr.	SS	59	.194	B	
		Toporcer, George (Specs) (SS27)	3B54	86	.248	B	

WON 95 — NATIONAL LEAGUE — FINISHED 1st.
LOST 59
TG 154 — 1928. — PCT. .617

ST. LOUIS

WM. BOYD McKECHNIE

WON	LOST	NAME	POS.	G.	BA	FROM	TO
16	9	Alexander, Grover Cleveland (Pete)	P	34	.291	B	
		Blades, Francis Raymond	OF19	51	.235	B	
		Bottomley, James LeRoy	1B148	149	.325	B	
		Davis, Virgil Lawrence (Spud)	C	2	+.200	A	Phil
		Douthit, Taylor Lee	OF	154	.295	B	
3	2	Frankhouse, Frederick Meloy	P21	22	.185	B	
		Frisch, Frank Francis Jr.	2B139	141	.300	B	
		Hafey, Chas. James (Chick)	OF133	138	.337	B	
2	2	Haid, Harold Augustine	P	27	.375	StLA19	
20	8	Haines, Jesse Joseph (Pop)	P	33	.184	B	
		Harper, George Washington	OF84	99	+.305	xN.Y.	
		High, Andrew Aird (2B19)	3B73	111	.285	Bos	
		Holm, Roscoe Albert (Wattie)	3B83	102	.277	B	
8	4	Johnson, Sylvester W.	P	34	.158	B	
0	0	Kaufmann, Anthony Chas. (Tony)	P	5	.000	B	
2	1	Littlejohn, Chas. Carlisle	P	12	.000	B	C
		Mancuso, August Rodney (Gus)	C	11	.184	A	
		Maranville, Walter James Vincent (Rabbitt)	SS	112	.240	B	
		Martin, John Leonard (Pepper)	OF1	39	.308	A	
8	9	Mitchell, Clarence Elmer	P	19	+.125	xPhil	
		O'Farrell, Robert Arthur	C14	16	+.212	B	N.Y.
		Orsatti, Ernest Ralph	OF17	27	.304	B	
4	6	Reinhart, Arthur Conrad	P23	27	.167	B	C
11	8	Rhem, Chas. Flint	P	28	.164	B	
		Roettger, Walter Henry	OF66	68	.341	B	
21	10	Sherdel, Wm. Henry	P	38	.226	B	
		Smith, Earl Sutton	C18	24	+.224	xPitt	
		Thevenow, Thomas Joseph Jr.	SS64	69	.205	B	
		Toporcer, George (Specs) (1B1)	2B1	8	.000	B	C
		Williamson, Nathaniel Howard Jr.		10	.222	A	C
		Wilson, James	C	120	+.258	xPhil	

WON 78 — NATIONAL LEAGUE — FINISHED 4th.
LOST 74
TG 152 — 1929. — PCT. .513

ST. LOUIS

WM. BOYD McKECHNIE — WM. HARRISON SOUTHWORTH

WON	LOST	NAME	POS.	G.	BA	FROM	TO
9	8	Alexander, Grover Cleveland (Pete)	P	22	.049	B	
0	2	Bell, Herman S.	P	7	.000	StL27	
		Bottomley, James LeRoy	1B145	146	.314	B	
		Butler, John Stephen (SS5)	3B7	17	.164	Chi	C
		Delker, Edward Albert (2B2 SS3)	3B3	22	.150	A	
1	2	Doak, Wm. Leopold	P	3	.000	Bkn	C
		Douthit, Taylor Lee	OF	150	.336	B	
7	2	Frankhouse, Frederick Meloy	P30	34	.288	B	
		Frisch, Frank Francis Jr. (3B13)	2B121	138	.334	B	
		Gelbert, Chas. Magnus	SS	146	.262	A	
0	0	Goldsmith, Harold Eugene	P	2	.000	Bos	C
3	2	Grabowski, Albert Francis	P	6	.250	A	
		Hafey, Chas. James (Chick)	OF130	134	.339	B	
9	9	Haid, Harold Augustine	P	38	.082	B	
13	10	Haines, Jesse Joseph (Pop)	P	28	.159	B	
4	4	Hallahan, Wm. Anthony (Wild Bill)	P	23	.154	StL26	
		Haney, Fred Girard	3B	10	.115	Chi27	
		High, Andrew Aird (2B22)	3B123	146	.295	B	
0	0	Hill, Carmen Proctor	P	3	+.000	xPitt	
0	1	Holland, Howard Arthur	P	8	.250	N.Y.27	C
		Holm, Roscoe Albert (Wattie)	OF44	64	.233	B	
13	7	Johnson, Sylvester W.	P	42	.117	B	
		Jonnard, Clarence James	C	18	.097	Phil27	
1	1	Lindsey, James Kendrick	P	2	.200	ClevA24	
8	11	Mitchell, Clarence Elmer	P25	26	.273	B	
		Orsatti, Ernest Ralph (1B10)	OF77	113	.332	B	
		Roettger, Walter Henry	OF69	79	.253	B	
		Selph, Carey Isom	2B16	25	.235	A	
10	15	Sherdel, Wm. Henry	P	33	.229	B	
		Smith, Earl Sutton	C50	57	.345	B	
		Southworth, Wm. Harrison MGR.	OF	19	.188	StL27	
		Wilson, James	C119	120	.325	B	

WON 92 | NATIONAL LEAGUE | FINISHED 1st.
LOST 62
TG 154 | 1930. | PCT. .597

ST. LOUIS

CHAS. EVARD STREET

WON	LOST	NAME	POS.	G.	BA	FROM	TO
		Adams, Earl John (Sparky) (2B25)	3B104	137	.314	Pitt	
4	3	Bell, Herman S.	P	39	.077	B	
		Blades, Francis Raymond	OF32	45	.396	StL28	
		Bottomley, James LeRoy	1B124	131	.304	B	
1	0	Dean, Jay Hanna (Dizzy)	P	1	.333	A	
		Douthit, Taylor Lee	OF	154	.303	B	
		Farrell, Edward Stephen	SS15	23	+.213	N.Y.	Chi
		Fisher, George Aloys	OF67	92	.374	WashA24	
2	3	Frankhouse, Frederick Meloy	P8	9	+.000	B	Bos
		Frisch, Frank Francis Jr. (3B10)	2B123	133	.346	B	
		Gelbert, Chas. Magnus	SS	139	.304	B	
6	4	Grabowski, Albert Francis	P33	35	.364	B	C
13	6	Grimes, Burleigh Arland	P22	23	+.263	xBos.	
		Hafey, Chas. James (Chick)	OF116	120	.336	B	
3	2	Haid, Harold Augustine	P20	21	.000	B	
13	8	Haines, Jesse Joseph (Pop)	P	29	.246	B	
15	9	Hallahan, Wm. Anthony (Wild Bill)	P	35	.123	B	
		High, Andrew Aird	3B48	72	.279	B	
0	1	Hill, Carmen Proctor	P	4	.333	B	C
12	10	Johnson, Sylvester W.	P	32	.214	B	
0	1	Kaufmann, Anthony Chas. (Tony)	P	2	.333	N.Y.	
7	5	Lindsey, James Kendrick	P	39	.286	B	
		Mancuso, August Rodney (Gus)	C61	76	.366	StL28	
		Martin, John Leonard (Pepper)	OF	6	.000	StL28	
1	0	Mitchell, Clarence Elmer	P	1	+.500	B	N.Y.
		Orsatti, Ernest Ralph (OF11)	1B22	48	.321	B	
		Peel, Homer Hefner	OF21	26	.164	Phil	
		Puccinelli, George Lawrence	OF2	11	.563	A	
12	8	Rhem, Chas. Flint	P	26	.231	StL28	
3	2	Sherdel, Wm. Henry	P	13	+.105	B	Bos
		Smith, Earl Sutton	C2	8	.000	B	C
		Watkins, George Archibald (1B13)	OF89	119	.373	A	
		Wilson, James	C99	107	.318	B	

WON 101 | NATIONAL LEAGUE | FINISHED 1st.
LOST 53
TG 154 | 1931. | PCT. .656

ST. LOUIS

CHAS. EVARD STREET

WON	LOST	NAME	POS.	G.	BA	FROM	TO
		Adams, Earl John (Sparky)	3B138	143	.293	B	
		Benes, Joseph Anthony (2B2 3B1)	SS2	10	.167	A	C
		Blades, Francis Raymond	OF20	35	.284	B	
		Bottomley, James LeRoy	1B93	108	.348	B	
		Collins, James Anthony (Rip)	1B68	89	.301	A	
		Cunningham, Raymond Lee	3B2	3	.000	A	
		Delker, Edward Albert	3B	1	.500	StL29	
18	8	Derringer, Samuel Paul	P	35	.097	A	
		Douthit, Taylor Lee	OF	36	+.331	B	Cin
		Flowers, D'Arcy Raymond (Jake) (2B20)	SS25	45	+.248	xBkn	
		Frisch, Frank Francis Jr.	2B129	131	.311	B	
		Gelbert, Chas. Magnus	SS130	131	.289	B	
		Gonzales, Miguel Angel Cordero	C12	15	.105	Chi29	
17	9	Grimes, Burleigh Arland	P	29	.184	B	
		Hafey, Chas. James (Chick)	OF118	122	.349	B	
12	3	Haines, Jesse Joseph (Pop)	P	19	.133	B	
19	9	Hallahan, Wm. Anthony (Wild Bill)	P	37	.099	B	
		High, Andrew Aird (2B19)	3B23	63	.267	B	
		Hunt, Oliver Joel	OF1	4	.000	A	
11	9	Johnson, Sylvester W.	P	32	.233	B	
1	1	Kaufmann, Anthony Chas. (Tony)	P15	20	.111	B	
6	4	Lindsey, James Kendrick	P	35	.111	B	
		Mancuso, August Rodney (Gus)	C56	67	.262	B	
		Martin, John Leonard (Pepper)	OF110	123	.300	B	
		Orsatti, Ernest Ralph	OF45	70	.291	B	
11	10	Rhem, Chas. Flint	P	33	.130	B	
		Roettger, Walter Henry	OF42	45	+.285	xCin	
6	0	Stout, Allyn McClelland	P	30	.105	A	
		Street, Chas. Evard (Gabby) MGR.	C	1	.000	B	
		Watkins, George Archibald	OF129	131	.288	B	
		Wilson, James	C110	115	.274	B	

WON 72 | NATIONAL LEAGUE | FINISHED 6th. (TIED WITH N.Y.)
LOST 82
TG 154 | 1932. | PCT. .468

ST. LOUIS

CHAS. EVARD STREET

WON	LOST	NAME	POS.	G.	BA	FROM	TO
		Adams, Earl John (Sparky)	3B30	31	.276	B	
		Blades, Francis Raymond	OF62	80	.229	B	
		Bottomley, James LeRpy	1B74	91	.296	B	
		Bressler, Raymond Bloom (Rube)	OF4	10	+.158	xPhil	C
10	13	Carleton, James Otto (Tex)	P	44	.150	A	

WON	LOST	NAME	POS.	G.	BA	FROM	TO
		Collins, James Anthony (Rip) (OF60)	1B81	149	.279	B	
		Cunningham, Raymond Lee (2B1)	3B3	11	.182	B	C
18	15	Dean, Jay Hanna (Dizzy)	P46	47	.258	StL30	
		DeLancey, Wm. Pinkney	C	8	.192	A	
		Delker, Edward Albert	2B10	20	+.119	B	Phil
11	14	Derringer, Samuel Paul	P	39	.178	B	
		Flowers, D'Arcy Raymond (Jake)	3B54	67	.255	B	
		Ford, Horace Hills	SS	1	+.000	Cin	Bos
0	2	Frey, Benjamin Rudolph	P	2	+.000	Cin	Cin
		Frisch, Frank Francis Jr. (3B37)	2B75	115	.292	B	
		Gelbert, Chas. Magnus	SS	122	.268	B	
		Gonzales, Miguel Angel Cordero	C	17	.143	B	
3	5	Haines, Jesse Joseph (Pop)	P	20	.185	B	
12	7	Hallahan, Wm. Anthony (Wild Bill)	P25	28	.214	B	
		Hendrick, Harvey (Gink)	3B12	28	+.250	Cin	Cin
		Holm, Roscoe Albert (Wattie)	OF3	11	.176	StL29	C
		Hunt, Oliver Joel	OF5	12	.190	B	C
5	14	Johnson, Sylvester W.	P	32	.196	B	
3	3	Lindsey, James Kendrick	P	33	.143	B	
		Mancuso, August Rodney (Gus)	C82	103	.284	B	
		Martin, John Leonard (Pepper) (3B15)	OF69	85	.238	B	
		Medwick, Joseoh Michael (Ducky)	OF	26	.349	A	
		Orsatti, Ernest Ralph	OF96	101	.336	B	
		Pepper, Raymond Watson	OF17	21	.246	A	
		Puccinelli, George Lawrence	OF30	31	.278	StL30	
		Reese, James Hymie	2B77	90	.265	NYA	C
4	2	Rhem, Chas. Flint	P	6	+.188	B	Phil
0	0	Sherdel, Wm. Henry	P	3	+1.000	xBos	C
1	1	Starr, Raymond Francis	P	3	.250	A	
4	5	Stout, Allyn McClelland	P	36	.100	B	
0	0	Teachout, Arthur John	P	1	.000	Chi	C
0	0	Terwilliger, Richard Martin	P	1	.000	A	C
		Watkins, George Archibald	OF120	127	.312	B	
		Webb, James LeVerne (Skeeter)	SS	1	.000	A	
		Wilson, Chas. Woodrow	SS	24	.198	Bos	
		Wilson, James	C75	92	.248	B	
1	1	Winford, James Harold	P	4	.667	A	

WON 82 NATIONAL LEAGUE FINISHED 5th.
LOST 71
TG 153 1933. PCT. .536

ST. LOUIS

CHAS. EVARD STREET FRANK FRANCIS FRISCH JR.

WON	LOST	NAME	POS.	G.	BA	FROM	TO
		Adams, Earl John (Sparky) (3B3)	SS5	8	+.167	B	Cin
17	11	Allen, Ethan Nathan	OF67	91	.241	N.Y.	
		Carleton, James Otto (Tex)	P44	46	.187	B	
		Collins, James Anthony (Rip)	1B123	132	.310	B	
		Crabtree, Estel Crayton	OF5	23	.265	Cin	
		Crawford, Clifford Rankin (2B15 3B7)	1B29	91	.268	Cin30	
20	18	Dean, Jay Hanna (Dizzy)	P48	51	.181	B	
0	2	Derringer, Samuel Paul	P	3	+.000	B	Cin
		Durocher, Leo Ernest	SS	123	+.258	xCin	
		Frisch, Frank Francis Jr. MGR. (SS15)	2B132	147	.303	B	
0	1	Grimes, Burleigh Arland	P	4	+.200	xChi	
9	6	Haines, Jesse Joseph (Pop)	P32	33	.067	B	
16	13	Hallahan, Wm. Anthony (Wild Bill)	P36	37	.150	B	
		Hornsby, Rogers (Rajah)	2B17	46	.325	Chi	StLA
3	3	Johnson, Sylvester W.	P	35	.238	B	
		Lewis, Wm. Henry	C	15	.400	A	
0	0	Lindsey, James Kendrick	P	1	.000	B	
		Martin, John Leonard (Pepper)	3B	145	.316	B	
		Medwick, Joseph Michael (Ducky)	OF147	148	.306	B	
2	5	Mooney, Jim Irving	P	21	.050	N.Y.	
		Moore, Eugene Jr. (Gene)	OF10	11	.395	Cin31	
		O'Farrell, Robert Arthur	C50	55	.239	N.Y.	
		Orsatti, Ernest Ralph (1B3)	OF107	120	.298	B	
		Pepper, Raymond Watson	OF	3	.222	B	
		Slade, Gordon Leigh (2B1)	SS31	39	.113	Bkn	
		Sprinz, Joseph Conrad	C	3	.200	ClevA31	C
0	0	Stout, Allyn McClelland	P	1	+.000	B	Cin
6	2	Vance, Clarence Arthur (Dazzy)	P	28	.179	Bkn	
9	10	Walker, Wm. Henry	P	29	.132	N.Y.	
		Watkins, George Archibald	OF135	138	.278	B	
		Whitehead, Burgess Urquhart (Whitey) (2B3)	SS9	12	.286	A	
		Wilson, Chas. Woodrow	SS	1	.000	B	
		Wilson, James	C107	113	.255	B	

WON 95 NATIONAL LEAGUE FINISHED 1st.
LOST 58
TG 153 1934. PCT. .621

ST. LOUIS

FRANK FRANCIS FRISCH JR.

WON	LOST	NAME	POS.	G.	BA	FROM	TO
16	11	Carleton, James Otto (Tex)	P40	41	.193	B	
		Collins, James Anthony (Rip)	1B	154	.333	B	
		Crawford, Clifford Rankin (3B2)	2B3	61	.271	B	C
		Davis, George Willis (Kiddo)	OF9	16	+.303	N.Y.	Phil
		Davis, Virgil Lawrence (Spud)	C94	107	.300	Phil	
30	7	Dean, Jay Hanna (Dizzy)	P	51	.246	B	
19	11	Dean, Paul Dee (Daffy)	P	39	.241	A	

WON	LOST	NAME	POS.	G.	BA	FROM	TO
		DeLancey, Wm. Pinkney	C77	93	.316	StL32	
		Durocher, Leo Ernest	SS	146	.260	B	
		Frisch, Frank Francis Jr. MGR. (3B25)	2B115	140	.305	B	
		Fullis, Chas. Philip (Chick)	OF56	69	+.261	xPhil	
2	1	Grimes, Burleigh Arland	P	4	+.000	B	Pitt
4	4	Haines, Jesse Joseph (Pop)	P	37	.158	B	
8	12	Hallahan, Wm. Anthony (Wild Bill)	P	32	.182	B	
		Healey, Francis Jeremiah	C1	15	.308	NY32	C
0	0	Heise, Clarence Edward	P	1	.000	A	C
0	1	Lindsey, James Kendrick	P	11	+.000	xCin	
0	0	Martin, John Leonard (Pepper) (P1)	3B107	110	.289	B	
		Medwick, Joseph Michael (Ducky)	OF	149	.319	B	
		Mills, Colonel Buster	OF18	29	.236	A	
2	4	Mooney, Jim Irving	P	32	.053	B	C
		Moore, Eugene Jr. (Gene)	OF	9	.278	B	
		Orsatti, Ernest Ralph	OF90	105	.300	B	
1	0	Rhem, Chas. Flint	P	5	+.000	Phil	Bos
		Riggs, Lewis Sidney (Lew)		2	.000	A	
		Rothrock, John Huston	OF	154	.284	ChiA32	
1	1	Vance, Clarence Arthur (Dazzy)	P	19	+.133	xCin	
12	4	Walker, Wm. Henry	P	24	.093	B	
		Whitehead, Burgess Urquhart (Whitey) (SS29 3B28)	2B48	100	.277	B	
0	2	Winford, James Harold	P	5	.000	StL32	
		Worthington, Robert Lee		1	+.000	xBos	C

WON 96
LOST 58
TG 154

NATIONAL LEAGUE

1935.

FINISHED 2nd.

PCT. .623

ST. LOUIS

FRANK FRANCIS FRISCH JR.

WON	LOST	NAME	POS.	G.	BA	FROM	TO
		Collins, James Anthony (Rip)	1B	150	.313	B	
7	6	Collins, Philip Eugene	P	26	+.160	xPhil	C
0	0	Copeland, Mays	P	1	.000	A	C
		Davis, Virgil Lawrence (Spud) (1B5)	C81	102	.317	B	
28	12	Dean, Jay Hanna (Dizzy)	P50	53	.234	B	
19	12	Dean, Paul Dee (Daffy)	P	46	.133	B	
		DeLancey, Wm. Pinkney	C83	103	.279	B	
		Durocher, Leo Ernest	SS142	143	.265	B	
0	0	Eckert, Albert George	P	2	.000	Cin31	C
		Frisch, Frank Francis Jr. MGR. (3B5)	2B89	103	.294	B	
		Gelbert, Chas. Magnus (2B3 SS21)	3B37	62	.292	StL32	
6	5	Haines, Jesse Joseph (Pop)	P	30	.273	B	
15	8	Hallahan, Wm. Anthony (Wild Bill)	P	40	.143	B	

WON	LOST	NAME	POS.	G.	BA	FROM	TO
1	1	Harrell, Raymond James (Ray)	P	11	.000	A	
5	5	Heusser, Edward Burlton	P	33	.118	A	
		Judy, Lyle LeRoy	2B5	8	.000	A	C
0	0	Kaufmann, Anthony Chas. (Tony)	P	7	.000	StL31	C
		King, Lynn Paul	OF	8	.182	A	
0	0	Kleinke, Norbert George	P	4	.000	A	
		Martin, John Leonard (Pepper) (OF16)	3B114	135	.299	B	
		Medwick, Joseph Michael (Ducky)	OF	154	.353	B	
		Moore, Eugene Jr. (Gene)		3	.000	B	
		Moore, Terry Buford (Bill)	OF117	119	.287	A	
1	0	McGee, Wm. Henry (B ill)	P	1	.333	A	
		Narron, Samuel	C1	4	.429	A	
		O'Farrell, Robert Arthur	C8	14	.000	Chi	C
		Orsatti, Ernest Ralph	OF60	90	.240	B	C
		Rothrock, John Huston	OF127	129	.273	B	
1	1	Ryba, Dominic Joseph (Mike)	P	2	.400	A	
0	0	Tinning, Lyle Forrest	P	4	.000	Chi	C
13	8	Walker, Wm. Henry	P37	38	.102	B	
0	0	Ward, Richard O.	P	1	.000	Chi	C
		Whitehead, Burgess Urquhart (Whitey) (SS6 3B8)	2B80	107	.263	B	
		Wilson, Chas. Woodrow	3B8	16	.323	StL33	C
0	0	Winford, James Harold	P	2	.000	B	
		Winsett, John Thomas (Tom)	OF2	7	.500	BosA33	

WON 87
LOST 67
TG 154

NATIONAL LEAGUE

1936.

FINISHED 2nd.
(TIED WITH CHI.)
PCT. .565

ST. LOUIS

FRANK FRANCIS FRISCH JR.

WON	LOST	NAME	POS.	G.	BA	FROM	TO
		Alston, Walter Emmons	1B	1	.000	A	C
		Ankenman, Frederick Norman Jr. (Pat)	SS	1	.000	A	
		Collins, James Anthony (Rip)	1B61	103	.292	B	
0	0	Cox, Wm. Donald	P	2	.000	A	
		Davis, Virgil Lawrence (Spud)	C103	112	.273	B	
24	13	Dean, Jay Hanna (Dizzy)	P	51	.223	B	
5	5	Dean, Paul Dee (Daffy)	P	17	.059	B	
		Durocher, Leo Ernest	SS	136	.286	B	
2	1	Earnshaw, George Livingston (Moose)	P	20	+.222	xBkn	C
		Frisch, Frank Francis Jr. MGR. (3B22)	2B60	93	.274	B	
		Fullis, Chas. Philip (Chick)	OF26	47	.281	StL34	C
		Garibaldi, Arthur E. (2B24)	3B46	71	.276	A	C
		Gelbert, Chas. Magnus (SS28)	3B60	93	.229	B	
		Gutteridge, Donald Joseph	3B23	23	.319	A	

7	5	Haines, Jesse Joseph (Pop)	P	25	.167	B	
2	2	Hallahan, Wm. Anthony (Wild Bill)	P	9	+.556	B	Cin
7	3	Heusser, Edward Burlton	P	42	.269	B	
5	3	Johnson, Silas Kenneth	P	12	+.190	xCin	
		King, Lynn Paul	OF34	78	.190	B	
0	0	Martin, John Leonard (Pepper) (P1 3B15)	OF127	143	.309	B	
		Martin, Stuart McGuire (Stu)	2B83	92	.298	A	
		Medwick, Joseph Michael (Ducky)	OF	155	.351	B	
		Mize, John Robert	1B97	126	.329	A	
		Moore, Terry Buford	OF133	143	.264	B	
		Morgan, Edwin Willis	OF4	8	.278	A	
0	3	Munns, Leslie Ernest	P	8	.111	Bkn	C
1	1	McGee, Wm. Henry (Bill)	P	7	.250	B	
		Ogrodowski, Ambrose Francis	C85	94	.228	A	
11	11	Parmelee, LeRoy Earl	P	37	.197	N.Y.	
0	2	Pippen, Henry Harold (Cotton)	P	6	.167	A	
0	0	Potter, Nelson Thomas	P	1	.000	A	
2	1	Rhem, Chas. Flint	P	10	.125	Bos	C
5	1	Ryba, Dominic Joseph (Mike)	P14	18	.167	B	
		Schuble, Henry George (Heinie)	3B1	2	.000	DetA	C
		Scoffic, Louis	OF3	4	.429	A	C
		Vergez, John Louis	3B	8	+.167	xPhil	C
5	6	Walker, Wm. Henry	P21	22	.280	B	C
11	10	Winford, James Harold	P	39	.085	B	

WON 81x
LOST 73
TG 154

NATIONAL LEAGUE — 1937. — FINISHED 4th. — PCT. .526

ST. LOUIS

FRANK FRANCIS FRISCH JR.

WON	LOST	NAME	POS.	G.	BA	FROM	TO
0	0	Andrews, Nathan Hardy	P	4	.000	A	
0	3	Blake, John Frederick (Sheriff)	P	14	.300	xStLA	C
		Bordagaray, Stanley George (OF27)	3B50	96	.293	Bkn	
		Bremer, Herbert T. Frederick	C10	11	.212	A	
		Brown, James Roberson (SS25)	2B112	138	.276	A	
0	0	Chambers, John Monroe	P	2	.000	A	C
13	10	Dean, Jay Hanna (Dizzy)	P	27	.227	B	
0	0	Dean, Paul Dee (Daffy)	P	1	.000	B	
		Durocher, Leo Ernest	SS134	135	.203	B	
		Frisch, Frank Francis Jr. MGR.	2B	17	.219	B	
		Gutteridge, Donald Joseph	3B105	119	.271	B	
3	3	Haines, Jesse Joseph (Pop)	P	16	.182	B	C
3	7	Harrell, Raymond James (Ray)	P	35	.045	StL35	
12	12	Johnson, Silas Kenneth	P	38	.138	B	
1	1	Kleinke, Norbert George	P	5	.000	StL35	C
3	1	Krist, Howard Wilbur	P	6	.000	A	
		Martin, John Leonard (Pepper)	OF82	98	.304	B	
		Martin, Stuart McGuire (Stu)	2B48	90	.260	B	
		Medwick, Joseph Michael (Ducky)	OF	156	.374	B	
		Mize, John Robert	1B144	145	.364	B	
		Moore, Randolph Edward (Randy)	OF1	8	+.000	xBkn	C
		Moore, Terry Buford	OF108	115	.267	B	
1	0	McGee, Wm. Henry (Bill)	P	4	.200	B	
		Ogrodowski, Ambrose Francis	C87	90	.233	B	C
		Owen, Arnold Malcolm (Mickey)	C78	80	.231	A	
		Padgett, Donald Wilson (Don)	OF109	123	.314	A	
9	6	Ryba, Dominic Joseph (Mike)	P38	41	.313	B	
		Siebert, Richard Walther (Dick)	1B	22	.184	Bkn	
0	0	Sunkel, Thomas Jacob	P	9	.111	A	
18	11	Warneke, Lonnie	P	36	.263	Chi	
15	14	Weiland, Robert George (Bob)	P	41	.169	StLA35	
2	4	Winford, James Harold	P	16	.125	B	
0	1	White, Adell Abe	P	5	1.000	A	C

xOne Game by Forfeit.

WON 71
LOST 80
TG 151

NATIONAL LEAGUE — 1938. — FINISHED 6th. — PCT. .470

ST. LOUIS

FRANK FRANCIS FRISCH JR. MIGUEL ANGEL CORDERO GONZALEZ

WON	LOST	NAME	POS.	G.	BA	FROM	TO
		Bordagaray, Stanley George	OF29	81	.282	B	
		Bremer, Herbert T. Frederick	C	50	.219	B	
		Brown, James Roberson (SS30 3B24)	2B49	108	.301	B	
		Bucher, James Quinter	2B14	17	.228	Bkn	
0	1	Bush, Guy Terrell	P	6	.000	Bos	
2	1	Cooper, Morton Cecil	P	4	.222	A	
		Crespi, Frank Angelo Joseph (Creepy)	SS	7	.263	A	
12	8	Davis, Curtis Benton (Curt)	P	40	.228	Chi	
3	1	Dean, Paul Dee (Daffy)	P	5	.182	B	
		Epps, Harold Franklin	OF10	17	.300	A	
		Gutteridge, Donald Joseph (SS68)	3B73	142	.255	B	
2	3	Harrell, Raymond James (Ray)	P	32	.000	B	
5	11	Henshaw, Roy John	P	27	.220	Bkn	
0	3	Johnson, Silas Kenneth	P	6	.000	B	
0	0	Krist, Howard Wilbur	P	2	.000	B	
0	3	Lanier, Hubert Max	P	18	.100	A	
4	11	Macon, Max Cullen	P38	46	.306	A	
		Martin, John Leonard (Pepper)	OF62	91	.294	B	
		Martin, Stuart McGuire (Stu)	2B99	114	.278	B	
		Medwick, Joseph Michael (Ducky)	OF144	146	.322	B	
		Mize, John Robert	1B140	149	.337	B	
		Moore, Terry Buford	OF75	94	.272	B	

WON	LOST	NAME	POS.	G.	BA	FROM	TO
		Myers, Lynnwood Lincoln	SS69	70	.242	A	
7	12	McGee, Wm. Henry (Bill)	P	47	.209	B	
		Owen, Arnold Malcolm (Mickey)	C116	122	.267	B	
		Padgett, Donald Wilson (Don) (1B16)	OF71	110	.271	B	
0	0	Roe, Elwin Chas.	P	1	.000	A	
1	1	Ryba, Dominic Joseph (Mike)	P	3	.000	B	
6	6	Shoun, Clyde Mitchell	P	40	.258	Chi	
		Siebert, Richard Walther (Dick)		1	1.000	B	PhilA
		Slaughter, Enos Bradsher (Country)	OF92	112	.276	A	
		Stainback, George Tucker (Tuck)	OF2	6	+.000	Chi	Phil
		Stripp, Joseph Valentine	3B51	54	+.286	Bkn	Bos
13	8	Warneke, Lonnie	P	31	.324	B	
16	11	Weiland, Robert George (Bob)	P	35	.138	B	

WON 92
LOST 61
TG 153

NATIONAL LEAGUE

1939.

FINISHED 2nd.

PCT. .601

ST. LOUIS

FRANCIS RAYMOND BLADES

WON	LOST	NAME	POS.	G.	BA	FROM	TO
		Adams, Elvin Clark		2	.000	A	
1	2	Andrews, Nathan Hardy	P	11	.000	StL37	
0	1	Barrett, Francis Joseph	P	1	.000	A	
13	5	Bowman, Robert James (Bob)	P	51	.085	A	
		Bremer, Herbert T. Frederick	C	9	.111	B	C
		Brown, James Roberson (2B50)	SS104	147	.298	B	
12	6	Cooper, Morton Cecil	P45	47	.232	B	
		Crespi, Frank Angelo Joseph (Creepy)		15	.172	B	
22	16	Davis, Curtis Benton (Curt)	P49	63	.381	B	
0	1	Dean, Paul Dee (Daffy)	P	16	.111	B	
0	0	Dickson, Murry Monroe	P	1	.000	A	
		Echols, John Gresham	2B	2	.000	A	C
		Franks, Herman Louis	C13	17	.059	A	
		Gutteridge, Donald Joseph	3B143	148	.269	B	
		Hopp, John Leonard	1B2	6	.500	A	
		King, Lynn Paul	OF44	89	.235	StL36	C
		Lake, Edward Erving	SS2	2	.250	A	
2	1	Lanier, Hubert Max	P	7	.286	B	
		Lary, Lynford Hobart (Lyn) (3B3)	SS30	34	+.187	xBkn	
		Martin, John Leonard (Pepper) (3B22)	OF51	88	.306	B	
		Martin, Stuart McGuire (Stu)	2B107	120	.268	B	
		Medwick, Joseph Michael (Ducky)	OF149	150	.332	B	
		Mize, John Robert	1B152	153	.349	B	
0	0	Moore, Terry Buford (Pl)	OF121	130	.295	B	
		Myers, Lynnwood Lincoln (3B13)	SS36	74	.239	B	C

WON	LOST	NAME	POS.	G.	BA	FROM	TO
12	5	McGee, Wm. Henry (Bill)	P	43	.145	B	
		Orengo, Joseph Chas.	SS	7	.000	A	
		Owen, Arnold Malcolm (Mickey)	C126	131	.259	B	
		Padgett, Donald Wilson (Don)	C61	92	.399	B	
0	0	Raffensberger, Kenneth David	P	1	.000	A	
		Repass, Robert Willis	2B2	3	.333	A	
3	1	Shoun, Clyde Mitchell	P	53	.115	B	
		Slaughter, Enos Bradsher (Country)	OF	149	.320	B	
4	4	Sunkel, Thomas Jacob	P	20	.321	StL37	
13	7	Warnede, Lonnie	P	34	.192	B	
10	12	Weiland, Robert George (Bob)	P	32	.065	B	

WON 84
LOST 69
TG 153

NATIONAL LEAGUE

1940.

FINISHED 3rd.

PCT. .549

ST. LOUIS

FRANCIS RAYMOND BLADES MIGUEL ANGEL CORDERO GONZALEZ
WM. HARRISON SOUTHWORTH

WON	LOST	NAME	POS.	G.	BA	FROM	TO
7	5	Bowman, Robert James (Bob)	P	28	.061	B	
0	0	Brecheen, Harry David	P	3	.000	A	
		Brown, James Roberson (SS28 3B41)	2B48	107	.280	B	
11	12	Cooper, Morton Cecil	P38	38	.157	B	
		Cooper, Wm. Walker 3B2	C	6	.316	A	
		Crespi, Frank Angelo Joseph (Creepy) (SS1)	3B2	3	.273	B	
0	4	Davis, Curtis Benton (Curt)	P	14	+.000	B	Bkn
		DeLancey, Wm. Pinkney	C12	15	.222	StL35	C
0	0	Dickson, Murry Monroe	P	1	.000	B	
3	3	Doyle, Wm. Carl	P	21	+.200	xBkn	C
		Epps, Harold Franklin	OF3	11	.200	StL38	
		Gillenwater, Carden Edison	OF	7	.160	A	
		Gutteridge, Donald Joseph	3B39	69	.269	B	
		Hopp, John Leonard (1B10)	OF39	80	.270	B	
4	2	Hutchinson, Ira Kendall	P	20	.222	Bkn	
		Jones, Maurice Morris	OF1	12	.091	A	C
1	0	Kimball, Newell W.	P	2	+.333	xBkn	
		Koy, Ernest Anyz (Chief)	OF91	93	+.310	xBkn	
		Lake, Edward Erving (SS6)	2B17	32	.212	B	
9	6	Lanier, Hubert Max	P	35	.200	B	
0	1	Lillard, Robert Eugene	P	2	.000	Chi	C
		Marion, Martin Whitford	SS	125	.278	A	
		Martin, John Leonard (Pepper) (3B2)	OF63	86	.316	B	
		Martin, Stuart McGuire (Stu) (2B33)	3B73	112	.238	B	
		Medwick, Joseph Michael (Ducky)	OF	37	+.304	B	Bkn
		Mize, John Robert	1B153	155	.314	B	
		Moore, Terry Buford	OF133	136	.304	B	
16	10	McGee, Wm. Henry (Bill)	P	38	.178	B	

WON	LOST	NAME	POS.	G.	BA	FROM	TO
		Orengo, Joseph Chas. (SS19 3B34)	2B77	129	.287	B	
		Owen, Arnold Malcolm (Mickey)	C113	117	.264	B	
		Padgett, Donald Wilson (Don) (1B2)	C72	93	.242	B	
3	4	Russell, Jack Erwin	P	26	.000	Chi	C
13	11	Shoun, Clyde Mitchell	P	54	.190	B	
		Slaughter, Enos Bradshaw (Country)	OF132	140	.306	B	
		Walker, Harry Wm.	OF	7	.185	A	
16	10	Warneke, Lonnie	P	33	.209	B	
0	0	Weiland, Robert George (Bob)	P	1	.000	B	C
1	1	White, Ernest Daniel	P8	9	.429	A	

WON 97 LOST 56 TG 153 — NATIONAL LEAGUE — FINISHED 2nd.

1941. — PCT. .634

ST. LOUIS

WM. HARRISON SOUTHWORTH

WON	LOST	NAME	POS.	G.	BA	FROM	TO
1	0	Beazley, John Andrew	P	1	.000	A	
		Brown, James Roberson (2B11)	3B123	132	.306	B	
13	9	Cooper, Morton Cecil	P	29	.186	B	
		Cooper, Wm. Walker	C63	68	.245	B	
		Crabtree, Estel Crayton (3B1)	OF50	77	.341	StL33	
		Crespi, Frank Angelo Joseph	2B145	146	.279	B	
1	2	Crouch, Wm. Elmer	P	18	+.000	xPhil	
		Dusak, Ervin Frank	OF4	6	.143	A	
1	0	Gornicki, Henry Frank	P	4	+.250	A	Chi
2	1	Grodzicki, John	P	5	.000	A	
11	5	Gumbert, Harry Edward	P33	34	+.321	xN.Y.	
		Hopp, John Leonard (1B39)	OF91	134	.303	B	
1	5	Hutchinson, Ira Kendall	P	29	.250	B	
		Koy, Ernest Anyz (Chief)	OF12	13	+.200	B	Cin
10	0	Krist, Howard Wilbur	P	37	.237	StL38	
		Kurowski, George John	3B4	5	.333	A	
		Lake, Edward Erving (2B5 3B15)	SS15	45	.105	B	
10	8	Lanier, Hubert Max	P	35	.192	B	
0	0	Lyons, Herschel Englebert	P	1	.000	A	C
		Mancuso, August Rodney (Gus)	C105	106	.229	Bkn	
		Marion, Martin Whitford	SS	155	.252	B	
		Marshall, Chas. Anthony	C	1	.000	A	C
		Mesner, Stephan Mathias (Steve)	3B22	24	.145	Chi39	
		Mize, John Robert	1B122	126	.317	B	
		Moore, Terry Buford	OF121	122	.294	B	
		Musial, Stanley Frank	OF11	12	.426	A	
0	1	McGee, Wm. Henry (Bill)	P	4	+.000	B	N.Y.
5	2	Nahem, Samuel Ralph	P	26	.174	Bkn38	

WON	LOST	NAME	POS.	G.	BA	FROM	TO
		Padgett, Donald Wilson (Don) (C18 1B2)	OF62	107	.247	B	
5	2	Pollet, Howard Joseph	P	9	.179	A	
		Sessi, Walter Anthony	OF3	5	.000	A	
3	5	Shoun, Clyde Mitchell	P	26	.182	B	
		Slaughter, Enos Bradsher (Country)	OF108	113	.311	B	
		Triplett, Herman Coaker	OF46	76	.286	Chi38	
		Walker, Harry Wm.	OF5	7	.267	B	
17	9	Warneke, Lonnie	P	37	.117	B	
17	7	White, Ernest Daniel	P32	33	.190	B	
		Young, Lemuel Floyd (Pep)		2	+.000	xCin	

WON 106 LOST 48 TG 154 — NATIONAL LEAGUE — FINISHED 1st.

1942. — PCT. .688

ST. LOUIS

WM. HARRISON SOUTHWORTH

WON	LOST	NAME	POS.	G.	BA	FROM	TO
21	6	Beazley, John Andrew	P	43	.137	B	
1	0	Beckmann, Wm. Aloysius	P	2	.000	xPhilA	C
		Blattner, Robert Garnett (2B3)	SS13	19	.043	A	
		Brown, James Roberson (SS12 3B66)	2B82	145	.256	B	
22	7	Cooper, Morton Cecil	P	37	.184	B	
		Cooper, Wm. Walker	C115	125	.281	B	
		Crabtree, Estel Crayton		10	.333	B	
		Crespi, Frank Angelo Joseph (Creepy) (SS5)	2B83	93	.243	B	C
		Cross, Joffre James	SS	1	.250	A	
6	3	Dickson, Murry Monroe	P36	37	.190	StL40	
		Dusak, Ervin Frank (3B1)	OF8	12	.185	B	
9	5	Gumbert, Harry Edward	P	38	.111	B	
		Hopp, John Leonard	1B88	95	.258	B	
13	3	Krist, Howard Wilbur	P34	35	.143	B	
		Kurowski, George John (SS1 OF1)	3B104	115	.254	B	
13	8	Lanier, Hubert Max	P	34	.255	B	
1	1	Lohrman, Wm. LeRoy (Bill)	P	5	+.667	N.Y.	N.Y.
		Mancuso, August Rodney (Gus)	C3	5	+.077	B	N.Y.
		Marion, Martin Whitford	SS	147	.276	B	
0	1	Moore, Lloyd Albert (Whitey)	P	9.	+.000	xCin	C
		Moore, Terry Buford (3B1)	OF126	130	.288	B	
		Musial, Stanley Frank	OF135	140	.315	B	
		Narron, Samuel	C2	10	.400	StL35	
		O'Dea, James Kenneth (Ken)	C49	58	.234	N.Y.	
7	5	Pollet, Howard Joseph	P	27	.226	B	
		Sanders, Raymond Floyd	1B77	95	.252	A	
0	0	Shoun, Clyde Mitchell	P	2	+.000	B	Cin
		Slaughter, Enos Bradsher (Country)	OF151	152	.318	B	
		Triplett, Herman Coaker	OF46	64	.273	B	

WON	LOST	NAME	POS.	G.	BA	FROM	TO
		Walker, Harry Wm. (2B2)	OF56	74	.314	B	
6	4	Warneke, Lonnie	P	12	+.333	B	Chi
7	5	White, Ernest Daniel	P26	27	.195	B	

WON 105 — NATIONAL LEAGUE — FINISHED 1st.
LOST 49
TG 154 — 1943. — PCT. .682

ST. LOUIS

WM. HARRISON SOUTHWORTH

WON	LOST	NAME	POS.	G.	BA	FROM	TO
		Adams, Elvin Clark	OF6	8	+.091	StL39	Phil
8	2	Brazle, Alpha Eugene	P	13	.281	A	
9	6	Breecheen, Harry David	P	29	.190	StL40	
		Brown, James Roberson (SS6 3B9)	2B19	34	.182	B	
1	0	Byerly, Eldred Wm.	P	2	.000	A	
21	8	Cooper, Morton Cecil	P	37	.170	B	
		Cooper, Wm. Walker	C112	122	.319	B	
		Demaree, Joseph Franklin (Frank)	OF23	39	.291	Bos	
8	2	Dickson, Murry Monroe	P	31	.265	B	
		Fallon, George Decatur	2B	36	.231	Bkn37	
		Garms, Debs C. (SS1 3B23)	OF47	90	.257	Pitt41	
10	5	Gumbert, Harry Edward	P	21	.156	B	
		Hopp, John Leonard (1B27)	OF52	91	.224	B	
		Klein, Louis Frank (SS51)	2B126	154	.287	A	
11	5	Krist, Howard Wilbur	P	34	.167	B	
		Kurowski, George John (SS2)	3B137	139	.287	B	
15	7	Lanier, Hubert Max	P	32	.164	B	
		Litwhiler, Daniel Webster	OF70	80	+.279	xPhil	
		Marion, Martin Whitford	SS128	129	.280	B	
9	5	Munger, George David	P	32	.214	A	
		Musial, Stanley Frank	OF155	157	.357	B	
		Narron, Samuel	C3	10	.091	B	C
		O'Dea, James Kenneth	C56	71	.281	B	
8	4	Pollet, Howard Joseph	P	16	.163	B	
		Sanders, Raymond Floyd	1B141	144	.280	B	
		Triplett, Herman Coaker	OF6	9	+.080	B	Phil
		Walker, Harry Wm. (2B1)	OF144	148	.295	B	
5	5	White, Ernest Daniel	P14	21	.214	B	

WON 105 — NATIONAL LEAGUE — FINISHED 1st.
LOST 49
TG 154 — 1944. — PCT. .682

ST. LOUIS

WM. HARRISON SOUTHWORTH

WON	LOST	NAME	POS.	G.	BA	FROM	TO
		Antonelli, John Lawrence (2B2 3B2)	1B3	8	.190	A	
		Bergamo, August Samuel (1B2)	OF50	80	.286	A	
16	5	Brecheen, Harry David	P30	31	.162	B	
2	2	Byerly, Eldred Wm.	P	9	.167	B	
22	7	Cooper, Morton Cecil	P	34	.202	B	
		Cooper, Wm. Walker	C97	112	.317	B	
2	1	Donnelly, Sylvester Urban (Blix)	P	27	.063	A	
		Fallon, George Decatur (SS24 3B6)	2B38	69	.199	B	
		Garms, Debs C. (3B21)	OF23	73	.201	B	
4	2	Gumbert, Harry Edward	P	10	+.190	B	Cin
		Hopp, John Leonard (1B6)	OF131	139	.336	B	
7	9	Jurisich, Alvin Joseph	P	30	.178	A	
		Keely, Robert Wm.	C	1	.000	A	
		Kurowski, George John (2B9 SS1)	3B146	149	.270	B	
17	12	Lanier, Hubert Max	P	33	.182	B	
		Litwhiler, Daniel Webster	OF136	140	.264	B	
		Marion, Martin Whitford	SS	144	.267	B	
		Martin, John Leonard (Pepper)	OF29	40	.279	StL40	C
11	3	Munger, George David	P	21	.114	B	
		Musial, Stanley Frank	OF	146	.347	B	
0	0	Naymick, Wm. Michael	P	1	.000	xClevA	C
		O'Dea, James Kenneth (Ken)	C69	85	.249	B	
		Sanders, Raymond Floyd	1B152	154	.295	B	
7	3	Schmidt, Frederick Albert	P	37	.206	A	
0	1	Trotter, Wm. Felix	P	2	.000	WashA42	C
		Verban, Emil Matthew	2B	146	.257	A	
17	4	Wilks, Theodore	P	36	.141	A	

WON 95 — NATIONAL LEAGUE — FINISHED 2nd.
LOST 59
TG 154 — 1945. — PCT. .617

ST. LOUIS

WM. HARRISON SOUTHWORTH

WON	LOST	NAME	POS.	G.	BA	FROM	TO
		Adams, Elvin Clark	OF	140	+.292	xPhil	
		Antonelli, John Lawrence	3B1	2	+.000	B	Phil
21	9	Barrett, Chas. Henry (Red)	P	36	+.112	xBos	
		Bartosch, David Robert	OF11	24	.255	A	C
		Bergamo, August Samuel (1B2)	OF77	94	.316	B	C
15	4	Brecheen, Harry David	P	24	.123	B	
18	8	Burkhart, Wm. Kenneth	P	42	.181	A	
4	5	Byerly, Eldred Wm.	P	33	.217	B	
2	0	Cooper, Morton Cecil	P	4	+.333	B	Bos
		Cooper, Wm. Walker	C	4	.389	B	

WON	LOST	NAME	POS.	G.	BA	FROM	TO
		Crawford, Glenn Martin	OF1	4	+.000	A	Phil
5	4	Creel, Jack Dalton	P26	35	.077	A	C
1	0	Crouch, Wm. Elmer	P	6	.000	StL41	C
		Crumling, Eugene Leon	C	6	.083	A	C
8	6	Dockins, George Woodrow	P	31	.176	A	
8	10	Donnelly, Sylvester Urban (Blix)	P	31	.130	B	
		Fallon, George Decatur (2B4)	SS20	24	.236	B	C
3	1	Gardner, Glenn Mileso	P	17	.333	A	C
		Garms, Debs C. (OF10)	3B32	74	.336	B	C
		Hopp, John Leonard (1B15)	OF104	124	.289	B	
3	3	Jurisich, Alvin Joseph	P	27	.087	B	
		Keely, Robert Wm.	C	1	.000	B	C
		Klein, Louis Frank (2B2 3B4 OF7)	SS7	19	.228	StL43	
		Kurowski, George John (SS6)	3B131	133	.323	B	
2	2	Lanier, Hubert Max	P	4	.182	B	
1	0	Lopatka, Arthur Joseph	P	4	.250	A	
		Mallory, James Baugh III	OF11	13	+.233	WashA40	N.Y.
		Marion, Martin Whitford	SS122	123	.277	B	
		O'Dea, James Kenneth (Ken)	C91	100	.254	B	
0	0	Partenheimer, Stanwood Wendell	P	8	.000	BosA	C
		Rebel, Arthur Anthony	OF18	26	.347	Phil38	C
		Rice, Delbert W.	C77	83	.261	A	
		Sanders, Raymond Floyd	1B142	143	.276	B	
		Schoendienst, Albert Fred (2B1 SS10)	OF118	137	.278	A	
		Verban, Emil Matthew	2B	155	.278	B	
4	7	Wilks, Theodore	P	18	.133	B	
		Young, Lemuel Floyd (Pep) (2B3 3B9)	SS11	27	.149	StL41	C

WON 98 — NATIONAL LEAGUE — FINISHED 1st.
LOST 58
TG 156 — 1946. — PCT. .628

ST. LOUIS

EDWIN HAWLEY DYER

WON	LOST	NAME	POS.	G.	BA	FROM	TO
		Adams, Elvin Clark	OF58	81	.185	B	
3	2	Barrett, Chas. Henry (Red)	P	23	.059	B	
7	5	Beazley, John Andrew	P	19	.242	StL42	
11	10	Brazle, Alpha Eugene	P	37	.212	StL42	
15	15	Brecheen, Harry David	P36	37	.133	B	
6	3	Burkhart, Wm. Kenneth	P	25	.147	B	
		Cross, Joffre James (2B8 3B1)	SS17	49	.217	StL42	
15	6	Dickson, Murry Monroe	P	47	.277	StL43	
1	2	Donnelly, Sylvester Urban (Blix)	P	13	+.000	B	Phil
		Dusak, Ervin Frank (2B2 3B11)	OF77	100	.240	StL42	
		Endicott, Wm. Franklin	OF2	20	.200	A	C
		Garagiola, Joseph Henry	C70	74	.237	A	
0	0	Grodzicki, John	P	3	.000	StL41	
		Jones, Vernal LeRoy	2B3	16	.333	A	
		Klein, Louis Frank	2B	23	.194	B	C
		Kluttz, Clyde Franklin	C49	52	+.265	xN.Y.	
0	2	Krist, Howard Wilbur	P	15	.000	StL43	C
		Kurowski, George John	3B138	142	.301	B	
6	0	Lanier, Hubert Max	P	6	.200	B	C
		Litwhiler, Daniel Webster		6	+.000	StL44	Bos
		Marion, Martin Whitford	SS145	146	.233	B	
2	1	Martin, Frederick Turner	P	6	.273	A	C
		Moore, Terry Buford	OF66	91	.263	StL42	
2	2	Munger, George David	P	10	.250	StL44	
		Musial, Stanley Frank (OF42)	1B114	156	.365	StL44	
		O'Dea, James Kenneth (Ken)	C	22	+.123	B	Bos
21	10	Pollet, Howard Joseph	P	40	.161	StL43	
		Rice, Delbert W.	C53	55	.273	B	
1	0	Schmidt, Frederick Albert	P	16	.000	StL44	
		Schoendienst, Albert Fred (SS4 3B12)	2B128	142	.281	B	
		Sessi, Walter Anthony		15	.143	StL41	C
		Sisler, Richard Allan (OF29)	1B37	83	.260	A	
		Slaughter, Enos Bradsher (Country)	OF	156	.300	StL42	
		Verban, Emil Matthew	2B	1	+.000	B	Phil
		Walker, Harry Wm. (1B8)	OF92	112	.237	StL43	
		Wilber, Delbert Quentin	C	4	.000	A	
8	0	Wilks, Theodore	P	40	.208	B	

WON 89 — NATIONAL LEAGUE — FINISHED 2nd.
LOST 65
TG 154 — 1947. — PCT. .578

ST. LOUIS

EDWIN HAWLEY DYER

WON	LOST	NAME	POS.	G.	BA	FROM	TO
14	8	Brazle, Alpha Eugene	P	44	.219	B	
16	11	Brecheen, Harry David	P	29	.241	B	
3	6	Burkhart, Wm. Kenneth	P	34	.125	B	
		Creger, Bernard Odell	SS13	15	.188	A	C
		Cross, Joffre James (2B2 SS14)	3B15	51	.102	B	
13	16	Dickson, Murry Monroe	P	47	.213	B	
		Diering, Chas. Edward Allen	OF75	105	.216	A	
		Dusak, Ervin Frank (3B7)	OF89	111	.284	B	
		Gargiole, Joseph Henry	C74	77	.257	B	
0	1	Grodzicki, John	P	16	.000	B	C
12	7	Hearn, James Tolbert	P	37	.145	A	
1	0	Johnson, Kenneth Carstensen	P	2	.500	A	
		Jones, Vernal LeRoy (OF2)	2B13	23	.247	B	
		Kurowski, George John	3B141	146	.310	B	
		Marion, Martin Whitford	SS141	149	.272	B	

WON	LOST	NAME	POS.	G.	BA	FROM	TO
		Medwick, Joseph Michael (Ducky)	OF43	75	.307	Bkn	
		Moore, Terry Buford	OF120	127	.283	B	
16	5	Munger, George David	P	40	.185	B	
		Musial, Stanley Frank	1B	149	.312	B	
		Northey, Ronald James (3B2)	OF94	110	+.293	xPhil	
9	11	Pollet, Howard Joseph	P	37	.231	B	
		Rice, Delbert W.	C94	97	.218	B	
0	0	Schmidt, Frederick Albert	P	2	+.000	B	Phil
		Schoendienst, Albert Fred (3B5 OF1)	2B142	151	.253	B	
		Sisler, Richard Allan (OF5)	1B10	46	.203	B	
		Slaughter, Enos Bradsher (Country)	OF142	147	.294	B	
1	0	Staley, Gerald Lee	P	18	.000	A	
		Walker, Harry Wm.	OF	10	+.200	B	Phil
		Wilber, Delbert Quentin	C34	51	.232	B	
4	0	Wilks, Theodore	P	37	.167	B	

WON 85 NATIONAL LEAGUE FINISHED 2nd.
LOST 69
TG 154 1948. PCT. .552

ST. LOUIS

EDWIN HAWLEY DYER

WON	LOST	NAME	POS.	G.	BA	FROM	TO
		Baker, Wm. Presley	C36	45	.294	Pitt46	
0	0	Beers, Clarence Scott	P	1	.000	A	C
10	6	Brazle, Alpha Eugene	P42	45	.145	B	
20	7	Brecheen, Harry David	P	33	.146	B	
		Bucha, John George	C1	2	.000	A	
0	0	Burkhart, Wm. Kenneth	P20	21	+.250	B	Cin
		Cross, Joffre James		2	+.000	B	Chi
12	16	Dickson, Murry Monroe	P42	43	.281	B	
		Diering, Chas. Edward Allen	OF5	7	.000	B	
0	0	Dusak, Ervin Frank (P1 2B29 SS1 3B9)	OF68	114	.209	B	
		Garagiola, Joseph Henry	C23	24	.107	B	
8	6	Hearn, James Tolbert	P34	36	.200	B	
2	4	Johnson, Kenneth Carstensen	P13	20	.300	B	
		Jones, Vernal LeRoy	1B128	132	.254	B	
		Kazak, Edward Terrance	3B	6	.273	A	
		Kurowski, George John	3B65	77	.214	B	
		Lang, Donald Chas. (2B2)	3B95	117	.269	Cin38	C
		LaPointe, Ralph John (SS25 3B1)	2B44	87	.225	Phil	C
		Marion, Martin Whitford	SS142	144	.252	B	
		Medwick, Joseph Michael (Ducky)	OF1	20	.211	B	C
		Miggins, Lawrence Edward		1	.000	A	
		Moore, Terry Buford	OF71	91	.232	B	
10	11	Munger, George David	P	39	.160	B	
		Musial, Stanley Frank (1B2)	OF155	155	.376	B	
		Northey, Ronald James	OF67	96	.321	B	

WON	LOST	NAME	POS.	G.	BA	FROM	TO
0	1	Papai, Alfred Thomas	P10	11	.000	A	
13	8	Pollet, Howard Joseph	P36	38	.118	B	
		Rice, Delbert W.	C99	100	.197	B	
		Rice, Harold Housten	OF	8	.323	A	
		Schoendienst, Albert Fred	2B96	119	.272	B	
		Slaughter, Enos Bradsher (Country)	OF	146	.321	B	
4	4	Staley, Gerald Lee	P	31	.222	B	
		Wilber, Delbert Quentin	C26	27	.190	B	
6	6	Wilks, Theodore	P	57	.167	B	
0	0	Yochim, Raymond Austin Aloysius	P	1	.000	A	
		Young, Norman Robert (Babe)	1B35	41	+.243	xCin	C
		Young, Robert George	3B1	3	.000	A	

WON 96 NATIONAL LEAGUE FINISHED 2nd.
LOST 58
TG 154 1949. PCT. .623

ST. LOUIS

EDWIN HAWLEY DYER

WON	LOST	NAME	POS.	G.	BA	FROM	TO
		Baker, Wm. Presley	C10	20	.133	B	C
		Bilko, Stephen Thomas	1B5	6	.294	A	
0	0	Boyer, Cloyd Victor	P	4	.000	A	
14	8	Brazle, Alpha Eugene	P	39	.134	B	
14	11	Brecheen, Harry David	P	32	.273	B	
		Derry, Alva Russell		2	.000	PhilA46	C
		Diering, Chas. Edward Allen	OF124	131	.263	B	
		Dusak, Ervin Frank		1	.000	B	
		Garagiola, Joseph Henry	C80	81	.261	B	
		Glaviano, Thomas Giatano (2B7)	3B73	87	.267	A	
1	3	Hearn, James Tolbert	P	17	.100	B	
		Hemus, Solomon Joseph	2B16	20	.333	A	
		Howerton, Wm. Ray	OF6	9	.308	A	
0	1	Johnson, Kenneth Carstensen	P14	21	.250	B	
		Jones, Vernal LeRoy	1B98	110	.300	B	
		Kazak, Edward Terrance (2B5)	3B80	92	.304	B	
		Klein, Louis Frank (2B9 3B7)	SS21	58	.219	StL46	
0	0	Krieger, Kurt Ferdinand	P	1	.000	A	
		Kurowski, George John	3B2	10	.143	B	C
5	4	Lanier, Hubert Max	P	15	.074	StL46	
		Marion, Martin Whitford	SS	134	.272	B	
6	0	Martin, Frederick Turner	P	21	.300	StL46	
15	8	Munger, George David	P	35	.258	B	
		Musial, Stanley Frank (1B1)	OF156	157	.338	B	
		Nelson, Glenn Richard	1B70	82	.221	A	
		Northey, Ronald James	OF73	90	.260	B	
20	9	Pollet, Howard Joseph	P	39	.195	B	
1	1	Reeder, Wm. Edgar	P	21	.000	A	C
		Rice, Delbert W.	C	92	.236	B	
		Rice, Harold Housten	OF10	40	.196	B	

WON	LOST	NAME	POS.	G.	BA	FROM	TO
		Sauer, Edward		24	+.222	Chi45	Bos
		Schoendienst, Albert Fred (SS14 3B6 OF2)	2B138	151	.297	B	
		Slaughter, Enos Bradsher (Country)	OF150	151	.336	B	
10	10	Staley, Gerald Lee	P	45	.122	B	
		Wilber, Delbert Quentin		2	.250	B	
10	3	Wilks, Theodore	P	59	.037	B	
0	0	Yochim, Raymond Austin Aloysius	P	3	.000	B	C

WON 78 — NATIONAL LEAGUE — FINISHED 5th.
LOST 75
TG 153 — 1950. — PCT. .510

ST. LOUIS

EDWIN HAWLEY DYER

WON	LOST	NAME	POS.	G.	BA	FROM	TO
		Bilko, Stephen Thomas	1B9	10	.182	B	
		Blatnik, John Louis	OF	7	+.150	xPhil	C
		Bollweg, Donald Raymond	1B	4	.182	A	
7	7	Boyer, Cloyd Victor	P	36	.182	B	
11	9	Bra zle, Alpha Eugene	P46	47	.213	B	
8	11	Brecheen, Harry David	P	27	.241	B	
		Bucha, John George	C17	22	.139	StL48	
0	0	Deal, Ellis Fergason	P	3	.000	BosA48	
		Diering, Chas. Edward Allen	OF81	89	.250	B	
0	2	Dusak, Ervin Frank (OF2)	P14	23	.083	B	
		Garagiola, Joseph Henry	C30	34	.318	B	
		Gardella, Daniel Lewis		1	.000	NY45	C
		Glaviano, Thomas Giatano (2B5 SS1)	3B106	115	.285	B	
0	1	Hearn, James Tolbert	P	6	+1.000	B	N.Y.
		Hemus, Solomon Joseph	3B5	11	.133	B	
		Howerton, Wm. Ray	OF94	110	.281	B	
0	0	Johnson, Kenneth Carstensen	P	2	+.000	B	Phil.
		Jones, Vernal LeRoy	1B8	13	.231	B	
		Kazak, Edward Terrance	3B48	93	.256	B	
11	9	Lanier, Hubert Max	P	27	.162	B	
		Lindell, John Harlan	OF33	36	.186	xNYA	
		Lowrey, Harry Lee (3B5 OF4)	2B6	17	+.268	xCin	
		Marion, Martin Whitford	SS101	106	.247	B	
4	2	Martin, Frederick Turner	P30	31	.267	B	C
		Mickelson, Edward Allen	1B4	5	.100	A	
		Mierkowicz, Edward Frank		1	.000	DetA48	C
		Miller, Edward Robert (2B1)	SS51	64	.227	Phil.	C
7	8	Munger, George David	P	32	.137	B	
		Musial, Stanley Frank (1B69)	OF77	146	.346	B	
		Nelson, Glenn Richard	1B70	76	.247	B	
1	0	Papai, Alfred Thomas	P	13	.000	xBosA	C
0	0	Poholsky, Thomas George	P	5	.000	A	
14	13	Pollet, Howard Joseph	P37	38	.143	B	

WON	LOST	NAME	POS.	G.	BA	FROM	TO
		Rice, Delbert W.	C	130	.244	B	
		Rice, Harold Housten	OF37	44	.211	B	
		Schoendienst, Albert Fred (SS10 3B1)	2B143	153	.276	B	
		Slaughter, Enos Bradsher	OF145	148	.290	B	
13	13	Staley, Gerald Lee	P	42	.145	B	
		Walker, Harry Wm. (1B2)	OF46	60	.207	Cin	
2	0	Wilks, Theodre	P	18	.000	B	

WON 81 — NATIONAL LEAGUE — FINISHED 3rd.
LOST 73
TG 154 — 1951. — PCT. .526

ST. LOUIS

MARTIN WHITFORD MARION

WON	LOST	NAME	POS.	G.	B A	FROM	TO
		Benson, Vernon Adair (OF4)	3B9	13	.261	PhilA46	
		Bilko, Stephen Thomas	1B19	21	.222	B	
3	3	Bokelmann, Richard Werner	P	20	.000	A	
		Bollweg, Donald Raymond	1B2	6	.111	B	
2	5	Boyer, Cloyd Victor	P	19	.200	B	
6	5	Brazle, Alpha Eugene	P	56	.109	B	
8	4	Brecheen, Harry David	P	24	.218	B	
11	6	Chambers, Clifford Day	P	21	+.163	xPitt	
		Ciaffone, Lawrence Thomas	OF1	5	.000	A	C
		Cole, Richard Roy	2B14	15	+.194	A	Pitt
2	1	Collum, Jack Dean	P	3	.429	A	
1	0	Crimian, John Melvin	P	11	.333	A	
		Diering, Chas. Edward Allen	OF44	64	.259	B	
0	0	Dusak, Ervin Frank	P	5	+.500	B	Pitt
		Garagiola, Joseph Henry	C23	27	+.194	B	Pitt
		Glaviano, Thomas Giatano (2B9)	OF17	54	.183	B	
0	0	Habenicht, Robert Julius	P	3	.000	A	
		Hemus, Solomon Joseph (2B12)	SS105	120	.281	B	
		Howerton, Wm. Ray	OF17	24	+.262	B	Pitt
		Johnson, Wm. Russell	3B	124	.262	xNYA	
		Jones, Vernal LeRoy	1B71	80	.263	B	
		Kazak, Edward Terrance	3B10	11	.182	B	
0	0	Krieger, Kurt Ferdinand	P	2	.000	StL49	C
11	9	Lanier, Hubert Max	P	31	.151	B	
0	1	Lewandowski, Daniel Wm.	P	2	.000	A	C
		Lowrey, Harry Lee (2B3 3B11)	OF85	114	.303	B	
4	6	Munger, George David	P	23	.172	B	
		Musial, Stanley Frank (1B60)	OF91	152	.355	B	
		Nelson, Glenn Richard (OF1)	1B4	9	+.222	B	Pitt
7	13	Poholsky, Thomas George	P	38	.209	B	
0	3	Pollet, Howard Joseph	P	6	+.000	B	Pitt
7	4	Presko, Joseph Edward	P	15	.162	A	
		Rice, Delbert W.	C120	122	.251	B	
		Rice, Harold Housten	OF63	69	.254	B	

WON	LOST	NAME	POS.	G.	BA	FROM	TO
		Richmond, Donald Lester	3B11	12	.088	PhilA47	C
		Rojek, Stanley Andrew	SS	51	+.274	xPitt	
		Sarni, Wm. F.	C35	36	.174	A	
		Scheffing, Robert Boden	C11	12	+.111	xCin	
		Schoendienst, Albert Fred (SS8)	2B124	135	.289	B	
		Slaughter, Enos Bradsher	OF106	123	.281	B	
19	13	Staley, Gerald Lee	P	42	.160	B	
		Van Noy, Jay Lowell	OF1	6	.000	A	C
		Walker, Harry Wm. (1B1)	OF6	8	.308	B	
		Westlake, Waldon Thomas	OF68	73	+.255	xPitt	
0	0	Wilks, Theodore	P	17	+.000	B	Pitt

WON 88
LOST 66
TG 154

NATIONAL LEAGUE — 1952. — FINISHED 3rd. PCT. .571

ST. LOUIS

EDWARD RAYMOND STANKY

WON	LOST	NAME	POS.	G.	BA	FROM	TO
		Benson, Vernon Adair	3B15	20	.191	B	
		Bilko, Stephen Thomas	1B	20	.264	B	
0	1	Bokelmann, Richard Werner	P	11	.000	B	
6	6	Boyer, Cloyd Victor	P23	24	.211	B	C
12	5	Brazle, Alpha Eugene	P	46	.125	B	
7	5	Brecheen, Harry David	P	25	.207	B	
4	4	Chambers, Clifford Day	P	26	.281	B	
2	0	Clark, Michael John	P	12	.000	A	
0	0	Collum, Jack Dean	P	2	.000	B	
0	0	Crimian, John Melvin	P	5	.000	B	
		Fusselman, Lester LeRoy	C	32	.159	A	
		Glaviano, Thomas Giatano (2B1)	3B52	80	.241	B	
		Gorman, Herbert Allen		1	.000	A	C
2	2	Haddix, Harvey (OF1)	P7	9	.214	A	
0	0	Hahn, Frederick Aloys	P	1	.000	A	C
		Hemus, Solomon Joseph (3B2)	SS148	151	.268	B	
		Hertweck, Neal Chas.	1B	2	.000	A	C
		Johnson, Wm. Russell	3B89	94	.252	B	
		Kazak, Edward Terrance	3B1	3	+.000	B	Cin
		Lowrey, Harry Lee (3B6)	OF106	132	.286	B	
		Mauch, Eugene Wm.	SS2	7	.000	Bos	
		Miggins, Lawrence Edward (1B1)	OF25	42	.229	StL48	C
6	3	Miller, Stuart Leonard	P	12	.120	A	
10	8	Mizell, Wilmer David	P	30	.044	A	
0	1	Munger, George David	P	1	+.000	B	Pitt
0	0	Musial, Stanley Frank (P1 1B25)	OF129	154	.336	B	
7	10	Presko, Joseph Edward	P	28	.093	B	
		Rice, Delbert W.	C	147	.259	B	
		Rice, Harold Housten	OF81	98	.288	B	
		Sarni, Wm. F.	C	3	.200	B	

WON	LOST	NAME	POS.	G.	BA	FROM	TO
2	3	Schmidt, Willard Raymond	P	18	.125	A	
		Schoendienst, Albert Fred (SS3 3B11)	2B142	152	.303	B	
		Sisler, Richard Allan	1B114	119	+.261	xCin	
		Slaughter, Enos Bradsher (Country)	OF137	140	.300	B	
17	4	Staley, Gerald Lee	P	35	.153	B	
		Stallcup, Thomas Virgil	SS12	29	+.129	xCin	
		Stanky, Edward Raymond MGR.	2B20	53	.229	N.Y.	
0	0	Tiefenauer, Bobby Gene	P	6	.000	A	
1	2	Werle, Wm. George	P	19	+.111	xPitt	
		Westlake, Waldon Thomas	OF15	21	+.216	B	Cin
12	2	Yuhas, John Edward	P	54	.190	A	

WON 83
LOST 71
TG 154

NATIONAL LEAGUE — 1953. — FINISHED 3rd. (TIED WITH PHILADELPHIA) PCT. .539

ST. LOUIS

EDWARD RAYMOND STANKY

WON	LOST	NAME	POS.	G.	BA	FROM	TO
		Anderson, Ferrell Jack	C12	18	.286	Bkn46	C
		Benson, Vernon Adair		13	.000	B	C
		Bilko, Stephen Thomas	1B	154	.251	B	
0	0	Bokelmann, Richard Werner	P	3	.000	B	C
6	7	Brazle, Alpha Eugene	P	60	.333	B	
		Castiglione, Peter Paul (2B9 SS3)	3B51	67	+.173	xPitt	
3	6	Chambers, Clifford Day	P	32	.118	B	C
1	0	Clark, Michael John	P	23	.000	B	C
0	0	Collum, Jack Dean	P	7	+.000	B	Cin
		Dunlap, Grant Lester	OF1	16	.353	A	C
		Elliott, Harry Lewis	OF17	24	.254	A	
3	1	Erautt, Edward Lorenz Sebastian	P	20	+.167	xCin	C
0	0	Faszholz, John Edward	P	4	.000	A	C
		Fusselman, Lester LeRoy	C	11	.250	B	C
20	9	Haddix, Harvey	P36	48	.289	B	
		Hemus, Solomon Joseph (2B3)	SS150	154	.279	B	
		Jablonski, Raymond Leo	3B	157	.268	A	
		Johnson, Wm. Russell	3B	11	.200	B	C
		Lowrey, Harry Lee (2B10 3B1)	OF38	104	.269	B	
		Marolewski, Fred Daniel	1B	1	.000	A	C
7	8	Miller, Stuart Leonard	P40	42	.186	B	
13	11	Mizell, Wilmer David	P	33	.084	B	
		Musial, Stanley Frank	OF	157	.337	B	
		Phillips, Howard Edward		9	.000	A	C
6	13	Presko, Joseph Edward	P34	35	.220	B	
		Rand, Richard Hilton	C	9	.290	A	
		Repulski, Eldon John	OF	153	.275	A	
		Rice, Delbert W.	C	135	.236	B	
		Rice, Harold Housten		8	+.250	B	Pitt

WON	LOST	NAME	POS.	G.	BA	FROM	TO
0	0	Romonosky, John	P	2	.000	A	
0	2	Schmidt, Willard Raymond	P	6	.000	B	
		Schoendienst, Albert Fred	2B140	146	.342	B	
		Schofield, John Richard	SS15	33	.179	A	
		Sisler, Richard Allan	1B10	32	.256	B	C
		Slaughter, Enos Bradsher	OF137	143	.291	B	
18	9	Staley, Gerald Lee	P	40	.103	B	
		Stallcup, Thomas Virgil		1	.000	B	C
		Stanky, Edward Raymond MGR.	2B8	17	.267	B	
6	5	White, Harold George	P	49	.000	xStLA	
0	0	Yuhas, John Edward	P	2	.000	B	C
		Yvars, Salvador Anthony	C26	30	+.246	xN.Y.	

WON 72 NATIONAL LEAGUE FINISHED 6th.
LOST 82 *
TG 154 1954. PCT. .468

ST. LOUIS

EDWARD RAYMOND STANKY

WON	LOST	NAME	POS.	G.	BA	FROM	TO
		Alston, Thomas Edison	1B65	66	.246	A	
0	4	Beard, Ralph Wm.	P	13	.059	A	C
		Bilko, Stephen Thomas	1B6	8	+.143	B	Chi
5	4	Brazle, Alpha Eugene	P	58	.000	B	C
		Burgess, Thomas Roland	OF4	17	.048	A	
		Castiglione, Peter Paul	3B	5	.000	B	C
		Cunningham, Joseph Roberts	1B	85	.284	A	
2	3	Deal, Ellis Fergason	P	33	.100	StL50	C
		Frazier, Joseph Filmore (1B1)	OF11	81	.295	ClevA47	
		Grammas, Alexander Peter (3B1)	SS142	142	.264	A	
0	1	Greason, Wm. Henry	P	3	.000	A	C
18	13	Haddix, Harvey	P43	61	.194	B	
		Hemus, Solomon Joseph (2B12 3B27)	SS66	124	.304	B	
		Jablonski, Raymond Leo (1B1)	3B149	152	.296	B	
4	4	Jones, Gordon Bassett	P	11	.125	A	
15	6	Lawrence, Brooks Ulysses	P	35	.189	A	
2	3	Lint, Royce James	P30	31	.100	A	C
		Lowrey, Harry Lee	OF12	74	.115	B	
0	1	Luna, Guillermo Romero	P	1	.000	A	C
2	3	Miller, Stuart Leonard	P19	20	.308	B	
		Moon, Wallace Wade	OF148	151	.304	A	
		Musial, Stanley Frank (1B10)	OF152	153	.330	B	
5	7	Poholsky, Thomas George	P	25	.148	StL51	
4	9	Presko, Joseph Edward	P37	38	.250	B	
8	9	Raschi, Victor Angelo John	P	30	.141	NYA	
		Repulski, Eldon John	OF	152	.283	B	
		Rice, Delbert W.	C52	56	.252	B	
		Sarni, Wm. F.	C118	123	.300	StL52	
0	1	Scheib, Carl Alvin	P	3	.000	xPhilA	C
		Schoendienst, Albert Fred	2B144	148	.315	B	
		Schofield, John Richard	SS11	43	.143	B	
7	13	Staley, Gerald Lee	P	48	.139	B	

WON	LOST	NAME	POS.	G.	BA	FROM	TO
0	0	Wade, Benjamin Styron	P	13	+.000	xBkn	
0	0	White, Harold George	P	4	.000	B	C
0	0	Wright, Melvin James	P	9	.000	A	
		Yvars, Salvador Anthony	C21	38	.246	B	C

*Lost one game by forfeit vs. Phila. July 18 (2nd game).

WON 68 NATIONAL LEAGUE FINISHED 7th.
LOST 86
TG 154 1955. PCT. .442

ST. LOUIS

EDWARD RAYMOND STANKY HARRY WM. WALKER

WON	LOST	NAME	POS.	G.	BA	FROM	TO
		Alston, Thomas Edison	1B7	13	.125	B	
11	8	Arroyo, Luis Enrique	P	35	.232	A	
		Blasingame, Donald Lee (SS2)	2B3	5	.375	A	
		Boyer, Kenton Lloyd (SS18)	3B139	147	.264	A	
		Burbrink, Nelson Edward	C55	58	.276	A	C
		Elliott, Harry Lewis	OF28	68	.256	StL53	C
1	0	Flowers, Bennett	P	4	.100	xDetA	
		Frazier, Joseph Filmore	OF14	58	.200	B	
1	0	Gettel, Allen Jones	P	8	.500	NY51	C
		Grammas, Alexander Peter	SS126	128	.240	B	
12	16	Haddix, Harvey	P	37	.164	B	
		Hemus, Solomon Joseph (2B10 SS2)	3B43	96	.243	B	
9	14	Jackson, Lawrence Curtis	P	37	.053	A	
0	0	Jacobs, Anthony Robert	P	1	.000	Chi48	C
1	4	Jones, Gordon Bassett	P	15	.071	B	
4	3	LaPalme, Paul Edmore	P	56	.211	Pitt	
3	8	Lawrence, Brooks Ulysses	P	46	.095	B	
0	1	Mackinson, John Joseph	P8	9	.000	PhilA53	C
1	1	Moford, Herbert	P	14	.000	A	
		Moon, Wallace Wade (1B51)	OF100	152	.295	B	
		Musial, Stanley Frank (OF51)	1B110	154	.318	B	
0	0	McDaniel, Lyndall Dale	P	4	.200	A	
9	11	Poholsky, Thomas George (OF1)	P30	30	.182	B	
		Rand, Richard Hilton	C	3	.300	StL53	
0	1	Raschi, Victor Angelo John	P	1	.000	B	KCA
		Repulski, Eldon John	OF141	147	.270	B	
		Rice, Delbert W.	C18	20	+.203	B	Mil
		Sarni, Wm. F.	C99	107	.256	B	
7	6	Schmidt, Willard Raymond	P	20	.119	StL53	
		Schoendienst, Albert Fred	2B142	145	.268	B	
		Schofield, John Richard	SS3	12	.000	B	
1	2	Schultz, George Warren	P	19	.000	A	
3	1	Smith, Frank Thomas	P	28	.000	Cin	
		Stephenson, Robert Loyd (2B7 3B1)	SS48	67	.243	A	C
1	4	Tiefenauer, Bobby Gene	P	18	.000	StL52	
		Virdon, Wm. Chas.	OF142	144	.281	A	
		Walker, Harry Wm. MGR.	OF1	11	.357	StL51	

WON	LOST	NAME	POS.	G.	BA	FROM	TO
		Whisenant, Thomas Peter	OF40	58	.191	Bos52	
2	4	Wooldridge, Floyd Lewis	P	18	.222	A	C
2	2	Wright, Melvin James	P	29	.000	B	

WON 76 NATIONAL LEAGUE FINISHED 4th.
LOST 78
TG 154 1956. PCT. .494

ST. LOUIS

FREDERICK CHAS. HUTCHINSON

WON	LOST	NAME	POS.	G.	BA	FROM	TO
		Alston, Thomas Edison	1B	3	.000	B	
		Blasingame, Donald Lee (SS49 3B2)	2B98	150	.261	B	
1	6	Blaylock, Robert Edward	P	14	.091	A	
		Boyer, Kenton Lloyd	3B149	150	.306	B	
		Brandt, John George	OF26	27	+.286	A	N.Y.
6	2	Collum, Jack Dean	P	38	.214	Cin	
		Cooper, Wm. Walker	C16	40	.265	Chi	
		Cunningham, Joseph Roberts	1B1	4	.000	StL54	
		Dark, Alvin Ralph	SS99	100	+.286	xN.Y.	
		Del Greco, Robert George	OF99	102	+.215	xPitt	
13	8	Dickson, Murry Monroe	P28	32	+.247	xPhil	
1	1	Flowers, Bennett	P	3	+.000	B	Phil
		Frazier, Joseph Filmore	OF3	14	+.211	B	Cin
		Grammas, Alexander Peter	SS5	6	+.250	B	Cin
1	0	Haddix, Harvey	P4	5	+.222	B	Phil
		Harmon, Chas. Byron (1B2 3B1)	OF11	20	+.000	xCin	
		Hatton, Grady Edgebert (3B1)	2B13	44	.247	xBosA	BaltA
		Hemus, Solomon Joseph		8	+.200	B	Phil
2	2	Jackson, Lawrence Curtis	P	51	.091	B	
0	2	Jones, Gordon Bassett	P	5	.000	B	
		Katt, Raymond Frederick	C	47	+.259	xN.Y.	
2	0	Kinder, Ellis Raymond	P	22	.000	BosA	ChiA
1	1	Konstanty, Casimer James	P	27	.000	xNYA	C
0	0	LaPalme, Paul Edmore	P	1	+.000	B	Cin
1	2	Liddle, Donald Eugene	P14	15	+.000	xN.Y.	C
0	2	Littlefield, Richard Bernard	P	3	+.000	xPitt	N.Y.
		Lockman, Carroll Walter (1B2)	OF57	70	+.249	xN.Y.	
0	1	Miller, Stuart Leonard	P3	4	+.000	StL54	Phil
14	14	Mizell, Wilmer David	P	33	.107	StL53	
		Moon, Wallace Wade (1B52)	OF97	149	.298	B	
		Morgan, Robert Morris (SS6 3B11)	2B13	61	+.195	xPhil	
		Musial, Stanley Frank (OF53)	1B103	151	.310	B	
7	6	McDaniel, Lyndall Dale	P	39	.219	B	
		Nelson, Glenn Richard (OF8)	1B14	38	+.232	xBkn	
		Peete, Chas.	OF21	23	.192	A	C
9	14	Poholsky, Thomas George	P	33	.159	B	
		Repulski, Eldon John	OF100	112	.277	B	
		Sarni, Wm. F.	C41	43	+.291	B	N.Y.
		Sauer, Henry John	OF37	75	.298	Chi	
6	8	Schmidt, Willard Raymond	P	33	.233	B	
		Schoendienst, Albert Fred	2B36	40	+.314	B	N.Y.
		Schofield, John Richard	SS9	16	.100	B	
		Smith, Harold Raymond	C66	75	.282	A	
0	0	Surkont, Maxim Constantine	P	5	+.000	xPitt	N.Y.
		Virdon, Wm. Chas.	OF	24	+.211	B	Pitt
12	9	Wehmeier, Herman Ralph	P34	42	+.224	xPhil	

WON 87 NATIONAL LEAGUE FINISHED 2nd.
LOST 67
TG 154 1957. PCT. .565

ST. LOUIS

FREDERICK CHAS. HUTCHINSON

WON	LOST	NAME	POS.	G.	BA	FROM	TO
		Alston, Thomas Edison	1B6	9	.294	B	C
0	1	Barnes, Frank	P3	4	.000	A	
		Blasingame, Donald Lee	2B	154	.271	B	
		Boyer, Kenton Lloyd (3B41)	OF105	142	.265	B	
0	1	Cheney, Thomas Edgar	P	4	.000	A	
		Cooper, Wm. Walker	C13	48	.269	B	C
		Dunningham, Joseph Roberts (OF46)	1B57	122	.318	B	
		Dark, Alvin Ralph (3B1)	SS139	140	.290	B	
0	1	Davis, James Bennett	P	10	+.000	Chi	N.Y.
5	3	Dickson, Murry Monroe	P	14	.222	B	
		Ennis, Delmer	OF127	136	.286	Phil	
		Green, Eugene LeRoy	OF3	6	.200	A	
		Harmon, Chas. Byron	OF8	9	+.333	B	Phil
15	9	Jackson, Lawrence Curtis	P	41	.181	B	
12	9	Jones, Samuel	P	28	.159	Chi	
		Kasko, Edward Michael (2B1 SS13)	3B120	134	.273	A	
		King, James Hubert	OF8	22	.314	Chi	
0	0	Kuzava, Robert LeRoy	P	3	.000	Phil55	C
		Landrith, Hobert Neal	C67	75	.243	Chi	
		Lassetter, Donald O'Neal	OF3	4	.154	A	C
0	1	Lovenguth, Lynn Richard	P2	3	.000	Phil55	C
0	0	Martin, Morris Webster	P	4	.000	BaltA	
15	9	McDaniel, Lyndall	P30	31	.257	B	
7	5	McDaniel, Max Von	P	17	.000	A	
1	2	Merritt, Lloyd Wesley	P	44	.000	A	C
		Miksis, Edward Thomas	OF31	49	.211	Chi	BaltA
0	0	Miller, Robert Lane	P5	7	.000	A	
8	10	Mizell, Wilmer David	P	33	.089	B	
		Moon, Wallace Wade	OF133	142	.295	B	
3	2	Muffett, Billy Arnold	P	23	.000	A	
		Musial, Stanley Frank	1B130	134	.351	B	
		Noren, Irving Arnold	OF8	17	.367	xKCA	
10	3	Schmidt, Willard Raymond	P	40	.212	B	
		Schofield, John Richard	SS23	65	.161	B	
		Smith, Bobby Gene	OF79	93	.211	A	

WON	LOST	NAME	POS.	G.	BA	FROM	TO
		Smith, Harold Raymond	C97	100	.279	B	
0	0	Smith, Robert Gilchrist	P	6	+.000	BosA55	Pitt
10	7	Wehmeier, Herman Ralph	P36	40	.203	B	
1	4	Wilhelm, James Hoyt	P	40	.000	N.Y.	ClevA

WON 72 LOST 82 TG 154

NATIONAL LEAGUE 1958.

FINISHED 5th. (TIED WITH CHICAGO) PCT. .468

ST. LOUIS

FREDERICK CHAS. HUTCHINSON STANLEY CAMFIELD HACK

WON	LOST	NAME	POS.	G.	BA	FROM	TO
		Amaro, Ruben Mora (2B1)	SS36	40	.224	A	
1	1	Barnes, Frank	P8	13	.167	B	
		Blasingame, Donald Lee	2B137	143	.274	B	
		Boyer, Kenton Lloyd	3B144	150	.307	B	
		(SS1 OF6)					
8	4	Brosnan, James Patrick	P	33	+.097	xChi	
		Burton, Ellis Narrington	OF7	8	.233	A	
0	1	Chittum, Nelson Boyd	P	13	.250	A	
0	1	Clark, Philip James	P7	8	.000	A	
		Cunningham, Joseph Roberts	1B67	131	.312	B	
		(OF66)					
		Dark, Alvin Ralph (3B8)	SS8	18	+.297	B	Chi
		Ennis, Delmer	OF84	106	.261	B	
0	0	Flanigan, Thomas Anthony	P	1	.000	ChiA54	C
		Flood, Curtis Chas. (3B1)	OF120	121	.261	Cin	
		Freese, Eugene Lewis	SS28	62	+.257	xPitt	
		(2B14 3B3)					
		Green, Eugene Leroy (C48)	OF75	137	.281	B	
13	13	Jackson, Lawrence Curtis	P49	50	.150	B	
14	13	Jones, Samuel	P	35	.100	B	
		Kasko, Edward Michael	SS77	104	.220	B	
		(2B12 3B1)					
		Katt, Raymond Frederick	C14	19	.171	N.Y.	
		Landrith, Hobert Neal	C45	70	.215	B	
3	9	Mabe, Robert Lee	P31	32	.042	A	
2	6	Maglie, Salvatore Anthony	P	10	.125	xNYA	C
3	1	Martin, Morris Webster	P	17	.000	B	ClevA
5	7	McDaniel, Lyndall Dale	P	26	.067	B	
0	0	McDaniel, Max Von	P	2	.000	B	C
10	14	Mizell, Wilmer David	P	30	.115	B	
		Moon, Wallace Wade	OF82	108	.238	B	
4	6	Muffett, Billy Arnold	P	35	.200	B	
		Musial, Stanley Frank	1B124	135	.337	B	
		Noren, Irving Arnold	OF77	117	.264	B	
0	0	O'Brien, John Thomas	SS5	12	+.000	xPitt	
		(P1 2B1)					
5	1	Paine, Phillips Steere	P	46	.286	Mil	C
		Schofield, John Richard	SS27	39	+.213	B	Pitt
		Smith, Bobby Gene	OF27	28	.284	B	
		Smith, Harold Raymond	C71	77	.227	B	
0	1	Smith, Wm. Garland	P	2	.000	A	
1	3	Stobbs, Chas. Klein	P	17	.250	xWashA	

WON	LOST	NAME	POS.	G.	BA	FROM	TO
		Tate, Lee Willie	SS9	10	.200	A	
		Taylor, Joe Cephus	OF5	18	.304	Cin	BaltA
		Valenzuela, Benjamin Baltran	3B3	10	.214	A	C
0	1	Wehmeier, Herman Ralph	P	3	.500	B	DetA
3	0	Wight, Wm. Robert	P	28	+.100	xCin	C

WON 71 LOST 83 TG 154

NATIONAL LEAGUE 1959.

FINISHED 7th. PCT. .461

ST. LOUIS

SOLOMON JOSEPH HEMUS

WON	LOST	NAME	POS.	G.	BA	FROM	TO
		Blasingame, Donald Lee	2B	150	.289	B	
4	5	Blaylock, Gary Nelson	P26	31	.118	A	NYA
0	1	Blaylock, Robert Edward	P	3	.000	StL56	C
		Boyer, Kenton Lloyd	3B143	149	.309	B	
		(SS12)					
6	3	Bridges, Marshall	P	27	.217	A	
7	12	Broglio, Ernest Gilbert	P	35	.098	A	
1	3	Brosnan, James Patrick	P	20	+.286	B	Cin
		Carmel, Leon James	OF	10	.130	A	
0	1	Cheney, Thomas Edgar	P	11	.000	StL57	
		Cimoli, Gino Nicholas	OF141	143	.279	L.A.	
0	1	Clark, Philip James	P	7	.000	B	C
		Crowe, George Daniel	1B14	77	.301	Cin	
		Cunningham, Joseph Roberts	OF121	144	.345	B	
		(1B35)					
0	1	Duliba, Robert John	P	11	.000	A	
		Durham, Joseph Vann	OF1	6	.000	BaltA57	C
		Essegian, Chas. Abraham	OF9	17	+.179	Phil	L.A.
		Flood, Curtis Chas. (2B1)	OF106	121	.255	B	
3	5	Gibson, Robert	P13	21	.115	A	
		Grammas, Alexander Peter	SS130	131	.269	Cin	
		Gray, Richard Benjamin	SS13	36	+.314	xL.A.	
		(2B2 3B6 OF1)					
		Green, Eugene Leroy (C11)	OF19	30	.189	B	
0	0	Grissom, Marvin Edward	P	3	.000	S.F.	C
		Hemus, Solomon Joseph MGR.	2B1	24	.235	Phil	
		(3B1)					
0	2	Hughes, Thomas Edward	P	2	.000	A	C
		Jablonski, Raymond Leo (SS1)	3B19	60	.253	S.F.	
14	13	Jackson, Lawrence Curtis	P40	54	.113	B	
0	1	Jeffcoat, Harold Bently	P11	12	+.000	xCin	C
		Katt, Raymond Frederick	C14	15	.292	B	C
2	1	Kellner, Alexander Raymond	P	12	.222	Cin	C
		King, Chas. Gilbert	OF4	5	+.429	xChi	C
		McCarver, James Timothy	C6	8	.167	A	
14	12	McDaniel, Lyndall Dale	P	62	.034	B	
4	3	Miller, Robert Lane	P	11	.208	StL57	
13	10	Mizell, Wilmer David	P	31	.187	B	
		Musial, Stanley Frank (OF3)	1B90	115	.255	B	
		Noren, Irving Arnold (1B1)	OF2	8	+.125	B	Chi
2	2	Nunn, Howard Ralph	P	16	.000	A	

WON	LOST	NAME	POS.	G.	BA	FROM	TO
		Oliver, Eugene George	OF42	68	.244	A	
		(C9 1B5)					
		O'Rourke, James Patrick		2	.000	A	C
		Porter, J. W. (1B1)	C19	23	.212	xWashA	C
1	6	Ricketts, Richard James	P	12	.056	A	C
		Shannon, Walter Chas. (2B10)	SS21	47	.284	A	
		Smith, Bobby Gene	OF32	43	.217	B	
		Smith, Harold Raymond	C141	142	.270	B	
0	0	Smith, Wm. Garland	P	6	.000	B	
0	1	Stone, Darrah Dean	P	18	.000	BosA57	
		Tate, Lee Willie	SS39	41	.140	B	C
		(2B2 3B2)					
0	0	Urban, Jack Elmer	P	8	.000	KCA	C
		White, Wm. DeKova (1B71)	OF92	138	.302	S.F.	

WON 86 — NATIONAL LEAGUE — FINISHED 3rd.
LOST 68
TG 154 — 1960. — PCT. .558

ST. LOUIS

SOLOMON JOSEPH HEMUS

WON	LOST	NAME	POS.	G.	BA	FROM	TO
0	1	Barnes, Frank	P	4	.000	StL58	C
0	0	Bauta, Eduardo Galvez	P	9	.000	A	
		Boyer, Kenton Lloyd	3B146	151	.304	B	
		Bridges, Everett Lamar	2B	3	.000	xClevA	
2	2	Bridges, Marshall	P	20	+.000	B	Cin
21	9	Broglio, Ernest Gilbert	P	52	.206	B	
0	0	Browning, Calvin Duane	P	1	.000	A	C
		Burton, Ellis Narrington	OF23	29	.214	StL58	
		Cannizzaro, Christopher John	C6	7	.222	A	
		Carmel, Leon James (OF1)	1B2	4	.000	B	
		Clemens, Douglas Horace	OF	1	.000	A	
		Crowe, George Daniel	1B5	73	.236	B	
		Cunningham, Joseph Roberts	OF116	139	.280	B	
		(1B15)					
4	4	Duliba, Robert John	P	27	.200	B	
		Flood, Curtis Chas. (3B1)	OF134	140	.237	B	
3	6	Gibson, Robert	P27	40	.179	B	
		Glenn, John	OF28	32	.258	A	C
		Gotay, Julio Enrique (3B1)	SS2	3	.375	A	
		Grammas, Alexander Peter	SS46	102	.245	B	
		(2B38 3B13)					
		Gray, Richard Benjamin (3B1)	2B4	9	.000	B	C
1	0	Grim, Robert Anton	P	15	+.000	xCin	
18	13	Jackson, Lawrence Curtis	P43	52	.211	B	
		James, Chas. Wesley	OF37	43	.180	A	
		Javier, Manuel Julien Liranzo	2B	119	.237	A	
		Johnson, Darrell Dean	C	8	.000	NYA58	
4	9	Kline, Ronald Lee	P	34	.143	Pitt	
		Kolb, Gary Alan	OF2	9	.000	A	
		Landrum, Donald Leroy	OF	13	.245	Phi157	
		McCarver, James Timothy	C5	10	.200	B	
12	4	McDaniel, Lyndall Dale	P	65	.231	B	

WON	LOST	NAME	POS.	G.	BA	FROM	TO
4	3	Miller, Robert Lane	P15	17	.143	B	
1	3	Mizell, Wilmer David	P	9	+.111	B	Pitt
		Moryn, Walter Joseph	OF62	75	+.245	xChi	
		Musial, Stanley Frank (1B29)	OF59	116	.275	B	
0	1	Nelson, Melvin Frederick	P	2	.500	A	
		Nieman, Robert Chas.	OF55	81	.287	BaltA	
		Olivares, Edward Balzac	3B1	3	.000	A	
		Rice, Delbert W.	C	1	+.000	xChi	BaltA
9	9	Sadecki, Raymond Michael	P26	29	.211	A	
		Sadowski, Robert Frank	2B	1	.000	A	
		Sawatski, Carl Ernest	C67	78	.229	Phil	
		Shannon, Walter Chas. (SS1)	2B15	18	.174	B	
7	4	Simmons, Curtis Thomas	P23	29	+.213	xPhil	
		Smith, Harold Raymond	C124	127	.228	B	
		Spencer, Daryl Dean (2B16)	SS138	148	.258	S.F.	
		Wagner, Leon Lamar	OF32	39	.214	S.F.	
		White, Wm. DeKova (OF29)	1B123	144	.283	B	

WON 80 — NATIONAL LEAGUE — FINISHED 5th.
LOST 74
TG 154 — 1961. — PCT. .519

ST. LOUIS

SOLOMON JOSEPH HEMUS — JOHN JOSEPH KEANE

WON	LOST	NAME	POS.	G.	BA	FROM	TO
4	3	Anderson, Norman Craig	P	25	.333	A	
2	0	Bauta, Eduardo Galvez	P	13	.500	B	
		Boyer, Kenton Lloyd	3B	153	.329	B	
9	12	Broglio, Ernest Gilbert	P	29	.145	B	
		Buchek, Gerald Peter	SS	31	.133	A	
		Cannizzaro, Christopher John	C5	6	.500	B	
2	6	Cicotte, Alva Warren	P	29	.286	ClevA59	
		Clemens, Douglas Horace	OF3	6	.167	B	
		Crowe, George Daniel		7	.143	B	C
		Cunningham, Joseph Roberts	OF86	113	.286	B	
		(1B10)					
		Flood, Curtis Chas.	OF119	132	.322	B	
13	12	Gibson, Robert	P35	40	.197	B	
		Gotay, Julio Enrique	SS	10	.244	B	
		Grammas, Alexander Peter	SS65	89	.212	B	
		(2B18 3B3)					
14	11	Jackson, Lawrence Curtis	P33	34	.176	B	
		James, Chas. Wesley	OF90	108	.255	B	
		Javier, Manuel Julien Liranzo	2B	113	.279	B	
		Landrum, Donald Leroy (2B1)	OF25	28	.167	B	
		Lillis, Robert Perry (2B24)	SS56	86	+.217	xL.A.	
		McCarver, James Timothy	C20	22	.239	B	
10	6	McDaniel, Lyndall Dale	P	55	.235	B	
1	0	McDermott, Maurice Joseph	P19	22	.071	DetA58	K.C.A
1	3	Miller, Robert Lane	P	35	.357	B	
		Moryn, Walter Joseph	OF7	17	+.125	B	Pitt
		Musial, Stanley Frank	OF103	123	.288	B	
		Nieman, Robert Chas.	OF4	6	.471	B	ClevA
		Olivares, Edward Balzac	OF10	21	.167	B	C

WON	LOST	NAME	POS.	G.	BA	FROM	TO
		Oliver, Eugene George (OF1)	C15	22	.269	StL59	
14	10	Sadecki, Raymond Michael	P31	36	.253	B	
		Sawatski, Carl Ernest (OF1)	C60	86	.299	B	
		Schaffer, Jimmie Ronald	C	68	.255	A	
		Schoendienst, Albert Fred	2B32	72	.300	Mil	
9	10	Simmons, Curtis Thomas	P30	32	.303	B	
		Smith, Harold Raymond	C	45	.248	B	
		Spencer, Daryl Dean	SS	37	+.254	B	L.A.
		Taussig, Donald Franklin	OF87	98	.287	SF58	
0	0	Tiefenauer, Bobby Gene	P	3	.000	ClevA	
		Warwick, Carl Wayne	OF48	55	+.250	xL.A.	
1	1	Washburn, Ray Clark	P	3	.125	A	
		White, Wm. DeKova	1B151	153	.286	B	

WON 84 NATIONAL LEAGUE FINISHED 6th.
LOST 78
TG 162 1962. PCT. .519

ST. LOUIS

JOHN JOSEPH KEANE

WON	LOST	NAME	POS.	G.	BA	FROM	TO
0	0	Anderson, John Chas.	P	5	+.000	BaltA60	Hous
1	0	Bauta, Eduardo Galvez	P	20	.250	B	
		Boyer, Kenton Lloyd	3B	160	.291	B	
0	1	Branch, Harvey Alfred	P	1	.000	A	C
12	9	Broglio, Ernest Gilbert	P	34	.139	B	
		Burda, Edward Robert	OF6	7	.071	A	
		Clemens, Douglas Horace	OF34	48	.237	B	
2	0	Duliba, Robert John	P	28	.000	StL60	
1	4	Ferrarese, Donald Hugh	P	38	+.200	xPhil	C
		Flood, Curtis Chas.	OF	151	.296	B	
15	13	Gibson, Robert	P32	42	.263	B	
		Gotay, Julio Enrique (2B8 OF2)	SS120	127	.255	B	
		Grammas, Alexander Peter (2B2)	SS16	21	+.111	B	Chi
16	11	Jackson, Lawrence Curtis	P	36	.169	B	
		James, Chas. Wesley	OF116	129	.276	B	
		Javier, Manuel Julien Liranzo (SS4)	2B151	155	.263	B	
		Kolb, Gary Alan	OF	6	.357	StL60	
		Landrum, Donald Leroy	OF26	32	+.314	B	Chi
0	0	Locke, Lawrence Donald	P	1	+.000	ClevA	Phil
		Maxvill, Chas. Dallan	SS76	79	.222	A	
3	10	McDaniel, Lyndall Dale	P	55	.095	B	
		Minoso, Saturnino Orestes Arrieta Armas	OF27	39	.196	ChiA	
		Musial, Stanley Frank	OF119	135	.330	B	
		Oliver, Eugene George (1B3 OF8)	C98	122	.258	B	
6	8	Sadecki, Raymond Michael	P22	24	.081	B	
		Sawatski, Carl Ernest	C70	85	.252	B	
		Schaffer, Jimmie Ronald	C69	70	.242	B	

WON	LOST	NAME	POS.	G.	BA	FROM	TO
		Schoendienst, Albert Fred (3B4)	2B21	98	.301	B	
		Shannon, Thomas Michael	OF7	10	.133	A	
5	3	Shantz, Robert Clayton	P	28	+.154	xHous	
10	10	Simmons, Curtis Thomas	P	31	.160	B	
		Smith, Bobby Gene	OF80	91	+.231	xChi	
1	0	Toth, Paul Louis	P	6	+.400	A	Chi
		Warwick, Carl Wayne	OF10	13	+.348	B	Hous
12	9	Washburn, Ray Clark	P	34	.179	B	
		White, Wm. DeKova (OF27)	1B146	159	.324	B	
		Whitfield, Fred Dwight	1B38	73	.266	A	

WON 93 NATIONAL LEAGUE FINISHED 2nd.
LOST 69
TG 162 1963. PCT. .574

ST. LOUIS

JOHN JOSEPH KEANE

WON	LOST	NAME	POS.	G.	BA	FROM	TO
		Altman, George Lee	OF124	135	.274	Chi	
3	4	Bauta, Eduardo Galvez	P	38	+.000	B	N.Y.
		Beauchamp, James Edward		4	.000	A	
		Bloomfield, Clyde Stalcup	3B	1	.000	A	
		Boyer, Kenton Lloyd	3B	159	.285	B	
18	8	Broglio, Ernest Gilbert	P	39	.112	B	
		Buchek, Gerald Peter	SS1	3	.250	StL61	
3	8	Burdette, Selva Lewis	P	21	+.097	xMil	
		Burke, Leo Patrick (3B5)	OF11	30	+.204	LAA	Chic.
		Carmel, Leon James (1B1)	OF38	57	+.227	StL60	N.Y.
		Clemens, Douglas Horace	OF3	5	.167	B	
		Damaska, Jack Lloyd (2B1)	OF1	5	.200	A	C
2	1	Fanok, Harry Michael	P	12	.400	A	
		Flood, Curtis Chas.	OF	158	.302	B	
		Gagliano, Philip Joseph (3B1)	2B3	10	.400	A	
18	9	Gibson, Robert	P36	41	.207	B	
		Groat, Richard Morrow	SS	158	.319	Pitt	
0	1	Humphreys, Robert Wm.	P	9	.000	DetA	
		James, Chas. Wesley	OF101	116	.268	B	
		Javier, Manuel Julien Liranzo	2B	161	.263	B	
2	0	Jones, Samuel	P	11	.000	DetA	
		Kolb, Gary Alan (C1 3B1)	OF58	75	.271	B	
		Long, Jeoffrey Keith		5	.200	A	
0	0	MacKenzie, Kenneth Purvis	P	8	+.000	xN.Y.	
		Maxvill, Chas. Dallan (2B9 3B3)	SS24	53	.235	B	
		McCarver, James Timothy	C126	127	.289	StL61	
		Musial, Stanley Frank	OF96	124	.255	B	C
		Oliver, Eugene George	C35	39	+.225	B	Mil
0	5	Olivo, Diomedes Antonio	P	19	.000	Pitt	C
		Ricketts, David Wm.	C	3	.250	A	
10	10	Sadecki, Raymond Michael	P36	39	.141	B	
		Sawatski, Carl Ernest	C27	56	.238	B	C
		Schoendienst, Albert Fred		6	.000	B	C
2	0	Schultz, George Warren	P	24	+.000	xChic.	
		Shannon, Thomas Michael	OF26	32	.308	B	

WON	LOST	NAME	POS.	G.	BA	FROM	TO
6	4	Shantz, Robert Clayton	P	55	.143	B	
15	9	Simmons, Curtis Thomas	P	32	.160	B	
9	7	Taylor, Ronald Wesley	P	54	.031	ClevA	
		Thacker, Morris Benton	C	3	.000	Chic.	C
5	3	Washburn, Ray Clark	P	11	.053	B	
		White, Wm. DeKova	1B	162	.304	B	
		Withrow, Raymond Wallace	OF2	6	.000	A	C

WON 93 NATIONAL LEAGUE FINISHED 1st.
LOST 69
TG 162 1964. PCT. .574

ST. LOUIS

JOHN JOSEPH KEANE

WON	LOST	NAME	POS.	G.	BA	FROM	TO
0	0	Bakenhaster, David Lee	P	2	.000	A	C
		Boyer, Kenton Lloyd	3B	162	.295	B	
		Brock, Louis Clark	OF102	103	+.348	xChic.	
3	5	Broglio, Ernest Gilbert	P	11	+.095	B	Chic
		Buchek, Gerald Peter (2B9 3B1)	SS20	35	.200	B	
1	0	Burdette, Selva Lewis	P	8	+.000	B	Chic
		Clemens, Douglas Horace	OF22	33	+.205	B	Chic
7	9	Craig, Roger Lee	P	39	.208	N.Y.	
5	5	Cuellar, Miguel Santana	P	32	.000	Cin59	
0	0	Dowling, David Barclay	P	1	.000	A	
0	0	Fanok, Harry Michael	P	4	.000	B	C
		Flood, Curtis Chas.	OF	162	.311	B	
		Gagliano, Philip Joseph (1B1 3B1 OF2)	2B12	40	.259	B	
19	12	Gibson, Robert	P	40	.156	B	
		Groat, Richard Morrow	SS160	161	.292	B	
1	2	Hobbie, Glen Frederick	P	13	+.154	xChic	C
2	0	Humphreys, Robert Wm.	P	28	.250	B	
		James, Chas. Wesley	OF60	88	.223	B	
		Javier, Manuel Julien Liranzo	2B154	155	.241	B	
		Lewis, John Joseph	OF36	40	.234	A	
		Long, Joeffrey Keith (1B3)	OF4	28	.233	B	ChicA
		Maxvill, Chas. Dallan (SS13 3B1 OF1)	2B15	37	.231	B	
		McCarver, James Timothy	C137	143	.288	B	
		Morgan, Joseph Michael		3	.000	ClevA61	C
4	2	Richardson, Gordon Clark	P	19	.077	A	
20	11	Sadecki, Raymond Michael	P37	39	.160	B	
1	3	Schultz, George Warren	P	30	.167	B	
		Shannon, Thomas Michael	OF	88	.261	B	
1	3	Shantz, Robert Clayton	P	16	+.000	B	Chic
18	9	Simmons, Curtis Thomas	P	34	.106	B	
		Skinner, Robert Ralph	OF31	55	+.271	xCin	
		Spiezio, Edward Wayne		12	.333	A	
0	0	Spring, Jack Russell	P	2	+.000	xChic	
8	4	Taylor, Ronald Wesley	P	63	.133	B	
		Uecker, Robert George	C	40	.198	Mil	

WON	LOST	NAME	POS.	G.	BA	FROM	TO
		Warwick, Carl Wayne	OF49	88	.259	Hous	
3	4	Washburn, Ray Clark	P	15	.133	B	
		White, Wm. DeKova	1B	160	.303	B	

CLUB RECORD

NATIONAL LEAGUE

SAN FRANCISCO

YEAR	TG	WON	LOST	PCT.	FINISHED	MANAGER
1958	154	80	74	.519	3	Wm. Joseph Rigney
1959	154	83	71	.539	3	Wm. Joseph Rigney
1960	154	79	75	.513	5	Wm. Joseph Rigney Thomas Clancy Sheehan
1961	154	85	69	.552	3	Alvin Ralph Dark
1962	165	103	62	.624	1	Alvin Ralph Dark
1963	162	88	74	.543	3	Alvin Ralph Dark
1964	162	90	72	.556	4	Alvin Ralph Dark

YEAR	TG	WON	LOST	TIED	PCT.	FINISHED	MANAGER
1965	163	95	67	1	.586	2	HERMAN LOUIS FRANKS
1966	161	93	68	0	.578	2	HERMAN LOUIS FRANKS
1967	162	91	71	0	.562	2	HERMAN LOUIS FRANKS
1968	163	88	74	1	.543	2	HERMAN LOUIS FRANKS
1969	162	90	72	0	.556	2W	CLYDE EDWARD KING
1970	162	86	76	0	.531	3W	CLYDE EDWARD KING CHARLES FRANCIS FOX
1971	162	90	72	0	.556	1W (LP)	CHARLES FRANCIS FOX
1972	155	69	86	0	.445	5W	CHARLES FRANCIS FOX

WON 80 — NATIONAL LEAGUE — FINISHED 3rd.
LOST 74
TG 154 — 1958. — PCT. .519

SAN FRANCISCO

WM. JOSEPH RIGNEY

WON	LOST	NAME	POS.	G.	BA	FROM	TO
		Alou, Felipe Rojas	OF70	75	.253	A	
16	13	Antonelli, John August	P41	47	.226	B	
1	0	Barclay, Curtis Cordell	P	6	.667	B	
		Brandt, John George	OF14	18	.250	NY56	
		Bressoud, Edward Francis (SS4 3B6)	2B57	66	.263	B	
0	0	Burnside, Peter Willits	P	6	.000	B	
		Cepeda, Orlando Manuel	1B147	148	.312	A	
1	0	Constable, James Lee	P	9	1.000	B	ClevA
1	2	Crone, Raymond Hayes	P	14	.000	B	C
		Davenport, James Houston (SS5)	3B130	134	.256	A	
		Finigan, James LeRoy (3B4)	2B8	23	.200	DetA	
0	0	Fitzgerald, John Francis	P	1	.000	A	C
4	5	Giel, Paul Robert	P	29	.074	NY55	
10	12	Gomez, Ruben Colon	P42	48	.200	B	
7	5	Grissom, Marvin Edward	P	51	.000	B	
		Jablonski, Raymond Leo	3B57	86	.230	B	
0	1	Johnson, Donald Roy	P	17	.000	BaltA55	C
3	1	Jones, Gordon Bassett	P	11	.000	B	
		King, James Hubert	OF15	34	.214	StL	
		Kirkland, Willie Chas.	OF115	122	.258	A	
		Lockman, Carroll Walter (1B7 2B15)	OF25	92	.238	B	
		Mays, Willie Howard	OF151	152	.347	B	
11	8	McCormick, Michael Francis	P	42	.222	B	
6	9	Miller, Stuart Leonard	P41	42	.120	B	
8	11	Monzant, Ramon Segundo	P43	44	.163	B	
		O'Connell, Daniel Francis (3B3)	2B104	107	.232	B	
		Rodgers, Kenneth Andre Ian	SS18	22	.206	B	
		Sauer, Henry John	OF67	88	.250	B	
		Schmidt, Robert Benjamin	C123	127	.244	A	
0	0	Shipley, Joseph Clark	P	1	.000	A	
		Speake, Robert Chas.	OF10	66	.211	Chi	
		Spencer, Daryl Dean (2B17)	SS134	148	.256	B	
		Taussig, Donald Franklin	OF36	39	.200	A	
		Testa, Nicholas	C	1	.000	A	C
		Thomas, Valmy	C61	63	.259	B	
		Wagner, Leon Lamar	OF57	74	.317	A	
		White, Wm. DeKova (OF2)	1B3	26	.241	NY56	
11	7	Worthington, Allan Fulton	P	54	.182	B	
1	0	Zanni, Dominick Thomas	P	1	.000	A	

WON 83 — NATIONAL LEAGUE — FINISHED 3rd.
LOST 71
TG 154 — 1959. — PCT. .539

SAN FRANCISCO

WM. JOSEPH RIGNEY

WON	LOST	NAME	POS.	G.	BA	FROM	TO
		Alou, Felipe Rojas	OF69	95	.275	B	
19	10	Antonelli, John August	P40	43	.158	B	
0	0	Barclay, Curtis Cordell	P	1	.000	B	C
		Brandt, John George	OF116	137	.270	B	
		(1B3 2B1 3B18)					
		Bressoud, Edward Francis	SS92	104	.251	B	
		(1B1 2B1 3B1)					
1	0	Byerly, Eldred Wm.	P	11	.000	BosA	
		Cepeda, Orlando Manuel	1B122	151	.317	B	
		(3B4 OF44)					
		Davenport, James Houston	3B121	123	.258	B	
		(SS1)					
2	6	Fisher, Eddie Gene	P	17	.000	A	
		Hegan, James Edward	C	21	+.133	xPhil	
3	2	Jones, Gordon Bassett	P	31	.000	B	
21	15	Jones, Samuel	P	50	.129	StL	
		Kirkland, Willie Chas.	OF117	126	.272	B	
		Landrith, Hobert Neal	C	109	.251	StL	
		Mays, Willie Howard	OF147	151	.313	B	
		McCardell, Roger Morton	C3	4	.000	A	C
12	16	McCormick, Michael Francis	P	47	.106	B	
		McCovey, Willie Lee	1B51	52	.354	A	
8	7	Miller, Stuart Leonard	P	59	.044	B	
0	0	Muffett, Billy Arnold	P	5	.000	StL	
		O'Connell, Daniel Francis	3B26	34	.190	B	
		(2B8)					
		Pagan, Jose Antonio	3B18	31	.174	A	
		(2B3 SS5)					
0	0	Renfroe, Marshall Daniel	P	1	.000	A	C
		Rhodes, James Lamar		54	.188	NY57	C
		Rodgers, Kenneth Andre Ian	SS66	71	.250	B	
15	12	Sanford, John Stanley	P	36	.111	Phil	
		Sauer, Henry John	OF1	13	.067	B	C
		Schmidt, Robert Benjamin	C70	71	.243	B	
0	0	Shipley, Joseph Clark	P	10	.000	B	
		Speake, Robert Chas.		15	.091	B	C
		Spencer, Daryl Dean (SS4)	2B151	152	.265	B	
		Wagner, Leon Lamar	OF28	87	.225	B	
2	3	Worthington, Allan Fulton	P	42	.077	B	
0	0	Zanni, Dominick Thomas	P	9	.000	B	

WON 79 NATIONAL LEAGUE FINISHED 5th.
LOST 75
TG 154 1960. PCT. .513

SAN FRANCISCO

WM. JOSEPH RIGNEY THOMAS CLANCY SHEEHAN

WON	LOST	NAME	POS.	G.	BA	FROM	TO
		Alou, Felipe Rojas	OF95	106	.264	B	
		Alou, Mateo Rojas	OF1	4	.333	A	
		Amalfitano, John Joseph	3B63	106	.277	NY55	
		(2B33 SS3 OF1)					
6	7	Antonelli, John August	P41	42	.235	B	
		Blasingame, Donald Lee	2B133	136	.235	StL	
		Bressoud, Edward Francis	SS115	116	.225	B	
1	0	Byerly, Eldred Wm.	P	19	.000	B	C
		Cepeda, Orlando Manuel	OF91	151	.297	B	
		(1B63)					
0	0	Choate, Donald Leon	P	4	.000	A	C
		Davenport, James Houston	3B103	112	.251	B	
		(SS7)					
1	0	Fisher, Eddie Gene	P	3	.600	B	
18	14	Jones, Samuel	P	39	.200	B	
1	1	Jones, Sherman Jarvis	P	16	.286	A	
		Kirkland, Willie Chas.	OF143	146	.252	B	
		Landrith, Hobert Neal	C70	71	.242	B	
3	2	Loes, Wm.	P	37	.250	BaltA	
		Long, Richard Dale	1B10	37	.167	Chi	N.Y.A
1	4	Maranda, Georges Henri	P	17	.167	A	
		Marshall, Rufus James	1B28	75	.237	Chi	
		(OF6)					
6	2	Marichal, Juan Antonio	P	11	.129	A	
		Sanchez					
		Mays, Willie Howard	OF152	153	.319	B	
15	12	McCormick, Michael Francis	P	40	.182	B	
		McCovey, Willie Lee	1B71	101	.238	B	
7	6	Miller, Stuart Leonard	P	47	.200	B	
0	0	Monzant, Ramon Segundo	P	1	.000	SF58	C
8	13	O'Dell, Wm. Oliver	P43	49	.107	BaltA	
		Pagan, Jose Antonio (3B1)	SS11	18	.286	B	
		Philley, David Earl (3B3)	OF10	39	+.164	xPhil	BaltA
		Rodgers, Kenneth Andre Ian	SS41	81	.244	B	
		(1B6 3B21 OF2)					
12	14	Sanford, John Stanley	P	37	.176	B	
		Schmidt, Robert Benjamin	C108	110	.267	B	
0	0	Shipley, Joseph Clark	P	15	.000	B	
		Wilson, Samuel O'Neil	C	6	.000	A	C

WON 85 NATIONAL LEAGUE FINISHED 3rd.
LOST 69
TG 154 1961. PCT. .552

SAN FRANCISCO

ALVIN RALPH DARK

WON	LOST	NAME	POS.	G.	BA	FROM	TO
		Alou, Felipe Rojas	OF122	132	.289	B	
		Alou, Mateo Rojas	OF58	81	.310	B	
		Amalfitano, John Joseph	2B95	109	.255	B	
		(3B6)					
		Bailey, Lonas Edgar (OF1)	C103	107	+.238	xCin	
		Blasingame, Donald Lee		3	+.000	B	Cin
2	2	Bolin, Bobby Donald	P	37	.286	A	

WON	LOST	NAME	POS.	G.	BA	FROM	TO
		Bowman, Ernest Ferrell (SS12 3B7)	2B13	38	.211	A	
		Bressoud, Edward Francis (2B1 3B3)	SS34	59	.211	B	
		Cepeda, Orlando Manuel (OF80)	1B81	152	.311	B	
		Davenport, James Houston	3B132	137	.278	B	
5	1	Duffalo, James Francis	P24	25	.294	A	
		Farley, Robert Jacob (1B1)	OF3	13	.100	A	
0	2	Fisher, Eddie Gene	P	15	.143	B	
		Haller, Thomas Frank	C25	30	.145	A	
		Hiller, Chas. Joseph	2B67	70	.238	A	
8	8	Jones, Samuel	P	37	.139	B	
		Kuenn, Harvey Edward (SS1 3B32)	OF93	131	.265	ClevA	
		Landrith, Hobert Neal	C30	43	.239	B	
3	6	LeMay, Richard Paul	P	27	.077	A	
6	5	Loes, Wm.	P	26	.156	B	C
13	10	Marichal, Juan Antonio Sanchez	P29	30	.119	B	
		Marshall, Rufus James (OF2)	1B4	44	.222	B	
		Mays, Willie Howard	OF153	154	.308	B	
13	16	McCormick, Michael Francis	P	40	.188	B	
		McCovey, Willie Lee	1B84	106	.271	B	
14	5	Miller, Stuart Leonard	P63	64	.200	B	
7	5	O'Dell, Wm. Oliver	P46	49	.103	B	
		Orsino, John Joseph	C	25	.277	A	
		Pagan, Jose Antonio (OF4)	SS132	134	.253	B	
13	9	Sanford, John Stanley	P38	39	.216	B	
		Schmidt, Robert Benjamin	C	2	+.167	B	Cin
1	0	Zanni, Dominick Thomas	P	8	.000	SF59	

WON 103 — NATIONAL LEAGUE — FINISHED 1st.
LOST 62
TG 165 — 1962. — PCT. .624

SAN FRANCISCO

ALVIN RALPH DARK

WON	LOST	NAME	POS.	G.	BA	FROM	TO
		Alou, Felipe Rojas	OF150	154	.316	B	
		Alou, Mateo Rojas	OF57	78	.292	B	
		Bailey, Lonas Edgar	C75	96	.232	B	
		Boles, Carl Theodore	OF7	19	.375	A	C
7	3	Bolin, Bobby Donald	P	41	.261	B	
		Bowman, Ernest Ferrell (SS10 3B11)	2B17	46	.190	B	
		Cepeda, Orlando Manuel (OF2)	1B160	162	.306	B	
		Davenport, James Houston	3B141	144	.297	B	
1	2	Duffalo, James Francis	P	24	.000	B	
0	0	Garibaldi, Rob Roy	P	9	.000	A	
		Haller, Thomas Frank	C91	99	.261	B	
		Hiller, Chas. Joseph	2B	161	.276	B	
		Kuenn, Harvey Edward (3B30)	OF105	130	.304	B	
5	4	Larsen, Donald James	P49	52	.200	ChiA	
0	1	LeMay, Richard Paul	P	9	.000	B	
18	11	Marichal, Juan Antonio Sanchez	P37	38	.236	B	
		Mays, Willie Howard	OF161	162	.304	B	
5	5	McCormick, Michael Francis	P28	29	.107	B	
		McCovey, Willie Lee (1B17)	OF57	91	.293	B	
5	8	Miller, Stuart Leonard	P59	60	.125	B	
		Mota, Manuel Rafael (2B3 3B7)	OF27	47	.176	A	
		Nieman, Robert Chas.	OF3	30	.300	xClevA	C
19	14	O'Dell, Wm. Oliver	P43	49	.133	B	
		Orsino, John Joseph	C16	18	.271	B	
		Pagan, Jose Antonio	SS	164	.259	B	
3	1	Perry, Gaylord Jackson	P	13	.231	A	
		Peterson, Chas. Andrew	SS2	4	.167	A	
		Phillips, Richard Eugene	1B1	5	.000	A	
16	6	Pierce, Walter Wm.	P	30	.214	ChiA	
		Pignatano, Joseph Benjamin	C	7	+.200	K.C.A	N.Y.
24	7	Sanford, John Stanley	P	39	.153	B	

WON 88 — NATIONAL LEAGUE — FINISHED 3rd.
LOST 74
TG 162 — 1963. — PCT. .543

SAN FRANCISCO

ALVIN RALPH DARK

WON	LOST	NAME	POS.	G.	BA	FROM	TO
		Alou, Felipe Rojas	OF153	157	.281	B	
		Alou, Jesus Maria Rojas	OF12	16	.250	A	
		Alou, Mateo Rojas	OF20	63	.145	B	
		Amalfitano, John Joseph (3B7)	2B37	54	.175	Hous	
		Bailey, Lonas Edgar	C88	105	.263	B	
10	6	Bolin, Bobby Donald	P	47	.143	B	
		Bowman, Ernest Ferrell (2B26 3B12)	SS40	81	.184	B	C
		Cardenal, Jose Domec	OF2	9	.200	A	
		Cepeda, Orlando Manuel (OF3)	1B150	156	.316	B	
		Coker, Jimmie Goodwin	C2	4	.200	Phil	
0	0	Constable, James Lee	P	4	.000	Mil.	C
		Davenport, James Houston (2B22 SS1)	3B127	147	.252	B	
4	2	Duffalo, James Francis	P	34	.111	B	
6	10	Fisher, John Howard	P	36	.103	BaltA	
0	1	Garibaldi, Rob Roy	P	4	.000	B	
		Haller, Thomas Frank (OF7)	C85	98	.255	B	
		Hart, James Ray	3B	7	.200	A	
0	0	Herbel, Ronald Samuel	P	2	.000	A	
		Hiller, Chas. Joseph	2B109	111	.223	B	
2	0	Hoeft, Wm. Frederick	P	23	1.000	BaltA	

WON	LOST	NAME	POS.	G.	BA	FROM	TO
		Kuenn, Harvey Edward (3B53)	OF64	120	.290	B	
		Larker, Norman Howard	1B11	19	+.071	Mil.	C
7	7	Larsen, Donald James	P	46	.181	B	
0	0	Linzy, Frank Alfred	P	8	.000	A	
25	8	Marichal, Juan Antonio Sanchez	P41	42	.179	B	
		Mays, Willie Howard (SS1)	OF157	157	.314	B	
		McCovey, Willie Lee (1B23)	OF135	152	.280	B	
14	10	O'Dell, Wm. Oliver	P36	47	.205	B	
		Pagan, Jose Antonio (2B1 OF1)	SS143	148	.234	B	
1	6	Perry Gaylord Jackson	P31	32	.222	B	
		Peterson, Chas. Andrew (SS1 3B5 OF3)	2B8	22	.259	B	
3	11	Pierce, Walter Wm.	P	38	.129	B	
0	0	Pregenzer, John Arthur	P	6	.000	A	
16	13	Sanford, John Stanley	P42	45	.138	B	
0	0	Stanek, Albert Wilfred	P	11	.000	A	C

WON 90 NATIONAL LEAGUE FINISHED 4th.
LOST 72
TG 162 1964. PCT. .556

SAN FRANCISCO

ALVIN RALPH DARK

WON	LOST	NAME	POS.	G.	BA	FROM	TO
		Alou, Jesus Maria Rojas	OF108	115	.274	B	
		Alou, Mateo Rojas	OF80	110	.264	B	
6	9	Bolin, Bobby Donald	P38	39	.100	B	
		Cardenal, Jose Domec	OF16	20	.000	B	
		Cepeda, Orlando Manuel (OF1)	1B139	142	.304	B	
		Crandall, Delmar Wesley	C65	69	.231	Mil.	
		Davenport, James Houston (2B30 3B41)	SS64	116	.236	B	
5	1	Duffalo, James Francis	P	35	.071	B	
1	2	Estelle, Richard Harry	P	6	.067	A	
		Garrido, Gilbert Gonzalo	SS	14	.080	A	
		Haller, Thomas Frank (OF3)	C113	117	.253	B	
		Hart, James Ray (OF6)	3B149	153	.286	B	
10	11	Hendley, Chas. Robert	P	30	.106	Mil.	
9	9	Herbel, Ronald Samuel	P40	41	.000	B	
		Hiller, Chas. Joseph (3B1)	2B60	80	.180	B	
		Hundley, Cecil Randolph	C	2	.000	A	
		Kuenn, Harvey Edward (1B11 3B2)	OF88	111	.262	B	
		Lanier, Harold Clifton (SS3)	2B93	98	.274	A	
0	1	Larsen, Donald James	P	6	+.000	B	Hous
0	0	MacKenzie, Kenneth Purvis	P	10	.000	StL	
21	8	Marichal, Juan Antonio Sanchez	P	33	.144	B	
		Mays, Willie Howard (1B1 SS1 3B1)	OF155	157	.296	B	
		McCovey, Willie Lee (1B26)	OF83	130	.220	B	
1	0	Murakami, Masanori	P	9	.000	A	
8	7	O'Dell, Wm. Oliver	P36	50	.000	B	
		Pagan, Jose Antonio (OF8)	SS132	134	.223	B	
12	11	Perry, Gaylord Jackson	P44	46	.054	B	
		Peterson, Chas. Andrew (1B2 2B1 3B1)	OF10	66	.203	B	
3	0	Pierce, Walter Wm.	P	34	.333	B	C
2	0	Pregenzer, John Arthur	P	13	.000	B	C
5	7	Sanford, John Stanley	P18	19	.133	B	
7	6	Shaw, Robert John	P	61	.000	Mil.	
		Snider, Edwin Donald	OF43	91	.210	N.Y.	C

CLUB RECORD

NATIONAL LEAGUE

SYRACUSE

YEAR	TG	WON	LOST	PCT.	FINISHED	MANAGER
1879	42	15	27	.357	DID NOT FINISH	George L. Smith

CLUB RECORD

OTHER MAJOR LEAGUES

SYRACUSE

YEAR	TG	WON	LOST	PCT.	FINISHED	MANAGER
AMERICAN ASSOCIATION						
1890	127	55	72	.433	7	Wallace C. Fessenden George Kasson Frazer

WON 15
LOST 27
TG 42

NATIONAL LEAGUE

1879

FINISHED 6th.
(DID NOT FINISH)
PCT. .357

SYRACUSE

GEORGE L. SMITH

WON	LOST	NAME	POS.	G.	BA	FROM	TO
		Adams, George (OF2)	1B2	4	.214	A	C
		Allen, Cyrus Alban (Dick) (OF3)	3B8	11	+.184	A	Clev
		Carpenter, Warren Wm. (Hick) (3B17 OF11)	1B32	63	.201	A	
		Creamer, George W. (SS2 OF3)	2B10	15	.213	Mil	
		Decker, Edward Harry (1B1 OF1)	C2	3	.100	A	
		Dorgan, Michael Cornelius (3B11 OF14)	1B21	59	.266	StL77	
		Farrell, John A.	2B	54	+.304	A	Prov.
		Holbert, Wm. H. (OF4)	C54	57	+.199	Mil	Troy
		Kelly, John Francis (1B2)	C7	9	.125	A	
		Macullar, James F. (OF24)	SS35	63	.213	A	
		Mansell, Michael R.	OF	66	.211	A	
		Mansell, Thomas E.	OF	1	+.250	xTroy	
11	13	McCormick, Patrick Henry	P49	55	.224	A	
		McGuinness, John J.	1B	12	.294	Lvlle76	
		Osterhout, Chas. H. (2B1)	C1	2	.000	A	C
4	14	Purcell, Wm. Aloysius (Blondy) (P22 C1)	OF45	62	+.265	A	Cin
		Richmond John H. (SS27)	OF33	61	.211	A	
		Woodhead, James	3B	34	.169	A	C

CLUB RECORD

NATIONAL LEAGUE

TROY

YEAR	TG	WON	LOST	PCT.	FINISHED	MANAGER
1879	75	19	56	.253	8(Last)	Robert V. Ferguson
1880	83	41	42	.494	4	Robert V. Ferguson
1881	84	39	45	.464	5	Robert V. Ferguson
1882	83	35	48	.422	7	Robert V. Ferguson

WON 19
LOST 56
TG 75

NATIONAL LEAGUE 1879

FINISHED 8th (LAST)
PCT. .253

TROY

ROBERT V. FERGUSON

WON	LOST	NAME	POS.	G.	BA	FROM	TO
13	40	Bradley, George Washington	P53	61	.245	Chi77	
0	2	Brouthers, Dennis (Dan) (P2)	1B37	39	.273	A	
		Caskin, Edward James (C20)	SS41	67	.259	A	
		Cassidy, John P. (1B2)	OF7	8	.176	Chi	
		Clapp, Aaron B. (OF10)	1B24	34	.272	A	C
		Doscher, John Herman Sr.	3B	46	.223	A	
		Evans, Jacob	OF	70	.230	A	
		Ferguson, Robert V. MGR.	3B24	29	.252	Chi	
0	2	Gardner, Franklin W.	P	2	.167	A	
2	4	Goldsmith, Frederick E. (1B1 OF2)	P8	9	.231	A	
		Hall, Archibald W.	OF	66	.255	A	
		Hawkes, Thorndike Proctor	2B	63	.206	A	
		Holbert, Wm. H.	C	4	+.267	xSyr	
		Mansell, Thomas E.	OF	39	+.242	A	Syr
0	2	McManus, P.	P	2	.125	A	C
		Nelson, Jackson W. (OF4)	SS24	28	.246	Indpls	
		Reilley, Chas. E. (1B10)	C49	61	.232	A	
4	6	Salisbury, Henry H. (OF1)	P10	10	.056	A	
		Shoup, John F.	SS	10	.097	A	
		Taylor, Wm. Henry	OF	24	.214	Hart77	

WON 41
LOST 42
TG 83

NATIONAL LEAGUE 1880.

FINISHED 4th.
PCT. .494

TROY

ROBERT V. FERGUSON

WON	LOST	NAME	POS.	G.	BA	FROM	TO
		Ahearn, Chas.	C	1	.250	A	C
		Briody, Chas. F.	C	1	.000	A	
		Brouthers, Dennis (Dan)	1B	3	.154	B	
		Caskin, Edward James (C1)	SS	82	.231	B	
		Cassidy, John P. (2B1)	OF82	83	.253	B	
		Cogswell, Edward	1B	47	.301	Bos	
		Connor, Roger	3B	83	.332	A	
		Dickerson, Lewis Pessano (SS1)	OF30	30	+.189	Cin	Wor
0	0	Evans, Jacob (P1 SS1)	OF46	47	.255	B	
		Ewing, Wm. (Buck) (OF4)	C10	13	.152	A	

WON	LOST	NAME	POS.	G.	BA	FROM	TO
		Ferguson, Robert V. MGR.	2B	82	.262	B	
		Gillespie, Patrick Peter	OF	82	.242	A	
		Haley, Fred	C	2	.000	A	C
		Harbidge, Wm. Arthur (OF1)	C8	8	.370	Chic	
		Higham, Richard (OF1)	C1	1	.200	Prov78	C
		Holbert, Wm. H. (OF4)	C57	60	.188	B	
6	6	Keefe, Timothy J.	P	12	.227	A	
0	5	Larkin, Frank (SS1 OF1)	P5	5	.118	Chi	
		Lawlor, Michael H.	C	4	.100	A	
1	1	Mountain, Frank H.	P	2	.222	A	
		Straub, Joseph	C	3	.231	A	
		Tobin, Wm.	1B	32	+.152	xWor	C
34	30	Welch, Michael F. (Mickey) (OF2)	P64	66	.286	A	

WON 39 NATIONAL LEAGUE FINISHED 5th.
LOST 45
TG 84 1881. PCT. .464

TROY

ROBERT V. FERGUSON

WON	LOST	NAME	POS.	G.	BA	FROM	TO
		Caskin, Edward James	SS	62	.226	B	
		Cassidy, John P.	OF	84	.219	B	
		Connor, Roger	1B	84	.288	B	
		Evans, Jacob	OF	81	.242	B	
		Ewing, Wm. (Buck) (SS21 3B1 OF1)	C43	65	.243	B	
		Ferguson, Robert V. MGR.	2B	84	.287	B	
		Gillespie, Patrick Peter	OF	83	.277	B	
		Hankinson, Frank Edward (SS1)	3B	84	.196	Clev	
		Holbert, Wm. H. (OF3)	C41	44	.274	B	
19	27	Keefe, Timothy J.	P	46	.230	B	
20	18	Welch, Michael F. (Mickey)	P	39	.279	B	

WON 35 NATIONAL LEAGUE FINISHED 7th.
LOST 48
TG 83 1882. PCT. .422

TROY

ROBERT V. FERGUSON

WON	LOST	NAME	POS.	G.	BA	FROM	TO
		Cassidy, John P. (3B12)	OF16	28	.176	B	
		Connor, Roger (3B14 OF24)	1B41	79	.327	B	
4	6	Egan, James (P14 C2)	OF15	29	.181	A	C
0	0	Ewing, Wm. (Buck) (P1 C25 1B1 2B4 OF1)	3B41	72	.273	B	
		%Ferguson, Robert V. MGR.	2B77	79	.254	B	
		Gillespie, Patrick Peter	OF	72	.265	B	
		*Harbidge, Wm. Arthur	OF23	32	.187	Troy80	
		#Holbert, Wm. H.	C53	68	.186	B	
		Holdsworth, James	OF	1	.000	Hart77	
17	26	Keefe, Timothy J. (3B3 OF8)	P43	51	.225	B	
		@Pfeffer, Nathaniel Frederick	SS81	83	.221	A	
		Roseman, James J.	OF	80	.236	A	
		Smith, Alexander Chas.	1B	34	+.236	A	Wor
14	16	Welch, Michael F. (Mickey) (OF7)	P30	37	.248	B	

%Ferguson also played 2 games at SS.
*Harbidge also played 2 games as C and 6 games at 1B.
#Holbert also played 1 game at 1B, 12 games at 3B and 3 games in the OF.
@Pfeffer also played 2 games at 3B.

CLUB RECORD

NATIONAL LEAGUE

WASHINGTON

YEAR	TG	WON	LOST	PCT.	FINISHED	MANAGER
1886	120	28	92	.233	8(Last)	Michael B. Scanlon John H. Gaffney
1887	122	46	76	.377	7	John H. Gaffney Walter L. Dennis Walter F. Hewitt
1888	134	48	86	.358	8(Last)	Theodore Paul Sullivan James E. Whitney
1889	124	41	83	.331	8(Last)	John Francis Morrill Arthur Albert Irwin
1890-1891	OUT OF LEAGUE					
1892	151	58	93	.384	10	Wm. S. Barnie Arthur Albert Irwin Daniel Richardson Jacob Earle Wagner
1893	129	40	89	.310	12(Last)	Jacob Earle Wagner James Henry O'Rourke
1894	132	45	87	.341	11	Gustavus Heinrich Schmelz
1895	128	43	85	.336	10	Gustavus Heinrich Schmelz
1896	131	58	73	.443	x9(Bkn)	Gustavus Heinrich Schmelz
1897	132	61	71	.462	x6(Bkn)	Gustavus Heinrich Schmelz Thomas T. Brown
1898	152	51	101	.335	11	Thomas T. Brown John Joseph Doyle James Thomas McGuire Arthur Albert Irwin
1899	148	53	95	.358	11	Arthur Albert Irwin

CLUB RECORD

OTHER MAJOR LEAGUES

WASHINGTON

YEAR	TG	WON	LOST	PCT.	FINISHED	MANAGER
AMERICAN ASSOCIATION						
1884	63	12	51	.190	DID NOT FINISH	John Samuel Hollingshead
1885-1890	OUT OF LEAGUE					
1891	135	44	91	.326	9(Last)	Samuel W. Trott Chas. N. Snyder Daniel W. Shannon Tobias Chas. Griffin
UNION ASSOCIATION (NATIONALS)						
1884	113	47	66	.416	7	Michael B. Scanlon

WON 28 LOST 92 TG 120 — NATIONAL LEAGUE — 1886. — FINISHED 8th (LAST) PCT. .233

WASHINGTON

MICHAEL B. SCANLON JOHN H. GAFFNEY

WON	LOST	NAME	POS.	G.	BA	FROM	TO
		Baker, Philip (OF21)	1B56	81	.221	WashUA84	C
4	18	Barr, Robert M.	P	22	.164	IndplsAA84	
		Carroll, Samuel (Clifford)	OF	111	.228	Prov	
0	1	Corcoran, Lawrence J. (Larry) (P1)	OF21	21	+.185	xN.Y.	
2	6	Crane, Edward Nicholas (Cannon-Ball) (P10)	OF68	80	.171	Buff	
0	6	Daly, Hugh I. (One-Arm)	P	6	.125	StL	
		Decker, Edward Harry (3B2)	C4	6	+.143	xDet	
		Farrell, John A.	2B	42	+.252	xPhil	
		Force, David W.	SS56	68	.181	Buff	C
0	1	Fox, John Joseph	P	1	.000	PittAA84	C
0	1	Fuller, Edward A.	P	1	.333	A	C
		Gallagher, James E.	SS	1	.200	A	C
		Gilligan, Andrew Bernard (Barney)	C71	82	.190	Prov	
4	4	Gilmore, Frank T.	P	9	.000	A	
		Gladman, John H.	3B	44	.138	WashAA84	C
		Goldsby, Walton Hugh	OF	6	.111	RichAA84	
		Hayes, John J.	C	26	.184	BknAA	
1	3	Henry, John Michael	P	4	.357	BaltAA	
		Hines, Paul A. (3B15)	OF90	121	.312	Prov	
		Houck, Stephen Arnold Douglas (Sadie)	SS50	51	.215	xBaltAA	
0	3	Keefe, George W.	P	4	.000	A	
		Kinslow, Thomas F.	C	3	.333	A	
		Knowles, James (3B53)	2B62	115	.212	BknAA84	
		Krieg, Wm. Frederick	1B	27	.255	BknAA	
		Mack, Connie	C	10	.361	A	
1	13	Madigan, Anthony J.	P	14	.068	A	C
		McGlone, John T.	3B	3	.091	A	
2	2	O'Day, Henry F. (Hank)	P	6	.167	PittAA	
		Oldfield, David	C	19	.158	xBknAA	C
		Shoch, George Quintus	OF25	26	.294	A	
14	31	Shaw, Frederick Lander (Dupee)	P	45	.087	Prov	
		Start, Joseph	1B	29	.229	Prov	C
		Whiting, Edward C.	C	6	.000	LvlleAA84	C
0	1	Winkelman, George Edward	P	1	.200	LvlleAA83	C
0	1	Wise, Wm. E.	P	1	.000	WashUA84	C
0	1	Yingling, Joseph	P	1	.000	A	

WON 46 LOST 76 TG 122 — NATIONAL LEAGUE — 1887. — FINISHED 7th. PCT. .377

WASHINGTON

JOHN H. GAFFNEY　　WALTER L. DENNIS

WON	LOST	NAME	POS.	G.	BA	FROM	TO
		Carroll, Samuel (Clifford)	OF	101	.276	B	
		Crane, Samuel Newhall	2B	7	.312	StL	
0	1	Daily, Edward M. (P1)	OF79	80	+.296	xPhil	
		Dealey, Patrick E. (SS20)	C27	56	.286	Bos	
		Donely, James B.	3B115	117	.229	K.C.	
		Farrell, John A. (2B38)	SS48	86	.264	B	
		Gilligan, Andrew Bernard (Barney)	C24	27	.242	B	
7	20	Gilmore, Frank T.	P	27	.130	B	
		Hines, Paul A.	OF109	123	.370	B	
		Irwin, John	SS	8	.382	AthAA	
0	1	Keefe, George W.	P	1	.000	B	
		Krieg, Wm. Frederick	1B16	24	.304	B	C
		Mack, Connie	C73	80	.220	B	
		Myers, Albert	2B78	105	.308	K.C.	
		O'Brien, Jeremiah	2B	1	.000	A	C
		O'Brien, Wm. Smith	1B103	113	.310	KCUA84	
8	19	O'Day, Henry F. (Hank)	P30	34	.244	B	
		Shoch, George Quintus	OF62	69	.294	B	
7	14	Shaw, Frederick Lander (Dupee)	P	21	.269	B	
24	21	Whitney, James E. (Grasshopper)	P46	52	.324	K.C.	
		Wright, Wm. H.	C	1	.667	A	C

WON 48　　NATIONAL LEAGUE　　FINISHED 8th (LAST)
LOST 86
TG 134　　1888.　　PCT. .358

WASHINGTON

WALTER F. HEWITT　　THEODORE PAUL SULLIVAN　　JAMES E. WHITNEY

WON	LOST	NAME	POS.	G.	BA	FROM	TO
		Arundel, John Thomas (Tug)	C	16	.196	Indpls	C
		Banning, James M.	C	1	.000	A	
2	4	Daily, Edward M. (P8)	OF100	110	.225	B	
		Deasley, Thomas H. (Pat)	C31	34	.157	N.Y.	C
		Donely, James B.	3B117	122	.201	B	
		Fuller, Wm. Benjamin	SS47	49	.182	A	
		Gardner, Franklin (Gid)	2B	2	.200	Indpls	C
1	10	Gilmore, Frank T.	P	13	.048	B	C
0	1	Greening, John A.	P	1	.000	A	C
0	2	Haddock, George Silas	P	2	.167	A	
		Hoy, Wm. Ellsworth (Dummy)	OF	136	.274	A	
		Irwin, John	SS27	37	.222	B	
6	7	Keefe, George W.	P	13	.237	B	
		Mack, Connie	C79	85	.186	B	
		Murray, Jeremiah J.	C	12	.098	LvlleAA85	
		Myers, Albert	2B	132	.207	B	
		O'Brien, Wm. Smith	1B132	133	.225	B	
16	31	O'Day, Henry F. (Hank)	P	47	.138	B	
		Shoch, George Quintus (OF35)	SS52	90	.183	B	
0	3	Shaw, Frederick Lander (Dupee)	P	3	.000	B	C
		Sweeney, Peter Jay	3B	11	.181	A	
		Werden, Percival Wheritt (Perry)	OF	3	.300	StLUA84	
19	21	Whitney, James E. (Grasshopper) MGR.	P39	42	.170	B	
4	7	Widner, Wm. Waterfield	P	15	.200	CinAA	
		Wilmot, Walter R.	OF	119	.224	A	

WON 41　　NATIONAL LEAGUE　　FINISHED 8th (LAST)
LOST 83
TG 124　　1889.　　PCT. .331

WASHINGTON

JOHN FRANCIS MORRILL　　ARTHUR ALBERT IRWIN

WON	LOST	NAME	POS.	G.	BA	FROM	TO
		Banning, James M.	C	2	.000	B	C
		Beecher, Edward C.	OF39	41	.296	Pitt87	
		Carney, John Joseph (OF16)	1B58	69	.230	A	
		Clark, Owen F.	C	37	.255	A	
		Clarke, Harry Corson	OF	1	.000	A	C
		Daly, Thomas Peter	C54	69	.300	Chi	
		Donely, James B.	3B	4	.154	B	
		Ebright, Hiram C. (Buck)	3B	15	.254	A	C
17	17	Ferson, Alexander	P	35	.114	A	
10	19	Haddock, George Silas	P	33	.223	B	
1	14	Healy, John J.(Egyptian)	P	15	+.283	Indpls	Chi
		Hoy, Wm. Ellsworth (Dummy)	OF	127	.282	B	
		Irwin, Arthur Albert MGR.	SS	85	+.233	xPhil	
		Irwin, John	3B	58	.289	B	
8	18	Keefe, George W.	P26	27	.163	B	
1	6	Krock, August H. (Gus)	P	7	+.100	xIndpls	
		Mack, Connie (1B21 OF33)	C43	97	.292	B	
		Morrill, John Francis MGR.	1B40	44	.185	Bos	
		Myers, Albert	2B	46	+.262	B	Phil
		McCoy, A. J.	OF	2	.000	A	C
		O'Brien, Wm. Smith	1B	2	.000	B	
4	5	O'Day, Henry F. (Hank)	P	13	+.170	B	N.Y.
		Riddle, John H.	C	11	.210	A	
		Shoch, George Quintus	OF29	30	.238	B	
0	3	Sullivan, Michael Joseph (Mike)	P	9	.050	A	
		Sweeney, Peter Jay	3B47	49	.228	B	StLAA
0	1	Thornton, John (Jack)	P	1	.000	A	
		Wilmot, Walter R.	OF	107	.301	B	
		Wise, Samuel Washington (SS26)	2B71	120	.250	Bos	

WON 58 NATIONAL LEAGUE FINISHED 10th.
LOST 93
TG 151 1892. PCT. .384

WASHINGTON

WM. S. BARNIE — ARTHUR ALBERT IRWIN
DANIEL RICHARDSON — JACOB EARLE WAGNER

WON	LOST	NAME	POS.	G.	BA	FROM	TO
6	15	Abbey, Bert Wood	P	19	.114	A	
		Berger, John Henry (Tun)	SS18	25	.142	Pitt	C
		Cooney, James John	SS	6	+.154	xChi	C
2	2	Dolan, Patrick Henry (Cozy)	P	5	.231	A	
		Donovan, Patrick Joseph	OF	40	+.252	WashAA	Pitt
		Dowd, Thomas Jefferson (3B17 OF22)	2B95	141	.246	WashAA	
		Dowse, Thomas Jefferson (OF3)	C3	6	+.261	xPhil	C
		Drauby, Jacob C.	3B	10	.205	A	C
		Duffee, Chas. Edward	OF121	129	.252	ColAA	
2	12	Duryea, James Whitney (Jesse)	P	16	+.106	xCin	
2	5	Foreman, Francis Isaiah	P	11	+.448	WashAA	Balt
2	6	Gastright, Henry Carl	P	12	.133	ColAA	
		Hoy, Wm. Ellsworth (Dummy)	OF	149	.279	StLAA	
2	4	Inks, Albert Preston (Bert)	P	8	+.300	xBkn	
1	2	Jones, Alexander H.	P	7	+.273	xLvlle	
29	25	Killen, Frank Bissell	P	54	.211	Mil AA	
1	1	Kilroy, Matthew Aloysius	P	4	.222	CinAA	
9	10	Knell, Philip H.	P	15	+.121	ColAA	Phil
		Larkin, Henry E.	1B114	116	.282	AthAA	
2	11	Meekin, Jouett	P	13	+.106	xLvlle	
		Miller, Frederick	SS	1	.000	A	C
		Milligan, John (Jack) (1B31)	C45	76	.277	AthAA	
		McGuire, James Thomas	C80	87	.241	WashAA	
		O'Hagan, Harold P.	C	1	.250	A	
		Potts, Daniel	C	1	.333	A	C
		Radford, Paul Revere (SS19 3B54)	OF59	134	.254	BosAA	
		Raymond, Harry H.	3B	4	+.067	xPitt	C
		Richardson, Arthur Harding	2B	9	+.114	BosAA	N.Y.
		Richardson, Daniel MGR. (SS11)	2B93	142	.240	N.Y.	
		Robinson, Wm. H. (Yank)	3B55	64	.180	CinAA	C
		Shannon, Frank E.	SS	1	.200	A	
		Twitchell, Lawrence Grant	OF48	51	.221	ColAA	
		Ulrich, George F.	SS	6	.291	A	

WON 40 NATIONAL LEAGUE FINISHED 12th (LAST)
LOST 89
TG 129 1893. PCT. .310

WASHINGTON

JACOB EARLE WAGNER — JAMES HENRY O'ROURKE

WON	LOST	NAME	POS.	G.	BA	FROM	TO
		Abbey, Chas. S.	OF	31	.277	A	
5	8	Duryea, James Whitney (Jesse)	P	17	.255	B	C
12	26	Esper, Chas. H.	P	40	.297	Pitt	
		Farrell, Chas. A. (Duke) (3B36)	C83	122	.296	Pitt	
0	1	Graff, John F.	P	2	.200	A	C
		Hoy, Wm. Ellsworth (Dummy)	OF	130	.259	B	
		Larkin, Henry E.	1B	81	.322	B	C
10	23	Maul, Albert Joseph	P34	39	.264	Pitt91	
10	17	Meekin, Jouett	P28	29	.254	B	
		Mulvey, Joseph H.	3B	55	.242	Phil	
		McGuire, James Thomas	C47	59	.262	B	
		O'Rourke, James Henry MGR. (1B33)	OF87	129	.305	N.Y.	
		Radford, Paul Revere	OF123	124	.228	B	
1	6	Stephens, George Benjamin	P	9	.120	Balt.	
2	8	Stocksdale, Otis H.	P	12	.333	A	
		Stricker, John A. (Cub)	2B39	59	.181	Balt	C
		Sullivan, Joseph Daniel	SS	127	.271	A	
		Wise, Samuel Washington (3B31)	2B90	121	.317	BaltAA91	C

WON 45 NATIONAL LEAGUE FINISHED 11th.
LOST 87
TG 132 1894. PCT. .341

WASHINGTON

GUSTAVUS HEINRICH SCHMELZ

WON	LOST	NAME	POS.	G.	BA	FROM	TO
		Abbey, Chas. S.	OF	129	.318	B	
0	2	Anderson, David S. (Varney)	P	2	.500	Pitt90	
0	3	Boyd, Frank C. (Jake)	P	6	.158	A	
		Campau, Chas. C.	OF	2	.142	StLAA90	C
		Cartwright, Edward H.	1B	132	.292	StLAA90	
		Dugdale, Daniel Edward	C30	33	.217	KC86	C
0	0	Egan, John Joseph (Rip)	P	1	.000	A	
6	9	Esper, Chas. H.	P	15	+.260	B	Balt
0	4	Haddock, George Silas (OF1)	P4	5	+.250	xPhil	C
		Hassamaer, Wm. Louis (3B30)	OF69	116	.326	A	
		Joyce, Wm. Michael (Scrappy)	3B	98	.344	Bkn92	
		Mohler, Ernest Follette (Kid)	SS	3	.125	A	C
2	1	Malarkey, John S.	P	4	.071	A	
11	15	Maul, Albert Joseph	P28	35	.233	B	
16	23	Mercer, George Marclay (Winnie)	P40	43	.294	A	
		McGuire, James Thomas	C	102	.304	B	
		O'Rourke, Timothy Patrick	1B	7	+.179	xStL	C
3	8	Petty, Chas. E.	P	15	+.205	N.Y.	Clev
		Radford, Paul Revere (2B24 OF22)	SS47	93	.233	B	C
		Scheibeck, Frank	SS	49	+.238	xPitt	

WON	LOST	NAME	POS.	G.	BA	FROM	TO
		Selbach, Albert Carl (Kip) (SS18)	OF76	96	.300	A	
0	3	Stephens, George Benjamin	P	3	.333	B	C
5	8	Stocksdale, Otis H.	P16	19	.306	B	
		Sullivan, Joseph Daniel (SS8 3B1)	2B8	17	+.239	B	Phil
2	10	Sullivan, Michael Joseph (Mike)	P	14	+.175	Cin	Clev
		Tebeau, George E.	OF	60	+.226	TolAA90	Clev
		Ward, Frank Gray (Piggy)	2B79	89	.303	Cin	C
0	1	Wynne, Wm. Avery	P	1	.000	A	C

WON 43 | NATIONAL LEAGUE | FINISHED 10th.
LOST 85
TG 128 | 1895. | PCT. .336

WASHINGTON

GUSTAVUS HEINRICH SCHMELZ

WON	LOST	NAME	POS.	G.	BA	FROM	TO
		Abbey, Chas. S.	OF	133	.275	B	
9	16	Anderson, David S. (Varney)	P	26	.301	B	
1	3	Boswell, Andrew Cottrell (1B1)	P6	7	+.231	xN.Y.	C
1	7	Boyd, Frank C. (Jake) (P14)	OF17	46	.284	B	
		Brown, Thomas T.	OF	31	+.227	xStL	
0	1	Buckingham, Edward Taylor	P	1	.000	A	C
		Cartwright, Edward H.	1B	121	.327	B	
		Coogan, Daniel George	SS16	21	.203	A	C
0	3	Corbett, Joseph	P	8	.067	A	
		Crooks, John Chas. (Jack)	2B	118	.291	StL93	
		DeMontreville, Eugene Napoleon	SS	12	.227	Pitt	
1	4	Gilroy, John N.	P	11	.269	A	
		Glasscock, John Wesley	SS	25	+.233	xLvlle	C
		Hassamaer, Wm. Louis	OF	89	+.278	B	Lvlle
		Joyce, Wm. Michael (Scrappy)	3B127	128	.308	B	
		Lush, Wm. Lucas	OF	5	.210	A	
		Mahaney, Daniel J.	C	6	.167	Cin92	C
0	8	Malarkey, John S.	P	22	.162	B	
11	6	Maul, Albert Joseph	P17	20	.253	B	
14	24	Mercer, George Barclay (Winnie)	P38	54	.254	B	
0	2	Molesworth, Carlton	P	4	.200	A	C
		McCauley, F. F.	SS	1	.000	A	C
		McGuire, James Thomas	C132	133	.330	B	
1	1	McJames, James McCutchen	P	3	.143	A	
		Nicholson, Thomas C.	SS	10	.184	TolAA90	C
0	0	Purner, Oscar	P	1	.000	A	C
		Shheibeck, Frank	SS44	48	.182	B	
		Selbach, Albert Carl (Kip)	OF118	129	.324	B	
		Shannon, Frank E.	SS	1	.200	Wash92	
5	10	Stocksdale, Otis H.	P	20	+.329	B	Bos
		Wesner,	SS	1	.000	A	C

WON	LOST	NAME	POS.	G.	BA	FROM	TO
		Woerlin,	SS	1	.333	A	C

WON 58 | NATIONAL LEAGUE | FINISHED 9th.
LOST 73 | | (TIED WITH BKLYN)
TG 131 | 1896. | PCT. .443

WASHINGTON

GUSTAVUS HEINRICH SCHMELZ

WON	LOST	NAME	POS.	G.	BA	FROM	TO
		Abbey, Chas. S.	OF	75	.255	B	
0	1	Anderson, David S. (Varney)	P	2	.600	B	C
1	2	Boyd, Frank C. (Jake)	P	4	.154	B	C
		Brown, Thomas T.	OF	113	.299	B	
		Cartwright, Edward H.	1B	131	.274	B	
		Crooks, John Chas. (Jack) (3B4)	2B19	24	+.280	B	Lvlle
		DeMontreville, Eugene Napoleon	SS	130	.349	B	
		Farrell, Chas. A. (Duke) (C13)	3B19	37	+.326	xN.Y.	
0	1	Flynn, Cornelius Francis Xavier	P	4	+.250	xN.Y.	C
2	18	German, Lester S.	P	23	+.229	xN.Y.	
0	0	Gilroy, John N.	P	1	.000	B	C
		Joyce, Wm. Michael (Scrappy)	3B	80	+.309	B	N.Y.
10	6	King, Chas. Frederick	P	16	.278	Cin93	
		Lush, Wm. Lucas	OF89	91	.245	B	
0	1	Malarkey, John S.	P	1	.500	B	
5	2	Maul, Albert Joseph	P	9	.250	B	
25	19	Mercer, George Barclay (Winnie)	P	44	.253	B	
		McCauley, Patrick M.	C	21	.247	StL93	
		McGuire, James Thomas	C	95	.325	B	
12	21	McJames, James McCutchen	P	34	.165	B	
3	2	Norton, Elisha S.	P	8	.158	A	
		O'Brien, John J.	2B	69	+.270	xLvlle	
		Rogers, James F. (2B6 OF1)	3B32	38	+.279	A	Lvlle
		Selbach, Albert Carl (Kip)	OF	121	.316	B	
		Smith, Harvey Fetterhoff	3B	34	.288	A	C
		Wrigley, George Watson	2B	5	.100	A	

WON 61 | NATIONAL LEAGUE | FINISHED 6th.
LOST 71 | | (TIED WITH BKLYN)
TG 132 | 1897. | PCT. .462

WASHINGTON

GUSTAVUS HEINRICH SCHMELZ THOMAS T. BROWN

WON	LOST	NAME	POS.	G.	BA	FROM	TO
		Abbey, Chas. S.	OF	78	.264	B	C
4	1	Bresnahan, Roger Philip	P	7	.333	A	

WON	LOST	NAME	POS.	G.	BA	FROM	TO
		Brown, Thomas T. MGR.	OF	116	.287	B	
		Cartwright, Edward H.	1B	33	.250	B	C
		DeMontreville, Eugene Napoleon (2B31)	SS101	132	.349	B	
		Farrell, Chas. A. (Duke)	C64	65	.327	B	
		Fox, Wm. H. (SS2)	2B2	4	.250	A	
4	3	German, Lester S. (P7)	2B12	19	.311	B	C
		Gettman, Jacob John	OF	37	.315	A	
9	9	King, Chas. Frederick	P	18	.193	B	C
		Leahy, Thomas Joseph (C1 2B1 3B5)	OF13	20	+.426	xPitt	
		Lush, Wm. Lucas	OF	2	.000	B	
0	0	Maul, Albert Joseph	P	1	+.000	B	Balt
24	21	Mercer, George Barclay (Winnie)	P	45	.333	B	
		McGuire, James Thomas	C76	82	.338	B	
14	24	McJames, James McCutchen	P	41	.160	B	
1	1	Norton, Elisha S.	P	8	.200	B	C
		O'Brien, John J.	2B	84	.242	B	
		Reilly, Chas. Thomas	3B	101	.275	Phi195	C
		Selbach, Albert Carl (Kip)	OF	126	.317	B	
0	0	Stanley, Joseph Bernard	P	1	.000	A	
5	12	Swaim, John Hillary	P20	24	.225	A	
		Tucker, Thomas Joseph	1B	96	+.333	xBos	
		Wrigley, George Watson (SS31 3B29)	OF33	102	.284	B	

WON 51 NATIONAL LEAGUE FINISHED 11th.
LOST 101
TG 152 1898. PCT. .335

WASHINGTON

THOMAS T. BROWN JOHN JOSEPH DOYLE
JAMES THOMAS McGUIRE ARTHUR ALBERT IRWIN

WON	LOST	NAME	POS.	G.	BA	FROM	TO
0	6	Amole, Morris George (Doc)	P	7	.111	Balt	
		Anderson, John Joseph	OF	108	+.305	xBkn (return)	Bkn
1	3	Baker, Kirtly	P	6	.278	Balt94	
		Brown, Thomas T. MGR.	OF	15	.164	B	C
		Carr, Chas. Carbitt	1B	20	.197	A	
		Casey, James Peter (Doc)	3B22	28	.270	A	
		Davis, Harry H.	1B	1	+.000	xLvlle	
9	16	Dinneen, Wm. Henry	P26	27	.118	A	
1	6	Donovan, Wm. Edward (Wild Bill) (P11)	OF19	30	.178	A	
		Doyle, John Joseph (Jack) MGR.	1B38	42	+.285	Balt	N.Y.
		Eagle, Wm.	OF	4	.333	A	C
3	3	Evans, LeRoy	P	7	.053	Lvlle	
		Farrell, Chas. A. (Duke) (1B28)	C60	88	.316	B	
		Field, James	1B	5	.095	RochAA90	C
		Freeman, John F. (Buck)	OF	29	.368	WashAA91	
		Gatins, Frank Anthony	SS	16	.250	A	

WON	LOST	NAME	POS.	G.	BA	FROM	TO
		Gettman, Jacob John	OF137	140	.279	B	
		Gilbert, John Robert	OF	2	+.167	A	N.Y.
7	9	Killen, Frank Bissell (OF3)	P17	20	+.268	xPitt	
		Kinslow, Thomas F.	C	3	+.111	Lvlle96	StL
		Leahy, Thomas Joseph	C	15	.182	B	
12	16	Mercer, George Barclay (Winnie) (SS21 OF19)	P29	73	.334	B	
		Meyers, J. Albert	3B	31	.261	StL96	
		McGuire, James Thomas MGR. (1B36)	C92	128	.273	B	
		McHale, Robert E.	OF	10	.171	A	C
		McQuaid, James H.	OF	1	.000	StLAA91	C
		Reitz, Henry P.	2B	132	.302	Balt	
		Selbach, Albert Carl (Kip)	OF130	131	.302	B	
		Smith, Judson Grant (Jud)	3B47	65	.302	Pitt96	
0	2	Sutthoff, John Gerhard	P	2	.333	A	
3	11	Swaim, John Hillary	P	15	.143	B	C
		Wagner, Albert Butts	3B	57	+.232	A	Bkn
0	1	Weber, Chas. P.	P	1	.000	A	C
15	26	Weyhing, August (Gus)	P	43	.181	Lvlle96	
0	2	Williams, Walter Merrill	P	2	.375	A	
		Wrigley, George Watson	SS98	111	.245	B	

WON 53 NATIONAL LEAGUE FINISHED 11th.
LOST 95
TG 148 1899. PCT. .358

WASHINGTON

ARTHUR ALBERT IRWIN

WON	LOST	NAME	POS.	G.	BA	FROM	TO
		Atherton, Chas. Morgan Herbert	3B	63	.240	A	
1	8	Baker, Kirtly	P	12	.176	B	C
		Barry, John C.	OF21	75	.303	A	
		Bonner, Frank J.	2B	85	.276	Bkn96	
		Butler, Richard H.	C	12	.263	Lvlle97	C
1	2	Carsey, Wilfred (Kid)	P	7	+.083	xClev	N.Y.
		Casey, James Peter (Doc)	3B	9	+.118	B	Bkn
		Cassidy, Peter Francis	1B	45	+.315	xBkn	C
		Coughlin, Wm. Paul	3B	5	.100	A	
		Davis, Harry H.	1B	18	.187	B	
		Decker, George A. (OF1)	1B2	4	+.000	xLvlle	C
14	18	Dinneen, Wm. Henry	P	36	.296	B	
		Duncan, James Wm.	C14	15	+.234	A	Clev
0	2	Dunkle, Edward Perks	P	4	.273	Phil	
3	2	Evans, Le Roy	P	7	.200	B	
		Farrell, Chas. A. (Duke)	C4	5	+.333	B	Bkn
2	4	Fifield, John Proctor (Jack) (3B1)	P6	7	+.200	xPhil	
		Freeman, John F. (Buck)	OF	155	.318	B	
		Gettman, Jacob John	OF	16	.226	B	
0	0	Herring, Silas Clarke	P	2	.500	A	
		Heydon, Michael Edward	C	3	.000	Balt	

		Hulen, Wm. Franklin	SS	19	.147	Phil96	C
0	2	Killen, Frank Bissell	P	5	+.250	B	Bos
		Kittredge, Malachi Jedediah	C	41	+.158	xLvlle	
		Latham, Walter Arlington (Arlie)	2B2	6	.143	StL96	
0	0	Leith, Wm.	P	1	.000	A	C
1	4	Magee, Wm. M.	P	5	+.188	xPhil	
7	14	Mercer, George Barclay (Winnie) (P21)	3B60	98	.303	B	
8	18	McFarlan, Anderson Daniel	P	29	+.190	xBkn	C
		McGann, Dennis L. (Dan)	1B	75	+.338	xBkn	
		McGuire, James Thomas	C	56	+.277	B	Bkn
		McManus, Francis E.	C	7	.400	A	
		O'Brien, John Joseph	OF	121	.279	A	
		Padden, Richard J. (2B48)	SS83	131	.272	Pitt	
		Powers, Michael Riley (1B1)	C12	14	+.333	xLvlle	
0	0	Riddlemoser, Dorsey Lee	P	1	.000	A	C
		Roach, James Michael	C	21	.237	A	C
		Scheibeck, Frank	SS	27	.287	Wash95	C
		Slagle, James Franklin (Shorty)	OF	146	.273	A	
		Stafford, James Joseph (SS13 3B2)	2B16	30	+.243	xBos	C
16	21	Weyhing, August (Gus)	P	40	.206	B	

CLUB RECORD

NATIONAL LEAGUE

WORCESTER

YEAR	TG	WON	LOST	PCT.	FINISHED	MANAGER
1880	83	40	43	.482	5	Frank Carter Bancroft Freeman Brown
1881	82	32	50	.390	8(Last)	Freeman Brown
1882	84	18	66	.214	8(Last)	Freeman Brown Thomas H. Bond John Curtis Chapman

WON 40 / LOST 43 / TG 83 — NATIONAL LEAGUE — FINISHED 5th.

1880. — PCT. .482

WORCESTER

FRANK CARTER BANCROFT FREEMAN BROWN

WON	LOST	NAME	POS.	G.	BA	FROM	TO
		Bennett, Chas. Wesley (OF5)	C45	50	.223	Mil78	
		Bushong, Albert John (OF1)	C37	37	.163	Ath76	
9	8	Corey, Frederick Harrison (P24 1B1 SS2)	OF30	41	.162	Prov78	
		Creamer, George W.	2B	83	.202	Syr	
		Dickerson, Lewis Pessano	OF	31	+.316	xTroy	
		Dignan, Stephen E.	OF	3	+.300	xBos	C
		Dorgan, Jeremiah F. (C1)	OF8	9	.229	A	
		Ellick, Joseph J.	3B	5	.053	Mil78	
		Geer, Wm. Henry Harrison (OF1)	SS1	2	.000	Cin78	
		Irwin, Arthur Albert (C1 3B3)	SS83	83	.260	A	
		Knight, Alonzo P. (Lon)	OF	48	.242	Ath76	
0	0	McGunnigle, Wm. Henry	P	1	+.000	xBuff	
0	2	Nichols, Frederick C. (Tricky)	P	2	.000	Prov78	
31	33	Richmond, John Lee (OF8)	P67	75	.224	Bos	
0	0	Stovey, Harry Duffield (P1 1B36)	OF45	81	.258	A	
		Sullivan, John Frank (Chubb)	1B	42	.267	Cin78	
		Tobin, Wm.	1B	5	+.125	A	Troy
		Whitney, Arthur Wilson	3B	75	.222	A	
		Wood, George A. (1B1)	OF78	79	.243	A	

WON 32 / LOST 50 / TG 82 — NATIONAL LEAGUE — FINISHED 8th (LAST)

1881. — PCT. .390

WORCESTER

FREEMAN BROWN

WON	LOST	NAME	POS.	G.	BA	FROM	TO
		Bushong, Albert John	C	75	.229	B	
		Carpenter, Warren Wm. (Hick)	3B	82	.209	Cin	
6	14	Corey, Frederick Harrison (P23 SS7)	OF25	51	.221	B	
		Creamer, George W.	2B	79	.209	B	
		Dickerson, Lewis Pessano	OF	80	.316	B	
		Dorgan, Michael Cornelius (SS2 OF23)	1B26	51	+.264	Prov	Det
		Flaherty, P. J.	OF	1	.000	A	C
		Hotaling, Peter James (C3)	OF73	76	.306	Clev	
		Irwin, Arthur Albert	SS	49	.266	B	
1	8	McCormick, Patrick Henry (OF3)	P12	12	.122	Syr79	
		Nelson, Jackson W.	SS	23	.275	Troy79	
		Pike, Lipman E.	OF	5	.091	Prov78	
		Quinn, Joseph C.	C	2	+.125	xBos	C
		Reilley, Chas. E.	C	2	+.375	xDet	C
25	27	Richmond, John Lee (OF9)	P52	60	.251	B	
		Smith, Chas. Marvin (Pap) (2B3)	OF8	11	+.068	xClev	Buff
		Stovey, Harry Duffield (OF18)	1B56	74	.270	B	
		Stratton, Asa Evans	SS	1	.250	A	C
		Sullivan, John Frank (Chubb)	(DID NOT PLAY)				C
0	1	Taylor, Wm. Henry (P1)	OF5	6	+.111	Troy79	Det

WON 18 / LOST 66 / TG 84 — NATIONAL LEAGUE — FINISHED 8th (LAST)

1882. — PCT. .214

WORCESTER

FREEMAN BROWN THOMAS HENRY BOND JOHN CURTIS CHAPMAN

WON	LOST	NAME	POS.	G.	BA	FROM	TO
0	0	Bond, Thomas Henry MGR. (P2)	OF8	8	.125	Bos	
		Bushong, Albert John	C	69	.152	B	
1	1	Clarkson, John Gibson (1B1)	P3	3	.364	A	
		Clinton, James Lawrence	OF	26	.163	Lvlle76	
		Cogswell, Edward	1B	13	.122	Troy80	C
1	15	Corey, Frederick Harrison (P16 1B6 3B5 OF10)	SS25	63	.247	B	
		Creamer, George W.	2B	81	.228	B	
0	1	Evans, Jacob (P1 2B1 SS11)	OF67	80	.212	Troy	
		Halpin, James Nathaniel	3B	2	.000	A	
		Hayes, John J. (C15 SS2 3B5)	OF56	78	.269	A	
		Irwin, Arthur Albert (SS33)	3B51	84	.220	B	
		Irwin, John	1B	1	.000	A	
		Mann, Frederick I. (1B1)	3B18	19	.241	A	AthAA
		Merrill, Edward S.	3B	2	.125	A	
0	5	Mountain, Frank H.	P	5	.056	Det	AthAA
2	11	Mountain, Frank H. (1B2 OF6)	P18	20	.264	xAthAA(return)	
		McLaughlin, Bernard (OF1)	SS14	15	.207	A	
		O'Brien, Thomas H. (2B2 3B1)	OF20	22	.202	A	
		O'Leary, Daniel	OF	6	.167	Det	
14	33	Richmond John Lee (OF10)	P47	55	.280	B	
		Smith, Alexander Chas.	1B	19	+.216	xTroy	C
		Stovey, Harry Duffield (OF41)	1B43	84	.288	B	

CLUB RECORD

AMERICAN LEAGUE

BALTIMORE

YEAR	TG	WON	LOST	TIED	PCT.	FINISHED	MANAGER
1901	133	68	65		.511	5	John Joseph McGraw
1902	138	50	88		.362	8(Last)	John Joseph McGraw Wilbert Robinson
1954	154	54	100		.351	7	James Joseph Dykes
1955	154	57	97		.370	7	Paul Rapier Richards
1956	154	69	85		.448	6	Paul Rapier Richards
1957	152	76	76		.500	5	Paul Rapier Richards
1958	153	74	79		.484	6	Paul Rapier Richards
1959	154	74	80		.481	6	Paul Rapier Richards
1960	154	89	65		.578	2	Paul Rapier Richards
1961	162	95	67		.586	3	Paul Rapier Richards Chalmer Luman Harris
1962	162	77	85		.475	7	Wm. Clyde Hitchcock
1963	162	86	76		.531	4	Wm. Clyde Hitchcock
1964	162	97	65		.599	3	Henry Albert Bauer
YEAR	TG	WON	LOST	TIED	PCT.	FINISHED	MANAGER
1965	162	94	68	0	.580	3	HENRY ALBERT BAUER
1966	160	97	63	0	.606	1	HENRY ALBERT BAUER
1967	161	76	85	0	.472	X6 (WAS)	HENRY ALBERT BAUER
1968	162	91	71	0	.562	2	HENRY ALBERT BAUER EARL SIDNEY WEAVER
1969	162	109	53	0	.673	1E (WP)	EARL SIDNEY WEAVER
1970	162	108	54	0	.667	1E (WP)	EARL SIDNEY WEAVER
1971	158	101	57	0	.639	1E (WP)	EARL SIDNEY WEAVER
1972	154	80	74	0	.519	3E	EARL SIDNEY WEAVER

WON 68
LOST 65
TG 133

American League

1901.

FINISHED 5th.
PCT. .511

BALTIMORE

JOHN JOSEPH McGRAW

WON	LOST	NAME	POS.	G.	BA	FROM	TO
0	0	Bresnahan, Roger Philip (P1)	C72	86	.262	ChiN	
		Brodie, Walter Scott	OF	84	.310	Chi	
		Donlin, Michael Joseph (1B43)	OF79	122	.340	StLN	
3	3	Dunn, John Joseph (Jack) (P6 SS17)	3B69	96	.247	xPhilN	
13	7	Foreman, Francis Isaiah	P	23	+.321	xBos	
		Foutz, Frank Hayes	1B	20	.236	A	C
		Hart, Warren F.	1B	58	.312	Buff	C
14	21	Howell, Harry	P38	54	.223	BknN	
		Jackson, James Benner	OF	97	.247	A	
		Jordan, Timothy Joseph	1B	1	+.000	xWash	
1	0	Kearns, W. A.	P	4	.143	A	C
		Keister, Wm. Hoffman	SS	114	.328	StLN	
		Latimer, Clifford Wesley	C	1	.250	PittN	
26	19	McGinnity, Joseph Jerome	P	48	.208	BknN	
		McGraw, John Joseph MGR.	3B69	73	.352	StLN	
11	12	Nops, Jeremiah H.	P	27	.216	BknN	C
		Robinson, Wilbert	C	71	.298	StLN	
		Rohe, George Anthony	3B	14	.294	A	
0	2	Schmidt, Frederick	P	4	.000	ClevN99	C
		Seymour, John Bentley (Cy)	OF	137	.302	NYN	
		Snodgrass, Walter Amzi	OF	2	.100	A	C
		Williams, James Thomas Williams	2B	131	.321	PittN	
0	1	Yerkes, Stanley	P	1	.333	A	StLN

WON 50
LOST 88
TG 138

AMERICAN LEAGUE

1902.

FINISHED 8th (LAST)
PCT. .362

BALTIMORE

JOHN JOSEPH McGRAW WILBERT ROBINSON

WON	LOST	NAME	POS.	G.	BA	FROM	TO
		Arndt, Harry A. (2B4 SS1 3B2)	OF60	67	+.257	xDet	
		Bresnahan, Roger Philip (C20 OF15)	3B30	66	.273	B	NYN
		Burns, Wm.		1	1.000	A	C
2	11	Butler, Isaac B. (OF3)	P15	18	.115	A	C
		Courtney, Ernest E.	3B	1	.500	xBosN	
2	5	Cronin, John J. (Jack)	P	9	+.182	xDet	NYN
		Dillon, Frank Edward	1B	2	+.286	xDet	
		Drill, Lewis L. (1B1)	C1	2	+.250	xWash (return)	Wash

WON	LOST	NAME	POS.	G.	BA	FROM	TO
0	2	Foreman, Francis Isaiah	P	2	.428	B	C
		Gilbert, Wm. Oliver	SS	130	.243	Mil	
0	1	Hale, Roy L.	P	3	.000	xBosN	C
0	3	Heismann, Christian Ernest	P	3	.142	xCinN	C
9	14	Howell, Harry	P25	96	.266	B	
		(1B1 2B22 SS11 3B19 OF19)					
7	8	Hughes, Thomas J.	P	15	+.136	ChiN	Bos
		Jones, Thomas (Tom) (2B1)	1B37	37	.283	A	
		Jordan, Timothy Joseph	OF	1	.000	B	
3	10	Katoll, John (OF2)	P13	15	+.152	xChi	C
		Kelley, Joseph James	OF47	60	.311	BknN	CinN
		(1B5 3B8)					
0	2	Lawson, Robert Baker	P	3	.200	BosN	C
		Mathison, I. I. (SS1)	3B27	28	.275	A	C
		Mellor, Wm. Harper	1B	10	.261	A	C
		McAllister, Lewis Wm.	1B1	3	+.091	xDet	Det
		(2B1 3B1)				(return)	
		McFarland, Hermus W.	OF	63	+.321	xChi	
		McGann, Dannis L. (Dan)	1B	68	.314	StLN	NYN
13	10	McGinnity, Joseph Jerome	P26	27	.295	B	NYN
		(OF2)					
		McGraw, John Joseph MGR.	3B19	20	.286	B	NYN
		Oyler, Andrew Paul	3B20	26	.227	A	C
		(2B1 SS2 OF3)					
3	3	Prentiss, George Pepper	P	6	+.000	xBos	C
		(George P. Wilson)					
		Robinson, Wilbert MGR.	C36	90	.292	B	
1	1	Ross, Eben B.	P	2	.000	A	C
		Selbach, Albert Carl (Kip)	OF	128	.321	NYN	
		Seymour, John Bentley (Cy)	OF	72	.278	B	CinN
		Sheckard, Samuel James	OF	4	.266	BknN	BknN
		Tilden					
3	9	Shields, Chas. Jessamine	P12	23	+.163	A	StL
		(OF1)					
		Smith, Alexander Benjamin	C25	40	.234	NYN	
		(1B7 2B3 3B1 OF4) (Broadway)					
		Thoney, John	3B	3	+.000	xClev	
		Williams, James Thomas	2B106	125	.311	B	
		Williams (1B1 3B18)					
7	9	Wiltse, Lewis DeWitt	P16	35	+.296	xPhil	
		(1B12 2B1 OF4)					
		Yeager, George E.	C	11	.184	xNYN	C

WON 54 AMERICAN LEAGUE FINISHED 7th.
LOST 100
TG 154 1954. PCT. .351

BALTIMORE

JAMES JOSEPH DYKES

WON	LOST	NAME	POS.	G.	BA	FROM	TO
		Abrams, Calvin Ross	OF	115	.293	xPittN	
		Berry, Cornelius John	SS	5	.111	Chi	C
0	1	Bickford, Vernon Edgell	P	1	.000	MilN	C
1	5	Blyzka, Michael John	P	37	.133	StL	C
		Brideweser, James Ehrenfeld	SS48	73	.265	N.Y.	
		(2B19)					
3	7	Chakales, Robert Edward	P	38	+.364	xClev	
		Coan, Gilbert Fitzgerald	OF67	94	.279	Wash	
13	17	Coleman, Joseph Patrick	P	33	.176	Phil	
		Courtney, Clinton Dawson	C111	122	.270	StL	
		Diering, Chas. Edward Allen	OF119	128	.258	NYN52	
0	0	Duren, Rinold George	P	1	.000	A	
		Durham, Joseph Vann	OF	10	.225	A	
1	2	Fox, Howard Francis	P	38	.250	PhilN52	C
		Fridley, James Riley	OF67	85	.246	Clev	
		Garcia, Vinicio Uzcanga	2B24	39	.113	A	C
0	0	Heard, Jehosie	P	2	.000	A	C
		Hunter, Gordon Wm.	SS124	125	.243	StL	
		Kellert, Frank Wm.	1B9	10	.206	StL	
		Kennedy, Robert Daniel	3B69	106	+.251	xClev	
		(OF23)					
		Kokos, Richard Jerome	OF1	11	.200	StL	C
0	1	Koslo, George Bernard	P	3	.000	NYN	MilN
6	11	Kretlow, Louis Henry	P	32	.157	StL	
		Kryhoski, Richard David	1B69	100	.260	StL	
1	3	Kuzava, Robert LeRoy	P	4	+.000	xN.Y.	
3	21	Larsen, Donald James	P29	44	.250	StL	
		Lenhardt, Donald Eugene	OF7	13	+.152	StL	Bos
		(1B2)					
0	0	Littlefield, Richard Bernard	P	3	.000	StL	PittN
		Mele, Sabath Anthony	OF62	72	+.239	Chi	Bos
		Moss, John Lester	C38	50	.246	StL	
		Murray, Raymond Lee	C21	22	.246	Phil	C
1	1	O'Dell, Wm. Oliver	P	7	.000	A	
10	14	Pillette, Duane Xavier	P	25	.132	StL	
		Stephens, Vernon Decatur	3B96	101	.285	StL	
1	2	Stuart, Marlin Henry	P	22	+.000	StL	N.Y.
14	15	Turley, Robert Lee	P	35	.136	StL	
		Waitkus, Edward Stephen	1B78	95	.283	PhilN	
		Wertz, Victor Woodrow	OF27	29	+.202	StL	Clev
		Young, Robert George	2B127	130	.245	StL	

WON 57 AMERICAN LEAGUE FINISHED 7th.
LOST 97
TG 154 1955. PCT. .370

BALTIMORE

PAUL RAPIER RICHARDS

WON	LOST	NAME	POS.	G.	BA	FROM	TO
		Abrams, Calvin Ross (1B4)	OF96	118	.243	B	
1	0	Alexander, Robert Somerville	P	4	.000	A	
0	4	Brown, Hector Harold	P15	25	+.000	xBos	
3	2	Byrd, Harry Gladwin	P	14	+.158	N.Y.	Chi
		Causey, James Wayne	3B55	68	.194	A	
		(2B7 SS1)					
		Coan, Gilbert Fitzgerald	OF43	61	+.238	B	Chi
0	1	Coleman, Joseph Patrick	P	6	+.667	B	Det

WON	LOST	NAME	POS.	G.	BA	FROM	TO
		Cox, Wm. Richard (2B18 SS6)	3B37	53	.211	BknN	C
		Dagres, Angelo George	OF5	8	.267	A	C
		Diering, Chas. Edward Allen (SS12 3B34)	OF107	137	.256	B	
3	3	Dorish, Harry	P	35	+.000	xChi	
		Dyck, James Robert (3B17)	OF45	61	.279	Clev	
		Evers, Walter Arthur	OF55	60	+.238	Det	Clev
0	0	Ferrarese, Donald Hugh	P	6	.000	A	
		Gastall, Thomas Everett	C15	20	.148	A	
1	2	Gray, Theodore Glenn	P	9	+.000	xN.Y.	C
		Hale, Robert Houston	1B44	67	.357	A	
0	0	Harrison, Robert Lee	P	1	.000	A	
2	4	Johnson, Donald Roy	P	31	.000	Chi	
		Kennedy, Robert Daniel (1B6 3B1)	OF14	26	+.143	B	Chi
0	4	Kretlow, Louis Henry	P	15	.091	B	
0	1	Kuzava, Robert LeRoy	P	6	.000	B	PhilN
		Leppert, Don Eugene	2B35	40	.114	A	C
0	0	Locke, Chas. Edward	P	2	.000	A	C
3	4	Lopat, Edmund Walter	P	10	+.176	xN.Y.	C
		Majeski, Henry (2B5)	3B8	16	+.171	xClev	C
		Marquis, Roger Julian	OF	1	.000	A	C
		Marsh, Fred Francis (SS16 3B18)	2B76	89	.218	Chi	
		Maxwell, Chas. Richard		4	+.000	Bos	Det
0	1	Miller, Wm. Paul	P	5	1.000	N.Y.	C
		Miranda, Guillermo Perez (2B1)	SS153	153	.255	N.Y.	
10	10	Moore, Raymond LeRoy	P	46	.136	BknN53	
		Moss, John Lester	C17	29	+.339	B	Chi
3	5	McDonald, James LeRoy	P	21	.182	N.Y.	
		Nelson, Robert Sidney (1B2)	OF6	25	.194	A	
5	11	Palica, Ervin Martin	P	33	.236	BknN	
		Philley, David Earl (3B2)	OF82	82	+.296	xClev	
0	3	Pillette, Duane Xavier	P	7	.167	B	
		Pope, David	OF73	86	+.248	xClev	
		Pyburn, James Edward (OF1)	3B33	39	.204	A	
		Robinson, Brooks Calbert	3B	6	.091	A	
1	8	Rogovin, Saul Walter	P14	15	.091	Chi53	PhilN
3	5	Schallock, Arthur Lawrence	P	30	+.105	xN.Y.	C
		Segrist, Kal Hill (1B1 2B1)	3B3	7	.333	NY52	C
		Smith, Harold Wayne	C125	135	.271	A	
		Stephens, Vernon Decatur	3B2	3	+.167	B	Chi
		Triandos, Gus (C36 3B1)	1B103	140	.277	N.Y.	
		Waitkus, Edward Stephen	1B26	38	.259	B	PhilN
		Westlake, Waldon Thomas	OF7	8	+.125	xClev	
6	8	Wight, Wm. Robert (1B1)	P19	19	+.083	xClev	
12	18	Wilson, James Alger	P	34	.169	MilN	
		Woodling, Eugene Richard	OF44	47	+.221	N.Y.	Clev
		Young, Robert George	2B58	59	+.199	B	Clev
4	3	Zuverink, George	P	28	+.217	xDet	

WON 69 — LOST 85 — TG 154

AMERICAN LEAGUE — 1956.

FINISHED 6th. — PCT. .448

BALTIMORE

PAUL RAPIER RICHARDS

WON	LOST	NAME	POS.	G.	BA	FROM	TO
		Adams, Robert Henry (2B18)	3B24	41	.225	Chi	
2	0	Beamon, Chas. Alonzo	P	2	.000	A	
1	0	Besana, Frederick Cyril	P	7	.000	A	C
0	0	Birrer, Werner Joseph	P	4	.000	Det	
		Boyd, Robert Richard (OF8)	1B60	70	.311	Chi54	
9	7	Brown, Hector Harold	P35	42	.190	B	
		Causey, James Wayne (2B7)	3B30	53	.170	B	
1	1	Consuegra, Sandalio Simeon Castellon	P	4	+.500	xChi	
		Diering, Chas. Edward Allen (3B2)	OF40	50	.186	B	C
0	0	Dorish, Harry	P	13	+.000	B	Bos
		Dyck, James Robert	OF9	11	.217	B	CinN
		Evers, Walter Arthur	OF36	48	+.241	xClev	C
4	10	Ferrarese, Donald Hugh	P	36	.036	B	
4	7	Fornieles, Jose Miguel Torres	P30	33	+.167	xChi	
		Francona, John Patsy (1B21)	OF122	139	.258	A	
		Frazier, Joseph Filmore	OF19	45	.257	xCinN	C
		Gardner, Wm. Frederick (SS25 3B6)	2B132	144	.231	NYN	
		Gastall, Thomas Everett	C20	32	.196	B	C
		Ginsberg, Myron Nathan	C8	15	+.071	xK.C.	
		Hale, Robert Houston	1B51	85	.237	B	
0	0	Harrison, Robert Lee	P	1	.000	B	C
		Hatton, Grady Edgebert (3B12)	2B15	27	.148	xStLN	
0	0	Held, Melvin Nicholas	P	4	.000	A	C
9	10	Johnson, Clifford	P	26	+.259	xChi	
		Kell, George Clyde (1B2 2B1)	3B97	102	+.261	xChi	
2	7	Loes, Wm.	P	21	.176	xBknN	
		Marsh, Fred Francis (2B5 3B8)	SS8	20	.125	B	C
1	1	Martin, Morris Webster	P	9	+.000	xChi	
		Miranda, Guillermo Perez	SS147	148	.217	B	
0	1	Moeller, Ronald Ralph	P	4	.000	A	
12	7	Moore, Raymond LeRoy	P	32	.271	B	
		Nelson, Robert Sidney	OF24	39	.206	B	
		Nieman, Robert Chas.	OF	114	+.322	xChi	
0	0	O'Dell, Wm. Oliver	P	4	.000	Balt54	
4	11	Palica, Ervin Martin	P29	30	.156	B	C
		Philley, David Earl (3B5)	OF31	32	+.205	B	Chi
		Pope, David	OF4	12	+.158	B	Clev
		Pyburn, James Edward	OF77	84	.173	B	
		Robinson, Brooks Calbert (2B1)	3B14	15	.227	B	
0	3	Schmitz, John Albert	P	18	+.000	xBos	C

WON	LOST	NAME	POS.	G.	BA	FROM	TO
		Smith, Harold Wayne	C71	78	+.262	B	K.C.
0	0	Sundin, Gordon Vincent	P	1	.000	A	C
		Triandos, Gus (1B52)	C89	131	.279	B	
0	0	Werley, George Wm.	P	1	.000	A	C
9	12	Wight, Wm. Robert	P	35	.200	B	
		Williams, Richard Hirshfeld	OF81	87	.286	xBknN	
		(1B10 2B10 3B4)					
4	2	Wilson, James Alger	P	7	+.267	B	Chi
7	6	Zuverink, George	P	62	.118	B	

WON 76
LOST 76
TG 152

AMERICAN LEAGUE — FINISHED 5th.

1957. — PCT. .500

BALTIMORE

PAUL RAPIER RICHARDS

WON	LOST	NAME	POS.	G.	BA	FROM	TO
0	0	Beamon, Chas. Alonzo	P	4	.000	B	
		Boyd, Robert Richard (OF1)	1B132	141	.318	B	
		Brideweser, James Ehrenfeld	SS74	91	.268	Det	C
		(2B1 3B3)					
7	8	Brown, Hector Harold	P25	30	.208	B	
		Busby, James Franklin	OF85	36	+.250	xClev	
		Causey, James Wayne (3B5)	2B6	14	.200	B	
0	5	Ceccarelli, Arthur Edward	P	20	.000	K.C.	
0	0	Consuegra, Sandalio Simeon	P	5	.000	B	NYN
		Castellon					
		Burham, Joseph Vann	OF59	77	.185	Balt54	
1	1	Ferrarese, Donald Hugh	P	8	.000	B	
2	6	Fornieles, Jose Miguel Torres	P15	16	+.278	B	Bos
		Francona, John Patsy (1B4)	OF73	97	.233	B	
		Gardner, Wm. Frederick	2B148	154	.262	B	
		(SS9)					
		Ginsberg, Myron Nathan	C66	85	.274	B	
		Goodman, Wm. Dale	3B54	73	+.308	xBos	
		(1B8 2B5 SS5 OF9)					
		Green, Leonard Chas.	OF15	19	.182	A	
		Hale, Robert Houston	1B5	42	.250	B	
0	0	Houtteman, Arthur Joseph	P	5	+.500	xClev	C
14	11	Johnson, Clifford	P	35	.135	B	
		Kell, George Clyde (1B22)	3B80	99	.297	B	C
8	3	Lehman, Kenneth Karl	P30	33	.200	xBknN	
12	7	Loes, Wm.	P	31	.080	B	
		Miksis, Edward Thomas		1	.000	xStLN	
		Miranda, Guillermo Perez	SS	115	.194	B	
11	13	Moore, Raymond LeRoy	P	34	.214	B	
		Nelson, Robert Sidney	OF8	15	.217	B	C
		Nieman, Robert Chas.	OF120	129	.276	B	
4	10	O'Dell, Wm. Oliver	P35	37	.147	B	
0	0	Pappas, Milton Stephen	P	4	.000	A	
		Patton, Thomas Allen	C	1	.000	A	C
		Peterson, Carl Francis	SS7	7	.176	Chi55	C
		Pilarcik, Alfred James	OF126	142	.278	K.C.	
		Powis, Carl Edgar	OF13	15	.195	A	C

WON	LOST	NAME	POS.	G.	BA	FROM	TO
		Pyburn, James Edward (C1)	OF28	35	.225	B	C
		Robinson, Brooks Calbert	3B47	50	.239	B	
		Robinson, Wm. Edward		4	+.000	xClev	C
		Triandos, Gus	C120	129	.254	B	
0	0	Trout, Paul Howard	P	2	.000	Bos52	C
1	0	Walker, Jerry Allen	P	13	.000	A	
6	6	Wight, Wm. Robert	P	27	.029	B	
		Williams, Richard Hirshfeld	OF26	47	.234	B	
		(1B12 3B15)					
		Zupo, Frank Joseph	C8	10	.083	A	
10	6	Zuverink, George	P	56	.130	B	

WON 74
LOST 79
TG 153

AMERICAN LEAGUE — FINISHED 6th.

1958. — PCT. .484

BALTIMORE

PAUL RAPIER RICHARDS

WON	LOST	NAME	POS.	G.	BA	FROM	TO
		Adair, Kenneth Jerry (2B1)	SS10	11	.105	A	
1	3	Beamon, Chas. Alonzo	P21	22	.000	B	C
		Boyd, Robert Richard	1B99	125	.309	B	
7	5	Brown, Hector Harold (3B2)	P19	21	.148	B	
		Burke, Leo Patrick (3B1)	OF3	7	.455	A	
		Busby, James Franklin (3B1)	OF103	113	.237	B	
		Castleman, Foster Ephraim	SS91	98	.170	NYN	C
		(2B4 3B4 OF1)					
		Gardner, Wm. Frederick	2B151	151	.225	B	
		(SS13)					
		Ginsberg, Myron Nathan	C39	61	.211	B	
		Green, Leonard Chas.	OF53	69	.231	B	
		Hale, Robert Houston	1B2	19	.350	B	
		Hamric, Odbert Herman		8	.125	BknN55	C
		Hansen, Ronald Lavern	SS	12	.000	A	
12	15	Harshman, John Elvin (OF1)	P34	47	.195	Chi	
6	9	Johnson, Clifford	P	26	.206	B	C
2	1	Lehman, Kenneth Karl	P	31	.071	B	
3	9	Loes, Wm.	P	32	.067	B	
		Marshall, Rufus James (OF8)	1B52	85	.215	A	ChiN
		Miksis, Edward Thomas	SS1	3	.000	B	CinN
		Miranda, Guillermo Perez	SS	102	.201	B	
0	0	Moeller, Ronald Ralph	P	4	.000	Balt56	
		Nieman, Robert Chas.	OF100	105	.325	B	
14	11	O'Dell, Wm. Oliver	P41	42	.111	B	
		Oertel, Chas. Frank	OF2	14	.167	A	C
10	10	Pappas, Milton Stephen (2B1)	P31	32	.143	B	
		Pilarcik, Alfred James	OF118	141	.243	B	
15	11	Portocarrero, Arnold Mario	P	32	.164	K.C.	
		Robinson, Brooks Calbert	3B140	145	.238	B	
		(2B16)					
1	0	Sleater, Louis Mortimer	P6	9	+.000	xDet	C
		Tasby, Willie	OF16	18	.200	A	
		Taylor, Joe Cephus	OF21	36	.273	xStLN	
		Triandos, Gus	C132	137	.245	B	

WON	LOST	NAME	POS.	G.	BA	FROM	TO
0	0	Walker, Jerry Allen	P	6	.000	B	
1	3	Wilhelm, James Hoyt	P	9	+.091	xClev	
		Williams, Richard Hirshfeld	OF70	128	.276	B	
		(1B26 2B7 3B45)					
		Woodling, Eugene Richard	OF116	133	.276	Clev	
		Zupo, Frank Joseph	C	1	.000	B	
2	2	Zuverink, George	P	45	.222	B	

WON 74 — AMERICAN LEAGUE — FINISHED 6th.
LOST 80
TG 154 — 1959. — PCT. .481

BALTIMORE

PAUL RAPIER RICHARDS

WON	LOST	NAME	POS.	G.	BA	FROM	TO
		Adair, Kenneth Jerry (SS1)	2B11	12	.314	B	
		Avila, Roberto Francisco	OF10	20	+.170	Clev	Bos
		Gonzalez (2B8 3B1)					
0	0	Bamberger, George Irvin	P	3	.000	NYN52	C
		Boyd, Robert Richard	1B109	128	.265	B	
11	9	Brown, Hector Harold	P	31	.048	B	
		Burke, Leo Patrick (3B2)	2B2	5	.200	B	
		Carrasquel, Alfonso Colon	SS89	114	.223	K.C.	C
		(1B1 2B22 3B2)					
0	0	Coleman, Walter Gary	P	3	+.000	xK.C.	
		Dropo, Walter (3B2)	1B54	62	.278	xCinN	
		Finigan, James LeRoy	3B42	48	.252	SFN	C
		(2B6 SS2)					
1	6	Fisher, John Howard	P	27	.130	A	
		Gardner, Wm. Frederick	2B139	140	.217	B	
		(SS1 3B1)					
		Ginsberg, Myron Nathan	C62	65	.181	B	
		Green, Leonard Chas.	OF22	27	+.292	B	Wash
		Hale, Robert Houston	1B8	40	.185	B	
		Hansen, Ronald Lavern	SS	2	.000	B	
0	6	Harshman, John Elvin	P14	15	+.200	B	Bos
1	1	Hoeft, Wm. Frederick	P	16	+.250	xBos	
4	1	Johnson, Ernest Thorwald	P	31	.333	MilN	C
		Klaus, Wm. Joseph	SS59	104	.249	Bos	
		(2B1 3B49)					
		Lockman, Carroll Walter	1B22	38	.217	SFN	CinN
		(2B5 OF1)					
4	7	Loes, Wm.	P	37	.125	B	
		Miranda, Guillermo Perez	SS47	65	.159	B	C
		(2B5 3B11)					
		Nieman, Robert Chas.	OF97	118	.292	B	
10	12	O'Dell, Wm. Oliver	P38	43	.083	B	
15	9	Pappas, Milton Stephen	P	33	.139	B	
		Pearson, Albert Gregory	OF49	80	+.232	xWash	
		Pilarcik, Alfred James	OF106	130	.282	B	
2	7	Portocarrero, Arnold Mario	P	27	.000	B	
		Robinson, Brooks Calbert	3B87	88	.284	B	
		(2B1)					
		Saverine, Robert Paul		1	.000	A	

WON	LOST	NAME	POS.	G.	BA	FROM	TO
		Shetrone, Barry Stevan	OF23	33	.203	A	
0	0	Stock, Wesley Gay	P	7	.000	A	
		Tasby, Willie	OF137	142	.250	B	
		Taylor, Joe Cephus	OF12	14	.156	B	C
		Triandos, Gus	C125	126	.216	B	
		Valentine, Fred Lee	OF8	12	.316	A	
11	10	Walker, Jerry Allen	P30	31	.169	B	
15	11	Wilhelm, James Hoyt	P	32	.053	B	
		Woodling, Eugene Richard	OF124	140	.300	B	
0	1	Zuverink, George	P	6	.000	B	C

WON 89 — AMERICAN LEAGUE — FINISHED 2nd.
LOST 65
TG 154 — 1960. — PCT. .578

BALTIMORE

PAUL RAPIER RICHARDS

WON	LOST	NAME	POS.	G.	BA	FROM	TO
		Adair, Kenneth Jerry	2B	3	.200	B	
0	0	Anderson, John Chas.	P	4	.000	PhilN58	
10	7	Barber, Stephen David	P	36	.056	A	
		Barker, Raymond Herrell	OF1	5	.000	A	
		Boyd, Robert Richard	1B17	71	.317	B	
		Brandt, John George	OF142	145	.254	SFN	
		(1B1 3B2)					
		Breeding, Marvin Eugene	2B	152	.267	A	
12	5	Brown, Hector Harold	P	30	.182	B	
		Busby, James Franklin	OF71	79	+.258	xBos	
0	2	Coleman, Walter Gary	P	5	.000	B	C
		Courtney, Clinton Dawson	C58	83	.227	Wash	
		Dropo, Walter (3B1)	1B67	79	.268	B	
18	11	Estrada, Chas. Leonard	P	36	.141	A	
12	11	Fisher, John Howard	P	40	.183	B	
		Gentile, James Edward	1B124	138	.292	LAN58	
		Ginsberg, Myron Nathan	C	14	+.267	B	Chi
		Green, Eugene Leroy	OF	1	.250	StLN	
		Hansen, Ronald Lavern	SS	153	.255	B	
2	1	Hoeft, Wm. Frederick	P	19	.000	B	
1	1	Jones, Gordon Bassett	P	29	.400	SFN	
		Klaus, Wm. Joseph	2B30	46	.209	B	
		(SS12 3B2)					
0	0	Mabe, Robert Lee	P	2	.000	CinN	C
		Nicholson, David Lawrence	OF44	54	.186	A	
15	11	Pappas, Milton Steven	P	30	.043	B	
		Pearson, Albert Gregory	OF32	48	.244	B	
		Philley, David Earl (3B1)	OF8	14	.265	xSFN	
		Pilarcik, Alfred James	OF75	104	.247	B	
3	2	Portocarrero, Arnold Mario	P	13	.000	B	C
		Powers, John Calvin	OF4	10	+.111	CinN	Clev
		Rice, Delbert W.	C	1	.000	xStLN	
		Robinson, Brooks Calbert	3B152	152	.294	B	
		(2B3)					
		Shetrone, Barry Stevan		1	.000	B	
		Stephens, Glen Eugene	OF77	84	+.238	xBos	

WON	LOST	NAME	POS.	G.	BA	FROM	TO
2	2	Stock, Wesley Gay	P	17	.000	B	
		Tasby, Willie	OF36	39	+.212	B	Bos
		Thomas, Valmy	C	8	.063	PhilN	
		Thomson, Robert Brown	OF2	3	+.000	xBos	C
		Triandos, Gus	C105	109	.269	B	
3	4	Walker, Jerry Allen	P29	35	.368	B	
11	8	Wilhelm, James Hoyt	P	41	.071	B	
		Woodling, Eugene Richard	OF124	140	.283	B	

WON 95 LOST 67 TG 162

AMERICAN LEAGUE 1961.

FINISHED 3rd. PCT. .586

BALTIMORE

PAUL RAPIER RICHARDS CHALMER LUMAN HARRIS

WON	LOST	NAME	POS.	G.	BA	FROM	TO
		Adair, Kenneth Jerry (SS27 3B2)	2B107	133	.264	B	
18	12	Barber, Stephen David	P	37	.163	B	
		Brandt, John George (3B1)	OF136	139	.297	B	
		Breeding, Marvin Eugene	2B80	90	.209	B	
10	6	Brown, Hector Harold	P	27	.140	B	
		Busby, James Franklin	OF71	75	.258	B	
		Courtney, Clinton Dawson	C16	22	+.267	xK.C.	C
		Dropo, Walter	1B12	14	.259	B	C
		Essegian, Chas. Abraham		1	+.000	LAN	K.C.
15	9	Estrada, Chas. Leonard	P	33	.114	B	
10	13	Fisher, John Howard	P	36	.089	B	
		Foiles, Henry Lee	C38	43	.274	Det	
		Gentile, James Edward	1B144	148	.302	B	
7	5	Hall, Richard Wallace	P29	30	.139	K.C.	
		Hansen, Ronald Lavern (2B7)	SS149	155	.248	B	
		Herzog, Dorrel Norman	OF98	113	.291	K.C.	
7	4	Hoeft, Wm. Frederick	P	35	.179	B	
1	2	Hyde, Richard Elde	P	15	1.000	Wash	C
0	0	Jones, Gordon Bassett	P	3	.000	B	
		Lau, Chas. Richard	C	17	.170	xMilN	
0	0	Lehew, James Anthony	P	2	.000	A	
0	0	Papa, John Paul	P	2	.000	A	
13	9	Pappas, Milton Stephen	P	26	.136	B	
		Philley, David Earl (1B1)	OF25	99	.250	B	
		Powell, John Wesley	OF3	4	.077	A	
		Robinson, Brooks Calbert (2B2 SS1)	3B163	163	.287	B	
		Robinson, Earl John	OF82	96	.266	LAN58	
		Shetrone, Barry Stevan	OF2	3	.143	B	
		Snyder, Russell Henry	OF108	115	.292	K.C.	
		Stephens, Glen Eugene	OF30	32	+.190	B	K.C.
5	0	Stock, Wesley Gay	P	35	.000	B	
		Thorneberry, Marvin Eugene (1B11)	OF15	56	+.208	xK.C.	
		Triandos, Gus	C114	115	.244	B	
9	7	Wilhelm, James Hoyt	P	51	.050	B	

WON	LOST	NAME	POS.	G.	BA	FROM	TO
		Williams, Richard Hirshfeld (1B20 3B2)	OF75	103	.206	K.C.	
		Zupo, Frank Joseph	C4	5	.500	Balt58	C

WON 77 LOST 85 TG 162

AMERICAN LEAGUE 1962.

FINISHED 7th. PCT. .475

BALTIMORE

WM. CLYDE HITCHCOCK

WON	LOST	NAME	POS.	G.	BA	FROM	TO
		Adair, Kenneth Jerry (2B34 3B1)	SS113	139	.284	B	
9	6	Barber, Stephen David	P	28	.071	B	
		Brandt, John George (3B2)	OF138	143	.255	B	
		Breeding, Marvin Eugene (SS1 3B1)	2B73	95	.246	B	
6	4	Brown, Hector Harold	P	22	+.286	B	N.Y.
9	17	Estrada, Chas. Leonard	P34	38	.152	B	
		Etchebarren, Andrew Auguste	C	2	.333	A	
7	9	Fisher, John Howard	P32	33	.102	B	
		Gentile, James Edward	1B150	152	.251	B	
6	6	Hall, Richard Wallace	P43	44	.167	B	
		Hansen, Ronald Lavern	SS64	71	.173	B	
		Herzog, Dorrel Norman	OF70	99	.266	B	
4	8	Hoeft, Wm. Frederick	P	57	.158	B	
		Johnson, Darrell Dean	C	6	.182	xCinN	C
		Landrith, Hobert Neal	C	60	.222	xNYN	
		Lau, Chas. Richard	C56	81	.294	B	
0	0	Lehew, James Anthony	P	6	.000	B	C
0	1	Luebke, Richard Raymond	P	10	.000	A	C
		McGuire, Mickey C.	SS5	6	.000	A	
1	0	McNally, David Arthur	P	1	.000	A	
1	1	Miller, John Ernest	P	2	.000	A	
		Nicholson, David Lawrence	OF80	97	.173	Balt60	
0	0	Papa, John Paul	P	1	.000	B	C
12	10	Pappas, Milton Stephen	P	35	.087	B	
		Powell, John Wesley (1B1)	OF112	124	.243	B	
2	2	Quirk, Arthur Lincoln	P	7	.143	A	
10	9	Roberts, Robin Evan	P	27	.192	PhilN	
		Robinson, Brooks Calbert (2B2 SS3)	3B162	162	.303	B	
		Robinson, Earl John	OF17	29	.286	B	C
		Savarine, Robert Paul	2B7	8	.238	Balt59	
		Shetrone, Barry Stevan	OF6	21	.250	B	
0	0	Short, Wm. Ross	P	5	.000	NY60	
		Smith, Nathaniel Beverly	C3	5	.222	A	C
		Snyder, Russell Henry	OF121	139	.305	B	
3	2	Stock, Wesley Gay	P	53	.000	B	
		Temple, John Ellis	2B71	78	.263	Clev	HousN
		Throneberry, Marvin Eugene	OF2	9	.000	B	NYN
		Triandos, Gus	C63	66	.159	B	
		Virgil, Osvaldo Jose		1	.000	K.C.	
		Ward, Peter Thomas	OF6	8	.143	A	

WON	LOST	NAME	POS.	G.	BA	FROM	TO
7	10	Wilhelm, James Hoyt	P	52	.125	B	
		Williams, Richard Hirshfeld (1B21 3B4)	OF29	82	.247	B	

WON 86 AMERICAN LEAGUE FINISHED 4th.
LOST 76
TG 162 1963. PCT. .531

BALTIMORE

WM. CLYDE HITCHCOCK

WON	LOST	NAME	POS.	G.	BA	FROM	TO
		Adair, Kenneth Jerry	2B103	109	.228	B	
		Aparicio, Luis Ernesto	SS145	146	.250	Chic.	
20	13	Barber, Stephen David	P	39	.138	B	
		Bowens, Samuel Edward	OF13	15	.333	A	
		Brandt, John George (3B1)	OF134	142	.248	B	
		Brown, Richard Ernest	C58	59	.246	Det	
0	1	Brunet, George Stuart	P	16	.000	xHousN	
0	1	Bunker, Wallace Edward	P	1	.500	A	C
0	1	Burnside, Peter Willets	P	6	+.000	Wash	Wash
1	3	Delock, Ivan Martin	P	7	+.000	xBos	C
3	2	Estrada, Chas. Leonard	P	8	.100	B	
		Gaines, Arnesta	OF39	66	.286	CinN	
		Gentile, James Edward	1B143	145	.248	B	
5	5	Hall, Richard Wallace	P47	48	.464	B	
		Johnson, Robert Wallace (1B8 SS7 3B5)	2B50	82	.295	Wash	
		Landrith, Hobert Neal	C1	2	+.000	B	Wash
		Lau, Chas. Richard	C8	29	+.188	B	K.C.
6	8	McCormick, Michael Francis	P	25	.174	SFN	
7	8	McNally, David Arthur	P	29	.053	B	
1	1	Miller, John Ernest	P	3	.000	B	
5	8	Miller, Stuart Leonard	P	71	.313	SFN	
0	0	Narum, Leslie Ferdinand	P	7	1.000	A	
		Orsino, John Joseph (1B3)	C109	116	.272	SFN	
16	9	Pappas, Milton Stephen	P34	36	.127	B	
		Powell, John Wesley (1B23)	OF121	140	.265	B	
14	13	Roberts, Robin Evan	P	35	.203	B	
		Robinson, Brooks Calbert (SS1)	3B160	161	.251	B	
		Savarine, Robert Paul (2B19 SS13)	OF59	115	.234	B	
		Smith, Alphonse Eugene	OF97	120	.272	Chic.	
		Snyder, Russell Henry	OF130	148	.256	B	
0	1	Starrette, Herman Paul	P	18	.000	A	
7	0	Stock, Wesley Gay	P	47	.000	B	
1	2	Stone, Darrah Dean	P	17	.000	Chic.	C
		Valentine, Fred Lee	OF10	26	.268	Balt59	

WON 97 AMERICAN LEAGUE FINISHED 3rd.
LOST 65
TG 162 1964. PCT. .599

BALTIMORE

HENRY ALBERT BAUER

WON	LOST	NAME	POS.	G.	BA	FROM	TO
		Adair, Kenneth Jerry	2B153	155	.248	B	
		Aparicio, Luis Ernesto	SS145	146	.266	B	
9	13	Barber, Stephen David	P	36	.149	B	
1	0	Bertaina, Frank Louis	P	6	.000	A	
		Blair, Paul L. D.	OF6	8	.000	A	
		Bowens, Samuel Edward	OF135	139	.263	B	
		Brandt, John George	OF134	137	.243	B	
		Brown, Richard Ernest	C84	88	.257	B	
19	5	Bunker, Wallace Edward	P	29	.069	B	
		Cimoli, Gino Nicholas	OF35	38	+.138	xK.C.	
3	2	Estrada, Chas. Leonard	P17	18	.143	B	
		Gaines, Arnesta	OF5	16	.154	B	HousN
		Green, Leonard Chas.	OF8	14	+.190	xL.A.	
5	5	Haddix, Harvey	P	49	.000	PittN	
9	1	Hall, Richard Wallace	P	45	.125	B	
		Jackson, Louis Clarence	OF1	4	.375	ChicN59	C
		Johnson, Robert Wallace (1B15 2B15 3B1 OF1)	SS18	93	.248	B	
0	0	Jones, Samuel	P	7	.000	StLN	C
		Kirkland, Willie Chas.	OF58	66	+.200	Clev	Wash
		Lau, Chas. Richard	C47	62	+.259	xK.C.	
0	2	McCormick, Michael Francis	P	4	.167	B	
9	11	McNally, David Arthur	P	30	.137	B	
7	7	Miller, Stuart Leonard	P	66	.111	B	
		Orsino, John Joseph (1B5)	C66	81	.222	B	
16	7	Pappas, Milton Stephen	P	37	.129	B	
		Piniella, Louis Victor		4	.000	A	
		Powell, John Wesley (1B5)	OF124	134	.290	B	
13	7	Roberts, Robin Evan	P	31	.132	B	
		Robinson, Brooks Calbert	3B	163	.317	B	
		Robinson, Earl John	OF34	37	.273	Balt62	C
1	0	Rowe, Kenneth Darrell	P	6	.000	LAN	
		Savarine, Robert Paul (OF2)	SS15	46	.147	B	
		Siebern, Norman Leroy	1B149	150	.245	K.C.	
		Snyder, Russell Henry	OF40	56	.290	B	
1	0	Starrette, Herman Paul	P	5	.000	B	
2	0	Stock, Wesley Gay	P	14	+.000	B	K.C.
2	5	Vineyard, David Kent	P	19	.167	A	C

CLUB RECORD

AMERICAN LEAGUE

BOSTON

YEAR	TG	WON	LOST	TIED	PCT.	FINISHED	MANAGER
1901	136	79	57		.581	2	James J. Collins
1902	137	77	60		.562	3	James J. Collins
1903	138	91	47		.659	1	James J. Collins
1904	154	95	59		.617	1	James J. Collins
1905	152	78	74		.513	4	James J. Collins
1906	154	49	105		.318	8(Last)	James J. Collins
							Chas. Sylvester Stahl
1907	149	59	90		.396	7	Denton True Young
							George A. Huff
							Robert Alexander Unglaub
							James Thomas McGuire
1908	154	75	79		.487	5	James Thomas McGuire
							Frederick L. Lake
1909	151	88	63		.583	3	Frederick L. Lake
1910	153	81	72		.529	4	Patrick Joseph Donovan
1911	153	78	75		.509	5	Patrick Joseph Donovan
1912	152	105	47		.691	1	Garland Stahl
1913	150	79	71		.527	4	Garland Stahl
							Wm. Francis Carrigan
1914	153	91	62		.595	2	Wm. Francis Carrigan
1915	151	101	50		.669	1	Wm. Francis Carrigan
1916	154	91	63		.591	1	Wm. Francis Carrigan
1917	152	90	62		.592	2	John Joseph Barry
1918	126	75	51		.595	1	Edward Grant Barrow
1919	137	66	71		.482	6	Edward Grant Barrow
1920	153	72	81		.471	5	Edward Grant Barrow
1921	154	75	79		.487	5	Hugh Duffy
1922	154	61	93		.396	8(Last)	Hugh Duffy
1923	152	61	91		.401	8(Last)	Frank LeRoy Chance
1924	154	67	87		.435	7	Leo Alexander Fohl
1925	152	47	105		.309	8(Last)	Leo Alexander Fohl
1926	153	46	107		.301	8(Last)	Leo Alexander Fohl
1927	154	51	103		.331	8(Last)	Wm. Francis Carrigan
1928	153	57	96		.373	8(Last)	Wm. Francis Carrigan
1929	154	58	96		.377	8(Last)	Wm. Francis Carrigan
1930	154	52	102		.338	8(Last)	Chas. F. Wagner
1931	152	62	90		.408	6	John Francis Collins
1932	154	43	111		.279	8(Last)	John Francis Collins
							Martin Joseph McManus
1933	149	63	86		.423	7	Martin Joseph McManus
1934	152	76	76		.500	4	Stanley Raymond Harris
1935	153	78	75		.510	4	Joseph Edward Cronin
1936	154	74	80		.481	6	Joseph Edward Cronin
1937	152	80	72		.526	5	Joseph Edward Cronin
1938	149	88	61		.591	2	Joseph Edward Cronin
1939	151	89	62		.589	2	Joseph Edward Cronin
1940	154	82	72		.532	x4(Chi)	Joseph Edward Cronin
1941	154	84	70		.545	2	Joseph Edward Cronin
1942	152	93	59		.612	2	Joseph Edward Cronin
1943	152	68	84		.447	7	Joseph Edward Cronin
1944	154	77	77		.500	4	Joseph Edward Cronin
1945	154	71	83		.461	7	Joseph Edward Cronin
1946	154	104	50		.675	1	Joseph Edward Cronin
1947	154	83	71		.539	3	Joseph Edward Cronin
1948	155	96	59		.619	2	Joseph Vincent McCarthy
1949	154	96	58		.623	2	Joseph Vincent McCarthy
1950	154	94	60		.610	3	Joseph Vincent McCarthy
							Stephen Francis O'Neill
1951	154	87	67		.565	3	Stephen Francis O'Neill
1952	154	76	78		.494	6	Louis Boudreau, Jr.
1953	153	84	69		.549	4	Louis Boudreau, Jr.
1954	154	69	85		.448	4	Louis Boudreau, Jr.
1955	154	84	70		.545	4	Michael Franklin Higgins
1956	154	84	70		.545	4	Michael Franklin Higgins
1957	154	82	72		.532	3	Michael Franklin Higgins
1958	154	79	75		.513	3	Michael Franklin Higgins
1959	154	75	79		.487	5	Michael Franklin Higgins
							Rudolph Preston York
							Wm. Frederick Jurges
1960	154	65	89		.422	7	Wm. Frederick Jurges
							Delmar David Baker
							Michael Franklin Higgins
1961	162	76	86		.469	6	Michael Franklin Higgins
1962	160	76	84		.475	8	Michael Franklin Higgins
1963	161	76	85		.472	7	John Michael Pesky
1964	162	72	90		.444	8	John Michael Pesky
YEAR	TG	WON	LOST	TIED	PCT.	FINISHED	MANAGER
1965	162	62	100	0	.383	9	WILLIAM JENNINGS HERMAN
1966	162	72	90	0	.444	9	WILLIAM JENNINGS HERMAN
							JAMES EDWARD RUNNELS *
1967	162	92	70	0	.568	1	RICHARD HIRSHFELD WILLIAMS
1968	162	86	76	0	.531	4	RICHARD HIRSHFELD WILLIAMS
1969	162	87	75	0	.537	3E	RICHARD HIRSHFELD WILLIAMS
							EDWARD JOSEPH POPOWSKI *
1970	162	87	75	0	.537	3E	EDWARD MICHAEL KASKO
1971	162	85	77	0	.525	3E	EDWARD MICHAEL KASKO
1972	155	85	70	0	.548	2E	EDWARD MICHAEL KASKO

WON 79 / LOST 57 / TG 136

AMERICAN LEAGUE 1901.

FINISHED 2nd. PCT. .581

BOSTON

JAMES JOSEPH COLLINS

WON	LOST	NAME	POS.	G.	BA	FROM	TO
0	2	Beville, Chas. E.	P	3	.250	A	C
		Collins, James Joseph MGR.	3B	138	.329	BosN	
		Criger, Louis	C	69	.240	StLN	
4	6	Cuppy, George Joseph (Nig)	P	17	.204	BosN	C
		Dowd, Thomas Jefferson	OF	138	.270	Mil	C
		Ferris, Albert Sayles (Hobe)	2B	138	.251	A	
0	1	Foreman, Francis Isaiah	P	1	+.000	Buff	Balt
		Freeman, John F. (Buck)	1B	120	.346	BosN	
		Gleason, Harry George	3B	1	1.000	A	
		Hemphill, Chas. Judson	OF	137	.269	K.C.	
		Jones, Chas. C.	OF	10	.119	Det	
2	3	Kellum, Winford Ansley	P	6	.150	Indps	
17	16	Lewis, Edward Morgan (Parson)	P	38	.168	BosN	C
6	9	Mitchell, Frederick Francis	P	20	.155	A	
0	0	Morrissey, Frank Frederick	P	1	.000	A	
		McLean, John Bannerman (Larry)	1B4	9	.210	A	
		Parent, Frederick Alfred	SS133	138	.318	StLN99	
		Schreckengost, Ossee Freeman	C75	83	.320	Buff	
		Slattery, John Thomas	C	1	.500	A	
		Stahl, Chas. Sylvester (Chick)	OF	130	.310	BosN	
1	0	Volz, Jacob Phillip	P	1	.000	A	
1	0	Wilson, George Pepper (George P. Prentiss)	P	2	.333	A	
17	10	Winter, George Lovington	P	28	.204	A	
31	10	Young, Denton True (Cy)	P42	45	.223	StLN	

WON 77 / LOST 60 / TG 137

AMERICAN LEAGUE 1902.

FINISHED 3rd. PCT. .562

BOSTON

JAMES JOSEPH COLLINS

WON	LOST	NAME	POS.	G.	BA	FROM	TO
1	1	Adkins, Merle Theron	P	4	.222	A	
1	2	Altrock, Nicholas (Nick)	P	3	.000	LvlleN98	
		Collins, James Joseph MGR.	3B	105	.324	B	
		Criger, Louis	C78	86	.259	B	
0	1	Deininger, Otto Chas.	P	2	.333	A	
21	20	Dinneen, Wm. Henry (OF2)	P42	44	.134	BosN	
		Dougherty, Patrick Henry (3B1)	OF103	106	.335	A	
		Ferris, Albert Sayles (Hobe)	2B	133	.251	B	
		Freeman, John F. (Buck)	OF	138	.311	B	
		Gleason, Harry George (2B4 OF22)	3B35	66	.224	B	
		Hickman, Chas. Taylor	OF	28	+.308	NYN	Clev
2	4	Hughes, Thomas J.	P	8	+.444	xBalt	
0	1	Husting, Berthold Juneau	P	1	+.250	Mil	Phil
		LaChance, George	1B	138	.275	Clev	
0	1	Mitchell, Frederick Francis	P	1	+.000	B	Phil
		Parent, Frederick Alfred	SS	139	.288	B	
2	2	Prentiss, George Pepper (Geo. P. Wilson)	P	6	+.250	B	Balt
7	8	Sparks, Tully Frank	P	17	.132	xNYN	
		Stahl, Chas. Sylvester (Chick)	OF126	127	.318	B	
		Warner, John Joseph	C63	64	.234	NYN	
0	0	Williams, David O.	P	3	.300	A	C
		Wilson, James Garrett	2B	3	.181	A	C
11	9	Winter, George Lovington	P	20	.159	B	
32	11	Young, Denton True (Cy)	P	45	.222	B	

WON 91 / LOST 47 / TG 138

AMERICAN LEAGUE 1903.

FINISHED 1st. PCT. .659

BOSTON

JAMES JOSEPH COLLINS

WON	LOST	NAME	POS.	G.	BA	FROM	TO
0	3	Altrock, Nicholas (Nick)	P	3	+.667	B	Chi
		Collins, James Joseph MGR.	3B	130	.296	B	
		Criger, Louis	C	96	.197	B	
21	11	Dinneen, Wm. Henry	P	34	.160	B	
		Dougherty, Patrick Henry	OF	139	.332	B	
		Farrell, Chas. A. (Duke)	C	17	.404	BknN	
		Ferris, Albert Sayles (Hobe)	2B	141	.250	B	
		Freeman, John F. (Buck)	OF	141	.285	B	
11	9	Gibson, Norwood R.	P	25	.262	KCA00	
21	7	Hughes, Thomas J.	P	32	.283	B	
		LaChance, George	1B	141	.258	B	
		O'Brien, John Joseph	OF74	96	.212	Clev01	C
		Parent, Frederick Alfred	SS	139	.304	B	
		Smith, Alexander Benjamin	C	12	.333	Balt	
		Stahl, Chas. Sylvester (Chick)	OF74	78	.279	B	
		Stahl, Garland	C26	38	.239	A	
		Stone, George Robert		2	.000	A	
10	8	Winter, George Lovington	P	23	.136	B	
28	9	Young, Denton True (Cy)	P40	41	.330	B	

WON 95 / LOST 59 / TG 154

AMERICAN LEAGUE 1904.

FINISHED 1st. PCT. .617

BOSTON

JAMES JOSEPH COLLINS

WON	LOST	NAME	POS.	G.	BA	FROM	TO
		Collins, James Joseph MGR.	3B	156	.265	B	
		Criger, Louis	C95	98	.217	B	
24	15	Dinneen, Wm. Henry	P	39	.212	B	
		Doran, Thomas J.	C	5	.000	A	
		Dougherty, Patrick Henry	OF	59	+.268	B	N.Y.
		Farrell, Chas. A. (Duke)	C56	67	.219	B	
		Ferris, Albert Sayles (Hobe)	2B	156	.221	B	
		Freeman, John F. (Buck)	OF	157	.278	B	
17	14	Gibson, Norwood R.	P	33	.065	B	
		LaChance, George	1B	157	.231	B	
		O'Neill, Wm. John	OF	18	+.192	A	Wash
		Parent, Frederick Alfred	SS	155	.296	B	
		Selbach, Albert Carl (Kip)	OF	98	+.268	xWash	
		Stahl, Chas. Sylvester (Chick)	OF	157	.300	B	
20	10	Tannehill, Jesse Niles	P33	45	+.205	N.Y.	
		Unglaub, Robert Alexander	3B5	7	+.182	xN.Y.	
8	4	Winter, George Lovington	P	20	.114	B	
26	16	Young, Denton True (Cy)	P	43	.211	B	

WON 78 AMERICAN LEAGUE FINISHED 4th.
LOST 74
TG 152 1905. PCT. .513

BOSTON

JAMES JOSEPH COLLINS

WON	LOST	NAME	POS.	G.	BA	FROM	TO
		Armbruster, Chas. A.	C	35	.198	A	
1	2	Barry, Edward	P	7	.191	A	
		Burkett, Jesse Cail	OF	149	.257	StL	C
		Collins, James Joseph MGR.	3B	131	.276	B	
		Criger, Louis	C	109	.198	B	
14	14	Dinneen, Wm. Henry	P	31	.148	B	
		Doran, Thomas J.	C	3	+.000	B	Det
		Farrell, Chas. A. (Duke)	C	7	.238	B	C
		Ferris, Albert Sayles (Hobe)	2B	141	.220	B	
		Freeman, John F. (Buck) (OF51)	1B72	130	.240	B	
5	10	Gibson, Norwood R.	P	24	.089	B	
		Godwin, John Henry	2B	16	.304	A	
		Grimshaw, Myron Frederick	1B74	85	.239	A	
1	2	Harris, Joseph White	P	3	.222	A	
3	0	Hughes, Edward H.	P	6	.200	A	
		LaChance, George	1B	12	.128	B	C
		McGovern, Arthur John	C	15	.114	A	C
1	2	Olmstead, Frederick D.	P	3	.125	A	
		Owens, Frank Walter	C	1	.000	A	
		Parent, Frederick Alfred	SS	153	.234	B	
		Rising, Perry Sumner	OF	11	.100	A	C
		Selbach, Albert Carl (Kip)	OF112	115	.246	B	
		Stahl, Chas. Sylvester (Chick)	OF	134	.258	B	
23	10	Tannehill, Jesse Niles	P	37	.226	B	
		Unglaub, Robert Alexander	3B21	43	.223	B	
14	16	Winter, George Lovington	P	34	.270	B	
16	18	Young, Denton True (Cy)	P	38	.150	B	

WON 49 AMERICAN LEAGUE FINISHED 8th (LAST)
LOST 105
TG 154 1906. PCT. .318

BOSTON

JAMES JOSEPH COLLINS CHAS. SYLVESTER STAHL

WON	LOST	NAME	POS.	G.	BA	FROM	TO
		Armbruster, Chas. A.	C66	72	.144	B	
0	3	Barry, Edward	P	3	.143	B	
		Carrigan, Wm. Francis	C35	37	.211	A	
		Chadbourne, Chester James	2B	11	.302	A	
		Collins, James Joseph MGR.	3B32	37	.275	B	
		Criger, Louis	C	6	.214	B	
8	19	Dinneen, Wm. Henry	P	28	.111	B	
		Doran, Thomas J.	C	2	.000	Det	C
		Ferris, Albert Sayles (Hobe)	2B126	130	.244	B	
		Freeman, John F. (Buck) (1B43)	OF65	121	.250	B	
0	2	Gibson, Norwood R.	P	5	.200	B	C
4	6	Glaze, Daniel Ralph	P19	22	.182	A	
		Godwin, John Henry	3B27	66	.187	B	C
		Graham, Chas. Henry	C27	30	.233	A	C
		Grimshaw, Myron Frederick	1B	110	.290	B	
2	21	Harris, Joseph White	P	30	.160	B	
		Hayden, John Francis (Jack)	OF	85	.248	Phi101	
		Hoey, John B.	OF	94	.244	A	
0	0	Hughes, Edward H.	P	2	.000	B	C
1	0	Kroh, Floyd H.	P	1	.000	A	
		Morgan, James Edward	3B	88	.215	A	C
1	3	Oberlin, Frank Rufus	P	4	.143	A	
		Parent, Frederick Alfred	SS143	149	.235	B	
		Peterson, Robert A.	C30	39	.203	A	
		Selbach, Albert Carl (Kip)	OF58	60	.211	B	C
		Stahl, Chas. Sylvester (Chick) MGR.	OF	155	.286	B	C
1	1	Swormstedt, Leonard Jordan	P	3	.125	CinN02	C
13	11	Tannehill, Jesse Niles	P26	31	.278	B	
		Wagner, Chas. F.	2B	9	.250	NYN02	
6	18	Winter, George Lovington	P	29	.246	B	
13	21	Young, Denton True (Cy)	P39	40	.154	B	

WON 59 AMERICAN LEAGUE FINISHED 7th.
LOST 90
TG 149 1907. PCT. .396

BOSTON

DENTON TRUE YOUNG GEORGE A. HUFF
ROBERT ALEXANDER UNGLAUB JAMES THOMAS McGUIRE

WON	LOST	NAME	POS.	G.	BA	FROM	TO

WON	LOST	NAME	POS.	G.	BA	FROM	TO
		Armbruster, Chas. A.	C	23	+.100	B	Chi
		Barrett, James Erigena	OF99	106	.243	CinN	
0	1	Barry, Edward	P	2	.000	B	C
0	1	Burchell, Frederick Duff	P	2	.167	PhilN03	
		Chadbourne, Chester James	OF	10	.289	B	
		Collins, James Joseph	3B	41	+.294	B	Phil
		Congalton, Wm. Millar (Bunk)	OF	124	+.286	xClev	C
		Criger, Louis	C74	75	.181	B	
0	4	Dinneen, Wm. Henry	P	7	+.000	B	StL
		Ferris, Albert Sayles (Hobe)	2B	143	.241	B	
		Freeman, John F. (Buck)	OF	4	.167	B	C
9	13	Glaze, Daniel Ralph	P	32	.180	B	
		Grimshaw, Myron Frederick (1B15)	OF23	64	.204	B	C
0	7	Harris, Joseph White	P	12	.190	B	C
		Hoey, John B.	OF21	39	.219	B	
0	0	Jacobson, Albert L. (Beany)	P	2	+.000	xStL	C
		Knight, John Wesley (Jack)	3B	98	+.215	xPhil	
0	4	Kroh, Floyd H.	P	7	.272	B	
		Lord, Harry Donald	3B	10	.184	A	
6	6	Morgan, Harry Richard (Cy)	P	13	+.057	xStL	
		McGuire, James Thomas MGR.	C	6	+.500	xN.Y.	
1	5	Oberlin, Frank Rufus	P	12	+.143	B	Wash
		Parent, Frederick Alfred (SS43)	OF47	114	.276	B	
		Peterson, Robert Alfred	C	4	.000	B	C
3	11	Pruiett, Chas. LeRoy	P	35	.157	A	
		Shaw, Alfred L.	C73	76	.192	Det01	
		Speaker, Tristram E. (Tris)	OF	7	.158	A	
0	1	Steele, Elmer Rae	P	4	.000	A	
		Sullivan, Dennis Wm.	OF143	144	.245	Wash05	
6	7	Tannehill, Jesse Niles	P18	21	.196	B	
		Unglaub, Robert Alexander MGR.	1B	139	.255	Bos05	
		Wagner, Chas. F.	SS109	111	.213	B	
		Whiteman, George	OF	4	.167	A	
12	15	Winter, George Lovington	P	35	.223	B	
22	15	Young, Denton True (Cy) MGR.	P44	45	.216	B	

WON 75 — AMERICAN LEAGUE — FINISHED 5th.
LOST 79
TG 154 — 1908. — PCT. .487

BOSTON

JAMES THOMAS McGUIRE — FREDERICK LOVETT LAKE

WON	LOST	NAME	POS.	G.	BA	FROM	TO
4	3	Arellanes, Frank Julian	P	12	.167	A	
		Barrett, James Erigena	OF	3	.125	B	C
1	0	Brady, James Ward	P	1	.000	PittN	
10	8	Burchell, Frederick Duff	P31	32	.246	B	
		Carlisle, Walter G.	OF	3	.100	A	C
		Carrigan, Wm. Francis	C47	57	.235	Bos06	
11	12	Cicotte, Edward Victor	P38	39	.229	Det05	
		Cravath, Glifford Carlton	OF77	94	.256	A	
		(Cactus)					
		Criger, Louis	C	84	.190	B	
		Donahue, Patrick Wm.	C32	35	.198	A	
		Gardner, Wm. Lawrence (Larry)	3B	3	.300	A	
		Gessler, Harry Homer	OF126	128	.308	ChiN06	
2	2	Glaze, Daniel Ralph	P	10	.077	B	C
0	0	Hartman, Chas. Otto	P	1	.000	A	C
		Hoey, John B.	OF	13	.139	B	C
		LaPorte, Frank B. (3B8)	2B12	60	+.245	N.Y.	N.Y.
		Lord, Harry Donald	3B144	145	.259	B	
13	14	Morgan, Harry Richard (Cy)	P	30	.127	B	
		McConnell, Ambrose Moses	2B127	140	.279	A	
		McFarland, Edward Wm.	C	19	.208	Chi	C
		McGuire, James Thomas MGR.	1B	1	+.000	B	Clev
		McHale, James Bernard	OF19	21	.224	A	C
1	0	McMahon, Henry John	P	1	.500	A	C
		Niles, Harry Clyde	2B	18	+.235	xN.Y.	
		Ostdiek, Henry Girard	C	1	.000	Clev04	C
0	0	Patten, Case L.	P	1	+.000	xWash	
1	7	Pruiett, Chas. LeRoy	P	13	.111	B	C
		Speaker, Tristram E. (Tris)	OF	31	.220	B	
		Stahl, Garland	1B	79	+.240	xN.Y.	
5	7	Steele, Elmer Rae	P	16	.051	B	
		Sullivan, Dennis Wm.	OF	100	+.241	B	Clev
1	0	Tannehill, Jesse Niles	P	1	+.500	B	Wash
1	0	Thielman, John Peter (Jake)	P	1	+.000	xClev	C
		Thoney, John	OF101	109	.255	NY04	
		Unglaub, Robert Alexander	1B	72	+.262	B	Wash
		Wagner, Chas. F.	SS	153	.247	B	
3	14	Winter, George Lovington	P	22	+.184	B	Det
1	1	Wood, Joseph (Smokey Joe)	P	6	.143	A	
21	11	Young, Denton True (Cy)	P	36	.226	B	

WON 88 — AMERICAN LEAGUE — FINISHED 3rd.
LOST 63
TG 151 — 1909. — PCT. .583

BOSTON

FREDERICK LOVETT LAKE

WON	LOST	NAME	POS.	G.	BA	FROM	TO
0	0	Anderson, John Frederick	P	1	.000	A	
16	12	Arellanes, Frank Julian	P45	46	.167	B	
3	3	Burchell, Frederick Duff	P	10	.158	B	C
		Carrigan, Wm. Francis	C77	94	.296	B	
7	6	Chech, Chas. Wm.	P	17	.083	Clev	C
0	2	Chesbro, John Dwight (Jack)	P	2	+.500	xN.Y.	C
13	5	Cicotte, Edward Victor	P	26	.224	B	
4	3	Collins, Raymond Williston	P	12	.130	A	
		Danzig, Harold P.	1B	6	.143	A	C
		Donahue, Patrick Wm.	C58	64	.239	B	
		French, Chas. Calvin (SS23)	2B28	51	.251	A	
		Gardner, Wm. Lawrence (Larry)	3B	19	.297	B	

WON	LOST	NAME	POS.	G.	BA	FROM	TO
		Gessler, Harry Homer	OF	111	+.299	B	Wash
6	4	Hall, Chas. Louis (Sea-Lion)	P	11	.158	CinN07	
		Hooper, Harry Bartholomew	OF	81	.282	A	
		Howard, Paul Joseph	OF	6	.230	A	C
5	2	Karger, Edwin	P	12	.125	xCinN	
		Lord, Harry Donald	3B134	136	.311	B	
		Madden, Thomas Francis	C	12	.168	A	
0	0	Mathews. Wm. C.	P	5	.000	A	C
3	9	Morgan, Harry Richard (Cy)	P	12	+.050	B	Phil
		McConnell, Ambrose Moses	2B	121	.238	B	
		Niles, Harry Clyde	OF117	145	.245	B	
0	0	Nourse, Chester Linwood	P	3	.000	A	C
2	0	Pape, Lawrence Albert (Larry)	P	11	.143	A	
0	0	Patten, Case L.	P	1	.000	B	C
4	3	Ryan, Jack	P13	14	.211	Clev	
2	2	Schlitzer, Victor Joseph	P	9	+.172	xPhil	
4	0	Smith, Chas. E.	P	5	+.300	xWash	
		Speaker, Tristram E. (Trie)	OF142	143	.309	B	
		Spencer, Edward Russell	C26	28	.162	StL	
		Stahl, Garland	1B126	127	.294	B	
4	2	Steele, Elmer Rae	P	15	.250	B	
		Thoney, John	OF	14	.184	B	
		Wagner, Chas. F.	SS123	124	.256	B	
4	3	Wolter, Harry Meigs (P10)	1B17	54	.244	StLN07	
11	7	Wood, Joseph (Smokey Joe)	P	24	.164	B	
		Yerkes, Stephen Douglass	SS	5	.286	A	

WON 81
LOST 72
TG 153

AMERICAN LEAGUE — FINISHED 4th.

1910. — PCT. .529

BOSTON

PATRICK JOSEPH DONOVAN

WON	LOST	NAME	POS.	G.	BA	FROM	TO
4	7	Arellanes, Frank Julian	P	18	.176	B	C
0	0	Barberich, Frank	P	2	.000	BosN07	C
		Bradley, Hugh Frederick	1B21	32	.169	A	
		Carrigan, Wm. Francis	C110	114	.249	B	
15	11	Cicotte, Edward Victor	P	36	.141	B	
13	11	Collins, Raymond Williston	P	35	.179	B	
		Donahue, Patrick Wm.	C	2	+.000	B	Phil
		Engle, Arthur Clyde	3B40	105	+.266	xNY	
		French, Chas. Calvin	2B	9	+.200	B	Chi
		Gardner, Wm. Lawrence (Larry)	2B	113	.283	B	
12	9	Hall, Chas. Louis (Sea-Lion)	P35	47	.207	B	
		Hearn, Edmund	3B	2	.000	A	C
		Hooper, Harry Bartholomew	OF	155	.267	B	
2	4	Hunt, Benjamin Franklin	P	7	.059	A	
11	7	Karger, Edwin	P	27	.294	B	
		Kleinow, John Peter	C	51	+.149	xN.Y.	
		Lerchen, Bertram Roe	SS	6	.067	A	C
0	0	LeRoy, Louis Paul	P	1	.000	NY06	C
		Lewis, George Edward (Duffy)	OF149	151	.283	A	

WON	LOST	NAME	POS.	G.	BA	FROM	TO
		Lord, Harry Donald	3B	77	+.243	B	Chi
		Madden, Thomas Francis	C	14	.400	B	
0	1	Mahoney, Christopher John	P	3	.143	A	C
		Myers, Ralph Edward	C	3	.333	A	
0	0	*Moskiman, Wm. Bankhead	P1	5	.111	A	C
		McConnell, Ambrose Moses	2B	12	+.125	B	Chi
0	2	McHale, Martin Joseph	P	2	.000	A	
		Niles, Harry Clyde	OF	18	+.214	B	Clev
		Pond, Ralph Benjamin	OF	1	.333	A	C
		Purtell, Wm. Patrick	3B	49	+.211	xChi	
11	6	Smith, Chas. E.	P	23	.097	B	
1	1	Smith, Frank Elmer	P	4	+.111	xChi	
		Speaker, Tristram E. (Tris)	OF140	141	.340	B	
		Stahl, Garland	1B142	144	.271	B	
		Wagner, Chas. F.	SS140	142	.273	B	
12	13	Wood, Joseph (Smokey Joe)	P	35	.261	B	

*Moskiman played 2 games at 1B and 1 in OF.

WON 78
LOST 75
TG 153

AMERICAN LEAGUE — FINISHED 5th.

1911. — PCT. .509

BOSTON

PATRICK JOSEPH DONOVAN

WON	LOST	NAME	POS.	G.	BA	FROM	TO
		Baker, Tracy Lee	1B	1	.000	A	C
		Bradley, Hugh Frederick	1B	12	.300	B	
0	1	Bushelman, John Francis	P	3	.000	CinN09	
		Carlstrom, Albin Oscar	SS	2	.167	A	C
		Carrigan, Wm. Francis	C62	72	.289	B	
11	14	Cicotte, Edward Victor	P	35	.141	B	
11	12	Collins, Raymond Williston	P	31	.150	B	
		Engle, Arthur Clyde (3B51)	1B65	146	.270	B	
		Gardner, Wm. Lawrence (Larry) (2B62)	3B72	138	.284	B	
		Giannini, Joseph Francis	SS	1	.500	A	C
		Gunning, Hyland	1B	4	.111	A	C
0	2	Hageman, Kurt R. Morris	P	2	.000	A	
8	7	Hall, Chas. Louis (Sea-Lion)	P32	39	.141	B	
		Henriksen, Olaf	OF25	27	.366	A	
		Hooper, Harry Bartholomew	OF	130	.311	B	
		Janvrin, Harold Chandler	3B	10	.153	A	
5	8	Karger, Edwin	P	25	.235	B	C
4	3	Killilay, John Wm.	P	14	.043	A	C
		Kleinow, John Peter	C	8	.214	B	PhilN
		Lewis, George Edward (Duffy)	OF125	130	.307	B	
		Lewis, John D.	2B	18	.271	A	
		Lonergan, Walter E. (2B7 SS1)	3B1	9	.269	A	C
		Madden, Thomas Francis	C	4	.200	B	PhilN
		Myers, Ralph Edward	1B	13	+.368	xStL	
0	1	Moser, Walter F.	P	6	+.000	PhilN06	StL

WON	LOST	NAME	POS.	G.	BA	FROM	TO
0	0	McHale, Martin Joseph	P	4	.000	B	
1	1	Nagle, Walter Harold	P	5	.100	xPittN	C
		Nunamaker, Leslie Grant	C59	62	.257	A	
5	1	O'Brien, Thomas Joseph	P	6	.125	A	
10	8	Pape, Lawrence Albert (Larry)	P	27	.203	Bos09	
		Purtell, Wm. Patrick	3B15	27	.280	B	
		Riggert, Joseph Aloysius	OF39	50	.212	A	
0	0	Smith, Chas. E.	P	1	.000	B	ChiN
0	0	Smith, Frank Elmer	P	1	.000	B	CinN
		Speaker, Tristram E. (Tris)	OF138	141	.327	B	
0	0	Thomas, Blaine M.	P	2	.500	A	C
		Thoney, John	OF	26	.250	Bos09	C
		Tonneman, Chas. Richard	C	2	.200	A	C
		Wagner, Chas. F.	2B40	80	.257	B	
		Williams, Alva Mitchel (C38)	1B57	95	.239	A	
		Wilson, Lester Wilbur	OF	4	.000	A	C
23	17	Wood, Joseph (Smokey Joe)	P	44	.261	B	
		Yerkes, Stephen Douglas	SS117	142	.279	Bos09	

WON 105 — AMERICAN LEAGUE — FINISHED 1st.
LOST 47
TG 152 — 1912. — PCT. .691

BOSTON

GARLAND STAHL

WON	LOST	NAME	POS.	G.	BA	FROM	TO
		Ball, Cornelius	2B	17	+.182	xClev	
20	10	Bedient, Hugh Carpenter	P	34	.192	A	
		Bradley, Hugh Frederick	1B	40	.190	B	
1	0	Bushelman, John Francis	P	3	.000	B	C
		Cady, Forrest LeRoy	C43	47	.259	A	
		Carrigan, Wm. Francis	C	87	.263	B	
1	2	Cicotte, Edward Victor	P	9	+.167	B	Chi
14	8	Collins, Raymond Williston	P	26	.169	B	
		Engle, Arthur Clyde (2B15)	1B25	57	.234	B	
		Gardner, Wm. Lawrence (Larry)	3B	143	.315	B	
0	0	Hageman, Kurt R. Morris	P	2	.000	B	
15	8	Hall, Chas. Louis (Sea-Lion)	P	32	.267	B	
		Henriksen, Olaf	OF	37	.321	B	
		Hooper, Harry Bartholomew	OF	147	.242	B	
		Krug, Martin John	SS8	15	.308	A	
		Lewis, George Edward (Duffy)	OF	154	.284	B	
		Nunamaker, Leslie Grant	C	35	.252	B	
18	13	O'Brien, Thomas Joseph	P	35	.138	B	
1	1	Pape, Lawrence Albert (Larry)	P	10	.235	B	C
0	0	Smith, Douglass Weldon	P	1	.000	A	C
		Speaker, Tristram E. (Tris)	OF	153	.383	B	
		Stahl, Garland MGR.	1B	95	.301	Bos10	
		Thomas, Chester David	C	13	.194	A	
1	0	VanDyke, Benjamin Harrison	P	3	.250	PhilN09	C
		Wagner, Chas. F.	SS	144	.274	B	
34	5	Wood, Joseph (Smokey Joe)	P	43	.290	B	
		Yerkes, Stephen Douglas	2B	131	.252	B	

WON 79 — AMERICAN LEAGUE — FINISHED 4th.
LOST 71
TG 150 — 1913. — PCT. .527

BOSTON

GARLAND STAHL — WM. FRANCIS CARRIGAN

WON	LOST	NAME	POS.	G.	BA	FROM	TO
0	6	Anderson, John Frederick	P	10	.050	Bos09	
		Ball, Cornelius	2B10	21	.172	B	C
15	14	Bedient, Hugh Carpenter	P	38	.125	B	
		Cady, Forrest LeRoy	C38	39	.242	B	
		Carrigan, Wm. Francis MGR.	C81	85	.242	B	
0	0	Chaney, Esty Cleon	P	1	.000	A	
19	8	Collins, Raymond Williston	P	30	.150	B	
		Engle, Arthur Clyde	1B134	143	.290	B	
3	4	Foster, George	P	20	.000	A	
		Gardner, Wm. Lawrence (Larry)	3B	131	.282	B	
4	4	Hall, Chas. Louis (Sea-Lion)	P26	33	.214	B	
		Henriksen, Olaf	OF	30	.375	B	
		Hooper, Harry Bartholomew	OF	148	.289	B	
		Janvrin, Harold Chandler (3B19)	SS48	86	.206	Bos11	
14	16	Leonard, Hubert Benjamin	P	39	.171	A	
		Lewis, George Edward (Duffy)	OF	149	.298	B	
0	0	Maloy, Paul Augustus	P	2	.000	A	C
9	5	Moseley, Earl Victor	P16	17	.081	A	
		Mundy, Wm. Edward	1B16	17	.255	A	C
		Nunamaker, Leslie Grant	C28	30	.227	B	
4	9	O'Brien, Thomas Joseph	P	13	+.156	B	Chi
		Rehg, Walter Phillip	OF26	30	.277	PittN	
		Snell, Walter Henry	C	6	.250	A	C
		Speaker, Tristram E. (Tris)	OF139	141	.366	B	
		Stahl, Garland MGR.	1B	1	.000	B	C
		Thomas, Chester David	C28	37	.286	B	
		Wagner, Chas. F.	SS105	109	.226	B	
11	5	Wood, Joseph (Smokey Joe)	P20	21	.268	B	
		Yerkes, Stephen Douglas	2B128	137	.267	B	

WON 91 — AMERICAN LEAGUE — FINISHED 2nd.
LOST 62
TG 153 — 1914. — PCT. .595

BOSTON

WM. FRANCIS CARRIGAN

WON	LOST	NAME	POS.	G.	BA	FROM	TO
8	12	Bedient, Hugh Carpenter	P	36	.100	B	
		Cady, Forrest LeRoy	C58	61	.258	B	
		Carrigan, Wm. Francis MGR.	C78	81	.253	B	
20	13	Collins, Raymond Williston	P	38	.139	B	
1	1	Cooper, Guy Evans	P	10	+.000	xN.Y.	

WON	LOST	NAME	POS.	G.	BA	FROM	TO
1	2	Coumbe, Frederick Nicholas (Fritz)	P	14	+.167	A	Clev
		Engle, Arthur Clyde	1B29	55	.194	B	BuffF
14	8	Foster, George	P	30	.175	B	
		Gainor, Delos Chas.	1B	38	+.238	xDet	
		Gardner, Wm. Lawrence (Larry)	3B153	155	.259	B	
3	4	Gregg, Sylveanus Augustus (Vean)	P	12	+.211	xClev	
		Henriksen, Olaf	OF27	61	.253	B	
		Holbitzell, Richard Carleton	1B	68	.319	xCinN	
		Hooper, Harry Bartholomew	OF140	141	.258	B	
		Janvrin, Harold Chandler (1B56 SS20)	2B57	143	.238	B	
4	9	Johnson, Adam Rankin	P	15	.133	A	ChiF
0	0	Kelly, Edward L.	P	3	.000	A	C
19	5	Leonard, Hubert Benjamin	P	32	.147	B	
		Lewis, George Edward (Duffy)	OF142	146	.278	B	
		Nunamaker, Leslie Grant	C	5	+.200	B	N.Y.
		Pratt, Lester John	C	5	.000	A	
		Rehg, Walter Phillip	OF42	84	.218	B	
2	1	Ruth, George Herman (Babe)	P	5	.200	A	
		Scott, Lewis Everett (Deacon)	SS143	144	.239	A	
10	4	Shore, Ernest Grady	P	19	.100	NYN12	
0	0	Speaker, Tristram E. (Tris) (P1)	OF157	158	.338	B	
		Swanson, Wm. Andrew	2B5	11	.211	A	C
		Thomas, Chester David	C61	63	.192	B	
		Wagner, Chas. F.	(did not play)				
		Wilson, George Frank	1B	1	.000	Det11	C
9	3	Wood, Joseph (Smokey Joe)	P18	20	.140	B	
		Yerkes, Stephen Douglas	2B91	92	.218	B	PittF
0	0	Zeiser, Matthew J.	P	2	.000	A	C

WON 101 — AMERICAN LEAGUE — FINISHED 1st.
LOST 50
TG 151 — 1915. — PCT. .669

BOSTON

WM. FRANCIS CARRIGAN

WON	LOST	NAME	POS.	G.	BA	FROM	TO
		Barry, John Joseph (Jack)	2B	78	+.265	xPhil	
		Cady, Forrest LeRoy	C77	78	.278	B	
		Carrigan, Wm. Francis MGR.	C44	46	.200	B	
5	7	Collins, Raymond Williston	P	25	.286	B	C
1	0	Comstock, Ralph Remick	P	3	.000	Det13	PittF
0	0	Cooper, Guy Evans	P	1	.000	B	C
20	9	Foster, George	P38	40	.277	B	
		Gainor, Delos Chas.	1B56	82	.295	B	
		Gardner, Wm. Lawrence (Larry)	3B	127	.258	B	
5	3	Gregg, Sylveanus Augustus (Vean)	P	18	.350	B	
		Haley, Raymond Timothy	C	5	.143	A	
		Henriksen, Olaf	OF25	73	.196	B	
		Hoblitzell, Richard Carleton	1B117	124	.283	B	
		Hooper, Harry Bartholomew	OF	149	.235	B	
		Janvrin, Harold Chandler (3B20)	SS64	99	.269	B	
15	7	Leonard, Hubert Benjamin	P	32	.264	B	
		Lewis, George Edward (Duffy)	OF	152	.291	B	
4	6	Mays, Carl Wm.	P	38	.237	A	
		McNally, Michael Joseph	3B18	23	.151	A	
0	0	Pennock, Herbert Jefferis	P	5	+.143	xPhil	
		Rehg, Walter Phillip	OF	5	.200	B	
		Rodgers, Wilbur Kincaid	2B	11	+.000	xClev	CinN
18	6	Ruth, George Herman (Babe) (OF10)	P32	42	.315	B	
		Scott, Lewis Everett (Deacon)	SS	100	.201	B	
19	7	Shore, Ernest Grady	P	38	.101	B	
		Shorten, Chas. Henry	OF	6	.214	A	
		Speaker, Tristram E. (Tris)	OF	150	.322	B	
		Thomas, Chester David	C82	86	.236	B	
		Wagner, Chas. F.	2B79	84	.239	B	
14	5	Wood, Joseph (Smokey Joe)	P25	29	.259	B	

WON 91 — AMERICAN LEAGUE — FINISHED 1st.
LOST 63
TG 154 — 1916. — PCT. .591

BOSTON

WM. FRANCIS CARRIGAN

WON	LOST	NAME	POS.	G.	BA	FROM	TO
		Agnew, Samuel Lester	C38	40	.209	StL	
		Barry, John Joseph (Jack)	2B	94	.203	B	
		Cady, Forrest LeRoy	C63	78	.191	B	
		Carrigan, Wm. Francis MGR.	C27	33	.270	B	
14	7	Foster, George	P34	38	.177	B	
		Gainor, Delos Chas.	1B48	56	.253	B	
		Gardner, Wm. Lawrence (Larry)	3B147	148	.308	B	
2	5	Gregg, Sylveanus Augustus (Vean)	P	21	.111	B	
		Haley, Raymond Timothy	C	1	+.000	B	Phil
		Henriksen, Olaf	OF31	68	.202	B	
		Hoblitzell, Richard Carleton	1B126	130	.259	B	
		Hooper, Harry Bartholomew	OF	151	.271	B	
		Janvrin, Harold Chandler (2B39)	SS59	117	.223	B	
0	1	Jones, Samuel Pond (Sad Sam)	P	13	.333	Clev	
18	12	Leonard, Hubert Benjamin	P	48	.200	B	
		Lewis, George Edward (Duffy)	OF	152	.268	B	
18	13	Mays, Carl Wm.	P44	48	.234	B	
0	1	McHale, Martin Joseph	P	2	+.000	N.Y.	Clev
		McNally, Michael Joseph	2B35	87	.171	B	
0	2	Pennock, Herbert Jefferis	P	11	.143	B	
23	12	Ruth, George Herman (Babe) (OF23)	P44	67	.272	B	

WON	LOST	NAME	POS.	G.	BA	FROM	TO
		Scott, Lewis Everett (Deacon)	SS121	123	.232	B	
16	10	Shore, Ernest Grady	P	38	.091	B	
		Shorten, Chas. Henry	OF33	53	.295	B	
		Thomas, Chester David	C90	99	.264	B	
		Wagner, Chas. F.	SS1	4	.500	B	
		Walker, Clarence Wm.	OF	128	.265	StL	
		Walsh, James Chas.	OF	15	+.348	xPhil	
0	0	Wyckoff, John Weldon	P	8	+.167	xPhil	

WON 90 AMERICAN LEAGUE FINISHED 2nd.
LOST 62
TG 152 1917. PCT. .592

BOSTON

JOHN JOSEPH BARRY

WON	LOST	NAME	POS.	G.	BA	FROM	TO
		Agnew, Samuel Lester	C	85	.208	B	
2	0	Bader, Loren Verne	P	15	.300	NYN12	
		Barry, John Joseph (Jack)	2B	116	.214	B	
		MGR.					
		Cady, Forrest LeRoy	C14	17	.152	B	
		Cooney, James Edward	2B9	11	.222	A	
8	7	Foster, George	P	17	.268	B	C
		Gainor, Delos Chas.	1B50	52	.308	B	
		Gardner, Wm. Lawrence	3B	146	.265	B	
		(Larry)					
		Henriksen, Olaf	OF	15	.083	B	C
		Hoblitzell, Richard Carleton	1B118	120	.257	B	
		Hooper, Harry Bartholomew	OF	151	.256	B	
		Janvrin, Harold Chandler	2B38	55	.197	B	
0	1	Jones, Samuel Pond (Sad Sam)	P	9	.000	B	
16	17	Leonard, Hubert Benjamin	P	37	.087	B	
		Lewis, George Edward (Duffy)	OF	150	.302	B	
		Mayer, Walter A.	C	4	.167	Chi15	
22	9	Mays, Carl Wm.	P	35	.252	B	
		McNally, Michael Joseph	3B14	42	.300	B	
5	5	Pennock, Herbert Jefferis	P	24	.167	B	
24	13	Ruth, George Herman (Babe)	P41	52	.325	B	
		(OF11)					
		Scott, Lewis, Everett (Deacon)	SS	157	.241	B	
13	10	Shore, Ernest Grady	P	29	.167	B	
		Shorten, Chas. Henry	OF43	69	.179	B	
		Thomas, Chester David	C77	83	.238	B	
		Walker, Clarence Wm.	OF96	106	.246	B	
		Walsh, James Charles	OF47	57	.265	B	C
0	0	Wyckoff, John Weldon	P	1	.000	B	

WON 75 AMERICAN LEAGUE FINISHED 1st.
LOST 51
TG 126 1918. PCT. .595

BOSTON

EDWARD GRANT BARROW

WON	LOST	NAME	POS.	G.	BA	FROM	TO
		Agnew, Samuel Lester	C	72	.166	B	
1	3	Bader, Loren Verne	P	5	.111	B	C
		Barbare, Walter Lawrence	3B11	13	.172	Clev16	
		Bluhm, Harvey Fred		1	.000	A	C
15	15	Bush, Leslie Ambrose	P	36	.276	Phil	
		(Bullet Joe)					
		Cochran, George Leslie	2B23	25	.127	A	C
		Coffey, John Francis	3B14	22	+.188	xDet	C
0	1	Dubuc, Jean Arthur	P	5	.167	Det16	
		Gonzales, Eusobio Miguel	SS2	3	.400	A	C
		(3B1)					
		Hoblitzell, Richard Carleton	1B19	25	.159	B	C
		Hooper, Harry Bartholomew	OF	126	.289	B	
16	5	Jones, Samuel Pond (Sad Sam)	P	24	.175	B	
0	0	Kinney, Walter Wm.	P	6	.000	A	
8	6	Leonard, Hubert Benjamin	P	16	.186	B	
		Mayer, Walter A.	C23	26	.224	B	
21	13	Mays, Carl Wm.	P35	38	.288	B	
		Miller, Lawrence H. (Hack)	OF10	12	.276	BknN16	
1	0	Molyneaux, Vincent L.	P	6	.000	StL	C
0	1	McCabe, Richard James	P	3	.000	A	
		McInnis, John Phaelen (Stuffy)	1B94	117	.272	Phil	
		(3B23)					
0	0	Pertica, Wm. Andrew	P	1	.000	A	
13	7	Ruth, George Herman (Babe)	OF58	95	.300	B	
		(P20 1B13)					
		Schang, Walter Henry (Wally)	C57	88	.245	Phil	
		(OF16)					
		Scott, Lewis, Everett (Deacon)	SS	126	.221	B	
		Shean, David Wm.	2B	115	.264	CinN	
		Stansbury, John James	3B18	20	.128	A	C
		Strunk, Amos Aaron	OF113	114	.256	Phil	
		Thomas, Frederick Harvey	3B41	44	.257	A	
		Truesdale, Frank D.	2B10	15	.278	NY14	C
		Wagner, Chas. F.	2B	3	.125	Bos16	
		Whiteman, George	OF69	71	.267	NY13	C
0	0	Wyckoff, John Weldon	P	1	.000	B	C

WON 66 AMERICAN LEAGUE FINISHED 6th.
LOST 71
TG 137 1919. PCT. .482

BOSTON

EDWARD GRANT BARROW

WON	LOST	NAME	POS.	G.	BA	FROM	TO
		Barry, John Joseph (Jack)	2B	31	.241	Bos17	C
0	0	Bush, Leslie Ambrose	P	5	.400	B	
		(Bullet Joe)					
5	4	Caldwell, Raymond Benjamin	P	31	+.271	N.Y.	Clev
0	4	Dumont, George Henry	P	13	.000	Wash	C
		Gainor, Delos Chas. (OF18)	1B21	47	.237	Bos17	

WON	LOST	NAME	POS.	G.	BA	FROM	TO
		Gilhooley, Frank Patrick	OF39	48	.241	N.Y.	C
		Hooper, Harry Bartholomew	OF	128	.267	B	
4	6	Hoyt, Waite Chas.	P	13	.131	NYN	
2	5	James, Wm. Henry	P	14	+.000	xDet	Chi
13	20	Jones, Samuel Pond (Sad Sam)	P	35	.136	B	
		Lamar, Wm. Harmong	OF39	48	+.291	xN.Y.	
8	12	Mays, Carl Wm.	P21	22	+.151	B	N.Y.
0	2	Musser, Paul	P	5	.000	Wash12	C
1	0	McGraw, Robert Emmett	P	10	+.100	xN.Y.	
		McInnis, John Phaelen (Stuffy)	1B118	120	.305	B	
		McNally, Michael Joseph	3B8	33	.262	Bos17	
		McNeil, Norman Francis	C	5	.273	A	C
17	8	Pennock, Herbert Jefferis	P	32	.173	Bos17	
		Roth, Robert Frank	OF	63	+.256	xPhil	
8	5	Russell, Allen E.	P	21	+.122	xN.Y.	
8	5	Ruth, George Herman (Babe) (P17)	OF111	130	.322	B	
		Schang, Walter Henry (Wally)	C104	113	.306	B	
		Scott, Lewis Everett (Deacon)	SS	138	.278	B	
		Shannon, Maurice Joseph	2B	80	+.259	xPhil	
		Shean, David Wm.	2B	29	.140	B	C
		Strunk, Amos Aaron	OF	48	+.271	B	Phil
		Vitt, Oscar Joseph	3B	133	.243	Det	
		Walters, Alfred John	C47	48	.193	N.Y.	
		Wilhoit, Joseph Wm.	OF	6	.333	NYN	C
0	0	Winn, George Benjamin	P	3	.000	A	

WON 72 — AMERICAN LEAGUE — FINISHED 5th.
LOST 81
TG 153 — 1920. — PCT. .471

BOSTON

EDWARD GRANT BARROW

WON	LOST	NAME	POS.	G.	BA	FROM	TO
		Bailey, Arthur Eugene	OF40	46	.230	xBosN	
		Brady, Clifford Francis	2B	53	.228	A	C
15	15	Bush, Leslie Ambrose (Bullet Joe)	P35	45	.245	B	
		Chaplin, Bert E.	C	4	.250	A	
		Devine, Wm. Patrick (Mickey)	C	8	.201	PhilN18	
0	0	DeViney, John Harold	P	1	1.000	A	C
0	0	Eibel, Henry H.	P	29	.186	Clev12	C
0	2	Fortune, Garrett Reese (Gary)	P	14	.167	PhilN18	C
		Foster, Edward Cunningham (2B21)	3B88	117	.259	Wash	
		Grimes, Oscar Ray	1B	1	.250	A	
5	14	Harper, Harry Clayton	P	27	.120	Wash	
		Hendryx, Timothy Green	OF98	99	.328	StL18	
		Hiller, Harvey Max	3B	17	.172	A	
		Hooper, Harry Bartholomew	OF	139	.312	B	
6	6	Hoyt, Waite Chas.	P	22	.116	B	
		Hunter, Herbert Harrison	OF	4	.083	ChiN17	
13	16	Jones, Samuel Pond (Sad Sam)	P37	44	.217	B	
3	8	Karr, Benjamin Joyce	P26	57	.280	A	

WON	LOST	NAME	POS.	G.	BA	FROM	TO
		Menosky, Michael Wm.	OF	141	.297	Wash	
9	1	Myers, Elmer Glen	P	12	+.316	xClev	
		McInnis, John Phaelen (Stuffy)	1B	148	.297	B	
		McNally, Michael Joseph	2B76	93	.256	B	
		Orme, George Wm.	OF	4	.323	A	C
		Paschal, Benjamin Edwin	OF	9	.250	Clev15	
16	13	Pennock, Herbert Jefferis	P37	38	.260	B	
5	6	Russell, Allen E.	P16	17	.122	B	
		Schang, Walter Henry (Wally) (OF40)	C73	122	.305	B	
		Scott, Lewis Everett (Deacon)	SS	154	.269	B	
		Smith, Lawrence Patrick (Paddy)	C	2	.000	A	C
		Statz, Arnold John (Jigger)	OF	2	.000	xNYN	
		Vitt, Oscar Joseph	3B64	87	.220	B	
		Walters, Alfred John	C85	88	.198	B	

WON 75 — AMERICAN LEAGUE — FINISHED 5th.
LOST 79
TG 154 — 1921. — PCT. .487

BOSTON

HUGH DUFFY

WON	LOST	NAME	POS.	G.	BA	FROM	TO
16	9	Bush, Leslie Ambrose (Bullet Joe)	P36	51	.325	B	
		Chaplin, Bert E.	C	3	.000	B	
		Collins, John Francis (Shano)	OF138	141	.286	Chi	
0	0	Dodge, Samuel Edward	P	1	.000	A	
		Foster, Edward Cunningham (2B22)	3B94	120	.284	B	
0	1	Fullerton, Curtis Hooper	P	4	.000	A	
		Hendryx, Timothy Green	OF41	49	.241	B	C
		Hiller, Harvey Max	OF	1	.000	B	C
23	16	Jones, Samuel Pond (Sad Sam)	P40	43	.240	B	
8	7	Karr, Benjamin Joyce	P26	43	.258	B	
		Leibold, Harry Loran (Nemo)	OF117	123	.306	Chi	
		Menosky, Michael Wm.	OF	133	.300	B	
8	12	Myers, Elmer Glen	P	30	.215	B	
		McInnis, John Phaelen (Stuffy)	1B	152	.307	B	
0	0	Nietzke, Ernest Frederick	P	11	.240	A	C
12	14	Pennock, Herbert Jefferis	P	32	.212	B	
		Perrin, John Stephenson	OF	4	.231	A	C
		Pittinger, Clark Alonzo	OF27	40	.198	A	
		Pratt, Derrill Burnham	2B134	135	.324	N.Y.	
		Ruel, Harold Dominic (Muddy)	C109	113	.277	N.Y.	
7	11	Russell, Allen E.	P	39	.123	B	
		Scott, Lewis Everett (Deacon)	SS	154	.262	B	
0	2	Sothoron, Allen Sutton	P	2	+.500	xStL	Clev
1	7	Thormahlen, Herbert Ehler	P	23	.174	N.Y.	
		Vick, Samuel Bruce	OF14	44	.260	N.Y.	C
		Vitt, Oscar Joseph	3B71	78	.190	B	
		Walters, Alfred John	C	54	.201	B	

WON 61
LOST 93
TG 154

AMERICAN LEAGUE

1922.

FINISHED 8th (LAST)

PCT. .396

BOSTON

HUGH DUFFY

WON	LOST	NAME	POS.	G.	BA	FROM	TO
		Burns, George Henry	1B140	147	.306	Clev	
		Chaplin, Bert E.	C21	28	.189	B	C
14	11	Collins, Harry Warren	P	32	.158	N.Y.	
		Collins, John Francis (Shano)	OF117	135	.271	B	
0	1	Dodge, Samuel Edward	P	3	.000	B	C
		Dugan, Joseph Anthony (Jumping Joe) (SS20)	3B64	84	+.281	Phil	N.Y.
9	16	Ferguson, James Alexander (Alex)	P	39	.092	N.Y.	
		Fewster, Wilson Lloyd	OF	23	+.316	xN.Y.	
		Foster, Edward Cunningham	3B	48	+.211	B	StL
1	4	Fullerton, Curtis Hooper	P30	31	.250	B	
		Harris, Joseph (1B21)	OF83	119	.316	Clev19	
5	12	Karr, Benjamin Joyce	P41	66	.214	B	
		Leibold, Harry Loran (Nemo)	OF71	81	.258	B	
		Lynch, Walter Edward	C	3	.667	A	C
		Maynard, LeRoy Evans	SS	12	.125	A	C
		Menosky, Michael Wm.	OF103	126	.283	B	
		Miller, Elmer	OF	44	+.172	xN.Y.	C
		Mitchell, John Franklin	SS	59	+.251	xN.Y.	
0	1	Myers, Elmer Glen	P	3	.000	B	C
		O'Rourke, Francis James (3B19)	SS48	67	.264	Wash	
10	17	Pennock, Herbert Jefferis	P	32	.138	B	
3	9	Piercy, Wm. Benton	P	29	.148	N.Y.	
		Pittinger, Clark Alonzo (SS28)	3B33	66	.259	B	
		Pratt, Derrill Burnham	2B	154	.302	B	
13	15	Quinn, John Picus	P	40	.099	N.Y.	
		Reichle, Richard Wendell	OF	6	.250	A	
		Ruel, Harold Dominic (Muddy)	C112	116	.255	B	
6	7	Russell, Allen E.	P	34	.079	B	
		Smith, Elmer John	OF	73	+.282	Clev	N.Y.
		Walters, Alfred John	C36	38	.194	B	

WON 61
LOST 91
TG 152

AMERICAN LEAGUE

1923.

FINISHED 8th (LAST)

PCT. .401

BOSTON

FRANK LEROY CHANCE

WON	LOST	NAME	POS.	G.	BA	FROM	TO
0	0	Black, David	P	2	.000	BaltF15	C
0	0	Blethen, Clarence Waldo	P	5	.000	A	
		Boone, Isaac Morgan	OF	5	.267	NYN	
		Burns, George Henry	1B	146	.328	B	
		Collins, John Francis (Shano)	OF89	97	.231	B	
		DeVormer, Albert E.	C55	74	.258	N.Y.	
		Donahue, John Francis	OF	10	.343	A	C
20	17	Ehmke, Howard John	P	43	.223	Det	
9	13	Ferguson, James Alexander (Alex)	P	34	.097	B	
		Fewster, Wilson Lloyd (SS36)	2B48	90	.236	B	
		Flagstead, Ira	OF102	109	+.312	xDet	
		Fuller, Frank Edward	2B	6	.238	Det16	C
2	15	Fullerton, Curtis Hooper	P	37	.297	B	
		Harris, Joseph	OF132	142	.335	B	
1	0	Howe, Lester Curtis	P	13	.000	A	
		Leibold, Harry Loran (Nemo)	OF	11	+.111	B	Wash
		Menosky, Michael Wm.	OF49	34	.229	B	C
		Mitchell, John Franklin	SS87	92	.225	B	
7	11	Murray, George King	P	39	.164	N.Y.	
		McMillan, Norman Alexis (2B34 SS28)	3B67	131	.253	N.Y.	
1	1	O'Doul, Frank Joseph (Lefty)	P23	36	.143	N.Y.	
		Picinich, Valentine John (Val)	C81	87	.276	Wash	
8	17	Piercy, Wm. Benton	P	30	.132	B	
		Pittinger, Clark Alonzo	2B42	60	.215	B	
13	17	Quinn, John Picus	P	42	.225	B	
		Reichle, Richard Wendell	OF93	122	.258	B	C
		Shanks, Howard Samuel (2B37)	3B83	131	.254	Wash	
		Skinner, Elisha Harrison Camp	OF	7	.230	N.Y.	C
0	0	Stimson, Carl Remus	P	2	.000	A	C
		Walters, Alfred John	C36	40	.250	B	

WON 67
LOST 87
TG 154

AMERICAN LEAGUE

1924.

FINISHED 7th.

PCT. .435

BOSTON

LEO ALEXANDER FOHL

WON	LOST	NAME	POS.	G.	BA	FROM	TO
		Boone, Isaac Morgan	OF	128	.333	B	
		Clark, Daniel Curran	3B94	104	.277	Det22	
		Collins, John Francis (Shano) (1B21)	OF56	89	.292	B	
		Connolly, Joseph George	OF	14	.100	Clev	C
19	17	Ehmke, Howard John	P45	46	.222	B	
		Ezzell, Homer Estell (SS21)	3B63	90	.271	StL	
14	17	Ferguson, James Alexander (Alex)	P	41	.140	B	
		Flagstead, Ira	OF	149	.304	B	
3	6	Fuhr, Oscar Lawrence	P	23	.182	Chi21	
7	12	Fullerton, Curtis Hooper	P	33	.071	B	
		Geygan, James Edward	SS	33	.256	A	
		Harris, Joseph	1B	133	.301	B	
		Heving, John Aloysius	C29	45	.284	StL20	
1	0	Howe, Lester Curtis	P	4	.500	B	C

WON	LOST	NAME	POS.	G.	BA	FROM	TO
0	0	Jamerson, Charley Dewey	P	1	.000	A	C
0	0	Kellett, Alfred Henry	P	1	.000	Phil	C
		Lee, Ernest Dudley	SS	94	.253	StL21	
2	9	Murray, George King	P	28	.182	B	
		O'Neill, Stephen Francis (Steve)	C92	106	.238	Clev	
		Picinich, Valentine John (Val)	C52	69	.273	B	
5	7	Piercy, Wm. Benton	P22	23	.154	B	
12	13	Quinn, John Picus	P	44	.179	B	
4	3	Ross, Chester Franklin	P	30	.200	A	
0	0	Ruffing, Chas. Herbert (Red)	P	8	.143	A	
		Shanks, Howard Samuel (3B22)	SS38	72	.259	B	
		Todt, Philip Julius	1B18	52	.262	A	
		Veach, Robert Hayes	OF130	142	.295	Det	
		Wambsganss, Wm. Adolph	2B	155	.275	Clev	
		Williams, Evon Daniel	OF	25	.365	CinN21	
0	2	Wingfield, Frederick David	P	4	+.333	xWash	
0	1	Winters, Clarence Jesse	P	4	.333	A	C
0	0	Woods, John Fulton	P	1	.000	A	C
0	0	Workman, Harry Hall	P	11	.000	A	C

WON 47
LOST 105
TG 152

AMERICAN LEAGUE 1925. FINISHED 8th (LAST) PCT. .309

BOSTON

LEO ALEXANDER FOHL

WON	LOST	NAME	POS.	G.	BA	FROM	TO
0	0	Adams, Robert Burdette	P	2	.333	A	C
		Bischoff, John George	C	41	+.278	xChi	
		Boone, Isaac Morgan	OF118	133	.330	B	
		Carlyle, Roy Edward	OF	93	+.326	xWash	
		Collins, John Francis (Shano)	OF1	2	.333	B	
		Connally, Mervin Thomas (3B2)	SS34	43	.261	A	C
9	20	Ehmke, Howard John	P	34	.148	B	
		Ezzell, Homer Estell (2B9)	3B47	58	.285	B	C
0	2	Ferguson, James Alexander (Alex)	P	5	+.000	B	N.Y.
		Flagstead, Ira	OF144	148	.280	B	
0	2	Francis, Raymond James	P	6	+.125	xN.Y.	C
0	6	Fuhr, Oscar Lawrence	P	33	.250	B	C
0	3	Fullerton, Curtis Hooper	P	4	.200	B	
		Geygan, James Edward	SS	3	.182	B	
		Gross, Ewell	SS	9	.094	A	C
		Harris, Joseph	1B	9	+.150	B	Wash
		Herrara, Ramon	2B	10	.385	A	
		Heving, John Aloysius	C34	45	.168	B	
		Jenkins, Thomas Griffith	OF	15	.297	A	
1	4	Kallio, Rudolph	P	7	.333	Det19	C
0	2	Kiefer, Joseph Wm.	P	2	.000	Chi20	
		Lee, Ernest Dudley	SS	84	.224	B	
0	1	Lucey, Joseph Earl (SS3)	P7	10	.133	NY20	C

WON	LOST	NAME	POS.	G.	BA	FROM	TO
1	0	Neubauer, Harold Chas.	P	7	.000	A	C
		Picinich, Valentine John (Val)	C74	90	.255	B	
		Prothro, James Thomson (Doc) (SS3)	3B108	119	.313	Wash	
7	8	Quinn, John Picus	P	19	+.094	B	Phil
		Rogell, Wm. George (Billy) (SS6)	2B49	58	.195	A	
		Rosenthal, Simon	OF17	19	.264	A	
3	8	Ross, Chester Franklin	P	33	.125	B	
		Rothrock, John Houston	SS	22	.345	A	
9	18	Ruffing, Chas. Herbert (Red)	P	37	.215	B	
		Stokes, Albert John	C	17	.212	A	
		Todt, Philip Julius	1B140	141	.278	B	
		Vache, Ernest Lewis	OF53	110	.313	A	C
		Veach, Robert Hayes	OF	1	+.200	B	N.Y.
		Wambsganss, Wm. Adolph (1B6)	2B103	111	.231	B	
		Welch, Herbert M.	SS	13	.289	A	C
		Williams, Evon Daniel	OF53	68	.229	B	
12	19	Wingfield, Frederick Davis	P	41	.245	B	
5	12	Zahniser, Paul Vernon	P	38	.133	Wash	

WON 46
LOST 107
TG 153

AMERICAN LEAGUE 1926. FINISHED 8th (LAST) PCT. .301

BOSTON

LEO ALEXANDER FOHL

WON	LOST	NAME	POS.	G.	BA	FROM	TO
		Bischoff, John George	C46	59	.260	B	C
		Bratchi, Frederick Oscar	OF37	72	.275	Chi21	
		Carlyle, Roy Edward	OF	45	+.285	B	N.Y.
0	0	Clowers, Wm. P.	P	2	.000	A	C
3	10	Ehmke, Howard John	P	14	+.147	B	Phil
		Fitzgerald, Howard Chumney	OF23	31	.258	ChiN24	C
		Flagstead, Ira	OF	98	.299	B	
0	0	Foreman, August (Gus)	P	3	.000	Chi24	C
		Fowler, Joseph Chester	3B	2	.125	CinN	C
		Gaston, Alexander Nathaniel	C	98	.223	NYN23	
		Geygan, James Edward	3B	4	.300	B	C
		Haney, Fred Girard	3B137	138	+.221	Det	
6	10	Harriss, Wm. Bryan	P	21	+.206	xPhil	
2	9	Heimach, Fred Amos	P	26	+.295	xPhil	
		Herrara, Ramon (3B16)	2B48	74	.257	B	C
		Jacobson, Wm. Chester	OF	98	+.302	xStL	
		Jenkins, Thomas Griffith	OF	21	+.180	B	Phil
0	3	Kiefer, Joseph Wm.	P	11	.143	B	C
		Langford, Elton	OF	1	.000	A	
		Lee, Ernest Dudley	SS	2	.143	B	C
0	2	Lundgren, Ebin Delmar	P	18	.000	PittN24	
0	1	MacFayden, Daniel Knowles (Danny)	P	3	.333	A	
		McCann, Robert Emmett	SS	6	.000	Phil21	C
		Moore, Wm. Henry	C	5	.167	A	

WON	LOST	NAME	POS.	G.	BA	FROM	TO
		Regan, Wm. Wright	2B106	108	.263	A	
		Rigney, Emory Elmo	SS146	148	.270	Det	
		Rosenthal, Simon	OF67	104	.267	B	C
0	1	Ross, Chester Franklin	P	1	.000	B	C
		Rothrock, John Huston	SS2	15	.294	B	
6	15	Ruffing, Chas. Herbert (Red)	P	37	.196	B	
0	5	Russell, Jack Erwin	P	37	.190	A	
		Shaner, Walter Dedaker	OF48	69	.283	Clev23	
0	0	Sommers, Rudolph	P	2	.000	BknF14	
		Stokes, Albert John	C29	30	.163	B	C
		Tobin, John Thomas	OF	51	+.273	xWash	
		Todt, Philip Julius	1B	154	.255	B	
4	2	Welzer, Anton Frank (Tony)	P	39	.211	A	
8	15	Wiltse, Harold James	P	37	.085	A	
11	16	Wingfield, Frederick Davis	P	43	.217	B	
6	18	Zahniser, Paul Vernon	P	30	.163	B	

WON 51 AMERICAN LEAGUE FINISHED 8th (LAST)
LOST 103
TG 154 1927. PCT. .331

BOSTON

WM. FRANCIS CARRIGAN

WON	LOST	NAME	POS.	G.	BA	FROM	TO
0	1	Bennett, Francis Allen	P	4	.000	A	
1	1	Bradley, Herbert Theodore	P	6	.429	A	
		Bratchi, Frederick Oscar		1	.000	B	C
0	0	Bushey, Francis Clyde	P	1	.000	A	
		Carlyle, Hiram Cleo	OF52	95	.234	A	C
0	0	Cremins, Robert Anthony	P	4	.000	A	C
0	0	Eggert, Elmer Albert	P	5	.000	A	C
		Flagstead, Ira	OF129	131	.285	B	
		Freeman, John Edward	OF1	4	.000	A	C
		Haney, Fred Girard	3B34	47	.276	B	ChiN
14	21	Harriss, Wm. Bryan	P	44	.121	B	
		Hartley, Grover Allen	C86	103	.275	NYN	
		Hofmann, Fred	C81	87	.272	NY25	
		Jacobson, Wm. Chester	OF	45	+.245	B	Clev
		Karow, Martin Gregory (SS1)	3B1	6	.200	A	C
5	12	Lundgren, Ebin Delmar	P	30	.159	B	C
5	8	MacFayden, Daniel Knowles (Danny)	P35	37	.283	B	
		Moore, Wm. Henry	C42	44	.217	B	C
		Myer, Chas. Solomon (Buddy)	SS116	133	+.288	xWash	
		Regan, Wm. Wright	2B121	129	.274	B	
		Rigney, Emory Elmo	3B2	7	+.118	B	Wash
		Rogell, Wm. George (Billy)	3B53	82	.266	Bos25	
		Rollings, Wm. Russell (1B10)	3B44	82	.266	A	
		Rothrock, John Huston (1B13 2B36 3B20)	SS40	117	.260	B	
5	13	Ruffing, Chas. Herbert (Red)	P26	29	.255	B	
4	9	Russell, Jack Erwin	P34	35	.125	B	
		Shaner, Walter Dedaker	OF108	122	.273	B	
0	0	Sommers, Rudolph	P	7	.500	B	C
		Tarbert, Wilbur Arlington (Arlie)	OF27	33	.189	A	
		Tobin, John Thomas	OF93	111	.310	B	C
		Todt, Philip Julius	1B139	140	.236	B	
		Wanninger, Paul Louis	SS15	18	.200	NY25	CinN
		Welch, Frank	OF7	15	.179	Phil	C
6	11	Welzer, Anton Frank (Tony)	P	37	.095	B	C
0	2	Wilson, John Samuel	P	5	.111	A	
10	18	Wiltse, Harold James	P	36	.208	B	
1	7	Wingfield, Frederick Davis	P20	22	.222	B	C

WON 57 AMERICAN LEAGUE FINISHED 8th (LAST)
LOST 96
TG 153 1928. PCT. .373

BOSTON

WM. FRANCIS CARRIGAN

WON	LOST	NAME	POS.	G.	BA	FROM	TO
		Asbjornson, Robert Anthony	C3	6	.187	A	
0	0	Bennett, Francis Allen	P	1	.000	B	C
		Berry, Chas. Francis	C63	80	.260	Phil25	
0	3	Bradley, Herbert Theodore	P	15	.154	B	
		Flagstead, Ira	OF135	140	.290	B	
0	0	Garrison, Clifford Garry	P	6	.000	A	C
		Gerber, Walter	SS	104	+.217	xStL	
0	3	Griffin, Martin John	P11	12	.308	A	C
8	11	Harriss, Wm. Bryan	P	27	.139	B	C
		Heving, John Aloysius	C62	82	.259	Bos25	
		Hinson, James Paul		3	.000	A	C
		Hofmann, Fred	C71	78	.226	B	C
		Loepp, George Herbert	OF14	15	.176	A	
9	15	MacFayden, Daniel Knowles (Danny)	P33	35	.143	B	
		Moncewicz, Frederick Alfred	SS1	3	.000	A	C
19	15	Morris, Edward	P	47	.154	ChiN22	
		Myer, Chas. Solomon (Buddy)	3B144	147	.313	B	
		Regan, Wm. Wright	2B137	138	.264	B	
		Rogell, Wm. George (Billy) (2B22)	SS67	102	.233	B	
		Rollings, Wm. Russell (2B1 3B1)	1B2	50	.229	B	
0	0	Rothrock, John Huston (P1 1B16 SS13 3B17)	OF53	117	.267	B	
10	25	Ruffing, Chas. Herbert (Red)	P42	60	.314	B	
11	14	Russell, Jack Erwin	P32	35	.210	B	
0	6	Settlemire, Edgar Merle	P30	33	.176	A	C
0	0	Shea, John Michael Joseph	P	1	.000	A	C
0	2	Simmons, Patrick Clement	P	31	.133	A	
0	0	Slayton, Foster Herbert	P	3	.000	A	C
		Sumner, Carl Rinedahl	OF10	16	.276	A	C
0	0	Taitt, Douglas John (P1)	OF139	143	.299	A	
		Tarbert, Wilbur Arlington (Arlie)	OF3	6	.176	B	C
		Todt, Philip Julius	1B	144	.252	B	

WON	LOST	NAME	POS.	G.	BA	FROM	TO
		Williams, Evon Daniel	OF1	16	.222	Bos25	C
		Williams, Kenneth Roy	OF127	133	.303	StL	
0	0	Wilson, John Samuel	P	2	.000	B	C
0	2	Wiltse, Harold James	P	2	+.000	B	StL

WON 58 — AMERICAN LEAGUE — FINISHED 8th (LAST)
LOST 96
TG 154 — 1929. — PCT. .377

BOSTON

WM. FRANCIS CARRIGAN

WON	LOST	NAME	POS.	G.	BA	FROM	TO
		Asbjornson, Robert Anthony	C15	17	.103	B	
		Barrett, Robert Schley	3B34	68	.270	BknN27	C
		Barrett, Wm. Joseph	OF	111	+.270	xChi	
5	5	Bayne, Wm. Lear	P	27	.320	Clev	
		Berry, Chas. Francis	C72	77	.242	B	
		Bigelow, Elliot Allardice	OF58	100	.285	A	C
0	0	Bradley, Herbert Theodore	P	3	.000	B	C
1	0	Carroll, Edgar Fleischer	P	24	.063	A	C
		Cicero, Joseph Francis	OF8	10	.313	A	
		Connolly, Edward Joseph	C1	5	.000	A	
0	0	Dobens, Raymond Joseph	P	11	.375	A	C
1	0	Durham, Edward Fant	P	14	.000	A	
		Flagstead, Ira	OF	16	+.325	B	Wash
		Gaston, Alexander Nathaniel	C49	55	.224	Bos26	C
12	19	Gaston, Nathaniel Milton	P	39	.193	Wash	
		Gerber, Walter (2B22)	SS30	61	.165	B	C
		Gillis, Grant	2B25	28	.247	Wash	C
		Heving, John Aloysius	C55	76	.319	B	
0	0	Lisenbee, Horace Milton	P	5	.000	Wash	
10	18	MacFayden, Daniel Knowles (Danny)	P	32	.176	B	
14	14	Morris, Edward	P	33	.232	B	
		Narleski, Wm. Edward (2B28)	SS51	96	.277	A	
		Reeves, Robert Edwin	3B132	140	.248	Wash	
		Regan, Wm. Wright (3B10)	2B91	104	.288	B	
		Rhyne, Harold (Hal)	SS114	120	.252	PittN27	
		Rothrock, John Huston	OF128	143	.300	B	
9	22	Ruffing, Chas. Herbert (Red)	P35	60	.307	B	
6	18	Russell, Jack Erwin	P35	37	.129	B	
		Ryan, John Francis (SS1)	OF1	2	.000	A	C
		Scarritt, Russell Mallory	OF145	151	.294	A	
0	0	Simmons, Patrick Clement	P	2	.000	B	C
		Standaert, Jerome John	1B10	19	.167	BknN26	C
		Taitt, Douglas John	OF	26	+.281	B	Chi
		Todt, Philip Julius	1B	153	.262	B	
		Williams, Kenneth Roy	OF36	74	.346	B	C

WON 52 — AMERICAN LEAGUE — FINISHED 8th (LAST)
LOST 102
TG 154 — 1930. — PCT. .338

BOSTON

CHAS. F. WAGNER

WON	LOST	NAME	POS.	G.	BA	FROM	TO
		Barrett, Wm. Joseph	OF4	6	+.176	B	Wash
0	0	Bayne, Wm. Lear	P	1	.500	B	C
		Berry, Chas. Francis	C85	88	.289	B	
0	1	Bushey, Francis Clyde	P	11	.111	Bos27	C
		Cicero, Joseph Francis (OF1)	3B2	18	.167	B	
		Connolly, Edward Joseph	C26	27	.188	B	
4	15	Durham, Edward Fant	P	33	.097	B	
		Durst, Cedric Montgomery	OF	102	+.243	xN.Y.	C
		Galvin, James Joseph		2	.000	A	C
13	20	Gaston, Nathaniel Milton	P	38	.204	B	
		Heving, John Aloysius	C71	75	.277	B	
0	0	Kline, Robert George	P	1	.000	A	
10	17	Lisenbee, Horace Milton	P	37	.266	B	
11	14	MacFayden, Daniel Knowles (Danny)	P	36	.141	B	
		Miller, Otis Louis (2B15)	3B83	112	.286	StL27	
4	9	Morris, Edward	P	18	.316	B	
0	1	Mulroney, Francis Joseph	P	2	.000	A	C
		Narleski, Wm. Edward (3B14)	SS19	39	.235	B	C
		Oliver, Thomas Noble	OF	154	.293	A	
		Reeves, Robert Edwin (2B11 SS15)	3B62	92	.217	B	
		Regan, Wm. Wright	2B127	134	.266	B	
		Rhyne, Harold (Hal)	SS	107	.203	B	
		Rothrock, John Huston (3B1)	OF6	45	.277	B	
0	3	Ruffing, Chas. Herbert (Red)	P	6	+.273	B	N.Y.
9	20	Russell, Jack Erwin	P35	41	.177	B	
		Scarritt, Russell Mallory	OF110	113	.289	B	
0	0	Shields, Benjamin Cowan	P	3	.000	NY25	
		Small, Chas. Albert	OF1	25	.167	A	C
1	2	Smith, George Selby	P27	29	.333	Det	C
		Sweeney, Wm. Joseph	1B56	88	.309	Det28	
		Todt, Philip Julius	1B104	111	.269	B	
		Warstler, Harold Burton (Rabbitt)	SS	54	.185	A	
		Webb, Earl Wm.	OF116	127	.323	ChiN28	
		Winsett, John Thomas (Tom)		1	.000	A	

WON 62 — AMERICAN LEAGUE — FINISHED 6th.
LOST 90
TG 152 — 1931. — PCT. .408

BOSTON

JOHN FRANCIS COLLINS

WON	LOST	NAME	POS.	G.	BA	FROM	TO
		Berry, Chas. Francis	C102	111	.283	B	
0	0	Brillheart, James Benson	P	11	.500	ChiN27	C
		Connolly, Edward Joseph	C41	42	.075	B	
		Creeden, Patrick Francis	2B2	5	.000	A	C
8	10	Durham, Edward Fant	P38	39	.056	B	
2	13	Gaston, Nathaniel Milton	P	23	.158	B	
5	5	Kline, Robert George	P	28	.333	B	
5	12	Lisenbee, Horace Milton	P	41	.226	B	
		Lucas, John Chas.	OF1	3	.000	A	
16	12	MacFayden, Daniel Knowles (Danny)	P	35	.123	B	
		Marquardt, Albert Ludwig	2B13	17	.179	A	C
		Marshall, Wm. Henry		1	.000	A	
		Miller, Otis Louis	3B75	107	.272	B	
11	13	Moore, Wm. Wilcy	P	53	.161	NY29	
5	7	Morris, Edward	P	37	.158	B	C
0	0	Murphy, Walter Joseph	P	2	.000	A	C
0	0	McLaughlin, Justin Theodore	P	9	.000	A	
		McManus, Martin Joseph (3B4)	2B13	17	+.276	xDet	
		McWilliams, Wm. Henry		2	.000	A	C
		Oliver, Thomas Noble	OF	148	.276	B	
		Olson, Marvin Clement	2B	15	.189	A	
		Pickering, Urbane Hugh (2B16)	3B74	103	.252	A	
0	0	Reeves, Robert Edwin (P1)	2B29	36	.167	B	C
		Rhyne, Harold (Hal)	SS	147	.273	B	
		Rothrock, John Huston (2B23)	OF79	133	.278	B	
		Ruel, Herold Dominic (Muddy)	C	33	+.301	Wash	Det
10	18	Russell, Jack Erwin	P36	41	.195	B	
		Rye, Eugene Rudolph	OF10	17	.179	A	C
		Scarritt, Russell Mallory	OF	10	.154	B	
		Smith, John Marshall	1B	4	.133	A	C
		Storie, Howard Edward	C	6	.118	A	
		Stumpf, George Frederick	OF	7	.250	A	
		Sweeney, Wm. Joseph	1B124	131	.295	B	C
		VanCamp, Albert Joseph (1B25)	OF59	101	.275	Clev28	
		Warstler, Harold Burton (Rabbitt) (SS19)	2B42	66	.243	B	
		Webb, Earl Wm.	OF	151	.333	B	
		Winsett, John Thomas (Tom)	OF4	64	.198	B	

WON 44 AMERICAN LEAGUE FINISHED 8th (LAST)
LOST 111
155 1932. PCT. .279

BOSTON

JOHN FRANCIS COLLINS MARTIN JOSEPH McMANUS

WON	LOST	NAME	POS.	G.	BA	FROM	TO
		Alexander, David Dale	1B	101	+.372	xDet	
8	6	Andrews, Ivy Paul	P25	27	+.137	xN.Y.	
		Berry, Chas. Francis	C	10	+.188	B	Chi
0	4	Boerner, Laurence Hyer	P	21	.000	A	C
		Connolly, Edward Joseph	C	75	.225	B	C
0	1	Donohue, Peter Joseph	P	4	.000	Clev	C
6	13	Durham, Edward Fant	P34	35	.123	B	
0	3	Gallagher, Edward Michael	P	9	.000	A	C
0	3	Jablonowski, Peter Wm. (Appleton)	P	11	+.176	xClev	
		Johnson, Roy Cleveland	OF85	94	+.296	xDet	
		Jolley, Smead Powell	OF126	137	+.309	xChi	
11	13	Kline, Robert George	P	47	.130	B	
0	0	Leheney, Regis Francis	P	2	.000	A	C
0	4	Lisenbee, Horace Milton	P	19	.048	B	
		Lucas, John Chas.	OF	1	.000	B	C
*2	10	MacFayden, Daniel Knowles (Danny)	P	12	+.120	B	N.Y.
1	6	Michaels, John Joseph	P28	29	.143	A	C
		Miller, Otis Louis	OF	2	.000	B	C
4	10	Moore, Wm. Wilcy	P	37	+.045	B	N.Y.
0	0	McLaughlin, Justin Theodore	P	1	.000	B	
		McManus, Martin Joseph MGR. (3B30)	2B49	93	.235	B	
0	1	McNaughton, Gordon Joseph	P	6	.250	A	C
		Oliver, Thomas Noble	OF116	122	.264	B	
		Olson, Marvin Clement	2B106	115	.248	B	
		Patterson, Henry Joseph	C	1	.000	A	C
		Pickering, Urban Hugh	3B126	132	.260	B	C
		Reder, John Anthony	1B10	17	.135	A	C
1	8	Rhodes, John Gordon	P	12	+.077	xN.Y.	
		Rhyne, Harold (Hal)	SS55	71	.227	B	
		Rothrock, John Huston	OF	12	+.208	B	Chi
1	7	Russell, Jack Erwin	P11	11	+.091	B	Clev
		Spognardi, Andrew Ettore (SS1 3B1)	2B7	17	.294	A	C
		Storie, Howard Edward	C1	6	.375	B	C
		Stumpf, George Frederick	OF51	79	.201	B	
		Tate, Henry Bennett	C76	81	+.245	xChi	
		VanCamp, Albert Joseph	1B25	34	.223	B	C
		Warstler, Harold Burton (Rabbitt)	SS107	115	.211	B	
		Watwood, John Clifford (1B18)	OF46	93	+.249	xChi	
		Webb, Earl Wm.	OF50	52	+.281	B	Det
6	16	Weiland, Robert George (Bob)	P	43	.148	Chi	
4	6	Welch, John Vernon	P20	23	.250	ChiN	

*Protest game of August 1st allowed crediting win to MacFayden see page 101 of Spalding Guide for 1933.

WON 63 AMERICAN LEAGUE FINISHED 7th.
LOST 86
TG 149 1933. PCT. .423

BOSTON

MARTIN JOSEPH McMANUS

WON	LOST	NAME	POS.	G.	BA	FROM	TO
		Alexander, David Dale	1B79	94	.281	B	C
		Almada, Melo Baidomero (Mel)	OF13	14	.341	A	
7	13	Andrews, Ivy Paul	P34	36	.214	B	
8	11	Brown, Lloyd Andrew	P	33	+.281	xStL	
		Cooke, Allen Lindsey (Dusty)	OF118	119	.291	N.Y.	
		Ferrell, Richard Benjamin (Rick)	C	118	+.297	xStL	
		Fothergill, Robert Roy	OF	28	.344	Chi	C
		Friberg, Bernard Albert (SS2 3B5)	2B6	17	.317	PhilN	C
0	2	Fullerton, Curtis Hooper	P	6	.222	Bos25	C
		Gooch, John Beverly	C26	37	.182	CinN30	C
		Hodapp, Urban John (1B10)	2B101	115	.312	Chi	C
8	6	Johnson, Henry Ward	P25	26	.231	N.Y.	
		Johnson, Roy Cleveland	OF125	133	.313	B	
		Jolley, Smead Powell	OF102	118	.282	B	C
		Judge, Joseph Ignatius Jr.	1B28	34	.288	BknN	
7	8	Kline, Robert George	P	46	.176	B	
		Legett, Louis Alfred	C	8	.200	BosN29	
0	0	Meola, Emile Michael	P	3	.000	A	
		Mulleavy, Gregory Thomas		1	.000	Chi	C
		Muller, Frederick Wm.	2B14	15	.188	A	
0	0	McLaughlin, Justin Theodore	P	6	.000	B	C
		McManus, Martin Joseph MGR. (1B4 2B26)	3B76	106	.284	B	
		Oliver, Thomas Noble	OF86	90	.258	B	C
		Olson, Marvin Clement	2B1	3	.000	B	C
9	8	Pipgras, George Wm.	P	22	+.196	xN.Y.	
12	15	Rhodes, John Gordon	P34	35	.267	B	
		Seeds, Robert Ira (Bob) (OF32)	1B41	82	.243	Chi	
		Shea, Mervyn David John	C	16	+.143	Det29	StL
		Stumpf, George Frederick	OF15	22	.341	B	
		Walters, Wm. Henry Jr. (Bucky) (2B7)	3B43	52	.256	BosN	
		Warstler, Harold Burton (Rabbitt)	SS87	92	.217	B	
		Watwood, John Clifford	OF	13	.133	B	
8	14	Weiland, Robert George (Bob)	P	39	.108	B	
4	9	Welch, John Vernon	P	47	.162	B	
		Werber, Wm. Murray (Bill) (3B39)	SS71	108	+.258	xN.Y.	
		Winsett, John Thomas (Tom)	OF	6	.083	Bos31	

WON 76
LOST 76
TG 152

AMERICAN LEAGUE

1934.

FINISHED 4th.

PCT. .500

BOSTON

STANLEY RAYMOND HARRIS

WON	LOST	NAME	POS.	G.	BA	FROM	TO
		Almada, Melo Baldomero (Mel)	OF	23	.233	B	
		Bishop, Max Frederick (1B15)	2B57	97	.261	Phil	
		Cissell, Chalmer Wm.	2B96	102	.267	Clev	
		Cooke, Allen Lindsey (Dusty)	OF44	74	.244	B	
		Ferrell, Richard Benjamin (Rick)	C128	132	.297	B	
14	5	Ferrell, Wesley Cheek (Wes)	P26	34	.282	Clev	
		Graham, Arthur Wm.	OF	13	.234	A	
8	8	Grove, Robert Moses (Lefty)	P	22	.173	Phil	
		Hinkle, Daniel Gordon	C26	27	.172	A	C
2	1	Hockette, George Edward	P	3	.273	A	
6	8	Johnson, Henry Ward	P	31	.233	B	
		Johnson, Roy Cleveland	OF137	143	.320	B	
		Judge, Joseph Ignatius Jr.	1B2	10	.333	B	C
		Kellett, Donald Stafford (2B1 SS1)	3B1	9	.000	A	C
		Lary, Lynford Hobart (Lyn) (1B1)	SS	129	+.241	xN.Y.	
		Legett, Louis Alfred	C17	19	.289	B	
1	2	Merena, John Joseph	P	4	.143	A	C
		Morgan, Edward Carre	1B137	138	.267	Clev	C
		Muller, Frederick Wm. (2B1)	3B1	2	.000	B	C
1	0	Mulligan, Joseph Ignatius	P	14	.000	A	C
		Niemiec, Alfred Joseph	2B	9	.219	A	
10	13	Ostermueller, Frederick Raymond (Fritz)	P	33	.167	A	
2	0	Pennock, Herbert Jefferis	P	30	.214	N.Y.	C
0	0	Pipgras, George Wm.	P	2	.000	B	
		Porter, Richard Twilley	OF	80	+.302	xClev	C
		Reynolds, Carl Nettles	OF100	113	.303	StL	
12	12	Rhodes, John Gordon	P	44	.133	B	
		Seeds, Robert Ira	OF	8	+.167	B	Clev
		Solters, Julius Joseph (Moose)	OF89	101	.299	A	
6	7	Walberg, George Elvin (Swede)	P	30	.188	Phil	
		Walters, Wm. Henry Jr. (Bucky)	3B	23	.216	B	PhilN
1	5	Weiland, Robert George (Bob)	P	11	+.105	B	Clev
13	15	Welch, John Vernon	P	41	.203	B	
		Werber, Wm. Murray (Bill) (SS22)	3B130	152	.321	B	

WON 78
LOST 75
TG 153

AMERICAN LEAGUE

1935.

FINISHED 4th.

PCT. .510

BOSTON

JOSEPH EDWARD CRONIN

WON	LOST	NAME	POS.	G.	BA	FROM	TO
		Almada, Melo Baldomero (Mel) (1B3)	OF149	151	.290	B	
		Berg, Morris (Moe)	C37	38	.286	Clev	
		Bishop, Max Frederick (1B11 SS2)	2B34	60	.230	B	C
2	1	Bowers, Stewart Cole Jr.	P10	11	.200	A	
0	3	Cascarella, Joseph Thomas	P	6	+.000	xPhil	

WON	LOST	NAME	POS.	G.	BA	FROM	TO
		Cooke, Allen Lindsey (Dusty)	OF82	100	.306	B	
		Cronin, Joseph Edward MGR. (1B2)	SS139	144	.295	Wash	
		Dahlgren, Ellsworth Tenney (Babe)	1B	149	.263	A	
		Dickey, George Willard	C	5	.000	A	
		Farrell, Edward Stephen	2B	4	.286	NY33	C
		Ferrell, Richard Benjamin (Rick)	C131	133	.301	B	
25	14	Ferrell, Wesley Cheek (Wes)	P41	75	.347	B	
		Graham, Arthur Wm.	OF2	8	.300	B	C
20	12	Grove, Robert Moses (Lefty)	P	35	.079	B	
2	3	Hockette, George Edward	P	23	.143	B	C
2	1	Johnson, Henry Ward	P	13	.000	B	
		Johnson, Roy Cleveland	OF142	145	.315	B	
		Kroner, John Harold	3B	2	.250	A	
		Legett, Louis Alfred		2	.000	B	C
		Melillo, Oscar Donald	2B	106	+.261	xStL	
		Miller, Edmund John (Bing)	OF29	78	.304	Phil	
7	8	Ostermueller, Frederick Raymond (Fritz)	P	22	.286	B	
0	1	Pipgras, George Wm.	P	5	.000	B	C
		Reynolds, Carl Nettles	OF64	78	.270	B	
2	10	Rhodes, John Gordon	P34	36	.146	B	
0	0	Ripley, Walter Franklin	P	2	.000	A	C
		Solters, Julius Joseph (Moose)	OF	24	+.241	B	StL
0	0	Vandenberg, Harold Harris	P	3	1.000	A	
5	9	Walberg, George Elvin (Swede)	P	44	.162	B	
10	9	Welch, John Vernon	P	31	.180	B	
		Werber, Wm. Murray (Bill)	3B123	124	.255	B	
		Williams, Edwin Dibrell (2B29 SS13)	3B30	75	+.211	xPhil	C
3	4	Wilson, John Francis (Jack)	P	23	.313	Phil	

WON 74 LOST 80 TG 154 — AMERICAN LEAGUE 1936. — FINISHED 6th. PCT. .481

BOSTON

JOSEPH EDWARD CRONIN

WON	LOST	NAME	POS.	G.	BA	FROM	TO
		Almada, Melo Baldomero (Mel)	OF8.	96	.253	B	
		Berg, Morris (Moe)	C	39	.240	B	
0	0	Bowers, Stewart Cole Jr.	P	6	.000	B	
0	2	Cascarella, Joseph Thomas	P	10	+.000	B	Wash
		Cooke, Allen Lindsey (Dusty)	OF91	111	.273	B	
		Cramer, Roger Maxwell (Flit)	OF	154	.292	Phil	
		Cronin, Joseph Edward MGR. (3B21)	SS60	81	.281	B	
		Dahlgren, Ellsworth Tenney (Babe)	1B	16	.281	B	
		Dickey, George Willard	C	10	.043	B	
0	0	Dickman, George Emerson Jr.	P	1	.000	A	

WON	LOST	NAME	POS.	G.	BA	FROM	TO
		Ferrell, Richard Benjamin (Rick)	C	121	.312	B	
20	15	Ferrell, Wesley Cheek (Wes)	P39	61	.267	B	
		Foxx, James Emory (Jimmie) (OF16)	1B139	155	.338	Phil	
		Gaffke, Fabian Sebastian	OF	15	.127	A	
17	12	Grove, Robert Moses (Lefty)	P	35	.138	B	
5	1	Henry, James Francis	P21	22	.115	A	
		Kroner, John Harold (SS18 3B28)	2B38	84	.292	B	
		Manush, Henry Emmett (Heinie)	OF72	82	.291	Wash	
8	13	Marcum, John Alfred	P31	48	.205	Phil	
		Melillo, Oscar Donald	2B93	98	.226	B	
0	2	Meola, Emile Michael	P	6	+.143	xStL	C
		Miller, Edmund John (Bing)	OF13	30	.298	B	C
		McNair, Donald Eric (2B35 3B11)	SS84	128	.285	Phil	
1	1	Olson, Theodore Otto	P	5	.143	A	
10	16	Ostermueller, Frederick Raymond (Fritz)	P	43	.234	B	
0	2	Poindexter, Chester Jennings	P	3	.000	A	
0	3	Russell, Jack Erwin	P	23	+.286	xWash	
5	4	Walberg, George Elvin (Swede)	P	24	.156	B	
2	1	Welch, John Vernon	P	9	.273	B	PittN
		Werber, Wm. Murray (Bill) (OF45)	3B101	145	.275	B	
6	8	Wilson, John Francis (Jack)	P43	44	.220	B	

WON 80 LOST 72 TG 152 — AMERICAN LEAGUE 1937. — FINISHED 5th. PCT. .526

BOSTON

JOSEPH EDWARD CRONIN

WON	LOST	NAME	POS.	G.	BA	FROM	TO
		Almada, Melo Baldomero (Mel)	OF	32	+.236	B	Wash
		Berg, Morris (Moe)	C	47	.255	B	
0	0	Bowers, Stewart Cole Jr.	P	1	.000	B	C
		Chapman, Wm. Benjamin	OF	113	+.307	xWash	
		Cramer, Roger Maxwell (Flit)	OF	133	.305	B	
		Cronin, Joseph Edward MGR.	SS	148	.307	B	
		Daughters, Robert Francis		1	.000	A	C
		Dallessandro, Nicholas Dominic	OF35	68	.231	A	
		DeSautels, Eugene Abraham	C94	96	.243	Det33	
		Doerr, Robert Pershing (Bobby)	2B47	55	.224	A	
		Ferrell, Richard Benjamin (Rick)	C	18	+.308	B	Wash
3	6	Ferrell, Wesley Cheek (Wes)	P	18	+.364	B	Wash
		Foxx, James Emory (Jimmie)	1B	150	.285	B	
		Gaffke, Fabian Sebastian	OF50	54	.288	B	
1	2	Gonzales, Joseph Madrid	P	3	.000	A	C
17	9	Grove, Robert Moses (Lefty)	P	32	.143	B	

WON	LOST	NAME	POS.	G.	BA	FROM	TO
1	0	Henry, James Francis	P	3	.000	B	
		Higgins, Michael Franklin (Pinkey)	3B152	153	.302	Phil	
13	11	Marcum, John Alfred	P37	51	.267	B	
		Melillo, Oscar Donald	2B19	26	.250	B	
		Mills, Colonel Buster	OF120	123	.295	BknN35	
8	8	McKain, Archie Richard (Happy)	P36	38	.265	A	
		McNair, Donald Eric	2B106	126	.292	B	
13	10	Newsom, Louis Norman	P	31	+.253	xWash	
0	0	Olson, Theodore Otto	P	11	.300	B	
3	7	Ostermueller, Frederick Raymond (Fritz)	P	25	.333	B	
		Peacock, John Gaston	C	9	.313	A	
0	2	Thomas, Alphonse Thomas Jr.	P	9	+.250	xStL	C
5	7	Walberg, George Elvin (Swede)	P	32	.147	B	C
16	10	Wilson, John Francis (Jack)	P	51	.165	B	

WON 88 — LOST 61 — TG 149

AMERICAN LEAGUE

1938.

FINISHED 2nd.

PCT. .591

BOSTON

JOSEPH EDWARD CRONIN

WON	LOST	NAME	POS.	G.	BA	FROM	TO
15	11	Bagby, James Chas. Jr.	P43	45	.191	A	
0	0	Baker, Albert Jones	P	3	.000	A	C
		Berg, Morris (Moe)	C	10	.333	B	
		Chapman, Wm. Benjamin	OF126	127	.340	B	
0	0	Cramer, Roger Maxwell (Flit) (P1)	OF148	148	.301	B	
		Cronin, Joseph Edward MGR.	SS142	143	.325	B	
		DeSautels, Eugene Abraham	C	108	.291	B	
5	5	Dickman, George Emerson Jr.	P	32	.286	Bos36	
		Doerr, Robert Pershing (Bobby)	2B	145	.289	B	
		Foxx, James Emory (Jimmie)	1B	149	.349	B	
		Gaffke, Fabian Sebastian (C1)	OF2	15	.100	B	
14	4	Grove, Robert Moses (Lefty)	P	24	.148	B	
5	5	Harris, Wm. Milton	P	13	.214	PittN34	C
8	1	Heving, Joseph Wm.	P	16	+.133	xClev	
		Higgins, Michael Franklin (Pinkey)	3B138	139	.303	B	
0	0	Humphreys, Wm. Byron	P	2	.000	A	C
0	0	LeFebvre, Wilfrid Henry	P	1	1.000	A	
5	6	Marcum, John Alfred	P15	19	.135	B	
1	1	Midkiff, Richard James	P	13	.200	A	C
5	4	McKain, Archie Richard (Happy)	P	37	.065	B	
		McNair, Donald Eric (2B14)	SS15	46	.156	B	
		Nonnenkamp, Leo Wm. (Red)	OF39	87	.283	PittN33	
0	0	Olson, Theodore Otto	P	2	.000	B	C
13	5	Ostermueller, Frederick Raymond (Fritz)	P31	33	.216	B	
		Peacock, John Gaston	C57	72	.303	B	
1	1	Rogers, Lee Otis	P	14	.000	A	BknN
		Tabor, James Reubin	3B11	19	.316	A	
		Vosmik, Joseph Franklin	OF	146	.324	StL	
1	3	Wagner, Chas. Thomas Jr. (Broadway)	P	13	.167	A	
15	15	Wilson, John Francis (Jack)	P	37	.221	B	

WON 89 — LOST 62 — TG 151

AMERICAN LEAGUE

1939.

FINISHED 2nd.

PCT. .589

BOSTON

JOSEPH EDWARD CRONIN

WON	LOST	NAME	POS.	G.	BA	FROM	TO
9	10	Auker, Eldon LeRoy	P	31	.226	Det	
5	5	Bagby, James Chas. Jr.	P	21	.294	B	
		Berg, Morris (Moe)	C13	14	.273	B	C
		Berger, Louis Wm. (Boze)	SS10	20	.300	Chi	C
		Carey, Thomas Francis Aloysius (SS10)	2B35	54	.242	StL37	
		Cramer, Roger Maxwell (Flit)	OF135	137	.311	B	
		Cronin, Joseph Edward MGR.	SS142	143	.308	B	
		DeSautels, Eugene Abraham	C73	76	.243	B	
8	3	Dickman, George Emerson Jr.	P	48	.056	B	
		Doerr, Robert Pershing (Bobby)	2B126	127	.318	B	
		Finney, Louis Klopsche (OF25)	1B32	95	+.325	xPhil	
0	0	Foxx, James Emory (Jimmie) (P1)	1B123	124	.360	B	
		Gaffke, Fabian Sebastian	OF	1	.000	B	
9	10	Galehouse, Dennis Ward (Denny)	P	30	.064	Clev	
15	4	Grove, Robert Moses (Lefty)	P23	25	.134	B	
11	3	Heving, Joseph Wm.	P	46	.188	B	
1	1	LeFabvre, Wilfrid Henry	P	7	.300	B	
		Nonnenkamp, Leo Wm. (Red)	OF15	58	.240	B	
11	7	Ostermueller, Frederick Raymond (Fritz)	P	34	.161	B	
		Peacock, John Gaston	C84	92	.277	B	
4	3	Rich, Woodrow Earl	P	21	.259	A	
0	0	Sayles, Wm. Nisbeth	P	5	.143	A	
		Tabor, James Reubin	3B148	149	.289	B	
		Vosmik, Joseph Franklin	OF144	145	.276	B	
1	4	Wade, Jacob Fields (Jake)	P	20	+.000	Det	StL
3	1	Wagner, Chas. Thomas Jr. (Broadway)	P	11	.071	B	
1	0	Weaver, Montgomery Morton	P	9	.000	Wash	C
		Williams, Theodore Samuel	OF	149	.327	A	
11	11	Wilson, John Francis (Jack)	P36	37	.159	B	

WON 82 — LOST 72 — TG 154

AMERICAN LEAGUE

1940.

FINISHED 4th. (TIED WITH CHICAGO)

PCT. .532

BOSTON

JOSEPH EDWARD CRONIN

WON	LOST	NAME	POS.	G.	BA	FROM	TO
10	16	Bagby, James Chas. Jr. (OF1)	P36	44	.203	B	
1	2	Butland, Wilburn Rue	P	3	.000	A	
		Carey, Thomas Francis Aloysius (2B4 3B4)	SS20	43	.323	B	
		Cramer, Roger Maxwell (Flit)	OF149	150	.303	B	
		Cronin, Joseph Edward MGR. (3B2)	SS146	149	.285	B	
		DeSautels, Eugene Abraham	C70	71	.225	B	
8	6	Dickman, George Emerson Jr.	P	35	.107	B	
		DiMaggio, Dominic Paul	OF94	108	.301	A	
		Doerr, Robert Pershing (Bobby)	2B	151	.291	B	
		Finney, Louis Klopsche (1B51)	OF69	130	.320	B	
1	2	Fleming, Leslie Fletcherd (Bill)	P	10	.000	A	
		Foxx, James Emory (Jimmie) (C42 3B1)	1B95	144	.297	B	
6	6	Galehouse, Dennis Ward (Denny)	P	25	.077	B	
		Gelbert, Chas. Magnus	3B	30	+.198	xWash	C
		Glenn, Joseph Chas.	C19	22	.128	StL	C
7	6	Grove, Robert Moses (Lefty)	P22	23	.151	B	
4	2	Harris, Maurice Chas.	P	13	.273	A	
7	7	Hash, Herbert Howard	P34	35	.175	A	
12	7	Heving, Joseph Wm.	P	39	.200	B	
6	2	Johnson, Earl Douglass	P17	18	.074	A	
		Lupien, Ulysses John	1B8	10	.474	A	
0	1	Mustaikis, Alexander Dominick	P	6	.333	A	C
		Nonnenkamp, Leo Wm. (Red)		9	.000	B	C
5	9	Ostermueller, Frederick Raymond (Fritz)	P31	33	.315	B	
		Owen, Marvin James (Freck) (1B8)	3B9	20	.211	Chi	C
		Peacock, John Gaston	C48	63	.282	B	
1	0	Rich, Woodrow Earl	P	3	.000	B	
		Spence, Stanley Orville	OF15	51	.279	A	
		Tabor, James Reubin	3B	120	.285	B	
1	0	Terry, Lancelot Yank	P	4	.250	A	
1	0	Wagner, Chas. Thomas Jr. (Broadway)	P12	13	.200	B	
0	0	Williams, Theodore Samuel (Ted) (P1)	OF143	144	.344	B	
12	6	Wilson, John Francis (Jack)	P	41	.273	B	

WON x84 AMERICAN LEAGUE FINISHED 2nd.
LOST 70
TG 154 1941. PCT. .545

BOSTON

JOSEPH EDWARD CRONIN

WON	LOST	NAME	POS.	G.	BA	FROM	TO
		Campbell, Paul McLaughlin		1	.000	A	
		Carey, Thomas Francis Aloysius (SS8)	2B9	24	.200	B	
		Cronin, Joseph Edward MGR. (3B22 OF1)	SS119	143	.311	B	
1	1	Dickman, George Emerson Jr.	P	9	.091	B	C
		DiMaggio, Dominic Paul	OF	144	.283	B	
12	5	Dobson, Joseph Gordon	P	27	.149	Clev	
		Doerr, Robert Pershing (Bobby)	2B	132	.282	B	
		Finney, Louis Klopsche (1B24)	OF92	127	.288	B	
		Flair, Albert Dell	1B8	10	.200	A	C
1	1	Fleming, Leslie Fletcherd (Bill)	P	16	.222	B	
		Fox, Ervin (Pete)	OF62	73	.302	Det	
		Foxx, James Emory (Jimmie) (3B5 OF1)	1B124	135	.300	B	
7	7	Grove, Robert Moses (Lefty)	P	21	.111	B	C
		Hale, Arvel Odell (Bad News) (2B1)	3B6	12	.208	Clev	NYN
8	14	Harris, Maurice Chas.	P	35	.109	B	
1	0	Hash, Herbert Howard	P	4	.000	B	C
5	3	Hughson, Cecil Carlton	P	12	.059	A	
4	5	Johnson, Earl Douglass	P	17	.294	B	
0	0	Judd, Thomas Wm. Oscar	P7	10	.500	A	
19	10	Newsome, Heber Hampton	P	36	.244	A	
		Newsome, Ashby Lamar (2B23)	SS69	93	.225	Phil39	
		Peacock, John Gaston	C70	79	.284	B	
2	0	Potter, Nelson Thomas	P	10	+.000	xPhil	
		Pytlak, Frank Anthony	C91	106	.271	Clev	
0	0	Rich, Woodrow Earl	P	2	.000	B	
7	3	Ryba, Dominic Joseph (Mike)	P	40	.216	StLN38	
		Spence, Stanley Orville (1B1)	OF52	86	.232	B	
		Tabor, James Reubin	3B125	126	.279	B	
12	8	Wagner, Chas. Thomas Jr. (Broadway)	P	29	.159	B	
		Williams, Theodore Samuel (Ted)	OF133	143	.406	B	
4	13	Wilson, John Francis (Jack)	P	27	.159	B	

xOne game won by forfeit.

WON 93 AMERICAN LEAGUE FINISHED 2nd.
LOST 59
TG 152 1942. PCT. .612

BOSTON

JOSEPH EDWARD CRONIN

WON	LOST	NAME	POS.	G.	BA	FROM	TO
9	3	Brown, Mace Stanley	P	34	.067	BknN	
7	1	Butland, Wilburn Rue	F	23	.036	Bos40	
		Campbell, Paul McLaughlin	OF4	26	.067	B	

WON	LOST	NAME	POS.	G.	BA	FROM	TO
		Carey, Thomas Francis Aloysius	2B	1	1.000	B	
5	1	Chase, Kendall Fay (Ken)	P	13	.182	Wash	
		Conroy, Wm. Gordon	C	83	.200	Phil37	
		Cronin, Joseph Edward MGR. (1B5 SS1)	3B11	45	.304	B	
		DiMaggio, Dominic Paul	OF	151	.286	B	
11	9	Dobson, Joseph Gordon	P	30	.145	B	
		Doerr, Robert Pershing (Bobby)	2B142	144	.290	B	
		Finney, Louis Klopsche (1B2)	OF95	113	.285	B	
		Fox, Ervin (Pete)	OF71	77	.262	B	
		Foxx, James Emory (Jimmie)	1B27	30	.270	B	ChiN
		Gilbert, Andrew	OF5	6	.091	A	
22	6	Hughson, Cecil Carlton	P	38	.176	B	
8	10	Judd, Thomas Wm. Oscar	P31	36	.269	B	
		Lupien, Ulysses John	1B121	128	.281	Bos40	
8	10	Newsome, Heber Hampton	P	24	.236	B	
		Newsome, Ashby Lamar (SS7 2B10)	3B12	29	.274	B	
		Peacock, John Gaston	C82	88	.266	B	
		Pesky, John Michael	SS	147	.331	A	
3	3	Ryba, Dominic Joseph (Mike) (C3)	P18	21	.294	B	
		Tabor, James Reubin	3B138	139	.252	B	
6	5	Terry, Lancelot Yank	P	20	.111	Bos40	
14	11	Wagner, Chas. Thomas Jr. (Broadway)	P	29	.077	B	
		Williams, Theodore Samuel (Ted)	OF	150	.356	B	

WON 68
LOST 84
TG 152

AMERICAN LEAGUE

FINISHED 7th.

1943.

PCT. .447

BOSTON

JOSEPH EDWARD CRONIN

WON	LOST	NAME	POS.	G.	BA	FROM	TO
		Barna, Herbert Paul	OF29	30	.170	xNYN	C
6	6	Brown, Mace Stanley	P	49	.059	B	
0	4	Chase, Kendall Fay (Ken)	P	7	.091	B	NYN
		Conroy, Wm. Gordon	C38	39	.180	B	
		Cronin, Joseph Edward MGR.	3B10	59	.312	B	
		Culberson, Delbert Leon	OF79	80	.272	A	
7	11	Dobson, Joseph Gordon	P	25	.096	B	
		Doerr, Robert Pershing (Bobby)	2B	155	.270	B	
		Doyle, Howard James	C	13	.209	A	C
		Fox, Ervin (Pete)	OF125	127	.288	B	
		Garrison, Robert Ford	OF32	36	.279	A	
12	15	Hughson, Cecil Carlton	P	35	.105	B	
11	6	Judd, Thomas Wm. Oscar	P23	27	.259	B	
1	1	Karl, Anton Andrew	P	11	.286	A	PhilN
		Lake, Edward Erving	SS63	75	.199	StLN41	
		Lazor, John Paul	OF63	83	.226	A	
3	4	Lucier, Louis Joseph	P	16	.200	A	
		Lupien, Ulysses John	1B153	154	.255	B	

WON	LOST	NAME	POS.	G.	BA	FROM	TO
		Metkovich, George Michael (1B2)	OF76	78	.246	A	
		Miles, Wilson Daniel (Dee)	OF25	45	.215	Phil	C
		McBride, Thomas Raymond	OF24	26	.240	A	
8	13	Newsome, Heber Hampton	P25	27	.146	B	C
		Newsome, Ashby Lamar (3B15)	SS98	114	.265	B	
		Olsen, Albert Wm.		1	.000	A	C
1	4	O'Neill, Robert Emmett	P	11	.188	A	
		Partee, Roy Robert	C91	96	.281	A	
		Peacock, John Gaston	C32	48	.202	B	
7	5	Ryba, Dominic Joseph (Mike)	P	40	.186	B	
		Simmons, Aloysius Harry (Al)	OF33	40	.203	Phil41	
		Tabor, James Reubin (OF2)	3B133	137	.242	B	
7	9	Terry, Lancelot Yank	P	30	.067	B	
5	6	Woods, George Rowland	P	23	.222	A	

WON 77
LOST 77
TG 154

AMERICAN LEAGUE

FINISHED 4th.

1944.

PCT. .500

BOSTON

JOSEPH EDWARD CRONIN

WON	LOST	NAME	POS.	G.	BA	FROM	TO
8	7	Barrett, Francis Joseph	P	38	.143	StLN39	
12	8	Bowman, Joseph Emil (Joe)	P26	59	.200	PittN41	
		Bucher, James Quinter (2B21)	3B44	80	.274	StLN38	
4	5	Cecil, Rex Rolston	P	11	.278	A	
		Conroy, Wm. Gordon	C	19	.213	B	C
		Cronin, Joseph Edward MGR.	1B49	76	.241	B	
		Culberson, Delbert Leon	OF72	75	.238	B	
		Doerr, Robert Pershing (Bobby)	2B	125	.325	B	
2	4	Dreisewerd, Clement John	P	7	.188	A	
		Finney, Louis Klopsche (OF2)	1B59	68	.287	Bos42	
		Fox, Ervin (Pete)	OF119	121	.315	B	
		Garrison, Robert Ford	OF12	13	+.245	B	Phil
4	7	Hausmann, Clemens Raymond	P	32	.079	A	
18	5	Hughson, Cecil Carlton	P	28	.152	B	
		Johnson, Robert Lee (Bob)	OF142	144	.324	Wash	
0	3	Johnson, Victor Oscar	P	7	.000	A	
1	1	Judd, Thomas Wm. Oscar	P9	10	.182	B	
0	0	Lake, Edward Erving (P6 2B3 3B1)	SS41	57	.206	B	
		Lazor, John Paul (C1)	OF6	16	.083	B	
0	0	Lucier, Louis Joseph	P	3	.000	B	PhilN
		Metkovich, George Michael (1B50)	OF82	134	.277	B	
		McBride, Thomas Raymond (1B5)	OF57	71	.245	B	
		Newsome, Ashby Lamar (2B8 3B1)	SS126	136	.242	B	
6	11	O'Neill, Robert Emmett	P	28	.182	B	
		Partee, Roy Robert	C85	89	.243	B	

WON	LOST	NAME	POS.	G.	BA	FROM	TO
0	0	Partenheimer, Stanwood Wendell	P	1	.000	A	
		Peacock, John Gaston	C2	4	.000	B	PhilN
12	7	Ryba, Dominic Joseph (Mike)	P	42	.146	B	
		Tabor, James Reubin	3B114	116	.285	B	
6	10	Terry, Lancelot Yank	P	27	.234	B	
		Wagner, Harold Edward	C64	66	+.332	xPhil	
0	1	Wood, Joseph Frank	P	3	.000	A	C
4	8	Woods, George Rowland	P	38	.146	B	

WON 71
LOST 83
TG 154

AMERICAN LEAGUE 1945. FINISHED 7th. PCT. .461

BOSTON

JOSEPH EDWARD CRONIN

WON	LOST	NAME	POS.	G.	BA	FROM	TO
4	3	Barrett, Francis Joseph	P	37	.250	B	
0	2	Bowman, Joseph Emil (Joe)	P3	9	.222	B	CinN
		Bucher, James Quinter (2B2)	3B32	52	.225	B	C
		Camilli, Adolph Louis	1B54	63	.212	BknN43	C
2	5	Cecil, Rex Rolston	P	7	.300	B	C
		Christopher, Loyd Eugene	OF3	8	.286	A	ChiN
4	4	Clark, Wm. Otis	P	12	.208	A	C
		Cronin, Joseph Edward MGR.	3B	3	.375	B	
		Culberson, Delbert Leon	OF91	97	.275	B	
0	1	Dreisewerd, Clement John	P	2	.000	B	
21	10	Ferriss, David Meadow	P35	61	.267	A	
		Finney, Louis Klopsche		2	+.000	B	StL
		Fox, Ervin (Pete)	OF57	66	.245	B	C
		Garbark, Robert Michael	C67	68	.261	Phil	C
5	7	Hausmann, Clemens Raymond	P	31	.103	B	C
4	10	Heflin, Randolph Rutherford	P	20	.086	A	
		Holm, Wm. Frederick	C57	58	.185	ChiN	C
		Johnson, Robert Lee (Bob)	OF140	143	.280	B	C
6	4	Johnson, Victor Oscar	P	26	.167	B	
0	1	Judd, Thomas Wm. Oscar	P	2	.500	B	PhilN
		LaForest, Byron Joseph (OF5)	3B45	52	.250	A	C
		Lake, Edward Erving (2B1)	SS130	133	.279	B	
		Lazor, John Paul	OF81	101	.310	B	
		McBride, Thomas Raymond (1B11)	OF81	100	.305	B	
		Metkovich, George Michael (OF42)	1B97	138	.260	B	
		Newsome, Ashby Lamar (SS33 3B11)	2B82	125	.290	B	
8	11	O'Neill, Robert Emmett	P	24	.180	B	
		Polly, Nicholas Joseph	3B2	4	.143	BknN37	C
		Pytlak, Frank Anthony	C6	9	.118	Bos41	
7	6	Ryba, Dominic Joseph (Mike)	P	34	.250	B	
		Steiner, Benjamin Saunders	2B77	78	.257	A	
		Steiner, James Harry	C24	26	+.207	xClev	C
0	4	Terry, Lancelot Yank	P	12	.111	B	C

WON	LOST	NAME	POS.	G.	BA	FROM	TO
		Tobin, John Patrick (2B5 OF1)	3B72	84	.252	A	C
		Walters, James Frederick	C38	40	.172	A	C
6	8	Wilson, James Alger	P23	25	.245	A	
4	7	Woods, George Rowland	P	24	.214	B	C

WON 104
LOST 50
TG 154

AMERICAN LEAGUE 1946. FINISHED 1st. PCT. .675

BOSTON

JOSEPH EDWARD CRONIN

WON	LOST	NAME	POS.	G.	BA	FROM	TO
		Andres, Ernest Henry	3B	15	.098	A	C
7	6	Bagby, James Chas. Jr.	P	21	.119	Clev	
3	1	Brown, Mace Stanley	P	18	.000	Bos43	C
1	0	Butland, Wilburn Rue	P	5	.250	Bos42	
		Campbell, Paul McLaughlin	1B5	28	.115	Bos42	
		Carey, Thomas Francis Aloysius	2B	3	.200	Bos42	C
		Culberson, Delbert Leon (3B4)	OF49	59	.313	B	
0	0	Deutsch, Melvin Elliott	P	3	.000	A	C
		DiMaggio, Dominic Paul	OF	142	.316	Bos42	
13	7	Dobson, Joseph Gordon	P	32	.100	Bos43	
		Doerr, Robert Pershing (Bobby)	2B	151	.271	Bos44	
4	1	Dreisewerd, Clement John	P	20	.000	B	
25	6	Ferriss, David Meadow	P40	45	.209	B	
		Gilbert, Andrew	OF1	2	.000	Bos42	C
		Gutteridge, Donald Joseph (3B8)	2B9	22	.234	StL	
17	9	Harris, Maurice Chas.	P	34	.231	Bos41	
0	1	Heflin, Randolph Rutherford	P	5	.667	B	C
		Higgins, Michael Franklin (Pinkey)	3B59	64	+.275	xDet	C
20	11	Hughson, Cecil Carlton	P	39	.132	Bos44	
5	4	Johnson, Earl Douglass	P	29	.227	Bos41	
3	2	Klinger, Robert Harold (Bob)	P	28	.313	PittN43	
		Lazor, John Paul	OF7	23	.138	B	C
		Metkovich, George Michael	OF81	86	.246	B	
		Moses, Wallace Jr.	OF44	48	+.206	xChi	
		McBride, Thomas Raymond	OF43	61	.301	B	
		McGah, Edward Joseph	C14	15	.216	A	
		Partee, Roy Robert	C38	40	.315	Bos44	
		Pellagrini, Edward Chas. (SS9)	3B14	22	.211	A	
		Pesky, John Michael	SS	153	.335	Bos42	
		Pytlak, Frank Anthony	C	4	.143	B	C
		Russell, Glen David (2B3)	3B70	80	.208	ChiN42	
0	1	Ryba, Dominic Joseph (Mike)	P	9	1.000	B	C
		Steiner, Benjamin Saunders	3B1	3	.250	B	
1	0	Wagner, Chas. Thomas Jr. (Broadway)	P	8	.091	Bos42	C
		Wagner, Harold Edward	C116	117	.230	Bos44	

WON	LOST	NAME	POS.	G.	BA	FROM	TO
		Williams, Theodore Samuel (Ted)	OF	150	.342	Bos42	
0	0	Wilson, James Alger	P	1	.000	B	
		York, Rudolph Preston (Rudy)	1B	154	.276	Det	
5	1	Zuber, Wm. Henry	P	15	+.111	xN.Y.	

WON 83
LOST 71
TG 154

AMERICAN LEAGUE

1947.

FINISHED 3rd.

PCT. .539

BOSTON

JOSEPH EDWARD CRONIN

WON	LOST	NAME	POS.	G.	BA	FROM	TO
		Aulds, Leycester Doyle	C	3	.250	A	C
		Batts, Matthew Daniel	C6	7	.500	A	
0	0	Butland, Wilburn Rue	P	1	.000	B	C
		Combs, Merrill Russell	3B	17	.221	A	
		Culberson, Delbert Leon (3B4)	OF25	47	.238	B	
0	1	Deal, Ellis Fergason	P5	6	.500	A	
		Dente, Samuel Joseph	3B	46	.232	A	
		DiMaggio, Dominic Paul	OF134	136	.283	B	
18	8	Dobson, Joseph Gordon	P	33	.208	B	
		Doerr, Robert Pershing (Bobby)	2B	146	.258	B	
7	8	Dorish, Harry	P	41	.143	A	
12	11	Ferriss, David Meadow	P33	52	.273	B	
1	2	Fine, Thomas Morgan	P	9	.333	A	
11	7	Galehouse, Dennis Ward (Denny)	P	21	+.096	xStL	
		Goodman, Wm. Dale	OF1	12	.182	A	
		Gutteridge, Donald Joseph (3B19)	2B20	54	.168	B	
5	4	Harriss, Maurice Chas.	P	15	.417	B	
		Hayes, Frank Witman (Blimp)	C4	5	.154	Chi	C
12	11	Hughson, Cecil Carlton	P	29	.033	B	
12	11	Johnson, Earl Douglass	P45	46	.273	B	
		Jones, James Murrell	1B	109	+.235	xChi	
1	1	Klinger, Robert Harold (Bob)	P	28	.111	B	C
		Mele, Sabath Anthony (1B1)	OF115	123	.302	A	
		Moses, Wallace Jr.	OF58	90	.275	B	
0	0	Murphy, John Joseph (Grandma)	P	32	.273	N.Y.	C
		McBride, Thomas Raymond	OF1	2	+.200	B	Wash
		McGah, Edward Joseph	C7	9	.000	B	C
2	3	Parnell, Melvin Lloyd	P	15	.056	A	
		Partee, Roy Robert	C54	60	.231	B	
		Pellegrini, Edward Chas. (SS26)	3B42	74	.203	B	
		Pesky, John Michael (3B22)	SS133	155	.324	B	
		Russell, Glen David	3B 13	26	.154	B	C
		Shofner, Frank Strickland	3B4	5	.154	A	C
1	3	Smith, Edgar	P	8	+.167	xChi	C
0	1	Stobbs, Chas. Klein	P	4	.000	A	
		Tebbetts, George Robert (Birdie)	C89	90	+.299	xDet	
		Wagner, Harold Edward	C	21	+.231	B	Det

WON	LOST	NAME	POS.	G.	BA	FROM	TO
0	0	Widmar, Albert Joseph	P	2	.000	A	
		Williams, Theodore Samuel (Ted)	OF	156	.343	B	
		York, Rudolph Preston (Rudy)	1B	48	+.212	B	Chi
1	0	Zuber, Wm. Henry	P	20	.154	B	C

WON 96
LOST 59
TG 155

AMERICAN LEAGUE

1948.

FINISHED 2nd.

PCT. .619

BOSTON

JOSEPH VINCENT McCARTHY

WON	LOST	NAME	POS.	G.	BA	FROM	TO
		Batts, Matthew Daniel	C41	46	.314	B	
1	1	Caldwell, Earl Welton	P	8	+.333	xChi	C
1	0	Deal, Ellis Fergason	P	4	.000	B	
		DiMaggio, Dominic Paul	OF	155	.285	B	
16	10	Dobson, Joseph Gordon	P	38	.202	B	
		Doerr, Robert Pershing (Bobby)	2B138	140	.285	B	
0	1	Dorish, Harry	P	9	.250	B	
7	3	Ferriss, David Meadow	P	31	.243	B	
8	8	Galehouse, Dennis Ward (Denny)	P	27	.167	B	
		Goodman, Wm. Dale (2B2 3B2)	1B117	127	.310	B	
7	10	Harriss, Maurice Chas.	P	20	.063	B	
		Hitchcock, Wm. Clyde (3B15)	2B15	49	.298	StL	
3	1	Hughson, Cecil Carlton	P	15	.000	B	
10	4	Johnson, Earl Douglass	P	35	.097	B	
		Jones, James Murrell	1B31	36	.200	B	C
10	7	Kinder, Ellis Raymond	P	28	.097	StL	
18	5	Kramer, John Henry	P	29	.151	StL	
		Martin, Boris Michael	C1	4	.500	StL46	
		Mele, Sabath Anthony	OF55	66	.233	B	
		Moses, Wallace Jr.	OF45	78	.259	B	
0	1	McCall, John Wm.	P	1	.000	A	
0	0	McDermott, Maurice Joseph	P	7	.375	A	
		Ostrowski, John Theodore		1	.000	ChiN46	
0	0	Palm, Richard Paul	P	3	.000	A	C
15	8	Parnell, Melvin Lloyd	P	35	.163	B	
		Pesky, John Michael	3B141	143	.281	B	
		Sheridan, Neill Rawlins		2	.000	A	C
		Spence, Stanley Orville (1B14)	OF92	114	.235	Wash	
		Stephens, Vernon Decatur	SS	155	.269	StL	
0	0	Stobbs, Chas. Klein	P	6	.000	B	
		Stringer, Louis Bernard	2B2	4	.091	ChiN46	
		Tebbetts, George Robert (Birdie)	C126	128	.280	B	
		Williams, Theodore Samuel (Ted)	OF134	137	.369	B	
		Wright, Thomas Everett		3	.500	A	

WON 96 | LOST 58 | TG 154

AMERICAN LEAGUE 1949. FINISHED 2nd. PCT. .623

BOSTON

JOSEPH VINCENT McCARTHY

WON	LOST	NAME	POS.	G.	BA	FROM	TO
		Batts, Matthew Daniel	C50	60	.242	B	
		Combs, Merrill Russell (SS1)	3B9	14	.208	Bos47	
		DiMaggio, Dominic Paul	OF144	145	.307	B	
14	12	Dobson, Joseph Gordon	P	33	.147	B	
		Doerr, Robert Pershing (Bobby)	2B	139	.309	B	
0	0	Dorish, Harry	P	5	.000	B	
		Dropo, Walter	1B	11	.146	A	
0	0	Ferriss, David Meadow	P	4	1.000	B	
0	0	Galehouse, Dennis Ward (Denny)	P	2	.000	B	C
		Goodman, Wm. Dale	1B117	122	.298	B	
2	3	Harris, Maurice Chas.	P	7	+.083	B	Wash
		Hitchcock, Wm. Clyde (2B8)	1B29	55	.204	B	
4	2	Hughson, Cecil Carlton	P	29	.045	B	C
3	6	Johnson, Earl Douglass	P	19	.000	B	
23	6	Kinder, Ellis Raymond	P	43	.130	B	
6	8	Kramer, John Henry	P	21	.257	B	
		Martin, Boris Michael	C1	2	.000	B	
3	4	Masterson, Walter Edward	P	18	+.118	xWash	
		Mele, Sabath Anthony	OF11	18	+.196	B	Wash
0	0	McCall, John Wm.	P	5	.667	B	
5	4	McDermott, Maurice Joseph	P	12	.212	B	
		O'Brien, Thomas Edward	OF32	49	.224	PittN45	
25	7	Parnell, Melvin Lloyd	P	39	.254	B	
		Pesky, John Michael	3B	148	.306	B	
0	0	Quinn, Frank Wm.	P	8	.167	A	
0	0	Robinson, John Edward	P	3	.000	A	C
		Spence, Stanley Orville	OF6	7	+.150	B	StL
		Stephens, Vernon Decatur	SS	155	.290	B	
11	6	Stobbs, Chas. Klein	P	26	.208	B	
		Stringer, Louis Bernard	2B9	35	.268	B	
		Tebbetts, George Robert (Birdie)	C118	122	.270	B	
		Williams, Theodore Samuel (Ted)	OF	155	.342	B	
0	0	Wittig, John Carl	P	1	.000	NYN43	C
		Wright, Thomas Everett		5	.250	B	
		Zarilla, Allen Lee	OF122	124	+.285	xStL	

WON 94 | LOST 60 | TG 154

AMERICAN LEAGUE 1950. FINISHED 3rd. PCT. .610

BOSTON

JOSEPH VINCENT McCARTHY STEPHEN FRANCIS O'NEILL

WON	LOST	NAME	POS.	G.	BA	FROM	TO
0	0	Atkins, James Curtis	P	1	.000	A	
		Batts, Matthew Daniel	C73	75	.273	B	
		Combs, Merrill Russell		1	+.000	B	Wash
		DiMaggio, Dominic Paul	OF140	141	.328	B	
15	10	Dobson, Joseph Gordon	P	39	.214	B	
		Doerr, Robert Pershing	2B	149	.294	B	
		Dropo, Walter	1B134	136	.322	B	
0	0	Ferriss, David Meadow	P	1	.000	B	C
0	0	Gillespie, Robert Wm.	P	1	.000	Chi48	C
		Goodman, Wm. Dale (1B21 2B5 SS1 3B27)	OF45	110	.354	B	
		Hatfield, Fred James	3B3	10	.250	A	
0	0	Johnson, Earl Douglass	P	11	.000	B	
		Keltner, Kenneth Frederick (Butch) (1B1)	3B8	13	.321	Clev	C
14	12	Kinder, Ellis Raymond	P	48	.183	B	
2	2	Littlefield, Richard Bernard	P	15	.000	A	
0	0	Marchildon, Philip Joseph	P	1	.000	Phil	C
8	6	Masterson, Walter Edward	P	33	.136	B	
		Maxwell, Chas. Richard	OF1	2	.000	A	
0	0	Mueller, Joseph Gordon	P	8	.000	A	C
7	3	McDermott, Maurice Joseph	P38	39	.364	B	
1	0	McDonald, James LeRoy	P	9	.333	A	
8	6	Nixon, Willard Lee	P	22	.139	A	
		O'Brien, Thomas Edward	OF	9	+.129	B	Wash
4	2	Papai, Alfred Thomas	P	16	.176	StL	StLN
18	10	Parnell, Melvin Lloyd	P	40	.194	B	
		Pesky, John Michael (SS8)	3B116	127	.312	B	
		Piersall, James Anthony	OF2	6	.286	A	
0	0	Quinn, Frank Wm.	P	1	.000	B	C
		Rosar, Warren Vincent	C25	27	.298	Phil	
3	2	Schanz, Charley Murrell	P	14	.091	PhilN47	C
		Scherbarth, Robert Elmer	C	1	.000	A	C
		Stephens, Vernon Decatur	SS146	149	.295	B	
12	7	Stobbs, Chas. Klein	P	32	.246	B	
		Stringer, Louis Bernard (2B1 SS1)	3B3	24	.294	B	C
0	0	Suchecki, James Joseph	P	4	.000	A	
2	0	Taylor, James Harry	P	3	.286	BknN48	
		Tebbetts, George Robert	C74	79	.310	B	
		Vollmer, Clyde Frederick	OF39	57	+.284	xWash	
		Williams, Theodore Samuel	OF86	89	.317	B	
		Wright, Thomas Everett	OF24	54	.318	B	
		Zarilla, Allen Lee	OF128	130	.325	B	

WON 87 | LOST 67 | TG 154

AMERICAN LEAGUE 1951. FINISHED 3rd. PCT. .565

BOSTON

STEPHEN FRANCIS O'NEILL

WON	LOST	NAME	POS.	G.	BA	FROM	TO
		Batts, Matthew Daniel	C	11	+.138	B	StL

WON	LOST	NAME	POS.	G.	BA	FROM	TO
		Boudreau, Louis (1B2 3B15)	SS52	82	.267	Clev	
		DiMaggio, Dominic Paul	OF	146	.296	B	
		DiPietro, Robert Louis Paul	OF3	4	.091	A	C
		Doerr, Robert Pershing (Bobby)	2B	106	.289	B	C
		Dropo, Walter	1B93	99	.239	B	
		Evans, Alfred Hubert	C10	12	.125	Wash	C
0	0	Evans, Wm. Lawrence	P	9	.000	Chi49	C
0	0	Flowers, Bennett	P	1	.000	A	
		Goodman, Wm. Dale (2B44 3B1 OF38)	1B62	141	.297	B	
		Guerra, Fermin Romero	C	10	+.156	Phil	Wash
		Hatfield, Fred James	3B49	80	.172	B	
0	0	Hinrichs, Paul Edwin	P	4	.000	A	C
0	1	Hisner, Harley Parnell	P	1	.500	A	C
		Hoderlein, Melvin Anthony (3B3)	2B3	9	.357	A	
7	7	Kiely, Leo Patrick	P17	18	.143	A	
11	2	Kinder, Ellis Raymond	P	63	.118	B	
3	0	Masterson, Walter Edward	P	30	.182	B	
		Maxwell, Chas. Richard	OF13	49	.188	B	
		Moss, John Lester	C69	71	+.198	xStL	
8	8	McDermott, Maurice Joseph	P34	43	.273	B	
7	4	Nixon, Willard Lee	P33	34	.289	B	
		Olson, Karl Arthur	OF	5	.100	A	
18	11	Parnell, Melvin Lloyd	P36	37	.309	B	
		Pesky, John Michael (2B5 3B11)	SS106	131	.313	B	
		Richter, Allen Gordon	SS3	5	.091	A	
		Robinson, Aaron Andrew	C25	26	+.203	xDet	C
		Rosar, Warren Vincent	C56	58	.229	B	C
12	9	Scarborough, Ray Wilson	P	37	.191	Chi	
		Stephens, Vernon Decatur	3B89	109	.300	B	
10	9	Stobbs, Chas. Klein	P	34	.180	B	
4	9	Taylor, James Harry	P	31	.103	B	
		Vollmer, Clyde Frederick	OF106	115	.251	B	
		White, Samuel Chas.	C	4	.182	A	
7	7	Wight, Wm. Robert	P	34	.073	Chi	
		Williams, Theodore Samuel	OF147	148	.318	B	
		Wright, Thomas Everett	OF18	28	.222	B	
		Zauchin, Norbert Henry	1B4	5	.167	A	C

WON 76 AMERICAN LEAGUE FINISHED 6th.
LOST 78
TG 154 1952. PCT. .494

BOSTON

LOUIS BOUDREAU

WON	LOST	NAME	POS.	G.	BA	FROM	TO
0	1	Atkins, James Curtis	P	3	.667	Bos50	C
4	3	Benton, John Alton	P	24	.000	Clev50	C
		Bevan, Joseph Harold	3B	1	+.000	A	Phil
		Bolling, Milton Joseph	SS	11	.222	A	
		Boudreau, Louis MGR. (3B1)	SS1	4	.000	B	

WON	LOST	NAME	POS.	G.	BA	FROM	TO
3	1	Brickner, Ralph Harold	P	14	.250	A	C
5	5	Brodowski, Richard Stanley	P	20	.205	A	C
4	9	Delock, Ivan Martin	P	39	.045	A	
		DiMaggio, Dominic Paul	OF123	128	.294	B	
		Dropo, Walter	1B35	37	+.265	B	Det
		Evers, Walter Arthur	OF105	106	+.262	xDet	
1	0	Freeman, Hershell Baskin	P	4	.500	A	
		Gernert, Richard Edward	1B99	102	.243	A	
		Goodman, Wm. Dale (1B23 3B5 OF4)	2B103	138	.306	B	
1	0	Gumpert, Randall Pennington	P	10	+.000	Chi	Wash
		Hatfield, Fred James	3B16	20	+.286	B	Det
5	4	Henry, Wm. Rodman	P13	14	.258	A	
7	9	Hudson, Sidney Chas.	P	21	+.174	xWash	
		Kell, George Clyde	3B73	75	+.319	xDet	
5	6	Kinder, Ellis Raymond	P	23	.000	B	
		Lehner, Paul Eugene	OF2	3	.667	Clev	C
		Lenhardt, Donald Eugene	OF27	30	+.295	Chi	Det
		Lepcio, Thaddeus Stanley (SS1 3B25)	2B57	84	.263	A	
		Lipon, John Joseph (3B7)	SS69	79	+.205	xDet	
1	1	Masterson, Walter Edward	P	5	+.000	B	Wash
		Maxwell, Chas. Richard (OF3)	1B3	8	.067	B	
10	9	McDermott, Maurice Joseph	P30	36	.226	B	
		Niarhos, Constantine Gregory	C25	29	.103	Chi	
5	4	Nixon, Willard Lee	P23	33	.208	B	
		Okrie, Leonard Joseph	C	1	.000	Wash	C
12	12	Parnell, Melvin Lloyd	P33	35	.095	B	
		Pesky, John Michael (SS2)	3B19	25	+.149	B	Det
		Piersall, James Anthony (3B1 OF22)	SS30	56	.267	Bos50	
1	5	Scarborough, Ray Wilson	P	28	+.222	B	N.Y.
0	0	Schmees, George Edward (P2 1B2)	OF29	42	+.203	xStL	C
		Stephens, Glen Eugene	OF13	21	.226	A	
		Stephens, Vernon Decatur (3B29)	SS53	92	.254	B	
1	0	Taylor, James Harry	P	2	.250	B	C
		Throneberry, Maynard Faye	OF86	98	.258	A	C
9	8	Trout, Paul Howard	P	26	+.136	xDet	
		Vollmer, Clyde Frederick	OF70	90	.264	B	
		White, Samuel Chas.	C110	115	.281	B	
2	1	Wight, Wm. Robert	P	10	+.143	B	Det
		Wilber, Delbert Quentin	C39	47	.267	xPhilN	
		Williams, Theodore Samuel	OF2	6	.400	B	
		Wilson, Archie Clifton	OF13	18	+.263	xWash	C
		Wood, Kenneth Lanier	OF13	15	+.100	StL	Wash
		Zarilla, Allen Lee	OF19	21	+.183	xStL	

WON 84 AMERICAN LEAGUE FINISHED 4th.
LOST 69
TG 153 1953. PCT. .549

BOSTON

LOUIS BOUDREAU

WON	LOST	NAME	POS.	G.	BA	FROM	TO
		Baker, Floyd Wilson (2B16)	3B37	81	+.273	xWash	
		Bolling, Milton Joseph	SS	109	.263	B	
11	6	Brown, Hector Harold	P	30	.293	Chi	
		Consolo, Wm. Angelo (2B11)	3B16	47	.215	A	
3	1	Delock, Ivan Martin	P	23	.100	B	
		DiMaggio, Dominic Paul		3	.333	B	C
		Evers, Walter Arthur	OF93	99	.240	B	
1	4	Flowers, Bennett	P	32	.158	Bos51	
1	4	Freeman, Hershell Baskin	P	18	.091	B	
		Gernert, Richard Edward	1B136	139	.253	B	
		Goodman, Wm. Dale (1B20)	2B112	128	.313	B	
2	6	Grissom, Marvin Edward	P	13	.000	Chi	NYN
5	5	Henry, Wm. Rodman	P	21	.188	B	
1	0	Holcombe, Kenneth Edward	P	3	.000	StL	C
6	9	Hudson, Sidney Chas.	P	30	.140	B	
		Kell, George Clyde (OF7)	3B124	134	.307	B	
0	0	Kennedy, Wm. Aulton	P	16	.500	Chi	
10	6	Kinder, Ellis Raymond	P	69	.379	B	
		Lepcio, Thaddeus Stanley (SS20 3B11)	2B34	66	.236	B	
		Lipon, John Joseph	SS58	60	+.214	B	StL
		Merson, John Warren	2B	1	.000	PittN	C
18	10	McDermott, Maurice Joseph	P32	45	.301	B	
		Niarhos, Constantine Gregory	C	16	.200	B	
4	8	Nixon, Willard Lee	P	23	.190	B	
		Olson, Karl Arthur	OF24	25	.123	Bos51	
21	8	Parnell, Melvin Lloyd	P	38	.223	B	
		Piersall, James Anthony	OF	151	.272	B	
		Richter, Allen Gordon	SS	1	.000	Bos51	C
		Stephens, Glen Eugene	OF72	78	.204	B	
1	1	Sullivan, Franklin Leal	P	14	.250	A	
		Umphlett, Thomas Mullen	OF136	137	.283	A	
		Vollmer, Clyde Frederick		1	+.000	B	Wash
0	1	Werle, Wm. George	P	5	.000	StLN	
		White, Samuel Chas.	C131	136	.273	B	
		Wilber, Delbert Quentin (1B2)	C28	58	.241	B	
		Williams, Theodore Samuel	OF26	37	.407	B	
		Zarilla, Allen Lee	OF18	57	.194	B	C

WON 69
LOST 85
TG 154

AMERICAN LEAGUE

1954.

FINISHED 4th.

PCT. .448

BOSTON

LOUIS BOUDREAU

WON	LOST	NAME	POS.	G.	BA	FROM	TO
		Agganis, Harry	1B119	132	.251	A	
		Baker, Floyd Wilson (2B1)	3B7	21	.200	B	PhilN
		Bolling, Milton Joseph (3B5)	SS107	113	.249	B	
10	9	Brewer, Thomas Austin	P33	37	.267	A	
1	8	Brown, Hector Harold	P	40	.125	B	
2	4	Clevenger, Truman Eugene	P23	25	.214	A	
		Consolo, Wm. Angelo (2B12 3B18)	SS50	91	.227	B	
0	0	Dobson, Joseph Gordon	P	2	.000	Chi	C
		Evers, Walter Arthur	OF1	6	.000	B	NYN
		Gernert, Richard Edward	1B6	14	.261	B	
		Goodman, Wm. Dale (1B27 3B12 OF13)	2B72	127	.303	B	
		Hatton, Grady Edgebert (1B1 SS1)	3B93	99	+.281	xChi	
3	7	Henry, Wm. Rodman	P24	25	.118	B	
1	2	Herrin, Thomas Edward	P	14	.125	A	C
3	4	Hudson, Sidney Chas.	P	33	.154	B	C
2	0	Hurd, Thomas Carr	P	16	.333	A	
		Jensen, Jack Eugene	OF151	152	.276	Wash	
		Kell, George Clyde	3B25	26	+.258	B	Chi
5	3	Kemmerer, Russell Paul	P	19	.143	A	
5	8	Kiely, Leo Patrick	P	28	.180	Bos51	
8	8	Kinder, Ellis Raymond	P	48	.185	B	
		Lenhardt, Donald Eugene (3B1)	OF13	44	+.273	xBalt	C
		Lepcio, Thaddeus Stanley (SS14 3B24)	2B80	116	.256	B	
		Maxwell, Chas. Richard	OF27	74	.250	Bos52	
		Mele, Sabath Anthony (OF13)	1B22	42	+.318	xBalt	
		Morton, Guy Jr.		1	.000	A	C
11	12	Nixon, Willard Lee	P	31	.265	B	
		Olson, Karl Arthur	OF78	101	.260	B	
		Owen, Arnold Malcolm	C30	32	.235	ChiN51	C
3	7	Parnell, Melvin Lloyd	P	19	.088	B	
		Piersall, James Anthony	OF126	133	.285	B	
15	12	Sullivan, Franklin Leal	P	36	.103	B	
0	1	Werle, Wm. George	P	14	.000	B	C
		White, Samuel Chas.	C133	137	.282	B	C
		Wilber, Delbert Quentin	C17	24	.131	B	
		Williams, Theodore Samuel	OF115	117	.345	B	

WON 84
LOST 70
TG 154

AMERICAN LEAGUE

1955.

FINISHED 4th.

PCT. .545

BOSTON

MICHAEL FRANKLIN HIGGINS

WON	LOST	NAME	POS.	G.	BA	FROM	TO
		Agganis, Harry	1B20	25	.313	B	C
2	1	Baumann, Frank Matthew	P	7	.231	A	
		Bolling, Milton Joseph	SS2	6	.200	B	
11	10	Brewer, Thomas Austin	P31	33	.151	B	
1	0	Brodowski, Richard Stanley	P	16	.500	Bos52	
1	0	Brown, Hector Harold	P	2	+1.000	B	Balt
		Consolo, Wm. Angelo	2B4	8	.222	B	
		Daley, Peter Harvey	C14	17	.220	A	
9	7	Delock, Ivan Martin	P	29	.143	Bos53	
0	0	Freeman, Hershel Baskin	P	2	.000	Bos53	CinN
		Friend, Owen Lacey (2B1)	SS14	14	.262	Clev53	ChiN

WON	LOST	NAME	POS.	G.	BA	FROM	TO
		Gernert, Richard Edward	1B5	7	.200	B	
		Goodman, Wm. Dale (1B5 OF1)	2B143	149	.294	B	
		Hatton, Grady Edgebert (2B1)	3B111	126	.245	B	
2	4	Henry, Wm. Rodman	P	17	.105	B	
8	6	Hurd, Thomas Carr	P	43	.071	B	
		Jensen, Jack Eugene	OF150	152	.275	B	
		Joost, Edwin David (2B17 3B2)	SS20	55	.193	Phil	C
1	1	Kemmerer, Russell Paul	P	7	.000	B	
3	3	Kiely, Leo Patrick	P	33	.192	B	
5	5	Kinder, Ellis Raymond	P	43	.250	B	
		Klaus, Wm. Joseph (3B8)	SS126	135	.283	MilN53	
		Lepcio, Thaddeus Stanley	3B45	51	.231	B	
		Malzone, Frank James	3B4	6	.350	A	
		Mele, Sabath Anthony	OF7	14	.129	B	CinN
12	10	Nixon, Willard Lee	P	31	.261	B	
		Olson, Karl Arthur	OF21	26	.250	B	
		Pagliarone, James Vincent	C	1	.000	A	
2	3	Parnell, Melvin Lloyd	P13	14	.316	B	
		Piersall, James Anthony	OF147	149	.283	B	
0	0	Smith, Robert Gilchrist	P	1	.000	A	
		Stephens, Glen Eugene	OF75	109	.293	Bos53	
18	13	Sullivan, Franklin Leal	P	35	.112	B	
		Sullivan, Haywood Cooper	C	2	.000	A	
9	7	Susce, George Daniel	P	29	.143	A	
		Throneberry, Maynard Faye	OF34	60	.257	Bos52	
0	0	Trimble, Joseph Gerard	P	2	.000	A	
		White, Samuel Chas.	C	143	.261	B	
		Williams, Theodore Samuel	OF93	98	.356	B	
		Zauchin, Norbert Henry	1B126	130	.239	Bos51	

WON 84 AMERICAN LEAGUE FINISHED 4th.
LOST 70
TG 154 1956. PCT. .545

BOSTON

MICHAEL FRANKLIN HIGGINS

WON	LOST	NAME	POS.	G.	BA	FROM	TO
2	1	Baumann, Frank Matthew	P	7	.333	B	
		Bolling, Milton Joseph (2B1 3B11)	SS26	45	.212	B	
19	9	Brewer, Thomas Austin	P32	38	.298	B	
		Buddin, Donald Thomas	SS113	114	.239	A	
		Consolo, Wm. Angelo	2B25	48	.182	B	
		Daley, Peter Harvey	C57	59	.267	B	
13	7	Delock, Ivan Martin	P	48	.103	B	
0	2	Dorish, Harry	P	15	+.000	xBalt	C
		Gernert, Richard Edward (1B37)	OF50	106	.291	B	
		Goodman, Wm. Dale	2B95	105	.293	B	
		Hatton, Grady Edgebert		5	.400	B	StLN
3	4	Hurd, Thomas Carr	P	40	.500	B	C
		Jensen, Jack Eugene	OF	151	.315	B	
		Keough, Richard Martin		3	.000	A	
2	2	Kiely, Leo Patrick	P	23	.167	B	
		Klaus, Wm. Joseph (SS26)	3B106	135	.271	B	
		Lepcio, Thaddeus Stanley (3B22)	2B57	83	.261	B	
		Malzone, Frank James	3B26	27	.165	B	
		Mauch, Eugene Wm.	2B6	7	.320	StLN52	
1	0	Minarcin, Rudy Anthony	P	3	.500	CinN	
9	8	Nixon, Willard Lee	P	23	.204	B	
7	6	Parnell, Melvin Lloyd	P	21	.152	B	C
		Piersall, James Anthony	OF	155	.293	B	
3	12	Porterfield, Erwin Coolidge	P	25	.326	Wash	
0	0	Schmitz, John Albert	P	2	+.000	Wash	Balt
9	8	Sisler, David Michael	P	39	.119	A	
		Stephens, Glen Eugene	OF71	104	.270	B	
14	7	Sullivan, Franklin Leal	P	34	.141	B	
2	4	Susce, George Daniel	P	21	.222	B	
		Throneberry, Maynard Faye	OF13	24	.220	B	
		Vernon, James Barton	1B108	119	.310	Wash	
		White, Samuel Chas.	C	114	.245	B	
		Williams, Theodore Samuel	OF110	136	.345	B	
		Zauchin, Norbert Henry	1B31	44	.214	B	

WON 82 AMERICAN LEAGUE FINISHED 3rd.
LOST 72
TG 154 1957. PCT. .532

BOSTON

MICHAEL FRANKLIN HIGGINS

WON	LOST	NAME	POS.	G.	BA	FROM	TO
		Aspromonte, Kenneth Joseph	2B	24	.269	A	
1	0	Baumann, Frank Matthew	P	4	.500	B	
		Bolling, Milton Joseph		1	+.000	B	Wash
16	13	Brewer, Thomas Austin	P32	45	.202	B	
0	2	Chakales, Robert Edward	P	18	+.667	xWash	C
		Consolo, Wm. Angelo (2B16 3B2)	SS61	68	.270	B	
		Daley, Peter Harvey	C77	78	.225	B	
9	8	Delock, Ivan Martin	P	49	.048	B	
8	7	Fornieles, Jose Miguel Torre	P25	26	+.136	xBalt	
		Gernert, Richard Edward (OF16)	1B71	99	.237	B	
		Goodman, Wm. Dale		18	+.063	B	Balt
		Jensen, Jack Eugene	OF144	145	.281	B	
0	0	Kemmerer, Russell Paul	P	1	+.000	Bos55	Wash
		Keough, Richard Martin	OF7	9	.059	B	
		Klaus, Wm. Joseph	SS118	127	.252	B	
		Lepcio, Thaddeus Stanley	2B68	79	.241	B	
		Malzone, Frank James	3B	153	.292	B	
		Mauch, Eugene Wm.	2B58	65	.270	B	C
0	0	Meyer, Russell Chas.	P	2	1.000	CinN	
0	0	Minarcin, Rudy Anthony	P	26	.000	B	C
12	13	Nixon, Willard Lee	P29	32	.293	B	
		Piersall, James Anthony	OF	151	.261	B	

WON	LOST	NAME	POS.	G.	BA	FROM	TO
4	4	Porterfield, Erwin Coolidge	P	28	.172	B	
7	8	Sisler, David Michael	P	22	.167	B	
0	0	Spring, Jack Russell	P	1	.000	PhilN55	
		Stephens, Glen Eugene	OF92	120	.266	B	
1	3	Stone, Darrah Dean	P	17	+.000	xWash	
14	11	Sullivan, Franklin Leal	P	31	.165	B	
		Sullivan, Haywood Cooper	C1	2	.000	Bos55	
7	3	Susce, George Daniel	P	29	.120	B	
		Throneberry, Maynard Faye		1	+.000	B	Wash
		Vernon, James Barton	1B70	102	.241	B	
3	0	Wall, Murray Wesley	P	11	.333	BosN50	
		White, Samuel Chas.	C	111	.215	B	
		Williams, Theodore Samuel	OF125	132	.388	B	
		Zauchin, Norbert Henry	1B36	52	.264	B	

WON 79   AMERICAN LEAGUE   FINISHED 3rd.
LOST 75
TG 154   1958.   PCT. .513

BOSTON

MICHAEL FRANKLIN HIGGINS

WON	LOST	NAME	POS.	G.	BA	FROM	TO
		Aspromonte, Kenneth Joseph	2B	6	+.125	B	Wash
2	2	Baumann, Frank Matthew	P	10	.214	B	
		Berberet, Louis Joseph	C49	57	+.210	xWash	
4	2	Bowsfield, Edward Oliver	P16	17	.154	A	
12	12	Brewer, Thomas Austin	P33	42	.195	B	
		Buddin, Donald Thomas	SS	136	.237	Bos56	
1	2	Byerly, Eldred Wm.	P	18	+.000	xWash	
0	0	Casale, Jerry Joseph	P	2	.000	A	
		Consolo, Wm. Angelo (SS11 3B1)	2B13	46	.125	B	
		Daley, Peter Harvey	C	27	.321	B	
14	8	Delock, Ivan Martin	P	31	.063	B	
4	6	Fornieles, Jose Miguel Torres	P	37	.207	B	
		Gernert, Richard Edward	1B114	122	.237	B	
		Jensen, Jack Eugene	OF153	154	.286	B	
		Keough, Richard Martin (1B2)	OF25	68	.220	B	
5	2	Kiely, Leo Patrick	P	47	.000	Bos56	
		Klaus, Wm. Joseph	SS27	61	.159	B	
		Lepcio, Thaddeus Stanley	2B40	50	.199	B	
		Malzone, Frank James	3B	155	.295	B	
3	4	Monbouquette, Wm. Chas.	P	10	.176	A	
1	7	Nixon, Willard Lee	P	10	.294	B	C
		Piersall, James Anthony	OF125	130	.237	B	
0	0	Porterfield, Erwin Coolidge	P	2	.000	B	PittN
		Renna, Wm. Beneditto	OF11	39	.268	KC56	
		Runnels, James Edward (1B42)	2B106	147	.322	Wash	
0	0	Schroll, Albert Bringhurst	P	5	1.000	A	
8	9	Sisler, David Michael	P	30	.196	B	
4	3	Smith, Robert Walkay	P	17	.105	A	
		Stephens, Glen Eugene	OF110	134	.219	B	
13	9	Sullivan, Franklin Leal	P	32	.164	B	
0	0	Susce, George Daniel	P	2	+.000	B	Det
8	9	Wall, Murray Wesley	P	52	.107	B	
		White, Samuel Chas.	C	102	.259	B	
		Williams, Theodore Samuel	OF114	129	.328	B	
0	0	Wilson, Duane Lewis	P	2	.000	A	C

WON 75   AMERICAN LEAGUE   FINISHED 5th.
LOST 79
TG 154   1959.   PCT. .487

BOSTON

MICHAEL FRANKLIN HIGGINS RUDOLPH PRESTON YORK WM. FREDERICK JURGES

WON	LOST	NAME	POS.	G.	BA	FROM	TO
		Avila, Roberto Francisco Gonzalez	2B11	22	+.244	xBalt	MilN
6	4	Baumann, Frank Matthew	P	26	.207	B	
0	1	Bowsfield, Edward Oliver	P	5	.000	B	
10	12	Brewer, Thomas Austin	P36	47	.111	B	
		Buddin, Donald Thomas	SS150	151	.241	B	
		Busby, James Franklin	OF34	61	.225	Balt	
13	8	Casale, Jerry Joseph	P	31	.169	B	
3	0	Chittum, Nelson Boyd	P	21	.200	StLN	
		Consolo, Wm. Angelo	SS2	10	+.214	B	Wash
		Daley, Peter Harvey	C58	65	.225	B	
11	6	Delock, Ivan Martin	P	28	.064	B	
5	3	Fornieles, Jose Miguel Torres	P	46	.158	B	
		Geiger, Gary Merle	OF95	120	.245	Clev	
		Gernert, Richard Edward (OF25)	1B75	117	.262	B	
		Gile, Donald Loren	C	3	.200	A	
		Green, Elijah Jerry (SS1)	2B45	50	.233	A	
2	3	Harshman, John Elvin	P8	9	+.143	xBalt	Clev
0	3	Hoeft, Wm. Frederick	P5	7	+.000	xDet	Balt
		Jensen, Jack Eugene	OF146	148	.277	B	
		Keough, Richard Martin (1B3)	OF69	96	.243	B	
3	3	Kiely, Leo Patrick	P	41	.000	B	
		Lepcio, Thaddeus Stanley	2B1	3	+.333	B	Det
		Mahoney, James Thomas	SS30	31	.130	A	
		Mallett, Gerald Gordon	OF	4	.267	A	C
		Malzone, Frank James	3B	154	.280	B	
0	2	Moford, Herbert	P	4	.000	Det	
7	7	Monbouquette, Wm. Chas.	P34	35	.065	B	
		Plews, Herbert Eugene		13	+.083	xWash	C
		Renna, Wm. Beneditto	OF7	14	.091	B	C
		Runnels, James Edward (1B44 SS9)	2B101	147	.314	B	
1	4	Schroll, Albert Bringhurst	P	14	.111	xPhilN	
0	0	Sisler, David Michael	P	3	+.500	B	Det
		Stephens, Glen Eugene	OF85	92	.278	B	
9	11	Sullivan, Franklin Leal	P	30	.200	B	
		Sullivan, Haywood Cooper	C2	4	.000	Bos57	
2	5	Wall, Murray Wesley	P	26	+.000	B	Wash
						(&return)	C

WON	LOST	NAME	POS.	G.	BA	FROM	TO
		Wertz, Victor Woodrow	1B64	94	.275	Clev	
		White, Samuel Chas.	C	119	.284	B	
		Williams, Theodore Samuel	OF76	103	.254	B	
2	6	Wills, Theodore Carl	P	9	.250	A	
1	1	Wilson, Earl Lawrence	P	9	.500	A	

WON 65 LOST 89 TG 154

AMERICAN LEAGUE 1960. FINISHED 7th. PCT. .422

BOSTON

WM. FREDERICK JURGES MICHAEL FRANKLIN HIGGINS

DELMAR DAVID BAKER

WON	LOST	NAME	POS.	G.	B A	FROM	TO
		Boone, Raymond Otis	1B22	34	.205	xMilN	C
0	4	Borland, Thomas Bruce	P	26	.000	A	
1	2	Bowsfield, Edward Oliver	P	17	+.250	B	Clev
10	15	Brewer, Thomas Austin	P34	45	.194	B	
		Buddin, Donald Thomas	SS	124	.245	B	
		Busby, James Franklin	OF	1	+.000	B	Balt
2	9	Casale, Jerry Joseph	P	29	.273	B	
0	0	Chittum, Nelson Boyd	P	6	.000	B	C
		Clinton, Lucîean Louis	OF89	96	.228	A	
		Coughtry, James Marlan (3B1)	2B13	15	.158	A	
9	10	Delock, Ivan Martin	P	24	.116	B	
0	1	Earley, Arnold Carl	P	2	.000	A	
10	5	Fornieles, Jose Miguel Torres	P	70	.400	B	
		Geirger, Gary Merle	OF66	77	.302	B	
		Gile, Donald Loren (1B11)	C15	29	.176	B	
		Green, Elijah Jerry (SS41)	2B69	133	.242	B	
		Hardy, Carroll Wm.	OF59	73	+.234	xClev	
0	3	Hillman, Darius Dutton	P	16	.000	ChiN	
		Jackson, Ronald Allen	1B9	10	.226	Chi	C
		Keough, Richard Martin	OF29	38	+.248	B	Clev
		Malzone, Frank James	3B151	152	.271	B	
14	11	Monbouquette, Wm. Chas.	P35	38	.092	B	
6	4	Muffett, Billy Arnold	P	23	.268	SFN	
0	2	Nichols, Chester Raymond Jr.	P	6	.000	MilN56	
		Nixon, Russell Eugene	C74	80	+.298	xClev	
		Pagliarone, James Vincent	C18	28	.306	Bos55	
		Repulski, Eldon John	OF33	73	.243	xLAN	
		Runnels, James Edward (1B57 3B3)	2B129	143	.320	B	
		Sadowski, Edward Roman	C36	38	.215	A	
0	0	Stallard, Evan Tracy	P	4	.000	A	
		Stephens, Glen Eugene	OF31	35	+.229	B	Balt
3	3	Sturdivant, Thomas Virgil	P	40	.182	K.C.	
6	16	Sullivan, Franklin Leal	P	40	.125	B	
		Sullivan, Haywood Cooper	C50	52	.161	B	
		Tasby, Willie	OF102	105	+.281	xBalt	
		Thomson, Robert Brown (1B1)	OF27	40	+.263	ChiN	Balt
		Webster, Raymond George	2B1	7	.000	Clev	C
		Wertz, Victor Woodrow	1B117	131	.282	B	

WON	LOST	NAME	POS.	G.	BA	FROM	TO
		Williams, Theodore Samuel	OF87	113	.316	B	C
1	1	Wills, Theodore Carl	P15	16	.250	B	
3	2	Wilson, Earl Lawrence	P13	15	.174	B	
0	1	Worthington, Allan Fulton	P	6	+.000	SFN	Chi

WON 76 LOST 86 TG 162

AMERICAN LEAGUE 1961. FINISHED 6th. PCT. .469

BOSTON

MICHAEL FRANKLIN HIGGINS

WON	LOST	NAME	POS.	G.	BA	FROM	TO
0	0	Borland, Thomas Bruce	P	1	.000	B	C
3	2	Brewer, Thomas Austin	P10	18	.286	B	C
		Buddin, Donald Thomas	SS109	115	.263	B	
2	4	Cisco,Galen Bernard	P17	18	.100	A	
		Clinton, Lucîean Louis	OF13	17	.255	B	
11	14	Conley, Donald Eugene	P	33	.219	PhilN	
6	9	Delock, Ivan Martin	P	28	.104	B	
2	4	Earley, Arnold Carl	P	33	.000	B	
9	8	Fornieles, Jose Miguel Torres	P	57	.156	B	
		Geiger, Gary Merle	OF137	140	.232	B	
		Gile, Donald Loren (C1)	1B6	8	.278	B	
		Ginsberg, Myron Nathan	C6	19	+.250	xChi	
		Green, Elijah Jerry (2B7)	SS57	88	.260	B	
		Hardy, Carroll Wm.	OF76	85	.263	B	
		Harrell, Wm. (1B3 SS7)	3B10	37	.162	Clev58	C
3	2	Hillman, Darius Dutton	P	28	.000	B	
		Jensen, Jack Eugene	OF131	137	.263	Bos59	
		Malzone, Frank James	3B149	151	.266	B	
14	14	Monbouquette, Wm. Chas.	P32	33	.130	B	
3	11	Muffett, Billy Arnold	P	38	.217	B	
3	2	Nichols, Chester Raymond Jr.	P	26	.111	B	
		Nixon, Russell Eugene	C66	87	.289	B	
		Pagliarone, James Vincent	C108	120	.242	B	
		Repulski, Eldon John	OF4	15	.280	B	C
		Runnels, James Edward (2B7 SS1 3B11)	1B113	143	.317	B	
		Schilling, Chas. Thomas	2B	158	.259	A	
15	7	Schwall, Donald Bernard	P25	27	.180	A	
2	7	Stallard, Evan Tracy	P	43	.083	B	
		Wertz, Victor Woodrow	1B86	99	+.262	B	Det
3	2	Wills, Theodore Carl	P	17	.000	B	
0	0	Wood, Wilbur Forrester	P	6	.000	A	
		Yastrzemski, Carl Michael	OF147	148	.266	A	

WON 76 LOST 84 TG 160

AMERICAN LEAGUE 1962. FINISHED 8th. PCT. .475

BOSTON

MICHAEL FRANKLIN HIGGINS

WON	LOST	NAME	POS.	G.	BA	FROM	TO
		Bressoud, Edward Francis	SS	153	.277	SFN	
4	7	Cisco, Galen Bernard	P	23	.080	B	NYN
		Clinton, Luciean Louis	OF103	114	.294	B	
15	14	Conley, Donald Eugene	P	34	.207	B	
4	5	Delock, Ivan Martin	P	17	.087	B	
4	5	Earley, Arnold Carl	P	38	.200	B	
3	6	Fornieles, Jose Miguel Torres	P	42	.188	B	
		Gardner, Wm. Frederick (SS4 3B7)	2B38	53	+.271	xN.Y.	
		Geiger, Gary Merle	OF129	131	.249	B	
		Gile, Donald Loren	1B14	18	.049	B	C
		Green, Elijah Jerry (SS5)	2B18	56	.231	B	
		Hardy, Carroll Wm.	OF105	115	.215	B	
0	2	Kolstad, Harold Everette	P	27	.056	A	
0	1	MacLeod, Wm. Daniel	P	2	.000	A	C
		Malzone, Frank James	3B	156	.283	B	
15	13	Monbouquette, Wm. Chas.	P	35	.096	B	
0	0	Muffett, Billy Arnold	P	1	.000	B	C
1	1	Nichols, Chester Raymond Jr.	P	29	.000	B	
0	0	Nippert, Merlin Lee	P	4	.000	A	C
		Nixon, Russell Eugene	C38	65	.278	B	
		Pagliarone, James Vincent	C73	90	.258	B	
		Philley, David Earl	OF4	38	.143	Balt	C
9	6	Radatz, Richard Raymond	P	62	.097	A	
		Runnels, James Edward	1B151	152	.326	B	
		Schilling, Chas. Thomas	2B118	119	.230	B	
9	15	Schwall, Donald Bernard	P33	34	.136	B	
0	1	Smith, Peter Luke	P	1	.000	A	
0	0	Stallard, Evan Tracy	P	1	.000	B	
		Tillman, John Robert	C66	81	.229	A	
0	0	Wills, Theodore Carl	P	1	.000	B	CinN
12	8	Wilson, Earl Lawrence	P31	35	.174	Bos60	
0	0	Wood, Wilbur Forrester	P	1	.000	B	
		Yastrzemski, Carl Michael	OF	160	.296	B	

WON 76 — AMERICAN LEAGUE — FINISHED 7th.
LOST 85
TG 161 — 1963. — PCT. .472

BOSTON

JOHN MICHAEL PESKY

WON	LOST	NAME	POS.	G.	BA	FROM	TO
		Bressoud, Edward Francis	SS137	140	.260	B	
		Clinton, Luciean Louis	OF146	148	.232	B	
3	4	Conley, Donald Eugene	P	9	.200	B	C
1	2	Delock, Ivan Martin	P	6	+.000	B	Balt
3	7	Earley, Arnold Carl	P	53	.278	B	
0	0	Fornieles, Jose Miguel Torres	P	9	+.333	B	Minn
		Gardner, Wm. Frederick (3B2)	2B21	36	.190	B	C
		Geiger, Gary Merle (1B6)	OF95	121	.263	B	
		Gosger, James Chas.	OF4	19	.063	A	
4	9	Heffner, Robert Frederick	P20	21	.116	A	
0	2	Kolstad, Harold Everette	P	7	.000	B	C
7	4	LaMabe, John Alexander	P	65	.094	A	
		Malzone, Frank James	3B148	151	.291	B	B
		Mantilla, Felix Lamela (2B5 OF11)	SS27	66	.315	NYN	
		Mejias, Roman Gomez	OF86	111	.227	HousN	
20	10	Monbouquette, Wm. Chas.	P	37	.114	B	
10	13	Morehead, David Michael	P	29	.105	A	
1	3	Nichols, Chester Raymond Jr.	P	21	.231	B	
		Nixon, Russell Eugene	C76	93	.268	B	
		Petrocelli, Americo	SS	1	.250	A	
15	6	Radatz, Richard Raymond	P	66	.069	B	
		Schilling, Chas. Thomas	2B143	146	.234	B	
0	0	Smith, Peter Luke	P	6	.000	B	C
0	0	Stephenson, Gerald Joseph	P	1	.000	A	
		Stuart, Richard Lee	1B155	157	.261	PittN	
		Tillman, John Robert	C95	96	.225	B	
1	4	Turley, Robert Lee	P	11	+.214	xL.A.	C
		Williams, Richard Hirshfeld (1B11 OF7)	3B17	79	.257	Balt	
11	16	Wilson, Earl Lawrence	P37	38	.208	B	
0	5	Wood, Wilbur Forrester	P	25	.000	B	
		Yastrzemski, Carl Michael	OF	151	.321	B	

WON 72 — AMERICAN LEAGUE — FINISHED 8th.
LOST 90
TG 162 — 1964. — PCT. .444

BOSTON

JOHN MICHAEL PESKY

WON	LOST	NAME	POS.	G.	BA	FROM	TO
		Bressoud, Edward Francis	SS	158	.293	B	
0	2	Charton, Frank Lane	P	25	.100	A	C
		Clinton, Luciean Louis	OF35	37	+.258	B	L.A.
		Conigliaro, Anthony Richard	OF106	111	.290	A	
4	11	Connolly, Edward Joseph	P	27	.167	A	
1	1	Earley, Arnold Carl	P	25	.111	B	
		Geiger, Gary Merle	OF4	5	.385	B	
0	0	Gray, David Alexander	P	9	1.000	A	C
		Guindon, Robert John (OF1)	1B1	5	.125	A	C
7	9	Heffner, Robert Frederick	P	55	.159	B	
		Horton, Anthony Darrin (1B8)	OF24	36	.222	A	
		Jones, James Dalton (SS1 3B1)	2B85	118	.230	A	
9	13	LaMabe, John Alexander	P	39	.115	B	
		Malzone, Frank James	3B143	148	.264	B	
		Mantilla, Felix Lamela (2B45 SS6 3B7)	OF48	133	.289	B	
		Mejias, Roman Gomez	OF37	62	.238	B	C
13	14	Monbouquette, Wm. Chas.	P36	39	.083	B	

WON	LOST	NAME	POS.	G.	BA	FROM	TO
8	15	Morehead, David Michael	P	32	.093	B	
		Nixon, Russell Eugene	C45	81	.233	B	
16	9	Radatz, Richard Raymond	P	79	.162	B	
1	1	Ritchie, Jay Seay	P	21	.111	A	
		Ryan, Michael James	C	1	.333	A	
		Schilling, Chas.Thomas	2B42	47	.196	B	
		Smith, Alphonse Eugene (OF8)	3B10	29	+.216	xClev	C
2	3	Spanswick, Wm. Henry	P	29	.286	A	C
		Stuart, Richard Lee	1B155	156	.279	B	
		Thomas James Leroy (1B1)	OF107	107	+.257	xL.A.	
		Tillman, John Robert	C	131	.278	B	
		Williams, Richard Hirshfeld (3B13 OF5)	1B21	61	.159	B	C
11	12	Wilson, Earl Lawrence	P33	54	.205	B	
0	0	Wood, Wilbur Forrester	P	4	.000	B	PittN
		Yastrzemski, Carl Michael (3B2)	OF148	151	.289	B	

WON 61 | AMERICAN LEAGUE | FINISHED 7th.
LOST 78
TG 139 | 1900. | PCT. .439

BUFFALO

DANIEL W. SHANNON

WON	LOST	NAME	POS.	G.	BA	FROM	TO
22	22	Amole, Morris George (Doc)	P	47	.179	WashN98	C
		Andrews, Jay A.	3B117	122	.250	A	C
		Atherton, Chas. Morgan Herbert	2B46	49	.336	WashN	C
2	5	Baker, Chas.	P	13	+.375	A	Clev
		Bierbauer, Louis W. (SS1 3B6)	2B33	40	+.295	xMil	C
		Broderick, Matthew L.	SS	45	.233	A	
		Burke, Edward D.	OF	7	+.103	xMinn	C
		Carey, George C.	1B116	135	.270	LvlleN98	
2	1	Carsey, Wilfred (Kid) (P4)	SS5	11	+.188	NYN	K.C.
0	2	Clarke, Wm. H. (Dad)	P	3	.143	LvlleN98	C
		Crooks, John Chas. (Jack)	2B	8	.100	StLN98	C
0	3	Fertsch, Edward P.	P	4	.100	A	C
		Flood, Timothy A.	2B	12	+.283	StLN	Clev
7	6	Foreman, Francis Isaiah	P15	18	.340	CinN96	
		Garry, James Thomas	OF	19	+.182	xMil	C
		Gettman, Jacob John	OF	121	.298	WashN	C
0	1	Gray, George Edward (Chummy)	P	1	+.000	PittN	K.C.
		Halligan, Wm. E. (Jocko)	OF126	127	.268	BaltN92	C
		Hallman, Wm. White (Billy) (2B20)	SS80	100	.279	BknN98	
		Hart, Warren F.	OF31	34	.234	A	
8	5	Hastings, Chas. Morton	P	15	+.184	xMinn	C
4	13	Hooker, Wm. E.	P	17	.177	A	
0	1	Jimeson, Jacob J.	P	1	.250	A	C
3	1	Kern, Archibald	P	8	+.154	A	Clev
12	14	Kerwin, John J.	P27	35	.277	A	C
		Knoll, Julius M. (Hub)	OF	14	.321	A	C
		Martin, Frank	2B	2	+.000	NYN	Clev
1	4	Milligan, Wm. J.	P	7	+.467	A	Inpls
		Schreckengost, Ossee Freeman (Ossie) (1B24)	C95	125	.282	StLN	
		Shearon, John M.	OF	80	+.274	ClevN96	Chi
		Smith, Judson Grant (Jud)	3B	14	.176	WashN98	
		Speer, George	C	57	.234	A	C

CLUB RECORD

AMERICAL LEAGUE

CHICAGO

YEAR	TG	WON	LOST	PCT.	FINISHED	MANAGER
1901	136	83	53	.610	1	Clarke Calvin Griffith
1902	134	74	60	.552	4	Clarke Calvin Griffith
1903	137	60	77	.438	7	James Joseph Callahan
1904	154	89	65	.578	3	James Joseph Callahan
						Fielder Allison Jones
1905	152	92	60	.605	2	Fielder Allison Jones
1906	151	93	58	.616	1	Fielder Allison Jones
1907	151	87	64	.576	3	Fielder Allison Jones
1908	154	88	64	.579	3	Fielder Allison Jones
1909	152	78	74	.513	4	Wm. Joseph Sullivan
1910	153	68	85	.444	6	Hugh Duffy
1911	151	77	74	.509	4	Hugh Duffy
1912	154	78	76	.506	4	James Joseph Callahan
1913	152	78	74	.513	5	James Joseph Callahan
1914	154	70	84	.455	6	James Joseph Callahan
1915	154	93	61	.604	3	Clarence Henry Rowland
1916	154	89	65	.578	2	Clarence Henry Rowland
1917	154	100	54	.649	1	Clarence Henry Rowland
1918	124	57	67	.460	6	Clarence Henry Rowland
1919	140	88	52	.629	1	Wm. J. Gleason
1920	154	96	58	.623	2	Wm. J. Gleason
1921	154	62	92	.403	7	Wm. J. Gleason
1922	154	77	77	.500	5	Wm. J. Gleason
1923	154	69	85	.448	7	Wm. J. Gleason
1924	153	66	87	.431	8(Last)	John Joseph Evers
1925	154	79	75	.513	5	Edward Trowbridge Collins
1926	153	81	72	.529	5	Edward Trowbridge Collins
1927	153	70	83	.458	5	Raymond Wm. Schalk
1928	154	72	82	.468	5	Raymond Wm. Schalk
						Russell Aubrey Blackburne
1929	152	59	93	.388	7	Russell Aubrey Blackburne
1930	153	62	92	.403	7	Owen Joseph Bush
1931	153	56	97	.366	8(Last)	Owen Joseph Bush
1932	151	49	102	.325	7	Lewis Albert Fonseca
1933	150	67	83	.447	6	Lewis Albert Fonseca
1934	152	53	99	.349	8(Last)	Lewis Albert Fonseca
						James Joseph Dykes
1935	152	74	78	.487	5	James Joseph Dykes
1936	151	81	70	.536	3	James Joseph Dykes
1937	154	86	68	.558	3	James Joseph Dykes
1938	148	65	83	.439	6	James Joseph Dykes
1939	154	85	69	.552	4	James Joseph Dykes
1940	154	82	72	.532	x4(Bos)	James Joseph Dykes
1941	154	77	77	.500	3	James Joseph Dykes
1942	148	66	82	.446	6	James Joseph Dykes
1943	154	82	72	.532	4	James Joseph Dykes
1944	154	71	83	.461	7	James Joseph Dykes
1945	149	71	78	.477	6	James Joseph Dykes
1946	154	74	80	.481	5	James Joseph Dykes
						Theodore Amar Lyons
1947	154	70	84	.455	6	Theodore Amar Lyons
1948	152	51	101	.336	8(Last)	Theodore Amar Lyons
1949	154	63	91	.409	6	John James Onslow
1950	154	60	94	.390	6	John James Onslow
						John Michael Corriden, Sr.
1951	154	81	73	.526	4	Paul Rapier Richards
1952	154	81	73	.526	3	Paul Rapier Richards
1953	154	89	65	.578	3	Paul Rapier Richards
1954	154	94	60	.610	3	Paul Rapier Richards
						Martin Whitford Marion
1955	154	91	63	.591	3	Martin Whitford Marion
1956	154	85	69	.552	3	Martin Whitford Marion
1957	154	90	64	.584	2	Alfonso Ramon Lopez
1958	154	82	72	.532	2	Alfonso Ramon Lopez
1959	154	94	60	.610	1	Alfonso Ramon Lopez
1960	154	87	67	.565	3	Alfonso Ramon Lopez
1961	162	86	76	.531	4	Alfonso Ramon Lopez
1962	162	85	77	.525	5	Alfonso Ramon Lopez
1963	162	94	68	.580	2	Alfonso Ramon Lopez
1964	162	98	64	.605	2	Alfonso Ramon Lopez

YEAR	TG	WON	LOST	TIED	PCT.	FINISHED	MANAGER
1965	162	95	67	0	.586	2	ALFONSO RAMON LOPEZ
1966	163	83	79	1	.512	4	EDWARD RAYMOND STANKY
1967	162	89	73	0	.549	4	EDWARD RAYMOND STANKY
1968	162	67	95	0	.414	X8 (CAL)	EDWARD RAYMOND STANKY
							JOHN LESTER MOSS *
							ALFONSO RAMON LOPEZ
1969	162	68	94	0	.420	5W	ALFONSO RAMON LOPEZ
							DONALD JOSEPH GUTTERIDGE
1970	162	56	106	0	.346	6W (LAST)	DONALD JOSEPH GUTTERIDGE
							MARION DANNE ADAIR *
							CHARLES WILLIAM TANNER
1971	162	79	83	0	.488	3W	CHARLES WILLIAM TANNER
1972	154	87	67	0	.565	2W	CHARLES WILLIAM TANNER

WON 82 | LOST 53 | TG 135

AMERICAN LEAGUE

1900.

FINISHED 1st. PCT. .608

CHICAGO

CHAS. ALBERT COMISKEY

WON	LOST	NAME	POS.	G.	BA	FROM	TO
		Brain, David Leonard (2B1)	3B7	8	.240	A	
		Brodie, Walter Scott	OF	64	.262	BaltN	
		Buckley, Richard D. (Dick)	C34	40	.201	PhilN95	C
		Burke, Edward D.		1	+.000	CinN97	Minn
		Clayton, G. E.	1B	2	.333	A	C
20	10	Denzer, Roger	P	36	.212	ChiN97	
		Dillard, Robert Lee	OF16	28	.193	xStLN	C
0	4	Doheny, Edward R.	P5	6	.214	xNYN	NYN (returned)
		Dowd, Thomas Jefferson	1B26	36	+.235	ClevN	Mil
19	9	Fisher, Chauncey Burr	P35	38	.225	BknN97	
		Hartman, Frederick Orrin	3B	116	.275	NYN	
		Hoy, Wm. Ellsworth (Dummy)	OF	137	.254	LvlleN	
5	2	Isbell, Wm. Frank (P7 3B15 OF18)	1B54	109	.249	ChiN98	
16	14	Katoll, John	P37	33	.155	ChiN	
0	1	Killen, Frank Bissell	P	1	.000	xChiN	C
		Lally, Daniel J. (OF4)	1B7	10	+.238	StLN97	Minn
		McFarland, Hermus W.	OF	120	.241	CinN98	
3	2	McGill, Wm. Vaness (Billy)	P	6	.200	PhilN96	C
		McManus, Francis E.	OF4	7	+.143	WashN	K.C.
		O'Leary, Chas. Timothy	SS	26	.163	A	
		Padden, Richard J.	2B	130	.284	WashN	
17	8	Pátterson, Roy Lewis	P29	33	.191	A	
1	1	Seymour, John Bentley (Cy)	P	2	.000	xNYN	NYN (returned)
		Shearon, John M.	OF	34	+.285	xBuff	C
		Shugart, Wm. Frank	SS	98	.283	PhilN97	
		Sugden, Joseph (1B43)	C74	121	.289	ClevN	
1	2	Thomas, Thomas W.	P	3	+.200	xK.C.	C
		Wood, Robert Lynn	C28	35	.307	xCinN	

WON 83 | LOST 53 | TG 136

AMERICAN LEAGUE

1901.

FINISHED 1st. PCT. .610

CHICAGO

CLARK CALVIN GRIFFITH

WON	LOST	NAME	POS.	G.	BA	FROM	TO
		Brain , David Leonard	2B	5	.350	B	
		Burke, James Timothy	3B	41	+.248	xMil	PittN
15	7	Callahan, James Joseph	P27	45	.344	ChiN	
0	0	Dupee, Frank Oliver	P	1	.000	A	C
		Foster, Clarence Francis (Pop)	OF8	11	+.281	xWash	C
24	8	Griffith Clark Calvin MGR.	P	35	.300	ChiN	
		Hartman, Frederick Orrin	3B	120	.313	B	
2	1	Harvey, Erwin K. (P3)	OF14	17	+.256	ChiN	Clev
		Hoy, Wm. Ellsworth (Dummy)	OF	130	.293	B	
		Isbell, Wm. Frank	1B	137	.261	B	
		Jones, Fielder Allison	OF	133	.325	BknN	
13	12	Katoll, John	P	27	.125	B	
		Mertes, Samuel Blair(Sandow)	2B132	137	.280	ChiN	
0	0	McAleese, John James	P	1	.000	A	
		McFarland, Hermus W.	OF	132	.265	B	
20	16	Patterson, Roy Lewis	P	40	.220	B	
3	5	Piatt, Wiley Harlan	P	8	+.118	xPhil	
		Shugart, Wm. Frank	SS	107	.251	B	C
6	4	Skopec, John(Lefty)	P	10	.345	A	
		Sugden, Joseph	C43	48	.283	B	
		Sullivan, Wm. Joseph (Billy)	C	98	.245	BosN	

WON 74 | LOST 60 | TG 134

AMERICAN LEAGUE

1902.

FINISHED 4th. PCT. .552

CHICAGO

CLARK CALVIN GRIFFITH

WON	LOST	NAME	POS.	G.	BA	FROM	TO
16	14	Callahan, James Joseph (SS1 OF22)	P34	68	.239	B	
		Daly, Thomas Peter	2B	137	.231	BknN	
		Davis, George Stacey (1B3)	SS130	132	.298	NYN	
1	1	Durham, James Garfield (OF3)	P3	5	.066	A	C
9	10	Garvin, Virgil Lee	P	23	.133	Mil	BknN
		Green, Edward (Danny)	OF120	129	.318	ChiN	
15	9	Griffith, Clark Calvin MGR. (OF3)	P28	34	.220	B	
		Hughes, Edward	C	1	.250	A	C
1	0	Isbell, Wm. Frank (P1 C1 SS4)	1B133	137	.256	B	
		Jones, Fielder Allison	OF	135	.318	B	
0	0	Katoll, John	P	1	+.000	B	Balt
0	0	Leitner, George Michael	P	1	+.000	xClev	C
0	0	Mertes, Samuel Blair (Sandow) (P1 C2 1B2 2B1 SS5 3B1)	OF123	129	.283	B	
		McFarland, Edward Wm. (1B1 OF7)	C69	71	.231	PhilN	
		McFarland, Hermus W.	OF	7	+.185	B	Balt
0	0	McMackin, Samuel	P	1	+.000	A	Det
20	13	Patterson, Roy Lewis	P	34	.190	B	
12	13	Piatt, Wiley Harlan	P	31	.205	B	
		Strang, Samuel Nicklin	3B	137	.273	NYN	ChiN
		Sullivan, Wm. Joseph (Billy) (1B2 OF2)	C73	78	.151	B	

WON 60 LOST 77 TG 137

AMERICAN LEAGUE 1903. FINISHED 7th. PCT. .438

CHICAGO

JAMES JOSEPH CALLAHAN

WON	LOST	NAME	POS.	G.	BA	FROM	TO
4	2	Altrock, Nicholas (Nick)	P	11	+.300	xBos	
1	2	Callahan, James Joseph MGR. (P3)	3B101	118	.290	B	
		Clark, Harry	3B	15	.308	Mil00	C
		Daly, Thomas Peter	2B	45	.201	B	CinN
		Dolan, Patrick Henry (Cozy)	1B19	28	.250	BknN	CinN
5	5	Dunkle, Edward Perks	P	11	+.306	WashN99	Wash
11	25	Flaherty, Patrick Joseph	P	39	.141	PittN00	
		Green, Edward (Danny)	OF	136	.313	B	
		Hallman, Wm. Harry	OF58	64	.213	Mil01	
		Holmes, James Wm. (Ducky)	OF	86	+.279	xWash.	
		Isbell, Wm. Frank (3B18)	1B120	138	.259	B	
		Jones, Fielder Allison	OF	137	.304	B	
		Magoon, George Henry	2B	94	.227	xCinN	C
		McFarland, Edward Wm.	C57	61	.210	B	
8	11	Owen, Frank Malcolm	P	26	.121	Det01	
14	16	Patterson, Roy Lewis	P	34	.105	B	
		Slattery, John Thomas (1B1)	C57	61	+.231	xClev	
		Sullivan, Wm. Joseph (Billy)	C31	32	.188	B	
		Tannehill, Lee Ford	SS	136	.220	A	
17	16	White, Guy Harris (Doc)	P	38	.200	PhilN	

WON 89 LOST 65 TG 154

AMERICAN LEAGUE 1904. FINISHED 3rd. PCT. .578

CHICAGO

JAMES JOSEPH CALLAHAN FIELDER ALLISON JONES

WON	LOST	NAME	POS.	G.	BA	FROM	TO
21	13	Altrock, Nicholas (Nick)	P	38	.207	B	
		Berry, Claude Elzy	C	3	.000	A	
		Callahan, James Joseph MGR. (2B28)	OF103	132	.263	B	
		Davis, George Stacey	SS	152	.256	NYN	
		Donahue, John Augustus (Jiggs)	1B	102	.251	StL02	
0	0	Dougherty, Thomas James	P	1	.000	A	C
		Dundon, Augustus J.	2B105	108	.234	A	
3	2	Flaherty, Patrick Joseph	P	5	.308	B	PittN
		Green, Edward (Danny)	OF146	148	.266	B	
		Heydon, Michael Edward	C	5	.100	StLN01	
		Holmes, James Wm. (Ducky)	OF62	67	.308	B	
		Huelsman, Frank Elmer	OF	3	+.167	StLN97	Det
				1	+.000	xDet	StL
		Isbell, Wm. Frank (2B27)	1B64	94	.208	B	
		Jones, Chas. C.	OF	5	.235	Bos01	
		Jones, Fielder Allison MGR.	OF	150	.245	B	
		McFarland, Edward Wm.	C49	50	.263	B	
21	15	Owen, Frank Malcolm	P	37	.215	B	
7	9	Patterson, Roy Lewis	P	22	.103	B	
16	10	Smith, Frank Elmer	P	26	.256	A	
0	1	Stricklett, Elmer Griffin	P	1	.000	A	
		Sullivan, Wm. Joseph (Billy)	C107	108	.235	B	
		Tannehill, Lee Ford	3B	153	.226	B	
5	5	Walsh, Edward Augustin	P	18	.214	A	
16	10	White, Guy Harris (Doc)	P	30	.139	B	

WON 92 LOST 60 TG 152

AMERICAN LEAGUE 1905. FINISHED 2nd. PCT. .605

CHICAGO

FIELDER ALLISON JONES

WON	LOST	NAME	POS.	G.	BA	FROM	TO
21	10	Altrock, Nicholas (Nick)	P40	41	.123	B	
		Callahan, James Joseph	OF93	96	.272	B	
		Davis, George Stacey	SS	151	.278	B	
		Donahue, John Augustus (Jiggs)	1B	149	.287	B	
		Dundon, Augustus J.	2B104	106	.192	B	
		Green, Edward (Danny)	OF107	112	.243	B	C
		Hart, James Henry	C	11	.125	A	
		Holmes, James Wm. (Ducky)	OF89	92	.201	B	C
		Isbell, Wm. Frank (OF40)	2B42	94	.296	B	
		Jones, Fielder Allison MGR.	OF	153	.245	B	
		McFarland, Edward Wm.	C70	80	.280	B	
22	14	Owen, Frank Malcolm	P	42	.145	B	
4	5	Patterson, Roy Lewis	P	13	.207	B	
		Rohe, George Anthony (2B16)	3B17	34	.212	Balt01	
19	12	Smith, Frank Elmer	P	39	.226	B	
		Sullivan, Wm. Joseph (Billy)	C94	98	.201	B	
		Tannehill, Lee Ford	3B	142	.200	B	
8	5	Walsh, Edward Augustin	P22	29	.155	B	
18	14	White, Guy Harris (Doc)	P	34	.163	B	

WON 93 LOST 58 TG 151

AMERICAN LEAGUE 1906. FINISHED 1st. PCT. .616

CHICAGO

FIELDER ALLISON JONES

WON	LOST	NAME	POS.	G.	BA	FROM	TO
20	13	Altrock, Nicholas (Nick)	P	38	.160	B	
		Davis, George Stacey	SS129	133	.277	B	
		Donahue, John Augustus (Jiggs)	1B	154	.257	B	
		Dougherty, Patrick Henry	OF	75	+.238	xN.Y.	
		Dundon, Augustus J.	2B18	33	.135	B	C
1	1	Fiene, Louis Henry	P	6	.200	A	

WON	LOST	NAME	POS.	G.	BA	FROM	TO
		Hahn, Edgar Wm.	OF	130	+.227	xN.Y.	
		Hart, James Henry	C15	17	.162	B	
		Hemphill, Frank Vernon	OF	13	.075	A	
		Isbell, Wm. Frank	2B132	143	.279	B	
		Jones, Fielder Allison MGR.	OF	144	.230	B	
		McFarland, Edward Wm.	C	12	.181	B	
		O'Neill, Wm. John	OF93	94	.248	Wash04	C
22	13	Owen, Frank Malcolm	P	42	.136	B	
10	7	Patterson, Roy Lewis	P	22	.061	B	
		Quillin, Lee	SS	3	.111	A	
		Rohe, George Anthony	3B57	74	.258	B	
		Roth, Frank Charles	C15	16	.196	StL	
5	5	Smith, Frank Elmer	P	20	.293	B	
		Sullivan, Wm. Joseph (Billy)	C	118	.214	B	
		Tannehill, Lee Ford (SS20)	3B92	112	.175	B	
		Towne, Jay King	C	13	.290	A	C
		Vinson, Ernest Augustus	OF	10	.250	Clev	C
17	13	Walsh, Edward Augustin	P41	42	.141	B	
18	6	White, Guy Harris (Doc)	P	28	.185	B	

WON 87 — AMERICAN LEAGUE — FINISHED 3rd.
LOST 64
TG 151 — 1907. — PCT. .576

CHICAGO

FIELDER ALLISON JONES

WON	LOST	NAME	POS.	G.	BA	FROM	TO
8	12	Altrock, Nicholas (Nick)	P	30	.181	B	
		Armbruster, Chas. A.	C	1	+.000	xBos	C
		Atz, Jacob Henry	3B	4	.125	Wash02	
		Davis, George Stacey	SS	132	.238	B	
		Donahue, John Augustus (Jiggs)	1B	157	.259	B	
		Dougherty, Patrick Henry	OF	148	.270	B	
0	1	Fiene, Louis Henry	P	4	.200	B	
		Hahn, Edgar Wm.	OF	156	.255	B	
		Hart, James Henry	C25	29	.271	B	C
		Hickman, Chas. Taylor	2B3	21	+.226	xWash	
0	0	Isbell, Wm. Frank (Pl)	2B119	125	.243	B	
		Jones, Fielder Allison MGR.	OF	154	.261	B	
		McFarland, Edward Wm.	C43	52	.283	B	
2	3	Owen, Frank Malcolm	P	11	.250	B	
4	6	Patterson, Roy Lewis	P	19	.097	B	C
		Quillin, Lee	3B48	49	.192	B	C
		Rohe, George Anthony (2B39 SS29)	3B73	144	.213	B	C
22	11	Smith, Frank Elmer	P41	42	.196	B	
		Sullivan, Wm. Joseph (Billy)	C109	112	.179	B	
		Tannehill, Lee Ford	3B31	33	.241	B	
24	18	Walsh, Edward Augustin	P56	57	.162	B	
		Welday, Lyndon Earl	OF15	24	.229	A	
27	13	White, Guy Harris (Doc)	P47	48	.222	B	

WON 88 — AMERICAN LEAGUE — FINISHED 3rd.
LOST 64
TG 152 — 1908. — PCT. .579

CHICAGO

FIELDER ALLISON JONES

WON	LOST	NAME	POS.	G.	BA	FROM	TO
3	7	Altrock, Nicholas (Nick)	P	23	.204	B	
		Anderson, John Joseph	OF90	123	.262	Wash	C
		Atz, Jacob Henry	2B46	83	.194	B	
		Davis, George Stacey (SS23)	2B95	128	.217	B	
		Donahue, John Augustus (Jiggs)	1B83	93	.204	B	
		Dougherty, Patrick Henry	OF128	138	.278	B	
0	1	Fiene, Louis Henry	P	1	.000	B	
		Hahn, Edgar Wm.	OF119	122	.251	B	
0	0	Isbell, Wm. Frank (Pl 2B18)	1B65	84	.247	B	
		Jones, Fielder Allison MGR.	OF	149	.253	B	
2	4	Manuel, Moxie	P	17	.067	Wash05	C
1	0	Nelson, Andrew	P	3	.000	A	C
1	0	Olmstead, Frederick D.	P	1	.000	Bos05	
6	7	Owen, Frank Malcolm	P	25	.180	B	
		Parent, Frederick Alfred	SS118	119	.207	Bos	
		Purtell, Wm. Patrick	3B25	26	.130	A	
		Schreckengost, Ossee Freeman	C	6	+.188	xPhil	C
		Shaw, Alfred L.	C29	32	.082	Bos	
16	17	Smith, Frank Elmer	P41	43	.189	B	
		Sullivan, Wm. Joseph (Billy)	C	137	.191	B	
		Tannehill, Lee Ford	3B136	141	.216	B	
40	15	Walsh, Edward Augustin	P	66	.172	B	
		Weaver, Arthur Coggshall	C	15	.200	StL05	C
19	13	White, Guy Harris (Doc)	P41	51	.229	B	

WON 78 — AMERICAN LEAGUE — FINISHED 4th.
LOST 74
TG 152 — 1909. — PCT. .513

CHICAGO

WM. JOSEPH SULLIVAN

WON	LOST	NAME	POS.	G.	BA	FROM	TO
		Altizer, David Tilden (1B45)	OF62	116	.233	Clev	
1	4	Altrock, Nicholas (Nick)	P	5	+.000	B	Wash
		Atz, Jacob Henry	2B114	119	.236	B	C
		Barrows, Roland	OF	4	.150	A	
7	13	Burns, Wm. Thomas	P	20	+.175	xWash	
		Cole, Willis Russel	OF	46	.236	A	
		Cravath, Clifford Carltone (Cactus)	OF	18	+.061	Bos	Wash
		Davis, George Stacey	1B17	28	.132	B	C
		Donahue, John Augustus (Jiggs)	1B	2	+.000	B	Wash

WON	LOST	NAME	POS.	G.	BA	FROM	TO
		Dougherty, Patrick Henry	OF138	139	.285	B	
2	2	Fiene, Louis Henry	P13	15	.069	B	C
		Hahn, Edgar Wm.	OF	76	.182	B	
		Isbell, Wm. Frank	1B101	120	.224	B	C
		Messenger, Chas. Walter	OF	31	.170	A	
3	2	Olmstead, Frederick D.	P	8	.095	B	
1	1	Owen, Frank Malcolm	P	3	.167	B	C
		Owens, Frank Walter	C57	64	.201	Bos05	
		Parent, Frederick Alfred (OF37)	SS98	136	.261	B	
		Patterson, Hamilton (Ham)	OF	1	+.000	xStL	C
		Payne, Frederick Thomas	C27	32	.244	Det	
		Purtell, Wm. Patrick (2B32)	3B71	103	.258	B	
		Reilly, Bernard Eugene	2B	12	.120	A	C
12	12	Scott, James	P	36	.106	A	
25	17	Smith, Frank Elmer	P51	53	.173	B	
		Sullivan, Wm. Joseph (Billy) MGR.	C	97	.162	B	
2	3	Sutor, Harry G.	P	18	.094	A	C
		Tannehill, Lee Ford (SS64)	3B91	155	.222	B	
15	11	Walsh, Edward Augustin	P31	32	.214	B	
		Welday, Lyndon Earl	OF	29	.189	Chi07	C
10	9	White, Guy Harris (Doc) (P23)	OF40	71	.238	B	

WON 68
LOST 85
TG 153

AMERICAN LEAGUE

FINISHED 6th.

1910.

PCT. .444

CHICAGO

HUGH DUFFY

WON	LOST	NAME	POS.	G.	BA	FROM	TO
		Barrows, Roland	OF	6	.200	B	
		Blackburne, Russell Aubrey (Lena)	SS74	75	.174	A	
		Block, James John	C47	55	.210	Wash07	
		Bowser, James H.	OF	1	.000	A	C
		Browne, George E.	OF	30	+.241	xWash	
0	0	Burns, Wm. Thomas	P	1	.000	B	CinN
		Chouinard, Felix George	OF23	24	.195	A	
0	0	Chouneau, Wm. (Chief)	P	1	.000	A	C
		Cole, Willis Russel	OF	22	.175	B	C
		Collins, John Francis (Shano) (1B27)	OF65	97	.197	A	
		Dougherty, Patrick Henry	OF121	127	.248	B	
		French, Chas. Calvin	2B	45	+.165	xBos	C
		Gandil, Chas. Arnold (Chick)	1B74	77	.193	A	
		Hahn, Edgar Wm.	OF	15	.113	B	C
		Kelly, Albert Michael (Red)	OF	14	.155	A	C
9	4	Lange, Frank H.	P23	33	.255	A	
		Lord, Harry Donald	3B	44	+.310	xBos	
		Meloan, Paul B.	OF	65	.243	A	
		Messenger, Chas. Walter	OF	9	.185	B	
		Mullen, Chas. George	1B37	41	.195	A	
		McConnell, Ambrose Moses	2B	32	+.296	xBos	
10	12	Olmstead, Frederick D.	P	32	.154	B	
		Parent, Frederick Alfred	OF62	81	.178	B	
		Payne, Frederick Thomas	C78	91	.222	B	
		Purtell, Wm. Patrick	3B	102	+.222	B	Bos
8	18	Scott, James	P	40	.208	B	
4	10	Smith, Frank Elmer	P	24	+.186	B	Bos
		Sullivan, Wm. Joseph (Billy)	C	45	.183	B	
		Tannehill, Lee Ford (1B23)	SS38	67	.222	B	
18	20	Walsh, Edward Augustin	P45	52	.217	B	
15	13	White, Guy Harris (Doc)	P33	56	.198	B	
4	8	Young, Irving Melrose (Young Cy)	P	27	.113	PittN08	
		Zeider, Rollie Hubert (SS45)	2B87	136	.217	A	
		Zwilling, Edward Harrison	OF	27	.184	A	

WON 77
LOST 74
TG 151

AMERICAN LEAGUE

FINISHED 4th.

1911.

PCT. .509

CHICAGO

HUGH DUFFY

WON	LOST	NAME	POS.	G.	BA	FROM	TO
2	7	Baker, Jesse Ormand	P	22	.103	A	C
		Barrows, Roland	OF	13	.195	B	
3	2	Benz, Joseph Louis	P	12	.059	A	
		Berghammer, Martin Andrew	2B	2	.000	A	
		Block, James John	C38	39	.304	B	
		Bodie, Frank L. (Ping) (2B16)	OF128	145	.288	A	
		Callahan, James Joseph	OF114	120	.281	Chi05	
		Chouinard, Felix George (2B5)	OF9	14	.157	B	
		Collins, John Francis (Shano)	1B96	106	.262	B	
		Corhan, Roy	SS	43	.213	A	
		Dougherty, Patrick Henry	OF56	76	.289	B	C
2	0	Hovlik, Joseph	P	12	.077	Wash	C
		Johnston, James Harle (Jimmy)	OF	1	.000	A	
		Jones, Wm. Roderick (Tex)	1B	9	.193	A	C
		Kreitz, Ralph Wesley	C	7	.176	A	C
8	8	Lange, Frank H.	P29	54	.289	B	
		Lord, Harry Donald	3B	141	.321	B	
		Mayer, Walter A.	C	1	.000	A	
		Meloan, Paul B.	OF	1	+.333	B	StL
		Messenger, Chas. Walter	OF	13	.133	B	
0	2	Mogridge, George Anthony	P	4	.400	A	
		Mullen, Chas. George	1B	20	.203	B	
		McConnell, Ambrose Moses	2B102	104	.280	B	C
		McIntyre, Matthew W. (Matty)	OF	146	.323	Det	
6	6	Olmstead, Frederick D.	P	25	.189	B	C
		Parent, Frederick Alfred	2B	3	.444	B	C
		Payne, Frederick Thomas	C56	66	.203	B	C
14	11	Scott, James	P	39	.155	B	
		Sullivan, Wm. Joseph (Billy)	C	89	.215	B	
		Tannehill, Lee Ford (2B27)	SS102	141	.254	B	

WON	LOST	NAME	POS.	G.	BA	FROM	TO
27	18	Walsh, Edward Augustin	P55	62	.206	B	
10	14	White, Guy Harris (Doc)	P34	39	.256	B	
5	6	Young, Irving Melrose (Young Cy)	P	24	.179	B	C
		Zeider, Rollie Hubert (SS17)	1B29	73	.254	B	

WON 78
LOST 76
TG 154

AMERICAN LEAGUE FINISHED 4th.

1912. PCT. .506

CHICAGO

JAMES JOSEPH CALLAHAN

WON	LOST	NAME	POS.	G.	BA	FROM	TO
		Barrows, Roland	OF	8	.231	B	C
0	0	Bell, Ralph A.	P	2	.000	A	C
13	17	Benz, Joseph Louis	P	38	.132	B	
		Berrens, Joseph	OF	2	.250	A	C
		Blackburne, Russell Aubrey (Lena)	SS	5	.000	Chi10	
		Block, James John	C	46	.257	B	
		Bodie, Frank L. (Ping)	OF	137	.294	B	
		Borton, Wm. Baker	1B	31	.371	A	
		Callahan, James Joseph MGR.	OF	111	.272	B	
9	8	Cicotte, Edward Victor	P	20	+.241	xBos	
		Collins, John Francis (Shano) (1B46)	OF107	153	.290	B	
0	0	Crabb, James Roy	P	2	+.000	A	Phil
0	0	Delhi, Lee Wm. (Flame)	P	1	.000	A	C
0	1	Douglas, Philip Brooks (Shufflin' Phil)	P	3	.000	A	
		Easterly, Theodore Harrison (Ted)	C	28	+.364	xClev	
		Ens, Anton (Mutz)	1B	3	.000	A	C
		Fournier, Jacques Frank	1B	35	.192	A	
0	0	Johnson, Ellis Watt	P	5	.000	A	
		Johnson, Ernest Rudolph	SS	18	.262	A	
0	0	Jordan, Raymond Willis	P	4	.000	A	
		Kuhn, Walter Chas.	C	75	.202	A	
0	0	Lamline, Frederick Arthur	P	1	.000	A	
10	10	Lange, Frank H.	P	36	.215	B	
		Lord, Harry Donald (OF45)	3B106	151	.267	B	
		Mattick, Walter Joseph	OF	88	.260	A	
		Mayer, Walter A.	C	9	.000	B	
3	4	Mogridge, George Anthony	P	9	.125	B	
		McIntyre, Matthew W. (Matty)	OF	45	.167	B	C
		McLarry, Paul Howard (Polly)		2	.000	A	
		Paddock, Delmar Harold		1	+.000	A	N.Y.
5	6	Peters, Oscar C.	P	23	.194	A	
		Rath, Maurice Chas.	2B	157	.272	Clev10	
		Russell, Ewell Albert (Reb)	(DID NOT PLAY)			A	
		Schalk, Raymond Wm.	C	23	.286	A	
2	2	Scott, James	P	5	.000	B	
1	0	Smith, Harry	P	1	.000	A	C

WON	LOST	NAME	POS.	G.	BA	FROM	TO
		Sullivan, Wm. Joseph (Billy)	C	39	.209	B	
		Tannehill, Lee Ford	3B	2	.000	B	C
0	1	Taylor, Wiley	P	3	.000	Det	
27	17	Walsh, Edward Augustin	P	61	.245	B	
		Weaver, George Davis (Buck)	SS	147	.224	A	
8	10	White, Guy Harris (Doc)	P	28	.125	B	
		Wolfe, Roy Chamberlain (Polly)	OF	1	.000	A	
		Zeider, Rollie Hubert (3B59)	1B69	129	.245	B	

WON 78
LOST 74
TG 152

AMERICAN LEAGUE FINISHED 5th.

1913. PCT. .513

CHICAGO

JAMES JOSEPH CALLAHAN

WON	LOST	NAME	POS.	G.	BA	FROM	TO
		Beall, John Woolf	OF	17	+.267	xClev	
7	10	Benz, Joseph Louis	P	28	.180	B	
		Berger, Joseph August	2B70	77	.215	A	
		Bodie, Frank L. (Ping)	OF123	127	.265	B	
		Borton, Wm. Baker	1B	28	+.275	B	NY
		Breton, James Frederick (3B2)	2B9	12	.173	A	
		Callahan, James Joseph MGR.	OF	6	.222	B	
		Chappell, Lawrence A. (Larry)	OF59	60	.229	A	
		Chase, Harold Homer (Hal)	1B	102	+.281	xNY	
18	12	Cicotte, Edward Victor	P	40	.142	B	
		Collins, John Francis (Shano)	OF147	148	.239	B	
		Daly, Thomas Daniel	C	1	.000	A	
		Easterly, Theodore Harrison (Ted)	C21	60	.235	B	
		Fournier, Jacques Frank (OF22)	1B29	68	.234	B	
		Jones, David Jefferson	OF	12	.288	Det	
		Kuhn, Walter Chas.	C24	26	.160	B	
1	4	Lange, Frank H.	P	16	.133	B	C
0	0	Lathrop, Wm. George	P	6	.000	A	
		Lord, Harry Donald	3B	150	.263	B	
		Mattick, Walter Joseph	OF64	68	.188	B	
		Meyer, Wm. Adam	C	1	1.000	A	
0	1	Miller, Frank Lee	P	1	.000	A	
0	3	O'Brien, Thomas Joseph	P	6	+.000	xBos	C
		Rader, Donald Russell (3B1)	OF3	4	.333	A	
		Rath, Maurice Chas.	2B86	90	.197	B	
		Roush, Edd J.	OF	9	.100	A	
22	16	Russell, Ewell Albert	P43	44	.189	B	
		Schalk, Raymond Wm.	C125	128	.244	B	
		Schaller, Walter (Biff)	OF29	34	.219	Det11	C
20	20	Scott, James	P	44	.072	B	
0	0	Scroggins, James Lynn	P	1	.000	A	C
0	1	Smith, Clarence Ossie	P	15	.000	A	
0	0	Smith, Robert A.	P	1	.000	A	
		Sullivan, Wm. Joseph (Billy)	(did not Play)			B	
8	3	Walsh, Edward Augustin	P13	16	.156	B	

WON	LOST	NAME	POS.	G.	BA	FROM	TO
		Weaver, George Davis (Buck)	SS	151	.272	B	
2	4	White, Guy Harris (Doc)	P16	17	.120	B	C
		Zeider, Rollie Hubert	2B	15	+.438	B	N.Y.

WON 70 AMERICAN LEAGUE FINISHED 6th.
LOST 84 (TIED WITH N.Y.)
TG 154 1914. PCT. .455

CHICAGO

JAMES JOSEPH CALLAHAN

WON	LOST	NAME	POS.	G.	BA	FROM	TO
		Alcock, John Forbes	3B48	54	.173	A	C
		Baker, Howard Francis	3B	15	.277	Clev12	
14	19	Benz, Joseph Louis	P	44	.130	B	
		Berger, Joseph August	SS27	47	.155	B	C
		Blackburne, Russell Aubrey (Lena)	2B143	144	.222	Chi12	
		Bodie, Frank L. (Ping)	OF95	107	.229	B	
		Breton, James Frederick	3B79	81	.212	B	
		Brown, E.		1	.000	A	C
		Chappell, Lawrence A. (Larry)	OF	21	.231	B	
		Chase, Harold Homer (Hal)	1B	58	.267	B	BuffF
11	16	Cicotte, Edward Victor	P	42	.163	B	
		Collins, John Francis (Shano)	OF	154	.274	B	
		Coombs, Cecil Lysander	OF	7	.173	A	C
		Daly, Thomas Daniel	OF23	61	.233	B	
		Demmitt, Chas. Raymond	OF	145	+.258	xDet	
10	9	Faber, Urban Chas. (Red)	P	33	.145	A	
		Fournier, Jacques Frank	1B97	109	.311	B	
1	0	Jasper, Harry W. (Hi)	P	16	.000	A	
		Kavanagh, Chas. Hugh	OF	5	.250	A	C
		Kuhn, Walter Chas.	C16	17	.275	B	C
1	2	Lathrop, Wm. George	P	16	.000	B	C
		Lord, Harry Donald	3B19	21	.189	B	
		Manda, Carl Alan	2B	9	.333	A	C
		Mayer, Walter A.	C33	39	.165	Chi12	
		Porter, Irving Marble	OF	1	.000	A	C
		Roth, Robert Frank	OF	34	.294	A	
8	12	Russell, Ewell Albert (Reb)	P33	39	.275	B	
		Schalk, Raymond Wm.	C124	135	.270	B	
		Schreiber, Henry Ward	OF	1	.000	A	
14	18	Scott, James	P	41	.163	B	
		Sullivan, Wm. Joseph (Billy)	C	1	.000	B	
2	3	Walsh, Edward Augustin	P	11	.062	B	
		Weaver, George Davis (Buck)	SS134	136	.246	B	
		Wolfe, Roy Chamberlain (Polly)	OF	8	.214	Chi12	C
9	5	Wolfgang, Meldon John	P	19	.175	A	

WON 93 AMERICAN LEAGUE FINISHED 3rd.
LOST 61
TG 154 1915. PCT. .604

CHICAGO

CLARENCE HENRY ROWLAND

WON	LOST	NAME	POS.	G.	BA	FROM	TO
		Baker, Howard Francis		2	.000	B	NYN
15	11	Benz, Joseph Louis	P	39	.127	B	
		Blackburne, Russell Aubrey (Lena)	3B83	96	.216	B	
		Breton, James Frederick	3B	16	.139	B	C
		Brief, Anthony Vincent (Bunny)	1B46	48	.214	StL13	
		Chappell, Lawrence A. (Larry)		1	.000	B	
13	11	Cicotte, Edward Victor	P39	40	.209	B	
		Collins, Edward Trowbridge	2B	155	.332	Phil	
		Collins, John Francis (Shano) (1B47)	OF104	153	.257	B	
		Daly, Thomas Daniel	C19	29	.191	B	
0	0	Davis, Frank Talmadge	P	2	.000	CinN12	
		Demmitt, Chas. Raymond	OF	9	.000	B	
24	13	Faber, Urban Chas. (Red)	P	49	.131	B	
		Felsch, Oscar Emil (Happy)	OF118	121	.248	A	
		Fournier, Jacques Frank (OF57)	1B65	126	.322	B	
		Jackson, Chas. Herbert		1	.000	A	
		Jackson, Joseph Jefferson	OF	46	+.269	xClev	
1	1	Jasper, Harry W. (Hi)	P	3	.333	B	
		Johns, Wm. R.	3B	28	.210	A	
0	0	Johnson, Ellis Watt	P	1	.000	Chi12	
0	0	Klepfer, Edward Lloyd	P	2	+.000	NY13	Clev
		Leibold, Harry Loran (Nemo)	OF	37	+.284	xClev	
		Mayer, Walter A.	C20	22	.222	B	
		Murphy, Joseph Edward	OF	78	+.315	xPhil	
		Quinlan, Thomas Finners	OF32	42	.193	StLN13	C
		Roth, Robert Frank (OF20)	3B27	69	+.257	B	Clev
11	12	Russell, Ewell Albert (Reb)	P42	45	.244	B	
		Schalk, Raymond Wm.	C134	135	.266	B	
24	11	Scott, James	P	48	.126	B	
3	0	Walsh, Edward Augustin	P	5	.363	B	
		Weaver, George Davis (Buck)	SS	148	.268	B	
2	2	Wolfgang, Meldon John	P	17	.118	B	

WON 89 AMERICAN LEAGUE FINISHED 2nd.
LOST 65
TG 154 1916. PCT. .578

CHICAGO

CLARENCE HENRY ROWLAND

WON	LOST	NAME	POS.	G.	BA	FROM	TO
9	5	Benz, Joseph Louis	P	28	.065	B	
15	7	Cicotte, Edward Victor	P	44	.212	B	
		Collins, Edward Trowbridge	2B	155	.308	B	
		Collins, John Francis (Shano)	OF136	143	.243	B	
6	5	Danforth, David Chas.	P	28	.087	Phil12	
17	9	Faber, Urban Chas. (Red)	P	35	.095	B	
0	0	Fautsch, Joseph R.	P	1	.000	A	C
		Felsch, Oscar Emil (Happy)	OF141	146	.301	B	

		Fournier, Jacques Frank	1B85	105	.240	B	
		Hasbrouck, Robert Lyndon	1B2	8	.125	A	
		Jackson, Joseph Hefferson	OF	155	.341	B	
		Jourdan, Theodore Chas.		3	.000	A	
		Lapp, John Walker (Jack)	C34	40	.208	Phil	C
		Leibold, Harry Loran (Nemo)	OF24	45	.244	B	
		Lynn, Byrd	C	31	.225	A	
		Moriarty, George Joseph	3B1	7	.200	Det	
		Murphy, Joseph Edward	OF24	51	.210	B	
		McMullin, Frederick Wm.	3B63	68	.257	Det14	
		Ness, John Chas.	1B69	75	.267	Det11	C
18	11	Russell Ewell Albert (Reb)	P	56	.142	B	
		Schalk, Raymond Wm.	C124	129	.232	B	
7	14	Scott, James	P	32	.115	B	
		Shook, Raymond Curtis		1	.000	A	C
		Terry, Zebulon Alexander (Zeb)	SS93	94	.190	A	
		VonKolnitz, Alfred Holmes (Fritz)	3B	24	.227	CinN	C
0	1	Walsh, Edward Augustin	P	2	.000	B	
		Weaver, George Davis (Buck) (SS66)	3B85	151	.227	B	
13	7	Williams, Claude Preston	P	43	.135	Det14	
4	6	Wolfgang, Meldon John	P	28	.225	B	
		Wright, Edward Yatman	SS	8	.000	A	C

WON 100 — AMERICAN LEAGUE — FINISHED 1st.
LOST 54
TG 154 — 1917. — PCT. .649

CHICAGO

CLARENCE HENRY ROWLAND

WON	LOST	NAME	POS.	G.	BA	FROM	TO
7	3	Benz, Joseph Louis	P	19	.167	B	
		Byrne, Robert Mathew	2B	1	.000	xPhilN	C
28	12	Cicotte, Edward Victor	P	49	.179	B	
		Collins, Edward Trowbridge	2B	156	.289	B	
		Collins, John Francis (Shano)	OF73	82	.234	B	
11	6	Danforth, David Chas.	P	50	.130	B	
16	13	Faber, Urban Chas. (Red)	P	41	.058	B	
		Felsch, Oscar Emil (Happy)	OF	152	.308	B	
		Fournier, Jacques Frank		1	.000	B	
		Gandil, Chas. Arnold (Chick)	1B	149	.273	Clev	
		Hasbrouck, Robert Lyndon	2B1	2	.000	B	C
		Jackson, Joseph Jefferson	OF145	146	.301	B	
		Jenkins, Joseph Daniel	C	10	.111	StL14	
		Jourdan, Theodore Chas.	1B14	17	.148	B	
		Leibold, Harry Loran (Nemo)	OF122	125	.236	B	
		Lynn, Byrd	C29	35	.222	B	
		Murphy, Joseph Edward	OF	53	.314	B	
		McMullin, Frederick Wm.	3B52	59	.237	B	
		Risberg, Chas. August (Swede)	SS146	149	.203	A	
15	5	Russell, Ewell Albert (Reb)	P35	39	.279	B	
		Schalk, Raymond Wm.	C139	140	.227	B	
6	7	Scott, James	P	24	.119	B	C

		Terry, Zebulon Alexander (Zeb)	SS1	2	.100	B	
		Weaver, George Davis (Buck) (SS10)	3B107	118	.284	B	
17	8	Williams, Claude Preston	P	45	.090	B	
0	0	Wolfgang, Meldon John	P	5	.000	B	

WON 57 — AMERICAN LEAGUE — FINISHED 6th.
LOST 67
TG 124 — 1918. — PCT. .460

CHICAGO

CLARENCE HENRY ROWLAND

WON	LOST	NAME	POS.	G.	BA	FROM	TO
7	8	Benz, Joseph Louis	P	29	.216	B	
12	19	Cicotte, Edward Victor	P	38	.163	B	
		Collins, Edward Trowbridge	2B96	97	.276	B	
		Collins, John Francis (Shano)	OF92	103	.274	B	
0	0	Corey, Edward N.	P	1	.000	A	C
6	15	Danforth, David Chas.	P	39	.143	B	
		DeVormer, Albert E.	C	8	.315	A	
5	1	Faber, Urban Chas. (Red)	P	11	.042	B	
		Felsch, Oscar Emil (Happy)	OF	53	.252	B	
		Gandil, Chas. Arnold (Chick)	1B	114	.271	B	
		Good, Wilbur David	OF	35	.250	PhilN16	C
		Hargrove, Wm. Patrick (Pat)		2	.000	A	C
		Jackson, Joseph Jefferson	OF	17	.354	B	
		Jacobs, Otto Albert	C20	29	.205	A	C
		Jourdan, Theodore Chas.	1B1	7	.100	B	
		Leibold, Harry Loran (Nemo)	OF114	116	.250	B	
		Lynn, Byrd	C	4	.142	B	
0	1	Mitchell, Albert Roy	P	2	.000	StL14	CinN
		Mostil, John Anthony	2B	10	.273	A	
		Murphy, Joseph Edward	OF63	91	.297	B	
		McMullin, Frederick Wm.	3B69	70	.276	B	
		Pinelli, Ralph Arthur (Babe)	3B	24	.231	A	
5	1	Quinn, John Picus	P	6	.222	BaltF15	
		Risberg, Chas. August (Swede) (2B12 3B24)	SS30	82	.256	B	
6	5	Russell, Ewell Albert (Reb)	P19	27	.140	B	
		Schalk, Raymond Wm.	C106	108	.219	B	
10	12	Schellenback, Frank Victor	P28	29	.130	A	
		Weaver, George Davis (Buck) (3B11)	SS98	112	.300	B	
6	4	Williams, Claude Preston	P	15	.132	B	
		Willson, Frank Hoxie		4	.000	A	
0	1	Wolfgang, Meldon John	P	5	.000	B	C

WON 88 — AMERICAN LEAGUE — FINISHED 1st.
LOST 52
TG 140 — 1919. — PCT. .629

CHICAGO

WM. J. GLEASON

WON	LOST	NAME	POS.	G.	BA	FROM	TO
0	0	Benz, Joseph Louis	P	1	.000	B	C
29	7	Cicotte, Edward Victor	P	40	.202	B	
		Collins, Edward Trowbridge	2B	140	.319	B	
		Collins, John Francis (Shano)	OF46	63	.279	B	
1	2	Danforth, David Chas.	P	15	.111	B	
11	9	Faber, Urban Chas. (Red)	P	25	.185	B	
		Felsch, Oscar Emil (Happy)	OF	135	.275	B	
		Gandil, Chas. Arnold (Chick)	1B	115	.290	B	C
		Jackson, Joseph Jefferson	OF	139	.351	B	
3	1	James, Wm. Henry	P	5	+.143	xBos	C
		Jenkins, Joseph Daniel	C	11	.167	Chi17	C
13	8	Kerr, Richard Henry (Dickey)	P	39	.250	A	
		Leibold, Harry Loran (Nemo)	OF	122	.302	B	
5	5	Lowdermilk, Grover Cleveland	P	20	+.088	xStL	
		Lynn, Byrd	C28	29	.227	B	
1	3	Mayer, James Erskine	P	6	.000	xPittN	C
		Murphy, Joseph Edward	OF	30	.486	B	
		McClellan, Harvey McDowell		7	.333	A	
0	0	McGuire, Thomas Patrick	P	1	.000	ChiF14	C
		McMullin, Frederick Wm.	3B40	60	.294	B	
0	0	Noyes, Winfield Chas.	P	1	+.500	xPhil	C
0	0	Ragan, Don Carlos Patrick (Pat)	P	1	.000	xNYN	
		Risberg, Chas. August (Swede) (1B22)	SS97	119	.256	B	
0	1	Robertson, Chas. Culbertson	P	1	.000	A	
0	0	Russell, Ewell Albert (Reb)	P	1	.000	B	
		Schalk, Raymond Wm.	C129	131	.282	B	
1	3	Shellenback, Frank Victor	P	8	.090	B	C
0	1	Sullivan, John Jeremiah	P	4	.333	A	C
		Weaver, George Davis (Buck) (SS43)	3B97	140	.296	B	
1	1	Wilkinson, Roy Hamilton	P	4	.375	Clev	
23	11	Williams, Claude Preston	P	41	.180	B	

WON 96 AMERICAN LEAGUE FINISHED 2nd.
LOST 58
TG 154 1920. PCT. .623

CHICAGO

WM. J. GLEASON

WON	LOST	NAME	POS.	G.	BA	FROM	TO
21	10	Cicotte, Edward Victor	P	37	.196	B	C
		Collins, Edward Trowbridge	2B	153	.369	B	
		Collins, John Francis (Shano)	1B	133	.303	B	
23	13	Faber, Urban Chas. (Red)	P	40	.106	B	
		Falk, Bibb August	OF	7	.294	A	
		Felsch, Oscar Emil (Happy)	OF	142	.338	B	C
0	0	Heath, Spencer Paul Jr.	P	4	.000	A	C
1	1	Hodge, Clarence Clemet	P	4	.000	A	
		Jackson, Joseph Jefferson	OF145	146	.382	B	C
		Jonnard, Clarence James	C	2	.000	A	
		Jourdan, Theodore Chas.	1B46	48	.240	Chi18	C
21	9	Kerr, Richard Henry (Dickey)	P45	46	.155	B	
0	1	Keifer, Joseph Wm.	P	2	.000	A	
		Leibold, Harry Loran (Nemo)	OF106	108	.220	B	
0	0	Lowdermilk, Grover Cleveland	P	3	.000	B	C
		Lynn, Byrd	C15	16	.320	B	C
		Murphy, Joseph Edward	OF19	58	.339	B	
		McClellan, Harvey McDowell	3B	10	.300	B	
		McMullin, Frederick Wm.	3B29	46	.197	B	C
1	1	Payne, George Washington	P	12	.125	A	C
		Risberg, Chas. August (Swede)	SS124	126	.266	B	C
		Schalk, Raymond Wm.	C	151	.270	B	
		Strunk, Amos Aaron	OF	52	+.220	xPhil	
		Weaver, George Davis (Buck) (SS25)	3B126	151	.333	B	C
7	9	Wilkinson, Roy Hamilton	P	34	.146	B	
22	14	Williams, Claude Preston	P	39	.218	B	C

WON 62 AMERICAN LEAGUE FINISHED 7th.
LOST 92
TG 154 1921. PCT. .403

CHICAGO

WM. J. GLEASON

WON	LOST	NAME	POS.	G.	BA	FROM	TO
0	0	Blackburn, Foster Edwin	P	1	.000	KCF15	C
		Bratchi, Frederick Oscar	OF	16	.286	A	
		Collins, Edward Trowbridge	2B136	139	.337	B	
0	1	Connally, George Walter	P	5	.500	A	
0	3	Davenport, Joubert Lum	P13	15	.412	A	
25	15	Faber, Urban Chas. (Red)	P	43	.148	B	
		Falk, Bibb August	OF149	152	.285	B	
0	0	Fenner, Horace Alfred	P	2	.000	A	C
6	8	Hodge, Clarence Clemet	P	36	.327	B	
		Hooper, Harry Bartholomew	OF	108	.327	Bos	
		Johnson, Ernest Rudolph	SS141	142	.295	StL18	
19	17	Kerr, Richard Henry (Dickey)	P44	45	.238	B	
		Lees, George Edward	C16	20	.214	A	C
		Leifer, Elmer Edwin	OF	9	.300	A	C
0	0	Michaelson, John August	P	2	.000	A	C
0	3	Morris, Joseph Bennett	P	4	+.400	StL18	StL
		Mostil, John Anthony	OF91	100	.301	Chi18	
		Mulligan, Edward Joseph	3B	152	.251	CinN16	
2	8	Mulrennan, Dominick Joseph	P	12	.150	A	C
		Murphy, Joseph Edward	OF	6	.200	B	
		McClellan, Harvey McDowell (SS15 OF15)	2B20	63	.179	B	
3	6	McWeeney, Douglas Lawrence	P	27	.032	A	
		Ostergard, Robert Lund	SS	12	.364	A	C
0	0	Pence, Russell Wm.	P	4	.000	A	C
		Pratt, Francis Bruce		1	.000	A	C
2	5	Russell, John Albert (Jack)	P	11	.400	BknN18	
		Schalk, Raymond Wm.	C126	128	.252	B	

WON	LOST	NAME	POS.	G.	BA	FROM	TO
		Sheely, Earl Homer	1B	154	.304	A	
		Strunk, Amos Aaron	OF111	121	.332	B	
0	3	Thompson, John Dudley	P	4	.286	A	C
1	2	Twombly, Edwin Parker (Cy)	P	7	.000	A	C
0	1	Wienecke, John	P	10	.100	A	C
4	20	Wilkinson, Roy Hamilton	P	36	.123	B	
		Yaryan, Clarence Everett	C34	45	.304	A	

WON 77 LOST 77 TG 154

AMERICAN LEAGUE

FINISHED 5th.

1922.

PCT. .500

CHICAGO

WM. J. GLEASON

WON	LOST	NAME	POS.	G.	BA	FROM	TO
0	2	Acosta, Jose	P	5	.200	Wash	C
0	0	Blankenship, Homer	P	4	.000	A	
8	10	Blankenship, Theodore (Ted)	P	24	.171	A	
0	0	Bowles, Emmett Jerome	P	1	.000	A	C
		Bubser, Harold Fred		3	.000	A	C
		Collins, Edward Trowbridge	2B	154	.324	B	
5	6	Courtney, Henry Seymour	P	18	+.273	xWash	C
0	0	Cox, Ernest Thompson	P	1	.000	A	C
1	1	Davenport, Joubert Lum	P	12	.000	B	
1	1	Duff, Cecil Elba	P	3	.400	A	C
		Evers, John Joseph	2B	1	.000	ChiN	
21	17	Faber, Urban Chas. (Red)	P	43	.200	B	
		Falk, Bibb August	OF129	131	.298	B	
		Graham, Roy Vincent	C	5	.000	A	
7	6	Hodge, Clarence Clemet	P	35	.207	B	C
		Hooper, Harry Bartholomew	OF149	152	.304	B	
		Jenkins, John Robert (SS1)	2B1	5	.000	A	C
		Johnson, Ernest Rudolph	SS141	145	.254	B	
13	10	Leverett, Gorham Vance (Dixie)	P	33	.253	A	
		Long, James Albert	C	3	.000	A	C
2	2	Mack, Frank George	P	8	.250	A	
		Mostil, John Anthony	OF123	132	.304	B	
		Mulligan, Edward Joseph	3B84	103	.234	B	
1	0	McCabe, Richard James	P	3	.000	Bos18	C
		McClellan, Harvey McDowell	3B71	91	.226	B	
0	1	McWeeney, Douglas Lawrence	P	4	.000	B	
		Pence, Elmer Clair	OF	1	.000	A	C
14	15	Robertson, Chas. Culbertson	P	37	.184	Chi19	
0	1	Russell, John Albert (Jack)	P	5	.000	B	C
		Schalk, Raymond Wm.	C	142	.281	B	
4	4	Schupp, Ferdinand Maurice	P17	18	.217	BknN	C
		Sheely, Earl Homer	1B	149	.317	B	
		Strunk, Amos Aaron	OF75	92	.289	B	
		Swentor, August Walter	3B	1	.000	A	C
0	1	Wilkinson, Roy Hamilton	P	4	.000	B	C
		Yaryan, Clarence Everett	C25	36	.197	B	C

WON 69 LOST 85 TG 154

AMERICAN LEAGUE

FINISHED 7th.

1923.

PCT. .448

CHICAGO

WM. J. GLEASON

WON	LOST	NAME	POS.	G.	BA	FROM	TO
		Archdeacon, Maurice John	OF20	22	.402	A	
		Barrett, Wm. Joseph	OF40	44	.271	Phi121	
1	1	Blankenship, Homer	P	4	.000	B	
9	14	Blankenship, Theodore (Ted)	P	44	.211	B	
0	1	Cadore, Leon Joseph	P	1	.000	xBknN	
0	0	Castner, Paul Henry	P	6	.000	A	C
		Collins, Edward Trowbridge	2B142	145	.360	B	
0	0	Connally, George Walter	P	3	.333	Chi21	
		Cortazzo, John Frank		1	.000	A	C
		Crouse, Clyde Ellsworth	C22	23	.257	A	
12	13	Cvengros, Michael John	P40	41	.203	NYN	
0	0	Davenport, Joubert Lum	P	2	1.000	B	
		Dorman, Chas. Frederick C.	C	1	.500	A	
		Elsh, Eugene Roy	OF57	81	.249	A	
0	0	Embrey, Chas. Akin	P	1	.000	A	C
14	11	Faber, Urban Chas. (Red)	P32	33	.217	B	
		Falk, Bibb August	OF80	87	.307	B	
1	3	Gillenwater, Claral Lewis	P	5	.000	A	C
		Graham, Roy Vincent	C33	36	.195	B	C
		Happenny, John Clifford	2B20	32	.221	A	C
		Hooper, Harry Bartholomew	OF143	145	.288	B	
		Johnson, Ernest Rudolph	SS	12	+.189	B	N.Y.
		Kamm, Wm. Edward	3B	149	.292	A	
10	13	Leverett, Gorham Vance (Dixie)	P	38	.267	B	
2	1	Lyons, Theodore Amar (Ted)	P	9	.200	A	
0	1	Mack, Frank George	P	12	.000	B	
		Mostil, John Anthony	OF143	153	.291	B	
		McClellan, Harvey McDowell	SS139	141	.235	B	
0	0	Proctor, Noah Richard	P	2	.000	A	C
		Rosenberg, Louis C. (OF1)	2B2	3	.250	A	C
13	18	Robertson, Chas. Culbertson	P	38	.247	B	
		Schalk, Raymond Wm.	C121	123	.228	B	
		Sheely, Earl Homer	1B	156	.296	B	
		Snipes, Wyatt Eure (Roxy)		1	.000	A	C
		Strunk, Amos Aaron	OF	54	.315	B	
		Taylor, Leo Thomas		1	.000	A	C
7	8	Thurston, Hollis John (Sloppy)	P	45	+.316	xStL	
0	1	Woodward, Frank Russell	P	2	.000	Wash	C

WON 66 LOST 87 TG 153

AMERICAN LEAGUE

FINISHED 8th (LAST)

1924.

PCT. .431

CHICAGO

JOHN JOSEPH EVERS

WON	LOST	NAME	POS.	G.	BA	FROM	TO
		Archdeacon, Maurice John	OF	95	.319	B	
0	0	Barnes, Robert Avery	P	2	.000	A	C
		Barrett, Wm. Joseph (OF27)	SS77	119	.271	B	
		Black, John Wm.	2B	6	.200	A	C
7	6	Blankenship, Theodore (Ted)	P	25	.326	B	
		Burns, Joseph Francis	C	8	.105	A	C
		Clancy, John Wm.	1B	13	.257	A	
		Collins, Edward Trowbridge	2B	152	.349	B	
7	13	Connally, George Walter	P	44	.220	B	
		Crouse, Clyde Ellsworth	C90	94	.259	B	
3	12	Cvengros, Michael John	P	26	.200	B	
		Dashiell, John Wallace	SS	1	.000	A	C
0	0	Davenport, Joubert Lum	P	1	.000	B	C
		Davis, Isaac Marion	SS	10	.242	Wash19	
		DeViveiros, Bernard John	SS	1	.000	A	
0	0	Dobb, John Kenneth	P	2	.000	A	C
		Elsh, Eugene Roy	OF14	60	.306	B	
9	11	Faber, Urban Chas. (Red)	P	21	.148	B	
		Falk, Bibb August	OF	138	.352	B	
0	0	Foreman, August (Gus)	P	5	.000	A	
		French, Raymond Edward	SS28	37	.179	BknN	C
		Grabowski, John Patrick	C19	20	.250	A	
		Hooper, Harry Bartholomew	OF123	130	.328	B	
		Kamm, Wm. Edward	3B145	147	.254	B	
0	0	Lawrence, Robert Andrew	P	1	.000	A	C
2	3	Leverett, Gorham Vance (Dixie)	P	21	.188	B	
12	11	Lyons, Theodore Amar (Ted)	P	41	.221	B	
1	4	Mangum, Leo Allen	P	13	.071	A	
		Morehart, Raymond Anderson	SS27	31	.200	A	
		Mostil, John Anthony	OF105	118	.325	B	
		McClellan, Harvey McDowell	SS21	32	.176	B	C
1	3	McWeeney, Douglas Lawrence	P	13	.000	Chi22	
		Naleway, Frank	SS	1	.000	A	C
4	10	Robertson, Chas. Culbertson	P	17	.182	B	
		Schalk, Raymond Wm.	C56	57	.196	B	
0	0	Schultz, Webb Carl	P	1	.000	A	C
		Sheely, Earl Homer	1B	146	.320	B	
0	0	Steengrafe, Milton Henry	P	3	.000	A	
		Strunk, Amos Aaron	OF	1	+.000	B	Phil
20	14	Thurston, Hollis John (Sloppy)	P39	51	.254	B	
		Wirts, Elwood Vernon	C	5	.083	ChiN	C

WON 79 — AMERICAN LEAGUE — FINISHED 5th.
LOST 75
TG 154 — 1925. — PCT. .513

CHICAGO

EDWARD TROWBRIDGE COLLINS

WON	LOST	NAME	POS.	G.	BA	FROM	TO
		Archdeacon, Maurice John	OF1	10	.111	B	C
0	0	Ash, Kenneth Lowther	P	2	.000	A	
		Barrett, Wm. Joseph (SS4 3B4 OF27)	2B41	81	.363	B	
0	0	Bender, Chas. Albert (Chief)	P	1	.000	PhilN17	C
		Bischoff, John George	C4	7	+.091	A	Bos
17	8	Blankenship, Theodore (Ted)	P	40	.205	B	
		Clancy, John Wm.	1B	4	.000	B	
		Collins, Edward Trowbridge MGR.	2B116	118	.346	B	
6	7	Connally, George Walter	P	40	.250	B	
		Crouse, Clyde Ellsworth	C48	54	.352	B	
3	9	Cvengros, Michael John	P	22	.152	B	
		Davis, Isaac Marion	SS144	146	.240	B	C
1	2	Edwards, James Corbette	P	9	+.118	xClev	
		Elsh, Eugene Roy (1B3)	OF16	32	.188	B	C
12	11	Faber, Urban Chas. (Red)	P	34	.103	B	
		Falk, Bibb August	OF	154	.301	B	
0	0	Freeze, Carl Alexander (Jake)	P	2	.000	A	C
		Grabowski, John Patrick	C	21	.304	B	
		Harris, Spencer Anthony	OF28	56	.283	A	
		Hooper, Harry Bartholomew	OF124	127	.265	B	C
		Kamm, Wm. Edward	3B	152	.279	B	
		Kane, John Francis (2B6)	SS8	14	.179	A	C
0	1	Kerr, Richard Henry (Dickey)	P12	13	.333	Chi21	C
21	11	Lyons, Theodore Amar (Ted)	P	43	.186	B	
0	0	Mack, Frank George	P	8	.333	Chi23	C
		Mallonee, Jules W.	OF1	2	.000	A	C
1	0	Mangum, Leo Allen	P	7	.500	B	
		Mostil, John Anthony	OF	153	.299	B	
0	0	Riviere, Arthur Bernard (Tink)	P	3	.000	StLN21	C
8	12	Robertson, Chas. Culbertson	P	24	.222	B	
		Schalk, Raymond Wm.	C	125	.274	B	
		Sheely, Earl Homer	1B	153	.315	B	
		Tankersley, Lawrence Wm.	C	1	.000	A	C
10	14	Thurston, Hollis John (Sloppy)	P36	44	.286	B	

WON 81 — AMERICAN LEAGUE — FINISHED 5th.
LOST 72
TG 153 — 1926. — PCT. .529

CHICAGO

EDWARD TROWBRIDGE COLLINS

WON	LOST	NAME	POS.	G.	BA	FROM	TO
		Barrett, Wm. Joseph	OF102	111	.307	B	
		Berg, Morris (Moe)	SS31	41	.221	BknN23	
13	10	Blankenship, Theodore (Ted)	P	29	.132	B	
		Clancy, John Wm.	1B10	12	.342	B	
		Collins, Edward Trowbridge MGR.	2B101	106	.344	B	
6	5	Connally, George Walter	P	31	.156	B	
0	1	Cox, Leslie Warren	P	2	.500	A	C
		Crouse, Clyde Ellsworth	C45	49	.237	B	
6	9	Edwards, James Corbette	P	32	.109	B	
15	8	Faber, Urban Chas. (Red)	P	27	.150	B	

WON	LOST	NAME	POS.	G.	BA	FROM	TO
		Falk, Bibb August	OF	155	.345	B	
		Grabowski, John Patrick	C38	48	.262	B	
		Gulley, Thomas Jefferson	OF12	16	.229	Clev24	C
		Harris, Spencer Anthony	OF63	80	.252	B	
		Hunnefield, Wm. Fenton (2B15 3B17)	SS98	131	.274	A	
		Kamm, Wm. Edward	3B142	143	.294	B	
1	1	Leverett, Gorham Vance (Dixie)	P	6	.143	Chi24	
18	16	Lyons, Theodore Amar (Ted)	P39	41	.212	B	
		Morehart, Raymond Anderson	2B48	73	.318	Chi24	
		Mostil, John Anthony	OF147	148	.328	B	
0	0	McBee, Pryor Edward	P	1	.000	A	C
		McCurdy, Harry Henry	C25	44	.326	StLN23	
		Purdy, Everett Virgil	OF	11	.182	A	
		Schalk, Raymond Wm.	C80	82	.265	B	
		Scott, Lewis Everett (Deacon)	SS39	40	.252	Wash	CinN
		Sheely, Earl Homer	1B144	145	.299	B	
1	2	Steengrafe, Milton Henry	P	13	.000	Chi24	C
15	12	Thomas, Alphonse Thomas Jr.	P	44	.186	A	
6	8	Thurston, Hollis John (Sloppy)	P31	38	.311	B	
		Veltman, Arthur Patrick (Pat)	OF	4	.000	A	

WON 70 LOST 83 TG 153

AMERICAN LEAGUE FINISHED 5th.

1927. PCT. .458

CHICAGO

RAYMOND WM. SCHALK

WON	LOST	NAME	POS.	G.	BA	FROM	TO
0	5	Barnabe, Chas. Edward	P17	18	.158	A	
		Barrett, Wm. Joseph	OF	147	.286	B	
		Battle, James Milton (SS1)	3B1	6	.375	A	C
		Berg, Morris (Moe) (2B10)	C10	35	.247	B	
		Blackburne, Russell Aubrey (Lena)		1	1.000	PhilN19	
12	17	Blankenship, Theodore (Ted)	P	38	.187	B	
		Boone, Isaac Morgan	OF11	29	.226	Bos25	
0	0	Brown, Joseph Henry	P	1	.000	A	C
		Clancy, John Wm.	1B123	130	.300	B	
1	4	Cole, Albert George (Bert)	P	27	.167	Clev25	C
10	15	Connally, George Walter	P	43	.328	B	
		Crouse, Clyde Ellsworth	C81	85	.239	B	
4	7	Faber, Urban Chas. (Red)	P	18	.270	B	
		Falk, Bibb August	OF	145	.327	B	
		Flaskamper, Raymond Harold	SS25	26	.221	A	C
		Hunnefield, Wm. Fenton (2B17)	SS78	112	.285	B	
2	4	Jacobs, Wm. Elmer	P	25	.150	ChiN25	C
		Kamm, Wm. Edward	3B146	148	.270	B	
22	14	Lyons, Theodore Amar (Ted)	P	41	.255	B	
		Metzler, Alexander	OF	134	.319	Phil	
		Moore, Randolph Edward (Randy)	OF3	6	.000	A	

WON	LOST	NAME	POS.	G.	BA	FROM	TO
		Mostil, John Anthony	OF2	13	.125	B	
		McCurdy, Harry Henry	C82	86	.286	B	
		Neis, Bernard Edmund	OF	45	+.289	xClev	C
		Peckinpaugh, Roger Thorpe	SS60	68	.295	Wash	
		Reynolds, Carl Nettles	OF13	14	.214	A	
		Schalk, Raymond Wm. MGR.	C15	16	.231	B	
		Sheely, Earl Homer	1B36	45	.209	B	
0	1	Stewart, Frank	P	1	.000	A	C
19	16	Thomas, Alphonse Thomas Jr.	P	40	.147	B	
		Ward, Aaron Lee	2B138	145	.270	N.Y.	
		Way, Robert Clinton	2B1	5	.333	A	C
		Willson, Frank Hoxie	OF2	7	.100	Chi18	C

WON 72 LOST 82 TG 154

AMERICAN LEAGUE FINISHED 5th.

1928. PCT. .468

CHICAGO

RAYMOND WM. SCHALK RUSSELL AUBREY BLACKBURNE

WON	LOST	NAME	POS.	G.	BA	FROM	TO
10	16	Adkins, Grady Emmett	P36	39	.143	A	
0	2	Barnabe, Chas. Edward	P	11	.500	B	C
		Barrett, Wm. Joseph (2B25)	OF37	76	.277	B	
		Berg, Morris (Moe)	C73	76	.246	B	
		Blackerby, George Francis	OF20	30	.253	A	C
9	11	Blankenship, Theodore (Ted)	P	27	.169	B	
		Cissell, Chalmer Wm.	SS123	125	.260	A	
		Clancy, John Wm.	1B128	130	.271	B	
2	5	Connally, George Walter	P	28	.105	B	
1	2	Cox, George Melvin	P	26	.077	A	C
		Crouse, Clyde Ellsworth	C76	78	.252	B	
0	0	Dugan, Daniel Philip	P	1	.000	A	
13	9	Faber, Urban Chas. (Red)	P	27	.114	B	
		Falk, Bibb August	OF78	98	.290	B	
0	0	Goodell, John Henry Wm.	P	2	.000	A	C
		Hunnefield, Wm. Fenton	2B83	94	.294	B	
		Kamm, Wm. Edward	3B	155	.308	B	
0	0	Leopold, Rudolph Matas	P	2	.000	A	C
15	14	Lyons, Theodore Amar (Ted)	P39	49	.253	B	
		Mann, John Leo	3B1	6	.286	A	C
		Metzler, Alexander	OF133	139	.304	B	
		Moore, Randolph Edward (Randy)	OF16	24	.213	B	
		Mostil, John Anthony	OF131	133	.270	B	
		McCurdy, Harry Henry	C34	49	.262	B	
		Redfern, George Howard (SS33)	2B45	86	.234	A	
		Reymonds, Carl Nettles	OF74	84	.323	B	
		Schalk, Raymond Wm. MGR.	C	2	1.000	B	
		Shires, Arthur Lee (The Great)	1B32	33	.341	A	
		Swanson, Karl Edward	2B21	22	.141	A	
17	16	Thomas, Alphonse Thomas Jr.	P	36	.219	B	
4	7	Walsh, Edward Arthur Jr.	P	14	.111	A	
1	0	Weiland, Robert George (Bob)	P	1	.333	A	

WON	LOST	NAME	POS.	G.	BA	FROM	TO
0	0	Williamson, Silas Albert	P	1	.000	A	C
0	0	Wilson, Roy Edward	P	1	.000	A	C

WON 59 LOST 93 TG 152 — AMERICAN LEAGUE 1929. — FINISHED 7th. PCT. .388

CHICAGO

RUSSELL AUBREY BLACKBURNE

WON	LOST	NAME	POS.	G.	BA	FROM	TO
2	11	Adkins, Grady Emmett	P31	37	.239	B	C
		Autry, Martin Gordon	C30	43	.208	Clev	
		Barrett, Wm. Joseph	OF	3	+.000	B	Bos
		Berg, Morris (Moe)	C106	107	.287	B	
0	0	Blackburne, Russell Aubrey (Lena) MGR.	P	1	.000	Chi27	C
0	2	Blankenship, Theodore (Ted)	P	8	.250	B	
0	1	Byrne, Gerald Wilfred	P	3	.000	A	C
		Cissell, Chalmer Wm.	SS	152	.280	B	
		Clancy, John Wm.	1B74	92	.283	B	
0	0	Connally, George Walter	P	11	.000	B	
		Crouse, Clyde Ellsworth	C40	45	.272	B	
1	4	Dugan, Daniel Philip	P	19	.150	B	C
13	13	Faber, Urban Chas. (Red)	P	31	.128	B	
1	0	Henry, Frank John	P	2	.143	xN.Y.N	
		Hoffman, Clarence Casper	OF89	107	.258	A	C
		Hunnefield, Wm. Fenton	2B26	47	.181	B	
		Kamm, Wm. Edward	3B145	147	.268	B	
		Kerr, John Francis	2B122	127	.258	Det24	
14	20	Lyons, Theodore Amar (Ted)	P37	40	.220	B	
		Metzler, Alexander	OF141	146	.275	B	
		Mostil, John Anthony	OF11	12	.229	B	C
6	9	McKain, Harold LeRoy	P	34	.227	Clev27	
		Redfern, George Howard	2B11	21	.130	B	C
		Reynolds, Carl Nettles	OF130	131	.317	B	
		Shires, Arthur Lee (The Great)	1B88	100	.312	B	
		Sigafoos, Francis Leonard		7	+.333	xDet	
		Swanson, Karl Edward		2	.000	B	C
		Taitt, Douglas John	OF	47	+.168	xBos	
14	18	Thomas, Alphonse Thomas Jr.	P36	37	.255	B	
6	11	Walsh, Edward Arthur Jr.	P24	25	.233	B	
		Watwood, John Clifford	OF77	85	.302	A	
2	4	Weiland, Robert George (Bob)	P	15	.111	B	

WON 62 LOST 92 TG 154 — AMERICAN LEAGUE 1930. — FINISHED 7th. PCT. .403

CHICAGO

OWEN JOSEPH BUSH

WON	LOST	NAME	POS.	G.	BA	FROM	TO
		Appling, Lucius Benjamin (Luke)	SS	6	.308	A	
		Autry, Martin Gordon	C29	34	.253	B	C
		Barnes, Emil Deering	OF	85	+.248	xWash	C
		Berg, Morris (Moe)	C	20	.115	B	
2	1	Blankenship, Theodore (Ted)	P	7	.200	B	C
4	10	Braxton, Edgar Garland	P	19	+.087	xWash	
		Campbell, Bruce Douglas	OF	5	.500	A	
10	10	Caraway, Cecil Patrick	P	38	.172	A	
		Cissell, Chalmer Wm. (SS10 3B24)	2B106	141	.271	B	
		Clancy, John Wm.	1B60	68	.244	B	
		Crouse, Clyde Ellsworth	C38	42	.254	B	C
8	13	Faber, Urban Chas. (Red)	P	29	.041	B	
		Fothergill, Robert Roy	OF	52	+.311	xDet	
		Harris, David Stanley	OF	33	+.235	BosN28	Wash
		Henline, Walter John (Butch)	C2	3	.125	BknN	
2	17	Henry, Frank John	P	35	.235	B	C
		Hunnefield, Wm. Fenton	SS22	31	.272	B	
		Jeffries, Irvine Franklin (SS13)	3B20	40	.237	A	
		Jolley, Smead Powell	OF151	152	.313	A	
		Kamm, Wm. Edward	3B105	111	.269	B	
		Kerr, John Francis (SS19)	2B51	70	.289	B	
		Klinger, Joseph John (C1)	1B1	4	.375	NYN27	C
22	15	Lyons, Theodore Amar (Ted)	P42	57	.311	B	
		Metzler, Alexander	OF	56	+.176	B	StL
2	1	Moore, James Stanford	P	9	.231	Clev	
		Moore, James Wm. Jr.	OF	16	+.205	A	Phil
		Mulleavy, Gregory Thomas	SS73	77	.263	A	
6	4	McKain, Harold LeRoy	P32	33	.419	B	
		Reynolds, Carl Nettles	OF132	138	.359	B	
		Riddle, John Ludy	C	25	.241	A	
		Ryan, John Collins (Blondy)	3B23	28	.207	A	
		Shires, Arthur Lee (The Great)	1B	37	+.260	B	Wash
		Smith, Ernest Henry	SS21	24	.241	A	C
		Tate, Henry Bennett	C	72	+.326	xWash	
5	13	Thomas, Alphonse Thomas Jr.	P	34	.125	B	
1	4	Walsh, Edward Arthur Jr.	P37	39	.265	B	
		Watwood, John Clifford (OF43)	1B62	133	.302	B	
0	0	Wehde, Wilbur	P	4	.000	A	
0	4	Weiland, Robert George (Bob)	P	14	.000	B	
		Willingham, Thomas Hugh	2B1	3	.250	A	

WON 56 LOST 97 TG 153 — AMERICAN LEAGUE 1931. — FINISHED 8th (LAST) PCT. .366

CHICAGO

OWEN JOSEPH BUSH

WON	LOST	NAME	POS.	G.	BA	FROM	TO
		Appling, Lucius Benjamin (Luke)	SS76	96	.232	B	
		Blue, Luzerne Atwell (Lou)	1B	155	.304	StL	

WON	LOST	NAME	POS.	G.	BA	FROM	TO
0	1	Bowler, Grant Tierney	P	13	.100	A	
0	3	Braxton, Edgar Garland	P	17	+.091	B	StL
		Campbell, Bruce Douglas	OF	4	.412	B	
10	24	Caraway, Cecil Patrick	P51	52	.194	B	
		Cissell, Chalmer Wm. (2B23)	SS83	109	.220	B	
		Eichrodt, Frederick George	OF32	34	.214	Clev27	C
10	14	Faber, Urban Chas. (Red)	P	44	.076	B	
		Fonseca, Lewis Albert (1B2 2B21)	OF95	121	+.299	xClev	
		Fothergill, Robert Roy	OF74	108	.282	B	
13	15	Frasier, Victor Patrick	P	46	.209	A	
0	2	Garland, Louis Lyman	P	7	.000	A	C
		Garrity, Francis Joseph	C3	8	.214	A	C
		Grube, Franklin Thomas	C81	88	.219	A	
		Henline, Walter John (Butch)	C2	11	.067	B	C
		Jeffries, Irvine Franklin	3B61	79	.224	B	
		Jolley, Smead Powell	OF23	54	.300	B	
		Kamm, Wm. Edward	3B	18	+.254	B	Clev
		Kerr, John Francis	2B117	128	.268	B	
4	6	Lyons, Theodore Amar (Ted)	P22	42	.152	B	
0	2	Moore, James Stanford	P	33	.063	B	
6	9	McKain, Harold LeRoy	P27	32	.119	B	
		Norman, Henry Willis Patrick	OF17	24	.182	A	
		Reynolds, Carl Nettles	OF109	118	.290	B	
		Simons, Melbern Ellis	OF59	68	.275	A	
		Sullivan, Wm. Joseph Jr.(Billy)	3B83	92	.275	A	
		Tate, Henry Bennett	C85	89	.267	B	
10	14	Thomas, Alphonse Thomas Jr.	P	43	.241	B	
		Watwood, John Clifford	OF102	128	.283	B	
1	0	Wehde, Wilbur	P	8	.000	B	C
2	7	Weiland, Robert George (Bob)	P	15	.182	B	

WON 49 LOST 102 TG 151 — AMERICAN LEAGUE — FINISHED 7th.

1932. — PCT. .325

CHICAGO

LEWIS ALBERT FONSECA

WON	LOST	NAME	POS.	G.	BA	FROM	TO
		Anderson, Harold	OF	9	.250	A	C
		Appling, Lucius Benjamin (Luke) (2B30 3B14)	SS85	139	.274	B	
0	0	Bartholomew, Lester Justin	P	3	.000	PittN28	C
		Berry, Chas. Francis	C70	72	+.305	xBos	
1	1	Biggs, Chas. Orval	P	6	.111	A	C
		Blue, Luzerne Atwell (Lou)	1B105	112	.249	B	
0	0	Bowler, Grant Tierney	P	4	.000	B	C
		Campbell, Bruce Douglas	OF6	7	+.222	B	StL
2	6	Caraway, Cecil Patrick	P	19	.143	B	C
0	5	Chamberlain, Wm. Vincent	P	12	.100	A	C
		Cissell, Chalmer Wm.	SS	12	+.256	B	Clev
2	4	Daglia, Peter George	P	12	.077	A	C
		English, Chas. Dewie	3B13	24	.317	A	
0	0	Evans, Wm. Arthur	P	7	.000	A	C

WON	LOST	NAME	POS.	G.	BA	FROM	TO
2	11	Faber, Urban Chas. (Red)	P	42	.222	B	
1	0	Fieber, Clarence Thomas	P	3	.000	A	C
0	0	Fonseca, Lewis Albert MGR. (P1)	OF6	18	.135	B	
		Fothergill, Robert Roy	OF86	116	.295	B	
3	13	Frasier, Victor Patrick	P	29	.091	B	
		Funk, Elias Calvin	OF120	122	.259	Det30	
1	3	Gallivan, Philip Joseph	P	13	.375	BknN	
7	17	Gaston, Nathaniel Milton	P	28	.233	Bos	
5	3	Gregory, Paul Edwin	P	33	.079	A	
		Grube, Franklin Thomas	C92	93	.282	B	
1	1	Hadley, Irving Darius (Bump)	P	3	+.167	Wash	StL
		Hayes, Minter Carney (Jackie) (SS10 3B10)	2B97	117	.257	Wash	
		Hodapp, Urban John	OF31	68	+.222	xClev	
		Jolley, Smead Powell	OF11	12	+.357	B	Bos
10	15	Jones, Samuel Pond (Sad Sam)	P30	39	.193	Wash	
1	1	Kimsey, Clyde Elias (Chad)	P	7	+.000	xStL	
0	1	Kowalik, Fabian Lorenz	P	6	.385	A	
		Kress, Ralph (Red) (SS53 3B19)	OF64	135	+.283	xStL.	
10	15	Lyons, Theodore Amar (Ted)	P33	49	.260	B	
0	0	Moore, James Tanford	P	1	.000	B	C
		Mulleavy, Gregory Thomas	2B	1	.000	Chi30	
0	0	McKain, Harold LeRoy	P	8	.000	B	C
		Norman, Henry Willis Patrick	OF	13	.229	B	C
0	0	Poser, John Falk	P	5	.000	A	
		Rothrock, John Huston	OF19	39	+.188	xBos	
		Seeds, Robert Ira	OF112	116	+.291	xClev	
		Selph, Carey Isom	3B71	116	.283	StLN29	C
		Simons, Melbern Ellis	OF1	7	.000	B	C
0	1	Smith, Arthur Laird	P	3	.000	A	C
		Sullivan, Wm. Joseph Jr.(Billy) (3B17)	1B52	93	.316	B	
		Swanson, Ernest Evar	OF	14	.308	CinN30	
		Tate, Henry Bennett	C	4	+.100	B	Bos
3	3	Thomas, Alphonse Thomas Jr.	P	12	+.077	B	Wash
0	2	Walsh, Edward Arthur Jr.	P	4	.286	Chi30	C
		Watwood, John Clifford	OF	13	+.296	B	Bos
0	0	Wise, Archibald Edwin	P	3	.000	A	C

WON 67 LOST 83 TG 150 — AMERICAN LEAGUE — FINISHED 6th.

1933. — PCT. .447

CHICAGO

LEWIS ALBERT FONSECA

WON	LOST	NAME	POS.	G.	BA	FROM	TO
		Appling, Lucius Benjamin (Luke)	SS	151	.322	B	
		Berry, Chas. Francis	C83	86	.255	B	
		Bocek, Milton Francis	OF	11	.364	A	
10	6	Durham, Edward Fant	P	24	.217	Bos	C
		Dykes, James Joseph	3B	151	.260	Phil	

WON	LOST	NAME	POS.	G.	BA	FROM	TO
		English, Chas. Dewie	2B	3	.444	B	
3	4	Faber, Urban Chas. (Red)	P	36	.000	B	C
		Fonseca, Lewis Albert MGR.	1B12	23	.203	B	
1	1	Frasier, Victor Patrick	P	10	+.000	B	Det
		Funk, Elias Calvin	OF	10	.222	B	C
8	12	Gaston, Nathaniel Milton	P	30	.154	B	
4	11	Gregory, Paul Edwin	P	23	.143	B	C
		Grube, Franklin Thomas	C83	85	.230	B	
		Haas, George Wm. (Mule)	OF	146	.287	Phil	
0	0	Haid, Harold Augustine	P	6	.250	BosN31	C
		Hayes, Minter Carney (Jackie)	2B	138	.258	B	
7	5	Heving, Joseph Wm.	P	40	.211	NYN31	
0	0	Hutchinson, Ira Kendall	P	1	.500	A	
10	12	Jones, Samuel Pond (Sad Sam)	P27	37	.155	B	
4	1	Kimsey, Clyde Elias (Chad)	P	28	.152	B	
		Kress, Ralph (Red) (OF8)	1B111	129	.248	B	
		Lovett, Merritt Marwood		1	.000	A	C
10	21	Lyons, Theodore Amar (Ted)	P36	51	.286	B	
5	6	Miller, Walter J.	P26	30	.189	Clev31	C
0	0	Murray, George King	P	2	.000	Wash27	C
		Rhyne, Harold (Hal) (SS2 3B13)	2B19	39	.265	Bos	C
		Simmons, Aloysius Harry (Al)	OF145	146	.331	Phil	
		Stoneham, John Andrew	OF	10	.120	A	C
		Sullivan, Wm. Joseph Jr. (Billy) (C8)	1B22	54	.192	B	
		Swanson, Ernest Evar	OF139	144	.306	B	
2	0	Tietje, Leslie Wm.	P	3	.125	A	
		Webb, Earl Wm.	OF12	58	+.308	xDet	C
3	4	Wyatt, John Whitlow (Whit)	P	26	+.214	xDet	

WON 53 LOST 99 TG 152

AMERICAN LEAGUE 1934.

FINISHED 8th (LAST) PCT. .349

CHICAGO

LEWIS ALBERT FONSECA JAMES JOSEPH DYKES

WON	LOST	NAME	POS.	G.	BA	FROM	TO
		Appling, Lucius Benjamin (Luke)	SS110	118	.303	B	
		Bocek, Milton Francis	OF10	19	.211	B	C
		Boken, Robert Anthony (SS22)	2B47	81	+.236	xWash	C
		Bonura, Henry John (Zeke)	1B	127	.302	A	
		Bordagaray, Stanley George	OF17	29	.322	A	
		Caithamer, George Theodore	C	5	.316	A	C
		Chamberlin, Joseph Jeremiah (3B14)	SS26	43	.241	A	C
		Conlan, John Bertrand (Jocko)	OF54	63	.249	A	
		Dykes, James Joseph MGR. (1B27 2B27)	3B74	127	.268	B	
14	11	Earnshaw, George Livingston (Moose)	P	33	.203	Phil	
		Fehring, Wm. Paul	C	1	.000	A	C
4	7	Gallivan, Philip Joseph	P	35	.225	Chi32	C
6	19	Gaston, Nathaniel Milton	P	29	.147	B	C
		Haas, George Wm. (Mule)	OF89	106	.268	B	
		Hayes, Minter Carney (Jackie)	2B61	62	.257	B	
1	7	Heving, Joseph Wm.	P	33	.185	B	
		Hopkins, Meredith Hilliard	3B63	67	.214	xPhilN	
8	12	Jones, Samuel Pond (Sad Sam)	P	31	.200	B	
0	2	Kennedy, Lloyd Vernon (Vern)	P	3	.286	A	
0	1	Kinzy, Harry Hersel	P	13	.300	A	C
0	2	Klaerner, Hugo Emil	P	3	.333	A	C
		Kress, Ralph (Red)	OF	8	+.286	B	Wash
11	13	Lyons, Theodore Amar (Ted)	P	50	.206	B	
		Madjeski, Edward Wm.	C	85	+.221	xPhil	
		Mauldin, Marshall Reese	3B	10	.263	A	C
		Pasek, John Paul	C2	4	.333	Det	C
0	0	Pomorski, John Leon	P	3	.000	A	C
		Radcliff, Raymond Allen (Rip)	OF	14	.268	A	
		Ruel, Herold Dominic (Muddy)	C21	22	.211	StL	
		Shea, Mervyn David John	C60	62	.159	StL	
		Simmons, Aloysius Harry (Al)	OF	138	.344	B	
0	0	Stine, Lee Elbert	P	4	.000	A	
0	0	Stratton, Monty Franklin Pierce	P	1	.000	A	
		Swanson, Mrnest Ernest	OF105	117	.298	B	C
5	14	Tietje, Leslie Wm.	P	34	.017	B	
		Uhalt, Bernard Bartholomew	OF40	57	.242	A	C
		Uhlir, Chas.	OF6	14	.148	A	C
4	11	Wyatt, John Whitlow (Whit)	P	23	.231	B	

WON 74 LOST 78 TG 152

AMERICAN LEAGUE 1935.

FINISHED 5th. PCT. .487

CHICAGO

JAMES JOSEPH DYKES

WON	LOST	NAME	POS.	G.	BA	FROM	TO
		Appling, Lucius Benjamin (Luke)	SS	153	.307	B	
		Bonura, Henry John (Zeke)	1B	138	.295	B	
0	0	Chelini, Italo Vincent	P	2	.500	A	
		Conlan, John Bertrand (Jocko)	OF37	65	.286	B	C
		Dykes, James Joseph MGR. (1B16 2B3)	3B98	117	.288	B	
1	2	Earnshaw, George Livingston (Moose)	P	3	.286	B	BknN
5	5	Fischer, Chas. Wm.	P	24	+.190	xDet	
		Grube, Franklin Thomas	C	9	+.368	xStL	
		Haas, George Wm. (Mule)	OF84	92	.291	B	
		Hafey, Daniel Albert		2	.000	A	PittN
		Hayes, Minter Carney (Jackie)	2B85	89	.267	B	
		Hopkins, Meredith Hilliard (2B5)	3B49	59	.222	B	C
8	7	Jones, Samuel Pond (Sad Sam)	P21	22	.167	B	C
11	11	Kennedy, Lloyd Vernon (Vern)	P	31	.247	B	
		Kreevich, Michael Andreas	3B	6	.435	ChiN31	

WON	LOST	NAME	POS.	G.	BA	FROM	TO
15	8	Lyons, Theodore Amar (Ted)	P23	29	.220	B	
4	8	Phelps, Raymond Clifford	P	27	.122	BknN32	
		Piet, Anthony Francis (Tony) (3B17)	2B59	77	.298	xCinN	
		Radcliff, Raymond Allen (Rip)	OF142	146	.286	B	
1	2	Salveson, John Theodore	P	20	.300	xPittN	
		Sewell, James Luther (Luke)	C112	118	.285	Wash	
		Shea, Mervyn David John	C43	46	.230	B	
		Simmons, Aloysius Harry (Al)	OF126	128	.267	B	
0	0	Stine, Lee Elbert	P	1	.000	B	
1	2	Stratton, Monty Franklin Pierce	P	5	.143	B	
		Tauby, Fred Joseph	OF	13	.125	A	
9	15	Tietje, Leslie Wm.	P	30	.197	B	
2	2	Vance, Joseph Albert	P	10	.182	A	
		Washington, Sloane Vernon	OF79	108	.288	A	
13	13	Whitehead, John Henderson	P	28	.146	A	
		Wright, Forest Glenn	2B	9	.120	BknN33	C
4	3	Wyatt, John Whitlow (Whit)	P	30	.231	B	

WON 81 — AMERICAN LEAGUE — FINISHED 3rd.
LOST 70
TG 151 — 1936. — PCT. .536

CHICAGO

JAMES JOSEPH DYKES

WON	LOST	NAME	POS.	G.	BA	FROM	TO
		Appling, Lucius Benjamin (Luke)	SS137	138	.388	B	
		Bonura, Henry John (Zeke)	1B146	148	.330	B	
6	2	Brown, Clinton Harold (Clint)	P	38	.160	Clev	
14	10	Cain, Merritt Patrick (Sugar)	P	31	+.103	xStL	
4	3	Chelini, Italo Vincent	P	18	.156	B	
4	4	Dietrich, Wm. John (Bill)	P	14	+.267	xWash	
		Dykes, James Joseph MGR.	3B125	127	.267	B	
0	3	Evans, Russell Earl (Red)	P17	18	.133	A	
		Grube, Franklin Thomas	C32	33	.161	B	
		Haas, George Wm. (Mule)	OF96	119	.284	B	
		Hayes, Minter Carney (Jackie) (SS13)	2B89	108	.312	B	
21	9	Kennedy, Lloyd Vernon (Vern)	P35	36	.283	B	
		Kreevich, Michael Andreas	OF133	137	.307	B	
10	13	Lyons, Theodore Amar (Ted)	P	26	.157	B	
		Morrissey, Joseph Anselm (2B1 SS4)	3B9	17	.184	CinN33	C
4	6	Phelps, Raymond Clifford	P	15	.231	B	C
		Piet, Anthony Francis (Tony) (3B32)	2B68	109	.273	B	
		Radcliff, Raymond Allen (Rip)	OF132	138	.335	B	
		Rock, Lester Henry	1B	2	.000	A	C
		Rosenthal, Lawrence John (Larry)	OF80	85	.281	A	
		Sewell, James Luther (Luke)	C126	128	.251	B	
		Shea, Mervyn David John	C	14	.125	B	

WON	LOST	NAME	POS.	G.	BA	FROM	TO
0	0	Shores, Wm. David	P	9	.200	NYN33	C
5	7	Stratton, Monty Franklin Pierce	P	16	.216	B	
		Stumpf, George Frederick	OF4	10	.273	Bos33	C
0	0	Tietje, Leslie Wm.	P	2	+.000	B	StL
		Walker, Fred (Dixie)	OF	26	+.271	xN.Y.	
		Washington, Sloane Vernon	OF12	20	.163	B	C
13	13	Whitehead, John Henderson	P	34	.241	B	
0	0	Wyatt, John Whitlow (Whit)	P	3	.000	B	

WON 86 — AMERICAN LEAGUE — FINISHED 3rd.
LOST 68
TG 154 — 1937. — PCT. .558

CHICAGO

JAMES JOSEPH DYKES

WON	LOST	NAME	POS.	G.	BA	FROM	TO
		Appling, Lucius Benjamin (Luke)	SS	154	.317	B	
		Berger, Louis Wm. (Boze)	3B40	52	.238	Clev	
		Bonura, Henry John (Zeke)	1B115	116	.345	B	
7	7	Brown, Clinton Harold (Clint)	P	53	.222	B	
4	2	Cain, Merritt Patrick (Sugar)	P	18	.182	B	
0	1	Chelini, Italo Vincent	P	4	.000	B	C
		Connors, Mervyn James	3B	28	.233	A	
1	0	Cox, Wm. Donald	P	3	.250	StLN	
8	10	Dietrich, Wm. John (Bill)	P	29	.182	B	
		Dykes, James Joseph MGR. (3B11)	1B15	30	.306	B	
0	0	Gick, George Edward	P	1	.000	A	
		Haas, George Wm. (Mule)	1B32	54	.207	B	
		Hayes, Minter Carney (Jackie)	2B	143	.229	B	
14	13	Kennedy, Lloyd Vernon (Vern)	P	32	.230	B	
		Kreevich, Michael Andreas	OF138	144	.302	B	
12	10	Lee, Thornton Starr (Lefty)	P	30	.211	Clev	
12	7	Lyons, Theodore Amar (Ted)	P22	23	.211	B	
		Piet, Anthony Francis (Tony) (2B13)	3B86	100	.235	B	
		Radcliff, Raymond Allen (Rip)	OF139	144	.325	B	
		Rensa, George Anthony	C23	26	.298	N.Y.33	
2	5	Rigney, John Dugan	P	22	.167	A	
		Rosenthal, Lawrence John (Larry)	OF25	58	.289	B	
		Sewell, James Luther (Luke)	C118	122	.269	B	
		Shea, Mervyn David John	C	25	.211	B	
		Steinbacher, Henry John	OF15	26	.260	A	
15	5	Stratton, Monty Franklin Pierce	P	22	.200	B	
		Walker, Fred (Dixie)	OF	154	.302	B	
11	8	Whitehead, John Henderson	P	26	.224	B	

WON 65 / LOST 83 / TG 148 — AMERICAN LEAGUE — 1938. — FINISHED 6th. PCT. .439

CHICAGO

JAMES JOSEPH DYKES

WON	LOST	NAME	POS.	G.	BA	FROM	TO
		Appling, Lucius Benjamin (Luke)	SS78	81	.303	B	
		Berger, Louis Wm. (Boze) (2B42)	SS67	118	.217	B	
0	4	Boyles, Harry	P	9	.125	A	
1	3	Brown, Clinton Harold (Clint)	P	8	.500	B	
0	1	Cain, Merritt Patrick (Sugar)	P	5	.000	B	C
		Connors, Mervyn James	1B16	24	.355	B	C
0	2	Cox, Wm. Donald	P	7	+.000	B	StL
2	4	Dietrich, Wm. John (Bill)	P	8	.063	B	
		Dykes, James Joseph MGR.	2B23	26	.303	B	
0	0	Ford, Eugene Matthew	P	4	.167	BosN36	C
1	7	Gabler, Frank Harold	P	18	.238	xBosN	C
		Gerlach, John Glenn	SS8	9	.280	A	
0	0	Gick, George Edward	P	1	.000	B	C
		Hayes, Minter Carney (Jackie)	2B61	62	.328	B	
5	10	Knott, John Henry Jr.	P	20	+.125	xStL	
		Kreevich, Michael Andreas	OF127	129	.297	B	
		Kuhel, Joseph Anthony (Joey)	1B111	117	.267	Wash	
		Landrum, Jesse Glenn	2B3	4	.000	A	C
13	12	Lee, Thornton Starr (Lefty)	P33	34	.258	B	
9	11	Lyons, Theodore Amar (Ted)	P23	24	.194	B	
		Martin, Wm. Joseph		1	.000	NYN36	C
		Meyer, George Francis	2B	24	.296	A	C
		Owen, Marvin James (Freck)	3B140	141	.281	Det	
		Radcliff, Raymond Allen (Rip) (1B23)	OF99	129	.330	B	
		Rensa, George Anthony	C57	59	.248	B	
9	9	Rigney, John Dungan	P	38	.145	B	
		Rosenthal, Lawrence John (Larry)	OF22	61	.286	B	
		Schlueter, Norman John	C34	35	.229	A	
		Sewell, James Luther (Luke)	C	65	.213	B	
		Steinbacher, Henry John	OF101	106	.331	B	
15	9	Stratton, Monty Franklin Pierce	P26	27	.266	B	C
		Thompson, Rupert Luckhart	1B1	19	.111	BosN36	
		Tresh, Michael Jr. (Mike)	C	10	.241	A	
0	0	Uhle, Robert Elwood	P	1	.000	A	
		Walker, Gerald Holmes (Gee)	OF107	120	.305	Det	
10	11	Whitehead, John Henderson	P	32	.100	B	

WON 85 / LOST 69 / TG 154 — AMERICAN LEAGUE — 1939. — FINISHED 4th. PCT. .552

CHICAGO

JAMES JOSEPH DYKES

WON	LOST	NAME	POS.	G.	BA	FROM	TO
		Appling, Lucius Benjamin (Luke)	SS	148	.314	B	
		Bejma, Aloysius Frank	2B81	90	.251	StL36	C
0	0	Boyles, Harry	P	2	.000	B	C
11	10	Brown, Clinton Harold (Clint)	P	61	.211	B	
7	8	Dietrich, Wm. John (Bill)	P	25	.216	B	
0	1	Dobernic, Andrew Joseph	P	4	.000	A	
		Dykes, James Joseph MGR.	3B	2	.000	B	
0	1	Eaves, Vallie Ennis	P	2	.333	Phi135	
0	1	Frasier, Victor Patrick	P	10	.286	BosN37	C
		Gerlach, John Glenn	3B1	3	1.000	B	C
		Hayes, Minter Carney (Jackie)	2B69	72	.249	B	
0	0	Herring, Arthur L.	P	7	.000	BknN34	
		Kennedy, Robert Daniel	3B2	3	.250	A	
11	6	Knott, John Henry Jr.	P	25	.151	B	
		Kreevich, Michael Andreas	OF139	145	.323	B	
		Kuhel, Joseph Anthony (Joey)	1B136	139	.300	B	
15	11	Lee, Thornton Starr (Lefty)	P	33	.165	B	
14	6	Lyons, Theodore Amar (Ted)	P	21	.295	B	
3	3	Marcum, John Alfred	P	38	+.281	xStL	C
		McNair, Donald Eric (2B19)	3B103	129	.324	Bos	
		Owen, Marvin James (Freck)	3B55	58	.237	B	
		Radcliff, Raymond Allen (Rip) (1B20)	OF78	113	.264	B	
		Rensa, George Anthony	C13	14	.200	B	C
15	8	Rigney, John Dungan	P	35	.200	B	
		Rosenthal, Lawrence John (Larry)	OF93	107	.265	B	
		Schlueter, Norman John	C32	34	.232	B	
		Silvestri, Kenneth Joseph	C20	22	.173	A	
9	11	Smith, Edgar	P	29	+.115	xPhil	
		Steinbacher, Henry John	OF22	71	.171	B	C
		Thompson, Rupert Luckhart	OF	1	+.000	B	StL
		Tresh, Michael Jr. (Mike)	C	119	.259	B	
		Walker, Gerald Holmes (Gee)	OF147	149	.291	B	
0	3	Whitehead, John Henderson	P	7	+.000	B	StL

WON 82 / LOST 72 / TG 154 — AMERICAN LEAGUE — 1940. — FINISHED 4th. (TIED WITH BOSTON) PCT. .532

CHICAGO

JAMES JOSEPH DYKES

WON	LOST	NAME	POS.	G.	BA	FROM	TO
		Appling, Lucius Benjamin (Luke)	SS	150	.348	B	
4	6	Brown, Clinton Harold (Clint)	P	37	.071	B	
10	6	Dietrich, Wm. John (Bill)	P	23	.240	B	
0	2	Eaves, Vallie Ennis	P	5	.000	B	
0	0	Grove, Orval LeRoy	P	3	.000	A	
1	1	Hallett, Jack Price	P	2	.400	A	

WON	LOST	NAME	POS.	G.	BA	FROM	TO
		Hayes, Minter Carney (Jackie)	2B15	18	.195	B	C
4	0	Jablonowski, Peter Wm. (Appleton)	P	25	.176	Wash	
		Kennedy, Robert Daniel	3B	154	.252	B	
11	9	Knott, John Henry Jr.	P	25	.088	B	
		Kolloway, Donald Martin	2B	10	.225	A	
		Kreevich, Michael Andreas	OF	144	.265	B	
		Kuhel, Joseph Anthony (Joey)	1B	155	.280	B	
12	13	Lee, Thornton Starr (Lefty)	P	28	.274	B	
12	8	Lyons, Theodore Amar (Ted)	P	22	.240	B	
		McNair, Donald Eric (3B1)	2B65	66	.227	B	
15	18	Rigney, John Dungan	P39	40	.215	B	
		Rosenthal, Lawrence John (Larry)	OF92	107	.301	B	
		Short, David Orvis		4	.333	A	
		Silvestri, Kenneth Joseph	C1	28	.250	B	
14	9	Smith, Edgar	P	32	.217	B	
		Solters, Julius Joseph (Moose)	OF107	116	.308	StL	
		Tresh, Michael Jr. (Mike)	C	135	.281	B	
		Turner, Thomas Richard	C29	37	.208	A	
		Webb, James Leverne (Skeeter) (SS7 3B1)	2B74	84	.237	Clev	
0	0	Weiland, Edwin Nicholas	P	5	.200	A	
		Wright, Taft Shedron	OF144	147	.337	Wash	

WON 77
LOST 77
TG 154

AMERICAN LEAGUE

1941.

FINISHED 3rd.

PCT. .500

CHICAGO

JAMES JOSEPH DYKES

WON	LOST	NAME	POS.	G.	BA	FROM	TO
0	3	Appleton, Peter Wm. (Jablonowski)	P	13	.250	B	
		Appling, Lucius Benjamin (Luke)	SS	154	.314	B	
		Chapman, Wm. Benjamin	OF	57	+.226	xWash	
		Dickey, George Willard	C17	32	.200	Bos36	
5	8	Dietrich, Wm. John (Bill)	P	19	.088	B	
		Goletz, Stanley		5	.600	A	C
0	0	Grove, Orval LeRoy	P	2	.000	B	
		Hajduk, Chester		1	.000	A	C
5	5	Hallett, Jack Price	P	22	.154	B	
0	0	Haynes, Joseph Walton	P	8	.273	Wash	
		Hoag, Myril Oliver	OF	106	+.255	xStL	
4	2	Humphries, John Wm.	P	14	.087	Clev	
		Jones, James Murrell	1B	3	.000	A	
		Kennedy, Robert Daniel	3B71	76	.206	B	
		Knickerbocker, Wm. Hart	2B88	89	.245	N.Y.	
		Kolloway, Donald Martin (1B4)	2B62	71	.271	B	
		Kreevich, Michael Andreas	OF113	121	.232	B	
		Kuhel, Joseph Anthony (Joey)	1B151	153	.250	B	
22	11	Lee, Thornton Starr (Lefty)	P	35	.254	B	

WON	LOST	NAME	POS.	G.	BA	FROM	TO
		Lodigiani, Dario Antonio (Lodi)	3B86	87	.239	Phil	
12	10	Lyons, Theodore Amar (Ted)	P	22	.270	B	
		Philley, David Earl	OF2	7	.222	A	
13	13	Rigney, John Dungan	P	30	.202	B	
		Rosenthal, Lawrence John (Larry)	OF	20	+.237	B	Clev
3	8	Ross, Lee Raven (Buck)	P	20	+.219	xPhil	
		Short, David Orvis	OF2	3	.000	B	C
13	17	Smith, Edgar	P	34	.216	B	
		Solters, Julius Joseph (Moose)	OF63	76	.259	B	
		Tresh, Michael Jr. (Mike)	C	115	.251	B	
		Turner, Thomas Richard	C35	38	.238	B	
		Webb, James Laverne (Skeeter) (SS5 3B3)	2B18	29	.190	B	
		Wright, Taft Shedron	OF134	136	.322	B	

WON 66
LOST 82
TG 148

AMERICAN LEAGUE

1942.

FINISHED 6th.

PCT. .446

CHICAGO

JAMES JOSEPH DYKES

WON	LOST	NAME	POS.	G.	BA	FROM	TO
0	0	Appleton, Peter Wm.	P	4	+.000	B	StL
		Appling, Lucius Benjamin (Luke)	SS141	142	.262	B	
		Dickey, George Willard	C29	59	.233	B	
6	11	Dietrich, Wm. John (Bill)	P	26	.104	B	
		Grant, James Chas.	3B10	12	.167	A	
4	6	Grove, Orval LeRoy	P	12	.227	B	
8	5	Haynes, Joseph Walton	P	40	.179	B	
		Heim, Val Raymond	OF12	13	.200	A	C
		Hoag, Myril Oliver	OF112	113	.240	B	
12	12	Humphries, John Wm.	P	28	.225	B	
		Jones, James Murrell	1B5	7	.150	B	
		Kennedy, Robert Daniel (OF16)	3B96	113	.231	B	
		Kolloway, Donald Martin (1B33)	2B116	147	.273	B	
		Kuhl, Joseph Anthony (Joey)	1B112	115	.249	B	
2	6	Lee, Thornton Starr (Lefty)	P	11	.200	B	
		Lodigiani, Dario Antonio (Lodi) (2B7)	3B43	59	.280	B	
14	6	Lyons, Theodore Amar (Ted)	P	20	.239	B	
		Moses, Wallace Jr.	OF145	146	.270	Phil	
		Mueller, Wm. Lawrence	OF	26	.165	A	
0	1	Perme, Leonard Joseph	P	4	.333	A	
3	3	Rigney, John Dungan	P	7	.053	B	
5	7	Ross, Lee Raven (Buck)	P	22	.158	B	
		Sketchley, Harry Clement	OF12	13	.194	A	C
7	20	Smith, Edgar	P	29	.123	B	
		Tresh, Michael (Mike) Jr.	C	72	.232	B	
		Tucker, Thurman Lowell	OF5	7	.125	A	

WON	LOST	NAME	POS.	G.	BA	FROM	TO
		Turner, Thomas Richard	C54	56	.242	B	
5	5	Wade, Jacob Fields (Jake)	P	15	.241	StL39	
		Webb, James Leverne (Skeeter)	2B29	32	.170	B	
0	0	Weiland, Edwin Nicholas	P	5	.000	Chi40	C
		Wells, Leo Donald	SS12	35	.194	A	
		West, Samuel Filmore	OF45	49	.232	Wash	C
		Wright, Taft Shedron	OF81	85	.333	B	

WON 82 — AMERICAN LEAGUE — FINISHED 4th.
LOST 72
TG 154 — 1943. — PCT. .532

CHICAGO

JAMES JOSEPH DYKES

WON	LOST	NAME	POS.	G.	BA	FROM	TO
		Appling, Lucius Benjamin (Luke)	SS	155	.328	B	
		Castino, Vincent Chas.	C30	33	.228	A	
		Cuccinello, Anthony Francis (Tony)	3B30	34	.272	xBosN	
		Culler, Richard Broadus (2B19 SS3)	3B26	53	.216	Phil36	
		Curtright, Guy Paxton	OF128	138	.291	A	
12	10	Dietrich, Wm. John (Bill)	P	26	.143	B	
		Grant, James Chas.	3B	58	+.259	B	Clev
15	9	Grove, Orval LeRoy	P	32	.182	B	
0	0	Hanski, Donald Thomas (P1)	1B5	9	.238	A	
7	2	Haynes, Joseph Walton	P	35	.265	B	
		Hodgin, Elmer Ralph (OF42)	3B56	117	.314	BosN39	
11	11	Humphries, John Wm.	P	28	.290	B	
		Kalin, Frank Bruno		4	.000	PittN40	C
		Kolloway, Donald Martin	2B	85	.216	B	
		Kuhel, Joseph Anthony (Joey)	1B	153	.213	B	
		Kwietniewski, Casimir Eugene	3B	2	.000	A	
5	9	Lee, Thornton Starr (Lefty)	P	19	.071	B	
7	4	Maltzberger, Gordon Ralph	P	37	.120	A	
		Moses, Wallace Jr.	OF148	150	.245	B	
11	7	Ross, Lee Raven (Buck)	P	21	.087	B	
11	11	Smith, Edgar	P	25	.159	B	
		Solters, Julius Joseph (Moose)	OF21	42	.155	Chi41	C
0	0	Speer, Floyd Vernie	P	1	.000	A	
0	2	Swift, Wm.	P	18	.100	BknN41	C
		Tresh, Michael Jr. (Mike)	C85	86	.215	B	
		Tucker, Thurman Lowell	OF132	139	.235	B	
		Turner, Thomas Richard	C49	51	.240	B	
3	7	Wade, Jacob Fields (Jake)	P	21	.148	B	
		Webb, James Leverne (Skeeter)	2B54	58	.235	B	

WON 71 — AMERICAN LEAGUE — FINISHED 7th.
LOST 83
TG 154 — 1944. — PCT. .461

CHICAGO

JAMES JOSEPH DYKES

WON	LOST	NAME	POS.	G.	BA	FROM	TO
0	0	Carnett, Edwin Elliott (P2 1B25)	OF88	126	.276	BosN41	
		Castino, Vincent Chas.	C26	29	.231	B	
		Clarke, Richard Grey	3B45	63	.260	A	C
		Cuccinello, Anthony Francis (Tony) (2B6)	3B30	38	.262	B	
		Curtright, Guy Paxton	OF51	72	.253	B	
		Dickshot, John Oscar	OF40	62	.253	NYN39	
16	17	Dietrich, Wm. John (Bill)	P	36	.117	B	
14	15	Grove, Orval LeRoy	P	34	.104	B	
0	0	Hanski, Donald Thomas	P	2	.000	B	C
5	6	Haynes, Joseph Walton	P	33	.200	B	
		Hoag, Myril Oliver	OF14	17	+.229	Chi42	Clev
		Hodgin, Elmer Ralph (OF33)	3B82	121	.295	B	
8	10	Humphries, John Wm.	P	30	.189	B	
		Jordan, Thomas Jefferson	C	14	.267	A	
3	9	Lee, Thornton Starr (Lefty)	P	15	.095	B	
11	10	Lopat, Edmund Walter	P27	30	.309	A	
10	5	Maltzberger, Gordon Ralph	P	46	.136	B	
		Metzig, Wm. Andrew	2B	5	.125	A	C
		Michaels, Casimir Eugene (3B3) (Kwietniewski)	SS21	27	.176	B	
		Moses, Wallace Jr.	OF134	136	.280	B	
2	7	Ross, Lee Raven (Buck)	P	20	.077	B	
		Schalk, LeRoy John (SS5)	2B142	146	.220	NY32	
0	0	Speer, Floyd Vernie	P	2	.000	B	C
		Tresh, Michael Jr. (Mike)	C	93	.260	B	
		Trosky, Harold Arthur (Hal)	1B130	135	.241	Clev41	
		Tucker, Thurman Lowell	OF120	124	.287	B	
		Turner, Thomas Richard	C	36	+.230	B	StL
2	4	Wade, Jacob Fields (Jake)	P	19	.292	B	
		Webb, James Leverne (Skeeter) (2B5)	SS135	139	.211	B	

WON 71 — AMERICAN LEAGUE — FINISHED 6th.
LOST 78
TG 149 — 1945. — PCT. .477

CHICAGO

JAMES JOSEPH DYKES

WON	LOST	NAME	POS.	G.	BA	FROM	TO
		Appling, Lucius Benjamin	SS17	18	.362	Chi43	
		Baker, Floyd Wilson (2B11)	3B58	82	.250	StL	
6	7	Caldwell, Earle Welton	P	27	.216	StL37	
		Castino, Vincent Chas.	C25	26	.216	B	C
		Cuccinello, Anthony Francis (Tony)	3B112	118	.308	B	C
		Curtright, Guy Paxton	OF84	98	.281	B	
		Dickshot, John Oscar	OF124	130	.302	B	C
7	10	Dietrich, Wm. John (Bill)	P	18	.167	B	

WON	LOST	NAME	POS.	G.	BA	FROM	TO
		Farrell, Major Kerby	1B97	103	.258	BosN43	
14	12	Grove, Orval LeRoy	P	33	.099	B	
5	5	Haynes, Joseph Walton	P14	15	.175	B	
		Hockett, Oris Leon	OF	106	.293	Clev	C
6	14	Humphries, John Wm.	P	22	.148	B	
3	0	Johnson, John Clifford	P	29	.286	N.Y.	C
15	12	Lee, Thornton Starr (Lefty)	P	29	.179	B	
10	13	Lopat, Edmund Walter	P26	32	.293	B	
		Michaels, Casimir Eugene (2B1) (Kwietniewski)	SS126	129	.245	B	
		Moses, Wallace Jr.	OF139	140	.295	B	
		Mueller, Wm. Lawrence	OF7	13	.000	Chi42	C
		Nagel, Wm. Taylor (3B1)	1B57	67	.209	PhilN41	C
		Orengo, Joseph Chas. (2B1)	3B7	17	.067	Det	C
4	4	Papish, Frank Richard	P	19	.231	A	
		Reynolds, Daniel Vance (2B11)	SS14	29	.167	A	C
1	1	Ross, Lee Raven (Buck)	P	13	.182	B	C
		Schalk, LeRoy John	2B	133	.248	B	C
0	0	Touchstone, Clayland Moffitt	P	6	.000	BosN29	C
		Tresh, Michael (Mike) Jr.	C	150	.249	B	

WON 74 AMERICAN LEAGUE FINISHED 5th.
LOST 80
TG 154 1946. PCT. .481

CHICAGO

JAMES JOSEPH DYKES THEODORE AMAR LYONS

WON	LOST	NAME	POS.	G.	BA	FROM	TO
		Appling, Lucius Benjamin	SS	149	.309	B	
		Baker, Floyd Wilson	3B6	9	.250	B	
13	4	Caldwell, Earle Welton	P	39	.167	B	
		Curtright, Guy Paxton	OF15	23	.200	B	C
		Dickey, George Willard	C30	37	.192	Chi42	
3	3	Dietrich, Wm. John (Bill)	P	11	.053	B	
		Fernandes, Edward Paul	C12	14	.250	PittN40	C
8	13	Grove, Orval LeRoy	P	33	.108	B	
2	7	Hamner, Ralph Conant	P	25	.167	A	
		Hayes, Frank Witman (Blimp)	C52	53	+.212	xClev	
7	9	Haynes, Joseph Walton	P	32	.246	B	
		Hodgin, Elmer Ralph	OF57	87	.252	Chi44	
3	2	Hollingsworth, Albert Wayne (Al)	P	21	+.000	xStL	C
		Jones, James Murrell	1B20	24	.266	Chi42	
		Jordan, Thomas Jefferson	C2	10	+.267	Chi44	Clev
		Kennedy, Robert Daniel (3B29)	OF75	113	.258	Chi42	
		Kolloway, Donald Martin (3B31)	2B90	123	.280	Chi43	
		Kuhel, Joseph Anthony (Joey)	1B63	64	+.273	xWash	
2	4	Lee, Thornton Starr (Lefty)	P	7	.267	B	
		Lodigiani, Dario Antonio (Lodi)	3B	44	.245	Chi42	C
13	13	Lopat, Edmund Walter	P29	30	.253	B	

WON	LOST	NAME	POS.	G.	BA	FROM	TO
1	4	Lyons, Theodore Amar (Ted) MGR.	P	5	.000	Chi42	
2	0	Maltzberger, Gordon Ralph	P	19	.000	Chi44	
		Michaels, Casimir Eugene (SS6 3B13) (Kwietniewski)	2B66	91	.258	B	
		Moses, Wallace Jr.	OF36	56	+.274	B	Bos
0	0	O'Neill, Robert Emmett	P	2	.000	xChiN	C
7	5	Papish, Frank Richard	P	31	.186	B	
0	0	Perme, Leonard Joseph	P	4	.000	Chi42	C
		Philley, David Earl	OF	17	.353	Chi41	
		Platt, Mizell George	OF61	84	.251	ChiN43	
5	5	Rigney, John Dungan	P	15	.154	Chi42	
		Smaza, Joseph P.	OF1	2	.200	A	C
8	11	Smith, Edgar	P	24	.178	Chi43	
		Tresh, Michael Jr. (Mike)	C79	80	.217	B	
		Trosky, Harold Arthur (Hal)	1B80	88	.254	Chi44	C
		Tucker, Thurman Lowell	OF110	121	.288	Chi44	
		Wells, Leo Donald (SS2)	3B38	45	.189	Chi42	C
		Whitman, Walter Franklin (1B1 2B1)	SS6	17	.063	A	
		Wright, Taft Shedron	OF107	115	.275	Chi42	

WON 70 AMERICAN LEAGUE FINISHED 6th.
LOST 84
TG 154 1947. PCT. .455

CHICAGO

THEODORE AMAR LYONS

WON	LOST	NAME	POS.	G.	BA	FROM	TO
		Appling, Lucius Benjamin (3B2)	SS129	139	.306	B	
		Baker, Floyd Wilson (2B1,SS1)	3B101	105	.264	B	
1	0	Bithorn, Hiram Gabriel	P	2	.000	ChiN	C
1	4	Caldwell, Earle Welton	P	40	.000	B	
		Christopher, Loyd Eugene	OF	7	.217	ChiN45	C
		Dickey, George Willard	C80	83	.223	B	C
2	3	Gebrian, Peter	P	27	.000	A	C
5	8	Gillespie, Robert Wm.	P	25	.061	Det44	
6	8	Grove, Orval LeRoy	P	25	.146	B	
3	8	Harrist, Earl	P	33	.208	CinN45	
14	6	Haynes, Joseph Walton	P	29	.262	B	
		Hodgin, Elmer Ralph	OF41	59	.294	B	
		Jones, James Murrell	1B43	45	+.240	B	Bos
		Kennedy, Robert Daniel (3B1)	OF106	115	.262	B	
		Kolloway, Donald Martin (1B11 3B8)	2B99	124	.278	B	
		Kuhel, Joseph Anthony (Joey)		4	.000	B	
3	7	Lee, Thornton Starr (Lefty)	P	21	.207	B	
16	13	Lopat, Edmund Walter	P31	35	.198	B	
1	4	Maltzberger, Gordon Ralph	P	33	.143	B	C
		Michaels, Casimir Eugene (3B44) (Kwietniewski)	2B60	110	.273	B	
12	12	Papish, Frank Richard	P	38	.086	B	
		Philley, David Earl (3B4)	OF133	143	.258	B	

WON	LOST	NAME	POS.	G.	BA	FROM	TO
2	3	Rigney, John Dungan	P	11	.000	B	C
3	5	Ruffing, Chas. Herbert (Red)	P9	14	.208	N.Y.	C
1	3	Smith, Edgar	P	15	+.167	B	Bos
		Stephenson, Joseph Chester	C13	16	.143	ChiN44	C
		Tresh, Michael Jr. (Mike)	C89	90	.241	B	
		Tucker, Thurman Lowell	OF65	89	.236	B	
		Wallaesa, John	SS27	81	.195	Phil	
		(3B1 OF22)					
		Wright, Taft Shedron	OF100	124	.324	B	
		York, Rudolph Preston (Rudy)	1B	102	+.243	xBos	

WON 51 LOST 101 TG 152

AMERICAN LEAGUE — FINISHED 8th (LAST)

1948. — PCT. .336

CHICAGO

THEODORE AMAR LYONS

WON	LOST	NAME	POS.	G.	BA	FROM	TO
		Adams, Herbert Loren	OF4	5	.273	A	
		Appling, Lucius Benjamin	3B72	139	.314	B	
		(SS64)					
		Baker, Floyd Wilson	3B71	104	.215	B	
		(2B18 SS1)					
0	0	Bradley, Frederick Langdon	P	8	.000	A	
1	5	Caldwell, Earle Welton	P	25	+.000	B	Bos
		Delsing, James Henry	OF15	20	.190	A	
8	10	Gettel, Allen Jones (2B1)	P22	24	+.241	xClev	
0	4	Gillespie, Robert Wm.	P	25	.000	B	
0	0	Goodwin, James Patrick	P	8	.500	A	C
2	10	Grove, Orval LeRoy	P	32	.095	B	
2	6	Gumpert, Randall Pennington	P	16	+.138	xN.Y.	
1	3	Harrist, Earl	P	11	+.000	B	Wash
9	10	Haynes, Joseph Walton	P	27	.160	B	
		Hodgin, Elmer Ralph	OF79	114	.266	B	C
4	5	Judson, Howard Kolls	P40	41	.103	A	
		Kennedy, Robert Daniel	OF	30	+.248	B	Clev
		Kolloway, Donald Martin	2B83	119	.273	B	
		(3B18)					
		Lupien, Ulysses John	1B	154	.246	PhilN45	C
		Michaels, Casimir Eugene	SS85	145	.248	B	
		(2B55 OF1) (Kwietniewski)					
3	6	Moulder, Glen Herbert	P	33	.300	StL	C
2	8	Papish, Frank Richard	P	32	.185	B	
2	3	Pearson, Isaac Overton	P	23	.200	PhilN46	C
		Philley, David Earl	OF128	137	.287	B	
8	10	Pieretti, Marino Paul	P21	32	+.179	xWash	
		Robinson, Aaron Andrew	C92	98	.252	N.Y.	
0	1	Rotblatt, Marvin Joseph	P	7	.000	A	
		Scala, Gerard Daniel	OF2	3	.000	A	
		Seerey, James Patrick	OF93	95	+.229	xClev	
		Tresh, Michael Jr. (Mike)	C34	39	.250	B	
		Wallaesa, John (OF1)	SS5	33	.188	B	C
		Weigel, Ralph Richard (OF2)	C39	66	.233	Clev46	
		Whitman, Walter Franklin	SS1	3	.000	Chi46	C

WON	LOST	NAME	POS.	G.	BA	FROM	TO
9	20	Wight, Wm. Robert	P	34	082	N.Y.	
		Wright, Taft Shedron	OF114	134	.279	B	

WON 63 LOST 91 TG 154

AMERICAN LEAGUE — FINISHED 6th.

1949. — PCT. .409

CHICAGO

JOHN JAMES ONSLOW

WON	LOST	NAME	POS.	G.	BA	FROM	TO
		Adams, Herbert Loren	OF48	56	.293	B	
		Appling, Lucius Benjamin	SS141	142	.301	B	
		Baker, Floyd Wilson	3B122	125	.260	B	
		(2B1 SS3)					
		Baumer, James Sloan	SS7	8	.400	A	
		Bowers, Grover Bill	OF20	26	.192	A	C
0	0	Bradley, Frederick Langdon	P	1	.000	B	C
1	2	Bruner, Jack Raymond	P	4	.000	A	
0	0	Cain, Robert Max	P	6	.000	A	
0	0	Carrasquel, Alejandro Alexander	P	3	.000	Wash45	C
0	1	Evans, Wm. Lawrence	P	4	.000	A	
2	5	Gettel, Allen Jones	P	19	+.167	B	Wash
		Goldsberry, Gordon Frederick	1B38	39	.248	A	
0	1	Groth, Ernest Wm.	P	3	.000	Clev	C
0	0	Grove, Orval LeRoy	P	1	.000	B	C
13	16	Gumpert, Randall Pennington	P	34	.190	B	
4	6	Haefner, Milton Arnold	P	14	+.261	xWash	
		Hancock, Fred James	SS27	39	.135	A	C
		(3B3 OF1)					
		Higdon, Wm. Travis	OF6	11	.304	A	C
1	14	Judson, Howard Kolls	P	26	.065	B	
2	0	Klieman, Edward Frederick	P	18	+.250	xWash	
		Kolloway, Donald Martin	3B2	4	+.000	B	Det
		Kress, Chas. Steven	1B95	97	.278	xCinN	
		Krsnich, Rocco Peter	3B	16	.218	A	
10	6	Kuzava, Robert LeRoy	P	29	.036	Clev47	
		Lane, Richard Harrison	OF11	12	.119	A	C
		Malone, Edward Russell	C51	55	.271	A	
		Metkovich, George Michael	OF87	93	.237	Clev47	
		Michaels, Casimir Eugene	2B	154	.308	B	
		(Kwietniewski)					
		Ostrowski, John Theodore	OF41	49	.266	Bos	
		(3B8)					
		Philley, David Earl	OF145	146	.286	B	
7	15	Pierce, Walter Wm.	P32	39	.176	Det	
4	6	Pieretti, Marino Paul	P39	48	.237	B	
		Rapp, Earl Wellington	OF13	19	+.259	xDet	
		Rhawn, Robert John (SS3)	3B19	24	.205	xPittN	C
		Scala, Gerard Daniel	OF	37	.250	B	
		Seerey, James Patrick	OF2	4	.000	B	C
1	1	Shoun, Clyde Mitchell	P	16	.200	xBosN	C
		Souchock, Stephen (1B30)	OF39	84	.234	N.Y.	
3	5	Surkont, Maxim Constantine	P	44	.045	A	
		Tipton, Joseph John	C53	67	.204	Clev	

WON	LOST	NAME	POS.	G.	BA	FROM	TO
		Wheeler, Donald Wesley	C58	67	.240	A	C
15	13	Wight, Wm. Robert	P	35	.165	B	
		Yankowski, George Edward	C6	12	.167	Phil42	C
		Zernial, Gus Edward	OF46	73	.318	A	

WON 60 AMERICAN LEAGUE FINISHED 6th.
LOST 94
TG 154 1950. PCT. .390

CHICAGO

JOHN JAMES ONSLOW JOHN MICHAEL CORRIDEN SR.

WON	LOST	NAME	POS.	G.	BA	FROM	TO
		Adams, Herbert Loren	OF33	34	.203	B	C
7	2	Aloma, Luis Barba	P	42	.067	A	
		Appling, Lucius Benjamin (1B13 2B1)	SS20	50	.234	B	C
		Baker, Floyd Wilson (2B3 OF2)	3B53	83	.317	B	
0	0	Bruner, Jack Raymond	P	9	+.000	B	StL
		Busby, James Franklin	OF12	18	.208	A	
9	12	Cain, Robert Max	P34	35	.197	B	
		Carrasquel, Alfonso Colon	SS	141	.282	A	
0	0	Connelly, Wm. Wirt	P	2	+.000	Phil45	Det
0	0	Cuellar, Chas. Jesus Patrick	P	2	.000	A	C
		Erautt, Joseph Michael	C5	16	.222	A	
		Fox, Jacob Nelson	2B121	130	.247	Phil	
		Goldsberry, Gordon Frederick (OF3)	1B40	82	.268	B	
5	12	Gumpert, Randall Pennington	P40	41	.071	B	
1	6	Haefner, Milton Arnold	P	24	.200	B	BosN
3	10	Holcombe, Kenneth Edward	P	24	.156	CinN48	
2	3	Judson, Howard Kolls	P	46	.100	B	
0	1	Keriazakos, Constantine Nicholas	P	1	1.000	A	
		Kirrene, Joseph John	3B	1	.250	A	
		Kozar, Albert Kenneth (3B1)	2B4	10	+.300	xWash	C
		Kress, Chas. Steven	1B2	3	.000	B	
0	0	Kretlow, Louis Henry	P	11	+.000	xStL	
1	3	Kuzava, Robert LeRoy	P	10	+.083	B	Wash
		Majeski, Henry	3B112	122	.309	Phil	
		Malone, Edward Russell	C21	31	.225	B	C
		Masi, Philip Samuel	C114	122	.279	PittN	
		Michaels, Casimir Eugene	2B35	36	+.312	B	Wash
		McCormick, Myron Winthrop	OF44	55	.232	xNYN	
		McGhee, Warren Edward	OF1	3	.167	A	
		Niarhos, Constantine Gregory	C36	41	+.324	xN.Y.	
		Ostrowski, John Theodore	OF14	1	+.500	B	Wash
				21	+.222	(and return)	C
0	0	Perkovich, John Joseph	P	1	.000	A	C
		Philley, David Earl	OF154	156	.242	B	
12	16	Pierce, Walter Wm.	P33	40	.260	B	
		Rickert, Marvin August (1B1)	OF78	84	.237	xPittN	C
		Robinson, Wm. Edward	1B	119	+.311	xWash	

WON	LOST	NAME	POS.	G.	BA	FROM	TO
0	0	Rotblatt, Marvin Joseph	P	2	.000	Chi48	
		Salkeld, Wm. Franklin	C	1	.000	BosN	C
		Scala, Gerard Daniel	OF23	40	.194	B	C
10	13	Scarborough, Ray Wilson	P	27	+.174	xWash	
10	16	Wight, Wm. Robert	P	30	.000	B	
		Wilson, Wm. Donald	OF2	3	.000	A	
		Zernial, Gus Edward	OF137	143	.280	B	

WON 81 AMERICAN LEAGUE FINISHED 4th.
LOST 73
TG 154 1951. PCT. .526

CHICAGO

PAUL RAPIER RICHARDS

WON	LOST	NAME	POS.	G.	BA	FROM	TO
6	0	Aloma, Luis Barba	P	25	.350	B	
		Baler, Floyd Wilson (2B5 SS3)	3B44	82	.263	B	
		Boyd, Robert Richard	1B6	12	.167	A	
0	0	Brown, Hector Harold	P3	4	1.000	A	
		Busby, James Franklin	OF139	143	.283	B	
1	2	Cain, Robert Max	P	4	+.333	B	Det
		Carrasquel, Alfonso Colon	SS	147	.264	B	
		Coleman, Raymond LeRoy	OF	51	+.276	xStL	
		DeMaestri, Joseph Paul (2B11 3B8)	SS27	56	.203	A	
		Dillinger, Robert Bernard	3B70	89	.301	xPittN	C
7	6	Dobson, Joseph Gordon	P	28	.065	Bos	
5	6	Dorish, Harry (3B1)	P32	32	.258	StL	
		Erautt, Joseph Michael	C12	16	.160	B	C
		Fox, Jacob Nelson	2B	147	.313	B	
		Goldsberry, Gordon Frederick	1B8	10	.091	B	
0	0	Grimsley, Ross Albert	P	7	.000	A	C
9	8	Gumpert, Randall Pennington	P33	37	.333	B	
		Haas, Berthold John (3B1 OF4)	1B7	23	.163	NYN49	C
		Hairston, Samuel	C2	4	.400	A	C
11	12	Holcombe, Kenneth Edward	P	28	.250	B	
5	6	Judson, Howard Kolls	P	27	.121	B	
6	9	Kretlow, Louis Henry	P	26	.083	B	
		Lehner, Paul Eugene	OF20	23	+.208	xPhil	StL
		Lenhardt, Donald Eugene (1B1)	OF53	64	+.266	xStL	
1	1	Littlefield, Richard Bernard	P	4	.000	Bos	
0	0	Mahoney, Robert Paul	P	3	+.000	A	StL
		Majeski, Henry	3B9	12	+.257	B	Phil
		Masi, Philip Samuel	C78	84	.271	B	
		Minoso, Saturnino Orestes Arrieta Armas (SS1 3B68)	OF82	138	+.324	xClev	
		Nelson, Glenn Richard		6	.000	xPittN	
		Niarhos, Constantine Gregory	C59	66	.256	B	
		Philley, David Earl	OF6	7	+.240	B	Phil
15	14	Pierce, Walter Wm.	P37	39	.203	B	
		Robinson, Wm. Edward	1B147	151	.282	B	

WON	LOST	NAME	POS.	G.	BA	FROM	TO
11	7	Rogovin, Saul Walter	P22	24	+.203	xDet	
4	2	Rotblatt, Marvin Joseph	P	26	.000	B	C
		Sheely, Hollis Kimball	C33	34	.180	A	
		Stewart, Edward Perry	OF63	95	.276	Wash	
		Wilson, Robert James	C	4	.273	A	
		Zarilla, Allen Lee	OF117	120	.257	Bos	
		Zernial, Gus Edward	OF	4	+.105	B	Phil

WON 81 LOST 73 TG 154 — AMERICAN LEAGUE 1952. — FINISHED 3rd. PCT. .526

CHICAGO

PAUL RAPIER RICHARDS

WON	LOST	NAME	POS.	G.	BA	FROM	TO
3	1	Aloma, Luis Barba	P	25	.000	B	
2	3	Brown, Hector Harold	P24	51	.158	B	
		Busby, James Franklin	OF	16	+.128	B	Wash
		Carrasquel, Alfonso Colon	SS99	100	.248	B	
		Coleman, Raymond LeRoy	OF72	85	+.215	B	StL
		Dente, Samuel Joseph (1B2 2B6 3B18 OF6)	SS27	62	.221	Wash	
14	10	Dobson, Joseph Gordon	P	29	.190	B	
8	4	Dorish, Harry	P	39	.091	B	
		Edwards, Henry Albert	OF3	8	.333	xCinN	
		Esposito, Samuel	SS	1	.250	A	C
		Fox, Jacob Nelson	2B151	152	.296	B	
12	10	Grissom, Marvin Edward	P	28	.151	Det49	
0	5	Holcombe, Kenneth Edward	P	7	+.000	B	StL
0	0	Hudson, Hal Campbell	P	2	+.000	xStL	
		Johnson, Darrell Dean	C20	22	+.108	xStL	
0	1	Judson, Howard Kolls	P	21	.000	B	
2	2	Kennedy, Wm. Aulton	P	47	.231	StL	
4	4	Kretlow, Louis Henry	P	19	.050	B	
		Krsnich, Rocco Peter	3B37	40	.231	Chi49	
		Landenberger, Kenneth Henry	1B1	2	.200	A	C
		Lollar, John Sherman	C120	132	.240	StL	
		Masi, Philip Samuel	C25	30	.254	B	C
		Mele, Sabath Anthony (1B3)	OF112	123	+.248	xWash	
		Minoso, Saturnino Orestes Arrieta Armas (SS1 3B9)	OF143	147	.281	B	
		Miranda, Guillermo Perez (2B2 3B5)	SS53	12	+.250	Wash	StL
				58	+.218	(& returned)	
		Nicholas, Donald Leigh		3	.000	A	
15	12	Pierce, Walter Wm.	P33	35	.187	B	
		Rivera, Manuel Joseph	OF	53	+.249	xStL	
		Robinson, Wm. Edward	1B	155	.296	B	
		Rodriguez, Hector Antonio	3B113	124	.265	A	C
14	9	Rogovin, Saul Walter	P	33	.202	B	
		Sheely, Hollis Kimball	C31	36	.240	B	
		Stewart, Edward Perry	OF60	92	.267	B	
7	12	Stobbs, Chas. Klein	P	38	.079	Bos	
		Thomas, Leo Raymond	3B9	19	+.167	xStL	C
0	0	Widmar, Albert Joseph	P	1	.000	StL	C

NAME	POS.	G.	BA	FROM	TO
Wilson, George Washington	OF1	8	.111	A	NYN
Wilson, Robert James	C	2	.000	B	
Wright, Thomas Everett	OF34	60	+.258	xStL	
Zarilla, Allen Lee	OF32	39	+.232	B	StL

WON 89 LOST 65 TG 154 — AMERICAN LEAGUE 1953. — FINISHED 3rd. PCT. .578

CHICAGO

PAUL RAPIER RICHARDS

WON	LOST	NAME	POS.	G.	BA	FROM	TO
2	0	Aloma, Luis Barba	P	24	.000	B	C
3	3	Bearden, Henry Eugene	P25	31	.190	StL	C
		Berry, Cornelius John	2B3	5	+.125	xStL	
		Boyd, Robert Richard (OF16)	1B29	55	.297	Chi51	
2	0	Byrne, Thomas Joseph	P6	18	+.167	StL	Wash
		Carrasquel, Alfonso Colon	SS	149	.279	B	
		Clark, Alfred Aloysius (OF1)	1B1	9	+.067	xPhil	C
7	5	Consuegra, Sandalio Simeon Castellon	P	29	+.057	xWash	
		Dente, Samuel Joseph	SS1	2	.000	B	
5	5	Dobson, Joseph Gordon	P	23	.069	B	
10	6	Dorish, Harry	P	55	.171	B	
		Elliott, Robert Irving (OF2)	3B58	67	+.260	xStL	
		Fain, Ferris Roy	1B127	128	.256	Phil	
8	7	Fornieles, Jose Miguel Torres	P	39	.098	Wash	
		Fox, Jacob Nelson	2B	154	.285	B	
1	0	Harrist, Earl	P	7	+.000	StL	Det
0	0	Hudson, Hal Campbell	P	1	.000	B	C
4	4	Johnson, Clifford	P14	15	.050	A	
7	5	Keegan, Robert Chas.	P	22	.321	A	
0	0	Kretlow, Louis Henry	P	9	+.000	B	StL
		Krsnich, Rocco Peter	3B57	64	.202	B	C
		Lollar, John Sherman (1B1)	C107	113	.287	B	
		Marsh, Fred Francis (1B5 2B2 SS17)	3B32	67	.200	StL	
		Mele, Sabath Anthony (1B2)	OF138	140	.274	B	
		Minoso, Saturnino Orestes Arrieta Armas (3B10)	OF147	151	.313	B	
18	12	Pierce, Walter Wm. (1B1)	P40	42	.126	B	
		Rivera, Manuel Joseph	OF	156	.259	B	
7	12	Rogovin, Saul Walter	P	22	.135	B	
		Ryan, Cornelius Joseph	3B16	17	.222	xPhilN	
		Sheely, Hollis Kimball	C17	31	.217	B	C
		Stephens, Vernon Decatur (SS3)	3B38	44	+.186	Bos	StL
		Stewart, Edward Perry	OF16	53	.271	B	
15	6	Trucks, Virgil Oliver	P	24	+.238	xStL	
		Wilson, Robert James	C63	71	.250	B	
		Wilson, Wm. Donald	OF3	9	.059	Chi50	
		Wright, Thomas Everett	OF33	77	.250	B	

WON 94
LOST 60
TG 154

AMERICAN LEAGUE 1954. FINISHED 3rd. PCT. .610

CHICAGO

PAUL RAPIER RICHARDS MARTIN WHITFORD MARION

WON	LOST	NAME	POS.	G.	BA	FROM	TO
		Batts, Matthew Daniel	C42	55	+.228	xDet	
		Boyd, Robert Richard (1B12)	OF13	29	.179	B	
		Cain, Robert Max		1	.000	StL	C
		Carrasquel, Alfonso Colon	SS	155	.255	B	
		Cavarretta, Philip Joseph (OF9)	1B44	71	.316	ChiN	
16	3	Consuegra, Sandalio Simeon Castellon (3B1)	P39	39	.229	B	
6	4	Dorish, Harry	P	37	.111	B	
		Fain, Ferris Roy	1B64	65	.302	B	
0	0	Flanigan, Thomas Anthony	P	2	.000	A	
1	2	Fornieles, Jose Miguel Torres	P15	16	.273	B	
		Fox, Jacob Nelson	2B	155	.319	B	
		Groth, John Thomas	OF	125	.275	StL	
14	8	Harshman, John Elvin (1B1)	P35	36	.143	NYN52	
		Hatton, Grady Edgebert (1B2)	3B10	13	+.167	xCinN	Bos
		Jackson, Ronald Allen	1B35	40	.280	A	
8	7	Johnson, Donald Roy	P	46	.029	Wash52	
		Jok, Stanley Edward	3B	3	.167	xPhilN	
16	9	Keegan, Robert Chas.	P31	32	.120	B	
		Kell, George Clyde (3B31 OF2)	1B32	71	+.283	xBos	
		Kirrene, Joseph John	3B	9	.304	Chi50	C
		Lollar, John Sherman	C93	107	.244	B	
		Marsh, Fred Francis (1B2 SS3 OF1)	3B36	62	.306	B	
		Marshall, Willard Warren	OF29	47	.254	CinN	
5	4	Martin, Morris Webster	P	35	+.133	xPhil	
		Michaels, Casimir Eugene (2B2)	3B91	101	.262	Phil	C
		Minoso, Saturnino Orestes Arrieta Armas (3B9)	OF146	153	.320	B	
		McGhee, Warren Edward	OF33	42	+.227	xPhil	
		Nicholas, Donald Leigh		7	.000	Chi52	C
9	10	Pierce, Walter Wm.	P36	38	.193	B	
		Rivera, Manuel Joseph	OF143	145	.286	B	
		Sawatski, Carl Ernest	C33	43	.183	ChiN	
0	1	Sima, Albert	P	5	+.000	Wash	Phil
		Stewart, Edward Perry	OF2	18	.077	B	C
0	0	Strahs, Richard Bernard	P	9	.000	A	C
19	12	Trucks, Virgil Oliver	P	40	.183	B	
0	0	Valentinetti, Vito John	P	1	.000	A	
		Wilson, Robert James	C	8	+.200	B	Det
		Wilson, Wm. Donald	OF19	20	+.171	B	Phil

WON 91
LOST 63
TG 154

AMERICAN LEAGUE 1955. FINISHED 3rd. PCT. .591

CHICAGO

MARTIN WHITFORD MARION

WON	LOST	NAME	POS.	G.	BA	FROM	TO
		Adams, Robert Henry (2B1)	3B9	28	.095	xCinN	
		Battey, Earl Jesse	C	5	.286	A	
		Brideweser, James Ehrenfeld (2B2 3B3)	SS26	34	.207	Balt	
		Busby, James Franklin	OF	99	+.243	xWash	
4	6	Byrd, Harry Gladwin	P	25	+.067	xBalt	
		Carrasquel, Alfonso Colon	SS144	145	.256	B	
		Cavarretta, Philip Joseph	1B3	6	.000	B	C
0	0	Chakales, Robert Edward	P	7	+.000	Balt	Wash
		Coan, Gilbert Fitzgerald	OF3	17	+.176	xBalt	
6	5	Consuegra, Sandalio Simeon Castellon	P	44	.103	B	
		Courtney, Clinton Dawson	C17	19	+.378	Balt	Wash
15	9	Donovan, Richard Edward	P29	40	.224	Det	
2	0	Dorish, Harry	P	13	+.333	B	Balt
		Dropo, Walter	1B140	141	.280	Det	
		Esposito, Samuel	3B2	3	.000	Chi52	
6	3	Fornieles, Jose Miguel Torres	P26	28	.103	B	
		Fox, Jacob Nelson	2B	154	.311	B	
0	0	Gray, Theodore Glenn	P	2	+.000	Det	Clev
		Groth, John Thomas	OF26	32	+.338	B	Wash
11	7	Harshman, John Elvin	P	32	.183	B	
8	3	Howell, Millard Fillmore	P	35	.381	CinN49	
		Jackson, Ronald Allen	1B29	40	.203	B	
7	4	Johnson, Clifford	P17	19	.152	Chi53	
		Jok, Stanley Edward (OF1)	3B3	6	.250	B	C
2	5	Keegan, Robert Chas.	P	18	.333	B	
		Kell, George Clyde (1B24 OF1)	3B105	128	.312	B	
		Kennedy, Robert Daniel (1B2 OF20)	3B56	83	+.304	xBalt	
		Lollar, John Sherman	C136	138	.261	B	
		Marshall, Willard Warren	OF12	22	.171	B	C
2	3	Martin, Morris Webster	P	37	.300	B	
		Merriman, Lloyd Archer		1	.000	CinN	ChiN
		Minoso, Saturnino Orestes Arrieta Armas (3B2)	OF138	139	.288	B	
		Moss, John Lester	C	32	+.254	xBalt	
		McGhee, Warren Edward	OF17	26	.077	B	C
		Nieman, Robert Chas.	OF78	99	.283	Det	
		Northey, Ronald James	OF2	14	.357	ChiN52	
0	0	Papai, Alfred Thomas	P	7	.000	StLN50	C
		Peterson, Carl Fr ancis	SS	6	.286	A	
15	10	Pierce, Walter Wm.	P33	34	.171	B	
		Powell, Robert Leroy		1	.000	A	
		Rivera, Manuel Joseph	OF143	147	.264	B	
		Stephens, Vernon Decatur	3B18	22	+.250	xBalt	C
13	8	Trucks, Virgil Oliver	P	32	.125	B	

WON	LOST	NAME	POS.	G.	BA	FROM	TO
		White, Edward Perry	OF2	3	.500	A	C

WON 85 LOST 69 TG 154

AMERICAN LEAGUE 1956. FINISHED 3rd. PCT. .552

CHICAGO

MARTIN WHITFORD MARION

WON	LOST	NAME	POS.	G.	BA	FROM	TO
		Abrams, Calvin Ross	OF2	4	.333	Balt	C
		Aparicio, Luis Ernesto	SS	152	.266	A	
		Battey, Earl Jesse	C3	4	.250	B	
		Brideweser, James Ehrenfeld	SS	10	+.182	B	Det
0	1	Byrd, Harry Gladwin	P	3	.000	B	
1	2	Consuegra, Sandalio Simeon Castellon	P	28	+.000	B	Balt
0	0	Dahlke, Jerome Alexander	P	5	.000	A	C
		Delsing, James Henry	OF30	55	+.122	xDet	
0	1	Derrington, Chas. James	P	1	.500	A	
		Doby, Lawrence Eugene	OF137	140	.268	Clev	
12	10	Donovan, Richard Edward	P34	44	.222	B	
		Dropo, Walter	1B117	125	.266	B	
		Esposito, Samuel (2B3 SS19)	3B61	81	.228	B	
0	0	Fischer, Wm. Chas.	P	3	.000	A	
0	1	Fornieles, Jose Miguel Torres	P	6	+.200	B	Balt
		Fox, Jacob Nelson	2B	154	.296	B	
15	11	Harshman, John Elvin	P34	36	.169	B	
		Hatfield, Fred James (2B1 SS3)	3B97	106	+.262	xDet	
5	6	Howell, Millard Fillmore	P	34	.235	B	
0	1	Johnson, Clifford	P.	5	+.000	B	Balt
		Jackson, Ronald Allen	1B19	22	.214	B	
5	7	Keegan, Robert Chas.	P	20	.125	B	
		Kell, George Clyde (1B3)	3B19	21	+.313	B	Balt
		Kennedy, Robert Daniel	3B6	8	+.077	B	Det
3	1	Kinder, Ellis Raymond	P	29	.000	xStLN	
3	1	LaPalme, Paul Edmore	P	29	.000	xCinN	
		Lollar, John Sherman	C132	136	.293	B	
0	0	Marlowe, Richard Burton	P	1	+.000	xDet	C
1	0	Martin, Morris Webster	P	10	+.200	B	Balt
		Minoso, Saturnino Orestes Arrieta Armas (1B1 3B8)	OF148	151	.316	B	
		Moss, John Lester	C49	56	.244	B	
0	2	McDonald, James Leroy	P	8	.000	Balt	
		Nieman, Robert Chas.	OF10	14	+.300	B	Balt
		Northey, Ronald James	OF4	53	.354	B	
		Philley, David Earl (OF30)	1B49	86	+.265	xBalt	
		Phillips, John Melvin (3B2)	OF35	67	.273	Det	
20	9	Pierce, Walter Wm.	P35	39	.157	B	
3	1	Pollet, Howard Joseph	P11	12	.375	ChiN	PittN
		Rivera, Manuel Joseph	OF134	139	.255	B	
8	3	Staley, Gerald Lee	P	26	+.094	xN.Y.	
9	12	Wilson, James Alger	P	28	+.306	xBalt	

WON 90 LOST 64 TG 154

AMERICAN LEAGUE 1957. FINISHED 2nd. PCT. .584

CHICAGO

ALFONSO RAMON LOPEZ

WON	LOST	NAME	POS.	G.	BA	FROM	TO
		Aparicio, Luis Ernesto	SS142	143	.257	B	
		Battey, Earl Jesse	C43	48	.174	B	
		Beard, Cramer Theodore	OF28	38	.205	PittN52	
0	1	Derrington, Chas. James	P	20	.000	B	C
		Doby, Lawrence Eugene	OF110	119	.288	B	
16	6	Donovan, Richard Edward	P28	30	.145	B	
		Dropo, Walter	1B69	93	.256	B	
		Esposito, Samuel (2B4 SS22 OF1)	3B53	94	.205	B	
7	8	Fischer, Wm. Chas.	P	33	.150	B	
		Fox, Jacob Nelson	2B	155	.317	B	
8	8	Harshman, John Elvin	P	30	.222	B	
		Hatfield, Fred James	3B44	69	.202	B	
6	5	Howell, Millard Fillmore	P37	42	.185	B	
0	0	Hughes, James Robert	P	4	.000	ChiN	C
		Jackson, Ronald Allen	1B	13	.317	B	
10	8	Keegan, Robert Chas.	P	30	.103	B	
		Kennedy, Robert Daniel		4	.000	B	BknN
0	0	Kinder, Ellis Raymond	P	1	.000	B	C
		Landis, James Henry	OF90	96	.212	A	
1	4	LaPalme, Paul Edmore	P35	36	.500	B	
1	2	Latman, Arnold Barry	P	7	.000	A	
		Lollar, John Sherman	C96	101	.256	B	
0	1	McDonald, James Leroy	P	10	.000	B	
0	0	McIlwain, Stover Wm.	P	1	.000	A	
		Minoso, Saturnino Orestes Arrieta Armas (3B1)	OF152	153	.310	B	
		Moss, John Lester	C39	42	.270	B	
		Northey, Ronald James		40	.185	B	PhilN
		Philley, David Earl (1B2)	OF17	22	+.324	B	Det
		Phillips, John Melvin (OF20)	3B97	121	.270	B	
20	12	Pierce, Walter Wm.	P37	41	.172	B	
		Powell, Robert Leroy		1	.000	Chi55	C
		Rivera, Manuel Joseph (1B31)	OF86	125	.256	B	
1	0	Rudolph, Frederick Donald	P	5	.500	A	
5	1	Staley, Gerald Lee	P	47	.045	B	
		Torgeson, Clifford Earl (OF1)	1B70	86	+.295	xDet	
15	8	Wilson, James Alger	P30	31	.147	B	

WON 82 LOST 72 TG 154

AMERICAN LEAGUE 1958. FINISHED 2nd. PCT. .532

ALFONSO RAMON LOPEZ

WON	LOST	NAME	POS.	G.	BA	FROM	TO
		Aparicio, Luis Ernesto	SS	145	.266	B	
		Battey, Earl Jesse	C49	68	.226	B	
		Beard, Cramer Theodore	OF15	19	.091	B	C
		Boone, Raymond Otis	1B64	77	+.244	xDet	
		Callison, John Wesley	OF	18	.297	A	
		Cash, Norman Dalton	OF4	13	.250	A	
15	14	Donovan, Richard Edward	P	34	.113	B	
		Dropo, Walter	1B16	28	.192	B	CinN
		Esposito, Samuel	3B63	98	.247	B	
		(2B2 SS22 OF1)					
2	3	Fischer, Wm. Chas.	P	17	+.143	B	Det
		Fox, Jacob Nelson	2B	155	.300	B	
		Francona, John Patsy	OF35	41	+.258	Balt	Det
		Goodman, Wm. Dale	3B111	116	.299	Balt	
		(1B3 2B1 SS1)					
0	0	Howell, Millard Fillmore	P	1	.000	B	C
		Jackson, Ronald Allen	1B38	61	.233	B	
0	2	Keegan, Robert Chas.	P	14	.000	B	C
		Landis, James Henry	OF	142	.277	B	
3	0	Latman, Arnold Barry	P	13	.083	B	
		Lindstrom, Chas. Wm.	C	1	1.000	A	C
		Lollar, John Sherman	C116	127	.273	B	
3	3	Lown, Omar Joseph	P	27	.333	xCinN	
		McAnany, James	OF3	5	.000	A	
0	0	McDonald, James Leroy	P	3	.000	B	C
0	0	McIlwain, Stover Wm.	P	1	.000	B	C
9	7	Moore, Raymond LeRoy	P	32	.205	Balt	
		Moss, John Lester		2	.000	B	C
		Mueller, Donald Frederick	OF43	70	.253	NYN	
		Phillips, John Melvin	3B47	84	.273	B	
		(OF37)					
17	11	Pierce, Walter Wm.	P	35	.205	B	
0	0	Qualters, Thomas Francis	P	26	.000	xPhilN	C
		Rivera, Manuel Joseph	OF99	116	.225	B	
		Romano, John Anthony	C2	4	.286	A	
1	0	Rudolph, Frederick Donald	P	7	.000	B	
4	2	Shaw, Robert John	P28	29	+.000	xDet	
		Smith, Alphonse Eugene (3B1)	OF138	139	.252	Clev	
4	5	Staley, Gerald Lee	P	50	.000	B	
		Torgeson, Clifford Earl	1B73	96	.266	B	
1	0	Trosky, Harold Arthur Jr.	P	2	.000	A	C
9	9	Wilson, James Alger	P	28	.078	B	C
14	16	Wynn, Early	P	40	.200	Clev	

WON 94 — AMERICAN LEAGUE — FINISHED 1st.
LOST 60
TG 154 — 1959. — PCT. .610

CHICAGO

ALFONSO RAMON LOPEZ

WON	LOST	NAME	POS.	G.	BA	FROM	TO
		Aparicio, Luis Ernesto	SS	152	.257	B	
2	0	Arias, Rodolfo Martinez	P	34	.000	A	C
		Battey, Earl Jesse	C20	26	.219	B	
		Boone, Raymond Otis	1B6	9	+.238	B	K.C.
		Callison, John Wesley	OF41	49	.173	B	
		Carreon, Camilo Garcia	C	1	.000	A	
		Cash, Norman Dalton	1B31	58	.240	B	
		Doby, Lawrence Eugene	OF12	21	+.241	xDet	C
		(1B2)					
9	10	Donovan, Richard Edward	P	31	.131	B	
		Ennis, Delmer	OF25	26	.219	xCinN	C
		Esposito, Samuel	3B45	69	.167	B	
		(2B2 SS14)					
		Fox, Jacob Nelson	2B	156	.306	B	
		Goodman, Wm. Dale (2B3)	3B74	104	.250	B	
		Hicks, Wm. Joseph	OF4	6	.429	A	
		Jackson, Ronald Allen	1B5	10	.214	B	
		Kluszewski, Theodore Bernard	1B29	31	.297	xPittN	
		Landis, James Henry	OF148	149	.272	B	
8	5	Latman, Arnold Barry	P	37	.128	B	
		Lollar, John Sherman (1B24)	C122	140	.265	B	
9	2	Lown, Omar Joseph	P	60	.250	B	
		Martin, Joseph Clifton	3B2	3	.250	A	
		McAnany, James	OF	67	.276	B	
0	1	McBride, Kenneth Faye	P	11	.167	A	
3	6	Moore, Raymond LeRoy	P	29	.087	B	
		Mueller, Donald Frederick		4	.500	B	C
0	0	Peters, Gary Chas.	P	2	.000	A	
		Phillips, John Melvin	3B100	117	.264	B	
		(OF23)					
14	15	Pierce, Walter Wm.	P	34	.191	B	
0	0	Raymond, Joseph Claude Marc	P	3	.000	A	
		Rivera, Manuel Joseph	OF69	80	.220	B	
		Romano, John Anthony	C38	53	.294	B	
0	0	Rudolph, Frederick Donald	P	4	.000	B	CinN
18	6	Shaw, Robert John	P	47	.123	B	
		Simpson, Harry Leon (1B1)	OF12	38	+.187	xK.C.	PittN
		Skizas, Louis Peter	OF6	8	.077	Det	C
		Smith, Alphonse Eugene	OF128	129	.237	B	
		(3B1)					
8	5	Staley, Gerald Lee	P	67	.154	B	
1	0	Stanka, Joe Donald	P	2	.333	A	C
		Torgeson, Clifford Earl	1B103	127	.220	B	
22	10	Wynn, Early	P	37	.244	B	

WON 87 — AMERICAN LEAGUE — FINISHED 3rd.
LOST 67
TG 154 — 1960. — PCT. .565

CHICAGO

ALFONSO RAMON LOPEZ

WON	LOST	NAME	POS.	G.	BA	FROM	TO
		Aparicio, Luis Ernesto	SS	153	.277	B	
		Averill, Earl Douglas	C5	10	.214	xChiN	
13	6	Baumann, Frank Matthew	P	47	.154	Bos	
		Brown, Richard Ernest	C14	16	.163	Clev	

WON	LOST	NAME	POS.	G.	BA	FROM	TO
		Carreon, Camilo Garcia	C7	8	.235	B	
6	1	Donovan, Richard Edward	P	33	.130	B	
		Esposito, Samuel (2B5 SS11)	3B37	57	.182	B	
0	1	Farrarese, Donald Hugh	P	5	.500	Clev	
		Fox, Jacob Nelson	2B149	150	.289	B	
		Freese, Eugene Lewis	3B122	127	.273	PhilN	
0	0	Garcia, Edward Miguel	P	15	.333	Clev	
		Ginsberg, Myron Nathan	C25	28	+.253	xBalt	
		Goodman, Wm. Dale (2B7)	3B20	30	.234	B	
		Hicks, Wm. Joseph	OF14	36	.191	B	
		Johnson, Stanley Lucius	OF2	5	.167	A	
6	3	Kemmerer, Russell Paul	P	36	+.000	xWash	
		Kluszewski, Theodore Bernard	1B39	81	.293	B	
		Landis, James Henry	OF147	148	.253	B	
		Lollar, John Sherman	C123	129	.252	B	
2	3	Lown, Omar Joseph	P	45	.200	B	
		Martin, Joseph Clifton (1B1)	3B5	7	.100	B	
		McAnany, James		3	.000	B	
0	1	McBride, Kenneth Faye	P	5	.000	B	
		Minoso, Saturnino Orestes Arrieta Armas	OF	154	.311	Clev	
1	1	Moore, Raymond LeRoy	P	14	+.000	B	Wash
0	0	Peters, Gary Chas.	P	2	.000	B	
14	7	Pierce, Walter Wm.	P	32	.179	B	
		Rivera, Manuel Joseph	OF24	48	.294	B	
		Robinson, Floyd Andrew	OF17	22	.283	A	
0	0	Rush, Robert Ransom	P	9	1.000	xMilN	C
5	10	Score, Herbert Jude	P	23	.100	Clev	
13	13	Shaw, Robert John	P	36	.138	B	
		Sievers, Roy Edward (OF6)	1B114	127	.295	Wash	
		Smith, Alphonse Eugene	OF141	142	.315	B	
13	8	Staley, Gerald Lee	P	64	.235	B	
0	0	Striker, Wilbur Scott	P	2	.000	Clev	C
		Torgeson, Clifford Earl	1B10	68	.263	B	
1	1	Worthington, Allan Fulton	P	4	+1.000	xBos	
13	12	Wynn, Early	P	36	.200	B	

WON 86 AMERICAN LEAGUE FINISHED 4th.
LOST 76
TG 162 1961. PCT. .531

CHICAGO

ALFONSO RAMON LOPEZ

WON	LOST	NAME	POS.	G.	BA	FROM	TO
		Aparicio, Luis Ernesto	SS	156	.272	B	
10	13	Baumann, Frank Matthew	P53	55	.262	B	
0	1	Brice, Alan Healey	P	3	.000	A	C
		Carey, Arthur Andrew	3B54	56	+.266	xK.C.	
		Carreon, Camilo Garcia	C71	78	.271	B	
		Covington, John Wesley	OF14	22	+.288	xMil.N	K.C.
0	0	DeGerick, Michael Arthur	P	1	.000	A	
		Esposito, Samuel (2B11 SS20)	3B28	63	.170	B	
		Fox, Jacob Nelson	2B	159	.251	B	
		Ginsberg, Myron Nathan	C2	6	+.000	B	Bos
		Goodman, Wm. Dale (1B2 2B1)	3B7	41	.255	B	
3	3	Hacker, Warren Louis	P	42	.111	PhilN58	C
9	6	Herbert, Raymond Ernest	P	21	+.226	xK.C.	
		Hershberger, Norman Michael	OF13	15	.309	A	
1	3	Horlen, Joel Edward	P	5	.000	A	
3	3	Kemmerer, Russell Paul	P	47	.200	B	
		Landis, James Henry	OF139	140	.283	B	
7	2	Larsen, Donald James	P	25	+.320	xK.C.	
		Lepcio, Thaddeus Stanley	3B1	5	+.000	PhilN	Minn
		Lollar, John Sherman	C107	116	.282	B	
		Look, Dean Zachary	OF1	3	.000	A	C
7	5	Lown, Omar Joseph	P59	60	.000	B	
		Martin, Joseph Clifton (3B36)	1B60	110	.230	B	
10	13	McLish, Calvin Coolidge	P	31	.167	CinN	
		Minoso, Saturnino Orestes Arrieta Armas	OF147	152	.280	B	
0	0	Peters, Gary Chas.	P	3	.333	B	
10	9	Pierce, Walter Wm.	P	39	.143	B	
		Pilarcik, Alfred James	OF17	47	+.177	xK.C.	C
14	7	Pizarro, Juan Cordova	P39	40	.246	MilN	
		Rivera, Manuel Joseph		1	+.000	B	K.C.
		Robinson, Floyd Andrew	OF106	132	.310	B	
		Roselli, Robert Edward	C10	22	.263	MilN58	
1	2	Score, Herbert Jude	P	8	.000	B	
3	4	Shaw, Robert John	P	14	+.000	B	K.C.
		Sievers, Roy Edward	1B132	141	.295	B	
		Smith, Alphonse Eugene (OF71)	3B80	147	.278	B	
0	3	Staley, Gerald Lee	P	16	+.000	B	K.C.
		Torgeson, Clifford Earl	1B1	20	+.067	B	N.Y.
8	2	Wynn, Early	P	17	.162	B	

WON 85 AMERICAN LEAGUE FINISHED 5th.
LOST 77
TG 162 1962. PCT. .525

CHICAGO

ALFONSO RAMON LOPEZ

WON	LOST	NAME	POS.	G.	BA	FROM	TO
		Aparicio, Luis Ernesto	SS152	153	.241	B	
7	6	Baumann, Frank Matthew	P	40	.267	B	
		Berry, Allen Kenneth	OF2	3	.333	A	
8	12	Buzhardt, John Wm.	P	28	.118	PhilN	
		Carreon, Camilo Garcia	C93	106	.256	B	
		Conde, Ramon Luis	3B7	14	.000	A	C
		Cunningham, Joseph Roberts (OF5)	1B143	149	.295	StLN	
0	0	DeBusschere, David Albert	P	12	.000	A	
0	0	DeGerick, Michael Arthur	P	1	.000	B	C

WON	LOST	NAME	POS.	G.	BA	FROM	TO
		Esposito, Samuel	3B41	75	.235	B	
		(2B7 SS20)					
		Farley, Robert Jacob	1B14	35	+.189	SFN	Det
9	5	Fisher, Eddie Gene	P	57	.130	SFN	
		Fox, Jacob Nelson	2B154	157	.267	B	
20	9	Herbert, Raymond Ernest	P	35	.195	B	
		Hershberger, Norman Michael	OF135	148	.262	B	
7	6	Horlen, Joel Edward	P	20	.053	B	
		Jones, Grover Wm.	1B6	18	.321	A	
2	1	Joyce, Michael Lewis	P	25	.429	A	
2	1	Kemmerer, Russell Paul	P	20	.500	B	HousN
		Kenworthy, Richard Lee	2B2	3	.000	A	C
0	0	Kreutzer, Franklin James	P	1	.000	A	
		Landis, James Henry	OF144	149	.228	B	
		Lollar, John Sherman	C66	84	.268	B	
4	2	Lown, Omar Joseph	P	42	.000	B	C
		Martin, Joseph Clifton	C6	18	.077	B	
		(1B1 3B1)					
		Maxwell, Chas. Richard	OF56	69	+.296	xDet	
		(1B6)					
		McCall, Brian Allen	OF1	4	.375	A	
0	1	Peters, Gary Chas.	P	5	.000	B	
12	14	Pizarro, Juan Cordova	P36	37	.159	B	
		Robinson, Floyd Andrew	OF155	156	.312	B	
		Roselli, Robert Edward	C20	35	.188	B	C
		Sadowski, Robert Frank	3B16	79	.231	PhilN	
		(2B12)					
0	0	Score, Herbert Jude	P	4	.000	B	C
		Smith, Alphonse Eugene	3B105	142	.292	B	
		(OF39)					
		Smith, Chas. Wm.	3B54	65	.207	PhilN	
1	0	Stone, Darrah Dean	P	27	.500	xHousN	
0	0	Tiefenthaler, Verle Mathew	P	3	.000	A	C
		Weis, Albert John	SS4	7	.083	A	
		(2B1 3B1)					
7	15	Wynn, Early	P	27	.130	B	
6	5	Zanni, Dominick Thomas	P	44	.278	SFN	

WON 94 — AMERICAN LEAGUE — FINISHED 2nd.
LOST 68
TG 162 — 1963. — PCT. .580

CHICAGO

ALFONSO RAMON LOPEZ

WON	LOST	NAME	POS.	G.	BA	FROM	TO
1	0	Ackley, Florian Frederick	P	2	.200	A	
2	1	Baumann, Frank Matthew	P	24	.091	B	
		Berry, Allen Kenneth (2B1)	OF2	4	.200	B	
3	8	Brosnan, James Patrick	P	45	.308	xCinN	C
		Buford, Don Alvin (2B2)	3B9	12	.286	A	
9	4	Buzhardt, John Wm.	P19	20	.083	B	
		Carreon, Camilo Garcia	C92	101	.274	B	
		Cunningham, Joseph Roberts	1B58	67	.286	B	
3	4	DeBusschere, David Albert	P	24	.045	B	C
		Esposito, Samuel		1	+.000	B	K.C.
9	8	Fisher, Eddie Gene	P	33	.139	B	
		Fox, Jacob Nelson	2B134	137	.260	B	
		Hansen, Ronald Lavern	SS	144	.226	Balt	
13	10	Herbert, Raymond Ernest	P	33	.222	B	
		Hershberger, Norman Michael	OF119	135	.279	B	
11	7	Horlen, Joel Edward	P	33	.225	B	
2	1	Howard, Bruce Ernest	P	7	.250	A	
		Jones, Grover Wm.	1B1	17	.188	B	
0	0	Joyce, Michael Lewis	P	6	.000	B	C
1	0	Kreutzer, Franklin James	P	1	.000	B	
		Landis, James Henry	OF124	133	.225	B	
		Lemon, James Robert	1B25	36	.200	xPhilN	C
		Lollar, John Sherman	C23	35	.233	B	C
		(1B2)					
		Martin, Joseph Clifton	C98	105	.205	B	
		(1B3 3B1)					
		Maxwell, Chas. Richard	OF24	71	.231	B	
		(1B17)					
		McCall, Brian Allen	OF2	3	.000	B	C
		McCraw, Tommy Lee	1B97	102	.254	A	
		Nicholson, David Lawrence	OF123	126	.229	Balt	
19	8	Peters, Gary Chas.	P41	50	.259	B	
0	0	Phillips, Wm. Taylor	P	9	.000	PhilN60	C
16	8	Pizarro, Juan Cordova	P	32	.178	B	
		Robinson, Floyd Andrew	OF137	146	.283	B	
0	1	Shipley, Joseph Clark	P	3	.000	S.F.N60	C
		Smith, Chas. Wm.	SS1	4	.286	B	
		Stephens, Glen Eugene	OF5	6	.389	K.C.	
0	0	Talbot, Fred Lealand	P	1	.000	A	
		Ward, Peter Thomas	3B154	157	.295	Balt	
		(2B1 SS1)					
		Weis, Albert John	2B48	99	.271	B	
		(SS27 3B1)					
5	8	Wilhelm, James Hoyt	P	55	.069	Balt	
0	0	Zanni, Dominick Thomas	P	5	.000	B	CinN

WON 98 — AMERICAN LEAGUE — FINISHED 2nd.
LOST 64
TG 162 — 1964. — PCT. .605

CHICAGO

ALFONSO RAMON LOPEZ

WON	LOST	NAME	POS.	G.	BA	FROM	TO
0	0	Ackley, Florian Frederick	P	3	1.000	B	C
0	3	Baumann, Frank Matthew	P	22	.000	B	
		Berry, Allen Kenneth	OF	12	.375	B	
		Buford, Donald Alvin	2B92	135	.262	B	
		(3B37)					
		Burgess, Forrest Harrill		7	.200	xPittN	
10	8	Buzhardt, John Wm.	P	31	.204	B	
		Carreon, Camilo Garcia	C34	37	.274	B	
		Cunningham, Joseph Roberts	1B33	40	+.250	B	Wash
6	3	Fisher, Eddie Gene	P	59	.167	B	

		Hansen, Ronald Lavern	SS	158	.261	B	
6	7	Herbert, Raymond Ernest	P	20	.139	B	
		Hershberger, Norman Michael	OF134	141	.230	B	
		Hicks, James Edward		2	.000	A	
13	9	Horlen, Joel Edward	P	32	.159	B	
2	1	Howard, Bruce Ernest	P	3	.000	B	
		Kenworthy, Richard Lee		2	.000	Chic62	
3	1	Kreutzer, Franklin James	P	17	+.125	B	Wash
		Landis, James Henry	OF101	106	.208	B	
		Long, Jeoffrey Keith (OF5)	1B5	23	.143	xStLN	C
		Martin, Joseph Clifton	C120	122	.197	B	
		Maxwell, Chas. Richard		2	.000	B	C
		McCraw, Tommy Lee (OF36)	1B84	125	.261	B	
		McNertney, Gerald Edward	C69	73	.215	A	
		Minoso, Saturnino Oresto Arrietta Armas	OF5	30	.226	Wash	C
3	1	Mossi, Donald Louis	P	34	.167	Det	
		Nicholson, David Lawrence	OF92	97	.204	B	
20	8	Peters, Gary Chas.	P37	54	.208	B	
19	9	Pizarro, Juan Cordova	P	33	.211	B	
		Robinson, Floyd Andrew	OF138	141	.301	B	
		Skowron, Wm. Joseph	1B70	73	+.293	xWash	
		Smith, Chas. Wm.	3B	2	.143	B	NYN
		Staehle, Marvin Gustav		6	.400	A	
		Stephens, Glan Eugene	OF59	82	.234	B	C
4	5	Talbot, Frederick Lealand	P17	18	.263	B	
		Ward, Peter Thomas	3B138	144	.282	B	
		Weis, Albert John (SS9 OF2)	2B116	133	.247	B	
12	9	Wilhelm, James Hoyt	P	73	.143	B	

CLUB RECORD

AMERICAN LEAGUE

CLEVELAND

YEAR	TG	WON	LOST	PCT.	FINISHED	MANAGER
1901	136	54	82	.397	7	James Robert McAleer
1902	136	69	67	.507	5	Wm. R. Armour
1903	140	77	63	.550	3	Wm. R. Armour
1904	151	86	65	.570	4	Wm. R. Armour
1905	154	76	78	.494	5	Napoleon Lajoie
1906	153	89	64	.582	3	Napoleon Lajoie
1907	152	85	67	.559	4	Napoleon Lajoie
1908	154	90	64	.584	2	Napoleon Lajoie
1909	153	71	82	.464	6	Napoleon Lajoie / James Thomas McGuire
1910	152	71	81	.467	5	James Thomas McGuire
1911	153	80	73	.523	3	James Thomas McGuire / George Thomas Stovall
1912	153	75	78	.490	5	Harry H. Davis / Joseph Leo Birmingham
1913	152	86	66	.566	3	Joseph Leo Birmingham
1914	153	51	102	.333	8(Last)	Joseph Leo Birmingham
1915	152	57	95	.375	7	Joseph Leo Birmingham / Leo Alexander Fohl
1916	154	77	77	.500	6	Leo Alexander Fohl
1917	154	88	66	.571	3	Leo Alexander Fohl
1918	127	73	54	.575	2	Leo Alexander Fohl
1919	139	84	55	.604	2	Leo Alexander Fohl / Tristram E. Speaker
1920	154	98	56	.636	1	Tristram E. Speaker
1921	154	94	60	.610	2	Tristram E. Speaker
1922	154	78	76	.507	4	Tristram E. Speaker
1923	153	82	71	.536	3	Tristram E. Speaker
1924	153	67	86	.438	6	Tristram E. Speaker
1925	154	70	84	.455	6	Tristram E. Speaker
1926	154	88	66	.571	2	Tristram E. Speaker
1927	153	66	87	.431	6	John McCallister
1928	154	62	92	.403	7	Roger Thorpe Peckinpaugh
1929	152	81	71	.533	3	Roger Thorpe Peckinpaugh
1930	154	81	73	.526	4	Roger Thorpe Peckinpaugh
1931	154	78	76	.506	4	Roger Thorpe Peckinpaugh
1932	152	87	65	.572	4	Roger Thorpe Peckinpaugh
1933	151	75	76	.497	4	Roger Thorpe Peckinpaugh / Walter Perry Johnson
1934	154	85	69	.552	3	Walter Perry Johnson
1935	153	82	71	.536	3	Walter Perry Johnson / Stephen Francis O'Neill
1936	154	80	74	.519	5	Stephen Francis O'Neill
1937	154	83	71	.539	4	Stephen Francis O'Neill
1938	154	86	68	.566	3	Oscar Joseph Vitt
1939	154	87	67	.565	3	Oscar Joseph Vitt
1940	154	89	65	.578	2	Oscar Joseph Vitt
1941	154	75	79	.487	x4(Det)	Roger Thorpe Peckinpaugh
1942	154	75	79	.487	4	Louis Boudreau, Jr.
1943	153	82	71	.536	3	Louis Boudreau, Jr.

1944	154	72	82	.468	x5(Phila)	Louis Boudreau, Jr.
1945	145	73	72	.503	5	Louis Boudreau, Jr.
1946	154	68	86	.442	6	Louis Boudreau, Jr.
1947	154	80	74	.519	4	Louis Boudreau, Jr.
1948	155	97	58	.626	1	Louis Boudreau, Jr.
1949	154	89	65	.578	3	Louis Boudreau, Jr.
1950	154	92	62	.597	4	Louis Boudreau, Jr.
1951	154	93	61	.604	2	Alfonso Ramon Lopez
1952	154	93	61	.604	2	Alfonso Ramon Lopez
1953	154	92	62	.597	2	Alfonso Ramon Lopez
1954	154	111	43	.721	1	Alfonso Ramon Lopez
1955	154	93	61	.604	2	Alfonso Ramon Lopez
1956	154	88	66	.571	2	Alfonso Ramon Lopez
1957	153	76	77	.497	6	Major Kirby Farrell
1958	153	77	76	.503	4	Robert Randall Bragan
						Joseph Lowell Gordon
1959	154	89	65	.578	2	Joseph Lowell Gordon
1960	154	76	78	.494	4	Joseph Lowell Gordon
						Joyner Clifford White
						James Joseph Dykes
1961	161	78	83	.484	5	James Joseph Dykes
						Melvin LeRoy Harder
1962	162	80	82	.494	6	Fred Melvin McGaha
1963	162	79	83	.488	x5(Det)	George Robert Tebbetts
1964	162	79	83	.488	x6(Minn)	George Bevan Strickland
						George Robert Tebbetts

YEAR	TG	WON	LOST	TIED	PCT.	FINISHED	MANAGER
1965	162	87	75	0	.537	5	GEORGE ROBERT TEBBETTS
1966	162	81	81	0	.500	5	GEORGE ROBERT TEBBETTS
							GEORGE BEVAN STRICKLAND
1967	162	75	87	0	.463	8	JOSEPH WILBUR ADCOCK
1968	162	86	75	1	.534	3	ALVIN RALPH DARK
1969	161	62	99	0	.385	6E (LAST)	ALVIN RALPH DARK
1970	162	76	86	0	.469	5E	ALVIN RALPH DARK
1971	162	60	102	0	.370	6E (LAST)	ALVIN RALPH DARK
							JOHN JOSEPH LIPON
1972	156	72	84	0	.462	5E	KENNETH JOSEPH ASPROMONTE

WON 63 AMERICAN LEAGUE FINISHED 6th.
LOST 73
TG 136 1900. PCT. .463

CLEVELAND

JAMES ROBERT McALEER

WON	LOST	NAME	POS.	G.	BA	FROM	TO
6	7	Baker, Chas.	P	17	+.231	xBuff	
		Bierbauer, Louis W.	2B35	43	+.217	StLN98	Mil
5	5	Braggins, Richard Realf (OF2)	P10	12	.200	A	
		Buelow, Chas. John	3B22	31	.353	A	
0	2	Chech, Chas. Wm. (OF2)	P5	7	.200	A	
		Crisham, Patrick Lewis (1B24 OF28)	C39	93	.254	BaltN	C
		Cross, Frank A.	C16	19	.234	A	
		Delehanty, Thomas James	2B	3	.200	LvlleN97	C
		Diggins, Wm. L.	C	13	+.170	A	Mil
1	1	Egan, John Joseph (Rip)	P	2	.250	WashN94	C
4	6	Fauver, Clayton King	P	10	.206	LvlleN	C
		Flood, Timothy A.	2B	91	+.247	xBuff	
		Frisbee, Chas. Augustus	OF	60	.231	xNYN	C
0	1	Gaston, Welcome Thornburg	P	1	+.667	xDet	C
		Genins, C. Frank	OF110	140	.293	PittN95	
18	15	Hart, Wm. Franklin	P34	37	.251	PittN98	
16	12	Hoffer, Wm. Leopold	P29	43	.190	PittN	
2	1	Jones, Chas. Leander (Bumpus)	P	3	.222	NYN93	C
		Jones, James Tilford	OF	27	.239	LvlleN97	
0	2	Kern, Archibald	P	2	+.143	xBuff	C
		LaChance, George	1B	116	.302	BaltN	
		Martin, Frank	3B	3	+.000	xBuff	C
		McAleer, James Robert MGR.	OF	20	.233	ClevN98	
8	10	McKenna, James Wm.	P	20	.147	BaltN	C
		Pickering, Oliver Dan	OF	140	.324	ClevN97	
2	4	Reust, S. A.	P	6	.190	A	C
		Shay, Daniel C.	SS	61	.224	A	
0	3	Smythe, Alfred Burns	P	6	.250	A	C
		Spies, Henry	C	74	+.216	LvlleN95	Mil
		Sullivan, Suter G.	3B	66	+.298	xDet	C
		Tamsett, James Edward	3B	24	.141	A	C
		Viox, Rooney	SS	48	.224	A	C
		Walters, John A. (Roxy)	3B	10	.151	A	C
		Weaver, Wm. B.	OF	8	.233	PittN94	C
		White, John F.	OF15	19	.277	A	
1	4	Wilson, Frank Ealton (Zeke)	P	6	.353	StLN	C

WON 54 AMERICAN LEAGUE FINISHED 7th.
LOST 82
TG 136 1901. PCT. .397

CLEVELAND

JAMES ROBERT McALEER

WON	LOST	NAME	POS.	G.	BA	FROM	TO
0	1	Baker, Chas.	P	1	+.000	B	Phil
		Beck, Erwin Thomas	2B	135	.283	BknN99	
4	8	Bracken, John James	P	12	.227	A	C
		Bradley, Wm. Joseph	3B	133	.296	ChiN	
1	2	Braggins, Richard Realf	P	4	.143	B	C
		Cermak, Edward	OF	1	.000	A	C
		Connor, Joseph Francis	C	38	+.138	xMil	
1	4	Cristall, Wm. A.	P	6	.350	A	C
		Cross, Frank A.	OF	1	.600	B	C
		Donovan, Thomas J.	OF	18	.253	A	C
8	15	Dowling, Henry Peter	P	34	+.162	xMil	C
		Eagan, Chas. Eugene (Truck) (3B1)	2B5	5	.176	xPittN	C
		Gallagher, D. F.	OF	2	.000	A	C
		Genins, C. Frank	OF	26	.232	B	C
		Hall, Russell P.	SS	1	.500	StLN98	C
		Hallman, Wm. White (Billy)	SS	5	.211	Buff	PhilN
6	12	Hart, Wm. Franklin	P	20	.218	B	C
0	7	Harvey, Erwin K. (P7)	OF37	44	+.351	xChi	
6	7	Hoffer, Wm. Leopold	P	17	.139	B	C
		Hogan, Harry S.	OF	1	.000	A	C
		LaChance, George	1B	133	.306	B	
		Livingston, Patrick Joseph (Paddy)	C	1	.000	A	
16	14	Moore, Earl Alonzo	P	31	.158	A	
		McAleer, James Robert MGR.	OF	3	.125	B	
		McCarthy, John A.	OF	86	.314	ChiN	
		Maguire, James A.	SS	18	.232	A	C
5	6	McNeal, John Harley	P	11	.162	A	C
		O'Brien, John Joseph	OF	91	+.236	xWash	
		Pickering, Oliver Dan	OF	138	.308	B	
7	6	Scott, Edward	P	16	.213	CinN	C
		Shay, Daniel C.	SS	19	.226	B	
		Scheibeck, Frank	SS92	93	.217	WashN99	
0	0	Weyhing, August	P	2	.000	BknN	CinN
		Wood, Robert Lynn	C84	96	.289	Chi	
		Woodruff, Orville Francis	OF	1	.250	NYN99	
		Yeager, George E.	C25	39	.226	Mil	PittN

WON 69 AMERICAN LEAGUE FINISHED 5th.
LOST 67
TG 136 1902. PCT. .507

CLEVELAND

WM. R. ARMOUR

WON	LOST	NAME	POS.	G.	BA	FROM	TO
		Bay, Harry Elbert	OF107	108	.287	xCinN	
		Bemis, Harry Parker (2B1 OF1)	C37	93	.311	A	
17	6	Bernhard, Wm. Henry	P	27	+.200	xPhil	
		Bonner, Frank J.	2B	34	+.278	WashN99	Phil
		Bradley, Wm. Joseph	3B	136	.341	B	
1	0	Clark, Harvey Daniel	P	1	.500	A	C
3	1	Dorner, Augustus	P	4	.384	A	
		Flick, Elmer Harrison	OF	110	+.293	xPhil	
		Gochnaur, John Peter	SS	126	.183	BknN	
		Graham, George Frederick (Peaches)	2B1	2	.333	A	
		Harvey Erwin K.	OF	12	.369	B	C
		Hemphill, Chas. Judson	OF	25	+.272	Bos	StL
2	3	Hess, Otto C.	P	7	.071	A	
0	1	Hickman, Chas. Taylor (P1)	1B102	102	+.376	xBos	
17	13	Joss, Adrian (Addie) (1B1)	P32	33	.116	A	
		Lajoie, Napoleon	2B	86	+.369	xPhil	
0	1	Leitner, George Michael	P	1	+.000	NYN	Chi
2	1	Lundbom, John Frederick	P	8	.250	A	C
17	18	Moore, Earl Alonzo	P	36	.212	B	
		McCarthy, John A.	OF	95	.276	B	
		O'Hagan, Harold P.	1B	3	.384	xNYN (return)	NYN
		Pickering, Oliver Dan (1B2)	OF58	60	.259	B	
0	1	Polchow, Louis Wm.	P	1	.000	A	C
		Schreckengost, Ossee Freeman	1B	18	+.338	Bos	Phil
0	1	Smith, Chas. E.	P	3	.125	A	
		Starnagle, George Henry	C	1	.000	A	C
0	7	Streit, Oscar W.	P	8	.210	BosN99	C
1	3	Taylor, Luther Haden	P	4	.100	NYN	NYN
		Thoney, John (SS11 OF2)	2B14	28	+.291	A	Balt
2	1	Varney, Lawrence Delano	P	3	.166	A	C
0	0	Vasbinder, Moses Calhoun	P	2	.500	A	C
0	1	Walker, Edward Harrison	P	1	.333	A	
		Wood, Robert Lynn (1B16 2B1 3B1 OF2)	C53	81	.286	B	
7	9	Wright, Clarence Eugene (1B1)	P22	24	.143	BknN	

WON 77 AMERICAN LEAGUE FINISHED 3rd.
LOST 63
TG 140 1903. PCT. .550

CLEVELAND

WM. R. ARMOUR

WON	LOST	NAME	POS.	G.	BA	FROM	TO
		Abbott, Frederick H.	C69	76	.271	A	
		Bay, Harry Elbert	OF	141	.310	B	
		Bemis, Harry Parker	C83	93	.258	B	
14	5	Bernhard, Wm. Henry	P	20	.185	B	
		Bradley, Wm. Joseph	3B	137	.315	B	
		*Clingman, Wm. Frederick	SS20	21	.286	Wash01	C
6	13	Donahue, Francis Rostell(Red)	P	19	+.151	xStL	
3	5	Dorner, Augustus	P	12	.080	B	
		Flick, Elmer Harrison	OF	142	.299	B	
1	2	Glendon, Martin H.	P	3	.000	CinN	C
		Gochnaur, John Peter	SS128	136	.181	B	C
		Hardy, John Doolittle	OF	5	.150	A	
		Hickman, Chas. Taylor	1B127	130	.330	B	

WON	LOST	NAME	POS.	G.	BA	FROM	TO
		Hill, Hugh Ellis		1	.000	A	
		Iott, John (Happy)	OF	3	.200	A	C
18	13	Joss, Adrian (Addie)	P32	34	.193	B	
3	5	Killian, Edwin Henry	P	10	.179	A	
		Lajoie, Napoleon (1B1)	2B124	126	.355	B	
22	7	Moore, Earl Alonzo	P	29	.098	B	
		McCarthy, John A.	OF100	109	.265	B	ChiN
1	2	Pearson, Alexander Franklin	P	4	.077	StLN	C
0	0	Pounds, Wm. Chas.	P	1	.500	A	BknN
2	3	Rhoades, Robert Bruce	P	5	.118	xStLN	
		Slattery, John Thomas	1B2	4	+.000	Bos01	Chi
5	1	Stovall, Jesse Cranmer	P	6	.045	A	
		Thoney, John	OF25	32	.213	Balt	
0	0	Walker, Edward Harrison	P	3	.000	B	C
2	7	Wright, Clarence Eugene	P	15	+.209	B	StL

*Clingman also played 5 games at 2B and 3 games at 3B.

WON 86 — LOST 65 — TG 151

AMERICAN LEAGUE — 1904. — FINISHED 4th. — PCT. .570

CLEVELAND

WM. R. ARMOUR

WON	LOST	NAME	POS.	G.	BA	FROM	TO
		Abbott, Frederick H.	C23	42	.168	B	
		Bay, Harry Elbert	OF	132	.260	B	
		Bemis, Harry Parker	C81	95	.225	B	
21	13	Bernhard, Wm. Henry	P	38	.176	B	
		Bradley, Wm. Joseph	3B	154	.300	B	
		Buelow, Frederick Wm.	C	42	+.180	xDet	
		Carr, Chas. Carbitt	1B	32	+.223	xDet	
18	14	Donahue, Francis Rostell(Red)	P	35	.168	B	
		Donovan, Michael B.	SS	2	.000	A	
		Flick, Elmer Harrison	OF145	149	.303	B	
9	7	Hess, Otto C.	P21	34	.120	Clev02	
0	3	Hickey, John W.	P	2	.000	A	C
		Hickman, Chas. Taylor	1B	85	+.415	B	Det
14	8	Joss, Adrian (Addie)	P25	28	.133	B	
		Lajoie, Napoleon (SS41)	2B99	140	.381	B	
		Lush, Wm. Lucas	OF	138	.272	Det	C
13	11	Moore, Earl Alonzo	P	26	.138	B	
		Ostdiek, Henry Girard	C	7	.157	A	
11	9	Rhoades, Robert Bruce	P22	29	.194	B	
		Rossman, Claude R.	OF	18	.190	A	
		Schwartz, Wm . Chas.	1B23	24	.151	A	C
		Stovall, George Thomas	1B38	51	.297	A	
		Turner, Terrence LaMont (Terry)	SS	111	.236	PittN01	
		Vinson, Ernest Augustus	OF	15	.269	A	

WON 76 — LOST 78 — TG 154

AMERICAN LEAGUE — 1905. — FINISHED 5th. — PCT. .494

CLEVELAND

NAPOLEON LAJOIE

WON	LOST	NAME	POS.	G.	BA	FROM	TO
		Barbeau, Wm. Joseph (Jap)	3B	12	.237	A	
		Bay, Harry Elbert	OF	143	.298	B	
		Bemis, Harry Parker	C58	69	.292	B	
6	14	Bernhard, Wm. Henry	P	22	.087	B	
		Bradley, Wm. Joseph	3B	145	.268	B	
		Buelow, Frederick Wm.	C60	74	.174	B	
		Carr, Chas. Carbitt	1B87	89	.235	B	
		Clarke, Jay Justin (Nig)	C	6	+.182	A	Det
				37	+.202	& recall	
		Congalton, Wm. Millar (Bunk)	OF	12	.369	ChiN02	
6	11	Donahue, Francis Rostell (Red)	P	20	.075	B	
0	0	Ferry, Alfred Joseph	P	1	.000	Det	C
		Flick, Elmer Harrison	OF	131	.306	B	
		Grant, Edward Leslie	2B	2	.375	A	
0	1	Halla, John Arthur	P	3	.200	A	C
10	12	Hess, Otto C. (OF27)	P27	54	.251	B	
		Jackson, James Benner	OF105	108	.257	NYN02	
19	12	Joss, Adrian (Addie)	P32	34	.138	B	
		Kahl, Nicholas Alexander	2B30	38	.221	A	C
		Lajoie, Napoleon MGR.	2B59	65	.329	B	
		Leber, Emil Bohmiel	3B	2	.000	A	C
16	14	Moore, Earl Alonzo	P	30	.106	B	
17	12	Rhoades, Robert Bruce	P29	33	.221	B	
		Stovall, George Thomas (2B45)	1B59	111	.272	B	
		Turner, Terrence LaMont (Terry)	SS151	154	.263	B	
		Vinson, Ernest Augustus	OF36	38	.195	B	
		Wakefield, Howard John	C	10	.111	A	
2	2	West, James	P	6	.077	A	

WON 89 — LOST 64 — TG 153

AMERICAN LEAGUE — 1906. — FINISHED 3rd. — PCT. .582

CLEVELAND

NAPOLEON LAJOIE

WON	LOST	NAME	POS.	G.	BA	FROM	TO
		Barbeau, Wm. Joseph (Jap)	3B32	42	.194	B	
		Bay, Harry Elbert	OF	68	.275	B	
		Bemis, Harry Parker	C81	93	.274	B	
16	15	Bernhard, Wm. Henry	P	31	.212	B	
		Birmingham, Joseph Leo	OF	10	.275	A	
		Bradley, Wm. Joseph	3B	82	.275	B	
		Buelow, Frederick Wm.	C	34	.163	B	

WON	LOST	NAME	POS.	G.	BA	FROM	TO
		Caffyn, Benjamin Thomas	OF29	30	.194	A	C
		Clarke, Jay Justin (Nig)	C54	57	.358	B	
		Congalton, Wm. Millar (Bunk)	OF114	117	.320	B	
4	5	Eells, Harry A.	P	14	.188	A	C
		Flick, Elmer Harrison	OF150	157	.311	B	
20	17	Hess, Otto C.	P42	53	.201	B	
		Jackson, James Benner	OF104	105	.214	B	C
21	9	Joss, Adrian (Addie)	P34	36	.210	B	
		Kittredge, Malachi Jedediah	C	5	+.100	xWash	C
		Lajoie, Napoleon MGR.	2B130	152	.355	B	
2	0	Liebhardt, Glenn John	P	2	.000	A	
1	1	Moore, Earl Alonzo	P	5	.000	B	
22	10	Rhoades, Robert Bruce	P	38	.161	B	
		Rossman, Claude R.	1B105	118	.308	Clev04	
		Shipke, Wm. M. (Tony)	3B	2	.000	A	
		Stovall, George Thomas (2B19 3B30)	1B55	116	.273	B	
3	7	Townsend, John	P	16	.133	Wash	C
		Turner, Terrence LaMont (Terry)	SS	147	.291	B	

WON 85 — AMERICAN LEAGUE — FINISHED 4th.
LOST 67
TG 152 — 1907. — PCT. .559

CLEVELAND

NAPOLEON LAJOIE

WON	LOST	NAME	POS.	G.	BA	FROM	TO
		Bay, Harry Elbert	OF31	34	.179	B	
		Bemis, Harry Parker	C21	65	.250	B	
3	3	Berger, Chas.	P	14	.179	A	
0	1	Bernhard, Wm. Henry	P	8	.125	B	C
		Birmingham, Joseph Leo	OF134	136	.235	B	
		Bradley, Wm. Joseph	3B	139	.223	B	
		Clarke, Jay Justin (Nig)	C115	120	.269	B	
5	7	Clarkson, Walter Hamilton	P	16	+.036	xN.Y.	
		Congalton, Wm. Millar (Bunk)	OF	9	+.182	B	Bos
		Delahanty, Frank George	OF	15	.173	N.Y.	
		Flick, Elmer Harrison	OF	147	.302	B	
6	6	Hess, Otto C.	P17	19	.138	B	
		Hinchman, Harry Sibley	2B	15	.216	A	C
		Hinchman, Wm. White	OF148	152	.228	CinN	
27	11	Joss, Adrian (Addie)	P	42	.114	B	
		Lajoie, Napoleon MGR.	2B128	137	.299	B	
18	14	Liebhardt, Glenn John	P	38	.161	B	
		Lister, Morris Elmer	1B	22	.277	A	C
0	3	Moore, Earl Alonzo	P	3	+.000	B	N.Y.
		Nill, George Chas.	2B	12	+.286	xWash	
		O'Brien, Peter J.	3B	43	+.244	StL	Wash
15	14	Rhoades, Robert Bruce	P	35	.185	B	
		Stovall, George Thomas	1B122	124	.236	B	
11	8	Thielman, John Peter (Jake)	P20	21	.203	StLN	
		Turner, Terrence LaMont (Terry)	SS141	142	.242	B	

WON	LOST	NAME	POS.	G.	BA	FROM	TO
		Wakefield, Howard John	C11	26	.135	Wash	C

WON 90 — AMERICAN LEAGUE — FINISHED 2nd.
LOST 64
TG 154 — 1908. — PCT. .584

CLEVELAND

NAPOLEON LAJOIE

WON	LOST	NAME	POS.	G.	BA	FROM	TO
		Altizer, David Tilden (SS8)	OF17	30	+.227	xWash	
		Bay, Harry Elbert		2	.000	B	C
		Bemis, Harry Parker	C76	91	.224	B	
13	8	Berger, Chas.	P	29	.108	B	
		Birmingham, Joseph Leo	OF121	122	.213	B	
		Bradley, Wm. Joseph (SS30)	3B118	148	.243	B	
11	7	Chech, Chas. Wm.	P	27	.104	CinN06	
		Clarke, Jay Justin (Nig)	C90	97	.241	B	
		Clarke, Joshua Baldwin (Josh)	OF	131	.242	StLN05	
0	0	Clarkson, Walter Hamilton	P	2	1.000	B	C
		Davidson, Homer Hurd (OF1)	C5	9	.000	A	C
2	5	Falkenberg, Frederick Peter (Cy)	P	8	+.059	xWash	
		Flick, Elmer Harrison	OF	9	.212	B	
1	0	Foster, Edward Lee	P	6	.000	A	C
		Good, Wilbur David	OF42	46	.279	NY05	
0	0	Graney, John Gladstone (Jack)	P	2	.000	A	
1	0	Hess, Otto C. (OF4)	P4	9	.000	B	
		Hichman, Chas. Taylor (1B20)	OF28	65	.234	Chi	C
		Hinchman, Wm. White (SS51)	OF75	137	.231	B	
24	11	Joss, Adrian (Addie)	P	42	.155	B	
		Lajoie, Napoleon MGR.	2B156	157	.289	B	
		Land, Grover Cleveland	C	7	.230	A	
1	2	Lattimore, Wm. Hershel	P	4	.400	A	C
15	16	Liebhardt, Glenn John	P	38	.175	B	
		McGuire, James Thomas		1	+.250	xBos	
		Nill, George Chas.	SS6	11	.215	B	C
		Perring, George Wilson (3B41)	SS48	89	.216	A	
18	12	Rhoades, Robert Bruce	P	37	.222	B	
1	0	Ryan, Jack	P	8	.091	A	
		Stovall, George Thomas	1B132	138	.292	B	
		Sullivan, Dennis Wm.	OF	4	+.000	xBos	
3	3	Thielman, John Peter (Jake)	P	11	+.304	B	Bos
		Turner, Terrence LaMont (Terry) (SS17)	OF36	60	.239	B	

WON 71 — AMERICAN LEAGUE — FINISHED 6th.
LOST 82
TG 153 — 1909. — PCT. .464

CLEVELAND

NAPOLEON LAJOIE JAMES THOMAS McGUIRE

WON	LOST	NAME	POS.	G.	BA	FROM	TO
1	1	Ables, Harry Terrell	P	6	.091	StL05	
		Ball, Cornelius	SS	96	+.255	xN.Y.	
		Bemis, Harry Parker	C36	42	.187	B	
13	14	Berger, Chas.	P	34	.132	B	
		Birmingham, Joseph Leo	OF98	100	.289	B	
0	1	Booles, Seabron James	P	4	.167	A	C
		Bradley, Wm. Joseph	3B87	95	.186	B	
		Clarke, Jay Justin (Nig)	C44	55	.274	B	
		Clarke, Joshua Baldwin (Josh)	OF	4	.000	B	
0	1	Doane, Walter Rudolph (P1)	OF3	4	.167	A	
		Easterly, Theodore Harrison (Ted)	C76	98	.261	A	
10	9	Falkenberg, Frederick Peter (Cy)	P	24	.173	B	
		Flick, Elmer Harrison	OF61	66	.255	B	
		Good, Wilbur David	OF80	94	.214	B	
		Higgins, Robert Stone	C	8	.087	A	
		Hinchman, Wm. White	OF131	139	.258	B	
14	13	Joss, Adrian (Addie)	P	33	.100	B	
		Lajoie, Napoleon MGR.	2B120	128	.324	B	
		Land, Grover Cleveland	C	1	.500	B	
1	5	Liebhardt, Glenn John	P	12	.000	B	C
		Lord, Bristol Robotham	OF67	69	.269	Phil07	
1	2	Mitchell, Wm.	P	3	.286	A	
		Netzel, Milo A. (OF3)	3B6	10	.189	A	C
2	2	Otis, Harry George	P	5	.000	A	C
		Perring, George Wilson	3B66	88	.223	B	
		Raftery, Thomas L.	OF	8	.269	A	C
		Reilley, Alexander Aloysius	OF18	20	.210	A	C
5	9	Rhoades, Robert Bruce	P	20	.163	B	C
3	2	Sitton, Cail Vedder	P	14	.133	A	C
		Stark, Monroe Randolph	SS	19	.200	A	
		Stovall, George Thomas	1B	145	.246	B	
		Sullivan, Dennis Wm.	OF1	3	.667	B	C
		Turner, Terrence LaMont (Terry) (SS26)	2B26	53	.250	B	
2	1	Upp, George Henry (Jerry)	P	7	.222	A	C
0	3	Winchell, Frederick Russell	P	4	.200	A	C
0	4	Wright, Wm. Simmons	P	5	.000	A	C
19	15	Young, Denton True (Cy)	P	34	.190	Bos	

WON 71 AMERICAN LEAGUE FINISHED 5th.
LOST 81
TG 152 1910. PCT. .467

CLEVELAND

JAMES THOMAS McGUIRE

WON	LOST	NAME	POS.	G.	BA	FROM	TO
		Adams, John Bertram	C	5	.230	A	
		Ball, Cornelius	SS27	53	.210	B	
		Bemis, Harry Parker	C46	61	.215	B	C
3	4	Berger, Chas.	P	13	.143	B	C
		Birmingham, Joseph Leo	OF103	104	.229	B	
2	2	Blanding, Fred James	P	6	.111	A	
		Bradley, Wm. Joseph	3B	61	.196	B	
		Bronkie, Herman Chas. (SS1)	3B3	5	.181	A	
		Callahan, David Joseph	OF	13	.181	A	
		Clarke, Jay Justin (Nig)	C17	21	.155	B	
0	3	DeMott, Benjamin Harrison	P	9	.167	A	
0	0	Doane, Walter Rudolph	P	6	.286	B	C
		Donahue, Patrick Wm.	C	2	+.167	xPhil	Phil
		Easterly, Theodore Harrison (Ted) (OF30)	C66	110	.306	B	
14	13	Falkenberg, Frederick Peter (Cy)	P	37	.183	B	
2	9	Fanwell, Harry Clayton	P	17	.033	A	C
		Flick, Elmer Harrison	OF18	24	.265	B	C
		Graney, John Gladstone (Jack)	OF114	116	.236	Clev08	
10	7	Harkness, Frederick Harvey	P	26	.140	A	
		Hohnhorst, Edward Henry	1B	17	.323	A	
		Jackson, Joseph Jefferson	OF	20	.387	Phil	
5	5	Joss, Adrian (Addie)	P	13	.111	B	C
6	4	Kahler, George Rannels	P	12	.143	A	
0	0	Kirsch, Harry	P	2	.000	A	C
		Knaupp, Henry Antone	SS	18	.236	A	
5	10	Koestner, Elmer Joseph	P	27	.313	A	
		Krueger, Arthur T.	OF	62	.170	CinN07 and return	BosN
		Lajoie, Napoleon	2B149	159	.384	B	
		Land, Grover Cleveland	C33	34	.207	B	
5	6	Linke, Frederick L.	P	22	+.167	A	StL
		Lord, Bristol Robotham	OF	57	+.226	B	Phil
12	8	Mitchell, Wm.	P	35	.157	B	
		McGuire, James Thomas MGR.	C	1	.000	B	
		Nicholls, Simon Burdette	SS	3	.000	Phil	C
		Niles, Harry Clyde	OF	70	+.212	xBos	C
		Peckinpaugh, Roger Thorpe	SS	15	.200	A	
		Perring, George Wilson	3B33	39	.221	B	
		Rath, Maurice Chas.	3B	27	+.191	xPhil	
		Rutherford, James Hollis	OF	1	.500	A	C
		Smith, Sydney	C	9	.346	StL08	
		Stovall, George Thomas	1B128	142	.261	B	
		Thomasen, Arthur Wilson	OF	17	.158	A	C
		Turner, Terrence LaMont (Terry) (3B46)	SS94	150	.230	B	
7	10	Young, Denton True (Cy)	P	21	.145	B	

#-Donohue was returned to Philadelphia by Cleveland.

WON 80 AMERICAN LEAGUE FINISHED 3rd.
LOST 73
TG 153 1911. PCT. .523

CLEVELAND

JAMES THOMAS McGUIRE GEORGE THOMAS STOVALL

WON	LOST	NAME	POS.	G.	BA	FROM	TO

WON	LOST	NAME	POS.	G.	BA	FROM	TO
		Adams, John Bertram	C	2	.250	B	
		Ball, Cornelius (3B17)	2B94	116	.296	B	
1	2	Baskette, James Blaine	P	4	.428	A	
		Birmingham, Joseph Leo (3B16)	OF102	125	.304	B	
7	11	Blanding, Fred James	P29	30	.262	B	
		Bronkie, Herman Chas.	3B	2	.167	B	
		Butcher, Henry Joseph	OF34	38	.240	A	
		Callahan, David Joseph	OF	6	.250	B	C
0	1	DeMott, Benjamin Harrison	P	2	.000	B	C
		Easterly, Theodore Harrison (Ted) (C23)	OF54	99	.324	B	
8	5	Falkenberg, Frederick Peter (Cy)	P15	16	.175	B	
		Fisher, August Harris	C58	70	.261	A	
		Graney, John Gladstone (Jack)	OF142	146	.269	B	
23	7	Gregg, Sylveanus Augustus (Vean)	P	34	.165	A	
		Griggs, Arthur J.	1B	27	.250	StL	
2	2	Harkness, Frederick Harvey	P	12	.316	B	C
		Hendryx, Timothy Green	OF	3	.285	A	
		Jackson, Joseph Jefferson	OF	147	.408	B	
3	4	James, Wm. Henry	P	8	.059	A	
9	8	Kahler, George Rannels	P	30	.167	B	
		Knaupp, Henry Antone	SS	13	.102	B	C
12	8	Krapp, Eugene	P35	36	.230	A	
		Lajoie, Napoleon (2B37)	1B41	90	.365	B	
		Land, Grover Cleveland	C34	35	.140	B	
		Lindsay, Wm. Gibbon	3B15	19	.242	A	C
		Mills, Abbott Paige (Jack)	SS	13	.294	A	C
7	14	Mitchell, Wm.	P31	32	.109	B	
		Olson, Ivan Massie	SS139	140	.261	A	
		O'Neill, Stephen Francis (Steve)	C	9	.111	A	
1	0	Paige, George L.	P	2	.143	A	C
0	1	Reisigl, Jacob	P	2	.000	A	C
		Smith, Sydney	C48	58	.299	B	
		Stovall, George Thomas MGR.	1B118	126	.271	B	
0	1	Swindell, Joel Ernest	P	4	.200	A	
		Turner, Terrence LaMont (Terry)	3B92	117	.252	B	
2	4	West, James	P	13	.130	Clev05	C
2	1	Yingling, Earl Hershey	P	6	.273	A	
3	4	Young, Denton True (Cy)	P	7	.063	B	BosN

WON 75 AMERICAN LEAGUE FINISHED 5th.
LOST 78
TG 153 1912. PCT. .490

CLEVELAND

HARRY H. DAVIS JOSEPH LEO BIRMINGHAM

WON	LOST	NAME	POS.	G.	BA	FROM	TO
		Adams, John Bertram	C	20	.204	B	
		Baker, Howard Francis	3B	11	.167	A	
		Ball, Cornelius	2B	38	+.233	B	Bos
8	4	Baskette, James Blaine	P	19	.125	B	
		Birmingham, Joseph Leo MGR.	OF	107	.255	B	
18	14	Blanding, Fred James	P	36	.226	B	
1	0	Brenner, Delbert Henry	P	2	.000	A	C
		Bronkie, Herman Chas.	3B	6	.000	B	
		Butcher, Henry Joseph	OF	24	.195	B	C
		Carisch, Frederick Behlmer	C	24	.275	PittN06	
		Carlock, John H.		1	.000	A	C
		Chapman, Raymond Johnson	SS	31	.312	A	
		Costello, J. A.	OF	1	.000	A	C
		Davis, Harry H. MGR.	1B	1	.000	Phil	
		Easterly, Theodore Harrison (Ted)	C	65	+.296	B	Chi
		Eibel, Henry H.	OF	1	.000	A	
0	5	George, Thomas Edward	P	9	.214	StL	
		Graney, John Gladstone (Jack)	OF	78	.242	B	
20	13	Gregg, Sylveanus Augustus (Vean)	P	33	.175	B	
		Griggs, Arthur J.	1B	89	.304	B	
		Grubb, Harvey Herbert	3B	1	.000	A	C
		Haugher, John Arthur	OF	15	.056	A	C
		Hendryx, Timothy Green	OF	23	.243	B	
		Hohnhorst, Edward Henry	1B	15	.209	Clev10	C
		Hunter, Wm. Ellsworth	OF	21	.165	A	C
		Jackson, Joseph Jefferson	OF	152	.395	B	
0	1	James Wm. A. (Lefty)	P	6	.000	A	
0	0	James, Wm. Henry	P	3	.000	B	
		Johnston, Wheeler Rogers	1B	43	.280	CinN09	
12	19	Kahler, George Rannels	P	32	.110	B	
		Kibble, John Westly (2B1)	3B4	5	.000	A	C
2	5	Krapp, Eugene	P	9	.333	B	
0	1	Krause, Harry Wm.	P	3	+.000	xPhil	C
		Lajoie, Napoleon (1B20)	2B97	117	.368	B	
		Livingston, Patrick Joseph (Paddy)	C	19	.234	Phil	
		Meixel, Merten Merrill (Moxie)	OF	3	.500	A	C
5	8	Mitchell, Wm.	P	22	.113	B	
		Nagelson, Louis Marcellis	C	2	.000	A	C
		Nash, Kenneth Leland	SS	9	.190	A	
0	0	Neher, James Gilmore	P	1	.000	A	C
		Olson, Ivan Massie (3B35)	SS56	123	.253	B	
		O'Neill, Stephen Francis (Steve)	C	68	.228	B	
		Peckinpaugh, Roger Thorpe	SS	69	.212	Clev10	
		Ryan, John Budd	OF	93	.271	A	
9	3	Steen, Wm. John	P	22	.271	A	
		Turner, Terrence LaMont (Terry)	3B	103	.308	B	
0	0	Walker, James Roy	P	2	.000	A	
0	0	Wolf, Emil	P	1	.000	A	C

WON 86 AMERICAN LEAGUE FINISHED 3rd.
LOST 66
TG 152 1913. PCT. .566

CLEVELAND

JOSEPH LEO BIRMINGHAM

WON	LOST	NAME	POS.	G.	BA	FROM	TO
0	0	Baskette, James Blaine	P	2	1 .000	B	C
		Bassler, John Landis	C	1	.000	A	
		Bates, Raymond	3B	20	.167	A	
		Beall, John Woolf		6	+.167	A	Chi
		Billings, John Augustus	C	1	.000	A	
		Birmingham, Joseph Leo MGR.	OF36	47	.282	B	
15	10	Blanding, Fred James	P	39	.244	B	
		Brady, (2B3) (Wm. Lorenz Kopf)	3B2	6	.300	A	
0	0	Brenton, Lynn Davis	P	1	.000	A	
		Carisch, Frederick Behlmer	C79	81	.216	B	
		Chapman, Raymond Johnson	SS138	140	.254	B	
3	7	Cullop, Norman Andrew	P	18	.143	A	
0	0	Dashner, Lee Claire	P	1	.000	A	C
		Dunlop, George Henry (3B3)	SS4	7	.222	A	
		Edmonson, Earl Edward (OF1)	1B	2	.000	A	C
23	10	Falkenberg, Frederick Peter (Cy)	P	36	.119	Clevll	
0	0	Glavenich, Luke Frank	P	1	.000	A	C
		Graney, John Gladstone (Jack)	OF	148	.267	B	
0	0	Gregg, David Chas.	P	1	.000	A	C
20	13	Gregg, Sylveanus Augustus (Vean)	P	37	.131	B	
		Jackson, Joseph Jefferson	OF	148	.373	B	
2	2	James, Wm. A. (Lefty)	P	11	.154	B	
		Johnston, Wheeler Rogers	1B	133	.255	B	
5	11	Kahler, George Rannels	P	24	.067	B	
		Krueger, Ernest George	C	5	.000	A	
		Lajoie, Napoleon	2B126	137	.335	B	
		Land, Grover Cleveland	C	17	.235	Clevll	
		Leibold, Harry Loran (Nemo)	OF72	84	.260	A	
		Lelivelt, John Frank (Jack)	OF	16	+.409	xN.Y.	
14	8	Mitchell, Wm.	P	29	.143	B	
		Olson, Ivan Massie (1B20)	3B74	104	.248	B	
		O'Neill, Stephen Francis (Steve)	C	78	.295	B	
		Peckinpaugh, Roger Thorpe	SS	1	+.000	B	N.Y.
		Ryan, John Budd	OF71	73	.296	B	C
		Southworth, Wm. Harrison	OF	1	.000	A	
4	5	Steen, Wm. John	P	18	.171	B	
		Swindell, Joel Ernest		1	.000	Clevll	C
		Turner, Terrence LaMont (Terry) (2B29 SS18)	3B68	120	.248	B	
		Young, George J.		2	.000	A	C

WON 51 AMERICAN LEAGUE FINISHED 8th (LAST)
LOST 102
TG 153 1914. PCT. .333

CLEVELAND

JOSEPH LEO BIRMINGHAM

WON	LOST	NAME	POS.	G.	BA	FROM	TO
		Barbare, Walter Lawrence	SS	15	.308	A	
		Bassler, John Landis	C25	43	.182	B	
0	0	Beck, George F.	P	1	.000	A	C
0	0	Benn, Henry Omer	P	1	.000	A	C
		Billings, John Augustus	C	10	.250	B	
		Birmingham, Joseph Leo MGR.	OF	19	.128	B	
0	1	Bishop, Lloyd Clifton	P	3	.000	A	C
		Bisland, Rivington Martin	SS15	18	.105	StL	C
3	9	Blanding, Fred James	P26	27	.102	B	C
2	7	Bowman, Alvah Edson	P	20	.047	A	
		Carisch, Frederick Behlmer	C38	40	.216	B	
1	3	Carter, Paul Warren	P	5	.000	A	
		Chapman, Raymond Johnson (2B33)	SS72	106	.275	B	
3	7	Collamore, Allan Edward	P	21	.094	Phil11	
1	5	Coumbe, Frederick Nicholas (Fritz)	P	15	+.217	xBos	
0	1	Cullop, Norman Andrew	P	1	.000	B	KCF
		Cypert, Alfred Boyd	3B	1	.000	A	C
0	1	Dillinger, Harley Hugh	P	10	.000	A	C
		Dunlop, George Henry	SS	1	.000	B	C
		Egan, Arthur Augustus	C27	29	.227	Phil12	
		Ginn, Tinsley Rucker	OF	2	.000	A	C
		Graney, John Gladstone (Jack)	OF127	130	.265	B	
9	3	Gregg, Sylveanus Augustus (Vean)	P	15	+.182	B	Bos
9	15	Hagerman, Zeriah Zequiel (Rip)	P	35	.016	ChiN09	
		Hartford, Bruce	SS	8	.181	A	C
		Jackson, Joseph Jefferson	OF119	122	.338	B	
0	3	James, Wm. A. (Lefty)	P	11	.000	B	C
		Johnston, Wheeler Rogers	1B90	103	.244	B	
0	0	Jones, Samuel Pond (Sad Sam)	P	1	.500	A	
0	1	Kahler, George Rannels	P	2	.000	B	C
		Kirke, Jay	OF42	67	.273	BosN	
		Lajoie, Napoleon (1B31)	2B80	121	.258	B	
		Leibold, Harry Loran (Nemo)	OF107	114	.264	B	
		Lelivelt, John Frank (Jack)	OF	32	.328	B	C
		Mills, Frank LeMoyne	C	4	.142	A	C
12	17	Mitchell, Wm.	P	35	.086	B	
1	13	Morton, Guy	P	20	.029	A	
		Olson, Ivan Massie (2B23 3B19)	SS31	89	.242	B	
		O'Neill, Stephen Francis (Steve)	C81	86	.253	B	
		Pezold, Lorenz J. (Larry)	3B	23	.226	A	C
		Reilly, Thomas H.		1	.000	StLN09	C
		Smith, Elmer John	OF	13	.333	A	
9	14	Steen, Wm. John	P	29	.200	B	
1	2	Tedrow, Allen Seymour	P	4	.200	A	C
		Turner, Terrence LaMont (Terry) (2B17)	3B103	120	.245	B	
		Wambsganss, Wm. Adolph	SS36	43	.217	A	
		Wood, Roy Winton (1B20)	OF40	72	.236	PittN	

WON 57
LOST 95
TG 152

AMERICAN LEAGUE

1915.

FINISHED 7th.

PCT. .375

CLEVELAND

JOSEPH LEO BIRMINGHAM LEO ALEXANDER FOHL

WON	LOST	NAME	POS.	G.	BA	FROM	TO
		Barbare, Walter Lawrence	3B68	77	.191	B	
		Billings, John Augustus	C	7	.266	B	
0	1	Bowman, Alvah Edson	P	2	.000	B	C
2	3	Brenton, Lynn Davis	P	11	.118	Clevl3	
1	2	Carter, Paul Warren	P11	12	.214	B	
		Chapman, Raymond Johnson	SS	154	.270	B	
2	5	Collamore, Allan Edward	P11	13	.174	B	C
4	7	Coumbe, Frederick Nicholas (Fritz)	P31	35	.270	B	
		Egan, Arthur Augustus	C40	42	.108	B	C
		Eschen, James Godrich	OF	15	.239	A	C
		Evans, Joseph Patton	3B30	42	.257	A	
2	2	Garrett, Clarence Raymond	P	4	.000	A	C
		Gooch, Lee Currin		2	.667	A	
		Graney, John Gladstone (Jack)	OF115	116	.260	B	
7	13	Hagerman, Zeriah Zequiel (Rip)	P	28	.105	B	
		Hammond, Water Chas.	2B19	35	.214	A	
3	6	Harstad, Oscar Theander	P	32	.125	A	C
		Haworth, Howard Homer	C	7	.142	A	C
0	0	Hill, Hubbell Johnson	P	1	.000	A	C
		Hoffman, Edward H. (Dutch)	3B	9	.153	A	C
		Jackson, Joseph Jefferson (1B28)	OF54	82	+.326	B	Chi
3	8	Jones, Samuel Pond (Sad Sam)	P	48	.156	B	
		Kirke, Jay	1B	87	.310	B	
2	6	Klepfer, Edward Lloyd	P	9	+.143	xChi	
		Leibold, Harry Loran (Nemo)	OF	56	+.246	B	Chi
11	14	Mitchell, Wm.	P	36	.127	B	
15	15	Morton, Guy	P	34	.146	B	
		O'Neill, Stephen Francis (Steve)	C115	121	.236	B	
		Paschal, Benjamin Edwin	OF	9	.111	A	
		Rodgers, Wilbur Kincaid	2B	16	+.298	A	Bos
		Roth, Robert Frank	OF	40	+.287	xChi	
		Shields, Francis LeRoy	1B	23	.208	A	C
		Smith, Elmer John	OF123	144	.248	B	
		Southworth, Wm. Harrison	OF44	60	.220	Clevl3	
0	4	Steen, Wm. John	P	10	+.125	B	Det
		Turner, Terrence LaMont (Terry) (3B29)	2B51	75	.252	B	
5	9	Walker, James Roy	P	25	.132	Clevl2	
		Wambsganss, Wm. Adolph (3B35)	2B78	121	.195	B	
		Wilie, Dennis Ernest	OF35	45	.252	StLN12	C
		Wood, Roy Winton	1B21	33	.193	B	C

WON 77
LOST 77
TG 154

AMERICAN LEAGUE

1916.

FINISHED 6th.

PCT. .500

CLEVELAND

LEO ALEXANDER FOHL

WON	LOST	NAME	POS.	G.	BA	FROM	TO
		Allison, Milo Henry	OF	14	.263	ChiN14	
16	15	Bagby, James Chas. Jacob (Sarge)	P48	51	.166	CinN12	
		Barbare, Walter Lawrence	3B9	13	.229	B	
5	3	Beebe, Frederick Leonard	P	21	.214	PhilN11	C
		Bergman, Alfred Henry	2B3	7	.214	A	C
		Billings, John Augustus	C	22	.160	B	
2	4	Boehling, John Joseph	P	11	+.294	xWash	
		Bradley, John Thomas	C	2	.667	A	C
		Chapman, Raymond Johnson (2B16 3B36)	SS52	109	.231	B	
		Chappell, Lawrence A. (Larry)	OF	3	.000	Chi	BosN
		Coleman, Robert Hunter	C	19	.214	PittN14	
7	5	Coumbe, Frederick Nicholas (Fritz)	P29	31	.057	B	
15	12	Coveleskie, Stanley Anthony	P	44	.173	Phil12	
		Daly, Thomas Daniel	C25	31	.219	Chi	
		DeBerry, John Herman (Hank)	C	15	.273	A	
0	0	DesJardien, Paul Raymond	P	1	.000	A	C
		Engle, Arthur Clyde	3B5	11	.133	BuffF	C
		Evans, Joseph Patton	3B28	33	.146	B	
		Gandil, Chas. Arnold (Chick)	1B145	146	.259	Wash	
5	7	Gould, Albert Frank	P	30	.103	A	
		Graney, John Gladstone (Jack)	OF154	155	.241	B	
		Guisto, Louis Joseph	1B	6	.158	A	
0	0	Gunkel, Woodward Wm.	P	1	.000	A	C
0	0	Hagerman, Zeriah Zequiel (Rip)	P	2	.000	B	C
		Howard, Ivan Chester	2B65	81	.187	StL	
		Kavanagh, Martin Joseph	2B	19	+.250	xDet	
6	7	Klepfer, Edward Lloyd	P	31	.025	B	
4	3	Lambeth, Samuel Otis	P15	16	.111	A	
		Leonard, Joseph Howard	3B	3	+.000	PittN14	Wash
		Lohr, Howard Sylvester	OF	3	.143	CinN14	C
1	5	Lowdermilk, Grover Cleveland	P	10	+.167	xDet	
2	5	Mitchell, Wm.	P	11	+.000	B	Det
		Moeller, Daniel Edward	OF	25	+.069	xWash	C
12	8	Morton, Guy	P	27	.212	B	
0	0	McHale, Martin Joseph	P	5	+.000	xBos	C
		O'Neill, Stephen Francis (Steve)	C128	130	.235	B	
1	0	Penner, Wm. Kenneth	P	4	.000	A	
		Roth, Robert Frank	OF112	125	.286	B	
1	3	Smith, Clarence Ossie	P	5	.286	Chi13	
		Smith, Elmer John	OF	79	+.277	B	Wash
		Speaker, Tristram E. (Tris)	OF	151	.386	Bos	
		Turner, Terrence LaMont (Terry) (2B42)	3B77	124	.262	B	
		Wambsganss, Wm. Adolph (2B24)	SS106	136	.246	B	

WON	LOST	NAME	POS.	G.	BA	FROM	TO
		Welf, Oliver Henry		1	.000	A	C

WON 88 — AMERICAN LEAGUE — FINISHED 3rd.
LOST 66
TG 154 — 1917. — PCT. .571

CLEVELAND

LEO ALEXANDER FOHL

WON	LOST	NAME	POS.	G.	BA	FROM	TO
		Allison, Milo Henry	OF	32	.143	B	C
23	13	Bagby, James Chas. Jacob (Sarge)	P	49	.231	B	
		Billings, John Augustus	C48	66	.178	B	
1	6	Boehling, John Joseph	P	14	.188	B	
		Chapman, Raymond Johnson	SS	156	.302	B	
8	6	Coumbe, Frederick Nicholas (Fritz)	P34	35	.154	B	
19	14	Coveleskie, Stanley Anthony	P45	46	.134	B	
		DeBerry, John Herman (Hank)	C3	25	.273	B	
0	0	Dickerson, George Clark	P	1	.000	A	C
		Eunick, Fernandas Bowen	3B	1	.000	A	C
		Evans, Joseph Patton	3B127	132	.190	B	
4	4	Gould, Albert Frank	P	27	.208	B	C
		Graney, John Gladstone (Jack)	OF145	146	.228	B	
		Guisto, Louis Joseph	1B59	73	.185	B	
		Harris, Joseph	1B95	112	.304	NY14	
		Howard, Ivan Chester	3B3	27	.102	B	C
		Kavanagh, Martin Joseph	2B1	14	.000	B	
14	4	Klepfer, Edward Lloyd	P	41	.032	B	
7	6	Lambeth, Samuel Otis	P	26	.188	B	
		Miller, Raymond P.	1B	19	.190	A	PittN
10	10	Morton, Guy	P	35	.085	B	
		O'Neill, Stephen Francis (Steve)	C127	129	.184	B	
		Roth, Robert Frank	OF135	145	.285	B	
0	1	Smith, Clarence Ossie	P	6	.000	B	C
		Smith, Elmer John	OF	64	+.261	xWash	
		Speaker, Tristram E. (Tris)	OF	142	.352	B	
2	1	Torkelson, Chester LeRoy	P	4	.222	A	C
		Turner, Terrence LaMont (Terry) (2B23)	3B40	69	.205	B	
		Wambsganss, Wm. Adolph	2B138	141	.255	B	
0	1	Wood, Joseph (Smokey Joe)	P	10	.000	Bos15	

WON 73 — AMERICAN LEAGUE — FINISHED 2nd.
LOST 54
TG 127 — 1918. — PCT. .575

CLEVELAND

LEO ALEXANDER FOHL

WON	LOST	NAME	POS.	G.	BA	FROM	TO
17	16	Bagby, James Chas. Jacob (Sarge)	P45	47	.212	B	
		Bescher, Robert Henry	OF17	25	.333	StLN	C
		Billings, John Augustus	C	2	.333	B	
0	0	Brennan, Addison Foster (Ad)	P	1	+.000	xWash	C
		Chapman, Raymond Johnson	SS	128	.267	B	
13	7	Coumbe, Frederick Nicholas (Fritz)	P30	32	.214	B	
22	13	Coveleskie, Stanley Anthony	P	38	.191	B	
5	7	Enzmann, John	P	30	.149	BknN14	
		Evans, Joseph Patton	3B74	79	.263	B	
		Farmer, John Floyd	OF	7	.222	PittN16	C
		Getz, Gustave	3B	6	.066	CinN	PittN
		Graney, John Gladstone (Jack)	OF45	70	.237	B	
2	2	Groom, Robert	P	14	.083	StL	C
		Halt, Alva Wm.	3B14	26	.174	BknF15	C
		Johnston, Wheeler Rogers	1B73	74	.227	PittN16	
		Kavanagh, Martin Joseph	1B	13	+.244	B	StLN
0	0	Lambeth, Samuel Otis	P	2	1.000	B	C
		Miller, Edward	1B22	32	.229	StL14	C
14	8	Morton, Guy	P	30	.156	B	
0	1	McQuillan, George Washington	P	5	.000	PhilN16	C
		O'Neill, Stephen Francis(Steve)	C113	114	.242	B	
		Onslow, Edward Joseph	OF	2	.200	Det13	
		Peters, John Wm.	C	1	.000	Det15	
		Roth, Robert Frank	OF	106	.283	B	
		Schaefer, Herman A. (Germany)	2B	1	.000	NY16	C
		Speaker, Tristram E. (Tris)	OF	127	.319	B	
		Thomas, Chester David	C24	32	.247	Bos	
		Turner, Terrence LaMont (Terry) (2B26)	3B46	74	.249	B	
		Wambsganss, Wm. Adolph	2B	87	.295	B	
0	0	Wilkinson, Roy Hamilton	P	1	.000	A	
		Williams, Alva Mitchel	1B21	28	.239	Wash16	C
		Wood, Joseph (Smokey Joe) (2B19)	OF95	119	.296	B	

WON 84 — AMERICAN LEAGUE — FINISHED 2nd.
LOST 55
TG 139 — 1919. — PCT. .604

CLEVELAND

LEO ALEXANDER FOHL TRISTRAM E. SPEAKER

WON	LOST	NAME	POS.	G.	BA	FROM	TO
17	11	Bagby, James Chas. Jacob (Sarge)	P35	37	.258	B	
7	1	Caldwell, Raymond Benjamin	P	8	+.348	xBos	
		Chapman, Raymond Johnson	SS109	115	.300	B	
1	1	Coumbe, Frederick Nicholas (Frist)	P	8	.500	B	
24	12	Coveleskie, Stanley Anthony	P	43	.213	B	
0	0	Engel, Joseph Wm.	P	1	.000	CinN17	
1	2	Enzmann, John	P	14	.133	B	
		Evans, Joseph Patton	SS2	21	.071	B	
0	0	Faeth, Anthony Joseph	P	6	.000	A	

WON	LOST	NAME	POS.	G.	BA	FROM	TO
		Gardner, Wm. Lawrence (Larry)	3B	139	.300	Phil	
		Graney, John Gladstone (Jack)	OF125	128	.234	B	
		Harris, Joseph	1B46	62	.375	Clevl7	
		Jamieson, Chas. Devine	OF	26	.353	Phil	
4	5	Jasper, Harry W. (Hi)	P	12	.103	StLN16	C
		Johnston, Wheeler Rogers	1B98	102	.305	B	
0	0	Klepfer, Edward Lloyd	P	5	.000	Clevl7	C
		Lunte, Harry August	SS24	26	.195	A	
9	9	Morton, Guy	P	26	.161	B	
8	7	Myers, Elmer Glen	P	23	.239	Phil	
		Nunamaker, Leslie Grant	C16	26	.256	StL	
		O'Neill, Stephen Francis (Steve)	C123	125	.289	B	
3	2	Phillips, Thomas Gerald	P	22	.364	StL15	
		Smith, Elmer John	OF111	114	.278	Clevl7	
		Speaker, Tristram E. (Tris) MGR.	OF	134	.296	B	
		Thomas, Chester David	C21	34	.109	B	
10	5	Uhle, George Ernest	P	26	.302	A	
		Wambsganss, Wm. Adolph	2B	139	.278	B	
0	0	Wood, Joseph (Smokey Joe) (Pl)	OF63	72	.255	B	

WON 98 LOST 56 TG 154

AMERICAN LEAGUE 1920.

FINISHED 1st. PCT. .636

CLEVELAND

TRISTRAM E. SPEAKER

WON	LOST	NAME	POS.	G.	BA	FROM	TO
31	12	Bagby, James Chas. Jacob (Sarge)	P48	49	.252	B	
0	1	Boehling, John Joseph	P	3	.500	Clevl7	C
		Burns, George Henry	1B	45	+.242	xPhil	
20	10	Caldwell, Raymond Benjamin	P34	41	.213	B	
		Chapman, Raymond Johnson	SS	111	.303	B	C
1	2	Clark, Robert Wm.	P	11	.167	A	
24	14	Coveleskie, Stanley Anthony	P	41	.225	B	
0	0	Ellison, George Russell	P	1	.000	A	C
		Evans, Joseph Patton	OF43	56	.349	B	
0	0	Faeth, Anthony Joseph	P	13	.000	B	C
		Gardner, Wm. Lawrence (Larry)	3B	154	.310	B	
		Graney, John Gladstone (Jack)	OF47	62	.296	B	
		Jamieson, Chas. Devine	OF98	.108	.319	B	
		Johnston, Wheeler Rogers	1B	147	.292	B	
		Lunte, Harry August	SS21	23	.197	B	C
7	0	Mails, John Walter (Duster)	P	9	.200	BknN16	
8	6	Morton, Guy	P	29	.217	B	
0	0	Murchison, Thomas Malcolm	P	2	.000	StLN17	C
2	4	Myers, Elmer Glen	P	16	+.240	B	Bos
1	2	Niehaus, Richard J.	P	19	.444	StLN15	C
		Nunamaker, Leslie Grant	C17	34	.333	B	
		O'Neill, Stephen Francis (Steve)	C148	149	.321	B	
		Sewell, Joseph Wheeler	SS	22	.329	A	
		Smith, Elmer John	OF	129	.316	B	
		Speaker, Tristram E. (Tris) MGR.	OF	150	.388	B	
		Thomas, Chester David	C	7	.333	B	
4	5	Uhle, George Ernest	P	27	.344	B	
		Wambsganss, Wm. Adolph	2B	153	.244	B	
0	0	Wood, Joseph (Smokey Joe) (Pl)	OF54	61	.270	B	

WON 94 LOST 60 TG 154

AMERICAN LEAGUE 1921.

FINISHED 2nd. PCT. .610

CLEVELAND

TRISTRAM E. SPEAKER

WON	LOST	NAME	POS.	G.	BA	FROM	TO
14	12	Bagby, James Chas. Jacob (Sarge)	P40	41	.198	B	
		Burns, George Henry	1B73	84	.361	B	
6	6	Caldwell, Raymond Benjamin	P	37	.208	B	C
0	0	Clark, Robert Wm.	P	5	.000	B	C
23	13	Coveleskie, Stanley Anthony	P	43	.155	B	
		Evans, Joseph Patton	OF47	57	.333	B	
		Gardner, Wm. Lawrence (Larry)	3B152	153	.319	B	
		Graney, John Gladstone (Jack)	OF32	68	.299	B	
		Guisto, Louis Joseph	1B	2	.500	Clevl7	
0	1	Henderson, Bernard	P2	3	.000	A	C
		Jamieson, Chas. Devine	OF137	140	.310	B	
		Jeanes, Ernest Lee	OF	4	.500	A	
		Johnston, Wheeler Rogers	1B116	118	.297	B	
14	8	Mails, John Walter (Duster)	P	34	.094	B	
8	3	Morton, Guy	P	30	.171	B	
		Nunamaker, Leslie Grant	C	46	.359	B	
1	0	Odenwald, Theodore Joseph	P	10	.000	A	
		O'Neill, Stephen Francis (Steve)	C105	106	.322	B	
0	0	Petty, Jesse Lee	P	4	.000	A	
		Sewell, James Luther (Luke)	C	3	.000	A	
		Sewell, Joseph Wheeler	SS	154	.318	B	
		Shinault, Enoch Erskine	C20	22	.378	A	
		Smith, Elmer John	OF128	129	.290	B	
12	4	Sothoron, Allen Sutton	P	22	+.276	xBos	
		Speaker, Tristram E. (Tris) MGR.	OF128	132	.362	B	
		Stephenson, Jackson Riggs	2B54	65	.330	A	
		Thomas, Chester David	C19	21	.257	B	C
16	13	Uhle, George Ernest	P41	48	.245	B	
		Wambsganss, Wm. Adolph	2B103	107	.285	B	
		Wilson, Arthur Earl	C	2	.000	BosN	C
		Wood, Joseph (Smokey Joe)	OF64	66	.366	B	

WON 78 LOST 76 TG 154

AMERICAN LEAGUE 1922.

FINISHED 4th. PCT. .507

CLEVELAND

TRISTRAM E. SPEAKER

WON	LOST	NAME	POS.	G.	BA	FROM	TO
4	5	Bagby, James Chas. Jacob (Sarge)	P	25	.262	B	
1	0	Bedgood, Philip Burdette	P	1	.000	A	
4	6	Boone, James Albert	P	11	.192	Det	
		Clanton, Eucal Curt	1B	1	.000	A	C
		Connolly, Joseph George	OF	12	.244	NYN	
17	14	Coveleskie, Stanley Anthony	P	35	.101	B	
		Doran, Wm. James	3B	3	.500	A	C
0	0	Drake, Logan Gaffney	P	1	.000	A	
0	0	Edmondson, George Henderson	P	2	.000	A	
3	8	Edwards, James Corbette	P	25	.087	A	
		Evans, Joseph Patton	OF49	75	.269	B	
		Gardner, Wm. Lawrence (Larry)	3B128	137	.285	B	
		Graney, John Gladstone (Jack)	OF13	37	.155	B	C
		Guisto, Louis Joseph	1B24	35	.250	B	
		Hammond, Walter Chas.	2B	1	.250	Clev15	PittN
0	0	Hamon, Frederick	P	1	.000	A	C
0	0	Jamieson, Chas. Devine (Pl)	OF144	145	.323	B	
0	0	Jeanes, Ernest Lee	P	1	.000	B	
0	0	Kahdot, Isaac Leonard	P	4	.000	A	C
0	0	Keefe, David Edwin	P	18	.333	Phil	C
4	5	Lindsey, James Kendrick	P	29	.167	A	
4	7	Mails, John Walter (Duster)	P	26	.160	B	
2	0	Metevier, George Dewey	P	2	.167	A	
0	1	Middleton, John Wayne	P	2	.333	A	C
14	9	Morton, Guy	P	38	.191	B	
		McInnis, John Phaelen (Stuffy)	1B140	142	.305	Bos	
		McNulty, Patrick Howard	OF	22	.271	A	
		Nunamaker, Leslie Grant	C	25	.302	B	C
0	0	Odenwald, Theodore Joseph	P	1	.000	B	C
		O'Neill, Stephen Francis (Steve)	C130	133	.311	B	
0	0	Pott, Nelson Alexander	P	2	.000	A	C
		Rabbitt, Joseph Patrick	OF	2	.333	A	C
		Sewell, James Luther (Luke)	C38	41	.264	B	
		Sewell, Joseph Wheeler (2B12)	SS139	153	.299	B	
0	0	Shaute, Joseph Benjamin	P	5	.000	A	
		Shinault, Enoch Erskine	C11	13	.133	B	C
1	0	Smith, Sherrod Malone (Sherry)	P	2	.333	xBknN	
		Sorrells, Raymond Edwin	SS	2	.000	A	C
1	3	Sothoron, Allen Sutton	P	6	.444	B	
		Speaker, Tristram E. (Tris) MGR.	OF110	131	.378	B	
		Stephenson, Jackson Riggs (2B24)	3B33	86	.339	B	
		Summa, Homer Wayne	OF	12	.348	PittN20	
22	16	Uhle, George Ernest	P51	56	.266	B	
		Wambsganss, Wm. Adolph (SS16)	2B124	143	.262	B	
1	2	Winn, George Benjamin	P	8	.333	Bos19	
		Wood, Joseph (Smokey Joe)	OF141	142	.297	B	C

WON 82 LOST 71 TG 153 — AMERICAN LEAGUE — FINISHED 3rd.

1923. — PCT. .536

CLEVELAND

TRISTRAM E. SPEAKER

WON	LOST	NAME	POS.	G.	BA	FROM	TO
0	2	Bedgood, Philip Burdette	P	9	.250	B	C
4	6	Boone, James Albert	P	27	.211	B	C
		Brower, Frank Willard	1B112	126	.285	Wash	
		Clarke, Sumpter Ellis	OF	1	.000	ChiN20	
		Connolly, Joseph George	OF39	52	.303	B	
13	14	Coveleskie, Stanley Anthony	P	33	.089	B	
0	0	Drake, Logan Gaffney	P	4	.000	B	
0	0	Edmondson, George Henderson	P	1	.000	B	
10	10	Edwards, James Corbette	P	38	.119	B	
0	0	Fry, Johnson	P	1	1.000	A	C
		Gallagher, Edward John	OF	1	1.000	A	C
		Gardner, Wm. Lawrence (Larry)	3B19	52	.253	B	
		Guisto, Louis Joseph	1B	40	.181	B	C
		Gulley, Thomas Jefferson	OF	3	.500	A	
		Hogan, Kenneth Timothy	OF	1	.000	CinN21	
		Jamieson, Chas. Devine	OF	152	.345	B	
		Knode, Robert Troxell	1B21	22	.289	A	
0	0	Levsen, Emil Henry	P	3	.000	A	
		Lutzke, Walter John	3B	143	.256	A	
4	2	Metevier, George Dewey	P	26	.150	B	
6	6	Morton, Guy	P32	33	.159	B	
		Myatt, Glenn Calvin	C69	92	.286	Phil21	
		O'Neill, Stephen Francis (Steve)	C111	113	.248	B	
		Sewell, James Luther (Luke)	C	10	.200	B	
		Sewell, Joseph Wheeler	SS151	153	.353	B	
		Shaner, Walter Dedaker	3B	3	.250	A	
10	8	Shaute, Joseph Benjamin	P33	34	.162	B	
9	6	Smith, Sherrod Malone (Sherry)	P	30	.244	B	
		Speaker, Tristram E. (Tris) MGR.	OF	150	.380	B	
		Stephenson, Jackson Riggs	2B66	91	.319	B	
0	1	Sullivan, James Richard Jr.	P	3	.000	Phil	C
		Summa, Homer Wayne	OF136	137	.328	B	
26	16	Uhle, George Ernest	P54	58	.361	B	
		Wambsganss, Wm. Adolph	2B88	101	.290	B	
0	0	Winn, George Benjamin	P	1	.000	B	C

WON 67 LOST 86 TG 153 — AMERICAN LEAGUE — FINISHED 6th.

1924. — PCT. .438

CLEVELAND

TRISTRAM E. SPEAKER

WON	LOST	NAME	POS.	G.	BA	FROM	TO
0	0	Brower, Frank Willard (Pl 1B26)	OF39	66	.280	B	C
		Burns, George Henry	1B	129	.310	Bos	
0	0	Cheeves, Virgil Earl	P	8	.142	ChiN	
1	3	Clark, Wm. Watson	P	12	.333	A	
0	0	Clarke, Sumpter Ellis	OF33	45	.227	B	C
15	16	Coveleskie, Stanley Anthony	P	37	.134	B	
1	2	Dawson, Ralph Fenton	P	4	.286	A	
0	1	Drake, Logan Gaffney	P	5	.000	B	C
0	0	Edmondson, George Henderson	P	5	.333	B	C
4	3	Edwards, James Corbette	P	10	.150	B	
		Ellerbe, Francis Rogers	3B	46	+.261	xStL	C
		Fewster, Wilson Lloyd	2B94	101	.267	Bos	
0	0	Fitzke, Paul Frederick Herman	P	1	.000	A	C
		Gardner, Wm. Lawrence(Larry)	3B	38	.200	B	C
		Gulley, Thomas Jefferson	OF	8	.150	B	
		Hogan, Kenneth Timothy	OF	1	.000	B	C
		Jamieson, Chas. Devine	OF	143	.358	B	
		Knode, Robert Troxell	1B10	11	.243	B	
0	1	Kuhn, Bernard Daniel	P	1	.000	A	C
1	1	Levsen, Emil Henry	P	4	.000	B	
0	0	Lindsay, James Kendrick	P	3	.000	Clev22	
		Lutzke, Walter John	3B103	106	.243	B	
2	0	Messenger, Andrew Warren	P	5	.125	A	C
1	5	Metevier, George Dewey	P	26	.125	B	C
0	1	Miller, Walter J.	P	2	.000	A	
0	1	Morton, Guy	P	9	.000	B	C
		Myatt, Glenn Calvin	C95	105	.342	B	
		McNulty, Patrick Howard	OF75	101	.268	Clev22	
0	5	Roy, Luther Franklin	P	16	.267	A	
		Sewell, James Luther (Luke)	C57	63	.291	B	
		Sewell, Joseph Wheeler	SS	153	.316	B	
20	17	Shaute, Joseph Benjamin	P	46	.318	B	
12	14	Smith, Sherrod Malone (Sherry)	P	40	.203	B	
		Speaker, Tristram E. (Tris) MGR.	OF128	135	.344	B	
		Spurgeon, Freddie	2B	2	.167	A	
		Stephenson, Jackson Riggs	2B58	71	.371	B	
		Summa, Homer Wayne	OF95	111	.290	B	
9	15	Uhle, George Ernest	P27	59	.308	B	
		Walters, Alfred John	C25	32	.257	Bos	
0	0	Wayneburg, Frank	P	2	.500	A	C
		Wyatt, Loral Joseph	OF	4	.166	A	C
		Yoter, Elmer Elsworth	3B	19	.273	Phil21	
1	1	Yowell, Carl Columbus	P	4	.191	A	

WON 70 AMERICAN LEAGUE FINISHED 6th.
LOST 84
TG 154 1925. PCT. .455

CLEVELAND

TRISTRAM E. SPEAKER

WON	LOST	NAME	POS.	G.	BA	FROM	TO
		Bedford, James Eldred	2B	2	.000	A	C
1	0	Benge, Raymond Adelphia	P	2	.400	A	
13	8	Buckeye, Garland Maiers	P	30	.226	Wash18	
		Burns, George Henry	1B126	127	.336	B	
1	1	Cole, Albert George (Bert)	P	13	+.154	xDet	
0	3	Edwards, James Corbette	P	13	+.222	B	Chi
		Eichrodt, Frederick George	OF13	15	.230	A	
		Fewster, Wilson Lloyd (3B10)	2B86	93	.248	B	
		Hendrick, Harvey (Gink) (1B3)	OF22	25	.286	N.Y.	
		Hodapp, Urban John	3B	37	.238	A	
		Jamieson, Chas. Devine	OF135	138	.296	B	
11	12	Karr, Benjamin Joyce	P32	46	.261	Bos22	
		Klugman, Joseph (1B4 3B2)	2B29	38	.333	BknN	C
		Knode, Robert Troxell	1B34	45	.250	B	
		Lee, Clifford Walker	OF70	77	.322	CinN	
1	2	Levsen, Emil Henry	P	4	.250	B	
		Lutzke, Walter John (2B10)	3B69	81	.219	B	
10	13	Miller, Walter J.	P	32	.183	B	
		Myatt, Glenn Calvin (OF1)	C98	106	.271	B	
		McCrea, Francis Wm.	C	1	.200	A	C
		McNulty, Patrick Howard	OF113	118	.314	B	
0	0	Roy, Luther Franklin	P	6	.000	B	
		Sewell, James Luther (Luke) (OF2)	C66	74	.232	B	
		Sewell, Joseph Wheeler (2B3)	SS153	155	.335	B	
4	12	Shaute, Joseph Benjamin	P	29	.302	B	
11	14	Smith, Sherrod Malone (Sherry)	P	31	.304		
		Speaker, Tristram E. (Tris) MGR.	OF109	117	.389	B	
3	5	Speece, Byron Franklin	P	28	.160	Wash	
		Spurgeon, Freddie (2B46 SS3)	3B56	107	.287	B	
		Stephenson, Jackson Riggs	OF16	19	.296	B	
		Summa, Homer Wayne (3B2)	OF54	75	.330	B	
		Tolson, Chas. Julius	1B	3	.250	A	
13	11	Uhle, George Ernest	P28	55	.287	B	
		Ussat, Wm. August	2B	1	.000	A	
		Walters, Alfred John	C	5	.200	B	C
2	3	Yowell, Carl Columbus	P	12	.125	B	C

WON 88 AMERICAN LEAGUE FINISHED 2nd.
LOST 66
TG 154 1926. PCT. .571

CLEVELAND

TRISTRAM E. SPEAKER

WON	LOST	NAME	POS.	G.	BA	FROM	TO
		Autry, Martin Gordon	C	3	.143	NY24	
1	0	Benge, Raymond Adelphia	P	8	.333	B	
6	9	Buckeye, Garland Maiers	P	32	.200	B	
		Burns, George Henry	1B	151	.358	B	
		Eichrodt, Frederick George	OF27	37	.313	B	
		Hodapp, Urban John		3	.200	B	
1	3	Judlin, George Willis	P	8	.125	A	
		Jamieson, Chas. Devine	OF	143	.299	B	
5	6	Karr, Benjamin Joyce	P30	31	.222	B	
		Knode, Robert Troxell	1B11	31	.333	B	C
		Lacy, Osceola Guy	2B11	13	.167	A	C
		Lee, Clifford Walker	OF	21	.175	B	C
0	0	Lehr, Norman Carl Michael	P	4	.000	A	C
16	13	Levsen, Emil Henry	P	33	.205	B	
		Lutzke, Walter John	3B	142	.261	B	
7	4	Miller, Walter J.	P	18	.083	B	
		Myatt, Glenn Calvin	C35	56	.248	B	
		McNulty, Patrick Howard	OF	48	.250	B	
		Padgett, Ernest Kitchen	3B29	36	.210	BosN	
		Sewell, James Luther (Luke)	C125	126	.238	B	
		Sewell, Joseph Wheeler	SS	154	.324	B	
14	10	Shaute, Joseph Benjamin	P	34	.274	B	
11	10	Smith, Sherrod Malone (Sherry)	P	27	.215	B	
		Speaker, Tristram E. (Tris) MGR.	OF149	150	.304	B	
0	0	Speece, Byron Franklin	P	2	.000	B	
		Spurgeon, Freddie	2B	149	.294	B	
		Summa, Homer Wayne	OF	154	.308	B	
27	11	Uhle, George Ernest	P39	50	.227	B	

WON 66 — AMERICAN LEAGUE — FINISHED 6th.
LOST 87
TG 153 — 1927. — PCT. .431

CLEVELAND

JACK McCALLISTER

WON	LOST	NAME	POS.	G.	BA	FROM	TO
		Autry, Martin Gordon	C14	16	.255	B	
0	2	Brown, Walter George (Jumbo)	P	8	.667	ChiN25	
10	17	Buckeye, Garland Maiers	P	35	.268	B	
		Burnett, John Henderson	2B1	17	.000	A	
		Burns, George Henry	1B139	140	.319	B	
0	0	Collard, Earl Clinton	P	4	.000	A	
0	0	Cullop, Henry Nicholas (P1)	OF31	32	+.235	xWash	
		Eichrodt, Frederick George	OF81	85	.221	B	
0	0	Ferrell, Wesley Cheek (Wes)	P	1	.000	A	
		Fonseca, Lewis Albert (1B13)	2B96	112	.311	PhilN25	
		Gerken, George Herbert	OF3	6	.214	A	
		Gill, John Wesley	OF17	21	.216	A	
4	6	Grant, George Addison	P	25	.095	StL25	
		Hodapp, Urban John	3B67	79	.304	B	
18	12	Hudlin, George Willis	P	43	.250	B	
		Jacobson, Wm. Chester	OF	32	+.252	xBos	Phil
		Jamieson, Chas. Devine	OF	127	.309	B	
3	3	Karr, Benjamin Joyce	P	22	.200	B	C
		Langford, Elton	OF	20	.269	Bos	
3	7	Levsen, Emil Henry	P	25	.200	B	
		Lind, Henry Carl	2B11	12	.135	A	
		Lutzke, Walter John	3B98	100	.251	B	C
10	8	Miller, Walter J.	P	34	.138	B	
		Myatt, Glenn Calvin	C26	55	.245	B	
0	1	McKain, Harold LeRoy	P	2	.000	A	
		McNulty, Patrick Howard	OF12	19	.317	B	C
		Neis, Bernard Edmund	OF	32	+.302	BosN	Chi
		Padgett, Ernest Kitchen	2B1	7	.286	B	C
		Sewell, James Luther (Luke)	C126	128	.293	B	
		Sewell, Joseph Wheeler	SS	153	.316	B	
9	16	Shaute, Joseph Benjamin	P	45	.325	B	
1	4	Smith, Sherrod Malone (Sherry)	P	11	.167	B	C
		Spurgeon, Freddie	2B52	57	.252	B	C
		Summa, Homer Wayne	OF	145	.286	B	
8	9	Uhle, George Ernest	P25	43	.266	B	
0	2	Underhill, Willie Vern	P	4	.000	A	
		Ussat, Wm. August	3B	4	.187	Clev25	C

WON 62 — AMERICAN LEAGUE — FINISHED 7th.
LOST 92
TG 154 — 1928. — PCT. .403

CLEVELAND

ROGER THORPE PECKINPAUGH

WON	LOST	NAME	POS.	G.	BA	FROM	TO
		Autry, Martin Gordon	C18	22	.300	B	
0	1	Barnhart, Leslie Earl	P	2	.500	A	
2	5	Bayne, Wm. Lear	P	37	.367	StL24	
		Bolton, Cecil Glenn	1B	4	.154	A	C
0	1	Brown, Clinton Harold (Clint)	P	2	.200	A	
0	1	Brown, Walter George (Jumbo)	P	5	.667	B	
1	5	Buckeye, Garland Maiers	P	9	.111	B	NYN
		Burnett, John Henderson	SS	3	.500	B	
		Burns, George Henry	1B	82	+.249	B	N.Y.
		Caldwell, Bruce	OF10	18	.222	A	
0	0	Collard, Earl Clinton	P	1	1.000	B	
		Dorman, Chas. Dwight	OF24	25	.364	A	C
0	2	Ferrell, Wesley Cheek (Wes)	P	2	.250	B	
		Fonseca, Lewis Albert (3B15)	1B56	75	.327	B	
		Gerken, George Herbert	OF34	38	.226	B	C
		Gill, John Wesley		2	.000	B	
		Goldman, Jonah John	SS	7	.238	A	
10	8	Grant, George Addison	P28	29	.182	B	

WON	LOST	NAME	POS.	G.	BA	FROM	TO
0	2	Harder, Melvin LeRoy (Mel)	P	23	.000	A	
		Harvel, Luther Raymond	OF39	40	.220	A	C
		Hodapp, Urban John	3B101	116	.323	B	
		(1B13)					
14	14	Hudlin, George Willis	P	42	.194	B	
		Jamieson, Chas. Devine	OF111	112	.307	B	
		Langford, Elton	OF107	110	.276	B	C
0	3	Levsen, Emil Henry	P	11	.000	B	C
		Lind, Henry Carl	2B	154	.294	B	
1	4	Miljus, John Kenneth	P	11	.200	xPittN	
8	9	Miller, Walter J.	P	25	.135	B	
		Montague, Edward Francis	SS15	32	.235	A	
0	1	Moore, James Stanford	P	1	.000	A	
		Morgan, Edward Carre	1B36	76	.313	A	
		(3B14 OF21)					
		Myatt, Glenn Calvin	C30	58	.288	B	
		Reinholz, Arthur August	3B1	2	.333	A	C
		Sewell, James Luther (Luke)	C118	122	.270	B	
		Sewell, Joseph Wheeler	SS137	155	.323	B	
		(3B19)					
13	17	Shaute, Joseph Benjamin	P	36	.228	B	
		Summa, Homer Wayne	OF132	134	.284	B	
		Tucker, Oliver Dinwiddie	OF	14	.128	Wash	C
12	17	Uhle, George Ernest	P31	55	.286	B	
1	2	Underhill, Willie Vern	P	11	.364	B	C
		Van Camp, Albert Joseph	1B	5	.235	A	
		Ward, Aaron Lee	3B1	6	.111	Chi	C
		(2B1 SS1)					
		Wilson, Francis Edward		2	+.000	BosN26	StL

WON 81 AMERICAN LEAGUE FINISHED 3rd.
LOST 71
TG 152 1929. PCT. .533

CLEVELAND

ROGER THORPE PECKINPAUGH

WON	LOST	NAME	POS.	G.	BA	FROM	TO
		Averill, Howard Earl	OF	152	.330	A	
0	2	Brown, Clinton Harold (Clint)	P	3	.000	B	
		Burnett, John Henderson	SS10	19	.152	B	
		Falk, Bibb August	OF121	126	.310	Chi	
21	10	Ferrell, Wesley Cheek (Wes)	P43	47	.236	B	
		Fonseca, Lewis Albert	1B147	148	.369	B	
		Gardner, Raymond Vincent	SS	82	.262	A	
0	2	Grant, George Addison	P	12	.000	B	
1	0	Harder, Melvin LeRoy (Mel)	P	11	.000	B	
		Hartley, Grover Allen	C13	24	.273	Bos27	
		Hauser, Joseph John	1B6	37	.250	Phil	C
		Hodapp, Urban John	2B72	90	.327	B	
6	5	Holloway, Kenneth Eugene	P	25	.171	Det	
17	15	Hudlin, George Willis	P	40	.196	B	
		Jamieson, Chas. Devine	OF93	102	.291	B	
		Jessee, Daniel Edward		1	.000	A	C
		Lind, Henry Carl	2B64	66	.240	B	
8	8	Miljus, John Kenneth	P	34	.255	B	C
14	12	Miller, Walter J.	P	29	.200	B	
0	0	Moore, James Stanford	P	2	.000	B	
		Morgan, Edward Carre	OF81	93	.318	B	
		Myatt, Glenn Calvin	C41	59	.233	B	
		Porter, Richard Twilley	OF30	71	.328	A	
		(2B22)					
		Sewell, James Luther (Luke)	C123	124	.236	B	
		Sewell, Joseph Wheeler	3B	152	.315	B	
8	8	Shaute, Joseph Benjamin	P	26	.298	B	
2	3	Shoffner, Milburn James	P	11	.000	A	
		Tavener, John Adam	SS89	92	.212	Det	C
4	6	Zinn, James Edward	P18	20	.380	PittN22	C

WON 81 AMERICAN LEAGUE FINISHED 4th.
LOST 73
TG 154 1930. PCT. .526

CLEVELAND

ROGER THORPE PECKINPAUGH

WON	LOST	NAME	POS.	G.	BA	FROM	TO
		Averill, Howard Earl	OF134	139	.339	B	
1	0	Barnhart, Leslie Earl	P	1	.000	Clev28	C
3	3	Bean, Belvedere Benton	P	23	.346	A	
11	13	Brown, Clinton Harold (Clint)	P	35	.247	B	
		Burnett, John Henderson	3B27	54	.312	B	
		(SS19)					
		Detore, George Francis	3B	3	.167	A	
		Falk, Bibb August	OF42	82	.325	B	
25	13	Ferrell, Wesley Cheek (Wes)	P43	53	.297	B	
		Fonseca, Lewis Albert	1B28	40	.279	B	
		Gardner, Raymond Vincent	SS22	33	.077	B	C
0	0	Gliatto, Salvador Michael	P	10	.000	A	C
		Goldman, Jonah John	SS93	111	.242	Clev28	
		(3B20)					
11	10	Harder, Melvin LeRoy (Mel)	P	36	.143	B	
		Hartley, Grover Allen	C	1	.750	B	
		Hodapp, Urban John	2B	154	.354	B	
1	1	Holloway, Kenneth Eugeue	P	12	+.000	B	N.Y.
13	16	Hudlin, George Willis	P	37	.219	B	
8	7	Jablonowski, Peter Wm.	P	39	.200	CinN28	
		(Appleton)					
		Jamieson, Chas. Devine	OF95	103	.301	B	
1	2	Lawson, Alfred Voyle (Roxie)	P	7	.091	A	
		Lind, Henry Carl	SS22	24	.247	B	C
4	4	Miller, Walter J.	P	24	.303	B	
		Montague, Edward Francis	SS46	58	.263	Clev28	
		(3B13)					
		Morgan, Edward Carre	1B129	150	.350	B	
		(OF19)					
		Myatt, Glenn Calvin	C71	86	.294	B	
		Porter, Richard Twilley	OF118	119	.350	B	
		Seeds, Robert Ira	OF70	85	.285	A	
		Sewell, James Luther (Luke)	C	76	.257	B	

WON	LOST	NAME	POS.	G.	BA	FROM	TO
		Sewell, Joseph Wheeler	3B97	109	.289	B	
0	0	Shaute, Joseph Benjamin	P	4	.000	B	
3	4	Shoffner, Milburn James	P	24	.212	B	
		Sprinz, Joseph Conrad	C	17	.178	A	
		Vosmik, Joseph Franklin	OF	9	.231	A	
		Winegarner, Ralph Lee	3B	5	.455	A	

WON 78
LOST 76
TG 154

AMERICAN LEAGUE FINISHED 4th.

1931. PCT. .506

CLEVELAND

ROGER THORPE PECKINAPUGH

WON	LOST	NAME	POS.	G.	BA	FROM	TO
		Averill, Howard Earl	OF	155	.333	B	
0	1	Bean, Belvedere Benton	P	4	.000	B	
		Berg, Morris (Moe)	C	10	.077	Chi	
11	15	Brown, Clinton Harold (Clint)	P	39	.172	B	
		Burnett, John Henderson (2B35 3B21)	SS63	111	.300	B	
5	5	Connally, George Walter	P	17	.185	Chi29	
		Connatser, Broadus Milburn	1B	12	.286	A	
0	0	Craghead, Howard Oliver	P	4	.000	A	
		Detore, George Francis (SS10)	3B13	30	.267	B	C
0	0	Donohue, Peter Joseph	P	2	.000	xNYN	
		Falk, Bibb August	OF33	79	.304	B	C
22	12	Ferrell, Wesley Cheek (Wes)	P40	48	.319	B	
		Fonseca, Lewis Albert	1B	26	+.370	B	Chi
		Goldman, Jonah John	SS	30	.129	B	C
		Hale, Arvel Odell (Bad News) (2B10)	3B15	25	.283	A	
13	14	Harder, Melvin LeRoy (Mel)	P	40	.253	B	
2	1	Hildebrand, Oral Clyde	P	5	.182	A	
		Hodapp, Urban John	2B121	122	.295	B	
15	14	Hudlin, George Willis	P	44	.200	B	
		Hunnefield, Wm. Fenton	SS	21	.239	Chi	BosN
4	4	Jablonowski, Peter Wm. (Appleton)	P29	30	.208	B	
		Jamieson, Chas. Devine	OF4	28	.302	B	
		Kamm, Wm. Edward	3B	114	+.295	xChi	
0	2	Lawson, Alfred Voyle (Roxie)	P	17	.143	B	
2	1	Miller, Walter J.	P	10	.077	B	
		Montague, Edward Francis	SS	64	.285	B	
		Morgan, Edward Carre	1B117	131	.351	B	
		Myatt, Glenn Calvin	C58	65	.247	B	
		Porter, Richard Twilley	OF109	114	.312	B	
		Seeds, Robert Ira	OF33	48	.306	B	
		Sewell, James Luther (Luke)	C105	108	.275	B	
2	3	Shoffner, Milburn James	P	12	.077	B	
		Sprinz, Joseph Conrad	C	1	.000	B	
2	4	Thomas, Fay Wesley	P	16	.154	NYN27	
		Vosmik, Joseph Franklin	OF147	149	.320	B	

WON 87
LOST 65
TG 152

AMERICAN LEAGUE FINISHED 4th.

1932. PCT. .572

CLEVELAND

ROGER THORPE PECKINPAUGH

WON	LOST	NAME	POS.	G.	BA	FROM	TO
		Averill, Howard Earl	OF	153	.314	B	
		Berger, Louis Wm. (Boze)	SS	1	.000	A	
		Boley, John Peter (Joe)	SS	1	+.250	xPhil	C
15	12	Brown, Clinton Harold (Clint)	P37	39	.250	B	
		Burnett, John Henderson (2B26)	SS103	129	.297	B	
		Cissell, Chalmer Wm. (SS6)	2B129	131	+.320	xChi	
8	6	Connally, George Walter	P	35	.175	B	
		Connatser, Broadus Milburn	1B14	23	.233	B	C
23	13	Ferrell, Wesley Cheek (Wes)	P38	55	.242	B	
15	13	Harder, Melvin LeRoy (Mel)	P	39	.181	B	
8	6	Hildebrand, Oral Clyde	P	27	.146	B	
		Hodapp, Urban John		7	+.188	B	Chi
12	8	Hudlin, George Willis	P	33	.203	B	
0	0	Jablonowski, Peter Wm. (Appleton)	P	4	+.000	B	Bos
		Jamieson, Chas. Devine	OF1	16	.063	B	C
		Kamm, Wm. Edward	3B	148	.286	B	
		Montague, Edward Francis (3B11)	SS57	66	.245	B	C
0	0	Moon, Leo	P	1	.500	A	C
		Morgan, Edward Carre	1B142	144	.293	B	
		Myatt, Glenn Calvin	C65	82	.246	B	
0	0	Pearson, Marcellus Monte	P	8	.000	A	
		Porter, Richard Twilley	OF145	146	.308	B	
		Powers, Ellis Foree	OF6	14	.182	A	
		Pytlak, Frank Anthony	C	12	.241	A	
5	7	Russell, Jack Erwin	P	20	+.300	xBos	
		Seeds, Robert Ira	OF1	2	+.000	B	Chi
		Sewell, James Luther (Luke)	C84	87	.253	B	
		Vosmik, Joseph Franklin	OF	153	.312	B	
1	0	Winegarner, Ralph Lee	P	7	.143	Clev30	

WON 75
LOST 76
TG 151

AMERICAN LEAGUE FINISHED 4th.

1933. PCT. .497

CLEVELAND

ROGER THORPE PECKINPAUGH WALTER PERRY JOHNSON

WON	LOST	NAME	POS.	G.	BA	FROM	TO
		Averill, Howard Earl	OF149	151	.301	B	
1	2	Bean, Belvedere Benton	P	27	.182	Clev31	
		Boss, Elmer Harley	1B110	112	.269	Wash30	C
11	12	Brown, Clinton Harold (Clint)	P33	34	.145	B	

WON	LOST	NAME	POS.	G.	BA	FROM	TO
		Burnett, John Henderson	SS41	83	.272	B	
		(2B17 3B12)					
		Cissell, Chalmer Wm.	2B62	112	.230	B	
		(SS46 3B1)					
5	3	Connally, George Walter	P	41	.231	B	
0	0	Craghead, Howard Oliver	P	11	.000	Clev31	C
11	12	Ferrell, Wesley Cheek (Wes)	P28	61	.271	B	
		(OF13)					
		Galatzer, Milton (1B5)	OF40	57	.238	A	
		Hale, Arvel Odell (Bad News)	2B73	98	.276	Clev31	
		(3B21)					
15	17	Harder, Melvin LeRoy (Mel)	P43	44	.190	B	
16	11	Hildebrand, Oral Clyde	P	36	.190	B	
5	13	Hudlin, George Willis	P	34	.146	B	
		Kamm, Wm. Edward	3B131	133	.282	B	
		Knickerbocker, Wm. Hart	SS	80	.226	A	
1	1	Lee, Thornton Starr (Lefty)	P	3	.375	A	
		Morgan, Edward Carre (OF1)	1B32	39	.264	B	
		Myatt, Glenn Calvin	C27	40	.234	B	
		Oulliber, John Andrew	OF18	22	.267	A	C
10	5	Pearson, Marcellus Monte	P	19	.260	B	
		Porter, Richard Twilley	OF124	132	.267	B	
		Powers, Ellis Foree	OF11	24	.277	B	C
		Pytlak, Frank Anthony	C69	80	.310	B	
		Spencer, Roy Hampton	C72	75	.203	Wash	
		Trosky, Harold Arthur (Hal)	1B	11	.295	A	
		Vosmik, Joseph Franklin	OF113	119	.263	B	

WON 85 — AMERICAN LEAGUE — FINISHED 3rd.
LOST 69
TG 154 — 1934. — PCT. .552

CLEVELAND

WALTER PERRY JOHNSON

WON	LOST	NAME	POS.	G.	BA	FROM	TO
		Averill, Howard Earl	OF	154	.313	B	
5	1	Bean, Belvedere Benton	P	21	.200	B	
		Berg, Morris (Moe)	C	29	+.258	xWash	
		Brenzel, Wm. Richard	C	15	.216	PittN32	
4	3	Brown, Clinton Harold (Clint)	P	17	.294	B	
5	10	Brown, Lloyd Andrew	P	38	.233	Bos	
		Burnett, John Henderson	3B42	72	.293	B	
		(OF2 SS9)					
		Carson, Walter Lloyd	OF4	5	.278	A	
0	0	Connally, George Walter	P	5	.000	B	C
		Galatzer, Milton	OF	49	.270	B	
0	0	Galehouse, Dennis Ward	P	1	.000	A	
		(Denny)					
		Garbark, Robert Michael	C2	5	.000	A	
		Hale, Arvel Odell (Bad News)	2B137	143	.302	B	
20	12	Harder, Melvin LeRoy (Mel)	P	44	.161	B	
11	9	Hildebrand, Oral Clyde	P	33	.171	B	
		Holland, Robert Clyde	OF31	50	.250	BosN	C
15	10	Hudlin, George Willis	P	36	.206	B	
		Kamm, Wm. Edward	3B118	121	.269	B	
		Knickerbocker, Wm. Hart	SS	146	.317	B	
1	1	Lee, Thornton Starr (Lefty)	P	24	.095	B	
		Moore, Graham Edward	2B18	27	.154	NYN32	C
		Myatt, Glenn Calvin	C34	36	.318	B	
18	13	Pearson, Marcellus Monte	P	39	.272	B	
0	1	Perrin, Wm. Joseph	P	1	.000	A	C
		Porter, Richard Twilley	OF	13	+.227	B	Bos
		Pytlak, Frank Anthony	C88	91	.260	B	
		Rice, Edgar Chas. (Sam)	OF78	97	.293	Wash	C
		Seeds, Robert Ira	OF	61	+.247	xBos	
		Spencer, Roy Hampton	C1	5	.143	B	
		Trosky, Harold Arthur (Hal)	1B	154	.330	B	
		Vosmik, Joseph Franklin	OF	104	.341	B	
1	5	Weiland, Robert George (Bob)	P	16	+.125	xBos	
5	4	Winegarner, Ralph Lee (OF1)	P22	32	.196	Clev32	

WON 82 — AMERICAN LEAGUE — FINISHED 3rd.
LOST 71
TG 153 — 1935. — PCT. .536

CLEVELAND

WALTER PERRY JOHNSON STEPHEN FRANCIS O'NEILL

WON	LOST	NAME	POS.	G.	BA	FROM	TO
		Averill, Howard Earl	OF139	140	.288	B	
0	0	Bean, Belvedere Benton	P	1	+.000	B	Wash
		Berger, Louis Wm. (Boze)	2B120	124	.258	Clev32	
		(1B2 SS3 3B1)					
		Brenzel, Wm. Richard	C51	52	.218	B	C
4	3	Brown, Clinton Harold (Clint)	P	23	.200	B	
8	7	Brown, Lloyd Andrew	P	42	.108	B	
		Campbell, Bruce Douglas	OF75	80	.325	StL	
		Carson, Walter Lloyd	OF4	16	.227	B	C
		Galatzer, Milton	OF81	93	.301	B	
1	0	Galehouse, Dennis Ward	P	5	.250	B	
		(Denny)					
		Garbark, Robert Michael	C	6	.333	B	
		George, Chas. Peter	C	2	.000	A	
		Hale, Arvel Odell (Bad News)	3B149	150	.304	B	
		(2B1)					
22	11	Harder, Melvin LeRoy (Mel)	P	42	.206	B	
9	8	Hildebrand, Oral Clyde	P	34	.164	B	
15	11	Hudlin, George Willis	P36	37	.279	B	
		Hughes, Roy John (Jeep)	2B40	82	.293	A	
		(SS29 3B1)					
		Kamm, Wm. Edward	3B	6	.333	B	C
		Knickerbocker, Wm. Hart	SS128	132	.298	B	
7	10	Lee, Thornton Starr (Lefty)	P	32	.197	B	
		Myatt, Glenn Calvin	C	10	.083	B	NYN
8	13	Pearson, Marcellus Monte	P	30	.177	B	
		Phillips, Edward David	C69	70	.273	Wash	C
		Pytlak, Frank Anthony	C48	55	.295	B	
6	6	Stewart, Walter Cleveland	P	24	+.200	xWash	C
		Trosky, Harold Arthur (Hal)	1B153	154	.271	B	

WON	LOST	NAME	POS.	G.	BA	FROM	TO
		Vosmik, Joseph Franklin	OF150	152	.348	B	
2	2	Winegarner, Ralph Lee (1B1 3B3 OF4)	P25	65	.310	B	
		Wright, Albert Owen	OF47	67	.238	A	

WON 80 — AMERICAN LEAGUE — FINISHED 5th.
LOST 74
TG 154 — 1936. — PCT. .519

CLEVELAND

STEPHEN FRANCIS O'NEILL

WON	LOST	NAME	POS.	G.	BA	FROM	TO
20	10	Allen, John Thomas (Johnny)	P36	37	.161	N.Y.	
		Averill, Howard Earl	OF150	152	.378	B	
		Becker, Joseph Edward	C15	22	.180	A	
		x Berger, Louis Wm. (Boze)	2B8	28	.173	B	
8	4	Blaeholder, George Franklin	P	35	.130	Phil	C
8	10	Brown, Lloyd Andrew	P	24	.222	B	
		Campbell, Bruce Douglas	OF47	76	.372	B	
5	3	Feller, Robert Wm. Andrew (Bob)	P	14	.136	A	
		Galatzer, Milton	OF42	49	.237	B	
8	7	Galehouse, Dennis Ward (Denny)	P	36	.170	B	
		George, Chas. Peter	C22	23	.195	B	
		Gleeson, James Joseph	OF33	41	.259	A	
		Hale, Arvel Odell (Bad News)	3B148	153	.316	B	
15	15	Harder, Melvin LeRoy (Mel)	P	36	.138	B	
		Heath, John Geoffrey (Jeff)	OF	12	.341	A	
10	11	Hildebrand, Oral Clyde	P	36	.190	B	
1	5	Hudlin, George Willis	P	27	.111	B	
		Hughes, Roy John (Jeep)	2B	152	.295	B	
0	0	Kardow, Paul Otto	P	2	.000	A	C
		Knickerbocker, Wm. Hart	SS	155	.294	B	
3	5	Lee, Thornton Starr (Lefty)	P	43	.122	B	
1	2	Milnar, Albert Joseph (Al)	P	4	.300	A	
		Pytlak, Frank Anthony	C58	75	.321	B	
		Sullivan, Wm. Joseph Jr. (Billy)	C72	93	.351	CinN	
		Trosky, Harold Arthur (Hal)	1B	151	.343	B	
0	1	Uhle, George Ernest	P	24	.381	N.Y.34	C
		Vosmik, Joseph Franklin	OF136	138	.287	B	
		Weatherly, Cyril Roy (Stormy)	OF	84	.335	A	
0	0	Winegarner, Ralph Lee	P	18	.125	B	C
1	1	Zuber, Wm. Henry	P	2	.200	A	

x Berger also played 8 games at 1B, 2 at SS and 7 at 3B.

WON 83 — AMERICAN LEAGUE — FINISHED 4th.
LOST 71
TG 154 — 1937. — PCT. .539

CLEVELAND

STEPHEN FRANCIS O'NEILL

WON	LOST	NAME	POS.	G.	BA	FROM	TO
		Alexander, Hugh	OF3	7	.091	A	C
15	1	Allen, John Thomas (Johnny)	P	24	.090	B	
3	4	Andrews, Ivy Paul	P	20	+.250	StL	N.Y.
		Averill, Howard Earl	OF	156	.299	B	
		Becker, Joseph Edward	C12	18	.333	B	C
2	6	Brown, Lloyd Andrew	P	31	.167	B	
		Campbell, Bruce Douglas	OF123	134	.301	B	
9	7	Feller, Robert Wm. Andrew (Bob)	P	26	.170	B	
0	1	Fischer, Chas. Wm.	P	2	+.000	Chi34	Wash
9	14	Galehouse, Dennis Ward (Denny)	P	36	.208	B	
		Hale, Arvel Odell (Bad News) (2B64)	3B90	154	.267	B	
15	12	Harder, Melvin LeRoy(Mel)	P	38	.174	B	
		Heath, John Geoffrey (Jeff)	OF14	20	.230	B	
8	4	Heving, Joseph Wm.	P	40	.263	Chi34	
12	11	Hudlin, George Willis	P	35	.169	B	
		Hughes, Roy John (Jeep) (2B32)	3B58	104	.277	B	
0	0	Jungels, Kenneth Peter	P	2	.000	A	
		Keltner, Kenneth Frederick (Butch)	3B	1	.000	A	
		Kroner, John Harold (3B11)	2B64	86	.237	Bos	
		Lary, Lynford Hobart (Lyn)	SS	156	.290	StL	
		Monaco, Blas	2B3	5	.286	A	
		Pytlak, Frank Anthony	C115	125	.315	B	
		Sodd, Wm.		1	.000	A	C
		Solters, Julius Joseph (Moose)	OF149	152	.323	StL	
		Sullivan, Wm. Joseph Jr. (Billy)	C38	72	.286	B	
		Trosky, Harold Arthur (Hal)	1B152	153	.298	B	
		Weatherly, Cyril Roy (Stormy)	OF38	53	.201	B	
8	8	Whitehill, Earl Oliver	P	33	.224	Wash	
2	3	Wyatt, John Whitlow (Whit)	P	29	.389	Chi	

WON 86 — AMERICAN LEAGUE — FINISHED 3rd.
LOST 66
TG 152 — 1938. — PCT. .566

CLEVELAND

OSCAR JOSEPH VITT

WON	LOST	NAME	POS.	G.	BA	FROM	TO
14	8	Allen, John Thomas (Johnny)	P	30	.253	B	
		Averill, Howard Earl	OF131	134	.330	B	
		Boudreau, Louis Jr.	3B	1	.000	A	
		Campbell, Bruce Douglas	OF122	133	.290	B	
17	11	Feller, Robert Wm. Andrew (Bob)	P	39	.181	B	

WON	LOST	NAME	POS.	G.	BA	FROM	TO
7	8	Galehouse, Dennis Ward (Denny)	P	36	.154	B	
		Grimes, Oscar Ray Jr. (1B1)	2B2	4	.200	A	
		Hale, Arvel Odell (Bad News)	2B127	130	.278	B	
17	10	Harder, Melvin LeRoy (Mel)	P38	39	.114	B	
		Heath, John Geoffrey (Jeff)	OF122	126	.343	B	
		Helf, Henry Hartz	C	6	.077	A	
		Hemsley, Ralston Burdett (Rollie)	C58	66	.296	StL	
1	1	Heving, Joseph Wm.	P	3	+.000	B	Bos
8	8	Hudlin, George Willis	P	29	.116	B	
9	8	Humphries, John Wm.	P	45	.103	A	
		Irwin, Thomas Andrew	SS	3	.111	A	C
1	0	Jungels, Kenneth Peter	P	9	.000	B	
		Keltner, Kenneth Frederick (Butch)	3B	149	.276	B	
		Kroner, John Harold	2B31	51	.248	B	C
		Lary, Lynford Hobart (Lyn)	SS	141	.268	B	
		Mack, Raymond James	2B	2	.333	A	
3	1	Milnar, Albert Joseph (Al)	P23	24	.154	Clev36	
		Pytlak, Frank Anthony	C99	113	.308	B	
		Russell, Lloyd Opal		2	.000	A	C
0	0	Smith, Clay Jamieson	P	4	.000	A	
		Solters, Julius Joseph (Moose)	OF46	67	.201	B	
0	0	Suche, Chas. Morris	P	1	1.000	A	C
		Trosky, Harold Arthur (Hal)	1B148	150	.334	B	
		Weatherly, Cyril Roy (Stormy)	OF55	83	.262	B	
		Webb, James Leverne (Skeeter)	SS13	20	.276	StLN32	
9	8	Whitehill, Earl Oliver	P	26	.125	B	
		Workman, Chas. Thomas	OF1	2	.400	A	
0	3	Zuber, Wm. Henry	P	15	.000	Clev36	

WON 87 — AMERICAN LEAGUE — FINISHED 3rd.
LOST 67
TG 154 — 1939. — PCT. .565

CLEVELAND

OSCAR JOSEPH VITT

WON	LOST	NAME	POS.	G.	BA	FROM	TO
9	7	Allen, John Thomas (Johnny)	P28	34	.225	B	
		Averill, Howard Earl	OF	24	+.273	B	Det
		Boudreau, Louis Jr.	SS	53	.258	B	
4	2	Broaca, John Joseph	P	22	.000	NY37	C
		Campbell, Bruce Douglas	OF115	130	.287	B	
		Chapman, Wm. Benjamin	OF146	149	.290	Bos	
2	3	Dobson, Joseph Gordon	P	35	.056	A	
0	1	Drake, Thomas Kendall	P	8	.000	A	
6	7	Eisenstat, Harry	P	26	+.250	xDet	
24	9	Feller, Robert Wm. Andrew (Bob)	P	39	.212	B	
		Grimes, Oscar Ray Jr. (1B43 SS37)	2B48	119	.269	B	
		Hale, Arvel Odell (Bad News)	2B73	108	.312	B	
15	9	Harder, Melvin LeRoy (Mel)	P	29	.139	B	
		Heath, John Geoffrey (Jeff)	OF108	121	.292	B	
		Hemsley, Ralston Burdett (Rollie)	C106	107	.263	B	
9	10	Hudlin, George Willis	P	27	.188	B	
2	4	Humphries, John Wm.	P	15	.000	B	
		Keltner, Kenneth Frederick (Butch)	3B	154	.325	B	
		Lary, Lynford Hobart (Lyn)	SS	3	.000	B	BknN
		Mack, Raymond James	2B34	36	.152	B	
14	12	Milnar, Albert Joseph (Al)	P37	41	.253	B	
0	1	Naymick, Wm. Michael	P	2	.000	A	
		Pytlak, Frank Anthony	C51	63	.268	B	
		Sewell, James Luther (Luke)	C15	16	.150	xBknN	
		Shilling, James Robert	2B27	31	.276	A	PhilN
		Solters, Julius Joseph (Moose)	OF	41	+.275	B	StL
0	1	Stromme, Floyd Marvin	P	5	.333	A	C
0	1	Sullivan, Paul Thomas	P	7	.000	A	C
		Trosky, Harold Arthur (Hal)	1B118	122	.335	B	
		Weatherly, Cyril Roy (Stormy)	OF76	95	.310	B	
		Webb, James Leverne (Skeeter)	SS	81	.264	B	
2	0	Zuber, Wm. Henry	P	16	.200	B	

WON 89 — AMERICAN LEAGUE — FINISHED 2nd.
LOST 65
TG 154 — 1940. — PCT. .578

CLEVELAND

OSCAR JOSEPH VITT

WON	LOST	NAME	POS.	G.	BA	FROM	TO
9	8	Allen, John Thomas (Johnny)	P	32	.208	B	
0	1	Andrews, Nathan Hardy	P	6	.000	StLN	
		Bell, Roy Chester (Beau) (1B14)	OF97	120	.279	Det	
		Boudreau, Louis Jr.	SS	155	.295	B	
		Campbell, Clarence Jr.	OF16	35	.226	A	
		Chapman, Wm. Benjamin	OF140	143	.286	B	
3	7	Dobson, Joseph Gordon	P	40	.125	B	
0	0	Dorsett, Calvin Leavell	P	1	.000	A	
1	4	Eisenstat, Harry	P	27	.273	B	
27	11	Feller, Robert Wm. Andrew (Bob)	P	43	.157	B	
		Grimes, Oscar Ray Jr. (3B1)	1B4	11	.000	B	
		Hale, Arvel Odell (Bad News)	3B3	48	.220	B	
12	11	Harder, Melvin LeRoy (Mel)	P	31	.177	B	
		Heath, John Geoffrey (Jeff)	OF90	100	.219	B	
		Helf, Henry Hartz	C	1	.000	Clev38	
		Hemsley, Ralston Burdett (Rollie)	C117	119	.267	B	
0	0	Howell, Millard Fillmore	P	3	.000	A	C
2	1	Hudlin, George Willis	P	4	+.125	B	Wash

WON	LOST	NAME	POS.	G.	BA	FROM	TO
0	2	Humphries, John Wm.	P	19	.000	B	
0	0	Jungels, Kenneth Peter	P	2	.000	Clev38	
		Keltner, Kenneth Frederick (Butch)	3B148	149	.254	B	
		Mack, Raymond James	2B	146	.283	B	
18	10	Milnar, Albert Joseph (Al)	P	37	.181	B	
1	2	Naymick, Wm. Michael	P	13	.167	B	
		Peters, Russell Dixon (1B1 SS6 3B6)	2B9	30	.239	Phil38	
		Pytlak, Frank Anthony (OF1)	C58	62	.141	B	
15	7	Smith, Alfred John	P	31	.306	PhilN	
		Trosky, Harold Arthur (Hal)	1B139	140	.295	B	
		Weatherly, Cyril Roy (Stormy)	OF	135	.303	B	
1	1	Zuber, Wm. Henry	P	17	.333	B	

WON 75 — AMERICAN LEAGUE — FINISHED 4th.
LOST 79 — (TIED WITH DETROIT)
TG 154 — 1941. — PCT. .487

CLEVELAND

ROGER THORPE PECKINPAUGH

WON	LOST	NAME	POS.	G.	BA	FROM	TO
0	0	Andrews, Nathan Hardy	P	2	.000	B	
9	15	Bagby, James Chas. Jr.	P33	35	.243	Bos	
		Bell, Roy Chester (Beau) (1B10)	OF14	48	.192	B	C
		Boudreau, Louis Jr.	SS147	148	.257	B	
3	3	Brown, Clinton Harold (Clint)	P	41	.118	Chi	
		Campbell, Clarence Jr.	OF78	104	.250	B	C
		Conway, Jack Clements	SS	2	.500	A	
1	4	Dean, Alfred Lovill (Chubby) (1B1)	P8	17	+.167	xPhil	
		DeSautels, Eugene Abraham	C	66	.201	Bos	
0	1	Dorsett, Calvin Leavell	P	5	.000	B	
		Edwards, Henry Albert	OF	16	.221	A	
1	1	Eisenstat, Harry	P	21	.333	B	
0	1	Embree, Chas. Willard	P	1	.000	A	
25	13	Feller, Robert Wm. Andrew (Bob)	P	44	.150	B	
		Fleming, Leslie Harvey	1B	2	.250	Det39	
		Freiberger, Vernon Donald	1B	2	.125	A	C
		Frierson, Robert Lawrence	OF3	5	.273	A	C
		Gaffke, Fabian Sebastian	OF2	4	.250	Bos39	
		Grimes, Oscar Ray Jr. (2B13 3B1)	1B62	77	.238	B	
1	1	Gromek, Stephen Joseph	P	9	.167	A	
5	4	Harder, Melvin LeRoy (Mel)	P	15	.080	B	
		Heath, John Geoffrey (Jeff)	OF	151	.340	B	
		Hegan, James Edward	C	16	.319	A	
		Hemsley, Ralston Burdett (Rollie)	C96	98	.240	B	
5	2	Heving, Joseph Wm.	P	27	.000	Bos	
		Hockett, Oris Leon	OF	2	.333	BknN39	
		Howell, Murray Donald		11	.286	A	C

WON	LOST	NAME	POS.	G.	BA	FROM	TO
0	0	Jungels, Kenneth Peter	P	6	.000	B	
		Keltner, Kenneth Frederick (Butch)	3B	149	.269	B	
1	2	Krakauskas, Joseph Victor Lawrence	P	12	.077	Wash	
		Lemon, Robert Granville	3B1	5	.250	A	
		Mack, Raymond James	2B	145	.228	B	
12	19	Milnar, Albert Joseph (Al)	P	35	.171	B	
		Peters, Russell Dixon (2B3 3B9)	SS11	29	.206	B	
		Rosenthal, Lawrence John (Larry) (1B1)	OF32	45	+.187	xChi	
12	13	Smith, Alfred John	P29	30	.155	B	
		Susce, George Cyril Methodius	C	1	.000	StL	
		Trosky, Harold Arthur (Hal)	1B85	89	.294	B	
		Walker, Gerald Holmes (Gee)	OF105	121	.283	Wash	
		Weatherly, Cyril Roy (Stormy)	OF88	102	.289	B	
		Workman, Chas. Thomas		9	.000	Clev38	

WON 75 — AMERICAN LEAGUE — FINISHED 4th.
LOST 79
TG 154 — 1942. — PCT. .487

CLEVELAND

LOUIS BOUDREAU

WON	LOST	NAME	POS.	G.	BA	FROM	TO
17	9	Bagby, James Chas. Jr.	P38	39	.189	B	
		Boudreau, Louis Jr. MGR.	SS146	147	.283	B	
1	1	Brown, Clinton Harold (Clint)	P	7	.000	B	C
0	0	Calvert, Leo Paul Emile	P	1	.000	A	
0	0	Center, Marvin Earl	P	1	.000	A	
8	11	Dean, Alfred Lovill (Chubby)	P27	70	.267	B	
		Denning, Otto George (OF2)	C78	92	.210	A	
		DeSautels, Eugene Abraham	C61	62	.247	B	
		Edwards, Henry Albert	OF12	13	.250	B	
2	1	Eisenstat, Harry	P	29	.250	B	C
3	4	Embree, Chas. Willard	P	19	.133	B	
3	2	Ferrick, Thomas Jerome	P	31	.211	Phil	
		Fleming, Leslie Harvey	1B	156	.292	B	
		Gaffke, Fabian Sebastian	OF16	40	.164	B	C
		Grimes, Oscar Ray Jr. (1B1 SS1 3B8)	2B24	51	.179	B	
2	0	Gromek, Stephen Joseph	P	14	.333	B	
13	14	Harder, Melvin LeRoy (Mel)	P	29	.119	B	
		Heath, John Geoffrey (Jeff)	OF146	147	.278	B	
		Hegan, James Edward	C66	68	.194	B	
5	3	Heving, Joseph Wm.	P	27	.000	B	
		Hockett, Oris Leon	OF145	148	.250	B	
		Keltner, Kenneth Frederick (Butch)	3B151	152	.287	B	
4	8	Kennedy, Lloyd Vernon (Vern)	P28	33	.200	Wash	
0	0	Krakauskas, Joseph Victor Lawrence (Kraky)	P	3	.000	B	

WON	LOST	NAME	POS.	G.	BA	FROM	TO
		Lemon, Robert Granville	3B1	5	.000	B	
		Mack, Raymond James	2B	143	.225	B	
		Mills, Colonel Buster	OF53	80	.277	NY40	
6	8	Milnar, Albert Joseph (Al)	P28	40	.171	B	
		Peters, Russell Dixon	SS24	34	.224	B	
		(2B1 3B1)					
1	3	Poat, Raymond Willis	P	4	.000	A	
0	0	Reynolds, Allie Pierce	P	2	.000	A	
		Robinson, Wm. Edward	1B1	8	.125	A	
		Sepkowski, Theodore Walter	2B2	5	.100	A	
10	15	Smith, Alfred John	P	30	.250	B	
		Susce, George Cyril Methodius	C	2	1.000	B	
		Weatherly, Cyril Roy (Stormy)	OF117	128	.258	B	

WON 82 — AMERICAN LEAGUE — FINISHED 3rd.
LOST 71
TG 153 — 1943. — PCT. .536

CLEVELAND

LOUIS BOUDREAU JR.

WON	LOST	NAME	POS.	G.	BA	FROM	TO
17	14	Bagby, James Chas. Jr.	P36	41	.268	B	
		(SS1)					
		Boudreau, Louis Jr. MGR.	SS152	152	.286	B	
		(C1)					
0	0	Calvert, Leo Paul Emile	P	5	.000	B	
1	2	Center, Marvin Earl	P	24	.000	B	
		Cullenbine, Roy Joseph	OF121	138	.289	N.Y.	
		(1B13)					
5	5	Dean, Alfred Lovill (Chubby)	P17	41	.196	B	C
		Denning, Otto George	1B34	37	.240	B	C
		DeSautels, Eugene Abraham	C66	68	.205	B	
		Doljack, Frank Joseph	OF2	3	.000	Det34	C
		Edwards, Henry Albert	OF74	92	.276	B	
		Grant, James Chas.	3B	15	+.136	xChi	
0	0	Gromek, Stephen Joseph	P	3	1.000	B	
8	7	Harder, Melvin LeRoy (Mel)	P	19	.213	B	
		Heath, John Geoffrey (Jeff)	OF111	118	.274	B	
1	1	Heving, Joseph Wm.	P	30	.071	B	
		Hockett, Oris Leon	OF139	141	.276	B	
		Keltner, Kenneth Frederick	3B107	110	.260	B	
		(Butch)					
10	7	Kennedy, Lloyd Vernon (Vern)	P28	38	.231	B	
0	1	Klieman, Edward Frederick	P	1	.000	A	
		Mack, Raymond James	2B	153	.220	B	
1	3	Milnar, Albert Joseph (Al)	P16	19	+.211	B	StL
		McDonnell, James Wm.	C1	2	.000	A	
4	4	Naymick, Wm. Michael	P	29	.188	Clev40	
		Peters, Russell Dixon	3B46	79	.219	B	
		(2B6 SS14 OF2)					
2	5	Poat, Raymond Willis	P	17	.154	B	
11	12	Reynolds, Allie Pierce	P34	39	.149	B	
		Rocco, Michael Dominic	1B	108	.240	A	
		Rosar, Warren Vincent (Buddy)	C114	115	.283	N.Y.	

WON	LOST	NAME	POS.	G.	BA	FROM	TO
5	3	Salveson, John Theodore	P	23	.231	Chi35	
		Seerey, James Patrick	OF16	26	.222	A	
17	7	Smith, Alfred John	P29	30	.206	B	
		Susce, George Cyril Methodius	C	3	.000	B	
		Turchin, Edward Lawrence	3B4	11	.231	A	C
		(SS2)					
		Woodling, Eugene Richard	OF6	8	.320	A	

WON 72 — AMERICAN LEAGUE — FINISHED 5th.
LOST 82 — (TIED WITH PHILA)
TG 154 — 1944. — PCT. .468

CLEVELAND

LOUIS BOUDREAU JR.

WON	LOST	NAME	POS.	G.	BA	FROM	TO
4	5	Bagby, James Chas. Jr.	P13	14	.226	B	
		Biras, Stephen Alexander	2B1	2	1.000	A	C
0	1	Bonness, Wm. John	P	2	.000	A	C
		Boudreau, Louis Jr. MGR.	SS149	150	.327	B	
		(C1)					
1	3	Calvert, Leo Paul Emile	P	35	.267	B	
		Cullenbine, Roy Joseph	OF151	154	.284	B	
		Devlin, James Raymond	C	1	.000	A	C
0	1	Embree, Chas. Willard	P	3	.000	Clev42	
		Grant, James Chas. (3B4)	2B20	61	.273	B	C
10	9	Gromek, Stephen Joseph	P35	44	.260	B	
12	10	Harder, Melvin LeRoy (Mel)	P	30	.216	B	
		Heath, John Geoffrey (Jeff)	OF37	60	.331	B	
1	1	Henry, Earl Clifford	P2	4	.000	A	
8	3	Heving, Joseph Wm.	P	63	.182	B	
		Hoag, Myril Oliver	OF66	67	+.285	xChi	
		Hockett, Oris Leon	OF110	124	.289	B	
		Keltner, Kenneth Frederick	3B	149	.295	B	
		(Butch)					
2	5	Kennedy, Lloyd Vernon (Vern)	P12	15	.087	B	PhilN
1	2	Kleine, Harold John	P11	14	.143	A	
11	13	Klieman, Edward Frederick	P	47	.105	B	
		Lyon, Russell Mayo	C3	7	.182	A	C
		Mack, Raymond James	2B	83	.232	B	
		McDonnell, James Wm.	C13	20	.233	B	
0	0	Naymick, Wm. Michael	P	7	.000	B	StLN
0	0	O'Dea, Paul (P3 1B3)	OF41	76	.318	A	
		Peters, Russell Dixon	2B63	88	.223	B	
		(SS13 3B8)					
4	8	Poat, Raymond Willis	P	36	.000	B	
11	8	Reynolds, Allie Pierce	P28	41	.123	B	
		Rocco, Michael Dominic	1B	155	.266	B	
		Rosar, Warren Vincent (Buddy)	C93	99	.263	B	
		Ruszkowski, Henry Alexander	C2	3	.375	A	
		Schlueter, Norman John	C43	49	.123	Chi39	C
		Seerey, James Patrick	OF86	101	.234	B	
7	13	Smith, Alfred John	P	28	.156	B	
		Susce, George Cyril Methodius	C	29	.230	B	C

WON 73 | LOST 72 | TG 145

AMERICAN LEAGUE 1945. FINISHED 5th. PCT. .503

CLEVELAND

LOUIS BOUDREAU JR.

WON	LOST	NAME	POS.	G.	BA	FROM	TO
8	11	Bagby, James Chas. Jr.	P	25	.293	B	
		Benjamin, Alfred Stanley	OF4	14	.333	PhilN42	C
		Boudreau, Louis Jr. MGR.	SS	97	.306	B	
0	0	Calvert, Leo Paul Emile	P	1	.000	B	C
0	0	Carnett, Edwin Elliott (P2)	OF28	30	.219	Chi	C
6	3	Center, Marvin Earl	P	31	.091	Clev43	
		Cihocki, Albert Joseph (2B23 3B29)	SS41	92	.212	A	C
		Cullenbine, Roy Joseph (3B3)	OF4	8	+.077	B	Det
		DeSautels, Eugene Abraham	C	10	.111	Clev43	
4	4	Embree, Chas. Willard	P	8	.143	B	
5	3	Feller, Robert Wm. Andrew (Bob)	P	9	.160	Clev41	
		Fleming, Leslie Harvey (1B5)	OF33	42	.329	Clev42	
19	9	Gromek, Stephen Joseph	P33	37	.231	B	
3	7	Harder, Melvin LeRoy (Mel)	P	11	.080	B	
		Hayes, Frank Witman (Blimp)	C	119	+.236	xPhil	
		Heath, John Geoffrey (Jeff)	OF101	102	.305	B	
0	3	Henry, Earl Clifford	P15	16	.500	B	C
0	0	Hoag, Myril Oliver (P2)	OF33	40	.211	B	C
0	0	Kleine, Harold John	P	3	.333	B	C
5	8	Klieman, Edward Frederick	P	38	.200	B	
		Mackiewicz, Felix Thaddeus	OF112	120	.273	Phil43	
		McDonnell, James Wm.	C23	28	.196	B	C
		Meyer, Lambert Dalton	2B	130	.292	Det42	
0	0	O'Dea, Paul (P1)	OF53	87	.235	B	C
18	12	Reynolds, Allie Pierce	P	44	.094	B	
		Rocco, Michael Dominic	1B141	143	.264	B	
		Ross, Donald Raymond	3B	106	+.262	xDet	
		Rothel, Robert Burton	3B	4	.200	A	C
		Ruszkowski, Henry Alexander	C	14	.204	B	
0	0	Salveson, John Theodore	P	19	.400	Clev43	C
		Seerey, James Patrick	OF117	126	.237	B	
5	12	Smith, Alfred John	P21	22	.293	B	C
		Steiner, James Harry	C4	12	+.143	A	Bos
		Weingartner, Elmer Wm.	SS	20	.231	A	C
		Wheeler, Edward Raymond (2B3 SS11)	3B33	46	.194	A	C
		Williams, Frederick	1B3	16	.211	A	C

WON 68 | LOST 86 | TG 154

AMERICAN LEAGUE 1946. FINISHED 6th. PCT. .442

CLEVELAND

LOUIS BOUDREAU JR.

WON	LOST	NAME	POS.	G.	BA	FROM	TO
		Becker, Heinz Reinhard	1B44	50	.299	xChiN	
3	6	Berry, Jonas Arthur	P	21	+.286	xPhil	C
1	2	Black, Donald Paul	P	18	.200	Phil	
		Boudreau, Louis Jr. MGR.	SS139	140	.293	B	
		Brewster, Chas. Lawrence	SS1	3	.000	ChiN44	C
		Case, George Washington	OF	118	.225	Wash	
0	2	Center, Marvin Earl	P	21	.000	B	C
		Conway, Jack Clements (SS14 3B3)	2B50	68	.225	Clev41	
		Edwards, Henry Albert	OF123	124	.301	Clev43	
8	12	Embree, Chas. Willard	P	28	.186	B	
26	15	Feller, Robert Wm. Andrew (Bob)	P	48	.129	B	
0	0	Ferrick, Thomas Jerome	P	9	+.667	Clev42	StL
0	1	Flanigan, Raymond Arthur	P	3	.500	A	C
		Fleming, Leslie Harvey (OF1)	1B80	99	.278	B	
1	1	Gassaway, Chas. Cason	P	13	.067	Phil	C
5	15	Gromek, Stephen Joseph	P29	37	.196	B	
5	4	Harder, Melvin LeRoy (Mel)	P	13	.086	B	
		Hayes, Frank Witman (Blimp)	C50	51	+.256	B	Chi
		Hegan, James Edward	C87	88	.236	Clev42	
0	1	Johnson, Victor Oscar	P	9	.000	Bos	C
		Jordan, Thomas Jefferson	C13	14	+.200	xChi	
		Keltner, Kenneth Frederick (Butch)	3B112	116	.241	Clev44	
0	0	Klieman, Edward Frederick	P	9	.000	B	
2	5	Krakauskas, Joseph Victor Lawrence (Kraky)	P	29	.000	Clev42	C
1	0	Kuzava, Robert LeRoy	P	2	.200	A	
4	5	Lemon, Robert Granville (OF12)	P32	55	.180	Clev42	
		Lollar, John Sherman	C24	28	.242	A	
		Mack, Raymond James	2B	61	.205	Clev44	
		Mackiewicz, Felix Thaddeus	OF72	78	.260	B	
		Meyer, Lambert Dalton	2B64	72	.232	B	C
		Mills, Colonel Buster	OF6	9	.273	Clev42	
		Mitchell, Loren Dale	OF	11	.432	A	
		Monaco, Blas		12	.000	Clev37	C
		Moss, Howard Glenn	3B	8	.063	xCinN	C
0	1	McCabe, Ralph Herbert	P	1	.000	A	C
		Peters, Russell Dixon	SS7	9	.286	Clev44	
0	0	Podgajny, John Sigmund	P	6	.000	PittN43	C
		Price, John Thomas Reid	SS4	7	.231	A	C
11	15	Reynolds, Allie Pierce	P31	35	.222	B	
		Robinson, Wm. Edward	1B	7	.467	Clev42	
		Rocco, Michael Dominic	1B27	34	.245	B	C
		Ross, Donald Raymond (OF2)	3B41	55	.268	B	C
		Sepkowski, Theodore Walter	3B	2	.500	Clev42	
		Seerey, James Patrick	OF115	117	.225	B	
		Wasdell, James Chas. (OF3)	1B4	32	.268	xPhilN	
1	1	Webber, Lester Elmer	P	4	.000	xBknN	

WON	LOST	NAME	POS.	G.	BA	FROM	TO
		Weigel, Ralph Richard	C	6	.167	A	
		Woodling, Eugene Richard	OF37	61	.188	Clev43	

WON 80
LOST 74
TG 154

AMERICAN LEAGUE

1947.

FINISHED 4th.

PCT. .519

CLEVELAND

LOUIS BOUDREAU JR.

WON	LOST	NAME	POS.	G.	BA	FROM	TO
0	0	Beardon, Henry Eugene	P	1	.000	A	
		Becker, Heinz Reinhard		2	.000	B	C
10	12	Black, Donald Paul	P	30	.182	B	
		Bockman, Joseph Edward	3B12	46	.258	N.Y.	
		(2B4 SS1 OF1)					
		Boudreau, Louis Jr. MGR.	SS148	150	.307	B	
		Conway, Jack Clements	SS24	34	.180	B	
		(2B5 3B1)					
		Doby, Lawrence Eugene	2B4	29	.156	A	
		(1B1 SS1)					
0	0	Dorsett, Calvin Leavell	P	2	.000	Clev41	C
		Edwards, Henry Albert	OF100	108	.260	B	
8	10	Embree, Chas. Willard	P27	28	.173	B	
20	11	Feller, Robert Wm. Andrew	P	42	.184	B	
		(Bob)					
		Fleming, Leslie Harvey	1B77	103	.242	B	
		Frazier, Joseph Filmore	OF5	9	.071	A	
11	10	Gettel, Allen Jones	P31	34	.294	N.Y.	
		Gordon, Joseph Lowell (Flash)	2B	155	.272	N.Y.	
3	5	Gromek, Stephen Joseph	P29	30	.318	B	
0	0	Groth, Ernest Wm.	P	2	.000	A	
6	4	Harder, Melvin LeRoy (Mel)	P	15	.179	B	C
		Hegan, James Edward	C133	135	.249	B	
		Klieman, Edward Frederick	3B150	151	.257	B	
		(Butch)					
5	4	Klieman, Edward Fredeick	P	58	.105	B	
1	1	Kuzava, Robert LeRoy	P	4	.111	B	
11	5	Lemon Robert Granville	P37	47	.321	B	
		(OF2)					
0	0	Linde, Lyman Gilbert	P	1	.000	A	
		Lopez, Alfonso Ramon (Al)	C57	61	.262	PittN	
		Mackiewicz, Felix Thaddeus	OF	2	+.000	B	Wash
		Metkovich, George Michael	OF119	126	.254	Bos	
		(1B1)					
		Mitchell, Loren Dale	OF115	123	.316	B	
		Peck, Harold Arthur	OF97	114	.293	Phil	
		Robinson, Wm. Edward	1B87	95	.245	B	
		Rosen, Albert Leonard (OF1)	3B2	7	.111	A	
		Ruszkowski, Henry Alexander	C16	23	.259	Clev45	C
		Sepkowski, Theodore Walter	OF1	10	+.125	B	N.Y.
		Seerey, James Patrick	OF68	82	.171	B	
5	10	Stephens, Bryan Maris	P	31	.111	A	
		Wasdell, James Chas.		1	.000	B	C

WON	LOST	NAME	POS.	G.	BA	FROM	TO
0	2	Willis, Lester Evans	P	22	.091	A	C
0	0	Wolff, Roger Francis	P	7	.000	Wash	PittN

WON 97
LOST 58
TG 155

AMERICAN LEAGUE

1948.

FINISHED 1st.

PCT. .626

CLEVELAND

LOUIS BOUDREAU JR.

WON	LOST	NAME	POS.	G.	BA	FROM	TO
20	7	Bearden, Henry Eugene	P	37	.256	B	
		Berardino, John	2B20	66	.190	StL	
		(1B18 SS12 3B3)					
2	2	Black, Donald Paul	P	18	.200	B	C
		Boone, Raymond Otis	SS4	6	.400	A	
		Boudreau, Louis Jr. MGR.	SS151	152	.355	B	
		(C1)					
3	2	Christopher, Russell Ormand	P	45	.000	Phil	C
		Clark, Alfred Aloysius	OF65	81	.310	N.Y.	
		(1B1 3B5)					
		Doby, Lawrence Eugene	OF114	121	.301	B	
		Edwards, Henry Albert	OF41	55	.269	B	
19	15	Feller, Robert Wm. Andrew	P	44	.095	B	
		(Bob)					
0	0	Garcia, Edward Miguel	P	1	.000	A	
0	1	Gettel, Allen Jones	P	5	+.000	B	Chic.
		Gordon, Joseph Lowell (Flash)	2B144	144	.280	B	
		(SS2)					
9	3	Gromek, Stephen Joseph	P	38	.146	B	
0	0	Groth, Ernest Wm.	P1	2	.000	B	
		Hegan, James Edward	C142	144	.248	B	
		Judnich, Walter Franklin	OF49	79	.257	StL	
		(1B20)					
		Keltner, Kenneth Frederick	3B	153	.297	B	
		(Butch)					
		Kennedy, Robert Daniel	OF50	66	+.301	xChi	
		(1B1 2B2)					
1	0	Kennedy, Wm. Aulton	P	6	+.667	A	StL
3	2	Klieman, Edward Frederick	P	44	.143	B	
20	14	Lemon, Robert Granville	P43	52	.286	B	
0	0	Linde, Lyman Gilbert	P	3	.000	B	C
		Mitchell, Loren Dale	OF140	141	.336	B	
5	4	Muncrief, Robert Cleveland Jr.	P	21	.111	StL	
		Murray, Raymond Lee		4	.000	A	
6	1	Paige, LeRoy	P	21	.087	A	
		Peck, Harold Arthur	OF9	45	.286	B	
		Robinson, Wm. Edward	1B131	134	.254	B	
		Rosen, Albert Leonard	3B2	5	.200	B	
		Seerey, James Patrick	OF7	10	+.261	B	Chi
		Tipton, Joseph John	C40	47	.289	A	
		Tucker, Thurman Lowell	OF66	83	.260	Chi	
0	0	Webber, Lester Elmer	P	1	.000	Clev46	C
0	1	Wensloff, Chas. Wm.	P	1	.000	N.Y.	C
9	6	Zoldak, Samuel Walter	P	23	+.139	xStL	

WON 89 LOST 65 TG 154

AMERICAN LEAGUE 1949. FINISHED 3rd. PCT. .578

CLEVELAND

LOUIS BOUDREAU JR.

WON	LOST	NAME	POS.	G.	BA	FROM	TO
		Avila, Roberto Francisco Gonzalez	2B5	31	.214	A	
8	8	Bearden, Henry Eugene	P	32	.111	B	
9	6	Benton, John Alton (Al)	P	40	.132	Det	
		Berardino, John (2B8 SS3)	3B25	50	.196	B	
		Boone, Raymond Otis	SS76	86	.252	B	
		Bourdreau, Louis Jr. MGR. (1B6 2B1 3B38)	SS88	134	.284	B	
		Clark, Alfred Aloysius (1B1)	OF17	35	.176	B	
		Doby, Lawrence Eugene	OF	147	.280	B	
		Easter, Luscious Luke	OF12	21	.222	A	
		Edwards, Henry Albert	OF	5	.267	B	ChiN
15	14	Feller, Robert Wm. Andrew (Bob)	P	36	.236	B	
14	5	Garcia, Edward Miguel	P	41	.235	B	
		Gordon, Joseph Lowell (Flash)	2B145	148	.251	B	
4	6	Gromek, Stephen Joseph	P	27	.167	B	
		Hegan, James Edward	C	152	.224	B	
		Keltner, Kenneth Frederick (Butch)	3B69	80	.232	B	
		Kennedy, Robert Daniel (3B21)	OF98	121	.276	B	
22	10	Lemon, Robert Granville	P37	46	.269	B	
		Marsh, Fred Francis		1	.000	A	
		Minoso, Saturnino Orestes Arrieta Armas	OF7	9	.188	A	
		Mitchell, Loren Dale	OF	149	.317	B	
		Nielsen, Milton Robert	OF	3	.111	A	
4	7	Paige, LeRoy	P	31	.063	B	
1	0	Papish, Frank Richard	P	25	.125	Chi	
		Peck, Harold Arthur	OF2	33	.310	B	C
		Reich, Herman Chas.	OF	1	+.500	xWash	ChiN
		Rosen, Albert Leonard	3B10	23	.159	B	
		Tresh, Michael Jr.	C	38	.216	Chi	C
		Tucker, Thurman Lowell	OF42	80	.244	B	
		Vernon, James Barton	1B	153	.291	Wash	
11	7	Wynne, Early Jr.	P26	35	.143	Wash	
1	2	Zoldak, Samuel Walter	P	27	.375	B	

WON 92 LOST 62 TG 154

AMERICAN LEAGUE 1950. FINISHED 4th. PCT. .597

CLEVELAND

LOUIS BOUDREAU JR.

WON	LOST	NAME	POS.	G.	BA	FROM	TO
1	0	Aber, Albert Julius	P	1	.000	A	
		Avila, Roberto Francisco Gonzalez (SS2)	2B62	80	.299	B	
1	3	Bearden, Henry Eugene	P	14	+.154	B	Wash
4	2	Benton, John Alton	P	36	.083	B	
		Berardino, John (3B1)	2B1	4	.400	B	PittN
		Boone, Raymond Otis	SS102	109	.301	B	
		Boudreau, Louis Jr. MGR. (1B8 2B2 3B2)	SS61	81	.269	B	
		Clark, Alfred Aloysius	OF41	59	.215	B	
		Conyers, Herbert LeRoy	1B1	7	.333	A	C
		Doby, Lawrence Eugene	OF140	142	.326	B	
		Easter, Luscious Luke (OF13)	1B128	141	.280	B	
16	11	Feller, Robert Wm. Andrew	P	35	.120	B	
3	3	Flores, Jesse Sandoval	P	28	.000	Phil47	C
11	11	Garcia, Edward Miguel	P	33	.200	B	
		Gordon, Joseph Lowell	2B105	119	.236	B	C
10	7	Gromek, Stephen Joseph	P	31	.158	B	
		Hegan, James Edward	C129	131	.219	B	
		Kennedy, Robert Daniel	OF144	146	.291	B	
		Lemon, James Robert	OF10	12	.176	A	
23	11	Lemon, Robert Granville	P44	72	.272	B	
		Mitchell, Loren Dale	OF127	130	.308	B	
		Murray, Raymond Lee	C45	55	.273	Clev48	
0	1	Pieretti, Marino Paul	P29	30	.286	Chi	C
		Rosen, Albert Leonard	3B154	155	.287	B	
0	0	Rozek, Richard Louis	P	12	.000	A	
		Tucker, Thurman Lowell	OF34	57	.178	B	
		Vernon, James Barton	1B25	28	+.189	B	Wash
1	3	Weik, Richard Henry	P	11	+.200	xWash	
18	8	Wynn, Early Jr.	P32	39	.234	B	
4	2	Zoldak, Samuel Walter	P	33	.188	B	

WON 93 LOST 61 TG 154

AMERICAN LEAGUE 1951. FINISHED 2nd. PCT. .604

CLEVELAND

ALFONSO RAMON LOPEZ

WON	LOST	NAME	POS.	G.	BA	FROM	TO
		Avila, Roberto Francisco Gonzalez	2B136	141	.305	B	
		Boone, Raymond Otis	SS	151	.233	B	
4	3	Brissie, Leland Victor	P	54	+.261	xPhil	
3	4	Chakales, Robert Edward	P	17	.350	A	
		Chapman, Samuel Blake (1B1)	OF84	94	.228	xPhil	C
		Clark, Alfred Aloysius	OF	3	+.300	B	Phil
		Combs, Merrill Russell	SS16	19	.179	Wash	
		Doby, Lawrence Eugene	OF132	134	.295	B	
		Easter, Luscious Luke	1B125	128	.270	B	
0	0	Fahr, Gerald Warren	P	5	.000	A	C

WON	LOST	NAME	POS.	G.	BA	FROM	TO
22	8	Feller, Robert Wm. Andrew (Bob)	P	33	.123	B	
20	13	Garcia, Edward Miguel	P	47	.212	B	
7	4	Gromek, Stephen Joseph	P	27	.296	B	
		Hansen, Douglas Wm.		3	.000	A	C
0	0	Harris, Chas.	P	2	+.000	xPhil	C
		Hegan, James Edward	C129	133	.238	B	
0	1	Jones, Samuel	P	2	.000	A	
		Kennedy, Robert Daniel	OF106	108	.246	B	
		Klein, Louis Frank		2	+.000	StLN49	Phil
		Lehner, Paul Eugene	OF1	12	+.231	xStL	
17	14	Lemon, Robert Granville	P42	56	.206	B	
		Maddern, James Clarence	OF1	11	.167	ChiN49	C
		Minoso, Saturnino Orestes Arrieta Armas	1B7	8	+.429	Clev49	Chi
		Mitchell, Loren Dale	OF124	134	.290	B	
		Murray, Raymond Lee	C	1	+1.000	B	Phil
		McCosky, Wm. Barney	OF16	31	.213	xCinN	
		Naragon, Harold Richard	C2	3	.250	A	
		Nielson, Milton Robert		16	.000	Clev49	C
		Rosen, Albert Leonard	3B	154	.265	B	
0	0	Rozek, Richard Louis	P	7	.333	B	
		Simpson, Harry Leon (1B50)	OF68	122	.229	A	
		Stirnweiss, George Henry (3B2)	2B25	50	.216	StL	
		Tebbetts, George Robert (Birdie)	C44	55	.263	Bos	
		Tucker, Thurman Lowell		1	.000	B	C
0	1	Vander Meer, John Samuel	P	1	.000	ChiN	C
20	13	Wynn, Early Jr.	P37	41	.185	B	
0	0	Zuverink, George	P	16	.000	A	

WON 93 AMERICAN LEAGUE FINISHED 2nd.
LOST 61
TG 154 1952. PCT. .604

CLEVELAND

ALFONSO RAMON LOPEZ

WON	LOST	NAME	POS.	G.	BA	FROM	TO
0	0	Abernathie, Wm. Edward	P	1	.000	A	C
		Avila, Roberto Francisco Gonzalez	2B149	150	.300	B	
		Berardino, John (1B2 SS8 3B4)	2B8	35	.094	StL	PittN
		Boone, Raymond Otis (2B1 3B2)	SS96	103	.263	B	
3	2	Brissie, Leland Victor	P	42	.250	B	
1	2	Chakales, Robert Edward	P	5	.500	B	
		Combs, Merrill Russell (2B3)	SS49	52	.165	B	C
		Doby, Lawrence Eugene	OF136	140	.276	B	
		Easter, Luscious Luke	1B118	127	.263	B	
9	13	Feller, Robert Wm. Andrew	P	30	.117	B	
		Fridley, James Riley	OF54	62	.251	A	
22	11	Garcia, Edward Miguel	P	46	.137	B	
		Glynn, Wm. Vincent	1B32	44	.272	PhilN49	
7	7	Gromek, Stephen Joseph	P29	30	.100	B	
3	0	Harris, Maurice Chas.	P	29	+.200	xWash	C
		Hegan, James Edward	C107	112	.225	B	
2	3	Jones, Samuel	P	14	.100	B	C
		Kennedy, Robert Daniel (3B3)	OF13	22	.300	B	
22	11	Lemon, Robert Granville	P42	54	.226	B	
		Majeski, Henry (2B3)	3B11	36	+.296	xPhil	
		Mitchell, Loren Dale	OF128	134	.323	B	
		McCosky, Wm. Barney	OF19	54	.213	B	
		Pope, David	OF10	12	.294	A	
		Reiser, Harold Patrick	OF10	34	.136	PittN	C
		Rosen, Albert Leonard (1B4 SS3)	3B147	148	.302	B	
1	0	Rozek, Richard Louis	P	10	.000	B	
		Simpson, Harry Leon (1B28)	OF127	146	.266	B	
		Stirnweiss, George Henry	3B	1	.000	B	C
		Strickland, George Bevan (2B1)	SS30	31	.216	xPittN	
		Tebbetts, George Robert	C37	42	.248	B	
		Tipton, Joseph John	C35	43	+.248	xPhil	
		Troupe, Quincy Thomas	C	6	.100	A	C
		Westlake, Waldon Thomas	OF28	29	.232	xCinN	
0	0	Wilks, Theodore	P	7	.000	xPittN	
23	12	Wynn Jr., Early	P42	44	.222	B	
0	0	Zuverink, George	P1	2	.000	B	

WON 92 AMERICAN LEAGUE FINISHED 2nd.
LOST 62
TG 154 1953. PCT. .597

CLEVELAND

ALFONSO RAMON LOPEZ

WON	LOST	NAME	POS.	G.	BA	FROM	TO
1	1	Aber, Albert Julius	P	6	+.000	Clev50	Det
		Avila, Roberto Francisco Gonzalez	2B140	141	.286	B	
		Aylward, Richard John	C	4	.000	A	C
		Boone, Raymond Otis	SS31	34	+.241	B	Det
0	0	Brissie, Leland Victor	P	16	.000	B	C
0	2	Chakales, Robert Edward	P	7	.286	B	
		Doby, Lawrence Eugene	OF146	149	.263	B	
		Easter, Luscious Luke	1B56	68	.303	B	
10	7	Feller, Robert Wm. Andrew	P	25	.107	B	
		Foiles, Henry Lee	C	7	.143	xCinN	
		Friend, Owen Lacey (SS8 3B1)	2B19	34	+.235	xDet	
18	9	Garcia, Edward Miguel	P	38	.250	B	
		Ginsberg, Myron Nathan	C38	46	+.284	xDet	
		Glynn, Wm. Vincent (OF2)	1B135	147	.243	B	
1	1	Gromek, Stephen Joseph	P	5	+.000	B	Det
		Hegan, James Edward	C106	112	.217	B	

WON	LOST	NAME	POS.	G.	BA	FROM	TO
5	4	Hooper, Robert Nelson	P	43	.083	Phil	
9	3	Hoskins, David Taylor	P26	38	.259	A	
7	7	Houtteman, Arthur Joseph	P22	23	+.147	xDet	
		Kennedy, Robert Daniel	OF89	100	.236	B	
		Lemon, James Robert (1B2)	OF11	16	.174	Clev50	
21	15	Lemon, Robert Granville	P41	51	.232	B	
		Majeski, Henry (3B7 OF1)	2B8	50	.300	B	
		Mitchell, Loren Dale	OF125	134	.300	B	
		McCosky, Wm. Barney		22	.190	B	C
		Rosen, Albert Leonard (1B1 SS1)	3B154	155	.336	B	
		Simpson, Harry Leon (1B2)	OF69	82	.227	B	
		Smith, Alphonse Eugene (3B2)	OF39	47	.240	A	
		Strickland, George Bevan (1B1)	SS122	123	.284	B	
		Tipton, Joseph John	C46	47	.229	B	
1	0	Tomanek, Richard Carl	P	1	.000	A	
		Weik, Richard Henry		1	+.000	Clev50	Det
		Westlake, Waldon Thomas	OF72	82	.330	B	
2	1	Wight, Wm. Robert	P	20	+.000	xDet	
0	0	Wilks, Theodore	P	4	.000	B	C
17	12	Wynn Jr., Early	P36	37	.275	B	

WON 111 — AMERICAN LEAGUE — FINISHED 1st.
LOST 43
TG 154 — 1954. — PCT. .721

CLEVELAND

ALFONSO RAMON LOPEZ

WON	LOST	NAME	POS.	G.	BA	FROM	TO
		Avila, Roberto Francisco Gonzalez (SS7)	2B141	143	.341	B	
2	0	Chakales, Robert Edward	P	3	+.333	B	Balt
		Dente, Samuel Joseph (2B7)	SS60	68	.266	Chi	
		Doby, Lawrence Eugene	OF	153	.272	B	
		Dyck, James Robert		2	1.000	StL	
		Easter, Luscious Luke		6	.167	B	C
13	3	Feller, Robert Wm. Andrew	P	19	.188	B	
19	8	Garcia, Edward Miguel	P	45	.136	B	
		Ginsberg, Myron Nathan	C1	3	.500	B	
		Glynn, Wm. Vincent (OF1)	1B96	111	.251	B	C
		Grasso, Newton Michael	C	4	.333	Wash	
		Hegan, James Edward	C137	139	.234	B	
0	0	Hooper, Robert Nelson	P	17	.000	B	
0	1	Hoskins, David Taylor	P14	15	.000	B	C
15	7	Houtteman, Arthur Joseph	P	32	.277	B	
		Kennedy, Robert Daniel	OF	1	+.000	B	Balt
23	7	Lemon, Robert Granville	P36	40	.214	B	
		Majeski, Henry (3B10)	2B25	57	.281	B	
		Mitchell, Loren Dale (1B1)	OF6	53	.283	B	

WON	LOST	NAME	POS.	G.	BA	FROM	TO
6	1	Mossi, Donald Louis	P	40	.158	A	
		Naragon, Harold Richard	C45	46	.238	Clev51	
3	3	Narleski, Raymond Edmond	P	42	.000	A	
		Nelson, Glenn Richard	1B2	4	.000	BknN52	
7	2	Newhouser, Harold	P	26	.154	Det	
		Philley, David Earl	OF129	133	.226	Phil	
		Pope, David	OF28	60	.294	Clev52	
		Regalado, Rudolph Valentino (2B2)	3B50	65	.250	A	
		Rosen, Albert Leonard (1B46 2B1 SS1)	3B87	137	.300	B	
0	0	Santiago, Jose Guillermo	P	1	.000	A	
		Smith, Alphonse Eugene (SS4 3B21)	OF109	131	.281	B	
		Strickland, George Bevan	SS	112	.213	B	
0	0	Tomanek, Richard Carl	P	1	.000	B	
		Wertz, Victor Woodrow (OF5)	1B83	94	+.275	xBalt	
		Westlake, Waldon Thomas	OF70	85	.263	B	
23	11	Wynn Jr., Early	P	40	.183	B	

WON 93 — AMERICAN LEAGUE — FINISHED 2nd.
LOST 61
TG 154 — 1955. — PCT. .604

CLEVELAND

ALFONSO RAMON LOPEZ

WON	LOST	NAME	POS.	G.	BA	FROM	TO
2	0	Aguirre, Henry John	P	4	.000	A	
		Altobelli, Joseph	1B40	42	.200	A	
		Avila, Roberto Francisco Gonzalez	2B	141	.272	B	
		Colavito, Rocco Domenico	OF2	5	.444	A	
0	1	Daley, Leavitt Leo	P	2	.000	A	
		Dente, Samuel Joseph (2B4 3B13)	SS53	73	.257	B	C
		Doby, Lawrence Eugene	OF129	131	.291	B	
		Evers, Walter Arthur	OF25	39	+.288	xBalt	
		Fain, Ferris Roy	1B51	56	+.254	xDet	C
4	4	Feller, Robert Wm. Andrew	P	25	.048	B	
		Foiles, Henry Lee	C41	62	.261	Clev53	
11	13	Garcia, Edward Miguel	P	38	.217	B	
0	0	Gray, Theodore Glenn	P	2	+.000	xChi	N.Y.
		Harrell, Wm.	SS11	13	.421	A	
		Hegan, James Edward	C111	116	.220	B	
10	6	Houtteman, Arthur Joseph	P	35	.158	B	
		Kiner, Ralph McPherran	OF87	113	.243	ChiN	C
		Kuhn, Kenneth Harold	SS	4	.333	A	
18	10	Lemon, Robert Granville	P35	49	.244	B	
		Locklin, Stuart Carlton	OF7	16	.167	A	
0	2	Maglie, Salvatore Anthony	P	10	.000	xNYN	
		Majeski, Henry (2B4)	3B9	36	+.188	B	Balt
		Mitchell, Loren Dale (OF3)	1B8	61	.259	B	
4	3	Mossi, Donald Louis	P	57	.111	B	
		Naragon, Harold Richard	C52	57	.323	B	

WON	LOST	NAME	POS.	G.	BA	FROM	TO
9	1	Narleski, Raymond Edmond	P	60	.292	B	
0	0	Newhouser, Harold	P	2	.000	B	C
		Pawloski, Stanley Walter	2B	2	.125	A	C
		Philley, David Edward	OF34	44	+.306	B	Balt Ba
		Pope, David	OF31	35	+.298	B	Balt
		Regalado, Rudolph Valentino	3B8	10	.240	B	
		(2B1)					
		Rosen, Albert Leonard	3B106	139	.244	B	
		(1B41)					
2	0	Santiago, Jose Guillermo	P	17	.500	B	
16	10	Score, Herbert Jude	P	33	.119	A	
		Simpson, Harry Leon		3	+.000	Clev53	K.C.
		Smith, Alphonse Eugene	OF120	154	.306	B	
		(2B1 SS5 3B45)					
		Strickland, George Bevan	SS128	130	.209	B	
		Wertz, Victor Woodrow (OF9)	1B63	74	.253	B	
		Westlake, Waldon Thomas	OF6	16	+.250	B	Balt
0	0	Wight, Wm. Robert	P	17	+.000	Cev53	Balt
		Woodling, Eugene Richard	OF70	79	+.278	xBalt	
17	11	Wynn, Early Jr.	P32	34	.179	B	
		Young, Robert George (3B1)	2B10	18	+.111	xBalt	

WON 88 AMERICAN LEAGUE FINISHED 2nd.
LOST 66
TG 154 1956. PCT. .571

CLEVELAND

ALFONSO RAMON LOPEZ

WON	LOST	NAME	POS.	G.	BA	FROM	TO
3	5	Aguirre, Henry John	P	16	.111	B	
		Averill, Earl Douglas	C34	42	.237	A	
		Avila, Roberto Francisco	2B135	138	.224	B	
		Gonzalez					
		Busby, James Franklin	OF133	135	.235	Chi	
		Caffie, Joseph Clifford	OF10	12	.342	A	
		Carrasquel, Alfonso Colon	SS141	141	.243	Chi	
		(3B1)					
		Colavito, Rocco Domenico	OF98	101	.276	B	
1	0	Daley, Leavitt Leo	P	14	.000	B	
		Evers, Walter Arthur		3	+.000	B	Balt
0	4	Feller, Robert Wm. Andrew	P	19	.000	B	C
		Foiles, Henry Lee	C	1	.000	B	PittN
11	12	Garcia, Edward Miguel	P	35	.115	B	
		Hegan, James Edward	C118	122	.222	B	
2	2	Houtteman, Arthur Joseph	P22	23	.167	B	
		Kuhn, Kenneth Harold	SS17	27	.273	B	
		(2B5)					
20	14	Lemon, Robert Granville	P39	43	.194	B	
		Locklin, Stuart Carlton	OF1	9	.167	B	C
0	0	Maglie, Salvatore Anthony	P	2	.000	B	BknN
		Mele, Sabath Anthony (1B8)	OF20	57	.254	CinN	C
		Mitchell, Loren Dale	OF1	38	.133	B	BknN
6	5	Mossi, Donald Louis	P	48	.150	B	
2	4	McLish, Calvin Coolidge	P37	39	.111	ChiN51	
		Naragon, Harold Richard	C48	53	.287	B	
3	2	Narleski, Raymond Edmond	P	32	.250	B	
		Pope, David	OF18	25	+.243	xBalt	C
		Regalado, Rudolph Valentino	3B14	16	.234	B	C
		(1B1)					
		Rosen, Albert Leonard	3B116	121	.267	B	C
20	9	Score, Herbert Jude	P	35	.184	B	
		Smith, Alphonse Eugene	OF122	141	.274	B	
		(2B1 3B28)					
		Strickland, George Bevan	2B28	85	.211	B	
		(SS28 3B26)					
		Ward, Preston Meyer	1B60	87	.253	xPittN	
		(OF17)					
		Wertz, Victor Woodrow	1B133	136	.264	B	
		Woodling, Eugene Richard	OF85	100	.262	B	
20	9	Wynn Jr., Early	P	38	.228	B	
		Young, Robert George		1	.000	B	

WON 76 AMERICAN LEAGUE FINISHED 6th.
LOST 77
TG 153 1957. PCT. .497

CLEVELAND

MAJOR KERBY FARRELL

WON	LOST	NAME	POS.	G.	BA	FROM	TO
1	1	Aguirre, Henry John	P	10	.000	B	
0	1	Alexander, Robert Somerville	P	5	.000	Balt55	C
		Altobelli, Joseph (OF7)	1B56	83	.207	Clev55	
		Avila, Roberto Francisco	2B107	129	.268	B	
		Gonzalez (3B16)					
		Brown, Richard Ernest	C33	34	.263	A	
		Busby, James Franklin	OF26	30	+.189	B	Balt
		Caffie, Joseph Clifford	OF19	32	.270	B	C
		Carrasquel, Alfonso Colon	SS122	125	.276	B	
		Colavito, Rocco Domenico	OF130	134	.252	B	
2	8	Daley, Leavitt Leo	P	34	.200	B	
12	8	Garcia, Edward Miguel	P	38	.160	B	
1	3	Gray, John Leonard	P	7	.000	KC55	
		Harrell, Wm.	SS14	22	.263	Clev55	
		(2B1 3B6)					
		Hegan, James Edward	C58	58	.216	B	
0	0	Houtteman, Arthur Joseph	P	3	+.000	B	Balt
		Kuhn, Kenneth Harold	2B14	40	.170	B	C
		(SS1 3B2)					
6	11	Lemon, Robert Granville	P21	25	.065	B	
		Maris, Roger Eugene	OF112	116	.235	A	
9	7	McLish, Calvin Coolidge	P42	44	.186	B	
11	10	Mossi, Donald Louis	P	36	.218	B	
		Naragon, Harold Richard	C39	57	.256	B	
11	5	Narleski, Raymond Edmond	P	46	.093	B	
		Nixon, Russell Eugene	C57	62	.281	A	
2	2	Pitula, Stanley	P23	24	.200	A	C
		Raines, Lawrence Glenn	3B27	96	.262	A	
		(2B10 SS25 OF8)					

WON	LOST	NAME	POS.	G.	BA	FROM	TO
		Robinson, Wm. Edward	1B7	19	+.222	xDet	Balt
2	1	Score, Herbert Jude	P	5	.091	B	
		Smith, Alphonse Eugene (OF58)	3B84	135	.247	B	
		Strickland, George Bevan (SS23 3B19)	2B48	89	.234	B	
2	1	Tomanek, Richard Carl	P	34	.231	Clev54	
		Usher, Robert Royce (3B1)	OF4	10	+.125	ChiN52	Wash
2	2	Valentinetti, Vito John	P	11	.200	xChiN	
		Ward, Preston Meyer	1B1	10	.182	B	
		Wertz, Victor Woodrow	1B139	144	.282	B	
1	0	Wilhelm, James Hoyt	P	2	.000	xStLN	
		Williams, Richard Hirshfeld (3B19)	OF37	67	+.283	xBalt	
		Woodling, Eugene Richard	OF113	133	.321	B	
14	17	Wynn Jr., Early	P	40	.116	B	

WON 77 AMERICAN LEAGUE FINISHED 4th.
LOST 76
TG 153 1958. PCT. .503

CLEVELAND

ROBERT RANDALL BRAGAN JOSEPH LOWELL GORDON

WON	LOST	NAME	POS.	G.	BA	FROM	TO
		Averill, Earl Douglas	3B	17	.182	Clev56	
		Avila, Roberto Francisco Gonzalez (3B33)	2B82	113	.253	B	
12	10	Bell, Gary	P	33	.196	A	
1	0	Brodowski, Richard Stanley	P	5	.000	Wash	
		Brown, Richard Ernest	C62	68	.237	B	
		Carrasquel, Alfonso Colon (3B16)	SS30	49	+.256	B	K.C.
0	0	Churn, Clarence Nottingham	P	6	.000	PittN	
0	0	Colavito, Rocco Domenico (P1 1B11)	OF129	143	.303	B	
0	1	Constable, James Lee	P	6	+1.000	xSFN	Wash
		Doby, Lawrence Eugene	OF68	89	.283	Chi	
3	4	Ferrarese, Donald Hugh	P	28	.115	Balt	
1	0	Garcia, Edward Miguel	P	6	.000	B	
0	0	Geiger, Gary Merle (P1 3B2)	OF53	91	.231	A	
		Graber, Rodney Blaine	OF2	4	.125	A	C
10	11	Grant, James Timothy	P44	54	.076	A	
		Hardy, Carroll Wm.	OF17	27	.204	A	
		Harrell, Wm. (2B7 SS45 OF1)	3B46	101	.218	B	
		Hatfield, Fred James	3B2	3	.125	Chi	CinN
		Held, Woodson George (SS14 3B4)	OF43	67	+.194	xK.C.	
		Hunter, Gordon Wm. (3B3)	SS75	76	+.195	xK.C.	C
		Jackson, Ransom Joseph	3B24	29	.242	xLAN	
0	2	Kelly, Robert Edward	P	13	.250	xCinN	C
0	1	Lemon, Robert Granville	P11	15	.231	B	C
		Maris, Roger Eugene	OF47	51	+.225	B	K.C.

WON	LOST	NAME	POS.	G.	BA	FROM	TO
2	0	Martin, Morris Webster	P	14	.000	xStLN	
16	8	McLish, Calvin Coolidge	P	39	.094	B	
		Minoso, Saturnino Orestes Arrieta Armas (3B1)	OF147	149	.302	Chi	
		Moran, Wm. Nelson (SS38)	2B74	115	.226	A	
7	8	Mossi, Donald Louis	P	43	.115	B	
		Naragon, Harold Richard		9	.333	B	
13	10	Narleski, Raymond Edmond	P	44	.204	B	
		Nixon, Russell Eugene	C101	113	.301	B	
		Porter, J. W. (1B4 3B1)	C20	40	.200	Det	
		Power, Victor Pellot (1B41 2B27 SS2 OF1)	3B42	93	+.317	xK.C.	
		Raines, Lawrence Glenn	2B2	7	.000	B	C
0	2	Ridzik, Stephen George	P	6	.000	NYN	
2	3	Score, Herbert Jude	P	12	.091	B	
2	3	Tomanek, Richard Carl	P18	20	+.118	B	K.C.
		Vernon, James Barton	1B96	119	.293	Bos	
		Ward, Preston Meyer (1B21)	3B24	48	+.338	B	K.C.
		Wertz, Victor Woodrow	1B8	25	.279	B	
2	7	Wilhelm, James Hoyt	P	30	+.095	B	Balt
6	6	Woodeshick, Harold Joseph	P	14	.167	Det56	

WON 89 AMERICAN LEAGUE FINISHED 2nd.
LOST 65
TG 154 1959. PCT. .578

CLEVELAND

JOSEPH LOWELL GORDON

WON	LOST	NAME	POS.	G.	BA	FROM	TO
		Baxes, Dimitrios S. (3B22)	2B48	77	.239	xLAN	C
16	11	Bell, Gary	P	44	.240	B	
		Bolger, James Cyril		8	.000	ChiN	PhilN
0	1	Briggs, John Tift	P	4	.000	ChiN	
2	2	Brodowski, Richard Stanley	P	18	.333	B	C
		Brown, Richard Ernest	C	48	.220	B	
3	1	Cicotte, Alva Warren	P	26	.333	Det	
		Colavito, Rocco Domenico	OF	154	.257	B	
		Coleman, Gordon Calvin	1B3	6	.533	A	
		Dillard, David Donald		10	.400	A	
5	3	Ferrarese, Donald Hugh	P	15	.259	B	
		Fitz Gerald, Edward Raymond	C45	49	+.271	xWash	C
		Francona, John Patsy (1B35)	OF64	122	.363	Det	
3	6	Garcia, Edward Miguel	P	29	.071	B	
10	7	Grant, James Timothy	P38	42	.200	B	
		Hamner, Granville Wilbur (2B7 3B5)	SS10	27	.164	xPhilN	
		Hardy, Carroll Wm.	OF15	32	.208	B	
5	1	Harshman, John Elvin	P13	21	+.206	xBos	
		Held, Woodson George (2B3 3B40 OF6)	SS103	143	.251	B	
		Jackson, Ransom Joseph	3B2	3	.143	B	ChiN

WON	LOST	NAME	POS.	G.	BA	FROM	TO
		Jones, Willie Edward	3B4	11	.222	xPhilN	CinN
		Leek, Eugene Harold (SS1)	3B13	13	.222	A	
3	2	Locke, Lawrence Donald	P	24	.333	A	
		Martin, Alfred Manuel (3B4)	2B67	73	.260	Det	
19	8	McLish, Calvin Coolidge	P	35	.189	B	
		Minoso, Saturnino Orestes Arrieta Armas	OF	148	.302	B	
		Moran, Wm. Nelson (SS5)	2B6	11	.294	B	
		Naragon, Harold Richard	C10	14	+.278	B	Wash
		Nixon, Russell Eugene	C74	82	.240	B	
12	10	Perry, James Evan	P	44	.300	A	
		Piersall, James Anthony (3B1)	OF91	100	.246	Bos	
0	1	Podbielan, Clarence Anthony	P	6	.000	CinN57	C
		Power, Victor Pellot (2B21 3B7)	1B121	147	.289	B	
1	0	Robinson, Humberto Valentino	P	5	.000	MilN	PhilN
9	11	Score, Herbert Jude	P	30	.096	B	
0	1	Smith, Robert Walkay	P	12	.000	xChiN	C
		Strickland, George Bevan (2B4 SS50)	3B80	132	.238	Clev57	
1	0	Striker, Wilbur Scott	P	1	.000	A	
		Tanner, Chas. Wm.	OF10	14	.250	ChiN	
		Valo, Elmer Wm.	OF2	34	.292	LAN	
		Webster, Raymond George (3B4)	2B24	40	.203	A	

WON 76 — AMERICAN LEAGUE — FINISHED 4th.
LOST 78
TG 154 — 1960. — PCT. .494

CLEVELAND

JOSEPH LOWELL GORDON — JOYNER CLIFFORD WHITE
JAMES JOSEPH DYKES

WON	LOST	NAME	POS.	G.	BA	FROM	TO
		Aspromonte, Kenneth Joseph (3B36)	2B80	117	+.290	xWash	
9	10	Bell, Gary	P28	30	.149	B	
		Bond, Walter Franklin	OF36	40	.221	A	
3	4	Bowsfield, Edward Oliver	P	11	+.100	xBos	
		Bridges, Everett Lamar	SS7	10	+.333	xDet	StLN
4	2	Briggs, John Tift	P	21	+.125	B	K.C.
		Cline, Tyrone Alexander	OF6	7	.308	A	
		de la Hoz, Miguel Angel (3B8)	SS38	49	.256	A	
		Demeter, Steven	3B3	4	.000	Det	C
		Dillard, David Donald	OF1	6	.143	B	
		Foiles, Henry Lee	C22	24	+.279	xK.C.	Det
		Francona, John Patsy (1B13)	OF138	147	.292	B	
4	2	Funk, Franklin Ray	P	9	.111	A	
9	8	Grant, James Timothy	P33	47	.281	B	
0	1	Grim, Robert Anton	P	3	.000	K.C.	CinN
		Hale, Robert Houston	1B5	70	.300	Balt	
		Hardy, Carroll Wm.	OF17	29	+.111	B	Bos
2	4	Harshman, John Elvin	P	15	.176	B	C
4	4	Hawkins, Wynn Firth	P	15	.100	A	
		Held, Woodson George	SS	109	.258	B	
		Keough, Richard Martin	OF42	65	+.248	xBos	
5	5	Klippstein, John Calvin	P	49	.143	LAN	
		Kuenn, Harvey Edward (3B5)	OF119	126	.308	Det	
7	7	Latman, Arnold Barry	P	31	.220	Chi	
0	0	Lee, Michael	P	7	.000	A	
3	5	Locke, Lawrence Donald	P32	35	.237	B	
0	1	Mathias, Carl Lynwood	P	7	.000	A	
		Morgan, Joseph Michael (OF2)	3B12	22	.298	xPhilN	
2	3	Newcombe, Donald	P20	24	.300	xCinN	C
		Nixon, Russell Eugene	C	25	+.244	B	Bos
18	10	Perry, James Evan	P41	42	.242	B	
		Phillips, John Melvin (OF25)	3B85	113	.207	Chi	
		Piersall, James Anthony	OF134	138	.282	B	
		Power, Victor Pellot (SS5 3B4)	1B147	147	.288	B	
		Powers, John Calvin	OF5	8	+.167	xBalt	C
		Romano, John Anthony	C99	108	.272	Chi	
5	11	Stigman, Richard Lewis	P	41	.222	A	
		Strickland, George Bevan (2B2 3B12)	SS14	32	.167	B	C
		Tanner, Chas. Wm.	OF4	21	.280	B	
		Temple, John Ellis (3B17)	2B77	98	.268	CinN	
1	0	Thomas, Carl Leslie	P4	5	.333	A	C
0	1	Tiefenauer, Bobby Gene	P	6	.000	StLN55	
		Whisenant, Thomas Peter	OF2	7	+.167	xCinN	Wash
		Wilson, Robert	C30	32	+.216	xDet	C

WON 78 — AMERICAN LEAGUE — FINISHED 5th.
LOST 83
TG 161 — 1961. — PCT. .484

CLEVELAND

JAMES JOSEPH DYKES — MELVIN LEROY HARDER

WON	LOST	NAME	POS.	G.	BA	FROM	TO
3	2	Allen, Robert Gray	P	48	.167	A	
0	4	Antonelli, John August	P11	12	.267	SFN	MilwN
		Aspromonte, Kenneth Joseph	2B21	22	+.229	xL.A.	
12	16	Bell, Gary	P	34	.198	B	
		Bond, Walter Franklin	OF12	38	.173	B	
		Cline, Tyrone Alexander	OF	12	.209	B	
1	0	Dailey, Wm. Garland	P	12	.000	A	
		de la Hoz, Miguel Angel (SS17 3B16)	2B17	61	.260	B	
		Dillard, David Donald	OF39	74	.272	B	
		Essegian, Chas. Abraham	OF49	60	+.289	xK.C.	

WON	LOST	NAME	POS.	G.	BA	FROM	TO
		Francona, John Patsy (1B14)	OF138	155	.301	B	
11	11	Funk, Franklin Ray	P	56	.059	B	
15	9	Grant, James Timothy	P35	48	.170	B	
		Hale, Robert Houston		42	+.167	B	N.Y.
0	0	Hamilton, Steve Absher	P	2	1.000	A	
7	9	Hawkins, Wynn Firth	P	30	.108	B	
		Held, Woodson George	SS144	146	.267	B	
0	0	Heman, Russell Frederick	P	6	+.000	A	L.A.
		Jones, Harold Marion	1B10	12	.171	A	
		Kirkland, Willie Chas.	OF138	146	.259	SFN	
		Kubiszyn, John Henry (2B2 SS7)	3B8	25	.214	A	
13	5	Latman, Arnold Barry	P	45	.073	B	
4	4	Locke, Lawrence Donald	P	37	.211	B	
		Luplow, Alvin David	OF	5	.056	A	
0	0	McDowell, Samuel Edward	P	1	.000	A	
		Morgan, Joseph Michael	OF2	4	.200	B	C
		Nieman, Robert Chas.	OF12	39	.354	xStLN	
10	17	Perry, James Evan	P	35	.164	B	
		Phillips, John Melvin	3B	143	.264	B	
		Piersall, James Anthony	OF120	121	.322	B	
		Power, Victor Pellot (2B7)	1B141	147	.268	B	
		Romano, John Anthony	C141	142	.299	B	
0	1	Schaffernoth, Joseph Arthur	P	15	.000	xChiN	C
2	5	Stigman, Richard Lewis	P	22	.125	B	
		Temple, John Ellis	2B	129	.276	B	
		Thomas, Valmy	C	27	.209	Balt	C

WON 80 — AMERICAN LEAGUE — FINISHED 6th.
LOST 82
TG 162 — 1962. — PCT. .494

CLEVELAND

FRED MELVIN McGAHA

WON	LOST	NAME	POS.	G.	BA	FROM	TO
		Agee, Thomas Lee	OF3	5	.214	A	
1	1	Allen, Robert Gray	P	30	.000	B	
		Alvis, Roy Maxwell	3B	12	.216	A	
		Aspromonte, Kenneth Joseph (3B3)	2B6	20	.143	B	MilN
10	9	Bell, Gary	P	57	.203	B	
		Bond, Walter Franklin	OF	12	.380	B	C
		Cline, Tyrone Alexander	OF107	113	.248	B	
0	0	Collum, Jack Dean	P	1	+.000	xMinn	C
		Coughtry, James Marlan		3	+.500	xK.C.	C
2	2	Dailey, Wm. Garland	P	27	.000	B	
		de la Hoz, Miguel Angel	2B2	12	.083	B	
		Dillard, David Donald	OF50	95	.230	B	
20	10	Donovan, Richard Edward	P	34	.180	Wash	
		Edwards, Howard Rodney	C39	53	.273	A	
		Essegian, Chas. Abraham	OF90	106	.274	B	
		Francona, John Patsy	1B	158	.272	B	
2	1	Funk, Franklin Ray	P	47	.067	B	

WON	LOST	NAME	POS.	G.	BA	FROM	TO
1	2	Gomez, Ruben Colon	P15	16	+.231	PhilN60	Minn
7	10	Grant, James Timothy	P26	30	.151	B	
		Green, Eugene Leroy (1B2)	OF33	66	.280	Wash	
0	1	Hartman, Robert Louis	P	8	.000	MilN59	C
1	0	Hawkins, Wynn Firth	P	3	.000	B	C
		Held, Woodson George (3B5 OF1)	SS133	139	.249	B	
		Jones, Harold Marion	1B4	5	.313	B	C
		Kindall, Gerald Donald	2B	154	.232	ChiN	
		Kirkland, Willie Chas.	OF125	137	.200	B	
		Kubiszyn, John Henry (3B1)	SS18	25	.169	B	C
8	13	Latman, Arnold Barry	P	45	.189	B	
		Luplow, Alvin David	OF86	97	.277	B	
		Mahoney, James Thomas (2B8 3B1)	SS23	41	.243	Wash	
3	7	McDowell, Samuel Edward	P	25	.154	B	
		Nieman, Robert Chas.		2	.000	B	S.F.N
12	12	Perry, James Evan	P	35	.183	B	
		Phillips, John Melvin (2B1 OF3)	3B145	148	.258	B	
10	12	Ramos, Pedro	P37	39	.147	Minn	
		Romano, John Anthony	C130	135	.261	B	
0	0	Rudolph, Frederick Donald	P	1	+.000	CinN59	Wash
		Tasby, Willie (3B1)	OF66	75	+.241	xWash	
2	2	Taylor, Ronald Wesley	P	8	.273	A	
0	0	Tyriver, David Burton	P	4	.000	A	C
1	0	Weaver, David Floyd	P	1	.500	A	

WON 79 — AMERICAN LEAGUE — FINISHED 5th.
LOST 83 — (TIED WITH DETROIT)
TG 162 — 1963. — PCT. .488

CLEVELAND

GEORGE ROBERT TEBBETTS

WON	LOST	NAME	POS.	G.	BA	FROM	TO
7	2	Abernathy, Theodore Wade	P	43	.400	Wash60	
		Adcock, Joseph Wilbur	1B78	97	.251	MilwN	
		Agee, Thomas Lee	OF	13	.148	B	
1	2	Allen, Robert Gray	P	43	.200	B	
		Alvis, Roy Maxwell	3B	158	.274	B	
		Azcue, Jose Joaquin	C91	94	+.284	xK.C.	
8	5	Bell, Gary	P	58	.115	B	
		Brown, Larry Leslie (2B27)	SS46	74	.255	A	
		Burton, Ellis Narrington	OF16	26	.194	StLN60	ChicN
		Chance, Robert	OF14	16	.288	A	
0	0	Curtis, Jack Patrick	P	4	.000	MilwN	C
		Davalillo, Victor Jose	OF89	90	.292	A	
		de la Hoz, Miguel Angel (SS2 3B6 OF2)	2B34	67	.267	B	
11	13	Donovan, Richard Edward	P30	31	.130	B	
		Edwards, Howard Rodney	C	10	+.258	B	K.C.

WON	LOST	NAME	POS.	G.	BA	FROM	TO
		Francona, John Patsy	OF122	142	.228	B	
		(1B11)					
13	14	Grant, James Timothy	P38	53	.188	B	
		Green, Eugene Leroy	OF18	43	.205	B	CinN
		Held, Woodson George	2B96	133	.248	B	
		(SS5 3B3 OF35)					
		Howser, Richard Dalton	SS44	49	+.247	xK.C.	
0	2	John, Thomas Edward	P	6	.000	A	
		Kindall, Gerald Donald	SS46	86	.205	B	
		(1B4 2B37)					
		Kirkland, Willie Chas.	OF112	127	.230	B	
13	9	Kralick, John Francis	P	28	+.183	xMinn	
7	12	Latman, Arnold Barry	P	38	.182	B	
		Lawrence, James Ross	C	2	.000	A	C
		Lipski, Robert Peter	C	2	.000	A	C
		Luplow, Alvin David	OF85	100	.234	B	
		Martinez, Antonio Gabriel	SS41	43	.156	A	
3	5	McDowell, Samuel Edward	P14	15	.211	B	
		Neeman, Calvin Amandus	C	9	+.000	PittN	Wash
0	2	Nischwitz, Ronald Lee	P	14	.000	Det	
0	0	Perry, James Evan	P	5	+.000	B	Minn
9	8	Ramos, Pedro	P36	54	.109	B	
		Romano, John Anthony	C71	89	.216	B	
		(OF4)					
0	1	Seyfried, Gordon Clay	P	3	.000	A	
		Tasby, Willie	OF37	52	.224	B	C
		(2B1)					
		Taylor, Samuel Douglas	C2	4	.300	xCinN	
6	6	Walker, Jerry Allen	P	39	.105	K.C.	
		Whitfield, Fred Dwight	1B92	109	.251	StLN	
1	2	Wynn Jr., Early	P	20	.273	Chic	C

WON 79 LOST 83 TG 162

AMERICAN LEAGUE 1964.

FINISHED 6th. (TIED WITH MINNESOTA) PCT. .488

CLEVELAND

GEORGE BEVAN STRICKLAND GEORGE ROBERT TEBBETTS

WON	LOST	NAME	POS.	G.	BA	FROM	TO
2	6	Abernathy, Theodore Wade	P	53	.000	B	
		Agee, Thomas Lee	OF12	13	.167	B	
		Alvis, Roy Maxwell	3B105	107	.252	B	
		Azcue, Jose Joaquin	C76	83	.273	B	
		Banks, George Edward	OF3	9	+.294	xMinn	
		(2B1 3B1)					
8	6	Bell, Gary	P	56	.375	B	
		Brown, Larry Leslie	2B103	115	.230	B	
		(SS4)					
		Chance, Robert	1B81	120	.279	B	
		(OF31)					
		Davilillo, Victor Jose	OF143	150	.270	B	
		Dicken, Paul Franklin		11	.000	A	
7	9	Donovan, Richard Edward	P30	31	.146	B	
		Francona, John Patsy	OF69	111	.248	B	
		(1B17)					
		Fuller, Vernon Gordon		2	.000	A	
3	4	Grant, James Timothy	P13	20	+.273	B	Minn
		Held, Woodson George	2B52	118	.236	B	
		(3B30 OF41)					
		Howser, Richard Dalton	SS	162	.256	B	
2	9	John, Thomas Edward	P	25	.208	B	
0	0	Kelley, Thomas Henry	P	6	.000	A	
		Kindall, Gerald Donald	1B	23	+.360	B	Minn
12	7	Kralick, John Francis	P	30	.156	B	
		Luplow, Alvin David	OF5	19	.111	B	
		Martinez, Antonio Gabriel	2B4	9	.214	B	
		(SS1)					
11	6	McDowell, Samuel Edward	P	31	.143	B	
6	4	McMahon, Donald John	P	70	.143	HousN	
		Moran, Wm. Nelson	3B42	69	+.205	xL.A.	
		(1B2 2B15)					
		Post, Walter Chas.	OF2	5	.000	Minn	C
7	10	Ramos, Pedro	P36	44	+.179	B	N.Y.
		Romano, John Anthony	C96	106	.241	B	
		(1B1)					
		Salmon, Ruthford Edward	OF53	86	.307	A	
		(1B13 2B32)					
0	0	Seyfried, Gordon Clay	P	2	.000	B	C
7	9	Siebert, Wilfred Chas	P41	42	.265	A	
		Sims, Duane B.	C1	2	.000	A	
		Smith, Alphonse Eugene	OF48	61	+.162	Balt	Bos
		(3B1)					
4	8	Stange, Albert Lee	P23	24	+.080	xMinn	
10	4	Tiant, Luis Clemente	P	19	.111	A	
		Wagner, Leon Lamar	OF	163	.253	L.A.	
0	1	Walker, Jerry Allen	P	6	.000	B	C
		Whitfield, Fred Dwight	1B79	101	.270	B	

CLUB RECORD

DETROIT

YEAR	TG	WON	LOST	PCT.	FINISHED	MANAGER
AMERICAN LEAGUE						
1900	138	71	67	.514	4	George Tweedy Stallings

CLUB RECORD

AMERICAN LEAGUE

DETROIT

YEAR	TG	WON	LOST	PCT.	FINISHED	MANAGER
1901	135	74	61	.548	3	George Tweedy Stallings
1902	135	52	83	.385	7	John Francis Dwyer
1903	136	65	71	.478	5	Edward Grant Barrow
1904	152	62	90	.408	7	Edward Grant Barrow Robert Lincoln Lowe
1905	153	79	74	.516	3	Wm. R. Armour
1906	149	71	78	.477	6	Wm. R. Armour
1907	150	92	58	.613	1	Hugh Ambrose Jennings
1908	153	90	63	.588	1	Hugh Ambrose Jennings
1909	152	98	54	.645	1	Hugh Ambrose Jennings
1910	154	86	68	.558	3	Hugh Ambrose Jennings
1911	154	89	65	.578	2	Hugh Ambrose Jennings
1912	153	69	84	.451	6	Hugh Ambrose Jennings
1913	153	66	87	.431	6	Hugh Ambrose Jennings
1914	153	80	73	.523	4	Hugh Ambrose Jennings
1915	154	100	54	.649	2	Hugh Ambrose Jennings
1916	154	87	67	.565	3	Hugh Ambrose Jennings
1917	153	78	75	.510	4	Hugh Ambrose Jennings
1918	126	55	71	.437	7	Hugh Ambrose Jennings
1919	140	80	60	.571	4	Hugh Ambrose Jennings
1920	154	61	93	.396	7	Hugh Ambrose Jennings
1921	153	71	82	.464	6	Tyrus Raymond Cobb
1922	154	79	75	.513	3	Tyrus Raymond Cobb
1923	154	83	71	.539	2	Tyrus Raymond Cobb
1924	154	86	68	.558	3	Tyrus Raymond Cobb
1925	154	81	73	.526	4	Tyrus Raymond Cobb
1926	154	79	75	.513	6	Tyrus Raymond Cobb
1927	153	82	71	.536	4	George Joseph Moriarty
1928	154	68	86	.442	6	George Joseph Moriarty
1929	154	70	84	.455	6	Stanley Raymond Harris
1930	154	75	79	.487	5	Stanley Raymond Harris
1931	154	61	93	.396	7	Stanley Raymond Harris
1932	151	76	76	.500	5	Stanley Raymond Harris
1933	154	75	79	.487	5	Stanley Raymond Harris Delmer David Baker
1934	154	101	53	.656	1	Gordon Stanley Cochrane
1935	151	93	58	.616	1	Gordon Stanley Cochrane
1936	154	83	71	.539	2	Gordon Stanley Cochrane
1937	154	89	65	.578	2	Gordon Stanley Cochrane
1938	154	84	70	.545	4	Gordon Stanley Cochrane Delmer David Baker
1939	154	81	73	.526	5	Delmer David Baker
1940	154	90	64	.584	1	Delmer David Baker
1941	154	75	79	.487	x4(Cleve)	Delmer David Baker
1942	154	73	81	.474	5	Delmer David Baker
1943	154	78	76	.506	5	Stephen Francis O'Neill
1944	154	88	66	.571	2	Stephen Francis O'Neill
1945	153	88	65	.575	1	Stephen Francis O'Neill
1946	154	92	62	.597	2	Stephen Francis O'Neill
1947	154	85	69	.552	2	Stephen Francis O'Neill

YEAR	TG	WON	LOST	TIED	PCT.	FINISHED	MANAGER
1948	154	78	76		.506	5	Stephen Francis O'Neill
1949	154	87	67		.565	4	Robert Abial Rolfe
1950	154	95	59		.617	2	Robert Abial Rolfe
1951	154	73	81		.474	5	Robert Abial Rolfe
1952	154	50	104		.325	8(Last)	Robert Abial Rolfe / Frederick Chas. Hutchinson
1953	154	60	94		.390	6	Frederick Chas. Hutchinson
1954	154	68	86		.442	5	Frederick Chas. Hutchinson
1955	154	79	75		.513	5	Stanley Raymond Harris
1956	154	82	72		.532	5	Stanley Raymond Harris
1957	154	78	76		.506	4	John Thomas Tighe
1958	154	77	77		.500	5	John Thomas Tighe / Henry Willis Patrick Norman
1959	154	76	78		.494	4	Henry Willis Patrick Norman / James Joseph Dykes
1960	154	71	83		.461	6	James Joseph Dykes / Wm. Clyde Hitchcock / Joseph Lowell Gordon
1961	162	101	61		.623	2	Robert Boden Scheffing
1962	161	85	76		.528	4	Robert Boden Scheffing
1963	162	79	83		.488	x5(Clev)	Robert Boden Scheffing / Chas. Walter Dressen
1964	162	85	77		.525	4	Chas. Walter Dressen
1965	162	89	73	0	.549	4	CHARLES WALTER DRESSEN
1966	162	88	74	0	.543	3	CHARLES WALTER DRESSEN / ROBERT VIRGIL SWIFT * / FRANCIS MICHAEL SKAFF *
1967	163	91	71	1	.562	X2 (MIN)	EDWARD MAYO SMITH
1968	164	103	59	2	.636	1	EDWARD MAYO SMITH
1969	162	90	72	0	.556	2E	EDWARD MAYO SMITH
1970	162	79	83	0	.488	4E	EDWARD MAYO SMITH
1971	162	91	71	0	.562	2E	ALFRED MANUEL MARTIN
1972	156	86	70	0	.551	1E (LP)	ALFRED MANUEL MARTIN

WON 71 LOST 67 TG 138

AMERICAN LEAGUE — 1900. — FINISHED 4th. PCT. .514

DETROIT

GEORGE TWEEDY STALLINGS

WON	LOST	NAME	POS.	G.	BA	FROM	TO
		Bay, Harry Elbert	OF	12	.200	A	
		Casey, James Peter (Doc)	3B	115	.260	xBknN	
19	22	Cronin, John J. (Jack)	P	46	.199	CinN	
		Dillon, Frank Edward	1B	123	.291	xPittN	
		Elberfeld, Norman Arthur (Kid)	SS	109	.262	CinN	
0	2	Fifield, John Proctor (Jack)	P	5	.167	WashN	C
6	9	Frisk, John Emil	P21	30	.286	CinN	
1	4	Gaston, Welcome Thornburg	P	8	+.167	BknN	Clev
		Grey, Wm. Tobin (2B3 SS4 3B7)	OF9	21	+.282	PittN98	Inpls
		Harley, Richard Joseph	OF	123	.325	ClevN	CinN
1	3	Hill, Wm. C.	P	5	.375	BknN	C
		Holmes, James Wm. (Ducky)	OF111	112	.291	BaltN	
		Jones, Chas. C.	OF	32	.231	A	
19	9	Miller, Roscoe Clyde	P	30	.163	A	
		McAllister, Lewis Wm. (2B32)	C48	109	.293	ClevN	
		Nicol, George Edward	OF	73	.258	LvlleN94	C
0	1	Owen, Frank Malcolm (1B1)	P3	4	.600	A	
		Ryan, John Bennett (Jack) (C20 1B15)	2B91	126	.258	BaltN	
		Shaw, Alfred L.	C87	88	.259	A	
		Sheehan, Daniel	SS19	22	.226	A	NYN
6	5	Siever, Edward T.	P	14	.263	A	
		Stallings, George Tweedy MGR.	OF	42	.251	PhilN98	
		Sullivan, Suter G.	3B12	22	+.226	ClevN	Clev
		Wheeler, Edward W.	3B	2	.000	A	
19	12	Yeager, Joseph F.	P33	45	.213	xBknN (returned)	BknN

WON 74 LOST 61 TG 135

AMERICAN LEAGUE — 1901. — FINISHED 3rd. PCT. .548

DETROIT

GEORGE TWEEDY STALLINGS

WON	LOST	NAME	POS.	G.	BA	FROM	TO
		Barrett, James Erigena	OF	136	.294	CinN	
		Buelow, Frederick Wm.	C	69	.229	StLN	
		Casey, James Peter (Doc)	3B130	131	.280	B	
		Crockett, Daniel Solomon	1B	28	.291	A	C
12	16	Cronin, John J. (Jack)	P	31	.244	B	

WON	LOST	NAME	POS.	G.	BA	FROM	TO
		Dillon, Frank Edward	1B	75	.298	B	
		Elberfeld, Norman Arthur (Kid)	SS	122	.309	B	
5	3	Frisk, John Emil	P12	19	.306	B	
		Gleason, Wm. J. (Kid)	2B	136	.278	NYN	
3	2	High, Edward	P	5	.000	A	C
		Holmes, James Wm. (Ducky)	OF	130	.294	B	
		Lockhead, Harry P.	SS	1	+.500	ClevN99	Phil
23	13	Miller, Roscoe Clyde	P36	39	.206	B	
		McAllister, Lewis Wm. (1B27)	C36	91	.287	B	
		Nance, Wm. G.	OF	133	.290	Minn	
1	4	Owen, Frank Malcolm	P	9	.050	B	
		Shaw, Alfred L.	C42	57	.275	B	
18	11	Siever, Edward T.	P	37	.163	B	
12	12	Yeager, Joseph F.	P	37	.301	BknN	

WON 52 — LOST 83 — TG 135

AMERICAN LEAGUE — FINISHED 7th.

1902. — PCT. .385

DETROIT

JOHN FRANCIS DWYER

WON	LOST	NAME	POS.	G.	BA	FROM	TO
		Arndt, Harry A.	1B1	10	+.135	A	Balt
		Barrett, James Erigena	OF	136	.304	B	
		Beck, Erwin Thomas (OF6)	1B36	41	.304	xCinN	C
		Buelow, Frederick Wm. (1B2)	C62	64	.223	B	
		Casey, James Peter (Doc)	3B	132	.275	B	
1	0	Cronin, John J. (Jack)	P	4	+.000	B	Balt
		Dillon, Frank Edward	1B	66	+.205	B	Balt
1	2	Egan, Aloysius Jerome	P	3	.250	A	
		Elberfeld, Norman Arthur (Kid)	SS130	139	.265	B	
0	0	Fisher, Thomas Chalmers	P	1	.000	A	
		Gleason, Wm. J. (Kid)	2B	118	.247	B	
		Harley, Richard Joseph	OF	124	.276	CinN	
		Holmes, James Wm. (Ducky)	OF	92	.253	B	
1	4	Kissinger, Chas. Samuel	P	5	.157	A	
		LePine, Louis Joseph (Pete) (1B8)	OF19	29	.202	A	C
15	18	Mercer, George Barclay (Winnie)	P	35	.180	Wash	C
6	11	Miller, Roscoe Clyde	P	20	.183	B	NYN
14	15	Mullin, George Joseph (OF4)	P33	37	.328	A	
		McAllister, Lewis Wm. (C2 2B4 SS5 3B3 OF4)	1B6	20	+.200	B (return)	Balt
		(on return) (C7 2B1 SS1 3B3 OF8)	1B22	44	+.209	xBalt	
1	7	McCarthy, Archibald J.	P	10	.071	A	C
		McGuire, James Thomas	C70	72	.229	BknN	
0	0	McMackin, Samuel	P	1	+.500	xChi	C

WON	LOST	NAME	POS.	G.	BA	FROM	TO
		O'Connell, John Joseph (1B2)	2B6	8	.136	BaltAA91	C
		Poste, E.	OF	3	.083	A	C
		Schiappacasse, Louis Joseph	OF	2	.000	A	C
8	13	Siever, Edward T.	P	25	.154	B	
0	1	Terry, John	P	1	.000	A	
5	12	Yeager, Joseph F. (2B12 SS3 3B1 OF13)	P19	48	.231	B	

WON 65 — LOST 71 — TG 136

AMERICAN LEAGUE — FINISHED 5th.

1903. — PCT. .478

DETROIT

EDWARD GRANT BARROW

WON	LOST	NAME	POS.	G.	BA	FROM	TO
		Barrett, James Erigena	OF	136	.315	B	
		Buelow, Frederick Wm.	C59	90	.222	B	
		Burns, John Joseph	2B	10	.256	A	
		Carr, Chas. Carbitt	1B	135	.282	Phi101	
		Courtney, Ernest E.	3B19	23	+.253	xN.Y.	
		Crawford, Samuel Earl	OF	137	.332	CinN	
3	8	Derring, John Thomas	P	11	+.318	A	N.Y.
17	15	Donovan, Wm. Edward (Wild Bill)	P36	39	.240	BknN	
2	4	Eason, Malcolm Wayne (Mal)	P	7	.167	BosN	
		Elberfeld, Norman Arthur (Kid)	SS	35	+.323	B	N.Y.
		Gessler, Harry Homer	OF	29	.238	A	BknN
		Greene, Patrick Joseph	3B	1	+.000	xN.Y.	C
0	2	Jones, Alexander H.	P	2	.000	PhilN94	C
0	2	Kane, Harry	P	3	.143	StL	
7	9	Kissinger, Chas. Samuel	P	16	.128	B	C
15	15	Kitson, Frank R.	P31	36	.191	BknN	
		Long, Herman C. (2B17)	SS52	69	+.218	xN.Y.	
		Lush, Wm. Lucas	OF103	117	.278	BosN	
19	14	Mullin, George Joseph	P40	46	.278	B	
		Murphy, John P.	SS	5	.182	StLN	C
		McAllister, Lewis Wm. (C17)	SS47	78	.264	B	C
		McGuire, James Thomas	C69	71	.241	B	
		Nicholls, Simon Burdette	SS	2	.375	A	
2	2	Skopec, John (Lefty)	P	6	.153	Chi01	C
		Smith, George Henry (Heinie)	2B92	93	.222	NYN	C
		Yeager, Joseph F.	3B106	109	.259	B	

WON 62 — LOST 90 — TG 152

AMERICAN LEAGUE — FINISHED 7th.

1904. — PCT. .408

DETROIT

EDWARD GRANT BARROW   ROBERT LINCOLN LOWE

WON	LOST	NAME	POS.	G.	BA	FROM	TO
		Barrett, James Erigena	OF	162	.264	B	
		Beville, Henry Monte	C	53	+.225	xN.Y.	C
		Buelow, Frederick Wm.	C	42	+.115	B	Clev
		Burns, John Joseph	2B	4	.125	B	C
		Carr, Chas. Carbitt	1B	91	+.270	B	Clev
		Coughlin, Wm. Paul	3B	56	+.355	xWash	
		Crawford, Samuel Earl	OF	150	.247	B	
17	16	Donovan, Wm. Edward	P34	44	.271	B	
		(Wild Bill)					
		Drennan, K. John	1B	1	.000	A	C
		Drill, Lewis L. (1B2)	C49	51	+.225	xWash	
0	1	Ferry, Alfred Joseph	P	3	.000	A	
		Gremminger, Lorenzo Edward	3B	82	.215	BosN	C
		Hickman, Chas. Taylor	1B	41	+.254	xClev	
		Huelsman, Frank Elmer	OF	4	+.333	xChi (return)	Chi
2	3	Jaeger, Chas. Thomas	P	8	.063	A	C
15	20	Killian, Edwin Henry	P	40	.143	Clev	
10	12	Kitson, Frank R.	P26	27	.205	B	
		Lowe, Robert Lincoln (Link)	2B	140	.205	xPittN	
		MGR.					
16	24	Mullin, George Joseph	P45	52	.305	B	
		McIntyre, Matthew W. (Matty)	OF	152	.254	Phil01	
		McManus, Francis E.	C	1	+.000	BknN	N.Y.
		O'Leary, Chas. Timothy	SS	135	.215	Chi00	
0	1	Raymond Arthur Lawrence	P	5	.000	A	
		(Bugs)					
		Robinson, Clyde	SS30	97	.204	Wash	
		(2B17 3B26 OF18)					
2	13	Stovall, Jesse Cranmer	P21	23	.196	Clev	C
		Wood, Robert Lynn	C47	49	.244	Clev02	

WON 79 — AMERICAN LEAGUE — FINISHED 3rd.
LOST 74
TG 153 — 1905. — PCT. .516

DETROIT

WM. R. ARMOUR

WON	LOST	NAME	POS.	G.	BA	FROM	TO
		Barrett, James Erigena	OF	18	.254	B	
0	0	Bruckmiller, Andrew	P	1	.000	A	C
4	0	Cicotte, Edward Victor	P	4	.300	A	
		Clark, Jay Justin (Nig)	C	2	+.400	xClev	Clev
		(Loaned to Detroit)					
		Cobb, Tyrus Raymond (Ty)	OF	41	.240	A	
		Cooley, Duff C. (Dick)	OF95	97	.247	BosN	C
		Coughlin, Wm. Paul	3B136	138	.252	B	
		Crawford, Samuel Earl	OF103	154	.297	B	
		(1B51)					
0	2	Disch, George Chas.	P	8	.157	A	C
18	14	Donovan, Wm. Edward	P34	46	.192	B	
		(Wild Bill)					
		Doran, Thomas J.	C	29	+.165	xBos	
		Drill, Lewis L.	C71	72	.261	B	C
2	0	Eubank, John Franklin	P	7	.294	A	
0	2	Ford, Eugene Wyman	P	7	.000	A	C
		Hickman, Chas. Taylor	OF40	59	+.221	B	Wash
		(1B19)					
0	2	Jackson, Chas. W.	P	2	.250	A	C
0	0	Justis, Walter	P	2	.000	A	C
22	14	Killian, Edwin Henry	P	39	.271	B	
8	17	Kitson, Frank R.	P	33	.184	B	
		Lindsay, Christian H.	1B	88	.267	A	
		Lowe, Robert Lincoln (Link)	OF24	58	.193	B	
		(3B22)					
22	18	Mullin, George Joseph	P44	47	.259	B	
		McIntyre, Matthew W. (Matty)	OF	131	.265	B	
		O'Leary, Chas. Timothy	SS	148	.213	B	
		Schaefer, Herman A.	2B151	153	.244	ChiN02	
		(Germany)					
		Sullivan, John Eugene	C	13	.176	KC00	
0	2	Thomas, Forrest	P	2	.000	A	C
		Warner, John Joseph	C	36	.202	xStLN	
3	3	Wiggs, James Alvin	P	6	.125	CinN03	
		Wood, Robert Lynn	C	8	.125	B	C

WON 71 — AMERICAN LEAGUE — FINISHED 6th.
LOST 78
TG 149 — 1906. — PCT. .477

DETROIT

WM. R. ARMOUR

WON	LOST	NAME	POS.	G.	BA	FROM	TO
		Cobb, Tyrus Raymond (Ty)	OF96	97	.320	B	
		Coughlin, Wm. Paul	3B	147	.235	B	
		Crawford, Samuel Earl	OF116	145	.295	B	
		(1B22)					
13	14	Donahue, Francis Rostell	P28	29	.123	Clev	C
		(Red)					
9	15	Donovan, Wm. Edward	P25	28	.121	B	
		(Wild Bill)					
4	10	Eubank, John Franklin	P23	26	.200	B	
		Hetling, August Julius (Gus)	3B	2	.143	A	C
		Jones, David Jefferson	OF83	84	.260	ChiN04	
9	6	Killian, Edwin Henry	P	20	.170	B	
		Lindsay, Christian H.	1B122	141	.224	B	C
		(2B17)					
		Lowe, Robert Lincoln (Link)	SS19	41	.207	B	
		(2B17)					
21	18	Mullin, George Joseph	P40	50	.225	B	
		McIntyre, Matthew W. (Matty)	OF	133	.260	B	
		O'Leary, Chas. Timothy	SS127	128	.219	B	
		Payne, Frederick Thomas	C47	72	.270	A	
		(OF17)					
0	1	Rowan, John Arthur	P	1	.250	A	
		Schaefer, Herman A.	2B114	124	.238	B	
		(Germany)					

		Schmidt, Chas.	C67	68	.218	A	
		Scheibeck, Frank	2B	3	.125	Clev01	C
14	10	Siever, Edward T.	P	29	.156	StL04	
		Thompson, Samuel L.	OF	8	.225	PhilN98	C
		Warner, John Joseph	C	49	+.242	B	Wash
1	1	Wiggs, James Alvin	P	4	.333	B	C
0	3	Willett, Robert Edgar	P	4	.000	A	

WON 92 AMERICAN LEAGUE FINISHED 1st.
LOST 58
TG 150 1907. PCT. .613

DETROIT

HUGH AMBROSE JENNINGS

WON	LOST	NAME	POS.	G.	BA	FROM	TO
		Archer, James Patrick	C17	18	.119	PittN04	
		Cobb, Tyrus Raymond (Ty)	OF	150	.350	B	
		Coughlin, Wm. Paul	3B133	134	.243	B	
		Crawford, Samuel Earl	OF	144	.323	B	
25	4	Donovan, Wm. Edward (Wild Bill)	P32	37	.266	B	
		Downs, Jerome Willis (OF20)	2B80	105	.219	A	
		Erwin, Ross Emil	C	4	.200	A	
2	3	Eubank, John Franklin	P	15	.129	B	C
		Jennings, Hugh Ambrose MGR.	SS1	2	.250	BknN03	
		Jones, David Jefferson	OF125	126	.273	B	
0	2	Jones, Elijah Albert	P	4	.000	A	
		Killefer, Wade Hampton	OF	1	.000	A	
25	13	Killian, Edwin Henry	P42	46	.320	B	
		Lowe, Robert Lincoln (Link)	3B	17	.243	B	C
0	1	Malloy, Herman	P	1	.250	A	
20	20	Mullin, George Joseph	P47	70	.217	B	
		McIntyre, Matthew W. (Matty)	OF	20	.284	B	
		O'Leary, Chas. Timothy	SS138	139	.241	B	
		Payne, Frederick Thomas	C46	53	.167	B	
		Rossman, Clude R.	1B	153	.277	Clev	
		Schaefer, Herman A. (Germany) (SS18)	2B74	109	.258	B	
		Schmidt, Chas.	C103	104	.244	B	
19	10	Siever, Edward T.	P	38	.154	B	
1	5	Willett, Robert Edgar	P	9	.091	B	

WON 90 AMERICAN LEAGUE FINISHED 1st.
LOST 63
TG 153 1908. PCT. .588

DETROIT

HUGH AMBROSE JENNINGS

WON	LOST	NAME	POS.	G.	BA	FROM	TO
		Bush, Owen Joseph (Owney)	SS	20	.294	A	
		Cobb, Tyrus Raymond (Ty)	OF	150	.324	B	
		Coughlin, Wm. Paul	3B	119	.215	B	C
		Crawford, Samuel Earl (1B17)	OF134	152	.311	B	
18	7	Donovan, Wm. Edward (Wild Bill)	P29	30	.159	B	
		Downs, Jerome Willis	2B82	84	.221	B	
		Jennings, Hugh Ambrose MGR.		1	.000	B	
		Jones, David Jefferson	OF32	56	.207	B	
		Killefer, Wade Hampton	2B16	28	.213	B	
11	10	Killian, Edwin Henry	P27	28	.137	B	
0	2	Malloy, Herman	P	3	.333	B	C
17	12	Mullin, George Joseph	P38	55	.256	B	
		McIntyre, Matthew W. (Matty)	OF	151	.295	B	
		O'Leary, Chas. Timothy	SS64	65	.251	B	
		Payne, Frederick Thomas	C15	20	.067	B	
		Perry, Clayton Shields	3B	7	.118	A	C
		Rossman, Clude R.	1B	138	.294	B	
		Schaefer, Herman A. (Germany) (2B58 3B29)	SS68	153	.259	B	
		Schmidt, Chas.	C	122	.265	B	
2	6	Siever, Edward T.	P	11	.167	B	C
1	0	Suggs, George Franklin	P	6	.333	A	
24	12	Summers, Oren Edgar	P	40	.124	A	
		Thomas, Ira Felix	C29	40	.307	N.Y.	
15	9	Willett, Robert Edgar	P	30	.164	B	
2	5	Winter, George Lovington	P	7	+.111	xBos	C

WON 98 AMERICAN LEAGUE FINISHED 1st.
LOST 54
TG 152 1909. PCT. .645

DETROIT

HUGH AMBROSE JENNINGS

WON	LOST	NAME	POS.	G.	BA	FROM	TO
		Beckendorf, Henry Ward	C	15	.259	A	
		Bush, Owen Joseph (Owney)	SS	157	.273	B	
		Casey, Joseph Felix	C	3	.200	A	
		Cobb, Tyrus Raymond (Ty)	OF	156	.377	B	
		Crawford, Samuel Earl (1B17)	OF139	156	.314	B	
		Delahanty, James Christopher Jr.	2B	48	+.253	xWash	
8	7	Donovan, Wm. Edward (Wild Bill)	P21	22	.200	B	
		Gainor, Delos Chas.	1B	2	.200	A	
		Jennings, Hugh Ambrose MGR.	1B1	2	.500	B	
		Jones, David Jefferson	OF57	69	.279	B	
1	1	Jones, Elijah Albert	P	2	.250	Det07	C
		Jones, Thomas (Tom)	1B	44	+.271	xStL	
		Killefer, Wade Hampton	2B	23	+.302	B	Wash
11	9	Killian, Edwin Henry	P	25	.161	B	
0	1	LaFitte, Edward Francis	P	3	.250	A	

WON	LOST	NAME	POS.	G.	BA	FROM	TO
0	2	Lelivelt, Wm. John	P	4	.400	A	
		Moriarty, George Joseph	3B106	133	.273	N.Y.	
29	8	Mullin, George Joseph	P40	52	.203	B	
		McIntyre, Matthew W. (Matty)	OF122	125	.244	B	
		O'Leary, Chas. Timothy	3B54	76	.203	B	
		Rossman, Claude R.	1B	80	+.246	B	StL
		Schaefer, Herman A. (Germany)	2B	87	+.250	B	Wash
		Schmidt, Chas.	C81	84	.209	B	
4	4	Speer, George Nathan	P	13	.120	A	C
		Stanage, Oscar Harland	C	77	.262	CinN06	
1	3	Suggs, George Franklin	P	9	.067	B	
19	9	Summers, Oren Edgar	P	35	.106	B	
22	9	Willett, Robert Edgar	P40	41	.202	B	
3	1	Works, Ralph Talmadge	P	16	.059	A	

WON 86 — AMERICAN LEAGUE — FINISHED 3rd.
LOST 68
TG 154 — 1910. — PCT. .558

DETROIT

HUGH AMBROSE JENNINGS

WON	LOST	NAME	POS.	G.	BA	FROM	TO
		Beckendorf, Henry Ward	C	3	+.429	B	Wash
2	2	Browning, Frank	P	11	.000	A	C
		Bush, Owen Joseph (Owney)	SS141	142	.262	B	
		Casey, Joseph Felix	C22	23	.194	B	
		Cobb, Tyrus Raymond (Ty)	OF137	140	.385	B	
		Crawford, Samuel Earl	OF153	154	.289	B	
		Delahanty, James Christopher Jr.	2B	106	.293	B	
18	7	Donovan, Wm. Edward (Wild Bill)	P	26	.145	B	
		Jones, David Jefferson	OF101	113	.265	B	
		Jones, Thomas (Tom)	1B	135	.255	B	C
4	3	Killian, Edwin Henry	P	11	.148	B	C
		Kirke, Jay	2B	8	.192	A	
		Lathers, Chas. Ten Eyck	3B13	41	.232	A	
0	1	Lelivelt, Wm. John	P	1	.500	B	C
0	1	Loudell, Arthur	P	5	.167	A	C
		Moriarty, George Joseph	3B134	136	.251	B	
21	12	Mullin, George Joseph	P38	50	.256	B	
		McIntyre, Matthew W. (Matty)	OF77	83	.236	B	
		O'Leary, Chas. Timothy (SS16)	2B38	65	.242	B	
0	1	Peasley, Marvin Warren	P	2	.000	A	C
4	3	Pernoll, Henry Hubbard	P	11	.063	A	
		Schmidt, Chas.	C66	71	.259	B	
		Simmons, George Washington	1B22	42	.191	A	
0	0	Skeels, David	P	1	.000	A	C
		Stanage, Oscar Harland	C84	88	.207	B	
5	9	Stroud, Ralph E.	P	28	.025	A	
13	12	Summers, Oren Edgar	P	30	.184	B	
16	11	Willett, Robert Edgar	P	38	.132	B	
3	6	Works, Ralph Talmadge	P	18	.267	B	

WON 89 — AMERICAN LEAGUE — FINISHED 2nd.
LOST 65
TG 154 — 1911. — PCT. .578

DETROIT

HUGH AMBROSE JENNINGS

WON	LOST	NAME	POS.	G.	BA	FROM	TO
		Baumann, Chas. John	2B23	26	.256	A	
		Bush, Owen Joseph (Owney)	SS	150	.232	B	
		Casey, Joseph Felix	C	15	.152	B	
0	0	Cavet, Tillar H. (Pug)	P	1	.000	A	
		Cobb, Tyrus Raymond (Ty)	OF	146	.420	B	
7	1	Covington, Wm. Wilkes (Tex)	P	17	.188	A	
		Crawford, Samuel Earl	OF	146	.378	B	
		Delahanty, James Christopher Jr. (2B59)	1B71	144	.339	B	
10	9	Donovan, Wm. Edward (Wild Bill)	P20	24	.200	B	
		Drake, Delos Daniel	OF83	95	.279	A	
		Gainor, Delos Chas.	1B69	70	.302	Det09	
		Jones, David Jefferson	OF92	98	.273	B	
11	8	LaFitte, Edward Francis	P29	31	.157	Det09	
		Lathers, Chas. Ten Eyck	3B5	29	.222	B	C
7	5	Lively, Henry Everett	P18	20	.255	A	C
1	0	Mitchell, Clarence Elmer	P	5	.500	A	
		Moriarty, George Joseph	3B129	130	.243	B	
18	10	Mullin, George Joseph	P30	40	.286	B	
		Ness, John Chas.	1B	12	.161	A	
		O'Leary, Chas. Timothy	2B66	74	.266	B	
		Schaller, Walter (Biff)	OF	40	.133	A	
		Schmidt, Chas.	C	28	.283	B	C
		Stanage, Oscar Harland	C	141	.264	B	
11	11	Summers, Oren Edgar	P	30	.254	B	
0	2	Taylor, Wiley	P	3	.000	A	
		Tutweiler, Guy Isbell (2B6)	OF7	13	.186	A	
13	14	Willett, Robert Edgar	P	39	.268	B	
		Wilson, George Frank	C	5	.187	A	
11	5	Works, Ralph Talmadge	P	31	.148	B	

WON 69 — AMERICAN LEAGUE — FINISHED 6th.
LOST 84
TG 153 — 1912. — PCT. .451

DETROIT

HUGH AMBROSE JENNINGS

WON	LOST	NAME	POS.	G.	BA	FROM	TO
		Bashang, Albert	OF	6	.167	A	

WON	LOST	NAME	POS.	G.	BA	FROM	TO
		Baumann, Chas. John (OF2)	3B10	13	.262	B	
1	2	Boehler, George Henry	P	4	.100	A	
1	4	Burns, Wm. Thomas	P	6	.231	PhilN	C
		Bush, Owen Joseph (Owney)	SS	144	.231	B	
		Cobb, Tyrus Raymond (Ty)	OF	140	.410	B	
		Coffey, John Joseph	3B	1	.000	A	C
		Corriden, John Michael (Red)	3B25	38	.203	StL10	
3	4	Covington, Wm. Wilkes (Tex)	P	9	.133	B	C
		Crawford, Samuel Earl	OF	149	.325	B	
0	1	Dauss, George August	P	2	.250	A	
		Deal, Chas. Albert	3B	41	.225	A	
		Delahanty, James Christopher Jr. (3B27 OF33)	2B45	78	.286	B	
1	0	Donovan, Wm. Edward (Wild Bill)	P	6	.077	B	
17	10	Dubuc, Jean Arthur	P	36	.276	CinN09	
		Gainor, Delos Chas.	1B	51	.240	B	
		Irvin, Wm. Edward	C	1	.667	A	C
		Jennings, Hugh Ambrose MGR.		1	.000	B	
1	2	Jensen, Wm.	P	4	.000	A	
		Jones, David Jefferson	OF	97	.294	B	
		Kocher, Bradley Wilson	C	24	.206	A	
0	0	LaFitte, Edward Francis	P	1	.000	B	
9	9	Lake, Joseph Henry	P	22	+.150	xStL	
		Leinhauser, Wm. Chas.	OF	1	.000	A	C
		Louden, Wm.	2B89	121	.241	NY07	
		Maharg, Wm.	3B	1	.000	A	
		Meany, Patrick	SS	1	.000	A	C
0	2	Moran, Harry Edwin	P	4	.200	A	
		Moriarty, George Joseph (3B33)	1B73	105	.248	B	
12	17	Mullin, George Joseph	P	37	.278	B	
		McDermott, Frank A.	OF	5	.250	A	C
		McGarr, James Vincent	OF	1	.000	A	C
		McGarvey, Daniel	OF	1	.000	A	C
0	1	McGehee, Patrick Henry	P	1	.000	A	C
		McGuire, James Thomas	C	1	.500	Clev	C
		O'Leary, Chas. Timothy	2B	3	.200	B	
		O'Mara, Oliver Edward	SS	1	.000	A	
		Onslow, Edward Joseph	1B	35	.227	A	
		Onslow, John James	C	31	.159	A	
0	0	Pernoll, Henry Hubbard	P	3	.000	Det10	C
		Perry, Wm. Henry	OF	13	.162	A	C
0	0	Remneas, Alexander	P	1	.000	A	
		Stanage, Oscar Harland	C	119	.261	B	
		Sugden, Joseph	1B	1	.333	StL05	C
2	1	Summers, Oren Edgar	P	3	.500	B	C
0	1	Travers, Aloysius Joseph	P	1	.000	A	C
0	1	Troy, Robert	P	1	.000	A	C
		Veach, Robert Hayes	OF	23	.342	A	
		Vitt, Oscar Joseph (2B15 3B24)	OF27	73	.245	A	
		Ward,	OF	1	.000	A	C
0	4	Wheatley, Chas.	P	5	.000	A	C
17	15	Willett, Robert Edgar	P	37	.165	B	
5	10	Works, Ralph Talmadge	P	22	.143	B	CinN

WON 66
LOST 87
TG 153

AMERICAN LEAGUE

FINISHED 6th.

1913.

PCT. .431

DETROIT

HUGH AMBROSE JENNINGS

WON	LOST	NAME	POS.	G.	BA	FROM	TO
		Baumann, Chas. John	2B48	49	.298	B	
0	1	Boehler, George Henry	P	1	.333	B	
		Burns, Joseph Francis	OF	4	.309	CinN10	C
		Bush, Owen Joseph (Owney)	SS	152	.251	B	
0	2	Clauss, Albert Stanley	P	4	.000	A	C
		Cobb, Tyrus Raymond (Ty) (2B1)	OF121	122	.390	B	
2	5	Comstock, Ralph Remick	P	9	.227	A	
		Crawford, Samuel Earl (1B13)	OF140	153	.316	B	
13	12	Dauss, George August	P	33	.177	B	
		Deal, Chas. Albert	3B15	16	.220	B	BosN
16	14	Dubuc, Jean Arthur	P30	66	.267	B	
0	0	Elder, Henry Knox	P	1	.000	A	C
		Gainor, Delos Chas.	1B103	104	.270	B	
		Gibson, Frank Gilbert	C19	20	.140	A	
0	0	Grover, Chas. Bert (Bugs)	P	2	.000	A	C
9	12	Hall, Marcus (Mark)	P	28	.091	StL10	
0	0	Harding, Chas. H.	P	1	.000	A	C
		Hennessey, Lester J.	2B	14	.133	A	C
		High, Hugh Jenkins	OF52	80	.230	A	
1	2	House, Wilfred E.	P	16	.000	A	C
1	2	Klawitter, Albert C.	P	6	.000	NYN10	C
8	7	Lake, Joseph Henry	P	24	.267	B	C
0	0	Lorenzen, Adolph Andreas	P	1	.500	A	C
		Louden, Wm.	2B32	72	.241	B	
		Moriarty, George Joseph	3B93	102	.239	B	
2	7	Mullin, George Joseph	P	12	+.350	B	Wash
		McKee, Raymond Ellis	C63	67	.283	A	
0	1	North, Louis Alexander	P	1	.000	A	
		Onslow, Edward Joseph	1B	17	.255	B	
		Partenheimer, Harold Philip	3B	1	.000	A	C
		Peploski, Joseph Aloysius	3B	2	.500	A	C
		Pipp, Walter Clement (Wally)	1B	11	.178	A	
		Platte, Alfred Frederick Joseph	OF	9	.111	A	C
		Powell, Raymond Reath	OF	2	.000	A	
0	1	Renfer, Erwin Arthur	P	1	.000	A	C
		Rondeau, Henri Joseph (1B4)	C14	35	.186	A	
		Stanage, Oscar Harland	C77	80	.224	B	
		Tutweiler, Guy Isbell	1B	14	.191	Det11	C
		Veach, Robert Hayes	OF	138	.269	B	
		Vitt, Oscar Joseph (3B16)	2B77	99	.240	B	
13	14	Willett, Robert Edgar	P33	34	.283	B	
0	1	Williams, Claude Preston	P	4	.100	A	
1	6	Zamloch, Carl Eugene	P	14	.182	A	C

WON 80
LOST 73
TG 153

AMERICAN LEAGUE

FINISHED 4th.

1914.

PCT. .523

DETROIT

HUGH AMBROSE JENNINGS

WON	LOST	NAME	POS.	G.	BA	FROM	TO
		Baker, Delmer David	C38	43	.214	A	
		Baumann, Chas. John	2B	3	.000	B	
2	3	Boehler, George Henry	P	13	.176	B	
		Burns, George Henry	1B	137	.291	A	
		Bush, Owen Joseph (Owney)	SS	157	.252	B	
7	7	Cavet, Tillar H. (Pug)	P	29	.106	Det11	
		Cobb, Tyrus Raymond (Ty)	OF96	97	.368	B	
22	12	Coveleskie, Harry Frank	P	42	.242	CinN10	
		Crawford, Samuel Earl	OF	157	.314	B	
18	15	Dauss, George August	P	43	.216	B	
		Demmitt, Chas. Raymond	OF	1	+.000	StL10	Chi
13	14	Dubuc, Jean Arthur	P35	69	.236	B	
		Gainor, Delos Chas.	1B	1	+.000	B	Bos
4	6	Hall, Marcus (Mark)	P	18	.045	B	C
		Heilmann, Harry Edwin (1B16)	OF29	67	.225	A	
		High, Hugh Jenkins	OF53	80	.266	B	
		Kavanagh, Martin Joseph	2B115	127	.248	A	
6	6	Main, Miles Grant	P	29	.100	A	
		Moriarty, George Joseph	3B126	130	.254	B	
1	0	McCreery, Edward P.	P	3	.000	A	C
		McKee, Raymond Ellis	C27	32	.187	B	
		McMullin, Frederick Wm.	SS	1	.000	A	
2	4	Oldham, John Cyrus	P	9	.267	A	
		Purtell, Wm. Patrick	3B16	26	.171	Bos11	C
5	3	Reynolds, E. Ross	P	20	.047	A	
		Stanage, Oscar Harland	C	122	.193	B	
		Veach, Robert Hayes	OF145	149	.275	B	
		Vitt, Oscar Joseph (3B16)	2B36	66	.251	B	
0	0	Williams, Claude Preston	P	3	.000	B	
0	3	Williams, John Brodie	P	4	.000	A	C

WON 100
LOST 54
TG 154

AMERICAN LEAGUE

FINISHED 2nd.

1915.

PCT. .649

DETROIT

HUGH AMBROSE JENNINGS

WON	LOST	NAME	POS.	G.	BA	FROM	TO
		Baker, Delmer David	C61	68	.246	B	
1	1	Boehler, George Henry	P	9	.750	B	
13	6	Boland, Bernard Anthony	P	47	.175	A	
		Burns, George Henry	1B104	105	.253	B	
		Bush, Owen Joseph (Owney)	SS	155	.228	B	
4	3	Cavet, Tillar H. (Pug)	P	17	.250	B	C
		Cobb, Tyrus Raymond (Ty)	OF	156	.370	B	
23	13	Coveleskie, Harry Frank	P	50	.175	B	
		Crawford, Samuel Earl	OF	156	.299	B	
23	13	Dauss, George August	P	46	.146	B	
17	12	Dubuc, Jean Arthur	P40	60	.205	B	
		Fuller, Frank Edward	2B	14	.156	A	
		Jacobson, Wm. Chester	OF	38	+.215	A	StL
7	3	James, Wm. Henry	P	11	+.267	xStL	
		Kavanagh, Martin Joseph (2B42)	1B44	113	.295	B	
0	0	Ledbetter, Ralph Overton	P	1	.060	A	C
4	1	Lowdermilk, Grover Cleveland	P	7	+.125	xStL	
		Moriarty,George Joseph	3B	31	.211	B	
		McKee, Raymond Ellis	C35	55	.274	B	
2	0	Oldham, John Cyrus	P	17	.143	B	
		Peters, John Wm.	C	1	.000	A	
0	1	Reynolds, E. Ross	P	4	.000	B	C
		Stanage, Oscar Harland	C	100	.223	B	
6	1	Steen, Wm. John	P	20	+.214	xClev	C
		Veach, Robert Hayes	OF	152	.313	B	
		Vitt, Oscar Joseph	3B151	152	.250	B	
		Young, Ralph Stuart	2B119	123	.244	NY13	

WON 87
LOST 67
TG 154

AMERICAN LEAGUE

FINISHED 3rd.

1916.

PCT. .565

DETROIT

HUGH AMBROSE JENNINGS

WON	LOST	NAME	POS.	G.	BA	FROM	TO
		Baker, Delmer David	C59	61	.153	B	
1	1	Boehler, George Henry	P	5	.000	B	
10	3	Boland, Bernard Anthony	P47	49	.250	B	
		Burns, George Henry	1B124	135	.286	B	
		Bush, Owen Joseph (Owney)	SS144	145	.225	B	
		Cobb, Tyrus Raymond (Ty)	OF143	145	.371	B	
21	10	Coveleskie, Harry Frank	P	44	.212	B	
		Crawford, Samuel Earl	OF79	100	.286	B	
7	10	Cunningham, George H. Jr.	P	35	.268	A	
		Dalton, Talbot Percy	OF	8	.182	BuffF	C
18	12	Dauss, George August	P	39	.222	B	
10	8	Dubuc, Jean Arthur	P36	52	.256	B	
		Dyer, Benjamin Franklin	SS	4	.308	NYN	
3	1	Ehmke, Howard John	P	5	.143	BuffF	
		Ellison, Herbert Spencer	3B	2	.125	A	
0	2	Erickson, Eric George	P	7	.000	NYN14	
		Fuller, Frank Edward	2B	20	.100	B	
2	3	Hamilton, Earl A.	P	5	+.077	xStL	StL
		Harper, George Washington	OF	44	.161	A	
		Heilmann, Harry Edwin (1B30)	OF77	136	.282	Det14	
7	12	James, Wm. Henry	P	30	.068	B	
0	0	Jones, Carroll Elmer	P	1	.000	A	

WON	LOST	NAME	POS.	G.	BA	FROM	TO
0	0	Jones, Carroll Elmer	P	1	.000	A	
		Kavanagh, Martin Joseph	2B5	58	+.141	B	Clev
0	0	Lowdermilk, Grover Cleveland	P	2	+.000	B	Clev
		Maisel, George John	3B1	8	.000	StL13	
8	4	Mitchell, Wm.	P	24	+.111	xClev	
		McKee, Raymond Ellis	C26	32	.211	B	C
0	1	McTigue, Wm. Percy	P	3	.000	BosN13	C
		Spencer, Edward Russell	C	19	.370	PhilN11	
		Stanage, Oscar Harland	C	94	.237	B	
		Sullivan, Wm. Joseph (Billy)	C	1	.000	Chi14	C
		Veach, Robert Hayes	OF	150	.306	B	
		Vitt, Oscar Joseph	3B151	153	.226	B	
		Young, Ralph Stuart	2B146	153	.263	B	

WON 78 — AMERICAN LEAGUE — FINISHED 4th.
LOST 75
TG 153 — 1917. — PCT. .510

DETROIT

HUGH AMBROSE JENNINGS

WON	LOST	NAME	POS.	G.	BA	FROM	TO
16	11	Boland, Bernard Anthony	P43	45	.056	B	
		Burns, George Henry	1B104	119	.226	B	
		Bush, Owen Joseph (Owney)	SS	147	.281	B	
		Cobb, Tyrus Raymond (Ty)	OF	152	.383	B	
0	0	Couch, John Daniel	P	3	.000	A	
4	6	Coveleskie, Harry Frank	P	16	.227	B	
		Crawford, Samuel Earl (1B15)	OF46	61	.173	B	C
2	7	Cunningham, George H. Jr.	P	44	.176	B	
17	14	Dauss, George August	P37	38	.126	B	
		DeFate, Clyde	2B1	3	.000	xStLN	C
		Dyer, Benjamin Franklin	SS14	30	.209	B	
10	15	Ehmke, Howard John	P	35	.247	B	
		Ellison, Herbert Spencer	1B	9	.172	B	
		Flagstead, Ira	OF	4	.000	A	
		Harper, George Washington	OF31	47	.205	B	
		Heilmann, Harry Edwin (1B27)	OF123	150	.281	B	
13	10	James, Wm. Henry	P	34	.212	B	
4	4	Jones, Carroll Elmer	P	24	.000	B	
		Jones, Robert Walter	2B18	46	.156	A	
12	8	Mitchell, Wm.	P30	31	.119	B	
		Nicholson, Frederick	OF	13	.286	A	
		Spencer, Edward Russell	C62	70	.239	B	
		Stanage, Oscar Harland	C95	99	.205	B	
		Veach, Robert Hayes	OF	154	.319	B	
		Vitt, Oscar Joseph	3B	140	.254	B	
		Walker, Chas. Franklin	OF	2	.000	A	
		Yelle, Archie Joseph	C24	25	.137	A	
		Young, Ralph Stuart	2B	141	.231	B	

WON 55 — AMERICAN LEAGUE — FINISHED 7th.
LOST 71
126 — 1918. — PCT. .437

DETROIT

HUGH AMBROSE JENNINGS

WON	LOST	NAME	POS.	G.	BA	FROM	TO
1	2	Bailey, Wm. F.	P	8	.077	ChiF15	
14	10	Boland, Bernard Anthony	P	29	.174	B	
		Bush, Owen Joseph (Owney)	SS	128	.234	B	
		Cobb, Joseph Stanley	C	1	.000	A	C
0	0	Cobb, Tyrus Raymond (Ty) (P1 1B13)	OF93	111	.382	B	
		Coffey, John Francis	2B	20	+.209	BosN09	Bos
0	1	Coveleskie, Harry Frank	P	3	.250	B	C
6	7	Cunningham, George H. Jr.	P25	56	.223	B	
		Curry, James L. (OF20)	2B	5	.250	NYA11	C
13	16	Dauss, George August	P	33	.182	B	
0	0	Donovan, Wm. Edward (Wild Bill)	P	2	.333	N.Y.	
		Dressen, Lee August	1B30	31	.178	StLN14	C
0	0	Dyer, Benjamin Franklin	P1	13	.278	B	
		Ellison, Herbert Spencer	2B4	7	.260	B	
4	5	Erickson, Eric George	P	12	.121	Det16	
1	2	Finneran, Joseph Ignatius	P	6	+.000	BknF15	N.Y.
		Griggs, Arthur J.	1B25	28	.364	BknF15	C
0	1	Hall, Chas. Louis (Sea-Lion)	P	6	.000	StLN16	C
		Hall, Herbert S.	OF	3	.000	A	C
		Harper, George Washington	OF68	69	.243	B	
		Heilmann, Harry Edwin (1B37)	OF40	79	.276	B	
6	11	James, Wm. Henry	P	19	.109	B	
		Jennings, Hugh Ambrose MGR.	1B	1	.000	B	
2	2	Jones, Carroll Elmer	P19	22	.185	B	C
		Jones, David Jefferson	OF	2	.000	PittF15	C
		Jones, Robert Walter	3B63	75	.275	B	
8	13	Kallio, Rudolph	P30	31	.161	A	
		Kavanagh, Martin Joseph	1B	13	.273	xStLN	C
0	1	Mitchell, Wm.	P	1	.000	B	
		Spencer, Edward Russell	C48	66	.219	B	C
		Stanage, Oscar Harland	C47	54	.253	B	
0	0	Veach, Robert Hayes (P1)	OF	127	.279	B	
		Vitt, Oscar Joseph	3B66	81	.239	B	
		Walker, Chas. Franklin	OF45	55	.198	B	
		Yelle, Archie Joseph	C52	56	.174	B	
		Young, Ralph Stuart	2B	91	.188	B	

WON 80 — AMERICAN LEAGUE — FINISHED 4th.
LOST 60
TG 140 — 1919. — PCT. .571

DETROIT

HUGH AMBROSE JENNINGS

WON	LOST	NAME	POS.	G.	BA	FROM	TO
		Ainsmith, Edward Wilbur	C106	114	.272	Wash	
4	3	Ayres, Yancey Wyatt	P	23	+.130	xWash	
14	16	Boland, Bernard Anthony	P	35	.108	B	
		Bush, Owen Joseph (Owney)	SS	129	.244	B	
		Cobb, Tyrus Raymond (Ty)	OF123	124	.384	B	
1	1	Cunningham, George H. Jr.	P17	26	.217	B	
21	9	Dauss, George August	P	34	.144	B	
		Dowd, Raymond Bernard		1	+.000	A	Phil
		Dyer, Benjamin Franklin	3B23	44	.247	B	C
17	10	Ehmke, Howard John	P	33	.253	Det17	
		Ellison, Herbert Spencer	2B25	56	.216	B	
0	2	Erickson, Eric George	P	3	+.200	B	Wash
		Flagstead, Ira	OF83	97	.331	Det17	
		Heilmann, Harry Edwin	1B	140	.320	B	
3	0	James, Wm. Henry	P	3	+1.000	B	Bos
		Jones, Robert Walter	3B	127	.260	B	
0	0	Kallio, Rudolph	P	12	.000	B	
14	13	Leonard, Hubert Benjamin	P	29	.155	Bos	
5	4	Love, Elmer Haughton	P	22	.222	N.Y.	
1	2	Mitchell, Wm.	P	3	.200	B	C
		Shorten, Chas. Henry	OF75	95	.315	Bos17	
		Stanage, Oscar Harland	C36	38	.242	B	
		Veach, Robert Hayes	OF138	139	.355	B	
		Yelle, Archie Joseph	C	6	.000	B	C
		Young, Ralph Stuart	2B121	125	.210	B	

WON 61 LOST 93 TG 154

AMERICAN LEAGUE

1920.

FINISHED 7th.

PCT. .396

DETROIT

HUGH AMBROSE JENNINGS

WON	LOST	NAME	POS.	G.	BA	FROM	TO
		Ainsmith, Edward Wilbur	C61	69	.231	B	
0	1	Alten, Ernest Matthias	P	14	.000	A	C
7	14	Ayres, Yancey Wyatt	P	46	.153	B	
0	1	Baumgartner, Harry E.	P	9	.250	A	C
2	1	Bogart, John Renzie	P	4	.250	A	C
0	2	Boland, Bernard Anthony	P	4	.142	B	
		Bush, Owen Joseph (Owney)	SS140	141	.263	B	
		Claire, David Matthew	SS	3	.000	A	C
		Cobb, Tyrus Raymond (Ty)	OF	112	.334	B	
2	1	Conkwright, Allen Howard	P	5	.250	A	C
0	0	Coombs, John Wesley (Jack)	P	2	.000	PhilN	C
0	0	Cox, Plateau Rex	P	3	.000	A	C
1	0	Crumpler, Ray Maxton	P	4	.333	A	
13	21	Dauss, George August	P	38	.169	B	
15	18	Ehmke, Howard John	P	38	.238	B	
		Ellison, Herbert Spencer	1B38	61	.219	B	C
		Flagstead, Ira	OF82	110	.235	B	
0	0	Fried, Arthur Edwin (Cy)	P	2	.000	A	C
0	0	Glaiser, John Burke	P	9	.000	A	C
		Hale, Samuel Douglas (3B16)	OF58	76	.293	A	
		Heilmann, Harry Edwin (OF21)	1B122	145	.309	B	
		Huber, Clarence Bill	3B	10	.205	A	
		Jones, Robert Walter	3B67	81	.249	B	
10	17	Leonard, Hubert Benjamin	P	28	.212	B	
0	0	Love, Elmer Haughton	P	1	.000	B	C
		Manion, Clyde Jennings	C30	32	.275	A	
1	1	Morrisette, Wm. Lee	P	8	.000	Phil16	C
1	2	Okrie, Frank Anthony	P	21	.200	A	C
8	13	Oldham, John Cyrus	P	39	.174	Det15	
		Pinelli, Ralph Arthur (Babe) (SS18)	3B74	102	.229	Chi18	
		Shorten, Chas. Henry	OF99	116	.288	B	
		Stanage, Oscar Harland	C77	78	.231	B	
		Veach, Robert Hayes	OF	154	.307	B	
0	0	Vedder, Louis Edward	P	1	.000	A	C
1	1	Wilson, Wm. Clarence	P	3	.250	A	C
		Woodall, Chas. Lawrence (Larry)	C15	18	.245	A	
		Young, Ralph Stuart	2B	150	.291	B	

WON 71 LOST 82 TG 153

AMERICAN LEAGUE

1921.

FINISHED 6th.

PCT. .464

DETROIT

TYRUS RAYMOND COBB

WON	LOST	NAME	POS.	G.	BA	FROM	TO
		Ainsmith, Edward Wilbur	C34	35	.276	B	StLN
0	0	Ayres, Yancey Wyatt	P	2	.000	B	C
		Barnes, Samuel Thomas Jr.	2B	7	.182	A	C
		Bassler, John Landis	C115	119	.307	Clev14	
		Blue, Luzerne Atwell (Lou)	1B152	153	.308	A	
0	0	Boone, James Albert	P	1	.000	Phil19	
		Bush, Owen Joseph (Owney)	SS	104	+.279	B	Wash
		Cobb, Tyrus Raymond (Ty)MGR.	OF121	128	.389	B	
7	4	Cole, Albert George (Bert)	P20	30	.283	A	
0	0	Cunningham, George H. Jr.	OF	1	.000	Det19	C
10	15	Dauss, George August	P	32	.261	B	
13	14	Ehmke, Howard John	P	30	.284	B	
		Flagstead, Ira (OF12)	SS55	85	.305	B	
		Hale, Samuel Douglas	OF	9	.000	B	
		Heilmann, Harry Edwin	OF147	149	.394	B	
3	7	Holling, Carl	P	35	.270	A	
		Huber, Clarence Bill	3B	1	.000	B	
		Jones, Robert Walter	3B	141	.303	B	
11	13	Leonard, Hubert Benjamin	P	36	.171	B	
		Manion, Clyde Jennings	C	11	.111	B	
		Merritt, Herman G.	SS17	20	.370	A	C
6	11	Middleton, James Blaine	P	38	.148	NYN17	C
11	14	Oldham, John Cyrus	P40	42	.224	B	
3	2	Parks, Vernon Henry	P	10	.111	A	C
1	0	Perritt, Wm. Dayton (Pol)	P	4	.400	xN.Y.N	C

WON	LOST	NAME	POS.	G.	BA	FROM	TO
		Sargent, Joseph Alexander Jr. (SS18 3B23)	2B24	66	.253	A	C
		Shorten, Chas. Henry	OF52	92	.272	B	
6	2	Sutherland, Harvey S.	P13	17	.407	A	C
0	0	Stewart, Walter Cleveland	P	5	.000	A	
		Tavener, John Adam (Jack)	SS	2	.000	A	
		Veach, Robert Hayes	OF149	150	.338	B	
0	0	Walsh, James Thomas	P	3	.000	A	C
		Woodall, Chas. Lawrence (Larry)	C24	46	.363	B	
		Young, Ralph Stuart	2B106	107	.299	B	

WON 79
LOST 75
TG 154

AMERICAN LEAGUE — FINISHED 3rd.

1922. — PCT. .513

DETROIT

TYRUS RAYMOND COBB

WON	LOST	NAME	POS.	G.	BA	FROM	TO
		Bassler, John Landis	C117	121	.323	B	
		Blue, Luzerne Atwell (Lou)	1B144	145	.300	B	
		Clark, Daniel Curran	2B38	83	.292	A	
		Cobb, Tyrus Raymond (Ty) MGR.	OF	137	.401	B	
1	6	Cole, Albert George (Bert)	P24	27	.160	B	
		Cutshaw, George Wm.	2B	132	.267	PittN	
13	13	Dauss, George August	P	39	.208	B	
17	17	Ehmke, Howard John	P	45	.157	B	
		Flagstead, Ira	OF31	44	.308	B	
		Fothergill, Robert Roy	OF39	42	.322	A	
		Gagnon, Harold Dennis	SS	9	.250	A	
		Haney, Fred Girard (1B11)	3B44	81	.352	A	
		Heilmann, Harry Edwin	OF115	118	.356	B	
1	1	Holling, Carl	P	7	.000	B	C
0	0	Holloway, Kenneth Eugene	P	1	.000	A	
7	3	Johnson, Sylvester W.	P	29	.222	A	
		Jones, Robert Walter	3B119	124	.257	B	
		Manion, Clyde Jennings	C21	42	.275	B	
		Mohardt, John Henry	OF	5	1.000	A	C
0	0	Moore, Roy Daniel	P	9	+.429	xPhil	
10	13	Oldham, John Cyrus	P	43	.260	B	
7	6	Olsen, Arthur Ole	P37	39	.179	A	
19	12	Pillette, Herman Polycarp	P	40	.172	CinN17	
		Rigney, Emory Elmo	SS	155	.300	A	
4	4	Stoner, Ulysses Simpson Grant (Lil)	P	17	.100	A	
		Veach, Robert Hayes	OF154	155	.327	B	
		Woodall, Chas. Lawrence (Larry)	C	50	.344	B	

WON 83
LOST 71
TG 154

AMERICAN LEAGUE — FINISHED 2nd.

1923. — PCT. .539

DETROIT

TYRUS RAYMOND COBB

WON	LOST	NAME	POS.	G.	BA	FROM	TO
		Bassler, John Landis	C128	135	.298	B	
		Blue, Luzerne Atwell (Lou)	1B	129	.284	B	
		Burke, Leslie Kingdon (2B1)	3B1	9	.090	A	
		Carisch, Frederick Behlmer	C	2	.000	Clev14	C
1	1	Clarke, Rufus Rivers	P	5	.000	A	
		Cobb, Tyrus Raymond (Ty) MGR.	OF141	145	.340	B	
13	5	Cole, Albert George (Bert)	P52	58	.255	B	
3	7	Collins, Harry Warren	P	17	.111	Bos	
		Cutshaw, George Wm.	2B43	45	.223	B	C
21	13	Dauss, George August	P	50	.231	B	
		Flagstead, Ira	OF	1	+.000	B	Bos
		Fothergill, Robert Roy	OF68	101	.315	B	
4	8	Francis, Raymond James	P33	37	.143	Wash	
		Haney, Fred Girard (SS16 3B55)	2B69	142	.282	B	
		Heilmann, Harry Edwin	OF130	144	.403	B	
11	10	Holloway, Kenneth Eugene	P	42	.123	B	
12	7	Johnson, Sylvester W.	P	37	.161	B	
		Jones, Robert Walter	3B97	100	.250	B	
		Kerr, John Francis	SS15	19	.214	A	
		Manion, Clyde Jennings	C	23	.136	B	
		Manush, Henry Emmett (Heinie)	OF79	109	.334	A	
0	0	Moore, Roy Daniel	P	4	.000	B	C
1	1	Olsen, Arthur Ole	P	17	.125	B	C
14	19	Pillette, Herman Polycarp	P	47	.247	B	
		Pratt, Derrill Burnham (1B17)	2B60	101	.310	Bos	
		Rigney, Emory Elmo	SS	129	.315	B	
		Veach, Robert Hayes	OF85	114	.321	B	
1	0	Wells, Edwin Lee	P	7	.000	A	
2	0	Whitehill, Earl Oliver	P	8	.364	A	
		Woodall, Chas. Lawrence (Larry)	C60	71	.277	B	

WON 86
LOST 68
TG 154

AMERICAN LEAGUE — FINISHED 3rd.

1924. — PCT. .558

DETROIT

TYRUS RAYMOND COBB

WON	LOST	NAME	POS.	G.	BA	FROM	TO
		Bassler, John Landis	C121	124	.346	B	
		Blue, Luzerne Atwell (Lou)	1B	108	.311	B	

WON	LOST	NAME	POS.	G.	BA	FROM	TO
		Burke, Leslie Kingdon	2B38	72	.253	B	
0	0	Clarke, Rufus Rivers	P	2	.000	B	C
		Cobb, Tyrus Raymond (Ty) MGR.	OF	155	.338	B	
3	9	Cole, Albert George (Bert)	P	33	.270	B	
14	7	Collins, Harry Warren	P34	37	.145	B	
12	11	Dauss, George August	P	40	.132	B	
		Fothergill, Robert Roy	OF45	54	.301	B	
		Gehringer, Chas. Leonard	2B4	5	.545	A	
		Haney, Fred Girard	3B59	86	.309	B	
		Heilmann, Harry Edwin	OF	153	.346	B	
14	6	Holloway, Kenneth Eugene	P	49	.190	B	
5	4	Johnson, Sylvester W.	P	29	.205	B	
0	0	Jones, Kenneth Frederick	P	1	.000	A	
		Jones, Robert Walter	3B106	110	.272	B	
		Kerr, John Francis (3B1)	OF1	17	.273	B	
3	2	Leonard, Hubert Benjamin	P	9	.211	Det21	
0	0	Ludolph, Wm. Francis	P	3	.000	A	C
		Manion, Clyde Jennings	C	14	.231	B	
		Manush, Henry Emmett (Heinie)	OF106	120	.289	B	
		O'Rourke, Francis James	2B39	47	.276	Bos22	
1	1	Pillette, Herman Polycarp	P18	19	.364	B	C
		Pratt, Derrill Burnham (1B51)	2B63	121	.303	B	C
		Rigney, Emory Elmo	SS	147	.289	B	
11	11	Stoner, Ulysses Simpson Grant (Lil)	P36	37	.195	Det22	
6	8	Wells, Edwin Lee	P	29	.212	B	
17	9	Whitehill, Earl Oliver	P35	37	.213	B	
		Wingo, Absalom Holbrook (Red)	OF43	78	.287	Phil19	
		Woodall, Chas. Lawrence (Larry)	C62	67	.309	B	

WON 81   AMERICAN LEAGUE   FINISHED 4th.
LOST 73
TG 154   1925.   PCT. .526

DETROIT

TYRUS RAYMOND COBB

WON	LOST	NAME	POS.	G.	BA	FROM	TO
		Bassler, John Landis	C118	121	.279	B	
		Blue, Luzerne Atwell (Lou)	1B148	150	.307	B	
		Burke, Leslie Kingdon	2B52	77	.289	B	
2	2	Carroll, Owen Thomas (OF1)	P10	11	.375	A	
0	0	Cobb, Tyrus Raymond (Ty) MGR. (P1)	OF105	121	.378	B	
2	3	Cole, Albert George (Bert)	P	14	+.273	B	Clev
6	11	Collins, Harry Warren	P	26	.119	B	
16	11	Dauss, George August	P	35	.185	B	
4	7	Doyle, Jess Herbert	P	45	.242	A	
		Fothergill, Robert Roy	OF57	71	.353	B	
		Gehringer, Chas. Leonard	2B6	8	.167	B	
		Haney, Fred Girard	3B107	114	.279	B	
		Harrington, Andrew Matthew	2B	1	.000	A	C
		Heilmann, Harry Edwin	OF148	150	.393	B	
13	4	Holloway, Kenneth Eugene	P	38	.229	B	
0	2	Johnson, Sylvester W.	P	6	.000	B	
		Jones, Robert Walter	3B46	50	.236	B	C
11	4	Leonard, Hubert Benjamin	P	18	.200	B	C
		Manush, Henry Emmett (Heinie)	OF74	99	.303	B	
0	0	Moore, Wm. Christopher	P	1	.000	A	C
		Neun, John Henry	1B13	60	.266	A	
		O'Rourke, Francis James (3B6)	2B118	124	.293	B	
		Rigney, Emory Elmo (3B4)	SS51	62	.247	B	
		Stanage, Oscar Harland	C	3	.200	Det20	C
10	9	Stoner, Ulysses Simpson Grant (Lil)	P	34	.291	B	
		Tavener, John Adam (Jack)	SS	134	.245	Det21	
		Warner, John Ralph	3B	10	.333	A	
6	9	Wells, Edwin Lee	P	35	.279	B	
11	11	Whitehill, Earl Oliver	P	36	.218	B	
		Wingo, Absalom Holbrook (Red)	OF124	130	.370	B	
		Woodall, Chas. Lawrence (Larry)	C	75	.205	B	

WON 79   AMERICAN LEAGUE   FINISHED 6th.
LOST 75
TG 154   1926.   PCT. .513

DETROIT

TYRUS RAYMOND COBB

WON	LOST	NAME	POS.	G.	BA	FROM	TO
1	2	Barfoot, Clyde Raymond	P	11	.200	StLN23	C
		Bassler, John Landis	C63	66	.305	B	
		Blue, Luzerne Atwell (Lou)	1B109	128	.287	B	
		Burke, Leslie Kingdon	2B15	38	.227	B	C
		Cobb, Tyrus Raymond (Ty) MGR.	OF55	79	.339	B	
8	8	Collins, Harry Warren	P30	31	.154	B	
0	4	Cooper, Arley Wilbur	P	8	.000	xChiN	C
12	7	Dauss, George August	P	35	.239	B	C
0	0	Doyle, Jess Herbert	P	2	1.000	B	
		Fothergill, Robert Roy	OF103	110	.367	B	
		Gehringer, Chas. Leonard	2B116	123	.277	B	
12	9	Gibson, Samuel Braxton	P35	36	.250	A	
		Hayworth, Raymond Hall	C	12	.273	A	
		Heilmann, Harry Edwin	OF134	141	.367	B	
4	5	Holloway, Kenneth Eugene	P	36	.239	B	
6	4	Johns, August Francis	P	35	.143	A	
0	1	Kneisch, Rudolph Frank	P	2	.000	A	C
		Manion, Clyde Jennings	C74	75	.198	Det24	
		Manush, Henry Emmett (Heinie)	OF120	136	.377	B	
		Mullen, Wm. John	3B	11	.077	BknN23	

WON	LOST	NAME	POS.	G.	BA	FROM	TO
		Neun, John Henry	1B49	97	.298	B	
		O'Rourke, Francis James (2B41 SS10)	3B60	111	.242	B	
1	2	Smith, George Selby	P	23	.000	A	
7	10	Stoner, Ulysses Simpson Grant (Lil)	P	32	.170	B	
		Tavener, John Adam (Jack)	SS	156	.265	B	
		Warner, John Ralph	3B95	100	.251	B	
12	10	Wells, Edwin Lee	P	36	.205	B	
16	13	Whitehill, Earl Oliver	P	36	.253	B	
		Wingo, Absalom Holbrook (Red)	OF74	108	.282	B	
		Woodall, Chas. Lawrence (Larry)	C59	67	.233	B	

WON 82
LOST 71
TG 153

AMERICAN LEAGUE — FINISHED 4th.

1927. — PCT. .536

DETROIT

GEORGE JOSEPH MORIARTY

WON	LOST	NAME	POS.	G.	BA	FROM	TO
		Bassler, John Landis	C67	81	.285	B	C
5	4	Billings, Haskell Clark	P	10	.259	A	
		Blue, Luzerne Atwell (Lou)	1B104	112	.260	B	
10	6	Carroll, Owen Thomas	P31	37	.174	Det25	
13	7	Collins, Harry Warren	P	30	.204	B	
		DeViveiros, Bernard John	SS14	24	.227	Chi24	C
0	0	Doyle, Jess Herbert	P	7	.333	B	
		Fothergill, Robert Roy	OF137	143	.359	B	
		Gehringer, Chas. Leonard	2B121	133	.317	B	
11	12	Gibson, Samuel Braxton	P	33	.212	B	
2	1	Hankins, Donald Wayne	P	20	.143	A	C
		Heilmann, Harry Edwin	OF135	141	.398	B	
11	12	Holloway, Kenneth Eugene	P	36	.129	B	
0	0	Johns, August Francis	P	1	.000	B	C
		Manion, Clyde Jennings		1	.000	B	
		Manush, Henry Emmett (Heinie)	OF150	152	.299	B	
		McManus, Martin Joseph (2B35 3B22)	SS39	108	.268	StL	
		Neun, John Henry	1B53	79	.323	B	
		Ruble, Wm. Arthur	OF43	56	.165	A	
		Shea, Mervyn David John	C31	34	.176	A	
4	1	Smith, George Selby	P	30	.318	B	
0	0	Smith, Rufus Frazier	P	1	.000	A	C
10	13	Stoner, Ulysses Simpson Grant (Lil)	P	38	.108	B	
		Tavener, John Adam (Jack)	SS114	116	.274	B	
0	0	Walkup, James Huey	P	2	.000	A	C
		Warner, John Ralph	3B138	139	.267	B	
0	1	Wells, Edwin Lee	P	8	.286	B	
16	14	Whitehill, Earl Oliver	P	41	.205	B	
		Wingo, Absalom Holbrook (Red)	OF34	75	.234	B	

WON	LOST	NAME	POS.	G.	BA	FROM	TO
		Woodall, Chas. Lawrence (Larry)	C86	88	.280	B	

WON 68
LOST 86
TG 154

AMERICAN LEAGUE — FINISHED 6th.

1928. — PCT. .442

DETROIT

GEORGE JOSEPH MORIARTY

WON	LOST	NAME	POS.	G.	BA	FROM	TO
5	10	Billings, Haskell Clark	P	21	.286	B	
16	12	Carroll, Owen Thomas	P34	43	.194	B	
		Easterling, Paul	OF34	43	.325	A	
		Fothergill, Robert Roy	OF90	111	.317	B	
		Galloway, Clarence Edward (Chick) (3B21)	SS22	53	.264	Phil	C
		Gehringer, Chas. Leonard	2B	154	.320	B	
5	8	Gibson, Samuel Braxton	P	20	.286	B	
		Hargrave, Wm. McKinley	C88	121	.275	StL26	
		Heilmann, Harry Edwin (1B25)	OF126	151	.328	B	
4	8	Holloway, Kenneth Eugene	P	30	.121	B	
		McManus, Martin Joseph (1B45)	3B92	139	.288	B	
		Neun, John Henry	1B25	36	.213	B	
2	0	Page, Philip Rausac Jr.	P	3	.222	A	
		Rice, Harry Francis	OF129	131	.302	StL	
		Shea, Mervyn David John	C30	39	.236	B	
1	1	Smith, George Selby	P	39	.111	B	
8	11	Sorrell, Victor Garland	P	29	.109	A	
		Stone, Jonathan Thomas	OF	26	.354	A	
5	8	Stoner, Ulysses Simpson Grant (Lil)	P	36	.179	B	
0	2	Sullivan, Chas. Edward	P	3	.000	A	
		Sweeney, Wm. Joseph	1B75	89	.252	A	
		Tavener, John Adam (Jack)	SS131	132	.260	B	
11	10	Vangilder, Elam Russell	P	38	.259	StL	
		Warner, John Ralph	3B52	75	.214	B	
11	16	Whitehill, Earl Oliver	P	31	.194	B	
		Wingo, Absalom Holbrook (Red)	OF71	87	.285	B	C
		Woodall, Chas. Lawrence (Larry)	C62	65	.210	B	

WON 70
LOST 84
TG 154

AMERICAN LEAGUE — FINISHED 6th.

1929. — PCT. .455

DETROIT

STANLEY RAYMOND HARRIS

WON	LOST	NAME	POS.	G.	BA	FROM	TO
		Akers, Wm.	SS	24	.265	A	

WON	LOST	NAME	POS.	G.	BA	FROM	TO
		Alexander, David Dale	1B	155	.343	A	
0	1	Barnes, Frank Samuel	P	4	.000	A	
0	1	Billings, Haskell Clark	P	8	.000	B	C
9	17	Carroll, Owen Thomas	P34	37	.230	B	
		Fothergill, Robert Roy	OF59	115	.350	B	
		Gehringer, Chas. Leonard	2B154	155	.339	B	
1	3	Graham, Kyle B.	P	13	.105	BosN26	C
		Hargrave, Wm. McKinley	C48	76	.330	B	
		Harris, Stanley Raymond (Bucky) MGR.	2B2	7	.091	Wash	
		Hayworth, Raymond Hall	C	14	.255	Det26	
		Heilmann, Harry Edwin	OF113	125	.344	B	
2	1	Herring, Arthur L.	P	4	.214	A	
1	2	Hogsett, Elon Chester (Chief)	P	4	.200	A	
		Johnson, Roy Cleveland	OF146	148	.314	A	
		McManus, Martin Joseph	3B150	154	.280	B	
0	2	Page, Philip Rausac Jr.	P	10	.125	B	
		Phillips, Edward David	C63	68	.235	BosN24	
1	6	Prudhomme, John Olgus	P	34	.238	A	C
		Rice, Harry Francis	OF127	130	.304	B	
		Richardson, Clifford Nolen	SS	13	.190	A	
		Schuble, Henry George (Heinie)	SS86	92	.233	StLN27	
		Shea, Mervyn David John	C46	50	.290	B	
		Sigafoos, Francis Leonard (2B2 SS2)	3B2	14	+.174	Phil26	Chi
3	2	Smith, George Selby	P	14	.417	B	
14	15	Sorrell, Victor Garland	P	36	.145	B	
		Stone, Jonathan Thomas	OF36	51	.260	B	
3	3	Stoner, Ulysses Simpson Grant (Lil)	P	24	.067	B	
15	11	Uhle, George Ernest	P32	40	.343	Clev	
0	1	Vangilder, Elam Russell	P	6	.000	B	C
14	15	Whitehill, Earl Oliver	P	38	.257	B	
		Woodall, Chas. Lawrence (Larry)		1	.000	B	C
		Wuestling, George	SS52	54	.200	A	
0	1	Wyatt, John Whitlow (Whit)	P	4	.100	A	
7	3	Yde, Emil Ogden	P29	46	.333	PittN27	C

WON 75 AMERICAN LEAGUE FINISHED 5th.
LOST 79
TG 154 1930. PCT. .487

DETROIT

STANLEY RAYMOND HARRIS

WON	LOST	NAME	POS.	G.	BA	FROM	TO
		Akers, Wm. (3B26)	SS49	85	.278	B	
		Alexander, David Dale	1B	154	.326	B	
3	2	Bridges, Thomas Jefferson Davis	P	8	.300	A	
1	5	Cantrell, Guy Dewey	P	16	.000	Phil27	C
0	5	Carroll, Owen Thomas	P	6	+.143	B	N.Y.
		DeSautels, Eugene Abraham	C	42	.190	A	
		Doljack, Frank Joseph	OF	20	.257	A	
		Easterling, Paul	OF25	29	.202	Det28	
		Fothergill, Robert Roy	OF	54	+.254	B	Chi
		Funk, Elias Calvin	OF129	140	.275	N.Y.	
		Gehringer, Chas. Leonard	2B	154	.330	B	
		Greenberg, Henry Benjamin (Hank)		1	.000	A	
		Hargrave, Wm. McKinley	C	55	+.286	B	Wash
		Hayworth, Raymond Hall	C76	77	.278	B	
3	3	Herring, Arthur L.	P	23	.130	B	
9	8	Hogsett, Elon Chester (Chief)	P	33	.293	B	
9	8	Hoyt, Waite Chas.	P	26	+.196	xN.Y.	
		Hughes, Thomas Franklin III	OF	17	.373	A	C
		Johnson, Roy Cleveland	OF118	125	.275	B	
0	1	Koenig, Mark Anthony (P2)	SS74	76	+.236	xN.Y.	
		McManus, Martin Joseph	3B130	132	.320	B	
0	1	Page, Philip Rausac Jr.	P	12	.000	B	
		Rensa, George Anthony	C18	20	.270	A	PhilN
		Rice, Harry Francis	OF	37	+.305	B	N.Y.
		Rogell, Wm. George (Billy) (3B13)	SS33	54	.166	Bos28	
0	0	Samuels, Joseph Jonas	P	2	.000	A	C
		Shevlin, James Cornelius	1B25	28	.143	A	
16	11	Sorrell, Victor Garland	P	35	.187	B	
		Stone, Jonathan Thomas	OF108	126	.313	B	
1	5	Sullivan, Chas. Edward	P	40	.292	Det28	
12	12	Uhle, George Ernest	P33	59	.308	B	
		Watson, John Thomas	SS	4	.250	A	C
17	13	Whitehill, Earl Oliver	P	34	.193	A	C
		Wise, Hugh Edward	C	2	.333	A	C
		Wuestling, George	SS	4	+.000	B	N.Y.
4	5	Wyatt, John Whitlow (Whit)	P21	22	.353	B	

WON 61 AMERICAN LEAGUE FINISHED 7th.
LOST 93
TG 154 1931. PCT. .396

DETROIT

STANLEY RAYMOND HARRIS

WON	LOST	NAME	POS.	G.	BA	FROM	TO
		Akers, Wm.	SS21	29	.197	B	
		Alexander, David Dale	1B126	135	.325	B	
8	16	Bridges, Thomas Jefferson Davis	P	35	.148	B	
		Brower, Louis Lester	SS20	21	.161	A	C
0	1	Collier, Orlin Edward	P	2	.000	A	C
		DeSautels, Eugene Abraham	C	3	.091	B	
		Doljack, Frank Joseph	OF54	63	.278	B	
		Dugan, Joseph Anthony (Jumping Joe)	3B3	8	.235	BosN29	C
		Gehringer, Chas. Leonard	2B78	101	.311	B	
		Grabowski, John Patrick	C39	40	.235	N.Y.29	C
		Harris, Stanley Raymond (Bucky) MGR.	2B	4	.125	B	
		Hayworth, Raymond Hall	C	88	.256	B	

WON	LOST	NAME	POS.	G.	BA	FROM	TO
7	13	Herring, Arthur L.	P	35	.200	B	
3	9	Hogsett, Elon Chester (Chief)	P	22	.235	B	
3	8	Hoyt, Waite Chas.	P	16	+.143	B	Phil
		Johnson, Roy Cleveland	OF150	151	.279	B	
0	0	Koenig, Mark Anthony (P3 SS35)	2B55	106	.253	B	
		McManus, Martin Joseph (2B17)	3B79	107	+.273	B	Bos
		Owen, Marvin James (Freck) (1B27 3B37)	SS37	105	.223	A	
		Quellich, George Wm.	OF	13	.222	A	C
		Richardson, Clifford Nolen	3B	38	.270	Det29	
		Rogell, Wm. George (Billy)	SS	48	.303	B	
		Ruel, Herold Dominic (Muddy)	C	14	+.120	xBos	
		Schang, Walter Henry (Wally)	C	30	.184	Phil	C
		Shiver, Ivey Merwin	OF	2	.111	A	
13	14	Sorrell, Victor Garland	P	35	.159	B	
		Stone, Jonathan Thomas	OF	147	.327	B	
3	2	Sullivan, Chas. Edward	P	31	.167	B	C
11	12	Uhle, George Ernest	P29	53	.244	B	
		Walker, Gerald Homes (Gee)	OF44	59	.296	A	
		Walker, Harvey Willos (Hub)	OF66	90	.286	A	
13	16	Whitehill, Earl Oliver	P	34	.155	B	
0	2	Wyatt, John Whitlow (Whit)	P	4	.286	B	

WON 76 AMERICAN LEAGUE FINISHED 5th.
LOST 76
TG 152 1932. PCT. .500

DETROIT

STANLEY RAYMOND HARRIS

WON	LOST	NAME	POS.	G.	BA	FROM	TO
		Alexander, David Dale	1B2	23	+.250	B	Bos
14	12	Bridges, Thomas Jefferson Davis	P	34	.164	B	
		Davis, Harry Albert	1B	140	.269	A	
		DeSautels, Eugene Abraham	C24	28	.236	B	
		Doljack, Frank Joseph	OF6	8	.385	B	
		Gehringer, Chas. Leonard	2B	151	.298	B	
3	2	Goldstein, Isidore	P	16	.294	A	C
		Heyworth, Raymond Hall	C105	108	.293	B	
1	2	Herring, Arthur L.	P	12	.000	B	
11	9	Hogsett, Elon Chester (Chief)	P47	48	.246	B	
		Johnson, Roy Cleveland	OF48	49	+.254	B	Bos
		Lawrence, Wm. Henry	OF15	25	.217	A	C
2	5	Marrow, Chas. Kennon	P	18	.158	A	
		Rhiel, Wm. Joseph (1B12)	3B36	84	.280	BosN30	
		Richardson, Clifford Nolen	3B65	69	.219	B	
		Rogell, Wm. George (Billy)	SS139	143	.271	B	
		Ruel, Herold Dominic (Muddy)	C48	50	.235	B	
		Schuble, Henry George (Heinie) (SS15)	3B76	101	.271	Det29	
0	0	Sewell, Truett Banks (Rip)	P	5	.500	A	
14	14	Sorrell, Victor Garland	P32	33	.118	B	

WON	LOST	NAME	POS.	G.	BA	FROM	TO
		Stone, Jonathan Thomas	OF141	144	.297	B	
		Susce, George Cyril Methodius	C	2	.000	PhilN29	
6	6	Uhle, George Ernest	P33	38	.182	B	
		Walker, Gerald Holmes (Gee)	OF116	126	.323	B	
		Webb, Earl Wm.	OF84	87	+.287	xBos	
		White, Joyner Clifford (Jo-Jo)	OF47	79	.260	A	
16	*13	Whitehill, Earl Oliver	P	32	.244	B	
9	13	Wyatt, John Whitlow (Whit)	P	42	.192	B	

*Protest game of August 1st allowed charging loss to Whitehill, see page 101 Spalding Guide for 1933.

WON 75 AMERICAN LEAGUE FINISHED 5th.
LOST 79
TG 154 1933. PCT. .487

DETROIT

STANLEY RAYMOND HARRIS DELMER DAVID BAKER

WON	LOST	NAME	POS.	G.	BA	FROM	TO
3	3	Auker, Eldon LeRoy	P	15	.118	A	
14	12	Bridges, Thomas Jefferson Davis	P	33	.205	B	
		Davis, Harry Albert	1B44	66	.214	B	
		DeSautels, Eugene Abraham	C	30	.143	B	
		Doljack, Frank Joseph	OF37	42	.286	B	
11	15	Fischer, Chas. Wm.	P	35	.145	StL	
		Fox, Ervin (Pete)	OF124	128	.288	A	
5	5	Frasier, Victor Patrick	P	20	+.189	xChi	
		Gehringer, Chas. Leonard	2B	155	.325	B	
		Greenberg, Henry Benjamin (Hank)	1B	117	.301	Det30	
1	0	Hamlin, Luke Daniel (Hot Potato)	P	3	.400	A	
		Hayworth, Raymond Hall	C133	134	.245	B	
1	2	Herring, Arthur L.	P	24	.077	B	
6	10	Hogsett, Elon Chester (Chief)	P	45	.211	B	
0	1	Lawson, Alfred Voyle (Roxie)	P	4	.000	Clev31	
16	11	Marberry, Frederick (Firpo)	P	37	.122	Wash	
0	0	Nekola, Francis Joseph (Bots)	P	2	.000	NY29	C
		Owen, Marvin James (Freck)	3B136	138	.262	Det31	
		Pasek, John Paul	C	28	.246	A	
		Reiber, Frank Bernard	C	13	.278	A	
		Rhiel, Wm. Joseph	OF1	19	.176	B	C
		Rogell, Wm. George (Billy)	SS	155	.295	B	
7	4	Rowe, Lynwood Thomas (Schoolboy)	P19	21	.220	A	
		Schuble, Henry George (Heinie) (2B1 SS2)	3B23	49	.219	B	
11	15	Sorrell, Victor Garland	P	36	.149	B	
		Stone, Jonathan Thomas	OF141	148	.280	B	
0	0	Uhle, George Ernest	P	1	+.000	B	NYN
		Walker, Gerald Holmes (Gee)	OF113	127	.280	B	
		Webb, Earl Wm.	OF	6	+.273	B	Chi

WON	LOST	NAME	POS.	G.	BA	FROM	TO
		White, Joyner Clifford (Jo-Jo)	OF54	91	.252	B	
0	1	Wyatt, John Whitlow (Whit)	P	10	+.000	B	Chi

WON 101 AMERICAN LEAGUE FINISHED 1st.
LOST 53
154 1934. PCT. .656

DETROIT

GORDON STANLEY COCHRANE

WON	LOST	NAME	POS.	G.	BA	FROM	TO
15	7	Auker, Eldon LeRoy	P	43	.149	B	
22	11	Bridges, Thomas Jefferson Davis	P	36	.122	B	
		Clifton, Herman Earl (Flea) (2B1)	3B1	16	.063	A	
		Cochrane, Gordon Stanley (Mickey) MGR.	C124	129	.320	Phil	
5	1	Crowder, Alvin Floyd (General)	P	9	+.133	xWash	
		Doljack, Frank Joseph	OF30	56	.233	B	
6	4	Fischer, Chas. Wm.	P	20	.065	B	
		Fox, Ervin (Pete)	OF121	128	.285	B	
1	3	Frasier, Victor Patrick	P	8	.286	B	
		Gehringer, Chas. Leonard	2B	154	.356	B	
		Goslin, Leon Allen (Goose)	OF149	151	.305	Wash	
		Greenberg, Henry Benjamin (Hank)	1B	153	.339	B	
2	3	Hamlin, Luke Daniel (Hot Potato)	P	20	.231	B	
		Hayworth, Raymond Hall	C	54	.293	B	
3	2	Hogsett, Elon Chester (Chief)	P	26	.231	B	
0	0	Larkin, Stephen Patrick	P	2	.333	A	C
15	5	Marberry, Frederick (Firpo)	P	38	.218	B	
		Owen, Marvin James (Freck)	3B	154	.317	B	
		Perkins, Ralph Foster (Cy)		1	.000	NY31	C
2	0	Phillips, Clarence Lemuel	P	7	.250	A	
		Reiber, Frank Bernard		3	.000	B	
		Rogell, Wm. George (Billy)	SS	154	.296	B	
24	8	Rowe, Lynwood Thomas (Schoolboy)	P45	51	.303	B	
		xSchuble, Henry George (Heinie)	3B1	11	.267	B	
6	9	Sorrell, Victor Garland	P	28	.108	B	
		Walker, Gerald Holmes (Gee)	OF80	98	.300	B	
		White, Joyner Clifford (Jo-Jo)	OF100	115	.313	B	
		Wilson, George Peacock		1	.000	A	C
		York, Rudolph Preston (Rudy)	C	3	.167	A	

x Schuble also played 1 game at SS and 1 game at 2B.

WON 93 AMERICAN LEAGUE FINISHED 1st.
LOST 58
TG 151 1935. PCT. .616

DETROIT

GORDON STANLEY COCHRANE

WON	LOST	NAME	POS.	G.	BA	FROM	TO
18	7	Auker, Eldon LeRoy	P	36	.216	B	
21	10	Bridges, Thomas Jefferson Davis	P	36	.239	B	
		Clifton, Herman Earl (Flea) (2B5 SS4)	3B21	43	.255	B	
		Cochrane, Gordon Stanley (Mickey) MGR.	C110	115	.319	B	
16	10	Crowder, Alvin Floyd (General)	P	33	.183	B	
0	1	Fischer, Chas. Wm.	P	3	+.000	B	Chi
		Fox, Ervin (Pete)	OF125	131	.321	B	
		Gehringer, Chas. Leonard	2B149	150	.330	B	
		Goslin, Leon Allen (Goose)	OF144	147	.292	B	
		Greenberg, Henry Benjamin (Hank)	1B	152	.328	B	
0	0	Hatter, Clyde Melno	P	8	.300	A	
		Hayworth, Raymond Hall	C48	51	.309	B	
6	6	Hogsett, Elon Chester (Chief)	P	40	.261	B	
3	1	Lawson, Alfred Voyle (Roxie)	P	7	.308	Det33	
0	1	Marberry, Frederick (Firpo)	P	5	.200	B	
		Morgan, Chester Collins	OF4	14	.174	A	
		Owen, Marvin James (Freck)	3B131	134	.263	B	
		Reiber, Frank Bernard	C	8	.273	B	
		Rogell, Wm. George (Billy)	SS	150	.275	B	
19	13	Rowe, Lynwood Thomas (Schoolboy)	P42	45	.312	B	
		Schuble, Henry George (Heinie) (2B1)	3B2	11	.250	B	
		Shelley, Herbert Leneirre	OF	7	.250	A	C
4	3	Sorrell, Victor Garland	P	12	.000	B	
6	6	Sullivan, Joseph	P	25	.163	A	
		Walker, Gerald Holmes (Gee)	OF85	98	.301	B	
		Walker, Harvey Willos (Hub)	OF	9	.160	Det31	
		White, Joyner Clifford (Jo-Jo)	OF93	114	.240	B	

WON 83 AMERICAN LEAGUE FINISHED 2nd.
LOST 71
TG 154 1936. PCT. .539

DETROIT

GORDON STANLEY COCHRANE

WON	LOST	NAME	POS.	G.	BA	FROM	TO
13	16	Auker, Eldon LeRoy	P	35	.308	B	
23	11	Bridges, Thomas Jefferson Davis	P	39	.212	B	
		Burns, John Irving	1B	138	+.283	xStL	C

WON	LOST	NAME	POS.	G.	BA	FROM	TO
		Clifton, Herman Earl (Flea) (2B1 3B2)	SS6	13	.192	B	
		Cochrane, Gordon Stanley (Mickey) MGR.	C42	44	.270	B	
4	3	Crowder, Alvin Floyd (General)	P	9	.150	B	C
		English, Gilbert Raymond	3B	1	.000	NYN32	
		Fox, Ervin (Pete)	OF55	73	.305	B	
		Gehringer, Chas. Leonard	2B	154	.354	B	
		Goslin, Leon Allen (Goose)	OF144	147	.315	B	
		Greenberg, Henry Benjamin (Hank)	1B	12	.348	B	
		Hayworth, Raymond Hall	C	81	.240	B	
0	1	Hogsett, Elon Chester (Chief)	P	3	+.000	B	StL
2	3	Kimsey, Clyde Elias (Chad)	P	22	.313	Chi33	C
8	6	Lawson, Alfred Voyle (Roxie)	P	41	.222	B	
		Myatt, Glenn Calvin	C	27	.218	NYN	C
		Owen, Marvin James (Freck)	3B153	154	.295	B	
		Parker, Francis James (Salty) (1B2)	SS7	11	.280	A	C
2	4	Phillips, Clarence Lemuel	P	22	.303	Det34	C
		Reiber, Frank Bernard	C17	20	.273	B	C
		Rogell, Wm. George (Billy)	SS	146	.274	B	
19	10	Rowe, Lynwood Thomas (Schoolboy)	P41	45	.256	B	
		Simmons, Aloysius Harry (Al)	OF138	143	.327	Chi	
6	7	Sorrell, Victor Garland	P	30	.154	B	
2	5	Sullivan, Joseph	P	26	.179	B	
		Tebbetts, George Robert (Birdie)	C	10	.303	A	
4	5	Wade, Jacob Fields (Jake)	P	13	.172	A	
		Walker, Gerald Holmes (Gee)	OF125	134	.353	B	
		White, Joyner Clifford (Jo-Jo)	OF18	58	.275	B	

WON 89　　AMERICAN LEAGUE　　FINISHED 2nd.
LOST 65
TG 154　　1937.　　PCT. .578

DETROIT

GORDON STANLEY COCHRANE

WON	LOST	NAME	POS.	G.	BA	FROM	TO
17	9	Auker, Eldon LeRoy	P	43	.198	B	
		Bolton, Wm. Clifton	C13	27	.263	Wash	
15	12	Bridges, Thomas Jefferson Davis	P	34	.240	B	
		Clifton, Herman Earl (Flea) (2B3 SS4)	3B7	15	.116	B	C
		Cochrane, Gordon Stanley (Mickey) MGR.	C	27	.306	B	
7	5	Coffman, George David (Slick)	P	28	.172	A	
		English, Gilbert Raymond	2B12	18	.262	B	BosN
		Fox, Ervin (Pete)	OF143	148	.331	B	
		Gehringer, Chas. Leonard	2B142	144	.371	B	
		Gelbert, Chas. Magnus	SS16	20	.085	xCinN	
11	4	Gill, George Lloyd	P	31	.140	A	
		Goslin, Leon Allen (Goose)	OF40	79	.238	B	
		Greenberg, Henry Benjamin (Hank)	1B	154	.337	B	
1	0	Hatter, Clyde Melno	P	3	.000	Det35	C
		Hayworth, Raymond Hall	C28	30	.269	B	
		Herman, Floyd Caves (Babe)	OF2	17	.300	CinN	
		Laabs, Chester Peter (Chet)	OF62	72	.240	A	
18	7	Lawson, Alfred Voyle (Roxie)	P	37	.259	B	
0	0	Logan, Robert Dean	P	1	.000	BknN35	ChiN
0	2	McLaughlin, Patrick Elmer	P	11	.100	A	
		Owen, Marvin James (Freck)	3B106	107	.288	B	
10	5	Poffenberger, Cletus Elwood (Boots)	P	29	.216	A	
		Rogell, Wm. George (Billy)	SS	146	.276	B	
1	4	Rowe, Lynwood Thomas (Schoolboy)	P	10	.200	B	
2	5	Russell, Jack Erwin	P	25	.000	Bos	
0	2	Sorrell, Victor Garland	P	7	.000	B	C
		Tebbetts, George Robert (Birdie)	C48	50	.191	B	
7	10	Wade, Jacob Fields (Jake)	P	33	.186	B	
		Walker, Gerald Holmes (Gee)	OF	151	.335	B	
		White, Joyner Clifford (Jo-Jo)	OF82	94	.246	B	
		York, Rudolph Preston (Rudy) (3B41)	C54	104	.307	Det34	

WON 84　　AMERICAN LEAGUE　　FINISHED 4th.
LOST 70
TG 154　　1938.　　PCT. .545

DETROIT

GORDON STANLEY COCHRANE　　DELMER DAVID BAKER

WON	LOST	NAME	POS.	G.	BA	FROM	TO
		Archie, George Albert		3	.000	A	
11	10	Auker, Eldon LeRoy	P	27	.088	B	
5	3	Benton, John Alton (Al)	P	19	.121	Phil35	
13	9	Bridges, Thomas Jefferson Davis	P	25	.130	B	
		Christman, Marquette Joseph (SS21)	3B69	95	.248	A	
4	4	Coffman, George David (Slick)	P	39	.167	B	
		Cullenbine, Roy Joseph	OF17	25	.284	A	
0	0	Davis, Woodrow Wilson	P	2	.000	A	C
9	6	Eisenstat, Harry	P	32	.139	BknN	
		Fox, Ervin (Pete)	OF	155	.293	B	
		Gehringer, Chas. Leonard	2B	152	.306	B	
12	9	Gill, George Lloyd	P	24	.105	B	
		Greenberg, Henry Benjamin (Hank)	1B	155	.315	B	
1	0	Harris, Robert Arthur	P	3	.333	A	
		Hayworth, Raymond Hall	C	8	.211	B	BknN
12	9	Kennedy, Lloyd Vernon (Vern)	P33	37	.291	Chi	

WON	LOST	NAME	POS.	G.	BA	FROM	TO
		Laabs, Chester Peter (Chet)	OF53	64	.237	B	
8	9	Lawson, Alfred Voyle (Roxie)	P	27	.044	B	
		Morgan, Chester Collins	OF	74	.284	Det35	C
		McCoy, Benjamin Jenison (3B1)	2B6	7	.200	A	
		Piet, Anthony Francis (Tony)	3B18	41	.213	Chi	C
6	7	Poffenberger, Cletus Elwood (Boots)	P	25	.182	B	
0	0	Rogalski, Joseph Anthony	P	2	.000	A	C
		Rogell, Wm. George (Billy)	SS134	136	.259	B	
		Ross, Donald Raymond	3B75	77	.260	A	
0	2	Rowe, Lynwood Thomas (Schoolboy)	P	4	.167	B	
		Tebbetts, George Robert (Birdie)	C	53	.294	B	
3	2	Wade, Jacob Fields (Jake)	P	27	.048	B	
		Walker, Fred (Dixie)	OF114	127	.308	Chi	
		White, Joyner Clifford (Jo-Jo)	OF55	78	.262	B	
		York, Rudolph Preston (Rudy) (OF14)	C116	135	.298	B	

WON 81 — AMERICAN LEAGUE — FINISHED 5th.
LOST 73
TG 154 — 1939. — PCT. .526

DETROIT

DELMER DAVID BAKER

WON	LOST	NAME	POS.	G.	BA	FROM	TO
		Averill, Howard Earl	OF	87	+.262	xClev	
		Bell, Roy Chester (Beau)	OF	54	+.239	xStL	
6	8	Benton, John Alton (Al)	P	37	.091	B	
17	7	Bridges, Thomas Jefferson Davis	P	29	.197	B	
		Christman, Marquette Joseph	SS	6	+.250	B	StL
2	1	Coffman, George David (Slick)	P	23	.000	B	
		Croucher, Frank Donald	SS93	97	.269	A	
		Cullenbine, Roy Joseph	OF46	75	.240	B	
2	2	Eisenstat, Harry	P	10	+.375	B	Clev
		Fleming, Leslie Harvey	OF3	8	.000	A	
		Fox, Ervin (Pete)	OF126	141	.295	B	
		Gehringer, Chas. Leonard	2B107	118	.325	B	
1	1	Giebell, Floyd Karl	P	9	.000	A	
0	1	Gill, George Lloyd	P	3	+.000	B	StL
		Greenberg, Henry Benjamin (Hank)	1B136	138	.312	B	
1	1	Harris, Robert Arthur	P	5	+.400	B	StL
		Higgins, Michael Franklin (Pinkey)	3B130	132	.276	Bos	
3	6	Hutchinson, Frederick Chas.	P	13	.382	A	
0	3	Kennedy, Lloyd Vernon (Vern)	P	4	+.286	B	StL
		Kress, Ralph (Red)	SS	51	+.242	xStL	
		Laabs, Chester Peter	OF	5	+.313	B	StL
1	1	Lawson, Alfred Voyle (Roxie)	P	2	+.000	B	StL
0	1	Lynn, Japhet Monroe	P	4	.000	A	NYN
		McCosky, Wm. Barney	OF145	147	.311	A	
		McCoy, Benjamin Jenison (SS16)	2B34	55	.302	B	
5	6	McKain, Archie Richard (Happy)	P	32	.220	Bos	
0	1	Newhouser, Harold	P	1	.000	A	
17	10	Newsom, Louis Norman (Buck)	P	35	+.186	xStL	
		Parsons, Edward Dixon	C	5	.000	A	
0	1	Pippen, Henry Harold (Cotton)	P	3	+.400	xPhil	
		Rogell, Wm. George (Billy) (3B21)	SS43	74	.230	B	
10	12	Rowe, Lynwood Thomas (Schoolboy)	P28	31	.246	B	
		Shea, Mervyn David John	C	4	.000	BknN	
		Tebbetts, George Robert (Birdie)	C100	106	.261	B	
7	0	Thomas, Luther Baxter (Bud)	P	27	+.111	xWash	
9	10	Trout, Paul Howard (Dizzy)	P33	35	.211	A	
		Walker, Fred (Dixie)	OF37	43	.305	B	BknN
0	1	Walkup, James Elton	P	7	+.500	xStL	C
		York, Rudolph Preston (Rudy) (1B19)	C67	102	.307	B	

WON 90 — AMERICAN LEAGUE — FINISHED 1st.
LOST 64
TG 154 — 1940. — PCT. .584

DETROIT

DELMER DAVID BAKER

WON	LOST	NAME	POS.	G.	BA	FROM	TO
		Averill, Howard Earl	OF22	64	.280	B	
		Bartell, Richard Wm.	SS	139	.233	ChiN	
6	10	Benton, John Alton (Al)	P	42	.000	B	
12	9	Bridges, Thomas Jefferson Davis	P	29	.176	B	
		Campbell, Bruce Douglas	OF74	103	.283	Clev	
1	0	Conger, Richard	P	2	.000	A	
		Croucher, Frank Donald (2B7 3B1)	SS26	37	.105	B	
		Fox, Ervin (Pete)	OF85	93	.289	B	
		Gehringer, Chas. Leonard	2B138	139	.313	B	
2	0	Giebell, Floyd Karl	P	2	.000	B	
7	7	Gorsica, John Joseph Perry	P	29	.194	A	
		Greenberg, Henry Benjamin (Hank)	OF	148	.340	B	
		Higgins, Michael Franklin (Pinkey)	3B129	131	.271	B	
3	7	Hutchinson, Frederick Chas.	P	17	.267	B	
		Kress, Ralph (Red) (SS12)	3B17	33	.222	B	
		Metha, Frank Joseph (3B6)	2B10	26	.243	A	C
		Meyer, Lambert Dalton	2B21	23	.259	ChiN37	
		Mullin, Patrick Joseph	OF1	4	.000	A	
		McCosky, Wm. Barney	OF141	143	.340	B	

WON	LOST	NAME	POS.	G.	BA	FROM	TO
5	0	McKain, Archie Richard (Happy)	P	27	.143	B	
1	1	Nelson, Lynn Bernard	P6	19	.348	Phil	C
9	9	Newhouser, Harold	P	28	.200	B	
21	5	Newsom, Louis Norman (Buck)	P	36	.215	B	
1	2	Pippen, Henry Harold (Cotton)	P	4	.000	B	C
16	3	Rowe, Lynwood Thomas (Schoolboy)	P	27	.269	B	
2	2	Seats, Thomas Edward	P	26	.083	A	
		Secory, Frank Edward		1	.000	A	
1	1	Smith, Clay Jamieson	P	14	.000	Clev38	C
		Stainback, George Tucker (Tuck)	OF9	15	.225	BknN	
		Sullivan, Wm. Joseph Jr. (Billy) (3B6)	C57	78	.309	StL	
		Tebbetts, George Robert (Birdie)	C107	111	.296	B	
0	1	Thomas, Luther Baxter (Bud)	P	3	.000	B	
3	7	Trout, Paul Howard (Dizzy)	P	33	.129	B	
0	0	Uhle, Robert Elwood	P	1	.000	Chi38	C
		York, Rudolph Preston (Rudy)	1B	155	.316	B	

WON 75
LOST 79
TG 154

AMERICAN LEAGUE

1941.

FINISHED 4th.
(TIED WITH CLEVE)
PCT. .487

DETROIT

DELMER DAVID BAKER

WON	LOST	NAME	POS.	G.	BA	FROM	TO
		Bartell, Richard Wm.	SS	5	.167	B	NYN
15	6	Benton, John Alton (Al)	P	38	.060	B	
9	12	Bridges, Thomas Jefferson Davis	P	25	.085	B	
		Campbell, Bruce Douglas	OF133	141	.275	B	
0	0	Cook, Earl Davis	P	1	.000	A	C
		Croucher, Frank Donald	SS	136	.254	B	
		Evers, Walter Arthur	OF	1	.000	A	
		Franklin, Murray Asher (3B1)	SS4	13	.300	A	
		Gehringer, Chas. Leonard	2B116	127	.220	B	
0	0	Giebell, Floyd Karl	P	17	.333	B	C
9	11	Gorsica, John Joseph Perry	P	33	.298	B	
		Greenberg, Henry Benjamin (Hank)	OF	19	.269	B	
		Harris, Robert Ned	OF12	26	.213	A	
		Higgins, Michael Franklin (Pinkey)	3B145	147	.298	B	
		Hutchinson, Frederick Chas.		2	.000	B	
1	0	Manders, Harold Carl	P	8	.000	A	
		Meyer, Lambert Dalton	2B40	46	.190	B	
0	0	Mueller, Leslie Clyde	P	4	.000	A	
		Mullin, Patrick Joseph	OF51	54	.345	B	
		McCosky, Wm. Barney	OF122	127	.324	B	

WON	LOST	NAME	POS.	G.	BA	FROM	TO
2	1	McKain, Archie Richard (Happy)	P	15	+.000	B	StL
		McNair, Donald Eric (SS3)	3B11	23	.186	Chi	
9	11	Newhouser, Harold	P	33	.150	B	
12	20	Newsom, Louis Norman (Buck)	P	43	.102	B	
		Patrick, Robert Lee	OF3	5	.286	A	
		Perry, Boyd Glenn (2B11)	SS25	36	.181	A	C
		Radcliff, Raymond Allen (Rip)	OF	96	+.317	xStL	
8	6	Rowe, Lynwood Thomas (Schoolboy)	P27	32	.273	B	
		Stainback, George Tucker (Tuck)	OF80	94	.245	B	
		Sullivan, Wm. Joseph Jr. (Billy)	C63	85	.282	B	
		Tebbetts, George Robert (Birdie)	C98	110	.284	B	
1	3	Thomas, Luther Baxter (Bud)	P	26	.105	B	C
9	9	Trout, Paul Howard (Dizzy)	P37	40	.180	B	
0	0	Trucks, Virgil Oliver	P	1	.000	A	
		Wakefield, Richard Cummings	OF1	7	.143	A	
0	0	White, Harold George	P	4	.000	A	
		York, Rudolph Preston (Rudy)	1B	155	.259	B	

WON 73
LOST 81
TG 154

AMERICAN LEAGUE

1942.

FINISHED 5th.

PCT. .474

DETROIT

DELMER DAVID BAKER

WON	LOST	NAME	POS.	G.	BA	FROM	TO
7	13	Benton, John Alton (Al)	P	35	.075	B	
		Bloodworth, James Henry (SS2)	2B134	137	.242	Wash	
9	7	Bridges, Thomas Jefferson Davis	P	23	.095	B	
		Cramer, Roger Maxwell (Flit)	OF150	151	.263	Wash	
		Franklin, Murray Asher (2B7)	SS32	48	.260	B	C
3	3	Fuchs, Chas. Thomas	P	9	.077	A	
		Gehringer, Chas. Leonard	2B3	45	.267	B	C
3	2	Gorsica, John Joseph Perry	P28	31	.100	B	
		Harris, Robert Ned	OF104	121	.271	B	
2	4	Henshaw, Roy John	P	23	.083	StLN38	
		Higgins, Michael Franklin (Pinkey)	3B137	143	.267	B	
		Hitchcock, Wm. Clyde (3B1)	SS80	85	.211	A	
		Lipon, John Joseph	SS	34	.191	A	
2	0	Manders, Harold Carl	P	18	.250	B	
		Meyer, Lambert Dalton	2B	14	.327	B	
		McCosky, Wm. Barney	OF	154	.293	B	
		McNair, Donald Eric	SS	26	+.162	B	Phil
8	14	Newhouser, Harold	P38	39	.154	B	
		Parsons, Edward Dixon	C62	63	.197	Det39	
		Patrick, Robert Lee	OF3	4	.250	B	C

WON	LOST	NAME	POS.	G.	BA	FROM	TO
		Radcliff, Raymond Allen (Rip) (1B4)	OF24	62	.250	B	
		Riebe, Harvey Donald	C	11	.314	A	
		Ross, Donald Raymond (3B20)	OF38	87	.274	BknN40	
1	0	Rowe, Lynwood Thomas (Schoolboy)	P	2	.000	B	BknN
		Tebbetts, George Robert (Birdie)	C97	99	.247	B	
12	18	Trout, Paul Howard (Dizzy)	P35	36	.213	B	
14	8	Trucks, Virgil Oliver	P	28	.123	B	
		Unser, Albert Bernard	C	4	.375	A	
12	12	White, Harold George	P	34	.169	B	
0	0	Wilson, John Francis (Jack)	P	9	+.000	xWash	C
		York, Rudolph Preston (Rudy)	1B152	153	.260	B	

WON 78
LOST 76
TG 154

AMERICAN LEAGUE — FINISHED 5th.

1943. PCT. .506

DETROIT

STEPHEN FRANCIS O'NEILL

WON	LOST	NAME	POS.	G.	BA	FROM	TO
		Bloodworth, James Henry	2B	129	.241	B	
12	7	Bridges, Thomas Jefferson Davis (Tom)	P	25	.219	B	
		Cramer, Roger Maxwell (Flit)	OF138	140	.300	B	
1	3	Gentry, James Ruffus	P	4	.000	A	
4	5	Gorsica, John Joseph Perry	P35	36	.174	B	
		Harris, Robert Ned	OF96	114	.254	B	
0	2	Henshaw, Roy John	P	26	.111	B	
		Higgins, Michael Franklin (Pinkey)	3B	138	.277	B	
		Hoover, Robert Joseph	SS	144	.243	A	
		Metro, Chas.	OF14	44	.200	A	
		McHale, John Joseph		4	.000	A	
8	17	Newhouser, Harold	P	37	.185	B	
3	2	Oana, Henry Kamehameha	P10	20	.385	PhilN34	
0	0	Orrell, Forrest Gordon	P	10	.250	A	
		Outlaw, James Paulus	OF16	20	.269	BosN39	
7	6	Overmire, Frank	P	29	.167	A	
		Parsons, Edward Dixon	C	40	.142	B	C
		Radcliff, Raymond Allen (Rip) (1B1)	OF19	70	.261	B	C
		Richards, Paul Rapier	C	100	.220	Phil35	
		Ross, Donald Raymond (2B7 SS18 3B1)	OF38	89	.267	B	
20	12	Trout, Paul Howard (Dizzy)	P44	45	.220	B	
16	10	Trucks, Virgil Oliver	P	33	.181	B	
		Unser, Albert Bernard	C37	38	.248	B	
		Wakefield, Richard Cummings	OF	155	.316	Det41	
7	12	White, Harold George	P	32	.140	B	
		Wood, Joseph Perry (3B18)	2B22	60	.323	A	C
		York, Rudolph Preston (Rudy)	1B	155	.271	B	

WON 88
LOST 66
TG 154

AMERICAN LEAGUE — FINISHED 2nd.

1944. PCT. .571

DETROIT

STEPHEN FRANCIS O'NEILL

WON	LOST	NAME	POS.	G.	BA	FROM	TO
1	2	Beck, Walter Wm. (Boom-Boom)	P	28	.318	PhilN	
		Borom, Edward Jones	2B4	7	.071	A	
		Cramer, Roger Maxwell (Flit)	OF141	143	.292	B	
0	0	Eaton, Zebulon Vance	P6	9	.100	A	
		Floyd, Leslie Roe		3	.444	A	C
12	14	Gentry, James Ruffus	P	37	.197	B	
0	1	Gillespie, Robert Wm.	P	7	.000	A	
6	14	Gorsica, John Joseph Perry	P34	40	.135	B	
		Heffner, Donald Henry (Jeep)	2B5	6	.211	Phil	C
0	0	Henshaw, Roy John	P	7	.000	B	C
		Higgins, Michael Franklin (Pinkey)	3B146	148	.297	B	
0	0	Hogsett, Elon Chester (Chief)	P	3	.000	Wash38	C
		Hoover, Robert Joseph (2B1)	SS119	120	.236	B	
		Hostetler, Chas. Cloyd	OF65	90	.298	A	
		Mayo, Edward Joseph (SS11)	2B143	154	.249	Phil	
		Metro, Chas.	OF20	38	+.192	B	Phil
		Miller, James Eldridge	C	5	.200	A	
0	0	Mooty, Jacob T. (Jake)	P	15	.143	ChiN	C
		McHale, John Joseph		1	.000	B	
29	9	Newhouser, Harold	P	47	.242	B	
		Orengo, Joseph Chas. (1B5 2B2 3B11)	SS29	46	.201	BknN	
2	1	Orrell, Forrest Gordon	P	10	.250	B	
		Outlaw, James Paulus	OF137	139	.273	B	
11	11	Overmire, Frank	P	32	.175	B	
		Richards, Paul Rapier	C90	95	.237	B	
		Ross, Donald Raymond (1B1)	OF37	66	.210	B	
		Sullivan, Carl Mancel	2B	1	.000	A	C
		Swift, Robert Virgil	C76	80	.255	Phil	
27	14	Trout, Paul Howard (Dizzy)	P49	51	.271	B	
		Unser, Albert Bernard (C1)	2B5	11	.120	B	
		Wakefield, Richard Cummings	OF	78	.355	B	
		York, Rudolph Preston (Rudy)	1B	151	.276	B	

WON 88
LOST 65
TG 153

AMERICAN LEAGUE — FINISHED 1st.

1945. PCT. .575

DETROIT

STEPHEN FRANCIS O'NEILL

WON	LOST	NAME	POS.	G.	BA	FROM	TO
13	8	Benton, John Alton (Al)	P	31	.063	Det42	

WON	LOST	NAME	POS.	G.	BA	FROM	TO
		Borom, Edward James (SS2 3B4)	2B28	55	.269	B	C
1	0	Bridges, Thomas Jefferson Davis (Tom)	P	4	.000	Det43	
5	1	Caster, George Jasper	P	22	+.182	xStL	
		Cramer, Roger Maxwell (Flit)	OF140	141	.275	B	
		Cullenbine, Roy Joseph	OF	146	+.277	xClev	
4	2	Eaton, Zebulon Vance	P17	26	.250	B	C
		Greenberg, Henry Benjamin (Hank)	OF72	78	.311	Det41	
		Hoover, Robert Joseph	SS68	74	.257	B	C
		Hostetler, Chas. Cloyd	OF8	42	.159	B	C
0	2	Houtteman, Arthur Joseph	P	13	.000	A	
		Kerms, Russell Eldon		1	.000	A	C
		Maier, Robert Philip (OF5)	3B124	132	.263	A	C
		Mayo, Edward Joseph	2B124	134	.285	B	
		McHale, John Joseph	1B3	19	.143	B	
0	0	McLaughlin, Patrick Elmer	P	1	.000	Phil40	C
		McNabb, Carl Mac		1	.000	A	C
		Mierkowicz, Edward Frank	OF6	10	.133	A	
		Miller, James Eldridge	C	2	.750	B	C
6	8	Mueller, Leslie Clyde	P	26	.182	Det41	C
25	9	Newhouser, Harold	P	40	.257	B	
0	0	Oana, Henry Kamehameha	P3	4	.200	Det43	C
2	3	Orrell, Forrest Gordon	P	12	.133	B	C
		Outlaw, James Paulus (3B21)	OF105	132	.271	B	
9	9	Overmire, Frank	P	31	.189	B	
0	0	Pierce, Walter Wm.	P	5	.000	A	
		Richards, Paul Rapier	C	83	.256	B	
		Ross, Donald Raymond	3B	8	+.379	B	Clev
		Swift, Robert Virgil	C94	95	.233	B	
4	5	Tobin, James Anthony	P14	17	.120	xBosN	C
18	15	Trout, Paul Howard (Dizzy)	P41	42	.245	B	
0	0	Trucks, Virgil Oliver	P	1	.000	Det43	
		Walker, Harvey Willos (Hub)	OF7	28	.130	CinN37	C
		Webb, James Leverne (Skeeter) (2B11)	SS104	118	.199	Chi	
		Welch, Milton Edward	C	1	.000	A	C
1	3	Wilson, Walter Wood	P	25	.053	A	C
		York, Rudolph Preston (Rudy)	1B	155	.264	B	

WON 92
LOST 62
TG 154

AMERICAN LEAGUE

1946.

FINISHED 2nd.

PCT. .597

DETROIT

STEPHEN FRANCIS O'NEILL

WON	LOST	NAME	POS.	G.	BA	FROM	TO
11	7	Benton, John Alton (Al)	P	28	.184	B	
		Bloodworth, James Henry	2B71	76	.245	Det43	
1	1	Bridges, Thomas Jefferson Davis (Tom)	P	9	.000	B	C
2	1	Caster, George Jasper	P	26	.143	B	C
		Cramer, Roger Maxwell (Flit)	OF50	68	.294	B	
		Cullenbine, Roy Joseph (1B21)	OF81	113	.335	B	
		Evers, Walter Arthur	OF76	81	.266	Det41	
0	0	Gentry, James Ruffus	P	2	.000	Det44	
0	0	Gorsica, John Joseph Perry	P	14	.667	Det44	
0	2	Gray, Theodore Glenn	P	3	.000	A	
		Greenberg, Henry Benjamin (Hank)	1B140	142	.277	B	
		Groth, John Thomas	OF	4	.000	A	
		Harris, Robert Ned		1	.000	Det43	C
		Higgins, Michael Franklin (Pinkey)	3B17	18	+.217	Det44	Bos
		Hitchcock, Wm. Clyde	2B1	3	+.000	Det42	Wash
0	1	Houtteman, Arthur Joseph	P	1	.500	B	
14	11	Hutchinson, Frederick Chas.	P28	40	.315	Det41	
		Kell, George Clyde (1B1)	3B104	105	+.327	xPhil	
1	0	Kretlow, Louis Henry	P	1	.500	A	
		Lake, Edward Erving	SS	155	.254	Bos	
		Lipon,John Joseph (3B1)	SS8	14	.300	Det42	
0	0	Manders, Harold Carl	P	2	.500	Det42	ChiN
		Mayo, Edward Joseph	2B49	51	.252	B	
		McCosky, Wm. Barney	OF24	25	+.198	Det42	Phil
		Moore, Anselm Winn	OF32	51	.209	A	C
		Mullin, Patrick Joseph	OF75	93	.246	Det41	
26	9	Newhouser, Harold	P	37	.126	B	
		Outlaw, James Paulus (3B38)	OF43	92	.261	B	
5	7	Overmire, Frank	P	24	.152	B	
		Richards, Paul Rapier	C54	57	.201	B	C
		Swift, Robert Virgil	C	42	.234	B	
		Tebbetts, George Robert (Birdie)	C	87	.243	Det42	
17	13	Trout, Paul Howard (Dizzy)	P38	40	.194	B	
14	9	Trucks, Virgil Oliver	P	32	.179	B	
		Wakefield, Richard Cummings	OF104	111	.268	Det44	
		Webb, James Leverne (Skeeter) (SS8)	2B50	64	.219	B	
1	1	White, Harold George	P	11	.000	Det43	

WON 85
LOST 69
TG 154

AMERICAN LEAGUE

1947.

FINISHED 2nd.

PCT. .552

DETROIT

STEPHEN FRANCIS O'NEILL

WON	LOST	NAME	POS.	G.	BA	FROM	TO
6	7	Benton, John Alton (Al)	P	36	.154	B	
		Cramer, Roger Maxwell (Flit)	OF35	73	.268	B	
		Cullenbine, Roy Joseph	1B138	142	.224	B	C
		Evers, Walter Arthur	OF123	126	.296	B	
0	0	Gentry, James Ruffus	P	1	.000	B	
2	0	Gorsica, John Joseph Perry	P	31	.200	B	C
		Groth, John Thomas	OF1	2	.250	B	
7	2	Houtteman, Arthur Joseph	P	23	.300	B	

WON	LOST	NAME	POS.	G.	BA	FROM	TO
18	10	Hutchinson, Frederick Chas.	P33	56	.302	B	
		Kell, George Clyde	3B	152	.320	B	
		Lake, Edward Erving	SS	158	.211	B	
		Mayo, Edward Joseph	2 B	142	.279	B	
		Mierkowicz, Edward Frank	OF10	21	.190	Det45	
		Mullin, Patrick Joseph	OF106	116	.256	B	
		McHale, John Joseph	1B25	39	.211	Det45	
17	17	Newhouser, Harold	P	40	.198	B	
		Outlaw, James Paulus (3B9)	OF37	70	.228	B	
11	5	Overmire, Frank	P	28	.149	B	
		Riebe, Harvey Donald	C3	8	.000	Det42	
		Steiner, Benjamin Saunders		1	.000	Bos	C
		Swift, Robert Virgil	C	97	.251	B	
		Tebbetts, George Robert (Birdie)	C	20	+.094	B	Bos
10	11	Trout, Paul Howard (Dizzy)	P32	34	.162	B	
10	12	Trucks, Virgil Oliver	P	36	.271	B	
		Wagner, Harold Edward	C	71	+.288	xBos	
		Wakefield, Richard Cummings	OF101	112	.283	B	
		Webb, James Leverne (Skeeter) (SS6)	2B30	50	.203	B	
		Wertz, Victor Woodrow	OF82	102	.288	A	
4	5	White, Harold George	P	35	.167	B	

WON 78 AMERICAN LEAGUE FINISHED 5th.
LOST 76
TG 154 1948. PCT. .506

DETROIT

STEPHEN FRANCIS O'NEILL

WON	LOST	NAME	POS.	G.	BA	FROM	TO
2	2	Benton, John Alton (Al)	P	30	.182	B	
		Bero, John George	2B2	4	.000	A	
		Berry, Cornelius John (2B26)	SS41	87	.266	A	
		Campbell, Paul McLaughlin	1B27	59	.265	Bos46	
		Cramer, Roger Maxwell (Flit)	OF1	4	.000	B	C
		Evers, Walter Arthur	OF138	139	.314	B	
0	0	Gentry, James Ruffus	P	4	1.000	B	C
		Ginsberg, Myron Nathan	C	11	.361	A	
6	2	Gray, Theodore Glenn	P	26	.241	Det46	
		Groth, John Thomas	OF4	6	.471	B	
2	16	Houtteman, Arthur Joseph	P	43	.196	B	
13	11	Hutchinson, Frederick Chas.	P33	76	.205	B	
		Kell, George Clyde	3B	92	.304	B	
2	1	Kretlow, Louis Henry	P	5	.500	Det46	
		Lake, Edward Erving (3B17)	2B45	64	.263	B	
		Lipon, John Joseph (2B1 3B1)	SS117	121	.290	Det46	
		Mayo, Edward Joseph (3B10)	2B86	106	.249	B	C
		McHale, John Joseph		1	.000	B	C
		Mierkowicz, Edward Frank	OF1	3	.200	B	

WON	LOST	NAME	POS.	G.	BA	FROM	TO
		Mullin, Patrick Joseph	OF131	138	.288	B	
21	12	Newhouser, Harold	P	39	.207	B	
		Outlaw, James Paulus (OF13)	3B47	74	.283	B	
3	4	Overmire, Frank	P	37	.071	B	
3	0	Pierce, Walter Wm.	P	22	.294	Det45	
		Riebe, Harvey Donald	C24	25	.194	B	
		Swift, Robert Virgil	C112	113	.223	B	
10	14	Trout, Paul Howard (Dizzy)	P	32	.217	B	
14	13	Trucks, Virgil Oliver	P	43	.165	B	
		Vico, George Steve	1B142	144	.267	A	
		Wagner, Harold Edward	C52	54	.202	B	PhilN
		Wakefield, Richard Cummings	OF86	110	.276	B	
		Wertz, Victor Woodrow	OF98	119	.248	B	
2	1	White, Harold George	P	27	.154	B	

WON 87 AMERICAN LEAGUE FINISHED 4th.
LOST 67
TG 154 1949. PCT. .565

DETROIT

ROBERT ABIAL ROLFE

WON	LOST	NAME	POS.	G.	BA	FROM	TO
		Berry, Cornelius John (SS4)	2B95	109	.237	B	
		Campbell, Paul McLaughlin	1B74	87	.278	B	
		Evers, Walter Arthur	OF123	132	.303	B	
10	10	Gray, Theodore Glenn	P34	36	.127	B	
2	4	Grissom, Marvin Edward	P	27	.222	NYN46	
		Groth, John Thomas	OF99	103	.293	B	
15	10	Houtteman, Arthur Joseph	P34	36	.244	B	
15	7	Hutchinson, Frederick Chas.	P33	38	.247	B	
		Kell, George Clyde	3B	134	.343	B	
		Kolloway, Donald Martin (1B57 3B7)	2B62	126	+.294	xChi	
3	2	Kretlow, Louis Henry	P	25	.000	B	
		Lake, Edwin Erving (2B19 3B18)	SS38	94	.196	B	
		Lipon, John Joseph	SS120	127	.251	B	
		Lund, Donald Andrew		2	.000	StL	
		Mavis, Robert Henry		1	.000	A	C
		Mullin, Patrick Joseph	OF79	104	.268	B	
18	11	Newhouser, Harold	P	38	.198	B	
		Outlaw, James Paulus		5	.250	B	C
1	3	Overmire, Frank	P	14	.333	B	
		Rapp, Earl Wellington		1	+.000	A	Chi
		Riebe, Harvey Donald	C11	17	.182	B	C
		Robinson, Aaron Andrew	C108	110	.269	Chi	
0	1	Rogovin, Saul Walter	P	5	.000	A	
0	2	Stuart, Marlin Henry	P14	15	.333	A	
		Swift, Robert Virgil	C69	74	.238	B	
3	6	Trout, Paul Howard (Dizzy)	P	33	.143	B	
19	11	Trucks, Virgil Oliver	P	41	.120	B	
		Vico, George Steve	1B53	67	.190	B	C

WON	LOST	NAME	POS.	G.	BA	FROM	TO
		Wakefield, Richard Cummings	OF32	59	.206	B	
		Wertz, Victor Woodrow	OF	155	.304	B	
1	0	White, Harold George	P9	10	.333	B	

WON 95 — AMERICAN LEAGUE — FINISHED 2nd.
LOST 59
TG 154 — 1950. — PCT. .617

DETROIT

ROBERT ABIAL ROLFE

WON	LOST	NAME	POS.	G.	BA	FROM	TO
		Berry, Cornelius John (2B2 3B1)	SS11	38	.256	B	
1	1	Borowy, Henry Ludwig	P	13	.143	xPittN	
2	2	Calvert, Leo Paul Emile	P	32	.000	Wash	
		Campbell, Paul McLaughlin		3	.000	B	C
0	0	Connelly, Wm. Wirt	P	2	+.000	xChi	
		Evers, Walter Arthur	OF139	143	.323	B	
		Ginsberg, Myron Nathan	C31	36	.232	Det48	
10	7	Gray, Theodore Glenn	P	27	.140	B	
		Groth, John Thomas	OF	157	.306	B	
1	2	Herbert, Raymond Ernest	P	8	.286	A	
		House, Henry Frank	C	5	.400	A	
19	12	Houtteman, Arthur Joseph	P	41	.151	B	
17	8	Hutchinson, Frederick Chas.	P39	44	.326	B	
		Kell, George Clyde	3B	157	.340	B	
		Keller, Chas. Ernest	OF6	50	.314	N.Y.	
		Kolloway, Donald Martin (2B1)	1B118	125	.289	B	
		Kryhoski, Richard David	1B47	53	.219	N.Y.	
		Lake, Edward Erving (3B1)	SS1	20	.000	B	C
		Lipon, John Joseph	SS	147	.293	B	
		Mullin, Patrick Joseph	OF32	69	.218	B	
15	13	Newhouser, Harold	P	35	.176	B	
		Priddy, Gerald Edward	2B	157	.277	StL	
		Robinson, Aaron Andrew	C103	107	.226	B	
2	1	Rogovin, Saul Walter	P	11	.188	B	
3	1	Stuart, Marlin Henry	P	19	.083	B	
		Swift, Robert Virgil	C66	67	.227	B	
13	5	Trout, Paul Howard (Dizzy)	P	34	.190	B	
3	1	Trucks, Virgil Oliver	P	7	.150	B	
		Wertz, Victor Woodrow	OF145	149	.308	B	
9	6	White, Harold George	P	42	.121	B	

WON 73 — AMERICAN LEAGUE — FINISHED 5th.
LOST 81
TG 154 — 1951. — PCT. .474

DETROIT

ROBERT ABIAL ROLFE

WON	LOST	NAME	POS.	G.	BA	FROM	TO
3	4	Bearden, Henry Eugene	P	37	+.188	xWash	
		Berry, Cornelius John (2B10 3B7)	SS38	67	.229	B	
2	2	Borowy, Henry Ludwig	P	26	.000	B	C
11	10	Cain, Robert Max	P	35	+.245	xChi	
0	0	Calvert, Leo Paul Emile	P	1	.000	B	C
		Daugherty, Harold Ray		1	.000	A	C
		Evers, Walter Arthur	OF108	116	.224	B	
		Federhoff, Alfred	2B1	2	.000	A	
		Ginsberg, Myron Nathan	C95	102	.260	B	
7	14	Gray, Theodore Glenn	P34	35	.143	B	
		Groth, John Thomas	OF112	118	.299	B	
4	0	Herbert, Raymond Ernest	P	5	.000	B	
		House, Henry Frank	C	18	.220	B	
10	10	Hutchinson, Frederick Chas.	P31	47	.188	B	
0	0	Johnson, Earl Douglass	P	6	.000	Bos	C
		Kell, George Clyde	3B	147	.319	B	
		Keller, Chas. Ernest	OF8	54	.258	B	
		Kolloway, Donald Martin	1B59	78	.255	B	
		Kryhoski, Richard David	1B112	119	.287	B	
		Lipon, John Joseph	SS125	129	.265	B	
0	1	Marlowe, Richard Burton	P	2	.000	A	
		Mullin, Patrick Joseph	OF83	110	.281	B	
0	1	McLeland, Wayne Gaffney	P	6	.000	A	
6	6	Newhouser, Harold	P15	17	.310	B	
		Priddy, Gerald Edward (SS1)	2B154	154	.260	B	
		Robinson, Aaron Andrew	C35	36	+.207	B	Bos
1	1	Rogovin, Saul Walter	P	5	+.286	B	Chi
		Souchock, Stephen (1B1 2B1 3B3)	OF59	91	.245	Chi49	
4	6	Stuart, Marlin Henry	P	29	.233	B	
		Sullivan, Russell Guy	OF	7	.192	A	
		Swift, Robert Virgil	C43	44	.192	B	
9	14	Trout, Paul Howard (Dizzy)	P	42	.269	B	
13	8	Trucks, Virgil Oliver	P	37	.236	B	
		Wertz, Victor Woodrow	OF131	138	.285	B	
3	4	White, Harold George	P	38	.250	B	

WON 50 — AMERICAN LEAGUE — FINISHED 8th (last)
LOST 104
TG 154 — 1952. — PCT. .325

DETROIT

ROBERT ABIAL ROLFE FREDERICK CHAS. HUTCHINSON

WON	LOST	NAME	POS.	G.	BA	FROM	TO
		Batts, Matthew Daniel	C55	56	.237	StL	
		Berry, Cornelius John (3B2)	SS66	73	.228	B	
0	1	Black, Wm. Carroll	P	2	.000	A	C
		Delsing, James Henry	OF32	33	+.274	xStL	
		Dropo, Walter	1B	115	+.279	xBos	
		Evers, Walter Arthur		1	+1.000	B	Bos

WON	LOST	NAME	POS.	G.	BA	FROM	TO
		Federoff, Alfred (SS7)	2B70	74	.242	B	C
		Garbowski, Alexander		2	.000	A	C
1	0	Garver, Ned Franklin	P	1	+.000	xStL	
		Ginsberg, Myron Nathan	C101	113	.221	B	
12	17	Gray, Theodore Glenn	P35	36	.171	B	
		Groth, John Thomas	OF139	141	.284	B	
		Hatfield, Fred James (SS9)	3B107	111	+.237	xBos	
2	7	Hoeft, Wm. Frederick	P	34	.150	A	
		Hopp, John Leonard (1B1)	OF4	42	+.217	xN.Y.	C
8	20	Houtteman, Arthur Joseph	P35	36	.101	Det50	
2	1	Hutchinson, Frederick Chas. MGR.	P12	17	.056	B	
0	0	Johnson, Kenneth Carstensen	P	9	.333	PhilN	C
		Kell, George Clyde	3B	39	+.296	B	Bos
		Kolloway, Donald Martin (2B8)	1B32	65	.243	B	
		Kuenn, Harvey Edward	SS	19	.325	A	
		Lenhardt, Donald Eugene	OF43	45	+.188	xBos	StL
		Lerchen, George Edward	OF7	14	.156	A	
		Linhart, Carl James		3	.000	A	C
		Lipon, John Joseph	SS	39	+.211	B	Bos
0	3	Littlefield, Richard Bernard	P	28	+.143	Chi	StL
		Lund, Donald Andrew	OF7	8	.304	Det49	
1	1	Madison, David Pledger	P	10	+.000	xStL	
		Mapes, Clifford Franklin	OF62	86	.197	StL	C
0	2	Marlowe, Richard Burton	P	4	.000	B	
		Mullin, Patrick Joseph	OF65	97	.251	B	
0	0	McLeland, Wayne Gaffney	P	4	.000	B	C
9	9	Newhouser, Harold	P25	26	.217	B	
		Pesky, John Michael (2B22 3B3)	SS41	69	+.254	xBos	
		Priddy, Gerald Edward	2B	75	.283	B	
		Souchock, Stephen (1B9 3B13)	OF56	92	.249	B	
3	2	Stuart, Marlin Henry	P	30	+.087	B	StL
		Sullivan, Russell Guy	OF14	15	.327	B	
		Swift, Robert Virgil	C	28	.138	B	
		Taylor, Eugene Benjamin	1B4	7	.167	StL	
1	5	Trout, Paul Howard	P	10	+.333	B	Bos
5	19	Trucks, Virgil Oliver	P	35	.188	B	
		Tuttle, Wm. Robert	OF6	7	.240	A	
		Wertz, Victor Woodrow	OF79	85	+.246	B	StL
1	8	White, Harold George	P	41	.182	B	
5	9	Wight, Wm. Robert	P	23	+.220	xBos	

WON 60
LOST 94
TG 154

AMERICAN LEAGUE — FINISHED 6th.

1953. — PCT. .390

DETROIT

FREDERICK CHAS. HUTCHINSON

WON	LOST	NAME	POS.	G.	BA	FROM	TO
4	3	Aber, Albert Julius	P	17	+.130	xClev	
		Baumgartner, John Edward	3B	7	.185	A	C
		Batts, Matthew Daniel	C103	116	.278	B	
		Bertoia, Reno Peter	2B	1	.000	A	
		Boone, Raymond Otis (SS3)	3B97	101	+.312	xClev	
4	7	Branca, Ralph Theodore Joseph	P	17	.118	xBknN	
		Bucha, John George	C56	60	.222	StLN50	C
		Carswell, Frank Willis	OF3	16	.267	A	C
		Delsing, James Henry	OF133	138	.288	B	
		Dropo, Walter	1B150	152	.248	B	
0	1	Erickson, Harold James	P	18	.000	A	C
0	0	Foytack, Paul Eugene	P	6	.000	A	
		Freese, George Walter		1	.000	A	
		Friend, Owen Lacey	2B26	31	+.177	StL50	Clev
11	11	Garver, Ned Franklin	P	30	.153	B	
		Ginsberg, Myron Nathan	C15	18	+.302	B	Clev
10	15	Gray, Theodore Glenn	P30	32	.230	B	
6	8	Gromek, Stephen Joseph	P	19	+.073	xClev	
0	2	Harrist, Earl	P	8	+.000	xChi	C
		Hatfield, Fred James (2B28 SS1)	3B54	109	.254	B	
4	6	Herbert, Raymond Ernest	P	43	.158	Det51	
		Hitchcock, Wm. Clyde (2B1 SS1)	3B12	22	.211	Phil	
9	14	Hoeft, Wm. Frederick	P29	30	.172	B	
2	6	Houtteman, Arthur Joseph	P	16	+.158	B	Clev
0	0	Hutchinson, Frederick Chas. MGR. (1B1)	P3	4	.167	B	
0	1	Jordan, Milton Mignot	P	8	.500	A	C
		Kaline, Albert Wm.	OF20	30	.250	A	
		Kuenn, Harvey Edward	SS	155	.308	B	
		Lund, Donald Andrew	OF123	131	.257	B	
3	4	Madison, David Pledger	P	32	.091	B	C
6	7	Marlowe, Richard Burton	P	42	.219	B	
1	2	Miller, Robert Gerald	P	13	.125	A	
		Mullin, Patrick Joseph	OF14	79	.268	B	C
0	1	Newhouser, Harold	P	7	.500	B	
		Nieman, Robert Chas.	OF135	142	.281	StL	
		Pesky, John Michael	2B73	103	.292	B	
		Priddy, Gerald Edward (1B11 3B2)	2B45	65	.235	B	C
0	2	Scarborough, Ray Wilson	P	13	+.000	xN.Y.	C
		Souchock, Stephen (1B1)	OF80	89	.302	B	
		Sullivan, Russell Guy	OF20	23	.250	B	C
		Swift, Robert Virgil	C	2	.333	B	C
0	1	Weik, Richard Henry	P	12	+.500	xClev	
0	3	Wight, Wm. Robert	P	13	+.429	B	Clev

WON 68
LOST 86
TG 154

AMERICAN LEAGUE — FINISHED 5th.

1954. — PCT. .442

DETROIT

FREDERICK CHAS. HUTCHINSON

WON	LOST	NAME	POS.	G.	BA	FROM	TO
5	11	Aber, Albert Julius	P	32	.128	B	
		Batts, Matthew Daniel	C8	12	+.286	B	Chi
		Belardi, Carroll Wayne	1B79	88	.236	xBknN	
		Bertoia, Reno Peter	2B15	54	.162	B	
		(SS3 3B8)					
		Bolling, Frank Elmore	2B113	117	.236	A	
		Boone, Raymond Otis (SS1)	3B148	148	.295	B	
3	3	Branca, Ralph Theodore	P	17	+.308	B	N.Y.
		Joseph					
		Bullard, George Donald	SS1	4	.000	A	C
		Delsing, James Henry	OF108	122	.248	B	
0	0	Donovan, Richard Edward	P	2	.000	BosN52	
		Dropo, Walter	1B95	107	.281	B	
		Evers, Walter Arthur	OF24	30	.183	xNYN	
14	11	Garver, Ned Franklin	P35	36	.165	B	
3	5	Gray, Theodore Glenn	P	19	.045	B	
18	16	Gromek, Stephen Joseph	P	36	.190	B	
		Hatfield, Fred James	2B54	81	.294	B	
		(3B15)					
3	6	Herbert, Raymond Ernest	P	42	.176	B	
7	15	Hoeft, Wm. Frederick	P34	35	.192	B	
		House, Henry Frank	C107	114	.250	Det51	
		Kaline, Albert Wm.	OF135	138	.276	B	
		King, Chas. Gilbert	OF7	11	.214	A	
		Kress, Chas. Steven (OF1)	1B7	24	.189	Chi50	BknN
		Kuenn, Harvey Edward	SS	155	.306	B	
		Lakeman, Albert Wesley	C4	5	.000	BosN49	C
0	0	Lary, Frank Strong	P	3	.000	A	
		Lund, Donald Andrew	OF31	35	.130	B	C
5	4	Marlowe, Richard Burton	P	38	.167	B	
1	1	Miller, Robert Gerald	P32	34	.133	B	
		Nieman, Robert Chas.	OF63	91	.263	B	
		Pesky, John Michael		20	+.176	B	Wash
		Souchock, Stephen (3B2)	OF9	25	.179	B	
		Streuli, Walter Herbert	C	1	.000	A	
		Tuttle, Wm. Robert	OF145	147	.266	Det52	
0	1	Weik, Richard Henry	P	9	.000	B	C
		Wilson, Robert James	C53	54	+.282	xChi	
9	13	Zuverink, George	P	35	.125	xCinN	

WON 79
LOST 75
TG 154

AMERICAN LEAGUE — FINISHED 5th.

1955. — PCT. .513

DETROIT

STANLEY RAYMOND HARRIS

3

WON	LOST	NAME	POS.	G.	BA	FROM	TO
6	3	Aber, Albert Julius	P	39	.059	B	
		Belardi, Carroll Wayne		3	.000	B	
		Bertoia, Reno Peter (SS5)	3B14	38	.206	B	
4	3	Birrer, Werner Joseph	P	36	.158	A	
1	1	Black, Wm. Carroll	P	3	.250	Det52	
		Boone, Raymond Otis	3B126	135	.284	B	
3	5	Bunning, James Paul	P	15	.200	A	
2	1	Coleman, Joseph Patrick	P	17	+.750	xBalt	C
0	1	Cristante, Leo Dante	P	20	.000	PhilN51	C
		Delsing, James Henry	OF101	114	.239	B	
		Fain, Ferris Roy	1B44	58	+.264	Chi	Clev
0	0	Fletcher, Vanoide	P	9	.000	A	C
0	0	Flowers, Bennett	P	4	.000	Bos53	StLN
		Foytack, Paul Eugene	P	22	.091	Det53	
0	0	Froats, Wm. John	P	1	.000	A	C
12	16	Garver, Ned Franklin	P	33	.224	B	
13	10	Gromek, Stephen Joseph	P	28	.167	B	
		Hatfield, Fred James	2B92	122	.232	B	
		(SS14 3B16)					
16	7	Hoeft, Wm. Frederick	P32	36	.207	B	
		House, Henry Frank	C93	102	.259	B	
		Kaline, Albert Wm.	OF	152	.340	B	
		King, Chas. Gilbert	OF6	7	.238	B	
		Kuenn, Harvey Edward	SS141	145	.306	B	
14	15	Lary, Frank Strong	P	36	.195	B	
5	6	Maas, Duane Frederick	P	18	.167	A	
		Malmberg, Harry Wm.	2B65	67	.216	A	C
1	0	Marlowe, Richard Burton	P	4	.000	B	
		Maxwell, Chas. Richard	OF26	55	+.266	xBalt	
		(1B2)					
2	1	Miller, Robert Gerald	P7	9	.222	B	
		Phillips, Jack Dorn (3B3)	1B35	55	.316	PittN52	
		Phillips, John Melvin (3B4)	OF65	95	.234	A	
		Porter, J. W. (C4 OF4)	1B6	24	.236	StL52	
		Samford, Ronald Edward	SS	1	.000	NYN	
0	0	Schultz, Robert Duffy	P	1	.000	PittN53	C
		Small, James Arthur	OF4	12	.000	A	
		Souchock, Stephen		1	1.000	B	C
		Streuli, Walter Herbert	C	2	.250	B	
		Torgeson, Clifford Earl	1B83	89	.283	xPhilN	
		Tuttle, Wm. Robert	OF	154	.279	B	
		Wilson, Robert James	C72	78	.220	B	
0	5	Zuverink, George	P	14	+.000	B	Balt

WON 82
LOST 72
TG 154

AMERICAN LEAGUE — FINISHED 5th.

1956. — PCT. .532

DETROIT

STANLEY RAYMOND HARRIS

WON	LOST	NAME	POS.	G.	BA	FROM	TO
4	4	Aber, Albert Julius	P	42	.300	B	
		Belardi, Carroll Wayne	1B31	79	.279	B	C
		(OF2)					
		Bertoia, Reno Peter (3B2)	2B18	22	.182	B	
1	1	Black, Wm. Carroll	P	5	.000	B	C
		Bolling, Frank Elmore	2B	102	.281	Det54	
		Boone, Raymond Otis	3B130	131	.308	B	
0	0	Brady, James Joseph	P	6	.000	A	C

WON	LOST	NAME	POS.	G.	BA	FROM	TO
		Brideweser, James Ehrenfeld (2B31 3B4)	SS32	70	+.218	xChi	
5	1	Bunning, James Paul	P	15	.333	B	
		Delsing, James Henry	OF4	10	+.000	B	Chi
15	13	Foytack, Paul Eugene	P	43	.122	B	
0	2	Garver, Ned Franklin	P	6	.000	B	
8	6	Gromek, Stephen Joseph	P	40	.148	B	
		Hatfield, Fred James	2B4	8	+.250	B	Chi
		Hicks, Clarence Walter (2B6 3B1)	SS16	26	.213	A	C
20	14	Hoeft, Wm. Frederick	P38	42	.250	B	
0	0	Host, Eugene Earl	P	1	.000	A	
		House, Henry Frank	C88	94	.240	B	
		Kaline, Albert Wm.	OF	153	.314	B	
		Kennedy, Robert Daniel (3B26)	OF28	69	+.232	xChi	
		King, Chas. Gilbert	OF4	7	.222	B	
		Kuenn, Harvey Edward (OF1)	SS141	146	.332	B	
21	13	Lary, Frank Strong	P	41	.184	B	
		Lau, Chas. Richard	C	3	.222	A	
0	7	Maas, Duane Frederick	P	26	.188	B	
1	1	Marlowe, Richard Burton	P	7	+.000	B	Chi
1	1	Masterson, Walter Edward	P	35	.250	Wash53	C
		Maxwell, Chas. Richard	OF136	141	.326	B	
0	2	Miller, Robert Gerald	P	11	.143	B	
		Phillips, Jack Dorn (2B1 OF1)	1B56	67	.295	B	
		Porter, J. W. (OF2)	C2	14	.095	B	
		Small, James Arthur	OF26	58	.319	B	
		Streuli, Walter Herbert	C	3	.250	B	C
		Torgeson, Clifford Earl	1B83	117	.264	B	
6	5	Trucks, Virgil Oliver	P	22	.244	Chi	
		Tuttle, Wm. Robert	OF137	140	.253	B	
		Wilson, Robert James	C	78	.289	B	
0	0	Wojey, Peter Paul	P	2	.000	BknN54	
0	2	Woodeshick, Harold Joseph	P	2	.000	A	

WON 78 AMERICAN LEAGUE FINISHED 4th.
LOST 76
TG 154 1957. PCT. .506

DETROIT

JOHN THOMAS TIGHE

WON	LOST	NAME	POS.	G.	BA	FROM	TO
3	3	Aber, Albert Julius	P	28	+.125	B	K.C.
		Bertoia, Reno Peter (2B3 SS7)	3B83	97	.275	B	
		Bolling, Frank Elmore	2B	146	.259	B	
		Boone, Raymond Otis (3B4)	1B117	129	.273	B	
		Boros, Steven (SS5)	3B9	24	.146	A	
20	8	Bunning, James Paul	P	45	.213	B	
4	3	Byrd, Harry Gladwin	P	37	.000	Chi	C
		Clark, Melvin Earl	OF2	5	.000	PhilN55	C
0	1	Crimian, John Melvin	P	4	.000	K.C.	C
0	0	Daniel, Chas. Edward	P	1	.000	A	C
		Dittmer, John Douglas (2B1)	3B3	16	.227	MilN	C
		Finigan, James LeRoy (2B3)	3B59	64	.270	K.C.	
14	11	Foytack, Paul Eugene	P	38	.222	B	
0	1	Gromek, Stephen Joseph	P	15	.000	B	C
		Groth, John Thomas	OF36	38	+.291	xK.C.	
9	11	Hoeft, Wm. Frederick	P34	42	.149	B	
		House, Henry Frank	C97	106	.259	B	
		Kaline, Albert Wm.	OF145	149	.295	B	
		Kuenn, Harvey Edward (1B1 3B17)	SS136	151	.277	B	
11	16	Lary, Frank Strong	P	40	.123	B	
1	3	Lee, Donald Edward	P	11	.167	A	
10	14	Maas, Duane Frederick	P	45	.085	B	
		Maxwell, Chas. Richard	OF137	138	.276	B	
		Olson, Karl Arthur	OF5	8	+.143	xWash	C
		Osborne, Lawrence Sidney (1B4)	OF5	11	.148	A	
		Philley, David Earl (3B1 OF12)	1B27	65	+.283	xChi	
		Phillips, Jack Dorn		1	.000	B	C
		Porter, J. W. (C12 1B3)	OF27	58	.250	B	
1	1	Presko, Joseph Edward	P	7	.000	StLN54	
		Robinson, Wm. Edward	1B1	13	+.000	K.C.	Clev
		Samford, Ronald Edward (2B11 3B4)	SS35	54	.220	Det55	
0	1	Shaw, Robert John	P	7	.000	A	
3	3	Sleater, Louis Mortimer	P	41	.250	MilN	
		Small, James Arthur	OF14	36	.214	B	
1	0	Stump, James Gilbert	P	6	.500	A	
		Taylor, Wm. Michael	OF5	9	.348	xNYN	
		Thomas, George Edward	3B	1	.000	A	
		Torgeson, Clifford Earl	1B17	30	+.240	B	Chi
1	0	Tsitouris, John Philip	P	2	.000	A	
		Tuttle, Wm. Robert	OF128	133	.251	B	
		Wilson, Robert James	C	59	.242	B	
0	0	Wojey, Peter Paul	P	2	.000	B	C
		Yewcic, Thomas	C	1	.000	A	C

WON 77 AMERICAN LEAGUE FINISHED 5th.
LOST 77
TG 154 1958. PCT. .500

DETROIT

JOHN THOMAS TIGHE HENRY WILLIS PATRICK NORMAN

WON	LOST	NAME	POS.	G.	BA	FROM	TO
3	4	Aguirre, Henry John	P	44	.214	Clev	
		Alusik, George Joseph	OF1	2	.000	A	
		Bertoia, Reno Peter (SS5 OF1)	3B68	131	.255	B	
		Bolling, Frank Elmore	2B	154	.269	B	

WON	LOST	NAME	POS.	G.	BA	FROM	TO
		Bolling, Milton Joseph (2B1 3B1)	SS13	24	.194	Wash	C
		Boone, Raymond Otis	1B31	39	+.237	B	Chi
		Boros, Steven A.	2B1	6	.000	B	
14	12	Bunning, James Paul	P35	36	.187	B	
3	1	Cicotte, Alva Warren	P14	15	+.176	xWash	
		Feller, Jack Leland	C	1	.000	A	C
2	4	Fischer, Wm. Chas.	P	22	+.000	xChi	Wash
15	13	Foytack, Paul Eugene	P	39	.240	B	
		Francona, John Patsy (1B1)	OF18	45	+.246	xChi	
		Groth, John Thomas	OF80	88	.281	B	
		Harris, Boyd Gail	1B122	134	.273	NYN	
		Hazle, Robert Sidney	OF12	43	.241	xMilN	C
		Hegan, James Edward	C	45	.192	Clev	PhilN
10	9	Hoeft, Wm. Frederick	P36	43	.273	B	
		Kaline, Albert Wm.	OF145	146	.313	B	
		Kuenn, Harvey Edward	OF138	139	.319	B	
16	15	Lary, Frank Strong	P	39	.170	B	
		Lau, Chas. Richard	C27	30	.147	Det56	
0	0	Lee, Donald Edward	P	1	.000	B	
		Martin, Alfred Manuel (3B41)	SS88	131	.255	K.C.	
		Maxwell, Chas. Richard (1B14)	OF114	131	.272	B	
0	0	McDermott Maurice Joseph	P2	4	.333	K.C.	
4	9	Moford, Herbert	P	25	.027	StLN55	
2	5	Morgan, Tom Stephen	P	39	.200	K.C.	
		Osborne, Lawrence Sidney		2	.000	B	
0	0	Presko, Joseph Edward	P	7	.000	B	C
1	2	Shaw, Robert John	P	12	+.375	B	Chi
		Skizas, Louis Peter (3B4)	OF5	23	.242	K.C.	
0	0	Sleater, Louis Mortimer	P	4	+1.000	B	Balt
1	0	Spencer, George Elwell	P	7	.000	NYN55	
4	3	Susce, George Daniel	P	27	+.125	xBos	
		Taylor, Wm. Michael	OF1	8	.375	B	C
		Thomas, George Edward	OF	1	.000	B	
		Thompson, Chas. Lemoine	C	4	.167	K.C.	C
1	0	Valentinetti, Vito John	P	15	+.000	Clev	Wash
		Veal, Orville Inman	SS	58	.256	A	
		Virgil, Osvaldo Jose	3B	49	.244	NYN	
1	0	Wehmeier, Herman Ralph	P	7	.000	xSt.LN	C
		Wilson, Robert James	C101	103	.299	B	
		Zernial, Gus Edward	OF24	66	.323	K.C.	

WON 76 | AMERICAN LEAGUE | FINISHED 4th.
LOST 78
TG 154 | 1959. | PCT. .494

DETROIT

HENRY WILLIS PATRICK NORMAN JAMES JOSEPH DYKES

WON	LOST	NAME	POS.	G.	BA	FROM	TO
0	0	Aguirre, Henry John	P	3	.000	B	
		Alvarez, Oswaldo Gonzales		8	.500	Wash	C
		Berberet, Louis Joseph	C95	100	.216	Bos	
		Bolling, Frank Elmore	2B126	127	.266	B	
		Bridges, Everett LaMar (2B5)	SS110	116	.268	Wash	
0	1	Bruce, Robert James	P	2	.000	A	
17	13	Bunning, James Paul	P	40	.191	B	
1	3	Burnside, Peter Willits	P	30	.000	SFN	
		Chrisley, Barbra O'Neil	OF21	65	.132	Wash	
2	2	Davie, Gerald Lee	P	11	.400	A	C
		Demeter, Steven	3B4	11	.111	A	
		Doby, Lawrence Eugene	OF16	18	+.218	Clev	Chi
14	14	Foytack, Paul Eugene	P	39	.111	B	
		Groth, John Thomas	OF41	55	.235	B	
		Harris, Boyd Gail	1B93	114	.221	B	
1	1	Hoeft, Wm. Frederick	P2	3	+.333	B	Bos
		Kaline, Albert Wm.	OF	136	.327	B	
		Kuenn, Harvey Edward	OF137	139	.353	B	
17	10	Lary, Frank Strong	P	32	.125	B	
		Lau, Chas. Richard	C	2	.167	B	
		Lepcio, Thaddeus Stanley (2B24 3B11)	SS35	76	+.279	xBos	
		Maxwell, Chas. Richard	OF136	145	.251	B	
1	4	Morgan, Tom Stephen	P	46	.391	B	
17	9	Mossi, Donald Louis	P34	36	.169	Clev	
4	12	Narleski, Raymond Edmond	P	42	.095	Clev	C
		Osborne, Lawrence Sidney (OF1)	1B56	86	.191	B	
0	1	Proctor, James Arthur	P	2	.000	A	C
1	2	Schultz, George Warren	P	13	1.000	StLN55	
		Shoop, Ronald Lee	C	3	.143	A	C
1	3	Sisler, David Michael	P	32	+.200	xBos	
0	3	Smith, Robert Gilchrist	P	9	.000	xPittN	C
0	0	Stump, James Gilbert	P	5	1.000	Det57	C
0	0	Susce, George Daniel	P	9	.000	B	C
		Veal, Orville Inman	SS72	77	.202	B	
		Wilson, Robert James	C64	67	.263	B	
		Yost, Edward Frederick (2B1)	3B146	148	.278	Wash	
		Zernial, Gus Edward (OF1)	1B32	60	.227	B	C

WON 71 | AMERICAN LEAGUE | FINISHED 6th.
LOST 83
TG 154 | 1960. | PCT. .461

DETROIT

JAMES JOSEPH DYKES WM. CLYDE HITCHCOCK JOSEPH LOWELL GORDON

WON	LOST	NAME	POS.	G.	BA	FROM	TO
5	3	Aguirre, Henry John	P	37	.036	B	
		Amoros, Edmundo Isasi	OF10	65	.149	xLAN	C
		Berberet, Louis Joseph	C81	85	.194	B	C
		Bilko, Stephen Thomas	1B62	78	.207	LAN58	
		Bolling, Frank Elmore	2B138	139	.254	B	
		Bridges, Everett Lamar (SS3)	3B7	10	+.200	B	Clev
4	7	Bruce, Robert James	P	34	.179	B	

WON	LOST	NAME	POS.	G.	BA	FROM	TO
11	14	Bunning, James Paul David	P36	38	.160	B	
7	7	Burnside, Peter Willits	P	31	.148	B	
		Cash, Norman Dalton (OF4)	1B99	121	.286	Chi	
		Chiti, Harry	C36	37	+.163	xK.C.	
		Chrisley, Barbra O'Neil (1B2)	OF47	96	.255	B	
		Colavito, Rocco Domenico	OF144	145	.249	Clev	
		Fernandez, Humberto Perez	SS130	133	.241	PhilN	
5	3	Fischer, Wm. Chas.	P	20	+.364	xWash	
		Foiles, Henry Lee	C22	26	+.250	xClev	
2	11	Foytack, Paul Eugene	P28	29	.280	B	
		Gernert, Richard Edward (OF6)	1B13	21	.300	xChiN	
		Groth, John Thomas	OF8	25	.368	B	C
		Harris, Boyd Gail	1B5	8	.000	B	C
		Kaline, Albert Wm.	OF142	147	.278	B	
0	3	Labine, Clement Walter	P	14	.000	xLAN	PittN
15	15	Lary, Frank Strong	P38	39	.183	B	
		Lindbeck, Emerit Desmond		2	.000	A	C
		Maxwell, Chas. Richard	OF120	134	.237	B	
		McAuliffe, Richard John	SS7	8	.259	A	
3	2	Morgan, Tom Stephen	P	22	+.000	B	Wash
9	8	Mossi, Donald Louis	P	23	.116	B	
0	4	Regan, Philip Raymond	P	17	.059	A	
3	0	Semproch, Roman Anthony	P	17	.000	PhilN	
7	5	Sisler, David Michael	P	41	.125	B	
0	1	Spencer, George Elwell	P	5	.000	Det58	C
		Veal, Orville Inman (2B1 3B3)	SS22	27	.297	B	
		Virgil, Osvaldo Jose (C1 2B8 SS5)	3B42	62	.227	Det58	
		Wilson, Robert James	C	45	+.216	B	Clev
		Wise, Kendall Cole (SS10 3B1)	2B17	30	.147	MilN	C
		Yost, Edward Frederick Joseph	3B142	143	.260	B	

WON 101 AMERICAN LEAGUE FINISHED 2nd.
LOST 61
TG 162 1961. PCT. .623

DETROIT

ROBERT BODEN SCHEFFING

WON	LOST	NAME	POS.	G.	BA	FROM	TO
4	4	Aguirre, Henry John	P	45	.000	B	
		Alusik, George Joseph	OF1	15	.143	Det58	
		Bertoia, Reno Peter (2B7 SS1)	3B13	24	+.217	xK.C.	
		Boros, Steven A.	3B	116	.270	Det58	
		Brown, Richard Ernest	C91	93	.266	Chi	
1	2	Bruce, Robert James	P	14	.111	B	
		Bruton, Wm. Haron	OF155	160	.257	MilN	
17	11	Bunning, James Paul	P	38	.130	B	
0	0	Casale, Jerry Joseph	P	3	+.000	xL.A.	
		Cash, Norman Dalton	1B157	159	.361	B	
		Chiti, Harry	C	5	.083	B	
		Colavito, Rocco Domenico	OF161	163	.290	B	
		Cottier, Chas. Keith (2B2)	SS8	10	+.286	MilN	Wash
1	1	Donohue, James Thomas	P	14	+.000	A	L.A.
		Fernandez, Humberto Perez (3B8)	SS121	133	.248	B	
3	2	Fischer, Wm. Chas.	P	26	+.000	B	K.C.
5	2	Fox, Terrence Edward	P	39	.167	MilN	
11	10	Foytack, Paul Eugene	P	32	.222	B	
		Freehan, Wm. Ashley	C3	4	.400	A	
		Gernert, Richard Edward		6	.200	B	CinN
1	0	Gladding, Fred Earl	P	8	.000	A	
1	0	Grzenda, Joseph Chas.	P	4	1.000	A	C
		House, Henry Frank	C14	17	.227	CinN	C
		Kaline, Albert Wm. (3B1)	OF147	153	.324	B	
5	3	Kline, Ronald Lee	P	10	+.167	xL.A.	
2	0	Koplitz, Howard Dean	P	4	.000	A	
23	9	Lary, Frank Strong	P36	42	.231	B	
		Maxwell, Chas. Richard	OF25	79	.229	B	
		McAuliffe, Richard John (3B22)	SS55	80	.256	B	
0	0	Montejo, Manuel	P	12	.000	A	C
		Morton, Wycliffe Nathaniel	OF30	77	.287	A	
15	7	Mossi, Donald Louis	P	35	.165	B	
0	1	Nischwitz, Ronald Lee	P	6	.000	A	
		Osborne, Lawrence Sidney (3B8)	1B11	71	.215	Det59	
10	7	Regan, Philip Raymond	P32	33	.075	B	
		Roarke, Michael Thomas	C85	86	.223	A	
1	1	Staley, Gerald Lee	P	13	+.000	xK.C.	C
		Thomas, George Edward (SS1)	OF2	17	+.000	Det58	L.A.
		Virgil, Osvaldo Jose (C3 2B1 SS1)	3B9	20	+.133	B	K.C.
		Wertz, Victor Woodrow		8	+.167	xBos	
		Wood, Jacob	2B	162	.258	A	
1	1	Woodeshick, Harold Joseph	P	12	+.000	xWash	

WON 85 AMERICAN LEAGUE FINISHED 4th.
LOST 76
TG 161 1962. PCT. .528

DETROIT

ROBERT BODEN SCHEFFING

WON	LOST	NAME	POS.	G.	BA	FROM	TO
		Alusik, George Joseph		2	+.000	B	K.C.
16	8	Aguirre, Henry John	P	42	.027	B	
		Bertoia, Reno Peter (SS1 3B1)	2B1	5	.000	B	C
		Boros, Steven A. (2B6)	3B105	116	.228	B	
		Brown, Richard Ernest	C132	134	.241	B	
		Bruton, Wm. Haron	OF145	147	.278	B	

WON	LOST	NAME	POS.	G.	BA	FROM	TO
		Buddin, Donald Thomas (2B5 3B2)	SS19	31	.229	xHousN	C
19	10	Bunning, James Paul David	P41	43	.242	B	
1	2	Casale, Jerry Joseph	P	18	.000	B	C
		Cash, Norman Dalton (OF3)	1B146	148	.243	B	
		Colavito, Rocco Domenico	OF	161	.273	B	
		Farley, Robert Jacob (1B6)	OF11	36	+.160	xChi	C
0	0	Faul, Wm. Alvan	P	1	.000	A	
		Fernandez, Humberto Perez (1B1 3B2)	SS138	141	.249	B	
0	0	Fletcher, Thomas Wayne	P	1	.000	A	C
3	1	Fox, Terrence Edward	P44	47	.250	B	
10	7	Foytack, Paul Eugene	P	29	.143	B	
0	4	Gallagher, Douglas Eugene	P	9	.333	A	C
0	0	Gladding, Fred Earl	P	6	.000	B	
		Goldy, Purnal Wm.	OF15	20	.229	A	
0	1	Humphreys, Robert Wm.	P	4	.000	A	
2	4	Jones, Samuel	P	30	.095	SFN	
		Kaline, Albert Wm.	OF	100	.304	B	
3	6	Kline, Ronald Lee	P	36	.125	B	
3	0	Koplitz, Howard Dean	P10	12	.231	B	C
		Kostro, Frank Joseph	3B11	16	.268	A	
2	6	Lary, Frank Strong	P17	22	.167	B	
		Maxwell, Chas. Richard (1B1)	OF15	30	+.194	B	Chi
		McAuliffe, Richard John (SS16 3B49)	2B70	139	.263	B	
		Morton, Wycliffe Nathaniel (1B3)	OF62	90	.262	B	
11	13	Mossi, Donald Louis	P35	36	.164	B	
4	5	Nischwitz, Ronald Lee	P	48	.417	B	
		Osborne, Lawrence Sidney (C1 1B7)	3B13	64	.230	B	
11	9	Regan, Philip Raymond	P	35	.206	B	
		Roarke, Michael Thomas	C53	56	.213	B	
		Wertz, Victor Woodrow	1B16	74	.324	B	
		Wood, Jacob	2B90	111	.226	B	

WON 79
LOST 83
TG 162

AMERICAN LEAGUE

1963.

FINISHED 5th.
(TIED WITH CLEV)
PCT. .488

DETROIT

ROBERT BODEN SCHEFFING CHAS. WALTER DRESSEN

WON	LOST	NAME	POS.	G.	BA	FROM	TO
14	15	Aguirre, Henry John	P	38	.132	B	
3	1	Anderson, Robert Carl	P	32	.444	ChicN	C
		Brown, Wm. Gates	OF16	55	.268	A	
		Bruton, Wm. Haron	OF138	145	.256	B	
12	13	Bunning, James Paul David	P39	41	.155	B	
		Cash, Norman Dalton	1B142	147	.270	B	
		Colavito, Rocco Domenico	OF159	160	.271	B	
0	1	Dustal, Robert Andrew	P	7	.000	A	C
0	1	Egan, Richard Wallis	P	20	.000	A	
5	6	Faul, Wm. Alvan	P	28	.148	B	
		Fernandez, Humberto Perez	SS14	15	.143	B	NYN
0	0	Foster, Lawrence Lynn	P	1	.000	A	C
8	6	Fox, Terrence Edward	P	46	.091	B	
0	1	Foytack, Paul Eugene	P	9	+.000	B	L.A.
		Freehan, Wm. Ashley (1B19)	C73	100	.243	Det61	
1	1	Gladding, Fred Earl	P	22	.000	B	
		Goldy, Purnal Wm.		9	.250	B	C
		Herzog, Dorrel Norman (OF4)	1B7	52	.151	Balt	C
		Horton, Wm. Wattison	OF9	15	.326	A	
		Kaline, Albert Wm.	OF140	145	.312	B	
1	1	Koch, Alan Goodman	P7	8	.667	A	
		Kostro, Frank Joseph (1B3 OF3)	3B6	31	+.231	B	L.A.
4	9	Lary, Frank Strong	P	16	.229	B	
5	9	Lolich, Michael Stephen	P	33	.056	A	
		McAuliffe, Richard John (2B15)	SS133	150	.262	B	
2	1	McLain, Dennis Dale	P	3	.200	A	
		Morton, Wycliffe Nathaniel	OF3	6	.091	B	MilN
7	7	Mossi, Donald Louis	P	24	.205	B	
		Phillips, John Melvin (OF5)	3B117	128	.246	Clev	
15	9	Regan, Philip Raymond	P	38	.143	B	
		Roarke, Michael Thomas	C16	23	.318	B	
		Smith, George Chas.	2B	52	.216	A	
1	0	Smith, Willie P.	P11	17	.125	A	
1	2	Sturdivant, Thomas Virgil	P	28	+.000	xPittN	K.C.
		Sullivan, John Peter	C2	3	.000	A	
		Thomas, George Edward (2B1)	OF40	49	+.239	xL.A.	
		Triandos, Gus	C90	106	.239	Balt	
		Veal, Orville Inman	SS12	15	.219	PittN	C
		Wert, Donald Ralph (2B21 SS8)	3B47	78	.259	A	
		Wertz, Victor Woodrow		6	+.000	B	Minn
		Wood, Jacob (3B1)	2B81	85	.271	B	

WON 85
LOST 77
TG 162

AMERICAN LEAGUE

1964.

FINISHED 4th.
PCT. .525

DETROIT

CHAS. WALTER DRESSEN

WON	LOST	NAME	POS.	G.	BA	FROM	TO
5	10	Aguirre, Henry John	P	32	.057	B	
		Brown, Wm. James	OF106	123	.272	B	
		Bruton, Wm. Haron	OF81	106	.277	B	C
		Cash, Norman Dalton	1B137	144	.257	B	
		Demeter, Donald Lee (1B17)	OF88	134	.256	PhilaN	

WON	LOST	NAME	POS.	G.	BA	FROM	TO
0	0	Egan, Richard Wallis	P	23	.000	B	
0	0	Faul, Wm. Alvan	P	1	.000	B	
0	0	Fisher, Frederick Brown	P	1	.000	A	C
4	3	Fox, Terrence Edward	P	32	.250	B	
		Freehan, Wm. Ashley (1B1)	C141	144	.300	B	
7	4	Gladding, Fred Earl	P	42	.000	B	
0	1	Hamilton, Jack Edwin	P	5	.000	PhilaN	
		Horton, Wm. Wattison	OF23	25	.163	B	
		Kaline, Albert Wm.	OF136	146	.293	B	
0	0	Koch, Alan Goodman	P	3	+.000	B	Wash
0	2	Lary, Frank Strong	P	6	.000	B	NYN
18	9	Lolich, Michael Stephen	P	44	.109	B	
		Lumpe, Jerry Dean	2B	158	.256	K.C.	
		McAuliffe, Richard John	SS160	162	.241	B	
4	5	McLain, Dennis Dale	P19	20	.135	B	
2	1	Navarro, Julio Ventura	P	26	+.000	xL.A.	
		Northrup, James Thomas	OF2	5	.083	A	
		Phillips, John Melvin (OF1)	3B22	46	.253	B	C
8	9	Rakow, Edward Chas.	P	42	.000	K.C.	
5	10	Regan, Philip Raymond	P32	33	.317	B	
		Roarke, Michael Thomas	C27	29	.232	B	C
		Roman, Wm. Anthony	1B2	3	.375	A	
1	0	Seale, John Ray	P	4	.000	A	
7	5	Sherry, Lawrence	P	38	.000	LAN	
		Smith, George Chas.	2B3	5	.286	B	
5	6	Sparma, Joseph Blase	P21	23	.160	A	
		Stanley, Mitchell Jack	OF	4	.273	A	
		Sullivan, John Peter	C	2	.000	B	
		Thomas, George Edward (3B1)	OF90	105	.286	B	
		Wert, Donald Ralph (SS4)	3B142	148	.257	B	
19	12	Wickersham, David Clifford	P	40	.073	K.C.	
		Wood, Jacob (2B10 3B6 OF2)	1B11	64	.232	B	

WON 71 — LOST 64 — TG 135

AMERICAN LEAGUE

1900.

FINISHED 3rd. — PCT. .526

INDIANAPOLIS

WM. HENRY WATKINS

WON	LOST	NAME	POS.	G.	BA	FROM	TO
13	10	Barnes, Frederick Edward	P25	32	.213	A	C
10	12	Damman, Wm. Henry A.	P26	27	.149	CinN	C
0	1	Doscher, John Herman Jr.	P	1	.000	A	
		Flynn, George A.	OF29	53	.217	ChiN96	C
8	8	Gardner, James Anderson	P20	23	.263	PittN	
		Geier, Philip Louis (OF27)	SS32	80	.322	xCinN	CinN (returned)
0	0	Gibson, Norwood R.	P	1	+.000	A	K.C.
7	2	Goar, Joshua Mercer (Jot)	P	10	.211	CinN98	C
		Grey, Wm. Tobin	SS	18	+.217	xDet	C
2	3	Guese, Theodore	P	9	.250	A	
		Hartsel, Tullos Frederick (Topsy)	OF101	104	.300	LvlleN	CinN
		Heydon, Michael Edward	C45	61	.250	WashN	
		Hickey, Michael Edward	3B	126	.244	BosN	
		Hogriever, George C.	OF	138	.252	CinN95	
		Kelley, Michael Joseph	1B	108	.206	LvlleN	C
20	18	Kellum, Winford Ansley	P	43	.205	A	
		Madison, Arthur M.	SS	98	.264	PittN	C
		Magoon, George Henry	2B	120	.309	ChiN	
6	6	Milligan, Wm. J.	P	13	+.225	xBuff	
		Powers, Michael Riley	C99	110	.298	WashN	
		Richter, John M.	OF	3	.000	LvlleN98	C
0	0	Sanders, Warren W. (War)	P	2	.667	A	
		Seybold, Ralph Orlando	OF107	115	.304	CinN	
		Stewart, Asa (Ace)	2B	1	+.333	ChiN95	K.C.
5	4	Stimmel, Archibald May	P	11	.118	xCinN	

CLUB RECORD

AMERICAN LEAGUE

KANSAS CITY

YEAR	TG	WON	LOST	PCT.	FINISHED	MANAGER
1900	139	69	70	.496	5	James H. Manning
1955	154	63	91	.409	6	Louis Boudreau
1956	154	52	102	.338	8(Last)	Louis Boudreau
1957	153	59	94	.386	7	Louis Boudreau / Harry Francis Craft
1958	154	73	81	.474	7	Harry Francis Craft
1959	154	66	88	.429	7	Harry Francis Craft
1960	154	58	96	.377	8(Last)	Robert Irving Elliott
1961	161	61	100	.379	x9(Wash) (Last)	Joseph Lowell Gordon / Henry Albert Bauer
1962	162	72	90	.444	9	Henry Albert Bauer
1963	162	73	89	.451	8	Edmund Walter Lopat
1964	162	57	105	.352	10(Last)	Edmund Walter Lopat / Fred Melvin McGaha

CLUB TRANSFERRED TO OAKLAND AFTER 1967 SEASON
NEW KANSAS CITY CLUB ADDED IN EXPANSION OF 1969

YEAR	TG	WON	LOST	TIED	PCT.	FINISHED	MANAGER
1965	162	59	103	0	.364	10 (LAST)	FRED MELVIN MC GAHA / HAYWOOD COOPER SULLIVAN
1966	160	74	86	0	.462	7	ALVIN RALPH DARK
1967	161	62	99	0	.385	10 (LAST)	ALVIN RALPH DARK / LUCIUS BENJAMIN APPLING *
1969	163	69	93	1	.426	4W	JOSEPH LOWELL GORDON
1970	162	65	97	0	.401	X4W (MIL)	CHARLES METRO / ROBERT GRANVILLE LEMON
1971	161	85	76	0	.528	2W	ROBERT GRANVILLE LEMON
1972	154	76	78	0	.494	4W	ROBERT GRANVILLE LEMON

WON 69 LOST 70 TG 139

AMERICAN LEAGUE 1900.

FINISHED 5th. PCT. .496

KANSAS CITY

JAMES H. MANNING

WON	LOST	NAME	POS.	G.	BA	FROM	TO
		Carroll,	OF	1	.000	A	C
1	0	Carsey, Wilfred (Kid)	P	3	+.286	xBuff	
2	5	Cates, Eli R.	P	11	.172	A	
		Clingman, Wm. Frederick	SS	41	.309	xChiN	
		Coughlin, Wm. Paul	3B	130	.263	WashN	
2	3	Daub, Daniel Wm. (OF1)	P7	8	.278	BknN97	C
		Dungan, Samuel Morrison	1B115	117	.337	xChiN	
		Farrell, John Stephen	OF124	125	.269	A	
		Ganzel, John Henry	1B	22	.391	PittN98	ChiN
19	11	Gear, Dale Dudley (OF34)	P35	79	.277	ClevN97	
2	4	Gibson, Norwood R.	P	8	+.111	xInpls	
		Gonding, John	C	73	.187	A	C
3	3	Gray, George Edward (Chummy)	P	13	+.190	xBuff	C
		Hemphill, Chas. Judson	OF	131	.319	ClevN	
23	22	Lee, Wyatt Arnold	P48	50	.227	A	
		McManus, Francis E.	C	33	+.297	xChi	
		Nagle,	OF	7	.233	A	C
		O'Brien, John Joseph	OF	140	.298	WashN	
17	20	Patten, Case L.	P	45	.206	A	
		Schaefer, Herman A. (Germany) (SS19)	2B84	110	.256	A	
		Stewart, Asa (Ace)	2B	54	+.179	xInpls	C
		Sullivan, John Eugene	C	7	.260	A	
		Thiel, Otto	3B	12	.111	A	C
0	2	Thomas, Thomas W.	P	2	+.250	xStLN	Chi
		Wagner, Albert Butts	SS	76	.275	BknN98	C
		Wilson, A. Parke	C39	42	.292	NYN	C

WON 63 LOST 91 TG 154

AMERICAN LEAGUE 1955.

FINISHED 6th. PCT. .409

KANSAS CITY

LOUIS BOUDREAU

WON	LOST	NAME	POS.	G.	BA	FROM	TO
		Astroth, Joseph Henry	C100	101	.252	Phil	
		Bevan, Joseph Harold	3B1	3	.000	Phil52	
1	0	Bishop, Chas. Tuller	P	4	.500	Phil	C
0	1	Blackwell, Ewell	P	2	.000	NY53	C

WON	LOST	NAME	POS.	G.	BA	FROM	TO
		Bollweg, Donald Raymond	1B3	12	.111	Phil	C
		Boyer, Cletis LeRoy (2B10 3B11)	SS12	47	.241	A	C
5	5	Boyer, Cloyd Victor	P	30	.069	StLN52	
2	0	Burtschy, Edward Frank	P	7	.333	Phil	
4	7	Ceccarelli, Arthur Edward	P	31	.079	A	
0	2	Cox, Glenn Melvin	P	2	.000	A	
0	2	Craddock, Walter Anderson	P	4	.000	A	
		DeMaestri, Joseph Paul	SS122	123	.249	Phil	
12	12	Ditmar, Arthur John	P	35	.210	Phil	
0	0	Dixon, John Craig	P	2	.000	Phil	
		Finigan, James LeRoy (3B59)	2B90	150	.255	Phil	
		George, Alexander Thomas	SS	5	.100	A	C
0	0	Fricano, Marion John	P	10	.667	Phil	C
7	6	Gorman, Thomas Aloysius	P	57	.083	N.Y.	
0	3	Gray, John Leonard	P	8	.125	Phil	
3	3	Harrington, Wm. Womble	P	34	.118	Phil53	
1	8	Herbert, Raymond Ernest	P23	24	.190	Det	
		Jacobs, Forrest Vandergrift	2B7	13	.261	Phil	
11	8	Kellner, Alexander Raymond	P	30	.214	Phil	
0	1	Keriazakos, Constantine Nicholas	P	5	.000	Wash	C
		Kryhoski, Richard David	1B14	28	.213	Balt	C
0	2	Kume, John Michael	P	6	.125	A	C
		Littrell, Jack Napier (1B6 2B4)	SS22	37	.200	Phil	
		Lopez, Hector Headley (2B36)	3B93	128	.290	A	
		MacKenzie, Eric Hugh	C	1	.000	A	C
		Plarski, Donald Joseph	OF6	8	.091	A	C
5	9	Portocarrero, Arnold Mario	P	24	.108	Phil	
		Power, Victor Pellot	1B144	147	.319	Phil	
4	6	Raschi, Victor Angelo John	P	20	.182	xStLN	C
		Renna, Wm. Beneditto	OF79	100	.213	Phil	
		Robertson, Alfred James	C4	6	.250	Phil	C
		Saffell, Thomas Judson	OF	9	.216	xPittN	C
2	5	Sain, John Franklin	P	25	+.000	xN.Y.	C
		Schypinski, Gerald Albert (2B2)	SS21	22	.217	A	C
5	10	Shantz, Robert Clayton	P23	26	.146	Phil	
		Shantz, Wilmer Ebert	C78	79	.258	Phil	
		Simpson, Harry Leon (1B3)	OF100	112	+.301	xClev	
		Slaughter, Enos Bradsher	OF97	108	+.322	xN.Y.	
1	1	Sleater, Louis Mortimer	P16	21	.154	Wash52	
0	0	Spicer, Robert Oberton	P	2	.000	A	
		Stewart, Wm. Wayne	OF6	11	.111	A	C
		Suder, Peter	2B24	26	.210	Phil	C
0	0	Trice, Robert Lee	P	4	.667	Phil	C
		Valo, Elmer Wm.	OF72	112	.364	Phil	
0	0	Van Brabant, Camille Oscar	P	2	.000	Phil	C
0	0	Wheat, Leroy Wm.	P	3	.000	Phil	C
0	0	Wilson, Wm. Donald (P1)	OF82	98	.223	Phil	C
		Zernial, Gus Edward	OF103	120	.254	Phil	

WON 52
LOST 102
TG 154

AMERICAN LEAGUE

1956.

FINISHED 8th (Last)

PCT. .338

KANSAS CITY

LOUIS BOUDREAU

WON	LOST	NAME	POS.	G.	BA	FROM	TO
		Astroth, Joseph Henry	C	8	.077	B	C
		Baxes, Michael (2B1)	SS62	73	.226	A	
		Boyer, Cletis LeRoy (3B7)	2B51	67	.217	B	
0	0	Bradford, Wm. D.	P	1	.000	A	C
0	0	Brunet, George Stuart	P	6	.000	A	
6	8	Burnette, Wallace Harper	P	18	.051	A	
3	1	Burtschy, Edward Frank	P	21	.125	B	C
0	1	Ceccarelli, Arthur Edward	P	3	.000	B	
0	2	Cox, Glenn Melvin	P	3	.000	B	
0	2	Craddock, Walter Andreson	P	2	.000	B	
4	8	Crimian, John Melvin	P54	55	.227	StLN52	
		DeMaestri, Joseph Paul (2B2)	SS132	133	.233	B	
12	22	Ditmar, Arthur John	P	44	.143	B	
1	1	Duser, Carl Robert	P	2	.000	A	
		Finigan, James LeRoy (3B32)	2B52	91	.216	B	
		Ginsberg, Myron Nathan	C57	71	+.246	Clev54	Balt
9	10	Gorman, Thomas Aloysius	P	52	.051	B	
		Groth, John Thomas	OF84	95	.258	Wash	
2	2	Harrington, Wm. Womble	P	23	.000	B	C
1	13	Herriage, Wm. Troy	P31	34	.120	A	C
		Jacobs, Forrest Vandergrift	2B31	32	.216	B	PittN
7	4	Kellner, Alexander Raymond	P20	21	.200	B	
4	9	Kretlow, Louis Henry	P	25	.061	Balt	C
0	4	LaSorda, Thomas Chas.	P18	19	.077	BknN	C
		Lopez, Hector Headley (2B8 SS4 OF20)	3B121	151	.273	B	
		Melton, David Olin	OF	3	.333	A	
0	5	McMahan, Jack Wally	P	23	.000	xPittN	C
		Pilarcik, Alfred James	OF67	69	.251	A	
		Pisoni, James Pete	OF9	10	.267	StL53	
		Pless, Rance (3B5)	1B15	48	.271	A	C
0	1	Portocarrero, Arnold Mario	P	3	.000	B	
		Power, Victor Pellot (2B47 OF7)	1B76	127	.309	B	
		Renna, Wm. Beneditto	OF25	33	.271	B	
		Robinson, Wm. Edward	1B47	75	+.198	xN.Y.	
1	2	Santiago, Jose Guillermo	P	9	.400	Clev	C
2	7	Shantz, Robert Clayton	P45	51	.091	B	
		Simpson, Harry Leon (1B32)	OF111	141	.293	B	
		Skizas, Louis Peter	OF74	83	+.316	xN.Y.	
		Slaughter, Enos Bradsher	OF57	91	+.278	B	N.Y.
		Smith, Harold Wayne	C	36	+.275	xBalt	
0	0	Spicer, Robert Oberton	P	2	.000	B	C
		Thompson, Chas. Lemoine	C68	92	.272	BknN54	

WON	LOST	NAME	POS.	G.	BA	FROM	TO
		Valo, Elmer Wm.	OF1	9	.222	B	PhilN
		Zernial, Gus Edward	OF69	109	.224	B	

WON 59 LOST 94 TG 153

AMERICAN LEAGUE

1957.

FINISHED 7th.

PCT. .386

KANSAS CITY

LOUIS BOUDREAU HARRY FRANCIS CRAFT

WON	LOST	NAME	POS.	G.	BA	FROM	TO
0	0	Aber, Albert Julius	P	3	+1.000	xDet	C
0	0	Blake, Edward James	P	2	.000	CinN53	C
		Boyer, Cletis LeRoy (3B1)	2B1	10	.000	B	
0	2	Brunet, George Stuart	P	4	.000	B	
7	11	Burnette, Wallace Harper	P	38	.250	B	
		Cerv, Robert Henry	OF89	124	.272	N.Y.	
0	7	Coleman, Walter Gary	P	19	.000	N.Y.	
1	0	Cox, Glenn Melvin	P	10	.000	B	
		DeMaestri, Joseph Paul	SS134	135	.245	B	
0	3	Duren, Rinold George	P	14	.071	Balt54	
6	13	Garver, Ned Franklin	P	24	.182	Det	
5	9	Gorman, Thomas Aloysius	P	38	.121	B	
		Graff, Milton Edward	2B53	56	.181	A	
		Groth, John Thomas	OF50	55	+.254	B	Det
		Held, Woodson George	OF	92	+.239	xN.Y.	
0	0	Hill, David Burnham	P	2	.000	A	C
0	2	Host, Eugene Earl	P	11	.000	Det	C
		Hunter, Gordon Wm. (SS35 3B17)	2B64	116	.191	N.Y.	
6	5	Kellner, Alexander Raymond	P	28	.234	B	
		Lopez, Hector Headley (2B4 OF3)	3B111	121	.294	B	
		Martin, Alfred Manuel (SS2 3B20)	2B52	73	+.257	xN.Y.	
		Martyn, Robert Gordon	OF49	58	.267	A	
1	4	McDermott, Maurice Joseph (1B2)	P29	58	.245	N.Y.	
9	7	Morgan, Tom Stephen	P	46	.091	N.Y.	
		Noren, Irving Arnold (OF6)	1B25	81	.213	N.Y.	StLN
		Pisoni, James Pete	OF	44	.237	B	
4	9	Portocarrero, Arnold Mario	P	33	.107	B	
		Power, Victor Pellot (2B4 OF6)	1B113	129	.259	B	
0	0	Raether, Harold Herman	P	1	.000	Phil54	C
		Simpson, Harry Leon (OF21)	1B27	50	+.296	B	N.Y.
		Skizas, Louis Peter (3B32)	OF76	119	.245	B	
		Smith, Harold Wayne	C103	107	.303	B	
0	0	Taylor, Harry Evans	P	2	.250	A	C
4	11	Terry, Ralph Willard	P21	22	+.143	xN.Y.	
		Thompson, Chas. Lemoine	C62	81	.204	B	
9	7	Trucks, Virgil Oliver	P	48	.143	Det	
7	4	Urban, Jack Elmer	P31	37	.282	A	

WON	LOST	NAME	POS.	G.	BA	FROM	TO
		Zernial, Gus Edward (1B1)	OF113	131	.236	B	

WON 73 LOST 81 TG 154

AMERICAN LEAGUE

1958.

FINISHED 7th.

PCT. .474

KANSAS CITY

HARRY FRANCIS CRAFT

WON	LOST	NAME	POS.	G.	BA	FROM	TO
		Baxes, Michael (SS4)	2B61	73	.212	KC56	C
1	1	Burnette, Wallace Harper	P	12	.167	B	C
		Carrasquel, Alfonso Colon (SS24)	3B30	59	+.213	xClev	
		Cerv, Robert Henry	OF136	141	.305	B	
		Chiti, Harry	C83	103	.268	ChiN56	
0	0	Cox, Glenn Melvin	P	2	.000	B	C
0	3	Craddock, Walter Anderson	P	23	.000	KC56	C
3	2	Daley, Leavitt Leo	P	26	.125	Clev	
0	4	Davis, Robert Edward	P	8	.167	A	
		DeMaestri, Joseph Paul	SS137	139	.219	B	
9	5	Dickson, Murry Monroe	P27	28	+.257	StLN	N.Y.
0	0	Duser, Carl Robert	P	1	.000	KC56	C
12	11	Garver, Ned Franklin	P	31	.174	B	
4	4	Gorman, Thomas Aloysius	P	50	.118	B	
		Graff, Milton Edward	2B1	5	.000	B	C
7	6	Grim, Robert Anton	P	26	+.188	xN.Y.	
		Hadley, Kent Wm.	1B2	3	.182	A	
		Held, Woodson George (SS1 3B4)	OF41	47	+.214	B	Clev
8	8	Herbert, Raymond Ernest	P	42	.192	KC55	
		Herzog, Dorrel Norman (1B22 3B1)	OF37	88	+.240	xWash	
		House, Henry Frank	C55	76	.252	Det	
		Hunter, Gordon Wm. (2B8)	SS12	22	+.155	B	Clev
0	0	Johnson, Kenneth Travis	P	2	.000	A	
0	2	Kellner, Alexander Raymond	P7	8	.091	B	CinN
		Klimchock, Louis Stephen	2B	2	.200	A	
		Lopez, Hector Headley (SS1 3B55 OF1)	2B96	151	.261	B	
4	5	Maas, Duane Frederick	P	10	+.176	Det	N.Y.
		Maris, Roger Eugene	OF	99	+.247	xClev	
		Martyn, Robert Gordon	OF63	95	.261	B	
		Melton, David Olin	OF2	9	.000	KC56	C
		Power, Victor Pellot (2B1)	1B50	52	+.302	B	Clev
1	0	Reed, Howard Dean	P	3	.000	A	
		Simpson, Harry Leon (OF11)	1B43	78	+.264	xN.Y.	
		Small, James Arthur	OF1	2	.000	Det	C
		Smith, Harold Wayne (C31 1B14)	3B43	99	.273	B	
11	13	Terry, Ralph Willard	P	40	.197	B	
5	5	Tomanek, Richard Carl	P	36	+.231	xClev	
0	1	Trucks, Virgil Oliver	P	16	+.000	B	N.Y.
0	0	Tsitouris, John Philip	P	1	.000	Det	

WON	LOST	NAME	POS.	G.	BA	FROM	TO
		Tuttle, Wm. Robert	OF145	148	.231	Det	
8	11	Urban, Jack Elmer	P30	31	.152	B	
		Ward, Preston Meyer (3B34 OF2)	1B39	81	+.254	xClev	

WON 66
LOST 88
TG 154

AMERICAN LEAGUE 1959.

FINISHED 7th.
PCT. .429

KANSAS CITY

HARRY FRANCIS CRAFT

WON	LOST	NAME	POS.	G.	BA	FROM	TO
		Bella, John (1B1)	OF25	47	.207	NY57	C
		Boone, Raymond Otis (3B3)	1B38	61	+.273	xChi	MilN
0	0	Brunet, George Stuart	P	2	.000	KC57	
		Carroll, Thomas Edward (3B3)	SS9	14	.143	NY56	C
		Cerv, Robert Henry	OF119	125	.285	B	
		Chiti, Harry	C47	55	.272	B	
2	10	Coleman, Walter Gary	P	29	+.080	KC57	Balt
16	13	Daley, Leavitt Leo	P	39	.295	B	
		DeMaestri, Joseph Paul	SS115	118	.244	B	
2	1	Dickson, Murry Monroe	P	38	.176	B	C
0	0	Freeman, Mark Price	P	3	+.000	A	N.Y.
10	13	Garver, Ned Franklin	P	32	.282	B	
1	0	Gorman, Thomas Aloysius	P	17	.000	B	C
6	10	Grim, Robert Anton	P	40	.094	B	
0	1	Grunwald, Alfred Henry	P6	8	.000	PittN55	C
		Hadley, Kent Wm.	1B95	113	.253	B	
11	11	Herbert, Raymond Ernest	P	37	.211	B	
		Herzog, Dorrel Norman (1B1)	OF34	38	.293	B	
		House, Henry Frank	C95	98	.236	B	
		Jablonski, Raymond Leo	3B17	25	.262	xStLN	
1	1	Johnson, Kenneth Travis	P	2	.000	B	
0	0	Kileen, Evans Henry	P	4	.000	A	C
		Klimchock, Louis Stephen	2B16	17	.273	B	
8	11	Kucks, John Chas.	P	33	+.085	xN.Y.	
0	0	Kutyna, Marion John	P	4	.000	A	
		Lopez, Hector Headley	2B33	35	+.281	B	N.Y.
		Lumpe, Jerry Dean (SS56 3B4)	2B60	108	+.243	xN.Y.	
		Maris, Roger Eugene	OF117	122	.273	B	
		Martyn, Robert Gordon		1	.000	B	C
1	0	Meyer, Russell Chas.	P	18	.000	Bos57	C
		Morgan, Joseph Michael	3B2	20	.190	xMilN	
0	3	Reed, Howard Dean	P	6	.000	B	
		Simpson, Harry Leon	1B4	8	+.286	B	Chi
		Smith, Harold Wayne (C22)	3B77	108	.288	B	
		Snyder, Russell Henry	OF64	73	.313	A	
2	6	Sturdivant, Thomas Virgil	P36	37	+.059	xN.Y.	
2	4	Terry, Ralph Willard	P	9	+.176	B	N.Y.
		Terwilliger, Willard Wayne (SS2 3B1)	2B63	74	.267	NYN56	
0	1	Tomanek, Richard Carl	P	16	.500	B	C
4	3	Tsitouris, John Philip	P	24	.150	B	
		Tuttle, Wm. Robert	OF121	126	.300	B	
		Ward, Preston Meyer (OF1)	1B22	58	.248	B	C
		Williams, Richard Hirshfeld (1B32 2B3 OF23)	3B80	130	.266	Balt	

WON 58
LOST 96
TG 154

AMERICAN LEAGUE 1960.

FINISHED 8th (Last)
PCT. .377

KANSAS CITY

ROBERT IRVING ELLIOTT

WON	LOST	NAME	POS.	G.	BA	FROM	TO
		Bauer, Henry Albert	OF67	95	.275	N.Y.	
0	0	Blemker, Raymond	P	1	.000	A	C
		Boak, Chester Robert	2B	5	.154	A	
0	2	Briggs, John Tift	P	8	+.000	xClev	C
0	2	Brunet, George Stuart	P	3	.000	B	MilN
		Carey, Andrew Arthur	3B91	102	+.233	xN.Y.	
		Cerv, Robert Henry	OF21	23	+.256	B	N.Y.
		Chiti, Harry	C52	58	+.221	B	Det
16	16	Daley, Leavitt Leo	P	37	.160	B	
		Daley, Peter Harvey (OF1)	C61	73	.263	Bos	
0	0	Davis, Robert Edward	P	21	.250	KC58	C
		Delsing, James Henry	OF10	16	.250	Chi56	C
		Foiles, Henry Lee	C2	6	+.571	PittN	Clev
4	9	Garver, Ned Franklin	P	28	.074	B	
1	0	Giggie, Robert Thomas	P	10	.000	xMilN	
8	13	Hall, Richard Wallace	P29	32	.107	PittN	
		Hamlin, Kenneth Lee	SS139	140	.224	PittN	
14	15	Herbert, Raymond Ernest	P	37	.171	B	
		Herzog, Dorrel Norman Elvert (1B2)	OF69	83	.266	B	
		Jablonski, Raymond Leo	3B6	21	.219	B	C
5	10	Johnson, Kenneth Travis	P	42	.167	B	
		Johnson, Robert Wallace (2B27 3B11)	SS30	76	.205	A	
1	2	Kiely, Leo Patrick	P	20	.000	Bos	C
		Klimchock, Louis Stephen	2B1	10	.300	B	
		Kravitz, Daniel	C47	59	.234	xPittN	C
4	10	Kucks, John Chas.	P	31	.133	B	C
3	2	Kutyna, Marion John	P	51	.200	B	
1	10	Larsen, Donald James	P22	23	.207	N.Y.	
		Lumpe, Jerry Dean (SS15)	2B134	146	.272	B	
		McManus, James Michael	1B3	5	.308	A	C
		Posada, Leopoldo Hernandez	OF9	10	.361	A	
0	0	Reed, Howard Dean	P	1	.000	B	C
		Siebern, Norman Leroy (1B69)	OF75	144	.279	N.Y.	
		Snyder, Russell Henry	OF91	125	.260	B	
		Terwilliger, Willard Wayne	2B	2	.000	B	C
		Throneberry, Marvin Eugene	1B71	104	.250	N.Y.	
1	3	Trowbridge, Robert	P	22	.056	MilN	C

WON	LOST	NAME	POS.	G.	BA	FROM	TO
0	2	Tsitouris, John Philip	P	14	.000	B	
		Tuttle, Wm. Robert	OF148	151	.256	B	
0	0	Wickersham, David Clifford	P	5	.000	A	
		Williams, Richard Hirshfeld	3B57	127	.288	B	
		(1B34 OF25)					

WON 61 AMERICAN LEAGUE FINISHED 9th.
LOST 100 (TIED WITH WASH)
TG 161 1961. PCT. .379

KANSAS CITY

JOSEPH LOWELL GORDON HANRY ALBERT BAUER

WON	LOST	NAME	POS.	G.	BA	FROM	TO
9	15	Archer, James Wm.	P	39	.063	A	
11	11	Bass, Norman Delaney	P40	41	.119	A	
		Bauer, Henry Albert MGR.	OF35	43	.264	B	C
		Bertoia, Reno Peter	3B29	39	+.242	xMinn	Det
		(2B6)					
		Boyd, Robert Richard	1B8	26	.229	Balt	MilwN
		Bryan, Billy Ronald	C4	9	.158	A	
		Carey, Andrew Arthur	3B	39	+.244	B	Chi
		Causey, James Wayne	3B88	104	.276	Balt57	
		(2B9 SS11)					
		Cipriani, Frank Dominick	OF11	13	.250	A	C
		Courtney, Clinton Dawson		1	+.000	Balt	Balt
		Covington, John Wesley	OF12	17	+.159	xChi	PhilN
4	8	Daley, Leavitt Leo	P	16	+.111	B	N.Y.
		Del Greco, Robert George	OF73	74	.230	xPhilN	
0	5	Ditmar, Arthur John	P	20	+.167	xN.Y.	
		Essegian, Chas. Abraham	OF1	4	+.333	xBalt	Clev
1	0	Fischer, Wm. Chas.	P	15	+.000	xDet	
0	0	Giel, Paul Robert	P	1	+.000	xMinn	C
		Hankins, Jay Nelson	OF65	76	.185	A	
3	6	Herbert, Raymond Ernest	P	13	+.107	B	Chi
		Howser, Richard Dalton	SS157	158	.280	A	
		Johnson, Deron Roger	OF59	83	+.216	xN.Y.	
		(1B3 3B19)					
0	4	Johnson, Kenneth Travis	P	6	.000	B	CinN
		Johnson, Stanley Lucius	OF2	3	.000	Chi	C
0	0	Keegan, Edward Chas.	P	6	.000	PhilN59	
0	0	Kirk, Wm. Partlemore	P	1	.000	A	C
		Klimchock, Louis Stephen	1B11	57	.215	B	
		(2B1 3B6 OF7)					
2	5	Krausse, Lewis Bernard Jr.	P12	13	.118	A	C
3	4	Kunkel, Wm. Gustave James	P	58	.125	A	
1	0	Larsen, Donald James	P8	18	+.300	B	Chi
		(OF1)					
		Lumpe, Jerry Dean	2B147	148	.293	B	
		MacKenzie, Henry Gordon	C7	11	.125	A	C
0	0	McDermott, Maurice Joseph	P4	7	.200	xStLN	C
5	8	Nuxhall, Joseph Henry	P37	56	.292	CinN	
0	0	Pfister, Daniel Albin	P	2	.000	A	
		Pignatano, Joseph Benjamin	C83	92	.243	LAN	
		(3B2)					
		Pilarcik, Alfred James	OF21	35	+.200	Balt	Chi
		Posada, Leopoldo Hernandez	OF102	116	.253	B	
		Prescott, George Bertrand	OF2	10	.083	A	C
2	8	Rakow, Edward Chas.	P	45	.103	LAN	
		Rivera, Manuel Joseph	OF43	64	+.241	xChi	C
9	10	Shaw, Robert John	P26	28	+.200	xChi	
		Shoemaker, Chas. Landis	2B6	7	.385	A	
		Siebern, Norman Leroy	1B109	153	.296	B	
		(OF47)					
1	1	Staley, Gerald Lee	P	23	+.000	xChi	Det
		Stephens, Glen Eugene	OF54	62	+.208	xBalt	
		Sullivan, Haywood Cooper	C88	117	.242	Bos	
		(1B16 OF5)					
		Throneberry, Marvin Eugene	1B30	40	+.238	B	Balt
		(OF10)					
		Tuttle, Wm. Robert	OF	25	+.262	B	Minn
		Virgil, Osvaldo Jose	3B4	11	+.143	xDet	
		(C3)					
8	14	Walker, Jerry Allen	P36	45	.250	Balt	
2	1	Wickersham, David Clifford	P	17	.667	B	
0	0	Wyatt, John Thomas	P	5	.000	A	

WON 72 AMERICAN LEAGUE FINISHED 9th.
LOST 90
TG 162 1962. PCT. .444

KANSAS CITY

HENRY ALBERT BAUER

WON	LOST	NAME	POS.	G.	BA	FROM	TO
		Alusik, George Joseph	OF50	90	+.273	xDet	
		(1B1)					
0	1	Archer, James Wm.	P	10	1.000	B	C
		Azcue, Jose Joaquin	C70	72	.229	CinN60	
2	6	Bass, Norman Delaney	P	22	.045	B	
		Bryan, Billy Ronald	C22	25	.149	B	
		Causey, James Wayne	SS51	117	.252	B	
		(2B9 3B26)					
		Charles, Edwin Douglas	3B140	147	.288	A	
		(2B2)					
		Cimoli, Gino Nicholas	OF147	152	.275	MilN	
		Consolo, Wm. Angelo	SS48	54	+.240	xL.A.	C
		Coughtry, James Marlan	3B3	6	+.182	xL.A.	Clev
		DelGreco, Robert George	OF124	132	.254	B	
0	2	Ditmar, Arthur John	P	6	.167	B	C
1	1	Drabowsky, Myron Walter	P	10	.167	xCinN	
4	12	Fischer, Wm. Chas.	P	34	.105	B	
1	1	Giggie, Robert Thomas	P	4	.000	KC60	C
0	1	Grim, Robert Anton	P	12	.000	StLN60	C
0	1	Hamner, Granville Wilbur	P	3	.000	Clev59	C
		Howser, Richard Dalton	SS72	83	.238	B	
		Jiminez, Manuel Emilio	OF122	139	.301	A	
		Johnson, Deron Roger	1B2	17	.105	B	C
		(3B2 OF2)					
3	2	Jones, Gordon Bassett	P	21	.000	Balt	C

WON	LOST	NAME	POS.	G.	BA	FROM	TO
		Kern, Wm. George	OF3	8	.250	A	C
0	0	Kunkel, Wm. Gustave James	P	9	.000	B	
		Lumpe, Jerry Dean	2B156	156	.301	B	
		(SS2)					
		Martinez, Hector		1	.000	A	
0	3	McDevitt, Daniel Eugene	P	33	.222	Minn	C
0	0	Norman, Fred Hubert	P	2	.000	A	
0	0	Osinski, Daniel	P	4	+.000	A	L.A.
6	4	Pena, Orlando Guevara	P	13	.161	CinN60	
4	14	Pfister, Daniel Albin	P41	52	.185	B	
		Posada, Leopoldo Hernandez	OF11	29	.196	B	C
14	17	Rakow, Edward Chas.	P	42	.098	B	
8	5	Segui, Diego Pablo	P	37	.235	A	
		Shoemaker, Chas. Landis	2B4	5	.182	B	C
		Siebern, Norman Leroy	1B	162	.308	B	
		Stephens, Glen Eugene		5	.000	B	
		Sullivan, Haywood Cooper	C94	95	.248	B	
		(1B1)					
		Tartabull, Jose	OF85	107	.277	A	
0	0	Toppin, Ruperto	P	2	1.000	A	C
8	9	Walker, Jerry Allen	P31	36	.263	B	
11	4	Wickersham, David Clifford	P	30	.057	B	
0	0	Williams, Donald Fred	P	3	.000	PittN59	
		Windhorn, Gordon Ray	OF7	14	+.158	LAN	L.A.
		Wojcik, John Joseph	OF12	16	.302	A	
10	7	Wyatt, John Thomas	P	59	.103	B	

WON 73 — AMERICAN LEAGUE — FINISHED 8th.
LOST 89
TG 162 — 1963. — PCT. .451

KANSAS CITY

EDMUND WALTER LOPAT

WON	LOST	NAME	POS.	G.	BA	FROM	TO
		Alusik, George Joseph	OF63	87	.267	B	
		Azcue, Jose Joaquin	C1	2	+.000	B	Clev
0	0	Bass, Norman Delaney	P	3	.000	B	C
5	7	Bowsfield, Edward Oliver	P41	43	.043	L.A.	
		Bryan, Billy Ronald	C	24	.169	B	
		Causey, James Wayne	SS135	139	.280	B	
		(3B2)					
		Charles, Edwin Douglas	3B	158	.267	B	
		Cimoli, Gino Nicholas	OF136	145	.263	B	
		Del Greco, Robert George	OF110	121	.212	B	
		(3B2)					
7	13	Drabowsky, Myron Walter	P	26	.161	B	
		Edwards, Howard Rodney	C63	71	+.250	xClev	
		Esposito, Samuel	2B7	18	+.200	xChic.	C
		(SS4 3B3)					
		Essegian, Chas. Abraham	OF53	101	.225	Clev	C
9	6	Fischer, Wm. Chas.	P	45	.067	B	
		Green, Richard Larry	SS6	13	.270	A	
		(2B4)					

WON	LOST	NAME	POS.	G.	BA	FROM	TO
		Harrelson, Kenneth Smith	1B34	79	.230	A	
		(OF28)					
		Hankins, Jay Nelson	OF9	10	.176	KC61	C
		Howser, Richard Dalton	SS10	15	+.195	B	Clev
		Jiminez, Manuel Emilio	OF40	60	.280	B	
0	0	Landis, Wm. Henry	P	1	.000	A	
		La Russa, Anthony	SS14	34	.250	A	
		(2B3)					
		Lau, Chas. Richard	C50	62	+.294	xBalt	
1	1	Lovrich, Peter	P	20	.000	A	C
		Lumpe, Jerry Dean	2B155	157	.271	B	
		Martinez, Hector	OF3	6	.286	B	C
0	0	Monteagudo, Aurelio Fautino	P	4	.000	A	
0	1	Norman, Fred Hubert	P	2	.000	B	
0	1	O'Donoghue, John Eugene	P	1	.000	A	
12	20	Pena, Orlando Guevara	P	35	.145	B	
1	0	Pfister, Daniel Albin	P3	4	.000	B	
9	10	Rakow, Edward Chas.	P	34	.105	B	
		Reynolds, Thomas D.	OF5	8	.053	A	
1	0	Santiago, Jose Rafael	P	4	.000	A	
9	6	Segui, Diego Pablo	P	38	.218	B	
		Siebern, Norman Leroy	1B131	152	.272	B	
		(OF16)					
1	2	Sturdivant, Thomas Virgil	P	17	+.000	xDet	
		Sullivan, Haywood Cooper	C37	40	.212	B	
		Tartabull, Jose	OF71	79	.240	B	
0	1	Thies, David Robert	P	9	.333	A	C
12	15	Wickersham, David Clifford	P	38	.138	B	
0	2	Willis, Dale Jerome	P25	26	.167	A	C
		Wojcik, John Joseph	OF17	19	.186	B	
6	4	Wyatt, John Thomas	P	63	.000	B	

WON 57 — AMERICAN LEAGUE — FINISHED 10th (LAST)
LOST 105
TG 162 — 1964. — PCT. .352

KANSAS CITY

EDMUND WALTER LOPAT FRED MELVIN McGAHA

WON	LOST	NAME	POS.	G.	BA	FROM	TO
0	1	Aker, Jack Delane	P9	10	.000	A	
		Alusik, George Joseph	OF44	102	.240	B	C
		(1B12)					
4	7	Bowsfield, Edward Oliver	P50	52	.095	B	C
		Bryan, Billy Ronald	C65	93	.241	B	
		Campaneris, Dagoberto Blanco	SS38	67	.257	A	
		(3B6 OF27)					
		Causey, James Wayne	SS131	157	.281	B	
		(2B17 3B9)					
		Charles, Edwin Douglas	3B147	150	.241	B	
		Cimoli, Gino Nicholas	OF	4	+.000	B	Balt
		Colavito, Rocco Domenico	OF159	160	.274	Det	
5	13	Drabowsky, Myron Walter	P53	54	.023	B	
		Duncan, David Edwin	C22	25	.170	A	

W	L	Name	Pos	G	Avg		
		Edwards, Howard Rodney (1B7)	C79	97	.224	B	
		Gentile, James Edward	1B128	136	.251	Balt	
		Green, Richard Larry	2B120	130	.264	B	
0	2	Grzenda, Joseph Chas.	P	20	.000	Det61	
0	1	Handrahan, James Vernon	P	18	.222	A	
		Harrelson, Kenneth Smith (1B15)	OF24	49	.194	B	
		Jiminez, Manuel Emilio	OF49	95	.225	B	
		Joseph, Ricardo Emelimo (3B3)	1B12	17	.222	A	
0	2	Krausse, Lewis Bernard Jr.	P5	8	.000	KC61	
		Lau, Chas. Richard	C35	43	+.271	B	Balt
		Mathews, Nelson Elmer	OF154	157	.239	ChicN	
1	4	Meyer, Robert Bernard	P9	12	+.000	xL.A.	
0	4	Monteagudo, Aurelio Fautino	P	11	.286	B	
1	2	Odom, John Lee	P	5	.000	A	
10	14	O'Donoghue, John Eugene	P39	40	.236	B	
12	14	Pena, Orlando Guevara	P40	42	.160	B	
1	5	Pfister, Daniel Albin	P19	20	.000	B	C
		Reynolds, Thomas D. (3B8)	OF25	31	.202	B	
0	2	Sanders, Kenneth George	P	21	.000	A	
0	6	Santiago, Jose Rafael	P	34	.000	B	
8	17	Segui, Diego Pablo	P	40	.155	B	
		Shoemaker, Chas. Landis	2B14	16	.212	KC62	C
		Stahl, Lawrence Floyd	OF10	15	.261	A	
6	3	Stock, Wesley Gay	P	50	+.200	xBalt	
0	0	Sturdivant, Thomas Virgil	P	3	1.000	B	NYN
		Tartabull, Jose	OF59	104	.200	B	
		Williams, George (SS2 3B2 OF2)	2B20	37	.209	HousN62	C
		Wojcik, John Joseph	OF	6	.136	B	C
9	8	Wyatt, John Thomas	P	81	.000	B	

CLUB RECORD

AMERICAN LEAGUE

LOS ANGELES

YEAR	TG	WON	LOST	PCT.	FINISHED	MANAGER
1961	161	70	91	.435	8	Wm. Joseph Rigney
1962	162	86	76	.531	3	Wm. Joseph Rigney
1963	161	70	91	.435	9	Wm. Joseph Rigney
1964	162	82	80	.506	5	Wm. Joseph Rigney

Club transferred to Anaheim after 1964 season, name changed to California

CALIFORNIA

YEAR	TG	WON	LOST	TIED	PCT.	FINISHED	MANAGER
1965	162	75	87	0	.463	7	WILLIAM JOSEPH RIGNEY
1966	162	80	82	0	.494	6	WILLIAM JOSEPH RIGNEY
1967	161	84	77	0	.522	5	WILLIAM JOSEPH RIGNEY
1968	162	67	95	0	.414	X8 (CHI)	WILLIAM JOSEPH RIGNEY
1969	163	71	91	1	.438	3W	WILLIAM JOSEPH RIGNEY HAROLD ROSS PHILLIPS
1970	162	86	76	0	.531	3W	HAROLD ROSS PHILLIPS
1971	162	76	86	0	.469	4W	HAROLD ROSS PHILLIPS
1972	155	75	80	0	.484	5W	DELBERT W. RICE

WON 70 | LOST 91 | TG 161

AMERICAN LEAGUE 1961. FINISHED 8th. PCT. .435

LOS ANGELES

WM. JOSEPH RIGNEY

WON	LOST	NAME	POS.	G.	BA	FROM	TO
		Ardell, Daniel Miers	1B1	7	.250	A	C
		Aspromonte, Kenneth Joseph	2B62	66	+.223	Clev	Clev
		Averill, Earl Douglas (2B1 OF9)	C88	115	.266	Chi	
		Becquer, Julio Vellegas	1B5	11	+.000	Wash	Minn
		Bilko, Stephen Thomas (OF3)	1B86	114	.279	Det	
11	8	Bowsfield, Edward Oliver	P41	46	.137	Clev	
		Brickell, Fritz Darrell	SS17	21	.122	NY59	C
		Bridges, Everett Lamar (SS25 3B4)	2B58	84	.240	StLN	C
		Burke, Leo Patrick		6	.000	Balt59	
1	5	Casale, Jerry Joseph	P	13	+.462	Bos	Det
		Cerv, Robert Henry	OF15	18	+.158	N.Y.	N.Y.
0	2	Chance, Wilmer Dean	P	5	.000	A	
2	1	Clevenger, Truman Eugene	P	12	+.000	Wash	N.Y.
4	6	Donohue, James Thomas	P	38	+.148	xDet	
6	12	Duren, Rinold George	P	40	+.040	xN.Y.	
5	8	Fowler, John Arthur	P	53	.077	LAN59	
		Fregosi, James Louis	SS	11	.222	A	
0	3	Garver, Ned Franklin	P	12	.000	K.C.	C
11	13	Grba, Eli	P40	42	.234	N.Y.	
		Hamlin, Kenneth Leo	SS39	42	.209	K.C.	
0	0	Heman, Russell Frederick	P	6	+.000	xClev	C
		Hunt, Kenneth Lawrence (2B1)	OF134	149	.255	N.Y.	
0	2	James, John Phillip	P36	43	+.000	xN.Y.	C
		Johnson, Louis Brown	OF	1	.000	Chi	
3	6	Kline, Ronald Lee	P	26	+.097	StLN	Det
		Kluszewski, Theodore Bernard	1B66	107	.243	Chi	C
		Koppe, Joseph (2B3 3B1)	SS88	91	.251	xPhilN	
		Leek, Eugene Harold (SS7 OF1)	3B49	57	.226	Clev59	
12	15	McBride, Kenneth Faye	P38	45	.084	Chi	
4	8	Moeller, Ronald Ralph	P33	35	.207	Balt58	
		Moran, Wm. Nelson (SS2)	2B51	54	.260	Clev59	
8	2	Morgan, Tom Sephen	P	59	.083	Wash	
		Pearson, Albert Gregory	OF113	144	.288	Balt	
		Rice, Delbert W.	C30	44	.241	Balt	C
		Rodgers, Robert Leroy	C14	16	.321	A	
		Sadowski, Edward Roman	C56	69	.232	Bos	
		Satriano, Thomas Victor (2B10 SS1)	3B23	35	.198	A	
0	0	Semproch, Roman Anthony	P	2	.000	Det	C
3	0	Spring, Jack Russell	P	18	.000	Wash58	
0	0	Sprout, Robert Samuel	P	1	.000	A	C
		Tanner, Chas. Wm.	OF1	7	.125	Clev	
		Thomas, George Edward (3B38)	OF45	79	+.280	xDet	
		Thomas, James Leroy (1B34)	OF86	130	+.284	xN.Y.	
		Throneberry, Maynard Faye	OF5	24	.194	Wash	
		Wagner, Leon Lamar	OF116	133	.280	StLN	
		Yost, Edward Frederick	3B67	76	.202	Det	

WON 86 | LOST 76 | TG 162

AMERICAN LEAGUE 1962. FINISHED 3rd. PCT. .531

LOS ANGELES

WM. JOSEPH RIGNEY

WON	LOST	NAME	POS.	G.	BA	FROM	TO
		Averill, Earl Douglas (C6)	OF49	92	.219	B	
10	11	Belinsky, Robert	P33	34	.167	A	
		Bilko, Stephen Thomas	1B50	64	.287	B	C
2	1	Botz, Robert Allen	P	35	.000	A	C
9	8	Bowsfield, Edward Oliver	P34	44	.162	B	
		Burgess, Thomas Roland (OF2)	1B35	87	.196	StLN54	C
		Burke, Leo Patrick (SS1 3B4)	OF12	19	.266	B	
14	10	Chance, Wilmer Dean	P	50	.062	B	
		Consolo, Wm. Angelo (2B1 SS4)	3B20	28	+.100	xPhilN	K.C.
		Coughtry, James Marlan (2B2)	3B5	11	+.182	Bos60	K.C.
0	1	Darwin, Arthur Bobby Lee	P	1	.000	A	
1	0	Donohue, James Thomas	P	12	+.250	B	Minn
2	9	Duren, Rinold George	P	42	.067	B	
4	3	Fowler, John Arthur	P	48	.273	B	
		Fregosi, James Louis	SS52	58	.291	B	
8	9	Grba, Eli	P40	42	.207	B	
		Hunt, Kenneth Lawrence	1B3	13	.182	B	
		Kirkpatrick, Edgar Leon	C1	3	.000	A	
		Koppe, Joseph (2B5 3B4)	SS118	128	.227	B	
8	8	Lee, Donald Edward	P	27	+.184	xMinn	
		Leek, Eugene Harold	3B4	7	.143	B	C
		Leja, Frank John	1B4	7	.000	NY55	C
11	5	McBride, Kenneth Faye	P	24	.164	B	
		Moran, Wm. Nelson	2B	160	.282		
5	2	Morgan, Tom Stephen	P	48	.000	B	
1	1	Navarro, Julio Ventura	P	9	.500	A	
0	1	Newman, Frederick W.	P	4	.000	A	
0	0	Nuxhall, Joseph Henry	P	5	.000	K.C.	CinN
6	4	Osinski, Daniel	P	33	+.000	xK.C.	
		Pearson, Albert Gregory	OF	160	.261	B	
		Rodgers, Robert Leroy	C150	155	.258	B	
		Sadowski, Edward Roman	C18	27	.200	B	
		Satriano, Thomas Victor	3B5	10	.421	B	

WON	LOST	NAME	POS.	G.	BA	FROM	TO
		Simpson, Richard Chas.	OF4	6	.250	A	C
4	2	Spring, Jack Russell	P	57	.091	B	
		Tanner, Chas. Wm.	OF2	7	.125	B	C
		Thomas, George Edward	OF51	56	.238	B	
		Thomas, James Leroy	1B90	160	.290	B	
		(OF74)					
		Torres, Felix	3B123	127	.259	A	
		Wagner, Leon Lamar	OF156	160	.268	B	
		Windhorn, Gordon Ray	OF27	40	+.178	xK.C.	C
1	1	Witt, George Adrian	P	5	.333	PittN̲	HousN̲
		Yost, Edward Frederick	3B28	52	.240	B	C
		Joseph (1B7)					

WON 70
LOST 91
TG 161

AMERICAN LEAGUE

FINISHED 9th.

1963.

PCT. .435

LOS ANGELES

WM. JOSEPH RIGNEY

WON	LOST	NAME	POS.	G.	BA	FROM	TO
2	9	Belinsky, Robert	P	13	.074	B	
13	18	Chance, Wilmer Dean	P	45	.150	B	
		Dees, Chas. Henry	1B56	60	.307	A	
1	1	Duliba, Robert John	P	6	.000	StLN̲	
		Foiles, Henry Lee	C30	41	.214	xCinN̲	
5	3	Fowler, John Arthur	P	57	.111	B	
5	5	Foytack, Paul Eugene	P25	26	+.267	xDet	
		Fregosi, James Louis	SS151	154	.287	B	
1	1	Gatewood, Aubrey Lee	P	4	.000	A	
1	2	Grba, Eli	P12	13	.000	B	C
		Hunt, Kenneth Lawrence	OF50	59	+.183	B	Wash
		Kirkpatrick, Edgar Leon	C14	34	.195	B	
		(OF10)					
		Koppe, Joseph	SS19	76	.210	B	
		(2B14 3B18 OF3)					
		Kostro, Frank Joseph	3B19	43	+.222	xDet	
		(1B5 OF3)					
8	11	Lee, Donald Edward	P	40	.156	B	
1	1	Lee, Michael R.	P	6	.000	Clev60	C
13	12	McBride, Kenneth Faye	P36	38	.172	B	
0	0	Moeller, Ronald Ralph	P	3	+.000	LA61	Wash
		Moran, Wm. Nelson	2B151	153	.275	B	
0	0	Morgan, Tom Stephen	P	13	.000	B	C
4	5	Navarro, Julio Ventura	P	57	.200	B	
2	3	Nelson, Melvin Frederick	P36	39	.091	A	
1	5	Newman, Frederick Wm.	P	12	.250	B	
8	8	Osinski, Daniel	P	47	.111	B	
		Pearson, Albert Gregory	OF148	154	.304	B	
		Perry, Melvin Gray	OF55	61	.253	A	
		Piersall, James Anthony	OF18	20	.308	xNYN̲	
		Rodgers, Robert Leroy	C85	100	.233	B	
		Sadowski, Edward Roman	C68	80	.172	B	
		Sadowski, Robert Frank	OF25	88	.250	Chic.	C
		(2B4 3B6)					

WON	LOST	NAME	POS.	G.	BA	FROM	TO
		Satriano, Thomas Victor	3B13	23	.180	B	
		(C2 1B1)					
3	0	Spring, Jack Russell	P	45	.333	B	
		Thomas, George Edward	OF39	53	+.210	B	Det
		(1B4 3B10)					
		Thomas, James LeRoy	1B104	149	.220	B	
		(OF43)					
		Torres, Felix	3B122	138	.261	B	
		(1B2)					
2	7	Turley, Robert Lee	P	19	+.160	N.Y.	Bos
		Wagner, Leon Lamar	OF141	149	.291	B	

WON 82
LOST 80
TG 162

AMERICAN LEAGUE

FINISHED 5th.

1964.

PCT. .506

LOS ANGELES

WM. JOSEPH RIGNEY

WON	LOST	NAME	POS.	G.	BA	FROM	TO
		Adcock, Joseph Wilbur	1B105	118	.268	Clev	
9	8	Belinsky, Robert	P	23	.095	B	
2	2	Brunet, George Stuart	P	10	.182	Balt	
20	9	Chance, Wilmer Dean	P	46	.079	B	
		Clinton, Luciean Louis	OF81	91	+.248	xBos	
		Dees, Chas. Henry	1B12	26	.077	B	
6	4	Duliba, Robert John	P	58	.000	B	
		Foiles, Henry Lee		4	.250	B	C
0	2	Fowler, John Arthur	P	4	.000	B	C
0	1	Foytack, Paul Eugene	P	2	.000	B	C
		Fregosi, James Louis	SS137	147	.277	B	
3	3	Gatewood, Aubrey Lee	P15	23	.100	B	
		Green, Leonard Chas.	OF23	29	+.250	xMinn	Balt
		Hiatt, Jack E. (1B2)	C3	9	.375	A	
2	0	Kelso, Wm. Eugene	P	10	.000	A	
		Kirkpatrick, Edgar Leon	OF63	75	.242	B	
		Knoop, Robert Frank	2B161	162	.216	A	
		Koppe, Joseph	SS31	54	.257	B	
		(2B13 3B3)					
6	10	Latman, Arnold Barry	P	40	.125	Clev	
5	4	Lee, Donald Edward	P	33	.261	B	
6	5	Lee, Robert Dean	P	64	.000	A	
4	13	McBride, Kenneth Faye	P	29	.214	B	
1	1	Meyer, Robert Bernard	P	6	+.000	xN.Y.	K.C.
		Moran, Wm. Nelson	3B47	50	+.268	B	Clev
		(2B3 SS1)					
0	0	Navarro, Julio Ventura	P	5	+.000	B	Det
13	10	Newman, Frederick Wm.	P32	39	.180	B	
3	3	Osinski, Daniel	P	47	.056	B	
		Pearson, Albert Gregory	OF66	107	.223	B	
		Perry, Melvin Gray	OF62	70	.276	B	C
		Piersall, James Anthony	OF72	87	.314	B	
		Power, Victor Pellott	1B48	68	+.249	xMinn	PhilaN̲
		(2B5 3B28)					
		Reichardt, Frederic Carl	OF	11	.162	A	

		Rodgers, Robert Leroy	C146	148	.243	B	
		Satriano, Thomas Victor (C25 1B32 2B1 SS2)	3B38	108	.200	B	
		Schaal, Paul (3B9)	2B9	17	.125	A	
		Simpson, Richard Chas.	OF16	21	.140	LA62	
1	4	Smith, Willie P. (P15)	OF87	118	.301	Det	
1	0	Spring, Jack Russell	P	6	.000	B	ChicN
0	1	Sukla, Edward Anthony	P	2	.000	A	
		Thomas, James LeRoy (1B1)	OF47	47	+.273	B	Bos
		Torres, Felix (1B3)	3B72	100	.231	B	C

CLUB RECORD

AMERICAN LEAGUE

MILWAUKEE

YEAR	TG	WON	LOST	PCT.	FINISHED	MANAGER
1900	137	79	58	.577	2	Connie Mack
1901	137	48	89	.350	8(Last)	Hugh Duffy

YEAR	TG	WON	LOST	TIED	PCT.	FINISHED	MANAGER
1970	163	65	97	1	.401	X4W (KC)	JAMES DAVID BRISTOL
1971	161	69	92	0	.429	6W (LAST)	JAMES DAVID BRISTOL
1972	156	65	91	0	.417	6W (LAST)	JAMES DAVID BRISTOL
							ROY DAVID MC MILLAN *
							DELMAR WESLEY CRANDALL

WON 79
LOST 58
TG 137

AMERICAN LEAGUE — 1900. — FINISHED 2nd. — PCT. .577

MILWAUKEE

CONNIE MACK

WON	LOST	NAME	POS.	G.	BA	FROM	TO
		Abbaticchio, Edward James (1B1)	2B13	16	+.180	xMinn	
		Anderson, John Joseph (OF44)	1B90	134	.309	BknN	
		Bierbauer, Louis W.	2B	45	+.183	xClev	Buff
		Burke, James Timothy	3B	127	.245	ClevN98	
		Carey, Thomas	OF78	79	.246	A	C
		Clark, Harry	1B	19	.263	A	
		Conroy, Wm. Edward (Wid)	SS89	116	.234	A	
		Diggins, Wm. L. (1B13)	C50	63	+.297	xClev	C
		Dowd, Thomas Jefferson (1B14)	OF48	62	+.278	xChi	
16	19	Dowling, Henry Peter	P37	38	.267	LvlleN	
		Fultz, David Lewis (SS49)	2B57	114	.298	BaltN	
		Garry, James Thomas	OF	60	+.264	BosN93	Buff
		Hallman, Wm. Harry	OF	29	.219	A	
4	1	Husting, Berthold Juneau	P	5	.118	A	PittN
		Ketcham, Frederick L.	OF	73	.231	LvlleN	
		O'Rourke,	SS	1	.000	A	C
		Raymer, Frederick Chas.	2B	1	.000	A	
19	9	Reidy, Wm. Joseph	P	32	.212	BknN	
		Reitz, Henry P.	2B	8	.370	PittN	C
7	11	Rettger, George Edward	P23	29	.207	CinN92	C
		Smith, Harry Thomas	C79	80	.260	A	
16	12	Sparks, Tu lly Frank	P	34	.231	PittN	
		Spies, Henry	C	17	+.317	xClev	C
10	3	Waddell, George Edward (Rube)	P	15	.244	xPittN (returned)	PittN
		Waldron, Irving	OF	139	.293	A	
7	3	Wheeler, George L.	P	16	.173	PhilN	C
		Yeager, George E.	C16	25	.387	BosN	

WON 48
LOST 89
TG 137

AMERICAN LEAGUE — 1901. — FINISHED 8th (LAST) — PCT. .350

MILWAUKEE

HUGH DUFFY

WON	LOST	NAME	POS.	G.	BA	FROM	TO
		Anderson, John Joseph	1B125	138	.339	B	
		Bone, George Drummond	SS	12	.292	A	C
		Bruyette, Edward	OF21	28	.180	A	C
		Burke, James Timothy	3B	64	+.207	B	Chi
		Connor, Joseph Francis (2B2 OF1)	C32	38	+.272	BosN	Clev
		Conroy, Wm. Edward (Wid)	SS	131	.269	B	
		Donahue, John Augustus (Jiggs)	C21	37	.305	xPittN	
3	5	Dowling, Henry Peter	P	10	+.182	B	Clev
		Duffy, Hugh MGR.	OF	78	.308	BosN	
		Friel, Wm. Edward (OF28)	3B61	106	.271	A	
8	21	Garvin, Virgil Lee	P	37	.107	ChiN	
		Geier, Philip Louis	OF	10	+.184	xPhil	
		Gertenrich, Louis Wilhelm	OF	2	.333	A	
		Gilbert, Wm. Oliver	2B	127	.269	A	
		Hallman, Wm. Harry	OF	139	.256	B	
7	13	Hawley, Emerson P. (Pink)	P24	28	.289	NYN	C
		Hogriever, George C.	OF	54	.243	Inpls	C
9	15	Husting, Berthold Juneau	P	35	.171	PittN	
		Jones, David Jefferson	OF	14	.169	A	
		King, Frederick	C	1	.500	A	C
		Leahy, Thomas Joseph	C	33	+.240	WashN98	Phil
		Maloney, Wm. Alphonse	C75	84	.297	A	
		McBride, George Florian	SS	1	.250	A	
15	18	Reidy, Wm. Joseph	P	36	.129	B	
6	17	Sparks, Tully Frank	P	30	.191	B	
		Waldron, Irving	OF	62	+.288	B	Wash

CLUB RECORD

MINNEAPOLIS

YEAR	TG	WON	LOST	TIED	PCT.	FINISHED	MANAGER
AMERICAN LEAGUE							
1900	139	53	86		.381	8(Last)	Walter R. Wilmot
MINNESOTA							
1961	160	70	90		.438	7	Harry Arthur Lavagetto Sabath Anthony Mele
1962	162	91	71		.562	2	Sabath Anthony Mele
1963	161	91	70		.565	3	Sabath Anthony Mele
1964	162	79	83		.488	x6(Cleve)	Sabath Anthony Mele
1965	162	102	60	0	.630	1	SABATH ANTHONY MELE
1966	162	89	73	0	.549	2	SABATH ANTHONY MELE
1967	164	91	71	2	.562	X2 (DET)	SABATH ANTHONY MELE CALVIN COOLIDGE ERMER
1968	162	79	83	0	.488	7	CALVIN COOLIDGE ERMER
1969	162	97	65	0	.599	1W (LP)	ALFRED MANUEL MARTIN
1970	162	98	64	0	.605	1W (LP)	WILLIAM JOSEPH RIGNEY
1971	160	74	86	0	.462	5W	WILLIAM JOSEPH RIGNEY
1972	154	77	77	0	.500	3W	WILLIAM JOSEPH RIGNEY FRANK RALPH QUILICI

WON 53
LOST 86
TG 139

AMERICAN LEAGUE

1900.

FINISHED 8th (LAST)

PCT. .381

MINNEAPOLIS

WALTER R. WILMOT

WON	LOST	NAME	POS.	G.	BA	FROM	TO
		Abbaticchio, Edward James	2B	101	+.238	PhilN98	Mil
14	11	Bailey, Harvey Francis	P	28	.253	xBosN	C
1	4	Bandeline, J. Oscar (P5)	OF16	22	.258	A	C
		Burke, Edward D.	OF	6	+.348	xChi	Buff
		Burns, John Thomas	OF	5	.237	A	C
		Campbell,	3B	2	.375	A	C
0	0	Corbett, Joseph	P	1	.000	BaltN97	
		Davis, Alfonzo DeFord	OF	101	.282	A	
		Dixon, Edward J.	C	16	.250	A	C
12	23	Ehret, Philip Sydney (Red)	P39	44	.252	LvlleN98	C
		Fisher, Newton	C114	118	.211	PhilN98	C
		Grim, John Helm (Jack)	1B	14	.318	BknN	C
7	14	Harvey, Erwin K. (P22)	OF26	51	.300	xChiN (returned)	ChiN
3	6	Hastings, Chas. Morton	P	12	+.219	PittN98	Buff
		Higgins, Daniel	2B	11	.175	A	C
		Jacklitsch, Frederick Lawrence	C25	32	.183	xPhilN (returned)	PhilN
		Krouse, Wm.	2B	9	.193	A	
		Lally, Daniel J.	OF127	128	+.264	xChi	C
		McAndrews, David Carr	3B	8	.093	A	C
4	13	McCann, Henry Eugene (Mike)	P23	24	.197	A	
		Nance, Wm. G.	3B	129	.268	LvlleN98	
		Nichols, Arthur Francis	2B23	44	.254	xChicN	ChicN
12	15	Parker, Harley Park (Dr)	P30	32	.237	ChiN96	
		Schrall, Joseph E.	OF	8	.167	A	C
		Smith, George J. (Germany)	SS	129	.258	StLN98	C
		Werden, Percival Wheritt (Perry)	1B	127	.316	LvlleN97	C
		Wilmot, Walter R. MGR.	OF	129	.267	NYN98	C

WON	70	AMERICAN LEAGUE	FINISHED 7th.
LOST	90		
TG	160	1961.	PCT. .438

MINNESOTA

HARRY ARTHUR LAVAGETTO SABATH ANTHONY MELE

WON	LOST	NAME	POS.	G.	BA	FROM	TO
		Allison, Wm. Robert (1B18)	OF150	159	.245	Wash	
		Altobelli, Joseph (1B2)	OF25	41	.221	Clev57	C
0	1	Arrigo, Gerald Wm.	P	7	.500	A	
		Battey, Earl Jesse	C131	133	.302	Wash	
0	0	Bacquer, Julio Vellegas (P1 OF5)	1B18	57	+.238	xL.A.	
		Bertoia, Reno Peter	3B32	35	+.212	Wash	K.C.
0	0	Bruckbauer, Frederick John	P	1	.000	A	C
		Consolo, Wm. Angelo (SS3 3B1)	2B3	11	.000	Wash	
1	3	Cueto, Dagoberto Concepcion	P	7	.000	A	C
		Dobbek, Daniel John	OF48	72	.168	Wash	C
0	0	Dotter, Gary Richard	P	2	.000	A	
		Gardner, Wm. Frederick (3B2)	2B41	45	+.234	Wash	N.Y.
1	0	Giel, Paul Robert	P12	15	+.500	Pitt	K.C.
		Green, Leonard Chas.	OF153	156	.285	Wash	
		Henry, Ronald Baxter (1B1)	C5	20	.143	A	C
		Jacobs, Lamar Gary	OF3	4	.250	Wash	C
9	17	Kaat, James Lee	P36	47	.238	Wash	
		Killebrew, Harmon Clayton (3B45 OF2)	1B119	150	.288	Wash	
13	11	Kralick, John Francis	P	33	.151	Wash	
3	6	Lee, Donald Edward	P	37	.067	Wash	
		Lemon, James Robert	OF120	129	.258	Wash	
		Lepcio, Thaddeus Stanley (2B22 SS6)	3B35	47	+.170	xChi	C
		Martin, Alfred Manuel (SS1)	2B105	108	.246	xMilN	C
1	0	McDevitt, Daniel Eugene	P	16	+.000	xN.Y.	
		Mincher, Donald Ray	1B29	35	.188	Wash	
4	4	Moore, Raymond LeRoy	P	46	.000	Wash	
		Naragon, Harold Richard	C36	57	.302	Wash	
1	1	Palmquist, Edwin Lee	P	9	.000	xLAN	C
15	16	Pascual, Camilo Alberto	P	35	.165	Wash	
4	2	Pleis, Wm.	P	37	.111	A	
11	20	Ramos, Pedro	P42	53	.172	Wash	
		Rollins, Richard John (3B4)	2B5	13	.294	A	
0	2	Sadowski, Theodore	P	15	.000	Wash	
4	4	Schroll, Albert Bringhurst	P	11	.278	ChiN	C
		Snyder, James Robert	2B	3	.100	A	
1	0	Stange, Albert Lee	P	7	.000	A	
2	3	Stobbs, Chas. Klein	P	24	.375	Wash	C
		Tuttle, Wm. Robert (2B2 OF64)	3B85	113	+.246	xK.C.	
		Valdivielso, Jose Lopez (2B15 3B14)	SS43	76	.195	Wash	C
		Versalles, Zoilo	SS	129	.280	Wash	
		Whisenant, Thomas Peter	OF5	10	.000	Wash	CinN
		Valo, Elmer Wm.	OF1	33	.156	Wash	PhiN

WON	91	AMERICAN LEAGUE	FINISHED 2nd.
LOST	71		
TG	162	1962.	PCT. .562

MINNESOTA

SABATH ANTHONY MELE

WON	LOST	NAME	POS.	G.	BA	FROM	TO
		Allen, Bernard Keith	2B158	159	.269	A	
		Allison, Wm. Robert	OF147	149	.266	B	
0	0	Arrigo, Gerald Wm.	P	1	.000	B	
		Banks, George Edward (3B6)	OF17	63	.252	A	
		Battey, Earl Jesse	C147	148	.280	B	
5	7	Bonikowski, Joseph Peter	P	30	.148	A	C
0	2	Collum, Jack Dean	P	8	+.000	LAN58	Clev
0	1	Donohue, James Thomas	P	6	+.000	xL.A.	C
1	1	Gomez, Ruben Colon	P	6	+.000	xClev	
		Goryl, John Albert (SS1)	2B4	37	.192	ChiN59	
		Green, Leonard Chas.	OF156	158	.271	B	
18	14	Kaat, James Lee	P39	48	.180	B	
		Killebrew, Harmon Clayton (1B4)	OF151	155	.243	B	
12	11	Kralick, John Francis	P	39	.202	B	
3	3	Lee, Donald Edward	P	9	+.211	B	L.A.
		Lemon, James Robert	OF3	12	.176	B	
0	0	Manning, James Benjamin	P	5	.000	A	C
1	3	Maranda, Georges Henri	P	32	.250	SFN60	C
		Martinez, Orlando (3B1)	SS11	37	.167	A	
		Mincher, Donald Ray	1B25	86	.240	B	
8	3	Moore, Raymond LeRoy	P	49	.000	B	
		Naragon, Harold Richard	C9	24	.229	B	C
		Oliva, Antonio Pedro	OF2	9	.444	A	
20	11	Pascual, Camilo Alberto	P	34	.268	B	
2	5	Pleis, Wm.	P	21	.286	B	
		Power, Victor Pellot (2B2)	1B142	144	.290	Clev	
0	0	Roland, James Ivan	P	1	.000	A	
		Rollins, Richard John (SS1)	3B159	159	.298	B	
1	1	Sadowski, Theodore	P	19	.500	B	C
		Snyder, James Robert (1B1)	2B5	12	.100	B	C
4	3	Stange, Albert Lee	P	44	.059	B	

WON	LOST	NAME	POS.	G.	BA	FROM	TO
12	5	Stigman, Richard Lewis	P	40	.044	Clev	
4	1	Sullivan, Franklin Leal	P	21	.000	xPhilN	
		Tuttle, Wm. Robert	OF104	110	.210	B	
		Versalles, Zoilo	SS	160	.241	B	
		Zimmerman, Gerald Robert	C	34	.274	CinN	

WON 91
LOST 70
TG 161

AMERICAN LEAGUE

1963.

FINISHED 3rd.

PCT. .565

MINNESOTA

SABATH ANTHONY MELE

WON	LOST	NAME	POS.	G.	BA	FROM	TO
		Allen, Bernard Keith	2B128	139	.240	B	
		Allison, Wm. Robert	OF147	148	.271	B	
1	2	Arrigo, Gerald Wm.	P	5	.000	B	
		Banks, George Edward	3B21	25	.155	B	
		Battey, Earl Jesse	C146	147	.285	B	
		Bacquer, Julio Villegas		1	.000	Minn61	C
6	3	Dailey, Wm. Garland	P	66	.238	Clev	
0	0	Dotter, Gary Richard	P	2	.000	Minn61	
1	1	Fornieles, Jose Miguel Torres	P	11	+.167	xBos	C
		Goryl, John Albert (SS7 3B11)	2B34	64	.287	B	
		Green, Leonard Chas.	OF119	145	.239	B	
		Hall, Jimmie Randolph	OF143	156	.260	A	
10	10	Kaat, James Lee	P31	36	.131	B	
		Killebrew, Harmon Clayton	OF137	142	.258	B	
1	4	Kralick, John Francis	P5	6	+.167	B	Clev
0	0	Lasher, Frederick Walter	P	11	.000	A	
		Lemon, James Robert	OF4	7	.118	B	PhilN
		Mincher, Donald Ray	1B60	82	.258	B	
1	3	Moore, Raymond LeRoy	P	31	.333	B	C
		Oliva, Antonio Pedro		7	.429	B	
21	9	Pascual, Camilo Alberto	P31	33	.250	B	
9	9	Perry, James Evan	P	35	+.216	xClev	
6	2	Pleis, Wm.	P	36	.125	B	
		Post, Walter Chas.	OF12	21	.191	xCinN	
		Power, Victor Pellott (2B18 3B5)	1B124	138	.270	B	
		Ratliff, Paul Hawthorne	C2	10	.190	A	
2	4	Roggenburk, Garry Earl	P	36	.143	A	
4	1	Roland, James Ivan	P	10	.000	B	
		Rollins, Richard John (2B1)	3B132	136	.307	B	
2	1	Siebler, Dwight Leroy	P	7	.133	A	
12	5	Stange, Albert Lee	P	32	.096	B	
15	15	Stigman, Richard Lewis	P	33	.107	B	
0	1	Sullivan, Franklin Leal	P	10	.000	B	C
		Tuttle, Wm.Robert	OF14	16	.000	B	C
		Versalles, Zoilo	SS	159	.261	B	
		Ward, John Francis (OF1)	3B4	9	.067	A	
		Wertz, Victor Woodrow	1B6	35	+.136	xDet	C
0	0	Williams, Donald Reid	P	3	.000	A	C
		Zimmerman, Gerald Robert	C	39	.232	B	

WON 79
LOST 83
TG 162

AMERICAN LEAGUE

1964.

FINISHED 6th.
(TIED WITH CLEVELAND)
PCT. .488

MINNESOTA

SABATH ANTHONY MELE

WON	LOST	NAME	POS.	G.	BA	FROM	TO
		Allen, Bernard Keith	2B71	74	.214	B	
		Allison, Wm. Robert (OF61)	1B93	149	.287	B	
7	4	Arrigo Gerald Wm.	P	41	.172	B	
		Battey, Earl Jesse	C125	131	.272	B	
		Banks, George Edward		1	+.000	B	Clev
		Bethea, Wm. Lamar (SS3)	2B7	10	.167	A	C
		Bloomfield, Clyde Stalcup (SS2)	2B3	7	.143	StLN	C
2	0	Boswell, David Wilson	P	4	.222	A	
1	2	Dailey, Wm. Garland	P	14	.000	B	C
0	0	Dotter, Gary Richard	P	3	.000	B	C
0	1	Fischer, Wm. Chas.	P	9	.000	K.C.	C
0	1	Fosnow, Gerald Eugene	P	7	.000	A	
		Goryl, John Albert (3B13)	2B28	58	.140	B	C
11	9	Grant, James Timothy	P26	39	+.167	xClev	
		Green, Leonard Chas.	OF7	26	+.000	B	L.A.
		Hall, Jimmie Randolph	OF137	149	.282	B	
		Henry, Ronald Baxter	C13	22	.122	Minn61	C
17	11	Kaat, James Lee	P36	46	.169	B	
		Killebrew, Harmon Clayton	OF157	158	.270	B	
		Kindall, Gerald Donald (1B1 SS7)	2B51	62	+.148	xClev	
0	4	Klippstein, John Calvin	P	33	.000	xPhilaN	
		Kostro, Frank Joseph (1B1 2B7 OF2)	3B12	59	.272	L.A.	
		McCabe, Joseph Robert	C12	14	.158	A	
		Mincher, Donald Ray	1B76	120	.237	B	
0	0	Nieson, Chas. Bassett	P	2	.000	A	C
		Nossek, Joseph Rudolph	OF2	7	.000	A	
		Oliva, Antonio Pedro	OF159	161	.323	B	
15	12	Pascual, Camilo Alberto	P	36	.181	B	
6	3	Perry, James Evan	P	42	.154	B	
4	1	Pleis, Wm.	P	47	.250	B	
		Power, Victor Pellott (2B1)	1B12	19	+.222	B	L.A.
		Reese, Richard Benjamin	1B1	10	.000	A	
2	6	Roland, James Ivan	P	30	.148	B	
		Rollins, Richard John	3B146	148	.270	B	
0	2	Shifflett, Garland Jessie	P	10	.000	Wash57	C
0	0	Siebler, Dwight Leroy	P	9	.000	B	
		Snyder, James Robert	2B25	26	.155	B	C
3	6	Stange, Albert Lee	P	14	+.040	B	Clev
6	15	Stigman, Richard Lewis	P	32	.101	B	
		Versalles, Zoilo	SS	160	.259	B	
		Ward, John Francis (OF3)	2B9	12	.226	B	
0	0	Whitby, Wm. Edward	P	4	.000	A	C
5	6	Worthington, Allan Fulton	P	41	.063	xCinN	
		Zimmerman, Gerald Robert	C	63	.200	B	

CLUB RECORD

AMERICAN LEAGUE

NEW YORK

YEAR	TG	WON	LOST	PCT.	FINISHED	MANAGER
1903	134	72	62	.537	4	Clark Calvin Griffith
1904	151	92	59	.609	2	Clark Calvin Griffith
1905	149	71	78	.477	6	Clark Calvin Griffith
1906	151	90	61	.596	2	Clark Calvin Griffith
1907	148	70	78	.473	5	Clark Calvin Griffith
1908	154	51	103	.331	8(Last)	Clark Calvin Griffith Norman Arthur Elberfeld
1909	151	74	77	.490	5	George Tweedy Stallings
1910	151	88	63	.583	2	George Tweedy Stallings Harold Homer Chase
1911	152	76	76	.500	6	Harold Homer Chase
1912	152	50	102	.329	8(Last)	Harry Sterling Wolverton
1913	151	57	94	.377	7	Frank LeRoy Chance
1914	154	70	84	.455	x6(Chi)	Frank LeRoy Chance Roger Thorpe Peckinpaugh
1915	152	69	83	.454	5	Wm. Edward Donovan
1916	154	80	74	.519	4	Wm. Edward Donovan
1917	153	71	82	.464	6	Wm. Edward Donovan
1918	123	60	63	.488	4	Miller James Huggins
1919	139	80	59	.576	3	Miller James Huggins
1920	154	95	59	.617	3	Miller James Huggins
1921	153	98	55	.641	1	Miller James Huggins
1922	154	94	60	.610	1	Miller James Huggins
1923	152	98	54	.645	1	Miller James Huggins
1924	152	89	63	.586	2	Miller James Huggins
1925	154	69	85	.448	7	Miller James Huggins
1926	154	91	63	.591	1	Miller James Huggins
1927	154	110	44	.714	1	Miller James Huggins
1928	154	101	53	.656	1	Miller James Huggins
1929	154	88	66	.571	2	Miller James Huggins Arthur Fletcher
1930	154	86	68	.558	3	James Robert Shawkey
1931	153	94	59	.614	2	Joseph Vincent McCarthy
1932	154	107	47	.695	1	Joseph Vincent McCarthy
1933	150	91	59	.607	2	Joseph Vincent McCarthy
1934	154	94	60	.610	2	Joseph Vincent McCarthy
1935	149	89	60	.597	2	Joseph Vincent McCarthy
1936	153	102	51	.667	1	Joseph Vincent McCarthy
1937	154	102	52	.662	1	Joseph Vincent McCarthy
1938	152	99	53	.651	1	Joseph Vincent McCarthy
1939	151	106	45	.702	1	Joseph Vincent McCarthy
1940	154	88	66	.571	3	Joseph Vincent McCarthy
1941	154	101	53	.656	1	Joseph Vincent McCarthy
1942	154	103	51	.669	1	Joseph Vincent McCarthy
1943	154	98	56	.636	1	Joseph Vincent McCarthy
1944	154	83	71	.539	3	Joseph Vincent McCarthy
1945	152	81	71	.533	4	Joseph Vincent McCarthy
1946	154	87	67	.565	3	Joseph Vincent McCarthy Wm. Malcolm Dickey John Henry Neun
1947	154	97	57	.630	1	Stanley Raymond Harris
1948	154	94	60	.610	3	Stanley Raymond Harris
1949	154	97	57	.630	1	Charles Dillon Stengel
1950	154	98	56	.636	1	Charles Dillon Stengel
1951	154	98	56	.636	1	Charles Dillon Stengel
1952	154	95	59	.617	1	Charles Dillon Stengel
1953	151	99	52	.656	1	Charles Dillon Stengel
1954	154	103	51	.669	2	Charles Dillon Stengel
1955	154	96	58	.623	1	Charles Dillon Stengel
1956	154	97	57	.630	1	Charles Dillon Stengel
1957	154	98	56	.636	1	Charles Dillon Stengel
1958	154	92	62	.597	1	Charles Dillon Stengel
1959	154	79	75	.513	3	Charles Dillon Stengel
1960	154	97	57	.630	1	Charles Dillon Stengel
1961	162	109	53	.673	1	Ralph George Houk
1962	162	96	66	.593	1	Ralph George Houk
1963	161	104	57	.646	1	Ralph George Houk
1964	162	99	63	.611	1	Lawrence Peter Berra

YEAR	TG	WON	LOST	TIED	PCT.	FINISHED	MANAGER
1965	162	77	85	0	.475	6	JOHN JOSEPH KEANE
1966	160	70	89	1	.440	10 (LAST)	JOHN JOSEPH KEANE RALPH GEORGE HOUK
1967	163	72	90	1	.444	9	RALPH GEORGE HOUK
1968	164	83	79	2	.512	5	RALPH GEORGE HOUK
1969	162	80	81	1	.497	5E	RALPH GEORGE HOUK
1970	163	93	69	1	.574	2E	RALPH GEORGE HOUK
1971	162	82	80	0	.506	4E	RALPH GEORGE HOUK
1972	155	79	76	0	.510	4E	RALPH GEORGE HOUK

WON 72 | LOST 62 | TG 134

AMERICAN LEAGUE 1903. FINISHED 4th. PCT. .537

NEW YORK

CLARK CALVIN GRIFFITH

WON	LOST	NAME	POS.	G.	BA	FROM	TO
0	1	Adkins, Merle Theron	P	2	.000	Bos	C
		Beville, Henry Monte	C77	82	.194	A	
1	0	Bliss, Elmer Ward	P	1	.000	A	
21	15	Chesbro, John Dwight (Jack)	P	40	.185	PittN	
		Conroy, Wm. Edward (Wid)	3B121	125	.277	PittN	
		Courtney, Ernest E.	SS23	25	+.241	Balt	Det
		Davis, Alfonzo DeFord	OF102	108	.245	PittN	
3	1	Derring, John Thomas	P	9	+.042	xDet	C
		Elberfeld, Norman Arthur (Kid)	SS	90	+.290	xDet	
		Fultz, David Lewis	OF76	78	.240	Phil	
		Ganzel, John Henry	1B	129	.285	NYN01	
		Greene, Patrick Joseph	3B	4	+.308	PhilN	Det
14	10	Griffith, Clark Calvin MGR.	P	25	.157	Chi	
		Holmes, Frederick	1B	1	.000	A	
10	7	Howell, Harry	P26	41	.229	Balt	
		Jordan, Timothy Joseph	1B	2	.125	Balt	
		Keeler, Wm. Henry	OF128	132	.318	BknN	
		Long, Herman C.	SS	22	+.225	BosN	Det
		McCauley, Patrick M.	C	6	.096	WashN96	C
		McFarland, Hermus W.	OF	103	.223	Balt	C
		O'Connor, John Joseph (Jack)	C	64	.197	PittN	
2	0	Puttman, Ambrose Nicholas	P	3	.143	A	
0	1	Quick, Edwin S.	P	1	.000	A	C
15	15	Tannehill, Jesse Niles	P32	39	.243	PittN	
		Williams, James Thomas Williams	2B	132	.281	Balt	
0	3	Wiltse, Lewis DeWitt	P	4	.222	Balt	C
6	9	Wolfe, Wm. O.	P	20	.074	A	
		Zalusky, John Francis	C	6	.267	A	C

WON 92 | LOST 59 | TG 151

AMERICAN LEAGUE 1904. FINISHED 2nd. PCT. .609

NEW YORK

CLARK CALVIN GRIFFITH

WON	LOST	NAME	POS.	G.	BA	FROM	TO
		Anderson, John Joseph (1B32)	OF110	143	.281	StL	
		Beville, Henry Monte (1B4)	C5	9	+.273	B	Det
0	0	Bliss, Elmer Ward	P	1	.000	B	C
41	13	Chesbro, John Dwight (Jack)	P	55	.233	B	
2	2	Clarkson, Walter Hamilton	P	13	.269	A	
		Collins, Orth Stein	OF	5	.352	A	
		Conroy, Wm. Edward (Wid) (SS24)	3B114	140	.249	B	
		Dougherty, Patrick Henry	OF	96	+.289	xBos	
		Elberfeld, Norman Arthur (Kid)	SS	122	.256	B	
		Fultz, David Lewis	OF90	96	.278	B	
		Ganzel, John Henry	1B118	129	.261	B	
0	1	Garvin, Virgil Lee	P	2	.250	xBknN	C
6	5	Griffith, Clark Calvin MGR.	P	16	.146	B	
7	11	Hughes, Thomas J.	P	23	+.444	Box	Wash
		Keeler, Wm. Henry	OF	143	.343	B	
		Kleinow, John Peter	C60	67	.200	A	
		McGuire, James Thomas	C97	100	.211	Det	
		McManus, Francis E.	C	4	+.000	xDet	C
11	5	Orth, Albert Lewis (OF6)	P18	24	+.365	xWash	
		O'Steen, James Champ	3B15	27	.202	Wash	
23	19	Powell, John Joseph	P	47	.170	StL	
2	0	Puttman, Ambrose Nicholas	P	10	.278	B	
		Thoney, John (OF11)	3B24	35	+.231	xWash	
		Unglaub, Robert Alexander	3B	6	+.211	A	Bos
		Williams, James Thomas Williams	2B	146	.259	B	
0	3	Wolfe, Wm. O.	P	7	+.000	B	Wash

WON 71 | LOST 78 | TG 149

AMERICAN LEAGUE 1905. FINISHED 6th. PCT. .477

NEW YORK

CLARK CALVIN GRIFFITH

WON	LOST	NAME	POS.	G.	BA	FROM	TO
		Anderson, John Joseph	OF	25	+.212	B	Wash
		Chase, Harold Homer (Hal)	1B122	126	.249	A	
20	13	Chesbro, John Dwight (Jack)	P	41	.188	B	
2	2	Clarkson, Walter Hamilton	P	8	.053	B	
		Cockman, James	3B	13	.076	A	C
		Connor, Joseph Francis (1B2)	C6	8	.271	Mil01	C
		Conroy, Wm. Edward (Wid) (SS18 OF21)	3B48	101	.273	B	
		Cooney, Philip	3B	1	.000	A	C
		Curtis, Frederick	1B	2	.222	A	C
		Delahanty, Frank George (1B3)	OF5	9	.240	A	
		Dougherty, Patrick Henry	OF111	116	.263	B	
		Doyle, John Joseph (Jack)	1B	1	.000	PhilN	C
		Elberfeld, Norman Arthur (Kid)	SS	108	.262	B	
		Fultz, David Lewis	OF	122	.232	B	C
0	0	Goodwin, Arthur Ingram	P	1	.000	A	C
0	1	Good, Wilbur David	P	5	.375	A	
6	5	Griffith, Clark Calvin MGR.	P	25	.219	B	
		Hahn, Edgar Wm.	OF	43	.319	A	
9	16	Hogg, Wm.	P	39	.060	A	

WON	LOST	NAME	POS.	G.	BA	FROM	TO
		Jacklitsch, Frederick Lawrence	C	1	.000	BknN	
		Keeler, Wm. Henry	OF139	149	.302	B	
		Kleinow, John Peter	C83	88	.221	B	
		LaPorte, Frank B.	2B	11	.375	A	
2	1	LeRoy, Louis Paul	P	3	.125	A	
		McCarthy, Joseph N.	C	1	.000	A	
		McGuire, James Thomas	C70	71	.219	B	
2	4	Newton, Eustace James (Doc)	P	12	.136	BknN02	
		Oldring, Reuben Noshier	SS	8	.300	A	
18	18	Orth, Albert Lewis	P	40	.183	B	
9	11	Powell, John Joseph	P	37	+.200	B	StL
		Powers, Michael Riley (Loaned to N.Y.)	C	11	+.083	xPhil	Phil
3	7	Puttman, Ambrose Nicholas	P	17	.313	B	
		Williams, James Thomas Williams	2B	129	.228	B	
		Yeager, Joseph F. (SS21)	3B90	115	.267	Det03	

WON 90 LOST 61 TG 151 — AMERICAN LEAGUE — FINISHED 2nd.

1906. — PCT. 596

NEW YORK

CLARK CALVIN GRIFFITH

WON	LOST	NAME	POS.	G.	BA	FROM	TO
0	0	Barger, Eros Bollivar	P	2	.000	A	
		Chase, Harold Homer (Hal)	1B150	151	.323	B	
24	16	Chesbro, John Dwight (Jack)	P	48	.208	B	
9	4	Clarkson, Walter Hamilton	P	32	.157	B	
		Conroy, Wm. Edward (Wid) (SS49)	OF97	148	.245	B	
		Delahanty, Frank George	OF86	92	.238	B	
		Dougherty, Patrick Henry	OF	12	+.170	B	Chi
2	2	Doyle, Judd Bruce	P	9	.071	A	
		Elberfeld, Norman Arthur (Kid)	SS98	99	.306	B	
2	2	Griffith, Clark Calvin MGR.	P	17	.111	B	
		Hahn, Edgar Wm.	OF	11	+.091	B	Chi
3	2	Hahn, Frank George	P	6	.333	CinN	C
		Hoffman, Daniel John	OF	100	+.257	xPhil	
14	13	Hogg, Wm.	P	28	.125	B	
0	0	Hughes, Thomas L.	P	3	.200	A	
		Keeler, Wm. Henry	OF	152	.304	B	
		Kleinow, John Peter	C95	96	.220	B	
		LaPorte, Frank B.	3B114	123	.264	B	
2	0	LeRoy, Louis Paul	P	11	.143	B	
		Moriarty, George Joseph	3B39	65	.234	ChiN04	
		McGuire, James Thomas	C49	51	.299	B	
7	5	Newton, Eustace James (Doc)	P	21	.220	B	
27	17	Orth, Albert Lewis	P45	47	.274	B	
		Thomas, Ira Felix	C42	44	.200	A	
		Williams, James Thomas Williams	2B	139	.277	B	

		Yeager, Joseph F.	SS22	57	.301	B	

WON 70 LOST 78 TG 148 — AMERICAN LEAGUE — FINISHED 5th.

1907. — PCT. .473

NEW YORK

CLARK CALVIN GRIFFITH

WON	LOST	NAME	POS.	G.	BA	FROM	TO
		Ball, Cornelius	SS	15	.205	A	
0	0	Barger, Eros Bollivar	P	1	.000	B	
		Bell, John (Beerwald)	OF	17	.212	A	C
		Blair, Walter Allan	C	7	.173	A	
1	3	Brockett, Louis Albert	P	10	.182	A	
1	1	Castleton, Roy J. C.	P	3	.000	A	
		Chase, Harold Homer (Hal)	1B121	125	.287	B	
9	10	Chesbro, John Dwight (Jack)	P	29	.208	B	
0	0	Clarkson, Walter Hamilton	P	6	+.286	B	Clev
		Conroy, Wm. Edward (Wid) (SS38)	OF100	140	.234	B	
11	11	Doyle, Judd Bruce	P	29	.138	B	
		Elberfeld, Norman Arthur (Kid)	SS118	120	.271	B	
0	0	Griffith, Clark Calvin MGR.	P	5	.000	B	
		Hoffman, Daniel John	OF135	136	.253	B	
11	8	Hogg, Wm.	P26	27	.172	B	
2	1	Hughes, Thomas L.	P	3	.167	B	
4	4	Keefe, Robert Francis	P	19	.053	A	
		Keeler, Wm. Henry	OF	107	.234	B	
3	2	Kitson, Frank R.	P	11	+.286	xWash	C
		Kleinow, John Peter	C86	90	.264	B	
		LaPorte, Frank B. (OF63)	3B64	130	.270	B	
		Louden, Wm.	3B	2	.167	A	
0	1	Manning, Walter S.	P	1	.000	A	
		McGuire, James Thomas		1	+.000	B	Bos
3	4	Moore, Earl Alonzo	P	12	+.273	xClev	
		Moriarty, George Joseph (1B22)	3B91	126	.277	B	
4	2	Neuer, John S.	P	7	.143	A	C
7	10	Newton, Eustace James (Doc)	P	19	.108	B	
14	21	Orth, Albert Lewis	P37	43	.324	B	
		Rickey, Wesley Branch (C11)	OF22	52	.182	StL	
		Thomas, Ira Felix	C61	80	.192	B	
0	0	Tift, Raymond Frank	P	4	.200	A	C
		Williams, James Thomas Williams	2B	139	.270	B	

WON 51 LOST 103 TG 154 — AMERICAN LEAGUE — FINISHED 8th (LAST)

1908. — PCT. .331

NEW YORK

CLARK CALVIN GRIFFITH NORMAN ARTHUR ELBERFELD

WON	LOST	NAME	POS.	G.	BA	FROM	TO
		Ball, Cornelius	SS130	132	.247	B	
0	0	Billiard, Harry P.	P	6	.167	A	
		Blair, Walter Allan	C60	76	.190	B	
		Chase, Harold Homer (Hal)	1B98	106	.257	B	
14	20	Chesbro, John Dwight (Jack)	P	44	.180	B	
		Conroy, Wm. Edward (Wid)	3B119	141	.237	B	
		Cree, Wm. Franklin	OF	21	.269	A	
		Delahanty, Frank George	OF36	37	.256	Clev	
		Donovan, Michael B.	3B	5	.157	Clev04	C
1	1	Doyle, Judd Bruce	P	12	.214	B	
		Elberfeld, Norman Arthur MGR. (Kid)	SS17	19	.196	B	
		Gardner, Earl M.	2B	20	.213	A	
0	4	Glade, Frederick Monroe	P	5	.000	StL	C
		Hemphill, Chas. Judson	OF	142	.297	StL	
4	16	Hogg, Wm.	P	24	.093	B	C
		Keeler, Wm. Henry	OF88	91	.263	B	
		Kleinow, John Peter	C89	96	.168	B	
9	21	Lake, Joseph Henry	P37	44	.188	A	
		LaPorte, Frank B.	2B	41	+.253	xBos	
13	16	Manning, Walter S.	P42	44	.187	B	
		Moriarty, George Joseph (3B28)	1B52	101	.236	B	
		McIlveen, Henry Cooke	OF	44	.213	PittN06	
4	5	Newton, Eustace James (Doc)	P	23	.160	B	
		Niles, Harry Clyde	2B	95	+.250	StL	Bos
0	1	O'Connor, Andrew James	P	1	.000	A	C
		*O'Rourke, James Stephen	SS23	34	.231	A	C
2	13	Orth, Albert Lewis	P21	38	.290	B	
		Stahl, Garland (1B14)	OF60	74	+.259	Wash06	Bos
		Sweeney, Edward Francis	C25	32	.146	A	
0	0	Vaughn, James Leslie (Big Jim)	P	2	.000	A	
1	3	Warhop, John Milton (Jack)	P	5	.071	A	
3	3	Wilson, A. Peter	P	7	.067	A	

*O'Rourke also played 3 games at 2B, 1 game at 3B and 7 games in the OF.

WON 74 AMERICAN LEAGUE FINISHED 5th.
LOST 77
TG 151 1909. PCT. .490

NEW YORK

GEORGE TWEEDY STALLINGS

WON	LOST	NAME	POS.	G.	BA	FROM	TO
		Austin, James Philip (SS23)	3B111	136	.231	A	
		Ball, Cornelius	SS	8	+.214	B	Clev
		Blair, Walter Allan	C	42	.209	B	
10	8	Brockett, Louis Albert	P	26	.283	NY07	
0	0	Carroll, Richard T.	P	2	.000	A	C
		Chase, Harold Homer (Hal)	1B	118	.283	B	
0	3	Chesbro, John Dwight (Jack)	P	8	+.167	B	Bos
		Cree, Wm. Franklin	OF77	104	.262	B	
		Demmitt, Chas. Raymond	OF109	119	.241	A	
8	6	Doyle, Judd Bruce	P	17	.167	B	
		Elberfeld, Norman Arthur (Kid) (3B44)	SS61	106	.237	B	
		Engle, Arthur Clyde	OF134	135	.278	A	
0	0	Ford, Russell Wm.	P	1	.000	A	
		Gardner, Earl M.	2B	22	.329	B	
		Hemphill, Chas. Judson	OF45	73	.243	B	
7	8	Hughes, Thomas L.	P	25	.128	NY07	
		Keeler, Wm. Henry	OF95	99	.264	B	
		Kleinow, John Peter	C77	78	.228	B	
		Knight, John Wesley (Jack) (1B19 2B17)	SS77	116	.236	Bos07	
14	11	Lake, Joseph Henry	P	32	.173	B	
		LaPorte, Frank B.	2B83	89	.298	B	
7	11	Manning, Walter S.	P	26	.182	B	
0	1	McConnell, George Neely (Pl)	1B12	13	.209	A	
		McIlveen, Henry Cooke		4	.000	B	C
0	3	Newton, Eustace James (Doc)	P	4	.200	B	C
1	0	Orth, Albert Lewis	P	22	.265	B	C
9	5	Quinn, John Picus	P	22	.156	A	
0	0	Schmidt, Chas. John	P	1	.000	A	
		Sweeney, Edward Francis	C62	67	.267	B	
		Tiemeyer, Edward Carl	1B	4	.363	CinN07	C
		Vaughn, Robert	2B	5	.143	A	
		Wanner, Clarence Mellert	SS	3	.125	A	C
		Ward, Joseph A.	2B	9	.179	PhilN06	PhilN
13	15	Warhop, John Milton (Jack)	P	36	.128	B	
5	6	Wilson, A. Peter	P	14	.118	B	C

WON 88 AMERICAN LEAGUE FINISHED 2nd.
LOST 63
TG 151 1910. PCT. .583

NEW YORK

GEORGE TWEEDY STALLINGS HAROLD HOMER CHASE

WON	LOST	NAME	POS.	G.	BA	FROM	TO
		Austin, James Philip	3B	133	.218	B	
		Blair, Walter Allan	C	6	.227	B	
1	0	Caldwell, Raymond Benjamin	P	6	.000	A	
		Channell, Lester Clark	OF	6	.263	A	
		Chase, Harold Homer (Hal) MGR.	1B	130	.290	B	
		Cree, Wm. Franklin	OF	134	.287	B	
		Criger, Louis	C	27	.189	StL	
		Daniels, Bertram Elmer (1B1 3B1)	OF85	95	.253	A	
0	2	Doyle, Judd Bruce	P	3	.250	B	CinN
		Engle, Arthur Clyde	3B	6	+.200	B	Bos

WON	LOST	NAME	POS.	G.	BA	FROM	TO
5	3	Fisher, Raymond Lyle	P	15	.103	A	
26	6	Ford, Russell Wm.	P	36	.208	B	
		Foster, Edward Cunningham	SS22	30	.132	A	
2	2	Frill, John Edmond	P	10	.111	A	
		Gardner, Earl M.	2B70	86	.244	B	
		Hamphill, Chas. Judson	OF94	102	.239	B	
7	9	Hughes, Thomas L.	P	23	.164	B	
		Kleinow, John Peter	C	5	+.455	B	Bos
		Knight, John Wesley (Jack) (1B23)	SS79	117	.312	B	
		LaPorte, Frank B. (OF24)	2B79	124	.264	B	
		Madden, Thomas J.	OF	1	.000	BosN06	C
2	4	Manning, Walter S.	P	16	.192	B	C
		Mitchell, Frederick Francis	C62	68	.230	BknN05	
		McClure, Lawrence Ledwith	OF	1	.000	A	C
18	12	Quinn, John Picus	P	35	.232	B	
		Roach, Wilbur C.	SS58	70	.214	A	
		Sweeney, Edward Francis	C77	78	.200	B	
13	11	Vaughn, James Leslie (Big Jim)	P	29	.133	NY08	
		Walsh, Joseph Francis	C	2	.333	A	
14	14	Warhop, John Milton (Jack)	P	37	.177	B	
		Wolter, Harry Meigs	OF130	135	.267	Bos	

WON 76 | AMERICAN LEAGUE | FINISHED 6th.
LOST 76
TG 152 | 1911. | PCT. .500

NEW YORK

HAROLD HOMER CHASE

WON	LOST	NAME	POS.	G.	BA	FROM	TO
0	1	Ables, Harry Terrell	P	3	.000	Clev09	C
		Bailey, Harry Louis	OF	5	.111	A	C
		Blair, Walter Allan	C84	85	.194	B	
2	4	Brockett, Louis Albert	P17	19	.308	NY09	C
14	14	Caldwell, Raymond Benjamin	P41	59	.212	B	
		Chase, Harold Homer (Hal) MGR.	1B124	133	.315	B	
0	1	Coakley, Andrew James	P	2	.250	ChiN09	C
		Cree, Wm. Franklin	OF132	137	.348	B	
		Curry, James L.	2B	4	.182	Phil09	
		Daniels, Bertram Elmer	OF120	131	.286	B	
		Dolan, Alvin James (Cozy)	3B18	19	.304	CinN09	
		Elliott, Eugene Birminghouse	3B2	5	.077	A	C
10	11	Fisher, Raymond Lyle	P	29	.119	B	
		Fitzgerald, Justin Howard	OF	16	.270	A	
22	11	Ford, Russell Wm.	P	37	.196	B	
		Gardner, Earl M.	2B101	102	.263	B	
		Handiboe, Aloysius James	OF	5	.067	A	C
		Hartzell, Roy Allen	3B122	144	.296	StL	
		Hemphill, Chas. Judson	OF55	69	.284	B	C
0	2	Hoff, Chester Cornelius	P	5	.286	A	
		Johnson, Otis L. (2B15)	SS46	71	.234	A	C
0	0	Klepfer, Edward Lloyd	P	2	.000	A	
		Knight, John Wesley (Jack) (1B27 2B21)	SS82	132	.268	B	
		Magner, Esmund Burke	2B	12	.194	A	C
		Priest, John Gooding	2B	8	.142	A	
8	9	Quinn, John Picus	P	39	.164	B	
		Roach, Wilbur C.	SS8	12	.250	B	
		Sweeney, Edward Francis	C	83	.231	B	
8	10	Vaughn, James Leslie (Big Jim)	P	26	.143	B	
		Walsh, Joseph Francis	C	4	.222	B	C
12	13	Warhop, John Milton (Jack)	P30	32	.160	B	
		Wilkinson, Edward E.	OF	10	.231	A	C
		Williams, Robert Elias	C	20	.191	A	
		Wolter, Harry Meigs	OF113	122	.304	B	
		Zinn, Guy	OF	9	.148	A	

WON 50 | AMERICAN LEAGUE | FINISHED 8th (LAST)
LOST 102
TG 152 | 1912. | PCT. .329

NEW YORK

HARRY STERLING WOLVERTON

WON	LOST	NAME	POS.	G.	BA	FROM	TO
		Batten, George Burnett	2B	1	.000	A	C
8	16	Caldwell, Raymond Benjamin	P	39	.237	B	
		Chase, Harold Homer (Hal)	1B123	131	.274	B	
		Coleman, Curtis Hancock	3B	12	.263	A	C
		Cree, Wm. Franklin	OF	50	.332	B	
		Daniels, Bertram Elmer	OF	133	.274	B	
1	5	Davis, George Allen Jr.	P	10	.111	A	
		Dolan, Alvin James (Cozy)	3B	17	.200	B	PhilN
		Fisher, August Harris	C	4	.200	Clev	C
2	8	Fisher, Raymond Lyle	P	16	.065	B	
13	21	Ford, Russell Wm.	P34	39	.286	B	
		Gardner, Earl M.	2B	43	.281	B	C
		Hartzell, Roy Allen (OF55)	3B56	123	.272	B	
0	1	Hoff, Chester Cornelius	P	5	.200	B	
		Kauff, Benjamin Michael	OF	5	.272	A	
0	3	Keating, Raymond Herbert	P	5	.375	A	
		Lelivelt, John Frank (Jack)	OF	36	.362	Wash	
		Little, Wm. Arthur	OF	3	.250	A	C
		Maloney, Patrick Wm.	OF	22	.215	A	C
		Martin, John Christopher	SS	69	.225	A	
		Midkiff, Ezra Millington	3B	21	.244	CinN09	
8	12	McConnell, George Neely	P	42	.297	NY09	
		McMillan, Thomas Law	SS	41	.228	CinN10	C
		O'Dowd, John Leo	SS	10	.194	A	C
		Otis, Paul Franklin	OF	4	.000	A	C
		Paddock, Delmar Harold	3B42	45	+.287	xChi	C

WON	LOST	NAME	POS.	G.	BA	FROM	TO
		Priest, John Gooding		2	.500	B	C
5	7	Quinn, John Picus	P	16	.210	B	
1	0	Schulz, Albert C.	P	3	.000	A	
0	0	Shears, George Penfield	P	4	.167	A	C
		Simmons, George Washington	2B93	110	.239	Det10	
		Smith, Frederick H.	OF	7	.185	A	C
		Sterrett, Chas. Hurlbut	OF38	66	.265	A	
		(1B17)					
		Street, Chas. Evard (Gabby)	C	28	.182	Wash	
		Stumpf, Wm. Frederick	SS27	40	.240	A	
		Sweeney, Edward Francis	C	110	.268	B	
0	2	Thompson, Thomas Carl	P	8	.300	A	C
		Thompson, Homer	C	1	.000	A	C
2	8	Vaughn, James Leslie	P	13	+.111	B	Wash
		(Big Jim)					
10	19	Warhop, John Milton (Jack)	P	37	.207	B	
		Williams, Robert Elias	C	20	.136	B	
		Wolter, Harry Meigs	OF	11	.393	B	
		Wolverton, Harry Sterling	OF	33	.300	BosN05	C
		MGR.					
		Zinn, Guy	OF	106	.264	B	

WON 57   AMERICAN LEAGUE   FINISHED 7th.
LOST 94
TG 151   1913.   PCT. .377

NEW YORK

FRANK LEROY CHANCE

WON	LOST	NAME	POS.	G.	BA	FROM	TO
		Boone, Lute Joseph	SS	6	.250	A	
		Borton, Wm. Baker	1B	33	+.121	xChi	
9	8	Caldwell, Raymond Benjamin	P23	51	.289	B	
		Chance, Frank LeRoy (Husk)	1B	11	.208	ChiN	
		MGR.					
		Chase, Harold Homer (Hal)	1B29	39	+.228	B	Chi
		(2B5 OF5)					
0	1	Clark, George Myron	P	11	.500	A	C
		Cook, Luther A.	OF	20	.264	A	
		Costello, Daniel Francis		2	.500	A	
		Cree, Wm. Franklin	OF	147	.271	B	
		Daniels, Bertram Elmer	OF90	93	.216	B	
		Derrick, Claude Lester	SS14	22	.292	Phil	
11	17	Fisher, Raymond Lyle	P	37	.278	B	
11	18	Ford, Russell Wm.	P	30	.162	B	
		Gilhooley, Frank Patrick	OF	24	.341	StLN	
		Gossett, John Star	C	39	.162	A	
0	0	Hanley, James Patrick	P	1	.000	A	C
		Hanson, Joseph	C	1	.000	A	C
		Hartzell, Roy Allen	2B93	141	.259	B	
		(3B24 OF28)					
0	0	Hoff, Chester Cornelius	P	2	.000	B	
		Holden, Wm. Paul	OF16	18	.302	A	
6	12	Keating, Raymond Herbert	P	22	.070	B	
0	1	Klepfer, Edward Lloyd	P	8	.250	NY11	

WON	LOST	NAME	POS.	G.	BA	FROM	TO
		Knight, John Wesley (Jack)	1B49	70	.236	Wash	C
		(2B20)					
		Lelivelt, John Frank (Jack)	OF4	18	+.214	B	Clev
		Maisel, Frederick Chas.	3B	51	.257	A	
		(Fritz)					
		Midkiff, Ezra Millington	3B67	68	.215	B	C
5	15	McConnell, George Neely	P34	35	.179	B	
2	4	McHale, Martin Joseph	P	7	.000	Bos11	
		McKechnie, Wm. Boyd	2B27	44	.134	xBosN	
		Peckinpaugh, Roger Thorpe	SS	95	+.268	xClev	
1	0	Pieh, Edwin John	P	4	.250	A	
		Reynolds, Wm. D.	C2	5	.000	A	
8	14	Schulz, Albert C.	P	33	.175	B	
		Smith, Joseph	C	14	.161	A	C
		Sterrett, Chas. Hurlbut	C	21	.171	B	C
		Stumpf, Wm. Frederick	SS6	12	.207	B	C
		Sweeney, Edward Francis	C113	117	.265	B	
4	4	Warhop, John Milton (Jack)	P	14	.217	B	
		Whiteman, George	OF	11	.343	Bos07	
		Williams, Harry P.	1B	27	.256	A	C
		Williams, Robert Elias	C	6	.158	B	
		Wolter, Harry Meigs	OF121	127	.256	B	
		Young, Ralph Stuart	SS	7	.067	A	
		Zeider, Rollie Hubert	SS22	46	+.227	xChi	

WON 70   AMERICAN LEAGUE   FINISHED 6th.
LOST 84   (TIED WITH CHICAGO)
TG 154   1914.   PCT. .455

NEW YORK

FRANK LEROY CHANCE   ROGER THORPE PECKINPAUGH

WON	LOST	NAME	POS.	G.	BA	FROM	TO
		Aragon, Angel Valdes Sr.	OF1	6	.142	A	
		Boone, Lute Joseph	2B90	106	.222	B	
5	5	Brown, Carroll Wm.	P	19	+.182	xPhil	
		Burr, Alexander Thomson	OF	1	.000	A	C
17	9	Caldwell, Raymond Benjamin	P30	58	.195	B	
		Chance, Frank LeRoy (Husk)	1B	1	.000	B	
		MGR.					
		Channell, Lester Clark	OF	1	1.000	NY10	C
11	9	Cole, Leonard Leslie (King)	P	25	.048	PittN12	
		Cook, Luther A.	OF126	131	.283	B	
0	0	Cooper, Guy Evans	P	1	+.000	A	Bos
		Cree, Wm. Franklin	OF76	77	.309	B	
		Daley, Thomas Francis (Pete)	OF	67	+.258	xPhil	
10	12	Fisher, Raymond Lyle	P	28	.138	B	
		Gilhooley, Frank Patrick	OF	1	.667	B	
		Gossett, John Star	C	10	.090	B	C
		Harris, Joseph	OF	2	.000	A	
		Hartzell, Roy Allen	OF128	137	.233	B	
		Holden, Wm. Paul	OF45	50	.182	B	CinN
7	11	Keating, Raymond Herbert	P32	33	.168	B	
		Kingman, Harry Lees	1B	4	.000	A	C
		Maisel, Frederick Chas.	3B148	149	.239	B	

WON	LOST	NAME	POS.	G.	BA	FROM	TO
		(Fritz)					
		Meara, Chas. Edward	OF	4	.286	A	C
		Mullen, Chas. George	1B85	93	.260	Chi11	
7	16	McHale, Martin Joseph	P29	30	.200	B	
		Nunamaker, Leslie Grant	C	86	+.265	xBos	
		Peckinpaugh, Roger Thorpe MGR.	SS	157	.223	B	
4	4	Pieh, Edwin John	P	13	.118	B	
		Reynolds, Wm. D.	C	4	.400	B	C
		Rogers, Jay Louis	C	5	.000	A	C
1	3	Schulz, Albert C.	P	4	.000	B	BuffF
		Schwartz, Wm. Dwight	C	1	.000	A	C
		Schwert, Pius Louis	C	2	.000	A	
		Sweeney, Edward Francis	C78	87	.212	B	
		Truesdale, Frank D.	2B67	77	.213	StL11	
		Walsh, James Charles	OF	43	+.207	Phil	Phil
8	15	Warhop, John Milton (Jack)	P31	35	.141	B	
		Williams, Robert Elias	1B58	59	.163	B	C

WON 69 — AMERICAN LEAGUE — FINISHED 5th.
LOST 83
TG 152 — 1915. — PCT. .454

NEW YORK

WM. EDWARD DONOVAN

WON	LOST	NAME	POS.	G.	BA	FROM	TO
		Alexander, Walter E.	C	25	+.250	xStL	
		Barney, Edmund J.	OF	11	.191	A	PittN
		Baumann, Chas. John (3B19)	2B43	76	.292	Det	
		Boone, Lute Joseph	2B115	130	.204	B	
0	0	Brady, Cornelius Joseph (Neal)	P	2	.000	A	
3	5	Brown, Carroll Wm.	P19	21	.188	B	C
19	16	Caldwell, Raymond Benjamin	P37	72	.243	B	
2	3	Cole, Leonard Leslie (King)	P	10	.077	B	C
		Cook, Luther A.	OF	132	.271	B	
0	1	Cottrell, Ensign Stover	P	7	.000	BosN	C
		Cree, Wm. Franklin	OF53	74	.214	B	C
		Daley, Thomas Francis (Pete)	OF	10	.250	B	C
0	3	Donovan, Wm. Edward (Wild Bill) MGR.	P	10	.083	B	
18	11	Fisher, Raymond Lyle	P	30	.108	B	
		Gilhooley, Frank Patrick	OF	1	.000	B	
		Hartzell, Roy Allen	OF107	119	.251	B	
		Hendryx, Timothy Green	OF	13	.200	Clev12	
		High, Hugh Jenkins	OF117	119	.258	Det	
3	6	Keating, Raymond Herbert	P	11	.153	B	
		Krueger, Ernest George	C	10	.172	Clev13	
		Layden, Eugene Francis	OF	3	.286	A	C
		Maisel, Frederick Chas. (Fritz)	3B134	135	.281	B	
2	0	Markle, Clifford Monroe	P	3	.000	A	
		Miller, Elmer	OF	26	.145	StLN12	

WON	LOST	NAME	POS.	G.	BA	FROM	TO
2	3	Mogridge, George Anthony	P	6	.083	Chi12	
		Mullen, Chas. George	1B27	40	.267	B	
3	7	McHale, Martin Joseph	P	13	.143	B	
		Nunamaker, Leslie Grant	C77	87	.226	B	
		Peckinpaugh, Roger Thorpe	SS	142	.225	B	
4	5	Pieh, Edwin John	P	21	.067	B	C
		Pipp, Walter Clement (Wally)	1B134	136	.246	Det13	
1	2	Russell, Allen E.	P	5	.250	A	
		Schwert, Pius Louis	C	9	.278	B	C
4	8	Shawkey, James Robert	P	16	+.241	xPhil	
		Shelton, Andrew Kemper	OF	10	.025	A	C
		Sweeney, Edward Francis	C	53	.190	B	
1	1	Tipple, Daniel Slaughter	P	3	.000	A	C
0	3	Vance, Clarence Arthur (Dazzy)	P	8	.600	xPittN	
		Walters, Alfred John	C	2	.333	A	
7	9	Warhop, John Milton (Jack)	P	21	.137	B	C

WON 80 — AMERICAN LEAGUE — FINISHED 4th.
LOST 74
TG 154 — 1916. — PCT. .519

NEW YORK

WM. EDWARD DONOVAN

WON	LOST	NAME	POS.	G.	BA	FROM	TO
		Alexander, Walter E.	C27	36	.256	B	
		Aragon, Angel Valdes Sr. (OF2)	3B9	12	.208	NY14	
		Baker, John Franklin (Home Run)	3B96	100	.269	Phil14	
		Baumann, Chas. John (3B26)	OF28	79	.287	B	
		Boone, Lute Joseph	3B25	46	.185	B	
		Brady, Cornelius Joseph	(DID NOT PLAY)			B	
0	0	Buckles, Jesse Robert	P	2	.000	A	C
5	12	Caldwell, Raymond Benjamin	P20	45	.204	B	
0	0	Cantwell, Michael Joseph	P	1	.000	A	
		Cook. Luther A.	OF	4	.100	B	C
13	6	Cullop, Norman Andrew	P	27	.111	KCF	
0	0	Donovan, Wm. Edward (Wild Bill) MGR.	P	1	.000	B	
11	8	Fisher, Raymond Lyle	P	31	.177	B	
		Gedeon, Elmer Joseph	2B	122	.211	Wash14	
		Gilhooley, Frank Patrick	OF51	58	.278	B	
		Hartzell, Roy Allen	OF28	33	.187	B	C
		Hendryx, Timothy Green	OF	15	.290	B	
		High, Hugh Jenkins	OF109	115	.263	B	
		Hofman, Arthur Frederich	OF	6	.296	BuffF	ChiN
5	6	Keating, Raymond Herbert	P	14	.200	B	
2	0	Love, Elmer Haughton	P	20	.000	Wash13	
		Magee, Leo Christopher (Lee)	OF128	131	.257	BknF	
		Maisel, Frederick Chas. (Fritz)	OF25	53	.228	B	
4	3	Markle, Clifford Monroe	P	11	.000	B	

WON	LOST	NAME	POS.	G.	BA	FROM	TO
		Miller, Elmer	OF42	43	.224	B	
6	12	Mogridge, George Anthony	P	31	.212	B	
		Mullen, Chas. George (1B17)	2B20	59	.267	B	C
		Nunamaker, Leslie Grant	C79	91	.296	B	
		Oldring, Reuben Noshier	OF	43	+.234	xPhil	
		Peckinpaugh, Roger Thorpe	SS	142	.255	B	
		Pipp, Walter Clement (Wally)	1B148	151	.262	B	
6	10	Russell, Allen E.	P	35	.044	B	
		Schaefer, Herman A. (Germany)	OF	1	.000	NwkF	
24	14	Shawkey, James Robert	P	53	.183	B	
4	3	Shocker, Urban James	P	12	.154	A	
		Walters, Alfred John	C65	66	.266	B	

WON 71 — AMERICAN LEAGUE — FINISHED 6th.
LOST 82
TG 153 — 1917. — PCT. .464

NEW YORK

WM. EDWARD DONOVAN

WON	LOST	NAME	POS.	G.	BA	FROM	TO
		Alexander, Walter E.	C	20	.137	B	C
		Aragon, Angel Valdes Sr. (SS1 OF5)	3B4	14	.067	B	C
		Baker, John Franklin (Home Run)	3B	146	.282	B	
		Baumann, Chas. John	2B18	49	.218	B	C
1	0	Brady, Cornelius Joseph (Neal)	P	2	.500	B	
13	16	Caldwell, Raymond Benjamin	P36	63	.258	B	
		Camp, Howard Lee	OF	5	.286	A	C
5	9	Cullop, Norman Andrew	P	30	.159	B	
0	1	Enright, John Percy	P	1	.000	A	C
		Fewster, Wilson Lloyd	2B9	11	.222	A	
8	9	Fisher, Raymond Lyle	P	23	.180	B	
		Gedeon, Elmer Joseph	2B31	33	.239	B	
		Gilhooley, Frank Patrick	OF46	54	.242	B	
		Hendryx, Timothy Green	OF107	125	.249	B	
		High, Hugh Jenkins	OF100	103	.236	B	
		Lamar, Wm. Harmong	OF	11	.244	A	
6	5	Love, Elmer Haughton	P	33	.167	B	
		Magee, Leo Christopher (Lee)	OF20	51	+.220	B	StL
		Maisel, Frederick Chas. (Fritz)	2B100	113	.198	B	
		Marsans, Armando	OF	25	+.227	xStL	
		Miller, Elmer	OF112	114	.251	B	
9	11	Mogridge, George Anthony	P	29	.159	B	
1	0	Monroe, Edward Oliver	P	9	.167	A	
0	1	McGraw, Robert Emmett	P	2	.000	A	
		Nunamaker, Leslie Grant	C91	104	.261	B	

WON	LOST	NAME	POS.	G.	BA	FROM	TO
		Peckinpaugh, Roger Thorpe	SS	148	.260	B	
0	1	Piercy, Wm. Benton	P	1	.000	A	
		Pipp, Walter Clement (Wally)	1B	155	.244	B	
		Ruel, Herold Dominic (Muddy)	C	6	.118	StL15	
7	8	Russell, Allen E.	P25	30	.323	B	
13	15	Shawkey, James Robert	P	32	.190	B	
8	5	Shocker, Urban James	P	26	.178	B	
0	0	Smallwood, Walter Clayton	P	2	.000	A	
0	1	Thormahlen, Herbert Ehler	P	1	.000	A	
		Vick, Samuel Bruce	OF	10	.278	A	
		Walters, Alfred John	C57	61	.263	B	
		Ward, Aaron Lee	SS	8	.115	A	

WON 60 — AMERICAN LEAGUE — FINISHED 4th.
LOST 63
TG 123 — 1918. — PCT. .488

NEW YORK

MILLER JAMES HUGGINS

WON	LOST	NAME	POS.	G.	BA	FROM	TO
		Baker, John Franklin (Home Run)	3B	126	.306	B	
		Beck, Zinn Bertram	1B2	11	.000	StLN16	C
0	0	Bernhardt, Walter Jacob	P	1	.000	A	C
		Bodie, Frank L. (Ping)	OF90	91	.256	Phil	
9	8	Caldwell, Raymond Benjamin (OF19)	P24	65	.291	B	
0	0	Ferguson, James Alexander (Alex)	P	1	.000	A	
		Fewster, Wilson Lloyd	2B1	5	.500	B	
3	6	Finneran, Joseph Ignatius	P	23	+.231	xDet	C
		Fournier, Jacques Frank	1B	27	.350	Chi	
		Gilhooley, Frank Patrick	OF111	112	.276	B	
		Hannah, James Harrison	C88	90	.220	A	
		High, Hugh Jenkins	OF	6	.000	B	C
		Hummel, John Edwin	OF14	22	.295	BknN15	C
		Hyatt, Robert Hamilton (Ham)	OF25	53	.229	StLN15	C
2	2	Keating, Raymond Herbert	P	15	.187	NY16	
		Lamar, Wm. Harmong	OF27	28	.227	B	
13	12	Love, Elmer Haughton	P	38	.230	B	
		Marsans, Armando	OF36	37	.236	B	C
		Miller, Elmer	OF62	67	.243	B	
15	13	Mogridge, George Anthony	P45	48	.190	B	
0	0	Monroe, Edward Oliver	P	1	.000	B	C
0	1	McGraw, Robert Emmett	P	1	.000	B	
		O'Connor, Patrick Francis	C	1	.333	PittF15	C
		Peckinpaugh, Roger Thorpe	SS	122	.231	B	
		Pipp, Walter Clement (Wally)	1B	91	.304	B	
		Pratt, Derrill Burnham	2B	126	.275	StL	
2	4	Robinson, John Henry	P	11	.000	StLN15	C
		Ruel, Herold Dominic (Muddy)	C	3	.333	B	

WON	LOST	NAME	POS.	G.	BA	FROM	TO
8	11	Russell, Allen E.	P27	29	.167	B	
0	2	Sanders, Roy L.	P	6	.000	A	
1	1	Shawkey, James Robert	P	3	.750	B	
7	3	Thormahlen, Herbert Ehler	P	16	.077	B	
0	0	Vance, Clarence Arthur (Dazzy)	P	2	.000	NY15	
		Vick, Samuel Bruce	OF	2	.667	B	
		Walters, Alfred John	C50	64	.199	B	
		Ward, Aaron Lee	SS11	20	.125	B	

WON 80 LOST 59 TG 139

AMERICAN LEAGUE 1919.

FINISHED 3rd. PCT. .576

NEW YORK

MILLER JAMES HUGGINS

WON	LOST	NAME	POS.	G.	BA	FROM	TO
		Baker, John Franklin (Home Run)	3B	141	.293	B	
		Bodie, Frank L. (Ping)	OF	134	.278	B	
		Fewster, Wilson Lloyd (SS23)	OF41	81	.283	B	
		Gleich, Frank Elmer	OF	4	.333	A	
		Halas, George Stanley	OF	12	.091	A	C
		Hannah, James Harrison	C73	75	.238	B	
		Hofmann, Fred	C	1	.000	A	
		Kane, Francis Thomas	OF	1	.000	BknF15	C
		Lamar, Wm. Harmong	OF	11	+.188	B	Bos
		Lewis, George Edward (Duffy)	OF	141	.272	Bos17	
5	2	Mays, Carl Wm.	P	13	+.311	xBos	
10	8	Mogridge, George Anthony	P	36	.125	B	
0	2	McGraw, Robert Emmett	P	6	+.000	B	Bos
3	0	Nelson, Luther Martin	P	9	.143	A	C
0	0	O'Doul, Frank Joseph (Lefty)	P	19	.250	A	
		Peckinpaugh, Roger Thorpe	SS121	122	.305	B	
		Pipp, Walter Clement (Wally)	1B	138	.275	B	
		Pratt, Derrill Burnham	2B	140	.292	B	
15	14	Quinn, John Picus	P	38	.209	Chi	
		Ruel, Herold Dominic (Muddy)	C	81	.240	B	
9	4	Russell, Allen E.	P	23	+.233	B	Bos
0	1	Schneider, Peter Joseph	P	7	.111	CinN	C
20	11	Shawkey, James Robert	P	41	.234	B	
5	8	Shore, Ernest Grady	P	20	.143	Bos17	
0	0	Smallwood, Walter Clayton	P	6	.000	NY17	C
13	9	Thormahlen, Herbert Ehler	P	30	.186	B	
		Vick, Samuel Bruce	OF100	106	.248	B	
		Walker, Wm. Curtis		1	.000	A	
		Ward, Aaron Lee (SS2)	1B4	27	.205	B	
		Wickland, Albert	OF15	26	.152	BosN	C

WON 95 LOST 59 TG 154

AMERICAN LEAGUE 1920.

FINISHED 3rd. PCT. .617

NEW YORK

MILLER JAMES HUGGINS

WON	LOST	NAME	POS.	G.	BA	FROM	TO
		Bodie, Frank L. (Ping)	OF	129	.295	B	
14	8	Collins, Harry Warren	P	36	.129	A	
		Connelly, Thomas Martin	OF	1	.000	A	
		Fewster, Wilson Lloyd	SS4	21	.286	B	
		French, Raymond Edward	SS	2	.000	A	
		Gleich, Frank Elmer	OF15	24	.122	B	C
		Hannah, James Harrison	C78	79	.247	B	C
		Hofmann, Fred	C	15	.292	B	
		Lewis, George Edward (Duffy)	OF99	107	.271	B	
		Lucey, Joseph Earl	2B1	3	.000	A	
26	11	Mays, Carl Wm.	P	45	.239	B	
		Meusel, Robert Wm. (3B45)	OF64	119	.328	A	
5	9	Mogridge, George Anthony	P	26	.167	B	
0	0	McGraw, Robert Emmett	P	15	.000	Bos	
0	0	O'Doul, Frank Joseph (Lefty)	P12	13	.167	B	
		Peckinpaugh, Roger Thorpe	SS137	139	.270	B	
		Pipp, Walter Clement (Wally)	1B	153	.280	B	
		Pratt, Derrill Burnham	2B	154	.314	B	
18	10	Quinn, John Picus	P	41	.091	B	
		Ruel, Herold Dominic (Muddy)	C80	82	.268	B	
1	0	Ruth, George Herman (Babe) (P1)	OF139	142	.376	Bos	
20	13	Shawkey, James Robert	P	38	.230	B	
2	2	Shore, Ernest Grady	P	14	.182	B	C
9	6	Thormahlen, Herbert Ehler	P	29	.222	B	
		Vick, Samuel Bruce	OF35	51	.220	B	
		Ward, Aaron Lee	3B114	127	.256	B	

WON 98 LOST 55 TG 153

AMERICAN LEAGUE 1921.

FINISHED 1st. PCT. .641

NEW YORK

MILLER JAMES HUGGINS

WON	LOST	NAME	POS.	G.	BA	FROM	TO
		Baker, John Franklin (Home Run)	3B83	94	.294	NY19	
		Bodie, Frank L. (Ping)	OF25	31	.172	B	C
11	5	Collins, Harry Warren	P	28	.196	B	
		Connelly, Thomas Martin	OF	4	.200	B	C
		DeVormer, Albert E.	C17	22	.347	Chi18	
3	1	Ferguson, James Alexander (Alex)	P	17	.211	NY18	

WON	LOST	NAME	POS.	G.	BA	FROM	TO
		Fewster, Wilson Lloyd (2B15)	OF43	66	.280	B	
4	3	Harper, Harry Clayton	P	8	.125	Bos	
		Hawks, Nelson Louis	OF15	41	.288	A	
		Hofmann, Fred	C18	23	.177	B	
19	13	Hoyt, Waite Chas.	P	43	.222	Bos	
27	9	Mays, Carl Wm.	P49	51	.343	B	
		Meusel, Robert Wm.	OF147	149	.318	B	
		Miller, Elmer	OF	56	.298	NY18	
		Mitchell, John Franklin	SS	13	.262	A	
		McNally, Michael Joseph (2B16)	3B47	71	.260	Bos	
		Peckinpaugh, Roger Thorpe	SS	149	.288	B	
5	4	Piercy, Wm. Benton	P	14	.214	NY17	
		Pipp, Walter Clement (Wally)	1B	153	.296	B	
8	7	Quinn, John Picus	P	33	.219	B	
0	1	Rogers, Thomas Andrew (Shotgun)	P5	6	.333	Phil19	C
		Roth, Robert Frank	OF37	43	.283	Wash	C
2	0	Ruth, George Herman (Babe) (P2)	OF152	152	.378	B	
		Schang, Walter Henry (Wally)	C132	134	.316	Bos	
18	12	Shawkey, James Robert	P	38	.300	B	
1	0	Sheehan, Thomas Clancy	P	12	.625	Phil16	
		Ward, Aaron Lee (3B31)	2B122	153	.306	B	

WON 94 AMERICAN LEAGUE FINISHED 1st.
LOST 60
TG 154 1922. PCT. .610

NEW YORK

MILLER JAMES HUGGINS

WON	LOST	NAME	POS.	G.	BA	FROM	TO
		Baker, John Franklin (Home Run)	3B60	69	.277	B	C
26	7	Bush, Leslie Ambrose (Bullet Joe)	P	39	.326	Bos	
		DeVormer, Albert E.	C17	24	.203	B	
		Dugan, Joseph Anthony (Jumping Joe)	3B40	60	+.294	xBos	
		Fewster, Wilson Lloyd (2B20)	OF20	44	+.228	B	Bos
		Hofmann, Fred	C28	37	.297	B	
19	12	Hoyt, Waite Chas.	P	37	.217	B	
13	13	Jones, Samuel Pond (Sad Sam)	P	45	.264	Bos	
1	0	Llewellyn, Clement Manley	P	1	.000	A	C
12	14	Mays, Carl Wm.	P34	35	.250	B	
		Meusel, Robert Wm.	OF	121	.319	B	
		Miller, Elmer	OF	51	+.286	B	Bos
		Mitchell, John Franklin	SS	4	+.000	B	Bos
3	2	Murray, George King	P	22	.278	A	
		McMillan, Norman Alexis	OF23	33	.256	A	
		McNally, Michael Joseph	3B34	52	.252	B	
0	0	O'Doul, Frank Joseph (Lefty)	P	8	.333	NY20	
		Pipp, Walter Clement (Wally)	1B	152	.329	B	
		Ruth, George Herman (Babe)	OF	110	.315	B	
		Schang, Walter Henry (Wally)	C119	124	.319	B	
		Scott, Lewis Everett (Deacon)	SS	154	.269	Bos	
20	12	Shawkey, James Robert	P	39	.183	B	
		Skinner, Elisha Harrison Camp	OF	27	.182	A	
		Smith, Elmer John	OF	21	+.208	xBos	
		Ward, Aaron, Lee	2B	154	.267	B	
		Witt, Lawton Walter (Whitey)	OF138	140	.297	Phil	

WON 98 AMERICAN LEAGUE FINISHED 1st.
LOST 54
TG 152 1923. PCT. .645

NEW YORK

MILLER JAMES HUGGINS

WON	LOST	NAME	POS.	G.	BA	FROM	TO
		Bengough, Bernard Oliver (Benny)	C	19	.132	A	
19	15	Bush, Leslie Ambrose (Bullet Joe)	P37	38	.274	B	
		Dugan, Joseph Anthony (Jumping Joe)	3B	146	.283	B	
		Gazella, Michael (2B1 SS1)	3B1	8	.077	A	
		Gehrig, Henry Louis (Lou)	1B	13	.423	A	
		Haines, Henry Luther	OF	28	.160	A	C
		Hendrick, Harvey (Gink)	OF	37	.273	A	
		Hofmann, Fred	C70	72	.290	B	
17	9	Hoyt, Waite Chas.	P	37	.190	B	
		Johnson, Ernest Rudolph	SS8	19	+.447	xChi	
21	8	Jones, Samuel Pond (Sad Sam)	P	39	.224	B	
5	2	Mays, Carl Wm.	P	23	.148	B	
		Meusel, Robert Wm.	OF121	132	.313	B	
		McNally, Michael Joseph (2B2)	3B3	30	.211	B	
19	6	Pennock, Herbert Jefferis	P	35	.193	Bos	
1	3	Pipgras, George Wm.	P	8	.000	A	
		Pipp, Walter Clement (Wally)	1B	144	.304	B	
0	0	Roettger, Oscar Frederick Louis	P	5	.000	A	
		Ruth, George Herman (Babe)	OF148	152	.393	B	
		Schang, Walter Henry (Wally)	C81	84	.276	B	
		Scott, Lewis Everett (Deacon)	SS	152	.246	B	
16	11	Shawkey, James Robert	P	36	.202	B	
		Smith, Elmer John	OF47	70	.306	B	
		Ward, Aaron Lee	2B	152	.284	B	
		Witt, Lawton Walter (Whitey)	OF144	146	.314	B	

WON 89
LOST 63
TG 152

AMERICAN LEAGUE 1924. FINISHED 2nd. PCT. .586

NEW YORK

MILLER JAMES HUGGINS

WON	LOST	NAME	POS.	G.	BA	FROM	TO
		Autry, Martin Gordon	C	2	.000	A	
2	0	Beall, Walter Esau	P	4	.142	A	
		Bengough, Bernard Oliver (Benny)	C	11	.312	B	
17	16	Bush, Leslie Ambrose (Bullet Joe)	P39	60	.339	B	
		Combs, Earle Bryan	OF11	24	.400	A	
		Dugan, Joseph Anthony (Jumping Joe)	3B	148	.302	B	
5	3	Gaston, Nathaniel Milton	P	28	.222	A	
		Gehrig, Henry Louis (Lou)	1B	10	.500	B	
		Hendrick, Harvey (Gink)	OF17	40	.263	B	
		Hillis, Malcolm David	2B	1	.000	A	
		Hofmann, Fred	C54	62	.175	B	
		Horan, Joseph Patrick	OF13	22	.290	A	C
18	13	Hoyt, Waite Chas.	P	46	.133	B	
		Johnson, Ernest Rudolph	2B27	64	.353	B	
9	6	Jones, Samuel Pond (Sad Sam)	P	36	.176	B	
1	1	Mamaux, Albert Leon	P	14	.077	BknN	C
0	3	Markle, Clifford Monroe	P	7	.000	CinN22	C
		Meusel, Robert Wm.	OF	143	.325	B	
		McNally, Michael Joseph (3B13)	2B25	49	.247	B	
		Paschal, Benjamin Edwin	OF	4	.272	Bos20	
21	9	Pennock, Herbert Jefferis	P	40	.158	B	
0	1	Pipgras, George Wm.	P	9	.333	B	
		Pipp, Walter Clement (Wally)	1B	153	.295	B	
0	0	Roettger, Oscar Frederick Louis	P	1	.000	B	
		Ruth, George Herman (Babe)	OF	153	.378	B	
		Schang, Walter Henry (Wally)	C106	114	.292	B	
		Scott, Lewis Everett (Deacon)	SS	153	.250	B	
16	11	Shawkey, James Robert	P	38	.319	B	
0	0	Shields, Benjamin Cowan	P	2	.000	A	
		Ward, Aaron Lee	2B	120	.253	B	
		Witt, Lawton Walter (Whitey)	OF143	147	.297	B	

WON 69
LOST 85
TG 154

AMERICAN LEAGUE 1925. FINISHED 7th. PCT. .448

NEW YORK

MILLER JAMES HUGGINS

WON	LOST	NAME	POS.	G.	BA	FROM	TO
0	1	Beall, Walter Esau	P	8	.000	B	
		Bengough, Bernard Oliver (Benny)	C94	95	.258	B	
1	1	Braxton, Edgar Garland	P	3	.333	BosN22	
0	0	Caldwell, Chas. Wm.	P	3	.000	A	C
		Combs, Earle Bryan	OF	150	.343	B	
		Dugan, Joseph Anthony (Jumping Joe)	3B96	102	.292	B	
		Durocher, Leo Ernest	SS	2	.000	A	
4	2	Ferguson, James Alexander (Alex)	P	21	+.133	xBos	Wash
0	0	Francis, Raymond James	P	4	+.000	Det23	Bos
		Gehrig, Henry Louis (Lou) (OF7)	1B120	126	.295	B	
		Hofmann, Fred	C1	3	.000	B	
11	14	Hoyt, Waite Chas.	P	46	.304	B	
		Johnson, Ernest Rudolph (SS28 3B2)	2B34	76	.282	B	C
1	3	Johnson, Henry Ward	P	24	.059	A	
15	21	Jones, Samuel Pond (Sad Sam) (OF1)	P43	46	.162	B	
		Koenig, Mark Anthony	SS	28	.205	A	
		Luebbe, Roy John	C	8	.000	A	C
0	0	Marquis, James Milburn	P	2	.000	A	C
		Merkle, Frederick Chas.	1B5	7	.385	ChiN20	
		Meusel, Robert Wm.	OF132	156	.292	B	
		Odom, Herman Boyd	3B	1	1.000	A	C
		O'Neill, Stephen Francis (Steve)	C31	35	.286	Bos	
		Paschal, Benjamin Edwin	OF66	89	.360	B	
16	17	Pennock, Herbert Jefferis	P	47	.202	B	
		Pipp, Walter Clement (Wally)	1B47	62	.230	B	
		Ruth, George Herman (Babe)	OF	98	.290	B	
		Schang, Walter Henry (Wally)	C58	73	.240	B	
		Scott, Lewis Everett (Deacon)	SS	22	+.217	B	Wash
		Shanks, Howard Samuel (2B21 OF4)	3B26	66	.258	Bos	C
6	14	Shawkey, James Robert	P	32	.136	B	
3	0	Shields, Benjamin Cowan	P	4	.125	B	
12	12	Shocker, Urban James	P	41	.172	StL	
		Veach, Robert Hayes	OF	56	+.353	xBos	Wash
		Wanninger, Paul Louis (2B1 3B3)	SS111	117	.236	A	
		Ward, Aaron Lee (3B10)	2B113	125	.246	B	
		Witt, Lawton Walter (Whitey)	OF10	31	.200	B	

WON 91
LOST 63
TG 154

AMERICAN LEAGUE 1926. FINISHED 1st. PCT. .591

NEW YORK

MILLER JAMES HUGGINS

WON	LOST	NAME	POS.	G.	BA	FROM	TO
		Adams, Spencer Dewey	2B4	28	.120	Wash	

WON	LOST	NAME	POS.	G.	BA	FROM	TO
		Barnes, John Francis	C	1	.000	A	C
2	4	Beall, Walter Esau	P	20	.136	B	
		Bengough, Bernard Oliver (Benny)	C35	36	.381	B	
5	1	Braxton, Edgar Garland	P	37	.300	B	
		Carlyle, Roy Edward	OF	35	+.385	xBos	C
		Collins, Tharon Patrick	C100	102	.286	StL24	
		Combs, Earle Bryan	OF	145	.299	B	
		Cullop, Henry Nicholas	OF	2	.500	A	
		Davis, George Willis (Kiddo)	OF	1	.000	A	
		Dugan, Joseph Anthony (Jumping Joe)	3B122	123	.288	B	
		Gazella, Michael (SS11)	3B45	66	.232	NY23	
		Gehrig, Henry Louis (Lou)	1B	155	.313	B	
16	12	Hoyt, Waite Chas.	P	39	.216	B	
0	0	Johnson, Henry Ward	P	1	.000	B	
9	8	Jones, Samuel Pond (Sad Sam)	P39	44	.205	B	
		Koenig, Mark Anthony	SS141	147	.271	B	
		Lazzeri, Anthony Michael (Tony)	2B145	155	.275	A	
		Merkle, Frederick Chas.	1B	1	.000	B	C
		Meusel, Robert Wm.	OF107	108	.315	B	
1	0	McQuaid, Herbert George	P	17	.000	CinN23	C
		Paschall, Benjamin Edwin	OF76	96	.287	B	
23	11	Pennock, Herbert Jefferis	P	40	.212	B	
2	3	Ruether, Walter Henry (Dutch)	P	13	+.143	xWash	
		Ruth, George Herman (Babe)	OF149	152	.372	B	
		Severeid, Henry Levai	C	41	+.266	xWash	C
8	7	Shawkey, James Robert	P	29	.257	B	
19	11	Shocker, Urban James	P	41	.171	B	
		Skiff, Wm. Franklin	C	6	.099	PittN21	C
6	6	Thomas, Myles Lewis	P	33	.116	A	
		Ward, Aaron Lee	1B4	22	.323	B	

WON 110 LOST 44 TG 154

AMERICAN LEAGUE 1927. FINISHED 1st. PCT. .714

NEW YORK

MILLER JAMES HUGGINS

WON	LOST	NAME	POS.	G.	BA	FROM	TO
0	0	Beall, Walter Esau	P	1	.000	B	
		Bengough, Bernard Oliver (Benny)	C30	31	.247	B	
		Collins, Tharon Patrick	C89	92	.275	B	
		Combs, Earle Bryan	OF	152	.356	B	
		Dugan, Joseph Anthony (Jumping Joe)	3B111	112	.269	B	
		Durst, Cedric Montgomery	OF36	65	.248	StL	
		Gazella, Michael	3B44	54	.278	B	
		Gehrig, Henry Louis (Lou)	1B	155	.373	B	
0	0	Giard, Joseph Oscar	P	16	.286	StL	C
		Grabowski, John Patrick	C68	70	.277	Chi	
22	7	Hoyt, Waite Chas.	P	36	.222	B	
		Koenig, Mark Anthony	SS122	123	.285	B	
		Lazzeri, Anthony Michael (Tony) (SS38)	2B113	153	.309	B	
		Meusel, Robert Wm.	OF131	135	.337	B	
19	7	Moore, Wm. Wilcy	P	50	.080	A	
		Morehart, Raymond Anderson	2B53	73	.256	Chi	C
		Paschal, Benjamin Edwin	OF27	50	.317	B	
19	8	Pennock, Herbert Jefferis	P	34	.217	B	
10	3	Pipgras, George Wm.	P	29	.239	NY24	
13	6	Ruether, Walter Henry (Dutch)	P28	35	.263	B	C
		Ruth, George Herman (Babe)	OF	151	.356	B	
2	3	Shawkey, James Robert	P10	19	.091	B	
18	6	Shocker, Urban James	P	31	.241	B	
7	4	Thomas, Myles Lewis	P	21	.333	B	
		Wera, Julian Valentine	3B19	38	.239	A	

WON 101 LOST 53 TG 154

AMERICAN LEAGUE 1928. FINISHED 1st. PCT. .656

NEW YORK

MILLER JAMES HUGGINS

WON	LOST	NAME	POS.	G.	BA	FROM	TO
		Bengough, Bernard Oliver (Benny)	C	58	.267	B	
		Burns, George Henry	1B	4	+.500	xClev	
0	1	Campbell, Archer Stewart (Archie)	P	13	.250	A	
		Collins, Tharon Patrick	C	70	.220	B	
		Combs, Earle Bryan	OF	149	.310	B	
5	1	Coveleskie, Stanley Anthony	P	12	.053	Wash	C
		Dickey, Wm. Malcolm	C	10	.200	A	
		Dugan, Joseph Anthony (Jumping Joe)	3B91	94	.276	B	
		Durocher, Leo Ernest (SS29)	2B66	102	.270	NY25	
		Durst, Cedric Montgomery	OF33	74	.252	B	
		Gazella, Michael	3B16	32	.232	B	C
		Gehrig, Henry Louis (Lou)	1B	154	.374	B	
		Grabowski, John Patrick	C	75	.238	B	
2	3	Heimach, Fred Amos	P13	18	.167	Bos26	
23	7	Hoyt, Waite Chas.	P	42	.257	B	
14	9	Johnson, Henry Ward	P	31	.241	NY26	
		Koenig, Mark Anthony	SS125	132	.319	B	
		Lazzeri, Anthony Michael (Tony)	2B110	116	.332	B	
		Meusel, Robert Wm.	OF	131	.297	B	
4	4	Moore, Wm. Wilcy	P	35	.143	B	
		Paschal, Benjamin Edwin	OF25	65	.316	B	
17	6	Pennock, Herbert Jefferis	P	28	.203	B	
24	13	Pipgras, George Wm.	P	46	.157	B	
		Robertson, Eugene Edward	3B70	83	.291	StL26	
		Ruth, George Herman (Babe)	OF	154	.323	B	
0	0	Ryan, Wilfred Patrick Dolan	P	3	.000	BosN26	

WON	LOST	NAME	POS.	G.	BA	FROM	TO
		(Rosy)					
8	6	Shealy, Albert Berley	P	23	.237	A	
0	0	Shocker, Urban James	P	1	.000	B	C
1	0	Thomas, Myles Lewis	P12	13	.400	B	
3	3	Zachary, Jonathan Thompson Walton (Tom)	P	7	+.133	xWash	

WON 88
LOST 66
TG 154

AMERICAN LEAGUE — FINISHED 2nd.

1929. — PCT. .571

NEW YORK

MILLER JAMES HUGGINS   ARTHUR FLETCHER

WON	LOST	NAME	POS.	G.	BA	FROM	TO
		Bengough, Bernard Oliver (Benny)	C	23	.194	B	
		Burns, George Henry	1B	9	+.000	B	Phil
		Byrd, Samuel Dewey	OF54	62	.312	A	
		Combs, Earle Bryan	OF141	142	.345	B	
		Dickey, Wm. Malcolm	C127	130	.324	B	
		Durocher, Leo Ernest	SS93	106	.246	B	
		Durst, Cedric Montgomery	OF72	92	.257	B	
		Funk, Elias Calvin		1	.000	A	
		Gehrig, Henry Louis (Lou)	1B	154	.300	B	
		Grabowski, John Patrick	C	22	.203	B	
11	6	Heimach, Fred Amos	P35	36	.184	B	
10	9	Hoyt, Waite Chas.	P	30	.224	B	
3	3	Johnson, Henry Ward	P12	13	.071	B	
		Jorgens, Arndt Ludwig	C15	18	.324	A	
		Koenig, Mark Anthony (3B37)	SS61	116	.292	B	
		Lary, Lynford Hobart (Lyn) (SS14)	3B55	80	309	A	
		Lazzeri, Anthony Michael (Tony)	2B	147	.354	B	
		Meusel, Robert Wm.	OF96	100	.261	B	
6	4	Moore, Wm. Wilcy	P	41	.067	B	
0	0	Nekola, Francis Joseph (Bots)	P	9	.500	A	
		Paschal, Benjamin Edwin	OF20	42	.208	B	C
9	11	Pennock, Herbert Jefferis	P	27	.176	B	
18	12	Pipgras, George Wm.	P	39	.143	B	
0	4	Rhodes, John Gordon	P	10	.300	A	
		Robertson, Eugene Edward	3B77	90	.298	B	BosN
		Ruth, George Herman (Babe)	OF133	135	.345	B	
6	6	Sherid, Roy Richard	P	33	.180	A	
0	2	Thomas, Myles Lewis	P	5	+.500	B	Wash
13	9	Wells, Edwin Lee	P	31	.230	Det27	
		Wera, Julian Valentine	3B3	5	.417	NY27	C
12	0	Zachary, Jonathan Thompson Walton (Tom)	P	26	.239	B	

WON 86
LOST 68
TG 154

AMERICAN LEAGUE — FINISHED 3rd.

1930. — PCT. .558

NEW YORK

JAMES ROBERT SHAWKEY

WON	LOST	NAME	POS.	G.	BA	FROM	TO
0	1	Barnes, Frank Samuel	P	3	.333	Det	C
		Bengough, Bernard Oliver (Benny)	C	44	.235	B	
		Byrd, Samuel Dewey	OF85	92	.284	B	
0	1	Carroll, Owen Thomas	P	11	+.200	xDet	CinN
		Chapman, Wm. Benjamin (2B45)	3B91	138	.316	A	
		Combs, Earle Bryan	OF135	137	.344	B	
		Cooke, Allen Lindsey (Dusty)	OF73	92	.255	A	
		Dickey, Wm. Malcolm	C101	109	.339	B	
		Durst, Cedric Montgomery	OF	8	+.188	B	Bos
0	0	Edwards, Foster Hamilton	P	2	.000	BosN28	C
		Gehrig, Henry Louis (Lou)	1B153	154	.379	B	
0	1	Gibson, Samuel Braxton	P	2	.333	Det28	
2	5	Gomez, Vernon Louis (Lefty)	P	15	.150	A	
		Hargrave, Eugene Franklin	C34	45	.278	CinN28	C
0	0	Henderson, Wm. Maxwell	P	3	.500	A	C
0	0	Holloway, Kenneth Eugene	P	16	+.231	xClev	C
2	2	Hoyt, Waite Chas.	P	8	+.063	B	Det
14	11	Johnson, Henry Ward	P44	51	.266	B	
		Jorgens, Arndt Ludwig	C	16	.367	B	
		Karlon, Wm. John	OF1	2	.000	A	C
		Koenig, Mark Anthony	SS	21	+.243	B	Det
		Lary, Lynford Hobart (Lyn)	SS113	117	.289	B	
		Lazzeri, Anthony Michael (Tony) (3B60)	2B77	143	.303	B	
1	3	McEvoy, Louis Anthony	P	28	.125	A	
11	7	Pennock, Herbert Jefferis	P	25	.182	B	
15	15	Pipgras, George Wm.	P	44	.150	B	
		Reese, James Hymie	2B48	77	.346	A	
0	0	Rhodes, John Gordon	P	3	.000	B	
		Rice, Harry Francis	OF	100	+.298	xDet	
15	5	Ruffing, Chas. Herbert (Red)	P34	52	+.374	xBos	
1	0	Ruth, George Herman (Babe) (P1)	OF144	145	.359	B	
12	13	Sherid, Roy Richard	P	37	.101	B	
12	3	Wells, Edwin Lee	P27	29	.259	B	
		Werber, Wm. Murray (Bill) (3B1)	SS4	4	.286	A	
		Wuestling, George	SS	25	+.190	xDet	C
1	1	Zachary, Jonathan Thompson Walton (Tom)	P	3	.250	B	BosN

WON 94
LOST 59
TG 153

AMERICAN LEAGUE — FINISHED 2nd.

1931. — PCT. .614

NEW YORK

JOSEPH VINCENT McCARTHY

WON	LOST	NAME	POS.	G.	BA	FROM	TO
2	0	Andrews, Ivy Paul	P	7	.182	A	
		Byrd, Samuel Dewey	OF88	115	.270	B	
		Chapman, Wm. Benjamin	OF137	149	.315	B	
		(2B11)					
		Combs, Earle Bryan	OF129	138	.318	B	
		Cooke, Allen Lindsey (Dusty)	OF11	27	.333	B	
		Dickey, Wm. Malcolm	C125	130	.327	B	
		Gehrig, Henry Louis (Lou)	1B154	155	.341	B	
21	9	Gomez, Vernon Louis (Lefty)	P	40	.132	B	
		Hoag, Myril Oliver	OF23	44	.143	A	
13	8	Johnson, Henry Ward	P	40	.195	B	
		Jorgens, Arndt Ludwig	C40	46	.270	B	
		Lary, Lynford Hobart (Lyn)	SS	155	.280	B	
		Lazzeri, Anthony Michael	2B90	135	.267	B	
		(Tony) (3B39)					
0	0	McEvoy, Louis Anthony	P	6	.000	B	C
11	6	Pennock, Herbert Jefferis	P	25	.152	B	
		Perkins, Ralph Foster (Cy)	C	16	.255	Phil	
7	6	Pipgras, George Wm.	P	36	.024	B	
		Reese, James Hymie	2B61	65	.241	B	
6	3	Rhodes, John Gordon	P	18	.214	B	
		Rolfe, Robert Abial (Red)	SS	1	.000	A	
16	14	Ruffing, Chas. Herbert (Red)	P37	48	.330	B	
		Ruth, George Herman (Babe)	OF142	145	.373	B	
		Sewell, Joseph Wheeler	3B121	130	.302	Clev	
5	5	Sherid, Roy Richard	P	17	.333	B	C
		Walker, Fred (Dixie)	OF	2	.300	A	
2	1	Weaver, James Dement	P	17	.050	Wash28	
2	2	Weinert, Phillip Walter	P	17	.000	ChiN28	C
9	5	Wells, Edwin Lee	P27	28	.222	B	

WON 107 AMERICAN LEAGUE FINISHED 1st.
LOST 47
TG 154 1932. PCT. .695

NEW YORK

JOSEPH VINCENT McCARTHY

WON	LOST	NAME	POS.	G.	BA	FROM	TO
17	4	Allen, John Thomas (Johnny)	P	33	.123	A	
2	1	Andrews, Ivy Paul	P	4	+.222	B	Bos
5	2	Brown, Walter George (Jumbo)	P	19	.174	Clev28	
		Byrd, Samuel Dewey	OF90	104	.297	B	
		Chapman, Wm. Benjamin	OF149	150	.299	B	
		Combs, Earle Bryan	OF138	143	.321	B	
		Cooke, Allen Lindsey (Dusty)	OF	3	.000	B	
		Crosetti, Frank Peter Joseph	SS83	115	.241	A	
		(3B33)					
1	0	Devens, Chas.	P	1	.000	A	
		Dickey, Wm. Malcolm	C	108	.310	B	
		Farrell, Edward Stephen	2B16	26	.175	ChiN30	
		Gehrig, Henry Louis (Lou)	1B	155	.349	B	
		Glenn, Joseph Chas.	C	6	.125	A	
24	7	Gomez, Vernon Louis (Lefty)	P	37	.173	B	
		Hoag, Myril Oliver	OF35	46	.370	B	
2	2	Johnson, Henry Ward	P	6	.231	B	
		Jorgens, Arndt Ludwig	C	55	.219	B	
		Lary, Lynford Hobart (Lyn)	SS80	91	.232	B	
		Lazzeri, Anthony Michael	2B133	141	.300	B	
		(Tony)					
7	5	Mac Fayden, Daniel Knowles	P	16	+.102	xBos	
		(Danny)					
2	0	Moore, Wm. Wilcy	P	10	+.000	xBos	
0	0	Murphy, John Joseph	P	2	1.000	A	
		(Grandma)					
9	5	Pennock, Herbert Jefferis	P	22	.151	B	
16	9	Pipgras, George Wm.	P	32	.220	B	
		Phillips, Edward David	C	9	.290	PittN	
1	2	Rhodes, John Gordon	P	10	+.250	B	Bos
18	7	Ruffing, Chas. Herbert (Red)	P35	55	.306	B	
		Ruth, George Herman (Babe)	OF127	132	.341	B	
		Saltzgaver, Otto Hamlin (Jack)	2B16	20	.128	A	
		Schalk, LeRoy John	2B	3	.250	A	
		Sewell, Joseph Wheeler	3B122	124	.272	B	
3	3	Wells, Edwin Lee	P22	24	.000	B	

WON 91 AMERICAN LEAGUE FINISHED 2nd.
LOST 59
TG 150 1933. PCT. .607

NEW YORK

JOSEPH VINCENT McCARTHY

WON	LOST	NAME	POS.	G.	BA	FROM	TO
15	7	Allen, John Thomas (Johnny)	P	25	.181	B	
5	1	Brennan, James Donald (Don)	P	18	.259	A	
7	5	Brown, Walter George (Jumbo)	P	21	.179	B	
		Byrd, Samuel Dewey	OF71	85	.280	B	
		Chapman, Wm. Benjamin	OF	147	.312	B	
		Combs, Earle Bryan	OF104	122	.298	B	
		Crosetti, Frank Peter Joseph	SS133	136	.253	B	
3	3	Devens, Chas.	P	14	.095	B	
		Dickey, Wm. Malcolm	C127	130	.318	B	
		Farrell, Edward Stephen	SS22	44	.269	B	
		(2B20)					
		Gehrig, Henry Louis (Lou)	1B	152	.334	B	
		Glenn, Joseph Chas.	C	5	.143	B	
16	10	Gomez, Vernon Louis (Lefty)	P	35	.113	B	
0	0	Jablonowski, Peter Wm.	P	1	.000	Bos	
		(Appleton)					
		Jorgens, Arndt Ludwig	C19	21	.220	B	
		Lary, Lynford Hobart (Lyn)	3B28	52	.220	B	
		(1B3 SS16 OF1)					
		Lazzeri, Anthony Michael	2B138	139	.294	B	
		(Tony)					

WON	LOST	NAME	POS.	G.	BA	FROM	TO
3	2	MacFayden, Daniel Knowles (Danny)	P	25	.029	B	
5	6	Moore, Wm. Wilcy	P	35	.133	B	C
7	4	Pennock, Herbert Jefferis	P	23	.238	B	
2	2	Pipgras, George Wm.	P	4	+.091	B	Bos
		Rensa, George Anthony	C	8	.310	PhilN31	
9	14	Ruffing, Chas. Herbert (Red)	P35	55	.252	B	
1	0	Ruth, George Herman (Babe) (P1)	OF132	137	.301	B	
		Sewell, Joseph Wheeler	3B131	135	.273	B	C
6	1	Uhle, George Ernest	P	12	+.400	xNYN	
12	4	VanAtta, Russell	P	26	.283	A	
		Walker, Fred (Dixie)	OF77	98	.274	NY31	
		Werber, Wm. Murray (Bill)		3	+.000	NY30	Bos

WON 94 AMERICAN LEAGUE FINISHED 2nd.
LOST 60
TG 154 1934. PCT. .610

NEW YORK

JOSEPH VINCENT McCARTHY

WON	LOST	NAME	POS.	G.	BA	FROM	TO
5	2	Allen, John Thomas (Johnny)	P	13	.192	B	
12	9	Broaca, John Joseph	P	26	.030	A	
		Byrd, Samuel Dewey	OF104	106	.246	B	
		Chapman, Wm. Benjamin	OF	149	.308	B	
		Combs, Earle Bryan	OF62	63	.319	B	
		Crosetti, Frank Peter Joseph (3B23)	SS119	138	.265	B	
6	7	DeShong, James Brooklyn	P	31	.190	Phi132	
1	0	Devens, Chas.	P	1	.500	B	C
		Dickey, Wm. Malcolm	C	104	.322	B	
		Gehrig, Henry Louis (Lou) (SS1)	1B153	154	.363	B	
26	5	Gomez, Vernon Louis (Lefty)	P	38	.131	B	
1	2	Grimes, Burleigh Arland	P	10	.000	xPittN	
		Heffner, Donald Henry (Jeep)	2B68	72	.261	A	
		Hoag, Myril Oliver	OF86	97	.267	NY32	
		Jorgens, Arndt Ludwig	C56	58	.208	B	
		Lary, Lynford Hobart (Lyn)	SS	1	+.000	B	Bos
		Lazzeri, Anthony Michael (Tony) (3B30)	2B92	123	.267	B	
4	3	MacFayden, Daniel Knowles (Danny)	P	22	.103	B	
14	10	Murphy, John Joseph (Grandma)	P	40	.099	NY32	
0	0	Newkirk, Floyd Elmo	P	1	.000	A	C
		Rolfe, Robert Abial (Red) (3B26)	SS46	89	.287	NY31	
19	11	Ruffing, Chas. Herbert (Red)	P36	45	.248	B	
		Ruth, George Herman (Babe)	OF111	125	.288	B	
		Saltzgaver, Otto Hamlin (Jack) (1B1)	3B84	94	.271	NY32	
		Selkirk, George Alexander (Twinkletoes)	OF	46	.313	A	
0	2	Smythe, Wm. Harry	P	8	.200	PhilN30	BknN
1	0	Tamulis, Vitautis Casimirus (Vito)	P	1	.250	A	
		Taylor, James Wren (Zack)	C1	4	.143	ChiN	
2	4	Uhle, George Ernest	P	10	.600	B	
3	5	VanAtta, Russell	P	28	.207	B	
		Walker, Fred (Dixie)	OF	17	.118	B	

WON 89 AMERICAN LEAGUE FINISHED 2nd.
LOST 60
TG 149 1935. PCT. .597

NEW YORK

JOSEPH VINCENT McCARTHY

WON	LOST	NAME	POS.	G.	BA	FROM	TO
13	6	Allen, John Thomas (Johnny)	P	23	.224	B	
15	7	Broaca, John Joseph	P	29	.150	B	
6	5	Brown, Walter George (Jumbo)	P	20	.313	NY33	
		Chapman, Wm. Benjamin	OF138	140	.289	B	
		Combs, Earle Bryan	OF70	89	.282	B	C
		Crosetti, Frank Peter Joseph	SS	87	.256	B	
4	1	DeShong, James Brooklyn	P	29	.071	B	
		Dickey, Wm. Malcolm	C118	120	.279	B	
		Gehrig, Henry Louis (Lou)	1B	149	.329	B	
		Glenn, Joseph Chas.	C16	17	.233	NY33	
12	15	Gomez, Vernon Louis (Lefty)	P	34	.120	B	
		Heffner, Donald Henry (Jeep)	2B	10	.306	B	
		Hill, Jesse Terrill	OF94	107	.293	A	
		Hoag, Myril Oliver (3B1)	OF37	48	.255	B	
		Jorgens, Arndt Ludwig	C33	36	.238	B	
		Lazzeri, Anthony Michael (Tony) (SS9)	2B118	130	.273	B	
3	5	Malone, Perce Leigh (Pat)	P	29	.000	ChiN	
10	5	Murphy, John Joseph (Grandma)	P	40	.156	B	
		Richardson, Clifford Nolen	SS	12	.217	Det32	
		Rolfe, Robert Abial (Red) (SS17)	3B136	149	.300	B	
16	11	Ruffing, Chas. Herbert (Red)	P30	50	.339	B	
		Ryan, John Collins (Blondy)	SS	30	.238	xPhilN	
		Saltzgaver, Otto Hamlin (Jack) (1B6 3B18)	2B25	61	.262	B	
		Selkirk, George Alexander (Twinkletoes)	OF127	128	.312	B	
10	5	Tamulis, Vitautis Casimirus (Vito)	P	30	.246	B	
0	0	VanAtta, Russell	P	5	+.000	B	StL
		Walker, Fred (Dixie)	OF2	8	.154	B	

WON 102
LOST 51
TG 153

AMERICAN LEAGUE — 1936. — FINISHED 1st. — PCT. .667

NEW YORK

JOSEPH VINCENT McCARTHY

WON	LOST	NAME	POS.	G.	BA	FROM	TO
12	7	Broaca, John Joseph	P	37	.110	B	
1	4	Brown, Walter George (Jumbo)	P	20	.000	B	
		Chapman, Wm. Benjamin	OF	36	+.266	B	Wash
		Crosetti, Frank Peter Joseph	SS	151	.288	B	
		Dickey, Wm. Malcolm	C107	112	.362	B	
		DiMaggio, Joseph Paul Jr. (Joe)	OF	138	.323	A	
		Gehrig, Henry Louis (Lou)	1B	155	.354	B	
		Glenn, Joseph Chas.	C	44	.271	B	
13	7	Gomez, Vernon Louis (Lefty)	P	31	.145	B	
14	4	Hadley, Irving Darius (Bump)	P	31	.235	Wash	
		xHeffner, Donald Henry (Jeep)	3B8	19	.229	B	
		Hoag, Myril Oliver	OF39	45	.301	B	
		Johnson, Roy Cleveland	OF33	63	.265	Bos	
		Jorgens, Arndt Ludwig	C30	31	.273	B	
1	1	Kleinhans, Theodore Otto	P	19	.167	CinN34	
		Lazzeri, Anthony Michael (Tony)	2B148	150	.287	B	
12	4	Malone, Perce Leigh (Pat)	P	35	.196	B	
9	3	Murphy, John Joseph (Grandma)	P	27	.361	B	
19	7	Pearson, Marcellus Monte	P	33	.253	Clev	
		Powell, Alvin Jacob (Jake)	OF	87	+.306	xWash	
		Rolfe, Robert Abial (Red)	3B133	135	.319	B	
20	12	Ruffing, Chas. Herbert (Red)	P33	53	.291	B	
		Saltzgaver, Otto Hamlin (Jack)	3B16	34	.211	B	
		Seeds, Robert Ira (Bob)	OF9	13	.262	Clev34	
		Selkirk, George Alexander (Twinkletoes)	OF135	137	.308	B	
0	0	Sundra, Stephen Richard (Steve)	P	1	.000	A	
		Walker, Fred (Dixie)	OF	6	+.350	B	Chi
1	2	Wicker, Kemp Caswell	P	7	.143	A	

xHeffner also played 3 games at 2B and 5 games at SS.

WON 102
LOST 52
TG 154

AMERICAN LEAGUE — 1937. — FINISHED 1st. — PCT. .662

NEW YORK

JOSEPH VINCENT McCARTHY

WON	LOST	NAME	POS.	G.	BA	FROM	TO
3	2	Andrews, Ivy Paul	P	11	+.067	xClev	
1	4	Broaca, John Joseph	P	7	.000	B	
7	4	Chandler, Spurgeon Ferdinand (Spud)	P	12	.133	A	
		Crosetti, Frank Peter Joseph	SS147	149	.234	B	
		Dahlgren, Ellsworth Tenney (Babe)		1	.000	Bos	
		Dickey, Wm. Malcolm	C137	140	.332	B	
		DiMaggio, Joseph Paul Jr. (Joe)	OF150	151	.346	B	
		Gehrig, Henry Louis (Lou)	1B	157	.351	B	
		Glenn, Joseph Chas.	C24	25	.283	B	
21	11	Gomez, Vernon Louis (Lefty)	P	34	.200	B	
11	8	Hadley, Irving Darius (Bump)	P	29	.169	B	
		Heffner, Donald Henry (Jeep) (SS13)	2B38	60	.249	B	
		Henrich, Thomas David	OF59	67	.320	A	
		Hoag, Myril Oliver	OF99	106	.301	B	
		Johnson, Roy Cleveland	OF	12	.294	B	BosN
		Jorgens, Arndt Ludwig	C11	13	.130	B	
		Lazzeri, Anthony Michael (Tony)	2B125	126	.244	B	
5	2	Makosky, Frank	P	26	.313	A	C
4	4	Malone, Perce Leigh (Pat)	P	28	.030	B	C
13	4	Murphy, John Joseph (Grandma)	P	39	.229	B	
9	3	Pearson, Marcellus Monte	P	22	.216	B	
		Powell, Alvin Jacob (Jake)	OF94	97	.263	B	
		Rolfe, Robert Abial (Red)	3B	154	.276	B	
20	7	Ruffing, Chas. Herbert (Red)	P31	54	.202	B	
		Saltzgaver, Otto Hamlin (Jack)	1B4	17	.182	B	
		Selkirk, George Alexander (Twinkletoes)	OF69	78	.328	B	
1	0	Vance, Joseph Albert	P	2	.000	Chi35	
7	3	Wicker, Kemp Caswell	P	16	.114	B	

WON 99
LOST 53
TG 152

AMERICAN LEAGUE — 1938. — FINISHED 1st. — PCT. .651

NEW YORK

JOSEPH VINCENT McCARTHY

WON	LOST	NAME	POS.	G.	BA	FROM	TO
1	3	Andrews, Ivy Paul	P	19	.167	B	C
3	2	Beggs, Joseph Stanley	P	14	.250	A	
14	5	Chandler, Spurgeon Ferdinand (Spud)	P	23	.203	B	
		Crosetti, Frank Peter Joseph	SS	157	.263	B	
		xDahlgren, Ellsworth Tenney (Babe)	3B8	27	.186	B	
		Dickey, Wm. Malcolm	C126	132	.313	B	
		DiMaggio, Joseph Paul Jr. (Joe)	OF	145	.324	B	
0	1	Donald, Richard Atley	P	2	.167	A	
2	2	Ferrell, Wesley Cheek (Wes)	P	5	+.167	xWash	
		Gehrig, Henry Louis (Lou)	1B	157	.295	B	

WON	LOST	NAME	POS.	G.	BA	FROM	TO
		Glenn, Joseph Chas.	C40	41	.260	B	
18	12	Gomez, Vernon Louis (Lefty)	P	32	.151	B	
		Gordon, Joseph Lowell (Flash)	2B126	127	.255	A	
9	8	Hadley, Irving Darius (Bump)	P	29	.093	B	
		Henrich, Thomas David	OF130	131	.270	B	
		Hoag, Myril Oliver	OF70	85	.277	B	
		Jorgens, Arndt Ludwig	C	9	.235	B	
		Knickerbocker, Wm. Hart	2B34	46	.250	StL	
8	2	Murphy, John Joseph (Grandma)	P	32	.063	B	
16	7	Pearson, Marcellus Monte	P	28	.171	B	
		Powell, Alvin Jacob (Jake)	OF43	45	.256	B	
		Rolfe, Robert Abial (Red)	3B	151	.311	B	
21	7	Ruffing, Chas. Herbert (Red)	P31	45	.224	B	
		Selkirk, George Alexander (Twinkletoes)	OF95	99	.254	B	
0	0	Stine, Lee Elbert	P	4	.500	CinN36	C
6	4	Sundra, Stephen Richard (Steve)	P	25	.182	N.Y.36	
0	0	Vance, Joseph Albert	P	4	.750	B	C
1	0	Wicker, Kemp Caswell	P	1	.000	B	

xDahlgren also played 6 games at 1B.

WON 106 — AMERICAN LEAGUE — FINISHED 1st.
LOST 45
TG 151 — 1939. — PCT. .702

NEW YORK

JOSEPH VINCENT McCARTHY

WON	LOST	NAME	POS.	G.	BA	FROM	TO
0	0	Breuer, Marvin Howard	P	1	.000	A	
3	0	Chandler, Spurgeon Ferdinand (Spud)	P	11	.400	B	
		Crosetti, Frank Peter Joseph	SS	152	.233	B	
		Dahlgren, Ellsworth Tenney (Babe)	1B	144	.235	B	
		Dickey, Wm. Malcolm	C126	128	.302	B	
		DiMaggio, Joseph Paul Jr. (Joe)	OF117	120	.381	B	
13	3	Donald, Richard Atley	P	24	.250	B	
1	2	Ferrell, Wesley Cheek (Wes)	P	3	.125	B	
		Gallagher, Joseph Emmett	OF	14	+.244	A	StL
		Gehrig, Henry Louis (Lou)	1B	8	.143	B	C
12	8	Gomez, Vernon Louis (Lefty)	P	26	.151	B	
		Gordon, Joseph Lowell (Flash)	2B	151	.284	B	
12	6	Hadley, Irving Darius (Bump)	P	26	.177	B	
		Henrich, Thomas David	OF88	99	.277	B	
10	4	Hildebrand, Oral Clyde	P	21	.182	StL	
		Jorgens, Arndt Ludwig	C	3	.000	B	C
		Keller, Chas. Ernest	OF105	111	.334	A	
		Knickerbocker, Wm. Hart (2B2)	SS2	6	.154	B	
3	6	Murphy, John Joseph (Grandma)	P	38	.182	B	
12	5	Pearson, Marcellus Monte	P	22	.321	B	
		Powell, Alvin Jacob (Jake)	OF23	31	.244	B	
		Rolfe, Robert Abial (Red)	3B	152	.329	B	
		Rosar, Warren Vincent (Buddy)	C35	43	.276	A	
21	7	Ruffing, Chas. Herbert (Red)	P28	44	.307	B	
8	3	Russo, Marius Ugo	P	21	.244	A	
		Selkirk, George Alexander (Twinkletoes)	OF124	128	.306	B	
11	1	Sundra, Stephen Richard (Steve)	P	24	.265	B	

WON 88 — AMERICAN LEAGUE — FINISHED 3rd.
LOST 66
TG 154 — 1940. — PCT. .571

NEW YORK

JOSEPH VINCENT McCARTHY

WON	LOST	NAME	POS.	G.	BA	FROM	TO
9	3	Bonham, Ernest Edward	P	12	.189	A	
8	9	Breuer, Marvin Howard	P	27	.037	B	
8	7	Chandler, Spurgeon Ferdinand (Spud)	P	27	.150	B	
		Chartak, Michael George	OF3	11	.133	A	
		Crosetti, Frank Peter Joseph	SS	145	.194	B	
		Dahlgren, Ellsworth Tenney (Babe)	1B	155	.264	B	
		Dickey, Wm. Malcolm	C102	106	.247	B	
		DiMaggio, Joseph Paul Jr. (Joe)	OF130	132	.352	B	
8	3	Donald, Richard Atley	P	24	.146	B	
3	3	Gomez, Vernon Louis (Lefty)	P	9	.000	B	
		Gordon, Joseph Lowell (Flash)	2B	155	.281	B	
0	0	Grissom, Leo Theo (Lee)	P	5	.000	CinN	BknN
3	5	Hadley, Irving Darius (Bump)	P	25	.111	B	
		Henrich, Thomas David (1B2)	OF76	90	.307	B	
1	1	Hildebrand, Oral Clyde	P	13	.000	B	C
		Keller, Chas. Ernest	OF136	138	.286	B	
		Knickerbocker, Wm. Hart (3B17)	SS19	45	.242	B	
		Mills, Colonel Buster	OF14	34	.397	StL38	
8	4	Murphy, John Joseph (Grandma)	P	35	.077	B	
7	6	Pearson, Marcellus Monte	P	16	.121	B	
		Powell, Alvin Jacob (Jake)	OF7	12	.185	B	
		Rolfe, Robert Abial (Red)	3B138	139	.250	B	
		Rosar, Warren Vincent (Buddy)	C63	73	.298	B	
15	12	Ruffing, Chas. Herbert (Red)	P30	33	.124	B	
14	8	Russo, Marius Ugo	P	30	.188	B	
		Selkirk, George Alexander (Twinkletoes)	OF111	118	.269	B	
4	6	Sundra, Stephen Richard (Steve)	P	27	.138	B	

WON 101 — AMERICAN LEAGUE — FINISHED 1st.
LOST 53
TG 154 — 1941. — PCT. .656

NEW YORK

JOSEPH VINCENT McCARTHY

WON	LOST	NAME	POS.	G.	BA	FROM	TO
9	6	Bonham, Ernest Edward	P	23	.160	B	
		Bordagaray, Stanley George	OF19	36	.260	CinN39	
5	1	Branch, Norman Downs	P	27	.000	A	
9	7	Breuer, Marvin Howard	P	26	.087	B	
10	4	Chandler, Spurgeon Ferdinand (Spud)	P	28	.183	B	
		Crosetti, Frank Peter Joseph (3B13)	SS32	50	.223	B	
		Dickey, Wm. Malcolm	C104	109	.284	B	
		DiMaggio, Joseph Paul Jr. (Joe)	OF	139	.357	B	
9	5	Donald, Richard Atley	P	22	.081	B	
15	5	Gomez, Vernon Louis (Lefty)	P	23	.153	B	
		Gordon, Joseph Lowell (Flash)	2B131	156	.276	B	
		Henrich, Thomas David	OF139	144	.277	B	
		Keller, Chas. Ernest	OF137	140	.298	B	
		Lindell, John Harlan		1	.000	A	
8	3	Murphy, John Joseph (Grandma)	P	35	.056	B	
4	2	Peek, Stephen George	P	17	.036	A	C
		Priddy, Gerald Edward (1B10 3B14)	2B31	56	.213	A	
		Rizzuto, Philip Francis	SS128	133	.307	A	
		Rolfe, Robert Abial (Red)	3B134	136	.264	B	
		Rosar, Warren Vincent (Buddy)	C60	67	.287	B	
15	6	Ruffing, Chas. Herbert (Red)	P23	38	.303	B	
14	10	Russo, Marius Ugo	P	28	.231	B	
		Selkirk, George Alexander (Twinkletoes)	OF47	70	.220	B	
		Silvestri, Kenneth Joseph	C13	17	.250	Chi	
3	3	Stanceu, Chas.	P	22	.000	A	
		Sturm, John Peter Joseph	1B	124	.239	A	C
0	1	Washburn, George Edward	P	1	.000	A	C

WON 103 — AMERICAN LEAGUE — FINISHED 1st.
LOST 51
TG 154 — 1942. — PCT. .669

NEW YORK

JOSEPH VINCENT McCARTHY

WON	LOST	NAME	POS.	G.	BA	FROM	TO
21	5	Bonham, Ernest Edward	P	28	.122	B	
15	4	Borowy, Henry Ludwig	P	25	.157	A	
0	1	Branch, Norman Downs	P	10	.333	B	C
8	9	Breuer, Marvin Howard	P	27	.056	B	
16	5	Chandler, Spurgeon Ferdinand (Spud)	P	24	.211	B	
		Chartak, Michael George	OF	5	+.000	NY40	Wash
		Crosetti, Frank Peter Joseph (2B2 SS8)	3B62	74	.242	B	
		Cullenbine, Roy Joseph (1B1)	OF19	21	+.364	xWash	
		Dickey, Wm. Malcolm	C80	82	.295	B	
		DiMaggio, Joseph Paul Jr. (Joe)	OF	154	.305	B	
11	3	Donald, Richard Atley	P	20	.148	B	
6	4	Gomez, Vernon Louis (Lefty)	P	13	.152	B	
		Gordon, Joseph Lowell (Flash)	2B	147	.322	B	
		Hassett, John Aloysius (Buddy)	1B	132	.284	BosN	C
		Hemsley, Ralston Burdett (Rollie)	C29	31	.294	xCinN	
		Henrich, Thomas David (1B7)	OF119	127	.267	B	
		Kearse, Edward Paul	C	11	.192	A	C
		Keller, Chas. Ernest	OF	152	.292	B	
		Levy, Edward Clarence	1B	13	.122	PhilN40	
2	1	Lindell, John Harlan	P23	27	.250	B	
4	10	Murphy, John Joseph (Grandma)	P	31	.154	B	
		Priddy, Gerald Edward (1B11 2B8 SS3)	3B35	59	.280	B	
1	0	Queen, Melvin Joseph	P	4	.000	A	
		Rizzuto, Philip Francis	SS	144	.284	B	
		Rolfe, Robert Abial (Red)	3B60	69	.219	B	
		Rosar, Warren Vincent (Buddy)	C58	69	.230	B	
14	7	Ruffing, Chas. Herbert (Red)	P24	30	.250	B	
4	1	Russo, Marius Ugo	P	9	.235	B	
		Selkirk, George Alexander (Twinkletoes)	OF19	42	.192	B	C
		Stainback, George Tucker (Tuck)	OF3	15	.200	Det	
1	1	Turner, James Riley	P	5	.000	xCinN	

WON 98 — AMERICAN LEAGUE — FINISHED 1st.
LOST 56
TG 154 — 1943. — PCT. .636

NEW YORK

JOSEPH VINCENT McCARTHY

WON	LOST	NAME	POS.	G.	BA	FROM	TO
15	8	Bonham, Ernest Edward	P	28	.197	B	
14	9	Borowy, Henry Ludwig	P	29	.203	B	
0	1	Breuer, Marvin Howard	P	5	.333	B	C
2	1	Byrne, Thomas Joseph	P11	13	.091	A	
20	4	Chandler, Spurgeon Ferdinand (Spud)	P	30	.258	B	
		Crosetti, Frank Peter Joseph	SS90	95	233	B	
		Dickey, Wm. Malcolm	C71	85	351	B	
6	4	Donald, Richard Atley	P	22	.128	B	

WON	LOST	NAME	POS.	G.	BA	FROM	TO
		Etten, Nicholas Raymond Thomas	1B	154	.271	PhilN	
		Gordon, Joseph Lowell (Flash)	2B	152	.249	B	
		Grimes, Oscar Ray Jr. (1B1)	SS3	9	.150	Clev	
		Hemsley, Ralston Burdett (Rollie)	C52	62	.239	B	
		Johnson, Wm. Russell	3B	155	.280	A	
		Keller, Chas. Ernest	OF	141	.271	B	
		Lindell, John Harlan	OF	122	.245	B	
		Metheny, Arthur Beauregard	OF91	103	.261	A	
12	4	Murphy, John Joseph (Grandma)	P	37	.053	B	
		Robinson, Aaron Andrew		1	.000	A	
5	10	Russo, Marius Ugo	P	24	.194	B	
		Sears, Kenneth Eugene	C50	60	.278	A	
		Stainback, George Tucker (Tuck)	OF61	71	.260	B	
		Stirnweiss, George Henry (2B4)	SS68	83	.219	A	
3	0	Turner, James Riley	P	18	.077	B	
		Weatherly, Cyril Roy (Stormy)	OF68	77	.264	Clev	
13	11	Wensloff, Chas. Wm.	P	29	.177	A	
8	4	Zuber, Wm. Henry	P	20	.184	Wash	

WON 83
LOST 71
TG 154

AMERICAN LEAGUE

1944.

FINISHED 3rd.

PCT. .539

NEW YORK

JOSEPH VINCENT McCARTHY

WON	LOST	NAME	POS.	G.	BA	FROM	TO
4	1	Bevens, Floyd Clifford	P	8	.063	A	
12	9	Bonham, Ernest Edward	P	26	.133	B	
17	12	Borowy, Henry Ludwig	P	35	.133	B	
0	0	Chandler, Spurgeon Ferdinand (Spud)	P	1	.000	B	
		Collins, Robert Joseph	C	3	.333	ChiN40	C
		Cooney, John Walter	OF2	10	.125	xBknN	C
		Crosetti, Frank Peter Joseph	SS	55	.239	B	
		Derry, Alva Russell	OF28	38	.254	A	
13	10	Donald, Richard Atley	P	30	.182	B	
		Drescher, Wm. Clayton	C1	4	.143	A	
13	13	Dubiel, Walter John	P30	31	.181	A	
		Etten, Nicholas Raymond Thomas	1B	154	.293	B	
		Garbark, Nathaniel Michael	C85	89	.261	A	
		Grimes, Oscar Ray Jr. (SS20)	3B97	116	.279	B	
		Hemsley, Ralston Burdett (Rollie)	C76	81	.268	B	
0	2	Johnson, John Clifford	P	22	.500	A	
		Levy, Edward Clarence	OF36	40	.242	NY42	C
		Lindell, John Harlan	OF	149	.300	B	

WON	LOST	NAME	POS.	G.	BA	FROM	TO
0	0	Lyons, Albert Harold	P11	19	.346	A	
		Martin, Hershel Ray	OF80	85	.302	PhilN40	
		Metheny, Arthur Beauregard	OF132	137	.239	B	
		Milosevich, Michael	SS91	94	.247	A	
5	7	Page, Joseph Francis	P	19	.156	A	
6	3	Queen, MelvinJoseph	P	10	.194	NY42	
		Rosenthal, Lawrence John (Larry)	OF25	36	+.198	Clev41	Phil
4	3	Roser, Emerson Corey	P	16	.100	A	
		Savage, Donald Anthony	3B60	71	.264	A	
		Stainback, George Tucker (Tuck)	OF24	30	.218	B	
		Stirnweiss, George Henry	2B	154	.319	B	
4	4	Turner, James Riley	P	35	.200	B	
		Waner, Paul Glee (Big Poison)		9	.143	xBknN	
5	7	Zuber, Wm. Henry	P	22	.129	B	

WON 81
LOST 71
TG 152

AMERICAN LEAGUE

1945.

FINISHED 4th.

PCT. .533

NEW YORK

JOSEPH VINCENT McCARTHY

WON	LOST	NAME	POS.	G.	BA	FROM	TO
13	9	Bevens, Floyd Clifford	P	29	.111	B	
8	11	Bonham, Ernest Edward	P	23	.238	B	
10	5	Borowy, Henry Ludwig	P	18	.220	B	ChiN
		Buzas, Joseph John	SS12	30	.262	A	C
2	1	Chandler, Spurgeon Frederick (Spud)	P	4	.333	B	
		Crompton, Herbert Bryan	C33	36	.192	Wash37	C
		Crosetti, Frank Peter Joseph	SS126	130	.238	B	
		Derry, Alva Russell	OF68	78	.225	B	
5	4	Donald, Richard Atley	P	9	.208	B	C
		Drescher, Wm. Clayton	C33	48	.270	B	
10	9	Dubiel, Walter John	P	26	.276	B	
		Etten, Nicholas Raymond Thomas	1B	152	.285	B	
		Garbark, Nathaniel Michael	C59	60	.216	B	C
9	8	Gettel, Allen Jones	P	27	.281	A	
		Grimes, Oscar Ray Jr. (1B1)	3B141	142	.265	B	
3	3	Holcombe, Kenneth Edward	P	23	.133	A	
		Keller, Chas. Ernest	OF	44	.301	NY43	
		Lindell, John Harlan	OF	41	.283	B	
		Martin, Hershel Ray	OF102	117	.267	B	C
		Metheny, Arthur Beauregard	OF128	133	.248	B	
		Milosevich, Michael (2B1)	SS22	30	.217	B	C
6	3	Page, Joseph Francis	P	20	.250	B	
		Robinson, Aaron Andrew	C45	50	.281	NY43	
0	0	Roser, Emerson Corey	P	11	.125	B	
7	3	Ruffing, Chas. Herbert (Red)	P11	21	.217	NY42	

WON	LOST	NAME	POS.	G.	BA	FROM	TO
		Savage, Donald Anthony (OF2)	3B14	34	.224	B	C
0	0	Schreiber, Paul Frederick	P	2	.000	BknN23	C
		Stainback, George Tucker (Tuck)	OF83	95	.257	B	
		Stirnweiss, George Henry	2B	152	.309	B	
3	4	Turner, James Riley	P	30	.091	B	C
		Waner, Paul Glee (Big Poison)		1	.000	B	C
5	11	Zuber, Wm. Henry	P	21	.167	B	

WON 87 LOST 67 TG 154 — AMERI CAN LEAGUE 1946. — FINISHED 3rd. PCT. .565

NEW YORK

JOSEPH VINCENT McCARTHY WM. MALCOLM DICKEY JOHN HENRY NEUN

WON	LOST	NAME	POS.	G.	BA	FROM	TO
		Berra, Lawrence Peter	C6	7	.364	A	
16	13	Bevens, Floyd Clifford	P	31	.083	B	
		Bockman, Joseph Edward	3B	4	.083	A	
5	8	Bonham, Ernest Edward	P	18	.129	B	
		Brown, Robert Wm. (3B2)	SS5	7	.333	A	
0	1	Byrne, Thomas Joseph	P4	14	.222	NY43	
20	8	Chandler, Spurgeon Frederick (Spud)	P	34	.149	B	
		Colman, Frank Loyd	OF	5	.267	xPittN	
		Crosetti, Frank Peter Joseph	SS24	28	.288	B	
		Dickey, Wm. Malcolm MGR.	C39	54	.261	NY43	C
		DiMaggio, Joseph Paul Jr. (Joe)	OF131	132	.290	NY42	
		Drescher, Wm. Clayton	C3	5	.333	B	C
0	1	Drews, Karl August	P	3	.000	A	
		Etten, Nicholas Raymond Thomas	1B84	108	.232	B	
6	7	Gettel, Allen Jones	P	26	.125	B	
		Gordon, Joseph Lowell (Flash)	2B108	112	.210	NY43	
		Grimes, Oscar Ray Jr. (2B5)	SS7	14	+.205	B	Phil
11	3	Gumpert, Randall Pennington	P	33	.128	Phil38	
		Henrich, Thomas David (1B41)	OF111	150	.251	NY42	
0	2	Hiller, Frank Walter	P	3	.250	A	
		Johnson, Wm. Russell	3B74	85	.260	NY43	
0	0	Karpel, Herbert	P	2	.000	A	C
		Keller, Chas. Ernest	OF149	150	.275	B	
		Lindell, John Harlan (1B14)	OF74	102	.259	B	
0	1	Lyons, Albert Harold	P	2	.000	NY44	
		Majeski, Henry	3B2	8	+.083	BosN41	Phil
3	4	Marshall, Clarence Westly	P	23	.143	A	
		Metheny, Arthur Beauregard		3	.000	B	C
4	2	Murphy, John Joseph (Grandma)	P	27	.000	NY43	
		Niarhos, Constantine Gregory	C29	37	.225	A	
9	8	Page, Joseph Francis	P31	32	.163	B	
1	1	Queen, Melvin Joseph	P	14	.143	NY44	
2	0	Raschi, Victor Angelo John	P	2	.250	A	
		Rizzuto, Philip Francis	SS125	126	.257	NY42	
		Robinson, Aaron Andrew	C95	100	.297	B	
1	1	Roser, Emerson Corey	P	4	.000	B	BosN
5	1	Ruffing, Chas. Herbert (Red)	P	8	.120	B	
0	2	Russo, Marius Ugo	P8	10	.000	NY43	C
		Silvestri, Kenneth Joseph	C12	13	.286	NY41	
		Souchock, Stephen	1B20	47	.302	A	
0	0	Stanceu Chas.	P	3	.000	NY41	PhilN
		Stirnweiss, George Henry (2B46 SS4)	3B79	129	.251	B	
2	1	Wade, Jacob Fields (Jake)	P	13	+.111	Chi44	Wash
		Weatherly, Cyril Roy (Stormy)		2	.500	NY43	
2	2	Wight, Wm. Robert	P	14	.000	A	
0	1	Zuber, Wm. Henry	P	3	+.000	B	Bos

WON 97 LOST 57 TG 154 — AMERICAN LEAGUE 1947. — FINISHED 1st. PCT. .630

NEW YORK

STANLEY RAYMOND HARRIS

WON	LOST	NAME	POS.	G.	BA	FROM	TO
0	0	Ardizola, Rinaldo Joseph	P	1	.000	A	C
		Berra, Lawrence Peter (OF24)	C51	83	.280	B	
7	13	Bevens, Floyd Clifford	P	28	.121	B	C
		Brown, Robert Wm. (SS11 OF3)	3B27	69	.300	B	
0	0	Byrne, Thomas Joseph	P	4	.000	B	
9	5	Chandler, Spurgeon Frederick (Spud)	P	17	.245	B	C
		Clark, Alfred Aloysius	OF16	24	.373	A	
		Colman, Frank Loyd	OF6	22	.107	B	C
		Crosetti, Frank Peter Joseph (SS1)	2B1	3	.000	B	
		DiMaggio, Joseph Paul Jr. (Joe)	OF139	141	.315	B	
6	6	Drews, Karl August	P	30	.037	B	
		Frey, Linus Reinhard (Lonny)	2B8	24	.179	xChiN	
4	1	Gumpert, Randall Pennington	P24	25	.071	B	
		Henrich, Thomas David (1B6)	OF132	142	.287	B	
		Houk, Ralph George	C	41	.272	A	
4	3	Johnson, Donald Roy	P	15	.000	A	
		Johnson, Wm. Russell	3B	132	.285	B	
		Keller, Chas. Ernest	OF43	45	.238	B	
		Lindell, John Harlan	OF113	127	.275	B	
		Lollar, John Sherman	C9	11	.219	Clev	

WON	LOST	NAME	POS.	G.	BA	FROM	TO
		Lucadello, John	2B5	12	.083	StL	C
1	0	Lyons, Albert Harold	P6	8	.667	B	PittN
		McQuinn, George Hartley (Mac)	1B142	144	.304	Phil	
		Mack, Raymond James		1	.000	Clev	ChiN
7	5	Newsom, Louis Norman (Buck)	P	17	+.095	xWash	
14	8	Page, Joseph Francis	P	56	.217	B	
		Phillips, Jack Dorn	1B10	16	.278	A	
0	0	Queen, Melvin Joseph	P	5	.000	B	PittN
7	2	Raschi, Victor Angelo John	P	15	.250	B	
19	8	Reynolds, Allie Pierce	P34	38	.146	Clev	
		Rizzuto, Philip Francis	SS151	153	.273	B	
		Robinson, Aaron Andrew	C74	82	.270	B	
		Sepkowski, Theodore Walter		2	+.000	xClev	C
14	5	Shea, Francis Joseph	P	27	.196	A	
		Silvestri, Kenneth Joseph	C	3	.200	B	
1	0	Starr, Richard Eugene	P	4	.333	A	
		Stirnweiss, George Henry	2B	148	.256	B	
3	1	Wensloff, Chas. Wm.	P	11	.263	NY43	
1	0	Wight, Wm. Robert	P	1	.000	B	

WON 94
LOST 60
TG 154

AMERICAN LEAGUE — FINISHED 3rd.

1948. — PCT. .610

NEW YORK

STANLEY RAYMOND HARRIS

WON	LOST	NAME	POS.	G.	BA	FROM	TO
		Bauer, Henry Albert	OF14	19	.180	A	
		Berra, Lawrence Peter (OF50)	C71	125	.305	B	
		Brown, Robert Wm. (2B17 SS26 OF4)	3B41	113	.300	B	
8	5	Byrne, Thomas Joseph	P	31	.326	B	
		Collins, Joseph Edward		5	.200	A	
		Crosetti, Frank Peter Joseph (SS5)	2B6	17	.286	B	C
		DiMaggio, Joseph Paul Jr. (Joe)	OF152	153	.320	B	
2	3	Drews, Karl August	P	19	+.000	B	StL
5	3	Embree, Chas. Willard	P	20	.148	Clev	
		Frey, Linus Reinhard (Lonny)		1	.000	B	NYN
1	0	Gumpert, Randall Pennington	P	15	+.000	B	Chi
		Henrich, Thomas David (1B46)	OF102	146	.308	B	
5	2	Hiller, Frank Walter	P	22	.375	NY46	
		Houk, Ralph George	C	14	.276	B	
		Johnson, Wm. Russell	3B118	127	.294	B	
		Keller, Chas. Ernest	OF66	83	.267	B	
		Lindell, John Harlan	OF79	88	.317	B	
		Lollar, John Sherman	C10	22	.211	B	
17	11	Lopat, Edmund Walter	P33	34	.173	Chi	
		Mapes, Clifford Franklin	OF21	53	.250	A	
0	0	Marshall, Clarence Westly	P	1	.000	NY46	

WON	LOST	NAME	POS.	G.	BA	FROM	TO
		McQuinn, George Hartley (Mac)	1B90	94	.248	B	C
		Niarhos, Constantine Gregory	C82	83	.268	NY46	
7	8	Page, Joseph Francis	P	55	.292	B	
		Phillips, Jack Dorn	1B	1	.000	B	
5	3	Porterfield, Erwin Coolidge	P	16	.250	A	
19	8	Raschi, Victor Angelo John	P	36	.235	B	
16	7	Reynolds, Allie Pierce	P39	41	.193	B	
		Rizzuto, Philip Francis	SS	128	.252	B	
9	10	Shea, Francis Joseph	P	28	.149	B	
		Silvera, Chas. Anthony Ryan	C	4	.571	A	
		Souchock, Stephen	1B32	44	.203	NY46	
0	0	Starr, Richard Eugene	P	1	.000	B	
		Stewart, Edward Perry		6	+.200	PittN42	Wash
		Stirnweiss, George Henry	2B	141	.252	B	

WON 97
LOST 57
TG 154

AMERICAN LEAGUE — FINISHED 1st.

1949. — PCT. .630

NEW YORK

CHAS. DILLON STENGEL

WON	LOST	NAME	POS.	G.	BA	FROM	TO
		Bauer, Henry Albert	OF95	103	.272	B	
		Berra, Lawrence Peter	C109	116	.277	B	
		Brown, Robert Wm. (OF3)	3B86	104	.283	B	
0	1	Buxton, Ralph Stanley	P	14	.000	Phil38	C
15	7	Byrne, Thomas Joseph	P32	35	.193	B	
1	0	Casey, Hugh Thomas	P	4	.000	xPittN	C
		Coleman, Gerald Francis (SS4)	2B122	128	.275	A	
		Collins, Joseph Edward	1B5	7	.100	B	
		Delsing, James Henry	OF5	9	.350	Chi	
		DiMaggio, Joseph Paul Jr. (Joe)	OF	76	.346	B	
0	2	Hiller, Frank Walter	P	4	.500	B	
		Henrich, Thomas David (1B52)	OF61	115	.287	B	
0	0	Hood, Wallace James Jr.	P	2	.000	A	C
		Houk, Ralph George	C	5	.571	B	
		Johnson, Wm. Russell (1B21 2B1)	3B81	113	.249	B	
		Keller, Chas. Ernest	OF31	60	.250	B	
		Kryhoski, Richard David	1B51	54	.294	A	
		Lindell, John Harlan	OF65	78	.242	B	
15	10	Lopat, Edmund Walter	P	31	.263	B	
		Mapes, Clifford Franklin	OF108	111	.247	B	
3	0	Marshall, Clarence Westly	P	21	.111	B	
		Mize, John Robert	1B6	13	.261	xNYN	
		Mole, Fenton LeRoy	1B8	10	.185	A	C
		Niarhos, Constantine Gregory	C30	32	.279	B	
13	8	Page, Joseph Francis	P	60	.175	B	
		Phillips, Jack Dorn	1B38	45	.308	B	PittN
2	4	Pillette, Duane Xavier	P	12	.000	A	
2	5	Porterfield, Erwin Coolidge	P	12	.053	B	

WON	LOST	NAME	POS.	G.	BA	FROM	TO
21	10	Raschi, Victor Angelo John	P	38	.157	B	
17	6	Reynolds, Allie Pierce	P35	37	.218	B	
		Rizzuto, Philip Francis	SS152	153	.275	B	
7	3	Sanford, John Frederick	P	29	.118	StL	
1	1	Shea, Francis Joseph	P	20	.250	B	
		Silvera, Chas. Anthony Ryan	C51	58	.315	B	
		Stirnweiss, George Henry (3B4)	2B51	70	.261	B	
		Witek, Nicholas Joseph (Mickey)		1	1.000	NYN47	C
		Woodling, Eugene Richard	OF98	112	.270	PittN47	

WON 98
LOST 56
TG 154

AMERICAN LEAGUE — FINISHED 1st.

1950. — PCT. .636

NEW YORK

CHAS. DILLON STENGEL

WON	LOST	NAME	POS.	G.	BA	FROM	TO
		Bauer, Henry Albert	OF110	113	.320	B	
		Berra, Lawrence Peter	C148	151	.322	B	
		Brown, Robert Wm.	3B82	95	.267	B	
0	0	Burdette, Selva Lewis	P	2	.000	A	
15	9	Byrne, Thomas Joseph	P31	34	.272	B	
		Coleman, Gerald Francis (SS6)	2B152	153	.287	B	
		Collins, Joseph Edward (OF2)	1B99	108	.234	B	
		Delsing, James Henry		12	+.400	B	StL
		DiMaggio, Joseph Paul Jr. (Joe) (1B1)	OF137	139	.301	B	
8	4	Ferrick, Thomas Jerome	P	30	+.143	xStL	
9	1	Ford, Edward Chas.	P	20	.194	A	
		Henrich, Thomas David	1B34	73	.272	B	C
		Hopp, John Leonard (OF6)	1B12	19	.333	xPittN	
		Houk, Ralph George	C9	10	.111	B	
		Jensen, Jack Eugene	OF23	45	.171	A	
1	0	Johnson, Donald Roy	P	8	+.000	NY47	StL
		Johnson, Wm. Russell (1B5)	3B100	108	.260	B	
		Lindell, John Harlan	OF6	7	.190	B	StLN
18	8	Lopat, Edmund Walter	P35	36	.232	B	
0	0	Madison, David Pledger	P	1	.000	A	
		Mapes, Clifford Franklin	OF102	108	.247	B	
		Martin, Alfred Manuel (3B1)	2B22	34	.250	A	
		Mize, John Robert	1B72	90	.277	B	
0	1	Nevel, Ernie Wrye	P	3	.000	A	
		Niarhos, Constantine Gregory		1	+.000	B	Chi
1	1	Ostrowski, Joseph Paul	P	21	+.111	xStL	
3	7	Page, Joseph Francis	P	37	.250	B	
0	0	Pillette, Duane Xavier	P	4	+.000	B	StL
1	1	Porterfield, Erwin Coolidge	P10	11	.333	B	
21	8	Raschi, Victor Angelo John	P	33	.198	B	
16	12	Reynolds, Allie Pierce	P35	36	.185	B	
		Rizzuto, Philip Francis	SS	155	.324	B	

WON	LOST	NAME	POS.	G.	BA	FROM	TO
5	4	Sanford, John Frederick	P	26	.229	B	
		Silvera, Chas. Anthony Ryan	C15	18	.160	B	
		Stirnweiss, George Henry (3B1)	2B4	7	+.000	B	StL
		Wakefield, Richard Cummings		3	.500	Det	
		Woodling, Eugene Richard	OF118	122	.283	B	
		Workman, Henry Kilgariff	1B1	2	.200	A	C

WON 98
LOST 56
TG 154

AMERICAN LEAGUE — FINISHED 1st.

1951. — PCT. .636

NEW YORK

CHAS. DILLON STENGEL

WON	LOST	NAME	POS.	G.	BA	FROM	TO
		Bauer, Henry Albert	OF107	118	.296	B	
		Berra, Lawrence Peter	C	141	.294	B	
		Brideweser, James Ehrenfeld	SS	2	.375	A	
		Brown, Robert Wm.	3B90	103	.268	B	
2	1	Byrne, Thomas Joseph	P	9	+.333	B	StL
		Cerv, Robert Henry	OF9	12	.214	A	
		Coleman, Gerald Francis (SS18)	2B102	121	.249	B	
		Collins, Joseph Edward (OF15)	1B114	125	.286	B	
		Courtney, Clinton Dawson	C	1	.000	A	
		DiMaggio, Joseph Paul Jr. (Joe)	OF113	116	.263	B	C
1	1	Ferrick, Thomas Jerome	P	9	+1.000	B	Wash.
1	0	Hogue, Robert Clinton	P	7	+.000	xStL	
		Hopp, John Leonard	1B25	46	.206	B	
		Houk, Ralph George	C	3	.200	B	
		Jensen, Jack Eugene	OF48	56	.298	B	
		Johnson, Wm. Russell	3B13	15	.300	B	StLN
1	3	Kramer, John Henry	P	19	.100	xNYN	C
8	4	Kuzava, Robert LeRoy	P23	24	+.136	xWash.	
21	9	Lopat, Edmund Walter	P	31	.179	B	
		Mantle, Mickey Chas.	OF86	96	.267	A	
		Mapes, Clifford Franklin	OF32	45	+.216	B	StL
		Martin, Alfred Manuel (SS6 3B2 OF1)	2B23	51	.259	B	
		Mize, John Robert	1B93	113	.259	B	
9	3	Morgan, Tom Stephen	P	27	.273	A	
0	0	Muncrief, Robert Cleveland	P	2	.000	ChiN49	C
		McDougald, Gilbert James (2B55)	3B82	131	.306	A	
0	0	Nevel, Ernie Wrye	P	1	.000	B	
6	4	Ostrowski, Joseph Paul	P	34	.107	B	
1	1	Overmire, Frank	P	15	+.143	xStL	
0	0	Porterfield, Erwin Coolidge	P	2	+.000	B	Wash.
21	10	Raschi, Victor Angelo John	P	35	.176	B	
17	8	Reynolds, Allie Pierce	P40	43	.184	B	
		Rizzuto, Philip Francis	SS	144	.274	B	

WON	LOST	NAME	POS.	G.	BA	FROM	TO
0	3	Sanford, John Frederick	P	11	+.000	B	Wash.
3	1	Schallock, Arthur Lawrence	P	11	.294	A	
5	5	Shea, Francis Joseph	P	25	.214	NY49	
		Silvera, Chas. Anthony Ryan	C	18	.275	B	
0	2	Wiesler, Robert George	P	4	.000	A	
		Wilson, Archie Clifton	OF2	4	.000	A	
		Woodling, Eugene Richard	OF116	120	.281	B	

WON 95 AMERICAN LEAGUE FINISHED 1st.
LOST 59
TG 154 1952. PCT. .617

NEW YORK

CHAS. DILLON STENGEL

WON	LOST	NAME	POS.	G.	BA	FROM	TO
		Babe, Loren Rolland	3B9	12	.095	A	
		Bauer, Henry Albert	OF139	141	.293	B	
		Berra, Lawrence Peter	C140	142	.273	B	
1	0	Blackwell, Ewell	P	5	.200	xCinN	
		Brideweser, James Ehrenfeld (2B4 3B1)	SS22	42	.263	B	
		Brown, Robert Wm.	3B24	29	.247	B	
		Carey, Andrew Arthur (SS1)	3B14	16	.150	A	
		Cerv, Robert Henry	OF27	36	.241	B	
		Coleman, Gerald Francis	2B	11	.405	B	
		Collins, Joseph Edward	1B119	122	.280	B	
6	2	Gorman, Thomas Aloysius	P	12	.087	A	
3	5	Hogue, Robert Clinton	P	27	+.273	B	StL
		Hopp, John Leonard	1B12	15	+.160	B	Det
		Houk, Ralph George	C	9	.333	B	
		Jensen, Jack Eugene	OF5	7	+.105	B	Wash
		Keller, Chas. Ernest	OF1	2	.000	Det	C
8	8	Kuzava, Robert LeRoy	P	28	.093	B	
10	5	Lopat, Edmund Walter	P	20	.173	B	
		Mantle, Mickey Chas. (3B1)	OF141	142	.311	B	
		Martin, Alfred Manuel	2B107	109	.267	B	
4	6	Miller, Wm. Paul	P	21	.214	A	
		Mize, John Robert	1B27	78	.263	B	
5	4	Morgan, Tom Stephen	P	16	.182	B	
3	4	McDonald, James LeRoy	P	26	.316	StL	
		McDougald, Gilbert James (2B38)	3B117	152	.263	B	
		Noren, Irving Arnold (1B19)	OF60	93	+.235	xWash	
2	2	Ostrowski, Joseph Paul	P	20	.000	B	C
16	6	Raschi, Victor Angelo John	P	31	.188	B	
20	8	Reynolds, Allie Pierce	P35	41	.153	B	
		Rizzuto, Philip Francis	SS	152	.254	B	
11	6	Sain, John Franklin	P35	47	.268	B	
5	1	Scarborough, Ray Wilson	P	9	+.357	xBos	
0	1	Schaeffer, Harry Edward	P	5	.000	A	C
0	0	Schallock, Arthur Lawrence	P	2	.000	B	
1	1	Schmitz, John Albert	P	5	.600	xBknN	CinN
		Segrist, Kal Hill (3B1)	2B11	13	.043	A	

WON	LOST	NAME	POS.	G.	BA	FROM	TO
		Silvera, Chas. Anthony Ryan	C	20	.327	B	
		Wilson, Archie Clifton		3	+.500	B	Wash
		Woodling, Eugene Richard	OF118	122	.309	B	

WON 99 AMERICAN LEAGUE FINISHED 1st.
LOST 52
TG 151 1953. PCT. .656

NEW YORK

CHAS. DILLON STENGEL

WON	LOST	NAME	POS.	G.	BA	FROM	TO
		Babe, Loren Rolland	3B	5	+.333	B	Phil
		Bauer, Henry Albert	OF126	133	.304	B	
		Berra, Lawrence Peter	C133	137	.296	B	
2	0	Blackwell, Ewell	P	8	.000	B	
		Bollweg, Donald Raymond (OF1)	1B43	70	.297	StLN51	
		Brideweser, James Ehrenfeld	SS3	7	1.000	B	
		Carey, Andrew Arthur (2B1 SS2)	3B40	51	.321	B	
		Cerv, Robert Henry		8	.000	B	
		Coleman, Gerald Francis (SS1)	2B7	8	.200	B	
		Collins, Joseph Edward (OF4)	1B113	127	.269	B	
18	6	Ford, Edward Chas.	P32	33	.267	NY50	
4	5	Gorman, Thomas Aloysius	P	40	.133	B	
		Houk, Ralph George	C	8	.222	B	
0	2	Kraly, Steve Chas.	P	5	.000	A	C
6	5	Kuzava, Robert LeRoy	P	33	.048	B	
16	4	Lopat, Edmund Walter	P25	26	.190	B	
		Mantle, Mickey Chas. (SS1)	OF121	127	.295	B	
		Martin, Alfred Manuel (SS18)	2B146	149	.257	B	
2	1	Miller, Wm. Paul	P	13	.200	B	
		Miranda, Guillermo Perez	SS44	48	+.224	xStL	
		Mize, John Robert	1B15	81	.250	B	C
9	7	McDonald, James LeRoy	P27	29	.098	B	
		McDougald, Gilbert James (2B26)	3B136	141	.285	B	
		Noren, Irving Arnold	OF96	109	.267	B	
13	6	Raschi, Victor Angelo John	P	28	.143	B	
		Renna, Wm. Beneditto	OF40	61	.314	A	
13	7	Reynolds, Allie Pierce	P41	42	.122	B	
		Rizzuto, Philip Francis	SS133	134	.271	B	
14	7	Sain, John Franklin	P40	41	.250	B	
2	2	Scarborough, Ray Wilson	P	25	+.083	B	Det
0	0	Schallock, Arthur Lawrence	P	7	.333	B	
0	0	Schmitz, John Albert	P	3	+.000	CinN	Wash
		Schult, Arthur Wm.		7	.000	A	
		Silvera, Chas. Anthony Ryan (3B1)	C39	42	.280	B	
		Triandos, Gus (C5)	1B12	18	.157	A	

WON	LOST	NAME	POS.	G.	BA	FROM	TO
		Verdi, Frank Michael	SS	1	.000	A	C
		Woodling, Eugene Richard	OF119	125	.306	B	

WON 103 LOST 51 TG 154

AMERICAN LEAGUE 1954.

FINISHED 2nd. PCT. .669

NEW YORK

CHAS. DILLON STENGEL

WON	LOST	NAME	POS.	G.	BA	FROM	TO
		Bauer, Henry Albert	OF108	114	.294	B	
		Berberet, Louis Joseph	C3	5	.400	A	
		Berra, Lawrence Peter (3B1)	C149	151	.307	B	
1	0	Branca, Ralph Theodore Joseph	P	5	+.500	xDet	
		Brown, Robert Wm.	3B17	28	.217	NY52	C
9	7	Byrd, Harry Gladwin	P	25	.196	Phil	
3	2	Byrne, Thomas Joseph	P5	7	.368	Wash	
		Carey, Andrew Arthur	3B120	122	.302	B	
		Cerv, Robert Henry	OF24	56	.260	B	
		Coleman, Gerald Francis (SS30 3B1)	2B79	107	.217	B	
		Collins, Joseph Edward	1B117	130	.271	B	
16	8	Ford, Edward Chas.	P	34	.161	B	
0	0	Gorman, Thomas Aloysius	P	23	.000	B	
20	6	Grim, Robert Anton	P	37	.143	A	
		Heid, Woodson George (3B1)	SS4	4	.000	A	
		Houk, Ralph George		1	.000	B	C
1	1	Konstanty, Casimer James	P	9	.000	xPhilN	
1	3	Kuzava, Robert LeRoy	P	20	+.000	B	Balt
		Leja, Frank John	1B6	12	.200	A	
12	4	Lopat, Edmund Walter	P	26	.018	B	
		Mantle, Mickey Chas. (2B1 SS4)	OF144	146	.300	B	
0	1	Miller, Wm. Paul	P	2	.000	B	
		Miranda, Guillermo Perez (2B4 3B1)	SS88	92	.250	B	
11	5	Morgan, Tom Stephen	P	32	.143	NY52	
4	1	McDonald, James LeRoy	P	16	.211	B	
		McDougald, Gilbert James (3B35)	2B92	126	.259	B	
		Noren, Irving Arnold (1B1)	OF116	125	.319	B	
13	4	Reynolds, Allie Pierce	P	36	.160	B	C
		Rizzuto, Philip Francis (2B1)	SS126	127	.195	B	
		Robinson, Wm. Edward	1B29	85	.261	Phil	
6	6	Sain, John Franklin	P	45	.353	B	
0	1	Schallock, Arthur Lawrence	P	6	.000	B	
		Silvera, Chas. Anthony Ryan	C18	20	.270	B	
		Skowron, Wm. Joseph (2B2 3B5)	1B61	87	.340	A	
		Slaughter, Enos Bradsher	OF30	69	.248	StLN	
3	0	Stuart, Marlin Henry	P	10	+.333	xBalt	C
		Triandos, Gus	C1	2	.000	B	

WON	LOST	NAME	POS.	G.	BA	FROM	TO
3	2	Wiesler, Robert George	P	6	.273	NY51	
		Woodling, Eugene Richard	OF89	97	.250	B	

WON 96 LOST 58 TG 154

AMERICAN LEAGUE 1955.

FINISHED 1st. PCT. .623

NEW YORK

CHAS. DILLON STENGEL

WON	LOST	NAME	POS.	G.	BA	FROM	TO
		Bauer, Henry Albert (C1)	OF133	139	.278	B	
		Berberet, Louis Joseph	C1	2	.400	B	
		Berra, Lawrence Peter	C145	147	.272	B	
		Blanchard, John Edwin	C	1	.000	A	
16	5	Byrne, Thomas Joseph	P27	45	.205	B	
		Carey, Andrew Arthur	3B	135	.257	B	
		Carroll, Thomas Edward	SS4	14	.333	A	
		Cerv, Robert Henry	OF20	55	.341	B	
		Coleman, Gerald Francis (2B13 3B1)	SS29	43	.229	B	
2	1	Coleman, Walter Gary	P	10	.200	A	
		Collins, Joseph Edward (OF27)	1B73	105	.234	B	
18	7	Ford, Edward Chas.	P	39	.163	B	
0	0	Gray, Theodore Glenn	P	1	+.000	xClev	Balt
7	5	Grim, Robert Anton	P	26	.120	B	
		Howard, Elston Gene (C9)	OF75	97	.290	A	
		Hunter, Gordon Wm.	SS	98	.227	Balt	
7	2	Konstanty, Casimer James	P	45	.125	B	
8	7	Kucks, John Chas.	P	29	.050	A	
9	2	Larsen, Donald James	P19	21	.146	Balt	
		Leja, Frank John	1B2	7	.000	B	
4	8	Lopat, Edmund Walter	P	16	+.138	B	Balt
		Mantle, Mickey Chas. (SS2)	OF145	147	.306	B	
		Martin, Alfred Manuel (SS3)	2B16	20	.300	NY53	
7	3	Morgan, Tom Stephen	P	40	.222	B	
		McDougald, Gilbert James (3B17)	2B126	141	.285	B	
		Noren, Irving Arnold	OF126	132	.253	B	
		Richardson, Robert Clinton (SS4)	2B6	11	.154	A	
		Rizzuto, Philip Francis (2B1)	SS79	81	.259	B	
		Robinson, Wm. Edward	1B46	88	.208	B	
0	0	Sain, John Franklin	P	3	+.000	B	K.C.
0	0	Schallock, Arthur Lawrence	P	2	+.000	B	Balt
		Silvera, Chas. Anthony Ryan	C11	14	.192	B	
		Skowron, Wm. Joseph (3B3)	1B74	108	.319	B	
		Slaughter, Enos Bradsher		10	+.111	B	K.C.
0	0	Staley, Gerald Lee	P	2	.000	xCinN	
1	3	Sturdivant, Thomas Virgil	P	33	.083	A	
		Tettelbach, Richard Morley	OF	2	.000	A	
		Throneberry, Marvin Eugene	1B	1	1.000	A	
17	13	Turley, Robert Lee	P	36	.134	Balt	

0	2	Wiesler, Robert George	P	16	.143	B	

WON 97
LOST 57
TG 154

AMERICAN LEAGUE

1956.

FINISHED 1st.

PCT. .630

NEW YORK

CHAS. DILLON STENGEL

WON	LOST	NAME	POS.	G.	BA	FROM	TO
		Bauer, Henry Albert	OF146	147	.241	B	
		Berra, Lawrence Peter (OF1)	C135	140	.298	B	
7	3	Byrne, Thomas Joseph	P37	44	.269	B	
		Carey, Andrew Arthur	3B131	132	.237	B	
		Carroll, Thomas Edward (SS1)	3B11	36	.353	B	
		Cerv, Robert Henry	OF44	54	.304	B	
0	0	Coates, James Alton	P	2	.000	A	
		Coleman, Gerald Francis (SS24 3B18)	2B41	80	.257	B	
3	5	Coleman, Walter Gary	P	29	.042	B	
		Collins, Joseph Edward (1B43)	OF51	100	.225	B	
0	1	Dixon, John Craig	P	3	.000	K.C.	C
19	6	Ford, Edward Chas.	P	31	.218	B	
6	1	Grim, Robert Anton	P	26	.063	B	
		Howard, Elston Gene (C26)	OF65	98	.262	B	
		Hunter, Gordon Wm.	SS32	39	.280	B	
0	0	Konstanty, Casimer James	P	8	.000	B	StLN
18	9	Kucks, John Chas.	P	34	.143	B	
11	5	Larson, Donald James	P38	45	.241	B	
		Lumpe, Jerry Dean (3B1)	SS17	20	.258	A	
		Mantle, Mickey Chas.	OF144	150	.353	B	
		Martin, Alfred Manuel (3B16)	2B105	121	.264	B	
6	7	Morgan, Tom Stephen	P	41	.154	B	
2	6	McDermott, Maurice Joseph	P23	46	.212	Wash	
		McDougald, Gilbert James (2B31 3B5)	SS92	120	.311	B	
		Noren, Irving Arnold (1B1)	OF10	29	.216	B	
		Richardson, Robert Clinton	2B	5	.143	B	
		Rizzuto, Philip Francis	SS30	31	.231	B	C
		Robinson, Wm. Edward	1B14	26	+.222	B	K.C.
		Siebern, Norman Leroy	OF51	54	.204	A	
		Silvera, Chas. Anthony Ryan	C	7	.222	B	
		Skizas, Louis Peter		6	+.167	A	K.C.
		Skowron, Wm. Joseph (3B2)	1B120	134	.308	B	
		Slaughter, Enos Bradsher	OF20	24	+.289	xK.C.	
0	0	Staley, Gerald Lee	P	1	+.000	B	Chi
16	8	Sturdivant, Thomas Virgil	P	32	.313	B	
1	2	Terry, Ralph Willard	P	3	.167	A	
8	4	Turley, Robert Lee	P	27	.174	B	
		Wilson, George Washington	OF6	11	.167	xNYN	C

WON 98
LOST 56
TG 154

AMERICAN LEAGUE

1957.

FINISHED 1st.

PCT. .636

NEW YORK

CHAS. DILLON STENGEL

WON	LOST	NAME	POS.	G.	BA	FROM	TO
		Bauer, Henry Albert	OF135	137	.259	B	
		Bella, John	OF4	5	.100	A	
		Berra, Lawrence Peter (OF6)	C121	134	.251	B	
4	6	Byrne, Thomas Joseph	P30	35	.189	B	C
		Carey, Andrew Arthur	3B81	85	.255	B	
2	2	Cicotte, Alva Warren	P	20	.150	A	
		Coleman, Gerald Francis (SS4 3B21)	2B45	72	.268	B	C
		Collins, John Edward (OF15)	1B32	79	.201	B	C
		Del Greco, Robert George	OF6	8	.429	xChiN	
8	3	Ditmar, Arthur John	P	46	.200	K.C.	
11	5	Ford, Edward Chas.	P	24	.143	B	
12	8	Grim, Robert Anton	P	46	.111	B	
		Held, Woodson George		1	+.000	NY54	K.C.
		Howard, Elston Gene (C32 1B2)	OF71	110	.253	B	
		Johnson, Darrell Dean	C20	21	.217	Chi52	
		Kubek, Anthony Christopher (2B1 SS41 3B38)	OF50	127	.297	A	
8	10	Kucks, John Chas.	P	37	.109	B	
10	4	Larsen, Donald James	P27	31	.250	B	
		Lumpe, Jerry Dean (SS6)	3B30	40	.340	B	
2	0	Maglie, Salvatore Anthony	P	6	.250	xBknN	
		Mantle, Mickey Chas.	OF139	144	.365	B	
		Martin, Alfred Manuel (3B13)	2B26	43	+.241	B	K.C.
		McDougald, Gilbert James (2B21 3B7)	SS121	141	.289	B	
		Richardson, Robert Clinton	2B93	97	.256	B	
11	5	Shantz, Robert Clayton	P30	33	.179	K.C.	
		Simpson, Harry Leon (1B21)	OF42	75	+.250	xK.C.	
		Skowron, Wm. Joseph	1B115	122	.304	B	
		Slaughter, Enos Bradsher	OF64	96	.254	B	
16	6	Sturdivant, Thomas Virgil	P	28	.183	B	
1	1	Terry, Ralph Willard	P	7	+.250	B	K.C.
13	6	Turley, Robert Lee	P	32	.088	B	

WON 92
LOST 62
TG 154

AMERICAN LEAGUE

1958.

FINISHED 1st.

PCT. .597

NEW YORK

CHAS. DILLON STENGEL

WON	LOST	NAME	POS.	G.	BA	FROM	TO
		Bauer, Henry Albert	OF123	128	.268	B	
		Berra, Lawrence Peter	C88	122	.266	B	
		(1B2 OF21)					
		Brickell, Fritz Darrell	2B	2	.000	A	
		Carey, Andrew Arthur	3B99	102	.286	B	
		Del Greco, Robert George	OF	12	.200	B	
1	2	Dickson, Murry Monroe	P	6	+.286	xK.C.	
9	8	Ditmar, Arthur John	P	38	.250	B	
6	4	Duren, Rinold George	P	44	.077	K.C.	
14	7	Ford, Edward Chas.	P	30	.205	B	
0	1	Grim, Robert Anton	P	11	+.000	B	K.C.
		Howard, Elston Gene	C67	103	.314	B	
		(1B5 OF24)					
0	0	James, John Phillip	P	1	.000	A	
		Johnson, Darrell Dean	C4	5	.250	B	
		Kubek, Anthony Christopher	SS134	138	.265	B	
		(1B1 2B1 OF3)					
8	8	Kucks, John Chas.	P	34	.125	B	
9	6	Larsen, Donald James	P19	28	.306	B	
		Lumpe, Jerry Dean (SS5)	3B65	81	.254	B	
7	3	Maas, Duane Frederick	P	22	+.088	xK.C.	
1	1	Maglie, Salvatore Anthony	P	7	.143	B	StLN
		Mantle, Mickey Chas.	OF	150	.304	B	
		McDougald, Gilbert James	2B115	138	.250	B	
		(SS19)					
4	2	Monroe, Zachary Chas.	P	21	.118	A	
		Richardson, Robert Clinton	2B51	73	.247	B	
		(SS2 3B13)					
7	6	Shantz, Robert Clayton (OF1)	P33	33	.229	B	
		Siebern, Norman Leroy	OF133	134	.300	NY56	
		Simpson, Harry Leon	OF15	24	+.216	B	K.C.
		Skowron, Wm. Joseph (3B2)	1B118	126	.273	B	
		Slaughter, Enos Bradsher	OF35	77	.304	B	
3	6	Sturdivant, Thomas Virgil	P	15	.190	B	
		Throneberry, Marvin Eugene	1B40	60	.227	NY55	
		(OF5)					
2	1	Trucks, Virgil Oliver	P	25	+.250	xK.C.	C
21	7	Turley, Robert Lee	P	33	.136	B	

WON 79 — AMERICAN LEAGUE — FINISHED 3rd.
LOST 75
TG 154 — 1959. — PCT. .513

NEW YORK

CHAS. DILLON STENGEL

WON	LOST	NAME	POS.	G.	BA	FROM	TO
		Bauer, Henry Albert	OF111	114	.238	B	
		Berra, Lawrence Peter	C116	131	.284	B	
		(OF7)					
		Blanchard, John Edwin	C12	49	.169	NY55	
		(1B1 OF8)					
0	1	Blaylock, Gary Nelson	P	15	.500	xStLN	C
		Boyer, Cletis LeRoy (3B16)	SS26	47	.175	KC57	
		Brickell, Fritz Darrell	SS15	18	.256	B	
		(2B3)					
0	3	Bronstad, James Warren	P	16	.000	A	
		Carey, Andrew Arthur	3B34	41	.257	B	
6	1	Coates, James Alton	P	37	.095	NY56	
13	9	Ditmar, Arthur John	P	38	.197	B	
3	6	Duren, Rinold George	P	41	.000	B	
16	10	Ford, Edward Chas.	P	35	.231	B	
0	0	Freeman, Mark Price	P	1	+.000	xK.C.	
1	1	Gabler, John Richard	P	3	.000	A	
2	5	Grba, Eli	P	19	.214	A	
		Howard, Elston Gene	1B50	125	.273	B	
		(C43 OF28)					
		Hunt, Kenneth Lawrence	OF5	6	.333	A	
		Kubek, Anthony Christopher	SS67	132	.279	B	
		(2B1 3B17 OF53)					
0	1	Kucks, John Chas.	P	9	+.000	B	K.C.
6	7	Larsen, Donald James	P25	29	.255	B	
		Lopez, Hector Headley	3B76	112	+.283	xK.C.	
		(OF35)					
		Lumpe, Jerry Dean	3B12	18	+.222	B	K.C.
		(2B1 SS4)					
14	8	Maas, Duane Frederick	P	38	.125	B	
		Mantle, Mickey Chas.	OF143	144	.285	B	
		McDougald, Gilbert James	2B53	127	.251	B	
		(SS52 3B25)					
0	0	Monroe, Zachary Chas.	P	3	.000	B	C
		Pisoni, James Pete	OF15	17	.176	xMilN	
		Richardson, Robert Clinton	2B109	134	.301	B	
		(SS14 3B12)					
7	3	Shantz, Robert Clayton	P33	40	.217	B	
		Siebern, Norman Leroy (1B2)	OF93	120	.271	B	
		Skowron, Wm. Joseph	1B72	74	.298	B	
		Slaughter, Enos Bradsher	OF26	74	.172	B	MilN
0	2	Sturdivant, Thomas Virgil	P	7	.000	B	
3	7	Terry, Ralph Willard	P	24	+.098	xK.C.	
		Throneberry, Marvin Eugene	1B54	80	.240	B	
		(OF13)					
8	11	Turley, Robert Lee	P	33	.087	B	
		Windhorn, Gordon Ray	OF4	7	.000	A	

WON 97 — AMERICAN LEAGUE — FINISHED 1st.
LOST 57
TG 154 — 1960. — PCT. .630

NEW YORK

CHAS. DILLON STENGEL

WON	LOST	NAME	POS.	G.	BA	FROM	TO
5	1	Arroyo, Luis Enrique	P	29	.000	CinN	
		Berra, Lawrence Peter	C63	120	.276	B	
		(OF36)					
		Blanchard, John Edwin	C28	53	.242	B	

WON	LOST	NAME	POS.	G.	BA	FROM	TO
		Boyer, Cletis Leroy (SS33)	3B99	124	.242	B	
		Carey, Andrew Arthur (OF1)	3B2	4	+.333	B	K.C.
		Cerv, Robert Henry (1B3)	OF51	87	+.250	xK.C.	
13	3	Coates, James Alton	P	35	.250	B	
		DeMaestri, Joseph Paul (SS17)	2B19	49	.229	K.C.	
15	9	Ditmar, Arthur John	P34	36	.159	B	
3	4	Duren, Rinold George	P	42	.000	B	
12	9	Ford, Edward Chas.	P	33	.151	B	
3	3	Gabler, John Richard	P	21	.091	B	
		Gonder, Jesse Lemar	C1	7	.286	A	
6	4	Grba, Eli	P24	27	.238	B	
		Hadley, Kent Wm.	1B24	55	.203	K.C.	C
		Howard, Elston Gene (OF1)	C91	107	.245	B	
		Hunt, Kenneth Lawrence	OF24	25	.273	B	
5	1	James, John Phillip	P	28	.000	NY58	
		Johnson, Deron Roger	3B5	6	.500	A	
0	1	Kipp, Fred Leo	P	4	.000	LAN	C
		Kubek, Anthony Christopher (OF29)	SS136	147	.273	B	
		Long, Richard Dale	1B11	26	.366	xSFN	
		Lopez, Hector Headley (2B5 3B1)	OF106	131	.284	B	
5	1	Maas, Duane Frederick	P	35	.000	B	
		Mantle, Mickey Chas.	OF150	153	.275	B	
		Maris, Roger Eugene	OF131	136	.283	K.C.	
		McDougald, Gilbert James (2B42)	3B84	119	.258	B	C
		Pisoni, James Pete	OF18	20	.111	B	C
		Richardson, Robert Clinton (3B11)	2B141	150	.252	B	
5	4	Shantz, Robert Clayton	P42	43	.100	B	
		Shantz, Wilmer Ebert	C	1	.000	KC55	C
3	5	Short, Wm. Ross	P	10	.200	A	
		Skowron, Wm. Joseph	1B142	146	.309	B	
3	1	Stafford, Wm. Chas.	P11	12	.045	A	
0	0	Stowe, Harold Rudolph	P	1	.000	A	C
10	8	Terry, Ralph Willard	P	35	.122	B	
9	3	Turley, Robert Lee	P	34	.073	B	
		Valo, Elmer Wm.	OF2	8	+.000	Clev	Wash

WON 109 AMERICAN LEAGUE FINISHED 1st.
LOST 53
TG 162 1961. PCT. .673

NEW YORK

RALPH GEORGE HOUK

WON	LOST	NAME	POS.	G.	BA	FROM	TO
15	5	Arroyo, Luis Enrique	P	65	.280	B	
		Berra, Lawrence Peter (C15)	OF87	119	.271	B	
		Blanchard, John Edwin (OF15)	C48	93	.305	B	
		Boyer, Cletis LeRoy (SS12 OF1)	3B141	148	.224	B	
		Cerv, Robert Henry (1B3)	OF30	58	+.271	xL.A.	
1	1	Clevenger, Truman Eugene	P	21	+.250	xL.A.	
11	5	Coates, James Alton	P	43	.029	B	
8	9	Daley, Leavitt Leo	P	23	+.133	xK.C.	
		DeMaestri, Joseph Paul (2B5 3B4)	SS18	30	.146	B	C
2	3	Ditmar, Arthur John	P	12	+.053	B	K.C.
0	1	Downing, Alphonse Erwin	P	5	.000	A	
0	1	Duren, Rinold George	P	4	+.000	B	L.A.
25	4	Ford, Edward Chas.	P	39	.177	B	
		Gardner, Wm. Frederick (2B6)	3B33	41	+.212	xMinn	
		Gonder, Jesse Lamar		15	.333	B	
		Hale, Robert Houston	1B5	11	+.154	xClev.	C
		Howard, Elston Gene (1B9)	C111	129	.348	B	
0	0	James, John Phillip	P	1	+.000	B	L.A.
		Johnson, Deron Roger	3B8	13	+.105	B	K.C.
		Kubek, Anthony Christopher	SS145	153	.276	B	
		Lopez, Hector Headley	OF72	93	.222	B	
0	0	Maas, Duane Frederick	P	1	.000	B	C
		Mantle, Mickey Chas.	OF150	153	.317	B	
		Maris, Roger Eugene	OF160	161	.269	B	
1	2	McDevitt, Daniel Eugene	P	8	+.000	LAN	Minn
		Reed, John Burwell	OF27	28	.154	A	
2	0	Reniff, Harold Eugene	P	25	.000	A	
		Richardson, Robert Clinton	2B161	162	.261	B	
11	5	Sheldon, Roland Frank	P35	36	.125	A	
		Skowron, Wm. Joseph	1B149	150	.267	B	
14	9	Stafford, Wm. Chas.	P	36	.179	B	
16	3	Terry, Ralph Willard	P	31	.227	B	
		Thomas, James Leroy		2	+.500	A	L.A.
		Torgeson, Clifford Earl	1B8	22	+.111	xChi	C
		Tresh, Thomas Michael	SS3	9	.250	A	
3	5	Turley, Robert Lee	P	15	.095	B	

WON 96 AMERICAN LEAGUE FINISHED 1st.
LOST 66
TG 162 1962. PCT. .593

NEW YORK

RALPH GEORGE HOUK

WON	LOST	NAME	POS.	G.	BA	FROM	TO
1	3	Arroyo, Luis Enrique	P	27	.500	B	
		Berra, Lawrence Peter (OF28)	C31	86	.224	B	
		Blanchard, John Edwin (C15 1B2)	OF47	93	.232	B	
7	7	Bouton, James Alan	P36	38	.063	A	
		Boyer, Cletis LeRoy	3B157	158	.272	B	
8	4	Bridges, Marshall	P	52	.000	CinN	
0	1	Brown, Hector Harold	P	2	+.000	xBalt	
		Cerv, Robert Henry	OF3	14	.118	B	HousN

WON	LOST	NAME	POS.	G.	BA	FROM	TO
2	0	Clevenger, Truman Eugene	P21	22	.000	B	C
7	6	Coates, James Alton	P	50	.125	B	
0	0	Cullen, John Patrick	P	2	.000	A	
7	5	Daley, Leavitt Leo	P	43	.185	B	
0	0	Downing, Alphonse Erwin	P	1	.000	B	
17	8	Ford, Edward Chas.	P	38	.118	B	
		Gardner, Wm. Frederick (3B1)	2B1	4	+.000	B	Bos
		Gibbs, Jerry Dean	3B1	2	.000	A	
		Howard, Elston Gene	C129	136	.279	B	
		Kubek, Anthony Christopher (OF6)	SS35	45	.314	B	
		Linz, Philip Francis (2B5 3B8 OF2)	SS21	71	.287	A	
		Long, Richard Dale	1B31	41	+.298	xWash	
		Lopez, Hector Headley (2B1 3B1)	OF84	106	.275	B	
		Mantle, Mickey Chas.	OF117	123	.321	B	
		Maris, Roger Eugene	OF154	157	.256	B	
		Pepitone, Joseph Anthony (1B16)	OF32	63	.239	A	
		Reed, John Burwell	OF75	88	.302	B	
0	0	Reniff, Harold Eugene	P	2	.000	B	
		Richardson, Robert Clinton	2B	161	.302	B	
7	8	Sheldon, Ronald Frank	P	34	.077	B	C
		Skowron, Wm. Joseph	1B135	140	.270	B	
14	9	Stafford, Wm. Chas.	P	35	.218	B	
23	12	Terry, Ralph Willard	P	43	.189	B	
		Tresh, Thomas Michael (OF43)	SS111	157	.286	B	
3	3	Turley, Robert Lee	P	24	.000	B	

WON 104 LOST 57 TG 161

AMERICAN LEAGUE 1963. FINISHED 1st. PCT. .646

NEW YORK

RALPH GEORGE HOUK

WON	LOST	NAME	POS.	G.	BA	FROM	TO
1	1	Arroyo, Luis Enrique	P	6	.000	B	C
		Berra, Lawrence Peter	C35	64	.293	B	
		Blanchard, John Edwin	OF64	76	.225	B	
21	7	Bouton, James Alan	P	40	.072	B	
		Boyer, Cletis LeRoy (2B1 SS9)	3B141	152	.251	B	
2	0	Bridges, Marshall	P	23	.000	B	
		Bright, Harry James (3B12)	1B35	60	.236	xCinN	
0	0	Daley, Leavitt Leo	P	1	.000	B	
13	5	Downing, Alphonse Erwin	P	24	.103	B	
24	7	Ford, Edward Chas.	P	38	.141	B	
		Gibbs, Jerry Dean	C1	4	.250	B	
		Gonzalez, Pedro	2B7	14	.192	A	
5	1	Hamilton, Steve Absher	P	34	+.286	xWash	
		Howard, Elston Gene	C132	135	.287	B	
		Kubek, Anthony Christopher (OF1)	SS132	135	.257	B	
3	2	Kunkel, Wm. Gustave James	P	22	.333	K.C.	C
		Linz, Philip Francis (2B6 3B13 OF12)	SS22	72	.269	B	
		Long, Richard Dale	1B2	14	.200	B	C
		Lopez, Hector Headley (2B1)	OF124	130	.249	B	
		Mantle, Mickey Chas.	OF52	65	.314	B	
		Maris, Roger Eugene	OF86	90	.269	B	
1	0	Metcalf, Thomas John	P	8	.000	A	C
		Pepitone, Joseph Anthony (OF16)	1B143	157	.271	A	
		Reed, John Burwell	OF89	106	.205	B	C
4	3	Reniff, Harold Eugene	P	48	.000	B	
		Richardson, Robert Clinton	2B150	151	.265	B	
4	8	Stafford, Wm. Chas.	P	28	.292	B	
17	15	Terry, Ralph Willard	P	40	.080	B	
		Tresh, Thomas Michael	OF144	145	.269	B	
9	8	Williams, Stanley Wilson	P	29	.102	LAN	

WON 99 LOST 63 TG 162

AMERICAN LEAGUE 1964. FINISHED 1st. PCT. .611

NEW YORK

LAWRENCE PETER BERRA

WON	LOST	NAME	POS.	G.	BA	FROM	TO
		Blanchard, John Edwin (1B3 OF14)	C25	77	.255	B	
18	13	Bouton, James Alan	P	38	.130	B	
		Boyer, Cletis LeRoy (SS21)	3B123	147	.218	B	
		Bright, Harry James	1B2	4	.200	B	
3	2	Daley, Leavitt Leo	P	13	.250	B	C
13	8	Downing, Alphonse Erwin	P37	40	.176	B	
17	6	Ford, Edward Chas.	P	39	.119	B	
		Gibbs, Jerry Dean	C2	3	.167	B	
		Gonzalez, Pedro (2B6 3B9 OF20)	1B31	80	.277	B	
7	2	Hamilton, Steve Absher	P30	32	.200	B	
		Hegan, James Michael	1B2	5	.000	A	
		Howard, Elston Gene	C146	150	.313	B	
		Jiminez, Felix Elvio	OF	1	.333	A	C
		Kubek, Anthony Christopher	SS99	106	.229	B	
		Linz, Philip Francis (2B5 3B41 OF3)	SS55	112	.250	B	
		Lopez, Hector Headley (3B1)	OF103	127	.260	B	
		Mantle, Mickey Chas.	OF132	143	.303	B	
		Maris, Roger Eugene	OF137	141	.281	B	
0	3	Meyer, Robert Bernard	P	7	+.000	A	L.A.

7	4	Mikkelsen, Peter James	P	50	.063	A
		Moore, Archie Francis (1B7)	OF8	31	.174	A
		Pepitone, Joseph Anthony (OF30)	1B155	160	.251	B
1	0	Ramos, Pedro	P	13	+.000	xClev
6	4	Reniff, Harold Eugene	P41	44	.100	B
		Repoz, Roger Allen	OF9	11	.000	A
		Richardson, Robert Clinton (SS1)	2B157	159	.267	B
5	2	Sheldon, Roland Frank	P	19	.088	NY62
5	0	Stafford, Wm. Chas.	P	31	.077	B
9	3	Stottlemyre, Melvin Leon	P13	14	.243	A
7	11	Terry, Ralph Willard	P	27	.200	B
		Tresh, Thomas Michael	OF146	153	.246	B
1	5	Williams, Stanley Wilson	P21	22	.143	B

CLUB RECORD

AMERICAN LEAGUE

PHILADELPHIA

YEAR	TG	WON	LOST	PCT.	FINISHED	MANAGER
1901	136	74	62	.544	4	Connie Mack
1902	136	83	53	.610	1	Connie Mack
1903	135	75	60	.556	2	Connie Mack
1904	151	81	70	.536	5	Connie Mack
1905	148	92	56	.621	1	Connie Mack
1906	145	78	67	.538	4	Connie Mack
1907	145	88	57	.607	2	Connie Mack
1908	153	68	85	.444	6	Connie Mack
1909	153	95	58	.621	2	Connie Mack
1910	150	102	48	.680	1	Connie Mack
1911	151	101	50	.669	1	Connie Mack
1912	152	90	62	.592	3	Connie Mack
1913	153	96	57	.627	1	Connie Mack
1914	152	99	53	.651	1	Connie Mack
1915	152	43	109	.283	8(Last)	Connie Mack
1916	153	36	117	.235	8(Last)	Connie Mack
1917	153	55	98	.359	8(Last)	Connie Mack
1918	128	52	76	.402	8(Last)	Connie Mack
1919	140	36	104	.257	8(Last)	Connie Mack
1920	154	48	106	.312	8(Last)	Connie Mack
1921	153	53	100	.346	8(Last)	Connie Mack
1922	154	65	89	.422	7	Connie Mack
1923	152	69	83	.454	6	Connie Mack
1924	152	71	81	.467	5	Connie Mack
1925	152	88	64	.579	2	Connie Mack
1926	150	83	67	.553	3	Connie Mack
1927	154	91	63	.591	2	Connie Mack
1928	153	98	55	.641	2	Connie Mack
1929	150	104	46	.693	1	Connie Mack
1930	154	102	52	.662	1	Connie Mack
1931	152	107	45	.704	1	Connie Mack
1932	154	94	60	.610	2	Connie Mack
1933	151	79	72	.523	3	Connie Mack
1934	150	68	82	.453	5	Connie Mack
1935	149	58	91	.389	8(Last)	Connie Mack
1936	153	53	100	.346	8(Last)	Connie Mack
1937	151	54	97	.358	7	Connie Mack
1938	152	53	99	.349	8(Last)	Connie Mack
1939	152	55	97	.362	7	Connie Mack
1940	154	54	100	.351	8(Last)	Connie Mack
1941	154	64	90	.416	8(Last)	Connie Mack
1942	154	55	99	.357	8(Last)	Connie Mack
1943	154	49	105	.318	8(Last)	Connie Mack
1944	154	72	82	.468	x5(Cleve)	Connie Mack
1945	150	52	98	.347	8(Last)	Connie Mack
1946	154	49	105	.318	8(Last)	Connie Mack
1947	154	78	76	.506	5	Connie Mack
1948	154	84	70	.545	4	Connie Mack
1949	154	81	73	.526	5	Connie Mack
1950	154	52	102	.338	8(Last)	Connie Mack

1951	154	70	84	.455	6	James Joseph Dykes
1952	154	79	75	.513	4	James Joseph Dykes
1953	154	59	95	.383	7	James Joseph Dykes
1954	154	51	103	.331	8(Last)	Edwin David Joost

WON 74 — AMERICAN LEAGUE — FINISHED 4th.
LOST 62
TG 136 — 1901. — PCT. .544

PHILADELPHIA

CONNIE MACK

WON	LOST	NAME	POS.	G.	BA	FROM	TO
0	1	Baker, Chas.	P	1	+.333	xClev	C
17	11	Bernhard, Wm. Henry	P30	31	.187	PhilN	
		Carr, Chas. Carbitt	1B	2	.125	WashN98	
		Cross, LaFayette Napoleon (Lave)	3B	100	.331	BknN	
		Davis, Harry H.	1B	117	.307	WashN99	
		Dolan, Joseph	SS64	97	.219	xPhilN	C
		Ely, Frederick Wm.	SS	45	.223	xPittN	
20	15	Fraser, Chas. Carrolton (Chick)	P40	43	.209	PhilN	
		Fultz, David Lewis (2B30)	OF93	132	.295	Mil	
		Geier, Philip Louis	OF	50	+.236	CinN	Mil
		Hayden, John Francis (Jack)	OF50	51	.266	A	
		Ketcham, Frederick L.	OF	5	.227	Mil	C
		Lajoie, Napoleon	2B130	131	.422	PhilN	
		Lauder, Wm.	3B	2	.125	PhilN99	
		Leahy, Thomas Joseph	C	3	+.294	xMil	
0	0	Leitner, George Michael	P	1	.000	A	NYN
		Lindermann, Robert J.	OF	3	.100	A	C
		Lockhead, Harry P.	SS	9	+.088	xDet	C
0	1	Loos, Peter	P	1	.000	A	C
0	3	Milligan, Wm. J.	P	7	.313	Inpls	
		Murphy, Morgan Edward (1B1)	C8	9	.179	PhilN	C
		McIntyre, Matthew W. (Matty)	OF	82	.283	A	
		McKinney, Robert Francis	2B	2	.000	A	C
0	1	McPherson, John Jacob	P	1	.000	A	
7	11	Piatt, Wiley Harlan	P	18	+.228	PhilN	Chi
16	14	Plank, Edward Stewart	P	33	.182	A	
		Powers, Michael Riley	C111	116	.248	Inpls	
		Seybold, Ralph Orlando (1B15)	OF99	114	.332	Inpls	
		Smith, Harry Thomas	C	11	.318	Mil	
		Steelman, Morris James	C	27	.267	xBknN	
14	5	Wiltse, Lewis DeWitt	P	19	.373	xPittN	

WON 83 — AMERICAN LEAGUE — FINISHED 1st.
LOST 53
TG 136 — 1902. — PCT. .610

PHILADELPHIA

CONNIE MACK

WON	LOST	NAME	POS.	G.	BA	FROM	TO
1	0	Bernhard, Wm. Henry	P	1	+.000	B	Clev
		Bonner, Frank J.	2B	11	+.182	xClev	

WON	LOST	NAME	POS.	G.	BA	FROM	TO
		Castro, Louis M. (SS1 3B1 OF3)	2B33	41	.248	A	C
		Cross, LaFayette Napoleon (Lave)	3B	137	.339	B	
		Cross, Montford Montgomery (Monte)	SS	137	.207	PhilN	
		Davis, Harry H. (OF5)	1B128	132	.308	B	
1	1	Duggleby, Wm. James	P	2	.000	PhilN	PhilN
		Flick, Elmer Harrison	OF	11	+.324	PhilN	Clev
		Fultz, David Lewis (2B18)	OF111	129	.300	B	
		Hartsel, Tullos Frederick (Topsy)	OF	137	.286	ChiN	
14	5	Husting, Berthold Juneau	P	32	+.165	xBos	C
1	1	Kenna, Edward Benninghaus	P2	3	.125	A	C
		Lajoie, Napoleon	2B	1	+.200	B	Clev
5	8	Mitchell, Frederick Francis (OF1)	P19	20	+.184	xBos	
		Murphy, Daniel Francis	2B	76	.313	NYN	
2	1	McAllister, Jack (Andrew James Coakley)	P	3	.125	A	
20	15	Plank, Edward Stewart	P	36	.296	B	
0	1	Porter, James	P	1	.000	A	C
0	1	Quinn, Clarence C.	P	1	.000	A	
		Powers, Michael Riley (1B3)	C68	71	.271	B	
		Schreckengost, Ossee Freeman (Ossie) (OF1)	C71	78	+.312	xClev	
		Seybold, Ralph Orlando	OF136	137	.317	B	
		Steelman, Morris James (OF5)	C5	10	.187	B	C
24	7	Waddell, George Edward (Rube)	P	33	.279	ChiN	
0	1	Walker, Thomas Wm.	P	1	.250	A	
7	4	Wilson, Howard P.	P	13	.171	ClevN99	
8	8	Wiltse, Lewis DeWitt	P	20	+.179	B	Balt

WON 75 | LOST 60 | TG 135

AMERICAN LEAGUE

1903.

FINISHED 2nd.

PCT. .556

PHILADELPHIA

CONNIE MACK

WON	LOST	NAME	POS.	G.	BA	FROM	TO
17	15	Bender, Chas. Albert (Chief)	P36	43	.182	A	
		Kalahan, John Joseph	C	1	.000	A	C
0	3	Coakley, Andrew James	P	6	.214	B	
		Cross, LaFayette Napoleon (Lave)	3B136	137	.292	B	
		Cross, Montford Montgomery (Monte)	SS	138	.245	B	
		Daly, Bert (SS3 3B1)	2B6	10	.190	A	C
		Davis, Harry H.	1B100	101	.298	B	
0	0	Fairbank, James Lee	P	1	.000	A	
		Hartsel, Tullos Frederick (Topsy)	OF97	98	.311	B	
12	9	Henley, Weldon	P29	30	.132	A	
		Hilley, Edward Garfield	3B	1	.333	A	C
		Hoffman, Daniel John	OF62	73	.235	A	
		Murphy, Daniel Francis	2B	133	.275	B	
1	0	McGeehan, Cornelius Bernard	P	6	.000	A	C
		Pickering, Oliver Dan	OF135	137	.281	Clev	
0	1	Pinnance, Edward D.	P	2	.000	A	C
23	16	Plank, Edward Stewart	P41	43	.193	B	
		Powers, Michael Riley	C66	74	.227	B	
0	0	Quinn, Clarence C.	P	2	.667	B	C
		Schreckengost, Ossee Freeman	C78	91	.222	B	
		Seybold, Ralph Orlando (1B16)	OF121	137	.299	B	
22	16	Waddell, George Edward (Rube)	P	38	.119	B	

WON 81 | LOST 70 | TG 151

AMERICAN LEAGUE

1904.

FINISHED 5th.

PCT. .536

PHILADELPHIA

CONNIE MACK

WON	LOST	NAME	POS.	G.	BA	FROM	TO
1	2	Applegate, Frederick Romaine	P	3	.286	A	C
0	1	Barthold, John Francis	P	4	.250	A	C
7	14	Bender, Chas. Albert (Chief)	P28	29	.228	B	
0	0	Bruce, Louis (P1)	OF25	30	.277	A	C
7	4	Coakley, Andrew James	P	11	.087	B	
		Cross, LaFayette Napoleon (Lave)	3B	155	.290	B	
		Cross, Montford Montgomery (Monte)	SS	153	.182	B	
		Davis, Harry H.	1B	102	.308	B	
0	1	Fairbank, James Lee	P	3	.000	B	C
		Hartsel, Tullos Frederick (Topsy)	OF	147	.249	B	
14	16	Henley, Weldon	P	36	.224	B	
		Hoffman, Daniel John	OF51	53	.305	B	
		Mullin, James Henry	1B26	26	+.415	A	Wash
			2B	17	+.157	& recalled	
		Murphy, Daniel Francis	2B	149	.286	B	
		Noonan, Peter John	C22	38	.202	A	
		Pickering, Oliver Dan	OF120	122	.224	B	
26	15	Plank, Edward Stewart	P41	45	.236	B	
		Powers, Michael Riley	C56	57	.187	B	
		Schreckengost, Ossee Freeman	C85	94	.189	B	
		Seybold, Ralph Orlando	OF129	143	.282	B	
26	17	Waddell, George Edward (Rube)	P	46	.130	B	

WON 92 — LOST 56 — TG 148

AMERICAN LEAGUE

1905.

FINISHED 1st. — PCT. .621

PHILADELPHIA

CONNIE MACK

WON	LOST	NAME	POS.	G.	BA	FROM	TO
		Barton, Harry Lamb	C	18	.167	A	C
15	10	Bender, Chas. Albert (Chief)	P	35	.217	B	
20	8	Coakley, Andrew James	P	34	.144	B	
		Cross, LaFayette Napoleon (Lave)	3B	146	.266	B	
		Cross, Montford Montgomery (Monte)	SS76	78	.270	B	
		Davis, Harry H.	1B	149	.284	B	
1	3	Dygert, James Henry	P	6	.267	A	
		Hartsel, Tullos Frederick (Topsy)	OF	148	.276	B	
4	12	Henley, Weldon	P	25	.169	B	
		Hoffman, Daniel John	OF117	119	.262	B	
		Knight, John Wesley (Jack)	SS81	88	.234	A	
		Lord, Bristol Robotham	OF60	66	.239	A	
		Murphy, Daniel Francis	2B	150	.278	B	
0	0	Myers, Joseph Wm.	P	1	.000	A	C
26	12	Plank, Edward Stewart	P	41	.231	B	
		Powers, Michael Riley	C	22	+.183	B	N.Y.
				19	+.161	& recall	
		Schreckengost, Ossee Freeman	C	114	.274	B	
		Seybold, Ralph Orlando	OF	132	.271	B	
26	11	Waddell, George Edward (Rube)	P	46	.172	B	

WON 78 — LOST 67 — TG 145

AMERICAN LEAGUE

1906.

FINISHED 4th. — PCT. .538

PHILADELPHIA

CONNIE MACK

WON	LOST	NAME	POS.	G.	BA	FROM	TO
		Armbruster, Herman	OF74	91	.238	A	C
0	0	Bartley, Wm. Jackson	P	3	.333	NYN03	
15	10	Bender, Chas. Albert (Chief)	P37	44	.253	B	
		Berry, Claude Elzy	C	10	.226	Chi04	
		Brouthers, Arthur H.	3B34	36	.208	A	C
		Byrnes, James Joseph	C	10	.167	A	C
7	8	Coakley, Andrew James	P	22	.143	B	
10	11	Coombs, John Wesley (Jack)	P23	24	.239	A	
		Cross, Montford Montgomery (Monte)	SS	134	.200	B	
0	0	Cunningham, Rudolph	P	6	.333	A	C
		Davis, Harry H.	1B	145	.292	B	
11	13	Dygert, James Henry	P	35	.176	B	
		Fetzer, Willy McKinnon	OF	1	.000	A	C
		Hannifan, John Joseph		1	.000	A	NYN
		Hartsel, Tullos Frederick (Topsy)	OF	144	.255	B	
		Hoffman, Daniel John	OF	7	+.217	B	N.Y.
0	1	Holmes, James Scott	P	3	.600	A	
		Knight, John Wesley (Jack)	3B67	74	.194	B	
		Lennox, James Edgar	3B	6	.059	A	
0	0	Lord, Bristol Robotham (Pl)	OF115	118	.233	B	
		Murphy, Daniel Francis	2B	119	.301	B	
		Nicholls, Simon Burdette	SS	12	.219	Det03	
		Oldring, Reuben Noshier	3B49	59	.241	N.Y.	
19	6	Plank, Edward Stewart	P	26	.233	B	
		Powers, Michael Riley	C57	58	.157	B	
		Schreckengost, Ossee Freeman	C89	98	.284	B	
0	2	Schumann, Carl J.	P	4	.000	A	C
		Seybold, Ralph Orlando	OF114	116	.316	B	
		Shean, David Wm.	2B	22	.213	A	
		Sullivan, (Edward Trowbridge Collins)	3B	6	.200	A	
16	16	Waddell, George Edward (Rube)	P	41	.163	B	

WON 88 — LOST 57 — TG 145

AMERICAN LEAGUE

1907.

FINISHED 2nd. — PCT. .607

PHILADELPHIA

CONNIE MACK

WON	LOST	NAME	POS.	G.	BA	FROM	TO
0	0	Bartley, Wm. Jackson	P	15	.090	B	C
16	8	Bender, Chas. Albert (Chief)	P33	45	.230	B	
		Berry, Claude Elzy	C	8	.291	B	
		Collins, Edward Trowbridge	SS	14	.320	B	
		Collins, James Joseph	3B	100	+.273	xBos	
6	9	Coombs, John Wesley (Jack)	P23	24	.167	B	
0	0	Craig, George McCarthy	P	2	.000	A	C
		Cross, Montford Montgomery (Monte)	SS74	77	.206	B	C
		Davis, Harry H.	1B	149	.266	B	
20	9	Dygert, James Henry	P	42	.128	B	
1	0	Fritz, Chas. Cornelius	P	1	.000	A	C
		Hartsel, Tullos Frederick (Topsy)	OF	143	.280	B	
0	0	Hope, Samuel	P	1	.000	A	C
		Knight, John Wesley (Jack)	3B	40	+.212	B	Bos
		Lord, Bristol Robotham	OF53	57	.182	B	
		Murphy, Daniel Francis	2B122	124	.271	B	
		Nicholls, Simon Burdette (2B28)	SS82	124	.302	B	
		Oldring, Reuben Noshier	OF	117	.286	B	
24	16	Plank, Edward Stewart	P	43	.211	B	
		Powers, Michael Riley	C	59	.182	B	
		Schreckengost, Ossee Freeman	C99	101	.272	B	

WON	LOST	NAME	POS.	G.	BA	FROM	TO
		Seybold, Ralph Orlando	OF	147	.271	B	
2	2	Vickers, Harry Porter (Rube)	P	10	.150	BknN03	
19	13	Waddell, George Edward (Rube)	P	43	.124	B	

WON 68 — AMERICAN LEAGUE — FINISHED 6th.
LOST 85
TG 153 — 1908. — PCT. .444

PHILADELPHIA

CONNIE MACK

WON	LOST	NAME	POS.	G.	BA	FROM	TO
		Baker, John Franklin (Home Run)	3B8	9	.290	A	
		Barr, Hyder Edward	2B	19	.143	A	
		Barry, John Joseph (Jack)	2B20	40	.222	A	
8	9	Bender, Chas. Albert (Chief)	P	20	.220	B	
		Blue, Bird Wayne	C	6	+.167	xStL	C
2	5	Carter, Conrad Powell	P	17	.100	A	C
		Collins, Edward Trowbridge (SS28)	2B47	102	.273	B	
		Collins, James Joseph	3B	115	.217	B	C
7	5	Coombs, John Wesley (Jack) (P26)	OF47	78	.255	B	
		Davis, Harry H.	1B	147	.248	B	
11	15	Dygert, James Henry	P	41	.080	B	
		Egan, Arthur Augustus	C	2	.143	A	
0	0	Files, Chas. Edward	P	2	.000	A	C
1	3	Flater, John Wm.	P	5	.133	A	C
		Fox, John Paul	OF	8	.209	A	C
		Hartsel, Tullos Frederick (Topsy)	OF	129	.243	B	
		Jackson, Joseph Jefferson	OF	5	.131	A	
0	2	Kellogg, Albert C.	P	3	.125	A	C
1	1	Krause, Harry Wm.	P	4	.000	A	
		Lapp, John Walter (Jack)	C	13	.143	A	
		Manush, Frank Benjamin	3B20	23	.156	A	C
0	1	Martin, Harold Winthrop (Doc)	P	1	.000	A	
0	0	Maxwell, J. Albert	P	4	.000	PittN06	
		Moran, Joseph Herbert	OF	19	.153	A	BosN
		Murphy, Daniel Francis (2B56)	OF83	142	.265	B	
		Nicholls, Simon Burdette (2B23)	SS120	150	.216	B	
		Oldring, Reuben Noshier	OF	116	.221	B	
14	16	Plank, Edward Stewart	P	36	.180	B	
		Powers, Michael Riley	C60	62	.180	B	
0	1	Salve, Augustus Wm.	P	2	.000	A	C
6	8	Schlitzer, Victor Joseph	P	23	.196	A	
		Schreckengost, Ossee Freeman	C	71	+.222	B	Chi
		Seybold, Ralph Orlando	OF34	48	.215	B	C
		Shaughnessy, Francis Joseph	OF	8	.321	Wash05	C
		Smith, Sydney	C	45	+.205	A	StL

WON	LOST	NAME	POS.	G.	BA	FROM	TO
		Strunk, Amos Aaron	OF	12	.222	A	
18	19	Vickers, Harry Porter (Rube)	P	53	.164	B	

WON 95 — AMERICAN LEAGUE — FINISHED 2nd.
LOST 58
TG 153 — 1909. — PCT. .621

PHILADELPHIA

CONNIE MACK

WON	LOST	NAME	POS.	G.	BA	FROM	TO
0	0	Atkins, Frank Montgomery	P	1	.000	A	
		Baker, John Franklin (Home Run)	3B146	148	.305	B	
		Barr, Hyder Edward	OF18	22	.079	B	C
		Barry, John Joseph (Jack)	SS	124	.215	B	
18	8	Bender, Chas. Albert (Chief)	P34	40	.215	B	
		Collins, Edward Trowbridge	2B152	153	.346	B	
12	11	Coombs, John Wesley (Jack)	P30	37	.169	B	
		Curry, James L.	2B	1	.250	A	
		Davis, Harry H.	1B	149	.268	B	
8	5	Dygert, James Henry	P	32	.214	B	
		Ganley, Robert Stephen	OF	83	+.207	xWash	C
		Hartsel, Tullos Frederick (Topsy)	OF74	83	.270	B	
		Heitmuller, Wm. Frederick	OF61	64	.286	A	
		Jackson, Joseph Jefferson	OF	5	.177	B	
18	8	Krause, Harry Wm.	P	32	.156	B	
1	0	Kull, John A.	P	1	1.000	A	C
		Lapp, John Walker (Jack)	C19	21	.336	B	
		Larkin, Edward Francis	C	2	.167	A	C
		Livingston, Patrick Joseph (Paddy)	C	64	.234	CinN06	
15	8	Morgan, Harry Richard (Cy)	P	27	+.108	xBos	
		Murphy, Daniel Francis	OF	149	.281	B	
		McInnis, John Phaelen (Stuffy)	SS	19	.239	A	
		Nicholls, Simon Burdette	3B	21	.211	B	
		Oldring, Reuben Noshier	OF89	90	.230	B	
19	10	Plank, Edward Stewart	P34	35	.219	B	
		Powers, Michael Riley	C	1	.250	B	C
		Rath, Maurice Chas. (3B2)	SS5	7	.269	A	
2	6	Schlitzer, Victor Joseph	P	9	+.250	B	Bos
		Strunk, Amos Aaron	OF	11	.114	B	
		Thomas, Ira Felix	C	84	.223	Det	
2	2	Vickers, Harry Porter (Rube)	P	18	.063	B	C

WON 102 — AMERICAN LEAGUE — FINISHED 1st.
LOST 48
TG 150 — 1910. — PCT. .680

PHILADELPHIA

CONNIE MACK

WON	LOST	NAME	POS.	G.	BA	FROM	TO
3	2	Atkins, Frank Montgomery	P	15	.118	B	C
		Baker, John Franklin (Home Run)	3B	146	.283	B	
		Barry, John Joseph (Jack)	SS	145	.259	B	
23	5	Bender, Chas. Albert (Chief)	P30	36	.269	B	
		Collins, Edward Trowbridge	2B	153	.322	B	
31	9	Coombs, John Wesley (Jack)	P45	46	.220	B	
		Davis, Harry H.	1B	139	.248	B	
		Derrick, Claude Lester	SS	2	.000	A	
		#Donahue, Patrick Wm.	C	16	+.143	xBos	C
4	4	Dygert, James Henry	P	19	.083	B	C
		Hartsel, Tullos Frederick (Topsy)	OF83	90	.221	B	
		Heitmuller, Wm. Frederick	OF28	31	.243	B	C
		Houser, Benjamin Franklin	1B29	34	.189	A	
6	6	Krause, Harry Wm.	P	16	.211	B	
		Lapp, John Walker (Jack)	C63	71	.234	B	
		Livingston, Patrick Joseph (Paddy)	C	37	.208	B	
		Lord, Bristol Robotham	OF	69	+.274	xClev	
		Mack, Earle Thaddeus	C	1	.500	A	
18	12	Morgan, Harry Richard (Cy)	P	36	.141	B	
		Murphy, Daniel Francis	OF	151	.300	B	
		McInnis, John Phaelen (Stuffy)	SS17	38	.301	B	
		Oldring, Reuben Noshier	OF	134	.308	B	
16	10	Plank, Edward Stewart	P	38	.128	B	
		Rath, Maurice Chas.	3B	15	+.160	B	Clev
1	0	Russell, Clarence Dickson	P	1	.000	A	
		Strunk, Amos Aaron	OF	16	.333	B	
		Thomas, Ira Felix	C	60	.277	B	

#-Donohue was returned to Philadelphia by Cleveland and finished the season with Philadelphia before closing his career.

WON 101 — AMERICAN LEAGUE — FINISHED 1st.
LOST 50
TG 151 — 1911. — PCT. .669

PHILADELPHIA

CONNIE MACK

WON	LOST	NAME	POS.	G.	BA	FROM	TO
0	1	Armstrong, Howard Elmer	P	1	.000	A	C
		Baker, John Franklin (Home Run)	3B	148	.334	B	
		Barry, John Joseph (Jack)	SS	127	.265	B	
17	5	Bender, Chas. Albert (Chief)	P31	32	.165	B	
0	1	Brown, Carroll Wm.	P	2	.000	A	
0	0	Collamore, Allan Edward	P	2	.000	A	
		Collins, Edward Trowbridge	2B	132	.365	B	
28	12	Coombs, John Wesley (Jack)	P47	52	.319	B	
5	2	Danforth, David Chas.	P	14	.167	A	
		Davis, Harry H.	1B53	57	.197	B	
		Derrick, Claude Lester	2B21	36	.230	B	
		Emerson, Chester Arthur	OF	7	.222	A	
		Hartsel, Tullos Frederick (Topsy)	OF	25	.237	B	C
		Hogan, Wm. Henry	OF	7	+.105	A	StL
11	7	Krause, Harry Wm.	P	28	.254	B	
		Lapp, John Walker (Jack)	C57	68	.353	B	
2	2	Leonard, Elmer Ellsworth	P	5	.286	A	C
		Livingston, Patrick Joseph (Paddy)	C26	27	.239	B	
0	0	Long, Lester	P	4	.000	A	C
		Lord, Bristol Robotham	OF132	134	.310	B	
		Mack, Earle Thaddeus	3B	2	.000	B	
1	3	Martin, Harold Winthrop (Doc)	P	11	.214	Phil08	
15	7	Morgan, Harry Richard (Cy)	P	38	.159	B	
		Murphy, Daniel Francis	OF136	141	.329	B	
		McInnis, John Phaelen (Stuffy) (SS24)	1B97	126	.321	B	
		Oldring, Reuben Noshier	OF119	121	.297	B	
22	8	Plank, Edward Stewart	P	40	.191	B	
0	2	Russell, Clarence Dickson	P	7	.357	B	
		Strunk, Amos Aaron	OF64	74	.256	B	
		Thomas, Ira Felix	C	103	.273	B	

WON 90 — AMERICAN LEAGUE — FINISHED 3rd.
LOST 62
TG 152 — 1912. — PCT. .592

PHILADELPHIA

CONNIE MACK

WON	LOST	NAME	POS.	G.	BA	FROM	TO
		Baker, John Franklin (Home Run)	3B	149	.347	B	
		Barry, John Joseph (Jack)	SS	139	.261	B	
0	0	Barry, Hardin	P	3	.000	A	C
13	8	Bender, Chas. Albert (Chief)	P	26	.150	B	
13	11	Brown, Carroll Wm.	P	30	.145	B	
0	0	Bush, Leslie Ambrose (Bullet Joe)	P	1	.500	A	
		Collins, Edward Trowbridge	2B	153	.348	B	
21	10	Coombs, John Wesley (Jack)	P	54	.255	B	
2	1	Coveleskie, Stanley Anthony	P	3	.143	A	
2	5	Crabb, James Roy	P	7	+.000	xChi	C
0	0	Danforth, David Chas.	P	3	.250	B	
		Derrick, Claude Lester	SS	21	.241	B	
		Egan, Arthur Augustus	C	48	.174	Phil08	
		Emerson, Chester Arthur		1.	.000	B	C
		Fahey, Howard Simpson	SS	5	.000	A	C
0	0	Harrell, Oscar Martin	P	1	.000	A	C
8	8	Houck, Byron Simon	P	25	.065	A	
0	1	Krause, Harry Wm.	P	3	+.000	B	Clev
		Lapp, John Walker (Jack)	C	90	.292	B	
		Lord, Briston Robotham	OF	96	.238	B	
		Maggert, Harl Vess	OF	72	.256	PittN07	C

WON	LOST	NAME	POS.	G.	BA	FROM	TO
0	0	Martin, Harold Winthrop (Doc)	P	2	.000	B	C
		Mathes, Joseph John	3B	4	.154	A	
3	8	Morgan, Harry Richard (Cy)	P	13	.033	B	
		Murphy, Daniel Francis	OF	36	.323	B	
		Murphy, Joseph Edward	OF	33	.317	A	
		McInnis, John Phaelen (Stuffy)	1B	153	.327	B	
		Oldring, Reuben Noshier	OF	98	.301	B	
1	2	Pennock, Herbert Jefferis	P	17	.125	A	
26	6	Plank, Edward Stewart	P	34	.267	B	
0	2	Russell, Clarence Dickson	P	3	.000	B	C
1	0	Salmon, Roger Elliott	P	1	.000	A	C
		Strunk, Amos Aaron	OF	120	.289	B	
		Thomas, Ira Felix	C	46	.216	B	
		Walsh, James Charles	OF	31	.252	A	

WON 96 — AMERICAN LEAGUE — FINISHED 1st.
LOST 57
TG 153 — 1913. — PCT. .627

PHILADELPHIA

CONNIE MACK

WON	LOST	NAME	POS.	G.	BA	FROM	TO
		Baker, John Franklin (Home Run)	3B	149	.336	B	
		Barry, John Joseph (Jack)	SS	135	.275	B	
19	9	Bender, Chas. Albert (Chief)	P	36	.154	B	
0	2	Boardman, Chas. Louis	P	2	.000	A	
0	1	Bohen, Leo J. (Pat)	P	1	.000	A	
		Brickley, George Vincent	OF	5	.166	A	C
18	11	Brown, Carroll Wm.	P	38	.167	B	
13	7	Bush, Leslie Ambrose (Bullet Joe)	P	33	.157	B	
		Carruthers, Chas. Preston	2B	5	.235	A	
		Collins, Edward Trowbridge	2B	148	.345	B	
0	0	Coombs, John Wesley (Jack)	P	1	.333	B	
0	0	Cottrell, Ensign Stover	P	1	.250	ChiN	
		Daley, Thomas Francis (Pete)	OF48	59	.260	CinN08	
		Davis, Harry H. (Cl)	1B	6	.444	Clev	
		Fritz, Harry Koch	3B	5	.000	A	
		Giebel, Joseph Henry	C	1	.333	A	C
15	6	Houck, Byron Simon	P	35	.082	B	
		Lapp, John Walker (Jack)	C82	84	.228	B	
		Lavan, John Leonard	SS	6	+.067	xStL	
0	0	Morey, David Beale	P	2	.000	A	C
		Murphy, Daniel Francis	OF	40	.322	B	
		Murphy, Joseph Edward	OF	136	.295	B	
		McAvoy, James Eugene	C	4	.111	A	
		McInnis, John Phaelen (Stuffy)	1B	148	.326	B	
		Oldring, Reuben Noshier	OF	136	.283	B	
		Orr, Wm. J.	SS9	27	.200	A	
		Peffer, Monte	SS	1	.000	A	C
4	1	Pennock, Herbert Jefferis	P	6	.111	B	
17	10	Plank, Edward Stewart	P	35	.080	B	
		Schang, Walter Henry (Wally)	C63	77	.266	A	
7	5	Shawkey, James Robert	P	17	.134	A	
		Strunk, Amos Aaron	OF82	93	.305	B	
0	1	Taff, John G.	P	5	.200	A	C
		Thomas, Ira Felix	C	21	.283	B	
		Walsh, James Charles	OF86	94	.255	B	
3	4	Wyckoff, John Weldon	P	10	.211	A	

WON 99 — AMERICAN LEAGUE — FINISHED 1st.
LOST 53
TG 152 — 1914. — PCT. .651

PHILADELPHIA

CONNIE MACK

WON	LOST	NAME	POS.	G.	BA	FROM	TO
		Baker, John Franklin (Home Run)	3B149	150	.319	B	
		Barry, John Joseph (Jack)	SS	140	.242	B	
17	3	Bender, Chas. Albert (Chief)	P	24	.145	B	
0	0	Boardman, Chas. Louis	P	2	.000	B	
10	4	Bressler, Raymond Bloom (Rube)	P	26	.216	A	
1	6	Brown, Carroll Wm.	P	15	+.000	B	N.Y.
16	12	Bush, Leslie Ambrose (Bullet Joe)	P	35	.189	B	
		Carruthers, Chas. Preston	2B	4	.200	B	C
		Collins, Edward Trowbridge	2B	152	.344	B	
0	1	Coombs, John Wesley (Jack)	P	5	.272	B	
		Coyne,	3B	1	.000	A	C
		Crane, Samuel Byren	SS	2	.000	A	
		Daley, Thomas Francis (Pete)	OF	28	+.241	B	N.Y.
1	0	Davies, Lloyd Garrison	P	19	.239	A	
		Davis, Harry H.	1B	7	.333	B	
0	0	Houck, Byron Simon	P	3	.333	B	BknF
0	1	Jensen, Wm.	P	2	.000	Det12	C
		Kopf, Wm. Lorenz (Larry)	2B	35	.189	Clev	
		Lapp, John Walker (Jack)	C67	69	.231	B	
		Mack, Earle Thaddeus	1B	2	.000	Phil11	C
		Moore, Ferdinand Henry	1B	2	.250	A	C
		Murphy, Joseph Edward	OF	148	.272	B	
		McAvoy, James Eugene	C	8	.111	B	
		McInnis, John Phaelen (Stuffy)	1B	149	.314	B	
		Oldring, Reuben Noshier	OF117	119	.277	B	
		Orr, Wm. J.	SS	10	.167	B	C
11	4	Pennock, Herbert Jefferis	P	27	.214	B	
16	6	Plank, Edward Stewart	P	30	.150	B	
		Rochefort, Bennett Harold	1B	1	.500	A	C
		Schang, Walter Henry (Wally)	C100	107	.287	B	
16	8	Shawkey, James Robert	P	34	.207	B	
		Strunk, Amos Aaron	OF120	122	.275	B	
		Sturgis, Dean Donnell	C	4	.250	A	C
		Sweeney,	OF	1	.000	A	C
		Thomas, Ira Felix	C	2	.000	B	
		Thompson, James Alfred	OF	16	.172	A	

WON	LOST	NAME	POS.	G.	BA	FROM	TO
		Walsh, James Charles	OF	67	+.226	xN.Y.	
0	0	Worden,	P	1	.000	A	C
11	8	Wyckoff, John Weldon	P30	32	.151	B	

WON 43 / LOST 109 / TG 152 — AMERICAN LEAGUE — FINISHED 8th (LAST)

1915. — PCT. .283

PHILADELPHIA

CONNIE MACK

WON	LOST	NAME	POS.	G.	BA	FROM	TO
0	1	Ancker, Walter	P	4	.000	A	C
		Bankston, Wilborn Everett	OF	11	.142	A	C
		Barry, John Joseph (Jack)	SS	54	+.218	B	Bos
		Bostick, Henry Landers	3B	2	.000	A	C
4	17	Bressler, Raymond Bloom (Rube)	P32	33	.145	B	
5	15	Bush, Leslie Ambrose (Bullet Joe)	P	25	.143	B	
0	0	Cone, H. B.	P	1	.000	A	C
		Conway, Owen Sylvester	3B	4	.067	A	C
		Corcoran, Arthur A.	3B	1	.000	A	C
		Crane, Samuel Byren	SS	8	.087	B	
2	6	Crowell, Minot Joy	P	10	.227	A	
		Damrau, Harry Robert	3B	16	.196	A	C
		Danner, Henry Frederick	SS	3	.250	A	C
0	2	Davies, Lloyd Garrison (P4)	OF32	56	.182	B	
		Davis, Harry H.	1B1	6	.167	B	
1	2	Davis, John Wilbur	P17	20	.348	A	
0	1	Eccles, Harry Josiah	P	5	.167	A	C
		Edwards, Albert	2B	2	.000	A	C
0	4	Fillingim, Dana	P	8	.167	A	
0	2	Haas, Bruno Philip	P	12	.051	A	C
		Haeffner, Wm. Bernard	C	3	.250	A	
0	1	Harper, John Wesley	P	3	.000	A	C
		Healy, Thomas Fitzgerald	3B17	23	.221	A	
4	7	Knowlson, Thomas H.	P	18	.083	A	C
		Kopf, Wm. Lorenz (Larry) (3B42)	SS74	118	.225	B	
		Lajoie, Napoleon	2B110	129	.280	Clev	
		Lapp, John Walker (Jack)	C89	112	.272	B	
		Lear, Frederick Francis	3B	2	.000	A	
		Malone, Lewis Aloysius	2B43	76	.204	A	
0	1	Meehan, Wm. Thomas	P	1	1.000	A	C
2	0	Morrisette, Wm. Lee	P	4	.286	A	
		Murphy, Joseph Edward	OF	60	+.231	B	Chi
1	0	Myers, Elmer Glen	P	1	.000	A	
		McAvoy, James Eugene	C64	68	.190	B	
		McConnell, Samuel Faulkner	3B	6	.191	A	C
		McInnis, John Phaelen (Stuffy)	1B	119	.314	B	
0	5	Nabors, John Jackson	P	10	.125	A	
		Oldring, Reuben Noshier	OF96	107	.248	B	
3	5	Pennock, Herbert Jefferis	P	11	+.294	B	Bos
0	0	Pepper, Robert Ernest	P	1	.000	A	C
		Perkins, Ralph Foster (Cy)	C	7	.190	A	
0	0	Pillon, Cecil Randolph	P	2	.000	A	C
0	1	Ray, Carl Grady	P	2	.000	A	
0	1	Richardson, John Wm.	P	3	.000	A	
		Schang, Walter Henry (Wally) (C26 OF41)	3B43	116	.248	B	
		Seibold, Harry (Socks)	SS6	10	.115	A	
6	5	Shawkey, James Robert	P	17	+.129	B	N.Y.
4	8	Sheehan, Thomas Clancy	P	15	.118	A	
1	0	Sherman, Joel Powers	P	2	.333	A	C
		Strunk, Amos Aaron	OF111	132	.297	B	
		Thomas, Ira Felix	C	1	.000	B	C
		Thompson, James Alfred	OF	17	.333	B	
0	1	Turner, Thomas Lovatt	P	1	.000	A	C
		Walsh, James Charles	OF109	117	.206	B	
0	2	Weaver, Harry A.	P	2	.167	A	
10	22	Wyckoff, John Weldon	P43	45	.125	B	

WON 36 / LOST 117 / TG 153 — AMERICAN LEAGUE — FINISHED 8th (LAST)

1916. — PCT. .235

PHILADELPHIA

CONNIE MACK

WON	LOST	NAME	POS.	G.	BA	FROM	TO
0	3	Bressler, Raymond Bloom (Rube)	P	4	.200	B	
		Brown, James Donaldson (Moose)	OF	14	.233	StLN	C
15	22	Bush, Leslie Ambrose (Bullet Joe)	P40	41	.140	B	
		Carroll, Ralph Arthur	C	10	.091	A	C
		Crane, Samuel Byren	SS	2	.250	B	
0	5	Crowell, Minot Joy	P	9	.000	B	C
		Davis, Harry H.	OF1	4	.167	B	
		Davis, John Wilbur	(did not play)			B	C
0	1	Driscoll, Michael Columbus	P	1	.000	A	C
		Grimm, Chas. John	OF	12	.091	A	
		Grover, Roy Arthur	2B	20	.272	A	
		Haley, Raymond Timothy	C33	34	+.220	xBos	
		Healy, Thomas Fitzgerald	3B	6	.261	B	C
0	4	Hesselbacher, George Edward	P	6	.125	A	C
2	9	Johnson, Russell Conwell	P	12	.074	A	
		Johnson, Wm. Lawrence	OF	4	.267	A	
		King, Edward Lee	OF22	42	.188	A	
		Lajoie, Napoleon	2B105	113	.246	B	C
0	3	Lanning, Lester Alfred (OF8)	P5	19	.182	A	C
		Lawry, Otis Carroll	2B29	41	.203	A	
0	0	Lindstrom, Axel Olaf	P	1	.500	A	C
		Malone, Lewis Aloysius	SS1	5	.000	B	
		Meyer, Wm. Adam	C48	50	.232	Chi13	
		Mitterling, Ralph	OF	13	.154	A	C

WON	LOST	NAME	POS.	G.	BA	FROM	TO
		Morgan, John P.	3B	1	.250	A	C
0	0	Morrisette, Wm. Lee	P	1	.000	B	
		Murphy, Michael Jerome	C	14	.107	StLN12	C
14	23	Myers, Elmer Glen	P44	53	.214	B	
		McElwee, Leland Stanford	3B30	54	.265	A	C
		McInnis, John Phaelen (Stuffy)	1B	140	.295	B	
1	21	Nabors, John Jackson	P	40	.101	B	
		Oldring, Reuben Noshier	OF	40	+.247	B	N.Y.
2	1	Parnham, James Arthur	P	4	.181	A	
		Picinich, Valentine John (Val)	C37	40	.195	A	
		Pick, Chas. Thomas	3B108	121	.241	Wash	
0	1	Ray, Carl Grady	P	3	.000	B	C
0	0	Richardson, John Wm.	P	1	.000	B	C
		Rowe, Harland Stimson	3B	17	.139	A	C
		Schang, Walter Henry (Wally) (C36)	OF61	110	.266	B	
1	2	Seibold, Harry (Socks)	P	5	.167	B	
1	15	Sheehan, Thomas Clancy	P	38	.125	B	
		Stellbauer, Wm. Jennings	OF	25	.270	A	C
		Strunk, Amos Aaron	OF143	150	.316	B	
		Thompson, James Alfred	OF	15	.000	B	C
		Thrasher, Frank Edward	OF	7	.310	A	
		Walsh, James Charles	OF	112	+.222	B	Bos
0	0	Weaver, Harry A.	P	3	.500	B	
0	0	Whitaker, Walter Elton	P	1	.000	A	C
0	6	Williams, Marshall McDiarmid	P	10	.105	A	C
		Witt, Lawton Walter (Whitey)	SS142	143	.245	A	
0	1	Wyckoff, John Weldon	P	8	+.375	B	Bos

WON 55
LOST 98
TG 153

AMERICAN LEAGUE

1917.

FINISHED 8th (LAST)

PCT. .359

PHILADELPHIA

CONNIE MACK

WON	LOST	NAME	POS.	G.	BA	FROM	TO
0	0	Anderson, Walter Carl	P	14	.428	A	
0	0	Bacon, Elmer	P	4	.600	A	C
		Bailey, Arthur Eugene	OF	5	.083	A	
		Bates, Raymond	3B124	127	.237	Clev13	C
		Bodie, Frank L. (Ping)	OF145	148	.291	Chi14	
		Bradshaw, Dallas Carl	2B	2	.000	A	C
11	17	Bush, Leslie Ambrose (Bullet Joe)	P	37	.200	B	
		Davis, Harry H.		1	.000	B	C
		Dugan, Joseph Anthony (Jumping Joe)	SS39	43	.194	A	
2	6	Falkenberg, Frederick Peter (Cy)	P	15	.185	BknF15	C
		French, Frank Alexander	OF1	4	.000	A	C
		Gooch, Lee Currin	OF16	17	.288	Clev15	C
		Griffin, Francis Arthur	1B3	18	.200	A	
		Grover, Roy Arthur	2B139	141	.224	B	
		Haley, Raymond Timothy	C34	41	.276	B	C

WON	LOST	NAME	POS.	G.	BA	FROM	TO
0	0	Hill, Clifford J.	P	1	.000	A	C
		Jamieson, Chas. Devine	OF	85	+.267	xWash	
0	2	Johnson, Ellis Watt	P	4	.000	Chi15	C
9	12	Johnson, Russell Conwell	P	35	.203	B	
		Johnson, Wm. Lawrence	OF30	48	.174	B	C
1	0	Keefe, David Edwin	P	3	.000	A	
		Lawry, Otis Carroll	2B17	30	.164	B	C
		Meyer, Wm. Adam	C55	62	.235	B	
9	16	Myers, Elmer Glen	P	38	.247	B	
		McAvoy, James Eugene	C	10	.250	Phil15	
		McInnis, John Phaelen (Stuffy)	1B	150	.303	B	
0	0	Nabors, John Jackson	P	2	.000	B	C
2	2	Naylor, Roleine Cecil (Rollie)	P	5	.091	A	
10	10	Noyes, Winfield Chas.	P	27	.127	BosN13	
		Palmer, Edwin Henry	3B13	16	.212	A	C
0	1	Parnham, James Arthur	P	2	.000	B	C
		Perkins, Ralph Foster (Cy)	C	6	.167	Phil15	
		Picinich, Valentine John (Val)	C	2	.333	B	
		Schang, Walter Henry (Wally)	C80	118	.285	B	
7	16	Schauer, Alexander John (Rube)	P	33	.145	NYN	C
4	16	Seibold, Harry (Socks)	P32	36	.220	B	
		Shannon, Maurice Joseph	SS	11	.257	BosN15	
		Sharman, Ralph Edward	OF	13	.297	A	C
		Strunk, Amos Aaron	OF146	148	.281	B	
		Thrasher, Frank Edward	OF22	23	.234	B	C
		Witt, Lawton Walter (Whitey)	SS110	128	.252	B	

WON 52
LOST 76
TG 128

AMERICAN LEAGUE

1918.

FINISHED 8th (LAST)

PCT. .402

PHILADELPHIA

CONNIE MACK

WON	LOST	NAME	POS.	G.	BA	FROM	TO
		Acosta, Balmadero Merito	OF	49	+.302	xWash	C
5	12	Adams, James Irwin	P	32	.140	PittF14	
0	0	Bauer, Louis Walter	P	1	.000	A	C
		Burns, George Henry	1B128	130	.352	Det	
		Davidson, Claude Boucher	2B15	31	.185	A	
		Dugan, Joseph Anthony (Jumping Joe) (2B35)	SS84	120	.195	B	
		Dykes, James Joseph	2B56	59	.188	A	
0	0	Fahey, Francis R.	P	10	.176	A	C
		Gardner, Wm. Lawrence (Larry)	3B	127	.285	Bos	
3	5	Geary, Robert Norton	P	16	.148	A	
8	14	Gregg, Sylveanus Augustus (Vean)	P	30	.168	Bos16	
0	0	Holmes, Edward M.	P	2	.000	A	C
1	1	Jamieson, Chas. Devine (P3)	OF93	110	.202	B	
1	5	Johnson, Roy	P	10	.067	A	
0	1	Keefe, David Edwin	P	1	.000	B	

WON	LOST	NAME	POS.	G.	BA	FROM	TO
1	0	Keen, Howard Victor	P	1	.000	A	
		Kopp, Merlin H.	OF	96	.234	Wash15	
		Munch, Jacob Ferdinand	1B	22	.267	A	C
4	8	Myers, Elmer Glen	P	18	.143	B	
		McAvoy, James Eugene	C74	83	.244	B	
		Oldring, Reuben Noshier	OF28	49	.233	NY16	C
		Perkins, Ralph Foster (Cy)	C61	68	.188	B	
21	19	Perry, Herbert Scott	P	44	.134	CinN	
0	1	Pierson, Wm. Morris	P	8	.200	A	
		Shannon, Maurice Joseph (2B26)	SS45	72	.240	B	
0	0	Shea, Patrick Henry	P	3	.000	A	
		Walker, Clarence Wm.	OF109	114	.294	Bos	
6	10	Watson, John Reeves	P	21	.135	A	
2	0	Zachary, Jonathan Thompson Walton (Tom)	P	2	.500	A	

WON 36
LOST 104
TG 140

AMERICAN LEAGUE

1919.

FINISHED 8th (LAST)

PCT. .257

PHILADELPHIA

CONNIE MACK

WON	LOST	NAME	POS.	G.	BA	FROM	TO
0	0	Adams, James Irwin	P	1	.000	B	C
		Allen, Robert	OF	11	.094	A	C
1	1	Anderson, Walter Carl	P	3	.000	Phil17	C
0	1	Boone, James Albert	P	3	.000	A	
		Burns, George Henry (OF34)	1B86	126	.296	B	
		Burrus, Maurice Lennon	1B38	70	.258	A	
		Dowd, Raymond Bernard (2B1 SS1)	3B1	13	+.158	xDet	
		Dugan, Joseph Anthony (Jumping Joe)	SS98	104	.271	B	
		Dykes, James Joseph	2B16	17	.184	B	
0	1	Eckert, Chas. Wm.	P	2	.200	A	
		Ewoldt, Arthur Lee	3B	9	.233	A	C
		Galloway, Clarence Edward (Chick)	SS	17	.143	A	
0	3	Geary, Robert Norton	P	9	.500	B	
0	0	Grevell, Wm.	P	5	.000	A	C
		Griffin, Ivy Moore	1B	17	.294	A	
		Groh, Lewis Carl	3B	4	.000	A	C
		Grover, Roy Arthur	2B	22	+.232	Phil17	Wash
0	2	Hasty, Robert Keller	P	2	.333	A	
		High, Chas. Edwin	OF	11	.077	A	
9	14	Johnson, Russell Conwell	P34	35	.194	Phil17	
0	1	Keefe, David Edwin	P	2	.000	B	
9	15	Kinney, Walter Wm.	P43	57	.284	Bos	
0	0	Kircher, Michael Andrew	P	2	.000	A	
		Kopp, Merlin H.	OF65	75	.226	B	C
0	2	Martin, Patrick Francis	P	2	.000	A	
		McAvoy, James Eugene	C57	62	.141	B	C
5	18	Naylor, Roleine Cecil (Rollie)	P	31	.168	Phil17	
1	5	Noyes, Winfield Chas.	P	10	+.125	Phil17	Chi
		Perkins, Ralph Foster (Cy)	C87	101	.252	B	
4	17	Perry, Herbert Scott	P	25	.136	B	
0	0	Pierson, Wm. Morris	P	2	.333	B	
0	2	Roberts, Raymond	P	3	.200	A	C
4	12	Rogers, Thomas Andrew (Shotgun)	P	23	+.234	xStL	
		Roth, Robert Frank	OF	48	+.323	Clev	Bos
2	3	Seibold, Harry (Socks)	P14	15	.154	Phil17	
		Shannon, Marucie Joseph	2B	39	+.271	B	Bos
		Strunk, Amos Aaron	OF	60	+.211	xBos	
		Styles, Wm. Graves (Lena)	C	8	.273	A	
		Thomas, Frederick Harvey	3B	124	.212	Bos	
0	1	Thompson, Harry	P	5	+.000	xWash	C
		Turner, Terrence LaMont (Terry)	SS25	38	.189	Clev	C
		Walker, Clarence Wm.	OF115	125	.292	B	
		Walker, John Miles	C	3	.000	A	
0	1	Watson, John Reeves	P	4	.000	B	
		Welch, Frank	OF	15	.167	A	
		Wingo, Absalom Holbrook (Red)	OF	15	.305	A	
		Witt, Lawton Walter (Whitey) (2B56)	OF59	122	.267	Phil17	
0	2	York, James E.	P	2	.000	A	
1	3	Zinn, James Edward	P	10	.400	A	

WON 48
LOST 106
TG 154

AMERICAN LEAGUE

1920.

FINISHED 8th (LAST)

PCT. .312

PHILADELPHIA

CONNIE MACK

WON	LOST	NAME	POS.	G.	BA	FROM	TO
0	3	Bigbee, Lyle Randolph	P	37	.186	A	
		Burns, George Henry	1B	21	+.259	B	Clev
		Burrus, Maruice Lennon	1B31	71	.185	B	
		Dugan, Joseph Anthony (Jumping Joe) (2B31 SS33)	3B59	123	.322	B	
		Dykes, James Joseph (3B44)	2B98	142	.256	B	
0	0	Eckert, Chas. Wm.	P	2	.000	B	
		Galloway, Clarence Edward (Chick)	SS84	98	.202	B	
		Griffin, Ivy Moore	1B126	129	.238	B	
9	14	Harriss, Wm. Bryan	P	31	.106	A	
1	3	Hasty, Robert Keller	P	19	.250	B	
0	1	Heimach, Fred Amos	P	1	.000	A	
		High, Chas. Edwin	OF	17	.308	B	C
		Johnson, Paul Oscar	OF	18	.208	BosN18	
6	7	Keefe, David Edwin	P31	32	.250	B	
		Kelly, Wm. Henry	1B	8	.181	A	
		Kerns, Daniel P		1	.000	A	C

WON	LOST	NAME	POS.	G.	BA	FROM	TO
2	4	Kinney, Walter Wm.	P	13	.346	B	
0	1	Knowlton, Wm. Young	P	1	.000	A	C
1	4	Martin, Patrick Francis	P	8	.400	B	C
1	13	Moore, Roy Daniel	P24	27	.200	A	
		Myatt, Glenn Calvin (C21)	OF37	70	.250	A	
		McCann, Robert Emmett	SS8	10	.286	A	
10	23	Naylor, Roleine Cecil (Rollie)	P	42	.163	B	
		Perkins, Ralph Foster (Cy)	C146	148	.260	B	
11	25	Perry, Herbert Scott	P	42	.157	B	
7	7	Rommel, Edwin Americus	P33	34	.216	A	
0	0	Shanner, W. W.	P	1	.000	A	C
		Shannon, Maurice Joseph	SS	24	+.167	xWash	
0	1	Slappey, John Henry	P	3	.500	A	C
		Strunk, Amos Aaron	OF	57	+.307	B	Chi
		Styles, Wm. Graves (Lena)	C8	24	.260	B	
		Thomas, Frederick Harvey	3B	77	+.233	B	Wash
		Walker, Chas. Franklin	OF	24	.231	Det18	
		Walker, Clarence Wm.	OF	149	.268	B	
		Walker, John Miles	C	6	.235	B	
		Welch, Frank	OF97	100	.258	B	
		Wingo, Edmond (LaRiviere)	C	1	.250	A	C
		Witt, Lawton Walter (Whitey)	OF50	65	.321	B	

WON 53
LOST 100
TG 153

AMERICAN LEAGUE 1921.

FINISHED 8th (LAST)
PCT. .346

PHILADELPHIA

CONNIE MACK

WON	LOST	NAME	POS.	G.	BA	FROM	TO
1	0	Barrett, Wm. Joseph	P4	14	.233	A	
0	0	Bishop, Wm. H.	P	2	.000	A	C
		Brazill, Frank Leo	1B36	66	.271	A	
		Callaway, Frank Burnett	SS	14	.240	A	
		Collins, John Edgar	OF21	24	.282	BosN17	C
		Dugan, Joseph Anthony (Jumping Joe)	3B	119	.295	B	
		Dykes, James Joseph	2B	155	.274	B	
1	4	Freeman, Harvey B.	P	18	.083	A	C
		Fulghum, James Lavoisier (Dot)	SS	2	.000	A	C
		Galloway, Clarence Edward (Chick) (3B20)	SS110	131	.265	B	
		Griffin, Ivy Moore	1B28	39	.321	B	C
11	16	Harriss, Wm. Bryan	P	39	.148	B	
5	16	Hasty, Robert Keller	P	35	.294	B	
1	0	Heimach, Fred Amos	P	1	.250	B	
		Johnson, Paul Oscar	OF32	48	.315	B	C
2	9	Keefe, David Edwin	P	44	.175	B	
		Mallonee, Howard Bennett	OF	7	.261	A	C
0	0	Miner, Raymond Theadore	P	1	.000	A	C
10	10	Moore, Roy Daniel	P29	31	.257	B	
		Myatt, Glenn Calvin	C27	44	.203	B	
		McCann, Robert Emmett	SS32	52	.223	B	
3	13	Naylor, Roleine Cecil (Rollie)	P32	33	.115	B	
		Perkins, Ralph Foster (Cy)	C	141	.288	B	
3	6	Perry, Herbert Scott	P	12	.038	B	C
16	23	Rommel, Edwin Americus	P	46	.191	B	
		Shannon, Maurice Joseph		1	.000	B	
		Styles, Wm. Graves (Lena)	C	4	.200	B	
0	2	Sullivan, James Richard Jr.	P	2	.000	A	
0	1	Taylor, Arliss W.	P	1	.000	A	C
		Walker, Chas. Franklin	OF	19	.227	B	
		Walker, Clarence Wm.	OF	142	.304	B	
		Walker, John Miles	1B99	113	.258	B	
		Welch, Frank	OF104	115	.285	B	
		Witt, Lawton Walter (Whitey)	OF	154	.315	B	
0	0	Wolf, Walter Francis	P	9	.250	A	C
		Yoter, Elmer Ellsworth		2	.000	A	

WON 65
LOST 89
TG 154

AMERICAN LEAGUE 1922.

FINISHED 7th.
PCT. .422

PHILADELPHIA

CONNIE MACK

WON	LOST	NAME	POS.	G.	BA	FROM	TO
		Berger, John Henne	C	2	1.000	A	
		Brazill, Frank Leo	3B	6	.077	B	C
		Bruggy, Frank Leo	C30	53	.279	PhilN	
		Callaway, Frank Burnett	2B11	29	.270	B	C
		Dykes, James Joseph	3B141	145	.275	B	
0	2	Eckert, Chas. Wm.	P	21	.091	Phil20	C
		Fuhrman, Alfred George (Ollie)	C	7	.333	A	C
		Galloway, Clarence Edward (Chick)	SS	155	.324	B	
9	20	Harriss, Wm. Bryan	P	47	.176	B	
9	14	Hasty, Robert Keller	P	28	.200	B	
		Hauser, Joseph John	1B94	111	.323	A	
7	11	Heimach, Fred Amos	P	37	.250	B	
		Johnston, Wheeler Rogers	1B65	71	.250	Clev	C
0	1	Ketchum, August Franklin	P	6	.000	A	C
		Miller, Edmund John (Bing)	OF139	143	.336	Wash	
0	3	Moore, Roy Daniel	P	15	+.263	B	Det
		McCue, Frank Aloysius	3B	2	.000	A	C
		McGowan, Frank Bernard	OF82	99	.230	A	
10	15	Naylor, Roleine Cecil (Rollie)	P35	36	.200	B	
1	4	Ogden, Warren Harvey (Curly)	P15	17	.241	A	
0	0	O'Neill, Joseph Henry	P	1	.000	A	
		Perkins, Ralph Foster (Cy)	C141	148	.267	B	
1	2	Rettig, Adolph John	P	4	.000	A	C
27	13	Rommel, Edwin Americus	P	51	.180	B	
		Scheer, Henry Wm. (3B10)	2B29	51	.171	A	
0	0	Schillings, Elbert Isiah	P	4	.000	A	C
0	2	Sullivan, James Richard Jr.	P	20	.091	B	

WON	LOST	NAME	POS.	G.	BA	FROM	TO
		Walker, Clarence Wm.	OF148	153	.283	B	
		Walker, John Miles	C	2	.000	B	C
		Welch, Frank	OF104	114	.259	B	
1	2	Yarrison, Byron Wordsworth	P	18	.167	A	
		Young, Ralph Stuart	2B120	125	.223	Det	C

WON 69 LOST 83 TG 152 — AMERICAN LEAGUE — FINISHED 6th.

1923. — PCT. .454

PHILADELPHIA

CONNIE MACK

WON	LOST	NAME	POS.	G.	BA	FROM	TO
		Bruggy, Frank Leo	C34	54	.210	B	
2	1	Burns, Dennis Jr.	P	3	.250	A	
		Dykes, James Joseph (SS20)	2B102	124	.252	B	
		French, Walter Edward	OF	16	.231	A	
		Galloway, Clarence Edward (Chick)	SS	134	.278	B	
		Hale, Samuel Douglas	3B107	115	.288	Det21	
10	16	Harriss, Wm. Bryan	P	46	.066	B	
13	15	Hasty, Robert Keller	P	44	.193	B	
		Hauser, Joseph John	1B	146	.307	B	
6	12	Heimach, Fred Amos	P40	63	.254	B	
0	1	Hulvey, James Hensel	P	1	.500	A	C
		Jones, John Wm.	OF	1	.250	A	
0	1	Kellett, Alfred Henry	P	5	.333	A	
0	0	Kelly, Reynolds Clarence	P	1	.000	A	C
0	1	Kinney, Walter Wm.	P	5	.167	Phi120	C
		Matthews, Wid Curry	OF127	129	.274	A	
3	0	Meeker, Chas. Roy	P	5	.111	A	
		Miller, Edmund John (Bing)	OF119	123	.299	B	
		McGowan, Frank Bernard	OF79	95	.254	B	
12	7	Naylor, Roleine Cecil (Rollie)	P	26	.244	B	
1	2	Ogden, Warren Harvey (Curly)	P18	19	.294	B	
0	0	O'Neill, Joseph Henry	P	3	.000	B	C
0	0	Ozmer, Horace Robert	P	1	.000	A	C
		Perkins, Ralph Foster (Cy)	C137	143	.270	B	
		Riconda, Harry Paul	3B47	55	.263	A	
18	19	Rommel, Edwin Americus	P	56	.237	B	
		Rowland, Chas. Leland	C	6	.000	A	C
		Scheer, Henry Wm.	2B51	69	.238	B	C
4	8	Walberg, George Elvin (Swede)	P	26	.317	xNYN̲	
		Walker, Clarence Wm.	OF26	52	.275	B	C
		Welch, Frank	OF117	125	.297	B	
0	0	Wolfe, Chas. Hunt	P	3	.333	A	C
		Wood, Chas. Spencer	SS	3	.333	A	C

WON 71 LOST 81 TG 152 — AMERICAN LEAGUE — FINISHED 5th.

1924. — PCT. .467

PHILADELPHIA

CONNIE MACK

WON	LOST	NAME	POS.	G.	BA	FROM	TO
13	6	Baumgartner, Stanwood Fulton	P	36	.216	PhilN̲22	
		Bishop, Max Frederick	2B80	91	.255	A	
		Bruggy, Frank Leo	C44	50	.265	B	
6	8	Burns, Dennis Jr.	P	37	.143	B	C
		Chapman, John Joseph	SS	19	.282	A	C
		Dykes, James Joseph (3B27)	2B77	110	.312	B	
		Galloway, Clarence Edward (Chick)	SS	129	.276	B	
		Gibson, Chas. Griffin	C	12	.133	A	C
8	7	Gray, Samuel David	P	34	.175	A	
		Green, Joseph Henry		1	.000	A	C
		Hale, Samuel Douglas	3B55	80	.318	B	
6	10	Harriss, Wm. Bryan	P	36	.167	B	
1	3	Hasty, Robert Keller	P	18	.077	B	C
		Hauser, Joseph John	1B	149	.288	B	
14	12	Heimach, Fred Amos	P40	58	.322	B	
		Lamar, Wm. Harmong	OF	87	.330	BknN̲21	
5	12	Meeker, Chas. Roy	P	30	.229	B	
		Miller, Edmund John (Bing)	OF94	113	.342	B	
0	5	Naylor, Roleine Cecil (Rollie)	P	10	.375	B	C
0	3	Ogden, Warren Harvey (Curly)	P	5	+.000	B	Wash
		Perkins, Ralph Foster (Cy)	C	128	.242	B	
0	0	Pierson, Wm. Morris	P	1	.000	Phil19	C
		Riconda, Harry Paul	3B73	83	.253	B	
18	15	Rommel, Edwin Americus	P43	45	.157	B	
		Sherling, Edward Creech		4	.500	A	C
		Simmons, Aloysius Harry (Al)	OF	152	.308	A	
		Strand, Paul Edward	OF	47	.228	BosN̲15	C
		Strunk, Amos Aaron	OF	30	+.143	xChi̲	C
0	0	Walberg, George Elvin (Swede)	P	6	.500	B	
		Welch, Frank	OF74	94	.290	B	

WON 88 LOST 64 TG 152 — AMERICAN LEAGUE — FINISHED 2nd.

1925. — PCT. .579

PHILADELPHIA

CONNIE MACK

WON	LOST	NAME	POS.	G.	BA	FROM	TO
0	0	Andrews, Elbert Devore Jr.	P	6	.000	A	C
		Bagwell, Wm. Mallory	OF4	36	.300	BosN̲23	C
6	3	Baumgartner, Stanwood Fulton	P	37	.233	B	
		Berry, Chas. Francis	C4	10	.214	A	

WON	LOST	NAME	POS.	G.	BA	FROM	TO
		Bishop, Max Frederick	2B104	105	.280	B	
		Cochrane, Gordon Stanley (Mickey)	C133	134	.331	A	
		Dykes, James Joseph (2B58 SS2)	3B64	122	.325	B	
		Engle, Chas.	SS	1	.000	A	
		Foxx, James Emory (Jimmy)	C1	10	.667	A	
		French, Walter Edward	OF19	67	.370	Phil23	
		Galloway, Clarence Edward (Chick)	SS148	149	.241	B	
		Gautreau, Walter Paul	2B	4	.000	A	BosN
1	0	Glass, Thomas Joseph	P	2	.000	A	C
16	8	Gray, Samuel David	P	32	.179	B	
10	12	Grove, Robert Moses (Lefty)	P	45	.123	A	
		Hale, Samuel Douglas (2B1)	3B96	110	.345	B	
19	12	Harriss, Wm. Bryan	P	46	.205	B	
0	1	Heimach, Fred Amos	P	15	.167	B	
		Holt, James Emmett Madison	1B25	27	.273	A	C
		Husta, Carl Lawrence	SS	6	.136	A	C
		Keesey, James Ward	1B2	5	.400	A	
		Lamar, Wm. Harmong	OF131	138	.356	B	
		Miller, Edmund John (Bing) (1B12)	OF96	124	.318	B	
		Perkins, Ralph Foster (Cy) (3B1)	C58	65	.307	B	
		Poole, James Ralph	1B123	133	.298	A	
6	3	Quinn, John Picus	P	18	+.097	xBos	
21	10	Rommel, Edwin Americus	P	52	.185	B	
		Simmons, Aloysius Harry (Al)	OF	153	.386	B	
		Smith, Marvin Harold (3B2)	SS16	20	.286	A	C
1	1	Stokes, Arthur Melton	P	12	.000	A	C
8	14	Walberg, George Elvin (Swede)	P	53	.156	B	
		Welch, Frank	OF57	85	.277	B	
0	0	Willis, Chas. Wm.	P1	3	.000	A	

WON 83 | LOST 67 | TG 150

AMERICAN LEAGUE — 1926. — FINISHED 3rd. — PCT. .553

PHILADELPHIA

CONNIE MACK

WON	LOST	NAME	POS.	G.	BA	FROM	TO
		Barbee, David Monroe	OF10	19	.170	A	
1	1	Baumgartner, Stanwood Fulton	P	10	.333	B	C
		Bishop, Max Frederick	2B119	122	.265	B	
		Cochrane, Gordon Stanley (Mickey)	C115	120	.273	B	
		Dykes, James Joseph (2B44)	3B77	124	.287	B	
12	4	Ehmke, Howard John	P	21	+.152	xBos	
		Engle, Chas.	SS16	19	.105	B	
		Foxx, James Emory (Jimmie)	C12	26	.313	B	
		French, Walter Edward	OF98	112	.305	B	
		Galloway, Clarence Edward (Chick)	SS	133	.240	B	
11	12	Gray, Samuel David	P	38	.216	B	
13	13	Grove, Robert Moses (Lefty)	P	45	.099	B	
		Hale, Samuel Douglas	3B77	111	.281	B	
3	5	Harriss, Wm. Bryan	P	12	+.059	B	Bos
		Hauser, Joseph John	1B65	91	.192	Phil24	
1	0	Heimach, Fred Amos	P	14	+.100	B	Bos
		Jenkins, Thomas Griffith	OF	6	+.174	xBos	
		Lamar, Wm. Harmong	OF107	116	.284	B	
		Metzler, Alexander	OF17	20	.242	ChiN	
		Miller, Edmund John (Bing)	OF	38	+.291	B	StL
9	0	Pate, Joseph Wm.	P	47	.148	A	
		Perkins, Ralph Foster (Cy)	C55	63	.291	B	
		Poole, James Ralph	1B101	112	.294	B	
10	11	Quinn, John Picus	P	31	.174	B	
11	11	Rommel, Edwin Americus	P	37	.098	B	
		Sigafoos, Francis Leonard	SS12	13	.255	A	
		Simmons, Aloysius Harry (Al)	OF	147	.343	B	
12	10	Walberg, George Elvin (Swede)	P	40	.152	B	
		Wambsganss, Wm. Adolph	SS15	54	.352	Bos	C
		Welch, Frank	OF49	75	.281	B	
0	0	Willis, Chas. Wm.	P	13	.222	B	

WON 91 | LOST 63 | TG 154

AMERICAN LEAGUE — 1927. — FINISHED 2nd. — PCT. .591

PHILADELPHIA

CONNIE MACK

WON	LOST	NAME	POS.	G.	BA	FROM	TO
0	0	Baker, Neal Vernon	P	5	.167	A	C
		Bates, Chas. Wm.	OF	9	.237	A	C
		Bishop, Max Frederick	2B106	117	.277	B	
		Boley, John Peter (Joe)	SS114	118	.311	A	
		Branom, Edgar Dudley	1B26	30	.234	A	C
0	2	Cantrell, Guy Dewey	P	2	.167	BknN	
		Cobb, Tyrus Raymond (Ty)	OF127	134	.357	Det	
		Cochrane, Gordon Stanley (Mickey)	C123	126	.338	B	
		Collins, Edward Trowbridge	2B56	95	.338	Chi	
0	0	Dykes, James Joseph (P2 3B25)	1B82	121	.324	B	
12	10	Ehmke, Howard John	P	30	.206	B	
		Foxx, James Emory (Jimmie)	1B32	61	.323	B	
		French, Walter Edward	OF94	109	.304	B	
		Galloway, Clarence Edward (Chick)	SS61	77	.265	B	C
9	6	Gray, Samuel David	P	37	.190	B	
20	13	Grove, Robert Moses (Lefty)	P	51	.125	B	
		Hale, Samuel Douglas	3B128	131	.313	B	

WON	LOST	NAME	POS.	G.	BA	FROM	TO
		Jacobson, Wm. Chester	OF	17	+.229	xClev	C
4	2	Johnson, Russell Conwell	P	17	.167	Phil19	
		Lamar, Wm. Harmong	OF79	84	.299	B	C
		Mellana, Joseph Peter	3B2	4	.286	A	C
0	3	Pate, Joseph Wm.	P	32	.300	B	C
		Perkins, Ralph Foster (Cy)	C54	59	.256	B	
		Poole, James Ralph	1B31	38	.222	B	C
1	1	Powers, John Lloyd	P	11	.400	A	
15	10	Quinn, John Picus	P	34	.091	B	
11	3	Rommel, Edwin Americus	P	30	.157	B	
		Saunders, Russell Collier	OF4	5	.133	A	C
		Simmons, Aloysius Harry (Al)	OF105	106	.392	B	
16	12	Walberg, George Elvin (Swede)	P46	47	.207	B	
0	0	Wetzel, Chas. E.	P	2	1.000	A	C
		Wheat, Zachary Davis (Zack)	OF62	88	.324	BknN	C
3	1	Willis, Chas. Wm.	P	14	.000	B	C
0	0	Yerkes, Chas. Carroll	P	1	.000	A	

WON 98
LOST 55
TG 153

AMERICAN LEAGUE

1928.

FINISHED 2nd.

PCT. .641

PHILADELPHIA

CONNIE MACK

WON	LOST	NAME	POS.	G.	BA	FROM	TO
		Bishop, Max Frederick	2B125	126	.316	B	
		Boley, John Peter (Joe)	SS	132	.264	B	
2	1	Bush, Leslie Ambrose (Bullet Joe)	P11	15	.067	NYN	C
		Cobb, Tyrus Raymond (Ty)	OF85	95	.323	B	C
		Cochrane, Gordon Stanley (Mickey)	C130	131	.293	B	
		Collins, Edward Trowbridge	SS	36	.303	B	
0	0	Daney, Arthur Lee	P	1	.000	A	C
		Dykes, James Joseph (SS21 3B20)	2B32	85	.277	B	
7	7	Earnshaw, George Livingston (Moose)	P	26	.246	A	
9	8	Ehmke, Howard John	P	23	.239	B	
		Foxx, James Emory (Jimmie) (C19 1B30)	3B60	118	.328	B	
		French, Walter Edward	OF20	49	.257	B	
24	8	Grove, Robert Moses (Lefty)	P	39	.170	B	
		Haas, George Wm. (Mule)	OF82	91	.280	PittN25	
		Hale, Samuel Douglas	3B79	88	.309	B	
		Hassler, Joseph Frederick	SS	28	.265	A	
		Hauser, Joseph John	1B88	95	.260	Phil26	
0	0	Johnson, Russell Conwell	P	3	.500	B	C
		Miller, Edmund John (Bing)	OF133	139	.329	StL	
6	5	Orwoll, Oswald Christian (P27)	1B34	64	.306	A	
		Perkins, Ralph Foster (Cy)	C	19	.172	B	
1	0	Powers, John Lloyd	P	9	.000	B	C
18	7	Quinn, John Picus	P	31	.165	B	
13	5	Rommel, Edwin Americus	P	43	.255	B	
1	1	Shores, Wm. David	P	3	.000	A	
		Simmons, Aloysius Harry (Al)	OF114	119	.351	B	
		Speaker, Tristram E. (Tris)	OF50	64	.267	Wash	C
17	12	Walberg, George Elvin (Swede)	P	38	.209	B	
0	1	Yerkes, Chas. Carroll	P	2	.000	B	

WON 104
LOST 46
TG 150

AMERICAN LEAGUE

1929.

FINISHED 1st.

PCT. .693

PHILADELPHIA

CONNIE MACK

WON	LOST	NAME	POS.	G.	BA	FROM	TO
		Bishop, Max Frederick	2B	129	.232	B	
		Boley, John Peter (Joe)	SS88	91	.251	B	
0	0	Breckinridge, Wm. Robertson	P	3	.000	A	C
		Burns, George Henry	1B	29	+.265	xN.Y.	C
		Cochrane, Gordon Stanley (Mickey)	C	135	.331	B	
		Collins, Edward Trowbridge		9	.000	B	
		Cramer, Roger Maxwell (Flit)	OF	2	.000	A	
		Cronin, James John	2B10	25	.232	A	C
		Dykes, James Joseph (2B12 3B45)	SS60	119	.327	B	
24	8	Earnshaw, George Livingston (Moose)	P	44	.172	B	
7	2	Ehmke, Howard John	P	11	.105	B	
		Foxx, James Emory (Jimmie)	1B142	149	.354	B	
		French, Walter Edward	OF6	45	.267	B	C
20	6	Grove, Robert Moses (Lefty)	P	42	.216	B	
		Haas, George Wm. (Mule)	OF	139	.313	B	
		Hale, Samuel Douglas	3B99	101	.277	B	
		Hassler, Joseph Frederick	SS1	4	.000	B	
		LeBourveau, DeWitt Wiley (Bevo)	OF2	12	.312	PhilN22	C
		Mattox, Cloy Mitchell	C1	3	.167	A	C
		Miller, Edmund John (Bing)	OF145	147	.335	B	
		Miller, Rudel Chas.	3B	2	.250	A	C
		Morse, Newell Obediah	2B	8	.074	A	C
		McNair, Donald Eric	SS	4	.500	A	
0	2	Orwoll, Oswald Christian	P12	30	.255	B	C
		Perkins, Ralph Foster (Cy)	C	38	.211	B	
11	9	Quinn, John Picus	P	35	.133	B	
12	2	Rommell, Edwin Americus	P	32	.205	B	
11	6	Shores, Wm. David	P	39	.125	B	
		Simmons, Aloysius Harry (Al)	OF142	143	.365	B	
		Summa, Homer Wayne	OF24	37	.272	Clev	
18	11	Walberg, George Elvin (Swede)	P	40	.223	B	
1	0	Yerkes, Chas. Carroll	P	19	.000	B	

WON 102 | AMERICAN LEAGUE | FINISHED 1st.
LOST 52
TG 154 | 1930. | PCT. .662

PHILADELPHIA

CONNIE MACK

WON	LOST	NAME	POS.	G.	BA	FROM	TO
		Bishop, Max Frederick	2B127	130	.252	B	
		Boley, John Peter (Joe)	SS120	121	.276	B	
		Cochrane, Gordon Stanley (Mickey)	C	130	.357	B	
		Collins, Edward Trowbridge		3	.500	B	C
		Cramer, Roger Maxwell (Flit)	OF21	30	.232	B	
		Dykes, James Joseph	3B123	125	.301	B	
22	13	Earnshaw, George Livingston (Moose)	P	49	.228	B	
0	1	Ehmke, Howard John	P	3	.333	B	C
		Foxx, James Emory (Jimmie)	1B	153	.335	B	
28	5	Grove, Robert Moses (Lefty)	P	50	.200	B	
		Haas, George Wm. (Mule)	OF131	132	.299	B	
		Harris, Spencer Anthony	OF13	22	.184	Wash	C
		xHiggins, Michael Franklin (Pinkey)	3B2	14	.250	A	
		Keesey, James Ward	1B1	11	.250	Phil25	C
0	1	Liebhardt, Glenn Ignatius	P	5	.000	A	
9	5	Mahaffey, Lee Roy	P	33	.119	PittN27	
0	0	Mahon, Alfred George	P	3	.000	A	C
		Miller, Edmund John (Bing)	OF	154	.303	B	
		Moore, James Wm. Jr.	OF	15	+.380	xChi	
		McNair, Donald Eric (3B29)	SS31	78	.266	B	
		Perkins, Ralph Foster (Cy)	C19	20	.158	B	
0	0	Perkins, Chas. Sullivan	P	8	.125	A	
9	7	Quinn, John Picus	P	35	.265	B	
9	4	Rommel, Edwin Americus	P	35	.263	B	
		Schang, Walter Henry (Wally)	C36	45	.174	StL	
12	4	Shores, Wm. David	P	31	.193	B	
		Simmons, Aloysius Harry (Al)	OF136	138	.381	B	
		Summa, Homer Wayne	OF15	25	.278	B	C
13	12	Walberg, George Elvin (Swede)	P	38	.164	B	
		Williams, Edwin Dibrell (SS19)	2B39	67	.262	A	

x Higgins also played 1 game at 2B and 1 game at SS.

WON 107 | AMERICAN LEAGUE | FINISHED 1st.
LOST 45
TG 152 | 1931. | PCT. .704

PHILADELPHIA

CONNIE MACK

WON	LOST	NAME	POS.	G.	BA	FROM	TO
		Bishop, Max Frederick	2B	130	.294	B	
		Boley, John Peter (Joe)	SS62	67	.228	B	
0	0	Carter, Solomon Mobley	P	2	.000	A	C
		Cochrane, Gordon Stanley (Mickey)	C117	122	.349	B	
		Cramer, Roger Maxwell (Flit)	OF55	65	.260	B	
		Dykes, James Joseph (SS15)	3B87	101	.273	B	
21	7	Earnshaw, George Livingston (Moose)	P	43	.263	B	
		Finney, Louis Klopsche	OF	9	.376	A	
		Foxx, James Emory (Jimmie) (3B26)	1B112	139	.291	B	
31	4	Grove, Robert Moses (Lefty)	P	41	.200	B	
		Haas, George Wm. (Mule)	OF	102	.323	B	
		Heving, John Aloysius	C40	42	.239	Bos	
10	5	Hoyt, Waite Chas.	P	16	+.289	xDet	
1	0	Krausse, Lewis Bernard	P	3	.000	A	
15	4	Mahaffey, Lee Roy	P	30	.190	B	
		Miller, Edmund John (Bing)	OF	137	.281	B	
		Moore, James Wm. Jr.	OF36	49	.223	B	C
2	4	McDonald, Henry M.	P	19	.095	A	
		McNair, Donald Eric (2B16 SS13)	3B47	79	.271	B	
		Palmisano, Joseph A.	C16	19	.227	A	C
0	1	Peterson, James Niels	P	6	.500	A	
7	5	Rommel, Edwin Americus	P25	29	.259	B	
0	3	Shores, Wm. David	P	6	.333	B	
		Simmons, Aloysius Harry (Al)	OF	128	.390	B	
		Todt, Philip Julius	1B52	62	.244	Bos	C
20	12	Walberg, George Elvin (Swede)	P44	45	.124	B	
		Williams, Edwin Dibrell (2B10)	SS72	86	.269	B	

WON 94 | AMERICAN LEAGUE | FINISHED 2nd.
LOST 60
TG 154 | 1932. | PCT. .610

PHILADELPHIA

CONNIE MACK

WON	LOST	NAME	POS.	G.	BA	FROM	TO
		Bishop, Max Frederick	2B106	114	.254	B	
		Boley, John Peter (Joe)	SS	10	+.206	B	Clev
0	1	Bowman, Joseph Emil (Joe)	P	7	1.000	A	
3	4	Cain, Merritt Patrick (Sugar)	P	10	.250	A	
		Cihocki, Edward Joseph	OF	1	.000	A	
		Cochrane, Gordon Stanley (Mickey)	C137	139	.293	B	
		Coleman, Parke Edward	OF16	26	.342	A	
		Cramer, Roger Maxwell (Flit)	OF86	92	.336	B	
0	0	DeShong, James Brooklyn	P	6	.000	A	

WON	LOST	NAME	POS.	G.	BA	FROM	TO
		Dykes, James Joseph (SS10)	3B141	153	.265	B	
19	13	Earnshaw, George Livingston (Moose)	P	36	.286	B	
		Foxx, James Emory (Jimmie) (3B13)	1B141	154	.364	B	
12	5	Freitas, Tony	P	23	.148	B	
25	10	Grove, Robert Moses (Lefty)	P	44	.168	B	
		Haas, George Wm. (Mule)	OF137	143	.305	B	
		Heving, John Aloysius	C28	33	.273	B	C
		Jones, John Wm.	OF1	4	.167	Phil23	C
4	1	Krausse, Lewis Bernard	P	20	.133	B	C
		Madjeski, Edward Wm.	C6	17	.229	A	
13	13	Mahaffey, Lee Roy	P	37	.172	B	
		Miller, Edmund John (Bing)	OF84	95	.295	B	
0	1	McKeithan, Emmett James	P	4	.000	A	
		McNair, Donald Eric	SS133	135	.285	B	
		Reiss, Albert Allen	SS1	9	.200	A	C
		Roettger, Oscar Frederick Louis	1B15	26	.233	BknN27	C
1	2	Rommel, Edwin Americus	P	17	.300	B	C
		Simmons, Aloysius Harry (Al)	OF	154	.322	B	
0	0	Stein, Irving Michael	P	1	.000	A	C
17	10	Walberg, George Elvin (Swede)	P	41	.170	B	
		Williams, Edwin Dibrell	2B53	62	.251	B	

WON 79 — AMERICAN LEAGUE — FINISHED 3rd.
LOST 72
TG 151 — 1933. — PCT. .523

PHILADELPHIA

CONNIE MACK

WON	LOST	NAME	POS.	G.	BA	FROM	TO
		Bishop, Max Frederick	2B113	117	.294	B	
13	12	Cain, Merritt Patrick (Sugar)	P38	39	.200	B	
		Cihocki, Edward Joseph	SS28	33	.144	B	C
2	0	Claset, Gowell Sylvester	P	8	.500	A	C
		Cochrane, Gordon Stanley (Mickey)	C128	130	.322	B	
		Coleman, Parke Edward	OF89	102	.281	B	
0	1	Coombs, Raymond Frank	P	21	.400	A	
		Cramer, Roger Maxwell (Flit)	OF	152	.295	B	
0	1	Dietrich, Wm. John (Bill)	P	8	.333	A	
5	10	Earnshaw, George Livingston (Moose)	P	21	.182	B	
		Finney, Louis Klopsche	OF63	74	.267	Phil31	
		Foxx, James Emory (Jimmie)	1B	149	.356	B	
2	4	Freitas, Tony	P	19	.063	B	
24	8	Grove, Robert Moses (Lefty)	P	45	.086	B	
		Hayes, Frank Witman (Blimp)	C	3	.000	A	
		Higgins, Michael Franklin (Pinkey)	3B	152	.314	Phil30	
		Johnson, Robert Lee (Bob)	OF	142	.290	A	
		Madjeski, Edward Wm.	C41	51	.282	B	
13	10	Mahaffey, Lee Roy	P	33	.215	B	
3	2	Marcum, John Alfred	P	5	.167	A	
		Miller, Edmund John (Bing) (1B6)	OF30	67	.275	B	
1	1	McDonald, Henry M.	P	4	+.000	Phil31	StL
1	0	McKeithan, Emmett James	P	3	.333	B	
		McNair, Donald Eric (2B27)	SS46	89	.261	B	
4	4	Oliver, Richard (Barrett)	P	15	.286	A	
2	5	Peterson, James Niels	P	32	.148	Phil31	
0	1	Roy, Emile Arthur	P	1	.000	A	C
9	13	Walberg, George Elvin (Swede)	P40	41	.132	B	
		Williams, Edwin Dibrell (2B29)	SS84	115	.289	B	
0	0	Winston, Henry Rudolph	P	1	.000	A	
		Zapustas, Joseph John	OF	2	.200	A	C

WON 68 — AMERICAN LEAGUE — FINISHED 5th.
LOST 82
TG 150 — 1934. — PCT. .453

PHILADELPHIA

CONNIE MACK

WON	LOST	NAME	POS.	G.	BA	FROM	TO
7	9	Benton, John Alton (Al)	P	32	.109	A	
		Berry, Chas. Francis	C	99	.268	Chi	
9	17	Cain, Merritt Patrick (Sugar)	P	36	.159	B	
12	15	Cascarella, Joseph Thomas	P	42	.094	A	
3	2	Casper, George Jasper	P	5	.267	A	
		Coleman, Parke Edward	OF86	101	.280	B	
		Cramer, Roger Maxwell (Flit)	OF152	153	.311	B	
11	12	Dietrich, Wm. John (Bill)	P39	40	.208	B	
		Finney, Louis Klopsche (1B15)	OF54	92	.279	B	
0	2	Flohr, Moritz Herman	P14	15	.333	A	C
		Foxx, James Emory (Jimmie)	1B140	150	.334	B	
		Hayes, Frank Witman (Blimp)	C89	92	.226	B	
		Higgins, Michael Franklin (Pinkey)	3B	144	.330	B	
		Johnson, Robert Lee (Bob)	OF139	141	.307	B	
6	2	Kline, Robert George	P	20	+.333	Bos	Wash
0	0	Lagger, Edwin Joseph	P	8	.000	A	C
		Madjeski, Edward Wm.	C	8	+.375	B	Chi
6	7	Mahaffey, Lee Roy	P	37	.271	B	
14	11	Marcum, John Alfred	P37	58	.268	B	
0	3	Matuzak, Harry George	P	11	.167	A	
		Miller, Edmund John (Bing)	OF46	81	.243	B	
		Moss, Chas. Crosby	C1	10	.200	A	
0	0	McKeithan, Emmett James	P	3	.000	B	C
		McNair, Donald Eric	SS	151	.280	B	

WON	LOST	NAME	POS.	G.	BA	FROM	TO
		McQuaig, Gerald Joseph	OF3	7	.063	A	C
0	0	Vaughn, Clarence LeRoy	P	2	.000	A	C
		Warstler, Harold Burton (Rabbitt)	2B107	117	.236	Bos	
		Williams, Edwin Dibrell	2B53	66	.273	B	
0	1	Wilson, John Francis (Jack)	P	2	.000	A	
0	1	Wilshere, Vernon Sprague	P	9	.000	A	

WON 58
LOST 91
TG 149

AMERICAN LEAGUE

1935.

FINISHED 8th (LAST)

PCT. .389

PHILADELPHIA

CONNIE MACK

WON	LOST	NAME	POS.	G.	BA	FROM	TO
3	4	Benton, John Alton (Al)	P	27	.040	B	
		Berry, Chas. Francis	C56	62	.253	B	
6	10	Blaeholder, George Franklin	P	23	+.043	xStL	
0	5	Cain, Merritt Patrick (Sugar)	P	6	+.000	B	StL
1	6	Cascarella, Joseph Thomas	P	9	+.125	B	Bos
1	4	Caster, George Jasper	P25	26	.227	B	
		Coleman, Parke Edward	OF	10	+.077	B	StL
		Conroy, Wm. Gordon	C	1	.250	A	
		Cramer, Roger Maxwell (Flit)	OF	149	.332	B	
7	13	Dietrich, Wm. John (Bill)	P43	44	.083	B	
2	7	Doyle, Wm. Carl	P	14	.133	A	
1	2	Eaves, Vallie Ennis	P	3	.000	A	
1	2	Ferrazzi, Wm. Joseph	P	3	.000	A	C
0	3	Fink, Herman Adam	P	5	.200	A	
		Finney, Louis Klopsche (1B18)	OF75	109	.273	B	
		Foxx, James Emory (Jimmie) (C26 3B2)	1B121	147	.346	B	
		Higgins, Michael Franklin (Pinkey)	3B131	133	.296	B	
		Hooks, Alexander Marcus	1B10	15	.227	A	C
1	0	Huckleberry, Earl Eugene	P	1	.000	A	C
		Johnson, Robert Lee (Bob)	OF	147	.299	B	
1	1	Lieber, Chas. Edwin	P18	19	.143	A	
8	4	Mahaffey, Lee Roy	P	27	.176	B	
17	12	Marcum, John Alfred	P39	64	.311	B	
0	2	Martini, Guido	P	3	.000	A	C
		Moses, Wallace Jr.	OF80	85	.325	A	
		Moss, Chas. Crosby	C	4	.333	B	
		McNair, Donald Eric (1B2 3B11)	SS121	137	.270	B	
		Newsome, Ashby Lamar (2B13 3B4 OF1)	SS24	59	.207	A	
		Owens, Furman Lee	C	2	.250	A	C
		Patton, George Wm.	C3	9	.300	A	C
		Peerson, Jack Chiles	SS4	10	.316	A	
		Richards, Paul Rapier	C79	85	.245	xN.Y.N	

WON	LOST	NAME	POS.	G.	BA	FROM	TO
		Snyder, Bernard Austin (SS4)	2B5	10	.344	A	C
0	3	Turbeville, George Edward	P	19	.105	A	
0	2	Upchurch, Jefferson Woodrow	P	3	.286	A	
0	2	Veach, Alvis Lindell	P	2	.000	A	C
		Warstler, Harold Burton (Rabbitt) (3B2)	2B136	138	.250	B	
		Williams, Edwin Dibrell (2B2)	SS2	4	+.100	B	Bos
9	9	Wilshere, Vernon Sprague	P	27	.093	B	

WON 53
LOST 100
TG 153

AMERICAN LEAGUE

1936.

FINISHED 8th (LAST)

PCT. .346

PHILADELPHIA

CONNIE MACK

WON	LOST	NAME	POS.	G.	BA	FROM	TO
2	3	Archer, Frederick Marvin	P	6	.267	A	
		Berry, Chas. Francis	C12	13	.059	B	
0	2	Bullock, Malton Joseph	P	12	.000	A	C
		Conroy, Wm. Gordon	C	1	.500	B	
		Culler, Richard Broadus (SS2)	2B7	9	.237	A	
		Dean, Alfred Lovill (Chubby)	1B77	111	.287	A	
4	6	Dietrich, Wm. John (Bill)	P	21	+.111	B	Wash
0	3	Doyle, Wm. Carl	P	8	.267	B	
8	16	Fink, Herman Adam	P	34	.125	B	
		Finney, Louis Klopsche (OF73)	1B78	151	.302	B	
0	0	Flythe, Stuart McGuire	P	17	.267	A	C
1	2	Gumpert, Randall Pennington	P	22	.273	A	
		Hayes, Frank Witman (Blimp)	C143	144	.271	Phil34	
		Higgins, Michael Franklin (Pinkey)	3B145	146	.289	B	
0	2	Johnson, Henry Ward	P	3	.250	Bos	
		Johnson, Robert Lee (Bob) (2B22)	OF131	153	.292	B	
15	12	Kelley, Harry LeRoy	P35	36	.198	Wash26	
0	1	Lieber, Chas. Edwin	P	3	.000	B	C
1	7	Lisenbee, Horace Milton	P	19	.120	Bos32	
		Luby, Hugh Max	2B	9	.184	A	
		Mailho, Emil Pierre	OF1	21	.056	A	C
0	1	Matuzak, Harry George	P	6	.000	Phil34	C
		Moses, Wallace Jr.	OF144	146	.345	B	
		Moss, Chas. Crosby	C19	33	.250	B	C
0	1	Naktenis, Peter Ernest	P	7	.200	A	
		Nicholson, Wm. Beck	OF	11	.000	A	
		Niemiec, Alfred Joseph	2B52	69	.197	Bos34	C
		Newsome, Ashby Lamar	SS123	127	.225	B	
		Oglesby, James Dorn	1B	3	.182	A	C
		Peerson, Jack Chiles (2B1)	SS7	8	.324	B	C
		Peters, Russell Dixon (3B10)	SS25	45	.218	A	

WON	LOST	NAME	POS.	G.	BA	FROM	TO
		Puccinelli, George Lawrence	OF117	135	.278	StL34	C
9	20	Rhodes, John Gordon	P	35	.213	Bos	C
9	14	Ross, Lee Raven (Buck)	P	30	.169	A	
1	1	Smith, Edgar	P	2	.125	A	
2	5	Turbeville, George Edward	P	12	.143	B	
0	2	Upchurch, Jefferson Woodrow	P	7	.143	B	C
		Warstler, Harold Burton (Rabbitt)	2B	66	.250	B	BosN
1	2	Wilshere, Vernon Sprague	P	5	.000	B	C

WON 54 LOST 97 TG 151

AMERICAN LEAGUE 1937. FINISHED 7th. PCT. .358

PHILADELPHIA

CONNIE MACK

WON	LOST	NAME	POS.	G.	BA	FROM	TO
		Ambler, Wayne Harper	2B50	56	.216	A	
0	0	Archer, Frederick Marvin	P	1	.000	B	C
		Barna, Herbert Paul		14	.389	A	
		Brucker, Earle Frank	C92	102	.259	A	
12	19	Caster, George Jasper	P34	37	.211	Phil35	
		Cissell, Chalmer Wm.	2B33	34	.265	Bos34	
		Conroy, Wm. Gordon	C18	26	.200	B	
1	0	Dean, Alfred Lovill (Chubby) (P2)	1B78	104	.262	B	
2	1	Fink, Herman Adam	P	28	.208	B	C
		Finney, Louis Klopsche (OF39)	1B50	92	.251	B	
0	0	Gumpert, Randall Pennington	P	10	.333	B	
		Hasson, Chas. Eugene	1B	28	.306	A	
		Hayes, Frank Witman (Blimp)	C56	60	.261	B	
		Hill, Jesse Terrill	OF	70	+.293	xWash	C
		Huston, Warren Llewellyn (SS15)	2B16	38	.130	A	
		Johnson, Robert Lee (Bob)	OF133	138	.306	B	
1	0	Kalfass, Wm. Philip	P	3	.000	A	C
13	21	Kelley, Harry LeRoy	P	41	.225	B	
		Morris, Doyt Theodore		6	.154	A	C
		Moses, Wallace Jr.	OF	154	.320	B	
4	9	Nelson, Lynn Bernard	P30	74	.354	ChiN34	
		Newsome, Ashby Lamar	SS	122	.253	B	
		Parker, Clarence McKay	SS19	38	.117	A	
		Peters, Russell Dixon (SS13 3B31)	2B70	116	.260	B	
5	10	Ross, Lee Raven (Buck)	P	28	.102	B	
		Rothrock, John Huston	OF58	88	.267	StLN35	C
4	17	Smith, Edgar	P38	40	.233	B	
8	15	Thomas, Luther Baxter (Bud)	P	35	.128	Wash33	
0	4	Turbeville, George Edward	P	31	.231	B	C
		Wagner, Harold Edward	C	1	.000	A	
		Werber, Wm. Murray (Bill)	3B125	128	.292	Bos	
4	1	Williams, Almon Edward	P	16	.083	A	
		Yount, Floyd Edwin		4	.286	A	

WON 53 LOST 99 TG 152

AMERICAN LEAGUE 1938. FINISHED 8th (LAST) PCT. .349

PHILADELPHIA

CONNIE MACK

WON	LOST	NAME	POS.	G.	BA	FROM	TO
		Ambler, Wayne Harper	SS116	120	.234	B	
		Barna, Herbert Paul	OF7	9	.133	B	
		Bartling, Irving Henry	SS13	14	.174	A	C
		Berry, Chas. Francis	C	1	.000	Phil36	C
		Brucker, Earle Frank	C44	53	.374	B	
0	1	Buxton, Ralph Stanley	P	5	.000	A	C
16	20	Caster, George Jasper	P	42	.198	B	
		Chapman, Samuel Blake	OF110	114	.259	A	
2	1	Dean, Alfred Lovill (Chubby)	P6	16	.300	B	
		Easterling, Paul	OF1	4	.286	Det30	C
		Etten, Nicholas Raymond Thomas	1B	22	.259	A	
		Finney, Louis Klopsche (OF46)	1B64	122	.275	B	
0	2	Gumpert, Randall Pennington	P	4	.250	B	
		Haas, George Wm. (Mule)	OF12	40	.205	Chi	C
		Hasson, Chas. Eugene	1B	19	.275	B	C
		Hayes, Frank Witman (Blimp)	C90	99	.291	B	
		Johnson, Robert Lee (Bob)	OF150	152	.313	B	
0	2	Kelley, Harry LeRoy	P	4	+.000	B	Wash
		Lodigiani, Dario Antonio (Lodi) (3B13)	2B80	93	.280	A	
		Moses, Wallace Jr.	OF139	142	.307	B	
10	11	Nelson, Lynn Bernard	P32	67	.277	B	
		Newsome, Ashby Lamar	SS15	17	.271	B	
		Parker, Clarence McKay	SS26	56	.230	B	C
		Peters, Russell Dixon	SS	2	.000	B	
2	12	Potter, Nelson Thomas	P35	38	.256	StLN36	
0	2	Reninger, James David	P	4	.000	A	
9	16	Ross, Lee Raven (Buck)	P	29	.190	B	
		Siebert, Richard Walther (Dick)	1B46	48	.284	xStLN	
2	1	Smith, David Merwin	P	21	.000	A	
3	10	Smith, Edgar	P	43	.286	B	
		Sperry, Stanley Kenneth	2B	60	.273	PhilN36	C
9	14	Thomas, Luther Baxter (Bud)	P	42	.130	B	
		Wagner, Harold Edward	C30	33	.227	B	
		Werber, Wm. Murray (Bill)	3B	134	.259	B	
0	7	Williams, Almon Edward	P	30	.040	B	C

WON 55 LOST 97 TG 152

AMERICAN LEAGUE 1939. FINISHED 7th PCT. .362

PHILADELPHIA

CONNIE MACK

WON	LOST	NAME	POS.	G.	BA	FROM	TO
		Ambler, Wayne Harper (2B19)	SS77	95	.211	B	C
7	11	Beckmann, Wm. Aloysius	P	27	.250	A	
		Brancato, Albert	3B20	21	.206	A	
		Brucker, Earle Frank	C47	62	.291	B	
9	9	Caster, George Jasper	P	28	.209	B	
		Chapman, Frederick Wm.	SS	15	.286	A	
		Chapman, Samuel Blake (1B19)	OF117	140	.269	B	
		Collins, Edward Trowbridge Jr.	OF6	32	.238	A	
5	8	Dean, Alfred Lovill (Chubby)	P54	80	.351	B	
		Etten, Nicholas Raymond Thomas	1B41	43	.252	B	
		Finney, Louis Klopsche	OF3	9	+.136	B	Bos
		Gantenbein, Joseph Stephen (3B14)	2B76	111	.290	A	
		Hayes, Frank Witman (Blimp)	C114	124	.283	B	
		Johnson, Robert Lee (Bob)	OF	150	.338	B	
3	5	Joyce, Robert Emmett	P	30	.086	A	
		Lillard, Wm. Beverly	SS	7	.316	A	
		Lodigiani, Dario Antonio (Lodi) (2B28)	3B89	121	.260	B	
0	0	Masters, Walter Thomas	P	4	.000	PhilN37	C
		Miles, Wilson Daniel (Dee)	OF77	106	.300	Wash36	
		Moses, Wallace Jr.	OF103	115	.307	B	
1	2	McCrabb, Lester Wm.	P	5	.000	A	
		McNamara, Robert Maxey	3B5	9	.222	A	C
0	0	Nagel, Wm. Taylor (P1 3B43)	2B56	105	.252	A	
10	13	Nelson, Lynn Bernard	P35	40	.188	B	
		Newsome, Ashby Lamar	SS93	99	.222	B	
		O'Neill, Harry Mink	C	1	.000	A	C
0	3	Page, Samuel Walter	P	4	.429	A	C
1	6	Parmelee, LeRoy Earl	P14	16	.133	ChiN37	C
4	11	Pippin, Henry Harold (Cotton)	P	25	+.086	StLN36	Det
8	12	Potter, Nelson Thomas	P	41	.179	B	
0	2	Reninger, James David	P	4	.167	B	C
6	14	Ross, Lee Raven (Buck)	P	29	.207	B	
0	0	Schelle, Gerard Anthony	P	1	.000	A	C
		Siebert, Richard Walther (Dick)	1B99	101	.294	B	
0	0	Smith, David Merwin	P	1	.000	B	C
1	0	Smith, Edgar	P	3	+.000	B	Chi
0	1	Thomas, Luther Baxter (Bud)	P	2	+.000	B	Wash
		Tipton, Eric Gordon	OF34	47	.231	A	
		Wagner, Harold Edward	C	5	.125	B	

WON 54
LOST 100
TG 154

AMERICAN LEAGUE FINISHED 8th (LAST)

1940. PCT. .351

PHILADELPHIA

CONNIE MACK

WON	LOST	NAME	POS.	G.	BA	FROM	TO
14	13	Babich, John Chas.	P	31	.116	BosN36	
8	4	Beckmann, Wm. Aloysius	P	34	.205	B	
0	3	Besse, Herman	P	17	.263	A	
		Brancato, Albert (3B25)	SS80	107	.191	B	
		Brucker, Earle Frank	C13	23	.196	B	
4	19	Caster, George Jasper	P	36	.129	B	
		Chapman, Frederick Wm.	SS25	26	.159	B	
		Chapman, Samuel Blake	OF129	134	.276	B	
		Davis, Lawrence Columbus (SS1)	2B19	23	.269	A	
6	13	Dean, Alfred Lovill (Chubby) (1B1)	P30	67	.289	B	
		Gantenbein, Joseph Stephen (1B6 SS3 OF1)	3B45	75	.239	B	C
		Hancken, Morris Medlock	C	1	.000	A	C
		Hayes, Frank Witman (Blimp) (1B2)	C134	136	.308	B	
6	13	Heusser, Edward Burlton	P	41	.167	PhilN38	
		Johnson, Robert Lee (Bob)	OF136	138	.268	B	
		Lillard, Wm. Beverly (2B1)	SS69	73	.238	B	C
		Lidigiani, Dario Antonio (Lodi)		1	.000	B	
0	2	Marchildon, Philip Joseph	P	2	.000	A	
		McCoy, Benjamin Jenison (3B1)	2B130	134	.257	Det	
0	0	McCrabb, Lester Wm.	P	4	.250	B	
0	0	McLaughlin, Patrick Elmer	P	1	.000	Det37	
0	0	Miles, Carl Thomas	P	2	.750	A	C
		Miles, Wilson Daniel (Dee)	OF50	88	.301	B	
		Moses, Wallace Jr.	OF133	142	.309	B	
9	14	Potter, Nelson Thomas	P	31	.254	B	
5	10	Ross, Lee Raven (Buck)	P	24	.132	B	
		Rubeling, Albert Wm. (2B10)	3B98	108	.245	A	
		Siebert, Richard Walther (Dick)	1B	154	.286	B	
		Simmons, Aloysius Harry(Al)	OF18	37	.309	CinN	
		Tipton, Eric Gordon	OF	2	.125	B	
		Valo, Elmer Wm.	OF	6	.348	A	
2	9	Vaughan, Cecil Porter	P	18	.235	A	
		Wagner, Harold Edward	C28	34	.253	B	
		Wallaesa, John	SS	6	.150	A	

WON 64
LOST 90
TG 154

AMERICAN LEAGUE FINISHED 8th (LAST)

1941. PCT. .416

PHILADELPHIA

CONNIE MACK

WON	LOST	NAME	POS.	G.	BA	FROM	TO
2	7	Babich, John Chas.	P	16	.400	B	C
5	9	Beckmann, Wm. Aloysius	P	22	.191	B	

WON	LOST	NAME	POS.	G.	BA	FROM	TO
2	0	Besse, Herman	P	6	.200	B	
		Brancato, Albert (3B7)	SS139	144	.234	B	
2	2	Caligiuri, Frederick John	P	5	.200	A	
		Chapman, Frederick Wm. (2B1 3B2)	SS28	35	.159	B	C
		Chapman, Samuel Blake	OF141	143	.322	B	
		Collins, Edward Trowbridge Jr.	OF50	80	.242	Phil39	
		Davis, Lawrence Columbus (1B12)	2B20	39	.219	B	
2	4	Dean, Alfred Lovill (Chubby) (1B1)	P18	27	+.237	B	Clev
8	10	Ferrick, Thomas Jerome	P	36	.205	A	
1	2	Fowler, Richard John	P	4	.000	A	
4	6	Hadley, Irving Darius (Bump)	P	25	.129	xNYN	C
4	4	Harris, Chalmer Luman	P	33	.275	A	
		Hayes, Frank Witman (Blimp)	C123	126	.280	B	
1	0	Johnson, Adam Rankin Jr.	P	7	.000	A	C
		Johnson, Robert Lee (Bob) (1B28)	OF122	149	.275	B	
13	11	Knott, John Henry Jr.	P	27	.077	Chi	
		Leovich, John Joseph	C	1	.500	A	C
		Mackiewicz, Felix Thaddeus	OF3	5	.286	A	
10	15	Marchildon, Philip Joseph	P	30	.167	B	
		Miles, Wilson Daniel (Dee)	OF35	80	.312	B	
		Moses, Wallace Jr.	OF109	116	.301	B	
		McCoy, Benjamin Jenison	2B135	141	.271	B	C
9	13	McCrabb, Lester Wm.	P	26	.143	B	
		Poole, Raymond Herman		2	.000	A	
1	1	Potter, Nelson Thomas	P	10	+.167	B	Bos
		Richmond, Donald Lester	3B	9	.200	A	
0	1	Ross, Lee Raven (Buck)	P	1	+.000	B	Chi
		Rubeling, Albert Wm.	3B	6	.263	B	
0	1	Shirley, Alvis Newman	P	5	.000	A	
		Siebert, Richard Walther (Dick)	1B	123	.334	B	
		Simmons, Aloysius Harry (Al)	OF5	9	.125	B	
		Suder, Peter (SS3)	3B136	139	.245	A	
		Tipton, Eric Gordon	OF	1	.500	B	
0	0	Tobin, Marion Brooks	P	1	.000	A	C
		Valo, Elmer Wm.	OF10	15	.420	B	
0	2	Vaughan, Cecil Porter	P	5	.143	B	
		Wagner, Harold Edward	C42	46	.221	B	
0	2	Wolff, Roger Francis	P	2	.200	A	

WON 55 | AMERICAN LEAGUE | FINISHED 8th (LAST)
LOST 99
TG 154 | 1942. | PCT. .357

PHILADELPHIA

CONNIE MACK

WON	LOST	NAME	POS.	G.	BA	FROM	TO
0	0	Abernathy, Talmadge LaFayette	P	1	.000	A	

WON	LOST	NAME	POS.	G.	BA	FROM	TO
		Adkins, Richard Earl	SS	3	.143	A	C
0	1	Beckmann, Wm. Aloysius	P	5	.500	B	StLN
2	9	Besse, Herman	P30	34	.226	B	
		Blair, Louis Nathan	3B126	137	.279	A	C
0	3	Caligiuri, Frederick John	P	13	.083	B	C
		Castiglia, James Vincent	C3	16	.389	A	C
4	13	Christopher, Russell Ormand	P	30	.089	A	
0	1	Coleman, Joseph Patrick	P	1	.000	A	
		Collins, Edward Trowbridge Jr.	OF9	20	.235	B	C
		Davis, Lawrence Columbus (1B3 SS26)	2B57	86	.224	B	C
		Eschen, Lawrence Edward (2B1)	SS7	12	.000	A	C
6	11	Fowler, Richard John	P31	32	.160	B	
11	15	Harris, Chalmer Luman	P	26	.161	B	
1	5	Harris, Robert Arthur	P	16	+.269	xStL	C
		Hayes, Frank Witman (Blimp)	C	21	+.238	B	StL
		Johnson, Robert Lee (Bob)	OF	149	.291	B	
		Knickerbocker, Wm. Hart (SS1)	2B81	87	.253	Chi	C
2	10	Knott, John Henry Jr.	P	20	.138	B	
		Konopka, Bruce Bruno	1B3	5	.300	A	
		Kreevich, Michael Andreas	OF107	116	.255	Chi	
0	0	Lowry, Samuel Joseph	P	1	.000	A	
		Mackiewicz, Felix Thaddeus	OF3	6	.214	B	
17	14	Marchildon, Philip Joseph	P	38	.238	B	
		Miles, Wilson Daniel (Dee)	OF81	99	.272	B	
0	0	McCrabb, Lester Wm.	P	1	.000	B	
		McNair, Donald Eric (2B1)	SS24	34	+.243	xDet	C
		Richardson, Kenneth Franklin (1B1 3B1)	OF3	6	.067	A	
0	1	Savage, John Robert	P	8	.111	A	
0	1	Shirley, Alvis Newman	P	15	.000	B	
		Siebert, Richard Walther (Dick)	1B152	153	.260	B	
		Suder, Peter (2B31 3B34)	SS69	128	.256	B	
		Swift, Robert Virgil	C	60	+.229	xStL	
		Valo, Elmer Wm.	OF122	133	.251	B	
		Wagner, Harold Edward	C94	104	.236	B	
		Wallaesa, John	SS	36	.256	Phil40	
12	15	Wolff, Roger Francis	P	32	.088	B	
		Yankowski, George Edward	C	6	.154	A	C

WON 49 | AMERICAN LEAGUE | FINISHED 8th (LAST)
LOST 105
TG 154 | 1943. | PCT. .318

PHILADELPHIA

CONNIE MACK

WON	LOST	NAME	POS.	G.	BA	FROM	TO
0	3	Abernathy, Talmadge LaFayette	P	5	.250	B	

WON	LOST	NAME	POS.	G.	BA	FROM	TO
4	13	Arntzen, Orie Edgar	P	32	.160	A	C
		Benson, Vernon Adair		2	.000	A	
1	1	Besse, Herman	P5	7	.000	B	
6	16	Black, Donald Paul	P	33	.188	A	
1	1	Bowles, Chas. James	P2	3	.125	A	
0	0	Brown, Norman	P	1	.000	A	
		Brucker, Earle Frank		1	.000	Phil40	C
		Burgo, Wm. Ross	OF	17	.371	A	
0	1	Burrows, John	P	4	.000	A	ChiN
		Busch, Edgar John	SS	4	.294	A	
5	8	Christopher, Russell Armand	P	24	.156	B	
1	3	Ciola, Louis Alexander	P	12	.167	A	C
0	0	Clyde, Thomas Knox	P	4	.000	A	C
		Estalella, Roberto Mendez	OF97	117	.259	Wash	
2	6	Fagan, Everett Joseph	P	18	.000	A	
		Flick, Lewis Miller	OF	1	.600	A	
12	14	Flores, Jesse Sandoval	P	31	.175	ChiN	
		Hall, Irvin Gladstone (2B1 3B1)	SS148	151	.256	A	
7	21	Harris, Chalmer Luman	P	32	.171	B	
		x Heffner, Donald Henry (Jeep)	2B47	52	+.208	xStL	
		Kell, George Clyde	3B	1	.200	A	
		Konopka, Bruce Bruno		2	.000	B	
0	1	Kucyznski, Bernard Carl	P	6	.000	A	C
0	0	Lowry, Samuel Joseph	P	5	.167	B	C
		Mackiewicz, Felix Thaddeus	OF3	9	.063	B	
0	1	Mains, James Royal	P	1	.000	A	C
		Mayo, Edward Joseph	3B123	128	.219	BosN38	
		Parisse, Louis Peter	C5	6	.176	A	
		Ripple, James Albert (Jimmy)	OF31	32	.238	CinN41	C
		Rullo, Joseph Vincent	2B	16	.291	A	
0	1	Scheib, Carl Alvin	P	6	.000	A	
		Siebert, Richard Walther (Dick)	1B145	146	.251	B	
		Skaff, Francis Michael (SS1 3B3)	1B18	32	.281	BknN35	C
		Staller, George Walborn	OF20	21	.271	A	C
		Suder, Peter (SS5 3B32)	2B95	131	.221	B	
		Swift, Robert Virgil	C	77	.192	B	
		Tyack, James Frederick	OF38	54	.258	A	C
		Valo, Elmer Wm.	OF63	77	.221	B	
		Wagner, Harold Edward	C99	111	.239	B	
		Welaj, John Ludwig	OF72	93	.242	Wash41	C
		Wheaton, Elwood Pierce	OF	7	.200	A	
		White, Joyner Clifford (Jo-Jo)	OF133	139	.248	Det38	
10	15	Wolff, Roger Francis	P	41	.122	B	

x Heffner also played one game at 1B.

WON 72
LOST 82
TG 154

AMERICAN LEAGUE

1944.

PHILADELPHIA

FINISHED 5th.
(TIED WITH CLEVE)
PCT. .468

CONNIE MACK

WON	LOST	NAME	POS.	G.	BA	FROM	TO
0	0	Abernathy, Talmadge LaFayette	P	1	.000	B	C
10	8	Berry, James Arthur	P	53	.120	ChiN42	
10	12	Black, Donald Paul	P	29	.186	B	
		Burgo, Wm. Ross	OF22	27	.239	B	C
		Burns, Joseph James (2B9)	3B17	28	.240	BosN	
		Busch, Edgar John (2B27 3B4)	SS111	140	.271	B	
14	14	Christopher, Russell Ormand	P	35	.222	B	
		Epps, Harold Franklin	OF60	67	+.262	xStL	C
		Estalella, Roberto Mendez (1B6)	OF128	140	.298	B	
		Flick, Lewis Miller	OF6	19	.114	B	C
9	11	Flores, Jesse Sandoval	P	27	.172	B	
		Garbark, Robert Michael	C15	18	.261	ChiN39	
		Garrison, Robert Ford	OF119	121	+.269	xBos	
		Hall, Irving Gladstone (1B4 SS40)	2B97	143	.268	B	
6	12	Hamlin, Luke Daniel (Hot Potato)	P	29	.232	PittN42	C
10	9	Harris, Chalmer Luman	P	23	.169	B	
		Hayes, Frank Witman (Blimp) (1B1)	C155	155	.248	StL	
		Kell, George Clyde	3B	139	.268	B	
		Metro, Chas. (2B2 3B5)	OF11	24	+.100	xDet	
		Mills, Wm. Henry	C1	5	.250	A	C
		McGhee, Wm. Harrison	1B75	77	.289	A	
0	0	McGillen, John Joseph	P	2	.000	A	C
13	15	Newsom, Louis Norman (Buck)	P	37	.114	Wash	
		Parisse, Louis Peter	C2	4	.000	B	C
		Peck, Harold Arthur	OF	2	.250	BknN	
		Pruett, James Calvin	C2	3	.250	A	
		Rosenthal, Lawrence John (Larry)	OF20	32	+.204	xN.Y.	
		Rullo, Joseph Vincent (1B1)	2B33	35	.167	B	C
0	0	Scheib, Carl Alvin	P	15	.300	B	
		Siebert, Richard Walther (Dick) (OF58)	1B74	132	.306	B	
		Simmons, Aloysius Harry (Al)	OF2	4	.500	Bos	C
		Wagner, Harold Edward	C1	5	+.250	B	Bos
0	1	Wheaton, Elwood Pierce (OF8)	P11	30	.186	B	C
		White, Joyner Clifford (Jo-Jo) (SS1)	OF74	85	.221	B	CinN
		Wilkins, Robert Linwood	SS9	24	.240	A	

WON 52
LOST 98
TG 150

AMERICAN LEAGUE

1945.

PHILADELPHIA

FINISHED 8th (LAST)

PCT. .347

CONNIE MACK

WON	LOST	NAME	POS.	G.	BA	FROM	TO
		Astroth, Joseph Henry	C8	10	.059	A	
8	7	Berry, Jonas Arthur	P	52	.143	B	
5	11	Black, Donald Paul	P	26	.162	B	
0	3	Bowles, Chas. James	P8	13	.238	Phil43	C
		Brancato, Albert	SS	10	.118	Phil41	C
		Burns, Joseph James (1B1 3B5)	OF19	31	.256	B	C
		Busch, Edgar John (1B1 2B2 3B5)	SS116	126	.250	B	C
		Chapman, Samuel Blake	OF8	9	.200	Phil41	
13	13	Christopher, Russell Ormand	P33	34	.171	B	
		Cicero, Joseph Francis	OF7	12	.158	Bos30	C
1	1	Connelly, Wm. Wirt	P	2	.000	A	
0	0	Crowson, Thomas Woodrow Wilson	P	1	.000	A	C
		Drake, Larry Francis	OF	1	.000	A	
		Estalella, Roberto Mendez	OF124	126	.299	B	C
7	10	Flores, Jesse Sandoval	P	29	.148	B	
1	2	Fowler, Richard John	P7	11	.444	Phil42	
		Garrison, Robert Ford	OF5	6	.304	B	
4	7	Gassaway, Chas. Cason	P	24	.154	ChiN	
		George, Chas. Peter	C46	51	.174	ChiN41	C
0	12	Gerkin, Stephen Paul	P	21	.059	A	C
		Hall, Irvin Gladstone	2B	151	.261	B	
		Hayes, Frank Witman (Blimp)	C	32	+.227	B	Clev
		Kell, George Clyde	3B	147	.272	B	
		Kish, Ernest Alexander	OF30	43	.245	A	C
5	11	Knerr, Wallace Luther	P27	28	.191	A	
0	1	Marchildon, Philip Joseph	P	3	.500	Phil42	
		Metro, Chas.	OF57	65	.210	B	C
		McGhee, Wm. Harrison (1B8)	OF48	93	.252	B	C
8	20	Newsom, Louis Norman (Buck)	P	36	.163	B	
		Peck, Harold Arthur	OF110	112	.276	B	
		Pruett, James Calvin	C4	6	.222	B	C
		Rosar, Warren Vincent (Buddy)	C85	92	.210	Clev	
		Rosenthal, Lawrence John (Larry)	OF21	28	.200	B	C
0	0	Scheib, Carl Alvin	P	4	.000	B	
		Siebert, Richard Walther (Dick)	1B	147	.267	B	C
		Smith, Edward Mayo	OF65	73	.212	A	C
		Wilkins, Robert Linwood (OF4)	SS40	62	.260	B	C

WON 49 AMERICAN LEAGUE FINISHED 8th (LAST)
LOST 105
TG 154 1946. PCT. .318

PHILADELPHIA

CONNIE MACK

WON	LOST	NAME	POS.	G.	BA	FROM	TO
		Armstrong, George Noble	C4	8	.167	A	C
		Astroth, Joseph Henry	C	4	.143	B	C
		Benson, Vernon Adair	OF2	7	.000	Phil43	
0	1	Berry, Jonas Arthur	P	5	+.333	B	Clev
0	2	Besse, Herman	P	7	.000	Phil43	C
0	1	Brown, Norman	P	4	.000	Phil43	C
		Caulfield, John Joseph (3B1)	SS31	44	.277	A	C
		Chapman, Samuel Blake	OF145	146	.261	B	
5	7	Christopher, Russell Ormand	P	30	.139	B	
0	2	Coleman, Joseph Patrick	P	4	.400	Phil42	
0	0	Cooper, Orge Patterson	P	1	.000	A	
		Derry, Alva Russell	OF50	69	.207	N.Y.	C
		DeSautels, Eugene Abraham	C	52	.215	Clev	C
0	1	Fagan, Everett Joseph	P	20	.286	Phil43	C
9	7	Flores, Jesse Sandoval	P	29	.250	B	
9	16	Fowler, Richard John	P	32	.183	B	
		Garrison, Robert Ford	OF8	9	.108	B	C
0	0	Griffeth, Leon Clifford	P	10	.000	A	C
		Grimes, Oscar Ray Jr. (SS4 3B6)	2B43	59	+.262	xN.Y.	C
		Hall, Irvin Gladstone (SS7)	2B40	63	.249	B	C
		Handley, Eugene Louis (SS1 3B4)	2B68	89	.251	A	
3	14	Harris, Chalmer Luman	P	34	.222	Phil44	
		Kell, George Clyde	3B	26	+.299	B	Det
3	16	Knerr, Wallace Luther	P	30	.180	B	
0	1	Knott, John Henry Jr.	P	3	.000	Phil42	C
		Konopka, Bruce Bruno (OF1)	1B20	38	.237	Phil43	C
		Majeski, Henry	3B72	78	+.250	xN.Y.	
13	16	Marchildon, Philip Joseph	P	36	.067	B	
1	1	McCahan, Wm. Glenn	P	4	.400	A	
		McCosky, Wm. Barney	OF85	92	+.354	xDet	
		McQuinn, George Hartley (Mac)	1B134	136	.225	StL	
3	5	Newsom, Louis Norman (Buck)	P	10	+.105	B	Wash
		Peck, Harold Arthur	OF35	48	.247	B	
		Richmond, Donald Lester	3B	16	.290	Phil41	
		Rosar, Warren Vincent (Buddy)	C117	121	.283	B	
3	15	Savage, John Robert	P	40	.122	Phil42	
		Stainback, George Tucker (Tuck)	OF66	91	.244	N.Y.	C
		Suder, Peter (1B3 2B12 3B33 OF2)	SS67	128	.281	Phil43	
		Valo, Elmer Wm.	OF90	108	.307	Phil43	
0	0	Vaughan, Cecil Porter	P	1	.000	Phil41	C
		Wallaesa, John	SS59	63	.196	Phil42	

WON 78 AMERICAN LEAGUE FINISHED 5th.
LOST 76
TG 154 1947. PCT. .506

PHILADELPHIA

CONNIE MACK

WON	LOST	NAME	POS.	G.	BA	FROM	TO
		Adams, Richard LeRoy	1B24	37	.202	A	C
		(OF3)					
		Binks, George Eugene	OF75	104	.258	Wash	
		(1B13)					
0	1	Brissie, Leland Victor	P	1	.000	A	
		Chapman, Samuel Blake	OF146	149	.252	B	
10	7	Christopher, Russell Ormand	P	44	.125	B	
6	12	Coleman, Joseph Patrick	P	32	.146	B	
		Cooper, Orge Patterson	1B1	13	.250	B	C
5	2	Dietrich, Wm. John (Bill)	P	11	.063	Chi	
		Fain, Ferris Roy	1B132	136	.291	A	
4	13	Flores, Jesse Sandoval	P	28	.227	B	
12	11	Fowler, Richard John	P	36	.171	B	
		Fox, Jacob Nelson	2B1	7	.000	A	
		Franks, Herman Louis	C4	8	.200	BknN41	
		Guerra, Fermin Romero	C62	72	.215	Wash	
		Handley, Eugene Louis	2B17	36	.256	B	C
		(SS1 3B10)					
		Joost, Edwin David	SS	151	.206	BosN45	
		Kirk, Thomas Daniel		1	.000	A	C
		Knickerbocker, Austin Jay	OF14	21	.250	A	C
		Laabs, Chester Peter (Chet)	OF7	15	.219	StL	C
		Majeski, Henry	3B134	141	.280	B	
		(2B1 SS4)					
19	9	Marchildon, Philip Joseph	P	35	.153	B	
10	5	McCahan, Wm. Glenn	P	29	.164	B	
		McCosky, Wm. Barney	OF136	137	.328	B	
		Poole, Raymond Herman		13	.231	Phil41	C
		Richmond, Donald Lester	3B4	19	.190	B	
		(2B1)					
		Rosar, Warren Vincent (Buddy)	C	102	.259	B	
		Rutner, Milton	3B11	12	.250	A	C
8	10	Savage, John Robert	P	44	.050	B	
4	6	Scheib, Carl Alvin	P21	22	.133	Phil45	
		Suder, Peter (SS3 3B2)	2B140	145	.241	B	
		Valo, Elmer Wm.	OF104	112	.300	B	

WON 84	AMERICAN LEAGUE	FINISHED 4th.
LOST 70		
TG 154	1948.	PCT. .545

PHILADELPHIA

CONNIE MACK

WON	LOST	NAME	POS.	G.	BA	FROM	TO
		Binks, George Eugene	OF14	17	+.098	B	StL
14	10	Brissie, Leland Victor	P	39	.237	B	
		Brucker, Earle Francis Jr.	C	2	.167	A	C
		Chapman, Samuel Blake	OF118	123	.258	B	
14	13	Coleman, Joseph Patrick	P	33	.122	B	
		Coleman, Raymond LeRoy	OF53	68	+.243	xStL	
		DeMars, Wm. Lester	SS9	18	.172	A	
		(2B1 3B1)					
1	2	Dietrich, Wm. John (Bill)	P	4	.000	B	C
		Fain, Ferris Roy	1B	145	.281	B	
15	8	Fowler, Richard John	P	29	.171	B	
		Fox, Jacob Nelson	2B	3	.154	B	
		Franks, Herman Louis	C27	40	.224	B	
		Guerra, Fermin Romero	C47	53	.211	B	
5	2	Harris, Chas.	P	45	.125	A	
1	2	Holborow, Walter Albert	P	5	.500	Wash45	C
		Joost, Edwin David	SS	135	.250	B	
0	0	Kellner, Alexander Raymond	P	13	.000	A	
		Majeski, Henry (SS8)	3B142	148	.310	B	
9	15	Marchildon, Philip Joseph	P	33	.069	B	
4	7	McCahan, Wm. Glenn	P	17	.258	B	
		McCosky, Wm. Barney	OF134	135	.326	B	
2	2	Potter, Nelson Thomas	P	8	+.250	xStL	BosN
		Rosar, Warren Vincent (Buddy)	C	90	.255	B	
5	1	Savage, John Robert	P	33	.077	B	
14	8	Scheib, Carl Alvin	P32	52	.298	B	
		(OF2)					
		Suder, Peter	2B	148	.241	B	
		Valo, Elmer Wm.	OF109	113	.305	B	
		Webb, James Leverne (Skeeter)	2B9	23	.148	Det	C
		(SS8)					
		Wellman, Robert Joseph	1B2	4	.200	A	
		(OF1)					
		White, Donald Wm. (3B17)	OF54	86	.245	A	
		York, Rudolph Preston (Rudy)	1B14	31	.157	Chi	C

WON 81	AMERICAN LEAGUE	FINISHED 5th.
LOST 73		
TG 154	1949.	PCT. .526

PHILADELPHIA

CONNIE MACK

WON	LOST	NAME	POS.	G.	BA	FROM	TO
		Astroth, Joseph Henry	C44	55	.243	Phil46	
		Biasatti, Henry Arcado	1B8	21	.083	A	C
16	11	Brissie, Leland Victor	P	34	.267	B	
		Chapman, Samuel Blake	OF	154	.278	B	
13	14	Coleman, Joseph Patrick	P	33	.177	B	
		Davis, Thomas Oscar	SS14	31	.267	A	
		(2B1 3B12)					
		Estalella, Roberto Mendez	OF6	8	.250	Phil45	C
		Fain, Ferris Roy	1B	150	.263	B	
15	11	Fowler, Richard John	P	31	.234	B	
		Fox, Jacob Nelson	2B77	88	.255	B	
		Galan, August John (Augie)	OF9	12	.308	xNYN	C
		Guerra, Fermin Romero	C95	98	.265	B	
1	1	Harris, Chas.	P	37	.125	B	
0	0	Housmann, Clemons Raymond	P	1	.000	Bos45	C
		Joost, Edwin David	SS	144	.263	B	

WON	LOST	NAME	POS.	G.	BA	FROM	TO
20	12	Kellner, Alexander Raymond	P	38	.217	B	
		Majeski, Henry	3B113	114	.277	B	
0	3	Marchildon, Philip Joseph	P	7	.167	B	
		Moses, Wallace Jr.	OF92	110	.276	Bos	
1	1	McCahan, Wm. Glenn	P	7	.200	B	C
		Rosar, Warren Vincent (Buddy)	C31	32	.200	B	
6	8	Shantz, Robert Clayton	P	33	.189	A	
9	12	Scheib, Carl Alvin	P38	47	.236	B	
		Suder, Peter (SS2 3B36)	2B89	118	.267	B	
		Valo, Elmer Wm.	OF	150	.283	B	
		White, Donald Wm. (3B4)	OF47	57	.213	B	C
0	0	Wilson, James Alger	P	2	.000	StL	
		Wright, Taft Shedron	OF35	59	.235	Chi	C

WON 52
LOST 102
TG 154

AMERICAN LEAGUE — 1950. — FINISHED 8th (LAST) — PCT. .338

PHILADELPHIA

CONNIE MACK

WON	LOST	NAME	POS.	G.	BA	FROM	TO
		Astroth, Joseph Henry	C38	39	.327	B	
7	19	Brissie, Leland Victor	P	46	.172	B	
0	1	Burtschy, Edward Frank	P	9	.000	A	
0	0	Byrd, Harry Gladwin	P	6	.000	A	
		Chapman, Samuel Blake	OF140	144	.251	B	
0	5	Coleman, Joseph Patrick	P	15	.059	B	
		Dillinger, Robert Bernard	3B	84	.309	StL	PittN
		Fain, Ferris Roy	1B	151	.282	B	
1	5	Fowler, Richard John	P	11	.192	B	
		Guerra, Fermin Romero	C78	87	.282	B	
		Guintini, Benjamin John	OF1	3	.000	PittN46	C
		Hitchcock, Wm. Clyde (SS1)	2B107	115	.273	Bos	
15	10	Hooper, Robert Nelson	P	45	.125	A	
		Joost, Edwin David	SS	131	.233	B	
8	20	Kellner, Alexander Raymond	P	36	.200	B	
0	0	Klieman, Edward Frederick	P	5	.000	Chi	C
1	1	Kucab, John Albert	P	4	.111	A	
		Lehner, Paul Eugene	OF101	114	.309	StL	
		Markland, Cleneth Eugene	2B	5	.125	A	C
		Moses, Wallace Jr.	OF62	88	.264	B	
0	3	Murray, Joseph Ambrose	P	8	.000	A	C
		McCosky, Wm. Barney	OF42	66	.240	Phil48	
0	0	McCrabb, Lester Wm.	P	2	.000	Phil42	C
		Ortiz, Roberto Gonzalo Nunez	OF3	6	+.071	xWash	C
		Rinker, Robert John	C1	3	.333	A	C
3	10	Scheib, Carl Alvin	P43	50	.250	B	
8	14	Shantz, Robert Clayton	P36	37	.167	B	
		Suder, Peter (1B4 SS10 3B11)	2B47	77	.246	B	
		Tipton, Joseph John	C59	64	.266	Chi	
		Valo, Elmer Wm.	OF117	129	.280	B	
		Wahl, Kermit Emerson (2B2 SS18)	3B61	89	.257	CinN47	
		Wellman, Robert Joseph	OF2	11	.333	Phil48	C
9	14	Wyse, Henry Washington	P	41	.153	ChiN47	

WON 70
LOST 84
TG 154

AMERICAN LEAGUE — 1951. — FINISHED 6th. — PCT. .455

PHILADELPHIA

JAMES JOSEPH DYKES

WON	LOST	NAME	POS.	G.	BA	FROM	TO
		Astroth, Joseph Henry	C57	64	.246	B	
0	2	Brissie, Leland Victor	P	2	+.200	B	Clev
0	0	Burtschy, Edward Frank	P	7	.333	B	
		Chapman, Samuel Blake	OF17	18	+.169	B	Clev
		Clark, Alfred Aloysius (3B10)	OF33	56	+.248	xClev	
1	6	Coleman, Joseph Patrick	P	28	.259	B	
		Davis, Thomas Oscar (3B1)	2B2	11	.067	Phil49	C
		Fain, Ferris Roy (OF11)	1B108	117	.344	B	
5	11	Fowler, Richard John	P	22	.190	B	
0	0	Harris, Chas.	P	3	+.000	Phil49	Clev
		Hitchcock, Wm. Clyde (1B1 2B23)	3B45	77	.306	B	
12	10	Hooper, Robert Nelson	P	38	.208	B	
		Joost, Edwin David	SS	140	.289	B	
11	14	Kellner, Alexander Raymond	P	33	.228	B	
		Klein, Louis Frank	2B42	49	+.229	xClev	C
4	3	Kucab, John Albert	P	30	.000	B	
		Lehner, Paul Eugene	OF6	9	+.143	B	Chi
		Limmer, Louis	1B58	94	.159	A	
		Majeski, Henry	3B88	89	+.285	xChi	
11	4	Martin, Morris Webster	P	35	.220	BknN49	
		Moses, Wallace Jr.	OF27	70	.191	B	C
		Murray, Raymond Lee	C39	40	+.213	xClev	
		McCosky, Wm. Barney	OF7	12	.296	B	CinN
		Philley, David Earl (3B2)	OF120	125	+.263	xChi	
		Samcoff, Edward Wm.	2B3	4	.000	A	C
1	12	Scheib, Carl Alvin	P46	48	.396	B	
18	10	Shantz, Robert Clayton	P32	36	.250	B	
		Suder, Peter (SS18 3B3)	2B103	123	.245	B	
		Tipton, Joseph John	C	72	.239	B	
		Valo, Elmer Wm.	OF116	123	.302	B	
		Wahl, Kermit Emerson	3B18	20	+.186	B	StL
1	2	Wyse, Henry Washington	P	9	+.250	B	Wash
		Zernial, Gus Edward	OF138	139	+.274	xChi	
6	10	Zoldak, Samuel Walter	P	26	.156	Clev	

WON 79 | LOST 75 | TG 154

AMERICAN LEAGUE 1952. FINISHED 4th. PCT. .513

PHILADELPHIA

JAMES JOSEPH DYKES

WON	LOST	NAME	POS.	G.	BA	FROM	TO
		Astroth, Joseph Henry	C102	104	.249	B	
		Bevan, Joseph Harold	3B6	8	+.353	xBos	C
2	2	Bishop, Chas. Tuller	P	6	.111	A	
15	15	Byrd, Harry Gladwin	P	37	.133	Phil50	
		Clark, Alfred Aloysius	OF48	71	.274	B	
		(1B2)					
		Fain, Ferris Roy	1B144	145	.327	B	
1	2	Fowler, Richard John	P	18	.000	B	C
1	0	Fricano, Marion John	P	2	.000	A	
		Hamilton, Thomas B.	1B5	9	.200	A	
		Hitchcock, Wm. Clyde	3B104	119	.246	B	
		(1B13)					
8	15	Hooper, Robert Nelson	P	43	.195	B	
0	0	Hoyle, Roland Edison	P	3	.000	A	C
		Joost, Edwin David	SS	146	.244	B	
		Kell, Everett Lee	2B68	75	.221	A	C
12	14	Kellner, Alexander Raymond	P	34	.207	B	
0	0	Kellner, Walter Joseph	P	1	.000	A	
0	1	Kucab, John Albert	P25	28	.200	B	C
		Littrell, Jack Napier (3B1)	SS2	4	.000	A	
		Majeski, Henry	3B	34	+.256	B	Clev
0	2	Martin, Morris Webster	P	5	.111	B	
0	0	Matarazzo, Leonard	P	1	.000	A	C
		Michaels, Casimir Eugene	2B	55	+.250	xStL	
		Murray, Raymond Lee	C42	44	.206	B	
3	3	Newsom, Louis Norman	P	14	+.133	xWash	
		Philley, David Earl (3B2)	OF149	151	.263	B	
		Robertson, Sherrard	2B8	43	+.200	xWash	C
		Alexander (3B2 OF7)					
11	7	Scheib, Carl Alvin	P30	44	.220	B	
24	7	Shantz, Robert Clayton	P33	34	.198	B	
		Suder, Peter	2B43	74	.241	B	
		(SS17 3B16)					
		Thomas, Keith Marshall	OF29	75	.250	A	
		Tipton, Joseph John	C	23	+.191	B	Clev
		Valo, Elmer Wm.	OF121	129	.281	B	
2	1	Wright, Henderson Edward	P	24	.143	BosN48	C
		Zernial, Gus Edward	OF141	145	.262	B	
0	6	Zoldak, Samuel Walter	P	16	.174	B	C

WON 59 | LOST 95 | TG 154

AMERICAN LEAGUE 1953. FINISHED 7th. PCT. .383

PHILADELPHIA

JAMES JOSEPH DYKES

WON	LOST	NAME	POS.	G.	BA	FROM	TO
		Astroth, Joseph Henry	C79	82	.296	B	
		Babe, Loren Rolland	3B93	103	+.224	xN.Y.	C
		(SS1)					
3	14	Bishop, Chas. Tuller	P39	40	.089	B	
11	20	Byrd, Harry Gladwin	P	40	.222	B	
		Clark, Alfred Aloysius	OF19	20	+.203	B	Chi
3	4	Coleman, Joseph Patrick	P	21	.286	Phil51	
		DeMaestri, Joseph Paul	SS108	111	.255	StL	
0	3	Fanovich, Frank Joseph	P	26	.182	CinN49	C
9	12	Fricano, Marion John	P39	46	.145	B	
		Giordano, Thomas Arthur	2B	11	.175	A	C
		Hamilton, Thomas Ball	1B7	58	.196	B	C
		(OF2)					
0	0	Harrington, Wm. Womble	P	1	.000	A	
		Joost, Edwin David	SS	51	.249	B	
11	12	Kellner, Alexander Raymond	P	25	.217	B	
0	0	Kellner, Walter Joseph	P	2	.000	B	C
		Kolloway, Donald Martin	3B1	2	.000	Det	C
0	0	Mackinson, John Joseph	P	1	.000	A	
10	12	Martin, Morris Webster	P	58	.095	B	
		Mauro, Carmen Louis	OF48	64	+.267	xWash	C
		(3B2)					
		Michaels, Casimir Eugene	2B110	117	.251	B	
0	0	Monahan, Edward Francis	P	4	.000	A	C
		Murray, Raymond Lee	C78	84	.284	B	
		McGhee, Warren Edward	OF99	104	.263	Chi50	
2	1	Newsom, Louis Norman	P	17	.167	B	C
		Philley, David Earl	OF157	157	.303	B	
		(3B1)					
		Robinson, Wm. Edward	1B155	156	.247	Chi	
0	0	Rozek, Richard Louis	P	2	.000	Clev	
3	7	Scheib, Carl Alvin	P28	35	.195	B	
5	9	Shantz, Robert Clayton	P16	21	.237	B	
		Suder, Peter	3B72	115	.286	B	
		(2B38 SS7)					
		Thomas, Keith Marshall	OF16	24	+.122	B	Wash
2	1	Trice, Robert Lee	P	3	.143	A	
		Valo, Elmer Wm.	OF25	50	.224	B	
		Watlington, Julius Neal	C9	21	.159	A	C
		Wilhelm, Chas. Ernest	SS6	7	.286	A	C
		Zernial, Gus Edward	OF141	147	.284	B	

WON 51 | LOST 103 | TG 154

AMERICAN LEAGUE 1954. FINISHED 8th (LAST) PCT. .331

PHILADELPHIA

EDWIN DAVID JOOST

WON	LOST	NAME	POS.	G.	BA	FROM	TO
		Astroth, Joseph Henry	C71	77	.221	B	
4	6	Bishop, Chas. Tuller	P20	22	.121	B	
		Bollweg, Donald Raymond	1B71	103	.224	N.Y.	

5	4	Burtschy, Edward Frank	P	46	.118	Phil51	
		DeMaestri, Joseph Paul (2B1 3B1)	SS142	146	.230	B	
1	4	Ditmar, Arthur John	P	14	.125	A	
5	7	Dixon, John Craig	P	38	+.250	xWash	
		Finigan, James LeRoy	3B	136	.302	A	
5	11	Fricano, Marion John	P37	42	.098	B	
3	12	Gray, John Leonard	P18	19	.029	A	
		Jacobs, Forrest Vandergrift	2B131	132	.258	A	
		Joost, Edwin David MGR. (2B1 3B5)	SS9	19	.362	B	
6	17	Kellner, Alexander Raymond	P	27	.182	B	
		Limmer, Louis	1B79	115	.231	Phil51	C
		Littrell, Jack Napier	SS	9	.300	Phil52	
2	4	Martin, Morris Webster	P	13	+.235	B	Chi
		McGhee, Warren Edward	OF13	21	+.208	B	Chi
0	1	Oster, Wm. Chas.	P	8	.333	A	C
9	18	Portocarrero, Arnold Mario	P	34	.107	A	
		Power, Victor Pellot (1B21 SS1 3B1)	OF101	127	.255	A	
0	0	Raether, Harold Herman	P	1	.000	A	
		Renna, Wm. Beneditto	OF117	123	.232	N.Y.	
		Robertson, Alfred James	C50	63	.184	A	
1	1	Romberger, Allen Irving	P	10	.000	A	C
0	0	Rozek, Richard Louis	P	2	.000	B	C
0	1	Scheib, Carl Alvin	P	1	.000	B	StLN
1	0	Shantz, Robert Clayton	P2	7	.333	B	
		Shantz, Wilmer Ebert	C	51	.256	A	
2	5	Sima, Albert	P	29	+.050	xChi	C
		Suder, Peter (SS2 3B20)	2B35	69	.200	B	
		Taylor, Joe Cephus	OF16	18	.224	A	
7	8	Trice, Robert Lee	P19	20	.286	B	
0	0	Upton, Wm. Ray	P	2	.000	A	C
		Valo, Elmer Wm.	OF62	95	.214	B	
0	2	Van Brabant, Camille Oscar	P	9	.200	A	
0	2	Wheat, LeRoy Wm.	P	8	.125	A	
		Wilson, Wm. Donald	OF91	94	+.238	xChi	
		Zernial, Gus Edward (1B2)	OF90	97	.250	B	

CLUB RECORD

AMERICAN LEAGUE

ST. LOUIS

YEAR	TG	WON	LOST	PCT.	FINISHED	MANAGER
1902	136	78	58	.574	2	James Robert McAleer
1903	139	65	74	.468	6	James Robert McAleer
1904	152	65	87	.428	6	James Robert McAleer
1905	153	54	99	.354	8(Last)	James Robert McAleer
1906	149	76	73	.510	5	James Robert McAleer
1907	152	69	83	.454	6	James Robert McAleer
1908	152	83	69	.546	4	James Robert McAleer
1909	150	61	89	.407	7	James Robert McAleer John O'Connor
1910	154	47	107	.305	8(Last)	John O'Connor
1911	152	45	107	.296	8(Last)	Rhoderick John Wallace
1912	154	53	101	.344	7	Rhoderick John Wallace George Thomas Stovall
1913	153	57	96	.373	8(Last)	George Thomas Stovall James Philip Austin Wesley Branch Rickey
1914	153	71	82	.464	5	Wesley Branch Rickey
1915	154	63	91	.409	6	Wesley Branch Rickey
1916	154	79	75	.513	5	Fielder Allison Jones
1917	154	57	97	.370	7	Fielder Allison Jones
1918	124	60	64	.484	5	Fielder Allison Jones James Philip Austin James Timothy Burke
1919	139	67	72	.482	5	James Timothy Burke
1920	153	76	77	.497	4	James Timothy Burke
1921	154	81	73	.526	3	Leo Alexander Fohl
1922	154	93	61	.604	2	Leo Alexander Fohl
1923	152	74	78	.487	5	Leo Alexander Fohl James Philip Austin
1924	152	74	78	.487	4	George Harold Sisler
1925	153	82	71	.536	3	George Harold Sisler
1926	154	62	92	.403	7	George Harold Sisler
1927	153	59	94	.386	7	Daniel Philip Howley
1928	154	82	72	.532	3	Daniel Philip Howley
1929	152	79	73	.520	4	Daniel Philip Howley
1930	154	64	90	.416	6	Wm. Lavier Killefer, Jr.
1931	154	63	91	.409	5	Wm. Lavier Killefer, Jr.
1932	154	63	91	.409	6	Wm. Lavier Killefer, Jr.
1933	151	55	96	.364	8(Last)	Wm. Lavier Killefer, Jr. Allen Sutton Sothoron Rogers Hornsby
1934	152	67	85	.441	6	Rogers Hornsby
1935	152	65	87	.428	7	Rogers Hornsby
1936	152	57	95	.375	7	Rogers Hornsby
1937	154	46	108	.299	8(Last)	Rogers Hornsby James LeRoy Bottomley
1938	152	55	97	.362	7	Chas. Evard Street Oscar Donald Melillo
1939	154	43	111	.279	8(Last)	Fred Girard Haney

1940	154	67	87	.435	6	Fred Girard Haney
1941	154	70	84	.455	x6(Wash)	Fred Girard Haney James Luther Sewell
1942	151	82	69	.543	3	James Luther Sewell
1943	152	72	80	.474	6	James Luther Sewell
1944	154	89	65	.578	1	James Luther Sewell
1945	151	81	70	.536	3	James Luther Sewell
1946	154	66	88	.429	7	James Luther Sewell James Wren Taylor
1947	154	59	95	.383	8(Last)	Harold Dominic Ruel
1948	153	59	94	.386	6	James Wren Taylor
1949	154	53	101	.344	7	James Wren Taylor
1950	154	58	96	.377	7	James Wren Taylor
1951	154	52	102	.338	8(Last)	James Wren Taylor
1952	154	64	90	.416	7	Rogers Hornsby Martin Whitford Marion
1953	154	54	100	.351	8(Last)	Martin Whitford Marion

WON 78 — LOST 58 — TG 136

AMERICAN LEAGUE — 1902.

FINISHED 2nd. — PCT. .574

ST. LOUIS

JAMES ROBERT McALEER

WON	LOST	NAME	POS.	G.	BA	FROM	TO
		Anderson, John Joseph (OF3)	1B126	126	.284	Mil	
0	1	Burkett, Jesse Cail (P1 SS1 3B1)	OF136	137	.306	StLN	
22	11	Donahue, Francis Rostell (Red)	P	35	.091	PhilN	
		Donahue, John Augustus (Jiggs) (1B5)	C22	29	.250	Mil	
0	0	Friel, Wm. Edward (P1 C1 1B10 2B20 SS3 3B8)	OF22	79	.239	Mil	
17	10	Harper, Chas. Wm. (Jack)	P	29	.205	StLN	
0	0	Heidrick, John Emmett (P1 SS1 3B1)	OF109	110	.288	StLN	
		Hemphill, Chas. Judson	OF	103	+.317	xClev	
		Jones, David Jefferson	OF	14	.224	Mil	ChiN
		Kahoe, Michael Joseph	C52	54	.251	xChiN	
0	1	Kane, Harry	P	4	.111	A	
		Maloney, Wm. Alphonse (C7)	OF23	30	.203	Mil	CinN
		McAleer, James Robert MGR.	OF	2	.666	Clev	
		McCormick, Wm. J. (Barry) (SS7 OF1)	3B130	139	.246	ChiN	
		Padden, Richard J.	2B	117	.265	StLN	
22	17	Powell, John Joseph (C1 1B1 OF2)	P43	44	.217	StLN	
3	5	Reidy, Wm. Joseph	P11	13	.195	Mil	
3	0	Shields, Chas. Jessamine	P	4	+.462	xBalt	
11	13	Sudhoff, John William (OF1)	P31	31	.171	StLN	
0	0	Sugden, Joseph (P1 1B3 OF1)	C63	69	.231	Chi	
0	0	Wallace, Rhoderick John (P1 OF1)	SS133	133	.287	StLN	

WON 65 — LOST 74 — TG 139

AMERICAN LEAGUE — 1903.

FINISHED 6th. — PCT. .468

ST. LOUIS

JAMES ROBERT McALEER

WON	LOST	NAME	POS.	G.	BA	FROM	TO
		Anderson, John Joseph	1B	139	.285	B	
		Bowcock, Benjamin F.	2B	14	.300	A	C
		Burkett, Jesse Cail	OF	133	.296	B	
6	4	Donahue, Francis Rostell (Red)	P	14	+.157	B	Clev
1	5	Evans, Le Roy	P	7	.105	xBknN	C
		Friel, Wm. Edward (3B25)	2B63	98	.223	B	C
		Gonzzle, Claude	2B	1	.000	A	C

WON	LOST	NAME	POS.	G.	BA	FROM	TO
		Heidrick, John Emmett	OF120	121	.281	B	
		Hemphill, Chas. Judson	OF105	106	.238	B	
		Hill, Hunter Benjamin	3B	86	.249	A	
		Kahoe, Michael Joseph	C70	74	.185	B	
		Martin, Joseph Samuel (OF16)	3B28	44	+.231	xWash	C
0	2	Morgan, Harry Richard (Cy)	P	2	.250	A	
		McCormick, Wm. J. (Barry)	2B	59	+.192	B	Wash
		Padden, Richard J.	2B	29	.202	B	
4	4	Pelty, Barney	P	8	.100	A	
15	19	Powell, John Joseph	P38	39	.208	B	
1	5	Reidy, Wm. Joseph	P	6	.067	B	BknN
		Shannon, Owen Dennis Ignatius	C	8	.200	A	
14	15	Siever, Edward T.	P31	32	.143	Det	
21	16	Sudhoff, John William	P38	41	.171	B	
		Sugden, Joseph	C66	79	.214	B	
		Swander, Edward O.	OF	14	.250	A	
1	0	Terry, John	P	3	.000	Det	C
		Wallace, Rhoderick John (Bobby)	SS	136	.245	B	
2	4	Wright, Clarence Eugene	P	8	+.136	xClev	

WON 65 — AMERICAN LEAGUE — FINISHED 6th.
LOST 87
TG 152 — 1904. — PCT. .428

ST. LOUIS

JAMES ROBERT McALEER

WON	LOST	NAME	POS.	G.	BA	FROM	TO
		Bader, Arthur Herman	OF	2	.000	A	C
		Burkett, Jesse Cail	OF	147	.273	B	
		DeMontreville, Eugene Napoleon	2B	4	.111	Wash	C
19	15	Glade, Frederick Monroe	P	36	.179	ChiN02	
		Gleason, Harry George (3B20)	SS20	45	.214	Bos02	
		Heidrick, John Emmett	OF	133	.269	B	
		Hemphill, Chas. Judson	OF	114	.253	B	
		Hill, Hunter Benjamin	3B	58	+.220	B	Wash
13	21	Howell, Harry	P34	35	.223	N.Y.	
		Huelsman, Frank Elmer	OF	20	+.221	xChi	Wash
1	0	Hynes, Patrick J. (P3)	OF63	66	.240	StLN	C
		Jones, Thomas (Tom) (2B17)	1B136	156	.241	Balt02	
		Kahoe, Michael Joseph	C	71	.215	B	
		Moran, Chas. Vincent	3B	81	+.241	xWash	
0	2	Morgan, Harry Richard (Cy)	P	8	.000	B	
		Nance, Wm. G.	C	1	.333	Det01	C
		O'Connor, John Joseph (Jack)	C	13	.178	N.Y.	
		Padden, Richard J.	2B	132	.238	B	
14	18	Pelty, Barney	P	40	.134	B	
11	16	Siever, Edward T.	P	30	.155	B	
7	14	Sudhoff, John William	P	29	.167	B	
		Sugden, Joseph (1B24)	C79	104	.262	B	
		Swander, Edward O.	OF	1	.000	B	C
		Varenhorst, H.		1	.000	A	C
		Wallace, Rhoderick John (Bobby)	SS	139	.273	B	
0	1	Wright, Clarence Eugene	P	1	.000	B	C

WON 54 — AMERICAN LEAGUE — FINISHED 8th (LAST)
LOST 99
TG 153 — 1905. — PCT. .354

ST. LOUIS

JAMES ROBERT McALEER

WON	LOST	NAME	POS.	G.	BA	FROM	TO
0	3	Ables, Harry Terrell	P	6	.000	A	
7	9	Buchanan, James F.	P	22	.152	A	C
		Frisk, John Emil	OF116	127	.261	Det01	
		Gibson, Chas. E.	C	1	.000	A	C
6	24	Glade, Frederick Monroe	P	32	.092	B	
		Gleason, Harry George	3B142	150	.217	B	C
14	21	Howell, Harry	P38	41	.193	B	
		Jones, Thomas (Tom)	1B	135	.242	B	
		Koehler, Bernard James	OF124	142	.237	A	
		Moran, Chas. Vincent	2B20	28	.195	B	C
2	6	Morgan, Harry Richard (Cy)	P	13	.258	B	
		Padden, Richard J.	2B	16	.172	B	C
13	14	Pelty, Barney	P	31	.153	B	
2	1	Powell, John Joseph	P	3	+.100	xN.Y.	
		Rickey, Wesley Branch	C	1	.000	A	
		Rockenfeld, Isaac B.	2B	95	.217	A	
		Roth, Frank Charles	C29	35	.262	PhilN	
		Spencer, Edward Russell	C34	35	.235	A	
		Starr, Chas. Watkin	2B16	24	.206	A	
		Stone, George Robert	OF	154	.296	Bos03	
10	20	Sudhoff, John William	P	32	.186	B	
0	1	Sugden, Joseph (P1)	C85	91	.173	B	
		VanZandt, Chas. Isaac	OF74	94	.233	ChiN	C
		Wallace, Rhoderick John (Bobby)	SS	156	.271	B	
		Weaver, Arthur Coggshall	C	28	.120	PittN03	

WON 76 — AMERICAN LEAGUE — FINISHED 5th.
LOST 73
TG 149 — 1906. — PCT. .510

ST. LOUIS

JAMES ROBERT McALEER

WON	LOST	NAME	POS.	G.	BA	FROM	TO
15	15	Glade, Frederick Monroe	P	35	.137	B	
		Hartzell, Roy Allen	3B103	113	.213	A	
		Hemphill, Chas. Judson	OF	154	.289	StL04	
15	13	Howell, Harry	P	36	.135	B	
9	9	Jacobson, Albert L. (Beany)	P	25	.086	Wash	

WON	LOST	NAME	POS.	G.	BA	FROM	TO
		Jones, Thomas (Tom)	1B143	144	.252	B	
		Koehler, Bernard James	OF52	66	.220	B	C
		Niles, Harry Clyde (3B31)	OF111	142	.229	A	
		Nordyke, Louis E.	1B	25	.245	A	C
		O'Brien, Peter J. (3B20)	2B120	151	.233	CinN01	
		O'Connor, John Joseph (Jack)	C54	58	.190	StL04	
17	12	Pelty, Barney	P	35	.168	B	
13	14	Powell, John Joseph	P	29	.234	B	
		Rickey, Wesley Branch	C55	64	.284	B	
		Rockenfeld, Isaac B.	2B26	27	.236	B	C
7	10	Smith, Rhesa Edward	P	19	.204	A	C
		Spencer, Edward Russell	C54	58	.176	B	
		Stone, George Robert	OF	154	.358	B	
		Wallace, Rhoderick John (Bobby)	SS138	139	.258	B	

WON 69 LOST 83 TG 152

AMERICAN LEAGUE 1907.

FINISHED 6th. PCT. .454

ST. LOUIS

JAMES ROBERT McALEER

WON	LOST	NAME	POS.	G.	BA	FROM	TO
4	1	Bailey, Wm. F.	P	6	.150	A	
		Buelow, Frederick Wm.	C25	26	.147	Clev	C
		Butler, Willis Everett	3B9	20	.220	A	C
		*Delahanty, James Christopher Jr.	3B13	33	+.219	CinN	Wash
7	11	Dinneen, Wm. Henry	P	22	+.204	xBos	
		Frisk, John Emil		5	.250	StL05	C
13	9	Glade, Frederick Monroe	P	32	.205	B	
		Hartzell, Roy Allen (2B15)	3B38	60	.236	B	
		Hemphill, Chas. Judson	OF	153	.259	B	
16	15	Howell, Harry	P42	44	.237	B	
1	5	Jacobson, Albert L. (Beany)	P	7	+.222	B	Bos
		Jones, Thomas (Tom)	1B	155	.250	B	
2	5	Morgan, Harry Richard (Cy)	P	13	+.100	StL05	Bos
1	0	McGill, Wm. John (Billy)	P	2	.000	A	C
		Niles, Harry Clyde	2B116	120	.289	B	
		O'Connor, John Joseph (Jack)	C	25	.157	B	
12	21	Pelty, Barney	P	36	.168	B	
		Pickering, Oliver Dan	OF	151	.276	Phil04	
13	16	Powell, John Joseph	P	35	.132	B	
		Spencer, Edward Russell	C63	71	.265	B	
		Stephens, James Walter	C56	58	.202	A	
		Stone, George Robert	OF	155	.320	B	
		Wallace, Rhoderick John (Bobby)	SS	147	.257	B	
		Yeager, Joseph F. (2B17)	3B91	123	.239	N.Y.	

*also played 12 games at 2B.

WON 83 LOST 69 TG 152

AMERICAN LEAGUE 1908.

FINISHED 4th. PCT . .546

ST. LOUIS

JAMES ROBERT McALEER

WON	LOST	NAME	POS.	G.	BA	FROM	TO
3	5	Bailey, Wm. F.	P	22	.088	B	
		Blue, Bird Wayne	C	11	+.375	A	Phil
0	1	Criss, Dode	P1	64	.341	A	
14	7	Dinneen, Wm. Henry	P	27	.203	B	
		Ferris, Albert Sayles (Hobe)	3B	148	.270	Bos	
6	7	Graham, Wm.	P	21	.119	A	
		Hartzell, Roy Allen (SS18)	OF82	115	.265	B	
		Heidrick, John Emmett	OF25	26	.215	StL04	C
		Hoffman, Daniel John	OF	99	.251	N.Y.	
18	18	Howell, Harry	P40	41	.183	B	
		Jones, Chas. C.	OF72	74	.232	Wash	C
		Jones, Thomas (Tom)	1B	155	.248	B	
7	4	Pelty, Barney	P20	21	.119	B	
16	13	Powell, John Joseph	P	33	.236	B	
		Schweitzer, Albert Caspar	OF55	64	.291	A	
		Smith, Sydney	C	28	+.182	xPhil	
		Spencer, Edward Russell	C88	91	.210	B	
		Stephens, James Walter	C45	47	.200	B	
		Stone, George Robert	OF	148	.281	B	
19	14	Waddell, George Edward (Rube)	P	43	.110	Phil	
		Wallace, Rhoderick John (Bobby)	SS	137	.253	B	
		Williams, James Thomas Williams	2B	148	.236	N.Y.	
		Yeager, Joseph F.	2B	10	.352	B	C

WON 61 LOST 89 TG 150

AMERICAN LEAGUE 1909.

FINISHED 7th. PCT. .407

ST. LOUIS

JAMES ROBERT McALEER JOHN JOSEPH O'CONNOR

WON	LOST	NAME	POS.	G.	BA	FROM	TO
9	11	Bailey, Wm. F.	P31	38	.286	B	
		Criger, Louis	C73	74	.170	Bos	
1	4	Criss, Dode	P10	35	.292	B	
		Crompton, Edward	OF	17	.157	A	
		Devoy, Walter Joseph	OF16	19	.247	A	C
6	7	Dinneen, Wm. Henry	P	17	.194	B	C
		Ferris, Albert Sayles (Hobe) (2B34)	3B114	148	.216	B	C
1	2	Gilligan, John Patrick	P	3	.111	A	
8	14	Graham, Wm.	P	34	.157	B	
		Griggs, Arthur J. (OF40)	1B49	108	.280	A	

WON	LOST	NAME	POS.	G.	BA	FROM	TO
		Hartzell, Roy Allen (SS65)	OF85	152	.271	B	
		Hoffman, Daniel John	OF	110	.269	B	
1	1	Howell, Harry	P10	18	.176	B	
		Jones, Thomas (Tom)	1B	97	+.254	B	Det
		Killefer, Wm. Lavier Jr.	C	11	.172	A	
0	3	Kusel, Edward	P	3	.200	A	C
		McAleese, John James	OF79	85	.213	Chi01	C
0	2	McCorry, Wm. Chas.	P	2	.000	A	C
		O'Connor, John Joseph MGR.	DID NOT PLAY			StL07	
		Patterson, Hamilton (Ham) (OF4)	1B6	17	+.204	A	Chi
11	11	Pelty, Barney	P27	37	.165	B	
12	16	Powell, John Joseph	P	34	.179	B	
1	2	Rose, Chas. Alfred	P	3	.000	A	C
		Rossman, Claude R.	1B	4	+.467	xDet	C
		Schweitzer, Albert Caspar	OF22	27	.224	B	
		Shotton, Burton Edwin	OF	17	.262	A	
		Smith, Wilbur Floyd	C	17	.190	A	C
		Stephens, James Walter	C72	79	.220	B	
		Stone, George Robert	OF81	83	.287	B	
0	2	Stremmel, Philip	P	2	.000	A	
11	14	Waddell, George Edward (Rube)	P	31	.067	B	
		Wallace, Rhoderick John (Bobby) (3B29)	SS87	116	.238	B	
		Williams, James Thomas Williams	2B109	110	.195	B	C

WON 47 — LOST 107 — TG 154

AMERICAN LEAGUE — FINISHED 8th (LAST)

1910. — PCT. .305

ST. LOUIS

JOHN JOSEPH O'CONNOR

WON	LOST	NAME	POS.	G.	BA	FROM	TO
		Abstein, Wm. Henry (Big Bill)	1B23	25	.149	PittN	C
		Allen, Fletcher Manson	C	14	.095	A	C
3	18	Bailey, Wm. F.	P	34	.206	B	
0	2	Boyd, Raymond C.	P	3	.200	A	
		Corriden, John Michael (Red)	SS	26	.155	A	
		Crisp, Joseph Shelby	C	1	.000	A	
2	1	Criss, Dode (P3)	OF67	70	.231	B	
0	0	Crouch, William Henry	P	1	.000	A	C
		Demmitt, Chas. Raymond	OF	10	.173	N.Y.	
		Fisher, John Gus	OF19	23	.125	A	C
0	3	Gilligan, John Patrick	P	9	.200	B	C
		Graham, Bert (2B2)	1B6	8	.115	A	C
0	8	Graham, Wm.	P	9	.143	B	C
		Griggs, Arthur J. (1B17 2B41)	OF49	123	.236	B	
1	7	Hall, Marcus (Mark)	P	8	.067	A	

WON	LOST	NAME	POS.	G.	BA	FROM	TO
		Hartzell, Roy Allen (SS38 OF23)	3B89	151	.218	B	
		Hoffman, Daniel John	OF	106	.237	B	
0	0	Howell, Harry	P	1	.000	B	C
		Jansen, Raymond W.	3B	1	.800	A	C
		Killefer, Wm. Lavier Jr.	C73	74	.124	B	
1	3	Kinsella, Edward Wm.	P	10	.250	PittN05	C
11	18	Lake, Joseph Henry	P35	37	.260	N.Y.	
0	1	Linke, Frederick L.	P	3	+.167	xClev	C
0	6	Malloy, Alexander	P	7	.063	A	C
		Mee, Thomas Wm.	SS	7	.167	A	C
4	2	Mitchell, Albert Roy	P	6	.211	A	
		McDonald, Joseph Malcolm	3B	10	.156	A	C
5	1	Nelson, Albert Francis	P	7	.261	A	
		Newnam, Patrick Henry	1B	103	.216	A	
		Northen, Hubbard Elwin	OF	26	.198	A	
		O'Connor, John Joseph MGR.	C	1	.000	B	C
5	10	Pelty, Barney	P	27	.089	B	
7	11	Powell, John Joseph	P	21	.163	B	
4	10	Ray, Robert Henry	P	21	.175	A	C
		Schweitzer, Albert Caspar	OF109	113	.230	B	
1	3	Spade, Robert	P	7	.273	xCinN	C
		Stephens, James Walter	C96	99	.241	B	
		Stone, George Robert	OF145	152	.256	B	C
0	2	Stremmel, Philip	P	5	.111	B	C
		Truesdale, Frank D.	2B122	123	.219	A	
3	1	Waddell, George Edward (Rube)	P	10	.111	B	C
		Wallace, Rhoderick John (Bobby) (3B39)	SS99	138	.258	B	

WON 45 — LOST 107 — TG 152

AMERICAN LEAGUE — FINISHED 8th (LAST)

1911. — PCT. .296

ST. LOUIS

RHODERICK JOHN WALLACE

WON	LOST	NAME	POS.	G.	BA	FROM	TO
2	1	Allison, Mack Pendleton	P	3	.100	A	
		Austin, James Philip	3B	148	.261	N.Y.	
0	4	Bailey, Wm. F.	P	5	.000	B	
		Black, John B.	1B	54	.150	A	C
0	2	Brown, Chas. Roy	P	3	.000	A	
2	1	Brown, Elmer Young	P	5	.125	A	
		Clancy, Albert Harrison	3B	3	.000	A	C
		Clarke, Jay Justin (Nig)	C73	82	.215	Clev	
		Compton, Albert Sebastian (Bash)	OF	28	.272	A	
		Crisp, Joseph Shelby	C	1	1.000	B	C
0	2	Criss, Dode (P4)	OF6	58	.253	B	C
0	3	Curry, George James	P	3	.000	A	C
		Duggan, James Elmer	1B	1	.000	A	C
3	10	George, Thomas Edward	P	27	.113	A	
0	1	Gregory Howard Watterson	P	3	.000	A	C

WON	LOST	NAME	POS.	G.	BA	FROM	TO
		Gust, Ernest	1B	3	.000	A	C
		Hallinan, Edward S. (2B15)	SS34	52	.207	A	
5	12	Hamilton, Earl A.	P	32	.107	A	
0	0	Harper, Wm. Homer	P	2	.000	A	C
1	4	Hawk, Edward	P	5	.154	A	C
		Hoffman, Daniel John	OF23	24	.210	B	C
		Hogan, Wm. Henry	OF	123	+.260	xPhil	
		Krichell, Paul Bernard	C25	28	.232	A	
		Kutina, Joseph Peter	1B	26	.259	A	
10	15	Lake, Joseph Henry	P	30	.263	B	
		LaPorte, Frank B.	2B133	136	.314	N.Y.	
		Meloan, Paul B.	OF	64	+.262	xChi	C
		Myers, Ralph Edward	1B	11	+.297	Bos	Bos
4	8	Mitchell, Albert Roy	P28	29	.224	B	
0	1	Moser, Walter F.	P	2	+1.000	xBos	C
		Moulton, Albert Theodore	2B	4	.067	A	C
		Murray, James O.	OF25	31	.186	ChiN02	
3	9	Nelson, Albert Francis	P	15	.125	B	
		Newnam, Patrick Henry	1B	20	.194	B	C
7	15	Pelty, Barney	P28	29	.138	B	
0	0	Pfeffer, Edward Joseph	P	2	.000	A	
8	19	Powell, John Joseph	P	32	.164	B	
		Rowan, David	1B	18	.384	A	C
		Schweitzer, Albert Caspar	OF68	76	.215	B	C
		Shotton, Burton Edwin	OF	139	.255	StL09	
		Southwick, Clyde Aubra	C	4	.250	A	C
		Stephens, James Walter	C66	70	.231	B	
		Truesdale, Frank D.	2B	1	.000	B	
		Wallace, Rhoderick John MGR.	SS123	125	.232	B	
		Williams, August Ray	OF	9	.269	A	
0	0	Willis, Joseph	P	1	.000	A	StLN

WON 53 — AMERICAN LEAGUE — FINISHED 7th.
LOST 101
TG 154 — 1912. — PCT. .344

ST. LOUIS

RHODERICK JOHN WALLACE GEORGE THOMAS STOVALL

WON	LOST	NAME	POS.	G.	BA	FROM	TO
2	3	Adams, James Irwin	P	13	.000	A	
		Aiton, George Wilson	OF	10	.235	A	C
		Alexander, Walter E.	C	37	.175	A	
6	17	Allison, Mack Pendleton	P	27	.137	B	
		Austin, James Philip	3B	149	.252	B	
0	0	Bailey, Wm. F.	P	3	.500	B	
11	14	Baumgartner, George Washington	P	28	.145	A	
		Brief, Anthony Vincent (Bunny) (1B4)	OF11	15	.310	A	
1	3	Brown, Chas. Roy	P	13	.190	B	
4	8	Brown, Elmer Young	P	21	.167	B	
		Brown, Wm. V.	OF	9	.200	A	C
		Compton, Albert Sebastian (Bash)	OF	100	.280	B	
		Criger, Louis	C	1	.000	NY10	C
		Crossin, Frank Patrick	C	7	.277	A	
		Daly, John Francis	SS	17	.173	A	C
1	0	Frill, John Edmond	P	3	.500	NY10	CinN
		Hallinan, Edward S.	SS	27	.221	B	C
11	14	Hamilton, Earl A.	P	36	.178	B	
		Hogan, Wm. Henry	OF	107	.214	B	C
		Jantzer, Walter C.	OF	31	.185	A	C
		Ketter, Philip	C	2	.333	A	C
		Krichell, Paul Bernard	C	57	.217	B	C
		Kutina, Joseph Peter	1B51	67	.205	B	C
3	10	Lake, Joseph Henry	P	15	+.136	B	Det
		LaPorte, Frank B. (3B35)	OF40	80	+.308	B	Wash
		Miller, C.	SS	1	.000	A	C
		Miller, Edward (SS4)	1B8	12	.155	A	
3	4	Mitchell, Albert Roy	P	9	.316	B	
0	2	Napier, Samuel LeRoy (Buddy)	P	6	.000	A	
0	3	Nelson, Albert Francis	P	8	.333	B	PhilN
0	3	Pelty, Barney	P	6	+.000	B	Wash
9	16	Powell, John Joseph	P	31	.183	B	C
		Pratt, Derrill Burnham (SS21)	2B121	151	.302	A	
		Proctor, L.		1	.000	A	C
		Shanley, Henry Roat	SS	5	.000	A	C
		Shotton, Burton Edwin	OF	154	.290	B	
		Smoyer, Henry Neitz (3B1)	SS3	6	.214	A	C
		Snell, Chas. A.	C	8	.222	A	C
0	0	Spencer, Frank G.	P	1	.000	A	C
		Stephens, James Walter	C	74	.249	B	C
		Stovall, George Thomas MGR.	1B	115	.254	Clev	
		Tennant, Thomas Francis		2	.000	A	C
		Walden, Frederick Thomas	C	1	.000	A	C
		Wallace, Rhoderick John MGR.	SS87	99	.241	B	
2	4	Weilman, Carl Woolworth	P	9	.118	A	
		Williams, August Ray	OF	64	.290	B	

WON 57 — AMERICAN LEAGUE — FINISHED 8th (LAST)
LOST 96
TG 153 — 1913. — PCT. .373

ST. LOUIS

GEORGE THOMAS STOVALL JAMES PHILIP AUSTIN
WESLEY BRANCH RICKEY

WON	LOST	NAME	POS.	G.	BA	FROM	TO
0	1	Adams, James Irwin	P	4	.000	B	
		Agnew, Samuel Lester	C	104	.208	A	
		Alexander, Walter E.	C	42	.141	B	
1	2	Allison, Mack Pendleton	P	11	.000	B	C
		Austin, James Philip MGR.	3B	142	.273	B	
		Balenti, Michael Richard	SS62	70	.181	CinN11	C
10	19	Baumgartner, George Washington	P	32	.167	B	

WON	LOST	NAME	POS.	G.	BA	FROM	TO
		Bisland, Rivington Martin	SS	12	.136	PittN	
		Bonin, Ernest Luther		1	.000	A	
		Brief, Anthony Vincent (Bunny)	1B62	84	.217	B	
1	1	Brown, Chas. Roy	P	2	.333	B	
		Compton, Albert Sebastian (Bash)	OF24	61	.180	B	
		Covington, Clarence Calvert	1B16	20	.150	A	
		Crossin, Frank Patrick	C	3	.333	B	
		Flanagan, Chas. James	3B	4	.000	A	C
		Graff, Frederick Gottleib	3B	4	.400	A	C
13	12	Hamilton, Earl A.	P	25	.121	B	
		Johnston, John Thomas	OF	109	.226	A	C
		Lavan, John Leonard	SS	46	+.147	A	Phil
6	17	Leverenz, Walter Frank (Tiny)	P	28	.176	A	
		Maisel, George John	OF	11	.157	A	
		Meinert, Walter Henry	OF	4	.375	A	C
13	16	Mitchell, Albert Roy	P	33	.148	B	
		McAllester, Wm. Lusk	C38	46	.153	A	C
0	0	Powell, Samuel	P	2	.000	A	C
		Pratt, Derrill Burnham	2B144	154	.296	B	
0	0	Schmidt, Herman	P	1	.000	A	C
1	0	Schwenk, Harold Edward	P	1	.333	A	C
		Shotton, Burton Edwin	OF	149	.293	B	
		Sloan, Yale Yeastman	OF	7	.269	A	
2	6	Stone, Dwight Ely	P	17	.273	A	
		Stovall, George Thomas MGR.	1B78	89	.287	B	
0	2	Taylor, Wiley	P	5	.000	Chi	
		Tomer, George		1	.000	A	C
		Walker, Clarence Wm.	OF	23	.294	Wash	
		Walker, Ernest Robert Sr.	OF	7	.214	A	
		Wallace, Rhoderick John (Bobby)	SS41	52	.211	B	
		Walsh, Thomas L.	SS22	23	.170	A	
		Wares, Clyde Ellsworth (Buzzy)	SS	10	.286	A	
10	20	Weilman, Carl Woolworth	P	39	.143	B	
		Williams, August Ray	OF146	149	.273	B	

WON 71 — AMERICAN LEAGUE — FINISHED 5th.
LOST 82
TG 153 — 1914. — PCT. .464

ST. LOUIS

WESLEY BRANCH RICKEY

WON	LOST	NAME	POS.	G.	BA	FROM	TO
		Agnew, Samuel Lester	C	113	.212	B	
		Austin, James Philip	3B127	130	.238	B	
0	0	Baichley, Grover	P	4	.000	A	C
14	13	Baumgartner, George Washington	P	38	.132	B	
		Bold, Chas. D. (Dutch)	1B	2	.000	A	C
		Bowden, David Timon	OF	6	.285	A	C
		Clemons, Robert E.	OF	8	.214	A	C
		Crossin, Frank Patrick	C41	43	.122	B	C
		Enzenroth, Clarence Herman	C	3	.167	A	KCF
		Hale, George Wagner	C	5	.271	A	
16	18	Hamilton, Earl A.	P	43	.176	B	
		Hemingway, Edson M.	3B	4	.000	A	
0	2	Hoch, Harry Keller	P	12	.056	PhilN08	
		Howard, Ivan Chester (1B28)	3B33	81	.244	A	
15	14	James, Wm. Henry	P	38	.113	Clev12	
		Jenkins, Joseph Daniel	C	19	.125	A	
		Kauffman, Howard Richard	1B	6	.333	A	
		Lavan, John Leonard	SS73	74	.263	Phil	
		Leary, John Louis	1B130	144	.265	A	
1	12	Leverenz, Walter Frank (Tiny)	P25	26	.182	B	
0	0	Manning, Ernest Devon	P	7	.000	A	C
		Messenger, Chas. Walter	OF	1	.000	Chill	C
		Miller, Edward	1B	34	.138	StL12	
4	5	Mitchell, Albert Roy	P	27	.205	B	
		Pratt, Derrill Burnham	2B152	158	.282	B	
		Rickey, Wesley Branch MGR.		2	.000	B	
		Rumler, Wm. George	C	33	.174	A	
		Schirick, Harry Ernest		1	.000	A	C
		Shotton, Burton Edwin	OF152	154	.269	B	
0	0	Sothoron, Allen Sutton	P	1	.000	A	
2	5	Taylor, Wiley	P	9	.167	B	C
		Walker, Clarence Wm.	OF145	151	.298	B	
		Walker, Ernest Robert Sr.	OF36	71	.298	B	
		Wallace, Rhoderick John (Bobby)	SS19	26	.219	B	
		Walsh, Thomas L.	SS	7	.087	B	
		Wares, Clyde Ellsworth (Buzzy)	SS68	81	.209	B	C
19	13	Weilman, Carl Woolworth	P	39	.149	B	
		Williams, August Ray	OF141	143	.253	B	

WON 63 — AMERICAN LEAGUE — FINISHED 6th.
LOST 91
TG 154 — 1915. — PCT. .409

ST. LOUIS

WESLEY BRANCH RICKEY

WON	LOST	NAME	POS.	G.	BA	FROM	TO
		Agnew, Samuel Lester	C102	104	.203	B	
		Alexander, Walter E.	C	1	+.000	StL13	N.Y.
		Austin, James Philip	3B	141	.266	B	
0	2	Baumgartner, George Washington	P	7	.000	B	
		Burkam		1	.000	A	C
0	0	Cook, Rollin Edward	P	5	.250	A	C
		Dalrymple, Michael	3B	3	.000	A	C
		Dee, Maurice F.	SS	1	.000	A	C
0	0	East, Carlton W.	P	1	.000	A	
9	17	Hamilton, Earl A.	P	35	.113	B	
0	3	Hoch, Harry Keller	P	12	.200	B	C
2	2	Hoff, Chester Cornelius	P	11	.176	N.Y.	C
		Howard, Ivan Chester (3B23 OF17)	1B48	113	.278	B	

WON	LOST	NAME	POS.	G.	BA	FROM	TO
		Jacobson, Wm. Chester	OF	33	+.209	xDet	
6	10	James, Wm. Henry	P	34	+.208	B	Det
		Kauffman, Howard Richard	1B32	37	.258	B	C
5	6	Koob, Ernest Gerald	P	28	.135	A	
		Lavan, John Leonard	SS	157	.218	B	
		Leary, John Louis	1B53	75	.243	B	C
		Lee, Wm. Joseph (3B1)	OF15	18	.186	A	
1	2	Leverenz, Walter Frank (Tiny)	P	5	.000	B	C
9	18	Lowdermilk, Grover Cleveland	P	38	+.125	ChiN12	Det
3	1	McCabe, Timothy	P	7	.133	A	
0	0	McKay, Reeves H.	P	1	.000	A	C
		O'Brien, George Joseph	C	3	.222	A	C
2	0	Park, James	P	3	.400	A	
		Parker, Clarence Perkins	OF	3	.167	A	C
0	0	Perry, Herbert Scott	P	1	.000	A	
2	3	Perryman, Emmett Key	P	24	.000	A	C
1	3	Phillips, Thomas Gerald	P	5	.111	A	
		Pratt, Derrill Burnham	2B158	159	.291	B	
0	0	Remneas, Alexander	P	2	.000	Det12	C
		Ruel, Herold Dominic (Muddy)	C	10	.000	A	
		Schmandt, Raymond Henry	1B	2	.000	A	
		Severeid, Henry Levai	C64	80	.222	CinN13	
		Shotton, Burton Edward	OF154	156	.283	B	
1	0	Sims, Clarence	P	3	1.000	A	C
4	5	Sisler, George Harold (P18 OF29)	1B37	81	.285	A	
0	1	Sothoron, Allen Sutton	P	3	.000	B	
0	0	Tillman, John L.	P	2	.000	A	C
		Walker, Clarence Wm.	OF139	144	.269	B	
		Walker, Ernest Robert Sr.	OF33	50	.211	B	C
		Wallace, Rhoderick John (Bobby)	SS7	9	.231	B	
0	0	Walsh, Thomas L. (P1)	OF45	59	.220	B	C
18	18	Weilman, Carl Woolworth	P	47	.230	B	
		Williams, August Ray	OF35	45	.202	B	C

WON 79
LOST 75
TG 154

AMERICAN LEAGUE — 1916.

FINISHED 5th.
PCT. .513

ST. LOUIS

FIELDER ALLISON JONES

WON	LOST	NAME	POS.	G.	BA	FROM	TO
		Austin, James Philip	3B124	129	.207	B	
1	0	Baumgartner, George Washington	P	4	.000	B	C
		Borton, Wm. Baker	1B22	66	.225	StLF	C
		Chapman, Harry E.	C	18	.097	StLF	C
		Clemons, Vernon James	C	3	.000	A	
0	0	Crandall, James Otis (Doc)	P	16	.083	StLF	
12	11	Davenport, Arthur David	P	59	.137	StLF	
		Deal, Chas. Albert	3B22	23	.135	StLF	ChiN
0	1	Fincher, Wm. Allen	P	12	.333	A	C
13	9	Groom, Robert	P	41	.111	StLF	
		Hale, George Wagner	OF	4	.000	StL14	
4	6	Hamilton, Earl A.	P	1	+.000	B	Det
				19	+.000	& recall	
		Hartley, Grover Allen	C75	89	.225	StLF	
		Johnson, Ernest Rudolph	SS60	74	.229	StLF	
		Kennedy, Raymond Lincoln	C	1	.000	A	C
11	8	Koob, Ernest Gerald	P	33	.000	B	
		Lavan, John Leonard	SS106	110	.236	B	
		Lee, Wm. Joseph	OF	7	.182	B	C
		Marsans, Armando	OF150	151	.254	StLF	
		Miller, Ward Taylor	OF135	146	.266	StLF	
3	0	McCabe, Timothy	P	13	.000	B	
1	4	Park, James	P	26	.100	B	
		Paulette, Eugene Edward		5	.500	NYN11	
16	15	Plank, Edward Stewart	P	37	.185	StLF	
		Pratt, Derrill Burnham	2B	158	.267	B	
		Rumler, Wm. George	OF	27	.324	StL14	
		Severeid, Henry Levai	C89	100	.273	B	
		Shotton, Burton Edwin	OF	157	.282	B	
1	3	Sisler, George Harold (P5 3B2)	1B140	151	.305	B	
		Tobin, John Thomas	OF41	77	.213	StLF	
		Wallace, Rhoderick John (SS2) (Bobby)	3B5	14	.278	B	
17	18	Weilman, Carl Woolworth	P	46	.154	B	

WON 57
LOST 97
TG 154

AMERICAN LEAGUE — 1917.

FINISHED 7th.
PCT. .370

ST. LOUIS

FIELDER ALLISON JONES

WON	LOST	NAME	POS.	G.	BA	FROM	TO
		Austin, James Philip	3B121	127	.239	B	
		Bigler, Ivan Edward	1B	1	.000	A	C
17	17	Davenport, Arthur David	P	47	.098	B	
		Demmitt, Chas. Raymond	OF	14	.283	Chi15	
		Gerber, Walter	SS	14	.308	PittN15	
8	19	Groom, Robert	P	38	.111	B	
		Hale, George Wagner	C28	38	.197	B	
0	9	Hamilton, Earl A.	P	27	.368	B	
		Hartley, Grover Allen	C	19	.231	B	
		Jacobson, Wm. Chester	OF131	148	.248	StL15	
		Johnson, Ernest Rudolph (2B18)	SS39	80	.248	B	
		Kenworthy, Wm. Jennings	2B2	5	.100	KCF15	C
6	14	Koob, Ernest Gerald	P	39	.114	B	
		Lavan, John Leonard	SS110	118	.239	B	
2	1	Lowdermilk, Grover Cleveland	P	3	.000	Clev	
		Magee, Leo Christopher (Lee)	OF10	36	+.165	xN.Y.	
		Marsans, Armando	OF	75	+.230	B	N.Y.
0	3	Martin, Elwood Goode	P	10	.000	A	
		Miller, Ward Taylor	OF25	43	.207	B	C
0	0	Molyneaux, Vincent L.	P	7	.000	A	

WON	LOST	NAME	POS.	G.	BA	FROM	TO
		Moore, Wm. Allen	3B3	4	.125	A	C
		Murray, Edward Francis	SS	1	.000	A	C
0	0	McCabe, Timothy	P	1	.000	B	
		Nye, Otto Adam		1	.000	A	C
1	1	Park, James	P	13	.000	B	C
		Paulette, Eugene Edward	1B4	12	.182	B	StLN
0	0	Pennington, George Louis	P	1	.000	A	C
5	6	Plank, Edward Stewart	P	20	.105	B	C
		Pratt, Derrill Burnham	2B119	123	.247	B	
		Richardson, Thomas Mitchell		1	.000	A	C
3	6	Rogers, Thomas Andrew (Shotgun)	P	24	.172	A	
		Rumler, Wm. George	OF9	78	.261	B	C
		Severeid, Henry Levai	C139	143	.265	B	
		Shotton, Burton Edwin	OF107	118	.224	B	
		Sisler, George Harold (2B3)	1B133	135	.353	B	
		Sloan, Yale Yeastman	OF77	109	.230	StL13	
		Smith, Earl Leonard	OF51	52	.281	ChiN	
14	19	Sothoron, Allen Sutton	P	49	.217	StL15	
1	2	Weilman, Carl Woolworth	P	5	.000	B	
0	0	Wright, Wayne Bromley	P3	16	.200	A	

WON 58 — AMERICAN LEAGUE — FINISHED 5th.
LOST 64
TG 122 — 1918. — PCT. .475

ST. LOUIS

FIELDER ALLISON JONES — JAMES PHILIP AUSTIN
JAMES TIMOTHY BURKE

WON	LOST	NAME	POS.	G.	BA	FROM	TO
		Austin, James Philip MGR. (3B48)	SS57	110	.264	B	
0	2	Bennett, Joseph Harley	P	4	.000	A	
10	11	Davenport, Arthur David	P	31	.135	B	
		Demmitt, Chas. Raymond	OF114	116	.281	B	
7	6	Gallia, Melvin Allys (Bert)	P	19	.130	Wash	
		Gedeon, Elmer Joseph	2B	123	.213	N.Y.	
		Gerber, Walter	SS	56	.240	B	
		Hale, George Wagner	C11	12	.133	B	C
		Hendryx, Timothy Green	OF65	88	.279	N.Y.	
2	4	Houck, Byron Simon	P	26	.150	BknF14	C
		Johns, Wm. R.	1B10	46	.180	Chi15	C
		Johnson, Ernest Rudolph	SS11	29	.265	B	
2	6	Leifield, Albert Peter (Lefty)	P	15	.053	ChiN13	
2	6	Lowdermilk, Grover Cleveland	P	13	.250	B	
		Maisel, Frederick Chas.	3B79	90	.232	N.Y.	C
0	0	McCabe, Timothy	P	2	.000	B	C
		Nunamaker, Leslie Grant	C80	85	.259	N.Y.	
8	10	Rogers, Thomas Andrew (Shotgun)	P	29	.245	B	
		Severeid, Henry Levai	C42	51	.256	B	

WON	LOST	NAME	POS.	G.	BA	FROM	TO
6	5	Shocker, Urban James	P	14	.324	N.Y.	
		Sisler, George Harold	1B	114	.341	B	
		Smith, Earl Leonard	OF81	89	.269	B	
13	12	Sothoron, Allen Sutton	P	29	.157	B	
		Tobin, John Thomas	OF	122	.277	StL16	
		Williams, Kenneth Roy	OF1	2	.000	CinN16	
8	2	Wright, Wayne Bromley	P	18	.294	B	

WON 67 — AMERICAN LEAGUE — FINISHED 5th.
LOST 72
TG 139 — 1919. — PCT. .482

ST. LOUIS

JAMES TIMOTHY BURKE

WON	LOST	NAME	POS.	G.	BA	FROM	TO
		Austin, James Philip	3B98	106	.237	B	
1	1	Bayne, Wm. Lear	P	2	.400	A	
		Billings, John Augustus	C27	38	.198	Clev	
		Bronkie, Herman Chas. (2B16)	3B34	67	.255	StLN	
		Collins, Tharon Patrick	C	11	.143	A	
2	11	Davenport, Arthur David	P	24	.077	B	C
		Demmitt, Chas. Raymond	OF49	79	.238	B	C
12	14	Gallia, Melvin Allys (Bert)	P	34	.153	B	
		Gedeon, Elmer Joseph	2B118	120	.254	B	
		Gerber, Walter	SS	140	.227	B	
0	0	Haid, Harold Augustine	P	1	.000	A	
		Jacobson, Wm. Chester	OF105	120	.323	StL17	
2	4	Koob, Ernest Gerald	P	24	.000	StL17	
6	4	Leifield, Albert Peter (Lefty)	P	19	.108	B	C
0	0	Lowdermilk, Grover Cleveland	P	7	+.000	B	Chi
0	3	Mapel, Rolla Hamilton	P	4	.167	A	C
		Mayer, Walter A.	C15	30	.226	Bos	C
0	1	Rogers, Thomas Andrew (Shotgun)	P	2	+.000	B	Phil
		Schepner, Joseph Martin	3B	14	.212	A	C
		Severeid, Henry Levai	C103	112	.248	B	
13	11	Shocker, Urban James	P	30	.138	B	
		Shovelin, John Joseph	2B	9	.212	PittN11	
		Sisler, George Harold	1B131	132	.352	B	
		Sloan, Yale Yeastman	OF20	27	.238	StL17	C
		Smith, Earl Leonard	OF68	88	.250	B	
20	12	Sothoron, Allen Sutton	P	39	.180	B	
		Tobin, John Thomas	OF123	127	.327	B	
1	0	Vangilder, Elam Russell	P	3	.667	A	
10	6	Weilman, Carl Woolworth	P	20	.191	StL17	
		Williams, Kenneth Roy	OF63	65	.300	B	
0	5	Wright, Wayne Bromley	P	24	.083	B	

WON 76 — AMERICAN LEAGUE — FINISHED 4th.
LOST 77
TG 153 — 1920. — PCT. .497

ST. LOUIS

JAMES TIMOTHY BURKE

WON	LOST	NAME	POS.	G.	BA	FROM	TO
		Austin, James Philip	3B75	83	.271	B	
5	6	Bayne, Wm. Lear	P	18	.171	B	
		Billings, John Augustus	C40	66	.278	B	
0	1	Boehler, George Henry	P	3	.000	Det16	
6	4	Burwell, Wm. Edwin	P33	35	.167	A	
		Collins, Tharon Patrick	C	23	.214	B	
18	12	Davis, Frank Talmadge	P	38	.266	PhilN18	
2	4	DeBerry, Joseph H.	P	10	.167	A	
		Dudley, Ernest (Ernest Dudley Lee)	SS	1	1.000	A	
0	1	Gallia, Melvin Allys (Bert)	P	2	.000	B	PhilN
		Gedeon, Elmer Joseph	2B	153	.292	B	C
		Gerber, Walter	SS	154	.279	B	
		Heving, John Aloysius	C	1	.000	A	
		Jacobson, Wm. Chester	OF	154	.355	B	
		Lamb, Lyman Raymond	OF	9	.375	A	
0	0	Leifield, Albert Peter (Lefty)	P	4	.000	B	C
0	2	Leverette, Horace Wm.	P	3	.000	A	C
2	0	Lynch, Adrian Ryan	P	5	.222	A	C
		Mullen, Wm. John	2B	2	.000	A	
		McManus, Martin Joseph	3B	1	.200	A	
		Pruess, Earl Henry	OF	1	.000	A	C
2	0	Richmond, Raymond S.	P	2	.167	A	
1	1	Sanders, Roy L.	P	8	.000	NY18	C
0	0	Scheneberg, John B.	P	1	.000	PittN13	C
		Severeid, Henry Levai	C117	123	.277	B	
20	10	Shocker, Urban James	P	38	.225	B	
		Shovelin, John Joseph	2B	7	.286	B	C
0	0	Sisler, George Harold (P1)	1B154	154	.407	B	
		Smith, Earl Leonard (OF15)	3B70	103	.306	B	
8	15	Sothoron, Allen Sutton	P	36	.222	B	
		Speraw, Paul Bachman	3B	1	.000	A	C
		Thompson, Frank E.	3B	22	.170	A	C
		Tobin, John Thomas	OF	147	.340	B	
3	8	Vangilder, Elam Russell	P	24	.133	B	
9	13	Weilman, Carl Woolworth	P	30	.175	B	C
		Wetzel, Franklin Burton	OF	7	.428	A	
		Williams, Kenneth Roy	OF138	141	.307	B	

WON 81 AMERICAN LEAGUE FINISHED 3rd.
LOST 73
TG 154 1921. PCT. .526

ST. LOUIS

LEO ALEXANDER FOHL

WON	LOST	NAME	POS.	G.	BA	FROM	TO
		Austin, James Philip	SS13	27	.273	B	
11	5	Bayne, Wm. Lear	P	47	.300	B	
		Billings, John Augustus	C12	20	.217	B	
0	0	Boehler, George Henry	P	1	.000	B	
1	4	Boland, Bernard Anthony	P	8	.100	Det	C
2	4	Burwell, Wm. Edwin	P	33	.240	B	
		Collins, Tharon Patrick	C31	58	.243	B	
0	2	Cullop, Norman Andrew	P	4	.000	NY17	C
16	16	Davis, Frank Talmadge	P	39	.217	B	
0	1	DeBerry, Joseph H.	P	10	.000	B	C
		Ellerbe, Francis Rogers	3B	105	+.288	xWash	
		Gerber, Walter	SS113	114	.278	B	
		Gleason, Wm. Patrick	2B25	26	.257	PittN17	C
0	0	Henry, Frank John	P	1	1.000	A	
		Jacobson, Wm. Chester (1B11)	OF141	151	.352	B	
8	7	Kolp, Raymond Carl	P37	39	.127	A	
		Lamb, Lyman Raymond	3B23	45	.253	B	C
		Lee, Ernest Dudley (2B30)	SS31	72	.167	B	
0	0	Morris, Joseph Bennett (Bennett)	P	1	+1.000	xChi	C
		Mullen, Wm. John	3B	4	.000	B	
		McManus, Martin Joseph (1B10 3B13)	2B96	121	.260	B	
4	7	Palmero, Emilio A.	P24	29	.216	NYN16	
0	1	Richmond, Raymond S.	P	6	.000	B	C
		Riley, James Norman	3B	4	.000	A	
		Severeid, Henry Levai	C126	143	.324	B	
27	12	Shocker, Urban James	P	47	.260	B	
		Sisler, George Harold	1B	138	.371	B	
		Smith, Earl Leonard (3B10)	OF10	25	+.333	B	Wash
1	2	Sothoron, Allen Sutton	P	5	+.111	B	Bos
		Stewart, John Franklin (Stuffy)		3	.333	StLN17	
		Stuart, Luther Lane (Luke)	2B	3	.333	A	C
		Tobin, John Thomas	OF	150	.352	B	
11	12	Vangilder, Elam Russell	P	31	.200	B	
		Wetzel, Franklin Burton	OF27	61	.210	B	C
		Williams, Kenneth Roy	OF145	146	.347	B	

WON 93 AMERICAN LEAGUE FINISHED 2nd.
LOST 61
TG 154 1922. PCT. .604

ST. LOUIS

LEO ALEXANDER FOHL

WON	LOST	NAME	POS.	G.	BA	FROM	TO
		Austin, James Philip	3B	15	.290	B	
4	5	Bayne, Wm. Lear	P	26	.233	B	
		Billings, John Augustus	C4	5	.429	B	
		Bronkie, Herman Chas.	3B18	23	.281	StL19	C
		Collins, Tharon Patrick	C27	63	.307	B	
5	2	Danforth, David Chas.	P	20	.087	Chi19	
11	6	Davis, Frank Talmadge	P	25	.136	B	

WON	LOST	NAME	POS.	G.	BA	FROM	TO
		Durst, Cedric Montgomery	OF	15	.333	A	
		Ellerbe, Francis Rogers	3B	91	.246	B	
		Foster, Edward Cunningham	3B	37	+.306	xBos	
		Gerber, Walter	SS152	153	.267	B	
0	0	Henry, Frank John	P	4	.000	B	
		Jacobson, Wm. Chester	OF137	145	.317	B	
14	4	Kolp, Raymond Carl	P	32	.298	B	
0	0	Meine, Henry Wm. (Heinie)	P	1	.000	A	
		McManus, Martin Joseph	2B	154	.312	B	
7	7	Pruett, Hubert Shelby (Hub)	P	39	.148	A	
		Robertson, Eugene Edward (SS2)	3B3	18	.296	A	
		Severeid, Henry Levai	C134	137	.321	B	
24	17	Shocker, Urban James	P	48	.191	B	
		Shorten, Chas. Henry	OF31	55	.275	Det	
		Sisler, George Harold	1B141	142	.420	B	
		Tobin, John Thomas	OF145	146	.331	B	
19	13	Vangilder, Elam Russell	P44	45	.344	B	
		Williams, Kenneth Roy	OF	153	.332	B	
9	7	Wright, Wayne Bromley	P	31	.140	StL19	

WON 74 AMERICAN LEAGUE FINISHED 5th.
LOST 78
TG 152 1923. PCT. .487

ST. LOUIS

LEO ALEXANDER FOHL JAMES PHILIP AUSTIN

WON	LOST	NAME	POS.	G.	BA	FROM	TO
		Austin, James Philip MGR.		1	.000	B	
2	2	Bayne, Wm. Lear	P	19	.231	B	
		Bennett, Herschel Emmett	OF	5	.000	A	
		Billings, John Augustus	C	4	.000	B	C
		Collins, Tharon Patrick	C47	85	.177	B	
16	14	Danforth, David Chas.	P	38	.211	B	
4	6	Davis, Frank Talmadge	P	19	.250	B	
		Durst, Cedric Montgomery (1B6)	OF8	45	.212	B	
		Ellerbe, Francis Rogers	3B	18	.184	B	
0	0	Elliott, James Thomas	P	1	.000	A	
		Ezzell, Homer Estell	3B73	88	.247	A	
		Foster, Edward Cunningham	2B20	27	.180	B	C
		Gerber, Walter	SS	154	.281	B	
0	0	Grant, George Addison	P	4	+.000	A	
		Jacobson, Wm. Chester	OF146	147	.309	B	
5	12	Kolp, Raymond Carl	P	34	.111	B	
		Mizeur, Wm.	OF	1	.000	A	
		McManus, Martin Joseph (1B20)	2B133	154	.309	B	
4	7	Pruett, Hubert Shelby (Hub)	P	32	.130	B	
		Rice, Harry Francis		4	.000	A	
		Robertson, Eugene Edward	3B74	78	.247	B	
0	4	Root, Chas. Henry	P	27	.077	A	
		Schleibner, Frederick Paul	1B	127	.275	xBknN	C
		Schulte, John Clement	C	7	.000	A	
		Severeid, Henry Levai	C116	122	.308	B	
20	12	Shocker, Urban James	P	43	.200	B	
		Simon, Sylvester Adam		1	.000	A	
0	0	Thurston, Hollis John (Sloppy)	P	2	+.000	A	Chi
		Tobin, John Thomas	OF	151	.317	B	
16	17	Vangilder, Elam Russell	P41	45	.218	B	
		Whaley, Wm. Carl	OF	23	.240	A	C
		Williams, Kenneth Roy	OF145	147	.357	B	
7	4	Wright, Wayne Bromley	P	20	.222	B	C

WON 74 AMERICAN LEAGUE FINISHED 4th.
LOST 78
TG 152 1924. PCT. .487

ST. LOUIS

GEORGE HAROLD SISLER

WON	LOST	NAME	POS.	G.	BA	FROM	TO
0	0	Barnhart, Edgar Vernon	P	1	.000	A	C
1	3	Bayne, Wm. Lear	P	22	.429	B	
0	0	Beck, Walter Wm. (Boom-Boom)	P	1	.000	A	
		Bennett, Herschel Emmett	OF21	41	.330	B	
		Burke, Patrick Edward	3B	1	.000	A	C
		Collins, Tharon Patrick	C20	32	.315	B	
15	12	Danforth, David Chas.	P	41	.171	B	
11	13	Davis, Frank Talmadge	P	29	.152	B	
		Ellerbe, Francis Rogers	3B	21	+.194	B	Clev
		Elmore, Verdo Wilson	OF	7	.176	A	C
		Evans, Joseph Patton	OF49	77	.254	Wash	
		Gerber, Walter	SS147	148	.272	B	
1	2	Grant, George Addison	P	22	.000	B	
		Jacobson, Wm. Chester	OF	152	.318	B	
5	7	Kolp, Raymond Carl	P	25	.200	B	
0	0	Lasley, Willard Almond	P	2	.000	A	C
3	2	Lyons, George Tony	P	26	.250	StLN20	C
		Mizeur, Wm.	OF	1	.000	B	C
		McManus, Martin Joseph	2B	123	.333	B	
		McMillan, Norman Alexis (3B19)	2B37	76	.279	Bos	
3	4	Pruett, Hubert Shelby (Hub)	P	33	.200	B	
		Rego, Anthony J.	C23	24	.220	A	
		Rice, Harry Francis	3B15	44	.279	B	
		Robertson, Eugene Edward	3B	121	.319	B	
		Severeid, Henry Levai	C130	137	.308	B	
16	13	Shocker, Urban James	P	40	.239	B	
		Simon, Sylvester Adam (3B3)	SS4	23	.250	B	C
		Sisler, George Harold MGR.	1B	151	.305	StL22	
		Tobin, John Thomas	OF134	136	.299	B	
5	10	Vangilder, Elam Russell	P	43	.295	B	
1	0	Voigt, Olen Edward	P	8	.250	A	C
		Williams, Kenneth Roy	OF108	114	.324	B	
13	12	Wingard, Ernest James	P36	37	.234	A	

WON 82 LOST 71 TG 153 — AMERICAN LEAGUE 1925. — FINISHED 3rd. PCT. .536

ST. LOUIS

GEORGE HAROLD SISLER

WON	LOST	NAME	POS.	G.	BA	FROM	TO
		Austin, James Philip	3B	1	.000	StL23	
		Bennett, Herschel Emmett	OF74	93	.279	B	
0	0	Blaeholder, George Franklin	P	2	.000	A	
14	14	Bush, Leslie Ambrose (Bullet Joe) (OF1)	P33	57	.254	N.Y.	
7	9	Danforth, David Chas.	P	38	.174	B	C
12	7	Davis, Frank Talmadge	P	35	.172	B	
		Dixon, Leo Michael	C75	76	.224	A	
		Evans, Joseph Patton	OF50	55	.314	B	C
0	0	Falk, Chester Emanuel	P13	17	.625	A	
15	14	Gaston, Nathaniel Milton	P	42	.263	N.Y.	
		Gerber, Walter	SS71	72	.272	B	
10	5	Giard, Joseph Oscar	P	30	.057	A	
0	2	Grant, George Addison	P	12	.250	B	
		Hargrave, Wm. McKinley	C	67	+.284	xWash	
		Jacobson, Wm. Chester	OF139	142	.341	B	
		LaMotte, Robert Eugene (3B3)	SS93	97	.273	Wash22	
1	1	Mogridge, George Anthony	P	2	+.000	xWash	
		McManus, Martin Joseph	2B	154	.288	B	
		Rego, Anthony J.	C19	20	.406	B	C
		Rice, Harry Francis (C1 1B3 2B1 3B1)	OF82	103	.359	B	
		Robertson, Eugene Edward (SS1)	3B154	154	.271	B	
		Severeid, Henry Levai	C31	34	+.358	B	Wash
0	0	Sisler, George Harold MGR. (P1)	1B150	150	.345	B	
0	0	Springer, Bradford Louis	P	2	.000	A	
0	1	Stauffer, Chas. Edward	P	20	.250	ChiN23	C
		Tobin, John Thomas (1B3)	OF40	77	.301	B	
14	8	Vangilder, Elam Russell	P	51	.183	B	
		Williams, Kenneth Roy	OF	102	.331	B	
9	10	Wingard, Ernest James (OF1)	P32	34	.288	B	

WON 62 LOST 92 TG 154 — AMERICAN LEAGUE 1926. — FINISHED 7th. PCT. .403

ST. LOUIS

GEORGE HAROLD SISLER

WON	LOST	NAME	POS.	G.	BA	FROM	TO
		Austin, James Philip	3B	1	.500	B	
10	10	Ballou, Noble Winfred (Win)	P	43	.048	Wash	
		Bennett, Herschel Emmett	OF50	80	.266	B	
0	0	Bolen, Stewart O'Neal	P	5	.500	A	
4	8	Davis, Frank Talmadge	P	27	.167	B	C
		Dixon, Leo Michael	C	33	.191	B	
		Durst, Cedric Montgomery	OF57	80	.237	StL23	
4	4	Falk, Chester Emanuel	P18	19	.194	B	
10	18	Gaston, Nathaniel Milton	P	32	.167	B	
		Gerber, Walter	SS129	131	.270	B	
3	10	Giard, Joseph Oscar	P	22	.276	B	
		Hargrave, Wm. McKinley	C58	92	.281	B	
		Jacobson, Wm. Chester	OF	50	+.290	B	Bos
0	2	Jonnard, Claude Alfred	P	12	.000	NYN24	
		LaMotte, Robert Eugene	SS30	36	.202	B	C
		Melillo, Oscar Donald (3B11)	2B88	99	.255	A	
		Miller, Edmund John (Bing)	OF	94	+.331	xPhil	
		McManus, Martin Joseph (2B61)	3B84	149	.284	B	
2	4	Nevers, Ernest Alonzo	P11	12	.185	A	
		Rice, Harry Francis	OF133	148	.313	B	
1	2	Robertson, Chas. Culbertson	P	8	.300	Chi	
		Robertson, Eugene Edward (SS10)	3B55	78	.251	B	
		Schang, Walter Henry (Wally)	C82	103	.330	N.Y.	
0	0	Sisler, George Harold MGR. (P1)	1B149	150	.289	B	
9	11	Vangilder, Elam Russell	P	42	.190	B	
		Williams, Kenneth Roy	OF92	108	.280	B	
5	8	Wingard, Ernest James	P39	42	.230	B	
14	15	Zachary, Jonathan Thompson Walton (Tom)	P	34	.268	Wash	

WON 59 LOST 94 TG 153 — AMERICAN LEAGUE 1927. — FINISHED 7th. PCT. .386

ST. LOUIS

DANIEL PHILIP HOWLEY

WON	LOST	NAME	POS.	G.	BA	FROM	TO
		Adams, Spencer Dewey (3B28)	2B54	88	.266	N.Y.	C
5	6	Ballou, Noble Winfred (Win)	P	21	.036	B	
1	0	Beck, Walter Wm. (Boom-Boom)	P	3	.250	StL24	
		Bennett, Herschel Emmett	OF55	93	.266	B	C
0	1	Blaeholder, George Franklin	P	1	.333	StL25	
0	1	Bolen, Stewart O'Neal	P	3	.333	B	
3	5	Crowder, Alvin Floyd (General)	P	21	+.261	xWash	
		Dixon, Leo Michael	C35	36	.194	B	
1	0	Falk, Chester Emanuel	P	9	.200	B	C
13	17	Gaston, Nathaniel Milton	P	37	.260	B	
		Gerber, Walter	SS141	142	.224	B	
8	14	Jones, Samuel Pond (Sad Sam)	P30	32	.109	N.Y.	

WON	LOST	NAME	POS.	G.	BA	FROM	TO
		Kress, Ralph (Red)	SS	7	.304	A	
		Melillo, Oscar Donald	2B101	107	.225	B	
		Miller, Edmund John (Bing)	OF128	144	.325	B	
		Miller, Otis Louis (3B11)	SS35	51	.224	A	
3	8	Nevers, Ernest Alonzo	P	27	.219	B	
		O'Neill, Stephen Francis (Steve)	C60	74	.230	NY25	
		O'Rourke, Francis James (2B16)	3B120	140	.268	Det	
		Rice, Harry Francis	OF130	137	.287	B	
		Schang, Walter Henry (Wally)	C75	97	.319	B	
		Schulte, Fred Wm.	OF49	60	.317	A	
		Sisler, George Harold	1B	149	.327	B	
8	11	Stewart, Walter Cleveland	P27	28	.306	Det21	
		Sturdy, Guy A.	1B	5	.429	A	
10	12	Vangilder, Elam Russell	P	44	.279	B	
		Williams, Kenneth Roy	OF113	131	.323	B	
2	13	Wingard, Ernest James	P35	42	.179	B	C
1	0	Wright, James	P	2	.000	A	
4	6	Zachary, Jonathan Thomas Walton (Tom)	P	13	+.107	B	Wash

WON 82 — AMERICAN LEAGUE — FINISHED 3rd.
LOST 72
TG 154 — 1928. — PCT. .532

ST. LOUIS

DANIEL PHILIP HOWLEY

WON	LOST	NAME	POS.	G.	BA	FROM	TO
2	3	Beck, Walter Wm. (Boom-Boom)	P	16	.429	B	
		Bennett, James Fred	OF1	7	.250	A	
		Bettencourt, Lawrence Joseph	3B41	67	.283	A	
10	15	Blaeholder, George Franklin	P	38	.211	B	
		Blue, Luzerne Atwell (Lou)	1B	154	.281	Det	
		Brannan, Otis Owen	2B	135	.244	A	
4	5	Coffman, Samuel Richard (Dick)	P	29	.043	Wash	
21	5	Crowder, Alvin Floyd (General)	P	41	.187	B	
		Danning, Ike	C	2	.500	A	C
		Gerber, Walter	SS	6	+.222	B	Bos
20	12	Gray, Samuel David	P	35	.188	Phil	
		Kress, Ralph (Red)	SS	150	.273	B	
		Manion, Clyde Jennings	C71	76	.226	Det	
		Manush, Henry Emmett (Heinie)	OF	154	.378	Det	
		Melillo, Oscar Donald (3B19)	2B28	51	.189	B	
		Mullen, Wm. John	3B4	15	.389	Det26	C
		McGowan, Frank Bernard	OF	47	.363	Phil23	
		McNeely, George Earl	OF120	127	.236	Wash	
1	0	Nevers, Ernest Alonzo	P	6	.000	B	C
15	16	Ogden, John Mahlon	P	38	.200	NYN18	
		O'Neill, Stephen Francis (Steve)	C	10	.292	B	
		O'Rourke, Francis James	3B96	99	.263	B	
		Sax, Erik Oliver	3B4	16	.176	A	C
		Schang, Walter Henry (Wally)	C82	91	.285	B	
		Schulte, Fred Wm.	OF143	146	.286	B	
7	9	Stewart, Walter Cleveland	P	29	.274	B	
0	2	Strelecki, Edward Harold	P	22	.200	A	
		Sturdy, Guy A.	1B1	54	.222	B	C
		Wilson, Francis Edward	OF1	6	+.000	xClev	C
2	5	Wiltse, Harold James	P	26	+.227	xBos	
0	0	Wright, James	P	2	.000	B	C

WON 79 — AMERICAN LEAGUE — FINISHED 4th.
LOST 73
TG 152 — 1929. — PCT. .520

ST. LOUIS

DANIEL PHILIP HOWLEY

WON	LOST	NAME	POS.	G.	BA	FROM	TO
		Austin, James Philip	3B	1	.000	StL26	C
		Badgro, Morris Hiram	OF37	54	.284	A	
14	15	Blaeholder, George Franklin	P	42	.121	B	
		Blue, Luzerne Atwell (Lou)	1B	151	.293	B	
		Brannan, Otis Owen	2B19	23	.294	B	C
0	0	Cobb, Herbert Edward	P	1	.000	A	C
1	1	Coffman, Samuel Richard (Dick)	P	27	.000	B	
11	6	Collins, Harry Warren	P	26	.275	Det27	
17	15	Crowder, Alvin Floyd (General)	P	40	.187	B	
		Dondero, Leonard Peter	3B10	19	.194	A	C
0	0	Estrada, Oscar	P	1	.000	A	C
		Ferrell, Richard Benjamin (Rick)	C45	64	.229	A	
18	15	Gray, Samuel David	P	43	.184	B	
0	0	Hopkins, Paul Henry	P	2	+.000	xWash	C
		Jenkins, Thomas Griffith	OF1	21	.182	Phil26	
3	6	Kimsey, Clyde Elias (Chad)	P24	29	.267	A	
		Kress, Ralph (Red)	SS146	147	.305	B	
		Manion, Clyde Jennings	C34	35	.243	B	
		Manush, Henry Emmett (Heinie)	OF141	142	.355	B	
		Melillo, Oscar Donald	2B	141	.296	B	
		McGowan, Frank Bernard	OF117	125	.254	B	
		McNeely, George Earl	OF62	69	.243	B	
4	8	Ogden, John Mahlon	P	34	.244	B	
		O'Rourke, Francis James	3B151	154	.251	B	
		Roetz, Edward Bernard (1B2 2B2)	SS7	16	.244	A	C
		Schang, Walter Henry (Wally)	C85	94	.237	B	
		Schulte, Fred Wm.	OF116	121	.307	B	
9	6	Stewart, Walter Cleveland	P	23	.118	B	

WON	LOST	NAME	POS.	G.	BA	FROM	TO
1	0	Stiely, Frederick Warren	P	1	.667	A	
1	1	Strelecki, Edward Harold	P	7	.000	B	

WON 64
LOST 90
TG 154

AMERICAN LEAGUE — FINISHED 6th.

1930. — PCT. .416

ST. LOUIS

WM. LAVIER KILLEFER JR.

WON	LOST	NAME	POS.	G.	BA	FROM	TO
		Badgro, Morris Hiram	OF61	89	.239	B	C
11	13	Blaeholder, George Franklin	P	37	.185	B	
		Blue, Luzerne Atwell (Lou)	1B111	117	.235	B	
		Burns, John Irving	1B	8	.300	A	
8	18	Coffman, Samuel Richard (Dick)	P	38	.136	B	
9	7	Collins, Harry Warren	P	35	.130	B	
		Crouch, Jack Albert	C3	6	.143	A	
3	7	Crowder, Alvin Floyd (General)	P	13	+.240	B	Wash
		Ferrell, Richard Benjamin (Rick)	C	101	.268	B	
		Goslin, Leon Allen (Goose)	OF	101	+.327	xWash	
4	15	Gray, Samuel David	P	27	.204	B	
		Gullic, Theodore Jasper	OF82	92	.250	A	
		Hale, Samuel Douglas	3B47	62	.274	Phil	C
		Hassler, Joseph Frederick	SS2	5	.250	Phil	C
0	1	Holshouser, Herman Alexander	P	25	.125	A	C
		Hungling, Bernard Herman	C	10	.323	BknN23	C
		Jenkins, Thomas Griffith	OF	2	.250	B	
6	10	Kimsey, Clyde Elias (Chad)	P42	60	.343	B	
		Kress, Ralph (Red) (3B31)	SS123	154	.313	B	
		Levey, James Julius	SS	8	.243	A	
		Manion, Clyde Jennings	C56	57	.216	B	
		Manush, Henry Emmett (Heinie)	OF	49	+.328	B	Wash
		Melillo, Oscar Donald	2B148	149	.256	B	
		Metzler, Alexander	OF	56	+.261	xChi	C
		McNeely, George Earl (1B27)	OF38	76	.272	B	
		O'Rourke, Francis James (SS23)	3B84	115	.268	B	
		Schulte, Fred Wm.	OF98	113	.278	B	
20	12	Stewart, Walter Cleveland	P	35	.244	B	
0	1	Stiely, Frederick Warren	P	5	.429	B	
3	6	Stiles, Rolland Mays	P	20	.270	A	
		Storti, Lindo Ivan	2B	7	.321	A	

WON 63
LOST 91
TG 154

AMERICAN LEAGUE — FINISHED 5th.

1931. — PCT. .409

ST. LOUIS

WM. LAVIER KILLEFER JR.

WON	LOST	NAME	POS.	G.	BA	FROM	TO
		Bengough, Bernard Oliver (Benny)	C37	40	.250	N.Y.	
		Bettencourt, Lawrence Joseph	OF58	74	.257	StL28	
11	15	Blaeholder, George Franklin	P	35	.143	B	
0	0	Braxton, Edgar Garland	P	11	+.667	xChi	
		Burns, John Irving	1B143	144	.260	B	
9	13	Coffman, Samuel Richard (Dick)	P	32	.079	B	
5	5	Collins, Harry Warren	P	17	.148	B	C
0	3	Cooney, Robert Daniel	P	5	.385	A	
		Crouch, Jack Albert	C3	8	.000	B	
0	0	Doyle, Jess Herbert	P	1	.000	Det27	C
		Ferrell, Richard Benjamin (Rick)	C108	117	.306	B	
		Goslin, Leon Allen (Goose)	OF	151	.328	B	
11	24	Gray, Samuel David	P	43	.177	B	
		Grimes, Edward Adelbert	3B22	43	.263	A	
6	7	Hebert, Wallace Andrew	P	23	.209	A	
		Jenkins, Thomas Griffith	OF58	81	.265	B	
4	6	Kimsey, Clyde Elias (Chad)	P42	47	.270	B	
		Kloza, John Clarence	OF1	3	.143	A	
		Kress, Ralph (Red) (1B10 SS38 OF40)	3B84	150	.311	B	
		Levey, James Julius	SS	139	.209	B	
		Melillo, Oscar Donald	2B	151	.306	B	
		McNeely, George Earl	OF36	49	.225	B	C
		O'Rourke, Francis James (1B1)	SS1	8	.222	B	C
		Schulte, Fred Wm.	OF	134	.304	B	
		Stanton, George Washington	OF1	13	.200	A	C
14	17	Stewart, Walter Cleveland	P	36	.250	B	
0	0	Stiely, Frederick Warren	P	4	.000	B	C
3	1	Stiles, Rolland Mays	P	34	.045	B	
		Storti, Lindo Ivan	3B67	86	.220	B	
		Waddey, Frank Orum	OF3	14	.273	A	C
		Young, Russell Chas.	C	16	.118	A	C

WON 63
LOST 91
TG 154

AMERICAN LEAGUE — FINISHED 6th.

1932. — PCT. .409

ST. LOUIS

WM. LAVIER KILLEFER JR.

WON	LOST	NAME	POS.	G.	BA	FROM	TO
		Bengough, Bernard Oliver (Benny)	C47	54	.252	B	C
		Bettencourt, Lawrence Joseph (3B1)	OF3	27	.133	B	C
14	14	Blaeholder, George Franklin	P	42	.136	B	
		Burns, John Irving	1B	150	.305	B	
		Campbell, Bruce Douglas	OF	139	+.285	xChi	

WON	LOST	NAME	POS.	G.	BA	FROM	TO
5	3	Coffman, Samuel Richard (Dick)	P	9	+.045	B	Wash
1	2	Cooney, Robert Daniel	P23	24	.000	B	C
		Ferrell, Richard Benjamin (Rick)	C120	126	.315	B	
3	7	Fischer, Chas. Wm.	P	24	+.265	xWash	
		Fisher, George Aloys	OF4	18	.182	StLN30	C
		Garms, Debs C.	OF33	34	.284	A	
		Goslin, Leon Allen (Goose)	OF149	150	.299	B	
7	12	Gray, Samuel David	P	52	.210	B	
		Grimes, Edward Adelbert	3B18	31	.235	B	C
13	20	Hadley, Irving Darius (Bump)	P	40	+.282	xChi	
1	12	Hebert, Wallace Andrew	P	35	.353	B	
		Jenkins, Thomas Griffith	OF12	25	.323	B	C
4	2	Kimsey, Clyde Elias (Chad)	P33	34	+.333	B	Chi
		Kloza, John Clarence	OF1	19	.154	B	C
		Kress, Ralph (Red)	3B	14	+.191	B	Chi
		Levey, James Julius	SS	152	.280	B	
		Melillo, Oscar Donald	2B153	154	.242	B	
		McLaughlin, James Robert	3B	1	.000	A	C
0	0	Polli, Louis Americo	P	5	.500	A	
		Scharein, Arthur Otto	3B77	81	.304	A	
		Schulte, Fred Wm.	OF129	146	.294	B	
		Schulte, John Clement	C3	15	.208	ChiN29	BosN
15	19	Stewart, Walter Cleveland	P	41	.146	B	
		Storti, Lindo Ivan	3B51	53	.259	B	

WON 55 — AMERICAN LEAGUE — FINISHED 8th (LAST)
LOST 96
TG 151 — 1933. — PCT. .364

ST. LOUIS

WM. LAVIER KILLEFER JR. ALLEN SUTTON SOTHORON ROGERS HORNSBY

WON	LOST	NAME	POS.	G.	BA	FROM	TO
15	19	Blaeholder, George Franklin	P	38	.182	B	
0	1	Braxton, Edgar Garland	P	5	.000	StL31	C
1	6	Brown, Lloyd Andrew	P	8	+.273	Wash	Bos
		Burns, John Irving	1B143	144	.288	B	
		Campbell, Bruce Douglas	OF144	148	.277	B	
3	7	Coffman, Samuel Richard (Dick)	P	21	.037	Wash	
		Crouch, Jack Albert	C	19	.167	StL31	CinN
		Ferrell, Richard Benjamin(Rick)	C	22	+.250	B	Bos
		Garms, Debs C.	OF47	78	.317	B	
7	4	Gray, Samuel David	P	38	.219	B	C
		Gullic, Theodore Joseph (1B14 3B33)	OF36	104	.243	StL30	C
15	20	Hadley, Irving Darius (Bump)	P	45	.156	B	
4	6	Hebert, Wallace Andrew	P	33	.391	B	
		Hemsley, Ralston Burdett (Rollie)	C27	32	.242	xCinN	
		Hornsby, Rogers (Rajah) MGR.		11	.333	xStLN	
1	8	Knott, John Henry Jr.	P	20	.304	A	
		Levey, James Julius	SS138	141	.195	B	C
		Melillo, Oscar Donald	2B130	132	.292	B	
0	4	McDonald, Henry M.	P	25	+.143	xPhil	C
		Reynolds, Carl Nettles	OF124	135	.286	Wash	
		Ruel, Herold Dominic (Muddy)	C28	36	.190	Det	
		Scharein, Arthur Otto	3B88	123	.204	B	
		Shea, Mervyn David John	C	94	+.262	xBos	
3	7	Stiles, Rolland Mayes	P	31	.061	StL31	C
		Storti, Lindo Ivan (3B27)	2B29	70	.195	B	C
6	14	Wells, Edwin Lee	P36	38	.197	N.Y.	
		West, Samuel Filmore	OF127	133	.300	Wash	

WON 67 — AMERICAN LEAGUE — FINISHED 6th.
LOST 85
TG 152 — 1934. — PCT. .441

ST. LOUIS

ROGERS HORNSBY

WON	LOST	NAME	POS.	G.	BA	FROM	TO
4	11	Andrews, Ivy Paul	P	43	.350	Bos	
		Bejma, Aloysius Frank (2B14 3B13 OF9)	SS32	95	.271	A	
14	18	Blaeholder, George Franklin	P	39	.093	B	
		Burns, John Irving	1B	154	.257	B	
		Campbell, Bruce Douglas	OF123	138	.279	B	
		Clark, Bailey Earl Jr.	OF9	13	.171	BosN	C
		Clift, Harlond Benton	3B141	147	.260	A	
9	10	Coffman, Samuel Richard (Dick)	P	40	.216	B	
		Garms, Debs C.	OF56	91	.293	B	
		Grube, Franklin Thomas	C55	65	.288	Chi	
10	16	Hadley, Irving Darius (Bump)	P	39	.203	B	
		Hartley, Grover Allen	C1	5	.333	Clev30	C
		Hemsley, Ralston Burdett (Rollie) (OF10)	C114	123	.309	B	
		Hornsby, Rogers (Rajah) MGR. (3B1)	OF1	24	.304	B	
10	3	Knott, John Henry Jr.	P	45	.133	B	
		Melillo, Oscar Donald	2B141	144	.241	B	
0	0	Mills, Howard Robinson (Lefty)	P	4	.333	A	
1	0	McAfee, Wm. Fort Jr.	P	28	.188	Wash	C
16	20	Newsom, Louis Norman (Buck)	P47	50	.183	ChiN32	
		O'Leary, Chas. Timothy		1	1.000	StLN13	C
		Pepper, Raymond Watson	OF136	148	.298	StLN	
		Puccinelli, George Lawrence	OF6	10	.231	StLN32	
		Scharein, Arthur Otto		1	.500	B	C
		Strange, Alan Cochrane (Inky)	SS125	127	.233	A	
0	0	Walkup, James Elton	P	3	.333	A	
2	0	Weaver, James Dement	P	5	.143	NY31	ChiN
1	7	Wells, Edward Lee	P	33	.045	B	C
		West, Samuel Filmore	OF120	122	.326	B	

WON 65 | LOST 87 | TG 152

AMERICAN LEAGUE — **1935.** — **FINISHED 7th.** PCT. .428

ST. LOUIS

ROGERS HORNSBY

WON	LOST	NAME	POS.	G.	BA	FROM	TO
13	7	Andrews, Ivy Paul	P	50	.132	B	
		Bejma, Aloysius Frank (SS8 3B2)	2B47	64	.192	B	
		• Bell, Roy Chester (Beau) (1B15 3B3)	OF37	76	.250	A	
1	1	Blaeholder, George Franklin	P	6	+.000	B	Phil
		Burnett, John Henderson (2B12 SS18)	3B31	70	.223	Clev	C
		Burns, John Irving	1B141	143	.286	B	
9	8	Cain, Merritt Patrick (Sugar)	P	31	+.193	xPhil	
3	2	Caldwell, Earl Welton	P	6	.182	PhilN28	
		Carey, Thomas Francis Aloysius	2B	76	.291	A	
		Clift, Harlond Benton (2B6)	3B127	137	.295	B	
5	11	Coffman, Samuel Richard (Dick)	P	41	.146	B	
		Coleman, Parke Edward	OF	108	+.287	xPhil	
		Garms, Debs C.	OF2	10	.267	B	
		Grube, Franklin Thomas	C	3	+.333	B	Chi
0	1	Hansen, Roy Emil	P	10	.143	xPhilN	C
		Heath, Thomas George	C37	47	.237	A	
		Hemsley, Ralston Burdett (Rollie)	C141	144	.290	B	
		Hornsby, Rogers (Rajah) MGR. (2B2 3B1)	1B3	10	.208	B	
11	8	Knott, John Henry Jr.	P	48	.115	B	
		Lary, Lynford Hobart (Lyn)	SS	93	+.288	xWash	
		Mazzera, Melvin Leonard (Mike)	OF10	12	.233	A	
		Melillo, Oscar Donald	2B	19	+.206	B	Bos
		Mueller, Clarence Franklin (OF2)	1B3	16	.185	BosN29	C
0	6	Newsom. Louis Norman (Buck)	P	7	+.091	B	Wash
		Pepper, Raymond Watson	OF57	92	.253	B	
1	1	Poser, John Falk	P	4	.250	Chi32	C
		Solters, Julius Joseph (Moose)	OF	127	+.330	xBos	
		Strange, Alan Cochrane (Inky)	SS	49	+.231	B	Wash
7	15	Thomas, Fay Wesley	P	49	.105	BknN32	C
9	16	VanAtta, Russell	P	53	+.214	xN.Y.	
6	9	Walkup, James Elton	P	55	.128	B	
		Warnock, Harold Chas.	OF	6	.286	A	C
0	2	Weiland, Robert George (Bob)	P	14	.000	Clev	
		West, Samuel Filmore	OF135	138	.300	B	

WON 57 | LOST 95 | TG 152

AMERICAN LEAGUE — **1936.** — **FINISHED 7th.** PCT. .375

ST. LOUIS

ROGERS HORNSBY

WON	LOST	NAME	POS.	G.	BA	FROM	TO
7	12	Andrews, Ivy Paul	P	36	.169	B	
		Bejma, Aloysius Frank	2B32	67	.259	B	
		Bell, Roy Chester (Beau) (1B17)	OF142	155	.344	B	
		Bottomley, James LeRoy	1B	140	.298	CinN	
		Burns, John Irving	1B	9	+.214	B	Det
1	1	Cain, Merritt Patrick (Sugar)	P	4	+.286	B	Chi
7	16	Caldwell, Earl Welton	P	41	.190	B	
		Carey, Thomas Francis Aloysius	2B128	134	.273	B	
		Clift, Harlond Benton	3B	152	.302	B	
		Coleman, Parke Edward	OF18	92	.292	B	C
		Giuliani, Angelo John (Tony)	C66	71	.217	A	
		Hemsley, Ralston Burdett (Rollie)	C114	116	.263	B	
13	15	Hogsett, Elon Chester (Chief)	P	43	+.143	xDet	
		Hornsby, Rogers (Rajah) MGR.	1B	2	.400	B	
0	3	Jakucki, Sigmund Jack	P	7	.000	A	
0	0	Kimberlin, Harry Liddle	P	13	.000	A	
9	17	Knott, John Henry Jr.	P	47	.070	B	
		Lary, Lynford Hobart (Lyn)	SS	155	.289	B	
0	0	Liebhardt, Glenn Ignatius	P	24	.000	Phil30	
2	6	Mahaffey, Lee Roy	P	21	.063	Phil	C
0	1	Meola, Emile Michael	P	9	+.500	Bos33	Bos
		Pepper, Raymond Watson	OF18	75	.282	B	C
		Solters, Julius Joseph (Moose)	OF147	152	.291	B	
11	9	Thomas, Alphonse Thomas Jr.	P	36	.138	PhilN	
3	5	Tietje, Leslie Wm.	P	16	+.067	xChi	
4	7	VanAtta, Russell	P52	53	.172	B	
0	3	Walkup, James Elton	P	5	.000	B	
		West, Samuel Filmore	OF148	152	.278	B	

WON 46 | LOST 108 | TG 154

AMERICAN LEAGUE — **1937.** — **FINISHED 8th (LAST)** PCT. .299

ST. LOUIS

ROGERS HORNSBY — JAMES LEROY BOTTOMLEY

WON	LOST	NAME	POS.	G.	BA	FROM	TO
		Allen, Ethan Nathan	OF78	103	.316	ChiN	
0	0	Baecht, Edward Joseph	P	3	.000	ChiN32	C
		Barkley, John Duncan	2B	31	.267	A	
		Bell, Roy Chester (Beau) (1B26)	OF131	156	.340	B	
0	1	Baldilli, Emil	P	4	.000	A	

2	2	Blake, John Frederick (Sheriff)	P	15	.100	PhilN31	StLN
4	11	Bonetti, Julio James Paul	P	28	.149	A	
		Bottomley, James LeRoy MGR.	1B24	65	.239	B	C
		Cafego, Thomas	OF1	4	.000	A	C
0	0	Caldwell, Earl Welton	P	9	.222	B	
		Carey, Thomas Francis Aloysius (SS44)	2B87	130	.275	B	
		Clift, Harlond Benton	3B	155	.306	B	
		Davis, Harry Albert	1B112	120	.276	Det33	C
		Giuliani, Angelo John (Tony)	C	19	.302	B	
		Harshaney, Samuel	C4	5	.091	A	
		Heath, Thomas George	C14	17	.233	StL35	
		Hemsley, Ralston Burdett (Rollie)	C94	100	.222	B	
0	1	Hennessey, George	P	5	.000	A	
8	17	Hildebrand, Oral Clyde	P	30	.200	Clev	
6	19	Hogsett, Elon Chester (Chief)	P37	40	.210	B	
		Hornsby, Rogers (Rajah) MGR.	2B17	20	.321	B	
		Huffman, Benjamin Franklin	C42	76	.273	A	C
0	2	Kimberlin, Harry Liddle	P	3	.200	B	
		Knickerbocker, Wm. Hart	SS115	121	.261	Clev	
8	18	Knott, John Henry Jr.	P	38	.140	B	
4	9	Koupal, Louis Laddie	P	26	.094	PhilN30	C
0	0	Lipscomb, Gerald (Jerry) (P3)	2B27	36	.323	A	C
		Mazzera, Melvin Leonard (Mike)		7	.286	StL35	
0	1	Miller, Wm. Francis	P	1	.000	A	C
1	1	Mills, Howard Robinson (Lefty)	P	2	.000	StL34	
0	0	Muncrief, Robert Cleveland Jr.	P	1	.000	A	
		Silber, Edward James	OF21	22	.313	A	
0	0	Strickland, Wm. Goss	P	9	.167	A	C
0	1	Thomas, Alphonse Thomas Jr.	P	17	+.000	B	Bos
1	2	Tietje, Leslie Wm.	P	5	.000	B	
2	9	Trotter, Wm. Felix	P	34	.030	A	
1	2	VanAtta, Russell	P	16	.462	B	
		Vosmik, Joseph Franklin	OF143	144	.325	Clev	
9	12	Walkup, James Elton	P	27	.241	B	
		West, Samuel Filmore	OF105	122	.328	B	

WON 55
LOST 97
TG 152

AMERICAN LEAGUE 1938. FINISHED 7th. PCT. .362

ST. LOUIS

CHAS. EVARD STREET OSCAR DONALD MELILLO

WON	LOST	NAME	POS.	G.	BA	FROM	TO
		Allen, Ethan Nathan	OF7	19	.303	B	C
		Almada, Melo Baldomero (Mel)	OF	102	+.342	xWash	
		Bell, Roy Chester (Beau)	OF132	147	.262	B	

1	2	Bildilli, Emil	P	5	.250	B	
2	3	Bonetti, Julio James Paul	P	17	.000	B	
		Clift, Harlond Benton	3B	149	.290	B	
1	5	Cole, Edward Wm. (Kisloski)	P	36	.143	A	
1	4	Cox, Wm. Donald	P	24	+.059	xChi	
		Grace, Joseph LaVerne	OF	12	.340	A	
		Gryska, Sigmund Stanley	SS	7	.476	A	
		Harshaney, Samuel	C10	11	.292	B	
		Heath, Thomas George	C65	70	.227	B	C
		Heffner, Donald Henry (Jeep)	2B	141	.245	N.Y.	
8	10	Hildebrand, Oral Clyde	P23	24	.254	B	
		Hughes, Roy John (Jeep)	2B21	58	.281	Clev	
3	7	Johnson, Frederick Edward	P	17	.240	NYN23	
0	0	Kimberlin, Harry Liddle	P	1	.000	B	
1	2	Knott, John Henry Jr.	P	7	+.100	B	Chi
		Kress, Ralph (Red)	SS	150	.302	Wash36	
0	0	Liebhardt, Glenn Ignatius	P	2	.000	StL36	C
1	7	Linke, Edward Karl	P	21	.200	Wash	C
		Lucadello, John	3B6	7	.150	A	
		Mazzera, Melvin Leonard (Mike)	OF47	86	.279	B	
		Mills, Colonel Buster	OF113	123	.285	Bos	
10	12	Mills, Howard Robinson (Lefty)	P	30	.091	B	
		McQuillen, Glenn Richard	OF30	43	.284	A	
		McQuinn, George Hartley (Mac)	1B	148	.324	CinN36	
20	16	Newsom, Louis Norman (Buck)	P44	46	.250	Bos	
		Sullivan, Wm. Joseph Jr. (Billy)	C99	111	.277	Clev	
0	3	Tamulis, Vitautas Casimirus (Vito)	P	3	.400	NY35	BknN
2	5	Tietje, Leslie Wm.	P17	18	.111	B	C
0	1	Trotter, Wm. Felix	P	1	.000	B	
4	7	VanAtta, Russell	P	25	.133	B	
1	12	Walkup, James Elton	P	18	.138	B	
0	1	Weaver, James Dement	P	1	.000	PittN	CinN
		West, Samuel Filmore	OF	44	+.309	B	Wash

WON 43
LOST 111
TG 154

AMERICAN LEAGUE 1939. FINISHED 8th (LAST) PCT. .279

ST. LOUIS

FRED GIRARD HANEY

WON	LOST	NAME	POS.	G.	BA	FROM	TO
		Almada, Melo Baldomero (Mel)	OF34	42	.239	B	BknN
		Bell, Roy Chester (Beau)	OF	11	+.219	B	Det
		Berardino, John	2B114	126	.256	A	
1	1	Bildilli, Emil	P	2	.000	B	
		Christman, Marquette Joseph	SS	79	+.216	xDet	
		Clift, Harlond Benton	3B149	151	.270	B	

WON	LOST	NAME	POS.	G.	BA	FROM	TO
0	2	Cole, Edward Wm. (Kisloski)	P	6	.000	B	C
0	2	Cox, Wm. Donald	P	4	.000	B	
		Gallagher, Joseph Emmett	OF	71	+.282	xN.Y.	
1	12	Gill, George Lloyd	P	27	+.154	xDet	C
		Glenn, Joseph Chas.	C82	88	.273	N.Y.	
		Grace, Joseph LaVerne	OF53	74	.304	B	
		Gryska, Sigmund Stanley	SS14	18	.265	B	C
0	1	Hanning, Loy Vernon	P	4	.000	A	
3	12	Harris, Robert Arthur	P	29	+.189	xDet	
		Harshaney, Samuel	C36	42	.241	B	
		Heffner, Donald Henry (Jeep) (2B32)	SS73	110	.267	B	
0	0	Hoag, Myril Oliver (P1)	OF117	129	.295	N.Y.	
		Hughes, Roy John (Jeep) (SS1)	2B6	17	.087	B	PhilN
0	1	Johnson, Frederick Edward	P	5	.000	B	C
9	17	Kennedy, Lloyd Vernon (Vern)	P	34	+.149	xDet	
1	2	Kimberlin, Harry Liddle	P	17	.333	B	C
9	16	Kramer, John Henry	P	40	.136	A	
		Kress, Ralph (Red)	SS	13	+.279	B	Det
		Laabs, Chester Peter (Chet)	OF	95	+.300	xDet	
3	7	Lawson, Alfred Voyle (Roxie)	P	37	+.186	xDet	
		Lucadello, John	2B7	9	.233	B	
2	5	Marcum, John Alfred	P	16	+.455	Bos	Chi
		Mazzera, Melvin Leonard (Mike)	OF25	34	.297	B	
4	11	Mills, Howard Robinson (Lefty)	P	34	.234	B	
0	0	Muncrief, Robert Cleveland Jr.	P	2	.000	StL37	
		McQuinn, George Hartley (Mac)	1B	154	.316	B	
		Neighbors, Robert Otis	SS5	7	.182	A	C
3	1	Newsom, Louis Norman (Buck)	P	6	+.222	B	Det
0	2	Pyle, Herbert Ewald	P	6	.000	A	
		Silber, Edward James		1	.000	StL37	C
		Solters, Julius Joseph (Moose)	OF	40	+.206	xClev	
		Spindel, Harold Stewart	C32	48	.269	A	
		Sullivan, Wm. Joseph Jr. (Billy) (C19)	OF59	118	.289	B	
		Thompson, Rupert Luckhart	OF	30	+.302	xChi	C
6	13	Trotter, Wm. Felix	P	41	.108	B	
0	0	VanAtta, Russell	P	2	.000	B	C
0	2	Wade, Jacob Fields (Jake)	P	4	+.000	xBos	
0	1	Walkup, James Elton	P	1	+.000	B	Det
1	3	Whitehead, John Henderson	P	26	+.059	xChi	

WON 67
LOST 87
TG 154

AMERICAN LEAGUE

1940.

FINISHED 6th.

PCT. .435

ST. LOUIS

FRED GIRARD HANEY

WON	LOST	NAME	POS.	G.	BA	FROM	TO
16	11	Auker, Eldon LeRoy	P	38	.213	Bos	
		Berardino, John (2B13 3B9)	SS112	142	.258	B	
2	4	Bildilli, Emil	P 28	29	.200	B	
		Clift, Harlond Benton	3B147	150	.273	B	
2	2	Coffman, George David (Slick)	P31	32	.200	Det	C
0	1	Cox, Wm. Donald	P12	13	.000	B	C
		Cullenbine, Roy Joseph (1B6)	OF57	86	.230	xBknN	
		Gallagher, Joseph Emmett	OF15	23	.271	B	BknN
		Grace, Joseph LaVerne (C12)	OF51	80	.258	B	
11	15	Harris, Robert Arthur	P	35	.250	B	
		Harshaney, Samuel	C2	3	.000	B	C
		Heffner, Donald Henry (Jeep)	2B125	126	.236	B	
		Hoag, Myril Oliver	OF46	76	.262	B	
0	1	Hudlin, George Willis	P	6	+.500	xWash	N.Y.N
		Judnich, Walter Franklin	OF133	137	.303	A	
12	17	Kennedy, Lloyd Vernon (Vern)	P34	35	.298	B	
3	7	Kramer, John Henry	P	16	.050	B	
		Laabs, Chester Peter (Chet)	OF63	105	.271	B	
		Lary, Lynford Hobart (Lyn) (2B1)	SS12	27	.056	StLN	C
5	3	Lawson, Alfred Voyle (Roxie)	P	30	.045	B	C
		Lucadello, John	2B16	17	.317	B	
0	6	Mills, Howard Robinson (Lefty)	P	26	.154	B	C
		McQuinn, George Hartley (Mac)	1B150	151	.279	B	
1	0	Newlin, Maurice Milton	P	1	.500	A	
7	11	Niggeling, John Arnold	P	28	.176	CinN	
		Radcliff, Raymond Allen (Rip) (1B4)	OF139	150	.342	Chi	
		Strange, Alan Cochrane (Inky) (2B4)	SS35	54	.186	Wash35	
		Susce, George Cyril Methodius	C	61	.212	PittN	
		Swift, Robert Virgil	C128	130	.244	A	
7	6	Trotter, Wm. Felix	P	36	.045	B	
		White, Albert Eugene		2	.000	A	
1	3	Whitehead, John Henderson	P	15	.167	B	

WON 70
LOST 84
TG 154

AMERICAN LEAGUE

1941.

FINISHED 6th.
(TIED WITH WASH)
PCT. .455

ST. LOUIS

FRED GIRARD HANEY JAMES LUTHER SEWELL

WON	LOST	NAME	POS.	G.	BA	FROM	TO
2	5	Allen, John Thomas (Johnny)	P	20	.136	Clev	BknN
		Archie, George Albert	1B	9	+.379	xWash	
14	15	Auker, Eldon LeRoy	P34	37	.125	B	
		Berardino, John (3B1)	SS123	128	.271	B	
0	0	Bildilli, Emil	P	2	.000	B	C
3	7	Caster, George Jasper	P	32	.103	Phil	
		Clift, Harlond Benton	3B	154	.255	B	

WON	LOST	NAME	POS.	G.	BA	FROM	TO
		Cullenbine, Roy Joseph (1B22)	OF120	149	.317	B	
		Estalella, Roberto Mendez	OF17	46	.241	Wash39	
		Ferrell, Richard Benjamin (Rick)	C	100	+.252	xWash	
9	10	Galehouse, Dennis Ward (Denny)	P	30	.191	Bos	
		Grace, Joseph LaVerne (C9)	OF88	115	.309	B	
		Grube, Franklin Thomas	C	18	.154	Chi36	C
12	14	Harris, Robert Arthur	P	34	.115	B	
		Heffner, Donald Henry (Jeep)	2B105	110	.233	B	
		Hoag, Myril Oliver	OF	1	+.000	B	Chi
0	0	Iott, Clarence Eugene	P	2	.000	A	
		Judnich, Walter Franklin	OF140	146	.284	B	
2	4	Kennedy, Lloyd Vernon (Vern)	P	6	+.400	B	Wash
4	3	Kramer, John Henry	P	29	.000	B	
		Laabs, Chester Peter (Chet)	OF100	118	.278	B	
		Lucadello, John (SS12 3B6 OF1)	2B70	107	.279	B	
13	9	Muncrief, Robert Cleveland Jr.	P	36	.237	StL39	
0	1	McKain, Archie Richard (Happy)	P	8	+.000	xDet	
		McQuillen, Glenn Richard	OF6	7	.333	StL38	
		McQuinn, George Hartley	1B125	130	.297	B	
0	2	Newlin, Maurice Milton	P	14	.000	B	C
7	9	Niggeling, John Arnold	P	24	.167	B	
0	3	Ostermueller, Frederick Raymond (Fritz)	P15	16	.214	Bos	
		Radcliff, Raymond Allen (Rip)	OF	19	+.282	B	Det
		Stephens, Vernon Decatur	SS1	3	.500	A	
		Stevens, Chas. Augustus	1B	4	.154	A	
		Strange, Alan Cochrane (Inky) (1B2 3B1)	SS32	45	.232	B	
		Swift, Robert Virgil	C58	63	.259	B	
4	2	Trotter, Wm. Felix	P	29	.000	B	

WON 82 — AMERICAN LEAGUE — FINISHED 3rd.
LOST 69
151 — 1942. — PCT. .543

ST. LOUIS

JAMES LUTHER SEWELL

WON	LOST	NAME	POS.	G.	BA	FROM	TO
1	1	Appleton, Peter Wm.	P	14	+.167	xChi	
14	13	Auker, Eldon LeRoy	P35	51	.161	B	C
		Berardino, John (1B5 2B4 3B6)	SS6	29	.284	B	
0	1	Biscan, Frank Stephen	P	11	.000	A	
8	2	Caster, George Jasper	P	39	.067	B	
		Chartak, Michael George	OF	73	+.249	xWash	
		Clift, Harlond Benton (SS1)	3B141	143	.274	B	
		Criscola, Anthony Paul	OF52	91	.297	A	

WON	LOST	NAME	POS.	G.	BA	FROM	TO
		Cullenbine, Roy Joseph	OF	38	+.193	B	Wash
		Dahlgren, Ellsworth Tenney (Babe)		2	.000	xChiN	BknN
3	4	Ferens, Stanley	P	19	.143	A	
		Ferrell, Richard Benjamin (Rick)	C95	99	.223	B	
12	12	Galehouse, Dennis Ward (Denny)	P	32	.194	B	
		Gutteridge, Donald Joseph (3B2)	2B145	147	.255	StLN40	
1	1	Hanning, Loy Vernon	P	11	.250	StL39	C
1	5	Harris, Robert Arthur	P	6	+.000	B	Phil
		Hayes, Frank Witman (Blimp)	C	56	+.252	xPhil	
		Hayworth, Raymond Hall		1	1.000	NYN39	
		Heffner, Donald Henry (Jeep) (1B4)	2B6	19	.167	B	
10	6	Hollingsworth, Albert Wayne (Al)	P33	36	.179	Wash40	
		Judnich, Walter Franklin	OF122	132	.313	B	
		Laabs, Chester Peter (Chet)	OF139	144	.275	B	
6	8	Muncrief, Robert Cleveland Jr.	P	24	.111	B	
		McQuillen, Glenn Richard	OF77	100	.283	B	
		McQuinn, George Hartley (Mac)	1B144	145	.262	B	
15	11	Niggeling, John Arnold	P	28	.139	B	
3	1	Ostermueller, Frederick Raymond (Fritz)	P	10	.188	B	
0	0	Pyle, Herbert Ewald	P	2	.000	StL39	
		Sewell, James Luther (Luke) MGR.	C	6	.083	B	
		Stephens, Vernon Decatur	SS144	145	.294	B	
		Strange, Alan Cochrane (Inky) (2B1 SS3)	3B10	19	.270	B	C
8	3	Sundra, Stephen Richard (Steve)	P	20	+.225	xWash	
		Swift, Robert Virgil	C	29	+.197	B	Phil
0	1	Trotter, Wm. Felix	P	3	+.000	B	Wash
0	0	Whitehead, John Henderson	P	4	.000	StL40	C

WON 72 — AMERICAN LEAGUE — FINISHED 6th.
LOST 80
TG 152 — 1943. — PCT. .474

ST. LOUIS

JAMES LUTHER SEWELL

WON	LOST	NAME	POS.	G.	BA	FROM	TO
		Baker, Floyd Wilson (3B1)	SS10	22	.174	A	
		Byrnes, Milton John	OF114	129	.280	A	
6	8	Caster, George Jasper	P	35	.136	B	
		Chartak, Michael George (1B18)	OF77	108	.256	B	
		Christman, Marquette Joseph (1B30 2B14 SS24)	3B37	98	.271	StL39	

WON	LOST	NAME	POS.	G.	BA	FROM	TO
		Clary, Ellis	3B	23	+.273	xWash	
		Clift, Harlond Benton	3B	105	+.232	B	Wash
		Criscola, Anthony Paul	OF13	29	.154	B	
0	0	Dean, Paul Dee (Daffy)	P	3	.000	NYN41	C
		Epps, Harold Franklin	OF	8	.286	StLN40	
		Ferrell, Richard Benjamin (Rick)	C70	74	.239	B	
0	0	Fuchs, Chas. Thomas	P	13	.000	xPhilN	
11	11	Galehouse, Dennis Ward (Denny)	P	31	.125	B	
		Gutteridge, Donald Joseph	2B	132	.273	B	
		Hayes, Frank Witman (Blimp) (1B1)	C76	88	.188	B	
		x Heffner, Donald Henry (Jeep)	2B13	18	+.121	B	Phil
6	13	*Hollingsworth, Albert Wayne (Al)	P35	36	.140	B	
0	0	Kramer, John Henry	P	3	.500	StL41	
		Kreevich, Michael Andreas	OF51	60	.255	Phil	
		Laabs, Chester Peter (Chet)	OF150	151	.250	B	
0	1	LaMacchia, Alfred Anthony	P	1	.000	A	
0	0	Miller, John Anthony	P	2	+.000	xWash	
1	2	Milnar, Albert Joseph (Al)	P	3	+.333	xClev	
13	12	Muncrief, Robert Cleveland Jr.	P	35	.152	B	
1	1	McKain, Archie Richard (Happy)	P	10	.000	StL41	C
		McQuinn, George Hartley (Mac)	1B122	125	.243	B	
1	6	Newsom, Louis Norman (Buck)	P	10	+.333	xBknN	Wash
6	8	Niggeling, John Arnold	P	20	+.061	B	Wash
0	2	Ostermueller, Frederick Raymond (Fritz)	P	11	.286	B	BknN
2	0	Peterson, Sidney Herbert	P	3	.000	A	C
10	5	Potter, Nelson Thomas	P	33	.145	Bos41	
0	0	Sanford, John Frederick	P	3	.000	A	
		Schmulbach, Henry Alrives		1	.000	A	C
		Schultz, Joseph Chas. Jr.	C26	46	.239	PittN41	
		Stephens, Vernon Decatur (OF11)	SS123	137	.289	B	
15	11	Sundra, Stephen Richard (Steve)	P	32	.219	B	
		Zarilla, Allen Lee	OF60	70	.254	A	

x-Heffner also played one game at 1B.

WON 89 — AMERICAN LEAGUE — FINISHED 1st.
LOST 65
TG 154 — 1944. — PCT. .578

ST. LOUIS

JAMES LUTHER SEWELL

WON	LOST	NAME	POS.	G.	BA	FROM	TO
		Baker, Floyd Wilson (SS16)	2B17	44	.175	B	
		Byrnes, Milton John	OF122	128	.295	B	
6	6	Caster, George Jasper	P	42	.250	B	
		Chartak, Michael George (OF7)	1B12	35	.236	B	C
		Christman, Marquette Joseph (1B3)	3B145	148	.271	B	
		Clary, Ellis (2B6)	3B11	25	.265	B	
		Demaree, Joseph Franklin (Frank)	OF	16	.255	StLN	C
		Epps, Harold Franklin	OF18	22	+.177	B	Phil
9	10	Galehouse, Dennis Ward (Denny)	P	24	.063	B	
		Gutteridge, Donald Joseph	2B146	148	.245	B	
		Hafey, Thomas Francis (1B1)	OF4	8	.357	NYN39	C
		Hayworth, Myron Claude	C86	89	.223	A	
5	7	Hollingsworth, Albert Wayne (Al)	P	26	.071	B	
0	1	Hudlin, George Willis	P	1	.000	NYN40	C
13	9	Jakucki, Sigmund Jack	P35	36	.151	StL36	
17	13	Kramer, John Henry	P	33	.165	B	
		Kreevich, Michael Andreas	OF100	105	.301	B	
		Laabs, Chester Peter (Chet)	OF55	66	.234	B	
		Mancuso, Frank Octavius	C87	88	.205	A	
		Martin, Boris Michael	OF1	2	.750	A	
		Moore, Eugene Jr. (1B1)	OF98	110	.238	Wash	
13	8	Muncrief, Robert Cleveland Jr.	P	33	.231	B	
		McQuinn, George Hartley (Mac)	1B	146	.250	B	
19	7	Potter, Nelson Thomas	P	32	.159	B	
		Schulte, Leonard Wm.		1	.000	A	
		Schultz, Joseph Chas. Jr.	C	3	.250	B	
5	4	Shirley, Alvis Newman	P23	30	.143	Phil42	
		Stephens, Vernon Decatur	SS143	145	.293	B	
2	0	Sundra, Stephen Richard (Steve)	P	3	.000	B	
		Turner, Thomas Richard	C10	15	+.320	xChi	
0	0	West, Weldon Edison	P	11	.143	A	
		Zarilla, Allen Lee	OF79	100	.299	B	
0	0	Zoldak, Samuel Walter	P	18	.333	A	

WON 81 — AMERICAN LEAGUE — FINISHED 3rd.
LOST 70
TG 151 — 1945. — PCT. .536

ST. LOUIS

JAMES LUTHER SEWELL

WON	LOST	NAME	POS.	G.	BA	FROM	TO
0	0	Appleton, Peter Wm.	P	2	+.000	StL42	Wash
		Byrnes, Milton John (1B2)	OF125	133	.249	B	C
1	2	Caster, George Jasper	P	10	+.333	B	Det
		Christman, Marquette Joseph	3B77	78	.277	B	
		Clary, Ellis (2B3)	3B16	26	.211	B	C
0	0	Fannin, Clifford Bryson	P	5	.000	A	

WON	LOST	NAME	POS.	G.	BA	FROM	TO
		Finney, Louis Klopsche (1B22 3B1)	OF36	57	+.277	xBos	
		Gray, Peter Wyshner	OF61	77	.218	A	C
		Gutteridge, Donald Joseph (OF14)	2B128	143	.238	B	
		Hayworth, Myron Claude	C55	56	.194	B	C
12	9	Hollingsworth, Albert Wayne (Al)	P26	28	.197	B	
12	10	Jakucki, Sigmund Jack	P	30	.186	B	C
0	0	Jones, Earl Leslie	P	10	.200	A	C
10	15	Kramer, John Henry	P	29	.148	B	
		Kreevich, Michael Andreas	OF80	84	+.237	B	Wash
		Laabs, Chester Peter (Chet)	OF	35	.239	B	
2	0	LaMacchia, Alfred Anthony	P	5	.000	StL43	
		Mancuso, Frank Octavius	C115	119	.268	B	
		Martin, Boris Michael (1B6)	OF48	54	.200	B	
		McQuinn, George Hartley (Mac)	1B136	139	.277	B	
2	1	Miller, John Anthony	P4	6	.182	StL43	
		Moore, Eugene Jr.	OF100	110	.260	B	C
13	4	Muncrief, Robert Cleveland Jr.	P27	28	.067	B	
15	11	Potter, Nelson Thomas	P	32	.304	B	
0	0	Sanders, Dee Wilma	P	2	.000	A	C
		Schulte, Leonard Wm. (2B37 SS14)	3B71	119	.247	B	
		Schultz, Joseph Chas. Jr.	C4	41	.295	B	
8	12	Shirley, Alvis Newman	P32	43	.286	B	
		Stephens, Vernon Decatur (3B4)	SS144	149	.289	B	
3	4	West, Weldon Edison	P	24	.074	B	C
3	2	Zoldak, Samuel Walter	P26	27	.050	B	

WON 66 LOST 88 TG 154 — AMERICAN LEAGUE 1946. — FINISHED 7th. PCT. .429

ST. LOUIS

JAMES LUTHER SEWELL JAMES WREN TAYLOR

WON	LOST	NAME	POS.	G.	BA	FROM	TO
		Archie, George Albert	1B3	4	.182	StL41	C
		Berardino, John	2B143	144	.265	StL42	
1	1	Biscan, Frank Stephen	P	16	.000	StL42	
		Bradley, George Washington	OF3	4	.167	A	C
		Christman, Marquette Joseph (SS47)	3B77	128	.258	B	
		Dahlgren, Ellsworth Tenney (Babe)	1B24	28	.175	PittN	C
		Dillinger, Robert Bernard (SS1)	3B54	83	.280	A	
5	2	Fannin, Clifford Bryson	P	27	.161	B	
2	9	Ferens, Stanley	P	34	.167	StL42	C

WON	LOST	NAME	POS.	G.	BA	FROM	TO
		Finney, Louis Klopsche	OF7	16	.300	B	
8	12	Galehouse, Dennis Ward (Denny)	P	30	.091	StL44	
		Grace, Joseph LaVerne	OF43	48	+.230	StL41	Wash
		Heath, John Geoffrey (Jeff)	OF83	86	+.275	xWash	
		Helf, Henry Hartz	C69	71	.192	Clev40	C
0	0	Hollingsworth, Albert Wayne (Al)	P	5	+.000	B	Chi
0	0	Johnson, Chester Lillis	P	5	.000	A	C
		Judnich, Walter Franklin	OF137	142	.262	StL42	
3	3	Kinder, Ellis Raymond	P	33	.053	A	
13	11	Kramer, John Henry	P	31	.136	B	
		Laabs, Chester Peter (Chet)	OF72	80	.261	B	
0	0	LaMacchia, Alfred Anthony	P	8	+.000	B	Wash
		Lehner, Paul Eugene	OF12	16	.222	A	
		Lucadello, John (2B19)	3B37	87	.248	StL41	
		Mancuso, Frank Octavius	C85	87	.240	B	
		Martin, Boris Michael	C2	3	.222	B	
		McQuillen, Glenn Richard	OF48	59	.241	StL42	
1	3	Miller, John Anthony	P	11	.286	B	
1	1	Milnar, Albert Joseph (Al)	P	4	.750	StL43	PhilN
		Moss, John Lester	C	12	.371	A	
3	12	Muncrief, Robert Cleveland Jr.	P	29	.031	B	
8	9	Potter, Nelson Thomas	P	23	.231	B	
2	1	Sanford, John Frederick	P	3	.286	StL43	
		Schulte, Leonard Wm. (3B1)	2B1	4	.400	B	C
		Schultz, Joseph Chas. Jr.	C17	42	.386	B	
		Sears, Kenneth Eugene	C4	7	.333	NY43	C
6	12	Shirley, Alvis Newman	P27	35	.196	B	C
0	0	Shore, Raymond Everett	P	1	.000	A	
		Stephens, Vernon Decatur	SS112	115	.307	B	
		Stevens, Chas. Augustus	1B120	122	.248	StL41	
0	0	Sundra, Stephen Richard (Steve)	P	2	.000	StL44	C
		Witte, Jerome Chas.	1B	18	.192	A	
		Zarilla, Allen Lee	OF107	125	.259	StL44	
9	11	Zoldak, Samuel Walter	P	35	.173	B	

WON 59 LOST 95 TG 154 — AMERICAN LEAGUE 1947. — FINISHED 8th (LAST) PCT. .383

ST. LOUIS

HEROLD DOMINIC RUEL

WON	LOST	NAME	POS.	G.	BA	FROM	TO
		Berardino, John	2B86	90	.261	B	
1	0	Brown, Walter Irving	P	19	.000	A	C
		Brown, Willard Jesse	OF18	21	.179	A	C
		Coleman, Raymond LeRoy	OF93	110	.259	A	
		Currin, Perry Gilmore	SS1	3	.000	A	C
0	0	Dean, Jay Hanna (Dizzy)	P	1	1.000	ChiN41	C
		Dillinger, Robert Bernard	3B	137	.294	B	

WON	LOST	NAME	POS.	G.	BA	FROM	TO
[illegible]	[illegible]	Fannin, Clifford Bryson	P	26	.190	B	
1	3	Galehouse, Dennis Ward (Denny)	P	9	+.000	B	Bos
		Heath, John Geoffrey (Jeff)	OF140	141	.251	B	
		Hitchcock, Wm. Clyde (1B5 SS7 3B17)	2B46	80	.222	Wash	
0	1	Iott, Clarence Eugene	P	4	.000	StL41	NYN̲
		Judnich, Walter Franklin (OF15)	1B129	144	.258	B	
8	15	Kinder, Ellis Raymond	P	34	.129	B	
11	16	Kramer, John Henry	P32	33	.113	B	
		Lehner, Paul Eugene	OF127	135	.248	B	
		Moss, John Lester	C	96	.157	B	
4	2	Moulder, Glen Herbert	P	32	.235	BknN̲	
8	14	Muncrief, Robert Cleveland Jr.	P	31	.105	B	
		McQuillen, Glenn Richard		1	.000	B	C
		Peters, Russell Dixon (SS2)	2B13	39	.340	Clev	C
4	10	Potter, Nelson Thomas	P	32	.257	B	
7	16	Sanford, John Frederick	P	34	.204	B	
		Schultz, Joseph Chas. Jr.		43	.184	B	
		Stephens, Vernon Decatur	SS149	150	.279	B	
0	0	Swartz, Sherwin Merle	P	5	1.000	A	C
		Thompson, Henry Curtis	2B19	27	.256	A	
		Witte, Jerome Chas.	1B27	34	.141	B	C
		Zarilla, Allen Lee	OF110	127	.224	B	
9	10	Zoldak, Samuel Walter	P	35	.172	B	

WON 59   AMERICAN LEAGUE   FINISHED 6th.
LOST 94
TG 153   1948.   PCT. .386

ST. LOUIS

JAMES WREN TAYLOR

WON	LOST	NAME	POS.	G.	BA	FROM	TO
		Anderson, Andy Holm (1B2 SS10)	2B21	51	.276	A	
		Arft, Henry Irven	1B	69	.238	A	
		Binks, George Eugene (1B4)	OF5	15	+.217	xPhil	C
6	7	Biscan, Frank Stephen	P	47	.192	StL46	C
		Coleman, Raymond LeRoy	OF5	17	+.172	B	Phil
		Dente, Samuel Joseph (3B6)	SS76	98	.270	Bos	
		Dillinger, Robert Bernard	3B	153	.321	B	
0	2	Dreisewerd, Clement John	P	13	.000	Bos46	NYN̲
3	2	Drews, Karl August	P	20	+.000	xN.Y.	
10	14	Fannin, Clifford Bryson	P34	48	.169	B	
7	11	Garver, Ned Franklin	P38	46	.288	A	
0	3	Gerheauser, Albert	P	14	.333	PittN46	C
		Jordan, Thomas Jefferson		1	.000	Clev̄46	C
7	8	Kennedy, Wm. Aulton	P	26	+.250	xClev	
		Kokos, Richard Jerome	OF	71	.298	A	

WON	LOST	NAME	POS.	G.	BA	FROM	TO
		Laydon, Peter John	OF30	41	.250	A	C
		Lehner, Paul Eugene (1B2)	OF89	103	.276	B	
		Lund, Donald Andrew	OF45	63	.248	xBknN̲	
		Moss, John Lester	C103	107	.257	B	
		McCarthy, Jerome Francis	1B	2	.333	A	C
4	6	Ostrowski, Joseph Paul	P	26	.222	A	
		Partee, Roy Robert	C76	82	.203	Bos	C
		Pellagrini, Edward Chas.	SS98	105	.238	Bos	
		Platt, Mizell George	OF114	123	.271	Chi46	
1	1	Potter, Nelson Thomas	P	2	+.500	B	Phil
		Priddy, Gerald Edward	2B146	151	.296	Wash	
12	21	Sanford, John Frederick	P42	43	.151	B	
		Schultz, Joseph Chas. Jr.		43	.189	B	C
1	1	Schwamb, Ralph Richard	P	12	.300	A	C
1	2	Shore, Raymond Everett	P	17	.000	StL46	
3	6	Stephens, Bryan Maris	P	43	.125	Clev	C
		Stevens, Chas. Augustus	1B	85	.260	StL46	C
2	6	Widmar, Albert Joseph	P	49	.300	Bos	
0	0	Wilson, James Alger	P	4	.000	Bos46	
		Wood, Kenneth Lanier	OF5	10	.083	A	
		Zarilla, Allen Lee	OF136	144	.329	B	
2	4	Zoldak, Samuel Walter	P	11	+.273	B	Clev

WON 53   AMERICAN LEAGUE   FINISHED 7th.
LOST 101
TG 154   1949.   PCT. .344

ST. LOUIS

JAMES WREN TAYLOR

WON	LOST	NAME	POS.	G.	BA	FROM	TO
1	0	Albrecht, Edward Arthur	P	1	.000	A	
		Anderson, Andy Holm (2B8 3B8)	SS44	71	.125	B	C
		Arft, Henry Irven		6	.200	B	
0	0	Bilbrey, James Melvin	P	1	.000	A	C
		Dillinger, Robert Bernard	3B133	137	.324	B	
4	12	Drews, Karl August	P	31	.000	B	
		Elder, George Rezin	OF10	41	.250	A	C
3	13	Embree, Chas. Willard	P35	40	.162	N.Y.	C
8	14	Fannin, Clifford Bryson	P30	37	.164	B	
6	4	Ferrick, Thomas Jerome	P50	51	.143	Wash	
		Friend, Owen Lacey	2B	2	.375	A	
12	17	Garver, Ned Franklin	P41	55	.187	B	
		Graham, John Bernard	1B136	137	.238	NYN̲46	C
4	11	Kennedy, Wm. Aulton	P	48	.150	B	
		Kokos, Richard Jerome	OF138	143	.261	B	
		Lehner, Paul Eugene (1B18)	OF55	104	.229	B	
		Lollar, John Sherman	C93	109	.261	N.Y.	
1	1	Malloy, Robert Paul	P	5	.000	CinN̲47	C
0	0	Medlinger, Irving John	P	3	.000	A	
		Moss, John Lester	C83	97	.291	B	
		Naples, Aloysius Francis	SS	2	.143	A	C
8	8	Ostrowski, Joseph Paul	P	40	.189	B	
		Pack, Frankie		1	.000	A	C

WON	LOST	NAME	POS.	G.	BA	FROM	TO
4	11	Papai, Alfred Thomas	P	42	.079	StLN	
		Pellagrini, Edward Chas.	SS76	79	.238	B	
		Platt, Mizell George (1B2)	OF59	102	.258	B	C
		Priddy, Gerald Edward	2B	145	.290	B	
1	2	Raney, Frank Robert	P	3	.000	A	
0	0	Savage, John Robert	P	4	.000	Phil	C
0	1	Shore, Raymond Everett	P	13	.000	B	C
		Sievers, Roy Edward (3B7)	OF125	140	.306	A	
		Spence, Stanley Orville (1B1)	OF84	104	+.245	xBos	C
1	7	Starr, Richard Eugene	P	30	.087	N.Y.	
		Sullivan, John Patrick	SS71	105	.226	Wash	C
		(2B6 3B23)					
0	0	Winegarner, Ralph Lee	P	9	.400	Clev36	C
		Wood, Kenneth Lanier	OF3	7	.000	B	
		Zarilla, Allen Lee	OF	15	+.250	B	Bos

WON 58   AMERICAN LEAGUE   FINISHED 7th.
LOST 96
TG 154   1950.   PCT. .377

ST. LOUIS

JAMES WREN TAYLOR

WON	LOST	NAME	POS.	G.	BA	FROM	TO
0	1	Albrecht, Edward Arthur	P	2	.000	B	C
		Arft, Henry Irven	1B84	98	.268	B	
0	0	Bauers, Russell Lee	P	1	.000	ChiN46	C
1	2	Bruner, Jack Raymond	P	13	+.000	xChi	C
		Coleman, Raymond LeRoy	OF98	117	.271	Phil48	
		Delsing, James Henry	OF53	69	+.263	xN.Y.	
		DeMars, Wm. Lester (3B5)	SS54	61	.247	Phil48	
4	9	Dorish, Harry	P29	30	.161	Bos	
5	9	Fannin, Clifford Bryson	P25	33	.176	B	
1	3	Ferrick, Thomas Jerome	P	16	+.250	B	N.Y.
0	1	Fine, Thomas Morgan	P14	16	.333	Bos47	C
		Friend, Owen Lacey	2B93	119	.237	B	
		(SS3 3B24)					
13	18	Garver, Ned Franklin (OF1)	P37	51	.286	B	
		Gustine, Frank Wm.	3B6	9	.158	ChiN	C
5	6	Johnson, Donald Roy	P	25	+.069	xN.Y.	
0	0	Kennedy, Wm. Aulton	P	1	.000	B	
		Kokos, Richard Jerome	OF127	143	.261	B	
0	2	Kretlow, Louis Henry	P9	10	+.000	Det	Chi
		Lenhardt, Donald Eugene	1B86	139	.273	A	
		(3B10 OF39)					
		Lollar, John Sherman	C109	126	.280	B	
1	3	Marshall, Clarence Westly	P	28	.333	N.Y.	C
		Moss, John Lester	C60	84	.266	B	
2	4	Ostrowski, Joseph Paul	P	9	+.222	B	N.Y.
9	12	Overmire, Frank	P	31	.167	Det	
3	5	Pillette, Duane Xavier	P24	27	+.136	xN.Y.	
0	1	Raney, Frank Robert	P	1	.000	B	C
0	0	Schacht, Sidney	P8	9	.000	A	
		Sievers, Roy Edward (3B21)	OF78	113	.238	B	

WON	LOST	NAME	POS.	G.	BA	FROM	TO
		Sommers, Wm. Dunn (2B21)	3B37	65	.255	A	C
7	5	Starr, Richard Eugene	P32	33	.139	B	
		Stirnweiss, George Henry	2B62	93	+.218	xN.Y.	
		(SS5 3B30)					
		Thomas, Leo Raymond	3B	35	.198	A	
		Upton, Thomas Herbert	SS115	124	.237	A	
		(2B2 3B1)					
7	15	Widmar, Albert Joseph	P	36	.149	StL48	
		Wood, Kenneth Lanier	OF94	128	.225	B	

WON 52   AMERICAN LEAGUE   FINISHED 8th (LAST)
LOST 102
TG 154   1951.   PCT. .338

ST. LOUIS

JAMES WREN TAYLOR

WON	LOST	NAME	POS.	G.	BA	FROM	TO
		Arft, Henry Irven	1B97	112	.261	B	
		Batts, Matthew Daniel	C64	79	+.302	xBos	
		Berardino, John	3B31	39	.227	PittN	
		(1B1 2B2 OF1)					
		Bero, John George (2B1)	SS55	61	.213	Det48	C
4	10	Byrne, Thomas Joseph	P19	34	+.263	xN.Y.	
		Coleman, Raymond LeRoy	OF87	91	+.282	B	Chi
		Delsing, James Henry	OF124	131	.249	B	
		DeMars, Wm. Lester	SS	1	.250	B	C
		Dyck, James Robert	3B	4	.067	A	
0	2	Fannin, Clifford Bryson	P7	8	.250	B	
		Gaedel, Edward Carl		1	.000	A	C
20	12	Garver, Ned Franklin	P33	49	.305	B	
		Goliat, Mike Mitchel	2B2	5	.182	xPhilN	
0	0	Herrera, Procopio Rodriguez	P	3	.000	A	C
1	1	Hogue, Robert Clinton	P	18	+.667	xBosN	N.Y.
		Jennings, Wm. Lee	SS	64	.179	A	C
0	1	Johnson, Donald Roy	P	6	+.333	B	Wash
1	5	Kennedy, Wm. Aulton	P	19	.125	B	
		Kluttz, Clyde Franklin	C1	4	+.500	PittN48	Wash
		Lehner, Paul Eugene	OF18	21	+.134	xChi	Clev
		Lenhardt, Donald Eugene	OF27	31	+.262	B	Chi
		(1B1)					
		Lollar, John Sherman (3B1)	C85	98	.252	B	
		Long, Richard Dale (OF1)	1B28	34	.238	xPittN	C
		Lutz, Rollin Joseph	1B11	14	.167	A	C
		Maguire, Jack	OF26	41	.244	xPittN	C
		(2B2 3B5)					
2	5	Mahoney, Robert Paul	P	30	+.222	xChi	
		Mapes, Clifford Franklin	OF53	56	+.274	xN.Y.	
1	1	Markell, Harry Duke	P	5	.167	A	C
		Marsh, Fred Francis	3B117	130	.243	Clev49	
		(2B2 SS3)					
0	0	Medlinger, Irving John	P	6	.000	StL49	C
		Moss, John Lester	C12	16	+.170	B	Bos
4	7	McDonald, James LeRoy	P16	17	.207	Bos	

WON	LOST	NAME	POS.	G.	BA	FROM	TO
1	6	Overmire, Frank	P	8	+.071	B	N.Y.
3	4	Paige, LeRoy	P	23	.125	Clev49	
6	14	Pillette, Duane Xavier	P35	41	.136	B	
		Rapp, Earl Wellington	OF25	26	.327	xNYN	
2	4	Sanford, John Frederick	P	9	+.286	xWash	C
		Saucier, Francis Field	OF3	18	.071	A	C
0	0	Schacht, Sidney	P	6	.000	B	BosN
		Sievers, Roy Edward	OF25	31	.225	B	
1	9	Sleater, Louis Mortimer	P20	25	.226	B	
2	5	Starr, Richard Eugene	P	15	+.222	B	Wash
0	6	Suchecki, James Joseph	P	29	.100	Bos	
		Taylor, Eugene Benjamin	1B25	33	.258	A	
		Thomas, John Tillman	SS	14	.350	A	C
0	1	Turley, Robert Lee	P	1	.000	A	
		Upton, Thomas Herbert	SS47	52	.198	B	
		Wahl, Kermit Emerson	3B6	8	+.333	xPhil	C
4	9	Widmar, Albert Joseph	P	26	.167	B	
		Wood, Kenneth Lanier	OF100	109	.237	B	
		Young, Robert George	2B	147	.260	StLN48	

WON 64 — AMERICAN LEAGUE — FINISHED 7th.
LOST 90
TG 154 — 1952. — PCT. .416

ST. LOUIS

ROGERS HORNSBY — MARTIN WHITFORD MARION

WON	LOST	NAME	POS.	G.	BA	FROM	TO
		Arft, Henry Irven	1B10	15	.143	B	C
7	8	Bearden, Henry Eugene	P34	45	.354	Det	
7	14	Byrne, Thomas Joseph	P29	40	.250	B	
12	10	Cain, Robert Max	P29	35	.138	Det	
		Coleman, Raymond LeRoy	OF16	20	+.196	xChi	C
		Courtney, Clinton Dawson	C113	119	.286	N.Y.	
		Crawford, Rufus	OF3	7	.182	A	C
		Delsing, James Henry	OF85	93	+.255	B	Det
		DeMaestri, Joseph Paul (2B1 3B1)	SS77	81	.226	Chi	
		Dyck, James Robert (OF48)	3B74	122	.269	B	
0	2	Fannin, Clifford Bryson	P10	11	.000	B	C
7	10	Garver, Ned Franklin	P21	24	+.184	B	Det
		Goldsberry, Gordon Frederick (OF2)	1B72	86	.229	Chi	C
		Goliat, Mike Mitchel	2B	3	.000	B	C
2	8	Harrist, Earl	P	36	.097	Wash48	
0	1	Hetki, John Edward	P	3	.000	CinN50	
0	1	Hogue, Robert Clinton	P	8	+.000	xN.Y.	C
0	2	Holcombe, Kenneth Edward	P	12	+.333	xChi	
0	0	Hudson, Hal Campbell	P	3	+.000	A	Chi
		Johnson, Darrell Dean	C22	29	+.282	A	Chi
		Kryhoski, Richard David	1B86	111	.243	Det	
		Lenhardt, Donald Eugene (1B2)	OF11	18	+.271	xDet	
2	3	Littlefield, Richard Bernard	P	7	+.063	xDet	
4	2	Madison, David Pledger	P	31	+.118	NY50	Det

WON	LOST	NAME	POS.	G.	BA	FROM	TO
0	0	Mahoney, Robert Paul	P	3	.000	B	C
		Marion, Martin Whitford MGR.	SS63	67	.247	StLN	
		Marsh, Fred Francis	SS60	11	+.217	B	Wash
		(2B9 3B21)		76	+.286	(& return)	
		Michaels, Casimir Eugene (2B8)	3B42	55	+.265	xWash	Phil
		Miranda, Guillermo Perez	SS	7	+.091	xChi (returned)	Chi
		Moss, John Lester	C39	52	.246	Bos	
		Nieman, Robert Chas.	OF125	131	.289	B	
0	3	Overmire, Frank	P	17	.182	N.Y.	C
12	10	Paige, LeRoy	P	46	.128	B	
10	13	Pillette, Duane Xavier	P30	35	.182	B	
		Porter, J. W. (3B2)	OF29	33	.250	A	C
		Rapp, Earl Wellington	OF7	30	+.143	B	Wash
		Rivera, Manuel Joseph	OF88	97	+.256	A	Chi
		Rojek, Stanley Andrew (2B1)	SS4	9	.143	StLN	C
		Schmees, George Edward (1B2)	OF19	34	+.131	A	Bos
		Sievers, Roy Edward	1B7	11	.200	B	
0	1	Sleater, Louis Mortimer	P	4	+.000	B	Wash
1	2	Stuart, Marlin Henry	P	12	+.000	xDet	
0	0	Taylor, Vernon Chas.	P	1	.000	A	C
		Thomas, Leo Raymond (2B1 SS3)	3B37	41	+.234	StL50	Chi
		Wertz, Victor Woodrow	OF36	37	+.346	xDet	
		Wright, Thomas Everett	OF18	29	+.242	Bos	Chi
		Young, Robert George	2B	149	.247	B	
		Zarilla, Allen Lee	OF35	48	+.238	xChi	Bos

WON 54 — AMERICAN LEAGUE — FINISHED 8th (LAST)
LOST 100
TG 154 — 1953. — PCT. .351

ST. LOUIS

MARTIN WHITFORD MARION

WON	LOST	NAME	POS.	G.	BA	FROM	TO
		Berry, Cornelius John (2B15 SS6)	3B17	57	+.283	Det	Chi
2	6	Blyzka, Michael John	P	33	.000	A	
5	13	Brecheen, Harry David	P26	27	.179	StLN	C
4	10	Cain, Robert Max	P32	34	.200	B	
		Courtney, Clinton Dawson	C103	106	.251	B	
		Dyck, James Robert (3B51)	OF55	112	.213	B	
		Edwards, Henry Albert	OF21	65	.198	Chi	C
		Elliott, Robert Irving	3B45	48	+.250	NYN	Chi
		Groth, John Thomas	OF	141	.253	Det	
0	0	Habenicht, Robert Julius	P	1	.000	StLN51	C
3	7	Holloman, Alva Lee	P	22	.105	A	C
		Hunter, Gordon Wm.	SS152	154	.219	A	
		Kellert, Frank Wm.	1B1	2	.000	A	

		Kokos, Richard Jerome	OF83	107	.241	StL50	
1	5	Kretlow, Louis Henry	P	22	+.200	xChi	
		Kryhoski, Richard David	1B88	104	.278	B	
0	1	Lanier, Hubert Max	P	10	.167	xNYN	C
7	12	Larsen, Donald James (OF1)	P38	50	.284	A	
		Lenhardt, Donald Eugene (3B6)	OF77	97	.317	B	
		Lipon, John Joseph (2B1)	3B6	7	+.222	xBos	
7	12	Littlefield, Richard Bernard	P36	38	.190	B	
		Marion, Martin Whitford MGR.	3B2	3	.000	B	
		Martin, Boris Michael	C1	4	.000	Bos49	C
		Mickelson, Edward Allen	1B3	7	.133	StLN50	
		Miranda, Guillermo Perez (3B6)	SS8	17	+.167	B	N.Y.
		Moss, John Lester	C71	78	.276	B	
3	9	Paige, LeRoy	P	57	.069	B	
7	13	Pillette, Duane Xavier	P	31	.132	B	
		Pisoni, James Pete	OF	3	.083	A	
		Sievers, Roy Edward	1B76	92	.270	B	
		Stephens, Vernon Decatur	3B	46	+.321	xChi	
8	2	Stuart, Marlin Henry	P	60	.192	B	
5	4	Trucks, Virgil Oliver	P	16	+.160	Det	Chi
2	6	Turley, Robert Lee	P	10	.278	StL51	
		Upright, R. T.		9	.250	A	C
		Wertz, Victor Woodrow	OF121	128	.268	B	
0	0	White, Harold George	P	10	.000	Det	StLN
		Young, Robert George	2B	148	.255	B	

CLUB RECORD

AMERICAN LEAGUE

WASHINGTON

YEAR	TG	WON	LOST	PCT.	FINISHED	MANAGER
1901	133	61	72	.459	6	James H. Manning
1902	136	61	75	.449	6	Thomas Joseph Loftus
1903	137	43	94	.314	8(Last)	Thomas Joseph Loftus
1904	151	38	113	.251	8(Last)	Malachi Jedediah Kittredge Patrick Joseph Donovan
1905	151	64	87	.421	7	Garland Stahl
1906	150	55	95	.367	7	Garland Stahl
1907	151	49	102	.325	8(Last)	Joe Cantillon
1908	152	67	85	.441	7	Joe Cantillon
1909	152	42	110	.276	8(Last)	Joe Cantillon
1910	151	66	85	.437	7	James Robert McAleer
1911	154	64	90	.416	7	James Robert McAleer
1912	152	91	61	.599	2	Clark Calvin Griffith
1913	154	90	64	.584	2	Clark Calvin Griffith
1914	154	81	73	.526	3	Clark Calvin Griffith
1915	153	85	68	.556	4	Clark Calvin Griffith
1916	153	76	77	.497	7	Clark Calvin Griffith
1917	153	74	79	.484	5	Clark Calvin Griffith
1918	128	72	56	.563	3	Clark Calvin Griffith
1919	140	56	84	.400	7	Clark Calvin Griffith
1920	152	68	84	.447	6	Clark Calvin Griffith
1921	153	80	73	.523	4	George Florian McBride
1922	154	69	85	.448	6	Jesse Clyde Milan
1923	153	75	78	.490	4	Owen Joseph Bush
1924	154	92	62	.597	1	Stanley Raymond Harris
1925	151	96	55	.636	1	Stanley Raymond Harris
1926	150	81	69	.540	4	Stanley Raymond Harris
1927	154	85	69	.552	3	Stanley Raymond Harris
1928	154	75	79	.487	4	Stanley Raymond Harris
1929	152	71	81	.467	5	Walter Perry Johnson
1930	154	94	60	.610	2	Walter Perry Johnson
1931	154	92	62	.597	3	Walter Perry Johnson
1932	154	93	61	.604	3	Walter Perry Johnson
1933	152	99	53	.651	1	Joseph Edward Cronin
1934	152	66	86	.434	7	Joseph Edward Cronin
1935	153	67	86	.438	6	Stanley Raymond Harris
1936	153	82	71	.536	4	Stanley Raymond Harris
1937	153	73	80	.477	6	Stanley Raymond Harris
1938	151	75	76	.497	5	Stanley Raymond Harris
1939	152	65	87	.428	6	Stanley Raymond Harris
1940	154	64	90	.416	7	Stanley Raymond Harris
1941	154	70	84	.455	x6(StL)	Stanley Raymond Harris
1942	151	62	89	.411	7	Stanley Raymond Harris
1943	153	84	69	.549	2	Oswald Louis Bluege
1944	154	64	90	.416	8(Last)	Oswald Louis Bluege
1945	154	87	67	.565	2	Oswald Louis Bluege
1946	154	76	78	.494	4	Oswald Louis Bluege
1947	154	64	90	.416	7	Oswald Louis Bluege
1948	153	56	97	.366	7	Joseph Anthony Kuhel
1949	154	50	104	.324	8(Last)	Joseph Anthony Kuhel

1950	154	67	87	.435	5	Stanley Raymond Harris
1951	154	62	92	.403	7	Stanley Raymond Harris
1952	154	78	76	.506	5	Stanley Raymond Harris
1953	152	76	76	.500	5	Stanley Raymond Harris
1954	154	66	88	.429	6	Stanley Raymond Harris
1955	154	53	101	.344	8(Last)	Chas. Walter Dressen
1956	154	59	95	.383	7	Chas. Walter Dressen
1957	154	55	99	.357	8(Last)	Chas. Walter Dressen Harry Arthur Lavagetto
1958	154	61	93	.396	8(Last)	Harry Arthur Lavagetto
1959	154	63	91	.409	8(Last)	Harry Arthur Lavagetto
1960	154	73	81	.474	5	Harry Arthur Lavagetto
1961	161	61	100	.379	x9(K.C.) (Last)	James Barton Vernon
1962	161	60	101	.373	10(Last)	James Barton Vernon
1963	162	56	106	.346	10(Last)	James Barton Vernon Gilbert Raymond Hodges
1964	162	62	100	.383	9	Gilbert Raymond Hodges

CLUB TRANSFERRED TO TEXAS AFTER 1971 SEASON

YEAR	TG	WON	LOST	TIED	PCT.	FINISHED	MANAGER
1965	162	70	92	0	.432	8	GILBERT RAYMOND HODGES
1966	159	71	88	0	.447	8	GILBERT RAYMOND HODGES
1967	161	76	85	0	.472	X6 (BAL)	GILBERT RAYMOND HODGES
1968	161	65	96	0	.404	10 (LAST)	JAMES ROBERT LEMON
1969	162	86	76	0	.531	4E	THEODORE SAMUEL WILLIAMS
1970	162	70	92	0	.432	6E (LAST)	THEODORE SAMUEL WILLIAMS
1971	159	63	96	0	.396	5E	THEODORE SAMUEL WILLIAMS

WON 61
LOST 72
TG 133

AMERICAN LEAGUE

FINISHED 6th.

1901.

PCT. .459

WASHINGTON

JAMES H. MANNING.

WON	LOST	NAME	POS.	G.	BA	FROM	TO
15	22	Carrick, Wm. Martin	P	42	.156	NYN	
		Clarke, Wm. Jones	C	109	.284	BosN	
		Clingman, Wm. Frederick	SS	137	.245	K.C.	
		Coughlin, Wm. Paul	3B	137	.277	K.C.	
		Dugan, Samuel Morrison (1B31)	OF104	137	.324	K.C.	C
		Everett, Wm. L.	1B	33	.189	ChiN	C
		Farrell, John Stephen (OF60)	2B74	135	.277	K.C.	
		Foster, Clarence Francis (Pop)	OF	104	+.271	NYN	Chi
3	11	Gear, Dale Dudley (P23)	OF32	58	.236	K.C.	C
		Grady, Michael Wm. (C50)	1B59	94	.286	NYN	
		Harrison, Leo J.	OF	1	.000	A	C
		Jordan, Timothy Joseph	1B	5	+.250	A	Balt
16	16	Lee, Wyatt Arnold	P	42	.269	K.C.	
		Luskey, Chas. Melton (C3)	OF8	11	.195	A	C
9	13	Mercer, George Barclay (Winnie)	P24	50	.300	NYN	
		O'Brien, John Joseph	OF	12	+.184	K.C.	Clev
18	10	Patten, Case L.	P	31	.137	K.C.	
		Quinn, Joseph J.	2B	66	.251	CinN	C
		Waldron, Irving	OF	79	+.321	xMil	C

WON 61
LOST 75
TG 136

AMERICAN LEAGUE

FINISHED 6th.

1902.

PCT. .449

WASHINGTON

THOMAS JOSEPH LOFTUS

WON	LOST	NAME	POS.	G.	BA	FROM	TO
		Atz, Jacob Henry	2B	3	.100	A	
		Carey, George C.	1B	120	.316	BuffA00	
12	17	Carrick, Wm. Martin (OF2)	P31	33	.187	B	C
		Clarke, Wm. Jones	C73	87	.262	B	
		Coughlin, Wm. Paul (2B25 SS31)	3B65	121	.298	B	
		Delahanty, Edward James (1B12)	OF110	123	.376	PhilN	
		Donahue, Timothy Cornelius	C	3	.250	ChiN00	C
		Doyle, John Joseph (Jack) (C1 1B7 OF4)	2B68	78	.238	xNYN	
		Drill, Lewis L. (2B2 SS1 OF4)	C62	37 32	+.272 .250	A (& return)	Balt
		Ely, Frederick Wm.	SS	105	.263	Phil	C

WON	LOST	NAME	POS.	G.	BA	FROM	TO
		Keister, Wm. Hoffman (SS2 3B14 OF39)	2B40	119	.303	Balt	
4	6	Lee, Wyatt Arnold (P12)	OF94	108	.261	B	
19	18	Orth, Albert Lewis (1B1 SS1 OF13)	P38	54	.218	PhilN	
17	17	Patten, Case L. (OF3)	P36	39	.095	B	
		Ryan, James E.	OF	120	.317	ChiN00	
		Stanley, Joseph Bernard	OF	3	.333	WashN97	
9	16	Townsend, John	P	27	.261	PhilN	
0	1	Vorhees, Henry Bert (Cy)	P	1	.667	xPhilN	C
		Wolverton, Harry Sterling	3B	59	.257	PhilN	PhilN

WON 43   AMERICAN LEAGUE   FINISHED 8th (LAST)
LOST 94
TG 137   1903.   PCT. .314

WASHINGTON

THOMAS JOSEPH LOFTUS

WON	LOST	NAME	POS.	G.	BA	FROM	TO
		Carey, George C.	1B47	48	.198	B	C
		Clarke, Wm. Jones (C37)	1B88	126	.239	B	
		Coughlin, Wm. Paul	3B121	125	.251	B	
		Delahanty, Edward James	OF42	43	.338	B	C
		DeMontreville, Eugene Napoleon	2B	11	.292	BosN	C
		Drill, Lewis L.	C48	51	.252	B	
5	8	Dunkle, Edward Perks	P	14	+.105	xChi	
		Hendricks, John Calhoun	OF	32	.183	ChiN	
		Holmes, James Wm. (Ducky) (2B2 3B4)	OF14	21	+.229	Det	Chi
		Kittridge, Malachi Jedediah	C	59	.218	xBosN	
8	13	Lee, Wyatt Arnold (P23)	OF49	76	.207	B	
		Martin, Joseph Samuel (3B11 OF8)	2B17	36	+.288	A	StL
		Moran, Chas. Vincent	SS96	98	.232	A	
		McCormick, Wm. J. (Barry)	2B	62	+.225	xStL	
10	21	Orth, Albert Lewis	P37	54	.318	B	
		O'Steen, James Champ	SS	10	.195	A	
10	23	Patten, Case L.	P	35	.165	B	
		Robinson, Clyde (2B25 OF27)	SS40	103	.219	A	
		Ryan, James E.	OF	114	.245	B	C
		Selbach, Albert Carl (Kip)	OF	141	.252	Balt	
2	11	Townsend, John	P	20	.044	B	
8	18	Wilson, Howard P.	P31	32	.207	Phil	

WON 38   AMERICAN LEAGUE   FINISHED 8th (LAST)
LOST 113
TG 151   1904.   PCT. .251

WASHINGTON

MALACHI JEDEDIAH KITTREDGE   PATRICK JOSEPH DONOVAN

WON	LOST	NAME	POS.	G.	BA	FROM	TO
		Cassidy, Joseph Phillip (3B23 OF51)	SS78	152	.234	A	
		Clarke, Wm. Jones (1B28)	C52	85	.213	B	
		Coughlin, Wm. Paul	3B	64	+.261	B	Det
		Donovan, Patrick Joseph MGR.	OF122	125	.239	StLN	
		Drill, Lewis L.	C	43	+.394	B	Det
2	9	Dunkle, Edward Perks	P12	13	.143	B	C
		Herring, Silas Clarke	OF	15	.174	WashN99	C
		Hill, Hunter Benjamin	3B	77	+.229	xStL	
		Hoffman, Harry C.	OF	10	.067	A	
		Huelsman, Frank Elmer	OF	84	+.331	xStL	
2	14	Hughes, Thomas J.	P	16	+.216	xN.Y.	
5	23	Jacobson, Albert L. (Beany)	P	33	.080	A	
		Kittredge, Malachi Jedediah MGR.	C79	80	.242	B	
0	3	Mason, Adelbert Wm. (Del)	P	5	.000	A	
		Moran, Chas. Vincent	SS	61	+.209	B	StL
		Mullin, James Henry	2B	26	+.168	xPhil (return)	Phil
		McCormick, Wm. J. (Barry)	2B	112	.219	B	C
		Nill, George Chas.	2B	15	.167	A	
		O'Neill, Wm. John	OF	94	+.277	xBos	
3	4	Orth, Albert Lewis (P10)	OF19	32	+.236	B	N.Y.
15	21	Patten, Case L.	P	44	.133	B	
		Selbach, Albert Carl (Kip)	OF	48	+.264	B	Bos
		Stahl, Garland (OF23)	1B118	141	.261	Bos	
		Thoney, John	OF	17	+.300	Clev	N.Y.
5	27	Townsend, John	P36	38	.167	B	
0	3	Wilson, Howard P.	Pq	4	.111	B	C
6	9	Wolfe, Wm. O.	P	18	+.149	xN.Y.	

WON 64   AMERICAN LEAGUE   FINISHED 7th.
LOST 87
TG 151   1905.   PCT. .421

WASHINGTON

GARLAND STAHL

WON	LOST	NAME	POS.	G.	BA	FROM	TO
2	6	Adams, Reuben Alexander (Rick)	P	8	.217	A	C
		Anderson, John Joseph	OF	100	+.295	xN.Y.	
		Cassady, Harry D.	OF	10	.128	PittN	C
		Cassidy, Joseph Phillip	SS	151	.215	B	C
4	4	Falkenberg, Frederick Peter (Cy)	P	12	.125	PittN03	
3	1	Hardy, Harry	P	8	.111	A	
		Heydon, Michael Edward	C	77	.192	Chi	
		Hickman, Chas. Taylor	2B	88	+.311	xDet	
		Hill, Hunter Benjamin	3B	103	.209	B	C
		Huelsman, Frank Elmer	OF116	121	.271	B	C
16	16	Hughes, Thomas J.	P	39	.211	B	
8	9	Jacobson, Albert L. (Beany)	P	22	.159	B	
		Jones, Chas. C.	OF	142	.208	Chi	

WON	LOST	NAME	POS.	G.	BA	FROM	TO
		Kittredge, Malachi Jedediah	C76	77	.163	B	
		Knoll, Chas. E. (Punch)	OF63	79	.213	A	C
0	0	Manuel, Moxie	P	3	.250	A	
		Mullin, James Henry	2B38	49	.190	B	C
		Nill, George Chas. (2B33)	3B54	103	.182	B	
16	20	Patten, Case L.	P	43	.151	B	
		Rothgeb, Claude James	OF	6	.133	A	C
		Shaughnessy, Francis Joseph	OF	1	.000	A	
		Stahl, Garland MGR.	1B	140	.250	B	
		Stanley, Joseph Bernard	OF27	28	.261	BosN	
		Sullivan, Dennis Wm.	OF	3	.000	A	
		Tate, Hugh Henry	OF	4	.230	A	C
6	17	Townsend, John	P	34	.181	B	
9	14	Wolfe, Wm. O.	P	27	.103	B	

WON 55
LOST 95
TG 150

AMERICAN LEAGUE 1906.

FINISHED 7th.
PCT. .367

WASHINGTON

GARLAND STAHL

WON	LOST	NAME	POS.	G.	BA	FROM	TO
		Altizer, David Tilden	SS113	115	.256	A	
		Anderson, John Joseph	OF	151	.271	B	
		Cross, LaFayette Napoleon (Lave)	3B	130	.263	Phil	
		Duff, Patrick Henry	C	1	.000	A	C
0	1	Edmondston, Samuel Sherwood	P	3	.333	A	
14	20	Falkenberg, Frederick Peter (Cy)	P	40	.170	B	
0	2	Goodwin, Clyde Samuel	P	3	.250	A	C
0	3	Hardy, Harry	P	5	.167	B	C
		Heydon, Michael Edward	C	49	.159	B	
		Hickman, Chas. Taylor (1B18)	OF95	120	.284	B	
7	17	Hughes, Thomas J.	P	30	.212	B	
		Jones, Chas. C.	OF128	131	.241	B	
6	14	Kitson, Frank R.	P32	33	.244	Det	
		Kittredge, Malachi Jedediah	C	22	+.191	B	Clev
		Nill, George Chas. (2B25 OF15)	SS31	89	.235	B	
19	16	Patten, Case L.	P	38	.117	B	
		Schlafly, Harry Lawrence	2B	123	.246	ChiN02	
		Shannabrook, W. H.	3B	1	.000	A	C
9	16	Smith, Chas. E.	P	33	.184	Clev02	
		Stahl, Garland MGR.	1B136	137	.222	B	
		Stanley, Joseph Bernard	OF63	73	.163	B	
0	0	Starkell, Conrad	P	1	.000	A	C
0	2	Sudhoff, John William	P	8	.429	StL	C
		Wakefield, Howard John	C60	77	.280	Clev	
		Warner, John Joseph	C	33	+.204	xDet	
		Williams, Otto George	2B	20	.137	ChiN04	C
0	1	Wilson, Howard Wm.	P	1	.000	A	C
0	3	Wolfe, Wm. O.	P	4	.286	B	C

WON 49
LOST 102
TG 151

AMERICAN LEAGUE 1907.

FINISHED 8th (LAST)
PCT. .325

WASHINGTON

JOE CANTILLON

WON	LOST	NAME	POS.	G.	BA	FROM	TO
		Altizer, David Tilden (1B50 OF26)	SS71	147	.269	B	
		Anderson, John Joseph (OF26)	1B61	87	.288	B	
		Blankenship, Clifford Douglas	C22	37	.225	CinN05	
		Block, James John	C21	24	.140	A	
		Clymer, Otis Edgar	OF51	57	.316	xPittN	
		Cross, LaFayette Napoleon (Lave)	3B	41	.199	B	C
		*Delehanty, James Christopher Jr.	2B61	108	+.293	xStL	
0	0	Durham, Louis G.	P	2	.000	BknN04	
0	0	Edmondston, Samuel Sherwood	P	1	.000	B	C
5	18	Falkenberg, Frederick Peter (Cy)	P32	33	.140	B	
		Ganley, Robert Stephen	OF	154	.276	PittN	
3	7	Gehring, Henry	P14	20	.205	A	
4	10	Graham, Oscar M.	P20	26	.229	A	C
		Heydon, Michael Edward	C57	62	.183	B	C
0	0	Hickman, Chas. Taylor (P1 2B12)	1B30	60	+.300	B	Chi
7	13	Hughes, Thomas J.	P34	36	.238	B	
5	9	Johnson, Walter Perry	P	14	.111	A	
		Jones, Chas. C.	OF111	121	.265	B	
		Kahoe, Michael Joseph	C15	17	.191	xChiN	
		Kay, Walter B. (Big Bill)	OF	25	.333	A	C
0	1	Kitson, Frank R.	P	5	+.100	B	N.Y.
0	0	Lanford, Lewis Grover	P	2	.333	A	C
		Milan, Jesse Clyde	OF47	48	.279	A	
0	0	McDonald, John J.	P	1	.333	A	C
		Nill, George Chas. (2B18 3B12)	SS36	66	+.218	B	Clev
2	6	Oberlin, Frank Rufus	P11	12	+.059	xBos	
		O'Brien, Peter J.	2B	39	+.185	xClev	C
12	17	Patten, Case L.	P	36	.126	B	
		Perrine, John Grover (Nig) (SS18)	2B24	44	.171	A	C
		Schlafly, Harry Lawrence	2B	24	.135	B	
		Shannon, Owen Dennis Ignatius	C	4	.143	StL03	C
		Shipke, Wm. M. (Tony)	3B63	64	.196	Clev	
		Smith, Anthony (Tony)	SS	51	.187	A	
11	21	Smith, Chas. E.	P36	37	.143	B	
0	0	Tonkin, Harry Glenville	P	1	1.000	A	C
		Warner, John Joseph	C64	72	.256	B	

*Also played 47 games at 3 B.

WON 67 LOST 85 TG 152

AMERICAN LEAGUE 1908.

FINISHED 7th. PCT. .441

WASHINGTON

JOE CANTILLON

WON	LOST	NAME	POS.	G.	BA	FROM	TO
		Altizer, David Tilden	OF40	66	+.218	B	Clev
6	11	Burns, Wm. Thomas	P	23	.148	A	
4	8	Cates, Eli R.	P19	40	.186	KC00	C
		Clymer, Otis Edgar	OF82	110	.253	B	
		Dehalanty, James Christopher Jr.	2B80	82	.317	B	
		Edmundson, Robert E.	OF	26	.188	A	C
6	1	Falkenberg, Frederick Peter (Cy)	P	17	+.259	B	Clev
		Freeman, James Jeremiah (Jerry)	1B	154	.252	A	
		Ganley, Robert Stephen	OF	150	.239	B	
0	1	Gehring, Henry	P	5	.600	B	C
18	15	Hughes, Thomas J.	P	43	.195	B	
14	14	Johnson, Walter Perry	P	36	.165	B	
		Kahoe, Michael Joseph	C	17	.185	B	
6	11	Keeley, Burton Elwood	P28	31	.102	A	
		Milan, Jesse Clyde	OF122	130	.239	B	
		McBride, George Florian	SS	155	.232	StLN06	
1	3	Patten, Case L.	P	10	+.200	B	Bos
		Pickering, Oliver Dan	OF98	113	.225	StL	C
		Shipke, Wm. M. (Tony)	3B110	111	.208	B	
9	13	Smith, Chas. E.	P26	30	.123	B	
		Street, Chas. Evard (Gabby)	C128	131	.206	CinN05	
1	4	Tannehill, Jesse Niles	P	26	+.256	xBos	
		Unglaub, Robert Alexander	3B42	72	+.307	xBos	
		Warner, John Joseph	C41	51	.241	B	C
2	4	Witherup, LeRoy Foster	P	6	.167	BosN06	

WON 42 LOST 110 TG 152

AMERIAN LEAGUE 1909.

FINISHED 8th (LAST) PCT. .276

WASHINGTON

JOE CANTILLON

WON	LOST	NAME	POS.	G.	BA	FROM	TO
1	3	Altrock, Nicholas (Nick) (OF3)	P9	12	+.053	xChi	
		Blankenship, Clifford Douglas	C17	39	.250	Wash07	C
		Browne, George E.	OF101	103	.272	xChiN	
2	0	Burns, Wm. Thomas	P	6	+.222	B	Chi
		Clymer, Otis Edgar	OF41	45	.196	B	
		Conroy, Wm. Edward (Wid)	3B120	139	.244	N.Y.	
		Cravath, Clifford Clarence (Cactus)	OF	4	+1.000	xChi	
0	0	Collins, Orth Stein (P1)	OF3	8	.000	NY04	C
		Crooks, Thomas	1B	3	.286	A	
		Delahanty, James Christopher Jr.	2B	88	+.221	B	Det
		Donahue, John Augustus (Jiggs)	1B	84	+.237	xChi	C
0	2	Foreman, Wm.	P	2	.333	A	
		Freeman, James Jeremiah (Jerry)	1B	19	.167	B	C
		Ganley, Robert Stephen	OF	16	+.209	B	Phil
		Gessler, Harry Homer	OF	17	+.182	xBos	
5	19	Gray, Wm. Denton (Dolly)	P36	47	.146	A	
6	26	Groom, Robert	P44	46	.091	A	
		Hardy, John Doolittle	C	10	.167	ChiN07	
		Hemphill, Frank Vernon	OF	1	.000	Chi06	C
0	0	Hovlik, Joseph	P	3	.000	A	
4	8	Hughes, Thomas J.	P	22	.083	B	
13	25	Johnson, Walter Perry	P	40	.129	B	
		Kahoe, Michael Joseph	C	4	.125	B	C
0	0	Keeley, Burton Elwood	P	2	.500	B	C
		Kelly, Robert Brown (Speed)	3B9	17	.143	A	C
		Killefer, Wade Hampton	OF30	40	+.160	xDet	
		Lelivelt, John Frank (Jack)	OF	91	.292	A	
		Milan, Jesse Clyde	OF120	130	.200	B	
		Miller, Warren W.	OF15	26	.216	A	
		McBride, George Florian	SS	155	.234	B	
1	3	Oberlin, Frank Rufus	P	10	.500	Wash07	
0	0	Ohl, Joseph Earl	P	4	.000	A	C
2	4	Reisling, Frank Carl	P10	12	.165	BknN05	
		Schaefer, Herman A. (Germany)	2B	37	+.155	xDet	
		Sebring, James Dennison	OF	1	.000	xBkn	C
		Shipke, Wm. M. (Tony)	3B	8	.154	B	C
		Slattery, John Thomas	C	32	.214	StLN06	
2	12	Smith, Chas. E.	P	21	+.156	B	Bos
		Street, Chas. Evard (Gabby)	C	137	.211	B	
1	1	Tannehill, Jesse Niles	P	16	.167	B	
		Unglaub, Robert Alexander (2B25 OF43)	1B57	130	.264	B	
3	1	Walker, Ewart Gladstone	P	4	.154	A	
2	6	Witherup, LeRoy Foster	P	12	.053	B	C
		Yohe, Wm. F.	3B19	21	.208	A	C

WON 66 LOST 85 TG 151

AMERICAN LEAGUE 1910.

FINISHED 7th. PCT. .437

WASHINGTON

JAMES ROBERT McALEER

WON	LOST	NAME	POS.	G.	BA	FROM	TO
		Ainsmith, Edward Wilbur	C30	33	.192	A	
		Beckendorf, Henry Ward	C	37	+.146	xDet	C
		Browne, George E.	OF	7	+.182	B	Chi
		Conroy, Wm. Edward (Wid) (OF46)	3B48	103	.254	B	

WON	LOST	NAME	POS.	G.	BA	FROM	TO
		Crooks, Thomas	1B	8	.182	B	C
		Cunningham, Wm. John	2B	22	.297	A	
		Elberfeld, Norman Arthur (Kid)	3B113	127	.250	N.Y.	
0	0	Foreman, Wm.	P	1	.000	B	C
		Gessler, Harry Homer	OF144	145	.259	B	
8	19	Gray, Wm. Denton (Dolly)	P34	35	.247	B	
12	17	Groom, Robert	P	34	.119	B	
		Hardy, John Doolittle	C	7	.375	B	C
		Henry, John Park	C18	29	.149	A	
0	1	Hinrichs, Wm. Louis	P	3	.000	A	C
0	0	Hovlik, Joseph	P	1	.000	B	
25	17	Johnson, Walter Perry	P	45	.176	B	
		Killefer, Wade Hampton	2B89	106	.229	B	
		Lelivelt, John Frank (Jack)	OF89	110	.265	B	
		Milan, Jesse Clyde	OF141	142	.279	B	
0	3	Moyer, Chas. Edward	P	6	.125	A	C
		McBride, George Florian	SS	154	.230	B	
1	6	Oberlin, Frank Rufus	P	8	.053	B	C
0	1	Otey, Wm. Tilford	P	9	.385	PittN07	
		Ralston, Samuel Beryl (Doc)	OF	22	.205	A	C
9	10	Reisling, Frank Carl	P30	31	.200	B	C
		Schaefer, Herman A. (Germany) (OF26)	2B35	74	.275	B	
		Somerlott, John Wesley	1B	16	.222	A	
		Street, Chas. Evard (Gabby)	C86	89	.203	B	
		Unglaub, Robert Alexander	1B123	124	.234	B	C
11	11	Walker, Ewart Gladstone	P	29	.130	B	

WON 64 — AMERICAN LEAGUE — FINISHED 7th.
LOST 90
TG 154 — 1911. — PCT. .416

WASHINGTON

JAMES ROBERT McALEER

WON	LOST	NAME	POS.	G.	BA	FROM	TO
		Ainsmith, Edward Wilbur	C47	61	.222	B	
3	5	Becker, Chas. S.	P	11	.227	A	
2	3	Cashion, Jay Carl	P	21	.324	A	
		Conroy, Wm. Edward (Wid) (OF15)	3B85	106	.232	B	C
		Conway, Chas. Connell	OF	2	.333	A	C
		Cunningham, Wm. John	2B93	94	.190	B	
		Elberfeld, Norman Arthur (Kid) (3B52)	2B68	127	.272	B	
		Gessler, Harry Homer	OF126	128	.282	B	
2	12	Gray, Wm. Denton (Dolly)	P	29	.227	B	C
13	17	Groom, Robert	P	38	.134	B	
		Henry, John Park (1B30)	C51	85	.203	B	
0	0	Herrell, Walter W.	P	1	.000	A	C
11	17	Hughes, Thomas J.	P	34	.185	Wash09	
23	15	Johnson, Walter Perry	P40	42	.234	B	
		Lelivelt, John Frank (Jack)	OF49	72	.320	B	
		Long, Thomas Augustus	OF	14	.208	A	
		Milan, Jesse Clyde	OF	154	.315	B	
		Miller, Warren W.	OF	21	.148	Wash09	C
		Morgan, Raymond Caryll	3B	25	.213	A	
		McBride, George Florian	SS	154	.236	B	
2	4	Otey, Wm. Tilford	P	12	.059	B	C
		Schaefer, Herman A. (Germany)	1B107	125	.334	B	
0	4	Sherry, Fred Peter	P	10	.158	A	C
		Smith, Louis O.		1	.000	ChiN06	C
		Somerlott, John Wesley	1B	13	.175	B	C
		Street, Chas. Evard (Gabby)	C71	72	.222	B	
		Walker, Clarence Wm.	OF98	09	.278	A	
8	13	Walker, Ewart Gladstone	P32	34	.303	B	

WON 91 — AMERICAN LEAGUE — FINISHED 2nd.
LOST 61
TG 152 — 1912. — PCT. .599

WASHINGTON

CLARK CALVIN GRIFFITH

WON	LOST	NAME	POS.	G.	BA	FROM	TO
		Agler, Joseph Abram	1B	2	.000	A	
		Ainsmith, Edward Wilbur	C	60	.226	B	
0	0	Ikers, Albert Earl (Jerry)	P	5	.250	A	C
0	0	Altrock, Nicholas (Nick)	P	1	.000	Wash09	
0	0	Becker, Chas. S.	P	4	.667	B	C
0	0	Boehling, John Joseph	P	3	.000	A	
11	6	Cashion, Jay Carl	P33	42	.214	B	
		Cunningham, Wm. John	2B	8	.185	B	C
1	5	Engel, Joseph Wm.	P	15	.059	A	
		Flynn, John Anthony	1B	20	.169	PittN	C
		Foster, Edward Cunningham	3B	154	.285	NY10	
0	0	Gallia, Melvin Allys (Bert)	P	2	.000	A	
		Gandil, Chas. Arnold (Chick)	1B	117	.305	Chi10	
0	0	Griffith, Clark Calvin MGR.	P	1	.000	CinN	
24	13	Groom, Robert	P	42	.117	B	
		Henry, John Park	C	63	.194	B	
0	0	Herring, Herbert Lee	P	1	.000	A	C
		Howard, David Austin		1	.000	A	
13	10	Hughes, Thomas J.	P	30	.194	B	
32	12	Johnson, Walter Perry	P	53	.264	B	
		Kenworthy, Wm. Jennings	OF	12	.289	A	
		Knight, John Wesley (Jack)	2B26	32	.161	N.Y.	
		LaPorte, Frank B.	2B	39	+.316	xStL	
		Long, Thomas Augustus	OF	1	.000	B	
		Milan, Jesse Clyde	OF	154	.306	B	
		Moeller, Daniel Edward	OF	132	.276	PittN08	
		Moran, Roy Ellis	OF	7	.077	A	C
		Morgan, Raymond Caryll	2B76	80	.238	B	
1	0	Musser, Paul	P	8	.000	A	
		McBride, George Florian	SS	152	.226	B	
2	6	Pelty, Barney	P	11	+.200	xStL	C
		Roach, Wilbur C.	SS	2	.500	N.Y.	
		Ryan, John Bennett (Jack)	3B	1	.000	StLN03	
		Schaefer, Herman A. (Germany) (1B15 2B16)	OF19	60	.247	B	

WON	LOST	NAME	POS.	G.	BA	FROM	TO
0	0	Schegg, (Lefty)	P	2	.000	A	C
		Shanks, Howard Samuel	OF	115	.236	A	
4	3	Vaughn, James Leslie (Big Jim)	P	9	+.182	xN.Y.	
		Walker, Clarence Wm.	OF33	36	.273	B	
3	6	Walker, Ewart Gladstone	P	9	.133	B	C
0	0	White, Stephen Vincent	P	1	.000	A	BosN
		Williams, Alva Mitchel	C	56	.318	Bos	

WON 90 — AMERICAN LEAGUE — FINISHED 2nd.
LOST 64
TG 154 — 1913. — PCT. .584

WASHINGTON

CLARK CALVIN GRIFFITH

WON	LOST	NAME	POS.	G.	BA	FROM	TO
		Acosta, Balmadero Merito	OF	12	.250	A	
		Ainsmith, Edward Wilbur	C	77	.210	B	
0	0	Altrock, Nicholas (Nick)	P	4	.000	B	
2	1	Ayres, Yancey Wyatt	P	4	.000	A	
0	0	Bentley, John Needles	P	3	.000	A	
17	7	Boehling, John Joseph	P	34	.227	B	
		Calvo, Jacinto	OF11	16	.242	A	
1	2	Cashion, Jay Carl (OF6)	P3	9	.294	B	
0	0	Dawson, Rexford Paul	P	1	.000	A	C
0	0	Drohan, Thomas F.	P	2	.000	A	C
8	9	Engel, Joseph Wm.	P	30	.061	B	
		Foster, Edward Cunningham	3B105	106	.247	B	
1	5	Gallia, Melvin Allys (Bert)	P	23	.087	B	
		Gandil, Chas.Arnold (Chick)	1B145	147	.318	B	
0	0	Gedeon, Elmer Joseph (Pl)	OF16	26	.188	A	
0	0	Griffith, Clark Calvin MGR.	P	1	1.000	B	
15	16	Groom, Robert	P	36	.163	B	
1	0	Harper, Harry Clayton	P	4	.250	A	
0	0	Hedgepeth, Harry Malcolm	P	1	.000	A	C
		Henry, John Park	C	96	.226	B	
4	12	Hughes, Thomas J.	P	28	.111	B	C
36	7	Johnson, Walter Perry	P	51	.263	B	
		LaPorte, Frank B. (2B14 OF11)	3B44	80	.250	B	
2	0	Love, Elmer Haughton	P	5	.200	A	
		Milan, Jesse Clyde	OF	154	.299	B	
		Moeller, Daniel Edward	OF	153	.236	B	
		Morgan, Raymond Carryll	2B133	137	.272	B	
		Morley, Wm. M.	2B	2	.000	A	C
2	4	Mullin, George Joseph	P	12	+.190	xDet	
		McBride, George Florian	SS	150	.214	B	
		Ryan, John Bennett (Jack)	C	1	.000	B	C
0	0	Schaefer, Herman A. (Germany) (Pl)	2B16	52	.320	B	
		Shanks, Howard Samuel	OF	109	.254	B	
0	1	Shaw, James Aloysius	P	2	.000	A	
		Spencer, L. Benjamin	OF	8	.300	A	C

WON	LOST	NAME	POS.	G.	BA	FROM	TO
		Williams, Alva Mitchel	C16	64	.283	B	
1	0	Williams, David Carter (Mutt)	P	1	.500	A	
0	0	Wilson, John Nicodemus	P	3	.000	A	C

WON 81 — AMERICAN LEAGUE — FINISHED 3rd.
LOST 73
TG 154 — 1914. — PCT. .526

WASHINGTON

CLARK CALVIN GRIFFITH

WON	LOST	NAME	POS.	G.	BA	FROM	TO
		Acosta, Balmadero Merito	OF22	38	.257	B	
		Ainsmith, Edward Wilbur	C51	58	.225	B	
0	0	Altrock, Nicholas (Nick)	P	1	.000	B	
12	16	Ayres, Yancey Wyatt	P	45	.169	B	
0	0	Barton, Carroll R.	P	1	.000	A	C
0	0	Barron, Frank John	P	1	.000	A	C
5	7	Bentley, John Needles	P	23	.275	B	
12	8	Boehling, John Joseph	P	27	.239	B	
0	1	Cashion, J. Carl	P	2	.000	B	C
7	5	Engel, Joseph Wm.	P	30	.111	B	
		Foster, Edward Cunningham	3B	156	.282	B	
0	0	Gallia, Melvin Allys (Bert)	P	2	.000	B	
		Gandil, Chas. Arnold (Chick)	1B	145	.259	B	
		Gedeon, Elmer Joseph	OF	4	.000	B	
0	0	Griffith, Clark Calvin MGR.	P	1	1.000	B	
2	1	Harper, Harry Clayton	P	22	.250	B	
		Henry, John Park	C	91	.169	B	
28	18	Johnson, Walter Perry	P50	54	.220	B	
		Meusel, Emil Frederick (Irish)	OF	1	.000	A	
		Milan, Jesse Clyde	OF113	115	.295	B	
		Mitchell, Michael Francis (Mike)	OF53	55	.285	xPittN	C
		Moeller, Daniel Edward	OF150	151	.250	B	
		Morgan, Raymond Caryll	2B146	147	.257	B	
		McBride, George Florian	SS	156	.203	B	
		Neff, Douglas Wm.	SS	3	.000	A	
		Pick, Chas. Thomas	OF	10	.347	A	
		Schaefer, Herman A.(Germany)	2B2	25	.241	B	
		Shanks, Howard Samuel	OF139	143	.224	B	
15	17	Shaw, James Aloysius	P	45	.119	B	
		Smith, Wallace H.	2B	45	.196	StLN12	C
0	0	Stevens, James Arthur	P	2	.000	A	C
		Williams, Alva Mitchel	C44	81	.278	B	
0	0	Williams, David Carter (Mutt)	P	5	.000	B	C
		Wilson, Thomas C.	C	1	.000	A	C

WON 85 — AMERICAN LEAGUE — FINISHED 4th.
LOST 68
TG 153 — 1915. — PCT. .556

WASHINGTON

CLARK CALVIN GRIFFITH

WON	LOST	NAME	POS.	G.	BA	FROM	TO
		Acosta, Balmadero Merito	OF53	72	.209	B	
		Ainsmith, Edward Wilbur	C42	47	.200	B	
0	0	Altrock, Nicholas (Nick)	P	1	.000	B	
15	9	Ayres, Yancey Wyatt	P	40	.190	B	
		Barber, Samuel Turner	OF19	20	.302	A	
0	2	Bentley, John Needles	P	4	.000	B	
13	13	Boehling, John Joseph	P40	41	.173	B	
		Connolly, Thomas Francis	3B24	50	.184	A	C
		(OF19)					
2	1	Dumont, George Henry	P	6	.166	A	
1	3	Engel, Joseph Wm.	P	11	.000	B	
		Foster, Edward Cunningham	3B79	154	.275	B	
		(2B75)					
16	10	Gallia, Melvin Allys (Bert)	P	43	.165	B	
		Gandil, Chas. Arnold (Chick)	1B134	136	.291	B	
5	4	Harper, Harry Clayton	P	19	.000	B	
		Henry, John Park	C94	95	.220	B	
0	1	Hopper, Wm. Booth	P	13	.200	StLN	C
		Jamieson, Chas. Devine	OF	17	.279	A	
27	13	Johnson, Walter Perry	P49	64	.231	B	
		Judge, Joseph Ignatius Jr.	1B	12	.353	A	
		Kopp, Merlin H.	OF	16	.250	A	
0	0	Mayer, Samuel Franklin	OF9	11	.231	A	C
		(P1 1B2)					
		Milan, Horace Robert	OF	10	.375	A	
		Milan, Jesse Clyde	OF151	153	.288	B	
		Moeller, Daniel Edward	OF116	118	.226	B	
		Morgan, Raymond Caryll	2B57	62	.233	B	
		McBride, George Florian	SS	146	.204	B	
		Neff, Douglas Wm.	3B8	30	.167	B	C
		(2B7 SS5)					
		Pick, Chas. Thomas		3	.000	B	
1	0	Rice, Edgar Chas. (Sam)	P	4	.375	A	
		Rondeau, Henri Joseph	OF	14	.154	Det13	
		Sawyer, Carl Everett	2B	10	.117	A	
		Shanks, Howard Samuel	OF80	141	.250	B	
		(3B49)					
5	12	Shaw, James Aloysius	P	25	.233	B	
		Williams, Alva Mitchel	C40	91	.244	B	
		(1B15)					

WON 76 AMERICAN LEAGUE FINISHED 7th.
LOST 77
TG 153 1916. PCT. .497

WASHINGTON

CLARK CALVIN GRIFFITH

WON	LOST	NAME	POS.	G.	BA	FROM	TO
		Acosta, Balmadero Merito	OF	5	.125	B	
		Ainsmith, Edward Wilbur	C46	51	.170	B	
5	9	Ayres, Yancey Wyatt	P	43	.140	B	
		Barber, Samuel Turner	OF	15	.212	B	
0	0	Bentley, John Needles	P	2	.000	B	
9	10	Boehling, John Joseph	P	28	+.163	B	Clev
0	1	Craft, Maurice M.	P	3	.000	A	
2	2	Dumont, George Henry	P	17	.071	B	
		Foster, Edward Cunningham	3B84	158	.253	B	
		(2B72)					
17	13	Gallia, Melvin Allys (Bert)	P	49	.194	B	
		Gharrity, Edward Patrick	C16	39	.228	A	
		(1B15)					
0	0	Goodwin, Marvin Mardo	P	3	.000	A	
15	10	Harper, Harry Clayton	P	36	.207	B	
		Henry, John Park	C116	117	.249	B	
0	0	Jamieson, Chas. Devine	OF41	64	.248	B	
		(P1)					
25	20	Johnson, Walter Perry	P50	59	.234	B	
		Judge, Joseph Ignatius Jr.	1B	103	.220	B	
		Leonard, Joseph Howard	3B	42	+.274	xClev	
		Menosky, Michael Wm.	OF	11	.162	PittF	
		Milan, Jesse Clyde	OF149	150	.273	B	
		Moeller, Daniel Edward	OF	78	+.245	B	Clev
		Morgan, Raymond Caryll	2B82	99	.267	B	
		McBride, George Florian	SS	139	.227	B	
0	1	Rice, Edgar Chas. (Sam)	OF46	58	.299	B	
		(P1)					
		Rondeau, Henri Joseph	OF48	50	.222	B	C
		Sawyer, Carl Everett	2B	16	.194	B	C
		Shanks, Howard Samuel	OF88	140	.253	B	
		(3B31)					
3	8	Shaw, James Aloysius	P	26	.156	B	
		Smith, Elmer John	OF	45	+.214	xClev	
0	3	Thomas, Claude Alfred	P	7	.100	A	C
		Williams, Alva Mitchel	1B34	76	.267	B	
		(C23)					

WON 74 AMERICAN LEAGUE FINISHED 5th.
LOST 79
TG 153 1917. PCT. .484

WASHINGTON

CLARK CALVIN GRIFFITH

WON	LOST	NAME	POS.	G.	BA	FROM	TO
		Ainsmith, Edward Wilbur	C119	125	.191	B	
11	10	Ayres, Yancey Wyatt	P	40	.206	B	
0	0	Craft, Maurice M.	P	8	.500	B	
		Crane, Samuel Byren	SS	32	.179	Phil	
5	14	Dumont, George Henry	P	37	.035	B	
		Foster, Edward Cunningham	3B86	143	.235	B	
		(2B57)					
9	13	Gallia, Melvin Allys (Bert)	P42	44	.209	B	
		Gharrity, Edward Patrick	1B46	76	.284	B	
11	12	Harper, Harry Clayton	P	31	.117	B	
		Henry, John Park	C59	65	.190	B	
0	0	Jamieson, Chas. Devine (P1)	OF9	20	+.171	B	Phil

WON	LOST	NAME	POS.	G.	BA	FROM	TO
23	16	Johnson, Walter Perry	P48	57	.254	B	
		Judge, Joseph Ignatius Jr.	1B100	102	.285	B	
		Leonard, Joseph Howard (1B20)	3B67	99	.192	B	
		Menosky, Michael Wm.	OF94	114	.258	B	
		Milan, Horace Robert	OF23	31	.288	Wash15	C
		Milan, Jesse Clyde	OF153	155	.294	B	
		Morgan, Raymond Caryll	2B95	101	.266	B	
		Murray, Wm. Allenwood	2B5	8	.143	A	C
		McBride, George Florian	SS41	50	.192	B	
		Rice, Edgar Chas. (Sam)	OF	155	.302	B	
		Shanks, Howard Samuel (OF26)	SS90	126	.202	B	
15	14	Shaw, James Aloysius	P	47	.154	B	
		Smith, Elmer John	OF	35	+.222	B	Clev
0	0	Waldbauer, Albert Chas.	P	2	.100	A	C

WON 72 AMERICAN LEAGUE FINISHED 3rd.
LOST 56
TG 128 1918. PCT. .563

WASHINGTON

CLARK CALVIN GRIFFITH

WON	LOST	NAME	POS.	G.	BA	FROM	TO
		Acosta, Balmadero Merito	OF	3	+.000	Wash16	Phil
		Ainsmith, Edward Wilbur	C89	96	.212	B	
1	2	Altrock, Nicholas (Nick)	P5	6	.125	Wash15	
10	12	Ayres, Yancey Wyatt	P	40	.152	B	
		Berman, Robert Leon	C	2	.000	A	C
0	0	Brennan, Addison Foster (Ad)	P	2	+.000	ChiF15	Clev
0	0	Buckeye, Garland Maiers	P	1	.000	A	
		Casey, Joseph Felix	C	8	.235	Det11	C
0	0	Craft, Maurice M.	P	3	.000	B	
1	1	Dumont, George Henry	P	4	.333	B	
		Foster, Edward Cunningham	3B127	129	.283	B	
		Gharrity, Edward Patrick	C	4	.250	B	
1	0	Hanson, Raymond	P	5	.000	A	C
11	10	Harper, Harry Clayton	P35	36	.134	B	
2	1	Hovlik, Edward C.	P	8	.125	A	
23	13	Johnson, Walter Perry	P39	65	.267	B	
		Judge, Joseph Ignatius Jr.	1B	130	.261	B	
		Lavan, John Leonard	SS	117	.278	StL	
5	3	Matteson, Henry Edson	P	14	.105	PhilN14	C
		Milan, Jesse Clyde	OF124	128	.290	B	
		Morgan, Raymond Caryll	2B80	88	.233	B	C
		McBride, George Florian	SS14	18	.132	B	
		Picinich, Valentine John (Val)	C46	47	.230	Phil	
1	0	Reese, Stanley Milton	P	2	.000	A	C
		Rice, Edgar Chas. (Sam)	OF	7	.348	B	
		Schulte, Frank	OF75	93	.288	PhilN	C
		Shanks, Howard Samuel (2B47)	OF63	120	.257	B	
16	12	Shaw, James Aloysius	P	41	.132	B	
		Shotton, Burton Edwin	OF122	126	.261	StL	
1	2	Yingling, Earl Hershey	P	8	.466	CinN14	C

WON 56 AMERICAN LEAGUE FINISHED 7th.
LOST 84
TG 140 1919. PCT. .400

WASHINGTON

CLARK CALVIN GRIFFITH

WON	LOST	NAME	POS.	G.	BA	FROM	TO
		Agnew, Samuel Lester	C36	42	.235	Bos	C
0	0	Altrock, Nicholas (Nick)	P	1	.000	B	
2	6	Ayres, Yancey Wyatt	P	12	+.385	B	Det
		Baker, Jesse	SS	1	.000	A	C
3	0	Courtney, Henry Seymour	P	4	.200	A	
0	3	Craft, Maurice M.	P	16	.111	B	C
		Davidson, Claude Boucher	3B	2	.375	Phil	C
		Davis, Isaac Marion	SS	7	.000	A	
		Ellerbe, Francis Rogers	SS	28	.276	A	
5	10	Erickson, Eric George	P	20	+.146	xDet	
0	0	Fisher, Clarence Henry	P	2	.000	A	
		Foster, Edward Cunningham	3B115	120	.263	B	
		Gharrity, Edward Patrick (OF33)	C60	111	.271	B	
1	1	Gill, Edward James	P	16	.000	A	C
		Grover, Roy Arthur	2B	24	+.187	xPhil	C
6	21	Harper, Harry Clayton	P	35	.169	B	
		Harris, Stanley Raymond (Bucky)	2B	8	.214	A	
0	0	Hovlik, Edward C.	P	3	.000	B	C
		Janvrin, Harold Chandler	2B56	61	.178	Bos17	StLN
20	14	Johnson, Walter Perry	P39	56	.192	B	
0	0	Jordan, Raymond Willis	P	1	.000	Chi12	C
		Judge, Joseph Ignatius Jr.	1B133	135	.288	B	
		Kelliher, Frank Mortimer		1	.000	A	C
		Leonard, Joseph Howard (3B25)	2B26	71	.258	Wash17	
		Menosky, Michael Wm.	OF103	116	.287	Wash17	
		Milan, Jesse Clyde	OF86	88	.287	B	
		Murphy, Robert R.	OF73	79	.262	BosN	C
		McBride, George Florian	SS	15	.200	B	
		Picinich, Valentine John (Val)	C69	80	.274	B	
		Rice, Edgar Chas. (Sam)	OF	141	.321	B	
0	2	Robertson, Richard J.	P	7	.000	BknN	C
2	0	Schacht, Alexander	P	2	.000	A	
		Shanks, Howard Samuel (2B34)	SS94	135	.248	B	
16	17	Shaw, James Aloysius	P	45	.160	B	
		Silva, Daniel James	3B	1	.250	A	C
0	1	Snyder, Wm. Nichols	P	2	.000	A	
0	3	Thompson, Harry	P	18	+.281	A	Phil
		Twombly, George Frederick	OF	1	.000	BosN17	C

WON	LOST	NAME	POS.	G.	BA	FROM	TO
0	1	Whitehouse, Chas. Evis	P	6	.000	NwkF15	C
1	5	Zachary, Jonathan Thompson Walton (Tom)	P	17	.333	Phil	

WON 68 — LOST 84 — TG 152

AMERICAN LEAGUE — 1920. — FINISHED 6th. — PCT. .447

WASHINGTON

CLARK CALVIN GRIFFITH

WON	LOST	NAME	POS.	G.	BA	FROM	TO
5	4	Acosta, Jose	P	17	.240	A	
1	0	Biemiller, Harry Lee	P	5	.000	A	
0	2	Bono, Adlai Wendell	P	4	.333	A	C
		Bowman, Elmari Wilhelm		2	.000	A	C
		Brower, Frank Willard	OF20	36	.311	A	
		Calvo, Jacinto	OF	17	.043	Wash13	
0	0	Carlson, Leon Alton	P	3	.167	A	C
0	0	Conway, Jerome Patrick	P	1	.000	A	C
8	11	Courtney, Henry Seymour	P	37	.232	B	
		Ellerbe, Francis Rogers (SS19)	3B75	101	.292	B	
0	0	Engel, Joseph Wm.	P	1	.000	Clev	C
12	16	Erickson, Eric George	P	39	.277	B	
0	1	Fisher, Clarence Henry	P	2	.000	B	C
		Gharrity, Edward Patrick (1B3)	C120	131	..245	B	C
0	0	Gleason, Joseph Paul	P	2	.000	A	
		Harris, Stanley Raymond (Bucky)	2B135	137	.300	B	
		Hollahan, Wm. Chas.	3B	3	.167	A	C
		Johnson, Edwin Cyril (1B2)	OF2	4	.230	A	C
8	10	Johnson, Walter Perry	P31	35	.261	B	
		Judge, Joseph Ignatius Jr.	1B124	126	.333	B	
		LaMotte, Robert Eugene	SS1	4	.000	A	
		Milan, Jesse Clyde	OF123	126	.322	B	
		McBride, George Florian	SS	14	.219	B	
		O'Neill, James Leo	SS80	86	.289	A	
		O'Rourke, Francis James	SS	14	.277	BknN18	
		Picinich, Valentine John (Val)	C45	48	.203	B	
		Prothro, James Thomson (Doc)	SS2	6	.385	A	
		Rice, Edgar Chas. (Sam)	OF	153	.338	B	
		Roth, Robert Frank	OF128	138	.290	Bos	
6	4	Schacht, Alexander	P	22	.192	B	
		Shanks, Howard Samuel (1B1 OF35)	3B63	128	.268	B	
		Shannon, Maurice Joseph	SS	63	+.288	Bos	Phil
11	18	Shaw, James Aloysius	P	38	.189	B	
0	1	Shirey, Clair Lee	P	2	.000	A	C
2	1	Snyder, Wm. Nichols	P	16	.316	B	C
		Thomas, Frederick Harvey	3B	2	+.000	xPhil	C
		Torres, Ricardo J. (1B7)	C9	16	.333	A	
		Watt, Albert Bailey	2B	1	1.000	A	C

WON	LOST	NAME	POS.	G.	BA	FROM	TO
15	16	Zachary, Jonathan Thompson Walton (Tom)	P44	51	.261	B	
		Leonard, Joseph Howard		1	.000	B	C

WON 80 — LOST 73 — TG 153

AMERICAN LEAGUE — 1921. — FINISHED 4th. — PCT. .523

WASHINGTON

GEORGE FLORIAN Mc BRIDE

WON	LOST	NAME	POS.	G.	BA	FROM	TO
5	4	Acosta, Jose	P	33	.067	B	
0	0	Bird, James Edwin	P	1	.000	A	C
		Brottem, Anton Christian	C	4	.147	StLN18	PittN
		Brower, Frank Willard	OF47	83	.261	B	
		Bush, Owen Joseph (Owney)	SS	23	+.238	xDet	
6	9	Courtney, Henry Seymour	P30	32	.298	B	
		Ellerbe, Francis Rogers	3B	10	+.200	B	StL
8	10	Erickson, Eric George	P	32	.150	B	
		Foss, George Dueward	3B	4	.000	A	C
0	0	Gaines, Willard Roland	P	4	.000	A	C
		Gharrity, Edward Patrick	C115	121	.310	B	
		Goslin, Leon Allen (Goose)	OF	14	.260	A	
		Harris, Stanley Raymond (Bucky)	2B	154	.289	B	
17	14	Johnson, Walter Perry	P35	38	.270	B	
		Judge, Joseph Ignatius Jr.	1B152	153	.301	B	
		LaMotte, Robert Eugene	SS12	16	.195	B	
		Lewis, George Edward (Duffy)	OF	27	.186	N.Y.	C
		Milan, Jesse Clyde	OF98	112	.288	B	
		Miller, Edmund John (Bing)	OF109	114	.288	A	
0	0	Miller, Ralph Henry	P	1	.000	A	C
18	14	Mogridge, George Anthony	P	38	.153	N.Y.	
0	0	McIlree, Vance Elmer	P	1	.000	A	C
		O'Rourke, Francis James	SS122	123	.234	B	
1	0	Phillips, Thomas Gerald	P	1	.000	Clev19	
		Picinich, Valentine John (Val)	C	45	.277	B	
		Rice, Edgar Chas. (Sam)	OF141	143	.330	B	
6	6	Schacht, Alexander	P29	30	.217	B	C
		Shanks, Howard Samuel	3B	154	.302	B	
1	0	Shaw, James Aloysius	P	15	.167	B	C
		Smith, Earl Leonard	OF	59	+.217	xStL	
		Torres, Ricardo J.	C	2	.333	B	
0	0	Woodward, Frank Russell	P	3	.333	StLN19	
18	16	Zachary, Jonathan Thompson Walton (Tom)	P	38	.257	B	

WON 69 — LOST 85 — TG 154

AMERICAN LEAGUE — 1922. — FINISHED 6th. — PCT. .448

WASHINGTON

JESSE CLYDE MILAN

WON	LOST	NAME	POS.	G.	BA	FROM	TO
		Bluege, Oswald Louis (Ossie)	3B54	84	.283	B	
4	6	Brillheart, James Benson	P	31	.083	A	
		Brower, Frank Willard	OF121	139	.293	B	
		Bush, Owen Joseph (Owney)	3B37	41	.238	B	
0	1	Courtney, Henry Seymour	P	5	+.000	B	Chi
4	12	Erickson, Eric George	P	30	.133	B	C
7	18	Francis, Raymond James	P	39	.167	A	
		Gharrity, Edward Patrick	C85	96	.256	B	
2	2	Gleason, Joseph Paul	P	8	.143	Wash20	C
		Goebel, Edwin	OF15	37	.271	A	C
		Goslin, Leon Allen (Goose)	OF92	101	.324	B	
		Harris, Stanley Raymond (Bucky)	2B	154	.269	B	
15	16	Johnson, Walter Perry	P41	43	.204	B	
		Judge, Joseph Ignatius Jr.	1B	148	.295	B	
		LaMotte, Robert Eugene	3B62	68	.252	B	
		Lapan, Peter Nelson	C	11	.324	A	
		Milan, Jesse Clyde MGR.	OF11	42	.230	B	C
18	13	Mogridge, George Anthony	P	34	.244	B	
0	0	McGrew, Walter Howard	P	1	.000	A	
		McNamara, George Francis	OF	3	.272	A	C
		Peckinpaugh, Roger Thorpe	SS	147	.254	N.Y.	
3	7	Phillips, Thomas Gerald	P	17	.150	B	C
		Picinich, Valentine John (Val)	C	76	.229	B	
		Rice, Edgar Chas. (Sam)	OF	154	.295	B	
		Shanks, Howard Samuel (OF27)	3B54	84	.283	B	
		Smith, Earl Leonard	OF49	65	.259	B	C
		Torres, Ricardo J.	C	4	.000	B	C
0	0	Turk, Lucas Newton	P	5	.250	A	C
1	0	Warmoth, Wallace Walter (Cy)	P	5	.147	StLN16	
0	0	Woodward, Frank Russell	P	1	.000	B	
0	0	Youngblood, Albert Clyde	P	2	.000	A	C
15	10	Zachary, Jonathan Thompson Walton (Tom)	P	32	.296	B	

WON 75 AMERICAN LEAGUE FINISHED 4th.
LOST 78
TG 153 1923. PCT. .490

WASHINGTON

OWEN JOSEPH BUSH

WON	LOST	NAME	POS.	G.	BA	FROM	TO
		Bluege, Oswald Louis (Ossie)	3B107	109	.245	B	
0	1	Brillheart, James Benson	P	12	.000	B	
		Bush, Owen Joseph (Owney) MGR. (2B2)	3B5	10	.409	B	
		Conroy, Wm. Frederick	3B	18	.133	A	C
		Evans, Joseph Patton (3B21)	OF72	106	.263	Clev	
		Fisher, George Aloys	OF	13	.240	A	
0	1	Friday, Grier Wm.	P	7	.222	A	C
		Gharrity, Edward Patrick (1B33)	C35	93	.207	B	
		Goslin, Leon Allen (Goose)	OF149	150	.300	B	
		Hargrave, Wm. McKinley	C	33	.288	A	
		Harris, Stanley Raymond (Bucky)	2B144	145	.282	B	
3	7	Hollingsworth, John Burnett	P	17	.090	PittN	
17	12	Johnson, Walter Perry	P	42	.194	B	
		Judge, Joseph Ignatius Jr.	1B112	113	.314	B	
		Lapan, Peter Nelson	C	2	.000	B	C
		Leibold, Harry Loran (Nemo)	OF	96	+.305	xBos	
4	0	Marberry, Frederick (Firpo)	P	11	.143	A	
2	4	Mitchell, Monroe Barr	P	10	.250	A	C
13	13	Mogridge, George Anthony	P	33	.227	B	
0	1	McGrew, Walter Howard	P	3	.000	B	
		Murray, Robert Hayes	3B	10	.162	A	C
		O'Neill, James Leo (SS1)	2B3	23	.273	Wash20	C
		Peckinpaugh, Roger Thorpe	SS	154	.264	B	
0	0	Potter, Robert H.	P	1	.000	A	C
		Propst, Wm. Jacob (Jake)		1	.000	A	C
		Prothro, James Thomson (Doc)	3B	6	.250	Wash20	
		Rice, Edgar Chas. (Sam)	OF147	148	.316	B	
		Riley, James Norman	1B	2	.000	StL21	C
0	1	Roe, Frederick Clay	P	1	.000	A	C
		Ruel, Herold Dominic (Muddy)	C133	136	.316	Bos	
10	7	Russell, Allen E.	P52	54	.200	Bos	
0	0	Schemanske, Frederick George	P	2	1.000	A	C
0	1	Sedgewick, Henry Kenneth	P	5	.000	PhilN21	C
		Smith, Carr E.	OF	5	.111	A	
		Wade, Richard Frank	OF19	33	.232	A	C
7	4	Warmoth, Wallace Walter (Cy)	P	21	.222	B	C
0	0	Wingfield, Frederick Davis	P	1	.000	A	
10	16	Zachary, Jonathan Thompson Walton (Tom)	P	35	.193	B	
9	10	Zahniser, Paul Vernon	P	33	.096	A	

WON 92 AMERICAN LEAGUE FINISHED 1st.
LOST 62
TG 154 1924. PCT. .597

WASHINGTON

STANLEY RAYMOND HARRIS

WON	LOST	NAME	POS.	G.	BA	FROM	TO
0	0	Altrock, Nicholas (Nick)	P	1	1.000	Wash19	
		Bluege, Oswalk Louis (Ossie)	3B102	117	.281	B	
		East, Carlton W.	OF	2	.333	StL15	C
		Fisher, George Aloys	OF11	15	.219	B	
		Gagnon, Harold Dennis	SS	4	.200	Det22	C
		Goslin, Leon Allen (Goose)	OF	154	.344	B	
		Griffith, Bert Joseph	OF	6	.111	BknN	C

WON	LOST	NAME	POS.	G.	BA	FROM	TO
		Hargrave, Wm. McKinley	C	24	.152	B	
		Harris, Stanley Raymond (Bucky) MGR.	2B	143	.268	B	
23	7	Johnson, Walter Perry	P38	39	.283	B	
		Judge, Joseph Ignatius Jr.	1B	140	.324	B	
		Lefler, Wade Hampton	OF	5	.625	xBosN	C
		Liebold, Harry Loran (Nemo)	OF70	84	.293	B	
11	12	Marberry, Frederick (Firpo)	P	50	.136	B	
6	8	Martina, Joseph John	P24	25	.326	A	C
		Matthews, Wid Curry	OF44	53	.302	Phil	
		Miller, Ralph Joseph	2B	9	.133	PhilN21	C
16	11	Mogridge, George Anthony	P	30	.176	B	
0	1	McGrew, Walter Howard	P	6	.000	B	C
		McNeely, George Earl	OF	43	.330	A	
9	5	Ogden, Warren Harvey (Curly)	P	14	+.295	xPhil	
		Peckinpaugh, Roger Thorpe	SS	155	.272	B	
		Prothro, James Thomson (Doc)	3B45	46	.333	B	
		Rice, Edgar Chas. (Sam)	OF	154	.334	B	
		Richbourg, Lancelot Clayton	OF	15	.281	PhilN21	
		Ruel, Herold Dominic (Muddy)	C147	149	.283	B	
5	1	Russell, Allen E.	P	37	.278	B	
		Shirley, Ernest Raeford (Mule)	1B	30	.234	A	
		Smith, Carr E.	OF	6	.191	B	C
2	1	Speece, Byron Franklin	P	21	.150	A	
		Tate, Henry Bennett	C14	21	.302	A	
		Taylor, Thomas Livingstone Carlton	3B16	26	.260	A	C
0	0	Wingfield, Frederick Davis	P	4	+.000	B	Bos
15	9	Zachary, Jonathan Thompson Walton (Tom)	P	32	.309	B	
5	7	Zahniser, Paul Vernon	P	23	.133	B	

WON 96 — AMERICAN LEAGUE — FINISHED 1st.
LOST 55
TG 151 — 1925. — PCT. .636

WASHINGTON

STANLEY RAYMOND HARRIS

WON	LOST	NAME	POS.	G.	BA	FROM	TO
		Adams, Spencer Dewey (SS8 3B3)	2B15	39	.272	PittN23	
1	1	Ballou, Noble Winfred (Win)	P	10	.143	A	
		Bluege, Oswalk Louis (Ossie) (SS4)	3B144	145	.287	B	
		Carlyle, Roy Edward	OF	1	+.000	A	Bos
20	5	Coveleskie, Stanley Anthony	P	32	.111	Clev	
5	1	Ferguson, James Alexander (Alex)	P	7	+.050	xN.Y.	
		Goslin, Leon Allen (Goose)	OF	150	.335	B	
2	2	Gregg, Sylveanus Augustus (Vean)	P	26	.214	Phil18	C
		Hargrave, Wm. McKinley	C1	5	+.500	B	StL
		Harris, Joseph (1B31)	OF41	99	+.324	xBos	
		Harris, Stanley Raymond (Bucky) MGR.	2B	144	.287	B	
		Jeanes, Ernest Lee	OF13	15	.263	Clev22	
20	7	Johnson, Walter Perry	P30	36	.433	B	
		Judge, Joseph Ignatius Jr.	1B109	112	.314	B	
1	1	Kelley, Harry LeRoy	P	6	.000	A	
		Leibold, Harry Loran (Nemo) (3B1)	OF26	56	.273	B	C
0	0	Lyle, James Claude	P	1	.000	A	C
8	6	Marberry, Frederick (Firpo)	P	55	.263	B	
		Matthews, Wid Curry	OF1	10	.444	B	C
4	3	Mogridge, George Anthony	P	10	+.105	B	StL
		Myer, Chas. Solomon (Buddy)	SS	4	.250	A	
		McGee, Francis D.	1B	2	.000	A	C
		McNally, Michael Joseph (2B1 SS2)	3B7	12	.143	N.Y.	C
		McNeely, George Earl	OF112	122	.285	B	
3	1	Ogden, Warren Harvey (Curly)	P	17	.250	B	
		Peckinpaugh, Roger Thorpe (1B1)	SS125	126	.294	B	
0	0	Pumpelly, Spencer Armstrong	P	1	.000	A	C
		Rice, Edgar Chas. (Sam)	OF	152	.350	B	
		Ruel, Herold Dominic (Muddy) (1B1)	C126	127	.310	B	
18	7	Ruether, Walter Henry (Dutch) (1B1)	P30	55	.333	BknN	
2	4	Russell, Allen E.	P	32	.143	B	C
		Scott, Lewis Everett (Deacon)	SS	33	+.272	xN.Y.	
		Severeid, Henry Levai	C	50	+.364	xStL	
		Shirley, Ernest Raeford (Mule)	1B9	14	.130	B	C
		Stewart, John Franklin (Stuffy) (2B1)	3B5	7	.353	BknN23	
		Tate, Henry Bennett	C14	16	.481	B	
0	2	Thomas, Clarence Franklin	P	2	.000	A	
		Veach, Robert Hayes	OF11	18	+.243	xN.Y.	C
12	15	Zachary, Jonathan Thompson Walton (Tom)	P	38	.174	B	

WON 81 — AMERICAN LEAGUE — FINISHED 4th.
LOST 69
TG 150 — 1926. — PCT. .540

WASHINGTON

STANLEY RAYMOND HARRIS

WON	LOST	NAME	POS.	G.	BA	FROM	TO
		Bluege, Oswalk Louis (Ossie)	3B134	139	.271	B	
1	8	Bush, Leslie Ambrose (Bullet Joe)	P12	17	.233	StL	PittN
14	11	Coveleskie, Stanley Anthony	P	36	.207	B	
7	4	Crowder, Alvin Floyd (General)	P	19	.237	A	
		Ennis, Russell Elwood	C	1	.000	A	C
3	4	Ferguson, James Alexander (Alex)	P	19	.182	B	
		Goslin, Leon Allen (Goose)	OF	147	.354	B	

WON	LOST	NAME	POS.	G.	BA	FROM	TO
0	0	Hadley, Irving Darius (Bump)	P	1	.000	A	
		Harris, Joseph (OF35)	1B36	92	.307	B	
		Harris, Stanley Raymond (Bucky) MGR.	2B	141	.283	B	
		Jeanes, Ernest Lee	OF14	21	.233	B	
15	16	Johnson, Walter Perry	P33	35	.194	B	
2	1	Jones, Decatur Poindexter	P	5	.200	A	
		Judge, Joseph Ignatius Jr.	1B128	134	.291	B	
0	0	Kelley, Harry LeRoy	P	7	.000	B	
0	0	Loftus, Francis Patrick	P	1	.000	A	C
11	7	Marberry, Frederick (Firpo)	P	64	.176	B	
3	3	Morrell, Willard Blackmer	P	26	.235	A	
6	3	Murray, George King	P	12	.139	Bos24	
		Myer, Chas. Solomon (Buddy)	SS117	132	.304	B	
		McNeely, George Earl	OF120	124	.303	B	
4	4	Ogden, Warren Harvey (Curly)	P	22	.185	B	C
2	2	Palmero, Emilio A.	P	7	.333	StL21	
		Peckinpaugh, Roger Thorpe	SS46	57	.238	B	
		Reeves, Robert Edwin	3B16	20	.224	A	
		Rice, Edgar Chas. (Sam)	OF	152	.337	B	
		Ruel, Herold Dominic (Muddy)	C	117	.299	B	
13	6	Ruether, Walter Henry (Dutch)	P	47	+.239	B	N.Y.
		Severeid, Henry Levai	C	22	+.212	B	N.Y.
		Stewart, John Franklin (Stuffy)	2B25	62	.270	B	
		Tate, Henry Bennett	C45	59	.267	B	
		Taylor, Daniel Turney	OF12	21	.300	A	
0	0	Thomas, Clarence Franklin	P	6	.000	B	C
		Tobin, John Thomas	OF	27	+.212	StL	Bos
0	0	Uchrinsko, James Emerson	P	3	.000	A	C

WON 85 AMERICAN LEAGUE FINISHED 3rd.
LOST 69
TG 154 1927. PCT. .552

WASHINGTON

STANLEY RAYMOND HARRIS

WON	LOST	NAME	POS.	G.	BA	FROM	TO
		Atkinson, Hubert Berley		1	.000	A	C
		Barnes, Emile Deering	OF	3	.364	A	
		Berger, John Henne	C4	9	.267	Phil22	C
		Bluege, Oswald Louis (Ossie)	3B	146	.274	B	
10	9	Braxton, Edgar Garland	P	58	.231	N.Y.	
3	2	Burke, Robert James	P	36	.125	A	
0	1	Coffman, Samuel Richard (Dick)	P	5	.333	A	
2	1	Coveleskie, Stanley Anthony	P	5	.333	B	
4	7	Crowder, Alvin Floyd (General)	P	15	+.136	B	StL
		Cullop, Henry Nicholas	OF	15	+.217	N.Y.	Clev
		Dear, Paul Stanford	2B1	2	.000	A	C
		Ganzel, Foster Pere	OF	13	.437	A	
		Gillis, Grant	SS	10	.222	A	
		Goslin, Leon Allen (Goose)	OF	148	.334	B	
14	6	Hadley, Irving Darius (Bump)	P	30	.271	B	

WON	LOST	NAME	POS.	G.	BA	FROM	TO
		Harris, Stanley Raymond (Bucky) MGR.	2B	128	.267	B	
		Hayes, Minter Carney (Jackie) (3B1)	SS6	10	.241	A	
1	0	Hopkins, Paul Henry	P	2	.667	A	
5	6	Johnson, Walter Perry	P18	26	.348	B	
0	0	Jones, Decatur Poindexter	P	2	.000	B	C
0	0	Judd, Ralph Wesley	P	1	.000	A	
		Judge, Joseph Ignatius Jr.	1B	137	.308	B	
18	9	Lisenbee, Horace Milton	P	39	.132	A	
10	7	Marberry, Frederick (Firpo)	P	56	.122	B	
1	1	Murray, George King	P	7	.167	B	
		Myer, Chas. Solomon (Buddy)	3B14	15	+.216	B	Bos
		McNeely, George Earl	OF47	73	.276	B	
		O'Neil, George Michael	C	5	.000	BknN	NYN
		Onslow, Edward Joseph	1B3	9	.222	Clev18	C
		Reeves, Robert Edwin (3B12)	SS96	112	.255	B	
		Rice, Edgar Chas. (Sam)	OF140	142	.297	B	
		Rigney, Emory Elmo (3B8)	SS33	46	+.271	xBos	C
		Ruel, Herold Dominic (Muddy)	C128	131	.308	B	
		Speaker, Tristram E. (Tris) (1B17)	OF121	141	.327	Clev	
		Stewart, John Franklin (Stuffy)	2B37	56	.240	B	
		Tate, Henry Bennett	C39	61	.313	B	
13	13	Thurston, Hollis John (Sloppy)	P29	42	.315	Chi	
		Tucker, Oliver Dinwiddie	OF2	20	.208	A	
0	0	VanAlstyne, Clayton Emory	P	2	.000	A	
		West, Samuel Filmore	OF18	38	.239	A	
4	7	Zachary, Jonathan Thompson Walton (Tom)	P	15	+.139	xStL	

WON 75 AMERICAN LEAGUE FINISHED 4th.
LOST 79
TG 154 1928. PCT. .487

WASHINGTON

STANLEY RAYMOND HARRIS

WON	LOST	NAME	POS.	G.	BA	FROM	TO
		Ballenger, Pelham Ashby (3B1)	2B2	3	.111	A	C
		Barnes, Emile Deering	OF104	114	.305	B	
		Bluege, Oswald Louis (Ossie)	3B144	146	.297	B	
		Bool, Albert J.	C	2	.143	A	
		Boss, Elmer Harley	1B3	12	.250	A	
13	11	Braxton, Edgar Garland	P	38	.125	B	
4	4	Brown, Lloyd Andrew	P	27	.160	BknN25	
2	4	Burke, Robert James	P	26	.250	B	
		Cronin, Joseph Edward	SS	63	.243	PittN	
		Crowley, Edgar Jewel	3B1	2	.000	A	C
		Ganzel, Foster Pere	OF5	10	.077	B	C
6	12	Gaston, Nathaniel Milton	P	28	.143	StL	
		Gillis, Grant	SS16	24	.253	B	
		Goslin, Leon Allen (Goose)	OF125	135	.379	B	

WON	LOST	NAME	POS.	G.	BA	FROM	TO
12	13	Hadley, Irving Darius (Bump)	P	33	.210	B	
		Harris, Stanley Raymond (Bucky) MGR.	2B96	99	.204	B	
		Hayes, Minter Carney (Jackie) (SS15)	2B41	60	.257	B	
17	7	Jones, Samuel Pond (Sad Sam)	P30	37	.253	StL	
		Judge, Joseph Ignatius Jr.	1B149	153	.306	B	
		Kenna, Edward Aloysius	C34	41	.297	A	C
2	6	Lisenbee, Horace Milton	P	16	.174	B	
13	13	Marberry, Frederick (Firpo)	P	48	.109	B	
		McMullen, Hugh Raphael		1	.000	NYN26	
		Reeves, Robert Edwin (2B22)	SS66	102	.303	B	
		Rice, Edgar Chas. (Sam)	OF147	148	.328	B	
		Ruel, Herold Dominic (Muddy)	C101	108	.257	B	
		Sisler, George Harold (OF4)	1B5	20	.245	StL	BosN
		Spalding, Chas. Harry (Dick)	OF11	16	.348	PhilN	C
		Tate, Henry Bennett	C30	57	.246	B	
0	0	VanAlstyne, Clayton Emory	P	4	.250	B	C
0	0	Weaver, James Dement	P	3	.000	A	
		West, Samuel Filmore	OF116	125	.301	B	
6	9	Zachary, Jonathan Thompson Walton (Tom)	P	20	+.303	B	N.Y.

WON 71 — AMERICAN LEAGUE — FINISHED 5th.
LOST 81
TG 152 — 1929 — PCT. .467

WASHINGTON

WALTER PERRY JOHNSON

WON	LOST	NAME	POS.	G.	BA	FROM	TO
		Altrock, Nicholas (Nick)	OF	1	1.000	Wash24	
		Barnes, Emile Deering	OF30	72	.200	B	
1	0	Beall, Walter Esau	P	3	.000	NY27	C
		Bluege, Oswald Louis (Ossie) (2B14 SS10)	3B34	64	.295	B	
		Boss, Elmer Harley	1B18	28	.273	B	
12	10	Braxton, Edgar Garland	P	37	.148	B	
8	7	Brown, Lloyd Andrew	P	40	.220	B	
6	8	Burke, Robert James	P	37	.140	B	
0	1	Campbell, Archer Stewart (Archie)	P	4	.000	N.Y.	
		Cronin, Joseph Edward	SS143	145	.282	B	
		Flagstead, Ira	OF	16	+.143	xBos	PittN
		Gharrity, Edward Patrick		3	.000	Wash23	
		Gooch, Chas. Furman (SS1 3B2)	1B4	39	.281	A	C
		Goslin, Leon Allen (Goose)	OF142	145	.288	B	
6	16	Hadley, Irving Darius (Bump)	P	37	.097	B	
		Harris, Spencer Anthony	OF3	6	.214	ChiA26	
		Hayes, Minter Carney (Jackie) (2B56)	3B63	123	.276	B	
0	1	Hopkins, Paul Henry	P	7	+.000	Wash27	StL

WON	LOST	NAME	POS.	G.	BA	FROM	TO
9	9	Jones, Samuel Pond (Sad Sam)	P24	28	.157	B	
		Judge, Joseph Ignatius Jr.	1B142	143	.315	B	
		Land, Wm. Gilbert	OF	1	.000	A	C
3	9	Liska, Adolph James (Ad)	P	24	.172	A	
19	12	Marberry, Frederick (Firpo)	P	49	.235	B	
		Myer, Chas. Solomon (Buddy) (3B53)	2B88	141	.300	Bos	
0	0	McCullough, Paul Willard	P	3	.000	A	C
		Rice, Edgar Chas. (Sam)	OF147	150	.323	B	
		Ruel, Herold Dominic (Muddy)	C63	69	.245	B	
0	0	Savidge, Donald Snyder	P	3	.000	A	C
		Spencer, Roy Hampton	C41	50	.155	PittN27	
		Stewart, John Franklin (Stuffy)	2B1	22	.000	Wash27	C
		Tate, Henry Bennett	C74	81	.294	B	
7	8	Thomas, Myles Lewis	P	22	+.264	xN.Y.	
		West, Samuel Filmore	OF139	142	.267	B	
0	0	Wineapple, Edward	P	1	.000	A	C

WON 94 — AMERICAN LEAGUE — FINISHED 2nd.
LOST 60
TG 154 — 1930. — PCT. .610

WASHINGTON

WALTER PERRY JOHNSON

WON	LOST	NAME	POS.	G.	BA	FROM	TO
		Barnes, Emile Deering	OF	12	+.167	B	Chi
		Barrett, Wm. Joseph		6	+.000	xBos	C
		Bluege, Oswald Louis (Ossie)	3B	134	.290	B	
		Boss, Elmer Harley	1B1	3	.000	B	
3	2	Braxton, Edgar Garland	P	15	+.000	B	Chi
16	12	Brown, Lloyd Andrew	P	38	.215	B	
3	4	Burke, Robert James	P	24	.174	B	
0	0	Child, Harry Stephen	P	5	.250	A	C
		Cronin, Joseph Edward	SS	154	.346	B	
15	9	Crowder, Alvin Floyd (General)	P	27	+.145	.145	xStL
1	1	Fischer, Chas. Wm.	P	8	.000	A	
		Gharrity, Edward Patrick	1B1	2	.000	B	C
		Goslin, Leon Allen (Goose)	OF	47	+.270	B	StL
15	11	Hadley, Irving Darius (Bump)	P	42	.226	B	
		Hargrave, Wm. McKinley	C	10	+.179	xDet	
		Harris, David Stanley	OF	73	+.320	xChi	
		Hayes, Minter Carney (Jackie)	2B29	51	.283	B	
15	7	Jones, Samuel Pond (Sad Sam)	P25	30	.148	B	
		Judge, Joseph Ignatius Jr.	1B117	126	.326	B	
		Kuhel, Joseph Anthony (Joey)	1B16	18	.286	A	
9	7	Liska, Adolph James (Ad)	P	32	.096	B	
		Loepp, George Herbert	OF48	50	.276	Bos28	C
		Manush, Henry Emmett (Heinie)	OF	88	+.362	xStL	
15	5	Marberry, Frederick (Firpo)	P	33	.329	B	
0	0	Moore, Carlos Witman	P	4	.000	A	C
		Myer, Chas. Solomon (Buddy)	2B134	138	.303	B	

WON	LOST	NAME	POS.	G.	BA	FROM	TO
		McLeod, Soule James	3B10	18	.265	A	
		Powell, Alvin Jacob (Jake)	OF	3	.000	A	
		Rice, Edgar Chas. (Sam)	OF145	147	.349	B	
		Ruel, Herold Dominic (Muddy)	C60	66	.253	B	
		Shires, Arthur Lee (The Great)	1B	33	+.365	xChi	
		Spencer, Roy Hampton	C	93	.255	B	
		Tate, Henry Bennett	C	14	+.231	B	Chi
2	2	Thomas, Myles Lewis	P12	14	.182	B	C
		Treadaway, Edgar Raymond	3B5	6	.211	A	C
		West, Samuel Filmore	OF118	120	.328	B	

WON 92 LOST 62 TG 154

AMERICAN LEAGUE

1931.

FINISHED 3rd. PCT. .597

WASHINGTON

WALTER PERRY JOHNSON

WON	LOST	NAME	POS.	G.	BA	FROM	TO
		Altrock, Nicholas (Nick)		1	.000	Wash29	
		Andrus, Wm. Morgan	3B2	3	.000	A	
		Bluege, Oswald Louis (Ossie)	3B	152	.272	B	
		Bolton, Wm. Clifton	C13	23	.255	A	
15	14	Brown, Lloyd Andrew	P	42	.229	B	
8	3	Burke, Robert James	P	30	.213	B	
		Cronin, Joseph Edward	SS155	156	.306	B	
18	11	Crowder, Alvin Floyd (General)	P	44	.216	B	
13	9	Fischer, Chas. Wm.	P	46	.121	B	
		Gill, John Wesley	OF	8	.267	Clev28	
11	10	Hadley, Irving Darius (Bump)	P	55	.167	B	
		Hargrave, Wm. McKinley	C25	40	.325	B	
		Harris, David Stanley	OF60	77	.312	B	
		Hayes, Minter Carney (Jackie)	2B19	38	.222	B	
9	10	Jones, Samuel Pond (Sad Sam)	P25	30	.313	B	
		Jordan, Baxter Byerly	1B	9	.222	N.Y.N29	
		Judge, Joseph Ignatius Jr.	1B15	35	.284	B	
		Kuhel, Joseph Anthony (Joey)	1B	139	.269	B	
0	1	Liska, Adolph James (Ad)	P	2	.000	B	
		Manush, Henry Emmett (Heinie)	OF143	146	.307	B	
16	4	Marberry, Frederick (Firpo)	P	45	.232	B	
0	0	Masters, Walter Thomas	P	3	.000	A	
		Myer, Chas. Solomon (Buddy)	2B137	139	.293	B	
		Phelps, Ernest Gordon (Babe)		3	.333	A	
		Rice, Edgar Chas. (Sam)	OF105	120	.310	B	
		Rice, Harry Francis	OF42	47	.265	N.Y.	
		Spencer, Roy Hampton	C	145	.275	B	
1	0	Tauscher, Walter Edward	P	6	.000	PittN28	C
1	0	Weaver, Montgomery Morton	P	3	.000	A	
		West, Samuel Filmore	OF127	132	.333	B	

WON 93 LOST 61 TG 154

AMERICAN LEAGUE

1932.

FINISHED 3rd. PCT. .604

WASHINGTON

WALTER PERRY JOHNSON

WON	LOST	NAME	POS.	G.	BA	FROM	TO
		Berg, Morris (Moe)	C	75	.236	Clev	
		Bluege, Oswald Louis (Ossie)	3B	149	.258	B	
15	12	Brown, Lloyd Andrew	P	46	.100	B	
3	6	Burke, Robert James	P22	23	.200	B	
1	6	Coffman, Samuel Richard (Dick)	P	22	+.091	xStL	
		Cronin, Joseph Edward	SS141	143	.318	B	
26	13	Crowder, Alvin Floyd (General)	P50	51	.221	B	
0	0	Edelen, Edward Joseph Jr.	P	2	.000	A	C
3	2	Fischer, Chas. Wm.	P	12	+.200	B	StL
0	0	Friedrich, Robert George	P	2	.000	A	C
		Harris, David Stanley	OF34	81	.327	B	
		Judge, Joseph Ignatius Jr.	1B78	82	.258	B	
		Kerr, John Francis (SS14)	2B17	51	.273	Chi	
		Kingdon, Westcott Wm. (Wes) (SS2)	3B3	18	.324	A	C
		Kuhel, Joseph Anthony (Joey)	1B85	101	.291	B	
		Manush, Henry Emmett (Heinie)	OF146	149	.342	B	
		Maple, Howard Albert	C41	44	.244	A	C
8	4	Marberry, Frederick (Firpo)	P	54	.167	B	
		Musser, Wm. Daniel	3B	1	.500	A	C
		Myer, Chas. Solomon (Buddy)	2B139	143	.279	B	
6	1	McAfee, Wm. Fort Jr.	P	8	.111	BosN	
		McLeod, Soule James	SS	7	.000	Wash30	
1	0	Ragland, Frank Roland	P	12	.273	A	
		Reynolds, Carl Nettles	OF95	102	.305	Chi	
		Rice, Edgar Chas. (Sam)	OF69	106	.323	B	
		Spencer, Roy Hampton	C98	102	.246	B	
8	7	Thomas, Alphonse Thomas Jr.	P	18	+.238	xChi	
0	0	Thomas, Luther Baxter (Bud)	P	2	.000	A	
22	10	Weaver, Montgomery Morton	P43	44	.287	B	
		West, Samuel Filmore	OF143	146	.287	B	

WON 99 LOST 53 TG 152

AMERICAN LEAGUE

1933.

FINISHED 1st. PCT. .651

WASHINGTON

JOSEPH EDWARD CRONIN

WON	LOST	NAME	POS.	G.	BA	FROM	TO
		Altrock, Nicholas (Nick)		1	.000	Wash31	C
		Berg, Morris (Moe)	C35	40	.185	B	
		Bluege, Oswald Louis (Ossie)	3B138	140	.261	B	

WON	LOST	NAME	POS.	G.	BA	FROM	TO
		Boken, Robert Anthony	2B31	55	.278	A	
		(SS10 3B19)					
		Bolton, Wm. Clifton (OF1)	C9	33	.410	Wash31	
4	3	Burke, Robert James	P	25	.235	B	
0	0	Campbell, John Millard	P	1	.000	A	C
0	0	Chapman, Edwin Volney	P	6	.000	A	C
		Cronin, Joseph Edward MGR.	SS	152	.309	B	
24	15	Crowder, Alvin Floyd (General)	P	52	.186	B	
		Goslin, Leon Allen (Goose)	OF128	132	.297	StL	
		Harris, David Stanley	OF45	82	.260	B	
		(1B6 3B2)					
		Kerr, John Francis (3B1)	2B16	28	.200	B	
		Kuhel, Joseph Anthony (Joey)	1B	153	.322	B	
1	0	Linke, Edward Karl	P	3	.167	A	
		Manush, Henry Emmett	OF150	153	.336	B	
		(Heinie)					
		Myer, Chas. Solomon (Buddy)	2B129	131	.302	B	
3	2	McAfee, Wm. Fort Jr. (2B1)	P27	27	.267	B	
1	0	McColl, Alexander Boyd	P	4	.333	A	
0	1	Prim, Raymond Lee	P	2	.000	A	
		Rice, Edgar Chas. (Sam)	OF39	73	.294	B	
12	6	Russell, Jack Erwin	P	50	.147	Clev	
		Schulte, Fred Wm.	OF142	144	.295	StL	
		Sewell, James Luther (Luke)	C	141	.264	Clev	
15	6	Stewart, Walter Cleveland	P34	35	.143	StL	
		(2B1)					
7	7	Thomas, Alphonse Thomas Jr.	P	35	.238	B	
0	0	Thomas, Luther Baxter (Bud)	P	2	.000	B	
		Travis, Cecil Howel	3B15	18	.302	A	
10	5	Weaver, Montgomery Morton	P	23	.125	B	
22	8	Whitehill, Earl Oliver (OF1)	P39	40	.222	Det	

WON 66 AMERICAN LEAGUE FINISHED 7th.
LOST 86
TG 152 1934. PCT. .434

WASHINGTON

JOSEPH EDWARD CRONIN

WON	LOST	NAME	POS.	G.	BA	FROM	TO
1	0	Armbrust, Orville Martin	P	3	.000	A	C
0	1	Benson, Allen Wilbert	P	2	.000	A	C
		Berg, Morris (Moe)	C	33	+.244	B	Clev
		Bluege, Oswald Louis (Ossie)	3B41	99	.246	B	
		(SS30 OF5)					
		Boken, Robert Anthony	2B	11	+.222	B	Chi
		Bolton, Wm. Clifton	C39	42	.270	B	
8	8	Burke, Robert James	P37	41	.228	B	
1	1	Cohen, Sydney Harry (OF1)	P4	4	.273	A	
		Cronin, Joseph Edward MGR.	SS	127	.284	B	
4	10	Crowder, Alvin Floyd (General)	P	29	+.219	B	Det
1	2	Diggs, Reese Wilson	P	4	.250	A	C
		Dugas, Augustin Joseph (Gus)	OF2	24	.053	PhilN	C
0	0	Filley, Marcus Lucius	P	1	.000	A	C
		Gill, John Wesley	OF	13	.245	Wash31	
		Harris, David Stanley	OF64	97	.251	B	C

WON	LOST	NAME	POS.	G.	BA	FROM	TO
		Kerr, John Francis	3B17	31	.272	B	C
1	0	Kline, Robert George	P	6	+.000	xPhil	C
		Klumpp, Elmer Edward	C11	12	.133	A	
		Kress, Ralph (Red) (OF5)	1B30	56	+.228	xChi	
		Kuhel, Joseph Anthony (Joey)	1B	63	.289	B	
2	2	Linke, Edward Karl	P	8	.182	B	
		Manush, Henry Emmett	OF131	137	.349	B	
		(Heinie)					
0	0	Milligan, John Alexander	P	2	.000	PhilN31	C
		Myer, Chas. Solomon (Buddy)	2B135	139	.305	B	
3	4	McColl, Alexander Boyd	P	42	.097	B	
		Phillips, Edward David	C53	56	.195	NY32	
		Powell, Alvin Jacob (Jake)	OF	9	.286	Wash30	
0	2	Prim, Raymond Lee	P	8	.000	B	
5	10	Russell, Jack Erwin	P	54	.159	B	
		Schulte, Fred Wm.	OF134	136	.298	B	
		Sewell, James Luther (Luke)	C50	72	.237	B	
		(1B6 2B1 3B1 OF7)					
		Sington, Frederic Wm.	OF	9	.286	A	
7	11	Stewart, Walter Cleveland	P24	25	.156	B	
		Stone, Jonathan Thomas	OF112	113	.315	Det	
		Susko, Peter John	1B	58	.286	A	C
8	9	Thomas, Alphonse Thomas Jr.	P	33	.184	B	
		Travis, Cecil Howel	3B99	109	.319	B	
11	15	Weaver, Montgomery Morton	P	31	.163	B	
14	11	Whitehill, Earl Oliver	P32	35	.200	B	

WON 67 AMERICAN LEAGUE FINISHED 6th.
LOST 86
TG 153 1935. PCT. .438

WASHINGTON

STANLEY RAYMOND HARRIS

WON	LOST	NAME	POS.	G.	BA	FROM	TO
2	0	Bean, Belvedere Benton	P	10	+.375	xClev	C
		Bluege, Oswald Louis (Ossie)	SS58	100	.263	B	
		(2B4 3B25)					
		Bolton, Wm. Clifton	C106	110	.304	B	
1	8	Burke, Robert James	P15	16	.182	B	
3	4	Coppola, Henry Peter	P	19	.071	A	
		Estalella, Roberto Mendez	3B	15	.314	A	
10	15	Hadley, Irving Darius (Bump)	P	35	.195	StL	
2	4	Hayes, James Millard	P	7	.250	A	C
0	3	Hensiek, Philip Frank	P	6	.667	A	C
		Holbrook, James Marbury	C47	52	.259	A	C
0	0	Kress, Ralph (Red)	SS53	84	.298	B	
		(P3 1B5 2B1 OF2)					
		Kuhel, Joseph Anthony (Joey)	1B	151	.261	B	
0	3	Lanahan, Richard Anthony	P	3	.167	A	
		Lary, Lynford Hobart (Lyn)	SS	39	+.194	Bos	StL
		Lewis, John Kelly Jr. (Buddy)	3B	8	.107	A	
11	7	Linke, Edward Karl	P	40	.294	B	

WON	LOST	NAME	POS.	G.	BA	FROM	TO
		Manush, Henry Emmett (Heinie)	OF111	119	.273	B	
		Marion, John Wyeth	OF	4	.182	A	
		Mihalic, John Jr.	SS	6	.227	A	
		Miles, Wilson Daniel (Dee)	OF45	60	.264	A	
		Myer, Chas. Solomon (Buddy)	2B	151	.349	B	
0	0	McLean, Albert Eldon	P	4	.000	A	C
11	12	Newsom, Louis Norman (Buck)	P	28	+.301	xStL	
8	5	Pettit, Leon Arthur	P	41	.080	A	
		Powell, Alvin Jacob (Jake) (2B2)	OF136	139	.312	B	
		Redmond, Jackson McKittrick	C15	22	.176	A	C
0	1	Rogers, Orlin Woodrow	P	2	.000	A	C
4	9	Russell, John Jack Erwin	P	43	.200	B	
		Schulte, Fred Wm.	OF55	75	.268	B	
		Sington, Frederic Wm.	OF4	20	.182	B	
		Starr, Wm.	C	12	.208	A	
0	1	Stewart, Walter Cleveland	P	1	+.000	B	Clev
		Stone, Jonathan Thomas	OF114	125	.315	B	
		Strange, Alan Cochrane (Inky)	SS	20	+.185	xStL	
0	0	Thomas, Alphonse Thomas Jr.	P	1	.000	B	PhilN
		Travis, Cecil Howel (OF16)	3B114	138	.318	B	
1	1	Weaver, Montgomery Morton	P	5	.333	B	
14	13	Whitehill, Earl Oliver	P	34	.183	B	

WON 82 — AMERICAN LEAGUE — FINISHED 4th.
LOST 71
TG 153 — 1936. — PCT. .536

WASHINGTON

STANLEY RAYMOND HARRIS

WON	LOST	NAME	POS.	G.	BA	FROM	TO
14	9	Appleton, Peter Wm. (Jablonowski)	P	38	.250	N.Y.33	
		Bluege, Oswald Louis (Ossie) (SS23 3B15)	2B52	90	.288	B	
0	2	Bokina, Joseph	P	5	.000	A	C
		Bolton, Wm. Clifton	C83	86	.291	B	
9	8	Cascarella, Joseph Thomas	P	22	+.143	xBos	
		Chapman, Wm. Benjamin	OF	97	+.332	xN.Y.	
0	0	Chase, Kendall Fay (Ken)	P	1	1.000	A	
0	2	Cohen, Sydney Harry	P	19	.000	Wash34	
0	0	Coppola, Henry Peter	P	6	.333	B	C
18	10	DeShong, James Brooklyn	P34	35	.190	N.Y.	
0	1	Dietrich, Wm. John (Bill)	P	5	+.000	xPhil	Chi
		Estalella, Roberto Mendez		13	.222	B	
		Hill, Jesse Terrill	OF60	85	.305	N.Y.	
		Hogan, James Francis (Shanty)	C	19	.323	BosN	
		Kress, Ralph (Red) (2B33)	SS64	109	.284	B	
		Kuhel, Joseph Anthony (Joey)	1B	149	.321	B	
		Lewis, John Kelly Jr. (Buddy)	3B139	143	.291	B	
1	5	Linke, Edward Karl	P	13	.400	B	
0	2	Marberry, Frederick (Firpo)	P	5	.000	xNYN	C
		Mihalic, John Jr.	2B	25	.239	B	
		Miles, Wilson Daniel (Dee)	OF10	25	.237	B	
		Millies, Walter Louis	C72	74	.312	BknN34	
		Myer, Chas. Solomon (Buddy)	2B43	51	.269	B	
17	15	Newsom, Louis Norman (Buck)	P43	44	.213	B	
0	0	Phebus, Raymond Wm.	P	2	.000	A	
		Powell, Alvin Jacob (Jake)	OF	53	+.290	B	N.Y.
		Reynolds, Carl Nettles	OF72	89	.276	Bos	
3	2	Russell, Jack Erwin	P	18	+.000	B	Bos
		Sabo, Alexander	C	4	.375	A	
		Sington, Frederic Wm.	OF	25	.319	B	
		Starr, Wm.	C	1	.000	B	C
		Stone, Jonathan Thomas	OF114	123	.341	B	
		Travis, Cecil Howel (OF53)	SS71	138	.317	B	
6	4	Weaver, Montgomery Morton	P	26	.200	B	
14	11	Whitehill, Earl Oliver	P	28	.169	B	

WON 73 — AMERICAN LEAGUE — FINISHED 6th.
LOST 80
TG 153 — 1937. — PCT. .477

WASHINGTON

STANLEY RAYMOND HARRIS

WON	LOST	NAME	POS.	G.	BA	FROM	TO
		Almada, Melo Baldomero (Mel)	OF	100	+.309	xBos	
0	1	Anderson, Arnold Revola	P	2	.000	A	
8	15	Appleton, Peter Wm. (Jablonowski)	P	35	.186	B	
		Bloodworth, James Henry	2B14	15	.220	A	
		Bluege, Oswald Louis (Ossie)	SS28	42	.283	B	
0	5	Cascarella, Joseph Thomas	P	10	.222	B	CinN
		Case, George Washington	OF	22	.289	A	
		Chapman, Wm. Benjamin	OF	35	+.262	B	Bos
4	3	Chase, Kendall Fay (Ken)	P	14	.034	B	
2	4	Cohen, Sydney Harry	P	33	.143	B	C
		Crompton, Herbert Bryan	C	2	.333	A	
14	15	DeShong, James Brooklyn	P	37	.202	B	
		Ferrell, Richard Benjamin (Rick)	C	86	+.229	xBos	
11	13	Ferrell, Wesley Cheek (Wes)	P	53	+.255	xBos	
4	5	Fischer, Chas. Wm.	P	17	+.136	xClev	C
		Gray, Milton Marshall	C	2	.000	A	C
		Guerra, Fermin Romero	C	1	.000	A	
		Hill, Jesse Terrill	OF	33	+.217	B	Phil
		Hogan, James Francis (Shanty)	C	21	.152	B	C
1	1	Jacobs, Newton Smith	P	11	.000	A	
1	0	Kohlman, Joseph James	P	2	.200	A	
4	1	Krakauskas, Joseph Victor Lawrence (Kraky)	P	5	.125	A	
		Kuhel, Joseph Anthony (Joey)	1B	136	.283	B	
0	1	Lanahan, Richard Anthony	P	6	.000	Wash35	
		Lewis, John Kelly Jr. (Buddy)	3B	156	.314	B	

WON	LOST	NAME	POS.	G.	BA	FROM	TO
6	1	Linke, Edward Karl	P36	37	.217	B	
		Lynn, Jerome	2B	1	.667	A	C
		Mihalic, John Jr.	2B28	38	.252	B	C
		Millies, Walter Louis	C56	59	.223	B	
		Myer, Chas. Solomon (Buddy)	2B119	125	.293	B	
3	4	Newsom, Louis Norman (Buck)	P	13	+.120	B	Bos
3	2	Phebus, Raymond Wm.	P	6	.000	B	
		Riddle, John Ludy	C	8	.269	Chi30	BosN
		Sabo, Alexander	C	1	.000	B	C
		Simmons, Aloysius Harry (Al)	OF	103	.279	Det	
		Sington, Frederic Wm.	OF64	78	.237	B	
		Stone, Jonathan Thomas	OF137	139	.330	B	
		Travis, Cecil Howel	SS129	135	.344	B	
		Trechock, Frank Adam	SS	1	.500	A	C
		Wasdell, James Chas.	1B21	32	.255	A	
12	9	Weaver, Montgomery Morton	P	30	.206	B	

WON 75 — AMERICAN LEAGUE — FINISHED 5th.
LOST 76
TG 151 — 1938. — PCT. .497

WASHINGTON

STANLEY RAYMOND HARRIS

WON	LOST	NAME	POS.	G.	BA	FROM	TO
		Almada, Melo Baldomero (Mel)	OF	47	+.244	B	StL
7	9	Appleton, Peter Wm. (Jablonowski)	P	43	.254	B	
		Bluege, Oswald Louis (Ossie) (SS10)	2B38	58	.261	B	
		Bonura, Henry John (Zeke)	1B129	137	.289	Chi	
		Case, George Washington	OF101	107	.305	B	
9	10	Chase, Kendall Fay (Ken)	P	32	.208	B	
5	8	DeShong, James Brooklyn	P	31	.261	B	
		Ferrell, Richard Benjamin (Rick)	C131	135	.292	B	
13	8	Ferrell, Wesley Cheek (Wes)	P	26	+.224	B	N.Y.
		Goslin, Leon Allen (Goose)	OF13	38	.158	Det	C
		Giuliani, Angelo John (Tony)	C	46	.217	StL	
5	6	Hogsett, Elon Chester (Chief)	P31	32	.304	StL	
9	8	Kelley, Harry LeRoy	P	38	+.250	xPhil	
0	0	Kohlman, Joseph James	P	7	.000	B	C
7	5	Krakauskas, Joseph Victor Lawrence (Kraky)	P	29	.182	B	
12	15	Leonard, Emil John (Dutch)	P	33	.232	BknN36	
		Lewis, John Kelly Jr. (Buddy)	3B	151	.296	B	
		Livingston, Thompson Orville	C	2	.750	A	
1	1	Monteagudo, Rene Miranda	P	5	.500	A	
		Myer, Chas. Solomon (Buddy)	2B121	127	.336	B	
0	0	Phebus, Raymond Wm.	P	5	.000	B	C
		Simmons, Aloysius Harry (Al)	OF117	125	.302	B	
		Stone, Jonathan Thomas	OF53	56	.244	B	C
		Travis, Cecil Howel	SS143	146	.335	B	
		Wasdell, James Chas.	1B26	53	.236	B	

WON	LOST	NAME	POS.	G.	BA	FROM	TO
7	6	Weaver, Montgomery Morton	P	31	.267	B	
		West, Samuel Filmore	OF	92	+.302	xStL	
		Wright, Taft Shedron	OF60	100	.350	A	

WON 65 — AMERICAN LEAGUE — FINISHED 6th.
LOST 87
TG 152 — 1939. — PCT. .428

WASHINGTON

STANLEY RAYMOND HARRIS

WON	LOST	NAME	POS.	G.	BA	FROM	TO
		Aderholt, Morris Woodrow	2B	7	.200	A	
5	10	Appleton, Peter Wm. (Jablonowski)	P	40	.160	B	
0	1	Bass, Richard Wm.	P	1	.000	A	C
		Bloodworth, James Henry	2B73	83	.289	Wash37	
		Bluege, Oswald Louis (Ossie)	1B11	18	.153	B	
5	9	Carrasquel, Alejandro Alexander	P	40	.167	A	
		Case, George Washington	OF123	128	.302	B	
10	19	Chase, Kendall Fay (Ken)	P	32	.169	B	
0	3	DeShong, James Brooklyn	P	7	.200	B	C
		Early, Jacob Willard	C24	32	.262	A	
		Estalella, Roberto Mendez	OF74	82	.275	Wash36	
		Evans, Alfred Hubert	C	7	.333	A	
		Ferrell, Richard Benjamin (Rick)	C83	87	.281	B	
		Gedeon, Elmer John	OF	5	.200	A	C
		Gelbert, Chas. Magnus (3B20)	SS28	68	.255	Det37	
		Giuliani, Angelo John (Tony)	C50	54	.250	B	
8	12	Haynes, Joseph Walton	P	27	.209	A	
0	1	Holland, Wm. David	P	3	.000	A	C
0	0	Jacobs, Newton Smith	P	2	.000	Wash37	
4	3	Kelley, Harry LeRoy	P	15	.267	B	C
11	17	Krakauskas, Joseph Victor Lawrence (Kraky)	P	39	.208	B	
		Leip, Edgar Ellsworth	2B8	9	.344	A	
20	8	Leonard, Emil John (Dutch)	P	34	.221	B	
		Lewis, John Kelly Jr. (Buddy)	3B134	140	.319	B	
		Loane, Robert Kenneth	OF	3	.000	A	
2	2	Masterson, Walter Edward	P	24	.154	A	
		Myer, Chas. Solomon Jr. (Buddy)	2B65	83	.302	B	
0	0	Palagyi, Michael Raymond	P	1	.000	A	C
		Pitko, Alexander	OF3	4	.125	PhilN	C
		Prichard, Robert Alexander	1B	26	.235	A	C
		Quick, James Harold	SS10	12	.244	A	C
0	0	Thomas, Luther Baxter (Bud)	P	4	+.000	xPhil	Det
0	0	Thuman, Louis Chas. Frank	P	3	.000	A	
		Travis, Cecil Howel	SS118	130	.292	B	
		Vernon, James Barton	1B75	76	.257	A	
		Wasdell, James Chas.	1B28	29	.303	B	
		Welaj, John Ludwig	OF55	63	.274	A	

WON	LOST	NAME	POS.	G.	BA	FROM	TO
		West, Samuel Filmore (1B17)	OF89	115	.282	B	
		Wright, Taft Shedron	OF123	129	.309	B	
0	2	Wynn, Early Jr.	P	3	.167	A	

WON 64 LOST 90 TG 154

AMERICAN LEAGUE

1940.

FINISHED 7th.

PCT. .416

WASHINGTON

STANLEY RAYMOND HARRIS

WON	LOST	NAME	POS.	G.	BA	FROM	TO
		Aderholt, Morris Woodrow	2B	1	.000	B	
1	1	Anderson, Arnold Revola	P	2	.600	Wash37	
		Bloodworth, James Henry (1B17 3B6)	2B96	119	.245	B	
		Bonura, Henry John (Zeke)	1B	79	.273	NYN	ChiN
6	2	Carrasquel, Alejandro Alexander	P	28	.000	B	
		Case, George Washington	OF	154	.293	B	
15	17	Chase, Kendall Fay (Ken)	P	35	.163	B	
		Early, Jacob Willard	C56	80	.257	B	
		Evans, Alfred Hubert	C9	14	.320	B	
		Ferrell, Richard Benjamin (Rick)	C99	103	.273	B	
0	0	Gelbert, Chas. Magnus	P2	22	+.370	B	Bos
		Hahn, Richard Frederick	C	1	.000	A	C
3	6	Haynes, Joseph Walton	P	22	.105	B	
1	0	Hollingsworth, Albert Wayne (Al)	P	3	.167	BknN	
1	2	Hudlin, George Willis	P	8	+.100	xClev	StL
17	16	Hudson, Sidney Chas.	P	38	.237	A	
0	1	Jacobs, Newton Smith	P	9	.000	B	C
1	6	Krakauskas, Joseph Victor Lawrence (Kraky)	P	32	.250	B	
14	19	Leonard, Emil John (Dutch)	P	35	.158	B	
		Lewis, John Kelly Jr. (Buddy) (3B36)	OF112	148	.317	B	
		Mallory, James Baugh III	OF3	4	.167	A	
3	13	Masterson, Walter Edward	P	31	.184	B	
2	6	Monteagudo, Rene Miranda	P	27	.182	Wash38	
		Myer, Chas. Solomon Jr. (Buddy)	2B54	71	.290	B	
		Pofahl, James Willard (2B4)	SS112	119	.234	A	
		Robertson, Sherrard Alexander	SS	10	.212	A	
		Sanford, John Doward	1B	34	.197	A	
0	1	Thuman, Louis Chas. Frank	P	2	.000	B	C
0	0	Torres, Don Gilberto	P	2	.000	A	
		Travis, Cecil Howel (SS23)	3B113	136	.322	B	
		Vernon, James Barton	1B4	5	.158	B	
		Walker, Gerald Holmes (Gee)	OF	140	.294	Chi	
		Wasdell, James Chas.	1B8	10	.086	B	BknN
		Welaj, John Ludwig	OF53	88	.256	B	
		West, Samuel Filmore (OF9)	1B12	57	.253	B	

WON 70 LOST x84 TG 154

AMERICAN LEAGUE

1941.

FINISHED 6th. (TIED WITH ST. L.)

PCT. .455

WASHINGTON

STANLEY RAYMOND HARRIS

WON	LOST	NAME	POS.	G.	BA	FROM	TO
		Aderholt, Morris Woodrow (3B1)	2B2	11	.143	B	
4	6	Anderson, Arnold Revola	P	32	.258	B	C
		Archie, George Albert (1B22)	3B63	105	+.269	Det38	StL
		Bloodworth, James Henry (SS1 3B6)	2B132	142	.245	B	
		Bolton, Wm. Clifton	C3	14	.000	Det37	C
6	2	Carrasquel, Alejandro Alexander	P	35	.095	B	
		Case, George Washington	OF151	153	.271	B	
		Chapman, Wm. Benjamin	OF	28	+.255	Clev	Chi
6	18	Chase, Kendall Fay (Ken)	P	33	.149	B	
		Cramer, Roger Maxwell (Flit)	OF152	154	.273	Bos	
0	0	Dean, James Harry	P	2	.000	A	C
		Early, Jacob Willard	C100	104	.287	B	
		Evans, Alfred Hubert	C51	53	.277	B	
		Ferrell, Richard Benjamin (Rick)	C	21	+.273	B	StL
13	14	Hudson, Sidney Chas.	P	33	.186	B	
1	7	Kennedy, Lloyd Vernon (Vern)	P17	18	+.143	xStL	
		Layne, Ivoria Hillis	3B	13	.280	A	
18	13	Leonard, Emil John (Dutch)	P	34	.102	B	
		Letchas, Charlie	2B	2	.125	PhilN39	
		Lewis, John Kelly Jr. (Buddy) (3B49)	OF96	149	.297	B	
0	1	MacFayden, Daniel Knowles (Danny)	P	5	.000	PittN	
4	3	Masterson, Walter Edward	P	34	.105	B	
0	0	Miller, Rolland Arthur	P	1	.000	A	C
0	1	Mulligan, Richard Chas.	P	1	.000	A	
		Myer, Chas. Solomon Jr. (Buddy)	2B24	53	.252	B	C
		Ortiz, Roberto Gonzalo Nunez	OF21	22	.329	A	
		Pofahl, James Willard	SS21	22	.187	B	
		Robertson, Sherrard Alexander	3B	1	.000	B	
		Sanford, John Doward	1B1	3	.400	B	
9	13	Sundra, Stephen Richard (Steve)	P	28	.217	N.Y.	
		Travis, Cecil Howel (3B16)	SS136	152	.359	B	
		Vernon, James Barton	1B132	138	.299	B	
		Welaj, John Ludwig	OF19	49	.208	B	
		West, Samuel Filmore	OF8	26	.270	B	
3	1	Wynn, Early Jr.	P	5	.133	Wash39	
6	4	Zuber, Wm. Henry	P	36	.000	Clev	

xOne game lost by forfeit.

WON 62 LOST 89 TG 151

AMERICAN LEAGUE 1942. FINISHED 7th. PCT. .411

WASHINGTON

STANLEY RAYMOND HARRIS

WON	LOST	NAME	POS.	G.	BA	FROM	TO
0	0	Adkins, John Dewey	P	1	.500	A	
0	1	Bevil, Louis Eugene	P	4	.000	A	C
		Campbell, Bruce Douglas	OF87	122	.278	Det	C
7	7	Carrasquel, Alejandro Alexander	P	35	.136	B	
		Case, George Washington	OF120	125	.320	B	
1	1	Cathay, Hardin	P	12	.375	A	C
		Chartak, Michael George	OF	24	+.217	xN.Y.	StL
		Clary, Ellis	2B69	76	.275	A	
		Croucher, Frank Donald	2B18	26	.277	Det	C
		Cullenbine, Roy Joseph	OF	64	+.286	xStL	N.Y.
		Early, Jacob Willard	C98	104	.204	B	
		Estalella, Roberto Mendez (OF36)	3B78	133	.277	StL	
		Evans, Alfred Hubert	C67	74	.229	B	
		Galle, Stanley Joseph	3B3	13	.111	A	C
		Gomez, Jose Luis Rodriguez	2B23	25	.192	PhilN36	C
		Hoffman, Raymond Lamont	3B6	7	.053	A	C
10	17	Hudson, Sidney Chas.	P35	36	.213	B	
0	1	Kennedy, Wm. Gorman	P	8	.000	A	
		Kvasnak, Alexander	OF3	5	.182	A	C
2	2	Leonard, Emil John (Dutch)	P	6	.100	B	
5	9	Masterson, Walter Edward	P25	26	.156	B	
		Moore, Eugene Jr.	OF	1	.000	BosN	
0	0	McCullough, Philip LaMar	P	1	.000	A	C
11	17	Newsom, Louis Norman (Buck)	P	30	.160	Det	BknN
		Ortiz, Roberto Gonzalo Nunez	OF9	20	.167	B	
		Pofahl, James Willard (2B15 3B14)	SS49	84	.208	B	C
		Repass, Robert Willis (SS11 3B29)	2B33	81	.239	StLN39	C
2	1	Scarborough, Ray Wilson	P	17	.190	A	
		Spence, Stanley Orville	OF	149	.323	Bos	
		Sullivan, John Patrick	SS92	94	.235	A	
1	3	Sundra, Stephen Richard (Steve)	P	6	+.167	B	StL
3	1	Trotter, Wm. Felix	P	17	+.000	xStL	
		Vernon, James Barton	1B	151	.271	B	
1	4	Wilson, John Francis (Jack)	P	12	+.118	Bos	Det
10	16	Wynn, Early Jr.	P	30	.217	B	
9	9	Zuber, Wm. Henry	P	37	.154	B	

WON 84 LOST 69 TG 153

AMERICAN LEAGUE 1943. FINISHED 2nd. PCT. .549

WASHINGTON

OSWALD LOUIS BLUEGE

WON	LOST	NAME	POS.	G.	BA	FROM	TO
0	0	Adkins, John Dewey	P	7	.000	B	C
		Barbary, Donald Odell		1	.000	A	C
		Butka, Edward Luke	1B	3	.333	A	
11	7	Candini, Mario Cain	P	28	.161	A	
0	0	Carpenter, Lewis Emmett	P	4	.000	A	C
11	7	Carrasquel, Alejandro Alexander	P	39	.186	B	
		Case, George Washington	OF140	141	.294	B	
		Clary, Ellis	3B	73	+.256	B	StL
		Clift, Harlond Benton	3B	8	+.300	xStL	
0	0	Curtis, Vernon Eugene	P	2	.000	A	
		Early, Jacob Willard	C122	126	.258	B	
		Giuliani, Angelo John (Tony)	C	49	.226	BknN41	C
0	1	Gomez, Vernon Louis (Lefty)	P	1	.000	N.Y.	C
11	5	Haefner, Milton Arnold	P	36	.133	A	
		Johnson, Robert Lee (Bob) (1B10 3B19)	OF88	117	.265	Phil	
		Kampouris, Alexis Wm. (2B10 OF1)	3B33	51	.207	xBknN	C
2	0	LeFebvre, Wilfried Henry	P6	7	.286	Bos39	
11	13	Leonard, Emil John (Dutch)	P	31	.104	B	
		Marion, John Wyeth	OF4	14	.176	Wash35	C
5	7	Mertz, James Verlin	P	33	.184	A	C
0	0	Miller, John Anthony	P	3	+.000	A	StL
		Moore, Eugene Jr. (1B1)	OF57	92	.268	B	
		Myatt, George Edward (SS2 3B2)	2B11	42	.245	NYN39	
3	3	Newsom, Louis Norman (Buck)	P	6	+.133	xStL	
4	2	Niggeling, John Arnold	P	6	+.278	xStL	
		Ortiz, Roberto Gonzalo Nunez	OF	1	.250	B	
		Padden, Thomas Francis	C2	3	.000	xPhilN	C
		Powell, Alvin Jacob (Jake)	OF33	37	.265	NY40	
		Priddy, Gerald Edward (SS15 3B1)	2B134	149	.271	N.Y.	
4	8	Pyle, Herbert Ewald	P	18	.100	StL	
		Roberts, Chas. Emory (3B1)	SS6	9	.261	A	C
		Robertson, Sherrard Alexander (SS1)	3B27	59	.217	Wash41	
4	4	Scarborough, Ray Wilson	P	24	.333	B	
0	0	Scheetz, Owen Franklin	P	6	.000	A	C
		Spence, Stanley Orville	OF148	149	.267	B	
		Sullivan, John Patrick	SS133	134	.208	B	
		Vernon, James Barton	1B143	145	.268	B	
18	12	Wynn, Early Jr.	P37	38	.296	B	

WON 64 LOST 90 TG 154

AMERICAN LEAGUE 1944. FINISHED 8th (LAST) PCT. .416

WASHINGTON

OSWALD LOUIS BLUEGE

WON	LOST	NAME	POS.	G.	BA	FROM	TO
		Binks, George Eugene	OF3	5	.250	A	
		Boland, Edward John	OF14	19	.271	PhilN35	C
		Butka, Edward Luke	1B14	15	.195	B	C
6	7	Candini, Mario Cain	P	28	.313	B	
8	7	Carrasquel, Alejandro Alexander	P	43	.194	B	
		Case, George Washington	OF114	119	.249	B	
		Clift, Harlond Benton	3B	12	.159	B	
0	1	Curtis, Vernon Eugene	P	3	.000	B	
		Evans, Alfred Hubert	C8	14	.091	Wash42	
		Ferrell, Richard Benjamin (Rick)	C96	99	.277	StL	
		Gomez, Pedro W. Martinez (SS2)	2B2	8	.286	A	C
		Guerra, Fermin Romero (OF1)	C58	75	.281	Wash37	
12	15	Haefner, Milton Arnold	P	31	.157	B	
0	0	Holborow, Walter Albert	P	1	.000	A	
		Kuhel, Joseph Anthony (Joey)	1B138	139	.278	Chi	
		Layne, Ivoria Hillis (2B3)	3B18	33	.195	Wash41	
2	4	LeFebvre, Wilfrid Henry (1B2)	P24	60	.258	B	C
14	14	Leonard, Emil John (Dutch)	P	32	.228	B	
		Monteagudo, Rene Miranda	OF9	10	.289	Wash40	
		Myatt, George Edward (SS15 OF3)	2B121	140	.284	B	
10	8	Niggeling, John Arnold	P	24	.130	B	
0	2	Ortiz, Oliverio Nunez	P	2	.167	A	C
		Ortiz, Roberto Gonzalo Nunez	OF80	85	.253	B	C
		Powell, Alvin Jacob (Jake) (3B1)	OF92	96	.240	B	
		Spence, Stanley Orville (1B3)	OF150	153	.313	B	
		Suarez, Luis Abelardo	3B	1	.000	A	C
		Sullivan, John Patrick	SS	138	.251	B	
0	0	Thesenga, Arnold Joseph	P	5	.000	A	C
		Torres, Don Gilberto (1B4 2B10)	3B123	134	.267	Wash40	
0	0	Ullrich, Carlos Santiago Castello	P	3	.333	A	
		Valdes, Armando Viera		1	.000	A	C
		Vaughn, Frederick Thomas (3B3)	2B26	30	.257	A	
		Vosmik, Joseph Franklin	OF12	14	.194	BknN41	C
4	15	Wolff, Roger Francis	P	33	.218	Phil	
8	17	Wynn, Early Jr.	P33	43	.207	B	
		Yost, Edward Frederick (SS2)	3B3	7	.143	A	
0	0	Zinser, Wm. Francis	P	2	.000	A	C

WON 87 AMERICAN LEAGUE FINISHED 2nd.
LOST 67
TG 154 1945. PCT. .565

WASHINGTON

OSWALD LOUIS BLUEGE

WON	LOST	NAME	POS.	G.	BA	FROM	TO
		Binks, George Eugene (1B20)	OF128	145	.278	B	
1	0	Appleton, Peter Wm. (Jablonowski)	P	6	+.200	xStL	C
7	5	Carrasquel, Alejandro Alexander	P	35	.083	B	C
		Case, George Washington	OF	123	.294	B	
		Chipple, Walter John	OF13	18	.136	A	C
0	0	Cleary, Joseph Christopher	P	1	.000	A	C
		Clift, Harlond Benton	3B111	119	.211	B	C
		Evans, Alfred Hubert	C41	51	.260	B	
		Ferrell, Richard Benjamin (Rick)	C83	91	.266	B	
		Guerra, Fermin Romero	C38	56	.210	B	
16	14	Haefner, Milton Arnold	P	37	.244	B	
1	1	Holborow, Walter Albert	P	15	.000	B	
		Kimble, Richard Louis	SS15	20	.245	A	C
		Kreevich, Michael Andreas	OF41	45	+.272	xStL	C
		Kuhel, Joseph Anthony (Joey)	1B141	142	.285	B	
		Layne, Ivoria Hillis	3B33	61	.299	B	C
17	7	Leonard, Emil John (Dutch)	P	31	.231	B	
		Lewis, John Kelly Jr. (Buddy)	OF	69	.333	Wash41	
1	2	Masterson, Walter Edward	P	4	.111	Wash42	
		McFarland, Howard Alexander	OF3	6	.091	A	C
		Myatt, George Edward (SS1 3B6 OF32)	2B94	133	.296	B	
7	12	Niggeling, John Arnold	P	26	.119	B	
14	13	Pieretti, Marino Paul	P	44	.222	A	
		Powell, Alvin Jacob (Jake)	OF27	31	.194	B	PhilN
0	0	Roche, Armando Baez	P	2	.000	A	C
0	0	Shepard, Bert Robert	P	1	.000	A	C
0	0	Stone, Chas. Richard	P	3	.000	A	C
		Torres, Don Gilberto (3B2)	SS145	147	.237	B	
		Travis, Cecil Howel	3B14	15	.241	Wash41	
3	3	Ullrich, Carlos Antiago Castello	P	28	.273	B	C
		Vaughn, Frederick Thomas (SS1)	2B76	80	.235	B	C
		Ventura, Vincent	OF15	18	.207	A	C
20	10	Wolff, Roger Francis	P	33	.107	B	
		Zardon, Jose Antonio	OF43	54	.290	A	C

WON 76 AMERICAN LEAGUE FINISHED 4th.
LOST 78
TG 154 1946. PCT. .494

WASHINGTON

OSWALD LOUIS BLUEGE

WON	LOST	NAME	POS.	G.	BA	FROM	TO
		Binks, George Eugene	OF28	65	.194	B	
2	0	Candini, Mario Cain	P	9	.333	Wash44	

WON	LOST	NAME	POS.	G.	BA	FROM	TO
		Coan, Gilbert Fitzgerald	OF29	59	.209	A	
0	0	Curtis, Vernon Eugene	P	11	.000	Wash44	C
		Early, Jacob Willard	C	64	.201	Wash43	
		Evans, Alfred Hubert	C81	88	.254	B	
		Goolsby, Raymond Daniel	OF1	3	.000	A	C
		Grace, Joseph LaVerne	OF74	77	+.302	xStL	
		Guerra, Fermin Romero	C27	41	.253	B	
14	11	Haefner, Milton Arnold	P	33	.203	B	
		Heath, John Goeffrey (Jeff)	OF47	48	+.283	Clev	StL
		Hitchcock, Wm. Clyde (3B46)	SS53	98	+.212	xDet	
8	11	Hudson, Sidney Chas.	P	31	.279	Wash42	
1	2	Kennedy, Wm. Gorman	P	21	.125	Wash42	
		Kuhel, Joseph Anthony (Joey)	1B5	14	+.150	B	Chi
0	1	LaMacchia, Alfred Anthony	P	2	+.000	xStL	C
10	10	Leonard, Emil John (Dutch)	P	26	.170	B	
		Lewis, John Kelly Jr. (Buddy)	OF145	150	.292	B	
5	6	Masterson, Walter Edward	P	29	.080	B	
		Myatt, George Edward (2B2)	3B7	15	.235	B	
11	8	Newsom, Louis Norman (Buck)	P	24	+.161	xPhil	
3	2	Niggeling, John Arnold	P	8	.182	B	BosN
2	2	Pieretti, Marino Paul	P	30	.214	B	
		Priddy, Gerald Edward	2B	138	.254	Wash43	
		Robertson, Sherrard Alexander (2B14 SS12 OF1)	3B38	74	.200	Wash43	
		Sanford, John Doward	1B6	10	.231	Wash41	C
7	11	Scarborough, Ray Wilson	P	32	.140	Wash43	
		Spence, Stanley Orville	OF150	152	.292	Wash44	
0	0	Torres, Don Gilberto (P3 2B7 3B18)	SS31	63	.254	B	C
		Travis, Cecil Howel (3B56)	SS75	137	.252	B	
		Vernon, James Barton	1B147	148	.353	Wash43	
0	0	Wade, Jacob Fields (Jake)	P	6	+.000	xN.Y.	C
0	1	Wilson, Chas. Max	P	9	.000	PhilN40	C
5	8	Wolff, Roger Francis	P	21	.103	B	
8	5	Wynn, Early Jr.	P17	25	.319	Wash44	
		Yost, Edward Frederick	3B7	8	.080	Wash44	

WON 64 — AMERICAN LEAGUE — FINISHED 7th.
LOST 90
TG 154 — 1947. — PCT. .416

WASHINGTON

OSWALD LOUIS BLUEGE

WON	LOST	NAME	POS.	G.	BA	FROM	TO
3	4	Candini, Mario Cain	P	38	.167	B	
3	1	Cary, Scott Russell	P	23	.077	A	C
		Case, George Washington	OF21	36	.150	Clev	C
		Christman, Marquette Joseph (2B1)	SS106	110	.223	StL	
		Coan, Gilbert Fitzgerald	OF	11	.500	B	
0	0	Dozier, Wm. Joseph	P	2	.000	A	
		Ermer, Calvin Coolidge	2B	1	.000	A	C
		Evans, Alfred Hubert	C94	99	.241	B	
		Ferrell, Richard Benjamin (Rick)	C	37	.303	Wash45	C
1	7	Ferrick, Thomas Jerome	P	31	.100	StL	
		Grace, Joseph LaVerne	OF67	78	.248	B	C
10	14	Haefner, Milton Arnold	P	31	.136	B	
0	0	Harris, Chalmer Luman	P	3	.000	Phil	C
6	9	Hudson, Sidney Chas.	P	20	.308	B	
0	0	Kennedy, Wm. Gorman	P	2	.000	B	C
0	0	Knerr, Wallace Luther	P	6	1.000	Phil	C
		Lewis, John Kelly Jr. (Buddy)	OF130	140	.261	B	
		Lyons, Edward Hoyt	2B	7	.154	A	C
		Mackiewicz, Felix Thaddeus	OF	3	+.167	xClev	C
		Mancuso, Frank Octavius	C35	43	.229	StL	C
12	16	Masterson, Walter Edward	P35	36	.133	B	
		Myatt, George Edward	2B1	12	.000	B	C
		McBride, Thomas Raymond (3B1)	OF51	56	+.271	xBos	
4	6	Newsom, Louis Norman (Buck)	P	14	+.241	B	N.Y.
2	4	Pieretti, Marino Paul	P	23	.231	B	
		Priddy, Gerald Edward	2B146	147	.214	B	
		Robertson, Sherrard Alexander (2B4 3B10)	OF55	95	.233	B	
6	13	Scarborough, Ray Wilson	P	33	.120	B	
		Spence, Stanley Orville	OF142	147	.279	B	
		Sullivan, John Patrick (2B1)	SS40	49	.256	Wash44	
0	1	Toenes, Wm. Harrell	P	3	.000	A	C
		Travis, Cecil Howel (SS15)	3B39	74	.216	B	C
		Vernon, James Barton	1B	154	.265	B	
		Wooten, Earl Hazell	OF	6	.083	A	
17	15	Wynn, Early Jr.	P33	54	.275	B	
		Yost, Edward Frederick	3B114	115	.238	B	

WON 56 — AMERICAN LEAGUE — FINISHED 7th.
LOST 97
TG 153 — 1948. — PCT. .366

WASHINGTON

JOSEPH ANTHONY KUHEL

WON	LOST	NAME	POS.	G.	BA	FROM	TO
2	3	Candini, Mario Cain	P	35	.364	B	
		Christman, Marquette Joseph (2B3 3B9)	SS102	120	.259	B	
		Clark, James (3B1)	SS1	9	.250	A	C
		Coan, Gilbert Fitzgerald	OF131	138	.232	B	
0	0	Cooper, Calvin Asa	P	1	.000	A	C
		Culberson, Delbert Leon	OF11	12	.172	Bos	C
		Difani, Clarence Joseph		2	.000	A	
		Drake, Larry Francis	OF2	4	.286	Phil45	C
		Early, Jacob Willard	C92	97	.220	StL	
		Evans, Alfred Hubert	C85	93	.259	B	
2	5	Ferrick, Thomas Jerome	P	37	.067	B	
		Fleitas, Angel Felix Husta	SS7	15	.077	A	C

WON	LOST	NAME	POS.	G.	BA	FROM	TO
0	0	Garcia, Ramon Garcia	P	4	1.000	A	C
		Gillenwater, Carden Edison	OF67	77	.244	BosN46	C
5	13	Haefner, Milton Arnold	P	28	.163	B	
3	3	Harrist, Earl	P	23	+.167	xChi	
4	16	Hudson, Sidney Chas.	P	39	.237	B	
		Kozar, Albert Kenneth	2B149	150	.250	A	
8	15	Masterson, Walter Edward	P	33	.193	B	
		Meeks, Samuel Mack (2B1)	SS10	24	.121	A	
		McBride, Thomas Raymond	OF55	92	.257	B	C
		Okrie, Leonard Joseph	C17	19	.238	A	
0	2	Pieretti, Marino Paul	P8	13	+.000	B	Chi
		Robertson, Sherrard Alexander	OF51	71	.246	B	
15	8	Scarborough, Ray Wilson	P	31	.219	B	
		Stewart, Edward Perry	OF114	118	+.279	xN.Y.	
		Sullivan, John Patrick (2B4)	SS57	85	.208	B	
6	10	Thompson, David Forrest	P	46	.286	A	
		Vernon, James Barton	1B	150	.242	B	
		Vollmer, Clyde Frederick	OF	1	.400	xCinN	
1	2	Weik, Richard Henry	P	3	.750	A	
2	1	Welteroth, Richard John	P	33	.100	A	
0	0	Wooten, Earl Hazell (P1 1B6)	OF73	88	.256	B	C
8	19	Wynn, Early Jr.	P33	73	.217	B	
		Yost, Edward Frederick	3B	145	.249	B	

WON 50 AMERICAN LEAGUE FINISHED 8th (LAST)
LOST 104
TG 154 1949. PCT. .324

WASHINGTON

JOSEPH ANTHONY KUHEL

WON	LOST	NAME	POS.	G.	BA	FROM	TO
6	17	Calvert, Leo Paul Emile	P34	35	.137	Clev45	
0	0	Candini, Mario Cain	P	3	1.000	B	
		Christman, Marquette Joseph (1B6 2B1 SS4)	3B23	49	.214	B	C
		Coan, Gilbert Fitzgerald	OF97	111	.218	B	
		Dente, Samuel Joseph	SS	153	.273	StL	
		Difani, Clarence Joseph	2B1	2	1.000	B	C
0	0	Dozier, Wm. Joseph	P	2	.000	Wash47	C
		Early, Jacob Willard	C	53	.246	B	C
		Evans, Alfred Hubert	C107	109	.271	B	
0	2	Gettel, Allen Jones	P	16	+.000	xChi	
0	0	Gonzales, Julio Enrique	P	13	.200	A	C
5	5	Haefner, Milton Arnold	P19	20	+.200	B	Chi
2	12	Harris, Maurice Chas.	P	23	+.205	xBos	
2	9	Haynes, Joseph Walton	P	37	.240	Chi	
5	7	Hittle, Lloyd Eldon	P	36	.143	A	
8	17	Hudson, Sidney Chas.	P	40	.239	B	
		Keller, Harold Kefauver		3	.333	A	
0	0	Klieman, Edward Frederick	P	2	+1.000	Clev	Chi
		Kozar, Albert Kenneth	2B102	105	.269	B	
		Lewis, John Kelly Jr.(Buddy)	OF67	95	.245	Wash47	C

WON	LOST	NAME	POS.	G.	BA	FROM	TO
3	2	Masterson, Walter Edward	P10	11	+.056	B	Bos
		Mele, Sabath Anthony (1B11)	OF63	78	+.242	xBos	
		Ortiz, Roberto Gonzalo Nunez	OF32	40	.279	Wash44	
0	1	Pearce, James Madison	P	2	.000	A	
		Reich, Herman Chas.		2	+.000	A	Clev
		Robertson, Sherrard Alexander (3B19 OF13)	2B71	110	.251	B	
		Robinson, Wm. Edward	1B	143	.294	Clev	
13	11	Scarborough, Ray Wilson	P	34	.194	B	
		Simmons, John Earl	OF26	62	.215	A	C
		Stewart, Edward Perry	OF105	118	.284	B	
0	1	Sutherland, Howard Alvin	P	1	.000	A	C
1	3	Thompson, David Forrest	P9	10	.600	B	C
		Vollmer, Clyde Frederick	OF114	129	.253	B	
		Weigel, Ralph Richard	C21	34	.233	Chi	C
3	12	Weik, Richard Henry	P27	28	.179	B	
2	5	Welteroth, Richard John	P	52	.059	B	
		Yost, Edward Frederick	3B122	124	.253	B	

WON 67 AMERICAN LEAGUE FINISHED 5th.
LOST 87
TG 154 1950. PCT. .435

WASHINGTON

STANLEY RAYMOND HARRIS

WON	LOST	NAME	POS.	G.	BA	FROM	TO
3	5	Bearden, Henry Eugene (1B1)	P12	14	+.227	xClev	
		Coan, Gilbert Fitzgerald	OF98	104	.303	B	
		Combs, Merrill Russell	SS30	37	+.245	xBos	
7	8	Consuegra, Sandalio Simeon Castellon	P21	24	.175	A	
		Dente, Samuel Joseph (2B29)	SS128	155	.239	B	
		Evans, Alfred Hubert	C88	90	.235	B	
		Genovese, George Michael		3	.000	A	C
		Grasso, Newton Michael	C 69	75	.287	NYN46	
5	9	Harris, Maurice Chas.	P	53	.235	B	
7	5	Haynes, Joseph Walton	P	27	.200	B	
2	4	Hittle, Lloyd Eldon	P	11	.077	B	C
14	14	Hudson, Sidney Chas.	P30	31	.215	B	
		Keller, Harold Kefauver	C8	11	.214	B	
		Kozar, Albert Kenneth	2B15	20	+.200	B	Chi
8	7	Kuzava, Robert LeRoy	P	22	+.100	xChi	
6	10	Marrero, Conrado Eugenio Ramos	P	27	.122	A	
0	1	Martinez, Rogelio Ulloa	P	2	.000	A	C
		Mele, Sabath Anthony (1B16)	OF99	126	.274	B	
		Michaels, Casimir Eugene	2B104	106	+.250	xChi	
1	1	Moreno, Julio Gonzales	P	4	.125	A	
2	5	Nagy, Stephen	P9	15	.227	PittN47	C
		Noren, Irving Arnold (1B17)	OF121	138	.295	A	
		O'Brien, Thomas Edward	OF	3	+.111	xBos	C
		Okrie, Leonard Joseph	C	17	.222	Wash48	

WON	LOST	NAME	POS.	G.	BA	FROM	TO
		Ortiz, Roberto Gonzalo Nunez	OF19	39	+.227	B	Phil
		Ostrowski, John Theodore	OF46	55	+.227	xChi (returned)	Chi
1	1	Pascual, Carlos Luis	P	2	.250	A	C
2	1	Pearce, James Madison	P	20	.154	B	
		Robertson, Sherrard Alexander (2B12 3B1)	OF14	71	.260	.260	B
		Robinson, Wm. Edward	1B	36	+.240	B	Chi
0	1	Ross, Floyd Robert	P	6	.000	A	
3	5	Scarborough, Ray Wilson	P	8	+.100	B	Chi
4	5	Sima, Albert	P	17	.115	A	
1	2	Singleton, Bert Elmer	P	21	.429	PittN48	
		Stewart, Edward Perry	OF100	118	.267	B	
		Taylor, Frederick Rankin	1B3	6	.125	A	
		Vernon, James Barton	1B85	90	+.306	xClev	
		Vollmer, Clyde Frederick	OF3	6	+.286	B	Bos
1	3	Weik, Richard Henry	P	14	+.154	B	Clev
0	0	Welteroth, Richard John	P	5	.000	B	C
		Yost, Edward Frederick	3B	155	.295	B	

WON 62 LOST 92 TG 154

AMERICAN LEAGUE 1951.

FINISHED 7th. PCT. .403

WASHINGTON

STANLEY RAYMOND HARRIS

WON	LOST	NAME	POS.	G.	BA	FROM	TO
0	0	Bearden, Henry Eugene	P	1	+.000	B	Det
0	0	Brown, Alton Leo	P	7	.000	A	C
		Campos, Francisco Jose Lopez	OF7	8	.423	A	
		Coan, Gilbert Fitzgerald	OF132	135	.303	B	
7	8	Consuegra, Sandalio Simeon Castellon	P	40	.233	B	
		Dente, Samuel Joseph (2B10 3B5)	SS65	88	.238	B	
2	0	Ferrick, Thomas Jerome	P	22	+.286	xN.Y.	
		Grasso, Newton Michael	C49	52	.206	B	
		Guerra, Fermin Romero	C66	72	+.200	xBos	C
6	8	Harris, Maurice Chas.	P	41	.188	B	
		Hawes, Roy Lee	1B1	3	.167	A	C
1	4	Haynes, Joseph Walton	P	26	.333	B	
5	12	Hudson, Sidney Chas.	P23	24	.273	B	
7	11	Johnson, Donald Roy	P	21	+.085	xStL	
		Kluttz, Clyde Franklin	C46	53	+.308	xStL	
3	3	Kuzava, Robert LeRoy	P	8	+.176	B	N.Y.
11	9	Marrero, Conrado Eugenio Ramos	P	25	.164	B	
		Mele, Sabath Anthony (1B15)	OF124	143	.274	B	
		Michaels, Casimir Eugene	2B128	138	.258	B	
		Miranda, Guillermo Perez (1B1)	SS2	7	.444	A	
5	11	Moreno, Julio Gonzales	P	31	.175	B	
		McCormick, Myron Winthrop	OF62	81	.288	Chi	C

WON	LOST	NAME	POS.	G.	BA	FROM	TO
		Noren, Irving Arnold	OF126	129	.279	B	
		Okrie, Leonard Joseph	C	5	.125	B	
		Porter, Daniel Edward	OF3	13	.211	A	C
9	8	Porterfield, Erwin Coolidge	P	19	+.130	xN.Y.	
		Robertson, Sherrard Alexander	OF22	62	.189	B	
0	1	Ross, Floyd Robert	P	11	.111	B	
		Runnels, James Edward	SS73	78	.278	A	
		Sacka, Frank	C6	7	.250	A	
2	3	Sanford, John Frederick	P	7	+.071	xN.Y.	StL
3	7	Sima, Albert	P	18	.176	B	
1	7	Starr, Richard Eugene	P	11	+.176	xStL	C
		Taylor, Frederick Rankin	1B2	6	.167	B	
		Verble, Gene Kermit (2B19 3B1)	SS28	68	.203	A	
		Vernon, James Barton	1B137	141	.293	B	
0	0	Wyse, Henry Washington	P	3	+.000	xPhil	C
		Yost, Edward Frederick (OF3)	3B152	154	.283	B	

WON 78 LOST 76 TG 154

AMERICAN LEAGUE 1952.

FINISHED 5th. PCT. .506

WASHINGTON

STANLEY RAYMOND HARRIS

WON	LOST	NAME	POS.	G.	BA	FROM	TO
		Baker, Floyd Wilson (SS7 3B1)	2B68	79	.262	Chi	
		Bradshaw, George Thomas	C9	10	.217	A	C
		Busby, James Franklin	OF128	129	+.244	xChi	
		Campos, Francisco Jose Lopez	OF23	53	.259	B	
		Coan, Gilbert Fitzgerald	OF86	107	.205	B	
6	0	Consuegra, Sandalio Simeon Castellon	P	30	.176	B	
4	3	Ferrick, Thomas Jerome	P	27	.200	B	C
2	2	Fornieles,Jose Miguel	P	4	.000	A	
		Grasso, Newton Michael	C114	115	.216	B	
0	0	Grossman, Harley Joseph	P	1	.000	A	
4	9	Gumpert, Randall Pennington	P	20	+.206	xBos	C
0	0	Harris, Maurice Chas.	P	1	+.000	B	Clev
0	3	Haynes, Joseph Walton	P	22	.105	B	C
		Hoderlein, Melvin Anthony	2B58	72	.269	Bos	
3	4	Hudson, Sidney Chas.	P	7	+.167	B	Bos
		Jensen, Jack Eugene	OF143	144	+.286	xN.Y.	
0	5	Johnson, Donald Roy	P	29	.077	B	
		Keller, Harold Kefauver	C	11	.174	Wash50	C
		Kluttz, Clyde Franklin	C52	58	.229	B	C
11	8	Marrero, Conrado Eugenio Ramos	P	22	.079	B	
		Marsh, Fred Francis (OF2)	2B5	9	+.042	xStL (returned)	StL
9	8	Masterson, Walter Edward	P	24	+.120	xBos	
		Mele, Sabath Anthony	OF7	9	+.429	B	Chi

WON	LOST	NAME	POS.	G.	BA	FROM	TO
		Michaels, Casimir Eugene	2B	22	+.233	B	StL
9	9	Moreno, Julio Gonzales	P	26	.122	B	
1	1	Newsom, Louis Norman	P	10	+.000	NYN48	Phil
		Noren, Irving Arnold	OF	12	+.245	B̲	N.Y.
13	14	Porterfield, Erwin Coolidge	P	31	.190	B	
		Rapp, Earl Wellington	OF10	46	+.284	xStL	C
		Robertson, Sherrard Alexander		1	+.000	B	Phil
		Runnels, James Edward (2B1)	SS147	152	.285	B	
1	1	Sanchez, Raul Guadalupe Rodriguez	P	3	.000	A	
11	7	Shea, Francis Joseph	P	22	.238	N.Y.	
4	2	Sleater, Louis Mortimer	P14	15	+.050	xStL	C
		Snyder, Jerry George (SS4)	2B19	36	.158	A	
0	0	Stewart, Veston Goff	P	1	.000	A	
		Taylor, Frederick Rankin	1B5	10	.263	B	C
		Upton, Thomas Herbert	SS3	5	.000	StL	C
		Varner, Glen Gann	OF1	2	.000	A	C
		Vernon, James Barton	1B153	154	.251	B	
		Wilson, Archie Clifton	OF24	26	+.208	xN.Y.	Bos
		Wood, Kenneth Lanier	OF56	61	+.238	xBos	
		Yost, Edward Frederick	3B	157	.233	B	

WON 76
LOST 76
TG 152

AMERICAN LEAGUE — FINISHED 5th.

1953. — PCT. .500

WASHINGTON

STANLEY RAYMOND HARRIS

WON	LOST	NAME	POS.	G.	BA	FROM	TO
		Baker, Floyd Wilson	3B1	9	+.000	B	Bos
		Barmes, Bruce Raymond	OF1	5	.200	A	C
		Busby, James Franklin	OF	150	.312	B	
0	5	Byrne, Thomas Joseph	P6	14	+.059	xChi	
		Campos, Francisco Jose Lopez		10	.111	B	C
		Coan, Gilbert Fitzgerald	OF46	68	.196	B	
0	0	Consuegra, Sandalio Simeon Castellon	P	4	+.000	B	Chi
		Davilillo, Pompeyo Romero	SS17	19	.293	A	C
5	8	Dixon, John Craig	P	43	.154	A	
		Fitz Gerald, Edward Raymond	C85	88	.250	xPittN̲	
		Grasso, Newton Michael	C59	61	.209	B	
		Hoderlein, Melvin Anthony (SS2)	2B11	23	.191	B	
		Jensen, Jack Eugene	OF146	147	.266	B	
1	4	Lane, Jerald Hal	P	20	.111	A	
8	7	Marrero, Conrado Eugenio Ramos	P	22	.125	B	
10	12	Masterson, Walter Edward	P	29	.137	B	
		Mauro, Carmen Louis	OF6	17	+.174	xBknN̲	Phil
3	1	Moreno, Julio Gonzales	P	12	.000	B̲	C
		Oldis, Robert Carl	C	7	.250	A	
0	1	Pearce, James Madison	P	4	.000	Wash50	

WON	LOST	NAME	POS.	G.	BA	FROM	TO
		Peden, Leslie Earl	C8	9	.250	A	C
22	10	Porterfield, Erwin Coolidge	P34	37	.255	B	
		Roig, Anton Ambrose	2B2	3	.125	A	
		Runnels, James Edward (2B11)	SS121	137	.257	B	
		Sacka, Frank	C6	7	.278	Wash51	C
2	7	Schmitz, John Albert	P	24	+.059	xN.Y.	
12	7	Shea, Francis Joseph	P	23	.177	B	
2	3	Sima, Albert	P	31	.118	Wash51	
		Snyder, Jerry George (2B4)	SS17	29	.339	B	
0	2	Stewart, Veston Goff	P	2	.200	B	
11	8	Stobbs, Chas. Klein	P	27	.227	Chi	
0	1	Stone, Darrah Dean	P	3	.000	A	
		Terwilliger, Willard Wayne	2B133	134	.252	BknN51	
		Thomas, Keith Marshall (C1)	OF8	38	+.293	xPhil	C
		Verble, Gene Kermit	SS8	13	.190	Wash51	C
		Vernon, James Barton	1B	152	.337	B	
		Vollmer, Clyde Frederick	OF106	118	+.260	xBos	
		Wood, Kenneth Lanier	OF7	12	.212	B	C
		Yost, Edward Frederick	3B	152	.272	B	

WON 66
LOST 88
TG 154

AMERICAN LEAGUE — FINISHED 6th.

1954. — PCT. .429

WASHINGTON

STANLEY RAYMOND HARRIS

WON	LOST	NAME	POS.	G.	BA	FROM	TO
		Busby, James Franklin	OF	155	.298	B	
		Dielzel, Leroy Louis (3B2)	2B7	9	.238	A	C
1	2	Dixon, John Craig	P	16	+.000	B	Phil
		Fitz Gerald, Edward Raymond	C107	115	.289	B	
		Hoderlein, Melvin Anthony (2B5)	SS6	14	.160	B	C
2	3	Keriazakos, Constantine Nicholas	P	22	.067	Chi50	
		Killebrew, Harmon Clayton	2B8	9	.308	A	
		Korcheck, Stephen Joseph	C	2	.143	A	
		Lemon, James Robert	OF33	37	.234	Clev	
		Levan, Jesse Roy (1B1)	3B4	7	.300	PhilN̲47	
3	6	Marrero, Conrado Eugenio Ramos	P	22	.000	B	C
7	15	McDermott, Maurice Joseph	P30	54	.200	Bos	
		Oldis, Robert Carl (3B2)	C8	11	.333	B	
4	7	Pascual, Camilo Alberto	P	48	.133	A	
		Paula, Carlos Conill	OF6	9	.167	A	
		Pesky, John Michael (SS1)	2B37	49	+.253	xDet	C
13	15	Porterfield, Erwin Coolidge	P	32	.102	B	
		Runnels, James Edward (2B27 OF1)	SS107	139	.268	B	
11	8	Schmitz, John Albert	P	29	.117	B	
2	9	Shea, Francis Joseph	P	23	.050	B	
		Sievers, Roy Edward (1B8)	OF133	145	.232	StL	

WON	LOST	NAME	POS.	G.	BA	FROM	TO
		Snyder, Jerry George (2B3)	SS48	64	.234	B	
0	2	Stewart, Veston Goff	P	29	.000	B	
11	11	Stobbs, Chas. Klein	P	31	.137	B	
12	10	Stone, Darrah Dean	P	31	.096	B	
		Terwilliger, Willard Wayne (SS3 3B10)	2B90	106	.208	B	
		Tipton, Joseph John	C52	54	.223	Clev	C
		Umphlett, Thomas Mullen	OF101	114	.219	Bos	
		Vernon, James Barton	1B148	151	.290	B	
		Vollmer, Clyde Frederick	OF26	62	.256	B	C
		Wright, Thomas Everett	OF43	76	.246	Chi	
		Yost, Edward Frederick	3B	155	.256	B	

WON 53
LOST 101
TG 154

AMERICAN LEAGUE

1955.

FINISHED 8th (LAST)

PCT. .344

WASHINGTON

CHAS. WALTER DRESSEN

WON	LOST	NAME	POS.	G.	BA	FROM	TO
5	9	Abernathy, Theodore Wade	P	40	.154	A	
		Becquer, Julio Vellegas	1B2	10	.214	A	
		Busby, James Franklin	OF	47	+.230	B	Chi
2	3	Chakales, Robert Edward	P	29	+.000	xChi	
0	0	Clarke, Vibert Ernesto	P	7	.167	A	C
		Courtney, Clinton Dawson	C67	75	+.298	xChi	
0	0	Currie, Wm. Cleveland	P	3	.000	A	C
		Delis, Juan Francisco (2B1 OF8)	3B24	54	.189	A	C
		Edwards, Chas. Bruce (3B5)	C22	30	.175	ChiN	
		Fitz Gerald, Edward Raymond	C72	74	.237	B	
0	0	Gonzales, Wenceslao O'Reilly	P	1	.000	A	C
		Groth, John Thomas	OF48	63	+.219	xChi	
0	0	Hyde, Richard Elde	P	3	.000	A	
		Killebrew, Harmon Clayton (2B3)	3B23	38	.200	B	
0	0	Kline, John Robert (P1 2B4 3B3)	SS69	77	.221	A	C
		Korcheck, Stephen Joseph	C12	13	.278	B	
		Lemon, James Robert	OF6	10	.200	B	
		Levan, Jesse Roy		16	.188	B	C
10	10	McDermott, Maurice Joseph	P31	70	.263	B	
		Oldis, Robert Carl	C	6	.000	B	
		Oravetz, Ernest Eugene	OF57	100	.270	A	
2	12	Pascual, Camilo Alberto	P	43	.219	B	
		Paula, Carlos Conill	OF86	115	.299	B	
10	17	Porterfield, Erwin Coolidge	P	30	.190	B	
5	11	Ramos, Pedro	P45	59	.079	A	
		Roig, Anton Ambrose (2B1 3B8)	SS21	29	.228	Wash53	
		Runnels, James Edward (SS2)	2B132	134	.284	B	
7	10	Schmitz, John Albert	P	32	.185	B	

WON	LOST	NAME	POS.	G.	BA	FROM	TO
		Schoonmaker, Jerald Lee	OF15	20	.152	A	
2	2	Shea, Francis Joseph	P	27	.400	B	C
		Sievers, Roy Edward (1B17 3B2)	OF129	144	.271	B	
		Snyder, Jerry George (SS20)	2B22	46	.224	B	
0	0	Stewart, Veston Goff	P	7	.000	B	
4	14	Stobbs, Chas. Klein	P	41	.171	B	
6	13	Stone, Darrah Dean	P	43	.043	B	
		Umphlett, Thomas Mullen	OF103	110	.217	B	C
		Valdivielso, Jose Lopez	SS	94	.221	A	
		Vernon, James Barton	1B144	150	.301	B	
		Wright, Thomas Everett		7	.000	B	
		Yost, Edward Frederick	3B107	122	.243	B	

WON 59
LOST 95
TG 154

AMERICAN LEAGUE

1956.

FINISHED 7th.

PCT. .383

WASHINGTON

CHAS. WALTER DRESSEN

WON	LOST	NAME	POS.	G.	BA	FROM	TO
1	3	Abernathy, Theodore Wade	P	5	.182	B	
		Berberet, Louis Joseph	C59	95	.261	N.Y.	
0	3	Brodowski, Richard Stanley	P	7	.000	Bos	
2	4	Byerly, Eldred Wm.	P	25	.091	CinN52	
4	4	Chakales, Robert Edward	P	43	.150	B	
0	0	Clevenger, Truman Eugene	P	20	.000	Bos54	
		Courtney, Clinton Dawson	C76	101	.300	B	
		Fitz Gerald, Edward Raymond	C50	64	.304	B	
1	6	Griggs, Harold Lloyd	P34	36	.000	A	
4	5	Grob, Conrad George	P	37	.333	A	C
1	1	Hernandez, Evelio Lopez	P	4	.182	A	
		Herzog, Dorrel Norman (1B5)	OF103	117	.245	A	
		Killebrew, Harmon Clayton (2B4)	3B20	44	.222	B	
		Lemon, James Robert	OF141	146	.271	B	
		Luttrell, Lyle Kenneth	SS37	38	.189	A	
		Olson, Karl Arthur	OF101	106	.246	Bos	
		Oravetz, Ernest Eugene	OF31	88	.248	B	C
6	18	Pascual, Camilo Alberto	P39	43	.138	B	
		Paula, Carlos Conill	OF20	33	.183	B	C
		Plews, Herbert Eugene (SS5 3B2)	2B66	91	.270	A	
12	10	Ramos, Pedro	P37	56	.205	B	
		Roig, Anton Ambrose (SS19)	2B27	44	.210	B	C
		Runnels, James Edward (2B69 SS3)	1B81	147	.310	B	
		Sievers, Roy Edward (1B76)	OF78	152	.253	B	
		Snyder, Jerry George (2B7)	SS35	43	.270	B	
5	7	Stewart, Veston Goff	P33	34	.250	B	C
15	15	Stobbs, Chas. Klein	P37	38	.179	B	
5	7	Stone, Darrah Dean	P41	42	.088	B	
		Tettelbach, Richard Morley	OF	18	.156	N.Y.	

WON	LOST	NAME	POS.	G.	BA	FROM	TO
		Valdivielso, Jose Lopez	SS	90	.236	B	
3	12	Wiesler, Robert George	P37	38	.091	N.Y.	
		Wright, Thomas Everett		2	.000	B	C
		Yost, Edward Frederick (OF8)	3B135	152	.231	B	

WON 55
LOST 99
TG 154

AMERICAN LEAGUE — FINISHED 8th (LAST)

1957. — PCT. .357

WASHINGTON

CHAS. WALTER DRESSEN   HARRY ARTHUR LAVAGETTO

WON	LOST	NAME	POS.	G.	BA	FROM	TO
2	10	Abernathy, Theodore Wade	P	26	.167	B	
		Becquer, Julio Vellegas	1B43	105	.226	Wash55	
		Berberet, Louis Joseph	C77	99	.261	B	
0	1	Black, Joseph	P	7	.000	CinN	C
		Bolling, Milton Joseph (SS37 3B1)	2B53	91	+.227	xBos	
		Bridges, Everett LaMar (2B14 3B1)	SS108	120	.228	xCinN	
0	1	Brodowski, Richard Stanley	P	6	.000	B	
6	6	Byerly, Eldred Wm.	P	47	.067	B	
0	1	Chakales, Robert Edward	P	4	+.143	B	Bos
		Chrisley, Barbra O'Neil	OF11	26	.157	A	
7	6	Clevenger, Truman Eugene	P	52	.212	B	
		Courtney, Clinton Dawson	C59	91	.267	B	
		Fitz Gerald, Edward Raymond	C37	45	.272	B	
0	1	Griggs, Harold Lloyd	P	2	.250	B	
0	3	Heise, James Edward	P	8	.000	A	C
0	0	Hernandez, Evelio Lopez	P	14	.000	B	C
		Herzog, Dorrel Norman	OF28	36	.167	B	
4	3	Hyde, Richard Elde	P	52	.167	Wash55	
7	11	Kemmerer, Russell Paul	P	39	+.067	xBos	
		Killebrew, Harmon Clayton (2B1)	3B7	9	.290	B	
		Lemon, James Robert (1B3)	OF131	137	.284	B	
0	1	Lumenti, Raphael Anthony	P	3	.000	A	
		Luttrell, Lyle Kenneth	SS17	19	.200	B	C
0	1	Minnick, Donald Athey	P	2	.000	A	C
		Olson, Karl Arthur	OF6	8	+.167	B	Det
8	17	Pascual, Camilo Alberto	P29	32	.140	B	
		Plews, Herbert Eugene (SS4 3B11)	2B79	104	.271	B	
12	16	Ramos, Pedro	P43	56	.171	B	
		Runnels, James Edward (2B23 3B32)	1B72	134	.230	B	
		Schoonmaker, Jerald Lee	OF13	30	.087	Wash55	C
		Schult, Arthur Wm. (OF31)	1B35	77	.263	xCinN	
0	0	Shifflett, Garland Jessie	P	6	.000	A	C
		Sievers, Roy Edward (1B21)	OF130	152	.301	B	
		Snyder, Jerry George (2B13 3B1)	SS15	42	.151	B	
8	20	Stobbs, Chas. Klein	P	42	.211	B	
0	0	Stone, Darrah Dean	P	3	+.000	B	Bos
		Tettelbach, Richard Morley	OF3	9	.182	B	C
		Throneberry, Maynard Faye	OF58	68	+.185	xBos	
		Usher, Robert Royce	OF95	96	+.261	xClev	C
1	1	Wiesler, Robert George	P	3	.167	B	
		Yost, Edward Frederick	3B107	110	.251	B	

WON 61
LOST 93
TG 154

AMERICAN LEAGUE — FINISHED 8th (LAST)

1958. — PCT. .396

WASHINGTON

HARRY ARTHUR LAVAGETTO

WON	LOST	NAME	POS.	G.	BA	FROM	TO
0	0	Albanese, Joseph Peter	P	6	.000	A	C
		Allison, Wm. Robert	OF	11	.200	A	
		Alvarez, Oswaldo Gonzalez (2B14 3B3)	SS64	87	.209	A	
		Aspromonte, Kenneth Joseph (SS1 3B11)	2B72	92	+.225	xBos	
		Becquer, Julio Vellegas (OF1)	1B42	86	.238	B	
		Berberet, Louis Joseph	C2	5	+.167	B	Bos
		Bridges, Everett LaMar (2B3 3B3)	SS112	116	.263	B	
2	0	Byerly, Eldred Wm.	P	17	+.000	B	Bos
0	3	Cicotte, Alva Warren	P8	9	+.200	N.Y.	Det
		Chrisley, Barbra O'Neil (3B1)	OF69	105	.215	B	
9	9	Clevenger, Truman Eugene	P	55	.136	B	
0	1	Constable, James Lee	P	15	+.250	xClev	
		Courtney, Clinton Dawson	C128	134	.251	B	
0	3	Fischer, Wm. Chas.	P	3	+.200	xDet	
		Fitz Gerald, Edward Raymond (1B5)	C21	58	.263	B	
3	11	Griggs, Harold Lloyd	P	32	.122	B	
		Herzog, Dorrel Norman	OF7	8	+.000	B	K.C.
10	3	Hyde, Richard Elde	P	53	.000	B	
6	15	Kemmerer, Russell Paul	P	40	.159	B	
		Killebrew, Harmon Clayton	3B9	13	.194	B	
		Korcheck, Stephen Joseph	C20	21	.078	Wash55	
		Lemon, James Robert	OF137	142	.246	B	
1	2	Lumenti, Raphael Anthony	P	8	.250	B	
		Malkmus, Robert Edward (SS1 3B2)	2B26	41	.186	MilN	
8	12	Pascual, Camilo Alberto	P	31	.158	B	
		Pearson, Albert Gregory	OF141	146	.275	A	
		Plews, Herbert Eugene (3B36)	2B64	111	.258	B	
14	18	Ramos, Pedro	P43	53	.239	B	
2	4	Romonosky, John	P18	27	.308	StLN53	
		Schaive, John Edward	2B6	7	.250	A	
		Sievers, Roy Edward (1B33)	OF114	148	.295	B	

WON	LOST	NAME	POS.	G.	BA	FROM	TO
		Snyder, Jerry George (SS1)	2B2	6	.111	B	C
0	0	Spring, Jack Russell	P	3	.000	Bos	
2	6	Stobbs, Chas. Klein	P	19	.000	B	StLN
		Throneberry, Maynard Faye	OF26	44	.184	B	
4	6	Valentinetti, Vito John	P	23	+.321	xDet	
0	0	Wiesler, Robert George	P	4	.000	B	C
		Yost, Edward Frederick (1B2 OF4)	3B114	134	.224	B	
		Zauchin, Norbert Henry	1B91	96	.228	Bos	

WON 63
LOST 91
TG 154

AMERICAN LEAGUE

1959.

FINISHED 8th (LAST)

PCT. .409

WASHINGTON

HARRY ARTHUR LAVAGETTO

WON	LOST	NAME	POS.	G.	BA	FROM	TO
		Allison, Wm. Robert	OF149	150	.261	B	
		Aspromonte, Kenneth Joseph (1B1 SS12 OF1)	2B52	70	.244	B	
		Becquer, Julio Vellegas	1B53	108	.268	B	
		Bertoia, Reno Peter (SS1 3B5)	2B71	90	.237	Det	
8	5	Clevenger, Truman Eugene	P	50	.174	B	
		Consolo, Wm. Angelo (2B4)	SS75	79	+.213	xBos	
		Courtney, Clinton Dawson	C53	72	.233	B	
		Dobbek, Daniel John	OF	16	.250	A	
9	11	Fischer, Wm. Chas.	P	34	.130	B	
		Fitz Gerald, Edward Raymond	C16	19	+.194	B	Clev
		Green, Leonard Chas.	OF58	88	+.242	xBalt	
2	8	Griggs, Harold Lloyd	P	37	.056	B	C
2	5	Hyde, Richard Elde	P	37	.000	B	
0	2	Kaat, James Lee	P	3	.000	A	
8	17	Kemmerer, Russell Paul	P	37	.133	B	
		Killebrew, Harmon Clayton (OF4)	3B150	153	.242	B	
		Korcheck, Stephen Joseph	C	22	.157	B	C
0	0	Kralick, John Francis	P	6	.000	A	
		Lemon, James Robert	OF142	147	.279	B	
0	0	Lumenti, Raphael Anthony	P	2	.000	B	C
		Malkmus, Robert Edward		6	.000	B	
0	0	McAvoy, Thomas John	P	1	.000	A	C
		Naragon, Harold Richard	C54	71	+.241	xClev	
17	10	Pascual, Camilo Alberto	P	32	.302	B	
		Pearson, Albert Gregory	OF22	25	+.188	B	Balt
		Plews, Herbert Eugene	2B8	27	+.225	B	Bos
		Porter, J. W. (1B2)	C34	37	.226	Clev	StLN
13	19	Ramos, Pedro	P37	45	.147	B	
1	0	Romonosky, John	P12	20	.182	B	C
		Samford, Ronald Edward (2B23)	SS64	91	.224	Det57	C
		Schaive, John Edward	2B	16	.153	B	
		Sievers, Roy Edward (OF13)	1B93	115	.242	B	

WON	LOST	NAME	POS.	G.	BA	FROM	TO
1	8	Stobbs, Chas. Klein	P	41	.105	B	
		Throneberry, Maynard Faye	OF86	117	.251	B	
		Valdivielso, Jose Lopez	SS21	24	.286	Wash56	
0	2	Valentinetti, Vito John	P	7	.000	B	C
		Versalles, Zoilo	SS	29	.153	A	
0	0	Wall, Murray Wesley	P	1	+.000	xBos	Bos
2	4	Woodeshick, Harold Joseph	P31	32	.000	Clev	
		Zauchin, Norbert Henry	1B	19	.211	B	C

WON 73
LOST 81
TG 154

AMERICAN LEAGUE

1960.

FINISHED 5th.

PCT. .474

WASHINGTON

HARRY ARTHUR LAVAGETTO

WON	LOST	NAME	POS.	G.	BA	FROM	TO
0	0	Abernathy, Theodore Wade	P	2	1.000	Wash57	
		Allison, Wm. Robert (1B4)	OF140	144	.251	B	
		Aspromonte, Kenneth Joseph		4	+.000	B	Clev
		Battey, Earl Jesse	C136	137	.270	Chi	
0	0	Becquer, Julio Vellegas (P1)	1B77	110	.252	B	
		Bertoia, Reno Peter (2B21)	3B112	121	.265	B	
5	11	Clevenger, Truman Eugene	P	53	.091	B	
		Consolo, Wm. Angelo (2B12 3B2)	SS82	100	.207	B	
		Dobbek, Daniel John	OF78	110	.218	B	
3	5	Fischer, Wm. Chas.	P	20	+.158	B	Det
		Gardner, Wm. Frederick (SS13)	2B145	145	.257	Balt	
		Green, Leonard Chas.	OF100	127	.294	B	
4	1	Hernandez, Rudolph Albert	P21	24	.167	A	
0	1	Hyde, Richard Elde	P	9	.000	B	
		Jacobs, Lamar Gary		6	.000	A	
1	5	Kaat, James Lee	P	13	.143	B	
0	2	Kemmerer, Russell Paul	P	3	+.000	B	Chi
		Killebrew, Harmon Clayton (3B65)	1B71	124	.276	B	
8	6	Kralick, John Francis	P	35	.122	B	
8	7	Lee, Donald Edward	P	44	.116	Det58	
		Lemon, James Robert	OF145	148	.269	B	
0	0	Maestri, Hector Anibal	P	1	.000	A	
		Mincher, Donald Ray	1B20	27	.241	A	
3	2	Moore, Raymond LeRoy	P	37	+.071	xChi	
1	3	Morgan, Tom Stephen	P	14	+.000	xDet	
		Naragon, Harold Richard	C29	33	.207	B	
12	8	Pascual, Camilo Alberto	P26	27	.176	B	
11	18	Ramos, Pedro	P43	53	.116	B	
1	0	Sadowski, Theodore	P	9	.000	A	
		Schaive, John Edward	2B4	6	.250	B	
12	7	Stobbs, Chas. Klein	P	40	.088	B	
		Throneberry, Maynard Faye	OF34	85	.248	B	
		Valdivielso, Jose Lopez (3B1)	SS115	117	.213	B	
		Valo, Elmer Wm.	OF6	76	+.281	xN.Y.	
		Versalles, Zoilo	SS	15	.133	B	

WON	LOST	NAME	POS.	G.	BA	FROM	TO
		Whisenant, Thomas Peter	OF47	58	+.226	xClev	
4	5	Woodeshick, Harold Joseph	P	41	.069	B	

WON 61
LOST 100
TG 161

AMERICAN LEAGUE

1961.

FINISHED 9th
(TIED WITH K.C.)
PCT. .379

WASHINGTON

JAMES BARTON VERNON

WON	LOST	NAME	POS.	G.	BA	FROM	TO
		Boak, Chester Robert	2B1	5	.000	K.C.	C
0	1	Bouldin, Carl Edward	P	2	.000	A	
		Bright, Harry James (C8 2B1)	3B40	72	.240	PittN	
		Brinkman, Edwin Albert	3B3	4	.091	A	
4	9	Burnside, Peter Willits	P	33	.059	Det	
1	3	Cheney, Thomas Edgar	P10	13	.500	xPittN	
		Cottier, Chas. Keith	2B100	101	+.234	xDet	
		Daley, Peter Harvey	C	72	.192	K.C.	C
12	11	Daniels, Bennie	P	32	.197	PittN	
10	10	Donovan, Richard Edward	P23	24	.179	Chi	
		Dotterer, Henry John	C	7	.263	CinN	C
3	8	Gabler, John Richard	P29	34	.200	N.Y.	C
0	1	Garcia, Edward Miguel	P	16	.000	Chi	C
		Green, Eugene Leroy (OF21)	C79	110	.280	Balt	
0	0	Heiser, LeRoy Barton	P	3	.000	A	C
0	1	Hernandez, Rudolph Albert	P	7	.000	B	C
		Hicks, Wm. Joseph	OF7	12	.172	Chi	
		Hinton, Chas. Edward	OF92	106	.260	A	
7	9	Hobaugh, Edward Russell	P26	27	.098	A	
		Johnson, Robert Wallace (2B2 3B2)	SS57	61	.295	K.C.	
		Keough, Richard Martin (1B10)	OF100	135	.249	Clev	
		King, James Hubert (C1)	OF91	110	.270	SFN58	
		Klaus, Wm. Joseph (2B1 SS18 OF1)	3B51	91	.227	Balt	
2	2	Klippstein, John Calvin	P	42	.143	Clev	
6	8	Kutyna, Marion John	P	50	.206	K.C.	
		Long, Richard Dale	1B95	123	.249	N.Y.	
0	1	Maestri, Hector Anibal	P	1	.000	B	C
		Mahoney, James Thomas (2B2)	SS31	43	.241	Bos59	
0	1	Mathias, Carl Lynwood	P	4	.200	Clev	C
8	18	McClain, Joseph Fred	P	33	.206	A	
		O'Connell, Daniel Francis (2B61)	3B73	138	.260	SFN59	
1	1	Osteen, Claude Wilson	P	3	.143	xCinN	
		Retzer, Kenneth Leo	C	16	.340	A	
2	8	Sisler, David Michael	P	45	.000	Det	
		Stevens, R. C.	1B25	33	.129	PittN	C
		Stillwell, Ronald Roy	SS5	8	.125	A	
2	6	Sturdivant, Thomas Virgil	P	15	.077	Bos	PittN
		Tasby, Willie	OF139	141	.251	Bos	
		Veal, Orville Inman	SS63	69	.202	Det	

WON	LOST	NAME	POS.	G.	BA	FROM	TO
3	2	Woodeshick, Harold Joseph	P	7	+.125	B	Det
		Woodling, Eugene Richard	OF90	110	.313	Balt	
		Zipfel, Marion Sylvester	1B44	50	.200	A	

WON 60
LOST 101
TG 161

AMERICAN LEAGUE

1962.

FINISHED 10th (LAST)
PCT. .373

WASHINGTON

JAMES BARTON VERNON

WON	LOST	NAME	POS.	G.	BA	FROM	TO
0	1	Baird, Robert Allen	P	3	.000	A	
1	2	Bouldin, Carl Edward	P6	7	.000	B	
		Bright, Harry James (C3 3B1)	1B99	113	.273	B	
		Brinkman, Edwin Albert (3B10)	SS38	54	.165	B	
5	11	Burnside, Peter Willits	P	40	.057	B	
7	9	Cheney, Thomas Edgar	P	37	.063	B	
		Cottier, Chas. Keith	2B134	136	.242	B	
7	16	Daniels, Bennie	P	44	.130	B	
0	1	Green, Fred Allan	P	5	.000	PittN	C
3	8	Hamilton, Steve Absher	P41	43	.077	Clev	
		Hamlin, Kenneth Lee (2B2)	SS87	98	.253	L.A.	
2	4	Hannan, James John	P	42	.091	A	
		Hicks, Wm. Joseph	OF42	102	.224	B	
		Hinton, Chas. Edward (2B12 SS1)	OF136	151	.310	B	
2	1	Hobaugh, Edward Russell	P	26	.167	B	
0	1	Jenkins, Warren Washington	P	3	.000	A	
		Johnson, Robert Wallace (2B3 SS50 OF1)	3B72	135	.288	B	
		Kennedy, John Edward (3B2)	SS9	14	.262	A	
		King, James Hubert	OF101	132	.243	B	
5	6	Kutyna, Marion John	P	54	.125	B	C
		Lock, Don Wilson	OF67	71	.253	A	
		Long, Richard Dale	1B51	67	+.241	B	N.Y.
0	4	McClain, Joseph Fred	P	10	.143	B	C
		O'Connell, Daniel Francis (2B22)	3B41	84	.263	B	C
8	13	Osteen, Claude Wilson	P28	37	.208	B	
		Piersall, James Anthony	OF132	135	.244	Clev	
		Retzer, Kenneth Leo	C99	109	.285	B	
1	2	Ripplemeyer, Raymond Roy	P	18	.500	A	C
8	10	Rudolph, Frederick Donald	P	37	+.175	xClev	
		Schaive, John Edward (2B6)	3B49	82	.253	Wash60	
		Schmidt, Robert Benjamin	C	88	.242	CinN	
11	12	Stenhouse, David Rotchford	P	34	.052	A	
		Stillwell, Ronald Roy (SS1)	2B6	6	.273	B	C
		Tasby, Willie	OF10	11	+.206	B	Clev
		Woodling, Eugene Richard	OF30	44	.280	B	NYN
		Zipfel, Marion Sylvester (OF23)	1B26	68	.239	B	C

WON 56
LOST 106
TG 162

AMERICAN LEAGUE 1963.

FINISHED 10th (LAST) PCT. .346

WASHINGTON

JAMES BARTON VERNON GILBERT RAYMOND HODGES

WON	LOST	NAME	POS.	G.	BA	FROM	TO
0	3	Baird, Robert Allen	P	5	.333	B	C
		Blasingame, Donald Lee	2B64	69	.256	xCinN	
2	2	Bouldin, Carl Edward	P	10	.000	B	
		Breeding, Marvin Eugene (2B22 SS2)	3B29	58	.274	Balt	LAN
		Brinkman, Edwin Albert	SS143	145	.228	B	
1	3	Bronstad, James Warren	P25	27	.000	NY59	
		Brown, Thomas Wm. (1B14)	OF16	61	.147	A	C
0	1	Burnside, Peter Willits	P	38	+.091	xBalt	
8	9	Cheney, Thomas Edgar	P23	26	.109	B	
2	4	Coates, James Alton	P	2	.000	N.Y.	CinN
		Cottier, Chas. Keith (SS24 3B1)	2B85	113	.205	B	
5	10	Daniels, Bennie (OF1)	P35	36	.152	B	
4	12	Duckworth, James Raymond	P	37	.000	A	
0	1	Hamilton, Steve Absher	P	3	+.000	B	N.Y.
2	2	Hannan, James John	P	13	.000	B	
		Hinton, Chas. Edward (1B6 SS2 3B19)	OF125	150	.269	B	
0	0	Hobaugh, Edward Russell	P	9	.500	B	C
		Hunt, Kenneth Lawrence	OF5	7	+.200	xL. A.	
0	2	Jenkins, Warren Washington	P	4	.333	B	
		Kennedy, John Edward (SS2)	3B26	36	.177	B	
		King, James Hubert	OF123	136	.231	B	
		Klimchock, Louis Stephen	2B3	9	.143	MilN	MilN
3	8	Kline, Ronald Lee	P	62	.091	Det	
		Landrith, Hobert Neal	C37	42	+.175	xBalt	C
		Leppert, Donald George	C60	73	.237	PittN	
		Lock, Don Wilson	OF146	149	.252	B	
		Minoso, Saturnino Orestes Arrietta Armas (3B8)	OF74	109	.229	StLN	
2	0	Moeller, Ronald Ralph	P	8	+.222	xL.A.	C
		Neeman, Calvin Amandus	C12	14	+.056	xClev	C
		Osborne, Lawrence Sidney (3B16)	1B81	125	.212	Det	C
9	14	Osteen, Claude Wilson	P40	49	.171	B	
		Phillips, Richard Eugene (2B5 3B4)	1B68	124	.237	A	
		Piersall, James Anthony	OF25	29	.245	B	NYN
1	0	Quirk, Arthur Lincoln	P	7	.250	Balt	C
		Retzer, Kenneth Leo	C81	95	.242	B	
5	6	Ridzik, Stephen George	P	20	.172	Clev58	
2	1	Roebuck, Edward Jack	P	26	.182	xLAN	
7	19	Rudolph, Frederick Donald	P	37	.178	B	
		Schaive, John Edward		3	.000	B	C
		Schmidt, Robert Benjamin	C6	9	.200	B	
		Shetrone, Barry Stevan		2	.000	Balt	C
3	9	Stenhouse, David Rotchford	P	16	.080	B	
		Zimmer, Donald Wm. (2B2)	3B78	83	.248	xLAN	

WON 62
LOST 100
TG 162

AMERICAN LEAGUE 1964.

FINISHED 9th. PCT. .383

WASHINGTON

GILBERT RAYMOND HODGES

WON	LOST	NAME	POS.	G.	BA	FROM	TO
		Blasingame, Donald Lee	2B135	143	.267	B	
0	3	Bouldin, Carl Edward	P9	10	.000	B	C
0	3	Bridges, Marshall	P	17	.000	N.Y.	
		Brinkman, Edwin Albert	SS125	132	.224	B	
0	1	Bronstad, James Warren	P	4	.000	B	C
		Brumley, Tony Mike	C132	136	.244	A	
1	3	Cheney, Thomas Edgar	P	15	.250	B	
		Cottier, Chas. Keith (SS2 3B3)	2B53	73	.168	B	
0	0	Craig, Peter Joel	P	2	.000	A	
		Cunningham, Joseph Roberts	1B41	49	+.214	xChic.	
8	10	Daniels, Bennie	P	33	.128	B	
1	6	Duckworth, James Raymond	P	30	.222	B	
4	7	Hannan, James John	P	49	.150	B	
		Hinton, Chas. Edward (3B2)	OF131	138	.274	B	
		Hunt, Kenneth Lawrence	OF37	51	.135	B	C
		Kennedy, John Edward (2B2 SS49)	3B101	148	.230	B	
		King, James Hubert	OF121	134	.241	B	
		Kirkland, Willie Chas.	OF27	32	+.216	xBalt	
10	7	Kline, Ronald Lee	P	61	.167	B	
3	10	Koch, Alan Goodman	P	32	+.250	xDet	C
0	0	Koplitz, Howard Dean	P	6	.000	Det62	
2	6	Kreutzer, Franklin James	P	13	+.000	xChic.	
		Leppert, Donald George	C43	50	.156	B	C
		Lock, Don Wilson	OF149	152	.248	B	
1	1	Loun, Donald Nelson	P	2	.000	A	C
9	15	Narum, Leslie Ferdinand	P	38	.061	Balt	
15	13	Osteen, Claude Wilson	P37	40	.156	B	
		Phillips, Richard Eugene (3B4)	1B61	109	.231	B	
		Retzer, Kenneth Leo	C13	17	.094	B	C
5	5	Ridzik, Stephen George	P	49	.222	B	
0	0	Roebuck, Edward Jack	P	2	.000	B	PhilaN
1	3	Rudolph, Frederick Donald	P	28	.067	B	C
		Sievers, Roy Edward	1B15	33	.172	xPhilaN	
		Skowron, Wm. Joseph	1B66	73	+.271	LAN	Chic.
2	7	Stenhouse, David Rotchford	P	26	.300	B	C
		Valentine, Fred Lee	OF57	102	.226	Balt	
		Zimmer, Donald Wm. (C2 2B1 OF4)	3B57	121	.246	B	

1965-1972 Rosters

ROSTER DATA FOR 1965 TO 1972

INFORMATION PRESENTED IN THIS SECTION IS THE SAME AS FOR 1876 TO 1964 WITH THE FOLLOWING ADDITIONS:

CLUB RECORDS - TIE GAMES ARE SHOWN AND TG (TOTAL GAMES) INCLUDES TIES. INTERIM MANAGERS ARE DENOTED BY AN ASTERISK. CLUB FRANCHISE SHIFTS ARE NOTED, AS ARE NEW CLUBS ADDED IN EXPANSION. BEGINNING IN 1969 THE AMERICAN AND NATIONAL LEAGUES WERE EACH DIVIDED INTO TWO SIX-CLUB DIVISIONS, EAST AND WEST. FINISHES FOR THESE YEARS INCLUDE AN "E" OR "W" DESIGNATING THE APPROPRIATE DIVISION. AFTER THE CONCLUSION OF THE REGULAR SEASON, THE WINNING TEAMS FROM EAST AND WEST PLAYED A BEST-OF-FIVE SERIES TO DETERMINE THE LEAGUE CHAMPION. PLAYOFF WINNERS ARE SHOWN BY "(WP)", WHILE LOSERS ARE DENOTED BY "(LP)".

ROSTER DATA - THE "TO" COLUMN HAS BEEN EXPANDED TO SHOW EACH PLAYER'S NEXT APPEARANCE IN THE MAJORS, IF ANY. THIS INFORMATION IS PRESENTED IN THE SAME MANNER AS IN THE "FROM" COLUMN, THAT IS:

"B" - INDICATES PLAYER PLAYED WITH THE SAME CLUB IN THE YEAR IMMEDIATELY FOLLOWING.
CLUB NAME, WITHOUT MARKING - INDICATES PLAYER PLAYED WITH CLUB SO DESIGNATED IN THE YEAR IMMEDIATELY FOLLOWING.
CLUB NAME, PRECEEDED BY "X" - INDICATES PLAYER MOVED TO CLUB SO DESIGNATED IN SAME YEAR.
CLUB NAME, WITH FIGURE - INDICATES CLUB AND YEAR OF PLAYER'S NEXT APPEARANCE IN MAJOR LEAGUES.
"C" - INDICATES PLAYER'S LAST APPEARANCE IN MAJOR LEAGUES.

NOTE: THE 1972 SEASON STARTED ONE WEEK LATER THAN PLANNED BECAUSE OF A DISAGREEMENT BETWEEN PLAYERS AND OWNERS WHICH RESULTED IN A PLAYER STRIKE. THUS EACH TEAM PLAYED ABOUT SEVEN GAMES LESS THAN THE 162 SCHEDULED.

WON 85
LOST 77
TIED 1
TG 163

NATIONAL LEAGUE

1966.

FINISHED 5

PCT. .525

ATLANTA

ROBERT RANDALL BRAGAN WILLIAM CLYDE HITCHCOCK

WON	LOST	NAME	POS.		G.	BA	FROM	TO
		AARON, HENRY LOUIS (2B2)	OF	158	158	.279	MIL	B
4	4	ABERNATHY, THEODORE WADE	P		38	+.250	XCHI	CIN
		ALOMAR, SANTOS (SS5)	2B	21	31	.091	MIL	NY
		ALOU, FELIPE ROJAS	1B	90	154	.327	MIL	B
		(SS1 3B3 OF79)						
		BALES, WESLEY OWEN (LEE)	2B	7	12	.063	A	HOU
		(3B3)						
3	7	BLASINGAME, WADE ALLEN	P	16	18	.217	MIL	B
		BOLLING, FRANK ELMORE	2B	67	75	.211	MIL	C
8	7	CARROLL, CLAY PALMER	P		73	.100	MIL	B
		CARTY, RICARDO ADOLFO JACOBO	OF	126	151	.326	MIL	B
		(C17 1B2 3B1)						
		CLINE, TYRONE ALEXANDER	OF	19	42	+.254	XCHI	B
		(1B6)						
14	11	CLONINGER, TONY LEE	P	39	47	.234	MIL	B
		DE LA HOZ, MIGUEL ANGEL	3B	30	71	.218	MIL	B
		(2B8 SS1)						
2	3	FISCHER, HENRY WILLIAM	P		14	+.000	MIL	XCIN
		GARRETT, HENRY ADRIAN (ADE)	OF	1	4	.000	A	CHI 70
		GEIGER, GARY MERLE	OF	49	78	.262	BOSA	B
		HERRNSTEIN, JOHN ELLETT	OF	5	17	+.222	XCHI	C
0	1	HIPPAUF, HERBERT AUGUST	P		3	.000	A	C
6	2	JARVIS, ROBERT PATRICK (PAT)	P		10	.000	A	B
0	4	JAY, JOSEPH RICHARD	P		9	+.125	XCIN	C
14	8	JOHNSON, KENNETH TRAVIS	P		32	.143	MIL	B
		JONES, MACK (1B1)	OF	112	118	.264	MIL	B
7	5	KELLEY, RICHARD ANTHONY	P		20	.036	MIL	B
		KEOUGH, RICHARD MARTIN (MARTY)	1B	4	17	+.059	CIN	XCHI
		(OF3)						
		KOPACZ, GEORGE FELIX	1B	2	6	.000	A	PIT 70
11	8	LEMASTER, DENVER CLAYTON	P		27	.119	MIL	B
		MATHEWS, EDWIN LEE	3B	127	134	.250	MIL	HOU
		MENKE, DENIS JOHN	SS	106	138	.251	MIL	B
		(1B7 3B39)						
		MILLAN, FELIX BERNARDO	2B	25	37	.275	A	B
		(SS1 3B1)						
4	3	NIEKRO, PHILIP HENRY	P		28	.000	MIL	B
2	3	O'DELL, WILLIAM OLIVER	P	24	26	+.250	MIL	XPIT
		OLIVER, EUGENE GEORGE	C	48	76	.194	MIL	B
		(1B5 OF2)						
5	4	OLIVO, FEDERICO EMILIO	P		47	.111	MIL	C
1	1	REED, RONALD LEE	P		2	.000	A	B
0	1	RITCHIE, JAY SEAY	P		22	.500	BOSA	B
		ROBINSON, WILLIAM HENRY	OF	5	6	.273	A	NY A
		SADOWSKI, EDWARD ROMAN	C		3	.111	LA A63	C
0	0	SCHNEIDER, DANIEL LOUIS	P		14	.500	MIL 64	HOU
3	3	SCHWALL, DONALD BERNARD	P		11	+.000	XPIT	B
		THOMAS, JAMES LEROY (LEE)	1B	36	39	+.198	BOSA	XCHI
		TORRE, JOSEPH PAUL (1B36)	C	114	148	.315	MIL	B
0	2	UMBACH, ARNOLD WILLAIM	P		22	.200	MIL 64	C
0	0	UPSHAW, CECIL LEE	P		1	1.000	A	B
1	0	VAUGHAN, CHARLES WAYNE	P		1	.250	A	ATL 69
		WOODWARD, WILLIAM FREDERICK	2B	79	144	.264	MIL	B
		(WOODY) (SS73)						

CLUB TRANSFERRED FROM MILWAUKEE AFTER 1965 SEASON.

WON 77 | LOST 85 | TIED 0 | TG 162

NATIONAL LEAGUE 1967.

FINISHED 7 | PCT. .475

ATLANTA

WILLIAM CLYDE HITCHCOCK KENNETH JOSEPH SILVESTRI

WON	LOST	NAME	POS.		G.	BA	FROM	TO
		AARON, HENRY LOUIS (2B1)	OF	152	155	.307	B	B
		ALOU, FELIPE ROJAS (OF56)	1B	85	140	.274	B	B
		BEAUCHAMP, JAMES EDWARD			4	.000	MIL 65	CIN
1	0	BLASINGAME, WADE ALLEN	P		10	+.143	B	XHOU
		BOYER, CLETIS LEROY (SS6)	3B	150	154	.245	NY A	B
0	2	BRITTON, JAMES ALAN	P		2	.000	A	B
2	3	BRUCE, ROBERT JAMES	P		12	.167	HOU	C
6	12	CARROLL, CLAY PALMER	P		42	.063	B	B
		CARTY, RICARDO ADOLFO JACOBO (1B9)	OF	112	134	.255	B	ATL 69
		CLARK, GLEN ESTER			4	.000	A	C
		CLINE, TYRONE ALEXANDER	OF	1	10	+.000	B	XSF
4	7	CLONINGER, TONY LEE	P		16	.200	B	B
		DE LA HOZ, MIGUEL ANGEL (SS1 3B22)	2B	23	74	.203	B	CIN 69
		FRANCONA, JOHN PATSY (TITO) (OF6)	1B	56	82	+.248	XPHI	B
		GASTON, CLARENCE EDWIN	OF	7	9	.120	A	SD 69
		GEIGER, GARY MERLE	OF	38	69	.162	B	HOU 69
		HERMOSO, ANGEL REMIGIO (REMY) (2B2)	SS	9	11	.308	A	MON 69
0	2	HERNANDEZ, RAMON GONZALEZ	P		46	.000	A	CHI
15	10	JARVIS, ROBERT PATRICK (PAT)	P		32	.085	B	B
13	9	JOHNSON, KENNETH TRAVIS	P		29	.127	B	B
		JONES, MACK	OF	126	140	.253	B	CIN
2	9	KELLEY, RICHARD ANTHONY	P		39	.250	B	B
		LAU, CHARLES RICHARD			52	.200	XBALA	C
9	9	LEMASTER, DENVER CLAYTON	P		31	.104	B	HOU
		LUM, MICHAEL KEN-WAI	OF	6	9	.231	A	B
		MARTINEZ, ORLANDO (MARTY) (C3 1B1 2B9 3B2)	SS	25	44	.288	MINA62	B
		MENKE, DENIS JOHN (3B3)	SS	124	129	.227	B	HOU
		MILLAN, FELIX BERNARDO	2B		41	.235	B	B
		NICHOLSON, DAVID LAWRENCE	OF	7	10	.200	HOU	C
11	9	NIEKRO, PHILIP HENRY	P		46	.123	B	B
		OLIVER, EUGENE GEORGE	C	14	17	+.196	B	XPHI
3	2	RAKOW, EDWARD CHARLES	P		17	.000	DETA65	C
4	1	RAYMOND, JOSEPH CLAUDE MARC	P		28	+.000	XHOU	B
1	1	REED, RONALD LEE	P		3	.000	B	B
4	6	RITCHIE, JAY SEAY	P		52	.300	B	CIN
0	0	SCHWALL, DONALD BERNARD	P		1	.000	B	C
0	0	STONE, GEORGE HEARD	P		2	.000	A	B
		TORRE, JOSEPH PAUL (1B23)	C	114	135	.277	B	B
		UECKER, ROBERT GEORGE	C	59	62	+.146	XPHI	C
2	3	UPSHAW, CECIL LEE	P		30	.167	B	B
		WOODWARD, WILLIAM FREDERICK (WOODY) (SS16)	2B	120	136	.226	B	B

COACH SILVESTRI SERVED AS INTERIM MANAGER NEAR CLOSE OF SEASON.

WON 81 | LOST 81 | TIED 1 | TG 163

NATIONAL LEAGUE 1968.

FINISHED 5 | PCT. .500

ATLANTA

CHALMER LUMAN HARRIS

WON	LOST	NAME	POS.		G.	BA	FROM	TO
		AARON, HENRY LOUIS (1B14)	OF	151	160	.287	B	B
		AARON, TOMMIE LEE (1B28 3B1)	OF	62	98	.244	MIL 65	B
		ALOU, FELIPE ROJAS	OF	158	160	.317	B	B
		BAKER, JOHNNIE B.	OF	3	6	.400	A	B
		BOYER, CLETIS LEROY	3B	69	71	.227	B	B
4	6	BRITTON, JAMES ALAN	P		34	.143	B	B
0	1	CARROLL, CLAY PALMER	P		10	+.000	B	XCIN
		CAUSEY, JAMES WAYNE (SS2 3B2)	2B	6	16	.108	XCALA	C
1	3	CLONINGER, TONY LEE	P		8	+.000	B	XCIN
0	0	DAVIDSON, THOMAS EUGENE (TED)	P		4	+.000	XCIN	C
		FRANCONA, JOHN PATSY (TITO) (1B33)	OF	65	122	.286	B	B
		GARR, RALPH ALLEN			11	.286	A	B
		GARRIDO, GIL GONZALO	SS	17	18	.208	SF 64	B
0	0	GUINN, DRANNON EUGENE (SKIP)	P	3	7	.000	A	HOU
		HRINIAK, WALTER JOHN	C		9	.346	A	B
		JACKSON, ROLAND THOMAS (SONNY)	SS	99	105	.226	HOU	B
16	12	JARVIS, ROBERT PATRICK (PAT)	P		34	.141	B	B
		JOHNSON, DERON ROGER (3B21)	1B	97	127	.208	CIN	PHI
5	8	JOHNSON, KENNETH TRAVIS	P		31	.175	B	B
		JOHNSON, ROBERT WALLACE (2B4)	3B	48	59	+.262	XCIN	STL
2	4	KELLEY, RICHARD ANTHONY	P		31	.043	B	SD
0	0	KESTER, RICHARD LEE	P		5	.000	A	B
		LUM, MICHAEL KEN-WAI	OF	95	122	.224	B	B
		MARTINEZ, ORLANDO (MARTY) (C14 2B16 3B37)	SS	54	113	.230	B	HOU
		MILLAN, FELIX BERNARDO	2B	145	149	.289	B	B
0	0	MILLER, STUART LEONARD	P		2	.000	BALA	C
14	12	NIEKRO, PHILIP HENRY	P		37	.104	B	B
		PAGE, MICHAEL RANDY	OF	6	20	.179	A	C
10	8	PAPPAS, MILTON STEPHEN	P		22	+.162	XCIN	B
3	5	RAYMOND, JOSEPH CLAUDE MARC	P		36	.143	B	B
11	10	REED, RONALD LEE	P		35	.161	B	B
0	1	SANTORINI, ALAN JOEL	P		1	.000	A	SD
7	4	STONE, GEORGE HEARD	P		17	.333	B	B
		TILLMAN, JOHN ROBERT (BOB)	C	75	86	.220	NY A	B
		TORRE, JOSEPH PAUL (1B29)	C	92	115	.271	B	STL
8	7	UPSHAW, CECIL LEE	P		52	.174	B	B
		VALDESPINO, HILARIO BORROTO (SANDY)	OF	20	36	.233	MINA	HOU
		WOODWARD, WILLIAM FREDERICK (WOODY) (2B1 3B2)	SS	6	12	+.167	B	XCIN

WON 93
LOST 69
TIED 0
TG 162

NATIONAL LEAGUE

1969.

FINISHED 1 W
(LOST LEAGUE PLAYOFF)
PCT. .574

ATLANTA

CHALMER LUMAN HARRIS

WON	LOST	NAME	POS.		G.	BA	FROM	TO
		AARON, HENRY LOUIS (1B4)	OF	144	147	.300	B	B
		AARON, TOMMIE LEE (OF8)	1B	16	49	.250	B	B
		ALOU, FELIPE ROJAS	OF	116	123	.282	B	OAKA
		ASPROMONTE, ROBERT THOMAS	OF	24	82	.253	HOU	B
		(2B2 SS18 3B23)						
		BAKER, JOHNNIE B.	OF		3	.000	B	B
		BOYER, CLETIS LEROY	3B	141	144	.250	B	B
		BREAZEALE, JAMES LEO	1B	1	2	.000	A	ATL 71
7	5	BRITTON, JAMES ALAN	P		24	.190	B	MON 71
		BROWN, OSCAR LEE	OF	3	7	.250	A	B
		CARTY, RICARDO ADOLFO JACOBO	OF	79	104	.342	ATL 67	B
		CEPEDA, ORLANDO MANUEL	1B	153	154	.257	STL	B
		DIDIER, ROBERT DANIEL	C		114	.256	A	B
2	0	DOYLE, PAUL SINNOTT	P		36	.000	A	CALA
		EVANS, DARRELL WAYNE	3B	6	12	.231	A	B
		FRANCONA, JOHN PATSY (TITO)	OF	15	51	.295	B	XOAKA
		(1B7)						
		GARR, RALPH ALLEN	OF	7	22	.222	B	B
		GARRIDO, GIL GONZALO	SS	81	82	.220	B	B
		GONZALEZ, ANDRES ANTONIO	OF	82	89	+.294	XSD	B
0	1	HILL, GARRY ALTON	P		1	.000	A	C
		HRINIAK, WALTER JOHN	C	6	7	+.143	B	XSD
		JACKSON, ROLAND THOMAS (SONNY)	SS	97	98	.239	B	B
13	11	JARVIS, ROBERT PATRICK (PAT)	P		37	.113	B	B
0	1	JOHNSON, KENNETH TRAVIS	P		9	.000	B	XNY A
0	0	KESTER, RICHARD LEE	P		1	.000	B	B
		LUM, MICHAEL KEN-WAI	OF	89	121	.268	B	B
0	0	MAXIE, LARRY HANS	P		2	.000	A	C
0	0	MC QUEEN, MICHAEL ROBERT	P		1	.000	A	B
		MILLAN, FELIX BERNARDO	2B		162	.267	B	B
1	2	NEIBAUER, GARY WAYNE	P		29	.000	A	B
23	13	NIEKRO, PHILIP HENRY	P		40	.211	B	B
6	10	PAPPAS, MILTON STEPHEN	P		26	.156	B	B
0	0	PRIDDY, ROBERT SIMPSON	P		1	.000	XCALA	B
2	2	RAYMOND, JOSEPH CLAUDE MARC	P		33	+.286	B	XMON
18	10	REED, RONALD LEE	P	36	37	.125	B	B
13	10	STONE, GEORGE HEARD	P		36	.186	B	B
		TILLMAN, JOHN ROBERT (BOB)	C		69	.195	B	B
6	4	UPSHAW, CECIL LEE	P		62	.238	B	ATL 71
0	0	VAUGHAN, CHARLES WAYNE	P		1	.000	ATL 66	C
2	0	WILHELM, JAMES HOYT	P		8	.000	XCALA	B

WON 76
LOST 86
TIED 0
TG 162

NATIONAL LEAGUE

1970.

FINISHED 5 W
PCT. .469

ATLANTA

CHALMER LUMAN HARRIS

WON	LOST	NAME	POS.		G.	BA	FROM	TO
		AARON, HENRY LOUIS (1B11)	OF	125	150	.298	B	B
		AARON, TOMMIE LEE (OF12)	1B	16	44	.206	B	B
		ASPROMONTE, ROBERT THOMAS	3B	30	62	.213	B	NY
		(1B1 SS4 OF1)						
		BAKER, JOHNNIE B.	OF	11	13	.292	B	B
0	1	BARBER, STEPHEN DAVID	P		5	+.250	XCHI	B
		BOYER, CLETIS LEROY (SS5)	3B	126	134	.246	B	B
		BROWN, OSCAR LEE	OF	25	28	.383	B	B
2	1	CARDWELL, DONALD EUGENE	P		16	+.400	XNY	C
		CARTY, RICARDO ADOLFO JACOBO	OF	133	136	.366	B	ATL 72
		CEPEDA, ORLANDO MANUEL	1B		148	.305	B	B
		DIDIER, ROBERT DANIEL	C		57	.149	B	B
		EVANS, DARRELL WAYNE	3B		12	.318	B	B
		GARR, RALPH ALLEN	OF	21	37	.281	B	B
		GARRIDO, GIL GONZALO (2B26)	SS	80	101	.264	B	B
0	0	GATEWOOD, AUBREY LEE	P		3	.000	CALA65	C
		GONZALEZ, ANDRES ANTONIO	OF	119	123	.265	B	XCALA
		HALL, JIMMIE RANDOLPH	OF	36	39	+.213	XCHI	C
		JACKSON, ROLAND THOMAS (SONNY)	SS	87	103	.259	B	B
16	16	JARVIS, ROBERT PATRICK (PAT)	P		36	.183	B	B
1	1	JASTER, LARRY EDWARD	P		14	.000	MON	ATL 72
0	0	KESTER, RICHARD LEE	P		15	.000	B	C
		KING, HAROLD	C	62	89	.260	HOU 68	B
0	0	KLINE, RONALD LEE	P		5	.000	BOSA	C
		LUM, MICHAEL KEN-WAI	OF	98	123	.254	B	B
1	5	MC QUEEN, MICHAEL ROBERT	P		22	.300	B	B
		MILLAN, FELIX BERNARDO	2B		142	.310	B	B
13	9	NASH, JAMES EDWIN	P		34	.087	OAKA	B
0	0	NAVARRO, JULIO VENTURA	P		17	.167	DETA66	C
0	3	NEIBAUER, GARY WAYNE	P		7	.000	B	B
12	18	NIEKRO, PHILIP HENRY	P		34	.152	B	B
2	2	PAPPAS, MILTON STEPHEN	P		11	+.000	B	XCHI
5	5	PRIDDY, ROBERT SIMPSON	P		41	.200	B	B
7	10	REED, RONALD LEE	P	21	22	.091	B	B
11	11	STONE, GEORGE HEARD	P		35	.236	B	B
		TILLMAN, JOHN ROBERT (BOB)	C	70	71	.238	B	C
6	4	WILHELM, JAMES HOYT	P		50	+.091	B	XCHI
		WILLIAMS, EARL CRAIG (3B3)	1B	4	10	.368	A	B

WON 82
LOST 80
TIED 0
TG 162

NATIONAL LEAGUE 1971. FINISHED 3 W PCT. .506

ATLANTA

CHALMER LUMAN HARRIS

WON	LOST	NAME		POS.		G.	BA	FROM	TO
		AARON, HENRY LOUIS	(OF60)	1B	71	139	.327	B	B
		AARON, TOMMIE LEE	(3B7)	1B	11	25	.226	B	C
		BAKER, JOHNNIE B.		OF	18	29	.226	B	B
3	1	BARBER, STEPHEN DAVID		P		39	.154	B	B
		BOYER, CLETIS LEROY	(SS1)	3B	25	30	.245	B	C
		BREAZEALE, JAMES LEO		1B	4	10	.190	ATL 69	B
		BROWN, OSCAR LEE		OF	15	27	.209	B	B
		CEPEDA, ORLANDO MANUEL		1B	63	71	.276	B	B
		DIDIER, ROBERT DANIEL		C	50	51	.219	B	B
		EVANS, DARRELL WAYNE	(OF3)	3B	72	89	.242	B	B
		FOSTER, LEONARD NORRIS		SS	3	9	.000	A	C
		GARR, RALPH ALLEN		OF	153	154	.343	B	B
		GARRIDO, GIL GONZALO		SS	32	79	.216	B	B
		(2B18 3B28)							
0	1	HERBEL, RONALD SAMUEL		P		25	.091	NY	C
1	0	HOUSE, THOMAS ROSS		P		11	.400	A	B
		JACKSON, ROLAND THOMAS	(SONNY)	OF	145	149	.258	B	B
6	14	JARVIS, ROBERT PATRICK	(PAT)	P		35	.106	B	B
9	5	KELLEY, THOMAS HENRY		P		28	.047	CLEA67	B
		KING, HAROLD		C	60	86	.207	B	TEXA
		LA RUSSA, ANTHONY		2B		9	.286	XOAKA	C
		LUM, MICHAEL KEN-WAI	(1B1)	OF	125	145	.269	B	B
4	1	MC QUEEN, MICHAEL ROBERT		P		17	.211	B	B
		MILLAN, FELIX BERNARDO		2B	141	143	.289	B	B
9	7	NASH, JAMES EDWIN		P	32	33	.149	B	B
1	0	NEIBAUER, GARY WAYNE		P		6	.000	B	B
15	14	NIEKRO, PHILIP HENRY		P		42	.152	B	B
		PEREZ, MARTIN ROMAN		SS	126	130	.227	CALA	B
4	9	PRIDDY, ROBERT SIMPSON		P		40	.182	B	C
13	14	REED, RONALD LEE		P		32	.149	B	B
		STAEHLE, MARVIN GUSTAVE		2B	7	22	.111	MON	C
		(3B1)							
6	8	STONE, GEORGE HEARD		P	27	30	.177	B	B
11	6	UPSHAW, CECIL LEE		P		49	.000	ATL 69	B
		VERSALLES, ZOILO		3B	30	66	.191	WASA69	C
		(2B1 SS24)							
0	0	WILHELM, JAMES HOYT		P		3	+.000	CHI	XLA
		WILLIAMS, EARL CRAIG		C	72	145	.260	B	B
		(1B31 OF42)							

WON 70
LOST 84
TIED 1
TG 155

NATIONAL LEAGUE 1972. FINISHED 4 W PCT. .455

ATLANTA

CHALMER LUMAN HARRIS EDWIN LEE MATHEWS

WON	LOST	NAME		POS.		G.	BA	FROM	TO
		AARON, HENRY LOUIS	(OF15)	1B	109	129	.265	B	
		BAKER, JOHNNIE B.		OF	123	127	.321	B	
0	0	BARBER, STEPHEN DAVID		P		5	.200	B	XCALA
		BLANKS, LARVELL	(SS4 3B2)	2B	18	33	.329	A	
		BREAZEALE, JAMES LEO	(3B1)	1B	16	52	.247	B	
		BROWN, OSCAR LEE		OF	59	76	.226	B	
		CARTY, RICARDO ADOLFO JACOBO		OF	78	86	.277	ATL 70	
		CASANOVA, PAULINO		C	43	49	.206	WASA	
		CEPEDA, ORLANDO MANUEL		1B	22	28	.298	B	XOAKA
		DIDIER, ROBERT DANIEL		C	11	13	.300	B	
		EVANS, DARRELL WAYNE		3B	123	125	.254	B	
2	2	FREEMAN, JIMMY LEE		P	6	8	.077	A	
		GARR, RALPH ALLEN		OF	131	134	.325	B	
		GARRIDO, GIL GONZALO		2B	21	40	.267	B	
		(SS10 3B3)							
		GILBREATH, RODNEY JOE	(3B4)	2B	7	18	.237	A	
5	2	HARDIN, JAMES WARREN		P		26	.095	NY A	
1	3	HOERNER, JOSEPH WALTER		P		25	+.000	XPHI	
0	0	HOUSE, THOMAS ROSS		P		8	.000	B	
		JACKSON, ROLAND THOMAS	(SONNY)	SS	17	60	.238	B	
		(3B6 OF10)							
11	7	JARVIS, ROBERT PATRICK	(PAT)	P		37	.125	B	
1	1	JASTER, LARRY EDWARD		P		5	.000	ATL 70	
5	7	KELLEY, THOMAS HENRY		P		27	.088	B	
		LUM, MICHAEL KEN-WAI	(1B2)	OF	109	123	.228	B	
3	5	MC LAIN, DENNIS DALE		P		15	.167	XOAKA	
0	5	MC QUEEN, MICHAEL ROBERT		P		23	.087	B	
		MILLAN, FELIX BERNARDO		2B	120	125	.257	B	
1	1	NASH, JAMES EDWIN		P		11	+.222	B	XPHI
0	0	NEIBAUER, GARY WAYNE		P		8	+.000	B	XPHI
16	12	NIEKRO, PHILIP HENRY		P		38	.194	B	
		OFFICE, ROWLAND JOHNIE		OF	1	2	.400	A	
		PEREZ, MARTIN ROMAN		SS		141	.228	B	
11	15	REED, RONALD LEE		P		31	.178	B	
5	8	SCHUELER, RONALD RICHARD		P		37	.190	A	
6	11	STONE, GEORGE HEARD		P	31	33	.200	B	
3	5	UPSHAW, CECIL LEE		P		42	.143	B	
		WILLIAMS, EARL CRAIG		C	116	151	.258	B	
		(1B20 3B21)							

WON 72 | LOST 90 | TIED 2 | TG 164

NATIONAL LEAGUE 1965.

FINISHED 8 PCT. .444

CHICAGO

ROBERT DANIEL KENNEDY LOUIS FRANK KLEIN

WON	LOST	NAME	POS.		G.	BA	FROM	TO
4	6	ABERNATHY, THEODORE WADE	P		84	.167	CLEA	B
		ALTMAN, GEORGE LEE (1B2)	OF	45	90	.235	NY	B
		AMALFITANO, JOHN JOSEPH (JOEY)	2B	24	67	.271	B	B
		(SS4)						
		BAILEY, LONAS EDGAR (ED)	C	54	66	+.253	XSF	CALA
		(1B3)						
		BANKS, ERNEST	1B	162	163	.265	B	B
0	1	BAUMANN, FRANK MATT	P		4	.000	CHIA	C
		BECKERT, GLENN ALFRED	2B	153	154	.239	A	B
		BERTELL, RICHARD GEORGE	C		34	+.214	B	XSF
		BOCCABELLA,JOHN DOMINIC	1B	2	6	.333	B	B
		(OF1)						
		BRIGHT, HARRY JAMES			27	.280	NY A	C
1	6	BROGLIO, ERNEST GILBERT	P		26	.000	B	B
		BROWNE, BYRON ELLIS	OF		4	.000	A	B
13	11	BUHL, ROBERT RAY	P		32	.060	B	B
0	2	BURDETTE, SELVA LEWIS (LEW)	P	7	8	+.333	B	XPHI
		BURKE, LEO PATRICK (OF1)	C	2	12	.200	B	C
		BURTON, ELLIS NARRINGTON	OF	12	17	.175	B	C
		CAMPBELL, RONALD THOMAS			2	.000	B	B
		CLEMENS, DOUGLAS HORACE	OF	105	128	.221	B	PHI
14	15	ELLSWORTH, RICHARD CLARK	P		36	.096	B	B
6	6	FAUL, WILLIAM ALVAN	P		17	.100	DETA	B
		GABRIELSON, LEONARD GARY	OF	14	28	+.250	B	XSF
		(1B1)						
		HARTENSTEIN, CHARLES OSCAR			1	.000	A	B
4	4	HENDLEY, CHARLES ROBERT (BOB)	P		18	+.000	XSF	B
2	2	HOEFT, WILLIAM FREDERICK	P		29	.273	MIL	B
0	0	HOLTZMAN, KENNETH DALE	P		3	.000	A	B
2	0	HUMPHREYS, ROBERT WILLIAM	P		41	.000	STL	WASA
14	21	JACKSON, LAWRENCE CURTIS	P	39	49	.128	B	B
		KESSINGER, DONALD EULON	SS	105	106	.201	B	B
7	9	KOONCE, CALVIN LEE	P		38	.102	B	B
		KRUG, EVERETT BEN (CHRIS)	C	58	60	.201	A	B
		KUENN, HARVEY EDWARD (1B1)	OF	35	54	+.217	XSF	B
		LANDRUM, DONALD LEROY	OF	115	131	.226	B	SF
5	6	MC DANIEL, LYNDALL DALE	P		71	.000	B	SF
		PENA, ROBERTO CESAR	SS	50	51	.218	A	B
		ROZNOVSKY, VICTOR JOSEPH	C	63	71	.221	B	BALA
		SANTO, RONALD EDWARD	3B		164	.285	B	B
		STEWART, JAMES FRANKLIN	OF	55	116	.223	B	B
		(SS48)						
0	1	WARNER, JACK DYER	P		11	.000	B	C
		WILLIAMS, BILLY LEO	OF		164	.315	B	B
		YOUNG, DONALD WAYNE	OF		11	.057	A	CHI 69

CHICAGO PILOT TITLED HEAD COACH DURING 1965 SEASON.

WON 59 | LOST 103 | TIED 0 | TG 162

NATIONAL LEAGUE 1966.

FINISHED 10 (LAST) PCT. .364

CHICAGO

LEO ERNEST DUROCHER

WON	LOST	NAME	POS.		G.	BA	FROM	TO
1	3	ABERNATHY, THEODORE WADE	P		20	+.000	B	XATL
		ALTMAN, GEORGE LEE (1B4)	OF	42	88	.222	B	B
		AMALFITANO, JOHN JOSEPH (JOEY)	2B	12	41	.158	B	B
		(SS2 3B3)						
		BANKS, ERNEST (3B8)	1B	130	141	.272	B	B
		BECKERT, GLENN ALFRED (SS1)	2B	152	153	.287	B	B
		BOCCABELLA,JOHN DOMINIC	OF	33	75	.228	B	B
		(C5 1B30)						
2	6	BROGLIO, ERNEST GILBERT	P		15	.368	B	C
		BROWNE, BYRON ELLIS	OF	114	120	.243	B	B
		BRYANT, DONALD RAY	C	10	13	.308	A	HOU 69
0	0	BUHL, ROBERT RAY	P		1	+.000	B	XPHI
		CAMPBELL, RONALD THOMAS	SS	11	24	.217	B	C
		(3B7)						
0	1	CHURCH, LEONARD	P		4	.000	A	C
		CLINE, TYRONE ALEXANDER	OF	5	7	+.353	MIL	XATL
0	1	CONNORS, WILLIAM JOSEPH	P		11	.000	A	NY
		COVINGTON, JOHN WESLEY (WES)	OF	1	9	+.091	PHI	XLA
1	0	DOWLING, DAVID BARCLAY	P		1	.000	STL 64	C
2	1	EARLEY, ARNOLD CARL	P		13	.000	BOSA	HOU
8	22	ELLSWORTH, RICHARD CLARK	P		38	.156	B	PHI
1	1	ESTRADA, CHARLES LEONARD	P		9	.000	BALA64	NY
1	4	FAUL, WILLIAM ALVAN	P		17	.000	B	SF 70
8	13	HANDS, WILLIAM ALFRED	P		41	.041	SF	B
0	0	HARTENSTEIN, CHARLES OSCAR	P		5	.000	B	B
4	5	HENDLEY, CHARLES ROBERT (BOB)	P		43	.167	B	B
		HERRNSTEIN, JOHN ELLETT	1B	4	9	+.176	XPHI	XATL
		(OF1)						
1	2	HOEFT, WILLIAM FREDERICK	P		36	+.250	B	XSF
11	16	HOLTZMAN, KENNETH DALE	P		34	.123	B	B
		HUNDLEY, CECIL RANDOLPH	C		149	.236	SF	B
0	2	JACKSON, LAWRENCE CURTIS	P		3	+.000	B	XPHI
6	8	JENKINS, FERGUSON ARTHUR	P		60	+.137	XPHI	B
		KEOUGH, RICHARD MARTIN (MARTY)	OF	5	33	+.231	XATL	C
		KESSINGER, DONALD EULON	SS	148	150	.274	B	B
5	5	KOONCE, CALVIN LEE	P		45	.130	B	B
		KRUG, EVERETT BEN (CHRIS)	C	10	11	.214	B	SD 69
		KUENN, HARVEY EDWARD	OF	1	3	+.333	B	XPHI
2	1	LEE, DONALD EDWARD	P		16	+.000	XHOU	C
0	0	NORMAN, FREDIE HUBERT	P		2	.000	CHI 64	B
0	2	NYE, RICHARD RAYMOND	P		3	.250	A	B
		PENA, ROBERTO CESAR	SS	5	6	.176	B	PHI 68
		PHILLIPS, ADOLFO EMILIO	OF	111	116	+.262	XPHI	B
		POPOVICH, PAUL EDWARD	2B		2	.000	CHI 64	B
		RAUDMAN, ROBERT JOYCE	OF		8	.241	A	B
2	3	ROBERTS, ROBIN EVAN	P		11	+.200	XHOU	C
		SANTO, RONALD EDWARD (SS8)	3B	152	155	.312	B	B
4	7	SIMMONS, CURTIS THOMAS	P		19	+.111	XSTL	B
		STEWART, JAMES FRANKLIN	OF	15	57	.178	B	B
		(2B4 SS2 3B2)						
		THOMAS, FRANK JOSEPH			5	.000	MIL	C
		THOMAS, JAMES LEROY (LEE)	1B	20	75	+.242	XATL	B
		(OF17)						
		WARWICK, CARL WAYNE	OF	10	16	.227	BALA	C
		WILLIAMS, BILLY LEO	OF		162	.276	B	B

WON 87 NATIONAL LEAGUE FINISHED 3
LOST 74
TIED 1 1967. PCT. .540
TG 162

CHICAGO

LEO ERNEST DUROCHER

WON	LOST	NAME	POS.		G.	BA	FROM	TO
		ALTMAN, GEORGE LEE (1B1)	OF	4	15	.111	B	C
		AMALFITANO, JOHN JOSEPH (JOEY)			4	.000	B	C
		BANKS, ERNEST	1B	147	151	.276	B	B
		BECKERT, GLENN ALFRED	2B	144	146	.280	B	B
		BERTELL, RICHARD GEORGE	C		2	.167	SF 65	C
		BOCCABELLA,JOHN DOMINIC	OF	9	25	.171	B	B
		(C1 1B3)						
		BROWNE, BYRON ELLIS	OF	8	10	.158	B	HOU
0	0	CALMUS, RICHARD LEE	P		1	.500	LA 63	C
		CAMPBELL, JOSEPH EARL	OF	1	1	.000	A	C
8	11	CULP, RAYMOND LEONARD	P		30	.098	PHI	BOSA
1	1	ELLIS, JAMES RUSSELL	P		8	.200	A	STL 69
0	2	GARDNER, RICHARD FRANK (ROB)	P		18	.000	NY	CLEA
		GIGON, NORMAN PHILIP	2B	12	34	.171	A	C
		(3B1 OF4)						
7	8	HANDS, WILLIAM ALFRED	P		49	.105	B	B
9	5	HARTENSTEIN, CHARLES OSCAR	P		45	.063	B	B
2	0	HENDLEY, CHARLES ROBERT (BOB)	P		7	+.000	B	XNY
9	0	HOLTZMAN, KENNETH DALE	P		12	.200	B	B
		HUNDLEY, CECIL RANDOLPH	C		152	.267	B	B
0	1	JAMES, RICHARD LEE	P		3	.000	A	C
20	13	JENKINS, FERGUSON ARTHUR	P	38	39	.151	B	B
		JONES, CLARENCE WOODROW	OF	31	53	.252	A	B
		(1B13)						
		KESSINGER, DONALD EULON	SS	143	145	.231	B	B
2	2	KOONCE, CALVIN LEE	P		34	+.000	B	XNY
0	0	LARSEN, DONALD JAMES	P		3	.000	BALA65	C
0	0	MIKKELSEN, PETER JAMES	P		7	+.000	XPIT	B
10	7	NIEKRO, JOSEPH FRANKLIN	P		36	.196	A	B
0	0	NORMAN, FREDIE HUBERT	P		1	.000	B	LA 70
13	10	NYE, RICHARD RAYMOND	P		35	.213	B	B
		PHILLIPS, ADOLFO EMILIO	OF	141	144	.268	B	B
		POPOVICH, PAUL EDWARD	SS	31	49	.214	B	LA
		(2B17 3B2)						
1	0	RADATZ, RICHARD RAYMOND	P		20	.250	XCLEA	DETA69
		RAUDMAN, ROBERT JOYCE	OF		8	.154	B	C
		SANTO, RONALD EDWARD	3B		161	.300	B	B
		SAVAGE, THEODORE E. (3B1)	OF	86	96	+.218	XSTL	B
0	2	SHAW, ROBERT JOHN	P		9	+.250	XNY	C
3	7	SIMMONS, CURTIS THOMAS	P		17	.143	B	XCALA
		SPANGLER, ALBERT DONALD	OF	41	62	.254	CALA	B
		STEPHENSON, JOHN HERMAN	C	13	18	.224	NY	B
		STEWART, JAMES FRANKLIN			6	.167	B	XCHIA
2	4	STONEMAN, WILLIAM HAMBLY	P		28	.000	A	B
		THOMAS, JAMES LEROY (LEE)	OF	43	77	.220	B	HOU
		(1B10)						
0	1	UPHAM, JOHN LESLIE	P	5	8	.667	A	B
		WILLIAMS, BILLY LEO	OF		162	.278	B	B

WON 84 NATIONAL LEAGUE FINISHED 3
LOST 78
TIED 1 1968. PCT. .519
TG 163

CHICAGO

LEO ERNEST DUROCHER

WON	LOST	NAME	POS.		G.	BA	FROM	TO
		ARCIA, JOSE RAIMUNDO	OF	17	59	.190	A	SD
		(2B10 SS7 3B1)						
		BANKS, ERNEST	1B	147	150	.246	B	B
		BECKERT, GLENN ALFRED	2B		155	.294	B	B
		BOBB, MARK RANDALL (RANDY)	C		7	.125	A	B
		BOCCABELLA,JOHN DOMINIC	C	4	7	.071	B	MON
		(OF1)						
0	0	BROWN, JOPHERY CLIFFORD	P		1	.000	A	C
		ELIA, LEE CONSTANTINE	SS	2	15	.176	CHIA66	C
		(2B1 3B1)						
0	1	FAST, DARCY RAE	P		8	.000	A	C
		FELSKE, JOHN FREDERICK	C	3	4	.000	A	MILA72
16	10	HANDS, WILLIAM ALFRED	P		38	.061	B	B
2	4	HARTENSTEIN, CHARLES OSCAR	P		28	.000	B	PIT
0	0	HERNANDEZ, RAMON GONZALEZ	P		8	.000	ATL	PIT 71
		HICKMAN, JAMES LUCIUS	OF	66	75	.223	LA	B
11	14	HOLTZMAN, KENNETH DALE	P	34	35	.125	B	B
		HUNDLEY, CECIL RANDOLPH	C		160	.226	B	B
20	15	JENKINS, FERGUSON ARTHUR	P		40	.160	B	B
		JOHNSON, LOUIS BROWN	OF	57	62	.244	LA	XCLEA
		JONES, CLARENCE WOODROW	1B	1	5	.000	B	C
		KESSINGER, DONALD EULON	SS	159	160	.240	B	B
3	2	LAMABE, JOHN ALEXANDER	P		42	.200	STL	C
		LA ROSE, VICTOR RAYMOND	2B	2	4	.000	A	C
		(SS2)						
		MC MATH, JIMMY LEE	OF	3	6	.143	A	C
0	0	MIKKELSEN, PETER JAMES	P		3+1	.000	B	XSTL
		NEN, RICHARD LEROY	1B	52	81	.181	WASA	WASA70
14	10	NIEKRO, JOSEPH FRANKLIN	P		34	.100	B	B
7	12	NYE, RICHARD RAYMOND	P		27	.182	B	B
		OLIVER, EUGENE GEORGE	1B	2	8	.364	XBOSA	B
		(C1 OF1)						
		PHILLIPS, ADOLFO EMILIO	OF	141	143	.241	B	B
		PLUMMER, WILLIAM FRANCIS	C	1	2	.000	A	CIN 70
0	1	REBERGER, FRANK BEALL	P		3	.000	A	SD
10	5	REGAN, PHILIP RAYMOND	P		68	+.150	XLA	B
0	1	REYNOLDS, ARCHIE EDWARD	P		7	.500	A	B
1	1	ROSS, GARY DOUGLAS	P		13	.091	A	B
		SANTO, RONALD EDWARD	3B		162	.246	B	B
		SAVAGE, THEODORE E.	OF	2	3	+.250	B	XLA
0	0	SMITH, WILLIE	OF	38	55	.275	XCLEA	B
		(P1 1B4)						
		SPANGLER, ALBERT DONALD	OF	48	88	.271	B	B
		STEPHENSON, JOHN HERMAN			2	.000	B	SF
0	1	STONEMAN, WILLIAM HAMBLY	P		18	.000	B	MON
0	1	TIEFENAUER, BOBBY GENE	P		9	.000	CLEA	C
0	0	UPHAM, JOHN LESLIE (OF2)	P	2	13	.200	B	C
		WILLIAMS, BILLY LEO	OF		163	.288	B	B

WON 92 LOST 70 TIED 1 TG 163

NATIONAL LEAGUE

1969.

FINISHED 2 E

PCT. .568

CHICAGO

LEO ERNEST DUROCHER

WON	LOST	NAME	POS.		G.	BA	FROM	TO
4	3	ABERNATHY, THEODORE WADE	P		56	.250	CIN	B
1	0	AGUIRRE, HENRY JOHN	P		41	.400	LA	B
		BANKS, ERNEST	1B	153	155	.253	B	B
		BECKERT, GLENN ALFRED	2B	129	131	.291	B	B
		BLADT, RICHARD ALAN	OF	7	10	.154	A	C
		BOBB, MARK RANDALL (RANDY)	C	2	3	.000	B	C
1	0	COLBORN, JAMES WILLIAM	P		6	.000	A	B
1	0	DECKER, GEORGE HENRY (JOE)	P		4	.000	A	B
0	0	DISTASO, ALEC JOHN	P		2	.000	A	C
		GAMBLE, OSCAR CHARLES	OF		24	.225	A	PHI
		HAIRSTON, JOHN LOUIS (OF1)	C	1	3	.250	A	C
		HALL, JIMMIE RANDOLPH	OF	5	11	.208	XNY A	B
20	14	HANDS, WILLIAM ALFRED	P		41	.092	B	B
		HEATH, WILLIAM CHRIS	C	9	27	.156	DETA67	C
		HICKMAN, JAMES LUCIUS	OF	125	134	.237	B	B
17	13	HOLTZMAN, KENNETH DALE	P		39	.150	B	B
		HUNDLEY, CECIL RANDOLPH	C		151	.255	B	B
21	15	JENKINS, FERGUSON ARTHUR	P		43	.139	B	B
		JIMENEZ, MANUEL EMILIO			6	.167	PIT	C
1	2	JOHNSON, KENNETH TRAVIS	P		9	.000	XNY A	MON
		KESSINGER, DONALD EULON	SS	157	158	.273	B	B
0	1	LEMONDS, DAVID LEE	P		2	.000	A	CHIA72
0	1	NIEKRO, JOSEPH FRANKLIN	P		4	+.200	B	XSD
1	1	NOTTEBART, DONALD EDWARD	P		16	.000	XNY A	C
3	5	NYE, RICHARD RAYMOND	P	34	36	.063	B	STL
		OLIVER, EUGENE GEORGE	C	6	23	.222	B	C
		OLIVER, NATHANIEL (PEEWEE)	2B	13	44	.159	XNY A	C
		PHILLIPS, ADOLFO EMILIO	OF	25	28	+.224	B	XMON
		POPOVICH, PAUL EDWARD	2B	25	60	+.312	XLA	B
		(SS7 3B6 OF1)						
		QUALLS, JAMES ROBERT (2B4)	OF	35	43	.250	A	MON
12	6	REGAN, PHILIP RAYMOND	P		71	.067	B	B
0	1	REYNOLDS, ARCHIE EDWARD	P		2	.000	B	B
0	0	ROSS, GARY DOUGLAS	P		2	+.000	B	XSD
		RUDOLPH, KENNETH VICTOR	C	11	27	.206	A	B
		(OF3)						
		SANTO, RONALD EDWARD	3B		160	.289	B	B
10	8	SELMA, RICHARD JAY	P		36	+.154	XSD	PHI
		SMITH, CHARLES WILLIAM			2	.000	NY A	C
		SMITH, WILLIE (1B24)	OF	33	103	.246	B	B
		SPANGLER, ALBERT DONALD	OF	58	82	.211	B	B
		WILLIAMS, BILLY LEO	OF	159	163	.293	B	B
		YOUNG, DONALD WAYNE	OF	100	101	.239	CHI 65	C

WON 84 LOST 78 TIED 0 TG 162

NATIONAL LEAGUE

1970.

FINISHED 2 E

PCT. .519

CHICAGO

LEO ERNEST DUROCHER

WON	LOST	NAME	POS.		G.	BA	FROM	TO
0	0	ABERNATHY, THEODORE WADE	P		11	+.000	B	XSTL
3	0	AGUIRRE, HENRY JOHN	P		17	.000	B	C
		BANKS, ERNEST	1B	62	72	.252	B	B
0	1	BARBER, STEPHEN DAVID	P		5	+.000	SEAA	XATL
		BECKERT, GLENN ALFRED (OF1)	2B	138	143	.288	B	B
		CALLISON, JOHN WESLEY	OF	144	147	.264	PHI	B
3	1	COLBORN, JAMES WILLIAM	P		34	.067	B	B
0	0	COSMAN, JAMES HENRY	P		1	.000	STL 67	C
		DAVIS, BRYSHEAR BARNETT	OF	1	6	.000	HOU 66	B
		(BROCK)						
		DAVIS, HERMAN THOMAS (TOMMY)	OF	10	11	+.262	XHOU	XOAKA
		DAY, CHARLES FREDERICK (BOOTS)	OF	7	11	+.250	STL	XMON
2	7	DECKER, GEORGE HENRY (JOE)	P		24	.176	B	B
0	2	DUNEGAN, JAMES WILLIAM	P	7	10	.250	A	C
		GAGLIANO, PHILIP JOSEPH	2B	16	26	+.150	XSTL	BOSA
		(1B1 3B1)						
		GARRETT, HENRY ADRIAN (ADE)			3	.000	ATL 66	OAKA
1	3	GURA, LAWRENCE CYRIL	P		20	.000	A	B
		HALL, JIMMIE RANDOLPH	OF	8	28	+.094	B	XATL
18	15	HANDS, WILLIAM ALFRED	P		39	.133	B	B
		HIATT, JACK E. (1B2)	C	63	66	+.242	XMON	HOU
		HICKMAN, JAMES LUCIUS (1B74)	OF	79	149	.315	B	B
17	11	HOLTZMAN, KENNETH DALE	P	39	40	.200	B	B
		HUGHES, TERRY WAYNE (OF1)	3B	1	2	.333	A	C
		HUNDLEY, CECIL RANDOLPH	C	73	73	.244	B	B
		JAMES, CLEO JOEL	OF	90	100	.210	LA 68	B
22	16	JENKINS, FERGUSON ARTHUR	P		40	.124	B	B
		KESSINGER, DONALD EULON	SS		154	.266	B	B
		MARTIN, JOSEPH CLIFTON (J.C.)	C	36	40	.156	NY	B
		(1B3)						
		METZGER, ROGER HENRY	SS		1	.000	A	HOU
0	0	MILLER, ROBERT LANE	P		7	.000	XCHIA	B
10	8	PAPPAS, MILTON STEPHEN	P		21	+.240	XATL	B
		PEPITONE, JOSEPH ANTHONY	OF	56	56	+.268	XHOU	B
		(1B13)						
0	0	PIZARRO, JUAN	P		12	.000	OAKA	B
		POPOVICH, PAUL EDWARD	2B	22	78	.253	B	B
		(SS17 3B16)						
5	9	REGAN, PHILIP RAYMOND	P		54	.000	B	B
0	2	REYNOLDS, ARCHIE EDWARD	P		7	.000	B	CALA
3	2	RODRIGUEZ, ROBERTO MUNOZ	P		26	+.125	XSD	C
		RUDOLPH, KENNETH VICTOR	C	16	20	.100	B	B
		SANTO, RONALD EDWARD (OF1)	3B	152	154	.267	B	B
		SKIDMORE, ROBERT ROE			1	1.000	A	C
		SMITH, WILLIE (OF1)	1B	43	87	.216	B	CIN
		SPANGLER, ALBERT DONALD	OF	6	21	.143	B	B
0	1	WILHELM, JAMES HOYT	P		3	+.000	XATL	ATL
		WILLIAMS, BILLY LEO	OF	160	161	.322	B	B

WON 83 | NATIONAL LEAGUE | FINISHED 3 E (TIED WITH NEW YORK)
LOST 79 | 1971. | PCT. .512
TIED 0
TG 162

CHICAGO

LEO ERNEST DUROCHER

WON	LOST	NAME	POS.		G.	BA	FROM	TO
		BANKS, ERNEST	1B	20	39	.193	B	C
		BECKERT, GLENN ALFRED	2B	129	131	.342	B	B
2	1	BONHAM, WILLIAM GORDON	P		33	.167	A	B
		BOURQUE, PATRICK DANIEL	1B	11	14	.189	A	B
		BREEDEN, DANNY RICHARD	C		25	.154	CIN 69	C
		BREEDEN, HAROLD NOEL	1B	8	23	.139	A	MON
		CALLISON, JOHN WESLEY	OF	89	103	.210	B	NY A
		CANNIZZARO, CHRISTOPHER JOHN	C	70	71	+.213	XSD	LA
0	1	COLBORN, JAMES WILLIAM	P		14	.000	B	MILA
		DAVIS, BRYSHEAR BARNETT (BROCK)	OF	93	106	.256	B	MILA
3	2	DECKER, GEORGE HENRY (JOE)	P	21	22	.250	B	B
		FANZONE, CARMEN (1B2 3B3)	OF	6	12	.186	BOSA	B
		FERNANDEZ, FRANK	C	16	17	.171	XWASA	B
0	0	GURA, LAWRENCE CYRIL	P		6	.000	B	B
12	18	HANDS, WILLIAM ALFRED	P		36	.083	B	B
		HICKMAN, JAMES LUCIUS (1B44)	OF	69	117	.256	B	B
		HISER, GENE TAYLOR	OF	9	17	.207	A	B
9	15	HOLTZMAN, KENNETH DALE	P		30	.130	B	OAKA
2	0	HOOTON, BURT CARLTON	P		3	.000	A	B
		HUNDLEY, CECIL RANDOLPH	C	8	9	.333	B	B
		JAMES, CLEO JOEL (3B2)	OF	48	54	.287	B	C
24	13	JENKINS, FERGUSON ARTHUR	P		39	.243	B	B
		JESTADT, GARRY ARTHUR	3B	1	3	+.000	MON 69	XSD
		KESSINGER, DONALD EULON	SS	154	155	.258	B	B
		MARTIN, JOSEPH CLIFTON (J.C.) (OF1)	C	43	47	.264	B	B
0	0	MILLER, ROBERT LANE	P		2	+.000	B	XSD
1	2	NEWMAN, RAYMOND FRANCIS	P		30	.000	A	MILA
		NORTH, WILLIAM ALEX	OF	6	8	.375	A	B
		ORTIZ, JOSE LUIS	OF	30	36	.295	CHIA	C
17	14	PAPPAS, MILTON STEPHEN	P		35	.154	B	B
		PEPITONE, JOSEPH ANTHONY (OF23)	1B	95	115	.307	B	B
7	6	PIZARRO, JUAN	P		16	.176	B	B
		POPOVICH, PAUL EDWARD (SS1 3B16)	2B	40	89	.217	B	B
5	5	REGAN, PHILIP RAYMOND	P		48	.000	B	B
		RUDOLPH, KENNETH VICTOR	C		25	.197	B	B
		SANTO, RONALD EDWARD (OF6)	3B	149	154	.267	B	B
		SPANGLER, ALBERT DONALD			5	.400	B	C
1	0	STEPHENSON, CHESTER EARL	P		16	.000	A	MILA
0	2	TOMPKINS, RONALD EVERETT	P		35	.000	KC A65	C
		TORRES, HECTOR EPITACIO (2B4)	SS	18	31	.224	HOU	MON
		WEBSTER, RAMON ALBERTO	1B	1	16	.313	XOAKA	C
		WILLIAMS, BILLY LEO	OF	154	157	.301	B	B

WON 85 | NATIONAL LEAGUE | FINISHED 2 E
LOST 70 | 1972. | PCT. .548
TIED 1
TG 156

CHICAGO

LEO ERNEST DUROCHER CARROLL WALTER LOCKMAN

WON	LOST	NAME	POS.		G.	BA	FROM	TO
6	6	AKER, JACK DELANE	P		48	.000	XNY A	
		BECKERT, GLENN ALFRED	2B	118	120	.270	B	
1	1	BONHAM, WILLIAM GORDON	P		19	.286	B	
		BOURQUE, PATRICK DANIEL	1B	7	11	.259	B	
		CARDENAL, JOSE DOMEC	OF	137	143	.291	MILA	
		COGGINS, FRANKLIN			6	.000	WASA68	
0	0	COMPTON, ROBERT CLINTON	P		1	.000	A	
		DAVIS, HERMAN THOMAS (TOMMY) (OF2)	1B	3	15	.269	OAKA	XBALA
1	0	DECKER, GEORGE HENRY (JOE)	P		5	.000	B	
		FANZONE, CARMEN (1B21 2B13 SS1 OF1)	3B	36	86	.225	B	
		FERNANDEZ, FRANK	C	1	3	.000	B	
0	0	GURA, LAWRENCE CYRIL	P		7	.000	B	
1	0	HAMILTON, STEVE ABSHER	P		22	.000	SF	
11	8	HANDS, WILLIAM ALFRED	P		32	.018	B	
		HENDRICKS, ELROD JEROME	C	16	17	.116	XBALA	
		HICKMAN, JAMES LUCIUS (OF27)	1B	77	115	.272	B	
		HISER, GENE TAYLOR	OF	15	32	.196	B	
11	14	HOOTON, BURT CARLTON	P		33	.125	B	
		HUNDLEY, CECIL RANDOLPH	C	113	114	.218	B	
20	12	JENKINS, FERGUSON ARTHUR	P		36	.183	B	
		KESSINGER, DONALD EULON	SS	146	149	.274	B	
		LA COCK, RALPH PIERRE (PETER)	OF	3	5	.500	A	
		MARTIN, JOSEPH CLIFTON (J.C.)	C	17	25	.240	B	
0	5	MC GINN, DANIEL MICHAEL	P	42	43	.250	MON	
		MONDAY, ROBERT JAMES (RICK)	OF	134	138	.249	OAKA	
		MONTREUIL, ALLAN ARTHUR	2B		5	.091	A	
		NORTH, WILLIAM ALEX	OF	48	66	.181	B	
17	7	PAPPAS, MILTON STEPHEN	P		29	.191	B	
		PEPITONE, JOSEPH ANTHONY	1B		66	.262	B	
3	3	PHOEBUS, THOMAS HAROLD	P	37	38	+.133	XSD	
4	5	PIZARRO, JUAN	P		16	.143	B	
		POPOVICH, PAUL EDWARD (SS8 3B1)	2B	36	58	.194	B	
0	1	REGAN, PHILIP RAYMOND	P		5	.000	B	XCHIA
10	8	REUSCHEL, RICKEY EUGENE	P		21	.136	A	
		ROSELLO, DAVID	SS		5	.250	A	
		RUDOLPH, KENNETH VICTOR	C	41	42	.236	B	
		SANTO, RONALD EDWARD (2B3 SS1 OF1)	3B	129	133	.302	B	
		SHAMSKY, ARTHUR LOUIS	1B	4	15	.125	NY	XOAKA
		TYRONE, JAMES VERNON	OF	4	13	.000	A	
		WARD, CHRIS GILBERT			1	.000	A	
		WILLIAMS, BILLY LEO (1B5)	OF	144	150	.333	B	

WON 89
LOST 73
TIED 0
TG 162

NATIONAL LEAGUE

1965.

FINISHED 4

PCT. .549

CINCINNATI

RICHARD ALLAN SISLER

WON	LOST	NAME	POS.		G.	BA	FROM	TO
2	4	ARRIGO, GERALD WILLIAM	P	27	28	.167	MINA	B
		BOROS, STEPHEN	3B		2	.000	B	C
		CARDENAS, LEONARDO ALFONSO	SS	155	156	.287	B	B
		COKER, JIMMIE GOODWIN	C	19	24	.246	B	B
		COLEMAN, GORDON CALVIN	1B	89	108	.302	B	B
1	4	CRAIG, ROGER LEE	P		40	.182	STL	PHI
4	3	DAVIDSON, THOMAS EUGENE (TED)	P		24	.000	A	B
0	1	DUFFALO, JAMES FRANCIS	P		22	+.000	XSF	C
		EDWARDS, JOHN ALBAN	C	110	114	.267	B	B
22	10	ELLIS, SAMUEL JOSEPH	P		44	.125	B	B
		HARPER, TOMMY (2B1 3B2)	OF	159	159	.257	B	B
		HELMS, TOMMY VANN	SS	8	21	.381	B	B
		(2B1 3B2)						
2	0	HENRY, WILLIAM RODMAN	P		3	+.000	B	XSF
		JAMES, CHARLES WESLEY	OF	7	26	.205	STL	C
9	8	JAY, JOSEPH RICHARD	P		37	.041	B	B
		JOHNSON, DERON ROGER	3B		159	.287	B	B
		KEOUGH, RICHARD MARTIN (MARTY)	1B	32	62	.116	B	ATL
		(OF4)						
0	1	LOCKE, LAWRENCE DONALD (BOBBY)	P		11	.000	PHI	CALA67
20	9	MALONEY, JAMES WILLIAM	P	33	35	.225	B	B
		MAY, LEE ANDREW			5	.000	A	B
9	10	MC COOL, WILLIAM JOHN	P		62	.037	B	B
11	4	NUXHALL, JOSEPH HENRY	P		32	.178	B	B
0	0	OSTEEN, MILTON DARRELL	P		3	.000	A	B
3	10	O'TOOLE, JAMES JEROME	P		29	.089	B	B
		PAVLETICH, DONALD STEPHEN	C	54	68	.319	B	B
		(1B9)						
		PEREZ, ATANASIO RIGAL (TONY)	1B	93	104	.260	B	B
		PINSON, VADA EDWARD	OF		159	.305	B	B
		QUEEN, MELVIN DOUGLAS	OF	1	5	.000	B	B
		ROBINSON, FRANK	OF	155	156	.296	B	BALA
		ROSE, PETER EDWARD	2B		162	.312	B	B
		RUIZ, HIRALDO SABLON (CHICO)	3B	4	29	.111	B	B
		(SS3)						
		SHAMSKY, ARTHUR LOUIS (1B1)	OF	18	64	.260	A	B
6	9	TSITOURIS, JOHN PHILIP	P		31	.070	B	B
0	0	ZANNI, DOMINICK THOMAS	P		8	.000	CIN 63	B

WON 76
LOST 84
TIED 0
TG 160

NATIONAL LEAGUE

1966.

FINISHED 7

PCT. .475

CINCINNATI

DONALD HENRY HEFFNER JAMES DAVID BRISTOL

WON	LOST	NAME	POS.		G.	BA	FROM	TO
0	0	ARRIGO, GERALD WILLIAM	P		3	+.000	B	XNY
1	5	BALDSCHUN, JACK EDWARD	P		42	.333	PHI	B
		CARDENAS, LEONARDO ALFONSO	SS		160	.255	B	B
		COKER, JIMMIE GOODWIN (OF2)	C	39	50	.252	B	B
		COLEMAN, GORDON CALVIN	1B	65	91	.251	B	B
5	4	DAVIDSON, THOMAS EUGENE (TED)	P		54	.000	B	B
		EDWARDS, JOHN ALBAN	C		98	.191	B	B
12	19	ELLIS, SAMUEL JOSEPH	P	41	43	.114	B	B
0	6	FISCHER, HENRY WILLIAM	P		11	+.091	XATL	XBOSA
		HARPER, TOMMY	OF	147	149	.278	B	B
		HELMS, TOMMY VANN (2B20)	3B	113	138	.284	B	B
6	2	JAY, JOSEPH RICHARD	P		12	+.115	B	XATL
		JOHNSON, DERON ROGER	OF	106	142	.257	B	B
		(1B71 3B18)						
16	8	MALONEY, JAMES WILLIAM	P	32	35	.222	B	B
		MAY, LEE ANDREW	1B	16	25	.333	B	B
8	8	MC COOL, WILLIAM JOHN	P		57	.167	B	B
5	4	NOTTEBART, DONALD EDWARD	P		59	.167	HOU	B
6	8	NUXHALL, JOSEPH HENRY	P		35	.100	B	C
0	2	OSTEEN, MILTON DARRELL	P	13	16	.500	B	B
5	7	O'TOOLE, JAMES JEROME	P		25	.128	B	CHIA
12	11	PAPPAS, MILTON STEPHEN	P	33	36	.107	BALA	B
		PAVLETICH, DONALD STEPHEN	C	55	83	.294	B	B
		(1B10)						
		PEREZ, ATANASIO RIGAL (TONY)	1B	75	88	.265	B	B
		PINSON, VADA EDWARD	OF	154	156	.288	B	B
0	0	QUEEN, MELVIN DOUGLAS (P7)	OF	32	56	.127	B	B
		ROSE, PETER EDWARD (3B16)	2B	140	156	.313	B	B
		RUIZ, HIRALDO SABLON (CHICO)	3B	27	82	.255	B	B
		(SS6 OF8)						
		SHAMSKY, ARTHUR LOUIS	OF	74	96	.231	B	B
		SIMPSON, RICHARD CHARLES	OF	64	92	.238	CALA	B
0	0	TSITOURIS, JOHN PHILIP	P		1	.000	B	B
0	0	ZANNI, DOMINICK THOMAS	P		5	1.000	B	C

WON 87 | LOST 75 | TIED 0 | TG 162

NATIONAL LEAGUE

1967.

FINISHED 4

PCT. .537

CINCINNATI

JAMES DAVID BRISTOL

WON	LOST	NAME	POS.		G.	BA	FROM	TO
6	3	ABERNATHY, THEODORE WADE	P		70	.059	ATL	B
6	6	ARRIGO, GERALD WILLIAM	P		32	.211	NY	B
0	0	BALDSCHUN, JACK EDWARD	P		9	.000	B	SD 69
		BENCH, JOHNNY LEE	C		26	.163	A	B
		BOEHMER, LEONARD JOSEPH	2B	1	2	.000	A	NY A69
		CARDENAS, LEONARDO ALFONSO	SS		108	.256	B	B
		COKER, JIMMIE GOODWIN	C	34	45	.186	B	C
		COLEMAN, GORDON CALVIN	1B	2	4	.000	B	C
1	0	DAVIDSON, THOMAS EUGENE (TED)	P		9	.000	B	B
		EDWARDS, JOHN ALBAN	C	73	80	.206	B	STL
8	11	ELLIS, SAMUEL JOSEPH	P		32	.082	B	CALA
		HARPER, TOMMY	OF	100	103	.225	B	CLEA
		HELMS, TOMMY VANN (SS46)	2B	88	137	.274	B	B
		JOHNSON, DERON ROGER (3B24)	1B	81	108	.224	B	ATL
3	3	LEE, ROBERT DEAN	P		27	+.375	XLA	B
15	11	MALONEY, JAMES WILLIAM	P	30	33	.159	B	B
		MAY, LEE ANDREW (OF48)	1B	81	127	.265	B	B
3	7	MC COOL, WILLIAM JOHN	P		31	.077	B	B
14	8	NOLAN, GARY LYNN	P		33	.104	A	B
0	3	NOTTEBART, DONALD EDWARD	P		47	.000	B	NY A69
0	2	OSTEEN, MILTON DARRELL	P	10	14	.000	B	OAKA70
16	13	PAPPAS, MILTON STEPHEN	P		34	.097	B	B
		PAVLETICH, DONALD STEPHEN	C	66	74	.238	B	B
		(1B6 3B1)						
		PEREZ, ATANASIO RIGAL (TONY)	3B	139	156	.290	B	B
		(1B18 2B1)						
		PINSON, VADA EDWARD	OF	157	158	.288	B	B
14	8	QUEEN, MELVIN DOUGLAS	P	31	49	.210	B	B
		ROBINSON, FLOYD ANDREW	OF	39	55	.238	CHIA	OAKA
		ROSE, PETER EDWARD (2B35)	OF	123	148	.301	B	B
		RUIZ, HIRALDO SABLON (CHICO)	2B	56	105	.220	B	B
		(SS11 3B13 OF5)						
		SHAMSKY, ARTHUR LOUIS	OF	40	76	.197	B	NY
		SIMPSON, RICHARD CHARLES	OF	26	44	.259	B	STL
1	0	TSITOURIS, JOHN PHILIP	P		2	.000	B	B
		WOOD, JACOB	OF	2	16	.118	XDETA	C

WON 83 | LOST 79 | TIED 1 | TG 163

NATIONAL LEAGUE

1968.

FINISHED 4

PCT. .512

CINCINNATI

JAMES DAVID BRISTOL

WON	LOST	NAME	POS.		G.	BA	FROM	TO
10	7	ABERNATHY, THEODORE WADE	P		78	.000	B	CHI
12	10	ARRIGO, GERALD WILLIAM	P		36	.075	B	B
		BEAUCHAMP, JAMES EDWARD	OF	13	31	.263	ATL	B
		(1B1)						
		BENCH, JOHNNY LEE	C		154	.275	B	B
		CARDENAS, LEONARDO ALFONSO	SS	136	137	.235	B	MINA
7	7	CARROLL, CLAY PALMER	P		58	+.250	XATL	B
4	3	CLONINGER, TONY LEE	P	17	21	+.206	XATL	B
		CORRALES, PATRICK	C		20	.268	STL 66	B
11	16	CULVER, GEORGE RAYMOND	P	42	49	.121	CLEA	B
1	0	DAVIDSON, THOMAS EUGENE (TED)	P		23	+.000	B	XATL
		HELMS, TOMMY VANN	2B	127	127	.288	B	B
		(SS2 3B1)						
		JOHNSON, ALEXANDER	OF	140	149	.312	STL	B
		JOHNSON, ROBERT WALLACE	SS	2	16	+.267	NY	XATL
		(1B1)						
		JONES, MACK	OF	60	103	.252	ATL	MON
4	1	KELSO, WILLIAM EUGENE	P		35	.000	CALA	C
2	4	LEE, ROBERT DEAN	P		44	.200	B	C
16	10	MALONEY, JAMES WILLIAM	P	33	38	.243	B	B
		MAY, LEE ANDREW (OF33)	1B	122	146	.290	B	B
3	4	MC COOL, WILLIAM JOHN	P		30	.125	B	SD
0	1	MC GINN, DANIEL MICHAEL	P		14	.000	A	MON
		MC RAE, HAROLD ABRAHAM	2B	16	17	.196	A	CIN 70
9	4	NOLAN, GARY LYNN	P		23	.130	B	B
2	5	PAPPAS, MILTON STEPHEN	P	15	16	+.063	B	XATL
		PAVLETICH, DONALD STEPHEN	1B	22	46	.286	B	CHIA
		(C5)						
		PEREZ, ATANASIO RIGAL (TONY)	3B		160	.282	B	B
		PINSON, VADA EDWARD	OF	123	130	.271	B	STL
0	1	QUEEN, MELVIN DOUGLAS	P	5	10	.125	B	B
2	3	RITCHIE, JAY SEAY	P		28	.000	ATL	C
		ROSE, PETER EDWARD	OF	148	149	.335	B	B
		(1B1 2B3)						
		RUIZ, HIRALDO SABLON (CHICO)	2B	34	85	.259	B	B
		(1B16 SS3 3B5)						
		SCHAFFER, JIMMIE RONALD	C	2	4	.167	PHI	C
0	3	TSITOURIS, JOHN PHILIP	P		3	.000	B	C
		WHITFIELD, FRED DWIGHT	1B	41	87	.257	CLEA	B
		WOODWARD, WILLIAM FREDERICK	SS	41	56	+.244	XATL	B
		(WOODY) (1B1 2B9)						

WON 89 LOST 73 TIED 1 TG 163

NATIONAL LEAGUE

1969.

FINISHED 3 W

PCT. .549

CINCINNATI

JAMES DAVID BRISTOL

WON	LOST	NAME	POS.		G.	BA	FROM	TO
4	7	ARRIGO, GERALD WILLIAM	P		20	.161	B	CHIA
		BEAUCHAMP, JAMES EDWARD	OF	9	43	.250	B	HOU
		(1B3)						
		BENCH, JOHNNY LEE	C	147	148	.293	B	B
		BREEDEN, DANNY RICHARD	C		3	.125	A	CHI 71
		CARBO, BERNARDO			4	.000	A	B
12	6	CARROLL, CLAY PALMER	P		71	.207	B	B
		CHANEY, DARREL LEE	SS	91	93	.191	A	B
11	17	CLONINGER, TONY LEE	P	35	36	.167	B	B
		CORRALES, PATRICK	C		29	.264	B	B
5	7	CULVER, GEORGE RAYMOND	P		32	.097	B	STL
		DE LA HOZ, MIGUEL ANGEL			1	.000	ATL 67	C
4	4	FISHER, JOHN HOWARD	P		34	.121	CHIA	C
9	6	GRANGER, WAYNE ALLAN	P		90	.095	STL	B
		HELMS, TOMMY VANN (SS4)	2B	125	126	.269	B	B
1	0	JACKSON, ALVIN NEIL	P		33	+.250	XNY	C
		JOHNSON, ALEXANDER	OF	132	139	.315	B	CALA
12	5	MALONEY, JAMES WILLIAM	P		30	.200	B	B
		MASHORE, CLYDE WAYNE			2	.000	A	MON
		MAY, LEE ANDREW (OF7)	1B	156	158	.278	B	B
17	9	MERRITT, JAMES JOSEPH	P		42	.143	MINA	B
8	8	NOLAN, GARY LYNN	P	16	17	.229	B	B
0	0	NORIEGA, JOHN ALAN	P		5	.000	A	B
0	0	PASCUAL, CAMILO ALBERTO	P		5	.000	XWASA	LA
1	1	PENA, JOSE	P		6	.000	A	LA
		PEREZ, ATANASIO RIGAL (TONY)	3B		160	.294	B	B
1	0	QUEEN, MELVIN DOUGLAS	P		2	.167	B	CALA
4	3	RAMOS, PEDRO	P		38	+.000	XPIT	WASA
0	0	RIBANT, DENNIS JOSEPH	P		7	+.000	XSTL	C
		ROSE, PETER EDWARD (2B2)	OF	153	156	.348	B	B
		RUIZ, HIRALDO SABLON (CHICO)	2B	39	88	.245	B	CALA
		(1B2 SS29 3B7 OF1)						
		SAVAGE, THEODORE E. (2B1)	OF	17	68	.227	LA	MILA
0	0	SHORT, WILLIAM ROSS	P		4	.000	NY	C
		STEWART, JAMES FRANKLIN	OF	66	119	.253	CHIA67	B
		(2B18 SS1 3B6)						
		TOLAN, ROBERT	OF	150	152	.305	STL	B
		WHITFIELD, FRED DWIGHT	1B	14	74	.149	B	MON
		WOODWARD, WILLIAM FREDERICK	SS	93	97	.261	B	B
		(WOODY) (2B2)						

WON 102 LOST 60 TIED 0 TG 162

NATIONAL LEAGUE

1970.

FINISHED 1 W (ALSO WON LEAGUE PLAYOFF)

PCT. .630

CINCINNATI

GEORGE LEE ANDERSON

WON	LOST	NAME	POS.		G.	BA	FROM	TO
0	2	BEHNEY, MELVIN BRIAN	P		5	.000	A	C
0	0	BELINSKY, ROBERT (BO)	P		3	1.000	PIT	C
		BENCH, JOHNNY LEE	C	140	158	.293	B	B
		(1B12 3B1 OF23)						
0	2	BORBON, PEDRO	P		12	.000	CALA	B
		BRAVO, ANGEL ALFONSO	OF	22	65	.277	CHIA	B
		CARBO, BERNARDO	OF	119	125	.310	B	B
9	4	CARROLL, CLAY PALMER	P		65	.071	B	B
		CHANEY, DARREL LEE	SS	30	57	.232	B	B
		(2B18 3B3)						
		CLINE, TYRONE ALEXANDER	OF	20	48	+.270	XMON	B
		(1B2)						
9	7	CLONINGER, TONY LEE	P		30	.213	B	B
		CONCEPCION, DAVID ISMAEL	SS	93	101	.260	A	B
		(2B3)						
		CORRALES, PATRICK	C	42	43	.236	B	B
		DUFFY, FRANK THOMAS	SS	5	6	.182	A	B
6	5	GRANGER, WAYNE ALLAN (OF1)	P	67	67	.100	B	B
5	2	GULLETT, DONALD EDWARD	P		44	.211	A	B
		HELMS, TOMMY VANN (SS12)	2B	148	150	.237	B	B
0	1	MALONEY, JAMES WILLIAM	P		7	.000	B	CALA
		MAY, LEE ANDREW	1B		153	.253	B	B
14	10	MC GLOTHLIN, JAMES MILTON	P		35	.121	CALA	B
		MC RAE, HAROLD ABRAHAM	OF	46	70	.248	CIN 68	B
		(2B1 3B6)						
20	12	MERRITT, JAMES JOSEPH	P		35	.169	B	B
18	7	NOLAN, GARY LYNN	P		37	.159	B	B
0	0	NORIEGA, JOHN ALAN	P		8	.250	B	C
		PEREZ, ATANASIO RIGAL (TONY)	3B	153	158	.317	B	B
		(1B8)						
		PLUMMER, WILLIAM FRANCIS	C		4	.125	CHI 68	B
		ROSE, PETER EDWARD	OF		159	.316	B	B
14	3	SIMPSON, WAYNE KIRBY	P	26	27	.094	A	B
		STEWART, JAMES FRANKLIN	OF	48	101	.267	B	B
		(C1 1B1 2B18 3B9)						
		TOLAN, ROBERT	OF	150	152	.316	B	CIN 72
		WARD, JOHN FRANCIS (JAY)	3B	2	6	.000	MINA64	C
		(1B1 2B1)						
4	4	WASHBURN, RAY CLARK	P		35	.000	STL	C
3	1	WILCOX, MILTON EDWARD	P		5	.200	A	B
		WOODWARD, WILLIAM FREDERICK	SS	77	100	.223	B	B
		(WOODY) (1B2 2B10 3B20)						

WON 79
LOST 83
TIED 0
TG 162

NATIONAL LEAGUE

1971.

FINISHED 4 W
(TIED WITH HOUSTON)
PCT. .488

CINCINNATI

GEORGE LEE ANDERSON

WON	LOST	NAME	POS.		G.	BA	FROM	TO
		BENCH, JOHNNY LEE	C	141	149	.238	B	B
		(1B12 3B3 OF12)						
0	0	BLATERIC, STEPHEN LAWRENCE	P		2	.000	A	NY A
0	0	BORBON, PEDRO	P		3	.000	B	B
		BRADFORD, CHARLES WM. (BUDDY)	OF	66	79	.200	XCLEA	CHIA
		BRAVO, ANGEL ALFONSO			5	+.200	B	XSD
		CARBO, BERNARDO	OF	90	106	.219	B	B
10	4	CARROLL, CLAY PALMER	P		61	.100	B	B
		CHANEY, DARREL LEE	SS	7	10	.125	B	B
		(2B1 3B1)						
		CLINE, TYRONE ALEXANDER	OF	28	69	.196	B	C
		(1B2)						
3	6	CLONINGER, TONY LEE	P		28	.259	B	STL
		CONCEPCION, DAVID ISMAEL	SS	112	130	.205	B	B
		(2B10 3B7 OF5)						
		CORRALES, PATRICK	C	39	40	.181	B	B
		DUFFY, FRANK THOMAS	SS	10	13	+.188	B	XSF
		FERRARA, ALFRED JOHN	OF	5	32	+.182	XSD	C
		FOSTER, GEORGE ARTHUR	OF	102	104	+.234	XSF	B
0	1	GARRETT, GREGORY	P		2	.333	CALA	C
5	6	GIBBON, JOSEPH CHARLES	P		50	.000	PIT	B
7	6	GRANGER, WAYNE ALLAN	P		70	.143	B	MINA
10	7	GRIMSLEY, ROSS ALBERT, II	P		26	.118	A	B
16	6	GULLETT, DONALD EDWARD	P	35	40	.120	B	B
		HELMS, TOMMY VANN	2B	149	150	.258	B	HOU
		MAY, LEE ANDREW	1B	143	147	.278	B	HOU
8	12	MC GLOTHLIN, JAMES MILTON	P		30	.137	B	B
		MC RAE, HAROLD ABRAHAM	OF	91	99	.264	B	B
1	11	MERRITT, JAMES JOSEPH	P	28	29	.138	B	B
12	15	NOLAN, GARY LYNN	P		35	.147	B	B
		PEREZ, ATANASIO RIGAL (TONY)	3B	148	158	.269	B	B
		(1B44 2B1)						
		PLUMMER, WILLIAM FRANCIS	C	4	10	.000	B	B
		(3B2)						
		ROSE, PETER EDWARD	OF	158	160	.304	B	B
4	7	SIMPSON, WAYNE KIRBY	P		22	.031	B	B
		SMITH, WILLIE	1B	10	31	.164	CHI	C
1	0	SPRAGUE, EDWARD NELSON	P		7	.000	OAKA69	B
		STEWART, JAMES FRANKLIN	OF	19	80	.232	B	HOU
		(2B6 3B9)						
2	2	WILCOX, MILTON EDWARD	P		18	.000	B	CLEA
		WOODWARD, WILLIAM FREDERICK	SS	85	136	.242	B	C
		(WOODY) (2B9 3B63)						

WON 95
LOST 59
TIED 0
TG 154

NATIONAL LEAGUE

1972.

FINISHED 1 W
(ALSO WON LEAGUE PLAYOFF)
PCT. .617

CINCINNATI

GEORGE LEE ANDERSON

WON	LOST	NAME	POS.		G.	BA	FROM	TO
		BENCH, JOHNNY LEE	C	130	147	.270	B	
		(1B6 3B4 OF17)						
12	12	BILLINGHAM, JOHN EUGENE	P		36	.070	HOU	
8	3	BORBON, PEDRO	P		62	.048	B	
		CARBO, BERNARDO	OF	4	19	+.143	B	XSTL
6	4	CARROLL, CLAY PALMER	P		65	.182	B	
		CHANEY, DARREL LEE	SS	64	83	.250	B	
		(2B12 3B10)						
		CONCEPCION, DAVID ISMAEL	SS	114	119	.209	B	
		(2B1 3B9)						
		CORRALES, PATRICK	C		2	+.000	B	XSD
		FOSTER, GEORGE ARTHUR	OF	47	59	.200	B	
		GERONIMO, CESAR FRANCISCO	OF	106	120	.275	HOU	
0	0	GIBBON, JOSEPH CHARLES	P		2	+.000	B	XHOU
14	8	GRIMSLEY, ROSS ALBERT, II	P		30	.121	B	
9	10	GULLETT, DONALD EDWARD	P		31	.211	B	
		HAGUE, JOE CLARENCE (OF19)	1B	22	69	+.246	XSTL	
10	1	HALL, TOM EDWARD	P		47	.100	MINA	
		JAVIER, MANUEL JULIAN	3B	19	44	.209	STL	
		(1B1 2B5)						
9	8	MC GLOTHLIN, JAMES MILTON	P		31	.174	B	
		MC RAE, HAROLD ABRAHAM (3B11)	OF	12	61	.278	B	
		MENKE, DENIS JOHN (1B11)	3B	130	140	.233	HOU	
1	0	MERRITT, JAMES JOSEPH	P		4	.000	B	
		MORGAN, JOSEPH LEONARD	2B		149	.292	HOU	
15	5	NOLAN, GARY LYNN	P		25	.117	B	
		PEREZ, ATANASIO RIGAL (TONY)	1B		136	.283	B	
		PLUMMER, WILLIAM FRANCIS	C	35	38	.186	B	
		(1B1 3B1)						
		ROSE, PETER EDWARD	OF		154	.307	B	
		RUBERTO, JOHN EDWARD	C		2	.000	SD 69	
8	5	SIMPSON, WAYNE KIRBY	P		24	.063	B	
3	3	SPRAGUE, EDWARD NELSON	P		33	.000	B	
		TOLAN, ROBERT	OF		149	.283	CIN 70	
0	0	TOMLIN, DAVID ALLEN	P		3	.000	A	
		UHLAENDER, THEODORE OTTO	OF	27	73	.159	CLEA	

WON 65
LOST 97
TIED 0
TG 162

NATIONAL LEAGUE

1965.

FINISHED 9

PCT. .401

HOUSTON

CHALMER LUMAN HARRIS

WON	LOST	NAME	POS.	G.	BA	FROM	TO
		ADLESH, DAVID GEORGE	C 13	15	.147	B	B
0	0	ARLICH, DONALD LOUIS	P	1	.000	A	B
		ASPROMONTE, ROBERT THOMAS	3B 146	152	.263	B	B
		(1B6 SS4)					
		BATEMAN, JOHN ALVIN	C 39	45	.197	B	B
		BEAUCHAMP, JAMES EDWARD	OF 9	24	+.189	B	XMIL
		(1B3)					
		BOND, WALTER FRANKLIN (OF38)	1B 74	117	.263	B	MINA67
		BRAND, RONALD GEORGE	C 102	117	.235	PIT 63	B
		(3B6 OF5)					
9	18	BRUCE, ROBERT JAMES	P	35	.122	B	B
0	2	COOMBS, DANIEL BERNARD	P	26	.111	B	B
1	4	CUELLAR, MIGUEL ANGEL	P	25	.000	STL	B
7	8	DIERKER, LAWRENCE EDWARD	P	26	.100	B	B
11	11	FARRELL, RICHARD JOSEPH (TURK)	P	33	.135	B	B
		FOX, JACOB NELSON (NELLIE)	3B 6	21	.268	B	C
		(1B2 2B1)					
		GAINES, ARNESTA JOE	OF 65	100	.227	B	B
		GENTILE, JAMES EDWARD	1B 68	81	.242	XKC A	B
8	7	GIUSTI, DAVID JOHN	P	38	.171	B	B
		HARRISON, CHARLES WILLIAM	1B 12	15	.200	A	B
		HOFFMAN, JOHN EDWARD	C	2	.333	B	C
		JACKSON, ROLAND THOMAS (SONNY)	SS 8	10	.130	B	B
		(3B1)					
3	2	JOHNSON, KENNETH TRAVIS	P	8	+.111	B	XMIL
0	0	JONES, GORDON BASSETT	P	1	.000	B	C
		KASKO, EDWARD MICHAEL (3B2)	SS 59	68	.247	B	BOSA
0	2	LAMABE, JOHN ALEXANDER	P	3	.250	XBOSA	CHIA
0	0	LARSEN, DONALD JAMES	P	1	.000	B	XBALA
0	0	LEE, DONALD EDWARD	P	7	.000	XCALA	B
		LILLIS, ROBERT PERRY	SS 104	124	.221	B	B
		(2B6 3B9)					
0	3	MAC KENZIE, KENNETH PURVIS	P	21	.273	SF	C
		MAHONEY, JAMES THOMAS	SS	5	.200	CLEA62	C
		MAYE, ARTHUR LEE	OF 103	108	+.251	XMIL	B
		MILLER, NORMAN CALVIN	OF 2	11	.200	A	B
		MORGAN, JOSEPH LEONARD	2B	157	.271	B	B
4	15	NOTTEBART, DONALD EDWARD	P	29	.104	B	CIN
6	5	OWENS, JAMES PHILIP	P	50	.125	B	B
		RATLIFF, KELLY EUGENE (GENE)		4	.000	A	C
0	2	RAY, JAMES FRANCIS	P	3	.000	A	B
7	4	RAYMOND, JOSEPH CLAUDE MARC	P 33	34	.115	B	B
5	2	ROBERTS, ROBIN EVAN	P	10	.238	XBALA	B
0	1	SEMBERA, CARROLL WILLIAM	P	2	.000	A	B
		SPANGLER, ALBERT DONALD	OF 33	38	.214	B	XCALA
		STAUB, DANIEL JOSEPH (RUSTY)	OF 112	131	.256	B	B
		(1B1)					
1	5	TAYLOR, RONALD WESLEY	P	32	+.000	XSTL	B
		THOMAS, FRANK JOSEPH	1B 16	23	+.172	XPHI	XMIL
		(3B2 OF1)					
		TRIANDOS, GUS	C 20	24	+.181	XPHI	C
0	0	VON HOFF, BRUCE FREDERICK	P	3	.000	A	HOU 67
		WHITE, JOYNER MICHAEL (MIKE)	3B 1	8	.000	B	C
3	4	WOODESHICK, HAROLD JOSEPH	P	27	+.167	B	XSTL
		WYNN, JAMES SHERMAN	OF 155	157	.275	B	B
0	2	ZACHARY, WILLIAM CHRIS	P	4	.000	B	B

WON 72
LOST 90
TIED 1
TG 163

NATIONAL LEAGUE

1966.

FINISHED 8

PCT. .444

HOUSTON

GRADY EDGEBERT HATTON

WON	LOST	NAME	POS.	G.	BA	FROM	TO
		ADLESH, DAVID GEORGE	C 1	3	.000	B	B
0	1	ARLICH, DONALD LOUIS	P	7	.000	B	C
		ASPROMONTE, ROBERT THOMAS	3B 149	152	.252	B	B
		(1B2 SS2)					
		BATEMAN, JOHN ALVIN	C 121	131	.279	B	B
		BRAND, RONALD GEORGE	C 25	56	.244	B	B
		(2B9 3B1 OF3)					
3	13	BRUCE, ROBERT JAMES	P	25	.077	B	ATL
1	0	CARPIN, FRANK DOMINIC	P	10	.000	PIT	C
		COLBERT, NATHAN		19	.000	A	HOU 68
0	0	COOMBS, DANIEL BERNARD	P	2	.000	B	B
12	10	CUELLAR, MIGUEL ANGEL	P	38	.113	B	B
		DAVIS, BRYSHEAR BARNETT	OF 7	10	.148	HOU 64	CHI 70
		(BROCK)					
		DAVIS, RONALD EVERETTE	OF	48	.247	HOU 62	B
10	8	DIERKER, LAWRENCE EDWARD	P	29	.149	B	B
6	10	FARRELL, RICHARD JOSEPH (TURK)	P	32	.146	B	B
		FREESE, EUGENE LEWIS	3B 4	21	.091	XCHIA	C
		(2B3 OF1)					
		GAINES, ARNESTA JOE	OF 3	11	.077	B	C
		GENTILE, JAMES EDWARD	1B 43	49	.243	B	XCLEA
15	14	GIUSTI, DAVID JOHN	P 34	41	.230	B	B
		GOTAY, JULIO SANCHEZ	3B 1	4	.000	CALA	B
		HARRISON, CHARLES WILLIAM	1B 114	119	.256	B	B
		HEATH, WILLIAM CHRIS	C 37	55	.301	CHIA	B
		JACKSON, ROLAND THOMAS (SONNY)	SS	150	.292	B	B
0	0	KROLL, GARY MELVIN	P	10	.000	NY	CLEA69
2	7	LATMAN, ARNOLD BARRY	P	31	.154	CALA	B
2	0	LEE, DONALD EDWARD	P	9+1	.000	B	XCHI
		LILLIS, ROBERT PERRY	2B 35	68	.232	B	B
		(SS18 3B6)					
		MANTILLA, FELIX LAMELA	1B 14	77	.219	BOSA	C
		(2B9 3B14 OF1)					
		MAYE, ARTHUR LEE	OF 97	115	.288	B	CLEA
		MILLER, NORMAN CALVIN (3B2)	OF 8	11	.147	B	B
0	0	MONTEAGUDO, AURELIO FAUSTINO	P	10	.000	XKC A	CHIA
		MORGAN, JOSEPH LEONARD	2B 117	122	.285	B	B
		NICHOLSON, DAVID LAWRENCE	OF 90	100	.246	CHIA	ATL
4	7	OWENS, JAMES PHILIP	P	40	.000	B	B
		POINTER, AARON ELTON	OF	11	.346	HOU 63	B
0	0	RAY, JAMES FRANCIS	P	1	.000	B	HOU 68
7	5	RAYMOND, JOSEPH CLAUDE MARC	P	62	.111	B	B
3	5	ROBERTS, ROBIN EVAN	P	13	+.063	B	XCHI
1	2	SEMBERA, CARROLL WILLIAM	P	24	.000	B	B
		SIMS, GREGORY EMMETT	OF 1	7	.167	A	C
		STAUB, DANIEL JOSEPH (RUSTY)	OF 148	153	.280	B	B
		(1B1)					
2	3	TAYLOR, RONALD WESLEY	P	36	.167	B	NY
		WATSON, ROBERT JOSE		1	.000	A	B
1	0	WILSON, DONALD EDWARD	P	1	.500	A	B
		WYNN, JAMES SHERMAN	OF 104	105	.256	B	B
3	5	ZACHARY, WILLIAM CHRIS	P	10	.222	B	B

WON 69
LOST 93
TIED 0
TG 162

NATIONAL LEAGUE

1967.

FINISHED 9

PCT. .426

HOUSTON

GRADY EDGEBERT HATTON

WON	LOST	NAME	POS.		G.	BA	FROM	TO
		ADLESH, DAVID GEORGE	C	31	39	.181	B	B
		ASPROMONTE, ROBERT THOMAS	3B	133	137	.294	B	B
		BALES, WESLEY OWEN (LEE)	2B	6	19	.111	ATL	C
		(SS1)						
		BATEMAN, JOHN ALVIN	C	71	76	.190	B	B
3	9	BELINSKY, ROBERT (BO)	P		27	.077	PHI	PIT 69
4	7	BLASINGAME, WADE ALLEN	P	15	16	+.182	XATL	B
		BRAND, RONALD GEORGE	C	67	84	.242	B	B
		(2B1 OF1)						
		BRANDT, JOHN GEORGE	1B	14	41	+.236	XPHI	C
		(3B1 OF6)						
0	0	BUZHARDT, JOHN WILLIAM	P		1	.000	XBALA	B
3	0	COOMBS, DANIEL BERNARD	P		6	.125	B	B
16	11	CUELLAR, MIGUEL ANGEL	P	36	38	.140	B	B
		DAVIS, RONALD EVERETTE	OF	80	94	.256	B	B
6	5	DIERKER, LAWRENCE EDWARD	P		15	.226	B	B
0	2	DUKES, THOMAS EARL	P		17	.500	A	B
0	0	EARLEY, ARNOLD CARL	P		2	.000	CHI	C
6	4	EILERS,DAVID LOUIS	P		35	.000	NY	C
1	0	FARRELL, RICHARD JOSEPH (TURK)	P		7	+.000	B	XPHI
11	15	GIUSTI, DAVID JOHN	P	37	43	.155	B	B
		GOTAY, JULIO SANCHEZ	2B	30	77	.282	B	B
		(SS20 3B3)						
		HARRIS, ALONZO			6	.000	A	C
		HARRISON, CHARLES WILLIAM	1B	59	70	.243	B	KC A69
		HEATH, WILLIAM CHRIS	C	5	9	.091	B	XDETA
		HERRERA, JOSE CONCEPCION			5	.250	A	B
1	0	HOUSE, PATRICK LORY	P		6	.000	A	B
		JACKSON, ROLAND THOMAS (SONNY)	SS	128	129	.237	B	ATL
		KING, HAROLD	C	11	15	.250	A	B
		LANDIS, JAMES HENRY	OF	44	50	.252	XBOSA	C
3	6	LATMAN, ARNOLD BARRY	P		39	.091	B	C
		LILLIS, ROBERT PERRY	SS	23	37	.244	B	C
		(2B3 3B2)						
		MATHEWS, EDWIN LEE (3B24)	1B	79	101	.238	ATL	XDETA
		MILLER, NORMAN CALVIN	OF	53	64	.205	B	B
		MORGAN, JOSEPH LEONARD (OF1)	2B	130	133	.275	B	B
		MURRELL, IVAN AUGUSTUS	OF	6	10	.310	HOU 64	B
0	1	OWENS, JAMES PHILIP	P		10	.000	B	C
		POINTER, AARON ELTON	OF	22	27	.157	B	C
		RADER, DOUGLAS LEE (3B7)	1B	36	47	.333	A	B
0	4	RAYMOND, JOSEPH CLAUDE MARC	P		21	+.200	B	XATL
1	1	REED, HOWARD DEAN	P		4	.000	CALA	MON 69
0	2	SCHNEIDER, DANIEL LOUIS	P	54	55	.200	ATL	HOU 69
2	6	SEMBERA, CARROLL WILLIAM	P		45	.143	B	MON 69
1	2	SHERRY, LAWRENCE	P		29	.000	XDETA	CALA
		STAUB, DANIEL JOSEPH (RUSTY)	OF	144	149	.333	B	B
0	3	VON HOFF, BRUCE FREDERICK	P		10	.067	HOU 65	C
		WATSON, ROBERT JOSE	1B	3	6	.214	B	B
10	9	WILSON, DONALD EDWARD	P		31	.091	B	B
		WYNN, JAMES SHERMAN	OF	157	158	.249	B	B
1	6	ZACHARY, WILLIAM CHRIS	P	9	10	.100	B	KC A69

WON 72
LOST 90
TIED 0
TG 162

NATIONAL LEAGUE

1968.

FINISHED 10 (LAST)

PCT. .444

HOUSTON

GRADY EDGEBERT HATTON HARRY WILLIAM WALKER

WON	LOST	NAME	POS.		G.	BA	FROM	TO
		ADLESH, DAVID GEORGE	C	36	40	.183	B	C
		ASPROMONTE, ROBERT THOMAS	3B	75	124	.225	B	ATL
		(1B1 SS1 OF36)						
		BATEMAN, JOHN ALVIN	C	108	111	.249	B	MON
1	2	BLASINGAME, WADE ALLEN	P		22	.000	B	B
		BRAND, RONALD GEORGE	C	29	43	.160	B	MON
		(3B1 OF1)						
		BROWNE, BYRON ELLIS	OF	2	10	.231	CHI	STL
4	4	BUZHARDT, JOHN WILLIAM	P		39	.250	B	C
		COLBERT, NATHAN (1B5)	OF	11	20	.151	HOU 66	SD
4	3	COOMBS, DANIEL BERNARD	P		40	.400	B	B
8	11	CUELLAR, MIGUEL ANGEL	P		28	.193	B	BALA
		DAVIS, RONALD EVERETTE	OF		52	+.212	B	XSTL
12	15	DIERKER, LAWRENCE EDWARD	P	32	33	.068	B	B
2	2	DUKES, THOMAS EARL	P		43	.000	B	SD
0	0	GILSON, HAROLD	P	2	3	+.000	XSTL	C
11	14	GIUSTI, DAVID JOHN	P	37	38	.183	B	STL
0	0	GLADDING, FRED EARL	P		7	.000	DETA	B
		GOTAY, JULIO SANCHEZ (3B1)	2B	48	75	.248	B	B
		HERRERA, JOSE CONCEPCION	OF	17	27	.240	B	MON
		(2B7)						
1	1	HOUSE, PATRICK LORY	P		18	.000	B	C
		KING, HAROLD	C	19	27	.145	B	ATL 70
10	15	LEMASTER, DENVER CLAYTON	P		33	.031	ATL	B
		MAYBERRY, JOHN CLAIBORN	1B	2	4	.000	A	B
		MC FADDEN, LEON	SS		16	.277	A	B
		MENKE, DENIS JOHN	2B	119	150	.249	ATL	B
		(1B5 SS35 3B4)						
		MILLER, NORMAN CALVIN	OF	74	79	.237	B	B
		MORGAN, JOSEPH LEONARD (OF1)	2B	5	10	.250	B	B
		MURRELL, IVAN AUGUSTUS	OF	15	32	.102	B	SD
		RADER, DOUGLAS LEE (1B5)	3B	86	98	.267	B	B
2	3	RAY, JAMES FRANCIS	P	41	42	.067	HOU 66	B
4	4	SHEA, STEVEN FRANCIS	P		30	.000	A	MON
		SIMPSON, RICHARD CHARLES	OF	49	59	+.186	XSTL	NY A
		STAUB, DANIEL JOSEPH (RUSTY)	1B	147	161	.291	B	MON
		(OF15)						
		THOMAS, JAMES LEROY (LEE)	OF	48	90	.194	CHI	C
		(1B2)						
		TORRES, HECTOR EPITACIO	SS	127	128	.223	A	B
		(2B1)						
		WALTON, DANIEL JAMES			2	.000	A	SEAA
		WATSON, ROBERT JOSE	OF	40	45	.229	B	B
13	16	WILSON, DONALD EDWARD	P	33	34	.214	B	B
		WYNN, JAMES SHERMAN	OF	153	156	.269	B	B

WON 81
LOST 81
TIED 0
TG 162

NATIONAL LEAGUE — 1969. — FINISHED 5 W — PCT. .500

HOUSTON

HARRY WILLIAM WALKER

WON	LOST	NAME	POS.	G.	BA	FROM	TO
		ALOU, JESUS MARIA ROJAS	OF 112	115	.248	SF	B
6	7	BILLINGHAM, JOHN EUGENE	P	52	.071	LA	B
0	5	BLASINGAME, WADE ALLEN	P 26	27	.000	B	B
		BLEFARY, CURTIS LEROY (OF1)	1B 152	155	.253	BALA	NY A
0	2	BOUTON, JAMES ALAN	P	16	.000	XSEAA	B
		BRYANT, DONALD RAY	C 28	31	.186	CHI 66	B
0	1	COOMBS, DANIEL BERNARD	P	8	.000	B	SD
		DAVIS, HERMAN THOMAS (TOMMY)	OF 21	24	.241	XSEAA	B
20	13	DIERKER, LAWRENCE EDWARD	P	39	.144	B	B
		EDWARDS, JOHN ALBAN	C	151	.232	STL	B
		GEIGER, GARY MERLE	OF 65	93	.224	ATL 67	B
		GERONIMO, CESAR FRANCISCO	OF 9	28	.250	A	B
4	8	GLADDING, FRED EARL	P	57	.100	B	B
		GOTAY, JULIO SANCHEZ (3B1)	2B 16	46	.259	B	C
11	10	GRIFFIN, THOMAS JAMES	P	31	.145	A	B
1	2	GUINN, DRANNON EUGENE (SKIP)	P	28	.000	ATL	HOU 71
0	0	HENRY, WILLIAM RODMAN	P	3	.000	PIT	C
		LAMPARD, CHRISTOPHER KEITH	OF 1	9	.250	A	B
13	17	LEMASTER, DENVER CLAYTON	P	38	.170	B	B
0	0	MARTINEZ, ORLANDO (MARTY)	OF 21	78	.308	ATL	B
		(P1 C7 2B1 SS17 3B15)					
		MAYBERRY, JOHN CLAIBORN		5	.000	B	B
		MC FADDEN, LEON (SS8)	OF 17	44	.176	B	B
		MENKE, DENIS JOHN	SS 131	154	.269	B	B
		(1B9 2B23 3B1)					
		MILLER, NORMAN CALVIN	OF 114	119	.264	B	B
		MORGAN, JOSEPH LEONARD (OF14)	2B 132	147	.236	B	B
		RADER, DOUGLAS LEE (1B4)	3B 154	155	.246	B	B
8	2	RAY, JAMES FRANCIS	P	40	.115	B	B
0	1	SCHNEIDER, DANIEL LOUIS	P	6	.000	HOU 67	C
0	0	SPINKS, SCIPIO RONALD	P	1	.000	A	B
		TORRES, HECTOR EPITACIO	SS 22	34	.159	B	B
		VALDESPINO, HILARIO BORROTO	OF 29	41	.244	ATL	XSEAA
		(SANDY)					
0	0	WATKINS, ROBERT CECIL	P	5	.000	A	C
		WATSON, ROBERT JOSE	OF 6	20	.275	B	B
		(C1 1B5)					
0	0	WILLIS, RONALD EARL	P	3	+.000	XSTL	SD
16	12	WILSON, DONALD EDWARD	P	34	.099	B	B
2	1	WOMACK, HORACE GUY (DOOLEY)	P	30	.167	NY A	XSEAA
		WYNN, JAMES SHERMAN	OF	149	.269	B	B

WON 79
LOST 83
TIED 0
TG 162

NATIONAL LEAGUE — 1970. — FINISHED 4 W — PCT. .488

HOUSTON

HARRY WILLIAM WALKER

WON	LOST	NAME	POS.	G.	BA	FROM	TO
		ALOU, JESUS MARIA ROJAS	OF 108	117	.306	B	B
		BEAUCHAMP, JAMES EDWARD	OF 16	31	+.192	CIN	XSTL
13	9	BILLINGHAM, JOHN EUGENE	P	46	.103	B	B
3	3	BLASINGAME, WADE ALLEN	P	13	.083	B	B
4	6	BOUTON, JAMES ALAN	P	29	.353	B	C
		BRYANT, DONALD RAY	C 13	15	.208	B	C
		CEDENO, CESAR	OF	90	.310	A	B
4	4	COOK, RONALD WAYNE	P 41	43	.235	A	B
3	3	CULVER, GEORGE RAYMOND	P	32	+.250	XSTL	B
		DAVIS, HERMAN THOMAS (TOMMY)	OF 53	57	+.282	B	XCHI
16	12	DIERKER, LAWRENCE EDWARD	P	37	.174	B	B
1	3	DI LAURO, JACK EDWARD	P 42	43	.000	NY	C
		EDWARDS, JOHN ALBAN	C 139	140	.221	B	B
1	2	FORSCH, KENNETH ROTH	P	4	.000	A	B
		GEIGER, GARY MERLE	OF 2	5	.250	B	C
		GERONIMO, CESAR FRANCISCO	OF 26	47	.243	B	B
7	4	GLADDING, FRED EARL	P	63	.000	B	B
3	13	GRIFFIN, THOMAS JAMES	P	23	.061	B	B
0	0	HARRIS, WALTER FRANCIS (BUDDY)	P	2	.000	A	B
		HOWARD, LAWRENCE RAYFORD	C 26	31	.307	A	B
		(1B2 OF1)					
		LAMPARD, CHRISTOPHER KEITH	OF 16	53	.236	B	C
		(1B2)					
7	12	LEMASTER, DENVER CLAYTON	P	39	.178	B	B
0	1	MARSHALL, MICHAEL GRANT	P	4	+.000	SEAA	XMON
		MARTINEZ, ORLANDO (MARTY)	SS 29	75	.220	B	B
		(C6 2B4 3B10)					
		MAYBERRY, JOHN CLAIBORN	1B 45	50	.216	B	B
		MC FADDEN, LEON		2	.000	B	C
		MENKE, DENIS JOHN	SS 133	154	.304	B	B
		(1B5 2B21 3B5 OF3)					
		MILLER, NORMAN CALVIN (C1)	OF 72	90	.239	B	B
		MORGAN, JOSEPH LEONARD	2B 142	144	.268	B	B
0	1	OSINSKI, DANIEL	P	3	.000	CHIA	C
		PEPITONE, JOSEPH ANTHONY	1B 50	75	+.251	NY A	XCHI
		(OF28)					
		RADER, DOUGLAS LEE (1B1)	3B 154	156	.252	B	B
6	3	RAY, JAMES FRANCIS	P	52	.185	B	B
0	1	SPINKS, SCIPIO RONALD	P 5	6	.000	B	B
		TORRES, HECTOR EPITACIO	SS 22	31	.246	B	CHI
		(2B6)					
		WATSON, ROBERT JOSE	1B 83	97	.272	B	B
		(C6 OF1)					
11	6	WILSON, DONALD EDWARD	P 29	30	.116	B	B
		WYNN, JAMES SHERMAN	OF 151	157	.282	B	B

WON 79	NATIONAL LEAGUE	FINISHED 4 W
LOST 83		(TIED WITH CINCINNATI)
TIED 0	1971.	PCT. .488
TG 162		

HOUSTON

HARRY WILLIAM WALKER

WON	LOST	NAME	POS.		G.	BA	FROM	TO
		ALOU, JESUS MARIA ROJAS	OF	109	122	.279	B	B
10	16	BILLINGHAM, JOHN EUGENE	P		33	.123	B	CIN
9	11	BLASINGAME, WADE ALLEN	P		30	.204	B	B
		BUSSE, RAYMOND EDWARD (3B3)	SS	5	10	.147	A	C
		CEDENO, CESAR (1B2)	OF	157	161	.264	B	B
		CHILES, RICHARD FRANCIS	OF	27	67	.227	A	B
0	4	COOK, RONALD WAYNE	P	5	6	.250	B	C
5	8	CULVER, GEORGE RAYMOND	P		59	.091	B	B
12	6	DIERKER, LAWRENCE EDWARD	P		24	.074	B	B
		EDWARDS, JOHN ALBAN	C	104	106	.233	B	B
8	8	FORSCH, KENNETH ROTH	P		33	.136	B	B
		GERONIMO, CESAR FRANCISCO	OF	64	94	.220	B	CIN
4	5	GLADDING, FRED EARL	P		48	.000	B	B
1	1	GREIF, WILLIAM BRILEY	P		7	.333	A	SD
0	6	GRIFFIN, THOMAS JAMES	P		10	.111	B	B
0	0	GUINN, DRANNON EUGENE (SKIP)	P		4	.000	HOU 69	C
1	1	HARRIS, WALTER FRANCIS (BUDDY)	P		20	.000	B	C
		HIATT, JACK E. (1B1)	C	65	69	.276	CHI	B
		HOWARD, LAWRENCE RAYFORD	C	22	24	.234	B	B
0	2	LEMASTER, DENVER CLAYTON	P		42	.167	B	MON
		MARTINEZ, ORLANDO (MARTY)	2B	9	32	.258	B	STL
		(1B4 SS7 3B3)						
		MAYBERRY, JOHN CLAIBORN	1B	37	46	.182	B	KC A
		MENKE, DENIS JOHN	1B	101	146	.246	B	CIN
		(2B5 SS17 3B32)						
		METZGER, ROGER HENRY	SS	148	150	.235	CHI	B
		MILLER, NORMAN CALVIN (C1)	OF	20	45	.257	B	B
		MORGAN, JOSEPH LEONARD	2B	157	160	.256	B	CIN
		RADER, DOUGLAS LEE	3B		135	.244	B	B
10	4	RAY, JAMES FRANCIS	P		47	.167	B	B
2	1	RICHARD, JAMES RODNEY	P		4	.000	A	B
		SCHLUETER, JAY D.	OF	2	7	.333	A	C
1	0	SPINKS, SCIPIO RONALD	P		5	.222	B	STL
		THOMAS, DERRELL OSBON	2B	1	5	.000	A	SD
		WATSON, ROBERT JOSE (1B45)	OF	87	129	.288	B	B
16	10	WILSON, DONALD EDWARD	P		35	.154	B	B
		WYNN, JAMES SHERMAN	OF	116	123	.203	B	B
0	0	YOUNT, LAWRENCE KING	P		1	.000	A	C

WON 84	NATIONAL LEAGUE	FINISHED 2 W
LOST 69		
TIED 0	1972.	PCT. .549
TG 153		

HOUSTON

HARRY WILLIAM WALKER   FRANCIS JAMES PARKER   LEO ERNEST DUROCHER

WON	LOST	NAME	POS.		G.	BA	FROM	TO
		ALOU, JESUS MARIA ROJAS	OF	23	52	.312	B	
0	0	BLASINGAME, WADE ALLEN	P		10	.000	B	XNY A
		CEDENO, CESAR	OF	137	139	.320	B	
		CHILES, RICHARD FRANCIS	OF	2	9	.273	B	
0	1	COSGROVE, MICHAEL JOHN	P		7	.000	A	
6	2	CULVER, GEORGE RAYMOND	P		45	.158	B	
15	8	DIERKER, LAWRENCE EDWARD	P		31	.167	B	
		EDWARDS, JOHN ALBAN	C	105	108	.268	B	
		FENWICK, ROBERT RICHARD	2B	17	36	.180	A	
		(SS4 3B2)						
6	8	FORSCH, KENNETH ROTH	P		30	.146	B	
0	0	GIBBON, JOSEPH CHARLES	P		9	+.000	XCIN	
5	6	GLADDING, FRED EARL	P		42	.000	B	
5	4	GRIFFIN, THOMAS JAMES	P		39	.280	B	
		HELMS, TOMMY VANN	2B		139	.259	CIN	
		HIATT, JACK E.	C		10	.200	B	XCALA
		HOWARD, LAWRENCE RAYFORD	C	53	54	.223	B	
		(OF1)						
		JOHNSON, CLIFFORD	C	1	5	.250	A	
		MAY, LEE ANDREW	1B	146	148	.284	CIN	
		METZGER, ROGER HENRY	SS		153	.222	B	
		MILLER, NORMAN CALVIN	OF	29	67	.243	B	
		RADER, DOUGLAS LEE	3B		152	.237	B	
10	9	RAY, JAMES FRANCIS	P		54	.063	B	
9	13	REUSS, JERRY	P		33	.106	STL	
1	0	RICHARD, JAMES RODNEY	P		4	.000	B	
12	7	ROBERTS, DAVID ARTHUR	P		35	.239	SD	
		STEWART, JAMES FRANKLIN	OF	11	68	.219	CIN	
		(1B9 2B8 3B2)						
		STINSON, GORRELL ROBERT	C	12	27	.171	STL	
		(OF3)						
		SUTHERLAND, GARY LYNN (3B1)	2B	1	5	.125	MON	
		WATSON, ROBERT JOSE (1B2)	OF	143	147	.312	B	
15	10	WILSON, DONALD EDWARD	P		33	.105	B	
		WYNN, JAMES SHERMAN	OF	144	145	.273	B	
0	1	YORK, JAMES HARLAN	P		26	.000	KC A	

COACH PARKER SERVED AS INTERIM MANAGER DURING CHANGEOVER.

WON 97 NATIONAL LEAGUE FINISHED 1
LOST 65
TIED 0 1965. PCT. .599
TG 162

LOS ANGELES

WALTER EMMONS ALSTON

WON	LOST	NAME	POS.		G.	BA	FROM	TO
3	2	BREWER, JAMES THOMAS	P	19	20	.000	B	B
		CRAWFORD, WILLIE MURPHY	OF	8	52	.148	B	B
		DAVIS, HERMAN THOMAS (TOMMY)	OF	16	17	.250	B	B
		DAVIS, WILLIAM HENRY	OF	141	142	.238	B	B
23	12	DRYSDALE, DONALD SCOTT	P	44	58	.300	B	B
		FAIRLY, RONALD RAY (1B13)	OF	148	158	.274	B	B
		FERRARA, ALFRED JOHN	OF	27	41	.210	LA 63	B
		GILLIAM, JAMES WM. (JUNIOR)	3B	80	111	.280	B	B
		(2B5 OF22)						
		GRIFFITH, ROBERT DERRELL	OF	11	22	.171	B	B
		JOHNSON, LOUIS BROWN	OF	128	131	.259	MIL 62	B
0	1	KEKICH, MICHAEL DENNIS	P		5	.000	A	LA 68
		KENNEDY, JOHN EDWARD (SS5)	3B	95	104	.171	WASA	B
26	8	KOUFAX, SANFORD	P		43	.177	B	B
		LEFEBVRE, JAMES KENNETH	2B	156	157	.250	A	B
		LE JOHN, DONALD EVERETT	3B	26	34	.256	A	C
6	7	MILLER, ROBERT LANE	P		61	.000	B	B
		MOON, WALLACE WADE	OF	23	53	.202	B	C
		OLIVER, NATHANIEL (PEEWEE)	2B	2	8	1.000	B	B
15	15	OSTEEN, CLAUDE WILSON	P	40	42	.121	WASA	B
		PARKER, MAURICE WESLEY (WES)	1B	154	154	.238	B	B
		(OF1)						
6	6	PERRANOSKI, RONALD PETER	P		59	.158	B	B
7	6	PODRES, JOHN JOSEPH	P		27	.178	B	B
2	1	PURDIN, JOHN NOLAN	P		11	.000	B	LA 68
7	5	REED, HOWARD DEAN	P		38	.000	B	B
		ROSEBORO, JOHN (3B1)	C	131	136	.233	B	B
0	0	SINGER, WILLIAM ROBERT	P		2	.000	B	B
		SMITH, RICHARD ARTHUR	OF	9	10	.000	NY	C
		TORBORG, JEFFREY ALLEN	C	53	56	.240	B	B
		TRACEWSKI, RICHARD JOSEPH	3B	53	78	.215	B	DETA
		(2B14 SS7)						
		VALLE, HECTOR JOSE	C	6	9	.308	A	C
		WERHAS, JOHN CHARLES	1B	1	4	.000	B	LA 67
2	2	WILLHITE, JON NICHOLAS (NICK)	P		15	.400	XWASA	B
		WILLS, MAURICE MORNING	SS	155	158	.286	B	B

WON 95 NATIONAL LEAGUE FINISHED 1
LOST 67
TIED 0 1966. PCT. .586
TG 162

LOS ANGELES

WALTER EMMONS ALSTON

WON	LOST	NAME	POS.		G.	BA	FROM	TO
		BARBIERI, JAMES PATRICK	OF	20	39	.280	A	C
0	2	BREWER, JAMES THOMAS	P		13	.000	B	B
		CAMPANIS, JAMES ALEXANDER	C		1	.000	A	B
		COVINGTON, JOHN WESLEY (WES)	OF	2	37	+.121	XCHI	C
		CRAWFORD, WILLIE MURPHY			6	.000	B	B
		DAVIS, HERMAN THOMAS (TOMMY)	OF	79	100	.313	B	NY
		(3B2)						
		DAVIS, WILLIAM HENRY	OF	152	153	.284	B	B
13	16	DRYSDALE, DONALD SCOTT	P	40	46	.189	B	B
		FAIRLY, RONALD RAY (1B25)	OF	98	117	.288	B	B
		FERRARA, ALFRED JOHN	OF	32	63	.270	B	B
		GILLIAM, JAMES WM. (JUNIOR)	3B	70	88	.217	B	C
		(1B2 2B2)						
		GRIFFITH, ROBERT DERRELL	OF	7	23	.067	B	C
		HUTTON, THOMAS GEORGE	1B		3	.000	A	LA 69
		JOHNSON, LOUIS BROWN	OF	148	152	.272	B	B
		KENNEDY, JOHN EDWARD	3B	87	125	.201	B	NY A
		(2B15 SS28)						
27	9	KOUFAX, SANFORD	P		41	.076	B	C
		LEFEBVRE, JAMES KENNETH	2B	119	152	.274	B	B
		(3B40)						
4	2	MILLER, ROBERT LANE	P		46	.077	B	B
2	4	MOELLER, JOSEPH DOUGLAS	P		29	.167	LA 64	B
		OLIVER, NATHANIEL (PEEWEE)	2B	68	80	.193	B	B
		(SS2 3B1)						
17	14	OSTEEN, CLAUDE WILSON	P		39	.211	B	B
		PARKER, MAURICE WESLEY (WES)	1B	140	156	.253	B	B
		(OF14)						
6	7	PERRANOSKI, RONALD PETER	P		55	.250	B	B
0	0	PODRES, JOHN JOSEPH	P		1	.000	B	XDETA
0	0	REED, HOWARD DEAN	P		1	.000	B	XCALA
14	1	REGAN, PHILIP RAYMOND	P		65	.143	DETA	B
		ROSEBORO, JOHN	C	138	142	.276	B	B
		SCHOFIELD, JOHN RICHARD (DICK)	3B	19	20	.257	XNY A	B
		(SS3)						
		SHIRLEY, BARTON ARVIN	SS	5	12	.200	LA 64	NY
0	0	SINGER, WILLIAM ROBERT	P		3	.000	B	B
		STUART, RICHARD LEE	1B	25	38	+.264	XNY	CALA69
12	12	SUTTON, DONALD HOWARD	P	37	38	.183	A	B
		TORBORG, JEFFREY ALLEN	C	45	46	.225	B	B
0	0	WILLHITE, JON NICHOLAS (NICK)	P		6	.000	B	CALA
		WILLS, MAURICE MORNING (3B4)	SS	139	143	.273	B	PIT

WON 73
LOST 89
TIED 0
TG 162

NATIONAL LEAGUE

1967.

FINISHED 8

PCT. .451

LOS ANGELES

WALTER EMMONS ALSTON

WON	LOST	NAME	POS.		G.	BA	FROM	TO
		ALCARAZ, ANGEL LUIS	2B		17	.233	A	B
		BAILEY, ROBERT SHERWOOD	3B	65	116	.227	PIT	B
		(1B4 SS1 OF27)						
5	4	BREWER, JAMES THOMAS	P		30	.045	B	B
0	0	BRUBAKER, BRUCE ELLSWORTH	P		1	.000	A	MILA70
		CAMPANIS, JAMES ALEXANDER	C	23	41	.161	B	B
		CRAWFORD, WILLIE MURPHY	OF	1	4	.250	B	B
		DAVIS, WILLIAM HENRY	OF	138	143	.257	B	B
		DEAN, TOMMY DOUGLAS	SS		12	.143	A	SD 69
13	16	DRYSDALE, DONALD SCOTT	P		38	.129	B	B
0	2	DUFFIE, JOHN BROWN	P		2	.000	A	C
1	1	EGAN, RICHARD WALLIS	P		20	.000	CALA	C
		FAIRLY, RONALD RAY (1B68)	OF	97	153	.220	B	B
		FERRARA, ALFRED JOHN	OF	94	122	.277	B	B
0	1	FOSTER, ALAN BENTON	P		4	.000	A	B
		GABRIELSON, LEONARD GARY	OF	68	90	.261	XCALA	B
0	0	HICKMAN, JAMES LUCIUS	OF	37	65	.163	NY	CHI
		(P1 1B2 3B2)						
		HUNT, RONALD KENNETH (3B8)	2B	90	110	.263	NY	SF
		JOHNSON, LOUIS BROWN	OF	91	104	.270	B	CHI
0	0	LEE, ROBERT DEAN	P		4	+.000	CALA	XCIN
		LEFEBVRE, JAMES KENNETH	3B	92	136	.261	B	B
		(1B5 2B34)						
		MICHAEL, EUGENE RICHARD	SS	83	98	.202	PIT	NY A
2	9	MILLER, ROBERT LANE	P		52	.125	B	MINA
0	0	MOELLER, JOSEPH DOUGLAS	P		6	.000	B	B
		OLIVER, NATHANIEL (PEEWEE)	2B	39	77	.237	B	SF
		(SS32 OF1)						
17	17	OSTEEN, CLAUDE WILSON	P	39	42	.178	B	B
		PARKER, MAURICE WESLEY (WES)	1B	112	139	.247	B	B
		(OF18)						
6	7	PERRANOSKI, RONALD PETER	P		70	.100	B	MINA
6	9	REGAN, PHILIP RAYMOND	P		55	.100	B	B
		ROSEBORO, JOHN	C	107	116	.272	B	MINA
		SCHOFIELD, JOHN RICHARD (DICK)	SS	69	84	.216	B	STL
		(2B4 3B2)						
12	8	SINGER, WILLIAM ROBERT	P	32	34	.090	B	B
11	15	SUTTON, DONALD HOWARD	P	37	43	.133	B	B
		TORBORG, JEFFREY ALLEN	C	75	76	.214	B	B
		WERHAS, JOHN CHARLES			7	.143	LA 65	XCALA

WON 76
LOST 86
TIED 0
TG 162

NATIONAL LEAGUE

1968.

FINISHED 7
(TIED WITH PHILADELPHIA)
PCT. .469

LOS ANGELES

WALTER EMMONS ALSTON

WON	LOST	NAME	POS.		G.	BA	FROM	TO
1	2	AGUIRRE, HENRY JOHN	P		25	.000	DETA	CHI
		ALCARAZ, ANGEL LUIS	2B	20	41	.151	B	KC A
		(SS1 3B13)						
		BAILEY, ROBERT SHERWOOD	3B	90	105	.227	B	MON
		(SS1 OF1)						
3	0	BILLINGHAM, JOHN EUGENE	P		50	.000	A	HOU
		BOYER, KENTON LLOYD (1B32)	3B	34	83	.271	XCHIA	B
8	3	BREWER, JAMES THOMAS	P		54	.222	B	B
		CAMPANIS, JAMES ALEXANDER	C		4	.091	B	KC A
		COLAVITO, ROCCO DOMENICO	OF	33	40	.204	CHIA	XNY A
		CRAWFORD, WILLIE MURPHY	OF	48	61	.251	B	B
		DAVIS, WILLIAM HENRY	OF	158	160	.250	B	B
14	12	DRYSDALE, DONALD SCOTT	P		31	.177	B	B
		FAIREY, JAMES BURKE	OF	63	99	.199	A	MON
		FAIRLY, RONALD RAY (1B36)	OF	105	141	.234	B	B
		FERRARA, ALFRED JOHN	OF		2	.143	B	SD
1	1	FOSTER, ALAN BENTON	P		3	.250	B	B
		GABRIELSON, LEONARD GARY	OF	86	108	.270	B	B
6	4	GRANT, JAMES TIMOTHY (MUDCAT)	P	37	43	.129	MINA	MON
		HALLER, THOMAS FRANK	C	139	144	.285	SF	B
		JAMES, CLEO JOEL	OF	2	10	.200	A	CHI 70
2	10	KEKICH, MICHAEL DENNIS	P		25	.081	LA 65	NY A
		LEFEBVRE, JAMES KENNETH	2B	62	84	.241	B	B
		(1B3 3B16 OF5)						
1	1	MOELLER, JOSEPH DOUGLAS	P		3	.000	B	B
12	18	OSTEEN, CLAUDE WILSON	P	39	40	.179	B	B
		PARKER, MAURICE WESLEY (WES)	1B	114	135	.239	B	B
		(OF28)						
		POPOVICH, PAUL EDWARD	2B	89	134	.232	CHI	B
		(SS45 3B7)						
2	3	PURDIN, JOHN NOLAN	P	35	36	.500	LA 65	B
2	0	REGAN, PHILIP RAYMOND	P		5	+.000	B	XCHI
0	0	ROMO, VICENTE	P		1	.000	A	XCLEA
		SAVAGE, THEODORE E.	OF	39	61	+.206	XCHI	CIN
		SHIRLEY, BARTON ARVIN (2B18)	SS	21	39	.181	NY	C
13	17	SINGER, WILLIAM ROBERT	P		37	.148	B	B
		SUDAKIS, WILLIAM PAUL	3B		24	.276	A	B
11	15	SUTTON, DONALD HOWARD	P	35	36	.177	B	B
		TORBORG, JEFFREY ALLEN	C		37	.161	B	B
		VERSALLES, ZOILO	SS	119	122	.196	MINA	CLEA

WON 85
LOST 77
TIED 0
TG 162

NATIONAL LEAGUE

1969.

FINISHED 4 W

PCT. .525

LOS ANGELES

WALTER EMMONS ALSTON

WON	LOST	NAME	POS.		G.	BA	FROM	TO
		BOYER, KENTON LLOYD	1B	4	25	.206	B	C
7	6	BREWER, JAMES THOMAS	P		59	.091	B	B
		BUCKNER, WILLIAM JOSEPH			1	.000	A	B
3	1	BUNNING,JAMES PAUL DAVID	P		9	+.111	XPIT	PHI
		CRAWFORD, WILLIE MURPHY	OF	113	129	.247	B	B
0	0	DARWIN, ARTHUR BOBBY LEE	P	3	6	.000	LA A62	LA 71
		DAVIS, WILLIAM HENRY	OF	125	129	.311	B	B
5	4	DRYSDALE, DONALD SCOTT	P		12	.136	B	C
		FAIRLY, RONALD RAY (OF10)	1B	12	30	+.219	B	XMON
3	9	FOSTER, ALAN BENTON	P		24	.074	B	B
		GABRIELSON, LEONARD GARY	OF	47	83	.270	B	B
		(1B2)						
		GARVEY, STEVEN PATRICK			3	.333	A	B
		GRABARKEWITZ, BILLY CORDELL	SS	18	34	.092	A	B
		(2B3 3B6)						
		HALLER, THOMAS FRANK	C	132	134	.263	B	B
		HUTTON, THOMAS GEORGE	1B		16	.271	LA 66	PHI 72
0	0	JENKINS, WARREN WASHINGTON	P		1	.000	WASA63	C
		JOSHUA, VON EVERETT	OF	8	14	.250	A	B
		KOSCO, ANDREW JOHN (1B3)	OF	109	120	.248	NY A	B
0	1	LAMB, RAYMOND RICHARD	P		10	.000	A	B
		LEFEBVRE, JAMES KENNETH	3B	44	95	.236	B	B
		(1B6 2B37)						
2	6	MC BEAN, ALVIN O'NEAL	P		31	+.000	XSD	B
7	5	MIKKELSEN, PETER JAMES	P		48	.167	STL	B
		MILLER, JOHN ALLEN	OF	6	26	.211	NY A66	C
		(1B5 2B1 3B2)						
1	0	MOELLER, JOSEPH DOUGLAS	P		23	.200	B	B
		MOTA, MANUEL RAFAEL	OF	80	85	+.323	XMON	B
20	15	OSTEEN, CLAUDE WILSON	P	41	44	.216	B	B
		PARKER, MAURICE WESLEY (WES)	1B	128	132	.278	B	B
		(OF2)						
		POPOVICH, PAUL EDWARD (SS3)	2B	23	28	+.200	B	XCHI
0	0	PURDIN, JOHN NOLAN	P		9	.000	B	C
		RUSSELL, WILLIAM ELLIS	OF	86	98	.226	A	B
20	12	SINGER, WILLIAM ROBERT	P		41	.102	B	B
		SIZEMORE, TED CRAWFORD	2B	118	159	.271	A	B
		(SS46 OF1)						
		STINSON, GORRELL ROBERT	C		4	.375	A	B
		SUDAKIS, WILLIAM PAUL	3B	121	132	.234	B	B
17	18	SUTTON, DONALD HOWARD	P		41	.153	B	B
		TORBORG, JEFFREY ALLEN	C	50	51	.185	B	B
		VALENTINE, ROBERT JOHN			5	.000	A	LA 71
		WILLS, MAURICE MORNING	SS		104	+.297	XMON	B

WON 87
LOST 74
TIED 0
TG 161

NATIONAL LEAGUE

1970.

FINISHED 2 W

PCT. .540

LOS ANGELES

WALTER EMMONS ALSTON

WON	LOST	NAME	POS.		G.	BA	FROM	TO
7	6	BREWER, JAMES THOMAS	P		58	.083	B	B
		BUCKNER, WILLIAM JOSEPH	OF	20	28	.191	B	B
		(1B1)						
		CRAWFORD, WILLIE MURPHY	OF	94	109	.234	B	B
		DAVIS, WILLIAM HENRY	OF	143	146	.305	B	B
		FERGUSON, JOSEPH VANCE	C	3	5	.250	A	B
10	13	FOSTER, ALAN BENTON	P		33	.109	B	CLEA
		GABRIELSON, LEONARD GARY	OF	2	43	.190	B	C
		(1B1)						
		GARVEY, STEVEN PATRICK (2B1)	3B	27	34	.269	B	B
		GRABARKEWITZ, BILLY CORDELL	3B	97	156	.289	B	B
		(2B20 SS50)						
		HALLER, THOMAS FRANK	C	106	112	.286	B	B
0	0	HOUGH, CHARLES OLIVER	P		8	.333	A	B
		JOSHUA, VON EVERETT	OF	41	72	.266	B	B
		KOSCO, ANDREW JOHN (1B1)	OF	58	74	.228	B	MILA
6	1	LAMB, RAYMOND RICHARD	P		35	.000	B	CLEA
		LEFEBVRE, JAMES KENNETH	2B	70	109	.252	B	B
		(1B1 3B21)						
0	0	MC BEAN, ALVIN O'NEAL	P		1	+.000	B	XPIT
4	2	MIKKELSEN, PETER JAMES	P		33	.333	B	B
7	9	MOELLER, JOSEPH DOUGLAS	P		31	.154	B	B
		MOORE, GARY DOUGLAS (1B1)	OF	5	7	.188	A	C
		MOTA, MANUEL RAFAEL (3B1)	OF	111	124	.305	B	B
2	0	NORMAN, FREDIE HUBERT	P		30	+.143	CHI 67	XSTL
16	14	OSTEEN, CLAUDE WILSON	P	37	39	.204	B	B
		PACIOREK, THOMAS MARIAN	OF	3	8	.222	A	B
		PARKER, MAURICE WESLEY (WES)	1B		161	.319	B	B
0	0	PASCUAL, CAMILO ALBERTO	P		10	.000	CIN	CLEA
4	3	PENA, JOSE	P		29	.125	CIN	B
		RUSSELL, WILLIAM ELLIS (SS1)	OF	79	81	.259	B	B
8	5	SINGER, WILLIAM ROBERT	P		16	.132	B	B
		SIZEMORE, TED CRAWFORD	2B	86	96	.306	B	STL
		(SS2 OF9)						
0	0	STEPHENSON, JERRY JOSEPH	P		3	.000	SEAA	C
		STINSON, GORRELL ROBERT	C	3	4	.000	B	STL
1	1	STRAHLER, MICHAEL WAYNE	P		6	.250	A	B
		SUDAKIS, WILLIAM PAUL	C	38	94	.264	B	B
		(1B1 3B37 OF3)						
15	13	SUTTON, DONALD HOWARD	P	38	40	.155	B	B
		TORBORG, JEFFREY ALLEN	C	63	64	.231	B	CALA
7	7	VANCE, GENE COVINGTON (SANDY)	P		20	.189	A	B
		WILLS, MAURICE MORNING (3B4)	SS	126	132	.270	B	B

WON 89
LOST 73
TIED 0
TG 162

NATIONAL LEAGUE — FINISHED 2 W

1971. — PCT. .549

LOS ANGELES

WALTER EMMONS ALSTON

WON	LOST	NAME	POS.		G.	BA	FROM	TO
6	6	ALEXANDER, DOYLE LAFAYETTE	P		17	.273	A	BALA
		ALLEN, RICHARD ANTHONY	3B	67	155	.295	STL	CHIA
		(1B28 OF60)						
6	5	BREWER, JAMES THOMAS	P		55	.333	B	B
		BUCKNER, WILLIAM JOSEPH	OF	86	108	.277	B	B
		(1B11)						
		CEY, RONALD CHARLES			2	.000	A	B
		CRAWFORD, WILLIE MURPHY	OF	97	114	.281	B	B
		DARWIN, ARTHUR BOBBY LEE	OF	4	11	.250	LA 69	MINA
		DAVIS, WILLIAM HENRY	OF	157	158	.309	B	B
20	9	DOWNING, ALPHONSO ERWIN	P		37	.174	MILA	B
		FERGUSON, JOSEPH VANCE	C	35	36	.216	B	B
		GARVEY, STEVEN PATRICK	3B	79	81	.227	B	B
		GRABARKEWITZ, BILLY CORDELL	2B	13	44	.225	B	B
		(SS1 3B10)						
		HALLER, THOMAS FRANK	C	67	84	.267	B	DETA
0	0	HOUGH, CHARLES OLIVER	P		4	.000	B	B
		JOSHUA, VON EVERETT	OF	5	11	.000	B	C
		LEFEBVRE, JAMES KENNETH	2B	102	119	.245	B	B
		(3B7)						
8	5	MIKKELSEN, PETER JAMES	P		41	.200	B	B
2	4	MOELLER, JOSEPH DOUGLAS	P		28	.000	B	C
		MOTA, MANUEL RAFAEL	OF	80	91	.312	B	B
2	2	O'BRIEN, ROBERT ALLEN	P		14	.111	A	C
14	11	OSTEEN, CLAUDE WILSON	P	38	39	.186	B	B
		PACIOREK, THOMAS MARIAN	OF	1	2	.500	B	B
		PARKER, MAURICE WESLEY (WES)	1B	148	157	.274	B	B
		(OF18)						
2	0	PENA, JOSE	P		21	.667	B	B
		RUSSELL, WILLIAM ELLIS	2B	41	91	.227	B	B
		(SS6 OF40)						
		SIMS, DUANE B. (DUKE)	C	74	90	.274	CLEA	B
10	17	SINGER, WILLIAM ROBERT	P		31	.103	B	B
0	0	STRAHLER, MICHAEL WAYNE	P		6	.000	B	B
		SUDAKIS, WILLIAM PAUL	C	19	41	.193	B	NY
		(1B1 3B3 OF1)						
17	12	SUTTON, DONALD HOWARD	P	38	39	.216	B	B
		VALENTINE, ROBERT JOHN	SS	37	101	.249	LA 69	B
		(2B21 3B23 OF11)						
2	1	VANCE, GENE COVINGTON (SANDY)	P		10	.000	B	C
0	1	WILHELM, JAMES HOYT	P		9	+.000	XATL	B
		WILLS, MAURICE MORNING (3B4)	SS	144	149	.281	B	B

WON 85
LOST 70
TIED 0
TG 155

NATIONAL LEAGUE — FINISHED 3 W

1972. — PCT. .548

LOS ANGELES

WALTER EMMONS ALSTON

WON	LOST	NAME	POS.		G.	BA	FROM	TO
8	7	BREWER, JAMES THOMAS	P		51	.000	B	
		BUCKNER, WILLIAM JOSEPH	OF	61	105	.319	B	
		(1B35)						
		CANNIZZARO, CHRISTOPHER JOHN	C	72	73	.240	CHI	
		CEY, RONALD CHARLES	3B		11	.270	B	
		CRAWFORD, WILLIE MURPHY	OF	74	96	.251	B	
		DAVIS, WILLIAM HENRY	OF	146	149	.289	B	
		DIETZ, RICHARD ALLEN	C	22	27	.161	SF	
9	9	DOWNING, ALPHONSO ERWIN	P		31	.121	B	
		FERGUSON, JOSEPH VANCE (OF2)	C	7	8	.292	B	
		GARVEY, STEVEN PATRICK (1B3)	3B	85	96	.269	B	
		GRABARKEWITZ, BILLY CORDELL	3B	24	53	.167	B	
		(2B19 SS2)						
0	0	HOUGH, CHARLES OLIVER	P		2	.000	B	
11	5	JOHN, THOMAS EDWARD	P		29	.159	CHIA	
		LACY, LEONDAUS	2B	58	60	.259	A	
		LEFEBVRE, JAMES KENNETH	2B	33	70	.201	B	
		(3B11)						
		LOPES, DAVID EARL	2B		11	.214	A	
		MC DERMOTT, TERRENCE MICHAEL	1B	7	9	.130	A	
5	5	MIKKELSEN, PETER JAMES	P		33	.000	B	
		MOTA, MANUEL RAFAEL	OF	99	118	.323	B	
20	11	OSTEEN, CLAUDE WILSON	P	33	36	.273	B	
		PACIOREK, THOMAS MARIAN	1B	6	11	.255	B	
		(OF6)						
		PARKER, MAURICE WESLEY (WES)	1B	120	130	.279	B	
		(OF5)						
0	0	PENA, JOSE	P		5	.000	B	
2	0	PERRANOSKI, RONALD PETER	P		9	.000	XDETA	
2	2	RAU, DOUGLAS JAMES	P		7	.143	A	
2	3	RICHERT, PETER GERARD	P		37	.500	BALA	
		ROBINSON, FRANK	OF	95	103	.251	BALA	
		RUSSELL, WILLIAM ELLIS (OF6)	SS	121	129	.272	B	
		SIMS, DUANE B. (DUKE)	C	48	51	.192	B	XDETA
6	16	SINGER, WILLIAM ROBERT	P		26	.073	B	
1	2	STRAHLER, MICHAEL WAYNE	P		19	.182	B	
19	9	SUTTON, DONALD HOWARD	P		33	.143	B	
		VALENTINE, ROBERT JOHN	2B	49	119	.274	B	
		(SS10 3B39 OF16)						
0	1	WILHELM, JAMES HOYT	P		16	.000	B	
		WILLS, MAURICE MORNING (3B26)	SS	31	71	.129	B	
		YEAGER, STEPHEN WAYNE	C		35	.274	A	

WON 86
LOST 76
TIED 0
TG 162

NATIONAL LEAGUE

1965.

FINISHED 5

PCT. .531

MILWAUKEE

ROBERT RANDALL BRAGAN

WON	LOST	NAME	POS.		G.	BA	FROM	TO
		AARON, HENRY LOUIS	OF	148	150	.318	B	ATL
		AARON, TOMMIE LEE	1B	6	8	.188	MIL 63	ATL 68
		ALOMAR, SANTOS (2B19)	SS	39	67	.241	B	ATL
		ALOU, FELIPE ROJAS	OF	91	143	.297	B	ATL
		(1B69 SS1 3B2)						
		BEAUCHAMP, JAMES EDWARD	1B	2	4	+.000	XHOU	ATL 67
		BLANCHARD, JOHN EDWIN	OF	1	10	.100	XKC A	C
16	10	BLASINGAME, WADE ALLEN	P		38	.185	B	ATL
		BOLLING, FRANK ELMORE	2B	147	148	.264	B	ATL
0	1	CARROLL, CLAY PALMER	P		19	.000	B	ATL
		CARTY, RICARDO ADOLFO JACOBO	OF	73	83	.310	B	ATL
		CLINE, TYRONE ALEXANDER	OF	86	123	.191	B	CHI
		(1B5)						
24	11	CLONINGER, TONY LEE	P	40	41	.162	B	ATL
		COWAN, BILLY ROLLAND	OF	10	19	+.185	XNY	PHI 67
		DE LA HOZ, MIGUEL ANGEL	SS	41	81	.256	B	ATL
		(1B1 2B10 3B22)						
		DILLARD, DAVID DONALD (DON)	OF	1	20	.158	MIL 63	C
0	0	EILERS,DAVID LOUIS	P		6	+.000	B	XNY
8	9	FISCHER, HENRY WILLIAM	P	31	32	.108	B	ATL
		GONDER, JESSE LEMAR	C	13	31	+.151	XNY	PIT
13	8	JOHNSON, KENNETH TRAVIS	P		29	+.115	XHOU	ATL
		JONES, MACK	OF	133	143	.262	MIL 63	ATL
1	1	KELLEY, RICHARD ANTHONY	P	21	22	.000	B	ATL
		KLIMCHOCK, LOUIS STEPHEN	1B	4	34	.077	B	NY
		KOLB, GARY ALAN	OF	13	24	+.259	B	XNY
7	13	LEMASTER, DENVER CLAYTON	P		32	.089	B	ATL
		MATHEWS, EDWIN LEE	3B	153	156	.251	B	ATL
		MAYE, ARTHUR LEE	OF	13	15	+.302	B	XHOU
		MENKE, DENIS JOHN	SS	54	71	.243	B	ATL
		(1B8 3B4)						
2	3	NIEKRO, PHILIP HENRY	P	41	42	.100	B	ATL
10	6	O'DELL, WILLIAM OLIVER (1B1)	P	62	62	.174	SF	ATL
		OLIVER, EUGENE GEORGE	C	64	122	.270	B	ATL
		(1B52 OF1)						
0	1	OLIVO, FEDERICO EMILIO	P		8	.000	B	ATL
0	3	OSINSKI, DANIEL	P		61	.167	LA A	BOSA
5	9	SADOWSKI, ROBERT	P		34	.086	B	BOSA
		THOMAS, FRANK JOSEPH (OF3)	1B	6	15	+.212	XHOU	CHI
0	1	TIEFENAUER, BOBBY GENE	P		6	.000	B	XNY A
		TORRE, JOSEPH PAUL (1B49)	C	100	148	.291	B	ATL
		WOODWARD, WILLIAM FREDERICK	SS	107	112	.208	B	ATL
		(WOODY) (2B8)						

CLUB TRANSFERRED TO ATLANTA AFTER 1965 SEASON.

CLUB RECORD

NATIONAL LEAGUE

MONTREAL

NEW CLUB ADDED IN EXPANSION OF 1969

YEAR	TG	WON	LOST	TIED	PCT.	FINISHED	MANAGER
1969	162	52	110	0	.321	6E (LAST)	EUGENE WILLIAM MAUCH
1970	162	73	89	0	.451	6E (LAST)	EUGENE WILLIAM MAUCH
1971	162	71	90	1	.441	5E	EUGENE WILLIAM MAUCH
1972	156	70	86	0	.449	5E	EUGENE WILLIAM MAUCH

WON 52 LOST 110 TIED 0 TG 162

NATIONAL LEAGUE 1969. FINISHED 6 E (LAST) PCT. .321

MONTREAL

EUGENE WILLIAM MAUCH

WON	LOST	NAME	POS.		G.	BA	FROM	TO
		BAILEY, ROBERT SHERWOOD	1B	85	111	.265	LA	B
		(3B1 OF12)						
		BATEMAN, JOHN ALVIN	C	66	74	.209	HOU	B
		BOCCABELLA,JOHN DOMINIC	C	32	40	.105	CHI	B
		BOSCH, DONALD JOHN	OF	32	49	.179	NY	C
		BRAND, RONALD GEORGE (OF2)	C	84	103	.258	HOU	B
		CLENDENON, DONN ALVIN (OF11)	1B	24	38	+.240	PIT	XNY
		CLINE, TYRONE ALEXANDER	OF	41	101	.239	SF	B
		(1B17)						
		COLLINS, KEVIN MICHAEL (3B16)	2B	20	52	+.240	XNY	DETA
4	2	FACE, ELROY LEON (ROY)	P		44	.500	DETA	C
		FAIREY, JAMES BURKE	OF	13	20	.286	LA	B
		FAIRLY, RONALD RAY (OF21)	1B	52	70	+.289	XLA	B
1	6	GRANT, JAMES TIMOTHY (MUDCAT)	P		11	+.125	LA	XSTL
		HAHN, DONALD ANTONE	OF	3	4	.111	A	B
		HERMOSO, ANGEL REMIGIO (REMY)	2B	18	28	.162	ATL 67	B
		(SS6)						
		HERRERA, JOSE CONCEPCION	OF	31	47	.286	HOU	B
		(2B2 3B1)						
1	6	JASTER, LARRY EDWARD	P		24	.421	STL	ATL
		JESTADT, GARRY ARTHUR	SS	1	6	.000	A	CHI 71
		JONES, MACK	OF	129	135	.270	CIN	B
		LABOY, JOSE ALBERTO (COCO)	3B	156	157	.258	A	B
0	0	MARENTETTE, LEO JOHN	P		3	.000	DETA65	C
7	10	MC GINN, DANIEL MICHAEL	P		74	.172	CIN	B
0	3	MORTON, CARL WENDLE	P		8	.000	A	B
		MOTA, MANUEL RAFAEL	OF	22	31	+.315	PIT	XLA
		PHILLIPS, ADOLFO EMILIO	OF	53	58	+.216	XCHI	B
0	4	RADATZ, RICHARD RAYMOND	P		22	.250	XDETA	C
1	2	RAYMOND, JOSEPH CLAUDE MARC	P		15	+.000	XATL	B
6	7	REED, HOWARD DEAN	P		31	.125	HOU 67	B
6	7	RENKO, STEVEN	P		18	.167	A	B
0	0	REYNOLDS, ROBERT ALLEN	P		1	.000	A	STL 71
5	16	ROBERTSON, JERRY LEE	P		38	.089	A	DETA
0	2	SEMBERA, CARROLL WILLIAM	P		23	.250	HOU 67	B
2	5	SHAW, DONALD WELLINGTON	P		35	.000	NY	STL 71
0	0	SHEA, STEVEN FRANCIS	P		10	.000	HOU	C
		STAEHLE, MARVIN GUSTAVE	2B	4	6	.412	CHIA67	B
		STAUB, DANIEL JOSEPH (RUSTY)	OF	156	158	.302	HOU	B
11	19	STONEMAN, WILLIAM HAMBLY	P		42	.055	CHI	B
		SUTHERLAND, GARY LYNN	2B	139	141	.239	PHI	B
		(SS15 OF1)						
3	7	WASLEWSKI, GARY LEE	P		30	+.033	XSTL	B
5	14	WEGENER, MICHAEL DENIS	P		32	.241	A	B
		WICKER, FLOYD EULISS	OF	11	41	.103	STL	MILA
		WILLS, MAURICE MORNING (2B1)	SS	46	47	+.222	PIT	XLA
		WINE, ROBERT PAUL (1B1 3B1)	SS	118	121	.200	PHI	B

NEW CLUB ADDED IN EXPANSION OF 1969.

WON 73 LOST 89 TIED 0 TG 162

NATIONAL LEAGUE 1970. FINISHED 6 E (LAST) PCT. .451

MONTREAL

EUGENE WILLIAM MAUCH

WON	LOST	NAME	POS.		G.	BA	FROM	TO
		BAILEY, ROBERT SHERWOOD	3B	48	131	.287	B	B
		(1B18 OF44)						
		BATEMAN, JOHN ALVIN	C	137	139	.237	B	B
		BOCCABELLA,JOHN DOMINIC	1B	33	61	.269	B	B
		(C24 3B1)						
		BRAND, RONALD GEORGE	SS	19	72	.238	B	B
		(C9 2B3 3B12)						
		CLINE, TYRONE ALEXANDER			2	+.500	B	XCIN
		DAY, CHARLES FREDERICK (BOOTS)	OF	35	41	+.269	XCHI	B
2	3	DILLMAN, WILLIAM HOWARD	P		18	.000	BALA67	C
		FAIREY, JAMES BURKE	OF	59	92	.242	B	B
		FAIRLY, RONALD RAY (OF4)	1B	118	119	.288	B	B
		GOSGER, JAMES CHARLES (1B19)	OF	71	91	.263	NY	B
		HAHN, DONALD ANTONE	OF	61	82	.255	B	NY
		HERMOSO, ANGEL REMIGIO (REMY)	2B	1	4	.000	B	C
		(3B1)						
		HERRERA, JOSE CONCEPCION			1	.000	B	C
		HIATT, JACK E. (1B2)	C	12	17	+.326	SF	XCHI
0	0	JOHNSON, KENNETH TRAVIS	P		3	.000	CHI	C
		JONES, MACK	OF	87	108	.240	B	B
		LABOY, JOSE ALBERTO (COCO)	3B	132	137	.199	B	B
		(2B3)						
3	7	MARSHALL, MICHAEL GRANT	P		24	+.091	XHOU	B
		MASHORE, CLYDE WAYNE	OF	10	13	.160	CIN	B
7	10	MC GINN, DANIEL MICHAEL	P		52	.114	B	B
0	2	MOORE, BALOR LILBON	P		6	.333	A	MON 72
18	11	MORTON, CARL WENDLE	P		43	.161	B	B
3	2	NYE, RICHARD RAYMOND	P	8	10	+.176	XSTL	C
2	3	O'DONOGHUE, JOHN EUGENE	P		9	.000	XMILA	B
		PHILLIPS, ADOLFO EMILIO	OF	75	92	.238	B	CLEA72
		QUALLS, JAMES ROBERT (OF2)	2B	2	9	.111	CHI	CHIA72
6	7	RAYMOND, JOSEPH CLAUDE MARC	P		59	.000	B	B
6	5	REED, HOWARD DEAN	P		57	.000	B	B
13	11	RENKO, STEVEN	P		41	.200	B	B
0	0	SEMBERA, CARROLL WILLIAM	P		5	.000	B	C
0	4	SPARMA, JOSEPH BLASE	P		9	.000	DETA	C
		STAEHLE, MARVIN GUSTAVE	2B	91	104	.218	B	ATL
		(SS1)						
		STAUB, DANIEL JOSEPH (RUSTY)	OF		160	.274	B	B
7	15	STONEMAN, WILLIAM HAMBLY	P	40	42	.100	B	B
3	1	STROHMAYER, JOHN EMERY	P		42	.167	A	B
		SUTHERLAND, GARY LYNN	2B	97	116	.206	B	B
		(SS15 3B1)						
0	2	WASLEWSKI, GARY LEE	P		6	.000	B	XNY A
3	6	WEGENER, MICHAEL DENIS	P		25	.118	B	C
		WHITFIELD, FRED DWIGHT	1B		4	.067	CIN	C
		WINE, ROBERT PAUL	SS		159	.232	B	B

WON 71
LOST 90
TIED 1
TG 162

NATIONAL LEAGUE

1971.

FINISHED 5 E

PCT. .441

MONTREAL

EUGENE WILLIAM MAUCH

WON	LOST	NAME	POS.		G.	BA	FROM	TO
		BAILEY, ROBERT SHERWOOD	3B	120	157	.251	B	B
		(1B9 OF51)						
		BATEMAN, JOHN ALVIN	C	137	139	.242	B	B
		BOCCABELLA,JOHN DOMINIC	C	37	74	.220	B	B
		(1B37 3B2)						
		BRAND, RONALD GEORGE	SS	22	47	.214	B	C
		(C1 2B1 3B4 OF4)						
2	3	BRITTON, JAMES ALAN	P		16	.000	ATL 69	C
		DAY, CHARLES FREDERICK (BOOTS)	OF	120	127	.283	B	B
		FAIREY, JAMES BURKE	OF	58	92	.245	B	B
		FAIRLY, RONALD RAY (OF10)	1B	135	146	.257	B	B
		GOSGER, JAMES CHARLES (1B6)	OF	23	51	.157	B	C
		HACKER, RICHARD WARREN	SS		16	.121	A	C
		HUMPHREY, TERRYAL GENE	C		9	.192	A	B
		HUNT, RONALD KENNETH (3B19)	2B	133	152	.279	SF	B
		JONES, MACK	OF	27	43	.165	B	C
		LABOY, JOSE ALBERTO (COCO)	3B	65	76	.252	B	B
		(2B2)						
5	8	MARSHALL, MICHAEL GRANT	P		66	.188	B	B
		MASHORE, CLYDE WAYNE (3B1)	OF	47	66	.193	B	B
11	12	MC ANALLY, ERNEST LEE	P		31	.117	A	B
		MC DONALD, DAVID BRUCE (OF1)	1B	8	24	.103	NY A69	C
1	4	MC GINN, DANIEL MICHAEL	P		28	.235	B	CHI
10	18	MORTON, CARL WENDLE	P		36	.182	B	B
0	0	O'DONOGHUE, JOHN EUGENE	P		13	.000	B	C
1	7	RAYMOND, JOSEPH CLAUDE MARC	P		37	.000	B	C
2	3	REED, HOWARD DEAN	P		43	.000	B	C
15	14	RENKO, STEVEN	P	40	41	.210	B	B
		STAUB, DANIEL JOSEPH (RUSTY)	OF		162	.311	B	NY
17	16	STONEMAN, WILLIAM HAMBLY	P	39	41	.129	B	B
7	5	STROHMAYER, JOHN EMERY	P		27	.229	B	B
		SUTHERLAND, GARY LYNN	2B	56	111	.257	B	HOU
		(SS46 3B2 OF4)						
		SWANSON, STANLEY LAWRENCE	OF	38	49	.245	A	C
		SWOBODA, RONALD ALAN	OF	26	39	.253	NY	XNY A
0	0	TORREZ, MICHAEL AUGUSTINE	P		1	+.000	XSTL	B
		WINE, ROBERT PAUL	SS		119	.200	B	B
		WOODS, RONALD LAWRENCE	OF	45	51	.297	XNY A	B

WON 70
LOST 86
TIED 0
TG 156

NATIONAL LEAGUE

1972.

FINISHED 5 E

PCT. .449

MONTREAL

EUGENE WILLIAM MAUCH

WON	LOST	NAME	POS.		G.	BA	FROM	TO
		BAILEY, ROBERT SHERWOOD	3B	135	143	.233	B	
		(1B3 OF4)						
		BATEMAN, JOHN ALVIN	C	7	18	+.241	B	XPHI
		BOCCABELLA,JOHN DOMINIC	C	73	83	.227	B	
		(1B7 3B1)						
		BREEDEN, HAROLD NOEL (OF1)	1B	26	42	.230	CHI	
		DAY, CHARLES FREDERICK (BOOTS)	OF	117	128	.233	B	
		FAIREY, JAMES BURKE	OF	37	86	.234	B	
		FAIRLY, RONALD RAY (1B68)	OF	70	140	.278	B	
		FOLI, TIMOTHY JOHN (2B1)	SS	148	149	.241	NY	
0	1	GILBERT, JOE DENNIS	P		22	.000	A	
		HUMPHREY, TERRYAL GENE	C	65	69	.186	B	
		HUNT, RONALD KENNETH (3B5)	2B	122	129	.253	B	
		JORGENSEN, MICHAEL (OF28)	1B	76	113	.231	NY	
		LABOY, JOSE ALBERTO (COCO)	3B	24	28	.261	B	
		(2B3 SS2)						
2	0	LEMASTER, DENVER CLAYTON	P		13	.333	HOU	
		MANGUAL, JOSE MANUEL	OF	3	8	.273	A	
14	8	MARSHALL, MICHAEL GRANT	P		65	.136	B	
		MASHORE, CLYDE WAYNE	OF	74	93	.227	B	
6	15	MC ANALLY, ERNEST LEE	P		29	.113	B	
		MC CARVER, JAMES TIMOTHY (TIM)	C	45	77	+.251	XPHI	
		(3B6 OF14)						
9	9	MOORE, BALOR LILBON	P		22	.145	MON 70	
7	13	MORTON, CARL WENDLE	P	27	35	.135	B	
1	10	RENKO, STEVEN (1B1)	P	30	32	.292	B	
		SINGLETON, KENNETH WAYNE	OF	137	142	.274	NY	
12	14	STONEMAN, WILLIAM HAMBLY	P	36	40	.080	B	
1	2	STROHMAYER, JOHN EMERY	P		48	.000	B	
0	0	TORRES, HECTOR EPITACIO	2B	60	83	.155	CHI	
		(P1 SS16 3B1 OF2)						
16	12	TORREZ, MICHAEL AUGUSTINE	P		34	.176	B	
2	2	WALKER, ROBERT THOMAS (TOM)	P		46	.000	A	
		WINE, ROBERT PAUL (2B1 SS4)	3B	21	34	.222	B	
		WOODS, RONALD LAWRENCE	OF	73	97	.258	B	

WON 50 | LOST 112 | TIED 2 | TG 164

NATIONAL LEAGUE 1965.

FINISHED 10 (LAST) PCT. .309

NEW YORK

CHARLES DILLON STENGEL WESLEY NOREEN WESTRUM

WON	LOST	NAME	POS.		G.	BA	FROM	TO
3	5	BEARNARTH, LAWRENCE DONALD	P		40	.111	B	B
		BERRA, LAWRENCE PETER (YOGI)	C	2	4	.222	NY A63	C
2	0	BETHKE, JAMES CHARLES	P		25	.000	A	C
		CANNIZZARO, CHRISTOPHER JOHN	C	112	114	.183	B	PIT 68
		CHRISTOPHER, JOSEPH O'NEAL	OF	112	148	.249	B	BOSA
4	8	CISCO, GALEN BERNARD	P		35	.259	B	BOSA67
		COLLINS, KEVIN MICHAEL (SS3)	3B	7	11	.174	A	NY 67
		COWAN, BILLY ROLLAND	OF	61	82	+.179	CHI	XMIL
		(2B2 SS1)						
1	1	EILERS, DAVID LOUIS	P		11	+1.000	XMIL	B
8	24	FISHER, JOHN HOWARD	P		43	.154	B	B
0	2	GARDNER, RICHARD FRANK (ROB)	P		5	.000	A	B
		GONDER, JESSE LEMAR	C	31	53	+.238	B	XMIL
		GOOSSEN, GREGORY BRYANT	C	8	11	.290	A	B
		HARRELSON, DERREL MCKINLEY	SS	18	19	.108	A	B
		(BUD)						
		HICKMAN, JAMES LUCIUS	OF	91	141	.236	B	B
		(1B30 3B14)						
		HILLER, CHARLES JOSEPH	2B	80	100	+.238	XSF	B
		(3B2 OF4)						
		HUNT, RONALD KENNETH (3B6)	2B	46	57	.240	B	B
8	20	JACKSON, ALVIN NEIL	P	37	56	.117	B	STL
		JONES, CLEON JOSEPH	OF	23	30	.149	NY 63	B
		KLAUS, ROBERT FRANCIS	2B	72	119	.191	B	C
		(SS28 3B25)						
		KOLB, GARY ALAN	OF	29	40	+.167	XMIL	PIT 68
		(1B1 3B1)						
		KRANEPOOL, EDWARD EMIL	1B	147	153	.253	B	B
6	6	KROLL, GARY MELVIN	P		32	.115	B	HOU
1	3	LARY, FRANK STRONG	P		14	.211	MIL	XCHIA
		LEWIS, JOHNNY JOE	OF	142	148	.245	STL	B
2	7	MC GRAW, FRANK EDWIN (TUG)	P	37	38	.130	A	B
		MC MILLAN, ROY DAVID	SS	153	157	.242	B	B
1	4	MILLER, LARRY DON	P		28	.182	LA	B
0	1	MOORHEAD, CHARLES ROBERT (BOB)	P		9	.000	NY 62	C
0	0	MUSGRAVES, DENNIS EUGENE	P		5	.000	A	C
		NAPOLEON, DANIEL (3B7)	OF	15	68	.144	A	B
1	10	PARSONS, THOMAS ANTHONY	P		35	.056	B	C
1	3	RIBANT, DENNIS JOSEPH	P		19	.000	B	B
2	2	RICHARDSON, GORDON CLARK	P		35	.000	STL	B
		SCHAFFER, JIMMIE RONALD	C	21	24	.135	XCHIA	PHI
2	1	SELMA, RICHARD JAY	P	4	7	.222	A	B
		SMITH, CHARLES WILLIAM	3B	131	135	.244	B	STL
		(2B1 SS6)						
4	12	SPAHN, WARREN EDWARD	P	20	21	+.114	MIL	XSF
		STEPHENSON, JOHN HERMAN	C	47	62	.215	B	B
		(OF2)						
3	1	SUTHERLAND, DARRELL WAYNE	P		18	.154	B	B
		SWOBODA, RONALD ALAN	OF	112	135	.228	A	B
		TAYLOR, ROBERT DALE (HAWK)	C	15	25	.152	B	B
		(1B1)						
1	2	WILLEY, CARLTON FRANCIS	P		13	.000	B	C

WON 66 | LOST 95 | TIED 0 | TG 161

NATIONAL LEAGUE 1966.

FINISHED 9 PCT. .410

NEW YORK

WESLEY NOREEN WESTRUM

WON	LOST	NAME	POS.		G.	BA	FROM	TO
3	3	ARRIGO, GERALD WILLIAM	P		17	+.500	XCIN	CIN
2	3	BEARNARTH, LAWRENCE DONALD	P		29	.111	B	MILA71
		BOYER, KENTON LLOYD (1B2)	3B	130	136	.266	STL	B
		BRESSOUD, EDWARD FRANCIS	SS	94	133	.225	BOSA	STL
		(1B9 2B7 3B32)						
		COLEMAN, CLARENCE (CHOO CHOO)	C	5	6	.188	NY 63	C
1	1	EILERS, DAVID LOUIS	P		23	.000	B	HOU
		ELLIOT, LAWRENCE LEE	OF	54	65	.246	NY 64	C
11	14	FISHER, JOHN HOWARD	P		38	.090	B	B
		FITZMAURICE, SHAUN EARLE	OF	5	9	.154	A	C
5	8	FRIEND, ROBERT BARTMESS	P		22	.034	XNY A	C
4	8	GARDNER, RICHARD FRANK (ROB)	P	41	43	.171	B	CHI
		GOOSSEN, GREGORY BRYANT	C	11	13	.188	B	B
0	0	GREEN, GEORGE DALLAS	P		4	.000	WASA	PHI
		GROTE, GERALD WAYNE (3B2)	C	115	120	.237	HOU 64	B
6	13	HAMILTON, JACK EDWIN	P		57	.132	DETA	B
		HARRELSON, DERREL MCKINLEY	SS	29	33	.222	B	B
		(BUD)						
3	3	HEPLER, WILLIAM LEWIS	P		37	.214	A	C
		HICKMAN, JAMES LUCIUS (1B17)	OF	45	58	.237	B	LA
		HILLER, CHARLES JOSEPH	2B	45	108	.280	B	B
		(3B14 OF9)						
		HUNT, RONALD KENNETH	2B	123	132	.288	B	LA
		(SS1 3B1)						
		JONES, CLEON JOSEPH	OF	129	139	.275	B	B
		KLIMCHOCK, LOUIS STEPHEN			5	.000	MIL	CLEA68
		KRANEPOOL, EDWARD EMIL (OF11)	1B	132	146	.254	B	B
		LEWIS, JOHNNY JOE	OF	49	65	.193	B	B
		LUPLOW, ALVIN DAVID	OF	101	111	.251	CLEA	B
2	9	MC GRAW, FRANK EDWIN (TUG)	P		15	.235	B	B
		MC MILLAN, ROY DAVID	SS	71	76	.214	B	C
0	2	MILLER, LARRY DON	P		4	.500	B	C
		MURPHY, WILLIAM EUGENE	OF	57	84	.230	A	C
		NAPOLEON, DANIEL	OF	10	12	.212	B	C
11	9	RIBANT, DENNIS JOSEPH	P	39	40	.197	B	PIT
0	2	RICHARDSON, GORDON CLARK	P		15	.000	B	C
1	2	RUSTECK, RICHARD FRANK	P		8	.000	A	C
0	1	RYAN, LYNN NOLAN	P		2	.000	A	NY 68
4	6	SELMA, RICHARD JAY	P	30	31	.071	B	B
11	10	SHAW, ROBERT JOHN	P		26	+.260	XSF	B
		STEPHENSON, JOHN HERMAN	C	52	63	.196	B	CHI
		(OF1)						
		STUART, RICHARD LEE	1B	23	31	+.218	PHI	XLA
2	0	SUTHERLAND, DARRELL WAYNE	P		31	.667	B	CLEA68
		SWOBODA, RONALD ALAN	OF	97	112	.222	B	B
		TAYLOR, ROBERT DALE (HAWK)	C	29	53	.174	B	B
		(1B13)						
0	1	TERRY, RALPH WILLARD	P		11	.167	XKC A	B

WON 61 LOST 101 TIED 0 TG 162

NATIONAL LEAGUE 1967. FINISHED 10 (LAST) PCT. .377

NEW YORK

WESLEY NOREEN WESTRUM FRANCIS JAMES PARKER

WON	LOST	NAME	POS.		G.	BA	FROM	TO
		ALOMAR, SANTOS (2B2 3B3)	SS	10	15	.000	ATL	XCHIA
1	1	BENNETT, DENNIS JOHN	P		8	.250	XBOSA	CALA
		BOSCH, DONALD JOHN	OF	39	44	.140	PIT	B
		BOSWELL, KENNETH GEORGE (3B4)	2B	6	11	.225	A	B
		BOYER, KENTON LLOYD (1B8)	3B	44	56	.235	B	XCHIA
		BUCHEK, GERALD PETER	2B	95	124	.236	STL	B
		(SS9 3B17)						
5	9	CARDWELL, DONALD EUGENE	P	26	27	.158	PIT	B
		CHARLES, EDWIN DOUGLAS	3B	89	101	.238	XKC A	B
		COLLINS, KEVIN MICHAEL	2B	2	4	.100	NY 65	B
0	0	CONNORS, WILLIAM JOSEPH	P		6	.000	CHI	B
		DAVIS, HERMAN THOMAS (TOMMY)	OF	149	154	.302	LA	CHIA
		(1B1)						
1	7	DENEHY, WILLIAM FRANCIS	P		15	.000	A	WASA
1	2	ESTRADA, CHARLES LEONARD	P		9	.000	CHI	C
9	18	FISHER, JOHN HOWARD	P		39	.100	B	CHIA
1	6	FRISELLA, DANIEL VINCENT	P		14	.087	A	B
		GOOSSEN, GREGORY BRYANT	C	23	37	.159	B	B
1	2	GRAHAM, WILLIAM ALBERT	P		5	.125	DETA	C
		GROTE, GERALD WAYNE	C	119	120	.195	B	B
0	0	GRZENDA, JOSEPH CHARLES	P		11	.000	KC A	MINA69
2	0	HAMILTON, JACK EDWIN	P		17	.200	B	XCALA
		HARRELSON, DERREL MCKINLEY	SS	149	151	.254	B	B
		(BUD)						
		HEISE, ROBERT LOWELL (SS3 3B2)	2B	12	16	.323	A	B
3	3	HENDLEY, CHARLES ROBERT (BOB)	P		15	+.111	XCHI	C
		HILLER, CHARLES JOSEPH	2B	14	25	+.093	B	XPHI
0	0	HINSLEY, JERRY DEAN	P		2	.000	NY 64	C
		JOHNSON, ROBERT WALLACE	2B	39	90	.348	XBALA	CIN
		(1B23 SS14 3B1)						
		JONES, CLEON JOSEPH	OF	115	129	.246	B	B
3	3	KOONCE, CALVIN LEE	P	11	13	+.154	XCHI	B
0	2	KOOSMAN, JEROME MARTIN	P		9	.000	A	B
		KRANEPOOL, EDWARD EMIL	1B	139	141	.269	B	B
0	3	LAMABE, JOHN ALEXANDER	P		16	+.000	XCHIA	XSTL
		LEWIS, JOHNNY JOE	OF	10	13	.118	B	C
		LINZ, PHILIP FRANCIS	2B	11	24	+.207	XPHI	B
		(SS8 3B1 OF1)						
		LUPLOW, ALVIN DAVID	OF	33	41	+.205	B	XPIT
0	3	MC GRAW, FRANK EDWIN (TUG)	P		4	.250	B	NY 69
		MOOCK, JOSEPH GEOFFREY	3B	12	13	.225	A	C
		OTIS, AMOS JOSEPH (3B1)	OF	16	19	.220	A	NY 69
3	3	RENIFF, HAROLD EUGENE	P		29	.000	XNY A	C
		REYNOLDS, TOMMIE D. (C1 3B5)	OF	72	101	.206	KC A65	OAKA69
2	1	ROHR, LESLIE NORVIN	P		3	.000	A	B
0	0	SCHMELZ, ALAN GEORGE	P		2	.000	A	C
16	13	SEAVER, GEORGE THOMAS (TOM)	P	35	36	.143	A	B
2	4	SELMA, RICHARD JAY	P	38	43	.091	B	B
4	5	SHAW, DONALD WELLINGTON	P		40	.000	A	B
3	9	SHAW, ROBERT JOHN	P		23	+.040	B	XCHI
		SHIRLEY, BARTON ARVIN	2B	3	6	.000	LA	LA
		STAHL, LARRY FLOYD	OF	43	71	.239	KC A	B
		SULLIVAN, JOHN PETER	C	57	65	.218	DETA65	PHI
		SWOBODA, RONALD ALAN (1B20)	OF	108	134	.281	B	B
		TAYLOR, ROBERT DALE (HAWK)	C	12	13	.243	B	XCALA
4	6	TAYLOR, RONALD WESLEY	P		50	.000	HOU	B
0	0	TERRY, RALPH WILLARD	P		2	.000	B	C
0	1	WILLHITE, JON NICHOLAS (NICK)	P		4	.000	XCALA	C
0	0	WYNNE, BILLY VERNON	P		6	.000	A	CHIA

WON 73 LOST 89 TIED 1 TG 163

NATIONAL LEAGUE 1968. FINISHED 9 PCT. .451

NEW YORK

GILBERT RAYMOND HODGES

WON	LOST	NAME	POS.		G.	BA	FROM	TO
		AGEE, TOMMIE LEE	OF	127	132	.217	CHIA	B
		BOSCH, DONALD JOHN	OF	33	50	.171	B	MON
		BOSWELL, KENNETH GEORGE	2B	69	75	.261	B	B
		BUCHEK, GERALD PETER	3B	37	73	.182	B	C
		(2B12 OF9)						
7	13	CARDWELL, DONALD EUGENE	P	29	30	.049	B	B
		CHARLES, EDWIN DOUGLAS (1B2)	3B	106	117	.276	B	B
		COLLINS, KEVIN MICHAEL	3B	40	58	.201	B	B
		(2B6 SS1)						
0	1	CONNORS, WILLIAM JOSEPH	P		9	1.000	B	C
		DYER, DON ROBERT (DUFFY)	C		1	.333	A	B
2	4	FRISELLA, DANIEL VINCENT	P		19	.083	B	B
		GOOSSEN, GREGORY BRYANT	1B	30	38	.208	B	SEAA
		(C2)						
		GROTE, GERALD WAYNE	C	115	124	.282	B	B
		HARRELSON, DERREL MCKINLEY	SS	106	111	.219	B	B
		(BUD)						
		HEISE, ROBERT LOWELL (2B1)	SS	6	6	.217	B	B
3	7	JACKSON, ALVIN NEIL	P	25	27	.250	STL	B
		JONES, CLEON JOSEPH	OF	139	147	.297	B	B
		JORGENSEN, MICHAEL	1B	4	8	.143	A	NY 70
6	4	KOONCE, CALVIN LEE	P		55	.000	B	B
19	12	KOOSMAN, JEROME MARTIN	P		35	.077	B	B
		KRANEPOOL, EDWARD EMIL (OF2)	1B	113	127	.231	B	B
		LINZ, PHILIP FRANCIS	2B	71	78	.209	B	C
		MARTIN, JOSEPH CLIFTON (J.C.)	C	53	78	.225	CHIA	B
		(1B14)						
4	7	MC ANDREW, JAMES CLEMENT	P		12	.045	A	B
0	2	ROHR, LESLIE NORVIN	P		2	.000	B	B
6	9	RYAN, LYNN NOLAN	P		21	.114	NY 66	B
16	12	SEAVER, GEORGE THOMAS (TOM)	P	36	38	.158	B	B
9	10	SELMA, RICHARD JAY	P	33	39	.207	B	SD
		SHAMSKY, ARTHUR LOUIS (1B17)	OF	82	116	.238	CIN	B
0	0	SHAW, DONALD WELLINGTON	P		7	.000	B	MON
0	3	SHORT, WILLIAM ROSS	P		34	.000	PIT	CIN
		STAHL, LARRY FLOYD (1B9)	OF	47	53	.235	B	SD
		SWOBODA, RONALD ALAN	OF	125	132	.242	B	B
1	5	TAYLOR, RONALD WESLEY	P		58	.000	B	B
		WEIS, ALBERT JOHN (2B29 3B2)	SS	59	90	.172	CHIA	B

WON 100
LOST 62
TIED 0
TG 162

NATIONAL LEAGUE

1969.

FINISHED 1 E
(ALSO WON LEAGUE PLAYOFF)
PCT. .617

NEW YORK

GILBERT RAYMOND HODGES

WON	LOST	NAME	POS.		G.	BA	FROM	TO
		AGEE, TOMMIE LEE	OF	146	149	.271	B	B
		BOSWELL, KENNETH GEORGE	2B	96	102	.279	B	B
8	10	CARDWELL, DONALD EUGENE	P		30	.170	B	B
		CHARLES, EDWIN DOUGLAS	3B	52	61	.207	B	C
		CLENDENON, DONN ALVIN (OF1)	1B	58	72	+.252	XMON	B
		COLLINS, KEVIN MICHAEL	3B	14	16	+.150	B	XMON
1	4	DI LAURO, JACK EDWARD	P		23	.000	A	HOU
		DYER, DON ROBERT (DUFFY)	C	19	29	.257	B	B
0	0	FRISELLA, DANIEL VINCENT	P		3	.000	B	B
		GARRETT, RONALD WAYNE (2B47 SS9)	3B	72	124	.218	A	B
		GASPAR, RODNEY EARL	OF	91	118	.228	A	B
13	12	GENTRY, GARY EDWARD	P		35	.081	A	B
		GOSGER, JAMES CHARLES	OF	5	10	.133	XSEAA	MON
		GROTE, GERALD WAYNE	C	112	113	.252	B	B
		HARRELSON, DERREL MCKINLEY (BUD)	SS	119	123	.248	B	B
		HEISE, ROBERT LOWELL	SS	3	4	.300	B	SF
0	0	HUDSON, JESSE JAMES	P		1	.000	A	C
0	0	JACKSON, ALVIN NEIL	P		9	+.000	B	XCIN
0	0	JOHNSON, ROBERT DALE	P		2	.000	A	KC A
		JONES, CLEON JOSEPH (1B15)	OF	122	137	.340	B	B
6	3	KOONCE, CALVIN LEE	P		40	.235	B	B
17	9	KOOSMAN, JEROME MARTIN	P		32	.048	B	B
		KRANEPOOL, EDWARD EMIL (OF2)	1B	106	112	.238	B	B
		MARTIN, JOSEPH CLIFTON (J.C.) (1B2)	C	48	66	.209	B	CHI
6	7	MC ANDREW, JAMES CLEMENT	P		27	.135	B	B
9	3	MC GRAW, FRANK EDWIN (TUG)	P	42	43	.167	NY 67	B
		OTIS, AMOS JOSEPH (3B3)	OF	35	48	.151	NY 67	KC A
		PFEIL, ROBERT RAYMOND (2B11 OF2)	3B	49	62	.232	A	PHI 71
0	0	ROHR, LESLIE NORVIN	P		1	.000	B	C
6	3	RYAN, LYNN NOLAN	P		25	.103	B	B
25	7	SEAVER, GEORGE THOMAS (TOM)	P	36	39	.121	B	B
		SHAMSKY, ARTHUR LOUIS (1B9)	OF	78	100	.300	B	B
		SWOBODA, RONALD ALAN	OF	97	109	.235	B	B
9	4	TAYLOR, RONALD WESLEY	P		59	.250	B	B
		WEIS, ALBERT JOHN (2B43 3B1)	SS	52	103	.215	B	B

WON 83
LOST 79
TIED 0
TG 162

NATIONAL LEAGUE

1970.

FINISHED 3 E

PCT. .512

NEW YORK

GILBERT RAYMOND HODGES

WON	LOST	NAME	POS.		G.	BA	FROM	TO
		AGEE, TOMMIE LEE	OF	150	153	.286	B	B
		BOSWELL, KENNETH GEORGE	2B	101	105	.254	B	B
0	2	CARDWELL, DONALD EUGENE	P		16	+.000	B	XATL
0	1	CHANCE, WILMER DEAN	P		3	.000	XCLEA	DETA
		CLENDENON, DONN ALVIN	1B	100	121	.288	B	B
		DYER, DON ROBERT (DUFFY)	C	57	59	.209	B	B
		FOLI, TIMOTHY JOHN (3B2)	SS	2	5	.364	A	B
0	2	FOLKERS, RICHARD NEVIN	P		16	.333	A	STL 72
		FOY, JOSEPH ANTHONY	3B	97	99	.236	KC A	WASA
8	3	FRISELLA, DANIEL VINCENT	P		30	.308	B	B
		GARRETT, RONALD WAYNE (2B45 SS1)	3B	70	114	.254	B	B
		GASPAR, RODNEY EARL	OF	8	11	.000	B	SD
9	9	GENTRY, GARY EDWARD	P		32	.068	B	B
		GROTE, GERALD WAYNE	C	125	126	.255	B	B
		HARRELSON, DERREL MCKINLEY (BUD)	SS	156	157	.243	B	B
2	2	HERBEL, RONALD SAMUEL	P		12	+.000	XSD	ATL
		JONES, CLEON JOSEPH	OF	130	134	.277	B	B
		JORGENSEN, MICHAEL (OF10)	1B	50	76	.195	NY 68	B
0	2	KOONCE, CALVIN LEE	P		13	.000	B	XBOSA
12	7	KOOSMAN, JEROME MARTIN	P		30	.086	B	B
		KRANEPOOL, EDWARD EMIL	1B	8	43	.170	B	B
		MARSHALL, DAVID LEWIS	OF	43	92	.243	SF	B
		MARTINEZ, TEODORO NOEL (TED) (SS1)	2B	4	4	.063	A	B
10	14	MC ANDREW, JAMES CLEMENT	P		32	.148	B	B
4	6	MC GRAW, FRANK EDWIN (TUG)	P		57	.308	B	B
7	11	RYAN, LYNN NOLAN	P		27	.178	B	B
8	4	SADECKI, RAYMOND MICHAEL	P		28	.205	SF	B
18	12	SEAVER, GEORGE THOMAS (TOM)	P	37	42	.179	B	B
		SHAMSKY, ARTHUR LOUIS (1B56)	OF	58	122	.293	B	B
		SINGLETON, KENNETH WAYNE	OF	51	69	.263	A	B
		STANTON, LEROY BOBBY	OF	1	4	.250	A	B
		SWOBODA, RONALD ALAN	OF	100	115	.233	B	MON
5	4	TAYLOR, RONALD WESLEY	P		57	.000	B	B
		WEIS, ALBERT JOHN (SS15)	2B	44	75	.207	B	B

WON 83 NATIONAL LEAGUE FINISHED 3 E
LOST 79 (TIED WITH CHICAGO)
TIED 0 1971. PCT. .512
TG 162

NEW YORK

GILBERT RAYMOND HODGES

WON	LOST	NAME	POS.		G.	BA	FROM	TO
		AGEE, TOMMIE LEE	OF	107	113	.285	B	B
		ASPROMONTE, ROBERT THOMAS	3B	97	104	.225	ATL	C
		BOSWELL, KENNETH GEORGE	2B	109	116	.273	B	B
0	1	CAPRA, LEE WILLIAM	P		3	.000	A	B
		CLENDENON, DONN ALVIN	1B	72	88	.247	B	STL
		DYER, DON ROBERT (DUFFY)	C	53	59	.231	B	B
		ESTRADA, FRANCISCO	C		1	.500	A	C
		FOLI, TIMOTHY JOHN	2B	58	97	.226	B	MON
		(SS12 3B36 OF1)						
8	5	FRISELLA, DANIEL VINCENT	P		53	.231	B	B
		GARRETT, RONALD WAYNE (2B9)	3B	53	56	.213	B	B
12	11	GENTRY, GARY EDWARD	P		32	.074	B	B
		GROTE, GERALD WAYNE	C	122	125	.270	B	B
		HAHN, DONALD ANTONE	OF	80	98	.236	MON	B
		HARRELSON, DERREL MCKINLEY	SS	140	142	.252	B	B
		(BUD)						
		JONES, CLEON JOSEPH	OF	132	136	.319	B	B
		JORGENSEN, MICHAEL (1B1)	OF	31	45	.220	B	MON
6	11	KOOSMAN, JEROME MARTIN	P		26	.160	B	B
		KRANEPOOL, EDWARD EMIL (OF11)	1B	108	122	.280	B	B
		MARSHALL, DAVID LEWIS	OF	64	100	.238	B	B
		MARTINEZ, TEODORO NOEL (TED)	SS	23	38	.288	B	B
		(2B13 3B3 OF1)						
0	3	MATLACK, JONATHAN TRUMPBOUR	P		7	.273	A	B
2	5	MC ANDREW, JAMES CLEMENT	P		24	.043	B	B
11	4	MC GRAW, FRANK EDWIN (TUG)	P		51	.222	B	B
		MILNER, JOHN DAVID	OF	3	9	.167	A	B
0	0	ROSE, DONALD GARY	P		1	.000	A	CALA
10	14	RYAN, LYNN NOLAN	P		30	.128	B	CALA
7	7	SADECKI, RAYMOND MICHAEL	P		34	.200	B	B
20	10	SEAVER, GEORGE THOMAS (TOM)	P	36	39	.196	B	B
		SHAMSKY, ARTHUR LOUIS (1B1)	OF	38	68	.185	B	CHI
		SINGLETON, KENNETH WAYNE	OF	96	115	.245	B	MON
		STANTON, LEROY BOBBY	OF		5	.190	B	CALA
2	2	TAYLOR, RONALD WESLEY	P		45	.250	B	SD
		WEIS, ALBERT JOHN (3B2)	2B	5	11	.000	B	C
5	6	WILLIAMS, CHARLES PROSEK	P		31	.087	A	SF

WON 83 NATIONAL LEAGUE FINISHED 3 E
LOST 73
TIED 0 1972. PCT. .532
TG 156

NEW YORK

LAWRENCE PETER BERRA

WON	LOST	NAME	POS.		G.	BA	FROM	TO
		AGEE, TOMMIE LEE	OF	109	114	.227	B	
		BARNES, LUTHER OWENS (SS6)	2B	14	24	.236	A	
		BEAUCHAMP, JAMES EDWARD	1B	35	58	.242	STL	
		(OF5)						
		BOSWELL, KENNETH GEORGE	2B	94	100	.211	B	
3	2	CAPRA, LEE WILLIAM	P		14	.250	B	
		DYER, DON ROBERT (DUFFY)	C	91	94	.231	B	
		(OF1)						
		FREGOSI, JAMES LOUIS	3B	85	101	.232	CALA	
		(1B3 SS6)						
5	8	FRISELLA, DANIEL VINCENT	P		39	.286	B	
		GARRETT, RONALD WAYNE (2B22)	3B	82	111	.232	B	
7	10	GENTRY, GARY EDWARD	P		32	.104	B	
		GROTE, GERALD WAYNE	C	59	64	.210	B	
		(3B3 OF1)						
		HAHN, DONALD ANTONE	OF	10	17	.162	B	
		HARRELSON, DERREL MCKINLEY	SS		115	.215	B	
		(BUD)						
		JONES, CLEON JOSEPH (1B20)	OF	84	106	.245	B	
11	12	KOOSMAN, JEROME MARTIN	P		34	.085	B	
		KRANEPOOL, EDWARD EMIL (OF1)	1B	108	122	.269	B	
		MARSHALL, DAVID LEWIS	OF	42	72	.250	B	
		MARTINEZ, TEODORO NOEL (TED)	2B	47	103	.224	B	
		(SS42 3B2 OF15)						
15	10	MATLACK, JONATHAN TRUMPBOUR	P		34	.128	B	
		MAYS, WILLIE HOWARD (1B11)	OF	49	69	+.267	XSF	
11	8	MC ANDREW, JAMES CLEMENT	P		28	.047	B	
8	6	MC GRAW, FRANK EDWIN (TUG)	P		54	.100	B	
		MILNER, JOHN DAVID (1B10)	OF	91	117	.238	B	
0	0	MOORE, TOMMY JOE	P		3	.333	A	
		NOLAN, JOSEPH WILLIAM	C	3	4	.000	A	
0	1	RAUCH, ROBERT JOHN	P		19	.000	A	
2	1	SADECKI, RAYMOND MICHAEL	P		34	.154	B	
		SCHNECK, DAVID LEE	OF	33	37	.187	A	
21	12	SEAVER, GEORGE THOMAS (TOM)	P	35	36	.146	B	
		STAUB, DANIEL JOSEPH (RUSTY)	OF	65	66	.293	MON	
0	3	STROM, BRENT TERRY	P		11	.000	A	
		SUDAKIS, WILLIAM PAUL (C5)	1B	7	18	.143	LA	
0	0	TAYLOR, CHARLES GILBERT	P		20	.000	STL	XMILA
0	0	WEBB, HENRY GAYLON MATTHEW	P		6	.000	A	

WON 85
LOST 76
TIED 1
TG 162

NATIONAL LEAGUE FINISHED 6

1965. PCT. .528

PHILADELPHIA

EUGENE WILLIAM MAUCH

WON	LOST	NAME	POS.		G.	BA	FROM	TO
		ALLEN, RICHARD ANTHONY (SS2)	3B	160	161	.302	B	B
		AMARO, RUBEN MORA	1B	60	118	.212	B	NY A
		(2B6 SS60)						
5	8	BALDSCHUN, JACK EDWARD	P		65	.000	B	CIN
4	9	BELINSKY, ROBERT (BO)	P	30	31	.188	LA A	B
		BRIGGS, JOHN EDWARD	OF	66	93	.236	B	B
19	9	BUNNING,JAMES PAUL DAVID	P		39	.214	B	B
3	3	BURDETTE, SELVA LEWIS (LEW)	P		19	+.300	XCHI	CALA
		CALLISON, JOHN WESLEY	OF	159	160	.262	B	B
		CORRALES, PATRICK	C	62	63	.224	B	STL
		COVINGTON, JOHN WESLEY (WES)	OF	64	101	.247	B	CHI
14	10	CULP, RAYMOND LEONARD	P		33	.088	B	B
		DALRYMPLE, CLAYTON ERROL	C	102	103	.213	B	B
		DEL GRECO, ROBERT GEORGE	OF	4	8	.000	KC A63	C
0	0	DUREN, RINOLD GEORGE	P		6	.000	CIN	XWASA
		GONZALEZ, ANDRES ANTONIO	OF	104	108	.295	B	B
5	8	HERBERT, RAYMOND ERNEST	P		25	.268	CHIA	B
		HERRNSTEIN, JOHN ELLETT	1B	18	63	.200	B	B
		(OF14)						
1	1	JACKSON, GRANT DWIGHT	P		6	.000	A	B
2	1	JENKINS, FERGUSON ARTHUR	P		7	.000	A	B
		JOHNSON, ALEXANDER	OF	82	97	.294	B	STL
2	5	MAHAFFEY, ARTHUR	P		22	.095	B	STL
		PHILLIPS, ADOLFO EMILIO	OF	32	41	.230	B	B
5	3	ROEBUCK, EDWARD JACK	P		44	.000	B	B
		ROJAS, OCTAVIO (COOKIE)	2B	84	142	.303	B	B
		(C2 1B1 SS11 OF55)						
18	11	SHORT, CHRISTOPHER JOSEPH	P		47	.131	B	B
		SORRELL, WILLIAM	3B	1	10	.385	A	SF 67
0	1	STEEVENS, MORRIS DALE	P		6	.000	B	C
		STUART, RICHARD LEE (3B1)	1B	143	149	.234	BOSA	NY
		TAYLOR, ANTONIO NEMESIO	2B	86	106	.229	B	B
		(3B5)						
		THOMAS, FRANK JOSEPH	OF	12	35	+.260	B	XHOU
		(1B11 3B1)						
		TRIANDOS, GUS	C	28	30	+.171	B	XHOU
7	7	WAGNER, GARY EDWARD	P		59	.077	A	B
		WINE, ROBERT PAUL (1B4)	SS	135	139	.228	B	B

WON 87
LOST 75
TIED 0
TG 162

NATIONAL LEAGUE FINISHED 4

1966. PCT. .537

PHILADELPHIA

EUGENE WILLIAM MAUCH

WON	LOST	NAME	POS.		G.	BA	FROM	TO
		ALLEN, RICHARD ANTHONY (OF47)	3B	91	141	.317	B	B
0	2	BELINSKY, ROBERT (BO)	P		9	.333	B	HOU
0	0	BOOZER, JOHN MORGAN	P		2	.000	PHI 64	B
		BRANDT, JOHN GEORGE	OF	71	82	.250	BALA	B
		BRIGGS, JOHN EDWARD	OF	69	81	.282	B	B
6	8	BUHL, ROBERT RAY	P		32	+.098	XCHI	B
19	14	BUNNING,JAMES PAUL DAVID	P		43	.179	B	B
		CALLISON, JOHN WESLEY	OF	154	155	.276	B	B
		CLEMENS, DOUGLAS HORACE	OF	28	79	.256	CHI	B
		(1B1)						
2	1	CRAIG, ROGER LEE	P		14	.000	CIN	C
7	4	CULP, RAYMOND LEONARD	P		34	.077	B	CHI
		DALRYMPLE, CLAYTON ERROL	C	110	114	.245	B	B
3	2	FOX, TERRENCE EDWARD	P	36	38	.000	XDETA	C
		GONZALEZ, ANDRES ANTONIO	OF	121	132	.286	B	B
		GROAT, RICHARD MORROW	SS	139	155	.260	STL	B
		(1B1 3B20)						
2	5	HERBERT, RAYMOND ERNEST	P		23	.077	B	C
		HERRNSTEIN, JOHN ELLETT	OF	2	4	+.100	B	XCHI
0	0	JACKSON, GRANT DWIGHT	P		2	.000	B	B
15	13	JACKSON, LAWRENCE CURTIS	P	35	36	+.146	XCHI	B
0	0	JENKINS, FERGUSON ARTHUR	P		1	+.000	B	XCHI
6	5	KNOWLES, DAROLD DUANE	P		69	.250	BALA	WASA
		KUENN, HARVEY EDWARD	OF	31	86	+.296	XCHI	C
		(1B13 3B1)						
		LINZ, PHILIP FRANCIS	3B	14	40	.200	NY A	B
		(2B3 SS6)						
1	1	MORRIS, JOHN WALLACE	P		13	.000	A	BALA68
		PHILLIPS, ADOLFO EMILIO	OF	1	2	+.000	B	XCHI
0	0	RIDZIK, STEPHEN GEORGE	P		2	.000	WASA	C
0	2	ROEBUCK, EDWARD JACK	P		6	.000	B	C
		ROJAS, OCTAVIO (COOKIE)	2B	106	156	.268	B	B
		(SS2 OF56)						
		SCHAFFER, JIMMIE RONALD	C	6	8	.133	NY	B
20	10	SHORT, CHRISTOPHER JOSEPH	P		42	.208	B	B
		SUTHERLAND, GARY LYNN	SS	1	3	.000	A	B
		TAYLOR, ANTONIO NEMESIO	2B	68	125	.242	B	B
		(3B52)						
		UECKER, ROBERT GEORGE	C	76	78	.208	STL	B
1	1	VERBANIC, JOSEPH MICHAEL	P		17	.000	A	NY A
0	1	WAGNER, GARY EDWARD	P		5	.000	B	B
		WHITE, WILLIAM DEKOVA	1B	158	159	.276	STL	B
		WINE, ROBERT PAUL (OF2)	SS	40	46	.236	B	B
5	6	WISE, RICHARD CHARLES	P	22	23	.000	PHI 64	B

WON 82
LOST 80
TIED 0
TG 162

NATIONAL LEAGUE

1967.

FINISHED 5

PCT. .506

PHILADELPHIA

EUGENE WILLIAM MAUCH

WON	LOST	NAME	POS.		G.	BA	FROM	TO
		ALLEN, RICHARD ANTHONY	3B	121	122	.307	B	B
		(2B1 SS1)						
5	4	BOOZER, JOHN MORGAN	P		28	.211	B	B
		BRANDT, JOHN GEORGE	OF	3	16	+.105	B	XHOU
		BRIGGS, JOHN EDWARD	OF	94	106	.232	B	B
0	0	BUHL, ROBERT RAY	P		3	.000	B	C
17	15	BUNNING,JAMES PAUL DAVID	P		40	.163	B	PIT
		CALLISON, JOHN WESLEY	OF	147	149	.261	B	B
		CLEMENS, DOUGLAS HORACE	OF	10	69	.178	B	B
		COWAN, BILLY ROLLAND	OF	20	34	.153	MIL 65	NY A69
		(2B1 3B1)						
		DALRYMPLE, CLAYTON ERROL	C	97	101	.172	B	B
6	7	ELLSWORTH, RICHARD CLARK	P		32	.108	CHI	BOSA
9	6	FARRELL, RICHARD JOSEPH (TURK)	P		50	+.105	XHOU	B
		FRANCONA, JOHN PATSY (TITO)	1B	24	27	+.205	STL	XATL
		(OF1)						
0	0	GOMEZ, RUBEN COLON	P		7	.000	MINA62	C
		GONZALEZ, ANDRES ANTONIO	OF	143	149	.339	B	B
0	0	GREEN, GEORGE DALLAS	P		8	.000	NY	C
		GROAT, RICHARD MORROW	SS	6	10	+.115	B	XSF
10	8	HALL, RICHARD WALLACE	P		48	.071	BALA	B
		HARMON, TERRY WALTER			2	.000	A	PHI 69
		HILLER, CHARLES JOSEPH	2B	6	31	+.302	XNY	PIT
2	3	JACKSON, GRANT DWIGHT	P		43	.133	B	B
13	15	JACKSON, LAWRENCE CURTIS	P	40	42	.161	B	B
		JOSEPH, RICARDO EMELINO	1B	13	17	.220	KC A64	B
		LINZ, PHILIP FRANCIS (3B1)	SS	7	23	+.222	B	XNY
		LOCK, DON WILSON	OF	97	112	.252	WASA	B
0	0	LOUGHLIN, LARRY JOHN	P		3	1.000	A	C
		OLIVER, EUGENE GEORGE (1B2)	C	79	85	+.224	XATL	BOSA
0	0	RAMOS, PEDRO	P		6	.000	NY A	PIT 69
0	0	ROJAS, OCTAVIO (COOKIE)	2B	137	147	.259	B	B
		(P1 C3 SS2 3B1 OF9)						
		SCHAFFER, JIMMIE RONALD	C	1	2	.000	B	CIN
9	11	SHORT, CHRISTOPHER JOSEPH	P		29	.091	B	B
		SUTHERLAND, GARY LYNN (OF25)	SS	66	103	.247	B	B
		TAYLOR, ANTONIO NEMESIO	1B	58	132	.238	B	B
		(2B42 SS3 3B44)						
0	0	THEONEN, RICHARD CRISPIN	P		1	.000	A	C
		UECKER, ROBERT GEORGE	C	17	18	+.171	B	XATL
0	0	WAGNER, GARY EDWARD	P		1	.000	B	B
		WHITE, WILLIAM DEKOVA	1B	95	110	.250	B	B
		WINE, ROBERT PAUL (1B2)	SS	134	135	.190	B	B
11	11	WISE, RICHARD CHARLES	P		36	.208	B	B

WON 76
LOST 86
TIED 0
TG 162

NATIONAL LEAGUE

1968.

FINISHED 7
(TIED WITH LOS ANGELES)
PCT. .469

PHILADELPHIA

EUGENE WILLIAM MAUCH GEORGE EDWARD MYATT ROBERT RALPH SKINNER

WON	LOST	NAME	POS.		G.	BA	FROM	TO
		ALLEN, RICHARD ANTHONY (3B10)	OF	139	152	.263	B	B
		BEDELL, HOWARD WILLIAM			9	.143	MIL 62	C
2	2	BOOZER, JOHN MORGAN	P		38	.111	B	B
		BRIGGS, JOHN EDWARD (1B36)	OF	65	110	.254	B	B
0	0	BROWN, PAUL DWAYNE	P		2	.000	PHI 63	C
		CALLISON, JOHN WESLEY	OF	109	121	.244	B	B
		CLEMENS, DOUGLAS HORACE	OF	17	29	.211	B	C
0	0	COLTON, LAWRENCE ROBERT	P		1	.000	A	C
		DALRYMPLE, CLAYTON ERROL	C	80	85	.207	B	BALA
4	6	FARRELL, RICHARD JOSEPH (TURK)	P		54	.167	B	B
12	14	FRYMAN, WOODROW THOMPSON	P		34	.085	PIT	B
		GONZALEZ, ANDRES ANTONIO	OF	117	121	.264	B	SD
4	1	HALL, RICHARD WALLACE	P		32	.333	B	BALA
		HISLE, LARRY EUGENE	OF	6	7	.364	A	B
1	6	JACKSON, GRANT DWIGHT	P	33	37	.300	B	B
13	17	JACKSON, LAWRENCE CURTIS	P	34	37	.141	B	C
4	4	JAMES, JEFFREY LYNN	P		29	.121	A	B
4	4	JOHNSON, JERRY MICHAEL	P		16	.080	A	B
		JOSEPH, RICARDO EMELINO	1B	30	66	.219	B	B
		(3B14 OF1)						
		LOCK, DON WILSON	OF	78	99	.210	B	B
		MONEY, DONALD WAYNE	SS		4	.231	A	B
		PENA, ROBERTO CESAR	SS	133	138	.260	CHI 66	SD
		ROJAS, OCTAVIO (COOKIE)	2B	150	152	.232	B	B
		(C1)						
		RYAN, MICHAEL JAMES	C		96	.179	BOSA	B
19	13	SHORT, CHRISTOPHER JOSEPH	P	42	43	.152	B	B
		SULLIVAN, JOHN PETER	C	8	12	.222	NY	C
		SUTHERLAND, GARY LYNN	2B	17	67	.275	B	MON
		(SS10 3B10 OF7)						
		TAYLOR, ANTONIO NEMESIO	3B	138	145	.250	B	B
		(1B1 2B5)						
4	4	WAGNER, GARY EDWARD	P		44	.083	B	B
		WHITE, WILLIAM DEKOVA	1B	111	127	.239	B	STL
		WINE, ROBERT PAUL (3B1)	SS	25	27	.169	B	MON
9	15	WISE, RICHARD CHARLES	P		30	.241	B	B

COACH MYATT SERVED AS INTERIM MANAGER DURING CHANGEOVER.

WON 63 | LOST 99 | TIED 0 | TG 162

NATIONAL LEAGUE 1969. PHILADELPHIA

FINISHED 5 E PCT. .389

ROBERT RALPH SKINNER GEORGE EDWARD MYATT

WON	LOST	NAME	POS.		G.	BA	FROM	TO
		ALLEN, RICHARD ANTHONY	1B	117	118	.288	B	STL
		BARRY, RICHARD DONOVAN	OF	9	20	.188	A	C
1	2	BOOZER, JOHN MORGAN	P		46	.333	B	C
		BRIGGS, JOHN EDWARD (1B2.)	OF	108	124	.238	B	B
		CALLISON, JOHN WESLEY	OF	129	134	.265	B	CHI
5	10	CHAMPION, BUFORD BILLY (BILL)	P		23	.171	A	B
3	4	FARRELL, RICHARD JOSEPH (TURK)	P		46	.000	B	C
12	15	FRYMAN, WOODROW THOMPSON	P		36	.118	B	B
		HARMON, TERRY WALTER	SS	38	87	.239	PHI 67	B
		(2B19 3B2)						
		HISLE, LARRY EUGENE	OF	140	145	.266	B	B
14	18	JACKSON, GRANT DWIGHT	P	38	40	.140	B	B
2	2	JAMES, JEFFREY LYNN	P		6	.182	B	C
		JOHNSON, DERON ROGER	OF	72	138	.255	ATL	B
		(1B18 3B50)						
6	13	JOHNSON, JERRY MICHAEL	P		33	.209	B	STL
		JOSEPH, RICARDO EMELINO	3B	58	99	.273	B	B
		(1B17 2B1)						
0	3	LERSCH, BARRY LEE	P		10	.000	A	B
		LOCK, DON WILSON	OF	1	4	.000	B	XBOSA
		MONEY, DONALD WAYNE	SS	126	127	.229	B	B
2	8	PALMER, LOWELL RAYMOND	P		26	.136	A	B
0	0	PERAZA, LUIS	P		8	.000	A	C
1	3	RAFFO, ALBERT MARTIN	P		45	.167	A	C
		REAMS, LEROY			1	.000	A	C
		REID, SCOTT DONALD	OF	5	13	.211	A	B
		ROJAS, OCTAVIO (COOKIE)	2B	95	110	.228	B	STL
		(OF2)						
		ROZNOVSKY, VICTOR JOSEPH	C	2	13	.231	BALA67	C
		RYAN, MICHAEL JAMES	C	132	133	.204	B	B
0	0	SHORT, CHRISTOPHER JOSEPH	P		2	.000	B	B
		STONE, EUGENE DANIEL	1B	5	18	.214	A	C
		STONE, HARRY RONALD (RON)	OF	69	103	.239	KC A66	B
		TAYLOR, ANTONIO NEMESIO	3B	71	138	.262	B	B
		(1B10 2B57)						
0	3	WAGNER, GARY EDWARD	P		9	.000	B	XBOSA
		WATKINS, DAVID ROGER	C	54	69	.176	A	C
		(3B1 OF5)						
2	5	WILSON, WILLIAM HARLAN	P		37	.000	A	B
15	13	WISE, RICHARD CHARLES	P		33	.270	B	B

COACH MYATT SERVED AS INTERIM MANAGER NEAR CLOSE OF SEASON.

WON 73 | LOST 88 | TIED 0 | TG 161

NATIONAL LEAGUE 1970. PHILADELPHIA

FINISHED 5 E PCT. .453

FRANK JOSEPH LUCCHESI

WON	LOST	NAME	POS.		G.	BA	FROM	TO
		BATES, DELBERT OAKLEY	C	20	22	.133	A	C
		BOWA, LAWRENCE ROBERT (2B1)	SS	143	145	.250	A	B
		BRIGGS, JOHN EDWARD	OF	95	110	.270	B	B
		BROWNE, BYRON ELLIS	OF	88	104	.248	STL	B
10	15	BUNNING,JAMES PAUL DAVID	P	34	35	.127	LA	B
0	2	CHAMPION, BUFORD BILLY (BILL)	P		7	.000	B	B
		COMPTON, MICHAEL LYNN	C	40	47	.164	A	C
		DOYLE, ROBERT DENNIS (DENNY)	2B	103	112	.208	A	B
		EDWARDS, HOWARD RODNEY (DOC)	C	34	35	.269	NY A65	C
8	6	FRYMAN, WOODROW THOMPSON	P		27	.128	B	B
		GAMBLE, OSCAR CHARLES	OF	74	88	.262	CHI	B
		HARMON, TERRY WALTER	SS	35	71	.248	B	B
		(2B14 3B2)						
		HISLE, LARRY EUGENE	OF	121	126	.205	B	B
9	5	HOERNER, JOSEPH WALTER	P		44	.200	STL	B
		HUTTO, JAMES NEAMON	OF	22	57	.185	A	C
		(C5 1B12 3B1)						
5	15	JACKSON, GRANT DWIGHT	P	32	52	.091	B	BALA
1	1	JACKSON, MICHAEL WARREN	P		5	1.000	A	STL
		JOHNSON, DERON ROGER (3B3)	1B	154	159	.256	B	B
		JOSEPH, RICARDO EMELINO	OF	12	71	.227	B	C
		(1B10 3B9)						
0	0	LAXTON, WILLIAM HARRY	P		2	.000	A	SD
6	3	LERSCH, BARRY LEE	P		42	.065	B	B
		LIS, JOSEPH ANTHONY	OF	9	13	.189	A	B
		LUZINSKI, GREGORY MICHAEL	1B	3	8	.167	A	B
		MC CARVER, JAMES TIMOTHY (TIM)	C		44	.287	STL	B
		MONEY, DONALD WAYNE (SS2)	3B	119	120	.295	B	B
		MONTANEZ, GUILLERMO (WILLIE)	OF	10	18	.240	CALA66	B
		(1B5)						
1	2	PALMER, LOWELL RAYMOND	P		38	.148	B	B
		PARRILLA, SAMUEL	OF	3	11	.125	A	C
		REID, SCOTT DONALD	OF	18	25	.122	B	C
0	0	REYNOLDS, KENNETH LEE	P		4	.000	A	B
		RYAN, MICHAEL JAMES	C		46	.179	B	B
8	9	SELMA, RICHARD JAY (1B1 3B2)	P	73	73	.150	CHI	B
9	16	SHORT, CHRISTOPHER JOSEPH	P		36	.049	B	B
		STONE, HARRY RONALD (RON)	OF	99	123	.262	B	B
		(1B6)						
		TAYLOR, ANTONIO NEMESIO	2B	59	124	.301	B	B
		(SS1 3B38 OF18)						
		VUKOVICH, JOHN CHRISTOPHER	SS	2	3	.125	A	B
		(3B1)						
2	0	WENZ, FREDERICK CHARLES	P		22	.000	BOSA	C
1	0	WILSON, WILLIAM HARLAN	P		37	.250	B	B
13	14	WISE, RICHARD CHARLES	P	35	37	.200	B	B

WON 67
LOST 95
TIED 0
TG 162

NATIONAL LEAGUE

1971.

FINISHED 6 E (LAST)

PCT. .414

PHILADELPHIA

FRANK JOSEPH LUCCHESI

WON	LOST	NAME	POS.		G.	BA	FROM	TO
		ANDERSON, MICHAEL ALLEN	OF		26	.247	A	B
		BOWA, LAWRENCE ROBERT	SS	157	159	.249	B	B
6	6	BRANDON, DARRELL G.	P		52	.154	MINA69	B
		BRIGGS, JOHN EDWARD	OF	8	10	.182	B	XMILA
		BROWNE, BYRON ELLIS	OF	30	58	.206	B	B
5	12	BUNNING,JAMES PAUL DAVID	P	29	31	.120	B	C
3	5	CHAMPION, BUFORD BILLY (BILL)	P		37	.111	B	B
		DOYLE, ROBERT DENNIS (DENNY)	2B	91	95	.231	B	B
		FREED, ROGER VERNON (C1)	OF	106	118	.221	BALA	B
10	7	FRYMAN, WOODROW THOMPSON	P		37	.189	B	B
		GAMBLE, OSCAR CHARLES	OF	80	92	.221	B	B
		HARMON, TERRY WALTER	2B	58	79	.204	B	B
		(1B2 SS9 3B3)						
		HISLE, LARRY EUGENE	OF	27	36	.197	B	C
4	5	HOERNER, JOSEPH WALTER	P		49	.100	B	B
		JOHNSON, DERON ROGER (3B22)	1B	136	158	.265	B	B
		KOEGEL, PETER JOHN (OF1)	C	7	12	.231	XMILA	B
5	14	LERSCH, BARRY LEE	P	38	44	.169	B	B
		LIS, JOSEPH ANTHONY	OF	35	59	.211	B	B
		LUZINSKI, GREGORY MICHAEL	1B		28	.300	B	B
		MC CARVER, JAMES TIMOTHY (TIM)	C	125	134	.278	B	B
		MONEY, DONALD WAYNE	3B	68	121	.223	B	B
		(2B20 OF40)						
		MONTANEZ, GUILLERMO (WILLIE)	OF	158	158	.255	B	B
		(1B9)						
0	1	MUNIZ, MANUEL	P		5	.000	A	C
0	0	PALMER, LOWELL RAYMOND	P		3	.200	B	STL
		PFEIL, ROBERT RAYMOND	3B	15	44	.271	NY 69	C
		(C4 1B1 2B1 SS1 OF3)						
5	9	REYNOLDS, KENNETH LEE	P	35	36	.200	B	B
		RYAN, MICHAEL JAMES	C		43	.164	B	B
0	2	SELMA, RICHARD JAY	P	17	18	1.000	B	B
7	14	SHORT, CHRISTOPHER JOSEPH	P		31	.083	B	B
		STONE, HARRY RONALD (RON)	OF	51	95	.227	B	B
		(1B3)						
		TAYLOR, ANTONIO NEMESIO	2B	14	36	.234	B	XDETA
		(1B2 3B11)						
1	0	TWITCHELL, WAYNE LEE	P		6	.000	MILA	B
		VUKOVICH, JOHN CHRISTOPHER	3B		74	.166	B	C
4	6	WILSON, WILLIAM HARLAN (3B1)	P	38	38	.100	B	B
17	14	WISE, RICHARD CHARLES	P	38	39	.237	B	STL

WON 59
LOST 97
TIED 0
TG 156

NATIONAL LEAGUE

1972.

FINISHED 6 E (LAST)

PCT. .378

PHILADELPHIA

FRANK JOSEPH LUCCHESI PAUL FRANCIS OWENS

WON	LOST	NAME	POS.		G.	BA	FROM	TO
		ANDERSON, MICHAEL ALLEN	OF	35	36	.194	B	
		BATEMAN, JOHN ALVIN	C	80	82	+.222	XMON	
		BOONE, ROBERT RAYMOND	C	14	16	.275	A	
		BOWA, LAWRENCE ROBERT	SS	150	152	.250	B	
7	7	BRANDON, DARRELL G.	P		42	.067	B	
		BROWNE, BYRON ELLIS	OF	9	21	.190	B	
27	10	CARLTON, STEVEN NORMAN	P		41	.197	STL	
4	14	CHAMPION, BUFORD BILLY (BILL)	P	30	32	.147	B	
1	1	DOWNS, DAVID RALPH	P		4	.250	A	
		DOYLE, ROBERT DENNIS (DENNY)	2B	119	123	.249	B	
		FREED, ROGER VERNON	OF	46	73	.225	B	
4	10	FRYMAN, WOODROW THOMPSON	P		23	.152	B	XDETA
		GAMBLE, OSCAR CHARLES (1B1)	OF	35	74	.237	B	
		HARMON, TERRY WALTER	2B	50	73	.284	B	
		(SS15 3B5)						
0	2	HOERNER, JOSEPH WALTER	P		15	+.000	B	XATL
		HUTTON, THOMAS GEORGE (OF48)	1B	87	134	.260	LA 69	
		JOHNSON, DERON ROGER	1B	62	96	.213	B	
		KOEGEL, PETER JOHN	1B	8	41	.143	B	
		(C5 3B4 OF2)						
4	6	LERSCH, BARRY LEE	P	36	37	.000	B	
		LIS, JOSEPH ANTHONY (OF14)	1B	30	62	.243	B	
		LUZINSKI, GREGORY MICHAEL	OF	145	150	.281	B	
		(1B2)						
		MC CARVER, JAMES TIMOTHY (TIM)	C	40	45	+.237	B	XMON
		MONEY, DONALD WAYNE (SS2)	3B	151	152	.222	B	
		MONTANEZ, GUILLERMO (WILLIE)	OF	130	147	.247	B	
		(1B14)						
0	8	NASH, JAMES EDWIN	P		9	+.100	XATL	
0	2	NEIBAUER, GARY WAYNE	P		9	+.250	XATL	
2	15	REYNOLDS, KENNETH LEE	P	33	48	.200	B	
		ROBINSON, CRAIG GEORGE	SS	4	5	.200	A	
		ROBINSON, WILLIAM HENRY	OF	72	82	.239	NY A69	
		RYAN, MICHAEL JAMES	C		46	.179	B	
1	2	SCARCE, GUERRANT MCCURDY (MAC)	P		31	.000	A	
		SCHMIDT, MICHAEL JACK (2B1)	3B	11	13	.206	A	
2	9	SELMA, RICHARD JAY	P	46	47	.200	B	
1	1	SHORT, CHRISTOPHER JOSEPH	P		19	.000	B	
		STONE, HARRY RONALD (RON)	OF	15	41	.167	B	
0	0	TERLICKI, ROBERT JOSEPH	P		9	.000	A	
5	9	TWITCHELL, WAYNE LEE	P		49	.071	B	
1	1	WILSON, WILLIAM HARLAN	P		23	.000	B	

WON 90 NATIONAL LEAGUE FINISHED 3
LOST 72
TIED 1 1965. PCT. .556
TG 163

PITTSBURGH

HARRY WILLIAM WALKER

WON	LOST	NAME	POS.		G.	BA	FROM	TO
		ALLEY, LEONARD EUGENE (GENE)	SS	110	153	.252	B	B
		(2B40 3B1)						
		BAILEY, ROBERT SHERWOOD	3B	142	159	.256	B	B
		(OF28)						
0	1	BUTTERS, THOMAS ARDEN	P		5	.000	B	C
13	10	CARDWELL, DONALD EUGENE	P		37	.162	B	B
3	1	CARPIN, FRANK DOMINIC	P		39	.000	A	HOU
		CLEMENTE, ROBERTO WALKER	OF	145	152	.329	B	B
		CLENDENON, DONN ALVIN (3B1)	1B	158	162	.301	B	B
		CRANDALL, DELMAR WESLEY	C		60	.214	SF	CLEA
5	2	FACE, ELROY LEON (ROY)	P		16	.000	B	B
		FREESE, EUGENE LEWIS	3B	19	43	.263	B	XCHIA
8	12	FRIEND, ROBERT BARTMESS	P		34	.042	B	NY A
4	9	GIBBON, JOSEPH CHARLES	P		31	.115	B	SF
17	9	LAW, VERNON SANDERS	P	29	34	.244	B	B
		LYNCH, GERALD THOMAS	OF	26	73	.281	B	B
		MAY, JERRY LEE	C		4	.500	B	B
		MAZEROSKI, WILLIAM STANLEY	2B	127	130	.271	B	B
6	6	MC BEAN, ALVIN O'NEAL (OF1)	P	62	62	.222	B	B
		MOTA, MANUEL RAFAEL	OF	95	121	.279	B	B
		OLIVER, ROBERT LEE	OF		3	.000	A	KC A69
		PAGAN, JOSE ANTONIO (SS7)	3B	15	42	+.237	XSF	B
		PAGLIARONI, JAMES VINCENT	C	131	134	.268	B	B
		RODGERS, KENNETH ANDRE IAN	SS	33	75	.287	CHI	B
		(1B6 2B1 3B15)						
		SCHOFIELD, JOHN RICHARD (DICK)	SS	28	31	+.229	B	XSF
9	6	SCHWALL, DONALD BERNARD	P		43	.000	B	B
7	3	SISK, TOMMIE WAYNE	P	38	39	.061	B	B
		SMITH, HAROLD RAYMOND	C		4	.000	STL 61	C
		SPRIGGS, GEORGE HERMAN	OF	1	9	.500	A	B
		STARGELL, WILVER DORNEL	OF	137	144	.272	B	B
		(1B7)						
17	12	VEALE, ROBERT ANDREW	P		39	.086	B	B
		VIRDON, WILLIAM CHARLES	OF	128	135	.279	B	PIT 68
		VIRGIL, OSVALDO JOSE	C	15	39	.265	BALA62	SF
		(2B5 3B7)						
0	0	WALKER, JAMES LUKE	P		2	.000	A	B
1	1	WOOD, WILBUR FORRESTER	P		34	.000	B	CHIA67

WON 92 NATIONAL LEAGUE FINISHED 3
LOST 70
TIED 0 1966. PCT. .568
TG 162

PITTSBURGH

HARRY WILLIAM WALKER

WON	LOST	NAME	POS.		G.	BA	FROM	TO
		ALLEY, LEONARD EUGENE (GENE)	SS	143	147	.299	B	B
		ALOU, MATEO ROJAS	OF	136	141	.342	SF	B
		BAILEY, ROBERT SHERWOOD	3B	96	126	.279	B	LA
		(OF20)						
11	7	BLASS, STEPHEN ROBERT	P		34	.231	PIT 64	B
		BOSCH, DONALD JOHN	OF	1	3	.000	A	NY
6	6	CARDWELL, DONALD EUGENE	P		32	.103	B	NY
		CLEMENTE, ROBERTO WALKER	OF		154	.317	B	B
		CLENDENON, DONN ALVIN	1B	152	155	.299	B	B
6	6	FACE, ELROY LEON (ROY)	P		54	.000	B	B
12	9	FRYMAN, WOODROW THOMPSON	P		36	.159	A	B
		GONDER, JESSE LEMAR	C	52	59	.225	MIL	B
12	8	LAW, VERNON SANDERS	P	31	34	.242	B	B
		LYNCH, GERALD THOMAS	OF	4	64	.214	B	C
		MAY, JERRY LEE	C	41	42	.250	B	B
		MAZEROSKI, WILLIAM STANLEY	2B		162	.262	B	B
4	3	MC BEAN, ALVIN O'NEAL	P	47	50	.100	B	B
		MICHAEL, EUGENE RICHARD	SS	8	30	.152	A	LA
		(2B2 3B1)						
9	8	MIKKELSEN, PETER JAMES	P		71	.150	NY A	B
		MOTA, MANUEL RAFAEL (3B4)	OF	96	116	.332	B	B
3	2	O'DELL, WILLIAM OLIVER	P		37	+.063	XATL	B
		PAGAN, JOSE ANTONIO	3B	83	109	.264	B	B
		(2B3 SS18 OF3)						
		PAGLIARONI, JAMES VINCENT	C	118	123	.235	B	B
0	1	PURKEY, ROBERT THOMAS	P	10	11	.000	STL	C
		ROBERTS, DAVID LEONARD	1B	2	14	.125	HOU 64	C
		RODGERS, KENNETH ANDRE IAN	SS	5	36	.184	B	B
		(1B2 3B3 OF3)						
3	2	SCHWALL, DONALD BERNARD	P		11	+.100	B	XATL
0	0	SHELLENBACK, JAMES PHILIP	P		2	.000	A	B
10	5	SISK, TOMMIE WAYNE	P		34	.098	B	B
		SPRIGGS, GEORGE HERMAN			9	.143	B	B
		STARGELL, WILVER DORNEL	OF	127	140	.315	B	B
		(1B15)						
16	12	VEALE, ROBERT ANDREW	P		38	.138	B	B
0	1	WALKER, JAMES LUKE	P		10	.000	B	PIT 68

WON 81 LOST 81 TIED 1 TG 163 — NATIONAL LEAGUE — 1967. — FINISHED 6 — PCT. .500

PITTSBURGH

HARRY WILLIAM WALKER   DANIEL EDWARD MURTAUGH

WON	LOST	NAME	POS.	G.	BA	FROM	TO
		ALLEY, LEONARD EUGENE (GENE)	SS 146	152	.287	B	B
		ALOU, MATEO ROJAS (1B1)	OF 134	139	.338	B	B
6	8	BLASS, STEPHEN ROBERT	P	32	.128	B	B
		CLEMENTE, ROBERTO WALKER	OF 145	147	.357	B	B
		CLENDENON, DONN ALVIN	1B 123	131	.249	B	B
2	1	DAL CANTON, JOHN BRUCE	P	8	.333	A	B
7	5	FACE, ELROY LEON (ROY)	P	61	.000	B	B
3	8	FRYMAN, WOODROW THOMPSON	P	28	.118	B	PHI
0	1	GELNAR, JOHN RICHARD	P	10	.167	PIT 64	SEAA69
		GONDER, JESSE LEMAR	C 18	22	.139	B	C
		JIMENEZ, MANUEL EMILIO	OF 6	50	.250	KC A	B
2	6	LAW, VERNON SANDERS	P 25	26	.111	B	C
		LUPLOW, ALVIN DAVID	OF 25	55	+.184	XNY	C
		MAY, JERRY LEE	C	110	.271	B	B
		MAZEROSKI, WILLIAM STANLEY	2B	163	.261	B	B
7	4	MC BEAN, ALVIN O'NEAL	P	51	.207	B	B
1	2	MIKKELSEN, PETER JAMES	P	32	+.000	B	XCHI
1	0	MOOSE, ROBERT RALPH	P	2	.333	A	B
		MOTA, MANUEL RAFAEL (3B2)	OF 99	120	.321	B	B
5	6	O'DELL, WILLIAM OLIVER	P 27	28	.115	B	C
		PAGAN, JOSE ANTONIO	3B 25	81	.289	B	B
		(C1 2B2 SS16 OF23)					
		PAGLIARONI, JAMES VINCENT	C 38	44	.200	B	OAKA
8	10	PIZARRO, JUAN	P	50	.259	CHIA	B
9	8	RIBANT, DENNIS JOSEPH	P 38	47	.267	NY	DETA
		ROBERTSON, ROBERT EUGENE	1B	9	.171	A	PIT 69
		RODGERS, KENNETH ANDRE IAN	1B 9	47	.230	B	C
		(2B2 SS3 3B5)					
		SANGUILLEN, MANUEL DEJESUS	C 28	30	.271	A	PIT 69
1	1	SHELLENBACK, JAMES PHILIP	P	6	.167	B	PIT 69
0	0	SHORT, WILLIAM ROSS	P	6	.000	BOSA	NY
13	13	SISK, TOMMIE WAYNE	P	37	.101	B	B
		SPRIGGS, GEORGE HERMAN	OF 13	38	.175	B	KC A69
		STARGELL, WILVER DORNEL	OF 98	134	.271	B	B
		(1B37)					
16	8	VEALE, ROBERT ANDREW	P	33	.043	B	B
		WILLS, MAURICE MORNING (SS2)	3B 144	149	.302	LA	B

WON 80 LOST 82 TIED 1 TG 163 — NATIONAL LEAGUE — 1968. — FINISHED 6 — PCT. .494

PITTSBURGH

LAWRENCE WILLIAM SHEPARD

WON	LOST	NAME	POS.	G.	BA	FROM	TO
		ALLEY, LEONARD EUGENE (GENE)	SS 109	133	.245	B	B
		(2B24)					
		ALOU, MATEO ROJAS	OF 144	146	.332	B	B
18	6	BLASS, STEPHEN ROBERT (OF1)	P 33	35	.137	B	B
4	14	BUNNING,JAMES PAUL DAVID	P	27	.098	PHI	B
		CANNIZZARO, CHRISTOPHER JOHN	C	25	.241	NY 65	SD
		CLEMENTE, ROBERTO WALKER	OF 131	132	.291	B	B
		CLENDENON, DONN ALVIN	1B 155	158	.257	B	MON
1	1	DAL CANTON, JOHN BRUCE	P	7	.000	B	B
6	5	ELLIS, DOCK PHILLIP	P 26	27	.069	A	B
2	4	FACE, ELROY LEON (ROY)	P	43	.000	B	XDETA
		HEBNER, RICHARD JOSEPH		2	.000	A	B
0	0	HENRY, WILLIAM RODMAN	P	10	+.000	XSF	HOU
		HILLER, CHARLES JOSEPH	2B 2	11	.385	PHI	C
		JIMENEZ, MANUEL EMILIO	OF 5	66	.303	B	CHI
12	5	KLINE, RONALD LEE	P	56	.000	MINA	B
		KOLB, GARY ALAN	OF 25	74	.218	NY 65	B
		(C10 2B1 3B4)					
		MAY, JERRY LEE	C 135	137	.219	B	B
		MAZEROSKI, WILLIAM STANLEY	2B 142	143	.251	B	B
9	12	MC BEAN, ALVIN O'NEAL	P 36	43	.194	B	SD
8	12	MOOSE, ROBERT RALPH	P	38	.093	B	B
		MOTA, MANUEL RAFAEL	OF 92	111	.281	B	MON
		(2B1 3B1)					
		OLIVER, ALBERT	OF 1	4	.125	A	B
		PAGAN, JOSE ANTONIO	3B 30	80	.221	B	B
		(1B1 2B2 SS8 OF19)					
		PATEK, FREDDIE JOE	SS 52	61	.255	A	B
		(3B1 OF5)					
1	1	PIZARRO, JUAN	P 12	13	.000	B	XBOSA
5	5	SISK, TOMMIE WAYNE	P	33	.083	B	SD
		STARGELL, WILVER DORNEL	OF 113	128	.237	B	B
		(1B13)					
		TAYLOR, CARL MEANS (OF2)	C 29	44	.211	A	B
13	14	VEALE, ROBERT ANDREW	P	36	.110	B	B
		VIRDON, WILLIAM CHARLES	OF 4	6	.333	PIT 65	C
0	3	WALKER, JAMES LUKE	P	39	.000	PIT 66	B
1	0	WICKERSHAM, DAVID CLIFFORD	P	11	.333	DETA	KC A
		WILLS, MAURICE MORNING (SS10)	3B 141	153	.278	B	MON

WON 88 LOST 74 TIED 0 TG 162

NATIONAL LEAGUE 1969. FINISHED 3 E PCT. .543

PITTSBURGH

LAWRENCE WILLIAM SHEPARD ALEXANDER PETER GRAMMAS

WON	LOST	NAME	POS.	G.	BA	FROM	TO
		ALLEY, LEONARD EUGENE (GENE)	2B 53	82	.246	B	B
		(SS25 3B5)					
		ALOU, MATEO ROJAS	OF	162	.331	B	B
0	3	BELINSKY, ROBERT (BO)	P	8	.000	HOU 67	CIN
16	10	BLASS, STEPHEN ROBERT	P 38	44	.250	B	B
0	0	BROSSEAU, FRANKLIN LEE	P	2	.000	A	PIT 71
10	9	BUNNING,JAMES PAUL DAVID	P	25	+.043	B	XLA
		CASH, DAVID	2B 17	18	.279	A	B
		CLEMENTE, ROBERTO WALKER	OF 135	138	.345	B	B
8	2	DAL CANTON, JOHN BRUCE	P	57	.300	B	B
		DAVIS, RONALD EVERETTE	OF 51	62	.234	STL	C
11	17	ELLIS, DOCK PHILLIP	P 35	37	.088	B	B
0	0	GARBER, HENRY EUGENE (GENE)	P	2	.000	A	B
5	1	GIBBON, JOSEPH CHARLES	P	35	+.000	XSF	B
5	4	HARTENSTEIN, CHARLES OSCAR	P	56	.071	CHI	B
		HEBNER, RICHARD JOSEPH (1B1)	3B 124	129	.301	B	B
		JETER, JOHN	OF 20	28	.310	A	B
1	3	KLINE, RONALD LEE	P	20	+.000	B	XSF
		KOLB, GARY ALAN	C 7	29	.081	B	C
		MANGUAL, ANGEL LUIS	OF 3	6	.250	A	OAKA71
1	1	MARONE, LOUIS STEPHEN	P	29	.000	A	B
		MARTINEZ, JOSE	2B 42	77	.268	A	B
		(SS20 3B5 OF2)					
		MAY, JERRY LEE	C 52	62	.232	B	B
		MAZEROSKI, WILLIAM STANLEY	2B 65	67	.229	B	B
14	3	MOOSE, ROBERT RALPH	P	44	.075	B	B
		OLIVER, ALBERT (OF21)	1B 106	129	.285	B	B
		PAGAN, JOSE ANTONIO	3B 44	108	.285	B	B
		(2B1 OF23)					
		PATEK, FREDDIE JOE	SS 146	147	.239	B	B
0	1	RAMOS, PEDRO	P	5	+.000	PHI 67	XCIN
		ROBERTSON, ROBERT EUGENE	1B 26	32	.208	PIT 67	B
		SANGUILLEN, MANUEL DEJESUS	C 113	129	.303	PIT 67	B
0	0	SHELLENBACK, JAMES PHILIP	P	8	.000	PIT 67	XWASA
		STARGELL, WILVER DORNEL	OF 116	145	.307	B	B
		(1B23)					
		TAYLOR, CARL MEANS (1B24)	OF 36	104	.348	B	STL
13	14	VEALE, ROBERT ANDREW	P	34	.051	B	B
4	6	WALKER, JAMES LUKE	P	31	.000	B	B

COACH GRAMMAS SERVED AS INTERIM MANAGER NEAR CLOSE OF SEASON.

WON 89 LOST 73 TIED 0 TG 162

NATIONAL LEAGUE 1970. FINISHED 1 E (LOST LEAGUE PLAYOFF) PCT. .549

PITTSBURGH

DANIEL EDWARD MURTAUGH

WON	LOST	NAME	POS.	G.	BA	FROM	TO
0	0	ACOSTA, EDUARDO ELIXBET	P	3	.000	A	SD
		ALLEY, LEONARD EUGENE (GENE)	SS 108	121	.244	B	B
		(2B8 3B2)					
		ALOU, MATEO ROJAS	OF 153	155	.297	B	STL
10	12	BLASS, STEPHEN ROBERT	P 31	32	.114	B	B
1	1	BRUNET, GEORGE STUART	P	12	.000	XWASA	STL
1	2	CAMBRIA, FREDERICK DENNIS	P	6	.200	A	C
		CASH, DAVID	2B 55	64	.314	B	B
		CLEMENTE, ROBERTO WALKER	OF 104	108	.352	B	B
		CLINES, EUGENE	OF 7	31	.405	A	B
1	0	COLPAERT, RICHARD CHARLES	P	8	.000	A	C
9	4	DAL CANTON, JOHN BRUCE	P	41	.000	B	KC A
13	10	ELLIS, DOCK PHILLIP	P 30	38	.100	B	B
0	3	GARBER, HENRY EUGENE (GENE)	P	14	.667	B	PIT 72
0	1	GIBBON, JOSEPH CHARLES	P	41	.000	B	CIN
9	3	GIUSTI, DAVID JOHN	P	66	.188	STL	B
2	1	GRANT, JAMES TIMOTHY (MUDCAT)	P	8	.000	XOAKA	B
1	1	HARTENSTEIN, CHARLES OSCAR	P	17	+.000	B	XSTL
		HEBNER, RICHARD JOSEPH	3B 117	120	.290	B	B
		JETER, JOHN	OF 56	85	.238	B	SD
		KOPACZ, GEORGE FELIX	1B 3	10	.188	ATL 66	C
0	1	LAMB, JOHN ANDREW	P	23	.000	A	B
0	0	MARONE, LOUIS STEPHEN	P	1	.000	B	C
		MARTINEZ, JOSE (2B4 SS1)	3B 7	19	.050	B	C
		MAY, JERRY LEE	C 45	51	.209	B	KC A
		MAY, MILTON SCOTT		5	.500	A	B
		MAZEROSKI, WILLIAM STANLEY	2B 102	112	.229	B	B
0	0	MC BEAN, ALVIN O'NEAL	P	7	+.000	XLA	C
11	10	MOOSE, ROBERT RALPH	P 28	29	.182	B	B
4	2	NELSON, JAMES LORIN	P	15	.200	A	B
		OLIVER, ALBERT (1B77)	OF 83	151	.270	B	B
		PAGAN, JOSE ANTONIO	3B 53	95	.265	B	B
		(1B1 2B1 OF4)					
		PATEK, FREDDIE JOE	SS 65	84	.245	B	KC A
2	1	PENA, ORLANDO	P	23	.000	CLEA67	BALA
		RICKETTS, DAVID WILLIAM	C 7	14	.182	STL	C
		ROBERTSON, ROBERT EUGENE	1B 99	117	.287	B	B
		(3B5 OF3)					
		SANGUILLEN, MANUEL DEJESUS	C 125	128	.325	B	B
		STARGELL, WILVER DORNEL	OF 125	136	.264	B	B
		(1B1)					
10	15	VEALE, ROBERT ANDREW	P	34	.164	B	B
15	6	WALKER, JAMES LUKE	P	42	.130	B	B

WON 97	NATIONAL LEAGUE	FINISHED 1 E	
LOST 65	1971.	(ALSO WON LEAGUE PLAYOFF)	
TIED 0		PCT. .599	
TG 162			

PITTSBURGH

DANIEL EDWARD MURTAUGH

WON	LOST	NAME	POS.	G.	BA	FROM	TO
		ALLEY, LEONARD EUGENE (GENE)	SS 108	114	.227	B	B
		(3B1)					
15	8	BLASS, STEPHEN ROBERT	P 33	34	.120	B	B
8	4	BRILES, NELSON KELLEY	P	37	.256	STL	B
0	0	BROSSEAU, FRANKLIN LEE	P	1	.000	PIT 69	C
		CASH, DAVID	2B 105	123	.289	B	B
		(SS3 3B24)					
		CLEMENTE, ROBERTO WALKER	OF 124	132	.341	B	B
		CLINES, EUGENE	OF 74	97	.308	B	B
		DAVALILLO, VICTOR JOSE (1B16)	OF 61	99	.285	STL	B
19	9	ELLIS, DOCK PHILLIP	P 31	44	.203	B	B
5	6	GIUSTI, DAVID JOHN	P	58	.059	B	B
5	3	GRANT, JAMES TIMOTHY (MUDCAT)	P	42	.250	B	XOAKA
		HEBNER, RICHARD JOSEPH	3B 108	112	.271	B	B
		HERNANDEZ, JACINTO (JACKIE)	SS 75	88	.206	KC A	B
		(3B9)					
0	1	HERNANDEZ, RAMON GONZALEZ	P	10	.500	CHI 68	B
9	10	JOHNSON, ROBERT DALE	P	31	.063	KC A	B
6	5	KISON, BRUCE EUGENE	P	18	.065	A	B
0	0	LAMB, JOHN ANDREW	P	2	.000	B	C
		LANIER, LORENZO		6	.000	A	C
		MAY, MILTON SCOTT	C 31	49	.278	B	B
		MAZEROSKI, WILLIAM STANLEY	2B 46	70	.254	B	B
		(3B7)					
1	2	MILLER, ROBERT LANE	P	16	+.000	XSD	B
11	7	MOOSE, ROBERT RALPH	P	30	.103	B	B
2	2	NELSON, JAMES LORIN	P	17	.500	B	C
		OLIVER, ALBERT (1B25)	OF 116	143	.282	B	B
		PAGAN, JOSE ANTONIO	3B 41	57	.241	B	B
		(1B2 OF3)					
		ROBERTSON, ROBERT EUGENE	1B 126	131	.271	B	B
		SANDS, CHARLES DUANE	C 3	28	.200	NY A67	B
		SANGUILLEN, MANUEL DEJESUS	C 135	138	.319	B	B
		STARGELL, WILVER DORNEL	OF 135	141	.295	B	B
		STENNETT, RENALDO ANTONIO	2B 36	50	.353	A	B
		TAVERAS, FRANKLIN		1	.000	A	B
		TAYLOR, CARL MEANS	OF 6	7	.167	STL	XKC A
6	0	VEALE, ROBERT ANDREW	P	37	.333	B	B
10	8	WALKER, JAMES LUKE	P	28	.022	B	B
		ZISK, RICHARD WALTER	OF 6	7	.200	A	B

WON 96	NATIONAL LEAGUE	FINISHED 1 E	
LOST 59	1972.	(LOST LEAGUE PLAYOFF)	
TIED 0		PCT. .619	
TG 155			

PITTSBURGH

WILLIAM CHARLES VIRDON

WON	LOST	NAME	POS.	G.	BA	FROM	TO
		ALLEY, LEONARD EUGENE (GENE)	SS 114	119	.248	B	
		(3B4)					
19	8	BLASS, STEPHEN ROBERT	P 33	35	.183	B	
14	11	BRILES, NELSON KELLEY	P	28	.157	B	
		CASH, DAVID	2B 97	99	.282	B	
		CLEMENTE, ROBERTO WALKER	OF 94	102	.312	B	
		CLINES, EUGENE	OF 83	107	.334	B	
		DAVALILLO, VICTOR JOSE (1B8)	OF 97	117	.318	B	
15	7	ELLIS, DOCK PHILLIP	P 25	36	.153	B	
0	0	GARBER, HENRY EUGENE (GENE)	P	4	.000	PIT 70	
7	4	GIUSTI, DAVID JOHN	P	54	.000	B	
		GOGGIN, CHARLES FRANCIS	2B 1	5	.286	A	
		GONZALEZ, JOSE FERNANDO	3B 1	3	.000	A	
		HEBNER, RICHARD JOSEPH	3B 121	124	.300	B	
		HERNANDEZ, JACINTO (JACKIE)	SS 68	72	.188	B	
		(3B4)					
5	0	HERNANDEZ, RAMON GONZALEZ	P	53	.167	B	
4	4	JOHNSON, ROBERT DALE	P	31	.143	B	
9	7	KISON, BRUCE EUGENE	P	32	.189	B	
		MAY, MILTON SCOTT	C 33	57	.281	B	
		MAZEROSKI, WILLIAM STANLEY	2B 15	34	.188	B	
		(3B3)					
1	0	MC KEE, JAMES MARION	P	2	.000	A	
5	2	MILLER, POBERT LANE	P	36	.000	B	
13	10	MOOSE, ROBERT RALPH	P 31	32	.169	B	
		OLIVER, ALBERT (1B3)	OF 138	140	.312	B	
		PAGAN, JOSE ANTONIO (OF2)	3B 32	53	.252	B	
		ROBERTSON, ROBERT EUGENE	1B 89	115	.193	B	
		(3B11 OF23)					
		SANDS, CHARLES DUANE		1	.000	B	
		SANGUILLEN, MANUEL DEJESUS	C 127	136	.298	B	
		(OF2)					
		STARGELL, WILVER DORNEL	1B 101	138	.293	B	
		(OF32)					
		STENNETT, RENALDO ANTONIO	2B 49	109	.286	B	
		(SS6 OF41)					
		TAVERAS, FRANKLIN	SS	4	.000	B	
0	0	VEALE, ROBERT ANDREW	P	5	.000	B	XBOSA
4	6	WALKER, JAMES LUKE	P	26	.083	B	
		ZISK, RICHARD WALTER	OF 12	17	.189	B	

WON 80 | NATIONAL LEAGUE | FINISHED 7
LOST 81
TIED 1 | 1965. | PCT. .497
TG 162

SAINT LOUIS

ALBERT FRED SCHEONDIENST

WON	LOST	NAME	POS.		G.	BA	FROM	TO
0	0	AUST, DENNIS KAY	P		6	.000	A	B
		BOYER, KENTON LLOYD	3B	143	144	.260	B	NY
3	3	BRILES, NELSON KELLEY	P		37	.133	A	B
		BROCK, LOUIS CLARK	OF	153	155	.288	B	B
		BUCHEK, GERALD PETER	2B	33	55	.247	B	B
		(SS18 3B1)						
0	0	CARLTON, STEVEN NORMAN	P		15	.000	A	B
2	3	DENNIS, DONALD RAY	P		41	.400	A	B
		FLOOD, CURTIS CHARLES	OF	151	156	.310	B	B
0	0	FRANCIS, EARL COLEMAN	P		2	.000	PIT	C
		FRANCONA, JOHN PATSY (TITO)	OF	34	81	.259	CLEA	B
		(1B13)						
		GAGLIANO, PHILIP JOSEPH	2B	57	122	.240	B	B
		(3B19 OF25)						
20	12	GIBSON, ROBERT	P	38	42	.240	B	B
		GROAT, RICHARD MORROW (3B2)	SS	148	153	.254	B	PHI
3	0	JASTER, LARRY EDWARD	P		4	.200	A	B
		JAVIER, MANUEL JULIAN	2B	69	77	.227	B	B
		KERNEK, GEORGE BOYD	1B	7	10	.290	A	B
		MAXVILL, CHARLES DALLAN (DAL)	2B	49	68	.135	B	B
		(SS12)						
		MC CARVER, JAMES TIMOTHY (TIM)	C	111	113	.276	B	B
10	9	PURKEY, ROBERT THOMAS	P		32	.029	CIN	PIT
		RICKETTS, DAVID WILLIAM	C		11	.241	STL 63	STL 67
6	15	SADECKI, RAYMOND MICHAEL	P		36	.200	B	B
		SAVAGE, THEODORE E.	OF	20	30	.159	PIT 63	B
2	2	SCHULTZ, GEORGE WARREN	P		34	.000	B	C
		(BARNEY)						
		SHANNON, THOMAS MICHAEL (MIKE)	OF	101	124	.221	B	B
		(C4)						
9	15	SIMMONS, CURTIS THOMAS	P		34	.047	B	B
		SKINNER, ROBERT RALPH	OF	33	80	.309	B	B
		SPIEZIO, EDWARD WAYNE	3B	3	10	.167	B	B
11	8	STALLARD, EVAN TRACY	P		40	.088	NY	B
2	1	TAYLOR, RONALD WESLEY	P		25	+.400	B	XHOU
		TOLAN, ROBERT	OF		17	.188	A	B
		UECKER, ROBERT GEORGE	C	49	53	.228	B	PHI
		WARWICK, CARL WAYNE (1B4)	OF	21	50	.156	B	XBALA
9	11	WASHBURN, RAY CLARK	P		28	.152	B	B
		WHITE, WILLIAM DEKOVA	1B	144	148	.289	B	PHI
3	2	WOODESHICK, HAROLD JOSEPH	P		51	+.000	XHOU	B

WON 83 | NATIONAL LEAGUE | FINISHED 6
LOST 79
TIED 0 | 1966. | PCT. .512
TG 162

SAINT LOUIS

ALBERT FRED SCHEONDIENST

WON	LOST	NAME	POS.		G.	BA	FROM	TO
0	1	AUST, DENNIS KAY	P		9	.000	B	C
4	15	BRILES, NELSON KELLEY	P		49	.079	B	B
		BROCK, LOUIS CLARK	OF	154	156	.285	B	B
		BUCHEK, GERALD PETER	2B	49	100	.236	B	NY
		(SS48 3B4)						
3	3	CARLTON, STEVEN NORMAN	P		9	.267	B	B
		CEPEDA, ORLANDO MANUEL	1B	120	123	+.303	XSF	B
		CORRALES, PATRICK	C	27	28	.181	PHI	CIN 68
1	0	COSMAN, JAMES HENRY	P		1	.000	A	B
4	2	DENNIS, DONALD RAY	P		38	.083	B	C
		FLOOD, CURTIS CHARLES	OF	159	160	.267	B	B
		FRANCONA, JOHN PATSY (TITO)	1B	30	83	.212	B	PHI
		(OF9)						
		GAGLIANO, PHILIP JOSEPH	3B	41	90	.254	B	B
		(1B8 2B1 OF5)						
21	12	GIBSON, ROBERT	P	35	46	.200	B	B
5	1	HOERNER, JOSEPH WALTER	P		57	.125	HOU 64	B
2	1	HUGHES, RICHARD HENRY	P		6	.400	A	B
13	15	JACKSON, ALVIN NEIL	P	36	51	.176	NY	B
11	5	JASTER, LARRY EDWARD	P		26	.178	B	B
		JAVIER, MANUEL JULIAN	2B	145	147	.228	B	B
		JOHNSON, ALEXANDER	OF	22	25	.186	PHI	B
		KERNEK, GEORGE BOYD	1B	16	20	.240	B	C
1	4	MAHAFFEY, ARTHUR	P		12	.000	PHI	C
		MAXVILL, CHARLES DALLAN (DAL)	SS	128	134	.244	B	B
		(2B5 OF1)						
		MC CARVER, JAMES TIMOTHY (TIM)	C	148	150	.274	B	B
1	3	PICHE, RONALD JACQUES	P		20	.000	CALA	C
2	1	SADECKI, RAYMOND MICHAEL	P	5	6	+.429	B	XSF
		SAVAGE, THEODORE E.	OF	7	16	.172	B	B
		SHANNON, THOMAS MICHAEL (MIKE)	OF	129	137	.288	B	B
		(C1)						
1	1	SIMMONS, CURTIS THOMAS	P		10	+.125	B	XCHI
		SKINNER, ROBERT RALPH			49	.156	B	C
		SMITH, CHARLES WILLIAM (SS1)	3B	107	116	.266	NY	NY A
		SPIEZIO, EDWARD WAYNE	3B	19	26	.219	B	B
1	5	STALLARD, EVAN TRACY	P		20	.000	B	C
		TOLAN, ROBERT (1B1)	OF	26	43	.172	B	B
11	9	WASHBURN, RAY CLARK	P		27	.093	B	B
		WILLIAMS, JAMES FRANCIS	SS	7	13	.273	A	B
		(2B3)						
0	0	WILLIS, RONALD EARL	P		4	.000	A	B
2	1	WOODESHICK, HAROLD JOSEPH	P		59	.200	B	B

WON 101 | NATIONAL LEAGUE | FINISHED 1
LOST 60
TIED 0 | 1967. | PCT. .627
TG 161

SAINT LOUIS

ALBERT FRED SCHEONDIENST

WON	LOST	NAME	POS.		G.	BA	FROM	TO
		BRESSOUD, EDWARD FRANCIS	SS	48	52	.134	NY	C
		(3B1)						
14	5	BRILES, NELSON KELLEY	P		49	.150	B	B
		BROCK, LOUIS CLARK	OF	157	159	.299	B	B
14	9	CARLTON, STEVEN NORMAN	P		30	.153	B	B
		CEPEDA, ORLANDO MANUEL	1B		151	.325	B	B
1	0	COSMAN, JAMES HENRY	P		10	.125	B	CHI 70
		FLOOD, CURTIS CHARLES	OF	126	134	.335	B	B
		GAGLIANO, PHILIP JOSEPH	2B	27	73	.221	B	B
		(1B4 SS2 3B25)						
13	7	GIBSON, ROBERT	P	24	27	.133	B	B
4	4	HOERNER, JOSEPH WALTER	P		57	.182	B	B
16	6	HUGHES, RICHARD HENRY	P	37	40	.128	B	B
		HUNTZ, STEPHEN MICHAEL	2B	2	3	.167	A	STL 69
9	4	JACKSON, ALVIN NEIL	P	38	41	.258	B	NY
9	7	JASTER, LARRY EDWARD	P	34	35	.100	B	B
		JAVIER, MANUEL JULIAN	2B	138	140	.281	B	B
		JOHNSON, ALEXANDER	OF	57	81	.223	B	CIN
3	4	LAMABE, JOHN ALEXANDER	P		23	+.200	XNY	CHI
		MARIS, ROGER EUGENE	OF	118	125	.261	NY A	B
		MAXVILL, CHARLES DALLAN (DAL)	SS	148	152	.227	B	B
		(2B7)						
		MC CARVER, JAMES TIMOTHY (TIM)	C	130	138	.295	B	B
		RICKETTS, DAVID WILLIAM	C	21	52	.273	STL 65	B
		ROMANO, JOHN ANTHONY	C	20	24	.121	CHIA	C
		SAVAGE, THEODORE E.			9	+.125	B	XCHI
		SHANNON, THOMAS MICHAEL (MIKE)	3B	122	130	.245	B	B
		(OF6)						
		SPIEZIO, EDWARD WAYNE (OF7)	3B	19	55	.210	B	B
		TOLAN, ROBERT (1B13)	OF	80	110	.253	B	B
0	1	TORREZ, MICHAEL AUGUSTINE	P		3	.000	A	B
10	7	WASHBURN, RAY CLARK	P		27	.091	B	B
		WILLIAMS, JAMES FRANCIS	SS		1	.000	B	C
6	5	WILLIS, RONALD EARL	P		65	.375	B	B
2	1	WOODESHICK, HAROLD JOSEPH	P		36	.000	B	C

WON 97 | NATIONAL LEAGUE | FINISHED 1
LOST 65
TIED 0 | 1968. | PCT. .599
TG 162

SAINT LOUIS

ALBERT FRED SCHEONDIENST

WON	LOST	NAME	POS.		G.	BA	FROM	TO
19	11	BRILES, NELSON KELLEY	P		33	.137	B	B
		BROCK, LOUIS CLARK	OF	156	159	.279	B	B
13	11	CARLTON, STEVEN NORMAN	P	34	35	.164	B	B
		CEPEDA, ORLANDO MANUEL	1B	154	157	.248	B	ATL
		DAVIS, RONALD EVERETTE	OF	25	33	+.177	XHOU	PIT
		EDWARDS, JOHN ALBAN	C	54	85	.239	CIN	HOU
		FLOOD, CURTIS CHARLES	OF	149	150	.301	B	B
		GAGLIANO, PHILIP JOSEPH	2B	17	53	.229	B	B
		(3B10 OF5)						
22	9	GIBSON, ROBERT	P	34	35	.170	B	B
0	2	GILSON, HAROLD	P		13	+.000	A	XHOU
4	2	GRANGER, WAYNE ALLAN	P		34	.200	A	CIN
		HAGUE, JOE CLARENCE (1B2)	OF	3	7	.235	A	B
8	2	HOERNER, JOSEPH WALTER	P		47	.000	B	B
2	2	HUGHES, RICHARD HENRY	P		25	.000	B	C
9	13	JASTER, LARRY EDWARD	P		31	.140	B	MON
		JAVIER, MANUEL JULIAN	2B		139	.260	B	B
		MARIS, ROGER EUGENE	OF	84	100	.255	B	C
		MAXVILL, CHARLES DALLAN (DAL)	SS		151	.253	B	B
		MC CARVER, JAMES TIMOTHY (TIM)	C	109	128	.253	B	B
0	0	MIKKELSEN, PETER JAMES	P		5	+.000	XCHI	LA
2	1	NELSON, MELVIN FREDERICK	P		18	.167	MINA	B
		RICKETTS, DAVID WILLIAM	C	1	20	.136	B	B
		SCHOFIELD, JOHN RICHARD (DICK)	SS	43	69	.220	LA	BOSA
		(2B23)						
		SHANNON, THOMAS MICHAEL (MIKE)	3B		156	.266	B	B
		SIMMONS, CURTIS THOMAS	C		2	.333	CALA	C
		SIMPSON, RICHARD CHARLES	OF	22	26	+.232	CIN	XHOU
		SPIEZIO, EDWARD WAYNE (3B2)	OF	11	29	.157	B	SD
		TOLAN, ROBERT (1B9)	OF	67	92	.230	B	CIN
2	1	TORREZ, MICHAEL AUGUSTINE	P		5	.286	B	B
14	8	WASHBURN, RAY CLARK	P		31	.083	B	B
		WICKER, FLOYD EULISS			5	.500	A	MON
2	3	WILLIS, RONALD EARL	P		48	.000	B	B

WON 87 / LOST 75 / TIED 0 / TG 162

NATIONAL LEAGUE — 1969. — FINISHED 4 E — PCT. .537

SAINT LOUIS

ALBERT FRED SCHEONDIENST

WON	LOST	NAME	POS.		G.	BA	FROM	TO
15	13	BRILES, NELSON KELLEY	P		36	.105	B	B
		BROCK, LOUIS CLARK	OF		157	.298	B	B
		BROWNE, BYRON ELLIS	OF	16	22	.226	HOU	PHI
1	0	CAMPISI, SALVATORE JOHN	P		7	.000	A	B
17	11	CARLTON, STEVEN NORMAN	P	31	32	.212	B	B
0	0	CLEVELAND, REGINALD LESLIE	P		1	.000	A	B
		COULTER, THOMAS LEE	2B		6	.316	A	C
0	0	DAVALILLO, VICTOR JOSE (P2)	OF	23	63	.265	XCALA	B
		DA VANON, FRANK GERALD (GERRY)	SS		16	+.300	XSD	B
		DAY, CHARLES FREDERICK (BOOTS)	OF	1	11	.000	A	CHI
0	0	ELLIS, JAMES RUSSELL	P		2	.000	CHI 67	C
		FLOOD, CURTIS CHARLES	OF	152	153	.285	B	WASA71
		GAGLIANO, PHILIP JOSEPH	2B	20	62	.227	B	B
		(1B9 3B9 OF2)						
20	13	GIBSON, ROBERT	P	35	37	.246	B	B
3	7	GIUSTI, DAVID JOHN	P		22	.200	HOU	PIT
7	5	GRANT, JAMES TIMOTHY (MUDCAT)	P	30	31	+.294	XMON	OAKA
0	1	GUZMAN, SANTIAGO DONOVAN	P		1	.333	A	B
		HAGUE, JOE CLARENCE (1B9)	OF	17	40	.170	B	B
		HICKS, JAMES EDWARD	OF	15	19	.182	CHIA66	XCALA
0	0	HILGENDORF, THOMAS EUGENE	P		6	1.000	A	B
2	3	HOERNER, JOSEPH WALTER	P		45	.000	B	PHI
		HUNTZ, STEPHEN MICHAEL	SS	52	71	.194	STL 67	SD
		(2B12 3B6)						
		JAVIER, MANUEL JULIAN	2B	141	143	.282	B	B
		JOHNSON, ROBERT WALLACE	3B	4	19	.207	ATL	XOAKA
		(1B1)						
		LEE, LERON	OF		7	.217	A	B
		MAXVILL, CHARLES DALLAN (DAL)	SS	131	132	.175	B	B
		MC CARVER, JAMES TIMOTHY (TIM)	C	136	138	.260	B	PHI
0	1	NELSON, MELVIN FREDERICK	P		8	.000	B	C
		NOSSEK, JOSEPH RUDOLPH	OF	1	9	.200	XOAKA	B
		PINSON, VADA EDWARD	OF	124	132	.255	CIN	CLEA
1	0	REUSS, JERRY	P		1	.333	A	B
0	0	RIBANT, DENNIS JOSEPH	P	1	2	+.000	CHIA	XCIN
		RICKETTS, DAVID WILLIAM	C	8	30	.273	B	PIT
		SHANNON, THOMAS MICHAEL (MIKE)	3B	149	150	.254	B	B
		SIMMONS, TED LYLES	C	4	5	.214	A	B
7	5	TAYLOR, CHARLES GILBERT	P		27	.179	A	B
		TORRE, JOSEPH PAUL (C17)	1B	144	159	.289	ATL	B
10	4	TORREZ, MICHAEL AUGUSTINE	P		24	.073	B	B
3	8	WASHBURN, RAY CLARK	P		28	.081	B	CIN
0	2	WASLEWSKI, GARY LEE	P		12	+.000	BOSA	XMON
		WHITE, WILLIAM DEKOVA	1B	15	49	.211	PHI	C
1	2	WILLIS, RONALD EARL	P		26	+1.000	B	XHOU

WON 76 / LOST 86 / TIED 0 / TG 162

NATIONAL LEAGUE — 1970. — FINISHED 4 E — PCT. .469

SAINT LOUIS

ALBERT FRED SCHEONDIENST

WON	LOST	NAME	POS.		G.	BA	FROM	TO
1	0	ABERNATHY, THEODORE WADE	P		11	+.000	XCHI	XKC A
		ALLEN, RICHARD ANTHONY	1B	79	122	.279	PHI	LA
		(3B38 OF3)						
		BEAUCHAMP, JAMES EDWARD	OF	10	44	+.259	XHOU	B
		(1B5)						
1	2	BERTAINA, FRANK LOUIS	P		8	.143	BALA	C
6	7	BRILES, NELSON KELLEY	P		30	.179	B	PIT
		BROCK, LOUIS CLARK	OF	152	155	.304	B	B
		CAMPBELL, JAMES ROBERT			13	.231	A	C
2	2	CAMPISI, SALVATORE JOHN	P		37	.000	B	MINA
		CARDENAL, JOSE DOMEC	OF	134	148	.293	CLEA	B
10	19	CARLTON, STEVEN NORMAN	P		34	.200	B	B
0	2	CHLUPSA, ROBERT JOSEPH	P		14	.000	A	B
0	4	CLEVELAND, REGINALD LESLIE	P		16	.250	B	B
		CROSBY, EDWARD CARLTON	SS	35	38	.253	A	STL 72
		(2B2 3B3)						
		CRUZ, JOSE	OF	4	6	.353	A	B
3	3	CULVER, GEORGE RAYMOND	P		11	+.176	CIN	XHOU
		DAVALILLO, VICTOR JOSE	OF	54	111	.311	B	PIT
		DA VANON, FRANK GERALD (GERRY)	3B	5	11	.111	B	BALA
		(2B3)						
		GAGLIANO, PHILIP JOSEPH	3B	6	18	+.188	B	XCHI
		(1B3 2B2)						
23	7	GIBSON, ROBERT	P	34	40	.303	B	B
1	1	GUZMAN, SANTIAGO DONOVAN	P		8	.200	B	B
		HAGUE, JOE CLARENCE (OF52)	1B	82	139	.271	B	B
0	0	HARTENSTEIN, CHARLES OSCAR	P		6	+.000	XPIT	XBOSA
0	4	HILGENDORF, THOMAS EUGENE	P		23	.000	B	CLEA72
2	1	HRABOSKY, ALAN THOMAS	P		16	.000	A	B
		JAVIER, MANUEL JULIAN	2B	137	139	.251	B	B
2	0	JOHNSON, JERRY MICHAEL	P		7	+.000	PHI	XSF
		KENNEDY, JAMES EARL (2B5)	SS	7	12	.125	A	C
		LEE, LERON	OF	77	121	.227	B	B
3	5	LINZY, FRANK ALFRED	P		47	+.000	XSF	B
		MAXVILL, CHARLES DALLAN (DAL)	SS	136	152	.201	B	B
		(2B22)						
0	3	MC COOL, WILLIAM JOHN	P		18	.000	SD	C
		MELENDEZ, LUIS ANTONIO	OF	18	21	.300	A	B
0	0	NORMAN, FREDIE HUBERT	P		1	+.000	XLA	B
		NOSSEK, JOSEPH RUDOLPH			1	.000	B	C
0	0	NYE, RICHARD RAYMOND	P		6	+.500	CHI	XMON
1	1	PARKER, HARRY WILLIAM	P		7	.250	A	B
		RAMIEREZ, MILTON (3B1)	SS	59	62	.190	A	B
7	8	REUSS, JERRY	P		20	.050	B	B
		ROJAS, OCTAVIO (COOKIE)	2B	10	23	.106	PHI	XKC A
		(SS2 OF3)						
		ROQUE, JORGE	OF	1	5	.000	A	B
		SHANNON, THOMAS MICHAEL (MIKE)	3B	51	55	.213	B	C
		SIMMONS, TED LYLES	C	79	82	.243	B	B
		TAYLOR, CARL MEANS	OF	46	104	.249	PIT	PIT
		(1B15 3B1)						
6	7	TAYLOR, CHARLES GILBERT	P		56	.115	B	B
		TORRE, JOSEPH PAUL	C	90	161	.325	B	B
		(1B1 3B73)						
8	10	TORREZ, MICHAEL AUGUSTINE	P		30	.270	B	B
		ZELLER, BARTON WALLACE	C		1	.000	A	C

WON 90
LOST 72
TIED 1
TG 163

NATIONAL LEAGUE

1971.

FINISHED 2 E

PCT. .556

SAINT LOUIS

ALBERT FRED SCHEONDIENST

WON	LOST	NAME	POS.		G.	BA	FROM	TO
		ALOU, MATEO ROJAS (1B57)	OF	94	149	.315	PIT	B
0	1	ARROYO, RUDOLPH	P		9	.000	A	C
		BEAUCHAMP, JAMES EDWARD	1B	44	77	.235	B	NY
		(OF1)						
		BROCK, LOUIS CLARK	OF		157	.313	B	B
0	1	BRUNET, GEORGE STUART	P		7	.333	PIT	C
		BURDA, EDWARD ROBERT (BOB)	1B	13	65	.296	MILA	BOSA
		(OF1)						
		CARDENAL, JOSE DOMEC	OF	83	89	.243	B	XMILA
20	9	CARLTON, STEVEN NORMAN	P		37	.177	B	PHI
0	0	CHLUPSA, ROBERT JOSEPH	P		1	.000	B	C
12	12	CLEVELAND, REGINALD LESLIE	P		34	.171	B	B
		CRUZ, JOSE	OF		83	.274	B	B
6	1	DRABOWSKY, MYRON WALTER (MOE)	P		51	.167	BALA	B
16	13	GIBSON, ROBERT	P		31	.172	B	B
0	0	GUZMAN, SANTIAGO DONOVAN	P		2	.000	B	B
		HAGUE, JOE CLARENCE (OF36)	1B	91	129	.226	B	B
1	0	HIGGINS, DENNIS DEAN	P		3	.000	CLEA	B
0	0	HRABOSKY, ALAN THOMAS	P		1	.000	B	B
0	0	JACKSON, MICHAEL WARREN	P		1	.000	PHI	KC A
		JAVIER, MANUEL JULIAN (3B1)	2B	80	90	.259	B	CIN
		KUBIAK, THEODORE RODGER	SS	17	32	.250	XMILA	TEXA
		(2B14)						
		LEE, LERON	OF	8	25	+.179	B	XSD
4	3	LINZY, FRANK ALFRED	P		50	.500	B	MILA
		MAXVILL, CHARLES DALLAN (DAL)	SS	140	142	.225	B	B
		MC NERTNEY, GERALD EDWARD	C	36	56	.289	MILA	B
		MELENDEZ, LUIS ANTONIO	OF	66	88	.225	B	B
0	0	NORMAN, FREDIE HUBERT	P		4	+.000	B	XSD
0	0	PARKER, HARRY WILLIAM	P		4	.000	B	C
0	1	PATTERSON, DARYL ALAN	P		13	.000	XOAKA	C
		RAMIEREZ, MILTON	SS		4	.273	B	C
14	14	REUSS, JERRY	P		36	.123	B	HOU
0	0	REYNOLDS, ROBERT ALLEN	P		4	.000	MON 69	XMILA
		ROQUE, JORGE	OF		3	.300	B	B
0	2	SANTORINI, ALAN JOEL	P		19	+.300	XSD	B
		SCHOFIELD, JOHN RICHARD (DICK)	SS	17	34	.217	XMILA	C
		(2B13 3B3)						
7	2	SHAW, DONALD WELLINGTON	P		45	.000	MON 69	B
		SIMMONS, TED LYLES	C	130	133	.304	B	B
		SIZEMORE, TED CRAWFORD	2B	93	135	.264	LA	B
		(SS39 3B1 OF15)						
		STINSON, GORRELL ROBERT	C	6	17	.211	LA	HOU
		(OF3)						
3	1	TAYLOR, CHARLES GILBERT	P		43	.167	B	NY
		TORRE, JOSEPH PAUL	3B		161	.363	B	B
1	2	TORREZ, MICHAEL AUGUSTINE	P		9	+.143	B	XMON
3	0	WILLIAMS, STANLEY WILSON	P		10	.000	XMINA	BOSA
3	10	ZACHARY, WILLIAM CHRIS	P	23	24	.242	KC A69	DETA

WON 75
LOST 81
TIED 0
TG 156

NATIONAL LEAGUE

1972.

FINISHED 4 E

PCT. .481

SAINT LOUIS

ALBERT FRED SCHEONDIENST

WON	LOST	NAME	POS.		G.	BA	FROM	TO
		ALLEN, RONALD FREDERICK	1B	5	7	.091	A	
		ALOU, MATEO ROJAS (OF39)	1B	66	108	.314	B	XOAKA
		ALYEA, GARRABRANT RYERSON	OF	3	13	.158	XOAKA	
		ANDERSON, DWAIN CLEAVEN	SS	43	57	.267	XOAKA	
		(2B1 3B13)						
0	1	BARE, RAYMOND DOUGLAS	P		14	.000	A	
1	3	BIBBY, JAMES BLAIR	P		6	.125	A	
		BROCK, LOUIS CLARK	OF	149	153	.311	B	
		CARBO, BERNARDO (3B1)	OF	92	99	+.258	XCIN	
0	1	CLEMONS, LANCE LEVIS	P		3	.000	KC A	
		CLENDENON, DONN ALVIN	1B	36	61	.191	NY	
14	15	CLEVELAND, REGINALD LESLIE	P		33	.239	B	
0	2	CLONINGER, TONY LEE	P		17	.000	CIN	
		CROSBY, EDWARD CARLTON	SS	43	101	.217	STL 70	
		(2B38 3B14)						
		CRUZ, JOSE	OF	102	117	.235	B	
1	1	CUMBERLAND, JOHN SHELDON	P		14	+.000	XSF	
1	1	DRABOWSKY, MYRON WALTER (MOE)	P		30	.000	B	XCHIA
2	7	DURHAM, DONALD GARY	P	10	14	.500	A	
		FIORE, MICHAEL GARRY JOSEPH	1B	6	17	+.100	BOSA	XSD
		(OF1)						
1	0	FOLKERS, RICHARD NEVIN	P		9	.000	NY 70	
19	11	GIBSON, ROBERT	P		34	.194	B	
1	0	GRZENDA, JOSEPH CHARLES	P		30	.000	WASA	
0	0	GUZMAN, SANTIAGO DONOVAN	P		1	.000	B	
		HAGUE, JOE CLARENCE (OF3)	1B	22	27	+.237	B	XCIN
1	2	HIGGINS, DENNIS DEAN	P		15	.000	B	
1	0	HRABOSKY, ALAN THOMAS	P		5	.000	B	
1	0	HUDSON, CHARLES	P		12	.000	A	
		JUTZE, ALFRED HENRY (SKIP)	C	17	21	.239	A	
		KELLEHER, MICHAEL DENNIS	SS		23	.159	A	
		MARTINEZ, ORLANDO (MARTY)	SS	3	9	.429	HOU	XOAKA
		(2B2 3B1)						
		MAXVILL, CHARLES DALLAN (DAL)	SS	95	105	.221	B	XOAKA
		(2B11)						
		MC NERTNEY, GERALD EDWARD	C	10	39	.208	B	
		MELENDEZ, LUIS ANTONIO	OF	105	118	.238	B	
0	3	PALMER, LOWELL RAYMOND	P	16	17	.000	PHI	XCLEA
0	0	PLODINEC, TIMOTHY ALFRED	P		1	.000	A	
		REITZ, KENNETH JOHN	3B	20	21	.359	A	
		ROQUE, JORGE	OF	24	32	.104	B	
8	11	SANTORINI, ALAN JOEL	P		30	.075	B	
3	1	SEGUI, DIEGO PABLO	P		33	.143	XOAKA	
0	1	SHAW, DONALD WELLINGTON	P		8	.000	B	XOAKA
		SIMMONS, TED LYLES (1B15)	C	135	152	.303	B	
		SIZEMORE, TED CRAWFORD	2B	111	120	.264	B	
5	5	SPINKS, SCIPIO RONALD	P	16	21	.167	HOU	
		STEIN, WILLIAM ALLEN (OF4)	3B	4	14	.314	A	
		TORRE, JOSEPH PAUL (1B27)	3B	117	149	.289	B	
		TYSON, MICHAEL RAY (SS2)	2B	11	13	.189	A	
		VOSS, WILLIAM EDWARD	OF	2	11	.267	XOAKA	
16	16	WISE, RICHARD CHARLES	P		35	.172	PHI	

CLUB RECORD

NATIONAL LEAGUE

SAN DIEGO

NEW CLUB ADDED IN EXPANSION OF 1969

YEAR	TG	WON	LOST	TIED	PCT.	FINISHED	MANAGER
1969	162	52	110	0	.321	6W (LAST)	PEDRO MARTINEZ GOMEZ
1970	162	63	99	0	.389	6W (LAST)	PEDRO MARTINEZ GOMEZ
1971	161	61	100	0	.379	6W (LAST)	PEDRO MARTINEZ GOMEZ
1972	153	58	95	0	.379	6W (LAST)	PEDRO MARTINEZ GOMEZ
							DONALD WILLIAM ZIMMER

WON 52
LOST 110
TIED 0
TG 162

NATIONAL LEAGUE

1969.

FINISHED 6 W (LAST)

PCT. .321

SAN DIEGO

PEDRO MARTINEZ GOMEZ

WON	LOST	NAME	POS.		G.	BA	FROM	TO
		ARCIA, JOSE RAIMUNDO	2B	68	120	.215	CHI	B
		(1B1 SS37 3B8 OF4)						
0	1	ARLIN, STEPHEN RALPH	P		4	.000	A	B
7	2	BALDSCHUN, JACK EDWARD	P		61	.250	CIN 67	B
		BROWN, OLLIE LEE	OF	148	151	.264	SF	B
		CANNIZZARO, CHRISTOPHER JOHN	C	132	134	.220	PIT	B
		COLBERT, NATHAN	1B	134	139	.255	HOU	B
1	3	CORKINS, MICHAEL PATRICK	P		6	.000	A	B
		DA VANON, FRANK GERALD (GERRY)	2B	15	24	+.136	A	XSTL
		(SS7)						
		DAVIS, ARTHUR WILLARD (BILL)	1B	14	31	.175	CLEA66	C
		DEAN, TOMMY DOUGLAS (2B2)	SS	97	101	.176	LA 67	B
1	0	DUKES, THOMAS EARL	P		13	.000	HOU	B
0	1	EVERITT, EDWARD LEON	P	5	6	.000	A	C
		FERRARA, ALFRED JOHN	OF	96	138	.260	LA	B
		GASTON, CLARENCE EDWIN	OF	113	129	.230	ATL 67	B
		GONZALEZ, ANDRES ANTONIO	OF	49	53	+.225	PHI	XATL
		HRINIAK, WALTER JOHN	C	19	31	+.227	XATL	C
4	8	KELLEY, RICHARD ANTHONY	P		27	.106	ATL	SD 71
		KELLY, VAN HOWARD (2B10)	3B	49	73	.244	A	B
		KENDALL, FRED LYN	C	9	10	.154	A	B
7	20	KIRBY, CLAYTON LAWS	P		35	.061	A	B
		KRUG, EVERETT BEN (CHRIS)	C	7	8	.059	CHI 66	C
		LIBRAN, FRANCISCO	SS	9	10	.100	A	C
0	1	MC BEAN, ALVIN O'NEAL	P		1	+.500	PIT	XLA
3	5	MC COOL, WILLIAM JOHN	P		54	.000	CIN	STL
		MORALES, JULIO RUBEN (JERRY)	OF		19	.195	A	B
		MURRELL, IVAN AUGUSTUS (1B2)	OF	72	111	.255	HOU	B
8	17	NIEKRO, JOSEPH FRANKLIN	P	37	38	+.118	XCHI	DETA
		PENA, ROBERTO CESAR	SS	65	139	.250	PHI	OAKA
		(1B12 2B33 3B27)						
5	6	PODRES, JOHN JOSEPH	P		17	.063	DETA67	C
1	2	REBERGER, FRANK BEALL	P		67	.200	CHI	SF
0	3	ROBERTS, DAVID ARTHUR	P	22	23	.267	A	B
		ROBLES, RAFAEL ORLANDO	SS		6	.100	A	B
3	12	ROSS, GARY DOUGLAS	P		46	+.000	XCHI	B
		RUBERTO, JOHN EDWARD	C	15	19	.143	A	CIN 72
8	14	SANTORINI, ALAN JOEL	P		32	.111	ATL	B
2	2	SELMA, RICHARD JAY	P		4	+.286	NY	XCHI
		SIPIN, JOHN WHITE	2B	60	68	.223	A	C
2	13	SISK, TOMMIE WAYNE	P		53	.120	PIT	CHIA
		SLOCUM, RONALD REECE	2B	4	13	.292	A	B
		(SS1 3B4)						
		SPIEZIO, EDWARD WAYNE (OF1)	3B	98	121	.234	STL	B
		STAHL, LARRY FLOYD (1B13)	OF	37	95	.198	NY	B
		WILLIAMS, JAMES ALFRED	OF	6	13	.280	A	B

NEW CLUB ADDED IN EXPANSION OF 1969.

WON 63
LOST 99
TIED 0
TG 162

NATIONAL LEAGUE

1970.

FINISHED 6 W (LAST)

PCT. .389

SAN DIEGO

PEDRO MARTINEZ GOMEZ

WON	LOST	NAME	POS.		G.	BA	FROM	TO
		ARCIA, JOSE RAIMUNDO	SS	67	114	.223	B	C
		(2B20 3B9 OF7)						
1	0	ARLIN, STEPHEN RALPH	P		2	.000	B	B
1	0	BALDSCHUN, JACK EDWARD	P		12	.000	B	C
		BARTON, ROBERT WILBUR	C	59	61	.218	SF	B
		BROWN, OLLIE LEE	OF	137	139	.292	B	B
		CAMPBELL, DAVID WILSON	2B	153	154	.219	DETA	B
		CANNIZZARO, CHRISTOPHER JOHN	C	110	111	.279	B	B
		COLBERT, NATHAN (3B1)	1B	153	156	.259	B	B
10	14	COOMBS, DANIEL BERNARD	P		35	.096	HOU	B
5	6	CORKINS, MICHAEL PATRICK	P	24	25	.216	B	B
		DEAN, TOMMY DOUGLAS	SS	55	61	.222	B	B
14	15	DOBSON, PATRICK EDWARD	P		40	.141	DETA	BALA
0	2	DOYLE, PAUL SINNOTT	P		9	.000	XCALA	CALA72
1	6	DUKES, THOMAS EARL	P		53	.000	B	BALA
		FERRARA, ALFRED JOHN	OF	96	138	.277	B	B
		GASTON, CLARENCE EDWIN	OF	142	146	.318	B	B
7	5	HERBEL, RONALD SAMUEL	P		64	+.000	SF	XNY
		HUNTZ, STEPHEN MICHAEL (3B51)	SS	57	106	.219	STL	CHIA
		KELLY, VAN HOWARD (2B1)	3B	27	38	.169	B	C
		KENDALL, FRED LYN	C	2	4	.000	B	B
		(1B1 OF1)						
10	16	KIRBY, CLAYTON LAWS	P		36	.149	B	B
		MORALES, JULIO RUBEN (JERRY)	OF	26	28	.155	B	B
		MURRELL, IVAN AUGUSTUS (1B1)	OF	101	125	.245	B	B
0	2	NYMAN, GERALD SMITH	P	2	3	.000	CHIA	C
8	14	ROBERTS, DAVID ARTHUR	P		43	.153	B	B
		ROBINSON, DAVID TANNER	OF	13	15	.316	A	B
		ROBLES, RAFAEL ORLANDO	SS		23	.213	B	SD 72
0	0	RODRIGUEZ, ROBERTO MUNOZ	P		10	+.000	XOAKA	XCHI
2	3	ROSS, GARY DOUGLAS	P		33	.500	B	B
1	8	SANTORINI, ALAN JOEL	P		21	.000	B	B
		SLOCUM, RONALD REECE	C	19	60	.141	B	B
		(2B9 SS17 3B11)						
		SPIEZIO, EDWARD WAYNE	3B	93	110	.285	B	B
		STAHL, LARRY FLOYD	OF	20	52	.182	B	B
		WEBSTER, RAMON ALBERTO (OF1)	1B	15	95	.259	OAKA	B
		WILLIAMS, JAMES ALFRED	OF	6	11	.286	B	C
2	2	WILLIS, RONALD EARL	P		42	.000	HOU	C
1	6	WILSON, ROBERT EARL	P		15	.059	XDETA	C

WON 61
LOST 100
TIED 0
TG 161

NATIONAL LEAGUE

1971.

FINISHED 6 W (LAST)

PCT. .379

SAN DIEGO

PEDRO MARTINEZ GOMEZ

WON	LOST	NAME	POS.		G.	BA	FROM	TO
3	3	ACOSTA, EDUARDO ELIXBET	P		8	.000	PIT	B
9	19	ARLIN, STEPHEN RALPH	P		36	.123	B	B
		BARTON, ROBERT WILBUR	C	119	121	.250	B	B
		BRAVO, ANGEL ALFONSO	OF	9	52	+.155	XCIN	C
		BROWN, OLLIE LEE	OF	134	145	.273	B	B
1	0	CALDWELL, RALPH MICHAEL (MIKE)	P		6	1.000	A	B
		CAMPBELL, DAVID WILSON	2B	69	108	.227	B	B
		(1B2 SS4 3B40 OF2)						
		CANNIZZARO, CHRISTOPHER JOHN	C	19	21	+.190	B	XCHI
		COLBERT, NATHAN	1B	153	156	.264	B	B
1	6	COOMBS, DANIEL BERNARD	P		19	.214	B	C
0	0	CORKINS, MICHAEL PATRICK	P		8	.000	B	B
		DEAN, TOMMY DOUGLAS	SS	28	41	.114	B	C
		(2B1 3B11)						
		FERRARA, ALFRED JOHN	OF	2	17	+.118	B	XCIN
0	1	FRANKLIN, JOHN WM. (JAY)	P		3	.000	A	C
		GASPAR, RODNEY EARL	OF	2	16	.118	NY	C
		GASTON, CLARENCE EDWIN	OF	133	141	.228	B	B
		HERNANDEZ, ENZO OCTAVIO	SS		143	.222	A	B
		IVIE, MICHAEL WILSON	C		6	.471	A	C
		JESTADT, GARRY ARTHUR	3B	49	75	+.291	XCHI	B
		(2B23 SS1)						
		JETER, JOHN	OF	17	18	.320	PIT	B
2	3	KELLEY, RICHARD ANTHONY	P		48	.333	SD 69	C
		KENDALL, FRED LYN	C	39	49	.171	B	B
		(1B1 3B1)						
15	13	KIRBY, CLAYTON LAWS	P	38	40	.093	B	B
0	2	LAXTON, WILLIAM HARRY	P		18	.000	PHI	C
		LEE, LERON	OF	68	79	+.273	XSTL	B
		MASON, DONALD STETSON (3B3)	2B	90	113	.212	SF	B
7	3	MILLER, ROBERT LANE	P		38	+.000	XCHI	XPIT
		MORALES, JULIO RUBEN (JERRY)	OF	7	12	.118	B	B
		MURRELL, IVAN AUGUSTUS	OF	72	103	.235	B	B
3	12	NORMAN, FREDIE HUBERT	P	20	25	+.237	XSTL	B
3	11	PHOEBUS, THOMAS HAROLD	P		29	.167	BALA	B
14	17	ROBERTS, DAVID ARTHUR	P	37	38	.221	B	HOU
		ROBINSON, DAVID TANNER			7	.000	B	C
1	3	ROSS, GARY DOUGLAS	P		13	.000	B	B
0	2	SANTORINI, ALAN JOEL	P		18	+.400	B	XSTL
2	5	SEVERINSEN, ALBERT HENRY	P		59	.000	BALA69	B
		SLOCUM, RONALD REECE	3B	6	7	.000	B	C
		SPIEZIO, EDWARD WAYNE (OF1)	3B	91	97	.231	B	B
		STAHL, LARRY FLOYD (1B7)	OF	75	114	.253	B	B
		WEBSTER, RAMON ALBERTO			10	.125	B	XOAKA

WON 58
LOST 95
TIED 0
TG 153

NATIONAL LEAGUE — 1972. — SAN DIEGO

FINISHED 6 W (LAST)
PCT. .379

PEDRO MARTINEZ GOMEZ DONALD WILLIAM ZIMMER

WON	LOST	NAME	POS.		G.	BA	FROM	TO
3	6	ACOSTA, EDUARDO ELIXBET	P		46	.083	B	
10	21	ARLIN, STEPHEN RALPH	P		38	.153	B	
		BARTON, ROBERT WILBUR	C		29	.193	B	
		BLEFARY, CURTIS LEROY	C	12	74	.196	XOAKA	
		(1B6 3B3 OF3)						
		BROWN, OLLIE LEE	OF	17	23	.171	B	XOAKA
7	11	CALDWELL, RALPH MICHAEL (MIKE)	P		42	.140	B	
		CAMPBELL, DAVID WILSON (2B1)	3B	31	33	.240	B	
		COLBERT, NATHAN	1B	150	151	.250	B	
6	9	CORKINS, MICHAEL PATRICK	P		47	.237	B	
		CORRALES, PATRICK	C	43	44	+.193	XCIN	
		ELLIOTT, RANDY LEE	OF	13	14	.204	A	
		FIORE, MICHAEL GARRY JOSEPH			7	+.000	XSTL	
0	0	GARCIA, RALPH	P		3	.000	A	
		GASTON, CLARENCE EDWIN	OF	94	111	.269	B	
		GODDARD, JOSEPH HAROLD	C		12	.200	A	
5	16	GREIF, WILLIAM BRILEY	P		34	.030	HOU	
		GRUBB, JOHN MAYWOOD	OF	6	7	.333	A	
		HERNANDEZ, ENZO OCTAVIO	SS	107	114	.195	B	
		(OF3)						
		HILTON, JOHN DAVID	3B		13	.213	A	
		JESTADT, GARRY ARTHUR	2B	48	92	.246	B	
		(SS3 3B25)						
		JETER, JOHN	OF	91	110	.221	B	
		KENDALL, FRED LYN (1B1)	C	82	91	.216	B	
0	0	KILKENNY, MICHAEL DAVID	P		5	.000	XOAKA	XCLEA
12	14	KIRBY, CLAYTON LAWS	P	34	35	.068	B	
		LEE, LERON	OF	96	101	.300	B	
		MASON, DONALD STETSON	2B	3	9	.182	B	
		MORALES, JULIO RUBEN (JERRY)	OF	96	115	.239	B	
		(3B4)						
		MURRELL, IVAN AUGUSTUS	OF	1	5	.143	B	
9	11	NORMAN, FREDIE HUBERT	P	42	43	.125	B	
0	1	PHOEBUS, THOMAS HAROLD	P		1	+.000	B	XCHI
		ROBERTS, DAVID WAYNE	3B	84	100	.244	A	
		(C1 2B20 SS3)						
		ROBLES, RAFAEL ORLANDO (3B1)	SS	15	18	.167	SD 70	
4	3	ROSS, GARY DOUGLAS	P		60	.154	B	
2	0	SCHAEFFER, MARK PHILIP	P		41	.000	A	
0	1	SEVERINSEN, ALBERT HENRY	P		17	.000	B	
0	2	SIMPSON, STEVEN EDWARD	P		9	.000	A	
		SPIEZIO, EDWARD WAYNE	3B	5	20	.138	B	XCHIA
		STAHL, LARRY FLOYD (1B1)	OF	76	107	.226	B	
		STANLEY, FREDERICK BLAIR	2B	21	39	.200	XCLEA	
		(SS17 3B4)						
0	0	TAYLOR, RONALD WESLEY	P		4	.000	NY	
		THOMAS, DERRELL OSBON	2B	83	130	.230	HOU	
		(SS49 OF3)						

WON 95
LOST 67
TIFD 1
TG 163

NATIONAL LEAGUE — 1965. — FINISHED 2 — PCT. .586

SAN FRANCISCO

HERMAN LOUIS FRANKS

WON	LOST	NAME	POS.		G.	BA	FROM	TO
		ALOU, JESUS MARIA ROJAS	OF	136	143	.298	B	B
0	0	ALOU, MATEO ROJAS (P1)	OF	103	117	.231	B	PIT
		BAILEY, LONAS EDGAR (ED)	C	12	24	+.107	MIL	XCHI
		(1B2)						
		BARTON, ROBFRT WILBUR	C	2	4	.571	A	B
		BERTELL, RICHARD GEORGE	C		22	+.188	XCHI	CHI 67
14	6	BOLIN, BOBBY DONALD	P		45	.167	B	B
		BROWN, OLLIE LEE	OF	4	6	.200	A	B
		BURDA, EDWARD ROBERT (BOB)	1B	11	31	.111	STL 62	B
		(OF1)						
		CEPEDA, ORLANDO MANUEL (OF2)	1B	4	33	.176	B	B
		DAVENPORT, JAMES HOUSTON	3B	39	106	.251	B	B
		(2B26 SS37)						
0	1	DUFFALO, JAMES FRANCIS	P		2	+.000	B	XCIN
0	0	ESTELLE, RICHARD HENRY	P		6	.000	B	C
		FUENTES, RIGOBERTO (TITO)	SS	18	26	.208	A	B
		(2B7 3B1)						
		GABRIFLSON, LEONARD GARY	OF	77	88	+.301	XCHI	B
		(1B5)						
		HALLER, THOMAS FRANK	C	133	134	.251	B	B
0	2	HANDS, WILLIAM ALFRED	P		4	.000	A	CHI
		HART, JAMES RAY (OF15)	3B	144	160	.299	B	B
		HENDERSON, KENNETH JOSEPH	OF	48	63	.192	A	B
0	0	HENDLEY, CHARLES ROBERT (BOB)	P		8	+.000	B	XCHI
2	2	HENRY, WILLIAM RODMAN	P		35	+.200	XCIN	B
12	9	HERBEL, RONALD SAMUEL	P		47	.020	B	B
		HIATT, JACK E. (1B7)	C	21	40	.284	LA A	B
		HILLER, CHARLES JOSEPH	2B	2	7	+.143	B	XNY
		HUNDLEY, CECIL RANDOLPH	C		6	.067	B	CHI
		KUENN, HARVEY EDWARD (1B7)	OF	14	23	+.237	B	XCHI
		LANIER, HAROLD CLIFTON (SS1)	2B	158	159	.226	B	B
9	3	LINZY, FRANK ALFRED	P		57	.222	SF 63	B
22	13	MARICHAL, JUAN ANTONIO	P		39	.173	B	B
		MAYS, WILLIE HOWARD	OF	151	157	.317	B	B
		MC COVFY, WILLIE LEE	1B	156	160	.276	B	B
4	1	MURAKAMI, MASANORI	P		45	.154	B	C
		PAGAN, JOSE ANTONIO	SS		26	+.205	B	XPIT
8	12	PERRY, GAYLORD JACKSON	P	47	49	.156	B	B
		PETERSON, CHARLES ANDREW (CAP)	OF	27	63	.248	B	B
1	0	PRIDDY, ROBERT SIMPSON	P	8	9	.000	PIT	B
4	5	SANFORD, JOHN STANLEY	P		23	.120	B	XCALA
		SCHOFIELD, JOHN RICHARD (DICK)	SS	93	101	+.203	XPIT	B
		SCHRODER, ROBERT JAMES (3B1)	2B	4	31	.222	A	B
16	9	SHAW, ROBERT JOHN	P		42	.101	B	B
3	4	SPAHN, WARREN EDWARD	P		16	+.143	XNY	C

WON 93
LOST 68
TIED 0
TG 161

NATIONAL LEAGUE — 1966. — FINISHED 2 — PCT. .578

SAN FRANCISCO

HERMAN LOUIS FRANKS

WON	LOST	NAME	POS.		G.	BA	FROM	TO
		ALOU, JESUS MARIA ROJAS	OF	100	110	.259	B	B
		BARTON, ROBERT WILBUR	C	39	43	.176	B	B
11	10	BOLIN, BOBBY DONALD	P		36	.171	B	B
		BROWN, OLLIE LEE	OF	114	115	.233	B	B
		BURDA, EDWARD ROBERT (BOB)	1B	7	37	.163	B	SF 69
		(OF4)						
		CEPEDA, ORLANDO MANUEL (1B6)	OF	8	19	+.286	B	XSTL
		DAVENPORT, JAMES HOUSTON	SS	58	111	.249	B	B
		(1B2 2B21 3B36)						
		DIETZ, RICHARD ALLEN	C	6	13	.043	A	B
		FUENTES, RIGOBERTO (TITO)	SS	76	133	.261	B	B
		(2B60)						
		GABRIELSON, LEONARD GARY	OF	67	94	.217	B	CALA
		(1B6)						
0	0	GARIBALDI, ROBERT ROY	P		1	.000	SF 63	SF 69
4	6	GIBBON, JOSEPH CHARLES	P		37	.200	PIT	B
		HALLER, THOMAS FRANK (1B4)	C	136	142	.240	B	B
		HART, JAMES RAY (OF17)	3B	139	156	.285	B	B
		HENDERSON, KENNETH JOSEPH	OF	10	11	.310	B	B
1	1	HENRY, WILLIAM RODMAN	P		35	.000	B	B
4	5	HERBEL, RONALD SAMUEL	P		32	.026	B	B
		HIATT, JACK F.	1B	7	18	.304	B	B
0	2	HOFFT, WILLIAM FREDERICK	P		4	+.000	XCHI	C
		JOHNSON, FRANK HERBERT	OF	13	15	.219	A	B
		LANDRUM, DONALD LEROY	OF	54	72	.186	CHI	C
		LANIER, HAROLD CLIFTON (SS41)	2B	112	149	.231	B	B
7	11	LINZY, FRANK ALFRED	P		51	.150	B	B
25	6	MAFICHAL, JUAN ANTONIO	P		37	.250	B	B
		MASON, DONALD STETSON	2B	9	42	.120	A	B
		MAYS, WILLIE HOWARD	OF	150	152	.288	B	B
		MC COVEY, WILLIE LEE	1B	145	150	.295	B	B
10	5	MC DANIEL, LYNDALL DALE	P		64	.091	CHI	B
21	8	PERRY, GAYLORD JACKSON	P		36	.186	B	B
		PETERSON, CHARLES ANDREW (CAP)	OF	51	89	.237	B	WASA
		(1B2)						
6	3	PRIDDY, ROBERT SIMPSON	P	38	39	.176	B	WASA
0	0	ROBERTSON, RICHARD PAUL	P		1	.000	A	B
3	7	SADECKI, RAYMOND MICHAEL	P		26	+.324	XSTL	B
		SCHOFIELD, JOHN RICHARD (DICK)	SS	8	11	.063	B	XNY A
		SCHRODER, ROBERT JAMES	SS	9	10	.242	B	B
1	4	SHAW, ROBERT JOHN	P		13	+.000	B	XNY
		VIRGIL, OSVALDO JOSE	C	13	42	.213	PIT	SF 69
		(1B5 2B2 3B13 OF2)						

WON 91 | LOST 71 | TIED 0 | TG 162

NATIONAL LEAGUE — 1967. — FINISHED 2 — PCT. .562

SAN FRANCISCO

HERMAN LOUIS FRANKS

WON	LOST	NAME	POS.	G.	BA	FROM	TO
		ALOU, JESUS MARIA ROJAS	OF 123	129	.292	B	B
		BARTON, ROBERT WILBUR	C	7	.211	B	B
6	8	BOLIN, BOBBY DONALD	P	37	.242	B	B
		BROWN, OLLIE LEE	OF 115	120	.267	B	B
0	0	BRYANT, RONALD RAYMOND	P	1	.000	A	SF 69
1	0	CHAVEZ, NESTOR ISAIAS	P	2	.000	A	C
		CLINE, TYRONE ALEXANDER	OF 37	64	+.270	XATL	B
		DAVENPORT, JAMES HOUSTON	3B 64	124	.275	B	B
		(2B12 SS28)					
		DIETZ, RICHARD ALLEN	C 43	56	.225	B	B
		ETHERIDGE, BOBBY LAMAR	3B 37	40	.226	A	SF 69
		FUENTES, RIGOBERTO (TITO)	2B 130	133	.209	B	SF 69
		(SS5)					
6	2	GIBBON, JOSEPH CHARLES	P	28	.042	B	B
		GROAT, RICHARD MORROW (2B1)	SS 24	34	+.171	XPHI	C
		GUTIERREZ, CESAR DARIO (2B1)	SS 15	18	.143	A	SF 69
		HALLER, THOMAS FRANK (OF1)	C 136	141	.251	B	LA
		HART, JAMES RAY (OF72)	3B 89	158	.289	B	B
		HENDERSON, KENNETH JOSEPH	OF 52	65	.190	B	B
2	0	HENRY, WILLIAM RODMAN	P	28	.000	B	B
4	5	HERBEL, RONALD SAMUEL	P	42	.107	B	B
		HIATT, JACK E.	1B 36	73	.275	B	B
		(C3 OF2)					
		JOHNSON, FRANK HERBERT	OF 3	8	.300	B	B
		LANIER, HAROLD CLIFTON (2B34)	SS 137	151	.213	B	B
7	7	LINZY, FRANK ALFRED	P	57	.000	B	B
14	10	MARICHAL, JUAN ANTONIO	P	26	.177	B	B
		MARSHALL, DAVID LEWIS		1	.000	A	B
		MASON, DONALD STETSON	2B 2	4	.000	B	B
		MAYS, WILLIE HOWARD	OF 134	141	.263	B	B
22	10	MC CORMICK, MICHAEL FRANCIS	P 40	41	.119	WASA	B
		MC COVEY, WILLIE LEE	1B 127	135	.276	B	B
2	6	MC DANIEL, LYNDALL DALE	P	41	.091	B	B
15	17	PERRY, GAYLORD JACKSON	P 39	42	.143	B	B
0	0	ROBERTSON, RICHARD PAUL	P	1	.000	B	B
12	6	SADECKI, RAYMOND MICHAEL	P 35	37	.247	B	B
		SCHRODER, ROBERT JAMES (3B4)	2B 45	62	.230	B	B
		SIEBERN, NORMAN LEROY (OF2)	1B 15	46	.155	CALA	XBOSA
		SORRELL, WILLIAM	OF 5	18	.176	PHI 65	KC A70

WON 88 | LOST 74 | TIED 1 | TG 163

NATIONAL LEAGUE — 1968. — FINISHED 2 — PCT. .543

SAN FRANCISCO

HERMAN LOUIS FRANKS

WON	LOST	NAME	POS.	G.	BA	FROM	TO
		ALOU, JESUS MARIA ROJAS	OF 105	120	.263	B	HOU
		BARTON, ROBERT WILBUR	C 45	46	.261	B	B
10	5	BOLIN, BOBBY DONALD	P	34	.091	B	B
		BONDS, BOBBY LEE	OF 80	81	.254	A	B
		BROWN, OLLIE LEE	OF 35	40	.232	B	SD
		CLINE, TYRONE ALEXANDER	OF 70	116	.223	B	MON
		(1B24)					
		DAVENPORT, JAMES HOUSTON	3B 82	113	.224	B	B
		(2B1 SS17)					
		DIETZ, RICHARD ALLEN	C 90	98	.272	B	B
1	2	GIBBON, JOSEPH CHARLES	P	29	.000	B	B
		HART, JAMES RAY (OF65)	3B 72	136	.258	B	B
		HENDERSON, KENNETH JOSEPH	OF 2	3	.333	B	B
0	2	HENRY, WILLIAM RODMAN	P	7	+.000	B	XPIT
0	0	HERBEL, RONALD SAMUEL	P	28	.000	B	B
		HIATT, JACK E. (1B10)	C 58	90	.232	B	B
		HUNT, RONALD KENNETH	2B 147	148	.250	LA	B
		JOHNSON, FRANK HERBERT	3B 36	67	.190	B	B
		(2B3 SS5 OF8)					
		LANIER, HAROLD CLIFTON	SS 150	151	.206	B	B
9	8	LINZY, FRANK ALFRED	P	57	.000	B	B
26	9	MARICHAL, JUAN ANTONIO	P	38	.163	B	B
		MARSHALL, DAVID LEWIS	OF 50	76	.264	B	B
		MASON, DONALD STETSON	2B 5	10	.158	B	B
		(SS4 3B2)					
		MAYS, WILLIE HOWARD (1B1)	OF 142	148	.289	B	B
12	14	MC CORMICK, MICHAEL FRANCIS	P	38	.103	B	B
		MC COVEY, WILLIE LEE	1B 146	148	.293	B	B
0	0	MC DANIEL, LYNDALL DALE	P	12	.000	B	XNY A
0	1	MONBOQUETTE, WILLIAM CHARLES	P	7	.000	XNY A	C
		OLIVER, NATHANIEL (PEEWEE)	2B 14	36	.178	LA	NY A
		(SS13 3B1)					
16	15	PERRY, GAYLORD JACKSON	P	39	.113	B	B
2	0	ROBERTSON, RICHARD PAUL	P	3	.500	B	B
12	18	SADECKI, RAYMOND MICHAEL	P 38	43	.094	B	B
		SCHRODER, ROBERT JAMES	2B 12	35	.159	B	C
		(SS4 3B2)					

WON 90
LOST 72
TIED 0
TG 162

NATIONAL LEAGUE FINISHED 2 W

1969. PCT. .556

SAN FRANCISCO

CLYDE EDWARD KING

WON	LOST	NAME	POS.		G.	BA	FROM	TO
		BARTON, ROBERT WILBUR	C		49	.170	B	SD
7	7	BOLIN, BOBBY DONALD	P		30	.154	B	MILA
		BONDS, BOBBY LEE	OF	155	158	.259	B	B
4	3	BRYANT, RONALD RAYMOND	P		16	.188	SF 67	B
		BURDA, EDWARD ROBERT (BOB) (OF19)	1B	45	97	.230	SF 66	B
		DAVENPORT, JAMES HOUSTON (1B1 SS1 OF1)	3B	104	112	.241	B	B
0	0	DAVISON, MICHAEL LYNN	P		1	.000	A	B
		DIETZ, RICHARD ALLEN	C	73	79	.230	B	B
		ETHERIDGE, BOBBY LAMAR (SS1)	3B	39	56	.260	SF 67	C
		FOSTER, GEORGE ARTHUR	OF	8	9	.400	A	B
		FUENTES, RIGOBERTO (TITO) (SS30)	3B	36	67	.295	SF 67	B
0	1	GARIBALDI, ROBERT ROY	P		1	.000	SF 66	C
1	3	GIBBON, JOSEPH CHARLES	P		16	+.000	B	XPIT
		GUTIERREZ, CESAR DARIO (SS4)	3B	7	15	.217	SF 67	XDETA
		HARRELL, JOHN ROBERT	C		2	.500	A	C
		HART, JAMES RAY (3B3)	OF	68	95	.254	B	B
		HENDERSON, KENNETH JOSEPH (3B3)	OF	111	113	.225	B	B
4	1	HERBEL, RONALD SAMUEL	P		39	.000	B	SD
		HIATT, JACK E. (1B3)	C	60	69	.196	B	MON
		HUNT, RONALD KENNETH (3B1)	2B	125	128	.262	B	B
		JOHNSON, FRANK HERBERT	OF		7	.100	B	B
0	2	KLINE, RONALD LEE	P		7	+.000	XPIT	XBOSA
		LANIER, HAROLD CLIFTON	SS		150	.228	B	B
14	9	LINZY, FRANK ALFRED	P		58	.267	B	B
21	11	MARICHAL, JUAN ANTONIO	P	37	38	.138	B	B
		MARSHALL, DAVID LEWIS	OF	87	110	.232	B	NY
		MASON, DONALD STETSON (SS7 3B21)	2B	51	104	.228	B	B
		MAYS, WILLIE HOWARD (1B1)	OF	109	117	.283	B	B
11	9	MC CORMICK, MICHAEL FRANCIS	P		32	.136	B	B
		MC COVEY, WILLIE LEE	1B	148	149	.320	B	B
3	1	MC MAHON, DONALD JOHN	P		13	.333	XDETA	B
19	14	PERRY, GAYLORD JACKSON	P		40	.120	B	B
1	3	ROBERTSON, RICHARD PAUL	P		17	.000	B	B
5	8	SADECKI, RAYMOND MICHAEL	P	29	30	.125	B	NY
		STEPHENSON, JOHN HERMAN (3B1)	C	9	22	.222	CHI	B
		VIRGIL, OSVALDO JOSE			1	.000	SF 66	C
		WAGNER, LEON LAMAR	OF	1	11	.333	CHIA	C

WON 86
LOST 76
TIED 0
TG 162

NATIONAL LEAGUE FINISHED 3 W

1970. PCT. .531

SAN FRANCISCO

CLYDE EDWARD KING CHARLES FRANCIS FOX

WON	LOST	NAME	POS.		G.	BA	FROM	TO
		BONDS, BOBBY LEE	OF		157	.302	B	B
5	8	BRYANT, RONALD RAYMOND	P		34	.111	B	B
		BURDA, EDWARD ROBERT (BOB) (OF1)	1B	8	28	.261	B	XMILA
2	1	CARRITHERS, DONALD GEORGE	P		11	.000	A	B
2	0	CUMBERLAND, JOHN SHELDON	P		7	.000	XNY A	B
		DAVENPORT, JAMES HOUSTON	3B	10	22	.243	B	C
3	5	DAVISON, MICHAEL LYNN	P		31	.000	B	C
		DIETZ, RICHARD ALLEN	C	139	148	.300	B	B
0	0	FAUL, WILLIAM ALVAN	P		7	.000	CHI 66	C
		FOSTER, GEORGE ARTHUR	OF	7	9	.316	B	B
		FUENTES, RIGOBERTO (TITO) (SS36 3B24)	2B	78	123	.267	B	B
		GALLAGHER, ALAN MITCHELL	3B	91	109	.266	A	B
		GIBSON, JOHN RUSSELL (RUSS)	C	23	24	.232	BOSA	B
		GOODSON, JAMES EDWARD (ED)	1B	2	7	.273	A	B
		HART, JAMES RAY (OF18)	3B	56	76	.282	B	B
		HEISE, ROBERT LOWELL (2B28 3B2)	SS	33	67	.234	NY	B
		HENDERSON, KENNETH JOSEPH	OF	146	148	.294	B	B
		HUNT, RONALD KENNETH (3B16)	2B	85	117	.281	B	MON
		JOHNSON, FRANK HERBERT (1B27)	OF	33	67	.273	B	B
1	0	JOHNSON, JAMES BRIAN	P		3	.000	A	C
3	4	JOHNSON, JERRY MICHAEL	P		33	+.067	XSTL	B
		LANIER, HAROLD CLIFTON (1B2 2B4)	SS	130	134	.231	B	B
2	1	LINZY, FRANK ALFRED	P		20	+.000	B	XSTL
12	10	MARICHAL, JUAN ANTONIO	P		34	.059	B	B
		MASON, DONALD STETSON	2B	14	46	.139	B	SD
		MAYS, WILLIE HOWARD (1B5)	OF	129	139	.291	B	B
3	4	MC CORMICK, MICHAEL FRANCIS	P		23	.160	B	XNY A
		MC COVEY, WILLIE LEE	1B	146	152	.289	B	B
9	5	MC MAHON, DONALD JOHN	P		61	.143	B	B
23	13	PERRY, GAYLORD JACKSON	P		41	.117	B	B
5	5	PITLOCK, LEE PATRICK	P		18	.080	A	C
1	3	PUENTE, MIGUEL ANTONIO	P		6	.000	A	C
7	8	REBERGER, FRANK BEALL	P	45	48	.234	SD	B
8	9	ROBERTSON, RICHARD PAUL	P		41	.102	B	B
		STEPHENSON, JOHN HERMAN (OF1)	C	9	23	.070	B	CALA
		TAYLOR, ROBERT LEE (C1)	OF	26	63	.190	A	C
		WHITAKER, STEPHEN EDWARD	OF	9	16	.111	SEAA	C
		WILLIAMS, BERNARD	OF	6	7	.313	A	B

WON 90
LOST 72
TIED 0
TG 162

NATIONAL LEAGUE

1971.

SAN FRANCISCO

CHARLES FRANCIS FOX

FINISHED 1 W
(LOST LEAGUE PLAYOFF)
PCT. .556

WON	LOST	NAME	POS.		G.	BA	FROM	TO
		ARNOLD, CHRISTOPHER PAUL	2B	3	6	.231	A	B
1	1	BARR, JAMES LELAND	P		17	.000	A	B
		BONDS, BOBBY LEE	OF	154	155	.288	B	B
7	10	BRYANT, RONALD RAYMOND	P		27	.200	B	B
5	3	CARRITHERS, DONALD GEORGE	P		22	.176	B	B
9	6	CUMBERLAND, JOHN SHELDON	P		45	.119	B	B
		DIETZ, RICHARD ALLEN	C	135	142	.252	B	LA
		DUFFY, FRANK THOMAS	SS	6	21	+.179	XCIN	CLEA
		(2B1 3B1)						
		FOSTER, GEORGE ARTHUR	OF	30	36	+.267	B	XCIN
		FUENTES, RIGOBERTO (TITO)	2B		152	.273	B	B
		GALLAGHER, ALAN MITCHELL	3B	128	136	.277	B	B
		GIBSON, JOHN RUSSELL (RUSS)	C	22	25	.193	B	B
		GOODSON, JAMES EDWARD (ED)	1B	14	20	.190	B	B
2	2	HAMILTON, STEVE ABSHER	P		39	.000	CHIA	CHI
		HART, JAMES RAY (OF3)	3B	3	31	.256	B	B
		HEALY, FRANCIS XAVIER	C	22	47	.280	KC A69	B
		HEISE, ROBERT LOWELL	SS	3	13	.000	B	XMILA
		(2B1 3B2)						
		HENDERSON, KENNETH JOSEPH	OF	138	141	.264	B	B
		(1B1)						
		HOWARTH, JAMES EUGENE	OF	6	7	.231	A	B
		JOHNSON, FRANK HERBERT (OF4)	1B	9	32	.082	B	C
12	9	JOHNSON, JERRY MICHAEL	P		67	.154	B	B
		KINGMAN, DAVID ARTHUR (OF14)	1B	20	41	.278	A	B
		LANIER, HAROLD CLIFTON	3B	83	109	.233	B	NY A
		(1B3 2B13 SS8)						
18	11	MARICHAL, JUAN ANTONIO	P		37	.133	B	B
		MAYS, WILLIE HOWARD (1B48)	OF	84	136	.271	B	B
		MC COVEY, WILLIE LEE	1B	95	105	.277	B	B
10	6	MC MAHON, DONALD JOHN	P		61	.000	B	B
16	12	PERRY, GAYLORD JACKSON	P	37	38	.102	B	CLEA
		RADER, DAVID MARTIN	C	1	3	.000	A	B
3	0	REBERGER, FRANK BEALL	P	13	16	.231	B	B
2	2	ROBERTSON, RICHARD PAUL	P		23	.067	B	C
		ROSARIO, ANGEL RAMON (JIM)	OF	67	92	.224	A	B
		SPEIER, CHRIS EDWARD	SS	156	157	.235	A	B
5	9	STONE, STEVEN MICHAEL	P		24	.000	A	B
		WICKER, FLOYD EULISS	OF	7	9	.143	XMILA	C
		WILLIAMS, BERNARD	OF	27	35	.178	B	B
0	1	WILLOUGHBY, JAMES ARTHUR	P		2	.000	A	B

WON 69
LOST 86
TIED 0
TG 155

NATIONAL LEAGUE

1972.

SAN FRANCISCO

CHARLES FRANCIS FOX

FINISHED 5 W

PCT. .445

WON	LOST	NAME	POS.		G.	BA	FROM	TO
		ARNOLD, CHRISTOPHER PAUL	3B	17	51	.226	B	
		(2B7 SS4)						
8	10	BARR, JAMES LELAND	P		44	.184	B	
		BLANCO, DAMASO (2B3 SS8)	3B	19	39	.350	A	
		BONDS, BOBBY LEE	OF		153	.259	B	
14	7	BRYANT, RONALD RAYMOND	P		35	.171	B	
4	8	CARRITHERS, DONALD GEORGE	P	25	26	.207	B	
0	4	CUMBERLAND, JOHN SHELDON	P		9	+.111	B	XSTL
		FUENTES, RIGOBERTO (TITO)	2B		152	.264	B	
		GALLAGHER, ALAN MITCHELL	3B	69	82	.223	B	
		GIBSON, JOHN RUSSELL (RUSS)	C		5	.167	B	
		GOODSON, JAMES EDWARD (ED)	1B	42	58	.280	B	
		HART, JAMES RAY	3B	20	24	.304	B	
		HEALY, FRANCIS XAVIER	C		45	.152	B	
		HENDERSON, KENNETH JOSEPH	OF	123	130	.257	B	
		HOWARTH, JAMES EUGENE (1B4)	OF	25	74	.235	B	
8	6	JOHNSON, JERRY MICHAEL	P		48	.000	B	
		KINGMAN, DAVID ARTHUR	3B	59	135	.225	B	
		(1B56 OF22)						
		MADDOX, GARRY LEE	OF	121	125	.266	A	
6	16	MARICHAL, JUAN ANTONIO	P		25	.196	B	
		MATTHEWS, GARY NATHANIEL	OF	19	20	.290	A	
		MAYS, WILLIE HOWARD	OF	14	19	+.184	B	XNY
		MC COVEY, WILLIE LEE	1B	74	81	.213	B	
10	8	MC DOWELL, SAMUEL EDWARD	P		28	.119	CLEA	
3	3	MC MAHON, DONALD JOHN	P		44	.250	B	
1	5	MOFFITT, RANDALL JAMES	P		40	.000	A	
0	0	MORRIS, JOHN WALLACE	P		7	.000	MILA	
		RADER, DAVID MARTIN	C	127	133	.259	B	
3	4	REBERGER, FRANK BEALL	P	20	22	.229	B	
		ROSARIO, ANGEL RAMON (JIM)	OF	1	7	.000	B	
0	1	SOSA, ELIAS	P		8	.000	A	
		SPEIER, CHRIS EDWARD	SS		150	.269	B	
6	8	STONE, STEVEN MICHAEL	P		27	.118	B	
		THOMASSON, GARY LEAH (OF2)	1B	7	10	.333	A	
		WILLIAMS, BERNARD	OF	15	46	.191	B	
0	2	WILLIAMS, CHARLES PROSEK	P		3	.000	NY	
6	4	WILLOUGHBY, JAMES ARTHUR	P		11	.185	B	

WON 94 LOST 68 TIED 0 TG 162

AMERICAN LEAGUE

1965.

FINISHED 3

PCT. .580

BALTIMORE

HENRY ALBERT BAUER

WON	LOST	NAME	POS.		G.	BA	FROM	TO
		ADAIR, KENNETH JERRY	2B		157	.259	B	B
		APARICIO, LUIS ERNESTO	SS	141	144	.225	B	B
15	10	BARBER, STEPHEN DAVID	P		37	.077	B	B
0	0	BARNOWSKI, EDWARD ANTHONY	P		4	.000	A	B
		BELANGER, MARK HENRY	SS	4	11	.333	A	B
0	0	BERTAINA, FRANK LOUIS	P		2	.000	B	B
		BLAIR, PAUL L. D.	OF	116	119	.234	B	B
		BLEFARY, CURTIS LEROY	OF	136	144	.260	A	B
		BOWENS, SAMUEL EDWARDS	OF	68	84	.163	B	B
		BRANDT, JOHN GEORGE	OF	84	96	.243	B	PHIN
		BROWN, RICHARD ERNEST	C	92	96	.231	B	C
10	8	BUNKER, WALLACE EDWARD	P		34	.073	B	B
		ETCHEBARREN, ANDREW AUGUSTE	C		5	.167	BAL 62	B
3	2	HADDIX, HARVEY	P		24	.000	B	C
11	8	HALL, RICHARD WALLACE	P	48	49	.333	B	B
		JOHNSON, DAVID ALLEN	3B	9	20	.170	A	B
		(2B3 SS2)						
		JOHNSON, ROBERT WALLACE	1B	34	87	.242	B	B
		(2B5 SS23 3B13)						
0	1	KNOWLES, DAROLD DUANE	P		5	.000	A	PHIN
1	2	LARSEN, DONALD JAMES	P		27	.273	XHOUN	CHIN67
		LAU, CHARLES RICHARD	C	35	68	.295	B	B
11	6	MC NALLY, DAVID ARTHUR	P		35	.092	B	B
6	4	MILLER, JOHN ERNEST	P		16	.100	BAL 63	B
14	7	MILLER, STUART LEONARD	P		67	.063	B	B
		ORSINO, JOHN JOSEPH (1B5)	C	62	77	.233	B	WAS
5	4	PALMER, JAMES ALVIN	P	27	29	.192	A	B
13	9	PAPPAS, MILTON STEPHEN	P		34	.071	B	CINN
		POWELL, JOHN WESLEY (BOOG)	1B	78	144	.248	B	B
		(OF71)						
5	7	ROBERTS, ROBIN EVAN	P		20	.171	B	XHOUN
		ROBINSON, BROOKS CALBERT	3B	143	144	.297	B	B
0	0	ROWE, KENNETH DARRELL	P		6	1.000	B	C
		SIEBERN, NORMAN LEROY	1B	76	106	.256	B	CAL
		SNYDER, RUSSELL HENRY	OF	106	132	.270	B	B
0	0	STARRETTE, HERMAN PAUL	P		4	.000	B	C
		WARWICK, CARL WAYNE	OF	3	9	.000	XSTLN	CHIN

WON 97 LOST 63 TIED 0 TG 160

AMERICAN LEAGUE

1966.

FINISHED 1

PCT. .606

BALTIMORE

HENRY ALBERT BAUER

WON	LOST	NAME	POS.		G.	BA	FROM	TO
		ADAIR, KENNETH JERRY	2B	13	17	+.288	B	XCHI
		APARICIO, LUIS ERNESTO	SS		151	.276	B	B
10	5	BARBER, STEPHEN DAVID	P		25	.068	B	B
0	0	BARNOWSKI, EDWARD ANTHONY	P		2	.000	B	C
		BELANGER, MARK HENRY	SS	6	8	.158	B	B
2	5	BERTAINA, FRANK LOUIS	P		16	.105	B	B
		BLAIR, PAUL L. D.	OF	127	133	.277	B	B
		BLEFARY, CURTIS LEROY (1B20)	OF	109	131	.255	B	B
		BOWENS, SAMUEL EDWARDS	OF	68	89	.210	B	B
4	3	BRABENDER, EUGENE MATTHEW	P		31	.077	A	B
10	6	BUNKER, WALLACE EDWARD	P	29	30	.104	B	B
		CARREON, CAMILO GARCIA	C	3	4	.222	CLE	C
6	0	DRABOWSKY, MYRON WALTER (MOE)	P		44	.364	KC	B
		EPSTEIN, MICHAEL PETER	1B	4	6	.182	A	B
		ETCHEBARREN, ANDREW AUGUSTE	C		121	.221	B	B
5	3	FISHER, EDDIE GENE	P		44	+.154	XCHI	B
6	2	HALL, RICHARD WALLACE	P		32	.167	B	PHIN
		HANEY, WALLACE LARRY	C		20	.161	A	B
		HELD, WOODSON GEORGE	OF	10	56	.207	WAS	B
		(2B5 SS3 3B3)						
		JOHNSON, DAVID ALLEN (SS3)	2B	126	131	.257	B	B
		JOHNSON, ROBERT WALLACE	2B	20	71	.217	B	B
		(1B17 3B3)						
		LAU, CHARLES RICHARD			18	.500	B	B
13	6	MC NALLY, DAVID ARTHUR	P		34	.195	B	B
4	8	MILLER, JOHN ERNEST	P		23	.118	B	B
9	4	MILLER, STUART LEONARD	P		51	.105	B	B
15	10	PALMER, JAMES ALVIN	P	30	36	.096	B	B
2	1	PHOEBUS, THOMAS HAROLD	P		3	.167	A	B
		POWELL, JOHN WESLEY (BOOG)	1B	136	140	.287	B	B
		ROBINSON, BROOKS CALBERT	3B		157	.269	B	B
		ROBINSON, FRANK (1B3)	OF	151	155	.316	CINN	B
		ROZNOVSKY, VICTOR JOSEPH	C	34	41	.237	CHIN	B
2	3	SHORT, WILLIAM ROSS	P		6	+.091	BAL 62	XBOS
		SNYDER, RUSSELL HENRY	OF	104	117	.306	B	B
9	7	WATT, EDWARD DEAN	P		43	.304	A	B

WON 76
LOST 85
TIED 0
TG 161

AMERICAN LEAGUE

1967.

FINISHED 6
(TIED WITH WASHINGTON)
PCT. .472

BALTIMORE

HENRY ALBERT BAUER

WON	LOST	NAME	POS.	G.	BA	FROM	TO
0	1	ADAMSON, JOHN MICHAEL (MIKE)	P	3	.500	A	B
		APARICIO, LUIS ERNESTO	SS 131	134	.233	B	CHI
4	9	BARBER, STEPHEN DAVID	P	15	+.091	B	XNY
		BELANGER, MARK HENRY	SS 38	69	.174	B	B
		(2B26 3B2)					
1	1	BERTAINA, FRANK LOUIS	P	5	+.111	B	XWAS
		BLAIR, PAUL L. D.	OF 146	151	.293	B	B
		BLEFARY, CURTIS LEROY (1B52)	OF 103	155	.242	B	B
		BOWENS, SAMUEL EDWARDS	OF 32	62	.183	B	WAS
6	4	BRABENDER, EUGENE MATTHEW	P	14	.071	B	B
3	7	BUNKER, WALLACE EDWARD	P	29	.077	B	B
0	1	BUZHARDT, JOHN WILLIAM	P	7	+.000	XCHI	XHOUN
5	9	DILLMAN, WILLIAM HOWARD	P 32	33	.161	A	MONN70
7	5	DRABOWSKY, MYRON WALTER (MOE)	P	43	.350	B	B
		EPSTEIN, MICHAEL PETER	1B 3	9	+.154	B	XWAS
		ETCHEBARREN, ANDREW AUGUSTE	C 110	112	.215	B	B
4	3	FISHER, EDDIE GENE	P	46	.200	B	CLE
0	0	FISHER, THOMAS GENE	P	2	.000	A	C
0	0	GILLIFORD, PAUL GANT	P	2	.000	A	C
		HANEY, WALLACE LARRY	C 57	58	.268	B	B
8	3	HARDIN, JAMES WARREN	P	19	.135	A	B
		HELD, WOODSON GEORGE	2B 9	26	+.146	B	XCAL
		(3B5 OF2)					
		JOHNSON, DAVID ALLEN (3B3)	2B 144	148	.247	B	B
		JOHNSON, ROBERT WALLACE		4	.333	B	XNY N
		LAU, CHARLES RICHARD		11	.125	B	XATLN
0	0	LEONHARD, DAVID PAUL	P	3	.000	A	B
1	0	LOPEZ, MARCELINO PONS	P 4	6	+.000	XCAL	BAL 69
		MAY, DAVID LAFRANCE	OF 19	36	.235	A	B
		MC GUIRE, MICKEY C.	2B 4	10	.235	BAL 62	C
7	7	MC NALLY, DAVID ARTHUR	P	24	.158	B	B
0	0	MILLER, JOHN ERNEST	P	2	.000	B	C
3	10	MILLER, STUART LEONARD	P	42	.000	B	ATLN
		MOTTON, CURTELL HOWARD	OF 18	27	.200	A	B
3	1	PALMER, JAMES ALVIN	P	9	.077	B	BAL 69
14	9	PHOEBUS, THOMAS HAROLD	P	33	.145	B	B
		POWELL, JOHN WESLEY (BOOG)	1B 114	125	.234	B	B
7	10	RICHERT, PETER GERARD	P 26	27	+.108	XWAS	B
		ROBINSON, BROOKS CALBERT	3B	158	.269	B	B
		ROBINSON, FRANK (1B2)	OF 126	129	.311	B	B
		ROZNOVSKY, VICTOR JOSEPH	C 23	45	.206	B	PHIN69
		SNYDER, RUSSELL HENRY	OF 69	108	.236	B	CHI
3	5	WATT, EDWARD DEAN	P	49	.182	B	B

WON 91
LOST 71
TIED 0
TG 162

AMERICAN LEAGUE

1968.

FINISHED 2

PCT. .562

BALTIMORE

HENRY ALBERT BAUER EARL SIDNEY WEAVER

WON	LOST	NAME	POS.	G.	BA	FROM	TO
0	2	ADAMSON, JOHN MICHAEL (MIKE)	P	2	.333	B	B
0	0	BEENE, FRED RAY	P	1	.000	A	B
		BELANGER, MARK HENRY	SS	145	.208	B	B
		BLAIR, PAUL L. D. (3B1)	OF 132	141	.211	B	B
		BLEFARY, CURTIS LEROY	OF 92	137	.200	B	HOUN
		(C40 1B12)					
6	7	BRABENDER, EUGENE MATTHEW	P	37	.086	B	SEA
		BUFORD, DONALD ALVIN	OF 65	130	.282	CHI	B
		(2B58 3B2)					
2	0	BUNKER, WALLACE EDWARD	P	18	.111	B	KC
4	4	DRABOWSKY, MYRON WALTER (MOE)	P	45	.286	B	KC
		ETCHEBARREN, ANDREW AUGUSTE	C 70	74	.233	B	B
		FERNANDEZ, LORENZO MARTO	SS 7	24	.111	A	C
		(2B4)					
		FIORE, MICHAEL GARRY JOSEPH	1B 5	6	.059	A	KC
		(OF1)					
		FLOYD, ROBERT NATHAN	SS 4	5	.111	A	B
		HANEY, WALLACE LARRY	C 32	38	.236	B	SEA
18	13	HARDIN, JAMES WARREN	P	35	.085	B	B
		HENDRICKS, ELROD JEROME	C 53	79	.202	A	B
0	2	HOWARD, BRUCE ERNEST	P	10	+.286	CHI	XWAS
		JOHNSON, DAVID ALLEN (SS34)	2B 127	145	.242	B	B
7	7	LEONHARD, DAVID PAUL	P 28	30	.129	B	B
		MAY, DAVID LAFRANCE	OF 61	84	.191	B	B
22	10	MC NALLY, DAVID ARTHUR	P	35	.128	B	B
2	0	MORRIS, JOHN WALLACE	P	19	.000	PHIN66	SEA
		MOTTON, CURTELL HOWARD	OF 54	83	.198	B	B
4	3	NELSON, ROGER EUGENE	P	19	.063	CHI	KC
0	0	O'DONOGHUE, JOHN EUGENE	P	16	.000	CLE	SEA
15	15	PHOEBUS, THOMAS HAROLD	P	36	.183	B	B
		POWELL, JOHN WESLEY (BOOG)	1B 149	154	.249	B	B
		RETTENMUND, MERVIN WELDON	OF 23	31	.297	A	B
6	3	RICHERT, PETER GERARD	P	36	.200	B	B
		ROBINSON, BROOKS CALBERT	3B	162	.253	B	B
		ROBINSON, FRANK (1B3)	OF 117	130	.268	B	B
		VALENTINE, FRED LEE	OF 26	47	+.187	XWAS	C
5	5	WATT, EDWARD DEAN	P	59	.000	B	B

WON 109
LOST 53
TIED 0
TG 162

AMERICAN LEAGUE

1969.

FINISHED 1 E
(ALSO WON LEAGUE PLAYOFF)
PCT. .673

BALTIMORE

EARL SIDNEY WEAVER

WON	LOST	NAME	POS.		G.	BA	FROM	TO
0	1	ADAMSON, JOHN MICHAEL (MIKE)	P		6	.000	B	C
0	0	BEENE, FRED RAY	P		2	.000	B	B
		BELANGER, MARK HENRY	SS	148	150	.287	B	B
0	0	BERTAINA, FRANK LOUIS	P		3	+1.000	XWAS	STLN
		BLAIR, PAUL L. D.	OF		150	.285	B	B
		BUFORD, DONALD ALVIN	OF	128	144	.291	B	B
		(2B10 3B6)						
		CROWLEY, TERRENCE MICHAEL	1B	3	7	.333	A	B
		(OF2)						
23	11	CUELLAR, MIGUEL ANGEL	P		39	.117	HOUN	B
		DALRYMPLE, CLAYTON ERROL	C	30	37	.238	PHIN	B
		ETCHEBARREN, ANDREW AUGUSTE	C	72	73	.249	B	B
		FLOYD, ROBERT NATHAN	2B	15	39	.202	B	B
		(SS15 3B9)						
5	2	HALL, RICHARD WALLACE	P		39	.286	PHIN	B
6	7	HARDIN, JAMES WARREN	P		30	.156	B	B
		HENDRICKS, ELROD JEROME	C	87	105	.244	B	B
		(1B4)						
		JOHNSON, DAVID ALLEN (SS2)	2B	142	142	.280	B	B
7	4	LEONHARD, DAVID PAUL	P	37	38	.095	B	B
5	3	LOPEZ, MARCELINO PONS	P		27	.214	BAL 67	B
		MAY, DAVID LAFRANCE	OF	40	78	.242	B	B
20	7	MC NALLY, DAVID ARTHUR	P		41	.085	B	B
		MOTTON, CURTELL HOWARD	OF	20	56	.303	B	B
16	4	PALMER, JAMES ALVIN	P	26	27	.203	BAL 67	B
14	7	PHOEBUS, THOMAS HAROLD	P		35	.200	B	B
		POWELL, JOHN WESLEY (BOOG)	1B	144	152	.304	B	B
		RETTENMUND, MERVIN WELDON	OF	78	95	.247	B	B
7	4	RICHERT, PETER GERARD	P		44	.125	B	B
		ROBINSON, BROOKS CALBERT	3B		156	.234	B	B
		ROBINSON, FRANK (1B19)	OF	134	148	.308	B	B
		SALMON, RUTHFORD EDUARDO	1B	17	52	.297	CLE	B
		(CHICO) (2B9 SS9 3B3 OF1)						
1	1	SEVERINSEN, ALBERT HENRY	P		12	.333	A	SD N71
5	2	WATT, EDWARD DEAN	P		56	.000	B	B

WON 108
LOST 54
TIED 0
TG 162

AMERICAN LEAGUE

1970.

FINISHED 1 E
(ALSO WON LEAGUE PLAYOFF)
PCT. .667

BALTIMORE

EARL SIDNEY WEAVER

WON	LOST	NAME	POS.		G.	BA	FROM	TO
		BAYLOR, DONALD EDWARD	OF	6	8	.235	A	B
0	0	BEENE, FRED RAY	P		4	.000	B	NY 72
		BELANGER, MARK HENRY	SS	143	145	.218	B	B
		(2B3 3B3)						
		BLAIR, PAUL L. D. (3B1)	OF	128	133	.267	B	B
		BUFORD, DONALD ALVIN	OF	130	144	.272	B	B
		CROWLEY, TERRENCE MICHAEL	OF	27	83	.257	B	B
		(1B23)						
24	8	CUELLAR, MIGUEL ANGEL	P	40	41	.089	B	B
		DALRYMPLE, CLAYTON ERROL	C	11	13	.219	B	B
4	2	DRABOWSKY, MYRON WALTER (MOE)	P		21	+.000	XKC	STLN
		ETCHEBARREN, ANDREW AUGUSTE	C	76	78	.243	B	B
		FLOYD, ROBERT NATHAN (2B1)	SS	2	3	+.000	B	XKC
		FREED, ROGER VERNON (OF1)	1B	3	4	.154	A	PHIN
		GRICH, ROBERT ANTHONY	SS	20	30	.211	A	B
		(2B9 3B1)						
10	5	HALL, RICHARD WALLACE	P		32	.083	B	B
6	5	HARDIN, JAMES WARREN	P		36	.067	B	B
		HENDRICKS, ELROD JEROME	C	95	106	.242	B	B
		JOHNSON, DAVID ALLEN (SS2)	2B	149	149	.281	B	B
0	0	LEONHARD, DAVID PAUL	P	23	25	.000	B	B
1	1	LOPEZ, MARCELINO PONS	P		25	.077	B	MIL
		MAY, DAVID LAFRANCE	OF	9	25	+.194	B	XMIL
24	9	MC NALLY, DAVID ARTHUR	P	40	41	.133	B	B
		MOTTON, CURTELL HOWARD	OF	21	52	.226	B	B
		OATES, JOHNNY LANE	C	4	5	.278	A	BAL 72
20	10	PALMER, JAMES ALVIN	P	39	44	.150	B	B
5	5	PHOEBUS, THOMAS HAROLD	P		27	.163	B	SD N
		POWELL, JOHN WESLEY (BOOG)	1B	145	154	.297	B	B
		RETTENMUND, MERVIN WELDON	OF	93	106	.322	B	B
7	2	RICHERT, PETER GERARD	P		50	.000	B	B
		ROBINSON, BROOKS CALBERT	3B	156	158	.276	B	B
		ROBINSON, FRANK (1B7)	OF	120	132	.306	B	B
		SALMON, RUTHFORD EDUARDO	SS	33	63	.250	B	B
		(CHICO) (1B2 2B12 3B11)						
7	7	WATT, EDWARD DEAN	P		53	.125	B	B

WON 101
LOST 57
TIED 0
TG 158

AMERICAN LEAGUE

1971.

FINISHED 1 E
(ALSO WON LEAGUE PLAYOFF)
PCT. .639

BALTIMORE

EARL SIDNEY WEAVER

WON	LOST	NAME	POS.		G.	BA	FROM	TO
		BAYLOR, DONALD EDWARD	OF		1	.000	B	B
		BELANGER, MARK HENRY	SS	149	150	.266	B	B
		BLAIR, PAUL L. D.	OF	138	141	.262	B	B
1	2	BOSWELL, DAVID WILSON	P		15	+.200	XDET	C
		BUFORD, DONALD ALVIN	OF	115	122	.290	B	B
		CROWLEY, TERRENCE MICHAEL	OF	6	18	.174	B	B
		(1B2)						
20	9	CUELLAR, MIGUEL ANGEL	P		38	.103	B	B
		DALRYMPLE, CLAYTON ERROL	C	19	23	.204	B	C
		DA VANON, FRANK GERALD (GERRY)	2B	20	38	.235	STLN	C
		(1B1 SS11 3B3)						
20	8	DOBSON, PATRICK EDWARD	P		38	.110	SD N	B
1	5	DUKES, THOMAS EARL	P		28	.143	SD N	CAL
		ETCHEBARREN, ANDREW AUGUSTE	C		70	.270	B	B
		GRICH, ROBERT ANTHONY (2B2)	SS	5	7	.300	B	B
6	6	HALL, RICHARD WALLACE	P		27	.400	B	C
0	0	HARDIN, JAMES WARREN	P		6	+.000	B	XNY
		HENDRICKS, ELROD JEROME	C	90	101	.250	B	B
		(1B3)						
4	3	JACKSON, GRANT DWIGHT	P		29	.091	PHIN	B
		JOHNSON, DAVID ALLEN	2B	140	142	.282	B	B
2	3	LEONHARD, DAVID PAUL	P	12	13	.278	B	B
21	5	MC NALLY, DAVID ARTHUR	P		30	.162	B	B
		MOTTON, CURTELL HOWARD	OF	16	38	.189	B	MIL
20	9	PALMER, JAMES ALVIN	P	37	38	.196	B	B
0	1	PENA, ORLANDO	P		5	.000	PITN	C
		POWELL, JOHN WESLEY (BOOG)	1B	124	128	.256	B	B
		RETTENMUND, MERVIN WELDON	OF	134	141	.318	B	B
3	5	RICHERT, PETER GERARD	P		35	.000	B	LA N
		ROBINSON, BROOKS CALBERT	3B		156	.272	B	B
		ROBINSON, FRANK (1B37)	OF	92	133	.281	B	LA N
		SALMON, RUTHFORD EDUARDO	1B	9	42	.179	B	B
		(CHICO) (2B9 SS5 3B6)						
		SHOPAY, THOMAS MICHAEL	OF	13	47	.257	NY 69	B
3	1	WATT, EDWARD DEAN	P		35	.000	B	B

WON 80
LOST 74
TIED 0
TG 154

AMERICAN LEAGUE

1972.

FINISHED 3 E

PCT. .519

BALTIMORE

EARL SIDNEY WEAVER

WON	LOST	NAME	POS.		G.	BA	FROM	TO
6	8	ALEXANDER, DOYLE LAFAYETTE	P		35	.080	LA N	
		BAYLOR, DONALD EDWARD (1B9)	OF	84	102	.253	B	
		BELANGER, MARK HENRY	SS	105	113	.186	B	
		BLAIR, PAUL L. D.	OF	139	142	.233	B	
		BUFORD, DONALD ALVIN	OF	105	125	.206	B	
		BUMBRY, ALONZA BENJAMIN	OF	2	9	.364	A	
		CABELL, ENOS MILTON	1B	1	3	.000	A	
		COGGINS, RICHARD ALLEN	OF	13	16	.333	A	
		CROWLEY, TERRENCE MICHAEL	OF	68	97	.231	B	
		(1B15)						
18	12	CUELLAR, MIGUEL ANGEL	P		35	.126	B	
		DAVIS, HERMAN THOMAS (TOMMY)	OF	18	26	.256	XCHIN	
		(1B3)						
16	18	DOBSON, PATRICK EDWARD	P		38	.141	B	
		ETCHEBARREN, ANDREW AUGUSTE	C	70	71	.202	B	
		GRICH, ROBERT ANTHONY	SS	81	133	.278	B	
		(1B16 2B45 3B8)						
3	4	HARRISON, RORIC EDWARD	P		39	.118	A	
		HENDRICKS, ELROD JEROME	C	28	33	.155	B	XCHIN
1	1	JACKSON, GRANT DWIGHT	P		32	.000	B	
		JOHNSON, DAVID ALLEN	2B	116	118	.221	B	
0	0	LEONHARD, DAVID PAUL	P	14	16	1.000	B	
		MATCHICK, JOHN THOMAS (TOMMY)	3B		3	.222	MIL	
13	17	MC NALLY, DAVID ARTHUR	P		36	.152	B	
		OATES, JOHNNY LANE	C	82	85	.261	BAL 70	
21	10	PALMER, JAMES ALVIN	P		36	.224	B	
		POWELL, JOHN WESLEY (BOOG)	1B	133	140	.252	B	
		RETTENMUND, MERVIN WELDON	OF	98	102	.233	B	
0	0	REYNOLDS, ROBERT ALLEN	P		3	.000	MIL	
		ROBINSON, BROOKS CALBERT	3B	152	153	.250	B	
		ROBLES, SERGIO	C	1	2	.200	A	
		SALMON, RUTHFORD EDUARDO	1B	2	17	.063	B	
		(CHICO) (3B1)						
0	1	SCOTT, RALPH ROBERT (MICKEY)	P		15	.000	A	
		SHOPAY, THOMAS MICHAEL	OF	3	49	.225	B	
2	3	WATT, EDWARD DEAN	P		38	.000	B	

WON 62
LOST 100
TIED 0
TG 162

AMERICAN LEAGUE

1965.

FINISHED 9

PCT. .383

BOSTON

WILLIAM JENNINGS HERMAN

WON	LOST	NAME	POS.		G.	BA	FROM	TO
5	7	BENNETT, DENNIS JOHN	P		34	.179	PHIN	B
		BRESSOUD, EDWARD FRANCIS	SS	86	107	.226	B	NY N
		(3B2 OF1)						
		CONIGLIARO, ANTHONY RICHARD	OF	137	138	.269	B	B
4	2	DULIBA, ROBERT JOHN	P		39	.000	LA	KC 67
0	1	EARLEY, ARNOLD CARL	P		57	.000	B	CHIN
		GEIGER, GARY MERLE	OF	16	24	.200	B	ATLN
		GOSGER, JAMES CHARLES	OF		81	.256	BOS 63	B
		GREEN, LEONARD CHARLES	OF	95	119	.276	BAL	B
0	2	HEFFNER, ROBERT FREDERICK	P		27	.000	B	CLE
		HORTON, ANTHONY DARRIN	1B	44	60	.294	B	B
		JONES, JAMES DALTON (2B8)	3B	81	112	.270	B	B
0	3	LAMABE, JOHN ALEXANDER	P		14	.000	B	XHOUN
9	17	LONBORG, JAMES REYNOLD	P		32	.136	A	B
		MALZONE, FRANK JAMES	3B	96	106	.239	B	CAL
		MANTILLA, FELIX LAMELA	2B	123	150	.275	B	HOUN
		(1B2 OF27)						
10	18	MONBOQUETTE, WILLIAM CHARLES	P	35	36	.059	B	DET
10	18	MOREHEAD, DAVID MICHAEL	P		34	.131	B	B
		MOSES, GERALD BRAHEEN			4	.250	A	BOS 68
		NIXON, RUSSELL EUGENE	C	38	59	.270	B	MIN
		PETROCELLI, AMERICO PETER	SS	93	103	.232	BOS 63	B
		(RICO)						
9	11	RADATZ, RICHARD RAYMOND	P		63	.185	B	B
1	2	RITCHIE, JAY SEAY	P		44	.200	B	ATLN
		RYAN, MICHAEL JAMES	C		33	.159	B	B
		SCHILLING, CHARLES THOMAS	2B	41	71	.240	B	C
		SCHLESINGER, WILLIAM CORDES			1	.000	A	C
1	5	STEPHENSON, JERRY JOSEPH	P		15	.231	BOS 63	B
		THOMAS, JAMES LEROY (LEE)	1B	127	151	.271	B	ATLN
		(OF20)						
		TILLMAN, JOHN ROBERT (BOB)	C	106	111	.215	B	B
13	14	WILSON, ROBERT EARL	P	36	47	.177	B	B
		YASTRZEMSKI, CARL MICHAEL	OF	130	133	.312	B	B

WON 72
LOST 90
TIED 0
TG 162

AMERICAN LEAGUE

1966.

FINISHED 9

PCT. .444

BOSTON

WILLIAM JENNINGS HERMAN JAMES EDWARD RUNNELS

WON	LOST	NAME	POS.		G.	BA	FROM	TO
		ANDREWS, MICHAEL JAY	2B		5	.167	A	B
3	3	BENNETT, DENNIS JOHN	P		16	.130	B	B
8	8	BRANDON, DARRELL G.	P	40	41	.182	A	B
		CHRISTOPHER, JOSEPH O'NEAL	OF	2	12	.077	NY N	C
		CONIGLIARO, ANTHONY RICHARD	OF	146	150	.265	B	B
		DEMETER, DONALD LEE (1B2)	OF	57	73	+.292	XDET	B
2	3	FISCHER, HENRY WILLIAM	P		6	.222	XCINN	B
		FOY, JOSEPH ANTHONY (SS13)	3B	139	151	.262	A	B
		GOSGER, JAMES CHARLES	OF	32	40	+.254	B	XKC
		GREEN, LEONARD CHARLES	OF	27	85	.241	B	DET
0	1	GRILLI, GUIDO JOHN	P		6	+.500	A	XKC
		HORTON, ANTHONY DARRIN	1B		6	.136	B	B
		JONES, JAMES DALTON (3B3)	2B	70	115	.234	B	B
		KASKO, EDWARD MICHAEL	SS	20	58	.213	HOUN	C
		(2B8 3B10)						
10	10	LONBORG, JAMES REYNOLD	P	45	46	.093	B	B
0	1	MAGRINI, PETER ALEXANDER	P		3	.000	A	C
8	7	MC MAHON, DONALD JOHN	P		49	+.091	XCLE	B
1	2	MOREHEAD, DAVID MICHAEL	P		12	.500	B	B
4	3	OSINSKI, DANIEL	P		44	.333	MILN	B
		PETROCELLI, AMERICO PETER	SS	127	139	.238	B	B
		(RICO) (3B5)						
0	2	RADATZ, RICHARD RAYMOND	P		16	+.000	B	XCLE
0	0	ROGGENBURK, GARRY EARL	P		1	+.000	XMIN	BOS 68
		RYAN, MICHAEL JAMES	C	114	116	.214	B	B
1	1	SADOWSKI, ROBERT	P		11	.000	MILN	C
3	6	SANDERS, KENNETH GEORGE	P		24	+.000	KC 64	XKC
12	13	SANTIAGO, JOSE RAFAEL	P	35	38	.196	KC	B
		SCOTT, GEORGE (3B5)	1B	158	162	.245	A	B
1	6	SHELDON, ROLAND FRANK	P		23	+.111	XKC	C
0	0	SHORT, WILLIAM ROSS	P		8	+.000	XBAL	PITN
		SMITH, CARL REGINALD (REGGIE)	OF		6	.154	A	B
		SMITH, GEORGE CORNELIUS	2B	109	128	.213	DET	C
		(SS19)						
7	9	STANGE, ALBERT LEE	P		28	+.063	XCLE	B
2	5	STEPHENSON, JERRY JOSEPH	P		15	.118	B	B
2	1	STIGMAN, RICHARD LEWIS	P		34	.118	MIN	C
		TARTABULL, JOSE	OF	46	68	+.277	XKC	B
		THOMAS, GEORGE EDWARD	OF	48	69	.237	DET	B
		(C2 1B2 3B6)						
		TILLMAN, JOHN ROBERT (BOB)	C	72	78	.230	B	B
5	5	WILSON, ROBERT EARL	P	15	18	+.250	B	XDET
3	4	WYATT, JOHN THOMAS	P		42	+.000	XKC	B
		YASTRZEMSKI, CARL MICHAEL	OF	158	160	.278	B	B

COACH RUNNELS SERVED AS INTERIM MANAGER NEAR CLOSE OF SEASON.

WON 92 | LOST 70 | TIED 0 | TG 162

AMERICAN LEAGUE

1967.

FINISHED 1

PCT. .568

BOSTON

RICHARD HIRSHFELD WILLIAMS

WON	LOST	NAME	POS.	G.	BA	FROM	TO
		ADAIR, KENNETH JERRY	3B 35	89	+.291	XCHI	B
		(2B23 SS30)					
		ANDREWS, MICHAEL JAY (SS6)	2B 139	142	.263	B	B
12	8	BELL, GARY	P	29	+.203	XCLE	B
4	3	BENNETT, DENNIS JOHN	P	13	.120	B	XNY N
5	11	BRANDON, DARRELL G.	P	39	.186	B	B
0	0	BRETT, KENNETH ALVEN	P	1	.000	A	BOS 69
0	1	CISCO, GALEN BERNARD	P	11	.000	NY N65	KC 69
		CONIGLIARO, ANTHONY RICHARD	OF	95	.287	B	BOS 69
		DEMETER, DONALD LEE (3B1)	OF 12	20	+.279	B	XCLE
1	2	FISCHER, HENRY WILLIAM	P	9	.143	B	C
		FOY, JOSEPH ANTHONY (OF1)	3B 118	130	.251	B	B
		GIBSON, JOHN RUSSELL (RUSS)	C 48	49	.203	A	B
		HARRELSON, KENNETH SMITH	OF 23	23	+.200	XKC	B
		(1B1)					
		HORTON, ANTHONY DARRIN	1B 6	21	+.308	B	XCLE
		HOWARD, ELSTON GENE	C 41	42	+.147	XNY	B
		JONES, JAMES DALTON	3B 30	89	.289	B	B
		(1B1 2B19)					
		LANDIS, JAMES HENRY	OF	5	+.143	XDET	XHOUN
1	0	LANDIS, WILLIAM HENRY	P 18	21	.000	KC 63	B
22	9	LONBORG, JAMES REYNOLD	P	39	.141	B	B
1	2	LYLE, ALBERT WALTER (SPARKY)	P	27	.250	A	B
1	2	MC MAHON, DONALD JOHN	P	11	+.000	B	XCHI
5	4	MOREHEAD, DAVID MICHAEL	P	10	.083	B	B
3	1	OSINSKI, DANIEL	P	34	.333	B	CHI 69
		PETROCELLI, AMERICO PETER	SS 141	142	.259	B	B
		(RICO) (1B1)					
		POULSEN, KEN STERLING (SS1)	3B 2	5	.200	A	C
2	3	ROHR, WILLIAM JOSEPH	P	10	.000	A	CLE
		RYAN, MICHAEL JAMES	C	79	.199	B	PHIN
12	4	SANTIAGO, JOSE RAFAEL	P	50	.190	B	B
		SCOTT, GEORGE (3B2)	1B 152	159	.303	B	B
		SIEBERN, NORMAN LEROY (OF1)	1B 13	33	.205	XSF N	B
		(2B6)					
		SMITH, CARL REGINALD (REGGIE)	OF 144	158	.246	B	B
8	10	STANGE, ALBERT LEE	P	35	.061	B	B
3	1	STEPHENSON, JERRY JOSEPH	P	8	.250	B	B
		TARTABULL, JOSE	OF 83	115	.223	B	B
		THOMAS, GEORGE EDWARD	OF 43	65	.213	B	B
		(C1 1B3)					
		TILLMAN, JOHN ROBERT (BOB)	C 26	30	+.188	B	XNY
2	2	WASLEWSKI, GARY LEE	P	12	.091	A	B
10	7	WYATT, JOHN THOMAS	P	60	.083	B	B
		YASTRZEMSKI, CARL MICHAEL	OF	161	.326	B	B

WON 86 | LOST 76 | TIED 0 | TG 162

AMERICAN LEAGUE

1968.

FINISHED 4

PCT. .531

BOSTON

RICHARD HIRSHFELD WILLIAMS

WON	LOST	NAME	POS.	G.	BA	FROM	TO
		ADAIR, KENNETH JERRY	SS 46	74	.216	B	KC
		(1B1 2B12 3B7)					
		ALVARADO, LUIS CESAR	SS	11	.130	A	B
		ANDREWS, MICHAEL JAY	2B 139	147	.271	B	B
		(SS4 3B1)					
11	11	BELL, GARY	P	35	.220	B	SEA
0	0	BRANDON, DARRELL G.	P	8	.000	B	SEA
16	6	CULP, RAYMOND LEONARD	P	35	.114	CHIN	B
16	7	ELLSWORTH, RICHARD CLARK	P	31	.056	PHIN	B
		FOY, JOSEPH ANTHONY (OF3)	3B 147	150	.225	B	KC
		GIBSON, JOHN RUSSELL (RUSS)	C 74	76	.225	B	B
		(1B1)					
		HARRELSON, KENNETH SMITH	OF 132	150	.275	B	B
		(1B19)					
		HOWARD, ELSTON GENE	C 68	71	.241	B	C
		JONES, JAMES DALTON	1B 56	111	.234	B	B
		(2B26 3B8)					
		LAHOUD, JOSEPH MICHAEL	OF 25	29	.192	A	B
3	3	LANDIS, WILLIAM HENRY	P	38	.000	B	B
6	10	LONBORG, JAMES REYNOLD	P	23	.282	B	B
6	1	LYLE, ALBERT WALTER (SPARKY)	P	49	.125	B	B
1	4	MOREHEAD, DAVID MICHAEL	P	11	.125	B	KC
		MOSES, GERALD BRAHEEN	C	6	.333	BOS 65	B
		NIXON, RUSSELL EUGENE	C 27	29	.153	MIN	C
		OLIVER, EUGENE GEORGE (OF1)	C 10	16	.143	PHIN	XCHIN
		PETROCELLI, AMERICO PETER	SS 117	123	.234	B	B
		(RICO)					
6	8	PIZARRO, JUAN	P 19	20	.161	XPITN	B
		ROBINSON, FLOYD ANDREW	OF 11	24	+.125	XOAK	C
0	0	ROGGENBURK, GARRY EARL	P	4	.000	BOS 66	B
9	4	SANTIAGO, JOSE RAFAEL	P 18	23	.163	B	B
		SCOTT, GEORGE (3B6)	1B 112	124	.171	B	B
		SIEBERN, NORMAN LEROY (OF2)	1B 2	27	.067	B	C
		SMITH, CARL REGINALD (REGGIE)	OF	155	.265	B	B
5	5	STANGE, ALBERT LEE	P	50	.133	B	B
2	8	STEPHENSON, JERRY JOSEPH	P	23	.353	B	SEA
		TARTABULL, JOSE	OF 43	72	.281	B	OAK
		THOMAS, GEORGE EDWARD	OF 9	12	.200	B	B
4	7	WASLEWSKI, GARY LEE	P 34	39	.038	B	STLN
0	0	WENZ, FREDERICK CHARLES	P	1	.000	A	B
1	2	WYATT, JOHN THOMAS	P	8	+.000	B	XNY
		YASTRZEMSKI, CARL MICHAEL	OF 155	157	.301	B	B
		(1B3)					

WON 87 | LOST 75 | TIED 0 | TG 162

AMERICAN LEAGUE

1969.

BOSTON

FINISHED 3 E

PCT. .537

RICHARD HIRSHFELD WILLIAMS EDWARD JOSEPH POPOWSKI

WON	LOST	NAME	POS.		G.	BA	FROM	TO
		ALVARADO, LUIS CESAR	SS	5	6	.000	B	B
		ANDREWS, MICHAEL JAY	2B	120	121	.293	B	B
		AZCUE, JOSE JOAQUIN	C		19	+.216	XCLE	XCAL
2	3	BRETT, KENNETH ALVEN	P		8	.300	BOS 67	B
		CONIGLIARO, ANTHONY RICHARD	OF	137	141	.255	BOS 67	B
		CONIGLIARO, WILLIAM MICHAEL	OF	24	32	.288	A	B
17	8	CULP, RAYMOND LEONARD	P		32	.152	B	B
0	0	ELLSWORTH, RICHARD CLARK	P		2	+.000	B	XCLE
		FISK, CARLTON ERNEST (PUDGE)	C	1	2	.000	A	BOS 71
1	0	GARMAN, MICHAEL DOUGLAS	P		2	.400	A	BOS 71
		GIBSON, JOHN RUSSELL (RUSS)	C	83	85	.251	B	SF N
		HARRELSON, KENNETH SMITH	1B		10	+.217	B	XCLE
5	6	JARVIS, RAYMOND ARNOLD	P		29	.069	A	B
		JONES, JAMES DALTON	1B	81	111	.220	B	DET
		(2B1 3B9)						
0	1	KLINE, RONALD LEE	P		16	.000	XSF N	ATLN
		LAHOUD, JOSEPH MICHAEL (1B1)	OF	66	101	.188	B	B
5	5	LANDIS, WILLIAM HENRY	P	45	46	.000	B	C
1	3	LEE, WILLIAM FRANCIS	P		20	.000	A	B
		LOCK, DON WILSON (1B4)	OF	28	53	.224	XPHIN	C
7	11	LONBORG, JAMES REYNOLD	P		29	.098	B	B
8	3	LYLE, ALBERT WALTER (SPARKY)	P		71	.118	B	B
		MOSES, GERALD BRAHEEN	C	36	53	.304	B	B
		MUSER, ANTHONY JOSEPH	1B		2	.111	A	CHI 71
12	2	NAGY, MICHAEL TIMOTHY	P	33	34	.077	A	B
		O'BRIEN, SYDNEY LLOYD	3B	53	100	.243	A	CHI
		(2B12 SS15)						
		PETROCELLI, AMERICO PETER	SS	153	154	.297	B	B
		(RICO) (3B1)						
0	1	PIZARRO, JUAN	P		6	+.333	B	XCLE
0	1	ROGGENBURK, GARRY EARL	P		7	+.000	B	XSEA
7	9	ROMO, VICENTE	P		52	+.129	XCLE	B
0	0	SANTIAGO, JOSE RAFAEL	P		10	.000	B	B
		SATRIANO, THOMAS VICTOR	C	44	47	+.189	XCAL	B
		(SS11 3B9 OF5)						
		SCHOFIELD, JOHN RICHARD (DICK)	2B	37	94	.257	STLN	B
		SCOTT, GEORGE (1B53)	3B	109	152	.253	B	B
14	10	SIEBERT, WILFRED CHAS. (SONNY)	P		43	+.151	XCLE	B
		SMITH, CARL REGINALD (REGGIE)	OF	139	143	.309	B	B
6	9	STANGE, ALBERT LEE	P		41	.086	B	B
		THOMAS, GEORGE EDWARD	OF	12	29	.353	B	B
		(C1 1B10 3B1)						
1	3	WAGNER, GARY EDWARD	P		6	.000	XPHIN	B
1	0	WENZ, FREDERICK CHARLES	P		8	.000	B	PHIN
		YASTRZEMSKI, CARL MICHAEL	OF	143	162	.255	B	B
		(1B22)						

COACH POPOWSKI SERVED AS INTERIM MANAGER NEAR CLOSE OF SEASON.

WON 87 | LOST 75 | TIED 0 | TG 162

AMERICAN LEAGUE

1970.

BOSTON

FINISHED 3 E

PCT. .537

EDWARD MICHAEL KASKO

WON	LOST	NAME	POS.		G.	BA	FROM	TO
		ALVARADO, LUIS CESAR (SS27)	3B	29	59	.224	B	CHI
		ANDREWS, MICHAEL JAY	2B	148	151	.253	B	CHI
2	0	BOLIN, BOBBY DONALD	P		6	+.000	XMIL	B
8	9	BRETT, KENNETH ALVEN	P		41	.317	B	B
		CONIGLIARO, ANTHONY RICHARD	OF		146	.266	B	CAL
		CONIGLIARO, WILLIAM MICHAEL	OF	108	114	.271	B	B
17	14	CULP, RAYMOND LEONARD	P		33	.124	B	B
0	0	CURTIS, JOHN DUFFIELD	P		1	.000	A	B
		DERRICK, JAMES MICHAEL (MIKE)	OF	2	24	.212	A	C
		(1B1)						
		FANZONE, CARMEN	3B	5	10	.200	A	CHIN
		FIORE, MICHAEL GARRY JOSEPH	1B	17	41	+.140	XKC	B
		(OF2)						
0	3	HARTENSTEIN, CHARLES OSCAR	P		17	.000	XSTLN	C
0	1	JARVIS, RAYMOND ARNOLD	P		15	.000	B	C
		KENNEDY, JOHN EDWARD (2B2)	3B	33	43	+.256	XMIL	B
3	4	KOONCE, CALVIN LEE	P		23	.095	XNY N	B
		LAHOUD, JOSEPH MICHAEL	OF	13	17	.245	B	B
2	2	LEE, WILLIAM FRANCIS	P		11	.000	B	B
4	1	LONBORG, JAMES REYNOLD	P		9	.444	B	B
1	7	LYLE, ALBERT WALTER (SPARKY)	P		63	.000	B	B
		MATCHICK, JOHN THOMAS (TOMMY)	3B	2	10	+.071	DET	XKC
		(2B1 SS1)						
0	0	MILLS, RICHARD ALAN	P		2	.000	A	C
		MONTGOMERY, ROBERT EDWARD	C		22	.179	A	B
1	0	MORET, ROGELIO	P		3	.000	A	B
		MOSES, GERALD BRAHEEN (OF1)	C	88	92	.263	B	CAL
6	5	NAGY, MICHAEL TIMOTHY	P		23	.250	B	B
		PAVLETICH, DONALD STEPHEN	1B	16	32	.138	CHI	B
		(C10)						
16	11	PETERS, GARY CHARLES	P	34	37	.244	CHI	B
		PETROCELLI, AMERICO PETER	SS	141	157	.261	B	B
		(RICO) (3B18)						
0	2	PHILLIPS, NORMAN EDWIN (ED)	P		18	.000	A	C
7	3	ROMO, VICENTE	P		48	.148	B	CHI
0	2	SANTIAGO, JOSE RAFAEL	P	8	9	.667	B	C
		SATRIANO, THOMAS VICTOR	C	51	59	.236	B	C
		SCHOFIELD, JOHN RICHARD (DICK)	2B	15	76	.187	B	MIL
		(SS3 3B15)						
		SCOTT, GEORGE (1B59)	3B	68	127	.296	B	B
15	8	SIEBERT, WILFRED CHAS. (SONNY)	P		33	.130	B	B
		SMITH, CARL REGINALD (REGGIE)	OF	145	147	.303	B	B
2	2	STANGE, ALBERT LEE	P		20	+.000	B	XCHI
		THOMAS, GEORGE EDWARD (3B6)	OF	26	38	.343	B	B
3	1	WAGNER, GARY EDWARD	P		38	.167	B	C
		YASTRZEMSKI, CARL MICHAEL	1B	94	161	.329	B	B
		(OF69)						

WON 85 | LOST 77 | TIED 0 | TG 162

AMERICAN LEAGUE

1971.

FINISHED 3 E

PCT. .525

BOSTON

EDWARD MICHAEL KASKO

WON	LOST	NAME	POS.		G.	BA	FROM	TO
		APARICIO, LUIS ERNESTO	SS	121	125	.232	CHI	B
		BENIQUEZ, JUAN JOSE	SS	15	16	.298	A	B
5	3	BOLIN, BOBBY DONALD	P		52	.250	B	B
0	3	BRETT, KENNETH ALVEN	P		29	.200	B	MIL
		CONIGLIARO, WILLIAM MICHAEL	OF	100	101	.262	B	MIL
		COOPER, CECIL CELESTER	1B	11	14	.310	A	B
14	16	CULP, RAYMOND LEONARD	P		35	.118	B	B
2	2	CURTIS, JOHN DUFFIELD	P		5	.111	B	B
		FIORE, MICHAEL GARRY JOSEPH	1B	12	51	.177	B	STLN
		FISK, CARLTON ERNEST (PUDGE)	C		14	.313	BOS 69	B
		GAGLIANO, PHILIP JOSEPH	OF	11	47	.324	CHIN	B
		(2B7 3B4)						
1	1	GARMAN, MICHAEL DOUGLAS	P		3	.333	BOS 69	B
		GRIFFIN, DOUGLAS LEE	2B	124	125	.244	CAL	B
		HUNTER, HAROLD JAMES (BUDDY)	2B	6	8	.222	A	C
		JOSEPHSON, DUANE CHARLES	C	87	91	.245	CHI	B
		KENNEDY, JOHN EDWARD	2B	37	74	.276	B	B
		(SS33 3B5)						
0	1	KOONCE, CALVIN LEE	P		13	.000	B	C
		LAHOUD, JOSEPH MICHAEL	OF	69	107	.215	B	MIL
9	2	LEE, WILLIAM FRANCIS	P		47	.217	B	B
10	7	LONBORG, JAMES REYNOLD	P		27	.170	B	MIL
6	4	LYLE, ALBERT WALTER (SPARKY)	P		50	1.000	B	NY
		MILLER, RICHARD ALAN	OF	14	15	.333	A	B
		MONTGOMERY, ROBERT EDWARD	C	66	67	.239	B	B
4	3	MORET, ROGELIO	P		13	.087	B	B
1	3	NAGY, MICHAEL TIMOTHY	P		12	.083	B	B
		OGLIVIE, BENJAMIN AMBROSIO	OF	11	14	.263	A	B
		PAVLETICH, DONALD STEPHEN	C	8	14	.259	B	C
14	11	PETERS, GARY CHARLES	P	34	53	.271	B	B
		PETROCELLI, AMERICO PETER	3B	156	158	.251	B	B
		(RICO)						
		SCOTT, GEORGE	1B	143	146	.263	B	MIL
16	10	SIEBERT, WILFRED CHAS. (SONNY)	P		32	.266	B	B
		SMITH, CARL REGINALD (REGGIE)	OF		159	.283	B	B
2	4	TATUM, KENNETH RAY	P		36	.300	CAL	B
		THOMAS, GEORGE EDWARD	OF	5	9	+.077	B	XMIN
1	7	TIANT, LUIS CLEMENTE	P		21	.158	MIN	B
		YASTRZEMSKI, CARL MICHAEL	OF	146	148	.254	B	B

WON 85 | LOST 70 | TIED 0 | TG 155

AMERICAN LEAGUE

1972.

FINISHED 2 E

PCT. .548

BOSTON

EDWARD MICHAEL KASKO

WON	LOST	NAME	POS.		G.	BA	FROM	TO
		APARICIO, LUIS ERNESTO	SS	109	110	.257	B	
		BENIQUEZ, JUAN JOSE	SS	27	33	.242	B	
0	1	BOLIN, BOBBY DONALD	P		21	.000	B	
		BURDA, EDWARD ROBERT (BOB)	1B	15	45	.164	STLN	
		(OF1)						
		CATER, DANNY ANDERSON	1B	90	92	.237	NY	
		COOPER, CECIL CELESTER	1B	3	12	.235	B	
		CORRELL, VICTOR CROSBY	C		1	.500	A	
5	8	CULP, RAYMOND LEONARD	P		16	.212	B	
11	8	CURTIS, JOHN DUFFIELD	P	26	27	.094	B	
		EVANS, DWIGHT MICHAEL	OF	17	18	.263	A	
		FISK, CARLTON ERNEST (PUDGE)	C		131	.293	B	
		GAGLIANO, PHILIP JOSEPH	OF	12	52	.256	B	
		(1B2 2B4 3B5)						
		GALLAGHER, ROBERT WILLIAM			7	.000	A	
0	1	GARMAN, MICHAEL DOUGLAS	P		3	.000	B	
		GRIFFIN, DOUGLAS LEE	2B		129	.260	B	
		HARPER, TOMMY	OF		144	.254	MIL	
		JOSEPHSON, DUANE CHARLES	1B	16	26	.268	B	
		(C6)						
		KENNEDY, JOHN EDWARD	2B	32	71	.245	B	
		(SS27 3B11)						
		KOSCO, ANDREW JOHN	OF	12	17	+.213	XCAL	
1	3	KRAUSSE, LEWIS BERNARD, JR.	P		24	.125	MIL	
7	4	LEE, WILLIAM FRANCIS	P		47	.188	B	
8	7	MC GLOTHEN, LYNN EVERATT	P		22	.189	A	
		MILLER, RICHARD ALAN	OF	75	89	.214	B	
		MONTGOMERY, ROBERT EDWARD	C	22	24	.286	B	
0	0	MORET, ROGELIO	P		3	.000	B	
0	0	NAGY, MICHAEL TIMOTHY	P		1	.000	B	
4	2	NEWHAUSER, DONALD LOUIS	P		31	.000	A	
		OGLIVIE, BENJAMIN AMBROSIO	OF	68	94	.241	B	
17	13	PATTIN, MARTIN WILLIAM	P		38	.140	MIL	
3	3	PETERS, GARY CHARLES	P		33	.200	B	
		PETROCELLI, AMERICO PETER	3B	146	147	.240	B	
		(RICO)						
12	12	SIEBERT, WILFRED CHAS. (SONNY)	P	32	33	.236	B	
		SMITH, CARL REGINALD (REGGIE)	OF	129	131	.270	B	
0	2	TATUM, KENNETH RAY	P		22	.000	B	
15	6	TIANT, LUIS CLEMENTE	P		43	.107	B	
2	0	VEALE, ROBERT ANDREW	P		6	.000	XPITN	
0	0	WILLIAMS, STANLEY WILSON	P		3	.000	STLN	
		YASTRZEMSKI, CARL MICHAEL	OF	83	125	.264	B	
		(1B42)						

WON 75 LOST 87 TIED 0 TG 162

AMERICAN LEAGUE 1965. FINISHED 7 PCT. .463

CALIFORNIA

WILLIAM JOSEPH RIGNEY

WON	LOST	NAME	POS.		G.	BA	FROM	TO
		ADCOCK, JOSEPH WILBUR	1B	97	122	.240	LA	B
9	11	BRUNET, GEORGE STUART	P		41	.054	LA	B
		CARDENAL, JOSE DOMEC	OF	129	134	.250	SF N	B
		(2B1 3B2)						
15	10	CHANCE, WILMER DEAN	P		36	.093	LA	B
		CIMOLI, GINO NICHOLAS	OF	1	4	.000	BAL	C
		CLINTON, LUCIEAN LOUIS	OF	73	89	+.243	LA	XKC
2	0	COATES, JAMES ALTON	P		17	.000	CINN63	B
		DEES, CHARLES HENRY	1B	8	12	.156	LA	C
		EGAN, THOMAS PATRICK	C	16	18	.263	A	B
		FREGOSI, JAMES LOUIS	SS	160	161	.277	LA	B
4	5	GATEWOOD, AUBREY LEE	P		46	.214	LA	ATLN70
		GOTAY, JULIO SANCHEZ	2B	23	40	.247	PITN	HOUN
		(SS1 3B9)						
		HERNANDEZ, JACINTO (JACKIE)	SS	2	6	.333	A	B
		(3B1)						
		KIRKPATRICK EDGAR LEON	OF		19	.260	LA	B
		KNOOP, ROBERT FRANK	2B		142	.269	LA	B
		KOPPE, JOSEPH	2B	10	23	.212	LA	C
		(SS4 3B4)						
1	1	LATMAN, ARNOLD BARRY	P		18	.000	LA	HOUN
0	1	LEE, DONALD EDWARD	P		10	.333	LA	XHOUN
9	7	LEE, ROBERT DEAN	P		69	.143	LA	B
14	13	LOPEZ, MARCELINO PONS	P	35	52	.203	PHIN63	B
4	9	MAY, RUDOLPH	P		30	.200	A	CAL 69
0	3	MC BRIDE, KENNETH FAYE	P		8	.000	LA	C
0	3	MC GLOTHLIN, JAMES MILTON	P		3	.000	A	B
14	16	NEWMAN, FREDERICK WILLIAM	P		36	.095	LA	B
		PEARSON, ALBERT GREGORY	OF	101	122	.278	LA	B
0	3	PICHE, RONALD JACQUES	P		14	.000	MILN63	STLN
		PIERSALL, JAMES ANTHONY	OF	41	53	.268	LA	B
		POWER, VICTOR PELLOT	1B	107	124	.259	PHIN	C
		(2B6 3B2)						
		RANEW, MERRITT THOMAS	C	24	41	.209	MILN	SEA 69
		REICHARDT, FREDERIC CARL	OF		20	.267	LA	B
		RODGERS, ROBERT LEROY	C	128	132	.210	LA	B
		ROOF, PHILLIP ANTHONY	C		9	+.136	MILN	XCLE
1	2	SANFORD, JOHN STANLEY	P		9	.143	XSF N	B
		SATRIANO, THOMAS VICTOR	3B	15	47	.165	LA	B
		(C12 1B3 2B12)						
		SCHAAL, PAUL (2B1)	3B	153	155	.224	LA	B
		SHOCKLEY, JOHN COSTEN (OF1)	1B	31	40	.187	PHIN	C
		SIMPSON, RICHARD CHARLES	OF		8	.222	LA	CINN
		SMITH, BOBBY GENE	OF	15	23	.228	STLN62	C
		SMITH, WILLIE (1B2)	OF	123	136	.261	LA	B
		SPANGLER, ALBERT DONALD	OF	24	51	.260	XHOUN	B
2	3	SULKA, EDWARD ANTHONY	P		25	.000	LA	B
0	0	WANTZ, RICHARD CARTER	P		1	.000	A	C

CLUB TRANSFERRED FROM LOS ANGELES TO ANAHEIM AFTER 1964 SEASON,
NAME CHANGED TO CALIFORNIA.

WON 80 LOST 82 TIED 0 TG 162

AMERICAN LEAGUE 1966. FINISHED 6 PCT. .494

CALIFORNIA

WILLIAM JOSEPH RIGNEY

WON	LOST	NAME	POS.		G.	BA	FROM	TO
		ADCOCK, JOSEPH WILBUR	1B	71	83	.273	B	C
		BAILEY, LONAS EDGAR (ED)			5	.000	CHIN	C
13	13	BRUNET, GEORGE STUART	P		41	.103	B	B
7	2	BURDETTE, SELVA LEWIS (LEW)	P		54	.125	PHIN	B
		CARDENAL, JOSE DOMEC	OF	146	154	.276	B	B
12	17	CHANCE, WILMER DEAN	P		41	.026	B	MIN
1	1	COATES, JAMES ALTON	P		9	.091	B	B
0	0	EGAN, RICHARD WALLIS	P		11	.000	DET 64	LA N
		EGAN, THOMAS PATRICK	C	6	7	.000	B	B
		FREGOSI, JAMES LOUIS (1B1)	SS	162	162	.252	B	B
		HERNANDEZ, JACINTO (JACKIE)	3B	11	58	.043	B	MIN
		(2B8 SS8 OF3)						
		JOHNSTONE, JOHN WM. (JAY)	OF		61	.264	A	B
1	1	KELSO, WILLIAM EUGENE	P		5	.000	LA 64	B
		KIRKPATRICK EDGAR LEON (1B3)	OF	102	117	.192	B	B
		KNOOP, ROBERT FRANK	2B		161	.232	B	B
5	4	LEE, ROBERT DEAN	P		61	.000	B	LA N
0	1	LOPEZ, JOSE RAMON	P	4	5	.000	A	C
7	14	LOPEZ, MARCELINO PONS	P	37	55	.190	B	B
		MALZONE, FRANK JAMES	3B	35	82	.206	BOS	C
3	1	MC GLOTHLIN, JAMES MILTON	P		19	.059	B	B
		MONTANEZ, GUILLERMO (WILLIE)	1B	2	8	.000	A	PHIN70
		MORTON, WYCLIFFE NATHANIEL	OF	14	15	.220	MILN63	B
		(BUBBA)						
4	7	NEWMAN, FREDERICK WILLIAM	P		21	.200	B	B
		PEARSON, ALBERT GREGORY	OF	1	2	.000	B	C
		PIERSALL, JAMES ANTHONY	OF	63	75	.211	B	B
0	1	REED, HOWARD DEAN	P		19	.000	XLA N	HOUN
		REICHARDT, FREDERIC CARL	OF	87	89	.288	B	B
		RODGERS, ROBERT LEROY	C		133	.236	B	B
7	4	ROJAS, MINERVINO ALEJANDRO	P		47	.071	A	B
2	1	RUBIO, JORGE JESUS	P		7	.000	A	B
13	7	SANFORD, JOHN STANLEY	P		50	.136	B	B
		SATRIANO, THOMAS VICTOR	C	43	103	.239	B	B
		(1B36 2B4 3B25)						
		SCHAAL, PAUL	3B	131	138	.244	B	B
		SIEBERN, NORMAN LEROY	1B	99	125	.247	BAL	SF N
		SMITH, WILLIE	OF	52	90	.185	B	CLE
		SPANGLER, ALBERT DONALD	OF	3	6	.667	B	CHIN
1	1	SULKA, EDWARD ANTHONY	P		12	.000	B	C
		VINSON, CHARLES ANTHONY	1B	11	13	.182	A	C
		WARNER, JOHN JOSEPH (JACKIE)	OF	37	45	.211	A	C
4	7	WRIGHT, CLYDE	P	20	24	.103	A	B

WON 84
LOST 77
TIED 0
TG 161

AMERICAN LEAGUE

1967.

FINISHED 5

PCT. .522

CALIFORNIA

WILLIAM JOSEPH RIGNEY

WON	LOST	NAME	POS.		G.	BA	FROM	TO
11	19	BRUNET, GEORGE STUART	P		40	.077	B	B
1	0	BURDETTE, SELVA LEWIS (LEW)	P		19	.000	B	C
		CARDENAL, JOSE DOMEC	OF	101	108	.236	B	CLE
3	3	CIMINO, PETER WILLIAM	P		46	.417	MIN	B
12	11	CLARK, RICKEY CHARLES	P		32	.040	A	B
1	2	COATES, JAMES ALTON	P		25	.333	B	C
		EGAN, THOMAS PATRICK	C		1	.000	B	B
		FREGOSI, JAMES LOUIS	SS		151	.290	B	B
		GABRIELSON, LEONARD GARY	OF	1	11	.083	SF N	XLA N
		HALL, JIMMIE RANDOLPH	OF	120	129	.249	MIN	B
9	6	HAMILTON, JACK EDWIN	P		26	.158	XNY N	B
		HELD, WOODSON GEORGE	3B	19	58	+.220	XBAL	B
		(2B3 SS13 OF17)						
		HIBBS, JAMES KERR			3	.000	A	C
		JOHNSTONE, JOHN WM. (JAY)	OF	63	79	.209	B	B
5	3	KELSO, WILLIAM EUGENE	P		69	.105	B	CINN
		KIRKPATRICK EDGAR LEON (OF1)	C	2	3	.000	B	B
		KNOOP, ROBERT FRANK	2B		159	.245	B	B
3	0	LOCKE, LAWRENCE DONALD (BOBBY)	P		9	.667	CINN65	B
0	2	LOPEZ, MARCELINO PONS	P	4	7	+.500	B	XBAL
		MC FARLANE, ORLANDO DEJESUS	C	6	12	.227	DET	B
12	8	MC GLOTHLIN, JAMES MILTON	P		32	.140	B	B
		MINCHER, DONALD RAY (OF1)	1B	142	147	.273	MIN	B
		MORTON, WYCLIFFE NATHANIEL	OF	61	80	.313	B	B
		(BUBBA)						
1	0	NEWMAN, FREDERICK WILLIAM	P		3	.000	B	C
		PIERSALL, JAMES ANTHONY	OF	1	5	.000	B	C
		REICHARDT, FREDERIC CARL	OF	138	146	.265	B	B
		REPOZ, ROGER ALLEN	OF	63	74	+.250	XKC	B
		RODGERS, ROBERT LEROY (OF1)	C	134	139	.219	B	B
		RODRIGUEZ, AURELIO	3B		29	.238	A	B
12	9	ROJAS, MINERVINO ALEJANDRO	P		72	.059	B	B
0	2	RUBIO, JORGE JESUS	P		3	.333	B	C
3	2	SANFORD, JOHN STANLEY	P		12	+.200	B	XKC
		SATRIANO, THOMAS VICTOR	3B	38	90	.224	B	B
		(C23 1B5 2B15)						
		SCHAAL, PAUL	3B	88	99	.188	B	B
		(2B1 SS2)						
2	1	SIMMONS, CURTIS THOMAS	P		14	.222	XCHIN	STLN
		SKOWRON, WM. JOSEPH (MOOSE)	1B	32	62	+.220	XCHI	C
		STUBING, LAWRENCE GEORGE			5	.000	A	C
		TAYLOR, ROBERT DALE (HAWK)	C	19	23	.308	XNY N	KC 69
1	2	TURNER, KENNETH CHARLES	P		13	.000	A	C
		WALLACE, DONALD ALLEN	2B	4	23	.000	A	C
		(1B1 3B1)						
3	0	WEAVER, JAMES BRIAN	P		13	.000	A	B
		WERHAS, JOHN CHARLES	3B	30	49	.160	XLA N	C
		(1B4 OF1)						
0	2	WILLHITE, JON NICHOLAS (NICK)	P		10	.000	LA N	XNY N
5	5	WRIGHT, CLYDE	P	20	23	.273	B	B

WON 67
LOST 95
TIED 0
TG 162

AMERICAN LEAGUE

1968.

FINISHED 8
(TIED WITH CHICAGO)
PCT. .414

CALIFORNIA

WILLIAM JOSEPH RIGNEY

WON	LOST	NAME	POS.		G.	BA	FROM	TO
0	5	BENNETT, DENNIS JOHN	P		16	.077	NY N	C
13	17	BRUNET, GEORGE STUART	P		39	.081	B	B
1	4	BURGMEIER, THOMAS HENRY	P	56	71	.000	A	KC
		(OF1)						
		CAUSEY, JAMES WAYNE	2B		4	+.000	XCHI	XATLN
0	0	CIMINO, PETER WILLIAM	P		4	.000	B	C
1	11	CLARK, RICKEY CHARLES	P		21	.107	B	B
		COTTIER, CHARLES KEITH (2B4)	3B	27	33	.194	WAS 65	B
		DAVALILLO, VICTOR JOSE	OF	86	93	+.298	XCLE	B
		EGAN, THOMAS PATRICK	C	14	16	.116	B	B
9	10	ELLIS, SAMUEL JOSEPH	P		42	.045	CINN	CHI
		FREGOSI, JAMES LOUIS	SS		159	.244	B	B
		HALL, JIMMIE RANDOLPH	OF	39	46	+.214	B	XCLE
3	1	HAMILTON, JACK EDWIN	P		21	.143	B	CLE
1	6	HARRELSON, WILLIAM CHARLES	P		10	.100	A	C
0	0	HEFFNER, ROBERT FREDERICK	P		7	.000	CLE 66	C
		HELD, WOODSON GEORGE	2B	5	33	+.111	B	XCHI
		(SS5 3B5 OF3)						
		HINTON, CHARLES EDWARD	1B	48	116	.195	CLE	CLE
		(2B9 3B13 OF37)						
		JOHNSTONE, JOHN WM. (JAY)	OF	29	41	.261	B	B
0	1	KEALEY, STEVEN WILLIAM	P		6	.000	A	B
		KIRKPATRICK EDGAR LEON	OF	45	89	.230	B	KC
		(C4 1B2)						
		KNOOP, ROBERT FRANK	2B	151	152	.249	B	B
		LLENAS, WINSTON ENRIQUILLO	3B	9	16	.128	A	B
2	3	LOCKE, LAWRENCE DONALD (BOBBY)	P		29	.000	B	C
		MC FARLANE, ORLANDO DEJESUS	C	9	18	.290	B	C
10	15	MC GLOTHLIN, JAMES MILTON	P		40	.111	B	B
4	2	MESSERSMITH, JOHN ALEXANDER	P	28	29	.100	A	B
		(ANDY)						
		MINCHER, DONALD RAY	1B	113	120	.236	B	SEA
		MORTON, WYCLIFFE NATHANIEL	OF	50	81	.270	B	B
		(BUBBA) (3B1)						
5	6	MURPHY, THOMAS ANDREW	P		15	.000	A	B
4	4	PATTIN, MARTIN WILLIAM	P		52	.083	A	SEA
		REICHARDT, FREDERIC CARL	OF	148	151	.255	B	B
		REPOZ, ROGER ALLEN	OF	114	133	.240	B	B
		RODGERS, ROBERT LEROY	C	87	91	.190	B	B
		RODRIGUEZ, AURELIO (2B2)	3B	70	76	.242	B	B
4	3	ROJAS, MINERVINO ALEJANDRO	P		38	.100	B	C
		SATRIANO, THOMAS VICTOR	C	85	111	.253	B	B
		(1B1 2B14 3B11)						
		SCHAAL, PAUL	3B	58	60	.210	B	KC
0	0	SHERRY, LAWRENCE	P		3	.000	HOUN	C
		SPENCER, JAMES LLOYD	1B		19	.191	A	B
		TATUM, JARVIS	OF	11	17	.176	A	B
		TREVINO, CARLOS (BOBBY)	OF	11	17	.225	A	C
0	1	WEAVER, JAMES BRIAN	P		14	.000	B	C
10	6	WRIGHT, CLYDE	P	41	51	.216	B	B

WON 71
LOST 91
TIED 1
TG 163

AMERICAN LEAGUE

1969.

FINISHED 3 W

PCT. .438

CALIFORNIA

WILLIAM JOSEPH RIGNEY HAROLD ROSS PHILLIPS

WON	LOST	NAME	POS.		G.	BA	FROM	TO
0	1	ALLEN, LLOYD CECIL	P		4	.500	A	B
		ALOMAR, SANTOS	2B		134	+.250	XCHI	B
		AMARO, RUBEN MORA	1B	18	41	.222	NY	C
		(2B9 SS5 3B2)						
		AZCUE, JOSE JOAQUIN	C		80	+.218	XBOS	B
2	3	BORBON, PEDRO	P		22	.000	A	CINN
0	1	BRADLEY, THOMAS WILLIAM	P		3	.000	A	B
		BROWN, EDWIN RANDOLPH (RANDY)	C	10	13	.160	A	B
		(OF1)						
6	7	BRUNET, GEORGE STUART	P		23	+.037	B	XSEA
		CHANCE, ROBERT	1B	1	5	.143	WAS 67	C
0	0	CLARK, RICKEY CHARLES	P		6	.500	B	CAL 71
		COTTIER, CHARLES KEITH	2B		2	.000	B	C
		COWAN, BILLY ROLLAND	OF	13	28	+.304	XNY	B
		DAVALILLO, VICTOR JOSE (1B3)	OF	22	33	.155	B	XSTLN
		EGAN, THOMAS PATRICK	C		46	.142	B	B
3	2	FISHER, EDDIE GENE	P		52	.000	CLE	B
		FREGOSI, JAMES LOUIS	SS	160	161	.260	B	B
1	1	GEISHERT, VERNON WILLIAM	P		11	.000	A	C
		HICKS, JAMES EDWARD (1B8)	OF	10	37	.083	XSTLN	B
		JOHNSON, LOUIS BROWN	OF	44	67	.203	CLE	C
		JOHNSTONE, JOHN WM. (JAY)	OF	144	148	.270	B	B
2	0	KEALEY, STEVEN WILLIAM	P		15	.000	B	B
		KNOOP, ROBERT FRANK	2B		27	+.197	B	XCHI
		LLENAS, WINSTON ENRIQUILLO	3B	9	34	.170	B	CAL 72
10	13	MAY, RUDOLPH	P	43	44	.082	CAL 65	B
8	16	MC GLOTHLIN, JAMES MILTON	P		37	.121	B	CINN
16	11	MESSERSMITH, JOHN ALEXANDER	P	40	42	.156	B	B
		(ANDY)						
		MORTON, WYCLIFFE NATHANIEL	OF	49	87	.244	B	C
		(BUBBA) (1B1)						
10	16	MURPHY, THOMAS ANDREW	P		36	.141	B	B
0	0	ORTEGA, FILOMENO CORONADO	P		5	.000	WAS	C
		PEREZ, MARTIN ROMAN	SS	7	13	.231	A	B
		(2B2 3B2)						
0	1	PRIDDY, ROBERT SIMPSON	P		15	+.000	XCHI	XATLN
		REICHARDT, FREDERIC CARL	OF	136	137	.254	B	B
		(1B3)						
		REPOZ, ROGER ALLEN (1B31)	OF	48	103	.164	B	B
		RODGERS, ROBERT LEROY	C		18	.196	B	C
		RODRIGUEZ, AURELIO	3B		159	.232	B	B
		SATRIANO, THOMAS VICTOR	C	36	41	+.259	B	XBOS
		(1B5 2B2)						
		SPENCER, JAMES LLOYD	1B	107	113	.254	B	B
		STUART, RICHARD LEE	1B	13	22	.157	LA N66	C
		TATUM, JARVIS	OF	5	10	.318	B	B
7	2	TATUM, KENNETH RAY	P		45	.286	A	B
		VOSS, WILLIAM EDWARD (1B2)	OF	111	133	.261	CHI	B
0	2	WASHBURN, GREGORY JAMES	P		8	.000	A	C
5	7	WILHELM, JAMES HOYT	P		44	.000	CHI	XATLN
0	0	WOLF, WALTER BECK	P		2	.000	A	B
1	8	WRIGHT, CLYDE	P	37	40	.182	B	B

WON 86
LOST 76
TIED 0
TG 162

AMERICAN LEAGUE

1970.

FINISHED 3 W

PCT. .531

CALIFORNIA

HAROLD ROSS PHILLIPS

WON	LOST	NAME	POS.		G.	BA	FROM	TO
1	1	ALLEN, LLOYD CECIL	P		8	.000	B	B
		ALOMAR, SANTOS (SS10 3B1)	2B	153	162	.251	B	B
		AZCUE, JOSE JOAQUIN	C	112	114	.242	B	CAL 72
2	5	BRADLEY, THOMAS WILLIAM	P		17	.167	B	CHI
		BROWN, EDWIN RANDOLPH (RANDY)	C		5	.000	B	C
		COWAN, BILLY ROLLAND	OF	27	68	.276	B	B
		(1B14 3B2)						
0	0	COX, TERRY LEE	P		3	.000	A	C
3	1	DOYLE, PAUL SINNOTT	P		40	.000	ATLN	XSD N
		EGAN, THOMAS PATRICK	C		79	.238	B	CHI
4	4	FISHER, EDDIE GENE	P		67	.091	B	B
		FREGOSI, JAMES LOUIS (1B6)	SS	150	158	.278	B	B
5	6	GARRETT, GREGORY	P		32	.067	A	CINN
		GONZALEZ, ANDRES ANTONIO	OF	24	26	.304	XATLN	B
		GRIFFIN, DOUGLAS LEE (3B8)	2B	11	18	.127	A	BOS
		HICKS, JAMES EDWARD			4	.250	B	C
		JOHNSON, ALEXANDER	OF		156	.329	CINN	B
		JOHNSTONE, JOHN WM. (JAY)	OF	100	119	.237	B	CHI
1	0	KEALEY, STEVEN WILLIAM	P		17	.250	B	CHI
4	1	LA ROCHE, DAVID EUGENE	P		38	.250	A	B
7	13	MAY, RUDOLPH	P		38	.087	B	B
		MC MULLEN, KENNETH LEE	3B	122	124	+.232	XWAS	B
11	10	MESSERSMITH, JOHN ALEXANDER	P	37	38	.157	B	B
		(ANDY)						
16	13	MURPHY, THOMAS ANDREW	P		39	.184	B	B
		OYLER, RAYMOND FRANCIS (3B2)	SS	13	24	.083	SEA	C
		PEREZ, MARTIN ROMAN	SS	2	3	.000	B	ATLN
3	6	QUEEN, MELVIN DOUGLAS	P	34	37	.250	CINN	B
		REICHARDT, FREDERIC CARL	OF	1	9	+.167	B	XWAS
		REPOZ, ROGER ALLEN (1B18)	OF	110	137	.238	B	B
		REYNOLDS, TOMMIE D. (3B1)	OF	32	59	.250	OAK	B
		RIVERS, JOHN MILTON (MICKEY)	OF	5	17	.320	A	B
		RODRIGUEZ, AURELIO	3B		17	+.270	B	XWAS
		RUIZ, HIRALDO SABLON (CHICO)	3B	27	68	.243	CINN	B
		(C1 1B2 2B3 SS3)						
0	0	SHANK, HARVEY TILLMAN	P		1	.000	A	C
		SILVERIO, TOMAS ROBERTO	OF	5	15	.000	A	B
		(1B1)						
		SPENCER, JAMES LLOYD	1B	142	146	.274	B	B
		TATUM, JARVIS	OF	58	75	.238	B	C
7	4	TATUM, KENNETH RAY	P		62	.182	B	BOS
		VOSS, WILLIAM EDWARD	OF	55	80	.243	B	MIL
0	0	WOLF, WALTER BECK	P		4	.000	B	C
22	12	WRIGHT, CLYDE	P	39	47	.171	B	B

WON 76
LOST 86
TIED 0
TG 162

AMERICAN LEAGUE — 1971. — FINISHED 4 W — PCT. .469

CALIFORNIA

HAROLD ROSS PHILLIPS

WON	LOST	NAME	POS.		G.	BA	FROM	TO
4	6	ALLEN, LLOYD CECIL	P		54	.294	B	B
		ALOMAR, SANTOS (SS28)	2B	137	162	.260	B	B
		BERRY, ALLEN KENT (KEN)	OF	101	111	.221	CHI	B
		CHRISTENSEN, BRUCE RAY	SS	24	29	.270	A	C
2	1	CLARK, RICKEY CHARLES	P		11	.267	CAL 69	B
		CONIGLIARO, ANTHONY RICHARD	OF	72	74	.222	BOS	C
		COWAN, BILLY ROLLAND (1B5)	OF	40	74	.276	B	B
10	8	FISHER, EDDIE GENE	P		57	.063	B	B
		FREGOSI, JAMES LOUIS	SS	74	107	.233	B	NY N
		(1B18 OF7)						
		GONZALEZ, ANDRES ANTONIO	OF	88	111	.245	B	C
0	3	HASSLER, ANDREW EARL	P		6	.000	A	C
		JOHNSON, ALEXANDER	OF	61	65	.260	B	CLE
		KUSNYER, ARTHUR WILLIAM	C		6	.154	CHI	B
5	1	LA ROCHE, DAVID EUGENE	P		56	.091	B	MIN
0	0	LASHER, FREDERICK WALTER	P		2	.000	CLE	C
0	3	MALONEY, JAMES WILLIAM	P		13	.200	CINN	C
11	12	MAY, RUDOLPH	P		32	.147	B	B
		MC MULLEN, KENNETH LEE	3B	158	160	.250	B	B
		MEOLI, RUDOLPH BART			7	.000	A	C
20	13	MESSERSMITH, JOHN ALEXANDER	P	38	39	.172	B	B
		(ANDY)						
		MOSES, GERALD BRAHEEN (OF1)	C	63	69	.227	BOS	CLE
6	17	MURPHY, THOMAS ANDREW	P		37	.173	B	B
		O'BRIEN, SYDNEY LLOYD	SS	52	90	.199	CHI	B
		(1B1 2B7 3B6 OF1)						
		PARKER, WILLIAM DAVID	2B		20	.229	A	B
2	2	QUEEN, MELVIN DOUGLAS	P	44	45	.000	B	B
		REPOZ, ROGER ALLEN (1B13)	OF	97	113	.199	B	B
0	3	REYNOLDS, ARCHIE EDWARD	P		15	.000	CHIN	MIL
		REYNOLDS, TOMMIE D. (3B1)	OF	26	45	.186	B	MIL
		RIVERS, JOHN MILTON (MICKEY)	OF	75	78	.265	B	B
		RUIZ, HIRALDO SABLON (CHICO)	3B	3	31	.263	B	C
		(2B2)						
		SILVERIO, TOMAS ROBERTO	OF	1	3	.333	B	B
		SPENCER, JAMES LLOYD	1B	145	148	.237	B	B
		STEPHENSON, JOHN HERMAN	C	88	98	.219	SF N	B
		TORBORG, JEFFREY ALLEN	C	49	55	.203	LA N	B
16	17	WRIGHT, CLYDE	P	37	40	.154	B	B
0	0	WYNNE, BILLY VERNON	P		3	.000	CHI	C

WON 75
LOST 80
TIED 0
TG 155

AMERICAN LEAGUE — 1972. — FINISHED 5 W — PCT. .484

CALIFORNIA

DELBERT W. RICE

WON	LOST	NAME	POS.		G.	BA	FROM	TO
3	7	ALLEN, LLOYD CECIL	P		42	.118	B	
		ALOMAR, SANTOS (SS4)	2B	154	155	.239	B	
		AZCUE, JOSE JOAQUIN	C	2	3	+.000	CAL 70	XMIL
4	4	BARBER, STEPHEN DAVID	P		34	.143	XATLN	
		BERRY, ALLEN KENT (KEN)	OF	116	119	.289	B	
		CARDENAS, LEONARDO ALFONSO	SS		150	.223	MIN	
4	9	CLARK, RICKEY CHARLES	P	26	27	.097	B	
		COLETTA, CHRISTOPHER MICHAEL	OF	7	14	.300	A	
		COWAN, BILLY ROLLAND			3	.000	B	
0	0	DOYLE, PAUL SINNOTT	P		2	.000	SD N70	
0	1	DUKES, THOMAS EARL	P		7	.000	BAL	
4	5	FISHER, EDDIE GENE	P		43	+.118	B	XCHI
0	1	FOSTER, ALAN BENTON	P		8	.000	CLE	
		HIATT, JACK E.	C	17	22	.289	XHOUN	
		HOWARD, DOUGLAS LYNN	OF	8	11	.263	A	
		(1B1 3B1)						
		KOSCO, ANDREW JOHN	OF	36	49	+.239	MIL	XBOS
		KUSNYER, ARTHUR WILLIAM	C	63	64	.207	B	
0	0	LANGE, RICHARD OTTO	P		2	.000	A	
		LLENAS, WINSTON ENRIQUILLO	3B	10	44	.266	CAL 69	
		(2B2 OF2)						
12	11	MAY, RUDOLPH	P		35	.113	B	
		MC MULLEN, KENNETH LEE	3B		137	.269	B	
8	11	MESSERSMITH, JOHN ALEXANDER	P	25	26	.189	B	
		(ANDY)						
		MOTTON, CURTELL HOWARD	OF	9	42	+.154	XMIL	
0	0	MURPHY, THOMAS ANDREW	P		6	+.000	B	XKC
		O'BRIEN, SYDNEY LLOYD	3B	8	36	+.179	B	XMIL
		(1B1 2B3 SS4)						
		OLIVER, ROBERT LEE (OF8)	1B	127	134	+.269	XKC	
		PARKER, WILLIAM DAVID	3B	21	36	.213	B	
		(2B9 SS1 OF5)						
		PINSON, VADA EDWARD (1B1)	OF	134	136	.275	CLE	
0	0	QUEEN, MELVIN DOUGLAS	P		17	.000	B	
		REPOZ, ROGER ALLEN			3	.333	B	
		RIVERS, JOHN MILTON (MICKEY)	OF	48	58	.214	B	
1	4	ROSE, DONALD GARY	P		16	.200	NY N	
19	16	RYAN, LYNN NOLAN	P		39	.135	NY N	
2	0	SELLS, DAVID WAYNE	P		10	.000	A	
		SILVERIO, TOMAS ROBERTO	OF	4	13	.167	B	
		SPENCER, JAMES LLOYD (OF24)	1B	35	82	.222	B	
		STANTON, LEROY BOBBY	OF	124	127	.251	NY N	
		STEPHENSON, JOHN HERMAN	C	56	66	.274	B	
		TORBORG, JEFFREY ALLEN	C	58	59	.209	B	
18	11	WRIGHT, CLYDE	P		35	.217	B	

WON 95 LOST 67 TIED 0 TG 162

AMERICAN LEAGUE 1965. FINISHED 2 PCT. .586

CHICAGO

ALFONSO RAMON LOPEZ

WON	LOST	NAME	POS.		G.	BA	FROM	TO
		AGEE, TOMMIE LEE	OF	9	10	.158	CLE	B
		BERRY, ALLEN KENT (KEN)	OF	156	157	.218	B	B
0	0	BOLLO, GREGORY GENE	P		15	.000	A	B
		BUFORD, DONALD ALVIN (3B41)	2B	139	155	.283	B	B
		BURGESS, FORREST HARRILL	C	5	80	.286	B	B
		(SMOKY)						
13	8	BUZHARDT, JOHN WILLIAM	P	32	34	.125	B	B
		CATER, DANNY ANDERSON	OF	127	142	.270	PHIN	B
		(1B3 3B11)						
15	7	FISHER, EDDIE GENE	P		82	.138	B	B
		FREESE, EUGENE LEWIS	3B	8	17	.281	XPITN	B
		HANSEN, RONALD LAVERN (2B1)	SS	161	162	.235	B	B
		HEATH, WILLIAM CHRIS			1	.000	A	HOUN
		HICKS, JAMES EDWARD	OF	5	13	.263	B	B
13	13	HORLEN, JOEL EDWARD (JOE)	P		34	.132	B	B
9	8	HOWARD, BRUCE ERNEST	P		30	.146	B	B
14	7	JOHN, THOMAS EDWARD	P		39	.169	CLE	B
		JOSEPHSON, DUANE CHARLES	C		4	.111	A	B
		KENWORTHY, RICHARD LEE			3	.000	B	B
1	0	LARY, FRANK STRONG	P		14	.500	XNY N	C
5	2	LOCKER, ROBERT AUTRY	P		51	.000	A	B
		MARTIN, JOSEPH CLIFTON (J.C.)	C	112	119	.261	B	B
		(1B4 3B2)						
		MC CRAW, TOMMIE LEE (OF64)	1B	72	133	.238	B	B
		NICHOLSON, DAVID LAWRENCE	OF	36	54	.153	B	HOUN
10	12	PETERS, GARY CHARLES	P	33	42	.181	B	B
6	3	PIZARRO, JUAN	P	18	19	.235	B	B
		ROBINSON, FLOYD ANDREW	OF	153	156	.265	B	B
		ROMANO, JOHN ANTHONY	C	111	122	.242	CLE	B
		(1B2 OF4)						
		SCHAFFER, JIMMIE RONALD	C	14	17	.194	CHIN	XNY N
		SKOWRON, WM. JOSEPH (MOOSE)	1B	145	146	.274	B	B
		STAEHLE, MARVIN GUSTAVE			7	.429	B	B
		VOSS, WILLIAM EDWARD	OF	10	11	.182	A	B
		WARD, PETER THOMAS (2B1)	3B	134	138	.247	B	B
		WEIS, ALBERT JOHN	2B	74	103	.296	B	B
		(SS7 3B2 OF2)						
7	7	WILHELM, JAMES HOYT	P		66	.000	B	B
2	0	WILLS, THEODORE CARL	P		15	.000	CINN62	C

WON 83 LOST 79 TIED 1 TG 163

AMERICAN LEAGUE 1966. FINISHED 4 PCT. .512

CHICAGO

EDWARD RAYMOND STANKY

WON	LOST	NAME	POS.		G.	BA	FROM	TO
		ADAIR, KENNETH JERRY (2B50)	SS	75	105	+.243	XBAL	B
		AGEE, TOMMIE LEE	OF	159	160	.273	B	B
		BERRY, ALLEN KENT (KEN)	OF	141	147	.271	B	B
0	1	BOLLO, GREGORY GENE	P		3	.000	B	C
		BRADFORD, CHARLES WM. (BUDDY)	OF	9	14	.143	A	B
		BUFORD, DONALD ALVIN	3B	133	163	.244	B	B
		(2B37 OF11)						
		BURGESS, FORREST HARRILL	C	2	79	.313	B	B
		(SMOKY)						
6	11	BUZHARDT, JOHN WILLIAM	P	33	34	.116	B	B
		CATER, DANNY ANDERSON	OF	18	21	+.183	B	XKC
		CAUSEY, JAMES WAYNE	2B	60	78	+.244	XKC	B
		(SS1 3B1)						
		ELIA, LEE CONSTANTINE	SS	75	80	.205	A	CHIN68
1	3	FISHER, EDDIE GENE	P		23	+.000	B	XBAL
		FREESE, EUGENE LEWIS	3B	34	48	.208	B	XHOUN
		HANSEN, RONALD LAVERN	SS		23	.176	B	B
		HICKS, JAMES EDWARD (1B2)	OF	10	18	.192	B	STLN69
1	0	HIGGINS, DENNIS DEAN	P		42	.176	A	B
10	13	HORLEN, JOEL EDWARD (JOE)	P	37	64	.067	B	B
9	5	HOWARD, BRUCE ERNEST	P		27	.070	B	B
14	11	JOHN, THOMAS EDWARD	P		34	.145	B	B
		JONES, GROVER WM. (DEACON)			5	.400	CHI 63	C
		JOSEPHSON, DUANE CHARLES	C		11	.237	B	B
		KENWORTHY, RICHARD LEE	3B	6	9	.200	B	B
1	0	KLAGES, FRED ANTHONY	P		3	.500	A	B
7	9	LAMABE, JOHN ALEXANDER	P		34	.057	HOUN	B
9	8	LOCKER, ROBERT AUTRY	P		56	.250	B	B
		MARTIN, JOSEPH CLIFTON (J.C.)	C	63	67	.255	B	B
		MC CRAW, TOMMIE LEE (OF41)	1B	121	151	.229	B	B
		MC NERTNEY, GERALD EDWARD	C	37	44	.220	CHI 64	B
12	10	PETERS, GARY CHARLES	P	30	38	.235	B	B
8	6	PIZARRO, JUAN	P		34	.154	B	PITN
		ROBINSON, FLOYD ANDREW	OF	113	127	.237	B	CINN
		ROMANO, JOHN ANTHONY	C	102	122	.231	B	STLN
		SKOWRON, WM. JOSEPH (MOOSE)	1B	98	120	.249	B	B
		STAEHLE, MARVIN GUSTAVE	2B	6	8	.133	B	B
		STROUD, EDWIN MARVIN	OF	11	12	.167	A	B
		VOSS, WILLIAM EDWARD	OF	1	2	.000	B	B
		WARD, PETER THOMAS	OF	59	84	.219	B	B
		(1B5 3B16)						
		WEIS, ALBERT JOHN (SS18)	2B	96	129	.155	B	B
5	2	WILHELM, JAMES HOYT	P		46	.125	B	B

WON 89
LOST 73
TIED 0
TG 162

AMERICAN LEAGUE

1967.

FINISHED 4

PCT. .549

CHICAGO

EDWARD RAYMOND STANKY

WON	LOST	NAME	POS.		G.	BA	FROM	TO
		ADAIR, KENNETH JERRY	2B	27	28	+.204	B	XBOS
		AGEE, TOMMIE LEE	OF	152	158	.234	B	NY N
		ALOMAR, SANTOS (2B2)	SS	8	12	.200	XNY N	B
		BERRY, ALLEN KENT (KEN)	OF	143	147	.241	B	B
		BOYER, KENTON LLOYD (1B18)	3B	33	57	.261	XNY N	B
		BRADFORD, CHARLES WM. (BUDDY)	OF	14	24	.100	B	B
		BUFORD, DONALD ALVIN	3B	121	156	.241	B	BAL
		(2B51 OF1)						
		BURGESS, FORREST HARRILL			77	.133	B	C
		(SMOKY)						
3	9	BUZHARDT, JOHN WILLIAM	P		28	+.200	B	XBAL
2	0	CARLOS, FRANCISCO MANUEL	P		8	.063	A	B
		CAUSEY, JAMES WAYNE (SS2)	2B	96	124	.226	B	B
		COLAVITO, ROCCO DOMENICO	OF	58	60	+.221	XCLE	LA N
		HANSEN, RONALD LAVERN	SS		157	.233	B	WAS
		HERRMANN, EDWARD MARTIN	C		2	.667	A	CHI 69
1	2	HIGGINS, DENNIS DEAN	P		9	.000	B	WAS
19	7	HORLEN, JOEL EDWARD (JOE)	P	35	51	.169	B	B
3	10	HOWARD, BRUCE ERNEST	P		30	.179	B	BAL
10	13	JOHN, THOMAS EDWARD	P		31	.157	B	B
2	2	JONES, STEVEN HOWELL	P		11	.250	A	WAS
		JOSEPHSON, DUANE CHARLES	C	59	62	.238	B	B
		KENWORTHY, RICHARD LEE	3B	35	50	.227	B	B
		KING, JAMES HUBERT	OF	12	23	+.120	XWAS	XCLE
4	4	KLAGES, FRED ANTHONY	P	11	12	.000	B	C
1	0	LAMABE, JOHN ALEXANDER	P		3	.000	B	XNY N
7	5	LOCKER, ROBERT AUTRY	P		77	.000	B	B
		MARTIN, JOSEPH CLIFTON (J.C.)	C	96	101	.234	B	NY N
		(1B1)						
		MC CRAW, TOMMIE LEE (OF6)	1B	123	125	.236	B	B
5	0	MC MAHON, DONALD JOHN	P		52	+.182	XBOS	B
		MC NERTNEY, GERALD EDWARD	C	52	56	.228	B	B
0	1	MONTEAGUDO, AURELIO FAUSTINO	P		1	.000	HOUN	KC 70
		MORALES, RICHARD ANGELO	SS	7	8	.000	A	B
		NASH, CHARLES FRANCIS (COTTON)	1B		3	.000	A	MIN 69
0	1	NELSON, ROGER EUGENE	P		5	.000	A	BAL
4	3	O'TOOLE, JAMES JEROME	P		15	.077	CINN	C
16	11	PETERS, GARY CHARLES	P	38	48	.212	B	B
		SKOWRON, WM. JOSEPH (MOOSE)			8	+.000	B	XCAL
		STAEHLE, MARVIN GUSTAVE	2B	17	32	.111	B	MONN69
		(SS5)						
		STEWART, JAMES FRANKLIN	OF	6	24	.167	XCHIN	CINN69
		(2B5 SS2)						
		STROUD, EDWIN MARVIN	OF	12	20	+.296	B	XWAS
		VOSS, WILLIAM EDWARD	OF	11	13	.091	B	B
		WARD, PETER THOMAS	OF	89	146	.233	B	B
		(1B39 3B22)						
		WEIS, ALBERT JOHN (SS13)	2B	32	50	.245	B	NY N
8	3	WILHELM, JAMES HOYT	P		49	.077	B	B
		WILLIAMS, WALTER ALLEN	OF	73	104	.240	HOUN64	B
4	2	WOOD, WILBUR FORRESTER	P		51	.063	PITN65	B

WON 67
LOST 95
TIED 0
TG 162

AMERICAN LEAGUE

1968.

FINISHED 8
(TIED WITH CALIFORNIA)
PCT. .414

CHICAGO

EDWARD RAYMOND STANKY JOHN LESTER MOSS ALFONSO RAMON LOPEZ

WON	LOST	NAME	POS.		G.	BA	FROM	TO
		ALOMAR, SANTOS	2B	99	133	.253	B	B
		(SS9 3B27 OF1)						
		APARICIO, LUIS ERNESTO	SS	154	155	.264	BAL	B
		BERRY, ALLEN KENT (KEN)	OF	151	153	.252	B	B
		BOOKER, RICHARD LEE (BUDDY)	C	3	5	.000	CLE 66	C
		BOYER, KENTON LLOYD (1B1)	3B	5	10	.125	B	XLA N
		BRADFORD, CHARLES WM. (BUDDY)	OF	99	103	.217	B	B
4	14	CARLOS, FRANCISCO MANUEL	P		29	.065	B	B
		CAUSEY, JAMES WAYNE	2B	41	59	+.180	B	XCAL
		CULLEN, TIMOTHY LEO	2B	71	72	+.200	WAS	XWAS
		DAVIS, HERMAN THOMAS (TOMMY)	OF	116	132	.268	NY N	SEA
		(1B6)						
8	13	FISHER, JOHN HOWARD	P		35	.113	NY N	CINN
		HANSEN, RONALD LAVERN (SS7)	3B	29	40	+.230	XWAS	B
		HELD, WOODSON GEORGE	OF	33	40	+.167	XCAL	B
		(2B1 3B5)						
		HOPKINS, GAIL EASON	1B	7	29	.216	A	B
12	14	HORLEN, JOEL EDWARD (JOE)	P	35	41	.104	B	B
10	5	JOHN, THOMAS EDWARD	P		25	.194	B	B
		JOSEPHSON, DUANE CHARLES	C	122	128	.247	B	B
		KENWORTHY, RICHARD LEE	3B	38	58	.221	B	C
0	1	LAZAR, JOHN DANIEL (DANNY)	P		8	.000	A	B
5	4	LOCKER, ROBERT AUTRY	P		70	.000	B	B
		MAY, CARLOS	OF		17	.179	A	B
		MC CRAW, TOMMIE LEE	1B	135	136	.235	B	B
2	1	MC MAHON, DONALD JOHN	P		25	+.333	B	XDET
		MC NERTNEY, GERALD EDWARD	C	64	74	.219	B	SEA
		(1B1)						
		MELTON, WILLIAM EDWIN	3B	33	34	.266	A	B
		MORALES, RICHARD ANGELO	SS	7	10	.172	B	B
		(2B5)						
2	1	NYMAN, GERALD SMITH	P		8	.154	A	B
4	13	PETERS, GARY CHARLES	P	31	46	.208	B	B
3	11	PRIDDY, ROBERT SIMPSON	P	35	42	.042	WAS	B
0	0	RATH, FRED HELSHER	P		5	.000	A	B
0	2	RIBANT, DENNIS JOSEPH	P		17	+.000	XDET	STLN
		SNYDER, RUSSELL HENRY	OF	22	38	+.134	BAL	XCLE
		VOSS, WILLIAM EDWARD	OF	55	61	.156	B	CAL
		WAGNER, LEON LAMAR	OF	46	69	+.284	XCLE	SF N
		WARD, PETER THOMAS	3B	77	125	.216	B	B
		(1B31 OF22)						
4	4	WILHELM, JAMES HOYT	P		72	.000	B	CAL
		WILLIAMS, WALTER ALLEN	OF	34	63	.241	B	B
13	12	WOOD, WILBUR FORRESTER	P		88	.091	B	B
0	0	WYNNE, BILLY VERNON	P		1	.000	NY N	B

COACH MOSS SERVED AS INTERIM MANAGER DURING CHANGEOVER.

WON 68
LOST 94
TIED 0
TG 162

AMERICAN LEAGUE

1969.

FINISHED 5 W

PCT. .420

CHICAGO

ALFONSO RAMON LOPEZ   DONALD JOSEPH GUTTERIDGE

WON	LOST	NAME	POS.		G.	BA	FROM	TO
		ADAMS, HAROLD DOUGLAS	C	4	8	.214	A	C
		ALOMAR, SANTOS	2B		22	+.224	B	XCAL
		APARICIO, LUIS ERNESTO	SS	154	156	.280	B	B
0	0	BELL, GARY	P		23	+.000	XSEA	C
		BERRY, ALLEN KENT (KEN)	OF	120	130	.232	B	B
		BRADFORD, CHARLES WM. (BUDDY)	OF	88	93	.256	B	B
		BRAVO, ANGEL ALFONSO	OF	25	27	.289	A	CINN
		BRINKMAN, CHARLES ERNEST	C		14	.067	A	B
4	3	CARLOS, FRANCISCO MANUEL	P		25	+.000	B	XWAS
		CHRISTIAN, ROBERT CHARLES	OF	38	39	.217	DET	B
1	6	EDMONDSON, PAUL MICHAEL	P		14	.172	A	C
0	3	ELLIS, SAMUEL JOSEPH	P		10	.167	CAL	C
0	3	HAMILTON, JACK EDWIN	P		8	+.000	XCLE	C
		HANSEN, RONALD LAVERN	2B	26	85	.259	B	NY
		(1B21 SS8 3B7)						
		HELD, WOODSON GEORGE	OF	18	56	.143	B	C
		(2B1 SS3 3B3)						
		HERRMANN, EDWARD MARTIN	C	92	102	.231	CHI 67	B
		HOPKINS, GAIL EASON	1B	101	124	.265	B	B
13	16	HORLEN, JOEL EDWARD (JOE)	P		36	.182	B	B
9	11	JOHN, THOMAS EDWARD	P		33	.114	B	B
1	3	JOHNSON, CLAIR BARTH (BART)	P		4	.167	A	B
		JOSEPHSON, DUANE CHARLES	C	47	52	.241	B	B
		KNOOP, ROBERT FRANK	2B		104	+.229	XCAL	B
0	0	LAZAR, JOHN DANIEL (DANNY)	P		9	.000	B	C
2	3	LOCKER, ROBERT AUTRY	P		17	+.000	B	XSEA
		MAY, CARLOS	OF		100	.281	B	B
		MC CRAW, TOMMIE LEE (OF41)	1B	44	93	.258	B	B
		MELTON, WILLIAM EDWIN (OF11)	3B	148	157	.255	B	B
		MORALES, RICHARD ANGELO	2B	38	55	.215	B	B
		(SS13 3B1)						
2	1	MURPHY, DANIEL FRANCIS	P		17	.000	CHIN62	B
4	4	NYMAN, GERALD SMITH	P	20	21	.050	B	SD N
		ORTIZ, JOSE LUIS	OF	8	16	.273	A	B
5	5	OSINSKI, DANIEL	P		51	.000	BOS 67	HOUN
0	0	O'TOOLE, DENNIS JOSEPH	P		2	.000	A	B
		PAVLETICH, DONALD STEPHEN	C	51	78	.245	CINN	BOS
		(1B13)						
10	15	PETERS, GARY CHARLES	P	36	37	.169	B	BOS
0	0	PRIDDY, ROBERT SIMPSON	P		4	+.000	B	XCAL
0	2	RATH, FRED HELSHER	P		3	.000	B	C
0	1	SECRIST, DONALD LAVERNE	P		19	.143	A	B
		SPENCE, ROBERT JOHN	1B	6	12	.154	A	B
		WARD, PETER THOMAS	1B	25	105	.246	B	NY
		(3B21 OF9)						
		WILLIAMS, WALTER ALLEN	OF	111	135	.304	B	B
10	11	WOOD, WILBUR FORRESTER	P		76	.000	B	B
7	7	WYNNE, BILLY VERNON	P		20	.122	B	B

WON 56
LOST 106
TIED 0
TG 162

AMERICAN LEAGUE

1970.

FINISHED 6 W (LAST)

PCT. .346

CHICAGO

DONALD JOSEPH GUTTERIDGE   MARION DANNE ADAIR   CHARLES WILLIAM TANNER

WON	LOST	NAME	POS.		G.	BA	FROM	TO
		APARICIO, LUIS ERNESTO	SS		146	.313	B	BOS
0	3	ARRIGO, GERALD WILLIAM	P		5	.0	CINN	C
		BERRY, ALLEN KENT (KEN)	OF	138	141	.276	B	CAL
		BLANCO, CARLOS OSVALDO (OSSIE)	1B	22	34	.197	A	C
		(OF1)						
		BRADFORD, CHARLES WM. (BUDDY)	OF	27	32	+.187	B	XCLE
		BRINKMAN, CHARLES ERNEST	C		9	.250	B	B
		CHRISTIAN, ROBERT CHARLES	OF	4	12	.267	B	C
4	7	CRIDER, JERRY STEPHEN	P		32	.083	MIN	C
0	0	EDDY, DONALD EUGENE	P		7	.000	A	B
0	0	HAMILTON, STEVE ABSHER	P		3	+.000	XNY	SF N
		HERRMANN, EDWARD MARTIN	C	88	96	.283	B	B
		HOPKINS, GAIL EASON (C8)	1B	77	116	.286	B	KC
6	16	HORLEN, JOEL EDWARD (JOE)	P		28	.115	B	B
10	17	JANESKI, GERALD JOSEPH	P		35	.076	A	WAS
12	17	JOHN, THOMAS EDWARD	P	37	38	.202	B	B
4	7	JOHNSON, CLAIR BARTH (BART)	P		18	.276	B	B
		JOSEPHSON, DUANE CHARLES	C	84	96	.316	B	BOS
		KNOOP, ROBERT FRANK	2B	126	130	.229	B	KC
		KUSNYER, ARTHUR WILLIAM	C	3	4	.100	A	CAL
1	5	MAGNUSON, JAMES ROBERT	P		13	.000	A	B
		MATIAS, JOHN ROY (1B18)	OF	22	58	.188	A	C
		MAY, CARLOS (1B7)	OF	141	150	.285	B	B
		MAYE, ARTHUR LEE			6	+.167	XWAS	B
		MC CRAW, TOMMIE LEE (OF49)	1B	59	129	.220	B	WAS
		MC KINNEY, CHARLES RICHARD	3B	23	43	.168	A	B
		(SS11)						
		MELTON, WILLIAM EDWIN (3B70)	OF	71	141	.263	B	B
4	6	MILLER, ROBERT LANE	P	15	16	+.174	XCLE	XCHIN
0	0	MOLONEY, RICHARD HENRY	P		1	.000	A	C
0	4	MOORE, ROBERT BARRY	P		24	+.263	XCLE	C
		MORALES, RICHARD ANGELO	SS	24	62	.161	B	B
		(2B12 3B20)						
2	3	MURPHY, DANIEL FRANCIS	P		51	.333	B	C
		O'BRIEN, SYDNEY LLOYD	3B	68	121	.247	BOS	CAL
		(2B43 SS5)						
		ORTIZ, JOSE LUIS	OF	8	15	.333	B	CHIN
0	0	O'TOOLE, DENNIS JOSEPH	P		3	.000	B	B
0	1	ROUNSAVILLE, VIRLE GENE	P		8	.000	A	C
0	0	SECRIST, DONALD LAVERNE	P		9	.000	B	C
1	1	SISK, TOMMIE WAYNE	P		17	.250	SD N	C
		SPENCE, ROBERT JOHN	1B	37	46	.223	B	B
1	0	STANGE, ALBERT LEE	P		16	+.000	XBOS	C
1	2	WEAVER, DAVID FLOYD	P		31	.000	CLE 65	MIL
		WILLIAMS, WALTER ALLEN	OF	79	110	.251	B	B
9	13	WOOD, WILBUR FORRESTER	P		77	.111	B	B
1	4	WYNNE, BILLY VERNON	P		12	.077	B	CAL

COACH ADAIR SERVED AS INTERIM MANAGER DURING CHANGEOVER.

WON	79	AMERICAN LEAGUE	FINISHED	3 W
LOST	83	1971.	PCT. .488	
TIED	0			
TG	162	CHICAGO		

CHARLES WILLIAM TANNER

WON	LOST	NAME	POS.		G.	BA	FROM	TO
		ALVARADO, LUIS CESAR (2B16)	SS	71	99	.216	BOS	B
		ANDREWS, MICHAEL JAY (1B25)	2B	76	109	.282	BOS	B
15	15	BRADLEY, THOMAS WILLIAM	P	45	48	.156	CAL	B
		BRINKMAN, CHARLES ERNEST	C	14	15	.200	B	B
0	2	EDDY, DONALD EUGENE	P		22	1.000	B	C
		EGAN, THOMAS PATRICK (1B1)	C	77	85	.239	CAL	B
2	3	FORSTER, TERRY JAY	P		45	.400	A	B
		HERRMANN, EDWARD MARTIN	C	97	101	.214	B	B
		HERSHBERGER, NORMAN MICHAEL	OF	59	74	.260	MIL	C
3	4	HINTON, RICHARD MICHAEL	P		18	.000	A	NY
8	9	HORLEN, JOEL EDWARD (JOE)	P	34	36	.100	B	OAK
		HOTTMAN, KENNETH ROGER	OF	5	6	.125	A	C
		HUNTZ, STEPHEN MICHAEL	2B	14	35	.209	SD N	C
		(SS7 3B6)						
0	0	JACQUEZ, PATRICK THOMAS	P		2	.000	A	C
13	16	JOHN, THOMAS EDWARD	P		38	.145	B	LA N
12	10	JOHNSON, CLAIR BARTH (BART)	P		53	.193	B	B
		JOHNSTONE, JOHN WM. (JAY)	OF	119	124	.260	CAL	B
2	2	KEALEY, STEVEN WILLIAM	P		54	.200	CAL	B
		KELLY, HAROLD PATRICK (PAT)	OF	61	67	.291	KC	B
		LOLICH, RONALD JOHN	OF		2	.125	A	CLE
1	1	MAGNUSON, JAMES ROBERT	P		15	.000	B	C
		MAY, CARLOS (OF9)	1B	130	141	.294	B	B
		MAYE, ARTHUR LEE	OF	10	32	.205	B	C
		MC KINNEY, CHARLES RICHARD	2B	67	114	.271	B	NY
		(3B5 OF25)						
		MELTON, WILLIAM EDWIN	3B	148	150	.269	B	B
		MORALES, RICHARD ANGELO	SS	57	84	.243	B	B
		(2B3 3B18 OF1)						
		MUSER, ANTHONY JOSEPH	1B	4	11	.313	BOS 69	B
0	0	O'TOOLE, DENNIS JOSEPH	P		1	.000	B	B
0	1	PERZANOWSKI, STANLEY	P		5	.000	A	C
		REICHARDT, FREDERIC CARL	OF	128	138	.278	WAS	B
		(1B9)						
		RICHARD, LEE EDWARD (BEEBEE)	SS	68	87	.231	A	B
		(OF16)						
1	7	ROMO, VICENTE	P		45	.364	BOS	B
		SPENCE, ROBERT JOHN	1B	7	14	.148	B	C
		STROUD, EDWIN MARVIN	OF	44	53	.177	WAS	C
		WILLIAMS, WALTER ALLEN (3B1)	OF	90	114	.294	B	B
22	13	WOOD, WILBUR FORRESTER	P		44	.052	B	B

WON	87	AMERICAN LEAGUE	FINISHED	2 W
LOST	67	1972.	PCT. .565	
TIED	0			
TG	154	CHICAGO		

CHARLES WILLIAM TANNER

WON	LOST	NAME	POS.		G.	BA	FROM	TO
3	0	ACOSTA, CECILIO	P		26	.000	A	
		ALLEN, HAROLD ANDREW (HANK)	3B	6	9	.143	MIL 70	
		ALLEN, RICHARD ANTHONY (3B2)	1B	143	148	.308	LA N	
		ALVARADO, LUIS CESAR	SS	81	103	.213	B	
		(2B16 3B2)						
		ANDREWS, MICHAEL JAY (1B5)	2B	145	148	.220	B	
21	16	BAHNSEN, STANLEY RAYMOND	P	43	44	.152	NY	
		BRADFORD, CHARLES WM. (BUDDY)	OF	28	35	.271	CINN	
15	14	BRADLEY, THOMAS WILLIAM	P	40	43	.132	B	
		BRINKMAN, CHARLES ERNEST	C	33	35	.135	B	
0	0	DRABOWSKY, MYRON WALTER (MOE)	P		7	.000	XSTLN	
		EGAN, THOMAS PATRICK	C	46	50	.191	B	
0	1	FISHER, EDDIE GENE	P		6	+.000	XCAL	
6	5	FORSTER, TERRY JAY	P	62	63	.526	B	
1	0	FRAILING, KENNETH DOUGLAS	P		4	.000	A	
0	0	GEDDES, JAMES LEE	P	5	6	.000	A	
7	1	GOSSAGE, RICHARD MICHAEL	P		36	.000	A	
		HERNANDEZ, RODOLPHO	SS	6	8	.190	A	
		HERRMANN, EDWARD MARTIN	C	112	116	.249	B	
0	3	JOHNSON, CLAIR BARTH (BART)	P		9	.000	B	
		JOHNSTONE, JOHN WM. (JAY)	OF	97	113	.188	B	
3	2	KEALEY, STEVEN WILLIAM	P		40	.000	B	
		KELLY, HAROLD PATRICK (PAT)	OF	109	119	.261	B	
4	7	LEMONDS, DAVID LEE	P	31	34	.120	CHIN69	
		LYTTLE, JAMES LAWRENCE	OF	21	44	.232	NY	
		MAY, CARLOS (1B5)	OF	145	148	.308	B	
		MELTON, WILLIAM EDWIN	3B	56	57	.245	B	
		MORALES, RICHARD ANGELO	SS	86	110	.206	B	
		(2B16 3B14)						
		MUSER, ANTHONY JOSEPH (OF1)	1B	29	44	.279	B	
0	0	NEUMEIER, DANIEL GEORGE	P		3	.000	A	
		ORTA, JORGE (2B14 3B9)	SS	18	51	.202	A	
0	0	O'TOOLE, DENNIS JOSEPH	P		3	.000	B	
		QUALLS, JAMES ROBERT	OF	1	11	.000	MONN70	
0	1	REGAN, PHILIP RAYMOND	P		10	1.000	XCHIN	
		REICHARDT, FREDERIC CARL	OF	90	101	.251	B	
		RICHARD, LEE EDWARD (BEEBEE)	OF	6	11	.241	B	
		(SS1)						
3	0	ROMO, VICENTE	P		28	.000	B	
		SPIEZIO, EDWARD WAYNE	3B		74	.238	XSD N	
		WILLIAMS, WALTER ALLEN (3B1)	OF	57	77	.249	B	
24	17	WOOD, WILBUR FORRESTER	P		49	.136	B	
		YANCY, HUGH	3B		3	.111	A	

WON 87 AMERICAN LEAGUE FINISHED 5
LOST 75
TIED 0 1965. PCT. .537
TG 162

CLEVELAND

GEORGE ROBERT TEBBETTS

WON	LOST	NAME	POS.		G.	BA	FROM	TO
		ALVIS, ROY MAXWELL (MAX)	3B	156	159	.247	B	B
		AZCUE, JOSE JOAQUIN	C	108	111	.230	B	B
		BANKS, GEORGE EDWARD	3B	1	4	.200	B	B
		BARKER, RAYMOND HERRELL	1B	3	11	+.000	BAL 60	XNY
6	5	BELL, GARY	P		60	.063	B	B
		BROWN, LARRY LESLIE (2B26)	SS	95	124	.253	B	B
		CARREON, CAMILO GARCIA	C		19	.231	CHI	BAL
		CLINTON, LUCIEAN LOUIS	OF	9	12	+.176	XKC	NY
		COLAVITO, ROCCO DOMENICO	OF		162	.287	KC	B
		DAVALILLO, VICTOR JOSE	OF	134	142	.301	B	B
		DAVIS, ARTHUR WILLARD (BILL)			10	.300	A	B
1	3	DONOVAN, RICHARD EDWARD	P		12	.000	B	C
		GAGLIANO, RALPH MICHAEL			1	.000	A	C
		GONZALEZ, PEDRO (3B2 OF3)	2B	112	116	+.253	XNY	B
4	3	HARGAN, STEVEN LOWELL	P		17	.053	A	B
0	0	HEDLUND, MICHAEL DAVID	P		6	.000	A	CLE 68
		HINTON, CHARLES EDWARD	OF	72	133	.255	WAS	B
		(1B40 2B23 3B1)						
		HOWSER, RICHARD DALTON (2B17)	SS	73	107	.235	B	B
2	1	KELLEY, THOMAS HENRY	P		4	.222	B	B
5	11	KRALICK, JOHN FRANCIS	P		30	.143	B	B
		LUPLOW, ALVIN DAVID	OF	6	53	.133	B	NY N
		MARTINEZ, GABRIEL ANTONIO			4	.000	B	B
17	11	MC DOWELL, SAMUEL EDWARD	P	42	43	.126	B	B
3	3	MC MAHON, DONALD JOHN	P		58	.222	B	B
		MORAN, WILLIAM NELSON (SS1)	2B	7	22	.125	B	C
		ROOF, PHILLIP ANTHONY	C	41	43	+.173	XCAL	KC
		SALMON, RUTHFORD EDUARDO	1B	28	79	.242	B	B
		(CHICO) (2B5 3B5 OF17)						
		SCHEINBLUM, RICHARD ALAN			4	.000	A	CLE 67
16	8	SIEBERT, WILFRED CHAS. (SONNY)	P	39	40	.106	B	B
		SIMS, DUANE B. (DUKE)	C	40	48	.178	B	B
1	2	SPRING, JACK RUSSELL	P		14	.333	STLN	C
8	4	STANGE, ALBERT LEE	P		41	.107	B	B
11	6	TERRY, RALPH WILLARD	P		30	.143	NY	KC
11	11	TIANT, LUIS CLEMENTE	P		41	.088	B	B
0	5	TIEFENAUER, BOBBY GENE	P		15	+.000	XNY	CLE 67
		WAGNER, LEON LAMAR	OF	134	144	.294	B	B
2	2	WEAVER, DAVID FLOYD	P		32	.091	CLE 62	CHI 70
		WHITFIELD, FRED DWIGHT	1B	122	132	.293	B	B
0	0	WILLIAMS, STANLEY WILSON	P		3	.000	NY	CLE 67

WON 81 AMERICAN LEAGUE FINISHED 5
LOST 81
TIED 0 1966. PCT. .500
TG 162

CLEVELAND

GEORGE ROBERT TEBBETTS GEORGE BEVAN STRICKLAND

WON	LOST	NAME	POS.		G.	BA	FROM	TO
2	2	ALLEN, ROBERT GRAY	P		36	.111	CLE 63	B
		ALVIS, ROY MAXWELL (MAX)	3B		157	.245	B	B
		AZCUE, JOSE JOAQUIN	C	97	98	.275	B	B
		BANKS, GEORGE EDWARD			4	.250	B	C
14	15	BELL, GARY	P		40	.132	B	B
		BOOKER, RICHARD LEE (BUDDY)	C	12	18	.214	A	CHI 68
		BROWN, LARRY LESLIE (2B10)	SS	90	105	.229	B	B
		COLAVITO, ROCCO DOMENICO	OF	146	151	.238	B	B
		CRANDALL, DELMAR WESLEY	C	49	50	.231	PITN	C
0	2	CULVER, GEORGE RAYMOND	P		5	.000	A	B
		CURRY, GEORGE ANTHONY (TONY)			19	.125	PHIN61	C
		DAVALILLO, VICTOR JOSE	OF	108	121	.250	B	B
		DAVIS, ARTHUR WILLARD (BILL)	1B	9	23	.158	B	SD N69
		DICKEN, PAUL FRANKLIN			2	.000	CLE 64	C
		FULLER, VERN GORDON	2B		16	.234	CLE 64	B
		GENTILE, JAMES EDWARD	1B	9	33	.128	XHOUN	C
		GONZALEZ, PEDRO (3B1 OF1)	2B	104	110	.233	B	B
13	10	HARGAN, STEVEN LOWELL	P		38	.121	B	B
0	1	HEFFNER, ROBERT FREDERICK	P		5	.000	BOS	CAL 68
		HINTON, CHARLES EDWARD	OF	104	123	.256	B	B
		(1B6 2B2)						
		HOWSER, RICHARD DALTON (SS26)	2B	26	67	.229	B	NY
4	8	KELLEY, THOMAS HENRY	P		31	.143	B	B
3	4	KRALICK, JOHN FRANCIS	P		27	.077	B	B
		LANDIS, JAMES HENRY	OF	61	85	.222	KC	DET
		MARTINEZ, GABRIEL ANTONIO	SS	5	17	.294	B	C
		(2B4)						
9	8	MC DOWELL, SAMUEL EDWARD	P	35	36	.200	B	B
1	1	MC MAHON, DONALD JOHN	P		12	+.000	B	XBOS
6	8	O'DONOGHUE, JOHN EUGENE	P		32	.152	KC	B
0	3	RADATZ, RICHARD RAYMOND	P		39	+.111	XBOS	B
		SALMON, RUTHFORD EDUARDO	SS	61	126	.256	B	B
		(CHICO) (1B24 2B28 3B6 OF10)						
16	8	SIEBERT, WILFRED CHAS. (SONNY)	P		34	.129	B	B
		SIMS, DUANE B. (DUKE)	C	48	52	.263	B	B
1	0	STANGE, ALBERT LEE	P		8	+.250	B	XBOS
12	11	TIANT, LUIS CLEMENTE	P		46	.111	B	B
		VIDAL, JOSE	OF	11	17	.188	A	B
		WAGNER, LEON LAMAR	OF	139	150	.279	B	B
		WHITFIELD, FRED DWIGHT	1B	132	137	.241	B	B

WON 75 | LOST 87 | TIED 0 | TG 162

AMERICAN LEAGUE — 1967. — FINISHED 8 — PCT. .463

CLEVELAND

JOSEPH WILBUR ADCOCK

WON	LOST	NAME	POS.		G.	BA	FROM	TO
0	5	ALLEN, ROBERT GRAY	P		47	.000	B	C
		ALVIS, ROY MAXWELL (MAX)	3B		161	.256	B	B
		AZCUE, JOSE JOAQUIN	C		86	.251	B	B
2	5	BAILEY, STEVEN JOHN	P		32	.000	A	B
1	5	BELL, GARY	P		9	+.000	B	XBOS
		BROWN, LARRY LESLIE	SS	150	152	.227	B	B
		COLAVITO, ROCCO DOMENICO	OF	50	63	+.241	B	XCHI
2	1	CONNOLLY, EDWARD JOSEPH	P		15	.182	BOS 64	C
7	3	CULVER, GEORGE RAYMOND	P		53	.250	B	CINN
		DAVALILLO, VICTOR JOSE	OF	125	139	.287	B	B
		DEMETER, DONALD LEE (3B1)	OF	35	51	+.207	XBOS	C
		FOSSE, RAYMOND EARL	C		7	.063	A	B
		FULLER, VERN GORDON (SS2)	2B	64	73	.223	B	B
		GIL, TOMAS GUSTAVO (GUS)	2B	49	51	.115	A	SEA 69
		(1B1)						
		GONZALEZ, PEDRO	2B	64	80	.228	B	C
		(1B4 SS3 3B4)						
14	13	HARGAN, STEVEN LOWELL	P		30	.164	B	B
		HINTON, CHARLES EDWARD (2B5)	OF	136	147	.245	B	CAL
		HORTON, ANTHONY DARRIN	1B	94	106	+.281	XBOS	B
0	0	KELLEY, THOMAS HENRY	P		1	.000	B	ATLN71
		KING, JAMES HUBERT	OF	1	19	+.143	XCHI	C
0	2	KRALICK, JOHN FRANCIS	P		2	.000	B	C
		LUND, GORDON THOMAS	SS	2	3	.250	A	SEA 69
		MAYE, ARTHUR LEE (2B1)	OF	77	115	.259	HOUN	B
13	15	MC DOWELL, SAMUEL EDWARD	P		37	.183	B	B
8	9	O'DONOGHUE, JOHN EUGENE	P		33	.100	B	BAL
0	3	PENA, ORLANDO	P		48	+.000	XDET	PITN70
0	0	RADATZ, RICHARD RAYMOND	P		3	.000	B	XCHIN
		SALMON, RUTHFORD EDUARDO	OF	28	90	.227	B	B
		(CHICO) (1B24 2B24 SS14 3B4)						
		SCHEINBLUM, RICHARD ALAN	OF		18	.318	CLE 65	B
10	12	SIEBERT, WILFRED CHAS. (SONNY)	P		34	.135	B	B
		SIMS, DUANE B. (DUKE)	C	85	88	.202	B	B
		SMITH, WILLIE (1B3)	OF	4	21	.219	CAL	B
12	9	TIANT, LUIS CLEMENTE	P		33	.254	B	B
0	1	TIEFENAUER, BOBBY GENE	P		5	.000	CLE 65	CHIN
		VIDAL, JOSE	OF	10	16	.118	B	B
		WAGNER, LEON LAMAR	OF	117	135	.242	B	B
		WHITFIELD, FRED DWIGHT	1B	66	100	.218	B	CINN
6	4	WILLIAMS, STANLEY WILSON	P		16	.091	CLE 65	B

WON 86 | LOST 75 | TIED 1 | TG 162

AMERICAN LEAGUE — 1968. — FINISHED 3 — PCT. .534

CLEVELAND

ALVIN RALPH DARK

WON	LOST	NAME	POS.		G.	BA	FROM	TO
		ALVIS, ROY MAXWELL (MAX)	3B	128	131	.223	B	B
		AZCUE, JOSE JOAQUIN	C	97	115	.280	B	B
0	1	BAILEY, STEVEN JOHN	P		2	.000	B	C
		BROWN, LARRY LESLIE	SS		154	.234	B	B
		CARDENAL, JOSE DOMEC	OF	153	157	.257	CAL	B
		DAVALILLO, VICTOR JOSE	OF	49	51	+.239	B	XCAL
4	2	FISHER, EDDIE GENE	P		54	.000	BAL	CAL
		FOSSE, RAYMOND EARL	C		1	.000	B	B
		FULLER, VERN GORDON	2B	73	97	.242	B	B
		(SS4 3B23)						
0	0	GARDNER, RICHARD FRANK (ROB)	P		5	.000	CHIN	NY 70
0	1	GRAMLY, BERT THOMAS (TOMMY)	P	3	4	.000	A	C
		HALL, JIMMIE RANDOLPH	OF	29	53	+.198	XCAL	B
8	15	HARGAN, STEVEN LOWELL	P		32	.176	B	B
		HARPER, TOMMY (2B2)	OF	115	130	.217	CINN	SEA
		HARRIS, JAMES WILLIAM (BILLY)	2B	27	38	.213	A	KC
		(SS1 3B10)						
0	0	HEDLUND, MICHAEL DAVID	P		3	.000	CLE 65	KC
		HORTON, ANTHONY DARRIN	1B	128	133	.249	B	B
		JOHNSON, LOUIS BROWN	OF	57	65	.257	XCHIN	CAL
		KLIMCHOCK, LOUIS STEPHEN	3B	4	11	.133	NY N66	B
		(1B1 2B1)						
1	0	KURTZ, HAROLD JAMES	P	28	30	.000	A	C
		LEON, EDUARDO ANTONIO	SS		6	.000	A	B
		MAYE, ARTHUR LEE (1B1)	OF	80	109	.281	B	B
15	14	MC DOWELL, SAMUEL EDWARD	P		38	.153	B	B
		NAGELSON, RUSSELL CHARLES			5	.333	A	B
		NELSON, DAVID EARL (SS14)	2B	59	88	.233	A	B
5	8	PAUL, MICHAEL GEORGE (1B1)	P	36	36	.167	A	B
1	1	PINA, HORACIO	P		12	.000	A	B
		PINIELLA, LOUIS VICTOR	OF	2	6	.000	BAL 64	KC
1	0	ROHR, WILLIAM JOSEPH	P		17	.000	BOS	C
5	3	ROMO, VICENTE	P		40	.143	XLA N	B
		SALMON, RUTHFORD EDUARDO	2B	45	103	.214	B	BAL
		(CHICO) (1B11 SS15 3B18 OF13)						
		SCHEINBLUM, RICHARD ALAN	OF	16	19	.218	B	B
12	10	SIEBERT, WILFRED CHAS. (SONNY)	P	31	33	.157	B	B
		SIMS, DUANE B. (DUKE)	C	84	122	.249	B	B
		(1B31 OF4)						
0	0	SMITH, WILLIE	1B	7	33	.143	B	XCHIN
		(P2 OF1)						
		SNYDER, RUSSELL HENRY (1B1)	OF	54	68	+.281	XCHI	B
		SUAREZ, KENNETH RAYMOND	C	12	17	.100	KC	B
		(2B1 3B1 OF1)						
0	0	SUTHERLAND, DARRELL WAYNE	P		3	.000	NY N66	C
21	9	TIANT, LUIS CLEMENTE	P		34	.080	B	B
		VIDAL, JOSE (1B1)	OF	26	37	.167	B	SEA
		WAGNER, LEON LAMAR	OF	10	38	+.184	B	XCHI
13	11	WILLIAMS, STANLEY WILSON	P		44	.161	B	B

WON 62 LOST 99 TIED 0 TG 161

AMERICAN LEAGUE 1969.

FINISHED 6 E (LAST) PCT. .385

CLEVELAND

ALVIN RALPH DARK

WON	LOST	NAME	POS.		G.	BA	FROM	TO
		ALVIS, ROY MAXWELL (MAX)	3B	58	66	.225	B	MIL
		(SS1)						
		AZCUE, JOSE JOAQUIN	C	6	7	+.292	B	XBOS
		BAKER, FRANK	OF	46	52	.256	A	CLE 71
0	2	BOYD, GARY LEE	P		8	.000	A	C
		BROWN, LARRY LESLIE	SS	101	132	.239	B	B
		(2B5 3B29)						
0	2	BURCHART, LARRY WAYNE	P		29	.000	A	C
		CAMILLI, LOUIS STEVEN	3B		13	.000	A	B
		CARDENAL, JOSE DOMEC (3B5)	OF	142	146	.257	B	STLN
6	9	ELLSWORTH, RICHARD CLARK	P		34	+.133	XBOS	B
		FOSSE, RAYMOND EARL	C		37	.172	B	B
		FULLER, VERN GORDON (3B7)	2B	102	108	.236	B	B
		HALL, JIMMIE RANDOLPH	OF	3	4	+.000	B	XNY
0	2	HAMILTON, JACK EDWIN	P		20	+.000	CAL	XCHI
5	14	HARGAN, STEVEN LOWELL	P	32	34	.159	B	B
		HARRELSON, KENNETH SMITH	OF	144	149	+.222	XBOS	B
		(1B16)						
		HEIDEMANN, JACK SEALE	SS		3	.000	A	B
2	1	HENNIGAN, PHILLIP WINSTON	P		9	.000	A	B
		HINTON, CHARLES EDWARD (3B14)	OF	40	94	.256	CAL	B
		HORTON, ANTHONY DARRIN	1B	157	159	.278	B	B
		KLIMCHOCK, LOUIS STEPHEN	3B	56	90	.287	B	B
		(C1 2B21)						
0	0	KROLL, GARY MELVIN	P		19	.000	HOUN66	C
3	4	LAW, RONALD DAVID	P		35	.143	A	C
		LEON, EDUARDO ANTONIO	SS		64	.239	B	B
		MAYE, ARTHUR LEE	OF	28	43	+.250	B	XWAS
18	14	MC DOWELL, SAMUEL EDWARD	P		39	.174	B	B
		NAGELSON, RUSSELL CHARLES	OF	3	12	.353	B	B
		(1B1)						
		NELSON, DAVID EARL (OF2)	2B	33	52	.203	B	WAS
5	10	PAUL, MICHAEL GEORGE	P		47	.000	B	B
		PETERSON, CHARLES ANDREW (CAP)	OF	30	76	.227	WAS	C
		(3B4)						
4	2	PINA, HORACIO	P		31	.500	B	WAS
3	3	PIZARRO, JUAN	P		48	+.200	XBOS	XOAK
1	1	ROMO, VICENTE	P		3	+.500	B	XBOS
		SCHEINBLUM, RICHARD ALAN	OF	50	102	.186	B	WAS 71
0	1	SIEBERT, WILFRED CHAS. (SONNY)	P		2	+.250	B	XBOS
		SIMS, DUANE B. (DUKE)	C	102	114	.236	B	B
		(1B1 OF3)						
		SNYDER, RUSSELL HENRY	OF	84	122	.248	B	MIL
		SUAREZ, KENNETH RAYMOND	C		36	.294	B	CLE 71
9	20	TIANT, LUIS CLEMENTE	P		38	.235	B	MIN
		VERSALLES, ZOILO	2B	46	72	+.226	LA N	XWAS
		(SS3 3B30)						
6	14	WILLIAMS, STANLEY WILSON	P		61	.100	B	MIN

WON 76 LOST 86 TIED 0 TG 162

AMERICAN LEAGUE 1970.

FINISHED 5 E PCT. .469

CLEVELAND

ALVIN RALPH DARK

WON	LOST	NAME	POS.		G.	BA	FROM	TO
2	5	AUSTIN, RICK GERALD	P		31	.111	A	B
		BRADFORD, CHARLES WM. (BUDDY)	OF	64	75	+.196	XCHI	B
		(3B1)						
		BROWN, LARRY LESLIE	SS	27	72	.258	B	B
		(2B16 3B17)						
		CAMILLI, LOUIS STEVEN	SS	3	16	.000	B	B
		(2B2 3B1)						
9	8	CHANCE, WILMER DEAN	P		45	.071	MIN	XNY N
1	1	COLBERT, VINCENT NORMAN	P		23	.000	A	B
4	9	DUNNING, STEVEN JOHN	P		19	.161	A	B
3	3	ELLSWORTH, RICHARD CLARK	P		29	+.000	B	XMIL
		FORD, THEODORE HENRY	OF	12	26	.174	A	B
		FOSSE, RAYMOND EARL	C		120	.307	B	B
		FOSTER, ROY	OF	131	139	.268	A	B
		FULLER, VERN GORDON	2B	16	29	.182	B	C
		(1B1 3B4)						
6	13	HAND, RICHARD ALLEN	P		35	.146	A	B
11	3	HARGAN, STEVEN LOWELL	P	23	28	.111	B	B
		HARRELSON, KENNETH SMITH	1B	13	17	.282	B	B
		HEIDEMANN, JACK SEALE	SS	132	133	.211	B	B
6	3	HENNIGAN, PHILLIP WINSTON	P		42	.143	B	B
4	6	HIGGINS, DENNIS DEAN	P		58	.250	WAS	STLN
		HINTON, CHARLES EDWARD	1B	40	107	.318	B	B
		(C4 2B3 3B2 OF35)						
		HORTON, ANTHONY DARRIN	1B	112	115	.269	B	C
		KLIMCHOCK, LOUIS STEPHEN	1B	5	41	.161	B	C
		(2B5)						
1	7	LASHER, FREDERICK WALTER	P		43	+.000	XDET	CAL
		LEON, EDUARDO ANTONIO	2B	141	152	.248	B	B
		(SS23 3B1)						
		LOWENSTEIN, JOHN LEE	2B	10	17	.256	A	B
		(SS1 3B2 OF2)						
20	12	MC DOWELL, SAMUEL EDWARD	P	39	40	.124	B	B
		(1B1 2B1)						
2	2	MILLER, ROBERT LANE	P		15	+.200	MIN	XCHI
1	0	MINGORI, STEPHEN BERNARD	P		21	.000	A	B
3	5	MOORE, ROBERT BARRY	P		13	+.095	WAS	XCHI
		NAGELSON, RUSSELL CHARLES	OF	4	17	+.125	B	XDET
		NETTLES, GRAIG (OF3)	3B	154	157	.235	MIN	B
2	8	PAUL, MICHAEL GEORGE	P		30	.154	B	B
		PINSON, VADA EDWARD (1B7)	OF	141	148	.286	STLN	B
1	1	RITTWAGE, JAMES MICHAEL	P	8	8	.375	A	C
		(3B1)						
		ROLLINS, RICHARD JOHN	3B	5	42	+.233	XMIL	C
		SIMS, DUANE B. (DUKE)	C	39	110	.264	B	LA N
		(1B29 OF36)						
		UHLAENDER, THEODORE OTTO	OF	134	141	.268	MIN	B

WON 60
LOST 102
TIED 0
TG 162

AMERICAN LEAGUE — 1971. — FINISHED 6 E (LAST) — PCT. .370

CLEVELAND

ALVIN RALPH DARK   JOHN JOSEPH LIPON

WON	LOST	NAME	POS.		G.	BA	FROM	TO
0	0	AUSTIN, RICK GERALD	P		23	.000	B	C
		BAKER, FRANK	OF	51	73	.210	CLE 69	C
1	2	BALLINGER, MARK ALAN	P		18	.200	A	C
		BEVACQUA, KURT ANTHONY (SS2 3B3 OF5)	2B	36	55	.204	A	B
		BRADFORD, CHARLES WM. (BUDDY)	OF	18	20	.158	B	XCINN
		BROWN, LARRY LESLIE	SS		13	+.220	B	XOAK
		CAMILLI, LOUIS STEVEN (2B16)	SS	23	39	.198	B	B
		CHAMBLISS, CARROLL CHRISTOPHER	1B	108	111	.275	A	B
		CLARK, JAMES EDWARD (1B1)	OF	3	13	.167	A	C
7	6	COLBERT, VINCENT NORMAN	P	50	52	.138	B	B
8	14	DUNNING, STEVEN JOHN	P	31	32	.182	B	B
5	4	FARMER, EDWARD JOSEPH	P		43	.071	A	B
		FORD, THEODORE HENRY	OF	55	74	.194	B	TEX
		FOSSE, RAYMOND EARL (1B4)	C	126	133	.276	B	B
8	12	FOSTER, ALAN BENTON	P	36	37	.039	LA N	CAL
		FOSTER, ROY	OF	107	125	.245	B	B
2	6	HAND, RICHARD ALLEN	P	15	16	.125	B	TEX
1	13	HARGAN, STEVEN LOWELL	P		37	.063	B	B
		HARRELSON, KENNETH SMITH (OF7)	1B	40	52	.199	B	C
		HEIDEMANN, JACK SEALE	SS		81	.208	B	B
4	3	HENNIGAN, PHILLIP WINSTON	P		57	.000	B	B
		HINTON, CHARLES EDWARD (C5 OF20)	1B	20	88	.224	B	C
		HODGE, HAROLD MORRIS (GOMER) (2B2 3B3)	1B	3	80	.205	A	C
0	0	KAISER, ROBERT THOMAS	P		5	.000	A	C
6	12	LAMB, RAYMOND RICHARD	P		43	.093	LA N	B
		LEON, EDUARDO ANTONIO (SS24)	2B	107	131	.261	B	B
		LOWENSTEIN, JOHN LEE (SS3 OF18)	2B	29	58	.186	B	B
0	2	MACHEMEHL, CHARLES WALTER	P		14	.500	A	C
13	17	MC DOWELL, SAMUEL EDWARD	P		35	.178	B	SF N
1	2	MINGORI, STEPHEN BERNARD	P		54	.500	B	B
		NETTLES, GRAIG	3B		158	.261	B	B
2	2	PASCUAL, CAMILO ALBERTO	P		9	.600	LA N	C
2	7	PAUL, MICHAEL GEORGE	P		17	.053	B	TEX
		PINSON, VADA EDWARD (1B3)	OF	141	146	.263	B	CAL
		STANLEY, FREDERICK BLAIR (2B3)	SS	55	60	.225	MIL	B
		SUAREZ, KENNETH RAYMOND	C	48	50	.203	CLE 69	TEX
		UHLAENDER, THEODORE OTTO	OF	131	141	.288	B	CINN

WON 72
LOST 84
TIED 0
TG 156

AMERICAN LEAGUE — 1972. — FINISHED 5 E — PCT. .462

CLEVELAND

KENNETH JOSEPH ASPROMONTE

WON	LOST	NAME	POS.		G.	BA	FROM	TO
		BELL, DAVID GUS (BUDDY) (3B6)	OF	123	132	.255	A	
		BEVACQUA, KURT ANTHONY (3B1)	OF	11	19	.114	B	
		BROHAMER, JOHN ANTHONY (3B1)	2B	132	136	.233	A	
0	0	BUTLER, WILLIAM FRANKLIN	P		6	.000	KC	
		CAMILLI, LOUIS STEVEN (2B2)	SS	8	39	.146	B	
		CHAMBLISS, CARROLL CHRISTOPHER	1B	119	121	.292	B	
1	7	COLBERT, VINCENT NORMAN	P	22	23	.200	B	
		DUFFY, FRANK THOMAS	SS	126	130	.239	SF N	
6	4	DUNNING, STEVEN JOHN	P	16	20	.273	B	
2	5	FARMER, EDWARD JOSEPH	P		46	.143	B	
		FOSSE, RAYMOND EARL (1B3)	C	124	134	.241	B	
		FOSTER, ROY	OF	45	73	.224	B	
0	3	HARGAN, STEVEN LOWELL	P		12	.000	B	
		HEIDEMANN, JACK SEALE	SS		10	.150	B	
5	3	HENNIGAN, PHILLIP WINSTON	P		38	.083	B	
3	1	HILGENDORF, THOMAS EUGENE	P		19	.077	STLN70	
		JOHNSON, ALEXANDER	OF	95	108	.239	CAL	
		JOHNSON, LARRY DOBY	C		1	.500	A	
4	1	KILKENNY, MICHAEL DAVID	P		22	+.071	XSD N	
5	6	LAMB, RAYMOND RICHARD	P		34	.000	B	
		LEON, EDUARDO ANTONIO (SS35)	2B	36	89	.200	B	
		LOLICH, RONALD JOHN	OF	22	24	.188	CHI	
0	0	LOPEZ, MARCELINO PONS	P		4	.000	MIL	
		LOWENSTEIN, JOHN LEE (1B2)	OF	58	68	.212	B	
		MC CRAW, TOMMIE LEE (1B38)	OF	84	129	.258	WAS	
0	6	MINGORI, STEPHEN BERNARD (OF1)	P	41	42	.125	B	
		MOSES, GERALD BRAHEEN (1B3)	C	39	52	.220	CAL	
		NETTLES, GRAIG	3B		150	.253	B	
0	0	PALMER, LOWELL RAYMOND	P		1	.000	XSTLN	
24	16	PERRY, GAYLORD JACKSON	P		41	.155	SF N	
		PHILLIPS, ADOLFO EMILIO	OF	10	12	.000	MONN70	
1	3	RIDDLEBERGER, DENNIS MICHAEL	P		38	.000	WAS	
		STANLEY, FREDERICK BLAIR (2B1)	SS	5	6	.167	B	XSD N
14	15	TIDROW, RICHARD WILLIAM	P		39	.100	A	
		UNSER, DELBERT BERNARD	OF	119	132	.238	WAS	
7	14	WILCOX, MILTON EDWARD	P		32	.200	CINN	

WON 89
LOST 73
TIED 0
TG 162

AMERICAN LEAGUE

1965.

FINISHED 4

PCT. .549

DETROIT

CHARLES WALTER DRESSEN

WON	LOST	NAME	POS.		G.	BA	FROM	TO
14	10	AGUIRRE, HENRY JOHN	P		32	.086	B	B
		BROWN, WM. JAMES (GATES)	OF	56	96	.256	B	B
		CASH, NORMAN DALTON	1B	139	142	.266	B	B
		DEMETER, DONALD LEE (1B34)	OF	81	122	.278	B	B
6	4	FOX, TERRENCE EDWARD	P		42	.000	B	B
		FREEHAN, WILLIAM ASHLEY	C	129	130	.234	B	B
6	2	GLADDING, FRED EARL	P		46	.000	B	B
1	1	HAMILTON, JACK EDWIN	P		4	.000	B	NY N
0	0	HILLER, JOHN FREDERICK	P		5	.000	A	B
0	0	HOLTGRAVE, LAVERN GEORGE	P		1	.000	A	C
		HORTON, WILLIAM WATTISON	OF	141	143	.273	B	B
		(3B1)						
		KALINE, ALBERT WILLIAM (3B1)	OF	112	125	.281	B	B
15	9	LOLICH, MICHAEL STEPHEN	P		43	.058	B	B
		LUMPE, JERRY DEAN	2B	139	145	.257	B	B
0	0	MARENTETTE, LEO JOHN	P		2	.000	A	MONN69
		MC AULIFFE, RICHARD JOHN	SS	112	113	.260	B	B
16	6	MC LAIN, DENNIS DALE	P		33	.054	B	B
		MOORE, JACKIE SPENCER	C	20	21	.094	A	C
0	2	NAVARRO, JULIO VENTURA	P		15	.000	B	B
1	0	NISCHWITZ, RONALD LEE	P		20	.000	CLE 63	C
		NORTHRUP, JAMES THOMAS	OF	54	80	.205	B	B
		OYLER, RAYMOND FRANCIS	SS	57	82	.186	A	B
		(1B1 2B11 3B1)						
4	6	PENA, ORLANDO	P		30	+.250	XKC	B
0	0	RAKOW, EDWARD CHARLES	P		6	.000	B	ATLN67
		REDMOND, HOWARD WAYNE	OF	2	4	.000	A	DET 69
1	5	REGAN, PHILIP RAYMOND	P		16	.083	B	LA N
		ROMAN, WILLIAM ANTHONY	1B	6	21	.074	B	C
0	0	SEALE, JOHNNY RAY	P		4	.000	B	C
3	6	SHERRY, LAWRENCE	P		39	.300	B	B
		SMITH, GEORGE CORNELIUS	2B	22	32	.094	B	BOS
		(SS3 3B3)						
13	8	SPARMA, JOSEPH BLASE	P		30	.135	B	B
		STANLEY, MITCHELL JACK	OF	29	30	.239	B	B
		SULLIVAN, JOHN PETER	C	29	34	.267	B	NY N67
		THOMAS, GEORGE EDWARD (2B1)	OF	59	79	.213	B	BOS
		WERT, DONALD RALPH	3B	161	162	.261	B	B
		(2B1 SS3)						
9	14	WICKERSHAM, DAVID CLIFFORD	P		34	.069	B	B
		WOOD, JACOB	2B	20	58	.288	B	B
		(1B1 SS1 3B1)						

WON 88
LOST 74
TIED 0
TG 162

AMERICAN LEAGUE

1966.

FINISHED 3

PCT. .543

DETROIT

CHARLES WALTER DRESSEN ROBERT VIRGIL SWIFT FRANCIS MICHAEL SKAFF

WON	LOST	NAME	POS.		G.	BA	FROM	TO
3	9	AGUIRRE, HENRY JOHN	P		30	.120	B	B
		BROWN, WM. JAMES (GATES)	OF	43	88	.266	B	B
		BRUNSBERG, ARLO ADOLPH	C		2	.333	A	C
		CASH, NORMAN DALTON	1B	158	160	.279	B	B
		DEMETER, DONALD LEE (1B4)	OF	27	32	+.212	B	XBOS
0	1	FOX, TERRENCE EDWARD	P		4	.000	B	XPHIN
		FREEHAN, WILLIAM ASHLEY	C	132	136	.234	B	B
		(1B5)						
5	0	GLADDING, FRED EARL	P		51	.000	B	B
0	0	GRAHAM, WILLIAM ALBERT	P		1	.000	A	NY N
0	0	HILLER, JOHN FREDERICK	P		1	.000	B	B
		HORTON, WILLIAM WATTISON	OF	137	146	.262	B	B
		KALINE, ALBERT WILLIAM	OF	136	142	.288	B	B
0	0	KORINCE, GEORGE EUGENE	P		2	.000	A	B
14	14	LOLICH, MICHAEL STEPHEN	P		40	.141	B	B
		LUMPE, JERRY DEAN	2B	95	113	.231	B	B
		MC AULIFFE, RICHARD JOHN	SS	105	124	.274	B	B
		(3B15)						
		MC FARLANE, ORLANDO DEJESUS	C	33	49	.254	PITN64	CAL
20	14	MC LAIN, DENNIS DALE	P		38	.183	B	B
7	8	MONBOQUETTE, WILLIAM CHARLES	P		30	.154	BOS	B
0	0	NAVARRO, JULIO VENTURA	P		1	.000	B	ATLN70
		NORTHRUP, JAMES THOMAS	OF	113	123	.265	B	B
		OYLER, RAYMOND FRANCIS	SS	69	71	.171	B	B
4	2	PENA, ORLANDO	P		54	.111	B	B
		PEPPER, DONALD HOYTE	1B	1	4	.000	A	C
4	5	PODRES, JOHN JOSEPH	P		36	.233	XLA N	B
8	5	SHERRY, LAWRENCE	P		55	.400	B	B
2	7	SPARMA, JOSEPH BLASE	P		29	.217	B	B
		STANLEY, MITCHELL JACK	OF	82	92	.289	B	B
		TRACEWSKI, RICHARD JOSEPH	2B	70	81	.194	LA N	B
		(SS3)						
		WERT, DONALD RALPH	3B		150	.268	B	B
8	3	WICKERSHAM, DAVID CLIFFORD	P		38	.044	B	B
13	6	WILSON, ROBERT EARL	P	23	27	+.234	XBOS	B
		WOOD, JACOB (1B2 3B4)	2B	52	98	.252	B	B

COACH SWIFT SERVED AS INTERIM MANAGER DURING ILLNESS OF DRESSEN.
COACH SKAFF SERVED AS INTERIM MANAGER DURING ILLNESS OF SWIFT.

WON 91
LOST 71
TIED 1
TG 163

AMERICAN LEAGUE

1967.

FINISHED 2
(TIED WITH MINNESOTA)
PCT. .562

DETROIT

EDWARD MAYO SMITH

WON	LOST	NAME	POS.		G.	BA	FROM	TO
0	1	AGUIRRE, HENRY JOHN	P		31	.500	B	LA N
		BROWN, WM. JAMES (GATES)	OF	20	51	.187	B	B
		CAMPBELL, DAVID WILSON	1B	1	2	.000	A	B
		CASH, NORMAN DALTON	1B	146	152	.242	B	B
		COMER, HARRY WAYNE	OF	1	4	.333	A	B
1	2	DOBSON, PATRICK EDWARD	P		28	.000	A	B
		FREEHAN, WILLIAM ASHLEY	C	147	155	.282	B	B
		(1B11)						
6	4	GLADDING, FRED EARL	P		42	.000	B	HOUN
		GREEN, LEONARD CHARLES	OF	44	58	.278	BOS	B
		HEATH, WILLIAM CHRIS	C	7	20	.125	XHOUN	CHIN69
4	3	HILLER, JOHN FREDERICK	P		23	.133	B	B
		HORTON, WILLIAM WATTISON	OF	110	122	.274	B	B
		KALINE, ALBERT WILLIAM	OF	130	131	.308	B	B
0	0	KLIPPSTEIN, JOHN CALVIN	P		5	.000	MIN	C
1	0	KORINCE, GEORGE EUGENE	P		9	.000	B	C
		LANDIS, JAMES HENRY	OF	12	25	+.208	CLE	XBOS
2	1	LASHER, FREDERICK WALTER	P		17	.111	MIN 63	B
14	13	LOLICH, MICHAEL STEPHEN	P	31	32	.197	B	B
		LUMPE, JERRY DEAN (3B6)	2B	54	81	.232	B	C
1	3	MARSHALL, MICHAEL GRANT	P		37	.222	A	SEA 69
		MATCHICK, JOHN THOMAS (TOMMY)	SS	1	8	.167	A	B
		MATHEWS, EDWIN LEE (1B13)	3B	21	36	.231	XHOUN	B
		MC AULIFFE, RICHARD JOHN	2B	145	163	.239	B	B
		(SS43)						
17	16	MC LAIN, DENNIS DALE	P	37	38	.118	B	B
0	0	MONBOQUETTE, WILLIAM CHARLES	P		2	+.000	B	XNY
		NORTHRUP, JAMES THOMAS	OF	143	144	.271	B	B
		OYLER, RAYMOND FRANCIS	SS	146	148	.207	B	B
0	1	PENA, ORLANDO	P		2	+.000	B	XCLE
3	1	PODRES, JOHN JOSEPH	P		21	.100	B	SD N69
		PRICE, JIMMIE WILLIAM	C	24	44	.261	A	B
0	1	SHERRY, LAWRENCE	P		20	.000	B	XHOUN
16	9	SPARMA, JOSEPH BLASE	P		37	.054	B	B
		STANLEY, MITCHELL JACK (1B8)	OF	128	145	.210	B	B
		TRACEWSKI, RICHARD JOSEPH	SS	44	74	.280	B	B
		(2B12 3B10)						
		WERT, DONALD RALPH (SS1)	3B	140	142	.257	B	B
4	5	WICKERSHAM, DAVID CLIFFORD	P		36	.000	B	PITN
22	11	WILSON, ROBERT EARL	P	39	52	.185	B	B
		WOOD, JACOB (2B2)	1B	2	14	.050	B	XCINN

WON 103
LOST 59
TIED 2
TG 164

AMERICAN LEAGUE

1968.

FINISHED 1

PCT. .636

DETROIT

EDWARD MAYO SMITH

WON	LOST	NAME	POS.		G.	BA	FROM	TO
		BROWN, WM. JAMES (GATES)	OF	17	67	.370	B	B
		(1B1)						
1	0	CAIN, LESLIE	P		8	.143	A	DET 70
		CAMPBELL, DAVID WILSON	2B	5	9	.125	B	B
		CASH, NORMAN DALTON	1B	117	127	.263	B	B
		CHRISTIAN, ROBERT CHARLES	1B	1	3	.333	A	CHI
		(OF1)						
		COMER, HARRY WAYNE (C1)	OF	27	48	.125	B	SEA
5	8	DOBSON, PATRICK EDWARD	P		47	.143	B	B
0	0	FACE, ELROY LEON (ROY)	P		2	.000	XPITN	MONN
		FREEHAN, WILLIAM ASHLEY	C	138	155	.263	B	B
		(1B21 OF1)						
		GREEN, LEONARD CHARLES	OF	2	6	.250	B	C
9	6	HILLER, JOHN FREDERICK	P		39	.081	B	B
		HORTON, WILLIAM WATTISON	OF	139	143	.285	B	B
		KALINE, ALBERT WILLIAM (1B22)	OF	74	102	.287	B	B
5	1	LASHER, FREDERICK WALTER	P		34	.111	B	B
17	9	LOLICH, MICHAEL STEPHEN	P	39	41	.114	B	B
		MATCHICK, JOHN THOMAS (TOMMY)	SS	59	80	.203	B	B
		(1B6 2B13)						
		MATHEWS, EDWIN LEE (3B6)	1B	6	31	.212	B	C
		MC AULIFFE, RICHARD JOHN	2B	148	151	.249	B	B
		(SS5)						
31	6	MC LAIN, DENNIS DALE	P	41	44	.162	B	B
3	1	MC MAHON, DONALD JOHN	P		20	+.000	XCHI	B
		NORTHRUP, JAMES THOMAS	OF	151	154	.264	B	B
		OYLER, RAYMOND FRANCIS	SS		111	.135	B	SEA
2	3	PATTERSON, DARYL ALAN	P		38	.000	A	B
		PRICE, JIMMIE WILLIAM	C	42	64	.174	B	B
2	2	RIBANT, DENNIS JOSEPH	P	14	16	+.200	PITN	XCHI
0	0	ROOKER, JAMES PHILLIP	P		2	.000	A	KC
10	10	SPARMA, JOSEPH BLASE	P		34	.133	B	B
		STANLEY, MITCHELL JACK	OF	130	153	.259	B	B
		(1B15 2B1 SS9)						
		TRACEWSKI, RICHARD JOSEPH	SS	51	90	.156	B	B
		(2B14 3B16)						
4	1	WARDEN, JONATHAN EDGAR	P		28	.000	A	C
		WERT, DONALD RALPH (SS2)	3B	150	150	.200	B	B
13	12	WILSON, ROBERT EARL	P	34	40	.227	B	B
1	0	WYATT, JOHN THOMAS	P		22	+.000	XNY	OAK

WON 90 AMERICAN LEAGUE FINISHED 2 E
LOST 72
TIED 0 1969. PCT. .556
TG 162

DETROIT

EDWARD MAYO SMITH

WON	LOST	NAME	POS.		G.	BA	FROM	TO
		BROWN, ISSAC	2B	45	70	.229	A	B
		(SS1 3B12 OF3)						
		BROWN, WM. JAMES (GATES)	OF	14	60	.204	B	B
		CAMPBELL, DAVID WILSON	1B	13	32	.103	B	SD N
		(2B5 3B1)						
		CASH, NORMAN DALTON	1B	134	142	.280	B	B
5	10	DOBSON, PATRICK EDWARD	P		49	.091	B	SD N
		FREEHAN, WILLIAM ASHLEY	C	120	143	.262	B	B
		(1B20)						
		GUTIERREZ, CESAR DARIO	SS	16	17	.245	XSF N	B
4	4	HILLER, JOHN FREDERICK	P	40	41	.286	B	B
		HORTON, WILLIAM WATTISON	OF	136	141	.262	B	B
		KALINE, ALBERT WILLIAM (1B9)	OF	118	131	.272	B	B
8	6	KILKENNY, MICHAEL DAVID	P		39	.054	A	B
2	1	LASHER, FREDERICK WALTER	P		32	.000	B	B
19	11	LOLICH, MICHAEL STEPHEN	P	37	38	.088	B	B
		MATCHICK, JOHN THOMAS (TOMMY)	2B	47	94	.242	B	BOS
		(1B2 SS6 3B27)						
		MC AULIFFE, RICHARD JOHN	2B	72	74	.262	B	B
24	9	MC LAIN, DENNIS DALE	P		42	.160	B	B
3	5	MC MAHON, DONALD JOHN	P		34	.000	B	XSF N
0	0	MC RAE, NORMAN	P		3	.000	A	B
		NORTHRUP, JAMES THOMAS	OF	143	148	.295	B	B
0	2	PATTERSON, DARYL ALAN	P		18	.000	B	B
		PRICE, JIMMIE WILLIAM	C	51	72	.234	B	B
2	2	RADATZ, RICHARD RAYMOND	P		11	.000	CHIN67	XMONN
		REDMOND, HOWARD WAYNE			5	.000	DET 65	C
0	0	REED, ROBERT EDWARD	P		8	.500	A	B
1	0	SCHERMAN, FREDERICK JOHN	P		4	.000	A	B
6	8	SPARMA, JOSEPH BLASE	P		23	.138	B	MONN
		STANLEY, MITCHELL JACK	OF	101	149	.235	B	B
		(1B4 SS59)						
0	1	TAYLOR, GARY WILLIAM	P		7	.000	A	C
4	3	TIMMERMAN, THOMAS HENRY	P		31	.111	A	B
		TRACEWSKI, RICHARD JOSEPH	SS	41	66	.139	B	C
		(2B13 3B6)						
		TRESH, THOMAS MICHAEL	SS	77	94	+.224	XNY	C
		(3B1 OF11)						
		WERT, DONALD RALPH	3B	129	132	.225	B	B
12	10	WILSON, ROBERT EARL	P	35	37	.132	B	B
		WOODS, RONALD LAWRENCE	OF	7	17	+.267	A	XNY

WON 79 AMERICAN LEAGUE FINISHED 4 E
LOST 83
TIED 0 1970. PCT. .488
TG 162

DETROIT

EDWARD MAYO SMITH

WON	LOST	NAME	POS.		G.	BA	FROM	TO
		BROWN, ISSAC	2B	23	56	.287	B	B
		(3B1 OF4)						
		BROWN, WM. JAMES (GATES)	OF	26	81	.226	B	B
12	7	CAIN, LESLIE	P		29	.162	DET 68	B
		CASH, NORMAN DALTON	1B	114	130	.259	B	B
		COLLINS, KEVIN MICHAEL	1B	1	25	.208	MONN	B
		FREEHAN, WILLIAM ASHLEY	C	114	117	.241	B	B
		GUTIERREZ, CESAR DARIO	SS		135	.243	B	B
6	6	HILLER, JOHN FREDERICK	P		47	.000	B	DET 72
		HORTON, WILLIAM WATTISON	OF		96	.305	B	B
		HOSLEY, TIMOTHY KENNETH	C	4	7	.167	A	B
		JONES, JAMES DALTON	2B	35	89	.220	BOS	B
		(1B10 3B18)						
		KALINE, ALBERT WILLIAM (1B52)	OF	91	131	.278	B	B
7	6	KILKENNY, MICHAEL DAVID	P	36	37	.077	B	B
0	1	LA GROW, LERRIN HARRIS	P		10	.000	A	DET 72
		LAMONT, GENE WILLIAM	C		15	.295	A	B
1	3	LASHER, FREDERICK WALTER	P		12	+.000	B	XCLE
14	19	LOLICH, MICHAEL STEPHEN	P	40	42	.134	B	B
		MADDOX, ELLIOTT	3B	40	109	.248	A	WAS
		(2B1 SS19 OF37)						
		MC AULIFFE, RICHARD JOHN	2B	127	146	.234	B	B
		(SS15 3B12)						
3	5	MC LAIN, DENNIS DALE	P		14	.065	B	WAS
0	0	MC RAE, NORMAN	P		19	.000	B	C
		NAGELSON, RUSSELL CHARLES	OF	4	28	+.188	XCLE	C
		(1B1)						
12	13	NIEKRO, JOSEPH FRANKLIN	P	38	39	.197	SD N	B
		NORTHRUP, JAMES THOMAS	OF	136	139	.262	B	B
7	1	PATTERSON, DARYL ALAN	P		43	.000	B	B
		PRICE, JIMMIE WILLIAM	C	38	52	.182	B	B
2	4	REED, ROBERT EDWARD	P	16	17	.083	B	C
0	0	ROBERTSON, JERRY LEE	P		11	.000	MONN	C
1	1	SAUNDERS, DENNIS JAMES	P		8	.000	A	C
4	4	SCHERMAN, FREDERICK JOHN	P		48	.167	B	B
		STANLEY, MITCHELL JACK (1B9)	OF	132	142	.252	B	B
		SZOTKIEWICZ, KENNETH JOHN	SS	44	47	.107	A	C
6	7	TIMMERMAN, THOMAS HENRY	P		61	.000	B	B
		WERT, DONALD RALPH (2B2)	3B	117	128	.218	B	WAS
4	6	WILSON, ROBERT EARL	P		18	.194	B	XSD N

WON 91
LOST 71
TIED 0
TG 162

AMERICAN LEAGUE

1971.

FINISHED 2 E

PCT. .562

DETROIT

ALFRED MANUEL MARTIN

WON	LOST	NAME	POS.		G.	BA	FROM	TO
0	0	BOSWELL, DAVID WILSON	P		3	+.000	MIN	XBAL
		BRINKMAN, EDWIN ALBERT	SS		159	.228	WAS	B
		BROWN, ISSAC	1B	17	59	.255	B	B
		(2B8 SS1 3B4 OF9)						
		BROWN, WM. JAMES (GATES)	OF	56	82	.338	B	B
10	9	CAIN, LESLIE	P	26	27	.145	B	B
		CASH, NORMAN DALTON	1B	131	135	.283	B	B
4	6	CHANCE, WILMER DEAN	P		31	.000	NY N	C
20	9	COLEMAN, JOSEPH HOWARD	P		39	.094	WAS	B
		COLLINS, KEVIN MICHAEL	3B	4	35	.268	B	C
		(2B1 OF2)						
0	3	DENEHY, WILLIAM FRANCIS	P		31	.000	WAS 68	C
0	0	FOOR, JAMES EMERSON	P		3	.000	A	B
		FREEHAN, WILLIAM ASHLEY	C	144	148	.277	B	B
		(OF1)						
2	1	GILBRETH, WILLIAM FREEMAN	P		9	.182	A	B
		GUTIERREZ, CESAR DARIO	SS	14	38	.189	B	C
		(2B2 3B5)						
1	0	HANNAN, JAMES JOHN	P		7	+.000	WAS	XMIL
		HORTON, WILLIAM WATTISON	OF	118	119	.289	B	B
		HOSLEY, TIMOTHY KENNETH	C	4	7	.188	B	C
		(1B1)						
		JONES, JAMES DALTON	OF	16	83	.254	B	B
		(1B3 2B1 3B13)						
		KALINE, ALBERT WILLIAM (1B5)	OF	129	133	.294	B	B
4	5	KILKENNY, MICHAEL DAVID	P		30	.083	B	B
		LAMONT, GENE WILLIAM	C		7	.067	B	B
		LANE, MARVIN	OF	6	8	.143	A	B
25	14	LOLICH, MICHAEL STEPHEN	P		45	.130	B	B
		MC AULIFFE, RICHARD JOHN	2B	123	128	.208	B	B
6	7	NIEKRO, JOSEPH FRANKLIN	P	31	32	.133	B	B
		NORTHRUP, JAMES THOMAS (1B32)	OF	108	136	.270	B	B
0	1	PATTERSON, DARYL ALAN	P		12	+.000	B	XOAK
0	1	PERRANOSKI, RONALD PETER	P		11	+.000	XMIN	B
		PRICE, JIMMIE WILLIAM	C	25	29	.241	B	C
		RODRIGUEZ, AURELIO (SS1)	3B	153	154	.253	WAS	B
11	6	SCHERMAN, FREDERICK JOHN	P		69	.208	B	B
0	0	SEELBACH, CHARLES FREDERICK	P		5	.000	A	B
		STANLEY, MITCHELL JACK	OF		139	.292	B	B
		TAYLOR, ANTONIO NEMESIO	2B	51	55	.287	XPHIN	B
		(3B3)						
7	6	TIMMERMAN, THOMAS HENRY	P		52	.053	B	B
0	2	WHILLOCK, JACK FRANKLIN	P		7	.000	A	C
		YOUNG, JOHN THOMAS	1B	1	2	.500	A	C
1	1	ZEPP, WILLIAM CLINTON	P		16	.000	MIN	C

WON 86
LOST 70
TIED 0
TG 156

AMERICAN LEAGUE

1972.

FINISHED 1 E
(LOST LEAGUE PLAYOFF)
PCT. .551

DETROIT

ALFRED MANUEL MARTIN

WON	LOST	NAME	POS.		G.	BA	FROM	TO
		BLESSITT, ISAIAH	OF	1	4	.000	A	
		BRINKMAN, EDWIN ALBERT	SS		156	.203	B	
		BROWN, ISSAC	OF	22	51	.250	B	
		(1B13 2B3 SS1 3B1)						
		BROWN, WM. JAMES (GATES)	OF	72	103	.230	B	
0	3	CAIN, LESLIE	P		5	.143	B	
		CASH, NORMAN DALTON	1B	134	137	.259	B	
19	14	COLEMAN, JOSEPH HOWARD	P		40	.110	B	
		COMER, HARRY WAYNE	OF	17	27	.111	WAS 70	
1	0	FOOR, JAMES EMERSON	P		7	.000	B	
		FREEHAN, WILLIAM ASHLEY	C	105	111	.262	B	
		(1B1)						
10	3	FRYMAN, WOODROW THOMPSON	P		16	.125	XPHIN	
		GAMBLE, JOHN ROBERT	SS	1	6	.000	A	
0	0	GILBRETH, WILLIAM FREEMAN	P		2	.000	B	
		HALLER, THOMAS FRANK	C	36	59	.207	LA N	
1	2	HILLER, JOHN FREDERICK	P		24	.000	DET 70	
0	1	HOLDSWORTH, FREDRICK WILLIAM	P		2	.333	A	
		HORTON, WILLIAM WATTISON	OF	98	108	.231	B	
		HOWARD, FRANK OLIVER (OF1)	1B	10	14	+.242	XTEX	
		JATA, PAUL (C1 OF10)	1B	12	32	.230	A	
		JONES, JAMES DALTON			7	+.000	B	XTEX
		KALINE, ALBERT WILLIAM (1B11)	OF	84	106	.313	B	
0	0	KILKENNY, MICHAEL DAVID	P		1	+.000	B	XOAK
		KNOX, JOHN CLINTON	2B	4	14	.077	A	
0	1	LA GROW, LERRIN HARRIS	P		16	.000	DET 70	
		LAMONT, GENE WILLIAM	C		1	.000	B	
		LANE, MARVIN	OF	3	8	.000	B	
0	0	LESHNOCK, DONALD LEE	P		1	.000	A	
22	14	LOLICH, MICHAEL STEPHEN	P		41	.067	B	
		MC AULIFFE, RICHARD JOHN	2B	116	122	.240	B	
		(SS3 3B1)						
0	1	MEELER, CHARLES RICHARD (DICK)	P		7	.000	A	
3	2	NIEKRO, JOSEPH FRANKLIN	P		18	.250	B	
		NORTHRUP, JAMES THOMAS (1B2)	OF	127	134	.261	B	
0	1	PERRANOSKI, RONALD PETER	P		17	.000	B	XLA N
		RODRIGUEZ, AURELIO (SS2)	3B	153	153	.236	B	
7	3	SCHERMAN, FREDERICK JOHN	P		57	.091	B	
9	8	SEELBACH, CHARLES FREDERICK	P		61	.143	B	
		SIMS, DUANE B. (DUKE) (OF4)	C	25	38	.316	XLA N	
5	6	SLAYBACK, WILLIAM GROVER	P		23	.174	A	
		STANLEY, MITCHELL JACK	OF	139	142	.234	B	
		STATON, JOSEPH	1B	2	6	.000	A	
0	0	STRAMPE, ROBERT EDWIN	P		7	.000	A	
		TAYLOR, ANTONIO NEMESIO	2B	67	78	.303	B	
		(1B1 3B8)						
8	10	TIMMERMAN, THOMAS HENRY	P	34	35	.136	B	
1	1	ZACHARY, WILLIAM CHRIS	P		25	.500	STLN	

WON 59
LOST 103
TIED 0
TG 162

AMERICAN LEAGUE

1965.

FINISHED 10 (LAST)

PCT. .364

KANSAS CITY

FRED MELVIN MC GAHA HAYWOOD COOPER SULLIVAN

WON	LOST	NAME	POS.		G.	BA	FROM	TO
4	3	AKER, JACK DELANE	P		34	.000	B	B
		BLANCHARD, JOHN EDWIN (C14)	OF	20	52	+.200	XNY	XMILN
		BRYAN, WILLIAM RONALD	C	95	108	.252	B	B
0	1	BUSCHHORN, DONALD LEE	P	12	13	.500	A	C
		CAMPANERIS, DAGBERTO (BERT)	SS	109	144	.270	B	B
		(P1 C1 1B1 2B1 3B1 OF39)						
		CAUSEY, JAMES WAYNE	SS	62	144	.261	B	B
		(2B45 3B35)						
		CHARLES, EDWIN DOUGLAS	3B	128	134	.269	B	B
		(2B1 SS1)						
		CLINTON, LUCIEAN LOUIS	OF		1	+.000	XCAL	XCLE
3	2	DICKSON, JAMES EDWARD	P		68	.000	CINN	B
1	5	DRABOWSKY, MYRON WALTER (MOE)	P		14	.091	B	BAL
		EDWARDS, HOWARD RODNEY (DOC)	C		6	+.150	B	XNY
		GENTILE, JAMES EDWARD	1B	35	38	.246	B	XHOUN
		GREEN, RICHARD LARRY	2B	126	133	.232	B	B
		HARRELSON, KENNETH SMITH	1B	125	150	.238	B	B
		(OF4)						
0	0	HARRISON, THOMAS JAMES	P	1	2	.000	A	C
		HERSHBERGER, NORMAN MICHAEL	OF	144	150	.231	CHI	B
0	1	HICKMAN, JESSE OWENS	P	12	14	.000	A	B
8	8	HUNTER, JAMES AUGUSTUS	P		32	.150	A	B
		(CATFISH)						
0	1	JOYCE, RICHARD EDWARD	P		5	.000	A	C
2	4	KRAUSSE, LEWIS BERNARD, JR.	P	7	10	.000	B	B
		LACHEMANN, RENE GEORGE	C	75	92	.227	A	B
		LANDIS, JAMES HENRY	OF	108	118	.239	CHI	CLE
0	1	LINDBLAD, PAUL AARON	P		4	.000	A	B
		LOCKWOOD, CLAUDE EDWARD (SKIP)	3B	7	42	.121	A	SEA 69
		MATHEWS, NELSON ELMER	OF	57	67	.212	B	C
0	0	MONTEAGUDO, AURELIO FAUSTINO	P	4	5	.000	B	B
5	8	MOSSI, DONALD LOUIS	P		51	.000	CHI	C
0	0	ODOM, JOHNNY LEE (BLUE MOON)	P		1	.000	B	B
9	18	O'DONOGHUE, JOHN EUGENE	P	34	39	.218	B	CLE
0	0	PAIGE, LEROY ROBERT (SATCHEL)	P		1	.000	STL 53	C
0	6	PENA, ORLANDO	P		12	+.111	B	XDET
		REYNOLDS, TOMMIE D. (3B1)	OF	83	90	.237	B	NY N67
		ROSARIO, SANTIAGO (OF3)	1B	31	81	.235	A	C
		SANDERS, JOHN FRANK			1	.000	A	C
0	0	SANTIAGO, JOSE RAFAEL	P		4	.000	B	BOS
		SCHWARTZ, DOUGLAS RANDALL	1B	2	6	.286	A	B
5	15	SEGUI, DIEGO PABLO	P	40	41	.191	B	WAS
10	8	SHELDON, ROLAND FRANK	P		32	+.078	XNY	B
		STAHL, LARRY FLOYD	OF	21	28	.198	B	B
0	4	STOCK, WESLEY GAY	P		62	.000	B	B
10	12	TALBOT, FRED LEALAND	P	39	47	.200	CHI	B
		TARTABULL, JOSE	OF	54	68	.312	B	B
0	0	TOMPKINS, RONALD EVERETT	P		5	.000	A	CHIN71
2	6	WYATT, JOHN THOMAS	P		65	.000	B	B

WON 74
LOST 86
TIED 0
TG 160

AMERICAN LEAGUE

1966.

FINISHED 7

PCT. .462

KANSAS CITY

ALVIN RALPH DARK

WON	LOST	NAME	POS.		G.	BA	FROM	TO
8	4	AKER, JACK DELANE	P		66	.095	B	B
		BANDO, SALVATORE LEONARD	3B	7	11	.292	A	B
2	4	BLANCO, GILBERT HENRY	P		11	.167	NY	C
		BLASINGAME, DON LEE	2B	4	12	+.158	XWAS	C
		BRYAN, WILLIAM RONALD (1B3)	C	21	32	+.132	B	XNY
		CAMPANERIS, DAGBERTO (BERT)	SS	138	142	.267	B	B
		CATER, DANNY ANDERSON	1B	53	116	+.292	XCHI	B
		(3B42 OF22)						
		CAUSEY, JAMES WAYNE (SS10)	3B	15	28	+.228	B	XCHI
		CHARLES, EDWIN DOUGLAS	3B	104	118	.286	B	B
		(1B1 OF1)						
		CHAVARRIA, OSVALDO	OF	26	86	.241	A	B
		(1B8 2B14 SS23 3B5)						
1	0	DICKSON, JAMES EDWARD	P		24	.250	B	C
4	6	DOBSON, CHARLES THOMAS	P		14	.115	A	B
		DONALDSON, JOHN DAVID	2B	9	15	.133	A	B
0	2	DUCKWORTH, JAMES RAYMOND	P		8	+.000	XWAS	C
0	1	EDGERTON, WILLIAM ALBERT	P		6	.000	A	B
		FAZIO, ERNEST JOSEPH (SS4)	2B	10	27	.206	HOUN63	C
		GOSGER, JAMES CHARLES	OF	77	88	+.224	XBOS	B
		GREEN, RICHARD LARRY (3B2)	2B	137	140	.250	B	B
0	1	GRILLI, GUIDO JOHN	P		16	+.000	XBOS	C
0	2	GRZENDA, JOSEPH CHARLES	P		21	.000	KC 64	NY N
0	1	HANDRAHAN, JAMES VERNON (VERN)	P		16	.000	KC 64	C
		HARRELSON, KENNETH SMITH	1B	58	63	+.224	B	XWAS
		(OF3)						
		HERSHBERGER, NORMAN MICHAEL	OF	143	146	.253	B	B
0	0	HICKMAN, JESSE OWENS	P		1	.000	B	C
9	11	HUNTER, JAMES AUGUSTUS	P		30	.153	B	B
		(CATFISH)						
		JIMENEZ, MANUEL EMILIO	OF	12	13	.114	KC 64	PITN
14	9	KRAUSSE, LEWIS BERNARD, JR.	P	36	40	.154	B	B
		LACHEMANN, RENE GEORGE	C	6	7	.200	B	OAK 68
5	10	LINDBLAD, PAUL AARON	P		38	.147	B	B
		MONDAY, ROBERT JAMES (RICK)	OF	15	17	.098	A	B
0	0	MONTEAGUDO, AURELIO FAUSTINO	P		6	.000	B	XHOUN
12	1	NASH, JAMES EDWIN	P		18	.102	A	B
		NOSSEK, JOSEPH RUDOLPH (3B1)	OF	78	87	+.261	XMIN	B
5	5	ODOM, JOHNNY LEE (BLUE MOON)	P	14	17	.097	B	B
		REPOZ, ROGER ALLEN (1B45)	OF	52	101	+.216	XNY	B
		ROOF, PHILLIP ANTHONY (1B2)	C	123	127	.209	CLE	B
3	4	SANDERS, KENNETH GEORGE	P		38	+.250	XBOS	OAK 68
		SCHWARTZ, DOUGLAS RANDALL	1B	2	10	.091	B	C
4	7	SHELDON, ROLAND FRANK	P		14	+.087	B	XBOS
0	4	STAFFORD, WILLIAM CHARLES	P		9	.000	NY	B
		STAHL, LARRY FLOYD	OF	94	119	.250	B	NY N
2	2	STOCK, WESLEY GAY	P		35	.000	B	B
		STONE, HARRY RONALD (RON)	OF	4	26	.273	A	PHIN69
		(1B3)						
		SUAREZ, KENNETH RAYMOND	C	34	35	.145	A	B
4	4	TALBOT, FRED LEALAND	P		11	+.150	B	XNY
		TALTON, MARION LEE (TIM)	C	14	37	.340	A	B
		(1B9)						
		TARTABULL, JOSE	OF	33	37	+.236	B	XBOS
1	5	TERRY, RALPH WILLARD	P		15	.214	CLE	XNY N
0	3	WYATT, JOHN THOMAS	P		19	+.000	B	XBOS

WON 62 — LOST 99 — TIED 0 — TG 161

AMERICAN LEAGUE — 1967. — FINISHED 10 (LAST) — PCT. .385

KANSAS CITY

ALVIN RALPH DARK   LUCIUS BENJAMIN APPLING

WON	LOST	NAME	POS.		G.	BA	FROM	TO
3	8	AKER, JACK DELANE	P		57	.125	B	OAK
		BANDO, SALVATORE LEONARD	3B	44	47	.192	B	OAK
		BOWLIN, LOIS WELDON	3B		2	.200	A	C
		CAMPANERIS, DAGBERTO (BERT)	SS	145	147	.248	B	OAK
		CATER, DANNY ANDERSON	3B	56	142	.270	B	OAK
		(1B44 OF55)						
		CHARLES, EDWIN DOUGLAS	3B		19	.246	B	XNY N
		CHAVARRIA, OSVALDO	2B	17	38	.102	B	C
		(SS2 3B7 OF3)						
10	10	DOBSON, CHARLES THOMAS	P	32	33	.181	B	OAK
		DONALDSON, JOHN DAVID (SS1)	2B	101	105	.276	B	OAK
0	0	DULIBA, ROBERT JOHN	P		7	.000	BOS 65	C
		DUNCAN, DAVID EDWIN	C	32	34	.188	KC 64	OAK
1	0	EDGERTON, WILLIAM ALBERT	P		7	.000	B	SEA 69
		GOSGER, JAMES CHARLES	OF	113	134	.242	B	OAK
		GREEN, RICHARD LARRY	3B	59	122	.198	B	OAK
		(1B1 2B50 SS1)						
		HARRELSON, KENNETH SMITH	1B	45	61	+.305	XWAS	XBOS
		HERSHBERGER, NORMAN MICHAEL	OF	130	142	.254	B	OAK
13	17	HUNTER, JAMES AUGUSTUS (1B1)	P	35	37	.196	B	OAK
		(CATFISH)						
		JACKSON, REGINALD MARTINEZ	OF	34	35	.178	A	OAK
7	17	KRAUSSE, LEWIS BERNARD, JR.	P	48	49	.146	B	OAK
		KUBIAK, THEODORE RODGER	SS	20	53	.157	A	OAK
		(2B10 3B5)						
0	2	LAUZERIQUE, GEORGE ALBERT	P		3	.000	A	OAK
		LEWIS, ALLAN SYDNEY			34	.167	A	OAK
5	8	LINDBLAD, PAUL AARON	P	46	48	.206	B	OAK
		MONDAY, ROBERT JAMES (RICK)	OF	113	124	.251	B	OAK
12	17	NASH, JAMES EDWIN	P		37	.100	B	OAK
		NOSSEK, JOSEPH RUDOLPH	OF	63	87	.205	B	OAK 69
3	8	ODOM, JOHNNY LEE (BLUE MOON)	P	29	33	.286	B	OAK
3	4	PIERCE, TONY MICHAEL	P		49	.000	A	OAK
		REPOZ, ROGER ALLEN	OF	31	40	+.241	B	XCAL
1	1	RODRIGUEZ, ROBERTO MUNOZ	P		15	.000	A	OAK 70
		ROOF, PHILLIP ANTHONY	C	113	114	.205	B	OAK
		RUDI, JOSEPH ODEN (OF6)	1B	9	19	.186	A	OAK
1	2	SANFORD, JOHN STANLEY	P		10	+.000	XCAL	C
3	4	SEGUI, DIEGO PABLO	P		36	.000	WAS	OAK
0	1	STAFFORD, WILLIAM CHARLES	P		14	.000	B	C
0	0	STOCK, WESLEY GAY	P		1	.000	B	C
		SUAREZ, KENNETH RAYMOND	C	36	39	.238	B	CLE
		TALTON, MARION LEE (TIM)	C	22	46	.254	B	C
		(1B1)						
		WEBSTER, RAMON ALBERTO (OF15)	1B	83	122	.256	A	OAK

COACH APPLING SERVED AS INTERIM MANAGER NEAR CLOSE OF SEASON.
CLUB TRANSFERRED TO OAKLAND AFTER 1967 SEASON.

WON 69 — LOST 93 — TIED 1 — TG 163

AMERICAN LEAGUE — 1969. — FINISHED 4 W — PCT. .426

KANSAS CITY

JOSEPH LOWELL GORDON

WON	LOST	NAME	POS.		G.	BA	FROM	TO
		ADAIR, KENNETH JERRY	2B	109	126	.250	BOS	B
		(SS8 3B1)						
		ALCARAZ, ANGEL LUIS	2B	19	22	.253	LA N	B
		(SS1 3B2)						
12	11	BUNKER, WALLACE EDWARD	P		35	.143	BAL	B
3	1	BURGMEIER, THOMAS HENRY	P	31	47	.167	CAL	B
		(OF1)						
9	10	BUTLER, WILLIAM FRANKLIN	P		34	.050	A	B
		CAMPANIS, JAMES ALEXANDER	C	26	30	.157	LA N	B
1	1	CISCO, GALEN BERNARD	P		15	.000	BOS 67	C
0	1	CRAM, GERALD ALLEN	P		5	.000	A	C
11	9	DRABOWSKY, MYRON WALTER (MOE)	P		52	.235	BAL	B
11	13	DRAGO, RICHARD ANTHONY	P		41	.058	A	B
		FIORE, MICHAEL GARRY JOSEPH	1B	91	107	.274	BAL	B
		(OF13)						
1	1	FITZMORRIS, ALAN JAMES	P		7	.000	A	B
		FOY, JOSEPH ANTHONY	3B	113	145	.262	BOS	NY N
		(1B16 2B3 SS5 OF16)						
		HARRIS, JAMES WILLIAM (BILLY)	2B	1	5	.286	CLE	C
		HARRISON, CHARLES WILLIAM	1B	55	75	.221	HOUN67	KC 71
		HEALY, FRANCIS XAVIER	C	5	6	.400	A	SF N71
3	6	HEDLUND, MICHAEL DAVID	P		34	.152	CLE	B
		HERNANDEZ, JACINTO (JACKIE)	SS	144	145	.222	MIN	B
2	3	JONES, STEVEN HOWELL	P		20	.125	WAS	C
		KELLY, HAROLD PATRICK (PAT)	OF	107	112	.264	MIN	B
		KEOUGH, JOSEPH WILLIAM (1B1)	OF	49	70	.187	OAK	B
		KIRKPATRICK EDGAR LEON	OF	82	120	.257	CAL	B
		(C8 1B2 2B1 3B2)						
		MARTINEZ, JOHN ALBERT (OF1)	C	55	72	.229	A	B
2	3	MOREHEAD, DAVID MICHAEL	P		21	.000	BOS	B
7	13	NELSON, ROGER EUGENE	P		29	.138	BAL	B
		NORTHEY, SCOTT RICHARD	OF	18	20	.262	A	C
		OLIVER, ROBERT LEE	OF	98	118	.254	PITN65	B
		(1B12 3B8)						
1	1	O'RILEY, DONALD LEE	P	18	19	.000	A	B
		PAEPKE, DENNIS RAY	C	8	12	.111	A	KC 71
		PINIELLA, LOUIS VICTOR	OF	129	135	.282	CLE	B
		RICO, ALFREDO CRUZ (3B1)	OF	9	12	.231	A	C
		RIOS, JUAN O. (SS32 3B4)	2B	46	87	.224	A	C
		RODRIGUEZ, ELISEO	C	90	95	.236	NY	B
4	16	ROOKER, JAMES PHILLIP	P	28	34	.281	DET	B
		SCHAAL, PAUL	3B	49	61	.263	CAL	B
		(2B6 SS6)						
		SPRIGGS, GEORGE HERMAN	OF	6	23	.138	PITN67	B
		TAYLOR, ROBERT DALE (HAWK)	OF	18	64	.270	CAL 67	B
		(C6)						
2	3	WICKERSHAM, DAVID CLIFFORD	P		34	.000	PITN	C
0	1	ZACHARY, WILLIAM CHRIS	P		8	.500	HOUN67	STLN71

NEW KANSAS CITY CLUB ADDED IN EXPANSION OF 1969.

WON 65 | LOST 97 | TIED 0 | TG 162

AMERICAN LEAGUE

1970.

FINISHED 4 W (TIED WITH MILWAUKEE) PCT. .401

KANSAS CITY

CHARLES METRO ROBERT GRANVILLE LEMON

WON	LOST	NAME	POS.		G.	BA	FROM	TO
9	3	ABERNATHY, THEODORE WADE	P		36	.214	XSTLN	B
		ADAIR, KENNETH JERRY	2B		7	.148	B	C
		ALCARAZ, ANGEL LUIS	2B	31	35	.167	B	C
2	11	BUNKER, WALLACE EDWARD	P		24	.065	B	B
6	6	BURGMEIER, THOMAS HENRY	P	41	42	.143	B	B
4	12	BUTLER, WILLIAM FRANKLIN	P		25	.045	B	B
		CAMPANIS, JAMES ALEXANDER	C	13	31	.130	B	C
		(OF1)						
1	2	DRABOWSKY, MYRON WALTER (MOE)	P		24	+.250	B	XBAL
9	15	DRAGO, RICHARD ANTHONY	P		35	.053	B	B
		FIORE, MICHAEL GARRY JOSEPH	1B	20	25	+.181	B	XBOS
8	5	FITZMORRIS, ALAN JAMES	P	43	45	.290	B	B
		FLOYD, ROBERT NATHAN (3B6)	SS	8	14	+.326	XBAL	B
2	3	HEDLUND, MICHAEL DAVID	P		9	.000	B	B
		HERNANDEZ, JACINTO (JACKIE)	SS	77	83	.231	B	PITN
8	13	JOHNSON, ROBERT DALE	P		40	.105	NY N	PITN
		KELLY, HAROLD PATRICK (PAT)	OF	118	136	.235	B	CHI
		KEOUGH, JOSEPH WILLIAM (1B18)	OF	34	57	.322	B	B
		KIRKPATRICK EDGAR LEON	C	89	134	.229	B	B
		(1B16 OF19)						
		MARTINEZ, JOHN ALBERT	C	5	6	.111	B	B
		MATCHICK, JOHN THOMAS (TOMMY)	SS	43	55	+.196	XBOS	MIL
		(2B10 3B1)						
1	1	MONTEAGUDO, AURELIO FAUSTINO	P		21	.000	CHI 67	C
3	5	MOREHEAD, DAVID MICHAEL	P		28	.167	B	C
0	2	NELSON, ROGER EUGENE	P		4	.000	B	B
		OLIVER, ROBERT LEE (3B46)	1B	115	160	.260	B	B
0	0	O'RILEY, DONALD LEE	P		9	.000	B	C
		OTIS, AMOS JOSEPH	OF		159	.284	NY N	B
		PINIELLA, LOUIS VICTOR (1B1)	OF	139	144	.301	B	B
		RODRIGUEZ, ELISEO	C	75	80	.225	B	MIL
		ROJAS, OCTAVIO (COOKIE)	2B	97	98	.260	XSTLN	B
10	15	ROOKER, JAMES PHILLIP (OF1)	P	38	41	.200	B	B
		SCHAAL, PAUL	3B	97	124	.269	B	B
		(2B6 SS10)						
		SEVERSON, RICHARD ALLEN	SS	50	77	.250	A	B
		(2B25)						
		SORRELL, WILLIAM (1B3 OF4)	3B	29	57	.267	SF N67	C
0	1	SPLITTORFF, PAUL WILLIAM	P		2	.500	A	B
		SPRIGGS, GEORGE HERMAN	OF	36	51	.208	B	C
		TAYLOR, ROBERT DALE (HAWK)	C	3	57	.164	B	C
		(1B1)						
1	2	WRIGHT, KENNETH WARREN	P		47	.000	A	B
1	1	YORK, JAMES HARLAN	P		4	.000	A	B

WON 85 | LOST 76 | TIED 0 | TG 161

AMERICAN LEAGUE

1971.

FINISHED 2 W PCT. .528

KANSAS CITY

ROBERT GRANVILLE LEMON

WON	LOST	NAME	POS.		G.	BA	FROM	TO
4	6	ABERNATHY, THEODORE WADE	P		63	.077	B	B
2	3	BUNKER, WALLACE EDWARD	P		7	.000	B	C
9	7	BURGMEIER, THOMAS HENRY	P	67	68	.250	B	B
1	2	BUTLER, WILLIAM FRANKLIN	P		14	.083	B	CLE
1	0	CLEMONS, LANCE LEVIS	P		10	.286	A	STLN
8	6	DAL CANTON, JOHN BRUCE	P		25	.087	PITN	B
17	11	DRAGO, RICHARD ANTHONY	P		35	.130	B	B
7	5	FITZMORRIS, ALAN JAMES	P		36	.250	B	B
		FLOYD, ROBERT NATHAN	SS	15	31	.152	B	B
		(2B8 3B1)						
		HARRISON, CHARLES WILLIAM	1B	39	49	.217	KC 69	C
15	8	HEDLUND, MICHAEL DAVID	P		32	.088	B	B
		HOPKINS, GAIL EASON	1B	83	103	.278	CHI	B
		KEOUGH, JOSEPH WILLIAM	OF	100	110	.248	B	B
		KIRKPATRICK EDGAR LEON (C59)	OF	61	120	.219	B	B
		KNOOP, ROBERT FRANK (3B1)	2B	52	72	.205	CHI	B
		MARTINEZ, JOHN ALBERT	C	21	22	.152	B	C
		MAY, JERRY LEE	C		71	.252	PITN	B
0	0	MC CORMICK, MICHAEL FRANCIS	P		4	.000	NY	C
3	0	MONTGOMERY, MONTY BRYSON	P		3	.000	A	B
0	1	NELSON, ROGER EUGENE	P		13	.333	B	B
		OLIVER, ROBERT LEE	1B	68	128	.244	B	B
		(3B2 OF48)						
		OTIS, AMOS JOSEPH	OF	144	147	.301	B	B
		PAEPKE, DENNIS RAY (OF17)	C	32	60	.204	KC 69	B
		PATEK, FREDDIE JOE	SS		147	.267	PITN	B
		PINIELLA, LOUIS VICTOR	OF	115	126	.279	B	B
		ROJAS, OCTAVIO (COOKIE)	2B	111	115	.300	B	B
		(SS2 OF1)						
2	7	ROOKER, JAMES PHILLIP	P	20	21	.000	B	B
		SAVAGE, THEODORE E.	OF	9	19	+.172	XMIL	C
		SCHAAL, PAUL	3B		161	.274	B	B
		SEVERSON, RICHARD ALLEN	2B	6	16	.300	B	C
		(SS6 3B1)						
8	9	SPLITTORFF, PAUL WILLIAM	P		22	.104	B	B
		TAYLOR, CARL MEANS	OF	12	20	.179	XPITN	B
		VALDESPINO, HILARIO BORROTO	OF	15	18	.317	MIL	C
		(SANDY)						
3	6	WRIGHT, KENNETH WARREN	P		21	.091	B	B
5	5	YORK, JAMES HARLAN	P		53	.118	B	HOUN

WON 76
LOST 78
TIED 0
TG 154

AMERICAN LEAGUE

1972.

FINISHED 4 W

PCT. .494

KANSAS CITY

ROBERT GRANVILLE LEMON

WON	LOST	NAME	POS.		G.	BA	FROM	TO
3	4	ABERNATHY, THEODORE WADE	P		45	.000	B	
2	1	ANGELINI, NORMAN STANLEY	P		21	.000	A	
6	2	BURGMEIER, THOMAS HENRY	P		51	.333	B	
3	1	BUSBY, STEVEN LEE	P		5	.200	A	
6	6	DAL CANTON, JOHN BRUCE	P		35	.098	B	
12	17	DRAGO, RICHARD ANTHONY	P	34	35	.059	B	
2	5	FITZMORRIS, ALAN JAMES	P	38	39	.174	B	
		FLOYD, ROBERT NATHAN	3B	30	61	.179	B	
		(2B2 SS29)						
		HANSEN, RONALD LAVERN	SS	6	16	.133	NY	
		(2B1 3B4)						
5	7	HEDLUND, MICHAEL DAVID	P		29	.188	B	
		HOPKINS, GAIL EASON (3B1)	1B	13	53	.211	B	
		HOVLEY, STEPHEN EUGENE	OF	68	105	.270	OAK	
1	2	JACKSON, MICHAEL WARREN	P		7	.000	STLN	
		KEOUGH, JOSEPH WILLIAM	OF	16	56	.219	B	
		KIRKPATRICK EDGAR LEON (1B1)	C	108	113	.275	B	
		KNOOP, ROBERT FRANK (3B4)	2B	33	44	.237	B	
		MAY, JERRY LEE	C	41	53	.190	B	
		MAYBERRY, JOHN CLAIBORN	1B	146	149	.298	HOUN	
3	3	MONTGOMERY, MONTY BRYSON	P		9	.176	B	
4	4	MURPHY, THOMAS ANDREW	P	18	21	+.000	XCAL	
11	6	NELSON, ROGER EUGENE	P		34	.093	B	
		OLIVER, ROBERT LEE	OF		16	+.270	B	XCAL
		OTIS, AMOS JOSEPH	OF	137	143	.293	B	
		PAEPKE, DENNIS RAY	C		2	.000	B	
		PATEK, FREDDIE JOE	SS		136	.212	B	
		PINIELLA, LOUIS VICTOR	OF	150	151	.312	B	
		ROJAS, OCTAVIO (COOKIE)	2B	131	137	.261	B	
		(SS2 3B6)						
5	6	ROOKER, JAMES PHILLIP	P		18	.100	B	
		SCHAAL, PAUL (SS1)	3B	123	127	.228	B	
		SCHEINBLUM, RICHARD ALAN	OF	119	134	.300	WAS	
12	12	SPLITTORFF, PAUL WILLIAM	P		35	.225	B	
		TAYLOR, CARL MEANS	C	21	63	.265	B	
		(1B6 3B5 OF7)						
		WOHLFORD, JAMES EUGENE	2B	8	15	.240	A	
1	2	WRIGHT, KENNETH WARREN	P		17	.000	B	

WON 65
LOST 97
TIED 1
TG 163

AMERICAN LEAGUE

1970.

FINISHED 4 W
(TIED WITH KANSAS CITY)
PCT. .401

MILWAUKEE

JAMES DAVID BRISTOL

WON	LOST	NAME	POS.		G.	BA	FROM	TO
		ALLEN, HAROLD ANDREW (HANK)	OF	14	28	+.230	XWAS	CHI 72
		(1B4 2B5)						
		ALVIS, ROY MAXWELL (MAX)	3B	36	62	.183	CLE	C
2	1	BALDWIN, DAVID GEORGE	P		28	.500	WAS	C
5	11	BOLIN, BOBBY DONALD	P		32	+.194	SF N	XBOS
6	15	BRABENDER, EUGENE MATTHEW	P		29	.098	SEA	C
0	0	BRUBAKER, BRUCE ELLSWORTH	P		1	.000	LA N67	C
		BURDA, EDWARD ROBERT (BOB)	OF	64	78	.248	XSF N	STLN
		(1B7)						
		COMER, HARRY WAYNE	OF	5	13	+.059	SEA	XWAS
2	10	DOWNING, ALPHONSO ERWIN	P		17	+.083	XOAK	LA N
0	0	ELLSWORTH, RICHARD CLARK	P		14	+.000	XCLE	B
		FRANCONA, JOHN PATSY (TITO)	1B	13	52	+.231	XOAK	C
4	3	GELNAR, JOHN RICHARD	P		53	.083	SEA	B
		GIL, TOMAS GUSTAVO (GUS)	2B	38	64	.185	SEA	B
		(3B14)						
		GOOSSEN, GREGORY BRYANT	1B	15	21	+.255	SEA	XWAS
		HARPER, TOMMY (2B22 OF13)	3B	128	154	.296	SEA	B
		HEGAN, JAMES MICHAEL (MIKE)	1B	139	148	.244	SEA	B
		(OF8)						
		HERSHBERGER, NORMAN MICHAEL	OF	35	49	.235	OAK	CHI
		HOVLEY, STEPHEN EUGENE	OF	38	40	+.281	SEA	XOAK
2	4	HUMPHREYS, ROBERT WILLIAM	P		23	+.000	XWAS	C
		KENNEDY, JOHN EDWARD	2B	16	25	+.255	SEA	XBOS
		(1B1 SS4 3B5)						
		KOEGEL, PETER JOHN	OF	1	7	.250	A	B
13	18	KRAUSSE, LEWIS BERNARD, JR.	P	37	38	.138	OAK	B
		KUBIAK, THEODORE RODGER	2B	91	158	.252	OAK	B
		(SS73)						
1	2	LAUZERIQUE, GEORGE ALBERT	P		11	.200	OAK	C
0	1	LOCKER, ROBERT AUTRY	P		28	+.000	SEA	XOAK
5	12	LOCKWOOD, CLAUDE EDWARD (SKIP)	P		27	.226	SEA	B
		MAY, DAVID LAFRANCE	OF	99	101	+.240	XBAL	B
		MC NERTNEY, GERALD EDWARD	C	94	111	.243	SEA	STLN
		(1B13)						
0	1	MEYER, ROBERT BERNARD	P		10	.333	SEA	C
4	3	MORRIS, JOHN WALLACE	P		20	.176	SEA	B
2	0	O'DONOGHUE, JOHN EUGENE	P		25	.000	SEA	XMONN
14	12	PATTIN, MARTIN WILLIAM	P	37	43	.129	SEA	B
		PENA, ROBERTO CESAR	SS	99	121	+.238	XOAK	B
		(1B7 2B15)						
0	2	PETERS, RAYMOND JAMES	P		2	.000	A	C
		ROLLINS, RICHARD JOHN	3B	7	14	+.200	SEA	XCLE
		ROOF, PHILLIP ANTHONY (1B1)	C	107	110	.227	OAK	B
5	2	SANDERS, KENNETH GEORGE	P		50	.231	OAK 68	B
		SAVAGE, THEODORE E. (1B1)	OF	82	114	.279	CINN	B
		SMITH, CALVIN BERNARD (BERNIE)	OF	39	44	.276	A	B
		SNYDER, RUSSELL HENRY	OF	106	124	.232	CLE	C
		STANLEY, FREDERICK BLAIR	2B	2	6	.000	SEA	CLE
0	0	TWITCHELL, WAYNE LEE	P		2	.000	A	PHIN
		VALDESPINO, HILARIO BORROTO	OF	1	8	.000	SEA	KC
		(SANDY)						
		WALTON, DANIEL JAMES	OF	114	117	.257	SEA	B
		WICKER, FLOYD EULISS	OF	12	15	.195	MONN	B

CLUB TRANSFERRED FROM SEATTLE AFTER 1969 SEASON.

WON 69
LOST 92
TIED 0
TG 161

AMERICAN LEAGUE 1971. MILWAUKEE

FINISHED 6 W (LAST) PCT. .429

JAMES DAVID BRISTOL

WON	LOST	NAME	POS.		G.	BA	FROM	TO
		AUERBACH, FREDERICK STEVEN	SS	78	79	.203	A	B
0	0	BEARNARTH, LAWRENCE DONALD	P		2	.000	NY N66	C
2	1	BELL, JERRY HOUSTON	P		8	.000	A	B
		BRIGGS, JOHN EDWARD (1B60)	OF	65	125	.264	XPHIN	B
		CARDENAL, JOSE DOMEC	OF	52	53	.258	XSTLN	CHIN
		ELLIS, ROBERT WALTER (OF15)	3B	19	36	.198	A	C
0	1	ELLSWORTH, RICHARD CLARK	P		11	.000	B	C
0	0	GELNAR, JOHN RICHARD	P		2	.000	B	C
		GIL, TOMAS GUSTAVO (GUS)	2B	8	14	.156	B	C
		(3B6)						
1	1	HANNAN, JAMES JOHN	P		21	+.000	XDET	C
		HARPER, TOMMY (2B1 3B70)	OF	90	152	.258	B	BOS
		HEGAN, JAMES MICHAEL (MIKE)	1B	45	46	+.221	B	XOAK
		HEISE, ROBERT LOWELL	SS	51	68	.254	XSF N	B
		(2B3 3B11 OF1)						
		KOEGEL, PETER JOHN	1B	1	2	.000	B	XPHIN
		KOSCO, ANDREW JOHN	OF	45	98	.227	LA N	CAL
		(1B29 3B12)						
8	12	KRAUSSE, LEWIS BERNARD, JR.	P		43	.023	B	BOS
		KUBIAK, THEODORE RODGER	2B	48	89	.227	B	XSTLN
		(SS39)						
10	15	LOCKWOOD, CLAUDE EDWARD (SKIP)	P	33	36	.081	B	B
2	7	LOPEZ, MARCELINO PONS	P	31	34	.059	BAL	CLE
		MATCHICK, JOHN THOMAS (TOMMY)	3B	41	42	.219	KC	BAL
		(2B1)						
		MAY, DAVID LAFRANCE	OF	142	144	.277	B	B
		MITCHELL, ROBERT VANCE	OF	19	35	.182	NY	C
2	2	MORRIS, JOHN WALLACE	P		43	.200	B	SF N
13	17	PARSONS, WILLIAM RAYMOND	P		36	.167	A	B
14	14	PATTIN, MARTIN WILLIAM	P		36	.084	B	BOS
		PENA, ROBERTO CESAR	1B	50	113	.237	B	C
		(2B1 SS23 3B37)						
		PORTER, DARRELL RAY	C		22	.214	A	B
		RATLIFF, PAUL HAWTHORNE	C	13	23	+.171	XMIN	B
0	1	REYNOLDS, ROBERT ALLEN	P		3	.000	XSTLN	BAL
		RODRIGUEZ, ELISEO	C	114	115	.210	KC	B
		ROOF, PHILLIP ANTHONY	C	39	41	+.193	B	XMIN
7	12	SANDERS, KENNETH GEORGE	P		83	.000	B	B
		SAVAGE, THEODORE E.	OF	6	14	+.176	B	XKC
		SCHOFIELD, JOHN RICHARD (DICK)	3B	12	23	.107	BOS	XSTLN
		(2B2 SS4)						
10	8	SLATON, JAMES MICHAEL	P		26	.109	A	B
		SMITH, CALVIN BERNARD (BERNIE)	OF	12	15	.139	B	C
		TEPEDINO, FRANK RONALD	1B	28	53	+.198	XNY	NY
		THEOBALD, RONALD MERRILL	2B	111	126	.276	A	B
		(SS1 3B1)						
		VOSS, WILLIAM EDWARD	OF	79	97	.251	CAL	B
		WALTON, DANIEL JAMES (3B1)	OF	19	30	+.203	B	XNY
0	1	WEAVER, DAVID FLOYD	P		21	.000	CHI	C
		WICKER, FLOYD EULISS			11	.125	B	XSF N
		YATES, ALBERT ARTHUR	OF	12	24	.277	A	C

WON 65
LOST 91
TIED 0
TG 156

AMERICAN LEAGUE 1972. MILWAUKEE

FINISHED 6 W (LAST) PCT. .417

JAMES DAVID BRISTOL   ROY DAVID MC MILLAN   DELMAR WESLEY CRANDALL

WON	LOST	NAME	POS.		G.	BA	FROM	TO
		AUERBACH, FREDERICK STEVEN	SS		153	.218	B	
		AZCUE, JOSE JOAQUIN	C	9	11	+.143	XCAL	
5	1	BELL, JERRY HOUSTON	P		25	.071	B	
7	12	BRETT, KENNETH ALVEN	P	26	31	.227	BOS	
		BRIGGS, JOHN EDWARD (1B28)	OF	106	135	.266	B	
		BROWN, OLLIE LEE (3B1)	OF	56	66	+.279	XOAK	
		CLARK, RONALD BRUCE (3B10)	2B	11	22	+.185	XOAK	
7	7	COLBORN, JAMES WILLIAM	P		39	.081	CHIN	
		CONIGLIARO, WILLIAM MICHAEL	OF	50	52	.230	BOS	
		DAVIS, BRYSHEAR BARNETT	OF	43	85	.318	CHIN	
		(BROCK)						
		FELSKE, JOHN FREDERICK (1B8)	C	23	37	.138	CHIN68	
		FERRARO, MICHAEL DENNIS	3B	115	124	.255	SEA 69	
		(2B1 SS1)						
		HEISE, ROBERT LOWELL	2B	49	95	.266	B	
		(SS9 3B24)						
		LAHOUD, JOSEPH MICHAEL	OF	97	111	.237	BOS	
2	2	LINZY, FRANK ALFRED	P		47	.111	STLN	
8	15	LOCKWOOD, CLAUDE EDWARD (SKIP)	P	29	31	.132	B	
14	12	LONBORG, JAMES REYNOLD	P		33	.145	BOS	
		MAY, DAVID LAFRANCE	OF	138	143	.238	B	
		MOTTON, CURTELL HOWARD	OF	3	6	+.167	BAL	XCAL
0	0	NEWMAN, RAYMOND FRANCIS	P		4	1.000	CHIN	
		O'BRIEN, SYDNEY LLOYD (2B7)	3B	9	31	+.207	XCAL	
13	13	PARSONS, WILLIAM RAYMOND	P		33	.164	B	
		PORTER, DARRELL RAY	C		18	.125	B	
		RATLIFF, PAUL HAWTHORNE	C	13	22	.071	B	
0	1	REYNOLDS, ARCHIE EDWARD	P		5	.500	CAL	
		REYNOLDS, TOMMIE D.	OF	41	72	.200	CAL	
		(1B1 3B1)						
		RODRIGUEZ, ELISEO	C	114	116	.285	B	
3	8	RYERSON, GARY	P		20	.042	A	
2	9	SANDERS, KENNETH GEORGE	P		62	.143	B	
		SCOTT, GEORGE (3B23)	1B	139	152	.266	BOS	
1	6	SLATON, JAMES MICHAEL	P		9	.091	B	
3	5	STEPHENSON, CHESTER EARL	P		35	.000	CHIN	
0	0	TAYLOR, CHARLES GILBERT	P		5	.500	XNY N	
		THEOBALD, RONALD MERRILL	2B	113	125	.220	B	
		VOSS, WILLIAM EDWARD	OF	11	27	+.083	B	XOAK

COACH MC MILLAN SERVED AS INTERIM MANAGER DURING CHANGEOVER.

WON 102 | LOST 60 | TIED 0 | TG 162

AMERICAN LEAGUE

1965.

MINNESOTA

FINISHED 1

PCT. .630

SABATH ANTHONY MELE

WON	LOST	NAME	POS.		G.	BA	FROM	TO
		ALLEN, BERNARD KEITH (3B1)	2B	10	19	.231	B	B
		ALLISON, WM. ROBERT (BOB) (1B3)	OF	122	135	.233	B	B
		BATTEY, EARL JESSE	C	128	131	.297	B	B
6	5	BOSWELL, DAVID WILSON	P	27	36	.316	B	B
0	0	CIMINO, PETER WILLIAM	P		1	.000	A	B
3	3	FOSNOW, GERALD EUGENE	P		29	.000	B	C
21	7	GRANT, JAMES TIMOTHY (MUDCAT)	P	41	50	.155	B	B
		HALL, JIMMIE RANDOLPH	OF	141	148	.285	B	B
18	11	KAAT, JAMES LEE	P	45	56	.247	B	B
		KILLEBREW, HARMON CLAYTON (3B44 OF1)	1B	72	113	.269	B	B
		KINDALL, GERALD DONALD (SS7 3B10)	2B	106	125	.196	B	C
9	3	KLIPPSTEIN, JOHN CALVIN	P		56	.000	B	B
		KOSCO, ANDREW JOHN (1B2)	OF	14	23	.236	A	B
		KOSTRO, FRANK JERRY (3B6 OF2)	2B	7	20	.161	B	MIN 67
5	4	MERRITT, JAMES JOSEPH	P		16	.136	A	B
		MINCHER, DONALD RAY (OF1)	1B	99	128	.251	B	B
0	4	NELSON, MELVIN FREDERICK	P		28	.111	LA 63	MIN 67
		NOSSEK, JOSEPH RUDOLPH (3B9)	OF	48	87	.218	B	B
		OLIVA, PEDRO (TONY)	OF	147	149	.321	B	B
9	3	PASCUAL, CAMILO ALBERTO	P		27	.200	B	B
12	7	PERRY, JAMES EVAN	P		36	.170	B	B
4	4	PLEIS, WILLIAM	P		41	.000	B	B
		QUILICI, FRANK RALPH (SS4)	2B	52	56	.208	A	MIN 67
		REESE, RICHARD BENJAMIN (OF1)	1B	6	14	.286	B	B
1	0	ROGGENBURK, GARRY EARL	P		12	.000	MIN 63	B
		ROLLINS, RICHARD JOHN (2B16)	3B	112	140	.249	B	B
		SEVCIK, JOHN JOSEPH	C	11	12	.063	A	C
0	0	SIEBLER, DWIGHT LEROY	P		7	.000	B	B
4	2	STIGMAN, RICHARD LEWIS	P		33	.133	B	BOS
		TOVAR, CESAR LEONARDO (SS1 3B2 OF2)	2B	4	18	.200	A	B
		UHLAENDER, THEODORE OTTO	OF	4	13	.182	A	B
		VALDESPINO, HILARIO BORROTO (SANDY)	OF	57	108	.261	A	B
		VERSALLES, ZOILO	SS		160	.273	B	B
10	7	WORTHINGTON, ALLAN FULTON	P		62	.100	B	B
		ZIMMERMAN, GERALD ROBERT	C	82	83	.214	B	B

WON 89 | LOST 73 | TIED 0 | TG 162

AMERICAN LEAGUE

1966.

MINNESOTA

FINISHED 2

PCT. .549

SABATH ANTHONY MELE

WON	LOST	NAME	POS.		G.	BA	FROM	TO
		ALLEN, BERNARD KEITH (3B2)	2B	89	101	.238	B	WAS
		ALLISON, WM. ROBERT (BOB)	OF	56	70	.220	B	B
		BATTEY, EARL JESSE	C	113	115	.255	B	B
12	5	BOSWELL, DAVID WILSON	P	28	32	.143	B	B
2	5	CIMINO, PETER WILLIAM	P		35	.000	B	CAL
		CLARK, RONALD BRUCE	3B	1	5	1.000	A	B
13	13	GRANT, JAMES TIMOTHY (MUDCAT)	P		35	.192	B	B
		HALL, JIMMIE RANDOLPH	OF	103	120	.239	B	CAL
25	13	KAAT, JAMES LEE	P	41	47	.195	B	B
0	0	KELLER, RONALD LEE	P	2	3	.000	A	MIN 68
		KILLEBREW, HARMON CLAYTON (1B42 OF18)	3B	107	162	.281	B	B
1	1	KLIPPSTEIN, JOHN CALVIN	P		26	.000	B	DET
		KOSCO, ANDREW JOHN (1B5)	OF	40	57	.222	B	B
7	14	MERRITT, JAMES JOSEPH	P		31	.103	B	B
		MINCHER, DONALD RAY	1B	130	139	.251	B	CAL
		MITTERWALD, GEORGE EUGENE	C		3	.200	A	MIN 68
		NIXON, RUSSELL EUGENE	C	32	51	.260	BOS	B
		NOSSEK, JOSEPH RUDOLPH	OF	2	4	+.000	B	XKC
		OLIVA, PEDRO (TONY)	OF		159	.307	B	B
0	0	OLLOM, JAMES DONALD	P		3	.000	A	B
8	6	PASCUAL, CAMILO ALBERTO	P		21	.216	B	WAS
11	7	PERRY, JAMES EVAN	P		33	.220	B	B
1	2	PLEIS, WILLIAM	P		8	.000	B	C
		REESE, RICHARD BENJAMIN			3	.000	B	B
1	2	ROGGENBURK, GARRY EARL	P		12	+.000	B	XBOS
0	0	ROLAND, JAMES IVAN	P		1	.000	MIN 64	B
		ROLLINS, RICHARD JOHN (2B2 OF1)	3B	65	90	.245	B	B
2	2	SIEBLER, DWIGHT LEROY	P		23	.000	B	B
		TOVAR, CESAR LEONARDO (SS31 OF24)	2B	76	134	.260	B	B
		UHLAENDER, THEODORE OTTO	OF	100	105	.226	B	B
		VALDESPINO, HILARIO BORROTO (SANDY)	OF	23	52	.176	B	B
		VERSALLES, ZOILO	SS	135	137	.249	B	B
6	3	WORTHINGTON, ALLAN FULTON	P		65	.273	B	B
		ZIMMERMAN, GERALD ROBERT	C	59	60	.252	B	B

WON 91
LOST 71
TIED 2
TG 164

AMERICAN LEAGUE

1967.

FINISHED 2
(TIED WITH DETROIT)
PCT. .562

MINNESOTA

SABATH ANTHONY MELE   CALVIN COOLIDGE ERMER

WON	LOST	NAME	POS.		G.	BA	FROM	TO
		ALLISON, WM. ROBERT (BOB)	OF	145	153	.258	B	B
		BATTEY, EARL JESSE	C	41	48	.165	B	C
		BOND, WALTER FRANKLIN	OF	3	10	.313	HOUN65	C
14	12	BOSWELL, DAVID WILSON	P	37	44	.219	B	B
		CAREW, RODNEY CLINE	2B	134	137	.292	A	B
20	14	CHANCE, WILMER DEAN	P		41	.033	CAL	B
		CLARK, RONALD BRUCE	3B	16	20	.167	B	B
5	6	GRANT, JAMES TIMOTHY (MUDCAT)	P		27	.179	B	LA N
		HARDY, CARROLL WILLIAM	OF	4	11	.375	HOUN64	C
		HERNANDEZ, JACINTO (JACKIE)	SS	15	29	.143	CAL	B
		(3B13)						
		IZQUIERDO, ENRIQUE ROBERTO	C		16	.269	A	C
16	13	KAAT, JAMES LEE	P	42	45	.172	B	B
		KELLY, HAROLD PATRICK (PAT)			8	.000	A	B
		KILLEBREW, HARMON CLAYTON	1B	160	163	.269	B	B
		(3B3)						
7	1	KLINE, RONALD LEE	P		54	.000	WAS	PITN
		KOSCO, ANDREW JOHN	OF	7	9	.143	B	NY
		KOSTRO, FRANK JERRY (3B1)	OF	3	32	.323	MIN 65	B
13	7	MERRITT, JAMES JOSEPH	P		37	.135	B	B
0	0	NELSON, MELVIN FREDERICK	P		1	.000	MIN 65	STLN
		NETTLES, GRAIG			3	.333	A	B
		NIXON, RUSSELL EUGENE	C	69	74	.235	B	BOS
		OLIVA, PEDRO (TONY)	OF		146	.289	B	B
0	1	OLLOM, JAMES DONALD	P		21	.200	B	C
8	7	PERRY, JAMES EVAN	P	37	39	.190	B	B
		QUILICI, FRANK RALPH	2B	13	23	.105	MIN 65	B
		(SS1 3B8)						
		REESE, RICHARD BENJAMIN	1B	36	95	.248	B	B
		(OF10)						
0	1	ROLAND, JAMES IVAN	P		25	.000	B	B
		ROLLINS, RICHARD JOHN	3B	97	109	.245	B	B
0	0	SIEBLER, DWIGHT LEROY	P		2	.000	B	C
		TOVAR, CESAR LEONARDO	OF	74	164	.267	B	B
		(2B36 SS9 3B70)						
		UHLAENDER, THEODORE OTTO	OF	118	133	.258	B	B
		VALDESPINO, HILARIO BORROTO	OF	65	99	.165	B	ATLN
		(SANDY)						
		VERSALLES, ZOILO	SS	159	160	.200	B	LA N
8	9	WORTHINGTON, ALLAN FULTON	P		59	.000	B	B
		ZIMMERMAN, GERALD ROBERT	C		104	.167	B	B

WON 79
LOST 83
TIED 0
TG 162

AMERICAN LEAGUE

1968.

FINISHED 7

PCT. .488

MINNESOTA

CALVIN COOLIDGE ERMER

WON	LOST	NAME	POS.		G.	BA	FROM	TO
		ALLISON, WM. ROBERT (BOB)	OF	117	145	.247	B	B
		(1B17)						
10	13	BOSWELL, DAVID WILSON	P	34	37	.233	B	B
		CAREW, RODNEY CLINE (SS4)	2B	117	127	.273	B	B
16	16	CHANCE, WILMER DEAN	P		43	.054	B	B
		CLARK, RONALD BRUCE	3B	52	104	.185	B	B
		(2B10 SS43)						
2	1	HALL, TOM EDWARD	P	8	11	.000	A	B
		HERNANDEZ, JACINTO (JACKIE)	SS	79	83	.176	B	KC
		(1B1)						
		HOLT, JAMES WILLIAM (1B1)	OF	38	70	.208	A	B
14	12	KAAT, JAMES LEE	P	30	36	.156	B	B
0	1	KELLER, RONALD LEE	P	7	8	.000	MIN 66	C
		KELLY, HAROLD PATRICK (PAT)	OF	10	12	.114	B	KC
		KILLEBREW, HARMON CLAYTON	1B	77	100	.210	B	B
		(3B11)						
		KOSTRO, FRANK JERRY (1B5)	OF	24	63	.241	B	B
		LOOK, BRUCE MICHAEL	C	41	59	.246	A	C
12	16	MERRITT, JAMES JOSEPH	P		38	.141	B	CINN
0	3	MILLER, ROBERT LANE	P		45	.143	LA N	B
		MITTERWALD, GEORGE EUGENE	C	10	11	.206	MIN 66	B
0	1	MORRIS, DANIEL WALKER	P		3	.000	A	B
		NETTLES, GRAIG (1B3 3B5)	OF	16	22	.224	B	B
		OLIVA, PEDRO (TONY)	OF	126	128	.289	B	B
8	7	PERRANOSKI, RONALD PETER	P		66	.000	LA N	B
8	6	PERRY, JAMES EVAN	P		32	.143	B	B
		QUILICI, FRANK RALPH	2B	48	97	.245	B	B
		(1B1 SS6 3B40)						
		REESE, RICHARD BENJAMIN	1B	87	126	.259	B	B
		(OF15)						
		RENICK, WARREN RICHARD (RICK)	SS	40	42	.216	A	B
4	1	ROLAND, JAMES IVAN	P	28	29	.000	B	OAK
		ROLLINS, RICHARD JOHN	3B	56	93	.241	B	SEA
		ROSEBORO, JOHN	C	117	135	.216	LA N	B
1	1	STEPHEN, LOUIS ROBERTS	P		2	.000	A	C
		TOVAR, CESAR LEONARDO	OF	78	157	.272	B	B
		(P1 C1 1B1 2B18 SS35 3B75)						
		UHLAENDER, THEODORE OTTO	OF	129	140	.283	B	B
4	5	WORTHINGTON, ALLAN FULTON	P		54	.000	B	B
		ZIMMERMAN, GERALD ROBERT	C		24	.111	B	C

WON 97
LOST 65
TIED 0
TG 162

AMERICAN LEAGUE

1969.

FINISHED 1 W
(LOST LEAGUE PLAYOFF)
PCT. .599

MINNESOTA

ALFRED MANUEL MARTIN

WON	LOST	NAME	POS.		G.	BA	FROM	TO
		ALLISON, WM. ROBERT (BOB)	OF	8	81	.228	B	B
		(1B3)						
20	12	BOSWELL, DAVID WILSON	P	39	40	.170	B	B
0	0	BRANDON, DARRELL G.	P		3	+.000	XSEA	PHIN71
		CARDENAS, LEONARDO ALFONSO	SS		160	.280	CINN	B
		CAREW, RODNEY CLINE	2B	118	123	.332	B	B
5	4	CHANCE, WILMER DEAN	P		20	.042	B	CLE
		CLARK, RONALD BRUCE	3B	2	5	+.125	B	XSEA
1	0	CRIDER, JERRY STEPHEN	P		21	.444	A	CHI
		DEMPSEY, JOHN RIKARD (RICK)	C	3	5	.500	A	B
4	1	GRZENDA, JOSEPH CHARLES	P		38	.000	NY N67	WAS
8	7	HALL, TOM EDWARD	P	31	32	.186	B	B
		HILL, HERMAN ALEXANDER	OF	5	16	.000	A	B
		HOLT, JAMES WILLIAM (1B1)	OF	5	12	.357	B	B
14	13	KAAT, JAMES LEE	P	40	43	.207	B	B
		KILLEBREW, HARMON CLAYTON	3B	105	162	.276	B	B
		(1B80)						
		KOSTRO, FRANK JERRY			2	.000	B	C
		MANUEL, CHARLES FUQUA	OF	46	83	.207	A	B
5	5	MILLER, ROBERT LANE	P		48	.000	B	CLE
		MITTERWALD, GEORGE EUGENE	C	63	69	.257	B	B
		(OF1)						
0	1	MORRIS, DANIEL WALKER	P		3	.000	B	C
		NASH, CHARLES FRANCIS (COTTON)	1B	6	6	.222	CHI 67	B
		(OF1)						
		NETTLES, GRAIG (3B21)	OF	54	96	.222	B	CLE
		OLIVA, PEDRO (TONY)	OF	152	153	.309	B	B
9	10	PERRANOSKI, RONALD PETER	P		75	.083	B	B
20	6	PERRY, JAMES EVAN	P	46	47	.172	B	B
		QUILICI, FRANK RALPH	3B	84	118	.174	B	B
		(2B36 SS1)						
		REESE, RICHARD BENJAMIN	1B	117	132	.322	B	B
		(OF5)						
		RENICK, WARREN RICHARD (RICK)	3B	30	71	.245	B	B
		(SS6 OF10)						
		ROSEBORO, JOHN	C	111	115	.263	B	WAS
		TISCHINSKI, THOMAS ARTHUR	C	32	37	.191	A	B
		TOVAR, CESAR LEONARDO	OF	113	158	.288	B	B
		(2B41 3B20)						
		UHLAENDER, THEODORE OTTO	OF	150	152	.273	B	CLE
0	0	WALTERS, CHARLES LEONARD	P		6	.000	A	C
7	5	WOODSON, RICHARD LEE	P		44	.074	A	B
4	1	WORTHINGTON, ALLAN FULTON	P		46	.000	B	C
0	0	ZEPP, WILLIAM CLINTON	P		4	.000	A	B

WON 98
LOST 64
TIED 0
TG 162

AMERICAN LEAGUE

1970.

FINISHED 1 W
(LOST LEAGUE PLAYOFF)
PCT. .605

MINNESOTA

WILLIAM JOSEPH RIGNEY

WON	LOST	NAME	POS.		G.	BA	FROM	TO
		ALLISON, WM. ROBERT (BOB)	OF	17	47	.208	B	C
		(1B7)						
		ALYEA, GARRABRANT RYERSON	OF	75	94	.291	WAS	B
0	0	BARBER, STEVEN LEE	P	18	19	.000	A	B
10	9	BLYLEVEN, RIK AALBERT (BERT)	P		27	.140	A	B
3	7	BOSWELL, DAVID WILSON	P	18	20	.160	B	DET
		BRYE, STEPHEN ROBERT	OF	6	9	.182	A	B
		CARDENAS, LEONARDO ALFONSO	SS		160	.247	B	B
		CAREW, RODNEY CLINE (1B1)	2B	45	51	.366	B	B
		DEMPSEY, JOHN RIKARD (RICK)	C	3	5	.000	B	B
11	6	HALL, TOM EDWARD	P	52	53	.182	B	B
0	2	HAMM, PETER WHITFIELD	P		10	.000	A	B
2	0	HAYDEL, JOHN HAROLD (HAL)	P		4	.667	A	B
		HILL, HERMAN ALEXANDER	OF	14	27	.091	B	C
		HOLT, JAMES WILLIAM (1B2)	OF	130	142	.266	B	B
14	10	KAAT, JAMES LEE	P	45	56	.197	B	B
		KILLEBREW, HARMON CLAYTON	3B	138	157	.271	B	B
		(1B28)						
		MANUEL, CHARLES FUQUA	OF	11	59	.188	B	B
		MENDOZA, CRISTOBAL RIGOBERTO	3B	5	16	.188	A	C
		(2B4)						
		MITTERWALD, GEORGE EUGENE	C		117	.222	B	B
		NASH, CHARLES FRANCIS (COTTON)	1B	2	4	.250	B	C
		NETTLES, JAMES WILLIAM	OF	11	13	.250	A	B
		OLIVA, PEDRO (TONY)	OF		157	.325	B	B
7	8	PERRANOSKI, RONALD PETER	P		67	.042	B	B
24	12	PERRY, JAMES EVAN (OF1)	P	40	41	.247	B	B
		QUILICI, FRANK RALPH	2B	73	111	.227	B	C
		(SS1 3B27)						
		RATLIFF, PAUL HAWTHORNE	C	53	69	.268	MIN 63	B
		REESE, RICHARD BENJAMIN	1B	146	153	.261	B	B
		RENICK, WARREN RICHARD (RICK)	3B	30	81	.229	B	B
		(SS1 OF25)						
		THOMPSON, DANNY LEON	2B	81	96	.219	A	B
		(SS6 3B37)						
7	3	TIANT, LUIS CLEMENTE	P		18	.406	CLE	BOS
		TISCHINSKI, THOMAS ARTHUR	C	22	24	.196	B	B
		TOVAR, CESAR LEONARDO	OF	151	161	.300	B	B
		(2B8 3B4)						
10	1	WILLIAMS, STANLEY WILSON	P		68	.000	CLE	B
1	2	WOODSON, RICHARD LEE	P		21	.000	B	MIN 72
9	4	ZEPP, WILLIAM CLINTON	P		43	.136	B	DET

WON 74 | LOST 86 | TIED 0 | TG 160

AMERICAN LEAGUE 1971. FINISHED 5 W PCT. .462

MINNESOTA

WILLIAM JOSEPH RIGNEY

WON	LOST	NAME	POS.		G.	BA	FROM	TO
		ALYEA, GARRABRANT RYERSON	OF	47	79	.177	B	OAK
1	0	BARBER, STEVEN LEE	P	4	6	.000	B	C
16	15	BLYLEVEN, RIK AALBERT (BERT)	P		38	.132	B	B
		BRAUN, STEPHEN RUSSELL	3B	73	128	.254	A	B
		(2B28 SS10 OF2)						
		BRYE, STEPHEN ROBERT	OF		28	.224	B	B
0	0	CAMPISI, SALVATORE JOHN	P		6	.000	STLN	C
		CARDENAS, LEONARDO ALFONSO	SS		153	.264	B	CAL
		CAREW, RODNEY CLINE (3B2)	2B	142	147	.307	B	B
8	11	CORBIN, ALTON RAY	P		52	.206	A	B
		DEMPSEY, JOHN RIKARD (RICK)	C		6	.308	B	B
1	2	GEBHARD, ROBERT HENRY	P		17	.000	A	B
4	7	HALL, TOM EDWARD	P	48	49	.265	B	CINN
2	4	HAMM, PETER WHITFIELD	P		13	.273	B	C
4	2	HAYDEL, JOHN HAROLD (HAL)	P		31	.333	B	C
		HOLT, JAMES WILLIAM (1B3)	OF	106	126	.259	B	B
13	14	KAAT, JAMES LEE	P	39	54	.161	B	B
		KILLEBREW, HARMON CLAYTON	1B	90	147	.254	B	B
		(3B64)						
2	5	LUEBBER, STEPHEN LEE	P	18	19	.053	A	B
		MANUEL, CHARLES FUQUA	OF	1	18	.125	B	B
		MITTERWALD, GEORGE EUGENE	C	120	125	.250	B	B
		NETTLES, JAMES WILLIAM	OF	62	70	.250	B	B
		OLIVA, PEDRO (TONY)	OF	121	126	.337	B	B
1	4	PERRANOSKI, RONALD PETER	P		36	+.000	B	XDET
17	17	PERRY, JAMES EVAN	P		40	.185	B	B
		POWELL, PAUL EDWARD	OF	15	20	.161	A	C
		RATLIFF, PAUL HAWTHORNE	C	15	21	+.159	B	XMIL
		REESE, RICHARD BENJAMIN	1B	95	120	.219	B	B
		(OF9)						
		RENICK, WARREN RICHARD (RICK)	3B	7	27	.222	B	B
		(OF7)						
		ROOF, PHILLIP ANTHONY	C	29	31	+.241	XMIL	B
		SODERHOLM, ERIC THANE	3B	20	21	.156	A	B
1	0	STRICKLAND, JAMES MICHAEL	P		24	.000	A	B
		THOMAS, GEORGE EDWARD	OF	11	23	+.267	XBOS	C
		(1B1 3B1)						
		THOMPSON, DANNY LEON	3B	17	48	.263	B	B
		(2B3 SS1)						
		TISCHINSKI, THOMAS ARTHUR	C		21	.130	B	C
		TOVAR, CESAR LEONARDO	OF	154	157	.311	B	B
		(2B2 3B7)						
4	5	WILLIAMS, STANLEY WILSON	P		46	.000	B	XSTLN

WON 77 | LOST 77 | TIED 0 | TG 154

AMERICAN LEAGUE 1972. FINISHED 3 W PCT. .500

MINNESOTA

WILLIAM JOSEPH RIGNEY FRANK RALPH QUILICI

WON	LOST	NAME	POS.		G.	BA	FROM	TO
		ADAMS, ROBERT MICHAEL (MIKE)	OF	1	3	.333	A	
17	17	BLYLEVEN, RIK AALBERT (BERT)	P		39	.160	B	
		BORGMANN, GLENN DENNIS	C		56	.234	A	
		BRAUN, STEPHEN RUSSELL	3B	74	121	.289	B	
		(2B20 SS11 OF9)						
		BRYE, STEPHEN ROBERT	OF	93	100	.241	B	
		CAREW, RODNEY CLINE	2B	139	142	.318	B	
8	9	CORBIN, ALTON RAY	P	31	34	.082	B	
		DARWIN, ARTHUR BOBBY LEE	OF	142	145	.267	LA N	
		DEMPSEY, JOHN RIKARD (RICK)	C	23	25	.200	B	
0	1	GEBHARD, ROBERT HENRY	P		13	.000	B	
3	3	GOLTZ, DAVID ALLAN	P		15	.103	A	
4	6	GRANGER, WAYNE ALLAN	P		63	.200	CINN	
		GUTH, CHARLES HENRY	SS	1	3	.000	A	
		HOLT, JAMES WILLIAM (1B1)	OF	7	10	.444	B	
10	2	KAAT, JAMES LEE	P	15	24	.289	B	
		KILLEBREW, HARMON CLAYTON	1B	130	139	.231	B	
5	7	LA ROCHE, DAVID EUGENE	P		62	.091	CAL	
0	0	LUEBBER, STEPHEN LEE	P		2	.000	B	
		MANUEL, CHARLES FUQUA	OF	28	63	.205	B	
		MITTERWALD, GEORGE EUGENE	C	61	64	.184	B	
		MONZON, DANIEL FRANCIS	2B	13	55	.273	A	
		(SS3 3B5 OF1)						
		NETTLES, JAMES WILLIAM (1B1)	OF	78	102	.204	B	
0	1	NORTON, THOMAS JOHN	P		21	.000	A	
		OLIVA, PEDRO (TONY)	OF	9	10	.321	B	
13	16	PERRY, JAMES EVAN	P		35	.155	B	
		REESE, RICHARD BENJAMIN	1B	98	132	.218	B	
		(OF13)						
		RENICK, WARREN RICHARD (RICK)	OF	21	55	.172	B	
		(1B6 SS1 3B4)						
		ROOF, PHILLIP ANTHONY	C		61	.205	B	
		SODERHOLM, ERIC THANE	3B	79	93	.188	B	
3	1	STRICKLAND, JAMES MICHAEL	P		25	.333	B	
		THOMPSON, DANNY LEON	SS		144	.276	B	
		TOVAR, CESAR LEONARDO	OF	139	141	.265	B	
14	14	WOODSON, RICHARD LEE	P		36	.080	MIN 70	

WON 77
LOST 85
TIED 0
TG 162

AMERICAN LEAGUE — FINISHED 6

1965. — PCT. .475

NEW YORK

JOHN JOSEPH KEANE

WON	LOST	NAME	POS.		G.	BA	FROM	TO
		BARKER, RAYMOND HERRELL	1B	61	98	+.254	XCLE	B
		(3B3)						
2	1	BECK, RICHARD HENRY	P		3	.000	A	C
		BLANCHARD, JOHN EDWIN	C		12	+.147	B	XKC
1	1	BLANCO, GILBERT HENRY	P		17	.000	A	KC
4	15	BOUTON, JAMES ALAN	P	30	31	.093	B	B
		BOYER, CLETIS LEROY (SS2)	3B	147	148	.251	B	B
0	0	BRENNEMAN, JAMES LEROY	P		3	.000	A	C
		CARMEL, LEON JAMES (DUKE)	1B	2	6	.000	NY N63	C
		CLARKE, HORACE MEREDITH	3B	17	51	.259	A	B
		(2B7 SS1)						
3	4	CULLEN, JOHN PATRICK	P		12	.150	NY 62	B
12	14	DOWNING, ALPHONSO ERWIN	P	35	36	.108	B	B
		EDWARDS, HOWARD RODNEY (DOC)	C	43	45	+.190	XKC	PHIN70
16	13	FORD, EDWARD CHARLES (WHITEY)	P	37	38	.183	B	B
		GIBBS, JERRY DEAN (JAKE)	C	21	37	.221	B	B
		GONZALEZ, PEDRO			7	+.400	B	XCLE
3	1	HAMILTON, STEVE ABSHER	P		46	.167	B	B
		HOWARD, ELSTON GENE	C	95	110	.233	B	B
		(1B5 OF1)						
0	0	JUREWICZ, MICHAEL ALLEN	P		2	.000	A	C
		KUBEK, ANTHONY CHRISTOPHER	SS	93	109	.218	B	C
		(1B1 OF3)						
		LINZ, PHILIP FRANCIS	SS	71	99	.207	B	PHIN
		(2B1 3B4 OF4)						
		LOPEZ, ARTURO	OF	16	38	.143	A	C
		LOPEZ, HECTOR HEADLEY (1B2)	OF	75	111	.261	B	B
		MANTLE, MICKEY CHARLES	OF	108	122	.255	B	B
		MARIS, ROGER EUGENE	OF	43	46	.239	B	B
4	9	MIKKELSEN, PETER JAMES	P		41	.100	B	PITN
		MOORE, ARCHIE FRANCIS	OF	5	9	.412	B	C
		MOSCHITTO, ROSS ALLEN	OF	89	96	.185	A	NY 67
		MURCER, BOBBY RAY	SS		11	.243	A	B
		PEPITONE, JOSEPH ANTHONY	1B	115	143	.247	B	B
		(OF41)						
5	5	RAMOS, PEDRO	P		65	.083	B	B
3	4	RENIFF, HAROLD EUGENE	P		51	.000	B	B
		REPOZ, ROGER ALLEN	OF	69	79	.220	B	B
		RICHARDSON, ROBERT CLINTON	2B	158	160	.247	B	B
		SCHMIDT, ROBERT BENJAMIN	C		20	.250	WAS 63	C
0	0	SHELDON, ROLAND FRANK	P		3	+.000	B	XKC
3	8	STAFFORD, WILLIAM CHARLES	P		22	.000	B	KC
20	9	STOTTLEMYRE, MELVIN LEON	P		37	.131	B	B
1	1	TIEFENAUER, BOBBY GENE	P		10	+.000	XMILN	XCLE
		TRESH, THOMAS MICHAEL	OF	154	156	.279	B	B
		WHITE, ROY HILTON (2B1)	OF	10	14	.333	A	B

WON 70
LOST 89
TIED 1
TG 160

AMERICAN LEAGUE — FINISHED 10 (LAST)

1966. — PCT. .440

NEW YORK

JOHN JOSEPH KEANE RALPH GEORGE HOUK

WON	LOST	NAME	POS.		G.	BA	FROM	TO
		AMARO, RUBEN MORA	SS		14	.217	PHIN	B
1	1	BAHNSEN, STANLEY RAYMOND	P		4	.143	A	NY 68
		BARKER, RAYMOND HERRELL	1B	47	61	.187	B	B
3	8	BOUTON, JAMES ALAN	P		24	.105	B	B
		BOYER, CLETIS LEROY (SS59)	3B	85	144	.240	B	ATLN
		BRYAN, WILLIAM RONALD (1B3)	C	14	27	+.217	XKC	B
		CLARKE, HORACE MEREDITH	SS	63	96	.266	B	B
		(2B16 3B4)						
		CLINTON, LUCIEAN LOUIS	OF	63	80	.220	CLE	B
1	0	CULLEN, JOHN PATRICK	P		5	.000	B	C
10	11	DOWNING, ALPHONSO ERWIN	P		30	.100	B	B
		FERRARO, MICHAEL DENNIS	3B		10	.179	A	NY 68
2	5	FORD, EDWARD CHARLES (WHITEY)	P		22	.000	B	B
1	4	FRIEND, ROBERT BARTMESS	P		12	.000	PITN	XNY N
		GIBBS, JERRY DEAN (JAKE)	C	54	62	.258	B	B
8	3	HAMILTON, STEVE ABSHER	P		44	.053	B	B
		HEGAN, JAMES MICHAEL (MIKE)	1B		13	.205	NY 64	B
0	0	HENRY, WILLIAM FRANCIS	P		2	.000	A	C
		HOWARD, ELSTON GENE (1B13)	C	100	126	.256	B	B
		LOPEZ, HECTOR HEADLEY	OF	29	54	.214	B	C
		MANTLE, MICKEY CHARLES	OF	97	108	.288	B	B
		MARIS, ROGER EUGENE	OF	95	119	.233	B	STLN
		MILLER, JOHN ALLEN (OF3)	1B	3	6	.087	A	LA N69
		MURCER, BOBBY RAY	SS	18	21	.174	B	NY 69
		PEPITONE, JOSEPH ANTHONY	1B	119	152	.255	B	B
		(OF55)						
12	11	PETERSON, FRED INGELS (FRITZ)	P		34	.224	A	B
3	9	RAMOS, PEDRO	P		52	.154	B	PHIN
3	7	RENIFF, HAROLD EUGENE	P		56	.286	B	B
		REPOZ, ROGER ALLEN	OF	30	37	+.349	B	XKC
		RICHARDSON, ROBERT CLINTON	2B	147	149	.251	B	C
		(3B2)						
		SCHOFIELD, JOHN RICHARD (DICK)	SS	19	25	.155	XSF N	XLA N
12	20	STOTTLEMYRE, MELVIN LEON	P		37	.137	B	B
7	7	TALBOT, FRED LEALAND	P		23	+.143	XKC	B
		TRESH, THOMAS MICHAEL (3B64)	OF	84	151	.233	B	B
		WHITAKER, STEPHEN EDWARD	OF		31	.246	A	B
		WHITE, ROY HILTON (2B2)	OF	82	115	.225	B	B
7	3	WOMACK, HORACE GUY (DOOLEY)	P		42	.200	A	B

WON 72
LOST 90
TIED 1
TG 163

AMERICAN LEAGUE 1967. FINISHED 9 PCT. .444

NEW YORK

RALPH GEORGE HOUK

WON	LOST	NAME	POS.		G.	BA	FROM	TO
		AMARO, RUBEN MORA	SS	123	130	.223	B	B
		(1B2 3B3)						
6	9	BARBER, STEPHEN DAVID	P		17	+.172	XBAL	B
		BARKER, RAYMOND HERRELL	1B	13	17	.077	B	C
1	0	BOUTON, JAMES ALAN	P		17	.000	B	B
		BRYAN, WILLIAM RONALD	C	1	16	.167	B	WAS
		CLARKE, HORACE MEREDITH	2B	140	143	.272	B	B
		CLINTON, LUCIEAN LOUIS	OF	1	6	.500	B	C
14	10	DOWNING, ALPHONSO ERWIN	P		31	.121	B	B
		FERNANDEZ, FRANK (OF2)	C	7	9	.214	A	B
2	4	FORD, EDWARD CHARLES (WHITEY)	P		7	.154	B	C
		GIBBS, JERRY DEAN (JAKE)	C	99	116	.233	B	B
2	4	HAMILTON, STEVE ABSHER	P		44	.111	B	B
		HEGAN, JAMES MICHAEL (MIKE)	1B	54	68	.136	B	SEA 69
		(OF10)						
		HOWARD, ELSTON GENE (1B1)	C	48	66	+.196	B	XBOS
		HOWSER, RICHARD DALTON	2B	22	63	.268	CLE	B
		(SS3 3B12)						
		KENNEDY, JOHN EDWARD	SS	36	78	.196	LA N	SEA 69
		(2B2 3B34)						
		KENNEY, GERALD T.	SS	18	20	.310	A	NY 69
		MANTLE, MICKEY CHARLES	1B	131	144	.245	B	B
6	5	MONBOQUETTE, WILLIAM CHARLES	P		33	+.156	XDET	B
		MOSCHITTO, ROSS ALLEN	OF	8	14	.111	NY 65	C
		PEPITONE, JOSEPH ANTHONY	OF	123	133	.251	B	B
		(1B6)						
0	1	PERKINS, CECIL BOYCE	P		2	.000	A	C
8	14	PETERSON, FRED INGELS (FRITZ)	P		36	.146	B	B
0	2	RENIFF, HAROLD EUGENE	P		24	.000	B	XNY N
0	0	ROBERTS, DALE	P		2	.000	A	C
		ROBINSON, WILLIAM HENRY	OF	102	116	.196	ATLN	B
		SANDS, CHARLES DUANE			1	.000	A	PITN71
		SHOPAY, THOMAS MICHAEL	OF	7	8	.296	A	NY 69
		SMITH, CHARLES WILLIAM	3B	115	135	.224	STLN	B
15	15	STOTTLEMYRE, MELVIN LEON	P		36	.098	B	B
6	8	TALBOT, FRED LEALAND	P	29	30	.158	B	B
		TEPEDINO, FRANK RONALD	1B	1	9	.400	A	NY 69
		TILLMAN, JOHN ROBERT (BOB)	C	15	22	+.254	XBOS	ATLN
3	9	TILLOTSON, THADDEUS ASA	P		43	.063	A	B
		TRESH, THOMAS MICHAEL	OF	118	130	.219	B	B
4	3	VERBANIC, JOSEPH MICHAEL	P		28	.111	PHIN	B
		WHITAKER, STEPHEN EDWARD	OF	114	122	.243	B	B
		WHITE, ROY HILTON (3B17)	OF	36	70	.224	B	B
5	6	WOMACK, HORACE GUY (DOOLEY)	P		65	.286	B	B

WON 83
LOST 79
TIED 2
TG 164

AMERICAN LEAGUE 1968. FINISHED 5 PCT. .512

NEW YORK

RALPH GEORGE HOUK

WON	LOST	NAME	POS.		G.	BA	FROM	TO
		AMARO, RUBEN MORA (1B22)	SS	23	47	.122	B	CAL
17	12	BAHNSEN, STANLEY RAYMOND	P		37	.049	NY 66	B
6	5	BARBER, STEPHEN DAVID	P		20	.051	B	SEA
1	1	BOUTON, JAMES ALAN	P		12	.000	B	SEA
		CLARKE, HORACE MEREDITH	2B	139	148	.230	B	B
1	0	COLAVITO, ROCCO DOMENICO	OF	28	39	.220	XLA N	C
		(P1)						
		COX, ROBERT JOE	3B	132	135	.229	A	B
0	0	CUMBERLAND, JOHN SHELDON	P		1	.000	A	B
3	3	DOWNING, ALPHONSO ERWIN	P		15	.176	B	B
		FERNANDEZ, FRANK (OF4)	C	45	51	.170	B	B
		FERRARO, MICHAEL DENNIS	3B	22	23	.161	NY 66	SEA
		GIBBS, JERRY DEAN (JAKE)	C	121	124	.213	B	B
2	2	HAMILTON, STEVE ABSHER	P		40	.000	B	B
		HOWSER, RICHARD DALTON	2B	29	85	.153	B	C
		(SS1 3B2)						
		KOSCO, ANDREW JOHN (1B28)	OF	95	131	.240	MIN	LA N
		MANTLE, MICKEY CHARLES	1B	131	144	.237	B	C
4	1	MC DANIEL, LYNDALL DALE	P		24	.000	XSF N	B
0	0	MICHAEL, EUGENE RICHARD	SS	43	61	.198	LA N	B
		(P1)						
5	7	MONBOQUETTE, WILLIAM CHARLES	P		17	.115	B	XSF N
		PEPITONE, JOSEPH ANTHONY	OF	92	108	.245	B	B
		(1B12)						
12	11	PETERSON, FRED INGELS (FRITZ)	P		36	.079	B	B
		ROBINSON, WILLIAM HENRY	OF	98	107	.240	B	B
		RODRIGUEZ, ELISEO	C		9	.208	A	KC
		SMITH, CHARLES WILLIAM	3B	13	46	.229	B	CHIN
		SOLAITO, TOLIA	1B		1	.000	A	C
21	12	STOTTLEMYRE, MELVIN LEON	P		36	.143	B	B
1	9	TALBOT, FRED LEALAND	P		29	.118	B	B
1	0	TILLOTSON, THADDEUS ASA	P		7	.000	B	C
		TRESH, THOMAS MICHAEL (OF27)	SS	119	152	.195	B	B
6	7	VERBANIC, JOSEPH MICHAEL	P		40	.080	B	NY 70
		WHITAKER, STEPHEN EDWARD	OF	14	28	.117	B	SEA
		WHITE, ROY HILTON	OF	154	159	.267	B	B
3	7	WOMACK, HORACE GUY (DOOLEY)	P		45	.200	B	HOUN
0	2	WYATT, JOHN THOMAS	P		7	+.000	XBOS	XDET

WON 80 LOST 81 TIED 1 TG 162

AMERICAN LEAGUE — 1969. — FINISHED 5 E — PCT. .497

NEW YORK

RALPH GEORGE HOUK

WON	LOST	NAME	POS.		G.	BA	FROM	TO
8	4	AKER, JACK DELANE	P		38	+.111	XSEA	B
9	16	BAHNSEN, STANLEY RAYMOND	P		40	.083	B	B
		BLOMBERG, RONALD MARK	OF	2	4	.500	A	NY 71
		BOEHMER, LEONARD JOSEPH	1B	21	45	.176	CINN67	NY 71
		(2B1 SS1 3B8)						
6	8	BURBACH, WILLIAM DAVID	P		31	.100	A	B
		CLARKE, HORACE MEREDITH	2B		156	.285	B	B
		COWAN, BILLY ROLLAND (1B6)	OF	14	32	+.167	PHIN67	XCAL
		COX, ROBERT JOE (2B6)	3B	56	85	.215	B	C
0	0	CUMBERLAND, JOHN SHELDON	P		2	.000	B	B
7	5	DOWNING, ALPHONSO ERWIN	P		30	.136	B	OAK
		ELLIS, JOHN CHARLES	C	15	22	.290	A	B
		FERNANDEZ, FRANK (OF14)	C	65	89	.223	B	OAK
		GIBBS, JERRY DEAN (JAKE)	C	66	71	.224	B	B
		HALL, JIMMIE RANDOLPH (1B7)	OF	50	80	+.236	XCLE	XCHIN
3	4	HAMILTON, STEVE ABSHER	P		38	.000	B	B
1	2	JOHNSON, KENNETH TRAVIS	P		12	.000	XATLN	XCHIN
4	6	KEKICH, MICHAEL DENNIS	P		28	.111	LA N	B
		KENNEY, GERALD T. (SS10 OF31)	3B	83	130	.257	NY 67	B
0	0	KLIMKOWSKI, RONALD BERNARD	P		3	.000	A	B
		LYTTLE, JAMES LAWRENCE	OF		28	.181	A	B
5	6	MC DANIEL, LYNDALL DALE	P		51	.000	B	B
		MC DONALD, DAVID BRUCE	1B	7	9	.217	A	MONN71
		MICHAEL, EUGENE RICHARD	SS	118	119	.272	B	B
		MUNSON, THURMAN LEE	C	25	26	.256	A	B
		MURCER, BOBBY RAY (3B31)	OF	118	152	.259	NY 66	B
0	0	NOTTEBART, DONALD EDWARD	P		4	.000	CINN67	XCHIN
		OLIVER, NATHANIEL (PEEWEE)			1	.000	SF N	XCHIN
		PEPITONE, JOSEPH ANTHONY	1B	132	135	.242	B	HOUN
17	16	PETERSON, FRED INGELS (FRITZ)	P		37	.112	B	B
		ROBINSON, WILLIAM HENRY	OF	62	87	.171	B	PHIN72
		(1B1)						
		SHOPAY, THOMAS MICHAEL	OF	11	28	.083	NY 67	BAL 71
		SIMPSON, RICHARD CHARLES	OF	5	6	+.273	HOUN	XSEA
20	14	STOTTLEMYRE, MELVIN LEON	P		39	.178	B	B
0	0	TALBOT, FRED LEALAND	P		8	+.000	B	XSEA
		TEPEDINO, FRANK RONALD	OF		13	.231	NY 67	B
		TRESH, THOMAS MICHAEL	SS	41	45	+.182	B	XDET
		WHITE, ROY HILTON	OF	126	130	.290	B	B
		WOODS, RONALD LAWRENCE	OF	67	72	+.175	XDET	B

WON 93 LOST 69 TIED 1 TG 163

AMERICAN LEAGUE — 1970. — FINISHED 2 E — PCT. .574

NEW YORK

RALPH GEORGE HOUK

WON	LOST	NAME	POS.		G.	BA	FROM	TO
4	2	AKER, JACK DELANE	P		41	.063	B	B
14	11	BAHNSEN, STANLEY RAYMOND	P		36	.149	B	B
		BAKER, FRANK WATTS	SS		35	.231	A	B
		BLEFARY, CURTIS LEROY (1B6)	OF	79	99	.212	HOUN	B
0	2	BURBACH, WILLIAM DAVID	P		4	.000	B	B
		CATER, DANNY ANDERSON	1B	131	155	.301	OAK	B
		(3B42 OF7)						
		CLARKE, HORACE MEREDITH	2B	157	158	.251	B	B
0	0	COLSON, LOYD ALBERT	P		1	.000	A	C
3	4	CUMBERLAND, JOHN SHELDON	P		15	.059	B	XSF N
		ELLIS, JOHN CHARLES	1B	53	78	.248	B	B
		(C2 3B5)						
1	0	GARDNER, RICHARD FRANK (ROB)	P		1	.333	CLE 68	OAK
		GIBBS, JERRY DEAN (JAKE)	C	44	49	.301	B	B
4	3	HAMILTON, STEVE ABSHER	P		35	+.000	B	XCHI
		HANSEN, RONALD LAVERN	SS	15	59	.297	CHI	B
		(2B1 3B11)						
0	0	JONES, GARY HOWELL	P		2	.000	A	B
6	3	KEKICH, MICHAEL DENNIS	P		26	.094	B	B
		KENNEY, GERALD T. (2B2)	3B	135	140	.193	B	B
6	7	KLIMKOWSKI, RONALD BERNARD	P		45	.053	B	OAK
6	6	KLINE, STEVEN JACK	P		16	.179	A	B
		LYTTLE, JAMES LAWRENCE	OF	70	87	.310	B	B
2	0	MC CORMICK, MICHAEL FRANCIS	P		9	.200	XSF N	KC
9	5	MC DANIEL, LYNDALL DALE	P		62	.167	B	B
		MICHAEL, EUGENE RICHARD	SS	123	134	.214	B	B
		(2B3 3B4)						
		MITCHELL, ROBERT VANCE	OF	7	10	.227	A	MIL
		MUNSON, THURMAN LEE	C	125	132	.302	B	B
		MURCER, BOBBY RAY	OF	155	159	.251	B	B
20	11	PETERSON, FRED INGELS (FRITZ)	P		39	.222	B	B
15	13	STOTTLEMYRE, MELVIN LEON	P	37	38	.188	B	B
		TEPEDINO, FRANK RONALD (OF1)	1B	1	16	.316	B	B
1	0	VERBANIC, JOSEPH MICHAEL	P		7	.333	NY 68	C
2	2	WASLEWSKI, GARY LEE	P		26	.100	XMONN	B
		WARD, PETER THOMAS	1B	13	66	.260	CHI	C
		WHITE, ROY HILTON	OF	161	162	.296	B	B
		WOODS, RONALD LAWRENCE	OF	78	95	.227	B	B

WON 82
LOST 80
TIED 0
TG 162

AMERICAN LEAGUE

1971.

FINISHED 4 E

PCT. .506

NEW YORK

RALPH GEORGE HOUK

WON	LOST	NAME	POS.		G.	BA	FROM	TO
4	4	AKER, JACK DELANE	P		41	.000	B	B
		ALOU, FELIPE ROJAS (1B42)	OF	83	131	+.289	XOAK	B
14	12	BAHNSEN, STANLEY RAYMOND	P		36	.152	B	CHI
		BAKER, FRANK WATTS	SS	38	43	.139	B	C
		BLEFARY, CURTIS LEROY (1B4)	OF	6	21	+.194	B	XOAK
		BLOMBERG, RONALD MARK	OF	57	64	.322	NY 69	B
		BOEHMER, LEONARD JOSEPH	3B	1	3	.000	NY 69	C
0	1	BURBACH, WILLIAM DAVID	P		2	.000	B	C
		CATER, DANNY ANDERSON (3B52)	1B	78	121	.276	B	BOS
		CLARKE, HORACE MEREDITH	2B	156	159	.250	B	B
2	2	CLOSTER, ALAN EDWARD	P		14	.000	WAS 66	B
		ELLIS, JOHN CHARLES (C2)	1B	65	83	.244	B	B
0	0	GARDNER, RICHARD FRANK (ROB)	P		2	+.000	XOAK	B
		GIBBS, JERRY DEAN (JAKE)	C	51	70	.218	B	C
3	1	HAMBRIGHT, ROGER DEE	P		18	.500	A	C
		HANSEN, RONALD LAVERN (2B9 SS3)	3B	30	61	.207	B	KC
0	2	HARDIN, JAMES WARREN	P		12	+.000	XBAL	ATLN
0	0	JONES, GARY HOWELL	P		12	.000	B	C
10	9	KEKICH, MICHAEL DENNIS	P		37	.154	B	B
		KENNEY, GERALD T. (1B1 SS5)	3B	109	120	.262	B	B
12	13	KLINE, STEVEN JACK	P		31	.136	B	B
0	0	LEY, TERRENCE RICHARD	P		6	.000	A	C
		LYTTLE, JAMES LAWRENCE	OF	29	49	.198	B	CHI
5	10	MC DANIEL, LYNDALL DALE	P		44	.111	B	B
		MICHAEL, EUGENE RICHARD	SS	136	139	.224	B	B
		MUNSON, THURMAN LEE (OF1)	C	117	125	.251	B	B
		MURCER, BOBBY RAY	OF	143	146	.331	B	B
15	13	PETERSON, FRED INGELS (FRITZ)	P		37	.082	B	B
16	12	STOTTLEMYRE, MELVIN LEON	P		35	.170	B	B
		SWOBODA, RONALD ALAN	OF	47	54	.261	XMONN	B
		TEPEDINO, FRANK RONALD	OF	1	6	+.000	B	XMIL
		TORRES, ROSENDO ANTONIO (RUSTY)	OF	5	9	.385	A	B
		WALTON, DANIEL JAMES	OF	4	5	+.143	XMIL	C
0	1	WASLEWSKI, GARY LEE	P		24	.000	B	OAK
		WHITE, ROY HILTON	OF	145	147	.292	B	B
		WOODS, RONALD LAWRENCE	OF	9	25	.250	B	XMONN

WON FORFEITED GAME FROM WASHINGTON ON SEPTEMBER 30TH,
NO PITCHER CREDITED WITH VICTORY.

WON 79
LOST 76
TIED 0
TG 155

AMERICAN LEAGUE

1972.

FINISHED 4 E

PCT. .510

NEW YORK

RALPH GEORGE HOUK

WON	LOST	NAME	POS.		G.	BA	FROM	TO
0	0	AKER, JACK DELANE	P		4	.000	B	XCHIN
		ALLEN, BERNARD KEITH (2B20)	3B	44	84	.227	WAS	
		ALOU, FELIPE ROJAS (OF15)	1B	95	120	.278	B	
1	3	BEENE, FRED RAY	P	29	30	.000	BAL 70	
0	1	BLASINGAME, WADE ALLEN	P		12	.000	XHOUN	
0	0	BLATERIC, STEPHEN LAWRENCE	P		1	.000	CINN	
		BLOMBERG, RONALD MARK	1B	95	107	.268	B	
		CALLISON, JOHN WESLEY	OF	74	92	.258	CHIN	
		CLARKE, HORACE MEREDITH	2B	143	147	.241	B	
0	0	CLOSTER, ALAN EDWARD	P		2	.000	B	
0	1	COX, JOSEPH CASEY	P		5	+.000	XTEX	
		ELLIS, JOHN CHARLES (1B8)	C	25	52	.294	B	
8	5	GARDNER, RICHARD FRANK (ROB)	P		20	.107	B	
0	1	GOWELL, LAWRENCE CLYDE	P		2	1.000	A	
1	0	HINTON, RICHARD MICHAEL	P		7	+.000	CHI	XTEX
10	13	KEKICH, MICHAEL DENNIS	P		29	.136	B	
		KENNEY, GERALD T. (3B1)	SS	45	50	.210	B	
0	3	KLIMKOWSKI, RONALD BERNARD	P		16	.000	OAK	
16	9	KLINE, STEVEN JACK	P		32	.092	B	
		LANIER, HAROLD CLIFTON (2B3 SS9)	3B	47	60	.214	SF N	
9	5	LYLE, ALBERT WALTER (SPARKY)	P		59	.190	BOS	
3	1	MC DANIEL, LYNDALL DALE	P		37	.286	B	
		MC KINNEY, CHARLES RICHARD	3B	33	37	.215	CHI	
0	0	MEDICH, GEORGE FRANCIS	P		1	.000	A	
		MICHAEL, EUGENE RICHARD	SS	121	126	.233	B	
		MUNSON, THURMAN LEE	C	132	140	.280	B	
		MURCER, BOBBY RAY	OF	151	153	.292	B	
17	15	PETERSON, FRED INGELS (FRITZ)	P		35	.232	B	
0	1	ROLAND, JAMES IVAN	P		16	+.000	XOAK	XTEX
		SANCHEZ, CELERINO	3B	68	71	.248	A	
		SPIKES, LESLIE CHARLES	OF	9	14	.147	A	
14	18	STOTTLEMYRE, MELVIN LEON	P	36	37	.200	B	
		SWOBODA, RONALD ALAN (1B2)	OF	35	63	.248	B	
		TEPEDINO, FRANK RONALD			8	.000	MIL	
		TORRES, ROSENDO ANTONIO (RUSTY)	OF	62	80	.211	B	
		WHITE, ROY HILTON	OF		155	.270	B	

CLUB RECORD

AMERICAN LEAGUE

OAKLAND

CLUB TRANSFERRED FROM KANSAS CITY AFTER 1967 SEASON

YEAR	TG	WON	LOST	TIED	PCT.	FINISHED	MANAGER
1968	163	82	80	1	.506	6	ROBERT DANIEL KENNEDY
1969	162	88	74	0	.543	2W	HENRY ALBERT BAUER
							JOHN FRANCIS MC NAMARA
1970	162	89	73	0	.549	2W	JOHN FRANCIS MC NAMARA
1971	161	101	60	0	.627	1W (LP)	RICHARD HIRSHFELD WILLIAMS
1972	155	93	62	0	.600	1W (WP)	RICHARD HIRSHFELD WILLIAMS

WON 82
LOST 80
TIED 1
TG 163

AMERICAN LEAGUE

1968.

OAKLAND

FINISHED 6

PCT. .506

ROBERT DANIEL KENNEDY

WON	LOST	NAME	POS.		G.	BA	FROM		TO
4	4	AKER, JACK DELANE	P		54	.143	KC		SEA
		BANDO, SALVATORE LEONARD	3B	162	162	.251	KC		B
		(OF1)							
0	0	BOGLE, WARREN FREDERICK	P		16	.000	A		C
		CAMPANERIS, DAGBERTO (BERT)	SS	155	159	.276	KC		B
		(OF3)							
		CATER, DANNY ANDERSON	1B	121	147	.290	KC		B
		(2B1 OF20)							
12	14	DOBSON, CHARLES THOMAS	P		35	.200	KC		B
		DONALDSON, JOHN DAVID	2B	98	127	.220	KC		B
		(SS1 3B5)							
		DUNCAN, DAVID EDWIN	C	79	82	.191	KC		B
0	0	FINGERS, ROLAND GLEN	P		1	.000	A		B
		GOSGER, JAMES CHARLES	OF	64	88	.180	KC		SEA
		GREEN, RICHARD LARRY	2B	61	76	.233	KC		B
		(C1 3B1)							
		HERSHBERGER, NORMAN MICHAEL	OF	90	99	.272	KC		B
13	13	HUNTER, JAMES AUGUSTUS	P	36	39	.232	KC		B
		(CATFISH)							
		JACKSON, REGINALD MARTINEZ	OF	151	154	.250	KC		B
		KEOUGH, JOSEPH WILLIAM (1B1)	OF	29	34	.214	A		KC
10	11	KRAUSSE, LEWIS BERNARD, JR.	P		36	.161	KC		B
		KUBIAK, THEODORE RODGER	2B	24	48	.250	KC		B
		(SS12)							
		LACHEMANN, RENE GEORGE	C	16	19	.150	KC	66	C
		LA RUSSA, ANTHONY			5	.333	A		B
0	0	LAUZERIQUE, GEORGE ALBERT	P		1	.000	KC		B
		LEWIS, ALLAN SYDNEY	OF	1	26	.250	KC		B
4	3	LINDBLAD, PAUL AARON	P		47	.375	KC		B
		MONDAY, ROBERT JAMES (RICK)	OF	144	148	.274	KC		B
13	13	NASH, JAMES EDWIN	P		34	.068	KC		B
16	10	ODOM, JOHNNY LEE (BLUE MOON)	P	32	42	.218	KC		B
		PAGLIARONI, JAMES VINCENT	C	63	66	.246	PITN		B
1	2	PIERCE, TONY MICHAEL	P		17	.000	KC		C
		ROBINSON, FLOYD ANDREW	OF	18	53	+.247	CINN		XBOS
		ROOF, PHILLIP ANTHONY	C	32	34	.188	KC		B
		RUDI, JOSEPH ODEN	OF	56	68	.177	KC		B
0	1	SANDERS, KENNETH GEORGE	P		7	.000	KC	66	MIL 70
6	5	SEGUI, DIEGO PABLO	P		52	.111	KC		SEA
3	4	SPRAGUE, EDWARD NELSON	P		47	.000	A		B
		WEBSTER, RAMON ALBERTO	1B	55	66	.214	KC		B

CLUB TRANSFERRED FROM KANSAS CITY AFTER 1967 SEASON.

WON 88 | LOST 74 | TIED 0 | TG 162

AMERICAN LEAGUE 1969. OAKLAND — FINISHED 2 W — PCT. .543

HENRY ALBERT BAUER   JOHN FRANCIS MC NAMARA

WON	LOST	NAME	POS.	G.	BA	FROM	TO
		BANDO, SALVATORE LEONARD	3B	162	.281	B	B
1	1	BLUE, VIDA	P	12	.000	A	B
		BROOKS, ROBERT	OF 21	29	.241	A	B
		CAMPANERIS, DAGBERTO (BERT)	SS 125	135	.260	B	B
		CATER, DANNY ANDERSON	1B 132	152	.262	B	NY
		(2B4 OF20)					
15	13	DOBSON, CHARLES THOMAS	P	35	.101	B	B
		DONALDSON, JOHN DAVID	2B 1	12	+.077	B	XSEA
		DUNCAN, DAVID EDWIN	C 56	58	.126	B	B
6	7	FINGERS, ROLAND GLEN	P	60	.200	B	B
		FRANCONA, JOHN PATSY (TITO)	1B 16	32	.341	XATLN	B
		(OF1)					
		GREEN, RICHARD LARRY	2B 131	136	.275	B	B
		HANEY, WALLACE LARRY	C	53	+.151	XSEA	B
		HERSHBERGER, NORMAN MICHAEL	OF 35	51	.202	B	MIL
12	15	HUNTER, JAMES AUGUSTUS	P 38	42	.224	B	B
		(CATFISH)					
		JACKSON, REGINALD MARTINEZ	OF 150	152	.275	B	B
		JOHNSON, ROBERT WALLACE	1B 7	51	.343	XSTLN	B
		(2B2)					
7	7	KRAUSSE, LEWIS BERNARD, JR.	P	43	.167	B	MIL
		KUBIAK, THEODORE RODGER	SS 42	92	.249	B	MIL
		(2B33)					
4	1	LACHEMANN, MARCEL ERNEST	P	28	.000	A	B
		LA RUSSA, ANTHONY		8	.000	B	B
3	4	LAUZERIQUE, GEORGE ALBERT	P	19	.100	B	MIL
		LEWIS, ALLAN SYDNEY		12	.000	B	B
9	6	LINDBLAD, PAUL AARON	P	60	.333	B	B
		MC NULTY, WILLIAM FRANCIS	OF 5	5	.000	A	OAK 72
		MONDAY, ROBERT JAMES (RICK)	OF 119	122	.271	B	B
8	8	NASH, JAMES EDWIN	P	26	.111	B	ATLN
		NOSSEK, JOSEPH RUDOLPH	OF 12	13	.000	KC 67	XSTLN
15	6	ODOM, JOHNNY LEE (BLUE MOON)	P 32	43	.266	B	B
		PAGLIARONI, JAMES VINCENT	C 7	14	+.148	B	XSEA
1	1	PIZARRO, JUAN	P	3	+.500	XCLE	CHIN
		REYNOLDS, TOMMIE D.	OF 89	107	.257	NY N67	CAL
5	1	ROLAND, JAMES IVAN	P	39	.095	MIN	B
		ROOF, PHILLIP ANTHONY	C	106	.235	B	MIL
		RUDI, JOSEPH ODEN (1B11)	OF 18	35	.189	B	B
1	1	SPRAGUE, EDWARD NELSON	P	27	.200	B	CINN71
1	2	TALBOT, FRED LEALAND	P	12	+.333	XSEA	B
		TARTABULL, JOSE	OF 63	75	.267	BOS	B
		TENACE, FURY GENE	C 13	16	.158	A	B
		WEBSTER, RAMON ALBERTO	1B 13	64	.260	B	SD N
0	1	WYATT, JOHN THOMAS	P	4	.000	DET	C

WON 89 | LOST 73 | TIED 0 | TG 162

AMERICAN LEAGUE 1970. OAKLAND — FINISHED 2 W — PCT. .549

JOHN FRANCIS MC NAMARA

WON	LOST	NAME	POS.	G.	BA	FROM	TO
		ALOU, FELIPE ROJAS (1B1)	OF 145	154	.271	ATLN	B
		BANDO, SALVATORE LEONARD	3B 152	155	.263	B	B
2	0	BLUE, VIDA	P	6	.200	B	B
		BROOKS, ROBERT	OF 5	7	.333	B	OAK 72
		CAMPANERIS, DAGBERTO (BERT)	SS 143	147	.279	B	B
		DAVIS, HERMAN THOMAS (TOMMY)	OF 45	66	.290	XCHIN	B
		(1B8)					
16	15	DOBSON, CHARLES THOMAS	P	41	.118	B	B
		DONALDSON, JOHN DAVID	2B 21	41	.247	SEA	C
		(SS6 3B1)					
3	3	DOWNING, ALPHONSO ERWIN	P	10	+.182	NY	XMIL
		DRISCOLL, JAMES BERNARD	2B 7	21	.192	A	TEX 72
		(SS7)					
		DUNCAN, DAVID EDWIN	C 73	86	.259	B	B
		FERNANDEZ, FRANK (OF1)	C 76	94	.214	NY	B
7	9	FINGERS, ROLAND GLEN	P	45	.103	B	B
		FRANCONA, JOHN PATSY (TITO)	1B 6	32	+.242	B	XMIL
		(OF1)					
6	2	GRANT, JAMES TIMOTHY (MUDCAT)	P	72	.222	STLN	XPITN
		GREEN, RICHARD LARRY	2B 127	135	.190	B	B
		(C1 3B5)					
		HANEY, WALLACE LARRY	C 1	2	.000	B	OAK 72
		HOVLEY, STEPHEN EUGENE	OF 42	72	+.190	XMIL	B
18	14	HUNTER, JAMES AUGUSTUS	P 40	43	.200	B	B
		(CATFISH)					
		JACKSON, REGINALD MARTINEZ	OF 142	149	.237	B	B
		JOHNSON, ROBERT WALLACE	3B 6	30	.174	B	C
		(1B1)					
3	3	LACHEMANN, MARCEL ERNEST	P	41	.000	B	B
		LA RUSSA, ANTHONY	2B 44	52	.198	B	B
		LEWIS, ALLAN SYDNEY	OF 2	25	.250	B	OAK 72
8	2	LINDBLAD, PAUL AARON	P	62	.000	B	B
3	3	LOCKER, ROBERT AUTRY	P	38	+.167	XMIL	B
		MINCHER, DONALD RAY	1B 137	140	.246	SEA	B
		MONDAY, ROBERT JAMES (RICK)	OF 109	112	.290	B	B
9	8	ODOM, JOHNNY LEE (BLUE MOON)	P 29	37	.241	B	B
1	0	OSTEEN, MILTON DARRELL	P	3	.000	CINN67	C
		PENA, ROBERTO CESAR (3B5)	SS 12	19	+.259	SD N	XMIL
0	0	RODRIGUEZ, ROBERTO MUNOZ	P	6	.000	KC 67	XSD N
3	3	ROLAND, JAMES IVAN	P	28	.000	B	B
		RUDI, JOSEPH ODEN (1B28)	OF 63	106	.309	B	B
10	10	SEGUI, DIEGO PABLO	P	47	.116	SEA	B
0	1	TALBOT, FRED LEALAND	P	1	.000	B	C
		TARTABULL, JOSE	OF 6	24	.231	B	C
		TENACE, FURY GENE	C 30	38	.305	B	B
0	0	WOMACK, HORACE GUY (DOOLEY)	P	2	.000	SEA	C

WON 101	AMERICAN LEAGUE	FINISHED 1 W
LOST 60		(LOST LEAGUE PLAYOFF)
TIED 0	1971.	PCT. .627
TG 161		

OAKLAND

RICHARD HIRSHFELD WILLIAMS

WON	LOST	NAME	POS.		G.	BA	FROM	TO
		ALOU, FELIPE ROJAS	OF		2	+.250	B	XNY
		ANDERSON, DWAIN CLEAVEN	SS	10	16	.270	A	B
		(2B5 3B1)						
		BANDO, SALVATORE LEONARD	3B		153	.271	B	B
		BLEFARY, CURTIS LEROY	C	14	50	+.218	XNY	B
		(2B2 3B5 OF14)						
24	8	BLUE, VIDA	P		39	.118	B	B
		BROWN, LARRY LESLIE	SS	31	70	+.196	XCLE	B
		(2B23 3B10)						
		CAMPANERIS, DAGBERTO (BERT)	SS	133	134	.251	B	B
		CLARK, RONALD BRUCE			2	.000	SEA 69	B
		DAVIS, HERMAN THOMAS (TOMMY)	1B	35	79	.324	B	CHIN
		(2B3 OF16)						
15	5	DOBSON, CHARLES THOMAS	P		30	.197	B	C
		DUNCAN, DAVID EDWIN	C	102	103	.253	B	B
		EPSTEIN, MICHAEL PETER	1B	96	104	+.234	XWAS	B
		FERNANDEZ, FRANK	C	3	4	+.111	B	XWAS
4	6	FINGERS, ROLAND GLEN	P		48	.212	B	B
0	0	GARDNER, RICHARD FRANK (ROB)	P		4	+.500	NY	XNY
		GARRETT, HENRY ADRIAN (ADE)	OF	5	14	.143	CHIN	B
1	0	GRANT, JAMES TIMOTHY (MUDCAT)	P		15	.333	XPITN	C
		GREEN, RICHARD LARRY (SS1)	2B	143	144	.244	B	B
		HEGAN, JAMES MICHAEL (MIKE)	1B	47	65	+.236	XMIL	B
		(OF2)						
		HENDRICK, GEORGE ANDREW	OF	36	42	.237	A	B
		HOVLEY, STEPHEN EUGENE	OF	11	24	.111	B	KC
21	11	HUNTER, JAMES AUGUSTUS	P	37	38	.350	B	B
		(CATFISH)						
		JACKSON, REGINALD MARTINEZ	OF	145	150	.277	B	B
2	2	KLIMKOWSKI, RONALD BERNARD	P		26	.400	NY	NY
5	2	KNOWLES, DAROLD DUANE	P		43	+.125	XWAS	B
0	0	LACHEMANN, MARCEL ERNEST	P		1	.000	B	C
		LA RUSSA, ANTHONY (SS4 3B2)	2B	7	23	.000	B	XATLN
1	0	LINDBLAD, PAUL AARON	P		8	+.333	B	XWAS
7	2	LOCKER, ROBERT AUTRY	P		47	.000	B	B
		MANGUAL, ANGEL LUIS	OF	81	94	.286	PITN69	B
		MINCHER, DONALD RAY	1B	27	28	+.239	B	XWAS
		MONDAY, ROBERT JAMES (RICK)	OF	111	116	.245	B	CHIN
10	12	ODOM, JOHNNY LEE (BLUE MOON)	P	25	37	.160	B	B
0	1	PANTHER, JAMES EDWARD	P		4	.000	A	TEX
0	0	PATTERSON, DARYL ALAN	P		4	+.000	XDET	XSTLN
1	3	ROLAND, JAMES IVAN	P		31	.000	B	B
		RUDI, JOSEPH ODEN (1B5)	OF	121	127	.267	B	B
10	8	SEGUI, DIEGO PABLO	P		26	.085	B	B
		TENACE, FURY GENE (OF1)	C	52	65	.274	B	B
		WEBSTER, RAMON ALBERTO	1B	1	7	.000	XSD N	XCHIN

WON 93	AMERICAN LEAGUE	FINISHED 1 W
LOST 62		(ALSO WON LEAGUE PLAYOFF)
TIED 0	1972.	PCT. .600
TG 155		

OAKLAND

RICHARD HIRSHFELD WILLIAMS

WON	LOST	NAME	POS.		G.	BA	FROM	TO
		ALOU, MATEO ROJAS (1B1)	OF	32	32	.281	XSTLN	
		ALYEA, GARRABRANT RYERSON	OF	8	20	.194	MIN	XSTLN
		ANDERSON, DWAIN CLEAVEN	SS	1	3	.000	B	XSTLN
		(3B1)						
		BANDO, SALVATORE LEONARD	3B	151	152	.236	B	
		(2B1)						
		BLEFARY, CURTIS LEROY	1B	1	8	.455	B	XSD N
		(2B1 OF1)						
6	10	BLUE, VIDA	P	25	27	.044	B	
		BROOKS, ROBERT	OF	11	15	.179	OAK 70	
		BROWN, LARRY LESLIE (3B1)	2B	46	47	.183	B	
		BROWN, OLLIE LEE	OF	15	20	+.241	XSD N	XMIL
		CAMPANERIS, DAGBERTO (BERT)	SS	148	149	.240	B	
		CEPEDA, ORLANDO MANUEL			3	.000	XATLN	
		CLARK, RONALD BRUCE (3B3)	2B	11	14	+.267	B	XMIL
		CULLEN, TIMOTHY LEO	2B	65	72	.261	WAS	
		(SS1 3B4)						
		DUNCAN, DAVID EDWIN	C	113	121	.218	B	
		EPSTEIN, MICHAEL PETER	1B	137	138	.270	B	
11	9	FINGERS, ROLAND GLEN	P		65	.316	B	
		GARRETT, HENRY ADRIAN (ADE)	OF	2	14	.000	B	
		GREEN, RICHARD LARRY	2B		26	.286	B	
6	6	HAMILTON, DAVID EDWARD	P		25	.154	A	
		HANEY, WALLACE LARRY (2B1)	C	4	5	.000	OAK 70	
		HEGAN, JAMES MICHAEL (MIKE)	1B	64	98	.329	B	
		(OF3)						
		HENDRICK, GEORGE ANDREW	OF	41	58	.182	B	
19	11	HOLTZMAN, KENNETH DALE	P	39	40	.178	CHIN	
3	4	HORLEN, JOEL EDWARD (JOE)	P		32	.176	CHI	
21	7	HUNTER, JAMES AUGUSTUS	P	38	39	.219	B	
		(CATFISH)						
		JACKSON, REGINALD MARTINEZ	OF		135	.265	B	
0	0	KILKENNY, MICHAEL DAVID	P		1	+.000	XDET	XSD N
5	1	KNOWLES, DAROLD DUANE	P		54	.250	B	
		KUBIAK, THEODORE RODGER	2B	49	51	+.181	XTEX	
		(3B1)						
		LEWIS, ALLAN SYDNEY	OF	6	24	.200	OAK 70	
6	1	LOCKER, ROBERT AUTRY	P		56	.000	B	
		MANGUAL, ANGEL LUIS	OF	74	91	.246	B	
		MARQUEZ, GONZALO ENRIQUE	1B	2	23	.381	A	
		MARTINEZ, ORLANDO (MARTY)	2B	17	22	+.125	XSTLN	XTEX
		(SS6 3B1)						
		MAXVILL, CHARLES DALLAN (DAL)	2B	24	27	.250	XSTLN	
		(SS4)						
1	2	MC LAIN, DENNIS DALE	P		5	.000	WAS	XATLN
		MC NULTY, WILLIAM FRANCIS	3B	3	4	.100	OAK 69	
		MINCHER, DONALD RAY	1B	11	47	+.148	XTEX	
15	6	ODOM, JOHNNY LEE (BLUE MOON)	P	31	59	.121	B	
0	0	ROLAND, JAMES IVAN	P		2	+.000	B	XNY
		RUDI, JOSEPH ODEN (3B1)	OF	147	147	.305	B	
0	1	SEGUI, DIEGO PABLO	P		7	.143	B	XSTLN
		SHAMSKY, ARTHUR LOUIS			8	.000	XCHIN	
0	1	SHAW, DONALD WELLINGTON	P		3	.000	XSTLN	
		TENACE, FURY GENE	C	49	82	.225	B	
		(1B7 2B2 3B2 OF9)						
		VOSS, WILLIAM EDWARD	OF	34	40	+.227	XMIL	XSTLN
0	3	WASLEWSKI, GARY LEE	P		8	.000	NY	

CLUB RECORD

AMERICAN LEAGUE

SEATTLE

NEW CLUB ADDED IN EXPANSION OF 1969
CLUB TRANSFERRED TO MILWAUKEE AFTER 1969 SEASON

YEAR	TG	WON	LOST	TIED	PCT.	FINISHED	MANAGER
1969	163	64	98	1	.395	6W (LAST)	JOSEPH CHARLES SCHULTZ, JR.

WON 64   AMERICAN LEAGUE   FINISHED 6 W (LAST)
LOST 98
TIED 1   1969.   PCT. .395
TG 163

SEATTLE

JOSEPH CHARLES SCHULTZ, JR.

WON	LOST	NAME	POS.		G.	BA	FROM	TO
0	2	AKER, JACK DELANE	P		15	+.000	OAK	XNY
1	0	BANEY, RICHARD LEE	P		9	.000	A	C
4	7	BARBER, STEPHEN DAVID	P		25	.200	NY	CHIN
0	0	BATES, CHARLES RICHARD (DICK)	P		1	.000	A	C
2	6	BELL, GARY	P		13	+.214	BOS	XCHI
2	1	BOUTON, JAMES ALAN	P		57	.000	NY	XHOUN
13	14	BRABENDER, EUGENE MATTHEW	P	40	41	.129	BAL	MIL
0	1	BRANDON, DARRELL G.	P		8	+.000	BOS	XMIN
2	5	BRUNET, GEORGE STUART	P		12	+.150	XCAL	WAS
		CLARK, RONALD BRUCE	SS	38	57	+.196	XMIN	OAK 71
		(1B1 2B5 3B15)						
		COMER, HARRY WAYNE (C1 3B1)	OF	139	147	.245	DET	MIL
		DAVIS, HERMAN THOMAS (1B1)	OF	112	123	.271	CHI	XHOUN
		DONALDSON, JOHN DAVID	2B	90	95	+.234	XOAK	OAK
		(SS1 3B2)						
0	1	EDGERTON, WILLIAM ALBERT	P		4	.000	KC 67	C
		FERRARO, MICHAEL DENNIS			5	.000	NY	MIL 72
1	3	FUENTES, MIGUEL	P		8	.333	A	C
3	10	GELNAR, JOHN RICHARD	P	39	40	.053	PITN67	MIL
		GIL, TOMAS GUSTAVO (GUS)	3B	38	92	.222	CLE 67	MIL
		(2B18 SS12)						
		GOOSSEN, GREGORY BRYANT (OF2)	1B	31	52	.309	NY N	MIL
		GOSGER, JAMES CHARLES	OF	26	39	.109	OAK	XNY N
		HANEY, WALLACE LARRY	C	20	22	+.254	BAL	XOAK
		HARPER, TOMMY (3B59 OF26)	2B	59	148	.235	CLE	MIL
		HEGAN, JAMES MICHAEL (1B19)	OF	64	95	.292	NY 67	MIL
		HOVLEY, STEPHEN EUGENE	OF	84	91	.277	A	MIL
		KENNEDY, JOHN EDWARD (3B23)	SS	33	61	.234	NY 67	MIL
3	3	LOCKER, ROBERT AUTRY	P		51	+.083	XCHI	MIL
0	1	LOCKWOOD, CLAUDE EDWARD (SKIP)	P		6	.000	KC 65	MIL
		LUND, GORDON THOMAS (2B1 3B1)	SS	17	20	.263	CLE 67	C
3	10	MARSHALL, MICHAEL GRANT	P	20	21	.259	DET 67	HOUN
		MC NERTNEY, GERALD EDWARD	C	122	128	.241	CHI	MIL
0	3	MEYER, ROBERT BERNARD	P		6	.091	KC 64	MIL
		MINCHER, DONALD RAY	1B	122	140	.246	CAL	OAK
0	0	MORRIS, JOHN WALLACE	P		6	1.000	BAL	MIL
2	2	O'DONOGHUE, JOHN EUGENE	P		55	.077	BAL	MIL
		OYLER, RAYMOND FRANCIS	SS		106	.165	DET	CAL
		PAGLIARONI, JAMES VINCENT	C	29	40	+.264	XOAK	C
		(1B2 OF1)						
7	12	PATTIN, MARTIN WILLIAM	P	34	39	.155	CAL	MIL
		RANEW, MERRITT THOMAS	C	13	54	.247	CAL 65	C
		(3B1 OF3)						
2	2	ROGGENBURK, GARRY EARL	P		7	+.125	XBOS	C
		ROLLINS, RICHARD JOHN (SS1)	3B	47	58	.225	MIN	MIL
12	6	SEGUI, DIEGO PABLO	P		66	.148	OAK	OAK
		SIMPSON, RICHARD CHARLES	OF	17	26	+.176	XNY	C
		STANLEY, FREDERICK BLAIR (2B1)	SS	15	17	.279	A	MIL
0	0	STEPHENSON, JERRY JOSEPH	P		2	.000	BOS	LA N
5	8	TALBOT, FRED LEALAND	P	25	27	+.162	XNY	XOAK
0	0	TIMBERLAKE, GARY DALE	P		2	.000	A	C
		VALDESPINO, HILARIO BORROTO	OF	7	20	.211	XHOUN	MIL
		(SANDY)						
		VELAZQUEZ, FEDERICO ANTONIO	C	5	6	.125	A	C
		VIDAL, JOSE	OF	6	18	.192	CLE	C
		WALTON, DANIEL JAMES	OF		23	.217	HOUN	MIL
		WHITAKER, STEPHEN EDWARD	OF	39	69	.250	NY	SF N
		WILLIAMS, WILLIAM	OF	3	4	.000	A	C
2	1	WOMACK, HORACE GUY (DOOLEY)	P		9	.000	XHOUN	OAK

CLUB RECORD

AMERICAN LEAGUE

TEXAS

CLUB TRANSFERRED FROM WASHINGTON AFTER 1971 SEASON

YEAR	TG	WON	LOST	TIED	PCT.	FINISHED	MANAGER
1972	154	54	100	0	.351	6W (LAST)	THEODORE SAMUEL WILLIAMS

WON 54
LOST 100
TIED 0
TG 154

AMERICAN LEAGUE

1972.

TEXAS

FINISHED 6 W (LAST)

PCT. .351

THEODORE SAMUEL WILLIAMS

WON	LOST	NAME	POS.		G.	BA	FROM		TO
		BITTNER, LAWRENCE DAVID	1B	65	137	.259	WAS		
		(OF65)							
		BILLINGS, RICHARD ARLIN	C	92	133	.254	WAS		
		(1B1 3B5 OF41)							
8	10	BOSMAN, RICHARD ALLEN	P		29	.094	WAS		
5	12	BROBERG PETER SVEN	P		39	.078	WAS		
		BURROUGHS, JEFFREY ALAN	OF	19	22	.185	WAS		
		(1B1)							
3	5	COX, JOSEPH CASEY	P		35	+.111	WAS		XNY
		DRISCOLL, JAMES BERNARD	2B	4	15	.000	OAK	70	
		(3B2)							
0	0	DUKES, NOBLE JAN	P		3	.000	WAS	70	
		FAHEY, WILLIAM ROGER	C		39	.168	WAS		
		FORD, THEODORE HENRY	OF	119	129	.235	CLE		
4	11	GOGOLEWSKI, WILLIAM JOSEPH	P		36	.125	WAS		
		GRIEVE, THOMAS ALAN	OF	49	64	.204	WAS	70	
10	14	HAND, RICHARD ALLEN	P		30	.154	CLE		
		HARRAH, COLBERT DALE (TOBY)	SS	106	116	.259	WAS		
		HARRIS, VICTOR LANIER (SS1)	2B	58	61	.140	A		
0	1	HINTON, RICHARD MICHAEL	P		5	+.500	XNY		
		HOWARD, FRANK OLIVER (OF21)	1B	66	95	+.244	WAS		XDET
0	1	JANESKI, GERALD JOSEPH	P		4	.000	WAS		
		JONES, JAMES DALTON	3B	23	72	+.159	XDET		
		(1B7 2B17 OF2)							
		KING, HAROLD	C	38	50	.180	ATLN		
		KUBIAK, THEODORE RODGER	2B	25	46	+.224	STLN		XOAK
		(SS15 3B1)							
0	0	LAWSON, STEVEN GEORGE	P		13	1.000	A		
5	8	LINDBLAD, PAUL AARON	P		66	.200	WAS		
		LOVITTO, JOSEPH	OF	103	117	.224	A		
		MADDOX, ELLIOTT	OF	94	98	.252	WAS		
		MARTINEZ, ORLANDO (MARTY)	SS	5	26	+.146	XOAK		
		(2B1 3B4)							
		MASON, JAMES PERCY (3B10)	SS	32	46	.197	WAS		
		MINCHER, DONALD RAY	1B	59	61	+.236	WAS		XOAK
		NELSON, DAVID EARL (OF15)	3B	119	145	.226	WAS		
5	9	PANTHER, JAMES EDWARD	P		58	.125	OAK		
8	9	PAUL, MICHAEL GEORGE	P		49	.167	CLE		
2	7	PINA, HORACIO	P		60	.200	WAS		
		RAGLAND, THOMAS (SS3 3B5)	2B	13	25	.172	WAS		
		RANDLE, LEONARD SHENOFF	2B	65	74	.193	WAS		
		(SS4 OF2)							
0	0	ROLAND, JAMES IVAN	P		5	+.000	XNY		
2	4	SHELLENBACK, JAMES PHILIP	P		22	.100	WAS		
2	9	STANHOUSE, DONALD JOSEPH	P	24	26	.129	A		
		SUAREZ, KENNETH RAYMOND	C	17	25	.152	CLE		

CLUB TRANSFERRED FROM WASHINGTON AFTER 1971 SEASON.

WON 70
LOST 92
TIED 0
TG 162

AMERICAN LEAGUE

1965.

FINISHED 8

PCT. .432

WASHINGTON

GILBERT RAYMOND HODGES

WON	LOST	NAME	POS.		G.	BA	FROM	TO
		ALYEA, GARRABRANT RYERSON	1B	3	8	.231	A	WAS 68
		(OF1)						
		BLASINGAME, DON LEE	2B	110	129	.223	B	B
1	2	BRIDGES, MARSHALL	P		40	.143	B	C
		BRINKMAN, EDWIN ALBERT	SS	150	154	.185	B	B
		BRUMLEY, TONY MIKE	C	66	79	.208	B	B
		CAMILLI, DOUGLAS JOSEPH	C	59	75	.192	LA N	B
		CASANOVA, PAULINO	C	4	5	.308	A	B
		CHANCE, ROBERT (OF3)	1B	48	72	.256	CLE	B
2	0	COLEMAN, JOSEPH HOWARD	P		2	.000	A	B
		COTTIER, CHARLES KEITH			7	.000	B	CAL 68
0	3	CRAIG, PETER JOEL	P		3	.667	B	B
		CUNNINGHAM, JOSEPH ROBERT	1B	59	95	.229	B	B
5	13	DANIELS, BENNIE	P		33	.133	B	C
2	2	DUCKWORTH, JAMES RAYMOND	P		17	.000	B	B
1	1	DUREN, RINOLD GEORGE	P		16	.000	XPHIN	C
		FRENCH, RICHARD JAMES (JIM)	C		13	.297	A	B
0	0	GREEN, GEORGE DALLAS	P		6	.000	PHIN	NY N
		HAMLIN, KENNETH LEE	2B	77	117	.273	WAS 62	B
		(SS47 3B1)						
1	1	HANNAN, JAMES JOHN	P		4	.000	B	B
		HELD, WOODSON GEORGE	OF	106	122	.247	CLE	BAL
		(2B4 SS2 3B5)						
		HOWARD, FRANK OLIVER	OF	138	149	.289	LA N	B
		KING, JAMES HUBERT	OF	88	120	.213	B	B
		KIRKLAND, WILLIE CHARLES	OF	92	123	.231	B	B
7	6	KLINE, RONALD LEE	P		74	.000	B	B
4	7	KOPLITZ, HOWARD DEAN	P		33	.100	B	B
2	6	KREUTZER, FRANKLIN JAMES	P		33	.045	B	B
		LOCK, DON WILSON	OF	136	143	.215	B	B
		MC CABE, JOSEPH ROBERT	C	11	14	.185	MIN	C
8	8	MC CORMICK, MICHAEL FRANCIS	P	44	45	.073	BAL	B
		MC MULLEN, KENNETH LEE	3B	142	150	.263	LA N	B
		(1B1 OF8)						
0	0	MOORE, ROBERT BARRY	P		1	.000	A	B
4	12	NARUM, LESLIE FERDINAND	P		46	.043	B	B
		(BUSTER)						
		NEN, RICHARD LEROY	1B	65	69	.260	LA N63	B
12	15	ORTEGA, FILOMENO CORONADO	P		35	.208	LA N	B
15	12	RICHERT, PETER GERARD	P	34	42	.156	LA N	B
6	4	RIDZIK, STEPHEN GEORGE	P		63	.167	B	PHIN
		SIEVERS, ROY EDWARD	1B	7	12	.190	B	C
		VALENTINE, FRED LEE	OF	11	12	.241	B	B
0	0	WILLHITE, JON NICHOLAS (NICK)	P		5	.000	LA N	XLA N
		ZIMMER, DONALD WILLIAM	C	33	95	.199	B	C
		(2B12 3B26)						

WON 71
LOST 88
TIED 0
TG 159

AMERICAN LEAGUE

1966.

FINISHED 8

PCT. .447

WASHINGTON

GILBERT RAYMOND HODGES

WON	LOST	NAME	POS.		G.	BA	FROM	TO
		ALLEN, HAROLD ANDREW (HANK)	OF		9	.387	A	B
0	0	BALDWIN, DAVID GEORGE	P		4	.000	A	B
		BLASINGAME, DON LEE (SS1)	2B	58	68	+.215	B	XKC
2	6	BOSMAN, RICHARD ALLEN	P		13	.250	A	B
		BRINKMAN, EDWIN ALBERT	SS		158	.229	B	B
		BRUMLEY, TONY MIKE	C	7	9	.111	B	C
		CAMILLI, DOUGLAS JOSEPH	C	39	44	.206	B	B
		CASANOVA, PAULINO	C	119	122	.254	B	B
		CHANCE, ROBERT	1B	13	37	.175	B	B
0	1	CHENEY, THOMAS EDGAR	P		3	.000	WAS 64	C
0	0	CLOSTER, ALAN EDWARD	P		1	.000	A	NY 71
1	0	COLEMAN, JOSEPH HOWARD	P		1	.000	B	B
4	5	COX, JOSEPH CASEY	P		66	.000	A	B
0	0	CRAIG, PETER JOEL	P		1	.000	B	C
		CULLEN, TIMOTHY LEO (2B5)	3B	8	18	.235	A	B
		CUNNINGHAM, JOSEPH ROBERT	1B		3	.125	B	C
0	3	DUCKWORTH, JAMES RAYMOND	P		5	+.000	B	XKC
		FRENCH, RICHARD JAMES (JIM)	C		10	.208	B	B
		HAMLIN, KENNETH LEE (3B1)	2B	50	66	.215	B	C
3	9	HANNAN, JAMES JOHN	P		30	.067	B	B
		HARRELSON, KENNETH SMITH	1B	70	71	+.248	XKC	B
		HOWARD, FRANK OLIVER	OF	135	146	.278	B	B
7	3	HUMPHREYS, ROBERT WILLIAM	P		58	.167	CHIN	B
		KING, JAMES HUBERT	OF	85	117	.248	B	B
		KIRKLAND, WILLIE CHARLES	OF	68	124	.190	B	C
6	4	KLINE, RONALD LEE	P		63	.167	B	MIN
0	0	KOPLITZ, HOWARD DEAN	P		1	.000	B	C
0	5	KREUTZER, FRANKLIN JAMES	P		9	.250	B	WAS 69
5	2	LINES, RICHARD GEORGE	P		53	.000	A	B
		LOCK, DON WILSON	OF	129	138	.233	B	PHIN
11	14	MC CORMICK, MICHAEL FRANCIS	P		41	.212	B	SF N
		MC MULLEN, KENNETH LEE	3B	141	147	.233	B	B
		(1B8 OF1)						
3	3	MOORE, ROBERT BARRY	P		12	.105	B	B
0	0	NARUM, LESLIE FERDINAND	P		3	.000	B	B
		(BUSTER)						
		NEN, RICHARD LEROY	1B	76	94	.213	B	B
		ORSINO, JOHN JOSEPH (C2)	1B	5	14	.174	BAL	B
12	12	ORTEGA, FILOMENO CORONADO	P		33	.056	B	B
		PHILLIPS, RICHARD EUGENE	1B	5	25	.162	WAS 64	C
14	14	RICHERT, PETER GERARD	P	36	43	.163	B	B
		SAVERINE, ROBERT PAUL	2B	70	120	.251	BAL 64	B
		(SS11 3B26 OF9)						
3	7	SEGUI, DIEGO PABLO	P		21	.111	KC	KC
		VALENTINE, FRED LEE (1B2)	OF	138	146	.276	B	B

WON 76
LOST 85
TIED 0
TG 161

AMERICAN LEAGUE

1967.

WASHINGTON

FINISHED 6
(TIED WITH BALTIMORE)
PCT. .472

GILBERT RAYMOND HODGES

WON	LOST	NAME	POS.		G.	BA	FROM	TO
		ALLEN, BERNARD KEITH	2B	75	87	.193	MIN	B
		ALLEN, HAROLD ANDREW (HANK)	OF	99	116	.233	B	B
2	4	BALDWIN, DAVID GEORGE	P		58	.000	B	B
6	5	BERTAINA, FRANK LOUIS	P	18	19	+.057	XBAL	B
3	1	BOSMAN, RICHARD ALLEN	P	7	8	.200	B	B
		BRINKMAN, EDWIN ALBERT	SS		109	.188	B	B
		CAMILLI, DOUGLAS JOSEPH	C	24	30	.183	B	WAS 69
		CASANOVA, PAULINO	C	137	141	.248	B	B
		CHANCE, ROBERT	1B	10	27	.214	B	CAL 69
		COGGINS, FRANKLIN	2B		19	.307	A	B
8	9	COLEMAN, JOSEPH HOWARD	P		28	.056	B	B
7	4	COX, JOSEPH CASEY	P		54	.000	B	B
		CULLEN, TIMOTHY LEO	SS	69	124	.236	B	CHI
		(2B46 3B15 OF1)						
		EPSTEIN, MICHAEL PETER	1B	80	96	+.229	XBAL	B
		FRENCH, RICHARD JAMES (JIM)	C		6	.063	B	B
1	1	HANNAN, JAMES JOHN	P		8	.000	B	B
		HARRELSON, KENNETH SMITH	1B	23	26	+.203	B	XKC
		HOWARD, FRANK OLIVER (1B4)	OF	141	149	.256	B	B
6	2	HUMPHREYS, ROBERT WILLIAM	P		48	.133	B	B
		KING, JAMES HUBERT (C1)	OF	31	47	+.210	B	XCHI
6	8	KNOWLES, DAROLD DUANE	P		61	.063	PHIN	B
2	5	LINES, RICHARD GEORGE	P		54	.111	B	C
		MC MULLEN, KENNETH LEE	3B	145	146	.245	B	B
7	11	MOORE, ROBERT BARRY	P		27	.130	B	B
1	0	NARUM, LESLIE FERDINAND	P		2	.000	B	C
		(BUSTER)						
		NEN, RICHARD LEROY (OF1)	1B	65	110	.218	B	CHIN
0	2	NOLD, RICHARD LEWIS	P		7	.000	A	C
		ORSINO, JOHN JOSEPH			1	.000	B	C
10	10	ORTEGA, FILOMENO CORONADO	P		34	.061	B	B
12	10	PASCUAL, CAMILO ALBERTO	P		28	.176	MIN	B
		PETERSON, CHARLES ANDREW (CAP)	OF	101	122	.240	SF N	B
3	7	PRIDDY, ROBERT SIMPSON	P	46	49	.182	SF N	CHI
2	6	RICHERT, PETER GERARD	P	11	12	+.059	B	XBAL
		SAVERINE, ROBERT PAUL	2B	48	89	.236	B	C
		(SS10 3B8 OF2)						
		STROUD, EDWIN MARVIN	OF	79	87	+.201	XCHI	B
		VALENTINE, FRED LEE	OF	136	151	.234	B	B

WON 65
LOST 96
TIED 0
TG 161

AMERICAN LEAGUE

1968.

WASHINGTON

FINISHED 10 (LAST)

PCT. .404

JAMES ROBERT LEMON

WON	LOST	NAME	POS.		G.	BA	FROM	TO
		ALLEN, BERNARD KEITH (3B2)	2B	110	120	.241	B	B
		ALLEN, HAROLD ANDREW (HANK)	OF	25	68	.219	B	B
		(2B11 3B16)						
		ALYEA, GARRABRANT RYERSON	OF	39	53	.267	WAS 65	B
0	2	BALDWIN, DAVID GEORGE	P		40	.000	B	B
7	13	BERTAINA, FRANK LOUIS	P		27	.132	B	B
		BILLINGS, RICHARD ARLIN	OF	8	12	.182	A	B
		(3B4)						
2	9	BOSMAN, RICHARD ALLEN	P		46	.200	B	B
		BOWENS, SAMUEL EDWARDS	OF	27	57	.191	BAL	B
		BRINKMAN, EDWIN ALBERT	SS	74	77	.187	B	B
		(2B2 OF1)						
		BRYAN, WILLIAM RONALD	C	28	40	.204	NY	C
		CASANOVA, PAULINO	C	92	96	.196	B	B
		COGGINS, FRANKLIN	2B	52	62	.175	B	CHIN72
12	16	COLEMAN, JOSEPH HOWARD	P	33	34	.129	B	B
0	1	COX, JOSEPH CASEY	P		4	.000	B	B
		CULLEN, TIMOTHY LEO	SS	33	47	+.272	XCHI	B
		(2B16 3B3)						
0	0	DENEHY, WILLIAM FRANCIS	P		3	.000	NY N	DET 71
		EPSTEIN, MICHAEL PETER	1B	110	123	.234	B	B
		FRENCH, RICHARD JAMES (JIM)	C	53	59	.194	B	B
10	6	HANNAN, JAMES JOHN	P		25	.064	B	B
		HANSEN, RONALD LAVERN (3B5)	SS	81	86	+.185	CHI	XCHI
0	0	HAYWOOD, WILLIAM KIERNAN	P		14	.000	A	C
4	4	HIGGINS, DENNIS DEAN	P		59	.133	CHI	B
		HOLMAN, GARY RICHARD (OF10)	1B	33	75	.294	A	B
1	4	HOWARD, BRUCE ERNEST	P		13	+.000	XBAL	C
		HOWARD, FRANK OLIVER (1B55)	OF	107	158	.274	B	B
5	7	HUMPHREYS, ROBERT WILLIAM	P		56	.400	B	B
1	2	JONES, STEVEN HOWELL	P		7	.000	CHI	KC
1	1	KNOWLES, DAROLD DUANE	P		32	.250	B	B
		MARTIN, THOMAS EUGENE (GENE)	OF	2	9	.364	A	C
		MC MULLEN, KENNETH LEE (SS11)	3B	145	151	.248	B	B
0	0	MILES, JAMES CHARLIE	P		3	.000	A	B
4	6	MOORE, ROBERT BARRY	P	32	34	.097	B	B
5	12	ORTEGA, FILOMENO CORONADO	P		31	.167	B	CAL
13	12	PASCUAL, CAMILO ALBERTO	P		31	.185	B	B
		PETERSON, CHARLES ANDREW (CAP)	OF	52	94	.204	B	CLE
0	1	SCHEON, GERALD THOMAS	P		1	.000	A	C
		STROUD, EDWIN MARVIN	OF	84	105	.239	B	B
		UNSER, DELBERT BERNARD (1B1)	OF	156	156	.230	A	B
		VALENTINE, FRED LEE	OF	27	37	+.238	B	XBAL

WON 86
LOST 76
TIED 0
TG 162

AMERICAN LEAGUE

1969.

FINISHED 4 E

PCT. .531

WASHINGTON

THEODORE SAMUEL WILLIAMS

WON	LOST	NAME	POS.		G.	BA	FROM	TO
		ALLEN, BERNARD KEITH (3B6)	2B	110	122	.247	B	B
		ALLEN, HAROLD ANDREW (HANK)	OF	91	109	.277	B	B
		(2B3 3B6)						
		ALYEA, GARRABRANT RYERSON	OF	69	104	.249	B	MIN
		(1B3)						
2	4	BALDWIN, DAVID GEORGE	P		43	.000	B	MIL
1	3	BERTAINA, FRANK LOUIS	P		14	+.364	B	XBAL
		BILLINGS, RICHARD ARLIN	OF	6	27	.135	B	B
		(3B1)						
14	5	BOSMAN, RICHARD ALLEN	P	31	32	.094	B	B
		BOWENS, SAMUEL EDWARDS	OF	30	33	.193	B	C
		BRINKMAN, EDWIN ALBERT	SS	150	151	.266	B	B
		CAMILLI, DOUGLAS JOSEPH	C		1	.333	WAS 67	C
1	1	CARLOS, FRANCISCO MANUEL	P		6	+.200	XCHI	B
		CASANOVA, PAULINO	C	122	124	.216	B	B
12	13	COLEMAN, JOSEPH HOWARD	P		40	.107	B	B
12	7	COX, JOSEPH CASEY	P		52	.106	B	B
		CULLEN, TIMOTHY LEO	2B	105	119	.209	B	B
		(SS9 3B1)						
0	2	DUKES, NOBLE JAN	P		8	.000	A	B
		EPSTEIN, MICHAEL PETER	1B	118	131	.278	B	B
		FRENCH, RICHARD JAMES (JIM)	C		63	.184	B	B
7	6	HANNAN, JAMES JOHN	P		35	.115	B	B
		HARRAH, COLBERT DALE (TOBY)	SS	1	8	.000	A	WAS 71
10	9	HIGGINS, DENNIS DEAN	P		55	.091	B	CLE
		HOLMAN, GARY RICHARD (OF3)	1B	11	41	.161	B	C
		HOWARD, FRANK OLIVER (1B70)	OF	114	161	.296	B	B
3	3	HUMPHREYS, ROBERT WILLIAM	P		47	.077	B	B
9	2	KNOWLES, DAROLD DUANE	P		53	.077	B	B
0	0	KREUTZER, FRANKLIN JAMES	P		4	.000	WAS 66	C
		MAYE, ARTHUR LEE	OF	65	71	+.290	XCLE	B
		MC MULLEN, KENNETH LEE	3B	154	158	.272	B	B
0	1	MILES, JAMES CHARLIE	P	10	12	.333	B	C
9	8	MOORE, ROBERT BARRY	P	31	32	.209	B	CLE
2	5	PASCUAL, CAMILO ALBERTO	P	14	17	.235	B	XCINN
4	7	SHELLENBACK, JAMES PHILIP	P		30	.185	XPITN	B
		SMITH, RICHARD KELLY	OF	9	21	.107	A	C
		STROUD, EDWIN MARVIN	OF	85	123	.252	B	B
		UNSER, DELBERT BERNARD	OF	149	153	.286	B	B
		VERSALLES, ZOILO	SS	13	31	+.267	XCLE	ATLN71
		(2B6 3B5)						

WON 70
LOST 92
TIED 0
TG 162

AMERICAN LEAGUE

1970.

FINISHED 6 E (LAST)

PCT. .432

WASHINGTON

THEODORE SAMUEL WILLIAMS

WON	LOST	NAME	POS.		G.	BA	FROM	TO
		ALLEN, BERNARD KEITH (3B12)	2B	80	104	.234	B	B
		ALLEN, HAROLD ANDREW (HANK)	OF	17	22	+.211	B	XMIL
		BIITTNER, LAWRENCE DAVID			2	.000	A	B
		BILLINGS, RICHARD ARLIN	C	8	11	.250	B	B
16	12	BOSMAN, RICHARD ALLEN	P		36	.137	B	B
		BRINKMAN, EDWIN ALBERT	SS	157	158	.262	B	DET
2	2	BROWN, JACKIE GENE	P		24	.154	A	B
8	6	BRUNET, GEORGE STUART	P		24	.158	SEA	XPITN
		BURROUGHS, JEFFREY ALAN	OF	3	6	.167	A	B
0	0	CARLOS, FRANCISCO MANUEL	P		5	.000	B	C
		CASANOVA, PAULINO	C	100	104	.229	B	B
8	12	COLEMAN, JOSEPH HOWARD	P		39	.119	B	DET
		COMER, HARRY WAYNE (3B1)	OF	58	77	+.233	XMIL	DET 72
8	12	COX, JOSEPH CASEY	P		37	.121	B	B
		CULLEN, TIMOTHY LEO (SS6)	2B	112	123	.214	B	B
0	0	DUKES, NOBLE JAN	P		5	.000	B	TEX 72
		EPSTEIN, MICHAEL PETER	1B	122	140	.256	B	B
		FRENCH, RICHARD JAMES (JIM)	C	62	69	.211	B	B
		(OF1)						
2	2	GOGOLEWSKI, WILLIAM JOSEPH	P		8	.000	A	B
		GOOSSEN, GREGORY BRYANT	OF	5	21	+.222	XMIL	C
		(1B2)						
		GRIEVE, THOMAS ALAN	OF	39	47	.198	A	TEX 72
3	6	GRZENDA, JOSEPH CHARLES	P		49	.000	MIN	B
9	11	HANNAN, JAMES JOHN	P		42	.129	B	DET
		HOWARD, FRANK OLIVER (1B48)	OF	120	161	.283	B	B
0	0	HUMPHREYS, ROBERT WILLIAM	P		5	+.000	B	XMIL
2	14	KNOWLES, DAROLD DUANE	P		71	.050	B	B
		MAYE, ARTHUR LEE (3B1)	OF	68	96	+.263	B	XCHI
		MC MULLEN, KENNETH LEE	3B		15	+.203	B	XCAL
		NELSON, DAVID EARL	2B	33	47	.159	CLE	B
		NEN, RICHARD LEROY	1B	1	6	.200	CHIN68	C
5	3	PINA, HORACIO	P		61	.000	CLE	B
0	0	RAMOS, PEDRO	P	4	5	.000	CINN	C
		REICHARDT, FREDERIC CARL	OF	79	107	+.253	XCAL	CHI
		(3B1)						
0	0	RIDDLEBERGER, DENNIS MICHAEL	P		8	.000	A	B
		RODRIGUEZ, AURELIO (SS7)	3B	136	142	+.247	XCAL	DET
		ROSEBORO, JOHN	C	30	46	.233	MIN	C
6	7	SHELLENBACK, JAMES PHILIP	P	39	40	.067	B	B
		STROUD, EDWIN MARVIN	OF	118	129	.266	B	CHI
1	5	SUCH, RICHARD STANLEY	P	21	22	.231	A	C
		UNSER, DELBERT BERNARD	OF	103	119	.258	B	B

WON 63 — AMERICAN LEAGUE — FINISHED 5 E
LOST 96
TIED 0 — 1971. — PCT. .396
TG 159

WASHINGTON

THEODORE SAMUEL WILLIAMS

WON	LOST	NAME	POS.		G.	BA	FROM	TO
		ALLEN, BERNARD KEITH (3B34)	2B	41	97	.266	B	NY
		BITTNER, LAWRENCE DAVID (1B3)	OF	41	66	.257	B	TEX
		BILLINGS, RICHARD ARLIN (3B2 OF32)	C	62	116	.246	B	TEX
12	16	BOSMAN, RICHARD ALLEN	P		35	.093	B	TEX
5	9	BROBERG PETER SVEN	P		18	.114	A	TEX
3	4	BROWN, JACKIE GENE	P		14	.133	B	C
		BURROUGHS, JEFFREY ALAN	OF	50	59	.232	B	TEX
		CASANOVA, PAULINO	C	83	94	.203	B	ATLN
5	7	COX, JOSEPH CASEY	P		54	.077	B	TEX
		CULLEN, TIMOTHY LEO (SS62)	2B	78	125	.191	B	OAK
		EPSTEIN, MICHAEL PETER	1B		24	+.247	B	XOAK
		FAHEY, WILLIAM ROGER	C		2	.000	A	TEX
		FERNANDEZ, FRANK (C1)	OF	6	18	+.100	XOAK	XCHIN
		FLOOD, CURTIS CHARLES	OF	10	13	.200	STLN69	C
		FOY, JOSEPH ANTHONY (2B3' SS1)	3B	37	41	.234	NY N	C
		FRENCH, RICHARD JAMES (JIM)	C		14	.146	B	C
6	5	GOGOLEWSKI, WILLIAM JOSEPH	P		27	.156	B	TEX
5	2	GRZENDA, JOSEPH CHARLES	P		46	.143	B	STLN
		HARRAH, COLBERT DALE (TOBY) (3B7)	SS	116	127	.230	WAS 69	TEX
		HOWARD, FRANK OLIVER (1B68)	OF	100	153	.279	B	TEX
1	5	JANESKI, GERALD JOSEPH	P		23	.214	CHI	TEX
2	2	KNOWLES, DAROLD DUANE	P		12	+.000	B	XOAK
6	4	LINDBLAD, PAUL AARON	P		43	+.158	XOAK	TEX
		MADDOX, ELLIOTT (3B12)	OF	103	128	.217	DET	TEX
		MASON, JAMES PERCY	SS		3	.333	A	TEX
		MC CRAW, TOMMIE LEE (1B30)	OF	60	122	.213	CHI	CLE
10	22	MC LAIN, DENNIS DALE	P		33	.103	DET	OAK
		MINCHER, DONALD RAY	1B	88	100	+.291	XOAK	TEX
		NELSON, DAVID EARL (2B1)	3B	84	85	.280	B	TEX
1	1	PINA, HORACIO	P		56	.000	B	TEX
		RAGLAND, THOMAS	2B		10	.174	A	TEX
		RANDLE, LEONARD SHENOFF	2B	66	75	.219	A	TEX
3	1	RIDDLEBERGER, DENNIS MICHAEL	P		57	.000	B	CLE
		SCHEINBLUM, RICHARD ALAN	OF	13	27	.143	CLE 69	KC
3	11	SHELLENBACK, JAMES PHILIP	P		40	.167	B	TEX
		STELMASZEK, RICHARD FRANCIS	C	3	6	.000	A	C
1	6	THOMPSON, MICHAEL WAYNE	P		16	.118	A	C
		UNSER, DELBERT BERNARD	OF	152	153	.255	B	CLE
		WERT, DONALD RALPH (2B1 3B7)	SS	7	20	.050	DET	C

FORFEITED GAME TO NEW YORK ON SEPTEMBER 30TH,
NO PITCHER CHARGED WITH LOSS.
CLUB TRANSFERRED TO TEXAS AFTER 1971 SEASON

Index

Abbreviations used in the Index stand for Leagues: A-American League; AA-American Association; F-Federal League; N-National League; P-Players League; and U-Union Association.

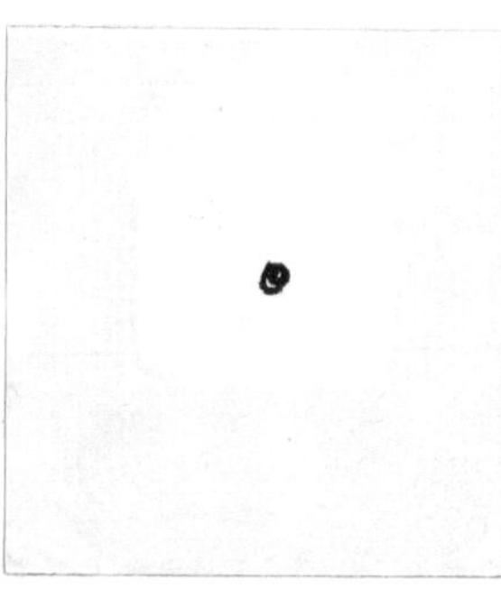